PUBLIC PAPERS OF THE PRESIDENTS
OF THE
UNITED STATES

PUBLIC PAPERS OF THE PRESIDENTS
OF THE
UNITED STATES

Ronald Reagan

1981

JANUARY 20 TO DECEMBER 31, 1981

UNITED STATES GOVERNMENT PRINTING OFFICE
WASHINGTON : 1982

Published by the
Office of the Federal Register
National Archives and Records Service
General Services Administration

For sale by the
Superintendent of Documents
U.S. Government Printing Office
Washington, D.C. 20402

Foreword

The first year of our administration, as chronicled in these pages, was a year of new hope for America. Beginning on Inauguration Day, as 52 brave Americans regained their freedom, our nation sought to recapture our unique spirit of pride and determination.

With the cooperation of the Congress, we moved forward on a bold and courageous course toward true prosperity for all Americans. We made significant progress in reducing the massive tax burden which had plagued our citizens for so many years, and we took the first real steps toward returning fiscal integrity to the Federal Government. We moved toward the goal of restoring our national defense to its position of prominence in the free world.

The United States reestablished its rightful position as the leader of the free world and the symbol of hope for peoples around the globe. In summit meetings at Ottawa and Cancún, we began an important dialog with our international partners, who voiced encouraging words of welcome for our role in world affairs. This year also heard the cries of hope of the courageous people of Poland, whose plight is never absent from our hearts.

The year 1981 was one of challenge and opportunity. It was a year, as these pages show, in which we met the challenges and seized the opportunities to truly make a New Beginning for America. I believe these documents are fitting testimony to the renewed spirit of hope and pride we all feel. They document a great start to the progress we will make together as a nation.

Ronald Reagan

Preface

This book contains the papers and speeches of the 40th President of the United States that were issued by the Office of the Press Secretary during the period January 20-December 31, 1981. The material has been compiled and published by the Office of the Federal Register, National Archives and Records Service, General Services Administration

The material is presented in chronological order, and the dates shown in the headings are the dates of the documents or events. In instances when the release date differs from the date of the document itself, that fact is shown in the textnote. Every effort has been made to ensure accuracy. Tape recordings of Presidential remarks are used to protect against errors in transcription, and signed documents are checked against the original to verify the correct printing. Textnotes, footnotes, and cross references have been provided by the editors for purposes of identification or clarity. Speeches were delivered in Washington, D.C., unless indicated. The times noted are local times. All materials that are printed full-text in the book have been indexed in the subject and name indexes.

The Public Papers series was begun in 1957 in response to a recommendation of the National Historical Publications Commission. An extensive compilation of messages and papers of the Presidents covering the period 1789 to 1897 was assembled by James D. Richardson and published under congressional authority between 1896 and 1899. Since then, various private compilations have been issued, but there was no uniform publication comparable to the Congressional Record or the United States Supreme Court Reports. Many Presidential papers could be found only in the form of mimeographed White House releases or as reported in the press. The Commission therefore recommended the establishment of an official series in which Presidential writings, addresses, and remarks of a public nature could be made available.

The Commission's recommendation was incorporated in regulations of the Administrative Committee of the Federal Register, issued under section 6 of the Federal Register Act (44 U.S.C. 1506), which may be found in Title I, Part 10, of the Code of Federal Regulations.

A companion publication to the Public Papers series, the Weekly Compilation of Presidential Documents, was begun in 1965 to provide a broader range of Presidential materials on a more timely basis to meet the needs of the contemporary reader. Beginning with the administration of Jimmy Carter, the Public Papers series expanded its coverage to include all material as printed in the Weekly Compilation. That coverage provides a listing of the President's daily schedule and meetings, when announced, and other items of general interest issued by the Office of the Press Secretary. Also included are lists of the President's nominations submitted to the Senate, materials released by the Office of the Press Secretary that are not printed full-text in the book, and acts approved by the President. This information appears in the appendixes at the end of the book.

Volumes covering the administrations of Presidents Hoover, Truman, Eisenhower, Kennedy, Johnson, Nixon, Ford, and Carter are also available.

This series is under the direction of John E. Byrne, Director, and Robert E. Lewis, Director of the Presidential Documents and Legislative Division, Office of the Federal Register, and is produced by the Presidential Documents Unit, Brenda A. Robeson, Chief. Editors of this book were Wilma P. Greene, Katherine A. Mellody, Kenneth R. Payne, and William K. Banks. The indexes were prepared by Judith B. Craine, Gwendolyn J. Henderson, Thomas D. Kevan, Walter W. Rice, and William M. Short.

White House liaison was provided by Larry M. Speakes, Deputy Assistant to the President and Deputy Press Secretary. The frontispiece and photographs used in the portfolio were supplied by the White House Photo Office. The frontispiece is from the White House ceremony welcoming home the freed American hostages, January 27.

The typography and design of the book were developed by the United States Government Printing Office under the direction of Danford L. Sawyer, Public Printer.

Robert M. Warner
Archivist of the United States

Gerald P. Carmen
Administrator of General Services
March 1982

Contents

Foreword . . . v

Preface . . . vii

Public Papers of Ronald Reagan,
January 20–December 31, 1981 . . . 1

Appendix A
Digest of Other White House Announcements . . . 1213

Appendix B
Nominations Submitted to the Senate . . . 1267

Appendix C
Checklist of White House Press Releases . . . 1301

Appendix D
Acts Approved by the President . . . 1321

Subject Index . . . A–1

Name Index . . . B–1

Administration of Ronald Reagan

1981

Inaugural Address
January 20, 1981

Senator Hatfield, Mr. Chief Justice, Mr. President, Vice President Bush, Vice President Mondale, Senator Baker, Speaker O'Neill, Reverend Moomaw, and my fellow citizens:

To a few of us here today this is a solemn and most momentous occasion, and yet in the history of our nation it is a commonplace occurrence. The orderly transfer of authority as called for in the Constitution routinely takes place, as it has for almost two centuries, and few of us stop to think how unique we really are. In the eyes of many in the world, this every-4-year ceremony we accept as normal is nothing less than a miracle.

Mr. President, I want our fellow citizens to know how much you did to carry on this tradition. By your gracious cooperation in the transition process, you have shown a watching world that we are a united people pledged to maintaining a political system which guarantees individual liberty to a greater degree than any other, and I thank you and your people for all your help in maintaining the continuity which is the bulwark of our Republic.

The business of our nation goes forward. These United States are confronted with an economic affliction of great proportions. We suffer from the longest and one of the worst sustained inflations in our national history. It distorts our economic decisions, penalizes thrift, and crushes the struggling young and the fixed-income elderly alike. It threatens to shatter the lives of millions of our people.

Idle industries have cast workers into unemployment, human misery, and personal indignity. Those who do work are denied a fair return for their labor by a tax system which penalizes successful achievement and keeps us from maintaining full productivity.

But great as our tax burden is, it has not kept pace with public spending. For decades we have piled deficit upon deficit, mortgaging our future and our children's future for the temporary convenience of the present. To continue this long trend is to guarantee tremendous social, cultural, political, and economic upheavals.

You and I, as individuals, can, by borrowing, live beyond our means, but for only a limited period of time. Why, then, should we think that collectively, as a nation, we're not bound by that same limitation? We must act today in order to preserve tomorrow. And let there be no misunderstanding: We are going to begin to act, beginning today.

The economic ills we suffer have come upon us over several decades. They will not go away in days, weeks, or months, but they will go away. They will go away because we as Americans have the capacity now, as we've had in the past, to do whatever needs to be done to preserve this last and greatest bastion of freedom.

In this present crisis, government is not the solution to our problem; government is the problem. From time to time we've been tempted to believe that society has become too complex to be managed by self-rule, that government by an elite group is superior to government for, by, and of the people. Well, if no one among us is capable of governing himself, then who among us has the capacity to govern someone else? All of us together, in and out of government, must bear the burden. The solutions we seek must be equitable, with no one group singled out to pay a higher price.

We hear much of special interest groups. Well, our concern must be for a special interest group that has been too long neglected. It knows no sectional boundaries or ethnic and racial divisions, and it crosses political party lines. It is made up of men and women who raise our food, patrol our streets, man our mines and factories, teach our children, keep our homes, and heal us when we're sick—professionals, industrialists, shopkeepers, clerks, cabbies, and truckdrivers. They are, in short, "We the people," this breed called Americans.

Well, this administration's objective will be a healthy, vigorous, growing economy that provides equal opportunities for all Americans, with no barriers born of bigotry or discrimination. Putting America back to work means putting all Americans back to work. Ending inflation means freeing all Americans from the terror of runaway living costs. All must share in the productive work of this "new beginning," and all must share in the bounty of a revived economy. With the idealism and fair play which are the core of our system and our strength, we can have a strong and prosperous America, at peace with itself and the world.

So, as we begin, let us take inventory. We are a nation that has a government—not the other way around. And this makes us special among the nations of the Earth. Our government has no power except that granted it by the people. It is time to check and reverse the growth of government, which shows signs of having grown beyond the consent of the governed.

It is my intention to curb the size and influence of the Federal establishment and to demand recognition of the distinction between the powers granted to the Federal Government and those reserved to the States or to the people. All of us need to be reminded that the Federal Government did not create the States; the States created the Federal Government.

Now, so there will be no misunderstanding, it's not my intention to do away with government. It is rather to make it work—work with us, not over us; to stand by our side, not ride on our back. Government can and must provide opportunity, not smother it; foster productivity, not stifle it.

If we look to the answer as to why for so many years we achieved so much, prospered as no other people on Earth, it was because here in this land we unleashed the energy and individual genius of man to a greater extent than has ever been done before. Freedom and the dignity of the individual have been more available and assured here than in any other place on Earth. The price for this freedom at times

has been high, but we have never been unwilling to pay that price.

It is no coincidence that our present troubles parallel and are proportionate to the intervention and intrusion in our lives that result from unnecessary and excessive growth of government. It is time for us to realize that we're too great a nation to limit ourselves to small dreams. We're not, as some would have us believe, doomed to an inevitable decline. I do not believe in a fate that will fall on us no matter what we do. I do believe in a fate that will fall on us if we do nothing. So, with all the creative energy at our command, let us begin an era of national renewal. Let us renew our determination, our courage, and our strength. And let us renew our faith and our hope.

We have every right to dream heroic dreams. Those who say that we're in a time when there are not heroes, they just don't know where to look. You can see heroes every day going in and out of factory gates. Others, a handful in number, produce enough food to feed all of us and then the world beyond. You meet heroes across a counter, and they're on both sides of that counter. There are entrepreneurs with faith in themselves and faith in an idea who create new jobs, new wealth and opportunity. They're individuals and families whose taxes support the government and whose voluntary gifts support church, charity, culture, art, and education. Their patriotism is quiet, but deep. Their values sustain our national life.

Now, I have used the words "they" and "their" in speaking of these heroes. I could say "you" and "your," because I'm addressing the heroes of whom I speak—you, the citizens of this blessed land. Your dreams, your hopes, your goals are going to be the dreams, the hopes, and the goals of this administration, so help me God.

We shall reflect the compassion that is so much a part of your makeup. How can we love our country and not love our countrymen; and loving them, reach out a hand when they fall, heal them when they're sick, and provide opportunity to make them self-sufficient so they will be equal in fact and not just in theory?

Can we solve the problems confronting us? Well, the answer is an unequivocal and emphatic "yes." To paraphrase Winston Churchill, I did not take the oath I've just taken with the intention of presiding over the dissolution of the world's strongest economy.

In the days ahead I will propose removing the roadblocks that have slowed our economy and reduced productivity. Steps will be taken aimed at restoring the balance between the various levels of government. Progress may be slow, measured in inches and feet, not miles, but we will progress. It is time to reawaken this industrial giant, to get government back within its means, and to lighten our punitive tax burden. And these will be our first priorities, and on these principles there will be no compromise.

On the eve of our struggle for independence a man who might have been one of the greatest among the Founding Fathers, Dr. Joseph Warren, president of the Massachusetts Congress, said to his fellow Americans, "Our country is in danger, but not to be despaired of . . . . On you depend the fortunes of America. You are to decide the important questions upon which rests the happiness and the liberty of millions yet unborn. Act worthy of yourselves."

Well, I believe we, the Americans of today, are ready to act worthy of ourselves, ready to do what must be done to ensure happiness and liberty for ourselves, our children, and our children's children. And as we renew ourselves here in our own land, we will be seen as having greater strength throughout the world. We will again be the exemplar of freedom and a beacon of hope for those who do not now have freedom.

To those neighbors and allies who share our freedom, we will strengthen our historic ties and assure them of our support and firm commitment. We will match loyalty with loyalty. We will strive for mutually beneficial relations. We will not use our friendship to impose on their sovereignty, for our own sovereignty is not for sale.

As for the enemies of freedom, those who are potential adversaries, they will be reminded that peace is the highest aspiration of the American people. We will negotiate for it, sacrifice for it; we will not surrender for it, now or ever.

Our forbearance should never be misunderstood. Our reluctance for conflict should not be misjudged as a failure of will. When action is required to preserve our national security, we will act. We will maintain sufficient strength to prevail if need be, knowing that if we do so we have the best chance of never having to use that strength.

Above all, we must realize that no arsenal or no weapon in the arsenals of the world is so formidable as the will and moral courage of free men and women. It is a weapon our adversaries in today's world do not have. It is a weapon that we as Americans do have. Let that be understood by those who practice terrorism and prey upon their neighbors.

I'm told that tens of thousands of prayer meetings are being held on this day, and for that I'm deeply grateful. We are a nation under God, and I believe God intended for us to be free. It would be fitting and good, I think, if on each Inaugural Day in future years it should be declared a day of prayer.

This is the first time in our history that this ceremony has been held, as you've been told, on this West Front of the Capitol. Standing here, one faces a magnificent vista, opening up on this city's special beauty and history. At the end of this open mall are those shrines to the giants on whose shoulders we stand.

Directly in front of me, the monument to a monumental man, George Washington, father of our country. A man of humility who came to greatness reluctantly. He led America out of revolutionary victory into infant nationhood. Off to one side, the stately memorial to Thomas Jefferson. The Declaration of Independence flames with his eloquence. And then, beyond the Reflecting Pool, the dignified columns of the Lincoln Memorial. Whoever would understand in his heart the meaning of America will find it in the life of Abraham Lincoln.

Beyond those monuments to heroism is the Potomac River, and on the far shore the sloping hills of Arlington National Cemetery, with its row upon row of simple white markers bearing crosses or Stars of David.

3

They add up to only a tiny fraction of the price that has been paid for our freedom.

Each one of those markers is a monument to the kind of hero I spoke of earlier. Their lives ended in places called Belleau Wood, The Argonne, Omaha Beach, Salerno, and halfway around the world on Guadalcanal, Tarawa, Pork Chop Hill, the Chosin Reservoir, and in a hundred rice paddies and jungles of a place called Vietnam.

Under one such marker lies a young man, Martin Treptow, who left his job in a small town barbershop in 1917 to go to France with the famed Rainbow Division. There, on the western front, he was killed trying to carry a message between battalions under heavy artillery fire.

We're told that on his body was found a diary. On the flyleaf under the heading, "My Pledge," he had written these words: "America must win this war. Therefore I will work, I will save, I will sacrifice, I will endure, I will fight cheerfully and do my utmost, as if the issue of the whole struggle depended on me alone."

The crisis we are facing today does not require of us the kind of sacrifice that Martin Treptow and so many thousands of others were called upon to make. It does require, however, our best effort and our willingness to believe in ourselves and to believe in our capacity to perform great deeds, to believe that together with God's help we can and will resolve the problems which now confront us.

And after all, why shouldn't we believe that? We are Americans.

God bless you, and thank you.

Note: The President spoke at 12 noon from a platform erected at the West Front of the Capitol. Immediately before the address, the oath of office was administered by Chief Justice Warren E. Burger.

In his opening remarks, the President referred to Rev. Donn D. Moomaw, senior pastor, Bel Air Presbyterian Church, Los Angeles, Calif.

The address was broadcast live on radio and television.

Remarks on Signing the Federal Employee Hiring Freeze Memorandum and the Cabinet Member Nominations
January 20, 1981

The President. This—for the benefit of the oral press—this is an order that I am signing, an immediate freeze on the hiring of civilian employees in the executive branch. I pledged last July that this would be a first step toward controlling the growth and the size of Government and reducing the drain on the economy for the public sector. And beyond the symbolic value of this, which is my first official act, the freeze will eventually lead to a significant reduction in the size of the Federal work force. Only rare exemptions will be permitted in order to maintain vital services.

Now, I am happy to be taking this action in this historic room, a sign of what I hope will be full cooperation between Congress and the executive branch.

This is a memorandum for the heads of executive departments and agencies, and then, of course, will be implemented by the Office of Management and Budget.

And now I shall sign the nominations for members of my Cabinet. This is for Alexander Haig, Jr., of Connecticut, Secretary of State. That will go to Alexander Haig.

Donald T. Regan, of New Jersey, to be Secretary of the Treasury. It's awfully hard for me to say Regan. [*Laughter*] I spent my life saying it the other way. But I found out that it's even because it's very difficult for him to call me Reagan. [*Laughter*]

Mr. Regan. It's getting easier. [*Laughter*]

The President. And this is for Caspar Willard Weinberger, Secretary of Defense.

William French Smith, of California, Attorney General.

James Watt, of Colorado, Secretary of the Interior.

John Block, of Illinois, Secretary of Agriculture—graduate of West Point, yes.

Malcolm Baldrige, of Connecticut, Secretary of Commerce. Avocation, rodeo riding. [*Laughter*] The first time I tried to get ahold of him on the phone his wife had to tell me he was in a calf-roping contest.

Raymond Donovan, of New Jersey, Secretary of Labor.

Richard Schweiker, Pennsylvania, Secretary of Health and Human Services.

Samuel R. Pierce, Jr., of New York, Secretary of Housing and Urban Development—already proved his quality in some of the meetings we've been having. He found the only washbasin in the washroom that you could get hot water out of. [*Laughter*]

Andrew L. Lewis, Pennsylvania, Secretary of Transportation.

And Governor James B. Edwards, of South Carolina, Secretary of Energy.

T. H. Bell, of Utah, Secretary of Education.

Jeane J. Kirkpatrick, of Maryland, to be Representative of the United States of America to the United Nations with the rank and status of Ambassador Extraordinary and Plenipotentiary and the Representative of the United States of America in the Security Council of the United Nations.

David A. Stockman, of Michigan, Director of the Office of Management and Budget.

William J. Casey, of New York, Director of Central Intelligence.

Darrell M. Trent, of California, to be Deputy Secretary of Transportation.

We've done it. All right.

Speaker O'Neill. Mr. President, on behalf of the leadership in the House, Jim Wright, John Rhodes, Bob Michel, this is the flag that flew over the Capitol of the United States on the day you were elected.

The President. Well, Mr. Speaker, thank you very much. Thank you.

Speaker O'Neill. I'm delighted to do it. We will also have the one that flew over the Capitol the day you were inaugurated. That will be preserved for you.

The President. Thank you very much.

Note: The President spoke at approximately 1 p.m. in the Presidents Room at the Capitol.

Memorandum Directing a Federal Employee Hiring Freeze
January 20, 1981

Memorandum for the Heads of Executive Departments and Agencies

Subject: Hiring Freeze

I am ordering today a strict freeze on the hiring of Federal civilian employees to be applied across the board in the executive branch.

This action is necessary because the national budget is out of control. Estimates of Federal spending for fiscal years 1981 and 1982 have—in a single year—increased by $100 billion.

Last July, during my campaign for the Presidency, I pledged that we would take this action as a first step towards controlling the growth and size of government and stopping the drain on the economy by the public sector.

Imposing a freeze now can eventually lead to a significant reduction in the size of the Federal work force. This begins the process of restoring our economic strength and returning the Nation to prosperity.

The Director of the Office of Management and Budget will issue detailed instructions concerning this freeze. I am delegating to him authority to grant exemptions in those rare and unusual circumstances where exemptions are necessary for the delivery of essential services.

I ask that in carrying out this directive you insure the smallest impact possible on those areas of your agencies' operations that vitally affect the public, such as the processing of social security claims and the payment of veterans and retirement benefits. You should seek efficient use of personnel and funds by making reallocations within your respective agencies to meet highest priority needs and to assure that essential services are not interrupted.

Obviously, contracting with firms and institutions outside the government to circumvent the intent of this directive must not be permitted.

This begins the process of revising and reducing the 1981 and 1982 budgets, a project that will occupy much of our time during the coming weeks and months.

This will be a demanding period for all of us; it is also a time of challenge and an unusual opportunity to serve our Nation well. I am relying upon you for strict implementation of this directive.

RONALD REAGAN

Nomination of Alexander M. Haig, Jr., To Be Secretary of State
January 20, 1981

The President today nominated Alexander Meigs Haig, Jr., of Hartford, Conn., to be Secretary of State.

General Haig is president and chief operating officer of United Technologies Corp., a position he has held since December 24, 1979.

General Haig was born on December 2, 1924. He received a B.S. from the United States Military Academy in 1947 and a M.A. from Georgetown University in 1961. He was graduated from the Naval War College in 1960 and the Army War College in 1966.

He received his commission as a second lieutenant in the United States Army in 1947. He served as staff officer in the Office of the Deputy Chief of Staff for Operations, Department of the Army, from 1962 to 1964 and as Military Assistant to the Secretary of the Army in 1964. From 1964 to 1965, he served as Deputy Special Assistant to the Secretary and Deputy Secretary of

Defense. He served in Vietnam from 1966 to 1967 and as Regimental Commander and Deputy Commandant of the U.S. Military Academy from 1967 to 1969. From 1969 to 1970, General Haig served as Military Assistant to the Assistant to the President for National Security Affairs and from 1970 to 1973 served as Deputy Assistant to the President for National Security Affairs.

In 1973 General Haig was commissioned general and served as Vice Chief of Staff of the U.S. Army. Later in 1973 he returned to the White House as Chief of Staff, a position in which he served until 1974 when he was appointed Commander in Chief of the U.S. European Command. He served in that capacity as well as Supreme Allied Commander, Europe SHAPE, until his retirement from the Army in 1978.

A trustee of Loyola College, General Haig is married to the former Patricia Antoinette Fox. They have three children: Alexander P., Brian F., and Barbara E.

Nomination of Donald T. Regan To Be Secretary of the Treasury
January 20, 1981

The President today nominated Donald T. Regan, of Colts Neck, N.J., to be the Secretary of the Treasury.

Mr. Regan is chairman and chief executive officer of Merrill Lynch and Co., Inc.,

the holding company formed in May 1973 by Merrill Lynch, Pierce, Fenner & Smith, Inc.

Mr. Regan was born on December 21, 1918. He was graduated from Harvard University with a B.A. in 1940. He joined the United States Marine Corps and retired at the end of World War II as a lieutenant colonel.

In 1946 Mr. Regan joined Merrill Lynch as an account executive trainee. Following his training, he worked as an account executive in Washington, D.C. In early 1952 he was named manager of the Over-the-Counter Department in New York. In 1954 Mr. Regan became a general partner in Merrill Lynch.

From 1955 until 1960, Mr. Regan served as manager of the Merrill Lynch office in Philadelphia. In 1960 he returned to New York as administrative division director.

In April 1964 Mr. Regan was elected executive vice president of Merrill Lynch, and in 1968 he became president. He was named chairman and chief executive officer of Merrill Lynch, Pierce, Fenner & Smith in January 1971. He relinquished those titles in January 1980 and continues as a

director and member of the executive committee of the company.

Mr. Regan is the author of "A View from the Street," an analysis of the events on Wall Street during the crisis years of 1969 and 1970, which was published in 1972 by The New American Library. He has also written many articles that have appeared in various financial and business publications.

Mr. Regan is a member of the Policy Committee of the Business Roundtable. He is also a trustee of the Committee for Economic Development and is a member of the Council on Foreign Relations. He served as chairman of the trustees of the University of Pennsylvania from 1974 to 1978 and is currently a life trustee of the university. He holds honorary degrees from four universities and is a trustee of the Charles E. Merrill Trust, a charitable foundation.

He is married to the former Ann Buchanan, and they have four children: Donna, Donald, Richard, and Diane.

Nomination of Caspar W. Weinberger To Be Secretary of Defense
January 20, 1981

The President today nominated Caspar Willard Weinberger, of Hillsborough, Calif., to be the Secretary of Defense.

Mr. Weinberger is general counsel, vice president, and director of the Bechtel Power Corp.

He was born on August 18, 1917. He was graduated magna cum laude with an A.B. from Harvard University in 1938 and in 1941 received an LL.B. from Harvard. He is a member of Phi Beta Kappa. In 1941 he entered the United States Army as a private and was honorably discharged as a captain in 1945. He served in the 41st Infantry Division in the Pacific Theatre and on the intelligence staff of Gen. Douglas MacArthur. He was awarded the Bronze Star.

Following his admission to the California Bar, Mr. Weinberger served as a law clerk to United States Judge William E. Orr from

1945 to 1947. He was elected to the California State Legislature from the 21st District in 1952 and was reelected without opposition in 1954 and 1956. From 1947 to 1969, Mr. Weinberger practiced law with the firm of Heller, Ehrman, White & McAuliffe and was a partner from 1959 to 1969. He served as vice chairman of the California Republican Central Committee from 1960 to 1962 and as chairman from 1962 to 1964. From 1968 to 1970, Mr. Weinberger served as director of finance for the State of California. In 1970 he served as Chairman of the Federal Trade Commission, and from 1970 to 1972, he served as Deputy Director of the Office of Management and Budget. Mr. Weinberger served as Director of the Office of Management and Budget from 1972 to 1973, and in 1973, served as Counsellor to the President. He served as Secretary of Health, Education, and Welfare from 1973 to 1975.

Mr. Weinberger is married to the former Jane Dalton. They have two children: Arlin Cerise and Caspar Willard, Jr.

Nomination of William French Smith To Be Attorney General of the United States
January 20, 1981

The President today nominated William French Smith, of Los Angeles, Calif., to be Attorney General of the United States.

Mr. Smith is a senior partner of Gibson, Dunn & Crutcher of Los Angeles.

Born in Wilton, N.H., on August 26, 1917, Mr. Smith attended the University of California, where he received his A.B. summa cum laude in 1939, and Harvard University, where he received his LL.B. in 1942. He served in the United States Naval Reserve from 1942 to 1946 and attained the rank of lieutenant.

He was admitted to the California Bar in 1942 and became a senior partner with Gibson, Dunn & Crutcher in 1946. Mr. Smith is a director of Pacific Lighting Corp., of San Francisco, Jorgensen Steel Co., and Pullman, Inc., of Chicago.

He has been a member of the U.S. Advisory Commission on International, Educational, and Cultural Affairs in Washington since 1971; a member of the board of directors of the Los Angeles World Affairs Council since 1970 and its president since 1975; a member of the Los Angeles Committee on Foreign Relations from 1954 to 1974; a member of the Executive Committee of the California Roundtable since 1975; a trustee of the Henry E. Huntington Library and Art Gallery since 1971; a trustee of Claremont Men's College since 1967; a trustee of the Cate School since 1971; and a trustee of the Northrop Institute of Technology from 1973 to 1975.

He has been a member of the Board of Regents of the University of California since 1968 and served as its chairman from 1970 to 1972, from 1974 to 1975, and in 1976. He has been a member of the Legal Aid Foundation of Los Angeles from 1963 to 1972; a member of the California Foundation for Commerce and Education since 1975; a member of the Advisory Council, Harvard University School of Government, since 1971; a member of the Advisory Board of the Center for Strategic and International Studies, Georgetown University, since 1978; a member of the Stanton Panel on International Information, Education, and Cultural Relations, Washington, since 1974; a member of the Board of Governors of the Performing Arts Council, Los Angeles Music Center, since 1978; a director of the California Chamber of Commerce since 1963 and served as its president in 1974 and 1975.

He was a member of the California delegation to the Republican National Convention in 1968, 1972, and 1976, serving as chairman of the delegation in 1968 and vice chairman of the delegation in 1972 and 1976.

He is a member of the American Bar Association, the State Bar of California, the Los Angeles County Bar, a fellow of the American Bar Foundation, the American Judicature Society, and the American Law Institute.

He is a member of Phi Beta Kappa, Pi Gamma Mu, and Pi Sigma Alpha.

He is married to the former Jean Webb, and they have four children: William French, Stephanie Oakes, Scott Cameron, and Gregory Hale.

Nomination of James G. Watt To Be Secretary of the Interior
January 20, 1981

The President today nominated James G. Watt, of Englewood, Colo., to be Secretary of the Interior.

Mr. Watt is president and chief legal officer of the Mountain States Legal Foundation, a public interest law center dedicated to bringing a balance to the courts in the defense of individual liberty and the private enterprise system. He has held that position since July 1977.

Mr. Watt was born on January 31, 1938. He received a B.S. with honors from the University of Wyoming College of Commerce and Industry in 1960 and a J.D. from the University of Wyoming College of Law in 1962.

From July to November 1962, Mr. Watt served as personal assistant to Milward L. Simpson, candidate for the United States Senate. Following Simpson's election, Mr. Watt served as legislative assistant and counsel to the Senator. From September 1966 to January 1969, he served as secretary to the Natural Resources Committee and the Environmental Pollution Advisory Panel, Chamber of Commerce of the United States. Mr. Watt served as special assistant to the Secretary and Under Secretary of the Interior from January to May 1969 and, following that, served as Deputy Assistant Secretary of the Interior. From July 1972 to November 1975, he served as director of the Bureau of Outdoor Recreation and, from November 1975 to July 1977, served with the Federal Power Commission as Commissioner and as Vice Chairman.

A member of the Wyoming Bar and the Bar of the United States Supreme Court, Mr. Watt was editor of the Wyoming Law Journal and is a member of Phi Kappa Phi, the national scholastic honor society.

He is married and has two children.

Nomination of John R. Block To Be Secretary of Agriculture
January 20, 1981

The President today nominated John R. Block, of Springfield, Ill., to be Secretary of Agriculture.

Mr. Block is Illinois Director of Agriculture and owns and operates his family farm near Galesburg, Ill.

Mr. Block was born on February 15, 1935. In 1957 he was graduated from the United States Military Academy at West Point. Since 1960, when he completed U.S. Army service as an infantry officer, he has guided the growth of Block Farms.

In September 1980 he led a 3-week people-to-people fact-finding mission to the Soviet Union, Poland, Hungary, Austria, and Switzerland. In 1978 and 1979 he served as a member of agricultural export teams traveling to China and Japan, and in 1977 represented Illinois at the Anuga Food Show in West Germany.

Mr. Block represents Illinois Governor James Thompson on the agricultural committee of the National Governors Association as well as the association's agricultural export task force. He has received numerous awards, including the Governor's Outstanding Achievement Award, the Cooperative Extension Service's Meritorious Service Award for outstanding contributions to Illinois agriculture, and the U.S. Jaycees Outstanding Young Farmer Award. He has served as president of the Mid-America International Agri-Trade Council and as chairman of a 11-State farm summit involving leaders of all major farm organizations. He is a trustee of the Farm Foundation and a former board member of the Illinois Farm Bureau.

Mr. Block and his wife, Sue, have a son and two daughters.

Nomination of Malcolm Baldrige To Be Secretary of Commerce
January 20, 1981

The President today nominated Malcolm Baldrige, of Woodbury, Conn., to be Secretary of Commerce.

Mr. Baldrige is chairman and chief executive officer of Scovill, Inc., of Waterbury, Conn.

Born October 4, 1922, Mr. Baldrige received his B.A. from Yale University in 1943. He served in the United States Army from 1943 to 1946 with the rank of captain.

Mr. Baldrige joined Eastern Co. in 1947 as a foundry foreman and became foundry superintendent, division manager, and group vice president before serving as president from 1960 to 1962. He joined Scovill, Inc., as executive vice president in 1962, became president and chief executive officer in 1963, and chairman and chief executive officer in 1969.

He is director of Scovill, Inc., AMF, Inc., ASARCO, Inc., Bendix Corp., Connecticut Mutual Life Insurance Co., Eastern Co., and Uniroyal, Inc. He holds membership on the Business Council, the Council on Foreign Relations, Inc., International Chamber of Commerce, and the Citizens Research Foundation.

He has served as chairman for National Corporate Giving for Yale University and is an ex officio member of the Yale Development Committee.

He served as a delegate to the Republican National Convention in 1968, 1972, and 1976, Connecticut cochairman of United Citizens for Nixon-Agnew, a member of the National Republican Finance Committee, and chairman of the Connecticut Bush for President Committee in 1980.

He is married to the former Margaret Trowbridge Murray, and they have two children: Megan Brewster and Mary Trowbridge.

Nomination of Raymond J. Donovan To Be Secretary of Labor
January 20, 1981

The President today nominated Raymond J. Donovan, of Short Hills, N.J., to be Secretary of Labor.

Mr. Donovan is executive vice president of Schiavone Construction Co. of Secaucus, N.J.

Born August 31, 1930, in Bayonne, N.J., he was graduated from Notre Dame Seminary in New Orleans in 1952 with a B.A. in philosophy.

From 1953 to 1958, he was associated with the American Insurance Co. in New Jersey, serving as a representative in Essex and Hudson Counties until 1955, when he joined the company's surety department.

In 1959 he joined Schiavone Construction Co. as a shareholder and vice president with responsibilities in all phases of construction and management. He became executive vice president in 1971 with broadened responsibilities in all subsidiary firms.

He became a member of the Ballantine Brewery Workers Union in 1950 when he was a summer employee of the brewery. In 1952 and 1953 he was a member of the Electrical Workers Union, IBEW.

During his association with Schiavone Construction Co., he had primary responsibility for labor relations, conducting negotiations on behalf of his company. In addition, he has been involved in labor-related activities in the maritime industry, as well as in newspaper publishing, serving as a negotiator and developer of labor contracts for the New York Herald Tribune.

He is chairman of the lay board of directors of the Shrine of St. Josephs in Stirling, N.J., and chairman of the lay board of advisers of Missionary Servants of the Most Holy Trinity, a charitable and social work order of the Catholic Church. From 1973 to 1965, he was chairman of the board of Honesty

House, a privately endowed home for treatment of alcoholics and addicts, in Stirling, N.J.

He is married to the former Catherine Sblendorio, and they have three children: Kenneth, Mary Ellen, and Keith.

Nomination of Richard S. Schweiker To Be Secretary of Health and Human Services
January 20, 1981

The President today nominated Richard Schultz Schweiker, of Worcester, Pa., to be the Secretary of Health and Human Services.

Mr. Schweiker was United States Senator from Pennsylvania.

He was born on June 1, 1926. During World War II, he enlisted in the United States Navy and served aboard an aircraft carrier from 1944 until his discharge as an electronics technician, second class, in 1946. He received his B.A. from Pennsylvania State University in 1950, where he was elected to Phi Beta Kappa.

He was a business executive from 1950 to 1960. In 1960 Mr. Schweiker was elected to the United States House of Representatives from the 13th Congressional District of Pennsylvania and served in the House from January 1961 to January 1969. In 1968 Mr. Schweiker was elected to the United States Senate. He was the ranking minority member of the Labor and Human Resources Committee and ranking minority member of its Health and Scientific Research Subcommittee. He was a member of the Appropriations Committee and ranking minority member of its Labor, Health, Human Services, and Education Subcommittee. He also served on the Rules and Administration Committee.

He is an honorary member of the National Council of the Boy Scouts of America and a member of the board of directors of the Schwenkfelder Library. He is the recipient of the Bringer of Light Award of the National Jewish Fund, the Samuel H. Daroff Humanitarian Award, the B'nai B'rith Anti-Defamation League Award, the National Mental Health Association Award, the Primo Minister of Israel's Medal, and the Opportunities Industrialization Center Key Award.

He is married to the former Claire Joan Coleman. They have five children: Malcolm, Lani, Kyle, Richard S., Jr., and Kristi.

Nomination of Samuel R. Pierce, Jr., To Be Secretary of Housing and Urban Development
January 20, 1981

The President today nominated Samuel R. Pierce, Jr., of Long Island, N.Y., to be Secretary of Housing and Urban Development.

Mr. Pierce is a senior partner in the New York City law firm of Battle, Fowler, Jaffin, Pierce & Kheel.

Mr. Pierce was born on September 8, 1922. He received his A.B. in 1947 from Cornell University and his J.D. in 1949 from Cornell Law University. In 1952 Mr. Pierce received an LL.M. in taxation from the New York University School of Law and from 1957 to 1958 did postgraduate study as a Ford Foundation fellow at the Yale Law School. On May 31, 1972, he was awarded an honorary doctor of laws (LL.D.) by New York University.

Admitted to the New York Bar in 1949, he began his law career as an assistant district attorney for New York County, an office he held until 1953. He was then appointed Assistant U.S. Attorney for the Southern District of New York. In 1955 he became the Assistant Under Secretary of Labor, then associate counsel and later counsel to the Judiciary Subcommittee on Antitrust of the U.S. House of Representatives. Mr. Pierce returned to New York City in 1957 where he practiced law and subsequently served as a judge of the Court of General Sessions (now part of the New York Supreme Court) in 1959 and 1960. In 1961 Mr. Pierce became a partner in the law firm of Battle, Fowler, Stokes & Kheel, where he has practiced until the present.

In 1970 Mr. Pierce was appointed General Counsel of the United States Treasury Department, a position he held until 1973. During this period he was also the Execu-

tive Director and General Counsel of the Emergncy Loan Guarantee Board, a Director of the Securities Investor Protection Corporation, General Counsel to the National Advisory Council, and Director of the Office of Equal Employment Opportunity in the Treasury. He is a director of the Prudential Insurance Company of America, General Electric Co., International Paper Co., U.S. Industries, First National Boston Corp., First National Bank of Boston, and a trustee of the Rand Corp. He is also a governor of the American Stock Exchange, chairman of the Impartial Disciplinary Review Board of the New York City Transit System, and the impartial arbitrator of the New York City Transit System.

Mr. Pierce is married to the former Barbara Wright, and they have one daughter, Mrs. Victoria Pierce Ransmeier.

Nomination of Andrew L. Lewis, Jr., To Be Secretary of Transportation
January 20, 1981

The President today nominated Andrew Lindsay Lewis, Jr., of Schwenksville, Pa., to be Secretary of Transportation.

Mr. Lewis is deputy chairman of the Republican National Committee. He also served as deputy director of the Office of the President-elect. Since 1974 he has been associated with the firm of Lewis & Associates, financial and management consultants, Plymouth Meeting, Pa.

Born November 3, 1931, Mr. Lewis received his B.S. from Haverford College in Pennsylvania in 1953, his M.B.A. from Harvard University in 1955, and did postgraduate work at Massachusetts Institute of Technology in 1968.

From 1955 to 1960, Mr. Lewis was foreman, job superintendent, production manager, and director of Henkels & McCoy, Inc., of Blue Bell, Pa. From 1960 to 1968, he was vice president for sales and director of American Olean Tile Company, Inc., a division of National Gypsum Co. in Lansdale, Pa.

In 1969 and 1970 he served as assistant to the chairman of National Gypsum Co. in Buffalo, N.Y. In 1970 he joined the Simplex Wire & Cable Co. in Boston as president and chief executive officer and served as its chairman until 1972. From 1970 to 1974, he was president and chief executive officer of Snelling & Snelling, Inc.

He is a director of Wawa, Inc., Henkels & McCoy, Inc., Tamaqua Wire & Cable Co., Provident National Corp., Provident National Bank, Philadelphia Suburban Water Co., and the Coleman Co.

He served as organizational chairman of the Dick Schweiker for Congress Committee in 1960 and the Pennsylvania State Committee for the 24th Senatorial District from 1964 to 1966 and from 1970 to 1973; Republican chairman of Montgomery County, Pa., from 1965 to 1968; a delegate to the Republican National Convention in 1968, 1972, 1976, and 1980; chairman of the Schweiker for Senator Committee in 1968; chairman of the Republican Financial Committee of Pennsylvania from 1971 to

1973; the Republican national committee-man for Pennsylvania from 1976 to the present. He was the Republican candidate for Governor in 1974.

He is married to the former Marilyn S. Stoughton, and they have three children: Karen Stoughton Sacks, Russell Shephard, and Andrew Lindsay IV.

Nomination of James B. Edwards To Be Secretary of Energy
January 20, 1981

The President today nominated James Burrows Edwards, of Charleston, S.C., to be Secretary of Energy.

Dr. Edwards, an oral surgeon, served as Governor of South Carolina from 1975 to 1978.

He was born on June 24, 1927. He received a B.S. in 1950 from the College of Charleston and a D.M.D. in 1955 from the University of Louisville School of Dentistry.

During World War II, he served with the U.S. Maritime Service. He began his service as a seaman and was discharged as a deck officer. He was on active duty with the United States Navy from 1955 to 1957 and remained in the Naval Reserve until 1967, holding the rank of lieutenant commander upon discharge.

Dr. Edwards was elected chairman of the Charleston County Republican Party in 1964, a post he held until 1969. He was elected the First Congressional District Republican Party chairman in 1970 and resigned that post in 1971 to become the Republican Party's candidate for election to the United States House of Representatives. He served as a member of the South Carolina State Senate from 1972 to 1974. As Governor of South Carolina, Dr. Edwards served as chairman of the National Governors Association Subcommittee on Nuclear Energy in 1978 and as chairman of the Southern Governors Conference in the same year.

He is a member of the American Dental Association and has served as a diplomate on the American Board of Oral Surgery since 1963. He is a member of Omicron Delta Kappa, a national honorary leadership fraternity, and of Phi Delta, the honorary dental fraternity. Dr. Edwards is a member of the board of trustees of Baker Hospital in Charleston and of the Charleston Council of the Navy League of the United States. He is also on the board of trustees of the College of Charleston Foundation.

Dr. Edwards is married to the former Ann Norris Darlington, and they have two children: James B. Edwards, Jr., and Catharine Darlington Edwards.

Nomination of Terrel H. Bell To Be Secretary of Education
January 20, 1981

The President today nominated Terrel H. Bell, of Salt Lake City, Utah, to be Secretary of Education.

Mr. Bell is Utah Commissioner of Higher Education and chief executive officer of the Utah State Board of Regents.

Mr. Bell received his B.A. in 1946 from the Southern Idaho College of Education, and in 1954 he received his M.S. in educational administration from the University of Idaho. In 1961 he received his doctorate in educational administration from the University of Utah.

He served in the United States Marines from 1942 to 1946, and from 1946 to 1947, he was athletic coach and science teacher at Eden Rural High School in Eden, Idaho. From 1947 to 1954, he served as superintendent of the Rockland Valley (Idaho) School, and from 1954 to 1955, he had a

Ford Foundation fellowship in school administration. From 1955 to 1957, he served as superintendent of Star Valley Schools in Afton, Wyo., and from 1957 to 1962, he seved as superintendent of the Weber County School District in Ogden, Utah. He served as professor and chairman of the department of educational administration at Utah State University from 1962 to 1963 and served as Utah State Superintendent of Public Instruction from 1963 to 1970. He served as Deputy Commissioner for School Systems with the U.S. Office of Education from 1970 to 1971 and from 1971 to 1974 served as superintendent of the Granite School District in Salt Lake City. From June of 1974 to July of 1976, he served as United States Commissioner of Education, a position to which he was appointed by the President of the United States.

Mr. Bell is the author of 6 books as well as 27 articles, and 3 of his major addresses have been published in "Vital Speeches of the Nation." He has received numerous awards including the Secretary's Special Citation from Caspar Weinberger (1975), a Certificate of Merit of State Boards of Education from Edinboro (Pa.) State College (1975), the Distinguished Service Award from the National Association of State Boards of Education (1973), the Distinguished Service Award from the National Council of Chief State School Officers (1971), and the Outstanding Service Award from the Utah School Boards Association (1970).

Mr. Bell is 59 years old. He is married and has four sons.

Nomination of Jeane J. Kirkpatrick To Be United States Representative to the United Nations
January 20, 1981

The President today nominated Jeane Jordan Kirkpatrick, of Bethesda, Md., to be United States Representative to the United Nations, with Cabinet rank.

Dr. Kirkpatrick is the Thomas and Dorothy Leavey professor at Georgetown University and resident scholar at the American Enterprise Institute for Public Policy Research (AEI).

Dr. Kirkpatrick was born on November 19, 1926. She received an A.A. from Stephens College in 1946, an A.B. from Barnard College in 1948, an M.A. in political science from Columbia University in 1950, and a Ph. D. in political science from Columbia in 1968.

From 1962 to 1967, Dr. Kirkpatrick served as an assistant professor at Trinity College. From January to June 1970, she served as a professorial lecturer at the Institute for American Universities, University of Aix-Marseilles, Aix-en-Provence, France. From 1967 to 1978, she served as a professor in the department of government at Georgetown University. Dr. Kirkpatrick joined AEI in May 1977. She became the Leavey professor at Georgetown University in September 1978.

Dr. Kirkpatrick is the author of three books: "The New Presidential Elite," "Political Women," and "Leader and Vanguard in Mass Society: A Study of Peronist Argentina." She has written numerous articles for many publications and has lectured extensively. She was a member of the Democratic National Convention's National Commission on Party Structure and Presidential Nomination and serves on the editorial boards of Regulation and of Public Opinion. She is a member of the executive council of the International Political Science Program and, from 1974 to 1976, served as a member of the Southern Political Science Association Committee on the Status of Women.

Dr. Kirkpatrick has received many awards and honors, including an honorary degree of Doctor of Humane Letters from Mt. Vernon College and the Distinguished Alumnae Award from Stephens College.

She is married and has three children.

Nomination of David A. Stockman To Be Director of the Office of Management and Budget
January 20, 1981

The President today nominated David Alan Stockman, of St. Joseph, Mich., to be the Director of the Office of Management and Budget and to be a member of the President's Cabinet.

Mr. Stockman is the United States Representative from the Fourth Congressional District of Michigan.

Mr. Stockman was born on November 10, 1946. He was graduated cum laude from Michigan State University in 1968 with a degree in U.S. history.

He served on the staff of Representative John Anderson as a special assistant from 1970 to 1972. In 1972 he was named executive director of the House Republican Conference Committee.

In 1976 Mr. Stockman was elected to the House of Representatives. He served on the Interstate and Foreign Commerce Committee and was a member of two of its subcommittees: Energy and Power, and Health and Environment. He also served on the House Administration Committee. Since 1977 Mr. Stockman has served as chairman of the Republican Economic Policy Task Force and is a member of the National Commission on Air Quality.

Nomination of William J. Casey To Be Director of Central Intelligence
January 20, 1981

The President today nominated William J. Casey, of Roslyn Harbor, N.Y., to be Director of Central Intelligence and to be a member of the President's Cabinet.

Mr. Casey was chairman of the executive committee of the Office of the President-elect, chairman of the Interim Foreign Policy Advisory Board, and a member of the Transition Appointments Committee. He is counsel to the law firm of Rogers & Wells of New York and Washington.

Born March 13, 1913, Mr. Casey attended Fordham University where he received his undergraduate and LL.B. degrees.

During World War II, Mr. Casey served as an aide to William B. Donovan in the Washington headquarters of the Office of Strategic Services, as Chief at OSS London headquarters, and as chief of secret intelli-gence for General Eisenhower's theater of war.

From April 1971 to January 1976, Mr. Casey served as President and Chairman of the Export-Import Bank of the United States, Under Secretary of State for Economic Affairs, and Chairman of the Securities and Exchange Commission. From 1969 to 1977, he served on a number of Presidential commissions, including the President's Foreign Intelligence Advisory Board, the Commission on Organization for the Conduct of Foreign Policy, the General Advisory Committee on Arms Control, and the Presidential Task Force on International Development.

Mr. Casey is a director of Capital Cities Communications, Long Island Lighting Co., and Long Island Trust Co., and chairman of the executive committee of the International Rescue Committee, and cochairman of the Citizen's Commission on Indo-Chinese Refugees.

Mr. Casey is married to the former Sophia Kurz, and they have a daughter, Bernadette.

Nomination of William E. Brock To Be United States Trade Representative
January 20, 1981

The President today nominated William E. Brock to be United States Trade Representative. Mr. Brock will be a member of the Cabinet, and he will report to the President.

Since 1977 Mr. Brock has been chairman of the Republican National Committee. From 1970 to 1977, he served as United States Senator from Tennessee, and from 1962 to 1970, he represented the Third Congressional District of Tennessee in the United States House of Representatives.

Mr. Brock was born in Chattanooga, Tenn., on November 23, 1930. He attended Washington and Lee University, where he earned a B.S. in 1953. Following his service as an officer in the United States Navy, Mr. Brock became associated with the Brock Candy Co. as a marketing executive.

He was elected to the Congress in 1962 and throughout his service was active in Republican Party building efforts, serving as head of the National Young Voters Programs in 1972. In 1974 Mr. Brock was selected to head the Republican Senatorial Campaign Committee.

Mr. Brock is married to the former Laura (Muffet) Handly, and they have four children: Bill, Oscar, Hutchey, and John.

Toast at the Inaugural Luncheon
January 20, 1981

Senator Mark Hatfield, Speaker O'Neill, the others here who are hosting this very beautiful luncheon:

I'm going to take the liberty of speaking for my partner, George, for Barbara and Nancy, in responding to this toast.

Twice this morning, in the ceremony, was mentioned the fact of the unusualness in this world of what has taken place here today, the orderly transfer, the continuity of government that has gone on, and that, I think, is the envy of the world.

Now, there's even more of unity represented here today. The crystalware Speaker Tip O'Neill graciously provided from the House side. The plates have come from the Senate. The wine is from California, but I didn't have a thing to do with that. [*Laughter*] It just turned out that way.

But I would like to drink to the idea that this great system that sometimes puts us in adversary relationships—and perhaps sometimes unnecessarily so—but was based on checks and balances to ensure that we do what is right for the people, that that kind of cooperation will continue. I'm delighted to be a guest here in the House of the Congress, and I look forward to coming back. I look forward to you being guests with us. I look forward to working with you on behalf of the people and that this partnership will continue.

And now, to conclude the toast, with thanks to Almighty God, I have been given a tag-line, the get-off line that everyone wants for the end of a toast or a speech or anything else. Some 30 minutes ago, the planes bearing our prisoners left Iranian airspace and are now free of Iran.

So, we can all drink to this one: To all of us, together, doing what we all know we can do to make this country what it should be, what it can be, what it always has been.

Thank you all.

Note: The President spoke at 2:15 p.m. in Statuary Hall at the Capitol.

Exchange With Reporters on the Release of the American Hostages in Iran
January 20, 1981

The President. One of the last official acts the President [Jimmy Carter] did, and which I am privileged to implement, is to restring the tree [National Community Christmas Tree]. And even though the holiday is over, the Christmas lights are going to be turned on.

Q. When?

The President. Just as soon as the word can get to them, for this evening. It's evening already. I think it's dark enough. They could be turned on. They've been waiting for quite——

Q. How do you feel about that and the fact that they're coming home?

The President. Oh, more pleased than anything I can say. It just was needed to make the day perfect.

They've had the refueling in Athens, which should put them by now on their way to Algiers. And whether they try and start immediately for Germany or not, that

I don't know. But they will switch to American planes in Algiers.

The President will be taking Air Force One, I believe early in the morning.

When we were watching the parade—well, at first, at lunch I learned that both planes had taken off and were in the air. And then I learned here, while we were watching the parade, that they had crossed the border and were out of Iranian airspace. And the next word I got, before the parade was over, was that they were refueling in Athens. The flight from there to Algiers is about 2½ hours.

Note: At approximately 5:20 p.m., members of the press went to the Oval Office at the White House for a photo session with the President. The remarks printed above are excerpted from the White House transcript of the President's exchange with reporters during the photo session.

Remarks at the Inaugural Balls
January 20, 1981

Capital Hilton Hotel (8:40 p.m.)

Hello, veterans and your ladies, and thank you for allowing Nancy and me to interrupt your evening here for just a few minutes. [*Laughter*] Well, it is for only a few minutes, because I understand, on the logistics they've gotten for our schedule tonight, that if we get in and out of each one of the parties in 10 minutes, it will only take us 4½ hours. [*Laughter*] But this is number one, and in more ways than one.

I've been told that you are honoring here tonight, as well any of us should, our Congressional Medal of Honor winners. And when I think of them, I remember a story I read once, and it was actually a novel, written by James Warner Bella, who used to write those great cavalry-Indian pictures that John Ford and John Wayne would do. [*Laughter*] He was called the Kipling of America for writing of that great era in American history.

17

But I remembered in this one story he had troops, a cavalry detachment out, a war party, and so forth. And the commanding officer fell mortally wounded, and he called the next in command over, who was to take over. And the lines I've never forgotten. He said to him as he was dying, "There may be only one time, one moment in your life when you will be called upon to do the nasty thing that has to be done, when you are the only one that can serve your country in that moment." He said, "Do it or the taste will be forever ashes in your mouth."

The men you honor tonight have no taste of ashes in their mouths. And [it is] because there were men and there are men today in this land of ours who are willing to do that thing that only they are in a position to do that we're able to meet as we meet tonight, we're able to have a day in which we continue 200 years of an orderly exchange of leadership and reigns of authority in our Government without military overthrow or force or violence, that we're able to still breathe free. And God help us, that must always remain.

When Alexander Haig, in the hearing the other day before the Senate committee said, and said with no uncertainty, "There are things for which we must be willing to fight," I think you're—[*applause*].

Thank you very much. Thank you.

Mayflower Hotel (8:50 p.m.)

Well, Nancy and I are delighted to be here, even if it is only for a few minutes, because, as you know, we're traveling the whole circuit and trying to get to all of them tonight. But we've looked forward to this one, because all during the months of the campaign, I was so thrilled and excited to see so many of you at the various campaign meetings, at the events that our party was putting on. It has not always been thus. But you, the young people, were there and were there in strength, and I think because, in the wisdom that comes with youth, you also recognized that it was time for a change and that we've got to go in a different direction. [*Applause*]

You are going to take turns at dancing, aren't you? [*Laughter*]

But, more than that, you know, there is a first this time in this inaugural. Maybe you

know about it; maybe you don't. But it was an idea—one of the cochairmen, maybe both of them, Bob Gray and—Charlie Wick—I knew the name; I was trying to swallow. [*Laughter*]

But that first inaugural, not quite 200 years ago, people came by stagecoach. This time people are actually attending it by satellite, because while there are 10 such balls here in Washington tonight—and Nancy and I are going to get to every one of them; they've given us 10 minutes in and out for each one—in somewhere in the neighborhood of 100 cities in the United States, by satellite they, too, are having inaugural balls in which the screens will be carrying what is happening in the balls here in Washington. And all the proceeds from those balls will go to their own particular local charities.

Nancy and I thank you very much for all that you've done in the months past and thank you for being here tonight, for making this such a wonderful occasion. Thank you very much. Thank you.

I'll have one get-off line. I don't know how long you've been here or how much you've been caught up on something. But if you haven't been out, you will find that the lights on the Christmas tree are now lighted.

Washington Hilton Hotel (9:15 p.m.)

The President. Ladies and gentlemen, Nancy, my Mike, his wife, Colleen:

We're delighted to be here. I know that it can only be for a few minutes, because there are 10 of these, and we're going to get to all of them. And the fellows that are engineering getting us around say it's only going to take 4½ hours. [*Laughter*] We're delighted to be here, and thank all of you for your being here.

I think you might like to have a little news bulletin. I have just learned that the planes have landed in Algiers. Fifty-two—and I just won't call them hostages; they were prisoners of war—but they are all hale and hearty and are now, and you can imagine their happiness, they're preparing to board the American planes for the last leg of the trip to Wiesbaden. So, I thought you'd like to hear that.

You know, thanks to Bob Gray, who introduced me here, and to Charlie Wick, the two of them as cochairmen of this inaugural, you agree that it's been a pretty fine inaugural so far? [*Cheers*] I think it's been wonderful right down to those beautiful fireworks tonight that I hope you saw. And, incidentally, the Christmas tree lights have gone on.

But almost 200 years ago at the first inaugural, people came by stagecoach. This time people all over America, millions of people, are attending this one by satellite, because in addition to these 10 balls here in Washington, there are in the neighborhood of 100 going on in various cities throughout the United States, and they are receiving, participating in these balls by large-screen television, that is being bounced off the satellite to them. And in each one of those cities, all of the proceeds are going to the charity of the choice of that community, in their own community, going to charity.

So, again, I know we have to move on. But Nancy and I again just want to thank you from the bottom of our hearts. This has been a wonderful day. Thank you very much. Thank you.

Audience. Mrs. Reagan!

Mrs. Reagan. Thank you. No, they just wanted me——

The President. They've got you saying something?

Mrs. Reagan. No, with them calling me to come up here.

The President. Oh, well, I'm glad you did. Thank you very much.

I have finally decided I'm not going to wake up. It isn't a dream. [*Laughter*] It really happened.

But again, God bless you all. Thank you very much.

Sheraton-Washington Hotel (9:42 p.m.)

The President. Well, ladies and gentlemen, thank you so very much, not only for that warm greeting but thank you also for being here, for being a part of what I think has been a very wonderful few days, thanks to the work of Bob Gray and Charlie Wick as cochairmen of this inaugural.

You have had a good time, haven't you? [*Cheers*] I was going to say I'd be sorry if you didn't, because Nancy and I have been enjoying it. [*Laughter*]

Audience [*chanting*]. Four more years! [*Laughter*]

The President. The wonderful entertainers who have donated their services to be here tonight, Ray Charles, all the others that are here—I know that if I start on names—I know that Wayne Newton is one. And I'm so grateful to him, because Wayne, throughout the whole campaign, was just constantly working in our behalf.

But could I, since they tell me that I don't have much time—we're on the circuit. We're getting to all 10 of these, and they have worked it out and told us that it's only going to take us 4½ hours—[*laughter*]—if we don't talk too long here.

But I thought maybe that we could give you a little update on the news, because, being here, you probably haven't had that. The latest word we have is that our Americans—and I never have felt comfortable calling them hostages; they are prisoners of war—all 52 of them, hale and hearty, have landed in Algeria and are preparing to board the American planes that will take them to Germany.

[*To Mrs. Reagan*] You look lovely, nice.

But one other bit of news; perhaps you're familiar with this. You know, that first inaugural almost 200 years ago, people arrived by horseback and stagecoach. Tonight all over America, there are Americans that are at the inaugural by satellite, because in addition to these 10 balls here in Washington, there are probably in the neighborhood of a hundred in that many different cities all over America who are a part of this by closed-circuit television, participating in these. And the proceeds from those are going to the charities of those local communities as named by the communities themselves. So, we're doing some good with that.

I think we've taken our quota of time here again, but——

Audience. No!

The President. Well, no, there are more to go. There's wonderful entertainment, and I know there's wonderful music for all of you. And Nancy and I, the music has been in our hearts. So, we'll get back on the road.

Viva, olé. You're singing our song.

If what I said this morning, and I feel even more like it tonight when I look out here at all of you, there isn't anything we can't do, and together we're going to do it.

Thank you very much. God bless you. Thank you.

Shoreham Hotel (10:14 p.m.)

The President. Our host and hostess, to Mrs. Shipley, and I know that you've met our son and Doria, his wife, earlier, Charlie and Mrs. Wick:

You know, I have to open this not only by thanking all of you for being here, for all that you've done and to make this such a wonderful time and then for those—to Bob Gray and Charlie Wick, who is cochairman, really put together what I think has been a very wonderful and enjoyable inaugural several days. I said several days; because it really has been going on, and it's been a wonderful thing.

I'm grateful to all the entertainers who are here, Bob Stack and all of them who are working so hard. I'm not going to try names, or I'll miss someone. And they have donated their services. They helped during the campaign, all of them. And we're grateful to them.

I thought that maybe I could just give you a little bit of a news item. Since you've been in here, you might not have heard this, known this. The latest word is—and as I said in the places we've visited already tonight, I refuse to call them hostages; they're prisoners of war—the last word I had, in Algeria they have deplaned from the Algerian planes, and they are preparing to get into the American planes, 52 of them, all of them hale and hearty, all of them just fine.

Now, we don't have very much time here, because they have us on the circuit. And they've told us that if we move right along that we can get to every ball, and it'll only take 4½ hours. [*Laughter*] So, we're delighted to—this is number five.

Someone just said that Nancy's beautiful, and I agree with him. They want to hear from you. I think it's a command performance.

Mrs. Reagan. Well, thank you. I've left this to my husband all along, so you've surprised me. But thank you all for coming. And we're delighted to see you, and we hope that you're having as good a time as we're having. Thank you for everything you've done for us in the past, and we appreciate it, and we never would be here without you. And we love you all.

The President. Let me just conclude, because I know they're signaling that we have to move on. But let me just tell you this one thing, and this, again, is due to the people, our two cochairmen there, their plan, something unusual that's never happened before.

The people who came to the first inaugural almost 200 years ago, of course, did so on horseback and stagecoach. Today all over America, there are people that are attending this inaugural by satellite, because in addition to the 10 balls here in Washington, there are in the neighborhood of a hundred in cities all over the United States who are attending these balls by closed-circuit television, by satellite. And all of the money that they have raised in those towns for those balls is going to a local charity in each one of those communities.

And having said that, I'd just add as a postscript to what I said this morning. When I look at you—and you're much closer—[*laughter*]—and I can see you better than I could this morning—but I am more than ever convinced we don't have a thing to worry about, not the American people, because between all of us, between us, we're going to straighten things out, and we're going to take the high road.

Thank you.

John F. Kennedy Center for the Performing Arts (10:40 p.m.)

Well, ladies and gentlemen, thank you all very much for being here.

And first of all, I think you will agree with me that our cochairmen of the inaugural, Charles Wick, Bob Gray, have done a magnificent job. And the people here, your host, Ed McMahon, the entertainers that are here, and this gentleman at my left—your name again—[*laughter*]—the great golfing friend—but all of you, there's no way to thank you for being here, for what you've done, and what you mean in all of this.

And I thought maybe to have something to say I could, in the little bit of time that is allotted us here, bring you up to date on a news bulletin that I know you're interested in. The latest report that I have received is that our—and I refuse to call them hostages—our prisoners of war have landed some time ago in Algeria and in the last bulletin were preparing to board the American planes that will take them to Wiesbaden, Germany. The other part of the report was that there are 52 of them, and they're all sound, hale, and hearty.

But now, I don't know whether you were aware of this or not, but there are others attending this ball and the others that are being held here in Washington, 10 in all. In that first inaugural almost 200 years ago, the people, the Americans went to that by horseback and stagecoach. Today all over America and even abroad, in Paris, France, Americans are attending these balls, dancing to the same music that you're hearing here, because they're going to them by satellite, by closed-circuit satellite.

Somewhere in the neighborhood of 100 cities, Paris, France, and here in the United States, these other cities are holding balls. They are connected, large-screen, closed-circuit television bounced off the satellite, hearing the same music. And in this particular moment that I'm speaking, I know that I am speaking also to them. We haven't hit on them at the same time or the right time at any of the other places we've been to tonight, but on this particular occasion.

So, I can say to all of them, to all of you who were there in Paris, France, in all those other cities in America, God bless all of you. And thank you for what you're doing, because in those cities, the proceeds are going to the local charities of those communities where the balls are being held.

[*To Mrs. Reagan*] You look very pretty tonight. I think she looks gorgeous, as a matter of fact. On the way over someone said, well, when we got here, we might even have a minute or two to dance, and I don't think so. Well, they've got us in public housing, and we'll dance when we get the heck there.

But, again, this morning was one thing, but you were all so far away. Tonight you're up close, and I can see you. And this is the sixth of the balls that we've attended. We have four more to go after this. But I want you to know, in looking at you and seeing you, I've never been more certain in my life that the things we want for America, the things that need doing for America, between us, we're going to get them done.

Thank you very much. Thank you.

Pension Building (11:09 p.m.)

Ladies and gentlemen, I don't think I have to tell you that Bob Gray, who just introduced me, Charlie Wick, his lovely lady, the cochairman of the whole inaugural ceremony and all of the events that have taken place, what a job they've done and what a several days they have given us in this inaugural.

And our host and hostess at this ball, Joe and Holly Coors, and the wonderful entertainers, the music, and the entertainers who have given of their services to be here and make these events successful, and especially all of you for being here and what you've contributed and what you've done to make this a success—we're very grateful.

I have been now—this is number seven. [*Laughter*] They tell us, by the time we get through, we'll only have spent 4½ hours doing this. But it's been great to see all of you and to see all of you up close.

And I've been trying to bring at the least the latest news bulletin that I have, and that is that our—and I've been refusing to call them hostages—our prisoners of war have been now for some time in Algiers. They have deplaned. And our last bulletin—and that was some time ago—was that they, 52 of them, healthy and sound, were getting ready to embark in the American planes for Wiesbaden, Germany.

You've been in here, so I don't know whether you've been outside to see that that Christmas tree, which for two Christmases has not been lighted, the lights are on tonight.

Now, your ball here is characterized by something else, also, and I want to pay recognition that the diplomatic corps, all the countries stationed here, Washington, D.C., are present at this ball. And I want to bid them welcome, look forward to a meeting with them in the days shortly ahead.

Now, there's something else about tonight that's kind of special. You're here in this inaugural ball. There are 10 of them going on in Washington, D.C. There was one, I guess, almost 200 years ago, when our first President was inaugurated, and at that time the people came by horseback and stagecoach. Tonight there are 10 in Washington, but there is one in Paris, and there are in the neighborhood of 100 in that many different cities throughout the United States who are attending these inaugural balls by satellite, not stagecoach. They are hearing the same music. They are seeing this on large-screen television. It is being bounced off a satellite and carried to them—a portion of each one of the balls that is going on here in Washington— hearing the same music and all.

And in those communities, the proceeds are going to the local charities of those communities in which they're being held. May I say, there's a certain amount of symbolism in that. That's the first step in seeing that some people are being able to keep their money in their own community. We'll see if we can't do more of that.

But they've told us that we only have a few minutes to interrupt, and I know that you have great entertainment in store for you. [*Shouting from audience*] I didn't hear what he said. [*Shouting from audience*] Well, I can't. We've got four more to go before we get back to our public housing. [*Laughter*]

So, I said earlier, it's so wonderful to see you up close, because this morning you were all quite a distance away. But seeing you up close just makes me believe my own words, spoken this morning, more than ever: Together, we're going to do what has to be done. I know that you can do it.

Thank you very much. Thank you.

[*At this point, the President and the First Lady danced.*]

That's our first dance at one of these inaugural balls.

National Air and Space Museum (11:33 p.m.)

Charles Wick and his lovely wife, Mary Jane, and Bob Gray, the cochairmen of this whole inaugural from the first event several days ago, right on up and through tonight, I think have done a magnificent job, and lovely Liz Taylor, Senator John Warner, her husband, Senator and Mrs. Jepsen of Iowa, and you, ladies and gentlemen:

We're so happy to be here. You're number seven so far—no, number eight, and they tell us that by the time we complete the circuit, it will have taken about 4 hours and a half.

But now, speaking of time, I have been figuring that I could take advantage of these meetings to give you a little update on the news. I think you'll be happy to know—and all evening I've been refusing to call them hostages; I refer to them as prisoners of war—but you'll be happy to know that they're in the American planes and roughly only an hour and a half away from touchdown in Wiesbaden, Germany.

And maybe you've been in here, and so you haven't noticed that that tree in Washington that hasn't been lighted for 2 years, the lights are on now.

But this is so wonderful to see all of you and to have a chance to thank you.

There is another thing that unusual, thanks to these chairmen that I have just spoken of and how hard they have worked on all of this inaugural. Almost 200 years ago there was an inauguration of the first President of the United States, and the people who came to that one inaugural ball and that inaugural ceremony came on horseback or by stagecoach. Tonight there are people all over America who are attending these balls by satellite, including in Paris, even—Americans there by closed-circuit, big-screen television. In somewhere near a hundred cities, there are people who are dancing to and hearing the same music that you are listening to, that are joining you and seeing all of you on that screen. The program is taking turns dropping in at each of the separate balls that are being held here and in each of those communities.

The proceeds are going to the charities that they have chosen in their own communities that they should go to. And I think there's something kind of symbolic in that. Here we are on the first night, and there are communities that are keeping their money at home. We're going to do our best to see that the idea catches on.

But I know we only have a few moments, because as I told you, we're on quite a circuit. But this morning it wasn't too easy to see you; you were quite a distance away. It's wonderful to be able to see you up close, because you reinforce my own belief in my own words more and more as I see you here, that together, we're going to do the things that have to be done. We're going to have a new beginning.

Thank you all very much, and God bless you. Thank you.

Museum of Natural History (11:47 p.m.)

Ladies and gentlemen, Bob Gray, just introducing me there, and with him Charles Wick. They are the cochairmen who have been working for months and months and put together what I think has been one of the most wonderful several days of inaugural parties and affairs that we've ever seen. I'm so grateful to the entertainers who have donated their services, to Hugh O'Brien and Carol Lawrence, Johnny "Scat" Davis, the others who are here, the music that we've been hearing, and seeing all of you.

And I want to thank all of you, because you, of course, without you there wouldn't be this successful inaugural. And thank you very much.

I've been trying to keep people apprised a little bit of one of the news bulletins that I think is of interest to all of us. And the latest word is, and I'm sure you'll be happy to know—I have been refusing all evening or before that to refer to them as hostages; they're prisoners of war. Well, these POW's are only minutes away from landing in Wiesbaden, Germany. I don't know whether you've been outside or not to see this, but that tree that hasn't been lighted for two Christmases is lighted tonight.

Well, it's wonderful to see you. And speaking of these gentlemen who put this together, this whole inaugural, I think it's kind of interesting and, in fact, it's exciting

and thrilling that once upon a time, almost 200 years ago at the first inaugural, the people arrived by horseback or stagecoach for the inauguration ceremony and the inaugural ball. Tonight all over the United States and even in Paris, Americans there are attending these balls by satellite. It's the first time it's ever been done. But they are holding balls somewhere in the neighborhood of a hundred cities—and large-screen television—they are participating in these balls. They are hearing the music that you are hearing. A portion of their total ball is coming from each one of the 10 balls that are being held here in Washington.

And what I think you'd like to know is that the proceeds in those balls is going to the local charities designated by the local people as to where they want the money to go in their community. And I like to think there's a little symbolism in that, that those communities are starting already on this first day to keep their money at home. We're going to see if we can't make that catch on a little.

This morning you were all so far away. Now you're up close, and I can see you. And I know we have to move on, because we have others that we've got to get to. But seeing you up close just reinforces my faith and belief in what I said this morning, that together, you bet we're going to do the job. We're going to solve these problems and have a new beginning.

God bless you, and thank you very much. Thank you.

Museum of American History (12:04 a.m.)

Ladies and gentlemen, I just have been touring all these balls tonight. I can't help but each time call attention to the fact that Charles Wick, his lovely wife, Mary Jane, Bob Gray, all of them, they have been the cochairmen of this whole inaugural program, every phase of it. And what they have done I think is most remarkable. And I'm deeply indebted to them, and I'm sure we all are. And my thanks to Hugh O'Brien, to Pat Boone, to Carol Lawrence, to all the other entertainers who've entertained here to the lovely music.

And I've tried as the evening has gone on and now—well, we started out last night to tour the balls, and now here we are this morning, here with yours. But I have tried to bring at least in my remarks a little update of a bulletin that I'm sure is of interest to all of us. And so, the last bulletin I can give tonight to you here is that—I don't call them hostages; I call them prisoners of war—earlier this evening I was able to announce that they had landed in Algeria and were preparing to board the American planes to go on to Germany. And I am happy to say now that they are only minutes away from landing in Wiesbaden, Germany.

How are you? Good to see you. My cousins from back in Illinois are all down there. Eureka?

Listen. Let me just go on and say, though, that it's wonderful—this morning you were all so far away. It's wonderful now to see you up close. And we've, as I say, we've been touring all of the balls here this evening. And there's somehting unusual about this inaugural, that, thanks to those chairmen I spoke about, that has never taken place before. In the first inaugural almost 200 years ago, the people who went to that went on horseback or by stagecoach. Tonight there are people in somewhere near a hundred cities in our country and in Paris,

Americans there who are attending these balls. They are going by satellite—it has never been done before—by closed-circuit television, including all of the 10 balls that are on here. Various periods of time they switch from ball to ball, and those people have been dancing to the same music that you've been hearing here. They have been actually seeing you and enjoying the ball with you at each one of them.

And it's also, I think, kind of symbolic, I like to feel, well, even though it is the next day now, this inaugural day, it's kind of symbolic that the proceeds of all those balls will stay in those communities and be distributed to the charities that they have chosen to receive them. Anyway, I think that that's kind of a good symbol, that money staying at home, and I hope the idea is going to catch on.

Now, as I say, you're closer, and I can see you. And I am just more convinced in my own mind of the truth of what I said this morning. When I see all of you, there isn't anything that's going to stop all of us together from doing what has to be done in this country. We're going to do it.

God bless you all, and thank you. Thank you very much.

Do you mind if I have the last dance with my lady?

Letter to the Speaker of the House and the President Pro Tempore of the Senate on the Inspector General Appointees of Certain Executive Agencies
January 20, 1981

Re: Notification Pursuant to Public Law 95–452 as Amended by Public Law 96–88 ("The Inspector General Act of 1978")

Dear Mr. Speaker: (Dear Mr. President:)

This is to advise the Senate that I have today exercised my power as President to remove from office the current appointees to the position of Inspector General in the following departments and agencies:

1. Department of Agriculture
2. Department of Commerce
3. Department of Education
4. Department of Housing and Urban Development
5. Department of the Interior
6. Department of Transportation
7. Community Services Administration
8. Environmental Protection Agency
9. General Services Administration
10. National Aeronautics and Space Administration
11. Small Business Administration
12. Veterans Administration

Some of these individuals may be involved in investigations which would be aided by some continued association with their offices. We will want to review these situations to consider asking such individuals to continue their participation on an appropriate basis.

Uncovering fraud, waste and mismanagement of federal funds as well as the promotion of economy, efficiency and effectiveness in the administration of federal programs and operations will be an important priority in my Administration. The Inspectors General will have critical roles in the achievement of this objective. As is the case with all positions where I, as President, have the power of appointment by and with the advice and consent of the Senate, it is vital that I have the fullest confidence in the ability, integrity and commitment of each appointee to the position of Inspector General.

I will be submitting to the Senate in the near future my nomination of an individual for each of these positions who has my confidence and who meets the appropriate qualifications. If any of these individuals wishes to be considered for reappointment, they may indicate their interest and they will be judged in competition with other applicants.

Sincerely,

RONALD REAGAN

Note: This is the text of identical letters addressed to Thomas P. O'Neill, Jr., Speaker of the House of Representatives, and Strom Thurmond, President pro tempore of the Senate.

The letter was announced by the Office of the Press Secretary on January 21.

Letter to the Speaker of the House and the President Pro Tempore of the Senate on the Inspector General Appointees of the Department of Energy
January 20, 1981

Re: Notification Pursuant to Public Law 95–91

Dear Mr. Speaker: (Dear Mr. President:)

This is to advise the House of Representatives that I have today exercised my power as President to remove from office the current appointees to the position of Inspector General and Deputy Inspector General for the Department of Energy. The removed appointees may be involved in investigations which would be aided by some continued association with their offices. We will want to review these situations to consider asking them to continue their participation on an appropriate basis.

Uncovering fraud, waste and mismanagement of federal funds as well as the promotion of economy, efficiency and effectiveness in the administration of federal programs and operations will be an important priority in my Administration. The Inspector General and Deputy Inspector General of the Department of Energy will have

critical roles in the achievement of this objective. As is the case with regard to all positions where I, as President, have the power of appointment by and with the advice and consent of the Senate, it is vital that I have the fullest confidence in the ability, integrity and commitment of the appointees to the position of Inspector General and Deputy Inspector General of the Department of Energy.

I will be submitting to the Senate in the near future my nomination of an individual for each of these positions who has my confidence and who meets the appropriate qualifications. If these individuals wish to be considered for reappointment, they may indicate their interest and they will be judged in competition with other applicants.

Sincerely,

RONALD REAGAN

Note: This is the text of identical letters addressed to Thomas P. O'Neill, Jr., Speaker of the House of Representatives, and Strom Thurmond, President pro tempore of the Senate.

The letter was announced by the Office of the Press Secretary on January 21.

Letter to the Speaker of the House and the President Pro Tempore of the Senate on the Inspector General Appointee of the Department of Health and Human Services
January 20, 1981

Re: Notification Pursuant to Public Law 94–505

Dear Mr. Speaker: (Dear Mr. President:)

This is to advise the Senate that I have today exercised my power as President to remove from office the current appointee to the position of Deputy Inspector General (Acting Inspector General) for the Department of Health And Human Services. The removed appointee may be involved in investigations which would be aided by some continued association with his office. We will want to review these situations to consider asking him to continue his participation on an appropriate basis.

Uncovering fraud, waste and mismanagement of federal funds as well as the promotion of economy, efficiency and effectiveness in the administration of federal programs and operations will be an important priority in my Administration. The Deputy Inspector General for the Department of Health and Human Services will have a critical role in the achievement of this objective. As is the case with regard to all positions where I, as President, have the power of appointment by and with the advice and consent of the Senate, it is vital that I have the fullest confidence in the ability, integrity and commitment of the appointee to the position of Deputy Inspector General for the Department of Health and Human Services.

I will be submitting to the Senate in the near future my nomination of an individual for this position who has my confidence and who meets the appropriate qualifications. If this individual wishes to be considered for reappointment, he may indicate his interest and he will be judged in competition with other applicants.

Sincerely,

RONALD REAGAN

Note: This is the text of identical letters addressed to Thomas P. O'Neill, Jr., Speaker of the House of Representatives, and Strom Thurmond, President pro tempore of the Senate.

The text of the letter was released by the Office of the Press Secretary on January 21.

Remarks at the Swearing-In Ceremony for Members of the White House Staff
January 21, 1981

I want you to know that I don't expect every morning to be greeted by the Marine Band. [*Laughter*]

I've just come down from breakfast. I'm happy to see you all here. I see a lot of faces of staff. They're staff of the gubernatorial period in Sacramento, and some of the faces are from the 1976 campaign staff, some from the 1980 staff. But now I'm happy, and I hope that they all are; we see the faces of the White House staff.

And I spoke yesterday about what we

faced and what we had to do—the renewal of the American spirit. And I used a number of times the word "we," and I want to reemphasize that, because that's the only way I know how to do it. We are a team. We're going to act as a team.

Now, a word about loyalty. I've had reason to learn from almost everyone here on this staff their great capacity for personal loyalty where I'm concerned. I'm deeply grateful for that, but we have a new kind of loyalty now.

Our loyalty must be only to this Nation and to the people that we represent. I've often said the only people in Washington who represent all the people are those, basically, that are found here, because we're beholden to no district, beholden to no particular section or State. And that loyalty is going to be translated in the judgments we make.

Every judgment will be made on the basis that no one's going to be seeking office ever again. Now, I don't say that we won't seek office ever again, but the decisions will be made on what is good for the people, what is right as against what is wrong, and with no political consideration entering in or even being discussed. And I'm sure that I can count on everyone here to do that.

I'm delighted to see so many of the families and friends that are here, also, for this swearing-in ceremony. And now I'm going to step back from the microphone and let the ceremony take place.

Note: The President spoke at 9:27 a.m. in the East Room at the White House.

Following the President's remarks, Chief Justice of the United States Warren E. Burger swore in the members of the White House staff.

Opening Remarks at a Meeting With the Cabinet
January 21, 1981

We might as well start. We have an agenda before us, but we won't start on that for obvious reasons for a moment or two.

But in case no one has given you an update, President Carter and Mondale, Muskie, and the others he took with him are due to land in Germany within the hour to greet our returning POWs. All last night I got out of the habit of calling them hostages. I called them prisoners of war.

To get down to things without getting into the agenda here—incidentally, George [Bush] is going to have to leave us before we get too far into the agenda, because he's got an important assignment. He will take the gavel and preside over the Senate for the first time. So, he'll be leaving us in a few minutes here.

But yesterday, just as a reminder—I know we've talked of this before—but yesterday after the oath, I went in and signed the directive regarding the freeze on the hiring of Federal employees. And while there will

be, I know, rare and exceptional circumstances where some particular individual will have to be replaced, I urge all of you to stick with that, because—I think Don Regan would second this—we've got to get control of the budget. It's increased virtually a hundred billion dollars in the last year, and it is out of control. And this, I think, is an important step. Through attrition we can reduce the size of government very drastically.

So, we may not run this like a quarter mile, but we're going to run it, the race, and we're going to make some changes for no other reason than they have to be made. But people are waiting for us to do it, and we'll do it.

Now, they keep right on clicking there. [*Laughter*] The next thing in mind is the agenda, but I'm going to be stubborn. [*Laughter*]

Note: The President spoke at 10:22 a.m. in the Cabinet Room at the White House.

In his remarks, the President referred to members of the press, who were present during the remarks.

Memorandum Requesting the Resignation of Noncareer Federal Employees
January 21, 1981

Memorandum for the Heads of Departments and Agencies

As President, I take office with the commitment to the American people to begin anew and undertake basic changes in government. Accordingly, it is important that non-career appointees occupying policy-making and confidential positions be committed to achieving these goals.

Therefore, I request that all Department and Agency heads and other proper personnel, where appropriate and in coordination with the Office of Presidential Personnel, obtain the resignation of PAS's and PA's (Presidential appointment with Senate confirmation and Presidential appointments).

In addition, I ask all Department and Agency heads to obtain the offer of resignation from non-career SES's (Senior Executive Service), NEA's (Non-career Executive Assignment) for appropriate determination as to removal or retention. (This request is not made to heads of independent regulatory agencies.) It is our intention to accept most such offers of resignation.

Sensitivity to providing for ongoing Government functions and complying with appropriate laws and regulations is required in the acceptance of resignations of persons holding the positions specified in the above two paragraphs.

I wish to thank all those who will be leaving government for their services to our country and know that they will understand that this step in no way reflects upon them personally. The new Administration wishes them well.

RONALD REAGAN

Remarks at a White House Reception for the Presidential Inaugural Committee
January 21, 1981

Well—[*laughter*]—I don't care what Rich Little says. If you've got a stage wait, that'll fill it as good as anything.[1] [*Laughter*]

You know, yesterday morning I spoke a great deal about the spirit of the American people, that America will prevail because that spirit is strong. But for Nancy and me, there are some other very special people whose spirit has made the past few days the very best of our lives.

Charlie Wick and Bob Gray—why don't you step right up here right now. Charles. Bob. And I know that with them—and they'd be the first to say—hundreds and hundreds of helpers, many of you, gave of themselves to make the inaugural ceremonies outstanding.

I had a little batch of phone calls to make today, and a number of them were out of the country. And you might be interested to know that one of the Prime Ministers I spoke to said that their whole nation watched our inaugural, and they said the reaction was, there will never again be one like it. [*Laughter*] That is due to Charlie

---

[1] *The President was referring to comedian Rich Little, who had performed an impersonation of the President at a pre-Inaugural event.*

and Bob and their helpers. And Mary Jane, I think, was very much a part of Bob in all of that help, full time.

Now, as one who went to all the balls last night—[*laughter*]—I can attest to the fact that the guests who came to Washington, in addition to not finding any dancing room—[*laughter*]—or in spite of that, they were caught up, as we were, in a time of great happiness and expectation. And those things don't happen by accident. It takes people who are devoted; it takes creative people and patient people. And I know what all of you who worked on this went through in these past few weeks. I know the kind of responsibilities you had. I know the multiple problems that descended on these two who were in charge.

And let me say that there may have been many toasts raised recently, but whether we've got a glass in our hand or not, it is time to toast the inaugural committee for a job well done and for gratitude that is well deserved.

And again, I know that I would have the agreement of these chairmen back here when I say there is another group connected with this, perhaps not specifically of the committee, but they couldn't have done it without them. And that's the group that through their generosity made possible, with their resources as well as their time, to make January 20th a very special day.

And I want you to know that this morning—General, how are you? It's wonderful to see you here. General Bradley. God bless you.

And I want you to know that there wasn't a minute off. We finally got home last night after making the full round. And just like that little girl, that 9-year-old girl, with her letter, said, this morning I got up and went to the Oval Office and went to work. [*Laughter*] That's what she told me to do, and I did it. [*Laughter*]

Well, God bless you all. And now, enough of this. We're going to get down and mingle. [*Laughter*]

Note: The President spoke at 6:10 p.m. in the East Room at the White House.

Remarks on Signing a Memorandum Directing Reductions in Federal Spending
January 22, 1981

Two days ago I signed a Federal hiring freeze, which started the process of bringing the runaway budget under control, and today that process continues in the form of four definite actions that I am taking today. One is cutting down on government travel; two is cutting back on government consultants and expensive contract studies; three is stopping the procurement of certain items; and four is calling for Federal appointees to exercise restraint on expenditures in their offices.

And no single action alone, I know, will get our economy back on the road to full recovery, but we must begin. And as with every other economic action we take, it's essential that we follow through on our commitments. Thus, I view the implementation of these orders as critical. The American people are determined, I believe, to have actions on the economic problems that we face. They're going to find out that we're listening to them. We're equally determined to see through every essential step that is needed to restore our economy.

So now, those four points that I made, that's what I am signing here today.

Note: The President spoke at 11:54 a.m. in the Oval Office at the White House.

Memorandum Directing Reductions in Federal Spending
January 22, 1981

Memorandum for the Heads of Executive Departments and Agencies

Subject: Reducing Unnecessary Federal Spending

Coping with runaway deficits in the current and pending budgets is one of the most urgent tasks before us. Thus, today I am taking four steps that will help reduce unnecessary Federal spending.

Effective immediately I am directing that, to the extent permitted under law, each Executive Department and Agency:

—Cut obligations for travel by 15 percent from the amounts available for the remainder of this fiscal year.

—Cut obligations for consulting, management and professional services, and special contract studies and analyses by 5 percent from the amounts shown for 1981 in the budget transmitted to Congress on January 15. (The cutback in consulting services is to be in addition to cutbacks ordered by the Carter Administration and the Congress.)

—Stop, until further notice, procurement of furniture, office machines and other equipment, except military equipment and equipment needed to protect human life and property.

—Finally, I am directing that Members of the Cabinet and other appointees set an example by avoiding unnecessary expenditures in setting up their personal offices. Appointees are not to redecorate their offices. This directive does not preclude reasonable and necessary cleaning, painting, and maintenance, or structural changes essential to the efficient functioning of an office.

The Director of the Office of Management and Budget will issue detailed instructions for carrying out the first three actions listed above. I am delegating to him authority to grant exemptions in those few cases where exemptions are necessary to provide essential services.

As with the hiring freeze, I ask that this directive not detract from agency operations that directly affect the delivery of vital public services. Again, you should establish a clear hierarchy of needs within your agencies and assure that essential services are not interrupted.

These four actions, together with the freeze on hiring of Federal civilian employees announced on January 20, will help redeem our pledge to the American people of a government that lives within its means.

RONALD REAGAN

Remarks Announcing the Establishment of the Presidential Task Force on Regulatory Relief
January 22, 1981

Well, ladies and gentlemen, I have a statement here that I want to make.

The regulatory reform, as you know, we've been talking about for a long time is one of the keystones in our program to return the nation to prosperity and to set loose again the ingenuity and energy of the American people.

Government regulations impose an enormous burden on large and small businesses in America, discourage productivity, and

contribute substantially to our current economic woes. To cut away the thicket of irrational and senseless regulations requires careful study, close coordination between the agencies and bureaus in the Federal structure.

Therefore, I am announcing today my intention to establish a Presidential Task Force on Regulatory Relief, a task force that will review pending regulations, study past regulations with an eye toward revising them, and recommend appropriate legislative remedies.

I intend that this be more than just another Presidential task force that files a report and is soon forgotten. We're seeking real reform and tangible results. And accomplishing this will take a vigorous leader, talented administrator, and absolutely, no doubt, a superb diplomat. And that person is Vice President George Bush, who's agreed to serve as Chairman of this task force and to coordinate an interagency effort to end excessive regulation.

I've asked him to get back to me prompt-

ly with recommended members of the task force and a detailed plan for its operations. And our goal is going to be to see if we cannot reverse the trend of recent years and see at the end of the year a reduction in the number of pages in the *Federal Register* instead of an increase.

And now I'm not taking any questions, and I'm going to leave, and George will take your questions here. George.

Note: The President spoke at 1:01 p.m. to reporters assembled in the Briefing Room at the White House.

Message to the Freed American Hostages
January 22, 1981

Welcome to Freedom.

While we at home cannot begin to know the depth of your feelings, we want you to know of our profound respect for your professionalism and patriotism under the most demanding circumstances.

I want you to know of our deep personal commitment to your future and the importance I attach to your return and to the restoration of both your family and professional relationships.

Our most immediate concern is to ensure that you are quickly reunited with your

families and that you are once again able to enjoy the precious blessings of freedom.

As difficult as this experience has been for each of you, it contains lessons for us all. Please know that we are with each of you, and that this episode in our history will be ever with us as, together, we look to the future.

Ronald Reagan

Note: The text of the message was read to the freed Americans in Wiesbaden, Germany.

Nomination of John O. Marsh, Jr., To Be Secretary of the Army
January 23, 1981

The President today announced his intention to nominate John O. Marsh, Jr., as Secretary of the Army.

Mr. Marsh was leader of the national security group and legal adviser to the Department of Defense transition team.

He is a partner with the firm of Mays, Valentine, Davenport & Moore and served as a Member of the House of Representatives from 1962 to 1970. From 1974 to

1977, Mr. Marsh served as Counsellor to President Ford, with Cabinet rank. From February 1974 to August 1974, Mr. Marsh served as assistant to the Vice President. From 1973 to 1974, Mr. Marsh served as Assistant Secretary of Defense for Legislative Affairs.

Mr. Marsh entered the Army in 1944 and was selected for infantry O.C.S. at Fort Benning at 18; commissioned at 19. He served in the Army of the Occupation of Germany. During 1947 to 1951, he was an officer in the Army Reserve. In 1951 he joined the 116th Infantry Regiment of the Virginia National Guard. He retired in 1976 with the rank of lieutenant colonel.

He has been awarded the Department of Defense Distinguished Public Service Medal, the American Legion Distinguished Service Medal, and the National Guard Distinguished Service Award.

Mr. Marsh is a native of Virginia and graduated from Washington and Lee University in 1952 (LL.B.). He is 54.

Nomination of John F. Lehman, Jr., To Be Secretary of the Navy
January 23, 1981

The President today announced his intention to nominate John F. Lehman, Jr., as Secretary of the Navy.

Mr. Lehman is currently president of the Abingdon Corp.

During the 1980 Presidential campaign, he served as a Reagan defense and foreign policy adviser. From 1977 to 1980, he was chairman of the defense advisory committee to the Republican National Committee. From 1975 to 1977, he was Deputy Director of the U.S. Arms Control and Disarmament Agency. From 1974 to 1975, Mr. Lehman served as counsel and senior staff member to Dr. Henry Kissinger and the National Security Council. He was a staff member between 1969 and 1971. From 1967 to 1969, Mr. Lehman was a staff member to the Foreign Policy Research Institute at the University of Pennsylvania.

He was an officer in the U.S. Naval Reserve. Mr. Lehman graduated from St. Joseph's College in 1964 (B.S.), Cambridge University in 1967 (B.A. and M.A.), and the University of Pennsylvania in 1974 (M.A. and Ph. D.).

Mr. Lehman is married to the former Barbara Thornton Wieland, and they have two children. He is 38.

Nomination of Verne Orr To Be Secretary of the Air Force
January 23, 1981

The President today announced his intention to nominate Verne Orr as Secretary of the Air Force.

Mr. Orr is currently an adjunct professor, Graduate School of Public Administration at the University of Southern California, director of the Huntington Memorial Hospital and the Huntington Institute of Medical Research, and a regent at the University of California.

From 1967 to 1969, Mr. Orr was director of the California Department of Motor Vehicles, and in 1969 was director of the California Department of General Services. From 1970 to 1975, Mr. Orr was director of the California Department of Finance.

Mr. Orr served active duty in the U.S. Naval Reserve during World War II and received an honorable discharge in 1952, with the rank of lieutenant commander.

Mr. Orr received a B.A. degree from Pomona College in 1937 and an M.B.A. degree from Stanford University in 1939. He is married, with two children.

Nomination of William P. Clark to be Deputy Secretary of State
January 23, 1981

The President today announced his intention to nominate William P. Clark as Deputy Secretary of State.

Mr. Clark is currently an associate justice on the California State Supreme Court. He was appointed to the court by Governor Ronald Reagan in 1973.

From 1971 to 1973, Mr. Clark was an associate justice for the California Court of Appeals. Previously he served as a Judge for the Superior Court of California from 1969 to 1971.

From 1967 to 1969, Mr. Clark was chief of staff to Governor Reagan in Sacramento. He was responsible for the reorganization of the executive branch of State government. At that time he was also chairman of the Chile-California program, a three-way contract among AID, Chile, and California.

Mr. Clark dealt extensively with several departments of the Federal Government's executive branch as well as the congressional delegation from California.

From 1959 to 1969, he was senior partner with the law firm of Clark, Cole and Fairfield in Oxnard, Calif. Following World War II he served in the counterintelligence corps in Western Europe. He has traveled extensively in Western Europe and Mexico. His law practice included representing clients in and from Western Europe and Mexico. He has lectured on comparative law in Budapest and Salzburg.

Mr. Clark attended Stanford and Santa Clara Universities and Loyola Night Law School. He is a fourth generation Californian and is married to the former Joan Brauner. They have five children.

Nomination of R. T. McNamar To Be Deputy Secretary of the Treasury
January 23, 1981

The President announced today the nomination of R. T. McNamar as Deputy Secretary of the Treasury.

Mr. McNamar has been executive vice president of Beneficial Standard Corp. since 1977.

From 1973 to 1977, Mr. McNamar was Executive Director of the Federal Trade Commission, exercising executive and administrative supervision over all offices and bureaus.

Mr. McNamar was an internal management consultant to the Cost of Living Council from February 1973 to November 1973. From 1972 to 1973, he served as Director of the Office of Case Management and Analysis to the Pay Board. Previously, from 1966 to 1972, he was a management consultant with McKinsey & Company, Inc., located in San Francisco, Calif.

Mr. McNamar is a member of the American Bar Association and the California State Bar. He has authored several articles on economics. He is married to the former Mary Ann Lyons, and they have two children.

Nomination of Edward C. Schmults To Be Deputy Attorney General
January 23, 1981

The President announced today the nomination of Edward C. Schmults as Deputy Attorney General of the United States, Department of Justice.

Mr. Schmults is a partner of the New York law firm of White & Case. His practice involves corporate and securities law matters. He is admitted to the New York and District of Columbia Bars.

Mr. Schmults was Under Secretary of the Treasury from July 1974 to October 1975, and General Counsel from June 1973 to July 1974. Mr. Schmults received the Alexander Hamilton Award, the Treasury's highest award.

From October 1975 to January 1977, he was Deputy Counsel to the President of the United States. As Cochairman of the Domestic Council Review Group on Regulatory Reform, Mr. Schmults was responsible at the White House for the development of President Ford's regulatory reform program.

In addition to his regular responsibilities at the Treasury Department, Mr. Schmults also served as a Director of the Securities Investors Protection Corporation, the Executive Director and General Counsel of the Energy Loan Guarantee Board, a Director of the United States Railway Association, and a Director of the Federal Financing Bank.

Mr. Schmults is a member of the Council of the Administrative Conference of the United States, having been appointed by President Ford in January 1977.

Mr. Schmults, 49, was born in Patterson, N.J. He received a bachelor of science degree from Yale University in 1953 and a bachelor of laws degree from Harvard Law School in 1958. After graduation from law school, he joined White & Case, and became a partner in July 1965. He was with the firm until his government service began in 1973.

He is married to the former Diane Beers, and they have three children.

Nomination of Richard E. Lyng To Be Deputy Secretary of Agriculture
January 23, 1981

The President announced today the nomination of Richard E. Lyng as Deputy Secretary of the Department of Agriculture.

Mr. Lyng has served as a consultant on food and agriculture since December 1979. From July 1973 to November 1979, he was president of the American Meat Institute, serving as chief executive officer representing meatpackers and meat processors.

From February 1969 to February 1973, Mr. Lyng was Assistant Secretary of the Department of Agriculture, responsible for marketing and consumer activities, including all USDA regulatory, animal and plant protection, and food agencies.

Mr. Lyng was director of the California State Department of Agriculture from February 1967 to February 1979. He has held directorships with the Tri/Valley Growers from 1975 to present, the Chicago Mercantile Exchange from 1975 to 1979, the Agribusiness Advisory Board from 1974 to present, the Commodity Credit Corporation from 1969 to 1973, and the USDA Graduate School from 1970 to 1973.

He was born on June 29, 1918, in San Francisco, Calif., and is married to the former Bethyl Ball and has two children.

Nomination of Murray L. Weidenbaum To Be a Member of the Council of Economic Advisers, and Designation as Chairman
January 23, 1981

The President today announced his intention to nominate Murray L. Weidenbaum as a member of the Council of Economic Advisers. Upon confirmation by the Senate, the President also intends to designate Mr. Weidenbaum as Chairman of the Council.

Mr. Weidenbaum is director of the Center for the Study of American Business and Mallinckrodt Distinguished University professor at Washington University in St. Louis, Mo. He has been a member of the faculty since 1964 and was chairman of the department of economics from 1966 to 1969.

From 1969 to 1971, Mr. Weidenbaum served as Assistant Secretary of the Treasury for Economic Policy. From 1963 to 1964, he was a senior economist at the Stanford Research Institute. From 1958 to 1963, Mr. Weidenbaum was a corporate economist with the Boeing Co. He was an economist with the U.S. Bureau of the Budget from 1949 to 1957.

His professional activities include serving as adjunct scholar for the American Enterprise Institute for Public Policy Research and a member of the board of directors of the American Council for Capital Formation.

Mr. Weidenbaum received his M.A. from Columbia University in 1949 and his Ph. D. at Princeton University in 1958.

Mr. Weidenbaum is the author of many books and articles on economics.

Remarks Announcing the Selection of Murray L. Weidenbaum as Chairman of the Council of Economic Advisers
January 23, 1981

The President. Good morning, all—my first morning without the Marine Band. It seemed very quiet getting down here.

I want to make an announcement, say a few words about the gentleman I'm about to introduce. This can't be a press conference, and, believe it or not—from purely a time schedule now—and we're already behind schedule. So, we won't be taking any questions but the gentleman I'm about to introduce—and Jim [Brady] will be with you at 2 o'clock this afternoon in the Briefing Room.

And now, the gentleman I'm speaking of is Dr. Murray L. Weidenbaum, whom I've appointed as Chairman of the economic advisory council. He's one of the country's most distinguished economists, a broad background in business and the academic world and government, and he has advised me economically for over 5 years. Now, a good share of that time he didn't know he was advising me, but I was following his writings and his utterances and many times referred to them and referred to him in my own weekly radio broadcast.

In the 1980 campaign, however, he was chairman of the task force on regulation and a member of the economic policy coordinating committee. And I'm looking forward with great eagerness to having him now as my chief economic adviser here and the Chairman of the economic council.

So, this is Dr. Murray Weidenbaum.

Dr. Weidenbaum. Thank you.

The President. Thank you for taking the position.

Dr. Weidenbaum. Thank you, Mr. President.

The President. And you will all see him at 2 o'clock this afternoon.

Note: The President spoke at 10:48 a.m. to reporters assembled in the Oval Office at the White House.

Nomination of Vice Admiral B. R. Inman To Be Deputy Director of Central Intelligence
January 24, 1981

The President announced today his intention to nominate Vice Admiral B. R. Inman as Deputy Director of Central Intelligence.

Since 1977 Admiral Inman has served as Director of the National Security Agency. From 1976 to 1977, he was Vice Director of the Defense Intelligence Agency.

From 1974 to 1976, Admiral Inman served as Director of the Naval Intelligence Department. He was Assistant Chief of Staff Intelligence to the Commander in Chief of the U.S. Pacific Fleet from 1973 to 1974.

From 1972 to 1973, he was executive assistant to the senior aide to the Vice Chief of Naval Operations.

Admiral Inman entered the Navy via the officer candidate school in 1952. He is a graduate of the University of Texas (B.A., 1950) and the National War College (1972).

He is married and has two children. The family currently resides at Ft. Meade, Md. Admiral Inman was born on April 4, 1931, and is a legal resident of California.

Nomination of Norman B. Ture To Be Under Secretary of the Treasury
January 24, 1981

The President announced today his intention to nominate Norman B. Ture as Under Secretary of the Treasury.

Since 1971 Mr. Ture has been president of Norman B. Ture, Inc., where he is an economic consultant. Since 1977 he has been president of the Institute for Research on the Economics of Taxation.

Mr. Ture is an adjunct scholar with the American Enterprise Institute for Public Policy Research. From 1968 to 1971, he was a principal of the Planning Research Corp.

From 1961 to 1969, he was director of tax studies, National Bureau of Economic Research, Inc.

From 1955 to 1961, Mr. Ture was with the Joint Economic Committee of the U.S. Congress. From 1951 to 1955, he served in the Office of the Secretary, Department of the Treasury.

Mr. Ture received his Ph. D. from the University of Chicago. He resides in Alexandria, Va., and is 57 years old.

Nomination of Roscoe L. Egger, Jr., To Be Commissioner of the Internal Revenue Service
January 24, 1981

The President announced today his intention to nominate Roscoe L. Egger, Jr., as Commissioner of the Internal Revenue Service, Department of the Treasury.

Since 1973 Mr. Egger has been partner-in-charge of Price Waterhouse and Co., Office of Government Services. Previously he served as partner-in-charge of the Tax Department from 1956 to 1973. Since joining Price Waterhouse and Co. in 1956, he has been engaged directly in the firm's tax practice as a specialist. He assumed responsibility for the firm's tax practice in Washington, D.C., from the beginning and continued in that role until 1973 when he assumed responsibility for the newly organized Office of Government Services.

He recently served as one of seven private sector members appointed to the Commission on Administrative Review of the U.S. House of Representatives. After months of study and analysis, the Commission submitted to the House of Representatives 42 proposed changes in rules or procedures dealing with such issues as accounting and management functions, committee reform, and congressional travel.

Mr. Egger is a member of the American Institute of CPA's and a member of the U.S. Chamber of Commerce board of directors. He is a member of the District of Columbia and American Bar Associations.

He is a graduate of Indiana University (B.S., 1942) and George Washington University Law School (J.D., 1950). Born in Jackson, Miss., on September 19, 1920, Mr. Egger resides in Washington, D.C.

Nomination of Robert W. Blanchette To Be Administrator of the Federal Railroad Administration
January 24, 1981

The President announced today his intention to nominate Robert W. Blanchette as Administrator of the Federal Railroad Administration, Department of Transportation.

Since 1976 Mr. Blanchette has been managing partner with the law firm of Alston, Miller and Gaines of Washington, D.C. Previously he served as a trustee of the Penn Central Transportation Co. and chairman of the board of trustees and chief executive officer from 1974 to 1978; from 1970 to 1976, he was counsel for trustees. He was attorney general in New England in 1969.

From 1969 to 1970, Mr. Blanchette was executive director of America's Sound Transportation Review Organization. He was general counsel to the New York, New Haven and Hartford Railroads from 1963 to 1968. From 1957 to 1962, he was a partner of the law firm of Adams, Blanchette and Evans in New Haven, Conn.

Mr. Blanchette was an officer in the U.S. Air Force from 1958 to 1960. He is a graduate of Yale Law School (LL.B., 1957) and is a member of the American and District of Columbia Bar Associations.

Mr. Blanchette was born in New Haven, Conn., on July 7, 1932. He is married and has two children. The family resides in Bethesda, Md.

Nomination of John M. Fowler To Be General Counsel of the Department of Transportation
January 24, 1981

The President announced today his intention to nominate John M. Fowler as General Counsel to the Department of Transportation.

Mr. Fowler is a lawyer who since 1979 has been vice president and chief financial officer of the Reading Co. in Philadelphia, Pa. He was responsible for the financial assets and reorganization of the railroad. Earlier he was the associate counsel for the company.

From 1974 to 1979, Mr. Fowler worked as a corporate lawyer for the White and Williams law firm in Philadelphia after graduating from the University of Pennsylvania Law School in 1974. He also has an economics degree from Yale University (1971).

Mr. Fowler is married and has one child, and the family resides in Philadelphia, Pa. Mr. Fowler was born on April 12, 1949.

Remarks at a White House Reception for the Families of the Freed American Hostages
January 25, 1981

Well, ladies and gentlemen—*[laughter]*—I can't start anymore since Rich Little got me started on that habit.[1] *[Laughter]*

We're delighted to have you all here. We know how happy you must be. And we all, of course, recognize the courage that has upheld those you're going to meet through these long 14 months. But I think it might be appropriate here to say a word about the courage of all of you, the dignity with which you have borne this, the courage when all you could do was wait through the many disappointments—and not only those who are coming home but all of you, too. America has to be very proud of you.

Now, we're not going to make any speeches here. As you know, there will be a welcome back here on Tuesday for all of you and all of them, and we're now going to just join you out there. But we want to explain we won't be going with you to New York, because we feel very deeply that you don't need any outsiders. This is a moment for you and for them.

Since we all didn't go to church this morning because of this—*[laughter]*—can we just say, dear God, thank You. Thank You for what You've done. And God give you the understanding and the patience that you need now with regard to this homecoming and get-together. Amen.

Note: The President spoke at 10:57 a.m. in the State Dining Room at the White House.

Following the reception, the families flew to Stewart Airport in Newburgh, N.Y., to await the arrival of Freedom One, which carried the former hostages from Wiesbaden, Germany. The reunited families then spent 2 days at the Hotel Thayer, on the campus of West Point Military Academy, before returning to Washington, D.C., for the official welcome.

---

[1] *See footnote on page 28.*

Appointment of Allen W. Locke as Deputy Staff Secretary of the White House
January 26, 1981

The President today announced the appointment of Allen W. Locke of Washington, D.C., as Deputy Staff Secretary of the White House.

Mr. Locke's previous government experience includes assignments in the Department of Defense and in the Department of State, where he most recently worked on international nuclear energy issues.

In his new post Mr. Locke will provide staff support to the President and help ensure effective communication and staffing among offices of the White House and the Executive Office of the President.

Mr. Locke, 42, was reared in Wellesley, Mass. He is a graduate of the University of Massachusetts (B.A., 1961; M.A., 1965). He is married to the former Elizabeth Gentry Heun of Washington, D.C. They have three children: Emily, Caroline, and William.

Remarks on Signing a Resolution Proclaiming a Day of Thanksgiving for the Freed American Hostages
January 26, 1981

The President. Good morning.

The resolution before me, here on the desk, is the proclamation of thanksgiving, a joint resolution from the Senate and the House, already signed by the Speaker and by the Vice President, as President of the Senate. I am going to affix my signature to it, also, to simply take advantage of this opportunity to share in it.

[*At this point, the President signed the joint resolution into law.*]

This resolution pays tribute to the strength of America. It recognizes the principle of public service, which 53 men and women fulfilled in the highest tradition of their calling. It recognizes the devotion and bravery of professional soldiers, the memories of those eight men and the long line of those who have given everything to preserve everything. It reminds us that "greater glory hath no man than that he lay down his life for another." It salutes the unity of the nation when we're confronted with threats to our freedom. And finally, it expresses what we must all remember, that God watched over His servants during this difficult time of testing.

I call on, as this resolution does, all Americans to join this Thursday in raising thanks that our sons and daughters have returned. They have shown by their example that the spirit of our country can never be broken.

I won't sign it again; I just have. But it seemed like that would have been a good——

Reporter. Thank you, Mr. President.

The President. I thank all of you. Nice to see you.

Note: The President spoke at 10:18 a.m. to reporters assembled in the Oval Office at the White House.

As enacted, S.J. Res. 16, proclaiming "A Day of Thanksgiving To Honor Our Safely Returned Hostages," is Public Law 97–1, approved January 26.

Nomination of W. Dennis Thomas To Be an Assistant Secretary of the Treasury
January 27, 1981

The President announced today his intention to nominate W. Dennis Thomas as Assistant Secretary for Legislative Affairs, Department of the Treasury.

Since 1976 Mr. Thomas has served as administrative assistant to Senator William V. Roth, Jr. (R-Del.). His responsibilities included work on the Finance Committee, Governmental Affairs Committee, and the Joint Economic Committee.

From 1974 to 1976, Mr. Thomas was administrative assistant to Senator J. Glenn Beall, Jr. (R-Md.). During that time he worked with the Budget Committee, Human Resources Committee, Commerce Committee, and the Small Business Committee. From 1971 to 1974, Mr. Thomas was executive assistant to Senator Beall, and from 1969 to 1970, he served as special assistant to then Congressman Beall.

Mr. Thomas was a member of the administrative staff of the Carroll County, Md., Board of Education from 1967 to 1968.

He graduated from Frostburg State College in Frostburg, Md., in 1965. He received his masters degree from the University of Maryland in 1967. Mr. Thomas is married and has one son. He lives with his family in Bethesda, Md. Mr. Thomas is 37 years old.

Nomination of Donald P. Hodel To Be Under Secretary of the Interior
January 27, 1981

The President announced today his intention to nominate Donald P. Hodel as Under Secretary of the Department of the Interior.

Since completing his legal training in 1960, Mr. Hodel has studied natural resource and energy issues from legal, industrial, government, and consulting perspectives.

He joined the law firm of Rockwood, Davies, Biggs, Strayer and Stoel in 1960 as an associate. From 1963 through 1969, Mr. Hodel was a member of the general counsel's staff at Georgia-Pacific Corp. In 1969 he was appointed Deputy Administrator of the Bonneville Power Administration by Secretary Hickel. Bonneville operates the largest high-voltage transmission system in the free world. He was subsequently appointed Administrator by Secretary Morton in 1972 and served until 1977.

After serving in government, Mr. Hodel formed his own consulting firm. In this capacity, he has served as a consultant to the president of the National Electric Reliability Council. He has been a delegate to the World Energy Conference.

Mr. Hodel is a graduate of the University of Oregon School of Law. He is married and resides in Lake Oswego, Oreg. He is 51 years old.

Nomination of Donald I. Hovde To Be Under Secretary of Housing and Urban Development
January 27, 1981

The President announced today his intention to nominate Donald I. Hovde as Under Secretary of Housing and Urban Development.

Recently Mr. Hovde was national senior vice president of Partners Real Estate, Inc. Previously he was owner and president of Hovde Realty, Inc., and president of 122 Building Corp.

Mr. Hovde was president of the National Association of Realtors in 1979. He has been a member of the board of directors since 1965.

Mr. Hovde graduated from the University of Wisconsin at Madison in 1953. He was commissioned second lieutenant in the U.S. Army in 1953, earned his pilot's wings in 1955, and joined the U.S. Army Reserve in 1956 and served until 1963.

Mr. Hovde is married and has five children. He lives with his family in Madison, Wis. He is 50 years old.

Remarks at the Welcoming Ceremony for the Freed American Hostages
January 27, 1981

The President. Cardinal Cooke, thank you, I think, for delivering this weather. We had been promised showers. We're most grateful.

Welcome to the Ambassadors of our friends in neighboring countries who are here today. And I can think of no better way to let you know how Nancy and I feel about your presence here today than to say on behalf of us, of the Vice President and Barbara, the Senators, the Members of Congress, the members of the Cabinet, and all of our fellow citizens, these simple words: Welcome home.

You are home, and believe me, you're welcome. If my remarks were a sermon, my text would be lines from the 126th Psalm: "We were like those who dreamed. Now our mouth is filled with laughter and our tongue with shouts of joy. The Lord has done great things for us. We are glad." You've come home to a people who for 444 days suffered the pain of your imprisonment, prayed for your safety, and most importantly, shared your determination that the spirit of free men and women is not a fit subject for barter.

You've represented under great stress the highest traditions of public service. Your conduct is symbolic of the millions of professional diplomats, military personnel, and others who have rendered service to their country.

We're now aware of the conditions under which you were imprisoned. Though now is not the time to review every abhorrent detail of your cruel confinement, believe me, we know what happened. Truth may be a rare commodity today in Iran; it's alive and well in America.

By no choice of your own, you've entered the ranks of those who throughout our history have undergone the ordeal of imprisonment: the crew of the *Pueblo*, the prisoners in two World Wars and in Korea and Vietnam. And like those others, you are special to us. You fulfilled your duty as you saw it, and now like the others, thank God you're home, and our hearts are full of gratitude.

I'm told that Sergeant Lopez here put up a sign in his cell, a sign that normally would have been torn down by those guards. But this one was written in Spanish, and his guards didn't know that "*Viva la roja, blanco, y azul*" means "Long live the red, white, and blue." They may not understand what that means in Iran, but we do, Sergeant Lopez, and you've filled our hearts with pride. *Muchas gracias.*

Two days ago, Nancy and I met with your families here at the White House. We know that you were lonely during that dreadful period of captivity, but you were never alone. Your wives and children, your mothers and dads, your brothers and sisters were so full of prayers and love for you that whether you were conscious of it or not, it must have sustained you during some of the worst times. No power on Earth could prevent them from doing that. Their courage, endurance, and strength were of heroic measure, and they're admired by all of us.

But to get down now to more mundane things, in case you have a question about your personal futures, you'll probably have less time to rest than you'd like. While you were on your way to Germany, I signed a hiring freeze in the Federal Government. In other words, we need you, your country needs you, and your bosses are panting to have you back on the job.

Now, I'll not be so foolish as to say forget what you've been through; you never will. But turn the page and look ahead, and do so knowing that for all who served their country, whether in the Foreign Service, the military, or as private citizens, freedom is indivisible. Your freedom and your individual dignity are much cherished. Those henceforth in the representation of this Nation will be accorded every means of protection that America can offer.

Let terrorists be aware that when the rules of international behavior are violated, our policy will be one of swift and effective retribution. We hear it said that we live in an era of limit to our powers. Well, let it also be understood, there are limits to our patience.

Now, I'm sure that you'll want to know that with us here today are families of the eight heroic men who gave their lives in the attempt to effect your rescue. "Greater glory hath no man than that he lay down his life for another." And with us also are Colonel Beckwith and some of the men who did return from that mission. We ask God's special healing for those who suffered wounds and His comfort to those who lost loved one. To them, to you, and to your families, again, welcome from all America and thank you for making us proud to be Americans.

And now, ladies and gentlemen, I call on, to speak for this wonderful group of returnees, Bruce Laingen, Deputy Chief of Mission [Chargé d'Affaires] in Tehran. Mr. Laingen.

Mr. Laingen. Mr. President, Mrs. Reagan, members of the Cabinet, Vice President and Mrs. Bush—I think I've got that out of order of priority in protocol terms—members of the diplomatic corps who are here, and all you beautiful people out there:

I'm not sure I'm capable of this after that emotionally draining, but beautiful experience that all of us have just had on the streets of this magnificent city, Mr. President. I hope you were watching TV, because I don't think any of us Americans have ever seen anything quite like it, quite so spontaneous, quite so beautiful in terms of the best qualities of our people. And we are deeply grateful for it.

Mr. President, our flight to freedom is now complete: thanks to the prayers and good will of countless millions of people, not just in this country but all around the world; the assistance of those many countries and governments who understood the values and principles that were at stake in this crisis; and the love and affection of our countrymen from all those tens of thousands out there on the streets today, to that lady that we saw standing on a hillside as we came in from Andrews, all alone, with no sign, no one around her, holding her hand to her heart—the enveloping love and affection of smalltown America of the kind we witnessed in that wonderful 2-day stop in New York State, West Point and its environs, and last, but not least, on this flight to freedom, the United States Air Force on Freedom I.

Mr. President, I give you now 52 Americans, supplemented by a 53d, today, Richard Queen sitting over here, overjoyed in reunion with our families, the real heroes in this crisis; 53 Americans, proud to rejoin their professional colleagues who had made their flight to freedom earlier—our 6 colleagues who came here with the great cooperation and friendship of our Canadian friends, and our 13 who came earlier. I give you now 53 Americans, proud, as I said earlier today, to record their undying respect and affection for the families of those brave 8 men who gave their lives so that we might be free, 53 of us proud today, this afternoon, and also to see and to meet with some of those families and Colonel Beckwith and some of those who came back. Fifty-three Americans who will always have a love affair with this country and who join with you in a prayer of thanksgiving for the way in which this crisis has strengthened the spirit and resilience and strength that is the mark of a truly free society.

Mr. President, we've seen a lot of signs along the road, here and up in New York. They are marvelous signs, as is the spirit and enthusiasm that accompanies this, what we've been calling "a celebration of freedom." They are signs that have not been ordered. They are spontaneous, sincere signs that reflect the true feelings of the hearts of those who hold them, even those, I suppose, like "IRS welcomes you"—[laughter]—which we saw today as we came into town, and another one that said, "Government workers welcome you back to work." Well, we're ready.

There was another sign that said, and I think that says it as well as any as far as we're concerned: "The best things in life are free." But even better than that was a sign that we saw as we left West Point today along a superhighway up there that someone had hastily put out: "And the world will be better for this." We pray, Mr. President, that this will be so.

Mr. President, in very simple words that come from the hearts of all of us, it is good to be back. Thank you, America, and God bless all of you.

Thank you very much.

The President. Thank you.

This is a flag, in this case bearing your name, and it is a symbol I will give to you now, because all the others you will each receive one when we get inside the building. Each one of you will have a flag symbolic of the 53 that are here in your honor.

And now—Nancy, come on up here—I think now a fit ending for all of this would be for all of us to participate in singing "God Bless America."

[*The audience sang "God Bless America."*]

Goodby. Thank you, and God bless you. We'll see you all inside.

Note: The President spoke at 3:11 p.m. on the South Lawn of the White House. His remarks were broadcast live on radio and television.

Prior to the ceremony, the President and Mrs. Reagan were introduced to the freed American hostages individually by Mr. Laingen in the Blue Room at the White House.

Remarks at a White House Reception for the Freed American Hostages and Their Families
January 27, 1981

Now, don't get worried. There's not going to be a lengthy speech here.

I've been in office now for 1 week, and one of the things I've found out is that there are a few orders that I can give. So, tonight I am officially ordering that all of you have a good rest, catch up with your families. And as much as Nancy and I and George and Barbara enjoy having you as our guests, we simply don't want to keep you from the privacy that you now deserve.

I know that a great many historic events have happened in this house and there have been many thousands of important people hosted here. But right at this moment I can't think of anyone more distinguished than you.

So, God bless all of you. Thank you again. Thank you for serving your country, for doing your duty. We're all very happy to have you back where you belong. And we're now going to go, and you have just received your second freedom. [*Laughter*]

Note: The President spoke at 3:46 p.m. in the East Room at the White House.

Executive Order 12287—Decontrol of Crude Oil and Refined Petroleum Products
January 28, 1981

By the authority vested in me as President by the Constitution and statutes of the United States of America, including the Emergency Petroleum Allocation Act of 1973, as amended (15 U.S.C. 751 *et seq.*), and notwithstanding the delegations to the Secretary of Energy in Executive Order No. 11790 as amended by Executive Order No. 12038, and in order to provide for an immediate and orderly decontrol of crude oil and refined petroleum products, it is hereby ordered as follows:

Section 1. All crude oil and refined petroleum products are exempted from the price and allocation controls adopted pursuant to the Emergency Petroleum Allocation Act of 1973, as amended. The Secretary of Energy shall promptly take such action as is necessary to revoke the price and allocation regulations made unnecessary by this Order.

Sec. 2. Notwithstanding Section 1 of this Order:

(a) All reporting and record-keeping requirements in effect under the Emergency Petroleum Allocation Act, as amended, shall continue in effect until eliminated or modified by the Secretary of Energy. The Secretary of Energy shall promptly review those requirements and shall eliminate them, except for those that are necessary for emergency planning and energy information gathering purposes required by law.

(b) The State set-aside for middle distillates (Special Rule 10, 10 CFR Part 211, Subpart A, Appendix A) shall remain in effect until March 31, 1981.

(c) The special allocation of middle distillates for surface passenger mass transportation (Special Rule 9, 10 CFR Part 211, Subpart A, Appendix A) shall remain in effect until March 31, 1981.

(d) The Buy-Sell lists and orders issued prior to this Order under the Buy-Sell Program and the Emergency Buy-Sell Program (10 CFR 211.65) shall remain in effect according to their terms and the Secretary of Energy may issue such further orders as may be necessary to give effect to lists and orders issued prior to this Order.

(e) The Canadian Allocation Program (10 CFR Part 214) shall remain in effect until March 31, 1981.

Sec. 3. The Secretary of Energy may, pursuant to Executive Order No. 11790, as amended by Executive Order No. 12038, adopt such regulations and take such actions as he deems necessary to implement this Order, including the promulgation of entitlements notices for periods prior to this Order and the establishment of a mechanism for entitlements adjustments for periods prior to this Order.

Sec. 4. The Secretary of Energy is authorized to take such other actions as he deems necessary to ensure that the purposes of this Order are effectuated.

Sec. 5. Because advance notice of and public procedure on the decontrol provided by this Order would be likely to cause actions that could lead to economic distortions and dislocations, and would therefore be contrary to the public interest, this Order shall be effective immediately.

RONALD REAGAN

The White House,
January 28, 1981.

[*Filed with the Office of the Federal Register, 4:38 p.m., January 28, 1981*]

Statement on Signing Executive Order 12287, Providing for the Decontrol of Crude Oil and Refined Petroleum Products
January 28, 1981

I am ordering, effective immediately, the elimination of remaining Federal controls on U.S. oil production and marketing.

For more than 9 years, restrictive price controls have held U.S. oil production below its potential, artificially boosted energy consumption, aggravated our balance of payments problems, and stifled technological breakthroughs. Price controls have also made us more energy-dependent on the OPEC nations, a development that has jeopardized our economic security and undermined price stability at home.

Fears that the planned phaseout of controls would not be carried out, for political reasons, have also hampered production. Ending these controls now will erase this uncertainty.

This step will also stimulate energy conservation. At the same time, the elimination of price controls will end the entitlements system, which has been in reality a subsidy for the importation of foreign oil.

This order also ends the gasoline allocation regulations which the Departments of Energy and Justice cite as important causes of the gas lines and shortages which have plagued American consumers on and off since 1974.

In order to provide for the orderly termination of petroleum controls, certain minor provisions of the current regulatory program will not end until March 31, 1981.

Ending price controls is a positive first step towards a balanced energy program, a program free of arbitrary and counter-productive constraints, one designed to promote prudent conservation and vigorous domestic production.

Toasts of the President and Prime Minister Edward Philip George Seaga of Jamaica
January 28, 1981

The President. Mr. Prime Minister, Mrs. Seaga, Mr. Shearer,[1] distinguished guests:

It's a pleasure for Nancy and me to welcome all of you here today. It's an honor of great significance to be host to the leader of a nation that is not only a close friend and a good neighbor of the United States but, with recent struggles to remain free of foreign interference, is an inspiration to the world.

Mr. Prime Minister, you are the first head of state to be our guest since I have taken office, and this tells me a great deal, because it speaks to the bond between our two countries. We share the commitment of free people around the world. We also share a personal bond, because we have

---

[1] *Hugh Lawson Shearer, Deputy Prime Minister of Jamaica and Minister of Foreign Affairs and Foreign Trade.*

come to office at nearly the same moment in history. We are both faced with problems, and we both perceive great opportunities for our countries.

Discussing some of our natural concerns during the meeting this morning made me even more mindful of the matters that bring us together. The times in which we find ourselves, the world in which our countries and the people exist require great courage. The trust given to every free individual, and particularly to you and me, is to protect and ensure for our children and our children's children liberty.

It's a special pleasure, Mr. Prime Minister, to welcome a leader of such unique and personal courage. That courage and the bold message that your people sent the world in electing you to lead them is testimony to the power of one man's dedication of the affirmation of free people, a democracy, and free enterprise. I pledge to you the good will, the cooperation, and the moral and material assistance of the United States as you are to meet the many challenges that you will face in the months ahead. Some of these challenges will come from forces hostile to our shared transitions and mutual interests. I'm confident that you will fulfill the trust that is placed in you by your country and embody the hope of all free people, not only in the Caribbean but in this hemisphere and around the world.

Those here today who believe in free enterprise have a great opportunity to put that belief into action. The Prime Minister shares that belief, and his country's greatest need is the development of business and industry to provide a sound private-sector economic base in his country.

Now, ladies and gentleman, I would ask that you join me in a toast to the Prime Minister of Jamaica and Mrs. Seaga, and to the friendship and alliance that we've renewed here today, and to the common endeavor to preserve the peace, independence, and the freedom of his country.

The Prime Minister. President Reagan, Mrs. Reagan, Vice President Bush and Mrs. Bush, Your Excellencies, Your Worship, distinguished guests, ladies and gentlemen:

It has been a great honor for my wife and myself and my delegation to have been the first invitees of your new administration to Washington on an official visit. This honor has in fact caused some degree of speculation as to why we have been selected as the first of many. And in pondering the many possibilities as to the reason for this honor on my country and on ourselves, I'm reminded of the story of a centipede that was suffering from arthritis. [*Laughter*]

And the centipede decided to consult with a doctor who was a stork. The stork made the obvious observation that he didn't have as much a problem in arthritis as the centipede did because he had only two legs, and therefore the solution to the problem was to reduce the centipede to two legs. The centipede considered this and realizing that there would be a 98-percent improvement immediately—[*laughter*]—decided that it would be worthwhile. But out of the caution of all those creatures that move slowly, he was prompted to ask, "Tell me, how are you going to make this transforma-

tion?" to which the stork replies, "I don't know. That's policy." [*Laughter*]

Well, we don't know whether we are here for reasons of policy, but we would like to think that there are policies being evolved surrounding our presence. We know that we too suffer from the problems of the centipede. As a nation, economically and politically, we are arthritic. We have inherited the malady, and it is a malady that is going to take time to cure. We know that you have policies that can assist us in curing them, and if there is one policy that ought to predominate in our thinking at this stage, it is the common outlook that we have in regards to how to deal with the difficult situations.

I say it here and now that although we are your guests, we are not guests who are here to take advantage of a situation by making enormous requests for assistance and for aid. That is not the purpose of our visit. Indeed, of the many issues that we are raising for discussion between the two administrations, aid plays a very minor role. Our concept of policy in this matter is one which directs to the possibility of developing greater flows in trade and in finance, the flows that will move capital and technology across the border to the economic development and betterment and mutual betterment of our people. This being our policy outlook, therefore, we hope that our arthritic problem may have the necessary injections, which won't be by surgical means, but by medicinal doses which will assist in helping us to overcome the problems we have inherited.

I would like to think also that our presence here is not only connected with the question of the transfusions between financial and trading movements of capital and goods. I would like to think that the signal that has been sent is a signal of the resumption of the great friendship that used to exist betwen the peoples of Jamaica and of the United States.

That great friendship had blossomed over many decades, cemented by bonds of migration, by bonds of investment, and by bonds of a commonality of interest among our people which have created a degree of inseparableness over which years we came to look at things together in like mind and in like manner. Over the past few years that bond was tested, tested severely, and indeed ruptured in many instances when this country and its people were being made the maligned butt and reason for the failures of the policies of the regime which ruled in Jamaica at that time. We hope that our being selected as your first visitors is a sign and a signal that we can resume the friendship in the strength of bonds that we used to know between the American and Jamaican people.

And as a token of that resumption, I would like to make reference to a matter of human compassion, something that has nothing to do whatsoever with our reception here, for which we have had the greatest expressions of warmth on both sides. We are cognizant of the fact that the American people have suffered through 444 days of captivity of 52 of their citizens as hostages in Iran. And at times you wondered who your friends were. Well, some of your friends were sitting by and waiting for the day when they would be able to assist and to share in any manner in which they could find possible towards the solution and towards all the recovery programs that must proceed after the solution.

And on behalf of my government I have the greatest pleasure in offering towards that recuperation and recovery some of our sunshine, some of our beaches, some of our climate, by offering 1 week's private vacation to each of the hostages and their families at any time that they may wish to take this up in the course of this year.

Mr. President, we have had your great friendship and your hospitality. We have had the warmth of your Cabinet ministers and a great deal of cordiality from all with whom we have met. It has been a delightful occasion and one which we hope will set the base for our future relations. We congratulate you on your magnificent victory, and we look forward to your party taking up the enormous task that it has on its shoulders of world leadership and domestic leadership and responding to the cause of world needs, responding to the cause of domestic needs in a balanced manner which will enhance your victory as a considerable achievement of the American people.

We thank you for the hospitality that you have offered, and we wish you the greatest success in your regime.

May I ask you all to rise and toast President and Mrs. Reagan, the government and the people of the United States.

Note: The President spoke at 12:25 p.m. in the State Dining Room at the White House.

Remarks on the Departure of Prime Minister Edward Philip George Seaga of Jamaica Following Their Meetings
January 28, 1981

The President. Prime Minister Seaga and I have found today that we have much in common, frankly because we both came into office about the same time. We've been exchanging stories about how similar our problems are, but I also think we share the view that our peoples are also strong enough to solve those problems. I found our discussions to be very helpful, and I'm convinced that this meeting will help strengthen the ties of friendship between Jamaica and the United States.

I told Prime Minister Seaga that our country noted with great pride his accomplishments at his election. The people of the United States take great hope from Prime Minister Seaga's election, and I am confident that we'll find ways to strongly support Jamaica. We are unrelaxed about the status of events in the Caribbean and the instability being inflicted on some countries in the Caribbean and in other places in the hemisphere from outside.

His election is a most hopeful event with which Americans can identify, and I'm delighted to start off my Presidency with this first visit. I can assure him and, indeed, all countries that the United States will continue to respect peaceful political change, change that in this instance offers great hope for freedom. I was impressed by the Prime Minister's strong commitment to rebuilding the Jamaican economy. I assured the Prime Minister that he could count on American support for his objectives, especially in his efforts to expand his country's private sector.

Mr. Prime Minister, we are honored to have you as America's first foreign visitor in our administration, and let me express my personal hope that the first shall not be the last.

The Prime Minister. President Reagan, we are very pleased to have been honored to be the first visitor in an official visit to the United States under your administration. This signal has many interpretations, but to our minds one of the interpretations which we would like to place on it is a new emphasis that may be developing in respect to Latin America and the Caribbean.

We have taken note of the fact that under the regime of former President Nixon there was a foreign policy thrust in the Far East and that under President Carter there was a foreign policy thrust in Africa. We are hopeful that my visit here is a signal that there will be a foreign policy thrust in Latin America and the Caribbean.

This does not mean that in making new thrusts all responsibilities in our mind are being abandoned. It simply means that new areas are being explored. And if that is so, then the policy of good neighbors once again comes to the front. And we can promise that we will be an effective part of any program of good neighbors, because there is a great deal of commonality of interests between our peoples and the objectives of our leadership.

We have taken great interest in the career of President Reagan and in his success and in the timeliness of his success which has coincided with similar events taking place in the Caribbean over the last year. Six Caribbean countries have all unilaterally decided to shift—indeed, to revolt—from the left to the center. This has presented a timely moment and one which a new administration coming into Washington at that time has an opportunity to capture in terms of a universality of thinking and of action.

We hope that we may be a part of the development process of this country's interest in the Caribbean and that you may be a part of our process in thinking out our own problems. In short, this means consultations. It means sharing our thinking as to what problems will arise in my country and in the Caribbean with you and seeking answers that can be effective and practical and mutually of interest. It means when your problems are sticky that we may be available for consultation. It is on the basis of this mutuality that we see a forward program, we see a position of mutual interest developing into policies of good neighborliness, policies which can help in the rebirth of influence and position of Latin America and the Caribbean in the spectrum of the world.

We have had an excellent visit, and we have had discussions with the President and his team which are far-reaching and are of great interest. And we sincerely hope that in the days to come that these will be renewed at other levels in a more practical sense. We thank you for the warm, cordial hospitality that you have offered us and for the sunshine. It only remains as to whose credit the sunshine is due, Jamaica's or California's. [*Laughter*]

The President. Mr. President [Prime Minister], normally I don't put a postscript on a tribute such as you've just paid, but I feel that all our people should know that one of the most gracious invitations has been extended by the Prime Minister, and that is that those that we honored here on the lawn yesterday, our returned, freed Americans and their families have been invited at any time that is suitable to them to come as his guests on a visit to Jamaica. It was a most gracious gesture, and I think all Americans owe him a "thank you" for that. It will be a private vacation for them. They will be his guests only to the extent that he has made it available.

Note: The President spoke at 1:25 p.m. at the South Portico of the White House.

Nomination of Walter J. Stoessel, Jr., To Be an Under Secretary of State
January 29, 1981

The President announced today his intention to nominate Walter J. Stoessel, Jr., as Under Secretary of State for Political Affairs.

Since 1976 Mr. Stoessel has served as Ambassador to the Federal Republic of Germany. From 1974 to 1976, he served as Ambassador to the U.S.S.R. From 1972 to 1974, Mr. Stoessel was Assistant Secretary of State for European Affairs. He was Ambassador to Poland from 1968 to 1972.

From 1965 to 1968, Mr. Stoessel was Deputy Assistant Secretary of State for European Affairs and served as Deputy Chief of Mission in Moscow from 1963 to 1965. He was a political officer in Paris from 1961 to 1963. From 1942 to 1961, Mr. Stoessel held a variety of diplomatic positions in Caracas, Moscow, Bad Nauheim, and Paris

Mr. Stoessel is a graduate of Stanford University (1941). He is 60 years old.

Nomination of Richard T. Kennedy To Be an Under Secretary of State
January 29, 1981

The President announced today his intention to nominate Richard T. Kennedy as Under Secretary of State for Management.

Mr. Kennedy served as Commissioner of the U.S. Nuclear Regulatory Commission from 1975 to 1980. From 1969 to 1975, he served as Deputy Assistant to the President for National Security Council Planning and was a senior member of the National Security Council staff. From 1964 to 1969, he served as Assistant Director, Deputy Director, and Director, Africa Region, Office of Assistant Secretary of Defense, International Security Affairs. And from 1961 to 1963, he served as a staff officer in the office of the assistant to the Secretary of Defense.

During the transition, Mr. Kennedy served as the team leader for the Nuclear Regulatory Commission transition team of the office of the President-elect.

In 1941 Mr. Kennedy received his B.A. degree (economics) from the University of Rochester and in 1953 received his M.B.A., with distinction, from Harvard University Graduate School of Business Administration. He served in the U.S. Army for 30 years, retiring in 1971 as colonel.

Mr. Kennedy is a member of the Service to Military Families Committee of the American Red Cross (D.C. chapter), a member of the National Association of Regulatory Utility Commissioners, and a member of the International Advisory Committee, American Nuclear Society. He was awarded the Distinguished Service Medal, the Legion of Merit, the Bronze Star, the Army Commendation Medal, and the Secretary of the Army Commendation. He has written many articles about civil use of nuclear energy, the worldwide energy problem, and regulatory matters.

He was born on December 24, 1919, and resides with his wife, Jean, in the District of Columbia.

Nomination of James L. Buckley To Be an Under Secretary of State
January 29, 1981

The President announced today his intention to nominate James L. Buckley for Under Secretary of State for Coordination of Security Assistance Programs.

Mr. Buckley has been a private business consultant and corporate director since 1977. From 1971 to 1977, he served as U.S. Senator from New York and was on the Public Works Committee, Commerce Committee, Budget Committee, and the Joint Committee on Atomic Energy.

Before serving in the U.S. Senate, Mr. Buckley was actively engaged in business negotiations in a number of countries, in such areas as Southeast Asia, Canada, Latin America, Europe, and Australia. In 1953 he was an officer and director of the Catawba Corp., a privately owned firm providing a variety of services to a group of oil and gas exploration companies operating primarily outside the United States. From 1949 to 1953, he practiced law with the Connecticut firm of Wiggin & Dana.

Mr. Buckley received his B.A. degree from Yale College in 1943 and his LL.B. degree from Yale Law School in 1949. He was an officer of the United States Naval Reserve and was honorably discharged from active duty with the rank of lieutenant in 1946.

Mr. Buckley is 57 years old and married to the former Ann Frances Cooley. They have five sons and one daughter and reside in Connecticut.

Nomination of Richard Fairbanks To Be an Assistant Secretary of State
January 29, 1981

The President today announced his intention to nominate Richard Fairbanks as Assistant Secretary of State for Congressional Relations.

Mr. Fairbanks is a partner in the law firm of Beveridge, Fairbanks and Diamond. From 1969 to 1971, he was an associate with Arnold and Porter, and in the summer of 1968, he was with Covington and Burling.

From January to June 1971, Mr. Fairbanks served as special assistant to the Administrator of the Environmental Protection Agency [EPA], and from July 1971 to December 1972, he served as a staff assistant at EPA. From December 1972 to April 1974, he served as Associate Director, Natural Resources, Energy, and Environment at EPA, and from July 1971 to April 1974, he served on the President's Domestic Council. From 1974 to 1977, Mr. Fairbanks served as a member of President Ford's Citizens' Advisory Committee on Environmental Quality.

In 1962 Mr. Fairbanks received his A.B. degree from Yale University, and in 1969 he received his J.D. degree from Columbia University School of Law. He served in the U.S. Navy from 1962 to 1966.

Mr. Fairbanks has been admitted to the District of Columbia Bar and to practice before the Supreme Court of the United States. He is a trustee of Meridian House International and a member of the Council on Natural Resources of the Republican National Committee. He is the founder of the American Refugee Committee of Washington, D.C.

He was born on February 10, 1941, in Indianapolis, Ind. He and his wife, Ann, have two children and reside in the District of Columbia.

Nomination of Robert C. McFarlane To Be Counselor of the Department of State
January 29, 1981

The President announced today his intention to nominate Robert C. McFarlane as Counselor, Department of State.

Since 1979 Mr. McFarlane has been a member of the professional staff of the Senate Committee on Armed Services. He was a senior research fellow at National Defense University in Washington, D.C., in 1977–78.

In 1976–77 he was Special Assistant to the President for National Security Affairs. Mr. McFarlane was executive assistant to the Assistant to the President for National Security Affairs in 1975–76. From 1973 to 1975, he was military assistant to Dr. Henry Kissinger at the White House. In 1971–72 he was a White House fellow and executive assistant to the Counsel to the President for Legislative Affairs.

Mr. McFarlane was a U.S. Marine officer. He is a graduate of the U.S. Naval Academy and studied international relations at the Institut des Hautes Etudes in Geneva, Switzerland. He is a recipient of the Distinguished Service Medal, the nation's highest peacetime military decoration.

Mr. McFarlane is married and has three children. He resides with his family in Bethesda, Md. He is 43 years old.

Nomination of M. Peter McPherson To Be Administrator of the Agency for International Development
January 29, 1981

The President announced today the nomination of M. Peter McPherson as Administrator of the Agency for International Development, United States International Development Cooperation Agency.

Mr. McPherson is serving as Acting White House Counsel and was the general counsel to the transition. Prior to that time, Mr. McPherson was a partner and head of the Washington office of the Ohio-based law firm of Vorys, Sater, Seymour and Pease.

He served as Special Assistant to President Ford and Deputy Director of Presidential Personnel in the Ford White House.

He was a tax law specialist for several years at the Internal Revenue Service, primarily working on international tax problems.

He was a Peace Corps volunteer in the middle sixties in Peru and at that time worked extensively with Food for Peace.

Previously he served on the Presidentially appointed Board for International Food and Agriculture Development, an advisory committee on AID agriculture activities. He was also the chairman of the Latin American work group of the Joint Committee on Agriculture Development, an advisory group to AID on Latin American agricultural matters.

Mr. McPherson is married and has two sons.

Nomination of Joseph F. Wright, Jr., To Be Deputy Secretary of Commerce
January 29, 1981

The President announced today his intention to nominate Joseph F. Wright, Jr., as Deputy Secretary of the Department of Commerce.

Currently Mr. Wright is president of both Citicorp Retail Services and Retail Consumer Services, Inc., and manages a wholly owned subsidiary of Citicorp, which consists of customer sales through 27 offices.

From 1971 to 1976, Mr. Wright served as Assistant Secretary of Administration at the U.S. Department of Agriculture, Deputy Director of the Social and Economic Statistics Administration, Department of Commerce, and Deputy Director of the Bureau of the Census. From 1966 to 1971, he was vice president and division head of Booz, Allen & Hamilton, Inc., and was responsible for new products and marketing.

Mr. Wright received his B.S. degree from the Colorado School of Mines in 1961 and an M.B.A. from Yale University in 1964.

Mr. Wright is 42 years old and resides in New York City.

Nomination of Beryl W. Sprinkel To Be an Under Secretary of the Treasury
January 29, 1981

The President today announced his intention to nominate Beryl W. Sprinkel as Under Secretary of Treasury for Monetary Policy.

Dr. Sprinkel has been executive vice president and economist at the Harris Trust and Savings Bank in Chicago, Ill., for 28 years. He heads the Economic Research Office and is a member of the bank's Management, Investment Guidance, Trust Investment, and Asset/Liability Committees.

In addition, Dr. Sprinkel is a publisher of Harris Economics, an economic and financial forecasting service. He is a member of TIME magazine's board of economists, chairman of the Economic Advisory Committee of the American Bankers Association, and has also served as consultant to various government agencies and congressional committees.

Dr. Sprinkel received a B.S. degree in public administration from the University of Missouri, and M.B.A. and Ph. D. degrees in finance and economics from the University of Chicago. He also received a C.F.A. from the Institute of Chartered Financial Analysts and an honorary degree, doctor of humane letters, from DePaul University.

Dr. Sprinkel is the author of three books and has contributed many articles to business and professional journals. He is 57 years old and resides in Flossmoor, Ill.

Nomination of C. W. McMillan To Be an Assistant Secretary of Agriculture
January 29, 1981

The President announced today his intention to nominate C. W. McMillan as Assistant Secretary of Agriculture for Marketing and Transportation Services.

Mr. McMillan has served as vice president, government affairs, of the National Cattlemen's Association since its formation through the merger of the American National Cattlemen's Association and the National Livestock Feeders in September 1977. Mr. McMillan had been executive vice president, Washington affairs, for the American National Cattlemen's Association since the Association opened its Washington office in 1970.

Prior to assuming the Washington post, he served for 11 years as ANCA's executive vice president in Denver, Colo. He was with the Swift and Co.'s Agricultural Research Department before joining the association.

Mr. McMillan was graduated from Colorado State University and served on the CSU resident faculty. Following service as a Navy lieutenant in the Pacific Theater during World War II, he returned to his native Colorado.

He is married and has three sons. He resides with his family in Alexandria, Va. Mr. McMillan was born February 9, 1926.

Nomination of Lee L. Verstandig To Be an Assistant Secretary of Transportation
January 29, 1981

The President announced today his intention to nominate Lee L. Verstandig as Assistant Secretary for Governmental Affairs, Department of Transportation.

Since 1977 Mr. Verstandig has served as administrative assistant and legislative director to U.S. Senator John H. Chafee. From 1970 to 1977, he was associate dean of academic affairs and dean for special studies at Brown University. Mr. Verstandig was a professor of history and political science at Roger Williams College from 1963 to 1970 and served as its department chairman from 1965 to 1967.

Mr. Verstandig received his B.A. degree from Franklin and Marshall College, his M.A. degree from the University of Tennessee, and his Ph. D. degree from Brown University.

Mr. Verstandig is the author of numerous articles and books on government, political history, education, and public policy. He has worked as a volunteer in many political campaigns, including the Reagan for President Committee.

Mr. Verstandig is 43 years old and resides in Washington, D.C.

Nomination of Raymond A. Peck, Jr., To Be Administrator of the National Highway Traffic Safety Administration
January 29, 1981

The President announced today his intention to nominate Raymond A. Peck, Jr., as Administrator, National Highway Traffic Safety Administration, Department of Transportation.

Since 1978 Mr. Peck has been vice president, director of regulatory affairs, National Coal Association, Washington, D.C. In 1977–78 he was a partner with Cotten, Day & Doyle law firm, specializing in energy and environmental litigation before Federal courts.

From 1975 to 1977, he was Deputy Assistant Secretary, Energy and Minerals, Department of the Interior. Mr. Peck was Director, Office of Energy Regulatory and Legislative Policy, Department of the Treasury in 1974–75. He was Environmental Counsel, Department of Commerce, from 1971 to 1974.

From 1964 to 1971, Mr. Peck was an associate in corporate litigation practice with the New York firms of Casey, Lane & Mittendorf and Norton, Sachs, Molineaux and Pastore.

Mr. Peck was graduated from the College of the Holy Cross in Worcester, Mass.

(1961). He was a Root-Tilden scholar at New York University School of Law (1964). He is a member of the New York, New Jersey, District of Columbia, and American Bar Associations.

Mr. Peck is married and has one daughter. He resides with his family in Washington, D.C. Mr. Peck was born on January 16, 1940.

Nomination of Ray A. Barnhart To Be Administrator of the Federal Highway Administration
January 29, 1981

The President announced today his intention to nominate Ray A. Barnhart as Administrator, Federal Highway Administration, Department of Transportation.

Since May 1979 Mr. Barnhart has served as a commissioner, Texas Highways and Public Transportation Department. He was appointed to a 6-year term on the three-member commission by Governor William Clements. He is a member of the Texas Turnpike Authority, which is the State agency responsible for construction and operation of major toll facilities in the State. Mr. Barnhart is an insurance agent with the Barmore Insurance Agency in Pasadena, Tex.

Mr. Barnhart has been active in politics for a number of years and is a former

member of the Pasadena City Council. He served in the Texas Legislature in 1973 and 1974. Mr. Barnhart is a former State chairman of the Texas Republican Party and also was chairman of the Harris County Republican Party. In 1976 he served as cochairman of the Reagan for President campaign in Texas, and was chairman of the Texas delegation to the 1976 Republican National Convention. In 1980 he was a member of the steering committee of the Reagan for President campaign.

Mr. Barnhart was graduated from Marietta College in Marietta, Ohio (B.A.), and received his M.A. from the University of Houston in Houston, Tex. He is married and has two children. Mr. Barnhart was born on January 12, 1928.

Appointment of Fred F. Fielding as Counsel to the President
January 29, 1981

The President announced today the appointment of Fred F. Fielding as Counsel to the President of the United States.

Mr. Fielding formerly served as Deputy Counsel to the President during the period 1970 to 1974. Prior to that time he was in the private practice of law in Philadelphia, Pa., from 1964 to 1970, with the firm of Morgan, Lewis and Bockius. Since 1974 he has been a partner of that same firm in its Washington, D.C., office.

He also served as conflict of interest counsel to the Reagan-Bush transition group, as well as heading the transition team for the Office of Government Ethics and being a member of the White House transition team.

A native of Mechanicsville (Bucks County), Pa., Mr. Fielding is a graduate of Gettysburg College (A.B., 1961) and the University of Virginia School of Law (J.D., 1964). He served 2 years active duty in the

United States Army, being discharged with the rank of captain.

Mr. Fielding, 41, is a member of the D.C. and Pennsylvania Bars and is admitted to practice before numerous Federal and State courts. He currently resides in Arlington, Va., with his wife, the former Maria Dugger, of Columbia, Tenn., and their two children: Adam, 5, and Alexandra, 3.

Appointment of Edwin W. Thomas, Jr., as Assistant Counsellor to the President
January 29, 1981

The President today announced the appointment of Edwin W. Thomas, Jr., of San Diego, Calif., as Assistant Counsellor to the President.

Mr. Thomas was formerly associate director, Center for Criminal Justice Planning and Policy, at the University of California, San Diego. He previously served as executive secretary to the California Highway Commission and as project director of the International Development and Direct Relief Foundation of Santa Barbara, Calif.

During the Reagan administration in California, Mr. Thomas served as special assistant to the Governor, assistant cabinet secretary, and administrative officer to the cabinet. During 1967 and 1968, he worked actively on the implementation and coordination of the Governor's survey on efficiency and cost control.

Born in Braddock, Pa., Mr. Thomas, 50, is a graduate of San Jose State University, completing postgraduate work at the University of California, San Francisco.

Mr. Thomas is married to the former Gretchen Wilson of East Liverpool, Ohio. The couple has two sons.

The President's News Conference
January 29, 1981

The President. How do you do? I have a brief opening statement here before I take your questions.

The National Economy

Yesterday Secretary of the Treasury Donald Regan sent to the Congress a request to raise the debt ceiling to $985 billion. This represents a dramatic jump of $50 billion over the previous debt ceiling. The administration took this action with great regret, because it's clear that the massive deficits our government runs is one of the root causes of our profound economic problems, and for too many years this process has come too easily for us. We've lived beyond our means and then financed our extravagance on the backs of the American people.

The clear message I received in the election campaign is that we must gain control of this inflationary monster.

Let me briefly review for the American people what we've already done. Within moments of taking the oath of office, I placed a freeze on the hiring of civilian employees in the Federal Government. Two days later I issued an order to cut down on government travel, reduce the number of consultants to the government, stopped the procurement of certain items, and called on my appointees to exercise restraint in their own offices. Yesterday I announced the elimination of remaining Federal controls on U.S. oil production and marketing.

Today I'm announcing two more actions to reduce the size of the Federal Government.

First, I'm taking major steps toward the elimination of the Council on Wage and Price Stability. This Council has been a failure. It has been totally ineffective in controlling inflation, and it's imposed unnecessary burdens on labor and business. Therefore, I am now ending the wage and price program of the Council. I am eliminating the staff that carries out its wage/pricing activities, and I'm asking Congress to rescind its budget, saving the taxpayers some $1½ million a year.

My second decision today is a directive ordering key Federal agencies to freeze pending regulations for 60 days. This action gives my administration time to start a new regulatory oversight process and also prevents certain last-minute regulatory decisions of the previous administration, the so-called midnight regulations, from taking effect without proper review and approval.

All of us should remember that the Federal Government is not some mysterious institution comprised of buildings, files, and paper. The people are the government. What we create we ought to be able to control. I do not intend to make wildly skyrocketing deficits and runaway government simple facts of life in this administration. As I've said, our ills have come upon us over several decades, and they will not go away in days or weeks or months. But I want the American people to know that we have begun.

Now I'll be happy to take your questions. Helen [Helen Thomas, United Press International].

U.S. Relations with Iran

Q. Mr. President, will your policy toward Iran be one of revenge or reconciliation? And will the United States honor the recent commitments to Iran, especially since you approved of most of them during the campaign?

The President. Well, I'm certainly not thinking of revenge, and I don't know whether reconciliation would be possible with the present government, or absence of a government, in Iran.

I think that the United States will honor the obligations. As a matter of fact, the most important of those were already put into effect by the preceding administration in negotiating the release. We are, however, studying, because there were four major agreements and there were nine Executive orders, and we are studying thoroughly what is a pretty complex matter, we've discovered, with regard to whether they are in keeping with international and our own national laws. And so, I won't be able to really answer your questions on specifics until we've completed that study.

Reductions in Federal Spending

Q. Mr. President, the Treasury Secretary said Monday that your budget cuts will be of a much higher magnitude than most people thought they would be. You said they would be across the board. Now that you've had some time to study the budget, can you say where these cuts will be made, what program will feel the cuts the most?

The President. They'll be made every place. Maybe across the board was the wrong decision, although it describes it. What I meant was that no one is exempt from being looked at for areas in which we can make cuts in spending.

And yes, they probably are going to be bigger than anyone has ever attempted, because this administration did not come here to be a caretaker government and just hope we could go along the same way and maybe do it a little better. We think the time has come where there has to be a change of direction of this country, and it's going to begin with reducing government spending.

U.S. Response to Terrorist Acts

Q. Mr. President, in your welcoming address to the freed Americans, you sounded a warning of swift and effective retribution in future terrorist situations. What kind of action are you prepared to take to back up this hard rhetoric?

The President. Well, that's a question that I don't think you can or should answer as to specifics. This is a big and it's a powerful nation. It has a lot of options open to it, and to try and specify now just particularly what you should do I think is one of the things that's been wrong.

People have gone to bed in some of these countries that have done these things to us in the past confident that they can go to sleep, wake up in the morning, and the United States wouldn't have taken any action. What I meant by that phrase was that anyone who does these things, violates our rights in the future, is not going to be able to go to bed with that confidence.

Walt [Walter Rodgers, Associated Press Radio].

Strategic Arms Limitation

Q. Mr. President, you campaigned rather vociferously against the SALT II treaty, saying it was slightly toward the Soviet Union. Yet I noticed your Secretary of State, Mr. Haig, now seems to suggest that for the time being, at least, the United States will abide by the limits of the SALT II treaty and he hopes the Soviet Union will, too. How long do you intend that the United States should abide by the terms of a SALT agreement which you consider inequitable, and what do you consider its greatest inequities to be?

The President. Well, the SALT treaty, first of all, I think, permits a continued buildup on both sides of strategic nuclear weapons but, in the main thing, authorizes an immediate increase in large numbers of Soviet warheads. There is no verification as to the number of warheads on the missile, no method for us to do this.

I don't think that a treaty—SALT means strategic arms limitation—that actually permits a buildup, on both sides, of strategic nuclear weapons can properly be called that. And I have said that when we can— and I am willing for our people to go in to negotiate or, let me say, discussions leading to negotiations—that we should start negotiating on the basis of trying to effect an actual reduction in the numbers of nuclear weapons. That would then be real strategic arms limitation.

And I happen to believe, also, that you can't sit down at a table and just negotiate that unless you take into account, in consideration at that table all the other things that are going on. In other words, I believe in linkage.

Sam [Sam Donaldson, ABC News].

Goals of the Soviet Union

Q. Mr. President, what do you see as the long-range intentions of the Soviet Union? Do you think, for instance, the Kremlin is bent on world domination that might lead to a continuation of the cold war, or do you think that under other circumstances détente is possible?

The President. Well, so far détente's been a one-way street that the Soviet Union has used to pursue its own aims. I don't have to think of an answer as to what I think their intentions are; they have repeated it. I know of no leader of the Soviet Union since the revolution, and including the present leadership, that has not more than once repeated in the various Communist congresses they hold their determination that their goal must be the promotion of world revolution and a one-world Socialist or Communist state, whichever word you want to use.

Now, as long as they do that and as long as they, at the same time, have openly and publicly declared that the only morality they recognize is what will further their cause, meaning they reserve unto themselves the right to commit any crime, to lie, to cheat, in order to attain that, and that is moral, not immoral, and we operate on a different set of standards, I think when you do business with them, even at a détente, you keep that in mind.

American Businesses and Iran

Q. Mr. President, what's your opinion of American companies that now want to resume business with Iran?

The President. My opinion of American companies that want to resume business with Iran? I hope they're going to do it by long distance. [*Laughter*] We wouldn't want to go back to having just a different cast of characters, but the same show going on. [*Laughter*]

I can understand that, particularly in the field of energy, their wanting to do that, but we are urging the people to think long and hard before they travel to Iran, because we don't think their safety can be guaranteed there.

American Prisoners in Iran

Q. Mr. President, three Americans are still incarcerated in Vietnam [Iran]. Can you tell us the status of their cases and whether the administration is doing anything to get them back?

The President. I have told our people about those three. They knew about them, of course, but I've told them that, yes, we continue and we want to get them back, also.

Now, I know I've been staying down front here too much. I've got to prove I can look at the back rows there. You, sir.

Affirmative Action Programs

Q. Okay. Mr. President, some administrative officials have promised adherence to the civil rights laws which are on the books, but there has been considerable discussion about dismantling the affirmative action aspect that gives those laws, to some people, greater meaning. And I'm wondering, Mr. President, that if there will be a retreat in the Federal Government on the government's advocacy of affirmative action programs generally and in Federal hiring of blacks and Hispanics specifically?

The President. No, there will be no retreat. This administration is going to be dedicated to equality. I think we've made great progress in the civil rights field. I think there are some things, however, that may not be as useful as they once were or that may even be distorted in the practice, such as some affirmative action programs becoming quota systems. And I'm old enough to remember when quotas existed in the United States for the purpose of discrimination, and I don't want to see that happen again.

Decontrol of Natural Gas Prices

Q. Mr. President, when and how will you seek the decontrol of natural gas prices?

The President. Well, we haven't dealt with that problem yet. We thought oil would do for a starter. But I can't really answer your question. That will be a matter for discussion in future Cabinet meetings.

Lou [Lou Cannon, Washington Post].

Soviet Grain Embargo

Q. Mr. President, during the campaign you repeatedly talked about the unfairness of the grain embargo, as you saw it. Do you have second thoughts now, or will you lift the grain embargo?

The President. Well, with the grain embargo, my quarrel with it from the first was that I thought it was asking only one group of Americans to participate, the farmers.

You only have two choices with an embargo: You either lift it, or you broaden it. And we have not made a decision except that, at the request of Secretary of Agriculture John Block, I have taken the matter of the embargo out of, you might say, the discussions of the National Security Council, and it, next week, is on the agenda for a full Cabinet meeting as to what our course will be. So, I can't answer what we do about it until next week.

As I say, it was asking one group of Americans to bear the burden and, I have always thought, was more of a kind of gesture than it was something real.

Yes, ma'am.

Atlanta Murders

Q. Mr. President, what will you do to honor the request from Atlanta officials for you and the Federal Government to intercede in the Atlanta case of 17 missing black children?

The President. Just a few minutes before I came in here, that message was handed to me that the Atlanta mayor wanted to talk, and we are going to get someone in touch with him immediately. Now, you recognize, of course, that possibly civil rights would be the only basis upon which we could have any jurisdiction down there in this. For FBI, for example, on any other thing, there's been no evidence of crossing State lines or anything. And yet we want to be helpful, because that is a most tragic case, and so we will be meeting on that very shortly. [1]

---

[1] *On January 30, Deputy Attorney General Charles B. Renfrew and Counselor to the Attorney General Kenneth Starr met with Mayor Maynard Jackson in Atlanta, Ga., to discuss the Federal role in helping to solve the cases.*

U.S. Policy Toward the Caribbean

Q. Mr. President, when the Jamaican Prime Minister was here yesterday, Mr. Seaga, he suggested publicly that now might be a good time for you, as the new President, to have a foreign policy initiative for Latin America and for the Caribbean. Do you intend to follow that suggestion, and if so, how would your policies differ from those of former President Carter?

The President. Well, I think we've seen a great reverse in the Caribbean situation, and it came about through Prime Minister Seaga's election. It was the turnover or turn-around of a nation that had gone, certainly, in the direction of the Communist movement; it was a protege of Castro. And his election was greeted by me with great enthusiasm, because it represented the people by their vote, having experienced that kind of government, turned another direction.

And I think this opens the door for us to have a policy in the Mediterranean [Caribbean] of bringing them back in—those countries that might have started in that direction—or keeping them in the Western World, in the free world. And so, we are looking forward to cooperation with Prime Minister Seaga.

Registration for the Draft

Q. Mr. President, I think you meant "Caribbean" in that last answer rather than "Mediterranean."

The President. What'd I say?

Q. "Mediterranean."

The President. Oh. I meant "Caribbean." I'm sorry.

Q. What do you intend to do, Mr. President, about the draft registration law that was passed during President Carter's administration? And in view of your opposition to it in the campaign, how is that consistent with your avowed intention to strengthen our national defenses?

The President. Well, to answer the last part first, I just didn't feel that the advance registration, on all the evidence we could get, would materially speed up the process if an emergency required the draft. It did create a bureaucracy. It caused, certainly, some unrest and dissatisfaction. And we were told that it would only be a matter of several days if we had to call up in a draft, that we could do that several days earlier with the registration than we would be able to if there was no registration at all.

This is one that's something to be looked at further down. I've only been here 9 days, and most of these 9 days have been spent in Cabinet meetings on the economy, getting ready to send our package up to the Hill. And so, I just have to tell you that we will be dealing with that, meet with that, and make a decision on what to do with it down the road someplace.

Gary [Cary Schuster, Detroit News].

Tax Reductions

Q. Mr. President, speaking of your economic package, can you give us your thoughts on an effective date for the tax cuts that you plan to recommend in your economic recovery plan, and specifying whether you prefer one effective date for business and another for personal cuts or whether you'd like to combine them?

The President. I'd like to see it all go forward all at once. As to date, I know there's been talk about whether it should be retroactive back or whether it should be as of that minute. That, to me, isn't as important as getting for individuals the principle of a 10-percent cut for each of 3 years in place and the business taxes, also, so that we can all look forward with some confidence of stability in the program. And we're going to strive for that. And I can't really answer you about what the date will be until we submit the package.

U.S. Relations with Iran

Q. Mr. President, I know you said earlier that you were not thinking of revenge toward Iran. But does that preclude any punishment whatsoever for what they've done?

The President. Well, again, I have to ask your forbearance and wait until we've finished our study of this whole situation as to what we're going to do. I don't think any of us have a friendly feeling toward the people that have done what they have done. But I think it's too complex for me to answer until we've had time to really study this.

Q. Mr. President, just one followup. Would you go so far as to encourage American businesses to resume commercial trade with Iran?

The President. At this point, no.

Departments of Energy and Education

Q. Mr. President, do you intend to follow through with your campaign pledges to abolish the Departments of Energy and Education?

The President. I have not retreated from that at all. Yes. The process, however, that I have asked for is for both Secretary Bell of Education and Secretary Jim Edwards of Energy to reorganize, to produce the most effective streamlining of their Departments that they can—in Education, to look at the appropriate role of the Federal Government in education, if there is one, and to report back. And then we will decide, making our recommendations. Much the same thing holds true with the Department of Energy. The reason for this being that while they were new Cabinet-level agencies, they incorporated government functions and programs that had been going on in them, and they came under that umbrella. And we have to find out which of those functions that have been a Federal Government function continue and where they would best fit.

But, yes, I'm determined, and I believe that it was wrong to have created the two agencies to begin with.

Dairy Price Supports

Q. Mr. President, during the campaign your chief farm spokesman put you on record as favoring, for the time being, continuation of the dairy price support level where it had been. Within the last couple of days, your budget director and your Secretary of Agriculture have indicated that the dairy program is too expensive and should be cut back. Could you reconcile those differences of approach for us?

The President. Well, I could only tell you that this, again, is something to wait for the next Cabinet meeting. All of these things are worked out between the appropriate Cabinet members and our Director of OMB, and then they come to the Cabinet for full discussion so that others who have

an interest in this can have their input. And so, I can't answer you, because that has not yet come to the Cabinet.

Stability in Persian Gulf Region

Q. Mr. President, Iran and the Soviet Union share a long border in a region vital to the future stability of the world. Given the anti-U.S. sentiment there, how do you best think the United States can ensure the stability of the region, the Persian Gulf region?

The President. Of the—you said Iran, the border between Iran and the Soviet Union.

Well, I think one of the first things that has to happen for stability, has got to be, in Iran itself, to establish a government that can speak as a government for Iran. And part of our problem in all these long 444 days has been the inability of anyone seemingly to speak for that nation, to have a government. Now, I think that any country would want to help another if they really showed an intent to have a government that would abide by international law and do what they could to help them in that regard. But until such a thing appears apparent there, I don't know that there's anything we can do.

U.S. Relations with Iran

Q. Mr. President, if it's your intention to signal the world that this country will respond with swift retribution in cases of international terrorism in the future, why is it your policy not to retaliate against Iran?

The President. Well, what good would just revenge do, and what form would that take? I don't think revenge is worthy of us. On the other hand, I don't think we act as if this never happened. And I'd rather wait until, as I say, we complete this study.

Who said—I know I've been on this side too long, but someone said, *"Por favor."* [*Laughter*]

Hispanics in Reagan Administration

Q. Mr. President, still I am impressed when I listened the other day, *"Viva la roja, la blanca, y azul."* [2]

[2] See page 41.

Mr. President, it is true that when Hispanics are given the opportunity to serve this country, they serve the country with diligence and dispatch. In view of this undisputed fact, when are you going to appoint Hispanic Americans to serve in your administration in policymaking positions?

The President. We are definitely recruiting and definitely trying to do that. I want an administration that will be representative of the country as a whole, and please don't judge us on the fact that we have only picked a hundred. There will be 1,700 positions to fill in the executive branch and the White House senior staff and staff. And the personnel committee in our administration that is talent hunting and looking for these people contains members of the minorities, Hispanics, and even a majority of women, and we want that very much. So, don't judge us now by the tip of the iceberg. Wait till it's all in.

Interest Rates and the Federal Reserve System

Q. Mr. President? Yes, thank you.

Mr. President, Paul Volcker, the Chairman of the Federal Reserve Board, has been implementing policies that are exactly opposite in basic thrust from what you recommend. He has been squeezing the productive sector of the economy in favor of the speculative sector. Now, I mean frankly, Mr. President, there are important sections of the American economy that are about to go under and won't even have an opportunity to benefit from the programs that you're putting forward because of the Federal Reserve policy.

I have a two-part question. First of all, do you think that objective economic conditions justify the interest rate levels that we now have? And I don't mean for your answer to imply criticism of the Fed; it's just an objective question. And the second question is, are you concerned that there might be a sabotage, so to speak, of your policies by programs that the Federal Reserve might be putting forward?

The President. No, I'm not concerned that there would be sabotage. I've met with Mr. Volcker, and not with the intention of trying to dictate, because it is an independent agency, and I respect that.

But I think that we have to face the fact that interest rates are not in themselves a cause of inflation; they're a consequence. And when you have, as we have had, double-digit inflation back to back for 2 solid years now—the last time that happened was in World War I—and when you have double-digit inflation there, that way there is no question that interest rates are going to have to go up and follow that inflation rate.

And so, the answer to the interest rates is going to be our program of reducing government spending, tied to the reduction of the tax rates that we've spoken of to bring down inflation, and you'll find that interest rates come down. We do want from the Fed and would ask for a moderate policy of money supply increasing relative to legitimate growth. All of these things have to work together. But I don't think that the Fed just deliberately raises interest rates.

The reason that we've got to tie taxes and we have to tie spending together is we, for all these decades, we've talked and we've talked about solving these problems, and we've acted as if the two were separate. So, one year we fight inflation and then unemployment goes up, and then the next year we fight unemployment and inflation goes up. It's time to keep the two together where they belong, and that's what we're going to do.

Yes, sir.

Reagan Administration Appointees

Q. Mr. President, a number of conservative leaders, among them some of your staunchest and most durable supporters, such as Senator Jesse Helms, are very concerned about some of your appointments.

The basis of the concern is that many people who have been longtime Reaganites and supporters of yours do not seem to be able to get jobs, like Bill Van Cleave, who played a key role on your defense transition team, whereas other individuals who have not supported you throughout the years or your philosophy, like Mr. Terrel Bell, the Secretary of Education, who was for the establishment of the Department which you've said you're going to abolish, when Mr. Frank Carlucci, Deputy Secretary of

Defense, who was not a supporter of yours, that they have gotten jobs.

My question is, why are these individuals in your administration? Why isn't Mr. Van Cleave? And how much of a problem do you think this conservative dissatisfaction with your appointments is?

The President. The only problem that I've had that is more difficult than knowing which hand raised to point to here—and believe me, it bothers me; I go home feeling guilty for all the hands that I couldn't point to. [*Laughter*] The only problem greater I've had is in the selection of personnel.

Now, in many instances some of the people that have been mentioned, whose names that have been mentioned by others did not want a position in the administration—helped, worked very hard, and wanted nothing for it. But you also have to recognize there aren't that many positions. After all, look how many votes I had. You can't reward them all.

Ms. Thomas. Thank you, Mr. President.

The President. Thank you. All right. Thank you all very much.

Note: The President's first news conference began at 4 p.m. in Room 450 of the Old Executive Office Building. It was broadcast live on radio and television.

Executive Order 12288—Termination of the Wage and Price Regulatory Program
January 29, 1981

By the authority vested in me as President and as Commander in Chief of the Armed Forces by the Constitution and laws of the United States of America, including Sections 2(c) and 3(a) of the Council on Wage and Price Stability Act, as amended (12 U.S.C. 1904 note), and Section 205(a) of the Federal Property and Administrative Services Act of 1949, as amended (40 U.S.C. 486(a)), and in order to terminate the regulatory burdens of the current wage and price program, it is hereby ordered as follows:

Section 1. Executive Order No. 12092, as amended, is revoked.

Sec. 2. The head of each Executive agency and military department, including the Council on Wage and Price Stability and the Office of Federal Procurement Policy, is authorized to take appropriate steps to terminate actions adopted in response to Executive Order No. 12092, as amended.

RONALD REAGAN

The White House,
January 29, 1981.

[*Filed with the Office of the Federal Register, 5:15 p.m., January 29, 1981*]

Message to the Congress Reporting a Budget Rescission
January 29, 1981

To the Congress of the United States:

In accordance with the Impoundment Control Act of 1974, I herewith report a proposal to rescind $1.5 million in funds appropriated for the Council on Wage and Price Stability. The details of this rescission proposal are contained in the attached report.

RONALD REAGAN

The White House,
January 29, 1981.

Note: The attachment detailing the rescission is printed in the Federal Register *of February 3, 1981.*

Memorandum Postponing Pending Federal Regulations
January 29, 1981

Memorandum for
The Secretary of the Treasury
The Attorney General
The Secretary of the Interior
The Secretary of Agriculture
The Secretary of Commerce
The Secretary of Labor
The Secretary of Health and Human Services
The Secretary of Housing and Urban Development
The Secretary of Transportation
The Secretary of Energy
The Secretary of Education
The Administrator of the Environmental Protection Agency

Subject: Postponement of Pending Regulations

Among my priorities as President is the establishment of a new regulatory oversight process that will lead to less burdensome and more rational federal regulation. I am now directing certain measures that will give this Administration, through the Task Force on Regulatory Relief, sufficient time to implement that process, and to subject to full and appropriate review many of the prior Administration's last-minute decisions that would increase rather than relieve the current burden of restrictive regulation. This review is especially necessary in the economic climate we have inherited.

1. Postponement of Pending Final Regulations. To the extent permitted by law, your agency shall, by notice in the *Federal Register,* postpone for 60 days from the date of this memorandum the effective date of all regulations that your agency has promulgated in final form and that are scheduled to become effective during such 60-day period.

2. Postponement of Proposed Regulations. To the extent permitted by law, your agency shall refrain, for 60 days following the date of this memorandum, from promulgating any final rule.

3. Emergency Regulations and Regulations Subject to Short-Term Deadlines. Your agency shall not postpone regulations that respond to emergency situations or for which a postponement pursuant to this memorandum would conflict with a statutory or judicial deadline.

4. Consultation with the Office of Management and Budget.

(a) Your agency shall report to the Director of the Office of Management and Budget all regulations that cannot legally be postponed under paragraphs 1 and 2 of this memorandum, and all regulations that will not be postponed under paragraph 3 of this memorandum, including a brief explanation of the legal or other reasons why the effective date of any such regulation will not be postponed.

(b) After consultation with the Director, or the Director's designee, your agency may decide to postpone the effective date or promulgation of a regulation for fewer than 60 days from the date of this memorandum, if circumstances warrant a shorter period of postponement.

5. Exemptions. This memorandum shall not apply to:

(a) regulations issued in accordance with the formal rule-making provisions of the Administrative Procedure Act, 5 U.S.C. 556, 557;

(b) regulations issued with respect to a military or foreign affairs function of the United States;

(c) regulations related to Federal government procurement;

(d) matters related to agency organization, management, or personnel; or

(e) regulations issued by the Internal Revenue Service.

6. *Definition.* For purposes of this memorandum, "regulation" or "rule" shall mean an agency statement of general applicability and future effect designed to implement, interpret, or prescribe law or policy or describing the procedure or practice requirements of an agency.

RONALD REAGAN

Nomination of Paul Craig Roberts To Be an Assistant Secretary of the Treasury
January 30, 1981

The President announced today his intention to nominate Paul Craig Roberts as Assistant Secretary of the Treasury for Economic Policy.

Dr. Roberts is currently a senior fellow in political economy at the Center for Strategic and International Studies at Georgetown University, professor of business administration and professor of economics at George Mason University, Wall Street Journal columnist for "Political Economy," and contributing editor to Harper's.

In the U.S. Congress, Dr. Roberts has served in the House of Representatives as economic counsel to Representative Jack Kemp, as staff associate with the Defense Appropriations Subcommittee, and as chief economist with the minority staff of the Committee on the Budget. In the U.S. Senate he has served as economic counsel to Senator Orrin Hatch. He managed the tax-cut movement in Congress during 1975–78 and drafted the original version of the Kemp-Roth bill.

Dr. Roberts was educated at the Georgia Institute of Technology (B.S., industrial management), the University of California at Berkeley, the University of Virginia (Ph. D., economics), and Oxford University, where he was a member of Merton College.

The author of two books, Dr. Roberts has also published many articles in the Wall Street Journal, the New York Times, and Harper's as well as other publications in the United States and Europe.

Dr. Roberts is 41 years old and resides in Alexandria, Va.

Statement on the Release of the Government's Index of Leading Economic Indicators
January 30, 1981

While no one set of economic reports is conclusive, this battery of bad economic news from last year's "inheritance" underscores the need to turn this economy around. We must deal simultaneously with inflation and a sluggish economy, and my comprehensive package is designed to do just that.

Announcement of the Formation of a Blind Trust To Manage the President's Personal Assets
January 30, 1981

The President has formed a blind trust under the Ethics in Government Act, as amended, to handle and invest his personal assets during his Presidency.

Under the arrangements, his investments, other than his ranch in Santa Barbara, Calif., and his personal residence in Pacific Palisades, Calif., have been converted to cash and will be placed in trust to be managed by an independent trustee, without his knowledge of the investments or control over them. His Pacific Palisades home has been placed on the market for sale, and it is contemplated that some or all of the proceeds from the sale of the home will also be placed in the blind trust.

The purpose for the trust is to allow an independent trustee to invest, manage, and control the President's assets without knowledge by the President of the investments of the trust, in order to avoid even the possibility of an appearance of any conflict of interest in the performance of his duties. The President will receive no information concerning the investments made by the trustee except periodic reports concerning the value of the assets in the trust and the income of the trust. The form of the trust and the selection of trustee has been approved by the Office of Government Ethics, to whom the trust agreement was submitted.

The trustee selected by the President is Raymond J. Armstrong, president of Starwood Corp., a New York-based, registered investment firm. Mr. Armstrong's firm manages investment portfolios for a variety of individuals and family groups and provides supervision and advice to charitable foundations, pension and profit-sharing plans, insurance companies, and other fiduciary accounts.

Message to the Congress Transmitting the 1982 Budget of the District of Columbia
January 30, 1981

To the Congress of the United States:

In accordance with the District of Columbia Self-Government and Governmental Reorganization Act, I am transmitting the 1982 Budget of the District of Columbia.

I am informed that the proposals for Federal payments to the District of Columbia reflected in this document are consistent with those shown in the 1982 Budget of the United States submitted to Congress by President Carter on January 15, 1981.

RONALD REAGAN

The White House,
January 30, 1981.

Message on the Observance of National Afro-American (Black) History Month, February 1981
February 2, 1981

All Americans can be proud of the accomplishments and goals of the Association for the Study of Afro-American Life and History. Knowledge of our past is one of our most treasured possessions, for only with an accurate picture of where we have been can we see where we must go.

The observance of Afro-American (Black) History Month serves to focus national attention on an endeavor of awareness that should follow us throughout the year. Understanding the history of black Americans is a key to understanding the strength of our nation. Their struggles, achievements and perseverance help us understand the moral fiber of America and our commitment to freedom, equality and justice.

This month's theme of "Black History: Role Model for Youth" goes to the very heart of our best hope for the future of our nation. We will hand to the youth of this nation the responsibility of preserving our heritage for future generations. The minds being shaped today in classrooms around the country must be fully enriched. The achievements and courage of individuals provide an inspiring example of the essence of the American spirit.

I urge all Americans, particularly those in our schools and civic groups, to study our history and incorporate in their activities projects to help us all understand those individuals who played so great a part in our development. We must ensure that the gains of the past are not lost in the future, and in so doing we can look to tomorrow with confidence.

RONALD REAGAN

Toasts of the President and President Chun Doo Hwan of the Republic of Korea
February 2, 1981

President Reagan. Nancy and I, Mr. President, are pleased to welcome you and Madame Chun to the White House. You are one of our first guests here. We haven't lived here very long, and in looking about, I can't help but contrast the peaceful and rather elegant setting with a meeting that took place in your country 30 years ago in a building in your capital in Seoul that was badly damaged by the war. It was just after the landing at Inchon. General Douglas MacArthur turned the command of the city over to President Rhee and the civilian authorities of the Republic of Korea. And General MacArthur spoke then of the special friendship that exists between our two countries and of our mutual commitment to democratic principles and individual liberty and personal dignity.

We've come a long way together since that meeting. You have a saying in your country that after the rain, the earth hardens. Well, the miracle of modern Korea is well known in the world. Nancy and I had the opportunity to see that miracle at first hand a few years ago when we visited your country. And we recall that visit with great warmth and great pleasure.

In the very short time, Mr. President, that you've had, you've done much to strengthen the traditions of 5,000 years of Korean history. We share your commitment to freedom. If there's one message that I have for the Korean people today, it is this: Our special bond of freedom and friendship is as strong today as it was in that meeting 30 years ago. Our young men have fought side by side, not only in Korea but in Vietnam. And again there, the cause was freedom. And today we are committed to each other's defense against aggression. We shall continue to search together for continued peace on the Korean peninsula, in the Pacific region, and throughout the world.

Now, will you all join in a toast celebrating the never-ending friendship of two nations and toasting the President of the Republic of Korea, President Chun, and Madame Chun.

President Chun. Mr. President, Mrs. Reagan, Excellencies, distinguished guests, ladies and gentlemen:

Allow me once more to express my very profound gratitude to you, Mr. President, for your and Mrs. Reagan's most gracious hospitality on this heart-warming occasion, and thank you, Mr. President, for your extremely kind words of welcome.

You have honored my country by inviting my wife and me today to the White House, and I thank you, Mr. President and Mrs. Reagan, for your invitation to me so soon after your inauguration as the President of the United States of America. With God's blessing, the United States will more than successfully achieve its national objectives under your great leadership. The new era of great renewal for America will certainly succeed because of your statesmanship and greatness in the American people that you will be serving and leading in the years ahead.

Incidentally, the Republic of Korea, too, embarked upon a new venture to open a new era for the country. The new era will be characterized by a renewal of the spirit of national harmony, replacing the old chronic and internecine battles between those who take rigid and extreme positions. We are determined and hopeful that we can usher in an era of dialog and consensus-building so that our national energy can be channeled to a far more constructive objective of building a freer, more abundant, and democratic society in our midst.

Next year, Mr. President, we will be observing the centennial of the first signing of the Treaty of Peace, Amity, Commerce and Navigation between the Kingdom of Korea and the United States of America. Since that time our two nations have maintained exceptionally close ties. In the more recent past when North Korean Communists invaded the Republic of Korea in 1950, Americans came to Korea to fight and make the supreme sacrifice in its defense of our liberty and independence.

After the armistice, the United States gave us generous assistance to rehabilitate our war-devastated economy. Mr. President, Korea has in recent years achieved rapid economic development despite countless difficulties. We are moving ahead vigorously in all sectors of society. Korea is now the 16th largest trading country in the world and ranks 11th among the trading partners of the United States. In other words, American assistance has not been in vain.

The Republic of Korea is now capable of joining with the United States to ensure the prosperity of mankind and peace in East Asia. Mr. President, you have aroused renewed hope, courage, and confidence within the United States and now lead the march toward an even greater future. I believe that your philosophy applies not only to the United States but to all free world nations.

I am convinced that our two nations will march forward as mature partners who will rely on and help each other through the complex and challenging decade of the 1980's.

Ladies and gentlemen, will you kindly join me in a toast to the good health of the President and Mrs. Reagan, to the prosperity of the United States, and to strong friendship between the Republic of Korea and the United States of America.

Note: The President spoke at 12:30 p.m. in the State Dining Room at the White House. President Chun spoke in Korean, and his remarks were translated by an interpreter.

Remarks of President Reagan and President Chun Doo Hwan of the Republic of Korea Following Their Meetings
February 2, 1981

President Reagan. Today we had a very warm and a very productive meeting with President Chun. Our meeting here today is a sign to all the people of Asia, as well as to the people of Korea, that the United States has a longstanding interest and enduring commitment to their part of the world.

I hope you'll understand that the United States will remain a reliable Pacific partner, and we shall maintain the strength of our forces in the Pacific area. I hope, too, that our Asian allies in Korea, Japan, Australia, New Zealand, and our friends in the ASEAN know that they will have—we'll have just as much alliance with them, and they will have our continued support as our European allies have.

Today at the luncheon, President Chun spoke of General MacArthur's wise admonition that we must never underestimate America's vital interests in the Pacific. So, it is my fervent hope in the years ahead that we can work together to make the great Pacific Basin a place of peace, prosperity, and stability for all who live there.

And we bid President Chun and Madame Chun goodby with a hope that their visit here will be as happy and successful as the visit that Nancy and I had some years ago in their country, a visit for which we are both grateful and deeply indebted to the Korean people.

President Chun. I am happy to be visiting in Washington at the kind invitation of His Excellency, the President of the United States, and Mrs. Reagan. I appreciated the opportunity I had this morning of exchanging views on matters of mutual interest with President Reagan in an atmosphere of warmth and mutual cordiality. I am happy to say that President Reagan gave me firm assurances that the United States has no intention of withdrawing the American forces in Korea. I am pleased that the present level of United States military presence in Korea will be maintained. This makes a vital and indispensable contribution toward not only peace in Korea but peace and tranquility of the Northeast Asia region.

In this great period of great renewal of America, I wish success and my best wishes to the Government of the United States and the country led and served by President Reagan.

Note: The President spoke at 1:50 p.m. at the South Portico of the White House. President Chun spoke in Korean, and his remarks were translated by an interpreter.

Joint Communique Following Discussions With President Chun Doo Hwan of the Republic of Korea
February 2, 1981

1. At the invitation of President Ronald W. Reagan, the President of the Republic of Korea and Mrs. Chun Doo Hwan made an official visit to Washington, D.C. from February 1 to 3, 1981.

2. The two Presidents met at the White House on February 2 to exchange views on the current international situation and to discuss matters of mutual interest in an atmosphere of friendship and cordial respect.

Among those present at the meeting were Vice President George Bush, Secretary of State Alexander Haig, Secretary of Defense Caspar Weinberger, United States Trade Representative William E. Brock, Jr., Counsellor to the President Edwin Meese III, Chief of Staff James Baker III, Assistant to the President for National Security Affairs Richard Allen, Deputy Chief of Staff Michael K. Deaver, and Ambassador William Gleysteen from the American side; and Deputy Prime Minister Shin Byong Hyun, Foreign Minister Lho Shin Yong, Minister of National Defense Choo Yong Bock, Ambassador Kim Yong Shik, and Secretary General to the President Kim Kyong Won from the Korean side.

3. The two Presidents reviewed the world situation and reaffirmed the critical importance of maintaining peace on the Korean peninsula and in Northeast Asia. President Reagan and President Chun pledged to uphold the mutual obligations embodied in the United States-Korea Mutual Defense Treaty of 1954. President Reagan affirmed that the United States, as a Pacific Power, will seek to ensure the peace and security of the region. President Chun expressed his full support for United States policies directed toward these ends and emphasized his view that the United States should continue to exercise firm leadership in world affairs.

4. President Reagan and President Chun reviewed the security situation on the Korean peninsula and the continuing threats to peace in the area. President Reagan assured President Chun that the United States has no plans to withdraw U.S. ground combat forces from the Korean peninsula. The two Presidents pledged to seek to strengthen US-Korean cooperation in deterring and defending against aggression as an indispensable contribution to peace and stability in Northeast Asia.

5. President Chun outlined the continuing efforts of the Republic of Korea to enhance its self-reliant defense capabilities through the modernization of its armed forces. President Reagan commended the Republic of Korea for its significant continuing efforts and confirmed that the United States will make available for sale appropriate weapons systems and defense industry technology necessary for enhancing Korea's capabilities to deter aggression.

6. President Chun was assured of United States support for the efforts of the Republic of Korea to resume a constructive dialogue with North Korea in order to ease tensions and build the framework for peaceful reunification of the peninsula. President Reagan commended President Chun for the

far-reaching proposal made on January 12, 1981 calling for an exchange of visits by the Presidents of the South and the North of Korea. President Reagan reaffirmed that the Republic of Korea must be a full participant in any United States negotiation with North Korea. The two Presidents shared the view that any unilateral steps toward North Korea which are not reciprocated toward South Korea by North Korea's principal allies would not be conducive to promoting stability or peace in the area.

7. Noting the strong ties of traditional friendship, alliance, and cooperation which have existed between the United States of America and the Republic of Korea, the two Presidents announced that they would resume immediately the full range of consultations between the two governments.

—US-ROK Security Consultative Meetings will be resumed promptly at a mutually convenient time later this spring.

—Annual U.S.-Korean economic Consultations covering the entire range of our economic relations will resume. The Under Secretary of State for Economic Affairs will lead a U.S. delegation to Korea to initiate these consultations before midyear.

—Annual U.S.-Korea policy planning talks will be resumed at a mutually convenient time this year.

8. President Reagan and President Chun expressed their satisfaction at the continuing expansion in the scope of economic relations between the two countries, and agreed to seek to foster a freer international trading system.

9. Presidents Reagan and Chun noted with satisfaction that mutually profitable U.S.-Korea trade had grown dramatically from $531 million in 1970 to $10 billion in 1980, and that the Republic of Korea is now the United States' twelfth largest trading partner. President Reagan emphasized in particular the importance of Korea as the fifth largest market for American agricultural exports. President Chun welcomed the positive response of the United States in meeting Korea's special needs this year for rice imports.

10. The two Presidents reaffirmed the close cooperation of the two countries on energy issues. The United States will seek to

assist Korea to obtain energy supplies in the event of an emergency affecting our mutual security interests. Korea will explore long term arrangements for importing American coal. President Reagan promised that the United States would remain a reliable supplier of nuclear fuel, generation equipment and power technology.

11. The two Presidents recognized that there remains a need for further promotion of mutual understanding and exchanges between the two peoples both through private and public channels, and they agreed to an early activation of the Korean-American Cultural Exchange Committee to be funded jointly by the two Governments.

12. President Reagan expressed special appreciation for the significant contribution to the Smithsonian Institution which President Chun presented on behalf of the Korean people for the construction of a new Museum of Eastern Art on the Mall in Washington. This museum will further enhance inter-cultural understanding and appreciation between the people of America and the peoples of Asia.

13. Pledging their mutual efforts to expand international cooperation throughout the Pacific Basin, the two Presidents expressed their intent to maintain close communication with each other and with other friends and allies in Asia. President Chun invited President Reagan to visit the Republic of Korea at a time of his convenience, and President Reagan accepted the invitation with pleasure.

14. President and Mrs. Chun, on behalf of themselves and the members of their party, expressed their deep appreciation to President and Mrs. Reagan and also to the people of the United States for the warmth of their friendly reception and the many courtesies extended to them both during the official visit to Washington and during their visits to other cities during their trip to the United States.

Appointment of Rear Admiral Robert M. Garrick as Deputy Counsellor to the President
February 2, 1981

The President announced today the appointment of Rear Adm. Robert M. Garrick as Deputy Counsellor to the President. Admiral Garrick will report to Edwin Meese III, Counsellor to the President.

Admiral Garrick is on leave from his position as senior vice president of Doremus & Co., an international public relations firm. He was deputy director of the transition for public affairs and served as director of research and policy development of the Reagan-Bush Campaign Committee.

Admiral Garrick attended Los Angeles City College, the University of Southern California, and the University of Hawaii, where he majored in journalism, radio, and aeronautical engineering. During World War II, he served as an enlisted combat correspondent in the U.S. Navy on the staff of Fleet Admiral Chester W. Nimitz. During his 4 years in the Navy, he advanced from yeoman 3/C to chief yeoman.

He was commissioned a lieutenant (j.g.) in the Naval Reserve in 1948 and in 1973 was promoted to the rank of rear admiral, as the Naval Reserve's first public affairs flag officer.

Following World War II, he returned to the Los Angeles Times-Mirror Corp. and served as assistant director of public relations. In 1947 he became director of public relations and advertising for the A. F. Gilmore Co. and the Hollywood Farmer's Market. He founded Robert M. Garrick Associates, a public relations consulting firm, in 1951, serving industrial and commercial firms and associations. In 1973 the firm was incorporated as Garrick Associates, Inc., and in 1975 the corporation merged with Doremus & Co.

Admiral Garrick retired from the Naval Reserve in March 1980 and was awarded the Legion of Merit. His other awards include two Navy Commendation medals, the

Asia-Pacific ribbon with 16 combat stars, and the World War II Victory, American Theatre, Naval Reserve Good Conduct, Philippines Liberation medals, and other citations. He is a member of the Public Relations Society of America and has been awarded the Society's Silver Anvil, the highest recognized award in the public relations field.

Admiral Garrick is married to the former Billie Clair Welsh of Kansas City, Mo. They have two children, Martin Welsh Garrick and Patti Kathleen Garrick. The Garricks reside in Pasadena and Bonsall, Calif.

Message on the Observance of the Chinese New Year
February 3, 1981

I am pleased to extend my warmest greetings and best wishes as millions of Chinese througout the world celebrate this New Year, the Year of the Rooster.

America is a strong and vibrant nation because its people are the people of many nations. They have given this land we love the inherited wisdom and strength of mankind's greatest civilizations, including that of China. Americans of Chinese ancestry can take pride in their cultural heritage and in the contributions they and their forebears have made to this country.

As we begin the New Year of 4679, we look forward with a vision of hope to a world where peace prevails and prosperity abounds.

Mrs. Reagan joins with me in extending our warmest regards to the Chinese American community.

RONALD REAGAN

Nomination of Charles M. Lichenstein To Be Alternate Representative for Special Political Affairs to the United Nations
February 3, 1981

The President announced today his intention to nominate Charles M. Lichenstein as Alternate Representative, [Special] Political Affairs, to the United Nations.

Since 1979 Mr. Lichenstein has been an independent consultant. His principal clients included the American Enterprise Institute for Public Policy Research, the Consortium for the Study of Intelligence, and the National Strategy Information Center. From 1975 to 1979, he was senior vice president with the Public Broadcasting Service in Washington, D.C. Mr. Lichenstein was Special Assistant to the President in 1974. He was special assistant and, later, administrative assistant to Chairman Dean Burch at the Federal Communications Commission from 1971 to 1974. From 1969 to 1971, Mr. Lichenstein was special assistant to Secretary Robert Finch at the Department of Health, Education, and Welfare and later Counsellor to the President.

From 1965 to 1968, he was a founding trustee, director of publications, and executive director of the Free Society Association in Washington, D.C. He was a freelance writer for Senator Goldwater and director of research for the Goldwater for President Committee and the Republican National Committee from 1963 to 1965. From 1959 to 1963, he was a research assistant to Richard Nixon. Mr. Lichenstein was an instructor in political science at the University of Notre Dame in 1958–59. He was a junior officer trainee, current intelligence analyst (Near East), and Special Projects Director (Office of Training) with the Central Intelligence Agency from 1952 to 1956.

Mr. Lichenstein received a B.A., M.A., and Ph. D. from Yale University. He served as an assistant instructor in political science at Yale and Albertus Magnus College in New Haven, Conn., in 1957–58. He resides in Washington, D.C., and was born on September 20, 1926.

Nomination of Marshall Brement To Be Deputy United States Representative to the United Nations
February 3, 1981

The President announced today his intention to nominate Marshall Brement as Deputy Representative to the United Nations.

In 1979 Mr. Brement was a staff member with the National Security Council, responsible for U.S.S.R., Eastern Europe, and East-West relations. In 1978-79 he was political counselor with the U.S. Embassy in Madrid, Spain. In 1977 he was with the RAND Corp.

From 1974 to 1976, he was political counselor with the U.S. Embassy in Moscow and was minister-counselor for public affairs with the U.S. Embassy in Saigon in 1973–74. From 1970 to 1973, he was counselor for public affairs with the U.S. Embassy in Djakarta. From 1967 to 1970, Mr. Brement was chief, political section, of the U.S. Embassy in Singapore.

In 1966 he was a National Institute of Public Affairs fellow at Stanford University. He served as second secretary with the U.S. Embassy in Moscow from 1964 to 1966. Mr. Brement was chief, internal political section, with the U.S. Consulate General in Hong Kong in 1961–63. In 1960–61 he was director of the press monitoring unit, U.S. Consulate General, in Hong Kong.

Mr. Brement in fluent in Russian, Mandarin, Cantonese, Indonesian, French, Spanish, and Hebrew. He was graduated from Brooklyn College (B.A., 1952) and the University of Maryland (M.A., 1955). He was in the United States Air Force from 1952 to 1954. Mr. Brement resides in Washington, D.C., and is 48 years old.

Nomination of Elliott Abrams To Be an Assistant Secretary of State
February 3, 1981

The President announced today his intention to nominate Elliott Abrams as Assistant Secretary of State for International Organizations. Mr. Abrams is currently an attorney with the Washington law firm of Verner, Lupert, Bernhard and McPherson.

From 1977 to 1979, Mr. Abrams served as special counsel to Senator Daniel Moynihan. In 1975–76 he served in the same capacity for Senator Henry Jackson. From 1970 to 1973, he was an attorney with the Boston firm of Breed, Abbott and Morgan.

Mr. Abrams received his B.A. degree from Harvard University in 1969, an M.Sc. degree from the London School of Economics in 1970, and his J.D. in 1973 from Harvard Law School.

Mr. Abrams is 33 years old and a resident of Washington, D.C.

Nomination of Thomas W. Pauken To Be Director of ACTION
February 3, 1981

The President announced today his intention to nominate Thomas Weir Pauken as Director of the ACTION agency. Since 1974 Mr. Pauken has been a practicing attorney and ran for the Texas State Senate in 1976 and the U.S. Congress in 1978 and 1980. He lost the races by small margins.

In 1967 he enlisted in the United States Army and served for 3 years on active duty. A year later he received a direct commission as a lieutenant in military intelligence and served in Vietnam. He was discharged with the rank of first lieutenant. Upon completing his military service, Mr. Pauken was Associate Director of the White House Fellowship program and a White House staff assistant.

In 1965 Mr. Pauken was elected national chairman of the College Republicans, and he served for 2 years as a chief spokesman for the Republican Party on campuses where he participated in hundreds of symposiums and debates.

In 1961 Mr. Pauken entered Georgetown University in Washington, D.C., on an academic scholarship. While in college, he worked for Senator John Tower and Representative Bill Stinson.

Mr. Pauken is married to the former Ida Ayala of Corpus Christi, Tex., and has five children. He resides with his family in Mesquite, Tex. Mr. Pauken was born on January 11, 1944.

Nomination of David S. Swoap To Be Under Secretary of Health and Human Services
February 3, 1981

The President today announced his intention to nominate David B. Swoap to be Under Secretary of Health and Human Services. Mr. Swoap is currently legislative director in the office of William Armstrong, United States Senator from Colorado, a position in which he has served since February 1979.

From October 1976 to February 1979, Mr. Swoap served as a professional staff member on the U.S. Senate Committee on Finance. He served as a senior research associate with the Republican Study Committee of the U.S. House of Representatives from February 1975 to October 1976, and from February 1974 to January 1975, Mr. Swoap served as director of the California State Department of Benefit Payments. From May 1973 to February 1974, he served as director of the California State Department of Social Welfare, and from March to May 1973, he served as chief deputy director and acting director of that department. Mr. Swoap served as assistant

secretary of the California State Personnel Board from February 1972 to March 1973, and from February 1967 to February 1972, he served as district coordinator for California State Senator Howard Way. Mr. Swoap served as a consultant to the California Senate Fact Finding Committee on Labor and Welfare from September 1965 to February 1967, and from September 1964 to August 1965, he served as assistant administrative analyst in the office of the legislative analyst of the joint legislative budget committee of the California State Legislature. Mr. Swoap was employed by the Conlin Travel Bureau (Ann Arbor, Mich.) from January to May 1964 and served as a legislative assistant to California Assemblyman Hoston Flournoy from September to December 1962. From 1956 to 1958, he served as clerk in the office of Congressman Donald E. Tewes (Wisconsin).

Mr. Swoap received a B.A. degree from Denison University in 1959 and an M.A. (in government) from Claremont Graduate

School in 1961. He is a member of Phi Beta Kappa and Omicron Delta Kappa. He served as a member of the U.S. Army Reserve from February 1963 to January 1969. Mr. Swoap is a member of the American Public Welfare Association and the National Welfare Fraud Association.

Mr. Swoap was born on August 12, 1937. He is single and resides in Fairfax, Va.

Nomination of Seeley Lodwick To Be an Under Secretary of Agriculture
February 4, 1981

The President announced today his intention to nominate Seeley Lodwick to be Under Secretary of Agriculture for International Affairs and Commodity Programs. Mr. Lodwick recently served as codirector of the farm and food division of the Reagan-Bush Committee. He organized the agriculture sector in 50 States and worked closely with farm organizations and agricultural firms.

In 1979–80 he served as Iowa administrator for U.S. Senator Roger W. Jepsen, responsible for the operation of each of the Senator's six Iowa district offices and for maintaining liaison with various State organizations. His government responsibilities have included 7 years as an Iowa State senator. He was elected president pro tempore of that body during his last year of service. His 5 years with the Federal Government began with the U.S. Department of Agriculture as Director of the Conservation and Land Use Division, later becoming Secretary of the Commodity Credit Corporation and leaving the Department after the election of 1976 as Associate Administrator of the Agricultural Stabilization and Conservation Service. He also served as director of government relations in the Washington office of the American Farm Bureau Federation.

Mr. Lodwick was appointed by Governor Robert Ray to the Iowa Agriculture Promotion Board and the Iowa Air Quality Commission. He served as a lieutenant in the First Marine Division during World War II. He is a member of the Iowa Farm Bureau, American Soybean Association, Iowa Corn Growers Association, Food and Agriculture Committee of the U.S. Chamber of Commerce, Soil Conservation Society of America, Society of American Farm Managers, Society of Agricultural Consultants, Rotary, and others.

He and his wife, Pat, are both graduates of Iowa State University. They have three daughters, all of whom are college graduates and now married. Mr. Lodwick lives with his wife on a farm near Wever, Iowa. He is 60 years old.

Appointment of Stephen M. Studdert as Special Assistant to the President and Director of the Advance Office
February 4, 1981

The President today announced the appointment of Stephen M. Studdert as Special Assistant to the President and Director of the Advance Office.

Since 1977 Mr. Studdert has been an independent businessman in the areas of residential housing and land development in Utah. During the 1980 campaign he took leave from business interests to direct the press advance office and served as deputy press secretary with the Reagan-Bush Committee.

From 1975 to 1977, he was Staff Assistant to the President and a member of the press advance staff at the White House. Mr. Studdert was chief of police in Brigham City, Utah, in 1973–75. From 1971 to 1973, he served as coordinator of State police planning for the State of Utah.

Civic activities include being elected a member of the Bountiful City Council and Jaycee president. He received the distinguished service award as the Outstanding Young Community Leader in two separate communities. Mr. Studdert has served on many local advisory commissions.

Mr. Studdert has been an active participant in Republican Party politics, including serving as a political consultant to the speaker of the Utah house of representatives and field advance coordinator to Vice-Presidential nominee Robert Dole in 1976.

Mr. Studdert is a graduate of Brigham Young University. He was a lecturer at Weber State College in 1973-75. He has been listed in Outstanding Young Men of America for 5 consecutive years. He is listed in Who's Who in the West and was named one of three Outstanding Young Men in Utah. He received the outstanding service award from the U.S. Indian Health Service for his work with Indian youth.

Mr. Studdert is married to the former Donnie Beck, and they have six children. He lives with his family in Bountiful, Utah. Mr. Studdert is 33 years old.

Appointment of Robert B. Carleson as Special Assistant to the President for Policy Development
February 4, 1981

The President announced today the appointment of Robert B. Carleson as Special Assistant to the President for Policy Development.

Mr. Carleson will be responsible for assisting in the formulation and coordination of plans to implement one of the President's major goals, the return of authority and responsibility for various programs from the Federal to State and local levels of government. He will report to Edwin J. Gray, Deputy Assistant to the President and Director of the White House Office of Policy Development.

Until his appointment, Mr. Carleson served as president of Robert B. Carleson and Associates, a management and public policy consulting firm which he founded in 1975.

From 1973 to 1975, Mr. Carleson served as U.S. Commissioner of Welfare. From 1971 to 1973, he was director of the California Department of Social Welfare, where he directed the design and implementation of then Governor Reagan's model welfare reform program.

From 1968 to 1971, he served as chief deputy director of the California Department of Public Works. From 1960 to 1968, Mr. Carleson was city manager of first, San Dimas and then Pico Rivera, Calif. From 1956 to 1960, he worked for the cities of Beverly Hills, Claremont, and Torrance, Calif.

Mr. Carleson attended the University of Utah and graduated from the University of Southern California with a degree (and postgraduate work) in public administration. He served as an officer in the navy during and after the Korean war, attached to the First Marine Division.

A second generation Californian, Mr. Carleson has three children living in California.

Remarks at the Annual Salute to Congress Dinner
February 4, 1981

The President. Madam Chairman, thank you very much, and thank you especially for not giving me a question. [*Laughter*]

I'm a little surprised to find myself at this podium tonight. I know your organization was founded by six Washington newspaperwomen in 1919—seems only yesterday. [*Laughter*] I know that it was Washington's National Press Club for over a half a century, so I thought that tonight's production would be equal time, right? A night for Nancy. Then I learned of your 1971 pioneering and coeducational Washington press corps. You changed the name. You admitted male members. You also encouraged male speakers. So, here I am, a poor but modest substitute for the former Nancy Davis, ready to defend myself and every other middle-aged male in America. [*Laughter*]

I can define "middle-aged." That's when you're faced with two temptations and you choose the one that'll get you home at 9 o'clock. [*Laughter*]

I do want to congratulate the Washington Press Club for forward-looking leadership, and I hope that Ann McFeatters and Carol Richards and all of you succeed quickly in your effort to acquire a clubhouse. [*Laughter*] And if we have our way and you wait a little bit there will be several public buildings that will be open to——[*laughter*].

But I tell you, it's good to be here with all my fellow classmates in the freshman class. Merv—you know that Merv and I came here by way of Sacramento. Merv was a Lieutenant Governor for Governor Brown. The difference you'll find here, Merv, is that the flakes are real. [*Laughter*] And if enough of them fall from heaven, it stops traffic for hours. And Senator D'Amato, if I could raise the kind of money with my pictures you're talking about, hell, I'd still be there. [*Laughter*]

Congressman Savage, I understand very well all that you were saying about Chicago. I had an uncle who was a Democrat in Chicago. He received a silver cup from the party for never having missed voting in 14 elections. He'd been dead for 15 of them. [*Laughter*] And I appreciated Senator Dodd's concern about those people from Eau Claire, Wisconsin, that couldn't get into some of the things at the Inaugural. We have taken care of that problem—just told them to hang on to them for about 4 more years. [*Laughter*]

But to get back to the view of the press club, I think that you're taking this honeymoon idea too seriously. I passed a Marriott drive-in and saw Helen Thomas trying to carry Jim Brady over the threshold. [*Laughter*] But it isn't all honeymoon. If I'm on a honeymoon, romance is dead in Washington. Jesse Helms wants me to move to the right; Lowell Weicker wants me to move to the left; Teddy Kennedy wants me to move back to California. [*Laughter*] And while I have the opportunity with so many of the press, I want you to know that it is not true that the Moral Majority has been trying to exert undue influence. That rumor started recently when Jerry Falwell called me with a suggestion for Ambassador to Iran: the publisher of Penthouse. [*Laughter*]

I've been spending some of my time trying to meet the Democratic Members of Congress half way, and the half-way house I found is Tip O'Neill's office. [*Laughter*]

But I am glad that you asked me here and seriously would like to explain that Nancy would have been with me. Maybe it was just the cold; I hope it was. She thought and felt like maybe she was coming down with something, and we're both scheduled very early in the morning for the Prayer Breakfast. And so, I was instrumental in telling her she should stay home by the fire and drink warm milk and maybe we'll be together in the morning.

So, I look forward to seeing all of you, the members particularly again, in a businesslike way. And please, for heaven's sake, don't stand up and wave and shout, or Jim Brady will take away my privileges. [*Laughter*]

Thank you.

Ms. McFeatters. Thank you, Mr. President.

And now before you leave, we would like to celebrate Friday the 6th, your birthday, 2 days early, before it's declared a national holiday. [*Laughter*] On behalf of the Washington Press Club, I would like to give you this poster, which shows you and Mrs. Reagan a year or so ago, and it's been titled "The Winning Team."

And now will you please all join me in a hearty rendition of "Happy Birthday, Mr. President."

[*The audience sang "Happy Birthday, Mr. President."*]

The President. Thank you very much.

I'm delighted to have this. And I just want to say that I don't mind at all any of the jokes or remarks about age, because Thomas Jefferson made a comment about the Presidency and age. He said that one should not worry about one's exact chronological age in reference to his ability to perform one's task. And ever since he told me that—[*laughter*]—I stopped worrying.

Thank you.

Note: The President spoke at 10:49 p.m. in the Sheraton Ballroom at the Sheraton Washington Hotel. Ann McFeatters is president of the Washington Press Club, which sponsored the dinner.

Remarks at the Annual National Prayer Breakfast
February 5, 1981

Mr. Chairman, Congressman Hefner, and all of you ladies and gentlemen:

Nancy and I are delighted to be here, and I want to thank you for the day in my life that you recognized in starting off my celebration of my 31st anniversary of my 39th birthday. [*Laughter*] But to all of you, to the many who are here from across the world and the different lands—and as the chairman told us earlier, I was surprised to learn that we are joined this morning by meetings of this kind in places that might be surprising to some: on naval vessels, military bases, even in penal institutions, all across our land.

You have taken Nancy and me back to a nostalgic time, because I have found myself remembering at occasions like this, in a hotel dining room not quite so grand or not quite so large, but the Governor's Breakfasts of Sacramento. And they were always enriching, spiritual experiences, and I think maybe—I haven't checked with Nancy about her—but I think for both of us I could say that this morning we are freed from the last vestige of homesickness.

I would like to tell just a little story. It was given to me by a friend on a printed card, author unknown. Now, I don't know how widely this has been distributed, or whether some of you or many of you are aware of it. I'm going to tell it anyway.

This unknown author wrote of a dream and in the dream was walking down the beach beside the Lord. And as they walked, above him in the sky was reflected each stage and experience of his life. Reaching the end of the beach, and of his life, he turned back and looked back down the beach and saw the two sets of footprints in the sand, except that he looked again and realized that every once in a while there was only one set of footprints. And each time there was only one set of footprints, it was when the experience reflected in the sky was one of of despair, of desolation, of great trial or grief in his life.

And he turned to the Lord and said, "You said that if I would walk with You, You would always be beside me and take my hand. Why did You desert me? Why are You not there in my times of greatest need?" And the Lord said, "My child, I did not leave you. Where you see only one set of footprints, it was there that I carried you."

Abraham Lincoln once said, "I would be the most foolish person on this footstool earth if I believed for one moment that I could perform the duties assigned to me without the help of one who is wiser than all." I know that in the days to come and the years ahead there are going to be many times when there will only be one set of footprints in my life. If I did not believe that, I could not face the days ahead.

Note: The President spoke at 8:58 a.m. in the International Ballroom at the Washington Hilton Hotel. In his opening remarks, he referred to Representative Elwood H. Hillis of Indiana, chairman of the National Prayer Breakfast Congressional Committee, which sponsored the breakfast.

Remarks to Delegates of the United States Senate Youth Program
February 5, 1981

The President. Is Charlie Gould here? Where's Charlie? Hey Charlie, how are you? Well, now you'll make me all homesick again. [*Laughter*] I know you've been welcomed and probably several times since you've been here. I'll just add mine to it.

You're now in the famous Rose Garden. Now, I have to confess something to you. When I came here to live a couple of weeks ago, I had always thought that the Rose Garden, the whole thing, was roses. [*Laughter*] I didn't know that it was a grass garden with a few roses along one side. I better not say that to Nancy or she'll get busy with a spade—[*laughter*]—and we'll have them.

Anyway, you are welcome, and I am so proud, first of all, of the Hearst Foundation doing this, the Senate sponsoring also at this end a visit of this kind. You've been chosen—very obviously have leadership qualities or you wouldn't be here—two from each State in our Union, and I know you must be very proud of having been selected for this. We're very proud of you.

For how many of you is this the first visit to Washington? If you haven't already, I know you will see all of the historic monuments and the places here that should be seen. Have you been to Lincoln's Monument yet—Lincoln's Memorial? You have. Then it won't do me any good to tip you off. [*Laughter*] I was going to tell you that I learned the first time I was here, someone told me that if you stand on one side of that massive statue and look up at his face, you see the compassion of Lincoln. If you go around to the other side and look—and the artist must have intended this—you see the strength of the man, a difference in his face

depending on which side you're standing. But you've been there now, and I know they won't want to interrupt the schedule for you to go back. Just take my word for it—it's there.

But seriously, I think you all know, or you wouldn't be here, the importance of leadership in our country—what you represent. Many years before your time there was—I know you've heard of him—there was a great cowboy philosopher and wit. Many people remember him more as a comedian than as a philosopher, but Will Rogers—and it's so easy to be cynical these days; you're bombarded with so many words every day—and Will Rogers responded once about the people who hold elective office. He said, "They are no better and no worse than the people who send them there. But they are all better than those who don't vote at all." So, use that leadership in the future. Use it to get your peers, your generation involved in public life. Ours is a government truly by the people, and we've tended many times in the past just through apathy on the part of our people to forget that and turn it over to someone else. You're going to run your lives, or politicians are going to run them for you. The choice is up to you. They are—and we—I forget every once in a while—[*laughter*]—we are your servants to make that system work.

I'm going to quit running off here now, because you'll all get cold from standing there.

Delegates. No!

The President. For a Californian it's cold.

But I had a copy of the Soviet Constitution, and I read it with great interest. And I saw all kinds of terms in there that sound just exactly like our own: "freedom of assembly" and "freedom of speech" and so forth. Of course, they don't allow them to have those things, but they're in there in the constitution. But I began to wonder about the other constitutions—everyone has one—and our own and why so much emphasis on ours. And then I found out, and the answer was very simple. That's why you don't notice it at first, but it is so great that it tells the entire difference. All those other constitutions are documents that say that "We, the government, allow the people the following rights," and our Constitution says "We, the people, allow the government the following privileges and rights."

We give our permission to government to do the things that it does. And that's the whole story of the difference—why we're unique in the world and why no matter what our troubles may be, we're going to overcome all of those troubles—and with your help and support, because it's an ongoing process.

God bless you all for being here, and thank you for being here.

Note: The President spoke at 11:20 a.m. in the Rose Garden at the White House. In his opening remarks, he greeted Charles L. Gould, vice president of the William Randolph Hearst Foundation, which sponsored the program.

Address to the Nation on the Economy
February 5, 1981

Good evening.

I'm speaking to you tonight to give you a report on the state of our Nation's economy. I regret to say that we're in the worst economic mess since the Great Depression.

A few days ago I was presented with a report I'd asked for, a comprehensive audit, if you will, of our economic condition. You won't like it. I didn't like it. But we have to face the truth and then go to work to turn things around. And make no mistake about it, we can turn them around.

I'm not going to subject you to the jumble of charts, figures, and economic jargon of that audit, but rather will try to explain where we are, how we got there, and how we can get back. First, however, let me just give a few "attention getters" from the audit.

The Federal budget is out of control, and we face runaway deficits of almost $80 billion for this budget year that ends September 30th. That deficit is larger than the entire Federal budget in 1957, and so is the almost $80 billion we will pay in interest this year on the national debt.

Twenty years ago, in 1960, our Federal Government payroll was less than $13 bil-

lion. Today it is 75 billion. During these 20 years our population has only increased by 23.3 percent. The Federal budget has gone up 528 percent.

Now, we've just had 2 years of back-to-back double-digit inflation—13.3 percent in 1979, 12.4 percent last year. The last time this happened was in World War I.

In 1960 mortgage interest rates averaged about 6 percent. They're 2½ times as high now, 15.4 percent.

The percentage of your earnings the Federal Government took in taxes in 1960 has almost doubled.

And finally there are 7 million Americans caught up in the personal indignity and human tragedy of unemployment. If they stood in a line, allowing 3 feet for each person, the line would reach from the coast of Maine to California.

Well, so much for the audit itself. Let me try to put this in personal terms. Here is a dollar such as you earned, spent, or saved in 1960. And here is a quarter, a dime, and a penny—36 cents. That's what this 1960 dollar is worth today. And if the present world inflation rate should continue 3 more years, that dollar of 1960 will be worth a quarter. What initiative is there to save? And if we don't save we're short of the investment capital needed for business and industry expansion. Workers in Japan and West Germany save several times the percentage of their income than Americans do.

What's happened to that American dream of owning a home? Only 10 years ago a family could buy a home, and the monthly payment averaged little more than a quarter—27 cents out of each dollar earned. Today, it takes 42 cents out of every dollar of income. So, fewer than 1 out of 11 families can afford to buy their first new home.

Regulations adopted by government with the best of intentions have added $666 to the cost of an automobile. It is estimated that altogether regulations of every kind, on shopkeepers, farmers, and major industries, add $100 billion or more to the cost of the goods and services we buy. And then another 20 billion is spent by government handling the paperwork created by those regulations.

I'm sure you're getting the idea that the audit presented to me found government policies of the last few decades responsible for our economic troubles. We forgot or just overlooked the fact that government—any government—has a built-in tendency to grow. Now, we all had a hand in looking to government for benefits as if government had some source of revenue other than our earnings. Many if not most of the things we thought of or that government offered to us seemed attractive.

In the years following the Second World War it was easy, for a while at least, to overlook the price tag. Our income more than doubled in the 25 years after the war. We increased our take-home pay in those 25 years by more than we had amassed in all the preceding 150 years put together. Yes, there was some inflation, 1 or 1½ percent a year. That didn't bother us. But if we look back at those golden years, we recall that even then voices had been raised, warning that inflation, like radioactivity, was cumulative and that once started it could get out of control.

Some government programs seemed so worthwhile that borrowing to fund them didn't bother us. By 1960 our national debt stood at $284 billion. Congress in 1971 decided to put a ceiling of 400 billion on our ability to borrow. Today the debt is 934 billion. So-called temporary increases or extensions in the debt ceiling have been allowed 21 times in these 10 years, and now I've been forced to ask for another increase in the debt ceiling or the government will be unable to function past the middle of February—and I've only been here 16 days. Before we reach the day when we can reduce the debt ceiling, we may in spite of our best efforts see a national debt in excess of a trillion dollars. Now, this is a figure that's literally beyond our comprehension.

We know now that inflation results from all that deficit spending. Government has only two ways of getting money other than raising taxes. It can go into the money market and borrow, competing with its own citizens and driving up interest rates, which it has done, or it can print money, and it's done that. Both methods are inflationary.

We're victims of language. The very word "inflation" leads us to think of it as just high prices. Then, of course, we resent the person who puts on the price tags, forgetting that he or she is also a victim of inflation. Inflation is not just high prices; it's a reduction in the value of our money. When the money supply is increased but the goods and services available for buying are not, we have too much money chasing too few goods. Wars are usually accompanied by inflation. Everyone is working or fighting, but production is of weapons and munitions, not things we can buy and use.

Now, one way out would be to raise taxes so that government need not borrow or print money. But in all these years of government growth, we've reached, indeed surpassed, the limit of our people's tolerance or ability to bear an increase in the tax burden. Prior to World War II, taxes were such that on the average we only had to work just a little over 1 month each year to pay our total Federal, State, and local tax bill. Today we have to work 4 months to pay that bill.

Some say shift the tax burden to business and industry, but business doesn't pay taxes. Oh, don't get the wrong idea. Business is being taxed, so much so that we're being priced out of the world market. But business must pass its costs of operations—and that includes taxes—on to the customer in the price of the product. Only people pay taxes, all the taxes. Government just uses business in a kind of sneaky way to help collect the taxes. They're hidden in the price; we aren't aware of how much tax we actually pay.

Today this once great industrial giant of ours has the lowest rate of gain in productivity of virtually all the industrial nations with whom we must compete in the world market. We can't even hold our own market here in America against foreign automobiles, steel, and a number of other products. Japanese production of automobiles is almost twice as great per worker as it is in America. Japanese steelworkers outproduce their American counterparts by about 25 percent.

Now, this isn't because they're better workers. I'll match the American working man or woman against anyone in the world. But we have to give them the tools and equipment that workers in the other industrial nations have.

We invented the assembly line and mass production, but punitive tax policies and excessive and unnecessary regulations plus government borrowing have stifled our ability to update plant and equipment. When capital investment is made, it's too often for some unproductive alterations demanded by government to meet various of its regulations. Excessive taxation of individuals has robbed us of incentive and made overtime unprofitable.

We once produced about 40 percent of the world's steel. We now produce 19 percent. We were once the greatest producer of automobiles, producing more than all the rest of the world combined. That is no longer true, and in addition, the "Big Three," the major auto companies in our land, have sustained tremendous losses in the past year and have been forced to lay off thousands of workers.

All of you who are working know that even with cost-of-living pay raises, you can't keep up with inflation. In our progressive tax system, as you increase the number of dollars you earn, you find yourself moved up into higher tax brackets, paying a higher

tax rate just for trying to hold your own. The result? Your standard of living is going down.

Over the past decades we've talked of curtailing government spending so that we can then lower the tax burden. Sometimes we've even taken a run at doing that. But there were always those who told us that taxes couldn't be cut until spending was reduced. Well, you know, we can lecture our children about extravagance until we run out of voice and breath. Or we can cure their extravagance by simply reducing their allowance.

It's time to recognize that we've come to a turning point. We're threatened with an economic calamity of tremendous proportions, and the old business-as-usual treatment can't save us. Together, we must chart a different course.

We must increase productivity. That means making it possible for industry to modernize and make use of the technology which we ourselves invented. That means putting Americans back to work. And that means above all bringing government spending back within government revenues, which is the only way, together with increased productivity, that we can reduce and, yes, eliminate inflation.

In the past we've tried to fight inflation one year and then, with unemployment increased, turn the next year to fighting unemployment with more deficit spending as a pump primer. So, again, up goes inflation. It hasn't worked. We don't have to choose between inflation and unemployment—they go hand in hand. It's time to try something different, and that's what we're going to do.

I've already placed a freeze on hiring replacements for those who retire or leave government service. I've ordered a cut in government travel, the number of consultants to the government, and the buying of office equipment and other items. I've put a freeze on pending regulations and set up a task force under Vice President Bush to review regulations with an eye toward getting rid of as many as possible. I have decontrolled oil, which should result in more domestic production and less dependence on foreign oil. And I'm eliminating that ineffective Council on Wage and Price Stability.

But it will take more, much more. And we must realize there is no quick fix. At the same time, however, we cannot delay in implementing an economic program aimed at both reducing tax rates to stimulate productivity and reducing the growth in government spending to reduce unemployment and inflation.

On February 18th, I will present in detail an economic program to Congress embodying the features I've just stated. It will propose budget cuts in virtually every department of government. It is my belief that these actual budget cuts will only be part of the savings. As our Cabinet Secretaries take charge of their departments, they will search out areas of waste, extravagance, and costly overhead which could yield additional and substantial reductions.

Now, at the same time we're doing this, we must go forward with a tax relief package. I shall ask for a 10-percent reduction across the board in personal income tax rates for each of the next 3 years. Proposals will also be submitted for accelerated depreciation allowances for business to provide necessary capital so as to create jobs.

Now, here again, in saying this, I know that language, as I said earlier, can get in the way of a clear understanding of what our program is intended to do. Budget cuts can sound as if we're going to reduce total government spending to a lower level than was spent the year before. Well, this is not the case. The budgets will increase as our population increases, and each year we'll see spending increases to match that growth. Government revenues will increase as the economy grows, but the burden will be lighter for each individual, because the economic base will have been expanded by reason of the reduced rates.

Now, let me show you a chart that I've had drawn to illustrate how this can be.

Here you see two trend lines. The bottom line shows the increase in tax revenues. The red line on top is the increase in government spending. Both lines turn upward, reflecting the giant tax increase already built into the system for this year 1981, and the increases in spending built into the '81 and '82 budgets and on into the future. As you

can see, the spending line rises at a steeper slant than the revenue line. And that gap between those lines illustrates the increasing deficits we've been running, including this year's $80 billion deficit.

Now, in the second chart, the lines represent the positive effects when Congress accepts our economic program. Both lines continue to rise, allowing for necessary growth, but the gap narrows as spending cuts continue over the next few years until finally the two lines come together, meaning a balanced budget.

I am confident that my administration can achieve that. At that point tax revenues, in spite of rate reductions, will be increasing faster than spending, which means we can look forward to further reductions in the tax rates.

Now, in all of this we will, of course, work closely with the Federal Reserve System toward the objective of a stable monetary policy.

Our spending cuts will not be at the expense of the truly needy. We will, however, seek to eliminate benefits to those who are not really qualified by reason of need.

As I've said before, on February 18th I will present this economic package of budget reductions and tax reform to a joint session of Congress and to you in full detail.

Our basic system is sound. We can, with compassion, continue to meet our responsibility to those who, through no fault of their own, need our help. We can meet fully the other legitimate responsibilities of government. We cannot continue any longer our wasteful ways at the expense of the workers of this land or of our children.

Since 1960 our government has spent $5.1 trillion. Our debt has grown by 648 billion. Prices have exploded by 178 percent. How much better off are we for all that? Well, we all know we're very much worse off. When we measure how harshly these years of inflation, lower productivity, and uncontrolled government growth have affected our lives, we know we must act and act now. We must not be timid. We will restore the freedom of all men and women to excel and to create. We will unleash the energy and genius of the American people, traits which have never failed us.

To the Congress of the United States, I extend my hand in cooperation, and I believe we can go forward in a bipartisan manner. I've found a real willingness to cooperate on the part of Democrats and members of my own party.

To my colleagues in the executive branch of government and to all Federal employees, I ask that we work in the spirit of service.

I urge those great institutions in America, business and labor, to be guided by the national interest, and I'm confident they will. The only special interest that we will serve is the interest of all the people.

We can create the incentives which take advantage of the genius of our economic system—a system, as Walter Lippmann observed more than 40 years ago, which for the first time in history gave men "a way of producing wealth in which the good fortune of others multiplied their own."

Our aim is to increase our national wealth so all will have more, not just redistribute what we already have which is just a sharing of scarcity. We can begin to reward hard work and risk-taking, by forcing this Government to live within its means.

Over the years we've let negative economic forces run out of control. We stalled the judgment day, but we no longer have that luxury. We're out of time.

And to you, my fellow citizens, let us join in a new determination to rebuild the foundation of our society, to work together, to act responsibly. Let us do so with the most profound respect for that which must be preserved as well as with sensitive understanding and compassion for those who must be protected.

We can leave our children with an unrepayable massive debt and a shattered economy, or we can leave them liberty in a land where every individual has the opportunity to be whatever God intended us to be. All it takes is a little common sense and recognition of our own ability. Together we can forge a new beginning for America.

Thank you, and good night.

Note: The President spoke at 9:02 p.m. from the Oval Office at the White House. His remarks were broadcast live on radio and television.

Remarks on Signing a Proclamation Designating 1981 as the International Year of Disabled Persons
February 6, 1981

I'm going to sign a proclamation here.

Few, if any, resources offer more potential, I think, than our 35 million disabled Americans. Too often they are relegated to the sidelines in spite of, in many cases, outstanding abilities. The International Year of Disabled Persons is an excellent example of how partnerships work.

Our Federal interagency task force of Government employees on special assignment has done an outstanding job. Alan Reich and David Kearns have demonstrated the best of American resourcefulness in establishing the private sector U.S. Council for the International Year of Disabled Persons. They've done this to assist the disabled in accomplishing their own goals.

I'm proud to participate in this International Year to help increase the awareness of each and every one of us, to commit that we'll make that extra effort in 1981 to assist our disabled in moving into the mainstream of American life. It takes so little, and it offers the promise of so much, because our most valuable resource is our people.

I was very proud in California that we started a program that did so much and to see people who had previously been sidelined actually involved and self-sufficient in contributing to our welfare and to society.

So, with that, I shall now with great pleasure sign this proclamation.

Note: The President spoke at 11:45 a.m. at the signing ceremony in the Oval Office at the White House.

Proclamation 4818—International Year of Disabled Persons
February 6, 1981

By the President of the United States of America

A Proclamation

We seek, in the 1980s, an era of national renewal, an era that will set loose again the energy and ingenuity of the American people.

Today there are 35 million disabled Americans who represent one of our most underutilized national resources. Their will, their spirit, and their hearts are not impaired, despite their limitations. All of us stand to gain when those who are disabled share in America's opportunities.

To increase the participation of disabled persons in our national life and in the lives of other nations the United Nations has designated 1981 the International Year of Disabled Persons. America has long been a world leader in this area, and the United States Council for the International Year of Disabled Persons and our Federal government have already responded to the United Nations challenge. Programs are underway throughout the Nation.

Through partnerships of disabled and nondisabled persons; of our private sector and our government; and of our national, state, and community organizations, we can expand the opportunities for disabled Americans to make a fuller contribution to our national life. I am proud to pledge the cooperation of my Administration and the Federal agencies under my jurisdiction, including the Federal Interagency Committee for the International Year of Disabled Persons.

Now, Therefore, in keeping with the goals of the International Year, I, *Ronald Reagan*, President of the United States of America, do hereby proclaim 1981 the International Year of Disabled Persons in the United States.

In Witness Whereof, I have hereunto set my hand this sixth day of February, in the year of our Lord nineteen hundred eighty-one, and of the Independence of the United States of America the two hundred and fifth.

RONALD REAGAN

[*Filed with the Office of the Federal Register, 2:13 p.m., February 9, 1981*]

Statement on the Death of Former Governor Ella T. Grasso of Connecticut
February 6, 1981

Governor Ella Grasso was a determined and spirited public servant who brought to her life the energies of the committed. She worked hard to make State government work, and her service to the people of Connecticut was unstinting.

Nancy joins me in extending our deepest sympathy to Governor Grasso's family.

Appointment of James H. Cavanaugh as Special Consultant to the President
February 6, 1981

The President today announced the appointment of James H. Cavanaugh as Special Consultant to the President. In this capacity he will provide advice and consultation on the management of the Presidential appointment process.

Dr. Cavanaugh is president of Allergan International, a unit of the Allergan Pharmaceutical Co. in Irvine, Calif. He was senior vice president for science and planning, having joined the company in 1977.

Prior to that he was on the White House staff, which he joined in 1971 as staff assistant to President Nixon for health affairs. He was named Associate Director of the Domestic Council staff in 1973, becoming Deputy Director of the Domestic Council staff the following year. In 1976 he was named Deputy Assistant to the President for Domestic Affairs and served as Deputy Chief of the White House staff under President Ford.

Prior to his White House service, he was Deputy Assistant Secretary for Health and Scientific Affairs at the U.S. Department of Health, Education, and Welfare. He was a member of the faculty of the Graduate College at the University of Iowa and has served as a consultant to various public and private health care organizations throughout North and South America.

He is a director of the Greater Irvine, Calif., Industrial League and a member of the executive committee of the board of directors of the Lincoln Club of Orange County, Calif. He is on the board of councilors of the School of Pharmacy of the University of Southern California.

He served as one of the President's economic and domestic advisers during the Presidential campaign and was deputy director of the Office of Presidential Personnel of the transition group.

Dr. Cavanaugh, 43, is a graduate of Fairleigh Dickinson University (B.S., 1959) and the University of Iowa (M.A., 1961; Ph. D., 1964).

He is a native of Madison, N. J. He resides with his wife, Esther, and two children in Newport Beach, Calif.

Memorandum on the Fiscal Year 1982 Budget
February 7, 1981

Memorandum for Heads of Non-Cabinet Agencies

Subject: Revisions of the 1982 Budget

The comprehensive economic program that I will present to the Congress on February 18, 1981, will describe spending reductions, tax reductions and actions to remove unnecessary regulatory burdens.

For the past several weeks, members of the Cabinet and I have been identifying major policy and program changes that must be made to begin bringing spending under control. These major changes will be outlined in my February 18th address.

In addition to these major items, reductions will have to made in virtually every agency for fiscal year 1981, 1982 and the future. This memorandum is to ask your cooperation in this second phase of our review and to outline the process and schedule that we must follow in order to submit a fully revised 1982 budget—including the details of the major changes I announce on February 18th and all other revisions of the budget submitted by President Carter on January 15th—to the Congress by March 10, 1981.

At my direction, the full review of the remainder of the Carter budget is already underway in the Office of Management and

Budget. The remaining steps in the revision process will of necessity be much more compressed than would normally be possible and the procedure will be very demanding for all of us. More specifically:

• During the next 9 days, OMB will complete its review, consult with my senior advisers and me as appropriate, and at my direction, will advise each agency of additional reductions that are needed from the Carter budget to achieve our spending and employment reduction goals.

• If you believe there are better ways of achieving the reductions, I ask that you convey your views to the Director of OMB in writing within 48 hours after receiving the revised budget and employment limits.

• I will look to you and the Office of Management and Budget to resolve any differences promptly and, in those few cases where they cannot be resolved, to bring those differences to me jointly for final decision. Of necessity, I need to receive such items within 4 days of the time that you receive the initial notification from OMB.

Some agencies will begin receiving the initial notification by February 9th. The entire process must be completed promptly for all departments and agencies to allow time for your preparation of supporting materials and for compiling and printing the revised budget. Your cooperation in this effort is appreciated.

RONALD REAGAN

Nomination of Fred C. Ikle To Be an Under Secretary of Defense
February 7, 1981

The President announced today his intention to nominate Fred C. Ikle to be Under Secretary of Defense for Policy.

Dr. Ikle was an adviser to the transition group on national security. Previously he served as a senior foreign policy adviser to the Reagan-Bush Committee.

Dr. Ikle was Director of the U.S. Arms

Control and Disarmament Agency and professor of political science at M.I.T. He was head of the social sciences department at the RAND Corp.

Dr. Ikle was graduated from the University of Chicago (M.A., 1948; Ph. D., 1950). Dr. Ikle is a resident of Bethesda, Md., and was born on August 21, 1924.

Appointment of Judy F. Peachee as Special Assistant to the President
February 9, 1981

The President announced today the appointment of Judy F. Peachee to be Special Assistant to the President. She will serve in the Intergovernmental Affairs Division of the White House.

Since 1976 Ms. Peachee has served as national committeewoman to the Republican National Committee. She has also served as special assistant for State affairs to Senator John W. Warner since 1979.

In 1978 she was campaign manager, Obenshain for U.S. Senate and Warner for U.S. Senate in Virginia. In 1977 she was State organization director, Dalton for Governor campaign. In 1976 Mrs. Peachee served as State organization director, President Ford Committee.

In 1973–76 she was, first, appointments secretary to Governor Mills E. Godwin, Jr., and then staff liaison to the Commission on the Status of Women. She was State organization director, Godwin for Governor campaign in 1973. In 1972 she was State organization director, Re-elect the President Committee.

Mrs. Peachee is a registered radiological technologist and a licensed real estate agent. She was graduated from St. Luke's Hospital School of Radiological Technology, Richmond, Va. Mrs. Peachee has three children and resides in Richmond.

Remarks on the Nation's Economy at a White House Meeting With State Legislators and County Executives
February 9, 1981

I'm not saying hello individually, except to those near at hand, because I understand we'll have a chance later when we leave here for some photos. But I am grateful that all of you came here today, and I hope that the meeting so far has been productive for you. I know that it's helpful for us.

The task before us is enormous. We are on the brink, as I said on the air, of an economic calamity—and I don't think that's too harsh a word—but it is not our economic system that is at fault. The system is sound, and it's proven itself time after time. We've just played fast and loose with the system, and it's time that we made it work the way it's supposed to. The first priority, I believe, is a return to the concept of federalism.

You, the State legislators, you who are in county and local government are the representatives that are closest to the people. You are the first to see which programs work and which don't, and you know what is best for the States, for your communities, and that means what's best for the people. I've long believed that State and local governments have a better chance to be efficient and responsive than does the Federal bureaucracy, which tries to fit solutions to problems that vary from one locale to another, and all too often they end up with their own bureaucracy the beneficiary of whatever program they administer. My goal is to transfer as many programs as are appropriate back to you, along with the tax resources to pay for them. And we can use your help in getting that done.

It'll take all of us working together to turn things around, and frankly, I've asked you here today to enlist you in this effort. I would like your guidance as we come down to the wire on our comprehensive economic program, which we'll be submitting to the Congress next week, and then I would like to continue working with you as we work to put that plan into operation.

I know that you've been spending a lot of time with our economic advisers this afternoon doing just that, but I'd like to hear from you myself. So, right now I think that's the end of the monolog. We can have a dialog, and the floor is open to hear your comments.

Note: The President spoke at 4:35 p.m. in the East Room at the White House.

The press release includes a transcript of the discussion session which followed the President's opening remarks.

Following the meeting, the President attended a reception for the State legislators and county executives.

Appointment of Richard S. Williamson as Assistant to the President for Intergovernmental Affairs
February 10, 1981

The President announced today the appointment of Richard S. Williamson to be the Assistant to the President for Intergovernmental Affairs. Mr. Williamson is presently Special Assistant to the President and Deputy to Chief of Staff James A. Baker III.

During the 1980 Presidential campaign, Mr. Williamson was deputy to the chairman, Reagan-Bush Committee. In 1977–80 he was a partner in the Washington office of Winston & Strawn, a Chicago-based law firm. He is a graduate of Princeton University (A.B., 1971) and the University of Virginia Law School. Mr. Williamson is a former administrative assistant to Congressman Philip M. Crane (R-Ill.).

Mr. Williamson is married to the former Jane Thatcher, and they have two children. Mr. Williamson was born on May 9, 1949, in Evanston, Ill. He resides with his family in McLean, Va.

White House Announcement on the Formation of the President's Economic Policy Advisory Board
February 10, 1981

The President announced today his intention to form the President's Economic Policy Advisory Board. The Board will be composed of economic experts from outside the Government and will meet every 3 or 4 months to advise the President with respect to the conduct and objectives of both domestic and international economic policy of the United States. The Board will work with Secretary of the Treasury Donald Regan, who will have principal responsibility for economic policy in the administration.

The members of the Board will be:

Arthur F. Burns, former Chairman of the Federal Reserve System, Counsellor to President Nixon, and Chairman of the Council of Economic Advisers under President Eisenhower.

Milton Friedman, senior research fellow, the Hoover Institution, and Nobel Laureate in economics.

Alan Greenspan, president, Townsend-Greenspan & Co., Inc., and former Chairman of the Council of Economic Advisers under President Ford.

Arthur Laffer, Charles B. Thornton Professor of Business Economics, University of Southern California; president, A. B. Laffer Associates.

James T. Lynn, managing partner, Jones, Day, Reavis, and Pogue; former Director, Office of Management and Budget; and former Secretary of Housing and Urban Development.

Paul McCracken, Edmund Ezra Day University Professor of Business Administration at the University of Michigan; former Chairman of the Council of Economic Advisers under President Nixon.

George Shultz, president, Bechtel Group, Inc.; former Secretary of the Treasury, Secretary of Labor, and Director of the Office of Management and Budget.

William E. Simon, former Secretary of the Treasury.

Thomas Sowell, senior fellow, the Hoover Institution.

Herbert Stein, senior fellow, American Enterprise Institute; former Chairman of the Council of Economic Advisers under President Nixon.

Charls E. Walker, chairman, Charls E. Walker Associates, Inc.; former Deputy Secretary of the Treasury.

Walter B. Wriston, chairman, Citibank/Citicorp.

George Shultz will serve as Chairman of the Board. Martin Anderson, Assistant to the President for Policy Development, will serve as Secretary to the Board.

The President stated: "I am grateful that this distinguished group of economists has volunteered to help monitor the progress of the economic policies we will be implementing to restore the vitality of the American economy. With their help, we will be better able to keep on course the efforts needed to reinvigorate production, spur growth and investment, stabilize prices, and create jobs."

Nomination of Carol E. Dinkins To Be an Assistant Attorney General
February 11, 1981

The President announced today his intention to nominate Carol E. Dinkins to be an Assistant Attorney General (Land and Resources Division), Department of Justice.

Mrs. Dinkins is currently a partner with the firm of Vinson & Elkins of Houston, Tex. She was chairman of the Governor's Task Force on Coastal Zone Management and chief negotiator for the Governor with the Federal Task Office of Coastal Zone Management in Texas in 1979. Mrs. Dinkins was chairman of the Governor's Flood Control Action Group in 1980.

Mrs. Dinkins was adjunct assistant professor of law at Bates College of Law, University of Houston, in 1972–73. In 1971–73 she was principal associate, Texas Law Institute of Coastal & Marine Resources, Bates College of Law, University of Houston.

She was graduated from the University of Texas (B.S., 1968) and the University of Houston (J.D., 1971). Mrs. Dinkins is a member of the Texas and American Bar Associations. She is married to O. Theodore Dinkins, and they have two children. Mrs. Dinkins is a native of Corpus Christi, Tex., and was born on November 9, 1945.

Nomination of William Gene Lesher To Be an Assistant Secretary of Agriculture
February 11, 1981

The President announced today his intention to nominate William Gene Lesher to be Assistant Secretary of Agriculture for Economics. Mr. Lesher has been serving in the position of Director of Economics, Policy Analysis and Budget, Department of Agriculture.

From August 1980 to January 1981, Mr. Lesher served as chief economist for the Senate Committee on Agriculture, Nutrition, and Forestry. He had served as an economist for the committee since 1978.

In 1977–78 he was agricultural legislative assistant to Senator Richard Lugar (R-Ind.).

In 1976–77 Mr. Lesher was acting assistant professor with the Department of Agricultural Economics at Cornell University. He had been with Cornell University since 1972.

Mr. Lesher was graduated from Purdue University in 1968. He received his M.S. from Oregon State University in 1970 and his Ph. D. from Cornell University in 1977.

He is the author of several publications on land use and agriculture. Mr. Lesher is married and has two children. He lives with his family in Burke, Va. Mr. Lesher is 34 years old.

Nomination of Albert Angrisani To Be an Assistant Secretary of Labor
February 11, 1981

The President announced today his intention to nominate Albert Angrisani to be an Assistant Secretary of Labor (Employment and Training).

Since August 1978 Mr. Angrisani has served as vice president of the Chase Manhattan Bank in New York. Previously he served as assistant vice president of the bank from August 1977 to July 1978, investments and product manager from May 1974 to July 1977, and investment assistant from August 1972 to April 1974.

He was graduated from Washington and Lee University (B.A., 1971), Fairleigh Dickinson University (M.B.A., 1974), and New York University (A.P.C., 1978). He was councilman and council president, Borough of Bernardsville, N.J., and a member of the Conrail Northeast United States Railroad Mass Transportation Revitalization Committee.

Mr. Angrisani is married to the former Caroline Purnell and resides in New Jersey. He was born on August 26, 1949.

Nomination of T. Timothy Ryan, Jr., To Be Solicitor of the Department of Labor
February 11, 1981

The President announced today his intention to nominate T. Timothy Ryan, Jr., to be Solicitor of the Department of Labor.

Since 1978 Mr. Ryan has worked exclusively in the labor and employment relations area with the firm of Pierson, Ball & Dowd, Washington, D.C. In 1971-78 he was with Loomis, Owen, Fellman & Coleman. In 1975–76 Mr. Ryan was deputy general counsel to the President Ford Committee. He was with Venable, Baetjer and Howard of Baltimore, Md., in 1974–75. In 1973–74 he served as an attorney to the National Labor Relations Board.

He was an adjunct professor of law at Georgetown University Law Center and a member of the board of visitors of George Mason University. He was graduated from Villanova University (B.A., 1967) and the American University School of Law (J.D., 1973). He is a member of the District of Columbia and American Bar Associations.

Nomination of Philip D. Winn To Be an Assistant Secretary of Housing and Urban Development
February 11, 1981

The President announced today his intention to nominate Philip D. Winn to be an Assistant Secretary of Housing and Urban Development (Housing). He will also serve as Federal Housing Commissioner.

Since 1976 Mr. Winn has served as chairman of the board of Philip D. Winn and Associates, a real estate development and property acquisition firm. He has also served as chairman of the board of Winn/Olson Marketing Group, a marketing and research and financial consulting firm which primarily dealt with residential real estate. In 1964–76 Mr. Winn was sales manager of Witkin Homes.

He is a former member of the board of directors of the Colorado Homeowner's Warranty Council, former board member of the Colorado Association for Housing and Building, former member of the board of directors, Homebuilders of Metropolitan Denver. He was president of that organiza- tion in 1975 and was elected "Man of the Year" in 1971.

Mr. Winn was elected chairman of the Colorado Republican Party in 1979. He is married and has two children. He was born on February 1, 1925, in New Britain, Conn.

Nomination of John B. Crowell, Jr., To Be an Assistant Secretary of Agriculture
February 11, 1981

The President announced today his intention to nominate John B. Crowell, Jr., to be an Assistant Secretary of Agriculture (Natural Resources and Environment).

Since 1972 Mr. Crowell has served as general counsel to the Louisiana-Pacific Corp. of Portland, Oreg. He was an attorney for the Georgia-Pacific Corp. in 1959–72. In 1957–59 Mr. Crowell served as law clerk to Judge Gerald McLaughlin, U.S. Court of Appeals for the Third Circuit.

Mr. Crowell was graduated from Dart- mouth College (1952) and Harvard Law School (LL.B., 1957). He is a member of the New Jersey, Oregon, and American Bar Associations. He is a member of the National Forest Products Association, the Western Timber Association, and the Public Timber Purchasers Group of Portland.

Mr. Crowell is married to the former Margaret McCue and has three children. He resides with his family in Lake Oswego, Oreg. Mr. Crowell was born in Elizabeth, N.J., on March 18, 1930.

Nomination of Thorne G. Auchter To Be an Assistant Secretary of Labor
February 11, 1981

The President announced today his intention to nominate Thorne G. Auchter to be an Assistant Secretary of Labor (Occupational Safety and Health).

Since 1975 Mr. Auchter has served as executive vice president of the Auchter Co. of Jacksonville, Fla. In 1968–75 he was jobsite construction supervisor. His responsibilities included corporate labor relations with 7 main crafts and 10 subcontractor crafts. In April-May 1975 Mr. Auchter was legislative coordinator, Senate Rules Committee, Tallahassee, Fla.

Mr. Auchter was graduated from Jacksonville University (B.A.,1968). He is a member of the board of directors of the Associated General Contractors and vice chairman, City of Jacksonville Economic Development Council. Mr. Auchter was born in Jacksonville, Fla., on March 6, 1945.

Nomination of James L. Malone To Be an Assistant Secretary of State
February 11, 1981

The President announced today his intention to nominate James L. Malone to be an Assistant Secretary of State for Oceans and International Environmental and Scientific Affairs.

Since 1978 Mr. Malone has practiced law with the Washington law firm of Doub and Muntzing, Chartered. The practice of the firm was principally devoted to energy law and international business and economic matters. Previously he was Ambassador and U.S. Representative to the Conference of the Committee on Disarmament (CCD) in 1976–77. In 1971–73 Mr. Malone served as Assistant General Counsel to the U.S. Arms Control and Disarmament Agency and from 1973 to 1976 served as General Counsel. He served as senior principal trial attorney for the Federal Maritime Commission in 1970–71.

He was a visiting professor of law, School of Law, University of Texas, in 1969; dean and professor of law, College of Law, Wilamette University in 1967–68; assistant dean and lecturer-in-law, School of Law, University of California, Los Angeles, in 1961–67. He was graduated from Pomona College (B.A., 1953), Stanford Law School (J.D., 1959).

Mr. Malone served as instructor, the Infantry School, Fort Benning, Ga., with the rank of first lieutenant in the U.S. Army from May 1954 to March 1956. He is a member of the District of Columbia, California, and American Bar Associations. He has authored various books and articles.

Mr. Malone is married and has three children and resides with his family in McLean, Va. He was born in Los Angeles, Calif., on December 22, 1931.

Nomination of Daniel J. Terra To Be United States Ambassador at Large for Cultural Affairs
February 11, 1981

The President announced today his intention to nominate Daniel J. Terra to be Ambassador at Large for Cultural Affairs, Department of State. Mr. Terra is founder and chairman and chief executive officer of Lawter Chemicals, Inc., Northbrook, Ill.

Mr. Terra will report to the Secretary of State and will represent the President at major national and international cultural events having significant American participation. He will act as adviser for the cultural programing functions of the U.S. International Communication Agency (ICA) and will serve as a liaison point between the State Department and ICA to plan cultural events abroad and to ensure harmonization with foreign policy objectives and priorities. Mr. Terra will make recommendations to the President and the Secretary of State regarding broad cultural policies and activities of the U.S. Government. He will provide guidance to the Art-in-Embassy program to ensure that American art displayed in Ambassadorial residences abroad is representative of our national cultural heritage and in concert with the President's goals and international policies of the Department of State. As the President's representative, Mr. Terra will act as adviser and coordinator of existing government cultural agencies and departments.

Mr. Terra serves on many cultural and civic committees. He was actively involved in the Reagan-Bush campaign.

He was graduated from Penn State University (B.S., 1931) and MacMurray College (J.D., 1973).

Mr. Terra is married and resides in Kenilworth, Ill. He was born in Philadelphia, Pa., on June 8, 1911.

Appointment of William A. Wilson as the Personal Representative of the President to the Holy See
February 11, 1981

The President announced today the appointment of William A. Wilson to be his Personal Representative to the Holy See. In this capacity, Mr. Wilson will visit the Vatican from time to time to exchange views with His Holiness Pope John Paul II and other Vatican officials on international and humanitarian subjects of interest and concern to the Holy See and the United States Government.

Born in Los Angeles, Calif., Mr. Wilson attended Stanford University and graduated with a degree in mechanical engineering. During World War II he served in the U.S. Army Ordnance Corps as a captain.

A registered mechanical and metallurgical engineer in California, Mr. Wilson was the president of Web Wilson Oil Tools, Inc., until 1960. He is also active in real estate development and has cattle interests in the United States and Mexico.

Among his civic activities, Mr. Wilson is a member of the board of trustees of St. John's Hospital in Santa Monica, Calif., serving on various committees. He is a member of the board of regents of the University of California and serves on the university's investment, finance, audit, and other committees. He also served as a member of the California Post Secondary Education Committee and the Commission of the Californias, an organization for the promotion of better understanding between California and Baja California. He is a member of the board of directors of the Earle M. Jorgensen Co.

Mr. Wilson is married to the former Elizabeth Johnson, and they have two children and six grandchildren.

Nomination of Leonore Annenberg To Have the Rank of Ambassador While Serving as Chief of Protocol for the White House
February 11, 1981

The President announced today that Leonore Annenberg will serve as Chief of Protocol for the White House and will be nominated to have the rank of Ambassador while so serving.

Mrs. Annenberg is a trustee of the Annenberg School of Communications, a graduate school with extensions at the University of Southern California and the University of Pennsylvania. Mrs. Annenberg has been active in the arts for many years. She serves on the board of directors of the Pennsylvania Academy of Fine Arts, board of directors of the Philadelphia Orchestra, board of trustees of the Academy of Music, and is a trustee of the Philadelphia Museum of Art.

Mrs. Annenberg is a member of the Philadelphia Society for the Preservation of Landmarks, the White House Preservation Fund, and former president of the Palm Springs Desert Museum.

She is an honorary trustee of the Performing Arts Council of the Music Center of Los Angeles County and is a director of the Metropolitan Opera Associates.

93

Mrs. Annenberg was graduated from Stanford University (B.A., 1940).

Mrs. Annenberg is married to Walter H. Annenberg and resides in Wynnewood, Pa. She was born in New York City on February 20, 1918.

Remarks to Reporters on Releasing an Audit of the United States Economy
February 12, 1981

The President. Today I'm releasing an audit of the American economy that's been prepared by my advisers and that I described to this Nation in the address last week.

And this audit confirms that the economy of the United States needs a profound and dramatic change in direction. There can no longer be a business-as-usual approach. Inflation and unemployment are threatening the American way of life as never before, and without a change of policy these intolerable conditions will get even worse.

This audit also suggests a sense of urgency that we must halt the growth of government and the corresponding burden of overspending, taxation, and regulation before they irreversibly alter the character of this Nation.

We're still the most productive people in the world, living in a nation with a potential that staggers the imagination. I'm confident with the facts before them, the American people will understand the need for the changes that we'll propose next week. And this audit shows us that our actions must put the nation on a fundamentally different course.

Now, I am due 5 minutes ago down at the Lincoln Memorial, so I am going to leave you now. But I am leaving you in the hands of Murray Weidenbaum, who can take all of your questions and explain this audit report to you, which I understand is going to be made available or already has been made available to you.

Thank you very much.

Mr. Weidenbaum. Thank you, Mr. President.

The purpose of this audit is to present the key facts and figures on the economic situation that President Reagan inherited. It shows that although the economy has in the past suffered either high inflation or high unemployment, what is unique today is the combination of sustained high inflation and sustained high unemployment.

We show that the basic source of most of our economic distress is the policies of government itself over the course of many previous administrations. Nevertheless, the fundamental strength of the private enterprise economy still shows through the dismal current statistics. To tap into this Nation's productive economic base requires a commitment to reduce tax and regulatory burdens and to increase incentives for working and saving.

The economy's various economic difficulties are closely interrelated. Any attempt to solve one, such as inflation, without taking the others, such as unemployment, into account is doomed to failure. In fact, it is the stop-and-go economic policies of the past that have been a major source of the problem.

A comprehensive solution aimed at the entire range of economic ills now facing the United States is required. That is the highlights, the essence of this economic presentation.

Note: The President spoke at 11:58 a.m. to reporters assembled in the Briefing Room at the White House. Following his remarks, Murray L. Weidenbaum, Chairman-designate of the Council of Economic Advisers, held a question-and-answer session with reporters.

Remarks at a Wreath-Laying Ceremony at the Lincoln Memorial
February 12, 1981

Ladies and gentlemen:

Of the millions who come to this city each year, there is always a stop to be made here at the base of the Reflecting Pool and a statue to be seen, of a backwoodsman who became a lawyer, a Congressman, and a President. It is said that by standing to one side of this statue there can be seen the profile of a man of strength and wisdom and by standing on the other side the profile of a man of compassion. These two views of Lincoln symbolize our own memory of him today: Lincoln, the national leader who in a time of crisis called his countrymen to greatness; and Lincoln, the man whose grace, compassion, and earnest commitment is remembered in countless biographies, folktales, and poetry.

Yet, there is more left to us of Lincoln than the ceremony, the monument, or even the memory of his greatness as a leader and a man. There are words, words he spoke and that speak in our time or to any time, words from the mind that sought wisdom and the heart that loved justice.

Today do our national leaders agonize over the dilemma between doing what is practical and what is right? Let us have faith in the right, that it makes might, Lincoln wrote, and in that faith let us to the end do our duty as we understand it.

Or do we ever fear failure of the defense of principle? "I am not bound to win," Lincoln said, "but am bound to be true. I am not bound to succeed, but I am bound by what light I have."

Do we sometimes question the commitment upon which this Nation was founded, the belief in the uncommon wisdom of the common people, the belief that in their right to render a final verdict on this Nation's course? "I appeal to you constantly," Lincoln said on his way to assume the Presidency, "bear in mind that not with politicians, not with a President, not with the office seekers, but with you is the question, 'Shall the liberties of this country be preserved to the latest generation?' "

In Lincoln's life there is ample testimony of the depth of his mind, to the compassion of his heart, to the breadth of his virtue, and above all, to the value of putting country above self-interest. But for today I will say only of him what he said so well of those who had fallen at Gettysburg, that the memory of his life and death are greater than any written or spoken tribute could ever be, the memory of Lincoln that belongs to us, but it belongs never only to us, for as it was said in the hour of his death, "Now he belongs to the ages."

Thank you.

Note: The President spoke at 12:20 p.m.

Nomination of Lionel H. Olmer To Be an Under Secretary of Commerce
February 12, 1981

The President today announced his intention to nominate Lionel H. Olmer to be Under Secretary of Commerce for International Trade.

For the past 4 years Mr. Olmer has developed and implemented international trade strategies for Motorola, Inc., Washington, D.C. Previous to joining Motorola, Mr. Olmer served for nearly 5 years on the President's Foreign Intelligence Advisory Board, established by President Eisenhower in 1956. He was a member of the board of directors of the International Rescue Committee and chairman of the executive committee's Washington advisory group.

Mr. Olmer has served in Governor James Thompson's Washington Volunteer Policy Group and has provided policy support during the transition period.

He was graduated from the University of Connecticut (1956) and American University Law School (1963). He is a member of the Connecticut and District of Columbia Bar Associations.

Mr. Olmer was a commander in the U.S. Navy and served on the staff of the Chief of Naval Operations in the late 1960's.

Mr. Olmer is married to the former Judith Sayler, and they have two children. He resides with his family in Rockville, Md. He was born in New Haven, Conn., on November 11, 1934.

Nomination of John E. Chapoton To Be an Assistant Secretary of the Treasury
February 12, 1981

The President announced today his intention to nominate John E. Chapoton to be Assistant Secretary of the Treasury (Tax Policy).

Since 1972 Mr. Chapoton has been a partner with the firm of Vinson & Elkins of Houston, Tex. In 1969 he served as associate tax legislative counsel to the Department of the Treasury and in 1970 served as deputy legislative counsel. In 1970–72 Mr. Chapoton was tax legislative counsel. Previously, from 1961 to 1969, Mr. Chapoton practiced law in Houston, Tex., specializing in Federal tax matters.

In 1960–61 Mr. Chapoton served in the U.S. Army as second lieutenant. He was graduated from the University of Texas (B.A., 1958) and the University of Texas School of Law (LL.B., 1960). He is a member of the Texas and American Bar Associations. In 1972 he received the U.S. Treasury Department Exceptional Service Award.

Mr. Chapoton was born in Galveston, Tex., on May 18, 1936. He resides in Houston, Tex.

Nomination of Angela M. Buchanan To Be Treasurer of the United States
February 12, 1981

The President announced today his intention to nominate Angela M. Buchanan to be Treasurer of the United States.

Recently Miss Buchanan served as national treasurer of the Reagan for President primary campaign and the Reagan-Bush general election campaign. In 1977–79 she was controller of Citizens for the Republic, a political action committee in Santa Monica, Calif. From January 1977 to April 1977, she was an accountant with H. M. Buchanan and Co. From January 1976 to December

1976, she was an accountant with Citizens for Reagan. In 1974–75 Miss Buchanan was an accountant with Bamfield and Co. Public Accountants in Sydney, Australia. She was a teacher of mathematics at Georgetown Visitation High School in 1973–74.

Miss Buchanan was graduated from Rosemont College, Philadelphia, Pa. (B.A., mathematics), and McGill University, Montreal, Canada (M.S., mathematics).

Miss Buchanan was born on December 20, 1948, and resides in Arlington, Va.

Nomination of R. Tenney Johnson To Be General Counsel of the Department of Energy
February 12, 1981

The President announced today his intention to nominate R. Tenney Johnson to be General Counsel of the Department of Energy.

Since 1978 Mr. Johnson has been a partner with the firm of Sullivan & Beauregard of Washington, D.C. In 1976–77 he was a member of the Civil Aeronautics Board. He was General Counsel of the Energy Research and Development Administration in 1975–76 and General Counsel of the National Aeronautics and Space Administration in 1973–75. In 1970–73 Mr. Johnson was General Counsel to the Civil Aeronautics Board. Mr. Johnson served as Deputy General Counsel to the Department of Transportation in 1967–70 and the Department of the Army in 1963–67. He was an attorney with the Office of the General Counsel, Department of Defense, in 1959–63.

In 1977 he was Chairman of the Organizational Integration Working Group, Department of Energy Activation Task Force. He was U.S. Cochairman, U.S./U.S.S.R. Joint Working Group on Intellectual Property, U.S./U.S.S.R. Agreements for Cooperation in 1975–79.

Mr. Johnson is a member of the District of Columbia and American Bar Associations. He received the Distinguished Service Award from the Energy Research and Development Administration in 1976. He was graduated from the University of Rochester (A.B., 1951) and Harvard Law School (LL.B., 1958). He was a lieutenant in the U.S. Navy in 1951–54.

Mr. Johnson is married and has three children. He resides with his family in Bethesda, Md. He was born in Evanston, Ill., on March 24, 1930.

Appointment of T. Kenneth Cribb, Jr., as Staff Assistant to the President and Assistant Director of the Office of Cabinet Administration
February 12, 1981

The President announced today the appointment of T. Kenneth Cribb, Jr., as Assistant Director, Office of Cabinet Administration, and Staff Assistant to the President.

During the transition, Mr. Cribb took a leave of absence from the firm of Dewey, Ballantine, Bushby, Palmer and Wood to serve as deputy director of the legal and administrative agencies group, office of executive branch management.

Mr. Cribb also served in the Presidential campaign as deputy to the chief counsel of the Reagan-Bush Committee.

From 1971 to 1977, he was national director of the Intercollegiate Studies Institute, with main offices in Bryn Mawr, Pa. He has also served as a consultant to the Heritage Foundation.

Mr. Cribb is a graduate of Washington and Lee University and the University of Virginia School of Law. He has recently been named a trustee of the Philadelphia Society. Mr. Cribb is a native of Spartanburg, S.C., and presently resides in Alexandria, Va. He is 32 years old.

Nomination of Edward N. Brandt, Jr., To Be an Assistant Secretary of Health and Human Services
February 13, 1981

The President announced today his intention to nominate Edward N. Brandt, Jr., to be an Assistant Secretary of Health and Human Services (for Health). It is the President's intention to see that this position is elevated to Under Secretary of Health in accordance with a reorganization plan that will be announced later.

Dr. Brandt has been vice chancellor for health affairs for the University of Texas since 1977. Prior to that, he was executive dean of the University of Texas medical branch at Galveston, Tex., and was affiliated with that school from 1970 to 1977. From 1962 to 1970, Dr. Brandt was at the University of Oklahoma Medical Center, first as director of the Medical Research Computer Center and later as associate dean. Dr. Brandt has also served since 1970 as a professor in the departments of preventive medicine and family medicine at the University of Texas.

Dr. Brandt has been active in various committees of the American Medical Association and the American Association of Medical Colleges. He is currently chairman of the AMA's section on medical schools. He is also a member of the American Academy of Family Physicians' Commission on Legislation and Governmental Affairs.

He was graduated from the University of Oklahoma (B.S., 1954), Oklahoma State University (M.S., 1955), and the University of Oklahoma Medical Center (M.D., 1960; Ph. D., 1963).

Dr. Brandt is married and has three children. He resides with his family in Austin, Tex. Dr. Brandt was born in Oklahoma City, Okla., on July 3, 1933.

Nomination of Donald J. Devine To Be Director of the Office of Personnel Management
February 13, 1981

The President announced today his intention to nominate Donald J. Devine to be Director of the Office of Personnel Management for a term of 4 years.

Dr. Devine was the transition team leader for the Office of Personnel Management (OPM) and related personnel agencies of the Federal Government within the office of the President-elect. He has been an associate professor of government and politics at the University of Maryland since 1967. During the 1980 Presidential campaign, Dr. Devine was a regional political director of the Reagan-Bush Committee. He also served as Maryland State chairman, deputy director of political planning and analysis, and coordinator for Delaware and the District of Columbia. In 1978 Dr. Devine was the Republican nominee for State Comptroller of Maryland.

Dr. Devine has been active in Republican Party politics for many years. He is the author of many publications and articles.

He was graduated from St. John's University (B.B.A., 1959), City University of New York (M.A., 1965), and Syracuse University (Ph. D., 1967).

Dr. Devine is married and has four children. He resides with his family in Wheaton, Md. Dr. Devine is 43.

Nomination of Loret M. Ruppe To Be Director of the Peace Corps
February 13, 1981

The President announced today his intention to nominate Loret M. Ruppe to be Director of the Peace Corps, ACTION.

Recently Mrs. Ruppe served as chairman of the Vice President-elect's inaugural reception. From August 1980 to November 1980, she served as cochairman of the Reagan-Bush Committee of Michigan. She was previously chairman of the George Bush for President campaign in Michigan from November 1979 to May 1980.

Mrs. Ruppe has spent most of her life in volunteer efforts. She has traveled extensively and shared ideals with past Peace Corps volunteers in many countries. She is a member of the International Neighbors Club IV and attended the Conference on Africa held in England in 1978.

Mrs. Ruppe attended Marymount College and Marquette University. She is married to former U.S. Representative Philip Ruppe and has five children. She lives with her family in Potomac, Md. She was born on January 3, 1936.

Proclamation 4819—National Agriculture Day
February 13, 1981

By the President of the United States of America

A Proclamation

Agriculture is among America's most vital and far-reaching industries. Its production, processing, and marketing segments together provide as many as 17 million jobs.

The productivity and efficiency of American agriculture are basic ingredients in our national strength. Agricultural productivity is a major weapon in the war against inflation and in the struggle to eliminate world hunger. The efficiency of the American farmer is the envy of the world.

American farmers are, in reality, fiercely independent businessmen whose job it is to provide food and fiber. With the profit motive and freedom of enterprise, these businessmen of the soil have supplied this Nation with an abundance never before witnessed in the history of man.

Today, our farmers are also making enormous contributions to America's trade balance. In the past year alone, farm exports amounted to $41 billion.

To achieve a better understanding of, and appreciation for, agriculture's role in the Nation's way of life and of each individual's stake in a reliable food and fiber supply, the Congress enacted a Joint Resolution, Public Law 96–416, to set aside March 19, 1981, as "National Agriculture Day."

Now, Therefore, I, Ronald Reagan, President of the United States of America, do hereby proclaim March 19, 1981, "National Agriculture Day" and do call upon the people of the United States to observe this day with appropriate ceremonies and activities.

In Witness Whereof, I have hereunto set my hand this thirteenth day of February in the year of our Lord nineteen hundred eighty-one, and of the Independence of the United States of America the two hundred and fifth.

RONALD REAGAN

[*Filed with the Office of the Federal Register, 4:53 p.m., February 13, 1981*]

Message on the Observance of National Brotherhood Week, February 15–21, 1981
February 13, 1981

"We The People"—these words, which helped forge a nation, still describe the spirit and meaning of America today.

Ours is a Nation of many heritages. Diverse religious, ethnic, and racial backgrounds find unity in our common belief in the dignity of the individual and our national commitment to the right of self-government.

All Americans share in this heritage. During National Brotherhood Week, I join the National Conference of Christians and Jews in asking everyone to make a special effort to reach across political, religious, and racial boundaries and extend to each other a warm hand of fellowship.

Let us also work this week to extend the hand of brotherhood to all the peoples and nations of the world. "The world is now too dangerous for anything but the truth," the Reverend A. Powell Davies once said, "and too small for anything but brotherhood."

Because we are made in the image and likeness of God—because we are as one on this planet—let us this week renew our commitment to a world where our Nation and all nations grow and prosper together in a spirit of love and brotherhood.

RONALD REAGAN

Message to the Congress Reporting Budget Rescissions and Deferrals
February 13, 1981

To the Congress of the United States:

I hereby withdraw the 33 rescission proposals transmitted to the Congress by the Carter Administration on January 15, 1981 totalling $1,142.4 million and temporarily convert them to deferrals. A list of the withdrawn rescission proposals is attached.

The conversion to temporary deferrals will provide my Administration with the opportunity to review and revise these proposals within the context of my overall plan to curtail the growth of government and reduce Federal spending.

In addition, I am reporting four other new deferrals totalling $8.0 million and a revision to a previously transmitted deferral increasing the amount deferred by $51.1 million. These four new items involve programs in the Departments of the Interior and Transportation and the International Communication Agency. The revision to the existing deferral involves the Department of the Treasury.

The details of the deferrals are contained in the attached reports.

RONALD REAGAN

The White House,
February 13, 1981.

Note: The attachments detailing the rescissions and deferrals are printed in the Federal Register of February 19, 1981.

The text of the message was released by the Office of the Press Secretary on February 14.

Executive Order 12289—Foreign Service Retirement and Disability System
February 14, 1981

By the authority vested in me as President of the United States of America by Section 827 of the Foreign Service Act of 1980 (22 U.S.C. 4067), and in order to conform further the Foreign Service Retirement and Disability System to the Civil Service Retirement and Disability System, it is hereby ordered as follows:

Section 1. (a) Section 826(c) of the Foreign Service Act of 1980 (22 U.S.C. 4066(c)) is deemed to be amended by striking out the first sentence of paragraph (1) thereof, and inserting in lieu thereof the following sentence:

"(1) The first increase (if any) made under this section to an annuity which is payable from the Fund to a participant or to the surviving spouse of a deceased participant who dies in service shall be equal to the product (adjusted to the nearest ¹⁄₁₀ of 1 percent) of—

"(a) ⅛ of the applicable percent change determined under Subsection (b) of this Section, multiplied by

"(b) the number of full months for which the annuity was payable from the Fund before the effective date of the increase (counting any portion of a month as a full month).".

Sec. 2. Section 808(a) of the Foreign Service Act of 1980 (22 U.S.C. 4048(a)) is deemed to be amended by adding at the end thereof the following:

"However, if a participant retiring under this section is receiving retired pay or re-tainer pay for military service (except that specified in Section 8332(c) (1) or (2) of title 5 of the United States Code) or Veterans' Administration pension or compensation in lieu of such retired or retainer pay, the annuity of that participant shall be computed under this chapter excluding extra credit authorized by this subsection and excluding credit for military service from that computation. If the amount of the annuity so computed, plus the retired or retainer pay which is received, or which would be received but for the application of the limitation in Section 5532 of title 5 of the United States Code, or the Veterans' Administration pension or compensation in lieu of such retired or retainer pay, is less than the annuity that would be payable under this chapter in the absence of the previous sentence, an amount equal to the difference shall be added to the annuity computed under this chapter.".

Sec. 3. The amendments to be deemed made by this Order shall take effect as of February 15, 1981.

RONALD REAGAN

The White House,
February 14, 1981.

[*Filed with the Office of the Federal Register, 10:50 a.m., February 17, 1981*]

Note: The text of the Executive order was released by the Office of the Press Secretary on February 17.

Nomination of William Howard Taft IV To Be General Counsel of the Department of Defense
February 17, 1981

The President today announced his intention to nominate William Howard Taft IV to be General Counsel, Department of Defense. Mr. Taft is an attorney with the firm of Leva, Hawes, Symington, Martin and Oppenheimer of Washington, D.C.

Prior to January 1977, Mr. Taft worked for 7 years with the Federal Trade Commission, the Office of Management and Budget, and the Department of Health, Education, and Welfare.

In April 1976 Mr. Taft was appointed by the President to serve as General Counsel of the Department of Health, Education, and Welfare. As such, he was the chief lawyer for the Department and the principal administrator of the Office of the General Counsel, which consisted of approximately 350 lawyers in Washington and 10 regional offices.

Prior to his appointment as General Counsel, Mr. Taft served 3 years as the executive assistant to the Secretary of HEW. From 1970 to 1973, he was the principal assistant to Caspar W. Weinberger, who was Deputy Director, then Director, of the

Office of Management and Budget in the Executive Office of the President. Mr. Taft assisted him in the management of the budgetary process, policy review, and program oversight for the entire Federal Government.

Mr. Taft served briefly as attorney adviser to the Chairman of the Federal Trade Commission in 1970.

A native of Washington, D.C., Mr. Taft earned his Ph. D. in English from Yale University in 1966 and his J.D. from Harvard Law School in 1969.

He is married and has three children. Mr. Taft resides in Lorton, Va., with his family. He was born in Washington, D.C., on September 13, 1945.

Nomination of G. Ray Arnett To Be an Assistant Secretary of the Interior
February 17, 1981

The President announced today his intention to nominate G. Ray Arnett to be Assistant Secretary of the Interior for Fish and Wildlife.

Mr. Arnett is an avid sportsman and outdoorsman who has devoted much of his life to the conservation, preservation, and enhancement of wildlife. He was appointed by Gov. Ronald Reagan to head the California Department of Fish & Game, where he served for 7 years.

Mr. Arnett was director of the National Wildlife Federation for 17 years, and served two terms as president, retiring from that position in 1978. He has been affiliated with many State and national conservation organizations. He was one of the founders and currently serves as chairman of the board of

the Wildlife Legislative Fund of America and its companion organization, the Wildlife Conservation Fund of America.

Mr. Arnett attended the University of California at Los Angeles and the University of Southern California, where he attended undergraduate and graduate school.

In 1942–46 Mr. Arnett served in the U.S. Marine Corps, South Central Pacific Theatre. He was recalled to active duty during the Korean conflict in 1950–52. He was honorably discharged with the rank of captain.

Mr. Arnett is married and has four children. He resides with his family in Stockton, Calif. He was born in Quantico, Va., on June 14, 1924.

Proclamation 4820—Rescission of Emergency Building Temperature Restrictions
February 17, 1981

By the President of the United States of America

A Proclamation

Emergency Building Temperature Restrictions were first implemented on July 16, 1979, by Proclamation No. 4667. They were twice extended, first by Proclamation No. 4750 and second by Proclamation No. 4813. Those restrictions set forth in Energy Conservation Contingency Plan No. 2 (44 FR 12911, March 8, 1979) are effective until October 16, 1981, unless earlier rescinded.

Although restrictions on building temperatures may result in reduced consumption of fuel, I have concluded that the regulatory scheme designed to accomplish that objective imposes an excessive regulatory burden and that voluntary restraint and market incentives will achieve substantially the same benefit without the regulatory cost.

Now, Therefore, I, Ronald Reagan, President of the United States of America, by the authority vested in me by the Constitution and laws of the United States, including Section 201(a) of the Energy Policy and Conservation Act (42 U.S.C. 6261(a)), do hereby proclaim that:

Section 1. The Energy Building Temperature Restrictions as provided for in Energy Conservation Contingency Plan No. 2 (44 FR 12911, March 8, 1979) are no longer required. Therefore, the effectiveness of that Plan as provided for in Proclamation No. 4813 is hereby rescinded.

Sec. 2. Proclamation No. 4813 is revoked.

Sec. 3. The Secretary of Energy shall take such action as may be necessary to ensure the implementation of this Proclamation.

In Witness Whereof, I have hereunto set my hand this seventeenth day of February, in the year of our Lord nineteen hundred and eighty-one, and of the Independence of the United States of America the two hundred and fifth.

RONALD REAGAN

[*Filed with the Office of the Federal Register, 3:17 p.m., February 17, 1981*]

Executive Order 12290—Federal Exports and Excessive Regulation
February 17, 1981

By the authority vested in me as President by the Constitution of the United States of America, and in order to ensure that the Export Administration Act of 1979 is implemented with the minimum regulatory burden, Executive Order No. 12264 of January 15, 1981, entitled "On Federal Policy Regarding the Export of Banned or Significantly Restricted Substances," is hereby revoked.

RONALD REAGAN

The White House,
February 17, 1981.

[*Filed with the Office of the Federal Register, 3:18 p.m., February 17, 1981*]

Executive Order 12291—Federal Regulation
February 17, 1981

By the authority vested in me as President by the Constitution and laws of the United States of America, and in order to reduce the burdens of existing and future regulations, increase agency accountability for regulatory actions, provide for presidential oversight of the regulatory process, minimize duplication and conflict of regulations, and insure well-reasoned regulations, it is hereby ordered as follows:

Section 1. Definitions. For the purposes of this Order:

(a) "Regulation" or "rule" means an agency statement of general applicability and future effect designed to implement, interpret, or prescribe law or policy or describing the procedure or practice requirements of an agency, but does not include:

(1) Administrative actions governed by the provisions of Sections 556 and 557 of Title 5 of the United States Code;

(2) Regulations issued with respect to a military or foreign affairs function of the United States; or

(3) Regulations related to agency organization, management, or personnel.

(b) "Major rule" means any regulation that is likely to result in:

(1) An annual effect on the economy of $100 million or more;

(2) A major increase in costs or prices for consumers, individual industries, Federal, State, or local government agencies, or geographic regions; or

(3) Significant adverse effects on competition, employment, investment, productivity, innovation, or on the ability of United States-based enterprises to compete with foreign-based enterprises in domestic or export markets.

(c) "Director" means the Director of the Office of Management and Budget.

(d) "Agency" means any authority of the United States that is an "agency" under 44 U.S.C. 3502(1), excluding those agencies specified in 44 U.S.C. 3502(10).

(e) "Task Force" means the Presidential Task Force on Regulatory Relief.

Sec. 2. General Requirements. In promulgating new regulations, reviewing existing regulations, and developing legislative proposals concerning regulation, all agencies, to the extent permitted by law, shall adhere to the following requirements:

(a) Administrative decisions shall be based on adequate information concerning the need for and consequences of proposed government action;

(b) Regulatory action shall not be undertaken unless the potential benefits to society from the regulation outweigh the potential costs to society;

(c) Regulatory objectives shall be chosen to maximize the net benefits to society;

(d) Among alternative approaches to any given regulatory objective, the alternative involving the least net cost to society shall be chosen; and

(e) Agencies shall set regulatory priorities with the aim of maximizing the aggregate net benefits to society, taking into account the condition of the particular industries affected by regulations, the condition of the national economy, and other regulatory actions contemplated for the future.

Sec. 3. Regulatory Impact Analysis and Review.

(a) In order to implement Section 2 of this Order, each agency shall, in connection with every major rule, prepare, and to the extent permitted by law consider, a Regulatory Impact Analysis. Such Analyses may be combined with any Regulatory Flexibility Analyses performed under 5 U.S.C. 603 and 604.

(b) Each agency shall initially determine whether a rule it intends to propose or to issue is a major rule, *provided that*, the Director, subject to the direction of the Task Force, shall have authority, in accordance with Sections 1(b) and 2 of this Order, to prescribe criteria for making such determinations, to order a rule to be treated as a major rule, and to require any set of related rules to be considered together as a major rule.

(c) Except as provided in Section 8 of this Order, agencies shall prepare Regulatory Impact Analyses of major rules and transmit them, along with all notices of proposed rulemaking and all final rules, to the Director as follows:

(1) If no notice of proposed rulemaking is to be published for a proposed major rule that is not an emergency rule, the agency shall prepare only a final Regulatory Impact Analysis, which shall be transmitted, along with the proposed rule, to the Director at least 60 days prior to the publication of the major rule as a final rule;

(2) With respect to all other major rules, the agency shall prepare a preliminary Regulatory Impact Analysis, which shall be transmitted, along with a notice of proposed rulemaking, to the Director at least 60 days prior to the publication of a notice of proposed rulemaking, and a final Regulatory Impact Analysis, which shall be transmitted along with the final rule at least 30 days prior to the publication of the major rule as a final rule;

(3) For all rules other than major rules, agencies shall submit to the Director, at least 10 days prior to publication, every notice of proposed rulemaking and final rule.

(d) To permit each proposed major rule to be analyzed in light of the requirements stated in Section 2 of this Order, each preliminary and final Regulatory Impact Analysis shall contain the following information:

(1) A description of the potential benefits of the rule, including any beneficial effects that cannot be quantified in monetary terms, and the identification of those likely to receive the benefits;

(2) A description of the potential costs of the rule, including any adverse effects that cannot be quantified in monetary terms, and the identification of those likely to bear the costs;

(3) A determination of the potential net benefits of the rule, including an evaluation of effects that cannot be quantified in monetary terms;

(4) A description of alternative approaches that could substantially achieve the same regulatory goal at lower cost, together with an analysis of this potential benefit and costs and a brief explanation of the legal reasons why such alternatives, if proposed, could not be adopted; and

(5) Unless covered by the description required under paragraph (4) of this subsection, an explanation of any legal reasons why the rule cannot be based on the requirements set forth in Section 2 of this Order.

(e)(1) The Director, subject to the direction of the Task Force, which shall resolve any issues raised under this Order or ensure that they are presented to the President, is authorized to review any preliminary or final Regulatory Impact Analysis, notice of proposed rulemaking, or final rule based on the requirements of this Order.

(2) The Director shall be deemed to have concluded review unless the Director advises an agency to the contrary under subsection (f) of this Section:

(A) Within 60 days of a submission under subsection (c)(1) or a submission of a preliminary Regulatory Impact Analysis or notice of proposed rulemaking under subsection (c)(2);

(B) Within 30 days of the submission of a final Regulatory Impact Analysis and a final rule under subsection (c)(2); and

(C) Within 10 days of the submission of a notice of proposed rulemaking or final rule under subsection (c)(3).

(f)(1) Upon the request of the Director, an agency shall consult with the Director concerning the review of a preliminary Regulatory Impact Analysis or notice of proposed rulemaking under this Order, and shall, subject to Section 8(a)(2) of this Order, refrain from publishing its preliminary Regulatory Impact Analysis or notice of proposed rulemaking until such review is concluded.

(2) Upon receiving notice that the Director intends to submit views with respect to any final Regulatory Impact Analysis or final rule, the agency shall, subject to Section 8(a)(2) of this Order, refrain from publishing its final Regulatory Impact Analysis or final rule until the agency has responded to the Director's views, and incorporated those views and the agency's response in the rulemaking file.

(3) Nothing in this subsection shall be construed to as displacing the agencies' responsibilities delegated by law.

(g) For every rule for which an agency publishes a notice of proposed rulemaking, the agency shall include in its notice:

(1) A brief statement setting forth the agency's initial determination whether the proposed rule is a major rule, together with the reasons underlying that determination; and

(2) For each proposed major rule, a brief summary of the agency's preliminary Regulatory Impact Analysis.

(h) Agencies shall make their preliminary and final Regulatory Impact Analyses available to the public.

(i) Agencies shall initiate reviews of currently effective rules in accordance with the purposes of this Order, and perform Regulatory Impact Anaylyses of currently effective major rules. The Director, subject to the direction of the Task Force, may designate currently effective rules for review in accordance with this Order, and establish schedules for reviews and Analyses under this Order.

Sec. 4. Regulatory Review. Before approving any final major rule, each agency shall:

(a) Make a determination that the regulation is clearly within the authority delegated by law and consistent with congressional intent, and include in the *Federal Register* at the time of promulgation a memorandum of law supporting that determination.

(b) Make a determination that the factual conclusions upon which the rule is based have substantial support in the agency record, viewed as a whole, with full attention to public comments in general and the comments of persons directly affected by the rule in particular.

Sec. 5. Regulatory Agendas.

(a) Each agency shall publish, in October and April of each year, an agenda of proposed regulations that the agency has issued or expects to issue, and currently effective rules that are under agency review pursuant to this Order. These agendas may be incorporated with the agendas published under 5 U.S.C. 602, and must contain at the minimum:

(1) A summary of the nature of each major rule being considered, the objectives and legal basis for the issuance of the rule, and an approximate schedule for completing action on any major rule for which the agency has issued a notice of proposed rulemaking;

(2) The name and telephone number of a knowledgeable agency official for each item on the agenda; and

(3) A list of existing regulations to be reviewed under the terms of this Order, and a brief discuission of each such regulation.

(b) The Director, subject to the direction of the Task Force, may, to the extent permitted by law:

(1) Require agencies to provide additional information in an agenda; and

(2) Require publication of the agenda in any form.

Sec. 6. The Task Force and Office of Management and Budget.

(a) To the extent permitted by law, the Director shall have authority, subject to the direction of the Task Force, to:

(1) Designate any proposed or existing rule as a major rule in accordance with Section 1(b) of this Order;

(2) Prepare and promulgate uniform standards for the identification of major rules and the development of Regulatory Impact Analyses;

(3) Require an agency to obtain and evaluate, in connection with a regulation, any additional relevant data from any appropriate source;

(4) Waive the requirements of Sections 3, 4, or 7 of this Order with respect to any proposed or existing major rule;

(5) Identify duplicative, overlapping and conflicting rules, existing or proposed, and existing or proposed rules that are inconsistent with the policies underlying statutes governing agencies other than the issuing agency or with the purposes of this Order, and, in each such case, require appropriate interagency consultation to minimize or eliminate such duplication, overlap, or conflict;

(6) Develop procedures for estimating the annual benefits and costs of agency regulations, on both an aggregate and economic or industrial sector basis, for purposes of compiling a regulatory budget;

(7) In consultation with interested agencies, prepare for consideration by the President recommendations for changes in the agencies' statutes; and

(8) Monitor agency compliance with the requirements of this Order and advise the President with respect to such compliance.

(b) The Director, subject to the direction of the Task Force, is authorized to establish procedures for the performance of all functions vested in the Director by this Order. The Director shall take appropriate steps to coordinate the implementation of the analysis, transmittal, review, and clearance provisions of this Order with the authorities and requirements provided for or imposed upon the Director and agencies under the Regulatory Flexibility Act, 5 U.S.C. 601 *et seq.,* and the Paperwork Reduction Plan Act of 1980, 44 U.S.C. 3501 *et seq.*

Sec. 7. Pending Regulations.

(a) To the extent necessary to permit reconsideration in accordance with this Order, agencies shall, except as provided in Section 8 of this Order, suspend or postpone the effective dates of all major rules that they have promulgated in final form as of the date of this Order, but that have not yet become effective, excluding:

(1) Major rules that cannot legally be postponed or suspended;

(2) Major rules that, for good cause, ought to become effective as final rules without reconsideration. Agencies shall prepare, in accordance with Section 3 of this Order, a final Regulatory Impact Analysis for each major rule that they suspend or postpone.

(b) Agencies shall report to the Director no later than 15 days prior to the effective date of any rule that the agency has promulgated in final form as of the date of this Order, and that has not yet become effective, and that will not be reconsidered under subsection (a) of this Section:

(1) That the rule is excepted from reconsideration under subsection (a), including a brief statement of the legal or other reasons for that determination; or

(2) That the rule is not a major rule.

(c) The Director, subject to the direction of the Task Force, is authorized, to the extent permitted by law, to:

(1) Require reconsideration, in accordance with this Order, of any major rule that an agency has issued in final form as of the date of this Order and that has not become effective; and

(2) Designate a rule that an agency has issued in final form as of the date of this Order and that has not yet become effective as a major rule in accordance with Section 1(b) of this Order.

(d) Agencies may, in accordance with the Administrative Procedure Act and other applicable statutes, permit major rules that they have issued in final form as of the date of this Order, and that have not yet become effective, to take effect as interim rules while they are being reconsidered in accordance with this Order, *provided that,* agencies shall report to the Director, no later than 15 days before any such rule is proposed to take effect as an interim rule, that the rule should appropriately take effect as an interim rule while the rule is under reconsideration.

(e) Except as provided in Section 8 of this Order, agencies shall, to the extent permitted by law, refrain from promulgating as a final rule any proposed major rule that has been published or issued as of the date of this Order until a final Regulatory Impact Analysis, in accordance with Section 3 of this Order, has been prepared for the proposed major rule.

(f) Agencies shall report to the Director, no later than 30 days prior to promulgating as a final rule any proposed rule that the agency has published or issued as of the date of this Order and that has not been considered under the terms of this Order:

(1) That the rule cannot legally be considered in accordance with this Order, together with a brief explanation of the legal reasons barring such consideration; or

(2) That the rule is not a major rule, in which case the agency shall submit to the Director a copy of the proposed rule.

(g) The Director, subject to the direction of the Task Force, is authorized, to the extent permitted by law, to:

(1) Require consideration, in accordance with this Order, of any proposed major rule that the agency has published or issued as of the date of this Order; and

(2) Designate a proposed rule that an agency has published or issued as of the date of this Order, as a major rule in accordance with Section 1(b) of this Order.

(h) The Director shall be deemed to have determined that an agency's report to the Director under subsections (b), (d), or (f) of this Section is consistent with the purposes of this Order, unless the Director advises the agency to the contrary:

(1) Within 15 days of its report, in the case of any report under subsections (b) or (d); or

(2) Within 30 days of its report, in the case of any report under subsection (f).

(i) This Section does not supersede the President's Memorandum of January 29, 1981, entitled "Postponement of Pending Regulations", which shall remain in effect until March 30, 1981.

(j) In complying with this Section, agencies shall comply with all applicable provisions of the Administrative Procedure Act, and with any other procedural requirements made applicable to the agencies by other statutes.

Sec. 8. Exemptions.

(a) The procedures prescribed by this Order shall not apply to:

(1) Any regulation that responds to an emergency situation, *provided that*, any such regulation shall be reported to the Director as soon as is practicable, the agency shall publish in the *Federal Register* a statement of the reasons why it is impracticable for the agency to follow the procedures of this Order with respect to such a rule, and the agency shall prepare and transmit as soon as is practicable a Regulatory Impact Analysis of any such major rule; and

(2) Any regulation for which consideration or reconsideration under the terms of this Order would conflict with deadlines imposed by statute or by judicial order, *provided that*, any such regulation shall be reported to the Director together with a brief explanation of the conflict, the agency shall publish in the *Federal Register* a statement of the reasons why it is impracticable for the agency to follow the procedures of this Order with respect to such a rule, and the agency, in consultation with the Director, shall adhere to the requirements of this Order to the extent permitted by statutory or judicial deadlines.

(b) The Director, subject to the direction of the Task Force, may, in accordance with the purposes of this Order, exempt any class or category of regulations from any or all requirements of this Order.

Sec. 9. Judicial Review. This Order is intended only to improve the internal management of the Federal government, and is not intended to create any right or benefit, substantive or procedural, enforceable at law by a party against the United States, its agencies, its officers or any person. The determinations made by agencies under Section 4 of this Order, and any Regulatory Impact Analyses for any rule, shall be made part of the whole record of agency action in connection with the rule.

Sec. 10. Revocations. Executive Orders No. 12044, as amended, and No. 12174 are revoked.

RONALD REAGAN

The White House,
February 17, 1981.

[Filed with the Office of the Federal Register, 3:19 p.m., February 17, 1981]

Address Before a Joint Session of the Congress on the Program for Economic Recovery
February 18, 1981

Mr. Speaker, Mr. President, distinguished Members of Congress, honored guests, and fellow citizens:

Only a month ago I was your guest in this historic building, and I pledged to you my cooperation in doing what is right for this Nation that we all love so much. I'm here tonight to reaffirm that pledge and to ask that we share in restoring the promise that is offered to every citizen by this, the last, best hope of man on Earth.

All of us are aware of the punishing inflation which has for the first time in 60 years held to double-digit figures for 2 years in a row. Interest rates have reached absurd levels of more that 20 percent and over 15 percent for those who would borrow to buy a home. All across this land one can see newly built homes standing vacant, unsold because of mortgage interest rates.

Almost 8 million Americans are out of work. These are people who want to be productive. But as the months go by, despair dominates their lives. The threats of layoff and unemployment hang over other millions, and all who work are frustrated by their inability to keep up with inflation.

One worker in a Midwest city put it to me this way: He said, "I'm bringing home more dollars than I ever believed I could possibly earn, but I seem to be getting worse off." And he is. Not only have hourly earnings of the American worker, after adjusting for inflation, declined 5 percent over the past 5 years, but in these 5 years, Federal personal taxes for the average family have increased 67 percent. We can no longer procrastinate and hope that things will get better. They will not. Unless we act forcefully—and now—the economy will get worse.

Can we, who man the ship of state, deny it is somewhat out of control? Our national debt is approaching $1 trillion. A few weeks ago I called such a figure, a trillion dollars, incomprehensible, and I've been trying ever since to think of a way to illustrate how big a trillion really is. And the best I could come up with is that if you had a stack of thousand-dollar bills in your hand only 4 inches high, you'd be a millionaire. A trillion dollars would be a stack of thousand-dollar bills 67 miles high. The interest on the public debt this year we know will be over $90 billion, and unless we change the proposed spending for the fiscal year beginning October 1st, we'll add another almost $80 billion to the debt.

Adding to our troubles is a mass of regulations imposed on the shopkeeper, the farmer, the craftsman, professionals, and major industry that is estimated to add $100 billion to the price of the things we buy, and it reduces our ability to produce. The rate of increase in American productivity, once one of the highest in the world, is among the lowest of all major industrial nations. Indeed, it has actually declined in the last 3 years.

Now, I've painted a pretty grim picture, but I think I've painted it accurately. It is within our power to change this picture, and we can act with hope. There's nothing wrong with our internal strengths. There has been no breakdown of the human, technological, and natural resources upon which the economy is built.

Based on this confidence in a system which has never failed us, but which we have failed through a lack of confidence and sometimes through a belief that we could fine-tune the economy and get it tuned to our liking, I am proposing a comprehensive four-point program. Now, let me outline in detail some of the principal parts of this program. You'll each be provided with a completely detailed copy of the entire program.

This plan is aimed at reducing the growth in government spending and taxing, reforming and eliminating regulations which are unnecessary and unproductive or counterproductive, and encouraging a consistent monetary policy aimed at maintaining the value of the currency. If enacted in full, this program can help America create 13 million new jobs, nearly 3 million more than we would have without these measures. It will also help us to gain control of inflation.

It's important to note that we're only reducing the rate of increase in taxing and spending. We're not attempting to cut either spending or taxing levels below that which we presently have. This plan will get our economy moving again, [create] productivity growth, and thus create the jobs that our people must have.

And I'm asking that you join me in reducing direct Federal spending by $41.4 billion in fiscal year 1982, and this goes along with another $7.7 billion in user fees and off-budget savings for a total of $49.1 billion. And this will still allow an increase of $40.8 billion over 1981 spending.

Now, I know that exaggerated and inaccurate stories about these cuts have disturbed many people, particularly those dependent on grant and benefit programs for their basic needs. Some of you have heard from constituents, I know, afraid that social security checks, for example, were going to be taken away from them. Well, I regret the fear that these unfounded stories have caused, and I welcome this opportunity to set things straight.

We will continue to fulfill the obligations that spring from our national conscience. Those who, through no fault of their own, must depend on the rest of us—the poverty stricken, the disabled, the elderly, all those with true need—can rest assured that the social safety net of programs they depend on are exempt from any cuts.

The full retirement benefits of the more than 31 million social security recipients will be continued, along with an annual cost-of-living increase. Medicare will not be cut, nor will supplemental income for the blind, the aged, and the disabled. And funding will continue for veterans pensions. School breakfasts and lunches for the children of low-income families will continue, as will nutrition and other special services for the aging. There will be no cut in Project Head Start or summer youth jobs.

All in all, nearly $216 billion worth of programs providing help for tens of millions of Americans will be fully funded. But government will not continue to subsidize individuals or particular business interests where real need cannot be demonstrated. And while we will reduce some subsidies to regional and local governments, we will at the same time convert a number of categorical grant programs into block grants to reduce wasteful administrative overhead and to give local governments and States more flexibility and control. We call for an end in duplication to Federal programs and reform of those which are not cost-effective.

Now, already some have protested that there must be no reduction in aid to schools. Well, let me point out that Federal aid to education amounts to only 8 percent of the total educational funding, and for this 8 percent, the Federal Government has insisted on tremendously disproportionate share of control over our schools. Whatever reductions we've proposed in that 8 percent will amount to very little in the total cost of education. They will, however, re-store more authority to States and local school districts.

Historically, the American people have supported by voluntary contributions more artistic and cultural activities than all the other countries in the world put together. I wholeheartedly support this approach and believe that Americans will continue their generosity. Therefore, I'm proposing a savings of $85 million in the Federal subsidies now going to the arts and humanities.

There are a number of subsidies to business and industry that I believe are unnecessary, not because the activities being subsidized aren't of value, but because the marketplace contains incentives enough to warrant continuing these activities without a government subsidy. One such subsidy is the Department of Energy's synthetic fuels program. We will continue support of research leading to development of new technologies and more independence from foreign oil, but we can save at least $3.2 billion by leaving to private industry the building of plants to make liquid or gas fuels from coal.

We're asking that another major industry—business subsidy I should say, the Export-Import Bank loan authority, be reduced by one-third in 1982. We're doing this because the primary beneficiaries of taxpayer funds in this case are the exporting companies themselves—most of them profitable corporations.

This brings me to a number of other lending programs in which government makes low-interest loans, some of them at an interest rate as low as 2 percent. What has not been very well understood is that the Treasury Department has no money of its own to lend; it has to go into the private capital market and borrow the money. So, in this time of excessive interest rates, the government finds itself borrowing at an interest rate several times as high as the interest it gets back from those it lends the money to. And this difference, of course, is paid by your constituents—the taxpayers. They get hit again if they try to borrow, because government borrowing contributes to raising all interest rates.

By terminating the Economic Development Administration, we can save hundreds of millions of dollars in 1982 and billions more over the next few years. There's a lack of consistent and convincing evidence that EDA and its Regional Commissions have been effective in creating new jobs. They have been effective in creating an array of planners, grantsmen, and professional middlemen. We believe we can do better just by the expansion of the economy and the job creation which will come from our economic program.

The Food Stamp program will be restored to its original purpose, to assist those without resources to purchase sufficient nutritional food. We will, however, save $1.8 billion in fiscal year 1982 by removing from eligibility those who are not in real need or who are abusing the program. But even with this reduction, the program will be budgeted for more than $10 billion.

We will tighten welfare and give more attention to outside sources of income when determining the amount of welfare that an individual is allowed. This, plus strong and effective work requirements, will save $520 million in the next year.

I stated a moment ago our intention to keep the school breakfast and lunch programs for those in true need. But by cutting back on meals for children of families who can afford to pay, the savings will be $1.6 billion in the fiscal year 1982.

Now, let me just touch on a few other areas which are typical of the kind of reductions we've included in this economic package. The Trade Adjustment Assistance program provides benefits for workers who are unemployed when foreign imports reduce the market for various American products, causing shutdown of plants and layoff of workers. The purpose is to help these workers find jobs in growing sectors of our economy. There's nothing wrong with that, but because these benefits are paid out on top of normal unemployment benefits, we wind up paying greater benefits to those who lose their jobs because of foreign competition than we do to their friends and neighbors who are laid off due to domestic competition. Anyone must agree that this is unfair. Putting these two programs on the same footing will save $1.15 billion in just 1 year.

Earlier I made mention of changing categorical grants to States and local governments into block grants. Now, we know of course that the categorical grant programs burden local and State governments with a mass of Federal regulations and Federal paperwork. Ineffective targeting, wasteful administrative overhead—all can be eliminated by shifting the resources and decision-making authority to local and State government. This will also consolidate programs which are scattered throughout the Federal bureaucracy, bringing government closer to the people and saving $23.9 billion over the next 5 years.

Our program for economic renewal deals with a number of programs which at present are not cost-effective. An example is Medicaid. Right now Washington provides the States with unlimited matching payments for their expenditures; at the same time, we here in Washington pretty much dictate how the States are going to manage those programs. We want to put a cap on how much the Federal Government will contribute, but at the same time allow the States much more flexibility in managing and structuring the programs. I know from our experience in California that such flexibility could have led to far more cost-effective reforms. Now, this will bring a savings of $1 billion next year.

The space program has been and is important to America, and we plan to continue it. We believe, however, that a reordering of priorities to focus on the most important and cost-effective NASA programs can result in a savings of a quarter of a million dollars.

Now, coming down from space to the mailbox, the Postal Service has been consistently unable to live within its operating budget. It is still dependent on large Federal subsidies. We propose reducing those subsidies by $632 million in 1982 to press the Postal Service into becoming more effective, and in subsequent years the savings will continue to add up.

The Economic Regulatory Administration in the Department of Energy has programs to force companies to convert to specific fuels. It has the authority to administer a gas rationing plan, and prior to decontrol it ran the oil price control program. With these and other regulations gone we can save several hundreds of millions of dollars over the next few years.

I'm sure there's one department you've been waiting for me to mention, the Department of Defense. It's the only department in our entire program that will actually be increased over the present budgeted figure. But even here there was no exemption. The Department of Defense came up with a number of cuts which reduce the budget increase needed to restore our military balance. These measures will save $2.9 billion in 1982 outlays, and by 1986 a total of $28.2 billion will have been saved—or perhaps I should say, will have been made available for the necessary things that we must do. The aim will be to provide the most effective defense for the lowest possible cost.

I believe that my duty as President requires that I recommend increases in defense spending over the coming years. I know that you're all aware—but I think it bears saying again—that since 1970 the Soviet Union has invested $300 billion more in its military forces than we have. As a result of its massive military buildup, the Soviets have made a significant numerical advantage in strategic nuclear delivery systems, tactical aircraft, submarines, artillery, and anti-aircraft defense. To allow this imbalance to continue is a threat to our national security. Notwithstanding our economic straits, making the financial changes beginning now is far less costly than waiting and having to attempt a crash program several years from now.

We remain committed to the goal of arms limitation through negotiation. I hope we can persuade our adversaries to come to realistic balanced and verifiable agreements. But, as we negotiate, our security must be fully protected by a balanced and realistic defense program.

Now, let me say a word here about the general problem of waste and fraud in the Federal Government. One government estimate indicated that fraud alone may account for anywhere from 1 to 10 percent— as much as $25 billion of Federal expenditures for social programs. If the tax dollars that are wasted or mismanaged are added

to this fraud total, the staggering dimensions of this problem begin to emerge.

The Office of Management and Budget is now putting together an interagency task force to attack waste and fraud. We're also planning to appoint as Inspectors General highly trained professionals who will spare no effort to do this job. No administration can promise to immediately stop a trend that has grown in recent years as quickly as government expenditures themselves, but let me say this: Waste and fraud in the Federal Government is exactly what I've called it before—an unrelenting national scandal, a scandal we're bound and determined to do something about.

Marching in lockstep with the whole program of reductions in spending is the equally important program of reduced tax rates. Both are essential if we're to have economic recovery. It's time to create new jobs, to build and rebuild industry, and to give the American people room to do what they do best. And that can only be done with a tax program which provides incentive to increase productivity for both workers and industry.

Our proposal is for a 10-percent across-the-board cut every year for 3 years in the tax rates for all individual income taxpayers, making a total cut in the tax-cut rates of 30 percent. This 3-year reduction will also apply to the tax on unearned income, leading toward an eventual elimination of the present differential between the tax on earned and unearned income.

Now, I would have hoped that we could be retroactive with this. But as it stands, the effective starting date for these 10-percent personal income tax rate reductions will call for as of July 1st of this year.

Again, let me remind you that while this 30-percent reduction will leave the taxpayers with $500 billion more in their pockets over the next 5 years, it's actually only a reduction in the tax increase already built into the system. Unlike some past "tax reforms," this is not merely a shift of wealth between different sets of taxpayers. This proposal for an equal reduction in everyone's tax rates will expand our national prosperity, enlarge national incomes, and increase opportunities for all Americans.

Some will argue, I know, that reducing tax rates now will be inflationary. A solid body of economic experts does not agree. And tax cuts adopted over the past three-fourths of a century indicate these economic experts are right. They will not be inflationary. I've had advice that in 1985 our real production in goods and services will grow by 20 percent and be $300 billion higher than it is today. The average worker's wage will rise in real purchasing power 8 percent, and this is in after-tax dollars. And this, of course, is predicated on a complete program of tax cuts and spending reductions being implemented.

The other part of the tax package is aimed directly at providing business and industry with the capital needed to modernize and engage in more research and development. This will involve an increase in depreciation allowances, and this part of our tax proposal will be retroactive to January 1st.

The present depreciation system is obsolete, needlessly complex, and economically counterproductive. Very simply, it bases the depreciation of plant machinery and vehicles and tools on their original cost, with no recognition of how inflation has increased their replacement cost. We're proposing a much shorter write-off time than is presently allowed—a 5-year-write-off for machinery, 3 years for vehicles and trucks, and a 10-year write-off for plant. In fiscal year 1982 under this plan, business would acquire nearly $10 billion for investment; by 1985, the figure would be nearly 45 billion.

These changes are essential to provide the new investment which is needed to create millions of new jobs between now and 1985 [1986], and to make America competitive once again in the world market. These won't be make-work jobs. They are productive jobs, jobs with a future.

I'm well aware that there are many other desirable and needed tax changes, such as indexing the income tax brackets to protect taxpayers against inflation; the unjust discrimination against married couples if both are working and earning; tuition tax credits; the unfairness of the inheritance tax, especially to the family-owned farm and the family-owned business; and a number of others. But our program for economic recovery is so urgently needed to begin to bring down inflation that I'm asking you to act on this plan first and with great urgency. And then, I pledge I will join with you in seeking these additional tax changes at the earliest date possible.

American society experienced a virtual explosion in government regulation during the past decade. Between 1970 and 1979, expenditures for the major regulatory agencies quadrupled. The number of pages published annually in the *Federal Register* nearly tripled, and the number of pages in the *Code of Federal Regulations* increased by nearly two-thirds. The result has been higher prices, higher unemployment, and lower productivity growth. Overregulation causes small and independent business men and women, as well as large businesses to defer or terminate plans for expansion. And since they're responsible for most of the new jobs, those new jobs just aren't created.

Now, we have no intention of dismantling the regulatory agencies, especially those necessary to protect environment and assure the public health and safety. However, we must come to grips with inefficient and burdensome regulations, eliminate those we can and reform the others.

I have asked Vice President Bush to head a Cabinet-level Task Force on Regulatory Relief. Second, I asked each member of my Cabinet to postpone the effective dates of the hundreds of new regulations which have not yet been implemented. Third, in coordination with the Task Force, many of the agency heads have already taken prompt action to review and rescind existing burdensome regulations. And finally, just yesterday I signed an Executive order that for the first time provides for effective and coordinated management of the regulatory process.

Much has been accomplished, but it's only a beginning. We will eliminate those regulations that are unproductive and unnecessary by Executive order where possible and cooperate fully with you on those that require legislation.

The final aspect of our plan requires a national monetary policy which does not allow money growth to increase consistently faster than the growth of goods and services. In order to curb inflation we need to slow the growth in our money supply.

Now, we fully recognize the independence of the Federal Reserve System and will do nothing to interfere with or undermine that independence. We will consult regularly with the Federal Reserve Board on all aspects of our economic program and will vigorously pursue budget policies that'll make their job easier in reducing monetary growth. A successful program to achieve stable and and moderate growth patterns in the money supply will keep both inflation and interest rates down and restore vigor to our financial institutions and markets.

This, then, is our proposal—America's new beginning: a program for economic recovery. I don't want it to be simply the plan of my administration. I'm here tonight to ask you to join me in making it our plan. Together we can embark on this road—— [*applause*].

Thank you very much. I should have arranged to quit right here. [*Laughter*]

Well, together we can embark on this road, not to make things easy, but to make things better. Our social, political, and cultural, as well as our economic institutions, can no longer absorb the repeated shocks that have been dealt them over the past decades. Can we do the job? The answer is yes. But we must begin now.

We're in control here. There's nothing wrong with America that together we can't fix. I'm sure there'll be some who raise the old familiar cry, "Don't touch my program; cut somewhere else." I hope I've made it plain that our approach has been evenhanded, that only the programs for the truly deserving needy remain untouched. The question is, are we simply going to go down the same path we've gone down before, carving out one special program here, another special program there? I don't think that's what the American people expect of us. More important, I don't think that's what they want. They're ready to return to the source of our strength.

The substance and prosperity of our nation is built by wages brought home from the factories and the mills, the farms, and the shops. They are the services provided in 10,000 corners of America; the interest on

the thrift of our people and the returns for their risk-taking. The production of America is the possession of those who build, serve, create, and produce.

For too long now, we've removed from our people the decisions on how to dispose of what they created. We've strayed from first principles. We must alter our course.

The taxing power of government must be used to provide revenues for legitimate government purposes. It must not be used to regulate the the economy or bring about social change. We've tried that, and surely we must be able to see it doesn't work.

Spending by government must be limited to those functions which are the proper province of government. We can no longer afford things simply because we think of them. Next year we can reduce the budget by $41.4 billion, without harm to government's legitimate purposes or to our responsibility to all who need our benevolence. This, plus the reduction in tax rates, will help bring an end to inflation.

In the health and social services area alone, the plan we're proposing will substantially reduce the need for 465 pages of law, 1,400 pages of regulations, 5,000 Federal employees who presently administer 7,600 separate grants in about 25,000 separate locations. Over 7 million man and woman hours of work by State and local officials are required to fill out government forms.

I would direct a question to those who have indicated already an unwillingness to accept such a plan: Have they an alternative which offers a greater chance of balancing the budget, reducing and eliminating inflation, stimulating the creation of jobs, and reducing the tax burden? And, if they haven't, are they suggesting we can continue on the present course without coming to a day of reckoning? If we don't do this, inflation and the growing tax burden will put an end to everything we believe in and our dreams for the future.

We don't have an option of living with inflation and its attendant tragedy, millions of productive people willing and able to work but unable to find a buyer for their work in the job market. We have an alternative, and that is the program for econom-ic recovery.

True, it'll take time for the favorable ef-fects of our proposal to be felt. So, we must begin now. The people are watching and waiting. They don't demand miracles. They do expect us to act. Let us act together.

Thank you, and good night.

Note: The President spoke at 9 p.m. in the House Chamber at the Capitol. He was in-troduced by Thomas P. O'Neill, Jr., Speaker of the House of Representatives. The ad-dress was broadcast live on radio and tele-vision.

Message to the Congress Transmitting the Proposed Package on the Program for Economic Recovery
February 18, 1981

To the Congress of the United States:

It is with pleasure that I take the oppor-tunity this evening to make my first major address to the Congress. The address briefly describes the comprehensive package that I am proposing in order to achieve a full and vigorous recovery for our economy. The key elements of that package are four in number:

—A budget reform plan to cut the rate of growth in Federal spending;

—A series of proposals to reduce personal income tax rates by 10 percent a year over three years and to create jobs by accelerating depreciation for business investment in plant and equipment;

—A far-reaching program of regulatory relief;

—And, in cooperation with the Federal Reserve Board, a new commitment to a monetary policy that will restore a stable currency and healthy financial markets.

Taken together, I believe these proposals will put the Nation on a fundamentally dif-ferent course—a course leading to less infla-tion, more growth, and a brighter future for all of our citizens.

To aid the Congress in acting promptly on these proposals, I am today forwarding the attached documents which describe the program in greater detail than I can in my address to you. Specifically, you will find the following documents in this package:

(1) An economic report—issued as a White House paper—that outlines all four of the elements in my program and sets forth the background to those elements.

(2) A lengthy report on my initial budget cut proposals that has been prepared by the Office of Management and Budget. It should be noted that this report will be fol-lowed by a complete budget submission to the Congress, addressing fiscal years 81 and 82. That report will be sent to you on March 10th.

(3) A report on my proposals for tax re-duction issued by the Department of the Treasury.

It is my hope that this combination of transmittals will allow the Congress to pro-ceed in accordance with timetables estab-lished in the Congressional Budget Act and will permit rapid consideration of this entire program.

My Cabinet and other members of my Administration have worked intensively and cooperatively with me in developing this program for economic recovery. All of us are now eager to work with the Congress as partners in an undertaking that is vital to the future of the Nation.

RONALD REAGAN

The White House,
February 18, 1981.

Note: The message is printed in the docu-ment entitled "America's New Beginning: A Program for Economic Recovery—February 18, 1981."

White House Report on the Program for Economic Recovery
February 18, 1981

I. *A Program for Economic Recovery*

Today the Administration is proposing a national recovery plan to reverse the debilitating combination of sustained inflation and economic distress which continues to face the American economy. Were we to stay with existing policies, the results would be readily predictable: a rising government presence in the economy, more inflation, stagnating productivity, and higher unemployment. Indeed, there is reason to fear that if we remain on this course, our economy may suffer even more calamitously.

The program we have developed will break that cycle of negative expectations. It will revitalize economic growth, renew optimism and confidence, and rekindle the Nation's entrepreneurial instincts and creativity.

The benefits to the average American will be striking. Inflation—which is now at double digit rates—will be cut in half by 1986. The American economy will produce 13 million new jobs by 1986, nearly 3 million more than if the status quo in government policy were to prevail. The economy itself should break out of its anemic growth patterns to a much more robust growth trend of 4 to 5 percent a year. These positive results will be accomplished simultaneously with reducing tax burdens, increasing private saving, and raising the living standard of the American family.

The plan is based on sound expenditure, tax, regulatory, and monetary policies. It seeks properly functioning markets, free play of wages and prices, reduced government spending and borrowing, a stable and reliable monetary framework, and reduced government barriers to risk-taking and enterprise. This agenda for the future recognizes that sensible policies which are consistently applied can release the strength of the private sector, improve economic growth, and reduce inflation.

We have forgotten some important lessons in America. High taxes are not the remedy for inflation. Excessively rapid monetary growth cannot lower interest rates. Well-intentioned government regulations do not contribute to economic vitality. In fact, government spending has become so extensive that it contributes to the economic problems it was designed to cure. More government intervention in the economy cannot possibly be a solution to our economic problems.

We must remember a simple truth. The creativity and ambition of the American people are the vital forces of economic growth. The motivation and incentive of our people—to supply new goods and services and earn additional income for their families—are the most precious resources of our Nation's economy. The goal of this Administration is to nurture the strength and vitality of the American people by reducing the burdensome, intrusive role of the Federal Government; by lowering tax rates and cutting spending; and by providing incentives for individuals to work, to save, and to invest. It is our basic belief that only by reducing the growth of government can we increase the growth of the economy.

The U.S. economy faces no insurmountable barriers to sustained growth. It confronts no permanently disabling tradeoffs between inflation and unemployment, between high interest rates and high taxes, or between recession and hyperinflation. We can revive the incentives to work and save. We can restore the willingness to invest in the private capital required to achieve a steadily rising standard of living. Most important, we can regain our faith in the future.

The plan consists of four parts: (1) a substantial reduction in the growth of Federal expenditures; (2) a significant reduction in Federal tax rates; (3) prudent relief of Federal regulatory burdens; and (4) a monetary policy on the part of the independent Federal Reserve System which is consistent with those policies. These four complementary policies form an integrated and comprehensive program.

It should be clear from the most cursory examination of the economic program of this Administration that we have moved from merely talking about the economic difficulties facing the American people to taking the strong action necessary to turn the economy around.

The leading edge of our program is the comprehensive reduction in the rapid growth of Federal spending. As shown in detail below, our budget restraint is more than "cosmetic" changes in the estimates of Federal expenditures. But we have not adopted a simple-minded "meat ax" approach to budget reductions. Rather, a careful set of guidelines has been used to identify lower-priority programs in virtually every department and agency that can be eliminated, reduced, or postponed.

The second element of the program, which is equally important asnd urgent, is the reduction in Federal personal income tax rates by 10 percent a year for 3 years in a row. Closely related to this is an incentive to greater investment in production and job creation via faster tax write-offs of new factories and production equipment.

The third key element of our economic expansion program is an ambitious reform of regulations that will reduce the government-imposed barriers to investment, production, and employment. We have suspended for 2 months the unprecedented flood of last-minute rulemaking on the part of the previous Administration. We have eliminated the ineffective and counterproductive wage and price standards of the Council on Wage and Price Stability, and we have taken other steps to eliminate government interference in the marketplace.

The fourth aspect of this comprehensive economic program is a monetary policy to provide the financial environment consistent with a steady return to sustained growth and price stability. During the first week of this Administration its commitment to the historic independence of the Federal Reserve System was underscored. It is clear, of course, that monetary and fiscal policy are closely interrelated. Success in one area can be made more difficult—or can be reinforced—by the other. Thus, a predictable and steady growth in the money supply at more modest levels than often experienced in the past will be a vital contribution to the achievement of the economic goals described in this *Report*. The planned reduction and subsequent elimination of Federal deficit financing will help the Federal Reserve System perform its important role in achieving economic growth and stability.

The ultimate importance of this program for sustained economic growth will arise not only from the positive effects of the individual components, important as they are. Rather, it will be the dramatic improvement in the underlying economic environment and outlook that will set a new and more positive direction to economic decisions throughout the economy. Protection against inflation and high tax burdens will no longer be an overriding motivation. Once again economic choices—involving working, saving, and investment—will be based primarily on the prospect for real rewards for those productive activities which improve the true economic well-being of our citizens.

II. *The Twin Problems of High Inflation and Stagnant Growth*

The policies this Administration is putting foward for urgent consideration by the Congress are based on the fact that this Nation now faces its most serious set of economic problems since the 1930s. Inflation has grown from 1 to 1½ percent a year in the early 1960s to about 13 percent in the past 2 years; not since World War I have we had 2 years of back-to-back double digit inflation. At the same time, the rate of economic growth has been slowing and the unemployment rate creeping upward. Productivity growth—the most important single measure of our ability to improve our standard of living—has been declining steadily for more than a decade. In the past 3 years our productivity actually fell.

The most important cause of our economic problems has been the government itself. The Federal Government, through tax, spending, regulatory, and monetary policies, has sacrificed long-term growth and price stability for ephemeral short-term goals. In particular, excessive government spending and overly accommodative monetary policies have combined to give us a climate of continuing inflation. That inflation itself has helped to sap our prospects for growth. In addition, the growing weight of haphazard and inefficient regulation has weakened our productivity growth. High marginal tax rates on business and individuals discourage work, innovation, and the investment necessary to improve productivity and long-run growth. Finally, the resulting stagnant growth contributes further to inflation in a vicious cycle that can only be broken with a plan that attacks broadly on all fronts.

THE ROLE OF THE GOVERNMENT IN
CAUSING INFLATION

Surges of inflation are not unusual in history; there were price explosions after both World Wars, as well as smaller outbursts in the 1920s and late 1930s. Therefore, in spite of the role played by food and energy prices in recent inflationary outbursts, it is misleading to concentrate on these transitory factors as fundamental causes of the inflationary bias in the American economy. Even when prices in these markets have been stable, inflation has continued with little relief.

What is unusual about our recent history is the *persistence of inflation*. Outbursts of high inflation in the last 15 years have not been followed by the customary price stability, but rather by long periods of continued high inflation. This persistence of inflation has crucially affected the way our economy works. People now believe inflation is "here to stay"; they plan accordingly, thereby giving further momentum to inflation. Since there are important long-term relationships between suppliers and customers and between workers and management, long-term contracts, sometimes unwritten, are often based on the view that inflation will persist. This robs the economy of flexibility which might otherwise contribute to reducing inflation.

The Federal Government has greatly contributed to the persistence of high inflation. Overly stimulative fiscal and monetary policies, on average, have financed excessive spending and thus pushed prices upward. Since government accommodation is widely expected to continue, inflation has become embedded in the economy.

When inflationary outbursts occur, policymakers all too often have made a quick turn toward restraint. Such turnabouts, however, have been short-lived and their temporary nature has increasingly been anticipated by savers, investors, and workers. Subsequent declines in employment and growth inevitably call forth stimulative policies before inflation can be brought under control. Such "stop-and-go" policies have only resulted in higher unemployment and lower real growth.

Finally, but equally important, government policies have increased inflation by reducing the potential of our economy to grow—directly through the increasing burdens of taxes and regulations, and indirectly through inflation itself. The result is a vicious circle. Its force can be measured by the statistics of our productivity slowdown, but it is seen more dramatically in the anxiety and concern of our people.

GOVERNMENT CONTRIBUTES TO THE
PRODUCTIVITY SLOWDOWN

Productivity, popularly measured as output per worker-hour, is an indicator of the efficiency of the economy and consequently of our ability to maintain the rate of improvement in our standard of living. Over the past 15 years, the rate of productivity improvement has slowed, and now virtually halted.

Government policies have been a major contributor to the slowdown but they can be an even more important contributor to the cure. The weight of regulation and the discouragement that results from high marginal tax burdens are key factors, but inflation itself also plays an important role. Reduced capital formation is the most important and visible, but not the only, channel by which this occurs.

By increasing uncertainty about the future, inflation discourages investors from undertaking projects that they would have considered profitable but which, with today's inflationary environment, they consider too risky. Inflation also diverts funds from productive investments into hedging and speculation.

Although recent statistics show that the share of our economy's production devoted to investment is high by historic standards, the magnitude is illusory—an illusion fostered by inflation. Accelerating prices, and the high interest rates and shifting economic policy associated with them, have contributed to an unwillingness to make long-lived investments. As a result, our stock of productive plant and equipment depreciates faster, so that more investment is needed simply to stand still.

The regulatory requirements imposed by the government have likewise served to discourage investment by causing uncertainty in business decisionmaking. In addition, investments to meet regulatory requirements have diverted capital from expanding productive capacity. Some estimates have put regulation-related investment at more than 10 percent of the total level of business investment in recent years. The expanding intrusiveness of the government into the private sector also inhibits innovation and limits the ability of entrepreneurs to produce in the most efficient way.

INFLATION, GROWTH, AND THE TAX SYSTEM

The role of the tax system in reducing our past growth, and its potential for improving the prospects for future growth, deserve special attention. By reducing the incentives for investment and innovation, both by individuals and by businesses, the tax system has been a key cause of our stagnation. Restoring the proper incentives will make a major contribution to the long-run vitality of our economy.

The progressivity of the personal income tax system levies rising tax rates on additions to income that merely keep pace with inflation. Households therefore find that even if their gross incomes rise with inflation, their after-tax real income declines. Some households respond to these higher marginal tax burdens by reducing their work effort. "Bracket creep" also encourages taxpayers to seek out "tax shelters," sources of income that offer higher after-tax returns but not necessarily higher before-tax returns than more productive sources, again contributing to economic inefficiency. In the last two decades the Congress has reduced personal income taxes seven times. Nevertheless, *average effective tax rates are now about 30 percent higher than their mid-1960's low.* Marginal tax rates have climbed in tandem with average rates.

Due to inflation, the rate of return on corporate assets, after tax, and the level of corporate earnings have been seriously eroded over the past decade and a half. That was a major factor stunting capital spending from what it otherwise would have been. The tax treatment of depreciation has been an important contributor to this lowering of returns. We now allow write-offs at the cost of purchase, rather than at more realistic prices. This creates phantom profits upon which taxes are paid.

Finally, unless the Congress takes frequent actions to offset the revenue generating effect of inflation on the progressive personal tax system, the Congress has available for spending unlegislated increases in funds. Inflation in tandem with the tax system thereby impairs the fiscal discipline of the budget process and facilitates higher levels of government spending than would result if the Congress were forced to vote on each tax increase. This offers further encouragement to inflation.

THE ECONOMY AS A WHOLE HAS SUFFERED

Because past policies have not reduced unemployment, even as they have encouraged rising inflation—the economy as a whole has suffered. Over the past two decades, we have seen the "misery index"—the sum of the inflation and unemployment rates—more than double, rising from 7.3 in 1960 to 17.2 in 1980. While unemployment rates have fluctuated over the business cycle, there has been no long-run tradeoff between unemployment and inflation. The upward movements in inflation have not brought us falling unemployment rates, nor has high unemployment brought lower inflation.

Thus trends of the past are clearly disturbing in that they have sapped our Nation's economic vitality. Of greater significance, however, is the danger we face if the policies of the 1970s are continued.

For the first time in American history financial markets reflect the belief that inflation will not retreat significantly from current high levels. The Nation's economy and financial system are on a dangerous course—one which, if not reversed, would lead to a prolonged stagnation of economic

growth and employment, ever higher inflation and interest rates, and potentially a financial crisis. The solution to this growing
economic threat calls for bold actions designed to reduce—dramatically and sharply—inflationary expectations. These policies
must restore fiscal integrity; increase incentives for saving, investment, and production; attain monetary and financial stability;
and enhance the role of the marketplace as
the principal force in the allocation of resources.

III. *Slowing the Growth of Government Spending*

The uncontrolled growth of government
spending has been a primary cause of the
sustained high rate of inflation experienced
by the American economy. Perhaps of
greater importance, the continued and apparently inexorable expansion of government has contributed to the widespread expectation of persisting—and possibly
higher—rates of inflation in the future.

Thus, a central goal of the economic program is to reduce the rate at which government spending increases. In view of the seriousness of the inflationary pressures facing
us, the proposed reductions in the Federal
budget for the coming fiscal year are the
largest ever proposed.

Despite the tendency to refer to "cutting" the budget, it is clear that an expanding population, a growing economy, and a
difficult international environment all lead
to the need for year-to-year rises in the
level of government spending. Thus, the
badly needed effort to "cut" the budget
really refers to reductions in the amount of
increase in spending requested from one
year to the next.

The magnitude of the fiscal problem
facing the United States can be seen when
we realize that, despite the $49.1 billion of
savings including $5.7 billion in off-budget
outlays that is being recommended for fiscal
1982, the total amount of Federal outlays
for the year is likely to be $41 billion higher
than the curent year. (A separate document
is being issued by the Office of Management and Budget that outlines the major
spending reductions in considerable detail.)

It is essential to stress the fundamental
principles that guided the development of
that program.

First, and most importantly, all members
of our society except the truly needy will be
asked to contribute to the program for
spending control.

Second, we will strengthen our national
defense.

Finally, these fundamental principles led
to nine specific guidelines that were applied in reducing the budget:

- Preserve "the social safety net."
- Revise entitlements to eliminate unintended benefits.
- Reduce subsidies to middle- and upper-
income groups.
- Impose fiscal restraint on other national interest programs.
- Recover costs that can be clearly allocated to users.
- Stretch-out and retarget public sector
capital investment programs.
- Reduce overhead and personnel costs
of the Federal Government.
- Apply sound economic criteria to subsidy programs.
- Consolidate categorical grant programs
into block grants.

The application of these guidelines has
required great care, judgment, and sensitivity. However, we are putting forward over
80 proposals that will carry out these guidelines and affect virtually every segment of
our economy except the truly needy. The
Administration's insistence on this fundamental principle has meant that programs
benefiting millions of truly needy beneficiaries have not been affected by the spending control effort. These programs include
social insurance benefits for the elderly,
basic unemployment benefits, cash benefits
for the chronically poor, and society's obligations to veterans.

The selection of specific reductions has
been a difficult task involving the entire
Administration as well as much consultation
with representatives of business, labor, agriculture, minority groups, and State and
local governments.

The spending reduction plan will shift
Federal budget priorities so that Federal resources are spent for purposes that are truly

the responsibility of the national government. As the table below indicates, our budget plans reflect the increased importance attached to national defense, maintain the Federal Government's support for the truly needy, and fulfill our responsibilities for interest payments on the national debt. The spending reductions will restrain Federal involvement in areas that are properly left to State and local governments or to the private sector.

SHIFT IN BUDGET PRIORITIES

	1962	1981	1984
Dollar amounts (in billions):			
DOD—Military	46.8	157.9	249.8
Safety net programs	26.2	239.3	313.0
Net interest	6.9	64.3	66.8
All other	26.9	193.2	142.0
Total	106.8	654.7	771.6
Outlay shares (percent):			
DOD—Military	43.8	24.1	32.4
Safety net programs	24.5	36.6	40.6
Net interest	6.4	9.8	8.6
All other	25.2	29.5	18.4
Total	100.0	100.0	100.0

Carrying out this program of budget restraint will also halt and begin to reverse the tendency of government to take an ever-larger share of our economic resources. From a high of 23 percent of the gross national product (GNP) in fiscal 1981, Federal outlays are now scheduled to decline to 21.8 percent in fiscal 1982 and to reach approximately 19 percent beginning in 1984.

THE FEDERAL BUDGET AND GNP

Fiscal year	Outlays as percent of GNP
1981	23.0
1982	21.8
1983	20.4
1984	19.3
1985	19.2
1986	19.0

In conjunction with the tax program that is being proposed, the present excessively high deficit in the budget will be reduced and, in a few years, eliminated. Because of the legacy of fiscal commitments that were inherited by this Administration, balancing the budget will require tough action over several years.

From a deficit of $59.6 billion in 1980—and of a similar deficit this year if past policies had continued—Federal expenditures are now estimated to exceed revenues by $45.0 billion in 1982, and $23.0 billion in 1983. By fiscal 1984—under the policy recommendations presented in this document—the Federal budget should be in balance. And that will not be a one-time occurrence. As shown in the table below, the Federal budget will actually generate a surplus in 1985 and 1986, for the first time since 1969.

FEDERAL REVENUES AND OUTLAYS

[IN BILLIONS OF DOLLARS]

Fiscal year	Revenues	Outlays	Deficit (−) or surplus (+)
1981	600.2	654.7	−54.5
1982	650.5	695.5	−45.0
1983	710.1	733.1	−23.0
1984	772.1	771.6	+0.5
1985	851.0	844.0	+7.0
1986	942.1	912.1	+30.0

THE FEDERAL BUDGET AND THE ECONOMY

The rewards that the economy will reap with enactment of the spending control plan are many and substantial. In the past, excessive deficit spending has been a major contributor to the initiation and persistence of inflation. Not only have Federal budget deficits at times of expanding private sector activity fueled inflationary pressures, but government's tendency to stop fighting inflation with the first signs of a slackening economy has persuaded firms and workers that they need not fear pricing themselves out of business with inflationary wage and price increases. With the plans for controlling government spending, the Federal budget will become a weapon against inflation, rather than one of its major causes.

During the decade of the 1970s, the Federal budget was in deficit every year. In 1970 the deficit was a relatively modest $2.8 billion; in 1980 it was nearly $60 billion. Outlays soared by almost 200 percent. When this Administration began, the prospect was for a continuation of these alarming trends.

Fiscal year	(In billions of dollars)		
	Receipts	Outlays	Deficit (−)
1970	193.7	196.6	−2.8
1971	188.4	211.4	−23.0
1972	208.6	232.0	−23.4
1973	232.2	247.1	−14.8
1974	264.9	269.6	−4.7
1975	281.0	326.2	−45.2
1976	300.0	366.4	−66.4
1977	357.8	402.7	−44.9
1978	402.0	450.8	−48.8
1979	465.9	493.6	−27.7
1980	520.0	579.6	−59.6

Many of the program reductions that are being proposed will contribute to a more efficient use of resources in the economy and thereby higher levels of production and income. No longer will the average American taxpayer be asked to contribute to programs that further narrow private interests rather than the general public interest. In many cases, such services are more appropriately paid for with user charges. By consolidating a variety of categorical grant programs into a few block grant programs, the resources spent will provide greater benefits because the levels of government closer to the people can better recongnize their needs than can Washington. And by reducing Federal deficits and off-budget Federal financing we will ensure that Federal borrowing requirements do not crowd more productive private activities out of the market.

The budget that is being proposed will restore the Federal Government to its proper role in American society. It will contribute to the health of the economy, the strength of our military, and the protection of the less fortunate members of society who need the compassion of the government for their support. Many special interests who had found it easier to look to the Federal Government for support than to the competitive market will be disappointed by this budget, but the average worker and businessman, the backbone of our Nation, will find that their interests are better served.

IV. *Reducing Tax Burdens*

An integral part of the comprehensive economic program is a set of tax proposals to improve the after-tax, after-inflation rewards to work, saving, and investment. Inflation inevitably increases the burden of taxes on individuals by pushing them into higher and higher marginal rates. In businesses, inflation makes the purchase of new equipment progressively more difficult by reducing the amount of cash flow available for capital investment. The tax package addresses both of these problems.

TAX RELIEF FOR INDIVIDUALS

Any increase in nominal income moves taxpayers into higher tax brackets, whether the increase is real or merely an adjustment for higher costs of living. As a consequence, taxes rise faster than inflation, raising average tax rates and tax burdens. In fact, every 10 percent increase in income—real or nominal—produces about a 15 percent increase in Federal personal income tax receipts. An average family requiring a $1,500 cost-of-living increase to maintain its standard of living must have $1,900 in wage increases to keep even after taxes.

Individual tax liabilities rose from 9.2 percent of personal income in 1965 to 11.6 percent last year. The average tax burden would have risen far more had not much of the inflation-related tax increases been offset by periodic tax cuts. Marginal tax rates, however, have been allowed to rise sharply for most taxpayers. In 1965, 6 percent of all taxpayers faced marginal rates of 25 percent of more. Today nearly one of every three taxpayers is in at least the 25 percent bracket.

As taxpayers move into higher brackets, incentives to work, save, and invest are reduced since each addition to income yields less after taxes than before. In the late 1960s and the early 1970s, Americans saved between 7 to 9 percent of personal disposable income. In 1979 and 1980, the saving rate was between 5 to 6 percent. The combination of inflation and higher marginal tax rates is undoubtedly a major factor in the lower personal saving rate.

To correct these problems and to improve the after-tax return from work and from saving, the President is asking the Congress to reduce the marginal tax rates for individuals across the board by 10 percent per year for the next 3 years starting July 1, 1981. This would reduce rates in stages from a range of 14 to 70 percent to a range of 10 to 50 percent effective January 1, 1984. These rate reductions will contribute materially above those which would be attained under present laws. At these higher income levels, the reductions in Federal tax revenues, compared with those which would be obtained under present law, are $6.4 billion in fiscal 1981, $44.2 billion in fiscal 1982, and rise to $162.4 billion in fiscal 1986.

The effect of these tax cuts on a 4-person family whose 1980 income is $25,000 would be a $153 tax reduction this year, and a $809 tax reduction for 1984, assuming no increase in income. If the family's nominal earnings rise to $30,300 in 1984, their tax reduction would be $1,112 in that year.

The Administration's proposals will bring down average individual tax receipts to 10.8 percent of personal income in 1984, still 1.6 percentage points above where it was in 1965. Without these marginal tax rate cuts, however, individual taxes would rise to 14.7 percent of personal income by 1984. Failure to enact these proposals is thus tantamount to imposing a tax increase on the average American taxpayer.

TAX INCENTIVES FOR INVESTMENT

Since the late 1960s the rate of net capital formation (excluding spending mandated to meet environmental standards) has fallen substantially. For the 5 years ending in 1979, increases in real net business fixed capital averaged just over 2 percent of the Nation's real net national product, or one-half the rate for the latter part of the 1960s.

One of the major tasks facing the U.S. economy in the 1980s is to reverse these trends and to promote more capital investment. To combat the decline in productivity growth, to hasten the replacement of energy-inefficient machines and equipment, to comply with government mandates that do not enhance production, we must increase the share of our Nation's resources going to investment. Both improvements in productivity and increases in productive jobs will come from expanded investment.

Inflation and an outdated capital equipment depreciation system have combined to lower the after-tax real rate of return on capital investments by business. High inflation causes a large discrepancy between the historic and the current replacement costs of physical assets of business. Thus, corporate financial records, utilizing historic costs and current dollar sales figures, significantly overstate nominal profits and understate true economic costs.

In 1980 alone, the replacement cost of inventories exceeded by over $43 billion the cost of the inventories claimed for tax purposes. Depreciation charges based on historical cost fell short of the replacement cost of capital assets consumed by another $17 billion. These arose from a failure to record inventory and capital assets at their true replacement cost.

On an inflation adjusted basis, many firms are now paying out more than their real income in the form of taxes and dividends. The result is that real investment in equipment, maintenance, modernization, and new technology is falling further behind the needs of our economy. Clearly, present incentives for business capital formation are inadequate.

As a consequence, the President is asking the Congress to provide for an accelerated cost recovery system for machinery and equipment and certain structures according to the following classes:

- Ten years on an accelerated write-off schedule for long-lived public utility property (with a 10 percent investment credit) and factories, stores, and warehouses used by their owners (no investment credit, consistent with present law).
- Five years on an accelerated write-off schedule (plus 10 percent investment credit) for all other machinery and equipment except long-lived utility property.
- Three years on an accelerated write-off schedule (plus 6 percent investment credit) for autos and light trucks and capital costs for research and development.

In addition, audit-proof recovery periods would be established for other depreciable real estate:

- Fifteen years straight line (and no investment credit) for other nonresidential buildings and low-income housing.
- Eighteen years straight line (and no investment credit) for other rental residential structures.

A 5-year phase-in of the accelerated recovery rates for the 5-year and 10-year classes is proposed, but the effective date would be January 1, 1981, so that no pending investment plans are deferred in anticipation of the new system. These tax changes will make important contributions to raising economic activity above the levels of which would be attained under present laws. At this higher income, Federal tax revenues would actually be less than those which would be obtained under present law, by $2.5 billion in fiscal 1981, $9.7 billion in fiscal 1982, and $59.3 billion in fiscal 1986.

DIRECT REVENUE EFFECTS OF PROPOSED TAX REDUCTIONS

[IN BILLIONS OF DOLLARS]

	(Fiscal years)					
	1981	1982	1983	1984	1985	1986
Individual:						
30 Percent phased rate reduction	−6.4	−44.2	−81.4	−118.1	−141.5	−162.4
Business:						
Accelerated cost recovery system after interaction with individual tax	−2.5	−9.7	−18.6	−30.0	−44.2	−59.3
Total	−8.8	−53.9	−100.0	−148.1	−185.7	−221.7

These changes will simplify accounting procedures and raise after-tax profits of businesses. For example, a manufacturer of glass products that buys new machinery for $100,000 in 1982 will, as a result of these new cost recovery allowances, reduce its tax liability by $1,798 in that year, $2,517 in 1983, and additional amounts in later years.

The basic differences between the present accelerated depreciation law and proposed accelerated capital cost recovery system are shown in the following chart:

PRESENT LAW DEPRECIATION AND ACCELERATED COST RECOVERY SYSTEM

COMPARISON OF MAJOR FEATURES

Item	Present law depreciation	Accelerated cost recovery system
General applicability	Option of "facts and circumstances" or guidelines (ADR).	Mandatory.
Recovery periods: Tangible personal property	Guidelines allow 2½ to 50 years depending on asset type or activity, with optional 20 percent variance for each.	3 years (autos, light trucks, and machinery and equipment used for research and development), 5 years (most machinery and equipment), or 10 years (long-lived public utility property).
Real estate	Determined by facts and circumstances or by guidelines ranging from 25 to 60 years depending on the type of building.	10 years for owner-occupied factories, stores, and warehouses; 15 years for other nonresidential and for low-income housing; 18 years for other residential.
Recovery method: Tangible personal property	Straight line; or for new property, taxpayer may elect declining balance up to 200 percent, or sum-of-years digits.	Accelerated write-off built into tables.

PRESENT LAW DEPRECIATION AND ACCELERATED COST RECOVERY SYSTEM—Continued

COMPARISON OF MAJOR FEATURES

Item	Present law depreciation	Accelerated cost recovery system
Real estate	Same for new residential; up to 150 percent declining balance for new, nonresidential; up to 125 percent declining balance for used residential; straight line for used nonresidential.	Same for 10-year property. Straight line for other.
Recapture provisions:		
Tangible personal property	Ordinary income recapture up to prior allowances (section 1245).	Ordinary income recapture up to prior allowances (section 1245).
Real estate	Ordinary income recapture up to excess over straight line (section 1250).	Same for 10-year real property. No recapture for others.
Asset accounting:		
General	Vintage accounting.	Vintage accounting.
First year	Rateably, or choice of conventions.	Half-year convention built into tables.
Investment tax credit	3⅓ percent for machinery and equipment written-off or held for 3–5 years, 6⅔ percent for 5–7 years, 10 percent if longer.	6 percent for 3-year class and 10 percent for 5-year and 10-year eligible property.
Carryovers	Choice of 20 percent shorter or longer lives; straight line or accelerated methods, where allowed. Deductions may add to net operating loss which can be carried over 7 years.	Extends net operating loss and investment credit carryover period from 7 to 10 years.
Timing of eligibility	When placed in service.	When placed in service, or for property with at least a 2 year construction period, as acquired.

V. *Providing Regulatory Relief*

The rapid growth in Federal regulation has retarded economic growth and contributed to inflationary pressures. While there is widespread agreement on the legitimate role of government in protecting the environment, promoting health and safety, safeguarding workers and consumers, and guaranteeing equal opportunity, there is also growing realization that excessive regulation is a very significant factor in our current economic difficulties.

The costs of regulation arise in several ways. First, there are the outlays for the Federal bureaucracy which administers and enforces the regulations. Second, there are the costs to business, nonprofit institutions, and State and local governments of complying with regulations. Finally, there are the longer run and indirect effects of regulation on economic growth and productivity.

The most readily identifiable of the costs are the administrative outlays of the regulatory agencies, since they appear in the Federal budget. These costs are passed on to individuals and businesses directly in the form of higher Federal taxes. Much larger than the administrative expenses are the costs of compliance, which add $100 billion per year to the costs of the goods and services we buy. The most important effects of regulation, however, are the adverse impacts on economic growth. These arise because regulations may discourage innovative research and development, reduce investment in new plant and equipment, raise unemployment by increasing labor costs, and reduce competition. Taken together, these longer run effects contribute significantly to our current economic dilemma of high unemployment and inflation.

In many cases the costs of regulation can be substantially reduced without significantly affecting worthwhile regulatory goals. Unnecessarily stringent rules, intrusive means of enforcement, extensive reporting and recordkeeping requirements, and other regulatory excesses are all too common.

During this Administration's first month in office, five major steps have been taken to address the problem of excessive and inefficient regulation. Specifically, we have:

- Established a Task Force on Regulatory Relief chaired by Vice President George Bush,
- Abolished the Council on Wage and Price Stability's ineffective program to control wage and price increases,
- Postponed the effective dates of pending regulations until the end of March,
- Issued an Executive order to strengthen Presidential oversight of the regulatory process, and
- Accelerated the decontrol of domestic oil.

PRESIDENTIAL TASK FORCE ON REGULATORY RELIEF

Previous efforts to manage the proliferation of Federal regulation failed to establish central regulatory oversight at the highest level. On January 22, the President announced the creation of a Task Force on Regulatory Relief to be chaired by the Vice President. The membership is to include the Secretary of the Treasury, the Attorney General, the Secretary of Commerce, the Secretary of Labor, the Director of the Office of Management and Budget, the Assistant to the President for Policy Development, and the Chairman of the Council of Economic Advisers.

The Task Force's charter is to:

- Review major regulatory proposals by executive branch agencies, especially those that appear to have major policy significance or involve overlapping jurisdiction among agencies.
- Assess executive branch regulations already on the books, concentrating on those that are particularly burdensome to the national economy or to key industrial sectors.
- Oversee the development of legislative proposals designed to balance and coordinate the roles and objectives of regulatory agencies.

TERMINATION OF CWPS'S WAGE-PRICE STANDARDS PROGRAM

The Council on Wage and Price Stability (CWPS) was created in 1974, and like many government agencies, rapidly grew in size and scope. But the CWPS program of wage-price standards proved to be totally ineffective in halting the rising rate of inflation.

On January 29, the President rescinded the CWPS's wage-price standards program. As a result, taxpayers will save about $1.5 million, employment in the Executive Office of the President will decline by about 135 people, and Federal requirements that businesses submit voluminous reports will end.

POSTPONING PENDING REGULATIONS

On January 29, the President also sent a memorandum to cabinet officers and the head of the Environmental Protection Agency (EPA), requesting that, to the extent permitted by law, they postpone the effective dates of those regulations that would have become effective before March 29 and that they refrain from issuing any new final regulations during this 60-day period.

This suspension of new regulations has three purposes: First, it allows the new Administration to review the "midnight" regulations issued during the last days of the previous Administration to assure that they are cost-effective. Second, the Administration's appointees now can become familiar with the details of the various programs for which they are responsible before the regulations become final.

Lastly, the suspension allows time for the Administration, through the Presidential Task Force, to develop improved procedures for management and oversight of the regulatory process.

THE EXECUTIVE ORDER ON FEDERAL REGULATION

The President has signed a new Executive order designed to improve management of the Federal regulatory process. It provides reassurance to the American people of the government's ability to control its regulatory activities. The Office of Management and Budget is charged with administering the new order, subject to the overall direction of the Presidential Task Force on Regulatory Relief.

The order emphasizes that regulatory decisions should be based on adequate information. Actions should not be undertaken unless the potential benefits to society outweigh the potential costs, and regulatory priorities should be set on the basis of net benefits to society. The order requires agencies to determine the most cost-effective approach for meeting any given regulatory objective, taking into account such factors as the economic condition of industry, the national economy, and other prospective regulations.

As part of the development of any important regulation, the order also requires that each agency prepare a Regulatory Impact Analysis to evaluate potential benefits and costs. The Task Force will oversee this process; OMB will make comments on regulatory analyses, help determine which new and existing regulations should be reviewed, and direct the publication of semiannual agendas of the regulations that agencies plan to issue or review.

DECONTROLLING DOMESTIC OIL PRICES

The President has also ordered the immediate decontrol of domestic oil prices, instead of waiting until October as originally scheduled. This has eliminated a large Federal bureaucracy which administered a cumbersome and inefficient system of regulations that served to stifle domestic oil production, increase our dependence on foreign oil, and discourage conservation.

INTEGRATING THE GOALS OF REGULATORY RELIEF WITH PAPERWORK REDUCTION

Our program to reduce regulatory burdens will dovetail with the efforts under the Paperwork Reduction Act of 1980. Lamentably, present regulations will require Americans to spend over 1.2 billion hours filling out government forms during 1981. This is equivalent to the annual labor input for the entire steel industry.

The Congress responded to the need for consistent management of Federal paperwork and regulatory issues by passing the Paperwork Reduction Act of 1980. The act creates an Office of Information and Regulatory Affairs within OMB with the power to review Federal regulations that contain a recordkeeping or reporting requirement and directs this agency to reduce the paperwork burden by 15 percent.

FUTURE TARGETS FOR REGULATORY REVIEW

The program of regulatory relief is just getting under way. Future regulatory reform efforts will be directed not only at proposed regulations, but also at existing regulations and regulatory statutes that are particularly burdensome. This process has already begun: in the first month of the Administration several cabinet departments and agencies—on their own initiative and in coordination with with the Task Force—have taken action on particularly controversial rules. For example, rules mandating extensive bilingual education programs, passive restraints in large cars, the labeling of chemicals in the workplace, controls on garbage truck noise, and increased overtime payments for executives have been withdrawn or postponed. The actions taken already are expected to save the American public and industry almost $1 billion annually. The Administration will be reviewing a host of other regulations in the near future.

LEGISLATIVE CHANGES

Not all of our regulatory problems can be resolved satisfactorily through more effective regulatory management and decision-making. Existing regulatory statutes too often preclude effective regulatory decisions. Many of the statutes are conflicting, overlapping, or inconsistent. Some force agencies to promulgate regulations while giving them little discretion to take into account changing conditions or new information. Other statutes give agencies extremely broad discretion, which they have sometimes exercised unwisely.

The Administration will examine all legislation that serves as the foundation for major regulatory programs. This omnibus review, spearheaded by the Presidential Task Force on Regulatory Relief, will result in recommendations to reform these statutes. The Task Force will initially concentrate its efforts on those laws scheduled for Congressional oversight or reauthorization, such as the Clean Air Act.

VI. *Controlling Money and Credit*

Monetary policy is the responsibility of the Federal Reserve System, an independent agency within the structure of the government. The Administration will do nothing to undermine that independence. At the same time, the success in reducing inflation, increasing real income, and reducing unemployment will depend on effective interaction of monetary policy with other aspects of economic policy.

To achieve the goals of the Administration's economic program, consistent monetary policy must be applied. Thus, it is expected that the rate of money and credit growth will be brought down to levels consistent with noninflationary expansion of the economy.

If monetary policy is too expansive, then inflation during the years ahead will continue to accelerate and the Administration's economic program will be undermined. Inflationary psychology will intensify. Wages, prices, and interest rates will reflect the belief that inflation—and the destructive effects of inflation—will continue.

By contrast, if monetary policy is unduly restrictive, a different set of problems arises, unnecessarily aggravating recession and unemployment. At times in the past, abruptly restrictive policies have prompted excessive reactions toward short-term monetary ease. As a result, frequent policy changes can send confusing signals, and the additional uncertainty undermines long-term investment decisions and economic growth.

With money and credit growth undergoing steady, gradual reduction over a period of years, it will be possible to reduce inflation substantially and permanently. In this regard, the Administration supports the announced objective of the Federal Reserve to continue to seek gradual reduction in the growth of money and credit aggregates during the years ahead. Looking back, it seems clear that if a policy of this kind had been successfully followed in the past, inflation today would be substantially lower and would not appear to be so intractable.

Until recently, the Federal Reserve had attempted to control money growth by setting targets for interest rates, particularly the rate on Federal funds. Experience here and abroad has shown repeatedly that this interest rate management approach is not sufficient to achieve reliable control. Mistakes in predicting movements in economic activity or tendencies on the part of policymakers to avoid large interest rate fluctuations can lead to undesirable gyrations in the rate of money growth.

Under new procedures the Federal Reserve adopted in October 1979, the Federal Reserve sets targets for growth of reserves considered to be consistent with the desired expansion in the monetary aggregates. Interest rates are allowed to vary over a much wider range in response to changes in the demand for money and credit. A number of factors—such as the introduction of credit controls and their subsequent removal and frequent shifts in announced fiscal policies—have contributed to pronounced fluctuations in interest rates and monetary growth over the past year. At the same time, we need to learn from the experience with the new techniques and seek further improvements. The Federal Reserve has undertaken a study of last year's experience. We look forward to the results and encourage them to make the changes that appear warranted.

In that connection, success in meeting the targets that the Federal Reserve has set will itself increase confidence in the results of policy. Otherwise, observers are likely to pay excessive attention to short-run changes in money growth and revise anticipations upward or downward unnecessarily. Without confidence in the long-term direction of policy, such short-run changes may lead to unwarranted but disturbing gyrations in credit, interest rates, commodity prices, and other sensitive indicators of inflation and economic growth.

Better monetary control is not consistent with the management of interest rates in the short run. But, with monetary policy focusing on long-term objectives, the resultant restraint on money and credit growth would interact with the tax and expenditure proposals to lower inflation as well as interest rates.

The Administration will confer regularly with the Federal Reserve Board on all aspects of our economic program. The policies that are proposed in the program will help to advance the efforts of the independent Federal Reserve System. In particular, the substantial reductions of the Federal Government's deficit financing and the achievement of a balanced budget in 1984 and the years that follow should enable the Federal Reserve System to reduce dramatically the growth in the money supply.

To that end, the economic scenario assumes that the growth rates of money and credit are steadily reduced from the 1980 levels to one-half those levels by 1986.

With the Federal Reserve gradually but persistently reducing the growth of money, inflation should decline at least as fast as anticipated. Moreover, if monetary growth rates are restrained, then inflationary expectations will decline. And since interest rate movements are largely a mirror of price expectations, reduction in one will produce reduction in the other.

VII. *A New Beginning for the Economy*

This plan for national recovery represents a substantial break with past policy. The new policy is based on the premise that the people who make up the economy—workers, managers, savers, investors, buyers, and sellers—do not need the government to make reasoned and intelligent decisions about how best to organize and run their own lives. They continually adapt to best fit the current environment. The most appropriate role for government economic policy is to provide a stable and unfettered environment in which private individuals can confidently plan and make appropriate decisions. The new recovery plan is designed to bring to all aspects of government policy a greater sense of purpose and consistency.

Central to the new policy is the view that expectations play an important role in determining economic activity, inflation, and interest rates. Decisions to work, save, spend, and invest depend crucially on expectations regarding future government policies. Establishing an environment which ensures efficient and stable incentives for work, saving, and investment now and in the future is the cornerstone of the recovery plan.

Personal tax reductions will allow people to keep more of what they earn, providing increased incentives for work and saving. Business tax reductions will provide increased incentives for capital expansion, resulting in increased productivity for workers. Spending reductions and elimination of unneeded regulation will return control over resources to the private sector where incentives to economize are strongest. Stable monetary policy, combined with expanding productive capacity, will bring about a reduction of the inflation rate.

Inflation control is best achieved with a two-edged policy designed both to limit the rate of increase in the money stock and to increase the productive capacity of the economy. Neither policy can be expected to achieve adequate results alone.

A stable monetary policy, gradually slowing growth rates of money and credit along a preannounced and predictable path, will lead to reductions in inflation. At the same time, the effects of supply-oriented tax and regulatory changes on work incentives, expansion and improvement of the capital stock, and improved productivity will boost output and create a "buyer's market" for goods and services.

As a result of the policies set forth here, our economy's productive capacity is expected to grow significantly faster than could be achieved with a continuation of past policies. Specifically, real economic activity is projected to recover from the 1980–81 period of weakness and move to a 4 or 5 percent annual growth path through 1986, as shown in the table below. Concurrently, the general rate of inflation is expected to decline steadily to less than 5 percent annually by 1986 from the current 10 percent plus rate.

ECONOMIC ASSUMPTIONS

	(Calendar years)					
	1981	1982	1983	1984	1985	1986
Nominal gross national product (billions)	$2,920.0	$3,293.0	3,700.0	$4,098.0	$4,500.0	$4,918.0
(Percent change)	11.1	12.8	12.4	10.8	9.8	9.3
Real gross national product (billions, 1972 dollars)	1,497.0	1,560.0	1,638.0	1,711.0	1,783.0	1,858.0
(Percent change)	1.1	4.2	5.0	4.5	4.2	4.2
Implicit price deflator	195.0	211.0	226.0	240.0	252.0	265.0
(Percent change)	9.9	8.3	7.0	6.0	5.4	4.9
Consumer Price Index,* 1967 = 100	274.0	297.0	315.0	333.0	348.0	363.0
(Percent change)	11.1	8.3	6.2	5.5	4.7	4.2
Unemployment rate (Percent)	7.8	7.2	6.6	6.4	6.0	5.6

*CPI for urban wage earners and clerical workers (CPI-W).

In contrast to the inflationary demand-led booms of the 1970s, the most significant growth of economic activity will occur in the supply side of the economy. Not only will a steady expansion in business fixed investment allow our economy to grow without fear of capacity-induced inflation pressures, but it will also increase productivity and reduce the growth of production costs by incorporating new and more high-efficient plants, machinery, and technology into our manufacturing base. The result will be revitalized growth in the real incomes and standards of living of our citizens and significantly reduced inflationary pressures. As our economy responds to a new era of economic policy, unemployment will be significantly reduced.

The Administration's plan for national recovery will take a large step toward improving the international economic environment by repairing domestic conditions. Improving expectations and slowing inflation will enhance the dollar as an international store of value and contribute to greater stability in international financial markets. As interest rates come down and faster U.S. growth contributes to rising world trade, economic expansion in other countries will also accelerate. This Administration will work closely with the other major industrial countries to promote consistency in economic objectives and policies so as to speed a return to noninflationary growth in the world economy. Finally, rising U.S. productivity will enhance our ability to compete with other countries in world markets, easing protectionist pressures at home and thus strengthening our ability to press other countries to reduce their trade barriers and export subsidies.

The economic assumptions contained in this message may seem optimistic to some observers. Indeed they do represent a dramatic departure from the trends of recent years—but so do the proposed policies. In fact, if each portion of this comprehensive economic program is put in place—quickly and completely—the economic environment could improve even more rapidly than envisioned in these assumptions.

But, if the program is accepted piecemeal—if only those aspects that are politically palatable are adopted—then this economic policy will be no more than a repeat of what has been tried before. And we already know the results of the stop-and-go policies of the past.

Indeed, if we as a Nation do not take the bold new policy initiatives proposed in this program, we will face a continuation and a worsening of the trends that have developed in the last two decades. We have a rare opportunity to reverse these trends: to stimulate growth, productivity, and employment at the same time that we move toward the elimination of inflation.

Note: The report is printed in the document entitled "America's New Beginning: A Program for Economic Recovery—February 18, 1981." As printed above, the item does not include the illustrative charts which were included as part of the report.

Remarks and a Question-and-Answer Session on the Program for Economic Recovery at a Breakfast for Newspaper and Television News Editors
February 19, 1981

The President. Those of you who haven't finished breakfast, go on eating, and I'll talk over you.

Welcome here. Delighted to have you all here this morning. Maybe some of you've noticed the helicopter was on the lawn in case my reception was somewhat different than it's been. [*Laughter*] You know, we're departing soon to make sure the west coast is still attached.

Again, as I say, we're pleased to have you here. We think that we can have a dialog instead of a monolog, and I'm going to, without any further remarks, introduce to you one of our Cabinet Secretaries who will introduce a couple of teammates, and then I will come back. And we will begin some question-and-answer which will be concluded with the gentleman you are about to meet.

And so, ladies and gentlemen, the Secretary of the Treasury, Don Regan.

Secretary Regan. Thank you, Mr. President.

Good morning, ladies and gentlemen. It's a pleasure to be here with you. I hope you are all as thrilled as I was last night in hearing the President's remarks. This program is really bold. It's innovative; it's new; it breaks with the past; and it is different. I think that it's going to be one of the most stimulating things that's ever happened to our economy. From the point of view of why we are being so abrupt in breaking with the past, is that we can no longer go on with what we have been doing. You take a look at what our economy has been doing

and consider that for the last 2 years we've had the greatest rates of inflation since the Civil War. And we apparently were going to continue down that road unless there was a break, so we have decided to make it.

We're doing it, as you know, as the President explained last night, with a four-part program. The first part of that program are the spending cuts. The second part of the program are the tax cuts. The third part of the program is deregulation, getting the government off the back of people. And the fourth part of it consists of having a stable monetary growth.

Now, during the morning, Dave Stockman, Murray Weidenbaum, and I will be explaining to you the details of this package. I won't take any longer except to say that as part of my program—that is, the tax part of it—I am going up on the Hill this morning at 10 o'clock to start explaining it. I have another session with a different part of the Hill at 2 o'clock. I'm back up there again tomorrow at 10 o'clock. We'll be explaining this program, I hope not ad nauseum, but at least with a great deal of clarity so that you'll all understand it. And we feel that it's exactly what the American people have wanted. It's been designed that way. We're going to give it to them that way. We're going to fight with them in Congress.

You can use any analogy you want. This is the kick-off in football. This is the first inning of a baseball game. We're right at the start of what promises to be a great victory for the Reagan forces. And that's the program that we're going to be developing over the next few months, working with the Congress.

Thank you very much.

Now, I'd like to introduce my colleague and sidekick for these past 6 weeks, a man that's well known to most of you, David Stockman, the Director of the Office of Management and Budget.

Dave.

Mr. Stockman. Well, thank you very much, Don. And ladies and gentlemen, I would like to welcome you to the President's new White House breakfast program this morning, the one new program that we didn't announce last night. But what we hope that we're offering to you this morning is not only a breakfast but some food for thought.

And what I would suggest today is the plan that the President announced last night contains more new ideas, more new approaches to the fundamental economic problems of this country than we've seen in the last 15 or 20 years in Washington. And when you look at the economic mess that we have today, the way that inflation is eroding the ability of our economy to operate, the way in which tax rates continue to creep up and destroy incentives, destroy investment, destroy savings, it's pretty clear to me and I think it's pretty clear to the President that the kind of bold changes on the spending side, on the tax side, on the regulatory side that he proposed last night are precisely what this country needs.

I'm in charge of the budget side in particular. And although the papers this morning, at least some of them, have suggested that this $41 billion cut that we're requesting in the Federal budget for next year is too draconian, is too deep, I would just take this opportunity to remind you that even after all those changes are made, and even after the Congress adopts the 83 different proposals that we presented last night, we will still have a budget next year that is $40 billion higher than it is this year.

The basic problem for 2 or 3 years now has been simply that the Federal budget has been growing at an astronomical, unsustainable rate. It's increased at 16 percent a year since fiscal year '79. That's far faster than the growth of our tax base. It's far faster than the growth of our economy as a whole. As a result, we're taking a larger and larger share of the output of our economy at the government level. And that explains basically the economic deterioration that we've had. So, we're proposing to shift direction sharply, to hold the growth rate of Federal spending to 6 percent next year and in the years thereafter.

It will be difficult to do. But we have proposed to slay some sacred cows, if you will. We have proposed to reduce or eliminate programs that simply can't be justified under the current fiscal and economic crisis conditions that we face in this country. But I think we're going to get a favorable response from the American people, and I think we're going to get a favorable response from the Hill.

I happened to spend 4 years on the Hill as a Member of Congress. And I know that during those 4 years, every Member of Congress knew in his mind and his heart that things were going too far, that things were out of hand. Now we have a President who's willing to propose a program to turn that around. We have a President who I think can rally the support of this country. And I think you're going to find on Capitol Hill, despite all the cynicism that you hear from some, that we're going to get a great deal of support and that we're going to get this job done.

Thank you.

Oh, excuse me. It's my pleasure now to introduce the third member of our economic team, Murray Weidenbaum, who's Chairman of the Council of Economic Advisers. He's the guy in charge of integrating and pulling this whole program together and explaining it in a lucid and convincing way, something that he's fully capable of doing. So, I would like to introduce Murray Weidenbaum, Chairman of the CEA.

Mr. Weidenbaum. Ladies and gentlemen, I would like to emphasize just one key point. The Reagan program is a program for a healthier economy which will provide real, solid benefits to every American citizen. I will not concentrate on the medicine, so to speak—the budget cuts, the regulatory restraint. I would like to emphasize the results, the positive results, in terms of bringing the inflation down by more than half, in terms of reducing the tax burden of every taxpayer, the creation of 3 million new jobs, all this between now and 1986—not a quick fix to be sure, but a constructive, balanced program which very frankly deserves the support, I think, of the American people.

And personally, it's a real pleasure to work for the number one economic communicator of our Nation, the President of the United States.

The President. Well, ladies and gentlemen, you obviously know that you are here because we believe that the main source of strength in this fight is going to be the people themselves. And we believe also that they are ready to support a great change and go along. And you are in a position to help with this.

I've been hearing some of the voices already, when I was getting dressed, on some of the morning shows, from those who would be expected to be against this program in government. And I almost sense that one of their plans is going to be to not criticize the cuts at all, but to see if they can't wipe out the tax part of the program. This tax part of the program we have tried to stress, and this is one of the reasons why we've gone out of our way to point out to the people that it is not a reducing of the amount of money that government is going to get, it is reducing that increase.

We found in California when I was Governor there that—and we had our great welfare reforms and all, and we had inherited a situation similiar to that of the Federal Government today. And during the campaign I was very frustrated when people would bring up and say, "Well, yes, he talks about saving money in California, but look, the budgets went up and they went up to such and such a figure by the time he left office." What they didn't realize was of course the budgets are going to go up. There's growth, there's inflation, there's growth in government to match the increase in population and so forth. What they didn't realize though was that that slant of going up, we reduced by 20 percent. And if you do the same with the taxes and change the steep rise, today there's virtually a hundred billion dollars of tax increase built into the present system that will take place in this coming year if we do not reduce that increase.

But for years now the two lines have been diverging. Even steep as the taxes are, they don't keep up with the increase in spending. If we can bring the those lines to more parallel and what we are, believe me, hoping for and we know we can do, is have the tax line begin to converge with the spending line. And when you reach that point and then if you keep going, the tax line will be bringing in revenues greater than the increase in government, that is when you go forward with further tax cuts of the kind to correct the inequities that I mentioned in my remarks last night.

And I believe the people are ready. But I believe that there's going to be a lot of misinformation released in the fights that might go on. And yet, we're optimistic. We think that across the aisle, in Congress today, there is a different feeling and there are more people than anyone realizes who are of the opinion that this has to go forward.

Now, rather than go on with any kind of a monolog, and since my time is limited here, and possibly yours also, maybe we can open this up to discussion or questions from you. And if you throw me one that I can't answer, you can see I've got three specialists here that I'll call on.

Q. Mr. President, in your list of inflationary forces last night, why did you not mention the increase in gasoline prices and home heating fuels?

The President. Why in the list of inflationary forces did I not mention gasoline prices and home heating fuel prices? Well, I have to believe that to a certain extent, I know that that's an unusual situation, prices are not so much the cause of inflation—price rises—they're the result. And when I say there is something different in that one, yes. When the OPEC nations with the near monopoly power now take advantage of that position and just simply raise the price to suit themselves, that is a price over and above the normal response to inflation.

One economist pointed out a couple of years ago—he didn't state this as a theory, but he just said it's something to look at—

when we started buying the oil over there, the OPEC nations, 10 barrels of oil were sold for the price of an ounce of gold. And the price was pegged to the American dollar. And we were about the only country left that still were on a gold standard. And then a few years went by, and we left the gold standard. And as this man suggested, if you looked at the recurrent price rises, were the OPEC nations raising the price of oil or were they simply following the same pattern of an ounce of gold, that as gold in this inflationary age kept going up, they weren't going to follow our paper money downhill? They stayed with the gold price. Of course, now, if we followed that, why, they should be coming down, because the price of gold's coming down. But I think that that's like the inflation-contributing factor that you'll have sometimes simply because of a poor crop. That is not based on the economy, that's simply supply and demand. And if there's a crop failure and you've got a bigger demand than you have supply, the price goes up.

But I believe that even though those things can be dealt with with the other factors that we're going to follow, and that is trying to increase the energy supply in our own country. I think we can talk conservation all we want, but there's a limit that you get below which you cannot get maintaining your level of comfort and your level of industry. And I think the best answer, while conservation is worthy in itself, is to try to make us independent of outside sources to the greatest extent possible for our energy, and I believe that we have the possibilities of that. We're not energy poor. There's energy yet to be found and developed in this country, including the biggest coal pile that any country in the world sits on.

So, if I didn't mention that, it was because I didn't mention a number of other things of the same kind in there. I wanted to get through in 30 minutes before my audience walked out on me. [*Laughter*]

Q. Mr. President, in your remarks last night you mentioned that you envisioned reductions in spending in some social services, and not only as a reduction in expenditures but as improving the efficiency in social services—[*inaudible*]—rather interesting. I was wondering if you feel that by cutting expenditures you do improve efficiency—the old theory that any job 10 men can do, 9 men can do, 8 men can do better—is that part of your thought on the governmental operation?

The President. Well, in social services—maybe part of my confidence in that and what we can do is based on what we did in California. We finally realized that all the savings we were making, all the economies, were all being eaten by welfare. And in good times and bad it bore no relation to the economy.

We saw that welfare in California was reaching a point of an increase of as much as 40,000 cases a month being added to the welfare rolls. We finally turned the task force loose to come back with a plan for reforming welfare. And we had a long fight. We could do the part administratively. We had two fights. We had a fight with our legislature to get some of it, because I had a hostile legislature at the time, and we had a fight with Washington, with the bureaucracy in HEW who had rules and regulations that for example—and this is still true today—that under those rules and regulations no one in the United States knows how many people are on welfare. They only know how many checks they're sending out, and then we turn up a woman in Chicago that's getting checks under 127 different names. And just recently in Pasadena, California, living in a lovely big home there, a woman was brought in and charged with collecting $300,000 in a welfare scheme.

Well, we set out to correct this. We finally got some waivers from HEW. We finally got the legislation, and again, we got it—one of the biggest single things that happened to turn the public on our side in that fight came from your profession—from the press. When a paper in San Francisco sent a reporter out to see if he could get on welfare—to see if our stories of the horrors of welfare were true—he got on welfare four times under four different names in the same office on the same day. And when he wrote that story, we had an ally.

When we finished our reforms, though—we hadn't been able to give a cost-of-living increase to the welfare recipients in California because we were spread so thin, this is

1958—we saved over a 3-year period, because the welfare reforms went in only in my last 3 years—we saved $2 billion for the California tax-payers in the program. The rolls were reduced by more than 350,000 people without us actually throwing anyone off. They just disappeared, and over and above that we had enough to increase the welfare grants to the deserving needy who remained by an average of 43 percent.

And when I say we didn't throw anyone off, we got permission that in 35 of our 58 counties, we could require able-bodied welfare recipients to work—to come and report for useful community projects—all of which we'd screened from school boards, from counties, from cities and towns, to make sure there were no boondoggles. And they had to report—they only had to work 20, not 40 hours a week; the other half was to be spent either in job training or looking for work. And then we assigned what we called job agents from our labor department to each group of these people and told these job agents their job was to look at these people doing these jobs and see how quickly they could get them out into private enterprise. And in the midst of the '73 and '74 recession, when unemployment was increasing in the nation, they funneled 76,000 welfare recipients through this program into private enterprise jobs—and free of welfare from there on out.

And we believe that this is what's going to happen, because we're very much determined to turn as much of welfare management as we can back to the States—give them the Federal revenue share, but more in the nature of a block grant, and give them the right to require able-bodied recipients to work and give them the right to administer this program without this layer of bureaucracy in Washington on top of it. And so, we think we're going to benefit rather than hurt the people that are getting these grants.

Q. Mr. President, is there any way you can get the Congress to vote this entire program up or down, or are you going to have to go program by program by program and get them to vote on each one?

The President. We're introducing five pieces of legislation. One will be the tax bill; the other one will be a reconciliation act—that will be one of the toughest ones—that is, to try and get them to simply submit the program to the major committees and not break it all up into fragments and fragment it out with all the subcommittees. Then there will be the rescissions for 1981. We didn't mention that last night, but our cuts have begun with the remainder of 1981, which has been going on since October 1st—this budget. We're going to make several billions of dollars of savings before the year is out in that program. That will take rescissions that have to be passed by Congress. And then, of course, the cuts in the 1982 budget which has been submitted by the previous administration. And that's the one where we're hoping to reduce $41.4 billion with our cuts.

So, that's as much as we could package it. We've emphasized and I've been meeting with legislative leaders from both sides of the aisle. We're going to continue to do that, urging them both to expedite this, but also to hold it together.

One of the reasons that we didn't add in any of the tax features that I mentioned later, as coming later on, is because we thought if we opened that door, then everyone with an idea might, and then would, begin to pick at the program with amendments and so forth. And we hope that they will just simply get the basic program passed. I believe, as I said earlier, that one of the things we must be most aware of will be the attempt—no one will want to stand up and oppose the cuts in today's climate, but they will then say, "Well, the tax part of it won't work." And we're sure it will.

Q. Mr. President, you said last night that your spending cuts and tax cuts would go in lockstep. What do you mean exactly by that? Do you mean that you won't sign tax cuts without the spending cuts you want?

The President. Now, now, wait a minute. I didn't——

Q. You said last night you wanted your tax cuts and spending cuts to go in lockstep.

The President. Yes.

Q. What exactly did you mean by that? Will you not sign the tax cuts unless you get the spending cuts you want?

The President. Well now, that's a problem I'm going to have to face. And I had a rule

I'll fall back on in California as Governor: I never talk about whether I'll sign or veto until whatever is there is before me on my desk. But the two must go together if we're to have the stimulant to the economy, because the main purpose of this is really to get the economy moving again. And to do that, we've seen the percentage of gross national product that the Federal Government is taking in taxes going up consistently. And if you go back to where it was hovering below 20 and down around anywhere from 17½ to 19 over the years. we didn't have inflation; we didn't have the problems we're having today. But we're on our way up to almost a fourth of the gross national product taken by government in taxes, and this is what we feel has to come down if the economy is to go forward. And of course, to do that, we've got to make—if we're going to cure inflation, which I believe stems in the main from government spending more than it takes in, we're going to have to bring government down to match the revenues.

Q. Mr. President, many people in Congress believe in the tax cuts—I mean, the budget cuts, but are very concerned about the tax cuts. They fear it will be inflationary. How do you plan to combat that fear among Congress?

The President. Well, I mentioned that last night, this fear that the tax cuts would be inflationary. First of all, a number of fine economists like Murray Weidenbaum and many of his associates don't think that that's so. But also we've got history on our side. Every major tax cut that has been made in this century in our country has resulted in even the government getting more revenue than it did before, because the base of the economy is so broadened by doing it.

We only have to look at the last few experiences with cuts in the capital gains tax, and you find that the very next year after the rate was lowered, the government got more revenue from capital gains tax than it's been getting at the higher rate. What happens? People up there who are now worried about and busying themselves with tax shelters, if it becomes profitable to move out into risk-taking adventure and investments, they then are encouraged to move out and into that.

Back when Calvin Coolidge cut the taxes across the board, and more than once, the government's revenues increased. When Jack Kennedy did it in the 2-year program and his economic advisers, they were all telling him—I can remember the figures—they told him that the government would lose $83 billion in revenue, and the government gained $54 billion in revenue, I think is the figure, that it actually went up. So, they had made quite a sizeable financial error in their estimates. Jack Kennedy's line about it was, "a rising tide lifts all boats." And this is what we believe that the tax proposals that we've made, what they're aimed at.

Business and industry in America today is investing the lowest percentage of any of the industrial nations in improvement in plant and equipment. We have the highest percentage of outmoded industrial plant and equipment of all the industrial nations. One of the reasons is the lack of capital. The government is competing in the private capital market to fund the government's deficits. The American people are saving at a lower percentage than the workers are in Japan, West Germany, and the other industrial nations, and that money that once went into savings accounts or insurance, as we all know it then, became a part of the capital pool that was reinvested by banks and insurance companies out in the free enterprise sector. And you could cite all sorts of figures of the increase in investment in tax-free municipal bonds and the reduction in industrial stocks that have taken place in America.

So, all of this is aimed, not at being inflationary, but the other way. And we're just convinced that what has happened before, every time, is going to happen again.

Q. Mr. President, the AFL-CIO meeting in Miami this week substantially opposes your program. I wonder if you consider this a serious impediment, and if so, how will you address it?

The President. Well, I can't say that I didn't expect it. I thought it was interesting that they kind of took a stand against it before they heard what it was. Now, whether they'll be converted or convinced by the things that they will now be able to understand or know about the program, I wish they would treat it with more of an open mind.

I happen to believe that sometimes they're out of step with their own rank and file. They certainly were in the last election. [*Laughter*] But I was a president of my own union once, an AFL-CIO union, and I think I know something about them. And it is true that they philosophically have tended for a number of years now to support the idea of government spending being good for the economy.

I remember once that as a union president representing not only my own but 32 other unions in the motion picture industry and management, I came to Washington to appear before the House Ways and Means Committee in support of a tax reform program that had been introduced. I was met by two of the lobbyists for the AFL-CIO and shown a rather sizable book labeled "The Tax Policy for the AFL-CIO" for that year, and it was completely the opposite of what I was here to say on behalf of those local unions that were all part of that organization. They frankly stated that the tax policy they favored would get the government $12 billion in additional revenue, and they wanted it to get that revenue because they had $12 billion worth of social welfare programs that they wanted the government to adopt.

Listen, I've been leaning to the right all the time—there must be people over here to the——[*laughter*].

Q. Mr. President, in cutting back Government support of the Synthetic Fuel Development Corporation [U.S. Synthetic Fuels Corporation], you express confidence that private enterprise will pick up that slack and do the job. In view of their failure to do so in the past, the energy companies' failure, what makes you think they'll do it here?

The President. Well, because if it's going to be done, they'll have to do it. Maybe they haven't done it in the past because there was so much promise of government standing there ready to do it. And you know, not that the giant companies are poor, but I keep remembering what Milton Friedman once said,"If you start paying people to be poor, there's going to be a lot

of poor people." And maybe the same thing was true of business, that human nature is the same in the board room as it is down there on the street.

But I think that with the price of fuel where it is—let me be practical about them and fair to them also—there was no incentive before, because what we were talking about, synthetic fuels, were going to be more costly than the natural fuels that we were using. Now with the price up where it is, there is an incentive for them to look at these because they may be cost-effective. They may even be cost-advantageous over fossil fuels. So, I believe that there is.

I've always preferred that if there is some stimulant in addition that is needed, I believe the tax incentives are a better route than outright subsidy.

Q. Mr. President, I believe last night you said that the spending cuts are the largest ever proposed. Are these the largest tax cuts ever proposed?

The President. Hmm. You know something? That's a question—I just looked over here, and I got a cue. Yes, Don Regan tells me they are. And that's fitting, because the tax increase that was adopted in the last year and that is built into the present system is the largest single tax increase in our Nation's history. So, we might as well match it with the largest single tax cut in our history.

I know that I've come to the end of my time and hear that helicopter take off pretty quickly, but don't think your questions won't be answered here. I am now going to get my trio back up here, and they will take your questions. And I think they'll be able to give you more indepth on anything that you might want to know about the program that we've been putting together.

So, Don Regan and Murray, Dave Stockman, it's your turn to come back up here and take the questions from these ladies and gentlemen. And if you'll forgive me, I am a few minutes late, and I'm going to have to run now. Now you can get down to the really deep questions with all of them. [*Laughter*]

Come on Dave, Murray, Don.

Note: The President spoke at 9:02 a.m. in the East Room at the White House.

Exchange With Reporters on the Program for Economic Recovery
February 19, 1981

Q. How are you, Mr. President?

The President. Hi. How are you?

Q. They tell us you're in good spirits today because of the reaction to the speech. We'd like to hear it from you.

The President. Well, yes, I'm in good spirits, but then you're always in good spirits when you figure you got by without losing your place or—[*laughter*]—forgetting your lines.

Q. How did you like the response to your program, and when do you think you'll actually get this program through? You're pretty confident, aren't you?

The President. Well, I don't know. Of course, now you can see the forces beginning to mobilize. But, no, I'm optimistic, because I think there is a widespread feeling that reflects the feeling of the people out there that they want this.

Q. Where do you think the big fight will come with the opposition?

The President. Possibly more over taxes than over the other.

Q. Is that right?

The President. There's still that belief on the part of many people that a cut in tax rates automatically means a cut in revenues. And if they'll only look at history, it doesn't. A cut in tax rates can very often be reflected in an increase in government revenues because of the broadening of the base of the economy.

Q. Are you going to try to keep those two programs together in a single bill?

The President. Well, they'll have to be single bills, but we are trying to keep the idea of the whole package together, to be treated as a package. We don't want to start fragmenting it up and then——

Q. Would you accept the tax cuts without the budget cuts?

The President. I can't give you a firm answer on that until I see that, but I have to point out that if they tried it—no, I think

it would be the other way around, that they are less apt to oppose the budget cuts than they are the tax cuts. But if you tried it the other way with the tax cuts of none, then I'm not sure that you'd have the same stimulant that you're going to have out of the whole program, and you could aggravate your situation.

Q. Are you saying, Mr. President, you don't expect a big battle over the spending cuts?

The President. Oh, I think here and there, there will be, yes; there will be battles here and there on some of them. But I've noticed that most of the immediate responses from those you would expect to oppose this have dealt with the taxes more than with the other.

Q. Will you be happy if you get some of what you want, but not all?

The President. Oh, 97 percent, I could live with. [*Laughter*]

Q. Do you have a timetable for getting it through actually? I mean, in your own mind—if it's years or 1 year?

The President. We want it through earlier than a year.

Q. A year? Do you have a deadline?

The President. No. I say, we've asked, and frankly, asked the leadership to act on it as expeditiously as possible. We're hoping for in a matter of months, a few months.

Q. What has been the thrust of the wires you've received, the telegrams?

The President. The big stack that I was handed last night less than an hour after the speech kind of put a lump in your throat with some of them. They were just totally in support.

Q. What did they mostly say? Did they agree with you?

The President. Oh, and yes, and "We've waited a long time for this," and things of that kind. And the calls—there have been over a thousand calls, and they run about 95 percent favorable.

Q. What are you going to be doing at the ranch? Are you going to be working anymore, or is this mainly a vacation for you?

The President. Well, I have a hunch that they will greet me with the same amount of reading material that they do in Washington; they have on the plane already. No, there'll be—leave the job behind, but I also think that I'll be able to haul some wood and ride some horses and do that.

Q. Are you going to ride a white stallion?

The President. Oh——

Q. That's not rideable.

The President. Yes, he really is. He's trained for what's known as high dressage.

But I have had to board him out for a little bit until we can get a facility for him if we're going to have him back up there, because the five geldings that I've got—that stallion was going to wind up being the only horse on the place if we didn't move him. So, until we can have a better facility, why, we've boarded him nearby.

Q. I can't print that in my newspaper. [*Laughter*]

The President. No, please don't.

Q. Thank you.

Note: The exchange took place on board Air Force One during the President's flight to California.

Remarks on Arrival at Point Mugu Naval Air Station, California
February 19, 1981

I know this is your lunch hour, and so time's a wasting. [*Laughter*] But I have to tell you, this is quite an overwhelming reception at a naval base for a former horse cavalryman. [*Laughter*]

Ladies and gentlemen, we are most grateful for this warm welcome, to come out here with two of our California Congressmen and their ladies—Congressmen Lagomarsino and Badham—and brought our lawyer along too, the Attorney General. We all just decided—well, it's only coincidence that I made a speech on inflation last night and turned up here this morning. [*Laughter*] We know that we will have to go back.

I know the ladies know about inflation. Once upon a time you used to put some money in your purse and go to the market and buy a bag full of groceries. Now you take a bag full of money, go to the market, and bring the groceries home in your purse. [*Laughter*] That's what we were talking about and what we are trying to correct.

Nancy and I are delighted to be back in California. This is the first time since the Inauguration, and I find that already I've become so much of a Washingtonian that I have a hard time keeping my eyes open in

the California Sun. [*Laughter*] But it's wonderful to be back. We've been very homesick. And while it is wonderful there and we're pleased to be there and doing what we're doing, I hope that we'll be seeing you again, and on a fairly regular basis.

Nancy, would you like to say how happy you are to be back in California? No? No? Well, she is. Well, we won't keep you any longer except to say that—incidentally, did you hear last night's speech? [*Applause*] Well, now I'm very much relieved. I wasn't going to mention it, because you were so friendly, and then I just kind of got curious as to whether you were friendly in spite of it or because of it.

We're grateful to be here and look forward to seeing you again and hope that some of the things that we said last night are going to take place and take place very quickly, because we think it's time to get America on the move again in the world. And we think it's time also for that which you represent here and the other branches of our service to take their rightful place in our society with the respect and the gratitude of the people extended to you for what you are all doing in our behalf, and we're going to see if that cannot happen too.

Thank you very much.

Note: The President spoke at 12:30 p.m. He then flew by helicopter to his ranch, Rancho del Cielo, near Santa Barbara.

Nomination of Judith T. Connor To Be an Assistant Secretary of Transportation
February 20, 1981

The President announced today his intention to nominate Judith T. Connor to be an Assistant Secretary of Transportation (Policy and International Affairs).

Miss Connor has been director of international affairs with Pan American World Airways since 1977 and was formerly with the Department of Transportation from 1973 to 1977 as an Assistant Secretary for Environment, Safety, and Consumer Affairs (October 1975 to January 1977). She was Acting Administrator, Urban Mass Transportation, from July 1975 to October 1975 and Special Assistant to the Administrator from May 1973 to June 1975. She has held the following positions in the Department of Commerce: Director, Public Policy Analysis Division, Domestic Commerce, from October 1971 to May 1973; policy analyst in the Office of the Secretary of Commerce from July 1971 to October 1971; policy adviser, U.S. Office of Economic Opportunity from February 1971 to July 1971.

Miss Connor was with Excalibur Associates from August 1969 to December 1970, Trans World Airlines from March 1968 to May 1969, and Pacific Telephone Co. from 1965 to 1968. She received a B.A. in English from Wellesley in 1961 and a M.B.A. in marketing from Columbia in 1965. Miss Connor is 42 years old and resides in New York City. She was born in Toronto, Canada, on March 6, 1939.

Nomination of Arlene Triplett To Be an Assistant Secretary of Commerce
February 20, 1981

The President announced today his intention to nominate Arlene Triplett to be an Assistant Secretary of Commerce (Administration).

Mrs. Triplett has served as director of administrative services with the Republican National Committee in Washington, D.C., since 1977. From 1976 to 1977, she was deputy controller with the President Ford Committee, and from 1975 to 1976, she was controller with Citizens for Reagan in Washington, D.C.

Mrs. Triplett was an independent financial consultant in Northern Virginia from 1973 to 1975 and was a budgets and reports analyst with Cutter Laboratories in Berkeley, Calif., from 1963 to 1966.

Arlene Triplett was born on January 21, 1942, and received a B.A. in business administration from the University of California at Berkeley in 1963. She is married and has two children.

Nomination of Raymond J. Waldmann To Be an Assistant Secretary of Commerce
February 20, 1981

The President announced today his intention to nominate Raymond J. Waldmann to be an Assistant Secretary of Commerce (International Economic Policy).

Since 1979 Mr. Waldmann was counsel with the firm of Schiff Hardin & Waite of Washington and Chicago. He specialized in international investment, corporate, transportation, communications, and technology law.

Previously he was president of Transnational Investments, Ltd., a Washington research and publishing firm. He was an executive consultant with Harbridge House, a management consulting group.

Mr. Waldmann was Special Counsel to the President for review of the intelligence community and a consultant on special foreign policy issues. In 1973–75 he was Deputy Assistant Secretary for Transportation and Telecommunications, coordinating U.S. policy in international aviation, shipping, and communications. He was chairman of the U.S. delegation to many negotiations and U.N. conferences, and chairman of first Intelsat Assembly. Mr. Waldmann was on the Domestic Council at the White House in 1970–73. He was staff assistant to the President for policy planning, with special responsibility for budgetary and economic issues. In 1967–70 he was a consultant on economic issues and regional development with Arthur D. Little, Ltd., of London. He was with Arthur D. Little, Inc., in Cambridge, Mass., in 1964–67, as a management consultant.

In 1962–64 he prepared presentations and edited technical reports on guidance and navigation systems for Moon landing flights for the NASA Apollo Project at M.I.T.

Mr. Waldmann is chairman, Committee on Foreign Investment in the U.S., American Bar Association; consultant to ABA Project on Law and Intelligence; editor, ABA Intelligence Law Newsletter; ABA Committee on Relations between the Executive and Legislative Branches; D.C. Bar Association International Division Steering Committee.

Mr. Waldmann was graduated from M.I.T. (S.B., 1960, '61) and Harvard (J.D., 1964). He resides in Bethesda, Md. Mr. Waldmann was born in Walton, N.Y., on November 28, 1938.

Nomination of William H. Morris, Jr., To Be an Assistant Secretary of Commerce
February 20, 1981

The President announced today his intention to nominate William H. Morris, Jr., to be an Assistant Secretary of Commerce (Trade Development).

Since August 1980 Mr. Morris has been president of William Morris and Associates, consultants in business management, government relations, and international marketing.

In 1979–80 he was deputy commissioner of economic and community development for the State of Tennessee, appointed by Gov. Lamar Alexander. He traveled overseas seeking reverse investment opportunities for the State and establishing foreign markets for Tenneessee products and negotiated the largest single purchase of Tennessee products by a foreign government, $439 million of industrial and agricultural products purchased by the Republic of China, April 1980.

In 1977–79 Mr. Morris was named executive vice president of the Southern Supply Co. of Jackson, Tenn., and from 1950 to

1976, he worked for Gooch–Edenton Wholesale Hardware Co., Jackson, Tenn., a firm he started with his father. He was deputy director of political programs and analysis for the Reagan–Bush campaign; served as coordinator of the program for the 1980 Republican National Convention; alternate delegate, Republican National Convention, 1976; served as executive assistant to U.S. Senator Bill Brock, 1970–76;

and Tennessee's Young Republican of the Year, 1969.

Mr. Morris is a member of the U.S. Department of Commerce District Export Council, Southern Industrial Development Council, and Tennessee Industrial Development Council.

He is married and has two children and resides in Nashville, Tenn. Mr. Morris was born on January 5, 1929.

Nomination of Ernest W. Lefever To Be an Assistant Secretary of State
February 20, 1981

The President announced today his intention to nominate Ernest W. Lefever to be an Assistant Secretary of State (Human Rights and Humanitarian Affairs).

Dr. Lefever was president of the Ethics and Public Policy Center, which he founded in 1976 at Georgetown University, which became independent in 1980. He is a professorial lecturer in the department of government and a faculty associate of the Center for Strategic and International Studies, both of Georgetown University.

From 1964 to 1976, Dr. Lefever was on the senior foreign policy studies staff of the Brookings Institution. IIis most recent Brookings book, "Nuclear Arms in the Third World," was published in 1979.

He was a member of the Values Education Commission of the State of Maryland.

He received an A.B. from Elizabethtown College and a B.D. and Ph. D. from Yale University. Dr. Lefever is a member of the International Institute for Strategic Studies (London), the Washington Institute of Foreign Affairs, and the Johns Hopkins University Society of Scholars. He served on the editorial boards of World Affairs and Policy Review.

Dr. Lefever has written, edited, or coauthored 14 books and has written for many American journals and newspapers.

He has done research at the Johns Hopkins School of Advanced International Studies, taught political science at the University of Maryland and American University, headed the Foreign Affairs Division of the Library of Congress, and was associated with the Washington Center of Foreign Policy Research. He has lectured at the National War College, the Army, Navy, and Air Force War Colleges, the Japan Defense College, the Foreign Service Institute, and many universities.

Dr. Lefever has traveled widely in Europe, Asia, Africa, and Latin America. He has visited and attended international conferences in many other countries.

Born in York, Pa., on November 12, 1919, Dr. Lefever is married and has two children. He resides with his family in Chevy Chase, Md.

Note: Mr. Lefever's nomination, which was submitted to the Senate on April 22, was withdrawn by the President on June 16.

Nomination of Rudolph W. Giuliani To Be an Associate Attorney General
February 20, 1981

The President today announced his intention to nominate Rudolph W. Giuliani to be an Associate Attorney General, Department of Justice.

Mr. Giuliani is a member of the New York law firm of Patterson, Belknap, Webb and Tyler. From 1975 to 1977, he served as Associate Deputy Attorney General at the U.S. Department of Justice, and from 1970 to 1975, he served in the following capacities: assistant U.S. attorney for the Southern District of New York; executive assistant U.S. attorney; chief, narcotics section; and chief, special prosecutions section. From 1968 to 1970, he served as a law clerk to Judge Lloyd F. McMahon, U.S. district judge in the Southern District of New York.

Mr. Giuliani received his A.B. degree (magna cum laude) from Manhattan College and his J.D. degree (magna cum laude) from the New York University School of Law, where he was elected to the Order of the Coif. He was a guest lecturer at the Harvard Law School Trial Advocacy Course (1975), a lecturer at New York County Lawyer's Association Program on the Federal Rules of Evidence (1975), and lecturer at the Attorney General's Advocacy Institute (summer and winter sessions, 1974).

In 1980 Mr. Giuliani published "The Potential Criminal Liability of a Professional Tax Adviser" in the 38th Annual New York University Institute on Federal Taxation. He was born on May 28, 1944, and resides in New York City.

Nomination of Theodore Bevry Olson To Be an Assistant Attorney General
February 20, 1981

The President announced today his intention to nominate Theodore Bevry Olson to be an Assistant Attorney General (Legal Counsel), Department of Justice.

Mr. Olson is a partner with the firm of Gibson, Dunn and Crutcher of Los Angeles, Calif. He joined the firm in 1965. Mr. Olson has extensive background in civil litigation including constitutional litigation for broadcasting and print media clients.

He was a delegate to the 1976 and 1980 Republican National Conventions.

Mr. Olson was graduated from the University of the Pacific (B.A., 1962) and the University of California (LL.B., 1965). At law school he was a member of the California Law Review. He is a member of the Los Angeles County and American Bar Associations. He was a member of the California Commission on Uniform State Laws in 1972–74.

Mr. Olson is married and has two children. He resides with his family in Palos Verdes Estates, Calif. Mr. Olson was born in Chicago, Ill., on September 11, 1940.

Nomination of William Francis Baxter To Be an Assistant Attorney General
February 20, 1981

The President announced today his intention to nominate William Francis Baxter to be an Assistant Attorney General (Antitrust Division), Department of Justice.

Mr. Baxter is a professor of law at Stanford University. He is a fellow at the Center for Advanced Study and Behavioral Sciences at Stanford. He has been at Stanford since 1960.

In 1964–65 he was visiting professor of law at Yale University, New Haven, Conn.

In 1958–60 Mr. Baxter was with Covington & Burling of Washington, D.C. In 1956–58 he was a member of the faculty at Stanford University Law School.

In 1968 Mr. Baxter was a member of the President's Task Force on Antitrust Policy.

Mr. Baxter was graduated from Stanford University (A.B., 1951; J.D., 1956). He is a resident of Atherton, Calif., and was born in New York, N.Y., on July 13, 1929.

Nomination of D. Lowell Jensen To Be an Assistant Attorney General
February 20, 1981

The President announced today his intention to nominate D. Lowell Jensen to be an Assistant Attorney General (Criminal Division), Department of Justice.

Mr. Jensen has served as district attorney in Oakland, Calif., since 1969. He was an assistant district attorney in 1966–69 and a deputy district attorney of Alameda County from 1955 to 1966.

Mr. Jensen was admitted to practice law in California in 1953 and was admitted to practice law in United States District Court in 1968.

He is a lecturer, panelist, and instructor on criminal law to many colleges and universities. He is assistant treasurer, National

District Attorneys Association Commission on Victim/Witness Assistance. He is a member of the California Council on Criminal Justice and the sentencing practices advisory committee of the Judicial Council. Mr. Jensen is on the National Crime Information Center Advisory Policy Board.

Mr. Jensen served in the U.S. Army in 1952–54. He was graduated from the University of California, Berkeley (A.B., 1949), and the University of California School of Law, Boalt (LL.B., 1952).

He is married and has three children. He resides with his family in Castro Valley, Calif. Mr. Jensen was born in Brigham, Utah, on June 3, 1928.

Nomination of Michael Cardenas To Be Administrator of the Small Business Administration
February 20, 1981

The President announced today his intention to nominate Michael Cardenas to be Administrator of the Small Business Administration.

Mr. Cardenas has been a partner with Fox & Co., a national CPA firm, since he merged in 1979 with his own firm, Michael Cardenas Accountancy Corp., which he started in 1967. In 1961–65 he was a staff accountant with Stoughton, Den Hartog & Davidson and became a certified public accountant in 1965.

Mr. Cardenas is a member of several CPA organizations. His participation in community services has included the regional advisory council of the Small Business Administration in the Fresno and San Francisco areas. He has also been a charter member of the Latin-American Businessmen's Association where he was selected Man of the Year in 1979. Mr. Cardenas has been active in various Republican campaigns at the local, State, and national level since 1967.

Mr. Cardenas is married and has two children. He is 47 years old and resides in Fresno, Calif.

Nomination of Ann McGill Gorsuch To Be Administrator of the Environmental Protection Agency
February 21, 1981

The President announced today his intention to nominate Ann McGill Gorsuch to be Administrator, Environmental Protection Agency.

Mrs. Gorsuch is an attorney with the corporate legal department of Mountain Bell in Denver, Colo. She also served as deputy district attorney for Denver.

Mrs. Gorsuch served 4 years as a Colorado State legislator. She served as vice chairman of the House Judiciary Committee from 1976 to 1978, chairman of the House State Affairs Committee in 1978–80, member of the House Transportation Committee in 1977, chairman of the House Legal Affairs Committee, and chairman of the Joint (House/Senate) Committee.

In 1977, as a member of the House Transportation Committee, she played a key role in the enactment of the Colorado stationary sources (air quality) bill.

Mrs. Gorsuch is a resident of Denver, Colo. She was born in Casper, Wyo., on April 21, 1942.

Nomination of John Whitlock Hernandez To Be Deputy Administrator of the Environmental Protection Agency
February 21, 1981

The President announced today his intention to nominate John Whitlock Hernandez to be Deputy Administrator, Environmental Protection Agency.

Since 1968 Dr. Hernandez has been professor of civil engineering at New Mexico State University. He has served as dean of the college of engineering, codirector of the New Mexico Environmental Institute and codirector of the Southwest Resources Center for Science and Engineering.

Dr. Hernandez has a B.S. in civil engineering from the University of New Mexico, an M.S. in sanitary engineering from Purdue University, and a Ph. D. in water resources from Harvard University. A registered professional engineer and land surveyor in New Mexico, Dr. Hernandez has written extensively in professional publications on water quality and waste treatment. He received a letter of commendation from President Nixon in 1970 for exceptional service in the field of air and water pollution. In 1978 he received the Engineer of the Year Award by the New Mexico Society of Professional Engineers.

Dr. Hernandez is married and resides in Las Cruces, N. Mex. He was born in Albuquerque, N. Mex., on August 17, 1929.

Nomination of Emanuel S. Savas To Be an Assistant Secretary of Housing and Urban Development
February 23, 1981

The President announced today his intention to nominate Emanuel S. Savas to be an Assistant Secretary of Housing and Urban Development (Policy Development and Research).

Since 1973 Dr. Savas has been professor of public systems management and director of the Center for Government Studies, Graduate School of Business, Columbia University. In 1970–72 he was first deputy city administrator, city of New York. In 1967–69 Dr. Savas was deputy city administrator, office of the mayor, city of New York. Previously he worked with the IBM Corp., first as control system consultant in 1959–65; assistant to the director of personnel in 1965–66; and manager of urban systems in 1966–67.

He has served on the editorial board of Urban Affairs Quarterly since 1978. He is a member of the American Public Works Association, American Society for Public Administration, Council of University Institutes of Urban Affairs, Urban and Regional Information Systems Association. He is the author of many books and articles.

Dr. Savas was graduated from the University of Chicago (B.A., 1951; B.S., 1953); Columbia University (M.A., 1956; Ph. D., 1960). He served in the U.S. Army in 1953–55.

Dr. Savas is married and has two children. He resides with his family in New York City.

Remarks at a White House Meeting With the National Governors' Association
February 23, 1981

Well, I just want to say this is a time for nostalgia for me. I see some familiar faces around here, and I want you to know that when you're all in town and around a hotel and walking down the corridor, I do the same thing that you do. Somebody says "Governor," and I turn around. [*Laughter*] But I appreciate this opportunity for some dialog with almost the entire membership of the National Governors' Association and look forward to working with you in a new approach to solving all the problems that, I think, we have together.

I am looking forward to having a coordinating task force on federalism and would appreciate your suggestions before you leave as to how we can organize this. In the meantime I'll be working with Rich Williamson[1] on the initial planning stages.

[1] *Assistant to the President for Intergovernmental Affairs Richard S. Williamson.*

As you know, this is a longtime dream of mine, this thing of balancing up the divisions of government. I think they've been badly distorted over the years. I've dreamed about it before and just today was going through some things that are still in the desk drawers from the old days. And I came across this set of figures—I don't know what they would be today, but back when I was Governor, that for every 10,000 Americans there are 12 doctors, 11 lawyers and judges, 40 gas station attendants, and 37 telephone employees. So, that's a total of 100 for every 10,000 people to keep us healthy and give us legal advice and sit in the courts and fill our cars with gas and take care of the telephones. But there were 130 Federal civilian employees for every 10,000 people, and I thought that was too many then, and I think it's too many now. But the Intergovernmental Affairs Office of the White House will be playing a part in our deliberations.

And I'd like also your thoughts on revenue sharing. Again, my dream has always been that, if possible, the ideal situation would be not the connection of Federal grants but of eventually turning over to the States—and turning, I'd say, back to the States, tax sources that more properly belong there and which would then help fund responsibilities that also properly belong at the State level instead of at the Federal level.

Now, we haven't made a final decision on some of the things with regard to revenue sharing, but I would like to hear from you and to hear your comments. But first I'm going to call on Governor Busbee for comments from chairmen of your standing committees.

Note: The President spoke at approximately 4 p.m. in the East Room at the White House.

Governor George Busbee of Georgia is chairman of the National Governors' Association.

Proclamation 4821—Save Your Vision Week
February 23, 1981

By the President of the United States of America

A Proclamation

Of all God's gifts, the ability to see is one of the most precious. It is the sense of sight that saves mankind from living in darkness. It is the sense of sight that permits individuals to communicate with each other and to future generations through literature and art. It enables man to enjoy the magnificence of a sunset and the promise of a rainbow.

Unfortunately, sight is often taken for granted. Few realize how many of our citizens lose their sight every year. Yet many forms of blindness can be cured if discovered soon enough, and many blinded by accident could have kept their sight had they taken only minor eye safety precautions.

Each of us has the responsibility to care for that which is ours. Our eyesight and the eyesight of our children should be paramount on the list of personal responsibilities. Money cannot but it, but a check-up and early care can preserve it.

To remind all Americans of the importance of good vision and of the ways we can safeguard our eyesight, the Congress, by joint resolution approved December 20, 1973 (77 Stat. 629, 26 U.S.C. 169a), has requested the President to proclaim the first week in March of each year as "Save Your Vision Week."

Now, Therefore, I, Ronald Reagan, President of the United States of America, do hereby designate the week beginning March 1, 1981, as Save Your Vision Week. I urge all of our citizens to join this observance by showing greater concern for preserving vision and preventing eye injury at home, at work, and at play. Also, I call upon educators and communicators, as well as eye care professionals, to stress to the public the importance of eye care and eye safety for Americans of all ages.

In Witness Whereof, I have hereunto set my hand this twenty-third day of February, in the year of our Lord nineteen hundred eighty-one, and of the Independence of the United States of America the two hundred and fifth.

RONALD REAGAN

[*Filed with the Office of the Federal Register, 10:52 a.m., February 24, 1981*]

Executive Order 12292—Foreign Service Act of 1980
February 23, 1981

By the authority vested in me as President by the Constitution and laws of the United States of America, including the Foreign Service Act of 1980 (94 Stat. 2071; 22 U.S.C. 3901 *et seq.*), and in order to conform existing Executive Orders to changes resulting from that Act, it is hereby ordered as follows:

Section 1. Section 1(k) of Executive Order No. 9154, as amended, is amended by inserting immediately before the period at the end thereof a comma and the words "or under authority of section 303 of the Foreign Service Act of 1980 (22 U.S.C. 3943)".

Sec. 2. Section 1 of Executive Order No. 10471 is amended as follows:

(a) strike out "section 202(c) of the Annual and Sick Leave Act of 1951, as added by the act of July 2, 1953, Public Law 102, 83rd Congress" and insert in lieu thereof "section 6305(b) of title 5 of the United States Code";

(b) strike out "said section 202 (c) (2)" and insert in lieu thereof "said section 6305(b)";

(c) strike out "section 411 of the Foreign Service Act of 1946" and insert in lieu thereof "section 401 of the Foreign Service Act of 1980 (22 U.S.C. 3961)".

Sec. 3. Section 2 of Executive Order No. 10624, as amended, is amended as follows:

(a) In clause (1), strike out "Title II of the Overseas Differentials and Allowances Act" and insert in lieu thereof "subchapter III of chapter 59 of title 5 of the United States Code";

(b) Clause (2) is amended to read as follows: "so much of the authority vested in the Secretary of State by chapter 9 of Title I of the Foreign Service Act of 1980, as relates to allowances and benefits under the said chapter 9 of Title I of the Foreign Service Act of 1980, as relates to allowances and benefits under the said chapter 9 of title I;"

Sec. 4. Executive Order No. 10903 is amended as follows:

(a) In the preamble, strike out "section 303 of the Foreign Service Act of 1946 (22 U.S.C. 843),";

(b) In section 1(a) strike out "section 111 (3) of the Overseas Differentials and Allowances Act (74 Stat. 792)" and insert in lieu thereof "section 5921 (3) of title 5, United States Code,";

(c) In Section 1(b):

(1) strike out "Title II of the Overseas Differentials and Allowances Act" and insert in lieu thereof "subchapter III of chapter 59 of title 5 of the United States Code,";

(2) strike out "202, 203, and 221(4)(B) of that Act" and insert in lieu thereof "5922(b), 5922(c), and 5924(4) (B) of that title";

(3) strike out "Title II of the Act" and insert in lieu thereof "said subchapter".

(d) In Section 1(c), strike out "section 22 of the Administrative Expenses Act of 1946 (added by section 311(a) of the Overseas Differentials and Allowances Act)" and insert in lieu thereof "5913 of title 5 of the United States Code".

(e) In Section 1(e):

(1) strike out "235(a) (2)" and insert in lieu thereof "235(2)"; and

(2) strike out "section 901 of the Foreign Service Act of 1946, as amended" and insert in lieu thereof "section 905 of the Foreign Service Act of 1980 (22 U.S.C. 4085)".

(f) strike out paragraphs (d) and (f) of Section 1 and redesignate paragraphs (e) and (g) thereof as paragraphs (d) and (e), respectively.

Sec. 5. Executive Order No. 11034 is amended by striking out in Section 5(c) after "provided by section" all that follows in that sentence and inserting in lieu thereof "310 of the Foreign Service Act of 1980 (22 U.S.C. 3950).".

Sec. 6. Executive Order No. 11219 is amended as follows:

(a) Section 1 is amended by striking out "officer or employee" and inserting in lieu thereof "member";

(b) Section 1 (b) is amended by inserting after "as amended," "the Foreign Service Act of 1980," and by striking out "that Act" and inserting in lieu thereof "the latter Act";

(c) Section 5 is amended by striking out "an officer or employee in"and inserting in lieu thereof "a member of" and by inserting after "as amended," "the Foreign Service Act of 1980," and by striking out "that Act" and inserting in lieu thereof "the latter Act".

Sec. 7. Executive Order No. 12137 is amended as follows:

(a) Section 1–111 is amended by striking out "1946, as amended" and inserting in lieu thereof "1980".

(b) Section 1–401 is amended by striking out "528 of the Foreign Service Act of 1946 (22 U.S.C. 928)" and inserting in lieu thereof, "310 of the Foreign Service Act of 1980 (22 U.S.C. 3950)".

Sec. 8. Executive Order No. 12163 is amended as follows:

(a) Section 1–201(a) (14) is revoked.

(b) Section 1–201(b) is amended by inserting "and" following "602(q)," and by striking out "and 625 (k) (l)";

(c) Section 1–602(a) is amended by striking out "625(d) (l)" each time it appears and inserting in lieu thereof "625(d)".

(d) Section 1–602(b) is amended by striking out "section 528 of the Foreign Service Act of 1946" and inserting in lieu thereof "section 310 of the Foreign Service Act of 1980 (22 U.S.C. 3950)".

(e) Section 1–603 is amended by striking out after "allowances", all that follows through "Foreign Service Act of 1946 (22 U.S.C. 801 *et seq.*)," and inserting in lieu thereof "authorized for a chief of mission as defined in section 102(a) (3) of the Foreign Service Act of 1980 (22 U.S.C. 3902(a) (3)),".

Sec. 9. Executive Order No. 12228 is amended as follows:

(a) Section 1–102(c) (1) is amended by striking out "Section 911 (9) of the Foreign Service Act of 1946, as amended (22 U.S.C. 1136(9))" and inserting in lieu thereof "Section 901 (6) of the Foreign Service Act of 1980 (22 U.S.C. 4081(6))";

(b) Section 1–103 is amended by striking out "Foreign Service Act of 1946, as amended" and inserting in lieu thereof "Foreign Service Act of 1980".

Sec. 10. The following are hereby revoked:

(a) Executive Order No. 9452 of June 26, 1944;

(b) Executive Order No. 9799 of November 8, 1946;

(c) Executive Order No. 9837 of March 27, 1947;

(d) Executive Order No. 9932 of February 27, 1948;

(e) Executive Order No. 10249 of June 4, 1951;

(f) Section 2 of Executive Order No. 10477 of August 1, 1953;

(g) Executive Order No. 10897 of December 2, 1960;

(h) Part III of Executive Order No. 11264 of December 31, 1965, as amended;

(i) Sections 1, 3, and 5 of Executive Order No. 11434 of November 8, 1968;

(j) Executive Order No. 11636 of December 17, 1971;

(k) Executive Order No. 12066 of June 29, 1978;

(l) Executive Order No. 12145 of July 18, 1979;

(m) Section 1–104(b) of Executive Order No. 12188 of January 2, 1980.

Sec. 11. This Order shall be effective as of February 15, 1981.

RONALD REAGAN

The White House,
February 23, 1981.

[Filed with the Office of the Federal Register, 10:53 a.m., February 24, 1981]

Executive Order 12293—Foreign Service of the United States
February 23, 1981

By the authority vested in me as President by the Constitution and laws of the United States of America, including the Foreign Service Act of 1980 (94 Stat. 2071, 22 U.S.C. 3901 *et seq.*), Section 202 of the Revised Statutes (22 U.S.C. 2656), and Section 301 of Title 3 of the United States Code, and in order to provide for the administration of the Foreign Service of the United States, it is hereby ordered as follows:

Section 1. There are hereby delegated to the Secretary of State those functions vested in the President by Sections 205, 401(a), 502(c), 613, and 801 of the Foreign Service Act of 1980, hereinafter referred to as the Act (22 U.S.C. 3925, 3942(a) (1), 3892(c), 4013, and 4041).

Sec. 2. The Secretary of State shall, in accord with Section 205 of the Act (22 U.S.C. 3925), consult with the Secretary of Agriculture, the Secretary of Commerce, the Director of the International Communication Agency, the Director of the United States International Development Cooperation Agency, the Director of the Office of Personnel Management, and the Director of the Office of Management and Budget, in order to ensure compatibility between the Foreign Service personnel system and other government personnel systems.

Sec. 3. The Secretary of State shall make recommendations to the President through the Director of the Office of Management and Budget whenever action is appropriate under Section 827 of the Act (22 U.S.C. 4067) to maintain existing conformity between the Civil Service Retirement and Disability System and the Foreign Service Retirement and Disability System.

Sec. 4. In accord with Section 402 of the Act (22 U.S.C. 3962), there are established the following salary classes with titles for the Senior Foreign Service (SFS), at basic rates of pay equivalent to that established from time to time for the Senior Executive Service (ES) under Section 5382 of Title 5 of the United States Code.

Career Minister
(a) Basic rate of pay equivalent to ES 6.

Minister-Counselor
(a) Basic rate of pay equivalent to ES 6, or
(b) Basic rate of pay equivalent to ES 5, or
(c) Basic rate of pay equivalent to ES 4.

Counselor
(a) Basic rate of pay equivalent to ES 6, or
(b) Basic rate of pay equivalent to ES 5, or
(c) Basic rate of pay equivalent to ES 4, or
(d) Basic rate of pay equivalent to ES 3, or
(e) Basic rate of pay equivalent to ES 2, or
(f) Basic rate of pay equivalent to ES 1.

Sec. 5. There is hereby delegated to the Secretary of State, without further action by the President, the authority vested in the President by Section 2107 of the Act to the extent necessary to implement the provisions of Section 2101 of the Act, relating to pay and benefits pending conversion.

Sec. 6. (a) Pursuant to Section 211 of the Act (22 U.S.C. 3931), there is established in the Department of State the Board of Examiners for the Foreign Service.

(b) The Board shall be appointed by, and in accordance with regulations prescribed by, the Secretary of State, except that not less than five shall be career members of the Foreign Service and not less than seven shall be appointed as follows.

(1) not less than five shall be appointed by the heads of the agencies utilizing the Foreign Service personnel system;

(2) not less that one shall be a representative appointed by the Director of the Office of Personnel Management; and

(3) not less than one shall be a representative appointed by the Secretary of Labor.

(c) The Secretary of State shall designate from among the members of the Board a Chairman who is a member of the Service.

(d) The Secretary of State shall provide all necessary administrative services and facilities for the Board.

Sec. 7. For the purpose of ensuring the accuracy of information used in the administration of the Foreign Service Retirement and Disability System, the Secretary of

151

State may request from the Secretary of Defense and the Administrator of Veterans Affairs such information as the Secretary deems necessary. To the extent permitted by law: (a) The Secretary of Defense shall provide information on retired or retainer pay provided under Title 10, United States Code; and, (b) the Administrator of Veterans Affairs shall provide information on pensions or compensation provided under Title 38 of the United States Code. The Secretary, in consultation with the officials from whom information is requested, shall ensure that information made available under this Order is used only for the purpose authorized.

Sec. 8. This Order shall be effective as of February 15, 1981.

RONALD REAGAN

The White House,
February 23, 1981.

[*Filed with the Office of the Federal Register, 10:54 a.m., February 24, 1981*]

Remarks During a White House Briefing on the Program for Economic Recovery
February 24, 1981

The President. I realize I'm interrupting here, and I did just drop by for a few minutes before today's briefing ends, that I thought I might add a few words of my own to those that you've already heard from members of the Cabinet.

Over the past 6 days since I addressed the Congress, the response to our economic program has been enormously encouraging. Several thousand Americans have already written to me or have sent telegrams expressing strong support. If you want the figures, the latest telegraph count is 2,490 favorable, 43 unfavorable. And I won't vouch for the arithmetic, but somebody that figured it out said that was 98 percent in our favor.

Yesterday, as you know, I had an opportunity to meet with the Nation's Governors, and they all recognize that this program will require some belt-tightening. But many of them also agreed that only if our Government grows less will our economy grow more.

And finally, I'm pleased that this morning Senators Pete Domenici of New Mexico and Fritz Hollings of South Carolina are together introducing a reconciliation resolution in the Senate so that the Congress can begin speedy and earnest deliberation on our proposals. Their bipartisan support for this resolution is very much in the spirit of what I said to Congress last week: that economic recovery must not be a concern of one party or one President, but of all parties and indeed all Americans. It shouldn't simply be my plan, it should be our plan.

So, I'm very pleased today that the legislative process to put America back on the road to economic health is now fully underway.

[Press Secretary] Jim Brady's told me that I can take a couple of questions before I leave.

Yes?

Reporter. Mr. President, on the defense budget, the rationale for it, in your increase, you believe that it's necessary in order to keep from falling behind the Russians. Now President Brezhnev has suggested a summit meeting with you to try to decrease tensions, and I presume down the line if it all worked, that might change the rationale for the defense budget. What are the chances that you'd have a summit meeting with Brezhnev, under what conditions, and what could you discuss?

The President. Well, I think the only answer to that question is I was most interested in his suggestion, and it's something that now we will discuss and discuss it with the State Department, with the Cabinet in general, and very particularly, discuss it in the days ahead with the leaders of our allies, which is—Margaret Thatcher coming here, Prime Minister of England, this week. That'll be part of the discussion, because I have pledged to them that we're not going to act on things like this unilaterally. We'll have a discussion with all of them as well as with our own people, and I have repeatedly said that I am willing to negotiate if it's a legitimate negotiation aimed at verifiable reductions, in particular, the strategic nuclear weapons.

And I also made it plain that I think that at such a negotiation table, if and when this takes place, there should be other considerations, what has been termed by Mr. Brezhnev as linkage. I think that you can't just deal with just one facet of the international relationship; you've got to deal with all of the problems that are dividing us.

Q. Would you have to agree to do certain things before you went? In other words, would the agenda have to be so complete that they would already have agreed to do things that we want them to do?

The President. Oh, no. I don't think anything of that kind, no.

Q. Mr. President, following up your linkage philosophy, what do the Soviets have to do to stop the shipment of these arms into El Salvador in order to qualify for such a summit conference?

The President. So far, at least publicly, they've been denying that they are involved in that, but I think the evidence that we have and that we've made public and that we've told our allies about makes it evident that they are involved.

I would think that this would be one of the things that should be straightened out—their participation in that kind of activity.

Q. Mr. President, is there any danger that we can become involved in El Salvador to the point that we might not be able to extricate ourselves easily?

The President. No, I don't think so. I know that this is a great concern. I think it's part of the Vietnam syndrome, but we have no intention of that kind of involvement. But there's no question but that we are in support of the government there against those who are attempting a violent overthrow of the government.

Mr. Brady. Thank you very much, Mr. President. Do you want to take one more question?

The President. Well, I'll take back there, and then he tells me I've got to go. [*Laughter*]

Q. Thank you, Mr. President. My question is about the summit meeting. If you appear to be delaying, won't that look like Brezhnev is the one seeking peaceful means, seeking a summit, and that the United States is the one holding off? Won't you be accused, won't it appear that way if you don't act quickly in giving him an answer?

The President. Oh, I don't think it's a case that we'll be obviously or intentionally dragging our feet. I think he's going to—or the world is going to see that this isn't something that you just say, "Well, you know, come on over. Let's talk."

We do have to put this up to our allies and to their leadership and wait for their consultation, as well as talking it over ourselves. So, I think that they would understand that. They've had experience dragging their feet.

Mr. Brady. Thank you, Mr. President.

Q. Mr. President, do you consider his invitation sincere, and do you think it comes from the heart—the Soviet invitation for a summit, or do you—are you suspecting——

The President. Helen [Helen Thomas, United Press International], I don't know that I could answer that. I wouldn't try to guess what's in his inner thinking, but let me just say I found it very interesting.

Mr. Brady. Thank you, Mr. President.

Q. How about these heartless budget cuts?

The President [*to the briefers*]. Back to you. [*Laughter*]

Note: The President spoke at 9:50 a.m. at the second of a series of briefings on the economic recovery program given by administration officials for reporters in Room 450 of the Old Executive Office Building.

Message to the Congress Transmitting the United States-Norway Fishery Agreement
February 24, 1981

To the Congress of the United States:

In accordance with the Fishery Conservation and Management Act of 1976 (Public Law 94–265; 16 USC 1801), I transmit herewith a governing international fishery agreement between the United States and Norway, signed at Washington on January 26, 1981.

This agreement is one of a series to be negotiated in accordance with that legislation. I urge that the Congress give favorable consideration to this agreement at an early date. Several U.S. fishing interests have urged prompt consideration of this agreement, and I therefore recommend that the Congress consider issuance of a joint resolution to bring this agreement into force.

RONALD REAGAN

The White House,
February 24, 1981.

Nomination of John S. R. Shad To Be a Member of the Securities and Exchange Commission, and Designation as Chairman
February 24, 1981

The President announced today his intention to nominate John S. R. Shad to be a member of the Securities and Exchange Commission for the remainder of the term expiring June 5, 1982. He will succeed Harold M. Williams, who is resigning. The President also announced his intention to designate him to serve as Chairman.

Mr. Shad is vice chairman of the board of directors of the E. F. Hutton Group, Inc., the second largest publicly owned investment banking and brokerage firm. He also serves as chairman of the finance, underwriting, investment and acquisition committees, and as a member of the executive committee.

Mr. Shad initiated Hutton's investment banking activities in 1963. He was named "Investment Banker of the Year" in 1972 by Finance magazine.

He served as chairman, Reagan/Bush New York Finance Committee during the 1980 Presidential election.

Mr. Shad was graduated from the University of Southern California (B.S., 1947); Harvard Business School (M.B.A., 1949); New York University Law School (LL.B., 1959). During World War II he served as lieutenant in the U.S. Naval Reserve.

Mr. Shad resides in New York City. He is 58.

Nomination of Louis O. Giuffrida To Be Director of the Federal Emergency Management Agency
February 24, 1981

The President announced today his intention to nominate Louis O. Giuffrida to be Director of the Federal Emergency Management Agency.

General Giuffrida is president of the Specialized Management Services Co. and director of the California Specialized Training Institute.

He has had a lengthy career as a military and civilian expert in crime prevention and investigation; industrial defense; physical security; civil disturbances and disasters; confinement and rehabilitation responsibilities. He attained the rank of colonel in the U.S. Army in 1968 and served in a variety of positions. In 1971 he left the Army and, at the request of Governor Ronald Reagan, organized the California Specialized Training Institute and has directed it since its inception. In addition, he served as an adviser on terrorism, emergency management, and other special topics for the office of the Governor of California. He was recently promoted to the rank of general in the California National Guard.

General Giuffrida was graduated from the University of Connecticut (B.A.) and Boston University (M.A.). He is an author and lecturer.

General Giuffrida resides in San Luis Obispo, Calif.

Remarks on Presenting the Medal of Honor to Master Sergeant Roy P. Benavidez
February 24, 1981

Men and women of the Armed Forces, ladies and gentlemen:

Several years ago, we brought home a group of American fighting men who had obeyed their country's call and who had fought as bravely and as well as any Americans in our history. They came home without a victory not because they'd been defeated, but because they'd been denied permission to win.

They were greeted by no parades, no bands, no waving of the flag they had so nobly served. There's been no "thank you" for their sacrifice. There's been no effort to honor and, thus, give pride to the families of more than 57,000 young men who gave their lives in that faraway war.

As the poet Laurence Binyon wrote, "They shall grow not old, as we that are left grow old: Age shall not weary them, nor the years condemn. At the going down of the sun and in the morning We will remember them." Pride, of course, cannot wipe out the burden of grief borne by their families, but it can make that grief easier to bear. The pain will not be quite as sharp if they know their fellow citizens share that pain.

There's been little or no recognition of the gratitude we owe to the more than 300,000 men who suffered wounds in that war. John Stuart Mill said, "War is an ugly thing, but not the ugliest of things. A man who has nothing which he cares about more than his personal safety is a miserable creature and has no chance of being free unless made and kept so by the exertions of better men than himself."

Back in 1970 Kenneth Y. Tomlinson wrote of what he had seen our young men do beyond and above the call of military duty in Vietnam—a marine from Texas on his way in at dawn from an all-night patrol stopping to treat huge sores on the back of an old Vietnamese man, an artilleryman from New Jersey spending his free time stacking sandbags at an orphanage to protect the children from mortar attacks, an Army engineer from California distributing toys he'd bought in Hong Kong to the orphans his unit had adopted. One senior military officer told Tomlinson, "My hardest task is keeping track of the incurable humanitarianism of our troops."

None of the recent movies about that war have found time to show those examples of humanitarianism. In 1969 alone, United States Army volunteers helped construct 1,253 schools and 597 hospitals and dispensaries, contributing $300,000 from their own pockets. Marines from the Third Amphibious Force helped build 268 classrooms, 75 dispensaries, 78 churches, temples, and pagodas. Marines contributed $40,000 to ensure an education for 935 children. Air Force men gave their money and their own labor to 1,218 schools, medical facilities, and orphanages. Air Force doctors, dentists, and medics treated 390,000 Vietnamese in volunteeer programs.

At Hoa Khanh, Children's Hospital treated in that one year some 16,000 children, many of whom might have died without the hospital. One of the finest and most modern in the Far East, it was built and financed with money raised by combat marines. An 11-year-old boy burned over three-quarters of his body was one of those saved. He interrupted the game he was playing with visiting marines to say, "All my life, I will never forget this place and these healing people. Some way, I will repay them."

A 27-year-old chaplain from Springfield, Missouri, came upon an orphanage where 60 children were sleeping on the floor of a school and subsisting on one or two bowls of rice a day. He told some men of the Americal Division's Fifth Battalion, 46th Infantry, about what he'd seen. A veteran sergeant said, "Don't worry, Chaplain. Those kids have just got themselves some new parents." And they had.

Army combat troops began sacking enemy food they had captured and shipping them back on returning helicopters. They found cots in a salvage dump, repaired them, and soon the children were sleeping in beds for the first time. One day, the cup was passed. Marines earmarked 10 percent of all poker winnings, and by the end of the year, the orphans were in a new building.

An Air Force pilot saw 240 lepers living in unimaginable filth. Soon there were volunteers from all branches of the military spending their weekends building houses at a hospital.

The stories go on and on. A Green Beret learned that a mother in a remote mountain village was having trouble in childbirth. He made his way to her home, carried her to a truck, and raced to Cam Ranh, where a Navy doctor delivered the baby. On Christmas he gave 1,500 orphans toothpaste, soap, candy, and nuts he'd collected from fellow servicemen.

Bob Hope, who visited our men there as he had in two previous wars, said of them, "The number of our GI's who devote their free time, energy, and money to aid the Vietnamese would surprise you." And then he added, "But maybe it wouldn't. I guess you know what kind of guys your sons and brothers and the kids next door are." Well, yes, we do know. I think we just let it slip our minds for a time. It's time to show our pride in them and to thank them.

In his book, "The Bridges of Toko-Ri," novelist James Michener writes movingly of the heroes who fought in the Korean conflict. In the book's final scene an admiral stands on the darkened bridge of his carrier waiting for pilots he knows will never return from their mission. And as he waits he asks in the silent darkness, "Where did we get such men?" Almost a generation later, I asked that same question when our POW's were returned from savage captivity in Vietnam: "Where did we find such men?" We find them where we've always found them, in our villages and towns, on our city streets, in our shops, and on our farms.

I have one more Vietnam story, and the individual in this story was brought up on a farm outside of Cuero in De Witt County, Texas, and he is here today. Thanks to the Secretary of Defense, Cap Weinberger, I learned of his story, which had been overlooked or buried for several years. It has to do with the highest award our Nation can give, the Congressional Medal of Honor, given only for service above and beyond the call of duty.

Secretary Weinberger, would you please escort Sergeant Benavidez forward.

Ladies and gentlemen, we are honored to have with us today Master Sergeant Roy P. Benavidez, U.S. Army, Retired. Let me read the plain, factual military language of the citation that was lost for too long a time.

"Master Sergeant Roy P. Benavidez, United States Army, Retired, for conspicuous gallantry and intrepidity in action at the risk of his life above and beyond the call of duty." Where there is a brave man, it is said, there is the thickest of the fight, there is the place of honor.

[*At this point, the President read the citation, the text of which follows.*]

The President of the United States of America, authorized by Act of Congress, March 3, 1863, has awarded in the name of the Congress the *Medal of Honor* to

Master Sergeant Roy P. Benavidez

United States Army, Retired

for conspicuous gallantry and intrepidity in action at the risk of his life above and beyond the call of duty:

On May 2, 1968, Master Sergeant (then Staff Sergeant) Roy P. Benavidez distinguished himself by a series of daring and extremely valorous actions while assigned to Detachment B-56, 5th Special Forces Group (Airborne), 1st Special Forces, Republic of Vietnam. On the morning of May 2, 1968, a 12-man Special Forces Reconnaissance Team was inserted by helicopters in a dense jungle area west of Loc Ninh, Vietnam to gather intelligence information about confirmed large-scale enemy activity. This area was controlled and routinely patrolled by the North Vietnamese Army. After a short period of time on the ground, the team met heavy enemy resistance, and requested emergency extraction. Three helicopters attempted extraction, but were unable to land due to intense enemy small arms and anti-aircraft fire. Sergeant Benavidez was at the Forward Operating Base in Loc Ninh monitoring the operation by radio when these helicopters returned to off-load wounded crewmembers and to assess aircraft damage. Sergeant Benavidez voluntarily boarded a returning aircraft to assist in another extraction attempt. Realizing that all the team members were either dead or wounded and unable to move to the pickup zone, he directed the aircraft to a nearby clearing where he jumped from the hovering helicopter, and ran approximately 75 meters under withering small arms fire to the crippled team. Prior to reaching the team's position, he was wounded in his right leg, face, and head. Despite these painful injuries, he took charge, repositioning the team members and directing their fire to facilitate the landing of an extraction aircraft, and the loading of wounded and dead team members. He then threw smoke cannisters to direct the aircraft to the team's position. Despite his severe wounds and under intense enemy fire, he carried and dragged half of the wounded team members to the awaiting aircraft. He then provided protective fire by running alongside the aircraft as it moved to pick up the remaining team members. As the enemy's fire intensified, he hurried to recover the body and the classified documents on the dead team leader. When he reached the team leader's body, Sergeant Benavidez was severely wounded by small arms fire in the abdomen and grenade fragments in his back. At nearly the same moment, the aircraft pilot was mortally wounded, and his helicopter crashed. Although in extremely critical condition due to his multiple wounds, Sergeant Benavidez secured the classified documents and made his way back to the wreckage, where he aided the wounded out of the overturned aircraft, and gathered the stunned survivors into a defensive perimeter. Under increasing enemy automatic weapons and grenade fire, he moved around the perimeter distributing water and ammunition to his weary men, reinstilling in them a will to live and fight. Facing a build-up of enemy opposition with a beleagured team, Sergeant Benavidez mustered his strength, and began calling in tactical air strikes and directing the fire from supporting gunships, to suppress the enemy's fire and so permit another extraction attempt. He was wounded again in his thigh by small arms fire while administering first aid to a wounded team member just before another extraction helicopter was able to land. His indomitable spirit kept him going as he began to ferry his comrades to the craft. On his second trip with the wounded, he was clubbed from behind by an enemy soldier. In the ensuing hand-to-hand combat, he sustained additional wounds to his head and arms before killing his adversary. He then continued under devastating fire to carry the wounded to the helicopter. Upon reaching the aircraft, he spotted and killed two enemy soldiers who were rushing the craft from an angle that prevented the aircraft door gunner from firing upon them. With little strength remaining, he made one last trip to the perimeter to ensure that all classified material had been collected or destroyed, and to bring in the remaining wounded. Only then, in extremely serious condition from numerous wounds and loss of blood, did he allow himself to be pulled into the extraction aircraft. Sergeant Benavidez' gallant choice to join voluntarily his comrades who were in critical straits, to expose himself constantly to withering enemy fire, and his refusal to be stopped despite numerous severe wounds, saved the lives of at least eight men. His fearless personal leadership, tenacious devotion to duty, and extremely valorous actions in the face of overwhelming odds were in keeping with the highest traditions of the military service, and reflect the utmost credit on him and the United States Army.

Ronald Reagan

Sergeant Benavidez, a nation grateful to you, and to all your comrades living and dead, awards you its highest symbol of gratitude for service above and beyond the call of duty, the Congressional Medal of Honor.

[At this point, the President presented the award to Master Sergeant Benavidez.]

Note: The President spoke at 1:45 p.m. at the ceremony held in the Inner Court of the Pentagon.

Prior to the ceremony, Secretary of Defense Caspar W. Weinberger and Master Sergeant Benavidez and members of his family met with the President in the Oval Office at the White House.

Executive Order 12294—Suspension of Litigation Against Iran
February 24, 1981

By the authority vested in me as President by the Constitution and statutes of the United States, including Section 203 of the International Emergency Economic Powers Act (50 U.S.C. 1702), Section 301 of Title 3 of the United States Code, Section 1732 of Title 22 of the United States Code, and Section 301 of the National Emergencies Act (50 U.S.C. 1631), in view of the continuing unusual and extraordinary threat to the national security, foreign policy and economy of the United States upon which were based the declarations of national emergency in Executive Order No. 12170, issued November 14, 1979, and in Executive Order No. 12211, issued April 17, 1980, in light of the agreement with the Government of Iran, as reflected in the Declarations of the Government of the Democratic and Popular Republic of Algeria dated January 19, 1981, relating to the release of United States diplomats and nationals being held as hostages and to the resolution of claims of United States nationals against Iran, in order to implement Article II of the Declaration of Algeria concerning the settlement of claims and to begin the process of normalization of relations between the United States and Iran, it is hereby ordered that as of the effective date of this Order:

Section 1. All claims which may be presented to the Iran-United States Claims Tribunal under the terms of Article II of the Declaration of the Government of the Democratic and Popular Republic of Algeria Concerning the Settlement of Claims by the Government of the United States of America and the Government of the Islamic Republic of Iran, and all claims for equitable or other judicial relief in connection with such claims, are hereby suspended, except as they may be presented to the Tribunal. During the period of this suspension, all such claims shall have no legal effect in any action now pending in any court of the United States, including the courts of any state or any locality thereof, the District of Columbia and Puerto Rico, or in any action commenced in any such court after the effective date of this Order. Nothing in this action precludes the commencement of an action after the effective date of this Order for the purpose of tolling the period of limitations for commencement of such action.

Sec. 2. Nothing in this Order shall require dismissal of any action for want of prosecution.

Sec. 3. Suspension under this Order of a claim or a portion thereof submitted to the Iran-United States Claims Tribunal for adjudication shall terminate upon a determination by the Tribunal that it does not have jurisdiction over such claim or such portion.

Sec. 4. A determination by the Iran-United States Claims Tribunal on the merits that a claimant is not entitled to recover on a claim shall operate as a final resolution and discharge of the claim for all purposes. A determination by the Tribunal that a claimant shall have recovery on a claim in a specified amount shall operate as a final resolution and discharge of the claim for all purposes upon payment to the claimant of the full amount of the award, including any interest awarded by the Tribunal.

Sec. 5. Nothing in this Order shall apply to any claim concerning the validity or payment of a standby letter of credit, performance or payment bond or other similar instrument.

Sec. 6. Nothing is this Order shall prohibit the assertion of a counterclaim or set-off by a United States national in any judicial proceeding pending or hereafter commenced by the Government of Iran, any political subdivision of Iran, or any agency, instrumentality, or entity controlled by the Government of Iran or any political subdivision thereof.

Sec. 7. The Secretary of the Treasury is authorized to employ all powers granted to me by the International Emergency Economic Powers Act and by 22 U.S.C.§1732 to carry out the purposes of this Order

Sec. 8. Executive Order Nos. 12276 through 12285 of January 19, 1981, are ratified.

This Order shall be effective immediately and copies shall be transmitted to the Congress.

RONALD REAGAN

The White House,
February 24, 1981.

[*Filed with the Office of the Federal Register, 3:04 p.m., February 24, 1981*]

Message to the Congress on the Suspension of Litigation Against Iran
February 24, 1981

To the Congress of the United States:

Pursuant to Section 204(b) of the International Emergency Economic Powers Act (IEEPA), 50 U.S.C. 1703(b), I have today exercised the authority granted by this Act to suspend certain litigation against Iran.

1. The circumstance necessitating the exercise of this authority is the implementation of the Claims Settlement Agreement between the United States and Iran. After a complete review of the agreements with Iran leading to the release of the hostages held by Iran I have decided to implement them.

This order is part of a series of actions necessary to resolve the national emergencies declared in Executive Order 12170 of November 14, 1979 and in Executive Order 12211 of April 17, 1980 and described in reports submitted to Congress under the IEEPA by President Carter on November 14, 1979; April 7, 1980; April 17, 1980; and January 19, 1981.

2. Although the hostages have been released, financial and diplomatic aspects of the crisis have not yet been resolved and continue to present an unusual and extraordinary threat to the national security, foreign policy and economy of the United States.

3. Thus claims which may be presented to the Iran-United States Claims Tribunal are suspended in accordance with the terms of the attached Executive Order pursuant to the terms of the Claims Settlement Agreement, and my powers under Article II of the Constitution, Section 1732 of Title 22, known as the Hostage Act, and Section 203 of IEEPA.

I am also ratifying earlier Executive Orders signed by President Carter on January 19, 1981 to remove any doubt as to their effect, an issue that has been raised in recent litigation challenging them. In this connection I note that Executive Orders 12276 through 12285 were all signed by President Carter and made effective while he was still in office. The Report to Congress required by IEEPA dated January 19, 1981 indicates that some of the Executive Orders were not signed until the release of the hostages, an event that did not occur until after the end of his term. The report, which was prepared in advance, did not, because of the press of circumstances, reflect events precisely as they occurred and to that extent it stands corrected.

4. The present Executive Order is neces-

sary for the United States to meet its obligations under the Claims Settlement Agreement to peacefully arbitrate certain claims.

5. The action is taken with respect to Iran

for the reasons outlined above.

RONALD REAGAN

The White House,
February 24, 1981.

Executive Order 12295—Nuclear Cooperation With EURATOM
February 24, 1981

By the authority vested in me as President by the Constitution and statutes of the United States of America, including Section 126a(2) of the Atomic Energy Act of 1954, as amended (42 U.S.C. 2155(a)(2)), and having determined that, upon the expiration of the period specified in the first proviso to Section 126a(2) of such Act and extended by Executive Order 12193, failure to continue peaceful nuclear cooperation with the European Atomic Energy Community would be seriously prejudicial to the achievement of United States non-prolifera-

tion objectives and would otherwise jeopardize the common defense and security of the United States, and having notified the Congress of this determination, I hereby extend the duration of that period to March 10, 1982.

RONALD REAGAN

The White House,
February 24, 1981.

[*Filed with the Office of the Federal Register, 3:05 p.m., February 24, 1981*]

Letter to the Speaker of the House and the President of the Senate on Continuing Nuclear Cooperation With EURATOM
February 24, 1981

Dear Mr. Speaker: (Dear Mr. President:)

The United States has been engaged in nuclear cooperation with the European Community for many years. This cooperation was initiated under agreements concluded over two decades ago between the United States and the European Atomic Energy Community (EURATOM) and extends until December 31, 1995. Since the inception of this cooperation, the Community has adhered to all its obligations.

The Nuclear Non-Proliferation Act of 1978 amended the Atomic Energy Act to establish nuclear export criteria, including a requirement that the United States have a right to consent to the reprocessing of fuel exported from the United States. Our present agreements for cooperation with EURATOM do not contain such a right. To avoid disrupting cooperation with EURATOM, a proviso was included in the law to enable

continued cooperation until March 10, 1980, and provide for negotiations concerning our cooperation agreements.

The law also provides that nuclear cooperation with EURATOM can be extended on an annual basis after March 10, 1980, upon determination by the President that failure to cooperate would seriously prejudice the achievement of United States non-proliferation objectives or otherwise jeopardize the common defense and security and after notification to the Congress. President Carter made such a determination last year and signed Executive Order 12193, permitting continued nuclear cooperation with EURATOM until March 10, 1981.

The United States has engaged in three rounds of talks with EURATOM regarding the renegotiation of the US-EURATOM agreements for cooperation. These were conducted in November 1978, September 1979, and April 1980. Progress has been made toward clarifying the issues relating to these agreements, and the talks will be continuing.

I believe that it is essential that cooperation between the United States and the Community continue and likewise that we work closely with our Allies to counter the threat of nuclear explosives proliferation. Accordingly, I have determined that failure to continue peaceful nuclear cooperation with EURATOM would be seriously prejudicial to the achievement of United States

non-proliferation objectives and would jeopardize the common defense and security of the United States. I intend to sign an Executive Order to extend the waiver of the application of the relevant export criterion of the NNPA for an additional twelve months from March 10, 1981.

Sincerely,

RONALD REAGAN

Note: This is the text of identical letters addressed to Thomas P. O'Neill, Jr., Speaker of the House of Representatives, and George Bush, President of the Senate.

Statement by the Press Secretary on the Formation of the United States Business Committee on Jamaica
February 24, 1981

The President and Prime Minister Seaga of Jamaica, in their talks here on January 28, stressed the central importance of new private sector investment for Jamaican economic recovery and agreed that the formation of action groups of outstanding business leaders in the two countries would contribute substantially to this end. The President therefore applauds and strongly endorses the formation of the U.S. Business Committee on Jamaica, which was announced today.

The Committee will be chaired by Mr. David Rockefeller, chairman, Chase Manhattan Bank, and have an initial steering group comprised of Frank Borman, chairman, Eastern Airlines; Charles Bludhorn, chairman, Gulf and Western Industries; John C. Duncan, chairman, St. Joe Minerals; W. H. Krome George, chairman, Alcoa; Howard C. Kauffmann, president, Exxon Corp.; Cornell C. Maier, chairman, Kaiser Aluminum and Chemical; Seymour Milstein, chairman, United Brands; David P. Reynolds, chairman, Reynolds Metal Co.; and Curt R. Strand, president, Hilton International.

The Committee will work together with a counterpart Jamaican group in seeking to stimulate and mobilize new investment, trade, and employment in Jamaica during this critical period of national economic recovery.

The Secretary of State has designated a senior adviser to assist the U.S. Committee and other private activities in support of Jamaican recovery and to help assure harmony with U.S. Government policies.

Revitalization of the private sector is an integral part of the overall economic program being developed by the Government of Jamaica. Discussions are underway between the Government of Jamaica and international financial institutions to establish a sound development and stabilization program over the next 3 years. The United States, other bilateral donors, and the multilateral development banks are coordinating increased levels of economic assistance to strengthen the productive capacity of the country. These efforts, and those of many other private and public bodies, will help alleviate the pressing social problems of poverty and unemployment.

161

Toasts at a Dinner Honoring the Nation's Governors
February 24, 1981

The President. Well, let me just say Nancy and I are both delighted that the first state dinner that we've had here should be this dinner on this occasion, to have you here in this room which traditionally is reserved for chiefs of state. It's been a nostalgic thing, as I said to some of you—ladies, to your husbands—the other day, because present are faces of men that I served with when we came here and sat as guests at the White House in the Governors' Conference and, of course, many new friends here also.

We've discussed in less pleasant surroundings some of the problems that confront us today. I'm sure that the Governors, whether they all agree or not, do realize that what we're trying to do is alter the economic situation in our country by changing one simple two-letter word, economic control *by* government to economic control *on* government. And I look forward to collaboration and cooperation with all of you because of my belief that our Constitution calls for the 50 sovereign States being the basis of our freedom here in this land.

You know, it isn't so different. I find sometimes that just in the short time that we've been here that I feel a little like I did many times and as you feel as Governor. Sometimes it's as Lincoln described the man that was being ridden out of town on a rail, tarred and feathered. He said, "If it wasn't for the honor I would really have preferred to walk." [*Laughter*]

But Bob Ray's State, the Des Moines Register and Tribune invited grade school children to write letters to the paper, which they guaranteed would be printed, as to what they would advise the President to do if they had the opportunity. And I was amazed at these letters from 9-, 10-, 11-, 12-year-old children, their grasp of the economic problems, the world situation, the things they recommended. But one letter that really moved me was from an 11-year-old boy who wrote and said, "When you get there, don't look to the past; look to the future. You won't have time to look to the past." And he said, "Make up your mind

that when you leave there you will be older, and tired, and there will be a few more gray hairs in your wise old head." [*Laughter*] And then he said, "Just get to the office, go to work, and be happy that you're only President, you don't have to be God." [*Laughter*] Out of the mouths of children.

Well, anyway, it's a great pleasure to have you here, and I look forward to contact as we've talked about in our previous meetings in the days ahead with all of you.

And now, I would like to propose a toast to the Right Honorable George Busbee, Governor of Georgia and chairman of the National Governors' Association.

And so that all can drink, including George, to the days ahead when between us we are going to see America solve its problems and have the cooperation that I think should properly exist between you, the chief executives of your States, and this Federal Government which was created by the States. So, a toast.

Thank you.

Governor Busbee. Thank you, Mr. President.

On behalf of the Governors of this Nation and their ladies, we would first like to express our appreciation to you and to Mrs. Reagan for your kind and your generous hospitality this evening. Listening to your remarks I reflect back to our meeting in Denver this past August when we looked at all the problems of our States, the problems of this Nation, formed by our States, and we said, "We need one priority to address the problems of all, and that is to relook at this question of federalism. And we adopted this as our number one priority. About that time we had a former Governor that was making speeches about the country espousing the same thoughts. Now, he's here with us. And those words have become acts and deeds.

You've asked, Mr. President, that the Governors of this Nation join with you in a partnership as you look at this great economic crisis that we as a nation face that demands immediate action, which you've taken. You have stated that you feel that we need to look at this system of government that we have, the levels of government we have that deliver the services to our people, and we need some realignment. You've asked for our imput, and you've provided access by meeting with the executive committee, with the standing committee chairmen, now with all of the Governors on yesterday. And I just would like to say to you, Mr. President, that we accept your invitation.

At this time, Mr. President, I would like to ask that we raise our glasses to the President of the United States.

The President. Now, if we'll all make our way to the Blue Room, the Green Room, and the Red Room for coffee and liqueurs, and then on to the East Room for entertainment, where a cast of 26 of the great Broadway musical, "A Chorus Line," are going to entertain. I think it is very fitting for them to entertain, because I have found out that the cast of 26 come from 18 separate States.

[The President spoke at 9:36 p.m. in the State Dining Room at the White House.

Following the entertainment in the East Room, the President spoke at 10:38 p.m., directing most of his remarks to the performers, as follows.]

I think you can tell by the happy faces how much you've done for—well, if a bomb should fall in this room right now, there'd be an awful strain on the country because here are most of the Governors of all the 50 States. [*Laughter*] And I understand you come from a spread of about 18 States, and show business would certainly have a terrific loss if something should happen to this room right now. [*Laughter*]

We want to thank you, and I'm sure you realize how happy you've made everyone here. And thank you very much for this, you've honored us greatly by being here. We appreciate it very much. Thank you.

And now I'm sure you almost feel like dancing yourselves, and out in the foyer there'll be an orchestra and there will be dancing. And thank you to the musicians who are here for all of this. Thank you very much.

I wish I'd started in show business. [*Laughter*]

Letter Accepting the Resignation of Max Cleland as Administrator of Veterans Affairs
February 25, 1981

Dear Mr. Cleland:

This letter is to accept your resignation as Administrator of Veterans' Affairs, effective today.

Your willingness to serve during this transition period has been greatly appreciated.

You have served our veterans and our Nation well. I know that in the years ahead you will be able to look back with pride on this experience.

As you return to private life, you take with you my very best wishes for every future success and happiness.

Sincerely,

RONALD REAGAN

[The Honorable Joseph Maxwell Cleland, Administrator of Veterans' Affairs, Washington, D.C. 20420]

Note: The text of the letter was made available by the Office of the Press Secretary on February 26. On the same day, the White House announced that Rufus H. Wilson, Deputy Administrator of the Veterans Administration, would serve as Acting Administrator until Mr. Cleland's successor was announced.

Remarks at the Welcoming Ceremony for Prime Minister Margaret Thatcher of the United Kingdom
February 26, 1981

The President. Prime Minister Thatcher, on behalf of the American people, Nancy and I extend to you and your family a warm welcome to the United States. Your visit here renews the personal friendship we began in your country just before you took office, and today as we meet in Washington at the start of my administration we also renew the friendship and alliance of our people.

Great Britain and the United States are kindred nations of like-minded people and must face their tests together. We are bound by common language and linked in history. We share laws and literature, blood, and moral fiber. The responsibility for freedom is ours to share.

When we talked in London just over 2 years ago—when neither of us was in office—I was impressed by the similar challenges our countries faced and by our determination to meet those challenges. You have said that we enter into a decade fraught with danger, and so we have. But the decade will be less dangerous if the West maintains the strength required for peace, and in achieving that goal, there is one element that goes without question: Britain and America will stand side by side.

Outside Cambridge curving rows of simple white markers testify to a time when peace was lost and Britons and Americans united to turn back threats to freedom. Our challenge today is to ensure that belligerance is not attempted again by the false perceptions of weakness. So long as our adversaries continue to arm themselves at a pace far beyond the needs of defense, so the free world must do whatever is necessary to safeguard its own security. A stronger, more vigilant NATO must be the background of that security and of our effort for equitable arms control.

The Atlantic Alliance will continue to be the steadfast center of our mutual security. But we're also both concerned with the totality of the East-West relationship. The Soviet invasion in Afghanistan was a brutal invasion, and you, Prime Minister, took a lead in rallying world opinion against it, and for that we commend you. The tension in Poland commands the attention of the world. Clearly, the Polish people must be allowed to work out their own solutions to their problems. Outside intervention there would affect profoundly and in the long term the entire range of East-West ties. There are problems in other parts of the world such as regions of Africa and Central America where Anglo-American cooperation is key to the success of Western efforts to find solutions.

Americans are grateful for British efforts to bring the American prisoners home from Iran. We remember and are grateful for the support you gave us when you visited here a little more than a year ago. We remember your words of encouragement. They gave us heart. And together we will work to continue to confront the scourge of international terrorism.

Finally, our two nations know that there is no true security unless there is economic stability. We have both suffered from substantial economic difficulties. They might be different in their complexities and require appropriately different solutions, but we know that we share one basic commitment: We believe that our solutions lie within the people and not the state. We are committed to unleashing the natural power of the individual to produce more and to make a better life for all. We believe that people will stay free when enterprise remains free, and we believe that there are no insurmountable problems when we let individuals make decisions outside the restricting confines of government.

Prime Minister Thatcher, I look forward to our discussions, to the pleasure of renewing our friendship, and to the opportunity to fortify the commitment between our countries. On behalf of all Americans I welcome you and your family to the United States.

The Prime Minister. Mr. President, I count it a double joy that I'm once again in the United States and that I'm being greeted here by you, Mr. President, newly in office, after a splendid victory but long since for me a trusted friend. Your warm welcome in this deeply moving ceremony will strike a chord in the hearts of British people everywhere.

Mr. President, these are not easy times in which to assume and to bear the responsibilities of national and international leadership. The problems are many, the dangers real, the decisions difficult. Indeed, weaker spirits might even be tempted to give way to gloom. But others like you, Mr. President, are stirred by the challenge. And that's why I value so greatly the opportunity to come to Washington to talk with you and to discuss the way ahead on so many of the problems of which you've spoken this morning.

We start from a common basis of understanding. For generations our two countries have cherished the same ideals. We've defended the same causes. We've valued the same friendships, and together we've faced the same dangers. Today, once again, our sense of common purpose and common resolution is being tested. It will not be found wanting.

The message I have brought across the Atlantic is that we in Britain stand with you. America's successes will be our successes. Your problems will be our problems, and when you look for friends we will be there.

Mr. President, the natural bond of interest between our two countries is strengthened by the common approach which you and I have to our national problems. You have mentioned some of the relevant things. We are both trying to set free the energies of our people. We are both determined to sweep away the restrictions that hold back enterprise. We both place our faith not so much in economic theory but in the resourcefulness and the decency of ordinary people.

Mr. President, you've spoken of a time for renewal. If we are to succeed in the battle of ideas, if we are to hold fast and extend the frontiers of freedom, we must first proclaim the truth that makes men free. We must have the courage to reassert our traditional values and the resolve to prevail against those who deny our ideals and threaten our way of life.

You, Mr. President, have understood the challenge. You've understood the need for leadership. In Britain you will find a ready response, an ally—valiant, staunch, and true.

Note: The President spoke at 10:11 a.m. on the South Lawn of the White House, where the Prime Minister was given a formal welcome with full military honors.

Following the ceremony, the President and the Prime Minister met privately in the Oval Office and then with their delegations in the Cabinet Room.

Remarks of the President and Prime Minister Margaret Thatcher of the United Kingdom Following Their Meetings
February 26, 1981

The President. I just have a few words here—both of us—but I also want to say that due to the schedule that has been arranged and the meetings of the Prime Minister yet to go to, there'll be no time for any questions.

It's both appropriate and timely, I think, that Prime Minister Thatcher should be the first West European leader to visit here in the new administration. Our deep ties and

perceptions we share give us much to talk about. Together we're confronting an extremely grave international situation. We do so with determination and optimism. We're both committed to safeguarding fundamental Western interests worldwide, including Europe, the Persian Gulf, Southwest Asia, and Central America.

Out partnership in NATO is a vital part of that effort. We're determined to consult closely with each other and with the rest of our allies on all matters involving our common security. In that connection, we affirmed our support for the Alliance's decision of December 1979 to modernize long-range theater nuclear forces and to pursue arms control efforts at the same time, in parallel.

We've also noted the Soviet proposal for a summit meeting. We believe this proposal needs to be carefully studied, and we will be consulting closely on this matter. For our part, we certainly have an interest in pursuing serious, constructive dialog with the Soviets on those issues which divide us.

And again, let me say, Madam Prime Minister, we're just delighted to have you here with us.

The Prime Minister. Thank you. Mr. President, friends, may I just add one or two things to what the President has said?

We're very sensible in Britain of the honor you do us, Mr. President, by asking us to make the first official visit of a head of government to see you here, and we have indeed taken advantage of the opportunity afforded us to discuss many things which will be extremely important in the coming months. The President and I had a tete-a-tete for some time, and then were joined by the Vice President and the foreign secretaries, when we discussed many of the wider issues the world over.

Of course, we take the same view in the United States and Britain that our first duty to freedom is to defend our own. And our second duty is to try somehow to enlarge the frontiers of freedom so that other nations might have the right to choose it. It is indeed a very difficult time the world over, and we have, of course, discussed the many problems, as the President said, including President Brezhnev's recent speech, the problems in Africa, the problems in the Middle East, and the problems in Central and South America.

I really regard it as the beginning of a process of consultation. We shall both of us be going to a number of summit meetings this year. It is absolutely vital that we coordinate our efforts and decide upon a common line for the many problems that will face us.

Mr. President, thank you very much for the wonderful welcome you've given us. Thank you for giving us so much time and for talking in so much detail about the things which concern us both, which concern our peoples, and which concern the peoples in the world everywhere. And I think, if I may—can I just end on a note of optimism? Yes, there are enormous problems. Yes, there have always been enormous problems, but I believe, together, we have the capacity to solve some of them. And those which we do not solve, I believe we can improve so that we can set them on their way to a solution in the end.

Ladies and gentlemen, thank you.

Note: The President spoke at 12:35 p.m. to reporters assembled on the South Grounds of the White House.

Statement by the Press Secretary on the Formation of the Cabinet Councils
February 26, 1981

The membership of each Cabinet Council has been finalized. The Cabinet Councils are designed to operate as subgroups of the full Cabinet, with the President presiding. Full Cabinet meetings will continue to focus on broad issues affecting the entire Government and on overall budgetary and fiscal matters.

Cabinet Council procedures have been developed and endorsed by the President. The procedures are intended to create an orderly process for reviewing issues requiring a decision by the President.

The Cabinet Council procedures are:

—Each Cabinet Council will be chaired by the President.

—Each Cabinet Council has a designated Chairman pro tempore who will guide the direction of the Council and will serve as the chairman of working sessions in which the President is not in attendance.

—An Executive Secretary will be appointed for each Cabinet Council from the Office of Policy Development. This individual, working with the Office of Cabinet Administration, will coordinate the activities of each Cabinet Council, including the preparation and distribution of agendas and meeting summaries. This activity will be supplemented by a secretariat for each Cabinet Council, composed of the Executive Secretary, representatives of the member departments, and other personnel as needed, to prepare background materials, refine policy options and recommendations, and otherwise assist the Cabinet Council.

—Issues will be sent to Cabinet Councils by the Office of Cabinet Administration. Notification of such assignments will be communicated immediately to all Cabinet members to assure full opportunity to participate in consideration of each issue.

—Presidential decisions, made in or after Cabinet Council meetings, will follow full discussion by any Cabinet member who wishes to participate. Council meetings are open to any member of the Cabinet. Decisions will be reported to the full Cabinet as they occur. When full Cabinet review is required, the matter will be set for a meeting of the full Cabinet.

Cabinet Council on Economic Affairs

Secretary of the Treasury, Chairman pro tempore
Secretary of State
Secretary of Commerce
Secretary of Labor
Secretary of Transportation
Director, Office of Management and Budget
U.S. Trade Representative
Chairman, Council of Economic Advisers
**The Vice President*
**Counsellor to the President*
**Chief of Staff*

---

*Ex officio member.

Cabinet Council on Natural Resources and Environment

Secretary of the Interior, Chairman pro tempore
Attorney General
Secretary of Agriculture
Secretary of Transportation
Secretary of Housing and Urban Development
Secretary of Energy
**The Vice President*
**Counsellor to the President*
**Chief of Staff*

Cabinet Council on Commerce and Trade

Secretary of Commerce, Chairman pro tempore
Secretary of State
Secretary of the Treasury
Attorney General
Secretary of Agriculture
Secretary of Labor
Secretary of Transportation
U. S. Trade Representative
Chairman, Council of Economic Advisers
**The Vice President*
**Counsellor to the President*
**Chief of Staff*

Cabinet Council on Human Resources

Secretary of Health and Human Services, Chairman pro tempore
Attorney General
Secretary of Agriculture
Secretary of Labor
Secretary of Housing and Urban Development
Secretary of Education
**The Vice President*
**Counsellor to the President*
**Chief of Staff*

Cabinet Council on Food and Agriculture

Secretary of Agriculture, Chairman pro tempore
Secretary of State
Secretary of the Interior
Secretary of Commerce
Secretary of Transportation
U. S. Trade Representative
**The Vice President*
**Counsellor to the President*
**Chief of Staff*

---

*Ex officio member.

Toasts of the President and Prime Minister Margaret Thatcher of the United Kingdom at the State Dinner
February 26, 1981

The President. Prime Minister Thatcher, Nancy and I welcome you, Mr. Thatcher, and your daughter, Carol, to this house, and it's my deep hope that as the leaders of two nations whose relationship is vital for the preservation of human freedom that we'll be in close and frequent consultation in the years ahead. Absolute trust between the Prime Minister of the United Kingdom and the President of the United States will continue to be the hallmark of Anglo-American cooperation.

Roosevelt and Churchill, Attlee and Truman, Eisenhower and Macmillan—these names inseparably linked in recent history—the legacy of their relationships is nothing less than the security and the freedom enjoyed by our nations today. We will continue in this great tradition, not only because it's essential but also because our two peoples expect and insist on it.

Our joint love of liberty was spawned by a common heritage. It was English history and tradition, with the Magna Carta and the Common Law, which gave birth to our Declaration of Independence. It was men of enormous intellectual capacity and courage—John Locke, Adam Smith, Thomas Jefferson, Alexander Hamilton, and John Stuart Mill—whose powerful ideas fed our notions of individual freedom and the dignity of all people.

In her London address last month to the Pilgrim Club the Prime Minister affirmed that her own political convictions are founded in that love of freedom, that rejection of tyranny and repression which inspired the Pilgrim Fathers and those who followed them to America. Well, it's widely known that I share many of your ideals and beliefs, Prime Minister Thatcher. My admiration for you was reinforced during today's productive meeting. I believe, however, that our relationship goes beyond cordiality and shared ideals. In these days the survival of our nations and the peace of the world are threatened by forces which are willing to exert any pressure, test any will, and destroy any freedom.

Survival in this era requires us, as those who preceded us, to take freedom in the palm of our hands and never to cower behind a veil of unrealistic optimism. We shall learn from those who spoke of the need for vigilance, even when speaking out was not popular. Winston Churchill was such a man, a man more than any other who symbolizes the link between our two nations. He was the son of Britain, but the child of a New World woman. His dedication to principle was not without hardship, yet his courage never wavered. We, undeniably, are the beneficiaries of the freedom he loved and the peace that he sought.

He had two nations in his soul, but he touched all nations with his spirit. But today peace, Churchill's peace, is in danger. It may serve us to look to the wisdom of his words. He said, and I shall quote him, "The peace will not be preserved without the virtues that make victory possible in war. Peace will not be preserved by pious sentiments expressed in terms of platitudes or by official grimaces and diplomatic correctitude, however desirable these may be from time to time. It will not be preserved by casting aside in dangerous years the panoply of warlike strength. There must be earnest thought; there must also be faithful perseverance and foresight. Great Heart must have his sword and armor to guard the pilgrims on their way. Above all, among the English-speaking peoples there must be the union of hearts based upon conviction and common ideals."

After our discussions today I'm confident that we too will be as Great Heart and guard the world's pilgrims on their way. Together we'll strive to preserve the liberty and peace so cherished by our peoples. No foe of freedom should doubt our resolve. We will prevail, because our faith is strong and our cause is just. And the same Winston Churchill that I quoted with that lovely passage also had the wit and humor that in

Canada in the dark days of World War II he could call attention to the fact that the enemy had threatened to wring the neck of the United Kingdom. And after the Battle of Britain, as he was speaking, who will ever forget him leaning over that podium and saying, "Some chicken. Some neck." [*Laughter*]

I ask you now to honor our most welcome guest this evening and and her country by joining me in a toast to Her Majesty, the Queen. The Queen.

You are very welcome here. We're delighted that you'd come.

The Prime Minister. Mr. President, ladies and gentlemen:

May I first thank you, Mr. President, for your wonderful hospitality this evening, for this remarkably beautiful banquet, and for the lovely music which you arranged for our delight.

I thought as I heard that song "I'll be seeing you in all the old familiar places," this is quite a nice, old familiar place in which to see you, Mr. President. [*Laughter*] And I hope we'll be able to sing that song for very, very many years. And what was the other? "There'll be bluebirds over the White Cliffs of Dover tomorrow when the dawn is free." Well, the dawn is free now. And you and I have to try to make something of it which would match the hopes of those who made it free.

We started this momentous day on your lawn, Mr. President, in weather that, when it occurs for some public occasion with us, we describe as royal weather. And it's a great pleasure to end the day in your house at this glittering dinner party as guests of you and Mrs. Reagan. We've heard so much of your oratory as a speaker, and it's been such a delight to hear you speak. And I've been very moved by what you've said.

I'm told, Mr. President, that when you and Mrs. Reagan were inspecting your new home, where we're dining this evening, to see what refurbishment was needed, you came across some charred areas, vestiges of certain heated events in 1812. [*Laughter*] I don't think I need apologize for them, because I'm relieved to hear that Mrs. Reagan saw in this not a source of historical reproach, but an opportunity for redecoration—[*laughter*]—and very beautiful it is.

This sense of renewal that's in the air is making itself felt far beyond this lovely house. You, Mr. President, won a massive victory in November after a marvelous campaign in which you made clear your determination to set your country on a fresh course. You underlined that determination last week in a budget speech which I very much admired and so it seemed to me did all those who heard it.

Mr. President, when you come to visit us in Britain—and I do hope it will be soon—you'll find that there's been change and renewal in the Old World too. Indeed, not long ago I was reading a book whose author had visited London shortly after the war. He wrote that "in spite of the homesickness, the hunger and annoyance at socialist bumbling, my farewell to London held its measure of regret. There were friendships made and cherished to this day."

Mr. President, you were that homesick and hungry author. You will remember the book which you wrote after, I think, you'd been making a film. Was it "The Hasty Heart" in London? Well, I doubt whether I'll be able to do much about your homesickness. You may even feel hunger if you're in search of a real American jellybean in London. [*Laughter*] But when you do come over, I can promise you two things. The first is the friendship of the British people, and the second, that the years of socialist bumbling are at an end.

I'm proud to lead a Conservative administration in Britain. For me, and I know for you, too, conservatism doesn't mean maintenance of the status quo. It means maintenance of the old values, the only background against which one could make the changes and adaptations which have to be made to keep abreast of the technological change that we need to embrace for a prosperous future. Conservatism means harnessing, but still more, the liberation of the fundamental strengths and resources which make a country great, which make its people prosperous and self-reliant.

As a Conservative I want determined and decisive government. But that's something very different from an all-powerful government. You and I, Mr. President, believe in strong governments in areas where only governments can do the job, areas where governments can and must be strong— strong in the defense of the nation, strong in protecting law and order, strong in promoting a sound currency. It we do these things very well, we shall indeed be leaders of strong government, doing the things that only government can do.

But for too long and in too many places we've seen government assume the role of universal provider and universal arbiter. In many areas of our daily life there are hard but essential choices to be made. But in a free society those choices ought not to be made by government, but by free men and women and managers and work force alike, whose lives and livelihood are directly affected.

Mr. President, wall-to-wall government is no substitute for that freedom of choice. Wall-to-wall government is economically inefficient and morally demeaning to the individual. Just take a look at those countries where the art has been brought to its cold, callous perfection to see where that leads.

Mr. President, in Britain's case we've set ourselves to reverse a process of industrial decline which has lasted decades. We too seek to release the real energies of the wealth-creating sector in the first place and, above all, by conquering the crippling forces of inflation. We're winning that battle. The cost is heavy, particularly in terms of the present levels of unemployment. But we won't solve that problem just by reflation, whatever the short-term attractions. The only true solution is a revitalized economy, providing real jobs of permanent economic viability. That is our goal, and we're going to stick to it.

Now above all is the time to stay on course. I say that, Mr. President, not least because only a firmly based economy can enable us to act as a strong and effective partner in an alliance—and that we are determined to be, because an enduring alliance with the United States is fundamental to our beliefs and our objectives. Never in the post-war years has that alliance been more essential to us all. You spoke of Winston Churchill. We all do. Nearly 50 years ago Winston told our two countries that together there is no problem we cannot solve.

We are together tonight. Together let us prove him right.

Mr. President, it is my very, very great pleasure to ask the assembled company to rise and drink a toast to our wonderful host, the new leader not only of the United States but of the whole of the Western World. I give you the toast: The President of the United States, President Reagan.

The President. Madam Prime Minister, thank you very much.

And now may I invite all of you to go to the Green and the Blue and the Red Rooms for coffee and liqueurs, and from there then make your way into the East Room, where you started this evening and where we are going to be entertained for a period by the Harlem Ballet.

So, I think we shall lead the way and all have our coffee in there.

[The President spoke at 9:24 p.m. in the State Dining Room at the White House.

Following the entertainment in the East Room, the president spoke at 10:30 p.m. as follows.]

Madam Prime Minister, Mr. Thatcher, Carol, Mr. Vice President, Barbara, all of you ladies and gentlemen:

I don't know how many of you know, this is the Harlem Ballet—12 years. Arthur Mitchell, would you stand up?

I think all of these young people here will agree, Arthur Mitchell is the man who had a dream 12 years ago and these young people from Harlem that he took and he put together in this very graceful and beautiful display that we've seen here. Nancy and I saw them a few weeks ago when they opened at the Kennedy Center in a full evening of ballet, and they have kindly come here to entertain us, and we are deeply grateful to them. And I think that what Arthur has done and the pride that he must have in seeing such beauty here on the stage and such grace—I just said to the Prime Minister while you were dancing, "Who could lack faith in the human race when they can produce such beauty and grace as we have seen here?"

We thank all of you. Now there's going to be dancing in the foyer, but again, our heartfelt thanks to all of you, and we hope we'll see you again soon.

Thank you.

Proclamation 4822—Red Cross Month, 1981
February 27, 1981

By the President of the United States of America

A Proclamation

This year we celebrate the 100th Anniversary of the American National Red Cross, a humanitarian movement born in Europe in time of war and founded in our Nation in 1881 by a small group headed by Clara Barton, a woman nearing the age of 60 who was known during the Civil War as the "Angel of the Battlefield."

With unfailing resourcefulness, zeal, and compassion, Red Cross volunteers have proved equal to the challenges of our time. In peace and in war, they have reflected the humanitarian instincts of the American people.

The Red Cross teaches individuals, families, and communities to avoid emergencies; prepares individuals, families, and communities for those emergencies that cannot be avoided; and helps individuals, families, and communities cope with crises when they do come.

The Red Cross serves beside our armed forces at home and abroad; provides blood and its components to our ill and injured; and helps those stricken by disaster.

The primary support of the American Red Cross always has been contributions, given voluntarily. This voluntary support reflects admirably the freedom and generosity of the American people. To insure that the Red Cross emblem continues to fly on banners across this Nation for another 100 years, I urge all Americans to continue this support with undiminished vigor.

Now, Therefore, I, Ronald Reagan, President of the United States of America and Honorary Chairman of the American National Red Cross, do hereby designate March 1981 as Red Cross Month, a month when every citizen is asked to join, serve, and contribute in the same example of unselfish spirit that has characterized the Red Cross since its founding a century ago.

In Witness Whereof, I have hereunto set my hand this twenty-seventh day of February, in the year of the Lord nineteen hundred eighty-one, and of the Independence of the United States of America the two hundred and fifth.

RONALD REAGAN

[*Filed with the Office of the Federal Register, 2:57 p.m., February 27, 1981*]

Memorandum Urging Support of the American National Red Cross
February 27, 1981

Memorandum for the Heads of Executive Departments and Agencies

The 100th Anniversary of the American National Red Cross is being celebrated this year and I have just affixed my signature to the document proclaiming the month of March as Red Cross Month.

The historic record of mercy and service of the Red Cross is known to us all. Its efforts this past year have alleviated suffering in this country and abroad, trained hundreds of thousands to deal effectively in matters of health and safety, and, through its blood services, saved the lives of untold numbers.

As President of the United States and Honorary Chairman of the American National Red Cross, I extend my personal support for the humanitarian efforts of this organization.

I know that you will join me in this support and encourage every Federal employee and member of our armed forces to assist the Red Cross by supporting their local chapters. It is essential to the Nation that the Red Cross continue to receive wide public voluntary support, both in funds and volunteer effort, to insure the organization's second century of service.

Let us all respond generously and help maintain the spirit of charity that has always been one of the hallmarks of the American character.

RONALD REAGAN

Appointment of Wendy H. Borcherdt as Associate Director of Presidential Personnel
February 27, 1981

The President today announced the appointment of Wendy H. Borcherdt to be Associate Director of Presidential Personnel, with responsibility for the recruitment of women. Mrs. Borcherdt will report to E. Pendleton James, Assistant to the President for Presidential Personnel.

Since 1977 Mrs. Borcherdt has been president, Training for Effective Management, a teaching and consulting firm specializing in organizational management, financial planning, and personnel. She was an associate with Teren and Co. of New York and Virginia Beach in 1976–77.

Mrs. Borcherdt has been involved with many volunteer organizations. Since 1974 she has served as a member of the finance committee of the Hoover Institution on War, Revolution, and Peace at Stanford University. She is vice chairman and trustee of the Independent Colleges of Southern California.

Since 1980 Mrs. Borcherdt has served as director of the Pacific Legal Foundation and director of Town Hall of California, a forum dedicated to civic education and to the discussion of public questions. Past volunteer activities have included: international director, Association of Junior Leagues, Inc.; president, Junior League of Los Angeles, Inc.; president, Symphonians to the Junior Philharmonic; president, Stanford Women's Club of Los Angeles County; member, City of Los Angeles Economic Advisory Council.

She has been active in Republican Party politics at the local, State, and national levels for many years. In 1979–80 she was regional finance director to the Reagan for President Committee in California.

Mrs. Borcherdt was graduated from Stanford University (B.A., political science and English, 1958). She is married and has two children. Mrs. Borcherdt resides with her family in Los Angeles, Calif. She was born on April 12, 1936.

Toasts of the President and Prime Minister Margaret Thatcher of the United Kingdom at the Dinner Honoring the President
February 27, 1981

The Prime Minister. Mr. President, Mr. Vice President, ladies and gentlemen:

Mr. President, an earlier visitor to the United States, Charles Dickens, described our American friends as by nature frank, brave, cordial, hospitable, and affectionate. That seems to me, Mr. President, to be a perfect description of the man who has been my host for the last 48 hours. And it's not surprising, therefore, that I've so much enjoyed all our talks together, whether the formal discussions in the Oval Office—and how very much it suits you, sir, to be there—or in the Cabinet Room or those less formal at the dinner table.

Mr. President, Henry David Thoreau once said that it takes two to speak the truth, one to speak and another to hear. Well, sometimes one of us has spoken and sometimes the other. But together, Mr. President, I would like to think that we have spoken the truth.

During the visit to which I've already referred, Charles Dickens, like me, also visited Capitol Hill. He described the Congressmen he met there as "striking to look at, hard to deceive, prompt to act, lions in energy, Americans in strong and general impulse." Having been there and agreeing with Dickens as I do, I'm delighted to see so many Members of Congress here this evening. And if Dickens was right, relations between the legislative and executive branches should be smooth indeed over the next 4 years. After all, "prompt to act and lions in energy" should mean, Mr. President, you'll get that expenditure-cutting program through very easily indeed. [*Laughter*]

In any event I hope, Mr. President, that in serving this evening wine from your own State of California, we British have done something to advance the cause of harmony. [*Laughter*] And I hope also that you'll think we've chosen well. I must confess that the Californian berries I've never seen growing on any tree, but of course they are none the worse for that. [*Laughter*] You see how much we try to attend to what has customarily become called "the supply side" in all aspects of life—[*laughter*]—not simply in economics.

California, of course, has always meant a great deal to my countrymen from the time, almost exactly 400 years ago, when one of our greatest national heroes, Sir Francis Drake, proclaimed it New Albion, in keeping with the bravado of the Elizabe-

than Age. This feeling of community and curiosity that we have about California exists in the present age when another of our household names made his career there, one of the greatest careers in show business. I refer to Mr. Bob Hope, who is here this evening, and whom we like to claim is partly ours because he was born in the United Kingdom, though he decided to leave when he was only 4 years old—[*laughter*]—presumably because he thought the golf courses in the United States were better than those in the United Kingdom. [*Laughter*] I'm glad that my husband, Denis, did not agree with him.

It's a great privilege, Mr. President, to welcome you this evening to this Embassy, and we're very sensible of the honor that you do us in coming here. I hope you didn't feel ill at ease as you came up the stairs and passed under the gaze of George III. [*Laughter*] I can assure you that we British have long since come to see that King George was wrong and that Thomas Jefferson was right when he wrote to James Madison that "a little rebellion now and then is a good thing." [*Laughter*]

Leaving history aside, I hope we've succeeded in making you feel at home. The Embassy has been described as being like a Queen Anne country house. At any rate, it's our own version of a Rancho del Cielo. [*Laughter*] It is, as they say, in a good neighborhood. After all, the Vice President and Mrs. Bush live next door. [*Laughter*] I'm told that they occasionally cast predatory glances on our excellent tennis court. But I fear there's little chance of persuading Nico and Mary Henderson to give it up. Too much useful business gets done on it, or so they claim. [*Laughter*]

It's a singular honor for me and, no less important, a great pleasure for all the other guests this evening that you should be here, Mr. President, not just because you are the free world's leading statesman but because you are a person who has got there by your own efforts and who retains that wonderful personality—natural, forthcoming, and wise, whatever the pomp and circumstance in which you find yourself surrounded. Emerson wrote that nothing astonishes men as much as common sense and plain dealing, but in you, Mr. President, to find these qualities is only what one would expect.

It's not the time, Mr. President, for me to talk at any length about the relations between our two countries, except to say that they are profoundly and deeply right. And beyond that, we perhaps don't have to define them in detail. But after these 2 days of talks with you and meetings with many of the United States ministerial and congressional leaders, I have realized what at any rate to me is exceptional about the dealings we two countries have with each other.

We honor the same values. We may not always have identical interests, but what we do have in common is the same way of looking at and doing things. We don't seek to score off the other. We don't seek to involve the other in some commitment against his will. We try rather, in discussing the whole range of world problems that affect us both, to find common ground and to find the way which protects for humanity that liberty which is the only thing which gives life dignity and meaning.

There will, of course, be times, Mr. President, when yours perhaps is the loneliest job in the world, times when you need what one of my great friends in politics once called "2 o'clock in the morning courage." There will be times when you go through rough water. There will be times when the unexpected happens. There will be times when only you can make a certain decision. It is at that time when you need the 2 o'clock in the morning courage. By definition it means courage. It requires also conviction. Even that is not enough. It requires wisdom. It requires a capacity to evaluate the varying advice that comes your way, the advice from those who say, "Yes, go on, go on, this is your great opportunity to prove what you're made of;" the advice which says, "This is the time to make a dignified retreat," and only you can weigh up that advice. Only you can exercise that judgment, and there's no one else. And it is the most lonely job, and what it requires is the most wonderful, profound understanding of human nature and the heights to which it can rise. And what it requires is a knowledge on your part that

whatever decision you make, you have to stick with the consequences and see it through until it be well and truly finished.

Those of us who are here realize what this 2 o'clock in the morning courage means, what a lonely job it is, and how in the end only one thing will sustain you, that you have total integrity and at the end of the day you have to live wih the decision you've made.

I want to say this to you, Mr. President, that when those moments come, we have, in this room, on both sides of the Atlantic, have in you total faith that you will make the decision which is right for protecting the liberty of common humanity in the future. You will make that decision which we as partners in the English-speaking world know that, as Wordsworth wrote, "We must be free or die, who speak the tongue that Shakespeare spake."

I'd like to thank you, Mr. President, for the hospitality you and your government have given to me, to my family, and to my party on this memorable visit. It's very early days in your administration, and you've very heavy preoccupations. But if these meetings have meant a tithe as much to you as they have meant to me and to my team, I shall leave with a pang of sorrow, but happy and contented, eager soon to see you on the shores of Britain.

It's in this spirit, Mr. President, that I would ask all our guests this evening to rise and drink a toast with affection, respect, and admiration to the President of the United States and Mrs. Reagan. The President of the United States.

The President. Prime Minister Margaret Thatcher, Mr. Vice President:

Prime Minister, Bob Hope will know what I mean when I speak in the language of my previous occupation and say you are a hard act to follow. [*Laughter*]

Nancy and I want to thank you for the warmth of those words that you spoke, as well as your gracious hospitality. And may I say that I do know something about that 2 o'clock courage, but I also know that you have already shown that 2 o'clock courage on too many occasions to name.

It's been delightful for Nancy and me to be here and with the Thatcher family in these 48 hours and to know them better, to know Mr. Thatcher, to know your daughter, Carol. I would also like to thank Sir Nicholas and Lady Henderson, who have made this house such a gracious center of hospitality in this city.

Winston Churchill is believed to have said that the three most difficult things a man can be asked to do is to climb a wall leaning toward him, kiss a woman leaning away from him, and give a good after-dinner speech. [*Laughter*]

This evening marks the first steps I've taken as a President on foreign soil. [*Laughter*] What an honor to visit Great Britain first and how symbolic of the close relationship between our two nations that I only had to go 15 city blocks to do it. I wonder if this is what is meant by the saying that the Sun never sets on the British Empire. [*Laughter*] I do hope you agree, Prime Minister, that this city is an excellent vantage point from which to see the brilliant sunlight that still falls upon the Empire.

I don't mean the empire of territorial possessions. I mean the empire of civilized ideas, the rights of man under God, the rule of law, constitutional government, parliamentary democracy, all the great notions of human liberty still so ardently sought by so many and so much of mankind. These are the enduring grandeur of the British heritage.

And you know, Prime Minister, that we have a habit of quoting Winston Churchill. Tell me, is it possible to get through a public address today in Britain without making reference to him? [*Laughter*] It is increasingly difficult to do so here, not just because we Americans share some pride in his ancestry but because there's so much to learn from him, his fearlessness. And I don't just mean physical courage; I mean he was, for instance, unafraid to laugh. I can remember words attributed to Churchill about one somber, straitlaced colleague in Parliament. Churchill said, "He has all the virtues I dislike and none of the vices I admire." [*Laughter*] He once said of one of our best known diplomats that he was the only case he knew of a bull who carries his own china closet with him. [*Laughter*]

The gift of humor can make a people see what they might ordinarily overlook, and it supplements that other gift of great leaders—vision. When he addressed Parliament in the darkest moments after Dunkirk, Churchill dared to promise the British their finest hour and even reminded them that they would someday enjoy "the bright, sunlit uplands" from which the struggle against Hitler would be seen as only a bad memory. Well, Madam Prime Minister, you and I have heard our share of somber assessments and dire predictions in recent months. I do not refer here to the painful business of ending our economic difficulties. We know that with regard to the economies of both our countries we will be home safe and soon enough. I do refer, however, to those adversaries who preach the supremacy of the state.

We've all heard the slogans, the end of the class struggle, the vanguard of the proletariat, the wave of the future, the inevitable triumph of socialism. Indeed, if there's anything the Marxist-Leninists might not be forgiven for, it is their willingness to bog the world down in tiresome cliches, cliches that rapidly are being recognized for what they are, a gaggle of bogus prophecies and petty superstitions. Prime Minister, everywhere one looks these days the cult of the state is dying, and I wonder if you and I and other leaders of the West should not now be looking toward bright, sunlit uplands and begin planning for a world where our adversaries are remembered only for their role in a sad and rather bizarre chapter in human history.

The British people, who nourish the great civilized ideas, know the forces of good ultimately rally and triumph over evil. That, after all, is the legend of the Knights of the Round Table, the legend of the man who lived on Baker Street, the story of London in the Blitz, the meaning of the Union Jack snapping briskly in the wind. Madam Prime Minister, I'll make one further prediction, that the British people are once again about to pay homage to their beloved Sir Winston by doing him the honor of proving him wrong and showing the world that their finest hour is yet to come. And how he would have loved the irony of that. How proud it would have made him.

So, ladies and gentlemen, I ask you to join

me in a toast to the memory of that great leader of free people, to his vision of bright, sunlit uplands, a toast to his Britannia and all that she's been, all that she is, and all that she will be, and to her finest hour, yet to come. Ladies and gentlemen, to Her Majesty, the Queen.

Note: The exchange of toasts began at 10:33 p.m. in the British Embassy ballroom.

Nomination of Gerald P. Carmen To Be Administrator of General Services
February 28, 1981

The President today announced his intention to nominate Gerald P. Carmen to be Administrator of General Services.

Mr. Carmen is a prominent New Hampshire businessman and civic leader. He was commissioner of the Manchester, N.H., Housing and Urban Renewal Authority, as well as the first State chairman of the New Hampshire Housing Authority. He also served on the State Vocational Education Committee.

Mr. Carmen was awarded the Retailer of the Year Award by the Downtown Manchester Association in recognition of his service to the business community as president of a wholesale service he formed in 1959 and sold in 1979.

Mr. Carmen has been active in civic and political activities in New Hampshire. He served as State chairman of the New Hampshire chapter, National Conference of Christians and Jews, and was awarded its Man of the Year Award in 1979; chairman of the New Hampshire Heart Fund campaign; director of the Merrimack Valley Region Association; member, Manchester Republican Committee; chairman, New Hampshire Republican Party; Republican National Committeeman for New Hampshire; delegate to the 1964 and 1980 Republican National Conventions.

During the 1980 Presidential campaign, Mr. Carmen was director of political programs and analysis for the Reagan-Bush Committee. He previously served as senior northeast adviser for the Reagan primary campaign in New Hampshire.

He was graduated from the University of New Hampshire (B.S., 1952). He is married to the former Anita J. Saidel, and they have two children. Mr. Carmen resides with his family in Manchester, N.H. He was born in Quincy, Mass., on July 8, 1930.

Remarks at the Mid-Winter Congressional City Conference of the National League of Cities
March 2, 1981

It's a pleasure to be with you today for your annual Congressional City Conference. The last time I was in this room, not too many weeks ago, was for the National Prayer Breakfast. And I hope that what was said then and what I did then has had some lasting effect. I'm especially pleased to have been introduced by my longtime personal friend, Mayor Bill Hudnut.

I understand and appreciate the part your organization has played in the Pennsylvania Avenue development plan here in Washington. The new 12-story building you've constructed overlooking Western Plaza is a fine example of what can be done to revitalize the inner city. It should serve to stimulate others to invest in such worthwhile efforts.

As you're well aware, rejuvenation of the American economy is the number one priority of my administration. This, I believe, was the mandate of the voters last November. It was a mandate that I sought, yet something all elected officials should understand, because it's a mandate for all of us. The election did not commission me to attempt economic reform alone, but to work with elected officials—Federal, State, and local—to put America's economic house in order. And that's why I'm here.

We've got a job to do together, and I believe we should open a clean, clear line of communication now. Our job, of course, is to get the economy of the United States moving again. It's essential for you as representatives of the cities; it's essential for all of us as Americans. One thing is certain: The time for business as usual has passed.

In the last two decades, Americans have suffered oppressively increased taxation, inflation, unemployment, and interest rates. The middle class, the life-blood of democracy and the American way of life, cannot withstand these pressures indefinitely. And the economic tremors rippling through our economy suggest that these people are near the breaking point. I don't know how many of you earlier this morning might have had an opportunity to watch on television as some citizens were being interviewed who publicly have stated they are simply going to rebel at paying their income tax, and they're going to appeal to others to do the same.

We're suffering the worst inflation in 60 years. Almost 8 billion—million—Americans are continuing to be out of work. I've been here only a month, and I'm beginning to talk in billions when I mean millions. [*Laughter*] Interest rates have climbed to an unprecedented 20 percent, with home mortgage rates of 15 percent destroying for millions the dream of home ownership. Investment in industry is lagging behind our major competitors, with too much of the personal savings of our people flowing into nonproductive inflation hedges instead of job-creating, long-term investment or savings.

Millions of Americans feel that for them the standard of living is actually going down, and it is. It's shocking and a depressing fact that after being adjusted for the continued cheapening of the dollar by inflation, the hourly earnings of American workers have dropped by 5 percent in the last 5 years. This is a complete reversal of the American experience and will have profound impact on the spirit of our people if something isn't done and done quickly.

And while our workers have been experiencing a decline in their standard of living, government has continued to spend money like there's no tomorrow. And come to think of it, that could be a self-fulfilling prophecy. In those same 5 years, those workers' taxes went up by 67 percent. Federal spending grew to 23 percent of the nation's gross national product, the highest peacetime share in our history. And the Federal Government has shown a deficit every year after 1969.

In fiscal year 1980 that deficit was $59.6 billion, the second largest in history. And we face another deficit of similar magnitude in this year of fiscal 1981. Now, this kind of irresponsibility can't go on. What most Federal officials have been afraid to admit is that Federal spending has been for some time increasingly out of control. If left unchecked, the current situation would lead to a redoubling of the Federal budget within 5 years.

For a time, it's appeared that Congress had more solutions than the country had problems; or, put another way, I've said before that cures were developed for which there were no known diseases. Just conceiving of a program that might help someone somewhere was itself reason enough to pass a law and appropriate money. Eventually, with so many programs, safeguarding public funds became an impossible task. One government estimate suggested that between 1 and 10 percent of all spending on social programs was, and probably still is, being lost to fraud alone, at a cost of up to $25 billion. When that cost or the cost of waste is added to that sum for fraud, the figures are even more appalling.

Of course, spending isn't the only aspect of government that seems out of control. In the last decade, American business and, yes, local government, has had to deal with an avalanche of Federal regulation. Between 1970 and 1979, expenditures for the major regulatory agencies quadrupled. The number of pages published annually in the *Federal Register* nearly tripled, and the number of pages in the *Code of Federal Regulations* increased by nearly two-thirds. The cost of this has been staggering. An estimated $100 billion per year—now I can say billion—is added on to the cost of everything we buy, just to pay for the cost of Federal regulations. And then there's the unseen cost which is harder to calculate but nonetheless devastating: Regulation tends to smother innovation, discourage new investment, increase labor costs, and reduce competition.

This Federal Goliath, unleashed and uncontrolled, brought us to the economic brink that is now confronting this Nation. Too many officials appear to feel totally helpless in the face of the monumental task of restoring order to the Federal Government's economic policies. Perhaps no one had the clout to get the job done. Whatever the reason, we now have much work to do. Together, we can put our economic house in order again and regain control of this situation.

We must realize that the economic crisis confronting America is not the result of a natural disaster or a catastrophe beyond our control. Inflation, unemployment—all of it—was basically caused by decisions that we, as a people, made. Now the only power needed to restore America's strength is willpower.

You may have heard a rumor to the effect that I've submitted a program to Congress, a four-part program which will get this country moving in the right direction again, I believe, increase the standard of living for our people, and cut the inflation and unemployment rates.

First, I've asked for a substantial reduction in the growth of Federal expenditures. Second, I've asked for a significant reduction in Federal tax rates. And third, I've asked for the prudent elimination of excessive regulation. Fourth, while recognizing the independence of the institution, I have pledged to work with the Federal Reserve

Board to develop a monetary policy which is consistent with those policies.

Let me refer back to the second of those points and just add this one fact. All of us must accept the fact which has been proven in this century, proven here in our own country several times, that a reduction in Federal tax rates does not necessarily result in a reduction in tax revenues. The economy expands, it reduces the burden for the individual, but the overall share goes up as the base of the economy is broadened.

Now, these four complementary policies form an integrated and comprehensive program, the details of which have been examined by the best economic minds in the country, people who are working with me on a daily basis. However, this program now faces a political gauntlet of interest groups. And, may I say, I know that in many instances there's legitimate concern, concern that some worthwhile program is now going to be unable to meet the purpose for which it was founded. And yet at the same time, I'm finding it increasingly difficult not to call some of the interest groups selfish interest groups, because we are not cutting at the muscle fiber of these programs.

And this is where you come in. You are not only important because of the power you wield on Capitol Hill, but also because you are looking out for the interests of millions of citizens who inhabit the great urban areas of America. You and I have shared goals. We both want what is best for those who live in our cities, just as I'm sure we both want what is best for the people of this country, wherever they reside.

Now, I know that you, like all Americans, recognize the importance of getting our economic house in order. The plague of inflation and stagnation is brutalizing this country. I don't have to remind you of the effects on local government: The cost of every service you provide skyrockets; tax revenue declines when businesses close their doors; and when coupled with the increased unemployment, the economic burden reaches a critical stage. Local government was not designed to withstand this kind of economic upheaval. Unless something is done to turn the economy around, local governments will suffer right along with many other respected American institutions.

On principle, we should never forget this: There is no better Federal program than an expanding American economy.

Even as our program for economic recovery awaits action by the Congress, we've already started to do what we can within the executive branch to cut back spending and regulation.

The Office of Management and Budget is now putting together an interagency task force to vigorously attack waste and fraud. Highly motivated and expertly trained professionals will be appointed as Inspectors General to the Cabinet departments.

We've suspended for 2 months the flood of last-minute rulemaking done by the previous administration so that we can look closely at it. We've eliminated the ineffective and counterproductive wage and price standards of the Council on Wage and Price Stability. We accelerated the decontrol of domestic oil. We have concentrated our efforts to enhance the effectiveness of the Paperwork Reduction Act of 1980. We placed a freeze on Federal hiring.

We've also begun taking action on particularly controversial rules. For example, rules mandating extensive bilingual education programs, passive restraints in large cars, the unnecessary labeling of chemicals in the workplace, controls on garbage truck noise, and increased overtime payments for executives have been withdrawn or postponed. These actions alone are expected to save the American public and industry almost $1 billion annually.

The administration will be reviewing a host of other regulations in the near future. Vice President Bush, who will be meeting with your executive committee this afternoon, is heading a special Presidential task force to clear away many regulatory roadblocks, as many as possible. His role in our regulatory reform effort should suggest the importance that we place on this issue. I'm aware that Bill Hudnut is circulating a questionnaire regarding regulatory relief which will be presented to the Vice President and the Task Force on Regulatory Relief this afternoon.

Now, all of this is being done to start us on the road toward recovery. What is important is that we begin. I'm sure we'll get there—if we work together.

Now, there are those who oppose almost everything in the economic program. They oppose the program, but for the most part they offer no alternative. Well, hoping things will get better won't make it so. I've been told that some Members of Congress disagree with my tax cut proposal. Well, you know it's been said that taxation is the art of plucking the feathers without killing the bird. [*Laughter*] It's time they realized the bird just doesn't have any feathers left. [*Laughter*] Maybe some of you have heard me put it a different way on several occasions when I've said that robbing Peter to pay Paul won't work anymore, because Peter's been bankrupt for some time now. [*Laughter*]

Nevertheless, the real threat to recovery comes from those who will oppose only a small part of the overall program, while supporting the overall effort. Needless to say, the small portion these parochial groups oppose always deals with the cuts that affect them directly. Those cuts they oppose. They favor cutting everybody else's subsidy as an important step in ending inflation and getting the country moving again. The accumulative effect of this shortsightedness can be damaging. We're all in the same boat, and we have to get the engines started before the boat goes over the falls.

Now, we've tried to be as fair and evenhanded in developing our package as was humanly possible. It's important to remember, when someone says that the administration is planning to cut the budget, what we really mean is we're planning to cut the growth in the fiscal year '82 budget from 16 percent to 7 percent. And even with our cuts, that 7 percent means that spending in fiscal year '82 will go up over fiscal year 1981 by about $40 billion.

Within this restructuring that we've proposed, some programs are eliminated, but others are strengthened. And we did nothing to weaken the social safety net which protects the truly needy in this society. As a matter of fact, when we reformed welfare in California, we discovered that the really truly deserving people that we were trying to help weren't helped as much as they should be helped, simply because of excesses administratively, duplication, and people who were not truly needy. We had spread ourselves so thin, that we didn't have the resources available to really take care of those with great need.

Full retirement benefits for more than 31 million social security recipients will be continued, along with an annual cost-of-living increase. The Medicare program will not be cut, nor will veterans pensions, nor supplemental income for the blind, aged, and disabled. The school lunch and breakfast programs will continue for the children of low-income families, as will nutrition and other special services for the aging. And, yes, there will be no cut in Project Head Start or summer youth jobs. When considering these essential programs, please remember the very best thing that can be done to strengthen things like social security is to get the American economy going and put people back to work, so they will be paying into the trust fund once again.

Now, I know there will be those who will charge that we're requiring sacrifices from the rest of the government, but not from the Defense Department. They'll suggest this proves we're not evenhanded as we promised. Well, I would remind those of you who wish to get beyond the slogans to examine my appointment to the job of Secretary of Defense. Cap Weinberger is anything but a big spender and was once given a nickname here in government to confirm that fact. So although the international situation dictates more spending for defense, it does not mean the Defense Department will be free from the cut-and-trim philosophy of this administration. I can assure you that Cap is going to do a lot of trimming over there in Defense to make sure the American taxpayer is getting more bang for every buck that is spent. I've even heard that there was a sigh of relief in several other departments when it was learned that Cap-the-Knife was going to Defense, and not to those other departments. [*Laughter*]

In our attempt to be evenhanded, we tried, whenever possible, to cushion the budget blows. In the case of money going to the cities, yes, undeniably, we're cutting the amount of money the cities could have expected had we continued through the economic crisis with a business-as-usual attitude. But while we are reducing some of these subsidies, we are at the same time converting many categorical grants into block grants, thus reducing wasteful Federal administrative overhead and giving local governments more flexibility and control. And corresponding to that, we're working to end duplication of Federal programs and reforming those that are not cost-effective.

Take, for example, the Urban Development Action Grants program, UDAG. I want to let you all know that we've decided to preserve the UDAG function in the Presidential program. But here's what we are doing. The UDAG function and the Community Development Grant program will be combined into a Community Development Support program, and we will be sending legislation up to the Hill in the near future to enable the UDAG function to continue.

As I said, we will be funding this new community support function at a slightly smaller amount than before, but we will be providing greater flexibility and autonomy to localities which show the ability to run these programs effectively. We believe the reduction will be largely covered by the elimination of administrative overhead. We're cutting fat, not muscle.

We're giving local government the power to decide what will be done with the money. Handled efficiently, the level of benefits may not suffer as might be suggested at first glance. However, there could well be something in local government that can and should be cut back during these times of economic hardship. If so, you will set your own priorities. You, not some Washington bureaucrat, will decide where the cuts will be made if cuts are necessary.

I know that accepting responsibility, especially for cutbacks, is not easy. But this package should be looked at by State and local governments as a great step toward not only getting America moving again but toward restructuring the power system which led to the economic stagnation and urban deterioration.

But for many of this country's major cities, economic stagnation is not a recent phenomenon. Increasingly, while power centralized in Washington, D.C., many great urban areas declined. I've always thought that Washington didn't have the same problems other cities did, to a certain extent because they grabbed hold of the fastest growing industry in America. [*Laughter*]

Many cities cannot even remember a time when they were economically healthy, but they were not always blighted with seemingly unsolvable problems. In the last century, American cities were shining examples of enterprise. They were places of optimism, where free men and women working together didn't know the meaning of the word "impossible." Alexis de Tocqueville noted the vitality of American cities when touring this country in the 1830's. He observed: "Towns are like great meeting houses with all the inhabitants as members. In them the people wield immense influence over their magistrates and often carry their desires into execution without intermediaries."

He described a land and a people which seem a far cry from those of today. But why? We're the same people. If we're not, what is different? Well, the answer to that is the increased intervention by Federal authority. Only 50 years ago, Americans still felt they could accomplish anything, and they did. Today, the descendants of these pathfinders peer through a maze of government regulations and often give up even before they've tried.

Local officials who once saw the local voters as boss now look to Washington, D.C., before considering a move. And what once was a Federal helping hand is quickly turning into a mailed fist. Instead of assistance, the Federal Government is giving orders. They call them mandates. More often that not the command comes from Washington, but few funds to implement the order can be found in the envelope. Mayor Koch of New York has detailed the problem of mandates better than anyone. Last year, he said his city was driven by 47 Federal and State mandates, with a total cost of $711 million in capital expenditures, 6.25 billion in expense-budget dollars, and

$1.66 billion in lost revenue. And people wonder why New York sings the blues.

Not only are the funds not available to meet all these mandates, often the mandates themselves are impossible to fulfill. In Fairfax County, Virginia, for example, students come from 50 different language backgrounds, 15 of which are spoken by more than 20 students. Were it able to follow the former HHS guidelines, the county would incur the expense of sponsoring bilingual programs in 15 different languages, including Urdu, Hindi, and Laotian.

Now, bilingual education—there is a need, but there is also a purpose that has been distorted, again at the Federal level. Where there are predominantly students speaking a foreign language at home, coming to school and being taught in English, and they fall behind or are unable to keep up in some subjects because of the lack of knowledge of the language, I think it is proper that we have teachers equipped who can get at them in their own language and understand why it is they don't get the answer to the problem and help them in that way. But it is absolutely wrong and against the American concept to have a bilingual education program that is now openly, admittedly dedicated to preserving their native language and never getting them adequate in English so they can go out into the job market and participate. [*Applause*] Thank you.

Today, I renew a pledge I made to your conference in Atlanta in December. I will examine the mandates issued by the Federal Government and take action to remove any undue burden placed upon local governments throughout this country.

Centralization of power in the hands of the Federal Government didn't happen by accident. Over the years local officials helped create this power flow by turning to the Federal Government for solutions to local problems. It appeared to be an easy way out. But now you're becoming more aware that to get a job done, the very last thing you should ask for is Federal money. [*Laughter*] First, there are so many strings attached that Federal projects take a lot longer to complete. And second, local money pays the bill anyway. Once the Federal vacuum cleaner gets through with the pockets of the local taxpayers, there isn't enough spare change left to run local government. [*Laughter*]

What we must do is strive to recapture the bounty of vigor and optimism de Tocqueville found in American cities. We can start by reestablishing the proper relationship between the Federal, State, and local governments. The block grant program in our package is the first step. It cuts considerable redtape and returns power and decisions to the cities for money taken by the Federal Government. It is something that we, in the years ahead, can build upon.

Shortly, my administration will announce the creation of a federalism task force to find out, specifically, what can be done to reestablish the balance between the levels of government. Your input and participation will be important in this process. Work-

ing together, we can establish a dialog about the proper functions of the respective levels of government and go about restructuring the federal system to maximize efficiency and freedom.

That is, as I've said, just a start. But it is a step, a first step, in the right direction. I hope in the years to come we'll be in direct communication. It'll take teamwork to get this country back on the right track, and it won't happen overnight. You can count on my cooperation to make the cities of America once again the thriving areas of commerce, culture, and freedom that once attracted the attention of people the world over. If we don't start now, who will, and when?

Thank you.

Note: The President spoke at 12:20 p.m. in the International Ballroom at the Washington Hilton Hotel.

Appointment of Three Members of the Board of Trustees of the Woodrow Wilson International Center for Scholars
March 2, 1981

The President today announced the appointments of William J. Baroody, Jr., and Robert A. Mosbacher to be private members of the Board of Trustees of the Woodrow Wilson International Center for Scholars (Smithsonian Institution). He also announced that James A. Baker III, White House Chief of Staff, will be the government member of the Board of Trustees.

Mr. Baroody is president of the American Enterprise Institute for Public Policy Research. He served as executive vice president of AEI in 1977–78. In 1973–74 Mr. Baroody was Special Assistant to the President, and later, Assistant to the President in 1974–76. From 1969 to 1973, he served as assistant to the Secretary of Defense. From 1961 to 1968, he was legislative assistant and press secretary to Representative Melvin Laird. Mr. Baroody was graduated from Holy Cross College (A.B., 1959). He served in the U.S. Navy in 1959–61. He is married and has nine children. He resides

with his family in Alexandria, Va. He was born in Manchester, N.H., on November 5, 1937.

Mr. Mosbacher has been an independent oil and gas producer since 1948, serving as chairman and chief executive officer of Mosbacher Production Co. of Houston, Tex. He has served as director or chairman of the following groups: the Texas Heart Institute, the Mid-Continental Oil and Gas Association, the American Petroleum Institute, the National Petroleum Council, the American Petroleum Landmen, and the All American Wildcatters Association. He has served as national finance chairman of the George Bush for President Committee, 1980, and the President Ford Committee in 1976. Mr. Mosbacher was graduated from Washington and Lee University (B.S., 1947). He is married and has four children. He resides in Houston, Tex. Mr. Mosbacher was born in Mt. Vernon, N.Y., on March 11, 1927.

Mr. Baker is Assistant to the President and White House Chief of Staff. He was previously with the firm of Andrews, Kurth, Campbell and Jones of Houston, Tex. In 1975–76 he was Under Secretary of Commerce. In May 1976 Mr. Baker was appointed deputy chairman for delegate operations of the President Ford Committee. In August 1976 he became chairman. Mr. Baker was the Republican nominee for attorney general of Texas in 1978. In 1979–80 he was chairman of the George Bush for President Committee. During the 1980 general election campaign, he acted as senior adviser to the Reagan-Bush Committee. In 1977 President Ford appointed Mr. Baker to serve a 5–year term on the Board of Trustees of the Woodrow Wilson International Center for Scholars. He was graduated from Princeton University (B.A., 1952) and the University of Texas Law School (J.D., 1957). He served in the U.S. Marine Corps in 1952–54. Mr. Baker is married and has eight children. He resides with his family in Washington, D.C. He was born in Houston, Tex., on April 28, 1930.

Executive Order 12296—President's Economic Policy Advisory Board
March 2, 1981

By the authority vested in me as President by the Constitution of the United States of America, and in order to establish, in accordance with the provisions of the Federal Advisory Committee Act, as amended (5 U.S.C. App. I), an advisory committee on the domestic and international economic policy of the United States, it is hereby ordered as follows:

Section 1. Establishment. (a) There is established the President's Economic Policy Advisory Board. The Board shall be composed of members from private life who shall be appointed by the President.

(b) The President shall designate a Chairman from among the members of the Board. The Assistant to the President for Policy Development shall serve as the Secretary to the Board.

Sec. 2. Functions. (a) The Board shall advise the President with respect to the objectives and conduct of the overall domestic and international economic policy of the United States.

(b) The Board shall work with the Cabinet Council on Economic Affairs (composed of the Secretaries of the Treasury, State, Commerce, Labor, and Transportation, and the United States Trade Representative, and the Chairman of the Council of Economic Advisers, and the Director of the Office of Management and Budget).

(c) In the performance of its advisory duties the Board shall conduct a continuing review and assessment of economic policy, and shall report thereon to the President whenever requested.

Sec. 3. Administration. (a) The heads of Executive agencies shall, to the extent permitted by law, provide the Board such information with respect to economic policy matters as it may require for the purpose of carrying out its functions. Information supplied to the Board shall, to the extent permitted by law, be kept confidential.

(b) Members of the Board shall serve without any compensation for their work on the Board. However, they shall be entitled to travel expenses, including per diem in lieu of subsistence, as authorized by law for persons serving intermittently in the government service (5 U.S.C. 5701–5707).

(c) Any expenses of the Board shall be paid from funds available for the Expenses of the Domestic Policy Staff.

Sec. 4. General. (a) Notwithstanding any other Executive order, the responsibilities of the President under the Federal Advisory Committee Act, as amended, shall be performed by the President, except that, the Administrator of General Services shall, on a reimbursable basis, provide such administrative services as may be required.

(b) The Board shall terminate on December 31, 1982, unless sooner extended.

RONALD REAGAN

The White House,
March 2, 1981.

[*Filed with the Office of the Federal Register, 11:33 a.m., March 3, 1981*]

Note: The text of the Executive order was released by the Office of the Press Secretary on March 3.

Nomination of Paul A. Vander Myde To Be an Assistant Secretary of Commerce
March 3, 1981

The President today announced his intention to nominate Paul A. Vander Myde to be an Assistant Secretary of Commerce (Congressional Affairs).

Since 1977 Mr. Vander Myde has served as Republican staff director, Committee on Science and Technology, U.S. House of Representatives. In 1973–77 he was Deputy Assistant Secretary of Agriculture (Conservation, Research and Education). Mr. Vander Myde was a staff member at the White House in 1977–73. He served as legislative assistant to Senator Bob Packwood (R-Oreg.)

in 1969–71. He was congressional fellow with Representative George Bush (R-Tex.) and Senator Bob Packwood in 1968–69. He was a staff assistant with the National Security Agency in 1962–68.

Mr. Vander Myde was graduated from the University of Minnesota (B.A., 1959) and the University of Iowa (M.A., 1966). He was a commander in the U.S. Naval Reserve in 1959–61. Mr. Vander Myde is married and resides in Alexandria, Va. He was born in Estherville, Iowa, on February 9, 1937.

Nomination of Lawrence J. Brady To Be an Assistant Secretary of Commerce
March 3, 1981

The President today announced his intention to nominate Lawrence J. Brady to be an Assistant Secretary of Commerce (Trade Administration).

In 1980 Mr. Brady was a candidate for the Republican nomination for the U.S. Senate in New Hampshire. He was also director of the New Hampshire Coalition for Peace Through Strength. From October 1974 to January 1980, he was Acting Director and Deputy Director of the Office of Export Administration of the U.S. Department of Commerce. In 1971–74 Mr. Brady was senior staff member and special advisor for congressional relations with the Council on International Economic Policy at the White House.

In 1970–71 he was senior international economist, Office of International Trade, Department of State. Mr. Brady was minority counsel to the Senate Judiciary Subcommittee on Separation of Powers in 1967–70. He previously worked as a legislative aide to the Senate Minority Secretary. He was a staff assistant with Senator Norris Cotton in 1958–63.

Mr. Brady received his Ph. D. in international affairs and economics from Catholic University. He is married and has three children. He resides with his family in Bedford, N.H. Mr. Brady was born in Berlin, N.H., on April 22, 1939.

Nomination of Richard D. DeLauer To Be an Under Secretary of Defense
March 3, 1981

The President today announced his intention to nominate Richard D. DeLauer to be Under Secretary of Defense for Research and Engineering.

Since 1970 Dr. DeLauer served as executive vice president of TRW, Inc. He was vice president and general manager of TRW Systems Group in 1968–71. Dr. DeLauer was vice president and general manager of the systems engineering and integration division in 1965–68. In 1963–65 Dr. DeLauer was director of ballistic missile program management, and in 1960–62 he was director of the Titan program office at TRW. In 1959–60 he was director of the vehicle development laboratory.

Dr. DeLauer was an aeronautical engineering officer in the U.S. Navy in 1943–58.

He is a member of the Defense Science Board and is a member of the board of governors of the Aerospace Industries Association.

Dr. DeLauer was graduated from Stanford University (A.B., 1940); U.S. Naval Postgraduate School (B.S., 1949); California Institute of Technology (A.E., 1950; Ph. D., 1953).

Dr. DeLauer resides in Los Angeles, Calif. He was born in Oakland, Calif., on September 26, 1918.

Nomination of William C. Clohan, Jr., To Be Under Secretary of Education
March 3, 1981

The President today announced his intention to nominate William C. Clohan, Jr., to be Under Secretary of Education.

Mr. Clohan is minority education counsel to the Education and Labor Committee, U.S. House of Representatives. He was formerly chief legislative assistant to two Members of Congress and an independent research and writing contractor.

As minority education counsel, Mr. Clohan had primary responsibility for issues concerning child nutrition, School

Lunch program, Community Schools program, education innovation and support, Fund for Improvement of Postsecondary Education, and many others.

He was graduated from the U.S. Air Force Academy (B.S., 1970); George Washington University (M.S.A., 1972); Georgetown University Law Center (J.D., 1976). He was an officer in the U.S. Air Force.

Mr. Clohan is married and resides in Washington, D.C. He was born in Martinsburg, W. Va., on July 29, 1948.

Nomination of Dorcas R. Hardy To Be an Assistant Secretary of Health and Human Services
March 3, 1981

The President today announced his intention to nominate Dorcas R. Hardy to be an

Assistant Secretary of Health and Human Services (Human Development Services).

Miss Hardy is currently associate director of the University of Southern California's Center for Health Services Research. The multidisciplinary research center addresses economic, social, and health policy issues.

In 1974 she was a health consultant with Media-Mark, Inc., specializing in the study of intergovernmental effectiveness of services for children. From January 1973 to April 1974, Miss Hardy was assistant secre-

tary of health for the State of California. From 1971 to 1973, she was executive director of the Health Services Industry Committee of the Cost of Living Council.

Miss Hardy received a B.A. degree in 1968 from Connecticut College and an M.B.A. degree from Pepperdine University in 1976. She resides in Washington, D.C., and was born in Newark, N.J., on July 18, 1946.

Nomination of John J. Knapp To Be General Counsel of the Department of Housing and Urban Development
March 3, 1981

The President today announced his intention to nominate John J. Knapp to be General Counsel of the Department of Housing and Urban Development.

Since 1971 Mr. Knapp has worked as chief legal officer for National Kinney Corp., a publicly held corporation engaged in building maintenance, construction, parking lot ownership, and housing development.

Prior to joining Kinney, Mr. Knapp was assistant secretary of Textron, Inc., and an associate at the law firm of Paul, Weiss, Rifkind, Wharton & Garrison, in New York.

Mr. Knapp received his B.S. in 1958 from Manhattan College and his J.D. degree in 1961 from Fordham Law School. He is married with two children and resides in Garden City, N.Y. Mr. Knapp was born September 15, 1934.

Nomination of James R. Harris To Be Director of the Office of Surface Mining Reclamation and Enforcement
March 3, 1981

The President today announced his intention to nominate James R. Harris to be Director of the Office of Surface Mining Reclamation and Enforcement, Department of the Interior.

In 1980 Mr. Harris was reelected to a second term in the Indiana State Senate. He served on and chaired the Senate Standing Committee on Natural Resources, Environment and Agriculture. He also served as ranking majority member of the Senate Standing Committee on Elections and Apportionment and as a member of the Senate Standing Committee on Finance.

He served as chairman of a 2-year Interim Study Committee on Surface Mining,

charged with the responsibility for drafting surface mining legislation to bring Indiana into compliance with the 1977 Federal Surface Mining Act. From 1978 to 1979, Mr. Harris chaired the Natural Resources Advisory Committee, a statutory legislative oversight committee for the Indiana Department of Natural Resources.

A certified professional geologist and former surface mine superintendent, Mr. Harris serves as Indiana's legislative representative to a 10-State interstate task force on more successful utilization of high sulphur coal.

Mr. Harris served in the Indiana House of Representatives in 1973–74. He was president and co-owner, Elberfeld Telephone Co., Inc., in 1969–74. In 1967–68 he was superintendent of the J.R. Coal Co. in Warrick County, Ind. Mr. Harris was a consulting geologist with the firm of Norrick & Harris in 1957–68.

He was graduated from the U.S. Navy Officer Candidate School (1955) and served on board the U.S.S. *Rehoboth*. He was also a student at Indiana University (A.B., 1951) and Evansville College (1947–49).

Mr. Harris is married and has four children. He resides with his family in Evansville, Ind. He is 51 years old.

Nomination of Robert F. Burford To Be Director of the Bureau of Land Management
March 3, 1981

The President today announced his intention to nominate Robert F. Burford to be Director of the Bureau of Land Management, Department of the Interior.

In 1974 Mr. Burford was elected to the Colorado House of Representatives. He was reelected to that office in 1976 and 1978. In 1979–80 he was elected to the office of the speaker.

Mr. Burford is a member of the Bureau of Land Management Grazing Advisory Board in Colorado. He is a member of the Colorado and National Cattleman's Association and the Colorado Farm Bureau.

Mr. Burford served in the U.S. Marine Corps during World War II. He attended the Colorado School of Mines.

He was born in Grand Junction, Colo., on February 5, 1923.

Nomination of Myer Rashish To Be an Under Secretary of State
March 3, 1981

The President today announced his intention to nominate Myer Rashish to be Under Secretary of State for Economic Affairs.

Mr. Rashish has been a private economist since 1963. He has served on the Advisory Committee for Trade Negotiations and was elected Chairman in 1980. From 1967 to 1971, Mr. Rashish was a consultant to the Joint Economic Committee. From 1961 to 1963, he served as an Assistant to the President for International Trade Policy.

Mr. Rashish has also served as special assistant to the Under Secretary of State for Economic Affairs, secretary of President-elect Kennedy's Task Force on Foreign Economic Policy and the Task Force on the Balance of Payments. In 1956–60 he was chief economist and staff director of the Subcommittee on Foreign Trade Policy and the Committee on Ways and Means, U.S. House of Representatives.

Mr. Rashish received his B.A. degree in 1941 from Harvard University and an M.A. degree in economics in 1947. He is married and has three children. Mr. Rashish was born in Cambridge, Mass., on November 10, 1924.

Nomination of Robert D. Hormats To Be an Assistant Secretary of State
March 3, 1981

The President today announced his intention to nominate Robert D. Hormats to be an Assistant Secretary of State (Economic Affairs).

Mr. Hormats is currently the Deputy U.S. Trade Representative. From 1977 to 1979, he served as Deputy Assistant Secretary of State for Economic and Business Affairs. Mr. Hormats also served on the National Security Council from 1974 to 1977 as a senior staff member for international economic affairs. From 1973 to 1974, he was an international affairs fellow, Council on Foreign Relations, and guest scholar of the Brookings Institution.

Mr. Hormats received his B.A. degree from Tufts University in 1965 and an M.A., M.A.L.D., and Ph. D. from the Fletcher School of International Law and Diplomacy at Tufts University.

Mr. Hormats resides in Chevy Chase, Md., and was born April 13, 1943, in Baltimore, Md.

Nomination of Chester Crocker To Be an Assistant Secretary of State
March 3, 1981

The President today announced his intention to nominate Chester Crocker to be an Assistant Secretary of State (African Affairs).

Since 1976 Dr. Crocker has been director of the African studies program, Center for Strategic and International Studies, Georgetown University. Since 1977 he has been associate professor of international relations, and in 1972–77 Dr. Crocker was assistant professor of international relations. In 1972–78 he was director, master of science in the foreign service program. In 1970–72 Dr. Crocker was staff officer (Africa, Middle East, and Indian Ocean), National Security Council.

He was graduated from Ohio State University (B.A., 1958) and Johns Hopkins School of Advanced International Studies (M.A., 1965; Ph. D., 1969).

Dr. Crocker is a resident of Washington, D.C. He was born in New York City on October 29, 1941.

Nomination of John H. Holdridge To Be an Assistant Secretary of State
March 3, 1981

The President today announced his intention to nominate John H. Holdridge to be an Assistant Secretary of State (East Asian and Pacific Affairs).

Since 1978 Mr. Holdridge has served with the Central Intelligence Agency. In 1975–78 he was U.S. Ambassador to the Republic of Singapore. Mr. Holdridge was Deputy Chief of Mission, U.S. Liaison Office in Peking, in 1973–75. In 1969–73 he served as Director of the Office of Research Analysis (East Asia), Bureau of Intelligence and Research, Department of State. He was Deputy Director of that office in 1966–68. Mr. Holdridge was chief, political section, Hong Kong, in 1962–69 and chief, political section, Office of Chinese Affairs, East Asia Bureau, in 1958–62.

He was graduated from the U.S. Military Academy (B.S., 1945). Mr. Holdridge resides in Bethesda, Md. He was born in New York City on August 24, 1924.

Nomination of Nicholas A. Veliotes To Be an Assistant Secretary of State
March 3, 1981

The President today announced his intention to nominate Nicholas A. Veliotes to be an Assistant Secretary of State (Near Eastern and South Asian Affairs).

Mr. Veliotes is a Career Minister. He was Deputy Assistant Secretary for Near Eastern and South Asian Affairs, Department of State, in 1977–78. In 1976–77 he was Deputy Director, Policy Planning Staff, and Special Assistant for Employee-Management Relations, Bureau of Personnel, in 1975–76.

Mr. Veliotes was Deputy Chief of Mission in Tel Aviv in 1973–75; Special Assistant to the Under Secretary of State in 1970–73;

international relations officer, African regional affairs; chief, political section in Vientiane in 1966–69; political officer in New Delhi in 1964-66; foreign affairs officer, Bureau of Cultural and Educational Affairs in 1962–64; international relations officer, executive secretariat staff; economic/general services officer in Rome in 1957–60; and consular/administrative officer in Naples in 1955–57.

Mr. Veliotes was graduated from the University of California (B.A., 1952; M.A., 1954). He resides in Amman, Jordan, and was born in Oakland, Calif., on October 28, 1928.

Nomination of Roger W. Mehle, Jr., To Be an Assistant Secretary of the Treasury
March 3, 1981

The President today announced his intention to nominate Roger W. Mehle, Jr., to be an Assistant Secretary of the Treasury (Domestic Finance).

In 1979 Mr. Mehle joined the firm of Dean Witter Reynolds Inc. as senior vice president and member of the board of directors to head the firm's public finance department. He was chosen as chairman of the municipal finance committee of the Securities Industry Association and elected to the SIA board of directors and executive committee. He began employment with the First Boston Corp. in its professional training program in 1969. After completion of the training program, he joined the public

finance department and was named cohead of the department in 1975. In 1976 Mr. Mehle was elected to the board of directors of the First Boston Corp. and in 1978 was named senior vice president of that firm.

Mr. Mehle was graduated from the U.S. Naval Academy (B.S., 1963) and attended night courses at New York University Graduate School of Business Administration (M.A., 1972) and at Fordham University School of Law (LL.B., 1976).

He served in the U.S. Navy in 1965–69. He is a member of the New York and American Bar Associations. He is a resident of New York City and was born in Long Beach, Calif., on December 28, 1941.

Nomination of John A. Svahn To Be Commissioner of Social Security
March 3, 1981

The President today announced his intention to nominate John A. Svahn to be Commissioner of Social Security, Department of Health and Human Services. Mr. Svahn is currently a private consultant specializing in public policy management problems.

From 1976 to 1979, Mr. Svahn was manager of government services for Deloitte Haskins & Sells, serving as a specialist in investigating Medicaid, welfare, and social services programs. In 1975 and 1976, he served as Administrator of the U.S. Social and Rehabilitation Service. In 1975 he directed the U.S. Office of Child Support En-

forcement. Mr. Svahn has also served as Deputy Administrator, U.S. Social and Rehabilitation Service; Commissioner, Assistance Payments Administration; Acting Commissioner, Community Services Administration; and chief deputy director and director of the California Department of Social Welfare.

Mr. Svahn received a B.A. degree in political science from the University of Washington in 1966. He is married, with two children, and resides in Severna Park, Md. Mr. Svahn was born in New London, Conn., on May 13, 1943.

Nomination of Philip F. Johnson To Be a Commissioner of the Commodity Futures Trading Commission, and Designation as Chairman
March 3, 1981

The President today announced his intention to nominate Philip F. Johnson to be Commissioner of the Commodity Futures Trading Commission. Upon confirmation the President intends to designate Mr. Johnson as Chairman for the term expiring April 13, 1984.

Mr. Johnson is a partner with the firm of Kirkland & Ellis of Chicago, Ill., where he has specialized in the Commodity Exchange Act and its regulations for 15 years. Mr. Johnson has been a speaker and a panelist at seminars and conferences on the Commodity Exchange Act sponsored by the Federal Bar Association, the Bureau of National Affairs, the American Law Institute, the Futures Industry Association, the Chicago Board of Trade, the American Bar Association, and other groups. He has served as a member of the Commodity Futures Trading Commission's Advisory Committee on

the Definition and Regulation of Market Instruments and is a member of the CFTC Advisory Committee on State Jurisdiction and Responsibilities.

Mr. Johnson is a member of the governing council of the American Bar Association's Section of Corporation, Banking and Business Law, the ABA's largest professional group, and has served as chairman of the ABA's Committee on Commodities Regulation since its creation in 1976.

Mr. Johnson has authored many articles on the Commodity Exchange Act. He serves as a member of the board of directors of the commodity industry's national trade association, the Futures Industry Association.

Mr. Johnson was graduated from Indiana University (A.B., 1959) and Yale Law School (LL.B., 1962). He resides in Chicago, Ill., and is 42 years old.

Nomination of J. Lynn Helms To Be Administrator of the Federal Aviation Administration
March 3, 1981

The President today announced his intention to nominate J. Lynn Helms to be Administrator of the Federal Aviation Administration, Department of Transportation.

Mr. Helms retired in 1980 as chairman of the board of Piper Aircraft Corp., having been elected to that post in September 1978. He served as president of Piper from July 1974 to September 1978 and as chief executive officer from July 1974 to September 1979.

Previously Mr. Helms was group vice president of the Bendix Corp. and president of the Norden Division of United Technologies.

In 1980 he served as chairman of the board of the General Aviation Manufacturers Association. Mr. Helms is active in many other aviation-related organizations. He is a member of the State of Arkansas National Advisory Board, a fellow in the American Institute of Aeronautics Association, a director of the Pennsylvania State Chamber of Commerce, and a member of the Society of Experimental Test Pilots. He was elected to the Pioneers Club for being the first aviator to exceed 1,000 mph in combat aircraft. Mr. Helms is a regular guest lecturer at the University of Michigan Graduate Business School and the Industrial College in Washington, D.C. He was selected for the General James H. Doolittle award and trophy in September 1980.

Mr. Helms has logged well over 10,000 hours of flight time and holds an active commercial certificate. He continues to log nearly 350 hours annually.

Born in DeQueen, Ark., on March 1, 1925, Mr. Helms attended Oklahoma University. During World War II, he completed U.S. Navy flight training and entered the U.S. Marine Corps. He resides in Westport, Conn.

Excerpts From an Interview With Walter Cronkite of CBS News
March 3, 1981

El Salvador

Mr. Cronkite. Mr. President, with your administration barely 6 weeks old, you're involved now in, perhaps, the first foreign policy crisis—if it can be called a crisis yet; probably cannot be, but it is being much discussed, of course—much concern about El Salvador and our commitment there. Do you see any parallel in our committing advisers and military assistance to El Salvador and the early stages of our involvement in Vietnam?

The President. No, Walter, I don't. I know that that parallel is being drawn by many people. But the difference is so profound. What we're actually doing is, at the request of a government in one of our neighboring countries, offering some help against the import or the export into the Western Hemisphere of terrorism, of disruption. And it isn't just El Salvador. That happens to be the target at the moment. Our problem is this whole hemisphere and keeping this sort of thing out.

Now, we have sent briefing teams to Europe, down to our Latin American neighbors with what we've learned of the actual involvement of the Soviet Union, of Cuba, of the PLO, of, even Qadhafi in Libya, and others in the Communist bloc nations to bring about this terrorism down there.

Now, you use the term "military advisers." You know, there's sort of technicality there. You could say they are advisers in that they're training, but when it's used as "adviser," that means military men who go in and accompany the forces into combat, advise on strategy and tactics. We have no one of that kind. We're sending and have sent teams down there to train. They do not accompany them into combat. They train recruits in the garrison area. And as a matter of fact, we have such training teams in more than 30 countries today, and we've always done that—the officers of the military in friendly countries and in our neighboring countries have come to our service schools—West Point, Annapolis, and so forth. So, I don't see any parallel at all.

And I think it is significant that the terrorists, the guerrilla activity in El Salvador was supposed to cause an uprising, that the government would fall because the people would join this aggressive force and support them. The people are totally against that and have not reacted in that way.

Mr. Cronkite. Well, that's one of the questions that's brought up about the wisdom of our policy right at the moment. Some Latin Americans feel that President Duarte has control of the situation. The people have not risen. This last offensive of the guerrillas did not work, and therefore aren't we likely to exacerbate the situation by American presence there now, therefore sort of promoting a self-fulfilling prophecy by coming down there and getting the guerrillas and the people themselves upset about "big brother" intervention, and therfore losing the game instead of winning it.

The President. Well, no, and we realize that our southern friends down there do have memories of the "great colossus of the North" and so forth—but no, his government has asked for this because of the need for training against terrorist and guerrilla activities, has asked for materiel such as helicopters and so forth that can be better at interdicting the supply lines where these illicit weapons are being brought in to the guerrillas, and this is what we've provided. And some of these teams that have been provided are also to help keep those machines in the air and on the water—patrol boats and so forth—to try to interdict the supply by water of weapons and ammunition. They need help in repair. They get laid up for repairs, and they don't have the qualified technicians.

Mr. Cronkite. What really philosophically is different from our going down to help a democratic government sustain itself against guerrilla activity promoted from the outside—Soviet and Cuban aid, as we believe it to be; your administration says it is—and Afghanistan? El Salvador is in our sort of geopolitical sphere of influence. Afghanistan, on the border of the Soviet Union, is certainly in their geopolitical sphere of influence. They went in with troops to support a Marxist government friendly to them. Why isn't that a parallel situation?

The President. Well, I don't think there can be a parallel there, because I was in Iran in '78 when the first coup came about, and it was the Soviet Union that put their man as President of Afghanistan. And then their man didn't work out to their satisfaction, so, they came in and got rid of him and brought another man that they'd been training in Moscow and put him in as their President. And then, with their armed forces, they are trying to subdue the people of Afghanistan who do not want this pro-Soviet government that has been installed by an outside force.

The parallel would be that without actually using Soviet troops, in effect, the Soviets are, you might say, trying to do the same thing in El Salvador that they did in Afghanistan, but by using proxy troops through Cuba and guerrillas. And they had hoped for, as I said, an uprising of the people that would then give them some legitimacy in the government that would be installed—the Communist government—but the people didn't rise up. The people have evidenced their desire to have the government they have and not be ruled by these guerrillas.

Mr. Cronkite. Secretary of State Haig has said that we'll not have a Vietnam in El Salvador, because the United States will direct its action toward Cuba, which is the main source of the intervention, in his words. But Cuba is a client state of the Soviet Union. It's not likely to stand by and let us take direct action against Cuba, is it?

The President. Well, that term "direct action," there are a lot of things open—diplomacy, trade, a number of things—and Secretary Haig has explained his use of the term, the source with regard to Cuba means the intercepting and stopping of the supplies coming into these countries—the export from Cuba of those arms, the training of the guerrillas as they've done there. And I don't think in any way that he was suggesting an assault on Cuba.

Mr. Cronkite. That intercepting and stopping means blockade. And isn't that an act of war?

The President. Well, this depends. If you intercept them when they're landing at the other end or find them where they're in the locale such as, for example, Nicaragua, and informing Nicaragua that we're aware of the part that they have played in this, using diplomacy to see that a country decides they're not going to allow themselves to be used anymore. There's been a great slowdown—we're watching it very carefully, Nicaragua—of the transfer of arms to El Salvador. This doesn't mean that they're not coming in from other guerrilla bases in other countries there.

Mr. Cronkite. You've said that we could extricate ourselves easily from El Salvador if that were required at any given point in this proceeding. I assume you mean at any given point. How could we possibly extricate ourselves? Even now, from this initial stage, how could we extricate ourselves without a severe loss of face?

The President. Well, I don't think we're planning on having to extricate ourselves from there. But the only thing that I could see that could have brought that about is if the guerrillas had been correct in their assessment and there had been the internal disturbance. Well, then it would be a case of we're there at the behest of the present government. If that government is no longer there, we're not going there without an invitation. We're not forcing ourselves upon them, and you'd simply leave—and there aren't that many people to be extricated.

Mr. Cronkite. Even if the Duarte forces begin to lose with whatever military materiel assistance we give them, whatever training advisers we give them, are you pledging that we will not go in with fighting forces?

The President. I certainly don't see any likelihood of us going in with fighting forces. I do see our continued work in the field of diplomacy with neighboring countries that are interested in Central America and South America to bring this violence to a halt and to make sure that we do not just sit passively by and let this hemisphere be invaded by outside forces.

U.S.-Soviet Relations

Mr. Cronkite. Moving on. Your hard line toward the Soviet Union is in keeping with your campaign statements, your promises. But there are some who, while applauding that stance, feel that you might have overdone the rhetoric a little bit in laying into the Soviet leadership as being liars and thieves, et cetera.

The President. Well, now, let's recap. I am aware that what I said received a great deal of news attention, and I can't criticize the news media for that. I said it. But the thing that seems to have been ignored—well, two things—one, I did not volunteer that statement. This was not a statement that I went in and called a press conference and said, "Here, I want to say the following." I was asked a question. And the question was, what did I think were Soviet aims? Where did I think the Soviet Union was going? And I had made it clear to them, I said, "I don't have to offer my opinion. They have told us where they're going over and over again. They have told us that their goal is the Marxian philosophy of world revolution and a single, one-world Communist state and that they're dedicated to that."

And then I said we're naive if we don't recognize in their performance of that, that they also have said that the only morality—remember their ideology is without God, without our idea of morality in the religious sense—their statement about morality is that nothing is immoral if it furthers their cause, which means they can resort to lying or stealing or cheating or even murder if it furthers their cause, and that is not immoral. Now, if we're going to deal with them, then we have to keep that in mind when we deal with them. And I've noticed that with their own statements about me and their attacks on me since I answered that question that way—it is the only statement I've made—they have never denied the truth of what I said.

Mr. Cronkite. You don't think that namecalling, if you could call it that, makes it more difficult when you do finally, whenever that is, sit down across the table from Mr. Brezhnev and his cohorts?

The Presdent. No, I've been interested to see that he has suggested having a summit meeting since I said that.

Mr. Cronkite. Let me ask another question about being tough with the Russians. When Ambassador Dobrynin of the Soviet Union drove over to the State Department for the first time after the administration came in, his car was turned away at the entrance to the basement garage, which he had been using, told that he had to use the street door like all the other diplomats had been doing. It was obviously tipped to the press that this was going to happen.

What advantage is there in embarrassing the Soviet Ambassador like that? A phone call would have said, "Hey, you can't use that door any longer." Was that just a macho thing for domestic consumption or——

The President. I have to tell you, I didn't know anything about it until I read it in the paper, saw it on television myself. I don't know actually how that came about or what the decision was, whether it was just one of those bureaucratic things in the——

Mr. Cronkite. You didn't ask Secretary Haig about it?

The President. No, and I just don't know——

Mr. Cronkite. Don't you think the Russians kind of think we're childish when we pull one like that?

The President. I don't know. I don't know, or maybe they got a message.

Mr. Cronkite. What conditions do have to be satisfied before you would agree to a summit meeting with Brezhnev?

The President. Well, I think it isn't a case of—well, there are some things that I think would help bring that about. The main thing is you don't just call up and say, "Yeah, let's get together and have lunch." A summit meeting of that kind takes a lot of preparation. And the first preparation from our standpoint is the pledge that we've made to our allies, that we won't take unilateral steps. We'll only do things after full consultation with them, because they're involved also. And I've had an opportunity to talk a little bit about it just—it only came to

light, his statement, a short time ago—with Prime Minister Thatcher when she was here. So, we haven't had the opportunity for the consultations about that that would be necessary.

I have said that I will sit and negotiate with them for a reduction in strategic nuclear weapons to lower the threshold of danger that exists in the world today. Well, one of the things—you say "conditions"—I think one of them would be some evidence on the part of the Soviet Union that they are willing to discuss that. So far, previous Presidents, including my predecessor, tried to bring negotiations to the point of actual reduction, and the Soviet Union refused. They refused to discuss that. I think that we would have to know that they're willing to do that.

I think it would help bring about such a meeting if the Soviet Union revealed that it is willing to moderate its imperialism, its aggression—Afghanistan would be an example. We could talk a lot better if there was some indication that they truly wanted to be a member of the peace-loving nations of the world, the free world.

Mr. Cronkite. Isn't that really what you have to negotiate? I mean, is it really conceivable that you're going to get such a change of heart, a change of statement that you could believe on that part of the Soviet Union before you ever sit down to talk with President Brezhnev?

The President. Well, is that subject a negotiation? If you sit at a table and say, "We want you to get out of Afghanistan," and they're going to say, "No," what do you do? Let them go in someplace else if they'll get out of there?

I remember when Hitler was arming and had built himself up—no one's created quite the military power that the Soviet Union has, but comparatively he was in that way—Franklin Delano Roosevelt made a speech in Chicago at the dedication of a bridge over the Chicago River. And in that speech he called on the free world to quarantine Nazi Germany, to stop all communication, all trade, all relations with them until they gave up that militaristic course and agreed to join with the free nations of the world in a search for peace.

Mr. Cronkite. That did a whale of a lot of good.

The President. Oh, but the funny thing was he was attacked so here in our own country for having said such a thing. Can we honestly look back now and say that World War II would have taken place if we had done what he wanted us to do back in 1938? I think there's a very good chance it wouldn't have taken place.

But again, as I say, some evidence from the Soviet Union, I think, would be very helpful in bringing about a meeting.

Mr. Cronkite. It sounds as if, sir, you're saying that there isn't going to be any summit meeting with Brezhnev.

The President. No, I haven't put that as a hard and fast condition. I'm just saying that in discussing with our allies, it would make it a lot easier if we were able to say, "Well now, look, they've shown some signs of moderating their real imperialistic course." You know, when we look at where they are and with their surrogates, Qadhafi in Chad, Cuba in Angola, Cuba and East Germans in Ethiopia, in South Yemen, and of course, now the attempt here in our own Western Hemisphere.

Mr. Cronkite. Well, I hate to belabor this, but since the whole world is looking forward, I think, to eventually some negotiations to stop the arms race, to get off of this danger point, it is an important thing, and I gather that the Soviet Union has to make a unilateral move—to their point, it would be backwards, that they'd, let's say, get out of Afghanistan. Do they have to get out of Afghanistan before you'd meet?

The President. No, I haven't said that. And, Walter, I can't really say a specific answer to any of these things unless and until I have met with and discussed this whole problem with allies who, you know, are only a bus ride from Russia.

Mr. Cronkite. They seem to be saying, as near as we can tell, in their press and elsewhere, that they're saying they're anxious for you to meet on arms control. They're anxious to get arms control discussions going. They're terribly concerned about that. They're fearful that you're not going to want to negotiate until such time as you get your defense program and your economic program through Congress and feel that you're negotiating from strength, and that they're fearful that that's going to be some time—and too late.

The President. Well, too late for what is the question. No, I don't know, but I do believe this: that it is rather foolish to have unilaterally disarmed, you might say, as we did by letting our defensive, our margin of safety deteriorate, and then you sit with the fellow who's got all the arms. What do you have to negotiate with? You're asking him to come down to where you are, or you to build up to where he is, but you don't have anything to trade.

So, maybe realistic negotiations could take place. When? We can say, "Well, all right, this thing we're building we'll stop if you'll stop doing whatever it is you're really doing."

Mr. Cronkite. You campaigned on lifting the grain embargo—the Soviet Union. You delayed doing that so far, because you, I gather, feel it would send the Russians the wrong message, perhaps, if you did. Senator Helms has suggested perhaps that the grain embargo should be extended to a general boycott of all U.S. trade with the Soviet Union. Is that an option that you're studying?

The President. Well, I don't think you rule out anything. Actually, my campaigning was more on my criticism that the embargo shouldn't have taken place the way it did in the first place, that if we were going to go that route, then it should have been a general embargo. We shouldn't have asked just one segment of our society—and not even agriculture, just the grain farmers—to bear the burden of this, when at the same time we knew we could not enforce or persuade friendly nations to us who would be tempted to take over that market. And many of them did, started supplying the grain that we weren't supplying. So, the question was: Were we hurting ourselves worse than we were hurting them? Certainly it didn't stop the invasion of Afghanistan. And I criticized this.

At the same time—and we have made no decision now on it—I would like to lift the embargo. I think all of us would. But at the same time, now and with Poland added, the situation in Poland to Afghanistan and all,

195

we have to think very hard as to whether we can just go forward unilaterally and do this.

Mr. Cronkite. Because in effect it has been effective. They are having problems with grain supply there, are they not?

The President. Well, I think they'll always have problems with supply, because they insist on that collective farm business, which never has worked and isn't going to work in the future.

You know, this is something that I've never been able to understand about the Russian leaders. Wouldn't you think sometime they would take a look at their system and say, "We can't provide enough food to feed our people," to say nothing of other consumer items that are still rationed and scarce in supply under that system? And yet, we can look at these other countries in the world, all the countries that chose this way—not only the United States but South Korea, Taiwan, all the countries that choose the free marketplace—their standard of living goes up and up. Our problem isn't one of not raising enough food; it's not finding enough places to sell it.

Human Rights

Mr. Cronkite. What place do you think human rights should have in our foreign policy?

The President. I think human rights is very much a part of our American idealism. I think they do play an important part. My criticism of them, in the last few years, was that we were selective with regard to human rights.

We took countries that were pro-Western, that were maybe authoritarian in government, but not totalitarian, more authoritarian than we would like, did not meet all of our principles of what constitutes human rights, and we punished them at the same time that we were claiming détente with countries where there are no human rights. The Soviet Union is the greatest violator today of human rights in all the world. Cuba goes along with it, and yet, previously, while we were enforcing human rights with others, we were talking about bettering relations with Castro's Cuba.

I think that we ought to be more sincere about our position of human rights.

Mr. Cronkite. Do you believe that our requirements for military allies and bases should take precedence over human rights considerations?

The President. No, I think what I'm saying is that where we have an alliance with a country that, as I say, does not meet all of ours, we should look at it that we're in a better position remaining friends, to persuade them of the rightness of our view on human rights than to suddenly, as we have done in some places, pull the rug out from under them and then let a completely totalitarian takeover that denies what human rights the people had had.

Mr. Cronkite. Doesn't that put us in the position rather of abetting the suppression of human rights for our own selfish ends, at least temporarily, until such time as we can make those persuasive changes?

The President. Well, what has the choice turned out to be? The choice has turned out to be they lose all human rights because there's a totalitarian takeover.

Mr. Cronkite. Your appointment to the head of the human rights section over at the State Department is Mr. Ernest Lefever, of course. He testified to the House Subcommittee in '79, "In my view, the United States should remove from the statute books all clauses that establish a human rights standard or condition that must be met by another sovereign nation." Do you agree with that flat statement?

The President. Well, I've never had a chance to discuss with him just how he views that or what he believes the course would take. I do, however, believe that contrary to some of the attacks against him, that he's as concerned about human rights as the rest of us. But I think what he means is that basic human rights and the violation of them are being ignored by us where they take place in the Communist bloc nations.

Mr. Cronkite. He says also that we should not be concerned with South Africa's racial policies, but should make the country a full-fledged partner of the United States in the struggle against Communist expansion. Should we drop all of our concerns about human rights in South Africa?

The President. No, no, and I think, though, that there's been a failure, maybe for political reasons in this country, to recognize how many people, black and white, in South Africa are trying to remove apartheid and the steps that they've taken and the gains that they've made. As long as there's a sincere and honest effort being made, based on our own experience in our own land, it would seem to me that we should be trying to be helpful. And can we, again, take that other course? Can we abandon a country that has stood beside us in every war we've ever fought, a country that strategically is essential to the free world in its production of minerals we all must have and so forth?

I just feel that, myself, that here, if we're going to sit down at a table and negotiate with the Russians, surely we can keep the door open and continue to negotiate with a friendly nation like South Africa.

Mr. Cronkite. The Argentinian Government has just arrested internationally respected heads of the principal human rights organization there, seized their list of 6,000 persons who've disappeared under this government. Is the United States going to protest that?

The President. I have not had an opportunity—that just happened, as you know, and I haven't had an opportunity to meet with Secretary Haig on this. In fact, the only information that so far has been presented to me is that it did happen.

Program for Economic Recovery

Mr. Cronkite. Let's move to some domestic affairs, which I think you're rather interested in these days—and the whole country is of course. Now that they face the stone-hard reality of it all, 150 liberal organizations have gotten together to campaign against your budget cuts in social welfare programs. Middle Western and Eastern, Northeastern States are concerned that the programs favor the Sunbelt. Some farm organizations are concerned that the subsidies are being cut, of course, all across the board. Now these people who are beginning to see that they're going to get hurt a little bit on these cuts. Are you still optimistic in the face of all of this opposition that it can be done?

The President. Yes, I expected that opposition. And one of the reasons, I'm optimistic is because we've received 100,000 letters and telegrams since I made the speech on the 18th. We so far have only been able to open and read and catalog about 5,339, I think the figure is. And of that first 5,000-plus messages, 92-and-a-fraction percent are totally in support of our program of what we want to do. I know that polls have been taken, and a national poll recently has shown an even higher percentage of people in support of the program. I know from my own experience in the few times that I get out of here and can meet the citizenry, I find the same thing. It just is true, you feel it, you sense it, you hear it among the people out there.

It's, I'm afraid, a little bit like Senator Long said, that when you start to cut in the budget the slogan in Washington had been for too many years, "Don't cut you and don't cut me, cut that fellow behind the tree." And I think these various groups are representing a lot of people behind the trees.

Mr. Cronkite. Your targeted ceiling on Federal spending is $695½ billion with a $45 billion deficit. How much higher than that in that budget can Congress go without seriously endangering your program?

The President. Well, I have to say that I believe our package has been so carefully worked out that they endanger it if they start picking off any parts of it. Our program is aimed not only at reducing a budget but, with the tax feature of it, at stimulating the economy, increasing productivity, which means more jobs for our people, and which will reduce inflation. And I believe in our program. Yes, there'll be a $45 billion deficit, but just think what that means. That means that that deficit would be double that without our program. And this is why we're presenting it literally in a package.

As a matter of fact, Prime Minister Thatcher told me that she regretted, in her own attempts, that she has been unable to cut government spending as she knew she would have to cure their ills. And she said one of the reasons was that she tried piecemeal, tried piece by piece to get this reduced, that reduced, and one by one, they just knocked it off and turned it down.

Mr. Cronkite. I'm just curious. Did she volunteer that, or did you ask her what went wrong with her program?

The President. No, she volunteered that, yes.

Mr. Cronkite. Well, do you see a parallel there? There is a conservative government, came in with much the same sort of a plan you did to turn back the clock on socialistic advances, a revolutionary approach to change, and it has failed miserably there. Unemployment is higher than any time since the Great Depression. Thousands of small businesses have folded.

The President. Yes.

Mr. Cronkite. Industrial production is low. Why isn't that a parallel to your problem?

The President. Well, you see, I think in her case, we have to recognize how much farther down the road England had gone. She has great industries now that are government-owned monopolies and losing their shirts as a result, because government doesn't run businesses very well. She was up against—well, we've now seen the Labor Party split in its own convention, and the left wing takeover—she was up against that powerful left wing element that was sabotaging. I don't think her experiment is over. I have confidence in her, and I admire her greatly and her courage, and she's still going at it.

I think we might have the same problems, but we still have the infrastructure. We still have this great industrial capacity of ours here. And if people would only look at it, what we're trying to correct that's gone wrong is: Some years ago when things were going better, government was only taking 19 percent of the gross national product; it's been increasing, it's on an upward line if we don't head it off. And so that cost of government plus the fact that the only way we can maintain that is by continued borrowing to the point that we're close to having a trillion dollar debt—a trillion.

Mr. Cronkite. I understand you're still trying to visualize a trillion dollars.

The President. Yes.

Mr. Cronkite. Mr. President, let me ask you about Congress again though. This is the whole core of the thing right now, of course, is getting that program through.

Now, you say you need 100 percent of it. Of course you do. That's what you're after. But realistically—and you're a realistic man—you can't really expect to get all of it through. I mean, there's got to be some failure somewhere along the line of getting it all through there. Are you going to be in the position, politically at any rate, of saying all those thousands out there who are for you to get the cuts made that if Congress cuts this one cent or adds one cent to it, that it's not your responsibility any longer. Congress has failed you and failed the people.

The President. Well, Walter, I virtually have to say that because if I said anything else—I played in the line when I played football—it's like giving the play away and indicating to your opponent where the play's going.

No, I can't—I have to stay with it. I think our package is designed—and the thing that is significant to me about all those people that you mentioned a moment ago that are opposed to the plan, as well as some of those on the Hill who are opposed: No one has brought up an alternative. Those are the people who have been dictating the policies of this country for the last three of four decades, that have put the country in the economic position it is in. Unless they can come up and say, " We are now recommending a change in this direction or that direction to cure what has happened," how can they stand and oppose a program that is designed to cure the economic chaos that they created?

Mr. Cronkite. The supply-siders feel that their program, your program, should get its first results through psychology, that the mere approach to these problems being made in a frontal assault by your administration will encourage people to get out and do the things necessary—invest and save and do the things necessary. The'll have faith in this. Do you see any early results of that yet?

The President. Well, one of the things that the mail we get and one of the things that I hear from pollsters and so forth is to the effect that there is a different attitude, that there is a kind of glow out there among the people and a confidence that things are going to be all right, where, a short time ago, polls were revealing that the people didn't think things were going to get better. Now, maybe that's what they meant.

But also there is this in our package that isn't just psychology. Maybe by a stretch you could call it that. But our program gives a stability down the road ahead. A person can say, "I know what's going to happen for the next few years," even in the 3-year implementing of the tax program. Someone can say, "I have confidence to do this, because I have been told and I know that this is what's going to happen to my tax situation in the years ahead." Business will know that they can invest in plant and that they're going to be allowed a better break in writing off the depreciation and so forth.

Mr. Cronkite. The cuts to be announced March 10th—we've seen some advance information on it. Whether it's entirely correct or not, we have no way of knowing, but the agricultural cuts to be announced, we understand, will cut back Agriculture Department's supplemental food programs, which include milk to children and pregnant women and that sort of thing, dairy products, fruit, to low-income families. Is that in there? Is that the cut?

The President. I can't tell you. We're still going at this, and the program is going to be presented. But, no, what we're talking about, though, in programs of that kind— and this has to do with food stamps too—is not taking those things away from the people who would have no other means of getting them. But program have a way to expand. Bureaucracy has to justify its existence. So, they spread and they accumulate barnacles, and what we're doing is taking a look at some of those barnacles. And you suddenly find and say, "Well, why are we, at taxpayers' expense, providing milk for this particular segment, who are perfectly able to provide it for themselves and other people of no better circumstances are providing it for themselves." The same [is] true of food stamps. These are where we're trying to make the cuts.

I believe that in our seven programs that we call the safety net, below which no one should be allowed to fall, we have not. We

have preserved that safety net. We have not cut that and——

Mr. Cronkite. How far below the present standard of living, even for the poverty groups in the country, is the safety net beyond where it is today?

The President. Well, the safety net is where it should be. But it isn't so much of lowering or raising it, it is a case of finding that around the edge of that safety net, we had acquired a group of people who were benefiting from it who didn't need to be there.

Mr. Cronkite. Well, they say in New York, now—of course, these figures are suspect too in a way because nobody knows precisely—but they're talking about a cut of 20,000 children off the Aid to Dependent Children; there's 30,000 old people off the help to the elderly. Is it your intention that that many people are on this fringe area? And even if they are, isn't it going to create a considerable hardship for them? They're not that much above poverty level.

The President. Walter, I hadn't seen those figures of people doing that. But let me just tell you an experience from California, again which is one that we're going to ride herd on very closely. The permanent structure of government, what we commonly call the bureaucracy, has a great ability of self-defense, to preserve itself. And we found sometimes in our own welfare reforms there that in an effort to focus attention and try to build a case against what we were trying to do, they would deliberately pick out the people who could be harmed the most and interpret what you were trying to do as denying aid to that particular person.

Now, we've had a little example of that: the so-called retroactive freeze on employment and suddenly the terrible stories—and I'm sure many of them true—about people who sold their homes, gave up their jobs, and came to Washington to get a job. But I can't deny the fact or overlook the fact that before November 4th I was saying that one of the first things I would do in the first 24 hours is put a freeze on the hiring of replacements—Federal employees. And, indeed, in the first hour, when after I took the oath and walked back into the Capitol building, I signed that Executive order [memorandum], and suddenly we find thousands of people who were recruited, beginning November 5th, and yet for some reason had not yet been put in their jobs by January 20th. And then the uproar that this was retroactive to November 5th—we didn't say anything about November 5th, but we also didn't realize that they could actually hold people for that long, leaving them to think they had jobs, and yet had not processed them and put them in the jobs. I have to be suspicious of this.

Now, the truth is, many of those people were victims, not of us, they were victims of what I think was a bureaucratic trick. And where we are finding real cases of distress because of that, we are making exceptions, because it wasn't their fault. They didn't know they were being victimized.

Now, I think, when I hear figures like this about who will have to be cut, this again, is the bureaucracy saying, "Okay, where can we make it?" It's like the old Washington story that if you cut the Park Service's budget, the first thing they fire is the elevator man at the Washington Monument and tell the people they've got to walk up 600 feet instead of ride. We're going to be on guard for that.

Mr. Cronkite. On your tax cuts, you cite the experience of the 1961 Kennedy tax cut to prove that it will hype up the economy. But that cut was specifically to stimulate buying, whereas your objective is to stimulate savings and investment. Now, how do you justify that?

The President. Well, whether he said to stimulate buying or not, remember he brought down the top bracket from 91 percent to 70 percent in that—it was over a 2-year period. Actually, he didn't implement the tax cuts, they followed his tragic death and were implemented, but they had been passed.

There is a page from a June issue of U.S. News and World Report, 1966, that I recommend as must reading, because the whole article on that page is about the strange paradox that the 2-year period of phased-in tax cuts, which is somewhat similar to what we're trying to do over 3 years, did not result, as the economists said they would, in an $83 billion loss of revenue to

government. They couldn't explain the paradox that ever since the cuts went into effect the government itself was getting more revenue, because the economy, the economic base, had been broadened and stimulated so each individual had the benefit of the cuts. But there were more individuals involved, so the government even profited. And as I say, that's 1966, in this 2-year program.

We can come up to 1978. The Steiger-Hansen bill that cut the capital gains tax, and the very first year, the government got more revenue from the capital gains tax at the lower rate than it had gotten at the higher. Why? Because suddenly capital gains, we'd removed some of the penalty, and capital gains, for those people who could invest and use capital gains for revenue, had become attractive again. And they did more of it.

Mr. Cronkite. But also, if I may pursue that issue, a 2-percent inflation, 1.2 percent, less than 2-percent inflation was the case in the sixties, mid-sixties. Now it's over 10 percent, it's double-digit. Certainly, with a 10-percent of the tax rate, which isn't a full 10-percent cut, as we know, 10 percent of 50 percent, 10 percent of 20 percent, whatever, 2-percent cut perhaps—but all of that certanly when you've got a 10-percent inflation or more, it's got to go into making up for the inflation among most of the population. Only the very rich can afford to save and invest under these circumstances.

The President. Well, no. Some polls have been taken on that, and they find at the very bottom of the ladder, yes, people say there are things that they will use it for in buying. But from there on up, the overwhelming majority in those polls reveal that they will use it for savings and investment.

Mr. Cronkite. Secretary of Treasury Regan argues that this is not so, because the tax cut will benefit the upper bracket, and the rich will be saving and investing. And yet, the propaganda has been, oh, now, it's going to benefit the lower brackets more than the upper. So, isn't there a dichotomy there?

The President. Well, it's across the board. And there's no question about it. If it's 10 percent, it's a reduction of the rates, the tax rates, 10 percent right from the basic rate of 14 percent now right on up to the top rate and then 10 percent the following, 10 percent the next. And a cut in the tax rates does not follow that dollar for dollar there will be a reduction in government's revenues as these other things that I've given illustrate. But, it's where you define the rich.

The simple truth is that in the income bracket between $10,000 and $60,000—now, I think you have to say, in today's inflated world, we're talking about the great middle class of America, the people who really make this country go—that bracket from ten to sixty thousand is paying today 72 percent of the income tax. They are going to get 73 percent, which I guess is about as close as you could get it, of the benefits of our tax bill. Now, I would say that in there, maybe when you get to 15, and from there up, you're going to be talking to people who will be able to save, invest, buy insurance, things that they're perhaps not able, and then that money becomes capital in the hands of the financial institutions for reinvestment.

Mr. Cronkite. Are you in favor of the Federal Reserve's tight money policy and high interest rates?

The President. I have to say that those high interest rates, I'm afraid, are the result of inflation, because it's as simple as this if you really look at it, although they're going to cooperate in a monetary policy that is geared to what we're trying to do. But if you're asking somone to lend money, when you look down the road and see nothing being done to curb inflation and inflation is running back to back now for 2 years, the person that's lending the money has to get an interest rate that will show that when he gets his money back he's getting back as much or more than he loaned. So, it is inflation that dictates that high interest rate. The interest rate has to be higher than the inflation rate or no one can afford to lend the money.

Mr. Cronkite. But if we cut the high interest rate then that would dampen inflation—if you could do it that way, but we can't do it.

The President. No, I think the other came first.

Mr. Cronkite. If I may, we are running kind of out of time. I've got a few that if we can keep it real short——

The President. All right.

Mr. Cronkite.——well, maybe we can still get a few more in.

Illegal Aliens

Mr. Cronkite. Illegal immigration is one of the major problems we have in the country today, and the congressional task force has just come in with a study on it. One of its recommendations, besides putting responsibility on employers not to hire illegal aliens, is to provide some means of identification for the aliens so that the employer will know who he's hiring. Would you support some form of national identification that could help attack this problem?

The President. Well, now, I'm very intrigued by a program that's been suggested by several border State Governors and their counterparts in the Mexican States on the other side of the border. They have met together on this problem. We have to remember we have a neighbor and a friendly nation on an almost 2,000-mile border down there. And they have an unemployment rate that is far beyond anything—a safety valve has to be some of that that we're calling "illegal immigration" right now. What these Governors have come up with—and I'm very intrigued with it—is a proposal that we and the Mexican Government get together and legalize this and grant visas, because it is to our interest also that that safety valve is not shut off and that we might have a breaking of the stability south of the border.

At the same time, that would then make these people in our country—an employer could not take advantage of them and work them at sweatshop wages and so forth under the threat of turning them in. They at the same time, then, would be paying taxes in this country for whatever they earned. They would be able to go legally back across the border if they wanted to, and come back across. But the border would become a two-way border for all people.

And I'm very intrigued with that. I'd like to talk about it and intend to, in April when I meet with President López Portillo.

Views on the Presidency

Mr. Cronkite. Final question. What's the greatest surprise that you've experienced in the Presidency?

The President. Walter, that's a—I know you're running out of time, and here I am hemming and hawing. I guess it's every once in a while realizing that you are—you know, it isn't as if suddenly something happens to you. I don't feel any different than I did before, and then now and then something happens, and you're caught by surprise. You say, "Well, why are they doing that?" And maybe that's it.

I'm not surprised by the amount of work. As I've often said, I'm not surprised about the confinement of living in the White House. I lived above the store when I was a kid, and it's much like that. So, I guess I can't find anything other than that.

Maybe it all started due to some of you gentlemen on the air on Election Day. You'd think that that'd be a very dramatic moment, and I was worrying that it was going to be a moment that would last all night, waiting for the returns to come in. I was in the shower and was called out of the shower, just getting ready to go out, late afternoon, when the President was on the other end of the phone. I was wrapped in a towel and dripping wet, and he told me that he was conceding. And that wasn't the way I'd pictured it.

Mr. Cronkite. That was the biggest surprise?

The President. Yes.

Mr. Cronkite. Thank you very much, Mr. President.

The President. Well, thank you, Walter. It's good to be here again. And I know you must be having a little nostalgia, the many Presidents that you've covered in this very room.

Mr. Cronkite. Indeed so, sir. It's been a long time now. I was counting back. It's eight Presidents. It's been a remarkable period in our history.

The President. Well, may I express appreciation. You've always been a pro.

Mr. Cronkite. I only regret that I'm stepping down from the evening news at the time when you are bringing such drama to our government again in your efforts to turn it around.

Thank you, sir.

The President. Thank you.

Note: The interview began at 1:22 p.m. in the Oval Office at the White House. It was taped for later broadcast on the CBS television network.

Proclamation 4832—World Trade Week, 1981
March 3, 1981

By the President of the United States of America

A Proclamation

International trade is an important means of furthering America's friendly international relations and of bettering the lives of all Americans.

Trade stimulates competition, stirs our creative energies, rewards individual initiative and increases national productivity. Among nations, it speeds the exchange of new ideas and technology.

As products made in this country compete successfully in world markets, we contribute to the strength and stability of our dollar, the expansion of our industry and fuller employment of our labor force.

For these reasons, the United States remains firmly committed to an active world trade role in the context of an increasingly interrelated international economy. A reciprocal spirit of world cooperation, permitting fair trade and investment between our country and the rest of the world, is indispensable to all of us.

Now, Therefore, I, Ronald Reagan, President of the United States of America, do hereby proclaim the week beginning May 17, 1981, as World Trade Week, and I urge the people of the United States to cooperate in observing that week with activities that promote the importance of trade to our national well-being at home and abroad.

In Witness Whereof, I have hereunto set my hand this third day of March in the year of our Lord nineteen hundred and eighty-one, and of the Independence of the United States of America the two hundred and fifth.

RONALD REAGAN

[*Filed with the Office of the Federal Register, 2:35 p.m., March 4, 1981*]

Note: The text of the proclamation was released by the Office of the Press Secretary on March 4.

Nomination of Stephen May To Be an Assistant Secretary of Housing and Urban Development
March 4, 1981

The President today announced his intention to nominate Stephen May to be an Assistant Secretary of Housing and Urban Development (Legislation).

Mr. May was with the firm of Branch, Turner and Wise of Rochester, N.Y., for the past 12 years. He served as mayor of Rochester in 1970–73. He was commissioner and chairman of the New York State Board of Elections in 1975–79, and a member of the Repblican State Platform Committee in 1978. He was a Rochester city councilman in 1966–73. Mr. May was executive assistant to Representative, and later, Senator Kenneth B. Keating in 1955-64.

Mr. May has been vice president, New York State Conference of Mayors; chairman of the Committee on Housing, White House Conference on Aging; and chairman of the board, Empire State Report (the journal of government and politics in New York State).

Mr. May is a graduate of Wesleyan University and Georgetown University. He is a veteran of the U.S. Army. Mr. May was born on July 30, 1931, in Rochester, N.Y.

Nomination of Arthur E. Teele, Jr., To Be Administrator of the Urban Mass Transportation Administration
March 4, 1981

The President today announced his intention to nominate Arthur E. Teele, Jr., to be Urban Mass Transportation Administrator, Department of Transportation.

Mr. Teele was team leader of the Department of Transportation transition group. He was national director of the voter groups division of the Reagan-Bush Committee in August–November 1980.

Mr. Teele practiced law in Tallahassee, Fla., from 1976 to 1980. He is an expert on tax, regulatory, and labor-management relations. He served as a congressional intern in the U.S. House of Representatives, and developed legislative and taxation proposals for the Florida State Legislature.

He is member of the Florida and American Bar Associations. Mr. Teele was an officer in the U.S. Army in 1967–76. He was awarded the Bronze Star for Valor, Bronze Star for Service, Purple Heart, Air Medal with two clusters, and Cross of Gallantry.

He was graduated from Florida A & M University (B.S.) and Florida State University College of Law (J.D.). He is a resident of Tallahassee, Fla.

Nomination of Lawrence S. Eagleburger To Be an Assistant Secretary of State
March 4, 1981

The President today announced his intention to nominate Lawrence S. Eagleburger to be an Assistant Secretary of State (European Affairs).

Since 1977 Mr. Eagleburger has served as Ambassador to Yugoslavia. He was Deputy Under Secretary for Management, Department of State, in 1975–77. Mr. Eagleburger was Executive Assistant to the Secretary of State in 1973–75.

In 1973 he was Deputy Assistant to the President for National Security Operations. Mr. Eagleburger was Deputy Assistant Secretary of the Department of Defense in 1971–73. He was political adviser to the Counselor for Political Affairs, U.S. Mission to NATO, in 1969–71. In 1969 he was executive assistant to the Assistant to the President for National Security Affairs. In 1967–69 Mr. Eagleburger was special assistant to the Under Secretary of State and a member of the National Security Council in 1966–67.

Mr. Eagleburger was graduated from the University of Wisconsin (B.S., 1952; M.S., 1957). His residence is in Daytona Beach, Fla. He was born in Milwaukee, Wis., on August 1, 1930.

Statement Announcing Additional Federal Aid for Programs Relating to the Murdered and Missing Youth in Atlanta, Georgia
March 5, 1981

One of the most tragic problems facing our nation is the murder of 19 children and the disappearance of 2 others in Atlanta.

As President, I have expressed in the strongest terms my outrage regarding this crisis, and as a citizen, I continue to share the boundless hurt suffered by the stricken families and the community at large.

Vice President Bush has been deeply involved, at my personal request, in overseeing the Federal efforts—now being coordinated by an Atlanta task force—in both the investigative aspects of the cases and in providing needed heatlh and community services.

To further support this continued Federal effort and the efforts of local officials and agencies, I am announcing that an additional $979,000 in Federal funds for a variety of programs requested by Mayor Maynard Jackson will be forthcoming from the Justice Department and other Federal agencies.

These funds will be used to provide after-school guidance and care for 1,000 youths in six areas where most of the murders have occurred, to establish a 24-hour hotline to provide counseling for parents and children, and to provide facilities to house disadvantaged or homeless teenage youths. Additional programs will be created to involve the city's youth in crime prevention projects.

Part of the money will be used also to effectively coordinate and administer the thousands of offers of aid that have been generously made from corporations, private citizens, State, Federal, and local agencies.

Of the total, $650,000 will be made available immediately from the Justice Department's Office of Juvenile Justice and Delinquency Prevention, and the remaining $329,000 will come from other Federal agencies with the juvenile justice agency coordinating that effort.

This aid is in addition to contributions of money or manpower from the Federal Bureau of Investigation, the Law Enforce-

ment Assistance Administration, the Community Relations Service, the Department of Education, and the Department of Health and Human Services.

The senseless and brutal murders of these children is deeply and painfully etched in the consciousness of our people.

Along with all Americans, we hope that this nightmare will soon end.

Nomination of Two Associate Judges of the Superior Court of the District of Columbia
March 5, 1981

The President has nominated Henry F. Greene and Ricardo M. Urbina to be Associate Judges of the Superior Court of the District of Columbia for terms of 15 years.

Mr. Greene graduated from Harvard College in 1963 (A.B.) and Columbia Law School in 1966 (LL.B.). Mr. Greene clerked for Chief Judge Bryant of the United States District Court and has served for over 13 years as an assistant United States attorney, including nearly 11 years as an attorney supervisor. He has served as deputy chief of the old Court of General Sessions division, teaching and directing the efforts of new trial assistants (1966–70); executive assistant United States attorney, the third highest ranking position in that office of over 160 lawyers (1972–77); and director of Superior

Court operations, supervising 79 assistant United States Attorneys (1977–present). He was born on June 17, 1941.

Mr. Urbina graduated from Georgetown University in 1967 (B.A.) and Georgetown University Law School in 1970 (J.D.). He was admitted to the District of Columbia Bar on November 23, 1970, and was a staff attorney for the Public Defender Service from 1970 until 1972. He was in private practice until 1974, when he left to begin a teaching career with Howard University School of Law. Mr. Urbina teaches torts and criminal procedure and has been supervisor and director of the Howard University Criminal Justice Clinic since 1974. He was born on January 31, 1946.

The President's News Conference
March 6, 1981

The President. How do you do? I have a brief opening statement before turning to your questions.

Reduction in Federal Employment

Today I'm instructing the Office of Management and Budget to include in the budget package that we will send to Congress next Tuesday a plan for the reduction of nondefense personnel in the Federal

Government. Under this plan we will replace the temporary hiring freeze with new, permanent ceilings that will reduce Federal employment by nearly 33,000 this fiscal year and another 63,100 in 1982 compared to the personnel projections of the last administration. In just 2 years these reductions will save the taxpayers $1.3 billion.

Millions of Americans today have had to tighten their belts because of the economic conditions, and it's time to put Washington on a diet, too. Gaining control of the size of govenment, getting our economy back on track, will not wait. We'll have to act now. And we'll continue to search for ways to cut the size of government and reduce the amount of Federal spending and achieve a trimmer, more efficient, more responsive government for all the people.

And now we shall get on with our first attempt at "Reagan roulette." [*Referring to a lottery that determined which reporters asked questions at the news conference*] [*Laughter*] Jim [Jim Gerstenzang, Associated Press].

El Salvador

Q. Mr. President, your Secretary of State has said that you would strongly oppose a right-wing takeover of the government in El Salvador, while your own White House spokesman has been less definite. Just how strongly would you oppose such a coup, and would it result in a complete cutoff of American aid, both economic and military?

The President. Well, I think what we're all intending to say is that we would have to view very seriously such an attempt and such a coup. We're there at the request of the government. We're supporting a government which we believe has an intention of improving the society there for the benefit of the people, and we're opposed to terrorism of the right or left. And so, we would have to view very seriously—I can't answer the last part of your question as to exactly what we would do, but it would be of the gravest concern to us if there were such a thing.

Helen [Helen Thomas, United Press International].

Tax Reduction

Q. Mr. President, we know you don't like to tip you hand on legislation before it arrives at your desk, but Mr. Stockman, who speaks with great authority for this administration, and others who've talked to you recently, say that you are considering a veto of the tax bill if it is changed substantially. Do they know whereof they speak?

The President. Well, the veto is a tool of government that belongs to the President, and I've never been reluctant to use it. But you were right in your first statement: I never talk about in advance whether I will

or will not veto.

First of all, I think I should say that I am reasonably optimistic. I'm not looking for a confrontation with the Congress, and I have, I think, sufficient reason to believe that there is great bipartisan support for our program in the Congress. And I'm going to keep trying to work with them so that we won't face that particular problem.

And now, Jim Gerstenzang. No, wait a minute. I'm sorry. I looked at one instead of three. Jim, sorry. Tom DeFrank [Newsweek].

El Salvador

Q. Mr. President, I'd like to ask you a two-part question on El Salvador. First, is a naval blockade an option you are considering? And second, given the fact that several Americans have been murdered in El Salvador in the last several weeks and the advisers you're sending there could well be a special target for terrorists, how do you intend to provide for the personal safety of those advisers? And do you envision the need for American troops as any sort of a security force for those advisers?

The President. Well, there almost were three parts to your question, so let me say the first part is, I won't comment on anything we might be considering in the line of an action with regard to the safety of our personnel. We're taking every precaution we can. We realize that there is a risk and a danger. None of them will be going into combat. None of them will be accompanying El Salvadoran troops on missions of that kind. They will be in what has to be considered as reasonably safe a place as there can be in that country in garrison.

They are there for training of the El Salvador personnel. We can't, I'm sorry to say, make it risk-free, but we shall do our utmost to provide for their safety.

Q. Just to follow up. Do you not see the need for American troops as security forces, in other words?

The President. No, that is not in our reckoning at all. We think we're abiding by what is—nor has it been requested. We've had requested the people that we have sent there already, and we don't foresee the need of any American troops.

Tim Schellhardt [Wall Street Journal].

Program for Economic Recovery

Q. Mr. President, several of your advisers say that you're going to be in deep political hot water if the public doesn't get conclusive evidence, at least by the end of the year, that your economic program is leading to a slowdown in inflation and in reducing unemployment. How long do you think Americans should wait before making a judgment on your program on your program, and to win a good mark from the public, in your mind, what specific progress must be made on the economic front?

The President. I think that one of the—and I hope that the public would understand this—that one of the things that must be realized is we're not promising any instant cure. We don't believe that in the matter of several months or probably even in the first year we're going to see more than beginning signs of recovery, because, remember, we have inherited one budget that still has never been passed—the Government is operating without a passed budget—but in a year that is pretty well gone. So, our first savings in this year are going to be reduced by that fact. October 1st the '82 fiscal year begins.

I think it would be premature, and I think no one should indicate that we are promising an instant cure of these problems. These problems have built up over several decades, and they're not going to go away overnight. But we do believe that as the—if the economies are passed, which—and they should be—and the tax program, we should begin to see some effects, I would think, by the end of the '82 year. First of all, we would see a drastic reduction in the deficit that will take place in the fiscal year '82.

But those things, as they take place, it takes some time before the effect of those is then felt out in the economy.

Steve Holt [Washington Broadcasting Company].

El Salvador

Q. Mr. President, I'd like to get back to El Salvador for a second.

The President. Must you? [*Laughter*]

Q. The United States role there is being compared with its role in Vietnam 15 to 20 years ago. Do you think that's a valid comparison? And also, how do you intend to avoid having El Salvador turn into a Vietnam for this country?

The President. I don't believe it is a valid parallel. I know that many people have been suggesting that. The situation here is, you might say, our front yard; it isn't just El Salvador. What we're doing, in going to the aid of a government that asked that aid of a neighboring country and a friendly country in our hemisphere, is try to halt the infiltration into the Americas by terrorists, by outside interference and those who aren't just aiming at El Salvador but, I think, are aiming at the whole of Central and possibly later South America—and, I'm sure, eventually North America. But this is what we're doing, is trying to stop this destabilizing force of terrorism and guerilla warfare and revolution from being exported in here, backed by the Soviet Union and Cuba and those others that we've named. And we have taken that evidence to some of our allies. So, I think the situation is entirely different.

We do not foresee the need of American troops, as I said earlier, in this, and we're sending, what, some 50-odd personnel for training. Well, we have such training squads in more than 30 countries today. So, this isn't an unusual thing that we are doing.

I keep waiting for someone else just to wave their—Charlotte Blount [Sheridan Broadcasting].

Reductions in Social Programs

Q. Thank you, Mr. President. Despite what Budget Director Stockman says about sharing the burden of the proposed budget cuts, I don't understand how the nation's poor are going to survive with almost across-the-board cuts in social programs. Can you explain this, since your proposed economic plan is not an immediate quick-fix?

The President. Yes, I think I can. We're not cutting into the muscle of a program where it is going to require taking aid away from those people that must have it. First of all, by putting many of the programs that are now categorical grants into block grants, we are getting rid of a rather expensive administrative overhead, which will account for part of the savings. Part of the savings also is going to be the manner in which these programs tend to expand. And then government loosens the regulations a little bit and says, "Well, we ought to include the benefits of the program to people over here or these people over here." And we find that we are giving the benefits of the program to people who do not have real need and for which the program was not originally intended.

I speak with some confidence of this, because this is very much what we did in California with our welfare reforms. We never had a single case turn up after our welfare reforms, and some 350,000 people in that one State disappeared from the welfare rolls. We never had a single case of anyone suddenly appearing and saying, "I am destitute. I've been cut off welfare." As a matter of fact, most of those people disappeared of their own free will, which led us to believe that under the regulations which bound us in our administrative ability, we were unable to really pin down how many people might be getting more than one welfare check. And when they just disappeared as the spotlight began to be turned on, possibly out of recognition that they were now going to be caught, the rolls just shrank. And it's this theory that is behind what we are doing.

Our safety net of programs, the seven we spoke of, is intact. I'm quite sure there will be attempts by those in the bureaucracy who are involved in some of these programs to suggest that there is great distress being caused by them. And we had the experience in California of seeing them actually attempt to penalize some of the truly needy until we could intervene simply to create cases of that kind. We'll be on guard for that.

John Hyde [Des Moines Register and Tribune].

Donations from Private Sources

Q. Sir, the White House is taking a somewhat unusual step of asking private groups to raise money to promote your economic program and to refurbish the White House. Could you tell us why the names of contributors to these programs are not being disclosed? Wouldn't disclosure of the names be a way of assuring the public that there is no conflict of interest?

The President. Well, there can't be any conflict of interest, because we didn't have anything to do with it. We know that such a program is going forward, and we have no contact with it all. But these are people that were so enthused after the presentation was made of the program that, apparently, they are enlisting support just as those who are opposed to it are massing their forces together to oppose the program.

Steve Neal [Chicago Tribune].

Automobile Imports

Q. Mr. President, there appears to be a debate within your administration over whether to have mandatory or voluntary limits on Japanese auto imports. Have you decided which you would recommend going with?

The President. We haven't reached a decision on this. We have a task force under Secretary of Transportation Drew Lewis. We've had one meeting with the task force, a Cabinet meeting, and the second meeting is scheduled for next week, and until then, no decisions have been made. Such things are part of the considerations as well as whatever special things we can do, mainly in the lifting of regulations that have made it more costly to build Amiercan cars and so forth. All of this is going to be discussed and a decision made when we have the final report in from the task force.

I think also that, again, we get back to our economic program. I think that in itself is one of the first steps in helping not only that industry but other industries.

Susan King [ABC News].

El Salvador

Q. Mr. President, I'd like to ask this question in context of the campaign. One of the major issues was what was called the "war issue" at that time, in fact the question of whether you would be more toward war than Mr. Carter. And in fact, exit polls showed that some of those who voted did feel that you might get us into one faster. The first major issue in foreign policy has been El Salvador, which has been called risky and reckless by some, and which the allies—who you have shown in your many times that are very important and key to any question—have not jumped on the bandwagon supporting you in El Salvador. In fact, in Canada there's some controversy. Aren't you worried about that fact, especially since you go to Canada this week?

The President. Not really, when you stop to think that I didn't start the El Salvador thing. I inherited it. And the previous administration, which probably was as vociferous as anyone in talking about my threat to peace, they were doing what we're doing, sending aid to El Salvador of the same kind of aid that we're sending. So, I don't think that I'm doing anything that warrants that charge, while I didn't think I warranted it before. And I've been here more than 6 weeks now and haven't fired a shot. [*Laughter*]

Diane Curtis [United Press International].

Q. Mr. President, in addition to your decision to send military aid and advisers to El Salvador, what specific steps have you taken to ensure that human rights violations there are not repeated?

The President. What steps to be sure that human rights violations will not be repeated? As you know, an investigation was going forward with regard to an episode that happened before I took office. But in addition to the military aid, we are also supplying general aid and they know our position with regard to the reforms that the Duarte government has been trying to implement—the land reform, creating of farms for the former tenants—and we support all of that. And one of our reasons for the support of this government is because we believe that they do hold out the best hope for improving the conditions of the people of El Salvador.

So, we're mindful of that, and we think that the—when the terrorists themselves, the guerrillas, boast of having killed—and they give a number somewhere above 6,000 people in the last year—and that's their own claim of what they've accomplished, we think that we are helping the forces that are supporting human rights in El Salvador.

Sarah McClendon [McClendon News Service].

Presidential Appointments

Q. Mr. President, sir, in the case of Mrs. Patricia Bailey, who was supposed to be named Chairman of the Federal Trade Commission and who 12 hours beforehand had the ill fate to make a speech criticizing the cutback in money for her agency, you participated in changing the papers on that proposed appointment which had been promised to Senator Baker and others and you went along with your money czar, Mr. Dave Stockman, in pulling her back. This involved money for an agency that would protect consumers. Did you mean to give a signal to other Republicans that if they don't conform, that off would go their heads? [*Laughter*]

The President. How can you say that about a sweet fellow like me? [*Laughter*]

No, Sarah, no. Ms. Bailey was one of the names under consideration, and she did have the backing of Senator Baker and some others on the Hill. But we also had forces that were supporting other candidates, and we hear everyone's case for— who recommends someone for a position, and then comparing them all we just make our decision based on who we believe should have the job. And there had been no decision made one way or the other until we made the final decision.

Michael Posner [Maclean's].

U.S.-Canadian Issues

Q. Mr. President, sir, in advance of your trip to Ottawa next week, the most serious bilateral tension between Canada and the United States remains the unratified east coast fishing and boundaries treaty. Are you committed to finding a solution acceptable to the Canadians, or are you prepared to see the fishing portions of the treaty, at least, put into diplomatic limbo?

The President. No, I don't want to see them in diplomatic limbo, and I want to see a settlement of this whole issue and have so informed our people on the Hill of that. But this meeting—there is going to be the first meeting, and it's going to be one of kind of establishing a base for future negotiations. I don't know whether we will get down to hard issues and make any settlements in a first meeting of this kind, but we'll certainly lay the groundwork for trying to eliminate anything that could divide us or remain a stumbling block to better relations. This is part of what I talked about all during the campaign, from my first announcement on, and that is to start here in the Western Hemisphere with building an accord between the three great countries of North America—Canada, the United States, and Mexico.

So, I'm sure that all of these things will be out on the table when we get there, but we'll set an agenda for trying to resolve them.

Donna Smith [Oil Daily].

Canadian Oil Production

Q. Mr. President, the Canadian Government has an energy plan calling for 50-percent Canadianization of oil interests in that country and also added taxation of their production. It's a plan that has caused some shift of production from Canada, I mean, of exportation from Canada to the United States. What will you be advising Mr. Trudeau next week when you visit with him on that plan? And how is it going to affect U.S. investments in that country?

The President. Well, again, I think—I wish you were asking me this after we'd had the meeting. Things of this kind, I would rather not state a case in advance. These are things that I would want to take up when I get there and see how we can, as I say, set an agenda for getting them resolved.

With regard to energy, I am determined that the proper goal for us must be energy independence in the United States, not that we would take advantage of either of our neighbors there with regard to energy supplies.

Q. May I follow that up? Would you advise Mr. Trudeau to follow in your footsteps and speed up decontrol of oil and gasoline in that country as you have done here?

The President. Well, there's a little touchy ground in a first meeting to try and advise somebody how to run their country. I don't know that I'll do that. I might talk about what we've done.

Forrest Boyd [International Media Service].

Drug Abuse Programs

Q. Mr. President, in light of what appears to be a growing concern about the drug abuse problem, especially among teenagers, what will your priorities be and specifically, do you expect to have a White House policy on drug abuse?

The President. Yes, I do. In fact, it can be stated as clearly as this: I think this is one of the gravest problems facing us internally in the United States. I've had people talk to me about increased efforts to head off the export into the United States of drugs from neighboring nations. With borders like ours, that, as the main method of halting the drug problem in America, is virtually impossible. It's like carrying water in a sieve.

It is my belief, firm belief, that the answer to the drug problem comes through winning over the users to the point that we take the customers away from the drugs, not take the drugs, necessarily—try that, of course—you don't let up on that. But it's far more effective if you take the customers away than if you try to take the drugs away from those who want to be customers.

We had a program in California—again, I call on that. We had an education program in the schools. We had former drug users who had straightened out. We found that they were most effective in talking to young people. You could go in, I could go in, anyone else and try to talk to these young people and tell them the harm in this and get nowhere. But when someone stood in front of them who said, "I've been there, and this what it was like, and this is why I'm standing here telling you today," we found they listened.

I envision whatever we can do at the national level to try and launch a campaign nationwide, because I think we're running the risk of losing a great part of a whole generation if we don't.

Tuna Koprulu [Hurriyet News]. Yes?

U.S. Assistance for Turkey

Q. Mr. President, as you well know, Turkey has been hit hard during the 3½ years' arms embargo from the United States. Do you consider to increase aid to Turkey on or above the amount President Carter suggested for fiscal year 1982 which is $700 million? And also, would you favor a military grant to Turkey?

The President. I—this is an awful thing to confess—I can't really out of all the programs remember where that figure stands.

Q. It stands, Mr. President, the $400 million is the military aid and the $300 million is the economic aid.

The President. Yes, but I mean I can't recall where our figures stand in comparison to that, but I know that basically our philosophy is one of continued aid. And knowing the problems that have existed between Turkey and another friend and ally of ours, Greece, we are hopeful that whatever we can do in resolving any of the differences there we want to do. But both countries are vital to us. I consider them the southern flank of the NATO line. And, yes, I think there will be improved relations.

Allan Cromley [Daily Oklahoman].

Tax Reductions

Q. Mr. President, if you get the personal income tax cuts that you want and if people use their tax savings to just simply pay their bills, as many of them may do, and make down payments on consumer goods instead of investing the money in things that increase productivity, where does that leave us? Wouldn't inflation then be worse than it is now?

The President. It might be if that happened. And we have done as much studying as we can of that, including a thorough study of the 2-year program of tax cuts under President Kennedy—well, President Kennedy started them, and they went into effect following his tragic death. And we have been very interested to note—because there is a parallel between that type of tax cut and what it is we're proposing—at the bottom of the ladder, spending, yes, there were people pressed as they are by inflation who found that they needed that money for purchases. But as you went up for the scale of earnings, there was a great savings—in following that 2-year program, during the program and following—a great increase in personal savings and investment by the American people.

Now, we have what I think has to include the total middle class of this country—from

$10,000 to $60,000 a year—pays 72 percent of all the income tax. They are going to get 73 percent of all the benefits. And it seems to me that in there, maybe at the 10 level or below, but as you begin to go up that ladder, that is where there is going to be savings and investment. And every indication we have from the past and from what we have been able to project now, indicates that will take place again under this plan. And that won't be inflationary; that will be helpful to the business cuts we're proposing in stimulating investment to increase productivity.

Bill Groody [Mutual Broadcasting System].

Oil Price Decontrol

Q. Mr. President, this morning's wholesale price figures seem to indicate that the fuel prices are still one of the prime motivating forces behind spiraling inflation. In light of this, are you having any second thoughts about your decision to decontrol the price of domestic oil, especially in light of some estimates by economists that it has caused the price of gasoline to rise as much as 14 cents a gallon?

The President. No, because we only advanced decontrol. It was supposed to take place in a few months anyway. And the increase in the price of gasoline today is only partly due to that decontrol. Part of it was due to the decontrol that had begun under the previous administration. The major part of it was the latest increase in OPEC prices, and our decontrolling now only amounts to 3 or 4 cents of the increase in the price of gasoline, and that would have taken place in October anyway, that same decontrol.

We do believe that as time goes on, though, we're going to see increased exploration and development of oil in this country, and that is the road toward lower prices when supply begins to match demand more. So, we don't see any reason, and I don't have any regrets about the change we made. I think the increase in drilling that has taken place, the wells that were unprofitable to pump—in 1976 we had some 400 wells in California that were closed down simply because at the price that the government would allow them to charge they could not bring the oil to the surface for that price and sell it. Well, wells like that now under decontrol go back into production.

Larry Barrett [Time, Inc.].

Soviet Grain Embargo

Q. Mr. President, at your first press conference you were asked about the Soviet grain embargo, and you said there were really only two options, either to abandon it or broaden it. Can you tell us which it's going to be, and if you haven't reached a decision yet, can you tell us what factors are still at play here?

The President. We haven't reached a decision. I think all of us would like to lift the embargo. I still think that it has been as harmful to the American farmer as it has been to the Soviet Union. But the situation has changed from the time when it was first installed.

I was against it at the time. I didn't think it should have been used as it was, that if we were to follow that road, we should have gone across the board and had a kind of quarantine. We didn't. But now we have to look at the international situation, the way it is, and see what would be the effect, not just on the use of grain but the whole effect and what would it say to the world now for us to just unilaterally move.

We're hopeful that we can arrive at a settlement and a decision on this and one that will benefit our farmers.

Lester Kinsolving [Globe Syndicate].

Abortions

Q. Mr. President, since you've become a strong supporter of the right-to-life movement whose leaders in Congress have introduced an amendment that human life begins at conception rather than birth, how can parents or election boards determine a person's date of conception for purposes of registration and eligibility for running for public office?

The President. Well, I think with the matter that's before the legislature now, there is going to be testimony by medical authorities, theologians, possibly, legal authorities also, and I think what is necessary in this whole problem and has been the least talked of in the whole question about abortion is determining when and what is a human being.

Now, I happen to have believed and stated many times that I believe in an abortion we are taking a human life. But if this is once determined, then there isn't really any need for an amendment, because once you have determined this, the Constitution already protects the right to human life.

Q. You said during your campaign you noticed that all the advocates of abortion are already born. Since this also applies to all the advocates in contraception, are you opposed to contraception, which also denies the right to life?

The President. No, I am not.

Ms. Thomas. Thank you. Do you want to explain it? [*Laughter*]

The President. Helen, you just got even.

No, as I·say, I think the idea of human life, once it has been created, and establishing that fact—and maybe I should have just taken your "thank you" and left here on this—is the whole issue that we have to determine.

It seems strange to me that we have a law, for example, in California, a law that says that if someone abuses or mistreats a pregnant woman to the point of causing the death of her unborn child, that individual will be tried for murder. We know that the law of the land gives an unborn child the right to inherit property, and the law protects property rights. Isn't it time we determined—if there was some question, if you found a body on the street and you didn't know whether it was dead or alive, wouldn't you opt on the basis that it was alive and not start shoveling dirt on it? This is what I feel about the other.

Until we determine and make to the best of our ability a determination of when life begins, we've been opting on the basis that, "Well, let's consider they're not alive." I think that everything in our society calls for opting that they might be alive.

Thank you.

Note: The President's second news conference began at 2 p.m. in Room 450 of the Old Executive Office Building. It was broadcast live on radio and television.

Nomination of Charles Z. Wick To Be Director of the International Communication Agency
March 6, 1981

The President today announced his intention to nominate Charles Z. Wick to be Director of the International Communication Agency.

Mr. Wick has been an independent businessman involved in the financing and operation of motion picture, television, radio, music, health care, and mortgage industries in the United States and abroad. He is president and chief executive officer of Wick Financial Corp., and Mapleton Enterprises, which he founded in the early 1960's. He

was cochairman of the 1981 Presidential Inaugural Committee.

Mr. Wick was graduated from the University of Michigan (B.M.) and Case Western Reserve University Law School (J.D.). He is a member of the California and Ohio Bar Associations.

Mr. Wick is married and has five children. He resides in Los Angeles, Calif. Mr. Wick was born in Cleveland, Ohio, on October 12, 1917.

Remarks and a Question-and-Answer Session During a White House Briefing for the National Association of Counties
March 9, 1981

The President. Well, the Vice President and I are delighted to be here. I know he's speaking to your entire group tomorrow, but I appreciate the opportunity for a dialog with you, who are county officials, and to reaffirm that, if you haven't been told already, that we really intend a working partnership with you as we attempt to solve our nation's economic problems.

Restoring a balance between the Federal Government and other levels of government is and will continue to be the policy of this administration. And the White House Intergovernmental Affairs Office, under the leadership of Rich Williamson, will be playing a key role as liaison with you. As a part of restoring the balance, we intend to establish a coordinating task force on federalism and have already been in touch with representatives of your organization to seek advice on how that task force should be organized.

In developing the economic package that—today's the day it goes up there— we've tried to be fair and evenhanded. We created a special safety net to protect the truly needy. And we have just one department that, as you well know—because it's

been heralded in the press a number of times—the Defense Department, that will not be cut back. But even there, Cap Weinberger—you can count on it—has already identified and gone to work to make cuts of $3 billion that he believes are unnecessary in there, which, thus, reduces the net increase that we would have for the improved weapons that we think are necessary.

I know there's been a great deal of talk and your concern about the UDAG function. That has not been eliminated. It's combined into a community development support program, and we're sending legislation up to the Hill to carry that out.

With respect to payments—if this hasn't come up this morning—in lieu of taxes, the Department of Interior has restructured its budget authority to allow for payments in lieu of taxes for counties which have Federal lands within their jurisdictions. We feel that making payments in lieu of taxes by the Federal Government is part of being a good neighbor. Responsibility of ownership requires landholders to pay their fair share

213

of the cost of local government, and Federal Government shouldn't be exempt.

Now, Vice President Bush will be addressing, as I said, tomorrow, and I'll jump the gun and tell you, he's in charge of a task force on regulatory relief, and I think that indicates the importance we place on that. Now, most of the attention seems to be given when this is discussed to what it's done to the private sector and to business and so forth, but you, county government, know how much unnecessary paperwork has been generated by the Federal Government, and we intend to change that.

I, having mentioned a dialog, I'd better stop having a monolog here now and whatever questions you have, be happy to field them.

Yes?

President's Advisory Committee for Women

Q. Katie Dixon, Salt Lake County, Utah. I'm chair of the elected women of NACO, and we would like to know if you are going to continue the President's Commission on Women?

The President. The President's Commission on Women—you know, I have to say I don't know whether that subject has even come up, so I would assume that we probably are. I think so, yes, because I have—being notorious for not supporting the amendment, during the campaign I made it plain, and I meant this very much—having passed 14 statutes in California where, to eliminate particular discriminations that we found in State law, I said then that we are going to have liaison with the States to pursue that course and someone in the White House to direct this and to help other levels of government find, where maybe in their own regulations without their realizing, they have such discriminatory practices. And it worked just fine for us—changing those 14 statutes.

Employment Programs

Q. Mr. President, we support your program to cut Federal spending, especially the CETA/PSC jobs, but we'd like to know what kind of programs you're proposing to take the disadvantaged off of welfare and to give them meaningful work.

The President. Well, one of the things that we're talking about now is based on something we did in California in our welfare reforms. As we give the States more authority in administering these programs by way of block grants, we are working on legislation right now that would further give flexibility to the States and allow them to require able-bodied welfare recipients to work at useful community projects in return for their welfare grants. And in California, even though the 1974 recession was coming on—in the '73, '74 recession—and unemployment increasing, in only 35 counties of California would they permit us to have an experiment of that kind. And we funneled 76,000 people through that program into private enterprise jobs.

What we did was not only require the work in useful community projects but then we assigned—and I throw this out for a suggestion—we assigned people from our labor department, State labor department, as what we called job agents to be given a list, a group of these people, to keep an eye on them, and then to go to work to see how quickly, based on what they saw of their abilities and so forth, they could move them out into private employment. And as I say, it was 76,000, and we think that this was the best thing that we had found in all the years that we were battling with this particular problem. So, if we can get that through, that will be one of the further flexibilities that you will all have. And, remember, we only had it in 35 counties. They wouldn't even let us have it in the great metropolitan areas like San Francisco and Los Angeles County.

Budget Reductions

Q. Mr. President, I don't know if sitting in the back is an advantage or not, but first of all, we appreciate very much your taking time to visit with us this morning. I'm Bob Eckels from Harris County. In the conference which we had with you, several of us, a few weeks ago, we mentioned two things: One was the creation of the position which Rich Williamson is doing now, and we appreciate that very much and look forward to working with him. The second thing that we were looking for was as these cuts are instituted, that they be done in a slow fashion, not a cold turkey, necessary situation, but allowing the local governments time to find a method for either substitution or elimination of the program without the catastrophic political effects that it can have on the local offices. Has anyone in the staff had an opportunity to review the time factors in coming into this?

The President. I'm sure that is being considered. I can't say that I participated in a meeting where that has been discussed, but I'll tell you now, I will look into that, see what I can find out about it. Because having been back there at the State level, I know what you mean.

Mass Transportation

Q. Al Delbello, Westchester County, New York. We're having a great deal of trouble in sustaining our mass transit system in that metropolitan New York area, particularly the commuter rail and the commuter bus services. I'm very unclear with regard to the direction you will be taking on commuter rail subsidization programs in the near future.

The President. Well, I have to tell you that I know, I can't give you the detail on all that—I know, however, that there are going to be cutbacks in that, and some features will be incorporated in the block grants for your own discretion about using those.

Federal Loans

Q. Mr. President, I'm Jack Brock from eastern North Carolina, and I understand the administration is going to give us a 10-percent interest on Farmers Home Administration money. It's been 5 for many years and most helpful. I wonder if there would be any chance of the administration reconsidering maybe 7 or 7½ percent money. This has a great effect on rural homes and our water and waste water treatment systems, and this money does flow back. I would like for the President, if you would, to respond to those interest rates.

The President. Let me say this one thing on those loans and where we felt that we had to come up closer to the market rate on them. At the time, the original 5 percent was in keeping with what was pretty much

the private interest rate, and no change was ever made. Now, the situation for us and for all the citizens is this: that when we approve those loans at that lower interest rate, the Treasury Department doesn't have any money to loan, running in a deficit situation, it has to go out into the market and borrow the interest at the high-interest rate and then turn around and lend it at this lower rate. And, perhaps not in this particular program, where homes and things are involved, we've actually found that there are some people that have discovered that it's just fine to get one of those loans, and then they go around on the other side and buy the government securities at the higher rate. And it makes a nice circle and a profitable one for them.

But we feel that what we're doing—whether that's the right figure or not, I'm sure that will be discussed and debated on the Hill—but to bring it up, because it always had been pretty much consistent with the going rate of interest. And the main purpose of it was not to give low-interest money; it was for those people that did not have the assets that they would need to cover going into the private fund market. Well, that provision still remains, but we believe that it is fair to bring that up closer to the going rate.

Agriculture Prices

Q. Mr. President, I'm Ray Nelson, chairman of the Rural Affairs Committee of NACO, from Kansas. And my biggest concern for the rural problem or the rural counties is that for the producers of food and fiber, the price has been—continuously since the first of the year, been going down. All the commodities and the prices of everything that they purchase has been going up considerably. We've had 10-percent and probably and average of 12-percent increase in everything they buy. And they feel that we sure need to open up some export markets or something to get this thing moving. For instance the price of wheat has dropped 75 cents since the first of the year back at the local elevators, and this is causing a lot of sale bills to go up on the wall. And I'm very concerned about the younger generation that's just trying to get into the operation of farming.

The President. Sir, I wish right now that I had John Block here, because we've got a working farmer today as Secretary of Agriculture, and he's completely aware of these problems. And all of us have been made aware that in food pricing, with all of the talk of prices up and down—it's an amazing thing that what happens from after it leaves the farm until it gets to the customer at the supermarket shelf, the fluctuations in price and so forth. But it hasn't been reflected for the farmer. And there's no question about him probably being caught the worst in the cost-price squeeze of anyone in this inflationary time.

I do a little ranching myself out there in California, and I realized one of the real problems of the farm when the second-hand 1953 tractor, which I bought 20 years ago for $1,200—someone in the tractor business told my wife that they thought I really ought to have something better than that, and they'd make me a great deal. So, they sent a man up, and he did. He offered a great deal on that $1,200, 20-year-old, 1953, secondhand tractor. He'd give me $4,000 in trade-in, and then it would only cost me $13,000 more to get a tractor. [*Laughter*] I'm still driving the 1953 Ford.

But I can tell you that we are—and opening up foreign markets is one of the things where we think government really does have a place for involvement.

Funding of Local Programs

Q. Bob Honts from Texas. Most local governments harvest most of their revenue from a regressive and inflexible property tax. We don't have a lot of room to go. We hear the good news: You're going to cut the budget and balance it at the Federal level. But the bad news is that it looks like those programs are headed our way, and we don't really see the revenue sources that were supposed to come with them yet.

The President. We think that the block grants and the flexibility they give you is going to be more helpful than we realize, because a lot of the cuts that are being made in the overall size are in administrative overhead that was accumulated from this end, and giving you the flexibility to set your own priorities without the rigid requirements of the past would help. But I only tell you what—and we can get over this hurdle and get this government back down to the size it should be and start.

No, I have a dream of my own. I think block grants are really only an intermediate step. I dream of the day when the Federal Government can substitute for those turning back to local and State governments the tax sources that we ourselves have preempted here at the Federal level so that you would have those tax sources.

Economic Development Grants

Q. President Reagan, I'm Tracey Owen from King County, Washington, president of the Western Region and chairman of a four-county district in economic development. You had made reference to UDAG being integrated with, perhaps, an expansion block grant. Is that similar approach in mind for at least funding of those things that are in the pipeline and had the communities' expectation raised that they would get funding for it—basic economic development grants?

The President. I don't know that I have the answer to that. We're dealing right now, of course, with 1981. We're making some cuts, but as far into the year that we are, it isn't anything like the cuts that we intend for the 1982 budget. So, I can't believe that there would be too much of a change for things that are already in the pipeline at all. You have a better answer to that?

Mr. Williamson. Yes, if I could just comment on that slightly. [*Laughter*]

The President. He's been working on it firsthand.

Mr. Williamson. That's right. See, eventually it'll percolate up to the man, but the work that's being done, that Ed Meese mentioned earlier with Dave Stockman, the UDAG function—the existing grants that have been committed and those applications in the pipeline would be funded enough within the ceiling that the President has established so that the administration would meet the existing commitments and be able to process the commitments that are now in the pipeline.

Q. Okay, I understand that with regard to UDAG. I think that was explained to the mayors or the city people when they met. I'm talking about the Economic Development Administration's funded programs that have been so important in helping to be the seed money for long-term productive employment in the private sector, because we know for every 1 percent of unemployment, it's going to cost the Federal Government maybe upwards to $25 billion a year. And I have a report of our four-county district which indicates that the seed money has been less than $1,000 per job created from the EDA grants. And there's about 15 projects that are in the pipeline that have been prioritized locally, and I'm sure that's true all across the country. And our concern is that they might not be able to all be funded out of the '81 allocations, and it might need to run into '82 before it's phased out.

Mr. Williamson. Well, just to respond to that quickly, and I'll sit back down. [*Laughter*] The task force that Ed Meese has together with Dave Stockman and Malcolm Baldrige and Sam Pierce working on the details of the community development support program for, hopefully, as soon as possible, to pass on to the President—that has been discussed with respect to the economic development grants and, in fact, met with the mayor of San Juan with respect to a particular problem they had just last week, and we're attempting to get a resolution. The only one that there's been a final signoff within the task force for recommendation to the President has to deal with the UDAG aspect. But there are three other aspects that will go into the larger block grant community development, and there's not been a resolution. It would be very helpful if at the end of today you would pass that on to me, because no decision finally has been made yet.

The President. Let me just say, if I seem to be flying blind here, it isn't that. We've had hours and hours of Cabinet meetings— and the major issue on each one of these cuts does come there, and all of the input and sometimes pro and con within the Cabinet discussion—and based on all of that input I finally make a decision. But coming from 739 billion down to 695, I have to tell

you honestly, some of the details on these things I can't remember. I just have to assume we've made the decision with the information that we have.

Interior Secretary Watt

Q. Mr. President, Cal Black from San Juan County, Utah. I don't have a question, but I want to compliment you on your appointment of Secretary of Interior, Jim Watt, and just encourage you to support him. Thank you.

The President. Well, thank you very much. He's a good man.

Programs for Minorities

Q. Mr. President, Chuck Williams, chairman of the National Association of Black County Officials. Since the thrust of the block grants has been directed toward the States, what kind of direction is going to be provided to the States to make sure that they filter down through local governments kinds of moneys that we need to provide the programs that we're most responsible for?

The President. Well, very obviously, I think I can say—if I interpret what might be your concern there—obviously, the State government, who wants to give all the flexibility it can, is certainly not going to hold still for anything being used at a different level of government in a discriminatory fashion. We won't permit that. And I think we have a right to say that.

So, I have every confidence that the flexibility that is given will be one that will allow the utmost in economies and so forth. But that will not allow any retreat from where we are and what we are and what we want to do for all the people of this country.

Mr. Williamson. One more question and then——

The President. Well, I was going to take this lady's question.

Education Programs

Q. Elizabeth Cofield, from Raleigh, North Carolina, county commissioner. And I haven't heard anything pertaining to education, and I'm very concerned about that. And I know that education in the terms of grants and loans have to suffer just as all others. But I would like to encourage you, Mr. President, to encourage those who will be making the reduction in loans and grants and other titles to look at it very carefully so that we don't throw the babies out with the wash water. Otherwise, we won't have anyone to be in this room 2 years from now.

The President. I couldn't agree more, and I assure you, we're not going to do that. Now, I just heard someone on the air yesterday and talking about tremendous cuts in educational funding and so forth. What they forget is that Federal funding of education only amounts to 10 percent of the cost of education, and they don't make that plain. This man was talking as if, why, there's going to be a 25-percent cut in the overall support for education. Well, 25 percent of 10 percent is 2½ percent. And we feel that a lot of the Federal Government's aid to education has resulted in unnecessary interference in education, which, in reality, has probably undone a lot of the help that the money would be by forcing added expense on the schools.

I had a college president tell me the other day that the paperwork, the administrative work required now for government help in his college has made his administrative cost for that go from $50,000 a year in his campus to $650,000 a year. Now, that'd hire a lot of professors that could teach. And so, we feel that we're not going to do anything to hurt education, and we think we are going to put it back in the hands of people that are closer to the scene and out of here. And I'm confident—we have an educator as the Secretary of that department right now. So, believe me, education has a good voice in our circles.

Mr. Williamson. Mr. President, this is Roy Orr. The president of the association will make a brief comment, and then I think we're going to have to move you on to your next appointment.

The President. All right.

Mr. Orr. I just want to say, Mr. President, on behalf of the National Association of Counties, that we appreciate you very much for taking your time. We realize that it's tough to face this many people—the directors of our national association, that reaches from the south to the north, to the east, to the west—and have all the answers that everybody wants. But we assure you that we want to be a good partner, and we will. And you thrill us when you say that you're going to return some of the authority back to the States and back to the local authorities and back to the counties, where we know that we're the government that's closest to the people.

You know, when you have a pothole in a road, they don't ask the President of the United States to patch that pothole; they ask a bunch of these people. So, consequently, we feel that we do know more about—whether it be Travis County or Dallas, Texas, or Sacramento, California, whatever—what it takes to please the people and to serve the people than maybe some bureaucrats in Washington. And we appreciate that partnership. The only thing we ask is that if it's not a good deal for both, it's not a good deal. That's a good county statement——

The President. That's right.

Mr. Orr. ——that we make. And we tell our State legislators, "If you're going to cut us, don't mandate us, because that's not a real good deal."

The President. No.

Mr. Orr. And we've often said that we can do more with half the money than the Federal bureaucrats can do with all the money, and is an alternative we've even talked about, is that we might even say, "Mr. President, cut all the grants and give us half of what you cut in general revenue sharing, and we'll serve more people than they're serving [with] all the rest, and you cut out a bunch of bureaucrats."

The President. Thank you. This is what we're counting on.

Mr. Orr. I want to take this minute to introduce my officers. Do you know Sandy Smoley, from the Farmers' Committee?

The President. Hi, Sandy, hi. How are you?

Ms. Smoley. Hi. It's nice to see you.

The President. Nice to see you.

Ms. Smoley. Thank you very much.

Mr. Orr. And this is Dick Conder, from North Carolina, our first vice president; Bill Murphy, from New York; and you know our great hired hand, Bernie Hillenbrand.

The President. I sure do. You bet. How do you do?

Mr. Orr. Again, we appreciate—we'll be looking for the Vice President tomorrow, and we appreciate it.

The President. Well, thank you. You've inspired me with that pothole. I'm just going to take one second and tell you my first—[*laughter*]—as a small boy, my first experience with hearing about county problems.

My brother, who was just a few years older than me, had gotten a job, he and another teenage kid, sitting on the back of a truck. And there was a fellow running for the Illinois State Legislature, and he was campaigning. And while he was speaking in each town, at outdoor rallies, they were to get off and pass out the leaflets in the town. He came home that night scared to death. They'd gotten out of town under a shower of rocks and paving stones and so forth.

It seems that this State legislator—they were building a State highway in Illinois at the time, and his district crossed a county line into two counties—and in each county he promised them that the State highway was going through their county. [*Laughter*] But my brother and the other kid got the leaflets mixed up and passed them out in the wrong county. [*Laughter*]

Thank you all very much.

Note: The President spoke at 11:33 a.m. in Room 450 of the Old Executive Office Building.

Nomination of Marc E. Leland To Be a Deputy Under Secretary of the Treasury, and Designation as an Assistant Secretary
March 9, 1981

The President today announced his intention to nominate Marc E. Leland to be a Deputy Under Secretary of the Treasury (International Affairs). Upon confirmation, the President will designate Mr. Leland to act as an Assistant Secretary of International Affairs.

Since 1978 Mr. Leland has served as a London resident partner with the firm of Proskauer Rose Goetz & Mendelsohn. He was senior adviser to the U.S. delegation to the mutual balanced force reduction talks in Vienna, Austria, in 1976–78. In 1972–73 Mr. Leland was a partner with the firm of Cerf, Robinson & Leland of San Francisco, Calif. He was an associate and partner of that firm in 1964–68.

Mr. Leland served as General Counsel to the ACTION agency in 1971–72. He was General Counsel to the Peace Corps in 1970–71. In 1968–70 he was a faculty fellow in foreign and comparative law at Harvard Law School. Mr. Leland was a Ford Foundation fellow at the Institute of Comparative Law, University of Paris, France, in 1963–64.

Mr. Leland was graduated from Harvard University (B.A., 1959); St. John's College, Oxford University (B.A., 1961); University of California at Berkeley (J.D., 1963).

Mr. Leland is married and has two children. He resides in London, England. Mr. Leland was born in San Francisco, Calif., on April 20, 1938.

Nomination of Robert C. Odle, Jr., To Be an Assistant Secretary of Energy
March 9, 1981

The President today announced his intention to nominate Robert C. Odle, Jr., to be an Assistant Secretary of Energy (Congressional, Intergovernmental and Public Affairs).

Mr. Odle joined International Paper Co. in 1976 as Washington corporate affairs representative. In this position, he has specialized in liaison with Federal departments and agencies and has represented the company's position on matters before the Congress, particularly energy, energy tax, environmental, regulatory, and wage-price issues. He is president of the firm of Manarin, Odle, and Rector, Inc., in Alexandria, Va.

In 1973–76 Mr. Odle served as Deputy Assistant Secretary and as Acting Assistant Secretary, Department of Housing and Urban Development. In 1971–73 he was director of administration, Committee to Reelect the President. Mr. Odle was a staff assistant to the President in 1969–71.

Mr. Odle was graduated from Wayne State University, Detroit, Mich. (B.A., 1966); Detroit College of Law (J.D., 1969). He is a member of the Michigan and American Bar Associations.

Mr. Odle is married to the former Lydia Ann Karpinol. He was born in Port Huron, Mich., on February 15, 1944.

Remarks on Signing Documents Transmitting Budget Revisions to the Congress
March 9, 1981

I'm going to make a statement here, but before I do, I just want to thank all of you. You're from the Office of Management and Budget, and you're the ones that have been working and slaving very hard, and all of us here are deeply grateful to you. And, at which time I shall now read a statement in which I'll take all the credit. [*Laughter*]

Today I'm signing a message to the Congress that adds hundreds of savings to the 83 major reductions that we announced on February 18th, and this brings our proposed budget outlay savings for 1982 to $48.6 billion. In addition, I'm proposing changes in user charges and off-budget payments that will save another $7.3 billion. Now, these are unprecedented cuts to meet an unprecedented situation, and they mark the end of an old era and the beginning of a new one. We're determined to enable the American people to gain control of the runaway government which threatens our economic vitality.

The details of this program, which have been drawn up and completed during the past 6 weeks, will be released tomorrow when the official budget goes to Congress. Like the first round of cuts, these reductions are evenhanded, and the safety net of basic income suport programs remains intact. Although it is now up to the Congress to act on these proposals, I believe that the Congress and the executive branch have a responsibility to involve the American people directly in these deliberations. We must see to it that the voice of the average American, not that of special interests or full-time lobbyists, is the dominant one.

Now, these cuts are not necessarily the last ones. We're committed to a 5-year spending program, and I am determined to stop the spending juggernaut. If more cuts are needed to keep within our spending ceilings, I will not hesitate to propose them. I would also stress what you already know:

If we can control spending and shave a few points off the inflation rate, we can do more good for the poor, the elderly, and the finances of State and local government than any package of Federal programs ever could. The reductions contained in this message are part of a longer term program designed to stop inflation, reward enterprise and initiative, and put America back on the road to prosperity. As I've said many times, our ultimate goal is to make government, again, the servant of the people by cutting its size and scope and ensuring that its legitimate functions are carried out efficiently and justly.

Now, what I'm signing there are three acts that must go up to the Congress. That is not the Federal budget; we couldn't get a truck in here with all of us here in the Rose Garden. So, I shall now sign.

[*At this point, the President signed a message to the Congress transmitting the fiscal year 1982 budget revisions, a message to the Congress on rescission proposals and deferrals for the fiscal year 1981 budget, and a letter to the Speaker of the House of Representatives transmitting proposed supplemental appropriations and amendments to the fiscal year 1981, 1982, and 1984 budgets.*]

All right. It's signed, and I think I have one little task here yet to do. There's been a lot of cartooning lately, and this is a cartoon. And maybe some of you are too far away to really see it—[*laughter*]—this is the original inscribed to Dave Stockman by the cartoonist. But I just had to add a little note over my own signature on the other side. For those who might be in the back, my desk is now an old door on four cement blocks, a crate for a seat, and my pens are kept in an empty bean can. So, I have just written, "Dear Dave, I hope you use second-hand cement blocks. The price of concrete is out of sight." [*Laughter*]

Well, thank you all again very much and, Dave, thank you very much. I appreciate it.

Note: The President spoke at 1:02 p.m. at the signing ceremony in the Rose Garden at the White House.

Message to the Congress Transmitting Fiscal Year 1982 Budget Revisions
March 10, 1981

To the Congress of the United States:

On February 18, I spoke to a Joint Session of Congress about the economic crisis facing America. I pledged then to take the action necessary to alleviate the grievous economic plight of our people. The plan I outlined will stop runaway inflation and revitalize our economy if given a chance. There is nothing but politics-as-usual standing in the way of lower inflation, increased productivity, and a return to prosperity.

Our program for economic recovery does not rely upon complex theories or elaborate Government programs. Instead, it recognizes basic economic facts of life and, as humanely as possible, it will move America back toward economic sanity. The principles are easily understood, but it will take determination to apply them. Nevertheless, if inflation and unemployment are to be curtailed, we must act.

First, we must cut the growth of Government spending.

Second, we must cut tax rates so that once again work will be rewarded and savings encouraged.

Third, we must carefully remove the tentacles of excessive Government regulation which are strangling our economy.

Fourth, while recognizing the independence of the Institution, we must work with the Federal Reserve Board to develop a monetary policy that will rationally control the money supply.

Fifth, we must move, surely and predictably, toward a balanced budget.

The budget reform plan announced on February 18 includes 83 major cuts resulting in $34.8 billion outlay savings for 1982, with greater future savings. With this message, over 200 additional reductions are proposed. An additional $13.8 billion in savings are now planned. Further, I am proposing changes in user charges and off-budget payments that will bring total fiscal savings to $55.9 billion. This compares with $49.1 billion in fiscal savings announced on February 18.

In terms of appropriations and other budget authority that will affect future spending, we are proposing elimination of $67 billion in 1982 and over $475 billion in the period 1981 to 1986.

These cuts sound like enormous sums— and they are—until one considers the overwhelming size of the total budget. Even with these cuts, the 1982 budget will total $695.3 billion, an increase of 6.1 percent over 1981.

The budget reductions we are proposing will, undoubtedly, face stiff opposition from those who are tied to maintaining the status quo. But today's status quo is nothing more than economic stagnation coupled with high inflation. Dramatic change is needed or the situation will simply get worse, resulting in even more suffering and misery, and possibly the destruction of traditional American values.

While recognizing the need for bold action, we have ensured that the impact of spending reductions will be shared widely and fairly by different groups and the various regions of the country. Also, we have, as pledged, maintained this society's basic social safety net, protecting programs for the elderly and others who rely on Government for their very existence.

Budget cuts alone, however, will not turn this economy around. Our package includes a proposal to reduce substantially the personal income tax rates levied on our people and to accelerate the recovery of business with capital investment. These rate reductions are essential to restoring strength and growth to the economy by reducing the existing tax barriers that discourage work, saving, and investment. Individuals are the ultimate source of all savings and invest-

ment. Lasting economic progress, which is our goal, depends on our success in encouraging people to involve themselves in this kind of productive behavior.

Our tax proposal will, if enacted, have an immediate impact on the economic vitality of the Nation, where even a slight improvement can produce dramatic results. For example, a 2 percent increase in economic growth will add $60 billion to our gross national product in one year alone. That $60 billion adds to the State and local tax base, to the purchasing power of the American family, and to the resources available for investment.

When considering the economic recovery package, I urge the Members of Congress to remember that last November the American people's message was loud and clear. The mandate for change, expressed by the American people, was not my mandate; it was our mandate. Together we must remember that our primary responsibility is to the Nation as a whole and that there is nothing more important than putting America's economic house in order.

The next steps are up to Congress. It has not been easy for my Administration to prepare this revised budget. I am aware that it will not be easy for the Congress to act upon it. I pledge my full cooperation. It is essential that, together, we succeed in again making this Nation a land whose expanding economy offers an opportunity for all to better themselves, a land where productive behavior is rewarded, a land where one need not fear that economic forces beyond one's control will, through inflation, destroy a lifetime of savings.

RONALD REAGAN

The White House,
March 10, 1981.

Note: The message is printed in the report entitled "Fiscal Year 1982 Budget Revisions, March 1981—Executive Office of the President, Office of Management and Budget" (Government Printing Office, 159 pages).

The message was signed by the President on March 9 for transmittal to the Congress on March 10.

Message to the Congress Reporting Budget Rescissions and Deferrals
March 10, 1981

To the Congress of the United States:

In accordance with the Impoundment Control Act of 1974, I herewith propose 3 new rescissions of budget authority previously provided by the Congress, totalling $128.0 million. In addition, I am reporting 24 new deferrals totalling $825.5 million, and revisions to five previously reported deferrals increasing the amount deferred by $876.4 million.

The rescission proposals affect programs of the Department of the Interior and the National Consumer Cooperative Bank. The deferrals affect Appalachian regional development programs, programs in the Departments of Commerce, Defense, Education, Energy, Housing and Urban Development, Justice, Labor, and Transportation, as well as the Veterans Administration, the General Services Administration, and the Small Business Administration.

The details of each rescission proposal and deferral are contained in the attached reports.

RONALD REAGAN

The White House,
March 10, 1981.

Note: The message was signed by the President on March 9 for transmittal to the Congress on March 10.

The attachments detailing the rescissions and deferrals are printed in the Federal Register of March 13, 1981.

Letter to the Speaker of the House Transmitting Proposed Supplemental Appropriations and Amendments
March 10, 1981

Sir:

I ask the Congress to consider proposed supplemental appropriations and amendments to pending supplemental appropriations for the fiscal year 1981 in the amount of $4,980,298,000 for program purposes, and reductions in the requests to cover the October 1980 Federal pay raise totalling $67,608,000; amendments reducing requests for appropriations for fiscal year 1982 by $22,134,673,463; and an amendment reducing a request for an advance appropriation for the fiscal year 1984 by $77,000,000.

These requests are part of my Economic Recovery Program.

The details of these proposals are set forth in the enclosed letter from the Director of the Office of Management and Budget. I concur with his comments and observations.

Respectfully,

RONALD REAGAN

Note: The letter was signed by the President on March 9 for transmittal to Thomas P. O'Neill, Jr., Speaker of the House of Representatives, on March 10.

Remarks of the President and Governor General Edward R. Schreyer of Canada at the Welcoming Ceremony in Ottawa
March 10, 1981

The Governor General. Mr. President, it is with great pleasure and warmth of feeling that we greet you and Mrs. Reagan on behalf of the people of Canada.

You come to us, Mr. President, representing the country that is both our nearest neighbor and also which the history of this twentieth century has made our closest ally. Through the long years of our association, Canada and the United States of America have met and overcome many challenges and problems together. We have, I believe, acted effectively as partners, confident that our differences make our combined efforts that much more effective.

Now, in a period of uncertainty in the world, Canada remains committed to working with the United States to further the fundamental ideals and values of freedom and of equality before the law, which we both share.

Mr. President, I am confident that your visit to Canada will serve to strengthen the firm and rational ties of friendship and practical cooperation which exist firmly and historically between our two countries. While here, I hope that beyond the sometimes formal aspects of state occasions that you will also encounter something of the human, kindred dimension which gives relations between Canada and the United States, and as between the millions of individual Americans and Canadians, their deeper meaning and their unique character.

Monsieur le Président, au nom de tous les Canadiens, je vous souhaite la bienvenue dans notre pays qui, comme le votre, compte parmi ces citoyens des personnes de souche ethnique et linguistique multiple et variée. [Mr. President, on behalf of all Canadians, I welcome you in our country, which, as yours, has among its citizens people of multiple and diverse ethnic and linguistic origins.]

Mr. President, if this is the era of the global village, then welcome to the house next door; welcome to Canada.

The President. Your Excellencies, Nancy and I are happy to be here. One can receive no warmer greeting than the heartfelt welcome of a trusted friend. And yes, we, the people of the United States and of Canada, are more than good neighbors; we're good friends. We citizens of North America, while respecting the sovereignty and independence of our respective national identities, are without question friends that can be counted upon. Whether in times of trial and insecurity or in times of peace and commerce, our relationship has never weakened. The faith between us has never wavered.

We each play a separate and important role in international affairs. We have economic interests that bind us in cooperation and, in some cases, put us into competition. But these separate roles are respected by our two peoples and have never diminished the harmony between us.

I hope this visit will make clear my commitment as President of the United States to work in close cooperation with the Government of Canada. Whether in trade or defense or protection of our environment and natural resources, our two nations shall continue the unique relationship that has been the envy of the world, a relationship that has enhanced the standard of living and the freedom of our people. Let us continue, and let us move forward.

It is a great pleasure to be here with you. *Merci.*

Note: The ceremony, which included full military honors, began at 9:59 a.m. at Hangar 11 at the Canadian Forces Base.

Remarks of the President and Prime Minister Pierre Elliott Trudeau of Canada Prior to Their Meetings in Ottawa
March 10, 1081

The Prime Minister. Canadians are simply delighted that you have come to visit us, and we're particularly pleased that in your first visit out of the United States you chose to visit our country.

Like Americans, Canadians are used to welcoming Americans. Last year, Mr. President, some 75 million border crossings were recorded between our two countries. That's about three times, more than three times, the entire population of Canada. So, Canadians know Americans, and Canadians like Americans. We like you because not only have we shared this continent together with our friends and neighbors, the Americans, with our friends and neighbors, the Mexicans, who have spanned this New World from one ocean to the other, but we also enjoy this neighborhood because we share the same values—individual liberty, justice, democratic values.

Mr. President, more than two centuries ago a great band of the brotherhood of man wrote the most revolutionary script since the New Testament. I'm talking of the American Constitution. And not content with that, they went on in the same sweet breath of humanity to write a Bill of Rights. Mr. President, those two documents, the words in there, the ideas in there, were heard around the world. Indeed, more than the shot fired at Lexington, it is these ideas and these values which have made America, the United States of America, the first great modern nation.

And that is why, Mr. President, the winds of freedom which first began to blow in your country and which then spread all over the world make that Canada and Canadians. As you can see from these signs and as you can hear from some of these lonely voices, Canadians expect much of Americans. But more important, Canadians have faith in the Americans. We know that our long relationship has been based on more than neighborhood; it's been based on friendship and on a sharing of these values. That is why we are happy you have come

to visit us, to exchange ideas with us, and to seek solutions to the problems that often develop between two great nations and two neighbors.

Mr. President, you are welcome here. *Les Canadiens qui comme moi connaissent bien les Etats-Unis parce qu'ils y vont souvent, parce qu'ils y ont passé, comme dans mon cas, plusieurs étés pendant leur enfance, ou qui vont pendant l'hiver pour trouver votre soleil plus chaud en Floride; ces Canadiens vous connaissent, ces Canadiens sont contents de vous accueillir.* [Canadians who, like me, know well the United States because they go often, because they have spent, as in my case, several summers during their youth, or because they go during wintertime to find your sun which is warmer in Florida; these Canadians know you, these Canadians are glad to welcome you.]

And this sense of excitement, this sense of expectation that we felt in anticipation of your visit, Mr. President, we owe it to this friendship between our nations—I love hecklers; I don't know about you, Mr. President. This could go on for a long while, because to each of these manifestations, to each of these concerns, there are answers. You and I, your government and ours, your people and ours, will find the answers because we have faith in the people of the United States. As you have said, Mr. President, the greatest asset of the United States is the freedom of its people. This freedom we enjoy and this freedom you will feel amongst us.

Thank you.

The President. Mr. Prime Minister, Mr. Speaker of the Senate, Madam Speaker of the House:

It is a pleasure to be here today, not only to hear such warm words of welcome but also to appreciate through a visitor's eyes these splendid halls of government.

It was said once of this place that it grasps and materializes the beauty of Canada, the vastness of its lands, its loneliness, its youth, and its hope. And yet Parliament Hill is more than an imposing symbol of your nation; it is also a landmark of the New World, a monument to the right of self-government and the value of human freedom that even sometimes, as you yourself have pointed out, makes raucous behavior permissible. This belief in self-rule and the rights of the individual springs from a common heritage that formed the backdrop for our discussions in the next 2 days.

Now, Mr. Prime Minister, there is important work on the agenda before us—improving our trade, protecting our environment, safeguarding our freedom. But before we begin our public business, I did want to address one other matter between us that should be dealt with early on.

You will remember a little while back when our national troubles were widely known, a journalist penned a testimony to our country that was entitled, simply, "Let's Hear It for the United States." It spoke with great affection about people of the United States, their generosity, their inner strength. That testimony in our land was reprinted many times in magazines and newspapers, played on radio stations and even in nightclubs in my country. It touched the American people deeply that anyone should think so kindly of us. But I don't think it surprised us to learn that the journalist who wrote those very kind words was a Canadian.

And so, Mr. Prime Minister, before we discuss the other important matters before us, I want to take this occasion not to talk about the affairs of state, but to speak from the heart to the heart, to say to the Canadian people, the people of the United States do not merely value your friendship, we cherish it. We are here today not just to seek friendly ties with a neighboring nation and a world power but to strengthen instead the deep, unbending bonds of trust between old and devoted friends.

Merci. C'est un plaisir to be here with you today. Thank you.

The Prime Minister. Hey, guys, when I go to the United States, I'm not met with these kind of signs. You know, the Americans have some beefs against us, too, but they receive them politely. Now, how about a great cheer for President Reagan? [*Cheers and applause*]

Note: The Prime Minister spoke at 11:10 a.m. outside the Centre Block on Parliament Hill. As printed above, the Prime Minister's remarks follow the text of the White House press release.

Following their remarks, the President and the Prime Minister met privately in the Prime Minister's office in the Centre Block. They then went to the Prime Minister's residence for a luncheon. Later in the afternoon, the President and the Prime Minister and their delegations held a meeting in the Cabinet Room at the Centre Block.

Remarks of the President and Governor General Edward R. Schreyer of Canada at the State Dinner in Ottawa
March 10, 1981

The Governor General. Mr. President, when such close neighbors as your charming wife and yourself come to visit, I've found that the planned protocol gives way, at least in part, to a natural hospitality. Only recently you and I both would probably have used the expression "good old western hospitality," but in current circumstances for you and me perhaps some other term is to be found. In any case, it is the

rapport that exists between the entirety of our two nations that matters and which obviously has motivated you to make such an early visit to Canada. For this we are greatly appreciative in all parts of the country, and that you have chosen to do so within the first 2 months of your new administration is something which compounds our feeling.

In addition to your discussions on specific items, there is, I suggest, a very powerful and positive symbolic purpose in this visit as well. For the past seven decades or more, which happens to coincide with the creation by your country and ours of the International Joint Commission, the relationship between our two countries has been a model for others. Despite occasional differences, the overwhelming momentum in all this time has been always toward positive, productive friendship.

In the past 60 years or so, every President of the United States, with only one or two rather circumstantial exceptions, has visited here and, may I say, obviously and hopefully for the future, with honorable and good mutual result. You are continuing in that tradition, which I believe has produced a bond which was unique and still is almost unique among sovereign states everywhere.

We on both sides of the border, I think, often refer to the 4,000 miles and more of virtually unpatrolled border, to the kindred cultures and affinities, to the scientific and technical cooperation—as in the space shuttle, to mention just one example—to our political systems which, despite interesting and intriguing and subtle differences, produce an impressively similar stability for fundamental freedoms and due process and equality before the law. Ironically, visits by their very nature often tend to focus greater attention on those far less numerous issues which divide us, on which we have differences. And I suppose this is a normal part of the day-to-day of the bilateral relations in this world of reality. But if that be so, then that is precisely why it is so ultimately important that this visit demonstrate to all, so there can be no misreading or misunderstanding, that beneath the complexity of some of the issues—and some of them, goodness knows, are complex enough—lies a very firm bond of friendship, proven to be so by history and based upon constitutional restraint of power and motivated by plain decency and love of freedom.

Given all this, Mr. President, we can surely withstand the differences and, I would suggest, even the occasional ribbing which we know very well goes on, both at

the officials' level and among the millions of our respective citizens. I won't try to relate some anecdote or examples of this ribbing that I refer to. In fact, I don't know if it's wise to relate any of them. But I think I could say as an aside that no one is excluded from this, including some present and former Prime Ministers and Presidents themselves.

Now, as between sisters, I'm not so sure; I don't really know. But those of you who have brothers will know very well how imaginative and descriptive some of this language can become in otherwise rather fraternal relations. Maybe it's just as well that I not elaborate further.

Still, I must mention that some Canadians are defensive about our winters, particularly since in very recent years the expression "Canadian snowbirds" became widespread in your country among some of your countrymen. But then our retort could well be to quote from a famous American poet, Walt Whitman. He said, and I quote, "I have often doubted whether there could be a great and sturdy people without the hardy influence of winter in due proportion." I don't know, Mr. President, what your response or sequel to that might be, but I don't urge you to come up with it tonight necessarily.

In closing, I should like to say—and with all the emphasis that I can muster—that a remarkable relationship indeed has been created between our two countries. And it has been sustained, despite some tangible differences, because of human decency and fair play and by the rational resorting in complex matters and circumstances to procedures and mechanisms that were once and are still today exemplary to the whole world. I have mentioned the IJC. I refer to the scientific and defense research cooperation arrangements, et cetera, et cetera.

Earlier today I tried with words *en français de même qu'en anglais* to express for the Canadian people the kind of welcome that they would want to extend to you. If, as I said, the planet is becoming a global village, then this is the house next door. You are both, both of you, as plainly and as fully welcome as that. And then to find that hosting you could be enjoyable as well, well, that's a bonus which we shall keep in our memory and treasure.

Thank you.

The President. Your Excellency, I think this matter of humor and laughing or ribbing that may take place—I know that in World War II, Winston Churchill said of your fighting men and ours and his own that we seemed to be the only people in the world that could laugh and fight at the same time. Now, I don't think he had in mind carrying that over into peacetime. So, we won't try to do that. But Nancy and I want to thank you for your warm words and generous welcome to this land of friends.

Friendship is not easily defined, but today I think I gained a better understanding of what our friendship means to each other. As we arrived this morning on Parliament Hill, we crossed Ottawa's Rideau Canal. The old canal, now nearly 150 years old, winds through Ottawa as a reminder of our relationship. I learned that it was built by an engineer who planned it as a military defense to protect Canada from the United States. [*Laughter*] Once intended to protect your nation from mine in war, it's now a place of serene peace. In the winter it becomes one of the longest skating rinks anywhere, and in the summer it charms visitors, I've been told, with the weeping willows that arch over it. But I didn't see that portion of it where there were weeping willows, but I trust they are there.

Canada's Gratin O'Leary once noted that this canal "tells the blessed thing that has come between these two countries and which today has roots deeper than before. That's friendship." An historian once described the vast and wealthy continent that we share as "a boundless vision of great forests, silent mountains and wilderness oceans mingling with the sky." Your national motto is *A Mari Usque Ad Mare*, from sea to sea. And in the United States, we sing of "America the Beautiful," "from sea to shining sea."

Our people know that our nations were forged in this like heritage. Our people inherited the resilience of those who first opened the mighty waterways which cross and thus give life to our continent—the Mississippi, the Columbia, the Saint Law-

rence, the Great Lakes. We've grown up with our own national characters, but we share the independence and self-reliance of courageous pioneers such as Cartier, LaSalle, Lewis and Clark, and Mackenzie. Yet we also share the frontiersman's dependence on his neighbor, a trait that came to us early when settlers turned to each other to clear a forest, to raise a house, barter their goods. This North American spirit is a bond between our people, and we must never take it for granted.

New ways must be found to reinforce our special relationship. We live on the strongest, most prosperous continent on Earth. But as we develop our resources, we must protect the environment around us. We will never shirk our responsibility to defend our way of life when it is threatened. Prime Minister Trudeau, while visiting the United States, said that our nation was once the hope of the New World. Well, he's right. And I would like to add that our New World of freedom and democracy is now the hope of the entire world.

Our strong defense is the foundation of freedom, peace, and stability, and our countries must continue to draw close in times of crisis as we always have. Together, we'll stand as an example. As we work to keep this spirit of cooperation fresh, we will continue to respect each other's sovereignty, recognize our distinct national interests, and maintain our individual commitments to greater self-sufficiency.

Robert W. Service lived in Canada for many years and wrote about the taming of our continent and about the wild Canadian northlands. The law of the Yukon Road is that only the strong shall thrive, only the fit will survive. This is the challenge to our nations in the world today. Our national characters were forged on such a frontier. I'm confident that Canada and the United States, independent but together, can meet the test.

Nancy and I are just delighted to be here and have had a wonderful day, and we shall look forward to returning.

Thank you very much.

Note: The Governor General spoke at 10:48 p.m. in the ballroom of Rideau Hall, the Governor General's residence.

Earlier in the evening, the President and Mrs. Reagan were the guests of the Prime Minister at a gala performance at the National Arts Centre.

Remarks of the President and Prime Minister Pierre Elliott Trudeau of Canada Before a Joint Session of the Parliament in Ottawa
March 11, 1981

The Prime Minister. Mr. Speaker of the Senate, Madam Speaker of the House, Mr. President, Mrs. Reagan, distinguished American visitors, honorable members of the Senate, members of the House of Commons, *Excellences, mesdames et messieurs:*

Mr. President, yesterday I welcomed you to Canada. Well, I repeat that welcome now because in this chamber Canada's democracy finds its ultimate expression. Here, in a special way, we speak on behalf of the people of Canada. And here, the people of Canada are honored to receive you, sir.

Nations do not choose their neighbors; geography does that. The sense of neighborhood, however, is more than a product of geography; it is a creation of people who may live as far apart as California and Quebec. It is what makes neighbors of Canada and Mexico, for instance. Canadians have noted this sense in you, Mr. President, and they know that it gives a particular meaning to your visit to Ottawa.

[*In French:*] Our neighborhood, Mr. President, is not only a place but a state of mind, not only North America but the New World. We share the dreams that have made this continent a beacon, a hope, and a haven for people everywhere. We share the courage and joy in hard work that enabled us to build two great federal states side by side, from our first landfalls on the Atlantic to our last frontiers on the Pacific. We cherish what we have made. We are determined to preserve it, but at the same time we have been glad to admit others to the bounty and freedom we have found here.

[*In English:*] It is right that we should celebrate what we hold in common. At the same time, it is necessary that we remember and respect what makes us different. More than 200 years ago our paths diverged although our goals remained the same. You created a great republic with a presidential system. We evolved as a constitutional monarchy under a parliamentary system. You placed yourselves from the outset under a written constitution that you continue to revere today. We are only now finishing the work of writing ours and bringing it home. You fought a tragic civil war. We have recently undergone the experience of a referendum that involved no violence, but nonetheless touched the very fiber of this country. The differences of history affect our relations today because they affect our perceptions, our approaches, our priorities.

You, Mr. President, would perhaps agree with Thoreau where he says of the United States Government, and I quote, ". . . this government of itself never furthered any enterprise, but by the alacrity with which it got out if its way. It does not settle the West. It does not educate. The character inherent in the American people has done all that has been accomplished . . .."

The character of the Canadian people, Mr. President, has also made Canada. But here in Canada, our own realities have sometimes made it necessary for governments to further enterprise. Those realities and that necessity are still with us today.

[*In French:*] Mr. President, you have come to Canada at a busy moment in our history. We are still engaged in the task of nation-making. As an American you will understand the challenge before us. We are seeking to perfect our democracy and strengthen our unity. Sometimes, the noise we make will reach your ears. I can assure you, however, that out of the tumult and heat of creation we are forging a stronger Canada. To borrow someone's definition of a megalopolis, we are determined that we will not emerge from our present debate as a "loose confederation of shopping centers."

In the years ahead, the United States will face a dynamic neighbor to the north. As we put our house in order, we in Canada will grow in self-confidence. We will see our interests more clearly and pursue them more vigorously. What will not change, however, is our deep friendship with the United States. Indeed, the relationship between our two countries will grow as Canada grows. Certainly, we will have some lively discussions over the back fence. But we have always spoken plainly to each other, plainly but with mutual respect, because that is the way sovereign equals and close friends should speak to each other. [*In English*:] Mr. President, you take on your awesome responsibilities at a time of stress and crisis in international affairs. The world badly needs the courage and wisdom of the United States, that courage that it can provide under your leadership, sir. I speak for all Canadians when I say we are ready to work with you in the cause of stability, security, and humanity.

Your task, our joint task, will not be an easy one. Many people fear that the world has become too complicated, that events have spiraled beyond the control of individuals or governments. They're tempted to give up, to opt out, and to hide from reality and responsibility. That way lies oblivion.

I believe that we must neither cower before reality nor oversimplify it. Yet complexity should not obscure plain truth. On this most favored of continents, we can not simply turn our gaze inwards and ignore poverty, ignorance, and injustice elsewhere.

To the East, Mr. President, we face a system that seems ill-designed to respond to change and growth. Nevertheless, the Soviet Union and the Eastern European states may come to accommodate themselves at least to the dynamics of their own region. If, for example, the Polish people are able to work out their own destiny within a framework accepted by their neighbors, then they will have matched

revolution with a no less remarkable evolution. Through courage and restraint they will have begun the process of making their reality more Polish and their system more responsive, more adaptable, and ultimately more stable.

In the West, Mr. President, we have a long familiarity with the pressures of change. In the past decade our economies have undergone a severe test, as trusted assumptions have been found wanting. In the 1970's we were buffeted by the rude shock of rapid energy price increases. We were forced to recognize that the old monopoly of economic power was coming to an end. And yet for all the strains upon us, our political and economic framework has survived, survived at least as well as the chicken and the neck to which Winston Churchill once referred in this chamber.

Each of the Western countries has met the challenge of change in its own way. Since all of us have our own distinctive economic strengths and weaknesses, our solutions have had to be diverse. We have found no simple answers. We've fashioned no single way. With cooperation and consultation, however, we've been able to complement our various approaches.

At another level, though, we do have a single approach. Let there be no doubt about our unity in the defense of our most precious heritage—that democracy which is envied by those who rightly crave it and feared by those who wrongly deny its force.

As to North and South, we are not dismayed by the complexity of the problems. The poverty of the developing countries does not have to be permanent, nor is it unalloyed. The gap between the two groups is neither racial nor unbridgeable. In the growth of the oil-producing states, in the vigor of the newly industrialized countries, there is convincing evidence of the dynamism and potential of the developing world. In the unity of the South, there's not so much an identity of circumstances as an idea, a point of view, a shared sense of injustice. The poorer peoples are at the mercy of circumstances that leave them out of balance, often out of hope, and too often vulnerable to opportunists who come poaching in troubled waters. The industrialized democracies have not only a human duty but a strategic obligation to help developing countries in their struggle, their survival, and their success.

Mr. President, humanity will prevail. We in the New World can never be pessimists, for we are, in a very real sense, the custodians of the future. You have reminded us of this, sir, on both sides of the 49th parallel. You've done so by evoking a past in which both our peoples have been the architects of change, not its victims. I wish you well in your task and comfort in your burden. May part of that comfort come from the assurance of Canada's abiding friendship for your country and for your people.

The President. Mr. Prime Minister, Mr. Speaker of the Senate, Madam Speaker of the House of Commons, the honorable Senators, members of the House of Commons, distinguished members of the diplomatic corps, ladies and gentlemen:

I came to this great capital of this great nation by crossing a border not which divides us, but a border which joins us.

Nous nous sommes souvent serré la main par dessus cette frontière et nous le faisons une fois encore aujourd-hui. For those of my own party who accompanied me, I have said we've often shaken hands across this border, and we're doing it once again today.

Nancy and I have arrived for this, the first state visit of my Presidency, in the spirit expressed so well by a Calgary writer and publisher some 60 years ago. He said, "The difference between a friend and an acquaintance is that a friend helps where an acquaintance merely advises." [*Laughter*] Well, we come here not to advise, not to lecture; we are here to listen and to work with you. We're here as friends, not as acquaintances.

Some years ago, Nancy and I both belonged to a very honorable profession in California. And as I prepared for these remarks today, I learned that among those in the motion picture industry in Hollywood, it has been estimated that perhaps as many as one out of five are of Canadian origin. Now, many of those whom I counted as close professional colleagues and, indeed, close personal friends did not come from America's heartland, as I did, but from the heart of Canada, as did most of you in this historic chamber. Art Linkletter, Glenn Ford, Raymond Massey, Walter Pidgeon, Raymond Burr are but a few of your countrymen who are celebrated in our entertainment industry.

I believe I know the very special relationship between Canada and the United States, but with all respect to those few that I have mentioned, I can do better than that. A young lady once came to Hollywood from Toronto, and before long little Gladys Smith was embraced by our entire nation. Gladys Smith of Toronto became Mary Pickford. And I know that you'll forgive us for adopting her so thoroughly that she became known the world over as "America's sweetheart." [*Laughter*] But "America's sweetheart" was Canadian. [*Laughter*]

Affinity, heritage, common borders, mutual interests—these have all built the foundation for our strong bilateral relationship. This relationship has grown to include some of the strongest economic links among the nations of this Earth. Some 16 percent of America's total world trade is done with Canada. Our joint trade amounts to about 90 billion Canadian dollars annually. This is greater than the gross national product of some 150 countries. It's estimated that three-quarters of a million United States workers are employed in exports to Canada and, in turn, Canadian exports to the United States account for one-sixth of your gross national product. Not only is the vast bulk of this trade conducted between private traders in two free economic systems, but more than half crosses our borders duty-free. Our seaways, highways, airways, and rails are the arteries of a massive, interconnecting trade network which has been critically important to both of us.

Thus, while America counts many friends across the globe, surely we have no better friend than Canada. And though we share bilateral interests with countries throughout the world, none exceeds the economic, cultural, and security interests that we share with you.

These strong and significant mutual interests are among the reasons for my visit here. Already, I have shared with Prime

Minister Trudeau very helpful discussions across a range of issues—to listen and to ensure that these important ties shall not loosen.

I'm happy to say that in the recent past we've made progress on matters of great mutual importance. Our governments have already discussed one of the largest joint private projects ever undertaken by two nations—the pipeline to bring Alaskan gas to the continental United States. We strongly favor prompt completion of this project based on private funds. We have agreed to an historic liberalization of our trade in the Tokyo Round of the multilateral trade negotiatons. We've continued our efforts, begun with the Great Lakes Water Quality Agreement of 1972, to protect our joint heritage in the Great Lakes. We want to continue to work cooperatively to understand and control the air and water pollution that respects no borders.

During my visit here, I've had the pleasure of participating in the conclusion of two other important agreements.

We are renewing the North American Aerospace Defense Command Agreement for 5 more years. For more than two decades now, NORAD has bound us together in our common defense with an integrated command structure symbolizing our interdependence. This agreement represents continued progress in our relations and mutual security.

And second, we have concluded an agreement regarding social security benefits between those of our citizens who combine work in both nations. And with this new agreement, these people who are employed in both countries, they can then be eligible for the combined benefits. And the workers will be eligible for those benefits in whichever country they choose to live.

Our deep and longtime bilateral economic interests lead me to depart from the norm today and to give to you a report on America's progress toward economic recovery.

Five weeks ago, I reported to the American people that the U.S. economy faced the worst economic mess since the great worldwide depression. We're a proud people, but we're also realists. The time has come for us to face up to what I described as a potential economic calamity.

I raise this issue today because America holds a genuine belief in its obligation to consult with its friends and neighbors. The economic actions that we take affect not just us alone but the relationships across our borders as well.

As we examined America's economic illness, we isolated a number of contributing factors. Our Federal Government has grown explosively in a very short period of time. We found that there had grown up a maze of stifling regulations, which began to crush initiative and deaden the dynamic industrial innovation which brought us to where we are. We saw unbelievable deficits—this year alone reaching up to nearly $80 billion, including off-budget items. And we found that these deficits got in no one's way, because the Government found it easy to fuel inflation by printing more money just to make up the difference.

The American taxing structure, the purpose of which was to serve the people, began instead to serve the insatiable appetite of government. If you will forgive me, you know someone has once likened government to a baby. It is an alimentary canal with an appetite at one end and no sense of responsibility at the other. [*Laughter*] But our citizens were being thrown into higher tax brackets for simply trying to keep pace with inflation. In just the last 5 years, Federal personal taxes for the average American household have increased 58 percent. The results: crippling inflation, interest rates which went above 20 percent, a national debt approaching a trillion dollars, nearly 8 million people out of work, and a steady 3-year decline in productivity.

We decided not just to complain, but to act. In a series of messages and actions, we have begun the slow process of stopping the assault on the American economy and returning to the strong and steady prosperity that we once enjoyed. It's very important for us to have friends and partners know and understand what we're doing. Let me be blunt and honest. The United States in the last few years has not been as solid and stable an ally and trading partner as it should be. How can we expect certain things of our friends if we don't have our own house in order?

Americans are uniting now as they always have in times of adversity. I have found there is a wellspring of spirit and faith in my country which will drive us forward to gain control of our lives and restore strength and vitality to our economic system. But we act not just for ourselves but to enhance our relationships with those we respect.

First, we're taking near revolutionary steps to cut back the growth in Federal spending in the United States. We're proposing that instead of having our national budget grow at the unacceptable rate of 14 percent per year, it should rise at a more sensible 6 percent. This enables us to maintain the kind of growth we need to protect those in our society who are truly dependent on government services. Just yesterday, I submitted our proposed budget for the coming year—and then immediately crossed the border. [*Laughter*] With extraordinary effort, we've isolated some 83 items for major savings and hundreds more for smaller savings, which together amount to $48.6 billion in the coming fiscal year.

Our second proposal is a 10-percent cut across the board every year for 3 years in the tax rates for all individual income tax payers, making a total cut in tax rates of 30 percent. This will leave our taxpayers with $500 billion more in their pockets over the next 5 years and create dramatic new incentives to boost productivity and fight inflation. When these personal cuts are combined with tax cuts to provide our business and industry with new capital for innovation and growth, we will be creating millions of new jobs, many of them ultimately on your side of the border.

Our third proposal is to eliminate those unproductive and unnecessary regulations which have slowed down our growth and added to our inflationary burdens. We shall do this with care, while still safeguarding the health and safety of the American people and, I might add, while mindful of our responsibility to have equal regard for the health and safety of our neighbors.

Finally, we'll be working closely with our Federal Reserve System to achieve stable and moderate growth patterns in our money supply.

As I said, America's program for economic recovery is designed not merely to solve an internal problem; it is viewed by my administration as part of an essential effort to restore the confidence of our friends and allies in what we're doing. When we gain control of our inflation, we can once again contribute more helpfully to the health of the world economy. We believe that confidence will rise, interest rates will decline, and investment will increase. As our inflation is reduced, your citizens and other world citizens will have to import less inflation from us.

As we begin to expand our economy once again and as our people begin to keep more control of their own money, we'll be better trading partners. Our growth will help fuel the steady prosperity of our friends. The control we regain over our tax and regulatory structures will have the effect of restoring steady growth in U.S. productivity. Our goods will go into markets not laden down with the drag of regulatory baggage or punitive levies, but with a competitive edge that helps us and those who trade with us.

Now, such new, sustained prosperity in an era of reduced inflation will also serve worldwide to help all of us resist protectionist impulses. We want open markets. We want to promote lower costs globally. We want to increase living standards throughout the world. And that's why we're working so hard to bring about this economic renewal.

There are, of course, other very important reasons for us to restore our economic vitality. Beyond our shores and across this troubled globe, the good word of the United States and its ability to remain stable and dependable rely in good part on our having a stable and dependable economy. Projecting solid internal strengths is essential to the West's ability to maintain peace and security in the world. Thus, our national interests, our bilateral interests, and our hemispheric interests are profoundly involved in truly international questions. That's why we must act now, why we can no longer be complacent about the consequences of economic deterioration. We've entered an era which commands the Alliance to restore its leadership in the world. And before we can be strong in the world, we must be once again strong at home.

Our friend, our ally, our partner, and our neighbor, Canada and the United States have always worked together to build a world with peace and stability, a world of freedom and dignity for all people.

Now, with our other friends, we must embark with great spirit and commitment on the path toward unity and strength. On this side of the Atlantic, we must stand together for the integrity of our hemisphere, for the inviolability of its nations, for its defense against imported terrorism, and for the rights of all our citizens to be free from the provocations triggered from outside our sphere for malevolent purposes. Across the oceans, we stand together against the unacceptable Soviet invasion into Afghanistan and against continued Soviet adventurism across the Earth. And toward the oppressed and dispirited people of all nations, we stand together as friends ready to extend a helping hand.

I say to you, our Canadian friends, and to all nations who will stand with us for the cause of freedom: Our mission is more than simply making do in an untidy world. Our mission is what it has always been—to lift the world's dreams beyond the short limits of our sights and to the far edges of our best hopes.

This will not be an era of losing liberty; it shall be one of gaining it. This will not be an era of economic pessimism, of restraint and retrenchment; it will be one of restoration, growth, and expanding opportunities for all men and women. And we will not be here merely to survive; we will be here, in William Faulkner's words, to "prevail," to regain our destiny and our mutual honor.

Sometimes it seems that because of our comfortable relationship, we dwell perhaps a bit too much on our differences. Now, I too have referred to the fact that we do not agree on all issues. We share so many things with each other; yet, for good reasons, we insist on being different to retain our separate identities.

This captured the imagination of Ernest Hemingway when he worked as a writer for the Toronto Star Weekly in 1922. Heming-

way was traveling in Switzerland, and he noted that the Swiss made no distinction between Canadians and citizens of the United States. And he wondered about this, and he asked a hotelkeeper if he didn't notice any difference between the people from the two countries. "Monsieur," he said to Hemingway, "Canadians speak English and always stay 2 days longer at any place than Americans do." [*Laughter*] Well, as you know, I shall be returning to Ottawa in July, and if you don't mind, I'll plan to stay as long as everyone else. [*Applause*]

I'm not here today to dwell on our differences. When President Eisenhower spoke from this spot in 1953, he noted his gratitude as Allied Commander in World War II for the Canadian contribution to the liberation of the Mediterranean. This touched my curiosity, and even though I'd participated in that war myself, I did a little research.

In the Second World War, there was something called the 1st Special Service Force, a unique international undertaking at the time. This force was composed of Canadians and Americans, distributed equally throughout its ranks, carrying the flags of both nations. They served under a joint command, were taught a hybrid close-order drill, and trained together as paratroopers, demolition experts, ski troops, and then as an amphibious unit.

The 1st Special Service Force became famous for its high morale, its rugged abilities, and tough fighting in situations where such reputations were hard earned. Alerted to their availability, General Eisenhower requested them for special reconnaissance and raiding operations during the winter advance up the Italian peninsula. They were involved in the Anzio beachhead campaign in Italy and were at the spearhead of the forces that captured Rome. The 1st Special Service Force made no distinctions when it went into battle. Its men had the common cause of freedom at their side and the common denominator of courage in their hearts. They were neither Canadian nor American. They were, in General Eisenhower's term, liberators.

So, let's speak no more of differences today. Certainly your Ambassador, Ken

Taylor, didn't when he first sheltered and then spirited six Americans out of the center of Tehran and brought them to their freedom. Their daring escape worked not because of our differences, but because of our shared likenesses.

A final word to the people of Canada: We're happy to be your neighbor. We want to remain your friend. We're determined to be your partner, and we're intent on working closely with you in a spirit of coopera-tion. We are much more than an acquaintance.

Merci. Thank you.

Note: The Prime Minister spoke at 11:15 a.m. in the House of Commons Chamber at the Centre Block.

Earlier in the day, the President met with former Canadian Prime Minister Joe Clark at Rideau Hall and then participated in a tree-planting ceremony near the Governor General's residence.

Remarks of the President and Prime Minister Pierre Elliott Trudeau of Canada on the United States-Canadian Discussions in Ottawa
March 11, 1981

The Prime Minister. The point has been made many times that we are happy to have received President Reagan and his ministers and officials. We want to report briefly this morning on the conversations and discussions that took place between us. I would merely preface them by saying that at the beginning of a new administration we were surprised and delighted that so much ground could be covered in such a positive way. There's no subject and no grievance, if I could use the word, which the United States wasn't prepared to discuss and indicate a will to settle.

We discussed, yesterday morning, mainly the area of international affairs, and we had a very wide-ranging *tour d'horizon. Nous avons parlé de l'Afghanistan, de la Pologne, du Proche-Orient.* [We discussed Afghanistan, Poland, the Near East.] We talked a fair amount of the Caribbean and Central America. And on El Salvador in particular there was agreement, as I could sense it, that the solution there should be a political solution and that we would work in whatever way we could to ensure that the moderates were those who took over and not the extremists of the right or of the left.

We, as you know, reached an agreement on NORAD, which will be signed imminently. We reached an agreement on social security, also. Much of the work in these two areas had been done before we even sat down to talk, because you realize, as we do, that every day of the week there are contacts between officials of both governments on a multitude of subjects. And what we concentrated on in our brief meetings was mainly in the area of disagreement or a need to clarify our respective positions, and I would say that on the two main areas of bilateral concern we were very pleased with the ultimate response of the President of the United States.

It began, of course, with an expression of our deep disappointment at the fact that the fisheries treaty had been withdrawn from the United States from ratification, because from the outset we had argued, when these discussions began several years ago, that linkage between the boundaries settlement and the fisheries was not only necessary, but it was obvious from the very nature of the two agreements. And we are disappointed at the delinkage, and that has been expressed very clearly to the United States. But as I said in the House of Commons a few days ago, I think it's fair to put the best possible light on this, and that is certainly in keeping with the attitude that the discussions assumed.

The fisheries treaty was bogged down for a couple of years in the Senate, and we view the United States gesture of withdrawing that treaty as an indication of their determination to solve the problem in other ways, because we made it quite clear that the two problems have to be solved. It is not just a matter of having the courts determine the boundaries; it is a matter of making sure that though there will be no fish war—we gave each other the assurance of that, and we will take measures to make sure it doesn't happen—no one would benefit if the fish ultimately were fished out by the extraordinary capacities of the Canadian fishermen to go ahead and fish if they see that there are no limits and that the Americans are not respecting them. So, in this sense, we are very happy that the United States administration has undertaken to assure fish conservation measures in that area. And we are hopeful that the problem will be settled in that way. Indeed, we're more than hopeful; we are confident that it will.

The other area, of course, of great concern to Canada was cross-boundary pollution, either through acid rain, Great Lakes water pollution, or the particular case of the Garrison diversion. And on all these matters I think it's fair to say that the United States, as the President had occasion to repeat in the House of Commons a few moments ago—we have the assurances that the United States has the will and the determination to cooperate with us in preserving the environment for ourselves and for posterity.

We talked about the pipeline, the northern gas pipeline, and you heard the President of the United States give us the assurance that they were determined to see it to its successful completion and therefore to carry on the undertakings we'd had from the previous administration. We talked about many other bilateral subjects in the area of trade. We said that the auto pact discussions should be pursued and continued. In the area of mass transit transportation, the United States has agreed to consider ways in which agreement and the buy-American provisions can be made to operate in a fair way to Canada.

We discussed other economic subjects. But I think it's important, in conclusion, to remind you that the impression that I got from our discussions with the American President and ministers was that we were doing this in the best possible of spirits and attitudes. We didn't approach this as a zero-sum game. We think that there can be beneficiaries on both sides in all these areas, whether it be from the environment or trade.

We don't see the negotiations as terminating in a victory for one and some losses for the other. On the contrary, the spirit and reality of these discussions and, I am convinced, of the future of our relations with President Reagan and his administration will be that both sides can come out the gainers if we solve problems of the environment, problems of boundaries or of fisheries, problems of trade, problems of social security, and that both sides have it to their advantage to look at international problems in that same light, too, because we share the main objectives of liberty and justice.

I expressed for my part that there might be some future meetings between the President of the United States and the President of Mexico and the Prime Minister of Canada, if we could have such meetings to try and share common views of people who inhabit the New World, particularly as we regard international developments.

We will be meeting again, the President and I and the other summiteers, in July. And I think that we have shown at least by our meeting in this past day and a half that we intend to continue our consultations. I did make the point—and I think the President agreed—that our reaction to tensions in Poland, as different from our reaction to events in Afghanistan more than a year ago, show that we had learned from the lesson of Afghanistan and that we understood that one of the most important things we could achieve as like-minded countries was to consult in order that we not react in disarray to crises or possible tensions in other parts of the world, but that we act, in fact as we are in spirit, with unison and with dedication to the spirit of freedom.

That's about all I think that I have to say, Mr. President, and it's up to you now to try and satisfy those that were not satisfied by me. [*Laughter*]

The President. Well, Mr. Prime Minister, I'm sure they are. You gave certainly a very thorough summing-up of the wonderful meetings we've held. I would like first, however, to remark on the kind of welcome that I have received here. That welcome went beyond careful planning and beyond a sincere and warm reception by the Governor General and the Prime Minister. It was truly a welcome, a meeting between neighbor and neighbor.

Our discussion showed that the United States and Canada stand together on many world issues. Understandably, on some issues, we see things differently. Each country has its own national interests and objectives. Each country brings to international issues a distinct point of view. But what has impressed me is the degree to which we are in agreement and, where we have differed, that we have discussed our differences with the kind of openness and understanding that exists between neighbors.

We discussed the major areas of instability in the world, as the Prime Minister told you, including Eastern Europe, the Middle East, Latin America. We considered carefully the Ottawa Summit, which will be held here in July. That meeting will be a very useful opportunity to share views on relationships between the industrialized democracies and the Soviet Union on energy cooperation and on economic relations within the developing nations.

In addition to discussing these world issues, we carefully considered the bilateral U.S.-Canadian relationship. We agreed wholeheartedly that consultation is vitally important to our close and cooperative relationship, and we agreed to foster frank and informal consultation at all levels and at all times. Our bilateral discussions took us into the areas where our two nations are closest. We discussed matters affecting the environment, fisheries, as you've been told, energy, trade, and defense. In each of these areas we were, I believe, able to deal with the issue squarely, in an atmosphere of frankness and understanding. And we did, yes, discuss the pipeline, the Canadian national energy program, took up the continuing

problems, as the Prime Minister told you, of east coast boundary and fisheries treaties.

On the environment we addressed the Garrison project and continued joint efforts to deal with both transboundary air pollution and the cleanup of the Great Lakes. We agreed to continue consultations on the auto industry and on reciprocal opportunities for urban mass transit trade. We discussed our defense production sharing agreements. We've had, in short, a busy time.

I look forward to continued contacts between us at the Prime Minister-President level, at the level of Cabinet officers, and at all levels below. To sum it up, our meetings have been, as he said, frank and constructive, and I intend to do all in my power to see that we continue to deal with each other in the same way in the years ahead.

And I would like to close by expressing my thanks to Governor General Schreyer, to Prime Minister Trudeau, and, through them, to the people of Canada for the warm welcome that I and my associates have received here this week. I can assure you we will not forget it. We will remember it with great warmth and pleasure.

Thank you, and I understand that——[*applause*].

The Prime Minister. We're going to see the signature of a couple of these agreements. I understand that Secretary Haig and Minister MacGuigan [Mark MacGuigan, Canadian Secretary of State for External Affairs] will stay on to answer any questions, and Madame Bégin [Monique Bégin, Minister for National Health and Welfare] also will answer questions. She may even ask some, if I know her. [*Laughter*] I personally will be giving a press conference tomorrow, and I'll be happy to answer any questions that may not have been dealt with today.

Note: The Prime Minister spoke at 12:08 p.m. to reporters assembled in the Railway Committee Room at the Centre Block.

Following the remarks, the President visited the U.S. Embassy and then returned to Washington, D.C.

Executive Order 12297—International Coffee Agreement 1976
March 12, 1981

By the authority vested in me as President by the International Coffee Agreement Act of 1980 (Public Law 96–599; 94 Stat. 3491) and Section 301 of Title 3 of the United States Code, and in order to carry out and enforce the International Coffee Agreement 1976, it is hereby ordered as follows:

Section 1. The functions vested in the President by Public Law 96–599 (94 Stat. 3491) are delegated to the United States Trade Representative.

Sec. 2. In carrying out the functions delegated to him, the United States Trade Representative shall consult with the Secretary of Agriculture and the Secretary of State. The United States Trade Representative may redelegate some or all of those functions to the head of another Executive agency with the consent of the head of such agency.

RONALD REAGAN

The White House,
March 12, 1981.

[*Filed with the Office of the Federal Register, 4:20 p.m., March 12, 1981*]

Executive Order 12298—Lake Tahoe Region
March 12, 1981

By the authority vested in me as President by the Constitution of the United States of America, and in order to eliminate unnecessary and duplicative Federal interference in the responsibilities of the Tahoe Regional Planning Agency (see Public Law 96–551 of December 19, 1980), it is hereby ordered that the Tahoe Federal Coordinating Council is terminated and Executive Order No. 12247 of October 15, 1980, is revoked.

RONALD REAGAN

The White House,
March 12, 1981.

[*Filed with the Office of the Federal Register, 4:21 p.m., March 12, 1981*]

Memorandum on Federal Cooperation With the Tahoe Regional Planning Agency
March 12, 1981

Memorandum for the Heads of Agencies Represented on the Western Federal Regional Council (Region IX)

Subject: Coordination with the Tahoe Regional Planning Agency

The States of California and Nevada have recently amended their bi-state compact to encourage the wise use and conservation of the waters of Lake Tahoe and of the resources of the area around the Lake. The Congress of the United States approved of that compact (Public Law 96–551). It is important that the Federal government cooperate with the bi-state efforts of that compact, not compete with it.

All Executive agencies shall cooperate with the Tahoe Regional Planning Agency with respect to their activities which take place within or affect the Lake Tahoe Region. All such cooperation should be coordinated through the Representative of the United States serving on the Governing Board of the Tahoe Regional Planning Agency, Zane G. Smith, Jr., Regional For-ester of the Pacific Southwest Region of the United States Forest Service.

RONALD REAGAN

Nomination of William H. Coldiron To Be Solicitor of the Department of the Interior
March 13, 1981

The President today announced his intention to nominate William H. Coldiron to be Solicitor of the Department of the Interior.

Since 1953 Mr. Coldiron has worked for the Montana Power Co. He has served as director and vice chairman of the board since 1979. He was executive vice president in 1975–70, elected director in 1974, vice president and general counsel in 1968–75. Previously he served as general counsel and adviser on all regulatory and business matters of the company.

He was director and president of Canadian-Montana Gas Co., Ltd., Canadian-Montana Pipe Line Co., and Roan Resources Co.

in 1974. He served as assistant attorney general of the State of Montana in 1950–51. He was a professor of law at the University of Montana Law School from 1947 to 1950 and from 1951 to 1954.

He served in the U.S. Army in 1942–46 and was discharged with the rank of captain. He was graduated from Morehead State University, Kentucky (B.A., 1938), and the University of Kentucky College of Law (J.D., 1947). He is a member of the Montana and American Bar Associations.

Mr. Coldiron is a resident of Butte, Mont. He was born in Catlettsburg, Ky., on August 12, 1916.

Nomination of Daniel Oliver To Be General Counsel of the Department of Education
March 13, 1981

The President today announced his intention to nominate Daniel Oliver to be General Counsel, Department of Education.

Since 1980 Mr. Oliver has served as president of Rincon Communications Corp. of New York. In 1980 he was involved in research and speechwriting for the James L. Buckley senatorial campaign in Connecticut. He was executive editor of National Review magazine in 1973–76 and editorial assistant in 1970–71. He was a candidate for the New York State Assembly in 1965, 1966, and 1968.

Mr. Oliver was with the firm of Alexander & Green of New York in 1971–73 and in 1976–79. In 1967–70 he was with Hawkins, Delafield & Wood of New York.

He was graduated from Harvard College (A.B., 1964) and Fordham Law School (LL.B., 1967). He was a Russian linguist in the U.S. Army in 1959–62.

Mr. Oliver is married and has five children. He resides with his family in Greenwich, Conn. He was born in New York City on April 10, 1939.

Nomination of Vincent E. Reed To Be an Assistant Secretary of Education
March 13, 1981

The President today announced his intention to nominate Vincent E. Reed to be Assistant Secretary for Elementary and Secondary Education, Department of Education.

Since 1976 Mr. Reed has served as superintendent of public schools in Washington, D.C. He was acting superintendent in 1975–76.

In 1974–75 Mr. Reed was associate superintendent for administration with the D.C. public schools. He was assistant superintendent for secondary schools in 1971–74 and executive assistant to the superintendent of schools in 1970–71. He held various other positions within the D.C. public school system prior to 1970.

Mr. Reed is affiliated with the American Association of School Personnel Administrators, National Association of Secondary School Principals, National Association for the Advancement of Colored People, Junior Achievement, and many other groups.

Mr. Reed attended the University of Pennsylvania, the Wharton School of Finance and Commerce. He was graduated from Howard University with an M.A. in education.

Mr. Reed is married and resides in Washington, D.C. He was born in St. Louis, Mo., on March 1, 1928.

Nomination of Mark S. Fowler To Be a Member of the Federal Communications Commission, and Designation as Chairman
March 13, 1981

The President today announced his intention to nominate Mark S. Fowler to be a member of the Federal Communications Commission for the unexpired term of 7 years from July 1, 1979. Upon confirmation, the President intends to designate Mr. Fowler as Chairman.

Since 1975 Mr. Fowler has been a senior partner with the firm of Fowler & Meyers of Washington, D.C. He specialized in representing radio, television, domestic and private radio stations throughout the United States before the Federal Communications Commission. He was a guest speaker over the past 5 years at more than 20 conventions of broadcasters, sponsored by the National Association of Broadcasters and various State broadcaster associations. He was codirector of the legal and administrative agencies group in the office of executive branch management during the transition.

He was FCC communications counsel to Citizens for Reagan in 1975–76 and to the Reagan for President Committee in 1979–80. He represented both committees before the Federal Communications Commission. Mr. Fowler was associate attorney with the firm of Smith & Pepper of Washington, D.C., in 1970–75. He was employed with various radio stations from 1959 to 1969.

Mr. Fowler was graduated from the University of Florida at Gainesville where he received both his undergraduate and law degrees. He is married and has two children. He resides with his family in Arlington, Va. Mr. Fowler was born in Toronto, Canada, on October 6, 1941.

Appointment of Peter M. Flanigan as a Member of the President's Economic Policy Advisory Board
March 13, 1981

The President today announced the appointment of Peter M. Flanigan to the President's Economic Policy Advisory Board. The Board is composed of economic experts from outside the government, and will meet every 3 or 4 months to advise the President with respect to the conduct and objectives of both the domestic and international economic policy of the United States.

Mr. Flanigan is a managing director of Dillon, Read & Co., Inc., in New York and is a member of the board of directors of Anheuser-Busch Co., Inc. In 1969 he served as Assistant to the President with responsi-

bility in the areas of domestic policy, commerce, and economics, was a Director of the Council of International Economic Policy in 1972, and served as deputy campaign manager in the 1968 Nixon Presidential campaign.

Other members of the President's Economic Policy Advisory Board are George P. Shultz, Chairman, James T. Lynn, Walter B. Wriston, Charls E. Walker, Herbert Stein, Thomas Sowell, Arthur F. Burns, William E. Simon, Paul W. McCracken, Alan Greenspan, Milton Friedman, and Arthur B. Laffer.

Remarks Announcing Additional Federal Aid for the Investigation of the Murdered and Missing Youth in Atlanta, Georgia
March 13, 1981

The President. I have a brief statement to read, and then I'm going to leave because of the Cabinet meeting that's scheduled, and the Vice President is going to remain for your questions.

Since the first days of this administration, we've been deeply concerned and involved in assisting the city of Atlanta and its citizens in attempting to bring an end to one of the most tragic situations that has ever confronted an American community. Twenty children have been murdered, and another is still missing. This nightmare has continued for more than 19 months, and I'm determined to continue to assist the city of Atlanta in bringing it to an end.

Today I'm directing that $1½ million be provided for the city of Atlanta for the increased costs of the investigation conducted by local law enforcement officials. This is in addition to the $979,000 in Federal funds that I asked be sent to the city on March 5th for the purpose of providing needed social and health services to the citizens of the area.

I want the people of Atlanta and the Nation to know that this administration is doing and will continue to do what we can to help bring an end to this tragedy. Presently we have nearly 40 FBI agents in the field working on the case along with scores of others throughout the country who are deeply involved. The Departments of Justice, Health and Human Services, and Education are providing investigative and social services requested by Mayor Maynard Jackson and other local officials.

Tomorrow Vice President George Bush will travel to Atlanta as my emissary to meet with the mayor, the members of the task force which we created nearly 4 weeks ago, and other concerned members of the community to convey the deep feelings and convictions that we both share regarding this crisis.

And finally, on a personal note, I'm deeply touched by the depth of concern and compassion being expressed by Americans in every area of our land. The American people are responding with offers of funds, personal commitments, and with other expressions of assistance. They've joined all of us with their prayers as they continue to display the kindness and the decency and the generosity of spirit that has historically been the hallmark of our people.

All of this that we've been doing so far, all of it has been managed by the Vice President. So, that's why I'm going to leave you in his hands now while I go back to the Cabinet meeting.

The Vice President. Thank you, sir.

Reporter. But, Mr. President, what do you have to say to people who say that Washington would have moved quicker if those children had been white than it did?

The President. Well, we moved as quickly as we could and were aware that there was a need for outside help. The mayor contacted us and asked, and we immediately went to work with these funds and appointed the Vice President right then, asked him to take charge. So, we've been doing it from the first that there was anything that we could do to help.

Q. The fact they were black didn't mean that we had less concern or you moved slower?

The President. No. Sam [Sam Donaldson, ABC News], I think there's one thing, and I want to make one thing very plain. This goes all the way back to the campaign. This administration is totally colorblind.

Q. Thank you, Mr. President.

Note: The President spoke at 12:57 p.m. to reporters assembled in the Briefing Room at the White House.

The Vice President's question-and-answer session with reporters also is included in the White House press release.

Statement on the National Defense Stockpile of Strategic and Critical Materials
March 13, 1981

I am today directing the Federal Emergency Management Agency (FEMA) to begin the first purchase program for the national defense stockpile of strategic and critical materials in over 20 years. These purchases of strategic materials, estimated initially at $100 million, are a step to restructure the existing $15 billion stockpile in critical areas of deficiency.

It is now widely recognized that our nation is vulnerable to sudden shortages in basic raw materials that are necessary to our defense production base. Our vulnerabilities have been highlighted in a number of congressional hearings and panels concerning the industrial base. Thus, this overdue addition to our stockpile constitutes a necessary hedge against any supply disruptions.

In addition to strategic stockpiling, I am considering other measures to decrease the Nation's vulnerability, including ways to expand domestic capacity to produce strategic and critical materials. This acquisition program is a necessary first step. It is expected that larger purchases will be made as funds from sales of excess materials build up in the stockpile fund.

Proclamation 4824—National Poison Prevention Week, 1981
March 13, 1981

*By the President of the United States
of America*

A Proclamation

The care and protection of children is a primary responsibility of all parents. This task should not be taken lightly because the stakes are high and, often, irreversible. Such is the case when dealing with poisons and other potentially hazardous material.

Thanks to child-protection packaging and greater awareness of parents, in the past two decades we have witnessed a reduction in the accidental poisoning of children. While progress has been made, we must remain vigilant. The death of even one child due to the ingesting of poison is too many.

A tragedy involving any family's child is a tragedy for us all. Parents around the Nation should be keenly aware that the danger of accidental poisoning knows no boundary and that only parental attention to the hazards around them will protect their children from needless suffering and possible death. Even heightened community awareness, even new safety packaging, even new laws on the books are less important than strict parental supervision when avoiding a tragedy from the misuse or abuse of common pharmaceutical and household products.

By Joint Resolution on September 26, 1961 (75 Stat. 681, 36 U.S.C. 165) Congress requested that the President issue an annual proclamation designating the third week in March as National Poison Prevention Week, to alert the American people to the problems of accidental poisoning among children and urge preventive measures for their solution.

Now, Therefore, I, Ronald Reagan, President of the United States of America, do hereby designate the week beginning March 15, 1981, as National Poison Prevention Week.

In Witness Whereof, I have hereunto set my hand this thirteenth day of March, in the year of our Lord nineteen hundred eighty-one, and of the Independence of the United States of America the two hundred and fifth.

RONALD REAGAN

[*Filed with the Office of the Federal Register, 8:45 a.m., March 16, 1981*]

Note: The text of the proclamation was released by the Office of the Press Secretary on March 14.

Exchange With Reporters in New York, New York
March 14, 1981

Q. Mr. President, are you going to do anything to help mass transit in New York City?

The President. Well, in the first place, New York City—there are some areas in the country that will probably—well, those that are trying to start new rapid transit that will not fare as well as New York will, where there is an established system. So, we don't think anyone's really going to be hurt too badly. And we've also given the green light to Westway.

Q. Is this a fence-mending trip, Mr. President?

The President. No. I didn't think there were any fences here to be mended. I came up here to—Nancy had some things to do here and some things she's interested in, the drug program and so forth. And while we're going to have some entertainment, why, this is, I think, business.

Q. Senator Byrd says the most you're going to get is a 1-year tax cut. How do you respond to that?

The President. I just hope with all my heart that Senator Byrd is wrong, as he's been so many times in the past.

Q. For example?

The President. I've found him wrong on most issues. I take it we're not talking about Harry Byrd. [*Laughter*]

Q. No, Senator Robert Byrd, the minority leader.

Q. How about the Russians in Poland?

Any movement there? The Russians in Poland?

The President. So far we see nothing, no evidence that this isn't just their exercise, the games.

Q. Thank you, Mr. President.

Note: The exchange began at 12 noon as the President departed the offices of the New York Daily News following an interview.

Statement on the Westway Highway Project in New York, New York
March 14, 1981

During the campaign, I spoke to local construction workers and pledged my support for the Westway Highway, a building project that will serve to restore and revitalize an area that sorely needs the help. I am pleased to announce today, on the occasion of my first visit to New York City as President, that many of the Federal financial and regulatory roadblocks that snarled the Westway Project have been cleared away.

Now that we've responded at the Federal level, any further action awaits decisions by State and local officials here in New York. I know there are differences among the various parties, but those differences are best resolved by the level of government closest to the people.

Washington is no longer standing in the way of this project. Westway has the green light, and it's up to New York to drive through.

Remarks Outside Angelo's Restaurant in New York, New York
March 14, 1981

Senator D'Amato and Congressman Molinari, your ladies, you ladies and gentlemen:

I just want to tell you I'm delighted to be here. And I want you to know that in these gentlemen beside me, you are well represented in Washington.

And Congressman Molinari has made a very great personal sacrifice to stay and help us with this program that we are trying to implement. I know you can hear all kinds of things about it and what it's going to do or not going to do. But is there anyone here that doesn't believe that we have to turn the direction around that

we've been going, in order to end inflation, end unemployment, and get this country back where it should be in the eyes of the world? [*Cheers*]

Well, that's what we're going to try to do. And as I say, it's really a great pleasure to be here. Between us, we'll all go to work, and we'll all try to do it there in Washington.

And now they tell me that they're going to take me inside and feed me. [*Laughter*] And I heard so much last night about how I'm going to be fed, I haven't had any breakfast yet. [*Laughter*] I've been waiting for this.

God bless you all. It's good to see you,. *Note: The President spoke at 12:29 p.m.*
and thank you for being here. Thank you.

Nomination of Mary Claiborne Jarratt To Be an Assistant Secretary of Agriculture
March 14, 1981

The President today announced his intention to nominate Mary Claiborne Jarratt to be Assistant Secretary of Agriculture (Food and Consumer Services).

Since 1975 Miss Jarratt has served as a professional staff member, Committee on Agriculture, U.S. House of Representatives. In 1972–75 she was executive secretary to William R. Haley, member of the National Transportation Safety Board. Miss Jarratt was executive assistant to Representative Richard H. Poff of Virginia in 1967–72. In 1966–67 she was assistant to professor, Harvard Graduate School of Business.

Miss Jarratt was graduated from Mary Baldwin College (B.A., 1964) and received a degree of business certification from the Katharine Gibbs School in Boston, Mass. Miss Jarratt was born in Clifton Forge, Va., on October 29, 1942. She is a resident of Alexandria, Va.

Nomination of Frederick Morris Bush To Be an Assistant Secretary of Commerce
March 14, 1981

The President today announced his intention to nominate Frederick Morris Bush to be Assistant Secretary of Commerce for Tourism.

Mr. Bush was assistant for administration in the Office of the Vice President-elect during the transition period. In August–November 1980, he was staff assistant to the Reagan-Bush Committee.

In 1979–80 Mr. Bush was national finance director of the George Bush for President Committee. In 1977–79 he was finance director of the Illinois Republican Party. Mr. Bush was assistant to the finance chairman of the Republican National Committee in 1977. He was national phone bank director of the President Ford Committee in 1975–76. In 1974–75 he was assistant to the finance chairman of the Republican National Committee. Mr. Bush was legislative aide to Representative Joe Skubitz in 1973. He served as a clerk to the Republican Policy Committee of the U.S. Senate in 1971–73.

Mr. Bush was graduated from the University of Colorado (B.A., 1971) and American University (M.A., 1974). Mr. Bush is married and has one child. He resides with his family in Houston, Tex. He was born in Newport News, Va., on February 6, 1949.

Nomination of Russell A. Rourke To Be an Assistant Secretary of Defense
March 14, 1981

The President today announced his intention to nominate Russell A. Rourke to be Assistant Secretary of Defense (Legislative Affairs).

Since 1977 Mr. Rourke has served as administrative assistant to Representative Harold S. Sawyer (R-Mich.). In 1976–77 he served as Special Assistant to the President (Legislative Affairs). Mr. Rourke was Deputy to Presidential Counsellor John O. Marsh, Jr., in 1974–76. In 1974 he was the Republican-Conservative nominee for Congress in the 36th District of New York.

Mr. Rourke served in 1965–74 as administrative assistant to Representative Henry P. Smith III (R-N.Y.). In 1960–64 he was administrative assistant to Representative John R. Pillion (R-N.Y.). Mr. Rourke was associated with the firm of Keogh, Carey and Costello in 1959–60. He is a member of the District of Columbia and American Bar Associations. He was graduated from the University of Maryland (B.A., 1953) and Georgetown University Law Center (LL.B., 1959).

Mr. Rourke was born in New York City on December 30, 1931. He is married to the former Judith Anne Muller, and they have three children. He resides with his family in Annapolis, Md.

Nomination of Henry E. Catto, Jr., To Be an Assistant Secretary of Defense
March 14, 1981

The President today announced his intention to nominate Henry E. Catto, Jr., to be Assistant Secretary of Defense (Public Affairs).

Since 1977 Mr. Catto has served as chairman of the IBIS Corp. of Washington, D.C. He has also served as chairman of the Washington Communications Corp.

In 1976–77 he was U.S. Permanent Representative to the European Office of the United Nations, with the rank of Ambassador, in Geneva. Mr. Catto was U.S. Chief of Protocol in 1974–76. In 1971–73 he was U.S. Ambassador to El Salvador. Mr. Catto was Deputy U.S. Representative to the Organization of American States, with the rank of Ambassador; U.S. member, Council on Education, Science and Culture; and U.S. member, Committee on Education, from 1969 to 1971. In 1952–69 Mr. Catto was involved with insurance, real estate, and banking interests in Texas.

Mr. Catto was a Republican candidate for the Texas Legislature in 1960 and 1961. He was national finance director, Citizens for Nixon, in 1968.

Mr. Catto was graduated from Williams College (B.A., 1952). He is married and has four children. He resides with his family in McLean, Va. Mr. Catto was born in San Antonio, Tex., on December 6, 1930.

Nomination of William S. Heffelfinger To Be an Assistant Secretary of Energy
March 14, 1981

The President today announced his intention to nominate William S. Heffelfinger to be Assistant Secretary of Energy (Administration, Procurement, Comptroller, and Finance).

Mr. Heffelfinger is currently serving as Director of Administration at the Department of Energy, where he has served since 1977. In 1977 he was Associate Administrator for Management and Administration, Federal Energy Administration. In 1971–77 Mr. Heffelfinger was Assistant Secretary of Transportation (Administration). He was Deputy Assistant Secretary of Transportation (Administration) in 1969–71.

Mr. Heffelfinger was staff assistant to the Assistant Secretary of the Interior for Water and Power Development in 1969. In 1962–69 he was director of program review with the Martin-Marietta Corp. Mr. Heffelfinger was Assistant Administrator of the Federal Civil Defense Administration in 1953–61. In 1961–62 he was Director of Administration of the Office of Emergency Preparedness in the Executive Office of the President. He was institutional business manager for the State of Kansas in 1946–53.

Mr. Heffelfinger is married and has three children. He was born in Effingham, Kans., on January 31, 1925. He resides with his family in McLean, Va.

Nomination of J. William Middendorf II To Be Permanent Representative of the United States to the Organization of American States
March 14, 1981

The President today announced his intention to nominate J. William Middendorf II to be Permanent Representative of the United States of America to the Organization of American States, with the rank of Ambassador.

Mr. Middendorf recently served as chairman of the finance committee of the Presidential Inaugural Committee. During the 1980 Presidential campaign, Mr. Middendorf served as coordinator of the International Economic Advisory Committee and the Naval Advisory Committee. He was also a member of the Strategic Minerals Task Force.

Mr. Middendorf was president and chief executive officer of Financial General Bankshares, Inc. He served as U.S. Ambassador to the Netherlands from 1969 to 1973 and as Under Secretary and Secretary of the Navy from 1973 to 1977. Mr. Middendorf's long career in investment banking culminated in 1962 with the formation of his own partnership, which he left in 1969 to enter government service.

He has been active in the Republican Party, serving as treasurer of the Republican National Committee, a delegate or alternate to three Republican National Conventions, and treasurer of the 1968 transition committee. He is the author of numerous articles, a frequent lecturer on major international security and economic issues, and is a member of several national and international organizations concerned with defense, trade, and monetary questions.

Mr. Middendorf was born in Baltimore, Md., on September 22, 1924. He received a bachelor of naval science degree from Holy Cross College in 1945 and a bachelor of arts degree from Harvard University in 1947. In 1954 he received an M.B.A. from New York

University Graduate School of Business Administration.

Mr. Middendorf is married to the former Isabelle Paine, and they have four children.

Remarks and a Question-and-Answer Session on the Program for Economic Recovery at a White House Luncheon for Congressional Women
March 16, 1981

The President. Well now, officially, welcome. This all resulted from a luncheon, a very enjoyable one we had on January 6th at Blair House. A number of you said that that was your first time to see Blair House, and I asked about this other house over here, and told you at the time that we'd do it again here. And I've been looking forward to this, and here we are.

There have been some changes, and I know there are several of you that sent regrets—as I said, Millicent[1] is across the hall in the Red Room. But I am pleased, also, by the fact that one of the things we discussed the first time was the position of women in government, and I told you what we were going to try and do. Now, I don't know whether we've completely satisfied you yet, but we're not through yet. But I'm just wondering how close we're coming now to having as many ladies present who are members of the administration as there are who are Members of the Congress.

So, I haven't had an opportunity to—I'll tell you what. [*Laughter*] I know you've all met each other at each table, but all of you who work in our end of the shop, in the executive branch, please just stand up and let the ladies see you. And there is one in particular who I'm going to ask to stand again so you'll be able to recognize her, because you may want to contact her, and that is Wendy Borcherdt,[2] who is here for the very purpose of seeing that your numbers increase.

So, maybe one day we'll do this again and we will outnumber you, and then you'll know we've really kept our word.

But it's been a very busy time. And someone told me the other day by actual count that I have met with, in these couple of months, more than 350 of the Members of Congress in an effort to have a liaison and—you notice I said liaison. I was taken to task in the press the other day for calling it *lay*-ison. And they thought that I just didn't know, but I'll tell you, I'm guilty. The Army has some words of its own, and when I was a reserve cavalry officer, the Army called it *lay*-ison, just like they call oblique ob-*like* in the Army. [*Laughter*] But now I'm a civilian, so I'll call it liaison.

You know the importance that we place on the economic program, and you weren't invited to lunch now for us to try and con you into anything. But maybe you might want to engage in a discussion or talk about any of the things that might be on your mind, as we did before in Blair House, and if so, we can have a dialog instead of a monolog here. At Blair House I was able to call on George Bush, but he is in Miami, Paula[3] tells me. I knew as far as Atlanta, because we had him there on that very tragic situation there. And he's delighted that he and Barbara went down and have met with some of the families that have known the tragedy of what's happening there, but also to make it plain that we're going to do everything we can from this end for what we think is the most unusual, tragic situation in the country. And while law enforcement is supposed to take place at the local level, we think this is the time

---

[1] *Representative Millicent Fenwick of New Jersey was attending a luncheon hosted by Mrs. Reagan in the Red Room.*
[2] *Associate Director of Presidential Personnel.*

---

[3] *Senator Paula Hawkins of Florida.*

when the whole country would like to have Washington doing whatever it could also to help. So, we are doing that.

Q. Mr. President, I appreciate very, very much our being able to be here and ask questions. And I think, as a working mother—I have always felt very strongly that all mothers are working mothers—one of the things that worries me a lot about the budget cuts is the fact that displaced homemakers and women who have done what we've really told them to do and tried to encourage them to do, stay home and take care of their family, may be running a tremendous risk. And it appears that the displaced homemaker program, allowing their getting back into the workplace if something should happen to their spouse or family that they need to and so forth, really is going to impact upon them. And I think when we tell them to do this, to say to them all you get for that is honor, it's hard to wear it or eat it—*[laughter]*—if you know what I'm saying.

And I'm just wondering, are you absolutely rigid on those specific programs? Is there going to be some flexibility where we can try to preserve those things that, I think, are so important?

The President. Well, and I will take some help if I can get it here, because with all the facets of all of these programs, I can't claim that I can keep everything in the front of my mind. But I think maybe we're talking about some programs that are not so much disappearing as are going to be part of block grant programs where, we believe, there could be more efficient administration of them and less administrative overhead.

You know, it's a very discouraging thing. If you would start at the very local level of government and compare the dollars it spends—it takes for a city or town to deliver a service to a community, then move up to the county level and find out how much higher the percentage is, move up to the State level and it's higher, and move up to the Federal level and it is the highest of all, the overhead in performing a service. And we believe that by transferring many of these things and incorporating them into block grants, where we give the local community the ability to set its priorities and to

operate without regulations that have been imposed from thousands of miles away, here by a group in Washington—I'm speaking now of the permanent employees of government, of bureaucracy that tries to make rules that will fit everything from New York and Chicago down to South Succotash—*[laughing]*—out there in the country. And, so, I don't think those programs are going to disappear.

Q. Well, I guess my fear is that sometimes when they go to the local level, you'll find that if you don't have any constraints on how they spend the block grant, very often the money that they save money on is women and children. Very often when there's budget cuts, it's kind of women and children first. And it happens at all different levels. And I would hope that we'd see some real direction; that if that's going to be the focus of the thing, that we make sure when they take the block grant money that they don't cut out displaced homemakers or something because they don't have the political clout in the city hall to fight back. And I guess that's what I'm really saying. Let's make sure people don't get hurt or that certain things don't totally disappear if we're going to restructure how they're administered.

The President. Yes, well, I think that is something to look at and be very sure of.

Q. Mr. President, I want to thank you for having us. I represent Cleveland, Ohio, the scene of your debate victory. And I was very pleased in the debate when you talked about and mentioned the inequities of poor women in the social security system, and I think millions of American women were. My focus of concern, of course, is older women and, in particular, problems that the Northeast and the Midwest are experiencing. In the State of Ohio, Mr. President, we get only 71 cents out of the dollar back to our State. And I'm wondering, if we go to a block grant approach to the States, like my own State, can we be assured that we'll get our share of jobs in the defense area and in energy and so on that by and large would help our State of Ohio and other Midwestern and Northeastern States? And then we'd have the money on a State level to do the kinds of things that you're suggesting we ought to be doing on a local area. Is there any concentration on bringing more jobs to our States so that we get one dollar for every dollar in taxation we give to the Federal Government?

The President. Well, I have to say with regard to jobs of that kind and government jobs, that we think the whole program is geared at the kind of jobs that really count, and that is the revitalization of industry, the renewal of industry. And I know that Ohio is hurt worse than a great many States represented here today. Your unemployment rate is way above the national average. But that's true also of Michigan and several other of the industrial States. And the whole function of the program is geared to increasing productivity, making it possible for business and industry to invest the capital that is necessary to be able to compete once again with our foreign competitors. So, that part will have—whether you can substitute with defense spending—actually there, I think, the first rule is what is the best and most efficient and economical way to build up our defenses.

I think that too often in the past we have confused military spending with, let's say, trying to attain a social aim at the same time. Now, I can see if there are two States or three States, that any one of them is in a position to meet the military contract, then I think you've got to use some fairness and honesty in spreading it around. But it is true that there are some States that are just heavier in defense—States along the coast with shipbuilding yards and so forth. And I can only say we try to be fair with the other. But the real thing that you need is the private industry put back on its feet to provide that kind of job for the people.

Q. Thank you, Mr. President. I want to assure you that we have all the skilled laborers in Ohio——[*inaudible*].

The President. Oh, I know you do.

Q. [*Inaudible*].

The President. I know they are. I know.

Q. Mr. President, first, I'd like to thank you for again giving us this opportunity to meet with you over this hour, and then I want to bring you two messages from the 61 counties in Nebraska that I represent.

In the first place, my mail is very, very heavy in favor of your program. Our folks

are in favor of the block grant program. We don't think that there's a monopoly on compassion nor on good judgment and efficiency here in Washington. We think that out in Nebraska, we can use those dollars better, and that the 75 or 80 percent of the money would do just as much for the programs that really are needed in Nebraska, and our folks will know better what is needed.

Our second message is our folks are saying, "Save on that budget across the board." Don't—let's try not to be distracted by—[*inaudible*]. This economy has got to be shaped up, and if we came here and are fairhanded across the board, we'll all be better off, and we'll all be glad to go home. Thank you.

The President. Well, thank you very much.

Ms. Collins.[4]

Q. Mr. President, I happen to represent a district in Illinois, and in Illinois, particularly in my district, we're not that pleased with your budget cuts. We find that many of our people feel that they're going to be hurt. My particular district has a lot of people who are very poor. We have a lot of people who are unemployed. We don't get a fair return on our tax dollars. So, I wish I could say the same as my colleague from Nebraska has said, but my remarks would be quite the contrary.

The President. Well, Ms. Collins, I appreciate that. But I think also that—and I'm aware of the feeling of a great many people that this is going to happen. It isn't. What we've called the safety net are the seven programs that really deal with the truly needy. They're not going to be hurt, and we're not going to permit them to be hurt. What we are trying to do is—well, let me just give you an example. I speak from a little personal history on this.

When we reformed welfare in California, there had not been a cost-of-living pay raise for the people on welfare in California for almost 20 years. And because we were spread so thin, what we reformed and reduced the rolls by, more than 350,000

---

[4] *Representative Cardiss Collins of Illinois.*

people, not by throwing people off, they just disappeared.

We found out, in our reforms, that we were spread thin because there were people that are attracted to and take advantage of regulations, complicated regulations, to get on programs they don't deserve to be on. And so, we were spread thin by trying to take care of these undeserving people.

And I just told at our table, and I told Ms. Boggs[5] here, about the one newspaper in our State that didn't know whether my horror stories that I was telling were true about what was going on in the line of undeserving people getting in these programs. They sent a reporter out to get on welfare. He got on welfare four times under four different names in the same office on the same day.

Q. Mr. President, with all due respect, that does not surprise me. Of course, there is fraud in everything. But I think that the stories we read about in the newspapers are the exceptions rather than the things that happen most of the time. I agree with you that to the extent that welfare can be cut down because of frauds and cheats, it should be. But I'm very concerned about those people who are recipients of AFDC, who are children, who cannot speak out for themselves. And that's a—*[inaudible]*—that I hope will be in your sacred seven. Unfortunately, it was not—*[inaudible]*—this side of the—*[inaudible]*—as well as the other, and I appreciate being given the opportunity to tell you about it.

The President. Well, I think you're going to be happily surprised. I think our situation has been greatly distorted. I want to remind all of you of one thing. We're not reducing government's cost down to below what they've been getting in the previous year. We're reducing the rate of increase that has been built into them. And, no, it will stop short of the needy. I should have added to that story about California, some 350,000 people disappeared from the rolls. But we were able to increase the grants to the truly needy by 43 percent, and that was the first raise they'd had since 1958. And I think you're going to find that—well, I have to

---

[5] *Representative Lindy Boggs of Louisiana.*

say that I think that some of the purveyors of these programs, the dispensers of the programs are more worried about losing their position than they are about the people they represent. And they're trying to create an image that we are picking on the poor, because they don't want to lose their clientele and possibly their position.

Q. Mr. President, if you give me your promise you won't hurt the poor, I'll sit down right now. [*Laughter*]

The President. We won't hurt the poor.

Q. Mr. President, I would like to thank you as well for your graciousness today, and certainly for what is, I think, a new beginning in terms of the relationship with the women in Congress. We've been invited to the White House on many occasions, and I've served over four administrations. This is the first time that we've had this kind of an open exchange, and I salute you for it. As for a report from Massachusetts, I'll say that the attitude there is to give the President a chance. That's great news—from Massachusetts. [*Laughter*]

The President [*laughing*]. Yes, yes it is.

Q. I feel very strongly. I feel that you have had a brilliant new beginning. I think that the morale of the free world has been increased, with reason, and that we have a very good and valid justification for holding our head high in terms of world leadership. And domestically, the confidence of the American people, now suddenly, is beginning to bud again. Certainly, we do not all agree on everything. But I think that we can find an accommodation that is a just one with our mutual goals.

I, personally, am very pleased that you saw fit to introduce us to the new women appointees of your administration. And I am very impressed with their caliber and their confidence and their concern. Because while we may differ on this or that, we certainly, I think, do desire and aspire to a fair and equal society. And the quality and the visibility and the involvement and the contribution of women in your administration is something that I very much applaud, and I think the American women will applaud as well, and many enlightened men. And I would hope that their ranks will continue to expand with the same degree of excellence that marks your initial selections. So, I believe that in all areas you have had a very good beginning. I wish you well, and I offer you my advice, counsel, support, and—[*inaudible*]—when the situation requires. [*Laughter*]

The President. Thank you.

Q. Mr. President, I'm Loret Ruppe, your Director-designate of the Peace Corps. We want to thank you very much for your most kind message of support that you sent to us on the occasion of our 20th anniversary. We are working hard on our budget. We realize that if the economy were in shreds, as it is in my home State of Michigan, there would be no money to send any volunteers overseas. And the Peace Corps and VISTA are doing the best job with what it has, and we're here at your service. Thank you.

The President. Thank you, very much.

Yes, Bobbi. [6]

Q. Mr. President, I read recently that the Speaker of the House, Tip O'Neill, has decided to try to organize those who oppose your economic package. I'm concerned about it, because when I was back in Los Angeles over the weekend, I began to see evidence of hearings that were to be held, and I believe the intent is to undermine it. What are we going to do to try to counter that kind of an effort?

The President. Well——

Q. May I help?

The President. Yes.

Q. I'm the Senator from Florida, and I'd like to tell you that we have all of your problems en masse. We have the refugees. We have the largest number of senior citizens. We have the largest influx of veterans. Those States here that are losing citizens and losing voters and losing congressional seats—Florida's gaining for it. So, we'd like to think they're the same people moving South.

I think that's a problem for the States to address. If you have taxed your people out of wanting to stay in those States, then it's a problem to address on your State—[*inaudible*]. I trust the State people to make those decisions; they're coming forward. But I have the same apprehension that you have.

---

[6] *Representative Bobbi Fiedler of California.*

I want to represent my people well. And with the largest number of senior citizens, the largest influx of veterans, I wanted to know, "How do you feel in light of the rhetoric we see every evening on television and every morning in the paper that this is going to hurt the poor, and the safety net is really full of holes. How you feel?" I ran an ad in six daily newspapers in the State of Florida. It cost $3,672. And I'd like you to know that in 2 days, we received 18,000 of them back in my office—90 percent supporting the President, 10 percent qualified, saying I support five, maybe not two. The largest two, of course, were supplying lunches for children—the one commodity that you consume and can't hurt. Everything else has a black market value, all of these other commodities. That's the one that there was some concern. But they're saying, "You support this President. You get behind him, and you do what you can."

Now, I think 18,000 is a fantastic sample. We're going to run it in the weeklies this week, and we're going to run it in the shoppers next week, because we have a tremendous number of citizens in our State cannot even afford a daily paper, so they take the shopper. It's a throwaway, and it has a lot of space in there. So, I'm going to deliver to the Congressmen in their district—we had six young people sorting them all weekend by congressional district. And when we run these ads, I'm going to deliver those to the Congress where I feel we're really going to have a problem.

And, indeed, the people in my State say, "Support this President. Give him a chance." And that's what I think we all should do. And I commend you from the bottom of my heart for being the first President I can remember in my lifetime that wants to make a payment on the national debt and not saddle my grandchildren with it. Thank you. [*Laughter*]

The President. Thank you very much.

Well, Bobbi, let me also just say with that regard, there is a movement afoot right now in people raising money to help mobilize an effort and to do this same thing of getting the public feeling. Our mail, from what we've opened so far in the White House, and it's been coming in in floods, is running about 100 to 1 in support. And as I told here, and I tell the rest of you, some of the letters are just—they're treasures. But one of them the other day that I opened— this was a retired civil service employee. And in there, endorsed over to the Department of the Treasury, was his whole month's check for his pension that he was contributing. He wants the program, and he just wanted to give this back to the Government to be of whatever help he could.

Bob Michel showed me a letter from Peoria, and you know, if it plays well in Peoria—[*laughter*] But Bob's letter was from a man—I went to school 20 miles away from Peoria, so I know about the Caterpillar Tractor Company. They have never before laid off employees. They now are having layoffs. He's laid off. His wife has lost her job. And yet, he wrote to tell Bob Michel that that was all right, and they'd do without their unemployment insurance if it would help get a program in that would put the country on the right track, so that we'd have the stability of knowing that the private jobs are out there.

There are things that need to be done. The other day in New York I counted up— we know the high unemployment rate here in Washington; we know in New York and their problems, and yet, how do I explain that in the Sunday Times, New York Times, there were 45½ pages of help wanted ads, and in the Washington Post Sunday, there were 33½ pages of help wanted ads? And these were jobs calling for people of every range that you could make. How does a person in any one of those skills justify calling themselves unemployed when there's a fellow spending money advertising and saying, "I've got a job; come fill my job"? And I've done this in other cities. Last time I did it in Los Angeles, there were 65½ pages in the Los Angeles Times of help wanted ads.

Now, someplace along the line, we're going to find that a lot of our problems maybe come from well-intentioned programs, but that have militated against solving the problems that we need to solve. If industry is out there with jobs to offer—and I know they're not in Ohio in the steel industry, and I know that the automobile plants are closed down and you've got to

solve those problems by restoring the whole economy, but maybe we've missed the boat someplace along the line, and maybe we're encouraging people to delay in taking jobs.

Q. Mr. President, I'm from New Jersey. And I think one of the most valuable aspects of this meeting here today, besides the lovely lunch, is the fact that we have the opportunity to speak directly to you. And if we're all doing our jobs correctly, we are speaking directly to our constituents. So, I want to give a little report, a person-to-person report, from my constituents in New Jersey. They are very much in support of this program. There is tremendous consensus for the cuts. They want them to be evenhanded and fair. They perceive them at this point in time to be, and they know that there are going to be modifications. They want tax reform. The size and the shape of that tax package is still an open question, but they are strongly supportive of the whole direction and the leadership that you're showing.

There is one area that—and I just returned from New Jersey an hour or two ago—one area that almost everyone in talking with me this weekend, and primarily the hardcore of my Republican support, that is being questioned. And that—and I think you should know it—and that is the area of the size of the defense request. It's not a question of whether we make up for our neglect in this area. I think there's broad consensus and agreement on that and, in fact, that was the heart of my campaign. But they're questioning whether we can absorb this size defense expenditure in a relatively short period of time.

And I think you should know that, and I think that you should know it because it is saying—word from the homefront—and also because you should have the opportunity, and your advisers and your secretaries of the departments involved should be planning extensive explanation of the need and the justification for the program.

The President. Thank you very much. And you make me wonder if—I wonder if, the figure that is given for the overall defense increase, how many people realize that that's a 5-year figure? I'm wondering if a great many people are saying, "Oh, that

30-odd billion dollars is going to be spent in 1 year." The net increase this year is going to be 4.8, I believe, but—about 4½—it would be double that if the Defense Department had not made savings in less important items to turn that money to weapons and to refurbishing the volunteer military. And I think one of the—part of the expense, of course, is we've got to do better by that volunteer military than we have done in the past. But I'm wondering if that might not be the cause. If they read this figure of 30-odd billion dollars and don't realize we're talking about the next 5 years for that——

Q. Well, that may very well be. I think there just needs to be a lot of work done in terms of understanding the program, the total numbers of dollars and how it will be phased in and how it will be targeted, in which areas. And certainly, they're all for the volunteer—putting those expenditures in the volunteer program.

The President. Let me, if I can, just for a second here. Come here. Let me—[*laughter*]—let me just say one thing. And I think the very terms we use—I was just saying here at the table—the very terms we've used, I think have made many people misunderstand. We say "budget cut." Automatically people think, "Well that means next year they're going to spend less money than they spent this year. They're actually reducing the size and cost of government." And as we all know, we're not. We're reducing the *increase* in cost. On the tax cuts, they think, "Well, how can the Government get along with less money than it's been

getting so far?" It isn't. The people of this country, even with our tax cuts, are going to face a tax increase. There's $100 billion tax increase built into 1982 that we have inherited, and all we're doing is reducing that increase. But the Government is going to have a budget next year that, even with the cuts, is going to be $45 or $50 billion higher than the present year. And I think you've touched on it, that all of these are things that we have not yet managed to make even the people who support us understand. And God bless them for supporting us in spite of that. [*Laughter*]

Q. Mr. President, I'm not nearly as effective as Mrs. Reagan in making you put your coat on. [*Laughter*] I really stood up to thank you for opening this dialog with us and making us feel that we can continue it. But we have to continue it at another time, because the President must leave. Thank you, Mr. President.

The President. All right. I won't argue. All right. Well, we shall do it again. And it has been wonderful to have you back here— back here?—here for the first time. The first time was at Blair House. I'm sorry we can't take any more, but good to talk to you, and thank you very much for coming.

Note: The President spoke at 1 p.m. in the Family Dining Room at the White House.

On the same day, Mrs. Anwar el-Sadat, wife of the President of Egypt, was a guest at a luncheon hosted by Mrs. Reagan in the Red Room. Prior to the question-and-answer session, Mrs. Reagan brought Mrs. Sadat to the Family Dining Room to meet the President and his guests.

Message on the Observance of St. Patrick's Day
March 16, 1981

Nancy and I are delighted to wish a most happy St. Patrick's Day to everyone.

It has been said that "the Irish, like the presence of God, are to be found everywhere." And that is certainly true. Even the Reagan family, with roots in Ballyporeen, County Tipperary, is rumored to have a

home in Washington, D.C.

In the name of every American, we gratefully honor the contributions of Irish Americans in every walk of life down through our nation's history. Just as St. Patrick brought the light of faith to Ireland, so

Ireland, in turn, has given many gifted men and women to America.

On this St. Patrick's Day, let us remember all our great Irish Americans. And let all sons and daughters of Erin keep green their Irish heritage, for their own sake and for the continued enrichment of American life.

RONALD REAGAN

Remarks at a Reception for Members of the Associated General Contractors of America
March 16, 1981

The President. Well, thank you very much. Now I have an Oscar. [*Laughter*]

Well, President Cianchette, members of the Associated General Contractors, this is indeed an honor. An award from you is much more than a recognition from the business community; it's a tribute from the people who literally built America. Your hard work and the hard work of builders before you took an American wilderness and turned it into a citadel of productivity and commerce. And I don't have to tell you that our country somehow then went astray somewhere along the line. But I pledge to you tonight, together we can get this country going again, and we're going to do that.

President Cianchette spoke of regulations. A fellow in my neighborhood, building his own home not too long ago, gave me a line for my campaign speeches. He got so fed up finally with the paperwork that he pasted them all together, just to build his house; strung them up on two poles. And he had a strip of paper 250 feet long. [*Laughter*] We're going to do something about that. We have a task force that's assigned to it.

We can bring inflation down, and we can get America building again. You know, if that sounds like we're asking for miracles, well, on this eve of St. Patrick's Day, someone with the name of Reagan I think is entitled to think in terms of miracles. [*Laughter*]

You know, there was a little tad that was in court in New York, bandaged from his toes to his chin, suing for $4 million as the result of an accident, and he won the suit. The lawyers for the insurance company went over to him, and they said, "You're never going to enjoy a penny of this. We're going to follow you 24 hours a day. We know you're faking, and the first time you move, we'll have you." He said, "Will you now? Well," he said, "Let me tell you what's going to happen to me." He said, "They're coming in here with a stretcher. They're taking me out, and downstairs they're putting me in an ambulance. They're driving me straight to Kennedy Airport, and they're putting me on the airplane on that stretcher. We're flying direct to Paris, France, and there they're taking me on the stretcher off the plane, putting me in another ambulance. We're going direct to the shrine of Lourdes, and there you're going to see the damndest miracle you ever saw." [*Laughter*]

Well, your endorsement of our economic recovery package is even more meaningful, because I'm aware that some of the proposed spending reductions affect your members directly. By thinking of the nation as a whole rather than monetary, financial interests, you're demonstrating the kind of spirit that made this country great. And it's the kind of spirit that will make it great once again.

But it's going to be a tough fight. There are those who would rather get theirs now than cure inflation. They're going to do everything they can to preserve the status quo. And I ask you, after 2 years of double-digit inflation and economic stagnation, do you really want to keep the status quo?

Audience. No!

The President. I didn't think so. Status quo, you know, that is Latin for "the mess we're in." [*Laughter*]

I appreciate your support, and I'm looking forward to a close working relationship with the Association of General Contractors. Americans are still a people with true grit, and your support suggests to me this kind of spirit is still out there.

Thank you again for the honor you've paid me tonight. And don't worry, we're going to get the job done. And let me just tell you something, an example of the spirit that's alive out there in America matching yours.

I got a check from a retiree the other day—I mean a letter from a retiree. I gave the punchline away. [*Laughter*] In there

was his check for civil service retirement, a full month's retirement endorsed over to the Treasury Department, because he said he just wanted to help us get the job done. So, we can't lose.

Thank you again. Thanks very much.

Note: The President spoke at 5:30 p.m. in the Grand Ballroom at the Washington Hilton Hotel. Prior to his remarks, president Ival Cianchette of the Associated General Contractors of America presented the President with the organization's Man of the Year Award for skill, integrity, and responsibility.

Proclamation 4825—National Farm Safety Week, 1981
March 16, 1981

By the President of the United States of America

A Proclamation

American farmers and ranchers are at the core of our Nation's economy, providing food not only for our own people, but for millions of others around the world.

Yet we must not take the miracle of American agricultural abundance for granted. An unacceptable number of farm accidents cripples people and threatens production. Last year, nearly 400,000 farmers and ranchers were injured or killed in accidents at work, at home, during recreation, or on roads.

Powerful equipment, chemicals and variable working conditions are potential agricultural hazards, but safe work practices, protective equipment and other measures can minimize the risks. Special vigilance by the agricultural community is also necessary to reduce the toll of off-the-job injuries.

Now, Therefore, I, Ronald Reagan, President of the United States of America, do hereby designate the week of July 25 through July 31, 1981, as National Farm Safety Week. I urge all persons engaged in farming and ranching and all persons and organizations allied with agriculture to redouble their personal and group efforts for farm, home, recreation and highway safety.

In Witness Whereof, I have hereunto set my hand this 16th day of March, in the year of our Lord nineteen hundred and eighty-one, and of the Independence of the United States of America the two hundred and fifth.

RONALD REAGAN

[*Filed with the Office of the Federal Register, 4:36 p.m., March 17, 1981*]

Note: The text of the proclamation was released by the Office of the Press Secretary on March 17.

Remarks on the Program for Economic Recovery at a Breakfast Meeting With the Republican Congressional Leadership
March 17, 1981

Well, I thank you both, and I thank you all. I think the very evidence of our meeting here this morning, in the eyes of the public, this early in the morning is an indication that we are prepared to work together, and I'm looking forward to it. And I also appreciate this opportunity to thank all of you, because you not only have been cooperating, you have put it on a fast track, this program of ours. A schedule already has been agreed to and set as to where we're going to go with it.

And I am optimistic, possibly because of what both you and Bob have said about the people. Every indication, every evidence— and I know this true in your own mail; it is in ours at the White House and anytime we go out among the people—we find that they are in support of this program. They know that something has to be done, different than we've been doing things from some time past.

So, I'm convinced that together we're going to be able to get this problem and get the economy of this country back on the upturn where it should be, take our rightful place once again out in world competition. And that means, for our people, bringing to an end the inflation that's been destroying them at every level and putting our people back to work who are out there who know now the indignity of unemployment.

So, I'll come up to the Hill as often as necessary. We've been busy down at our end, as you well know, sending things here. We thought every once in a while we'd better come down here. [*Laughter*] But actually we're here now because now we've passed that stage, and we're at the stage where together we must go forward and get this program for the people of this country.

Note: The President spoke at 8:15 a.m. in Room S–207 of the Capitol. He was introduced by Senator Howard H. Baker, Jr., of Tennessee, majority leader of the Senate, and Representative Robert H. Michel of Illinois, minority leader of the House of Representatives.

Statement on St. Patrick's Day
March 17, 1981

St. Patrick's Day is not only the feast day of a great man of God, it is a symbol of the commitment of the Irish people to freedom, to justice, and to the values upon which Western civilization is built.

We in the United States know the great contribution made by citizens of Irish ancestry. From our Revolution to the present day, Irish Americans have been at the forefront of the defense of freedom. By their labor and by their sacrifices, they have been a major force in building our nation.

It is therefore gratifying on this St. Patrick's Day to be able to pay tribute to the great role Ireland and the Irish have played in defending and renewing the values we cherish.

But we are also conscious of the violence, bloodshed, and despair which now haunt all of the people of Northern Ireland. This tragedy cannot go unnoticed by the United States, which owes so much and has such close ties to the Irish.

As an American proud of his Irish ancestry and as President, I recognize the vital importance to our nation and the Western alliance of a peaceful, just, and swift solution to current problems in Northern Ireland.

The United States will continue to urge the parties to come together for a just and peaceful solution. I pray and hope that the day will come when the tragedy of history which now afflicts Northern Ireland will be overcome by faith, the courage and the love of freedom and justice of the Irish.

We will continue to condemn all acts of terrorism and violence, for these connot solve Northern Ireland's problems. I call on all Americans to question closely any appeal for financial or other aid from groups in-volved in this conflict to ensure that contributions do not end up in the hands of those who perpetuate violence, either directly or indirectly.

I add my personal prayers and the good offices of the United States to those Irish—and indeed to all world citizens—who wish fervently for peace and victory over those who sow fear and terror.

Toast at a St. Patrick's Day Luncheon Hosted by the Irish Ambassador
March 17, 1981

Well, I came not bearing gifts of such value, but I did bring a Waterford glass filled with completely green jellybeans. [*Laughter*]

Mr. Minister, Mr. Ambassador, Mrs. Donlon, honored guests:

It goes without saying that I'm delighted to be here on this very special day for the Irish and all who wish they were—[*laughter*]—and for the lovely music and the young lady who sang so beautifully, your daughter, Mr. Ambassador. You know, it's been said and I've heard it all my life that when the Irish sing an Irish song, all who listen wish they were Irish, too.

I don't know whether what I'm going to say now could be called a gift or not, and he doesn't know that he is going to be the gift, but I think this is the most appropriate occasion I can think of to introduce to you the designate as Ambassador to Ireland for the United States, Bill McCann. Bill, why don't you stand up?

I'm honored to have received your traditional shamrocks, which symbolize this day and the friendship between our two countries, and I'm especially pleased and most grateful for the beautiful scroll of the Reagan family tree. Up on the Hill this morning at a meeting with some of the legislative leadership—Mr. Speaker, on our side of the aisle—[*laughter*]—Senator Laxalt presented me with a great green button that he thought I should wear, which said, "Honorary Irishman." And I said to that son of the Basques—[*laughter*]—"I'm not honorary; I *am*." [*Laughter*] And I now have the proof of it here.

I have to tell you, though, if you don't mind, a personal note. I am deeply grateful for this, because my father was orphaned at age 6, and I grew up never having heard anything or knowing anything about my family tree. And I would meet other people of the name Reagan or Regan—[*laughter*]—we're all of the same clan, all cousins. But I tried to say to the Secretary[1] one day that his branch of the family just couldn't handle that many letters—[*laughter*]—and then received a paper from Ireland that told me that in the clan to which we belong, those who said Regan and spelled it that way were the professional people and the educators, and only the common laborers called it Reagan. [*Laughter*] So, meet a common laborer. [*Laughter*] But anyway, I am delighted to now finally know what I've never known all my life—the line and the heritage and to where it goes in Ireland.

My father also, at the same time, used to tell me and my brother when we were boys that, very proudly he would say that in this country the Irish built the jails and then filled them. [*Laughter*] And I was kind of disturbed at the note of pride in his voice, because I pictured this in a little different way until I finally learned what he was im-

---

[1] *Donald T. Regan, Secretary of the Treasury.*

plying, and that was the great, high percentage of the police officers in our land who were Irish. [*Laughter*]

But I wonder how many realize, even here where you are so versed in the background, how many realize how far back in our history of this country the contribution of the Irish to this land really goes.

George Washington, the first President of the United States, said,"When our friendless standard was first unfurled for resistance, who were the strangers who first mustered around our staff? And when it reeled in the fight, who more bravely sustained it than Erin's generous sons?"

I remember hearing some years ago and the first time that I ever had occasion to visit Ireland was right after World War II, and I was told of how Winston Churchill several times went on British Broadcasting radio to complain of Ireland's official neutrality in that war. And each time, he grew a little more stern and harsh in his words about that until finally Eamon de Valera went on radio and replied and said that if Winston didn't stop that kind of carping, he would withdraw the British Eighth Army from North Africa and bring it back to Ireland. [*Laughter*]

Mr. Ambassador, I know the courage with which you've worked to help bring peace to your land, and we here, in this land, have no deeper wish than that by the next St. Patrick's Day, if not before, the conflict and violence in North Ireland will have been replaced with reason and good will. And your efforts and those of others in bringing this about will have the full backing of the American people and their President.

Now, in the words of a poet, Dion Boucicault—I have it, I think, right—"When the law can stop the blades of grass from growing as they grow and when the leaves in summertime their colour dare not show, then will I change my colour too, the colour I wear in my caubeen; but till that day, plaze God, I'll stick to wearin' o' the green."

Now, Mr. Ambassador, Mrs. Donlon, Mr. Minister, the honored guests here today, I ask you to join me in a toast to the enduring friendship between the Irish and American peoples.

Note: The President spoke at 1:03 p.m. at the residence of Irish Ambassador to the United States Sean Donlon in response to toasts by the Ambassador and Minister of Finance Eugene Fitzgerald.

Nomination of William Edward McCann To Be United States Ambassador to Ireland
March 17, 1981

The President today announced his intention to nominate William Edward McCann to be Ambassador to Ireland.

Since 1968 Mr. McCann has served as president, chief executive officer, and director of operations of the Foundation Life Insurance Company of America, Chatham, N.J. He held the same positions with the Associated Life Insurance Company of Wilmington, Del., prior to 1968.

He has been active in the Republican Party, including serving as national chairman of the Reagan-Bush Pioneers during

1980. He was a delegate to the 1980 Republican National Convention.

Mr. McCann served in the U.S. Army during the Korean conflict. He was graduated from Bradshaw College in Lowell, Mass. (1957). He also attended Boston University.

Mr. McCann is married to the former Virginia Ann Blouin, and they have two children. He resides with his family in Short Hills, N.J. Mr. McCann was born on September 27, 1930.

Nomination of Richard T. Pratt To Be a Member of the Federal Home Loan Bank Board, and Designation as Chairman
March 17, 1981

The President today announced his intention to nominate Richard T. Pratt to be a member of the Federal Home Loan Bank Board for the remainder of the term expiring June 30, 1981. In addition, Mr. Pratt will be nominated for a new term of 4 years expiring June 30, 1985. Upon confirmation, the President intends to designate Mr. Pratt as Chairman.

Since 1970 Mr. Pratt has served as president of Richard T. Pratt Associates, Inc. He has also been a partner with the firm of Johnson, Pratt and Stewart since 1975. He is a professor of finance, College of Business, University of Utah, and has served in that position since 1973.

Mr. Pratt has consulted with many businesses and the government on financial matters. He was public interest director of the Seattle Federal Home Loan Bank and a member of its Executive Bank Board in 1970–79. He was associate professor of finance, College of Business, University of Utah, in 1966–73 and assistant professor of finance, University of Iowa, in 1965–66.

Mr. Pratt was graduated from the University of Utah (B.S., M.B.A.) and Indiana University (Ph. D.). He was in the Air Force Reserve in 1959. Mr. Pratt is married and has four children. He resides with his family in Salt Lake City, Utah. Mr. Pratt was born in Salt Lake City on February 5, 1937.

Appointment of Frank A. Whetstone as a United States Commissioner of the International Boundary Commission, United States and Canada
March 17, 1981

The President announced today his intention to appoint Frank A. Whetstone to be Commissioner on the part of the United States on the International Boundary Commission, United States and Canada.

Mr. Whetstone is former president of Lack Jack Gas and Oil Co. and publisher and president of Cut Bank Pioneer Press in Montana. He is chairman of the board of radio station KLCB in Libby, Mont. He was chief executive officer and chairman of the Cut Bank Gas Co., Cut Bank, Mont. He also served as chairman of the board of the Coeur D'Alene Co., with offices in Montana, Idaho, and Washington States. He is president of IMPEX, an import-export firm.

Mr. Whetstone is active in many civic organizations in Montana. He initiated an annual "Good Neighbor Day" for observance by Montana and Alberta, Canada, citizens. He chaired a highway committee to build better roads between Montana and Canada and initiated good will tours from Montana to Canada.

Mr. Whetstone is an active Republican in Montana. He served as a senior adviser to the transition group and as Western States coordinator to the Reagan for President Committee.

Mr. Whetstone is a native of Cut Bank, Mont. He was born on June 19, 1914.

Appointments to the White House Office of Public Liaison
March 17, 1981

The President today announced the following appointments to the Office of Public Liaison:

Red Cavaney to be Deputy Assistant to the President and Deputy to Elizabeth H. Dole, Assistant to the President for Public Liaison. Formerly president and chief executive officer of Ericson Yachts, Inc., of Irvine, Calif. Mr. Cavaney served as a volunteer advance representative during the 1980 general election campaign. In 1973–77 he served as Special Assistant to the President and Director of the Advance Office. Previously he was commercial loan vice president for Security National Bank in Newport Beach, Calif. He was graduated from the University of Southern California (1964). Mr. Cavaney is married and has two children. He resides in Balboa, Calif. He is 37 years old.

Jack Burgess to be Special Assistant to the President and Deputy Director for Public Liaison, with management responsibilities for the business, labor, and agriculture sectors. He served as Peace Corps country director in Micronesia in 1975–78 and for several years prior to that was the executive assistant to the Director of ACTION. Mr. Burgess is a former assistant dean of the Georgetown University School of Foreign Service and was dean of freshmen of the College of Arts and Sciences. Mr. Burgess was graduated from Georgetown University (A.B., 1963; M.A., 1966). He was ethnic media liaison of the Reagan-Bush Committee's nationalities division and was director of the nationalities division of the Republican National Committee in 1968.

Diana Lozano to be Special Assistant to the President and Deputy Director for Public Liaison, with management responsibility for human services. Miss Lozano was national account marketing representative with the IBM Corp. in New York. In 1973–77 she was executive assistant to the Director of the Minority Business Development Administration of the U.S. Department of Commerce. In 1972 Miss Lozano was a member of the White House staff. In 1971–72 she served as special assistant to the Chairman of the Cabinet Committee on Opportunities for Spanish-Speaking People. She was graduated from the University of California (B.A., 1970). She was born on October 30, 1947, in San Jose, Calif. Miss Lozano resides in Great Neck, N.Y.

Aram Bakshian, Jr., to be Special Assistant to the President for Public Liaison, with responsibilities including maintaining liaison with leaders in the arts, humanities, and private foundations. An author, critic, and essayist, Mr. Bakshian served as consultant to former Treasury Secretary William Simon in 1976–77. He was Deputy Special Assistant to the President in 1972–75. In 1971 Mr. Bakshian was special assistant to the chairman of the Republican National Committee. In 1966–70 he was an aide to former Representative William E. Brock (R-Tenn.). A native of Washington, D.C., Mr. Bakshian was educated in local public and private schools and in the autumn of 1975 was appointed a fellow of Harvard University's Institute of Politics.

Thelma Duggin to be Deputy Special Assistant to the President for Public Liaison. Formerly Ms. Duggin served as a field coordinator with Wright McNeill & Associates. During the 1980 general election she was a volunteer in the national black voters program as a liaison from the Republican National Committee. In 1973–77 Ms. Duggin was a senior merchandise manager with the J. C. Penney Co. in Columbus, Ga. In 1971–73 she worked with the Catholic school system in Mobile, Ala., as a teacher at Holy Family Elementary School. She has served as a member of the mayor's Community Relations Commission, Columbus, Ga., and served on the board of governors for the Georgia Health System Agency. She was graduated from Edgewood College in Madison, Wis. (1971). Ms. Duggin was born in Mobile, Ala., on December 23, 1949. She resides in Alexandria, Va.

Morton C. Blackwell to be Special Assistant to the President for Public Liaison, with responsibilities for veterans, fraternal organizations, Native Americans, religious affairs, and limited government organizations. Formerly policy director for Senator Gordon Humphrey (R-N.H.), Mr. Blackwell has also served recently as deputy director of congressional clearance in the office of the President-elect. Mr. Blackwell oversaw the Youth for Reagan effort in the 1980 campaign. He founded and was chairman of the Committee for Responsible Youth Politics in 1972–79. In 1973–79 he was editor of The New Right Report and a contributing editor of Conservative Digest in 1974–81. Mr. Blackwell has held a number of posts in Republican youth organizations, including executive director of the College Republican National Committee and national vice chairman of the Young Republican National Federation. He is married and has one child. He resides with his family in Arlington, Va. Mr. Blackwell was born in LaJara, Colo., on November 16, 1939.

Virginia H. Knauer to be Special Assistant to the President for Public Liaison, with responsibilities for consumers, aging, health care, and the disabled. Mrs. Knauer was founder and president of Virginia Knauer and Associates, Inc., a consulting firm specializing in consumer issues. In 1969 she was appointed Special Assistant to the President for Consumer Affairs. In addition, she was Executive Secretary of the President's Committee on Consumer Interests, Director of the U.S. Office of Consumer Affairs, and U.S. Representative and Vice Chairman of the Consumer Policy Committee of the Organization for Economic Cooperation and Development (OECD). Mrs. Knauer has been chairman of the Council for the Advancement of Consumer Policy, a nonprofit, nonpartisan educational organization, and served as a member of the executive committee of the Board of the Council of Better Business Bureaus, Inc., and many other consumer organizations. Mrs. Knauer was the consumer adviser to the Reagan-Bush Committee and was a transition adviser on the Federal Government's consumer programs and policies. Mrs. Knauer was graduated from the University of Pennsylvania. She has two children and she resides in Washington, D.C. She was born in Philadelphia, Pa., on March 28, 1915.

Robert F. Bonitati to be Special Assistant to the President for Public Liaison, with responsibilities for labor, public services, and natural resources. Mr. Bonitati was director of public affairs for the Air Line Pilots Association, responsible for government relations and political activities of the pilot's union since 1975. He was assistant to the Director of the Office of Management and Budget in 1973–74 and Associate Director of the Cost of Living Council in 1973–74. He served as campaign director for Senator Howard Baker (R-Tenn.) in 1966 and 1972 and as executive assistant to Senator Baker in 1966–67. Mr. Bonitati was assistant dean of students for the University of Tennessee in 1964–66 and

assistant dean of men at Arizona State University in 1962–64. He was graduated from the University of Connecticut (B.A., 1960). Mr. Bonitati resides in Alexandria, Va. He was born in Bridgeport, Conn., on September 19, 1938.

Ernest Eugene Garcia to be Director of Resources, Office of Public Liaison, and Deputy Director, Office of Consumer Affairs. In addition, Mr. Garcia will serve as liaison with the Hispanic community. He was administrative assistant and legislative coordinator to Elizabeth H. Dole during the transition. He has previously worked for Senator Robert Dole (R-Kans.) as legislative assistant and administrative assistant in 1977–80. In 1976–77 he was a policy analyst with the division of State planning and research, policy research/intergovernmental relations section, State of Kansas. He was a research analyst with InterAmerica Research Associates in 1975–76. In 1974–76 Mr. Garcia was assistant to the dean of men at the University of Kansas. He was leadership training coordinator, El Centro de Servicios Para Mexicanos, in 1973–74. Mr. Garcia is a member of the U.S. Marine Corps Reserve. He is married and has one child. He resides with his family in Lawrence, Kans. Mr. Garcia was born in Garden City, Kans., on July 12, 1946.

Wayne H. Valis to be Special Assistant to the President for Public Liaison, with responsibilities for trade associations, corporations, small business, and chambers of commerce. Since 1977 Mr. Valis has served as special assistant to the president of the American Enterprise Institute. In 1973–77 he was first Staff Assistant to the President and then Director of Planning and Research, Office of Public Liaison. In 1976 he was director of opposition research for the President Ford Committee. Mr. Valis was assistant to the director for legislative analysis of the American Enterprise Institute in 1972–73. In 1966–72 he was editor, the Intercollegiate Review, Intercollegiate Studies Institute, Bryn Mawr, Pa. Mr. Valis has written many articles and books, including "The Future Under President Reagan." Mr. Valis was graduated from Rutgers University (B.A., 1966). He resides in Falls Church, Va., with his daughter. Mr. Valis was born in Somerville, N.J., on June 14, 1944.

Nomination of Willard Kenneth Davis To Be Deputy Secretary of Energy
March 17, 1981

The President today announced his intention to nominate Willard Kenneth Davis to be Deputy Secretary of Energy.

Since 1973 Mr. Davis has served as vice president, planning and advanced development, Bechtel Power Corp. He was vice president, nuclear projects, in 1971–73; vice president, Vernon Division, in 1970–71; vice president and manager, IPIM Division, in 1967–70; vice president and manager, scientific development department, in 1963–67; and vice president, science and nuclear development department, in 1958–62.

Mr. Davis was Director of Reactor Development, Atomic Energy Commission, in 1954–58. He was chief development engineer and manager of the research department, California Research and Development Co., in 1951–54. In 1949–53 Mr. Davis was associate professor and professor of engineering at the University of California (Los Angeles).

Mr. Davis was graduated from MIT (B.S., 1940; M.S., 1942). Mr. Davis is actively involved in many private energy-related societies and committees.

Mr. Davis is married and has three children. He resides with his family in San Rafael, Calif. Mr. Davis was born in Seattle, Wash., on July 26, 1918.

Message to the Congress Reporting Budget Rescissions and a Deferral
March 17, 1981

To the Congress of the United States:

In accordance with the Impoundment Control Act of 1974, I herewith report 81 proposals to rescind a total of $11.1 billion in budget authority previously provided by the Congress. In addition, I am proposing to reduce authority to incur obligations for direct loans by a total of $751.8 million and I am reporting one new deferral of $3.4 million. These proposals are an integral part of my plan to reduce government spending.

The details of the rescission proposals and the deferral are contained in the attached reports.

RONALD REAGAN

The White House,
March 17, 1981.

Note: The attachments detailing the rescission proposals and the deferral are printed in the Federal Register of March 23, 1981.

Letter to the Speaker of the House and the President of the Senate Announcing the Intention to Amend the Generalized System of Preferences for Developing Countries
March 17, 1981

Dear Mr. Speaker: (Dear Mr. President:)
In accordance with section 502(a) of the

Trade Act of 1974, as amended, I herewith notify the House (Senate) of my intention to issue an Executive order proclaiming that all member countries of the Andean Group (Bolivia, Colombia, Ecuador, Peru, and Venezuela) and of the Association of South East Asian Nations (ASEAN) (Indonesia, Malaysia, Philippines, Singapore, and Thailand) shall be treated, respectively, as one country under section 502(a) (3) for purposes of the Generalized System of Preferences. I have determined that the Andean Pact and ASEAN and the respective member countries of each meet all the requirements of a beneficiary developing country set forth in section 502.

My decision was made after giving due consideration to the following factors as required by section 502(c):

(1) The requests of the Andean Group and ASEAN that they each be designated as an association of countries which is contributing to comprehensive regional economic integration among its members through appropriate means, including *inter alia*, the reduction of duties;

(2) The level of economic development of the member countries of each of the associations, including their per capita gross national product, the general living standards of their populations, the levels of health, nutrition, education and housing of their populations, and the degree of industrialization of the countries;

(3) The fact that other major developed countries (specifically, the European Community and Japan) are treating such associations as one country under their generalized tariff preference schemes;

(4) The fact that these associations provide the United States with equitable and reasonable access to their markets and my

expectation that these policies will continue.

In making the decision to designate each of these associations, I have also considered Congressional interest in encouraging regional economic integration among the developing countries as a means of fostering the political and economic viability of these countries and fulfilling their development goals. (See House Report 96–317, p. 200; Senate Report 96–249, pp. 271–273.)

All member countries of the Andean Group and of ASEAN are currently designated beneficiaries of the Generalized System of Preferences. Bolivia, Colombia, Peru, Malaysia, Philippines, Singapore, and Thailand were designated as beneficiary developing countries in Executive Order 11888 of November 24, 1975, effective January 1, 1976. Ecuador, Indonesia and Venezuela were named beneficiary developing countries in Executive Order 12204 of March 27, 1980, following fulfillment of the requirements specified in section 502(e) (2) of the Trade Act of 1974, as amended. The provisions of that Executive order became effective March 30, 1980. As a result, all member countries of the Andean Group and of ASEAN, respectively, may be treated as one country with respect to eligible articles for purposes of the Generalized System of Preferences, as provided for in section 503(b) (1) (B) as amended.

Sincerely,

RONALD REAGAN

Note: This is the text of identical letters addressed to Thomas P. O'Neill, Jr., Speaker of the House of Representatives, and to George Bush, President of the Senate.

Statement on the Meeting With President-designate Roberto Viola of Argentina
March 17, 1981

I am glad to have had this chance to meet and talk wih President-designate Viola on the eve of his inauguration as President

of Argentina. We have had a good discussion on bilateral and multilateral issues of concern to our respective countries. I look forward to efforts by both governments to further improve our relations, and I have

extended to General Viola my best wishes for his tenure as President.

Remarks at the National Association of State Departments of Agriculture Dinner Honoring Secretary of Agriculture Block
March 17, 1981

The President. I learned in public speaking you're never supposed to open with an apology, but my schedule has kind of gotten jammed up with two things happening almost simultaneously, so I only have a few minutes. But I did want to come here and, first of all, thank you and commend you for you who selected to honor tonight, Secretary of Agriculture John Block and his lovely lady.

You know, I have to tell you that it's been quite a day. I had lunch at the Irish Embassy. It happened to be an appropriate occasion for that today. [*Laughter*] It's the most infectious brogue in the world. Before I left, I was talking just like, well, you know. [*Laughter*]

But we changed gears here, and I've tried to warn John about some of the things—I remember when Ezra Taft Benson was Secretary of Agriculture. And he was out in the country and hearing reports from people in the farm areas and talking to them, and at one place there was a fellow that was giving him a really bad time, really complaining. And Ezra turned around and looked at some notes that someone handed him and then turned back and said, "Now, wait a minute." He said, "You didn't have it so bad." He said, "You had 26 inches of rain this last year." And the fellow said, "Yes, I remember the night it happened." [*Laughter*]

All of you are engaged in what is really the energy industry that is the most important of all, because the energy you produce or that you have to do with that is produced—if it isn't, we are out of business.

And I know once when I was out on the mashed potato circuit before I—well, that was when I was unemployed—[*laughter*]—I was speaking to a farm group in Las Vegas.

And on the way in to where I was to speak, there was one of those fellows that was there for the action, and he recognized me. And he said, "What are you doing here?" And I told him why. He said, "What are a bunch of farmers doing in Las Vegas?" And I just couldn't help it. I said, "Buster, they're in a business that makes a Las Vegas crap table look like a guaranteed annual income." [*Laughter*]

I am so happy at the kind words that you were saying about our selection for Secretary of Agriculture on the way through the room. It gladdened my heart, because I can tell you, already you've heard that we have a kind of Cabinet system of government; we do. And they don't just come in, or one at a time speak on their particular problem and no one else does this. We really debate all the issues around the table, everybody's department, and get a consensus and find out all the various opinions, and we don't take a vote. Then I know the monkey gets on my back, and I have to make a decision. But I can assure you, farming and agriculture in America is darn well represented in this administration by John Block.

So, I am pleased to be here and to just add my voice to yours in honoring him tonight, to thank all of you for being here. And naturally, we know that you're all going to be in total support of our economic package. [*Laughter*] With that, thank you all.

And I—yes. Is he all right?

Mrs. Dole. He's doing fine. Thank you.

The President. Mrs. Bob Dole. She and I have been conspiring to try and keep him from doing too much—[*laughter*]—after his operation.

Well, it's good to see all of you. And thank you for letting me join you for even just this few minutes.

Note: The President spoke at 6:40 p.m. in the ballroom at the Hotel Washington.

In his remarks, the President referred to Senator Robert Dole of Kansas, who was recuperating from surgery.

Executive Order 12299—Presidential Advisory Board on Ambassadorial Appointments
March 17, 1981

By virtue of the authority vested in me as President by the Constitution of the United States of America, and in order to terminate the Presidential Advisory Board on Ambassadorial Appointments established on February 5, 1977, it is hereby ordered that Executive Order No. 11970, as amended, and Section 1–101(f) of Executive Order No. 12258, as amended, are revoked.

RONALD REAGAN

The White House,
March 17, 1981.

[Filed with the Office of the Federal Register, 4:16 p.m., March 18, 1981]

Note: The text of the Executive order was released by the Office of the Press Secretary on March 18.

Nomination of A. James Barnes To Be General Counsel of the Department of Agriculture
March 18, 1981

The President today announced his intention to nominate A. James Barnes to be General Counsel of the Department of Agriculture.

Mr. Barnes is a partner with the firm of Beveridge, Fairbanks & Diamond of Washington, D.C. He is an adjunct professor, School of Business Administration, Georgetown University. In 1973 Mr. Barnes served as assistant to the Deputy Attorney General. In 1970–73 he was assistant to the Administrator of the Environmental Protection Agency. Mr. Barnes was trial attorney and special assistant to the Assistant Attorney General, Civil Division of the Department of Justice, in 1969–70. In 1967–69 he was assistant professor, Graduate School of Business, Indiana University.

Mr. Barnes was graduated from Michigan State University (B.A., 1964) and Harvard Law School (J.D., 1967). Mr. Barnes is married to the former Sarah Jane Hughes, and they have one child. He resides with his family in Washington, D.C. Mr. Barnes was born in Napoleon, Ohio, on August 30, 1942.

Nomination of Loren A. Smith To Be Chairman of the Administrative Conference of the United States
March 18, 1981

The President today announced his intention to nominate Loren A. Smith to be Chairman of the Administrative Conference of the United States for a term of 5 years.

Mr. Smith has been an associate professor of law at Delaware Law School, Widener University, since November 1976. Prior to that, he served as special assistant to the U.S. attorney for the District of Columbia. In 1973–74 he was assistant to the Special Counsel to the President. Mr. Smith was general attorney, Office of the General Counsel, Federal Communications Commission, in 1973. In 1973–74 he also was adjunct professor of law, International School of Law, Washington, D.C.

Mr. Smith was general counsel and member of the board of directors of the executive committee of Robert Suggs, Inc.,
an Illinois corporation, in 1971–73. In 1972–73 he was a research consultant to Sidley & Austin, a Chicago law firm. Mr. Smith was host and coproducer of a nightly radio interview program on radio station WEEF-AM and FM in Highland Park, Ill., in 1972.

Mr. Smith was deputy director of the office of executive branch management, legal and administrative agencies, in the office of the President-elect. He was chief counsel to the Reagan for President Committee in 1979–80.

Mr. Smith was graduated from Northwestern University (B.A. and J.D.). He is married and has two children. He resides with his family in Yorklyn, Del. Mr. Smith was born in Chicago, Ill., on December 22, 1944.

Nomination of William H. Draper III To Be President and Chairman of the Export-Import Bank of the United States
March 18, 1981

The President today announced his intention to nominate William H. Draper III to be President and Chairman of the Export-Import Bank.

Mr. Draper is founder and general partner of Sutter Hill Ventures of Palo Alto, Calif. Sutter Hill Ventures has provided equity capital to 150 young manufacturing companies throughout the United States. Mr. Draper was an associate of Draper, Gaither & Anderson in 1959–62. He was a sales representative with the Inland Steel Co. of Chicago, Ill., in 1954–59.

Mr. Draper is director, National Venture Capital Association, and is a former president of the Western Association of Venture Capitalists and the Western Association of Small Business Investment Companies. He was director of the Measurex Corp., Plantronics, Inc., of San Jose, Calif., and a variety of other companies.

Mr. Draper has been active in Republican politics for many years. He was a fundraiser for the Reagan-Bush campaign in California in 1980; national cochairman of the finance committee for the Bush for President campaign (1980); candidate for U.S. Congress (1967); director and former chairman, Republican Alliance. He has also been involved in community activities including serving as chairman of the board, California Association for American Conservatory Theater, San Francisco, Calif.

Mr. Draper was graduated from Yale University (B.A., 1950) and Harvard Graduate School of Business Administration (M.B.A., 1954). He is married and has three children. Mr. Draper was born in White Plains, N.Y., on January 1, 1928. He resides with his family in Atherton, Calif.

Nomination of Donald E. Sowle To Be Administrator for Federal Procurement Policy
March 19, 1981

The President today announced his intention to nominate Donald E. Sowle to be Administrator for Federal Procurement Policy, Office of Management and Budget.

Mr. Sowle is president of Don Sowle Associates, Inc., a diversified management consulting firm specializing in the fields of acquisition management, procurement, logistics, contract administration, business organization and planning, and management information systems.

Mr. Sowle was the Director of Studies for the Commission on Government Procurement. He was a group vice president, Gulf & Western Industries, Inc., with full management responsibility for three operating divisions engaged in commercial and defense work, primarily related to the aerospace industry. He was also assistant director of the Jet Propulsion Laboratory, California Institute of Technology, with responsibilities for the direction of JPL's divisions of financial management, procurement, material services, and the management systems and data analysis office. Mr. Sowle was Director, Contract Administration Services, Office of the Secretary of Defense.

He was graduated from Central Michigan University and the University of Chicago. He is a trustee of the National Contract Management Association and former Executive Director of the Government Procurement Commission. Mr. Sowle is an adjunct professor at American University.

Mr. Sowle resides in McLean, Va. He was born in Mt. Pleasant, Mich., on May 27, 1915.

Proclamation 4826—National Day of Prayer, 1981
March 19, 1981

By the President of the United States of America

A Proclamation

Our Nation's motto—"In God We Trust"—was not chosen lightly. It reflects a basic recognition that there is a divine authority in the universe to which this Nation owes homage.

Throughout our history Americans have put their faith in God and no one can doubt that we have been blessed for it. The earliest settlers of this land came came in search of religious freedom. Landing on a desolate shoreline, they established a spiritual foundation that has served us ever since.

It was the hard work of our people, the freedom they enjoyed and their faith in God that built this country and made it the envy of the world. In all of our great cities and towns evidence of the faith of our people is found: houses of worship of every denomination are among the oldest structures.

While never willing to bow to a tyrant, our forefathers were always willing to get to their knees before God. When catastrophe threatened, they turned to God for deliverance. When the harvest was bountiful the first thought was thanksgiving to God.

Prayer is today as powerful a force in our Nation as it has ever been. We as a Nation should never forget this source of strength. And while recognizing that the freedom to choose a Godly path is the essence of liberty, as a Nation we cannot but hope that more of our citizens would, through prayer, come into a closer relationship with their Maker.

Recognizing our great heritage, the Congress, by Joint Resolution approved April 17, 1952 (36 U.S.C. 169h; 66 Stat. 64), has called upon the President to set aside a suitable day each year as a National Day of. Prayer.

Now, Therefore, I, Ronald Reagan, President of the United States of America, do hereby proclaim Thursday, May 7, 1981, National Day of Prayer. On that day I ask all who believe to join with me in giving thanks to Almighty God for the blessings He has bestowed on this land and the protection He affords us as a people. Let us as a Nation join together before God, fully aware of the trials that lie ahead and the need, yes, the necessity, for divine guid-

ance. With unshakeable faith in God and the liberty which is heritage, we as a free Nation will surely survive and prosper.

In Witness Whereof, I have hereunto set my hand this nineteenth day of March, in year of our Lord nineteen hundred and eighty-one, and of the Independence of the United States of America the two hundred and fifth.

RONALD REAGAN

[*Filed with the Office of the Federal Register, 10:33 a.m., March 20, 1981*]

Message to the Congress Reporting Budget Rescissions and a Deferral
March 19, 1981

To the Congress of the United States:

In accordance with the Impoundment Control Act of 1974, I herewith report 33 proposals to rescind a total of $2.8 billion in budget authority previouly provided by the Congress, and one new deferral of $8.0 million

The details of the recission proposals and

the deferral are contained in the attached reports.

RONALD REAGAN

The White House,
March 19, 1981.

Note: The attachments detailing the rescission proposals and the deferral are printed in the Federal Register *of March 24, 1981.*

Statement by the Press Secretary on the President's Meeting With the Auto Task Force
March 19, 1981

The President today met with members of the Auto Task Force. He was presented with a series of options. The discussion focused in part on the current situation in the auto industry, pending legislation on Capitol Hill, the overall U.S. trade posture, principles underlying American trade, and U.S. relations with Japan.

The question of how to proceed with regard to imports was left open for further discussion by the President. The President told the group he wanted to have an opportunity to meet with others before making a decision on the import issue. The earliest possible time we could expect that would be late next week.

The President reemphasized he remains committed to the principles of free trade and, in general, he believes the Government should not become deeply entangled with the economic fortunes of any company or industry. He believes the auto industry is now involved in a situation that is not entirely of its own making and the forces of

Government bear some degree of responsibility. The Government must now bear part of the responsibility for helping the auto industry back on its feet.

Appointment of John F. W. Rogers as Special Assistant to the President for Administration and Director of the Office of Administration
March 20, 1981

The President today announced the appointment of John F. W. Rogers to be Special Assistant to the President for Administration and Director of the Office of Administration. Mr. Rogers was most recently Special Assistant for Management and Acting Director of the Office of Administration.

In his new position, Mr. Rogers will be responsible for the day-to-day administrative operation of the White House, including finance, facilities, personnel information management, correspondence, and central records. He will also supervise the operations of the White House Visitors Office.

In addition to his White House responsibilities, Mr. Rogers will be Director of the Office of Administration, a separate agency of the Executive Office of the President. In this position, he will be responsible for providing common administrative support to the entire Executive Office of the President, including such functions as library support, personnel, and financial and management information systems. He will act as liaison with the General Services Administration for the White House and the Executive Office of the President.

During the transition period, Mr. Rogers was executive assistant to the director on the White House transition team and was responsible for the administrative side of the White House.

Before joining the White House transition team, Mr. Rogers was executive assistant to the president for administration at the American Enterprise Institute for Public Policy Research. He joined AEI in 1977 to help launch a new periodical, Public Opinion. He served on the editorial staff until he moved into the administrative ranks of the Institute. In 1974 he joined the White House staff as a researcher and later became an assistant to the Director of the Office of White House Communications, a post he held until January 1977.

Mr. Rogers is a graduate of George Washington University and recipient of the Trautman Scholarship. He was born in Seneca Falls, N.Y., on April 15, 1956.

Nomination of Sherman E. Unger To Be General Counsel of the Department of Commerce
March 20, 1981

The President today announced his intention to nominate Sherman E. Unger to be General Counsel, Department of Commerce.

Since 1972 Mr. Unger has practiced law in Cincinnati, Ohio, and Washington, D.C., specializing in complex commercial litigation and corporate finance. In 1971–72 he was vice president of American Financial Corp., a Cincinnati-based diversified financial holding company. In 1969–70 Mr. Unger was General Counsel, Department of Housing and Urban Development. In addition, he was General Counsel, Government National Mortgage Association; a member of the Administrative Conference of the

United States; a member of the Office of Economic Opportunity National Advisory Committee for the Legal Services Program; and served as a member of the Board of Directors of the Federal National Mortgage Association from 1969 to 1971. In 1971 he was appointed by the President as a member of the National Advisory Council on Economic Opportunity for a term of 3 years.

Prior to his appointment as General Counsel of HUD, Mr. Unger was in 1956–69 an associate, then partner, in the Cincinnati law firm of Frost & Jacobs, with a corporate practice emphasizing antitrust, finance, and trial.

Mr. Unger served in the U.S. Army in 1946 and 1947 and the U.S. Air Force as a judge advocate from 1953 to 1956. He was graduated from Miami University, Oxford, Ohio (A.B., 1950) and the University of Cincinnati College of Law (J.D., 1953).

Mr. Unger is married and has four children. He resides with his family in Cincinnati, Ohio. He was born in Chicago, Ill., on October 9, 1927.

Nomination of Francis J. West To Be an Assistant Secretary of Defense
March 20, 1981

The President today announced his intention to nominate Francis J. West to be an Assistant Secretary of Defense (International Security Affairs).

Since 1977 Mr. West has served as consultant to the Secretary of the Navy and Chief of Naval Operations. He is Dean of Advanced Research, The Naval War College. He was visiting professor of international politics at the Fletcher School, Tufts University, and made regular lecture appearances at the Georgetown Center for Strategic and International Studies. In 1974–75 he was assistant to the Secretary and Deputy Secretary of Defense. Mr. West was professor of management, The Naval War College in 1973–74. In 1971–72 he was Director, Program Planning, Office of the Assistant Secretary of Defense for Systems Analysis. Mr. West served as an analyst with the Rand Corp. in 1968–70.

Mr. West served in the U.S. Marine Corps in 1962–67. He was graduated from Georgetown University (B.A., 1961) and Princeton University (M.A., 1967).

Mr. West is married and has four children. He resides with his family in Newport, R.I., and was born in Boston, Mass., on May 2, 1940.

Nomination of Rosslee Green Douglas To Be Director of the Office of Minority Economic Impact
March 20, 1981

The President today announced his intention to nominate Rosslee Green Douglas to be Director, Office of Minority Economic Impact, Department of Energy.

Since 1978 Mrs. Douglas has been commissioner, South Carolina Industrial Commission. In 1973–78 she was administrator/ supervisor, Franklin C. Fetter Family Health Center, Charleston, S.C. Mrs. Douglas was director of outreach of the Center in 1969–73. In 1968 she was an assistant teacher, reading laboratory for slow learners, Corey Elementary School, Greensboro, Ga. Previously, from 1952 to 1968, she served in various nursing capacities including serving as a consultant to health care groups.

Mrs. Douglas was graduated from Dillard University, New Orleans, La. (1948); New York University (1967); and the Medical University of South Carolina (1972).

Mrs. Douglas has two children. She resides in Mount Pleasant, S.C., and was born in Florence County, S.C., on August 12, 1928.

Nomination of Joseph J. Tribble To Be an Assistant Secretary of Energy
March 20, 1981

The President today announced his intention to nominate Joseph J. Tribble to be an Assistant Secretary of Energy (Conservation and Renewable Energy).

Since 1946 Mr. Tribble has been engineer and supervisor of the Union Camp Corp. in Savannah, Ga. He has held positions as assistant powerplant superintendent and powerplant superintendent. In 1942–43 he was with the Bethlehem Steel Co.

Mr. Tribble has been involved in civic and political activities, including having served as chairman of the Savannah Junior Chamber of Commerce Public Affairs Committee; elected State senator in Georgia in 1963; chairman of the Republican Party of Georgia in 1964–65; and chairman of the Reagan for President campaign in the First Congressional District of Georgia in 1980. He has served as a delegate to the 1964, 1968, 1976, and 1980 Republican National Conventions.

He was graduated from the Georgia Institute of Technology (B.S., 1942). Mr. Tribble is married and has four children. He resides with his family in Savannah, Ga. He was born in Forsyth, Ga., on August 30, 1920.

Nomination of Stephen J. Bollinger To Be an Assistant Secretary of Housing and Urban Development
March 20, 1981

The President today announced his intention to nominate Stephen J. Bollinger to be an Assistant Secretary of Housing and Urban Development (Community Planning and Development).

Since 1977 Mr. Bollinger has served as executive director of the Columbus, Ohio, Metropolitan Housing Authority. In 1976–77 he was vice president of Laws Insurance Co. of Cincinnati. Mr. Bollinger was president of WNOP Radio in Newport, Ky., in 1975–76. In 1973–75 he was vice president of the Caral Corp. Mr. Bollinger was legislative assistant to Representative Gene Snyder (R-Ky.) in 1970–71.

Mr. Bollinger is affiliated with the National Association of Housing & Redevelopment Association. He serves on the National Presidents Committee; the Large Housing Authorities Working Group; the North Central Regional Council; and the National Housing Committee. He was vice president and cofounder of the Public Housing Authorities Director Association and was a member of the Housing Task Force of the Mid-Ohio Regional Planning Commission. He was a candidate for the Cincinnati city council in 1975 and in 1977.

Mr. Bollinger was graduated from Harvard College (B.A., 1970). He is married and has two children. He resides with his family in Columbus, Ohio. Mr. Bollinger was born in Louisville, Ky., on April 11, 1948.

Nomination of Gerald J. Mossinghoff To Be Commissioner of Patents and Trademarks
March 20, 1981

The President today announced his intention to nominate Gerald J. Mossinghoff to be Commissioner of Patents and Trademarks, Department of Commerce.

Since 1976 Mr. Mossinghoff has been Deputy General Counsel, National Aeronautics and Space Administration (NASA). He was Assistant General Counsel for General Law in 1974–76; Deputy Assistant Administrator for Legislative Affairs in 1971–74; and Director of Congressional Liaison in 1967–71. Mr. Mossinghoff was Director, Office of Legislative Planning, U.S. Patent and Trademark Office in 1965–67. He was patent attorney with that office in 1963–65 and first joined the Patent Office in 1957. Mr. Mossinghoff was a patent attorney in private practice in 1961–63. In 1954–57 he was assistant project engineer with Sachs Electric Corp., St. Louis, Mo.

Mr. Mossinghoff was graduated from St. Louis University (B.S., 1957) and George Washington University (J.D., 1961). Mr. Mossinghoff is married and has three children. He resides with his family in Fairfax Station, Va. He was born in St. Louis, Mo., on September 30, 1935.

Nomination of Donald Allan Derman To Be an Assistant Secretary of Transportation
March 20, 1981

The President today announced his intention to nominate Donald Allan Derman to be an Assistant Secretary of Transportation (Budget and Programs).

Since 1976 Mr. Derman has served as Deputy Associate Director, Human Resources, Office of Management and Budget. In 1973–76 he was Deputy Associate Director, Community and Veterans Affairs, and in 1972–73 he was Deputy Chief, Human Resources Division. Mr. Derman was Deputy Chief, Economics, Science, and Tecnology Division, Bureau of the Budget, in 1970–72. In 1969–70 he was Assistant Division Director, Space Programs; and budget examiner in the Bureau in 1968–69.

Mr. Derman served as senior program analyst in the Office of Economic Opportunity in 1965–68. He was with the Atomic Energy Commission in 1960–65.

Mr. Derman was graduated from the University of Connecticut (B.A., 1959; M.A., 1960). He served in the U.S. Air Force in 1952–56.

Mr. Derman is married and has one child. He resides with his family in Washington, D.C. He was born in Fairfield, Conn., on May 27, 1933.

Appointment of Herbert E. Ellingwood as Deputy Counsel to the President
March 20, 1981

The President today announced the appointment of Herbert E. Ellingwood as Deputy Counsel to the President.

Mr. Ellingwood is a partner with the firm of Caldwell and Toms of Sacramento, Calif. During the period 1960 to 1966, he was

273

deputy assistant attorney for Alameda County, Calif., and from 1966 to 1969 was legislative advocate for law and legislative committees, District Attorneys' and Peace Officers' Associations. Mr. Ellingwood was the legal affairs secretary to then-Governor Ronald Reagan from 1969 to 1974 and served as special assistant to the attorney general, State of California, from 1975 to 1979. From 1953 to 1956, he served in the United States Army, being discharged as first lieutenant.

Mr. Ellingwood was graduated from Yale University (B.A., 1953) and Stanford University Law School (LL.B., 1960). Mr. Ellingwood has been active in numerous civic, religious, and professional organizations at the Federal, State, and local levels.

Mr. Ellingwood is married to the former Audrey Kesler, and they have two children. He resides with his family in Sacramento, Calif. Mr. Ellingwood was born in Ordway, Colo., on March 5, 1931.

Appointment of Richard A. Hauser as Deputy Counsel to the President
March 20, 1981

The President today announced the appointment of Richard A. Hauser as Deputy Counsel to the President.

Mr. Hauser formerly served in the Office of the Counsel to the President during the period 1973 to 1974. From 1968 to 1970, he served as law clerk to the chief judge of the United States District Court for the Southern District of Florida, and from 1970 to 1971, as an assistant United States attorney in the same district. Mr. Hauser served as attorney-adviser to the Deputy Attorney General and later as the Associate Director of the Office of Justice Policy and Planning.

Since 1975 Mr. Hauser has been in the private practice of law, most recently with the firm of Brodsky and Hauser P.C.

A native of Litchfield, Ill., Mr. Hauser is a graduate of the University of Pennsylvania (Wharton, 1965) and the University of Miami School of Law (J.D., cum laude, 1964).

Mr. Hauser, 38, is a member of the D.C., Virginia, and Florida Bars and is active on committees of both the American and Federal Bar Associations. He currently resides in Alexandria, Va., with his wife, the former Karen Rollow Allen of Washington, D.C.

Nomination of David R. MacDonald To Be a Deputy United States Trade Representative
March 20, 1981

The President today announced his intention to nominate David R. MacDonald to be Deputy United States Trade Representative, with the rank of Ambassador.

Since 1977 Mr. MacDonald has served on the board of directors of the Chicago Association of Commerce and Industry. He has served since 1978 as a member of the board of directors of the Chicago Crime Commission, and in 1980 he was a member of the executive committee of the World Trade

Conference. Since 1979 he has been a member of the Policy Board, Economic Affairs Council, and cochairman, tax subcommittee, Republican National Committee. In 1974–76 Mr. MacDonald was Assistant Secretary of the Treasury, specializing in international trade statutes. He was Under Secretary of the Navy in 1976–77.

Mr. MacDonald was a partner with the firm of Baker & McKenzie beginning in

1962. He was a partner with Kirkland & Ellis in 1957–62.

Mr. MacDonald was graduated from Cornell University (B.S., 1952) and Michigan Law School (J.D., 1955). Mr. MacDonald is married and has five children. He resides with his family in Winnetka, Ill. He was born in Chicago, Ill., on November 1, 1930.

Nomination of Michael B. Smith To Be a Deputy United States Trade Representative
March 20, 1981

The President today announced his intention to nominate Michael B. Smith to be Deputy United States Trade Representative, with the rank of Ambassador. Mr. Smith is currently serving in that position.

In 1975–79 Mr. Smith was Chief Textile Negotiator with the Office of the U.S. Trade Representative. In 1973–75 he served in the Textiles and Fibers Division of the State Department. He was Chief of the White House Correspondence Section in 1971–73.

Mr. Smith was a principal officer in the Office of the American Consulate General in Lyon, France. He was deputy principal officer with the American Consulate General in Strasbourg, France, in 1967–68. Mr. Smith has served in American Embassies in N'Djamema, Chad, and Tehran, Iran.

Mr. Smith was graduated from Harvard College (A.B., 1958). He is married and has two children. Mr. Smith was born on June 16, 1936.

Remarks at the Conservative Political Action Conference Dinner
March 20, 1981

Mr. Chairman and Congressman Mickey Edwards, thank you very much. My goodness, I can't realize how much time has gone by, because I remember when I first knew Mickey, he was just a clean-shaven boy. [*Laughter*] But thank you for inviting me here once again. And as Mickey told you, with the exception of those 2 years, it is true about how often I've been here. So, let me say now that I hope we'll be able to keep this tradition going forward and that you'll invite me again next year.

And in the rough days ahead, and I know there will be such days, I hope that you'll be like the mother of the young lad in camp when the camp director told her that he was going to have to discipline her son. And she said, "Well, don't be too hard on him. He's very sensitive. Slap the boy next to him, and that will scare Irving." [*Laughter*] But let us also, tonight, salute those with vision who labored to found this group—the American Conservative Union,

the Young Americans for Freedom, National Review and Human Events.

It's been said that anyone who seeks success or greatness should first forget about both and seek only the truth, and the rest will follow. Well, fellow truthseekers, none of us here tonight—contemplating the seal on this podium and a balanced budget in 1984—can argue with that kind of logic. For whatever history does finally say about our cause, it must say: The conservative movement in 20th century America held fast through hard and difficult years to its vision of the truth. And history must also say that our victory, when it was achieved, was not so much a victory of politics as it was a victory of ideas, not so much a victory for any one man or party as it was a victory for a set of principles—principles that were protected and nourished by a few unselfish Americans through many grim and heartbreaking defeats.

Now, you are those Americans that I'm talking about. I wanted to be here not just to acknowledge your efforts on my behalf, not just to remark that last November's victory was singularly your victory, not just to mention that the new administration in Washington is a testimony to your perseverance and devotion to principle, but to say, simply, "Thank you," and to say those words not as a President, or even as a conservative; thank you as an American. I say this knowing that there are many in this room whose talents might have entitled them to a life of affluence but who chose another career out of a higher sense of duty to country. And I know, too, that the story of their selflessness will never be written up in Time or Newsweek or go down in the history books.

You know, on an occasion like this it's a little hard not to reminisce, not to think back and just realize how far we've come. The Portuguese have a word for such recollection—*saudade*—a poetic term rich with the dreams of yesterday. And surely in our past there was many a dream that went aglimmering and many a field littered with broken lances.

Who can forget that July night in San Francisco when Barry Goldwater told us that we must set the tides running again in the cause of freedom, and he said, "until our cause has won the day, inspired the world, and shown the way to a tomorrow worthy of all our yesteryears"? And had there not been a Barry Goldwater willing to take that lonely walk, we wouldn't be here talking of a celebration tonight.

But our memories are not just political ones. I like to think back about a small, artfully written magazine named National Review, founded in 1955 and ridiculed by the intellectual establishment because it published an editorial that said it would stand athwart the course of history yelling, "Stop!" And then there was a spritely written newsweekly coming out of Washington named Human Events that many said would never be taken seriously, but it would become later "must reading" not only for Capitol Hill insiders but for all of those in public life.

How many of us were there who used to go home from meetings like this with no thought of giving up, but still find ourselves wondering in the dark of night whether this much-loved land might go the way of other great nations that lost a sense of mission and a passion for freedom?

There are so many people and institutions who come to mind for their role in the success we celebrate tonight. Intellectual leaders like Russell Kirk, Friedrich Hayek, Henry Hazlitt, Milton Friedman, James Burnham, Ludwig von Mises—they shaped so much of our thoughts.

It's especially hard to believe that it was only a decade ago, on a cold April day on a small hill in upstate New York, that another of these great thinkers, Frank Meyer, was buried. He'd made the awful journey that so many others had: He pulled himself from the clutches of "The God That Failed," and then in his writing fashioned a vigorous new synthesis of traditional and libertarian thought—a sythesis that is today recognized by many as modern conservatism.

It was Frank Meyer who reminded us that the robust individualism of the American experience was part of the deeper current of Western learning and culture. He pointed out that a respect for law, an appreciation for tradition, and regard for the social consensus that gives stability to our public and private institutions, these civilized ideas must still motivate us even as we seek a new economic prosperity based on reducing government interference in the marketplace.

Our goals complement each other. We're not cutting the budget simply for the sake of sounder financial management. This is only a first step toward returning power to the States and communities, only a first step toward reordering the relationship between citizen and government. We can make government again responsive to people not only by cutting its size and scope and thereby ensuring that its legitimate functions are performed efficiently and justly.

Because ours is a consistent philosophy of government, we can be very clear: We do not have a social agenda, separate, separate economic agenda, and a separate foreign agenda. We have one agenda. Just as surely as we seek to put our financial house in order and rebuild our nation's defenses, so too we seek to protect the unborn, to end the manipulation of schoolchildren by utopian planners, and permit the acknowledgement of a Supreme Being in our classrooms just as we allow such acknowledgements in other public institutions.

Now, obviously we're not going to be able to accomplish all this at once. The American people are patient. I think they realize that the wrongs done over several decades cannot be corrected instantly. You know, I had the pleasure in appearing before a Senate committee once while I was still Governor, and I was challenged because there was a Republican President in the White House who'd been there for several months why we hadn't then corrected everything that had been done. And the only way I could think to answer him is I told him about a ranch many years ago that Nancy and I acquired. It had a barn with eight stalls in it in which they had kept cattle, and we wanted to keep horses. And I was in there day after day with a pick and a shovel, lowering the level of those stalls, which had accumulated over the years. [*Laughter*] And I told this Senator who'd asked that question that I discovered that you did not undo in weeks or months what it had taken some 15 years to accumulate.

I also believe that we conservatives, if we mean to continue governing, must realize that it will not always be so easy to place the blame on the past for our national difficulties. You know, one day the great baseball manager Frankie Frisch sent a rookie out to play center field. The rookie promptly dropped the first fly ball that was hit to him. On the next play he let a grounder go between his feet and then threw the ball to the wrong base. Frankie stormed out of the dugout, took his glove away from him and said, "I'll show you how to play this position." And the next batter slammed a line drive right over second base. Frankie came in on it, missed it completely, fell down when he tried to chase it, threw down his glove, and yelled at the rookie, "You've got center field so screwed up nobody can play it." [*Laughter*]

The point is we must lead a nation, and that means more than criticizing the past. Indeed, as T. S. Eliot once said, "Only by

acceptance of the past will you alter its meaning."

Now, during our political efforts, we were the subject of much indifference and often times intolerance, and that's why I hope our political victory will be remembered as a generous one and our time in power will be recalled for the tolerance we showed for those with whom we disagree.

But beyond this, beyond this we have to offer America and the world a larger vision. We must remove government's smothering hand from where it does harm; we must seek to revitalize the proper functions of government. But we do these things to set loose again the energy and the ingenuity of the American people. We do these things to reinvigorate those social and economic institutions which serve as a buffer and a bridge between the individual and the state—and which remain the real source of our progress as a people.

And we must hold out this exciting prospect of an orderly, compassionate, pluralistic society—an archipelago of prospering communities and divergent institutions—a place where a free and energetic people can work out their own destiny under God.

I know that some will think about the perilous world we live in and the dangerous decade before us and ask what practical effect this conservative vision can have today. When Prime Minister Thatcher was here recently we both remarked on the sudden, overwhelming changes that had come recently to politics in both our countries.

At our last official function, I told the Prime Minister that everywhere we look in the world the cult of the state is dying. And I held out hope that it wouldn't be long before those of our adversaries who preach the supremacy of the state were remembered only for their role in a sad, rather bizarre chapter in human history. The largest planned economy in the world has to buy food elsewhere or its people would starve.

We've heard in our century far too much of the sounds of anguish from those who live under totalitarian rule. We've seen too many monuments made not out of marble or stone but out of barbed wire and terror.

277

But from these terrible places have come survivors, witnesses to the triumph of the human spirit over the mystique of state power, prisoners whose spiritual values made them the rulers of their guards. With their survival, they brought us "the secret of the camps," a lesson for our time and for any age: Evil is powerless if the good are unafraid.

That's why the Marxist vision of man without God must eventually be seen as an empty and a false faith—the second oldest in the world—first proclaimed in the Garden of Eden with whispered words of temptation: "Ye shall be as gods." The crisis of the Western world, Whittaker Chambers reminded us, exists to the degree in which it is indifferent to God. "The Western world does not know it," he said about our struggle, "but it already possesses the answer to this problem—but only provided that its faith in God and the freedom He enjoins is as great as communism's faith in man."

This is the real task before us: to reassert our commitment as a nation to a law higher than our own, to renew our spiritual strength. Only by building a wall of such spiritual resolve can we, as a free people, hope to protect our own heritage and make it someday the birthright of all men.

There is, in America, a greatness and a tremendous heritage of idealism which is a reservoir of strength and goodness. It is ours if we will but tap it. And, because of this—because that greatness is there—there is need in America today for a reaffirmation of that goodness and a reformation of our greatness.

The dialog and the deeds of the past few decades are not sufficient to the day in which we live. They cannot keep the promise of tomorrow. The encrusted bureaucracies and the engrained procedures which have developed of late respond neither to the minority or the majority. We've come to a turning point. We have a decision to make. Will we continue with yesterday's agenda and yesterday's failures, or will we reassert our ideals and our standards, will we reaffirm our faith, and renew our purpose? This is a time for choosing.

I made a speech by that title in 1964. I said, "We've been told increasingly that we must choose between left or right." But we're still using those terms—left or right. And I'll repeat what I said then in '64. "There is no left or right. There's only an up or down:" up to the ultimate in individual freedom, man's age old dream, the ultimate in individual freedom consistent with an orderly society—or down to the totalitarianism of the ant heap. And those today who, however good their intentions, tell us that we should trade freedom for security are on that downward path.

Those of us who call ourselves conservative have pointed out what's wrong with government policy for more than a quarter of a century. Now we have an opportunity to make policy and to change our national direction. All of us in government—in the House, in the Senate, in the executive branch—and in private life can now stand together. We can stop the drain on the economy by the public sector. We can restore our national prosperity. We can replace the overregulated society with the creative society. We can appoint to the bench distinguished judges who understand the first responsibility of any legal system is to punish the guilty and protect the innocent. We can restore to their rightful place in our national consciousness the values of family, work, neighborhood, and religion. And, finally, we can see to it that the nations of the world clearly understand America's intentions and respect for resolve.

Now we have the opportunity—yes, and the necessity—to prove that the American promise is equal to the task of redressing our grievances and equal to the challenge of inventing a great tomorrow.

This reformation, this renaissance will not be achieved or will it be served, by those who engage in political claptrap or false promises. It will not be achieved by those who set people against people, class against class, or institution against institution. So, while we celebrate our recent political victory we must understand there's much work before us: to gain control again of government, to reward personal initiative and risk-taking in the marketplace, to revitalize our system of federalism, to strengthen the private institutions that make up the independent sector of our society, and to make our own spiritual affirmation in the face of those who would deny man has a place before God. Not easy tasks perhaps. But I would remind you as I did on January 20th, they're not impossible, because, after all, we're Americans.

This year we will celebrate a victory won two centuries ago at Yorktown, the victory of a small, fledgling nation over a mighty world power. How many people are aware—I've been told that a British band played the music at that surrender ceremony because we didn't have a band. [*Laughter*] And they played a tune that was very popular in England at the time. Its title was "The World Turned Upside Down." I'm sure it was far more appropriate than they realized at that moment. The heritage from that long difficult struggle is before our eyes today in this city, in the great halls of our government and in the monuments to the memory of our great men.

It is this heritage that evokes the images of a much-loved land, a land of struggling settlers and lonely immigrants, of giant cities and great frontiers, images of all that our country is and all that we want her to be. That's the America entrusted to us, to stand by, to protect, and yes, to lead her wisely.

Fellow citizens, fellow conservatives, our time is now. Our moment has arrived. We stand together shoulder to shoulder in the thickest of the fight. If we carry the day and turn the tide, we can hope that as long as men speak of freedom and those who have protected it, they will remember us, and they will say, "Here were the brave and here their place of honor."

Thank you.

Note: The President spoke at 9:25 p.m. in the Grand Ballroom at the Mayflower Hotel. In his opening remarks, he referred to James Lacey, national chairman of the Young Americans for Freedom, and Representative Mickey Edwards of Oklahoma, chairman of the American Conservative Union.

Remarks at a White House Reception for Performers in and Sponsors of the Ford's Theatre Benefit Gala
March 21, 1981

It's our pleasure to host you all here tonight, and I know that we all look forward to the performance that's going to follow at Ford's Theatre.

You know, one of the great benefits we found of living here is you get to be a part of the great history of this beautiful city. Now, I used the word "benefit" there. For some who are among us tonight—[*laughter*]—you realize that that word has a very singular meaning. A benefit in the entertainment world is any occasion where the actors are performing without pay. [*Laughter*] And I learned at first hand that on such occasions, if you don't sing or dance, you usually wind up introducing someone who does. [*Laughter*]

I remember one such occasion when there were seven of us lined up to introduce Nelson Eddy singing "Shortenin' Bread." [*Laughter*] And if you did that enough, that usually led to your being an after-dinner speaker. And as that went on, you could talk your way right out of show business into another line of work. [*Laughter*]

Tonight, in this room, everyone is deserving of a thank you—not only these fine talented artists who are going to perform for us tonight but all the rest of you who are here because you are generous patrons, not alone of charities but of cultural and artistic activities and in the preservation of historic treasures. And you're carrying on a tradition that is uniquely American, because in this land we have maintained by private and voluntary contributions more orchestras, more opera, more ballet, more non-profit theater, more libraries, and other cultural activities than all the rest of the world put together.

So, may I just take advantage of this moment and my position to thank you on behalf of all Americans. And Nancy and I are greatly honored to welcome you to your national home. Thank you all very much for what you're doing.

Note: The President spoke at 5:25 p.m. in the East Room at the White House.

Remarks at a "Roast" In Honor of Press Secretary Brady
March 21, 1981

The President. Well, I just have to tell you that, Jim, we've been looking all over for you. [*Laughter*] Headline news breaking all around us—I've declared martial law, dismissed the Congress—[*laughter*]—and here I find you fraternizing. [*Laughter*]

I understand that this is something in the nature of, well, shall we say "a roast," and I don't know whether Jim is prepared for that yet or not. Here you are. And therefore, I would like to ask all of you—you know—there's still a long way to go on our honeymoon, and Nancy says he's "Y and H." [*Laughter*] So, even though it's a roast——

Audience Member. You have to explain what that means.

The President. That means young and handsome. [*Laughter*] So, please be gentle. [*Laughter*] And, Jim, you're not to take seriously anything they say.

Mr. Brady. I never do.

The President. As a matter of fact, don't take anything seriously that I've said so far. [*Laughter*] But I will be serious for a minute. I think that this is borne out of a respect and affection that is widespread among these people and which you have earned. And let's cancel the lottery. [*Laughter*] Or were you going to promise that later? [*Laughter*]

Mr. Brady. I didn't want to make any unilateral concessions, and now you've given it away. [*Laughter*]

The President. Well, that's one of the major decisions we've made. We've got some minor things going on like El Salvador—[*laughter*]—Afghanistan, and so forth. But you can see that when it comes to the big decisions, we make them fast and hard. [*Laughter*]

Well, anyway, I'm glad that we could drop by here, and I'm glad that you're all doing this, and I'm very glad that Jim is where he is, and I mean that seriously, in our administration. [*Cheers*]

Enjoy it. We're on our way to Ford's Theatre. [*Laughter*]

Mr. Brady. Thank you, Mr. President.

Note: The President spoke at 7:28 p.m. at the Georgetown Club.

In his remarks, the President referred to a lottery that determined which reporters asked questions at the March 6 news conference.

Remarks at the Conclusion of the Ford's Theatre Benefit Gala
March 21, 1981

Nancy and I have been very honored to be a part of this, and I think that I speak for everyone here when I say a heartfelt thanks to these fine artists who have given their time and their talent to make this evening so wonderful.

You know, some people were mentioned, some credits given; you couldn't name all of the people here in this theater that have had a hand in making this very wonderful evening. One was mentioned, Frankie Hewitt, and she certainly deserves it. There were two ladies that I don't think any of the others will mind if I mention, who worked long and tirelessly together to make this a success—Mrs. Tip O'Neill and Mrs. Howard Baker. They worked so well together that I've got a couple of projects I'm going to suggest to their husbands. [*Laughter*] It's worth a try.

But here in this place that is so much a part of our heritage, reminds us so much of our traditions—and, incidentally, it is not true I used to play this theater before it closed. [*Laughter*] But it just reminds me of a tradition I spoke to—I said this earlier this evening to a number of these people and to some of you in the audience, and that is a tradition that I think all of us want to see

upheld, and I was so pleased tonight to hear the opening remarks and know how some of you here in this audience are upholding it. And that is, as I told them earlier, a tradition in this land that we have supported with voluntary contributions, more musical groups, more orchestras, more ballet, more opera, more nonprofit theater, more cultural institutions like libraries, than all the rest of the world put together. And I think we can continue to do that in the years to come.

Now, again, I'll say a thank you myself to all of you who have made this possible—and not only this evening but the restoration of this theater. And for all of you, a heartfelt thanks again to these wonderful people. Thank you.

Note: The President spoke at 11 p.m. at Ford's Theatre.

Proclamation 4827—Pan American Day and Pan American Week, 1981
March 20, 1981

By the President of the United States of America

A Proclamation

Since its first observance fifty years ago, Pan American Day has served as an annual reminder of the common ideals of the nations of this hemisphere, further strengthening our peoples' bonds.

Commitment to such common goals among nations is an example for the world. Such cooperation has as its first priority the resolution of differences through peaceful conciliation and arbitration. The Organization of American States has provided a valuable framework for such progress to be made.

Through increased awareness and mutual cooperation, the Pan American nations strive to promote peace and stability in the region, as well as economic, social and cultural development. Pan American Day commemorates the voluntary cooperation of our countries in achieving solidarity of purpose

while maintaining individuality of culture and tradition.

On this Pan American Day of 1981, the people of the United States extend warm greetings to their neighbors in the Americas, and reaffirm their commitment to the spirit of solidarity, the ideals and purposes of the Inter-American system, and their active support of the Organization of American States.

Now, Therefore, I, Ronald Reagan, President of the United States of America, do hereby proclaim Tuesday, April 14, 1981, as Pan American Day, and the week beginning on April 12, 1981, as Pan American Week; and I urge the Governors of the fifty States, and the Governor of the Commonwealth of Puerto Rico, and officials of the other areas under the flag of the United States of America to honor these observances with appropriate activities and ceremonies.

In Witness Whereof, I have hereunto set my hand this 20th day of March in the year of our Lord nineteen hundred eighty-one, and of the Independence of the United States of America the two hundred and fifth.

RONALD REAGAN

[*Filed with the Office of the Federal Register, 11:05 a.m., March 24, 1981*]

Note: The text of the proclamation was released by the Office of the Press Secretary on March 23.

Proclamation 4828—Cancer Control Month
March 20, 1981

By the President of the United States of America

A Proclamation

This year an estimated 805,000 Americans will be diagnosed as having cancer. About 134,000 cancer patients will die who might have been saved by earlier diagnosis and prompt treatment.

While cancer is often called the disease Americans fear most, it is also now one of the most manageable chronic diseases in our country. We are approaching the day when, through surgery, chemotherapy and radiotherapy, half of the most serious forms of cancer can be cured.

Although we still face an enormous struggle in treating this disease, we must reaffirm today our ultimate goal—the cure of all those struck by this dread disease.

In addition to improving treatment for cancer patients, we must also reduce the incidence of this disease. In view of increasing evidence that a majority of cancers are related to environment and lifestyle, the major effect of Federal research today is in these areas.

Vigorous cancer research, directed to both treatment and prevention, must continue. All of us look to the day when this disease has been eradicated as a major threat to American lives.

Now, Therefore, I, Ronald Reagan, President of the United States of America, do hereby proclaim the month of April 1981 as Cancer Control Month, and I invite the Governors of the States and the Commonwealth of Puerto Rico, and the appropriate officials of all other areas of the United States flag to issue similar proclamations.

To give emphasis to this serious problem and to encourage the determination of the American people to meet it, I also ask the medical and health professions, the communications industries, and all other interested persons and groups to unite during this appointed time in public reaffirmation of our Nation's abiding commitment to control cancer.

In Witness Whereof, I have hereunto set my hand this 20th day of March, in the year of our Lord nineteen hundred and eighty-one, and of the Independence of the United States of America the two hundred and fifth.

RONALD REAGAN

[*Filed with the Office of the Federal Register, 11:06 a.m., March 24, 1981*]

Note: The text of the proclamation was released by the Office of the Press Secretary on March 23.

Message to the Congress Transmitting a Report on the Community Impact of New Military Facilities
March 23, 1981

To the Congress of the United States:

Section 803(b) of the Military Construction Authorization Act of 1980 (PL 96–418) called for "a thorough study of the adverse impact on communities in areas in which major, new military facilities are constructed with a view to determining the most effective and practicable means of promptly mitigating such impact."

I am submitting herewith a preliminary report of this study which is being conducted by an interagency task force of the President's Economic Adjustment Committee. Additional portions of the study are underway, and will be reflected in a final report which I will forward to the Congress as early as practicable. I will defer offering any recommendations on organizational and budgeting approaches to community and impact assistance until that time.

The study's initial findings suggest that the near-term local economic benefits of a major new military base may not be sufficient to offset the cost of required additional community facilities and services, and that special Federal assistance to affected States and localities may sometimes be justified. At the same time, States and localities should be expected to meet their share of community facility and service costs in defense growth areas.

As a general proposition, therefore, any special Federal community assistance should be limited to the minimum level required to mitigate the adverse effects of extraordinary growth directly resulting from major new bases. In addition, I would oppose any such assistance taking the form of Federal guarantees of State or municipal indebtedness where the interest is not subject to Federal income tax.

With specific reference to the MX weapon system and the East Coast Trident base, Section 802 of the Military Construction Authorization Act contains a wide range of authorities to provide impact assistance for affected areas. If additional legislation is required, I will request it at a later date.

I am pleased to note that representatives of the States and affected communities of Nevada, Utah, Georgia, and Florida have participated fully in preparation of this report. I am confident that, working together, we can meet legitimate State and local concerns about defense growth impacts, while at the same time satisfying national security requirements.

RONALD REAGAN

The White House,
March 23, 1981.

Proclamation 4829—Small Business Week, 1981
March 23, 1981

By the President of the United States of America

A Proclamation

Two centuries ago in this country, small business owners—the merchants, the builders, the traders—rebelled against excessive taxation and government interference and helped found this Nation. Today we are working to bring about another revolution, this time against the intolerable burdens inflation, over-regulation, and over-taxation have placed upon the Nation's 12 million small businesses, which provide the livelihood for more than 100 million of our people.

To revitalize the Nation, we must stimulate small business growth and opportunity. Small business accounts for over 60 percent of our jobs, half of our business output, and at least half of the innovations that keep American industry strong. The imagination, skills, and willingness of small business men and women to take necessary risks symbolize the free enterprise foundation of the American economy and must be encouraged.

I urge all Americans who own or work in a small business to continue their resourcefulness and successes, for these efforts contribute so much to the entrepreneurial spirit which made this Nation great. It is with justifiable pride that the American small business man can point to himself as the backbone of our Nation.

Now, Therefore, I, Ronald Reagan, President of the United States of America, do hereby proclaim the week beginning May 10, 1981, as Small Business Week. I call upon every American to join me in this tribute.

In Witness Whereof, I have hereunto set my hand this 23rd day of March, in the year of our Lord nineteen hundred eighty-one, and of the Independence of the United States of America the two hundred and fifth.

RONALD REAGAN

[*Filed with the Office of the Federal Register, 3:53 p.m., March 24, 1981*]

Note: The text of the proclamation was released by the Office of the Press Secretary on March 24.

Executive Order 12300—Exceptions From the Competitive Service
March 23, 1981

By the authority vested in me as President of the United States of America by Sections 3301 and 3302 of Title 5 of the United States Code, and having determined that it is necessary and warranted by conditions of good administration that certain positions in the Department of Agriculture ought to be excluded from the coverage of Section 2302 of Title 5 of the United States Code, and excepted from the competitive service because of their confidential, policy-determining, policy-making, or policy-advocating character, in order to ensure their deep involvement in the development and advocacy of Administration proposals and policies and to ensure their effective and vigorous implementation, it is hereby ordered that Section 6.8 of Civil Service Rule VI (5 CFR 6.8) is amended by adding thereto the following new subsection: "(c) Within the Department of Agriculture, positions in the Agricultural Stabilization and Conservation Service the incumbents of which serve as State Executive Directors and positions in the Farmers Home Administration the incumbents of which serve as State Directors or State Directors-at-Large shall be listed in Schedule C for all grades of the General Schedule.".

RONALD REAGAN

The White House,
March 23, 1981.

[*Filed with the Office of the Federal Register, 3:54 p.m., March 24, 1981*]

Note: The text of the Executive order was released by the Office of the Press Secretary on March 24.

Message to President Constantine Karamanlis of Greece on the Anniversary of the Greek War of Independence
March 24, 1981

The Greek War of Independence which was launched on March 25, 1821, had a special significance for Americans of that time. Only forty-five years before, the American colonies, too, had declared their independence. For Americans, the Greek struggle was that of a people whose ancient heritage was the source of fundamental ideas of free government on which the American Republic was founded.

Our friendship has continued to flourish and to strengthen, immeasurably enriched by the millions of Greeks who have come to our country to add their unique heritage to the fabric of American life. I am confident that Greek-American friendship will continue to grow and to produce even greater mutual benefits in the future.

Mr. President, on behalf of the American Government and the American people, I wish to extend my sincere congratulations on the anniversary of Greek independence.

RONALD REAGAN

Statement by the Press Secretary on Foreign and Domestic Crisis Management
March 24, 1981

I am confirming today the President's decision to have the Vice President chair the administration's crisis management team, as a part of the National Security Council system.

The purpose of this team is to coordinate and control all appropriate Federal resources in responding to emergency situations both foreign and domestic. The type of incident that might be involved ranges from an isolated terrorist attack to an attack upon United States territory by a hostile power.

During any emergency, the President would of course be available to make all critical decisions and to chair the crisis management team as his presence may be needed. Vice President Bush's role is to chair the team in the absence of the President. Of great importance, he will also engage in forward planning for emergency responses, develop options for Presidential consideration, and take the lead in the implementation of those decisions.

President Reagan's choice of the Vice President was guided in large measure by the fact that management of crises has traditionally—and appropriately—been done within the White House.

As in the past, the National Security Council staff will provide the administrative and other staff support to the President and the Vice President for the crisis management team.

Exchange With Reporters on Foreign and Domestic Crisis Management
March 25, 1981

Q. Sir, could we ask you if—*[inaudible]*—Secretary Haig—*[inaudible]*—and do you have a meeting of the minds on his role in your administration?

The President. Yes. As a matter of fact, as you see, I have a piece of paper in my hand.

Q. What was it that you wanted to tell us?

Q. Answer any question.

The President. Well, you are going to have a press briefing in just a few minutes in there, I understand, with my friend Mr. Brady, and this is a statement that I have left with him to read to you. But I will read it to you now, myself or give it to you—my own statement. And then he will take the questions there in the press briefing that you might have.

"One of the principal responsibilities of a President, as we all know, is the conduct of foreign policy. In meeting this responsibility, let me say what I said a number of times before: The Secretary of State is my primary adviser on foreign affairs, and in that capacity, he is the chief formulator and spokesman for foreign policy for this administration. There is not, nor has there ever been any question about this."

Q. *[Inaudible]*—about his testimony yesterday about making public his unhappiness on Capitol Hill, Mr. President?

The President. *[Inaudible]*—further questions.

Q. Mr. President, why, when you're in charge of foreign policy and you're in charge of Government, do you need a crisis manager? I mean, aren't you the ultimate crisis manager?

The President. Yes. That is why I have authorized such an office. It has no conflict whatsoever with what I just said. Crisis having to do—it could be with an earthquake, it could be with a flood in any one of our States, a disaster of that kind. There has always been such an office in the White House, and normally the White House adviser, the national security adviser, has chaired that. We thought it was more appropriate to have the Vice President, if I am not present—to have the Vice President do that.

Q. *[Inaudible]*—for the Secretary of State yesterday?

The President. Well, as I say, there is no conflict between what I have just said and between that.

Q. Did Haig ever threaten to resign, Mr. President?

The President. No, never once threatened me.

Q. Mr. President, can't you give us your own reaction to what you read about the Secretary's testimony on the Hill yesterday? You said before that you're not happy about airing public unhappiness——

The President. You've got my reaction.

Q. Well.

The President. My reaction was that maybe some of you were trying to make the news instead of reporting it.

Press Secretary Brady. Thank you, Mr. President.

Note: The exchange began at 1:40 p.m. at the South Portico of the White House as the President was leaving for several hours of horseback riding at Quantico Marine Base, Va.

Message to the Senate Transmitting the United States-New Zealand Maritime Boundary Treaty
March 25, 1981

To the Senate of the United States:

I transmit herewith, for the advice and consent of the Senate to ratification, the Treaty between the United States of America and New Zealand on the Delimitation of the Maritime Boundary between the United States of America and Tokelau. Also transmitted for the information of the Senate is the report of the Department of State with respect to the Treaty.

This Treaty is necessary to settle the overlapping claims of jurisdiction resulting from the establishment of a 200 nautical mile fishery conservation zone off the coasts of American Samoa in accordance with the Fishery Conservation and Management Act of 1976, and the establishment by the Government of New Zealand of a 200 nautical mile zone around Tokelau.

In this connection, the status of three Tokelauan islands has also been resolved and the sovereignty of the United States over Swains Island has been confirmed.

The Treaty satisfies the interest of the peoples of Tokelau and New Zealand that the Tokelauan claim to sovereignty over three of these islands, inhabited by natives of Tokelau and administered by New Zealand, will not be encumbered by a conflicting but inferior claim by the United States. The Treaty protects United States interests by confirming United States sovereignty over Swains Island, which had been claimed by Tokelau, and by securing a maritime boundary in accordance with equitable principles. It further serves United States foreign policy interests in the area by promoting friendly relations with New Zealand and with Tokelau.

I am transmitting for the information of the Senate a document from the Government of New Zealand vesting the Tokelauan signatories with authority to sign the Treaty on behalf of New Zealand and a separate exchange of letters between the United States and New Zealand, signed on December 2, 1980, setting forth the understanding of each side that New Zealand is willing to make arrangements for United States fishermen to have access to the Tokelauan 200 mile zone.

I recommend that the Senate give early consideration to the Treaty and give its advice and consent to ratification.

RONALD REAGAN

The White House,
March 25, 1981.

Statement on Signing Executive Order 12301, Concerning Integrity and Efficiency in Federal Programs
March 26, 1981

Today, I am announcing two actions to respond to the demand of the American people for honesty in government.

While hundreds of thousands of government employees are working honestly and competently to serve their nation, there is also a very small minority of dishonest—and some frankly incompetent—individuals who are costing the taxpayers perhaps billions of dollars in fraud and waste.

This is not my money; it is not the Congress' money; it is the people's money. Our failure to stop this fraud, waste, and mismanagement has led to growing public cynicism about the ability of government to control itself. It raises fundamental questions about the integrity of government.

My first action is the issuance of an Executive order establishing the President's Council on Integrity and Efficiency. This action signals everyone who works for or does business with the Government that we mean business.

This Executive order I have signed brings together in one body the Inspectors General of the various agencies of Government so that they can focus their total efforts in the places that will do the most good. This will also include the efforts of the Justice Department and its resources in the FBI.

Bringing together these efforts will permit all agencies to share knowledge of fraudulent and wasteful activities. They will exchange information on the kinds of investigations which will provide the most promising results. And they will be ready to move in quickly with tough and effective criminal prosecutions where such prosecutions are warranted.

I have asked Edwin Harper, Assistant to the President and Deputy Director of the Office of Management and Budget, to chair the new Council. Mr. Harper will be reporting directly to me, and, Ed, I am confident that you will have a lot to report.

I am also announcing the appointments of the first 6 of the 16 Inspectors General that are authorized by law. When I exercised my prerogative as a new President to terminate the appointments of the incumbent inspectors, I announced that we would seek the very best people we could find, includ-

ing those who previously held these positions. Five of the six individuals I am announcing today were previously serving as Inspectors General, and I hope this puts to rest suspicions that have been voiced that politics has anything to do with these appointments. We sought the best people available—individuals with experience who have uncovered cases of fraud and waste in government and have saved or recovered millions of dollars.

I am pleased to announce that the FBI has just concluded a major investigation in New York relating to fraud in the summer lunch program. FBI Director William Webster will be here later today to give you a complete briefing on this matter.

We will not rest with today's announcement. We will not simply tuck this event away and go on with business as usual. The American people are demanding action, and they are going to get it. Believe me, we are out to get control of our lives—and we are going to follow every lead, root out every incompetent, and prosecute any crook we find who's cheating the people of this Nation. This I promise.

Note: The President read the statement at a signing ceremony which began at approximately 11:30 a.m. in the Roosevelt Room at the White House.

Executive Order 12301—Integrity and Efficiency in Federal Programs
March 26, 1981

By the authority vested in me as President by the Constitution and statutes of the United States of America, and in order to coordinate and implement Government policies with respect to integrity and efficiency in Federal programs, it is hereby ordered as follows:

Section 1. Establishment of the President's Council on Integrity and Efficiency. (a) There is established as an interagency committee the President's Council on Integrity and Efficiency.

(b) The Council shall be composed of the following members:

(1) The Deputy Director of the Office of Management and Budget who shall be the Chairman of the Council;

(2) The Deputy Attorney General;

(3) The Director of the Office of Personnel Management;

(4) The Executive Assistant Director of Investigations of the Federal Bureau of Investigation;

(5) Inspector General, Department of Energy;

(6) Inspector General, Department of Agriculture;

(7) Inspector General, Department of Housing and Urban Development;

(8) Inspector General, Department of Labor;

(9) Inspector General, Department of Transportation;

(10) Inspector General, Veterans Administration;

(11) Inspector General, Department of Health and Human Services;

(12) Inspector General, Department of Education;

(13) Inspector General of the Department of State and the Foreign Service;

(14) Inspector General, Department of Commerce;

(15) Inspector General, Department of Interior;

(16) Inspector General, Community Services Administration;

(17) Inspector General, Environmental Protection Agency;

(18) Inspector General, General Services Administration;

(19) Inspector General, National Aeronautics and Space Administration;

(20) Inspector General, Small Business Administration;

(21) A designee of the Secretary of the Treasury;

(22) A designee of the Secretary of Defense, and

(23) A designee of the Director of the United States International Development Cooperation Agency.

(c) The Chairman shall, from time to time, invite the following to participate in the meetings of the Council:

(1) The Comptroller General of the United States, and

(2) The Postmaster General of the United States.

Sec. 2. Functions of the Council. (a) The Council shall develop plans for coordinated government-wide activities which attack fraud and waste in government programs and operations.

(b) In order to ensure coordinated relationships between Federal, State and local government agencies, and nongovernment entities with respect to all matters relating to the promotion of economy and efficien-

cy, the Council shall develop standards for the management, operation, and conduct of inspector general-type acitivities.

(c) Policies shall be developed by the Council which will ensure the establishment of a corps of well-trained and highly skilled auditors and investigators.

(d) The Council shall develop interagency audit and investigation programs and projects to deal efficiently and effectively with those problems concerning fraud and waste which exceed the capability or jurisdiction of an individual agency. The Council will recognize the pre-eminent role of the Department of Justice in matters involving law enforcement and litigation.

(e) The Council membership shall, to the extent of their own authority to do so, implement those coordinated plans, standards, policies, programs, and projects, (1) in order to conduct and supervise audits and investigations relating to programs and operations of the Government, and (2) in order to promote economy, efficiency, and effectiveness in the administration of programs and operations of the Government, as well as to detect fraud and abuse in such programs and operations.

(f) The creation and operation of the Council shall not interfere with existing lines of authority and responsibility in the departments and agencies.

Sec. 3. Responsibilities of the Chairman. (a) The Chairman shall, in consultation with the members of the Council, establish procedures for the Council; and, he shall establish the agenda for Council activities.

(b) The Chairman shall, on behalf of the Council, report to the President on the activities of the Council. The Chairman shall advise the Council with respect to the reaction of the President on the Council's activities.

(c) The Chairman shall provide agency heads with summary reports of the activities of the Council.

(d) The Chairman shall establish such committees of the Council, including an executive committee, as he deems necessary or appropriate for the efficient conduct of Council functions. Committees of the Council may act for the Council in those areas that affect the membership of the committee.

(e) The Chairman shall be supported by the Associate Director for Management of the Office of Management and Budget who shall advise and assist the Chairman in the execution of the entire range of responsibilities set forth above.

Sec. 4. Coordinating Conference. (a) There is established as an interagency committee the Coordinating Conference of the President's Council on Integrity and Efficiency.

(b) The Conference shall be composed of the Chairman of the Council and one representative of each Executive agency not represented on the Council. The head of each such agency shall designate as the agency's representative the official who is responsible for coordinating the agency's efforts to eliminate fraud and waste in the agency's programs and operations.

(c) The Chairman shall convene meetings of the Conference at least quarterly. The Chairman provide for the dissemination to the Conference of appropriate information

on the activities of the Council, in order to enable the Conference membership, to the extent of their own authority to do so, to implement the coordinated plans, standards, policies, programs, and projects developed by the Council.

Sec. 5. Administrative Provisions. (a) The Director of the Office of Management and Budget shall provide the Council and the Conference with such administrative support as may be necessary for the performance of the functions of the Council and the Conference.

(b) The head of each agency represented on the Council or the Conference shall provide its representative with such administrative support as may be necessary, in accordance with law, to enable the agency representative to carry out his responsibilities.

RONALD REAGAN

The White House,
March 26, 1981.

[*Filed with the Office of the Federal Register, 3:34 p.m., March 26, 1981*]

Memorandum on the Reduction of Fraud and Waste in Federal Programs
March 26, 1981

Memorandum for

The Secretary of State
The Secretary of the Treasury
The Secretary of Defense
The Attorney General
The Secretary of the Interior
The Secretary of Agriculture
The Secretary of Commerce
The Secretary of Labor
The Secretary of Health and Human Services
The Secretary of Housing and Urban Development
The Secretary of Transportation
The Secretary of Energy
The Secretary of Education

The Director of the Community Services Administration
The Administrator of the Environmental Protection Agency
The Administrator of General Services
The Director of the United States International Development Cooperation Agency
The Director of the Office of Management and Budget
The Director of the Office of Personnel Management
The Administrator of the National Aeronautics and Space Administration
The Administrator of the Small Business Administration
The Administrator of Veterans Affairs

Subject: Government-Wide Anti-Fraud
and Waste Efforts

The reduction of fraud and waste in all
Federal programs is a major commitment
and priority of my Administration. Today, I
am establishing, by Executive Order, the
President's Council on Integrity and Efficiency to focus and improve our efforts to
deal with the problem. The Deputy Director of the Office of Management and
Budget will chair this Council which will
include all of the statutory Inspectors General and other key officials.

The commitment to reduce fraud and
waste cannot be met simply by appointing
Inspectors General and establishing a Presidential Council. Each of you is responsible
for taking the initiative to reduce fraud and
waste wherever they are found in the programs which you administer.

The establishment of this Council is an
integral part of a broader plan to attack
fraud, waste and inefficiency in Federal
programs. This plan will involve a combination of key officials and organizations, coordinating mechanisms, and priority projects operating under active OMB leadership on my behalf.

I expect each of you to provide the necessary support and cooperation to assure that
our objective is accomplished. One specific
action I am asking you to take is to designate an individual at the Assistant Secretary
level or higher who will have the responsibility for following up on the recommendations of your Inspector General and the
General Accounting Office.

RONALD REAGAN

Memorandum on the Reduction of Fraud and Waste in Federal Programs
March 26, 1981

*Memorandum for the Heads of
Departments and Agencies*

Subject: Government-Wide Anti-Fraud
and Waste Efforts

The reduction of fraud and waste in the
operation of all Federal programs is a major
commitment and priority of my Administration. Today, I am establishing by Executive
Order, the President's Council on Integrity
and Efficiency to focus and improve our
efforts to deal with the problem. The
Deputy Director of the Office of Management and Budget will chair this Council
which will include all of the statutory Inspectors General and other key officials.

The commitment to reduce fraud and
waste cannot be limited to those departments and agencies where statutory IGs
have been established. I have asked the
Chairman of the Council to ensure that
other departments and agencies are actively involved in this most important undertaking. The Executive Order directs the

Chairman to convene all of the agencies not
on the Council at least four times a year to
share information on Council policy initiatives.

The establishment of this Council is an
integral part of a broader plan to attack
fraud, waste and inefficiency in Federal
programs. This plan will involve a combination of key officials and organizations, coordinating mechanisms, and priority projects operating under active OMB leadership on my behalf.

I expect each of you to provide the necessary support and cooperation to assure that
our objective is accomplished. One specific
action I am asking you to take is to designate a top level individual who will have
the responsibility for following up on the
recommendations of your official who is responsible for coordinating efforts to eliminate fraud and waste and the recommendations of the General Accounting Office.

RONALD REAGAN

Appointment of Six Inspectors General
March 26, 1981

The President announced today the appointment of six Inspectors General for Government departments and agencies. Five of the six have previously served as Inspectors General. Three of those appointed today will resume their positions at the same agency as before and two will be in different agencies.

The appointments are:

Robert L. Brown as Inspector General of the Department of State and the Foreign Service. Mr. Brown is a retired Foreign Service officer who has been recalled to serve as Inspector General of the Department of State and the Foreign Service under existing authority. The Secretary has nominated him to fill this position, with the advice and consent of the Senate, under the provisions of the New Foreign Service Act. Prior to his retirement in 1980, Mr. Brown served as a senior inspector in the Office of the Inspector General. When Secretary of State Haig was Supreme Allied Commander in Europe, Mr. Brown was his political adviser. He served Secretaries Rusk and Rogers as Deputy Executive Secretary of the Department. Among his Foreign Service assignments, Mr. Brown has served as Deputy Director of Personnel, economic counselor to the Republic of China, and has served in Japan, Morocco, Belgium, and New Caledonia. Mr. Brown graduated from Syracuse University and has done graduate work at Northwestern and George Washington Universities. In 1962–63 he attended the State Department's senior seminar in foreign policy. He holds the Secretary of State's Superior Honor Award and the Secretary of Defense's Civilian Defense Medal. Born in Dayton, Ohio, in 1920, Mr. Brown now resides in the Washington, D.C., metropolitan area with his wife, Marion Jean. They have one son, a Washington businessman.

Paul R. Boucher as Inspector General of the Small Business Administration. Mr. Boucher was born April 13, 1942, in Cambridge, Mass. He received a B.S. from Merrimack College in 1963 and a J.D. from Suffolk University Law School in 1969. From 1964 to 1970, Mr. Boucher was a special agent and assistant senior resident agent for U.S. Naval Intelligence in Boston. From 1970 to 1972, he was staff assistant for legal matters at Naval Investigative Headquarters in Alexandria, Va. From 1972 to 1974, he was a trial attorney with the Criminal Division of the Justice Department. From 1974 to 1975, he was Assistant General Counsel of the U.S. Government Printing Office. From 1975 to 1979, he was Deputy Section Chief of the General Crimes Section at the Justice Department's Criminal Division. In that capacity, he was selected to organize and direct task forces created by the Attorney General to investigate allegations of violations of Federal criminal law by United States intelligence agencies.

Charles L. Dempsey as Inspector General of the Department of Housing and Urban Development. Mr. Dempsey was born June 7, 1928, in Morristown, N.J. He received a B.S. from Georgetown University in 1960. He served in the U.S. Army in 1952 and 1953. He joined the Department of Housing and Urban Development in 1968, where he served as Acting Director of Investigation (1970–1972), Assistant Inspector General for Administration (1972–1975), Acting Inspector General (1975), and Assistant Inspector General for Investigation (1975–1977). From 1977 to 1979, he was Inspector General of the Department, serving on a nonstatutory basis.

Thomas F. McBride as Inspector General of the Department of Labor. He previously was the Inspector General at the Department of Agriculture. Mr. McBride was born February 8, 1929, in Elgin, Ill. He received a B.A. from New York University in 1952 and an LL.B. from Columbia Law School in 1956. He served in the U.S. Army from 1946 to 1947. From 1956 to 1959, he was assistant district attorney of New York County, and from 1959 to 1960, he was assistant counsel to the New York State Commission on Government Operations of the City of New York. In 1960 and 1961 he was an attorney and supervisory investigator for the Labor Department, and from 1961 to 1965, he was a trial attorney for the Justice Department. From 1965 to 1968, Mr. McBride was Deputy Director of the Peace Corps for the Latin America Region. From 1968 to 1969, he was associate director of the Urban Coalition. In 1969 he was deputy chief counsel to the U.S. House of Representatives Select Committee on Crime. In 1970 he was chief of the Center for Demonstrations and Professional Services of the National Institute of Law Enforcement and Criminal Justice. From 1970 to 1973, he was associate director and staff director of the Police Foundation, a Ford Foundation-funded program to support innovation and experimentation in police and criminal justice services. From 1973 to 1975, McBride was Associate Special Prosecutor with the Watergate Special Prosecution Force. From 1975 to 1977, he was Director of the Bureau of Enforcement at the Civil Aeronautics Board, directing all economic enforcement activities in the field of the U.S. air transport. From 1977 to 1979, he served as Inspector General of the Agriculture Department on a nonstatutory basis.

Frank S. Sato as Inspector General of the Environmental Protection Agency. He previously was Inspector General at the Department of Transportation. Mr. Sato was born March 16, 1929, in Puyallup, Wash. He received a B.A. in accounting from the University of Washington in 1953. From 1953 to 1965, he was with the U.S. Air Force Auditor General's Office, serving in various positions, finally as Chief of the Logistics Audits Division. From 1965 to 1974, he was with the Office of the Assistant Secretary of Defense (Comptroller), serving as Director for Special Activities Audits, Director for Audit Operations, Director for Defense Agencies Audits, and Deputy Comptroller for Audit Operations. From 1974 to 1979, he was Deputy Assistant Secretary of Defense for Audit. He also served as Director of the Defense Audit Service. Mr. Sato has been national president of the Association of Government Accountants and is active in accounting and auditing associations.

James B. Thomas, Jr., as Inspector General of the Department of Education. Mr. Thomas is a career civil servant who came to the Department from the Interstate Commerce Commission (ICC), where he had been Director of the Bureau of Accounts since October 1977. In that post he was responsible for all ICC accounting, auditing, and financial analysis of the country's surface transportation system. In 1971 he worked for the ICC's Bureau of Accounts as an accounting officer, and from 1972 to 1975, he served as Assistant Bureau Director. From

1960 to 1971, he worked at the Department of Housing and Urban Development as an auditor, audit supervisor, audit manager, and Assistant Director for Audit Operations. From 1975 to 1977, he served as HUD's Inspector General. Prior to his Federal service, he was a senior auditor for the State of Florida and, earlier, a junior auditor with the Tallahassee accounting firm of J.D.A. Holley & Co. Mr. Thomas graduated from Florida State University in 1957 with a bachelor of science degree in business administration. He did graduate work in accounting, economics, and finance, and has been a certified public accountant since 1962 and a certified internal auditor since 1973. He is a native of Aucilla, Fla., and currently lives in McLean, Va.

There are 16 statutory Inspectors General, including that of the State Department, which has a slightly different statutory basis. President Reagan announced that the remaining 10 positions will be filled shortly and that previously serving Inspectors General are under consideration for some of those positions.

Shortly after assuming office, the President terminated the appointments of all the incumbent Inspectors General, exercising the prerogative of a newly inaugurated President. He announced at that time that he would seek the most qualified appointees for these important positions and that the former incumbents would be among those considered.

Each of the IG's appointed today has compiled an excellent record of uncovering fraud and other abuses in the programs under their surveillance. In some cases, their investigations have led to criminal indictments, and in all cases they have produced recoveries of moneys falsely expended or other savings.

Statement by the Press Secretary on the Situation in Poland
March 26, 1981

The White House issued the following statement at the conclusion of today's National Security Council meeting. This statement reflects the views of the President of the United States.

The United States has watched with growing concern indications that Polish authorities may be preparing to use force to deal with continuing differences in that country between the authorities and labor unions. We are similarly concerned that the Soviet Union may intend to undertake repressive action in Poland.

Our position on the situation in Poland has been clear and consistent from the outset. We believe Poland should be allowed to resolve its own problems without outside interference of any kind. We have scrupulously implemented that policy in our statements, while acting generously in response to Poland's requests to us for economic assistance.

We have welcomed past assurances by the Polish Government and Polish labor organizations that they intended to resolve their differences peaceably and in a spirit of compromise and conciliation. We continue to believe that this path offers the only hope of resolving Poland's difficulties on a basis acceptable to all parties concerned.

We would like to make clear to all concerned our view that any external intervention in Poland, or any measures aimed at suppressing the Polish people, would necessarily cause deep concern to all those interested in the peaceful development of Poland, and could have a grave effect on the whole course of East-West relations.

At the same time, we would emphasize our continuing readiness to assist Poland in its present economic and financial troubles, for as long as the Polish people and authorities continue to seek through a peaceful process of negotiation the resolution of their current problems. It is in this spirit that we shall receive Deputy Prime Minister Jagielski in Washington next week.

Remarks at a White House Reception for Delegates to the Young Republican Leadership Conference
March 26, 1981

The President. Well, I'm delighted to be here—and so is Nancy—and to have all of you here in your national home. And I know that we're celebrating the 50th birthday of YR's. Maybe you'd prefer now that you've reached that point that I refer to it as the 11th anniversary of your 50th—[*laughter*]. I found it very satisfactory where I'm concerned. [*Laughter*]

I know, also, all that's gone on in these years since you started out. I know the delegations that you've sent to Europe and to Africa and to Latin America, the interaction that you've had with youth groups in the rest of the world; forums, exchange of literature, and how you sponsored groups of young people from those other countries to come here. And you've raised over $600,000 in—not in, but for campaign training schools, literature, and for direct assist-

ance to candidates. And I speak as one of those who benefited from that direct assistance. I will say there have been a few days in the couple of months we've been here when I didn't know whether I was happy that you did that or not. [*Laughter*]

But incidentally I know, and I hope this is true—I've been told that there's an old friend of mine from Iowa here, but also one of yours—General George Olmstead who was that first—well, he's Chairman now of the Board of the International Bank here in Washington, but he was the first Chairman of YR's in 1931. George are you here? There he is. We're old friends and near neighbors in our working days out there.

Well, it's been almost 17 years since I told a group of Young Republicans once that we had a rendezvous with destiny, and now here we are. [*Laughter*] But you've helped, you've added representatives at every level of government to strengthen our forces, and now for us to go forward and try to realize our ideals and the things that we've been talking about all these years. One of those things is, of course, the economic program that we have submitted.

The battle is on; lines are being drawn. I believe we've got a better chance of getting the cuts in the budget that we've proposed. There seems to be more general agreement on the need to reduce government spending, but the other half of the program is equally important. That is the half that is designed to stimulate productivity to make us once again the industrial giant that we should be, to put our people back to work— almost 8 million unemployed today—and that is the tax part of the program, tax cuts across the board.

And let me warn you now, you're going to have to help, because they're going to have to realize that the people of this country want what you have just applauded. And some of those who have evidenced their dislike of this program, whether it had to do with the cuts or the tax reductions, have fuzzed up the issue to the place that we have got to convey to the people that first of all, those who have brought about the present economic crisis are not automatically, by virtue of doing that, qualified to bring an end to it.

And the other thing they must realize is that in our tax cuts, we are faced—and as of January 1st, it began, last January 1st—that the American people today are burdened with the biggest single tax increase that has ever been imposed on the people of this country. And our tax cuts, major as they may seem to some, are actually not reducing the tax burden below what it was before January 1st. We are simply reducing the increase. The people will still be facing an increase, and we have to make that plain to everyone that these tax cuts are not taking us back to some poverty level of government. As a matter of fact, the tax in-crease that I've mentioned, unless we get our cuts, in the next 5 years will take an added $500 billion out of the pockets of the American people. And we're just trying to reduce that—although, I'll tell you this, we've got a second package in mind that when it begins to show some effect and we can afford it, we'll be going back until we get rid of the rest of that increase too, later on.

Well, thank you very much.

Mr. Abell. It's such an honor to be here on behalf of all the Young Republicans across the country and about a half a million of us that wished we could all have been here today, and we're glad we're here. And Mr. President, thank you for having us, and I'd like to say that—I'd like to thank you for having us and especially on our 50th anniversary. And I'd like to have our national chairman present you a bowl from Tiffany's that we got for you so you might be able to use it in your home in California.

Thank you again.

The President. Well, thank you very much.

Mrs. Reagan. Just right for jellybeans.

The President. Nancy says it's just right for jellybeans. [*Laughter*] And, well, I've said this before: We won't have to wait until we get back to California. We live above the store. [*Laughter*] Thank you all very much.

Thank you for being here, and thank you for all that you've done. I know you didn't start with the organization 50 years ago— [*laughter*]—but for all that YR's means— and you certainly are keeping alive the tradition and the level of activity, and we're all grateful to you.

Thank you.

Note: The President spoke at 5:35 p.m. in the East Room at the White House. Richard Abell is the chairman of the Young Republican National Federation, which sponsored the leadership conference.

Nomination of John J. Louis, Jr., To Be United States Ambassador to the United Kingdom
March 27, 1981

The President today announced his intention to nominate John J. Louis, Jr., of Winnetka, Ill., as Ambassador to the United Kingdom of Great Britain and Northern Ireland. He would succeed Kingman Brewster, Jr., who has resigned.

Mr. Louis served in the U.S. Army Air Force (1943–45) as second lieutenant, aircraft pilot. From 1951 to 1958, he was account executive with the advertising firm of Needham, Louis, and Brorby, Inc., and from 1958 to 1961, he was director of international marketing of the S. C. Johnson and Son, Inc. He was chairman of KTAR Broadcasting Co. (radio and television) from 1961 to 1968. Since 1968 he has been chairman of Combined Communications Corp., a division of Gannett Co., Inc., of Rochester, N.Y.

In 1972 he was Personal Representative of the President, with the rank of Special Ambassador, to head the United States Delegation at the ceremonies commemorating the 12th anniversary of the independence of the Gabon Republic.

Mr. Louis was born June 10, 1925, in Evanston, Ill. He was graduated from Williams College (B.A., 1947) and Dartmouth College (M.B.A., 1949). He is married to the former Josephine Peters, and they have three children.

Appointment of Frank A. Ursomarso as Director of the White House Office of Communications
March 27, 1981

The President today announced the appointment of Frank A. Ursomarso to be Director of the White House Office of Communications.

Among its responsibilities, the Office of Communications is to coordinate the activities of public affairs officers of government agencies or departments, provide research and information services to the President and White House staff, and to assist the television networks in their coverage of the President.

From 1973 to 1976, Mr. Ursomarso was an advance representative for President Nixon and President Ford. He was television production coordinator for the 1976 Presidential debates, and during the 1980 Presidential campaign, served Governor Reagan as television production coordinator and advance coordinator for the Presidential debates.

Before assuming his present White House post, Mr. Ursomarso was in the automobile business in Wilmington, Del. He was also a member of the Pennsylvania Public Television Network and the Pennsylvania Securities Commission.

During his service in the U.S. Army as a military police officer, he was a member of the task force on domestic disturbances. He served 1 year in Vietnam and was awarded the Bronze Star Medal.

Mr. Ursomarso was born in Philadelphia, Pa., on September 19, 1942. He received his B.A. in 1964 from Gettysburg College and his J.D. in 1967 from the University of California at Los Angeles.

Mr. Ursomarso is married to the former Catherine Sanders, and they have three children. The family resides in Unionville, Chester County, Pa.

Remarks at a White House Luncheon for Members of the Baseball Hall of Fame
March 27, 1981

The President. Gentlemen, go ahead with your coffee and all, but I know that time is getting by and we have a few remarks.

I'm delighted—well, I can't tell you how thrilled to have you all here. And over there at the other table is a ballplayer who is delighted to be here, Vice President George Bush, and he did play. But I want to tell you, you span the years for me, and all these young gentlemen here that are growing up as ballplayers. It's a delight to have all of you here.

The nostalgia is bubbling within me, and I may have to be dragged out of here because of all the stories that are coming up in my mind. Baseball—I had to finally confess over here, no, I didn't play when I was young. I went down the football path. But I did play in a way, as Bob Lemon well knows, I was old Grover Cleveland Alexander, and I've been very proud of that. It was a wonderful experience.

There were quite a few ballplayers, including Bob Lemon, who were on the set for that picture. And I remember one day when they wanted some shots of me pitching, but kind of close up—so, they wanted me to throw past the camera, and they had a fellow back there—well, Al Lyons, one of the ballplayers that was there, was going to catch the ball back there and then toss it back over the camera to me. And the cam was getting these close shots for use wherever they could use them. And he was on one side of the camera, and my control wasn't all that it should be at one point, and I threw it on the other side of the camera. And he speared it with his left hand with no glove on. He was a left-hander, and after he brought the ball to me, and he said, "Alex, I'm sorry I had to catch your blazer bare-handed." [*Laughter*] He didn't suffer any pain, I am sure of it.

But I remember we had a fellow that I'm sure some of you know and remember, Metkovitch. And Metkovitch, during the day's shooting, would memorize everyone's lines. And then if we were on location and

get in the bus to go back in from location, he would now play all the scenes for us on the bus. [*Laughter*] So, thinking about this, one day, on the process screen, an umpire behind him, he was at the plate, and they wanted a shot of a ballplayer at the plate. And the director said, "There are no lines, but you'll know what to say." He said, "The umpire's going to call it a strike," and he said, " You don't think it's a strike. So, do what you do in a ballgame when you think it's a bad call." And extroverted Metkovitch, who was so happy to play all the scenes, was standing up at the plate and if you looked closely, you could see that the bat was beginning to shake a little bit— [*laughter*]—and the ball came by on an after play and the umpire bellowed out, "Strike one!" And Metkovitch lowered the bat and he says, "Gee, that was no strike." [*Laughter*] The picture wasn't a comedy, so we could't leave it in.

But you know, I've always been sorry about one thing. Alex is in the Hall of Fame and deservedly so. Everyone knows that great 1926 World Series, when he had won two games, received the greatest ovation anyone's ever received, and then was called on in the 7th inning with the bases loaded, no one out, and one of the most dangerous hitters in baseball at the plate. And he came in and saved the game. The tragedy that I've always regretted is that the studio was unwilling to reveal in the picture, was afraid to reveal what I think was the best kept secret in sports.

A bad habit of Alex's was widely heralded and took something away from his luster. But they wouldn't let us use the actual word of what was behind, maybe, his bad habit. Alex was an epileptic. And when he was arrested and picked up for being drunk in a gutter, as he once was, he wasn't at all. But he would rather take that than admit to the disease that plagued him all his life.

But he also, early in his baseball career, was hit in the head going from first base down to second on a throw from second;

they caught him right in the head. And he was out of baseball for a while, and they didn't know whether forever, because he had double vision. And he kept experimenting, trying to find out if there wasn't some way that he could pitch. And he went to a minor league club and asked for a tryout, and the manager got up at the plate and said, "Well, go on out on the mound and throw me a few." Alex broke three of his ribs on the first pitch. [*Laughter*] His experiment had been that he thought that if he closed one eye and threw, he'd only—[*laughter*]—and the friend that was with him when they were thrown out of the ballpark said, " What happened?" And he said, "I closed the wrong eye." [*Laughter*]

But there are men in this room that were playing when I was broadcasting, and I promised to say something here to a great Cub fan that we have at the table that would make him feel good. I was broadcasting the Cubs when the only mathematical possibility—and Billy Herman will remember this very well—that the Cubs had of winning the pennant was to win the last 21 games of the season. And they did. And I was so imbued with baseball by that time that I know you're not supposed to talk about a no-hitter while it's going on because you'll jinx them. So, there I was, a broadcaster, and never mentioned once in the 21 games—and I was getting as uptight as they were—and never mentioned the fact that they were at 16, they were at 17, and that they hadn't lost a game, because I was afraid I'd jinx them. But anyway, they did it and it's still in the record books.

What isn't in the record books is Billy Jurges staying at the plate, I think, the longest of any ballplayer in the history of the game. I was doing the games by telegraphic report, and the fellow on the other side of a window with a little slit underneath, the headphones on, getting the dot-and-dash Morse code from the ballpark, would type out the play. And the paper would come through to me—it would say, "S1C." Well, you're not going to sell any Wheaties yelling "S1C!" [*Laughter*] So, I'd say, "And so-and-so comes out of the wind-up, here's the pitch, and it's a called strike, breaking over the outside corner to so-and-so, who'd

rather have a ball someplace else and so forth and backed out there."

Well, I saw him start to type, and I started—Dizzy Dean was on the mound—and I started the ball on the way to the plate—or him in the wind-up and he, Curly, the fellow on the other side, was shaking his head, and I thought he just—maybe it was a miraculous play or something. But when the slip came through it said, "The wire's gone dead." Well, I had the ball on the way to the plate. [*Laughter*] And I figured real quick, I could say we'll tell them what had happened and then play transcribed music. But in those days there were at least seven or eight other fellows that were doing the same ballgame. I didn't want to lose the audience.

So, I thought real quick, "There's one thing that doesn't get in the score book," so I had Billy foul one off. And I looked at Curly, and Curly just went like this; so I had him foul another one. And I had him foul one back at third base and described the fight betwen the two kids that were trying to get the ball. [*Laughter*] Then I had him foul one that just missed being a home run, about a foot and a half. And I did set a world record for successive fouls or for someone standing there, except that no one keeps records of that kind. And I was beginning to sweat, when Curly sat up straight and started typing, and he was nodding his head, "Yes." And the slip came through the window, and I could hardly talk for laughing, because it said, "Jurges popped out on the first ball pitch." [*Laughter*]

But those were wonderful days, not only playing the part, but some of you here, I think, will—I'm going to tell another story here that has been confirmed for me by Waite Hoyt. Those of you who played when the Dodgers were in Brooklyn, know that Brooklynese have a tendency to refer to someone by the name of Earl as "oil." But if they want a quart of oil in the car, they say, "Give me a quart of earl." And Waite was sliding into second. And he twisted his ankle. And instead of getting up, he was lying there, and there was a deep hush over the whole ballpark. And then a Brooklyn voice was heard above all that silence and said, "Gee, Hurt is hoyt." [*Laughter*]

But, I can't take any more time doing this or we'd be here all day. They tell me that I'm supposed to go out there in front of the door to the Blue Room, and because I haven't been able to say hello to all of you in here and, as I say, there are many of you that were playing when I broadcast in those telegraphic report games, and not only re-created but—as I just told you—now and then created some of the ballgame. But I understand that we're going to have a chance outside here—kind of a line where I can say hello and goodby at the same time to each one of you.

And now I'm going to present—the Commissioner has something here that I think should be said. Commissioner, come on up here.

Mr. Kuhn.[1] Okay, fine. I just wanted to take a moment on behalf of all of us gathered here together to thank the President for his great kindness in having us all here today.

I'm going to borrow a line from the man I talked to yesterday who's sitting here in the room, Mr. President, Bob Howsam. When Bob and I were talking, I said, "I'll see you there tomorrow, won't I?" And Bob's a member of our executive council from the Cincinnati Reds sitting over here, and he said, "Commissioner, I will never be so proud or so old that I won't be thrilled to set foot in the White House and say hello to the President of the United States." And I think on behalf of us all, I can say we're very thrilled to be here, to be with you, to share with you some anecdotes about the game of baseball.

I want to just do one little thing that I found. I want to say to the President on behalf of baseball that I think we have contributed mightily to the President's situation here in Washington, because he was a Cubs fan, as you can tell. And I've got an article I found in the Chicago Tribune which plainly indicates that baseball has prepared him for his career here. It says, "For four years, Ronald Reagan broadcast games of the Cubs and in the process

---

[1] *Bowie Kuhn, Commissioner of the American Baseball Association.*

became that rarest of nature's noblemen," Dave Broder, "a Cub fan. Nothing before or since those four years has prepared him more fully to face with fortitude the travails of the Oval Office. As a Cub fan, he learned that virtue will not necessarily prevail over chicanery, that swift failure follows closely on the heels of even the most modest success, that the world mocks those who are pure in heart, but slow of foot. But"—and here's the good news, Mr. President—"but that the bitterest disappointment will soon yield to the hope and promise of a new season."

We thank you from the bottoms of our heart for your kindness and generosity here today.

Mr. Stack. I'm Ed Stack, the president of the Baseball Hall of Fame, and I have a couple presentations I'd like to make.

Before the luncheon, the President greeted the commissioner and myself in the Oval Office and was very gracious to sign our historic Presidential baseball, which we have on display at the Baseball Hall of Fame in Cooperstown. He added his signature to the baseballs that have been signed by all the Presidents since William Howard Taft. And tomorrow morning, it'll be on display in Cooperstown for the millions of visitors to see when they come through the shrine.

Also, we presented the President with a lifetime gold pass to the Baseball Hall of Fame, and we hope that he will use it many times in the future.

I'd like to ask the President to accept from us a couple gifts. The first gift that we have to present is something that Billy Martin sent from Oakland. Bill heard about the luncheon and asked that I present this to the President. And if he could open it and show the audience, I think he'll enjoy it.

[*The President was presented with an Oakland A's team jacket.*]

The President. Hey, look, Ma, I made the team! [*Laughter*] I hope he hasn't got this too big. [*Laughter*] A little big.

Well, I thank him very much. I thank all of you.

Mr. Stack. The veterans' committee of the Hall of Fame met recently in Tampa, Florida, to elect new members to the Hall of Fame: Johnny Mize, who's in the room today, was elected just a couple weeks ago. At the meeting, the veterans' committee wrestled with other candidates, the many candidates to the Hall of Fame. President Reagan's name came up, because we all knew that he was a baseball player in the movie "Grover Cleveland Alexander." But he didn't make it on this go around. So, the veterans' committee asked me to arrange for the Hall of Fame to present to the President today a remembrance from the Hall of Fame.

[*Mr. Stack presented the President with a painting.*]

It's Grover Cleveland Alexander.

The President. Hey!

Mr. Kuhn. And on the back we have an inscription of what it's all about.

The President. Oh, believe me, I'm delighted to have this. This is just wonderful. I never had more fun or enjoyed anything more in my life than when we were making that picture. And I remember Nancy and I—we were engaged and waiting for the picture to end to get married. And she came out on the set one day, and I said, "How would you like to have a baseball autographed by all these fellows that are— all these ballplayers?" And, oh, she thought that would be great. And I started out, and I looked back, and there were tears in her eyes, and she was standing there. And I said, "What?" And she said, "Can't I go get them?" [*Laughter*]

Well, I'm more pleased—delighted to have this. Thank you very much.

Mr. Kuhn. I'd like to make just one announcement. The Baseball Hall of Famers who are here, after the receiving line, if you could remain for a minute, we will have a group photograph. I'm pleased to announce that this is the largest assembled group of Hall of Famers that ever been in one place together at any time.

The President. See you all outside.

Note: The President spoke at 12:57 p.m. in the State Dining Room at the White House.

Remarks to Representatives of the Sister Cities International Program
March 27, 1981

The President. Greetings to all of you— and I see it's [the rain] holding off. [*Laughter*]

Well, I am most pleased. I understand that I'm the honorary chairman now. Well, I'm very proud to be here with you who are on the board of directors of this wonderful, international cities program—702 American cities with—some of them have got more than one sister, because there's 951 foreign cities in 77 nations, and it totals about 86 million people in population. But the greatest thing is, what an evidence it is on this, the 25th anniversary of this, that you've come that far and done that—I'll have to start saying "we" now—in 25 years. But what an evidence it is of what people in their home communities and at the local level can accomplish that I think should give all of us confidence that there aren't any problems we can't lick if we go at them that way. With the people doing it, we don't have to wait for someone to hand it down to us as an accomplished fact. And bless you all for what you're doing.

So, happy 25th.

Mayor Wilson.[1] Thank you, Mr. President.

This is indeed an honor, Mr. President, for us to be here today and to thank you personally for accepting honorary membership in Sister Cities International. I just can't tell you how much this is going to mean to the thousands of people that volunteer their time and their money to help in

---

[1] *Betty Wilson, mayor pro tem of Santa Fe Springs, Calif.*

spreading world understanding and peace. It's really going to be a big boost in our program. And you mentioned 700 cities. As a fellow Californian, I want you to know how proud I am that 166 of those are from California.

But this a great occasion and we are celebrating our 25th anniversary. We'll have the big celebration in August in Kansas City, Missouri. And on behalf of the board, I would like to invite you or a delegate to attend our conference.

The President. Well, I hope I can. I've learned in 66 days that I don't have an awful lot to say about where I go or what I do. [*Laughter*]

Mayor Wilson. Is it all right if I talk to Eve [Eve Baskowitz, Staff Assistant to the President for Intergovernmental Affairs]? [*Laughter*]

But we are very delighted, and we just can't thank you enough. And on behalf of the board, I would like to make a presentation. This is the "Treasures of the Library of Congress." It's a limited edition. And it's presented to you on occasion of the 25th anniversary of this great program that was started by President Eisenhower, and I'm sure that he is looking down on us today and being very happy with what we have accomplished since he started this program.

The President. And he has every reason to be happy.

Mayor Wilson. And then from all of the thousands and thousands of people that are working in Sister Cities, this book on Eisenhower and his paintings in honor of your being our honorary chairman.

The President. Oh, thank you very much.

Mayor Wilson. And again, thank you so much.

The President. Thank you all. I've sometimes said, "Now has come that moment." Sometime ago, a newspaper sent me a whole stack of letters from grade school children that had been asked to write to the newspapers what they would like to say to the President if they had a chance. And I was reading them, and I came to one from a 9-year-old girl. And she had some very good suggestions about inflation and unemployment and everything else. But she wound up with what now has to happen to me. She said, "Now, get back to the Oval Office and go to work." [*Laughter*] So, I'll do that.

But bless you all again. And I'm very proud to have these, proud to have the honorary chairmanship that you've offered. And you're confirming with this a very deep-seated belief of mine. I have always believed that a lot of the problems in the world would disappear if people would start talking *to* each other instead of about each other.

Mayor Wilson. Thank you again, Mr. President.

The President. Thank you.

Note: The President spoke at 1:34 p.m. in the Rose Garden at the White House.

Nomination of Antonio Monroig To Be an Assistant Secretary of Housing and Urban Development
March 28, 1981

The President today announced his intention to nominate Antonio Monroig to be an Assistant Secretary of Housing and Urban Development (Fair Housing and Equal Opportunity).

Since 1977 Mr. Monroig has served as administrator of the Municipal Services Administration, appointed by the Governor of Puerto Rico. In 1977 he was special assistant to the mayor of San Juan. In 1973–75 Mr. Monroig was deputy director of San Juan Legal Services Inc. He was trial attorney, Land Affairs Division, Department of Justice, in 1972–73. He was Legal Counsel, Cooperative Development Administration, in 1971–72.

Mr. Monroig was graduated from the University of Puerto Rico (B.A., 1965) and

Catholic University of Puerto Rico (J.D., 1968). He also received a certificate from the Harvard Senior Managers in Government Programs in 1978.

He is married and has two children. He was born in San Juan, P.R., on February 7, 1944.

Nomination of William A. Niskanen, Jr., To Be a Member of the Council of Economic Advisers
March 28, 1981

The President today announced his intention to nominate William A. Niskanen, Jr., to be a member of the Council of Economic Advisers.

Mr. Niskanen will have the primary responsibility within the Council for the analysis of policies, such as regulations, subsidies, labor, and trade policies, that affect selected sectors of the economy. He will report to Murray Weidenbaum, Chairman of the Council.

Previously Mr. Niskanen was a professor at the Graduate School of Management at the University of California, Los Angeles.

In 1975–80 Mr. Niskanen was the director of economics of the Ford Motor Co. He was a professor at the Graduate School of Public Policy at the University of California,

Berkeley, from 1972–75. He was Assistant Director for Evaluation of the Office of Management and Budget from 1970 to 1972 and Director of Special Studies of the Office of the Secretary of Defense in the early 1960's.

Mr. Niskanen is a founder of the National Tax Limitation Committee and has contributed to the drafting of several tax limitation amendments. He also participated in several of the President's economic task forces during the 1980 campaign.

Mr. Niskanen is a graduate of Harvard College and received his masters and doctorate degrees in economics from the University of Chicago.

A native of Oregon, Mr. Niskanen is married to the former Anne Pardee and has three children.

Designation of Secretary of the Interior Watt as Chairman of the Water Resources Council
March 28, 1981

The President today announced his intention to designate James G. Watt to serve as Chairman of the Water Resources Council.

Mr. Watt was nominated by President-elect Reagan to serve as Secretary of the Interior on December 22, 1980. He was confirmed by the Senate on January 22, 1981. In 1977–80 he was president and chief legal officer, Mountain States Legal Foundation. In 1977 he served as Vice Chairman of the Federal Power Commission and served as a Commissioner in 1975–77.

In 1972–75 Mr. Watt was Director, Bureau of Outdoor Recreation, Department of the Interior. He served as Deputy Assistant Secretary of the Interior in 1969–72, and special assistant to the Secretary and Under Secretary of the Interior in 1969. He was secretary to the Natural Resources Committee and the Environmental Pollution Advisory Panel, Chamber of Commerce of the United States, in 1966–69. In 1962–66 he was legislative assistant and counsel to former U.S. Senator Simpson (R-Wyo.).

Mr. Watt was graduated from the University of Wyoming (B.S., 1960; J.D., 1962). He is married and has two children and resides in Englewood, Colo. Mr. Watt was born in Lusk, Wyo., on January 31, 1938.

Nomination of Alex Kozinski To Be Special Counsel of the Merit Systems Protection Board
March 28, 1981

The President today announced his intention to nominate Alex Kozinski to be Special Counsel of the Merit Systems Protection Board for a term of 5 years.

Mr. Kozinski was deputy legal counsel to the office of the President-elect from November 1980 to January 1981. He was an associate of the firm of Covington & Burling of Washington, D.C., in 1979–81. He specialized in appellate litigation. Previously, in 1977–79, he was an associate with the firm of Forry, Golbert, Singer & Gelles of Los Angeles, Calif.

In 1976–77 Mr. Kozinski was clerk to the Chief Justice of the United States. He was clerk to Judge Anthony M. Kennedy, Court for the Ninth Circuit, Sacramento, Calif., in 1975–76. Mr. Kozinski is a member of the California and District of Columbia Bar Associations.

Mr. Kozinski was graduated from the University of California at Los Angeles (A.B., 1972; J.D., 1975). He was managing editor and an associate editor of the UCLA Law Review.

He was born in Bucharest, Romania, on July 23, 1950. He is married and resides in Washington, D.C.

Nomination of Frank Wesley Naylor, Jr., To Be an Assistant Secretary of Agriculture
March 30, 1981

The President today announced his intention to nominate Frank Wesley Naylor, Jr., to be an Assistant Secretary of Agriculture (Rural Development).

Since 1976 Mr. Naylor has served as senior vice president of the 11th Farm Credit District in Sacramento, Calif. He was Associate Administrator and Administrator of the Farmers Home Administration in 1973–76. In 1972–73 he was Executive Assistant to the Administrator, Veterans Administration. Mr. Naylor was Deputy Administrator of the Federal Crop Insurance Corporation in 1969–72.

Mr. Naylor was graduated from the University of Kansas (B.A., 1961). He served in the U.S. Navy during the Vietnam war and was awarded the Navy Commendation Medal. He was national chairman of the Vietnam Veterans Committee.

Mr. Naylor is married and has two children. He resides with his family in Shingle Springs, Calif. He was born in Kansas City, Kans., on February 7, 1939.

Nomination of Pamela Needham Bailey To Be an Assistant Secretary of Health and Human Services
March 30, 1981

The President today announced his intention to nominate Pamela Needham Bailey to be an Assistant Secretary of Health and Human Services (Public Affairs).

Since 1979 Mrs. Bailey has served as director, government relations, American Hospital Supply Corp. She previously served as manager, government and consumer affairs, in 1975–79. In 1970–75 Mrs. Bailey was a member of the White House staff, responsible for the analysis, development, and implementation of the President's health, welfare, and social security policies. She was Assistant Director of the Domestic Council in 1975; staff assistant to the Domestic Council in 1974–75; staff assistnat to the President and Director of Research in 1973–74; research assistant to the President in 1971–73; research assistant to the Vice President in 1970–71.

Mrs. Bailey was assistant director of the office of personnel, office of the President-elect in 1980. She was a member of the Reagan-Bush Campaign Advisory Task Force on Welfare Reform.

She was graduated from Mount Holyoke College (A.B., 1970). She is married to William W. Bailey and has three children. Mrs. Bailey was born in Reading, Pa., on May 24, 1948. She resides in Annandale, Va.

Nomination of Warren S. Richardson To Be an Assistant Secretary of Health and Human Services
March 30, 1981

The President today announced his intention to nominate Warren S. Richardson to be an Assistant Secretary of Health and Human Services (Legislation).

Mr. Richardson is a professional lobbyist who has been involved in a number of lobbying campaigns. He was chief lobbyist for the Associated General Contractors, the Liberty Lobby, the National Right-to-Work Committee, and the National Lumber Manufacturers' Association. For the past 3½ years he has managed his own independent lobbying firm, Richardson, Randall and Associates. Previously he served as an attorney in the Justice Department and the General Accounting Office.

Mr. Richardson was graduated from the University of Rochester (A.B., B.S.) and the Catholic University of America (LL.B.). He is married and has four children. He was born in Rochester, N.Y., on December 20, 1923.

Nomination of Kenneth L. Smith To Be an Assistant Secretary of the Interior
March 30, 1981

The President today announced his intention to nominate Kenneth L. Smith to be an Assistant Secretary of the Interior (Indian Affairs).

Since 1972 Mr. Smith has served as general manager of the Warm Springs Tribe in Oregon. He was acting general manager in 1969–71. He began work with the tribe in 1959.

Mr. Smith served on the American Indian Policy Review Commission Task Force on Reservation Resource Development and Protection in 1974. He was a board member of the Oregon State Board of Education in 1973–79. Since 1975 Mr. Smith has served on the board of directors of the Oregon Historical Society. He is president of the Intertribal Timber Council and also served as chairman of the steering committee of the National Indian Timber Sympo-

sium.

Mr. Smith was graduated from the University of Oregon (B.A., 1959). He was named Outstanding Junior Citizen (Jaycee) in 1960 and was named one of Oregon's Five Outstanding Young Men (Jaycee) in 1970.

Mr. Smith is married and has four children. He was born in The Dalles, Oreg., on March 29, 1935.

Nomination of Garrey Edward Carruthers To Be an Assistant Secretary of the Interior
March 30, 1981

The President today announced his intention to nominate Garrey Edward Carruthers to be an Assistant Secretary of the Interior (Land and Water Resources).

Since 1979 Mr. Carruthers has been professor, department of agricultural economics and agricultural business at New Mexico State University. He was previously assistant and associate professor in 1968–74 and 1978–79. In 1976–78 he was acting director of the New Mexico Water Resources Research Institute. Mr. Carruthers was Special Assistant to the Secretary of Agriculture in 1974–75.

Mr. Carruthers was cochairman of the President Ford Committee in Dona Ana County, N. Mex., in 1976. He served as chairman of the New Mexico Republican Party in 1977–79. He was chairman of the John Connally Presidential campaign in New Mexico in 1980.

Mr. Carruthers was graduated from New Mexico State University (B.S., M.S.) and Iowa State University (Ph. D.). He is the author of many publications and papers on economics and agricultural economic policy.

Mr. Carruthers was born in Aztec, N. Mex., on August 29, 1939.

Message to the Congress Transmitting the Annual Report on Federal Advisory Committees
March 30, 1981

To the Congress of the United States:

In accordance with the provisions of Section 6(c) of the Federal Advisory Committee Act, I am pleased to transmit the Ninth Annual Report on Federal Advisory Committees.

This Report, which was prepared by the General Services Administration, summarizes the activities, status, and changes in

the composition of Federal Advisory Committees for calendar year 1980.

On January 22, 1981, I directed all Executive departments and agencies to reduce obligations for advisory committees by five percent for 1981. As part of the annual review of advisory committees, which will begin in April, we will scrutinize the activities and responsibilities of each advisory committee to determine whether it should be renewed or abolished.

RONALD REAGAN

The White House,
March 30, 1981.

Note: The report is entitled "Federal Advisory Committees—Ninth Annual Report of the President Covering the Calendar Year 1980—March 1981" (Government Printing Office, 140 pages).

Remarks at the National Conference of the Building and Construction Trades Department, AFL-CIO
March 30, 1981

Mr. President, reverend clergy, gentlemen here on the dais, and you ladies and gentlemen:

There's been a lot of talk in the last several weeks here in Washington about communication and the need to communicate, and the story that I haven't told for a long time—but somehow it's been brought back to me since I've been here— about communication and some of the basic rules of communication.

It was told to me the first time by Danny Villanueva who used to placekick for the Los Angeles Rams, and then later became a sports announcer, and Danny told me that one night as a sports announcer, he was having a young ballplayer with the Los Angeles Dodgers over to the house for dinner. And the young wife was bustling about getting the dinner ready while he and the ballplayer were talking sports, and the baby started to cry. And over her shoulder, the wife said to her husband, "Change the baby." And this young ballplayer was embarrassed in front of Danny, and he said to his wife, "What do you mean change the baby? I'm a ballplayer. That's not my line of work." And she turned around, out her hands on her hips and she communicated. [*Laughter*] She said, "Look, buster, you lay the diaper out like a diamond, you put second base on home plate, put the baby's bottom on the pitcher's mound, hook up first and third, slide home underneath, and if it starts to rain, the game ain't called, you start all over again." [*Laughter*] So, I'm going to try to communicate a little bit today.

I'm pleased to take part in this national conference of the Building and Construction Trades Department of the AFL-CIO. And I hope you'll forgive me if I point with some pride to the fact that I'm the first President of the United States to hold a lifetime membership in an AFL-CIO union. And, Mr. President, I'm very grateful for your words about cooperation. Now, if I can only persuade certain individuals up on the Hill to do the same thing, we won't have any trouble at all.

But members of your organization have played and do play a great part in the building of America. They also are an important part of the industry in which my union plays a part. Now, it's true that grease paint and make-believe are not tools of your members' trade, but we all know the meaning of work and of family and of country.

For two decades or more, I participated in renegotiating our basic contract when it came renewal time. And here, too, we have much in common. Sitting at the negotiating table, we were guided by three principles in our demands: Is it good for our people? Is it fair to the other fellow and to the customer? And is it good for the industry?

Samuel Gompers, who founded the American Federation of Labor and who literally gave his life to that cause, said, "Doing for people what they can and ought to do for themselves is a dangerous experiment. In the last analysis the welfare of the workers depends upon their own initiative. Whatever is done under the guise of philanthropy or social morality which in any way lessens initiative is the greatest crime that can be committed against the toilers. Let social busybodies and professional public morals experts in their fads reflect upon the perils they rashly invite under the pretense of social welfare."

Samuel Gompers was repudiating the socialist philosophy when he made that statement. No one worked harder to get or believed more in a fair shake for the people who sweat as the fuel of our country, but he didn't believe that this should or could come from government compulsion.

America depends on the work of labor, and the economy we build should reward and encourage that labor as our hope for the future. We've strayed far from the path that was charted by this man who believed so much in the freedom and dignity of the worker. We are in today's economic mess precisely because our leaders have forgotten that we built this great Nation on rewarding the work ethic instead of punishing it.

We've gone astray from first principles. We've lost sight of the rule that individual freedom and ingenuity are at the very core of everything that we've accomplished. Government's first duty is to protect the people, not run their lives. What have been some of the results of this straying from basic principles? Well, for one, violent crime has surged 10 percent, making neighborhood streets unsafe and families fearful in their homes. We've been left with a legacy of almost 8 million people out of work—666,000 of them construction workers. All of these people have been robbed of a basic human dignity and forced into the humiliation of unemployment. The annual inflation rate has soared to nearly 12 percent, making a mockery of hard work and savings. And our national debt has grown to more than $950 billion despite taxes that eat up an ever-increasing share of the family dollar.

This deficit has particular meaning for you, because when government has to borrow to pay its bills, it competes for private capital, driving interest rates up and construction starts down. So, when people ask me why we have to cut down the budget deficit, I think the answer is pretty clear. If we don't get control of the budget and stop wild and irresponsible spending,

we will repeat past intolerable prime interest rates of more than 20 percent, rates which have played havoc with the lives of your fellow workers. And when we do not have economic security at home, our national security is threatened. We've let our defense spending fall behind and our capability to defend ourselves against foreign aggressors is not what it should be. These trends not only must stop, believe me, they will be stopped.

Every American and especially all the working people of our country have an enormous stake in what we do. You pay the most taxes. You believe in a work ethic but subsidize a government that does not. You, who have traditionally saved to provide for your futures, today cannot save. You, who most want to work, are most likely to be laid off. You, through taxes on your hard-earned wages, pay for what could be as much as $25 billion each year in Federal waste, abuse, and outright fraud in government programs. Franklin Delano Roosevelt spoke of "the forgotten man at the bottom of the economic pyramid." Well, today it's safe to say that the people at both ends of the pyramid are getting attention. The man who's forgotten is the fellow who built it.

Such a man wrote his Congressman a few weeks back, and that letter landed on my desk. I've gotten tens of thousands of letters about our plan for economic recovery. I appreciate all of them, but a few of them really stand out, and this man's letter is one of them.

He's an unemployed factory worker from Illinois, the Peoria area, but he worked in construction for 10 years before that. His income right now is totally dependent on unemployment and supplemental benefits from the company he worked for. He and his wife have only been married three months, but she's been laid off too. He wrote to say that if spending cuts in government affect his benefits, it'll be hard for his family, but they'll make it. And shades of Sam Gompers, he ended his letter saying that when the opponents of our economic plan start lobbying against it—and let me quote—he said, "Let me know that there is someone out here who's seen what they can do and is willing to stake his future on trying a different approach."

That man has faith in America and faith in what the American people can do if the government will only let them do it. And that man, like most of America, wants a change.

Right now we have the highest peacetime deficit in living memory. Federal personal taxes for the average American family have gone [up] 58 percent in the last 5 years, and regulations by the government cost consumers an estimated hundred billion dollars a year. The man in Peoria is right. Across the country, there are millions of people like him yearning for a different approach. They're yearning for us to reach for our hopes and make room for our dreams, and to put it bluntly, they want something different for a change. Instead of halfway solutions, jerry-built programs tied together with redtape, they're ready for an overhaul to make the engine work again.

I've heard the complaints coming often from those who had a hand in creating our present situation. They demand proof in advance that what we've proposed will work. Well, the answer to that is we're living with the proof that what they want to continue doing hasn't worked and won't work. I believe what we proposed will work simply because it always has. We must get control of the budget monster, get control of our economy, and I assure you, get control of our own lives and our own destinies.

What has been submitted to the Congress is a four-point comprehensive program or package for economic recovery. If only part of the package is passed by Congress, we'll only ease some of our problems, and that isn't a solution at all.

We must first get government spending under control. And let me make something plain. We're not asking that government spend less than it has been spending, although that might not be the worst idea in the world. We're simply proposing that government increase its spending in 1982 over 1981 by 6.1 percent, not 14 percent, as has been advocated. If we keep spending at the present rate of increase, our budget will double again in 6 years.

Now, I propose cutting $48.6 billion from the Federal budget in fiscal year '82. Now

it's true these are the largest spending cuts ever proposed. But even with these cuts, that budget will still increase by $40 billion next year, and there will probably be a $45 billion deficit. Without our cuts, that deficit will be more than $90 billion.

The second point is a 10-percent across-the-board tax rate cut every year for the next three years. This is the most sweeping tax incentive program in the last 20 years, the largest tax rates cuts ever proposed. And again, we're not asking government to get along on less money than it's been accustomed to. Our largest-in-history tax cut will only reduce the largest-in-history tax increase that was imposed on all of us at the beginning of this year.

Now, I have a feeling that in all the arguing and rhetoric, many Americans have lost sight of the fact that they're not facing taxes as usual, but a gigantic tax increase that will take $770 billion extra out of our pockets over the next 6 years. We think that's too much. This Government, without taking a single vote in Congress, has raised billions of dollars from taxpayers in the last few years, just through inflation. The system keeps kicking people up into higher brackets, that they try to keep up with the cost-of-living increase, bleeding their earnings, sapping their incentive, and quite frankly, making a mockery out of the tax system. Not too long ago, only 3 percent of the people who work and earn in this country were in a 30-percent tax bracket. Today, 33 percent are in that bracket, and they have no more purchasing power now than they had before when they were in a much lower bracket.

There are just too many people in this town who think this money belongs to the Government. Well, it doesn't. It's your money. It's your sons' and daughters' money that they're hoping to use for a new home. It's your parents' money that they need for a decent retirement. And if we do nothing else in this administration, we're going to convince this city that the power, the money, and the responsibility in this country begins and ends with the people and not with some cinderblock building in Washington, D.C.

The third measure we've called for is elimination of excessive regulation. Now, I know you have no experience with regulation. [*Laughter*] Overregulation affects every industry. Many of you know people who are out of work because of the way it affects yours. It's estimated that total regulations have added as much as 20 percent to the cost of a home. Indeed, I've seen the figure more recently put at 22 percent, as the cost.

I've told before, I have a neighbor out in my neighborhood in California who was building his own home. And he got so fed up with all the paperwork and the regulations required that he pasted them all together into one strip of paper, put up two poles in front of the half-finished house, and strung them up across there. The strip of paper was 250 feet long.

And, finally, we're determined to work with the Federal Reserve Board to develop a monetary policy consistent with the economic program designed to stabilize the money supply, reduce inflation, and allow interest rates to come down.

People who hold down jobs in the building trades probably understand better than anyone—well, that is, better than anyone except someone who's just lost his job in the building trade—the need for a stable monetary policy. Fewer than 1 in 11 American families can afford to buy a new home. Housing starts are down by 36 percent from what they were in 1978. Mortgage rates for this year are averaging 13½ percent, although I'm told in some parts of the country they're currently running in excess of 15 percent.

The main source of strength in this fight is going to be the people themselves. The idea is to unleash the American worker, encourage the American investor, and let each of us produce more to make a better life for all. After all, why should we pay for some luxuries that are not truly essential to our well-being, pay by way of a subsidy when the man and his wife in Peoria are out of work? Why should we subsidize increased production of some things that we already have in surplus? And why should we go in debt to pay for school lunches for children of upper-income families when borrowing by government may cost you

your job? We not only shouldn't do those things, we no longer can afford to do them.

We'll continue to fulfill our obligations to those who must depend on the rest of us. Those who are deserving can rest assured that they'll not be cut adrift, but the rest of us will feel the impact of the budget cuts, which have been distributed through the economy, as evenly as possible.

There is one area, however, where we must spend more and that is for our national defense. Now, don't get me wrong. Cap Weinberger, Secretary of Defense, has shown me programs in his department where we can and will realize substantial savings. We'll cut $2.9 billion in next year's budget alone, and the cuts will accumulate to more than $28 billion by 1986 in the Defense Department. But those savings will be applied to the necessary things we must do, thus reducing the amount of additional spending that we'll need.

Since 1970 the Soviet Union has undergone a massive military buildup, far outstripping any need for defense. They've spent $300 billion more than we have for military forces resulting in a significant numerical advantage in strategic nuclear delivery systems, tactical aircraft, submarines, artillery, and anti-aircraft defense. And to allow this defense or this imbalance to continue is a threat to our national security. It's my duty as President, and all of our responsibility as citizens, to keep this country strong enough to remain free.

As union members and as concerned citizens of the world, we watch with great interest the struggle of our fellow workers in Poland. Their courage reminds us not only of the precious liberty that is ours to nourish and protect but of the spirit in each of us everywhere. The Polish workers stand as sentinels on behalf of universal human principles, and they remind us that on this good Earth, the people will always prevail. They serve to show us how trust and unity keep alive the very purpose of our existence and to remind us that man's work is not only directed at providing physical sustenance but that the toil of men and women everywhere must also have the goal of feeding the spirit of freedom.

As we work to solve our economic problems, let us tap that well of human spirit. We'll find more than strength of numbers and strength of resources, we'll find strength of individual determination. We may even find strength in mutual trust. For too many years now, we've trusted numbers and computers. We've trusted balance sheets, organization charts, policies, and systems. We've placed trust in rules, regulations in government, government dictates. Well, I think it's about time that we placed trust in ourselves.

I'm here today because I salute what you've done for America. In your work you build. In your personal lives, you sustain the core of family and neighborhood. In your faith, you sustain our religious principles. And with your strong patriotism, you're the bulwark which supports an America second to none in the world. I believe the American people are with us in our cause. I'm confident in our ability to work together, to meet and surmount our problems, and to accomplish the goals that we all seek.

Now, I know that we can't make things right overnight. But we will make them right. Our destiny is not our fate. It is our choice. And I'm asking you as I ask all Americans, in these months of decision, please join me as we take this new path. You and your forebears built this Nation. Now, please help us rebuild it, and together we'll make America great again.

Thank you very much.

Note: The President spoke at 2:03 p.m. in the International Ballroom at the Washington Hilton Hotel. In his opening remarks, he referred to Robert A. Georgine, president of the AFL-CIO.

Statement by Assistant to the President David R. Gergen About the Attempted Assassination of the President
March 30, 1981

Good afternoon. This is to confirm the statements made at George Washington Hospital that the President was shot once in the left side, this afternoon, as he left the hotel. His condition is stable.

A decision is now being made whether or not to operate to remove the bullet. The White House and the Vice President are in communication, and the Vice President is now en route to Washington. He is expected to arrive in the city this afternoon.

Mrs. Reagan is currently with the President at the hospital.

I'd like to add two notes. We have been informed by [Chief of Staff and Assistant to the President] Jim Baker that the President walked into the hospital.

I would also like to inform you that in the building [the White House] as of the moment are the Secretary of State, the Secretary of the Treasury, the Secretary of Defense, and the Attorney General, as well as other Assistants to the President.

Note: Mr. Gergen, Assistant to the President and Staff Director, made the statement at 3:37 p.m. to reporters assembled in the Briefing Room at the White House, following initial reports that the President had left the hotel unharmed by the assassination attempt.

The President was shot at 2:25 p.m. outside the Washington Hilton Hotel, after addressing the national conference of the Building and Construction Trades Department, AFL-CIO. Immediately following the shooting, the President was taken to George Washington University Hospital in his limousine.

Press Secretary to the President James S. Brady, Timothy J. McCarthy, a Secret Service agent, and Thomas K. Delahanty, a District of Columbia policeman, also were wounded in the incident. Mr. Brady and Mr. McCarthy were taken to George Washington University Hospital; Officer Delahanty was taken to the Washington Hospital Center.

Secret Service agents at the scene apprehended John W. Hinckley, Jr., 25, of Evergreen, Colo. He initially was charged with attempting to assassinate the President and assaulting a special agent and an employee of the Secret Service.

Remarks by Secretary of State Alexander M. Haig, Jr., About the Attempted Assassination of the President
March 30, 1981

Ladies and gentlemen, I just wanted to touch upon a few matters associated with today's tragedy. First, as you know, we are in close touch with the Vice President, who is returning to Washington. We have in the Situation Room all of the officials of the Cabinet who should be here and ready at this time.

We have informed our friends abroad of the situation, the President's condition as we know it—stable, now undergoing surgery. And there are absolutely no alert measures that are necessary at this time or contemplated.

Note: Secretary Haig spoke at 4:14 p.m. to reporters assembled in the Briefing Room at the White House. Later in the afternoon, the White House announced that the President went into surgery at approximately 4 p.m. and that doctors' preliminary reports to Mrs. Reagan, who was at the hospital, indicated that the President's condition was good and stable.

Statement by the Vice President About the Attempted Assassination of the President
March 30, 1981

Well, I have a very brief statement that I would like to read. I am deeply heartened by Dr. O'Leary's report on the President's condition, that he has emerged from this experience with flying colors and with the most optimistic prospects for a complete recovery. I can reinsure this Nation and a watching world that the American Government is functioning fully and effectively. We've had full and complete communication throughout the day, and the officers of the Federal Government have been fulfilling their obligations with skill and with care.

I know I speak on behalf of the President and his family when I say that we are very grateful to all the many people from across this country who've expressed their concern at this act of violence. And finally, let me add our profound concern on behalf of two brave law enforcement officers who served to protect the President and then, of course, for a friend of everybody here, dedicated public servant, Jim Brady. We're going to watch their progress with all our prayers and with all our hopes.

Now, I'm going to walk over and speak briefly to Mrs. Reagan, who's returned to the Residence.

Thank you all very much.

Note: The Vice President read the statement at 8:20 p.m. to reporters assembled in the Briefing Room at the White House.

The Vice President arrived at Andrews Air Force Base, Md., from Texas at 6:30 p.m. At 7 p.m. he met with members of the Cabinet and White House staff in the Situation Room at the White House.

Prior to the Vice President's statement, Dr. Dennis O'Leary, dean of clinical affairs, George Washington University Hospital, briefed reporters at the hospital on the condition of the President, Press Secretary Brady, and Agent McCarthy.

Dr. O'Leary reported that the President had been wounded by a single bullet which penetrated his left lung, that the President was awake and in stable condition following surgery, and that the prognosis for his recovery was excellent.

Dr. O'Leary reported that Mr. Brady was shot in the forehead and that he was still in surgery and in critical condition.

Dr. O'Leary also reported that Mr. McCarthy had been wounded by a bullet which entered his right chest and, following surgery, he was doing extremely well.

See page 1224 for additional medical reports.

Exchange Between the Vice President and Reporters on the President's Recovery Following the Attempted Assassination *March 31, 1981*

The Vice President. The medical reports were very good. I had a very short visit with him. He'd taken a nap. When I walked in there he was awake, and I had a very good talk with him. What he really needs is rest. I tell you, the report from [Physician to the President] Dr. Ruge, when he briefed the Cabinet and briefed the leadership, was extraordinarily good. The President, to me, looked well and was very responsive, asked with his unfailing courtesy about Barbara, my wife. And Nancy Reagan, Mrs. Reagan, was there.

So, I feel the same thing the country feels, a great sense of relief and feeling that he is on the road to recovery. It's a turmoil around there. I thought in intensive care that everybody would be whispering, but it's like Grand Central Station.

But he's doing very well. Very well. And everything seems to be proceeding. I just want to go up and walk out on the Senate floor, chat with some of my friends there, and tell them about this visit, and then go back. I have to get back to meet with The Netherlands Prime Minister.

Q. There is a report that there's something of a rift among some of the Cabinet members, particularly Secretary Haig and Secretary Weinberger. Is your role in any way involved in trying to heal that rift?

The Vice President. No, and I don't detect any such rift. And I think—the thing, I think, from my vantage point, which admittedly, with some of it at 30,000 feet traveling back, was that things proceeded smoothly, in an orderly fashion. I sense a real, calm determination to go ahead. The President—there's no need for any emergency procedures, the power of the Vice President to do anything. And I have not detected, nor do I believe there's any such rift.

Q. Thank you, sir.

Q. You won't be assuming any special powers, Mr. Vice President?

The Vice President. No. Absolutely not. And it's orderly, and just to do what I can to assist, I will be taking over some of the meetings that the President would have participated in. But I'm in most of them anyway, so, business as usual to the best we can do it.

Note: The Vice President spoke at 11:09 a.m. in a hallway of the Capitol.

Prior to his visit with the President, the Vice President chaired a meeting of the Cabinet and then met with the bipartisan congressional leadership.

Remarks of the Vice President and Prime Minister Andreas A. M. van Agt of The Netherlands Following Their Meetings
March 31, 1981

The Vice President. We've just had a delightful visit with Prime Minister van Agt, and I told him how much the President had been looking forward to seeing him. And I know from having visited the President in the hospital, prior to this visit, that today how much our President regrets not being able to receive this very, very distinguished visitor on this beautiful day here at the White House.

Our talks, we think, on the American side, have been extremely useful, despite the overlying concerns that everybody feels about our President. But these talks do testify to the continuing importance which the United States places on our transatlantic ties, including those with all of the members of NATO.

In that connection, the President asked me to extend through the Prime Minister, to extend to Her Majesty Queen Beatrix our hope that she will come to the United States in 1982. A visit by Her Majesty would be a fitting culmination of our joint celebration during that year of our bicentennial of the U.S.-Dutch relations.

And the Prime Minister also comes to us as Chairman of the European Council. I have welcomed this opportunity to exchange views on issues of concern to the Community and, of course, bilateral concerns to the United States. And I know we feel—and I'm sure I speak for Secretary Haig and all that were privileged to meet with the Prime Minister—that there is a mutual understanding on many issues.

There is a mutual understanding, for example, in the Middle East and of our efforts there, efforts in which they have played a key role. The Netherlands and the United States are also allies in NATO, which I mentioned, and which, of course, remains the backbone of our mutual security. In our talks, I reiterated the U.S. determination as President Reagan has made clear, to pursue vigorously the two tracks of NATO's December '79 decision on theater nuclear weapons, both modernization and arms control.

We discussed Poland and were in strong agreement that the Polish people must be allowed to work out a solution to their own problems. Outside intervention or internal suppression in Poland would have severely—you'd have severe negative effects on East-West relations.

We discussed a little bit, to some degree, the crisis in Afghanistan, brought about by this illegal invasion and occupation of the country. We talked about the regional security of the Caribbean. We discussed, to some degree, El Salvador. I explained that American policy is designed to help that country defend itself against attacks from Marxist guerrillas that are supported and trained by Communist countries. The Duarte government must be given the opportunity to institute its reform programs.

And so these are some of the subjects. We had a very fruitful meeting. I expressed my regrets to the Prime Minister that he did not have the opportunity to be received and to meet and to discuss these issues with our President. But it was a tribute to our friendship that, our President being absent, the Prime Minister was willing to accord us every courtesy and come here and to have these fruitful discussions.

Mr. Prime Minister.

The Prime Minister. Mr. Vice President, let me first say again how much we were shocked by the events of yesterday. We wish, again, the President, wholeheartedly, a speedy and full recovery.

The meetings we had today have no doubt further contributed to the excellent relations between the United States and Europe. Our historic relationship has proved to be essential at the most crucial moments in our past and will continue to be so in the future. Today we are strongly united in an alliance aimed at our common, single goal—preserving peace and freedom in the world. At the same time, we are dedicated to contribute to national and in-

313

ternational efforts to improve the quality of life for the millions in the world who are in the most serious need.

The European Council meeting in The Netherlands last week further emphasized the need for the closest possible cooperation between the European Communities and the United States in solving the extremely serious economic problems we are facing. The only way to win the economic fight is through well-coordinated, joint efforts.

Mr. Vice President, you mentioned the fact that our countries are preparing for the celebration next year of the 200th anniversary of our diplomatic and trade relations. They are the oldest, unbroken, continuously peaceful relations between the United States and any other foreign power.

Mr. Vice President, the announcement you just made to extend an invitation to Her Majesty Queen Beatrix to visit your great country in 1982 fills us with a great sense of gratitude. Your gracious invitation will enable our Queen to continue a tradition which has become a symbol of our friendship in all times. We regard your invitation as a seal on that unalterable and unique relationship between our countries across the ocean.

Mr. Vice President, I'm convinced that these celebrations, highlighted by your visit of our Queen, will serve their high purpose in contributing to an increased recognition of our respective shares in efforts to improve the lot of mankind.

May I, repeatedly, thank you, Mr. Vice President, for your willingness to receive us today under such extraordinary, exceptional circumstances. I said to you already, we would not have been surprised in case you would have canceled entirely, or at least partly, the program which had been prepared for the visit long before. Now, the gratitude is ours. We had very valuable and instructive talks. We spoke as allies and friends. And I'm sure these talks will contribute to our common efforts.

Again, I ask you, we'll convey our best wishes, friendship, respect, and sympathy to your President.

The Vice President. May I just share, Mr. Prime Minister, with the people here on the lawn what I told you. I did visit the President in the hospital this morning, a very short visit, but I was very pleased at the way he looked. He, in his typical, unfailing thoughtfulness, asked me to convey his regards here and then also asked about my wife, and everything seemed so normal. And I just thought I'd tell this group what I've told you, that we feel very relieved in this country at what appears to be a very speedy recovery. And I know he would want me to say, as you leave these grounds, farewell and Godspeed and come back, sir.

Thank you very much.

Note: The Vice President spoke at 1:38 p.m. to reporters assembled at the South Portico of the White House.

Earlier the Vice President and the Prime Minister met in the Roosevelt Room, and then they and their delegations held a working luncheon in the Cabinet Room at the White House.

Statement by Deputy Press Secretary Speakes About United States Consultations Concerning Southern Africa
March 31, 1981

Assistant Secretary of State-designate for African Affairs Chester A. Crocker will leave next month for an extensive round of consultations with African governments concerning the problems of southern Africa.

He will report to Secretary Haig when he returns.

The President believes it is important to make clear the administration's objectives in southern Africa. The broad objective we seek is to strengthen the security of southern Africa, a region of growing importance to our interests. The United States strongly supports negotiated solutions to the problems of this region. The path of violence serves no one's interest except that of our global adversary. We seek a peaceful solution of the Namibian problem leading to a genuinely independent and democratic Namibia recognized by the international community. To this end, we will work with all interested parties.

This administration intends to maintain and strengthen ties with the states of Africa. We wish to strengthen mutual understanding and cooperation between the United States and all African states. There can be no question of American support for apartheid, which is repugnant to our multiracial and democratic society. We intend to make our views plainly known, not in a spirit of confrontation, but of constructive help.

Remarks at the Annual Academy Awards Presentation Ceremonies
March 31, 1981

Good evening to my fellow Americans, eagerly awaiting the presentation of the 53d annual Academy Awards.

It's surely no state secret that Nancy and I share your interest in the results of this year's balloting. We're not alone; the miracle of American technology links us with millions of moviegoers around the world. It is the motion picture that shows us all not only how we look and sound but—more important—how we feel. When it achieves its most noble intent, film reveals that people everywhere share common dreams and emotions.

Tonight I applaud all who create, make, distribute, exhibit, and attend movies. I salute the Academy for the influence its work has on the world's most enduring art form. Film is forever—I've been trapped in some film forever myself. And as a former member of the Academy, I ask you now to join Nancy and me in enjoying this year's ceremonies.

Note: The President's remarks were videotaped in the Library at the White House on March 5 for broadcast at the televised ceremonies on March 31.

Executive Order 12302—Amending the Generalized System of Preferences
April 1, 1981

By virtue of the authority vested in me by the Constitution and statutes of the United States of America, including Title V of the Trade Act of 1974 (88 Stat. 2066, 19 U.S.C. 2461 *et seq.*) as amended, Section 604 of the Trade Act of 1974 (88 Stat. 2073, 19 U.S.C. 2483), and Section 503 (a) (2) (A) of the Trade Agreements Act of 1979 (93 Stat. 251), and as President of the United States of America, in order to modify, as provided by Sections 504 (a) and (c) of the Trade Act of 1974 (88 Stat. 2070, 19 U.S.C.

2464(a) and (c)), the limitations on peferential treatment for eligible articles from countries designated as beneficiary developing countries, to adjust the original designation of eligible articles taking into account information and advice received in fulfillment of Sections 503(a) and 131–134 of the Trade Act of 1974 (88 Stat. 2069, 19 U.S.C. 2463; 88 Stat. 1994, 19 U.S.C. 2151 *et seq.*) and to modify the designations of beneficiary developing countries in accord with my notification to the Congress of March 17,

1981, and in accord with technical changes in the identification of certain beneficiary developing countries, it is hereby ordered as follows:

Section 1. In order to subdivide existing items for purposes of the Generalized System of Preferences (GSP), the Tariff Schedules of the United States (TSUS) (19 U.S.C. 1202) are modified as provided in Annex I, attached hereto and made a part hereof.

Sec. 2. Annex II of Executive Order No. 11888 of November 24, 1975, as amended, listing articles that are eligible for benefits of the GSP when imported from any designated beneficiary developing country, is amended by substituting therefor the new Annex II attached hereto and made a part hereof.

Sec. 3. Annex III of Executive Order No. 11888, as amended, listing articles that are eligible for benefits of the GSP when imported from all designated beneficiary countries except those specified in General Headnote 3(c) (iii) of the TSUS, is amended by substituting therefor the new Annex III, attached hereto and made a part hereof.

Sec. 4. General Headnote 3(c) (iii) of the TSUS, listing articles that are eligible for benefits of the GSP except when imported from the beneficiary countries listed opposite those articles, is amended by substituting therefor the General Headnote 3(c) (iii) set forth in Annex IV, attached hereto and made a part hereof.

Sec. 5. In order to provide staged reductions in the rates of duty for those new TSUS items created by Annex I to this Order, Annex III to Proclamation 4707 of December 11, 1979, and Annex III to Proclamation 4768 of June 28, 1980, are amend-

ed by Annex V to this Order, attached hereto and made a part hereof.

Sec. 6. General Headnote 3(c) (i) of the TSUS is modified as provided in Annex VI, attached hereto and made a part hereof.

Sec. 7. In order to provide special treatment for the least developed developing countries (LDDC's) with regard to TSUS items 387.25 and 387.35, Annex IV of Proclamation 4707 of December 11, 1979, is amended by Annex VII to this Order, attached hereto and made a part hereof.

Sec. 8. Whenever the column 1 rate of duty in the TSUS for any item specified in Annex I to this Order is reduced to the same level as, or to a lower level than, the corresponding rate of duty inserted in the column entitled "LDDC" by Annex I or VII of this Order, the rate of duty in the column entitled "LDDC" for such item shall be deleted from the TSUS.

Sec. 9. Annexes III and IV of Proclamation 4707 of December 11, 1979, and Annex III of Proclamation 4768 of June 28, 1980, are superseded to the extent inconsistent with this Order.

Sec. 10. The amendments made by this Order shall be effective with respect to articles both: (1) imported on and after January 1, 1976, and (2) entered, or withdrawn from warehouse for consumption, on and after March 31, 1981.

RONALD REAGAN

The White House,
April 1, 1981.

[Filed with the Office of the Federal Register, 10:43 a.m., April 1, 1981]

Note: The annexes are printed in the Federal Register *of April 2, 1981.*

Nomination of Lawrence J. Korb To Be an Assistant Secretary of Defense
April 1, 1981

The President today announced his intention to nominate Lawrence J. Korb to be an Assistant Secretary of Defense (Manpower, Reserve Affairs and Logistics).

Mr. Korb is director of defense policy studies of the American Enterprise Institute in Washington, D.C. In 1975–80 he was professor of management, U.S. Naval War College. Mr. Korb was associate professor of government, U.S. Coast Guard Academy, in 1971–75. He has been adjunct scholar for Federal budget analysis with the American Enterprise Institute since 1972 and consultant to the Office of the Secretary of Defense since 1975. He was an adviser to the Reagan-Bush committee in 1980 and served as a member of the Arms Control and Disarmament Agency transition team.

Mr. Korb was graduated from Athenaeum of Ohio (B.A., 1961); St. John's University (M.A., 1962); and State University of New York at Albany (Ph. D., 1969). He was in the U.S. Navy in 1962–66. He is currently a commander in the Naval Air Reserve.

Mr. Korb resides in Reston, Va., and was born in New York City on July 9, 1939.

Nomination of William R. Gianelli To Be an Assistant Secretary of the Army
April 1, 1981

The President today announced his intention to nominate William R. Gianelli to be Assistant Secretary of the Army (Civil Works).

Since 1973 Mr. Gianelli has been a consulting civil engineer in California. He has served as chairman, Monterey Peninsula Water Management District, in 1978–80 and California director of the National Water Resources Association in 1967–73. In 1973–76 he was appointed by the President as a member of the National Commission on Water Quality.

In 1960–67 Mr. Gianelli was senior partner, Gianelli and Murray, consulting engineers. In 1959–60 he was district engineer, southern district, California State Department of Water Resources. Mr. Gianelli was staff engineer and special assistant to the director of the California State Department of Water Resources in 1956–59.

In 1941–45 he served in the U.S. Army Corps of Engineers. He was graduated from the University of California (B.S., 1941). He received the Distinguished Service Award of the California Council of Civil Engineers and Land Surveyors in 1972 and received the Citizen Award from the Department of the Interior in 1975 in recognition of outstanding leadership in the effective development of the nation's water resources.

Mr. Gianelli is married and has two children. He resides with his family in Monterey, Calif. Mr. Gianelli was born in Stockton, Calif., on February 19, 1919.

Nomination of Shelby Templeton Brewer To Be an Assistant Secretary of Energy
April 1, 1981

The President today announced his intention to nominate Shelby Templeton Brewer to be an Assistant Secretary of Energy (Nuclear Energy).

Since 1977 Mr. Brewer has served as Director of the Office of Program Planning and Evaluation and Assistant Secretary for Nuclear Energy, Department of Energy. In 1975–77 he was Chief, Program Planning and Assessment, Division of Reactor Development and Demonstration, Energy Research and Development Agency, Atomic Energy Commission (ERDA/AEC). Mr. Brewer was special technical assistant to the Director (ERDA/AEC) in 1971–75. In 1968–71 he was a consultant on nuclear reactor engineering. Mr. Brewer has served on various committees on nuclear energy

317

including serving as Chairman, Task Force on Light Water Reactor Technology, Department of Energy.

Mr. Brewer was graduated from Columbia University (B.A., 1960) and Massachusetts Institute of Technology (M.S., 1966, Ph. D., 1970). He has authored many articles on nuclear energy.

Mr. Brewer is married and has two children. He resides with his family in Gaithersburg, Md. Mr. Brewer was born in Little Rock, Ark., on February 19, 1937.

Nomination of Warren T. Lindquist To Be a Member of the Board of Directors of the New Community Development Corporation, and Designation as General Manager
April 1, 1981

The President today announced his intention to nominate Warren T. Lindquist to be a member of the Board of Directors of the New Community Development Corporation, Department of Housing and Urban Development. Upon appointment by the President, he will automatically become General Manager of the Corporation and serve as Chief Executive Officer under the Board's general direction.

Mr. Lindquist is currently chairman and director of SCETAM, Inc., a management consulting firm concerned with regional economic development. He is also a general partner in Q-L Partners, a New York real estate investment and management firm.

From 1951 until he founded SCETAM in 1977, Mr. Lindquist was a senior associate with David Rockefeller. He originated and supervised Mr. Rockefeller's interest in such commerical investment ventures as L'Enfant Plaza in Washington, D.C.; Embarcadero Center in San Francisco, Calif.; and Interstate North in northwest Atlanta, Ga. In addition, Mr. Lindquist was executive director or chief executive officer of such organizations as the Downtown-Lower Manhattan Association in New York City and the New York City Community Preservation Corp.

Mr. Lindquist served as a member of the Technical Subcommittee on Housing of the White House Conference on the Aging and of the Panel on Government and the Management of Growth of the White House Conference on Balanced National Growth and Economic Development. He was a member of the National Public Advisory Committee on Regional Economic Development and chaired its finance subcommittee.

Mr. Lindquist was graduated from Lafayette College (B.A., 1940) and did graduate study in finance and investment at New York University.

Mr. Lindquist resides in New York City and Seal Harbor, Maine. He was born in New York City on June 18, 1919.

Nomination of Fred Joseph Villella To Be Deputy Director of the Federal Emergency Management Agency
April 1, 1981

The President today announced his intention to nominate Fred Joseph Villella to be Deputy Director of the Federal Emergency Management Agency.

Since 1978 Mr. Villella has been chief, academic division, California Specialized Training Institute; chief, administrative division; and chief of staff, Emergency Management Institute. He has been a member of the faculty of the California Specialized

Training Institute since 1976.

In 1974–76 Mr. Villella was Commander, Law Enforcement Command, Fort Carson, Colo. He served 20 years with the U.S. Military. In 1972–73 Mr. Villella served in Vietnam, responsible for international law enforcement, security, and investigations. He served as Battalion Commander for law enforcement and support services at Fort Dix, N.J., in 1971–72. In 1955–69 he served in various posts in the U.S. Army in Europe, Panama, Latin America, and Vietnam.

Mr. Villella was graduated from Gannon College in Erie, Pa. (B.A., 1955) and Indiana University (M.P.A., 1974).

Mr. Villella is married and has six children. He resides with his family in Pismo Beach, Calif. He was born in Punxsutawney, Pa., on June 21, 1933.

Note: Mr. Villella's nomination, which was submitted to the Senate on May 1, was withdrawn by the President on May 12.

Nomination of Kieran O'Doherty To Be a Commissioner of the Postal Rate Commission, and Designation as Chairman
April 1, 1981

The President today announced his intention to nominate Kieran O'Doherty to be a Commissioner of the Postal Rate Commission for a term expiring October 16, 1986. Upon confirmation by the Senate, the President intends to designate Mr. O'Doherty Chairman.

Mr. O'Doherty has been an attorney-at-law and a member of the New York State and Federal Bar Associations since 1957. He was a Commissioner of the Postal Rate Commission in 1975–80. In 1972–73 Mr. O'Doherty was a Commissioner, Foreign Claims Settlement Commission. In 1971–72 he was consultant to the Secretary of Commerce and special assistant to the General Counsel, Department of Commerce.

Mr. O'Doherty is a cofounder and first State chairman of the Conservative Party of New York. He was a candidate for the United States Senate (1962), United States Congress (1964), and Lieutenant Governor of New York (1966).

Mr. O'Doherty was graduated from City College of New York (A.B., 1950) and Columbia Law School (LL.B., 1953). He served in the U.S. Army in 1944–46. He is married and resides in New York City and Arlington, Va. He was born in New York City on August 8, 1926.

Remarks of the Vice President and Deputy Prime Minister Mieczyslaw Jagielski of Poland Following Their Meeting
April 2, 1981

The Vice President. Well, let me say that we've had a very good discussion with the Deputy Prime Minister Jagielski of Poland. He is the First Deputy. We had a broad range of discussions of U.S.-Polish relations. Secretary of State Haig was there throughout. And Secretary Regan and Secretary Baldrige took place in the meeting also—took part in it. I should say at the very beginning that the Deputy Prime Minister expressed his concern over our President, and I told him that after my visit today to the hospital that I could report to him, firsthand, that our President was, indeed, doing very well.

The U.S. values its constructive relations with Poland, and we want to develop those relations further on the basis of mutual respect and reciprocity. We're following a policy of nonintervention in Poland's internal affairs; and of course we are anxious that others do the same, and we're doing what we can to ensure that. We support the policy of the Polish Government, which is to use peaceful means to resolve Poland's internal problem. And we also welcome the Polish leadership's policy of renewal and economic reform.

We talked a good deal about that, the Deputy Prime Minister explaining in considerable detail the concerns of the Polish people and of his government. And we recognize that these economic problems can only be resolved through an economic program which does have the full support of the people. We're very sympathetic to Poland's economic difficulties. And the American people have, as I told him, a very strong, compatible, humanitarian interest in the welfare of the Polish people.

For these reasons, I had the pleasure of confirming what Secretary Haig had told the Deputy Prime Minister, and that is that the United States Government will sell at concessionary prices certain dairy products, surplus dairy products to Poland. This food, consisting of dried milk and butter, was requested by the government, and we were pleased to be able to reach agreement on that. There are other matters that the Deputy Prime Minister raised with us in terms of things that we might do to help further the economy of Poland. Those matters are being considered with a matter of some urgency, because he impressed upon us the problems facing his country.

We hope that the assistance that we can give will help relieve the current difficulties. And from our standpoint we had a most cordial and productive visit.

Thank you, sir, for coming our way.

The Deputy Prime Minister. Just as the Vice President has said it, I would like on my own part to confirm that our meeting was very interesting and that it was very fruitful, above all, and very advantageous. This allows us to present a wide spectrum of matters very important to our country, for Poland, from economic problems of general meaning and about the means that we in our own country, Poland, to solve the problems with which we are faced and confronted in our country in the most effective way, in the interest of the whole of our people.

I have emphasized once again that the will of my highest authorities is the consistent implementation of the Polish Socialist renewal and the solution of all swelling problems by political means. It is clear that the essential role is assigned to economic matters. And in their solution we expect assistance on the part of our friends, the United States. We are fully cognizant that we must solve these matters, referring at this point to economic matters, by means of our own resources and forces by our own work; increasing its productivity, reinforcing law and order. But we expect also to have assistance from our friends. This will be a subsequent consecutive demonstration of efforts to expand our economic cooperation as much as the historically shaped ties of friendship.

I wish to extend my thanks to the Vice President and to other interlocutors and for the cordial and warm reception accorded us.

Once again, thank you for your attention.

Note: The Vice President spoke at 3:28 p.m. to reporters assembled outside the West Wing Lobby at the White House. The Deputy Prime Minister spoke in Polish, and his remarks were translated by an interpreter.

Proclamation 4830—Law Day, U.S.A., 1981
April 2, 1981

By the President of the United States of America

A Proclamation

America was founded on the principles of liberty and the rule of law. And throughout our Nation's history, the preservation of individual rights has been dependent upon the dedication of our people to liberty and the institutionalization of its principles in the law of the land.

Our forefathers' dedication to liberty is clearly expressed in this Nation's great Charters of Freedom: the Declaration of Independence, the Constitution and the Bill of Rights. These documents, which are the very foundation of American law, guarantee certain inalienable rights and privileges to every citizen. Among these are: freedom of speech, freedom of the press, freedom of religion, freedom of contract, the right to assemble and petition, the right of property ownership, and the right to due process of law.

This year marks the Nation's twenty-fourth annual celebration of Law Day, U.S.A.—a special day for reflection on our heritage of individual freedom and for re-dedication to maintaining, through law, the principles of liberty which govern this land.

Now, Therefore, I, Ronald Reagan, President of the United States of America, invite the American people to celebrate Friday, May 1, 1981, as Law Day, U.S.A., and to mark its observance with programs and ceremonies as befits our great heritage of liberty under law.

I urge clergymen of all faiths to bring to public attention through sermons and suitable programs the moral and ethical dimensions of law and liberty.

I also urge schools, civic, service and fraternal organizations, public bodies, libraries, the courts, the legal profession, all media of public information and interested individuals and organizations to participate in the observance through programs which will focus on the Law Day 1981 theme: Law—the Language of Liberty. To that end, I call upon all public officials to display the flag of the United States on all government buildings on that day.

In Witness Whereof, I have hereunto set my hand this second day of April in the year of our Lord nineteen hundred and eighty-one, and of the Independence of the United States of America the two hundred and fifth.

RONALD REAGAN

[*Filed with the Office of the Federal Register, 10:29 a.m., April 2, 1981*]

Note: On April 6 at a ceremony in the Roosevelt Room at the White House, the Vice President made remarks concerning the proclamation and the importance of the rule of law in our society. See page 328.

Nomination of Craig A. Nalen To Be President of the Overseas Private Investment Corporation
April 2, 1981

The President today announced his intention to nominate Craig A. Nalen to be President of the Overseas Private Investment Corporation, United States International Development Cooperation Agency.

Mr. Nalen has been director of Barnett Bank of Palm Beach County, Fla., since 1978; director of Firan-Glendale Corp. of Ontario, Canada, since 1976; chairman of the board of the Griswold Companies of Minneapolis, Minn., since 1975; and director and founder of Children's World of Denver, Colo., since 1969.

In 1975–80 he was member, management committee, of Esmark, Inc., of Chicago, Ill. During that same period he was chairman, president, and director, STP Corp., Fort Lauderdale, Fla. In 1972–75 Mr. Nalen was chairman, president, and director, American Photograph Corp. He was divisional general manager, corporate vice president, and member of the executive council of General Mills, Inc., in 1964–72. He was marketing executive of Foremost-McKesson in 1962-64 and marketing executive at Proctor & Gamble in 1957–62.

Mr. Nalen served in the U.S. Navy in 1952–55. He was graduated from Princeton University (B.A., 1952) and Stanford University Graduate School of Business (M.B.A., 1957).

Mr. Nalen is married and has three children. He resides with his family in Ocean Ridge, Fla., and Wayzata, Minn. Mr. Nalen was born in Montclair, N.J., on April 17, 1930.

Nomination of Edward E. Noble To Be Chairman of the Board of Directors of the United States Synthetic Fuels Corporation
April 2, 1981

The President today announced his intention to nominate Edward E. Noble to be Chairman of the Board of Directors of the United States Synthetic Fuels Corporation for a term of 7 years.

Mr. Noble has been involved in various businesses, including serving as director of Noble Affiliates, Inc., an oil-related company in Oklahoma. He was involved in the development of Lenox Square Shopping Center, a 1,500,000-square-foot shopping center located in Atlanta, Ga.

He also developed Noble Inns Corp., a motor hotel company operating motor hotels in Georgia, Florida, and Ohio. He is presently chairman of the board and director. He is director of Auto Crane Co. of Tulsa, Okla., a manufacturer of heavy cranes used by oil and heavy equipment industries in the United States.

Mr. Noble was graduated from the University of Oklahoma in 1951. He is a director of the Hoover Institute and a trustee of the Samuel Roberts Foundation, Inc., in Ardmore, Okla. Mr. Noble was active during the 1980 election in the Reagan campaign.

Mr. Noble was born in Ardmore, Okla., on March 19, 1928.

White House Statement on the Vice President's Meeting With Minister of Foreign Affairs Ilter Turkmen of Turkey
April 2, 1981

Vice President Bush today met with Ilter Turkmen, the Foreign Minister of Turkey, who has come to the United States at the invitation of Secretary Haig. The meeting included senior officials from both Turkey and the United States Government.

The Vice President and the Foreign Minister reviewed in a cordial way a number of bilateral and international issues. They discussed in particular the need for all NATO allies to continue concerted efforts to enhance their defense posture in response to existing threats in Southwest Asia and Europe. The Vice President also noted with satisfaction Turkish efforts to improve bilateral relations with Greece and Turkish support for the ongoing intercommunal talks on Cyprus.

The Vice President took special note of the excellent state of the Turkish-American relationship and the significance of this year, which marks the centennial of the birth of Mustafa Kemal Ataturk, the founder of modern Turkey.

White House Statement Concerning the Centennial Anniversary of the Birth of Mustafa Kemal Ataturk of Turkey
April 2, 1981

Beginning on May 19, Turkey will launch a year of celebration to commemorate the Centennial Anniversary of the birth of Mustafa Kemal Ataturk, the founder of the Republic of Turkey. Ataturk was a great national leader in times of war and peace. He was, and he remains, first in the hearts of his countrymen. For Turkey and its people, the Ataturk Centennial Year is as important an event as the 1976 Bicentennial was for us.

In observance of this centennial year, events are being planned in the United States and other countries to acknowledge the significance of Ataturk to the Western World. Indeed, the turbulence of our era calls to mind the enduring wisdom of Ataturk's goal—"Peace at Home, Peace Abroad."

The visit of Turkish Foreign Minister Turkmen in this centennial year gives us cause to take note of the great value and importance of Turkish-American relations.

The United States of America and the Republic of Turkey have been firm friends and allies for more than a generation. Beginning with Harry Truman, every American President has viewed a strong and stable Turkey as an essential goal of American policy. This is no less the case in the Reagan administration. In recent years, the United States has been working vigorously with other nations to provide Turkey the resources necessary to regain economic health and to meet its important goals as a member of the North Atlantic Treaty Organization. The United States fully supports the efforts of the Turkish Government to eradicate terrorism and to carry out basic reforms that will assure the long-term stability of Turkish democracy and the well-being of the Turkish people.

In commemorating the Ataturk Centennial, the United States and its people extend best wishes to the Republic of Turkey and its people.

Remarks of the Vice President on Presenting the Annual Cancer Courage Award to Karen Eakens Anderson
April 3, 1981

I know I speak for everybody here that we wish the President were standing right here on this beautiful day. I know that if he were here, he would first express his deep appreciation to the American Cancer Society, to Dr. Scanlon, who's president, to Mr. Jonas, his chairman, and the others who do such magnificent work. But today, we here at the White House want to join with the Cancer Society in presenting to Karen An-

derson the 1981 Cancer Courage Award. Karen's personal courage in overcoming leukemia—I guess, got it at 18, and now 26 and totally recovered—is a great inspiration. And it shows what research has done. It shows what the Cancer Society has contributed to in such a magnificent way. And we view you, in a sense, as a symbol of victory. The volunteers and the staff of the Cancer Society, by their hard work and commitment, show us also what Americans can do when they work together to tackle tough problems, in this instance, this insidious problem of cancer.

And so, I would simply say good luck on the educational and fundraising activities planned for Cancer Control Month. My family was hit with leukemia 30 years ago, and I just can't tell you what this magnificent progress means, personally. And I know I express to you, Karen, our congratulations, and I know I speak for the President on this one.

Thank you all very much.

Note: The Vice President spoke at 11:30 a.m. at the ceremony in the Rose Garden at the White House.

Remarks of the Vice President on Senate Passage of Federal Budget Legislation
April 3, 1981

I just have a brief statement. First, an expression of appreciation from the President to the Senators here and to the Senate itself for its performance yesterday. But let me just briefly make some comments that there is in the administration clearly—and the President has asked the Chief of Staff to have me convey this deep gratification by the Senate's action on the budget yesterday.

The 88-to-10 vote dramatically began the process of saving $36 billion for the American people in '82. And it's clear that this was bipartisan—Republicans and Democrats alike responding to the demands of the American people to get the economic house in order, and the overwhelming bipartisan vote is a heartwarming indication that elected officials really do mean business. And it's significant that during the Senate debate there were a lot of very popular amendments—popular on both sides of the aisle. But they would have watered down the economic package and the economic effect of the package, and they were beaten back. And this kind of responsiveness to the national interest is really in the great spirit of cooperation between the two branches of government.

We hope that it will serve—speaking for the administration, and I'm sure the Senate feels that way, having responded overwhelmingly on that vote—we hope it will be an example to the Members of the House of Representatives, who now have the same responsibility ahead of them in the future weeks here.

So, I express the President's congratulations, and I commend the Senate for its thorough examination, open debate, on the important issue of economic recovery. Obviously, the debate was spirited at times, but bipartisan cooperation prevailed and that was the encouraging thing. Yesterday's vote, we recognize, was simply an important initial step, but combined with tax reduction and relief from overregulation and stable money supply, we are confident that there will be a restoration of our economic vitality in this country.

I am particularly grateful, of course, to the majority leader of the Senate and to Senator Domenici and his counterpart on the important committee that handled all of this, Senator Fritz Hollings. The Senate really behaved magnificently in the view of the administration, and I really came up here today to simply say, "Thank you."And if you would convey that to others—we caught the Senate at a rather quiet time, but after what you've been through, why, it's appropriate there be a little lull.

Thank you all very, very much. And now I am going to go down and see the President, and I know that the Senators have agreed to respond to any questions, if anybody would like to ask them.

Thank you.

Note: The Vice President spoke at 12:10 p.m. to reporters assembled outside the Capitol.

Letter to the Chairmen of the Senate Foreign Relations Committee and the House Foreign Affairs Committee on the Situation in Zimbabwe
April 3, 1981

Dear Mr. Chairman:

In accordance with the provisions of Section 720 of the International Security and Development Cooperation Act of 1980, I am submitting the following report on the internal situation in Zimbabwe.

There is considerable evidence to indicate that the transition to majority rule in Zimbabwe, which was consummated at Lancaster House and came into effect on April 18, 1980, is now gathering momentum both economically and politically.

Economically, Zimbabwe has made considerable progress in the 11 months since independence. Real growth for 1980 is estimated to have been 8–10 percent. Inflation averaged between 12 percent and 15 percent for the year. With the announcement of a high pre-planting price and a good rainy season, Zimbabwe is expecting a million ton maize surplus this harvest. The mining sector remains solidly prosperous despite some uncertainty about a possibly increased government role.

In the July 1980 budget and the February 1981 economic policy statement, "Growth with Equity", the government has committed itself to the maintenance of a mixed economy aimed at satisfying black aspirations and assuring white confidence by attracting foreign investment and aid to generate continued economic growth.

Zimbabwe's economic success is partly associated with the fact that more than 90 percent of the country's white population, about 200,000 people, have chosen to stay in Zimbabwe. We estimate that about 20,000 whites have left, 15,000 of them have gone to South Africa. Nevertheless, white emigration has led to some dislocations in areas of the economy dependent upon mechanical and technical expertise, e.g. railroad maintenance and telecommunications. The country's 5,000 white commercial farmers have almost all stayed in Zimbabwe.

Politically, the dire predictions which were heard at the same time of independence have not come to pass. Black-white political conflict has been inconsequential. The expected Ndebele-Shona political conflict has materialized; however, despite two bloody clashes in Bulawayo, the tension has been contained by the existing political and military structures and senior leaders on both sides have responded to the problems which have arisen with a view toward the long-term best interests of the country. On the whole, the political scene has been marked by increasing stability and the enhancement of the authority of Prime Minister Robert Mugabe.

The process of military integration of ZIPRA and ZANLA continues to move forward slowly despite the collapse of three of the eleven integrated battalions in last month's difficulties. Most observers now believe that Zimbabwe will for at least the near term have a larger army than was initially anticipated, due to the fact that most of the remaining 25,000 guerrillas will probably be incorporated into the new national army.

As noted in detail in the 1981 "Country Reports on Human Rights Practices", independent Zimbabwe on the whole has a good record in living up to the guarantees on civil liberties contained in the Lancaster House accords, in particular those contained in Annex C. Zimbabwe continues to be a functioning, multi-party, parliamentary democracy in which the rights of the population as set forth in the constitution are respected.

The basic rights called for in the agreement such as the right to life, personal liberty, freedom from torture and inhuman treatment, freedom from deprivation of property, privacy and freedom of conscience, expression, and assembly are in effect. Thus, for example, at the time of this report, there are no persons under detention in Zimbabwe because of their political views. In order to end South African control of the press, the government purchased controlling interest from the Argus Groups and invested it in a national press board which appears so far to operate independently. The electronic media are sometimes criticized for being overly enthusiastic about government policies.

The House of Assembly and the Senate which were set up pursuant to the Lancaster House agreement have proven to be active political bodies in which substantive and frank debate is the order of the day. Regularly scheduled elections continue to be held, most recently at the local level. Nevertheless, disturbances led to the postponement of local government elections in Bulawayo following clashes between partisans of competing political parties.

The court system recognized in the Lancaster House agreement functions as set forth in the agreement. Thus, for example, ZANU-PF Secretary General Edgar Tekere, who was charged with the murder of a white farmer, was freed by the court under a law passed by the former regime to protect government officials. While many Zimbabweans may have lamented Tekere's release, it was widely noted that, as promised, Prime Minister Mugabe's government did not interject itself in any way into the judicial process. The public service and the police also operate as set forth in the Lancaster House agreement.

Sincerely,

RONALD REAGAN

Note: This is the text of identical letters addressed to Charles H. Percy, chairman of the Senate Foreign Relations Committee, and Clement J. Zablocki, chairman of the House Foreign Affairs Committee.

Nomination of Donald J. Senese To Be an Assistant Secretary of Education
April 3, 1981

The President today announced his intention to nominate Donald J. Senese to be Assistant Secretary for Educational Research and Improvement, Department of Education.

Since 1976 Dr. Senese has been senior research associate, Republican Study Committee, U.S. House of Representatives. In 1973–76 he was chief legislative assistant to Representative William Archer (R-Tex.). Dr. Senese served as legislative assistant and newsletter editor to Senator William Scott (R-Va.) in 1973. In 1969–72 he was associate professor of history at Radford University, Radford, Va.

Dr. Senese was a member of the General Administration Board of the Department of Agriculture Graduate School in 1975–80. He was elected to the national board of directors and also to the executive committee of the University Professors for Academic Order in 1978.

Dr. Senese was graduated from Loyola University of Chicago (B.S., 1964) and the University of South Carolina (M.A., 1966; Ph. D., 1970). He was named an Outstanding Young Man in America in 1976 and 1978.

Dr. Senese resides in Alexandria, Va. He was born in Chicago, Ill., on April 6, 1942.

Nomination of Gary L. Jones To Be a Deputy Under Secretary of Education
April 3, 1981

The President today announced his intention to nominate Gary L. Jones to be Deputy Under Secretary for Planning and Budget, Department of Education.

Since 1980 Dr. Jones has been director of the general grants program for the Chicago-based MacArthur Foundation. He served the Reagan for President campaign as director of research and policy coordination during the initial phase of the campaign. Before joining the campaign, Dr. Jones was vice president for administration at the American Enterprise Institute for Public Policy Research. He also served as associate editor of two of AEI's periodical publications, Regulation, and Public Opinion, and was active in AEI's academic outreach program.

Previously Dr. Jones served as assistant to U.S. Senator Robert Griffin (R-Mich.). From 1966 to 1970, he served in the admissions office at Albion College, the last 2 years as assistant director.

Dr. Jones is active in the field of education, currently serving as a member of the Fairfax County School Board in Fairfax, Va., and on the Visiting Committee for Student Affairs at Case Western Reserve University. He is a member of the American Association for Higher Education, the American Association of School Administrators, and the National School Boards Association.

Dr. Jones was graduated from Albion College (A.B., 1966) and Michigan State University (M.A., Ph. D.).

Dr. Jones resides in Fairfax, Va. He was born in Jackson, Miss., on May 6, 1944.

Nomination of Winifred Ann Pizzano To Be Deputy Director of ACTION
April 3, 1981

The President today announced the nomination of Winifred Ann Pizzano to be Deputy Director of the ACTION agency.

Since 1975 Ms. Pizzano has served as a principal in Arthur Young and Co., directing the company's Federal health care practice. In 1972–75 she was executive administrator, Division of Emergency Medical Services, Illinois Department of Public Health. Ms. Pizzano was assistant to the Governor, State of Illinois, in 1971–72, with responsibility as chief of liaison with the Department of Public Health and other health-related agencies. In 1966–70 she was legisla-

tive assistant to Representative Robert H. Michel (R-Ill.).

Ms. Pizzano is a member of the governing board and chairman of the program section on Emergency Health Services, American Public Health Association. She is a past member of the board of directors, Northern Virginia Health Systems Agency. Ms. Pizzano has authored articles on health care and medical systems.

Ms. Pizzano is a resident of Arlington, Va. She was born in Harrisburg, Pa., on March 24, 1942.

Nomination of John A. Gavin To Be United States Ambassador to Mexico
April 3, 1981

The President today announced his intention to nominate John A. Gavin, of California, to be Ambassador to Mexico, vice Julian Nava, resigned.

Mr. Gavin served in the United States Navy in 1952–55. In 1956 he began his acting career and has appeared in many films and television series. He is a past president of the Screen Actors Guild.

In 1961–63 he was a member of a special task force in the Department of State and special adviser to the Organization of American States in 1961–65.

Since 1968 he has been president of Gamma Services Corp. of Los Angeles, Calif. He is a trustee of Villanova Preparatory School.

Mr. Gavin was graduated from Stanford University (B.A., 1952). He is married to the former Constance Towers and has four children. He was born in Los Angeles, Calif., on April 8, 1931.

Remarks of the Vice President Concerning Law Day, U.S.A., 1981
April 6, 1981

Let me just read a brief statement.

President Reagan has proclaimed May 1st as Law Day, U.S.A. The proclamation follows a 24-year tradition of annual reflection on the importance of rule of law in our society. And the theme this year is "Law—the Language of Liberty." This is especially appropriate for the first Law Day proclamation of a President whose eloquent articulation of the principles of individual liberty and freedom has been one of the hallmarks of his public service, public life.

The theme of law as the language of liberty calls to mind several points of particular current significance. One is the problem of violent crime. The rule of law represents the civil discourse of a free people. Violent crime is the uncivilized shout that threatens to drown out and ultimately silence the language of liberty. The events of last Monday were a tragic reminder as the violent act of one man sought tho hush the voice of the Nation as to who its leader would be. But no less tragic are the daily, less dramatic acts of violence inflicted upon our citizens by a criminal few.

Attorney General Smith has stated that reduction of violent crime is his number one priority, and under the direction of the President, he's established a task force to determine the ways that Federal, State, and local governments and officials can work together to fight violent crime. This work is vital if the language of liberty is to continue to be spoken in our land.

President Reagan's proclamation emphasizes our nation's great charters of freedom—the Declaration of Independence, the Constitution, and the Bill of Rights. These founding documents remind us that the language of liberty in America has a particularly rich heritage, but they tell us something else about law as the language of liberty. They are legal documents, but they are really much more than that. Their language is central, fundamental, inspiring, rather than narrow and technical and legalistic. These charters of freedom truly speak the language of liberty, a language addressed to free men and women who know its vocabulary, its tone, its emphasis, and its objectives. Its message is muted and distorted when law becomes too technical, too regulatory, too great an interference in the lives of free citizens. President Reagan's emphasis on our charters of freedom encourages each of us to redouble our efforts to make our laws consistent with the principles these great documents, the cardinal statement of our freedom, express.

And finally, the theme of law as the language of liberty underscores that the rule of law is the common language of free people. Our Founding Fathers knew that our freedoms depended, in the final analysis, on the virtue of the American people, people to whom the laws of civilized existence were second nature, whose instincts for decency provided the necessary forum in which the language of liberty could be spoken and heard by all. This is no less true today. Our laws cannot make us good and decent citizens and human beings. To the contrary, we must be a good and decent people if law is to survive.

President Reagan's proclamation of Law Day, U.S.A., 1981, refocuses our attention on this basic truth and calls each of us to strive to live and act in ways that will keep the language of liberty clear, not only for us but for generations of Americans yet unborn.

Thank you, Mr. Smith, and thank you, Mr. Attorney General and others.

Note: The Vice President spoke at 10:05 a.m. in the Roosevelt Room at the White House. William R. Smith, president of the American Bar Association, Attorney General William French Smith, State attorneys general, Members of Congress, and administration officials were present at the ceremony.

For the text of Proclamation 4830, signed April 2, see page 321.

Nomination of Arthur H. Woodruff To Be United States Ambassador to the Central African Republic
April 6, 1981

The President today announced his intention to nominate Arthur H. Woodruff, of Florida, to be Ambassador to the Central African Republic, vice Goodwin Cooke, resigned.

Mr. Woodruff entered the Foreign Service in 1955 as consular officer in Casablanca. In 1957–60 he was consular officer, then political officer in Lubumbashi. In the Department, he was international relations officer, then personnel placement specialist in 1960–63. He was political officer in London in 1962–68 aand political-military officer, U.S.-NATO, Brussels, in 1968–73. He attended the Canadian Defense College in 1973–74. In the Department, he was international relations officer, the Deputy Director of the Office of Policy Planning, Public and Congressional Affairs in 1974–77; member of the Board of Examiners for the Foreign Service, Bureau of Personnel, in 1977–78; and Deputy Director of the Office of Foreign Service Career Development and Assignments in the Bureau of Personnel in 1978–80. Since 1980 he has been assigned to the Office of the Director General of the Foreign Service. He is fluent in French.

Mr. Woodruff was born September 26, 1928, in Philadelphia, Pa. He was graduated from Harvard College (B.A., 1950) and Harvard University (M.P.A., 1960). He served in the United States Marine Corps in 1950–52. Mr. Woodruff is married and has four children.

Nomination of Deane R. Hinton To Be United States Ambassador to El Salvador
April 6, 1981

The President today announced his intention to nominate Deane R. Hinton, of Illinois, to be Ambassador to El Salvador, vice Robert E. White, resigned.

Mr. Hinton entered the Foreign Service in 1946 as chief of political section in Damascus. From 1949 to 1951, he was principal officer in Mombasa. He attended economic studies at the Fletcher School of Law and Diplomacy and Harvard University from 1951 to 1952. In 1955–58 he was Chief of the West European Branch, then Chief of Regional European Research, Bureau of Intelligence, in the Department. In 1958–61 he was chief of overseas development and finance section in Brussels/USEC. He attended the National War College in 1961–62. In the Department, he was Chief of Commodity/Programming Division in the Bureau of Economic Affairs (1962–63) and Director of the Office of Atlantic Political-Economic Affairs in the Bureau of European Affairs (1963–67). In 1967–69 he was Director of the USAID Mission and counselor for economic affairs in Guatemala. In 1969–71 he was Director of the USAID mission and counselor for economic affairs in Santiago.

He served at the White House as Assistant Executive Director of the Council on International Economic Policy (1971–73) and Deputy Executive Director of the Council on Economic International Policy (1973–74).

From 1974 to 1975, Mr. Hinton was Ambassador to the Republic of Zaire. In 1975 he was senior adviser to the Under Secretary of State for Economic Affairs. In 1975–79 he was United States Representative to the European Communities, with rank and status of Ambassador, Brussels. And since 1979 he has been Assistant Secretary of State for Economic and Business Affairs. He is fluent in French and Spanish.

Mr. Hinton, a widower, was born March 12, 1923, in Missoula, Mont. He was graduated from the University of Chicago (A.B., 1943). He served in the United States Army in 1943–45 as a second lieutenant.

Nomination of John A. Burroughs, Jr., To Be United States Ambassador to Malawi
April 6, 1981

The President today announced his intention to nominate John A. Burroughs, Jr., of Maryland, to be Ambassador to the Republic of Malawi, vice Harold Horan, resigned.

From 1959 to 1960, Mr. Burroughs was a social science teacher in the public schools of Washington, D.C. He was with the Department of State and served successively as passport examiner in 1960–63, Assistant Chief of Special Services Branch of the Passport Office in 1963–64, and administrative assistant in the Bureau of Economic and Business Affairs in 1964–66. He was employee relations specialist in 1966–70 and special assistant for equal opportunity to the Assistant Secretary of the Navy in 1970–77. In 1977–80 he was Deputy Assistant Secretary of State for Equal Employment Opportunity, Department of State, and since 1980 has been assigned to the Office of the Director General of the Foreign Service.

Mr. Burroughs received the Superior Civilian Service Award in 1977.

He was born July 31, 1936, in Washington, D.C. He was graduated from the University of Iowa (B.A., 1959). He attended George Washington University in 1962 and Stanford University in 1974. Mr. Burroughs is married.

Nomination of Jay Fleron Morris To Be an Assistant Administrator of the Agency for International Development
April 6, 1981

The President today announced his intention to nominate Jay Fleron Morris to be Assistant Administrator of the Agency for International Development (External Affairs), United States International Development Cooperation Agency.

Mr. Morris is presently executive recruiter, Office of Presidential Personnel, the White House. He was deputy director of administration during the transition. In August-November 1980 he was a member of the Reagan-Bush planning task force and regional finance director of the Reagan for President Committee in 1979–80.

In 1979–80 Mr. Morris was government relations advisor with the firm of Vorys, Sater, Seymour and Pease of Washington, D.C. He was Executive Director of the President's Commission on Personnel Interchange in 1976–78. In 1975–76 he was manager of Federal transportation programs of Motorola, Inc. Mr. Morris was senior administrative assistant to the county executive, Prince Georges County, Md., in 1971–74. He was research and legislative assistant to Senator James B. Pearson (R-Kans.) in 1967–71.

Mr. Morris was graduated from the University of Maryland (B.S., 1963; M.S., 1965) and Johns Hopkins School of Advanced International Studies (Ph. D., 1967).

Mr. Morris is married, has one child, and resides in Adelphi, Md. He was born in Honolulu, Hawaii, on February 21, 1941.

Nomination of John H. Rodriguez To Be a Deputy Under Secretary of Education
April 6, 1981

The President today announced his intention to nominate John H. Rodriguez to be Deputy Under Secretary for Intergovernmental and Interagency Affairs, Department of Education.

In 1974–80 Dr. Rodriguez was Associate Commissioner for Compensatory Educational Programs, U.S. Office of Education. He was Associate Deputy Commissioner for School Systems in 1972–74. In 1970–72 Dr. Rodriguez was superintendent, Upland School District, Upland, Calif. He served previously as superintendent of Perris School District in Perris, Calif., and principal of Rialto Unified School District in Rialto, Calif.

He is an instructor and consultant to many school districts and colleges in California and has lectured on educational topics before various educational associations throughout the country.

Dr. Rodriguez was graduated from San Diego State College (B.A., 1953) and Claremont Graduate School (M.A., 1959; Ph. D., 1973). He is married, has two children, and resides with his family in McLean, Va. Dr. Rodriguez was born in San Diego, Calif., on November 28, 1926.

Nomination of Judith L. Tardy To Be an Assistant Secretary of Housing and Urban Development
April 6, 1981

The President today announced his intention to nominate Judith L. Tardy to be an Assistant Secretary of Housing and Urban Development (Administration).

In 1979–80 Ms. Tardy was Director, Administrative Programs and Services, Department of Labor. She was a member of the transition team for the Export-Import Bank. In 1976–79 she was Director, Executive Secretariat, Department of Labor, and in 1975–76 she was Director for Management, Commodity Futures Trading Commission. Ms. Tardy was special assistant to the Administrator, Federal Energy Administration

in 1974–75. In 1972–74 she was special assistant to the Deputy Director, Cost of Living Council. In 1971–72 she was personnel management specialist, Department of Labor. Ms. Tardy was personnel management specialist, Department of Transportation, in 1969–71. Previously she was a teacher in Fairfax County, Va., in 1968–69 and in Hawaii in 1967–68.

Ms. Tardy was graduated from the University of Hawaii (B.A., 1966). She resides in Arlington, Va., and was born in Carlisle, Pa., on February 7, 1944.

Nomination of Daniel N. Miller To Be an Assistant Secretary of the Interior
April 6, 1981

The President today announced his intention to nominate Daniel N. Miller to be an Assistant Secretary of the Interior (Energy and Minerals).

Since 1969 Mr. Miller has been State geologist and executive director of the Geological Survey of Wyoming and commissioner with the Wyoming Oil and Gas Conservation Commission. He has served as adjunct professor to the department of geology, University of Wyoming.

In 1963–69 he was professor and chairman, department of geology, Southern Illinois University. Mr. Miller was a geological consultant with the firm of Barlow and Haun, Inc., of Casper, Wyo., in 1961–63. In 1960–61 he was senior exploration geologist,

Lion Oil Division, Monsanto Chemical Co. of Casper, Wyo. He was previously senior exploration geologist and Rocky Mountain division research coordinator, Pan American Petroleum Corp. in 1955–60. In 1951–52 Mr. Miller was intermediate geologist in petroleum exploration on the Texas gulf coast with Stanolind Oil and Gas Co.

Mr. Miller served in the U.S. Army Air Force in 1943–46. He was graduated from Missouri School of Mines and Metallurgy at Rolla, Mo. (B.S., 1949) and the University of Texas (Ph. D., 1955).

He is married, has two children, and resides in Laramie, Wyo. Mr. Miller was born in St. Louis, Mo., on August 22, 1924.

Statement on Assistance for the Domestic Automobile Industry
April 6, 1981

The American automobile industry is in serious trouble. Our national economic con-

dition and strangling regulations have helped cause the layoff of an estimated

500,000 workers in automobile and related industries. Last year, domestic production dropped to a 19-year low, and American auto firms lost an unprecedented $4.3 billion.

I believe in the American worker, in American innovation, and in our free marketplace. Today I am announcing steps that can help the automobile industry restore its competitive position both here and abroad. The industry must solve its own problems, but the Government must not unnecessarily hamper its efforts through excessive regulation and interference.

The first step to be taken in aid of this industry is to create a stronger and more stable economy. It is therefore essential that the Congress act quickly to pass our comprehensive package for economic recovery.

The second step is to reduce unnecessary regulations by the Environmental Protection Agency and the National Highway Traffic Safety Administration. Our proposals for these two areas will save the industry and consumers more than $9 billion during the next 5 years. Our Task Force on Regulatory Relief is considering additional regulatory changes which could result in even greater savings.

Third, the Department of Labor is proposing revisions in its programs to make more effective use of assistance to unemployed autoworkers.

Fourth, I have proposed an acceleration in the rate of government purchases of motor vehicles. The U.S. Government will spend about $100 million more on government vehicles this fiscal year, which, while helping the industry, will also lower the government's operating costs.

Fifth, the Attorney General has pledged a quick response to the industry's request that he seek the lifting of certain prohibitions against cooperative ventures and joint presentations before regulatory agencies.

He will respond to that request immediately following the resolution of a related action now pending in the Court of Appeals.

And sixth, we will monitor the effect of international trade on our domestic automobile industry. We are committed to free trade and believe free trade benefits all nations concerned. In observing the principles of free trade, however, we expect our trading partners to do so, as well.

At the invitation of the Japanese Government, a briefing delegation is being sent to Japan. We believe this closely coordinated exchange of information will lead to a greater understanding and cooperation between our two countries, and will ultimately strengthen our economic relationship with Japan.

It should be understood that real recovery will not be accomplished by government alone. We only can remove the Federal shackles and improve the economic environment within which the automobile industry operates. It is up to automobile management and unions to take the strong necessary steps to restore our competitiveness with other nations.

The automobile industry is vital to our nation's economy. Business, labor, and government must work together to restore our traditional leadership in this field.

Note: Vice President Bush read the statement at 2:10 p.m. at a news conference in Room 450 of the Old Executive Office Building.

On April 9 the White House announced that with the issuance of the statement, the work of the Auto Task Force had been completed and that Secretary of Commerce Malcolm Baldrige would be primarily responsible for implementing the recommendations of the Task Force.

Nomination of Thomas L. Lias To Be an Assistant Director of ACTION
April 6, 1981

The President today announced his intention to nominate Thomas L. Lias to be Assistant Director for Voluntary Citizen Participation of the ACTION agency.

In 1980 Mr. Lias was director, Professionals for Reagan-Bush. In 1979 he was deputy director of the George Bush for President campaign. Mr. Lias was consultant to the University of Alabama and aided in setting up its Washington office in 1977–78. In 1976 he was Assistant Secretary for Legislation, Department of Health, Education, and Welfare. He served as executive assistant to the Secretary of Health, Education, and Welfare in 1975.

Mr. Lias was executive director of the Republican National Committee in 1973–74. In 1971–72 he was executive assistant to the U.S. Permanent Representative to the United Nations. He previously served as Deputy Special Assistant to the President in 1969–71. He held various staff positions with the Republican Congressional Committee in 1965–70.

Mr. Lias was graduated from the University of Iowa (B.A., 1956). He resides in Washington, D.C., and was born in Akron, Iowa, on September 27, 1934.

Nomination of Mary Ann Weyforth Dawson To Be a Commissioner of the Federal Communications Commission
April 6, 1981

The President today announced his intention to nominate Mary Ann Weyforth Dawson to be Commissioner, Federal Communications Commission, for a term of 7 years from July 1, 1981, vice Robert E. Lee, term expiring June 30, 1981.

Since 1973 Mrs. Dawson has served as chief of staff/administrative assistant, legislative director, and press secretary to Senator Robert Packwood (R-Oreg.). In 1973 she was legislative assistant and press secretary to Representative Richard Ichord (D-Mo.). Mrs. Dawson was legislative assistant to Representative James W. Symington (D-Mo.) in 1969–72.

In her position as chief of staff/administrative assistant to Senator Packwood, Mrs.

Dawson has had primary responsibility for the operation of the Senator's personal staff, the Senate Committee on Commerce, Science, and Transportation, and the National Republican Senatorial Committee, both chaired by the Senator. Commerce Committee jurisdiction included communications, including telephone, telegraph, radio, television, cable television, and satellite communications.

Mrs. Dawson was graduated from Washington University, St. Louis, Mo. (A.B., 1966). She is married and resides in Washington, D.C. Mrs. Dawson was born in St. Louis, Mo., on August 31, 1944.

Nomination of A. Alan Hill To Be a Member of the Council on Environmental Quality, and Designation as Chairman
April 6, 1981

The President today announced his intention to nominate A. Alan Hill to be a member of the Council on Environmental Quality. Upon confirmation, the President intends to designate Mr. Hill Chairman.

Since 1976 Mr. Hill has served as president of Hill Building Specialties, Inc., of San Francisco, Calif. He was division manager of the Purves Supply Co. in 1974–76. During the period 1969–74, Mr. Hill worked for the State of California in various capacities. He most recently was deputy secretary, Agriculture and Services Agency. He was previously deputy director, Department of Conservation, and assistant to the secretary, Resources Agency.

In 1965–69 Mr. Hill was State information officer of the Republican State Central Committee of California. He was assistant to the minority leader, California State Senate.

Mr. Hill was graduated from the College of the Pacific (B.A., 1960). He is married, has three children, and resides with his family in San Rafael, Calif. Mr. Hill was born in San Francisco, Calif., on February 1, 1938.

Nomination of Charles M. Butler III To Be a Member of the Federal Energy Regulatory Commission, and Designation as Chairman
April 6, 1981

The President today announced his intention to nominate Charles M. Butler III, to be a member of the Federal Energy Regulatory Commission, Department of Energy, for the remainder of the term expiring October 20, 1983. Upon confirmation, the President intends to designate Mr. Butler Chairman.

Since 1979 Mr. Butler has served as administrative assistant to Senator John Tower (R-Tex.). In 1976–79 he was senior attorney with the American National Resources Co., Detroit, Mich. He was an attorney with the firm of Kendrick, Kendrick & Bradley of Dallas, Tex., in 1975–76. In 1974–75 Mr. Butler was chief legislative assistant to Senator Tower. He was an attorney with the firm of Baker & Botts of Houston, Tex., in 1971–73.

Mr. Butler was graduated from the University of Houston (B.A., 1969) and the University of Texas (J.D., 1971). He is married, has three children, and resides with his family in Bethesda, Md. Mr. Butler was born in Midland, Tex., on February 6, 1943.

Message to the Congress Transmitting Additional Details on Fiscal Year 1982 Budget Revisions
April 7, 1981

To the Congress of the United States:

On March 10, 1981, I forwarded to the Congress a fully revised 1982 Budget with specific proposals for fiscal year 1981 and 1982 and clearly stated targets for 1983 through 1986. I have already submitted to the Congress the supplemental budget requests, rescissions and deferrals for 1981 and budget amendments for 1982 necessary for the Congress to act upon my proposals.

My Budget Reform plan, first presented February 18th and submitted in detail on March 10th, was one of four parts of my comprehensive program for the Nation's economic recovery. The Budget plan called for substantial budget savings and a redirection of Federal Government activities. It included more than 200 proposals for spending reductions, user charges and off-budget savings that are necessary to put the Federal Government on a path toward fiscal responsibility.

We have already provided extensive information on the proposed budget savings. However, I want to be sure that the Congress and the American people fully understand the reasons for the planned budget savings. Accordingly, I have directed the Office of Management and Budget to compile a document to make available additional details on the specific savings proposals.

I hope that this information will be useful to the various committees and subcommittees of the Congress as they consider my proposals.

RONALD REAGAN

The White House,
April 7, 1981.

Note: The message is printed in the report entitled "Fiscal Year 1982 Budget Revisions: Additional Details on Budget Savings, April 1981—Executive Office of the President, Office of Management and Budget" (Government Printing Office, 435 pages).

Remarks of the Vice President at the Annual Republican Senate-House Dinner
April 7, 1981

Thank you, Senator Packwood. And first let me just express my deep appreciation to Joe Rodgers, the chairman, to Bob Packwood and to Guy Vander Jagt for this spectacular dinner, for the enormous effort that so many people out there put in to making this the obvious success that it is.

I also want to thank Ambassador Brock, Chairman Bill Brock, if you will, and John Heinz, who, though not in their political offices now in terms of the Senate and National Committee, both of whom did this magnificent job in shaping the victories that were ours last November, and also to convey my best wishes to our new, very able chairman, Dick Richards, the new chairman of the Republican National Committee, who has a tough act to follow in following Bill Brock, but whom I'm confident will do a magnificent job.

All of these people have made a tremendous contribution, not just to this dinner but to the results we're all here complimenting ourselves on for what happened in both the House and the Senate. They're fantastic leaders, and I want to pay my respects to every one of them.

You know, being asked to substitute for President Reagan as a guest speaker at a gathering of Republicans is like pinch hitting for George Brett out there in Kansas City. You know, it's almost impossible, and there's no way that you can possibly do the job as well as the person you're filling in for. But it is a pleasure to be here in front of this distinguished audience and to thank so many solid party supporters who helped make the great Republican victory of 1980 possible and now and are hard at work, as you've heard from previous speakers, laying the groundwork for 1982.

And thanks to your efforts we now have a Republican President, and thanks to your efforts we now have a Republican Senate. But two out of three, while it may be pretty good—.666 in baseball—may be okay, but it isn't good enough when it comes to turning this country around completely. We have Howard Baker as Senate Majority Leader, and now we need, and President Reagan needs, Bob Michel as Speaker of the House of Representatives. That is our objective.

Every American, regardless of party, regardless of where you come from, is heartened by the magnificent progress that our President is making on his road to recovery. I stopped over there just for a couple of minutes on the way to this dinner, and I must say that he looks well. That fantastic humor and spirit is there, and I'll tell you, here's one guy that just can't wait for him to get out of that hospital and get back to the Oval Office. The country needs it so much. We need his strength, we need his resilience, we need his articulation about division of our country's future, and we need his will and his determination to make the decade of the eighties one of a great new beginning for our country.

And while we're at it, I expect I express the sentiments of everybody here when I say the same goes for Jim Brady, the same goes for Secret Service Agent McCarthy, who did get out of the hospital today, and the same goes for that heroic policeman, Mr. Delahanty. We need them. We need them back at what they were all doing, each in their own way, so very well indeed.

It's been only 2 months since the President launched what Joe talked about, this new beginning for the Nation, but the signal is clear for everybody to see—in President Reagan we have a leader now who inspires new confidence, who inspires new hope in our country's future. I see it at home, and I see it abroad, as we meet with leader after leader from overseas. Ten days ago, speaking here, the President outlined the basic philosophy that guides his administration, the philosophy that those of us who work with him day to day have heard him express in various ways whenever key issues are being discussed.

This is what the President told members of the National Conference of Building and Construction Trades, and here's the quote, "We've gone astray from our first principles. We've lost sight of the rule that individual freedom and ingenuity are at the very core of everything that we've accomplished." And then, summing up the meaning of the Reagan mandate, the President had this to say: "Government's first duty is to protect the people, not run their lives."

And let me repeat that: "Government's first duty is to protect the people, not run their lives."

We Republicans, as Guy Vander Jagt put it, we believe in the American people. We have faith in the people's ability, through exercising individual freedom and their God-given ingenuity, to make better lives for themselves, their families, and their communities. And the record of the past half century shows that under Democratic leadership we've had ever expanding, ever more centralized government trying to run the lives of our citizens. And the Reagan mandate of 1980 was a clear and unmistakable message from the people to turn that trend around, to make America once again a government of, by, and for the people, and not of, by, and for the bureaucrats.

Until this year the opposition party had held control over both Houses of the Congress for 46 years out of the last 50 years. And last November, thanks to the help of many here, we broke that monopoly by winning a majority in the Senate. And next year, 1982, with your help, we're going to finish the job on Capitol Hill by electing a Republican majority in the House. And we're going to strengthen the Republican majority that now exists in the Senate. I feel that deep down inside me. If this program, and I want to mention briefly, is successful, we are going to win control of the House of Representatives and get this country back to work again.

The mandate of 1980 was only a beginning. It was the birth of a new coalition in American politics, a major realignment, if you will, of the Nation's electorate. This new coalition, the Reagan coalition, created that mandate last November. It repudiated the old and discredited opposition philosophy, and it endorsed a real, not simply a rhetorical, program to restore our country's economic stability at home. And that program calls for several things.

First, a reduction in the growth of Federal Government spending. And if we're going to curb inflation and unconscionable interest rates, we've got to begin by curbing the excessive, wasteful spending policies and programs inspired and supported by the opposition leadership year in and year

337

out, fighting the very concept that we must control the growth of spending. That is the first ingredient of the Reagan program. And last week, under the great leadership of Senator Howard Baker and Pete Domenici, the inspired leadership in that Senate, we took a major step in that direction with the Senate cutting some $40 billion odd from the fiscal '82 budget.

And I'm happy to note that many members of the opposition, Democrats, joined in, responding to the people's wishes—joined the Republican majority in supporting the President. The vote was, I believe, 88 to 10. And we all owe a tremendous debt to Howard Baker and to Pete Domenici for spearheading this legislative effort to make that victory possible.

Let me tell you something about that vote. Amendment after amendment, I believe Howard told me today at lunch, there were 43 amendments—and a lot of them popular amendments, a lot of them molded so you could try to pull away a vote or two, voting for something that had a very attractive label on it. And under the leadership of Howard Baker and of Pete Domenici and others, we held that line firm in the United States Senate, and thus set the pattern saying to the people, "We are going to do what we were elected to do—control the growth of Federal spending"—a masterful job by the majority leader and by the chairman of the Budget Committee.

Now, we hope that that same approach will have the same results in the House of Representatives. And, believe me, if the people are heard from, if the people that vote out there across this country are heard from, I believe those same results are possible.

Secondly, the Reagan program for economic recovery calls for creating new jobs for millions of unemployed Americans who want to work by revitalizing our nation's productive capacity and encouraging investment in the private sector. And to do this the President's economic program calls for a bold, innovative tax program providing for a 10-percent, across-the-board rate cut every year for the next 3 years, and that next 3 years is important. We've got to be able to plan ahead so that we can invest and so that we can build and so we can put

this country back to work again. This program is the program that President Reagan campaigned on, was elected on last November, and its enactment is absolutely essential if we're going to make the promise of the Reagan mandate a reality and pull America out of this quagmire of economic stagnation.

And thirdly, the program for economic recovery calls for the elimination of excessive, wasteful Federal regulation. Within 24 hours after he took office, the President created a Regulatory Task Force and let it be known that he wanted that Task Force to go forward full speed toward one goal—getting the Federal Government off the backs of the American people in their daily lives and livelihood. We have regulated ourselves to death in the United States, and President Reagan is going to change it.

The President made me Chairman of that Task Force, and I can tell you his leadership is continual. That pressure is on us to perform, and we recognize the responsibility of government in protecting the environment. Of course we do. We recognize the Government's responsibility in the safety of the workingplace. Of course we do. But unrealistic, overzealous regulators have made a mockery of the good intentions, and by their arbitrary actions they've added tens of thousands of workers to the unemployment rolls, and they've threatened the very existence of some of these small businesses. Large businesses can cope, with big computers, a lot of people out there. But small businesses are being driven to their knees by the excesses of Federal regulation, and our Task Force has already taken action in several key areas of the economy.

Yesterday we moved to eliminate needless, burdensome regulations that have held down the productive capacity of the American automotive industry, and we're going to put unemployed Americans back to work. And our first step must be to free this economy from the shackles of unneeded bureaucratic regulation, and I just can't tell you how much I enjoy my job when it comes to this Regulatory Task Force. Something's going to happen out there, and it's going to be good for the working man in this country.

And fourth, as the President told the National Conference of Building and Construction Trades, we intend to cooperate with the overall economic program and have with it also, working with it, a monetary policy designed to stabilize the money supply, reduce inflation, and bring down interest rates.

And a fifth element of the program, though not directly related to economic recovery, is also fundamental to the meaning of the Reagan mandate, and we're determined to reverse the trend of recent decades where bureaucratic decisionmakers in Washington increase power at the expense of State, local, and county governments. The Founding Fathers created a Federal system based on the premise that the closer the government is to the people, the more responsive government will be to the needs and desire of the people. And that idea, untested in recent years as powers gravitated to Washington, is as true today as it was two centuries ago. And restoring that concept to relations between the national, State, local, and county governments is an integral part of the way President Reagan views his November mandate.

He feels strongly about getting those answers closer to the people and not having them all done right here in Washington, D.C. And as this federalism unfolds, I believe that those local governments will increase in excellence and increase in their responsiveness to the people if they feel they can have, through block grants, the funds to make possible their own priorities, take care of their own priorities at these various levels of government.

These are five ingredients, and three of them—the control of the growth of spending and the tax thing and the regulatory thing—are all part of it. But let me tell you what concerns me tonight, and I don't want to assign guilt to anybody that puts out a thousand bucks for a plate. That gets you in, and you shouldn't be harassed. But I'll tell you something about my own office.

I've had business guys come in, and they come down to the office and they say, "George, please tell the President down the hall we're all for him." And I say, "Oh, well, great. Thank you, sir," show them to the door. But, "While I have your attention, don't cut the XYZ Bank, because every dollar we spend on the XYZ Bank gets $10 down the road." "Thank you, sir, very much for your support." He goes out. Some guy from the university comes in. He says, "George, please tell the President that we're all for him. We are being clobbered by regulations." I had one president of a college tell me, $3 million for one medium-sized college and wrote, "Please tell him down the hall, we think he's doing a magnificent job." "Oh, thank you, sir." Start showing him to the door. "But while I have your attention, please don't touch student loans. Please don't tighten up on student loans. It's going to kill us." You cannot nickel and dime this program to death, and let me tell you something—we've got to hold it together.

We get this country back to work and produce and create and innovate and save, and then we'll have plenty of time to second guess the President of the United States. But for now, we need your help in holding this program together and getting it through the House and getting it through the Senate, so the people will say at last, "We have a President who did, after elected, what he said he was going to do." And that President, my friends, is Ronald Reagan.

Thank you very, very much.

Note: The Vice President spoke at 9:57 p.m. in the International Ballroom at the Washington Hilton Hotel.

Earlier in the evening, the Vice President attended a reception for the dinner chairmen in the East Room at the White House.

As printed above, the item follows the text of the White House press release.

Proclamation 4831—Victims Rights Week, 1981
April 8, 1981

By the President of the United States of America

A Proclamation

For too long, the victims of crime have been the forgotten persons of our criminal justice system. Rarely do we give victims the help they need or the attention they deserve. Yet the protection of our citizens—to guard them from becoming victims—is the primary purpose of our penal laws. Thus, each new victim personally represents an instance in which our system has failed to prevent crime. Lack of concern for victims compounds that failure.

Statistics reported by the Federal Bureau of Investigation and other law enforcement agencies indicate that crime continues to be a very serious national problem. But statistics cannot express the human tragedy of crime felt by those who are its victims. Only victims truly know the trauma crime can produce. They have lived it and will not soon forget it. At times, whole families are entirely disrupted—physically, financially and emotionally. Lengthy and complex judicial processes add to the victim's burden. Such experiences foster disillusionment and, ultimately, the belief that our system cannot protect us. As a Nation, we can ill afford this loss of faith on the part of innocent citizens who have been victimized by crimes.

We need a renewed emphasis on, and an enhanced sensitivity to, the rights of victims. These rights should be a central concern of those who participate in the criminal justice system, and it is time all of us paid greater heed to the plight of victims.

Now, Therefore, I, Ronald Reagan, President of the United States of America, do hereby proclaim the week beginning April 19, 1981, as Victims Rights Week. I urge all Federal, state and local officials involved in the criminal justice system to devote special attention to the needs of victims of crime, and to redouble their efforts to make our system responsive to those needs. I urge all other elected and appointed officials to join in this effort to make our justice system more helpful to those whom it was designed to protect. And I urge all citizens, from all walks of life, to remember that the personal tragedy of the victim is their own tragedy as well.

In Witness Whereof, I have hereunto set my hand this eighth day of April, in the year of our Lord nineteen hundred and eighty-one, and of the Independence of the United States of America the two hundred and fifth.

RONALD REAGAN

[*Filed with the Office of the Federal Register, 3:01 p.m., April 8, 1981*]

Executive Order 12303—Presidential Advisory Committee on Federalism
April 8, 1981

By the authority vested in me as President by the Constitution of the United States of America, and in order to establish, in accordance with the provisions of the Federal Advisory Committee Act, as amended (5 U.S.C. App. I), an advisory committee on federalism policy of the United States, it is hereby ordered as follows:

Section 1. Establishment. (a) There is established the Presidential Advisory Committee on Federalism. The Committee shall be composed of members from among private citizens of the United States, public officials from State and local governments, and members of the Legislative and Executive branches of the Federal government, who shall be appointed by the President. The members shall serve at the pleasure of the President.

(b) The President shall designate a Chairman from among the members of the Committee.

Sec. 2. Functions. The Committee shall advise the President with respect to the objectives and conduct of the overall federalism policy of the United States.

Sec. 3. Administration. (a) The heads of Executive agencies shall, to the extent permitted by law, provide the Committee such information with respect to federalism issues as it may require for the purpose of carrying out its functions.

(b) Members of the Committee shall serve without any compensation for their work on the Committee. However, they may be allowed travel expenses, including per diem in lieu of subsistence, as authorized by law for persons serving intermittently in the government service (5 U.S.C. 5701–5707), to the extent funds are available therefor.

(c) Any administrative support expenses of the Committee shall be paid from funds available to the White House Office.

Sec. 4. General. (a) Notwithstanding any other Executive order, the responsibilities of the President under the Federal Advisory Committee Act, as amended, shall be performed by the President, except that, the Administrator of General Services shall, on a reimbursable basis, provide such administrative services as may be requested.

(b) The Committee shall terminate on December 31, 1982, unless sooner extended.

RONALD REAGAN

The White House,
April 8, 1981.

[Filed with the Office of the Federal Register, 4:29 p.m., April 8, 1981]

Statement on Signing the Executive Order Establishing the Presidential Advisory Committee on Federalism
April 8, 1981

The Presidential federalism advisory committee that I am forming today is a first step in helping me to restore a proper constitutional relationship between the Federal, State, and local governments. Unfortunately, our decentralized system of government has over the years been bent out of shape. The Federal Government too often has treated elected State and local officials as if they were nothing more than administrative agents for Federal authority. I will look to this Advisory Committee to help me find ways to return towards a proper balance.

The people who make up State and local governments are as capable as any in Washington, D.C. My administration looks forward to working with them in concrete ways. We need to provide for greater authority and responsibility in the States, counties, cities, and towns—to return government to those closest to the people most affected.

I am particularly pleased that my good friend Senator Paul Laxalt, who served in county government before being elected Lieutenant Governor and then Governor of the State of Nevada, has agreed to serve as Chairman of this Committee. I am further pleased that a bipartisan cross section of Governors, State legislators, mayors, county officials, and Members of Congress have agreed to serve on this Committee.

Appointment of the Membership of the Presidential Advisory Committee on Federalism and the Coordinating Task Force on Federalism
April 8, 1981

The President today announced the creation of the Presidential Advisory Committee on Federalism to be chaired by Senator Paul Laxalt.

The purposes of the Committee are to provide for:
—full and adequate input to him on Federal legislative proposals impacting on the States and localities;
—advice for the administration in implementing its federalism proposals; and
—assistance in developing long-term policies to reverse the current trend of greater control over State and local programs by the Federal Government.

The Presidential Advisory Committee on Federalism also will have a Coordinating Task Force on Federalism chaired by Senator Laxalt.

The Federal, State, and local officials and private citizens who will serve on the Presidential Advisory Committee on Federalism and the Coordinating Task Force on Federalism are:

Presidential Advisory Committee on Federalism

Governors:

Gov. George Busbee (D-Georgia)
Gov. Scott M. Matheson (D-Utah)
Gov. Lamar Alexander (R-Tennessee)
Gov. James R. Thompson (R-Illinois)
Gov. Pierre S. DuPont IV (R-Delaware)
Gov. Richard A. Snelling (R-Vermont)

State Legislators:

Representaitve T. W. (Tom) Stivers (R-Idaho)
Senator Ross O. Doyen (R-Kansas)
Senator Ann Lindeman (R-Arizona)
Speaker Benjamin L. Cardin (D-Maryland)
Speaker John J. Hainkel, Jr. (D-Louisiana)
Assemblyman Dean Rhoads (R-Nevada)

Mayors:

Mayor Edward I. Koch (D-New York City)
Mayor William H. Hudnut III (R-Indianapolis)
Mayor Margaret Hance (R-Phoenix)
Mayor Ferd Harrison (R-Scotland Neck, N.C.)
Mayor Tom Moody (R-Columbus, Ohio)

County Officials:

J. Richard Conder (D-Richmond County, N.C.)
Roy Orr (D-Dallas County, Tex.)
William Murphy (R-Rensselaer County, N.Y.)
Sandra Smoley (R-Sacramento County, Calif.)
Bruce Nestande (Nonpartisan-Orange County, Calif.)
Donald L. Smith (R-Anchorage Municipality, Alaska)

Members of the U.S. Senate:

Senator William V. Roth, Jr. (R-Delaware)
Senator David Durenberger (R-Minnesota)
Senator Pete V. Domenici (R-New Mexico)
Senator David L. Boren (D-Oklahoma)
Senator Ernest F. Hollings (D-South Carolina)
Senator Paul Laxalt (R-Nevada)

Members of the House of Representatives:

Representative Richard T. Schulze (R-Pennsylvania)
Representative Richard Bolling (D-Missouri)
Representative L. H. Fountain (D-North Carolina)
Representative Clarence Brown (R-Ohio)
Representative Frank Horton (R-New York)
Representative Jack Brooks (D-Texas)

Private Citizens:

F. Clifton White
Dr. Robert B. Hawkins
C. D. Ward
Former Senator Clifford Hansen
Former Gov. Otis Bowen

The Coordinating Task Force on Federalism

Senator Paul Laxalt, Chairman
Secretary Terrel Bell
Secretary Samuel Pierce
Secretary Donald Regan
Secretary Richard Schweiker
Secretary James Watt

Director David Stockman
Edwin Meese III
James A. Baker III
Richard S. Williamson
Martin Anderson
Robert Carleson

Letter to the House Minority Leader Concerning the Program for Economic Recovery
April 8, 1981

Dear Bob:

I've been delighted by the progress in moving our economic recovery program forward. I'm sure you regret as I do the House Budget Committee's recent actions, however. I fear that too many of our colleagues in the House prefer that we return to business as usual—that we can solve the problems of the future by continuing the economic mistakes of the past.

On my behalf, would you please convey my strongest concern that we redouble our efforts to enact *all* the key elements of our plan for economic recovery. Together, we can gain a significant victory for the American people.

Sincerely,

RON

P.S. I promise to "suit up" and come off the bench as soon as possible.

[The Honorable Robert H. Michel, House of Representatives, Washington, D.C. 20515]

Note: The text of the letter was made available by the Office of the Press Secretary on April 9.

Statement on the Death of General Omar N. Bradley
April 9, 1981

I join all Americans in mourning the death of General of the Army Omar N. Bradley. For 69 years he wore the colors of an American soldier—with courage, integrity, professionalism, and, above all, honor. Even as he rose in rank, humility never left his side. He was the "GI's General" because he was, always, a GI.

In World War II his conspicuously brilliant leadership thrust him to the top of the U.S. military command. Whether at Normandy, North Africa, or Sicily, the Bradley command always meant good fortune for freedom's defenders.

General Bradley's memory will be revered by his countrymen. He left to us exemplary qualities that long will be the standard of every soldier who takes the solemn pledge to defend this Nation.

Nancy and I were honored to have Omar Bradley as our friend, and honored that one of his last public appearances was at my Inauguration. Both of us extend to General Bradley's family our deepest sympathies.

Proclamation 4832—Death of General Bradley
April 9, 1981

*By the President of the United States
of America*

A Proclamation

To the People of the United States:

With sadness, I announce the death of General of the Army Omar Nelson Bradley, who died yesterday in New York City.

For sixty-nine years General Bradley wore the colors of an American soldier—with courage, integrity, professionalism and, above all, honor. Even as he rose in rank, humility never left his side. He was the "G.I.'s General" because he was, always, a G.I.

In World War II his conspicuously brilliant leadership thrust him to the top of the U.S. military command. Whether at Normandy, North Africa, or Sicily, the Bradley command always meant good fortune for freedom's defenders.

General Bradley's memory will be revered by his countrymen. He left to us exemplary qualities that long will be the standard of every soldier who takes the solemn pledge to defend this Nation.

As a mark of respect for the memory of General Bradley, I hereby order that the flag of the United States shall be flown at half-staff upon all public buildings and grounds, at all military posts and naval stations, and on all naval vessels of the Federal Government in the District of Columbia and throughout the United States and its Territories and possessions until his interment. I also direct that the flag shall be flown at half-staff for the same length of time at all United States embassies, legations, consular offices, and other facilities abroad, including all military facilities and naval vessels and stations.

In Witness Whereof, I have hereunto set my hand this ninth day of April, in the year of our Lord nineteen hundred and eighty-one, and of the Independence of the United States of America the two hundred and fifth.

RONALD REAGAN

[*Filed with the Office of the Federal Register, 4:20 p.m., April 9, 1981*]

Statement by Deputy Press Secretary Speakes About the NATO Defense Ministers Position on Poland
April 9, 1981

The President is very pleased by this strong expression of allied unity. It reflects the results of the full and extensive consultations which the administration has had with our European allies since January 20. The President, the Secretaries of State and Defense, and other senior administration officials have met frequently with European leaders both here and abroad. This series of talks has resulted in common understandings on the key problems facing the Alliance. The President is gratified that that sense of understanding has been made dramatically clear by the statement of the NATO Defense Ministers. He believes the statement has made a significant contribution to the prospects for world peace.

Note: Deputy Press Secretary Speakes read the statement at the daily press briefing in the Briefing Room at the White House.

On April 8 the NATO Defense Ministers, meeting as the Nuclear Planning Group in Bonn, Federal Republic of Germany, issued a statement which supported the linking of Soviet intervention in Poland with effective arms control negotiations.

Nomination of Kenneth Albert Gilles To Be Administrator of the Federal Grain Inspection Service
April 9, 1981

The President today announced his intention to nominate Kenneth Albert Gilles to be Administrator of the Federal Grain Inspection Service, Department of Agriculture.

Since 1961 Dr. Gilles has been associated with the North Dakota State University. In 1961–70 he was professor and chairman, Department of Cereal Technology; vice president for agricultural affairs since 1969; acting director, Cooperative Extension Service in 1972–74; acting director, Agricultural Experiment Station in 1978–79.

Previously Dr. Gilles served as a senior biochemist with General Mills, Inc., and a research engineer with the Pillsbury Co.

He was editor-in-chief of Cereal Chemistry; president of the American Association of Cereal Chemists; chairman of the Great Plains Agricultural Council; and chairman of the legislative committee for USDA budget, division of agriculture, National Association of State Universities and Land Grant Colleges. He is the author or coauthor of more than 100 publications. In August 1979 he was selected to address the Wheat Chemistry and Technology Seminar in Tokyo, sponsored by the American Association of Cereal Chemists, the Japan Flour Millers Association, and the Canadian and Australian Wheat Boards.

Dr. Gilles was graduated from the University of Minnesota (B.S., Ph. D.). He is married, has two children, and resides in Fargo, N. Dak. He was born in Minnesota, Minn., on March 6, 1922.

Nomination of Harold V. Hunter To Be Administrator of the Rural Electrification Administration
April 9, 1981

The President today announced his intention to nominate Harold V. Hunter to be Administrator of the Rural Electrification Administration, Department of Agriculture, for a term of 10 years.

Mr. Hunter has been owner and operator of HVH Farms in Waukomis, Okla. He was chairman of the national board of directors of the American Polled Hereford Association in 1972 and was a member of the board in 1969–74. In 1972 Mr. Hunter was United States delegate to the World Hereford Congress, Union of South Africa. He was president of the Oklahoma Polled Hereford Association for four terms.

Since 1965 Mr. Hunter has served on the board of directors of the Waukomis State Bank. He was a member of the Oklahoma House of Representatives in 1962–69 and served as Republican assistant floor leader. In 1969–77 he was Oklahoma State executive director of the Agricultural Stabilization and Conservation Service. In 1973 Mr. Hunter was a Department of State team member to the Government Wheat Stabilization Program in Afghanistan.

Mr. Hunter is married, has two children, and resides in Waukomis, Okla. He was born in Waukomis on August 14, 1917.

Nomination of Michael J. Fenello To Be Deputy Administrator of the Federal Aviation Administration
April 9, 1981

The President today announced his intention to nominate Michael J. Fenello to be Deputy Administrator, Federal Aviation Administration, Department of Transportation.

Since 1943 Mr. Fenello has held various positions with Eastern Airlines. He was a pilot with Eastern in 1943 and 1946–63. In 1963 Mr. Fenello joined Eastern Airlines management as assistant operations manager in New York. He was director of administration flight operations in Miami, Fla., in 1963–68. Mr. Fenello was division vice president, operations coordination, and assistant to the vice president of the operations group in 1968–72. In 1972–76 he was vice president of operational control. In 1976–81 he was vice president of systems operations and safety. He is currently retired.

Mr. Fenello has flown over 12,000 hours. While an active pilot, he served as master chairman, Air Line Pilots Association, and on ALPA national committees. He is responsible for the development of the present Eastern Control Center.

Mr. Fenello was graduated from Buffalo State College (B.S., 1938) and New York University (M.A., 1941). He attended U.S. Navy Flight School in 1943. He was also a U.S. Navy pilot during World War II in 1943–46.

Mr. Fenello is married, has three daughters, and resides with his family in Eustis, Fla. He was born in Rochester, N.Y., on January 22, 1916.

Nomination of Jean Tufts To Be an Assistant Secretary of Education
April 9, 1981

The President today announced his intention to nominate Jean Tufts to be Assistant Secretary for Special Education and Rehabilitative Services, Department of Education.

Mrs. Tufts has served as president of the National School Boards Association since 1980 and has been on the board of directors of that organization since 1970. She was a member of the New Hampshire State Board of Education in 1970–75 and also served on the New Hampshire Library Commission. Mrs. Tufts has been a consultant, preschool programs for the handicapped, New Hampshire State Department of Education.

In 1974–79 Mrs. Tufts was executive director, Rehabilitation Center, Portsmouth, N.H. She was senior project officer, New England Program in Teacher Education, in 1973–79; and executive director, Greater Manchester Child Care Association.

Mrs. Tufts was principal of Rockingham School for Special Children in 1961–70. She has been involved in other national, State, and local services, including the Council of Exceptional Children; delegate to the National Conference on Children and Youth in 1972–73; and the Governor's Task Force on Education, Special Education, in 1970.

Mrs. Tufts was graduated from Boston University (B.S., 1945; M.A., 1963). She is married, has four children, and resides with her family in Exeter, N.H. She was born in Melrose, Mass., on October 7, 1927.

Nomination of George A. Conn To Be Commissioner of the Rehabilitation Services Administration
April 9, 1981

The President today announced his intention to nominate George A. Conn to be Commissioner of the Rehabilitation Services Administration, Department of Education.

Mr. Conn has worked with the Paralyzed Veterans of America since 1979. From March 1979 to March 1980, he was national research director and recently served as national legislative director of the organization. In 1978 he was a self-employed consultant with the design and engineering section of the General Services Administration at the National Institutes of Health on structural remediation of the Lister Hill Bio-Medical Communication Systems Center. Mr. Conn was special assistant to the Executive Director and Director of Planning, White House Conference on Handicapped Individuals, in 1975–77. He was Director, Office of Public Information, Rehabilitation Services Administration (RSA), of the De-

partment of Health, Education, and Welfare in 1972–75. In 1963–66 he was assistant director of public relations, Morton Salt Co., Chicago, Ill.

Mr. Conn was a member of the RSA task force on implementation of the Rehabilitation Act of 1973; special sections on the Office on Handicapped Individuals, Architectural and Transportation Barriers Compliance Board. He was a member of the recreation subcommittee of the President's Committee on Employment of the Handicapped.

Mr. Conn has served as president of the League of Disabled Voters and vice president of the National Paraplegia Foundation. He was graduated from Northwestern University, School of Speech (B.S., 1955). He is married and has four children. He resides with his family in Millersville, Md. He was born in Evanston, Ill., on April 24, 1933.

Proclamation 4833—African Refugee Relief Day
April 9, 1981

By the President of the United States of America

A Proclamation

The American people are blessed with freedom and material abundance, yet they are not deaf to the cries of agony from those who suffer deprivation. Today, cries for help are heard from Africa where more than 4 million of our fellow human beings have been displaced.

The United States applauds the humanitarian efforts of the nations which take in these refugees. Host nations are often themselves poor in resources and their willingness to accept refugees is exemplary of the best in the human spirit.

Americans are a compassionate people and will do their part, either through government or through voluntary contributions.

With this in mind, Congress has, by joint resolution, requested me to designate April 9, 1981, as African Refugee Relief Day and to call upon the people of the United States to observe that day by increasing their awareness of the plight of the African refugee. Further, I call on Americans of all faiths to involve themselves directly in this problem with their prayers and with contributions to recognized private voluntary agencies which provide care and relief to African refugees.

Now, Therefore, I, Ronald Reagan, President of the United States of America, do

347

hereby designate April 9, 1981, as African Refugee Relief Day.

In Witness Whereof, I have hereunto set my hand this ninth day of April, in the year of our Lord nineteen hundred and eighty-one, and of the Independence of the United States of America the two hundred and fifth.

RONALD REAGAN

[*Filed with the Office of the Federal Register, 4:21 p.m., April 9, 1981*]

Message to the *Columbia* Astronauts on the Inaugural Flight of the Space Shuttle
April 9, 1981

Commander John W. Young and Captain Robert L. Crippen, you go forward this morning in a daring enterprise, and you take the hopes and prayers of all Americans with you. You go in the hand of God and draw on the courage of life.

Our countryman and poet William Cullen Bryant said America is where mankind throws its last fetters. With your exploits, we loosen one more. Who, he said, shall place a limit to the giant's strength, or curb his swiftness in the forward race?

Through you, today, we all feel as giants once again. Once again we feel the surge of pride that comes from knowing we are the best, and we are so because we are free.

For all Americans, Nancy and I thank you and the 50,000 others who have worked to make this day possible. As you hurtle from Earth in a craft unlike any other ever constructed, you will do so in a feat of American technology and American will.

May God bless you, and may God bring you safely home to us, again.

Note: The flight, originally scheduled for Friday morning, April 10, was postponed because of equipment malfunction. The Columbia was successfully launched on Sunday morning, April 12.

Nomination of Thomas Patrick Melady To Be an Assistant Secretary of Education
April 10, 1981

The President today announced his intention to nominate Thomas Patrick Melady to be Assistant Secretary for Postsecondary Education, Department of Education.

Since 1976 Dr. Melady has been president of Sacred Heart University where he is also a professor of political science. He has been serving as chairman of the Connecticut Conference of Independent Colleges.

He served previously as Ambassador to Burundi and to Uganda. He was a member of the U.S. delegation to the United Nations. Dr. Melady was executive vice president of St. Joseph's University, Philadelphia, Pa., prior to his position at Sacred Heart

University. He was chairman of the department of Asian studies and nonwestern civilization at Seton Hall University.

Dr. Melady is a member of the board of directors of the National Conference of Christians and Jews, the International League of Human Rights, and the International Institute of Connecticut.

Dr. Melady was graduated from Duquesne University (B.A.) and Catholic University of America (M.A., Ph. D.).

Born in Norwich, Conn., on March 4, 1927, Dr. Melady is married and has two children. He resides with his family in Fairfield, Conn.

Appointment of Anna C. Chennault as a Member and Vice Chairman of the President's Export Council
April 10, 1981

The President today announced his intention to appoint Anna C. Chennault as a member and Vice Chairman of the President's Export Council.

Mrs. Chennault began her career as a war correspondent for the Central News Agency in 1944–48 and became their special Washington correspondent in 1965, a position she still holds today. She was a feature writer with Hsin Ming Daily News in Shanghai in 1944–49; with the Civil Air Transport in Taipai, Taiwan, in 1946–57 and served as public relations officer in 1947–57. In 1958–63 she was chief, Chinese section, machine translation research, Georgetown University. In 1963–66 Mrs. Chennault was a broadcaster for Voice of America and U.S. correspondent for Hsin Shen Daily News in Washington. She became vice president of the Flying Tiger Line, Inc., in 1968. She currently serves as president, TAC International of Washington, D.C.

She is the author of "Chennault and the Flying Tigers; Way of a Fighter," 1949, and "A Thousand Springs," 1962.

Mrs. Chennault has been very active in the Republican Party, serving as chairman of the National Republican Heritage Council, member of the Republican Finance Committee and, since 1960, has served as the committeewoman for the Washington, D.C., Republican Party.

Mrs. Chennault was graduated from Ling Nan University, Hong Kong (B.A., 1944); Lincoln University (LL.D.).

She is a widow and has two children. She resides in Washington, D.C. Mrs. Chennault was born in Peking, China, on June 23, 1925.

Appointments to the White House Office of Intergovernmental Affairs
April 10, 1981

The President today announced the following appointments to the Office of Intergovernmental Affairs:

Alan F. Holmer to be Deputy Assistant to the President and Deputy to Richard S. Williamson, Assistant to the President for Intergovernmental Affairs. Formerly he was an attorney with the Washington, D.C., law firm of Steptoe & Johnson. From 1972 to 1978, Mr. Holmer was administrative assistant to Senator Bob Packwood (R-Oreg.). During the 1980 primaries, he was an adviser to the Reagan campaign on natural resource issues and was a volunteer in Oregon during the 1980 general election campaign. Mr. Holmer was graduated from Princeton University Law Center (J.D., 1978). He is married and has one child. Mr. Holmer resides in McLean, Va.

Judy F. Peachee to be Special Assistant to the President for Intergovernmental Affairs, with management responsibilities for liaison with State legislatures. In addition, she will be responsible for working with State and local officials to eliminate sex discrimination in State laws. From 1978 to 1981, she was special assistant for State affairs for Senator John W. Warner (R-Va.) and from 1974 to 1977, was appointments secretary to Governor Mills E. Godwin, Jr. (R-Va.) and staff liaison to the Virginia Commission on the Status of Women. She served from 1976 to 1980 as Virginia's Republican national committeewoman. Mrs. Peachee attended Madison College in Harrisonburg, Va., and graduated from St. Lukes Hospital School of Technology. She has three children and resides in Richmond, Va.

James M. Medas to be Special Assistant to the President for Intergovernmental Affairs, with responsibilities including maintaining liaison with Governors and other statewide elected officials. He was formerly chief of staff for the California State Senate minority leader and a practicing attorney in Los Angeles. Mr. Medas is a graduate of Miami University (B.A., 1965) and Harvard Law School (J.D., 1968). In 1980 he served as director of voter activities in California for the Reagan-Bush campaign and the California Republican Party.

J. Steven Rhodes to be Special Assistant to the President for Intergovernmental Affairs, with management responsibility for liaison with city and county officials. From 1973 to 1981, Mr. Rhodes was associated with Dart Industries, Inc., in Los Angeles, most recently as director of government and public affairs. He was graduated from Loyola Marymount University (B.A., 1973) and Pepperdine University (M.B.A., 1977). Mr. Rhodes was born in New Orleans, La. He is married and has one child.

Penny L. Eastman to be special assistant to Richard S. Williamson, Assistant to the President for Intergovernmental Affairs, with responsibilities including work relating to the Regulatory Relief Task Force. Most recently, Ms. Eastman was employed by the law firm of Winston & Strawn. From 1973 to 1978, she was a congressional aide to Representatives Larry Winn (R-Kans.), William H. Hudnut III (R-Ind.), and Philip M. Crane (R-Ill.). During the primary and general election campaign, she was an assistant to the campaign chairman, Senator Paul Laxalt. She attended high school and college in the Washington, D.C., area. Ms. Eastman was born in Washington, D.C., and currently resides in Falls Church, Va.

Susan Hawkes to be deputy to James M. Medas, Special Assistant to the President for Intergov-

ernmental Affairs. She was previously an attorney with the law firm of Patmont & Myers in San Francisco. Recently she served as counsel to the senior policy advisor for intergovernmental affairs in the Office of the President-elect. Ms. Hawkes is a graduate of Mills College (B.A., 1976) and Golden Gate University School of Law (J.D., 1980). She was born in Washington, D.C., and is currently a resident of Arlington, Va.

Eve Baskowitz to be deputy to J. Steven Rhodes, Special Assistant to the President for Intergovernmental Affairs. Formerly Miss Baskowitz was employed in the Washington office of the law firm of Winston & Strawn. During the 1980 Presidential election campaign, she was coordinator of the business advisory task force. She graduated from Sweet Briar College. Miss Baskowitz was born in St. Louis, Mo., and resides in Alexandria, Va.

Robert R. Gleason, Jr., to be deputy to Judy F. Peachee, Special Assistant to the President for Intergovernmental Affairs. He was formerly executive assistant to the cochairman of the Republican National Committee and from 1971 to 1976, was assistant to the executive director of the National Association of Trade & Technical Schools. He was site coordinator for the 1980 Republican election night activities in Washington, D.C., and was transportation coordinator for the 1980 Republican National Convention. A graduate of Tri-State College, Indiana (B.S., 1969), Mr. Gleason is married and has lived in Washington, D.C., for 11 years. He was born in Jersey City, N.J.

Statement Upon Leaving George Washington University Hospital
April 11, 1981

As my stay at the George Washington University Hospital reaches its end, I want to express my deep and heartfelt appreciation to all who have contributed to my care. The entire staff at the hospital contributed to my comfort and recovery, and I will always remember their special efforts on my behalf.

I look forward, of course, to returning to the White House. And I return with a new respect for the men and women who serve in the medical profession and with tremendous gratitude for their dedication, professionalism, and genuine concern for their

fellow man. They represent the best of America, and I am proud to know them.

Tim McCarthy and Tom Delahanty have returned home to their families and friends, and Jim Brady continues to make great progress. All of us have much to be thankful for, and we join in a salute to those who have made their life's work the care of their fellow man.

Note: The President returned to the White House by motorcade late Saturday morning after greeting and thanking hospital staff members assembled in the hospital.

Nomination of Kent Lloyd To Be a Deputy Under Secretary of Education
April 13, 1981

The President today announced his intention to nominate Kent Lloyd to be Deputy Under Secretary for Management, Department of Education.

Since 1967 Dr. Lloyd has served as president, Center for Leadership Development, a private management development corporation. He was recently special consultant for reorganization and management to Secretary of Education Terrel Bell.

He was project director, Management Performance Seminars for Vocational Education Directors, funded and cosponsored by Utah and Arizona State Departments of Education. Since 1977 Dr. Lloyd was project codirector, Management Performance Seminars for Principals in California School Districts.In 1976 he served as project codirector, Management Performance Seminars for Bilingual Education Administrators in California School Districts.

In 1971 Dr. Lloyd was senior associate, Planned Organization Change Through Executive Consulting and Management Team Building, Office of the Comptroller, Federal Housing Administration.

Dr. Lloyd was professor of management, Graduate School of Business and Management, Pepperdine University, in 1970–74. He was visiting professor, political science department, University of California at Los Angeles, in 1970. Dr. Lloyd was graduated from Brigham Young University (B.S., 1955); Wayne State University (M.P.A., 1959); and Stanford University (Ph. D., 1964).

Dr. Lloyd is married, has seven children, and resides with his family in La Jolla, Calif. He was born in Grace, Idaho, on March 5, 1931.

Statement on the Death of Former World Heavyweight Boxing Champion Joe Louis
April 13, 1981

I was privileged and will always be grateful to have had Joe Louis as my friend.

The son of an Alabama sharecropper, Joe Louis fought his way to the top of professional boxing and into the hearts of millions of Americans. Out of the ring, he was a considerate and soft-spoken man; inside the ring, his courage, strength, and consummate skill wrote a unique and unforgettable chapter in sports history.

But Joe Louis was more than a sports legend—his career was an indictment of racial bigotry and a source of pride and inspiration to millions of white and black people around the world.

All of America mourns his loss, and we convey our sympathy to his family and friends. But we also share their pride in his professional achievements, his service to his country, and his strength of heart and spirit.

Note: On April 16 the White House announced that at the request of Mrs. Louis, the President waived the burial requirements for Arlington National Cemetery to allow Joe Louis to be buried there.

Statement Honoring the Freed American Hostages
April 13, 1981

I am pleased to join the Department of State in honoring those members of the Foreign Service who were held captive in Iran and those who worked on their behalf during their 444-day ordeal. Every American remembers with pride the dignity, determination, and quiet courage with which they withstood the abuse of their captors. We remember the joy and thanksgiving that united the Nation on their release.

We must be resolved that this cruel episode in our history shall not be forgotten—that we will ensure our professional diplomats and military personnel every means of protection that America can offer.

We also owe thanks to the families of those held captive and of their fellows in the Foreign Service who worked and prayed so hard for their return. But the deepest debt of all is to those eight Americans who gave their lives in an effort to win freedom for their fellow citizens. All these citizens, with their dedication, are the basis of America's strength.

Note: Secretary of State Alexander M. Haig, Jr., read the statement during ceremonies at the Department of State honoring the diplomatic and U.S. Marine personnel who had been held captive in Iran.

Proclamation 4834—Mother's Day, 1981
April 13, 1981

By the President of the United States of America

A Proclamation

Each year our Nation designates Mother's Day as a moment of special tribute and appreciation for the mothers of America.

Recent years have brought many changes to the lives of American mothers. Today they are increasingly involved in business, politics, education, arts, sciences, and government as well as the vital work of the home and family. Yet, whether they seek careers outside the home or work as homemakers, they remain the heart of the American family.

They shape the character of our people through the love and nurture of their children. It is the strength they give their families that keeps our Nation strong.

On this Mother's Day, we express our deep personal gratitude to our own mothers and thank all those women whose devotion to their families helps sustain a healthy and productive citizenry.

Now, Therefore, I, Ronald Reagan, President of the United States of America, do hereby designate Sunday, May 10, 1981, as Mother's Day. I direct Government officials to display the flag of the United States on all Federal Government buildings, and I urge all citizens to display the flag at their homes and other suitable places on that day.

In Witness Whereof, I have hereunto set my hand this thirteenth day of April, in the year of our Lord nineteen hundred eighty-one, and of the Independence of the United States of America the two hundred and fifth.

RONALD REAGAN

[*Filed with the Office of the Federal Register, 4:44 p.m., April 13, 1981*]

Statement on the Landing of the Space Shuttle *Columbia* Following Its Inaugural Flight
April 14, 1981

Your brave adventure has opened a new era in space travel. You put new worlds within closer reach and more knowledge within our grasp.

We thank God for your safe return.

You were right, Captain Crippen, when you said the *Columbia* and her voyage would mean much to this country and to the world. Today the world watched us in triumph. Today our friends and our adversaries are reminded that we are a free people capable of great deeds. We are a free people in search of progress for mankind, and today we found a little more.

We are grateful to you and to those who have worked with you. We are proud of you, and we are proud of our country.

Welcome home.

Note: Assistant to the President James A. Baker III read the statement at welcoming ceremonies for Comdr. John W. Young and Capt. Robert L. Crippen, who had earlier landed the Columbia *at Edwards Air Force Base, Calif. The ceremonies were held at Ellington Air Force Base near the Johnson Space Center in Houston, Tex.*

Proclamation 4835—Import Quota on Peanuts
April 14, 1981

By the President of the United States of America

A Proclamation

By Proclamation No. 4807 of December 4, 1980, the quantity of certain peanuts permitted entry into the customs territory of the United States during a quota year was increased 200 million pounds on a temporary and emergency basis.

The increase of quantity was to be effective pending further action; specifically, after receipt of a report of findings and recommendations of the United States International Trade Commission, which was scheduled to conduct an investigation into this matter pursuant to section 22 of the Agricultural Adjustment Act of 1933, as amended (7 U.S.C. 624). The Commission has conducted an investigation and reported its findings and recommendations.

On the basis of the Commission's investigation and report, I find and declare that through July 31, 1981, the entry of 300 million pounds of peanuts—which would otherwise be under the terms and conditions specified in item 951.01 of part 3 of the Appendix to the Tariff Schedules of the United States—in addition to the quota quantity specified for such peanuts in item 951.00 of part 3 of the Appendix to the Tariff Schedules of the United States, will not render or tend to render ineffective, or materially interfere with, the price support operations now being conducted by the Department of Agriculture for peanuts, or reduce substantially the amount of any product processed in the United States from domestic peanuts with respect to which such program is now being undertaken.

Now, Therefore, I, Ronald Reagan, President of the United States of America, by the authority vested in me by section 22 of the Agricultural Adjustment Act, as amended, do hereby proclaim: that item 951.01 of part 3 of the Appendix to the Tariff Schedules of the United States, as added by Proclamation No. 4807, is hereby amended by changing the figure "200 million" to read "300 million" and by changing the date

"June 30, 1981" to read "July 31, 1981"; and, that section (2) of Proclamation No. 4807 is amended by changing "July 1, 1981" to read "August 1, 1981."

In Witness Whereof, I have hereunto set my hand this fourteenth day of April, in the year of our Lord nineteen hundred eighty-one, and of the Independence of the United States of America the two hundred fifth.

RONALD REAGAN

[*Filed with the Office of the Federal Register, 11 a.m., April 15, 1981*]

Proclamation 4836—Loyalty Day, 1981
April 14, 1981

By the President of the United States of America

A Proclamation

One of the great treasures of America is the unity of its people. No nation is composed of citizens with such diverse cultural, racial and religious backgrounds as is the United States of America. And while the unique contributions of each segment of our population are important, the significant fact remains that each of us, whatever background, remains loyal to the Nation and to the ideals of freedom for which it stands.

Throughout our history, all Americans have toiled together to build this land into the freest and most prosperous Nation on earth. And when the times required it, our people stood shoulder-to-shoulder proclaiming to any in the world who would threaten, that all were Americans and proud of it.

Seldom are we called upon to consciously consider and express loyalty to our Nation and its ideals of liberty. It would be well to do so. The world is filled with tyranny and deprivation. Each of us can thank God that we are living in this blessed land. And when differences arise among us, which is only natural in a free society, we should always remain aware that we are one people, together and indivisible.

As we strive to solve the problems confronting us, it is appropriate to stop for a moment and reflect upon our national institutions, our heritage of freedom and what it means to be an American.

To encourage such reflection, a joint resolution of the Congress was enacted on July 18, 1958 (72 Stat. 369, 36 U.S.C. 162), designating the first day of May of each year as Loyalty Day, and requesting that the President issue an annual proclamation inviting public observance.

Now, Therefore, I, Ronald Reagan, President of the United States of America, call upon all Americans and upon patriotic, civic, and educational organizations to observe Friday, May 1, 1981, as Loyalty Day, with appropriate ceremonies.

I call upon officials of the Government to display the flag of the United States on all Government buildings and grounds on that day in testimony of our loyalty.

In Witness Whereof, I have hereunto set my hand this fourteenth day of April, in the year of our Lord nineteen hundred eighty-one, and of the Independence of the United States of America the two hundred and fifth.

RONALD REAGAN

[*Filed with the Office of the Federal Register, 2:44 p.m., April 15, 1981*]

Note: The text of the proclamation was released by the Office of the Press Secretary on April 15.

Message to the Congress Transmitting a Report of the United States Sinai Support Mission
April 15, 1981

To the Congress of the United States:

I am pleased to transmit herewith the Eleventh Report of the United States Sinai Support Mission. It covers the Mission's activities during the six-month period ending April 1, 1981. This report is provided in accordance with Section 4 of Public Law 94 110 of October 13, 1975.

The Sinai Support Mission was established in January 1976 to implement the United States Proposal in the September 1975 Second Sinai Disengagement Agreement to install and operate a tactical early warning system in the Sinai Peninsula. The United States continued to operate the early warning system until January 25, 1980, under the 1979 Egyptian-Israeli Peace Treaty.

Because it was not possible to gain United Nations Security Council agreement to assume responsibility for supervising the security arrangements called for by the Peace Treaty, the United States agreed during September 1979 talks with Egypt and Israel to monitor adherence to the Treaty's military limitations. Verification inspections, conducted by the Sinai Field Mission, began in April 1980 and will continue until April 25, 1982, the scheduled date for total Israeli withdrawal from the Sinai.

My Administration has initiated bilateral discussions with both Parties on the security arrangements to be implemented in the Sinai following Israel's final withdrawal. The United States intends to carry out its commitment to ensure the establishment and maintenance of an acceptable alternative multinational force if it proves impossible for the United Nations to support the security arrangements under the Treaty. We share the desire of both Parties to move forward expeditiously on this question. We will keep the Congress fully informed and will consult as our discussions of this matter progress.

Funding of the Sinai Support Mission for Fiscal Year 1981 is authorized under Chapter 6, Part II of the Foreign Assistance Act, "Peacekeeping Operations," at $16 million. For Fiscal Year 1982, only $10 million is being requested, a level that will fund both the Mission's operations during its final months and the projected costs of its phase-out after April 25, 1982.

Our nation has contributed substantially to the promotion of peace in this critical part of the Middle East, and the Congress can be proud of the accomplishments of the Sinai Support and Field Missions. I am counting on your continued support for this aspect of our efforts to achieve a lasting peace in the Middle East.

RONALD REAGAN

The White House,
April 15, 1981.

Note: The report is entitled "Report to the Congress—SSM: United States Sinai Support Mission" (14 pages plus annexes).

Nomination of Robert Melvin Worthington To Be an Assistant Secretary of Education
April 15, 1981

The President today announced his intention to nominate Robert Melvin Worthington to be Assistant Secretary for Vocational and Adult Education, Department of Education.

Since 1979 Mr. Worthington has served as associate commissioner of higher education, Utah State Board of Regents. In 1974–79 he was chairman and senior research associate, Career Development Associated, Inc., Princeton, N.J. He was a visiting professor of education, Rutgers University Graduate School of Education in 1973–74. In 1971–73 Mr. Worthington was Associate U.S. Commissioner of Education; Director, Bureau of Adult, Vocational and Technical Education, Department of Health, Education, and Welfare. He was assistant commissioner of education; director, Division of Vocational Education, New Jersey State Department of Education in 1965–71. In 1958–65 Mr. Worthington was professor and chairman, Department of Industrial Education and Technology, Trenton State College, Trenton, N.J. He previously served as an instructor and teaching assistant at Purdue University and the University of Minnesota.

Mr. Worthington was graduated from Eastern Kentucky State University (B.S., 1948) and the University of Minnesota (M.A., 1949; Ph. D., 1958).

Mr. Worthington resides in Salt Lake City, Utah. He was born in Saskatchewan, Canada, on May 31, 1922. He is a naturalized American citizen. He served as an officer in the U.S. Army Air Corps in 1942–47. He is a recipient of many educational honors, including the University of Minnesota Board of Regents Outstanding Achievement Award in 1975.

Nomination of Tidal W. McCoy To Be an Assistant Secretary of the Air Force
April 15, 1981

The President today announced his intention to nominate Tidal W. McCoy to be Assistant Secretary of the Air Force (Manpower, Reserve Affairs & Installations). Since 1979 Mr. McCoy has served as assistant for national security affairs to Senator Jake Garn (R-Utah).

After graduation from West Point in 1967, he spent almost 5 years as an Army field artillery officer in command and staff assignments in the United States, Europe, and Vietnam. Mr. McCoy was assigned by the Army to the Defense Intelligence Agency and the National Security Agency and was employed as a civilian by the Central Intelligence Agency as an intelligence officer. For 5 years Mr. McCoy worked full- or part-time as staff assistant in the immediate office of five Secretaries of Defense. He has also served as a staff member of the National Security Council; as scientific assistant to the Assistant Secretary of the Navy for Research, Engineering, and Systems; and as the Director of Policy Research in the Office of the Under Secretary of Defense for Policy. Mr. McCoy's work in his various assignments has covered a wide range of U.S. foreign and defense policy issues and intelligence subjects. His awards are numerous, they include the Secretary of Defense Meritorious Civilian Service Medal.

Mr. McCoy has a master's degree in business finance from George Washington University. He was born in Gainesville, Fla., on April 25, 1945. He currently resides in McLean, Va.

Nomination of Jon D. Holstine To Be an Assistant Administrator of the Agency for International Development
April 15, 1981

The President today announced his intention to nominate Jon D. Holstine to be Assistant Administrator of the Bureau for Asia, Agency for International Development, United States International Development Cooperation Agency.

Since 1975 Dr. Holstine has served as minority staff consultant, House Foreign Affairs Committee, with responsibilities in several areas, including international development and security assistance, international communications, and weapons transfers. He was an instructor at Thiel College in 1973–75, Russell Sage College in 1967–73, Indiana University in 1965–67, and Ball State University in 1964–65. Dr. Holstine served with the U.S. Information Agency in 1962–64.

Dr. Holstine was graduated from Purdue University (B.S., 1959), the American University (M.A., 1964), and Indiana University (Ph. D., 1971).

Dr. Holstine is married, has two children, and resides in Alexandria, Va. He was born in Danville, Ill., on September 23, 1937.

Nomination of Samuel R. Martinez To Be an Assistant Administrator of the Agency for International Development
April 15, 1981

The President today announced his intention to nominate Samuel R. Martinez to be Assistant Administrator of the Bureau for Latin America and the Caribbean, Agency for International Development, United States International Development Cooperation Agency.

Since January 1980 Mr. Martinez has served as director, public affairs, Adolph Coors Co., Golden, Colo. In 1977–80 he formed, operated, and later sold Mountain Plains Energy Conservation (MPEC). During that time he was a part-time instructor with the Graduate School of Public Administration, University of Northern Colorado. In 1976–77 Mr. Martinez was Director, Community Services Administration, within the Executive Office of the President. He was Regional Director (Region VIII), Department of Labor in 1973–76. In 1974—76 he was Chairman, Federal Regional Council (Region VIII). In 1969–73 Mr. Martinez was Regional Director, Office of Economic Opportunity, Executive Office of the President. He was special assistant to the Governor of Colorado in 1965–69.

Mr. Martinez is married and has three children. He resides with his family in Lakewood, Colo. Mr. Martinez was born in Del Norte, Colo., on April 30, 1933.

Statement on Federal Income Tax Reductions
April 15, 1981

Today is the last day for filing income tax returns—a day that reminds us that taxpayers pay too much of their earnings to the Federal Government.

And Americans will continue to pay too much money to the Federal Government until the Congress acts on our proposals to reduce tax rates across the board. Without these reductions, there will be an automatic $200 billion tax increase over the next 2 years.

While April 15 serves as a reminder, the people of the United States truly do not need to be reminded. They are victims of inflation, which pushes them into higher tax brackets. They are robbed daily of a better standard of living. They are discouraged from work and investment.

There are a few other alternative tax proposals now before the Congress, but compared to our proposals, they will result in higher taxes for the American people. In fact, these alternatives are not the answer; they are the problem.

Taxes are much too high to deal in half measures. In 1965 less than 6 percent of all taxpayers faced marginal rates of 25 percent or more. Today, more than one of every three taxpayers is in at least the 25–percent bracket. In addition, since 1965 the marginal tax rate for a median-income family of four has jumped from 17 percent to 24 percent in 1980. And under current law it would grow to a crushing 32 percent in 1984. We simply can't allow our already overburdened and demoralized taxpayers to suffer this unacceptable increase.

By comparison, our tax reduction program will reduce the marginal tax rate to 23 percent in 1984, a very important step in the right direction; a step that will play a significant role in rejuvenating the economy.

Our plan treats Americans at all income levels evenly and fairly. Three-fourths of the tax cuts will go to middle-income taxpayers. Under present law, these middle-income citizens—who make between $10,000 and $60,000—pay 72 percent of all income taxes and will receive 73 percent of the benefits of our proposal.

The choice before us is clear. I strongly feel that the great majority of Americans believe that nothing would better encourage economic growth than leaving more money in the hands of the people who earn it. It's time to stop stripping bare the productive citizens of America and funneling their hard-earned income into the Federal bureaucracy.

Today is a day when the people reaffirm their commitment to our system by contributing a portion of their income to the Government. Americans have always been prepared to pay their fair share, but today they should make it clear to all elected officials that government has gone beyond its bounds and that the people will not tolerate the ever-increasing tax burden they have experienced in recent years.

I ask all Americans to join me in changing our tax system so that next April 15 we shall begin to celebrate tax reductions instead of simply one more predictable and painful tax increase.

Note: Secretary of the Treasury Donald T. Regan read the statement at 1:55 p.m. at a news conference with regional reporters, editors, and news directors in Room 450 of the Old Executive Office Building.

Statement on Granting Pardons to W. Mark Felt and Edward S. Miller
April 15, 1981

Pursuant to the grant of authority in article II, section 2 of the Constitution of the United States, I have granted full and unconditional pardons to W. Mark Felt and Edward S. Miller.

During their long careers, Mark Felt and Edward Miller served the Federal Bureau of Investigation and our nation with great distinction. To punish them further—after 3 years of criminal prosecution proceedings—would not serve the ends of justice.

Their convictions in the U.S. District Court, on appeal at the time I signed the pardons, grew out of their good-faith belief that their actions were necessary to preserve the security interests of our country. The record demonstrates that they acted not with criminal intent, but in the belief that they had grants of authority reaching to the highest levels of government.

America was at war in 1972, and Messrs. Felt and Miller followed procedures they believed essential to keep the Director of the FBI, the Attorney General, and the President of the United States advised of the activities of hostile foreign powers and their collaborators in this country. They have never denied their actions, but, in fact, came forward to acknowledge them publicly in order to relieve their subordinate agents from criminal actions.

Four years ago, thousands of draft evaders and others who violated the Selective Service laws were unconditionally pardoned by my predecessor. America was generous to those who refused to serve their country in the Vietnam war. We can be no less generous to two men who acted on high principle to bring an end to the terrorism that was threatening our nation.

Nomination of Georgiana Sheldon To Be a Member of the Federal Energy Regulatory Commission
April 15, 1981

The President today announced his intention to nominate Georgiana Sheldon to be a member, Federal Energy Regulatory Commission, Department of Energy, for a term expiring October 20, 1984.

Since 1977 Mrs. Sheldon has served as a member of the Federal Energy Regulatory Commission. In 1976–77 she was Acting Chairman and Vice Chairman of the U.S. Civil Service Commission. Mrs. Sheldon was Director, Office of Foreign Disaster Relief, and Deputy Coordinator for International Disaster Assistance, Agency for International Development in 1975–76. In 1969–75 she was Deputy Director, Defense Civil Preparedness Agency. Mrs. Sheldon was a special recruiter for the Peace Corps in 1969. She served as executive secretary and personal assistant to Representative Rogers C. B. Morton in 1963–69. Previously she was executive secretary to the Foundation for Specialized Group Housing in 1961 62; vice president of Sorin-Hall, Inc., in 1961; assistant to the special assistant to the chairman of the Republican National Committee in 1956–61; and registrar and director of admissions, Stetson University College of Law in 1954–56.

Mrs. Sheldon was graduated from Keuka College, Keuka Park, N.Y. (B.A., 1945) and Cornell University (M.S., 1949).

Mrs. Sheldon is married and resides in Arlington, Va. She was born in Lawrenceville, Pa., on December 2, 1923.

Statement on Actions Taken Against Waste, Fraud, and Abuse in the Federal Government
April 16, 1981

A study released yesterday reveals startling statistics that confirm much of what this administration has said about the "national scandal" of waste, fraud, and abuse in government.

Forty-five percent of Federal employees who responded to the survey said that in the last 12 months they had observed or had evidence of waste or illegality; 17 percent have personal knowledge of Federal property being stolen; 11 percent have personal knowledge of ineligible recipients getting funds, goods, or services. These are far from trivial matters. Indeed, 9 percent of the employees in the survey claimed to have observed specific incidents each involving over $100,000 of waste or mismanagement.

The study, conducted by the Merit Systems Protection Board and the Inspectors General, also found that much of the wasteful or illegal activities have gone unreported because of the belief that "nothing would be done."

This administration means to change that attitude. As I said when I announced the appointment of the President's Council on Integrity and Efficiency on March 26: "We are going to follow every lead, root out every incompetent, and prosecute any crook we find who's cheating the people of this Nation."

Today the Council on Integrity and Efficiency is publicizing a series of "hotline" numbers that will be available to Federal employees who want to report wrongdoing in their departments.

But, more important, the Council is reasserting a point I want understood throughout the Government: Federal employees or private citizens who wish to report incidents of illegal or wasteful activities are not only encouraged to do so but will be guaranteed confidentiality and protected against reprisals.

I also want every member of this administration—from those in the Cabinet, to the sub-Cabinet, to Federal employees beginning their careers today—to understand that we will not tolerate fraud, waste, and abuse of the taxpayers' dollars. Every allegation of wrongdoing, every investigative lead will be pursued thoroughly and objectively.

The vital element in any program designed to fight fraud and waste is the willingness of employees to come forward when they see this sort of activity. They must be assured that when they "blow the whistle" they will be protected and their information properly investigated.

I want it made clear that today this administration is providing that assurance to every potential whistleblower in the Federal Government.

Since I appointed the Council on Integrity and Efficiency, we have already begun to develop momentum in the fight against waste and fraud. Let me cite a few examples.

—Hundreds of additional investigative leads, some of great significance, on incidents of waste, fraud, and abuse in government have been developed. Our Inspectors General are vigorously pursuing these leads.

—The Inspector General's office at AID secured a guilty plea from a former AID employee accused of extorting $138,000 for channeling a rice-seed contract to a firm in the Far East. The individual also agreed to resign from AID immediately and to return to the Government, in the form of criminal and civil fines, some $40,000 of the funds he allegedly extorted. In addition, he received a 2-year suspended sentence and 5 years of probation.

—This administration has announced its support of legislation creating additional Inspectors General who will have powers tailored to the specific needs of the Departments of Defense, Treasury, and Justice.

—I have also approved six more individuals to be nominated as IG's. Their names will be announced as soon as they have successfully completed the initial clearance process.

During the past few decades, government programs have multiplied and expenditures have grown by quantum leaps. But during this time little attention has been paid to the serious problems of mismanagement and criminal fraud. One Department of Justice study has revealed that in social programs fraud alone could be as much as 1 to 10 percent of the expenditures for those programs.

It is time to put a halt to this waste and wrongdoing. These steps I have mentioned today represent only a beginning in one of the toughest and most important programs this administration will undertake: eliminating waste and fraud, and restoring the public's faith in the integrity of government.

Note: On the same day, the White House released a fact sheet which includes the following hotline numbers:

Department of Agriculture, 800–424–4488 and in Washington, D.C., 202–546–1441

Department of Commerce, 202–724–3519

Department of Defense, 202–693–5080 or 800–424–9098

Department of Education, 202–755–2770

Department of Energy, 202–252–4073

Department of Health and Human Services, 202–472–4222

Department of Housing and Urban Development, 202–472–4200

Department of the Interior, 202–343–2424

Department of Justice, 202–633–3365

Department of Labor, 202–357–0027 or 800–424–5409

Department of State, 202–632–3320

Department of Transportation, 202–755–1855 or 800–424–9071

Department of the Treasury, 202–566–6900

Community Services Administration, 202–653–5430

Environmental Protection Agency, 202–245–3090; after business hours 202–245–3132

General Services Administration, 800–424–5210 or 202–566–1780

National Aeronautics and Space Administration, 202–755–8304 (Investigation); 202–755–3481 (Audit)

Small Business Administration, 202–653–7557

Veterans Administration, 202–389–5394

General Accounting Office, 800–424–5454

Statement on the Celebration of Passover and Easter
April 17, 1981

This weekend, people across the world will join in holy celebrations, drawing spiritual sustenance from their worship. Here in America, religious beliefs are central to our founding principles. We draw special strength from our unity as a people who trust in God, and from the lessons for us and our children in our rituals.

Saturday night, Jewish people everywhere will sit with their families and friends for the celebration of Passover—a celebration of freedom.

Beginning with the traditional *Seder* meal, Passover is rich with tradition and symbolism. Its observance reminds us that the fight for freedom and the battle against oppression, waged by Jews throughout their history, is one of which all free people are a part.

Beginning today and culminating on Sunday morning, Christians will celebrate with their families the resurrection of Christ, His victory over death. We will remember that He gave His body and His blood—washing clean the faults and the shortcomings of the world. In our rejoicing we will renew the hope that is ours through the risen Lord.

Nancy joins me in extending to all who celebrate Passover or Easter our warmest wishes for a time filled with joy and spiritual fulfillment and our hope that one day men and women everywhere will be able to worship God in the manner of their choosing.

Nomination of Russell D. Hale To Be an Assistant Secretary of the Air Force
April 17, 1981

The President today announced his intention to nominate Russell D. Hale to be Assistant Secretary of the Air Force (Financial Management).

Since 1978 Mr. Hale has been a member of the professional staff of the House Committee on Armed Services. In 1975–78 he was a member of the professional staff of the House Committee on the Budget, national defense function. He was an account executive to defense/aerospace corporations with IBM's data processing division in 1973–75. Mr. Hale was special assistant to the Assistant Secretary of Defense for budget review, acquisition strategies, and procurement policies in 1971–73. In 1969–71 he was operation research analyst to the Comptroller of the U.S. Air Force.

Mr. Hale was graduated from the U.S. Naval Academy (B.S., 1966); Georgia Institute of Technology (M.S., 1969).

Mr. Hale is married and has three children. He resides with his family in Arlington, Va. He was born in Sherman, Tex., on August 8, 1944.

361

Nomination of John V. Byrne To Be Administrator of the National Oceanic and Atmospheric Administration
April 17, 1981

The President today announced his intention to nominate John V. Byrne to be Administrator of the National Oceanic and Atmospheric Administration, Department of Commerce.

Dr. Byrne has held various positions with Oregon State University since 1960. He was an associate professor in 1960–65; professor and chairman, Department of Oceanography in 1968–72; dean, School of Oceanography in 1972–76; acting director, Marine Science Center in 1972–77; dean of research (acting) in 1976–77; dean of research in 1977–80; dean of graduate school (acting) in 1979–80; and vice president for research and graduate studies since 1980.

Dr. Byrne was program director for physical oceanography, National Science Foundation, in 1966–67. In 1966–68 he was a geologist with the U.S. Geological Survey.

He has been a member of many scientific and professional societies including: American Society for Oceanography, Marine Technology Society, Society of Economic Paleontologists and Mineralogists, American Association of Petroleum Geologists, and the University Corporation for Atmospheric Research. He is the author of many articles and papers on geology and oceanography.

Dr. Byrne was graduated from Hamilton College (B.A., 1951), Columbia College (M.A., 1953), and the University of Southern California (Ph. D., 1957).

Dr. Byrne is married, has four children, and resides in Corvallis, Oreg. He was born in Hempstead, N.Y., on May 9, 1928.

Nomination of Juan A. del Real To Be General Counsel of the Department of Health and Human Services
April 17, 1981

The President today announced his intention to nominate Juan A. del Real to be General Counsel of the Department of Health and Human Services.

Since April 1980 Mr. del Real has served as Assistant General Counsel, Health Care Financing and Human Development Services Divisions, Department of Health and Human Services. He was mainly responsible for providing legal services to the Health Care Financing Administration (HCFA) and the Office of the Secretary with respect to the Medicare and Medicaid programs. In 1968–80 he was a partner with the firm of Hill, Christopher and Phillips of Washington, D.C. Mr. del Real was special assistant to the president of Central Aguirre Sugar

Co. of San Juan, P.R., in 1967–68. In 1966–67 he was assigned to the international financing department of Surrey, Karasik, Gould & Greene of Washington, D.C.

Mr. del Real attended Tulane University (1957–59); Havana University Law School (1959–60) and was graduated from St. Louis University Law School (J.D., 1966). He is a member of the American, District of Columbia, and Missouri Bar Associations.

Mr. del Real is married, has three children, and resides with his family in Potomac, Md. He was born in Cuba on November 4, 1939, and became a naturalized American citizen of the United States on January 5, 1967.

Nomination of Donald L. Dotson To Be an Assistant Secretary of Labor
April 17, 1981

The President today announced his intention to nominate Donald L. Dotson to be Assistant Secretary of Labor (Labor Management Relations).

Since 1976 Mr. Dotson has served as chief labor counsel to the Wheeling-Pittsburgh Steel Corp. He was labor attorney, Western Electric Co., Inc., in 1975–76. In 1973–75 Mr. Dotson was labor counsel to the Westinghouse Electric Corp. and subsidiaries. He was an attorney to the National Labor Relations Board in 1968–73.

Mr. Dotson is a member of the Pennsylvania, North Carolina, and American Bar Associations. He served in the U.S. Navy in 1960–65 and was honorably discharged with the rank of lieutenant commander.

He was graduated from the University of North Carolina (B.A., 1960) and Wake Forest University (J D , 1968).

Mr. Dotson resides in Pittsburgh, Pa., and was born in Rutherford County, N.C., on October 8, 1938.

Nomination of Robert Dean Nesen To Be United States Ambassador to Australia and Nauru
April 17, 1981

The President today announced his intention to nominate Robert Dean Nesen, of Thousand Oaks, Calif., to be Ambassador to Australia and to serve concurrently as Ambassador to the Republic of Nauru.

Mr. Nesen served in the United States Navy from 1942 to 1946 and was in the Naval Reserve from 1946 to 1966, lieutenant commander. In 1941 he was with Air-Research Corp. of Los Angeles, Calif. From 1946 to 1947, he was the owner-manager of Coast Aero Flying Service of Oxnard, Calif. Since 1948 he has been founder-chairman of the board, R. D. Nesen Oldsmobile-Cadillac, Inc., of Thousand Oaks, Calif. Also, since 1971 he has been founder-chairman of the board, Nesen Leasing Corp.

From 1972 to 1974, Mr. Nesen served as Assistant Secretary of the Navy in Washington, D.C. He was appointed by Governor Reagan to the California New Car Dealers Policy and Appeals Board (elected first president), California State Board of Education, and as chairman, then cochairman of the California delegation to the National Convention. He served as a member of the Executive Committee of the National Review Board, Department of State, from 1970 to 1973.

Mr. Nesen was born January 22, 1918, in St. Louis, Mich. He attended Tri-State Engineering College and graduated as an aeronautical engineer in 1941 from Curtis-Wright Technical School. He is married to the former Delta Hudson and has three children.

Appointment of Three Members of the Iran-United States Claims Tribunal
April 17, 1981

The President today appointed the following individuals to serve on the Iran-U.S. Claims Tribunal, pursuant to the Claims Settlement Agreement of January 19, 1981. The United States and Iran are each to appoint three arbitrators to the Claims Tribunal by April 19; those six arbitrators are to appoint three "neutral" arbitrators by May 19, 1981.

Malcolm R. Wilkey, appointed to the U.S. Court of Appeals for the District of Columbia Circuit in 1970. He was general counsel, Kennecott Copper Corp. in 1967–70; Assistant Attorney General of the United States in 1958–61; and U.S. attorney, Southern District of Texas in 1954–58. He was graduated from Harvard (A.B., 1940; LL.B., 1948). Mr. Wilkey was born in Murfreesboro, Tenn., on December 6, 1918.

Richard M. Mosk, partner in the Los Angeles firm of Mitchell, Silberberg & Knupp, specializing in litigation. He was special deputy Federal public defender, in 1975–76, handling Federal criminal cases. He is a member of the Los Angeles County Commission on Judicial Procedures and was a member of the staff of the President's Commission on the Assassination of President Kennedy. He has been a member of the California Bar since 1964. Mr. Mosk is married and has two children. He was graduated from Stanford University (A.B.) and Harvard (J.D.). He is 41 years old and resides in Beverly Hills, Calif.

Howard M. Holtzmann, partner in the New York firm of Holtzmann, Wise & Shepard, specializing in arbitration and international private law. He was a member of the U.S. delegation to the United Nations Commission on International Trade Law since 1975; member of a study group on arbitration of the Secretary of State's Advisory Committee on Private International Law; past chairman of the board of the American Arbitration Association, and currently chairman of its international arbitration committee. Previously he served as director of the Syntex Corp., the Ogden Corp., and CF & I Steel Corp. Mr. Holtzmann was graduated from Yale University (A.B., 1942) and St. Bonaventure University (J.D., 1947). He is married and resides in New York City. He was born in New York on December 10, 1921.

Statement on Federal Audiovisual Aids and Publications
April 20, 1981

Today, I'm asking the heads of all Federal departments and agencies to impose an immediate moratorium on the production and procurement of new audiovisual aids and Government publications. The Federal Government is spending too much money on public relations, publicity, and advertising. Much of this waste consists of unnecessary and expensive films, magazines, and pamphlets.

I am keeping the pledge I made to this country to cut out wasteful spending by the Federal Government. While we have a duty to keep the citizens of this country accurately and fully informed about government programs and activities, we should not use this as a license to produce films, pamphlets, and magazines that do not truly serve the public interest.

Over the past few months, many of you have sent examples to us of publications and pamphlets, most of them unsolicited, that you felt were useless and a waste of the taxpayers' dollars. We are grateful for this contribution to our efforts to eliminate waste in this area. Additionally, some Federal agencies have already conducted their own reviews of public relations activity. Their investigations indicate that there is potential for significant savings from a review of this type in all our departments and agencies.

I am asking the heads of agencies and departments to impose a government-wide moratorium on these activities so that a comprehensive review of current and planned spending may be conducted. I am asking the head of each department and agency to develop specific plans to prevent abuses in the future. I have instructed the Director of the Office of Management and Budget to issue procedures and guidelines to carry out the directive, to assist agencies in developing plans, and to monitor the savings. I am requesting that all departments

and agencies begin their reviews immediately and report their progress and plans no later than July 15, 1981.

During these difficult economic times, we cannot afford to waste time and money on activities that have limited benefit to the people of this country. Controlling spending on public relations, publicity, and advertising is an important contribution to our overall goal of cutting out waste in the Federal Government.

Proclamation 4837—Asian/Pacific American Heritage Week, 1981
April 20, 1981

By the President of the United States of America

A Proclamation

The United States is a Nation comprised almost entirely of immigrants and their descendents. The interaction of different cultures, each of which has become a vital part of a culture uniquely American, constantly revitalizes our national spirit and heritage.

Among the most significant components of the American cultural blend are the ancient Asian-Pacific cultures. Asians have brought to the United States values and traditions that profoundly enrich American life. In a variety of fields that span the spectrum of human endeavor—including art, dance, agriculture, the sciences, medicine, commerce, government and philosophy—Asian and Pacific Americans have made outstanding contributions to the cultural and technological development of their adopted Nation. Their hard work, creativity and intelligence have inspired their fellow citizens, added new dimensions to our national life and strengthened the social fabric of our land.

Commonly, immigrants have come to American shores with few material possessions, relying on initiative, hard work and opportunity as the keys to success and pros-

perity in their new Nation. Asian and Pacific Americans have been squarely within this tradition. Overcoming great hardships, they have lived the American dream, and continue as exemplars of hope and inspiration not only to their fellow Americans, but also to the new groups of Asian and Pacific peoples who even now are joining the American family.

The United States owes a debt of gratitude to Asian and Pacific Americans for their contributions to the culture, heritage and freedom of the Nation we together love and serve.

Now, Therefore, I, Ronald Reagan, President of the United States of America, do hereby declare the seven days beginning May 4, 1981, as Asian/Pacific American Heritage Week, and call upon all people of the United States to observe this week with appropriate ceremonies and activities.

In Witness Whereof, I have hereunto set my hand this 20th day of April in the year of our Lord nineteen hundred and eighty-one, and of the Independence of the United States of America the two hundred and fifth.

RONALD REAGAN

[*Filed with the Office of the Federal Register, 4:34 p.m., April 20, 1981*]

Nomination of Robert Gerhard Neumann To Be United States Ambassador to Saudi Arabia
April 20, 1981

The President today announced his intention to nominate Robert Gerhard Neumann of Culver City, Calif., to be Ambassador to the Kingdom of Saudi Arabia, vice John C. West, resigning.

Mr. Neumann was an instructor at State Teachers College in Oshkosh, Wis., from 1941 to 1942, and a lecturer of political science at the University of Wisconsin from 1946 to 1947. From 1947 to 1970, he was with the University of California at Los Angeles serving successively as assistant, associate, and professor. Also he was director of the Institute of International and Foreign Studies (1958–65), and chairman of the Atlantic and West European Program (1965–66). He was granted a leave of absence in 1966–70. Since 1976 he has been with Georgetown University in Washington, D.C., as director of the Institute for the Study of Diplomacy (1976–77), senior associate for parliamentary/congressional relations of the Center for Strategic and International Studies (1976–present), and since 1980 as vice chairman, Center for Strategic and International Studies.

From 1966 to 1973, Mr. Neumann was Ambassador to Afghanistan and Ambassador to Morocco from 1973 to 1976. He was the director of the Department of State transition team.

Mr. Neumann was born January 2, 1916, in Vienna, Austria. He received diplomas from the University of Rennes, France (1936), Consular Academy, Austria (1937), and Geneva School of International Studies, Switzerland (1937). He graduated in 1940 (M.A.) from Amherst College and received his Ph. D. in 1946 from the University of Minnesota. He is married to the former Marlen Eldredge and has two grown children.

Message to the Senate on the United States-Canada Maritime Boundary Treaty and Fishery Agreement
April 21, 1981

To the Senate of the United States:

On March 6, 1981, I asked the Chairman of the Committee on Foreign Relations to uncouple two pending treaties, signed March 29, 1979, relating to East Coast fishery and maritime boundary matters. I made this request after members of the Senate leadership advised me the treaties could not be ratified as they were.

My goal, as I am sure is yours, is to resolve the fishery problem and at the same time fortify our strong and close relationship with Canada.

Our two nations have built a friendship based on good will and mutual respect, recognizing that we both have independent, national interests to pursue. I believe that the proposed course of action will ensure the settlement of the maritime boundary by an impartial and binding procedure, and that it will allow a future fisheries relationship with Canada to be based on better known facts and circumstances.

Therefore, I recommend that the Senate give advice and consent to ratification of the Treaty Between the Government of the United States of America and the Government of Canada to Submit to Binding Dispute Settlement the Delimitation of the Maritime Boundary in the Gulf of Maine Area, signed at Washington, March 29, 1979, subject to technical amendments including an amendment which would allow it to be brought into force without the entry into force of the accompanying fishery agreement. And, I request that the

Senate return to me without further action the Agreement Between the Government of the United States of America and the Government of Canada on East Coast Fishery Resources, signed at Washington, March 29, 1979.

I believe that the course of action outlined above is in the best interest of the United States and will contribute to the close and cooperative relationship with Canada that we seek.

RONALD REAGAN

The White House,
April 21, 1981.

Message to the Senate Transmitting the United States-British Virgin Islands Convention on Taxation and Fiscal Evasion
April 21, 1981

To the Senate of the United States:

I am transmitting for Senate advice and consent to ratification, a Convention between the Government of the United States of America and the Government of the British Virgin Islands for the Avoidance of Double Taxation and the Prevention of Fiscal Evasion with respect to Taxes on Income (the Convention). I am also transmitting a related note from the Government of the British Virgin Islands, signed at Washington on February 18, 1981.

The Convention will replace the 1945 income tax convention between the United States and the United Kingdom which was applied to the British Virgin Islands in 1959. The Convention takes into account the modernization of tax treaties which has taken place since that time and is based primarily on the United States and OECD model tax treaties published in 1977. The most important differences from the model tax treaties are the rates of tax at source on investment income. Because of the positive rates at source, the use of the Convention by third country residents in deriving investment income from the United States will decline substantially.

An important feature of the Convention, which benefits the United States in particular, is found in the provisions of Article 25 which provide for the exchange of information. The note of the Government of the British Virgin Islands confirms that financial information will be made available, on request, to the United States. It also confirms that, under the terms of the Convention, the United States may terminate the Convention if, as a result of a change in law or practice in the British Virgin Islands, such information is not made available.

I recommend that the Senate give early and favorable consideration to the Convention and give advice and consent to its ratification.

RONALD REAGAN

The White House,
April 21, 1981.

Nomination of Joel E. Bonner To Be an Assistant Secretary of the Army
April 21, 1981

The President today announced his intention to nominate Joel E. Bonner to be an Assistant Secretary of the Army (Installations, Logistics and Financial Management).

Since 1972 Mr. Bonner has been a member of the professional staff of the Senate Committee on Appropriations with primary responsibility for defense appropriations. In 1981 he was assigned as majority staff director for the Defense Appropriations Subcommittee. In 1971–72 he was Deputy Director, Office of the Assistant Secretary of Defense for Legislative Affairs.

Mr. Bonner was commissioned a second lieutenant in the Marine Corps and designated a naval aviator in January 1943. He participated in World War II, the Korean war, and the Vietnam war. He retired from the Marine Corps as a colonel in 1971. He is a recipient of the Legion of Merit with Combat V and gold star, Distinguished Flying Cross, Air Medal with seven stars, Presidential Unit Citation, Navy Unit Commendation, and the Vietnamese Cross of Gallantry with palm.

Mr. Bonner was graduated from the University of Maryland (B.S., 1961). He is married, has three children, and resides in Alexandria, Va. Mr. Bonner was born in Dallas, Tex., on March 23, 1922.

Nomination of Robert G. Dederick To Be an Assistant Secretary of Commerce
April 21, 1981

The President today announced his intention to nominate Robert G. Dederick to be an Assistant Secretary of Commerce (Economic Affairs).

Since 1970 Dr. Dederick has served as senior vice President and chief economist, the Northern Trust Co., Chicago, Ill. He has been with that firm since 1964. In 1957–64 he worked for the New England Mutual Life Insurance Co. He has had teaching experience at Cornell, Harvard, and Boston Universities.

Dr. Dederick is a fellow and past president, National Association of Business Economists; member, banking, monetary and fiscal affairs committtee, U.S. Chamber of Commerce; member, finance committee, American Economic Association; and member, executive committee, Illinois Council on Economic Education.

Dr. Dederick was graduated from Harvard University (A.B., A.M., and Ph. D.). He is married, has three children, and resides in Hinsdale, Ill. Dr. Dederick was born in Keene, N.H., on November 18, 1929.

Nomination of Joseph P. Welsch To Be Inspector General of the Department of Transportation
April 21, 1981

The President today announced his intention to nominate Joseph P. Welsch to be Inspector General, Department of Transportation.

Since 1978 Mr. Welsch has served as Vice President for Finance of the United States Railway Association and was responsible for monitoring the financial operations of the Consolidated Rail Corp. (Conrail), Delaware and Hudson and Missouri-Kansas-Texas railroads. In 1974–78 he was Deputy Assistant Secretary of Defense for Management Systems in the Office of the Assistant Secretary of Defense (Controller). Mr. Welsch was Deputy Assistant Secretary of Defense for Audit in 1971–74. In 1962–71 he directed the Management Audit organization in the Office of the Secretary of Defense. Previously he worked for the Air Force Auditor General.

Mr. Welsch was graduated from Pace College, New York City, and attended Colorado University. He resides in Arlington, Va., and was born in Bayonne, N.J., on October 2, 1928.

Nomination of Ann Dore McLaughlin To Be an Assistant Secretary of the Treasury
April 21, 1981

The President today announced his intention to nominate Ann Dore McLaughlin to be an Assistant Secretary of the Treasury (Public Affairs).

Since 1977 Mrs. McLaughlin has been president of McLaughlin & Co. of Washington, D.C., and Washington manager of Braun and Co. of Los Angeles, Calif. Both firms are public affairs companies.

In 1974–77 she was with the Union Carbide Corp. She was Director, Office of Public Affairs, Environmental Protection Agency, in 1973–74. Mrs. McLaughlin was assistant to the chairman and press secretary, Presidential Inaugural Committee in 1972–73. In 1971–72 she was director of communications, Presidential Election Committee. Previously she served as an account executive with Myers-Infoplan International, Inc., of New York City. Mrs. McLaughlin was a consultant and literary agent with Perla Meters International Kitchen in 1970–71; director, alumnae relations, Marymount College, in 1966–69; and supervisor, network commercial scheduling, American Broadcasting Co., in 1963–66.

Mrs. McLaughlin was graduated from Marymount College (B.A., 1963) and attended the University of London, Queen Mary College, in 1961–62.

Mrs. McLaughlin is married and resides in Washington, D.C. She was born in Chatham, N.J., on November 16, 1941.

Nomination of Donna Pope To Be Director of the Mint
April 21, 1981

The President today announced his intention to nominate Donna Pope to be Director of the Mint, Department of the Treasury, for a term of 5 years.

Since 1972 Mrs. Pope has been a member of the Ohio House of Representatives. She represents the 12th district and was elected minority whip in 1978. Current legislative assignments include the judiciary, rules, ethics and legislative service commission committees. In 1979–80 Mrs. Pope served as cochairman of the Ohio Reagan campaign and was cochairman of the Ohio delegation to the 1980 Republican National Convention. In 1968–72 she was supervisor, Cuyahoga County Board of Elections.

Mrs. Pope was named one of the outstanding women legislators in the Nation by Rutgers University Institute of Politics. She was honored by the Women's Institute of Politics, Mt. Vernon College, Washington, D.C. (1978), as one of five of the Nation's most influential women legislators.

Mrs. Pope is married, has two children, and resides in Parma, Ohio. She was born in Cleveland, Ohio, on October 15, 1931.

369

Question-and-Answer Session With Reporters Helen Thomas and Jim Gerstenzang on the President's Recovery Period
April 22, 1981

Ms. Thomas. All the reports seem to be true, rosy-cheeked and——

The President [*laughing*]. No, I'm feeling fine.

Ms. Thomas. Can you tell us a little bit about how you felt at the time of the shooting? Did you ever feel you were in mortal danger? I know you didn't even know you were hit, but——

The President. No, that's right, and as a matter of fact, it still seems unreal. I knew there had to be shots, and my first instinct was to take a look and see what was going on from where they were. But the Secret Service man behind me had a different idea, and the next thing I knew I found myself pushed into the car. But it still seems kind of unreal.

Ms. Thomas. It's unreal to us, too, because we've come out of that hotel so many times and——

The President. Yeah.

Ms. Thomas. ——nothing——

Mr. Gerstenzang. What were your first thoughts when you realized that you had been hit?

The President. Actually, I can't recall too clearly. I knew I'd been hurt, but I thought that I'd been hurt by the Secret Service man landing on me in the car. And it was, I must say, it was the most paralyzing pain. I've described it as if someone had hit you with a hammer.

But that sensation, it seemed to me, came after I was in the car, and so I thought that maybe his gun or something, underneath, when he had come down on me, had broken a rib. But when I sat up on the seat and the pain wouldn't go away, and suddenly I found that I was coughing up blood, we both decided that maybe I'd broken a rib and punctured a lung. So, that's when we headed for the hospital. And I walked in and gave them my own diagnosis, and the next thing I knew I was on a cart and it was then, I guess, that they found the wound and that I actually had been shot.

Ms. Thomas. Then, you were awake and everything? I mean——

The President. Oh, yes.

Ms. Thomas. ——but had lost a lot of blood and——

The President. Yes. And my main concern, even as I was getting to the hospital, was that—and I voiced this several times to them—that the more I tried to breathe and the deeper I tried to breathe, it kept seeming as if I was getting less air—and you know that panic that you can get if you're strangling on something. I almost had the feeling that it was going to diminish to the place where I wouldn't be getting any. And then they shut me up by sticking a pipe down by throat and oxygen on, and that's when I had to start writing notes—[*laughter*]—because I couldn't talk with that pipe in there.

Ms. Thomas. But you always felt that you were alert enough to know what was going on and——

The President. Oh, yes. Yeah, I knew that in the manner in which I was unclothed that I probably wouldn't wear that suit again.

Ms. Thomas. Do you have any feelings about going out again? I mean, are there any—is there trauma or instants that you say, "Oh, God, do I have to face this again?" Or do you feel that, you know——

The President. I have a hunch I'll be more alert in going again.

Ms. Thomas. We will, too.

The President. That's the other thing.

I look back now in some of these reviews that they've shown of the first few months and so forth. I see some of the milling in crowds and so forth that we've done, and I find myself wondering, "Well, why didn't this happen 27 times before?" But, no, there's not going to be any change in the way we do things.

Mr. Gerstenzang. Do you have any recurrent thoughts about it? Does it become a nightmare or a dream?

The President. No. That's where I say, the whole unreality of it.

Ms. Thomas. How do you actually feel? I mean, do you hurt at times and you feel good at times?

The President. Well, as the doctors will tell you, I have never had a chest injury before. They will tell you that it is one of the longest enduring discomforts, and it doesn't go away. There is just that kind of pain or discomfort there constantly that you hope day by day is getting less, and I think is getting less and less. But other than that—I've resumed at a little slower pace my regimen of exercises that I've always done for keeping fit. And I don't think I'm going to hurdle any tables in the room here for a while, but, really, the recovery is astonishing to me as I think it is, in the reaction, to the doctors, because the only comparison I have to go by is I once had pneumonia, and that was 36 years ago when I was making a picture. And I lost 17 pounds at the time and was months in regaining strength or anything. And I'm so far ahead in this than I was then, that I have to——

Ms. Thomas. You are. I know we keep pushing because we keep forgetting what a short time it's actually been.

Mr. Deaver.[1] Thank you, Helen.

The President. 3 weeks and 2 days.

Ms. Thomas. And 2 days? You haven't counted lately. Who's counting? I mean—[*laughing*]——

The President. Yes.

Ms. Thomas. When do you think you'll be feeling well enough to go back to the Oval Office, or do you like working in the family quarters or——

The President. Well, actually, I don't think I'd be doing anything different. And I'm just going to, you know, I'm going to do it my way. It's convenient this way, because there still are calls by the doctors who want to come and check. There is the convenience of being able to get up and, for example, the telephone calling that I've been doing, which I'd be doing from the office, but I can get up in the morning without bothering to get dressed yet, put on a robe, and sit and do the calls.

---

[1] *Assistant to the President Michael K. Deaver.*

So this, you know, with the Congress on recess, I don't think there'd be anything different or I'd be doing anything different than I've done other than possibly some appearances that have been scheduled and which had to be canceled or which George Bush substituted for me. But other than that I've been doing what I'd be doing. Remember, the schedule actually called for me to be in California for a few days.

Ms. Thomas. Going to a wedding and——

The President. Yes.

Ms. Thomas. ——making a speech and meeting the Mexican——

The President. Uh-huh——

Ms. Thomas. When do you think you'll be able to——

The President. ——and going to the ranch.

Ms. Thomas. Going to the ranch, right. But going to the ranch won't be so much fun unless you can ride a horse and——

The President. Well, I think that'll come along pretty soon.

Ms. Thomas. Do you think your first travel will be Notre Dame?

The President. I don't know whether that's the first trip on the schedule or not.

Mr. Deaver. Well, we haven't confirmed anything yet, Helen.

Ms. Thomas. How about your program itself? Do you think that everything's been sort of on hold or slowed down because of——

The President. No, I really don't. As I say, the Congress is on recess. I'd be doing the same thing, telephoning them while they're back there, with things that I think might be helpful in meeting their constituents. There isn't anything more that we could do in pushing up on the Hill. So, no, I think everything's going along all right.

Mr. Gerstenzang. Could you, maybe in describing how you are working up there each day, sort of show how your day goes?

The President. Well, they vary from day to day. Usually we start with a staff meeting, and we do that—which was normal before. Yesterday I had a series of meetings, finishing up with almost an hour's meeting with those Governors who came to see me. We have security briefings.

So, that some days—now, today, for example, has been—well, there's been some sizable amount of paper signing and so forth that went on, and then mainly after the staff meeting, the telephone calling, which I've been doing. And that will continue, because you don't get them the first call.

Ms. Thomas. You might find them at a radio station. [*Laughter*]

The President. And believe me, that was a total accident. They didn't make it sound exactly that way. Usually I say to them, "Where did we find you?" And I'll tell you why I say that, because early in the calls, I called a Congressman and we'd found him in New Zealand at 4 a.m. [*Laughter*]

Ms. Thomas. You mean recently?

The President. Yes.

Ms. Thomas. Oh, my God.

The President. I wanted to tell him that I was somebody else. [*Laughter*] It was too late. He knew who it was. [*Laughter*]

Ms. Thomas. Was he awake?

The President. Yes, I must say he was most pleasant about the whole thing. So, I usually ask that. And yesterday I asked that question, "Where'd I find you?" and he told me, "In Beaver Falls, at this radio station." He said, "I'm on a talk show here." And I said, "You mean, we're on the talk show now?" And he said, "Well, no, they've put me on another phone for this call." But he said, "I think they'd appreciate it very much if you'd say hello to their"—well, his forum. "They know you're on the phone." And I said, "Well, okay."

So, they put him on the other phone, the one that is audible to the radio audience, and we carried on our conversation there on the talk show.

Ms. Thomas. Do you go to bed earlier now? Do you take naps? Do you sort of try to ease into it?

The President. The only routine that I'm continuing is an afternoon nap. And that was never—in spite of some stories to the contrary—that was never a habit of mine. As a matter of fact, I've never been one who naps very well in the daytime. Everybody else sacks out on the plane and everything else, and I don't.

But I have found that I do go to sleep and sleep for a brief period. So, I guess that is part of the recovery.

Ms. Thomas. Do you think your life has changed?

The President. Only temporarily, such as not getting on a horse for a while yet.

Ms. Thomas. It's not like in the movies.

The President. Oh, I thought you meant just changed in——

Ms. Thomas. I mean the impact itself, of everything that's happened in terms of the Presidency, yourself——

The President. Well, of course, you know, I had 8 years of a job that was similar enough that there hasn't been any great surprises to me in this. But I'm enjoying it, to be able to deal directly with the things I've heretofore talked about. I enjoy doing that.

Ms. Thomas. You don't want to hang up your cleats or anything because of this incident?

The President. No, no.

Ms. Thomas. Does it give you any kind of new sense of—I mean, I think the country's kind of worried about your security and——

The President. Well, again, you get—maybe this is part of it—that you get a little used to it. In all those 8 years and those hectic times when I was Governor, I was aware that there were constant threats. And I could usually tell when there was a slight difference in the security precautions and the normal—something new must have been suggested. And in the two campaigns, having had national-type security, Secret Service, no, I've been—you're aware of that. And you sometimes wonder in your mind when and how it's going to happen or any attempt or what it would be like.

You remember '76; there was that fellow with the toy gun. Well, I never saw that; I was busy saying hello to someone. And I didn't see this.

Ms. Thomas. Do you have any feelings about your assailant? Of course there's nothing you can really feel, I guess. It's something that's senseless.

The President. Well, yes, the feeling is I hope, indeed I pray, that he can find an answer to his problem. He seems to be a very disturbed young man. He comes from a fine family. They must be devastated by this. And I hope he'll get well too.

Ms. Thomas. That's very kind of you. You don't have any feelings of real anger, then, or——

The President. Well, I don't know how I could ask for help for myself and feel that way about someone else.

Mr. Gerstenzang. If you were to speak to his parents, what would you tell them?

The President. Well, I think I'd tell them that I understand and—[*pause*]—hope for a good outcome there, to end their problem.

Ms. Thomas. Do you think that you will get your budget and taxes through now?

The President. Well, I still continue to be optimistic. After all, the argument from whether we should have a plan or not has become an argument of——

Ms. Thomas. How much.

The President. ——how much and where. So, I think we've gained some ground.

Mr. Gerstenzang. Has this in any way changed your thinking on gun control at all?

The President. No, and let me explain why. I'm not just being closed-minded or stubborn.

We have the laws now. Granted that all States aren't uniform. But I don't know of any place—there may be some—but I don't know of any place in the country where it is now not against the law to carry a concealed weapon. Now, we've found that that can't prevent someone. Your District of Columbia here has such a law. But a man was carrying a concealed weapon. So, I don't see where we believe that adding another law that probably will be just as unenforceable as this one is going to make a difference.

In fact, if anything, I'm a little disturbed that focusing on gun control as an answer to the crime problem today could very well be diverting us from really paying attention to what needs to be done if we're to solve the crime problem.

Ms. Thomas. Which is?

The President. Well, I do think we're showing the results of several decades of growing permissiveness, unwillingness to hold individuals responsible for their misdeeds, blaming society instead. In other words, quicker, more effective justice.

Mr. Deaver. One more.

Ms. Thomas. One more. We've got to make this one good. [*Laughter*]

In terms of [Press Secretary] Brady, will he continue on? Are you going to keep the slot open for him?

The President. Oh, you bet. And I think all of us—as I say, when I finally did learn that three others had been hit, including the agent who deliberately placed himself between me and the gunman—but Jim, of course, was the most serious, and I am so gratified by the optimism about his recovery that that's a daily prayer.

Ms. Thomas. A miracle.

The President. Yes. For him.

Ms. Thomas and Mr. Gerstenzang. Thank you very much.

Note: The question-and-answer session with Helen Thomas of United Press International and Jim Gerstenzang of Associated Press began at 12 noon in the Map Room at the White House.

Nomination of Sherman Maxwell Funk To Be Inspector General of the Department of Commerce
April 22, 1981

The President today announced his intention to nominate Sherman Maxwell Funk to be Inspector General, Department of Commerce.

For the past 11 years, Mr. Funk has served in a variety of capacities related to the fostering of minority and other small business in both the Department of Com-

merce and the Department of Energy. His service has included responsibilities in planning and evaluation, program design, budgeting, and procurement. Working closely with Commerce Secretary Maurice Stans in launching the Federal minority business program, Mr. Funk earned the Commerce Department's Silver Medal for his efforts.

Since 1980 he has served as Special Assistant to the Director, Office of Small and Disadvantaged Business Utilization, at the Department of Energy. He was a member of the Secretary's Task Force on Minority Business and Special Assistant to the Director, Office of Minority Economic Impact. In 1970–79 he was Assistant Director for Planning and Evaluation; Assistant Director for Administration and Program Development; Deputy Assistant Director for Field Operations; and Chief, Program Research and Development at the Department of Commerce. In 1958–70 he served in the Headquarters, U.S. Air Force, in capacities including Chief, Air Force Cost Reduction Office; Chairman, Air Force Industry Cost Reduction Program; and Chief, Air Force Management Improvement Program.

Mr. Funk was graduated from Harvard University (A.B.) and the University of Arizona (M.A.). Mr. Funk is married, has two children, and resides in Chevy Chase, Md. He was born in New York City on November 13, 1925.

Nomination of Thomas O. Enders To Be an Assistant Secretary of State
April 22, 1981

The President today announced his intention to nominate Thomas O. Enders to be Assistant Secretary of State (Inter-American Affairs), vice William G. Bowdler, retired.

Mr. Enders began his Foreign Service career in 1958 as intelligence research specialist in the Department of State. From 1960 to 1963, he was visa officer, then economic officer in Stockholm. In the Department he was supervisory international economist in the Bureau of European Affairs (1963–66), Special Assistant in the Office of Under Secretary for Political Affairs (1966–68), and Deputy Assistant Secretary for International Monetary Affairs (1968–69). From 1969 to 1971, he was Deputy Chief of Mission in Belgrade, and in Phnom Penh from 1971 to 1974. From 1974 to 1976, he was Assistant Secretary of State for Economic and Business Affairs in the Department. He was Ambassador to Canada in 1976–79, and from 1979 to 1981, he was United States Representative to the European Communities with rank and status of Ambassador Extraordinary and Plenipotentiary in Brussels.

Mr. Enders was born November 28, 1931, in Hartford, Conn. He received his B.A. (1953) from Yale University, M.A. (1955) from the University of Paris, and M.A. (1957) from Harvard University. He received the Arthur S. Flemming Award in 1970. He is married to the former Gaetana Marchegiano and has four children.

Nomination of Lawrence F. Davenport To Be an Associate Director of ACTION
April 22, 1981

The President today announced his intention to nominate Lawrence F. Davenport to be Associate Director of the ACTION agency (Domestic and Anti-Poverty Operations).

Since 1979 Dr. Davenport has been provost of the San Diego Community College District. In that position he served as the chief academic officer of the second largest district in the State of California and the third largest district in the United States. In 1974–79 he was president of the San Diego Community College Educational Cultural Complex. Dr. Davenport served as vice president for development of Tuskegee Institute in 1972–74. In 1969–72 he was director of special projects at the University of Michigan (Flint) and in 1972 was assistant dean for special projects. In 1968–69 he was assistant director of student activities at Lansing Community College in Michigan.

In 1970 he was appointed by President Nixon to serve on the National Advisory Council on Vocational Education and in 1971 was appointed Chairman. In 1972 Dr.

Davenport was appointed by the Secretary of Labor to the National Manpower Advisory Council. He was appointed by President Nixon to the National Advisory Council on Equality of Educational Opportunity in 1973.

Dr. Davenport was graduated from Michigan State University (B.A., 1968) and Farleigh Dickinson (Ph. D., 1975). He resides in Spring Valley, Calif. He was born on October 13, 1944.

Nomination of Elise R. W. du Pont To Be an Assistant Administrator of the Agency for International Development
April 22, 1981

The President today announced his intention to nominate Elise R. W. du Pont to be an Assistant Administrator of the Agency for International Development (Bureau for Private and Development Cooperation), United States International Development Cooperation Agency.

In 1978–80 Mrs. du Pont worked in the corporate law department of the firm of Montgomery, McCracken, Walker & Rhoads of Philadelphia, Pa. In 1980 she led the Department of Commerce's first officially sponsored State Trade Mission of business leaders to the People's Republic of China. Since 1973 Mrs. du Pont has developed several properties in the District of Columbia, including renovations on Capitol Hill.

In 1966–68 Mrs. du Pont was vice president of the New Castle Young Republicans

and chaired the GOP Congressional Candidates Wives Seminar in 1969. In 1974–75 she founded and chaired the Women's Campaign Fund, a group which funded women candidates for Federal and statewide offices through direct mail. She has been an active campaigner for her husband, Governor Pierre S. du Pont, in five statewide campaigns for U.S. Congress and Governor. She is a member of the Delaware World Affairs Council and served on the Delaware State Board of Health in 1969–72.

Mrs. du Pont was graduated from Temple University (B.A., 1976) and the University of Pennsylvania Law School (J.D., 1979). The Governor and Mrs. du Pont have four children and reside in Rockland, Del. Mrs. du Pont was born in New York City on December 27, 1935.

Proclamation 4838—Days of Remembrance of Victims of the Holocaust
April 22, 1981

By the President of the United States of America

A Proclamation

The Congress of the United States established the United States Holocaust Memorial Council to create a living memorial to

the victims of the Nazi Holocaust. Its purpose: So mankind will never lose memory of that terrible moment in time when the awful spectre of death camps stained the history of our world.

When America and its allies liberated those haunting places of terror and sick destructiveness, the world came to a vivid and tragic understanding of the evil it faced in those years of the Second World War. Each of those names—Auschwitz, Buchenwald, Dachau, Treblinka and so many others—became synonymous with horror.

The millions of deaths, the gas chambers, the inhuman crematoria, and the thousands of people who somehow survived with lifetime scars are all now part of the conscience of history. Forever must we remember just how precious is civilization, how important is liberty, and how heroic is the human spirit.

Like the genocide of the Armenians before it, and the genocide of the Cambodians which followed it—and like too many other such persecutions of too many other peoples—the lessons of the Holocaust must never be forgotten.

As part of its mandate, the Holocaust Memorial Council has been directed to designate annual Days of Remembrance as a national, civic commemoration of the Holocaust, and to encourage and sponsor appropriate observances throughout the United States. This year, the national Days of Remembrance will be observed on April 26 through May 3.

Now, Therefore, I, Ronald Reagan, President of the United States of America, do hereby ask the people of the United States to observe this solemn anniversary of the liberation of the Nazi death camps, with appropriate study, prayers and commemoration, as a tribute to the spirit of freedom and justice which Americans fought so hard and well to preserve.

In Witness Whereof, I have hereunto set my hand this 22nd day of April, in the year of our Lord nineteen hundred and eighty-one, and of the Independence of the United States of America the two hundred and fifth.

RONALD REAGAN

[*Filed with the Office of the Federal Register, 10:52 a.m., April 23, 1981*]

Note: The President's remarks at the first annual commemoration of the Days of Remembrance of Victims of the Holocaust begin on page 396.

Proclamation 4839—National Defense Transportation Day and National Transportation Week, 1981
April 22, 1981

By the President of the United States of America

A Proclamation

From the Boston Post Road to the Pony Express to the golden spike that joined together the transcontinental railroads . . . from the flight at Kitty Hawk and the appearance of the first horseless carriage to the advent of jet travel and the development of the interstate highway system . . . transportation in America has played a vital and historical role in our development as a Nation.

Today, transportation is still vital to our economy, necessary to our defense, essential to our personal mobility and leisure.

Transportation keeps America moving, producing, and growing.

Among the Americans who contribute to transportation are the hundreds of thousands who build machines, construct the facilities, operate and maintain the equipment, and provide the services that make our transportation systems work. Countless others labor to make transportation better and to meet the needs of our changing times.

In their honor and in recognition of the indispensable role transportation plays in our lives, we set aside one week each year as National Transportation Week.

By joint resolution, the Congress on May 16, 1957, requested the President to proclaim the third Friday in each May as National Defense Transportation Day, and by joint resolution of May 14, 1962, requested the President to designate the week in which that Friday falls as National Transportation Week.

Now, Therefore, I, Ronald Reagan, President of the United States of America, do hereby designate Friday, May 15, 1981, as National Defense Transportation Day, and the week beginning May 10, 1981, as National Transportation Week.

In Witness Whereof, I have hereunto set my hand this twenty-second day of April in the year of our Lord nineteen hundred and eighty-one, and of the Independence of the United States of America the two hundred and fifth.

RONALD REAGAN

[*Filed with the Office of the Federal Register, 10:53 a.m., April 23, 1981*]

Proclamation 4840—National Maritime Day, 1981
April 22, 1981

By the President of the United States of America

A Proclamation

The maritime industry has been a key contributor to our economic strength and security since our Nation was founded. Its continued growth and prosperity is necessary for the economic renewal we all seek.

As the leader in world trade and the principal military power of the free world, the United States conveys goodwill through its Merchant Marine, serving the cause of international peace. The Merchant Marine also stands ready to provide logistical support in military emergencies.

In recognition of the importance of the American Merchant Marine and the men and women serving aboard our merchant ships, Americans have observed National Maritime Day on May 22 for the last 49 years. This observance commemorates the

same date in 1819, when the SS Savannah began the first steamship, transatlantic voyage from the port of Savannah, Georgia.

Now, Therefore, I, Ronald Reagan, President of the United States of America, do hereby urge the people of the United States to honor our American Merchant Marine on May 22, 1981, by displaying the flag of the United States at their homes and other suitable places, and I request that all ships under the American flag dress ship on that day.

In Witness Whereof, I have hereunto set my hand this twenty-second day of April in the year of our Lord nineteen hundred and eighty-one, and of the Independence of the United States of America the two hundred and fifth.

RONALD REAGAN

[*Filed with the Office of the Federal Register, 10:54 a.m., April 23, 1981*]

Nomination of Eugene V. Rostow To Be Director of the United States Arms Control and Disarmament Agency
April 22, 1981

The President today announced his intention to nominate Eugene V. Rostow to be Director of the United States Arms Control and Disarmament Agency.

Since 1976 Mr. Rostow has been Sterling

Professor of Law and Public Affairs, Yale University Law School. He was visiting professor, Balliol College, Oxford University, in 1970–71. In 1966–69 Mr. Rostow was Under Secretary of State for Political Affairs. He was Sterling Professor of Law and Public Affairs at Yale University Law School in 1964, dean of Yale Law School in 1955–65, and professor of law at Yale in 1950–54.

Mr. Rostow is currently Chairman, Executive Committee on the Present Danger. He served on the Advisory Council for the Peace Corps in 1961 and was on the Attorney General's National Committee for the Study of Anti-trust Laws in 1954–55.

Mr. Rostow was graduated from Yale University (A.B., 1933; LL.B., 1937; A.M., 1944); Cambridge University (M.A., 1959; LL.D., 1962); Boston University (LL.D., 1976). He is married, has three children, and resides in New Haven, Conn. He was born in Brooklyn, N.Y., on August 25, 1913.

Statement on Federal Credit Management
April 23, 1981

The burden of delinquent debts owed to the Federal Government continues to grow every year and is contributing to our problems of inflation. More that $25 billion of the $175 billion in debts owed the Federal Government is either delinquent or in default. The interest on the delinquent debt alone, at a 15-percent rate, is almost $10.3 million per day. This abnormally high delinquency rate is another example of the abuse and mismanagement in the Federal Government. Allowing uncollected debt to grow increases the cost of government and adds to the inflation that hurts every one of us.

We must make it clear that debts owed to the Federal Government must be repaid. These debts are due from all segments of our society: college graduates whose tuition was paid for by Government loans; homeowners who have defaulted on loans from the Veterans Administration, Farmers Home Administration, and Federal Housing Administration; businesses who have used Government funds to finance export sales; farmers who have used Government loans to finance farm operations; and individuals and businesses who have not settled their tax accounts with the Internal Revenue Service.

It is not right that responsible, honest citizens should suffer because of those who do not honor their obligations or pay their taxes.

We must immediately pursue the current overdue debt to reduce that $25 billion burden. We must institute better Federal credit management to prevent debt delinquencies and defaults and use more aggressive debt collection practices to recover the delinquencies that do occur.

I am directing the heads of Federal agencies and departments to institute more effective debt collection practices and better credit management. I am asking them to designate an official in each agency or department who will have direct responsibility for debt collection. Additionally, I am calling for a detailed review of the current overdue debt and asking for a plan to collect those debts. Each agency and department must also provide a plan for improved credit management and debt collection in the future.

A progress report on the results of the detailed review of backlogged debt, along with the credit management plans, will be due by September 30, 1981. As a further step in establishing better discipline in this area, an annual report on debt collection will be due every September when the Federal budgets are being reviewed.

Administrative action alone is not enough to solve this massive problem. Accordingly, this administration will support legislation to facilitate debt collection and allow the Federal agencies and departments to practice better credit management.

We will not allow mismanagement and abuses in the Federal Government to contribute to the burden already being carried by the American people.

Memorandum on Federal Credit Management
April 23, 1981

Memorandum for the Heads of Executive Departments and Agencies

Subject: Strengthening Federal Credit Management

The burden of delinquent debts owed to the Federal Government continues to grow every year and is contributing to our serious problem of inflation. We must again establish the principle that debts to the Federal Government must be paid. Recent studies by the Executive Branch Debt Collection Project and the General Accounting Office reveal that more than $25 billion of the $175 billion in debts owed the Federal Government are either delinquent or in default.

We must institute better credit management to prevent debt delinquencies and defaults and use more aggressive debt collection procedures to recover the delinquencies that do occur. We must take firm action now to reduce that portion of the $25 billion debt backlog that is collectible.

As first steps, I am directing you to designate an official with responsibility and authority for debt collection and submit the name of this official to the Office of Management and Budget by May 15, 1981. Additionally, each department and agency is to complete a review of their agencies debt situation and prepare a detailed plan and schedule for resolving identified problems. This is due by June 15, 1981 to the Office of Management and Budget.

To slow the expansion of delinquent debt, each agency and department will provide a plan for improved credit management and more efficient debt collection. A progress report on the results of your reviews and the development of credit management plans will be due by September 30, 1981 to the Office of Management and Budget. Hereafter, an annual report on debt collection will be submitted in September.

I am instructing the Director of the Office of Management and Budget to issue procedures and guidelines to assist you in carrying out this directive.

Administrative actions are not sufficient to resolve this critical problem. Accordingly, this Administration will support legislation to facilitate better credit management and more effective debt collection.

We cannot afford to allow debt to grow and add to the burden of inflation. Immediate action is required now to restore sound credit management to the Federal Government.

RONALD REAGAN

Nomination of James Montgomery Beggs To Be Administrator of the National Aeronautics and Space Administration
April 23, 1981

The President today announced his intention to nominate James Montgomery Beggs to be Administrator of the National Aeronautics and Space Administration.

Since 1974 Mr. Beggs has been executive vice president, aerospace, General Dynamics Corp. In 1973–74 he was managing director of operations, Summa Corp. He served as Under Secretary of Transportation in 1969–73 and was Associate Administrator, Office of Advanced Research and Technology (NASA) in 1968–69. Mr. Beggs was with the Westinghouse Electric Corp. in 1955–68, serving as general manager, underseas division, in 1955–60; general manager systems operations division, in 1960–63; vice president, defense and space center; and general manager, surface division, in 1963–67; and corporate director, purchases and traffic, in 1967–68.

Mr. Beggs served in the United States Navy, serving in various assignments as a line officer from ensign to lieutenant commander. He was graduated from the United States Naval Academy (B.S., 1947) and Harvard Graduate School of Business Administration (M.B.A., 1955).

Mr. Beggs is married and resides in St. Louis, Mo. He was born in Pittsburgh, Pa., on January 9, 1926.

Nomination of Hans M. Mark To Be Deputy Administrator of the National Aeronautics and Space Administration
April 23, 1981

The President today announced his intention to nominate Hans M. Mark to be Deputy Administrator of the National Aeronautics and Space Administration.

Dr. Mark has served as Secretary of the Air Force since 1979. He was Under Secretary in 1977–79. He was Director of NASA's Ames Research Center in 1969–77. Previously he was a professor of nuclear engineering, and chairman of the department, at the University of California at Berkeley. He is a recipient of the Distinguished Service Award from both NASA and the Department of Defense. Dr. Mark is a member of the National Academy of Sciences.

He was graduated from MIT (Ph. D., physics). Dr. Mark resides in Alexandria, Va. He was born in Mannheim, Germany, on June 17, 1929.

Nomination of L. Keith Bulen To Be United States Commissioner of the International Joint Commission—United States and Canada
April 23, 1981

The President today announced his intention to nominate L. Keith Bulen to be Commissioner on the part of the United States on the International Joint Commission—United States and Canada.

Mr. Bulen was elected to the Indiana State House of Representatives in 1960 and was reelected in 1962. Since 1969 Mr. Bulen has been an attorney with the firm of Bulen, Castor, Robinette and Nickels. In 1972–74 he was chairman of the board of Campaign Communicators, Inc., involved in Presidential, State, and local campaigns. Mr. Bulen was director of political liaison at the office of the President-elect. He was eastern coordinator for the Reagan-Bush Committee during the Presidential campaign. He has been an active Republican for the past 30 years.

Mr. Bulen was graduated from Indiana University (B.A., 1949; J.D., 1952). He served in the Army Air Force during World War II.

Mr. Bulen is married, has four children, and resides in Indianapolis, Ind. He was born in Pendleton, Ind., on December 31, 1926.

Proclamation 4841—National Day of Recognition for Veterans of the Vietnam Era
April 23, 1981

By the President of the United States of America

A Proclamation

The decade which has come to be known as the Vietnam era was a time of trial for our Nation. Nearly every citizen was touched in some way by the war in Southeast Asia.

As in all wars, the brunt of the conflict was borne by the soldiers, sailors, airmen, and marines who served in our Armed Forces during that time, particularly the millions who saw duty in Vietnam. Beyond the 57,000 who died during the Vietnam war, we have among us millions of veterans who have yet to receive the full measure of thanks for having accepted the call to arms when such service was not popular with all Americans. More than 300,000 of these were wounded in Vietnam, many suffering permanent disabilities.

The cold statistics are empty, however, unless we keep in mind the individual and personal drama which accompanies each Vietnam-era veteran and casualty. Much has been said about the sacrifice made by those who served, but full recognition of the Nation's debt of gratitude to them is long overdue.

Our first national commemoration of the Vietnam-era veteran was in 1974, when Vietnam Veterans Day was proclaimed pursuant to a joint resolution of the Congress. I believe it is appropriate again to recognize and commemorate those men and women who did their duty in a time of crisis. No one should doubt the nobility of the effort they made.

By their demonstrations of loyalty and courage, Vietnam veterans have earned our esteem. A recent survey revealed that the American public overwhelmingly admires the Vietnam-era veteran. Certainly, those veterans who suffer from physical and psychic aftereffects can look to their fellow citizens for understanding and help.

In these times of economic hardship and budget restriction every citizen should be aware that showing our gratitude to the Vietnam veteran will take more than leaving it up to the Federal Government to provide money and programs. Each of us must do his or her part in reaching out in a personal way to these brave men and women. This recognition will mean much to the Vietnam veterans who never received the thanks they deserved when they originally returned home from war.

In honor of those who deserve the profound gratitude of their countrymen, the Congress, by joint resolution, has requested the President to issue a proclamation designating Sunday, April 26, 1981, as a National Day of Recognition for Veterans of the Vietnam Era.

Now, Therefore, I, Ronald Reagan, President of the United States of America, call upon all Americans, and upon patriotic and civic organizations, to observe Sunday, April 26, 1981, as a National Day of Recognition for Veterans of the Vietnam Era. I urge my fellow citizens to observe this day with appropriate programs, ceremonies, and activities dedicated to those issues of concern to Vietnam veterans.

I call upon officials of the Government to display the flag of the United States on all Government buildings and grounds on that day in testimony of our respect for the contributions of Vietnam veterans.

In Witness Whereof, I have hereunto set my hand this 23rd day of April, in the year of our Lord nineteen hundred and eighty-one, and of the Independence of the United States of America the two hundred and fifth.

RONALD REAGAN

[*Filed with the Office of the Federal Register, 3:47 p.m., April 23, 1981*]

Statement on Terminating United States Restrictions on Agricultural Sales to the Soviet Union
April 24, 1981

I am today lifting the U.S. limitation on additional agricultural sales to the Soviet Union as I promised to do during last year's Presidential campaign. My administration has made a full and complete study of this sales limitation, and I reached my decision after weighing all options carefully and conferring fully with my advisers, including members of the Cabinet and the National Security Council. We have also been consulting with our allies on this matter.

As a Presidential candidate, I indicated my opposition to the curb on sales, because American farmers had been unfairly singled out to bear the burden of this ineffective national policy. I also pledged that when elected President I would "fully assess our national security, foreign policy, and agricultural needs to determine how best to terminate" the decision made by my predecessor.

This assessment began as soon as I entered office and has continued until now. In the first few weeks of my Presidency, I decided that an immediate lifting of the sales limitation could be misinterpreted by the Soviet Union. I therefore felt that my decision should be made only when it was clear that the Soviets and other nations would not mistakenly think it indicated a weakening of our position.

I have determined that our position now cannot be mistaken: The United States, along with the vast majority of nations has condemned and remains opposed to the Soviet occupation of Afghanistan and other aggressive acts around the world. We will react strongly to acts of aggression wherever they take place. There will never be a weakening of this resolve.

Note: Deputy Press Secretary Larry M. Speakes read the statement at the regular press briefing in the Briefing Room at the White House.

Memorandum Directing the Termination of United States Restrictions on Agricultural Sales to the Soviet Union
April 24, 1981

Memorandum for the Secretary of Commerce

I hereby direct that you, in consultation with the Secretary of Agriculture and other appropriate officials, immediately terminate the current restrictions on the export of agricultural commodities and products to the Soviet Union imposed under authority of the Export Administration Act pursuant to the Presidential Memorandum to the Secretary of Commerce of January 7, 1980. I also direct that you terminate restrictions imposed on the export of phosphate rock and related commodities by virtue of the regulations of the Department of Commerce published on February 7, 1980.

RONALD REAGAN

Memorandum on Terminating United States Restrictions on Agricultural Sales to the Soviet Union
April 24, 1981

Memorandum for the Secretary of Agriculture

I have today directed the Secretary of Commerce, in consultation with you and other appropriate officials, to immediately terminate the current restrictions on the export of agricultural commodities and products to the Soviet Union imposed under authority of the Export Administra- tion Act pursuant to the Presidential Memorandum to the Secretary of Commerce of January 7, 1980. I have also directed that the restrictions be terminated which were imposed on the export of phosphate rock and related commodities by virtue of the regulations of the Department of Commerce published on February 7, 1980.

RONALD REAGAN

Nomination of Alan Green, Jr., To Be a Commissioner of the Federal Maritime Commission, and Designation as Chairman
April 24, 1981

The President today announced his intention to nominate Alan "Punch" Green, Jr., to be a Federal Maritime Commissioner for a term expiring June 30, 1984, vice Leslie Lazar Kanuk. Upon confirmation, the President intends to designate Mr. Green Chairman.

Mr. Green is president and commissioner, Port of Portland, Portland, Oreg. He has been president since 1974 and a member since 1970.

Previously he was a member of the board of directors of Equitable Savings & Loan, Portland, Oreg.; secretary-treasurer of the Southern Oregon Battery & Supply Co., Inc.; member of the board of directors of Comprehensive Care, Inc., Newport Beach, Calif.; chairman of the board, Western Batteries, Inc., Beaverton, Oreg.; and chairman of the board, Tom Bonoon Class Co., Inc., Portland, Oreg.

Mr. Green was graduated from Stanford University (B.A., 1949). He served in the U.S. Army in 1943–45. Mr. Green is married, has three children, and resides with his family in Portland, Oreg. He was born in Portland on May 1, 1925.

Proclamation 4842—Memorial Day, May 25, 1981
April 24, 1981

By the President of the United States of America

A Proclamation

Over one hundred years ago, Memorial Day was established to commemorate those who died in the defense of our national ideals. Our ideals of freedom, justice, and equal rights for all have been challenged many times since then, and thousands of Americans have given their lives in many parts of the world to secure those same ideals and insure for their children a lasting peace. Their sacrifice demands that we, the living, continue to promote the cause of peace and the ideals for which they so valiantly gave of themselves.

Today, the United States stands as a beacon of liberty and democratic strength before the community of nations. We are resolved to stand firm against those who would destroy the freedoms we cherish. We are determined to achieve an enduring peace—a peace with liberty and with honor. This determination, this resolve, is the highest tribute we can pay to the many who have fallen in the service of our Nation.

In recognition of those Americans whom we honor today, the Congress, by joint resolution of May 11, 1950 (64 Stat. 158), has requested the President to issue a proclamation calling upon the people of the United States to observe each Memorial Day as a day of prayer for permanent peace and a period during such day when the people of the United States might unite in prayer.

Now, Therefore, I, Ronald Reagan, President of the United States of America, do hereby designate Memorial Day, Monday, May 25, 1981, as a day of prayer for permanent peace, and I designate the hour beginning in each locality at 11 o'clock in the morning of that day as a time to unite in prayer.

I urge the press, radio, television, and all other information media to cooperate in this observance.

I also request the Governors of the United States and the Commonwealth of Puerto Rico and the appropriate officials of all local units of Government to direct that the flag be flown at half-staff during this Memorial Day on all buildings, grounds, and naval vessels throughout the United States and in all areas under its jurisdiction and control, and I request the people of the United States to display the flag at half-staff from their homes for the customary forenoon period.

In Witness Whereof, I have hereunto set my hand this twenty-fourth day of April, in the year of our Lord nineteen hundred and eighty-one, and of the Independence of the United States of America the two hundred and fifth.

RONALD REAGAN

[*Filed with the Office of the Federal Register, 10:59 a.m., April 27, 1981*]

Note: The text of the proclamation was released by the Office of the Press Secretary on April 25.

Remarks by Telephone at the Annual Dinner of the White House Correspondents Association
April 25, 1981

Mr. Pierpoint. Mr. President, this is Bob Pierpoint at the podium.

The President. Bob, I hope you don't mind, but David Stockman is making me call collect. [*Laughter*]

Mr. Pierpoint. Well, I do mind, Mr. President, but he's a hard man to talk out of it, so we'll take the call.

The President [*laughing*]. Okay. Well, I'm happy to be speaking to the White House correspondents' spring prom. [*Laughter*] I'm sorry that I can't be there in person.

Mr. Pierpoint. We're very sorry you can't also, Mr. President.

The President. Well, I'm up at Camp David. We're getting a little used to it now, but I have to tell you the first time I came to this place, to Camp David, Ed Meese sewed nametags in all my undershorts and T-shirts. [*Laughter*]

But, Bob, I'm sure your fellow correspondents have already praised you or will soon do so for your year in office. Mark Twain is supposed to have said there's nothing harder to put up with than the annoyance of a good example, and you certainly have been that to the White House press corps.

Mr. Pierpoint. Thank you, Mr. President.

The President. I know that Cliff Evans must be there somewhere.

Mr. Pierpoint. Yes.

The President. And, Cliff, let me send my congratulations to you as one new president to another. If you enjoy your office as much as I do mine, you'll be a very happy and fulfilled man.

Mr. Evans. Well, you stay well, Mr. President, and we'll take care of the pressroom, Pierpoint and I and all of my colleagues. Stay well.

The President. Okay. If I could give you just one little bit of advice, when somebody tells you to get in a car quick, do it. [*Laughter*]

Mr. Pierpoint. Mr. President, we know now that you are really recovering. You sound terrific.

The President [*laughing*]. Well, I am. believe me, well on the road and feeling just fine.

Mr. Pierpoint. That's wonderful. Well, let me tell you, Mr. President, there are about—well, over 1,800 people assembled in this room tonight listening to you. And I told the Vice President that they are actually here for him, but you know the truth. [*Laughter*] We all hoped that you would make it. We well understand that you could not.

Among these people are many of your Cabinet Secretaries. There's only really one that I think is very noticeable by his absence. I haven't seen Secretary Haig. I wondered if you've been watching television tonight. We are a little worried who's in the Situation Room and who's in control. [*Laughter*]

The President. Well, I'll tell you, wherever he is, I have every confidence in him. [*Laughter*]

Mr. Pierpoint. Very good, Mr. President. We really appreciate your call.

The President. Well, if I could be serious for just a moment, there's someone who isn't there tonight and yet, in a sense, I'm sure in all our hearts is. And I'd like to give the phone to Nancy for a moment to say something, and you'll understand when she does.

Mr. Pierpoint. Thank you.

Mrs. Reagan. Hello. I really want to say— this is a message to Sarah, and Sarah, I hope you're there.

Mr. Pierpoint. And Sarah is here, Mrs. Reagan. I believe she's over at table 45. [*Applause*]

Mrs. Reagan. Oh, good.

Mr. Pierpoint. Sarah Brady is now standing up, Mrs. Reagan. And as you can imagine, she's receiving a very warm round of applause.

Mrs. Reagan. Sarah, you remember those days in the hospital when you and I had many conversations. And we both agreed that you and I, from now on, had a bond that was very special and that nobody could ever break. It was just something between you and me that was ours. And I want you to know that you've never left my thoughts and my prayers, and all my love and all my prayers are with you as they always have been. And I know that both our fellows are going to make it, and I send you and Jim all my love.

Mr. Pierpoint. And we all join you, Mrs. Reagan in those thoughts to the Bradys. [*Applause*]

The President. Bob, thank you very much. Could I just say——

Mr. Pierpoint. Mr. President, the entire room is standing and applauding Sarah Brady.

The President. Well, could I then suggest something?

Mr. Pierpoint. We're having a little trouble hearing you because the applause is so loud in this room for Sarah and Jim Brady.

The President. All right.

Mr. Pierpoint. I think the President would like to sign off if you'll all be seated.

The President. Yes, I'd like to say just one thing before you sit down, and that is, as long as you're standing, I know how close to all of you is "The Bear," and certainly Nancy said it, there isn't an hour that he isn't in our prayers. Why don't we raise a glass to "The Bear's" health and to Sarah?

Mr. Pierpoint. That's certainly a fine idea. Everyone stand, please, and let's raise a glass to"The Bear" and to Sarah. To their good health.

We've done it, Mr. President.

The President. Thank you very much.

Mr. Pierpoint. Thank you for calling.

The President. Well, I'm looking forward to the next news conference. I have so many questions to ask you all. *[Laughter]*

Mr. Pierpoint. We've got a few for you too. And have a very pleasant weekend, and don't work too hard on that speech for Tuesday night.

The President. All right, and good night and enjoy yourselves. God bless all of you.

Mr. Pierpoint. Thank you.

The President. Thank you.

Note: The exchange of remarks began at approximately 8:15 p.m. in the International Ballroom at the Washington Hilton Hotel. Also speaking were Robert C. Pierpoint of CBS News, president, and Clifford Evans of RKO General Broadcasting, incoming president, White House Correspondents Association.

Nomination of Bernard J. Wunder, Jr., To Be an Assistant Secretary of Commerce
April 27, 1981

The President today announced his intention to nominate Bernard J. Wunder, Jr., to be Assistant Secretary of Commerce for Communications and Information.

Since February 1981 Mr. Wunder has been associate minority counsel, Committee on Energy and Commerce, House of Representatives. In 1980–81 he was chief counsel and staff director, Subcommittee on Communication, Committee on Energy and Commerce. Mr. Wunder was associate minority counsel, Subcommittee on Oversight and Investigations, Committee on Interstate and Foreign Commerce, in 1979–80. He served as minority counsel in 1975–79.

In 1973–75 Mr. Wunder was an attorney with the firm of Hull, Towill, Norman, Barrett & Johnson of Augusta, Ga. He was administrative assistant to Representative James M. Collins (R-Tex.) in 1970 and legislative assistant in 1969–70.

Mr. Wunder was graduated from The Citadel (B.A., 1965) and University of South Carolina School of Law (J.D., 1973). He served in the United States Air Force in 1965–69 and was awarded the Bronze Star Medal and two Air Force Commendation Medals.

Mr. Wunder is married, has two children, and resides in Dumfries, Va. He was born in Baltimore, Md., on December 13, 1943.

Nomination of Herman E. Roser To Be an Assistant Secretary of Energy
April 27, 1981

The President today announced his intention to nominate Herman E. Roser to be an Assistant Secretary of Energy (Defense Programs).

Mr. Roser has been Manager of the Department of Energy's Albuquerque Operations (ALO) since 1975. He had been Deputy Manager in 1972–75. As Manager of ALO, Mr. Roser was responsible for field coordination and direction of the nation's

nuclear weapons production program as well as for energy research and development programs at Sandia National Laboratories and Los Alamos National Scientific Laboratory.

On September 17, 1980, Mr. Roser was one of the first recipients of the Presidential rank awards as Meritorious Executive from the Department of Energy. In August 1979, he was awarded the DOE Exceptional Service Award. He is also the recipient of the DOE Special Achievement Award and the Atomic Energy Commission's Distinguished Service Award.

Mr. Roser joined the Atomic Energy Commission at Los Alamos, N. Mex., in 1961 as Assistant Area Manager for Community Affairs. He was Deputy Manager from 1964 to 1967 and was named Area Manager in 1967. From 1948 until he joined the AEC, Mr. Roser was with the Zia Co. of Los Alamos.

Mr. Roser is married, has two children, and resides in Albuquerque, N. Mex. He was born in San Marcial, N. Mex., on August 5, 1922.

Nomination of J. Erich Evered To Be Administrator of the Energy Information Administration
April 27, 1981

The President today announced his intention to nominate J. Erich Evered to be Administrator of the Energy Information Administration, Department of Energy.

Mr. Evered is a petroleum engineer and geologist, currently geotechnical division manager for CER Corp., an energy resource consulting and project management company based in Las Vegas, Nev. He joined CER in 1978. His responsibilities included management of the firm's oil and gas consulting business, as well as management of a multimillion dollar research program in unconventional natural gas supply.

In 1976–78 Mr. Evered served in Washington as energy adviser to Senator Dewey F. Bartlett (R-Okla.). He was previously with Phillips Petroleum Co. and C & K Petroleum, Inc., in Oklahoma and Texas.

Mr. Evered was graduated from the University of Oklahoma (B.S., 1974). He is married and was born in Webb City, Mo., on August 27, 1953.

Nomination of Robert J. Rubin To Be an Assistant Secretary of Health and Human Services
April 27, 1981

The President today announced his intention to nominate Robert J. Rubin to be Assistant Secretary of Health and Human Services (Planning and Evaluation).

Dr. Rubin is a physician, specializing in nephrology. He was chief of the renal division of Lemuel Shattuck Hospital in Boston, Mass., and also served as assistant dean for government affairs, Tufts University School of Medicine. Since 1979 Dr. Rubin has been a consultant to the U.S. Senate Committee on Human Resources, where he worked closely with Senator Schweiker in developing health legislation. In 1972–74 he was epidemic intelligence officer, Respiratory Disease and Special Pathogens Viral Diseases Division, Center for Disease Control.

Dr. Rubin was graduated from Williams College (A.B., 1966) and Cornell University Medical College (M.D., 1970).

Dr. Rubin is married, has two children, and resides in Lexington, Mass. He was born in Brooklyn, N.Y., on February 7, 1946.

Nomination of Richard D. Erb To Be United States Executive Director of the International Monetary Fund
April 27, 1981

The President today announced his intention to nominate Richard D. Erb to be United States Executive Director of the International Monetary Fund for a term of 2 years.

Dr. Erb is currently resident fellow, American Enterprise Institute for Public Policy Research. In addition to his work at AEI, he also serves as a consultant to the Comptroller of the Currency.

In 1976–77 he was Deputy Assistant Secretary for Developing Nations Finance, Department of the Treasury. Dr. Erb was international affairs fellow, Council on For-eign Relations, and resident economist, American Enterprise Institute for Public Policy Research, in 1974–76. In 1971–74 he served as staff assistant to the president and director for international monetary affairs, Council on International Economic Policy. Dr. Erb was a consultant with Arthur D. Little, Inc., in 1969–71.

He was graduated from State University of New York at Buffalo (B.A., 1963) and Stanford University (Ph. D., 1967).

Dr. Erb is married to the former Joanna Reed Shelton. He was born in Wantagh, N.Y., on April 15, 1941.

Message to the Congress Reporting Budget Rescissions and Deferrals
April 27, 1981

To the Congress of the United States:

In accordance with the Impoundment Control Act of 1974, I herewith report six revisions to previously transmitted rescission proposals. Three of the revisions decrease the total amount proposed for rescission by $3.7 million. The other revisions to proposed rescissions make technical changes to appropriation language which do not affect the amounts proposed for rescission. In addition, I am reporting two new deferrals totaling $6.4 million and revisions to five previously reported deferrals.

The revisions to rescission proposals affect programs in the Departments of Agriculture and Energy, as well as ACTION and the National Science Foundation. The new deferrals and revisions to existing deferrals involve programs in the Departments of Agriculture, Commerce, Energy, Health and Human Services, and Transportation, as well as the Board for International Broadcasting and the International Communication Agency.

The details of each rescission proposal and deferral are contained in the attached reports.

RONALD REAGAN

The White House,
April 27, 1981.

Note: The attachments detailing the rescission proposals and deferrals are printed in the Federal Register *of May 1, 1981.*

Nomination of Toni Ford To Be an Assistant Administrator of the Agency for International Development
April 28, 1981

The President today announced his intention to nominate Toni Ford to be Assistant Administrator of the Agency for International Development (Near East), United States International Development Cooperation Agency.

Mrs. Ford is production supervisor, General Motors Corp., Fisher Body Division. Previously she spent almost 2 years in personnel with General Motors. Mrs. Ford was formerly a White House Fellow and served as assistant to Secretary of Treasury John Connally. She was Deputy Director of the Office of Federal Contract Compliance and was appointed by President Ford to the Clemency Board.

Mrs. Ford was graduated from Chestnut Hill College, Philadelphia, Pa. (B.S.) and American University (M.S.). She is a National Science Foundation fellow at Stanford University and a fellow at the Institute of Politics at Harvard.

Mrs. Ford is married, has one child, and resides in Detroit, Mich. She was born in Philadelphia on December 14, 1941.

Nomination of Robert W. Karpe To Be President of the Government National Mortgage Association
April 28, 1981

The President today announced his intention to nominate Robert W. Karpe to be President, Government National Mortgage Association, Department of Housing and Urban Development.

Mr. Karpe has been associated with Karpe Real Estate Center since 1959, serving as president in 1959–71, and as chairman of the board from 1976 to present. The center is a firm offering full real estate services, including sales, financing, escrow, appraisal, investment, and real estate development.

In 1971–75 Mr. Karpe served as commissioner of the California Department of Real Estate. He has been active in real estate affairs, serving as president of the California Association of Realtors (1968); director of the National Association of Realtors (1968–71 and 1979–81) and vice president of the National Association of Real Estate Licensed Law Officials (1974–75).

Mr. Karpe was graduated from the University of California at Berkeley. He is married, has three children, and resides in Bakersfield, Calif. He was born in Bakersfield on November 3, 1930.

Nomination of Danford L. Sawyer To Be Public Printer
April 28, 1981

The President today announced his intention to nominate Danford L. Sawyer to be Public Printer, Government Printing Office, vice John J. Boyle, resigned.

Since 1979 Mr. Sawyer has served as director of Presidential Savings and Loan, Sarasota, Fla. In 1964–80 he was president of Sawyer & Associates Advertising, Inc., and president of Area Guides, Inc., a Sarasota publishing firm. He was publisher of

Sarasota South, a community news magazine serving the southern part of Sarasota County, Fla.

Mr. Sawyer began his business career as a cost accountant for Cone Brothers Contracting Co. in Tampa, Fla. He then became the advertising manager of Newsmonth magazine and joined the display advertising staff of the Sarasota Herald-Tribune & Journal. He later became the commercial manager of WSPB Radio in Sarasota.

Mr. Sawyer was graduated from the University of the South, Sewanee, Tenn. He is married, has three children, and resides in Sarasota, Fla. He was born in New York City on November 11, 1939.

Nomination of Richard P. Kusserow To Be Inspector General of the Department of Health and Human Services
April 28, 1981

The President today announced his intention to nominate Richard P. Kusserow to be Inspector General, Department of Health and Human Services.

Since 1969 Mr. Kusserow has been a special agent with the FBI. In 1969–70 he was assigned to the Pittsburgh Division and since 1970 has been assigned to the Chicago Division, specializing in white collar crime—embezzlement, bribery, and public corruption. Mr. Kusserow coordinated many task force investigations, including Department of Housing and Urban Development, real estate broker fraud, in 1978; Health, Education, and Welfare, welfare fraud, 1976; Veterans Administration, school fraud, 1975; and Housing and Urban Development, single family fraud, in 1974. In 1967–68 he was an intelligence officer with the Central Intelligence Agency.

Mr. Kusserow served in the U.S. Marine Corps as a captain in 1965–67. He was graduated from the University of California at Los Angeles (B.A., 1963) and California State University (M.A., 1964).

Mr. Kusserow is married, has one child, and resides with his family in Aurora, Ill. He was born in San Jose, Calif., on December 9, 1940.

Statement on Action by the Senate Budget Committee on a Fiscal Year 1982 Budget Resolution
April 28, 1981

I want to congratulate and express sincere appreciation to Chairman Domenici and his colleagues on the Senate Budget Committee upon completion of work on the first budget resolution for fiscal year 1982. Their vote is a welcome display of a strong bipartisan spirit and puts our economic recovery program firmly on track. Together with the reconciliation instructions passed by the Senate on April 2, this resolution will provide the basis for achieving the budget savings and the tax relief needed for the revitalization of the nation's economy.

I look forward to working with the Members of both the House and the Senate, of both political parties, as they proceed with additional actions necessary for recovery. Together we can accomplish the things the people elected us to do. And today we have no greater task, no more important job, than putting America's economic house in order. I thank Senator Domenici and the other members of the Senate Budget Committee for taking this important and constructive step.

Address Before a Joint Session of the Congress on the Program for Economic Recovery
April 28, 1981

You wouldn't want to talk me into an encore, would you? [*Laughter*]

Mr. Speaker, Mr. President, distinguished Members of the Congress, honored guests, and fellow citizens:

I have no words to express my appreciation for that greeting.

I have come to speak to you tonight about our economic recovery program and why I believe it's essential that the Congress approve this package, which I believe will lift the crushing burden of inflation off of our citizens and restore the vitality to our economy and our industrial machine.

First, however, and due to events of the past few weeks, will you permit me to digress for a moment from the all-important subject of why we must bring government spending under control and reduce tax rates. I'd like to say a few words directly to all of you and to those who are watching and listening tonight, because this is the only way I know to express to all of you on behalf of Nancy and myself our appreciation for your messages and flowers and, most of all, your prayers, not only for me but for those others who fell beside me.

The warmth of your words, the expression of friendship and, yes, love, meant more to us than you can ever know. You have given us a memory that we'll treasure forever. And you've provided an answer to those few voices that were raised saying that what happened was evidence that ours is a sick society.

The society we heard from is made up of millions of compassionate Americans and their children, from college age to kindergarten. As a matter of fact, as evidence of that I have a letter with me. The letter came from Peter Sweeney. He's in the second grade in the Riverside School in Rockville Centre, and he said, "I hope you get well quick or you might have to make a speech in your pajamas." [*Laughter*] He added a postscript. "P.S. If you have to make a speech in your pajamas, I warned you." [*Laughter*]

Well, sick societies don't produce men like the two who recently returned from outer space. Sick societies don't produce young men like Secret Service agent Tim McCarthy, who placed his body between mine and the man with the gun simply because he felt that's what his duty called for him to do. Sick societies don't produce dedicated police officers like Tom Delahanty or able and devoted public servants like Jim Brady. Sick societies don't make people like us so proud to be Americans and so very proud of our fellow citizens.

Now, let's talk about getting spending and inflation under control and cutting your tax rates.

Mr. Speaker and Senator Baker, I want to thank you for your cooperation in helping to arrange this joint session of the Congress. I won't be speaking to you very long tonight, but I asked for this meeting because the urgency of our joint mission has not changed.

Thanks to some very fine people, my health is much improved. I'd like to be able to say that with regard to the health of the economy.

It's been half a year since the election that charged all of us in this Government with the task of restoring our economy. Where have we come in this 6 months? Inflation, as measured by the Consumer Price Index, has continued at a double-digit rate. Mortgage interest rates have averaged almost 15 percent for these 6 months, preventing families across America from buying homes. There are still almost 8 million unemployed. The average worker's hourly earnings after adjusting for inflation are lower today than they were 6 months ago, and there have been over 6,000 business failures.

Six months is long enough. The American people now want us to act and not in half-measures. They demand and they've earned a full and comprehensive effort to clean up our economic mess. Because of the extent of our economy's sickness, we know that the cure will not come quickly and that even with our package, progress will come in inches and feet, not in miles. But to fail to act will delay even longer and more painfully the cure which must come. And that cure begins with the Federal budget. And the budgetary actions taken by the Congress over the next few days will determine how we respond to the message of last November 4th. That message was very simple. Our government is too big, and it spends too much.

For the last few months, you and I have enjoyed a relationship based on extraordinary cooperation. Because of this cooperation we've come a long distance in less than 3 months. I want to thank the leadership of the Congress for helping in setting a fair timetable for consideration of our recommendations. And committee chairmen on both sides of the aisle have called prompt and thorough hearings.

We have also communicated in a spirit of candor, openness, and mutual respect. Tonight, as our decision day nears and as the House of Representatives weighs its alternatives, I wish to address you in that same spirit.

The Senate Budget Committee, under the leadership of Pete Domenici, has just today voted out a budget resolution supported by Democrats and Republicans alike that is in all major respects consistent with the program that we have proposed. Now we look forward to favorable action on the Senate floor, but an equally crucial test involves the House of Representatives.

The House will soon be choosing between two different versions or measures to deal with the economy. One is the measure offered by the House Budget Committee. The other is a bipartisan measure, a substitute introduced by Congressmen Phil Gramm of Texas and Del Latta of Ohio.

On behalf of the administration, let me say that we embrace and fully support that bipartisan substitute. It will achieve all the essential aims of controlling government spending, reducing the tax burden, building a national defense second to none, and stimulating economic growth and creating millions of new jobs.

At the same time, however, I must state our opposition to the measure offered by the House Budget Committee. It may appear that we have two alternatives. In reality, however, there are no more alternatives left. The committee measure quite simply falls far too short of the essential actions that we must take.

For example, in the next 3 years, the committee measure projects spending $141 billion more than does the bipartisan substitute. It regrettably cuts over $14 billion in essential defense spending, funding required to restore America's national security. It adheres to the failed policy of trying to balance the budget on the taxpayer's back. It would increase tax payments by over a third, adding up to a staggering quarter of a trillion dollars. Federal taxes would increase 12 percent each year. Taxpayers would be paying a larger share of their income to government in 1984 than they do at present.

In short, that measure reflects an echo of the past rather than a benchmark for the future. High taxes and excess spending growth created our present economic mess; more of the same will not cure the hardship, anxiety, and discouragement it has imposed on the American people.

Let us cut through the fog for a moment. The answer to a government that's too big is to stop feeding its growth. Government spending has been growing faster than the economy itself. The massive national debt which we accumulated is the result of the government's high spending diet. Well, it's time to change the diet and to change it in the right way.

I know the tax portion of our package is of concern to some of you. Let me make a few points that I feel have been overlooked. First of all, it should be looked at as an integral part of the entire package, not something separate and apart from the budget reductions, the regulatory relief, and the monetary restraints. Probably the most common misconception is that we are proposing to reduce Government revenues to less than what the Government has been receiving. This is not true. Actually, the discussion has to do with how much of a tax increase should be imposed on the taxpayer in 1982.

Now, I know that over the recess in some informal polling some of your constituents have been asked which they'd rather have, a balanced budget or a tax cut, and with the common sense that characterizes the people of this country, the answer, of course, has been a balanced budget. But may I suggest, with no inference that there was wrong intent on the part of those who asked the question, the question was inappropriate to the situation.

Our choice is not between a balanced budget and a tax cut. Properly asked, the question is, "Do you want a great big raise in your taxes this coming year or, at the worst, a very little increase with the prospect of tax reduction and a balanced budget down the road a ways?" With the common sense that the people have already shown, I'm sure we all know what the answer to that question would be.

A gigantic tax increase has been built into the system. We propose nothing more than a reduction of that increase. The people have a right to know that even with our plan they will be paying more in taxes, but not as much more as they will without it.

The option, I believe, offered by the House Budget Committee, will leave spending too high and tax rates too high. At the same time, I think it cuts the defense budget too much, and by attempting to reduce the deficit through higher taxes, it will not create the kind of strong economic growth and the new jobs that we must have.

Let us not overlook the fact that the small, independent business man or woman creates more than 80 percent of all the new jobs and employs more than half of our total workforce. Our across-the-board cut in tax rates for a 3-year period will give them much of the incentive and promise of stability they need to go forward with expansion plans calling for additional employees.

Tonight, I renew my call for us to work as a team, to join in cooperation so that we find answers which will begin to solve all our economic problems and not just some of them. The economic recovery package that I've outlined to you over the past weeks is, I deeply believe, the only answer that we have left.

Reducing the growth of spending, cutting marginal tax rates, providing relief from overregulation, and following a noninflationary and predictable monetary policy are interwoven measures which will ensure that we have addressed each of the severe dislocations which threaten our economic future. These policies will make our economy stronger, and the stronger economy will balance the budget which we're committed to do by 1984.

When I took the oath of office, I pledged loyalty to only one special interest group— "We the people." Those people—neighbors and friends, shopkeepers and laborers, farmers and craftsmen—do not have infinite patience. As a matter of fact, some 80 years ago, Teddy Roosevelt wrote these instructive words in his first message to the Congress: "The American people are slow to wrath, but when their wrath is once kindled, it burns like a consuming flame." Well, perhaps that kind of wrath will be deserved if our answer to these serious problems is to repeat the mistakes of the past.

The old and comfortable way is to shave a little here and add a little there. Well, that's not acceptable anymore. I think this great and historic Congress knows that way is no longer acceptable. [*Applause*]

Thank you very much.

I think you've shown that you know the one sure way to continue the inflationary spiral is to fall back into the predictable patterns of old economic practices. Isn't it time that we tried something new?

When you allowed me to speak to you here in these chambers a little earlier, I told you that I wanted this program for economic recovery to be ours—yours and mine. I think the bipartisan substitute bill has achieved that purpose. It moves us toward economic vitality.

Just 2 weeks ago, you and I joined millions of our fellow Americans in marveling at the magic historical moment that John Young and Bob Crippen created in their space shuttle, *Columbia*. The last manned effort was almost 6 years ago, and I remembered on this more recent day, over the years, how we'd all come to expect technological precision of our men and machines.

And each amazing achievement became commonplace, until the next new challenge was raised.

With the space shuttle we tested our ingenuity once again, moving beyond the accomplishments of the past into the promise and uncertainty of the future. Thus, we not only planned to send up a 122-foot aircraft 170 miles into space, but we also intended to make it maneuverable and return it to Earth, landing 98 tons of exotic metals delicately on a remote, dry lakebed. The space shuttle did more than prove our technological abilities. It raised our expectations once more. It started us dreaming again.

The poet Carl Sandburg wrote, "The republic is a dream. Nothing happens unless first a dream." And that's what makes us, as Americans, different. We've always reached for a new spirit and aimed at a higher goal. We've been courageous and determined, unafraid and bold. Who among us wants to be first to say we no longer have those qualities, that we must limp along, doing the same things that have brought us our present misery?

I believe that the people you and I represent are ready to chart a new course. They look to us to meet the great challenge, to reach beyond the commonplace and not fall short for lack of creativity or courage.

Someone you know has said that he who would have nothing to do with thorns must never attempt to gather flowers. Well, we have much greatness before us. We can restore our economic strength and build opportunities like none we've ever had before.

As Carl Sandburg said, all we need to begin with is a dream that we can do better than before. All we need to have is faith, and that dream will come true. All we need to do is act, and the time for action is now.

Thank you. Good night.

Note: The President spoke at 9:05 p.m. in the House Chamber at the Capitol. He was introduced by Thomas P. O'Neill, Jr., Speaker of the House of Representatives. The address was broadcast live on radio and television.

Proclamation 4843—Older Americans Month, 1981
April 29, 1981

By the President of the United States of America

A Proclamation

Older Americans, a resource of talent, knowledge and judgment, are essential to our effort for national renewal. As a Nation, we should recognize our debt to older Americans and the leadership they can provide for the future.

As we move into this era of renewal, we must remember that all Americans are interdependent. We must maintain our commitment to the integrity of the Social Security system. We must work together for economic recovery, mindful that while our economic ills hurt us all, their burdens fall most heavily on those with fixed incomes. We must ensure the dignity of our Nation's older citizens through programs such as

Medicare, aging services and the Older Americans Act.

In addition to recognizing the vital importance of older Americans to our society, we must acknowledge the voluntary efforts of millions of citizens, young and old alike, to enhance the lives of older Americans.

I urge all Americans to help older citizens continue to enrich our society by realizing their aspirations and fulfilling their potential.

Now, Therefore, I, Ronald Reagan, President of the United States of America, do hereby designate the month of May 1981 as Older Americans Month.

In Witness Whereof, I have hereunto set my hand this twenty-ninth day of April, in the year of our Lord nineteen hundred eighty-one, and of the Independence of the

United States of America the two hundred and fifth.

RONALD REAGAN

[*Filed with the Office of the Federal Register, 11:12 a.m., April 30, 1981*]

Executive Order 12304—Seal for the Panama Canal Commission
April 29, 1981

By the authority vested in me as President of the United States of America, it is hereby ordered as follows:

Section 1. There is approved for the official use of the Panama Canal Commission a seal approved by the Board of Directors of the Panama Canal Commission, and described as follows:

A view of a lower lock chamber of the Panama Canal, showing the bow end of a ship in an upper chamber, behind a closed gate, flanked on the left by a control house and on the right by a towing locomotive and three lamp standards. The ship colors to be dull red hull with white trim, white superstructure, white kingposts, and gray funnel. The lock walls, control house and lamp standards to be white. The control house roof to be dull red. The lock gate and towing locomotive to be gray. The sky to be light blue and the water to be azure blue. All to be encircled with a white band edged in navy blue and containing the inscription "PANAMA CANAL COMMISSION * COMISION DEL CANAL DE PANAMA *" in navy blue letters.

Sec. 2. The design of the seal is attached hereto and made a part of this Order.

RONALD REAGAN

The White House,
April 29, 1981.

[*Filed with the Office of the Federal Register, 11:13 a.m., April 30, 1981*]

Note: The design of the seal is printed in the Federal Register *of May 1, 1981.*

Nomination of Jonathan C. Rose To Be an Assistant Attorney General
April 29, 1981

The President today announced his intention to nominate Jonathan C. Rose to be an Assistant Attorney General (Office of Legal Policy), Department of Justice.

Since 1978 Mr. Rose has been in the practice of law with the firm of Jones, Day, Reavis and Pogue. Prior to joining this firm, he was with the Department of Justice in various positions from 1974 to 1977; as General Counsel, Council on International Economic Policy, Executive Office of the President from 1972 to 1974; as Special Assistant to the President from 1971 to 1972; and was a law clerk to Justice R. Ammi Cutter of the Supreme Court of Massachusetts from 1967 to 1968.

Mr. Rose served in the U.S. Army from 1969 to 1971, when he was honorably discharged. He graduated from Yale University in 1963 with an A.B. degree, and from Harvard Law School in 1967 with an LL.B. degree, cum laude. He was admitted to the Bars for the Commonwealth of Massachusetts and the District of Columbia in 1971 and the Ohio State Bar in 1978.

Mr. Rose is married and resides in Alexandria, Va. He was born in Cleveland, Ohio, on June 8, 1941.

Remarks at the First Annual Commemoration of the Days of Remembrance of Victims of the Holocaust
April 30, 1981

I feel a little unnecessary, because I don't know that anyone could say anything that would add to those words that we've just heard. It is a particular pleasure for me to be here with you today. This ceremony has meaning not only for people of the Jewish faith, those who have been persecuted, but for all who want to prevent another Holocaust.

Jeremiah wrote of the days when the Jews were carried off to Babylon and Jerusalem was destroyed. He said, "Jerusalem weeps in the night and tears run down her cheeks." Today, yes, we remember the suffering and the death of Jews and of all those others who were persecuted in World War II. We try to recapture the horror of millions sent to gas chambers and crematoria. And we commemorate the days of April in 1945 when American and Allied troops liberated the Nazi death camps.

The tragedy that ended 36 years ago was still raw in our memories, because it took place, as we've been told, in our lifetime. We share the wounds of the survivors. We recall the pain only because we must never permit it to come again. And yet, today, in spite of that experience, as an entire generation has grown to adulthood, who never knew the days of World War II, and we remember ourselves, when we were younger, how distant history seemed, anything that came before our time—and so the signs do exist: the ugly graffiti, the act of violence, the act of terrorism here and there, scattered throughout the world and not quite large enough in dimension for us to rally as we once did in that war.

I'm horrified today when I know and hear that there are actually people now trying to say that the Holocaust was invented, that it never happened, that there weren't 6 million people whose lives were taken cruelly and needlessly in that event, that all of this is propaganda. Well, the old cliche that a picture's worth a thousand words—in World War II, not only do we have the survivors today to tell us at first hand, but in World War II, I was in the military and assigned to a post where every week, we obtained from every branch of the service all over the world the combat film that was taken by every branch. And we edited this into a secret report for the general staff. We, of course, had access to and saw that secret report.

And I remember April '45. I remember seeing the first film that came in when the war was still on, but our troops had come upon the first camps and had entered those camps. And you saw, unretouched—no way that it could have ever been rehearsed—what they saw, the horror they saw. I felt the pride when, in one of those camps, there was a nearby town, and the people were ordered to come and look at what had been going on, and to see them. And the reaction of horror on their faces was the greatest proof that they had not been conscious of what was happening so near to them.

And that film still, I know, must exist in the military, and there it is, living motion pictures, for anyone to see, and I won't go into the horrible scenes that we saw. But it remains with me as confirmation of our right to rekindle these memories, because we need always to guard against that kind of tyranny and inhumanity. Our spirit is strengthened by remembering, and our hope is in our strength.

There is an American poem that says humanity, with all its fears and all its hopes, depends on us. As a matter of fact, it was the Pope, at the end of World War II, when the world was so devastated, and yet, we alone remained so strong, who said: America has a genius for great and unselfish deeds, and into the hands of America, God has placed an afflicted mankind.

I think that that was a trust given to us that we should never betray. It is this responsibility as free people that we face today. It's this commitment among free people that we celebrate.

The hope of a ceremony such as this is that even a tortured past holds promise if we learn its lessons. According to Isaiah, there will be a new heaven and a new earth and the voice of weeping will be heard no more. Together, with the help of God, we can bear the burden of our nightmare. It is up to us to ensure that we never live it again.

Theodore Roosevelt said that the Presidency was a bully pulpit. Well, I, for one, intend that this bully pulpit shall be used on every occasion, where it is appropriate, to point a finger of shame at even the ugliness of graffiti, and certainly wherever it takes place in the world, the act of violence or terrorism, and that even at the negotiating table, never shall it be forgotten for a moment that wherever it is taking place in the world, the persecution of people, for whatever reason—persecution of people for their religious belief—that is a matter to be on that negotiating table, or the United States does not belong at that table.

Note: The President spoke at 10:22 a.m. in the East Room at the White House. The ceremony was sponsored by the United States Holocaust Memorial Council.

Nomination of Charles H. Dean, Jr., To Be a Member of the Board of Directors of the Tennessee Valley Authority, and Designation as Chairman
April 30, 1981

The President today announced his intention to nominate Charles H. Dean, Jr., to be a member of the Board of Directors of the Tennessee Valley Authority for a term of 9 years, expiring May 5, 1990, to succeed Robert N. Clement, whose term is expiring May 18, 1981. Upon confirmation the President intends to designate Mr. Dean as Chairman to succeed Simon David Freeman.

Since 1959 Mr. Dean has held various engineering and administrative positions with the Knoxville Utilities Board. He has served as general manager since 1971. In 1977 he was president of the Tennessee Valley Public Power Association and director of the American Public Power Association in 1977–80. In 1951–59 Mr. Dean was factory representative with the Knoxville Fertilizer Co.

Mr. Dean is a licensed professional engineer and served in the U.S. Marine Corps for 3 years and the U.S. Marine Corps Reserve for 10 years as commanding officer of the 6th Engineers. He was graduated from the U.S. Naval Academy (B.S., 1947).

Mr. Dean is married, has three children, and resides in Knoxville, Tenn. He was born in Knoxville on October 22, 1925.

Nomination of James G. Stearns To Be Director of the Office of Alcohol Fuels
April 30, 1981

The President today announced his intention to nominate James G. Stearns to be Director of the Office of Alcohol Fuels, Department of Energy.

Mr. Stearns was appointed secretary of the Agriculture and Services Agency and a member of the Governor's cabinet in 1972 by Governor Ronald Reagan. Prior to his appointment as a cabinet officer, Mr. Stearns served as director of the State Department of Conservation. Mr. Stearns served as county supervisor for Modoc County in 1951–67. In 1965 he served as president of the Supervisors Association of California, following terms as president of the Northern California County Supervisors Association and the western regional district of the National Association of Counties. Mr. Stearns was member and vice chairman of the California Klamath River Compact Commission.

Mr. Stearns attended Oregon State University, leaving to enter World War II service as a flight instructor. He holds a commercial pilot's license. In connection with his farming operations near Tule Lake, Calif., he flew for a crop-dusting firm.

Mr. Stearns is married, has three children, and resides in Reno, Nev. He was born in Lapine, Oreg., on January 29, 1922.

Nomination of Francis Stephen Ruddy To Be an Assistant Administrator of the Agency for International Development
April 30, 1981

The President today announced his intention to nominate Francis Stephen Ruddy to be Assistant Administrator of the Agency for International Development (African Affairs), United States International Development Cooperation Agency.

Since 1978 Dr. Ruddy has been counsel, Exxon Corp., in Houston, Tex. He has been associated with Exxon since 1974. In 1973–74 Dr. Ruddy was Deputy General Counsel and Congressional Liaison, United States Information Agency (USIA). He was senior Attorney with the Office of Telecommunications Policy, Executive Office of the President, in 1972–73. In 1969–72 Dr. Ruddy was Assistant General Counsel at USIA.

Dr. Ruddy was graduated from Holy Cross College (A.B., 1959), Loyola University (LL.B., 1965), New York University (LL.M., 1967) and Cambridge University (Ph. D., 1969).

Dr. Ruddy is married, has three children, and resides in Houston, Tex. He was born in New York City on September 15, 1937.

Nomination of Edward L. Rowny To Be Special Representative for Arms Control and Disarmament Negotiations
April 30, 1981

The President today announced his intention to nominate Edward L. Rowny to be Special Representative for Arms Control and Disarmament Negotiations. General Rowny will serve as the Chief Negotiator and head of the U.S. Delegation for Arms Control Negotiations. The President also announced his intention to nominate General Rowny to have the rank of Ambassador while serving in this capacity.

Lieutenant General Rowny was born in Baltimore, Md., on April 3, 1917. He was graduated from Johns Hopkins University (B.S., 1937) and entered the United States Military Academy, graduating as a second lieutenant in the Corps of Engineers in 1941.

During World War II he served as company commander and later as Operations Officer of the 41st Engineer Regiment in Liberia, Africa. In 1942 he was a member of the cadre of the 92d Infantry Division, Fort McClellan, Ala., where he served as Assistant Division G3 Operations Officer and later as commander of the 317th Engineer Combat Battalion. He commanded an infantry battalion and subsequently a regimental task force of the 92d Division in Italy.

In 1945–47 General Rowny served with the Operations Division of the War Department General Staff in Washington, D.C. In 1947 he attended Yale University, where in 1949 he received two masters degrees. Subsequently, he was assigned to the Far East Headquarters in Tokyo, Japan, as a planning officer.

In the early stages of the Korean conflict, he helped plan the Inchon invasion and acted as official spokesman for Geneal MacArthur. During the final stages he commanded the 38th Infantry. Altogether, he fought in seven Korean campaigns.

In 1952 General Rowny was assigned to the Infantry School at Fort Benning, Ga. He then became Chief of the Advanced Tactics Group and later Assistant Director of the Tactical Department.

He attended the Armed Forces Staff College, Norfolk, Va., in 1955, and in July was assigned to SHAPE in France. There he served as Secretary of the Joint Staff for Generals Cruenther and Norstad. In 1959 he became the Army member of the Chairman's Staff Group, Joint Chiefs of Staff, a position he held until 1961. General Rowny was the Assistant Division Commander of the 82d Airborne Division in 1961–62.

In 1962 he was sent to Vietnam, where he established the Army Concept Team, charged with testing and evaluating new Army concepts for counterinsurgency operations. In 1963 he returned to the United States to serve as the Special Assistant for Tactical Mobility as a deputy to the Assistant Chief of Staff for Force Development, Department of the Army.

In 1965 General Rowny assumed command of the 24th Infantry Division, Augsburg, Germany. In 1966 he became the Deputy Chief of Staff for Logistics, Headquarters, U.S. Army, Europe and Seventh Army, Heidelberg, Germany. In 1968–69 he was Deputy Chief of Staff, Headquarters, U.S. European Command, Stuttgart, Germany. In 1969 he assumed duties as the Deputy Chief of Research and Development in Washington. In 1970 he assumed command of I Corps, Camp Red Cloud, Korea, a position he held until 1971. He was promoted to lieutenant general in 1970.

In 1971 General Rowny was assigned as the Deputy Chairman, NATO Military Committee in Brussels, Belgium. He established and chaired the Mutual Balance Force Reductions Group. General Rowny was the Joint Chiefs of Staff representative for the Strategic Arms Limitation Talks in 1973–79. He retired from the Army on June 30, 1979.

General Rowny was awarded a doctor of philosophy degree in international studies by the American University in 1977. He is currently a fellow at the Wilson Center, Smithsonian Institution.

Nomination of Robert P. Nimmo To Be Administrator of Veterans Affairs
April 30, 1981

The President today announced his intention to nominate Robert P. Nimmo to be Administrator of Veterans Affairs.

Since 1976 Mr. Nimmo has served as a member of the California State Senate. He was a member of the California State Assembly in 1973–76. Mr. Nimmo served on the Senate rules, finance, agriculture, and revenue and taxation committees. In 1970– 73 he was appointed by Gov. Ronald Reagan to serve as United States property and fiscal officer for the State of California, with responsibility for receipt and accounting for all Federal property and Federal funds furnished the State of California for support of the Army and Air National Guard. Mr. Nimmo was employed by the California State Military Department in various military assignments in 1955–70. Previously he was engaged in livestock raising and grain farming in Terrebonne, Oreg.

In 1950–52 Mr. Nimmo served as Company Commander, 161st Ordnance Company, and in 1943–46 served as a pilot in the U.S. Army Air Corps. During that time he was with the 8th U.S. Air Force in England. He recently retired with the rank of colonel.

Mr. Nimmo was graduated from the United States Army Command and General Staff College in 1964. He is an active Republican and was honorary chairman of the Reagan for President Committee in San Luis Obispo County, Calif., in 1980.

Mr. Nimmo is married, has three children, and resides in Atascadero, Calif. He was born in Balboa, Calif., on February 5, 1922.

Nomination of Clarence Thomas To Be an Assistant Secretary of Education
May 1, 1981

The President today announced his intention to nominate Clarence Thomas to be Assistant Secretary for Civil Rights, Department of Education.

Since 1979 Mr. Thomas has been serving as legislative assistant to Senator John C. Danforth (R-Mo.). In 1977–79 he was an attorney at the Monsanto Co. Mr. Thomas was assistant attorney general of Missouri in 1974–77.

Mr. Thomas was graduated from Holy Cross College and is a member of the board of trustees of that institution. He attended Yale Law School and received a J.D. degree in June 1974.

Mr. Thomas was born in Savannah, Ga., on June 23, 1948.

Nomination of Dwight A. Ink To Be Director of the Community Services Administration
May 1, 1981

The President today announced his intention to nominate Dwight A. Ink to be Director of the Community Services Administration.

Mr. Ink is vice president for management, National Consumer Cooperative Bank. In 1976–80 he was director, Office of Sponsored Research and Continuing Education, the American University. Mr. Ink served as Deputy Administrator of the General Services Administration in 1973–76. In 1969–73 he was Assistant Director for Executive Management, Office of Management and Budget. Mr. Ink was First Assistant Secretary for Administration, Department of Housing and Urban Development, in 1966–69. In 1959–66 he was Assistant General Manager, U.S. Atomic Energy Commission. He was Assistant to the Chairman of the AEC in 1958–59; Management Assistant in 1955–58; Chief, Reports and Statistics Branch, Savannah River Operations Office, in 1952–55; and program analyst, Office of Community Affairs, Oak Ridge Operations Office, in 1951–52.

Mr. Ink is a recipient of many awards, including the Flemming Award for Ten Outstanding Young Men in Government, U.S. Chamber of Commerce, 1961; Career Service Award, National Civil Service League, 1966; Distinguished Service Award, U.S. Atomic Energy Commission, 1966; and

Commissioners Award for Distinguished Service, Civil Service Commission.

Mr. Ink was graduated from Iowa State University (B.S.) and the University of Minnesota (M.A.). In 1942–46 he served in the U.S. Air Force.

Mr. Ink is married and resides in Washington, D.C. He was born in Des Moines, Iowa, on September 9, 1922.

Appointment of Janet Colson as Special Assistant to the President for National Security Affairs
May 1, 1981

The President today announced the appointment of Janet Colson to be Special Assistant to the President for National Security Affairs. Ms. Colson has been Executive Assistant to the Assistant to the President for National Security Affairs.

A native Californian, Ms. Colson earlier served as the Associate Director of the President's Commission on White House Fellowships (1975–77). Prior to joining the National Security Council staff, she served as a senior national security policy analyst on the Reagan-Bush transition team and held positions with the University of California (San Francisco) and Hastings College

of the Law. In 1965–70 she served as a research associate in Asian studies at the Hoover Institution on War, Revolution and Peace at Stanford University, where she worked on the Yearbook on International Communist Affairs, as well as other selected research projects.

Ms. Colson received a B.A. degree and M.A. degree from Stanford University, where she was elected to Phi Beta Kappa. She currently is completing requirements for an MBA degree at the University of Santa Clara (California).

Ms. Colson was born in San Jose, Calif., on December 7, 1940.

Proclamation 4844—Jewish Heritage Week
May 1, 1981

By the President of the United States of America

A Proclamation

The vitality of the United States derives in great measure from the richness of our cultural heritage. The values and ideals brought to these shores by people of many races and religions are woven deeply into the fabric of America.

American Jews have contributed significantly to the spiritual and cultural elevation of our society since the founding of our Nation. Jewish immigrants and their descendants have brought dignity and distinction to every field of American endeavor. Our Jewish citizens have served America by

fighting for her freedom, building her industry, striving for her goals, and nurturing her dreams.

Yet, Jewish heritage reaches far and deeply into the dawn of history, when America was but a wilderness. The Jewish people still firmly carry these ancient and revered traditions, which have been harshly tested over the centuries.

In the spring of each year, through special celebrations and observances, American Jewry remembers its past and renews its dedication to the challenges that remain. Beginning with the observance of Passover, recalling the passage from bondage to freedom, through the anniversary of the Warsaw Ghetto Uprising and the Days of

Remembrance honoring the victims and survivors of the Holocaust, Jews all over the world pay tribute to their past. In the celebration of Israeli Independence Day, Jerusalem Day, and Solidarity Day for Soviet Jews, Jewish people reflect upon their common heritage.

In recognition of the special significance of this time of year to American Jewry, in homage to the significant contributions made by the Jewish community to the United States, and to foster appreciation of the cultural diversity of the American people, the Congress of the United States, by joint resolution, has requested the President to proclaim May 3 through May 10, 1981, as Jewish Heritage Week.

Now, Therefore, I, Ronald Reagan, President of the United States of America, do hereby proclaim the week beginning May 3, 1981, as Jewish Heritage Week.

I call upon the people of the United States, Federal and local government officials, and interested organizations to observe that week with appropriate ceremonies, activities, and reflection.

In Witness Whereof, I have hereunto set my hand this first day of May, in the year of our Lord nineteen hundred and eighty-one, and of the Independence of the United States of America the two hundred and fifth.

RONALD REAGAN

[*Filed with the Office of the Federal Register, 4:46 p.m., May 1, 1981*]

Note: The text of the proclamation was released by the Office of the Press Secretary on May 2.

Message on the 60th Birthday of Andrei Sakharov
May 2, 1981

I am pleased to add my congratulations to Academician Andrei Sakharov on the occasion of his 60th birthday. Sakharov is one of the true spiritual heroes of our time. An outstanding scientist whose position insured him all the security and comfort he might desire, he was willing to risk all to speak out on behalf of human rights and freedom. He persisted in this mission even after being subjected to increasingly harsh penalties.

Mr. Sakharov is a Russian patriot in the best sense of the word because he perceived his peoples' greatness to lie not in militarism and conquests abroad but in building a free and lawful society at home. His principled declarations on behalf of freedom and peace reinforce our belief in these ideals. We hope and pray that his exile will be ended and that he will enjoy a long and creative life on behalf of science and humanity.

Note: The message was read to a group of scientists attending a conference in New York City on May 2.

Nomination of Robert A. McConnell To Be an Assistant Attorney General
May 4, 1981

The President today announced his intention to nominate Robert A. McConnell to be an Assistant Attorney General, Department of Justice.

Since 1978 Mr. McConnell has been a partner with the firm of Steiger, Helm, Kyle & McConnell of Tempe, Ariz. He also served as special counsel to the attorney general of Arizona in certain specific lawsuits. Since 1976 he has been director and officer with the Program Development Corp., a consulting firm specializing in campaign management, fundraising, and governmental relations. In 1975–78 Mr. McConnell was an attorney in private practice and was with the firm of Sparks, Siler and McConnell in 1973–75 in Scottsdale,

Ariz. In 1970–73 he was legislative assistant to Representative John J. Rhodes (R-Ariz.).

Mr. McConnell was graduated from Arizona State University (B.A., 1967; J.D., 1970).

Mr. McConnell is married and resides in Tempe, Ariz. He was born in Long Beach, Calif., on August 29, 1944.

Nomination of Reese H. Taylor, Jr., To Be a Member of the Interstate Commerce Commission, and Designation as Chairman
May 4, 1981

The President today announced his intention to nominate Reese H. Taylor, Jr., to be a member of the Interstate Commerce Commission for a term of 7 years from January 1, 1977, vice Robert J. Corber. Upon confirmation, the President intends to designate Mr. Taylor Chairman.

In 1971 Mr. Taylor became a partner in the law firm of Laxalt, Berry & Allison of Carson City, Nev. In 1978 the firm was reorganized and incorporated as Allison, Brunetti, MacKenzie & Taylor, Ltd. His work with the firm consisted primarily of an administrative law practice, with particular emphasis on regulatory matters pertaining to public utilities and transportation

companies.

In 1967–71 he was chairman of the Public Service Commission of Nevada and in 1967–69 was also vice chairman of the Nevada Tax Commission. In 1967–71 he was also a member of the Governor's Cabinet and his Civil Defense Advisory Council. Previously he was associated with law firms in Las Vegas, Nev., and Los Angeles, Calif.

Mr. Taylor was graduated from Stanford University (1949) and Cornell Law School (1952).

Mr. Taylor is married, has three children, and resides in Carson City, Nev. He was born in Los Angeles, Calif., on May 6, 1928.

Nomination of Carleton S. Coon, Jr., To Be United States Ambassador to Nepal
May 4, 1981

The President today announced his intention to nominate Carleton S. Coon, Jr., of New Hampshire, as Ambassador to the Kingdom of Nepal, vice Phillip R. Trimble, resigned.

Mr. Coon entered the Foreign Service in 1949 and was assigned to Frankfurt am Main. He was consular-economic officer in Damascus in 1952–56 and economic officer in New Delhi in 1956–59. In the Department, he was foreign affairs officer in 1959–

61 and officer in charge of Cyprus affairs, then international relations officer in 1961–63. In 1963–65 he was principal officer in Tabriz. He was officer in charge of India, Nepal, Ceylon affairs in the Department, in 1965–68. He attended the National War College in 1968–69. He was Chief of Presidential Appointments staff in the Office of Director General of the Foreign Service in 1969–70. In 1970–73 Mr. Coon was Deputy Chief of Mission in Kathmandu. He was dip-

lomat in residence at Carleton College in 1973–74. He was Deputy Chief of Mission (Minister-Counselor) in Rabat in 1974–76. In 1976–79 he was Deputy Director of the Foreign Service Institute, and since 1979 he has been country director of the Office of

North African Affairs in the Bureau of Near Eastern and South Asian Affairs.

Mr. Coon was born April 27, 1927, in Paris, France. He graduated from Harvard University (B.A., 1949). He is married, has six children, and resides in Weare, N.H.

Executive Order 12305—Termination of Certain Federal Advisory Committees
May 5, 1981

By the authority vested in me as President by the Constitution of the United States of America, and in accordance with the provisions of the Federal Advisory Committee Act, as amended (5 U.S.C. App. I), the following Executive Orders establishing advisory committees, are hereby revoked and the committees terminated:

(a) Executive Order No. 12059 of May 11, 1978, as amended, establishing the United States Circuit Judge Nominating Commission;

(b) Executive Order No. 11992 of May 24, 1977, establishing the Committee on Selection of Federal Judicial Officers;

(c) Executive Order No. 12084 of September 27, 1978, as amended by Executive

Order 12097 of November 8, 1978, establishing the Judicial Nominating Commission for the District of Puerto Rico; and

(d) Executive Order No. 12064 of June 5, 1978, establishing the United States Tax Court Nominating Commission.

Subsections (g), (i), (j) and (k) of Section 1–101 of Executive Order No. 12258, extending these committees, are also revoked.

RONALD REAGAN

The White House,
May 5, 1981.

[*Filed with the Office of the Federal Register, 4:49 p.m., May 5, 1981*]

Nomination of K. William O'Connor To Be Inspector General of the Community Services Administration
May 6, 1981

The President today announced his intention to nominate K. William O'Connor to be Inspector General, Community Services Administration.

Since April 1980 Mr. O'Connor has served as Special Counsel for Interagency Coordination and Staff Director of the Executive Group Staff. His duties included advising the Deputy Attorney General on policy, programs, and matters affecting the Executive Group. In 1978–80 he was Senior Trial Attorney (Prosecutor/GSA Task Force) and led teams of investigators and lawyers in grand jury investigations of fraud

schemes at the General Services Administration. In 1976–78 he was Associate Justice and then Chief Justice, High Court of American Samoa. Mr. O'Connor was vice president and counsel, Association of Motion Picture and Television Producers, Inc., in 1975–76; Special Counsel, Intelligence Coordination, Department of Justice, in 1975; Deputy Assistant Attorney General, Civil Rights Division, in 1971–75; Chief, Criminal Section, Civil Rights Division, in 1970–71; assistant to the Assistant Attorney General, Civil Rights Division, in 1967–70.

Previously he held various positions with the Job Corps.

Mr. O'Connor was graduated from the University of Virginia (B.A., 1952; LL.B., 1958). He served in the U.S. Marine Corps and was discharged in 1955 as first lieutenant.

Mr. O'Connor is married, has four children, and resides in Falls Church, Va. He was born in Washington, D.C., on August 1, 1931.

Nomination of John V. Graziano To Be Inspector General of the Department of Agriculture
May 6, 1981

The President today announced his intention to nominate John V. Graziano to be Inspector General, Department of Agriculture.

Since 1979 Mr. Graziano has been Assistant Inspector General for Investigations, Department of Commerce. In 1978–79 he was Special Coordinator for Grain Elevator Safety and Security, Office of the Secretary, Department of Agriculture. In 1974–79 Mr. Graziano was Director, Office of Investigation, Department of Agriculture, and was Chief, Cargo Security Division, Department of Transportation, in 1971–74. In 1970–71

he was Chief, Air Security Guard Division, Federal Aviation Administration; Chief, Investigations Division, FAA; Chief, Compliance & Security Staff, and Chief, Civil Rights Staff, FAA Aeronautical Center in Oklahoma City, Okla. Previously he was an investigator with the U.S Civil Service Commission.

Mr. Graziano was graduated from St. John's University (B.S., 1951).

Mr. Graziano resides in Annandale, Va. He was born in Brooklyn, N.Y., on July 3, 1927.

Nomination of Joseph A. Sickon To Be Inspector General of the General Services Administration
May 6, 1981

The President today announced his intention to nominate Joseph A. Sickon to be Inspector General, General Services Administration.

Mr. Sickon is presently Assistant Inspector General for Audit at the Department of Housing and Urban Development. In 1979–80 Mr. Sickon was Director, Office of Procurement and ADP Management, Department of Commerce, and in 1977–79 he was Director, Office of Audits. In 1975–77 he was Director, Office of Financial Management, Maritime Administration. Previously, in 1972–75, he was Director of the Office of Financial Analysis. In 1971–72 Mr. Sickon

was Special Assistant for System Studies to the Deputy Assistant Secretary for Maritime Affairs; Chief, Division of External Audits and Financial Analysis, in 1969–71; and Assistant Chief, Division of External Affairs, in 1964–69. In 1958–64 he was Supervisory Auditor, U.S. General Accounting Office.

Mr. Sickon was graduated from the University of Detroit (1954) and George Washington University (1971). He attended Detroit College of Law and the University of Virginia.

Mr. Sickon is married, has five children, and resides in Alexandria, Va. He was born in Cleveland, Ohio, on October 14, 1930.

Nomination of Jose S. Sorzano To Be United States Representative on the Economic and Social Council of the United Nations
May 6, 1981

The President today announced his intention to nominate Jose S. Sorzano to be the Representative of the United States of America on the Economic and Social Council of the United Nations, with the rank of Ambassador.

Dr. Sorzano has been associate professor of government at Georgetown University since 1979 and also held that position in 1969–76. He has conducted lectures and seminars at Georgetown University's School of Foreign Service. In 1976–79 Dr. Sorzano was Director of the Peace Corps in Bogotá, Colombia, and supervised the largest Peace Corps program in Latin America. He was escort/interpreter with the Department of State in 1963–65.

Dr. Sorzano is the recipient of many honors and awards, including the Superior Achievement Award for outstanding performance of the duties and responsibilities of a Peace Corps Country Director (1977) and a two-step meritorious increase in recognition of having tripled Peace Corps programs in Colombia without increasing administrative and managerial costs (1979).

He was graduated from Georgetown University School of Foreign Service (B.S.F.S., 1965; Ph. D., 1972).

Dr. Sorzano is married, has two children, and resides with his family in Arlington, Va. He was born in Havana, Cuba, on November 9, 1940, and is a naturalized United States citizen.

Appointment of John S. Herrington as Deputy Assistant to the President for Presidential Personnel
May 6, 1981

The President today announced the appointment of John S. Herrington to be Deputy Assistant to the President for Presidential Personnel.

In 1965–67 Mr. Herrington was deputy district attorney in the Ventura County District Attorney's Office in California. In 1967 he opened his own law office in Walnut Creek, Calif., specializing in real estate, corporate law, taxation, and contracts. He was recently involved in property management.

During the 1980 Presidential campaign, Mr. Herrington was a full-time volunteer advanceman with the Reagan for President committee. Following the Republican National Convention he was named western regional director for advance.

Mr. Herrington was graduated from Stanford University (A.B., 1961) and the University of California, Hastings College of Law (LL.B., J.D.; 1964). He served in the U.S. Marine Corps.

Mr. Herrington is married, has two children, and resides with his family in Walnut Creek, Calif. He was born in Los Angeles on May 31, 1939.

Announcement of the Establishment of the Presidential Task Force on the Arts and Humanities
May 6, 1981

The President today announced the creation of a Task Force on the Arts and Humanities. Named to head the Task Force as the Chairman for the Arts is actor and American Film Institute chairman, Charlton Heston. Dr. Hanna H. Gray, president of the University of Chicago, will serve as Chairman for the Humanities. Chairman for the Federal Government will be the Ambassador at Large for Cultural Affairs-designate, Daniel J. Terra, Chicago arts patron. Barnabas McHenry, of New York City, was named as Vice Chairman.

The Task Force will recommend to the President ways in which private support might offset the cuts in the budgets of the National Endowments for the Arts and Humanities. The Task Force will, however, direct its inquiry to all of the activities of both Endowments, as well as other Federal arts and humanities programs. Special attention will be paid to three areas: First is the possibility of increasing support to State and local programs; second is increasing the role of nongovernmental, professional judgment in award making; and third is the desirability of converting the Endowments into public corporations.

Statement on the Establishment of the Presidential Task Force on the Arts and Humanities
May 6, 1981

I am naming this Task Force because of my deep concern for the arts and humanities in America. Our cultural institutions are an essential national resource; they must be kept strong. While I believe firmly that the Federal Government *must* reduce its spending, I am nevertheless sympathetic to the very real needs of our cultural organizations and hope the Task Force will deliver to my desk by Labor Day a plan to make better use of existing Federal resources and to increase the support for the arts and humanities by the private sector.

Nomination of Gilbert A. Robinson To Be Deputy Director of the International Communication Agency
May 6, 1981

The President today announced his intention to nominate Gilbert A. Robinson to be Deputy Director, International Communication Agency.

Since 1960 Mr. Robinson has been chairman, Gilbert A. Robinson, Inc., a public relations firm. He is presently chairman, International Management of Capital & Assets Corp. In 1970 he was vice president and head of corporate communications for Gulf & Western Industries, Inc. In 1953–55 he was assistant to the chairman of the Ford Foundation project which initiated educational television in the United States.

Mr. Robinson's Government service has included serving as consultant to the Director of the Peace Corps in 1971–72, Special Assistant to the Secretary of Commerce in

1955–59, Special Assistant for Reciprocal Trade Agreements Legislation in 1958, coordinator of the American National Exhibition in Moscow in 1959, and analyst with the National Security Agency in 1950–52.

Mr. Robinson was graduated from Roanoke College (B.S., 1950). He is married, has one child, and resides in Carmel, N.Y. He was born in New York City on May 25, 1928.

Remarks on the Meeting Between Secretary of State Haig and the NATO Foreign Ministers
May 6, 1981

The President. Well, thank you all for coming here. Sorry that we delayed you for a few minutes, and let me explain—we won't have time to take any questions because we're due in to a major briefing meeting now. But I wanted to welcome the Secretary of State back from his trip to the meeting in Rome, NATO, and to be able to tell you—having had about a half-hour's briefing this morning, and we'll go in now for a much more thorough briefing—he comes home in triumph from a most successful meeting, in a situation that could have been critical for us with regard to our allies and their reactions, and it is a triumphal return.

I think that we have a better relationship with our NATO allies now and resolved many points of difference that might have existed there and erased their worries about our relationship with the Soviet Union.

The Secretary of State. By and large, Mr. President, all I would add to that is that this meeting, which the Secretary General describes as perhaps the most important that has occurred in recent years, served to underline the most important object of American foreign policy, and that's solidarity within the Alliance and especially the transatlantic aspects of it. And secondly, this meeting enabled me to present President Reagan's foreign policy to the North Atlantic Council, and it received unanimous, enthusiastic endorsement by all of the member states. And I think that's a major achievement of which we're all very proud.

Note: The President spoke at 11:54 a.m. to reporters assembled outside the Oval Office at the White House.

Statement on the Death of Frank Fitzsimmons, President of the International Brotherhood of Teamsters
May 6, 1981

Frank Fitzsimmons was an important and powerful voice in the American labor movement. His death is a sad moment not only for the millions of Teamster union members he so diligently represented but for our nation as well.

Affable and humorous, Frank Fitzsimmons was also—from his earliest days as a labor organizer in the 1930's—a hard bargainer who won the respect of both business and political leaders throughout the Nation.

Frank was here at the White House recently. I expressed gratitude then for his kind words of support. All of us were deeply impressed with the courage and dignity with which he bore his illness.

I was personally very fond of Frank and will miss him. Nancy and I convey our deepest sympathy to his family and to the members of the Teamsters union.

Remarks at the Welcoming Ceremony for Prime Minister Zenko Suzuki of Japan
May 7, 1981

The President. Mr. Prime Minister, Madam Suzuki:

It's a great honor for Nancy and me in behalf of the American people to welcome you to the United States. We're delighted to be your hosts during your first visit in both our administrations.

The people of Japan and the people of America are friends of separate pasts. We have a different language, different ancestry, and yet together, our actions have helped to shape the future. Today, we have a chance to bring freshness and a new direction to the deep friendship between our peoples.

The custom when leaders of our two nations meet is to look back, to measure how far we've come. It's true that we've accomplished much in a relatively short period of time. Today, however, you and I will look forward. We'll chart the future course of our friendship for peace.

You and I hold a sacred trust, a sacred trust of two of the world's greatest nations. Our countries are economic leaders in the world of sophisticated technology, industry, and science. And because we're leaders, great tides swirl around us, forces of independence, progress, and friendly competition. As you have said, the choices we make will determine the fate of generations. What we create must blend into the future as the poet Shelley described the west wind—a "tumult of [thy] mighty harmonies."

You have said that harmony is the keynote of your government's philosophy, and harmony is a philosophy I admire very much. Harmony requires differences to be joined in pursuit of higher ideals. It is the philosophy that you have said you want to share with the world. It is the foundation of a philosophy necessary to mold strength into greatness. Japan has been a harmonious and loyal ally whose people understand that free societies must bear the responsibility of freedom together. And Japan and the United States understand and work with each other because of the strong ties that we have built upon the principles of a harmonious relationship.

We in America are grateful for the strong measures that you have taken to penalize the Soviet Union for its violent aggression in Afghanistan. You have come to the aid of countries resisting Soviet expansion. You have rescued refugees, imposed sanctions against tyrants, and offered economic assistance to the oppressed. The people of Japan stand with Americans, Europeans, and people of other democracies in a community of free powers. But even in this world community of leadership, Japan and the United States stand out in their achievements.

The economic forces at our command are the basis of a powerful guarantee of progress in peace. They are the essential tools with which we can help others to advance and to ensure freedom. Our most valuable resource, our people, have the strength to carry out their dreams, and in our dreams, we both yearn to be the best. Our mutual search for excellence, for achievement, for genuine security is conducted in the spirit of harmony.

There is a hill in Boston where dreams are made and sometimes shattered. Runners beaded in sweat and panting for breath must conquer that hill to win—demanding foot race known as the Boston Marathon. It is called Heartbreak Hill. About 2 weeks ago, a young man from Japan raced up that hill and won. His name: Toshihiko Seko, a sales clerk from Tokyo. After the race, he told us that he was motivated by respect for the American who had won last year. In Japan, he said, when you respect somebody, you show it by going beyond his achievements. Well, Mr. Seko is not only an awesome athlete, he is a gracious and wise man. And let me say, Mr. Seko has earned the respect of a pack of American runners who look forward to the pleasure of meeting him again next year.

Let us continue to be challenged by our accomplishments, by the accomplishments of each other. Let us compete in the same contests with each victory becoming the next goal to conquer. But let us also always remember and let the world be aware— Japan and America will go forward together.

The Prime Minister. Mr. President, thank you very much for your very warm welcome. Let me express my heartfelt thankfulness for your truly remarkable recovery from the unfortunate incident and my delight that you are now standing here in very good health and with that winning smile that is now known throughout the world.

Mr. President, the world is now beset by unprecedentedly complex political, economic, and social challenges. I am convinced, however, that the industrialized democracies, by strengthening their cooperation and solidarity and by addressing these challenges with firm determination, can dispel misery, oppression, and violence from the face of this Earth and can bring peace, justice, freedom, and prosperity to the international community. Japan and the United States are great powers whose combined national products account for one-third of the world's total. Close coordination between our two countries can contribute immeasurably to the peace and security of the entire world.

I have come, Mr. President, to hold a candid exchange of views with you about the responsibilities Japan and the United States should discharge and the roles we should play in the current international situation. It is also my earnest desire to consolidate the bond of friendship and expand further the horizons of cooperation between our two countries. I must add that the opportunity to talk with you so soon after you have assumed the Presidency in such trying times, but with the full and sacred trust and mandate of the American people, I regard as very timely and significant.

Mr. President, the moment I set foot on American soil this time, I sensed the aspirations of the American people to build a society filled with vitality. The Japanese people have profound respect for the American people who are now embarked on the new beginning under your leadership. We wish to advance hand in hand with you toward realizing the aspirations of the international community by expanding our cooperation with your country and by strengthening the ties between our two peoples, both of whom aspire to peace and to societies filled with vigor and vitality.

I know that the talks that will begin shortly will mark an important step forward in our common enterprise.

Thank you.

Note: The President spoke at 10:05 a.m. on the South Lawn of the White House, where the Prime Minister was given a formal welcome with full military honors. The Prime Minister spoke in Japanese, and his remarks were translated by an interpreter.

Following the ceremony, the President and the Prime Minister met privately in the Oval Office and then with their delegations in the Cabinet Room.

Statement on Approval by the House of Representatives of a Fiscal Year 1982 Budget Resolution
May 7, 1981

I am extremely grateful to the Members of the House of Representatives, both Democratic and Republican, for their vote today on the 1982 budget. This is a resounding victory—not only for our economy but for a spirit of bipartisanship that we can build upon in the months and years ahead.

In my conversations with Members of the House over the past several days, they have repeatedly told me how serious they are about bringing the Federal budget under control. This budget resolution is a major step in that process. It sets responsible spending limits within which we must now work together.

There is another message here that is equally important: When the people speak, Washington will now listen—and will act. For years, the American people have been asking the the Federal Government put its house in order. Today, the people have been heard.

As we move forward toward economic recovery, let us never forget this historic moment of commitment: to a government that can both serve the people and live within its means.

Toasts of the President and Prime Minister Zenko Suzuki of Japan at the State Dinner
May 7, 1981

The President. It's been a pleasure for Nancy and me to welcome the Prime Minister and Mrs. Suzuki to Washington. Our discussions today have been positive and constructive and I think have served to deepen the understanding between our two countries. As we talked, I thought again about the differences and the similarities between Japan and America, and I was struck by how much more profound the similarities are. We are two nations based on freedom, free enterprise, private industry, and democracy. We have become principal trading partners and chief competitors. [*Laughter*]

There's a legend in Japan about two villages separated by a river, and on moonlight nights a man from one town would come out and sing. And his voice would resound farther and farther, floating out across the river until it reached the other town. Meanwhile, the people of the second town decided to compete. They looked for a singer who could surpass the excellence of the man across the river. And then it happened that one night another voice was heard, and the second was fully as rich as the first. And when the original singer heard it, he realized he was faced with a strong rival, and he sang and sang at the top of his voice. And the singing grew more and more beautiful as each singer found depths to his talent that he hadn't known were there.

Well, Japan and America are like those singers. We each seek great achievements, and the standards we set for each other are marks of excellence. And yet we do not exhaust ourselves in the contest, but rather, pursue our respective goals as friends and allies.

The Japanese-American relationship is the anchor of American policy in East Asia. It is a pillar of strength in a world where democratic values are always under challenge. Our friendship is based on respect and mutual trust. America will honor her commitments to Japan, and we will continue to consult fully as true partners. Together we confront a serious world situation.

Energy supplies are uncertain. Economies are fragile. The Soviet Union continues its aggression, and the dynamics of the Persian Gulf are precarious. And the United States will play an active role in addressing these challenges, and we welcome Japan's determination to participate as a full partner in behalf of world peace. Just as we will count on Japan, Japan can count on America.

We will continue our respective search for excellence, and we shall cooperate with each other, bringing to the world the high standards of the future a little more quickly. The voices that call to each other across the Pacific will remain in harmony.

And with that goal in mind I ask all of you to join me in a toast to the Prime Minister and to Mrs. Suzuki and to the strong and growing and enduring friendship between Japan and the United States.

The Prime Minister. President and Mrs. Reagan, ladies and gentlemen:

Let me first express my sincere gratitude to President Reagan for this splendid ban-

411

quet and for your warm greetings to my wife and me and the Japanese people. Though I have met with you only this morning for the first time, Mr. President, this gathering tonight and your warm hospitality make me feel as if we have known each other for many years.

I was born on the Pacific coast of the northern part of Japan and grew up beside the roaring surf coming from the east. California, which has been your home for so many years, is facing my home country across the Pacific. I spent my youth dreaming of America, the land of liberty, lying far across the sea. Belonging as we do to the same generation, Mr. President, I expect that you and I share a similar experience of the vicissitudes of our times. Add to that the fact that Japan and the United States have a long history of helping each other as true friends, and it is natural that I should feel a deep sense of friendship for you, Mr. President, as if we had known each other for many, many years.

Mr. President, allow me to mention two recent events in the United States which have moved me very deeply. The first has to do with the unfortunate incident you came across a short time ago. My colleagues and I, and indeed the people of Japan as a whole, were all deeply distressed to learn of that regrettable event. What struck us most of all, however, was the fortitude and devotion with which Mrs. Reagan supported you and the calm presence of mind and admirable sense of humor which you, Mr. President, displayed in dealing with the situation. The affairs of state, in the meantime, remained in firm and reliable hands, and at no time was there any cause for concern among your allies about the United States leadership capability. Japan's faith in the United States of America has been greatly enhanced.

The second event is the heroic achievement of the space shuttle *Columbia*. Despite the fact that it was after 3 a.m. local time, over 3 million Japanese sat glued to their television sets to watch the *Columbia's* successful return to Earth. The frontier spirit of the American people has been a constant source of courage and inspiration to the Japanese people, and frontier spirit is in perfect harmony with our traditional spirit of enterprise.

Ladies and gentlemen, President Reagan and I have today reaffirmed how important solidarity and cooperation between Japan and the United States is to the prosperity of mankind in the years to come. We have also affirmed that Japan-U.S. partnership has grown to be an indispensable element in the peace and stability of the Asian-Pacific region, as well as that of the international community as a whole.

The present turbulent international situation makes me intensely aware of the precious value of freedom that Japan, the United States, and other democracies have consistently defended over the years. We must cooperate in pooling our wisdom to build still more peaceful and vigorous societies imbued with the spirit of freedom. As the Prime Minister of Japan, I am determined to do everything I can to join hands with you, Mr. President, and to work together for the sake of the future generations of the 21st century.

The success of the space shuttle inspires us to challenge the unknown. Tireless effort to build a better world for the future is a common task for the people of all nations. I would like to share with you this spirit of challenge.

Ladies and gentlemen, I would like to mention one more reason why I feel as if President Reagan is an old friend. We were born in the same year and are both proud of being a youthful 70. [*Laughter*] I have to admit, however, Mr. President, that I cannot match your health and vitality. This is because I was born, unfortunately, 26 days before you, which gives you that much edge. [*Laughter*]

More seriously, Mr. President, I wish to congratulate you on the great victory sign for your administration today as your budget has passed Congress.

Let me conclude by offering a toast to the health of the President and Mrs. Reagan and to the prosperity of the people of the United States of America.

Note: The President spoke at 9:37 p.m. in the State Dining Room at the White House. The Prime Minister spoke in Japanese, and his remarks were translated by an interpreter.

Remarks of the President and Prime Minister Zenko Suzuki of Japan Following Their Meetings
May 8, 1981

The President. Well, ladies and gentlemen of the press, I won't take too much of your time, but I just want to say first, and before the Prime Minister is heard, that this has been a most fruitful meeting for both our countries. We have established a bond of friendship. In fact, last night, the Prime Minister referred to it that we were buddies. And we have come to an agreement, or at least discovered, perhaps I should say, that we're in agreement on a number of broad issues—economic, political, military— and have established a base whereby we can have full consultation, and any possible difference or misunderstanding that might arise that we can be in instant contact to resolve it. So, we're most grateful and honored that the Vice President [Prime Minister] has been here. And as I say, I think we're all much better for what has been decided in the meetings we've held.

Mr. Prime Minister.

The Prime Minister. Mr. President, thank you very much for your kind words. As you've just said, through the 2 days of talks with you, Mr. President, we have been able to establish between us an unshakable basis of friendship and mutual trust. And this is the greatest treasure that I take home from my visit to the United States to Japan.

Also, in the course of our 2 days of talks, we touched on a broad range of issues— political, economic, and other issues, including the questions of the relationship between the developing and the developed parts of the world and also including the question of how the countries in the West should cooperate together in securing, in a comprehensive manner, the security of the West as a whole.

We did engage in very forthright and open exchanges of views and, as a result, we were able to confirm that we have a basic convergence of views and perceptions about the important matters that face the international community today. We were also able to reaffirm that we are both dedicated to the common goal of securing world peace and stability and prosperity, and we reaffirmed our common resolve to join our hands together and move vigorously forward to that end.

We also agreed that we will always be in very close touch. We will communicate with each other very closely, consult very closely on these global issues, as well as on the problems that we may have in our bilateral relations. On the basis of mutual trust and friendship that I have been able to establish with you, Mr. President, as true partners and as true friends, we can certainly contribute together to the further advancement of the relations between our two countries.

My visit this time has been very, very fruitful, thanks to your kind cooperation. And I'm happy to report to you that I'm perfectly satisfied with the very fruitful visit that I've been able to have.

Thank you very much.

Note: The President spoke at 12:03 p.m. to reporters assembled on the South Grounds of the White House. The Prime Minister spoke in Japanese, and his remarks were translated by an interpreter.

Earlier, the President and the Prime Minister met privately in the Oval Office and then with their delegations in the Cabinet Room.

Joint Communique Following Discussions With Prime Minister Zenko Suzuki of Japan
May 8, 1981

At the invitation of the Government of the United States, the Prime Minister and Mrs. Suzuki paid an official visit to the United States from May 4 through 9. President Reagan and Prime Minister Suzuki met in Washington on May 7 and 8 for a comprehensive and fruitful review of the current international situation and U.S.-Japan relationship. They pledged that they would work closely together in pursuit of world peace and prosperity. The President and the Prime Minister, recognizing that the alliance between the United States and Japan is built upon their shared values of democracy and liberty, reaffirmed their solidarity, friendship and mutual trust.

The President and the Prime Minister viewed with concern the Soviet military build-up and the Soviet activities in the Third World as seen in its military intervention into Afghanistan and its behavior elsewhere. They reaffirmed their position that the Soviet intervention into Afghanistan cannot be condoned and that the immediate, unconditional and total withdrawal of the Soviet troops should be realized. They restated their view that the problems of Poland should be resolved by the Polish people themselves without any external interference and that any intervention in Poland would have a serious adverse effect on world peace. They shared the view that should intervention in Poland occur, the Western industrialized democracies should cooperate and implement their policies in concert.

Affirming their interest in the peace and stability of Asia, the President and the Prime Minister agreed:

—to continue respectively to expand cooperative relations with the People's Republic of China,

—to promote the maintenance of peace on the Korean Peninsula as important for peace and security in East Asia, including Japan,

—to continue their cooperation in support of the solidarity of ASEAN and its quest for the greater resilience and development of its members.

The President and the Prime Minister placed high value on the respective role each country is playing in this regard as exemplified recently by the President's decision to maintain U.S. ground forces in Korea and by the Prime Minister's visit to ASEAN countries this January.

They agreed that an early and comprehensive political settlement of the Kampuchean problem, including the withdrawal of foreign forces, through an international conference based on the resolutions of the General Assembly of the United Nations is important for the restoration of a durable peace in Indochina.

The President and the Prime Minister affirmed that the maintenance of peace and security in the Middle East, particularly in the Gulf region, is highly important for the peace and security of the entire world. They agreed that the determined efforts of the United States in the face of fragile security conditions in the region contribute to restoring stability, and that many countries, including Japan, are benefiting from them. They also agreed that the process of achieving a comprehensive peace in the Middle East should be further promoted to strengthen the security of the area.

In the process of reviewing the international situation, the President and the Prime Minister took note of the presence of various elements of instability in other areas of the world, and particularly with respect to some parts of Africa and Central America, they expressed their concern about the existence of conditions affecting peace and stability.

The President and the Prime Minister recognized the role that international efforts toward genuine arms control and disarmament should play in advancing world peace ansd stability, encouraging restraint and responsibility in international affairs, and promoting the security of the West as a whole.

The Prime Minister stated his view that it is important for the industrialized democracies to have a shared recognition of the various political, military and economic problems of the world and to cope with them in a consistent manner in order comprehensively to provide for the security of the West as a whole.

In meeting these international challenges to their peace and security, the President and the Prime Minister recognized that all Western industrialized democracies need to make greater efforts in the areas of defense, world economic improvement, economic cooperation with the Third World, and mutually supportive diplomatic initiatives.

The President and the Prime Minister reaffirmed their belief that the U.S.-Japan Treaty of Mutual Cooperation and Security is the foundation of peace and stability in the Far East and the defense of Japan. In insuring peace and stability in the region and the defense of Japan, they acknowledged the desirability of an appropriate division of roles between Japan and the United States. The Prime Minister stated that Japan, on its own initiative and in accordance with its Constitution and basic defense policy, will seek to make even greater efforts for improving its defense capabilities in Japanese territories and in its surrounding sea and air space, and for further alleviating the financial burden of U.S. forces in Japan. The President expressed his understanding of the statement by the Prime Minister. They recognized their common interest in contributing to the defense of Japan, and expressed the hope for even more fruitful dialogue between the two countries on security matters. In this regard, they looked forward to the scheduled meetings in June on security matters by representatives of the two Governments both at the ministerial and working levels.

The President and the Prime Minister agreed upon the importance of the relationship between the industrialized countries and the developing countries. They expressed their hope that constructive progress will be made in dealing with the countries of the south through various means, in particular through the discussion scheduled for Ottawa and Mexico.

They affirmed that political, economic and social stability of developing countries is indispensable for the maintenance of peace and stability of the world. The Prime Minister stated that the Government of Japan will strive to expand and improve its official development assistance under the New Medium Term Target and that the Government will strengthen its aid to those areas which are important to the maintenance of peace and stability of the world.

They also stated that they will continue to assist the victims of international instability through their aid to Indochinese, Afghan and African refugees.

The President and the Prime Minister discussed various problems facing the world economy. In this connection, they expressed their concern about the rising pressure toward protectionism in many countries and affirmed that the United States and Japan are determined to continue their efforts to maintain and strengthen free and open trade principles embodied in the GATT framework. In this regard, the President expressed his appreciation for the voluntary action taken by the Government of Japan to restrain the export of automobiles to the United States at a time when the United States automobile industry is passing through a difficult adjustment period.

The President and the Prime Minister highly valued the role the Summit Meeting of the Seven Industrialized Nations plays in securing the stability and development of the world economy.

The President and the Prime Minister expressed their satisfaction with the close bilateral economic relationship and noted the prospects for a further expansion of these ties. They shared the view that economic issues between the two countries have been and should continue to be given early and mutually satisfactory solutions in the spirit of goodwill and cooperation.

The President and the Prime Minister highly valued the report of the Japan-United States Economic Relations Group which contains recommendations that will contribute to the long term development of the United States-Japan economic relations. They agreed that the two governments should address the various recommendations for possible implementation. They also expressed the hope that the recommendations would be studied in such fora as the U.S.-Japan Businessmen's Conference.

They reconfirmed the importance of the dialogue between the two countries through various fora including the United States-Japan sub-cabinet group.

The President and the Prime Minister, noting that the energy problem continues to be critical to the healthy development of the world economy, reaffirmed the need for the two countries to make further efforts, together with other industrialized countries, in such fields as increase of energy production, promotion of development and use of alternative energy sources, and conservation of energy.

The President and the Prime Minister, in recognition of vital importance of preventing nuclear weapons proliferation, reaffirmed the need to continue to promote international efforts to this end. They shared the view, on the other hand, that the role of nuclear energy ought to be further expanded under appropriate safeguards to meet the increasing energy needs of the world and that the United States and Japan have special responsibility to cooperate further in promoting the peaceful uses of nuclear energy. In this connection, the President endorsed the view of the Prime

Minister that reprocessing is of particular importance to Japan. The President and the Prime Minister thus agreed that the two governments should promptly start consultations with a view to working out a permanent solution at an early date on such pending issues as the continued operation of the Tokai Reprocessing Facility and the construction of an additional reprocessing plant in Japan.

Underscoring their belief that cultural exchange is an important element in fostering mutual understanding and friendship, the President welcomed the announcement of the Prime Minister that the Government of Japan has made a financial contribution to the Japan-U.S. Friendship Commission and that it has announced its intention to give substantial financial assistance respectively to the Japan Society of New York and, in a continuing manner, to the Special Japan-U.S. Exchange Program of "Youth for Understanding" which is to commence next fiscal year.

Finally, the Prime Minister expressed his sincere appreciation to the President for the warm reception he has received during his visit to the United States. The Prime Minister extended an invitation to the President to visit Japan. The President thanked the Prime Minister for his gracious invitation, and said that he hoped to visit Japan at a mutually convenient time.

Nomination of Four Members of the Board of Directors of the United States Synthetic Fuels Corporation
May 8, 1981

The President today announced his intention to nominate four individuals to be members of the Board of Directors of the United States Synthetic Fuels Corporation.

Robert A. G. Monks has been chairman of the board of directors of the Boston Co., Inc., Boston, Mass., since 1975. In 1975–76 he was president of the Maine Wood Fuel Co., Portland, Maine. He has been president of Ram & Co., a real estate investment firm since 1972. In 1967–71 Mr. Monks was president of C. H. Sprague & Son Co., a coal and oil distribution firm in Boston. During 1967–71, Mr. Monks

held directorships with Westmoreland Coal Co., Winding Gulf Coal Co., and Penn-Virginia Corp. In 1973–76 he was chairman of the finance committee of Sulpetro of Canada, Ltd., a natural gas company. Mr. Monks was graduated from Harvard College (1954) and Harvard Law School (1958). He is married, has two children, and resides in Cape Elizabeth, Maine, and Boston, Mass. He was born in Boston on December 4, 1933.

Victor Schroeder has been manager of development for the Atlanta Apparel Mart and executive director of the Peachtree Center since

1978. He has also been president and chief executive officer of Aplomb, Inc., consulting in real estate analysis, planning, leasing, operating, management and building of real estate development. In 1975–78 he was a consultant and contract manager to various business clients. In 1971–74 Mr. Schroeder was senior vice president for development of the Phipps Land Co. In 1970–71 he was president of Resort Properties, Jasper, Ga. Mr. Schroeder attended Oklahoma State University and graduated from Officer Candidate School at Fort Benning, Ga. He is married, has five children, and resides in Atlanta, Ga. Mr. Schroeder was born in Rosedale, Kans., on July 29, 1921.

V. M. Thompson, Jr., is chairman of the board and chief executive officer of Utica National Bank & Trust Co. and Utica Bankshares Corp., Tulsa, Okla. He was president and chief executive officer of Utica National Bank & Trust Co. in 1970–77. In 1973–77 Mr. Thompson was vice chairman of the board, First National Bank & Trust Co., Stillwater, Okla. In 1957—73 he was president and chief executive officer. He recently served on the Oklahoma City branch of the Federal Reserve Board. Mr. Thompson was graduated from the University of Oklahoma (1948) and served in the U.S. Marine Corps in 1942–46. He is married, has three children, and resides in Tulsa, Okla. He was born in Thomas, Okla., on November 12, 1924.

C. Howard Wilkins is founder and managing partner of the Maverick Co. In 1966 he built, owned, and operated 13 Pizza Hut restaurants in the State of Kentucky and acted as president of Pizza Huts of Louisville, Inc. Later he merged his Kentucky-based Pizza Hut franchises into Pizza Corporation of America, a $50-million corporation that eventually became Pizza Hut, Inc., in September 1974. He served as vice chairman of the board of Pizza Huts, Inc., until leaving to found the Maverick Co. Mr. Wilkins was graduated from Yale University (1960). He is married, has five children, and resides in Wichita, Kans. He was born in Wichita on February 19, 1938.

Nomination of Anne Graham To Be an Assistant Secretary of Education
May 8, 1981

The President today announced his intention to nominate Anne Graham to be Assistant Secretary for Legislation and Public Affairs, Department of Education.

Ms. Graham is currently Deputy Special Assistant to the President for Communications. During the 1980 Presidential campaign, Ms. Graham was assistant press secretary to the Reagan-Bush campaign, responsible for media activities for the Reagan family members. In 1976–79 she was press secretary to Senator Harrison Schmitt (R-

N. Mex.). Ms. Graham worked for Secretary of the Treasury Simon in 1974–75 and served in the White House News Summary Office in 1973. She was special assistant to the Deputy Director for Communications, Republican National Committee, in 1971.

Ms. Graham was graduated from Bradford College, Bradford, Mass., and attended Columbia University. She resides in McLean, Va., and was born in Annapolis, Md., on December 28, 1949.

Nomination of Anthony G. Sousa To Be a Member of the Federal Energy Regulatory Commission
May 8, 1981

The President today announced his intention to nominate Anthony G. Sousa to be a member of the Federal Energy Regulatory Commission, Department of Energy, vice George Hall, for a term of 4 years.

Since 1973 Mr. Sousa has been vice president and general counsel of the Hawaiian Telephone Co., a subsidiary of General Telephone & Electronics Corp. In 1968–73 he was counsel, later senior counsel, and finally administrative law judge with the California Public Utilities Commission. Mr. Sousa worked with U.S. Steel Corp. in 1967. Previously, in 1959–67, Mr. Sousa worked in the traffic department and was later Western regional distribution manager with Thomas J. Lipton, Inc., of San Francisco, Calif. Prior to 1959 he was manager of trade promotion and documentation at Hong Kong General Chamber of Commerce in Hong Kong.

He was graduated from St. Luiz Gonzaga College (B.A., 1945) and the University of San Francisco Law School (J.D., 1966).

Mr. Sousa is married, has three children, and resides in Honolulu, Hawaii. He was born in Hong Kong, China, on August 8, 1927.

Message of Congratulations to François Mitterrand on His Election as President of France
May 10, 1981

Dear Mr. Mitterrand:

I speak for myself and for the American people in extending to you my warmest congratulations on your election as President of France. In personal terms, I am especially impressed by your victory; only those who have devoted the hard work and years-long dedication to winning the presidency can fully appreciate what today's reaffirmation of the democratic process in France represents.

Together we face serious challenges to the security and well-being of our peoples and to the cause of peaceful progress worldwide. I am confident that the centuries-old tradition of Franco-American friendship, together with the democratic values our two nations deeply share, will enable us to meet these challenges and preserve the spirit of Western cooperation on which the constructive future of the world increasingly depends.

I look forward to working closely with you and to the pleasure of meeting you in person.

Sincerely,

RONALD REAGAN

Note: The text of the message was released by the Office of the Press Secretary on May 11.

Remarks on the Program for Economic Recovery at a White House Reception for Members of the House of Representatives
May 11, 1981

Before my remarks, I have a brief announcement. Anyone that hasn't gotten his cufflinks or tickets to the Kennedy Center, please see Max Friedersdorf. [*Laughter*]

Well, ladies and gentlemen, members of the Cabinet and staff and all of you who are here, I don't think the East Room has ever seen exactly this kind of meeting here before. And I think last week we saw an extraordinary example of cooperation between the legislative and executive branches of government, and I want all of you Members of the House to know how deeply grateful I am for what you did last week.

During these past 112 days we've worked well together, and I think we've made a little history. Thanks to you, we've made it clear that spending can be controlled and that our system works. The voice of the people can be heard here in the Capital, and in so doing, we've restored their confidence of our people in their government and in the institutions of this Government. I know that what we did was only the first step, but I have confidence that in the weeks and months ahead we'll continue to put country ahead of partisanship.

Yes, we have a big job ahead of us putting tax cuts into effect that are really the other half of returning America's prosperity. I believe the reduction in the tax rates, as I know I've said to many of you, is essential to restoring the spirit of enterprise.

You know, some years ago there was an economist at Harvard, now deceased, Sumner Schlichter. And he said once that if a visitor from Mars came to Earth, he would conclude that our tax policy had been created to make private enterprise unworkable. [*Laughter*] And, you know, maybe what he was talking about, sometimes in a business or a sports team or an army, will outperform its competitor even though the material assets of the two seem to be roughly equal.

Now, some academicians have commented—well, they've referred to this as the x factor in human affairs, a confidence or a spirit that makes men and women dream and dare and take greater risks. Well, for too long a time our tax structure has stifled that x factor and that spirit of confidence and daring in our economic doings here in our land. Those who have the means to invest have sought tax shelters instead. And workers have been discouraged from saving or even trying to increase their earnings by increasing their productivity. I think the people have told us they want to see America return to the can-do spirit that made this country an industrial and economic giant.

Would I be wrong in suggesting that all of us here today feel a kind of special closeness? It's a feeling, I think, born of standing together for something we believed in. And I appreciate the courage it took for some of you to take that stand. I hope that we can maintain this bond established so far in the days to come. And again, I thank you from the bottom of my heart.

Note: The President spoke at 5:35 p.m. in the East Room at the White House.

In his remarks, the President referred to Assistant to the President for Legislative Affairs Max L. Friedersdorf.

Nomination of William E. Mayer To Be Administrator of the Alcohol, Drug Abuse, and Mental Health Administration
May 12, 1981

The President today announced his intention to nominate William E. Mayer to be Administrator of the Alcohol, Drug Abuse, and Mental Health Administration, Department of Health and Human Services.

Since 1980 Dr. Mayer has been medical director, Department of Health Services, in San Diego, Calif. In 1977–80 he was Chief, U.S. Army Europe Alcoholism Treatment Facility, Stuttgart, Germany. Dr. Mayer served as associate clinical professor of psychiatry, University of California (Irvine) College of Medicine, and associate chief of staff, Veterans Administration Hospital (Long Beach). In 1973–75 he was director, California State Department of Health, and in 1971–73 was director, California State Department of Mental Hygiene. Dr. Mayer was director, Community Mental Health Programs, in Contra Costa, Humboldt, and Del Norte Counties, Calif., in 1965–71.

Dr. Mayer served in the U.S. Navy in 1946–52 and in the U.S. Army in 1952–58 and 1960–65. He was awarded many decorations including the Bronze Star (twice) and the Army Commendation Medal. He was graduated from Northwestern University (B.S., 1943; B.M., 1946; M.D., 1947).

Dr. Mayer is married, has four children, and resides in Coronado, Calif. He was born in Chicago, Ill., on September 24, 1923.

Nomination of Everett Alvarez, Jr., To Be Deputy Director of the Peace Corps
May 12, 1981

The President today announced his intention to nominate Everett Alvarez, Jr., to be Deputy Director of the Peace Corps, ACTION.

Mr. Alvarez is currently a law clerk with the firm of Finnegan, Henderson, Farabow, Garrett & Dunner of Washington, D.C. He was assistant program manager for the U.S. Navy's A–4 aircraft program in 1976–80.

Mr. Alvarez is a career aviator and was a Navy pilot in 1963–80. He was the longest held prisoner of war in North Vietnam (8½ years). Upon his return, he established the Everett Alvarez, Jr., Scholarship Foundation with personal funds raised by lecturing. The foundation is now administered by the University of Santa Clara, California.

Mr. Alvarez was graduated from the University of Santa Clara (B.S., 1960) and Naval Postgraduate School in Monterey, Calif. (M.S., 1976). He is currently enrolled at the National Law Center, George Washington University.

Mr. Alvarez is married, has two children, and resides in Rockville, Md. He was born in Salinas, Calif., on December 23, 1937.

Statement on National Nursing Home Week
May 12, 1981

During National Nursing Home Week, we are particularly reminded of the needs of nursing home residents. They require special medical and health-related services delivered by individuals dedicated to their care in safe and healthful settings.

People in nursing homes also need contact with the community—often possible only when the community itself reaches out to those who have no families or whose families are far away.

Let us remember the elderly and dedicate our efforts to enabling these citizens to remain healthy and independent while at the same time ensuring that the care provided them in nursing homes fulfills the human needs of the people whom they are committed to serve.

Statement on Action by the Senate on a Fiscal Year 1982 Budget Resolution
May 12, 1981

The people of this country won another great victory tonight when Members of the Senate passed the 1982 budget resolution. With the Senate vote, we are closer to achieving our goal of fiscal responsibility and a government that lives within its means.

Senator Pete Domenici, chairman of the Budget Committee that so promptly reported the resolution to the floor, put it well when he said that, in the past, we have been spending the blessings of America while forgetting where the blessings came from. Tonight, we are putting that kind of habit behind us, thanks to his able leadership and that of Majority Leader Howard Baker.

Just as Members of the House of Representatives did a few days ago, Senators of both parties worked together to shape and pass this resolution. This was an example of bipartisan cooperation and representative democracy at its best.

On behalf of all Americans, I thank the Senators who heard the voice of the people and found the courage to commit themselves seriously to budgetary restraint, tax rate reduction, and renewed national prosperity.

Nomination of Nyle C. Brady To Be an Assistant Administrator of the Agency for International Development
May 13, 1981

The President today announced his intention to nominate Nyle C. Brady to be an Assistant Administrator of the Agency for International Development (Bureau for Technology), United States International Development Cooperation Agency.

Since 1976 Dr. Brady has been professor of soil science, Cornell University, and director general, the International Rice Research Institute, since 1973. In 1970–73 he was associate dean, New York State College of Agriculture and Life Sciences. Dr. Brady was director, Cornell University Agricultural Experiment Station, in 1965–73 and Director of Science and Education, Department of Agriculture, in 1963–65. He was assistant to the Director of Agricultural Relations, Tennessee Valley Authority, in 1959. In 1947–63 he held various positions with Cornell University.

Dr. Brady was graduated from Brigham Young University (B.S., 1941) and North Carolina State University (Ph. D., 1947). He has served on many boards and national panels, including the President's Science Advisory Committee; Agricultural Board of the National Research Council; and the

Board on Science and Technology, National Academy of Sciences Foreign Secretary's Office.

Dr. Brady is married, has four children, and resides in Ithaca, N.Y. He was born in Manassa, Colo., on October 25, 1920.

Nomination of John M. Walker, Jr., To Be an Assistant Secretary of the Treasury
May 13, 1981

The President today announced his intention to nominate John M. Walker, Jr., to be an Assistant Secretary of the Treasury (Enforcement and Operations).

Since 1975 Mr. Walker has been a partner with the firm of Carter, Ledyard & Milburn of New York, N.Y. In 1970–75 he was assistant U.S. attorney for the Southern District of New York. Mr. Walker was an associate with the firm of Davis, Polk and Wardwell in 1969–70, and in 1966–68 was assigned to the Attorney General, Republic of Botswana, through the Africa-Asia Fellowship Program, administered by the Maxwell School, Syracuse University. He previously served as a staff aide to Senator John Sherman Cooper (R-Ky.).

Mr. Walker was graduated from Yale University (B.A., 1962) and the University of Michigan Law School (J.D., 1966). He served in the U.S. Marine Corps Reserve in 1963–67.

Mr. Walker is married and resides in New York City. He was born on December 26, 1940, in New York.

Nomination of Paul J. Manafort, Jr., To Be a Member of the Board of Directors of the Overseas Private Investment Corporation
May 13, 1981

The President today announced his intention to nominate Paul J. Manafort, Jr., to be a member of the Board of Directors of the Overseas Private Investment Corporation, United States International Development Cooperation Agency.

Mr. Manafort is currently a partner with the firm of Black, Manafort & Stone, specializing in government relations, public affairs, and political consulting. He was personnel coordinator, Office of Executive Management, during the transition period. In 1978–80 he was southern coordinator, Reagan for President Committee, and deputy political director, Republican National Committee. In 1977–80 Mr. Manafort was an attorney with the firm of Vorys, Sater, Seymour and Pease in Washington, D.C. He was Associate Director of the Presidential Personnel Office at the White House in 1975–77. In 1976 he served as a delegate-hunt coordinator for eight States for the President Ford Committee. In 1974–75 he was general counsel and executive officer of Family Realty.

Mr. Manafort was graduated from Georgetown University (B.S., B.A., 1971) and Georgetown University Law School (J.D., 1974).

Mr. Manafort is married and resides in Alexandria, Va. He was born in New Britain, Conn., on April 1, 1949.

Message to Pope John Paul II Following an Attempt on His Life
May 13, 1981

Your Holiness:

I have just received the shocking news of the attack on you. All Americans join me in hopes and prayers for your speedy recovery from the injuries you have suffered in the attack. Our prayers are with you.

RONALD REAGAN

Note: The White House announced that on hearing of the shooting incident, the President spoke by telephone with Terence Cardinal Cooke, Archbishop of New York. The President expressed the sorrow of the American people and his personal concern and prayers for the Pope.

Statement on the Attempted Assassination of Pope John Paul II
May 13, 1981

Pope John Paul II, a man of peace and goodness—an inspiration to the world—has been struck today by a would-be assassin's bullet. The world is horrified, and all of us grieve over this terrible act of violence.

Pope John Paul II was wounded today while doing what he had done so well and so often throughout his travels—reaching out to others, offering hope, light, and the peace of God.

We are grateful that he has been spared. We pray that all of us will heed Pope John Paul's call for a "world of love, not of hate;" that we will hear his words reminding us that all men are brothers, that they must forever forsake the ways of violence and live together in peace.

The people of the United States, whose unbounded affection for Pope John Paul II was shown in our city streets a year and a half ago, join millions throughout the world in fervent prayer for his full and rapid recovery.

Remarks on the Program for Economic Recovery at a White House Reception for Members of the Senate
May 14, 1981

Nancy and I are delighted to have you here this evening and particularly delighted because of the occasion that this marks. Not too long ago we had a slightly bigger crowd—I guess the other House has more Members than you—in hailing the House's passage of the economic program. And I'm not going to try to get into any jokes or anything about the two Houses. I did that once when I was Governor.

We were having the prayer breakfast, and there was a part of the prayer breakfast that was a little less sacred and a little more informal than most. And a senator—our lower house in California is called the Assembly—and a senator asked me something that he might be able to say a little light-hearted about the other House. And it being a prayer breakfast, I referred him to the scriptures—the verse that says, ". . . the assembly was confused; and the more part knew not wherefore they were brought [come] together." [*Laughter*] They used this to the delight of all the senators. And the speaker of the Assembly stood up, and he too had referred to the scriptures—to that portion which reveals that Pontius Pilate was a senator. [*Laughter*]

423

But anyway, I want to thank you very much for not only what you did with regard to the legislation which we have been pushing but for something else on a bigger scale that you did, I think, for all the people of this country. I think a certain faith was restored for a lot of people in our institutions of government. And with this evidence that when the events justified, the people came ahead of partisanship, and I hope it is something that we can continue in the years ahead. I know we're not going to always agree on everything or every single issue, but as long as we have the bond that you can almost feel in this room and that I felt in that other room and can talk *to* each other instead of *about* each other—I'm sure the people will be justified in their confidence, and all of us will feel a lot better about this land of ours.

So, now, we'll just come down and mingle, but Nancy and I will just say to all of you, thank you from the bottom of our hearts.

Note: The President spoke at 5:53 p.m. in the State Dining Room at the White House.

Nomination of James R. Richards To Be Inspector General of the Department of Energy
May 15, 1981

The President today announced his intention to nominate James R. Richards to be Inspector General of the Department of Energy.

Since 1980 Mr. Richards has served as general counsel and vice president of the National Legal Center for the Public Interest in Washington, D.C. In 1977–80 he was vice president and legal director of Capital Legal Foundation. Mr. Richards was Director of Office of Hearings and Appeals, Department of the Interior, in 1973–77, and in 1969–73 he was assistant U.S. attorney for Colorado. In 1963–65 Mr. Richards was legislative and executive assistant to Senator Peter H. Dominick (R–Colo.). Previously he was engaged in the private practice of law in Colorado for 3 years. He served 2 years as Colorado assistant attorney, acting as counsel to the State Highway and Patrol Departments, and was active politically as a member of the State Republican Central Committee.

Mr. Richards is a member of the District of Columbia, Colorado, and American Bar Associations. He was graduated from Western State College, Gunnison, Colo. (B.A., 1955) and the University of Colorado School of Law (LL.B., 1960).

Mr. Richards resides in Arlington, Va. He was born on November 21, 1933, in Kinder Post, Mo.

Nomination of Peter J. Wallison To Be General Counsel of the Department of the Treasury
May 15, 1981

The President today announced his intention to nominate Peter J. Wallison to be General Counsel for Department of the Treasury.

Since 1977 Mr. Wallison has been a partner with the firm of Rogers & Wells of New York City, specializing in general corporate, securities, and financial law. In 1974–77 he was Counsel to the Vice President of the United States. He was Counsel to the Commission on Critical Choices for Americans in 1973–74, and was special assistant to Governor Nelson A. Rockefeller in 1972–73. Mr. Wallison was a Senior Staff Associate,

President's Advisory Council on Executive Organization, in 1969–70.

Mr. Wallison is a member of the New York, District of Columbia, and American Bar Associations. He was graduated from Harvard College (B.A., 1963) and Harvard Law School (LL.B., 1966).

Mr. Wallison is married, has three children, and resides in Scarsdale, N.Y. He was born on June 6, 1941, in New York, N.Y.

Nomination of Vinton DeVane Lide To Be Inspector General of the Environmental Protection Agency
May 15, 1981

The President today announced his intention to nominate Vinton DeVane Lide to be Inspector General, Environmental Protection Agency.

Since 1979 Mr. Lide has been general counsel, South Carolina Department of Social Services. In 1979 he was assistant attorney general, State of South Carolina, in charge of the establishment of the White Collar Crime Unit. Mr. Lide was executive assistant to the Governor, James B. Edwards, in 1978–79, with responsibility for the Governor's manpower division. In 1965–78 he was managing partner with the firm of Shand, Lide & Stanton in Hartsville, S.C. He was previously an associate and later partner with that firm in 1962–65.

Mr. Lide is a member of the South Carolina, Virginia, and American Bar Associations. He was graduated from Davidson College, Davidson, N.C. (B.S., 1959) and the University of Virginia School of Law (J.D., 1962).

Mr. Lide is married, has two children, and resides in Lexington, S.C. He was born on May 4, 1937, in Greenville, S.C.

Nomination of Alfred E. Eckes, Jr., To Be a Member of the United States International Trade Commission
May 15, 1981

The President today announced his intention to nominate Alfred E. Eckes, Jr., to be a member of the United States International Trade Commission for the remainder of the term expiring June 16, 1981, and for a term expiring June 16, 1990.

Since 1979 Dr. Eckes has been executive director, House Republican Conference Committee. In 1977–79 he was editorial page editor of the Columbus Dispatch, Columbus, Ohio. Previously Dr. Eckes was associate professor, history department, Ohio State University in 1969–78.

Dr. Eckes was graduated from Washington and Lee University (B.A., 1964); Fletcher School of Law and Diplomacy, Tufts University (M.A., 1966); University of Texas at Austin (Ph. D., 1969). He is the author of several articles and three books.

Dr. Eckes resides in Alexandria, Va. He was born on July 11, 1942, in North Conway, N.H.

Nomination of Eugene J. Frank To Be a Member of the United States International Trade Commission
May 15, 1981

The President today announced his intention to nominate Eugene J. Frank to be a member of the United States International Trade Commission for the remainder of the term expiring December 16, 1982.

Mr. Frank's 30-year business career has been spent as an investment banker, economist, and financial consultant. As an investment banker he primarily served as a general partner of Singer Deane & Scribner and its director of research (now Butcher Singer), also vice president of Shearson Hayden Stone for research and investment banking, and president of E. J. Frank Associates. He is currently a consultant and vice president with M. Waddell and Towne, Inc., Pittsburgh, Pa.

Through the years Mr. Frank has undertaken a wide variety of financial and economic studies for numerous companies and financial institutions. He has published articles and papers on economic and financial subjects.

Mr. Frank was graduated from Western Maryland College (B.A., 1950) and the University of Pittsburgh (M.A., 1956). He is married, has four children, and resides in Pittsburgh, Pa. He was born on October 13, 1927, in Wanamie, Pa.

Nomination of James F. McAvoy To Be a Member of the Council on Environmental Quality
May 15, 1981

The President today announced his intention to nominate James F. McAvoy to be a member of the Council on Environmental Quality.

Since 1979 Mr. McAvoy has been director of the Department of Environmental Protection, State of Ohio. In 1977–79 he was assistant director, Department of Mental Health and Mental Retardation, and in 1975–77 served as deputy director. Mr. McAvoy was nuclear construction manager, Newport News Shipbuilding & Drydock Co., Newport News, Va., in 1962–64.

Mr. McAvoy has served on many committees in Ohio including, chairman, Governor's Task Force on Nuclear Plant Safety; chairman, Governor's Hazardous Waste Siting Board; chairman, Vehicle Emissions Inspection and Maintenance Safety Board; member, Ohio Water Development Authority; and member, Ohio Air Quality Development Authority.

Mr. McAvoy was graduated from the Maine Maritime Academy, Castine, Maine, (B.S.); Certificate in Advanced Administrative Management, University of Virginia Graduate School of Business; Certificate in Executive Development, Harvard Graduate Business School; Certificate in Nuclear Engineering/Reactor Theory, Carnegie Technical Extension Program.

Mr. McAvoy is married, has four children, and resides in Columbus, Ohio. He was born on November 24, 1931, in Elizabeth, N.J.

Nomination of W. Ernst Minor To Be a Member of the Council on Environmental Quality
May 15, 1981

The President today announced his intention to nominate W. Ernst Minor to be a member of the Council on Environmental Quality.

In 1972–80 Mr. Minor was director of public affairs at the Environmental Research Center in Cincinnati, Ohio. In 1980 he resigned his position to work for the Reagan-Bush Committee as director of family scheduling. Following the election, Mr. Minor served as a member of the Environmental Protection Agency transition team. Since January 20, he has been the Executive Assistant to the EPA Acting Administrator.

Prior to his government service, Mr. Minor managed a Cincinnati printing concern for 6 years and a broadcasting company owning radio stations in Ohio and California for 4 years. Mr. Minor served on the board of directors of America's first public broadcasting station, WCET–TV Cincinnati.

Mr. Minor was graduated from Brown University (1955), Providence, R.I. He served in the U.S. Navy in 1955–57. He is married, has three children, and resides in Cincinnati, Ohio. He was born in Cincinnati on April 25, 1931.

Appointment of the Membership and Principal Officials of the President's Commission on White House Fellowships
May 15, 1981

The President today announced the appointment of the new members of the President's Commission on White House Fellowships. The Commission is bipartisan. Its purpose is to recommend to the President the White House fellows who serve for a 1-year period on the White House staff, in the Executive Office of the President, Office of the Vice President, or the offices of members of the Cabinet.

The new Chairman of the Commission is Vice Adm. James B. Stockdale (USN–Ret.). A native of Abington, Ill., Admiral Stockdale completed a distinguished Naval career in 1979. He is the recipient of more than 25 combat decorations, including the Congressional Medal of Honor, which was awarded to him for valor during the 8 years he spent as the senior American Naval prisoner of war in North Vietnam. Admiral Stockdale served as President of the Naval War College from 1977 to 1979 and as the president of the Citadel from 1979 to 1980. He is the recipient of seven honorary degrees and is currently a senior research

fellow at the Hoover Institution on War, Revolution and Peace at Stanford University.

The other members of the Commission are:

Dennis L. Bark, deputy director and senior fellow, the Hoover Institution, Stanford, Calif.

Dr. James E. Bostic, Jr., corporate executive, Riegel Textile Corp., Greenville, S.C.

Bruce L. Bower, attorney at law, Winston & Strawn, Chicago, Ill.

Marva Nettles Collins, founder and teacher, Westside Preparatory, Chicago, Ill.

Midge Decter, executive director, Committee for the Free World, New York, N.Y.

Ada E. Deer, legislative liaison, Native Americans Study Commission, Washington, D.C.

Donald J. Devine, Director, Office of Personnel Management, Washington, D.C.

Edwin J. Fuelner, president, Heritage Foundation, Washington, D.C.

Lt. Gen. Andrew Jackson Goodpaster, Superintendent, U.S. Military Academy, West Point, N.Y.

Edith Green, retired Congresswoman, Wilsonville, Oreg.

Michel T. Halbouty, independent oil producer, Houston, Tex.

Bruce H. Hasenkamp, director of government and industrial relations, The Shaklee Corp., San Francisco, Calif.

Susan C. Herter, founder and former president of Volunteer Opportunities Inc., New York, Santa Fe, N. Mex.

Richard Hinojosa, attorney at law, Evers & Toothaker, McAllen, Tex.

Francis S. M. Hodsoll, Deputy Assistant to the President, Washington, D.C.

Author E. Hughes, president, University of San Diego, San Diego, Calif.

Nancy Landon Kassebaum, United States Senator, Washington, D.C.

Irving Kristol, coeditor, The Public Interest, New York, N.Y.

Sammy Lee, medical doctor and former Olympic diver, Santa Ana, Calif.

James T. Lynn, attorney at law, Jones, Day, Reavis & Pogue, Washington, D.C., and former Director of the Office of Management and Budget

Dana G. Mead, vice president for human resources, International Paper Co., New York, N.Y.

Rita Moreno, actress, Pacific Palisades, Calif.

Martha Peterson, president, Beloit College, Beloit, Wis.

Nancy Clark Reynolds, vice president, Bendix Corp., Washington, D.C.

Jean Smith (Mrs. William French), officer and member of numerous volunteer organizations, San Marino, Calif.

Robert S. Strauss, attorney at law, Akin, Gump, Strauss, Hauer & Field, Washington, D.C., and Dallas, Tex., and former chairman of the Democratic National Committee

Deanell Reece Tacha, associate vice chancellor, University of Kansas, Lawrence, Kans.

Shannon J. Wall, president, National Maritime Union, New York, N.Y.

Margaret Bush Wilson, attorney at law, Wilson, Smith & McCullin, St. Louis, Mo., and former chairman of the board of NAACP National Housing Corp.

In addition, James C. Roberts, 34, of Great Falls, Va., was named Director of the Commission. Roberts previously was president of James C. Roberts and Associates, a Washington-based public relations firm.

Named Deputy Director of the Commission was Lt. Comdr. Marsha A. Johnson-Evans, 33, of Springfield, Ill. Lieutenant Commander Johnson-Evans is a former White House fellow and is on detail from the Navy.

Nomination of Nunzio J. Palladino To Be a Member of the Nuclear Regulatory Commission, and Designation as Chairman
May 15, 1981

The President today announced his intention to nominate Nunzio J. Palladino to be a member of the Nuclear Regulatory Commission. Upon confirmation the President intends to designate Dr. Palladino Chairman.

Dr. Palladino is dean of the College of Engineering and professor of nuclear engineering at the Pennsylvania State University. He worked for the Westinghouse Electric Corp. for 20 years before going to Penn State, including 4 years on loan to the Oak Ridge National Laboratory and the Argonne National Laboratory. In 1950–59 while working at Westinghouse, Dr. Palladino was

in charge of reactor core design for the submarine prototype reactor, Mark I; for the Nautilus reactor; and for the Shippingport Atomic Power Station. In 1958 he was awarded the Westinghouse Order of Merit for technical direction of reactor designs of the Nautilus and Shippingport powerplants; in 1956 he received the Prime Movers Award of the American Society of Mechanical Engineers for his work on the Shippingport plant.

Dr. Palladino served as the first head of the Department of Nuclear Engineering at the Pennsylvania State Unversity in 1959–66, when he was appointed dean of the

College of Engineering. As head of the Nuclear Engineering Department, he was responsible for development and implementation of course work and graduate programs and research in nuclear engineering.

Dr. Palladino has served on many committees, including the Governor's Energy Council and the Governor's Science Advisory Committee, for which he chaired the Energy Management Subcommittee; member and chairman of both the Pennsylvania Advisory Committee on Atomic Energy Development and Radiation Control and the U.S. Advisory Committee on Reactor Safeguards, which reviews all nuclear plants proposed for construction and operation in the United States. More recently, he has been a member of the Governor's Commission on Three Mile

Island, and participated on a Nuclear Regulatory Commission special task force to evaluate the cleanup activities at Three Mile Island, which culminated in the preparation of a report submitted to the NRC Commissioners.

Dr. Palladino is a native of Allentown, Pa., and received his B.S. and M.S. degrees in mechanical engineering from Lehigh University in 1938 and 1939. In addition, he did graduate work in nuclear engineering at the University of Tennessee and in business and management at the University of Pittsburgh. Lehigh University awarded him the honorary degree of doctor of engineering in 1964. He is married, has three daughters, and resides in State College, Pa. He was born on November 10, 1916.

Nomination of Kenneth W. Gideon To Be an Assistant General Counsel of the Department of the Treasury
May 15, 1981

The President today announced his intention to nominate Kenneth W. Gideon to be an Assistant General Counsel in the Department of the Treasury (Chief Counsel for the Internal Revenue Service).

Mr. Gideon has been associated with the firm of Fulbright & Jaworski, Houston, Tex., since 1971. He became a partner of the firm in 1978. Mr. Gideon has been active in the areas of Federal and State taxation since 1971, including substantial tax litigation and controversy work. In 1979–81 he was chairman, committee on court procedure, American Bar Association taxation section. Since 1979 he has been chairman, commit-

tee on administrative practice, and liaison with the comptroller of public accounts, taxation section, State Bar of Texas. In 1980 Mr. Gideon was chairman, subcommittee on capital and financial structure, legal, tax and accounting committee, National Council of Farmer Cooperatives.

Mr. Gideon is a member of the Texas and American Bar Associations. He was graduated from Harvard University (B.A., 1968) and Yale Law School (J.D., 1971).

Mr. Gideon is married, has three children, and resides in Houston, Tex. He was born on July 25, 1946, in Lubbock, Tex.

Statement on Armed Forces Day
May 16, 1981

Today is Armed Forces Day, and on behalf of millions of Americans I want to send to our men and women in uniform a personal message of thanks and gratitude.

Today their job is vitally important—their sacrifice and patriotism makes it possible for those of us who are civilians to go about our everyday lives. Their commitment keeps our nation strong and our future free.

You know, James Michener writes in one of his novels about a commanding officer who thinks about the self-sacrifice of those who served under him and wonders, "Where do we get such men?"

Today millions of Americans are asking themselves that same question about the dedicated men and women who serve in our Armed Forces. Like me, they're asking that question with gratitude, with respect and affection in their hearts. Today, I want all those wearing American uniforms around the globe to know: America is grateful to you—and proud of you, too.

Note: The statement was released by the Office of the Press Secretary on May 15.

Appointment of Philip A. Lacovara as the Presidential Appointee to the District of Columbia Judicial Nomination Commission
May 16, 1981

The President today announced the appointment of Philip A. Lacovara as the Presidential appointee to the District of Columbia Judicial Nomination Commission. Mr. Lacovara will fill the unexpired 5-year term of William A. Borders, Jr., who was appointed by President Carter on July 2, 1980.

Mr. Lacovara is currently resident partner of the Washington, D.C., office of the law firm Hughes, Hubbard & Reed, where he is engaged in the general practice of law. In 1976 and 1977 he served as special counsel, House Committee on Standards of Official Conduct, for the Korean influence investigation. In 1973 and 1974 he served as Counsel to the Special Prosecutor, Watergate Special Prosecution Force. Prior to that, in 1972–73 and 1967–69, he served in the capacities of Deputy Solicitor General of the United States and Assistant to the Solicitor General of the United States, respectively. In 1971–72 he served as special counsel to the police commissioner of New York. Mr. Lacovara served as Special Assistant to the Attorney General in 1970. From 1969 to 1971, he was associated with Hughes, Hubbard & Reed. Prior to that, in 1968 and 1969 he served as consultant to the U.S. Representative to the Organization of American States.

Immediately following his graduation from law school in 1966, Mr. Lacovara served a judicial clerkship with Judge Harold Leventhal of the United States Court of Appeals for the District of Columbia Circuit. Mr. Lacovara graduated summa cum laude from Columbia University School of Law, where he was first in his class for each of 3 years. He received his bachelor's degree magna cum laude from Georgetown University in 1963, where he graduated in 3 years.

Mr. Lacovara has been actively involved in District of Columbia legal affairs throughout his distinguished career, which has included service since 1976 on the board of trustees of the Public Defender Service of the District of Columbia, and since 1979 on the committee on admissions and grievances, United States Court of Appeals for the District of Columbia Circuit. Additionally, he has served since 1973 on the Judicial Conference of the District of Columbia Circuit, and since 1976 on the Advisory Committee on Procedure, Judicial Council of the District of Columbia Circuit, and the Legal Ethics Committee, District of Columbia Bar. From 1978 through 1980, he was delegate from the District of Columbia to the American Bar Association House of Delegates. He is a member of the American Law Institute.

Mr. Lacovara has served as an adjunct professor of law at Georgetown University Law Center and lecturer in law at Columbia University School of Law. He has been a frequent author and lecturer in many areas of the law, including the criminal justice system, constitutional law, antitrust law, and professional responsibility.

Mr. Lacovara is married, has seven chil-

dren, and resides in Washington, D.C. He was born on July 11, 1943.

Address at Commencement Exercises at the University of Notre Dame
May 17, 1981

Father Hesburgh, I thank you very much and for so many things. The distinguished honor that you've conferred upon me here today, I must say, however, compounds a sense of guilt that I have nursed for almost 50 years. I thought the first degree I was given was honorary. [*Laughter*] But it's wonderful to be here today with Governor Orr, Governor Bowen, Senators Lugar and Quayle, and Representative Hiler, these distinguished honorees, the trustees, administration, faculty, students, and friends of Notre Dame and, most important, the graduating class of 1981.

Nancy and I are greatly honored to share this day with you, and our pleasure has been more than doubled because I am also sharing the platform with a longtime and very dear friend, Pat O'Brien.

Pat and I haven't been able to see much of each other lately, so I haven't had a chance to tell him that there is now another tie that binds us together. Until a few weeks ago I knew very little about my father's ancestry. He had been orphaned at age 6. But now I've learned that his grandfather, my great-grandfather, left Ireland to come to America, leaving his home in Ballyporeen, a village in County Tipperary in Ireland, and I have learned that Ballyporeen is the ancestral home of the O'Briens.

Now, if I don't watch out, this may turn out to be less of a commencement than a warm bath in nostalgic memories. Growing up in Illinois, I was influenced by a sports legend so national in scope, it was almost mystical. It is difficult to explain to anyone who didn't live in those times. The legend was based on a combination of three elements: a game, football; a university, Notre Dame; and a man, Knute Rockne. There has been nothing like it before or since.

My first time to ever see Notre Dame was to come here as a sports announcer, 2 years out of college, to broadcast a football game. You won or I wouldn't have mentioned it. [*Laughter*]

A number of years later I returned here in the company of Pat O'Brien and a galaxy of Hollywood stars for the world premiere of "Knute Rockne—All American" in which I was privileged to play George Gipp. I've always suspected that there might have been many actors in Hollywood who could have played the part better, but no one could have wanted to play it more than I did. And I was given the part largely because the star of that picture, Pat O'Brien, kindly and generously held out a helping hand to a beginning young actor.

Having come from the world of sports, I'd been trying to write a story about Knute Rockne. I must confess that I had someone in mind to play the Gipper. On one of my sports broadcasts before going to Hollywood, I had told the story of his career and tragic death. I didn't have very many words on paper when I learned that the studio that employed me was already preparing a story treatment for that film. And that brings me to the theme of my remarks.

I'm the fifth President of the United States to address a Notre Dame commencement. The temptation is great to use this forum as an address on a great international or national issue that has nothing to do with this occasion. Indeed, this is somewhat traditional. So, I wasn't surprised when I read in several reputable journals that I was going to deliver an address on foreign policy or on the economy. I'm not going to talk about either.

But, by the same token, I'll try not to belabor you with some of the standard rhet-

431

oric that is beloved of graduation speakers. For example, I'm not going to tell you that "You know more today that you've ever known before or that you will ever know again." [*Laughter*] The other standby is, "When I was 14, I didn't think my father knew anything. By the time I was 21, I was amazed at how much the old gentleman had learned in 7 years." And then, of course, the traditional and the standby is that "A university like this is a storehouse of knowledge because the freshmen bring so much in and the seniors take so little away." [*Laughter*]

You members of the graduating class of 18—or 1981—[*laughter*]—I don't really go back that far—[*laughter*]—are what behaviorists call achievers. And while you will look back with warm pleasure on your memories of these years that brought you here to where you are today, you are also, I know, looking at the future that seems uncertain to most of you but which, let me assure you, offers great expectations.

Take pride in this day. Thank your parents, as one on your behalf has already done here. Thank those who've been of help to you over the last 4 years. And do a little celebrating; you're entitled. This is your day, and whatever I say should take cognizance of that fact. It is a milestone in life, and it marks a time of change.

Winston Churchill, during the darkest period of the "Battle of Britain" in World War II said: "When great causes are on the move in the world . . . we learn we are spirits, not animals, and that something is going on in space and time, and beyond space and time, which, whether we like it or not, spells duty."

Now, I'm going to mention again that movie that Pat and I and Notre Dame were in, because it says something about America. First, Knute Rockne as a boy came to America with his parents from Norway. And in the few years it took him to grow up to college age, he became so American that here at Notre Dame, he became an All American in a game that is still, to this day, uniquely American.

As a coach, he did more than teach young men how to play a game. He believed truly that the noblest work of man was building the character of man. And maybe that's

why he was a living legend. No man connected with football has ever achieved the stature or occupied the singular niche in the Nation that he carved out for himself, not just in a sport, but in our entire social structure.

Now, today I hear very often, "Win one for the Gipper," spoken in a humorous vein. Lately I've been hearing it by Congressmen who are supportive of the programs that I've introduced. [*Laughter*] But let's look at the significance of that story. Rockne could have used Gipp's dying words to win a game any time. But 8 years went by following the death of George Gipp before Rock revealed those dying words, his deathbed wish.

And then he told the story at halftime to a team that was losing, and one of the only teams he had ever coached that was torn by dissension and jealousy and factionalism. The seniors on that team were about to close out their football careers without learning or experiencing any of the real values that a game has to impart. None of them had known George Gipp. They were children when he played for Notre Dame. It was to this team that Rockne told the story and so inspired them that they rose above their personal animosities. For someone they had never known, they joined together in a common cause and attained the unattainable.

We were told when we were making the picture of one line that was spoken by a player during that game. We were actually afraid to put it in the picture. The man who carried the ball over for the winning touchdown was injured on the play. We were told that as he was lifted on the stretcher and carried off the field he was heard to say, "That's the last one I can get for you, Gipper."

Now, it's only a game. And maybe to hear it now, afterward—and this is what we feared—it might sound maudlin and not the way it was intended. But is there anything wrong with young people having an experience, feeling something so deeply, thinking of someone else to the point that they can give so completely of themselves? There will come times in the lives of all of us when we'll be faced with causes bigger than ourselves, and they won't be on a playing field.

This Nation was born when a band of men, the Founding Fathers, a group so unique we've never seen their like since, rose to such selfless heights. Lawyers, tradesmen, merchants, farmers—56 men achieved security and standing in life but valued freedom more. They pledged their lives, their fortunes, and their sacred honor. Sixteen of them gave their lives. Most gave their fortunes. All preserved their sacred honor.

They gave us more than a nation. They brought to all mankind for the first time the concept that man was born free, that each of us has inalienable rights, ours by the grace of God, and that government was created by us for our convenience, having only the powers that we choose to give it. This is the heritage that you're about to claim as you come out to join the society made up of those who have preceded you by a few years, or some of us by a great many.

This experiment in man's relation to man is a few years into its third century. Saying that may make it sound quite old. But let's look at it from another viewpoint or perspective. A few years ago, someone figured out that it you could condense the entire history of life on Earth into a motion picture that would run for 24 hours a day, 365 days—maybe on leap years we could have an intermission—[*laughter*]—this idea that is the United States wouldn't appear on the screen until 3½ seconds before midnight on December 31st. And in those 3½ seconds not only would a new concept of society come into being, a golden hope for all mankind, but more than half the activity, economic activity in world history, would take place on this continent. Free to express their genius, individual Americans, men and women, in 3½ seconds, would perform such miracles of invention, construction, and production as the world had never seen.

As you join us out there beyond the campus, you know there are great unsolved problems. Federalism, with its built in checks and balances, has been distorted. Central government has usurped powers that properly belong to local and State governments. And in so doing, in many ways that central government has begun to fail

to do the things that are truly the responsibility of a central government.

All of this has led to the misuse of power and preemption of the prerogatives of people and their social institutions. You are graduating from a great private, or, if you will, independent university. Not too many years ago, such schools were relatively free from government interference. In recent years, government has spawned regulations covering virtually every facet of our lives. The independent and church-supported colleges and universities have found themselves enmeshed in that network of regulations and the costly blizzard of paperwork that government is demanding. Thirty-four congressional committees and almost 80 subcommittees have jurisdiction over 439 separate laws affecting education at the college level alone. Almost every aspect of campus life is now regulated—hiring, firing, promotions, physical plant, construction, recordkeeping, fundraising and, to some extent, curriculum and educational programs.

I hope when you leave this campus that you will do so with a feeling of obligation to your alma mater. She will need your help and support in the years to come. If ever the great independent colleges and universities like Notre Dame give way to and are replaced by tax-supported institutions, the struggle to preserve academic freedom will have been lost.

We're troubled today by economic stagnation, brought on by inflated currency and prohibitive taxes and burdensome regulations. The cost of stagnation in human terms, mostly among those least equipped to survive it, is cruel and inhuman.

Now, after those remarks, don't decide that you'd better turn your diploma back in so you can stay another year on the campus. I've just given you the bad news. The good news is that something is being done about all this because the people of America have said, "Enough already." You know, we who had preceded you had just gotten so busy that we let things get out of hand. We forgot that we were the keepers of the power, forgot to challenge the notion that the state is the principal vehicle of social change, forgot that millions of social interactions among free individuals and institutions can do more to foster economic and social progress than all the careful schemes of government planners.

Well, at last we're remembering, remembering that government has certain legitimate functions which it can perform very well, that it can be responsive to the people, that it can be humane and compassionate, but that when it undertakes tasks that are not its proper province, it can do none of them as well or as economically as the private sector.

For too long government has been fixing things that aren't broken and inventing miracle cures for unknown diseases.

We need you. We need your youth. We need your strength. We need your idealism to help us make right that which is wrong. Now, I know that this period of your life, you have been and are critically looking at the mores and customs of the past and questioning their value. Every generation does that. May I suggest, don't discard the time-tested values upon which civilization was built simply because they're old. More important, don't let today's doomcriers and cynics persuade you that the best is past, that from here on it's all downhill. Each generation sees farther than the generation that preceded it because it stands on the shoulders of that generation. You're going to have opportunities beyond anything that we've ever known.

The people have made it plain already. They want an end to excessive government intervention in their lives and in the economy, an end to the burdensome and unnecessary regulations and a punitive tax policy that does take "from the mouth of labor the bread it has earned." They want a government that cannot only continue to send men across the vast reaches of space and bring them safely home, but that can guarantee that you and I can walk in the park of our neighborhood after dark and get safely home. And finally, they want to know that this Nation has the ability to defend itself against those who would seek to pull it down.

And all of this, we the people can do. Indeed, a start has already been made. There's a task force under the leadership of the Vice President, George Bush, that is to look at those regulations I've spoken of. They have already identified hundreds of them that can be wiped out with no harm to the quality of life. And the cancellation of just those regulations will leave billions and billions of dollars in the hands of the people for productive enterprise and research and development and the creation of jobs.

The years ahead are great ones for this country, for the cause of freedom and the spread of civilization. The West won't contain communism, it will transcend communism. It won't bother to dismiss or denounce it, it will dismiss it as some bizarre chapter in human history whose last pages are even now being written.

William Faulkner, at a Nobel Prize ceremony some time back, said man "would not only [merely] endure: he will prevail" against the modern world because he will return to "the old verities and truths of the heart." And then Faulkner said of man, "He is immortal because he alone among creatures . . . has a soul, a spirit capable of compassion and sacrifice and endurance."

One can't say those words—compassion, sacrifice, and endurance—without thinking of the irony that one who so exemplifies them, Pope John Paul II, a man of peace and goodness, an inspiration to the world, would be struck by a bullet from a man towards whom he could only feel compassion and love. It was Pope John Paul II who warned in last year's encyclical on mercy and justice against certain economic theories that use the rhetoric of class struggle to justify injustice. He said, "In the name of an alleged justice the neighbor is sometimes destroyed, killed, deprived of liberty or stripped of fundamental human rights."

For the West, for America, the time has come to dare to show to the world that our civilized ideas, our traditions, our values, are not—like the ideology and war machine of totalitarian societies—just a facade of strength. It is time for the world to know our intellectual and spiritual values are rooted in the source of all strength, a belief in a Supreme Being, and a law higher than our own.

When it's written, history of our time won't dwell long on the hardships of the recent past. But history will ask—and our answer determine the fate of freedom for a thousand years—Did a nation born of hope lose hope? Did a people forged by courage find courage wanting? Did a generation steeled by hard war and a harsh peace forsake honor at the moment of great climactic struggle for the human spirit?

If history asks such questions, it also answers them. And the answers are to be found in the heritage left by generations of Americans before us. They stand in silent witness to what the world will soon know and history someday record: that in the [its] third century, the American Nation came of age, affirmed its leadership of free men and women serving selflessly a vision of man with God, government for people, and humanity at peace.

A few years ago, an Australian Prime Minister, John Gorton, said, "I wonder if anybody ever thought what the situation for the comparatively small nations in the world would be if there were not in existence the United States, if there were not this · giant country prepared to make so many sacrifices." This is the noble and rich heritage rooted in great civil ideas of the West, and it is yours.

My hope today is that in the years to come—and come it shall—when it's your time to explain to another generation the meaning of the past and thereby hold out to them their promise of the future, that you'll recall the truths and traditions of which we've spoken. It is these truths and traditions that define our civilization and make up our national heritage. And now, they're yours to protect and pass on.

I have one more hope for you: when you do speak to the next generation about these things, that you will always be able to speak of an America that is strong and free, to find in your hearts an unbounded pride in this much-loved country, this once and future land, this bright and hopeful nation whose generous spirit and great ideals the world still honors.

Congratulations, and God bless you.

Note: The President spoke at 3:11 p.m. at the 136th commencement ceremony of the university, which was held in the Notre Dame Athletic and Convocation Center at the campus in South Bend, Ind. The President was introduced by Rev. Theodore M. Hesburgh, president of the university, who had presented the President with an honorary doctor of laws degree prior to the commencement address.

In his remarks, the President referred to Governor Robert Orr, former Governor Otis R. Bowen, Senators Richard G. Lugar and Dan Quayle, and Representative John P. Hiler, all of Indiana. The President also referred to the movie "Knute Rockne—All American," which was filmed at Notre Dame in 1940. The President played the part of All American halfback George Gipp, who died of pneumonia.

The occasion marked the first trip by the President outside of Washington, D.C., since the assassination attempt on March 30. Four former Presidents—Franklin D. Roosevelt, Dwight D. Eisenhower, Gerald R. Ford, and Jimmy Carter—addressed convocations or commencement exercises at the university and were awarded honorary degrees.

Nomination of Harry N. Walters To Be an Assistant Secretary of the Army
May 18, 1981

The President today announced his intention to nominate Harry N. Walters to be an Assistant Secretary of the Army (Manpower and Reserve Affairs).

Since 1977 Mr. Walters has been presi-

dent and chief executive officer of Potsdam Paper Corp., Potsdam, N.Y. In 1976–77 he was a management consultant with Howard Paper Mills, Inc., Dayton, Ohio. Mr. Walters was executive vice president of Standard

Paper Manufacturing Co., Richmond, Va., in 1975–76. He previously held positions with the Kimberly Clark Corp. in Neenah, Wis., and New York City. In 1959–63 he served in the U.S. Army.

Mr. Walters was graduated from the U.S. Military Academy at West Point in 1959. He is married, has two children, and resides in Hannawa Falls, N.Y. He was born on June 4, 1936.

Nomination of George A. Sawyer To Be an Assistant Secretary of the Navy
May 18, 1981

The President today announced his intention to nominate George A. Sawyer to be an Assistant Secretary of the Navy (Shipbuilding and Logistics).

Since 1976 Mr. Sawyer has been president and chief executive officer of John J. McMullen Associates, Inc. In 1969–76 he was with Bechtel, Inc., of San Francisco, Calif. He served as environmental systems manager in the Scientific Development Department in 1969–71; manager of Business Development in 1971–75; and manager of Eastern Operations and vice president of International Bechtel, Inc., in 1975–76.

In 1967–69 Mr. Sawyer was manager of Marine Systems, Batelle Memorial Institute,

Richland, Wash. He was manager, Marine Systems, NUS Corp., in 1965–67. And in 1963–65 he was nuclear power coordinator of Marine Projects with Babcock & Wilcox. In 1953–62 he was a submarine engineer officer in the U.S. Navy.

Mr. Sawyer was graduated from Yale University and studied nuclear engineering at Knolls Atomic Power Laboratories in Schenectady, N.Y. He is a member of the American Society of Naval Engineers and the Society of Naval Architects and Marine Engineers.

Mr. Sawyer resides in Red Bank, N.J. He was born in New York City on April 20, 1931.

Nomination of Nora Walsh Hussey To Be Superintendent of the United States Mint at Denver
May 18, 1981

The President today announced his intention to nominate Nora Walsh Hussey to be Superintendent of the Mint of the United States, Department of the Treasury, at Denver.

Since 1952 Mrs. Hussey has been manager of Hussey Trucking Co. of Sturgis, S. Dak. She serves on the board of directors of the Black Hills Fine Arts Council and was South Dakota chairman of the Reagan-Bush

Committee during the 1980 Presidential campaign. She has also served as Republican National Committeewoman for South Dakota. Mrs. Hussey was named Outstanding Republican Woman in South Dakota in 1980.

Mrs. Hussey attended New York University and Amherst College. She is married and resides in Sturgis, S. Dak. She was born in New York City on March 25, 1915.

Nomination of James B. Conkling To Be an Associate Director of the International Communication Agency
May 18, 1981

The President today announced his intention to nominate James B. Conkling to be Associate Director of the International Communication Agency (Broadcasting).

Since 1978 Mr. Conkling has been president of BEI Productions, Inc., a subsidiary of Bonneville International Corp. BEI Productions specializes in the development of motion picture and television concepts. He has been director of Bonneville International Corp. since 1965. BEI, Inc. has advised the China Record Co. of Beijing in the development of recording equipment.

In 1975–77 Mr. Conkling was producer of a major traveling musical play "Threads of Glory," a Bicentennial production. He was cofounder and vice president of the Raymar Book Co., Inc., Monrovia, Calif., in 1970–80. In 1968–74 he constructed, owned, and operated a winter/summer resort in California. Mr. Conkling was a performing member of the King Family singers in 1965–68. In 1961–65 he was president of the International Educational Broadcasting Corp. and was founder and president of Warner Brothers Records, Inc., in 1958–61. He was one of the original six founders of the National Academy of Recording Arts and Sciences and was its first national chairman. He was president of Columbia Records in 1951–56, and vice president of Capitol Records in 1942–51.

Mr. Conkling was graduated from Dartmouth College (1936) and the University of Pennsylvania (1938). He served in the U.S. Naval Reserve in 1942–43.

Mr. Conkling is married, has five children, and resides in Sherman Oaks, Calif. He was born on March 1, 1915, in East Orange, N.J.

Nomination of Jan W. Mares To Be an Assistant Secretary of Energy
May 18, 1981

The President today announced his intention to nominate Jan W. Mares to be an Assistant Secretary of Energy (Fossil Energy).

Since 1963 Mr. Mares has held various positions with the Union Carbide Corp. Since 1979 he has been vice president and general manager of the Ethylene Oxide Derivatives Division. He was operations manager, Ethylene Oxide Derivatives and Industrial Chemicals Departments in 1976–79; business financial task force manager, Hydrocarbons Department, in 1977–78; business manager, OPEC program, Hydrocarbons Department, in 1973–75; chief international counsel, Law Department, in 1972–73; European, African, and Middle Eastern area attorney, Law Department, in 1968–72; assistant international attorney in 1966–67; and attorney in 1963–66. Mr. Mares is also director, Energy Resources Co., Inc., an energy and environmental services and technology development company.

Mr. Mares graduated from Harvard University (B.A., 1958; LL.B., 1963) and MIT (1960).

Mr. Mares is married, has two children, and resides in New Canaan, Conn. He was born December 12, 1936, in St. Louis, Mo.

Appointment of Robert N. Broadbent as Commissioner of the Bureau of Reclamation
May 18, 1981

The President today announced the appointment of Robert N. Broadbent to be Commissioner of the Bureau of Reclamation, Department of the Interior.

Mr. Broadbent is currently a Federal bankruptcy trustee. Previously he was a pharmacist in 1950–75. Since 1968 he has served as an elected member of the board of county commissioners, Clark County, Nev. In 1959–68 he was mayor and member of the Boulder City Council.

He was graduated from Idaho State University (B.S., 1950). He served in the U.S. Air Force in 1945–46.

Mr. Broadbent is married, has four children, and resides in Las Vegas, Nev. He was born June 19, 1926, in Ely, Nev.

Nomination of Ronald DeWayne Palmer To Be United States Ambassador to Malaysia
May 18, 1981

The President today announced his intention to nominate Ronald DeWayne Palmer, of Maryland, as Ambassador to Malaysia.

Mr. Palmer entered the Foreign Service in 1957 as intelligence research specialist in the Department of State. In 1959–60 he attended Indonesian language training at the Foreign Service Institute. He was economic officer in Djakarta (1960–62) and in Kuala Lumpur (1962–63). In the Department, he was Foreign Affairs Officer (1963–64) and staff assistant (1964–65). He was cultural attaché in Copenhagen, on detail to the International Communication Agency in 1965–67, and was faculty member at the United States Military Academy in 1967–70.

He was international relations officer in the Department in 1975–76. In 1976–78 he was Ambassador to the Republic of Togo. In the Department, he has been Director of Foreign Service Career Development and Assignments (1978–79), and since 1979 he has been Deputy Assistant Secretary for Personnel. He speaks Indonesian, French, and Danish.

Mr. Palmer was born May 22, 1932, in Uniontown, Pa. He graduated from Howard University (B.A., 1955) and Johns Hopkins University (M.A., 1957). He is married to the former Euna Scott, and they have two children.

Letter to the Speaker of the House and the Chairman of the Senate Foreign Relations Committee Reporting on the Cyprus Conflict
May 19, 1981

Dear Mr. Speaker: (Dear Mr. Chairman:)

In accordance with the provision of Public Law 95–384, I am submitting the following report on progress made during the past sixty days toward reaching a negotiated settlement of the Cyprus problem.

The intercommunal negotiations between Greek Cypriot and Turkish Cypriot representatives continue under the chairmanship of the Secretary General's Special Representative on Cyprus, Ambassador Hugo Gobbi. The two sides are proceeding in their detailed review of the four basic, mutually agreed-upon issues and continuing to devote each session to one topic.

Meetings were held on March 18, April 2, 15, and 29, and May 6. The pace of weekly sessions has slowed somewhat as both Greek and Turkish Cypriots prepare for elections. A reduced schedule in May and June is anticipated with resumption of a regular schedule in July. Both sides have continued their talks in a congenial negotiating atmosphere.

Although not directly connected to the intercommunal talks, the problem of missing persons in Cyprus has been a significant issue dividing the communities. Consequently, we are pleased to note a significant, positive development in this area. Ambassador Gobbi announced on April 22 that an intercommunal agreement had been reached on the terms of reference for a Committee on Missing Persons (text attached). The date for the first meeting of the Committee will be fixed soon following coordination with the International Committee of the Red Cross and appointment of members of the Committee.

The issue of setting up a Committee on Missing Persons could, in our view, only be resolved with the cooperation of both Cypriot communities. Consequently, we are gratified by the United Nations' announcement and hope that subsequent discussion in the Committee will be productive and lead to a resolution of this important, humanitarian question.

We also believe the formation of a Committee will contribute to a positive negotiating atmosphere facilitating progress in the intercommunal talks. The agreement reached to form a Committee suggests that patient, persistent negotiating between both communities, under United Nations aegis, holds the potential for success even on the most difficult of issues. I am confident that the productive attitudes charac-

terized by the formation of a Committee on Missing Persons can be employed in the pursuit of a just and lasting settlement of the Cyprus question.

Sincerely,

RONALD REAGAN

Statement of Agreement on Missing Persons Committee

Following is the text of a statement made April 22 by SRSG Gobbi at the Ledra Palace in Nicosia, Cyprus:

"On behalf of the Secretary-General, I am very pleased to announce that agreement has been reached by the two sides on the terms of reference for the establishment of a committee on missing persons in Cyprus.

"The Secretary-General has asked me to thank both sides for their important cooperation which has made this agreement possible. In particular, I wish to thank the representatives of the two sides who, over the past few months, were engaged in intensive efforts to bring about the setting up of this committee. The Secretary-General also wishes to thank the International Committee of the Red Cross for its cooperation in facilitating this significant achievement. On the basis of this agreement it is possible now to proceed to the establishment of the committee. This development represents a very important step forward in the solution of a long-standing issue of great concern to the two sides.

"Furthermore, we hope the efforts of the committee on missing persons will strengthen the spirit of cooperation and the joint endeavor undertaken in the framework of the intercommunal talks."

Note: This is the text of identical letters addressed to Thomas P. O'Neill, Jr., Speaker of the House of Representatives, and Charles H. Percy, chairman of the Senate Foreign Relations Committee.

Nomination of Cecilia Aranda Frantz To Be Director of the National Institute of Handicapped Research
May 19, 1981

The President today announced his intention to nominate Cecilia Aranda Frantz to be Director of the National Institute of Handicapped Research, Department of Education.

Since 1979 Mrs. Frantz has been superintendent for the Wilson School District in Phoenix, Ariz. In 1975–79 she served as the Wilson School psychologist and director of special education. Previously, in 1972–75, Mrs. Frantz was associated with Arizona State University. She assisted in and taught graduate-level counseling classes in 1972–73; practicum supervisor in 1979; co-leader in self-awareness seminar conducted at Phoenix Union District for their faculty; psychologist, Child Evaluation Center, in 1973–75.

Since 1975 Mrs. Frantz has been a participant in the Arizona Diagnostic Development Project. She participated in a counseling project for minority people in Chicanos Por La Causa and serves as one of their consultants. She is also a member of the board of directors of the Saguaro chapter of the March of Dimes (1978–79) and a member of the Mayor's Community Services Commission (1980).

Mrs. Frantz was graduated from the University of Arizona at Tucson (B.A., 1966); and Arizona State University at Tempe (M.A., 1972; Ph. D., 1975).

She is married and has one child. She was born August 6, 1941, in Nogales, Ariz.

Nomination of Clifford M. Barber To Be Superintendent of the United States Assay Office at New York
May 19, 1981

The President today announced his intention to nominate Clifford M. Barber to be Superintendent of the United States Assay Office, Department of the Treasury, at New York, N.Y.

Since 1977 Mr. Barber has been senior partner of Barber and Gross of Montgomery, N.Y. He had been in private practice since 1948.

Mr. Barber was village trustee, village of Walden, in 1949–51; appointed acting police justice in 1951–67; elected town justice, town of Montgomery, in 1955 and reelected to four terms, retiring in 1975. He is an active Republican and served as a delegate to the Republican National Convention in 1976 and 1980.

Mr. Barber was graduated from Rutgers University (B.A., 1940) and Cornell Law School (LL.D., 1947).

Mr. Barber is married, has eight children, and resides in Walden, N.Y. He was born October 8, 1917, in Elizabeth, N.J.

Remarks at a White House Luncheon Honoring the Astronauts of the Space Shuttle *Columbia*
May 19, 1981

The President. Ladies and gentlemen, welcome. And before we say anything at all or I make any remarks—because there are many here who probably don't know that in addition to the men we're honoring today, that there are in our midst, as a great part of this audience, many who have been those pioneers out into space, our astronauts going back to the very beginning of the program. Could I ask that all of you who fit that description, all of you, to please stand up?

Well, we're in very distinguished company, believe me. Commander Young and Captain Crippen, all the world held its breath in the silent moments of your reentry, and when we finally heard your voices again, all the world knew America had begun a new age.

A few moments ago, I had the privilege of decorating Commander Young and Captain Crippen for their personal courage and the honor they have brought to our nation, and also honored Dr. Alan Lovelace, who is here with us today, but more about that later. I presented to John Young the Congressional Space Medal of Honor, our highest award for achievements in space, and to both him and Bob Crippen, the NASA Distinguished Service Medal, the highest award the space agency can bestow.

These men have traveled across the country since their shuttle flight, and I think they now must be conscious of and realize that to all America they have now become John and Bob. The American people have welcomed them with tremendous affection, and no wonder. Through them, we've all been part of a greatness pushing wider the boundaries of our freedom. As I told them before they took off, through them we all felt as giants once again. And once again, we felt the surge of pride that comes from knowing that we're the first and we're the best—and we are so because we're free.

The space shuttle is the world's first true space transportation system. It will be the space workhorse for many years to come, and soon we'll have the operational capability that will place cargo in orbit for a variety of users. Because we lead the world in science and space travel, we're on the cutting edge of technology and discovery. The shuttle will affect American life in both subtle and dramatic ways, bringing energy and excitement into our national renewal.

The flight of the *Columbia* was a victory for the American spirit. John Young and Bob Crippen both made us very proud. Their deeds reminded us that we, as a free people, can accomplish whatever we set out to do. Nothing binds our abilities except our expectations, and given that, the farthest star is within our reach.

To paraphrase John Greenleaf Whittier: We are the people who have thrown the windows of our souls wide open to the sun. We will follow as we can where our hearts have long since gone, and progress will be ours for all mankind to share. Americans have shown the world that we not only dream great dreams, we dare to live those great dreams.

And now, I would like to introduce a man whose leadership and high standards have made the success of the *Columbia* possible. Ladies and gentlemen, the acting director of NASA, Dr. Alan M. Lovelace.

Dr. Lovelace. I'd like to ask John and Bob to join me. And, Vice President Bush, would you please join me at the podium?

Mr. President, I'd like to just say one brief remark—and I know I speak for myself, I think I speak for everybody in NASA—and that is, we thank you for the opportunity to serve the country, and we are prepared to continue to do that.

I would like now to present to you, Mr. President, your flag that was flown on the first flight of the *Columbia*.

The President. Thank you very much.

Dr. Lovelace. And, Mr. Vice President, a flag for you, sir.

The Vice President. Thank you very much.

Dr. Lovelace. Mr. President, we had the pleasure of hosting Vice President Bush at the Kennedy Space Center some weeks ago, and on that occasion, we presented him with a flight jacket. We brought yours here to Washington, and I'd like to present it to you today. Suitable for flying or riding. [*Laughter*]

Mr. Young. It's a great honor for Bob and I to be here today. And we'd also like to make a presentation to the President that tells, for all of you who contributed so much to this program, just exactly what it's all about. Could you unveil that, please?

[*A plaque detailing the history of the space shuttle program was unveiled.*]

It's always significant to me that the United States flag is the biggest thing on there. Let's never forget that. And this, to the Vice President, the same kind of memento.

The President. You won't mind if I only wear this within Earth's atmosphere. [*Laughter*] But, thank you all very much.

And now, I think there's two individuals here that you'd like to meet also, because I think they have to be just as courageous or even more so than those who make the flight. I think you'd like to see Mrs. Young and Mrs. Crippen. Would you stand, please?

And we're back at ground zero; we have landed successfully. Thank you.

Note: The President spoke at 1:30 p.m. in a tent constructed for the luncheon in the Rose Garden at the White House.

In an Oval Office ceremony prior to the luncheon, the President presented the NASA Distinguished Service Medal to John W. Young and Capt. Robert L. Crippen, the Congressional Space Medal of Honor to Mr. Young for his 16-year service in the space program, and the Presidential Citizens Medal to Dr. Alan M. Lovelace, Acting Administrator of the National Aeronautics and Space Administration. The Vice President, Secretary of State Alexander M. Haig, Jr., and members of the White House staff also attended the ceremony.

Nomination of Arthur F. Burns To Be United States Ambassador to the Federal Republic of Germany
May 19, 1981

The President today announced his intention to nominate Arthur F. Burns to be Ambassador of the United States of America to the Federal Republic of Germany.

Mr. Burns has been distinguished scholar-in-residence, American Enterprise Institute, since 1978 and distinguished professorial lecturer at Georgetown University in Washington, D.C. Since 1969 he has been John Bates Clark professor of economics emeritus at Columbia University in New York. In 1970–78 he was Chairman of the Board of Governors of the Federal Reserve System. He served as Counsellor to the President in 1969–70 and was Chairman of the President's Council of Economic Advisers in

1953–56. Mr. Burns was associated with the National Bureau of Economic Research in 1930–69 and currently serves as honorary chairman. He was previously a professor of economics with Rutgers University.

Mr. Burns graduated from Columbia University (A.B., 1925; A.M., 1925; Ph. D., 1934) and Lehigh University (LL.D., 1952). He has received many other degrees from Brown University, Dartmouth College, Oberlin College, Wesleyan University, and others.

Mr. Burns is married, has two children, and resides in Washington, D.C. He was born April 27, 1904, in Stanislau, Austria.

Nomination of George A. Keyworth II To Be Director of the Office of Science and Technology Policy
May 19, 1981

The President today announced his intention to nominate George A. Keyworth II to be Director of the Office of Science and Technology Policy.

Since 1968 Dr. Keyworth has been associated with the Los Alamos National Laboratory in Los Alamos, N. Mex. In 1968–73 he was staff member, Neutron Physics; assistant group leader, Neutron Physics, in 1973–74; group leader, Neutron Physics, in 1974–77; alternate physics division leader in 1978; acting laser fusion division leader in 1980–81; and since 1978 has been physics division leader.

In 1963–68 Dr. Keyworth was research assistant and later research associate at Duke University. He is a member of various organizations, including the American Physical Society, American Association for the Advancement of Science, and the Cosmos Club of Washington, D.C.

Dr. Keyworth was graduated from Yale University (B.S., 1963) and Duke University (Ph. D., 1968). He is married, has two children, and resides in Santa Fe, N. Mex. He was born November 30, 1939, in Boston, Mass.

Nomination of James A. Belson To Be an Associate Judge of the District of Columbia Court of Appeals
May 19, 1981

The President today announced the nomination of James A. Belson to be an Associate Judge of the District of Columbia Court of Appeals, filling the vacancy created by the retirement of Associate Judge George P. Gallagher.

James A. Belson is currently an Associate Judge of the Superior Court of the District of Columbia. He was appointed on March 11, 1968, by President Johnson and reappointed on March 11, 1978, upon a rating of "exceptionally well-qualified," by the District of Columbia Commission on Judicial Disabilities and Tenure. Judge Belson received an A.B. degree cum laude from Georgetown University in 1953 and a J.D. from Georgetown Law Center in 1956. He also received an LL.M. from Georgetown Law Center in 1962. He served as law clerk to the Honorable E. Barrett Prettyman, U.S.

Court of Appeals for the D.C. Circuit, during the period 1956–57, and as an officer, Judge Advocate U.S.A., from 1957 to 1960. He was an associate and later a partner with the firm of Hogan and Hartson, Washington, D.C., from 1960 until 1968, when he was appointed to the Superior Court.

Judge Belson has served as chairman of the Court's Rules Committee since 1972 and has chaired the Court's Advisory Committee on Rules of Civil Procedure since 1970. He has served on the faculty of the National Judicial College since 1973, and he is a member of the board of directors of the American Judicature Society.

Judge Belson was born in Milwaukee, Wis., on September 23, 1931. He and his wife, Rosemary, reside in Washington, D.C.

Nomination of F. E. DuBois III To Be an Assistant Secretary of Labor
May 20, 1981

The President today announced his intention to nominate F. E. "Bill" DuBois III to be Assistant Secretary of Labor for Mine Safety and Health.

Mr. DuBois' background encompasses 23 years of diversified experience in the mining industry. Since 1975 he has been Nevada State Inspector of Mines, Carson City, Nev. In this position he was responsible for enforcement and industry compliance with Nevada revised statutes regulating mine health and safety. Mr. DuBois began his career in 1958 as a surveyor with Isbell Construction Co., Reno, Nev., and has taken an active role in mine activities at a variety of levels including exploration, land-use engineer, metallurgical consultant, mine lease operator, right-of-way consultants, and general manager of a mine exploration company.

Mr. DuBois was graduated from the University of Nevada at Reno, Mackay School of Mines (B.S., 1964). He is a member of the American Institute of Mining Engineers.

Mr. DuBois is married, has two children, and resides in Fallon, Nev. He was born May 9, 1933, in La Jolla, Calif.

Nomination of Charles E. Lord To Be First Vice President of the Export-Import Bank of the United States
May 20, 1981

The President today announced his intention to nominate Charles E. Lord to be First Vice President of the Export-Import Bank of the United States. Mr. Lord will also serve as Vice Chairman.

Since 1979 Mr. Lord has served as Senior Advisor to the Comptroller of the Currency. He was director of institutional relations and alumni programs, Yale University, in 1976-79. Previously he held various positions with the Hartford National Bank and Trust Co. Mr. Lord was assistant vice president in 1957; vice president in 1959; manager of Constitution Plaza office and the international department in 1962; senior vice president, loan and investment division, in 1966; president in 1967; and chief executive officer in 1972. In addition, Mr. Lord was elected president of Hartford National Corp. in 1969; vice chairman in 1972; president and chief executive officer in 1975.

Mr. Lord is a member of the Banker's Association for Foreign Trade and served as director in 1969–71. He was also chairman of the Connecticut Regional Export Expansion Council of the Department of Commerce in 1969–71.

Mr. Lord was graduated from Yale University (B.A., 1949; M.A.H., 1976). He is married, has four children, and resides in Washington, D.C. He was born April 26, 1928, in New York City.

Nomination of Robert A. Rowland To Be a Member of the Occupational Safety and Health Review Commission
May 20, 1981

The President today announced his intention to nominate Robert A. Rowland to be a member of the Occupational Safety and Health Review Commission.

Since 1962 Mr. Rowland has been in private law practice in Austin, Tex. He was assistant attorney general of Texas in 1958–62.

Mr. Rowland was State vice chairman of the Reagan for President Committee during the 1980 Presidential primary campaign and was a member of the State steering committee for the Reagan–Bush Committee during the general election campaign.

Mr. Rowland was graduated from the University of Texas (B.S., LL.B., 1958). He served in the U.S. Marine Corps Reserve.

Mr. Rowland is married, has two children, and resides in Austin, Tex. He was born March 23, 1932, in Houston, Tex.

Nomination of Walter D. Weaver To Be Federal Insurance Administrator
May 20, 1981

The President today announced his intention to nominate Walter D. Weaver to be Federal Insurance Administrator, Federal Emergency Management Agency.

Since 1977 Mr. Weaver has been director, Department of Insurance, State of Nebraska. In 1974–77 he was corporate secretary and general counsel to Blue Cross and Blue Shield of Nebraska in Omaha. During that time he also served as acting president, corporate transportation officer, and senior vice president, legal and customer service division. Mr. Weaver was professor, College of Public Affairs, University of Nebraska at Omaha, in 1971–73. In 1968–71 he served as executive director, Nebraska Commission on Law Enforcement and Criminal Justice. He was deputy prosecuting attorney, Lancaster County, Nebr., in 1962–68.

Mr. Weaver was graduated from the University of Nebraska (B.S., 1960) and Creighton University School of Law (J.D., 1962). He served in the U.S. Marine Corps in 1945–49 and in 1950–51.

Mr. Weaver is married, has three children, and resides in Plattsmouth, Nebr. He was born December 31, 1927, in Callaway, Nebr.

Proclamation 4845—Father's Day, 1981
May 20, 1981

By the President of the United States of America

A Proclamation

There is no institution more vital to our Nation's survival than the American family. Here the seeds of personal character are planted, the roots of public virtue first nourished. Through love and instruction, discipline, guidance and example, we learn from our mothers and fathers the values that will shape our private lives and our public citizenship.

The days of our childhood forecast our lives, as poets and philosophers long have told us. "The childhood shows the man as morning shows the day," John Milton wrote. "Train up a child in the way he should go: and when he is old, he will not depart from it," Solomon tells us. Clearly, the future is in the care of our parents. Such is the responsibility, promise and hope of fatherhood. Such is the gift that our fathers give us.

Our fathers bear an awesome responsibility—one that they shoulder willingly and fulfill with a love that asks no recompense. By turns both gentle and firm, our fathers guide us along the path from infancy to adulthood. We embody their joy, pain and sacrifice, and inherit memories more cherished than any possession.

On Father's Day each year, we express formally a love and gratitude whose roots go deeper than conscious memory can recite. It is only fitting that we have this special day to pay tribute to those men— our natural fathers, adoptive fathers and foster fathers—who deserve our deepest respect and devotion. It is equally fitting, as we recall the ancient and loving command to honor our fathers, that we resolve to do so by becoming ourselves parents and citizens who are worthy of honor.

Now, Therefore, I, Ronald Reagan, President of the United States of America, do hereby proclaim, in accordance with the joint resolution of Congress (36 U.S.C., §142a), that Sunday, June 21, 1981 be observed as Father's Day. I call upon all citizens to mark this day with appropriate public and private expressions of the honor we owe our fathers, and invite the States and local communities throughout the Nation to observe Father's Day with appropriate ceremonies.

In Witness Whereof, I have hereunto set my hand this 20th day of May, in the year of our Lord nineteen hundred eighty-one, and of the Independence of the United States of America the two hundred and fifth.

RONALD REAGAN

[*Filed with the Office of the Federal Register, 4:23 p.m., May 20, 1981*]

Remarks at a White House Reception for Members of the Advertising Council
May 20, 1981

I'm still not getting used to the fact that in my own house, somebody has to tell me whether I can come in a room or not. [*Laughter*]

Well, anyway, good afternoon. I'm very pleased to welcome you here to the White House. You may not know this, but the Advertising Council is a pretty popular group with my administration. As a matter of fact, you may be too popular. I've just looked at your schedule, and I saw the list of our people who will be speaking to you tomorrow. And it includes about half the Cabinet—[*laughter*]—which means that while you're getting briefed, I won't be. [*Laughter*]

That's all right. By the time they've given you all the latest information—or they have, I'm sure, on spending and taxes, we may just ask you to go on up to Capitol Hill then and give the word that I'm still hanging tough for a good tax bill. [*Laughter*] I'm just as eager for this as I was for the bill on cutting spending. So, we'd just like to have them just get it over with and give us the tax cuts, and we'll go forward from there.

Let me say on behalf of Nancy, who couldn't be here but who wanted to be— she's got a schedule too, I found out. I used to just come home and open the front door and say, "I'm home." And now I come home, look through 132 rooms, and then look at her schedule—[*laughter*]—to know where she is. But on her behalf—you who worked on that great Foster Grandparents spot, and on behalf of our administration and millions of our citizens, I'm very honored to continue the tradition that has been observed by every President since F.D.R. I salute you and your organization on this, your 37th annual conference. My goodness, I was only a small boy when you started. [*Laughter*] And may I add a simple, "Thank you, " for all that you've done.

Through the years you've done this both for peace and in wartime, and your public service work has provided an indispensable source of communication between our Government and the American people. Your ad campaigns have educated, have motivated, have united, have improved the quality of our lives. And you've demonstrated what is really the American spirit, and that is what voluntarism is all about. As you've probably suspected, I'm a great believer in this spirit of voluntary service, cooperation of the private and community initiatives. And that spirit flows like a deep, mighty river through the history of our nation.

In recent years, we've seen the river go down a little bit as government has steadily expanded its own influence over our economic and our personal lives. And as government did this more and more, Americans developed an attitude of, "Well, why should I worry or get involved? Let the government handle it. That's their business." And it really isn't. It's ours, as I think you've always known. So, we know that letting government handle it, as it has done, has done to our economy just about what Mrs. O'Leary's cow did to the city of Chicago—[*laughter*]—which makes organizations like yours all the more important.

I was very gratified to hear that once again you were planning to take action. And this, together with the National Association of Broadcasters, that you're preparing a giant public service ad campaign to educate Americans on the need to improve productivity—nothing could be more welcome. And if it will help cut through any redtape, let me pledge to you right now the full enthusiastic support of our administration.

Improving productivity, you know, really only requires two things: people who have better ideas and people who have savings and want to invest in those ideas. Now, we have the first. Our problem is today we don't have the second. So, this need for greater savings and investment is why our administration insists that while reducing excessive spending, monetary growth, and regulation, we must also enact tax rate reductions across the board.

I was just looking at some figures up there, and we have doubled the taxes of the people of this country since 1976. What we're asking in our tax cut actually is only the prevention of a gigantic tax increase that is built into the system for the coming year, and we're not really reducing them, we just want to reduce the increase. And I think if the people get to know that, then I think maybe up on the Hill they'll get to know that.

So, we're willing to enact the total recovery program—economic recovery program, which I think is what the people of this country want. Then we'll provide incentives for greater economic growth than we've had in more than a decade. And when that happens, we'll not only restore strong productivity, we'll reduce inflation, and we'll save that American dream that we all love. The ultimate objective in everything that we're trying to do is to give this economy back to the American people, where it belongs, because they are the most valuable resource of our nation.

You know, America's revolutionary gift to the world is the idea that individual freedom is the inalienable right granted by God to all of us as a birthright, and this is at the core of everything that we've accomplished so far. Now, I know that some call this idea old-fashioned, even reactionary. Well, it's still the most unique, the newest and the most exciting and successful idea the world has ever know.

Albert Einstein, one of the greatest of geniuses, probably summed it up best when he said, "Everything that is really great and inspiring is created by individuals who labor in freedom." Now, this is the message that all of us, and that you and your Advertising Council, we in this administration, must give to our countrymen and the world beyond, because when we do, they'll be telling millions of people the true story about hope and a better tomorrow. And we'll be telling them about America.

So, now, thank you very much, and I'll have a chance for a minute or two to say hello. Thank you all.

Note: The President spoke at 5:37 p.m. in the East Room at the White House.

Remarks at the Welcoming Ceremony for Chancellor Helmut Schmidt of the Federal Republic of Germany
May 21, 1981

The President. Chancellor Schmidt, one of the warmest greetings that Americans can offer in welcoming a guest into their midst is to say, "Make yourself at home." On behalf of our fellow citizens, Nancy and I hope that you and Mrs. Schmidt will make yourselves at home during your visit to the United States. We remember with great pleasure how welcome and at home you made us feel on our visit to Germany in 1978.

As you know, millions of German immigrants over the years have made America their home. With strong hands and good hearts, these industrious people helped build a strong and good America. But as proud as they were of this country, they didn't forget their German heritage. They named towns in the New World after those in the Old. The Federal Republic of Germany has just one Bremen; the Federal Republic has one, but we have Bremens in Indiana, in Georgia, and Ohio. And our States are dotted with Hamburgs and Berlins. In honor of Baron von Steuben, the Prussian officer who aided our revolution, we have cities and towns in a number of States named after him. But I hope you'll forgive us, over the years we've sort of anglicized the pronunciation. We call them now Steubens and Steubensvilles. And the list goes on from Heidelberg, Mississippi, to Stuttgart, Arkansas.

But the Federal Republic of Germany and the United States of America share more than a common background and a well-established friendship. We share values about the importance of liberty. This year marks the 20th anniversary of the Berlin Wall, a border of brutality that assaults the human spirit and the civilized mind. On one side of the wall, people live in dignity and democracy; on the other side, in domination and defeat. We of the United States are aware of the relentless pressure on the Federal Republic and her citizens, and we admire you for your courage in the face of such grim realities.

The Federal Republic is perched on the cliff of freedom that overlooks Soviet dependents to the East. While the dominated peoples in these lands cannot enjoy your liberties, they can look at your example and hope. The United States is proud to stand beside you as your beacon shines brightly from that cliff of freedom.

We both recognize the challenges posed to our security by those who do not share our beliefs and our objectives. And together, we will act to counter those dangers. The United States will work in partnership with you and with our other European allies to bolster NATO and to offset the disturbing buildup of Soviet military forces. At the same time, we will work toward meaningful negotiations to limit those very weapons.

Mr. Chancellor, under your thoughtful and responsible leadership, the Federal Republic has sought to ease tensions in a world taut and quivering with the strains of instability—not only between East and West but between North and South. And we're aware of the Federal Republic's other contributions as well. Americans remember that when the United States sought support in freeing American prisoners in Iran, the Federal Republic stood firmly by us, and we thank you for that support.

Although the Federal Republic, like the United States, is not immune to economic difficulties, the Communist countries cannot help but compare your well-being to their own shortages and hardships.

Our economic policies should be as closely allied as our defense policies, for in the end, our military capabilities are dependent on the strengths of our economies. Sound fiscal management was the hallmark of the Federal Republic's economic miracle, and we in the United States intend to import some of that responsibility to gain control of our own economy.

Chancellor Schmidt, I began these remarks speaking of German immigrants who came to America. Let me mention one immigrant in particular—Johann Augustus Roebling, the man who built the Brooklyn Bridge, which at its opening in 1883 was called the eighth wonder of the world. Well, Mr. Roebling spanned more than the East River with his accomplishment; he spanned two countries and two peoples. The discussions we have today will span our common goals and bridge our joint concerns. They will set the scene for the closest possible consultations in the future.

We have come to rely on one another in times of calm and in times of crisis, and that certainly is the basis of a true friend-partnership. It is in that spirit that I look forward to the important talks ahead.

And again, *herzlich willkommen* [a hearty welcome].

The Chancellor. Mr. President, Mrs. Reagan, ladies and gentlemen:

Thank you very much, Mr. President, for your cordial reception and your most friendly words of welcome.

This is not the first time I've been here, but on each occasion I'm impressed by the authority and dignity which radiates from this seat of government of the mighty United States of America. I am very glad to have this opportunity for an exchange of views with you, Mr. President, on major issues which both of us have much on our minds.

I cannot tell you how happy I am to know that you have recovered so well from the treacherous attempt on your life on the 30th of March. We in Germany have followed your rapid progress with much feeling, sir, and with a great sense of relief.

My visit to Washington is taking place against the background of a serious international situation. At the beginning of the eighties, we are confronted with a whole range of problems and challenges. I need only mention the excessive Soviet arms buildup, the challenge toward the community of nations resulting from the continuing Soviet intervention in Afghanistan, the threat to the non-alignment of the Third World countries stemming from unresolved political conflicts and as a result of East-West conflicts being transferred to their part of the world. And I need only mention, also, the impact of the oil price explosion on the whole world economy.

The Western democracies will be able to cope with these challenges if they show their determination, if they do take joint action, and if they let themselves be guided by the principles of consistency, predictability, and reliability.

Three weeks ago in Rome, Italy, our Alliance gave a clear signal for the continuity of our common policies. I regarded this as a proof of the Alliance's political strength. And as I said in the German Parliament 2 weeks ago, I also regard it as a success for your new administration, sir, here in Washington, D.C.

German-American partnership is today again manifest in the wide-ranging consultations between you, Mr. President, and the German head of government. Good and reliable relations between the Federal Republic of Germany and the United States of America are, in my view, a major factor for the security of the West and for international stability. I am confident that this visit will help us to fulfill our common responsibilities.

Thank you very much.

Note: The President spoke at 10:12 a.m. on the South Lawn of the White House, where Chancellor Schmidt was given a formal welcome with full military honors. Following the ceremony, the President and the Chancellor met privately in the Oval Office.

Letter to Congressional Leaders on the Social Security System
May 21, 1981

Dear————:

Over the past several weeks, all Americans have been proud of the bipartisan spirit that we have created in working on the nation's economic recovery. Today I am writing to you to ask that we now bring that same spirit to bear on another issue threatening our public welfare.

As you know, the Social Security System is teetering on the edge of bankruptcy. Over the next five years, the Social Security trust fund could encounter deficits of up to $111 billion, and in the decades ahead its unfunded obligations could run well into the trillions. Unless we in government are willing to act, a sword of Damocles will soon hang over the welfare of millions of our citizens.

Last week, Secretary Richard Schweiker presented a series of Administration proposals that we believe are sound, sensible solutions, both in the short and long term. We recognize that Members of Congress on both sides of the aisle have alternative answers. This diversity is healthy—so long as it leads to constructive debate and then to an honest legislative response.

As Secretary Schweiker has pointed out on several occasions, we believe that all of us owe an obligation to our senior citizens to work together on this issue. This Administration is not wedded to any single solution; this Administration welcomes the opportunity to consult with Congress and with private groups on this matter. Our sole commitment—and it is a commitment we will steadfastly maintain—is to three basic principles:

—First, this nation must preserve the integrity of the Social Security trust fund and the basic benefit structure that protects older Americans.

—Second, we must hold down the tax burden on the workers who support Social Security.

—Finally, we must eliminate all abuses in the system that can rob the elderly of their rightful legacy.

It is clear that the half–actions of the past are no longer sufficient for the future. It is equally clear that we must not let partisan differences or political posturing prevent us from working together.

Therefore, I have today asked Secretary Schweiker to meet with you and other leaders of the Congress as soon as possible to launch a bipartisan effort to save Social Security. I have also asked him to make the full resources of his department available for this undertaking. And of course, you can count on my active support of this effort.

None of us can afford to underestimate the seriousness of the problems facing Social Security. For generations of Americans, the future literally rests upon our actions. This should be a time for statesmanship of the highest order, and I know that no one shares that desire more strongly than you.

With every good wish,

Sincerely,

RONALD REAGAN

Note: This is the text of identical letters addressed to Senate Majority Leader Howard H. Baker, Jr., Speaker of the House of Representatives Thomas P. O'Neill, Jr., Senate Minority Leader Robert C. Byrd, House Majority Leader Jim Wright, House Minority Leader Robert H. Michel, and Senator Strom Thurmond of South Carolina.

Toasts of the President and Chancellor Helmut Schmidt of the Federal Republic of Germany at the State Dinner
May 21, 1981

The President. Chancellor Schmidt, Mrs. Schmidt:

It's a genuine pleasure to welcome you and your guests to the White House this evening.

Mr. Chancellor, your visit today has been a most welcome and productive one. We've discussed significant issues that affect us— our NATO and security commitments, our economy and foreign policy, our desire for greater stability in the world. I must tell everyone here tonight, though, that one important matter was left off our agenda. I had hoped that we could resolve once and for all the relative advantages of Rhine wines versus California wines. [*Laughter*]

Earlier today I spoke of America's debt to German immigrants who settled here. Many of their names are easily recognizable: a piano craftsman, Heinrich Steinway; a space scientist, Werner von Braun; Levi Strauss, who created bluejeans—[*laughter*]—and a brewer, Adolphus Busch. But one of our most notable German Americans is the caricaturist Thomas Nast, who made some very special contributions. He gave us our images of Santa Claus, the Republican elephant, the Democratic donkey, and he even created the character of Uncle Sam, the personification of America all around the world.

Now, these symbols have been important to Americans and their self-image. Today I hope we've dealt in both symbol and substance. The arrival ceremony and this state dinner are symbols of a respect and a friendship for the Federal Republic of Germany and its Chancellor. Our discussions, on the other hand, dealt with the substance of our economy and our defense partnership. From these talks, we have a better understanding of our common goals and aspirations.

Mr. Chancellor, the American people have a high regard for the vitality and the future of the Federal Republic. We agree with the German poet Heinrich Heine, who wrote, "Germany will ever stand. It is a hale and hearty land."

And so, ladies and gentlemen, I ask you to join me in a toast to Chancellor and Mrs. Schmidt, to their hale and hearty land, and to our continued hale and hearty friendship.

The Chancellor. Mr. President, ladies and gentlemen:

The kind words you have just spoken, Mr. President, for which I'm most grateful, underscore the warm hospitality that you have extended to us here in Washington.

My wife and I and the members of my delegation are being touched by this manifestation of the close bonds of friendship between our two countries. And we even are thankful that you saved us from a contest between Californian and Rhine wine. I mentioned to the neighbors at my table that we had jellybeans instead, and they were not so bad. [*Laughter*]

Let me frankly say that in a way, I regard this evening as a kind of homecoming after having been in your great country so many times, after working with political leaders of both sides of the aisle in America, so many long years, and with four American Presidents, and seeing, of course, so many old friends as your guests tonight, Mr. President. We deem it a great pleasure to be able to end this day, a day of important political discussion here in the White House, as you and Mrs. Reagan's guests.

My wife and I wish you both success and happiness in the years ahead, and I say this with specific emphasis, because we are still feeling the shock of the attempt made on your life, in which you were seriously wounded. We all are grateful and relieved to see that you have recovered so quickly, and I cannot tell you how much I was relieved this morning in getting out of the car and seeing you there, standing upright, and smiling a little and seeming strong and vigorous. We felt deeply sorry about that attempt, and we deeply admired your courage, you circumspection, your unbroken energy. And I'm also glad that the other

451

members of your staff who were wounded are well again or are recovering. And if some of your staff would care, please give them our regards, transmitted to them.

Mr. President, under your leadership the United States is now embarking on a steady course of confidence and self-assuredness. You have set about the task of resolving your country's economic problems with new ideas, exceptional vigor. And I followed with interest how you have applied yourself with great energy, personal commitment to your program for America's economic renewal. And the interest of us Europeans, of us Germans, in your economic renewal is, of course, only too understandable, because the economic well-being of the United States is of direct importance for us in Europe and for us in Germany. It is also for this reason that we hope that your administration will soon meet with success in its efforts to overcome the economic difficulties.

The United States and the Federal Republic are allies whose close cooperation has proved its value in difficult times over more than a quarter of a century now, and I guess it will continue to stand the test in an international environment that is becoming increasingly difficult and also increasingly dangerous. In view of the instability around the world, the partnership between Western Europe and North America, I think, is the prime factor of stability. That partnership remains a constant feature of our policy. It is at no one's disposal. Our American friends can rely on us just as we do rely on the United States.

And we, in particular, welcome the self-confidence, the self-assuredness, of the American Nation under your leadership, Mr. President. We Europeans know that it is crucial for the United States to live up to its responsibilities as a world power allied with Western Europe. We believe that Europe and America have a common destiny. America's political and military presence in Europe is not only an indispensable condition for the security of West Europeans, it's also an essential element of global security, and German-American friendship is one cornerstone of that Euro-American partnership.

The present generation on both sides of the Atlantic know this from past experience. Meanwhile, a new generation is in the process of assuming the responsibility for the destiny of our countries. It is, I feel, one of the foremost tasks of our generation to make sure that the next generation will appreciate the decisive role of this close and trustful partnership—better still that they themselves experience it. Only then will they be in a position to cherish, defend, and further develop this precious legacy.

The talks and meetings I've had today have proved that we continue with fresh confidence the successful cooperation for the benefit of our peoples and for the preservation of peace. It is on this note, ladies and gentlemen, that I would like to ask you to drink with me to the health of the President of the United States of America and Mrs. Reagan, and to the well-being of the great American Nation.

Note: The President spoke at 9:46 p.m. in the State Dining Room at the White House.

Remarks of the President and Chancellor Helmut Schmidt of the Federal Republic of Germany Following Their Meetings
May 22, 1981

The President. Ladies and gentlemen of the press, the time has come to me to say goodby to our visitor here. I just want to tell you that we have had fine meetings, and we have an understanding that there will be full consultation and cooperation between us, as there properly should be between friends and allies.

We have been in agreement on the various issues that confront us, ranging from the matters of the problems in Eastern Europe, Poland, of the theater nuclear forces, and the fact that we are going forward with arms limitation talks also, with the Warsaw Pact and with the Soviet Union. All of these things and all of these problems were discussed, and I think we've established a cordial relationship and a friendship that bodes very well for the future and for the West.

Mr. Chancellor, it's been a great pleasure to have you here and Mrs. Schmidt here, and we hope that there will be repeated visits and exchanges.

The Chancellor. Thank you very much, sir.

Mr. President, ladies and gentlemen, I would like to agree with every line that the President just relayed to you. The amount of mutual understanding you can measure by the secret which I'm going to disclose right now. The President had a lengthy speech—a lengthy paper prepared for him by the White House staff, and I was without any such paper. And I said, "This is unfair." And he dropped it immediately.

So, you see, we really did not only agree on such more peripheral issues, but we did agree on the substance of policies whether it is, as the President said, vis-a-vis the Soviet Union and their allies, whether it is in concern of such specific problems as Eastern Europe right now or Afghanistan or the Gulf or the Middle East or Africa or Latin America, Central America, or whether it is in the other fields in which we have mutual interests and shall cooperate in the future.

I would like, Mr. President, also on behalf of my delegation and also on behalf of my wife, to thank you personally, to thank the Vice President, to thank the Secretary of Foreign Affairs, the Secretary of Defense, the Secretary of the Treasury, and the other Cabinet members, to thank all of the hosts in Washington for the warm and cordial welcome not only but also regarding the free uninhibited exchange of views.

I'm not so sure, it's about my 45th or 46th or 47th visit to the United States. It was the fourth time that I had the privilege of meeting you, Mr. President, the first time in your new capacity as the head of state and head of government of the most important nation of the world, the greatest nation. I, to some degree, feel at home in the United States and at home in Washington, D.C. I felt very much at home these 2 days, and I will get back to my people, get back to my parliament, will report to the German Parliament Tuesday next week on how much did we agree on very difficult matters in worldwide politics.

It is due to my lacking a paper, ladies and gentlemen—and I apologize, Mr. President—of speaking so long, but what I really want to project towards the ladies and gentlemen of the press is how deeply satisfied I am about this visit.

Thank you very much again, Mr. President.

Note: The President spoke at 12:05 p.m. to reporters assembled on the South Grounds of the White House.

Joint Statement Following Discussions With Chancellor Helmut Schmidt of the Federal Republic of Germany
May 22, 1981

During the official visit of Chancellor Helmut Schmidt of the Federal Republic of Germany to the United States from May 20–23, 1981, President Reagan and the Federal Chancellor held detailed talks on a wide range of political and economic questions. They noted with satisfaction that they share a common assessment of the international situation and its implications for the Western Alliance. They agreed that their two countries have a common destiny founded on joint security interests and firmly rooted in their shared values of liberty, a democratic way of life, self-determination and belief in the inalienable rights of man.

They regard the reliable and proven U.S.-German partnership as an essential factor in international stability and Western security based on the North Atlantic Alliance. They agreed that substantive and effective consultations are a mainstay of the relations between Western Europe and the United States.

The President and the Federal Chancellor welcomed and reaffirmed the results of the recent NATO Ministerial meetings in Rome and Brussels as renewed proof of the political strength of the Alliance and the continuity of Alliance policy. They stressed the determination of Alliance members to take the necessary steps to work with their NATO partners to strengthen the Western defense posture and to address adverse trends due to the Soviet military buildup. Together with deterrence and defense, arms control and disarmament are integral parts of Alliance security policy.

The President and the Federal Chancellor affirmed in this connection their resolve to implement both elements of the NATO decision of December 1979 and to give equal weight to both elements. The Federal Chancellor welcomed the U.S. decision to begin negotiations with the Soviet Union on the limitation of theater nuclear weapons within the SALT framework by the end of this year. He also welcomed the fact that the U.S. Secretary of State has initiated preparatory discussions on theater nuclear forces with the Soviet Union, looking toward an agreement to begin formal negotiations. The President and the Federal Chancellor agreed that TNF modernization is essential for Alliance security and as a basis for parallel negotiations leading to concrete results on limitations of theater nuclear forces. They further agreed that the preparatory studies called for in the Rome Communique should be undertaken as matters of immediate priority by the relevant NATO bodies.

The President and the Federal Chancellor assessed very favorably the close cooperation between the Federal Republic of Germany and the Three Powers in matters relating to Berlin and Germany as a whole. The Federal Chancellor thanked the President for his reaffirmation of the pledge that the United States will continue to guarantee the security and viability of Berlin. They agreed that the maintenance of the calm situation in and around Berlin is of crucial significance for European security and stability.

The European Community plays an important part in maintaining international political and economic stability. The U.S. will continue to support the process of European unification.

Both sides noted that a serious international situation has been created by Soviet expansionism and armaments efforts. To meet this challenge and to secure peace, they are determined to respond with firmness and to maintain a dialog with the Soviet Union.

The President and the Federal Chancellor agreed that it is important for the stabilization of East-West relations that the current CSCE Review Conference in Madrid agree on a balanced substantive concluding document which includes enhanced respect for human rights, increased human contacts, a freer flow of information, and cooperation among and security for all of the participants. In this regard, and as part of such a balanced result, the President and the Chancellor favor agreement on a precise mandate for a conference on disarmament in Europe, providing for the application of militarily significant, binding and verifiable confidence-building measures covering all of the continent of Europe from the Atlantic to the Urals.

Poland must be allowed to solve its problems peacefully and without external interference. The President and the Federal Chancellor reaffirmed unequivocally their view that any external intervention would have the gravest consequences for international relations and would fundamentally change the entire international situation.

Genuine nonalignment of the states of the developing world is an important stabilizing factor in international relations. The Chancellor and the President support the independence and the right of self-determination of the states of the developing world. They will, in concert with their Allies and the countries affected, oppose any attempts, direct or indirect, by the Soviet Union to undermine the independence and stability of these states. They confirmed their willingness to continue their cooperaion with these states on the basis of equal partnership and to continue their support of their economic development.

The President and the Federal Chancellor reaffirmed their view that the Soviet occupation of Afghanistan is unacceptable. They demanded the withdrawal of Soviet troops from Afghanistan and respect for that country's right to return to independence and nonalignment. The destabilizing effects which the Soviet intervention in Afghanistan has on the entire region must be countered.

Both sides stressed the importance of broad-based cooperation with the states of the Gulf Region.

The President and the Federal Chancellor agreed that the United States and the Federal Republic of Germany, the latter within the framework of European political cooperation, should continue the search for a comprehensive, just, and lasting peace in the Middle East. Their efforts should continue to be complementary and build upon what has been achieved so far.

Both sides reaffirmed the determination to strengthen further the open system of world trade and to oppose pressure for protectionist measures.

They stressed the vital importance for political and economic stability of further energy conservation and diversification measures to reduce the high degree of dependence on oil. The pressing energy problems can only be mastered on the basis of worldwide cooperative efforts that strengthen Western energy security and reduce the vulnerability of the West to potential supply cutoffs from any source. The supply problems of the developing countries require particular attention.

The President and the Federal Chancellor agreed on the need in framing their economic policies to give high priority to the fight against inflation and to the creation of improved conditions for renewed economic growth and increased productivity. Both sides stressed the need for a close coordination of economic policies among the industrial countries.

Both sides stressed the need for close and comprehensive exchange of views on the United Nations Conference on the Law of the Sea while the U.S. Government reviews its position.

The President and the Federal Chancellor noted that their talks once more demonstrated the friendly and trusting relationship that has linked their two countries for over 30 years. They welcomed all efforts which serve to broaden mutual contacts and underlined the responsibility of the coming generation for maintaining and developing German-American friendship.

Nomination of Ernest Henry Preeg To Be United States Ambassador to Haiti
May 22, 1981

The President today announced his intention to nominate Ernest Henry Preeg, of Virginia, to be Ambassador of the United States of America to Haiti. He would succeed Henry L. Kimelman, who has resigned.

Mr. Preeg was a Merchant Marine officer with the American Export Lines of Hoboken, N.J., in 1956–61, and lecturer in economics at Brooklyn College in 1962–63.

He entered the Foreign Service in 1963 as international economist in the Department of State. In 1968–69 he was economic officer in London. He was international relations officer in the Department in 1969–72 and attended economic studies at the National Planning Association in 1972–73. In the Department, he was Director of the Office of OECD, European Community and Atlantic Political-Economic Affairs (1973–

76), and Deputy Assistant Secretary of State for International Finance and Development (1976–77). In 1977 he was on detail to the White House as Executive Director of the Economic Policy Group. In 1977–80 he was Deputy Chief of Mission in Lima. Since 1980 he has been senior adviser on Jamaica.

Mr. Preeg was born July 5, 1934, in Englewood, N.J. He received his B.S. (1956) from New York State Maritime College; M.A. (1961) and Ph. D. (1964) from the New School for Social Research. He is married to the former Florence Tate and has one daughter.

Nomination of Three Associate Judges of the Superior Court of the District of Columbia
May 22, 1981

The President today announced the nominations of Reggie Barnett Walton, Richard Stephen Salzman, and Warren Roger (Willie) King to be Associate Judges of the Superior Court of the District of Columbia, each for a term of 15 years.

Reggie Walton was nominated to fill the vacancy created by the retirement of Associate Judge Leonard Braman. Mr. Walton served in the Army Reserve Officers Training Corps while attending West Virginia State College, where he received a B.A. degree in 1971. His J.D. degree was awarded by American University, Washington College of Law, in 1974. On January 8, 1975, Mr. Walton was admitted to the D.C. Bar and, thereafter, was employed as a staff attorney for the Defender Association of Philadelphia, Appellate Division. Since March 1976, he has served as an Assistant United States Attorney for the District of Columbia. From June 1979 until July 1980, he held the title, Chief, Career Criminal Unit, and currently is the Executive Assistant United States Attorney, the third highest ranking position in that office of over 160 attorneys. Mr. Walton was born in North Charlerio, Pa., on February 8, 1949, and resides in Washington, D.C.

Richard Salzman was nominated to fill the position of retiring Associate Judge William S. Thompson. Mr. Salzman graduated from Columbia University (A.B., 1954; LL. B., 1959) and actively served in the U.S. Navy before entering law school. He has been admitted to both the New York and D.C. Bars. From 1959 until 1960, he clerked for the U.S. Court of Appeals for

the D.C. Circuit in a position which is now referred to as Clerk to the Court. In 1960 he became associated with the New York firm of Hays, Sklar & Herzberg (now Botein, Hays, Sklar & Herzberg). He left in 1962 for employment as a trial attorney in the Civil Division, Appellate Section of the Justice Department. In 1967 he became Assistant Chief Counsel of the Federal Highway Administration and returned to private practice in 1970 with the D.C. firm of Kominers, Fort, Schlefer and Boyer. Since 1974 he has served as Administrative Judge and member of the Atomic Safety and Licensing Appeal Panel, Nuclear Regulatory Commission. Mr. Salzman was born in New York City on April 6, 1933. He and his wife, Lois, reside in Washington, D.C.

Willie King was nominated to fill the vacancy created by the retirement of Associate Judge Fred L. McIntyre. Mr. King served in the U.S. Navy on active duty and in the reserves from 1960 until 1974. He received a bachelor of aeronautical engineering degree in 1960 from the Rensselaer Polytechnic Institute and a J.D. degree from American University, Washington College of Law, in 1967. He was admitted to the D.C. Bar on February 29, 1968, and received an LL.M. degree from Yale Law School in 1969. From 1969 until 1975, Mr. King practiced law as an Assistant United States attorney for the District of Columbia, the last 5 years of which were served exclusively in the D.C. Superior Court. He left to become a law professor at Antioch School of Law in Washington, where he remained for 3 years. Mr. King returned to government service in October 1977 at the Justice Department as an attorney-adviser. He served on the Attorney General's task force on the new code of ethics promulgated by the Kutak Commission and is currently the chairman of the Justice Department Committee on Amendments to the Federal Rules of Civil Procedure. Mr. King was born on May 9, 1937, in Takoma Park, Md., and he and his wife, Joyce, reside in Washington, D.C.

Nomination of Lennie-Marie P. Tolliver To Be Commissioner of the Administration on Aging
May 23, 1981

The President today announced his intention to nominate Lennie-Marie P. Tolliver to be Commissioner on Aging, Department of Health and Human Services.

Since 1964 Dr. Tolliver has been professor, associate director, and graduate program coordinator, School of Social Work, University of Oklahoma. In 1961–64 she was assistant professor of field work, School of Social Service Administration, University of Chicago. She worked as a caseworker in 1961–62 for the Family Service Bureau, United Charities, Chicago, Ill. In 1959 Dr. Tolliver was supervisor and acting director, Department of Social Work, Johnstone Training and Research Center, Bordentown, N.J. She was instructor and acting supervisor, Psychiatric Social Work, Duke University Medical Center, in 1956–58.

Dr. Tolliver is former chairperson of the Health and Welfare Committee and vice president of the Oklahoma City Urban League. She was chairperson of the Oklahoma Black Republican Council in 1972–78 and alternate delegate to the 1980 Republican National Convention.

Dr. Tolliver was graduated from the Hampton Institute (B.S., 1950; A.M., 1952); University of Chicago (P.M., 1961); and Union Graduate School, Union for Experimental Colleges and Universities (Ph. D., 1979).

Dr. Tolliver is married and resides in Oklahoma City, Okla. She was born December 1, 1928, in Cleveland, Ohio.

Nomination of Rex E. Lee To Be Solicitor General of the United States
May 23, 1981

The President today announced his intention to nominate Rex E. Lee, of Provo, Utah, to be Solicitor General of the United States, Department of Justice. Mr. Lee is currently dean of Brigham Young University, a position he has held since 1977.

Mr. Lee attended Brigham Young University, where he received his B.A. in 1960 and the University of Chicago, where he was awarded the juris doctor degree in 1964.

He served as law clerk for United States Supreme Court Justice Byron R. White in 1963 and 1964. He joined the firm of Jennings, Strouss, Salmon & Trask in Phoenix, Ariz., as an associate in 1964, and in 1967 became a partner in the firm. In 1971 he was appointed founding dean of Brigham Young University's J. Reuben Clark Law School. From 1975 to 1977, he was Assistant Attorney General, Civil Division, United States Department of Justice.

He was born February 27, 1935, in Los Angeles, Calif.

Nomination of Anthony H. Murray, Jr., To Be Superintendent of the United States Mint at Philadelphia
May 23, 1981

The President today announced his intention to nominate Anthony H. Murray, Jr., to be Superintendent of the Mint of the United States at Philadelphia, Department of the Treasury.

Since 1974 Mr. Murray has been an attorney at law in Pennsylvania. From February 1980 until May 1980, he was the regional administrator of the Philadelphia office of the Pennsylvania Department of Revenue on a special assignment to reorganize the regional office. Mr. Murray was vice president, community development, with The Korman Corp. from 1967 to 1974. From 1960 to 1967, he was executive vice president and general counsel with Walker & Murray Associates, Inc.

Mr. Murray graduated from St. Joseph's College in 1950 with a B.S. degree in business administration. He graduated from Temple University School of Law in June 1957.

Mr. Murray has also served as rear admiral, Navy Reserves, from 1944 to the present. He is married, with five children, and resides in Philadelphia, Pa. Mr. Murray was born June 7, 1926.

Message to Vice President Oswaldo Hurtado Larrea of Ecuador on the Death of the Ecuadorean President and Minister of Defense
May 25, 1981

The American people and I have been shocked and saddened to learn of the tragic death of President and Mrs. Jaime Roldós Aguilera and the Minister of Defense and his wife, Major General and Mrs. Marco Subía Martínez.

Please accept our deepest condolences and our sympathy as we join the Educadorian people in mourning this terrible loss.

RONALD REAGAN

Note: President and Mrs. Roldós, Defense Minister and Mrs. Subía, and five other persons were killed on May 24, when the plane in which they were traveling crashed in the mountains near the Peruvian border with Ecuador.

Nomination of Jerry L. Jordan To Be a Member of the Council of Economic Advisers
May 25, 1981

The President today announced his intention to nominate Jerry L. Jordan to be a member of the Council of Economic Advisers.

Since July 1980, Mr. Jordan has been the dean of the Robert O. Anderson School of Management at the University of New Mexico in Albuquerque. Since October 1975, Mr. Jordan was senior vice president and chief economist at the Pittsburgh National Bank.

From 1967 to 1975, Mr. Jordan was employed by the Federal Reserve Bank of St. Louis. In 1969 Mr. Jordan was appointed a Vice President of the St. Louis Federal Reserve and was given responsibility for the data processing, data systems, and planning departments. In 1971 Mr. Jordan returned to the research department of the Federal Reserve Bank where he was appointed Senior Vice President and Director of Research in 1975. From December 1, 1971 to May 31, 1972, Mr. Jordan was on leave from his responsibilities in the research department in order to serve as a consultant to the German central bank in Frankfurt, West Germany, in matters relating to economic policies and computer operations.

Mr. Jordan is past-president of the Economic Club of Pittsburgh and served for 3 years as a member of the Economic Advisory Committee of the American Bankers Association.

Mr. Jordan, who resides in Albuquerque, N. Mex., is married and has three children. He was born on December 12, 1941, in California.

Nomination of James Hackett To Be an Associate Director of the International Communication Agency
May 25, 1981

The President today announced his intention to nominate James Hackett to be an Associate Director of the International Communication Agency (Management).

Since 1973 Mr. Hackett has been Administrative Director of the U.S. Arms Control and Disarmament Agency. From 1971 to 1973, he was Deputy Executive Secretary, National Security Council. In 1970–71 he was personnel officer, Department of State.

Mr. Hackett graduated from the University of Southern California with a B.A. degree in international relations in 1959. He was also a distinguished graduate at the Armed Forces Staff College in Norfolk, Va., in 1969–70.

Mr. Hackett is married, with two sons, and resides in Sterling, Va. He was born in Boston, Mass., in 1931.

Nomination of Jose Manuel Casanova To Be Executive Director of the Inter-American Development Bank
May 26, 1981

The President today announced his intention to nominate Jose Manuel Casanova to be Executive Director of the Inter-American Development Bank.

Since 1979 Mr. Casanova has been president of Agro-Com Exports in Miami, Fla., and a real estate broker with Presto Realty. Since 1977 he has also been a private consultant in the financial and management area. In 1976 Mr. Casanova was senior vice president of the Flagship National Bank of Miami. In 1974–76 he was the president of Flagship National Bank of Westland, in Hialeah, Fla.

Mr. Casanova attended Babson Institute in Wellesley Hills, Mass., Flagship College (banking courses), and the University of Miami. Mr. Casanova holds licenses in securities and real estate.

Mr. Casanova is married, with seven children, and resides in Miami, Fla. He was born August 14, 1930.

Statement by Deputy Press Secretary Larry M. Speakes on Consultations With Ambassador Habib Concerning the Situation in Lebanon
May 27, 1981

The President has asked Ambassador [Philip C.] Habib to return to Washington for consultations about the progress and future of his mission in the Middle East. As the President's special representative, Ambassador Habib has been engaged in talks with the leaders of Lebanon, Syria, Israel, and Saudi Arabia during the last 3 weeks. The President believes that this is an appropriate moment to receive firsthand Ambassador Habib's views and to discuss with him the future of his continuing mission in the context of efforts peacefully to resolve the crisis involving events in Lebanon.

Exchange With Reporters on Consultations With Ambassador Habib Concerning the Situation in Lebanon
May 27, 1981

Q. Tell us about Mr. [Philip C.] Habib's return.

The President. Well, I think it's time for a little consultation. He agreed, and I've called him home for consultation of what he's done. I think that he's done a remarkable job so far.

Q. Would you call the mission a failure?

The President. Oh, no, no. They were on the verge of war, and that has not happened in these several weeks. But now I think it's time for us to have a talk, and then he'll go back.

Q. But the fact that he is not now going on to shuttle in Syria, doesn't that indicate there's an impasse?

The President. No—well, you know, there's a kind of a pause while everybody considers where they are. But we felt that it was necessary now for him to come back here to see us, and then he'll go back.

Q. You do expect him to return and continue the mission?

The President. Yes.

Q. Thank you.

Note: The exchange began at 8:19 a.m. on the South Lawn of the White House as the President was leaving for a trip to the U.S. Military Academy in West Point, N.Y.

Address at Commencement Exercises at the United States Military Academy
May 27, 1981

General Goodpaster; reverend clergy; General Means [Meyer]; the Members of the United States Senate and House of Representatives who are here; the officers on the platform; you, the family, the friends, the Corps and, above all, this graduating class:

Nancy and I consider it a great pleasure to be here today to congratulate you who have successfully completed your education and training at the United States Military Academy. I'm a little self-conscious being introduced as your Commander when I began my military career as a second lieutenant in the Cavalry, the horse Cavalry, that is. [*Laughter*] I have threatened on occasion that that was the reason I got this job was so that I could reinstitute the horse Cavalry. [*Laughter*]

But we honor you for the responsibility that you're willing to accept. Today you become officers in the Armed Forces of the United States, guardians of freedom, protectors of our heritage. But more than that you become the keepers of the peace.

Those shrill voices that would have us believe the defenders of our nation are somehow the enemies of peace are as false as they are shrill. A Chinese philosopher, Sun Tzu, 2,500 years ago, said, "Winning a hundred victories in a hundred battles is not the acme of skill. To subdue the enemy without fighting is the acme of skill." A truly successful army is one that because of its strength and ability and dedication will not be called upon to fight, for no one will dare to provoke it.

There have been four wars in my lifetime. None of them came about because the United States was too strong. At the end of World War II we alone were at the peak of our military strength. Our great industrial capacity was untouched by war's destruction, and it was then that in those dark days that Pope Pius XII said, "America has a great genius for great and unselfish deeds. Into the hands of America God has placed an afflicted mankind."

We set out to restore the war-ravaged lands of our erstwhile enemies as well as our friends. We prevented what could have been a retreat into the Dark Ages. Unfortunately another great power in the world was marching to a different drumbeat, creating a society in which everything that isn't compulsory is prohibited. The citizens in that society have little more to say about their government than a prison inmate has to say about the prison administration.

About 10 days ago I addressed the graduating class at the University of Notre Dame. Young men and women of your generation were facing a future in which they wonder what jobs will be available and who their employers will be. You don't have that problem. [*Laughter*] You know what your job will be, and your employers will be those Notre Dame graduates as well as the rest of your fellow citizens.

Now, of course, they won't be directly and personally in charge. That's left to those of us that they've chosen to represent them—Secretary Marsh, who is here, Secretary of the Army. But speaking on behalf of all the people, those employers of yours, may I say that we intend that you shall find better working conditions, tools adequate to the tasks you're expected to perform, and pay somewhat more commensurate with the responsibilities you assume than has been the case in recent years.

Now you may have heard rumors to the effect that increasing government spending is not something I'm prone to do, and to tell the truth, there's a certain substance to those rumors. At the same time, I accept without question the words of George Washington: "To be prepared for war is one of the most effectual means of preserving peace." Now, in spite of some things you may have heard, he didn't tell me that personally—[*laughter*]—still, I'm in full agreement and believe that he did say it.

But let me seriously speak about your employers. We've been through a period in which it seemed that we the people had forgotten that government is a convenience of, for, and by the people. And while we were busy with our own affairs, government began to grow beyond the consent of the governed. Its growth was nourished by an ever-larger share of the people's earnings that it took by taxation which became more and more confiscatory. At the same time government neglected one of its prime responsibilities, national security, as it engaged more and more in social experimentation. Our margin of safety in an increasingly hostile world was allowed to diminish, and for a time it seemed that there was an erosion of respect for the honorable profession that you have chosen.

All of this has led to an economic crisis. Deficit spending, an almost trillion dollar debt resulted in runaway inflation, lowered productivity, and great unemployment. And the tools of your trade were given a very low priority.

Well, I'm happy to tell you that the people of America have recovered from what can only be called a temporary aberration. There is a spiritual revival going on in this country, a hunger on the part of the people to once again be proud of America—all that it is and all that it can be.

Now, the first step in restoring our margin of safety must be the rejuvenation of our economy. A vibrant and expanding economy is necessary if we're to have the research, the technology, and the industry and capacity to provide you with what you need to practice your profession.

Reflecting the will of the people, the government has returned to our long-time tradition of bipartisanship—not only where national security is concerned but with regard to the economic needs of our people. In recent weeks one could say there were no Democrats or Republicans in Congress—just Americans.

Yes, there are and will be disagreements, but they are legitimate differences of opinion on how best to reduce government costs, what tax changes will provide incentive to increase productivity, and how best to restore our defense capability. Already the Congress has voted the greatest reduction in the budget ever attempted and, at the same time, has mightily increased spending for the military. The argument, if there is any, will be over which weapons, not whether we should forsake weaponry for treaties and agreements.

My good friend Laurence Beilenson authored a book a few years ago called, "The Treaty Trap." It was the result of years of research, and it makes plain that no nation that placed its faith in parchment or paper, while at the same time it gave up its protective hardware, ever lasted long enough to write many pages in history. Now this is not to say that we shouldn't seek treaties and understandings and even mutual reduction of strategic weapons. The search for peace must go on, but we have a better chance of finding it if we maintain our strength while we're searching. Mr. Beilenson has recently authored a new thought-provoking book called "Survival and Peace in the Nuclear Age."

But weaponry alone does not mean security. General George Patton said, "Wars may be fought with weapons, but they are won by men. It is the spirit of the men who

follow and of the man who leads that gains the victory." Now, today we seek to make one change in that statement. It is, "The men and women who follow and the men and women who lead." Now—I meant to ask the General before I got up here, and I forgot to do it, because I've been given two figures—I know that there are either 58 or 68 women in this graduating class. And I do know that women do constitute more than 9 percent of the Army today.

The indispensable factor for protection for all that we hold dear is leadership, a leadership of you and young men and women like you, that you offer to this Nation. You will be the individuals who most inspire and lead those who are called upon to do the hard and sometimes thankless job.

There's a writer, James Warner Bellah, sometimes called our Rudyard Kipling because of his stories of our Army on the frontier as we pushed westward. And in one of his stories he described a poignant scene. A commanding officer lay dying on the field of battle. As he passed the command to a younger officer he said, "There may be only one time in your life when your country will call upon you and you will be the only one who can do the nasty job that has to be done—do it or forever after there will be the taste of ashes in your mouth."

A torch of leadership is being handed to you in this commencement ceremony today, a ceremony that in all this land is duplicated only in the several other service academies. I know that you've learned the principles of leadership here in this historic place. You know that it requires one to command respect of those who follow by deserving that respect, by dedication and total commitment to the defense of our country and all that it represents.

You've had an excellent example to follow. General Goodpaster, who is, I know, an honorary member of your graduating class now, he arrived as Superintendent almost at the same time as you enrolled as plebes, and he retires now as you graduate. He served his country well, retired as a four-star general, but was willing to leave retirement and give up a star to return to West Point.

You are part of a great tradition. It's overused, I know, but the term "the long gray line" is descriptive of the tradition of which you are now a part. In that line have been men who turned defeat into victory, who stood in the breach till citizen armies could be raised. For a time West Point was the nation's principal source of professionally trained engineers. The West was explored and mapped by members of the long gray line. A West Point graduate helped design the Panama Canal and the Holland Tunnel. Two were Presidents. Two are presently Cabinet members in this administration. Others have been giants of commerce and industry—Henry du Pont, class of 1833; Robert E. Wood, class of 1900.

Dwight Eisenhower said, "Even in the event of a complete disarmament there is a role for West Point. Even if we just turned our graduates back into the body politic it would be good. The graduates are trained people who understand their duty and who do it."

Six of the astronauts are graduates of West Point, among them the first man to walk in space, Colonel Edward White, who then lost his life in 1967 in a tragic fire that swept the Apollo spacecraft.

But let us look ahead to the force of which you will be an important and significant part. I doubt there will be many surprises, because in a way you've been "Army" for the last 4 years. There's little chance that you'll be like that recruit in World War II who asked in some bewilderment why the Army did certain things in the way it did. And a long-time Regular Army sergeant said, "Well, let me explain it to you, son. If you were in charge of a brand new country and creating an army for that country, you finally got a division organized, what would you call it?" And the recruit said, "Well, I guess I'd call it the 1st Division." "Well," he said, "in the United States Army when they did that, they called it the 2d Division." And he said, "When you understand that, you'll know everything about the Army and why it does things the way—[*laughter*]——

But our country has a unique tradition among the nations. Unlike the other powers with armies of conscripts, our military was always composed of citizen volunteers. In times past, the standing Army was a skeleton force that expanded in wartime to absorb the draftees, the conscripts. We also counted on a National Guard, a trained reserve to bridge the period when the draftees were undergoing basic training. We must still have that reserve, and we're taking steps to upgrade it to a state of immediate readiness.

We once had the luxury of time provided by the two great oceans—a luxury we no longer have. At the end of World War II we continued the draft into peacetime even though the peacetime draft was counter to American tradition. We had always believed that only in the most severe national emergency did a government have a claim to mandatory service of its younger citizens.

But we returned to that tradition in 1973—a volunteer military. Some proclaimed it a failure from the start. I'm not going to take your time by reciting the pros and cons of the debate, which still goes on, except to say that some express the belief that patriotism alone should be cause enough to serve. Well, George Washington, to quote him again, once said of patriotism: "It must be aided by a prospect of Interest or some reward. For a time it may, of itself push Men to Action; to bear much, to encounter difficulties; but it will not endure unassisted by interest."

Now, it's true that patriotism can't be bought; neither can it be coerced. Any you here today are living proof of that. Obviously you did not choose this profession with the thought of making a fortune. Samuel Johnson, 200 years ago, said, "An officer is much more respected than any other man who has so little money." [*Laughter*]

Young men and women volunteered for duty in our Armed Forces and then found that too much of their reward was expected to be patriotism. And in recent years even here they were shortchanged. In much of the seventies there was a widespread lack of respect for the uniform, born perhaps of what has been called the Vietnam syndrome. The result was inevitable—a fall-off of enlistments, but even worse, a drop in reenlistment, resulting in a great loss of experienced noncommissioned officers. The cry for a draft arose to a crescendo.

Well, I still believe there is another way, one more in keeping with our system of rewarding those who work and serve, on a scale commensurate with what we ask of them. I don't suppose we could put an exact price on the sacrifice that we ask of those who guarantee our safety, but one thing is certain: They deserve better than a bare subsistence level.

I have asked Secretary of Defense Weinberger to form a Defense Manpower Task Force to review the entire military manpower question and to make proposals which will increase the effectiveness of the active and reserve all-volunteer forces.

Last year's pay increase was a step in the right direction, but we're asking for another one in the fiscal year that begins October 1st. We seek to channel pay increases and bonuses to those in the most needed skill areas. We're studying proposals for a merit pay system and increased flexibility in personnel practices.

A few years ago the GI bill was eliminated and replaced with a program having fewer benefits. At the same time we were expanding Federal aid to college students. The Federal Government, in effect, provided more benefits to those who were not serving their country and reduced them for those who were. The Defense Manpower Task Force will be studying ways in which we can make enlistment more attractive to the kind of young people we need in our military forces.

Already enlistments are up, and so are reenlistments. And surprisingly—well, maybe we shouldn't be surprised—many who have already left the service are now returning. There's also been a decided rise in quality as measured by educational and testing attainment. Something other than pay and benefits contributed to this.

I mentioned earlier the new spirit that is abroad in our land. The era of self-doubt is over. We've stopped looking at our warts and rediscovered how much there is to love in this blessed land. All of us together and you very definitely in the posts you go to can help restore the sense of pride our men and women are entitled to have in wearing the uniform.

Let friend and foe alike be made aware of the spirit that is sweeping across our land, because it means we will meet our responsibility to the free world. Very much a part of this new spirit is patriotism, and with that goes a heartfelt appreciation for the sacrifices of those in uniform.

You are a prime ingredient that keeps us free, that protects all we cherish and hold dear. You can transmit the historic heritage which is in the very air of West Point. The first Purple Heart medal was awarded here. It was the first decoration ever given to an enlisted man.

At Trophy Point I'm told there are links of a great chain that was forged and stretched across the Hudson to prevent the British fleet from penetrating further into the valley. Today you are that chain holding back an evil force that would extinguish the light we've been tending for 6,000 years.

Now, before I finish, there is one thing that I should say on behalf of you directly. And that is that in keeping with what I understand is a tradition, I have asked the Superintendent to grant an amnesty. [*Applause*] I knew I should have saved that for the last—[*laughter*]—but seriously, I wanted to close with some other remarks.

Almost two decades ago in the sunset of his life, a West Point graduate, Douglas MacArthur, returned to this place to address the Cadet Corps. No one who ever heard him that day can ever forget his call to duty, honor, country, nor his declaration that so long as there was a breath in his body, he would hear the words "the Corps, the Corps, the Corps."

Do your duty. Keep untarnished your honor, and you of the Corps will preserve this country for yourselves, for all of us, for your children, and for your children's children.

God bless you and keep you.

Note: The President spoke at 10:12 a.m. at the ceremonies, which were held in Michie Stadium on the campus at West Point, N.Y. In his opening remarks, he referred to Lt. Gen. Andrew J. Goodpaster, Superintendent of the U.S. Military Academy, and Gen. Edward C. Meyer, Army Chief of Staff.

Following his remarks, the President awarded the Defense Distinguished Service Medal to General Goodpaster.

Nomination of Theodore E. Cummings To Be United States Ambassador to Austria
May 27, 1981

The President announced today his intention to nominate Theodore E. Cummings, of Beverly Hills, Calif., as Ambassador to Austria. He succeeds Philip M. Kaiser, who has resigned.

From 1960 to 1972, Mr. Cummings served as chairman of the board of Pacific Coast Properties, a firm specializing in real estate development, of Beverly Hills, Calif. From 1967 to 1969, he was president of the California division and vice chairman of the board of Vornado, Inc., Santa Fe Springs, Calif. From 1944 to 1968, Mr. Cummings served as president and chief executive officer of Food Giant Markets, Foster Freeze, Unimart, Builders Emporium of Santa Fe Springs, Calif.

Mr. Cummings, a philanthropist who has been long involved in civic and community affairs, has been a member of the board of directors or trustees of: Cedars-Sinai Medical Center; University of Southern California; the Joseph H. Hirshhorn Museum and Sculpture Garden. He was founder of the Theodore E. Cummings Humanitarian Award, the Eleanor Roosevelt Cancer Foundation, the Los Angeles Museum of Art, and the Los Angeles Music Center. He served on the Commission on Judicial Qualification of the State of California, California Hospital Commission, and in 1971 was appointed by the President as a member of the Committee on the Health Services Industry, Cost of Living Council.

In addition, Mr. Cummings has been the recipient of numerous honors, including the degree of honorary doctor of law from the University of Southern California, the degree of doctor of humane letters from the University of San Fernando, and the degree of doctor of laws from Pepperdine University of Los Angeles.

Mr. Cummings was born December 25, 1907, in Brzzany, Austria. He is married and has two daughters.

Remarks and a Question-and-Answer Session With State and Local Officials During a White House Briefing on the Program for Economic Recovery
May 28, 1981

The President. I am pleased that you're here because I think, in large part, one of the things underlying the program upon which you've been briefed and are going to continue to be briefed today is the balance between State and Federal and local government. And I think that balance is the key to economic recovery in our country and recovery of a lot of other things that you have to deal with every day.

You know what's best for your States; you know what's best for your communities. You are the closest to the people; you hear them. And we in this administration want a partnership with you, and I think with such a partnership there'd be no limit to what we can accomplish.

We need your help in getting the consolidation of categorical grants into block grants. Granted, there are going to be reductions in the budget, as you've been told. But I think if you were given the flexibility to use those block grants with your judgment, the way they should be, set your priorities, that I don't think that you'll feel the pain of those cuts as much as maybe somebody in the bureaucracy up here's going to feel them.

Now, I know that this afternoon that's going to be the subject that you hear, so I'm not going to get into great detail about it.

There is one other thing that I think—if you haven't heard today—that you would be interested in—our task force on regulations. So far, more than 100 of them have been targeted for elimination, and more than a third of that 100 will remove the restrictions that are presently imposed on local and State government entities. And having been in State government myself, I've got some experience with some of those regulations and restrictions and the additional paperwork that they call for.

You know what's happening in the country. You're closer to the people, and you hear the cry of the people for some reform. We hope that we'll soon have—I'm hoping anyway; I know Don Regan has spoken to you this morning already about it—but I hope that very shortly we'll have a bipartisan tax policy similar to the Gramm-Latta bill, one that we can all go forward together on.

One last point here: Senator Paul Laxalt is chairing a task force and an advisory committee, chairing both of them, and they're on federalism. This, if we'll only look at it, is the secret of America's success. We're unique in all the world in that we were set up to be a federation of sovereign States with as much law as possible kept at the local level.

Now, you hear a lot of jokes every once in a while about silent Cal Coolidge. But I think the joke is on the people that make jokes, because if you look at his record, he cut the taxes four times. We had probably the greatest growth in prosperity that we've ever known. And I have taken heed of that, because if he did that by doing nothing, maybe that's the answer that the Federal Government better—[*laughter*]——

But I have a quote—1926, from Cal Coolidge. He said, "No method of procedure has ever been devised by which liberty could be divorced from local self-government. No plan of centralization has ever been adopted which did not result in bureaucracy, tyranny, inflexibility, reaction and decline. Of all forms of government, those administered by bureaus are about the least satisfactory to an enlightened and

progressive people. Being irresponsible, they become autocratic. And being autocratic, they resist all development. Unless bureaucracy is constantly resisted, it breaks down representative government and overwhelms democracy. It is the one element in our institutions that sets up the pretense of having authority over everybody and being responsible to nobody."

Now, I know that time is limited, but we can have some dialog, at least, here before they grab me.

Q. Mr. President, Joe Malone from Boydentown City, New Jersey. Much has been said about the possibility of a national workfare program. Will the administration be getting involved in a national workfare program?

The President. This is what we are hoping we can achieve. It was an experiment that we tried in California, when we reformed welfare out there, of getting the able-bodied welfare recipients to work at useful community projects in return for their welfare grants. And the way we operated it there—I don't know what the plans are that are going forward over in Senator Schweiker's office now, but I know he's heart and soul in favor of this, in support of it.

What we did was, they worked 20 hours a week, not 40. And we assigned representatives from the State labor department to them as, what we called, job agents. In other words, we did not want them as permanent. We started first by getting every element of local government, from school districts to communities, counties, whatever, to submit to us those things that, as we defined it, they would be doing if they had the manpower and the money, but which they were otherwise not able to do. In other words, don't invent, make work.

And we screened all those to make sure they were legitimate undertakings. Then these people were sent for to go to work, report for work in those projects. And the job agents watched them, and on the basis of what they saw, they actually acted as agents and went out and tried as quickly as possible to move them from those jobs into private enterprise jobs. And this was most successful in putting tens of thousands of people through that program out into private enterprise jobs at a time when unemployment was increasing in the '73–'74 recession.

There was another sideline benefit. Thousands of those people who were notified didn't report, and we stopped sending the checks, and we never heard from them again. [*Laughter*]

Q. Mr. President, I'm Virgil Brown from Cuyahoga County, Cleveland, Ohio. How do you propose to get fair treatment for, let's say, in a State like Ohio, where we have Cleveland, which is a very urban area, and you have rural areas, and if the block grants are going to come through the State, how do we get fair treatment out of that?

The President. Well, again, I just have to feel and have faith that a State government has got to be fair in this or there will be a different State government. And we haven't had an opportunity—I haven't had yet—in the arranging of this program to talk about whether there would be any recourse kept available for the Federal Government if someone tried unfair tactics. But I've met with all the Governors on this, and I know a number of them are very supportive, and I believe these are honorable men who are not going to let that happen. They think they represent all the people.

Q. Jim Long from Indianapolis, Indiana. Mr. President, I have a question on Federal revenue sharing. I feel, and I'm sure a lot of other local officials feel, that we should be helping ourselves, like you do here at the national level. And at the same time, I think some of us are going to have to be prepared enough to know what's going to happen with regards to Federal revenue sharing and whether it's going to be done away with in the near future or not.

The President. Well, you mean Federal revenue sharing; you mean by way of the block grants that we're talking about. Let me tell you, we need your help, because this is going to be probably one of the most difficult of all the parts of our reform program to bring about. There is a great reluctance on the part of the Federal Government to trust the people out there, and they believe that inhaling the fogs off the Potomac imparts a wisdom that is not generally shared. [*Laughter*] But we are going

to need help to get that. There's a reluctance to give up that authority.

I have to tell you that I think the block grants—my long distance dream is that the block grants are only a bridge, that the real ultimate goal should be to transfer the actual sources of taxation to State and local governments.

Q. Gary Thalen, Mr. President, and I'd like to thank you for this afternoon here, and appreciate the administration's effort in their deregulation program and the bureaucracy that causes so many problems on counties and municipal governments. Thank you, sir.

The President. Thank you.

Q. Mr. President, this is just a little change in the procedure here, but one of our constituents in Cape May County, New Jersey, wrote a poem. And I think he might have sent it to you, and I said I was going to read it if I got the opportunity. [*Laughter*]

"Faith and a dream is all that we need to carry us on like a galloping steed. With eyes to the future, let us pray, God bless America and the American way." Andrea Lippia wrote this from Cape May County, and I'd like you to have it.

The President. Thank you very much. Thank you. And I agree, this country started with a dream.

Q. Mr. President, we're going through the same process—I'm Marie Muhler from New Jersey—on our budget as the Federal Government is. The only information that we are getting from our bureaucrats in every area in government at the State level is a list of all the cuts. What we would like to know is the information about the block grants, some idea. If there's a billion dollar cut, we want to know just what portion—is it 20 percent that can be restored in block grants, is it 70 percent?—or some way to lobby our congressional delegation so that those of us that are in a minority have the ammunition to say, fine, maybe those are the cuts, we make these decisions, and this is where we have to trim before we adopt our budgets.

The President. Well, I think very possibly this afternoon you might get an answer to that in the briefing that will be on block grants. If not, I certainly will make sure that that is a consideration. I think all of us are aware that most of the screams of pain that we're hearing are coming from the bureaucracy and not from the supposed victims of our cuts.

Q. Mr. President, my name is Hazel Gluck. I'm an assemblywoman from New Jersey. I know one of the cornerstones of your economic recovery program is your tax cut plan. I read with great concern, through the media, through the New York media and the New Jersey media, that Wall Street, the financial community, is resisting the tax cut plan because they feel it's inflationary. How do you address that?

The President. Well, one thing that I address it on is that I have never found Wall Street a source of good economic advice. [*Laughter*] They are sitting there watching anything that they think may change the interest rates and the bond market and so forth, and it is true that they have not recognized history, for that matter.

John F. Kennedy proposed a broad, across-the-board income tax cut over a 2-year period, and it was implemented after he was gone. But the economists were rising up and telling him that this was going to reduce Federal revenues by $83 billion, and he had some very good answers, such as he said, "A rising tide raises all boats." And he stuck to his guns.

Well, they made about a $143 billion mistake, because when the score was finally in, the government had actually increased its revenues at the lower rates by more than $50 billion. In other words, proper tax cuts can stimulate the economy. The individual pays less tax but there are more individuals paying it, and the economy is broadened at every level.

This happened with regard to the cut in the capital gains tax. They reduced the rates in the capital gains tax, and the next year the government got more money from the lower rate. Now, what was the answer to that? The answer was that when the tax rates are at a certain level, those people with money to invest start looking for tax shelters, and they're not going to increase productivity with tax shelters. And once you make it more profitable, they bring that money out of the tax shelters and start investing in industry, in America, and back-

ing entrepreneurs with commercial ideas and so forth.

You can go all the way back. I mentioned the tax cuts in Coolidge's era. Every one of those tax cuts resulted in more revenues for the Government because of the increased prosperity of the country as a whole.

As I say, I think that Wall Street, in all due respect, I think they're looking through a very narrow glass, and they've only seeing one facet.

Q. My name is Emily Morris, and I reside in a county that is three to one Democrat registration. I want to applaud you on your program, to let you know that I support it and many of my race support the program as well, and also to let you know that direct services to people do not have to be phased out or eliminated. We can look for other options and other alternatives, and I want you to know that in Delaware that's the way we're going to be going.

Thank you very much.

The President. Oh, bless you, and thank you. Thank you very much. I could take advantage of this. They said that I could only take one more question. That would be a great one to quit on. If you'll all forgive me, I'll take this gentleman here. I know you've had your hand up before.

Q. I'm Chuck Hebner, speaker of the house, in Delaware, also. I applaud your practical approach to the regulation problem, but I'd like to call your attention, if I may, to one of the most pervasive regulatory bodies we face. That is the Federal courts and the Federal judges, particularly. I don't want you to try to fetter them, sir, but I wish there was a way to channel their practicality, and I just ask you to take a look at that problem.

The President. We are aware of that problem and, of course, probably the best thing I can do is wait until it's my turn to appoint some. [*Laughter*]

Thank you all very much.

Note: The President spoke at 11:34 a.m. in Room 450 of the Old Executive Office Building. The briefing was given for State, county, and city officials.

Message to the Polish Council of Bishops on the Death of Stefan Cardinal Wyszynski of Poland
May 28, 1981

The American people join me in extending our deepest condolences over the passing of a great leader and a great son of the Polish nation, Cardinal Wyszynski. Americans nurtured a deep respect and admiration for Cardinal Wyszynski as Primate of Poland. He played a vital role in helping to safeguard deep and enduring values which both our peoples share, and in the development of close relations between our two countries over the past quarter-century. My compatriots and I fully share Poland's deep sense of loss.

RONALD REAGAN

Message to the Senate Transmitting the United States-Colombia Treaty on Extradition
May 28, 1981

To the Senate of the United States:

With a view to receiving the advice and consent of the Senate to ratification, I transmit herewith the Treaty of Extradition between the United States of America and the Republic of Colombia, signed at Washington on September 14, 1070.

I transmit also, for the information of the Senate, the report of the Department of State with respect to the treaty.

The treaty is one of a series of modern extradition treaties being negotiated by the United States. It expands the list of extraditable offenses to include narcotics violations, aircraft hijacking, bribery, and obstruction of justice, as well as many other offenses not covered by our existing extradition treaty with Colombia. Upon entry into force, it will terminate and supersede the existing Extradition Treaty and Supplementary Convention between the United States and Colombia.

This treaty will make a significant contribution to international cooperation in law enforcement. I recommend that the Senate give early and favorable consideration to the treaty and give its advice and consent to ratification.

RONALD REAGAN

The White House,
May 28, 1981.

Message to the Senate Transmitting the United States-Netherlands Treaty on Extradition
May 28, 1981

To the Senate of the United States:

With a view to receiving the advice and consent of the Senate to ratification, I transmit herewith the Treaty of Extradition between the United States of America and the Kingdom of the Netherlands, signed at The Hague on June 24, 1980.

I transmit also, for the information of the Senate, the report of the Department of State with respect to the treaty.

The treaty is one of a series of modern extradition treaties being negotiated by the United States. It expands the list of extraditable offenses to include narcotics violations, aircraft hijacking, bribery, and obstruction of justice, as well as many other offenses not covered by our existing extradition treaty with the Netherlands. Upon entry into force, it will terminate and supersede the existing Extradition Treaty and Supplementary Treaty between the United States and the Netherlands.

This treaty will make a significant contribution to international cooperation in law enforcement. I recommend that the Senate give early and favorable consideration to the treaty and give its advice and consent to ratification.

RONALD REAGAN

The White House,
May 28, 1981.

Nomination of William Bradford Reynolds To Be an Assistant Attorney General
May 28, 1981

The President today announced his intention to nominate William Bradford Reynolds to be an Assistant Attorney General (Civil Rights Division), Department of Justice.

Mr. Reynolds has been a litigation partner with the law firm of Shaw, Pittman, Potts & Trowbridge, Washington, D.C., since 1973. From 1970 to 1973, he was assistant to the Solicitor General of the United States, Erwin Griswold. In 1967–70 he was an associate with the law firm of Sullivan & Cromwell, New York, N.Y. In 1966 he was assistant to the U.S. Attorney for the Eastern District of Tennessee, Nashville, Tenn.

Mr. Reynolds received his B.A. degree from Yale University in 1964 and his law degree from Vanderbilt University School of Law in 1967.

Mr. Reynolds is married, with four children, and resides in Potomac, Md. He was born June 21, 1942, in Bridgeport, Conn.

Nomination of Charles H. Price II To Be United States Ambassador to Belgium
May 28, 1981

The President today announced his intention to nominate Charles H. Price II as Ambassador to Belgium. He would succeed Anne Cox Chambers, who has resigned.

Mr. Price served in the U.S. Air Force from 1953 to 1955. He is presently chairman of the board of the American Bank and Trust Co., of Kansas City, Mo. From 1955 to the present, he has been with the Price Candy Co. and is serving as president or chairman of the board of American Mortgage Co., Price Bank Building Corp., American Bancorporation, Inc., Linwood Securities Co., Twenty-one Central United, Inc. Since 1976 he has also been chairman of several businesses in Boise, Idaho.

He has received the Alumni Award from the University of Missouri School of Business and Public Administration; Award of Appreciation, Midwest Research Institute; and Outstanding Achievement Award, University of Missouri-Kansas City, Performing Arts Center.

Mr. Price was born April 1, 1931, in Kansas City, Mo. He attended Wentworth Military Academy and the University of Missouri.

Nomination of Charles W. Bray III To Be United States Ambassador to Senegal
May 28, 1981

The President announced today his intention to nominate Charles W. Bray III, of Maryland, as Ambassador to the Republic of Senegal. He would succeed Walter C. Carrington, who has resigned.

Mr. Bray entered the Foreign Service in 1958 was and information specialist in the Bureau of East Asian and Pacific Affairs in the Department of State. He was consular officer in Cebu (1961–63) and political officer in Bangui (1963–65). From 1965 to 1966, he was personnel officer in the Bureau of African Affairs. He attended economic studies at the University of Maryland from 1966 to 1967. He was special assistant to the Under Secretary of State for Political Affairs from 1967 to 1968. From 1968 to 1969, he took a leave of absence to become program director of the American Foreign Service Association in Washington, D.C.

Since 1969 he has served in the Department as Deputy Director of the Office of North African Affairs (1969–70), Director of Public Affairs in the Bureau of African Affairs (1970–71), Spokesman for the Department of State and Special Assistant to the Secretary of State for Press Relations (1971–73), Deputy Assistant Secretary of State for Inter-American Affairs (1976–77). From 1977 to 1981, he was Deputy Director of the International Communication Agency.

Mr. Bray served in the United States Army from 1956 to 1958. He was adjunct lecturer at the School of Foreign Service, Georgetown University, from 1973 to 1974.

He was born October 24, 1933, in New York, N.Y. He received his A.B. degree in 1955 from Princeton University.

Nomination of Maxwell M. Rabb To Be United States Ambassador to Italy
May 28, 1981

The President announced today his intention to nominate Maxwell M. Rabb, of New York, as Ambassador to Italy. He would succeed Richard N. Gardner, who has resigned.

Mr. Rabb served in the United States Navy as a lieutenant from 1944 to 1946. From 1935 to 1937 and from 1946 to 1951, he was a partner in the law firm of Rabb and Rabb, Boston, Mass. Since 1958 he has been senior partner in the law firm of Stroock, Stroock and Lavan, New York, N.Y.

His government experience began in 1937 when he was administrative assistant to United States Senator Henry Cabot Lodge until 1943. In 1944 he was administrative assistant to United States Senator Sinclair Weeks. He was legal and legislative consultant to Secretary of the Navy Forrestal in 1946, and in 1952 he was consultant to the United States Rules Committee. From 1953 to 1958, he served as Presidential Assistant and Secretary of the Cabinet of the United States and from January-October 1953 was also Associate Counsel to the President. He has actively served on numerous committees and commissions since 1958.

Mr. Rabb was born September 28, 1910, in Boston, Mass. He graduated (A.B.) in 1932 from Harvard College and received his law degree from Harvard Law School in 1935.

Nomination of Jane Abell Coon To Be United States Ambassador to Bangladesh
May 28, 1981

The President announced today his intention to nominate Jane Abell Coon, of New Hampshire, as Ambassador to the People's Republic of Bangladesh. She would succeed David T. Schneider, who is resigning.

Mrs. Coon began her government career in 1951 in the State Department as foreign affairs officer, then intelligence research analyst. She was appointed a Foreign Service officer in 1956 and served in Karachi, Bombay, New Delhi, and the Department, prior to resigning in 1967. She returned to the Department in 1976 as international re-lations officer in the Bureau of Oceans and International Environmental and Scientific Affairs. From 1977 to 1979, she was Director of Pakistan, Afghanistan, and Bangladesh Affairs. Since 1979 she has been Deputy Assistant Secretary of State for Near Eastern and South Asian Affairs.

Mrs. Coon was born May 9, 1929, in Durham, N.H. She graduated (B.A.) in 1951 from the College of Wooster. She is married to Carleton S. Coon, Jr., and has six stepchildren.

Statement by Deputy Press Secretary Larry M. Speakes on Federal Tax Reductions
May 28, 1981

The administration as of this hour has received only secondhand reports on the Democratic caucus this afternoon. Treasury Secretary Regan looks forward to a more complete, firsthand report from Chairman Rostenkowski in the near future.

In the meantime, President Reagan's position remains firm: Across-the-board, mul-tiyear tax cuts are just as essential to economic recovery as across-the-board, multiyear budget cuts. The President remains hopeful that a bipartisan coalition can be built in Congress to give the American people the tax cuts that they so clearly need, want, and deserve.

Nomination of Allen B. Clark, Jr., To Be Deputy Administrator of Veterans Affairs
May 29, 1981

The President today announced his intention to nominate Allen B. Clark, Jr., to be Deputy Administrator of Veterans Affairs.

Mr. Clark served in the United States Army Green Berets in Vietnam and retired as a captain due to wounds received in combat action. His military service awards include the Silver Star for Gallantry in Action, the Bronze Star, the Air Medal, the Purple Heart, two battle stars for Vietnam service, the Combat Infantryman's Badge, and Airborne Wings.

He served as president of the West Point Society of North Texas in 1973, as president of the Young Executives Group of the Dallas Council on World Affairs in 1977, as chairman of the Horizons Committee of the Dallas American Revolution Bicentennial Committee in 1976, and as chairman of the

Special Gifts Division of the Dallas American Heart Association Fund Drive in 1978.

Mr. Clark attended Gonzaga Jesuit High School in Washington, D.C., and is a graduate of Phillips Exeter Academy in New Hampshire. He earned a bachelor of science degree from the United States Military Academy (West Point) in 1963, where he

was in the top 10 percent of his class and served as a cadet platoon leader. He earned a master of business administration from the Southern Methodist University.

Mr. Clark was born on June 20, 1942, in McAllen, Tex. He is married to the former Jacklyn Adell McAdams of Dallas, Tex., and they have two daughters.

Message to Acting President Abdus Sattar of Bangladesh on the Death of President Ziaur Rahman
May 31, 1981

Your Excellency:

I was shocked and deeply grieved to learn of the assassination of President Ziaur Rahman. The United States—indeed the world—had come to respect President Zia's profound and compassionate commitment to a better life for his people and his dedication to the rule of law. His wisdom in international affairs will be sorely missed. I am confident that the people of Bangladesh are united in their determination to assure

that the stability and progress of recent years will survive this tragedy. Please extend to Begum Zia and her children my sincere condolences on this sad occasion.

Sincerely,

RONALD REAGAN

Note: President Rahman was killed during an attempted coup d'etat by Army officers in Chittagong on May 30.

Message to the Congress Recommending Extension of the Veterans Education Assistance Program
May 30, 1981

To the Congress of the United States:

In 1976, the Congress established, in Public Law 94–502, a new contributory education program under which individuals entering military service on and after January 1, 1977, would, on a voluntary basis, have funds withheld from their military pay for their future education. These contributions would, under the law, be matched by the Veterans Administration on a $2 for $1 basis.

The law provides for this Veterans' Education Assistance Program (VEAP) to be conducted on a test basis and requires termination of new enrollments by service personnel after December 31, 1981, unless

I recommend continuation of the program before June 1, 1981.

Last year, the Congress enacted the Department of Defense Authorization Act, 1981, and the Veterans' Rehabilitation and Education Amendments of 1980. These two laws included revisions to the VEAP program and established a new, second test program under which service personnel, who enlist or reenlist after September 30, 1980, and before October 1, 1981, may be eligible for education benefits after serving for a specified period of time.

The conference report on the Department of Defense Authorization Act, 1981, recommended that the VEAP program be extended to June 30, 1982, in order to provide sufficient time for the Department of Defense to test and evaluate the new pilot program. That program is currently undergoing testing and evaluation.

As of the end of February 1981, a total of 3,872 individuals had commenced education training under the VEAP program. The relatively low training rate reflects, in part, the fact that under the law an individual may not begin to use his or her educational entitlement until completion of the first obligated period of active duty or 6 years of active duty, whichever period is less. Since the law did not become effective until January 1, 1977, the number of persons eligible to pursue training has thus far been minimal.

Over the next several months the Administration will be continuing its evaluation and review of both the VEAP and Department of Defense test programs, with a view towards developing legislative recommendations regarding education programs for servicemembers and veterans. In view of this effort, I am recommending that the VEAP program be continued beyond its current termination date of December 31, 1981. This will permit the Administration to complete its review and will provide time for submission of legislative recommendations that I anticipate will be submitted in early 1982.

Recently, the Veterans Administration submitted legislation to the Congress that would authorize a 1-year extension of the Veterans' Educational Assistance Program and make certain other adjustments in Public Law 94–502. I urge the Congress to enact this legislation.

RONALD REAGAN

The White House,
May 30, 1981.

Note: The text of the message was released by the Office of the Press Secretary on June 1.

Nomination of Richard Mulberry To Be Inspector General of the Department of the Interior
June 1, 1981

The President today announced his intention to nominate Richard Mulberry as Inspector General at the Department of the Interior.

Mr. Mulberry has more than 30 years of public accounting experience and, since 1963, has been executive partner with Fox & Co. in Dallas, Tex. From 1960 to 1963, he was with the accounting firm of La-France, Walker, Jockley & Saville, which later merged with Fox & Co. From 1956 to 1960, he was with Smith, Mulberry & Saville (cofounder).

Mr. Mulberry graduated from George Washington University with a B.A. degree in 1948. He received his M.B.A. from Wharton Graduate School, University of Pennsylvania, in 1949. He served in the U.S. Marine Corps Reserve for more than 30 years, including combat during World War II, Korea, and in Vietnam on special assignments. Mr. Mulberry attained the rank of major general, the highest rank possible in the Reserve.

Mr. Mulberry was born March 14, 1920, in Scott County, Ky. He is married, with two daughters, and resides in Dallas, Tex.

Nomination of Robert Sherwood Dillon To Be United States Ambassador to Lebanon
June 1, 1981

The President today announced his intention to nominate Robert Sherwood Dillon as Ambassador to Lebanon. He would succeed John Gunther Dean, who is resigning.

Mr. Dillon was a research analyst with the Department of Defense from 1951 to 1956. From 1956 to 1958, he was consular officer in Puerto La Cruz (Department of State). He attended economic studies at Princeton University from 1958 to 1959. In the Department he was economic officer in the Bureau of Near Eastern and South Asian Affairs and attended Turkish language training (1959–60) at the Foreign Service Institute. He was economic officer in Izmir (1960–62) and political officer in Ankara (1962–66). He was personnel officer in the Department (1966–68), special assist-

ant to the Under Secretary of State for Political Affairs (1968–69), and attended French language training at the Foreign Defense College in Rome. From 1970 to 1971, he was deputy principal officer in Istanbul. He was Director of Turkish Affairs in the Department from 1971 to 1974. From 1974 to 1977, he was Deputy Chief of Mission in Kuala Lampur, in Ankara (1977–80), and since 1980 as Deputy Chief of Mission in Cairo.

Mr. Dillon was born January 7, 1929, in Chicago, Ill. He received his B.A. in 1951 from Duke University. In 1971 he received the Meritorious Honor Award and Group Superior Honor Award. He is a resident of Arlington, Va.

Executive Order 12306—Amendments to the Manual for Courts-Martial, United States, 1060 (Revised Edition)
June 1, 1981

By the authority vested in me as President by Chapter 47 of Title 10 of the United States Code (the Uniform Code of Military Justice), in order to prescribe an amendment to the Military Rules of Evidence of the Manual for Courts-Martial, United States, 1969 (Revised edition), prescribed by Executive Order No. 11476, as amended by Executive Order 11835, Executive Order No. 12018, Executive Order No. 12198, and Executive Order No. 12233, it is hereby ordered as follows:

Section 1. Rule 410 of Chapter 27 of the Manual for Courts-Martial, United States, 1969 (Revised edition), is amended to read as follows:

"Rule 410. *Inadmissibility of pleas, plea discussions, and related statements.*

"(a) *In general.* Except as otherwise provided in this rule, evidence of the following is not admissible in any court-martial proceeding against the accused who made the

plea or was a participant in the plea discussions:

(1) a plea of guilty which was later withdrawn;

(2) a plea of nolo contendere;

(3) any statement made in the course of any judicial inquiry regarding either of the foregoing pleas; or

(4) any statement made in the course of plea discussions with the convening authority, staff judge advocate, trial counsel or other counsel for the Government which do not result in a plea of guilty or which result in a plea of guilty later withdrawn.

However, such a statement is admissible (i) in any proceeding wherein another statement made in the course of the same plea or plea discussions has been introduced and the statement ought in fairness be considered contemporaneously with it, or (ii) in a court-martial proceeding for perjury or false statement if the statement was made by the accused under oath, on the record and in the presence of counsel.

"(b) *Definitions*. A "statement made in the course of plea discussions" includes a statement made by the accused solely for the purpose of requesting disposition under an authorized procedure for administrative action in lieu of trial by court-martial; "on the record" includes the written statement submitted by the accused in furtherance of such request.".

Sec. 2. Notwithstanding Military Rule of Evidence 1102, Military Rule of Evidence 410, as prescribed by Executive Order No. 12198, shall remain in effect until the amendment prescribed by Section 1 of this Order takes effect.

Sec. 3. The amendment of Military Rule of Evidence 410 prescribed by Section 1 of this Order shall take effect on August 1, 1981. That amendment applies to all court-martial processes taken on or after August 1, 1981: Provided, that nothing contained in that amendment shall be construed to invalidate any investigation, trial in which arraignment has been completed, or other action begun prior to that date; and any such investigation, trial, or other action may be completed in accordance with applicable laws, Executive Orders, and regulations in the same manner and with the same effect as if that amendment had not been prescribed.

Sec. 4. The Secretary of Defense, on behalf of the President, shall transmit a copy of this Order to the Congress of the United States in accord with Section 836 of Title 10 of the United States Code.

RONALD REAGAN

The White House,
June 1, 1981.

[*Filed with the Office of the Federal Register, 11:41 a.m., June 2, 1981*]

Proclamation 4846—Flag Day and National Flag Week, 1981
June 1, 1981

By the President of the United States of America

A Proclamation

On June 14, 1777, the Continental Congress adopted the Stars and Stripes as our national flag. Ever since, the American flag has embodied the continuity of our original ideals and principles.

The stars in varying constellations and the stripes of alternating red and white have accompanied Americans from the Marne to the Moon. The flag was flying when the British surrendered to General Washington at Yorktown, when Admiral Peary reached the North Pole, and when our soldiers battled at Iwo Jima. Recently, we saw the American flag proudly on the side of the Space Shuttle Columbia as she circled the Earth.

Yet the flag flies not only over the great events our history but also over the more personal moments of American life. Who cannot recall the vivid images of children at parades waving small flags in patriotic delight, of immigrants solemnly reciting the oath of allegiance before a flag in a judge's chambers, or of a grieving military widow clutching the folded Stars and Stripes?

The American clergyman Henry Ward Beecher conveyed the full meaning of the flag when he wrote, "A thoughtful mind, when it sees a nation's flag, sees not the flag only, but the nation itself; and whatever may be its symbols, its insignia, he reads chiefly in the flag the government, the principles, the truths, the history which belongs to the nation that sets it forth."

When we honor our flag we honor what we stand for as a Nation—freedom, equality, justice, and hope. Flag Day and National Flag Week are our traditional means to commemorate the Nation's beliefs as symbolized by the Stars and Stripes. In more recent times, the twenty-one days from Flag Day through Independence Day have been set aside as a period to honor America during which Americans reflect upon the Nation's character, heritage, fortifying principles and future well-being.

Now, Therefore, I, Ronald Reagan, President of the United States of America, do hereby designate the week beginning Sunday, June 14, 1981, as National Flag Week, and I direct the appropriate officials of the Government to display the flag on all Government buildings during that week. I urge all Americans to observe Flag Day, June 14, and National Flag Week by flying the Stars and Stripes from their porches, windows and storefronts. I further urge the people of America to observe Honor America Days, from Flag Day through Independ-ence Day, by appropriate activities which reflect upon our good fortune at being Americans.

In Witness Whereof, I have hereunto set my hand this 1st day of June, in the year of our Lord nineteen hundred and eighty-one, and of the Independence of the United States of America the two hundred and fifth.

RONALD REAGAN

[*Filed with the Office of the Federal Register, 11:40 a.m., June 2, 1981*]

Note: The text of the proclamation was released by the Office of the Press Secretary on June 2.

Nomination of June Gibbs Brown To Be Inspector General of the National Aeronautics and Space Administration
June 2, 1981

The President today announced his intention to nominate June Gibbs Brown as Inspector General of the National Aeronautics and Space Administration.

Mrs. Brown has been Inspector General at the Department of Interior since May 1979. In 1976–79 she was Project Manager, Pay-Personnel System Design, Bureau of Reclamation in Denver, Colo. From 1975 to 1976, she was Chief, Financial Systems Design, Bureau of Land Management in Denver. From 1972 to 1975, she was Director, Internal Audit, at the Navy Finance Center in Cleveland, Ohio. From 1971 to 1972, she was accounting instructor at Cleveland State University and Dyke College in Cleveland.

Mrs. Brown is a certified public accountant. She received her law degree in 1978 from the University of Denver, College of Law; an M.B.A. degree from Cleveland State University in 1972; and a B.B.A. degree (summa cum laude) from Cleveland State University in 1971.

Mrs. Brown was born October 5, 1933, in Cleveland, Ohio. She is married, with six children, and resides in Arlington, Va.

Appointment of Two Members of the Advisory Commission on Intergovernmental Relations, and Designation of Vice Chairman
June 2, 1981

The President today announced his intention to appoint Robert Boone Hawkins, Jr., as private citizen member, Advisory Commission on Intergovernmental Relations, for a term of 2 years.

In 1980 Mr. Hawkins became president of Trendsetter Energy Systems, Inc. Since 1979 he has been a fellow with the Center for the Study of Federalism. In 1978 he was president of the Sequoia Institute in Sacramento. Since 1976 he has been the president of Capital Resource Development Corp. and has also been program coordinator of the Woodrow Wilson Institute for Scholars. In 1975 he was a visiting research fellow at the Hoover Institution. In March of 1974 he was cofounder and board member of the Institute of Contemporary Studies in San Francisco until 1978.

Mr. Hawkins received his B.S. degree in 1965 from San Francisco State College and his Ph. D. in 1969 from the University of Washington. He is the author of numerous publications on federalism.

Mr. Hawkins was born September 6, 1941, in Berkely, Calif. He is married, with two children, and resides in Vacaville, Calif.

The President today also announced his intention to appoint Governor Lamar Alexander (R–Tenn.) as a member of the Advisory Commission on Intergovernmental Relations for a term of 2 years. He will also be designated as Vice Chairman of the Commission.

Message to the Congress on Trade With Romania, Hungary, and the People's Republic of China
June 2, 1981

To the Congress of the United States:

In accordance with subsection 402(d)(5) of the Trade Act of 1974, I transmit herewith my recommendation for a further 12-month extension of the authority to waive subsections (a) and (b) of section 402 of the Act.

I include as part of my recommendation my determination that further extension of the waiver authority, and continuation of the waivers applicable to the Socialist Republic of Romania, the Hungarian People's Republic, and the People's Republic of China will substantially promote the objectives of section 402.

This recommendation also includes my reasons for recommending the extension of waiver authority and for my determination that continuation of the three waivers currently in effect will substantially promote the objectives of section 402.

RONALD REAGAN

The White House,
June 2, 1981.

Recommendation for Extension of Waiver Authority

I recommend to the Congress that the waiver authority granted by subsection 402(c) of the Trade Act of 1974 (hereinafter "the Act") be further extended for twelve months. Pursuant to subsection 402(d)(5) of the Act, I have today determined that further extension of such authority, and continuation of the waivers currently applicable to the Socialist Republic of Romania, the Hungarian People's Republic, and the People's Republic of China will substantially promote the objectives of section 402 of the Act. My determination is attached to this Recommendation and is incorporated herein.

The general waiver authority conferred by section 402(c) of the Act is an important means for the strengthening of mutually beneficial relations between the United States and certain countries of Eastern Europe and the People's Republic of China. The waiver authority has permitted us to conclude and maintain in force bilateral trade agreements with Romania, Hungary, and the People's Republic of China. These agreements are fundamental elements in our political and economic relations with those countries, including our important productive exchanges on human rights and emigration matters. Moreover, continuation of the waiver authority might permit future expansion of our bilateral relations with other countries now subject to subsection 402 (a) and (b) of the Act, should circumstances permit. I believe that these considerations clearly warrant this recommendation for expansion of the general waiver authority.

I also believe that continuing the current waivers applicable to Romania, Hungary and the People's Republic of China will substantially promote the objectives of section 402 of the Act.

Romania—Emigration from Romania to the United States has increased substantially since the waiver has been in effect. In 1980, more than 2,800 persons emigrated from Romania to the United States. This is nearly seven times the pre-MFN level of emigration and almost twice the 1979 level. Continuation of the waiver will also contribute to maintaining a framework for dialogue with the Romanian Government on emigration procedures, emigration to Israel, binational marriages, and other humanitarian problems.

Hungary—In March 1978 the Hungarian Government stressed to the U.S. Government that it intended to deal with emigration matters in a responsible and humanitarian way. Since that time the actions of Hungarian authorities have been consistent with this policy. A large majority of Hungarians seeking to emigrate are able to do so without undue difficulty. Very few problem cases arise, and U.S. officials are able to discuss these constructively with the Hungarian Government. Most problem cases ultimately are favorably resolved.

People's Republic of China—During the past year, China has continued its commitment to open emigration, exemplified by its undertaking in the September 1980 U.S.-China Consular Convention to facilitate family reunification. Our posts in China issued over 3,400 immigrant visas in FY-1980, and over 12,800 nonimmigrant visas for business, study and family visits. More than 5,000 Chinese now have come to the United States since 1979 for long term study and research. As has been the case for the past several years, the numerical limits imposed on entry to the U.S. by our immigration law continue to be a more significant impediment to immigration from China than Chinese Government exit controls. The Chinese Government is aware of our interest in open emigration, and extension of the waiver will encourage the Chinese to maintain its present travel and emigration policies.

In light of these considerations, I have determined that continuation of the waivers applicable to Romania, Hungary, and the People's Republic of China will substantially promote the objectives of section 402 of the Act.

Memorandum on Trade With Romania, Hungary, and the People's Republic of China
June 2, 1981

Presidential Determination No. 81–8

Memorandum for the Secretary of State

Subject: Determination under Subsection 402(d)(5) and (d)(5)(C) of the Trade Act of 1974—Continuation of Waiver Authority

Pursuant to the authority vested in me under the Trade Act of 1974 (Public Law 93–618, January 3, 1975; 88 Stat. 1978) (hereinafter "the Act"), I determine, pursuant to Subsections 402(d)(5)(C) of the Act, that the further extension of the waiver authority granted by Subsection 402(c) of the Act will substantially promote the objec- tives of Section 402 of the Act. I further determine the continuation of the waivers applicable to the Socialist Republic of Romania, the Hungarian People's Republic and the People's Republic of China will substantially promote the objectives of Section 402 of the Act.

This determination shall be published in the *Federal Register*.

RONALD REAGAN

[*Filed with the Office of the Federal Register, 4:23 p.m., June 9, 1981*]

Memorandum on Trade With Romania and Hungary
June 2, 1981

Presidential Determination No. 81–9

Memorandum for the United States Trade Representative

Subject: Renewal of Trade Agreements with Romania and Hungary—Findings and Determinations under Subsection 405(b)(1) of the Trade Act of 1974

Pursuant to my authority under the Trade Act of 1974 (Public Law 93–618, January 3, 1975; 88 Stat. 1978), I find, pursuant to subsection 405(b)(1) of that Act, that a satisfactory balance of concessions in trade and services has been maintained during the lives of the Agreements on Trade Rela-
tions between the United States and the Socialist Republic of Romania and the Hungarian People's Republic. I further determine that actual or foreseeable reductions in United States tariffs and non-tariff barriers to trade resulting from multilateral negotiations have been satisfactorily reciprocated by the Socialist Republic of Romania and by the Hungarian People's Republic.

These findings and determinations shall be published in the *Federal Register*.

RONALD REAGAN

[*Filed with the Office of the Federal Register, 11:36 a.m., June 3, 1981*]

Nomination of Alton Gold Keel, Jr., To Be an Assistant Secretary of the Air Force
June 3, 1981

The President today announced his intention to nominate Alton Gold Keel, Jr., to be an Assistant Secretary of the Air Force (Research, Development & Logistics).

From 1978 to the present, Dr. Keel was professional staff member of the Senate Armed Services Committee and is currently senior professional staff member of the committee. In 1977 Dr. Keel was selected as a Congressional Science Fellow by the American Institute of Aeronautics and Astronautics. He began serving in Senator Howard Cannon's (D–Nev.) office as a defense and technical adviser. From 1971 to 1977, he was with the Naval Surface Weapons Center, White Oak Laboratory, in Silver Spring, Md. In 1976 he became scientific staff assistant to the Associate Technical Director of the White Oak Laboratory.

Dr. Keel was a postdoctoral scholar (1971) at the University of California at Berkeley. In 1970 he received his Ph. D. in engineering physics from the University of Virginia. He received his bachelor of aerospace engineering in 1966 from the University of Virginia.

Dr. Keel was born September 8, 1943, in Newport News, Va. He is a resident of Washington, D.C.

Nomination of H. Monroe Browne To Be United States Ambassador to New Zealand and Western Samoa
June 3, 1981

The President today announced his intention to nominate H. Monroe Browne, of
California, as Ambassador to New Zealand and to serve concurrently as Ambassador to

Western Samoa. He would succeed Anne C. Martindell, who is resigning.

Mr. Browne was dean of boys, history teacher, and football coach at Delano High School from 1939 to 1942. He was a businessman in Bakersfield, Calif., as president and owner of McCoy Truck and Tire Co. (1945–60), of Browne Cattle Co., Inc. (1948–81), and of Hartman Concrete Materials Co. (1950–70). From 1951 to 1960, he was vice president and stockholder of Bakersfield Cattle Feeding Co. From 1975 to 1981, he was president and chief executive officer of the Institute for Contemporary Studies of San Francisco, Calif.

From 1972 to 1974, he served as a member of California's first appeals board of the California Occupational Safety and Health Administraton, appointed by Governor Reagan and confirmed by the California Senate. He also served as a member of the Reagan transition team and chairman of the small business task force (October 1980–January 1981).

Mr. Browne graduated (A.B.) in 1938 from the University of California at Los Angeles and attended graduate studies in 1939 and at Berkeley from 1940 to 1941. He served in the United States Navy as lieutenant from 1943 to 1945.

Nomination of Dean E. Fischer To Be an Assistant Secretary of State
June 4, 1981

The President today announced his intention to nominate Dean E. Fischer, of Virginia, to be an Assistant Secretary of State (Public Affairs). He would succeed William J. Dyess, who is resigning.

Mr. Fischer was a reporter with the Des Moines Register of Des Moines, Iowa, from 1960 to 1964. From 1964 to 1981, he has been with Time magazine, first as correspondent and most recently as news editor of the Washington bureau.

Since 1981 he has been Spokesman of the Department of State.

Mr. Fischer received his B.A. in 1958 from Monmouth College and M.A. from the University of Chicago in 1960. In 1959 he attended the University of Calcutta (India). He is married to the the former Marina Farwagi and has four children.

Exchange With Reporters Following a Luncheon With Mother Teresa of Calcutta
June 4, 1981

Q. How was your visit, Mr. President?

The President. Just wonderful. You can't be in the presence of someone like that without feeling better about the world.

Q. What do you think about the tax plan?

The President. Well, I can't talk about that now.

Q. What did you talk about with Mother Teresa?

The President. Her work, what she's doing. And just as I said, really, here is someone who's so optimistic about all of us, mankind, and what she's trying to do is very inspiring.

Q. What impressed you most about her, sir?

The President. I guess she's just the soul of kindness and great humility, because in all of her work and all that she's done, she expresses thanks for having had the opportunity to do it.

Q. Thank you, sir.

Note: The exchange began at 1:35 p.m. at the South Portico of the White House following Mother Teresa's departure.

Mother Teresa was awarded the 1979 Nobel Peace Prize for outstanding human rights missionary service in underdeveloped nations.

Nomination of Vernon A. Walters To Be United States Ambassador at Large
June 4, 1981

The President today announced his intention to nominate Vernon A. Walters, of Palm Beach, Fla., as Ambassador at Large.

General Walters was in the United States Army from 1941 to 1976, when he retired as lieutenant general. His special assignments included serving directly under Presidents Truman, Eisenhower, and Nixon; as aide to Averell Harriman at the Marshall plan in Paris; Assistant to General Eisenhower to set up SHAPE Headquarters in Paris; staff assistant to President Eisenhower on all his foreign trips; accompanied Vice President Nixon on his trip to South America in 1957; military attaché in Italy, Brazil, and France. He conducted negotiations with the North Vietnamese and Chinese in Paris from 1969 to 1972. From 1972 to 1976, he was Deputy Director of the Central Intelligence Agency.

From 1976 to 1981, he has been consultant, lecturer, and author. Since 1981 he has been senior adviser to Secretary of State Haig.

General Walters was born January 3, 1917, in New York, N.Y. He attended the St. Louis de Gonzague in Paris, and Stoneyhurst College (United Kingdom). His languages are French, Spanish, Portuguese, Italian, German, Dutch, and Russian.

Remarks on Federal Tax Reductions Following Meetings With Members of Congress
June 4, 1981

The President. Ladies and gentlemen, thank you very much for being here. I have an announcement to make.

First of all, I'd like to explain—here with me, the Vice President; Don Regan, the Secretary of the Treasury—but with me also are—and I will not attempt to do these in seniority or anything—but Senators Howard Baker, Robert Dole, Bill Roth, Harry Byrd, Lloyd Bentsen, David Boren; and from the House, Barber Conable, Kent Hance, Bob Michel, and Trent Lott.

And the statement that I'd like to make is that last November, the American people sent a clear and resounding message to Washington that the highest order of business before the nation is to restore our economic prosperity. In recent weeks, as votes have been cast on the Federal budget, we, the elected representatives, have tried to send an equally clear message back home that we're listening and we're acting.

Today I'm pleased to announce that we're prepared to move ahead on a second front—to reduce the burden of Federal taxes. And just as we did on the budget, we're moving ahead with a bipartisan coalition in the Congress. We believe that on economic recovery, there can be no Republicans and no Democrats, only Americans. And with me here this afternoon, these gentlemen that I have just introduced, are many of the leaders of the bipartisan coalition that we're building.

In the course of the past several days, we're reached agreement in principle on a tax plan that all of us can support, and the main elements are these: First, the plan provides for a 5-percent cut in the personal income tax rates, across the board, beginning this October. That will be followed by a 10-percent cut in mid-1982 and another 10-percent cut in mid-1983—for a total cut in tax rates of 25 percent over 3 years. Second, the plan provides relief from the marriage tax penalty. Third, it lowers estate and gift taxes. Fourth, it provides incentives for individuals to save and invest. Fifth, it provides for accelerated appreciation for business investment so that we can have more jobs and our products can be more competitive overseas.

Now, these tax cuts, along with others to be incorporated in our plan, are an essential companion to the budget cuts now moving through the Congress. Taken together, tax cuts and budget cuts, this package will put us back on the road to a sound economy, with lower inflation, more growth, and a government that lives within its means. Our goal is a very simple one: to rebuild this Nation so that individual Americans can once again be the masters of their own destiny. Congressmen Conable and Hance will be introducing the tax bill in the House that we fully endorse.

And now let me express a word of special appreciation to those who are with me here today from the Congress. These gentlemen and others that they represent from Capitol Hill are the leaders of a new bipartisan coalition that we're forging on behalf of the American people. We come from different backgrounds. We even come from different parties. But we're united in the belief that we must work together to rebuild this economy. The American people have suffered economically for too long, and we just want to tell them help is on the way.

And now, the great majority of us—as a matter of fact, all but one of us—are going to leave this podium and throw to the kind mercy of all of you for whatever questions you may have of the Secretary of the Treasury, Don Regan.

Reporter. I take it you think you have the votes, Mr. President?

The President. I said we wouldn't take any question—[*laughter*]—and I'm glad I said it.

Q. I assume you wouldn't be here announcing this if you didn't have the votes?

Secretary Regan. That's correct.

Note: The President spoke at 4:46 p.m. to reporters assembled in the Rose Garden at the White House.

The press release also includes the transcript of the question-and-answer session with Secretary Regan.

Proclamation 4847—National Safe Boating Week, 1981
June 4, 1981

By the President of the United States of America

A Proclamation

Americans enjoy a multitude of sports and recreational activities that serve to refresh the body and spirit. For many of our citizens, recreation means boating.

Those involved in recreational boating should always remember that the primary responsibility for safety rests with the individual. And while a cruise can be a wonderful experience for one person or an entire family, it can also result in tragedy.

Aware of the need for boating safety, the Congress enacted the joint resolution of June 4, 1958 (36 U.S.C. 161) as amended, requesting that the President proclaim a National Safe Boating Week.

Now, Therefore, I, Ronald Reagan, President of the United States of America, do hereby designate the week beginning on June 7, 1981 as National Safe Boating Week.

All Americans who utilize our waterways for recreation should possess at least a minimum knowledge of safety afloat. I urge all Americans who engage in recreational boating to take advantage of the numerous safe boating courses sponsored by governmental and private organizations. I particularly urge inexperienced operators of small boats to enroll in these safety and educational programs. Learning the fundamentals of safe boating can do nothing but add to the potential pleasure and excitement of recreational boating.

I also invite the Governors of the States, Puerto Rico, the Northern Mariana Islands, the Virgin Islands, Guam, and American Samoa, and the Mayor of the District of Columbia to provide for the observance of this week.

In Witness Whereof, I have hereunto set my hand this 4th day of June in the year of our Lord nineteen hundred and eighty-one, and of the Independence of the United States of America the two hundred and fifth.

RONALD REAGAN

[Filed with the Office of the Federal Register, 4:55 p.m., June 5, 1981]

Note: The text of the proclamation was released by the Office of the Press Secretary on June 5.

Executive Order 12307—President's Commission on Hostage Compensation
June 4, 1981

By the authority vested in me as President by the Constitution and statutes of the United States of America, in accordance with the Federal Advisory Committee Act, as amended (5 U.S.C. App. I), and to give the President's Commission on Hostage Compensation time to complete its work, it is hereby ordered that Executive Order No. 12285 (January 19, 1981) is amended as follows:

The first sentence of Section 1–202 of the Order is amended to read: "The Commission shall submit a report to the President no later than August 20, 1981."

The second sentence of Section 1–301 of the Order is amended to read: "In addition to conducting open meetings in accordance with the Federal Advisory Committee Act, the Commission may conduct public hearings to identify critical issues and possible solutions related to compensation."

RONALD REAGAN

The White House,
June 4, 1981.

[Filed with the Office of the Federal Register, 3:26 p.m., June 5, 1981]

Note: The text of the Executive order was released by the Office of the Press Secretary on June 5.

Appointment of Five Members of the President's Commission on Hostage Compensation, and Designation of Chairman
June 5, 1981

The President today announced the appointment of the following to be members of the President's Commission on Hostage Compensation and the designation of James S. Dwight, Jr., as Chairman:

James S. Dwight, Jr., currently a partner with the public accounting firm of Deloitte, Haskins and

Sells in Washington, D.C. From 1973 to 1975, he was Administrator, Social and Rehabilitation Services, at HEW. From 1972 to 1973, he was Associate Director of the Office of Management and Budget. From 1966 to 1972, he was the chief deputy director of finance for the State of California. Mr. Dwight was born March 9, 1934, in Pasadena, Calif., and resides with his wife and children in Arlington, Va.

Jeanne H. Ferst, presently a member of several civic organizations, including membership in the Atlanta Urban League, the Jewish Committee, and the International Human Assistance Foundation. From 1977 to 1980, she was a member of the Advisory Council on National Security and Foreign Affairs, Republican National Committee. From 1973 to 1978, she was a member of the Advisory Committee on Voluntary Foreign Aid, AID. From 1971 to 1973, she was appointed member of the President's Panel on South Asian Relief Assistance, and from 1969 to 1970, she was selected as a member of the U.S. Delegation to the U.N. Development Program's Governing Council in Geneva. Mrs. Ferst was born September 6, 1918, in Chicago, Ill. She resides with her husband in Atlanta, Ga.

Constance D. Armitage, associate professor of art history at Wofford College in Spartanburg, S.C. From 1972 to 1975, she was president of the National Federation of Republican Women and campaign chairman in 1980. From 1977 to 1979, she served on the board of directors and steering committee of the American Conservative Union. Mrs. Armitage was born May 13, 1920, in San Francisco, Calif. She resides in Inman, S.C.

Anderson Carter, a self-employed businessman who has been involved in politics since 1960. He was director of field operations for the Reagan for President Committee and also served as political director. Mr. Carter was born October 10, 1926, in Roswell, N. Mex. He resides with his wife in Lovington, N. Mex.

Henry Lucas, Jr., a doctor of dental surgery in San Francisco, Calif. He is also founder and member of the board of directors of Time Savings and Loan Association and is a lecturer at the University of California School of Dentistry. Dr. Lucas was born February 27, 1932, in Rahway, N.J. He and his wife reside in San Francisco, Calif.

Nomination of Charles Wilson Shuman To Be Administrator of the Farmers Home Administration
June 5, 1981

The President today announced his intention to nominate Charles Wilson Shuman to be Administrator of the Farmers Home Administration, Department of Agriculture.

Since 1977 Mr. Shuman has been with Blunt, Ellis and Loewi, Inc., in Decatur, Ill. From 1971 to 1977, he was with the Farmers Home Administration in Champaign,

Ill., as Illinois State Director. From 1958 to 1971, Mr. Shuman was a self-employed farmer in Sullivan, Ill.

Mr. Shuman graduated from the University of Illinois, College of Agriculture, in 1957.

Mr. Shuman was born June 16, 1935, and resides in Sullivan, Ill.

Nomination of Edward J. Philbin To Be a Deputy Assistant Secretary of Defense
June 5, 1981

The President today announced his intention to nominate Edward J. Philbin to be Deputy Assistant Secretary of Defense for Reserve Affairs.

Since 1979 Dr. Philbin has been Commander AFIS/RE Detached Training Site 10 at March Air Force Base in California. From 1978 to 1979, he was visiting professor of international law, Air War College, Maxwell Air Force Base in Alabama. From 1972 to 1976, he was Training Officer, Operations and Executive Officer, Air Force Intelligence Service Detachment Training Site 10, March A.F.B. In civilian life, he is a tenured professor of law and former assistant dean at the University of San Diego School of Law.

Dr. Philbin graduated from San Diego State University in 1957 and from the University of San Diego School of Law in 1965. He was born August 7, 1932, in New York, N.Y., and resides in San Diego, Calif.

Nomination of Edward C. Aldridge, Jr., To Be Under Secretary of the Air Force
June 5, 1981

The President today announced his intention to nominate Edward C. Aldridge, Jr., to be Under Secretary of the Air Force.

Since 1977 Mr. Aldridge has been vice president of the Strategic Systems Group and is responsible for the management and direction of the strategic analyses and policy planning functions of the corporation. From 1974 to 1977, he was with the Office of the Secretary of Defense as Director of Planning and Evaluation (1976–77) and Deputy Assistant Secretary of Defense for Strategic Programs (1974–76). From 1973 to 1974, he was Senior Management Associate with the Office of Management and Budget. From 1972 to 1973, he was manager, advanced concepts, with LTV Aerospace Corp. From 1967 to 1972, he was Director, Strategic Defense Division, with the Office of the Secretary of Defense. From 1962 to 1967, he was with the Douglas Aircraft Co. as manager of the Missile and Space Division.

Mr. Aldridge graduated from Texas A&M University (B.S) in 1960. He received his M.S. from Georgia Institute of Technology in 1962.

Mr. Aldridge was born August 18, 1938, in Houston, Tex. He resides in Vienna, Va.

Nomination of Frank S. Swain To Be Chief Counsel for Advocacy of the Small Business Administration
June 5, 1981

The President today announced his intention to nominate Frank S. Swain to be Chief Counsel for Advocacy, Small Business Administration.

Since 1977 Mr. Swain has been legislative counsel of the National Federation of Independent Business and has represented them on such legislation as the Regulatory Flexibility Act, Equal Access to Justice Act, the Motor Carrier Act of 1980, and the Omnibus Regulatory Reform legislation.

From 1975 to 1977, he was an attorney with the law firm of Sayles, Evans, Brayton, Palmer and Tifft in Elmira, N.Y. From 1973 to 1975, he was law clerk with the firm of O'Connor and Hannan in Washington, D.C.

Mr. Swain received his B.A. from Colgate University in 1972 and his J.D. from Georgetown University Law Center in 1975.

Mr. Swain was born January 4, 1951, in Elmira, N.Y. He resides in Washington, D.C.

Nomination of Donald Eugene Santarelli To Be a Member of the Board of Directors of the United States Synthetic Fuels Corporation
June 5, 1981

The President today announced his intention to nominate Donald Eugene Santarelli to be a member of the Board of Directors, U.S. Synthetic Fuels Corporation.

Mr. Santarelli has had a general law practice, in Washington, D.C., concentrating on government affairs. Since 1975 he has been a member of the Board of Directors of the Corporation for Public Broadcasting and is currently serving as Chairman of the Program Advisory Committee of the Board. From 1973 to 1974, he served as Administrator of the Law Enforcement Assistance Administration, Department of Justice. From 1969 to 1972, he was Associate Deputy Attorney General at the Department. From 1968 to 1969, he served as special counsel to the Senate Judiciary Committee on Constitutional Rights, Senator Sam Ervin, chairman. From 1967 to 1968, he was minority counsel to the U.S. House of Representatives Committee on the Judiciary. From 1966 to 1967, he served as assistant U.S. attorney for the District of Columbia.

Mr. Santarelli graduated from Mount St. Mary's College in 1955 and from the University of Virginia Law School in 1962.

Mr. Santarelli was born July 22, 1937, in Hershey, Pa. He resides in Alexandria, Va.

Nomination of Paul Heron Robinson, Jr., To Be United States Ambassador to Canada
June 5, 1981

The President today announced his intention to nominate Paul Heron Robinson, Jr., of Illinois, to be Ambassador to Canada. He would succeed Kenneth M. Curtis, who has resigned.

In 1960 Mr. Robinson founded and is president of Robinson Incorporated of Chicago, Ill. (broker/administrators for banks and professional institutions). He is also the principal owner of Robinson Incorporated: Washington, D.C., Boston, Mass., and San Francisco, Calif.; Robinson Coulter Limited, London, England; Robinson (Australia) Limited, Sydney, Australia; Robinson Thomson Limited, Wellington, New Zealand; and Latitude Club (a group travel club), Chicago, Ill.

Mr. Robinson was born June 22, 1930, in Chicago, Ill. He graduated (B.S.) in 1953 from the University of Illinois. From 1953 to 1955, he served in the U.S. Navy as lieutenant. He is the author of numerous financial articles.

Nomination of Richard Noyes Viets To Be United States Ambassador to Jordan
June 5, 1981

The President today announced his intention to nominate Richard Noyes Viets, of Vermont, to be Ambassador to the Hashemite Kingdom of Jordan. He would succeed Nicholas A. Veliotes, who has been named Assistant Secretary of State for Near Eastern and South Asian Affairs.

Mr. Viets was with Bank of America in

Los Angeles, Calif., in 1955 and, from 1960 to 1962, Mobil International Oil Co. in New York, N.Y.

He was with the International Communication Agency (formerly United States Information Agency) as Public Affairs Assistant from 1955 to 1957, and from 1957 to 1960, he was Assistant Exhibit Manager with the Department of Commerce. He came to the Department of State in 1962 as commerical officer in Tokyo and was commercial officer in Madras from 1965 to 1967. In New Delhi he was political and economic officer (1967–69) and special as-

sistant to the Ambassador (1969–72). In the Department he was international relations officer from 1972 to 1973 and Director of the Executive Secretariat from 1973 to 1974. From 1974 to 1977, he was Deputy Chief of Mission in Bucharest and in Tel Aviv from 1977 to 1979. Since 1979 he has been Ambassador to the United Republic of Tanzania. He is fluent in Romanian and French.

Mr. Viets was born November 10, 1930, in Burlington, Vt. He received his A.B. in 1955 from the University of Vermont. He served in the U.S. Army from 1950 to 1952.

Remarks on Presenting the Robert F. Kennedy Medal to Mrs. Ethel Kennedy
June 5, 1981

The President. Mrs. Kennedy, the Congress has authorized the presentation of a medal for you in recognition of the distinguished and dedicated service which your husband, Robert Kennedy, gave to the government and to the people of the United States.

Robert Kennedy's service to his country, his commitment to his great ideals, and his devotion to those less fortunate than himself are matters now for history and need little explanation from me. The facts of Robert Kennedy's public career stand alone. He roused the comfortable. He exposed the corrupt, remembered the forgotten, inspired his countrymen, and renewed and enriched the American conscience.

Those of us who had our philosophical disagreements with him always appreciated his wit and his personal grace. And may I say I remember very vividly those last days of the California primary and the closeness that had developed in our views about the growing size and unresponsiveness of government and our political institutions. Among the last words he spoke to this Nation that night in Los Angeles were, "What I think is quite clear is that we can work together in the last analysis, and that is what has been going on within the

United States—the division, the violence, the disenchantment with our society; the divisions, whether it's between blacks and whites, between poor and more affluent, or between age groups or on the war in Vietnam—is that we can start to work together. We are a great country, an unselfish country, and a compassionate country."

Obviously, many of you here knew him better than most. You knew him as husband, as brother, as father, and uncle. He wrote to his son, Joseph, on the day of President Kennedy's death, "Remember all the things that Jack started. Be kind to others that are less fortunate than we and love our country." And it is in the final triumph of Robert Kennedy that he used his personal gifts to bring this message of hope and love to the country, to millions of Americans who supported and believed in him. "Come my friends," he liked to quote the Tennyson lines, "it's not too late to seek a newer world." And this is how we should remember him, beyond the distinguished public service or our own sadness that he is gone.

His friend, composer John Stuart, said about him what he said about the first fallen Kennedy and about us: that when a chill wind takes the sky, we should remember the years he gave us hope, for they can never die.

So, Mrs. Kennedy, this medal has been waiting patiently to be presented.

Mrs. Kennedy. Thank you so much.

Senator Kennedy. Mr. President and Mrs. Reagan and friends of my brother here at this ceremony and everywhere, on behalf of Ethel and her children and all the members of our family, let me thank you, Mr. President, for this great honor that you have given to Robert Kennedy. And it is appropriate that he should receive it from you, for he understood so well that the common love of our country transcends all party identification and all partisan difference. And you should know that after he debated you on international television in 1967, my brother Bob said that Ronald Reagan was the toughest debater he ever faced and, obviously, he was right. [*Laughter*]

Robert Kennedy was a man of action but also of vision. From memory, he so often quoted Shaw's words that they were finally his own bywords. And so he dreamed things that never were and said, "Why not?" And I hope that when we think of him now, we will think as he did of all those who have no one else to care for their concerns. He gave his strength for those who were weak. He gave his voice for those who had no special interest to speak for them, and he always remembered those who were forgotten. He had an uncommon feeling for the common people who make America work. He had often walked the corridors of power in this White House and conferred with the mighty here, but he could walk with equal grace through migrant camps or talk with utter ease to workers on an assembly line.

There was at once an intensity and a gentleness in him that made him a unique spark of hope in a dark time. The violence that struck him down has threatened and touched so many others. The nation and the world have felt the pain so recently. Those of us who were with Robert Kennedy when he died in 1968 felt a special sense of relief

this year, Mr. President, at your own recovery from the attack against you.

And today, all the Kennedys feel a special sense of pride in the brother, husband, father, and son who went before us. He was often misunderstood in life. But people everywhere know how much he meant, for they have missed him so much all the years since his loss.

To you, Mr. President, to the Congress, and to our fellow citizens, we are grateful for this gracious tribute today. Our family is grateful to Ethel, the light of his life, who stood with him on countless platforms around the nation and around the world, a friend who has sustained our spirits in dark passages and bright days.

And I speak here for many others who loved Robert Kennedy as well. How proud our remarkable mother is of what he did and of this recognition. And if they were here, that pride would be shared by my father, by Joe and Jack and Kathleen, who always knew that while Bobby was the smallest, he had the biggest heart.

Thirteen years ago at this hour, Robert Kennedy lay dying of his wounds. And accepting this medal in his memory, I would say again what I said when we took leave of him. He was a good and decent man who saw wrong and tried to right it, saw suffering and tried to heal it, saw war and tried to stop it.

And my prayer would be the same. Those of us who loved and who took him to his rest that day continue to pray that what he was for us and what he wished for others will some day come to pass for all the world.

Thank you.

Note: The President spoke at 11:40 a.m. at the presentation ceremony in the Rose Garden at the White House. Prior to the ceremony, the President met in the Oval Office with Senator Edward M. Kennedy and Ethel Kennedy and her children.

The gold medal was authorized by the 95th Congress on November 1, 1978.

Executive Order 12308—Presidential Task Force on the Arts and Humanities
June 5, 1981

By the authority vested in me as President by the Constitution of the United States of America, and to establish in accordance with the provisions of the Federal Advisory Committee Act, as amended (5 U.S.C. App. I), an advisory committee on arts and humanities of the United States, it is hereby ordered as follows:

Section 1. Establishment. (a) There is hereby established the Presidential Task Force on the Arts and Humanities. The Task Force shall be composed of no more than 36 members appointed by the President. No more than one member shall be a full-time Federal officer or employee. The remaining members shall not represent Executive agencies.

(b) The President shall designate three Cochairmen and one Vice Chairman from among the members of the Task Force.

Sec. 2. Functions. (a) The Task Force shall advise the President with respect to:

(1) methods to increase private support for the arts and humanities;

(2) ways in which Federal decisions regarding arts and humanities projects can rely more on the judgments of nongovernmental professionals, private sector groups, and individuals; and

(3) potential improvements in the management, organization and structure of (i) the National Foundation on the Arts and the Humanities (including the National Endowment for the Arts, the National Endowment for the Humanities and the Federal Council on the Arts and the Humanities) and (ii) other Federal arts and humanities programs.

(b) The Task Force shall report its findings and recommendations to the President, the Chairman of the National Endowment for the Arts, and the Chairman of the National Endowment for the Humanities.

Sec. 3. Administration. (a) The heads of Executive agencies shall, to the extent permitted by law, provide the Task Force with such information with respect to arts and humanities issues as may be necessary for the effective performance of its functions.

(b) Members of the Task Force shall receive no compensation for their work on the Task Force. However, while engaged in the work of the Task Force, members may be allowed travel expenses, including per diem in lieu of subsistence, as authorized by law for persons serving intermittently in the government service (5 U.S.C. 5701-5707).

(c) The National Endowment for the Humanities shall, to the extent permitted by law and subject to the availability of funds, provide the Task Force with such administrative services, funds, facilities, staff and other support services as may be necessary for the effective performance of its functions.

Sec. 4. General Provisions. (a) Notwithstanding the provisions of any other Executive order, the responsibilities of the President under the Federal Advisory Committee Act, as amended, except that of reporting annually to the Congress, which are applicable to the advisory committee established by this Order, shall be performed by the Chairman of the National Endowment for the Humanities, in accordance with the guidelines and procedures established by the Administrator of General Services.

(b) The Task Force shall terminate on September 30, 1981, unless sooner extended.

RONALD REAGAN

The White House,
June 5, 1981.

[*Filed with the Office of the Federal Register, 4:56 p.m., June 5, 1981*]

Appointment of the Membership of the Presidential Task Force on the Arts and Humanities
June 5, 1981

The President today announced the membership of the Presidential Task Force on the Arts and Humanities. The members will serve with Cochairmen Hanna H. Gray, Charlton Heston, and Daniel J. Terra, and Vice Chairman W. Barnabas McHenry. The Task Force will recommend to the President ways in which private support for the arts and humanities might be enhanced.

The members of the Task Force are:

Margo Albert, actress, member, National Council on the Arts

Dr. Edward C. Banfield, author, professor of government, Harvard University

Anne Bass, trustee, Fort Worth Art Museum

Dr. Daniel J. Boorstin, Librarian of Congress

Dr. William G. Bowen, president, Princeton University

Joseph Coors, president, Adolph Coors Co.

Armand Deutsch, member, board of directors, Center Theatre Group, Los Angeles Music Center

Virginia B. Duncan, Bechtel Corp.

Robert Fryer, artistic director, Ahmanson Theatre, Los Angeles Music Center

Henry Geldzahler, commissioner of cultural affairs, New York City

Gordon Hanes, chairman of the board, Hanes Corp.

Nancy Hanks, former Chairman, National Endowment for the Arts

Dr. Paul R. Hanna, Hoover Institution

Ernest J. Kump, architect

June Noble Larkin, trustee, Edward John Noble Foundation

Dr. Robert M. Lumiansky, president, American Council of Learned Societies

Angus MacDonald, president, Angus MacDonald & Co., founder, cochairman, MIT Council on the Arts

Nancy Mehta, former vice president, Four Hundred Group, Los Angeles Music Center

Arthur Mitchell, choreographer, Dance Theater of Harlem

Dr. Franklin D. Murphy, chairman of the board, Times Mirror Corp.

David Packard, chairman of the board, Hewlett-Packard Co.

Edmund Pillsbury, director, Kimbell Art Museum

Dr. George C. Roche, president, Hillsdale College

Richard Mellon Scaife, chairman of the board, Tribune Review Publishing Co.

Franklin Schaffner, film producer and director, member, National Council on the Arts

Beverly Sills, general director, New York City Opera

Leonard Silverstein, chairman of the executive committee, National Symphony Orchestra, Washington, D.C.

Robert I. Smith, president, Glen Meade Trust

Roger Stevens, Chairman of the Board of Trustees, John F. Kennedy Center for the Performing Arts

John Swearingen, chairman of the board, Standard Oil Co.

Lucien Wulsin, chief executive officer, Baldwin United Corp.

Rawleigh Warner, Jr., chairman of the board, Mobil Oil Corp.

Nomination of Davis R. Robinson To Be Legal Adviser of the Department of State
June 5, 1981

The President today announced his intention to nominate Davis R. Robinson to be Legal Adviser, Department of State.

Since 1971 Mr. Robinson has been an associate and, since 1975, a partner in the law firm of Leva, Hawes, Symington, Martin and Oppenheimer in Washington, D.C. From 1969 to 1971, he was an associate with the law firm of Sullivan & Cromwell in New York. From 1961 to 1969, he was a Foreign Service officer with the Department of State.

Mr. Robinson graduated from Yale College (B.A.) in 1961 and from Harvard Law School in 1967.

Mr. Robinson was born July 11, 1940, in New York, N.Y. He resides in Washington, D.C.

Nomination of Henry M. Rivera To Be a Member of the Federal Communications Commission
June 5, 1981

The President today announced his intention to nominate Henry M. Rivera to be a member of the Federal Communications Commission for the term expiring June 30, 1987, succeeding James H. Quello, whose term has expired.

Since 1973 Mr. Rivera has been an attorney with the law firm of Sutin, Thayer & Browne and is currently a partner of that firm. From 1968 to 1970, Mr. Rivera served in the U.S. Army in Vietnam.

Mr. Rivera graduated from the University of New Mexico (B.A.) in 1968 and from the University of New Mexico (J.D.) in 1973.

He was born September 25, 1947, in New Mexico. Mr. Rivera is married, with one child, and resides in Albuquerque, N. Mex.

Nomination of James Henry Quello To Be a Member of the Federal Communications Commission
June 5, 1981

The President today announced his intention to nominate James Henry Quello to be a member of the Federal Communications Commission for the remainder of the term expiring June 30, 1984, succeeding Charles D. Ferris, who is resigning.

Since 1974 Mr. Quello has been a member of the Federal Communications Commission. From 1972 to 1974, he was a communications consultant in Michigan. From 1947 to 1972, he was vice president and station manager for Goodwill Stations, Inc., in Detroit, Mich.

Mr. Quello has been a member of the Governor's Special Commisssion on Urban Problems, Governor's Special Study Committee on Legislative Compensation, Mayor's Committee on Human Relations, and assistant national public relations chairman for the VFW. He has served as TV-radio chairman of the United Foundation, executive board member of the Boy Scouts of America, and a member of the board of the American Negro Emancipation Centennial.

He was born in Laurium, Mich., on April 21, 1914, and resides in Alexandria, Va.

Statement by Deputy Press Secretary Speakes on the Withdrawal of the Nomination of Ernest W. Lefever To Be an Assistant Secretary of State
June 5, 1981

The President this evening reaffirmed his confidence in the integrity and competence of Dr. Lefever. The President was prepared to stand behind his nomination until final disposition by the Senate, and he deeply regrets that the nation will lose the benefit of his services.

Note: The statement was released in response to Dr. Lefever's letter to the President requesting that his nomination to be Assistant Secretary of State for Human Rights and Humanitarian Affairs be withdrawn. Earlier in the day, the Senate Foreign Relations Committee had voted 13–4 against favorable consideration of the nomination in the Senate.

Mr. Lefever's nomination was withdrawn by the President on June 16.

Remarks at the Welcoming Ceremony for President José López Portillo of Mexico
June 8, 1981

President Reagan. I warmly welcome President López Portillo on behalf of the people of the United States. But I also want to convey my personal greetings because of my personal respect and affection. The relationship we've built as individuals is indicative of a new dimension that we are bringing to the friendship between our two countries.

Our planned meeting of 2 months ago, which I was looking forward to with great anticipation, was abruptly canceled. And I want to thank you, Mr. President, for the consideration you've shown in visiting us here in Washington. You've done us a great honor in your visit to the White House.

You'll recall, Mr. President, the last time we met was in the Museum of Art, part of Mexico's rich cultural past—that was in Ciudad Juarez. We were surrounded there by magnificent pieces of art, part of Mexico's rich cultural past. It was appropriate that we should meet in such a place, for art transcends time and material consideration.

The same is true of the friendship between the peoples of Mexico and the United States. In a world filled with neighbors who resort to violence, neighbors who've lost sight of the shared values and mutual interests, the good will between Mexico and the United States is a blossom whose beauty we meet here to cherish and protect.

God made Mexico and the United States neighbors, but it is our duty and the duty of generations yet to come to make sure that we remain friends. I welcome you today with the pledge that this administration will sincerely and diligently strive to maintain a relationship of mutual respect and cooperation between our two nations and that decisions which affect both sides of our border will be made only after the closest consultation between our governments. Our very proximity is an opportunity to demonstrate to the world how two nations, talking together as equals, as partners, as friends, can solve their problems and deepen their mutual respect.

Mr. President, you are a scholar, a man of art, and a political leader of a proud and independent nation. There are many items of importance on our agenda. I look forward to a far-reaching exchange of views that will cement the ties between us. The personal friendship that we're developing must be equaled by the closeness between our two peoples.

President López Portillo. Mr. President, under the sign of friendship which began in Ciudad Juarez, it is now for me a great pleasure to be here in the Capital City of your great country.

We are sorry that we did not meet in Tijuana as we had planned. But I am very happy that we are meeting now here at the White House, and it also pleases me enormously to see that you have totally recovered from the attempt that was brought on by absurd violence. I am very happy to see that you have enormous capacity of recovery. And in your good health and in your strength, I can see the good health and the strength of your nation.

There are few countries in the world that have so many items to deal with among themselves as the United States and Mexico. We're not only neighbors, we are also the representatives of two worlds. Literally and geographically speaking, we represent the North and the South along 3,000 kilometers of border. Therefore, there are structural matters between us that have been shaped by our history and our geography.

We also represent the relationship between the developing world and the world that has already been developed. And we're also immersed in a regional context that shapes our relationship. I come here now, sir, as a friend without any prejudice, to talk over these matters with you and to prove with my coming that there can be friendship among friends and that this friendship can have as its main pillar and basis the rule of reason.

In an absurd world, the reasonable thing to do can be the possible thing to do. And what is reasonable is based on respect and on the law. There are many problems that we have to deal with. We will be very happy to find our similarities. And when we do not have coinciding opinions—and it is very possible that in this world of plurality there may be times when we do not have coinciding opinions—then we will talk things over without arrogance.

Arrogance is a dangerous deviation of they who are in a weaker position. The other very dangerous aspect is submission. We will select the road of respect and the rule of reason without any submission and without any arrogance.

I believe that few times in our history has there been an opportunity for good understanding as there is today to understand each other well and to deepen and make headway in our relationship.

I feel, Mr. President, that you have great good will and a friendly feeling. I feel that you are a decent individual and an honest one. I shall make a great effort to respond to the kindnesses that you have with me.

We have established a friendship which no doubt will be both symbolic and solid. I am absolutely certain that we will [be] able to achieve what our two peoples and nations want of us. We want to be understood, and in turn, we want to understand. We want to respect, and we want to be respected. We want a solid relationship that will seek out the mutual interests of two countries that are neighbors and friends.

I am very certain, Mr. President, that if we go beyond rhetoric and prejudice, we shall be able to achieve our goals. And this will be for the good of both countries.

I thank you very much.

Note: President Reagan spoke at 10:35 a.m. at the South Portico of the White House. President López Portillo spoke in Spanish, and his remarks were translated by an interpreter.

Following their remarks, the two Presidents met briefly in the Yellow Oval Room, and then they left the White House for an overnight stay at Camp David, Md. Following their arrival there, they met for discussions, first privately and then with their delegations.

In the evening, President Reagan hosted a dinner for President López Portillo and his delegation.

Nomination of Samuel J. Cornelius To Be Deputy Director of the Community Services Administration
June 8, 1981

The President today announced his intention to nominate Samuel J. Cornelius to be Deputy Director of the Community Services Administration.

Mr. Cornelius is president of Cornelius-Wiggins Internationale, Inc., a business management and public relations firm. From 1979 to April 10, 1981, he was director, Economic Development Assistance Center. Previously, in 1974–77, he served as Deputy Director of the Office of Minority Business Enterprise, Department of Commerce. Mr. Cornelius was Regional Director, Office of Economic Opportunity, Kansas City, Mo., in 1970–74. In 1967–70 he was director, Nebraska Technical Assistance Agency, and assistant to the Governor, State of Nebraska. He previously held various positions with the Young Men's Christian Association (YMCA) in Nebraska, California, Kansas, and Oklahoma.

Mr. Cornelius was graduated from Anderson College (B.S., 1953), Anderson, Ind. He is married, has five children, and resides in Silver Spring, Md. He was born April 14, 1928, in Kansas City, Mo.

Nomination of Lawrence Y. Goldberg To Be an Assistant Director of the Community Services Administration
June 8, 1981

The President today announced his intention to nominate Lawrence Y. Goldberg to be an Assistant Director of the Community Services Administration (External Affairs).

Mr. Goldberg was president of Lawrence Y. Goldberg Associates, Inc. During the 1980 Presidential campaign, he served as executive director of Coalition for Reagan-Bush. Previously, in 1974–77, Mr. Goldberg was Assistant Director of the Federal Preparedness Agency. In 1973–74 he was vice president, Brandeis University, Waltham, Mass. In 1973 he was special advisor to the Counsellor to the President for Community Development. In 1957–71 Mr. Goldberg was executive vice president, American Leisure Products, Warwick, R.I. He was Legislative Counsel, Small Business Administration, in 1959–60.

In 1974–75 Mr. Goldberg was a member of the U.S. Advisory Commission on International Education and Cultural Affairs. He also served on the Stanton Commission on International Information, Education and Cultural Affairs.

Mr. Goldberg was graduated from Brown University (A.B., 1953) and Harvard Law School (J.D., 1956). He is married, has two children, and resides in Pawtucket, R.I. He was born July 21, 1931, in Providence, R.I.

Nomination of Thomas Morgan Roberts To Be a Member of the Nuclear Regulatory Commission
June 8, 1981

The President today announced his intention to nominate Thomas Morgan Roberts to be a member of the Nuclear Regulatory Commission.

Mr. Roberts was with the Southern Boiler & Tank Works, Inc., from 1962 to 1978 and was president and chief executive officer from 1969 to 1978. He has been an underwriting member of Lloyd's of London; director of the Boyle Investment Co., a real estate sales and development firm; and a former member of the employee benefits committee of the National Association of Manufacturers.

Mr. Roberts received his B.S. degree in industrial engineering from the Georgia Institute of Technology in 1959.

He was born April 14, 1937, in Memphis, Tenn. He is married, with three children, and resides in Washington, D.C.

Message to the Congress Reporting Budget Rescissions
June 8, 1981

To the Congress of the United States:

In accordance with the Impoundment Control Act of 1974, I herewith report four proposals to rescind a total of $114.1 million in budget authority previously provided by the Congress. The rescission proposals affect programs in the Environmental Protection Agency and the National Endowments for the Arts and Humanities. These proposals are a part of my continuing effort to help reduce government spending.

The details of the rescission proposals are contained in the attached reports.

RONALD REAGAN

The White House,
June 8, 1981.

Note: The attachments detailing the rescission proposals are printed in the Federal Register *of June 11, 1981.*

Nomination of Alvin W. Trivelpiece To Be Director of the Office of Energy Research
June 9, 1981

The President today announced his intention to nominate Alvin W. Trivelpiece to be Director of the Office of Energy Research, Department of Energy.

Dr. Trivelpiece is a physicist with extensive experience in various areas of plasma physics and fusion research. Since 1978 he has been corporate vice president of Science Applications, Inc., of La Jolla, Calif. Dr. Trivelpiece's responsibilities at SAI include exploration of business opportunities in new technical areas. In 1976–78 he was vice president for engineering and research at Maxwell Laboratories, San Diego, Calif. Dr. Trivelpiece was Assistant Director for Research, Division of Controlled Thermonuclear Research, Atomic Energy Commission, in 1973–75. In 1966–76 he was professor of physics at the University of Maryland. Previously he was professor, electrical engineering department, University of California (Berkeley) in 1959–65.

Dr. Trivelpiece is the author or coauthor of over 100 technical papers and reports. He is a fellow of the American Association for the Advancement of Science, the American Physical Society, and the Institute of Electrical and Electronic Engineers.

Dr. Trivelpiece was graduated from California State Polytechnic College (B.S., 1953) and California Institute of Technology (M.S., 1955; Ph. D., 1958). He is married, has three children, and resides in California. He was born March 15, 1931, in Stockton, Calif.

Nomination of Dallas Lynn Peck To Be Director of the Geological Survey
June 9, 1981

The President today announced his intention to nominate Dallas Lynn Peck to be Director of the Geological Survey, Department of the Interior.

Since 1951 Dr. Peck has held various positions with the U.S. Geological Survey. In 1951–53 he was a geologic field assistant, geologist in 1954–77, and Chief Geologist since 1977.

He has served as an adviser to the National Science Foundation (Earth Sciences Advisory Committee) in 1960–72; National Research Council (Fullbright-Hays Program, Advisory Screening Committee for Earth Sciences) in 1974–77; National Research Council (advisory board to the Office of

Earth Sciences) in 1975–79. In 1972 Dr. Peck was a delegate to Moscow as a member of the US/USSR Joint Commission on Scientific and Technical Cooperation—Energy Working Group. He is a recipient of the Department of the Interior Meritorious Award (1970), Distinguished Service Award (1979), and Presidential Meritorious Executive Award (1980).

Dr. Peck was graduated from the California Institute of Technology (B.S., 1951; M.S., 1953) and Harvard University (Ph. D., 1960). He is married, has three children, and resides in Reston, Va. He was born March 28, 1929, in Cheney, Wash.

Nomination of William M. Otter To Be Administrator of the Wage and Hour Division
June 9, 1981

The President today announced his intention to nominate William M. Otter to be Administrator of the Wage and Hour Division, Department of Labor.

Mr. Otter is an attorney and has been in private practice for 19 years, mostly involved in negotiating collective bargaining contracts with labor unions. He served as a consultant and analyst to the Occupational Safety and Health Administration in 1971–

76. In 1968-71 Mr. Otter was director, Department of Labor, State of Kentucky.

Mr. Otter was graduated from Washington & Lee University (A.B., 1946), University of Louisville (J.D., 1948), and University of Michigan Law School (J.S.D., A.B.D., 1952–53). He is married, has four children, and resides in Prospect, Ky. He was born April 2, 1923, in Louisville, Ky.

Toasts of the President and President José López Portillo of Mexico at the Luncheon Honoring the Mexican President
June 9, 1981

President Reagan. President López Portillo, some years ago when I was Governor of California, I was inspecting areas in our State which had been enormously damaged by one of those natural catastrophes that we

sometimes see on the Pacific coast—great mudslides that can sweep away a man's home in a matter of moments.

One of these belonged to an old gentleman from your country, who was standing

497

in the middle of what, before the slide, had been his living room. We were both knee-deep in mud. It must have been heartbreaking for him, because his home had obviously been newly furnished. Now it was a scene of ruin. With quiet dignity and the utmost sincerity, he said, "Governor Reagan, *mi casa es su casa*"—my house is your house. I was deeply moved, and I realized that I was witness to what was purely and traditionally Hispanic—personal pride and courage in the face of adversity.

Today, Mr. President, the entire nation is happy to have you with us here in the White House. And since this house belongs to all of them, may I say on behalf of my fellow citizens, "*Mi casa es su casa.*"

From the moment of our meeting on the Friendship Bridge at Ciudad Juarez last January, I was certain that we would make our relationship more than symbolic, not only because our peoples expect certain cordiality between their leaders but because the leader of the Mexican people exemplifies so well the proud culture and heritage of his people. When you took that highly symbolic step across the boundary to grasp my hand, I knew that our future relationship would be that of personal friends.

Your concern and good wishes during my period of hospitalization were deeply appreciated. The Vice President told me of your concern for my health and of your most generous offer to travel to Washington for this meeting even though protocol called for me to visit you.

At our first meeting, you gave me a splendid example of your own artistry, drawings of horses etched on glass, drawn by you, that are now proudly displayed behind my desk in the Oval Office. And I value greatly the volumes on beautiful art of your country. But it would be difficult to match the gift that arrived at our ranch shortly before my Inauguration—El Alamain, a magnificent horse, your personal mount. Now, that was more than friendship; you took me into your family.

But I remember, too, that you presented me with a bound volume of a book that you wrote on Quetzalcoatl—almost had trouble there. [*Laughter*] It has much to say about your people. It also says much about the man who leads them today. I found especially relevant to your land the words of Quetzalcoatl to his newborn son: "You are made with the fibers of joy and sorrow, of laughter and tears. You are at the edge of all the possibilities and soon you will have the strength to choose. You will be the course and the measure of the richness and misery. You will be the eagle and the serpent. With your pain, you will maintain the conscience of the universe, with your laughter, the dignity of Man."

Later in the book, Quetzalcoatl, perplexed by the problems of governing, said something we can both relate to: "Despite its regularity, this world is a confused sphere of arbitrary things." The art of politics is sometimes frustrating, but there are other times of confidence and optimism, and your visit has been such a time.

I listened very carefully to you in our meetings, Mr. President, noting the content and the spirit with which you spoke. Your presence inspires confidence that we can calm any of the tensions that inevitably arise between two such close neighbors.

During your election campaign in 1976, you traveled through all 31 of Mexico's states, spreading new hope. The message you brought to the Mexican people is something that can serve as a cornerstone for our relationship as well. If problems arise between us, we must always remember we are the solution. There is nothing that with mutual respect and honest communication we cannot work out together.

I look forward to our next meeting in Cancún, Mexico, in October. In saluting you today, I thank you for your generosity, but more, I thank you for the continued good will between our two peoples that your visit represents.

And so, I ask all of you to join me in a toast to José López Portillo, the President of Mexico.

President López Portillo. Mr. President, Mrs. Reagan, my friends:

I must confess that I am moved. I must confess that I have spoken in this same place three times before, and I have never done so as moved as I feel today.

It is true that I had always been sincere, but also cautious. I had always spoken frankly, but I have always measured the weight of each one of my words, because the relationship, for some reason or another, had always been a tense one. A relationship between neighbors that are so different are always difficult. It is difficult for the one side and for the other. But I confess for the first time now I have felt totally relaxed.

For the first time a President of the United States has used with me that very generous formula of "my home is your home." And for we who understand the greatness and dignity that there is behind that expression, what I have heard from the President today has deeply moved me—as I can understand very well that he felt deeply moved also when he heard that old man that had no roof over his head and who was offering him his home, because a home is the environment of respect for the intimacy of the human being. And when one gives one's intimacy in friendship, it is that that he is giving.

We understand this to be so, Mr. President, and we thank you for this. But I must also say that it has not only been the external behavior but also the substantive part of our relationship that has always been generous, kind, and affectionate.

If all the powerful people in the world were to truly understand what respect means to the weak people, the world would totally change. It is not only to give, not only to help; the most important thing of all is to respect. He who gives without respect is usually offensive. Very frequently I am reminded, and I remind others, that the first civic expression that we learn as children is the one that was said by one our great men and Presidents [Benito Juarez], the counterpart, so to speak, of Abraham Lincoln. He said, "Respect for the rights of others is peace." The first word that we Mexicans learn in our civic behavior is the word "respect." And this is the way, ladies and gentlemen, which we have been treated. We have been treated with respect and with friendship, and these are basic qualities to us.

On that basis, everything can be built. One can coincide, one can dissent; human beings are made in many and various different ways and shapes. And in our plurality, we should learn to coexist and to tolerate

one another. Tolerance in itself is respect. And when a human relationship is built on respect, it is indestructible. We have spoken about many things. Fortunately, we have agreed on most of them. We have dissented on some. But with the greatest respect, we have agreed to talk about the matters on which we dissent in order to find appropriate solutions.

Intolerance has not come to cancel out opportunity, and that is very important for a good relationship between countries such as ours. It is important, because it is a representative sample of what is happening in the world—the relationship between the countries that have been able to develop and the developing nations. And in a geographic analogy, we could say that this is an expression of the North-South relationship.

We are the most significant relationship between the North and the South. That is why, Mr. President, I have felt so happy and so grateful that you have accepted our invitation to come to Cancún, because we do not only have concepts in mind, but we have direct experiences and reciprocal experiences. I am very certain that the special characteristics of our relationship, North-South relationship, that is, United States-Mexico, can be taken to generalization and that it will be useful, that it can be useful. And this is what we fervently wish—it can be useful for the rest of mankind.

We want appropriate communication so that political will can be expressed. And political will has been expressed here and now today in the United States as regards Mexico and with reference to Mexico as regards the United States within an environment of good will, peace, respect, and consideration for each other.

I believe, Mr. President, that in Cancún we can be a stimulating example to help and participate in the détente of this world which is so complex and at times so absurd, because if the disasters brought on by nature that create all these things for human beings are absurd in themselves— these disasters that leave old men without a roof over their heads but still with their dignity—nature, in that case, nature that has its own strength and will, cannot be controlled by us. But there is something that leaves man without a roof over his head and which is not nature—and I'm talking about passions, ambition, intolerance, violence—vices all of human will. And it is up to the will of the human being to correct these mistakes. Perhaps we can do nothing against nature, but we can do a great deal with our will if we're talking about good will, and I do believe that good will is possible. And I believe that in Cancún, we shall have the opportunity to say that is possible and to confirm that we're speaking the truth.

I would hope, Mr. President, that we will know how to lay bridges that will make it possible for all men and women in the world to say to each other, "My friends, this is your home."

Thank you.

I would like to propose a toast to the health of President Reagan and his beautiful wife, to the friendship of Mexico and the United States. To your health.

Note: President Reagan spoke at 2:06 p.m. in the East Room at the White House. President López Portillo spoke in Spanish, and his remarks were translated by an interpreter.

Earlier in the day, the two Presidents and members of their delegations held a breakfast meeting at Camp David. Following their return to the White House, President Reagan, President López Portillo, Secretary of State Alexander M. Haig, Jr., Mexican Secretary of Foreign Relations Jorge Castañeda de la Rose, and Richard V. Allen, Assistant to the President for National Security Affairs, met in the Oval Office. The two Presidents and their delegations then met in the Cabinet Room.

Remarks on the Departure of President José López Portillo of Mexico
June 9, 1981

Ladies and gentlemen of the press, thank you very much for being here.

I just want to express my appreciation for President López Portillo's changing his schedule and coming to Washington to accommodate us. The talks that we've had were frank, they were valuable, and they lead to a closer relationship between our two countries. In addition to that, I'm very proud, personally, to say that we have a warm and a close personal relationship between the two of us.

Our frank discussion revealed basic agreement on the need to strengthen the economies of the less developed nations, to bring about social and economic development of their peoples. We agreed that this was the best way to assure the region's future stability, and we'll be exchanging ideas on how best to bring about such development.

We agreed that the special nature of our relations required a special framework for doing business. We decided to form a bilateral Foreign Secretaries commission to assure integrated handling of matters of common concern. It will be cochaired by Secretary Haig and Secretary Castañeda. They will submit a report by December 31st, 1981.

Because trade problems are essentially and especially urgent, we also decided to set up immediately a Cabinet-level trade committee to recommend how to go about dealing with outstanding bilateral trade questions. The committee will be cochaired by the Mexican and United States Secretaries of Commerce and the United States Trade Representative. The committee will begin work as soon as possible. We also agreed to address outstanding fisheries problems on a similar urgent basis.

An important agreement providing for supply of substantial quantities of United States grain to Mexico during 1982 was signed by Secretary Block for the United States and Secretary de la Vega for Mexico. Attorney General Smith briefed the Mexican party in detail on the various options we're now considering to deal with the undocumented migrant problem. And I assured the President that the United States would take Mexico's interest in this problem fully into consideration, as well as the interests and rights of the individual migrants themselves.

I had the great pleasure of informing the President that the legislature has acted, the Congress has acted, and we are going forward with construction of the Otay Mesa additional border crossing to relieve the logjam that we have at the San Ysidro crossing there. It is badly needed on the California Baja border. And we agreed that it would be an important boost to tourism in both directions.

President López Portillo formally invited me to participate in a meeting of heads of government, an international meeting to be held in Cancún, Mexico, in October, and I happily accepted that invitation. I look forward to the informal discussion of North-South questions which will occur at that meeting, as well as additional meetings that we have spoken of.

And now comes the—I shall present President López Portillo for his farewell, but it is a sad moment now. We have had a fine, warm, friendly, and productive meeting

Note: President Reagan spoke at 2:43 p.m. to reporters assembled at the North Portico of the White House.

Statement on the Introduction of Federal Tax Reduction Legislation in the House of Representatives
June 9, 1981

I want to commend Congressmen Barber Conable and Kent Hance for the introduction of a new bipartisan tax bill [H.R. 3849] this afternoon. This bill, carefully crafted during hours of discussion with members of both parties, brings with it fresh hope of economic progress for all Americans.

My administration is fully committed to this bill, and I trust that in coming weeks we will build a strong, national, bipartisan consensus for its passage.

In recent weeks, the American people have heard a great deal about taxes, some of it perhaps confusing, but there is now only one bill before the House—the bill introduced today—that offers true tax relief and a new economic beginning.

Executive Order 12309—President's Economic Policy Advisory Board
June 9, 1981

By the authority vested in me as President by the Constitution of the United States of America, and in order to amend the limitations on membership for the President's Economic Policy Advisory Board, it is hereby ordered that the second sentence of Section 1(a) of Executive Order No. 12296 of March 2, 1981, is amended by deleting "from private life who shall be."

RONALD REAGAN

The White House,
June 9, 1981.

[*Filed with the Office of the Federal Register, 3:23 p.m., June 10, 1981*]

Note: The text of the Executive order was released by the Office of the Press Secretary on June 10.

Appointment of the 1981–82 White House Fellows
June 10, 1981

The President today announced the appointments of the 1981–82 White House fellows. This is the 17th class of Fellows since the program began in 1964.

The 15 Fellows were chosen from among 1,650 applicants and screened by 11 regional panels. The President's Commission on White House Fellowships, chaired by Vice Adm. James B. Stockdale, USN (Ret.), interviewed the 33 national finalists before recommending the 15 persons to the President. Their year of government service will begin on September 1, 1981.

The 1981-82 White House fellows are:

Paul V. Applegarth, 35, of McLean, Va., Chief of the Financial Analysis Division, World Bank, Washington, D.C.;

Joe Linus Barton, 31, of Ennis, Tex., assistant to the vice president, Ennis Business Forms, Ennis, Tex.;

Richard Eugene Birney, 32, of Marietta, Ga., assistant for technology, information systems division, International Business Machines, Atlanta, Ga.;

Wayne Dale Collins, 29, of New York, N.Y., attorney, Shearman & Sterling, New York, N.Y.;

Priscilla Harriet Douglas, 33, of Cambridge, Mass., research fellow, Joint Center for Urban Studies, MIT/Harvard, Cambridge, Mass.;

Ellen Elizabeth Heineman, 33, of Arlington, Va., lieutenant commander, U.S. Navy Office of Program Appraisal, Office of the Secretary of the Navy, the Pentagon, Washington, D.C.;

David Kemp Karnes, 32, of Omaha, Nebr., attorney, partner, Morsman, Fike, Davis and Schumacher, P.C., Omaha, Nebr.;

Mary Elisabeth Lupo Ricci, 33, of Palm Beach Gardens, Fla., county court judge, Fifteenth Judicial Circuit, West Palm Beach, Fla.;

Thomas Counter Shull, 29, of Somerville, Mass., infantry captain, U.S. Army, who is currently scheduled to teach in the Department of Behavioral Sciences and Leadership at West Point, N.Y.;

James K. Stewart, 38, of Orinda, Calif., captain, commanding, criminal investigation division, Oakland Police Department, Oakland, Calif.;

Howard Patrick Sweeney, 37, of Springfield, Va., major, U.S. Air Force, attorney-adviser, Office of the General Counsel, Office of the Secretary of Defense, the Pentagon, Washington, D.C.;

George Lee Thomas, 34, of Englewood, Colo., chairman, American Science and Engineering Society, Englewood, Colo.;

Myron Edward Ullman III, 34, of Cincinnati, Ohio, vice president for business affairs, University of Cincinnati, Ohio;

Mary Anne O. Wood, 35, of Provo, Utah, associate professor of law, J. Reuben Clark Law School, Brigham Young University, Provo, Utah;

Michael Esa Zacharia, 29, of Falls Church, Va., attorney, participating associate, Fulbright & Jaworski, Washington, D.C.

Message to the Senate Transmitting Protocols for the Extension of the 1971 International Wheat Agreement Conventions
June 11, 1981

To the Senate of the United States:

With a view to receiving the advice and consent of the Senate to ratification, I trans-

mit herewith the Protocols for the Extension of the Wheat Trade Convention, 1971 (WTC), and the Food Aid Convention, 1980

(FAC), which Conventions constitute the International Wheat Agreement, 1971. The Protocols were adopted by a conference which met in London on March 6, 1981 and were open for signature in Washington from March 24 through May 15, 1981. They were signed by the United States on May 8, 1981.

I transmit also, for the information of the Senate, the report of the Secretary of State with respect to the Protocols.

The Protocols extend both Conventions through June 30, 1983. They maintain the framework for international cooperation in wheat trade matters, continue the existence of the International Wheat Council, and extend the parties' commitments to provide minimum annual quantities of cereals aid to developing countries.

I ask that the Senate give early and favorable consideration to the two Protocols so that ratification by the United States can be effected at an early date. Doing so will demonstrate our continued commitment to cooperation on international wheat trade matters and to providing food aid to needy developing nations.

RONALD REAGAN

The White House,
June 11, 1981.

Message to the Senate Transmitting the United States-Argentina Convention on Taxation and Fiscal Evasion
June 11, 1981

To the Senate of the United States:

I transmit herewith, for Senate advice and consent to ratification, a Convention between the Government of the United States of America and the Government of the Republic of Argentina for the Avoidance of Double Taxation and the Prevention of Fiscal Evasion with respect to Taxes on Income and Capital (the Convention), together with a related Protocol, signed at Buenos Aires on May 7, 1981. I also transmit the report of the Department of State on the Convention.

The Convention, based on the United States and OECD model income tax conventions published in 1977, is the first of its kind to be entered into by the United States with a Latin American country.

Argentina taxes all income derived in Argentina, but does not tax any income derived by residents of Argentina from foreign sources. Thus, the usual treaty practice of reciprocal reductions in withholding taxes at source on dividends, interest, and royalties paid to residents of the other country has little appeal to Argentina. Argentina is reluctant to reduce its own tax at source, incurring a revenue cost for which it sees no offsetting benefit. The negotiators believe that the Convention represents a fair and reasonable compromise between the Argentine position that tax should be imposed only at source and the broader view of the United States and most other countries that tax may also be imposed on the basis of residence.

I recommend that the Senate give early and favorable consideration to the Convention and related Protocol and give advice and consent to their ratification.

RONALD REAGAN

The White House,
June 11, 1981.

503

Message to the Senate Transmitting the United States-Colombia Treaty on Mutual Legal Assistance
June 11, 1981

To the Senate of the United States:

With a view to receiving the advice and consent of the Senate to ratification, I transmit herewith the Treaty on Mutual Legal Assistance between the United States of America and the Republic of Colombia, together with a related exchange of notes, signed at Washington on August 20, 1980.

I transmit also, for the information of the Senate, the report of the Department of State with respect to the treaty.

The treaty is one of a series of modern mutual assistance treaties being negotiated by the United States. The treaty is self-executing and utilizes existing statutory authority.

The new treaty provides for a broad range of cooperation in criminal matters. Mutual assistance available under the treaty includes: (1) executing requests relating to criminal matters; (2) taking of testimony or statements of persons; (3) effecting the production, preservation, and authentication of documents, records, or articles of evidence; (4) returning to the requesting Party any objects, articles, or other property or assets belonging to it or obtained by an accused through offenses; (5) serving judicial documents, writs, summonses, records of judicial verdicts, and court judgments or decisions; (6) effecting the appearance of a witness or expert before a court of the requesting Party; (7) locating persons; and (8) providing judicial records, evidence, and information.

I recommend that the Senate give early and favorable consideration to the treaty and give its advice and consent to ratification.

RONALD REAGAN

The White House,
June 11, 1981.

Statement by Deputy Press Secretary Speakes on the Situation in the Middle East
June 11, 1981

The President today is meeting with the Ambassadors to discuss his initiatives for peace in the Middle East. He wants the Ambassadors of the various countries to be aware of his commitment and the commitment of the United States to the furtherance of the peace process in that critical region of the world. He wishes the Ambassadors to convey this to their respective governments. The President will welcome their views on this matter.

The mission of Ambassador Habib continues today with the important goals as outlined by the President when he asked the Ambassador to undertake this important venture. This is to seek a reduction of the tensions and a lessening of the possibility of conflict arising out of developments in Lebanon which affect the entire region. The President regards this goal to be of utmost importance. He wishes that the Habib mission will continue in cooperation with the concerned parties, whom we hope share our sense of the mission's continued importance.

[The President said,] "The incident [*referring to the Israeli bombing of the Osirak nuclear facility near Baghdad, Iraq*] earlier this week is evidence the only answer in the Middle East is to achieve a true peace. As long as there is suspicion among the nations, the specter of further tragedies will hang over us."

Note: Deputy Press Secretary Larry M. Speakes read the statement at the daily press briefing in the Briefing Room at the White House.

Prior to reading the statement, Mr. Speakes announced that the President would be holding afternoon meetings at the Oval Office with, first, Ambassadors Abdulaziz Abdulrahman Buali of Bahrain, Sheikh Faisal Alhegelan of Saudi Arabia, Ali Bengelloun of Morocco, Al-Sharif Fawaz Sharaf of Jordan, and Omer Salih Eissa of Sudan and, then, Ambassador Ephraim Evron of Israel.

Remarks on the Program for Economic Recovery at a White House Reception for Business and Government Leaders
June 11, 1981

I bring you apologies from Nancy. It seems that she has a schedule too. [*Laughter*] As a matter of fact, that was one thing I didn't know about this job—and I should have anticipated it after being Governor—that there is somebody that tells us what we're going to be doing every 15 minutes all day long. [*Laughter*] It's a little bit like Irving Berlin in that World War I song about the bugler. When I find out who's doing that—[*laughter*]——

But I've been looking forward to meeting with you today, welcoming you here to the White House. You know, around the turn of the century there was an English gentleman, Samuel Butler, who remarked that the advantage of doing one's praising of one's self is that I can lay it on so thick and in exactly the right places—[*laughter*]. Well, I did come to give generous praise, but not to myself or anyone in our administration, although I must say for them, I'm very proud of them and of the work that they've been doing. But I came to pay tribute to you, the new superstars of American grassroots politics. [*Applause*] I'll join in that applause. [*Laughter*]

No, you represent a cross section of Americans from all backgrounds, different regions across this country. In fact, you remind me very much of that one special interest group that I mentioned on Inauguration Day—the one special interest group that has been neglected and needs help—that is, we the people.

Thanks to your efforts in supporting the Gramm-Latta spending resolution, you gave all of the people of this country, I think, a tremendous victory. Not a victory for one party, but for more bipartisan cooperation and less inflation for a government that will finally begin living within its means. The bottom line is that millions of Americans are renewing their faith in our political system, and all of those people have waited so long for someone in Washington to listen and care and take action. So, from all of them to all of you, simply, thank you for what you've done for your country.

Now, before you start feeling too good, let me warn you. You're not going to get out of here scot-free. [*Laughter*] We need your help with another vital bipartisan piece of legislation. Now, you have no idea of what I'm talking about. [*Laughter*] We absolutely must have across the board a 3-year, 25-percent reduction for every American taxpayer, and we're not going to settle for less.

Now, there are those who are insisting that we settle for less. They demand proof in advance that what we've proposed will work, and they refuse to accept the record of history which clearly demonstrates that tax rate reductions do work. I think we can prove that what they've been doing in the last few decades hasn't worked and never will. And I don't think it automatically follows that those who brought about the present economic mess are, simply by virtue of having done that, the best qualified to clean it up.

They never answer one question that I keep asking—and you've probably heard me ask it. Why is it inflationary if the people keep their own money and spend it the way they want to and it's not inflationary if the government takes it and spends it the way it wants to? So, we're asked to believe that their proposal is more compassionate to the working people. But their proposal won't even match the built-in tax increase that they themselves are responsible for.

As a matter of fact, let's be honest about it. Our 25-percent, across-the-board tax cut actually is not that much of a tax cut at all. It is simply removing the imposition over the next 3 years by way of inflation which moves people up in brackets and built-in tax increases of the tax increase that will be imposed on the people without that across-the-board reduction. And theirs doesn't match that. The people over the next 3 years will get a tax increase unless this is adopted.

Now, it's that simple. Our opponents want more money from your family budgets so they can spend it on the Federal budget and make it remain high. Maybe it's time that you and millions like you remind them of a few simple facts. It's your money, not theirs. You earned it. They didn't. You have every right to keep a bigger share than you've been allowed to keep for a great many years now. When they insist we can't reduce taxes and spending and balance the budget too, one 6-word answer will do: "Yes, we can, and yes, we will."

For too long, government has stood in the way of taking more of what our people earn, no matter how hard they try. It's almost become economics without a soul. And that's why the ultimate goal in everything that we're trying to do is to give this economy back to the American people.

Now, you're the most valuable resource we have, and you're the ones who can save our future. Some say the future is looking impossible, filled with danger and uncertainty and scarcity. Well, the future's always looked bleak til people with brains and faith and courage who dreamed and dared to take great risks found a way to make it better—people like Robert Fulton and Eli Whitney and Thomas Edison and Henry Ford and Albert Einstein. Einstein himself gave us the formula—everything that is really great and inspiring was created by individuals who labor in freedom.

So, our message today is simply help us pass these incentives so we can help you. We want nothing more than to turn you loose so you can make the 1980's the most exciting, successful decade our nation has ever known—years of renaissance for American entrepreneurs, years when millions of free men and women went out and found the energy to make us secure and created a revolutionary technological breakthrough on every front, years when they rebuilt our cities and, in the process, created millions of new jobs, stronger families, and a real hope for young Americans everywhere. That's the kind of country I want to leave for our children, and I know it's what you want, too. Now, if we keep working together, just like we have, we're going to succeed and save that American dream that we all love.

Thank you all, and God bless you. And I'm going to get off of here and come down and say hello.

Note: The President spoke at 5:32 p.m. in the East Room at the White House.

Nomination of John P. Horton To Be an Assistant Administrator of the Environmental Protection Agency
June 12, 1981

The President today announced his intention to nominate John P. Horton to be an Assistant Administrator of the Environmental Protection Agency (Administration).

Since 1957 Mr. Horton has been president, Danline, Inc., manufacturer of power brushes for road and runway cleaning. In addition, since 1970 he has been treasurer of Growth Enterprises, Inc., a restaurant company. In 1970–78 he was president, Ecolotec, Inc., a manufacturer of vacuum street sweepers sold throughout the United States. In 1954–57 he was assistant director of development, Virginia-Carolina Chemical

Corp. He was assistant to the president, National Dairy Research Laboratories, in 1951–54.

Mr. Horton has served as a member and chairman of the New Jersey Clean Air Council. He also served on the State Planning Task Force and the State Council on the Future.

Mr. Horton attended Swarthmore College (1943–44), University of Pennsylvania (1944–45), and the U.S. Naval Academy (1945–47). He is married, has four children, and resides in Bernardsville, N.J. He was born February 16, 1925, in Orange, N.J.

Nomination of William M. Bell To Be a Member of the Equal Employment Opportunity Commission, and Designation as Chairman
June 12, 1981

The President today announced his intention to nominate William M. Bell to be a member of the Equal Employment Opportunity Commission. Upon confirmation, the President intends to designate Mr. Bell Chairman.

Since 1976 Mr. Bell has been president, Bold Concepts, Inc., a personnel consulting firm specializing in placement of women and minorities located in Detroit, Mich. In 1975–76 he was a special consultant with the Equal Employment Opportunity Commission. Mr. Bell was previously president,

William M. Bell & Associates, a financial counseling and public relations firm, from 1958 to 1975.

Mr. Bell is an active Republican. He was an unsuccessful candidate for Michigan State senator, Detroit City Council, and U.S. Congress. He served on the Michigan Reagan for President Commmittee in 1980.

Mr. Bell graduated from the University of Michigan (B.A., 1948; M.B.A., 1954). He is married and resides in Detroit, Mich. He was born August 31, 1926.

Nomination of Robert John Hughes To Be an Associate Director of the International Communication Agency
June 12, 1981

The President today announced his intention to nominate Robert John Hughes to be

an Associate Director of the International Communication Agency (Programs).

Since 1979 Mr. Hughes has been president, publisher, and editor of Hughes Newspapers, Inc., Orleans, Mass. He founded the company in 1977. He was director and consultant, News-Journal, Wilmington, Del., in 1975–78; radio correspondent from the Far East for Westinghouse Broadcasting Co. in 1964–70; weekly television commentator, WBZ–TV, Boston, Mass., in 1962–64. In 1954–79 Mr. Hughes held a wide variety of positions with the Christian Science Monitor. He was Africa correspondent in 1955–61, assistant overseas news editor in 1962–64, Far East correspondent in 1964–70, managing editor in 1970, editor in 1970–76, and editor and manager in 1976–79. In 1952–54 he was South African correspondent for the Daily Express in London. Mr. Hughes was a reporter with the London Daily Mirror in 1950–51.

Mr. Hughes attended Stationers' Company's School in London, England, in 1941–46. He was a Nieman Fellow, Harvard University, in 1961–62. Mr. Hughes was a recipient of the Pulitzer Prize for international reporting in 1967. He was director and president of the American Society of Newspaper Editors in 1972–80.

Mr. Hughes is married, has two children, and resides in Orleans, Mass. He was born April 28, 1930, in Neath, south Wales.

Remarks on Signing a Resolution and a Proclamation Declaring National P.O.W.-M.I.A. Recognition Day, 1981
June 12, 1981

Ladies and gentlemen, welcome to what I think is a very important and worthwhile little signing ceremony here in the Rose Garden. I am pleased that I'm going to sign a joint resolution and a proclamation designating July 17th, 1981 National P.O.W.-M.I.A. Recognition Day.

The brave men and women who fought for our country should all know that America does remember and is grateful and will always be proud of their courage and honor on the battlefield. And it's fitting that we pay this special tribute to those who so heroically endured the hardships and torture of enemy captivity—unusual in any war in our history, because it was the longest period that American fighting men have ever been held in captivity. Just the thought of the terrible pain that they suffered and endured should be seared in our memories forever. And let us remember, too, that 6 years after American involvement in Vietnam, in the war, we still don't have a full accounting of our missing servicemen from that conflict, an accounting that was guaranteed in the Paris peace accords that brought the fighting there to an end, an agreement which has been violated.

Recently there have been reports that Americans are still being held captive in Indochina. None of these reports, I'm sorry to say, has been verified, but the world should know that this administration continues to attach the highest priority to the problem of those missing in action. We intend to seek the fullest possible account from the governments involved.

I'm grateful that we have with us here today one of America's outstanding heroes from the Vietnam war, one of the former prisoners of war, and now the Senator from Alabama, Jeremiah Denton, accompanied by his lovely wife Jane. July 17th, it is just 16 years—or that will be—to the day that he was shot down over Southeast Asia. Now, lest someone think that there's a little confusion there, he was shot down on July 18th, 1965, but when it was the 18th there, on this side of the dateline it was the 17th. Jeremiah Denton. Who will ever forget on that first night in that first plane that arrived at Clark Field in the Philippines, and he was the first man we saw come down the ramp from the plane, salute our flag, ask God's blessing on America, and then thank us for bringing them home.

They're joined here by leaders of the House and Senate, many of their colleagues, Cap Hollenbeck and Bob Dornan, John LeBoutillier and Bill Hendon and John Paul Hammerschmidt and Tom Lantos from the House, and Senators Dennis DeConcini and Bob Dole, along with Senator Jeremiah Denton.

And now, I'm going to have the happy task of signing the proclamation and the bill.

Note: The President spoke at 3:02 p.m. at the signing ceremony in the Rose Garden at the White House.

As enacted, S.J. Res. 50 is Public Law 97–13, approved June 12.

Proclamation 4848—National P.O.W.-M.I.A. Recognition Day, 1981
June 12, 1981

By the President of the United States of America

A Proclamation

Throughout American history our prisoners of war have been called upon to make uncommon sacrifices. In fulfilling their duty as citizens of the United States they have defended American ideals while suffering unimaginable indignities under the absolute control of the enemy. They remained steadfast even while their treatment contravened international understandings and violated elementary consideration of compassion and morality.

All Americans ought to recognize the special debt we owe to our fellow citizens who, in the act of serving our Nation, relinquished their freedom that we might enjoy the blessings of peace and liberty. Likewise, we must remember the unresolved casualties of war—our servicemen who are still missing. The pain and bitterness of war endure for their families, relatives and friends—and for all of us. Our Nation will continue to seek answers to the many questions that remain about their fate.

Now, Therefore, I, Ronald Reagan, President of the United States of America, do hereby proclaim Friday, July 17, 1981, as National P.O.W.–M.I.A. Recognition Day, a day dedicated to all former American prisoners of war, to those still missing, and to their families. I urge all Americans to join in honoring those who made the uncommon sacrifice of being held captive in war, and to honor as well their loved ones who have also suffered valiantly and patiently. I also call on appropriate officials of the Federal, State and local governments, as well as private organizations, to observe this day with appropriate ceremonies and activities.

In Witness Whereof, I have hereunto set my hand this twelfth day of June, in the year of our Lord nineteen hundred and eighty-one, and of the Independence of the United States of America the two hundred and fifth.

RONALD REAGAN

[*Filed with the Office of the Federal Register, 5:02 p.m., June 12, 1981*]

Remarks at a White House Reception for the Republican National Committee
June 12, 1981

The President. Nancy and I are both delighted that you're all here. We are kind of happy that we're here. [*Laughter*]

I know you've been reading a lot about what's going on here in Washington. Some of it's true. [*Laughter*] We've been trying to follow the advice of Mark Twain, which was "Do what's right and you'll please some of the people and astound the rest." [*Laughter*] There's been some criticism, however, that we don's have a definite foreign policy, that we haven't been doing enough about that, and that's not true at all. Just the other day, before he left for China, Al Haig sent a message to Brezhnev that said, "Roses are red, violets are blue, stay out of El Salvador and Poland, too." [*Laughter*]

But you know, this has been a great day and this tops it off just fine. This is George Bush's birthday. We have a great relationship, and George was very tactful; he hasn't told me how young he is. [*Laughter*]

But I thank all of you, seriously, for the work that you've done, not only in the last election but also throughout the years of even our losing campaigns, when we were winning those moral victories. [*Laughter*] And our victory in November was due to the accumulated efforts that you've made, and it just took a little while for the message to get through.

The victory at the polls leaves us with a tremendous responsibility to do the things that we've talked about for so long. I think I've learned in the last 5 months how important it is that we, as Republicans, continue to work together as a team to accomplish our objective. And thanks to your help in keeping the heat on at the State and local level, we've succeeded in getting our budget cuts through Congress. I worried for a while when that happened that maybe Dave Stockman was too young—he rushed right out and got a giant piggybank. [*Laughter*]

But I can tell you right now that we're going to get the tax cuts also. And I jotted down here in my notes that that's because

the American people are with us. And then I just happened to remember that wonderful line that Joe Louis said once during the war about the Lord, and I think maybe we ought to reverse that. We got them through because we're with the American people.

I know you've heard some of the arguments that they're using over on the other side about why we shouldn't do this, and you've probably run into some of them yourself. And when they do, just tell them that our true choice is not between tax reduction on the one hand and avoidance of large Federal deficits on the other. An economy that's stifled by restrictive tax rates will never produce enough revenue to balance the budget, just as it will never produce enough jobs or enough profits. And when they try to argue that one with you, remind them that's what John F. Kennedy said when he passed his 2-year, 23-percent tax cut. It wound up with an increase in personal savings, an increase in investment, an increase in productivity and jobs, and even an increase in the total amount of revenues that the Federal Government received at the lower rates. And that's what we think is going to happen when we get our tax cut across the board.

America is on the edge—I think we're all aware of it—of an era of good feelings. Our budget proposals, with the pruning of excessive regulations, steady monetary policy, can and will restore vitality to our economy. And, believe me, the better America is, the better it'll be for the Republican Party.

You know, recent accounts have described sometimes the Democrats as being in disarray. So, what else is new? [*Laughter*] Will Rogers, a number of years ago, made the point that he did not belong to any organized political party; he was a Democrat. [*Laughter*] But we mustn't be lulled into self-confidence. We've got a great chairman, Dick Richards, and his primary goal is to build our party into a strong, efficient, and majority party—and I think that can happen in 1982.

Some historians are suggesting that the election of 1980 was a turning point, a watershed election which rearranged party loyalties for some time to come. And I think that you and I just don't want to embarrass those historians. [*Laughter*] Let's make that come true.

But looking around this room I see old friends—Tommy Thomas right there.

Mr. Thomas. Last night.

The President. Saw him last night out— we were out at a thrilling thing that I wish all America could see.

Mr. Thomas. Everybody should see it.

The President. It's a great ceremony by the Marine Corps. And you looked at them, and you just couldn't help but want to stand up and salute and sing the National Anthem. It was a very wonderful, wonderful ceremony to see.

Mr. Thomas. Mr. President, we feel the same way about you. [*Applause*]

The President. Thank you very much.

Well, I'm not going to try to go on with anything after that. [*Laughter*] We've been through too much together, and I'm anxious

to have at least a few minutes here to chat with you down there on the floor. And I'll anticipate one question so I'll only have to answer it once. I feel just great. [*Laughter*] And, as a matter of fact, during the last visit to California, over Decoration Day, we did some horseback riding. And the other day up at Camp David the Mexican President, President López Portillo, and I played hooky from the business meeting and went horseback riding again. And that fixed things up just fine. [*Laughter*]

So, now if our finance chairman is within reach someplace—[*laughter*]—I just want to buy a ticket as a sustaining member of the Republican National Committee.

Mr. DeVos. Well, I have a membership card for you—card number one. And the Vice President has card number two. [*Inaudible*]

The President. Well, thank you all for being here and, as I say, we're going to try and say hello at least to a few of you down here in the crowd.

Note: The President spoke at 5:15 p.m. in the East Room at the White House.

Nomination of J. Robinson West To Be an Assistant Secretary of the Interior
June 13, 1981

The President today announced his intention to nominate J. Robinson West to be an Assistant Secretary of the Interior (Policy, Budget and Administration).

Mr. West was a member of the Presidential personnel transition staff. In 1977–80 he was vice president and subsequently first vice president of Blyth, Eastman, Dillon and Co., an investment banking firm. Mr. West served as Deputy Assistant Secretary of Defense for International Economic Affairs in 1976–77, assistant to the Secretary of Defense in 1976, and as a member of the White House staff in 1974–76. He has served on a number of advisory commmissions, including the National Advisory Com-

mittee on Oceans and Atmosphere in 1977. He was elected a member and secretary of the Chester County Government Study Commission and served as a trustee of the United Fund of Greater Philadelphia. He was also director of the Health and Welfare Council of Chester County. He is a member of the Council on Foreign Relations. Mr. West was selected as one of the Ten Outstanding Young Men in Pennsylvania.

Mr. West graduated from the University of North Carolina (B.A., 1968) and Temple University (J.D., 1973). He resides in Unionville, Pa., and was born in Bryn Mawr, Pa., on September 16, 1946.

Nomination of Arthur W. Hummel, Jr., To Be United States Ambassador to the People's Republic of China
June 13, 1981

The President today announced his intention to nominate Arthur W. Hummel, Jr., to be Ambassador to the People's Republic of China. He would succeed Leonard Woodcock, who has resigned.

Mr. Hummel, 61, is currently U.S. Ambassador to Pakistan. A career Foreign Service officer who was born in China of American missionary parents and speaks fluent Chinese, Mr. Hummel has emerged as the Department's senior sinologist in a career spanning 30 years.

Mr. Hummel received an M.A. in international studies from the University of Chicago in 1949. He has served as Deputy Assistant Secretary (1972–75) and Assistant Secretary (1976) of the Department of State's Bureau of East Asian and Pacific Affairs. In addition to his current Ambassadorial post in Pakistan, he has served as U.S. Ambassador to Ethiopia (1975–76) and to Burma (1968–71). Previously he was Deputy Assistant Secretary in the Bureau of Educational and Cultural Affairs (1963–65), and Deputy Director of the Voice of America (1961–63), after attending the National War College in 1960.

Mr. Hummel was born June 1, 1920, is married to the former Betty Lou Firstenberger, and resides in Maryland. Mr. and Mrs. Hummel have two sons, Timothy and William.

Statement on the Reduction of Federal Regulations
June 13, 1981

Excessive and inefficient Federal regulations place an undue burden on our society. They limit job opportunities, raise prices, and reduce the incomes of all Americans.

During the Presidential campaign, I promised quick and decisive action. Since taking office, I have made regulatory relief a top priority. It is one of the cornerstones of my economic recovery program.

Thanks to the constructive work of my Task Force on Regulatory Relief, chaired by Vice President Bush, many needless and unproductive regulations have been eliminated. Other officials in my administration are moving forward with equal vigor and are producing tangible results. Regulatory relief actions to date have resulted in billions of dollars in savings to the American people.

The materials in this volume document some of our progress. But more needs to be done, and will be done. I am confident that the legitimate purposes of regulation can be met at considerably lower costs. We shall not rest until that goal is achieved.

Note: The statement is printed in the 122-page report entitled "Materials on President Reagan's Program for Regulatory Relief."

Announcement of Additional Federal Aid for Programs Relating to the Murdered and Missing Youth in Atlanta, Georgia
June 15, 1981

The President today is announcing the approval of $1.160 million for the Safe Summer Parks and Recreation Program for Atlanta, Fulton and DeKalb Counties, Ga. This brings to a total of $4.1 million that the Federal Government has provided Atlanta in the situation regarding the number of young people that are missing or dead.

[The President said,] "The people of Atlanta and the surrounding communities have endured grief and suffering in a manner that touches the hearts and minds and souls of millions of our countrymen. The American people are united in a collective effort to bring an end to this devastation of human life, to eliminate family suffering, and to restore a new spirit to a beleaguered community."

Note: Deputy Press Secretary Larry M. Speakes read the announcement at the daily press briefing in the Briefing Room at the White House.

Letter to the Attorney General Directing an Assessment of the Voting Rights Act
June 15, 1981

Dear Bill:

As you are aware, certain provisions of the Voting Rights Act are due to expire in August of 1982. In its 15-year history, the Act has made a massive contribution to the achievement of full constitutional and political equality for black Americans. And by virtue of amendments added in 1975, the Act has helped to insure greater equality for other minorities, especially Mexican-Americans.

I am sensitive to the controversy which has attached itself to some of the Act's provisions, in particular those provisions which impose burdens unequally upon different parts of the nation. But I am sensitive also to the fact that the spirit of the Act marks this nation's commitment to full equality for all Americans, regardless of race, color, or national origin. Because my Administration intends to maintain that commitment, the question before us in the months ahead will not be whether the rights which the Act seeks to protect are worthy of protection, but whether the Act continues to be the most appropriate means of guaranteeing those rights.

Before making a final determination on the Act's extension or revision, I want to be assured that we have received and evaluated the considered opinions of all concerned parties. Accordingly, I would like the Department to undertake, at your direction, a comprehensive assessment of the Act's history to date; extant or likely abuses of voting rights that may require special scrutiny; the adequacy of the Department's powers under the Act; your suggestions as to whether any changes in the Act may be desirable; and the feasibility of extending the Act's coverage to voting rights infringements not now covered by the Act.

Finally, in the course of developing your assessment, I would like you to consult with concerned citizen groups, state, local, and federal officials, and others whose thoughtful views will contribute to the development of a just and sound Administration position.

I understand that you have already begun this deliberative and consultative process, and I am pleased by this. It will be necessary, however, to complete our review in sufficient time to enable Congress to enact a bill prior to the expiration of the Act's special provisions. I would therefore like to receive your report not later than October 1, 1981.

Sincerely,

RON

[The Honorable William French Smith, The Attorney General, Washington, D.C. 20530]

Nomination of Herbert Rudolph Lippold, Jr., To Be Director of the National Ocean Survey
June 15, 1981

The President today announced his intention to nominate Herbert Rudolph Lippold, Jr., to be Director of the National Ocean Survey, National Oceanic and Atmospheric Administration, Department of Commerce.

Rear Admiral Lippold joined the Coast and Geodetic Survey, now the National Ocean Survey, National Oceanic and Atmospheric Administration, in 1950. During the last 29 years, he has conducted research and surveying on land and sea in the Atlantic, Pacific, and Arctic Oceans, and in most of the conterminous United States, Alaska, and Hawaii. This was highlighted by 9 years of sea suty on eight vessels, three of which he commanded. He surveyed the north Arctic coast by cat train, spent 8 years in geodesy accomplishing basic surveys, established a satellite triangulation worldwide network, and served as liaison with the Air Force, bringing horizontal and vertical control to intercontinental ballistic missile sites in the United States. He conducted liaison with the Navy at Pearl Harbor on the Pacific tide and seismic sea wave warning system, supervised ship construction at Pt. Pleasant, W. Va., and served as Director of the NOS Pacific Marine Center, Seattle, Wash. As Associate Director, Office of Fleet Operations, in Rockville, Md., he directed the operations of NOAA's research and hydrographic survey fleet of 25 vessels. During 1965–66 he was a Department of Commerce Scientific and Technical Fellow, assigned to the National Bureau of Standards.

Admiral Lippold graduated from New England College, Henniker, N.H. (B.S., 1949) and the University of New Hampshire (B.C.E., 1950). He is married, has four children, and resides in New Hampshire. He was born April 9, 1926, in Methuen, Mass.

Nomination of Lilla Burt Cummings Tower To Be Director of the Institute of Museum Services
June 15, 1981

The President today announced his intention to nominate Lilla Burt Cummings Tower to be Director of the Institute of Museum Services, Department of Education.

Since 1960 Mrs. Tower has been an attorney in private practice. In 1973 she was appointed by D.C. Mayor Walter Washington to the Board of Zoning Adjustment, an independent agency of the District of Columbia Government having both appellate and original jurisdiction. She was reappointed by Mayor Washington in 1974. Previously Mrs. Tower was an economist and assistant to chief economist, Rand Corp., in 1950–53; assistant director of political and legislative research, Congressional Quarterly News Features, Inc., in 1949–50; and graduate and undergraduate assistant in economics, George Washington University, in 1948–50.

Mrs. Tower graduated from George Washington University (A.B., 1949) and George Washington University National Law Center (J.D., 1960; LL.M., 1965). She was a recipient of the Certificate of Meritorious Service, Law Review, in 1957–58 and 1958–59.

Mrs. Tower is married to Senator John G. Tower (R–Tex.), has one son, and resides in Washington, D.C. She was born October 6, 1928, in Philadelphia, Pa.

Nomination of William Addison Vaughan To Be an Assistant Secretary of Energy
June 15, 1981

The President today announced his intention to nominate William Addison Vaughan to be an Assistant Secretary of Energy (Environmental Protection, Safety and Emergency Preparedness).

Since 1976 Mr. Vaughan has been director, energy management, manufacturing staff, General Motors Corp. In 1971–76 he was attorney-in-charge, Environmental & Energy Law Section, General Motors legal staff and was an attorney in 1970–71. Previously Mr. Vaughan was instructor and assist-ant professor of civil engineering, Virginia Military Institute, in 1960–70. He served as deputy commandant of cadets at VMI in 1964–67.

Mr. Vaughan served as an officer in the U.S. Army in 1957–60. He graduated from the Virginia Military Institute (B.S., 1957), Purdue University (M.S.C.E., 1964), and Washington and Lee University (J.D., 1970). He is married, has three children, and resides in Grosse Pointe Farms, Mich. He was born April 19, 1935, in Richmond, Va.

Nomination of Clarence Eugene Hodges To Be an Assistant Director of the Community Services Administration
June 15, 1981

The President today announced his intention to nominate Clarence Eugene Hodges to be an Assistant Director of the Community Services Administration (Community Action).

Since 1977 Mr. Hodges has served on the staff of Senator Richard G. Lugar (R–Ind.), acting as assistant State director. In 1976–77 he served with the Indianapolis Housing Authority and in 1973–76, was director, Department of Human Resources, and assistant to the mayor of Indianapolis. He was executive director, Concentrated Employment Program, St. Lois, Mo., in 1967–73. Previously Mr. Hodges was director of social services, Kinloch School District, St. Louis County, in 1966–67, and casework supervi-sor, division of welfare, State of Missouri, in 1962–66.

Mr. Hodges served in the U.S. Air Force in 1956–60. He was a candidate for the U.S. Congress in 1980 from Indiana's 11th District. He has been active in community affairs including serving as chairman, Committee on Conflict, Indianapolis Urban League Task Force on School Violence, and president and chairman of the board of directors, Community Action Against Poverty.

Mr. Hodges graduated from Upper Iowa University (B.A.) and Occidental College (M.A.). He is married, has four children, and resides in Indianapolis, Ind. He was born October 1, 1939, in Princeton, N.C.

Nomination of Wilson E. Schmidt To Be United States Executive Director of the International Bank for Reconstruction and Development
June 15, 1981

The President today announced his intention to nominate Wilson E. Schmidt to be United States Executive Director of the International Bank for Reconstruction and Development.

Since 1966 Dr. Schmidt has been professor of economics, Virginia Polytechnic Institute, and was head of the department of economics in 1966–77. He was Deputy Assistant Secretary of the Treasury in 1970–72. In 1963–65 he was visiting professor of economics, Johns Hopkins Bologna Center, Italy. He was also visiting professor of economics, School of Advanced International Studies, Johns Hopkins University, in 1960. In 1950–67 he was instructor to professor, Economics Department, George Washington University. He has served intermittently as consultant to the Agency for International Development.

Dr. Schmidt graduated from the University of Maryland (B.S., 1947), the University of Pittsburgh (M.A., 1948), and the University of Virginia (Ph. D., 1952). He is married, has three children, and resides in Blacksburg, Va. He was born March 22, 1927, in Madison, Wis.

Nomination of Frederic Andre To Be a Member of the Interstate Commerce Commission
June 15, 1981

The President today announced his intention to nominate Frederic Andre to be a member of the Interstate Commerce Commission.

Mr. Andre has been serving as executive director, Medical Liability Commission, Chicago, Ill. Previously he was assistant director of field service, American Medical Association, acting as legislative liaison and membership services director for the southern region. Mr. Andre was chief deputy commissioner of the Indiana Bureau of Motor Vehicles, Indianapolis, Ind., and was staff director of the Indiana Public Service Commission. He was legislative assistant to Representative Henry C. Schadeberg (Wisconsin).

Mr. Andre graduated from Calvin College (A.B., 1955), Stanford Business School (M.B.A., 1962), and Valparaiso School of Law (J.D., 1970). He resides in Paoli, Ind., and was born June 25, 1933, in Grand Rapids, Mich.

Nomination of Malcolm M. B. Sterrett To Be a Member of the Interstate Commerce Commission
June 15, 1981

The President today announced his intention to nominate Malcolm M. B. Sterrett to be a member of the Interstate Commerce Commission.

Since January 1980 Mr. Sterrett has been Vice President and General Counsel, United States Railway Association. In that position he was responsible for the administration of a 150-member staff, managing litigation, corporate affairs and congressional relations activities, and planning future rail service in the Northeast. In 1976–80 he was minority staff director and counsel, U.S. Senate Committee on Commerce, Science, and Transportation. Mr. Sterrett was minority staff counsel, Senate Committee on Commerce, in 1972–76. In 1967–72 he was attorney-advisor, Interstate Commerce Commission.

Mr. Sterrett graduated from Princeton University (B.A., 1964) and Vanderbilt University School of Law (J.D., 1967). He is married, has one child, and resides in Bethesda, Md. He was born September 21, 1942, in Norwalk, Conn.

Nomination of John A. Bohn, Jr., To Be United States Director of the Asian Development Bank
June 15, 1981

The President today announced his intention to nominate John A. Bohn, Jr., to be United States Director of the Asian Development Bank.

Since 1980 Mr. Bohn has been vice president, Correspondent Banking Division, and manager, International Personal Banking Department, Wells Fargo International Banking Group. He is a member of the Wells Fargo Legislative Policy Committee, Country Risk Evaluation Committee, and the International Advisory Council. In 1979–80 Mr. Bohn was manager, administration and development; division manager, North American division, in 1974–79; manager, International Group, in 1972–74; and vice president and Far East representative in 1967–72. Before joining Wells Fargo, Mr. Bohn was an attorney.

Mr. Bohn graduated from Stanford University (A.B., 1959) and Harvard Law School (LL.B., 1963). He also attended London School of Economics (1959–60). He is married, has four children, and resides in Belvedere, Calif. He was born October 31, 1937, in Oakland, Calif.

Message to the Senate Transmitting the Inter-American Convention on Commercial Arbitration
June 15, 1981

To the Senate of the United States:

I transmit herewith the Inter-American Convention on Commercial Arbitration, adopted by the First Specialized Conference on Private International Law of the Organization of American States at Panama City on January 30, 1975, for the purpose of receiving the advice and consent of the Senate to ratification. This Convention was signed on behalf of the United States on June 9, 1978.

The provisions of the Inter-American Convention are explained in the report of the Secretary of State which accompanies this letter. In broad terms, the Inter-American Convention is designed to facilitate the settlement of international commercial disputes by arbitration rather than by court proceeding where the parties so desire, by providing that courts will enforce in appropriate cases both the agreement to arbitrate and any resulting arbitral award.

This Convention is similar in purpose and effect to the New York Convention on the Recognition and Enforcement of Arbitral Awards, adopted at the United Nations on June 10, 1958, which the United States ratified in 1970. The Inter-American Convention has, however, been ratified by a greater number of Member States of the Organization of American States than the New York Convention. We are thus hopeful that ratification of the Inter-American Convention by the United States and by OAS Member States will make possible greater recognition and enforcement of arbitral agreements and arbitral awards among the countries of the Western Hemisphere.

New legislation will be required as part of Title 9 (Arbitration) of the United States Code in order to implement the provisions of the Convention within the United States. The United States' instrument of ratification will be executed only after the necessary legislation has been enacted.

There is substantial support for ratification among members of the legal and business community concerned with international trade and investment. You will find enclosed as an attachment to the report of the Secretary of State letters recommending ratification of this Convention by the United States which have been received from the American Arbitration Association, the American Bar Association, the United States Chamber of Commerce, the Association of American Chambers of Commerce in Latin America, the American Foreign Law Association, and a number of state and local bar associations. We are aware of no opposition to ratification.

I recommend that the Senate give its advice and consent to ratification of this Convention, subject to the three reservations which are described in the accompanying report of the Secretary of State.

RONALD REAGAN

The White House,
June 15, 1981.

Nomination of Joan M. Clark To Be Director General of the Foreign Service
June 16, 1981

The President today announced the nomination of Joan M. Clark, of the District of Columbia, to be Director General of the Foreign Service, Department of State.

Since 1979 Miss Clark has served as United States Ambassador to the Republic of Malta. In 1977–79 she was Director, Office of Management Operations, Department of State. Miss Clark was Executive Director, Bureau of European Affairs, in 1972–77; Deputy Executive Director, Bureau of European Affairs, in 1971–72; personnel officer, then administrative officer, Bureau of Inter-American Affairs, in 1969–71; coordinator for administrative training, School of Professional Studies, in 1968–69; administrative officer, Luxembourg, in 1962–68; placement officer, then administrative officer, at the Department; administrative assistant, Belgrade, in 1953–57; economic assistant, London, in 1951–53; clerk, then administrative assistant, Berlin, in 1945–51.

Miss Clark attended Katharine Gibbs School in New York City. She is a recipient of the Superior Honor Award (1970) and the Luther I. Replogle Award for Management Improvement (1975).

Miss Clark resides in Washington, D.C. She was born March 27, 1922, in Ridgefield Park, N.J.

The President's News Conference
June 16, 1981

Program for Economic Recovery

The President. Good afternoon.

Last November the American people gave the elected representatives in Washington an overwhelming mandate to rescue the economy from high inflation and high unemployment. That was last November. Today, 7 months later, people are still watching, and they're still waiting. And there's no longer any reason to delay.

Two major pieces of economic legislation are now before the Congress.

The first, an omnibus bill to reduce spending. A month ago, the House of Representatives approved by a 77-vote margin a long overdue and unprecedented budget resolution. That resolution ordered House committees to cut $36 billion for spending next year, some $140 billion over the next 3 years. And yet there is now clear danger of congressional backsliding and a return to spending as usual.

Some House committees have reported spending cuts they know can't be made, closing, for example, one-third of the nation's post offices. One House committee claims to have achieved savings by eliminating a day care program to provide suppers, but it also slipped into the change of the law to say that lunches can be served at suppertime.

This practice is unconscionable. The hard work of Congress in passing the bipartisan budget resolution was not an academic exercise. It was a solemn commitment that transforms a mandate from the people into a compact with the people. The Congress and the administration together must protect the integrity of that compact.

I urge the House leaders to revise the committee work so that it honestly and responsibly achieves the original spending goals. But if that proves impossible, let me be clear: My administration will have no other choice than to support the proposal of a number of Representatives in the House to offer a budget substitute on the floor that matches the resolution they voted for in May.

The second major economic item on the agenda is a cut in the tax rates that we promised the American people.

Some 12 days ago, I outlined the basic elements of a bipartisan tax plan that provides multiyear, across-the-board cuts in individual tax rates, and it is an essential feature of our overall economic program. A bill incorporating these principles was introduced last week by [Republican] Congressman Barber Conable and Democratic Congressman Kent Hance. I'm pleased to report from conversations with Senators and Congressmen, I'm convinced there is a gathering bipartisan consensus for this tax bill.

But, once again, time is fleeting. Just to take care of the paperwork associated with the tax changes that would be effective on October 1st, we must quickly have the legislation on the books.

More important, let us never forget the mandate of November. The people of this Nation have asked for action—and they deserve it now, not somewhere down in a misty future.

Therefore, I'm asking Congress today to live up to its original commitment and deliver to my desk before the August recess, not one but two bills—a spending bill and a tax bill. Only then can we say as elected representatives that we truly deserve a rest.

Now, the first question. Dean Reynolds [United Press International].

Communism

Q. Mr. President, last month you told graduates at Notre Dame that Western civilization will transcend communism and that communism is, in your words, "A sad, bizarre chapter in human history whose last pages are even now being written."

In that context, sir, do the events of the last 10 months in Poland constitute the beginning of the end of Soviet domination of Eastern Europe?

The President. Well, what I meant then in my remarks at Notre Dame and what I believe now about what we're seeing tie together. I just think that it is impossible—and history reveals this—for any form of government to completely deny freedom to people and have that go on interminably. There eventually comes an end to it. And I think the things we're seeing, not only in Poland but the reports that are beginning to come out of Russia itself about the younger generation and its resistance to long-time government controls, is an indication that communism is an aberration. It's not a normal way of living for human beings, and I think we are seeing the first, beginning cracks, the beginning of the end.

Israeli Attack Against Iraq

Q. Mr. President, have you learned anything in the past 10 days that would support Israel's contention that its attack on the Iraqi nuclear plant was defensive? If it was defensive, was it proper? If it wasn't defensive, what action should the United States take beyond condemnation?

The President. Well, I did make a statement in which I condemned that and thought that there were other options that might have been considered—that we would have welcomed an opportunity, for example, to try and intervene with the French who were furnishing the nuclear fuel and so forth.

I can't answer the last part of your question there about future action, because this is still under review. Under the law I had to submit to the Congress the fact that this did appear to be a violation of the law regarding American weapons that were sold for defensive purposes. But I've not heard back yet from the Congress, and that review is not yet complete.

On the other hand, I do think that one has to recognize that Israel had reason for concern in view of the past history of Iraq, which has never signed a cease-fire or recognized Israel as a nation, has never joined in any peace effort for that—so, in other words, it does not even recognize the existence of Israel as a country.

But I think the biggest thing that comes out of what happened is the fact that this is further evidence that a real peace, a settlement for all of the Mideast problems, is long overdue, that the area is torn by tension and hostility. We have seen Afghani-

stan invaded with the Soviets, Iran invaded by Iraq, and that was in violation of a treaty. Lebanon's sovereignty has been violated routinely. Now this latest act. And I think that what it should be is a compelling move—and this I have stated to the representatives of several Arab countries—a compelling reason why we should once and for all settle this matter and have a stable peace.

Q. But in this case, can you say was it—do you think now that it was a defensive move? Are there any—anything which indicates that yet?

The President. No, I can't answer that, because, as I say, this review has not been completed. But what I would have to say is I think, in looking at the circumstances that I outlined earlier, that we can recognize that very possibly in conducting that mission, Israel might have sincerely believed it was a defensive move.

Foreign Policy

Q. Mr. President, a couple of times in recent weeks your staff has told us that you were not quite ready to make a major foreign policy address and declined the opportunity to do so. In light of recent events in the Middle East and in Eastern Europe, have you given some serious thought to a foreign policy program across the board, and, if so, could you give us today some of the outlines of your foreign policy beyond your often-expressed determination to stand up to the Soviets?

The President. Well, there seems to be a feeling as if an address on foreign policy is somehow evidence that you have a foreign policy, and until you make an address, you don't have one. And I challenge that. I'm satisfied that we do have a foreign policy.

I have met with eight heads of state already, representatives of nine other nations. The Secretary of State is making his second trip and is now in China and is going to meet with the ASEAN nations in the Philippines and then go on for a meeting in New Zealand. The Deputy Secretary of State has been in Africa and is now returning by way of Europe. I have been in personal communication by mail with President Brezhnev.

I don't necessarily believe that you must, to have a foreign policy, stand up and make a wide declaration that this is your foreign policy. I've spoken about a number of areas. We are going forward with a program, a tripartite program, dealing with Central America and the Caribbean. We have tried to deal with various areas of the world—both Asia, Africa, and in Europe. And so as to an address, I definitely did not do one at commencements, because I happen to believe, as I said at Notre Dame, that it has been traditional for people in my position to go and use a graduation ceremony as a forum for making an address that was of no interest particularly or no connection to the occasion, but just for wide dissemination. And I thought that the young people who were graduating deserved a speech, whether good or bad, that was aimed at them.

Gary [Gary Schuster, Detroit News].

The Middle East

Q. Mr. President, can we return to the Mideast situation for a moment? Several of the Mideast leaders, most particularly Syria, say that because of the Israeli raid and the U.S. response to it that envoy Habib's peace mission is virtually eliminated, that it's permanently damaged. Do you agree with that, and if so, why not?

The President. I hope it isn't. I know that he's still there, and he has left Saudi Arabia now for Damascus. And I think that he's done a miraculous job so far when you stop to think that when we sent him there, they literally had the weapons cocked and ready for war. And it's been several weeks now, and no war has happpened. It would be just further tragic evidence if this latest happening should turn this off. But till he comes home and says, "I give up," why, I'm going to believe that we can do it.

Nuclear Nonproliferation

Q. Mr. President, how appropriate do you believe is Israel's decision not to sign the Nuclear Non-Proliferation Treaty and not to submit to inspections by the International Atomic Energy Agency? And I have a followup.

The President. Well, I haven't given very much thought to that particular question there, the subject about them not signing

that treaty or, on the other hand, how many countries do we know that have signed it that very possibly are going ahead with nuclear weapons? It's, again, something that doesn't lend itself to verification.

It is difficult for me to envision Israel as being a threat to its neighbors. It is a nation that from the very beginning has lived under the threat from neighbors that they did not recognize its right to exist as a nation.

I'll have to think about that question you asked.

Q. What do you think the proper role of the United States is in preventing the spread of nuclear weapons and nuclear weapons technology?

The President. Well, our position is—and it is unqualified—that we're opposed to the proliferation of nuclear weapons and do everything in our power to prevent it. I don't believe, however, that that should carry over into the development of nuclear power for peaceful purposes. And so, it increases the difficulty, if you're going to encourage the one, because you have at least opened a crack in the door where someone can proceed to the development of weapons.

But I'm not only opposed to the proliferation of nuclear weapons, but, as I've said many times, I would like to enter into negotiations leading toward a definite, verifiable reduction of strategic nuclear weapons worldwide.

I'd better abandon the front row here for a minute.

Handgun Control

Q. Mr. President, at a recent White House meeting Senator Edward Kennedy asked if you'd refuse to lead the fight against his legislation on handgun control, or Saturday night specials, sales of Saturday night specials. What was your answer?

The President. Would I lead the fight against his——

Q. No, he asked that you not lead the fight against his legislation.

The President. Oh.

Q. What was your answer?

The President. Well, we had a very nice talk. And I told him that I believe that some of the things that we had tried in California served better, and that is to make the penalties for the carrying of a weapon, particularly in the commission of a crime, much stiffer than they are. California—we added 5 to 15 years to the prison sentence for anyone carrying a gun in the commission of a crime—convicted of that crime, whether they used the gun or not. And since, that's been augmented to include no probation—mandatory prison sentence.

I believe in that, because my concern about gun control is that it's taking our eyes off what might be the real answers to crime. It's diverting our attention. There are today more than 20,000 gun control laws in effect—Federal, State, and local—in the United States. Indeed, some of the stiffest gun control laws in the nation are right here in the District, and they didn't seem to prevent a fellow a few weeks ago from carrying one down by the Hilton Hotel. In other words, they are virtually unenforceable.

So, I would like to see us directing our attention to what has caused us to have the crime that continues to increase as it has and is one of our major problems in the country today.

Undocumented Aliens

Q. Muchas gracias, Señor Presidente. Su causa es mi causa, su casa es mi casa [Your cause is my cause, your home is my home]—I wonder when I will be able to tell to the undocumented aliens in this country these same words. You spoke with López Portillo the other day, and he said that you are going to agree in order to give some opportunity to those undocumented workers. I would like that you clarify to the nation what is the status of this situation.

The President. If I understand your question—are you talking about visiting the White House or me visiting you? [*Laughter*] Either way it would be a pleasure. [*Laughter*]

Sam [Sam Donaldson, ABC News].

Nuclear War

Q. Mr. President, every President since Dwight Eisenhower seems to believe that if the Soviet Union and the United States actually get into a shooting war, say, in

Europe, can't be contained and it would spread to a thermonuclear war. Do you agree?

The President. Well, it's a frightening possibility, and history bears it out. If we want to look for one little bit of optimism anyplace, the only time that I can recall in history that a weapon possessed by both sides was never used was in World War II—the use of poison gas. And possibly it was because the weapon was available to both sides. But the weapons are there, and they do extend to the battlefield use as well—the tactical weapons as well as the strategic.

And I have to believe that our greatest goal must be peace, and I also happen to believe that that will come through our maintaining enough strength that we can keep the peace.

Q. Sir, I have a followup. I ask the question, because I suppose that your defense strategy depends on whether you think if the Soviets invade Western Europe, a tactical nuclear war could be fought there and contained, or whether you think that it would spread inevitably to a thermonuclear exchange. What do you think?

The President. I thought I answered it. I try to be optimistic and think that the threat of both sides would keep it from happening, and yet, at the same time, as I say, history seems to be against that, that there comes a moment in desperation when one side tries to get an advantage over the other.

Candidacy for Second Term

Q. Mr. President, about 10 days ago your Chief of Staff said on a television interview program that he thought you were committed to running for a second term. And another aide of yours, Lyn Nofziger, has said virtually the same thing. Can you tell us, sir, if you are committed to running for a second term?

The President. I think that having only been here 5 months, no one should be making a decision about what they're going to do 3 years and 7 months from now.

Q. Can you tell us why your aides are making such statements in public? Is it to prevent you being regarded at this stage as a possible lameduck?

The President. No, but I've neither ruled in or ruled out whether I would run again, and it's something that for the first 4 years in Sacramento I always refused to answer about. And one of the reasons I refuse to answer is because I, myself, am determined that any decisions that we make in this administration are not going to be made based on whether they might have an effect on a coming election. There will be no political ramifications to them. But I'll make that decision when we get closer to that.

Actually, I suppose what I'm saying is the people make that decision. They let you know whether you're going to run again or whether you should or not.

Federal Tax Reduction

Q. Mr. President, for months you said you wouldn't modify your tax cut plan, and then you did. And when the business community vociferously complained, you changed your plan again. I just wondered whether Congress and other special interest groups might get the message that if they yelled and screamed loud enough, you might modify your tax plan again?

The President. No, the 3-year, across-the-board spread which I did modify—to the extent of making it 5–10–10 instead of 10–10–10, and which I moved up to October 1st instead of retroactive back through the year in going into effect—was done in an effort to create, as we did with the spending law, a bipartisan package.

And the suggestions that were offered in the negotiations that led to that were suggestions that I had to admit were good ones. The marriage penalty tax, the making it possible for workers to save money for their own retirement and have an income tax break for that reason, the adjustment of the investment funds, the 70-percent ceiling to 50 and so forth—all of these things, I thought, were worth—and to put them into the bill, they were all things—and that including the estate tax, which you've heard me in the campaign say many times I wanted to eventually eliminate—all of those were things that we had said would be in a second tax package when we could do it. By making the change that I made in that across-the-board cut, that provided most of

the revenue that made it possible to move those up into the first.

I can't retreat, and I don't think the people want us to. The latest polls that we have show that 79 percent of the people approve of the individual tax cut and approve of it over a 3-year span. And that, I think, should be a message to anyone who's elected to office on the Hill or elsewhere.

The gentleman there.

Minority Businesses

Q. Thank you, Mr. President. Your administration to some extent has been called an administration or a Presidency of the wealthy. I'm wondering if you have laid out any programs in your administration, currently, that will provide for increasing the viability of minority business and other programs that relate to business development for minorities?

The President. All of these things that you just mentioned there, increasing the viability of minority business and so forth, all of these are matters of the policy of an administration and what we intend to do.

I've heard these charges about our supposedly being an administration for the wealthy. I don't see where they fit. We have watched the so-called social reforms for three of four decades now fail in trying to lift people that are not in the mainstream and that don't have their foot on the ladder of opportunity, and they failed.

As a matter of fact, what they've created is a kind of bondage in which the people are made subservient to the government that is handing out the largesse, and the only people who prosper from them is that large bureaucracy that administers them. And I believe that our economic package is aimed at stimulating the economy, providing incentive, increasing productivity so as to create new jobs. And those jobs will make it possible for those people who are now economically below the norm to get a foot on the ladder and improve themselves. And, as some of the other programs, that is a case of how you direct the administering of the programs, such as aid to small business. And I would think, for one, the minority community and the black community has the most to gain from the development of small business within their neighborhoods.

If you will compare those communities to other ethnic communities of various kinds, you will find that the money that is spent in those communities almost from the first dollar—there is no turnover. It is spent outside that community. In the others the dollars turn over as much as five and six times before they leave that community and go out into the general economy. And it is that turnover that multiplies the effect. And right now the black community has about $140 billion that is not basically, even from the first dollar, being spent in their own communities.

So, this is one of the big targets—is to have an improvement of business there.

Syrian Missiles in Lebanon

Q. Mr. President, as you know, the Israeli Government has made the threat that it might take military action to wipe out the Syrian missiles in Lebanon. If that were to be done against our wishes, would you consider that a violation of the terms of the laws under which the Israelis have obtained those weapons?

The President. Well, this one's going to be one, I'm afraid, that I can't answer now as to how—I would hate to see this happen. They're offensive[1] weapons. There's no question about the direction in which they're aimed. I'm speaking now of the Syrian weapons. This would end our prospects for trying to bring peace to Lebanon, I know.

We're going to use every effort we can to see that they, on either side, that there isn't a firing of those missiles.

The young lady next to you.

The Assassination Attempt

Q. Thank you, Mr. President. As everyone knows, this is your first news conference since you were shot, and I think everybody has the impression that you have fully recovered. My first question is, have you fully recovered? And secondly, can you tell us how having been shot has changed

---

[1] *The White House later announced that the President had meant to say "defensive."*

you? Have you become more cautious, or are there any differences?

The President. I have recovered. I feel fine. And the doctors say I've recovered. So, if I'm a medical miracle, I'm a happy one.

No, you can't spend your life worrying about that. I'm quite sure that there will be and have been changes in—I look back now and wonder why it didn't happen 30 times before—changes in alertness on the part of security and so forth. But it hasn't made too much of a change in how we do, and I still want to be able to see the people and meet them.

Weapons Sales to China

Q. Mr. President, Secretary Haig, as you know, announced in China today that the United States is lifting its ban against lethal weapons sales to the People's Republic of China. I want to know if you would explain to the American people, please, why you've decided to help the People's Republic of China rearm militarily and how you think the Soviet Union will react to your action?

The President. Well, I don't know how the Soviet Union will react, but all we have done is—with the People's Republic of China, we've wanted—and I've said for a long time—to improve relations with them, move them to the same status of many other countries and not necessarily military allies of ours, in making certain technology and defensive weapons available to them. And I think this is a normal part of the process of improving our relations there.

Political Action Committees

Q. Mr. President, do you approve of conservative fundraising groups such as NCPAC [National Conservative Political Action Committee] making these expensive television commercials targeting liberal Democrats for defeat in the next election?

The President. I don't really know how to answer that, because the game of politics is trying to win an election. And I've never seen the time when both parties have not been doing everything they can to win an election.

I think one of the things that does not set too well with me is that to campaign before there is a candidate on your side means that you're campaigning totally in a negative way. And I've always believed that you campaign by stressing what it is your candidate would do and your approval of it.

Q. If I may follow up on that, sir, is it really a sense of fair play that these groups with all their money are, in effect, ganging up on one Member of Congress to make him an object lesson for other wavering Congressmen who might not see things their way?

The President. Well, I thought they were going after a gang of them—*[laughter]*—just one won't do us much good. *[Laughter]*

Pakistan

Q. Mr. President, you said earlier that you strongly oppose the proliferation of nuclear weapons. Yet at the same time, you are asking Congress to waive an American law so that Pakistan, which has refused to sign the Nuclear Non-Proliferation Treaty, can receive $3 billion in American aid.

Do we have any assurances from Pakistan that they will not seek to build an atomic bomb?

The President. Let me just say with regard to Pakistan—and I won't answer the last part of the question—we have had a long-time treaty with Pakistan in a mutual aid pact. But Pakistan is also in a very strategic position now in view of what has happened to Afghanistan. And I believe it is in our best interest to be supportive of Pakistan.

Impact Aid to Schools

Q. Mr. President, sir, I wonder, you don't want inferior schools for soldiers, do you?

The President. Inferior schools for soldiers? No.

Q. For their children?

The President. No.

Q. Well, I didn't think you would. I call your attention to what's happening to the school impacted aid program under your reductions, and you're going to have some schools near military bases that are supposed to educate the children of soldiers that are going to be in a very hard-hit way unless some new formula——

I was wondering if you couldn't find a new formula for taking care of the children of the poor soldiers?

The President. Well, Ms. McClendon [Sarah McClendon, McClendon News Service], I think what you're going to find is this is one of the things I talked about in my opening statement. This is one of the things in the committee in Congress that has been a cut that we did not put in our program. While we were going to reduce impacted aid in those areas where—see, impacted aid is for, like a military base, where the people are not taxpayers, not property owners, where they come in temporarily and their children then are put as an added burden on the local system. But we have been having impacted aid for a long time to areas where the people are permanent residents, but government employees, but they are homeowners, and they are property taxpayers and so forth.

What has happened now is in this same way we see them putting into effect cuts that they know cannot last. In other words, we think it is designed to really destroy, in a sense, the program that we're trying to implement in putting these cuts in—this drastic cut that has been proposed in impact aid, which would do what you have said. We're hoping that the Congressmen in the Budget Committee—they will correct some of those things that have been done, and if not then, as I said, we'll go along with those Congressmen, many of them Democrats, who want to put in a substitute bill, and we would then meet the Senate bill in a conference committee.

Poland

Q. Mr. President, how do you assess the current situation in Poland? And the second part of that is whether the warming up on relations, especially in the strategic military area with China, has any connection in your mind with events in Poland?

The President. No, I don't see any connection between China and what's going on in Poland. I think the Poland situation is going to be very tense for quite some time now. The Soviet Union is faced with a problem of this crack in their once Iron Curtain and what happens if they let it go. But on the other hand, what is going to be the impact if they take a forceful action? The impact on the rest of the world, I think, would be tremendous in the reaction that would come from all the——

Q. The point of my question, sir, was that there was a list being made up by the Pentagon of weapons which might be supplied to China in the event that the Soviets invaded Poland. There has been a connection drawn by General Haig and others that one way to deter the Soviets in Poland is to make it clear that they might have to pay by increased American aid to China. Does that exist in——

The President. Well, now, these might have been contingencies that were discussed. Certainly they are not policy in our administration.

Now you, sir.

Taiwan

Q. Thank you, Mr. President. Returning once to that question of lifting of the lethal arms sales shipments to China, does that affect in any way our relationship with Taiwan, and if so, how? Does that move us in any direction either to or away from the Government of Taiwan?

The President. No, and I have not changed my feeling about Taiwan. We have an act, a law, called the Taiwan Relations Act, that provides for defensive equipment being sold to Taiwan as well as other things in the relationship. And I intend to live up to the Taiwan Relations Act.

Mr. Reynolds. Thank you, Mr. President.

The President. We're out? Sam, you told me that it was all right about walking away from all those upraised hands, and I have to tell you, it still bothers me very much. I'm sorry that we can't answer all the questions.

Q. We'll stay if you will, sir.

The President. No. I know I can't. I know I can't, and I'm sorry.

Q. Do you like it better than the lottery, Mr. President.

The President. Yes.

Program for Economic Recovery

Q. [House Speaker] Tip O'Neill says you don't know anything about the working people, that you have just a bunch of wealthy and selfish advisers.

The President. One more. Just one. [*Laughter*] Wouldn't you know that Sam Donaldson would be the one? Sam says, quoted—why didn't you do that earlier?—said that Tip O'Neill has said that I don't know anything about the working man.

I'm trying to find out something about his boyhood, because we didn't live on the wrong side of the railroad tracks, but we lived so close to them we could hear the whistle real loud. And I know very much about the working group. I grew up in poverty and got what education I got all by myself and so forth, and I think it is sheer demagoguery to pretend that this economic program which we've submitted is not aimed at helping the great cross section of people in this country that have been burdened for too long by big government and high taxes. From 10 to 50 to 60 thousand dollars covers, certainly, all the middle class, and they pay 72 percent of the tax. And 73 percent of our tax relief or more is going to that bracket of workers. And we're going to do our utmost to keep that bottom rung of the ladder clear for those people that haven't yet started to climb.

Q. Did you mean to suggest in your opening statement that you might ask Congress to stay through August and—[*inaudible*]?

The President. That's something we could think about.

Note: The President's third news conference began at 2 p.m. in Room 450 of the Old Executive Office Building. It was broadcast live on radio and television.

Remarks on Presenting the Congressional Gold Medal to Kenneth Taylor, Former Canadian Ambassador to Iran
June 16, 1981

The President. I wonder what would happen if I said that in trying to express our gratitude, I was now going to talk for about 55 minutes. [*Laughter*] No, I'm not. But the 444 days of the hostage crisis were trying times for this country, and they were not a time of which any world citizen can be proud. What the Iranians did was a breach of international law and the rules by which states live together.

Against the background of those difficult days, however, several acts of individual heroism reminded us of man's nobler sides. There was the courage of those participating in the daring rescue mission, some of whom gave their lives.

We're today honoring another act of courage, this one with a happier ending in which the courage and ingenuity were rewarded by success after 79 days. I'd like to sketch briefly the events of those 79 days, to describe not only Ambassador Taylor's courage but also the contribution of all the Canadian Embassy personnel in Tehran and the Canadian Government in Ottawa.

Four days after the storming of the American Embassy, Ambassador Taylor received a call from five Americans who had escaped from the Embassy when it was overrun. They were hiding, but they were afraid that they'd soon be discovered and captured. Ambassador Taylor immediately recommended to his government in Ottawa that Americans be given shelter. Without any hesitation, the Canadian Government granted the permission. Two days later, the Americans were taken to Ambassador Taylor's residence and that of another Canadian Embassy family, the John Sheardowns. Two weeks later, another American joined his five compatriots. For 79 days, they lived there pretending to be visitors. I understand they're the best-read and the most skilled Scrabble players in all of North America.

There were several tense moments in the weeks that followed. At one point, an article was imminent in a Montreal paper which would have disclosed the story of the sheltered Americans. In an admirable display of responsibility, the journalist who had written the article agreed to withdraw it from publication. However, from this article, and more immediately from an anonymous phone call to the Taylor's residence asking to speak to two of the escapees, Ambassador Taylor knew that the chances of his guests being discovered were high.

At this point, the Canadian Government in Ottawa and the Embassy began the ingenious preparations for an escape. The Canadian Government agreed to issue fictitious passports to the Americans. The Canadian Embassy staff began making flights in and out of Tehran to establish a travel pattern and to learn airport procedures.

Finally, on January 28th, 1980, the Americans packed the bags that were given them by their Canadian hosts with the clothes also given to them. Using their Canadian passports, they flew out of the country. Ambassador Taylor and three others of his staff saw them off and then left themselves. Even this brief outline of those 79 days highlights what a team effort it was.

The Canadian Department of External Affairs in Ottawa and the Canadian Cabinet responded with speed and decisiveness to help an ally. Ambassador Towe is here today representing the Canadian Government. The U.S. State Department is represented today by Ambassador Stoessel, and there were others who were working at the State Department during the crisis who played a part with discretion and skill. And here today also is Representative Daniel Akaka, the sponsor, and several of his cosponsors, of the legislation which resulted in the gold medal which I am going to present today.

Also present today is Lee Schatz, one of the six whom the Taylors rescued, as well as Bruce Laingen and Victor Tomseth, who had to wait a little longer before they could come home.

Mrs. Taylor is here with her husband and was directly involved with him in this deed. She shared the risks. She did much of the work. It was at her residence that several of the Americans were actually staying. And, finally, it's my great honor to present the medal to Kenneth Taylor whose valor, ingenuity, and steady nerves made possible this one happy chapter in the agony of those 444 days of hostage crisis.

Major Kline. The medal is inscribed by an "Act of Congress, March 6, 1980. *Entre amis*, appreciation for the noble and heroic effort in the harboring of six United States diplomats and safe return to America. Thank you, Canada."

The President. Ambassador Taylor, it's a great pleasure to present this medal to you on behalf of the American people, who are grateful to you and grateful to our neighbor, Canada.

Ambassador Taylor. Thank you. Thank you very much, President Reagan. I'm very honored to receive this recognition on behalf of all Canadians who participated in whatever we could contribute to the welfare of the U.S. citizens.

I think what I'd like to say is best expressed by Honorable Frank Annunzio, chairman of the committee, during the course of Representative Akaka's resolution. That is, he said, "To me, the medal represents the gratitude and thanks of every American not only to Ambassador Taylor but to his staff, the Government of Canada, and indeed every Canadian." And it's in that sense that I'm very honored to receive the medal.

At this time, it's a very perplexing and unique situation to be a diplomat. At the same time as serious questions are being asked as to the validity of the career as opposed to earlier times, there are some who are challenging the very right of diplomats to convey their country's message and attempt to create international disorders such as we experienced in Tehran. It's therefore very reassuring and a sense of pride to all diplomats to have seen the dignity and professionalism with which U.S. citizens in Tehran conducted themselves and also the unselfish courage and heroism of the eight who lost their lives attempting to right the balance.

The presentation of the Congressional Gold Medal, President Reagan, not only means a great deal to myself and my family, but I think it underlines the very unique and very special relationship between Canada and the United States.

The United States faces the rebuffs of history with patience, determination, and a search for justice. For this, you have gained the everlasting respect of all Canadians. Moreover, your generosity, great generosity to all, your tolerance, cements the long-lasting and precious friendship which Canadians and United States citizens share.

Thank you, again, for this recognition. I speak on behalf of Canada, and I can say and sum it up that we're very fortunate, and we relish that, cherish our neighborhood relationship with you.

Thank you, again, Mr. President.

Note: The President spoke at 3:35 p.m. at the presentation ceremony in the Rose Garden at the White House. Maj. John P. Kline, Jr., Marine Corps Aide to the President, read the inscription on the medal. Peter M. Towe is the Canadian Ambassador to the United States, and Walter J. Stoessel, Jr., is Under Secretary of State for Political Affairs.

Executive Order 12310—President's Commission on Housing
June 16, 1981

By the authority vested in me as President of the United States, and in order to establish, in accordance with the provisions of the Federal Advisory Committee Act, as amended (5 U.S.C. App. I), a Presidential advisory committee on national housing policies and Federal programs in furtherance thereof, it is hereby ordered as follows:

Section 1. Establishment. (a) There is established the President's Commission on Housing. The Commission shall be composed of not more than twenty-two (22) members from private life and from State and local governments who shall be appointed by the President.

(b) The President shall designate a Chairman and Vice-Chairman from among the members of the Commission.

Sec. 2. Functions. The Commission shall advise the President and the Secretary of Housing and Urban Development with respect to options for the development of a national housing policy consistent with the President's Economic Recovery Program and the role and objectives of the government in future housing availability. Consistent with these general functions, the Commission shall:

a. Analyze the relationship of homeownership to political, social, and economic stability within the nation;

b. review all existing federal housing policies and programs;

c. assess those factors which contribute to the cost of housing as well as the current housing finance structure and practices in the country;

d. seek to develop housing and mortgage finance options which strengthen the ability of the private sector to maximize opportunities for homeownership and provide adequate shelter for all Americans;

e. detail program options for basic reform of federally-subsidized housing; and,

f. utilize such private and public sector expertise available in the housing field as the Commission, in its discretion, deems appropriate.

The Commission shall provide information and advice to the President or to the Secretary of Housing and Urban Development whenever requested and shall provide the President and the Secretary of Housing and Urban Development with an interim report not later than October 30, 1981 and a final report not later than April 30, 1982.

Sec. 3. Administration. (a) Members of the Commission shall serve without compensation. However, they shall be entitled to travel expenses, including per diem in lieu of subsistence, as authorized by law for persons serving intermittently in the government service (5 U.S.C. 5701–5707), to the extent funds are available therefor.

(b) The Heads of the Executive agencies shall, to the extent permitted by law, provide the Commission such information as it may require for the purpose of carrying out its functions.

(c) Any expenses of the Commission shall be paid from funds available to the Secretary of Housing and Urban Development.

Sec. 4. General. (a) Notwithstanding any other Executive Order, the responsibilities of the President under the Federal Advisory Committee Act, as amended, except that of reporting annually to the Congress, which are applicable to the advisory committee established by this Order, shall be performed by the Secretary of Housing and Urban Development in accordance with guidelines and procedures established by the Administrator of General Services.

(b) The Commission shall terminate upon presenting its final report and recommendations to the President and the Secretary of Housing and Urban Development.

RONALD REAGAN

The White House,
June 16, 1981.

[*Filed with the Office of the Federal Register, 12:15 p.m., June 17, 1981*]

Note: The text of the Executive order was released by the Office of the Press Secretary on June 17.

Remarks on Signing a Veterans Medical Care Bill
June 17, 1981

The President. I'm pleased today to be signing into law this House resolution 2156. This legislation is aimed at maintaining the quality of medical care for our veterans.

Five State medical schools have been established under the Veterans Administration Medical School Assistance and Health Manpower Training Act of 1972, but due to some unavoidable delays, they may lose some of the funds that were allocated to them.

House resolution 2156 provides an additional year for the medical schools to use the moneys that were allocated by the original act. These moneys allocated to improve the health care of veterans will not be withdrawn simply because of unavoidable delays that prevented meeting of artificial deadlines set within the original legislation. We owe more than money to those who wore their country's uniform and sacrificed in our behalf, and will not waiver in our obligation to them.

So, I am particularly pleased to sign this bill which represents a sound and productive program for helping American people. So saying, I'll sign it.

[At this point, the President signed the bill.]

Reporter. Mr. President, why won't you meet with the Vietnam veteran hunger strikers?

The President. This is the only question I'll take on that. Let me explain something about that. We did have—it wasn't possible for me to get out there. We did have representatives who met with the original group that came in protesting and were demonstrating, you might say. And they were satisfied that we were doing the things that they were there asking for with regard to Agent Orange and the doubling of money for research on that, helping the veterans increasing the—we're doubling the amount also for the Veterans Treatment Centers, the Vietnam Veterans Treatment Centers, and we are also going forward witha program for what is known as effects of delayed stress. And this latter group then came in and apparently were unwilling to accept that these things had already been agreed to.

So, this was the only reason. The others who had come in and heard the case that was presented left satisfied.

Q. Thank you.

Note: The President spoke at 10:48 a.m. at the signing ceremony in the Roosevelt Room at the White House.

As enacted, H.R. 2156 is Public Law 97–15, approved June 17.

Remarks Following a Meeting With the Chairman and Vice Chairman of the President's Commission on Housing
June 17, 1981

The President. I know that Secretary Pierce shares my delight that Bill McKenna has accepted the Chairmanship and Carla Hills the Vice Chairmanship of the President's Commission on Housing. And they, along with the 20 members of the Commission who'll be named today, represent a great reservoir of experience and background in this field.

Homeownership is the symbol of the family unit, the neighborhood, and is essential if we're going to have social, economic, and political stability in our land. The industry has been suffering from economic ups and downs, a roller coaster for the past two decades, and is suffering today. Our economic recovery program is the key, I think, to long-term recovery for that particular industry and for homeownership in the land.

This Commission is going to be taking a hard look at all aspects of housing—financing, costs, construction, the Federal housing programs—and in addition, is going to look at how much government should be in housing, and come up with options for a national housing policy, and what we can do to maximize in the private sector homeownership.

Well, Bill and Carla, you have a big job ahead of you, and I'm delighted that you'd take on that job.

Mr. McKenna. Mr. President, I appreciate your trust, and the job will be done.

Mrs. Hills. Thank you, Mr. President.

Note: The President spoke at 11:18 a.m. to reporters assembled in the Oval Office at the White House.

Appointment of the Membership of the President's Commission on Housing, and Designation of Chairman and Vice Chairman
June 17, 1981

The President has established by Executive order the President's Commission on Housing.

The Commission will advise the President and the Secretary of Housing and Urban Development with respect to options for the development of a national housing policy and the role and objectives of the government in future housing availability.

The Executive order requests the Commission to:

—Analyze the relationship of homeownership to political, social, and economic stability within the nation;

—Review all existing Federal housing policies and programs;

—Assess those factors which contribute to the cost of housing;

—Assess the current housing finance structure and practices in the country;

—Seek to develop housing and mortgage finance options which strengthen the ability of the private sector to maximize opportunities for homeownership and provide adequate shelter for all Americans;

—Detail program options for basic reform of federally subsidized housing.

The Commission will provide information to the President and the Secretary of HUD whenever requested, as well as an interim report not later than October 30, 1981, and a final report not later than April 30, 1982. Members will serve without compensation but will be entitled to expenses.

The President designated William F. McKenna, a Los Angeles attorney, as Chairman, and Washington, D.C., attorney Carla Anderson Hills as Vice Chairman. Mr. McKenna is an expert in housing finance. Mrs. Hills served as Secretary of the Department of Housing and Urban Development from 1975 to 1977.

The members of the Commission are:

William F. McKenna, Chairman. Mr. McKenna, a resident of Los Angeles, is a distinguished attorney and senior partner of the national law firm of McKenna, Conner & Cuneo (Los Angeles, San Francisco, and Washington, D.C.). From 1948 to 1951, he served as litigation counsel for the Federal Home Loan Bank System and the Federal Savings & Loan Insurance Corporation. He was the Republican counsel to the House Committee on Expenditures in the Executive Departments, predecessor to the House Government Operations Committee, in 1951. Two years later, he served as general counsel for the House Government Operations Committee and was chief counsel to several of its subcommittees, including the Government Reorganization Subcommittee. Also in 1953, he served as chief counsel of the Joint Anti-racketeering Subcommittee of the House Government Operations and House Education and Labor Committees. In 1954 McKenna set up the Organized Crime Unit of the U.S. Department of Justice. Also in 1954, at President Eisenhower's request, McKenna served as Deputy Administrator of the U.S. Housing and Home Finance Agency, predecessor of HUD. In this role, he was asked to clean up a myriad of problems and scandals in these housing agencies with emphasis on solving problems at FHA. From 1962 to 1970, at the request of the U.S. Department of State, he advised the Government of Brazil on housing finance matters. He is a graduate of Yale University Law School (1939) and was awarded an LL.D. degree at Providence College, Providence, R.I., in 1969. He is a fellow of the American College of Trial Lawyers and is a founder of the Free Clinic for the Aged Poor (Knights of Malta) in downtown Los Angeles.

Carla Anderson Hills, Vice Chairman. Mrs. Hills, a resident of Los Angeles, Calif., is a partner in the Washington, D.C., law firm of Latham, Watkins & Hills. A graduate of Stanford University and Yale Law School, she served as Secretary of the Department of Housing and Urban Development from 1975 to 1977. She began her legal career in 1958 as an assistant U.S. attorney, Civil Division, Los Angeles. From 1962 to 1974, she was a partner in the Los Angeles law firm of Munger, Tolles, Hills & Rickershauser. She returned to government service in 1974 as Assistant Attorney General, Civil Division, Department of Justice, Washington, D.C. Since 1978 she has served as a member of the MIT-Harvard Joint Center for Urban Studies and as a director of the American Council for Capital Formation. She served as the chairman of the Reagan-Bush housing task force in 1980.

Garry E. Brown. A resident of Washington, D.C., Mr. Brown was a Michigan State senator from 1962 to 1966 and served as a Member of Congress from 1967 to 1979. While in Congress, he was the second ranking member on the House Banking, Finance and Affairs Committee (served 12 years) and the ranking member on Housing and Community Development Subcommittee. Mr. Brown also was a senior ranking member on the Government Operations Committee and ranking member on its Commerce, Consumer and Monetary Affairs Subcommittee. In addition, he was the second ranking House Member on the Joint Economic Committee and a member of three of its subcommittees. Mr. Brown is a partner and director in the Washington, D.C., law firm of Hill, Christopher, and Phillips. He is a graduate of Kalamazoo College, Mich., and received his law degree from George Washington Law School in 1954.

Edward W. Brooke. A resident of Washington, D.C., he served two terms in the U.S. Senate from the State of Massachusetts. A graduate of Howard University, he received his LL.B. and LL.M. degrees from Boston University. As a Senator, he served as the ranking Republican member of the Senate Banking, Housing and Urban Affairs Committee. He also held other key committee assignments, including seats on the Armed Services Committee, the Joint Committee on Defense Production, and the Appropriations Committee. He is a partner in the Washington, D.C., law firm of O'Connor and Hannan and serves as counsel to Csaplar & Bok in Boston, a partner in Bear, Stearns & Co. in New York, and a consultant to E. F. Hutton in New York. Senator Brooke is a fellow of the American Bar Association and of the American Academy of Arts and Sciences.

Bernard J. Carl. A resident of Washington, D.C., Mr. Carl is a partner in the Washington, D.C., law firm of Williams and Connolly. Prior to joining the firm in 1977, he served as Acting Assistant Secretary for Policy Development and Research (1976–1977) and Deputy Assistant Secretary for Policy Development and Program Evaluation (1975–1976) at the U.S. Department of Housing and Urban Department. He was the principal author of HUD's 1976 Presidential White Paper on the Future Role of FHA. He also was the principal author of HUD's 1976 Housing Assistance Block Grant Proposal and the 1976 Counter-Cyclical Community Development Block Grant Proposal. In addition, he was policy adviser to the October 1976 Interim Report of the President's Committee on Urban Development and Neighborhood Revitalization. He was a member of the Reagan-Bush committee housing task force in 1980 and was the HUD project program director for the Reagan transition. Carl is a graduate of Wesleyan University, Conn., and received his law degree from the University of Virginia in 1972.

Richard E. Carver. Currrently the mayor of Peoria, Ill. (since 1973), Mr. Carver also is president of Carver Lumber Co. in Peoria, Ill. A graduate of Bradley University, he now serves as a director of the University's Urban Affairs Institute, the Illinois State Chamber of Commerce, and the National League of Cities. He is president of the National Conference of Republican Mayors and is immediate past president of the U.S. Conference of Mayors and is presently a member of its executive committee. Mr. Carver is also a member of the President's Advisory Commission on Intergovernmental Relations and serves on the Mayors Advisory Board of the Federal Home Loan Bank Board Community Reinvestment Program. Mr. Carver is chairman of the Illinois Department of Local Government Affairs Energy Advisory Committee. He has served as a delegate to the U.N. Center for Human Settlements in 1976.

Stuart A. Davis. A resident of Webster Groves, Mo., Mr. Davis is president of Laurene Davis, Inc., a St. Louis area realty firm. He is a graduate of Washington University, St. Louis, and was selected "Realtor of the Year" in 1980 by the Missouri Association of Realtors. A member of the executive committee of the National Association of Realtors (NAR) and a former chairman of the NAR resolutions committee (1979), Mr. Davis also was president of the Missouri Association of Realtors in 1977 and has served on its board of directors since 1968. He is a past president (1974) of the Real Estate Board of Metropolitan St. Louis, has been a director since 1968, and a member of the executive committee for 5 years. He was, for six terms, chairman of the Board's Committee on Professional Standards. Mr. Davis was the 1980–81 chairman of the board of the Better Business Bureau of Greater St. Louis.

G. Richard Dunnels. A resident of Bethesda, Md., Mr. Dunnels has been a partner in the Washington, D.C., law firm of Dunnels, Duvall, Bennett & Porter since 1977. A graduate of Dartmouth College, he took his law degree from the University of Virginia in 1967. He began his legal career with the Washington, D.C., law firm of Hogan & Hartson and 2 years later (1969) joined the Nixon administration. From 1970 to 1973, he had various assignments at the U.S. Department of Housing and Urban Development, Washington, D.C., first, as special assistant to the Under Secretary (1970) then as Deputy Assistant Secretary for Housing and Urban Renewal (1970–1971), and as Deputy Assistant Secretary for Housing Management (1971–1973).

Richard L. Fore. A resident of Glenbrook, Nev., Mr. Fore has been a managing partner of Lincoln Property Co., Carson City, Nev., since 1977. He was vice president and general manager of the Donald L. Huber Corp., Dayton, Ohio, from 1975 to 1976. Mr. Fore was Executive Assistant to the General Manager of the New Community Development Corporation and Deputy Administrator of the New Communities Administration, U.S. Department of Housing and Urban Development, from 1973 to 1975, and also was administrative assistant to the Secretary of HUD during that period. A graduate of Florida State University, he received his MPA from Arizona State University in 1970. Mr. Fore was a member of President-elect Reagan's transition staff and was a member of the Reagan-Bush housing task force in 1980.

Lee Goodwin. A resident of Southampton, N.Y., Mrs. Goodwin has been a senior vice president for Merrill Lynch Huntoon-Page, New York

City, since 1976. A graduate of Barnard College, she took graduate courses in public law at Brown University. From 1957 to 1962, she was assistant to the chairman, New York State Senate Committee on New York City Affairs, and also was assistant to the chairman of the Joint Legislation Committee on Housing, New York State Legislature. From 1962 to 1963, she was executive assistant to the State Commission on Housing and served as assistant director of the New York State Housing Financial Authority from 1962 to 1973. From 1973 to 1976, she was a member of the New York Commission on Housing.

Richard K. Helmbrecht. A resident of Okemos, Mich., Mr. Helmbrecht has served as executive director of the Michigan State Housing Development Authority since 1977. He was director of the Michigan State Department of Commerce from 1972 to 1977 and held various positions in the office of the Governor of the State of Michigan from 1962 to 1972, including responsibility for new program development, legislative affairs, and special housing assignments. In 1977 he served as chairperson of the Governor's Urban Action Group. He is a graduate of Pennsylvania State University and took an MA in political science from the University of Chicago in 1963. Mr. Helmbrecht is president of the Council of State Housing Agencies.

Peter D. Herder. A resident of Tucson, Ariz., Mr. Herder serves as president of three construction firms: Herder Construction Co., Villa Catalina Building Corp., and Herder Commercial Development Corp. He also is vice president and owner of Arizona Brick Co. A graduate of San Jose State University, he took his masters degree from the University of Southern California. He has served as three-term president of Southern Arizona Home Builders Association (1969, 1975, 1976) and was named "Inspirational Leader of the Decade" in 1977. From 1978 to 1979, he served as vice president, Area 13, of the National Association of Home Builders (Arizona, Colorado, New Mexico, Nevada, Utah, Wyoming). He also is a director of the U. S. Chamber of Commerce, and was president of Tucson Economic Development Corp. from 1977 to 1979. Mr. Herder is a director of the United Bank of Arizona (Phoenix), and was a commissioner of Arizona Power Authority from 1972 to 1980. He was a director of the Tucson Airport Authority from 1979 to 1980.

Samuel C. Jackson. A resident of Washington, D.C., Mr. Jackson is a member of the New York and Washington, D.C., law firm of Stroock & Stroock & Lavan. He is a graduate of Washburn University, Topeka, Kans., where he also received a law degree in 1954. From 1969 to 1973, he served at the Department of Housing and Urban Development as Assistant Secretary for Community Planning and Development. Prior to his appointment as Assistant Secretary of HUD, he served as vice president of the American Arbitration Association and director of its National Center for Dispute Settlement from 1968 to 1969. He was one of five U.S. Commissioners of the U.S. Equal Employment Opportunity Commission from 1965 to 1968. He has held legal positions with the NAACP at local, State, and national levels. Formerly a member of the Administrative Conference of the United States, he has lectured and written extensively in legal and urban affairs journals.

Gordon C. Luce. A resident of San Diego, Calif., Mr. Luce is chairman of the board and chief executive officer of San Diego Federal Savings and Loan Association. He is a 1950 graduate of Stanford University, where he received his M.B.A. 2 years later. Mr. Luce served as secretary of business and transportation in the cabinet of Governor Reagan from 1967 to 1969. He has twice served as a delegate to the International Building Societies IES conference in Europe. He was the founding chairman of San Diego Economic Corp. Mr. Luce is a member of the board of overseers of the Hoover Institution (Stanford University). He also serves as an adviser to the University of Southern California Center for the Study of Financial Institutions. He is a director of the Federal Home Loan Bank of San Francisco and the U.S. League of Savings Associations. He also is a former president of the California Savings and Loan League.

Maurice Mann. A resident of San Francisco, Calif., Dr. Mann is vice chairman of A.G. Becker-Warburg Paribas Becker, Inc., a major U.S. investment banking and financial services firm. A graduate of Northeastern University, Boston, with a M.A. degree at Boston University, he received his Ph. D. at Syracuse University in 1955. From 1973 to 1978, he was president and chief executive officer of the Federal Home Loan Bank of San Francisco. Earlier he was executive vice president of the Western Pennsylvania National Bank and was Assistant Director of the Office of Management and Budget in Washington, D.C., from 1969 to 1970. He currently serves as chairman of the economic advisory board of the National Savings and Loan League and is chairman of the Federal Savings and Loan Advisory Council. He also is a chairman of the policy advisory board of the Real Estate and Urban Economics

Program at the University of California, Berkeley.

Preston Martin. A resident of Chicago, Ill., Mr. Martin is chairman and chief executive officer of the Seraco Group, a division of Sears Roebuck and Co. A graduate of the University of Southern California, where he also received his M.B.A., Mr. Martin received his Ph. D. in economics from Indiana University in 1952. He served as commissioner of the California Savings and Loan Department under Governor Reagan from 1967 to 1969. President Nixon named him Chairman of the Federal Home Loan Bank Board in Washington, D.C., in 1969, where he served until 1972. He is a member of the advisory board of the Joint Center of Urban Studies at MIT-Harvard University. He also is a member of the advisory committee of the Wharton School of Business. In 1977 he was a member of the Housing and Urban Development Task Force, whose mission was the "Future of FHA." In 1959 he authored the book "Principles and Practices of Real Estate" (Macmillan).

Robert V. Mathison. A resident of Hilton Head Island, S.C., Mr. Mathison is an inventor. He holds 30 U.S. patents, plus 26 patents in foreign lands. He currently is a consultant with Kimberly-Clarke and is a director of Rowe Furniture Corp., Salem, Va. From 1976 to 1980, he served as a member of the South Carolina State Housing Authority and was its vice chairman for 3 years. Previously he served as chairman of the City of Asheville Housing Authority, Asheville, N.C., from 1967 to 1970. He was vice president of Transcon Investment and Financial Limited (1971–1974), a private housing corporation. Mr. Mathison attended Carleton College, Minn., and Northwestern University, Evanston, Ill.

Martin P. Mayer. A resident of New York City, Mr. Mayer is a writer. He has authored 23 books, some of which are: "Wall Street, Men and Money" (1955), "Madison Avenue, USA" (1958), "The Schools" (1961), "The Lawyers" (1967), "About Television" (1972), "The Bankers" (1975), and "The Builders" (1978). He also has written articles on various aspects of American life in such publications as TV Guide, Cosmopolitan, Better Homes and Gardens, American Scholar, Commentary, and Musical America. Mr. Mayer is currently doing research for a book which will deal with the future of banking, growing out of a study on the subject for the 20th Century Fund. He is a graduate of Harvard College and holds honorary D. Lit(t). degrees from Lake Forest University and Adelphi University. Mr. Mayer worked as a reporter for the New York Journal of Commerce from 1947 to 1948 and was an associate editor of Esquire magazine from 1951 to 1954.

Richard F. Muth. A resident of Stanford, Calif., Dr. Muth has been a professor of economics at Stanford University since 1970. He is a graduate of Washington University, St. Louis, Mo., where he took his MA in 1950. Dr. Muth received his Ph. D. in economics at the University of Chicago in 1958. He served as a member of the President's Task Force on Urban Renewal in 1969. He was a member of the Reagan-Bush housing task force in 1980. He is the author of numerous articles and publications, some of which are: "Cities and Housing" (1969), and a monograph on "Public Housing" (1974), and "Urban Economic Problems" (1975).

Bernard H. Siegan. A resident of La Jolla, Calif., Mr. Siegan serves as distinguished professor of law and director of law and economic studies at the University of San Diego Law School. A graduate of the University of Chicago Law School, he was a practicing attorney in Chicago for 23 years before moving to Southern California. He was a research fellow in law and economics at the University of Chicago Law School from 1968 to 1969. Mr. Siegan was a member of the Reagan-Bush housing task force in 1980. He has authored and served as editor of seven books, including "Land Use Without Zoning" (1972), "Other People's Property" (1976), and "Economic Liberties and the Constitution," University of Chicago Press (1981). He also was the editor and contributor to the following books: "Planning Without Prices" (1977), "Regulation, Economics, and the Law" (1979), and "Government, Regulation and the Economy" (1980). Mr. Siegan has written numerous articles for professional journals and publications.

Kenneth J. Thygerson. A resident of Englewood, Colo., Dr. Thygerson is vice president of mortgage banking for Western Federal Savings and Loan Association, Denver, and is chairman of the board of First Capital Mortgage. A graduate of Northwestern University, Evanston, Ill., he also took a Ph. D. in economics from Northwestern in 1973. He was chief economist and director, division of economics and research, for the U.S. League of Savings Associations, Washington, D.C., from 1975 to 1981. The author of numerous books, publications, and articles on housing and housing finance, he was assistant director of human services in the office of policy coordination, Reagan transition, Washington, D.C. Dr. Thygerson is a former director of the American Real Estate and Urban Economic Association. He is currently a member of the advisory council, Credit Research Center, at Purdue University.

Charles J. Urstadt. A resident of Bronxville, N.Y., Mr. Urstadt is chairman, president, and chief executive officer of Pearce, Urstadt, Mayer & Greer, Inc., New York City, a mortgage and sales brokerage, building leasing, management, and insurance firm. A graduate of Dartmouth College where he also received an M.B.A. in 1951, Mr. Urstadt holds an LL.B. degree from Cornell University and also studied taxation at New York University Graduate Law School. From 1973 to 1978, he was chairman and chief executive officer, Battery Park City Authority, in New York. From 1967 to 1973, he was commissioner of Housing and Community Renewal, State of New York. He was chairman of the New York State Housing Finance Commission from 1969 to 1973 and served as chairman of the New York State Building Code Council from 1969 to 1973. He is former chairman of New York Construction Users Council and is a member of the advisory board of the Real Estate Institute of New York University.

Appointment of David R. Gergen as Assistant to the President for Communications
June 17, 1981

The President today announced the appointment of David R. Gergen to be Assistant to the President for Communications. Mr. Gergen has been serving since January as Assistant to the President and Staff Director of the White House.

Under this reassignment, Mr. Gergen will be filling a new post at the White House that will place him in charge of the White House Press Office, the Office of Communications, and the Speechwriting Office.

Mr. Gergen, 39, came to the White House

staff from the American Enterprise Institute for Public Policy Research, where he had been serving as a resident fellow and managing editor of Public Opinion, a magazine he helped to cofound. He is currently on leave from AEI.

Mr. Gergen has served on the White House staffs of two previous Presidents. In 1971 he joined the staff of President Nixon and in 1973–74 served as a Special Assistant to the President and chief of the White House writing and research team. In 1975, after a year at the Treasury Department under Secretary William Simon, he re- turned to the White House under President Ford and became Special Counsel to the President and Director of the White House Office of Communications, a post he held until early 1977.

Mr. Gergen is an honors graduate of both Yale University (A.B., 1963) and the Harvard Law School (1967) and is a member of the D.C. Bar Association.

He was born and raised in Durham, N.C. He currently resides with his wife Anne and two children in McLean, Va. Mr. Gergen was born May 9, 1942.

Appointment of Larry M. Speakes as Deputy Assistant to the President and Principal Deputy Press Secretary to the President
June 17, 1981

The President today announced the appointment of Larry Speakes to be Deputy Assistant to the President and principal Deputy Press Secretary to the President. Mr. Speakes is currently serving as Deputy Press Secretary.

Prior to joining the White House staff on January 20, 1981, Mr. Speakes was vice president of the international public relations firm of Hill and Knowlton in 1977–81. He served as deputy spokesman in the office of the President-elect during transition, and Mr. Speakes was liaison director for the Reagan-Bush Committee with former President Ford.

Mr. Speakes started his newspaper career in 1961 as editor of the Oxford (Mississippi) Eagle and was managing editor of the Bolivar Commercial in Cleveland, Miss., in 1962–66. He was general manager and editor of Progress Publishers of Leland, Miss., publishing weekly newspapers in four cities, in 1966–68. His newspapers won top awards from the Mississippi Press Association for 6 straight years.

Mr. Speakes came to Washington in 1968 as Press Secretary to Senator James O. East- land (D-Miss.), serving as spokesman for the Committee on the Judiciary and a coordinator for Senator Eastland's 1972 reelection campaign. During his service with Senator Eastland, Mr. Speakes directed press relations for major Judiciary Committee hearings, including the confirmation of four Supreme Court Justices.

In 1974 Mr. Speakes joined the Nixon administration as a Staff Assistant to the President and was later appointed Press Secretary to the Special Counsel to the President. In August 1974, he became Assistant Press Secretary to the President in the Ford administration. During the 1976 Presidential campaign, he was press secretary to Senator Bob Dole (R-Kans.), the Republican candidate for Vice President. When President Ford left office in 1977, Mr. Speakes became his press secretary, serving until June 1, 1977.

Mr. Speakes is a graduate of the University of Mississippi, where he majored in journalism. He is married to the former Laura Crawford, has three children, and resides in Annandale, Va.

Appointment of Peter Roussel as Deputy Press Secretary
June 17, 1981

The President today announced the appointment of Peter Roussel to be Deputy Press Secretary.

Mr. Roussel is currently director of governmental relations with the Houston (Tex.) Chamber of Commerce. In 1976 Mr. Roussel served on the President Ford Committee as special assistant to the campaign director, James Baker. In 1975 he was appointed as Assistant to White House Chief of Staff Donald Rumsfeld. In 1973–74 Mr. Roussel served as personal press officer to Republican National Committee Chairman George Bush. Following Mr. Bush's appointment as U.S. Ambassador to the United Nations in 1971, he was named his personal press officer. In 1969 he served as press secretary to U.S. Congressman George Bush and, in 1970, returned to Texas to serve as campaign press secretary to Bush in the U.S. Senate race of that year.

Mr. Roussel graduated from the University of Houston (B.S.) in 1965. He was born October 23, 1941, in Houston, Tex., and resides in Houston.

Nomination of Richard N. Perle To Be an Assistant Secretary of Defense
June 17, 1981

The President today announced his intention to nominate Richard N. Perle to be an Assistant Secretary of Defense (International Security Planning).

Mr. Perle was a professional staff member, Select Permanent Subcommittee on Investigations, and a staff member, Subcommittee on Arms Control, Senate Armed Services Committee, 1972–80. He was a consultant to the Special Assistant to the Secretary of Defense in 1969. He also served as an adviser to Senator Henry Jackson (D-Wash.).

Mr. Perle graduated from the University of California at Los Angeles (B.A., 1964) and Princeton University (M.A., 1967).

Mr. Perle resides in Chevy Chase, Md. He was born September 16, 1941, in New York, N.Y.

Nomination of Joan D. Aikens To Be a Member of the Federal Election Commission
June 17, 1981

The President today announced his intention to nominate Joan D. Aikens to be a member of the Federal Election Commission for the remainder of the term expiring April 30, 1983, vice Vernon Thomson.

Since 1975 Mrs. Aikens has served as a Republican member on the Federal Election Commission. In 1974–75 she was vice president of Lew Hodges/Communications, Inc., a public relations firm in Valley Forge, Pa. Mrs. Aikens was a fashion consultant with the Park Avenue Shop, Swarthmore, Pa., in 1971–74.

Mrs. Aikens graduated from Ursinus College (B.A., 1950), Collegeville, Pa. She is a recipient of an honorary doctor of laws degree (1969) from that institution. She has been active in the Republican Party in Pennsylvania including serving as president of the Pennsylvania Council of Republican Women in 1972 and 1974.

Mrs. Aikens has one son and resides in Washington, D.C. She was born January 1, 1928.

Nomination of Lee Ann Elliott To Be a Member of the Federal Election Commission
June 17, 1981

The President today announced his intention to nominate Lee Ann Elliott to be a member of the Federal Election Commission for the term expiring April 30, 1987, vice Joan Aikens.

Since 1979 Mrs. Elliott has been vice president, Bishop, Bryant & Associates, Inc., of Washington, D.C. She has also been associate editor, Political Action Report, Tyke Research Associates. In 1970–79 she was associate executive director, American Medical Political Action Committee, and served as assistant director in 1961–70.

Mrs. Elliott is a member of the board of directors of the American Association of Political Consultants, Public Affairs Committee of the Chamber of Commerce of the United States, and board of directors and past president of the Chicago Area Public Affairs Group. She is a recipient of the Award of Excellence in Serving Corporate Public Affairs from the National Association of Manufacturers (1979).

Mrs. Elliot graduated from the University of Illinois (B.A.) and attended Northwestern University. She resides in Skokie, Ill., and was born June 26, 1927.

Letter Accepting the Retirement of Potter Stewart as Associate Justice of the United States Supreme Court
June 18, 1981

Dear Mr. Justice:

It is with the deepest regret and appreciation for your long and outstanding service to our Nation that, at your request, I accept your retirement as Associate Justice of the Supreme Court of the United States, effective July 3, 1981.

Throughout your distinguished judicial career you have shown unfailing dedication to the Court, to the highest standards of the legal profession, and to the fundamental principles and protections of our Constitution. Your opinions have reflected concern for striking appropriate balances between federal and state authority, between individual freedoms and the legitimate interests of community and government, and between preservation of our timeless values and the need to allow for reform and change. And you have expressed your views with special grace and lucidity, which will help make yours an enduring presence in our law.

When you came to the Court you swore to "administer justice without respect to persons," and to "do equal right to the poor and to the rich . . . agreeably to the Constitution and laws of the United States." You can leave with the assurance that you have kept your solemn oath.

I hope that the Nation can continue to call on your services, and I wish you and Mrs. Stewart a long and happy retirement.

Sincerely,

RONALD REAGAN

Note: On the same day, the White House announced that the President and Justice Stewart had met at the White House on May 18, at which time the Justice gave the President a letter which expressed his intention to retire.

Nomination of John R. Van de Water To Be a Member of the National Labor Relations Board, and Designation as Chairman
June 18, 1981

The President today announced his intention to nominate John R. Van de Water to be a member of the National Labor Relations Board, for the remainder of the term expiring August 27, 1981, vice John A. Penello. He will also be nominated for the full 5-year term expiring August 27, 1986. Upon confirmation, the President intends to designate Dr. Van de Water Chairman.

Since 1949 Dr. Van de Water has been president of Van de Water Associates, Inc., consultants to management. He is also executive vice president of Promanent International, Inc., specializing in the audiovisual presentation of professional management development programs. Dr. Van de Water created and served as the first director of the California State Bar Program for the Continuing Education of the Legal Profession. He has served as director of the executive program for UCLA's Graduate School of Management and as a member of that school's faculty for 20 years, and as adjunct professor of industrial relations and management at the Graduate School of Business Administration, University of Southern California.

Dr. Van de Water is an attorney at law and member of the California Bar. He has served as a representative of management for North American Aviation, Inc. and the Ford Motor Co. He has served on the labor arbitration and collective bargaining law committee of the American Bar Association and the labor relations committee of the United States Chamber of Commerce.

Dr. Van de Water graduated from the University of Chicago (A.B., 1939) and the University of Chicago Law School (J.D., 1941). He is the author of many articles and publications in the areas of management, labor law, and industrial production.

Dr. Van de Water is married, has seven children, and resides in San Pedro, Calif. He was born March 26, 1917, in Long Beach, Calif.

Nomination of Robert P. Hunter To Be a Member of the National Labor Relations Board
June 18, 1981

The President today announced his intention to nominate Robert P. Hunter to be a member of the National Labor Relations Board, term expiring August 27, 1985, vice John C. Truesdale.

Since January 1981 Mr. Hunter has been serving as chief counsel and chief of staff for the Senate Labor and Human Resources Committee. He was responsible for development of all policy issues which fall within the Committee's broad jurisdiction, including labor law. In 1977–81 he was legislative director and Labor Committee counsel to Senator Orrin Hatch (R-Utah). Mr. Hunter was Senate Labor Committee counsel to Senator Robert Taft, Jr., (R-Ohio) in 1974–76. In 1969–74 he was an attorney with the National Labor Relations Board in the Buffalo, N.Y., and Cincinnati, Ohio, regional offices. Prior to this time he was an attorney with the firm of Coffman and Jones, Jacksonville, Fla.

Mr. Hunter graduated from the University of Connecticut (B.S., 1962); Vanderbilt Law School (J.D., 1965); and New York University Graduate Law School (LL.M. 1966).

He served as a captain in the U.S. Air Force Judge Advocate Corps in 1966–69.

Mr. Hunter is married, has three children, and resides in Vienna, Va. He was born August 23, 1940, in Bridgeport, Conn.

Nomination of Loretta Cornelius To Be Deputy Director of the Office of Personnel Management
June 18, 1981

The President today announced his intention to nominate Loretta Cornelius to be Deputy Director of the Office of Personnel Management, vice Jule Sugarman, resigned.

Mrs. Cornelius is currently vice president for administration, PRC Data Services Co., McLean, Va. Since joining the company in 1967, she has held positions as department manager, division manager, then vice president. In 1967–74 she was on the technical staff at PRC as an analyst. In 1960–61 she was the administrative manager for the

firm of Keith & Noland, Clarksville, Tenn. Mrs. Cornelius was administrative assistant to the president, Bass & Co., Hopkinsville, Ky., in 1954–59.

Mrs. Cornelius graduated from Bowie State College (B.A.); George Washington University (M.A.); and Draughons College (A.A.). She is a member of the American Society of Personnel Administrators.

She is married, has three children, and resides in Warrenton, Va. She was born April 1, 1936, in Hopkinsville, Ky.

Statement on Action by the Senate Finance Committee on Federal Tax Reduction Legislation
June 18, 1981

The votes taken today by the Senate Finance Committee are important first steps toward passage of a bipartisan tax reduction bill. On both votes there was widespread support from both sides of the aisle for administration objectives. I was especially gratified by the support shown for our pro-

posed 5–10–10 reductions in individual income tax rates.

I am deeply grateful to the members of the Senate Finance Committee, and I am especially grateful to Committee Chairman Robert Dole for his leadership and wise counsel.

Nomination of J. Raymond Bell To Be a Member of the Foreign Claims Settlement Commission of the United States, and Designation as Chairman
June 19, 1981

The President today announced his intention to nominate J. Raymond Bell to be a member of the Foreign Claims Settlement Commission of the United States, Department of Justice, for a term expiring September 30, 1982, vice Richard W. Yarborough. Upon confirmation, the President intends to designate Mr. Bell Chairman.

Mr. Bell is an attorney and public relations professional. He was appointed by President Nixon, reappointed by President Ford, as Chairman, Foreign Claims Settlement Commission of the United States. Previously, he was vice president, Columbia Pictures Industries, Inc.; attorney with the firm of Wyman, Bautzer, Rothman and Kuchel in California; vice president, advertising and public relations, Capital Airlines; eastern publicity manager, Metro-Goldwyn-Mayer; director, advertising and publicity, Loew's Theatres; and a reporter for the Detroit Times.

He was president, New York and Washington chapters, Public Relations Society of America, and chairman, public relations advisory committee, Air Transport Association, for two terms. Mr. Bell graduated from Atlanta Law School (LL.B., 1930).

Mr. Bell is married, has six children, and resides in Washington, D.C. He was born January 7, 1908, in New Orleans, La.

Nomination of Frank H. Conway To Be a Member of the Foreign Claims Settlement Commission of the United States
June 19, 1981

The President today announced his intention to nominate Frank H. Conway to be a member of the Foreign Claims Settlement Commission of the United States, Department of Justice, for the remainder of the term expiring September 30, 1981, vice Ralph W. Emerson. The President intends to reappoint Mr. Conway for a term expiring September 30, 1984.

Since 1975 Mr. Conway has been an attorney with the firm of Jameson, Locke and Fullerton, of Wellesley, Mass. Previously, since 1935, he was associated with the New England Telephone and Telegraph Co., where he served as a management consultant, general labor relations supervisor, and division manager.

Mr. Conway served in the U.S. Army in 1942–46. He is an active Republican and was a delegate to the 1980 Republican National Convention. He was cochairman of the Reagan-Bush committee (Massachusetts).

Mr. Conway graduated from Boston University School of Law (J.D., 1952) and Providence College (Ph. D., 1953). He is married, has four children, and resides in Wellesley, Mass. He was born May 2, 1913, in Providence, R.I.

Nomination of L. Ebersole Gaines To Be Executive Vice President of the Overseas Private Investment Corporation
June 19, 1981

The President today announced his intention to nominate L. Ebersole Gaines to be Executive Vice President of the Overseas Private Investment Corporation, United States International Development Cooperation Agency, vice Dean R. Axtell, resigned.

Since 1972 Mr. Gaines has been self-employed. Previously he was executive vice president and director, Diversa-Graphics, Inc., New York and Chicago, in 1969–72; marketing manager, Nationwide Papers, U.S. Plywood-Champion Paper, Chicago and New York, in 1967–69; sales manager,

central metal division, Continental Can Co., New York and Chicago, in 1960–67; district manager, Cincinnati district, Plax Corp., Hartford, Conn., in 1953–60; and with the American Arbitration Association in 1951–53.

Mr. Gaines served in the U.S. Navy in 1945–46. He graduated from Princeton University (A.B., 1951). He is married, has four children, and resides in Ketchum, Idaho. He was born April 21, 1927, in Charleston, W. Va.

Nomination of Bevis Longstreth To Be a Member of the Securities and Exchange Commission
June 19, 1981

The President today announced his intention to nominate Bevis Longstreth to be a member of the Securities and Exchange Commission for the remainder of the term expiring June 5, 1982, vice John S. R. Shad.

Since 1962 Mr. Longstreth has practiced law with the firm of Debevoise, Plimpton, Lyons & Gates, New York, N.Y. He was admitted to partnership in that firm in 1970. Mr. Longstreth has served as secretary on the Special Committee on Science and Law of the Association of the Bar of the City of New York in 1962–67. In 1967–79 he served as a member of the Committee

on Professional Responsibility of the Bar Association. In 1963–73 he was a member, and later chairman, of the board of directors of Union Settlement Association, a neighborhood service and action agency.

Mr. Longstreth has written several publications on investment and behavioral research. He graduated from Princeton University (B.S.E., 1956) and Harvard Law School (LL.B., 1961). He served in the U.S. Marine Corps in 1956–58. He is married, has three children, and resides in New York, N.Y. He was born January 29, 1934, in Princeton, N.J.

Nomination of Parker W. Borg To Be United States Ambassador to Mali
June 19, 1981

The President today announced his intention to nominate Parker W. Borg to be United States Ambassador to the Republic of Mali, vice Anne F. Holloway, resigned.

Mr. Borg was a Peace Corps volunteer, teaching English in the Philippines in 1961–63. He entered the Foreign Service in 1965 as Foreign Service officer-general in Kuala

Lumpur. In 1967–70 he was on detail to the Agency for International Development with the CORDS program in Vietnam. In the Department he was staff officer in the Executive Secretariat (1972–74), Special Assistant to the Director General of the Foreign Service (1972–74), and Special Assistant to the Secretary of State (1974–75). He was principal officer in Lubumbashi in 1976–78. In 1978–79 he was on detail to the Council on Foreign Relations in New York, N.Y.

Since 1979 he has been director of the Office of West African Affairs in the Department.

Mr. Borg graduated from Dartmouth College (A.B., 1961) and Cornell University (M.P.A., 1965). His languages are French, Vietnamese, and Malay. He received the Department's Superior Honor Award in 1978. Mr. Borg resides in Washington, D.C. He was born May 25, 1939, in Minneapolis, Minn.

Nomination of Robert Strausz-Hupé To Be United States Ambassador to Turkey
June 19, 1981

The President today announced his intention to nominate Robert Strausz-Hupé to be United States Ambassador to the Republic of Turkey, vice James W. Spain, resigned.

Since 1977 Mr. Strausz-Hupé has been diplomat in residence, then consultant, Foreign Policy Research Institute, University of Pennsylvania (Philadelphia). In 1976–77 he was United States Permanent Representative on the Council of the North Atlantic Treaty Organization, with the rank of Ambassador, Brussels. Previously he served as Ambassador to Sweden in 1974–76, Ambassador to Belgium in 1972–74, and Ambassador to Sri Lanka and to the Republic of Maldives in 1970–72. Mr. Strausz-Hupé was

professor of political science, University of Pennsylvania, in 1952–70; associate professor of political science in 1946–52; and special lecturer in 1940–46.

Mr. Strausz-Hupé has authored many publications on foreign policy. He was editor of Orbis in 1957–69 and a guest professor at the University of Munich (1978–79 and 1979–80) and the University of Munster (1980–81). He was graduated from the University of Pennsylvania (M.A., 1945; Ph. D., 1946). He is fluent in German and French.

Mr. Strausz-Hupé is married and resides in Newton Square, Pa. He was born March 25, 1903, in Vienna, Austria.

Remarks of the President and Prime Minister Lee Kuan Yew of Singapore Following Their Meetings
June 19, 1981

The President. Ladies and gentlemen, I've been delighted to have a chance to renew a dialog with a man who I think is one of the most dynamic and experienced leaders on the world scene today. Prime Minister Lee deserves much credit not only for the outstanding progress that his country, Singapore, has made, but also for helping to forge the association of the Southeast Asian nations, what we call ASEAN, forge it into a

strong and durable organization that it has become.

I count the Prime Minister as a longtime friend. We've had previous meetings, beginning with 10 years ago, and I know that he has an excellent understanding of what it is that we're trying to accomplish here in America.

We've had wide-ranging discussions involving events in several parts of the world, including Asia and Europe and the Middle East. And the Prime Minister welcomes our efforts to reinvigorate our alliances, strengthen our friendships, to consolidate the free world as we move through a very difficult period.

It's been my honor and pleasure to have him here as a distinguished visitor but also as a very good friend, and I count him among my closest associates and friends and have unlimited admiration for him.

Mr. Prime Minister?

The Prime Minister. Mr. President, I was greatly privileged more than 10 years ago to have met you, and I count myself fortunate to have done so, because I thereby avoided the mistake of accepting the caricature that was purveyed up till the time the world decided that you were more than just a Governor and an actor. My admiration for you and the fact that I took your views seriously 10 years ago has been my good fortune.

I enjoyed the confidence you showed by sounding off on a wide range of issues, particularly on Asia, on ASEAN, on the evolving relationships between the United States and the countries of the West Pacific, the multiple implications of change in relationships between the countries of the Pacific Basin. Change is an inevitable facet of any dynamic world, and as we view it in historic perspective, I feel great confidence that this country, that has seen a President assassinated, has gone through the throes of 2 years of Watergate and a President that was being hounded and besieged, was able, through its constitutional processes, to throw up someone who has brought such a state of grace and confidence to Washington, to America, and to the world. And confidence in your ability to stand up for what you believe in and to find a way to overcome your economic difficulties, your inflation, your unemployment, in a way that makes it possible for you to live up to your defense commitments—that is the crux to a safe and secure future for all of us, including the countries of ASEAN and Southeast Asia.

I feel greatly reassured at your robust, your quiet confidence that nothing has changed. Your friendships are enduring. Your principles are abiding. Your friends can ask for no more.

Thank you.

Note: The President spoke at 1:25 p.m. to reporters assembled at the South Portico of the White House.

Earlier, the President and the Prime Minister had met in the Oval Office, and then they attended a working luncheon in the Blue Room.

Remarks on Action by the House of Representatives on Federal Budget Legislation
June 19, 1981

The President. Ladies and gentlemen, I have a statement that I think is being or will be distributed, but I will, for the sound media, read it, not in its entirety, but enough of it for you to get the idea.

Forty-five days ago, the House of Representatives joined in a bipartisan commitment to bring runaway Federal spending under control. And that was an essential step toward national economic recovery, toward reducing inflation, creating more jobs, and lowering interest rates. But that was only a step. It required faithful implementation by the committees of the Congress.

And now we're approaching the crucial test. Next week, the House plans to vote on the single largest economic and budget reform package in history. During recent weeks, many House committees have made a good faith effort to help bring this Federal spending under control. And I applaud them for their efforts. But in two major instances, the bill that is emerging in the House Budget Committee has serious shortcomings.

First, many of the measures that are needed to curb the automatic spending programs have not been adopted. These reforms would target programs more directly toward the truly needy while they help to eliminate waste and abuse.

Unfortunately, the House committee has adopted only one-third of the savings that these reforms would bring. And the result, if unchallenged, will be $23 billion in additional red ink and inflationary pressure in the next several years. Doing only one-third of the job is not good enough.

Secondly, certain House committees have not yet received the message of last November that the American people want less bureaucratic overhead in Washington and less redtape tying up State and local government. Consequently, these committees rejected my proposed consolidation of 86 duplicative, regulated-ridden Federal programs into block grants.

Now, I believe that we should permit many social programs to be administered by State and local governments, which best know the needs of their people and the priorities for meeting them. Instead, some of the House committees want to hang on to the strings and the Washington bureaucracy. And this means extra administrative costs at the expense of services for the people.

I have spoken to most of the Governors in the country and many of the mayors, to the National Association of State Legislators. All of them have told me they can absorb the cuts in the categorical grants that were made if they have the flexibility that block grants would bring. And now they're going to get the cuts but without that flexibility if some in the Congress or some committees have their way.

Now, our nation's needs are too important to tolerate this "business as usual" attitude on Capitol Hill. For these reasons, three leaders in the House, earlier this afternoon, announced plans to offer a bipartisan amendment that would fulfill the commitment of the original Gramm-Latta resolution.

The American people have waited patiently and for 8 months for the full-scale attack on runaway spending. Adoption by the House of the bipartisan Gramm-Latta amendment next week will be a major step toward ensuring that the will of the people is carried out. And there can be no doubt that we can and we will stop this fiscal joyride in Washington. And I am going to be in full support and help of that amendment.

Now, at 4:30 this afternoon, Dave Stockman will be giving a complete briefing on the entire package to all of you.

Reporter. How do you plan to help personally, Mr. President?

The President. Well, by dint of persuasion and reason, pointing out the messages that have been brought to me already from industry in the United States of billions of dollars of planned expansion and modernization that is going to take place, the kind of thing that will increase productivity and provide more jobs. And they have stated to me voluntarily that they are planning these billions of dollars of spending based on the expectations of the program that we presented.

Q. Do you have the votes, Mr. President?

The President. I don't know. That's why I'll be working.

Q. Did you talk to the Speaker today by telephone?

The President. This morning, to tell him how much—that I could go along with the bulk of what came out of the committees, but that there was just this narrow area in the entire program and asked if he would permit a one-time vote on a single amendment so that we could have a vote by the Congress one way or the other on this amendment.

Q. And he will?

The President. The instructions? I have received no answers yet, so I don't know.

Q. Do you have a way of getting it to the floor for a vote if he says no?

The President. Well, I'll tell you; take that up with Dave Stockman today. He's been dealing more on the strategy field than I have.

Q. Any other message for the Speaker?

The President. Just my best wishes. [*Laughter*]

Q. Thank you.

Note: The President spoke at 3:18 p.m. to reporters assembled at the South Portico of the White House.

Statement on Action by the House of Representatives on Federal Budget Legislation
June 19, 1981

Forty-three days ago the House of Representatives joined in a bipartisan commitment to bring runaway Federal spending under control. That was an essential step toward national economic recovery—toward reducing inflation, creating more jobs, and lowering interest rates. But that was only a step. It required faithful implementation by the committees of the Congress.

Now we are approaching a crucial test. Next week, the House plans to vote on the single largest economic and budget reform package in history. During recent weeks many House committees have made a good faith effort to help bring Federal spending under control. I applaud them for their efforts. But in two major instances, the bill that is emerging in the House Budget Committee has serious shortcomings.

First, many of the measures needed to curb automatic spending programs have not been adopted. These reforms would target programs more directly toward the truly needy while they help to eliminate waste and abuse.

Unfortunately, the House committees adopted only one-third of the savings that these reforms would bring. The result, if unchallenged, will be $23 billion in additional red ink and inflationary pressure in the next several years. Doing only one-third of the job is not good enough.

Secondly, certain House committees have not yet received the message of last November that the American people want less bureaucratic overhead in Washington and less redtape tying up State and local government. Consequently, these committees rejected my proposed consolidation of 88 duplicative, regulation-ridden Federal programs into block grants.

I believe we should permit many social programs to be administered by State and local governments—which best know the needs of their people and the priorities for meeting them. Instead, some House committees want to hang onto the strings and Washington bureaucracy. This means extra administrative costs at the expense of services for people.

Our nation's needs are too important to tolerate this "business as usual" attitude on Capitol Hill. For these reasons, three leaders in the House earlier this afternoon announced plans to offer a bipartisan amendment that would fulfill the commitment of the original Gramm-Latta resolution. After consultation with Hill leaders, I have decided today to throw my full support behind this amendment.

This amendment will ensure:

—that the budget reduction and reform goals adopted by Congress last month will be translated into new laws and concrete steps to implement my economic recovery program.

—that the runaway growth of automatic spending programs will be contained and abuse of Federal programs eliminated.

—that long overdue pruning of Federal overhead and redtape will permit social needs to be met at less cost to the taxpayers.

—and that today's punishing interest rates and inflation will come down as Federal spending is brought under control.

The American people have waited patiently 8 months for a full-scale attack on runaway spending. Adoption by the House of the bipartisan Gramm-Latta amendment next week will be a major step toward ensuring that the will of the people is carried out. Let there be no doubt: We can and we will put a stop to the fiscal joyride in Washington.

Message to the Congress Reporting Budget Rescissions and Deferrals
June 19, 1981

To the Congress of the United States:

In accordance with the Impoundment Control Act of 1974, I herewith report 6 new proposals to rescind a total of $321.0 million in budget authority previously provided by the Congress. In addition, I am reporting 13 new deferrals totalling $220.1 million, and revisions to five previously reported deferrals increasing the amount deferred by $78.1 million.

The rescission proposals affect programs in the Departments of Agriculture, Education, Health and Human Services, and Housing and Urban Development as well as the Environmental Protection Agency. The deferrals affect programs in the Departments of Agriculture, Defense, Health and Human Services, Interior, and State as well as the National Foundation on the Arts and Humanities.

The details of each rescission proposal and deferral are contained in the attached reports.

RONALD REAGAN

The White House,
June 19, 1981.

Note: The attachments detailing the rescission proposals and deferrals are printed in the Federal Register *of July 1, 1981.*

Remarks at a White House Reception Opening the "Champions of American Sport" Exhibition
June 22, 1981

It's a pleasure to welcome you all to the White House. I know that I used to talk about some of you on my broadcast when I was sports-announcing, and now I get to meet you in the flesh. I'm trying to remember what all I said about all of you. [*Laughter*]

The champion of American sports exhibit was a champion idea, and I think we all owe Dennis O'Toole a debt of gratitude for his origination of the concept. And thanks to Beverly Cox and Marc Pachter and Ken Yellis for all the work they did to make it come alive. [1]

Sports have played an indispensable role in the development of American character.

---

[1] *The President was referring to the former Curator of Education, the Curator of Exhibits, an historian, and the Curator of Education, respectively, all of the National Portrait Gallery, Smithsonian Institution, where the "Champions of American Sport" exhibition was being shown.*

You who were participants have provided, especially for young Americans, I think, an inspiration, something to look up to. It was sports heroes in my day that created in me the ambition to participate in sports—first in high school and then in college. Indeed, if it hadn't been for football, track, and swimming, I might not have been able to go to college. We didn't have athletic scholarships in those days. We had to do things like wind the clock in the gym. [*Laughter*] But I loved it when it was plain and simple and honorable. [*Laughter*]

I maybe shouldn't admit this, but I went to a very small school in the Midwest, and my senior year—it was the conference that this school was in, had a rule which you could employ someone as an athletic instructor and still leave them eligible to play—in my senior year, on the starting 11, there were 7 physical ed instructors, and I was the swimming coach. [*Laughter*] For 8 years, I will also confess though that I didn't know very much about grades like A's and B's, scholastically. The eligibility requirement was a C average, and that became my top goal.

I know there are some in the room—you know, there's a little nostalgia beginning to creep in here, as you can see. And George here must be champion, because his was baseball. I couldn't play baseball, because I couldn't see good enough. [*Laughter*] That's why I turned to football. The ball was bigger, and so were the fellows. [*Laughter*]

Speaking of that, there was one that I know—there are some people, if I read the guest list correctly—there are some people here who know this particular fellow. I found myself in football—I was a guard—right guard—[*laughter*]—and I was playing against a fellow who later was All-Pro Tackle with the Chicago Bears for 8 years—George Musso. And as you will recall, in those days you played both offense and defense. So, for 60 minutes I was opposite him. He outweighed me 100 pounds—[*laughter*]—and it was a busy time. I couldn't go under him. I wouldn't do that. [*Laughter*] And I certainly couldn't go over him. I tried going around him once and ran into one of our men coming around him from the other side. [*Laughter*] It liked to kill me.

But enough of that. The men and women of sports have done much to bring this country together. One of our first great sports heroes was John L. Sullivan at a time when there was a great discrimination in this country against the Irish. And when Jim Corbett finally took his world title away from him, Sullivan won the hearts of the Nation with his words: "I have fought once too often, but if I had to get licked, I'm glad it was by an American."

Years later, another champ, the Brown Bomber, Joe Louis, would capture our hearts. And what American can forget the pride that swept this country last year when our U.S. ice hockey team beat the Russians? The image of those boys after the victory on the ice with their country's flag in their hand, I think, is a national treasure.

We owe something else, seriously, to the world of sports. When I was broadcasting major league baseball, there was a rule barring some Americans from playing in organized baseball. And I'm proud that I was one of those in the sports-reporting fraternity who continually editorialized against that rule, that baseball was for Caucasian gentlemen only. And finally, thanks to Branch Rickey and Jackie Robinson, baseball became truly the American sport.

And I'm sure many people have forgotten any feelings of prejudice they might have had as they've cheered black athletes who were bringing home victory for their favorite team. Those players have made baseball better, they've made America better, and so have the great black athletes in all the other major sports.

If there was ever a golden age of sports, this is it. More people are attending sporting events than ever before, and there are a wider variety of sports events today. And just as important, there are more people involving themselves directly in sports. We can be proud of our country's sports tradition. And as spokesman of all our citizens, I want to thank all of you—the sports men and women this afternoon—for adding a bit of joy and inspiration to our lives with the achievements that you've made.

So, welcome here to your house, which you're letting me live in for a while. [*Laughter*] God bless all of you.

Thank you.

Note: The President spoke at 5:38 p.m. in the East Room at the White House.

Remarks on the Program for Economic Recovery at a White House Breakfast for Democratic Members of the House of Representatives
June 23, 1981

I'm going to say a few words here first, and them we're going to have breakfast. And then we'll have a dialog instead of a monolog by me, and I'll try to make the monolog very brief.

Over the last several weeks, I think we'll all agree the American people have begun to believe in the President and the Congress and believe that we can really solve the problems that face this Nation. And your vote on the Gramm-Latta measure, I think, was the principal reason for them feeling that way, and I want to thank you for that. I think I understand the courage it took for all of you to support that resolution, and I think you have the gratitude of your fellow citizens today. But the people may be disappointed. Reconciliation, which has a lot of meanings but the particular one where we're concerned right now, may turn out to be the difference between what you voted for in Gramm-Latta and what the people are actually going to get if the budget committee package goes through.

The new Gramm-Latta bipartisan reconciliation bill is true to the principles of the original resolution. It is a compromise accepting the majority of the committee recommendations—and I must say, I think that in the majority that most of the committees did do a fine job, and there was no problem at all in accepting what they brought forth. But there were a few that brought down things that would make us fall more than $20 billion short of what we need over the next 3 years. And what we're talking about, of course, in the son of Gramm-Latta, is how to correct these so that those with the majority reports that came out of the committees could be put before the House.

I think it deserves to be put before the House for an up-or-down vote. And I called the Speaker and asked him if he would permit either a substitute or an amendment containing that package to be added to those, the majority that we would accept. I've had no answer. And apparently I know what the answer is.

Another bipartisan effort—and I think probably we should mention this morning—is the effort representing, again, a compromise between congressional proposals and the administration's original proposal, and that's the Conable-Hance tax reduction bill.

I have retreated from 10–10–10 retroactive to last January 1st to 5–10–10 to be effective as of this coming October 1st, but accepted—and very willingly—a number of changes, particularly around the business tax and others that were recommended even by some of you, but in the negotiations that have been going on. And I believe that proposal will restore the economy, stimulate savings, investment, and increase productivity.

I've just received a report the last few days from 15 of the major steel companies in the United States. These 15 companies, between them, are planning a number of modernization and rehabilitation and expansion projects that total $3.2 billion. Now, I know that some are concerned that maybe the business tax is going to inspire plants to leave where they are and move to other areas and so forth. So, I've broken down the projects to just see if there might be anything to that.

These 15 companies, with their $3.2 billion proposed spending, 12 of them will be in the Northeast in the already existing plants, 15 will be in the Midwest, and I'm including Ohio and Arkansas in the Midwest. I'm sometimes not sure whether they're in border areas, whether the East considers one East and the South considers the other South, but if you consider them Midwest, there are 15 there. Six will be in the South, three in the West, and only one project unspecified as yet. And all of this was planned and decided upon, in their report they say, with the expectation that the economic package is going to be passed. Now, what are we going to do with that package for the economy if just simply the promise of it has brought that about after all the years of the deterioration and the aging in that very basic industry?

The Conable-Hance tax program targets 70 percent of the income tax relief to the people in the $5,000 to $50,000 earning bracket, who presently pay 67 percent of the tax. I simply throw that in as an answer to those who are still attacking the bill as somehow being slanted to the more affluent. And of course we know the income tax cut isn't really very much of a cut, because there is built into the system an increase that will amount to 22 percent over the next 3 years. And our tax calls for 25-percent reduction, so we're basically just eliminating this enormous tax increase.

So, with that as an appetizer—[*laughter*]—we'll have breakfast, and then we'll have some conversation.

Note: The President spoke at 9:10 a.m. in the State Dining Room at the White House.

Appointment of Seven Members of the Advisory Council on Historic Preservation, and Designation of Chairman and Vice Chairman
June 23, 1981

The President today announced the appointments of the following individuals to serve on the Advisory Council on Historic Preservation for the terms indicated:

Alexander Aldrich to be Chairman, term expiring June 10, 1985. Since 1979 he has been president of Aldrich Management, Inc., a cultural resource planning and consulting firm in Saratoga Springs, N.Y. He has also served as town attorney of Greenfield, N.Y., and city attorney of Saratoga Springs, N.Y. He has been an attorney with the firm of Helm, Shapiro, Ayers, Anito & Aldrich since 1975. Mr. Aldrich was commissioner of parks and recreation and State historic preservation officer, State of New York, in 1971–75. He was president, Long Island University Brooklyn Center, in 1968–71. Previously Mr. Aldrich was first director, New York State Hudson River Valley Commission, in 1966–68; executive assistant to Gov. Nelson Rockefeller and chairman of the State Cabinet Committee for Civil Rights, in 1963–68; first director, New York State Division for Youth, in 1960–63; and an attorney with the firm of Milbank, Tweed, Hope & Hadley, in 1953–56. Mr. Aldrich graduated from Harvard University (A.B.) and Harvard Law School (J.D.). He was a member of the National Council on Historic Preservation as one of the 10 at-large members of the Council, which advises the President and the Congress on national preservation policy (1976–78). Mr. Aldrich is married and resides in Saratoga Springs, N.Y. He was born March 14, 1928, in New York, N.Y.

Armand S. Deutsch to be Vice Chairman and member, term expiring June 10, 1982. Mr. Deutsch is currently chairman of the board of the Starwood Corp. of New York City. He was previously director for approximately 25 years. He was also director of the Frances Denney Corp. of New York City and the Geneve Corp. of Greenwich, Conn., since 1977. Mr. Deutsch served on the board of directors of Warner Brothers-Seven Arts Limited in 1964–68 and was film producer with MGM Studios in 1946–53. Mr. Deutsch has been a member of the board of the Performing Arts Council, Los Angeles Music Center, since 1973. He also serves on the board of directors of the Center Theatre Group, Los Angeles Music Center. Mr. Deutsch graduated from the University of Chicago (B.A.). He is married, has four children, and resides in Beverly Hills, Calif. He was born January 25, 1913, in Chicago, Ill.

Thomas B. Muths to be an expert member, term expiring June 10, 1982. Mr. Muths is an architect and has served as an architectural consultant to determine historic architectural value for restoration projects in Wyoming, Montana, South Dakota, Arizona, and Colorado. In 1976 he was appointed to a 2-year term to the Advisory Council on Historic Preservation, serving as chairman of the Gettysburg Task Force. He is a member of the national board of directors of the American Institute of Architects. Mr. Muths graduated from the University of Washington (B.A.) and served in the U.S. Army in 1951–54. He is married, has one child, and resides in Jackson, Wyo. He was born October 11, 1931, in Mobile, Ala.

The following four officials were appointed to serve at the pleasure of the President:

Donald Regan, Secretary of the Treasury.

Samuel Pierce, Secretary of Housing and Urban Development.

Drew Lewis, Secretary of Transportation.

Gerald Carmen, Administrator of General Services.

Nomination of Rayburn D. Hanzlik To Be Administrator of the Economic Regulatory Administration
June 23, 1981

The President today announced his intention to nominate Rayburn D. Hanzlik to be Administrator of the Economic Regulatory Administration, Department of Energy, vice Hazel R. Rollins.

Since 1979 Mr. Hanzlik has been a self-employed attorney and counsel to the firm of Darling, Rae & Gute of Los Angeles, Calif. He was counsel to the firm of Akin, Gump, Hauer & Feld of Washington, D.C., and Dallas, Tex., in 1978–79. In 1977–78 Mr. Hanzlik was counsel to Danzansky, Dickey, Tydings, Quint & Gordon of Washington, D.C. Previously, in 1976–77, he served as Associate Director for Intergovernmental Relations at the White House. He was Staff Director, Public Forums on Domestic Policy, Office of the Vice Presi

dent, in 1975–76; partner, Robert Finch and Associates of Los Angeles, Calif., and Washington, D.C., in 1974–75; junior partner, E. Del Smith and Co., of Washington, D.C., in 1973–74; Executive Assistant to the Counselor to the President in 1971–73, Director, 1971 White House Conference on Youth; and assistant to the director, Center for the Study of Science, Technology and Public Policy, University of Virginia, in 1968–70.

Mr. Hanzlik graduated from the Principia College (B.S.), Woodrow Wilson School of Government and Foreign Affairs (M.A.), and the University of Virginia School of Law (J.D.). He is married, has four children, and resides in Pasadena, Calif. He was born June 7, 1938, in Los Angeles, Calif.

Nomination of Rosemary M. Collyer To Be a Member of the Federal Mine Safety and Health Review Commission, and Designation as Chairman
June 23, 1981

The President today announced his intention to nominate Rosemary M. Collyer to be a member of the Federal Mine Safety and Health Review Commission for a term of 6 years, expiring August 30, 1986, vice Jerome R. Waldie. Upon confirmation, the President intends to designate Mrs. Collyer Chairman.

Since 1977 Mrs. Collyer has served as labor attorney with the firm of Sherman & Howard of Denver, Colo. She was an instructor with Personnel Predictions & Re-

search, Inc., in 1973–74; creative director, Pennington & Richard Associates, in 1972–73; director of public relations of the Manlius Pebble Hill School, Manlius, N.Y., in 1971–72; and reporter for the Canadian Register in Toronto, Canada, in 1969–70.

She graduated from Trinity College (B.A., 1968) and the University of Denver College of Law (J.D., 1977). She is married, has one child, and resides in Denver, Colo. She was born November 19, 1945, in Port Chester, N.Y.

Remarks at a White House Reception for Delegates to the National Leadership Conference of Teen Age Republicans
June 23, 1981

The President. Good afternoon, and welcome to the White House.

You know, it's always heartening to see young people in politics, and it is especially for me, because when I first became active and ran for Governor in California, it was in those riotous days of the sixties. Now, during the last election, the difference was that I couldn't help but notice that wherever we went, there was a large contingent of Teen Age Republicans who were working their hearts out in the campaign.

You had a significant impact on the outcome in the last election in a number of areas. You walked the precincts, you licked stamps, stuffed envelopes, got senior citizens to the polls, and babysat while mothers voted. It may not sound very glamorous, but it's absolutely essential and especially in this era of campaign spending limitations. And it very often, what you did, makes the difference between winning and losing. It happens on election day—*[applause]*——

You know, during the last decade there was a vocal minority of American young people who were attracted to, let us say, alien ideologies. And they got the lion's share of the public attention, while many good things were accomplished by young people such as Teen Age Republicans, and that went unacknowledged because the attention was being paid the other way. That's nothing new, however. President Woodrow Wilson noted the same thing way back in 1914. When he was speaking of young people, he said, "They're generally thought of to be arch-radicals. As a matter of fact, they're the most conservative people I've ever dealt with."

You Teen Age Republicans are doing a tremendous job, and I think that's tremendous testimony to Barbie Wells,[1] who's really made the TARs the vibrant organization that it is today. There she is, back there. Barbie, bless you and thank you.

---

[1] *National Teen Age Republican director.*

Somebody even mentioned that you've got a club in Dixon, Illinois, and they have a delegation here today. That's my hometown. Dixon, well—oh, there's one of those hats from the Inaugural, yes. Well, welcome. That's where I spent my Huck Finn days and grew up and lifeguarded on the Rock River every summer for seven summers——

Audience member. How about Geneseo?

The President. I played football down at Geneseo. As a matter of fact, it snowed that day. *[Laughter]*

I understand that your organization has almost 120,000 members with clubs spread throughout the 50 States. Our country does offer an opportunity to participate in the political process. Remember, it's the activists, the ones who put out the time and effort, who determine the future. And your activities are certainly a chance to learn about government, but more than that, you're actually making history.

I want you to spread the word that there's opportunity for young people in the Republican Party, and we want young people to play a vital role, because our party believes in America's future. And sometimes I'm inclined to believe that there are others around that have a very dim view of the future. Well, don't you believe it. You're going to have better opportunities than we had. You're going to know finer things. And there is a very bright future out there; we just have to quit listening to the doom-criers and getting government off our backs and out of our pockets, and then you'll have that—*[applause]*——

I want to thank you for all that you've done and what you will do for our party. And one can't help but have renewed confidence in seeing all of you today. So, good luck at your leadership conference.

And now, before I have to get back in there for some things that have still to be done today, I think you should know, if you don't already know, that some congratulations are in order. And I'm delighted to have this chance to announce today Paul Findley's—Paul, where are you? Where's Congressman Paul Findley? Way in the back? Well, I can't ask him then if it's all right for me to tell him how many—but let me just show how easy it is. Today Paul Findley celebrates his 60th birthday. Yes, that makes him a lot younger than the President, who also happens to be in good health. And, incidentally, Paul Findley's from Pittsfield, Illinois, represents the 20th District and is serving his 11th term here in the House.

Well, as I say—I'm stalling now because I hate to have to leave and go back in there—[*laughter*]—but you've brightened the day considerably by being here, and you've brightened a lot of other days.

I can tell you one of the other reasons I hate to go back in there. You can hear this crack in my voice. That doesn't have anything to do with an incident of several weeks ago. I have found out that I have an allergic reaction to air-conditioning, and we're in the season in Washington where you can't live without air-conditioning and closing the windows. So, I guess I'll be this way till I get to California, which I'm going to do, beginning tomorrow morning. I'm starting on some speaking trips and will wind up in California. So, maybe I'll at least have a few days in which I can talk normally.

God bless you all, and thank you very much for all that you've done and all you're doing and for all—[*applause*]. Okay, regards to Dixon, and I'll give my own to California

Note: The President spoke at 5:04 p.m. in the Rose Garden at the White House.

Remarks on the Program for Economic Recovery at a White House Reception for Republican Members of the House of Representatives
June 23, 1981

The President. You know, I've just finished meeting a little while ago out there with the Teen Age Republicans, the TAR's. And for some reason or other, I had it in mind that one of you, Paul Findley, from my old State of Illinois, Pittsfield—there you are—was going to be there. And I called, and you weren't there. [*Laughter*] And now I've found you, because I just wanted to say that this was kind of a special day in addition to just being here. And I could announce that—can I tell them how many?

Representative Findley. Go ahead. I'm proud of it.

The President. Okay, see how easy it is today. He is 60 years old today. And just by way of encouragement, I want to tell you that's a lot younger than the President, and the President feels just fine. [*Laughter*]

Well, welcome all of you here. I'm a little surprised. My schedule said that I was supposed to meet with the House Members of the minority party. You don't act like a minority party. You act more like people who know that the ideas, your ideas, are shared and supported by the majority of the American people, and I think they are. And we're delighted to have you here.

It's no secret that we've been trying hard, as you know, to build a strong, bipartisan support for the economic recovery program. I don't doubt that's what the American people want, and I think that we know that that's what the American economy needs. But it's just as important that every one of you knows how positive and decisive your own contribution has become. Because you stuck together and refused to break ranks, we succeeded in passing the tightest spending ceiling and the largest budget reduction in the history of this country on May 7th. But now we need your help, your unity more than ever.

As you know, not all of the House committees have fully implemented the spending reductions in Gramm-Latta. So, just to hit the $695 billion spending target next year and achieve a balanced budget in 1984, we need $46 billion in savings in automatic spending programs over the next 3 years. And we can do that if we're just given a fair chance to vote on the new son of Gramm-Latta amendment and if all of you will stand with us shoulder to shoulder.

Now, it isn't easy to restrict benefits, I know, in food stamps, subsidized housing, student loans, or other programs. But if we ever again want to see low inflation, low interest rates, a sound dollar, and a prosperous people, we have no choice but to make these tough decisions now. And believe me, Americans do want and will remember your leadership.

The same holds true with the block grant proposals. I can't, in good conscience, believe that we should cut over 80 health, education, and social programs by 25 percent and then leave the Federal overhead and the bureaucratic redtape intact. It's the wrong approach. I know that the 50 Governors are ready to go with us all the way on the block grants and take the cut. And they say they'll make it work if we'll give them the flexibility to run those programs as they believe they should be run when they get to their level. And I speak with some experience from having been in that spot. And I know how much of the total spending is just sheer administrative overhead and waste.

Now, let's also make it plain that we're determined to reduce tax rates over the next 3 years by 25 percent across the board for every American taxpayer. And we won't settle for less, because anything less than that is no tax cut at all. It won't provide the incentive needs to create new jobs, to make our economy grow, and to renew the feelings of hope and optimism throughout America.

I know a few shrill voices criticize the tax bill as benefits for the wealthy. Well, in point of fact, we're cutting taxes for people who pay taxes—the people earning between 5 thousand and 50 thousand dollars now pay 67 percent of all of the income tax. They'll receive 70 percent of the total cut. It's ironic to me that some of those who now are criticizing us are the very people who approve doubling the taxes on the American people in just the last 5 years. They've actually doubled.

So, let me just remind you not to take your eye off the ball. We're trying to give the economy back to the American people. That's what they deserve, and I think they'll support us if we continue to hang tough.

Lincoln, that first Republican President, once said, "I am not bound to win but am bound to be true." He said that because he believed in the uncommon wisdom of the common people. I know you do too, and that's why if all of us remain true to our principles, we can be confident that America's greatest days are still to come.

This morning I told some Democratic Congressmen—I know that some of you have concerns that maybe some of our business cuts are going to stimulate leaving areas like the industrial Northeast and Midwest and fleeing to the Sun Belt. Well, I've just received a report from 15 steel companies, the major steel producers in this country, and those 15 steel producers have many more than 15 expansion and modernization programs that they have given the go-ahead to—in their own plants, already established plants, not building new plants. And of all of those, 13 of them are in plants in the Northeast, 15 of them are in plants in the Midwest, if all of you agree with me that Ohio and Arkansas are in the Midwest. [*Laughter*] I'm never quite sure. I debated a little whether to put them in the East or Midwest and decided, being a Midwesterner, I'll settle for the Midwest. And there are five, I believe, in the West and three in the South and only one that is actually not specified as yet. But that's the total number of $3.2 billion worth of modernization and expansion in the steel industry. And they made the decision to go ahead. They have said in that report on the basis of the economic package and their belief that it is going to be adopted and that that gives them the confidence to go forward and expand in this way.

Now, what you're hearing in my voice does not have anything to do with the state of my health. I think it has to do with—this is about the 18th time today that I've had to stand up and speak, and I'm going to get the—well, I'm going to get off of here—

[*laughter*]—and mingle. I think that'll be a lot more fun.

So, thank you all for being here.

Note: The President spoke at 5:50 p.m. in the East Room at the White House.

Remarks at the Annual Convention of the United States Jaycees in San Antonio, Texas
June 24, 1981

Gib, would you mind going on the road with me and doing all the introductions? You're a mighty hard act to follow. In fact, I can't remember anyone saying such kind things about me. Oh, there was one time during the campaign. There was a very prominent Democrat who reportedly told a large group, he said, "Don't worry. I've seen Ronald Reagan, and he looks like a million." He was talking about my age. [*Laughter*]

But Gib Garrow, Gary Nagao, Jan Zook, and Christi Bartlett, my little friend—hi. We met sometime ago in Washington. But I'm happy to be here this afternoon. All of the distinguished ladies and gentlemen here on the platform, the Jaycees deserve a thanks, I think, from all of us, for your incredible outpouring of creative participation in more than 8,000 local communities. You have sponsored programs touching everything from the assistance to the elderly, the handicapped, the mentally retarded, to sponsoring junior athletics, organizing energy conservation efforts, conducting cardiopulmonary resuscitation—200 lives saved just last year alone. And, Christi, I understand the Jaycees have set their goal for raising $2½ million for muscular dystrophy in the campaign this year. And if they say they're going to do it, they'll do it.

Well, these are just a few of the reasons why the Jaycees have always been a very special group for me. So, I'm delighted to have this chance to meet with you again and here in San Antonio. I know that Texas is first in a lot of things, but I'm glad to see it's still first in hospitality.

Now, you know, I didn't come here today to bear bad tidings. You know, if you're a fisherman, the best day to go fishing is yesterday; that's when they were biting. [*Laughter*] But that's only true for fishing.

The good news I bring is that tomorrow will be better, and for one very good reason. You believe in America and so do I. And I believe that your Jaycee spirit has become the American spirit. It's even making inroads in one of the most remote, protected areas of our country—the Federal bureaucracy in Washington, D.C.

Now, you might have heard a rumor to the effect that we've been suggesting a few changes in Washington in recent months. All we're really trying to do is return to some basic principles which have never failed us when we've lived up to them. For example, only by making government live within its means and restricting its role in our personal lives can we unleash the spirit of individual enterprise so essential to prosperity and the preservation of freedom itself. And the way we're doing this is by changing just one little two-letter word: control *by* government to control *of* government.

Now, we've made some progress, but the advocates of a different philosophy are manning the barricades in these puzzle palaces on the Potomac. But let's be clear about where the real credit goes for our progress to date. It goes to that great group of people with a much greater force than our own, the group comprising tens of millions of people, from every profession, every background, every region of this land. They don't consider themselves Democrats or Republicans so much as just deeply patriotic Americans, concerned about their country and determined to save its future while there's still time.

I spoke of them on Inauguration Day, and I'm looking at nearly 10,000 of them right now. You know who I mean. It's the really special interest group in this country—the one that's known as "We the people."

It isn't easy to thank you for all you've done, but I'll try. Back when nearly everyone was still talking about the need for a change, the Jaycees put together a grassroots plan, then went out and made it happen. Just like Thomas Edison said: "Genius is one percent inspiration and ninety-nine percent perspiration."

When your entire membership decided for the first time 30 years to rally around a single political issue—the support of our economic recovery program—millions of Americans followed your lead and sent a loud, clear message to Washington that "Enough is enough!" I think the Congress heard you—which just proves that Washington is still the only city where sound travels faster than light. [*Laughter*]

But now that you've tasted victory and heard some words of praise and are beginning to feel good, I'd better warn you I have a little favor to ask. Please understand it's strictly in the national interest. I simply ask you this: Are you willing to sit back, rest on your laurels, and retire from action with the battle only half won?

Audience. No!

The President. I expected that answer. [*Laughter*]

I think you want spending reductions that you approved in the bipartisan budget resolution of last month, May 7th. I think you want the 3-year across-the-board tax rate reduction for every American taxpayer— and nothing less. And as I've said before, when Congress passed that bipartisan budget resolution, they took an historic step toward bringing spending and inflation under control.

I've been criticized for saying that spending was out of control. Well, what else describes it? Consider, for example, those programs which have spending increases built into them directly by the law.

In 1967 those automatic spending programs, what we called entitlements, amounted to $57 billion—1967. Next year, they'll amount to a staggering $428 billion, and our elected representatives don't have any control over them. If we do nothing to change these laws, the uncontrollable spending will grow to an unbelievable level of more than half a trillion dollars by 1984.

The food stamp program in 1970 cost 577 million. Today, because of the built-in growth, the automatic growth, that program now costs us $11.5 billion. That is 20 times as much just in these recent years. Federal housing subsidies were $500 million just 11 years ago. Today, they're $6.5 billion, and without adding even one single new subsidy, that sum will jump to over $10.5 billion by 1985—21 times as much as it was 11 years ago.

Now, these programs have truly turned out to be good intentions run amok, budgetary time bombs set to explode in the years ahead. Their effect is to pile an enormous new debt on the backs of our children, heavily mortgage their future for the sake of temporary social cures. Any economic solution which ignores the reforms of this automatic spending program is really no solution at all.

But let me also take a moment to give credit where credit is due. I can report to the American people that this Congress made enormous progress, and for most of what they've done they deserve the gratitude of the nation. In fact, the majority of committees in the House of Representatives have taken the necessary steps which followed that resolution. They then had to take the individual programs that were contained in that single resolution and implement them, and the majority have taken the necessary steps to help us gain control of the excessive spending by reporting out of their committees the changes that we needed.

Now I'm asking those remaining committees not in that majority group and the House leadership to join me in going that last mile. Together we can take those final steps toward a balanced budget in 1984 and save our economy from the roller coaster extremes that have caused the mess we're in.

While much progress has been made, there are too many automatic spending programs that still have not been reduced sufficiently, and without those added reductions, we will have given up just on the brink of a great national victory. Without those reductions, we will have nearly $22 billion of added red ink, an unbalanced budget, and more inflationary pressure in the next few years. But more important, without those reductions, we can't guarantee the success of our economic program, and that would be the biggest tragedy of all.

I'm not here to criticize the Congress. I'm here to say that you and I and the rest of the Nation will support them if they act responsibly and courageously. We'll help them shoulder the burden of taking tough but necessary action. We can succeed only if they finish the job that's almost complete. But if they don't finish the job, America will have merely delayed the day of reckoning, a day which will cause us to slip once again into the terrible quicksand of built-in inflation, high interest rates, and government out of control.

Now, once these critically important actions on which the Congress committees have not taken action—one of them is cutting Federal redtape and wasteful spending by consolidating 83 confusing and duplicative Federal programs into block grants. It's not fair to ask the taxpayers to send their earnings to Washington and then charge them billions of dollars more to have this same money turned around and sent right back to the local communities and the States with strings attached that make it expensive. We can cut out the middleman by putting funds in the hands of State and local governments, where the citizens of America can have greater control.

Now, I want to pause here, because there's something that's been bothering me the last few days. I read a report that the chairman of the Democratic Party says that he would like to kick Congressman Phil Gramm, the coauthor of the Gramm-Latta resolution, out of the party.

As you know, Phil Gramm has been a tireless supporter of our efforts to restore economic sanity. Controlling spending and restoring economic sanity is not just a Republican issue or a Democratic issue; it's an American issue. And I don't think it's our way to threaten to kick people out of any party for doing what they believe is right.

I can't advise Mr. Gramm what to do, but I want to assure him this: There are millions of Democrats, Republicans, and Independents who are wholeheartedly in support of what he's doing.

Now, cutting the increase in the rate of spending is only one part of our economic program. Government is also taking too great a percentage of our earnings, taking it in taxes. And this percentage must be reduced if we're going to have the incentive we need to increase productivity. And we're not going to have economic recovery till we increase productivity, which means capital investment in American business and industry.

What we've proposed is not just a tax rate cut to relieve the over-burdened citizenry. In fact, in some ways we aren't proposing a tax cut at all. We're proposing to reduce or eliminate a tax increase that is already built into our system, just as those spending increases are built in—the biggest single tax increase in our nation's history. And it comes on top of the fact that our Federal taxes have already doubled just since 1976. How many of us have been aware of that? In these 5 years, we have doubled the tax burden in this country.

If I could paraphrase Will Roger's line about never having met a man he didn't like, it seems that some in government have never met a tax they didn't hike. [*Laughter*] We're living with a social security payroll tax that was increased a short time ago and which is scheduled to automatically increase several times over the next 5 years. And these increases hasve a double whammy. The rate increases, but at the same time the percentage of earnings that the rate is applied to also goes up. Thus, like the graduated income tax, we have bracket creep that penalizes workers whose wage goes up just to keep pace with the cost of living. That tax is now 13.3 percent on the first $29,700 of earnings, and the law already adopted calls for it to go to 15.3 percent of $66,900 of earnings.

Like the budget reforms, we seek a tax package that will help stimulate the economy by providing capital for investment to modernize and expand our industrial machine.

Individuals—even where the husband and wife are both working—have no surplus to put in savings or in insurance. Investors with capital to invest have been driven to tax shelters because of the low after-tax return on investments. There's less money for research and development. The number of patents issued to American companies has been declining for the past decade, while the Japanese patent activity here in America has increased in each of the 53 U.S. patent fields.

Ironically, some of those who helped pass these tax increases of which I've spoken are now the first and largest in charging that our proposal is designed to benefit the wealthy. Well, it's not true. Those who will get the biggest percentage of reduction in their total tax burden will be the lower- and middle-income families. Our program provides incentives so that more people can share in America's prosperity.

Their other charge is that it's too risky to cut tax rates while we're running a giant budget deficit. Well, I hope I'll be forgiven for pointing out they're also the same people who helped create those deficits.

But I'm happy to say there are others in the Congress on both sides of the aisle who have come together in a coalition supporting a bipartisan tax bill coauthored by Republican Barber Conable and Democrat Kent Hance. And this bill is the result of negotiations between the people in Congress and our own administration. It's a good bill. It deserves the kind of support you gave the Gramm-Latta budget proposal.

The principle of across-the-board cuts in marginal tax rates over a 3-year period has been maintained. Now, it's true we moved back from a 30-percent cut to 25 percent over the 3 years for personal income, but this did make possible other tax cuts which I believe will be great stimulants to savings, investment, and increased productivity.

I don't feel that I can accept any further changes even though those who are unenthusiastic about tax cuts generally want to settle for a 15-percent cut in the income tax only over 2 years. In the first place, that built-in tax increase I described will amount to 22 percent over the next 3 years. And our proposal to eliminate that will give at least a small reduction over and above it of what the tax burden is today.

Now, in addition, I believe the third year is important, particularly for small business, which creates 80 percent of the new jobs and which pays the individual tax rather that the corporate tax. Individual entrepreneurs would be able to look ahead and make plans better with the assurance of 3 years of stability in the tax picture.

Now let me say a word about marginal tax rates, rates that we propose to reduce across the board. These, as you know, are the brackets above the base income tax. They dictate how much more of every extra dollar you get—whether from a pay raise or interest on savings or income from your profession, shop, or whatever—must go to government.

In this land, born of the desire to be free, middle-income Americans are being pushed into punitive tax brackets that were once reserved for the wealthy. Not too many years ago, only 3 percent of those who work and earn were in a 30-percent tax bracket. Today a full one-fourth of the work force is paying that marginal tax rate. And when your social security and State income taxes, where there are such, are included in the total tax burden, the average family is facing 40 to 44 percent in marginal tax rates.

No wonder a middle-class family can't find money to put aside and have the means to send their children to college. The worker finds that it's not worthwhile to put in for overtime or try to upgrade him or herself, so productivity drops and we become less competitive in the world market. We must have a change from the practice of tax and tax, spend and spend, elect and elect, and we must have it now.

It's economic nonsense to say that lowering the tax rates will add to our deficits. We've had, as I have pointed out, giant tax increases, and the deficits kept right on increasing, because government doesn't tax to get the money it needs. Government will always find more needs for the money it gets.

By contrast, we find that every time that government has a broad reduction in the tax rates, the boost in prosperity is so immediate that while the taxpayers pay less individually, government revenues go up because of that increased prosperity. And the latest example, not too many years ago, in the early sixties, when John F. Kennedy, against all the advice of the same kind of people who are opposing us now, proposed an across-the-board tax cut, and the result was exactly what we've said. Even government's income in the gross went up because of the increased prosperity.

The Conable-Hance tax bill will give almost three-quarters of the income tax relief to those earning between 10 and 60 thousand dollars a year—three-quarters. They presently are paying 72 percent of the total income tax. In addition, the unjust penalty imposed on married couples where husband and wife are both working will be relieved. Individuals will be allowed to take a deduction of a thousand dollars a year for personal retirement programs, even if they're participating in some pension plan at the present. And of special interest to farmers and family businesses—the estate tax exemption will be raised to $600,000, and of even greater help, there will be no estate tax for a surviving spouse.

Now, this is just a hasty sketch, and I haven't mentioned all of the tax changes for individuals. The plan will also provide incentive, because people don't work just so they can pay taxes. They work to earn more after-tax income. To the doubters I address one question that I've asked over and over again and never received an answer—and they say its inflationary: "Why is it inflationary for you to spend your money the way you want to spend it and it isn't inflationary if government takes it away from you and spends it the way government wants to spend it?"

The Conable-Hance tax tax bill calls for lowering the 70-percent ceiling on so-called unearned income to 50 percent. Capital gains tax will be lowered. And business will get the biggest tax reduction in our nation's history—some $60 billion in depreciation allowances, et cetera.

To those who say we can't cut spending, lower tax rates, reduce inflation, and, yes, rebuild the defenses we need in this dangerous world, I have a six-word answer: "Yes we can and yes we must!"

You know, it was with sadness that I watched someone last night on the TV news suggest that our program was going to destroy America. When someone makes that kind of charge, I have another question to ask: Where on Earth has he been for the last few years? And strangely enough, the answer is right in Washington, D.C., in a most responsible leadership position in government. Inflation rates didn't reach 18 percent because of our program. Nearly 8 million people didn't get thrown out of work because of anything that happened in the last 5 months. Twenty percent interest and 15 percent mortgages didn't begin on the morning of January 20th, 1981.

Those who make such charges want to return to the same old, discredited policies that set off America's economic high fever in the first place. I ask you, if you're better off with the repeated red ink, high taxes, and monster government of the past, then you go ahead and oppose our new program. But if you're ready to try something new, come with us. Lend us your help and commit your lives. Send a powerful message to those people who live in the past and tell them, "No more business as usual and no more repeat performances, because we're going to make America great again."

You know, we survived a great depression that toppled governments. We came back from Pearl Harbor to win the greatest military victory in world history. Today's living Americans have fought harder, paid a higher price for freedom, and done more to advance the dignity of man than any people who ever lived. We have in my lifetime gone from the horse and buggy to putting men on the Moon and bringing them safely home. Don't tell us that we can't be trusted with an increased share of our own earnings.

You know, it's your money, not theirs. You earned it, they didn't. And it's time they let you keep more of it. All over America, people are yearning for the opportunity to produce once again, to save their money and to have saving it mean something, to live without the constant pressures of higher and higher prices. They don't ask for much, just for a chance to make a better life for themselves and their children.

Now, some have accused me of fighting too hard for these reforms and for not wanting to compromise on key principles. Well, to some of these accusations I plead guilty. For too long the government has stood in the way, taking more of what the people earn no matter how hard they are trying to get ahead. Who can blame our people for fearing that they're trapped inside an economy with no bright tomorrows, an economy that has lost its soul?

I happen to believe that our free country was not put on this Earth simply to make a government bigger. Families shouldn't have to work only to achieve survival. America was put here to extend freedom and to create richer and fuller lives for its people, and this is why our administration wants more than anything else to give the economy back to you, the American people.

Nearly a year ago, as I accepted my nomination—or the nomination of my party for President—I asked that we embark on a national crusade to make America great again. I never meant to do that alone. I need your help, the help of every American to lighten the burden of taxes, which are too high, and to stop feeding the government Goliath.

We must complete the task that we set out to do when we voted for Gramm-Latta. Let's remember this: America is not a second-best society. We've never accepted anything that is less than what is right. And we, with our complete economic packages, we have a chance to succeed, a chance—without that full package, however, that we can't guarantee will end the terrible cycle of economic retreat.

If you believe, as I do, that we must end this cycle, then may I suggest that Members of Congress might be interested in hearing from you and a few million of your fellow citizens again now. Why? Well, I regret to report to you that I just learned on the way down here that a few hours ago, while I was flying down, the House Rules Committee, dominated by those who suggest that I'm destroying America, ruled that our package of amendments to correct the failure of some committees to make budget cuts necessary for the success of the program, cannot be submitted to the House on the floor for the Representatives to give a yes or no vote.

It's a sad commentary on the state of our opposition when they have to resort to a parliamentary gimmick to thwart the will of the people. It is in the hands of Congress now to decide which road we shall take, and if we take the right road, once again we can dare to do great deeds and reach for the impossible.

And again I say with all my heart to you, thank you, God bless you.

Note: The President spoke at 1:16 p.m. at the Henry B. Gonzales Convention Center. He was introduced by Gilbert Garrow, outgoing president of the U.S. Jaycees.

In his opening remarks, the President also referred to Genichi Nagao of Tokyo, Japan, president of Jaycees International, Jan Zook, president of the U.S. Jaycettes, and Christi Bartlett, the 1981 National Muscular Dystrophy Poster Child.

Statement on Action by the House of Representatives on Federal Budget Legislation
June 24, 1981

As I have been traveling today, very distressing news has reached me from Washington, D.C.

In my absence, it seems that the Democratic leaders of the House of Representatives have agreed to go forward with a scheme tomorrow morning that would effectively sabotage our attempts to cut Federal spending.

I have asked the House leadership to let us have a single up-or-down vote on our bipartisan package of spending cuts.

Instead, the leaders want to splinter that package into pieces. They are pursuing a divide and conquer strategy—a strategy that would once again allow special interest groups to triumph over the general economic interest of the nation.

This parliamentary scheme is unacceptable to me and, I am sure, to the great majority of the American people.

We now have the best opportunity in years to achieve real change in this country. We just can't surrender it to backroom politics in the Halls of Congress.

Time is now short; the House promises to bring this issue to a vote as early as tomorrow morning.

I want the American people to understand that if they want to bring real change in Washington—if they want real reductions in spending—this is the time to speak up. This is the time to be heard.

Telegram to Members of the House of Representatives on Federal Budget Legislation
June 24, 1981

Urgently request your support for Rule to permit single up-or-down vote on our bipartisan budget package to save additional $20 billion consistent with Gramm-Latta I. I consider this vote on the previous question vital to our Economic Recovery Program. Gag rule to deny House consideration of our entire package is unacceptable and denies American people opportunity to be heard on runaway Federal spending. Our previous efforts will be badly damaged unless we can stay together on this issue. Therefore, I seek your support to reconfirm your vote on the May 7 Budget Resolution.

Note: The President sent the telegram to 190 Republican and 63 Democratic Members of the Congress who had voted in favor of the Gramm-Latta amendment.

Nomination of James E. Burnett, Jr., To Be a Member and the Chairman of the National Transportation Safety Board
June 25, 1981

The President today announced his intention to nominate James E. Burnett, Jr., of Arkansas, to be a member of the National Transportation Safety Board for a term expiring December 31, 1985, vice Elwood Driver. He also announced his intention to nominate Mr. Burnett to be Chairman of the Board for a term of 2 years, to succeed James B. King.

Mr. Burnett is a practicing attorney and serves as Special Associate Justice of the Supreme Court of Arkansas. He has been a juvenile judge, Van Buren County, since 1973 and city judge, Damascus, Ark., since 1979. He was the youngest judge in the State of Arkansas when elected.

Mr. Burnett is a member of the Arkansas Bar Association, the American Bar Association, and the National Conference of Special Court Judges. He graduated from the University of Arkansas (B.A., J.D.).

Mr. Burnett resides in Clinton, Ark. He was born September 20, 1947.

Nomination of Henry E. Thomas IV To Be an Assistant Secretary of Energy
June 25, 1981

The President today announced his intention to nominate Henry E. Thomas IV to be an Assistant Secretary of Energy (International Affairs).

Mr. Thomas is currently Director, Standards and Regulations Division, Air, Noise and Radiation, Environmental Protection Agency. Previously Mr. Thomas was Senior Policy Officer, Radiation, Hazardous Materials, Noise Resource Recovery, at EPA in 1973–75. He was Director, Compliance and Enforcement, Cost of Living Council, Executive Office of the President, in 1971–73.

Mr. Thomas served in the U.S. Marine Corps and graduated from the Virginia Military Institute (B.A., 1959) and the University of New Mexico (M.A., 1970).

Mr. Thomas is married, has one child, and resides in Alexandria, Va. He was born October 15, 1937, in Charlotte, N.C.

Nomination of Lee M. Thomas To Be an Associate Director of the Federal Emergency Management Agency
June 25, 1981

The President today announced his intention to nominate Lee M. Thomas to be an Associate Director of the Federal Emergency Management Agency (State and Local Programs and Support).

Since 1980 Mr. Thomas has been director, Division of Public Safety, Governor's Office, South Carolina. He was an independent consultant in 1978–80; director, Office of Criminal Justice, Governor's Office, South Carolina, in 1972–78; research analyst, South Carolina Department of Corrections, in 1970–71; and probation officer, Richland County, South Carolina, in 1968–70.

Mr. Thomas graduated from the University of the South (B.A.) and the University of South Carolina (M.E.D.). He has two children and resides in Ridgeway, S.C. He was born June 13, 1944, in South Carolina.

Nomination of Robert N. Smith To Be an Assistant Secretary of Defense
June 25, 1981

The President today announced his intention to nominate Robert N. Smith to be an Assistant Secretary of Defense (Health Affairs).

Since 1954 Dr. Smith has been a practicing anesthesiologist with the Katchka, Friedman, Crider Medical Center in Toledo, Ohio. He was Assistant Secretary of Defense (Health Affairs) in 1976–78.

Dr. Smith served as Chairman of the Department of Defense Health Council; Chairman, Armed Forces Institute of Pathology Board of Governors; member, National Advisory Mental Health Council; and member, National Advisory Council on Aging.

Dr. Smith graduated from the United States Military Academy (B.S., 1943), Massachusetts Institute of Technology (M.S., 1945), and the University of Nebraska (M.D., 1952). He served in the U.S. Air

Force in 1943–48.

    Dr. Smith is married, has six children, and resides in Toledo, Ohio. He was born April 2, 1920, in Toledo, Ohio.

Remarks in Los Angeles at the Luncheon of the Central City and California Taxpayers' Associations
June 25, 1981

Thank you for a very kind introduction, Mr. Chairman, and the gentlemen and lady who are here at the head table. She was a surprise guest to me. She had other appointments. She heard about the telephone calls to Washington, too. So, I'm delighted that she's here.

I also am meeting you with mixed emotions only about my own situation. Normally, you stand up here well prepared in your mind as to what you're going to say, but I think that any more I will only accept speaking engagements when the Congress is in recess. [*Laughter*] First, I was late and caused the whole luncheon to be late, and therefore I'm late in getting started here. And I'm not quite sure now as to—well, I know that the speech I intended to make is hardly appropriate, because I was really going to go all out on a real stern message about the games that were being played in Washington and how I needed your help because of those games.

You might have heard a rumor to the effect that we've been suggesting a few changes back there. [*Laughter*] And the rumor is correct. But now as a result of all those telephone calls, you know that you helped, with your support, in getting adopted someting called the Gramm-Latta bipartisan budget reduction resolution. And it was a great victory to get Congress to vote the greatest reduction in Government spending that has ever been attempted.

In learning the ways of Washington, I discovered that was just a resolution and meant that the total figure was supposed to be the budget. But then it was all going to be broken up and delivered to all the various congressional committees for them to look at each program and see whether they came back with the proper figure and what they wanted to do with it. And so it became a bill of 4,000 pages, and the committees reported in, and most of the committees in the House, of course, are dominated by, literally, those of another philosophy. But the bulk of the committee reports back were very acceptable and went with the spirit of Gramm-Latta. Phil Gramm is the Democrat Congressman who helped coauthor that measure.

And there were a few committees that in a very important part of the program made changes which literally would have broken the budget before the year was out. And I came here intending to speak about the fact that through a parliamentary procedure, they were going to present—to prevent a vote on Gramm-Latta II. That was the amendment that would remedy what that little handful of committees had done, but which would amount to more than $20 billion of increased deficit and prevent us from balancing the budget by 1984.

I'm extremely pleased and gratified to report to you that just today, in fact within the last hour or two, the American people have won two great victories in the Congress of the United States. First of all, on the House floor, Republican Congressmen joined by 31 courageous members of the Democrat party have joined together to defeat the gag rule that would have seriously damaged our plans for reducing the budget.

Twenty-four hours ago our defeat seemed almost certain; indeed, it was being openly predicted by the other side. But we have, since that first vote, won the second one now also, which means that the next order of business for the Congress is the voting on the Gramm-Latta amendment—the son of Gramm-Latta. The simple truth is that Congress heard the voice of the people, and they acted to carry out the will of the people.

Even as we're gathering here now, I've been informed by the most recent call that the House leadership is engaged in an internal debate on what next step they should take. Well, it's my hope that the House will move quickly now to put our package of spending cuts to a vote. Certainly, there's no reason to delay or postpone beyond their July 4th recess. But let me just reemphasize here today just how important this vote earlier this afternoon is. It means that in the crunch of heavy pressure from all sides, the Congress of the United States seems ready and eager to join in the fight to curb runaway spending.

It means that in both Houses of the Congress and, indeed, on both sides of the aisle, there are enough Members who have the wisdom and courage to cast their vote in favor of America's overall economic interest, not just our special interests. It means that for the first time in many years, we have the opportunity to forge a new coalition in this country—a coalition built upon people from all parties and from every background who will work together for the good of the Nation. It means, in fact, that we can have a new beginning in America, a new beginning toward economic progress for all of our people.

There's good news on the second front today, too, and that is with regard to the subject near and dear to all of you here— the struggle to reduce taxes. Just a little while ago, the Senate Finance Committee, by a margin of 19–1, voted resoundingly for the package of tax changes that are virtually identical to those that I embraced earlier this year. That was another victory for the Nation, and I salute Chairman Bob Dole and the other Republican and Democrat members of his committee for their very swift and judicious action.

Let me just say from the bottom of my heart that we would never have come as far as we have today without the support of you—the American people. I know from the many phone calls and personal visits that I've had with the Members of Congress over the past few months, and even over the past few hours, just how important

grassroots support is to the passage of our economic recovery program. It's your support, it's your help that has been crucial from the day that I arrived in Washington. And when it comes, let me just say, victory will belong to you—the people.

All we're really trying to do is return to some basic principles which have never failed us when we've lived up to them. For example, only by making government live within its means and restricting its role in our personal lives can we unleash the spirit of individual enterprise so essential to prosperity and the preservation of freedom itself. And the way we're doing this is by changing just one little two-letter word— control *by* government to control *of* government.

Now, this doesn't mean it's clear sailing. There are some advocates of a different philosophy that are manning the barricades there in those puzzle palaces on the Potomac. [*Laughter*] But let's be clear about where the real credit goes for our progress to date. It goes to a group with a much greater force than our own, a group comprising tens of millions of people from every profession, every background, every region in this land. They don't consider themselves Democrats or Republicans so much as just deeply patriotic Americans, concerned about their country, determined to save its future while there's still time. We've summed it up in many of our most sacred documents—it is simply, "We the people."

It isn't easy to thank you for all you've done, but I'll try. It's like Thomas Edison said, "Genius is one percent inspiration and 99 percent perspiration." When we announced our economic plan, millions of Americans sent a loud, clear message to Washington that enough is enough. And I think the Congress heard you, which just proves that Washington is still the only city where sound travels faster than light. [*Laughter*]

But now that you've tasted victory and are beginning to feel good, I'd better warn you I have a little favor to ask, and its strictly in the national interest. I simply want to ask you not to sit back and retire from action, as the battle still is not definitely won. I think you want spending reductions that you approved in that bipartisan budget resolution last month. I think you want a 3-year across-the-board tax rate reduction for every American taxpayer and nothing less.

Now, you know, I've been criticized for saying that Federal spending is out of control. But what else describes it? Consider, for example, those programs which have spending increases built into them directly by law. In 1967, the automatic spending program—those are the things called entitlement programs, the redistribution of income—they amounted to $57 billion dollars. Next year, they will amount to a staggering $428 billion, and our elected representatives don't have control over them. If we do nothing to change the laws, this uncontrollable spending will grow to the unbelievable level, by 1984, of more than a half a trillion dollars.

The food stamp program, just back a decade ago, 1970, cost $577 million. Today, again because of the automatic built-in growth, that program costs us $11½ billion. That's 20 times as much in 10 years.

Federal housing subsidies were $500 million just 11 years ago. Today, the cost is $6½ billion and without even adding one single new subsidy, the sum will jump over $10½ billion by 1985. That's 21 times as much as it was 11 years ago.

These programs have truly turned out to be good intentions run amok, budgetary time bombs set to explode in the years ahead, and the effect is to file enormous debts on the backs of our children, heavily mortgaging their future for some sake of temporary social cure. The American economic solution, which ignores reforms in these automatic spending programs, is really no solution at all.

Now, one of those critically important actions on which the Congress can now take action—that was in that little package that they were trying to block—is to cut the Federal redtape and wasteful spending by consolidating 83 confusing and duplicative Federal programs into block grants. It's not fair to ask the taxpayers to send their earnings to Washington and then charge them billions of dollars more to have this same money turned around and sent right back with strings attached. We can do better

than that, and we can do it by cutting out the middleman and putting those funds in the hands of State and local governments where the citizens of America can have greater control of it.

Now, I mentioned Phil Gramm, one of those courageous Democrats. I was saddened to learn the other day that the Chairman of the Democratic National Party has said that he would like to kick Congressman Phil Gramm, coauthor of that Gramm-Latta bill, out of the party. As you know, Phil's been a tireless supporter, as I've told you, and it's not a Democrat or Republican issue. It's an American issue. And I don't think it's our way to threaten to kick people out of any party for doing what they believe is right.

I can't advise Mr. Gramm what to do, but I want to assure him this: There are millions of Democrats, Republicans, and Independents who support what he does. They don't like the idea of partisan threats, and I do advise him, having been a Democrat once myself, I'll tell him to come on over, the water's fine. [*Laughter*]

But, you know, cutting the increase in spending, that's only one part of the program, and this is where I get down to that further request. The Government is taking too great a percentage of the gross national product in taxes. This percentage must be reduced if we're going to have the incentive we need to increase productivity. And we're not going to have recovery till we increase productivity, which requires capital investment of American business and industry.

Now, before I go on with that tax thing, let me just tell you something that's happened in the last few days. Fifteen of the major steel-producing companies in the United States have sent me a report, voluntarily, that they're going forward, all of them together—well, not together, but I mean individually, but together in collection of what they're doing for the steel industry—with improvement and modernization of existing plants to the extent of $3 billion, 200 million. And they have already done that, and they said they are going forward with it simply on the expectation of our recovery program. People who doubt whether the program will work: It's working before it's even been voted into effect. And I'm most grateful to them for what they're doing, and I know that it's going to mean a great deal. And it must be a reflection of what's happening in industry all over the country.

Now, we haven't proposed just a tax rate cut to relieve the over-burdened citizenry. In fact, in some ways we aren't proposing a tax cut at all. We're proposing to reduce or eliminate the tax increase that's already built in to our system, the biggest single tax increase in our nation's history, and it comes on top of the fact that Federal taxes have already doubled just since 1976. If I could paraphrase Will Rogers' line about never having met a man he didn't like, it seems that some in government have never met a tax they didn't hike. [*Laughter*]

We're living with a social security payroll tax that was increased some short time ago, which is scheduled to increase automatically several times in the next 5 years, and those increases have a kind of double whammy. At the same time that the percentage or that the rate increases, the percentage of earnings that that rate is applied to also goes up, so that like the income tax, we have a bracket creep, penalizing workers whose wages go up to keep pace with the cost of living. That social security payroll tax now is 13.3 percent of $29,700. In 1937 they said it would never be greater than $3,000 that would be taxed. The law, already adopted, calls for it to go to 15.3 percent of $66,900 of income.

Like the budget reforms that we seek, the tax package that will help stimulate the economy by providing capital investment to modernize and expand our industrial machine, individuals, even with husband and wife both working, have no surplus to put in savings accounts or insurance. Investors with capital to invest have been driven to tax shelters because of the low after-tax return on investment. There's less money for research and development. The number of patents issued to American companies has been declining for the past decade, while Japanese patent activity, here in America, has increased in each of the 53 United States patent fields.

Now, ironically, some of those who helped pass the tax increases of which I've spoken are now the first and the loudest in charging that our proposal is designed to benefit the wealthy. Well, that's not true. Those who will get the biggest percentage of reduction in their total tax burden will be the lower- and the middle-income families. Our program provides incentives so that more people can share in our prosperity.

The other charge is that it's too risky to cut tax rates when we're running a giant budget deficit. Well, I hope I'll be forgiven for pointing out that they are also the same people who helped create those deficits. But I'm happy to say there are others, as we've learned today, on both sides of the aisle, who can come together and support the bipartisan tax bill that's coauthored by Republican Barber Conable and Democrat Kent Hance. And this bill is the result of negotiations between Members of Congress and our own administration.

The principle of across-the-board cuts and the marginal tax rates over a 3-year period has been maintained in that bill. Now, it's true that I slid back from a 30-percent cut to 25 percent in 3 years for personal income, but this made possible the other tax cuts which I believe will be great stimulants to saving, investment, and increased productivity.

Some of the other tax cuts—I could have won an Oscar for my appearance of reluctance in giving into them. [*Laughter*] But I don't feel I can accept any further changes, even though those who are unenthusiastic about the tax cuts have said they would settle for a 15-percent cut over 2 years. Well, in the first place, that built-in tax increase will amount to 22 percent over 3 years. Our proposal will eliminate that and give at least a small reduction.

In addition, I believe the third year is important particularly for small and independent business, which creates 80 percent of the new jobs and which pays the individual tax rather than the corporate tax. Individual entrepreneurs can look ahead and make plans better with the assurance of 3 years of stability in the tax picture.

Now, let me say just a word about those marginal tax rates that we propose to reduce. In this land, born of a desire to be free, middle-income Americans are being pushed into punitive tax brackets once reserved for the wealthy. Not too many years ago, only 3 percent of those who work and earn were in a 30-percent bracket. Today, a full one-fourth of the work force is paying that marginal tax rate. And when your social security and State income taxes are included in the total tax burden, the average family finds they're facing a 40- to 44-percent marginal tax rate. No wonder middle-class families find they can't put money aside or have means to send their children to college. The worker finds it isn't worthwhile to put in overtime or to try to upgrade him or herself. Productivity drops, and we become less competitive in the world market.

We have to change what has been in existence since the Great Depression, and that is the philosophy of tax and tax, spend and spend, elect and elect.

Now, it's economic nonsense to say that lowering the tax rates will add to our deficits. We've been having tax increases—the most recent, the biggest in our history, as I said—but we're also running the biggest deficits, because government doesn't tax to get the money it needs. Government will always find needs for the money it gets.

By contrast, we find that every time government has had a broad reduction in tax rates, the boost in prosperity is so immediate that while taxpayers pay less individually, government revenues actually go up because of the increased prosperity. And the latest example, in the early sixties, was John F. Kennedy's program, and the same voices were raised against that tax reduction that are raised today.

The Conable-Hance tax bill will give almost three-fourths of the income tax relief to those earning between $10,000 and $60,000 a year. They presently pay 72 percent of the total income tax. So, it sounds like it's a fairly even thing across-the-board.

In addition, the unjust penalty imposed on married couples where husband and wife are both working will be relieved. Individuals will be allowed to deduct $1,000 a year for personal retirement programs even if they are already involved in another pension program. And of special interest to farmers and family-owned businesses, the estate tax exemption will be raised to $600,000, and of even greater help, there will be no estate tax at all for a surviving spouse.

Well now, this is just a hasty sketch of the tax changes for individuals. The plan will provide incentive, because people don't work so they can pay taxes, they work to earn more after-tax income. To the doubters, I address one question I've asked over and over again and I never have gotten an answer once in Washington: "Why is it inflationary for you to keep and spend more of your own money and it isn't inflationary if government takes it and spends it the way it wants to?"

The Conable-Hance bill calls for lowering the 70-percent ceiling on so-called unearned income to the 50-percent ceiling. Capital gains will be lowered, and business will get the biggest tax reduction in our nation's history—some $60 billion in depreciation allowances, et cetera.

To those who say we can't cut spending, lower taxes and, yes, rebuild the defenses we need in this dangerous world, I have a six-word answer: "Yes we can, and yes we must."

It was with some sadness the other night that I watched an individual on TV news suggest that our program was going to destroy America. Now, when someone makes that kind of charge, I have another question to ask: "Where has he been for the last few years?" And the answer to that in this particular case is, "Right in Washington, D.C., in a responsible leader position in the Congress."

Inflation rates didn't rise 18 percent because of our program. Nearly 8 million people didn't get thrown out of work because of anything that happened in these past 5 months. Twenty percent interest and 15-percent mortgage rates didn't begin on the morning of January 20th, 1981. Those who make such charges want to return to some of the old, discredited policies that set off America's high economic fever in the first place. If you're better off with the repeat of red ink every year, continued high taxes and higher taxes, and the monster government of the past, then oppose our program. But if you're ready to try something new, come with us. Send a powerful message to those people who live in the past and tell them, "No more business as usual and no more repeat performances, because we're going to make America great again."

You know, for those doom-criers to try and scare us—and I know I've said this before—but we survived, we the living Americans, a great depression that toppled governments; we came back from Pearl Harbor to win the greatest military victory in world history. Today's living Americans have fought harder, paid a higher price for freedom, and done more to advance the dignity of man than any people who ever lived. We have in my lifetime gone from the horse and buggy to putting a man on the Moon and bringing him safely home. Now, don't tell us that we can't be trusted with an increased share of our own earnings.

All over America people are yearning for the opportunity to produce once again, to save their money and have their savings mean something, to live without the constant pressures of higher and higher prices. They don't ask for much, just a chance to make a better life for themselves and their children. Some have accused me of fighting too hard for these reforms and for not wanting to compromise on key principles. Well, to some of those charges I plead guilty. But for too long, government has stood in the way by taking more of what our people earn no matter how hard they try to get ahead. Who can blame our people for fearing they're trapped inside an economy with no bright tomorrows, an economy that has lost its soul?

And that's why we have to revive the spirit of America, the American Revolution, the spirit of another revolution right here a few years ago, of Propositon 13. We're not demanding the impossible. You're just demanding, I think, some of the same opportunities the Founding Fathers risked their lives, property, and sacred honor for more than 200 years ago—a commitment that if you work and save more tomorrow than you did today, your reward will be higher than it was today. More of every dollar's earnings will be yours to keep, more of your added wages, your added interest. And those are what we mean by incentives. Those are what will unlock the spirit and the energy of our people, to drive Americans to dream and dare to take greater risks for a greater good, unlock the spirit of a Fulton and a Ford and the Wright brothers and Lindberg and all of our astronauts.

We did it before, and we can do it again. We can solve the energy crisis and pioneer technological breakthroughs and rebuild our cities and, in the process, strengthen our families and create new jobs and a real hope for young Americans everywhere.

Yes, we can do all that and save the American dream, but only on one condition—that we always remember we owe our progress to the unique form of government that allows us the freedom to choose our own destiny, a government that answers to "We the people." And with your help, I think that we're going to do that in Washington.

I've never felt better in these last 5 months than I feel in this particular moment today. And for that, thank you, and God bless you.

Note: The President spoke at 1:14 p.m. in the Los Angeles Ballroom at the Century Plaza Hotel. Prior to the luncheon, the President attended a reception with members of the associations in the Sherman Oaks Room at the hotel.

Nomination of Frank Shakespeare To Be a Member of the Board for International Broadcasting, and Designation as Chairman
June 26, 1981

The President today announced his intention to nominate Frank Shakespeare to be a member of the Board for International Broadcasting, term expiring May 20, 1983, vice Frank Markoe, Jr. Upon confirmation, the President intends to designate Mr. Shakespeare Chairman.

Mr. Shakespeare is president, RKO General, Inc., of New York City. Previously he served as president of CBS–TV Services and was senior vice president of the CBS–TV

Network. He was Director of the United States Information Agency (USIA) in 1969–73. Mr. Shakespeare was executive vice president of the Westinghouse Electric Corp. in 1973–75.

Mr. Shakespeare graduated from Holy Cross College (B.S., 1945). He served in the U.S. Navy in 1943–46. Mr. Shakespeare is married, has three children, and resides in Greenwich, Conn. He was born April 9, 1925, in New York, N.Y.

Nomination of Two Members of the Board for International Broadcasting
June 26, 1981

The President today announced his intention to nominate Mark Goode and Ben J. Wattenberg to be members of the Board for International Broadcasting, terms expiring April 28, 1983. They will succeed Rita E. Hauser and John A. Gronouski.

Mr. Goode served in the U.S. Army in 1954–57. After his service in the Army he became a staff associate director with ABC–TV in Los Angeles, Calif., and became director before leaving in 1967 to become a freelance television producer and director in Los Angeles until 1971. His shows included "The Johnny Cash Show," "Pat Paulsen's Half A Comedy Hour," and "Barney Miller." He also produced coverage of political conventions and elections. In 1977–80 he became the co-owner and general manager for Goode Ideas, Inc., manufacturers of active sportswear for women. From July 1980 to November 1980, Mr. Goode was television adviser to the Reagan-Bush campaign. He served as a member of the transition team for the International Communication Agency after the 1980 election. Mr. Goode was a member of the Advisory Board for the John F. Kennedy Center for the Performing Arts in 1973–77 and a member of the communications advisory

committee for the Republican National Committee in 1977–79. He served as a Special Assistant to the President in 1971–73 and Consultant to the President in 1970–76. Mr. Goode graduated from Northwestern University (1954). He is married, has three children, and resides in Hidden Hills, Calif. He was born March 25, 1932, in Steubenville, Ohio.

Mr. Wattenberg is a senior fellow at the American Enterprise Institute in Washington, D.C., and coeditor of AEI's bimonthly magazine Public Opinion. Throughout his career he has served as a narrator-essayist for the Public Broadcasting Service (PBS). Mr. Wattenberg was an aide and speechwriter to President Johnson in 1966–68. In 1970 he was a campaign adviser to Senator Hubert Humphrey (D-Minn.) and an adviser to Senator Henry Jackson (D-Wash.) in 1972 and 1976. He was one of the cofounders and is now chairman of the Coalition for a Democratic Majority. In 1977 Mr. Wattenberg was appointed by President Carter to serve on the Presidential Advisory Board on Ambassadorial Appointments. In 1980 he was chosen as public member of the American delegation to the Madrid

Conference on Human Rights. Mr. Wattenberg is a writer, editor, and publisher. He was a professor-at-large at Mary Washington College. He graduated from Hobart College (1955). Mr. Wattenberg is married, has three children, and resides in Washington, D.C. He was born August 26, 1933, in New York, N.Y.

Nomination of James C. Miller III To Be a Member of the Federal Trade Commission, and Designation as Chairman
June 26, 1981

The President today announced his intention to nominate James C. Miller III to be a member of the Federal Trade Commission. Upon confirmation, the President intends to designate Dr. Miller Chairman. Dr. Miller will continue to fulfill his duties on the Presidential Task Force on Regulatory Relief until his designation as Chairman of the FTC.

Dr. Miller is currently serving as Administrator for Information and Regulatory Affairs, Office of Management and Budget. He is also Executive Director of the Presidential Task Force on Regulatory Relief. Previously, since 1977, Dr. Miller has been a resident scholar at the American Enterprise Institute and was codirector of AEI's Center for the Study of Government Regulation. He was a member of the board of editors of AEI's journal Regulation and served on the board of editorial advisers of the AEI Economist. Dr. Miller was an elected member of the executive committee of the Southern Economic Association and also holds memberships in the American Association for the Advancement of Science, the American Economic Association, the Public Choice Society, and the Western Economic Association. In 1974–75 Dr. Miller served as a Senior Staff Economist with the Council of Economic Advisers, where he specialized in matters relating to transportation, regulation and antitrust policy. In 1975 he was appointed the Council on Wage and Price Stability's Assistant Director for Government Operations and Research. He has also served as a member of President Ford's Domestic Council Regulatory Review Group, which directed the administration's program in regulatory reform. In 1972–74 Dr. Miller was an associate professor of economics at Texas A&M University and served as a consultant to the Department of Transportation and the National Bureau of Standards. Previously, in 1972, he was research associate at the Brookings Institution and at AEI. In 1969–72 he was a senior staff economist at the Department of Transportation.

Dr. Miller graduated from the University of Georgia (B.B.A., 1964) and the University of Virginia (Ph. D., 1969). He is married, has three children, and resides in Washington, D.C. He was born June 25, 1942, in Atlanta, Ga.

Nomination of F. Keith Adkinson To Be a Member of the Federal Trade Commission
June 26, 1981

The President today announced his intention to nominate F. Keith Adkinson to be a member of the Federal Trade Commission for the unexpired term of 7 years from September 26, 1975, vice Robert Pitofsky, resigned.

Since 1979 Mr. Adkinson has been an attorney with the firm of Seyfarth, Shaw,

Fairweather & Geraldson of Washington, D.C. In 1974–79 he was counsel, Senate Permanent Subcommittee on Investigations, and chief assistant to Senator Sam Nunn (D-Ga.) Mr. Adkinson was associate attorney with the firm of Wyman, Bautzer, Rothman & Kuchel of Century City, Los Angeles, Calif., and Washington, D.C., in 1969–73.

Mr. Adkinson graduated from the University of Virginia (B.A., 1966) and the University of Virginia Law School (J.D., 1969). He was a member of the Fairfax County, Va., Democratic Committee, and was the Democratic nominee for election to the Virginia General Assembly from the 19th legislative district.

Mr. Adkinson resides in Harpers Ferry, W. Va. He was born May 26, 1944, in New York, N.Y.

Statement on Approval of Federal Budget Reconciliation Legislation by the House of Representatives
June 26, 1981

Today the House of Representatives gave the American people a major victory in the war against inflation. By passing the Gramm-Latta spending control amendment, despite intense political pressure, an emerging coalition of Democrats and Republicans demonstrated that bipartisan cooperation is for real and that America can once again have a government that lives within its means.

Today's vote was a profile in political courage and should inspire the gratitude of us all. It will renew the faith of millions of Americans who have waited so long just for those in Washington to listen and care and take action.

Let there be no misunderstandings: The victory of the Gramm-Latta amendment was absolutely essential in order to meet our spending targets next year and balance the budget by 1984. There will be a need for additional spending restraints in the future, but without this vote today, we would have faced more than $20 billion in additional deficits over the next 3 years.

The Senate has already produced a spending bill that is highly satisfactory. So, while we must still await a House-Senate conference, today's vote ensures that the final outcome will carry us a long way toward our budgetary goals.

Nomination of Richard L. Walker To Be United States Ambassador to the Republic of Korea
June 27, 1981

The President today announced his intention to nominate Richard L. Walker, of South Carolina, to be Ambassador to the Republic of Korea. He would succeed William H. Gleysteen, Jr., who is resigning.

Mr. Walker was assistant professor of history at Yale University in 1950–57. Since 1957 he has been professor of international relations at the University of South Carolina. He also was head of the department of international studies in 1957–72 and, since 1961, has been the director of the Institute of International Studies. He has served as visiting professor at the National Taiwan University, Kyoto Sangyo University (Japan), the National Chengchi University, and the Far Eastern and Russian Institute at the University of Washington. In 1960–61 he was professor of international politics at National War College.

Mr. Walker has written many articles and books, from his first in 1949, "Western Language Periodicals on China," to the most recent in 1975, "Ancient Japan and Its Influence in Modern Times."

Mr. Walker received his B.A. in 1944 from Drew University and his M.A. in 1947 and Ph. D. in 1950 from Yale University. He served in the United States Army in 1943–46. He is married, has three children, and resides in Columbia, S.C. He was born April 13, 1922, in Bellefonte, Pa.

Nomination of Julius Waring Walker, Jr., To Be United States Ambassador to Upper Volta
June 27, 1981

The President today announced his intention to nominate Julius Waring Walker, Jr., of Texas, to be Ambassador to the Republic of Upper Volta. He would succeed Thomas D. Boyatt, who is now serving as Ambassador to Colombia.

In 1950–56 Mr. Walker was employed in Texas with private industry, serving successively as assistant manager of a grocery store, claims adjuster of an insurance company, a newspaper reporter, and television announcer.

He entered the Foreign Service in 1956 as information officer with the News Division in the Department. In 1958–61 he was consular officer in Valletta, and political officer in Bujumbura in 1961–63. In the Department he was personnel officer in the Bureau of Personnel in 1963–65 and international relations officer in 1965–66. In 1966–69 he was Deputy Chief of Mission in Fort Lamy and political officer in London in 1969–72. He attended the National War College from 1972–73. In the Department he was Director of the Office of African Regional Affairs in 1973–75, Director of the Office of Directorate for Transportation and Communication Agencies in 1975–76, and Director of the Office of International Conferences in 1976–78. Since 1978 he has been Deputy Chief of Mission in Monrovia.

Mr. Walker received his B.F.A. (1950) from the University of Texas and M.S. (1973) from George Washington University. He is married to the former Savannah Tunnell and has three children. Mr. Walker was born February 21, 1927, in Plainview, Tex.

Nomination of Frederic V. Malek To Be a Governor of the United States Postal Service
June 27, 1981

The President today announced his intention to nominate Frederic V. Malek to be a Governor of the United States Postal Service for a term expiring December 8, 1989, vice Wallace Hyde.

Mr. Malek has been with Marriott Corp. since 1975 and serves as executive vice president. He is responsible for Marriott's hotel business, its architecture and construction division, and Sun Line Cruises. He served as Deputy Director of the Office of Management and Budget in 1973–74, and, prior to that, served as Special Assistant to the President and as Deputy Under Secretary of the Department of Health, Education, and Welfare. Mr. Malek has been a management consultant with McKinsey and Co. and in 1967 founded and became chairman of the Triangle Corp.

Mr. Malek has previously served as a member of the President's Domestic Council, the President's Commission on White House Fellows, and the President's Commission on Personnel Interchange. He currently serves on the board of directors of three NYSE companies: Automatic Data

Processing, Inc., Mark Controls Corp., and Sargent-Welch Scientific Co.; and serves on the national advisory council of the National Center of Economic Education for Children. He has published many articles which have appeared in the Harvard Business Review, the Wall Street Journal, the New York Times, and the Los Angeles Times. He is the author of "Washington's Hidden Tragedy," published in 1978.

Mr. Malek is a graduate of West Point and a former Green Beret in Vietnam. He received his M.B.A. degree from the Harvard Business School in 1964. He is married, has two children, and resides in McLean, Va. He was born December 22, 1936, in Berwyn, Ill.

Remarks in Denver, Colorado, at the Annual Convention of the National Association for the Advancement of Colored People
June 29, 1981

Chairwoman Margaret Bush Wilson, I thank you very much for that introduction and that explanation also of my year's tardiness in getting here.

I remember a year ago I was in California when I received your invitation at the same time that I received a clipping that I had not answered your invitation. Now, at that moment it was almost impossible for me—well, it was impossible to find a way—not even Air Force One could have bridged from California to Florida. But I'm delighted that this time, as you say, there was better staff work and I was able to get the invitation in plenty of time.

President Cobb, Vice Chairman Kelly Alexander, and Executive Director Benjamin Hooks, the ladies and gentlemen here on the platform, the members of the board of directors, and you, ladies and gentlemen, representatives to this convention:

I'm very happy to be talking to the NAACP's 72d annual convention.

There are many things that we need to discuss, and I thank you for the invitation to do so. Let us talk today about the needs of the future, not the misunderstandings of the past; about new ideas, not old ones; about what must become a continuing dialog, not a dialog that flows only at intermittent conventions that we both attend.

Part of that continuing dialog took place last Tuesday when I met with Ben Hooks and Margaret Bush Wilson in the Oval Office. Our discussion was candid and useful. The wide range of our conversation showed that there is a great deal to be gained when we take time to share our views. And while our communication should always deal with current issues of importance, it must never stray far from our national commitment to battle against discrimination and increase our knowledge of each other.

A few isolated groups in the backwater of American life still hold perverted notions of what America is all about. Recently in some places in the nation there's been a disturbing reoccurrence of bigotry and violence. If I may, from the platform of this organization, known for its tolerance, I would like to address a few remarks to those groups who still adhere to senseless racism and religious prejudice, to those individuals who persist in such hateful behavior.

If I were speaking to them instead of to you, I would say to them, "You are the ones who are out of step with our society. You are the ones who willfully violate the meaning of the dream that is America. And this country, because of what it stands for, will not stand for your conduct." My administration will vigorously investigate and prosecute those who, by violence or intimidation, would attempt to deny Americans their constitutional rights.

Another kind of terror has recently plagued the city of Atlanta. Not long ago in a speech before the Congress I read the now famous "pajama letter" from Peter

573

Sweeney. If only my letters from children could all be as lighthearted as Peter's. Other letters are more poignant. When little girls in Atlanta write asking that I make things right so they won't be scared anymore, even a President of the United States can feel a little helpless.

We committed the resources of the FBI and a number of Federal agencies to help Mayor Jackson. I appointed Vice President Bush to head this Federal task force, and its work will continue until this tragic episode is over. Not counting manpower and equipment, we've provided over $4 million to this cause. I know that all of us wish we could tell the children of Atlanta that they need no longer fear, and until we can say that, however, we will not be satisfied until those children can once again play safely in their schoolyards and parks.

Our dialog must also include discussions on how we can best protect the rights and privileges of all our citizens. My administration will root out any case of government discrimination against minorities and uphold and enforce the laws that protect them. I emphasize that we will not retreat on the nation's commitment to equal treatment of all citizens. Now, that, in my view, is the primary responsibility of National Government. The Attorney General is now carefully studying the decennial redistricting plans being submitted under the current Voting Rights Act. As soon as we have all the information there will be a decision regarding extension of the act.

Until a decision is announced, you should know this: I regard voting as the most sacred right of free men and women. We have not sacrificed and fought and toiled to protect that right so that now we can sit back and permit a barrier to come between a secret ballot and any citizen who makes a choice to cast it. Nothing—nothing will change that as long as I am in a position to uphold the Constitution of the United States.

In the months ahead, our dialog also will include tough and realistic questions about the role of the Federal Government in the black community. I'm not satisfied with its results, and I don't think you are either. And the failures of the past have been particularly hard on the minority poor, because

their hopes have failed as surely as the Federal programs that built those hopes. But I must not be the only one who questions about government policies.

Can the black teenager who faces a staggering unemployment rate feel that government policies are a success? Can the black wage earner who sees more and more of his take-home pay shrinking because of government taxes feel satisfied? Can black parents say, despite a massive influx of Federal aid, that educational standards in our schools have improved appreciably? Can the women I saw on television recently—whose family had been on welfare for three generations and who feared that her children might be the fourth—can she believe that current government policies will save her children from such a fate?

We ask these tough questions, because we share your concerns about the future of the black community. We ask these questions, because the blacks of America should not be patronized as just one more voting bloc to be wooed and won. You are individuals as we all are. Some have special needs. I don't think the Federal Government has met those needs.

I've been listening to the specific needs of many people—blacks, farmers, refugees, union members, women, small business men and women, and other groups—they're commonly referred to as special-interest groups. Well, in reality they're all members of the interest group that I spoke of the day I took the oath of office. They are the people of America. And I'm pleased to serve that special-interest group.

The people of the inner cities will be represented by this administration every bit as much as the citizens of Flagstaff, Arizona, Ithaca, New York, or Dixon, Illinois, where I grew up. Anyone who becomes President realizes he must represent all the people of the land, not just those of a home State or a particular party. Nor can he be just President of those who voted for him.

But it doesn't matter what groups we belong to, what area we live in, how much or how little we earn; the economy affects every single one of us regardless of our other interests and affiliations. We have proceeded full throttle on our economic recovery program, because a strong, growing economy without inflation is the surest, most equitable way to ease the pressures on all the segments of our society.

The well-being of blacks, like the well-being of every other American, is linked directly to the health of the economy. For example, industries in which blacks had made sufficient gains in employment—substantial gains, like autos and steel—have been particularly hard hit. And "last hired, first fired" is a familiar refrain in too many black workers. And I don't need to tell this group what inflation has done to those who can least afford it. A declining economy is a poisonous gas that claims its first victims in poor neighborhoods, before floating out into the community at large.

Therefore, in our national debate over budget and tax proposals, we shall not concede the moral high ground to the proponents of those policies that are responsible in the first place for our economic mess—a mess which has injured all Americans. We will not concede the moral high ground to those who show more concern for Federal programs than they do for what really determines the income and financial health of blacks—the nation's economy.

Now, I know you've been told that my proposal for economic recovery is designed to discriminate against all who are economically deprived. Now, those who say that could be confused by the misstatements that have been made by some who are either ignorant of the facts or those who are practicing, for political reasons, pure demagoguery.

Rebuilding America's economy is an absolute moral imperative if we're to avoid splitting this society in two with class against class. I do not intend to let America drift further toward economic segregation. We must change the economic direction of this country to bring more blacks into the mainstream, and we must do it now.

And [in] 1938, before we had the equality we know today, Langston Hughes wrote "Let America Be America Again." And he wrote:

Oh, yes, I see [say] it plain
America never was America to me.
And yet I swear this oath—
America will be!

America will be. That is the philosophy the people proclaimed in last November's election. America will be. And this time, she will be for everyone. Together, we can recreate for every citizen the same economic opportunities that we saw lift up a land of immigrant people, the kind of opportunities that have swept the hungry and the persecuted into the mainstream of our life since the American experiment began.

To a number of black Americans, the U.S. economy has been something of an underground railroad; it has spirited them away from poverty to middle-class prosperity and beyond. But too many blacks still remain behind. A glance at the statistics will show that a large proportion of the black people have not found economic freedom. Nationwide, for example, 43 percent of black families in 1979 had money incomes under $10,000.

Harriet Tubman, who was known as the "conductor" of that earlier underground railroad, said on her first escape from slavery, "When I found I had crossed that line, I looked at my hands to see if I was the same person. There was such a glory over everything." Even after a century the beauty of her words is powerful. We can only imagine the soaring of her soul, what a feeling that must have been when she crossed into freedom and the physical and mental shackles fell from her person.

Harriet Tubman's glory was the glory of the American experience. It was a glory which had no color or religious preference or nationality. It was simply, eloquently, the universal thirst that all people have for freedom.

Well, there are poor people in this country who should experience just such an elation if they found the economic freedom of a solid job, a productive job—not one concocted by government and dependent on Washington winds; a real job where they could put in a good day's work, complain about the boss, and then go home with confidence and self-respect. Why has this Nation been unable to fill such a basic, admirable need?

The government can provide subsistence, yes, but it seldom moves people up the economic ladder. And as I've said before, you

575

have to get on the ladder before you can move up on it. I believe many in Washington, over the years, have been more dedicated to making needy people government-dependent rather than independent. They've created a new kind of bondage, because regardless of how honest their intention in the beginning, those they set out to help soon became clients essential to the well-being of those who administered the programs.

An honest program would be dedicated to making people independent, no longer in need of government assistance. But then what would happen to those who made a career of helping? Well, Americans have been very generous, with good intentions and billions of dollars, toward those they believed were living in hardship. And yet, in spite of the hopes, the government has never lived up to the dreams of poor people. Just as the Emancipation Proclamation freed black people 118 years ago, today we need to declare an economic emancipation.

I genuinely and deeply believe the economic package we've put forth will move us toward black economic freedom, because it's aimed at lifting an entire country and not just parts of it. There's a truth to the words spoken by John F. Kennedy that a rising tide lifts all boats. Yes, I know it's been said, "What about the fellow without a boat who can't swim?" Well, I believe John Kennedy's figure of speech was referring to the benefits which accrue to all when the economy is flourishing.

Now, much has been said and written—not all of it flattering—about the savings I've proposed in the budget which were adopted by the House last Friday. I can assure you that the budget savings we've advocated are much more equitable than the tremendous cuts in social programs, made by inflation and the declining economy, which can't find jobs for almost 8 million men and women who are unemployed.

Those cuts are exacted without regard to need or age. Let me give some examples. In the prosperity of the 1960's, an era of only a few Federal programs costing very little, the number of people living in poverty was reduced by nearly 50 percent. During the "stagflation" of the 1970's with

many Federal programs with huge budgets, the number living in poverty was reduced by only 6 percent.

In the 1960's black unemployment fell from 10.7 percent to 6.4 percent. In the 1970's it increased from 6.4 percent to 11.3 percent. What is more, relative to the white unemployment rate, black unemployment fell more in the 1960's but rose more in the 1970's. The declining economy has cut black family income. From 1959 to 1969, the median family income of blacks, after adjusting for inflation, rose at 5 percent per year, but from 1969 to 1979, income actually dropped.

Now, these are hard economic facts which are hard to take, because they show massive amounts of government aid and intervention have failed to produce the desired results. A strong economy returns the greatest good to the black population. It returns a benefit greater than that provided by specific Federal programs. By slowing the growth of government and by limiting the tax burden and thus stimulating investment, we will also be reducing inflation and unemployment. We will be creating jobs, nearly 3 million additional new jobs by 1986. We will be aiding minority businesses, which have been particularly hard hit by the scarcity of capital and the prohibitive interest rates. And these concerns are what the bipartisan tax cut proposal currently before the Congress is all about.

I said the other day in our conversation in the Oval Office that the income a year or two ago—I don't have the most recent figure—for the black community was something like $140 billion. Now, in most neighborhoods what really brings prosperity is when the income of that neighborhood is then multiplied by turning over several times within that community. I must tell you that in the black communities in America the turnover is less than once before the dollars, those $140 billion, go out into the community at large. And that has to be changed.

In the convention last summer Benjamin Hooks—the one that I missed—well, no, this was the Republican Convention; I made that one—[*laughter*]—Benjamin Hooks said to the assembled delegates, "We must decide as a nation if we're to become prisoners of our past or possessors of an enlightened and progressive future." Those are the very words I want to say to you today.

We cannot be tied to the old ways of solving our economic and racial problems. But it is time we looked to new answers and new ways of thinking that will accomplish the very ends the New Deal and the Great Society anticipated. We're not repealing the gains of black people. We're solidifying those gains and making them safe for your children and grandchildren.

It's time that we found ways to make the American economic pie bigger instead of just cutting an ever smaller pie into more but smaller slices. It's time we welcomed those Americans into the circle of prosperity to let them share in the wonders of our society, and it's time to break the cycle of dependency that has become the legacy of so many Federal programs that no longer work—indeed, some of which never did work.

Let me give you an idea of how bountiful this famous economic pie could have been by now. If productivity had not stopped growing and then started downhill after 1965, the gross national product today would be $850 billion bigger—enough to balance the budget, cut personal and social security taxes in half, and still provide every American with an extra $2,500 in spending money. And all of this would have happened with the compliments of the private sector.

Now, you wisely learned to harness the Federal Government in the hard pull toward equality, and that was right, because guaranteeing equality of treatment is government's proper function. But as the last decade of statistics I just read indicated, government is no longer the strong draft horse of minority progress, because it has attempted to do too many things it's not equipped to do. I ask you if it isn't time to hitch up a fresh horse to finish the task. Free enterprise is a powerful workhorse that can solve many problems of the black community that government alone can no longer solve.

The black leadership of this Nation has shown tremendous courage, both physical and intellectual, and great creativity as it sought to bring equality to its people. You in this audience are the inheritors of that proud black heritage. You are the black leaders of today, and I believe you possess the very same courage and creativity. I ask you to use that courage and creativity to examine the challenges that are facing not just blacks but all of America.

I ask you to question the status quo as your predecessors did and look for new and imaginative ways to overcome minority problems. I'm talking about the kind of courage and questioning your chairman, Margaret Bush Wilson, showed in taking the heat for the NAACP's controversial 1978 energy statement—a statement which shook the elitists of our country back into the real world, at least for a time. What I'm asking you to consider requires not so much a leap of faith, but a realization that the Federal Government alone is just not capable of doing the job we all want done for you or any other Americans.

In the months ahead, as the administration is free to turn attention from the economic program to other needs of America, we'll be advancing proposals on a number of issues of concern to this convention. The inner cities, for example, should be communities, neighborhoods, not warehouses of despair where children are bused out and ineffectual Federal funds are bused in. I believe that with the aid of commonsense government assistance and the use of free enterprise zones, with less reliance on busing and more reliance on better, basic education, and with an emphasis on local activism, such as you represent, communities can be reinvigorated.

Certainly, we're all inspired by the wonderful example of Marva Collins in Chicago, the gallant lady who has the educational grit to make Shakespeare admirers out of inner-city children. She just proves to me what a friend of mine, Wilson Riles, California's superintendent of education, used to say: "The concept that black children can't learn unless they're sitting among white children is utter and complete nonsense." Now, Dr. Riles was not suggesting that integration isn't a good and proper thing; it is. And it's good for all of us when it's brought about with commonsense and attention to what is best for the children.

We plan to take a look, a comprehensive look, at the education of blacks from primary school upward and strengthen the base of black colleges, which are a sound educational investment. They are more than that. They're a proud tradition, a symbol of black determination and accomplishment, and I feel deeply they must be preserved. We've increased the share of Department of Education Title III funds spend on black colleges, and that trend will continue.

We have equal concern for the black business leaders of today. Minority business development, as I indicated earlier, is a key to black economic progress. Black-owned businesses are especially important in neighborhood economies where the dollars, as I said, spent have a beneficial multiplier effect.

We want your input. I expect my domestic advisers to be in regular touch with you as our policies evolve. We may not always agree, but new ideas are often sparked by opinions clashing.

I didn't come here today bearing the promises of government handouts, which others have brought and which you've rightly learned to mistrust. Instead, I ask you to join me to build a coalition for change.

Seventy-two years ago the famous call went forth, the call for a conference emphasizing the civil and political rights of blacks. And the result of that call, of course, was the National Association for the Advancement of Colored People. Well, today let us issue a call for new perspectives on the economic challenges facing black Americans. Let us issue a call for exciting programs to spring America forward toward the next century, an America full of new solutions to old problems.

We will link hands to build an era where we can put fear behind us and hope in front of us. It can be an era in which programs are less important than opportunities. It can be an era where we all reach out in reconciliation instead of anger and dispute.

In the war in Vietnam several years ago, a live grenade fell among a group of American soldiers. They were frozen with horror knowing they were only seconds away from death. Then one young soldier, a black, threw himself on the grenade, covering it with his helmet and his body. He died to save his comrades. Greater glory hath no man. Congressional Medal of Honor winner, posthumously presented, Garfield Langhorn's last whispered words were, "You have to care."

Let us care. Let us work to build a nation that is free of racism, full of opportunity, and determined to loosen the creative energies of every person of every race, of every station, to make a better life. It will be my honor to stand alongside you to answer this call.

Thank you.

Note: The President spoke at 1:10 p.m. in Currigan Hall "B" of the Denver Convention Complex.

Following his appearance before the NAACP, the President went to Buckley Air National Guard Base, Aurora, Colo. Prior to leaving for Washington, D.C., he met with former President Gerald R. Ford and Children's Diabetes Foundation Poster Children Heidi Koehler and Brock Vincent Ryan.

Proclamation 4849—National Clean-Up and Flag-Up America's Highways Week, 1981
June 27, 1981

By the President of the United States of America

A Proclamation

Americans enjoy the use of our Nation's highway system, which is one of the finest systems in the world, both for business and pleasure. Our highways are a source of pride for this Nation and they directly or indirectly affect and serve every American. Highways are our lifelines—providing us with food and other necessities, the opportunity to explore this vast, beautiful country, and a great freedom of choice in selecting our home and work areas. Highways have contributed significantly to employment, provided us improved lifestyles, and aided in our defense. Our highways should be recognized as a national asset and our citizens should be urged to clean up and rehabilitate them. Clean and litter-free highways will contribute to national pride and road safety.

To remind all Americans of the importance of national pride and road safety, the Congress, by an Act approved June 5, 1981

(Public Law 97–12), has requested the President to proclaim June 28 through July 4 as National Clean-up and Flag-up America's Highways Week.

Now, Therefore, I, Ronald Reagan, President of the United States of America, do hereby designate the week beginning June 28 through July 4, 1981, as National Clean-up and Flag-up America's Highways Week. I call upon the people of the United States to observe that week with appropriate ceremonies and activities.

In Witness Whereof, I have hereunto set my hand this 27th day of June, in the year of our Lord nineteen hundred and eighty-one, and of the Independence of the United States of America the two hundred and fifth.

RONALD REAGAN

[*Filed with the Office of the Federal Register, 1:01 p.m., June 30, 1981*]

Note: The text of the proclamation was released by the Office of the Press Secretary on June 30.

Executive Order 12311—Amending the Generalized System of Preferences
June 29, 1981

By virtue of the authority vested in me by the Constitution and statutes of the United States of America, including Title V of the Trade Act of 1974 (88 Stat. 2066, 19 U.S.C. 2461 *et seq.*) as amended, Section 604 of the Trade Act of 1974 (88 Stat. 2073, 19 U.S.C. 2483), and as President of the United States of America, in order to modify the limitations on preferential treatment for eligible articles from countries designated as beneficiary developing countries and to adjust the original designation of eligible articles taking into account information and advice received in fulfillment of

Sections 503(a) and 131–134 of the Trade Act of 1974 (88 Stat. 2069, 19 U.S.C. 2463; 88 Stat. 1994, 19 U.S.C. 2151 *et seq.*), it is hereby ordered as follows:

Section 1. In order to subdivide and amend the nomenclature of existing items for purposes of the Generalized System of Preferences (GSP), the Tariff Schedules of the United States (TSUS) (19 U.S.C. 1202) are modified as provided in Annex I, attached hereto and made a part hereof.

Sec. 2. Annex II of Executive Order No. 11888 of November 24, 1975, as amended, listing articles that are eligible for benefits of the GSP when imported from any designated beneficiary developing country is amended:

(a) by adding in numerical sequence the following TSUS item numbers created by Annex I of this Order: 170.12, 170.13 and 170.70,

(b) by deleting TSUS item 408.52, and

(c) by adding in numerical sequence TSUS items 603.45, 687.42 and 727.29.

Sec. 3. Annex III of Executive Order No. 11888, as amended, listing articles that are eligible for benefits of the GSP when imported from all designated beneficiary countries except those specified in General Headnote 3(c)(iii) of the TSUS, is amended by deleting TSUS items 603.45, 687.42, and 727.29 therefrom.

Sec. 4. General Headnote 3(c)(iii) of the TSUS, listing articles that are eligible for benefits of the GSP except when imported from the beneficiary countries listed opposite those articles, is modified by deleting Mozambique opposite TSUS item 155.20, and also deleting "603.45. . . . Chile", "687.42. . . . Taiwan", and "727.29. . . . Yugoslavia" therefrom.

Sec. 5. In order to provide staged reductions in the rates of duty for the new TSUS items created by Annex I to this Order, Annex III to Proclamation 4768 of June 28, 1980, is amended by Annex II to this Order, attached hereto and made a part hereof.

Sec. 6. (a) The amendment made by Section 2(b) of this order is effective with respect to articles both: (1) imported on and after January 1, 1976, and (2) entered, or withdrawn from warehouse for consumption, on and after December 2, 1980;

(b) The amendments made by sections 2(c), 3, 4, and Annex I(A) are effective with respect to articles both: (1) imported on and after January 1, 1976, and (2) entered, or withdrawn from warehouse for consumption, on and after March 31, 1981; and

(c) The amendments made by the remaining sections of this order are effective with respect to articles both: (1) imported on and after January 1, 1976, and (2) entered, or withdrawn from warehouse for consumption, on and after the third day following the date of publication of this Order in the *Federal Register*.

RONALD REAGAN

The White House,
June 29, 1981.

[Filed with the Office of the Federal Register, 1:02 p.m., June 30, 1981]

Note: The annexes are printed in the Federal Register of July 1, 1981.

The text of the Executive order was released by the Office of the Press Secretary on June 30.

Remarks at the Welcoming Ceremony for Prime Minister J. Malcolm Fraser of Australia
June 30, 1981

The President. Prime Minister Fraser, the American people welcome you to our country with a deep and a heartfelt warmth reserved for only the best of friends. Nancy and I are pleased to be able to welcome you and Mrs. Fraser as representatives of a country with whom we are proud to be allied and the American people are grateful to have as friends.

Robert Louis Stevenson wrote, "We are all travelers in what John Bunyan calls the wilderness of this world. And the best that we find in our travels is an honest friend—they keep us worthy of ourselves." The people of Australia are honest and loyal friends, independent of mind and will, who bring strength of character and courage to the international community. America's proud to have such an ally in a world where freedom and democracy are constantly challenged.

Australians have fought side by side with Americans in every major war in this century. They've opened their hearts and homes to us when we were away from home, and they have stood with us in good times and bad. And America is grateful to have such steadfast friends.

You, Mr. Prime Minister, are a world leader who has made Australia a force for peace. Under your government Australia has done much to bring independence and economic growth to developing countries as close to you as Southeast Asia and as far away as Africa. And there you played the key role in Commonwealth consultations leading to the independence of Zimbabwe. Together with New Zealand, Australia and America have shared a bond of the tripart ANZUS alliance, for 30 years working together to maintain peace and security in the East Asian and Pacific regions.

As Sir Robert Menzies said, "We work for the same kind of free world. We see the world from similar perspectives, though no two countries could be on more opposite ends of the globe. We share values shaped on the new world frontier passed on to us as our heritage. We live in freedom and will accept no other life. We govern ourselves in democracy and will not tolerate anything less. We cherish liberty and hold it safe, providing hope for the rest of the world. We were born in the same era, sprang from the same stock, and live for the same ideals. Australia and America share an affinity that reaches to our souls."

You have said, Mr. Prime Minister, that the liberty we enjoy has no guarantee. And most importantly, liberty requires an understanding by ordinary people of what is at stake. The survival of the whole way of life depends on their commitment.

I was particularly impressed, deeply so, when, Mr. Prime Minister, I heard your powerful declaration in your speech before the B'nai B'rith here in Washington last September. You reminded us that a people without an objective are a people lost. A people without faith are a people destroyed. A people without conviction will not survive. It is liberty which provides the objective, liberty which allows faith, liberty which sustains conviction. But liberty is not an inevitable state, and there is no law which guarantees that once achieved it will survive. Its preservation requires skill, determination, and strength.

Mr. Prime Minister, the Australian example is an inspiration for free people everywhere. You may be assured that America will remain vigilant, will keep herself strong, and will always be a dependable partner in the quest for stability, freedom, and peace. Australia is indeed a friend who keeps us worthy of ourselves.

Prime Minister Fraser, I look forward to our meetings today as an opportunity to enhance our cooperation with one of our closest allies, but it will also be a pleasure to get to know the Frasers—get to know them better, strengthening the personal friendship between our two lands.

So, on behalf of all Americans, I welcome you to the United States.

The Prime Minister. Mr. President, for my wife and myself, the Australian party who are with me, thank you very much indeed for your warm and generous welcome. I'm looking forward, indeed, to the discussions that we shall be having.

Australia and the United States, as you've pointed out, Mr. President, share a commitment to the values of freedom and of democracy. And we know that these values are not mere words; they stand for our way of life, for the attitudes we have towards people and the kind of opportunities we want for our children.

We share a faith in the enterprise and judgment of free men and women. Both our countries were built by immigrants from across the seas, pursuing dreams of liberty and of independence. The dream of freedom can have the same powerful good in the world today as it had at the foundation of this great Republic. And the world certainly needs strong and confident voices speaking for freedom.

You have come, Mr. President, to your great office at the end of what has been, in many ways, a decade of adversity. You embody through your eloquence and courage the determination to overcome that adversity. In your Inaugural Address you urged America to begin an era of renewal. The energy and ingenuity of the American people, their capacity to rise to a challenge give me confidence that they will respond, are responding, to your call. Indeed the clear evidence that they're doing so already must be encouraging to all of us.

The future of the course of freedom around the world depends so greatly on the leadership of the United States. There are so many things that will not be done unless the United States is prepared to do them. There is so much that only the world's greatest democracy can do. But we're well aware that powerful as you are, other countries also have a role and a duty. All the democracies need that confidence in themselves, that sense of larger purpose, that willingness to play a part which can create the will to work together and to prevail.

There are obvious limits, Mr. President, to what a nation of 14 million people can do. But, Mr. President, Australians are a people given to forming our own views, and it's this spirit of independence that makes us determined to be active in improving the condition of mankind and to contribute effectively to the cause of peace and of freedom.

The relationships between Americans and Australians have always been warm and spontaneous, and the alliance between our countries reflects that friendship. But it does, I suggest, more than that. It is built on the bedrock of mutual interests. As countries whose people fought and died in two World Wars, we share an abiding commitment to world peace. As countries bordering the same ocean, we share a central concern for stability and prosperity in the Asia-Pacific region. And as two of the world's democracies, we share a concern for liberty and the open society.

Mr. President, it used to be said of one great democratic statesman, that he was at his most effective and formidable on the rebound. I trust that far before the end of your Presidency as Western economies recover, as Western defenses strengthen, as Western will is remobilized, we will have demonstrated that the same is true of democracy itself.

We in Australia, along with the rest of the civilized world, admired greatly the courage and composure that you showed, Mr. President, throughout the ordeal that followed the attempt on your life some weeks ago. And you have shown by personal demonstration that given old-fashioned strength of character, it is possible to dominate events, rather than to surrender to those events. In doing so, you transformed an ugly and potentially tragic event into one from which decent men and women could draw confidence and strength.

I thank you again, very much, Mr. President, for your welcome to Tammy and to myself and to the Australian party today. I'm looking forward very much to getting to know you and Mrs. Reagan and to having our discussions.

Note: The President spoke at 10:11 a.m. on the South Lawn of the White House, where the Prime Minister was given a formal welcome with full military honors.

Following the ceremony, the President and the Prime Minister met in the Oval Office. Also present at that meeting were Secretary of State Alexander M. Haig, Jr., Australian Minister for Foreign Affairs Anthony A. Street, Assistant to the President for National Security Affairs Richard V. Allen, and Sir Geoffrey Yeend, Secretary, Department of the Prime Minister and Cabinet. The President and the Prime Minister and their delegations then met in the Cabinet Room.

Remarks of the President and Prime Minister J. Malcolm Fraser of Australia Following Their Meetings
June 30, 1981

The President. Ladies and gentlemen, our talks this morning have been wide-ranging. We've touched on the defense strategies in Southeast Asia, the Indian Ocean; peace-keeping efforts in the Middle East; need for richly endowed countries, such as ours, to be sensitive and helpful toward other nations not as blessed with natural resources, space, and security; nuclear nonproliferation; and some of the legal issues resulting from extraterritorial application of our own United States laws. But all of our discussions left me with two enduring feelings: that Australia is a friend for the long pull, where people see things basically as we do, but who will always have the courage and the friendship to tell us when they think we're wrong.

Prime Minister Malcolm Fraser and I lead countries whose best days lie in the future. Our friendship and cooperation will hasten the day when more of the people of the world can share what we're so fortunate to enjoy—freedom, strength, and confidence in the future.

It's been a pleasure meeting with the Prime Minister, and I certainly thank him for coming to visit our country. Mr. Prime Minister, thank you very much.

The Prime Minister. Mr. President and ladies and gentlemen, the discussions that we've had this morning I regard as being particularly useful and constructive, quite clearly from the policies that have been implemented in the United States under the President's charge. You'd expect, I think, that Australia would be in a fair measure of agreement on a number of those policies, the economic policies and the strengthening of the dollar and the strengthening of the economy of this country. We'd like to say all strength to your arm, Mr. President, because an economically strong United States is important to the entire free world.

And the policies in relation to East-West, and again, a strong United States is impor-

tant not only to the American people but to Australian people and to free people everywhere. And so again, Mr. President, all strength to your arm.

We've discussed, as you've indicated, a wide range of issues. And I was particularly delighted, Mr. President, with your willingness to see what can be done to remove the rough edges at the extraterritorial reach of United States law, and we have agreed that as—when it will be convenient for both our Attorneys General, for them to consult to see how this might best be achieved. And thank you very much for directing that that review take place.

We've discussed at length major North-South issues—economic relationships between wealthy countries, such as the United States and Australia and many others, and the developing countries or the least developed countries of this world. And I hope I'm not putting words into your mouth, Mr. President, in saying that I believe that we both recognize that it's important for the peace and stability of the world that we try and make progress in these major issues, that we try and see that more and more peoples of the world have opportunities to live a decent life in dignity and self-esteem. And you have told me of some of the things that you have in mind to help achieve that particular objective.

We're meeting again this evening, Mr. President, and I'll be looking forward to discussions with your Secretary of State and Secretary of Defense and other members of your administration.

Again, may I say how much my wife and I and the entire Australian party are delighted to be here. And may I say how delighted we are to see what is happening in the United States right at this time.

Note: The President spoke at 12:13 p.m. to reporters assembled on the South Grounds of the White House.

Toasts of the President and Prime Minister J. Malcolm Fraser of Australia at the State Dinner
June 30, 1981

The President. Mr. Prime Minister and Mrs. Fraser, our Australian friends, and our friends from America:

Today has been a great pleasure. As Prime Minister Fraser and I discussed bilateral issues and world questions, it was clear that the bonds between us and the bonds between our two countries are strong. We're both committed to growth economies based on free enterprise. As the Prime Minister said, "A philosophy can't be mere words. It must guide policy and be expressed in action." And this he has done—bringing down inflation, spurring growth by cutting government spending, limiting bureaucracy, abolishing unnecessary regulations, and cutting taxes. You know, we ought to try something like that here. [*Laughter*]

But in his words, Australia has "passed the ball to private enterprise which has now picked it up and is running hard." Well, we in America are on our way to doing the same thing. And internationally, our ideas are also similar. We both recognize the responsibility of freedom and are prepared to shoulder it squarely. In culture and business, our societies cooperate to share opportunities, understanding, and friendships. We've hit on only one minor snag, and that happens to be sporting competition. Now, the America's Cup I understand; that's friendly—we always win. [*Laughter*] But the U.S. Open is something else again. [*Laughter*] And David Graham says he isn't through with us yet. [*Laughter*]

But Australia, like America, is a country where anything can happen and where anything can be achieved because people are free. "Australian history," Mark Twain wrote, "is full of surprises and adventures and incongruities and contradictions and incredibilities, but they're all true. They all happened." [*Laughter*] Well it's the same way here, but that's our secret. We do not stagnate in a planned and withering government-dominated existence. We're free to be all that we can imagine.

A few moments ago at the table, I was asking Mrs. Fraser—just checking out my memory to make sure it was correct, and that is a very wonderful day that is observed annually in Australia in commemoration of the Battle of the Coral Sea, the turning point in World War II, where once again, as we've been so often, we were allied. And I have on my desk the tribute that was rendered at one of those particular days of commemoration by an Australian and his recognition of the blood bond between Americans and Australians who died together to turn that war around and to make Australia safe. I didn't dare read it here because I don't think I could have gotten through it tonight.

But the dynamics of the Australian way of life make her an even more powerful ally, and the vitality of her people make her an even stronger friend. So I would like to propose a toast to the Prime Minister of Australia and Mrs. Fraser, to the continued friendship and cooperation between our two countries, and to Her Majesty the Queen.

The Queen.

The Prime Minister. Mr. President, Mrs. Reagan, ladies and gentlemen:

Thank you very much, Mr. President, for your kind and gracious remarks. But may I first, with your permission, let your guests here this evening into a small secret between us, which is a source of special pleasure to me? Ladies and gentlemen, the President is exploiting one of my weaknesses, and I freely confess it. He's given me a magnificent fishing rod. [*Laughter*] I'm not sure whether there's some message in this. I don't know whether he should be encouraging me to wade in deep waters. But I'm sure that if I do, he'd want me to make a big catch. And when I catch a fish with this particular rod, I'll always be wondering who it is on the end of it. [*Laughter*] That's got a particular relevance for certain people in Australia. Mr. President, it's a splendid gift, and I thank you very much indeed for it.

I speak as one dedicated to the principles of small government, low inflation, and short afterdinner speeches. [*Laughter*] And fortunately, what I have to say can be said simply and briefly. It's been a great pleasure to meet you, Mr. President, and to exchange views with you today. We weren't able to raise many arguments. I wasn't altogether surprised at that, because I had watched from afar and read what you'd had to say and had seen what you'd been doing, and I applaud it.

You and I, your government and mine, your country and mine share basic values and principles. We have confidence in the enterprise and judgment of free men and women living in open societies and conducting their own affairs without too much government interference. We maintain that the role of governments we lead and of all other governments should be a limited one and wish that that were more widely recognized in more countries, I think, around the world.

We know that the market economy has delivered the goods in the past and believe that it can continue to deliver them while allowing people the greatest freedom of choice. We believe that liberty is worth defending, and we're not inhibited in saying so. We believe that nothing is gained and a good deal is lost by pretending that tyranny is not tyranny, even if we have to deal with those who perpetrate it. And we know that in an imperfect world, those who wish to remain free must also remain strong and united. This, I suggest, is not a bad basis of agreement to be getting on with.

I happen to believe that the future of free societies is going to depend crucially on the quality of leadership they produce in the immediate future. That leadership must both recognize danger and stimulate confidence, for in recent years, our societies have simultaneously suffered from comforting illusions about their enemies and from doubt and uncertainty about themselves.

The feeling of these illusions and doubts has become, I suspect in both our countries in past years, a major intellectual growth industry. The trend must be reversed, and

reversing will require courage, imagination, and staying power.

Leadership is more than a matter of position papers, options, and management. It is a matter of poise, of inner conviction, of the self-assurance that comes from being at ease with one's self—of what Ernest Hemingway summed up as "grace under pressure." It is also being able to embody and express the deepest aspirations of ordinary men and women, because that is what our kind of governments is all about, and that is what we stand for and that is our purpose.

It is that sort of leadership that free people throughout the world are looking for, and it is that sort of leadership that you, Mr. President, just by being yourself, have begun to provide. And this is clear from the spirit beginning to show in this United States.

Mr. President, we in Australia have arrived at our own independent conclusions as to what is needed if peace, freedom, and prosperity are to be maintained in the world. We've done so living far from the centers of Western intellectual and cultural fashions which, given the nature of those fashions in recent years, has perhaps given us an unfair advantage. [*Laughter*]

We've been prepared to advance our views when they were somewhat less popular than they are now. But the fact that they have become more accepted will not cause us to put them less vigorously or to change course. I have nothing against being in a majority occasionally. [*Laughter*]

Mr. President, until today I've observed your Presidency from a considerable distance. And they say that distance, or should I say a long shot, lends color to the view. But in this instance, I'm feeling that things look much better even closeup.

For your own sake and for the sake of the free world, I wish you well, Mr. President, over the next 3½ years. And I ask everyone here to join me in drinking to your health and to the health of this great country and of all the American people.

Mr. President.

Note: The President spoke at 9:33 p.m. in the State Dining Room at the White House.

Proclamation 4850—Captive Nations Week, 1981
June 30, 1981

By the President of the United States of America

A Proclamation

Twenty-two years ago, by a joint resolution approved July 17, 1959 (73 Stat. 212), the Congress authorized and requested the President to proclaim the third week in July as Captive Nations Week.

Last January 20 saw again a change in Administration under our Constitution, the oldest written document of its type in continuous force in the world. The peaceful and orderly transfer of power in response to the sovereign will of our people is sometimes taken for granted by Americans. Yet events in some other areas of the world should remind us all of the vital, revolutionary ideal of our Founding Fathers: that governments derive their legitimacy from the consent of the peoples they govern.

During Captive Nations Week, Americans should realize our devotion to the ideal of government by consent, a devotion that is shared by millions who live in nations dominated today by a foreign military power and an alien Marxist-Leninist ideology.

This week, Americans should recall the series of historical tragedies—beginning with the broken promises of the Yalta Conference—that led to the denial of the most elementary forms of personal freedom and human dignity to millions in Eastern Europe and Asia.

In recent years, we have seen successful attempts to extend this oppression to Africa, Latin America and Asia—most recently in the brutal suppression of national sovereignty in Afghanistan and attempts to intimidate Poland.

During Captive Nations Week, we Americans must reaffirm our own tradition of self-rule and extend to the peoples of the Captive Nations a message of hope—hope founded in our belief that free men and women will ultimately prevail over those who deny individual rights and preach supremacy of the state; hope in our conviction that the human spirit will ultimately triumph over the cult of the state.

While we can be justly proud of a government that is responsive to our people, we cannot be complacent. Captive Nations Week provides us with an opportunity to reaffirm publicly our commitment to the ideals of freedom and by so doing maintain a beacon of hope for oppressed peoples everywhere.

Now, Therefore, I, Ronald Reagan, President of the United States of America, do hereby designate the week beginning on July 19, 1981, as Captive Nations Week.

I invite the people of the United States to observe this week with appropriate ceremonies and activities and to reaffirm their dedication to the ideals which unite us and inspire others.

In Witness Whereof, I have hereunto set my hand this 30th day of June, in the year of our Lord nineteen hundred and eighty-one, and of the Independence of the United States of America the two hundred and fifth.

RONALD REAGAN

[*Filed with the Office of the Federal Register, 2:30 p.m., July 1, 1981*]

Note: The text of the proclamation was released by the Office of the Press Secretary on July 1.

Message to the Senate Transmitting the United States-Canada Treaty on Pacific Albacore Tuna Vessels
July 1, 1981

To the Senate of the United States:

I transmit herewith, for the advice and consent of the Senate, the Treaty between the Government of the United States and the Government of Canada on Pacific Albacore Tuna Vessels and Port Privileges. Also transmitted for the information of the Senate is the report of the Department of State with respect to the Treaty.

This Treaty is necessary to resolve difficulties which have arisen between the United States and Canada concerning albacore tuna fishing on the Pacific Coast. In the past Canada has seized vessels of the United States fishing albacore tuna off the Canadian coast, and the United States has retaliated by prohibiting the import of tuna from Canada.

The Treaty solves these problems by securing free and unlimited access for vessels of both countries off the Pacific coasts of the United States and Canada. It provides reciprocal port access and rights to land tuna in specified ports. The Treaty will also assure that circumstances will not arise which would lead to Canadian seizures of American vessels in the albacore tuna fishery or require another United States embargo of Canadian tuna. This approach was suggested by and has the support of the United States albacore fishing industry.

Not only will this Treaty benefit the fishing industries of both countries, but it represents important progress in the resolution of the fisheries issues which have been troubling the United States and Canada.

I recommend that the Senate give early consideration to the Treaty and give its advice and consent to ratification.

RONALD REAGAN

The White House,
July 1, 1981.

Nomination of William Lacy Swing To Be United States Ambassador to Liberia
July 1, 1981

The President today announced his intention to nominate William Lacy Swing, of North Carolina, to be Ambassador to the Republic of Liberia, vice Robert P. Smith, resigned.

In 1961 Mr. Swing was a schoolteacher in Germany, and in 1961–63 he was associate director, Council on Religion in Independent Schools (New York). He entered the Foreign Service in 1963, attending consular and African area studies at the Foreign Service Institute. He was Vice Consul in Port Elizabeth in 1964–66. In 1966–67 he was international economist in the Bureau of Economic and Business Affairs in the Department, and in 1968–72 he was head of visa section then chief of consular section in Hamburg. In the Department he was desk officer for the Federal Republic of Germany in 1972–74. He was Deputy Chief of Mission in Banqui in 1974–76. He attended the Harvard University Center for International Affairs in 1976–77. In the Department he was Alternate Director of the Office of Central African Affairs in 1977–79. Since 1979 he has been Ambassador to the People's Republic of the Congo.

Mr. Swing graduated from Catawba College and Yale University. In 1961 he attended postgraduate studies at Tuebingen University in Germany. Mr. Swing has one child and resides in Lexington, N.C. He was born September 11, 1934, in Lexington, N.C.

Nomination of John R. Countryman To Be United States Ambassador to Oman
July 1, 1981

The President today announced his intention to nominate John R. Countryman, of Washington, D.C., to be Ambassador to the Sultanate of Oman, vice Marshall W. Wiley, resigned.

Mr. Countryman was a reporter and feature writer for the News-Times of Danbury, Conn., in 1961–62 prior to entering the Foreign Service. In 1963–65 he was a Foreign Service officer-general in Istanbul and served as staff assistant in the Department in 1965–66. He studied Arabic language in Beirut in 1966–68 and was economic and commercial officer in Dhahran (1968–71), in Tripoli (1971–73), and Deputy Chief of Mission in Libreville (1973–75). In 1975–76 he attended the Army War College. In the Department he was Deputy Director of the Office of Regional Affairs in the Bureau of Near Eastern and South Asian Affairs (1976–78), and since 1979 he has been Director of Arabian Peninsula Affairs.

Mr. Countryman graduated from Fordham University (B.S., 1954) and the University of Miami (M.A., 1961). He was a Fulbright Scholar at the University of Berlin (Germany) in 1954–55. He served in the U.S. Air Force as a pilot in 1956–58. Mr. Countryman is married and has one child. He was born January 25, 1933, in Brooklyn, N.Y.

Nomination of John A. Todhunter To Be an Assistant Administrator of the Environmental Protection Agency
July 1, 1981

The President today announced his intention to nominate John A. Todhunter to be Assistant Administrator for Toxic Substances of the Environmental Protection Agency, vice Steven D. Jellinek, resigned.

Since 1978 Dr. Todhunter has been chairman, Biochemistry Program, and assistant professor of biology, the Catholic University of America, Washington, D.C. He was a fellow in the Department of Biochemistry, Roche Institute of Molecular Biology, Hoffman LaRoche, Inc., Nutley, N.J., in 1976–78. Dr. Todhunter was teaching assistant, research assistant, and regent's fellow at the University of California (Santa Barbara) in 1974–76. Previously he was an instructor at California State University (Los Angeles).

Dr. Todhunter graduated from the University of California (B.S., 1971); California State University (M.S., 1973); and the University of California (Ph. D., 1976).

Dr. Todhunter is married, has two children, and resides in Maryland. He was born October 9, 1949, in Cali, Colombia, South America.

Nomination of Charles M. Girard To Be an Associate Director of the Federal Emergency Management Agency
July 1, 1981

The President today announced his intention to nominate Charles M. Girard to be an Associate Director of the Federal Emergency Management Agency (Resources Management and Administration), vice Richard J. Green.

Since 1980 Dr. Girard has been director of human resources, Public Technology, Inc., of Washington, D.C. In 1971–80 he was president, International Training, Research & Evaluation Council, in Fairfax, Va. Dr. Girard was assistant to the director of the Southeast Michigan Council of Governments, Detroit, Mich., in 1969–71. He was an instructor and training coordinator at Wayne State University, Detroit, Mich., in 1967–69. Previously Dr. Girard was assistant to the city manager, city of Port Huron, Mich., in 1966–67 and a part-time employment and management trainee with the Ford Motor Co. in 1961–65.

Dr. Girard was a member of the Director-Nominee's Reorganization Task Force, Federal Emergency Management Agency. He was also a member of the first national advisory board, National Crime Prevention Institute, University of Louisville, Louisville, Ky.

Dr. Girard graduated from Park College, Parkville, Mo. (B.A.); University of Pennsylvania (M.A.); and Wayne State University, Detroit, Mich. (Ph. D.).

Dr. Girard is married, has one child, and resides in Fairfax, Va. He was born February 3, 1943, in Detroit, Mich.

Nomination of Vernon R. Wiggins To Be Federal Cochairman of the Alaska Land Use Council
July 1, 1981

The President today announced his intention to nominate Vernon R. Wiggins to be Federal Cochairman of the Alaska Land Use Council.

Since 1978 Mr. Wiggins has been executive director and secretary to the board of directors, Citizens for the Management of Alaska Lands, Inc., Anchorage, Alaska. Previously, he was planning services manager with Tryck, Nyman & Hayes (Engineers, Planners & Surveyors) in 1973–77; associate planner, senior planner, assistant planning director, and director of planning, municipality of Anchorage, in 1967–72; assistant planner and director of planning, charter township of Waterford (Mich.) in 1963–67; and planning technician, Northern Kentucky Area Planning Commission, in 1962–63.

Mr. Wiggins graduated from the University of Cincinnati (B.A., 1962). He is married, has two children, and resides in Anchorage, Alaska. He was born June 15, 1939, in Norwood, Ohio.

Nomination of Richard L. Wagner, Jr., To Be Chairman of the Military Liaison Committee to the Department of Energy
July 2, 1981

The President today announced his intention to nominate Richard L. Wagner, Jr., to be Chairman of the Military Liaison Committee to the Department of Energy, vice James P. Wade, Jr.

Since 1963 Mr. Wagner has been associated with the University of California's E. O. Lawrence Livermore National Laboratory (LLNL) in Livermore, Calif. LLNL and its companion laboratory at Los Alamos, N. Mex., carry out the U.S. research and development effort on nuclear weapons. Mr. Wagner currently serves as associate director for nuclear testing. He has served on many committees and study groups outside the laboratory, including the advanced munitions study sponsored by the Department of Defense's Defense Nuclear Agency and Advanced Research Projects Agency; science advisory group to Joint Strategic Target Planning Staff; Energy Research and Development Administration/Department of Defense Transfer Study; member, U.S. Army Science Advisory Panel; and the Defense Science Board.

Mr. Wagner graduated from Williams College (B.A., 1958) and the University of Utah (Ph. D., 1963). He is married, has three children, and resides in Livermore, Calif. He was born July 7, 1936, in Oklahoma City, Okla.

Nomination of Pedro A. Sanjuan To Be an Assistant Secretary of the Interior
July 2, 1981

The President today announced his intention to nominate Pedro A. Sanjuan to be an Assistant Secretary of the Interior (Territorial and International Affairs), vice John Henry Kyl, resigned.

Mr. Sanjuan is currently resident fellow and director of the Hemispheric Center at the American Enterprise Institute for Public Policy Research. He recently served as policy coordinator for the State Department transition team. In 1977–78 he served on the White House staff, detailed from the Arms Control and Disarmament Agency (ACDA). He was Public Affairs Adviser, ACDA, in 1975–77. In 1973–75 Mr. Sanjuan was Assistant for Strategic and Economic Analysis and Director of Energy Task Force, Office of the Secretary of Defense. In 1971–73 he was Deputy Director, Policy Plans for Negotiations and Arms Control,

Office of the Secretary of Defense. Mr. Sanjuan was special assistant to the Principal Deputy Assistant Secretary of Defense in 1971. He was executive director, CLOSE-UP, 1970–71; president of Interlandia Corp. in 1969–71; member of the Department of State Inter-American Policy Coordinating Committee in 1963–66; Director, Office of Chancery Affairs, Department of State, in 1963–64; Director, Office for Special Representational Services, Department of State, in 1962–63; and Deputy of Chief of Protocol, in 1962.

Mr. Sanjuan graduated from Wofford College (B.A.) and Harvard University (M.A.). He has attended Rutgers University and Columbia University. He served in the U.S. Naval Reserve in 1956–59.

Mr. Sanjuan resides in Washington, D.C. He was born August 10, 1930.

Nomination of Robert Carlton Horton To Be Director of the Bureau of Mines
July 2, 1981

The President today announced his intention to nominate Robert Carlton Horton to be Director of the Bureau of Mines, Department of the Interior, vice Lindsay D. Norman, Jr.

Since 1976 Mr. Horton has been with Bendix Field Engineering Corp., serving as director of the geology division since 1977

and regional geologist, Reno, Nev., in 1976–77. He was a private consultant and examined mines in the Western United States, Canada, and Mexico in 1972–76. He was vice president, Transcon Industries, Inc., in 1967–71. Mr. Horton was associate director, Nevada Bureau of Mines and Nevada

Mining Analytical Laboratory, University of Nevada, in 1965–66. He was assistant and associate mining engineer, Nevada Bureau of Mines, University of Nevada, in 1955–65. Previously he served as a geological assistant with the U.S. Geological Survey.

Mr. Horton has authored many articles on mining. He was Engineer of the Year (1967), Reno Chapter, National Society of Professional Engineers. He served on the Governor's Advisory Mining Board in 1967–73.

Mr. Horton attended the University of Gonzaga, Spokane, Wash., in 1944–46, and graduated from Mackay School of Mines, University of Nevada (B.S., 1949). He served in the U.S. Navy in 1944–46 and 1953–55.

Mr. Horton is married, has three children, and resides in Grand Junction, Colo. He was born July 25, 1926, in Tonopah, Nev.

Nomination of Kathleen M. Bennett To Be an Assistant Administrator of the Environmental Protection Agency
July 2, 1981

The President today announced his intention to nominate Kathleen M. Bennett to be Assistant Administrator of the Environmental Protection Agency for Air, Noise and Radiation, vice David G. Hawkins, resigned.

Since 1977 Mrs. Bennett has served as Federal affairs representative, Crown Zellerbach Corp. She was a member of the American Paper Institute Air Quality Committee, and chairman, Air Quality Subcommittee on Prevention of Significant Deterioration. Since 1978 she served as faculty member of Executive Enterprises, Inc., environmental law series, lecturing on the Clean Air Act and on congressional environmental policymaking. In 1974–77 Mrs. Bennett was director of legislative affairs, American Paper Institute. She was Washington representative, Public Affairs Analysts, Inc., in 1972–74, and Administrative Assistant, Office of Congressional Affairs, General Services Administration, in 1971–72. Previously she was executive secretary, Office of the Governor, Chicago, Ill., in 1970–71, and executive secretary to the director, Citizens to Elect Senator Ralph Tyler Smith in 1970.

Mrs. Bennett graduated from Manhattanville College, Purchase, N.Y. (B.A., 1970). She is married, has three children, and resides in Alexandria, Va. She was born May 11, 1948, in New York, N.Y.

Nomination of Major General Thomas K. Turnage To Be Director of Selective Service
July 2, 1981

The President today announced his intention to nominate Maj. Gen. Thomas K. Turnage to be Director of Selective Service.

General Turnage was commissioned as an infantry officer in 1942 and later entered active duty and was assigned to the 386th Infantry Regiment of the 97th Division. He served in Germany and Czechoslovakia. Later he was redeployed with the Division to Japan where he served as a commander during occupation duties until 1946. Returning to college after World War II, he joined the California Army National Guard in 1949 and was recalled to active duty with the 223d Infantry Regiment, 40th Infantry Division, in 1950. During subsequent training in Japan and combat in Korea, he served as an infantry battalion operations officer and executive officer. General Turnage remained active with the California

National Guard after returning from Korea in 1952.

In 1967 he was transferred to the State of California military department headquarters in Sacramento. His 7-year tenure there was served principally as the deputy adjutant general, Army, and later as the deputy commanding general of the California Army National Guard.

General Turnage returned to active duty in November 1979 to assume his current duties as Special Assistant for Training and Readiness to the Deputy Assistant Secretary of Defense (Reserve Affairs).

General Turnage graduated from the University of California at Los Angeles (B.S.)

and George Washington University (M.S.) He also graduated from the Infantry School Basic, Armor School Advanced, Command and General Staff College, and the Army War College. His decorations and awards include the Legion of Merit with Oak Leaf Cluster, Bronze Star Medal, Meritorious Service Medal, Army Commendation Medal, Korean Presidential Unit Citation, and the California Medal of Merit with three Oak Leaf Clusters.

General Turnage is married, has two children, and resides in Alexandria, Va. He was born June 27, 1923, in Conroe, Tex.

Nomination of Monteagle Stearns To Be United States Ambassador to Greece
July 2, 1981

The President today announced his intention to nominate Monteagle Stearns to be Ambassador to Greece, vice Robert J. McCloskey, resigned.

Since 1979 Mr. Stearns has been vice president of the National Defense University in Washington, D.C. In 1976–79 he was Ambassador to the Republic of the Ivory Coast. In 1974–76 he was Deputy Chief of Mission in Athens. Mr. Stearns was Deputy Assistant Secretary of State for East Asian and Pacific Affairs in 1973–74. In 1972–73 he attended the Bowie seminar at the Harvard University Center for International Af-

fairs. In 1969–72 he was Deputy Chief of Mission in Vientiane and in 1967–69 served as political officer in London. In 1965–67 Mr. Stearns was special assistant to the Ambassador at Large in the Department of State. In 1963–65 he served as political officer in Leopoldville and in 1957–63 as political officer in Athens.

Mr. Stearns graduated from Columbia University (B.A., 1948). He is fluent in French and Greek.

Mr. Stearns is married, has six children, and resides in Pasadena, Calif. He was born December 5, 1924, in Cambridge, Mass.

Executive Order 12312—The Meritorious Service Medal
July 2, 1981

By the authority vested in me as President of the United States of America and as Commander-in-Chief of the Armed Forces, and to permit the award of the Meritorious Service Medal to members of the armed forces of friendly foreign nations, it is hereby ordered that Section 1 of Executive Order Number 11448 of January 16, 1969,

is amended to read as follows:

"Section 1. There is hereby established a Meritorious Service Medal, with accompanying ribbons and appurtenances, for award by the Secretary of a Military Department or the Secretary of Transportation with regard to the Coast Guard when not operating as a service in the Navy, or by such military commanders or other appropriate officers as the Secretary concerned may designate, to any member of the armed forces of the United States, or to any member of the armed forces of a friendly foreign nation, who has distinguished himself by outstanding meritorious achieve-ment or service.".

RONALD REAGAN

The White House,
July 2, 1981.

[*Filed with the Office of the Federal Register, 2:29 p.m., July 6, 1981*]

Memorandum on the Combined Federal Campaign
July 2, 1981

Memorandum for the Heads of Executive Departments and Agencies

The Honorable Malcolm Baldrige, Secretary of Commerce, has agreed to serve this year as Chairman of the Combined Federal Campaign for the National Capital Area.

Combined in this campaign are the annual fundraising efforts of the United Way, the National Health Agencies, local non-federated voluntary agencies and the American Red Cross. Through the CFC, Federal Employees have the opportunity to help our neighbors and fellow citizens without going through government channels. We have the chance to prove what people can do on their own.

In America, we have traditionally accepted the responsibility of individual giving for good causes. The values that cause us to care for our neighbors, our countrymen and people in faraway lands are the values that make us great.

I request that you serve personally as Chairman of the Combined Campaign in your organization and appoint a top assistant as your Vice Chairman. Please advise Secretary Baldrige of the person you designate as your Vice Chairman.

RONALD REAGAN

Message on the Observance of Independence Day
July 3, 1981

Today, all over America, families and friends are reuniting to renew ties, enjoy each other's company, and celebrate our Nation's birthday. It is a day when liberty and laughter go hand in hand—when we can acknowledge that, oh yes, we have our faults, and lots of problems, too, but we're happy and proud because we're free, and we know the best of America is yet to be.

If you close your eyes and try to picture our country, chances are the first thing you'll see is your own hometown. I always see mine, Dixon and Tampico in Illinois. Today it is the hometowns of America, both big and small, that remind us what a diverse yet united country we are. Each in its own special way will carry out a wish expressed by one of the Founding Fathers 205 years ago.

Back in 1776, John Adams wrote his wife Abigail that the anniversary of our independence should be observed with great fanfare: ". . . with pomp and parades . . . shows and games . . . and sports and guns and bells . . . with bonfires and illuminations, from one end of this continent to the other, and from this time forevermore."

Well, Mr. Adams, rest assured that what you wanted is being done. Your traditions are now ours, and we guard them like national treasures. And you know why. When we unfurl our flags, strike up the bands, and light up the skies each July 4th, we celebrate the most exciting, ongoing adventure in human freedom the world has ever known.

It began in 1620 when a group of courageous families braved a mighty ocean to build a new future in a new world. They came not for material gain, but to secure liberty for their souls within a community bound by laws.

A century-and-a-half later, their descendants pledged their lives, their fortunes and their sacred honor to found this Nation. Some would forfeit their fortunes and their lives, but none sacrificed honor.

Thomas Jefferson wrote that on that day of America's birth, in the little hall in Philadelphia, debate raged for hours, but the issue remained in doubt. These were honorable men; still, to sign a Declaration of Independence seemed such an irretrievable act that the walls resounded with cries of "treason" and "the headsman's axe."

Then, it is said, one unknown man rose to speak. He was neither young, nor strong in voice; yet, he spoke with such conviction that he mesmerized the hall. He cited the grievances that had brought them to this moment. Then, his voice failing, he said: "They may turn every tree into a gallows, every hole into a grave, and yet the words of that parchment can never die. To the mechanic in the workshop, they will speak hope, to the slave in the mines, freedom. Sign that parchment. Sign if the next moment the noose is around your neck, for that parchment will be the textbook of freedom, the bible of the rights of man forever." And sign they did.

What makes our revolution unique and so exciting, then, is that it changed the very concept of government. Here was a new nation telling the world that it was conceived in liberty; that all men are created equal with God-given rights, and that power ultimately resides in "We the people."

We sometimes forget this great truth, and we never should, because putting people first has always been America's secret weapon. It's the way we've kept the spirit of our revolution alive—a spirit that drives us to dream and dare, and take great risks for a greater good. It's the spirit of Fulton and Ford, the Wright brothers and Lindbergh, and of all our astronauts. It's the spirit of Joe Louis, Babe Ruth, and a million others who may have been born poor, but who would not be denied their day in the Sun.

Well, I'm convinced that we're getting that spirit back. The Nation is pulling together. We're looking to the future with new hope and confidence—and we know we can make America great again by putting the destiny of this Nation back in the hands of the people. And why shouldn't we? Because, after all, we are Americans.

As Dwight Eisenhower once said: "There is nothing wrong with America that the faith, love of freedom, intelligence and energy of her citizens cannot cure."

He was right. If we just stick together, and remain true to our ideals, we can be sure that America's greatest days lie ahead.

Happy Fourth of July!

Message to the Congress Transmitting the United States-Egypt Agreement on Nuclear Energy
July 6, 1981

To the Congress of the United States:

I am pleased to transmit to the Congress, in accordance with Section 123d of the Atomic Energy Act of 1954, as amended (42 U.S.C. 2153(d)), the text of the proposed Agreement for Cooperation Between the Government of the United States of America and the Government of the Arab Republic of Egypt Concerning Peaceful Uses of Nuclear Energy and accompanying annex and agreed minute; my written approval, authorization and determination concerning the agreement; and the memorandum of the Director of the United States Arms Control and Disarmament Agency with the Nuclear Proliferation Assessment Statement concerning the agreement. The joint memorandum submitted to me by the Secretaries of State and Energy, which includes a summary of the provisions of the agreement, and the views and recommendations of the Director of the Arms Control and Disarmament Agency and the Members of the Nuclear Regulatory Commission, is also enclosed.

The Atomic Energy Act sets forth certain requirements for new agreements for peaceful nuclear cooperation with other countries. In my judgment, the proposed agreement for cooperation between the United States and Egypt, together with its accompanying agreed minute, meets all statutory requirements.

The proposed bilateral agreement reflects the desire of the Governments of the United States and Egypt to establish a framework for peaceful nuclear cooperation between our two countries in a manner

which recognizes our shared non-proliferation objectives, the economic and energy development needs of Egypt, and the friendly and harmonious relations between the United States and Egypt.

In February, Egypt ratified the Treaty on the Non-Proliferation of Nuclear Weapons. This is an important step toward controlling the dangers of the spread of nuclear weapons, and is a reaffirmation of Egypt's long-standing commitment to the objectives of this Treaty and its commitment to peace and stability in the Middle East and Africa. This proposed agreement fully recognizes this important step.

I believe that this agreement will further the non-proliferation and other foreign policy interests of the United States. I have considered the views and recommendations of the interested agencies in reviewing it and have determined that its performance will promote, and will not constitute an unreasonable risk to, the common defense and security. Accordingly, I have approved the agreement and authorized its execution, and urge that the Congress give it favorable consideration.

RONALD REAGAN

The White House,
July 6, 1981.

Appointment of James R. Nelson as United States Alternate Representative on the Council of the International Civil Aviation Organization
July 6, 1981

The President today announced the appointment of James R. Nelson, of Virginia, as the Alternate Representative of the United States on the Council of the International Civil Aviation Organization. He would succeed Clyde W. Pace, Jr., who has retired.

Mr. Nelson served in the United States Air Force in 1944–67, when he retired as lieutenant colonel. His assignments included: multiengine flying instructor, instrument flying instructor, aero engineer, pilot,

project officer, instrument check pilot, and staff officer.

He came to the Federal Aviation Administration in 1967 and has successively served as Chief of Category III Landing Section (1969–71), Chief of Terminal Navigation Branch (1972–73), International Program Manager (1975–78), Chief of Helicopter Program Staff (1978–80), and since 1980 as Assistant Chief of the Navigation and Landing Division. He was Project Manager and Civil Aviation Adviser in Ankara with the

International Civil Aviation Organization of Montreal in 1973–75.

Mr. Nelson graduated from the U.S. Military Academy (B.S., 1944) and the University of Michigan (B.S.E., 1953). He attended the Air War College in 1963–64. Mr. Nelson is a commercial pilot of airplane, rotorcraft, instrument, single and multiengine jet type ratings.

He is married, has three children, and resides in Arlington, Va. He was born January 20, 1924, in Lawton, Okla.

Remarks Announcing the Intention To Nominate Sandra Day O'Connor To Be an Associate Justice of the Supreme Court of the United States
July 7, 1981

The President. Ladies and gentlemen, I have a statement to make. And then following that statement, if there are any questions you might have, I shall refer you to the Attorney General.

As President of the United States, I have the honor and the privilege to pick thousands of appointees for positions in Federal Government. Each is important and deserves a great deal of care for each individual called upon to make his or her contribution, often at personal sacrifice, to shaping the policy of the Nation. Thus each has an obligation to you, in varying degrees, has an impact on your life.

In addition, as President, I have the privilege to make a certain number of nominations which have a more lasting influence on our lives, for they are the lifetime appointments of those men and women called upon to serve in the judiciary in our Federal district courts and courts of appeals. These individuals dispense justice and provide for us these most cherished guarantees of protections of our criminal and civil laws. But, without doubt, the most awesome appointment is a guarantee to us of so many things, because it is a President—as a President, I can make an appointment to the United States Supreme Court.

Those who sit in the Supreme Court interpret the laws of our land and truly do leave their footprints on the sands of time. Long after the policies of Presidents and Senators and Congressmen of any given era may have passed from public memory, they'll be remembered.

After very careful review and consideration, I have made the decision as to my nominee to fill the vacancy on the United States Supreme Court created by the resignation of Justice Stewart. Since I am aware of the great amount of speculation about this appointment, I want to share this very important decision with you as soon as possible.

Needless to say, most of the speculation has centered on the question of whether I would consider a woman to fill this first vacancy. As the press has accurately pointed out, during my campaign for the Presidency I made a commitment that one of my first appointments to the Supreme Court vacancy would be the most qualified woman that I could possibly find.

Now, this is not to say that I would appoint a woman merely to do so. That would not be fair to women nor to future generations of all Americans whose lives are so deeply affected by decisions of the Court. Rather, I pledged to appoint a woman who meets the very high standards that I demand of all court appointees. I have identified such a person.

So today, I'm pleased to announce that upon completion of all the necessary checks by the Federal Bureau of Investigation, I will send to the Senate the nomination of Judge Sandra Day O'Connor of Arizona Court of Appeals for confirmation as an Associate Justice of the United States Supreme Court.

She is truly a person for all seasons, possessing those unique qualities of temperament, fairness, intellectual capacity, and devotion to the public good which have characterized the 101 brethren who have preceded her. I commend her to you, and I urge the Senate's swift bipartisan confirmation so that as soon as possible she may take her seat on the Court and her place in history.

Reporter. Do you agree with her position on abortion, Mr. President?

The President. I said that I was going to turn over all questions to the Attorney General here and let him answer the questions.

Q. But the right-to-life people object, and we just wonder if——

The President. All those questions the Attorney General is prepared to answer.

Q. But, Mr. President, you have such a firm position on that. Can you give us your feelings about her position on that?

The President. I am completely satisfied.

Q. On her right-to-life position?

The President. Yes.

Q. And did you interview her personally?

The President. Yes.

Note: The President spoke at 10:46 a.m. to reporters assembled in the Briefing Room at the White House. His remarks were broadcast live on radio and television.

The Office of the Press Secretary also released a transcript of Attorney General William French Smith's question-and-answer session with the reporters.

Later in the day, Deputy Press Secretary Larry M. Speakes announced that the President and Judge O'Connor had met in the Oval Office on July 1. Also attending the meeting were the Attorney General and members of the White House staff.

Nomination of Sandra Day O'Connor To Be an Associate Justice of the Supreme Court of the United States
July 7, 1981

The President today announced his intention to nominate Judge Sandra Day O'Connor to be an Associate Justice of the Supreme Court of the United States, filling the vacancy created by the resignation of Justice Potter Stewart. Judge O'Connor presently serves on the Arizona Court of Appeals. The President will forward to the Senate his nomination of Judge O'Connor upon completion of the required background check by the Federal Bureau of Investigation.

Judge O'Connor, age 51, earned both her undergraduate and law degrees at Stanford University. She received her B.A. magna cum laude in 1950 and her LL.B. with high honors in 1952. She was a member of the board of editors of the Stanford Law

Review and a member of the Order of the Coif. Judge O'Connor was admitted to the Bar of the State of California in the year of her graduation and to the Bar of the State of Arizona in 1957.

Judge O'Connor practiced law in Phoenix, Ariz., for a number of years. She served as assistant attorney general of Arizona from 1965 to 1969 and served in the Arizona State Senate from 1969 to 1975.

In 1974 Judge O'Connor was elected to the superior court for Maricopa County, Ariz. She served on that court until she was appointed to the Arizona Court of Appeals in 1979.

Judge O'Connor is married to John Hay O'Connor III. They have three children.

Letter to the Chairmen of the Senate Foreign Relations Committee and the House Foreign Affairs Committee Reporting on the Situation in Zimbabwe
July 7, 1981

Dear Mr. Chairman:

In accordance with the provisions of Section 720 of the International Security and Development Cooperation Act of 1980, I am submitting the following report on the internal situation in Zimbabwe.

In the period that has elapsed since the last Report to Congress on Zimbabwe, the country has continued to gain political and economic momentum in an atmosphere that can be characterized as both dynamic and stable.

The overwhelming response from Western donor nations and international organizations at the March Donors' Conference, which resulted in $2 billion pledged over the next three to five years, will allow the government to move forward immediately with its economic development program and its plans for reconstruction and land resettlement. The success of the conference vindicated Prime Minister Mugabe's decision to turn to the West for economic and political support and allows the West to play a role in the emerging political/economic structure.

Recently there has been a significant increase in the volume and stridency of public exchanges between the governments of South Africa and Zimbabwe. The exchanges derive primarily from a concern of both countries that the other is giving support to anti-government groups. Despite this development, there remains a strong basis for cooperation, given the extensive interrelationship between the two countries in trade and communications.

The disarmament process in Zimbabwe is now well on its way to being completed. Approximately 18,000 former guerrillas in seven camps around the country have been completely disarmed. While it is likely that arms caches and illegally armed men are still present in the country, the disarmament that has occurred represents one of the most significant achievements since independence.

There has been some concern expressed by the business community lately on the foreign investment climate in Zimbabwe, with particular reference to the possibility that the government may decide to participate in the sale of Zimbabwe's minerals through a Minerals Marketing Board. Prime Minister Mugabe has publicly stated that his Government's policy is to provide an acceptable and effective marketing system for all minerals and metals produced in Zimbabwe with a view to increasing sales and profits. The Prime Minister made a general reference to the Marketing Board again in his May 1 speech but no determination has yet been made about the functions the Board will perform.

Sincerely,

RONALD REAGAN

Note: This is the text of identical letters addressed to Charles S. Percy, chairman of the Senate Foreign Relations Committee and Clement J. Zablocki, chairman of the House Foreign Affairs Committee.

Nomination of Ford Barney Ford To Be an Assistant Secretary of Labor
July 7, 1981

The President today announced his intention to nominate Ford Barney Ford to be Assistant Secretary of Labor for Mine Safety and Health, vice Robert B. Lagather, retired.

Since 1978 Mr. Ford has been vice president of the California Institute for Industrial and Governmental Relations in Sacramento, Calif. He was chairman and public member of the California Occupational Safety and Health Appeals Board in 1973–78; deputy secretary, California Resources Agency, in 1967–73; executive director and chief consultant, the Senate Fact Finding Committee on Natural Resources, in 1959–67; associate administrative analyst, Joint Legislative Committee, in 1955–59; and an inspector with the Coca-Cola Bottling Co. in 1948–55.

Mr. Ford graduated from the University of California (B.S., 1948) and attended the Virginia Military Institute. He served in the U.S. Army in 1943–46.

Mr. Ford is married, has two grown children, and resides in Citrus Heights, Calif. He was born November 19, 1922, in Norton, Va.

Nomination of Tom C. Korologos To Be a Member of the United States Advisory Commission on Public Diplomacy
July 7, 1981

The President today announced his intention to nominate Tom C. Korologos to be a member of the United States Advisory Commission on Public Diplomacy for a term expiring July 1, 1984, vice John Hope Franklin, term expired.

Since 1975 Mr. Korologos has been vice president and director of legislative affairs of Timmons and Co., Inc., a consulting firm representing corporate and association clients in the area of government relations. He was director of congressional relations in the office of the President-elect in 1980–81.

Mr. Korologos was Deputy Assistant to the President for Senate Relations for 4 years under Presidents Nixon and Ford. Previously he served as assistant to Senator Wallace Bennett (R-Utah) for 8 years.

Mr. Korologos graduated from the University of Utah (B.A., 1956) and Columbia University Graduate School of Journalism (M.A., 1958). He served in the U.S. Air Force in 1956–57.

Mr. Korologos is married, has three children, and resides in Great Falls, Va. He was born April 6, 1933, in Salt Lake City, Utah.

Nomination of Michael J. Connally To Be General Counsel of the Equal Employment Opportunity Commission
July 7, 1981

The President today announced his intention to nominate Michael J. Connally to be General Counsel of the Equal Employment Opportunity Commission for a term of 4 years, vice Leroy D. Clark, resigned.

Since 1977 Mr. Connally has served as labor counsel to the General Motors Corp., Detroit, Mich. In 1973–76 he was with the

599

firm of Berry, Moorman, King, Lott & Cook of Detroit, Mich. He specialized in labor law representing both large and small employers.

Mr. Connally has published various guides on equal employment. He graduated from Regis College, Denver, Colo. (B.A., 1970), University of Mississippi (J.D., 1973), and Wayne State University Law School (LL.M., 1976).

Mr. Connally resides in Grosse Point Park, Mich. He was born March 26, 1949, in Detroit, Mich.

Nomination of James E. Yonge To Be a Member of the Board of Directors of the Export-Import Bank of the United States
July 7, 1981

The President today announced his intention to nominate James E. Yonge to be a member of the Board of Directors of the Export-Import Bank of the United States, vice Thibaut de Saint Phalle.

Mr. Yonge has been a partner with the firm of Yonge & Halpern of Ft. Lauderdale, Fla., since 1979. Since 1978 he has been vice chairman, secretary, and director of Q-Masters, Inc., a Florida corporation which owns and operates restaurants, and director of North Ridge Bank in Ft. Lauderdale. Prior to 1978 Mr. Yonge was a partner with the firm of Scruby, Yonge, Cobb & Waite of Orange Park, Fla. He has been actively involved in property development and home construction in Florida. In 1959–61 he was, first, general counsel to the Florida Senate Committee on Finance and Taxation, then general counsel to the Florida House Committee on Finance and Taxation. Mr. Yonge was assistant attorney general, State of Florida, in 1957.

Mr. Yonge organized the Bank of Orange Park, a Florida banking corporation, and First Federal Savings and Loan Association of Clay County, Fla.

Mr. Yonge graduated from Stetson University, De Land, Fla. (B.S., 1954) and the University of Florida (LL.B., 1957). He resides in Ft. Lauderdale, Fla. He was born January 12, 1932, in Miami, Fla.

Remarks at a Fundraising Dinner for Governor James R. Thompson, Jr., in Chicago, Illinois
July 7, 1981

Mr. Chairman, reverend clergy, and Governor Jim Thompson—I thank you very much, Jim, for your hospitality and for those kind words—Senator Percy and the Members of Congress, the members of your legislature, the officials of our party, all who have been introduced here tonight:

I don't know whether I'm the latest after-lunch speaker or the earliest after-dinner speaker that's ever been at an affair like this, but I am grateful that you've made it possible for me to speak early, because we have made a 2,000-mile round trip for dinner.

It's been very thrilling to come back here. I have met people on the way in from Tampico, where I was born, and those people with the white hats over there are from Dixon, where I grew up. But your welcome is so warm that I'm sorry we have to return to the Capital this evening. Its just a case of from one windy city to another— only Washington doesn't have the excuse of a lake. [*Laughter*] That isn't all we have in common. Your mayor moved into public housing, she said, to draw attention to the conditions there. Well, Nancy and I have done the same thing and for the same reason. [*Laughter*]

You know, back a few years ago—and I'm not going to say how many—I used to broadcast Chicago Cubs games. Now, of course, there's a baseball strike. But every dark cloud has a silver lining. You can look at it this way: For almost a month now the Cubs haven't lost a single game. [*Laughter*]

But I'd like to preface my remarks by saying that this has been a very happy day for me and, I hope, for our country.

As I said during the campaign, I have long believed that the time has come for the highest court in our land to include not only distinguished men but distinguished women as well. And thus, when Justice Potter Stewart reported his retirement to us earlier this year, we began a search for a highly qualified woman who would serve this Nation well. And today I announced my intention to nominate just such an individual—Judge Sandra O'Connor of Arizona.

I had the pleasure of meeting with Mrs. O'Connor last week, and I can report to you that she not only has a long and brilliant record as a legislator and jurist, but she also impressed me as a thoughtful, capable woman whose judicial temperament is highly appropriate for the Court. After listening to her and examining her whole record in public life, I am fully satisfied that her appointment is consistent with the principles enunciated in our party platform this past year.

Judge O'Connor, in my view, will bring new lustre and new strength to the Supreme Court, and I feel certain that her term upon the bench will be one of the proudest legacies of my Presiden[cy].

But tonight we're here to honor a big man in Illinois. Now, there's no doubt that Jim Thompson's tall, but Jim built his fame and a different kind of size as a courageous prosecutor fighting corruption in places people said could never be rid of it. He restored the people's faith in those who hold public office, and he sought justice in government in the name of the governed. He brings to the office of Governor that same integrity and competence—the qualities that build coalitions, the qualities that

capture public support, the qualities of a great leader.

And I can tell you that he's been one of our strongest supporters in the fight to cut Federal spending. He knows that we have to balance the budget in Washington, because he's balanced the budget in Illinois for the last 4 years. Now, Jim Thompson knows that America has to compete in world markets, and he's worked hard to make Illinois the largest dollar-volume exporter of agricultural products in America. He knows people of different parties can work together, because that's how you do things in Illinois. I rely on his advice and counsel and am grateful for his friendship.

Now, there's someone who couldn't be here tonight that I would like to thank—the colleague of those fine Congressmen you've already met—Bob Michel. He's been the point man for our cause in the House of Representatives. Without his unfailing and able help, the victories we've won these past few weeks would never have been possible. Bob has our thanks and admiration.

And of course, there is another man missing who should be here—Jim Brady. But Jim's parents are here, Mr. and Mrs. Brady, I want you to know I spoke with Jim just before I left. He's getting better every day, and his humor is as outrageously funny as ever. His job is waiting for him, and we all hope and pray that he'll be back soon, because we miss him very much.

My fellow Republicans, one year ago in a Midwestern city only a few hundred miles from here, those of us in the party of Lincoln met in convention. At that time and place, we pledged an end to those economic policies that had sparked double-digit inflation, soaring unemployment, and declining economic growth.

We pledged to end the unnecessary intrusions of government into the everyday lives of American workers. We pledged to end disrespect for America abroad and to rebuild our national defense so as to make America respected again among the nations. And yes, we pledged to rescue America from 4 years of malaise caused not by the American people, but by those who failed to give America leadership. We pledged, in short, to reopen all those roads to greatness that led America to unrivaled freedom and unparalleled strength in the world.

Now, we acknowledged that we couldn't undo all the harmful effects of misguided policy and special-interest politics in a few months or even a few years, but that early in our Republican administration, no matter how hard the decisions, we would stand by our commitment to get government under control and to put America back on the road to prosperity. And we're keeping that pledge.

We have moved to cut Federal spending, to eliminate excessive regulations, and to reduce the steadily growing tax burden on working men and women. You might have heard some talk of that lately. We've moved to reinvigorate our private institutions and to renew the confidence of the American people in the greatness of their nation and in their values of family, work, and neighborhood—values responsible for that greatness.

This new national confidence isn't just reflected in opinion polls at home. Ten of our major steel producers and eleven other steel producers are spending $3.6 billion on modernization of plant and equipment. And then there is the new-found strength of the American dollar in the money markets. And certainly it's reflected in the new respect and deference shown American leadership by both friend and foe around the globe.

Now, some in the press have been overly concerned because I haven't made a "major foreign policy address." Their automatic assumption is that until I do, we don't have a foreign policy.

Well, to begin with, I just don't happen to believe it necessary to spell out in detail and in advance a formula which will guide our every move in international relations. Basically, good foreign policy is the use of good commonsense in dealing with friends and potential adversaries. Now, I assure you, we know where we're going, and we think it might be counter-productive to make a speech about it.

Over and over again in last year's campaign, it was emphasized that renewal of America's economic might and a return to a stable and sound prosperity was the first step to a credible foreign policy. During the

last few months, in a startling and heartwarming display of national unity, Republicans and discerning Democrats have worked together toward that end. We've laid the foundation for a long-range buildup of our Armed Forces, bringing us nearer the day when Americans can once again enjoy a margin of safety and peace will be made more secure.

I received a letter the other day from an enlisted man in our Navy. He wrote that he was speaking for his almost 200 shipmates. "I am beginning to see a rebirth throughout the Navy of pride and professionalism," he wrote. "It feels good to be an American again. We may not be the biggest navy in the world, but we're certainly the best."

We've begun to solidify, after years of tension and softness, sometimes often discord, our ties with Japan and our European allies. Through the Habib mission, we have helped avert war in the Middle East. And the mission continues; he's on his way back there. We've further developed our relationship with China, while we've stood by and will continue to stand by our commitments to Taiwan.

In Southwest Asia we have reinvigorated our strategically important relationship with Pakistan. In southern Africa we have initiated work on a realistic Namibian solution. And in the Caribbean we've launched an effort to attack the root causes, of instability, while we're making it clear the United States will not tolerate interference by Cuba with the lives and freedoms of other nations in this hemisphere.

At home and abroad, in less than 6 months, we've worked quietly and effectively to set our agenda and give priority to our problems, addressing them headon. And this has been accomplished in a manner consistent with the promises made last year to the American people. We're keeping our promise to all of those millions of Americans who heard the call sounded last July and who responded last November with an overwhelming mandate. We're responding to that mandate not by politics of division or envy, but by claiming a share of the moral high ground, by summoning every American from every walk of life, from every ethnic and racial group, to a future of national prosperity, of expanded opportunity, and greater personal freedom.

Last year we were deeply distressed about the direction our country had taken. Our country faced grave threats. How, in these past few days, we've all known the joy of a great bipartisan victory! Well now, maybe not all of us knew the joy. The moment Members of the House affirmed the Gramm-Latta budget resolution and the people at last began to regain control of their government, there were some immediate cries of pain. It was even said that I was trying to destroy America.

You wonder where some of these people have been for the last few years. Well, the answer to that is: right in Washington, D.C., in responsible leadership positions in government. Double-digit inflation rates, unemployment rates of more than 7 percent, interest rates of 20 percent, mortgage rates of over 15 percent did not begin on the afternoon of January 20th, 1981.

They began when this Nation started down the path of government intervention, of "tax and tax, spend and spend, elect and elect." Let no one fault the motives of those who implemented such policies. They only intended to help, but they based their efforts on an impossible equation. If I can't pay for my needs, and you can't pay for yours, we can't solve our problem by hiring the government to take money from both of us to give to each other.

So-called entitlement programs—the redistribution of funds from one group of citizens to another—has risen by 453 percent in the last 13 years, going from $63 billion to $346 billion in the proposed budget for 1982. Now, we called for reducing that 1982 budget amount by 5.2 percent—$17.9 billion.

I submit that a 5.2-percent reduction of funding for those programs can be made without penalizing the truly needy or any of those people that the programs are intended to help. The reduction is based on knowledge of recipients who are unfairly receiving benefits through loopholes and loose management of entitlement funds. And so it is with the other proposed budget cuts.

Truly needy people, including our senior citizens, are being cruelly and unnecessarily frightened by those who contributed to our economic mess in the first place. The planned march on Washington this autumn will be far more representative of those who administer the benefits than of those who are really dependent on government help.

We Americans are a generous and a compassionate people, and no particular segment of our society has a monopoly on those traits. Jim Thompson, Bob Michel, and all these others who are here tonight who've been leading and helping secure the budget reductions in the Gramm-Latta bill have compassion for those who must be helped. They also have compassion for those long-suffering Americans who've been providing that help and whose voices have finally been heard in Washington, D.C.

Within the last few weeks the Congress of the United States has been an arena of ideas and courage, where elected representatives summoned strength born not of politics, but of statesmanship. Led by Republicans and joined by, as I've called them, discerning Democrats, the Congress voted to turn away from the established pattern of more and more spending and bigger and bigger government. Men and women of both parties are coming together with a spirit and drive that can only mean great things for all Americans.

The American people are taking their lives and their livelihoods back into their own hands. They are regaining control of their political institutions and making them respond again to their will. Now, this means that for a change the American people are winning.

We've begun the job, but this is no time to rest, for just ahead of us lies the largest and most difficult and most important step of all, to reduce the escalating tax burden that is crushing the spirit of enterprise.

Our punishing tax structure has the effect of discouraging people from earning more, taking away incentives to work harder and accept more responsibility. Our tax structure, coupled with inflation, is locking families and people rigidly in place as the cost of living, the pricetag on the American dream, passes out of reach. This always happens when policymakers lose faith.

603

For too long we've been burdened with people in Washington who wanted to spend more but had no faith that our economy could produce more. So what did they do? They taxed more and more and more, to the point that last year they approved the largest single tax increase in the history of this country.

Such a government-dominated economy can only be a withering economy. We need only look around us for evidence of what is happening. What is happening in Poland today is a classic example. There are probably few people as strong and as valiant as the people of Poland, and yet their economy is described as being in a vicious downward spiral. Now, this isn't the fault of the Polish people. It is the logical result of an illogical system, a system that has no trust, no belief or faith in people. And when government has no respect for its citizens, the citizens lose respect for government.

The problems with the American economy are not the fault of the American people. They're responding as you might expect. Consumers and businessmen are making decisions based on how to avoid burdensome and unnecessary regulations and punitive taxes. Decisions on investment are made not from maximum return, but on tax strategy. There's a growing underground economy, which is a deeply disturbing trend. And this kind of deliberate dishonesty can never be condoned. But even honest taxpayers are feeling a growing resentment toward inflation and a tax system that profits by that inflation. Continuing as we are is the greatest danger we face. The American people must have tax relief, and they must have it now.

Thursday morning in Washington a Congressman from Illinois will reconvene the Committee on Ways and Means of the United States House of Representatives. All tax legislation must begin in that committee. That Congressman from Illinois, Representative Dan Rostenkowski, must provide the leadership necessary to report a tax bill to the House floor in time for the Congress to debate it and for both Houses to agree—and time is running out. The Congress must act by early August, when both Houses recess, so that new tax tables can be made. If there's no tax bill sent to my desk for

signature by early August, there won't be a tax cut this year.

The Senate is ready, and you and I can take pride in that. Last November the people of this country elected a Republican majority in the Senate, and the Senate Finance Committee already has agreed on a tax cut bill. But let's be fair as well as proud of our Republican leadership. Democratic and Republican Senators on that committee worked together. The vote was 19 to 1 for a bipartisan bill that comes very close to what we had proposed.

Senator Bob Dole, chairman of the Finance Committee, tells me the Senate will act on that bill next week. That puts the ball, as the saying goes, in the court of Chairman Danny Rostenkowski and the House Ways and Means Committee. In the meantime, if all of you will join with your neighbors to send the same message to Washington, we'll have that tax cut, and we'll have it this year.

Whatever your faith might be in the post office, take a chance and send a letter to Congress. [*Laughter*] And I'm convinced that once debate is allowed to begin on the House floor, we'll have a tax-cut bill like the bipartisan bill announced at the White House last month.

We need a tax bill, but we need the right tax bill. Our proposal is not a "rich man's windfall" as some have falsely charged. It is fair, it is equitable, and it is compassionate. And three-quarters of the relief will go to those who are paying just about three-quarters of the tax.

Our tax cut proposal reduces taxes in proportion to the taxes paid. Nothing less would be fair. Our tax cut proposal reduces tax rates across the board by the same percentage for everyone who pays taxes. Nothing less would be equitable. Our tax-cut program will provide jobs in the private sector—jobs that will last. Our program will provide opportunities for all. Nothing less would be compassionate.

The bipartisan tax cut bill that we support includes a 25-percent, across-the-board marginal rate cut over a 3-year period, a reduction in the marriage penalty, estate, and gift taxes, along with the elimination of any estate tax at all on a surviving spouse.

We propose reducing the tax on investment income from 70 down to the top of 50 percent, such as an accelerated—and also for business—an accelerated recovery system.

Now, some of these features, I'm happy to say, are included in the tax proposals that are being talked of in the House Ways and Means Committee. At the same time, however, let me point out a very crucial difference—a difference that makes all the difference in the proposal being bandied about by some of the Democratic leadership—for it is no tax cut at all; it is a tax increase. They only propose a 15-percent reduction in the personal income tax.

There is presently an already built-in tax increase plus the bracket creep of inflation, which amounts to a tax increase of nearly 22 percent in the course of the next 3 years. Our tax proposal counters this 22-percent, built-in increase with a 25-percent decrease over those 3 years in addition to the other additional features such as the tax deductions for personal retirement plans, correction of the marriage penalty, et cetera. In other words, the present choice is between our tax cut or no tax cut at all—indeed, a tax increase.

Now, there are those who oppose the bipartisan tax cut, because frankly they're afraid the Government will lose revenue. Now, somehow that doesn't strike me as a national disaster. [*Laughter*] I've said many times, government doesn't tax to get the money it needs; government always finds a need for the money it gets. Many years ago, when the imposition of an income tax was first being debated in the Congress, one of the proponents declared—and, oh my, how we should have listened—he said, "We must have this tax not for government's needs, but for government's wants."

Well, we must cut the growth of spending this year, next year, and the next after that. We must also reduce the excessive percentage of the gross national product that the government is taking [in] taxes. Government has become a drag on the economy. Now, it's true that I believe, as President Kennedy did, that our kind of tax cut will so stimulate our economy that we will actually increase government revenue, but the gross national product will be increased

even more so that government's excessive percentage will be reduced.

Plainly and simply, our tax plan, while it will reduce the burden for each one of us, is intended to stimulate the economy, increase productivity, and provide jobs. President Kennedy put it very well when he said that "an economy hampered by restrictive tax rates will never produce enough revenue to balance our budget."

You know, I'm tired of hearing our opponents justify their opposition by saying they're the party of the working people. Well, as you well know, for a long time I believed they were. In fact, I think some of their past leaders not only believed they were but dedicated themselves to that cause. But today, there's a disenchantment with the leadership of the Democratic Party on the part of millions of patriotic Democrats who see that leadership stubbornly clinging to the belief that only more and bigger government is the answer to our problems.

It's significant that at last year's Democratic National Convention an inordinate percentage of delegates were not rank-and-file working people, but public employees, who had a personal stake in continued big government. They were the majority.

Just the other week a former Democratic Congressman, recently elected to a liberal leadership position, said free enterprise could be too cruel. What we need, he said, is "the gentle force of government." The gentle force of government? For the working men and women who can't get a job, can't buy a house, or can't keep up with the cost of living, that force of government has all the gentleness of a runaway bulldozer.

Which really is the party of the people? The party that embraces the failed policies that will continue high inflation, or the party that wants to stop it? The party whose only answer to unemployment is temporary make-work, or the party that is working to produce private-sector jobs, jobs with a future? The party that sees government as the benevolent master of the people, or the party that says the people are the master of government? The party that, as I said before, last year gave us the largest single tax increase in the history of this Nation, or the party that's fighting hard to reduce tax rates?

Carl Sandburg wrote of the days when our party was formed, tense and restless days of growth in the 1850's. America was torn by the issue of slavery. Neighbors were turning against neighbors in Kansas and Missouri. Liberty and freedom for all men was at stake. Political elements in Illinois and in other States were holding conventions to establish State parties and create a national Republican Party.

Illinois delegates met in Bloomington, in Major's Hall, upstairs over a store near the courthouse square. All stripes of political belief were there—Whigs, bolting Democrats, Free-Soilers, and abolitionists. After several delegates spoke, there were calls for Lincoln. He stood up. There were cries, "Take the platform," and he did. He observed that we were in a trying time and that unless popular opinion made itself very strongly felt and a change was made in, as he put it, "our present course," the nation would turn against itself.

He gave the convention a rousing speech that was the tongue and voice of those present, a speech against slavery, but a speech about liberty and freedom. He told those present that if the safeguards of liberty are broken down for some, they're broken down for all. He called on Americans to be true to themselves and to protect their freedom with their ballot. He was telling why the Republican Party was being organized.

Later, a delegate to the second national convention of the new party, where Lincoln had been nominated for President, reporting on the convention to the folks back home in Wisconsin, said, "We kept in mind that the Republican Party had sprung from the indignation of the people and had gained its strength by the uprising of the popular heart for a great positive idea; that it is a party of volunteers held together not by drill and command, but by the moral power of a great common cause."

Ours is that party still building and expanding a coalition drawn from the heart of this land, a coalition that will again change a course we've been on for far too many years.

We are a coalition of Americans willing to be true to ourselves, willing to invest ourselves in "a great common cause," the future of America. Our country needs our minds and our energies. There can be no wealth unless we create it, no new discoveries unless we find them, and we'll not create or discover until we're willing to risk a little.

We've inherited from our forefathers and possessed by our freedom the strength of will that enables us to thrive. We believe tomorrow will be better. We're willing to take a chance on ourselves.

If we're free to dare—and we are—if we're free to give—and we are—then we're free to shape the future and have within our grasp all that we dream that future will be.

We've tried the "gentle force of government" for almost 40 years. May I simply say, it's time for a change.

Thank you very much.

Note: The President spoke at 7:58 p.m. in the Main Exhibit Hall at McCormick Place.

Following his appearance at the dinner, the President returned to Washington, D.C.

Remarks at a Meeting With Disabled Climbers Following Their Ascent of Mount Rainier
July 8, 1981

The President. I thank you very much. I'm afraid to ask—I know the flag—but I'm afraid to ask if jellybeans helped nourish you on the climb.[1] [*Laughter*]

You'd be surprised, though, we're beginning to run the government with them. They get us through a lot of late afternoon meetings, and you'd be surprised at the very important affairs that are being discussed and the jar of jellybeans is going around the table. I'm always interested in seeing the different styles. Some just grab a handful and some pick each one out one at a time—[*laughter*]—or it's passed on.

You know, the poet William Blake once wrote, "Great things are done when men and mountains meet." Well now, I would add "women" to that statement and then say all of you certainly proved him correct—and even more than correct. And so, it is with great pride that I accept this flag. By carrying it each step of your climb and planting it on top of Mount Rainier, you also planted courage and the capabilities of disabled people firmly in the minds of all Americans. Your triumph on Independence Day, during this International Year of Disabled Persons, clearly illustrated the independence disabled people can achieve when given the opportunity.

I take particular pride in the fact that we have on our White House staff someone who also serves as an example of that independence and self-confidence that disabled people can attain. I'm talking about Hal Krents, who carried this flag to you on our behalf, and I know he would have liked to have been on the mountain with you. Your 11-hour battle with snow, ice, and altitude, while carrying 40-pound backpacks, demonstrated to all of us that with spirit and determination, challenges are made to be met. We sometimes hear of the faith to move mountains. Well, you have the faith to climb mountains, and that faith is in yourselves.

When you came down from that mountain, it wasn't the experienced leading the disabled, but rather those who could see leading those who could not, those who could hear helping those who could not. And the tremendous bond that was forged by this experience, where you complemented each other and joined together to accomplish a great goal, is a significant lesson on what all of us as Americans can accomplish if we work together.

Nancy and I followed your progress, and when you reached the top, we, with the rest of America, shared your joy and were inspired by your courage. And we also must acknowledge the courage of your families, because we saw you, too, on television and, on television, heard through the radios, the walkie-talkies that you were carrying, the joy from the top of the mountain, all of you and your shouts as they were heard down below.

I know there must have been some tense moments during the climb and that the support you received from your families was an important element in your success. And I'm sure that Chuck O'Brien's twins will celebrate their birthdays with more than the usual sense of pride.

The corporations which sponsored this event believed in you. We must all work toward seeing that all businesses appreciate the possibilities of the disabled as fully as those gathered here today. As I stated in my February 6th proclamation of the International Year of Disabled Persons, disabled Americans represent one of our most underutilized resources. Your successful Mount Rainier ascent speaks more about the capabilities of our disabled citizens than any words can possibly state.

So, congratulations, and thanks to all of you for what you have shown and given to all of us. And I shall be very proud to keep this flag.

---

[1] *The group had presented the President with a bag of jellybeans and a flag which had been carried to the mountain's summit.*

Thank you all for being here. I think I'd better let you get into some shade now. [*Laughter*] It's warm—a slightly different climate than Mount Rainier. [*Laughter*]

Participant. We should have brought you back part of the glacier. [*Laughter*]

The President. Right here in the Rose Garden.

Well, God bless you all.

Note: The President spoke at 12:05 p.m. in the Rose Garden at the White House.

Nomination of Guy W. Fiske To Be Under Secretary of Energy
July 8, 1981

The President today announced his intention to nominate Guy W. Fiske to be Under Secretary of Energy, vice John Mark Deutch, resigned.

Since 1977 Mr. Fiske has been executive vice president and director of the General Dynamics Corp., St. Louis, Mo. He was also chairman of the Asbestos Corp., Ltd. In 1972–77 he was corporate vice president and group executive of the International Telephone and Telegraph Corp. He was product line manager-worldwide in 1969–72 and product line manager-worldwide,

controls and instruments, electrical and electronic devices, electronic components and plastics, in 1968–69. Mr. Fiske was manager, specialty equipment operation and computer support services, information systems equipment division, General Electric Co., Phoenix, Ariz. He was with General Electric for 20 years.

Mr. Fiske graduated from Brown University (B.A., 1943). He is married, has three children, and resides in St. Louis, Mo. Mr. Fiske was born September 28, 1924, in Upton, Mass.

Nomination of Kenneth L. Adelman To Be United States Deputy Representative to the United Nations
July 8, 1981

The President today announced his intention to nominate Kenneth L. Adelman, of Virginia, as the Deputy Representative of the United States to the United Nations, with the rank of Ambassador. He would succeed William J. vanden Heuvel, who has resigned.

Dr. Adelman was Legislative Officer at the Department of Commerce in 1968–70. In 1970–72 he was with the Office of Economic Opportunity as Special Assistant to the Director of VISTA, and also to the Director of Congressional Relations. He was Congressional Liaison Officer at the Agency for International Development in 1975–76, and in 1976–77 he was Assistant to the Secretary of Defense.

Dr. Adelman was researching for his dissertation at Georgetown University and at Kinshasa, Zaire, in 1972–75. Since 1977 he has been senior political scientist at the Strategic Studies Center of SRI International in Arlington, Va. He has also done freelance writing since 1977.

Dr. Adelman graduated from Grinnell College (B.A., 1967) and Georgetown University (M.S., 1969; Ph. D., 1975). He is the author of "African Realities" and a member of the International Institute for Strategic Studies. Dr. Adelman is married, has two children, and resides in Arlington, Va. He was born June 9, 1946, in Chicago, Ill.

Nomination of Marshall Brement To Be United States Ambassador to Iceland
July 8, 1981

The President today announced his intention to nominate Marshall Brement, of Arizona, to be Ambassador to Iceland. He would succeed Richard A. Ericson, Jr., who has retired.

Mr. Brement entered the Foreign Service in 1956 as staff assistant in the Bureau of East Asian and Pacific Affairs. He attended Chinese language training in Taichung in 1958–60, and was political officer in Hong Kong in 1960–63. In 1963–64 he attended Russian language training at the Foreign Service Institute. He was political officer in Moscow in 1964–66. He attended the National Institute of Public Affairs at Stanford University in 1966–67. He was chief of the political section in Singapore (1967–70),

counselor for public affairs in Jakarta (1970–73), counselor for public affairs in Saigon (1973–74), counselor for political affairs in Moscow (1974–76), and in Madrid (1977–79). In 1979–80 Mr. Brement was staff member, National Security Council at the White House. He served in the U.S. Air Force in 1952–54.

Mr. Brement graduated from Brooklyn College (B.A., 1952) and the University of Maryland (M.A., 1955). His foreign languages are Russian, Chinese (Mandarin and Cantonese), French, Spanish, and Indonesian. Mr. Brement is married, has three children, and resides in Washington, D.C. He was born January 10, 1932, in New York, N.Y.

Nomination of David Eugene Zweifel To Be United States Ambassador to the Yemen Arab Republic
July 8, 1981

The President today announced his intention to nominate David Eugene Zweifel, of Maryland, to be Ambassador to the Yemen Arab Republic. He would succeed George M. Lane, who is being assigned as diplomat-in-residence at Portland State University.

Mr. Zweifel entered the Foreign Service in 1962 as political officer in Rio de Janeiro. In 1965–67 he was personnel officer in the Department. He attended Arabic language training in Beirut in 1967–68. He was Consul in Amman (1969–70), political officer in Mexico City (1971–74), and Deputy Chief of Mission in Muscat (1974–76). He attended the National War College in 1976–

77. Mr. Zweifel was Deputy Director for Egyptian Affairs in the Department in 1977–79, and since 1979 he has been Deputy Chief of Mission in Amman.

Mr. Zweifel graduated from Oregon State University (B.S., 1957). He served in the U.S. Navy as lieutenant in 1957–62, serving as Naval ROTC instructor at Princeton University in 1960–62. His foreign languages are Portuguese, Arabic, Spanish, and French. Mr. Zweifel is married, has two children, and resides in Chevy Chase, Md. He was born September 13, 1934, in Denver, Colo.

Nomination of David Anderson To Be United States Ambassador to Yugoslavia
July 8, 1981

The President today announced his intention to nominate David Anderson, of New York, to be Ambassador to the Socialist Federal Republic of Yugoslavia. He would succeed Lawrence S. Eagleburger, who has been named Assistant Secretary of State for European Affairs.

Mr. Anderson entered the Foreign Service in 1959 as intelligence research analyst, then management analyst in the Department. In 1961–62 he attended Serbo-Croatian language training at the Foreign Service Institute. He was political officer in Belgrade (1962–65), in Bamako (1965–67), in the United States Mission at Berlin (1967–

70), in Brussels-US-NATO (1970–71), and in Bonn (1971–75). In the Department, he was Director of the Office of Central European Affairs (1975–77), and Deputy Executive Secretary (1977–78). Since 1978 he has been assistant chief of mission in the United States Mission at Berlin.

Mr. Anderson graduated from Union College (B.A., 1958) and Fletcher School of Law and Diplomacy (M.A., 1959). His languages are French, German, Serbo-Croatian, and some knowledge of Russian. Mr. Anderson was born January 3, 1937, in Kirkcaldy, Scotland.

Announcement of the Establishment of the Military Manpower Task Force
July 8, 1981

The President today announced the establishment of a Military Manpower Task Force, to be chaired by Secretary of Defense Caspar W. Weinberger.

The Task Force will review all aspects of manpower requirements and conditions in the Armed Forces, including such matters as the adequacy of the military compensation and incentives; educational benefits; current manpower readiness of the Armed Forces; effectiveness of training, leadership, and discipline; enlistment standards; recruiting and retention efforts; and Selective Service registration.

The Task Force will evaluate the total manpower situation and will provide recommendations to the President to increase the effectiveness of the active and reserve all-volunteer services.

Members of the Task Force will include Edwin Meese III, Counsellor to the Presi-

dent; David A. Stockman, Director of the Office of Management and Budget; John O. Marsh, Secretary of the Army; John F. Lehman, Secretary of the Navy; Verne Orr, Secretary of the Air Force; Richard V. Allen, Assistant to the President for National Security Affairs; Martin Anderson, Assistant to the President for Policy Development; Murray L. Weidenbaum, Chairman of the Council of Economic Advisers; and Gen. David Jones, Chairman of the Joint Chiefs of Staff.

The Executive Officer of the Task Force will be Maj. Gen. Thomas K. Turnage, who is also Director-designate of the Selective Service System.

An interagency working group to support the Task Force will be chaired by Lawrence J. Korb, Assistant Secretary of Defense (Manpower, Reserve Affairs and Logistics).

Remarks Following a Concert by the Mostly Mozart Festival Orchestra
July 8, 1981

[*To the orchestra*] The applause is for you.

The only thing that I have in common with them that would cause you applauding me is that I've got a white coat on, too. [*Laughter*]

Wasn't that lovely? I think it was. [*Applause*]

Speaking for Nancy and, I'm sure, for all of you, it was a thrill to hear the American premiere of this long-lost Mozart symphony performed here on the South Lawn of the White House and performed so beautifully by you, the Mostly Mozart Festival Orchestra of Lincoln Center. And I thank you, Leonard Slatkin, and all of you fine musicians, you very wonderful musicians, for bringing this traditional New York City Mostly Mozart Festival to Washington.

And thank you for allowing us to hear what Mozart meant when he said, "Music should never be painful to the ear, but should flatter and charm it." And you certainly did that.

Someone once wrote that whether the angels play only Bach while praising God, we can't be sure, but we do know that when they play for themselves, they play Mozart. [*Laughter*] And now we know why.

But, you know, when we talk about this incredible genius—and Haydn, Mozart's instructor, called him the greatest composer ever—we sometimes forget that important part that we were reminded of him, that Mozart was really a child prodigy. He played the klavier when he was three, and he composed a symphony—the symphony you just heard—as you've been told, when he was only nine. Now, personally I never forget little facts like that, because no one appreciates youth more than I do. [*Laughter*] I've had quite a while to appreciate it—[*laughter*]—but I mention this, because in a sense this afternoon is our way of saluting youth in arts.

You see, in addition to Mozart, we're doubly honored today to be able to pay tribute to another young prodigy—one of our own. On June 25th, 17-year-old Amanda McKerrow, from Rockville, Maryland, made ballet history by winning the gold medal at the Moscow International Ballet Competition. No American has ever won this award before. And just to give you an idea how sensational she was, one of Amanda's performances drew eight curtain calls from one of the world's most partisan and knowledgeable audiences.

And now, Amanda, I hope you won't mind if we ask you and your parents, Mr. and Mrs. Alan McKerrow, to all stand for a moment so we can let you know how proud and how happy we are and how happy you've made all of us, too. [*Applause*]

So, today we honor history and those who make it. And, come to think of it, I've made just a little bit of history here myself. I've nearly completed an entire public appearance without even once mentioning our tax proposal. [*Laughter*] And it's not the place for it. I'm not going to tell you that we need a 25-percent, personal rate reduction across the board for 3 years—[*laughter*]—or that we need it now. I won't mention that. [*Laughter*]

Before I take the spotlight off where it belongs, let me just invite all of you now— and incidently, this is a very special audience, too, because this concert might have been played in this same way in this same place with a different cast of characters, both in the audience and myself, if it hadn't been for so many of you and what you did.

But now, it is warm in here, and to escape the summer heat, the state rooms in the Residence are prepared with nice cool refreshments for all of you.

And again, our heartfelt thanks to all of you for honoring us as you have. Thank you very much.

Note: The President spoke at 5:57 p.m. inside a tent constructed on the South Lawn for the concert.

The performance included Mozart's Symphony in F, K. 19a, which was composed in 1765 and thought to be lost until its discovery in 1980 in the Federal Republic of Germany.

Remarks on Receiving the First Consolidated Report on the Inspectors General Program
July 9, 1981

Mr. Harper. Mr. President, we're pleased to present this, the first consolidated report of the Inspectors General, to you this morning. And, as I mentioned, we're going to be having a press briefing in a few minutes with other members of the press to tell them about your plans for the program, the commitments that you've made. And then these three Inspectors General are going to be telling the press about specific projects we've undertaken to improve the effectiveness of the Inspector General program.

We appreciate your interest.

The President. Well, you have more than my interest; you have my support and enthusiastic backing in this. I think it is high time. We've spoken of this over a period of time—going clear back to the campaign—of fraud, waste, and abuse. And I never was in sympathy with the way one department in government, some time ago, eliminated fraud, waste, and abuse. As I understand it, they called a staff meeting and said they would no longer use those words. They would now call it mismanagement and something else. [*Laughter*] Therefore, fraud, waste, and abuse disappeared.

But this is the way to go at it, and you sure do have our backing, and go get them.

Mr. Harper. Thank you very much, Mr. President. We know you have a very busy schedule, and we've got to get over to our meeting with the press. Thank you for your time.

The President. Well, thank you for what you're doing.

Note: The exchange began at 9:43 a.m. in the Oval Office at the White House. Edwin L. Harper is Deputy Director of the Office of Management and Budget.

Also attending the meeting were Thomas F. McBride, Inspector General of the Department of Labor, Joseph P. Welsch, Inspector General-designate of the Department of Transportation, and Paul R. Boucher, Inspector General of the Small Business Administration.

Remarks Announcing the Intention To Nominate Charles A. Bowsher To Be Comptroller General of the United States
July 9, 1981

The President. Ladies and gentlemen of the press, Members of the Congress who are here with us today, and our former Comptroller General, Elmer Staats—retired recently:

The Comptroller General holds a unique and critically important post in the Federal Government. His term of office is 15 years, and he's charged with overseeing the legal, accounting, and auditing functions of the General Accounting Office, which is the right arm of the Congress.

It's obvious that in this post a strong and effective leader can have an enduring impact on our political institutions. Such a leader can do much to restore the faith of the people in the integrity and efficiency of government. This is one of the most important appointments that I shall make as President, and that's why I'm especially pleased to announce today the appointment of Charles A. Bowsher as Comptroller General.

Mr. Bowsher is uniquely qualified for this position. He has served in the Pentagon as an Assistant Secretary of Navy for Financial Management, as a managing partner of Arthur Andersen, and an official of the American Institute of Certified Public Accountants. He has spent the last decade working with and advising government leaders on financial and management problems. Mr. Bowsher's specialty has been financial systems in the Federal Government. He has supervised several notable studies in this area, including one comprehensive survey of Federal financial reporting. In addition, Mr. Bowsher has worked closely with several committees of the Congress and served on advisory boards of departments in the Federal Government too numerous to mention.

Mr. Bowsher, in short, has the expertise of an insider with the perspective of an outsider. He will need these qualities in great abundance. The problem of waste and fraud in the Federal Government is, as I said in my first speech to the Congress, an unrelenting national scandal. This administration has already taken action to deal with this problem. We'll continue to move methodically, but vigorously, in this area.

We've chosen our Inspectors General with deliberate speed and in consultation with the Congress. Our Council on Integrity and Efficiency at OMB, which coordinates the activities of our Inspectors General, is the major innovation, and its work is now underway.

By the way, I thought some of you would like to know that each week the desk officers at the Office of Management and Budget submit reports on recent government actions in the area of waste and fraud. During only one week last month, these reports showed projections of between $270,000 and $400,000 in questionable payments in one student assistance program; $36 million in bloated rental costs for Federal agencies; and more than $249,000 in invalid welfare payment claims. In the criminal area, the Project Match has produced indictments of 22 persons for allegedly defrauding the government of

$100,000 in the Food Stamp program. In a Treasury sweep, three other persons were indicted in an alleged attempt to defraud the Customs Service of $1.6 million. And I want to stress to you—these are only highlights from a single week's report.

So, Chuck, it's clear that your work is cut out for you. You'll have to be practical. You'll have to work in harmony with the branches and agencies of the Federal Government. But at the same time, I hope you never lose that sense of indignation that any private citizen feels at the spectacle of waste and fraud in the Federal Government.

You'll need the support of those of us who are here today. The Congress must give you the resources you need; the executive branch must cooperate and respond to your requests. Nothing has disturbed me more than the failure of some Federal agencies to enact fiscal reforms recommended in the General Accounting Office audits. If you have difficulties here, believe me, I'll want to know about it.

A word of gratitude is also in order to Congressman Jack Brooks and Senator Roth and Speaker O'Neill and these others on the congressional commission who worked so diligently to find a suitable candidate for this position.

When Lincoln Steffens wrote "The Shame of the Cities" earlier in this century, political power was centered in the big city political machines, many of which were corrupt. Today that locus of power—with the staggering increase in Federal expenditures during the past two decades—has moved to the National Government. Waste, fraud, corruption, and abuse are severe problems. All of us in government have a moral responsibility to meet them head on.

I believe that today's appointment is a major step in fulfilling our responsibility. Comptroller General Bowsher has not only my congratulations but my pledge of wholehearted support.

Mr. Bowsher. Thank you very much, Mr. President, and I want to thank also the congressional leaders here today that sent my nomination to you, Mr. President. And I hope that I can carry on the fine tradition that my predecessor Elmer Staats performed as a great Comptroller General for 15 years, just prior to stepping down this past March.

It's a great challenge to work and to try to achieve efficiency and effectiveness in the government, and that's what I dedicate myself to today. And as soon as I'm through with the confirmation process, I would then be happy to take substantive questions, but at this time I would like to beg off until we get through the confirmation process.

Thank you.

Note: The President spoke at 9:45 a.m. in the Rose Garden at the White House.

Nomination of Charles A. Bowsher To Be Comptroller General of the United States
July 9, 1981

The President today announced his intention to nominate Charles A. Bowsher to be Comptroller General of the United States.

Since 1971 Mr. Bowsher has been managing partner with the firm of Arthur Andersen & Co. of Washington, D.C., specializing in government financial and general management problems at the National, State, and local levels. He has been associated with the company since 1956.

In 1967–71 he was Assistant Secretary of the Navy (Financial Management). Mr. Bowsher's responsibilities included direct supervision of an annual budget of over $20 billion and an accounting and systems department of 4,500 people. In addition, he had the coordination responsibility for both the Senate and House Appropriations Committees, the Office of Management and Budget, and the General Accounting Office.

Mr. Bowsher served in the U.S. Army in 1953–55. He is a recipient of the Navy Distinguished Public Service Award (1969 and 1971) and the Department of Defense Distinguished Public Service Award (1971). He was graduated from the University of Illinois (B.S. 1953) and the University of Chicago (M.B.A., 1956).

Mr. Bowsher resides in Washington, D.C. He was born May 30, 1931, in Elkhart, Ind.

Nomination of Nancy H. Steorts To Be a Member of the Consumer Product Safety Commission, and Designation as Chairman
July 9, 1981

The President today announced his intention to nominate Nancy H. Steorts to be a member and Chairman of the Consumer Product Safety Commission.

Since 1977 Mrs. Steorts has been a private consultant and consumer adviser. In 1973–77 she was Special Assistant to the Secretary of Agriculture for Consumer Affairs. She served at the request of the Secretary of Agriculture as Chairman of the Department's Committee on Consumer Responsiveness, Vice Chairman of the Department's Committee on Food Safety and Quality, and Chairman of the USDA National Consumer Advisory Committee. Prior to these positions, she was U.S. Expositions Officer, Department of Commerce, in 1973. Mrs. Steorts was assistant national director of volunteers and national director of women's speakers bureau with the Committee for the Re-Election of the President in 1971–72. She served as a staff associate to the Committee for Executive Reorganization of the Government in 1971. She was a sales associate with Naomi B. Faison, Inc., Realtors, in 1967–68 and home economist with the Washington Gas Light Co. in 1961–64.

Mrs. Steorts graduated from Syracuse University (B.S., 1959). She has one daugh-

ter and resides in Bethesda, Md. Mrs. Steorts was born November 28, 1936, in Manlius, N.Y.

Message to the Congress Transmitting the Annual Report of the National Science Foundation
July 9, 1981

To the Congress of the United States:

I am pleased to transmit the annual report of the National Science Foundation for Fiscal Year 1980. I have long maintained an interest in the vitality of our scientific and technological capabilities. I consider these capabilities as crucial to the economic well-being of our Nation, a mainstay of our national security, and a beneficial influence on the quality of life of our citizens.

As this report is issued, we find ourselves at a turning point in our history, a time when we must make difficult choices. This Administration is committed to revitalizing the economy. Our success in this endeavor will depend greatly upon how well we can improve the productivity and competitiveness of our industrial sector. As we look for ways to enhance technological innovation—a key to increase productivity and competitiveness—we remember that the ultimate source of innovation is new knowledge. The National Science Foundation is unique among Federal agencies in that its primary responsibility is to promote advances in knowledge through encouragement and support of basic research. Such research,

properly executed, is an essential investment in our future and one we must wisely and responsibly nurture.

When the National Science Foundation was created in 1950, the United States led all other nations in economic productivity, military power, the sciences, and technology. Today we face challenges in all these areas. But as the Foundation Director, John Slaughter, notes in his opening statement in this report, challenges also bring with them opportunities.

I know we have the talent and dedication to pursue and apply scientific knowledge to meet our present and future needs. We will continue to maintain our support of scientific research in a wise and responsible manner as a critical investment in our Nation's future.

RONALD REAGAN

The White House,
July 9, 1981.

Note: The report is entitled "National Science Foundation—Thirtieth Annual Report for Fiscal Year 1980" (Government Printing Office, 146 pages).

Announcement Concerning a Presidential Directive on United States Conventional Arms Transfer Policy
July 9, 1981

On July 8, the President signed a directive on conventional arms transfer policy, which superseded Presidential Directive 13 of May 13, 1977. The new arms transfer

policy follows:

The challenges and hostility toward fundamental United States interests, and the interests of its friends and allies, have grown significantly in recent years. These trends threaten stability in many regions and impede progress toward greater political and economic development.

The United States cannot defend the free world's interests alone. The United States must, in today's world, not only strengthen its own military capabilities, but be prepared to help its friends and allies to strengthen theirs through the transfer of conventional arms and other forms of security assistance. Such transfers complement American security commitments and serve important United States objectives. Prudently pursued, arms transfers can strengthen us.

The United States therefore views the transfer of conventional arms and other defense articles and services as an essential element of its global defense posture and an indispensable component of its foreign policy. Applied judiciously, arms transfers can:

—help deter aggression by enhancing the states of preparedness of allies and friends;

—increase our own armed forces effectiveness by improving the ability of the United States, in concert with its friends and allies, to project power in response to threats posed by mutual adversaries;

—support efforts to foster the ability of our forces to deploy and operate with those of our friends and allies, thereby strengthening and revitalizing our mutual security relationships;

—demonstrate that the United States has an enduring interest in the security of its friends and partners, and that it will not allow them to be at a military disadvantage;

—foster regional and internal stability, thus encouraging peaceful resolution of disputes and evolutionary change; and

—help to enhance United States defense production capabilities and efficiency.

Attainment of these objectives in turn requires effective United States Government control and direction over arms transfers. Because of the diversity of United States security interests, this administration will tailor its approach to arms transfer requests to specific situations and exercise sufficient flexibility to respond promptly to changes affecting the mutual interests of the United States and its allies and friends. We will review such requests with care.

The United States will evaluate requests primarily in terms of their net contribution to enhanced deterrence and defense. It will accord high priority to requests from its major alliance partners and to those nations with whom it has friendly and cooperative security relationships. In making arms transfer decisions the United States will give due consideration to a broad range of factors including:

—the degree to which the transfer responds appropriately to the military threats confronting the recipient;

—whether the transfer will enhance the recipient's capability to participate in collective security efforts with the United States;

—whether the transfer will promote mutual interests in countering externally supported aggression;

—whether the transfer is consistent with United States interests in maintaining stability within regions where friends of the United States may have differing objectives;

—whether the transfer is compatible with the needs of United States forces, recognizing that occasions will arise when other nations may require scarce items on an emergency basis;

—whether the proposed equipment transfer can be absorbed by the recipient without overburdening its military support system or financial resources; and

—whether any detrimental effects of the transfer are more than counterbalanced by positive contributions to United States interests and objectives.

All requests will be considered on a case-by-case basis. Those for coproduction, or the transfer of sensitive or advanced technology, will receive special scrutiny, taking into account economic and industrial factors for both the United States and other participating countries, the importance of arms cooperation with NATO and other close friends and allies, potential third party transfers, and the protection of sensitive technology and military capabilities.

Particular care must be taken to avoid any adverse impact on allied and friendly nations by encouraging them to assume burdens for which their economies are ill-prepared Therefore, careful consideration will be given to lower-cost alternatives including adaptations of military equipment for sale abroad, recognizing that first-line systems may not suit the needs of many countries. This consideration of the full range of available American alternatives will take place at every stage of review.

United States Government representatives overseas will be expected to provide the same courtesies and assistance to firms that have obtained licenses to market items on the United States Munitions List as they would to those marketing other American products.

The policy changes being initiated should not be seen as heralding a period of unrestrained military transfers. The United States retains a genuine interest in arms

transfer restraint and remains prepared to consider specific proposals directed toward that end. There has been, however, little or no interest in arms transfer limitations manifested by the Soviet Union, or the majority of other arms-producing nations. In the absence of such interest, the United States will not jeopardize its own security needs through a program of unilateral restraint. At the same time, recognizing the special role that its major allies can play in strengthening common friends, it will seek to develop complementary policies with those allies.

The realities of today's world demand that we pursue a sober, responsible, and balanced arms transfer policy, a policy that will advance our national security interests and those of the free world. Both in addressing decisions as to specific transfers and opportunities for restraint among producers, we will be guided by principle as well as practical necessity. We will deal with the world as it is, rather than as we would like it to be.

Statement on Signing a Bill To Approve a Constitution for the United States Virgin Islands
July 10, 1981

I take great pleasure in signing into law House Joint Resolution 238, an act to "approve a Constitution for the United States Virgin Islands."

There have been many important moments in the history of Virgin Islands self-government since the King of Denmark ceded sovereignty over the islands to the United States in 1917. In 1937 the Legislative Assembly of the Virgin Islands was established for the territory; in 1970 the territory inaugurated its first elected Governor; and in 1972, the first Virgin Islands delegate to Congress was sworn in. These were significant events for Virgin Islands self-government. All were accomplished, not by Virgin Islanders, but rather for Virgin Islanders through enactments by the United States Congress. Now, however, a locally

written constitution, if adopted by the people of the Virgin Islands, will be the capstone of local self-government.

This legislation approves referring the constitution to the voters of the Virgin Islands for referendum. It does not represent a Federal endorsement of the constitution's substantive provisions. That task is reserved to the voters of the Virgin Islands.

The draft constitution represents a great deal of hard work and serious thought on the part of Virgin Islands constitution drafters. It is the product of the democratic process at work in the territory.

This resolution will further advance the progress of self-government in the Virgin Islands. It is, indeed, a privilege for me to play a role in this constitution-making process.

Note: As enacted, H.J. Res. 238 is Public Law 97–21, approved July 9.

Nomination of Julia Chang Bloch To Be an Assistant Administrator of the Agency for International Development
July 10, 1981

The President today announced his intention to nominate Julia Chang Bloch to be an Assistant Administrator of the Agency for International Development (Food and Peace), United States International Development Cooperation Agency, vice Calvin H. Raullerson, resigned.

Since 1980 Mrs. Bloch has been a fellow of the Institute of Politics, Kennedy School of Government, Harvard University. She was Deputy Director, Office of African Affairs, U.S. International Communication Agency, in 1977–80; chief minority counsel, Senate Select Committee on Nutrition and Human Needs, in 1976–77; professional staff member, minority staff, Senate Select Committee on Nutrition and Human Needs, in 1971–76; evaluation officer, Peace Corps, in 1968–70; training officer, East Asia and Pacific Region, Peace Corps, 1967–68; and Peace Corps volunteer in Sabah, Malaysia, in 1964–66.

Mrs. Bloch graduated from the University of California at Berkeley (B.A., 1964) and Harvard University (M.A., 1967). She is a recipient of the Hubert H. Humphrey Award for International Service. She is married and resides in Washington, D.C. She was born March 2, 1942, in Chefoo, China.

Nomination of John Langeloth Loeb, Jr., To Be United States Ambassador to Denmark
July 10, 1981

The President today announced his intention to nominate John Langeloth Loeb, Jr., of New York, to be Ambassador to Denmark, vice Warren Damian Manshel, resigned.

Mr. Loeb has been with Loeb, Rhoades and Co. of New York City since 1956, as general partner (1959–73) and limited partner (1973–present). Since 1979 he has been president of John L. Loeb, Jr., Associates of New York, N.Y. He has also served as special adviser to Gov. Nelson A. Rockefeller on environmental matters (1967–73); chairman of New York State Council on Environmental Advisors (1970–75) and of the Governor's Keep New York State Clean program (1971–75); and chairman of the Holly Sugar Corp. (1969–71). He has served as director of John Morrell and Co., Atlantico del Golfo, the American Star Insurance Co., International Rescue Committee, Denver and Rio Grande Western Railroad, Metro-Goldwyn-Mayer, and Rio Grande Industries.

Mr. Loeb graduated from Harvard College (B.A., 1952) and Harvard Business School (M.B.A., 1954). He served in the U.S. Air Force as first lieutenant in 1954–56. He has two children and resides in Purchase, N.Y. He was born May 2, 1930, in New York, N.Y.

Nomination of Keith Foote Nyborg To Be United States Ambassador to Finland
July 10, 1981

The President today announced his intention to nominate Keith Foote Nyborg, of Idaho, to be Ambassador to Finland, vice James E. Goodby, resigned.

Mr. Nyborg has been with Finlandia Ranch since 1957 as manager, owner, and operator (1961–78), and since 1978 as president and general manager. He was personnel administration specialist with the United States Army in 1954–56. In 1952 he served as interpreter and guide for the United States Olympic Team in Helsinki. He was a missionary for the Church of Jesus Christ of Latter-Day Saints in Helsinki in 1950–52. He served with the Department of Agriculture Forest Service (1966–67), the Farmers Home Administration (1977–80), and Bureau of Reclamation in the Department of Interior (1978–80). He has been an instructor of the Finnish language at Ricks College in Rexburg, Idaho.

Mr. Nyborg attended Ricks College and is fluent in Finnish. He is married, has three children, and resides in Ashton, Idaho. He was born March 4, 1930, in Ashton, Idaho.

Nomination of Frederic L. Chapin To Be United States Ambassador to Guatemala
July 10, 1981

The President today announced his intention to nominate Frederic L. Chapin, of New Jersey, to be Ambassador to Guatemala, vice Frank V. Ortiz, Jr., resigned.

Mr. Chapin was economic analyst in Paris with the Economic Cooperation Administration in 1950–52. In 1952 he became a Foreign Service officer and served as economic officer in Vienna. He was international relations officer in the Department of State in 1956–59. In 1959–61 he was political-labor officer in Managua, and chargé d'affaires, then Deputy Chief of Mission in Fort Lamy in 1961–62. In the Department he was foreign affairs officer (1962–63), Special Assistant to Under Secretary of State for Political Affairs (1963–65), Executive Secretary with the Agency for International Development (1965–66), Foreign Service examiner (1966–67), Foreign Service inspector (1967–68), Country Director for Bolivia and Chile (1968–70), and Deputy Assistant Secretary for Management in the Bureau of Inter-American Affairs (1970–72). In 1972–78 he was Consul General in São Paulo, and Ambassador to Ethiopia from 1978–80. In 1980–81 he was Deputy Assistant Secretary of Defense for Inter-American Affairs. In 1981 he was chargé d'affaires ad interim in San Salvador.

Mr. Chapin graduated from Harvard University (A.B., 1950). His foreign languages are German, French, Spanish, and Portuguese. He is married, has four children, and resides in New Brunswick, N.J. He was born July 13, 1929, in New York, N.Y.

Nomination of Abraham Katz To Be United States Representative to the Organization for Economic Cooperation and Development
July 10, 1981

The President today announced his intention to nominate Abraham Katz, of Florida, to be the Representative of the United States of America to the Organization for Economic Cooperation and Development, with the rank of Ambassador, vice Herbert Salzman, resigned.

In 1950 Mr. Katz began his government career as foreign affairs officer in the Department of State. In 1951–53 he was principal officer in Merida and in 1953–55 economic officer in Mexico, D.F. In 1956 he attended Russian language training at the Foreign Service Institute, and in 1956–57 he attended graduate studies in Soviet affairs at Harvard University. He was intelligence research specialist in the Department in 1957–59. He was Secretary of Delegation in Paris/USRO (1959–64), and Counselor for Economic Affairs in Moscow (1964–66). He attended the Center for International Affairs at Harvard University in 1966–67. In 1967–74 he was Director of the Office of OECD, European Communities and Atlantic Political Economic Affairs in the Department. In 1974 he was head of the Task Force on International Energy Policy. In 1974–78 he was Deputy Chief of Mission to the United States Mission to the Organization for Economic Cooperation and Development in Paris. He was on detail to the Department of Commerce as Deputy Assistant Secretary of Commerce for International Economic Policy and Research (1978–80) and Assistant Secretary of Commerce for International Economic Policy (1980–81).

Mr. Katz graduated from Brooklyn College (B.A., 1948); Columbia University (M.I.A., 1950); and Harvard University (Ph. D., 1968). His foreign languages are French, Spanish, Russian, and Hebrew. Mr. Katz is married, has three children, and resides in Hollywood, Fla. He was born December 4, 1926, in Brooklyn, N.Y.

Remarks of the President and Prime Minister Pierre Elliott Trudeau of Canada Following Their Meeting
July 10, 1981

The President. Ladies and gentlemen, it's a pleasure this afternoon to meet once again with Prime Minister Trudeau, and our discussion covered a number of bilateral and multilateral issues. As you know, the Prime Minister has just returned from Europe, and he brought a very good report on Europe's preparations for the economic summit in Ottawa that begins some 9 days from now.

I told the Prime Minister how much we're looking forward to those Ottawa talks. They come at a very opportune time for the seven industrial democracies that will be in attendance. All of our nations now face a common task of reducing inflation, increasing employment, and improving long-term economic prospects for our people.

It's clear that achieving economic recovery now poses one of the greatest challenges to the free world, and it's this challenge that shall lie at the heart of our summit in Ottawa. We must discuss not just our problems there but our own national policies to cope with them and what we must do together to restore general prosperity.

I also hope from this summit will come a new sense of confidence and community among the industrial nations that economic recovery can be achieved. And I hope, further, that in our meetings, our countries will reaffirm our fundamental partnership with each other. For many years we've shared democratic political institutions, market economic systems, and a belief and faith in human dignity and freedom. By meeting at this summit, we will express our quiet determination to defend those institutions against any threat.

Finally, let me say I look forward to the summit for personal reasons. I believe it's important to the vitality of our foreign policy that I have the opportunity to renew friendships with world leaders who've already visited here in Washington and also have an opportunity to forge new relationships with those who've recently been elected to office.

Prime Minister Trudeau and I, as well as others who will join us in Ottawa, all agree that we can achieve both progress and peace only through a close and continuous cooperation, which this meeting symbolizes. That's the basis of our partnership, and partnership is the basis of our common task.

So, Mr. Prime Minister, I look forward to seeing you again when I arrive in your country for what we consider a very important meeting.

The Prime Minister. Mr. President, ladies and gentlemen of the press:

I want to express my thanks to President Reagan for having made my job as Chairman of the Ottawa Summit easier by accepting to meet me today and discussing frankly not so much the areas of agreement, which are many, but the areas of possible disagreement amongst those seven industrialized democracies, which realized way back at the beginning of these summits that we are interdependent, that our policies do affect each other, that much of the world is watching us to see how democracies solve their difficult economic problems. They're waiting to see if we are successful in meeting the economic challenges, the difficult ones that are posed in every one of our countries, and whether we will be able to lead the democracies in the solutions of these problems.

As Chairman, I have found it important to meet with the President of the United States so that we could become acquainted with the areas of discussion. And I want to report that I am as optimistic as the President is that we will find the solutions by the discussions we will have together.

If I had any grudge with the President it would be that the way he spoke just now, he sounded as though he wanted to be the Chairman in Ottawa, and I don't think I'll let that happen. [*Laughter*] It'll be your turn some other time, Mr. President. But there was great value in meeting in preparation for the summit.

[*At this point, the Prime Minister spoke in French. The White House press release contained the following translation.*]

I would like to say in French that this meeting that will take place in Ottawa will permit us to explore not only the points of similarity, but the differences. I still have the hope, as Chairman of this summit, that we will find the way to form a consensus and reach solutions that we can all agree upon.

[*In English:*] There is just one bilateral that I think it is important that I mention here, Mr. President. You were gracious enough to give me, as we left your luncheon table, the flag that had flown on your spaceship which landed so majestically some months ago. And I'm very happy to say that beyond all the multilateral problems, and there are many, we have so many areas of common agreement and we have so many ways in which we look to the future together, and there could be none more exciting, I think, than the cooperation that we have been embarked upon for some time now in the area of space technology. I'm very grateful for the gesture of handing that flag to me, which is the witness of one of the United States great triumphs in space technology, and even more important, a sign and a guarantee of the close cooperation between our countries in the advancement of that technology for the benefit of our peoples and the benefit of mankind.

Thank you very much for your very welcome hospitality.

Note: The President spoke at 1:42 p.m. to reporters assembled at the North Portico of the White House.

Earlier, the President and the Prime Minister met in the Oval Office. Also attending the meeting were Secretary of State Alexander M. Haig, Jr., Assistant to the President for National Security Affairs Richard V. Allen, Canadian Under Secretary for External Affairs Allan Gottlieb, and Canadian Ambassador to the United States Peter Towe. Following that meeting, the President and the Prime Minister and their delegations held a working luncheon in the Blue Room.

Designation of Michael K. Deaver as Presidential Liaison for the 1984 Olympic Games
July 13, 1981

The President today announced that Michael K. Deaver, Assistant to the President and Deputy Chief of the White House staff, will serve as the Presidential Liaison to the 1984 Olympic Games, the U.S. Olympic Committee, and the International Olympic Committee.

Mr. Deaver will be the principal point of contact in the executive branch for all matters relating to the 1984 Olympic Games in Los Angeles, Calif., and to the U.S. and International Olympic Committees. He will work directly with Peter V. Ueberroth, president of the Los Angeles Olympic Organizing Committee, and with F. Don Miller, executive director of the U.S. Olympic Committee.

The President looks forward to the 1984 Olympic Games in Los Angeles and has asked Mr. Deaver to provide all appropriate assistance and guidance. Mr. Deaver will report directly to the President.

Nomination of Bruce Chapman To Be Director of the Census
July 13, 1981

The President today announced his intention to nominate Bruce Chapman to be Director of the Census, Department of Commerce, vice Vincent P. Barabba, resigned.

Since January 1981, Mr. Chapman has been a consultant to the Cascade Institute for Public Policy. In 1975–81 he was secretary of state, State of Washington. Prior to 1975, he was a member of the Seattle City Council in 1971–75; a public affairs consultant in 1966–71; an editorial writer for the New York Herald Tribune in 1965–66; and publisher of Advance magazine (Cambridge, Mass.) in 1960–64. Mr. Chapman has served on various boards and commissions, including the President's Advisory Council on Historic Preservation, Washington Trust on Historic Preservation, and the World Affairs Council in Seattle.

Mr. Chapman graduated from Harvard College (B.A., 1962). He served in the U.S. Air Force Reserve in 1965–69.

Mr. Chapman is married, has one child, and resides in Seattle, Wash. He was born December 1, 1940, in Chicago, Ill.

Nomination of Luis Victor Hurtado To Be Assayer of the United States Mint at Denver, Colorado
July 13, 1981

The President today announced his intention to nominate Luis Victor Hurtado to be Assayer of the Mint of the United States at Denver, Department of the Treasury, vice Michael E. Witt.

Mr. Hurtado is currently serving as Special Assistant to the Treasurer of the United States. In this position he has participated in the formulation of Mint policies, plans, and programs. During the 1980 general election, Mr. Hurtado was assistant treasurer to the Reagan-Bush committee. He was deputy director, matching funds, to the Reagan for President Committee during the primary campaign in 1979–80. In 1978–79 he was a realtor associate with Corliss & Associates Realtors of Los Angeles, Calif. Previously he was associated with the University of California at Los Angeles.

Mr. Hurtado graduated from the University of California (B.S., 1977). He resides in Washington, D.C., and was born April 1, 1954, in Los Angeles, Calif.

Nomination of Everett George Rank, Jr., To Be a Member of the Board of Directors of the Commodity Credit Corporation
July 13, 1981

The President today announced his intention to nominate Everett George Rank, Jr., to be a member of the Board of Directors of the Commodity Credit Corporation, Department of Agriculture, vice Howard W. Hjort, resigned.

Mr. Rank has been a lifelong farmer in Fresno, Calif. He is currently serving as Administrator, Agriculture Stabilization and Conservation Service (ASCS), Department of Agriculture. Mr. Rank has been a leader in agribusiness in Fresno County, Calif., for many years. He was director, Huron Cotton Ginning Co.; Director, Western Region, ASCS; director, Ranchers Cotton Oil Co.; and director, Fresno County Farm Bureau.

Mr. Rank served in the U.S. Navy in 1943–45. He is married, has three children, and was born December 1, 1921, in Fresno, Calif.

Nomination of Elizabeth Jones To Be Engraver of the United States Mint at Philadelphia, Pennsylvania
July 13, 1981

The President today announced his intention to nominate Elizabeth Jones to be Engraver of the Mint of the United States at Philadelphia, Department of the Treasury, vice Frank Gasparro, resigned.

Miss Jones is a freelance medalist and artist. She has participated in various one-man and group shows, including five Tiffany & Co. exhibitions, H. Stern Jewellers exhibitions in Rio de Janeiro and São Paulo, Brazil, in 1967, and other exhibitions in Washington, D.C., New York City, Rome, Paris, Prague, Athens, Madrid, and Helsinki. She has been commissioned to design many medals for various groups and individuals, including medals commissioned by the Franklin Mint. She is a recipient of the Outstanding Sculptor of the Year Gold Medal from the American Numismatic Association (1972) and the Louis Bennett Award from the National Sculpture Society (1978).

Miss Jones graduated from Vassar College (B.A., 1957). She resides in Chatham, N.J., and was born May 31, 1935, in Montclair, N.J.

Appointment of Five Members of the Board of Directors of the Federal National Mortgage Association
July 13, 1981

The President today announced his intention to appoint the following individuals to be members of the Board of Directors of the Federal National Mortgage Association for terms ending on the date of the annual meeting of the stockholders in 1982.

Merrill Butler is currently president of Butler Housing Corp. (Irvine, Calif.) and Bullard Homes Corp. (Fresno, Calif.). He began his home building career in 1956 when he founded the Butler-Harbour Construction Co. in Anaheim, Calif. Mr. Butler is president of the National Association of Home Builders and is a member of the advisory committee of the Federal Home Loan Mortgage Corporation. He is a past president of the Building Industry Association of Southern California. He was named Southern California Builder of the Year by that association in 1978. Mr. Butler graduated from the University of Southern California (1948) and served during World War II as a combat officer and earned a Silver Star, Bronze Star, Purple Heart, Presidential Unit Citation, and Army Commendation Ribbon. Mr. Butler is married, has three children, and resides in Corona Del Mar, Calif. He was born February 18, 1925, in Los Angeles, Calif.

James B. Coles has been engaged as a general contractor and owner and chairman of the board of James B. Coles, Inc., and the Coles Development Co., Inc. (San Diego, Calif.), since 1972. He is a member of the National Association of Home Builders and serves on the executive board and board of directors of San Diego State University. Mr. Coles was Reagan for President finance chairman for San Diego, Imperial, and Riverside Counties in 1979–80. He graduated from San Diego State University (B.A., 1967) and served in the U.S. Army in 1960–63. Mr. Coles is married, has two daughters, and resides in Del Mar, Calif. He was born September 29, 1941, in Camden, N.J.

Bert A. Getz has been president and director of the Globe Corp., a family-owned holding company (Scottsdale, Ariz.) since 1959. He has also served as director of the Arizona Bank since 1970, and the First National Bank of Winnetka (Winnetka, Ill.) since 1968. Mr. Getz graduated from the University of Michigan (B.B.A., 1959). He is married, has three children, and resides in Scottsdale, Ariz. He was born May 7, 1937, in Chicago, Ill.

Dianne E. Ingels is currently an independent real estate broker, investor, and consultant in Colorado Springs, Colo. In 1965–68 she was a licensed realtor with Weidman and Co. and was a partner of Villa de Mesa development project. Miss Ingels was a partner with Smartt-Ingels & Associates, Realtors, in 1968–75. She was appointed to the Colorado Springs Urban Renewal Commission in 1972 and was elected chairman of the Commission in 1974. In 1976–77 Miss Ingels was president and broker, Ingels Co. She then created Dianne Ingels and Associates. She is a member of the National Association of Realtors and the Colorado Association of Realtors. She served on the board of directors of Columbia Savings and Loan Association. Miss Ingels graduated from the University of Colorado (B.S., 1963) and New York University (M.S., 1964). She resides in Colorado Springs, Colo., and was born August 8, 1941, in Denver, Colo.

James E. Lyon is currently chairman of the board and chief executive officer of the River Oaks Bank & Trust Co., the River Oaks Financial Corp., and Ruska Instruments Corp. He also is a member of the World Business Council, American Institute of Banking, Houston Bankers Association, National Board of Realtors, Texas Real Estate Association, Houston Board of Realtors, and the Houston Home Builders Association. Mr. Lyon has been actively involved in the Republican Party in Texas. He was Texas finance chairman for Citizens for Reagan in 1976 and was involved in fundraising activities during the 1980 Reagan-Bush campaign. Mr. Lyon attended Rice University in Houston and the University of Houston. He served in the U.S. Marine Corps in 1945–47.

Mr. Lyon has three children and resides in Houston, Tex. He was born August 25, 1927, in Houston.

Executive Order 12313—Specification of Hostage Return Date Under Hostage Relief Act of 1980
July 13, 1981

By the authority vested in me as President of the United States of America by sections 101(2)(A) and 205(b)(1) of the Hostage Relief Act of 1980 (Public Law 96–449; 94 Stat. 1967, 1972; 5 U.S.C. 5561 note) (the "Hostage Act"), it is hereby ordered, for the purposes of these sections of the Hostage Act, that January 21, 1981, is specified as the date on which all citizens and resident aliens of the United States who were placed in a captive status due to the seizure of the

United States Embassy in Iran have been returned to the United States or otherwise accounted for, and were no longer under foreign control.

RONALD REAGAN

The White House,
July 13, 1981.

[*Filed with the Office of the Federal Register, 10:56 a.m., July 14, 1981*]

White House Statement on the President's Meeting with Gaston Thorn, President of the Commission of European Communities
July 13, 1981

The President met with Gaston Thorn, President of the Commission of European Communities, from 2:30 p.m. to 2:55 p.m. in the Oval Office and Cabinet Room.

The meeting was the culmination of a series of meetings Mr. Thorn has had with officials of the United States. These include sessions with the Vice President, Secretary of State, the Secretary of the Treasury, the U.S. Trade Representative, and the Deputy Secretary of State.

The meeting with the President included discussion of a number of issues that will be presented by the United States and other countries at the economic summit in Ottawa. Mr. Thorn spoke of the interrelation between United States' economic policies and those of Europe and urged close consultation with European nations on the formulation and implementation of these policies. The meeting was described as warm and cordial.

Remarks at a Senate Republican Policy Committee Luncheon
July 14, 1981

Thank you, John and Howard. I appreciate that, and I appreciate your very warm welcome. I want to thank you all for accommodating to my schedule. It's nice to be on the end of a welcome for a change instead

of doing it the other way in the Oval Office, especially when it's a welcome from the leadership of the new majority party in the United States Senate.

So, Mr. Vice President, the gentlemen

I've recognized already, and Ted, Strom—I don't think I've had a chance to congratulate you yet, Strom, on being the President Pro Tem, and I do so now. I think all of you remember that just a few years ago we were not only an endangered species, there were some who said we had become extinct. And if that's true, an awful lot of you must be awfully stubborn elephants, because as far as I'm concerned, the most exciting story in politics today is the resurgence of the Grand Old Party, and we're the emerging majority party in America.

We all know why that's happening. We're convincing more and more Americans to come under our tent, not just because we're Republicans, but because we're offering better, more secure, and more exciting visions of the future. What we're saying, and what more and more citizens, I think, are saying, is that it's time to give this economy and this government back to the people. And let me tell you, after watching the phenomenal progress that you've made in just 5½ months, I'm more convinced than ever that we can, and we will, give it back to the people.

Howard Baker, Ted Stevens, Bob Dole, Pete Domenici, all the rest of you, thanks to your tremendous leadership and, let me add, thanks to the tremendous leadership by your counterparts on the House side, we've done more in a shorter period of time to put the economy of this country back on a sound footing than any government in the past 50 years. And I think you can be proud of that. But remember, we're still a long way from home. Three obstacles stand between us and the victory we want to give the people this summer—a victory they deserve and they've been waiting for so long.

First, we need a successful conference on the budget bill. And if you can give us that and pave the way for a final passage of more than $140 billion in budget savings, you will have demonstrated that reconciliation really works, and you'll have proved to the public that you really meant business when you promised to begin making this government live within its means.

Second, we have to have a good tax bill— I'm sure you knew I'd mention that— [*laughter*]—completed and ready to sign before Congress leaves for recess in August. Unless that happens, the new incentives the economy so badly needs to encourage more savings and investment will once again be in doubt.

Now, the so-called tax bill that is being peddled by the Democratic leadership in the House is actually something of a wolf in sheep's clothing, if I can coin a cliche. How can they look Americans in the eye and say that "we're reducing you taxes" when they know they're offering only a 15-percent tax cut against a 22-percent built-in tax increase with no tax cut at all for 1984? They say it's too dangerous to give individuals a commitment for 3 years ahead. And yet, when they talk about the business tax, they're planning to give them a cut that extends for 7 years ahead—continuous cuts. And it's a funny thing, too, how you can compare their approach to tax cuts with tax increases, because in 1977 they were responsible for the biggest single tax cut in our nation's history, and it extends in stages 9 years ahead, all the way up to 1986 when the last tax increase goes into effect.

Of course, they're offering the poor man's tax bill, and we're out to favor the rich. That's why they've gone out of their way to offer 2,500 commodities speculators a tax break of some $400 million. [*Laughter*]

The bottom line is that our bill reduces taxes in word and in deed while theirs deals in make-believe. The irony is, so many in Congress who now criticize our proposed tax reductions as inadequate for the workers are the very people who approved the terrible tax increases on the working Americans a few years ago in the first place. And yet, those same people are unwilling to go far enough to get the huge future tax increases reduced.

They offer the mirage of tax reduction while working to lock in a tax increase so they'll have more and more money, I suppose, to spend on more and more government. But it won't work, because I don't think you're fooled. And the American people aren't fooled; and they want us to start protecting their family budgets by giving less to the Federal budget, and we agree.

Our present tax system exerts a heavy

drag on the growth that it siphons out of the private economy—too large a share of personal and business purchasing power—and it reduces the financial incentives for personal effort, investment, and risktaking. The next time you're in a discussion with one of our friends across the aisle, you might quote that, because those are the words of John F. Kennedy when he gave us the last tax cut, real tax cut, that we've had in this government, almost 20 years ago.

Thank you all very much for inviting me to lunch.

Note: The President spoke at 12:19 p.m. in Room S–207 at the Capitol.

Prior to the luncheon, the President met in the Senate majority leader's office with the Vice President, Senator Strom Thurmond, Senator John Tower, chairman of the Republican Policy Committee, and Senator Howard H. Baker, Jr., Senate majority leader. Following the luncheon, the President visited briefly with Senator Robert C. Byrd, Senate minority leader.

Nomination of Dominick L. DiCarlo To Be an Assistant Secretary of State
July 14, 1981

The President today announced his intention to nominate Dominick L. DiCarlo to be an Assistant Secretary of State for International Narcotics Matters, vice K. Mathea Falco, resigned.

Mr. DiCarlo has been a member of the New York State Assembly since 1965, and a practicing attorney since 1954. In 1959–62 he was an Assistant U.S. Attorney for the Eastern District of New York, during the last 2 years of which he was Chief of the Organized Crime and Racketeering Section. Mr. DiCarlo was vice chairman of the New York Joint Legislative Committee on Crime in 1969–70 and the Select Committee on Correctional Institutions and Programs

(Attica Investigation) in 1972–73. In 1971–74 he chaired the New York State Assembly Standing Committee on Codes and was an ex-officio member of the New York State Law Revision Commission and the New York State Judicial Conference. In 1975–78 he was deputy minority leader of the New York State Assembly.

Mr. DiCarlo graduated from St. John's College, Brooklyn (B.A., 1950); St. John's University School of Law (LL.B., 1953); and New York University School of Law (LL.M., 1957).

Mr. DiCarlo is married, has four children, and resides in Brooklyn, N.Y. He was born March 11, 1928, in Brooklyn.

Nomination of Thomas R. Donnelly, Jr., To Be an Assistant Secretary of Health and Human Services
July 14, 1981

The President today announced his intention to nominate Thomas R. Donnelly, Jr., to be an Assistant Secretary of Health and Human Services (Legislation), vice William B. Welsh.

Since 1974 Mr. Donnelly has been managing partner with the Washington firm of

Louis C. Kramp & Associates, government relations counselors. He was president and chairman, TRD Associates, Inc., a public affairs counseling firm, in 1972–74; executive vice president, National Center for Voluntary Action, in 1970–72; and executive vice president, the United States Jaycees, in

627

1967–70. Prior to that position, Mr. Donnelly was with Air Products & Chemicals (Pittsburgh, Pa.) in 1963–65 and the Johns Manville Corp. in 1961–63.

Mr. Donnelly graduated from Princeton University (B.S.E., 1961). He is married, has three children, and resides in Springfield, Va. He was born May 23, 1939, in Steubenville, Ohio.

Nomination of William J. Dyess To Be United States Ambassador to the Netherlands
July 14, 1981

The President today announced his intention to nominate William J. Dyess, of Alabama, to be Ambassador to the Kingdom of the Netherlands, vice Geri M. Joseph, resigned.

Mr. Dyess entered the Foreign Service in 1958 and served in the Department as exchange program officer, and then intelligence research specialist. In 1960–61 he attended Serbo-Croatian language training at the Foreign Service Institute. He was political officer in Belgrade (1961–63) and in Copenhagen (1963–65). In 1965 he attended Russian language training at the Foreign Service Institute. In 1966–68 he was administrative officer, then political officer, in Moscow and political officer at the United States Mission Berlin, in 1968–70. In the Department, he was international relations officer (1970–75), Executive Director of the Bureau of Public Affairs (1975–77), and Deputy Assistant Secretary of State for Public Affairs (1977–80). Since 1980 he has been Assistant Secretary of State for Public Affairs.

Mr. Dyess graduated from the University of Alabama (B.A., 1950; M.A., 1951). He served in the U.S. Army in 1953–56. He received the Meritorious Honor Award in 1973. Mr. Dyess is married, has one child, and resides in Washington, D.C. He was born August 1, 1929, in Troy, Ala.

Appointment of George Allen as a Member of the President's Council on Physical Fitness and Sports
July 14, 1981

The President today announced the appointment of George Allen as a member of the President's Council on Physical Fitness and Sports, vice Alfred J. McGuire, resigned. The President also intends to appoint Mr. Allen Chairman.

Mr. Allen began his sports career as head football coach for Morningside College in Sioux City, Iowa, and Whittier College in California, then becoming the defensive coach for the Chicago Bears. He was the head coach of the Los Angeles Rams until 1971 when he become head coach, vice president, and general manager of the Washington Redskins. He is currently a football commentator and analyst with CBS Sports.

Mr. Allen has been actively involved in civic affairs. He served as the national chairman of the National Alliance of Business' Summer Job Program and in 1974 was the recipient of the Department of Justice Drug Enforcement Award. In 1978 he received the Award for Patriotism from the American Law Enforcement Officers Association. He is the recipient of three Presidential commendations.

Mr. Allen graduated from the University of Michigan (B.A., 1947; M.A., 1948). Mr.

Allen and his wife, Etty, have been married 28 years. They have four children and reside in Palos Verdes Estates, Calif. He was born April 29, 1922, in Detroit, Mich.

Nomination of Donald Eugene Santarelli To Be a Member of the Board of Directors of the Overseas Private Investment Corporation
July 15, 1981

The President today announced his intention to nominate Donald Eugene Santarelli to be a member of the Board of Directors of the Overseas Private Investment Corporation, United States International Development Cooperation Agency, for a term expiring December 17, 1983, vice Edward R. Marcus, term expired.

Mr. Santarelli has had a general law practice in Washington, D.C., concentrating on government affairs. Since 1975 he has been a member of the board of directors of the Corporation for Public Broadcasting and is currently serving as chairman of the Program Advisory Committee of the board. In 1973–74 he served as Administrator of the Law Enforcement Assistance Administration, Department of Justice. In 1969–72 he was Associate Deputy Attorney General at the Department. In 1968–69 he served as special counsel to the Senate Judiciary Committee on Constitutional Rights, Senator Sam Ervin, chairman. In 1967–68 he was minority counsel to the U.S. House of Representatives Committee on the Judiciary. In 1966–67 he served as Assistant U.S. Attorney for the District of Columbia.

Mr. Santarelli graduated from Mount St. Mary's College in 1955 and from the University of Virginia Law School in 1962. Mr. Santarelli was born July 22, 1937, in Hershey, Pa. He resides in Alexandria, Va.

Note: On June 5, the White House announced the President's intention to nominate Mr. Santarelli to be a member of the Board of Directors of the U.S. Synthetic Fuels Corporation. His name was withdrawn for that post.

Nomination of Carlos C. Campbell To Be an Assistant Secretary of Commerce
July 15, 1981

The President today announced his intention to nominate Carlos C. Campbell to be an Assistant Secretary of Commerce (Economic Development Administration), vice Jerry J. Jasinowski, resigned.

Since 1976 Mr. Campbell has been a management consultant. In 1975–76 he was Deputy Assistant Administrator, Department of the Interior, American Revolution Bicentennial Administration. Previously he was Director, Bicentennial Sports Programs, in 1974–76; Deputy Director, Program Review and Evaluation Division; and Director, Horizons Program, in 1974–75 in the Department. Mr. Campbell was a research fellow and management consultant in 1972–74. In 1969–72 he was special assistant to the Assistant Secretary of Housing and Urban Development (Community Planning and Management).

Mr. Campbell graduated from Michigan State University (B.S., 1959), U.S. Naval Post Graduate School (1965), and the Catholic University of America (1968).

Mr. Campbell is married, has two children, and resides in Reston, Va. He was born July 19, 1937, in Harlem, N.Y.

Statement on United States Nuclear Nonproliferation Policy
July 16, 1981

Our nation faces major challenges in international affairs. One of the most critical is the need to prevent the spread of nuclear explosives to additional countries. Further proliferation would pose a severe threat to international peace, regional and global stability, and the security interests of the United States and other countries. Our nation has been committed on a bipartisan basis to preventing the spread of nuclear explosives from the birth of the atomic age over 35 years ago. This commitment is shared by the vast majority of other countries. The urgency of this task has been highlighted by the ominous events in the Middle East.

The problem of reducing the risks of nuclear proliferation has many aspects, and we need an integrated approach to deal with it effectively. In the final analysis, the success of our efforts depends on our ability to improve regional and global stability and reduce those motivations that can drive countries toward nuclear explosives. This calls for a strong and dependable United States, vibrant alliances and improved relations with others, and a dedication to those tasks that are vital for a stable world order.

I am announcing today a policy framework that reinforces the longstanding objectives of our nation in nonproliferation and includes a number of basic guidelines.

The United States will:

• seek to prevent the spread of nuclear explosives to additional countries as a fundamental national security and foreign policy objective;

• strive to reduce the motivation for acquiring nuclear explosives by working to improve regional and global stability and to promote understanding of the legitimate security concerns of other states;

• continue to support adherence to the Treaty on the Non-Proliferation of Nuclear Weapons and to the Treaty for the Prohibition of Nuclear Weapons in Latin America (Treaty of Tlatelolco) by countries that have not accepted those treaties;

• view a material violation of these treaties or an international safeguards agreement as having profound consequences for international order and United States bilateral relations, and also view any nuclear explosion by a nonnuclear-weapon state with grave concern;

• strongly support and continue to work with other nations to strengthen the International Atomic Energy Agency to provide for an improved international safeguards regime;

• seek to work more effectively with other countries to forge agreement on measures for combating the risks of proliferation;

• continue to inhibit the transfer of sensitive nuclear material, equipment and technology, particularly where the danger of proliferation demands, and to seek agreement on requiring IAEA safeguards on all nuclear activities in a nonnuclear-weapon state as a condition for any significant new nuclear supply commitment.

I am also announcing that I will promptly seek the Senate's advice and consent to ratification of Protocol I of the Treaty of Tlatelolco.

The United States will cooperate with other nations in the peaceful uses of nuclear energy, including civil nuclear programs to meet their energy security needs, under a regime of adequate safeguards and controls. Many friends and allies of the United States have a strong interest in nuclear power and have, during recent years, lost confidence in the ability of our nation to recognize their needs.

We must reestablish this Nation as a predictable and reliable partner for peaceful nuclear cooperation under adequate safeguards. This is essential to our nonproliferation goals. If we are not such a partner, other countries will tend to go their own ways, and our influence will diminish. This would reduce our effectiveness in gaining the support we need to deal with proliferation problems.

To attain this objective, I am:

• instructing the executive branch agencies to undertake immediate efforts to ensure expeditious action on export requests and approval requests under agreements for peaceful nuclear cooperation where the necessary statutory requirements are met;

• requesting that the Nuclear Regulatory Commission act expeditiously on these matters.

The administration will also not inhibit or set back civil reprocessing and breeder reactor development abroad in nations with advanced nuclear power programs where it does not constitute a proliferation risk.

The United States will support IAEA programs and other international cooperative efforts in the areas of nuclear safety and environmentally sound nuclear waste management.

To carry out these policies, I am instructing the Secretary of State, working with the other responsible agencies, to give priority attention to efforts to reduce proliferation risks, to enhance the international nonproliferation regime and, consistent with United States security interests, to reestablish a leadership role for the United States in international nuclear affairs.

Message to the Congress Reporting Budget Deferrals and a Rescission
July 16, 1981

To the Congress of the United States:

In accordance with the Impoundment Control Act of 1974, I herewith report a new proposal to rescind $173.0 million in budget authority previously provided by the Congress. In addition, I am reporting ten new deferrals totaling $495.1 million, and revisions to four previously reported deferrals increasing the amount deferred by $76.4 million.

The rescission proposal affects a program in the Department of Energy. The deferrals affect programs in the Departments of Agriculture, Commerce, Defense, Health and

Human Services, Justice, and Labor, as well as the Railroad Retirement Board and the United States Railway Association.

The details of each rescission proposal and deferral are contained in the attached reports.

RONALD REAGAN

The White House,
July 16, 1981.

Note: The attachments detailing the rescission proposal and deferrals are printed in the Federal Register *of July 21, 1981.*

Appointment of Rita Ricardo-Campbell as a Member of the President's Economic Policy Advisory Board
July 16, 1981

The President today announced the appointment of Rita Ricardo-Campbell to be a member of the President's Economic Policy Advisory Board.

Since 1968 Dr. Campbell has been a senior fellow at the Hoover Institution, Stanford, Calif. In 1973–78 she received a

courtesy appointment from the Health Services Administration, Stanford University Medical Center. In 1961–68 Dr. Campbell was archivist and research associate, Hoover Institution. She was visiting professor, San Jose State University in 1960–61. She was a consulting economist in 1957–60; economist, House of Representatives Ways and Means Committee, in 1953; economist, Wage Stabilization Board, in 1951–53; assistant professor, Tufts College, in 1948–51; instructor, Harvard University, in 1946–48; and teaching fellow and tutor, Harvard University, in 1945–46.

Dr. Campbell graduated from Simmons College, Boston, Mass. (B.A., 1941) and Harvard University (M.A., 1945; Ph. D., 1946). She has authored many books and articles on health issues.

Dr. Campbell is married, has three children, and resides in Los Altos Hills, Calif. She was born March 16, 1920, in Boston, Mass.

Remarks on Signing the Steel Industry Compliance Extension Act of 1981
July 17, 1981

Well, we're here for a bill signing and regulation reform, I'm sure we've made plain, is an essential part of putting America's economic house in order.

Today, I'm proud to sign this legislation which represents the kind of regulatory common sense that is needed to achieve enduring economic progress.

The steel industry has always been, of course, one of the vital components of our nation's economy, employing nearly 600,000 people with annual wages and salaries amounting to over $12 billion. But much like the economy as a whole, the steel industry has been abused by a decade of irrational taxation and overregulation. At a time when other nations nurtured their basic industries, our companies found themselves in an adversary relationship with their own government. H.R.—House Resolution 3520 permits the steel industry to stretch out compliance with the Clean Air Act, providing regulatory relief without discarding our goals. Its phased-in program of compliance will, in the long run, improve the efficiency and productivity of the steel industry and will provide clean air as well.

This legislation uses the word "reasonable" twice. The dictionary says that word means "being within the bounds of reason."

Another definition says, "not extreme, or to be moderate or fair." This Nation has been suffering from regulation that is not within the bounds of reason, regulation that is neither fair nor moderate. The bipartisan support given this legislation underscores that the American people, Republicans and Democrats alike, understand the need for a new balanced approach to regulation. In the years ahead, we intend to maintain a responsible working relationship with business and labor, ensuring that jobs and progress go hand-in-hand with necessary regulation.

This act, affecting one of America's most vital industries, is a symbol of the administration's commitment—a commitment to cast aside the over-zealous and unnecessary regulation that has shackled most productive forces in our economy. And with that said, I shall now sit down and affix my signature to that piece of legislation.

Note: The President spoke at 11:07 a.m. in the Rose Garden at the White House. The signing ceremony was attended by Members of Congress and a group of steel industry representatives.

As enacted, H.R. 3520 is Public Law 97–23, approved July 17.

Message to the Congress Transmitting the National Energy Policy Plan
July 17, 1981

To the Congress of the United States:

The National Energy Policy Plan that I am sending you, as required by Section 801 of the Department of Energy Organization Act (Public Law 95–91), represents a break from the format and philosophy of the two National Energy Plans that preceded it.

Our national energy plan should not be a rigid set of production and conservation goals dictated by Government. Our primary objective is simply for our citizens to have *enough* energy, and it is up to them to decide how much energy that is, and in what form and manner it will reach them. When the free market is permitted to work the way it should, millions of individual choices and judgments will produce the proper balance of supply and demand our economy needs.

Overall, the outlook for this country's energy supplies is not nearly as grim as some have painted it, although our problems are not all behind us. The detailed projections, along with the supplementary documents on environmental and economic questions, are being submitted separately by the Secretary of Energy.

The approach explained in the basic National Energy Policy Plan cannot be divorced from the Administration's program for national economic recovery. Energy is one important aspect of our society, but it is only one.

This Administration's actions to end oil price controls and to dismantle the cumbersome regulatory apparatus associated with those controls demonstrate the intent stated in my February 18 economic message to minimize Federal intervention in the marketplace. Reforms in leasing policies and the removal of unnecessary environmental restrictions upon the production, delivery, and use of energy are part of this same effort to reduce bureaucratic burdens on all Americans.

This does not mean that the Federal government is withdrawing from all involvement in energy. It cannot and should not. The Government itself is directly responsible for lands which contain a major share of our resource wealth.

There is also an appropriate Federal role in certain long-term research and development related to energy production and distribution. The goal of these projects is to develop promising technological innovations to the point where private enterprise can reasonably assess their risks.

Given our continued vulnerability to energy supply disruptions, certain emergency preparations—such as rapid filling of the Strategic Petroleum Reserve—remain principally a Government responsibility. But our basic role is to provide a sound and stable economic and policy environment that will enable our citizens, businesses, and governmental units at all levels to make rational decisions on energy use and production—decisions that reflect the true value, in every sense, of all the Nation's resources.

RONALD REAGAN

The White House,
July 17, 1981.

Note: The Plan is entitled "Securing America's Energy Future, The National Energy Policy Plan, A Report to the Congress Required by Title VIII of the Department of Energy Organization Act (Public Law 95–91)—July 1981, U.S. Department of Energy."

Message to the International Whaling Commission
July 17, 1981

I want to take this opportunity to affirm the United States Government's continuing commitment to whale protection and to urge you to support our proposal for an indefinite moratorium on commercial whaling.

Throughout human history, whales have evoked awe and wonder. They are the largest creatures ever to have lived on this earth; yet they are also among the most mysterious. It is this mysterious quality that gives whales their appeal and increases the importance of effective management that could assure whale populations for the future.

The United States has long supported scientific research and efforts to strengthen management procedures used by the International Whaling Commission. We believe that further revisions to management procedures are essential to reflect the inadequate information on whale biology, behavior, population dynamics, and, most importantly, abundance. Even such revisions, however, will probably not secure the necessary protection. Our cooperative efforts in the past to regulate whaling have been tragically unsuccessful and species after species has been successfully over-exploited and reduced to protected status. Indeed, the International Whaling Commission prohibits all commercial whaling on the majority of whale stocks because of their reduced abundance. We have no basis to believe that commercial whaling will not continue to reduce whale stocks.

It is time to recognize the errors of the past. Available information is inadequate to protect the whales while commercial whaling continues, and it is for this reason as well as others that the United States has proposed an indefinite moratorium on commercial whaling. I urge you to join with us and other people throughout the world to secure the protection of these magnificent creatures and wish you success in your important work.

RONALD REAGAN

Note: The text of the message was made available by the Office of the Press Secretary on July 20. It was not issued as a White House press release.

Letter to Congressional Leaders About the Social Security System
July 18, 1981

The highest priority of my Administration is restoring the integrity of the Social Security System. Those 35 million Americans who depend on Social Security expect and are entitled to prompt bipartisan action to resolve the current financial problem.

At the same time, I deplore the opportunistic political maneuvering, cynically designed to play on the fears of many Americans, that some in the Congress are initiating at this time. These efforts appear designed to exploit an issue rather than find a solution to the urgent Social Security problem. They would also have the unfortunate effect of disrupting the budget conference and reversing the actions of a majority of both Houses of the Congress. Such a result would jeopardize our economic recovery program so vital to the well-being of the Nation.

In order to tell the American people the facts, and to let them know that I shall fight to preserve the Social Security System and protect their benefits, I will ask for time on television to address the Nation as soon as possible.

During this address, I will call on the Congress to lay aside partisan politics, and join me in a constructive effort to put Social Security on a permanently sound financial basis as soon as the 97th Congress returns in September.

Sincerely,

RONALD REAGAN

Note: This is the text of identical letters addressed to Senate Majority Leader

Howard H. Baker, Jr., Senate Minority Leader Robert C. Byrd, Speaker of the House of Representatives Thomas P. O'Neill, Jr., and House Minority Leader Robert H. Michel.

The text of the letter was released by the Office of the Press Secretary on July 20.

Nomination of Donald L. Totten To Be a United States Commissioner of the International Joint Commission—United States and Canada
July 20, 1981

The President today announced his intention to nominate Donald L. Totten to be a Commissioner on the part of the United States on the International Joint Commission—United States and Canada.

Since 1980 Mr. Totten has served in the Illinois State Senate after serving 8 years in the Illinois State House of Representatives. He served on the Appropriations, Higher Education, and Elections Committees.

Before his legislative career, Mr. Totten was assistant to the director of the Department of Transportation for the State of Illinois. He spent 15 years in the engineering and business fields.

In addition to his business and legislative experience, he was elected Republican committeeman of Schaumburg Township in 1966 and reelected in 1970, 1974, and 1978. In 1976 he was State chairman of Illinois Citizens for Reagan and a member of the steering committee of the Illinois President Ford Committee. He served as regional political director for the Reagan for President Committee and State chairman for the Reagan for President Committee in Illinois in 1980.

Mr. Totten graduated from the University of Notre Dame (1955). He is married, has three children, and resides in Hoffman Estates, Ill. He was born February 19, 1933, in Brooklyn, N.Y.

Summary of Political Issues by the Chairman of the Ottawa Economic Summit Conference
July 20, 1981

1. Our discussion of international affairs confirmed our unity of view on the main issues that confront us all. We are determined to face them together in a spirit of solidarity, cooperation and responsibility.

2. We all view with concern the continuing threats to international security and stability. Lasting peace can only be built on respect for the freedom and dignity of nations and individuals. We appeal to all governments to exercise restraint and responsi-

bility in international affairs and to refrain from exploiting crises and tensions.

3. In the Middle East, we remain convinced that a solution must be found to the Arab-Israeli dispute. We all deplore the escalation of tension and continuing acts of violence now occurring in the region. We are deeply distressed by the scale of destruction, particularly in Lebanon, and the heavy civilian loss of life on both sides. We call on all states and parties to exercise re-

straint, in particular to avoid retaliation which only results in escalation; and to forego acts which could lead, in the current tense situation in the area, to further bloodshed and war.

4. We are particularly concerned, in this respect, by the tragic fate of the Lebanese people. We support the efforts now in progress to permit Lebanon to achieve a genuine national reconciliation, internal security and peace with its neighbours.

5. In East-West Relations, we are seriously concerned about the continuing build-up of Soviet military power. Our concern is heightened by Soviet actions which are incompatible with the exercise of restraint and responsibility in international affairs. We ourselves, therefore, need a strong defense capability. We will be firm in insisting on a balance of military capabilities and on political restraint. We are prepared for dialogue and cooperation to the extent that the Soviet Union makes this possible. We are convinced of the importance of working towards balanced and verifiable arms control and disarmament agreements in pursuit of undiminished security at lower levels of armament and expenditure.

6. We welcome the fact that, at the Madrid Conference on Security and Cooperation in Europe, Western countries have just taken another major initiative aimed at defining the area to be covered by the measures the proposed European Disarmament Conference would negotiate. Equally important, they have proposed a number of human rights provisions that would give new hope for individuals deprived of their freedom. We believe that Soviet acceptance of these initiatives would enable a balanced conclusion of the Madrid meeting and a substantial reduction of tension in Europe.

7. As regards Afghanistan, about which we publicly stated our firm and unanimous position at last year's Venice Summit, we note that the situation remains unchanged. Therefore, with the overwhelming majority of nations, we continue to condemn the Soviet military occupation of Afghanistan. We support international efforts to achieve the complete withdrawal of Soviet troops and to restore to the Afghan people, who are fighting a war of liberation, their right to determine their own future. We note with approval the constructive proposal of the European Council for an international conference to bring about this result and call upon the Soviet Union to accept it. We are grateful for the report given us by Foreign Secretary Carrington on his recent visit to Moscow, and his discussions there, on behalf of the Ten, on the international conference proposal.

8. Believing as we do that the Kampuchean people are entitled to self-determination, we welcome and support the Declaration of the International Conference on Kampuchea.

9. Together with other states and regional organizations, we are resolved to do what is necessary to enhance regional security and to ensure a peace built on the independence and dignity of sovereign nations. All peoples should be free to chart their own course without fear of outside intervention. To that end, we shall continue to promote peaceful resolution of disputes and to address underlying social and economic problems. We reaffirm our conviction that respect for independence and genuine non-alignment are important for international peace and security.

10. Recalling the statement on refugees adopted at the Venice Summit, we are seriously concerned over the growing plight of refugees throughout the World. We reaffirm our support for international relief efforts and our appeal to all governments to refrain from actions which can lead to massive flows of refugees.

Note: As printed above, the summary follows the text issued at the summit conference and made available by the Office of the Press Secretary. It was not issued as a White House press release.

Ottawa Economic Summit Conference Statement on Terrorism
July 20, 1981

1. The Heads of State and Government, seriously concerned about the active support given to international terrorism through the supply of money and arms to terrorist groups, and about the sanctuary and training offered terrorists, as well as the continuation of acts of violence and terrorism such as aircraft hijacking, hostage-taking and attacks against diplomatic and consular personnel and premises, reaffirm their determination vigorously to combat such flagrant violations of international law. Emphasizing that all countries are threatened by acts of terrorism in disregard of fundamental human rights, they resolve to strengthen and broaden action within the international community to prevent and punish such acts.

2. The Heads of State and Government view with particular concern the recent hijacking incidents which threaten the safety of international civil aviation. They recall and reaffirm the principles set forth in the 1978 Bonn Declaration and note that there are several hijackings which have not been resolved by certain states in conformity with their obligations under international law. They call upon the governments concerned to discharge their obligations promptly and thereby contribute to the safety of international civil aviation.

3. The Heads of State and Government are convinced that, in the case of the hijacking of a Pakistan International Airlines aircraft in March, the conduct of the Babrak Karmal government of Afghanistan, both during the incident and subsequently in giving refuge to the hijackers, was and is in flagrant breach of its international obliga-

tions under the Hague Convention to which Afghanistan is a party, and constitutes a serious threat to air safety. Consequently the Heads of State and Government propose to suspend all flights to and from Afghanistan in implementation of the Bonn Declaration unless Afghanistan immediately takes steps to comply with its obligations. Furthermore, they call upon all states which share their concern for air safety to take appropriate action to persuade Afghanistan to honour its obligations.

4. Recalling the Venice Statement on the Taking of Diplomatic Hostages, the Heads of State and Government approve continued cooperation in the event of attacks on diplomatic and consular establishments or personnel of any of their governments. They undertake that in the event of such incidents, their governments will immediately consult on an appropriate response. Moreover, they resolve that any state which directly aids and abets the commission of terrorist acts condemned in the Venice Statement, should face a prompt international response. It was agreed to exchange information on terrorist threats and activities, and to explore cooperative measures for dealing with and countering acts of terrorism, for promoting more effective implementation of existing anti-terrorist conventions, and for securing wider adherence to them.

Note: As printed above, the statement follows the text issued at the summit conference and made available by the Office of the Press Secretary. It was not issued as a White House press release.

Concluding Statements of the Ottawa Economic Summit Conference Participants
July 21, 1981

Prime Minister Trudeau. Good afternoon, ladies and gentlemen. I should wish first on behalf of my colleagues at the table here to express our welcome to the press here and in accordance with the practices, established practices, and as Chairman of the summit meeting this year, I must make a statement summarizing the main points we have dealt with in the course of the last few days, and each of my colleagues will in turn speak to you.

The Ottawa Summit was met at a time of rapid change and great challenge to world economic progress and peace. East-West relations have been affected by the increase in the armed forces of the U.S.S.R. and its ever-increasing presence in the world. The political and economic situation of many countries has made it difficult for them to adapt to the new changes. The members of the summit meeting have also been victims of these changes and whatever we have attempted to do in the course of the last years was not necessarily carried out. We have had to reexamine the situation and restructure our activities so that, of course, there has been some pessimism about this summit.

Of course, it seemed to have been a difficult one but in my dual capacity as a participant and Chairman I am able to say, "No, the pessimists were not justified." We have met for many hours, and these contacts, of course, promote mutual trust and confidence in facing the crises we may have to—which challenge us. We've had very comprehensive discussions and frank discussions during our meetings. We have not tried to hide our divergences. We realize that we are dealing with economies which have different structures and have different reactions to the evolving situation. We have agreed that we could not revitalize our economies by isolating ourselves from one another. We have agreed on the fundamentals and realize we must take into account in our politics the impact it may have on our partners.

The whole burden of that fight cannot be made on monetary policy alone. And third, levels and movements of interest rates in one country can make life more difficult for other countries by influencing the exchange rates. This is something to which we must all remain sensitive and which we must try to minimize.

We must also pursue responsible trade policies. Over the years, as summit partners, we have warned against succumbing to the temptation of protection. These warnings have served us well. If we had drifted into protectionism, we might have conjured up an economic crisis similar to that of the 1930's. We have reiterated our strong commitment to an open, liberal, and multilateral trading system. We have agreed to deal with trade distortions. But we are determined not to lay the burdens of adjustment at the doorstep of our neighbors. We are looking forward to working with others on a trade agenda for the 1980's.

I regard this consensus about trade policy as one of the most important to have emerged from our meeting, not least for a major trading nation like Canada.

One of the uncertainties hovering over this summit was how it would deal with the North-South relationship. It's no secret to anyone that I attach very great importance to that relationship as an element of fundamental equity of mutual interests and benefits, and of global security.

The Ottawa Summit was the first of a series of important meetings this year where the North-South relationship will be at the center of the agenda. It seemed important to me, therefore, that the signal emanating from Ottawa should be clear and that it could be positive. For such a signal to be persuasive, it had to come from all of us jointly. That was the purpose of much of the travel, that as Chairman of this year's meetings I undertook in the weeks immediately preceding the summit.

The world looked to the Ottawa Summit for some sign of movement, some basis for hope that progress is possible, that the logjam can be broken. I'm very pleased with what we've been able to achieve. Our discussions showed a common appreciation of the magnitude of the problem and a common readiness to respond to it. There is now a disposition on the part of all summit countries to pursue any opportunity for meaningful progress, including what are known as global negotiations. That openness to the process of global negotiations represents a consensus which did not exist before our summit and seemed very remote not too many months ago.

The message we send from this meeting to the developing countries is the following: First, we respect your independence and support genuine nonalignment as a contribution to international peace and stability and as a basis for cooperation. Second, we look to you to play a full part in the international economic system and to become closely integrated to it. Third, we are ready to participate with you in preparations for a process of global negotiations. Fourth, we appreciate the problems of energy supply which you are encountering and are prepared to join with the surplus oil-exporting countries in examining how best we might jointly help you in developing your indigenous energy reserves. Five, we recognize the importance of more food production in your countries and of greater world food security and will try to make increased resources available for these purposes. Six, we will maintain our strong multilateral commitment to the international financial institutions and to the role they have played in alleviating the problems of development. And lastly, we will direct the major portion of our aid to the poorer countries.

On the occasion of this year's summit meeting, it seemed to us we could not ignore the fact that the strengthening of the armed forces in the Soviet Union has had an impact on the resources of our country and on the orientations which we have had to follow. We are convinced of the need for a strong defense capability, but we're also open to the possibility of dialog and negotiation with the Soviet Union, particularly as regards the nuclear armaments and security with less armaments and diminished cost.

I should wish, in conclusion, as Prime Minister of Canada, to say that we were very happy to be the host nation of this summit meeting. I am particularly grateful to all those who have accepted the challenge for this great endeavor and have provided the maximum of effort in assuring success. May I be permitted also to express deep gratitude to my colleagues at this table for having made my task so easy and to wish them Godspeed as they return to their own countries.

I will now call on the President of the United States, President Reagan.

President Reagan. Prime Minister Trudeau, I am sure I speak for all of us in thanking you for the welcome we've had and the hospitality that we've enjoyed during our 2 days together in Montebello. *Merci.* You've been a most gracious host, and my fellow countrymen and I shall long be grateful.

Not long ago, the conventional wisdom was that our seven nations were more sharply divided than any time in years. Only three of us had attended an economic summit before, and the rest of us are still in the first grade, the first-year class.

To the outside world this looked like it would be a difficult summit. Inflation rates are running at incredible levels. Unemployment, I should say, disrupts the lives of millions of people, and new fears of protectionism are sweeping across our continents. The agenda of Montebello represented an enormous challenge for all of us. The true measure of these past 2 days, days filled with candid but always friendly talks, is that we leave with a true sense of common understanding and common purpose. We've discussed at great length how each one of us is addressing economic problems at home while working in concert to assure that we are sensitive to the impact of our actions upon our partners.

I'm grateful to the other leaders here for their degree of understanding and support for the economic policies we're embarked upon in the United States. We have also resolved that we shall resist protectionism and support an open, expanding system for multilateral trade. And, as you have been told by the Prime Minister, we shall work together in helping the developing nations move toward full partnership in that system.

As Chancellor Schmidt has told us, our unity in economic matters is the best insurance we have against a return to the disastrous "beggar-thy-neighbor" policies of another era. Economic unity and political unity are two great goals we must continue to pursue. All our nations share democratic insitutions based on a belief in human dignity, freedom, and the preeminence of the individual. I believe that we depart with fresh confidence and optimism about the future of democratic values and our societies.

Many uncertainties still lie ahead; much remains to be done. But, as an American, I would like to recall for you an inspiring story of my native land. It's the story of young Franklin Roosevelt, who was struck down by polio in the prime of life and then, struggling to cover and to scale new heights. I mention it because much of that struggle took place on a little island not too far from here in New Brunswick, Canada, and the story is remembered by a very appropriate title, "Sunrise at Campobello."

Now, today, as we leave Montebello, I just can't resist the suggestion that over the past few years our nations have suffered from an affliction too, an economic affliction. I hope sometime in the future people will look back and say that here, in these talks, we began to put our nations back on the road to economic recovery and that a new Sun rose at Montebello.

That is a hope I know all of us share. Thank you very much.

Prime Minister Trudeau. Thank you, President Reagan. I now give the floor to the President of the French Republic, President Mitterrand.

President Mitterrand. I, too, would like to express my thanks to Mr. Pierre Elliott Trudeau, Prime Minister, and I would like to thank the Canadian Government for their excellent welcome and for the very favorable conditions under which the Ottawa or Montebello Summit was carried out. These conditions were so favorable that we were able to progress, to achieve work, and even to achieve some conclusions.

You know that France has an original policy, a new policy, if you like, within this framework, as compared to the theme generally put forward. Now, I call this an original policy. It is our own peculiar policy. We have our own objectives, and it was important for us to see whether it was possible—and I had no doubt this was possible—for us to fulfill this policy in harmony with the others. By the others, I mean our main partners, those represented here and a few others as well. This has been possible partly because everybody participated, partly because everybody has realized what elements in our own policies can harm other

countries' policies and what must, therefore, be set aside.

We have all realized what can be favorable to our common success and should, thus, be supported. But this has succeeded also because France is in favor of solidarity. We support, first of all, our friends. We think of history—particularly the history of the past half century in which we have seen disruptions, crises, and war—and we, thus, are united behind a certain number of fundamental changes, particularly freedom—freedom concerning the international level and freedom concerning democracy and democratic values within each of our countries.

We stand solidly behind our friends, and we also fully support those who, without being represented here, have been kept in mind in many of our discussions, and in many, in fact, of our decisions. I'm thinking more particularly of the countries of the Third World, more particularly the poorer among the countries of the Third World.

Right from the beginning, I wanted to emphasize the fact that we have to cooperate, to restrict as much as possible erratic exchange rates in our currencies, and to avoid as much as possible, as well, high interest rates. This is not a French problem; it is a European problem. In fact, I can say that this is a worldwide problem. I can say this taking into account possible consequences of present trends.

If you have a look at the text of our communique, you will see that there are a certain number of points being put forward concerning these issues. Similarly, right from the start, our position was in favor of everything that is able to bring down protectionism provided, of course, that right from the start we are all familiar with the whole set of existing mechanisms—mechanisms which mean that here and there protectionism is much too present.

Concerning trade with East bloc countries, as the communique says, a new examination of the situation will be carried out shortly. I have expressed the hope that, concerning this issue as concerning all the others, we take stock very precisely of the state of trade with those countries and that we take stock of the strategic consequences that might arise. This is also a point included in the communique.

In addition to this, priority had to be given during our talks to a policy towards countries of the Third World, what we call North-South relations. This is necessary not simply because it is our duty, but also because it is in our own interest. We must be distrustful of any attitude that I would term paternalistic. It is when we will be able to expand trade on stable bases, when we will be able to stabilize raw material prices—once this is done—it will be possible for those countries to set up lasting development plans. And once they have done this, we, the industrialized countries, will be able to fulfill our tasks.

And I think that along the lines of what we call the energy affiliate and along the lines of global negotiations which will be referred to again at Cancún, and also concerning international relations, I would say that on all these points progress has been achieved. We have been able to outline our objectives clearly.

And then, particularly during our informal meetings, we discussed problems concerning international relations, concerning the balance of forces. The position of France has always been as follows: equilibrium above anything else. Of course, equilibrium has to dominate not simply the matter of forces, but it should determine the nature, the type of negotiation to be opened up—the aim being to ensure disarmament and peace.

In conclusion, I would like to say that in Paris, or perhaps I should say in France, the next summit will be held. As you know, we have reached the end of a first cycle here in Canada. This was the seventh summit. So a new cycle of such summit meetings will begin, and I am very happy that the first element, the first step in this cycle, will take place in France. I will be happy to welcome there, my friends and partners, gathered here today. And since it is my task, I will continue to put forward and defend the interests of my country, but I will make sure that the summit of the industrialized countries will make it possible for us to continue along the path of understanding of our common interests and of our common tasks.

Thank you, very much. Thank you, Mr. President.

Prime Minister Trudeau. The Chancellor of the Federal Republic of Germany, Chancellor Schmidt, now has the floor.

Chancellor Schmidt. Thank you, Mr. Chairman, ladies and gentlemen. First of all, I, too, would like to thank you very warmly for the welcome, the hospitality of your country, and for the way you have acted as Chairman. You have been a very fair, very just Chairman. Thank you very much, Mr. Trudeau.

I think that we have found many areas in which we have been able to agree, and there were also many other areas or sectors in which close cooperation is possible and in which I think we can achieve or have already achieved a compromise. We have all expressed our desire to fight inflation and unemployment and to achieve competent and strong world trade and world economy.

I would like to stress these points because this time, even more so than in the past, the countries were represented by heads of state who use different economic policies or recipes, if I can call them this, in their own countries, in the range between monetarism and Keynesian theory.

I would like to bring up four points. Firstly, the main role played by trade policy. We agreed here that we do not wish to adopt any policies that take account only of national goals and do not take account of the repercussions they may have on the world economy. We do not wish to pursue such national policies.

I'd like to refer you to points 21 through 24 of the communique more particularly. We all face considerable pressure towards protectionism in our own governments, and we have all here expressed the desire to avoid such protectionism with a view to maintaining the strength and freedom of world trade.

Secondly, another important subject was that concerning the problems caused by high interest rates. We had a very detailed and interesting discussion without any accusations from one of the other parties, and several participants mentioned what negative repercussions a longlasting, high interest rate would have on their national economies. This is true in any case for the German economy, particularly if you keep in mind the fact that the European economies have already been more strongly affected by the second oil price rise than was expected a couple of years ago.

We also welcome the fact that the United States of America has expressed the intention to do their very best to bring down these high interest rates. President Reagan, too, has told us that the American economy is also suffering from high interest rates.

It has not yet been able to see whether the fight against inflation in the United States might take certain different paths, which is why I have had to point out that my government, when I go back to Bonn, will begin to take certain decisions concerning the fact that, unfortunately for the time being, we will still have to deal with high interest rates and that we will thus have to take certain measures.

The third point, North-South relations, I would like to emphasize what Prime Minister Trudeau said a moment ago, and I would like to say, quite clearly, that we have full respect towards truly nonaligned countries, towards genuine nonalignment, which we consider to be an essential element of stability throughout the world.

I would also like to announce that the Federal Government in Bonn will support the organization of global negotiations in the near future. I am happy that we have already been able to hold discussions on the upcoming summit in Cancún.

Fourthly, I would like to emphasize the importance of the exchange of views involving the basic agreement concerning East-West relations where we are talking about equilibrium in military forces, dialog, and preparedness to cooperation. An exchange of views about present-day problems, about arms limitation and arms control, more particularly, were particularly important to me.

And I was also very much interested in the exchange of views about the present-day situation in the Middle East. We have expressed the common desire to see peace be established in that part of the world in the near future. We all want the vicious circle of the use of violence in that part of the world to be ended.

In conclusion, I would like to thank very warmly President Reagan, President Mitterrand, my colleagues Prime Minister Thatcher, Mr. Spadolini, Mr. Suzuki, and more particularly, to our host, Prime Minister Pierre Trudeau. I would like to thank you all for the openness, the frankness with which you all spoke.

As far as I am concerned, I have been very much enriched by this summit meeting, and I have to say that I'm happy to note that we have become better acquainted and that we are all determined not to accept that we should act without taking account of each other's problems. But quite on the contrary, we have said strongly that we will take into account everybody else's interests and problems. These are two essential points for me.

Thank you.

Prime Minister Trudeau. Thank you very much, Chancellor. From Great Britain, Prime Minister Thatcher.

Prime Minister Thatcher. Mr. Chairman, can I join my colleagues in paying a very warm tribute to your skilled chairmanship and thorough preparations. I think our success at this summit owes a great deal to those two things. I'd like also to say thank you to our Canadian hosts for the excellent arrangements they made, both in Montebello and in Ottawa.

It is my third economic summit. And over that period, we've increasingly given time in our discussions to the major political issues of the day such as Afghanistan and the Middle East, as well as to the economic problems that face us. I think this development reflects reality, because political issues and economic matters can't be isolated from one another and treated separately. They interact at every level, national and international. And I think this reality was recognized more at this summit than at any other. And the result, I think, was a workmanlike, balanced discussion which comprehended all of the major problems, whether economic or political, that face the Western world.

On these substantive issues, I'd like to confine my comments to four points: First, the world economy. At the last two summits in Tokyo and Venice, our work was dominated by the impact of the second oil price shock on the world economy. We then considered the impact it would have and how we should react to it. This time, of course, we met in the trough of the recession which that shock produced. But we've had to look at the whole range of economic questions, at the twin evils of inflation and unemployment, the need to adopt our economies and attitudes in order to beat unemployment, and of monetary disorders producing high interest rates and volatile exchange rates.

We all agreed on the need to fight inflation as the precondition for defeating unemployment as you have emphasized, Mr. Chairman, and on the need for low monetary growth, on the need for containing public borrowing, and for tight control of government expenditure. We are all giving effect to these principles in our own policies according to our own different circumstances.

Now, the second substantive issue on which I'd like to comment is developing countries. I think I take away three salient thoughts from our discussions on relations with developing countries. The first is that we share many of the problems of the world economy with them—the need to develop energy resources, to encourage investment, to fight inflation and unemployment, and to expand trade. All of these things we share with them. The second thing that we share is that we welcome discussion with them in whatever ways or groups are useful. And the third is, we must pay particular regard to the needs of the poorer countries. We agreed to direct a major portion of our aid to the poorer countries, and I would like to stress that the United Kingdom has a particularly good record on that.

Thirdly, a few comments about the Middle East. We have been meeting in the shadow of a further outbreak of fierce fighting in the Middle East. Once again, the unfortunate people of Lebanon are bearing the brunt of a conflict that is not of their seeking. And whatever any of us may think about the causes, we all agree on the need for an urgent cease-fire in Lebanon, for an end to the loss of innocent civilian life there and, above all, for a solution to the conflict

between Arabs and Israel from which this violence flows. In the United Kingdom, we shall continue to use all our influence for this purpose.

And the last issue on which I'd like to comment—East-West relations. We discussed this scene and the concern that we all feel about the extent of the Soviet military threat to our interests. Speaking for Britain, I've been heartened by the strength of common purpose that I sensed in our discussions. We all agreed, and we agreed with real determination, on the need to maintain a strong defense capability and to insist on the need for military balance. Of course, that goes hand-in-hand with our readiness to negotiate arms control agreements that will ensure genuine security at a lower level of weaponry and resources.

So, Mr. Chairman, our discussions have linked the two aspects of the preservation of the free world and the free market economy which sustains it, namely, defense and the maintenance of peace and the health and soundness of the world economy. Altogether, a very successful summit on which you, Mr. Chairman, and Canada deserve our thanks and congratulations.

Thank you.

Prime Minister Trudeau. Ms. Thatcher, thank you. I will now call on the Prime Minister of Japan, Prime Minister Suzuki.

Prime Minister Suzuki. Thank you, Mr. Chairman. For this most successful conclusion of this Ottawa Summit, we are indebted to the outstanding chairmanship of Prime Minister Trudeau and the most generous cooperation by the Government of Canada. I am grateful, Mr. Prime Minister, beyond expression.

The fundamental task of summitry, particularly this summit, is for us to deal with political and economic difficulties that threaten the peace and the prosperity of the world. It is in this sense that as the sole representative having crossed the Pacific Ocean to join this summitry, to say that the nations of Asia and the Pacific also have much expectation of and interest in this summit.

Now, as regards the fruits of this summit, there have been many fruits—on East-West relations, North-South issues, and various problems that face all of us in the West within us. We have committed ourselves and expressed this commitment that we should tackle these problems with a common perception and sense of common objectives in a way that befits our respective nations and its strength and circumstances.

Another fruit is that we have felt strongly that we should demonstrate that the Western political, economic, and social institutions are superior to those in the East. And also to step up our cooperation with the Third World and pledging ourselves to the steadfast maintenance of free trade institutions is a most important fruit out of this summit. I believe this is indeed the message from Ottawa to the world.

Our participants have expressed our solidarity and cooperation and this strong expression, I believe, is a most valuable and irreplaceable achievement of this summit.

Above all, I am satisfied that we have been able to build friendship and mutual confidence among us, the leaders of these summit nations.

The North-South question was an important item on our agenda. We have been united in recognition that our interdependence in international community is becoming more important than ever, and we have committed to further expand official development assistance.

In conclusion, I would like to say that for this most successful summit conference, I am again grateful to Prime Minister Trudeau personally and to the people of Canada for their most generous support and cooperation and, with that note of thanks, I would like to conclude my comments.

Thank you.

Prime Minister Trudeau. I now give the floor to the President of the Council of the Italian Republic, Mr. Spadolini.

Prime Minister Spadolini. The Government of the Italian Republic is very grateful to the Canadian Government and in particular to Prime Minister Trudeau, who was the animator and coordinator of our discussion, for the perfect organization of this summit meeting of the main industrial countries of the Western world—a summit meeting which has coincided with one of the most difficult periods of the Western industrial countries and after many events which have affected our countries, which has had an impact on all our countries and which have made it necessary to search for new points of view and coordinated views.

In this case, also, as in the past, the work of the summit meeting developed in a spirit of civil and constructive confrontation and a frame of tolerance and a mutual understanding within a frame of a common understanding of our pluralistic, complex society, which is shaken by serious events. In a short period of time, the societies we have constructed on the basis of a reliance on and a firm belief in our values have gone over to uncertainty and doubt. And it is our responsibility to interpret and to understand the reasons for these upheavals, which are affecting the very foundation of our societies, in order to revitalize our societies and to broaden consensus and trust in our political democratic institutions based on stability of our economy and the social progress.

The Italian Government has explained its own policy in the field of economics, and social policies as well, which is aimed at controlling inflation through a range of initiatives and activities aimed at reducing the cost—government costs—and conciliating the interests of unions and management, just as all of the nations participating in these matters. We are convinced that we must defeat this monster of inflation and unemployment since they absorb ever-increasing resources and leave very little room for productive investments.

We consider it very significant that the joint communique refers explicitly to the common desire of the seven governments that the fluctuations of interest rates cause difficulties for other countries in pursuing their affairs. The problem of foreign exchange and stability of markets is considered very important for the proper and consistent development of our economies.

We have also dealt with the problems of energy and the dialog—the North-South dialog. We have emphasized our interest in developing alternative sources of energy, starting with nuclear energy.

As regards the problems affecting our societies, many derived from the need to find a common measure between industrialized countries and developing countries, mindful of the mutual interdependence of the summit, has made forward progress in this. We are well aware that developing countries, that is to say, the Third World, their public debt has reached proportions which can no longer be sustained, and therefore, there is an urgent need to provide aid to those countries so that they will not be burdened with further debts. And we have given appropriate priority to the harmonious development of relations between the North and South. And if we forego this need, we would be abdicating our own responsibility as regards peoples who are faced with those problems of underdevelopment and hunger. That is why we have proposed that Italy should assume, as soon as possible, in concert with the European economy, the development of specific proposals for action in the field of food and agriculture, in coordination with the international agencies in Rome and that should—priority interest should be devoted to those countries. One of the results of our summit meeting has been to unite our bonds even stronger on the basis of effective common activities and pursuits beyond all rhetoric and ritual. And this is a battle which, as Chancellor Schmidt indicated, is of essential importance.

Italy reaffirms, just as France, as Prime Minister Mitterrand, its solidarity with the Western powers in the knowledge and that there is a close link between Europe and the United States, and this has been again confirmed by President Reagan. And we may say that this is a great satisfaction for us to observe that we have—there are many common points on which we have agreed—social justice, international peace, and other items are all indivisible problems for us.

Prime Minister Trudeau. I now give the floor to the President of the European Community, Mr. Gaston Thorn.

President Thorn. Thank you, Mr. Chairman. I'm sure it's no exaggeration to be the seventh to thank you. And I would like to say that the heads of state and of governments represented here have decided to start up a new cycle, a second cycle of summits. And they have done so because the results quite justify such a second cycle. This is because the conference was very well prepared, of course, and also because the welcome extended by Canada and the beautiful site at which the conference took place favored such success. Moreover, Prime Minister Trudeau had taken up the pilgrim staff and had made sure that debates be restricted as much as possible, that as many results be achieved as possible.

Speaking on behalf of the Community, on behalf of the Commission of the European Communities, I'm not speaking at the same level and not speaking on behalf—for example, I'm not wishing to take the place of Mrs. Thatcher, who's President of the Council at the time being.

But I would like to say that the Community, particularly countries not represented at the summit, wish to be heard, wish to speak. And we have been heard. It has been sufficiently often said that times are very hard. They are particularly hard for the European Community. Why is this so? Well, because in terms of trade, we are more vulnerable than anybody else—we depend much more on foreign trade—and also because, in monetary terms, our interdependence is greater and, thus, perhaps we suffer more greatly from the repercussions of policies carried out in other industrialized countries. Moreover, perhaps our commitment is greater towards the Third World, since we are committed to the Lomé Convention, for example, which binds us to a large number of Third World countries.

It has been said that it was important for us to get to know each other. It was particularly important through personal contact to become aware of the limits of everybody, to understand why perhaps each of us have adopted somewhat different attitudes. I think that once this understanding exists, there should no longer be any unclarity among ourselves. We understand the essential points. We agree, although we do, all of us, understand that sometimes we have to act differently. We agree that trade at the world level must remain open, that protectionism is something we all should avoid, it being fully understood that free trade is a common rule that has to be respected by everybody, and this is why another conference at the ministerial level will perhaps be organized.

Now, we also understand why the United States follows a certain policy while other countries adopt another policy, and we have to see, as the Chancellor of Germany has just said, we have to—we will have to see how each of us will have to react to the results of this conference between us. You will have to react as well, of course.

Finally, I would like to say that I'm very happy that during this summit of the industrialized nations we did not concern ourselves only with industrialized nations. We dealt also with other countries, with the developing countries, not for reasons of charity but because we know that the future of those countries will play an important part in our own future. And I am happy on behalf of the European Community to be able to see that on this point people have moved closer together and that dialog, perhaps even global negotiations, and perhaps even the energy affiliate, on all these points I think that we have achieved greater agreement. We are happy to see that concerning substantive matters we all agree. And once again, I would like to thank Canada warmly for their excellent organization of this summit.

Thank you.

Prime Minister Trudeau. Thank you, Mr. President of the European Community.

Ladies and gentlemen, this ends the meeting we have with the press. I believe the press of the various countries will have some occasion to meet the heads of state or government of its own country. At this time, however, we adjourn this meeting.

Merci beaucoup.

Note: Prime Minister Pierre Elliott Trudeau of Canada, Chairman of the summit meeting, spoke at 5:05 p.m. in the Opera House at the National Arts Centre in Ottawa, Ontario, Canada. Some participants spoke in their native languages, and their remarks were translated by interpreters.

The concluding statements were made to members of the press following the 2½ days of the summit conference between President Reagan, Prime Minister Trudeau, President François Mitterrand of France, Chancellor Helmut Schmidt of the Federal Republic of Germany, Prime Minister Zenko Suzuki of Japan, Prime Minister Margaret Thatcher of the United Kingdom, Prime Minister Giovanni Spadolini of Italy, and Gaston Thorn, President of the Commission of the European Communities.

Declaration Issued at the Conclusion of the Ottawa Economic Summit Conference
July 21, 1981

1. We have met at a time of rapid change and great challenge to world economic progress and peace. Our meeting has served to reinforce the strength of our common bonds. We are conscious that economic issues reflect and affect the broader political purposes we share. In a world of interdependence, we reaffirm our common objectives and our recognition of the need to take into account the effects on others of policies we pursue. We are confident in our joint determination and ability to tackle our problems in a spirit of shared responsibility, both among ourselves and with our partners throughout the world.

The Economy

2. The primary challenge we addressed at this meeting was the need to revitalize the economies of the industrial democracies, to meet the needs of our own people and strengthen world prosperity.

3. Since the Venice Summit the average rate of inflation in our countries has fallen, although in four of them inflation remains in double figures. In many countries unem-

ployment has risen sharply and is still rising. There is a prospect of moderate economic growth in the coming year but at present it promises little early relief from unemployment. The large payments deficits originating in the 1979–80 oil price increase have so far been financed without imposing intolerable adjustment burdens but are likely to persist for some time. Interest rates have reached record levels in many countries and, if long sustained at these levels, would threaten productive investment.

4. The fight to bring down inflation and reduce unemployment must be our highest priority and these linked problems must be tackled at the same time. We must continue to reduce inflation if we are to secure the higher investment and sustainable growth on which the durable recovery of employment depends. The balanced use of a range of policy instruments is required. We must involve our peoples in a greater appreciation of the need for change: change in expectations about growth and earnings, change in management and labour relations and practices, change in the pattern of industry, change in the direction and scale of investment, and change in energy use and supply.

5. We need in most countries urgently to reduce public borrowing; where our circumstances permit or we are able to make changes within the limits of our budgets, we will increase support for productive investment and innovation. We must also accept the role of the market in our economies. We must not let transitional measures that may be needed to ease change become permanent forms of protection or subsidy.

6. We see low and stable monetary growth as essential to reducing inflation. Interest rates have to play their part in achieving this and are likely to remain high where fears of inflation remain strong. But we are fully aware that levels and movements of interest rates in one country can make stabilization policies more difficult in other countries by influencing their exchange rates and their economies. For these reasons, most of us need also to rely on containment of budgetary deficits, by means of restraint in government expenditures as necessary. It is also highly desirable to minimize volatility of interest rates and

exchange rates; greater stability in foreign exchange and financial markets is important for the sound development of the world economy.

7. In a world of strong capital flows and large deficits it is in the interests of all that the financial soundness of the international banking system and the international financial institutions be fully maintained. We welcome the recently expanded role of the IMF in financing payments deficits on terms which encourage needed adjustment.

8. In shaping our long term economic policies, care should be taken to preserve the environment and the resource base of our planet.

Relations With Developing Countries

9. We support the stability, independence and genuine non-alignment of developing countries and reaffirm our commitment to cooperate with them in a spirit of mutual interest, respect and benefit, recognizing the reality of our interdependence.

10. It is in our interest as well as in theirs that the developing countries should grow and flourish and play a full part in the international economic system commensurate with their capabilities and responsibilities and become more closely integrated in it.

11. We look forward to constructive and substantive discussions with them, and believe the Cancún Summit offers an early opportunity to address our common problems anew.

12. We reaffirm our willingness to explore all avenues of consultation and cooperation with developing countries in whatever forums may be appropriate. We are ready to participate in preparations for a mutually acceptable process of global negotiations in circumstances offering the prospect of meaningful progress.

13. While growth has been strong in most middle income developing countries, we are deeply conscious of the serious economic problems in many developing countries, and the grim poverty faced especially by the poorer among them. We remain ready to support the developing countries in the efforts they make to promote their economic and social development within the frame-

work of their own social values and traditions. These efforts are vital to their success.

14. We are committed to maintaining substantial and, in many cases, growing levels of Official Development Assistance and will seek to increase public understanding of its importance. We will direct the major portion of our aid to poorer countries, and will participate actively in the United Nations Conference on the Least Developed Countries.

15. We point out that the strengthening of our own economies, increasing access to our markets, and removing impediments to capital flows contribute larger amounts of needed resources and technology and thereby complement official aid. The flow of private capital will be further encouraged in so far as the developing countries themselves provide assurances for the protection and security of investments.

16. The Soviet Union and its partners, whose contributions are meagre, should make more development assistance available, and take a greater share of exports of developing countries, while respecting their independence and non-alignment.

17. We will maintain a strong commitment to the international financial institutions and work to ensure that they have, and use effectively, the financial resources for their important responsibilities.

18. We attach high priority to the resolution of the problems created for the non-oil developing countries by the damaging effects on them of high cost of energy imports following the two oil price shocks. We call on the surplus oil-exporting countries to broaden their valuable efforts to finance development in non-oil developing countries, especially in the field of energy. We stand ready to cooperate with them for this purpose and to explore with them, in a spirit of partnership, possible mechanisms, such as those being examined in the World Bank, which would take due account of the importance of their financial contributions.

19. We recognize the importance of accelerated food production in the developing world and of greater world food security, and the need for developing countries to pursue sound agricultural and food policies; we will examine ways to make increased resources available for these purposes. We

note that the Italian Government has in mind to discuss within the European Community proposals to be put forward in close cooperation with the specialized U.N. institutions located in Rome for special action in this field primarily directed to the poorest countries.

20. We are deeply concerned about the implications of world population growth. Many developing countries are taking action to deal with that problem, in ways sensitive to human values and dignity; and to develop human resources, including technical and managerial capabilities. We recognize the importance of these issues and will place greater emphasis on international efforts in these areas.

Trade

21. We reaffirm our strong commitment to maintaining liberal trade policies and to the effective operation of an open multilateral trading system as embodied in the GATT.

22. We will work together to strengthen this system in the interest of all trading countries, recognizing that this will involve structural adaptation to changes in the world economy.

23. We will implement the agreements reached in the Multilateral Trade Negotiations and invite other countries, particularly developing countries, to join in these mutually beneficial trading arrangements.

24. We will continue to resist protectionist pressures, since we recognize that any protectionist measure, whether in the form of overt or hidden trade restrictions or in the form of subsidies to prop up declining industries, not only undermines the dynamism of our economies but also, over time, aggravates inflation and unemployment.

25. We welcome the new initiative represented by the proposal of the Consultative Group of Eighteen that the GATT Contracting Parties convene a meeting at Ministerial level during 1982, as well as that of the OECD countries in their programme of study to examine trade issues.

26. We will keep under close review the role played by our countries in the smooth functioning of the multilateral trading system with a view to ensuring maximum

openness of our markets in a spirit of reciprocity, while allowing for the safeguard measures provided for in the GATT.

27. We endorse efforts to reach agreement by the end of this year on reducing subsidy elements in official export credit schemes.

Energy

28. We are confident that, with perseverance, the energy goals we set at Venice for the decade can be achieved, enabling us to break the link between economic growth and oil consumption through structural change in our energy economies.

29. Recognizing that our countries are still vulnerable and energy supply remains a potential constraint to a revival of economic growth, we will accelerate the development and use of all our energy sources, both conventional and new, and continue to promote energy savings and the replacement of oil by other fuels.

30. To these ends we will continue to rely heavily on market mechanisms, supplemented as necessary by government action.

31. Our capacity to deal with short-term oil market problems should be improved, particularly through the holding of adequate levels of stocks.

32. In most of our countries progress in constructing new nuclear facilities is slow. We intend in each of our countries to encourage greater public acceptance of nuclear energy, and respond to public concerns about safety, health, nuclear waste management and non-proliferation. We will further our efforts in the development of advanced technologies, particularly in spent fuel management.

33. We will take steps to realize the potential for the economic production, trade and use of coal and will do everything in our power to ensure that its increased use does not damage the environment.

34. We also intend to see to it that we develop to the fullest possible extent sources of renewable energy such as solar, geothermal and biomass energy. We will work for practical achievements at the fourthcoming United Nations Conference on New and Renewable Sources of Energy.

35. We look forward to improved understanding and cooperation with the oil exporting countries in the interests of the world economy.

East-West Economic Relations

36. We also reviewed the significance of East-West economic relations for our political and security interests. We recognized that there is a complex balance of political and economic interests and risks in these relations. We concluded that consultations and, where appropriate, coordination are necessary to ensure that, in the field of East-West relations, our economic policies continue to be compatible with our political and security objectives.

37. We will undertake to consult to improve the present system of controls on trade in strategic goods and related technology with the U.S.S.R.

Conclusion

38. We are convinced that our democratic, free societies are equal to the challenges we face. We will move forward together and with all countries ready to work with us in a spirit of cooperation and harmony. We have agreed to meet again next year and have accepted the invitation of the President of the French Republic to hold this meeting in France. We intend to maintain close and continuing consultation and cooperation with each other.

Remarks About Federal Tax Reduction Legislation at a White House Luncheon for Out-of-Town Editors and Broadcasters
July 22, 1981

Ladies and gentlemen, please go on eating your dessert. It won't bother me a bit; I got mine already. I want to take a moment just to welcome you to the White

House and tell you how delighted we are to have you here. Actually, we were thinking of inviting Tip O'Neill to be here with us, too, but then I remembered that my good friend, the Speaker, just can't stomach the idea of a free lunch. [*Laughter*]

Anyway, it's good to see you all. You know, I always realized that each of you, your group, command great respect, but I never realized how much until today. You've corralled nearly half our top people and arranged it so that you were getting all the briefings on taxes, and I wasn't. [*Laughter*] So, finally I decided if you can't lick 'em, join 'em. So, you'll get a little more briefing here.

As you'll notice, I didn't come unprepared. I brought along a little art work to highlight what we believe is the single most important part of this entire tax debate. Our bipartisan coalition offers a real tax reduction, while the House Democratic leadership, I think, is offering still another make-believe tax cut that dissolves into a huge tax increase.

As you can see—the first chart on the right—they're offering only a 15-percent tax cut against nearly a 22-percent built-in tax increase. Now, of course, we're being told that there's—I should say, in 1984 they offer no tax cut at all. Now, of course, we're being told there's a possibility of triggering a third-year tax cut if the economic conditions improve. But by holding the people's tax reduction hostage to future economic events, we'll be removing the certainty that they need to begin saving or investing more of their money, precisely what is needed to get our economy back in shape.

I have said before, and will repeat: Government does not tax to get the money it needs; government always finds a need for the money it gets. And so that third possible tax cut would be dangling out there. A trigger will do far more to preclude a third-year tax cut than to promote one. And that's why, on this chart on the right, I like that line marking the break-even point on taxes at about 22 percent. It's colored ocean-blue because, obviously, that's the line every taxpayer must remain above to stay afloat. But under the other proposal you won't, you're sunk.

Now, maybe that's why when I asked their leadership last week how they can look the American public in the eye and say, "We're reducing your taxes," I got no answer. They had no answer. And then I wondered why they're willing to give a business tax cut for at least 7 years, staged out in advance, but they think it's too dangerous to give individuals a commitment for 3 years. We're still waiting for an answer to that one, too, but we shouldn't hold our breath. It seems they rest their entire case on just one claim—that their bill does more for middle-income Americans. And today, we're going to bury that fairytale also. To paraphrase a wise Englishman, Samuel Johnson, these fellows have had only one idea their whole life long, and what a pity because it's dead wrong.

You see, if we're sincere about giving the American people real tax reduction, then we have to do better than the typical one-shot, here today and gone tomorrow rebates of old. We must make the people a commitment, the kind of commitment that says if you work or save more tomorrow than you did today, then your reward will be higher. More of every added dollar that you earn will be yours to keep. And that's why it's so important to reduce tax rates.

Now, for all those who will work hard for their families, and who could succeed over time in raising their incomes, we must make a commitment that they won't be punished by tax rates designed only to feed the already bloated Federal budget. So, this is why in addition to reducing tax rates, we must also reduce those rates across the board. Only then can we look the public in the eye and say we're providing real incentives that will help all Americans create, build, and share in growing prosperity. And only then can we truthfully say we're making a commitment to your future and not just to the next election. We think that's the real difference between our bill and the House leadership bill.

We make this commitment without qualifications. They offer half a loaf and a vague promise. Take a look at these charts on the left which show what the real tax payments will be for income earners between $15,000 and $30,000 under the two bills. The dotted line is theirs. Yes, it goes down and, as they have boasted, a little bit more sharply in the first year than ours. But you come to this point down here where their tax cut stops and starts going back up again, not only in the form of social security taxes that have already been adopted, but in the form of bracket creep through inflation. And you will notice that our tax line does not go down as steeply beyond there but continues to go on down. And that orange space in there is the money that you'll have in your pocket, differing—between which tax you'll have in your pocket or out of your pocket, depending on which one of those tax programs we choose.

By 1983, under their bill, your tax cut as you can see is already a thing of the past. Your taxes are rising again, and they'll begin shooting higher and higher as time goes on. They want to rig the tax code to take back their tax cut as quickly as possible, and that way they'll be able to spend more and more. Under our proposal working Americans do much better, because the bipartisan bill makes a commitment to get rates down, and we're going to keep them down.

I believe these charts speak wonders about two very different views of the world. And we're going to do everything we can to be sure the public sees them, because while they show the bipartisan bill making a genuine commitment to the future of middle-income Americans, they show the Democrat leadership bill throwing the public a bone now, knowing they'll get it back—if you'll forgive the expression, with an arm and a leg attached.

The bottom line then is not a choice between two different versions of a tax cut as so many have said. It's a choice between reducing taxes on the American people or increasing them. And that's why we're so determined to hang tough on our bill.

The simple truth is that there is a gigantic tax increase presently built into the tax system, and what we're really talking about with our tax bill is eliminating that tax increase. We go a few percentage points beyond. The tax increase that's built in is 22 percent. Our tax cut is about 25 percent. And we look forward, when we get out of the hole and have some leeway, we're already talking about a second tax cut bill in which we'll correct some more of the inequities that still exist. But we have to get that rate of growth up there.

I don't have a chart for this. You'll have to just look at my arms. The simple truth is we're not, in our budget cuts, trying to do that line of growth in government down that way; we just want to lower it. And we want the tax bill that is being taken from the people lowered. And there will be the legitimate growth built-in that we will need for our increase in size, for just normal growth that takes place. The difference will be that where we have been increasing spending in the government about 14 percent a year, we seek to bring it down to half that, to about a 7 percent increase a year.

And now, I have to apologize. I'm running late, but I've got a cousin here who's going to take over for me, Don Regan, with any questions that you may have. And I'm sorry that I can't stay to hear those. But one of these days, I'm going to find where that place is here where they tell me what I'm doing every 15 minutes a day. And heads will roll. [*Laughter*]

Thank you all very much for being here.

Don Regan, Secretary of the Treasury.

Note: The President spoke at 1:15 p.m. in the State Dining Room at the White House.

Nomination of Three Members of the Mississippi River Commission, and Designation of President
July 22, 1981

The President today announced his intention to nominate the following individuals to be members of the Mississippi River Commission:

Brig. Gen. Richard S. Kem is Division Engineer, United States Army Engineer Division, Ohio River, Cincinnati, Ohio. He was Deputy Director of Civil Works, Office of the Chief of Engineers, in 1980; Deputy Assistant Chief of Engineers, Office of the Chief of Engineers, in 1979–80; Assistant Deputy Chief of Staff, Engineer, Headquarters, United States Army Europe, in 1979; Chief Installation and Construction Division, Office, Deputy Chief of Staff, Engineer, Headquarters, United States Army Europe, in 1978–79; Commander, 7th Engineer Brigade, and Commander, Ludwigsburg-Kornwestheim Military Community, United States and Europe, in 1976–78; Chief, Public Affairs, Office of the Chief of Engineers, Washington, in 1975–76; Assistant to the Director of the Army Staff, Office, Chief of Staff, Washington, in 1974–75; Personnel Management Officer, Colonels Division, Officer, Personnel Management Directorate, United States Army Military Personnel Center, Alexandria, Va., in 1972–74. General Kem graduated from the United States Military Academy (B.S.), the University of Illinois (M.S.), and George Washington University (M.S.). He is a recipient of the Legion of Merit, Bronze Star Medal, Meritorious Service Medal, Army Commendation Medal, and Air Medal. General Kem was born August 9, 1934, in Richmond, Ind.

Maj. Gen. William E. Read, to be designated President of the Mississippi River Commission, is Division Engineer, United States Army Engineer Division, Lower Mississippi Valley, Vicksburg, Miss. He was Assistant Chief of Engineers, Office of the Chief of Engineers, Washington, in 1978–80; Division Engineer, United States Army Engineer Division, Missouri River, Omaha, Nebr., in 1976–78; Deputy Command-ing General, United States Army Aviation Systems Command, St. Louis, in 1974–76; Director, Procurement and Production, United States Army Aviation Systems Command, St. Louis, in 1972–74; District Engineer, United States Army Engineer District, Tulsa, Okla., in 1971–72; Commander, Task Force Ivy, United States Army, Pacific-Vietnam, in 1970–71; Commander, Division Support Command, 4th Infantry Division, United States Army, Pacific-Vietnam, in 1970; and member, Civil Engineering Branch, Services Division, J–4 Directorate, Organization, Joint Chiefs of Staff, Washington, in 1969–70. General Read graduated from the United States Military Academy (B.S.) and the University of Illinois (M.S.). He is a recipient of the Legion of Merit, Bronze Star Medal, Air Medals, and the Army Commendation Medal. General Read was born May 17, 1927, in Charlotte, N.C.

Maj. Gen. Hugh G. Robinson is Division Engineer, United States Army Engineer Division, Southwestern, Dallas, Tex. He was Deputy Director of Civil Works, Office, Chief of Engineers, Washington, in 1978–80; District Engineer, Army Engineer District, Los Angeles, Calif., in 1976–78; Commander, Army Engineer School Brigade, Ft. Belvoir, Va., in 1974–76; Commander, 3d Regiment, United States Corps of Cadets, United States Military Academy, in 1973–74; Executive Officer/Operations Officer, 3d Regiment, United States Corps of Cadets, United States Military Academy, in 1972–73; and Staff Officer, Regional Capabilities Branch, War Plans for Military Operations, Washington, in 1969–70. General Robinson graduated from the United States Military Academy (B.S.) and the Massachusetts Institute of Technology (M.S.). He is a recipient of the Legion of Merit, Bronze Star Medal, Joint Service Commendation Medal, Air Medals, and the Army Commendation Medal. General Robinson was born August 4, 1932, in Washington, D.C.

Nomination of Three Members of the California Debris Commission
July 22, 1981

The President today announced his intention to nominate the following individuals to be members of the California Debris Commission:

Col. Paul Bazilwich, Jr., is District Engineer, United States Army Engineer District, San Francisco, Calif. He was Deputy Division Engineer, United States Army Engineer Division, North Atlantic, New York, N.Y., in 1978–80; Staff Officer, School Brigade, United States Army Engineer School, Ft. Belvoir, Va., in 1976–78; Battalion Commander, 11th Engineer Battalion, in 1976; Deputy Commander/Director, United States Army Facilities Engineering Support Agency, Ft. Belvoir, in 1974–76; and Deputy District Engineer, United States Army Engineer District, Anchorage, Alaska, in 1970–74. Colonel Bazilwich graduated from the United States Military Academy (B.S.) and the University of Illinois (M.S.). He is a recipient of the Bronze Star Medal, Meritorious Service Medal, and the Parachutist Badge. Colonel Bazilwich was born January 21, 1933, in Belle Vernon, Pa.

Brig. Gen. Homer Johnstone, Jr., is Division Engineer, United States Army Engineer Division, South Pacific, San Francisco, Calif. He was Commander, Defense Contract Administration Services Region, New York, in 1979–80; Engineer, United Nations Command/Combined Forces Command, Korea/United States Forces Korea/Eighth United States Army, in 1977–79; Engineer, United States Army Engineer District, Wilmington, N.C., in 1974–77; Operations Research Analyst, Wheels Study Group, Office of the Chief of Staff, United States Army,

Washington, in 1972–73; Commander, 8th Engineer Battalion, 1st Cavalry Division, Vietnam, in 1970–71; and Civil Engineer Staff Officer, Engineer Division, Logistics Directorate, United States Strike Command, MacDill Air Force Base, Fla., in 1968–70. General Johnstone graduated from the United States Military Academy (B.S.), the University of California (M.S.), Command and General Staff College (M.M.S.), and George Washington University (D.B.A.). He is a recipient of the Bronze Star Medal, Meritorious Service Medal, Joint Service Commendation Medal, Army Commendation Medal, and the Legion of Merit. General Johnstone was born August 23, 1935, in Los Angeles, Calif.

Col. Paul F. Kavanaugh is District Engineer, United States Army Engineer District, Sacramento, Calif. He was Chief, Concepts and Organization Branch, Combat Development and Force Modernization Division, Deputy Chief of Staff, Operations, United States Army Forces Command, Ft. McPherson, Ga., in 1976–79; Engineer Staff Officer, United States Army Pacific Support Office, Defense Nuclear Agency, Honolulu, in 1975–76; Commander, 84th Engineer Battalion (Construction), Schofield Barracks, Hawaii, in 1973–75; Nuclear Weapons Officer, Defense Intelligence Agency, Washington, in 1970–73; and Assistant Division Engineer, 1st Cavalry Division, Vietnam, in 1969–70. Colonel Kavanaugh is a recipient of the Bronze Star Medal, Meritorious Service Medal, Air Medal, and the Army Commendation Medal. He was graduated from Norwich University (B.S.) and Oklahoma State University (M.S.). Colonel Kavanaugh was born August 19, 1934, in Boston, Mass.

Nomination of J. Paul McGrath To Be an Assistant Attorney General
July 22, 1981

The President today announced his intention to nominate J. Paul McGrath to be an Assistant Attorney General (Civil Division), Department of Justice, vice Alice Daniel.

Since his graduation from law school, Mr. McGrath has been in the general practice

of law with the firm of Dewey, Ballantine, Bushby, Palmer and Wood in New York City. He concentrated mainly on litigation, especially antitrust, securities, and various other Federal court litigation for major corporate clients.

Mr. McGrath graduated from Holy Cross

College, Worcester, Mass. (A.B., 1962) and Harvard Law School (LL.B., 1965). He re-sides in Montclair, N.J. He was born September 9, 1940, in Rochester, N.Y.

Nomination of Matthew N. Novick To Be Inspector General of the Environmental Protection Agency
July 22, 1981

The President today announced his intention to nominate Matthew N. Novick to be Inspector General, Environmental Protection Agency, vice Inez Smith Reid.

Since 1980 Mr. Novick has been Director, Office of Technical Assistance, Department of the Interior. He was Deputy Director for Finance and Administration with the Department in 1978–80; Financial Manager and Budget Officer under the Deputy Assistant Secretary for Management in 1974–78; and Budget Analyst, Office of the Director of Procurement, Department of Defense, in 1971–74. Previously he served as an auditor in the United States Army.

Mr. Novick graduated from Benjamin Franklin University (B.C.S., 1963) and the Industrial College of the Armed Forces (1971). He resides in Washington, D.C., and was born December 3, 1933, in Brooklyn, N.Y.

Executive Order 12314—Federal Regional Councils
July 22, 1981

By the authority vested in me as President by the Constitution and statutes of the United States of America, and in order to establish interagency coordinating groups structured to respond to opportunities for promoting Federal policies and to support interagency and intergovernmental cooperation, it is hereby ordered as follows:

Section 1. Establishment of Federal Regional Councils.

(a) There is hereby restructured a Federal Regional Council for each of the ten standard Federal regions (Office of Management and Budget Circular No. A–105). Each Council shall be composed of a principal policy official in the region at the Administrator, Director, Secretarial Representative, or equivalent level, from each of the following agencies:

(1) The Department of the Interior.
(2) The Department of Agriculture.
(3) The Department of Labor.
(4) The Department of Health and Human Services.
(5) The Department of Housing and Urban Development.
(6) The Department of Transportation.
(7) The Department of Energy.
(8) The Department of Education.
(9) The Environmental Protection Agency.

(b) The President shall designate a Chairman for each Council. Representatives of the Office of Management and Budget may participate in the deliberations of the Councils.

(c) Each member of each Council shall designate an alternate to serve whenever the regular member is unable to attend any meeting of the Council. The alternate shall be a principal official in the region at the Deputy or equivalent level, or the head of an operating unit of the agency.

(d) Whenever matters are to be considered by a Council which significantly affect the interests of agencies not represented on that Council, the Regional Director or other appropriate representative of the affected agency shall participate in the deliberations of the Council.

Sec. 2. Federal Regional Council Functions.

(a) Each Council shall, upon request, establish liaison with State, tribal, regional, and local offices, and shall inform elected officials, including State legislators, concerning Government policies and initiatives, through such mechanisms as are appropriate in individual cases.

(b) Each Council shall respond to State, tribal, regional, and local concerns or inquiries about major agency policy and budgeting decisions, in order to ensure that the total effect of those actions and related actions of other agencies are explained and understood.

(c) Each Council shall assist in explaining the following federalism initiatives:

(1) Reform of the Federal aid system through block grants.

(2) Devolution of Federal programs and functions.

(3) Reduction in the number and impact of Federal regulations and administrative requirements.

(d) Each Council shall coordinate the Federal response to social and economic impacts resulting from Federal actions.

(e) Each Council shall identify significant problems with Federal regulations, policies and actions for resolution in the field or refer such problems to the appropriate agency for resolution in a timely fashion, to ensure that problems which are of interest to State and local governments are acted upon expeditiously.

Sec. 3. Oversight.

(a) The Office of Management and Budget will provide policy guidance to the Councils in consultation with the White House Office of Policy Development; establish policy with respect to Federal Regional Council procedural matters; respond to Council initiatives; seek to resolve policy issues referred to it by the Councils; coordinate Federal Regional Council activities relating to State and local governments with the White House Office of Intergovernmental Affairs; and, coordinate Council activities relating to specific programmatic areas with the appropriate Federal agencies.

(b) The Office of Management and Budget shall provide direction for, and oversight of, the implementation by the Councils of Federal management improvement actions and of Federal aid reforms.

Sec. 4. General Provisions.

(a) Each agency represented on a Council shall provide, to the extent permitted by law, appropriate staff for common or joint interagency activities as requested by the Chairman of the Council.

(b) Executive Order No. 12149 is revoked.

RONALD REAGAN

The White House,
July 22, 1981.

[Filed with the Office of the Federal Register, 2:17 p.m., July 23, 1981]

Note: The text of the Executive order was released by the Office of the Press Secretary on July 23.

Letter to the Speaker of the House and the Chairman of the Senate Foreign Relations Committee Reporting on the Cyprus Conflict
July 23, 1981

Dear Mr. Speaker: (Dear Mr. Chairman:)

In accordance with the provision of Public Law 95–384, I am submitting the following report on progress made during the past sixty days toward reaching a negotiated settlement of the Cyprus problem.

The intercommunal negotiations between Greek Cypriot and Turkish Cypriot representatives are continuing under the chairmanship of the United Nations Secretary General's Special Representative on Cyprus, Ambassador Hugo Gobbi. During the period since my last report, the Greek and

Turkish Cypriots prepared for and held elections, and the pace of intercommunal negotiations slowed with one negotiating session held on June 2. Elections having been completed, regular intercommunal sessions resumed on July 8 and we anticipate the parties will continue meetings on a regular basis. Both sides have continued to negotiate in a congenial atmosphere.

We also note with pleasure that the Committee on Missing Persons held its inaugural meeting on July 14. Although procedural questions delayed the initial session, these now appear largely to have been overcome. As I noted in my report of May 19, although the problem of missing persons in Cyprus is not officially an issue for the intercommunal negotiations, it is an important humanitarian concern for both communities. Consequently, progress on this issue could be conducive to facilitating a positive negotiating atmosphere and we hope the Committee will be able to proceed with its substantive mandate in the near term.

More importantly we hope that during the coming months the parties, under the *aegis* of United Nations Secretary General Waldheim, will seek to move vigorously on the issues dividing them. During almost a year of steady negotiating, the parties have examined in detail the complex issues separating them. We hope they can now begin with imagination and flexibility to attack the problems and advance toward a just, fair and lasting resolution of the Cyprus question.

Sincerely,

RONALD REAGAN

Note: This is the text of identical letters addressed to Thomas P. O'Neill, Jr., Speaker of the House of Representatives, and Charles H. Percy, chairman of the Senate Foreign Relations Committee.

Remarks About Federal Tax Reduction Legislation at a Meeting With State Legislators and Local Government Officials
July 23, 1981

I'm glad to have this chance to talk with you all today, although I must say I stand here with kind of mixed emotions. I know that you've been briefed, and I know that others have addressed you, and the Vice President, I know, has been talking to you about regulations, and I wonder if there's anything that I can say that won't have been said before. But I'll try for just a few minutes, and then we'll get to a dialog instead of a monolog from me.

I think the American people are on the verge of making some historic changes in the way their government is run—changes that will return this country to the way that it was supposed to be run all along—and your help is a key to making sure these changes are made.

Today in the Congress, the Senators and Representatives from your States and districts are negotiating on the final dimensions of the largest budget cuts in our history. And they're also determining how much flexibility you'll have in deciding how money in your communities is to be spent. They're also reaching the crucial stages in the struggle to give the American people a meaningful tax cut—a struggle that will leave more money where it's earned—to offset the largest single tax increase in the history of our country, an increase that was passed last year.

Now, the tax debate may have gotten confusing and differences have begun to blur. Yesterday in this room we met with a number of newspaper editors, and I was amazed at how little they understood of what really is going on in the debate. And it concerned me, because when some of them suggested to me that, well, maybe I ought to explain this, I wanted to say. "Well, you can help." [*Laughter*]

There is a blur about it, but there's one indisputable fact in the fight that's going on now, or the debate, about the tax bill. The

House leadership is offering the American people a tax increase, no matter what we may say about it or how many cuts may be enclosed in their bill. We think that our bipartisan bill, in fact we know, offers a real tax cut. The proposal coming out of the Ways and Means Committee provides for a 15-percent cut during the time when your real tax burden will go up by nearly 22 percent due to that built-in tax increase. Now, that is a tax increase, no matter how much they reduce it or somewhat.

We would offset that 22-percent climb with a 25-percent cut to actually eliminate the tax increase and at least have a few points below the present level. The Democratic leadership talks magically of a mystical trigger that would, after the second year, provide enough of a cut to match ours in that third year. But that trigger was designed by people who don't really believe in cutting taxes. And they're the ones who raised the taxes on the American people in the first place.

And I have a feeling our tax program is designed to stimulate the economy, to offer optimism to people to where they will move forward and begin expanding productivity in this country. I have a hunch that the American people are just cynical enough that a trigger that 3 years from now is supposed to, maybe, cut the taxes again—they'll figure no one is ever going to pull that trigger. So, we think of it as avoiding a long-term commitment to the American people to cut taxes decisively and permanently.

And our bipartisan bill, supported by an overwhelming majority of Democrats and Republicans in the Senate and supported by members of both parties in the House, makes that kind of commitment. And I'd like to say a word to you about my own strong personal commitment to this. Let there be no doubt I'll go any place, any time, to ensure that the working people of this country get their first real tax reduction in nearly 20 years. Anything less will not get the economy back on track.

The economic mess that we're in doesn't mean there's something wrong with our American system. Our economic system is sound, and our way of government is the best yet devised. But we've abandoned basic principles of that system. Of everyone in government, you know best what is happening in the workplaces of this country, to family budgets, and to savings accounts. You know what's happening to the productivity and what is not happening in investment. You're closer to the people, and you hear their cry for reform. With your help, the Members of the Congress may also hear that cry.

Our program of budget cuts will discipline the Federal Government to live within its means, and the bipartisan tax rate cuts will once again reward the hard work and the spirit of enterprise that is the foundation of our economic program.

We've also taken important steps to reduce the burden of overregulation, as I'm sure the Vice President told you, and established a coordinating task force on federalism and a federalism advisory committee, both chaired by Senator Paul Laxalt, who was Governor of Nevada, to restore power and authority to local governments.

Thomas Jefferson wrote that "Were we directed from Washington when to sow and when to reap, we would soon be wanting for bread." Well, figuratively speaking, I'm afraid that's exactly what's been happening. To return America to prosperity, we must call on the people at the local level, on the talent in our State legislatures, in our county seats, and our city halls. We must respond to the needs and the dreams of our people, and you are the officials who know best in government what they are.

I believe as our Founding Fathers did that local governments should do as much as they can, because they can do so much so much better than distant officials in some faraway bureaucracy. We're unique in all the world. I had this borne in on me at the summit meeting in Ottawa the other day. We are a federation of sovereign states with as much law as possible kept at the local level. And federalism has been the secret of America's success, and it will be a priority again. America must return to her first and well-charted course. And with your help, that's exactly what we're going to do.

Thank you.

Note: The President spoke at 11:36 a.m. in the State Dining Room at the White House.

Remarks About Federal Tax Reduction Legislation at a Meeting of the House Republican Conference
July 24, 1981

Jack and Bob and Trent, thanks to your efforts and those of the rest of you, we're on the brink of fulfilling the promise we made to the American people. And today we take the last historic steps to provide the first real tax cut for all Americans in nearly 20 years. We have this chance because many of you have been working very hard. But I think our special thanks go to people like Barber Conable and Dick Cheney and Stan Parris and Newt Gingrich.

This tax cut is the most crucial item left on our agenda for prosperity. Last fall, most of us in this room stood out on the steps of the Capitol and pledged to work as a team, united in the goals of our party. We pledged that within the year we would not only cut Federal spending that had grown out of control, we would cut taxes that had stolen the hope for a better tomorrow. We made a solemn covenant with the American people, and today we're within striking distance of those goals.

You and other members of the House and Senate are working out the final details of the largest budget cuts the Congress has ever considered. And today you and your colleagues will begin an historic debate as our final tax cut proposal is introduced.

This is a good and a fair tax bill. It includes incentives to further stimulate our economy. I promise my enthusiastic support, and I think it'll have yours. The choice is between a tax increase or this bipartisan tax cut. The choice is clear, and the momentum is with us. We've gotten this far because we've all stood together. If we remain together during these last critical days, we'll realize the goal to which we pledged ourselves, a goal the people said, actually, they didn't think could ever be reached. Together, we can change the course of history, reverse the decline of America's economic strength, and start her on the road to recovery again.

Now, I said the choice before us is a tax cut or a tax increase. The Speaker boasts that this tax cut of 15 percent gives a bigger break to the worker than our bill. And if you're only planning on living for 2 years, it does. [*Laughter*] But then bracket creep takes over, and the taxes start going up again.

The other day—to a bunch of newspaper editors—I had a chart to show them about this. And of every bracket, from the bottom right on up, those tax brackets—and their line was dotted and our line was a solid line; I thought that was more appropriate that way. [*Laughter*] But our line kept on going down in the tax cut. Their line, dotted line, started down and then turned up. And it turns up when they come to the end of that 15 percent, and bracket creep continues to take over.

Now, our bill goes on for 3 years, and then that reduction of 25 percent in the tax rate becomes permanent, because from then on, we index the brackets against inflation.

Now, they claim it's too risky to cut taxes for 3 years ahead; you just can't figure that far ahead. That's for individuals. But it's perfectly all right for business, to offer them a tax cut every year for the next 7 years, which is in their proposal.

In the last 10 years, the majority leadership in the House has given the American people five tax cuts. But in those same 10 years, taxes have increased by more than $400 billion. That's a kind of sleight of hand at which you and I have no talent. That all belongs to them. When is a tax cut not a tax cut? When they do it.

Now, some things that I know you already know: Our bipartisan tax bill, Conable-Hance bill, targets three-fourths of the tax relief to the middle-income wage earners, indexing to eliminate bracket creep, and estate tax relief that will keep family farms and family-owned businesses in the family. Now, which bill really sounds like a bill for the working people?

I've been concerned lately that rhetoric has begun to blur the sharp edge in this debate, and many people are unaware of the clear choice before them. Now, everyone should know that their taxes are already doomed to rise by 22 percent during the next 3 years because of the built-in tax increase and the bracket creep of inflation. The committee bill offers a 15-percent cut; we offer 25.

It's been said that government performs its highest duty when it restores to its citizens taxes oppressively collected. Well, let us respond to that duty call that we have sounded and rally others here and across America. Let us point out a simple truth. We have worked out between us, all of us here, a tax bill that we believe will provide incentive and stimulate productivity, thus reducing inflation and producing jobs for the unemployed. That is the one and only purpose of the tax bill that we're proposing. What is it that they are proposing? What is their purpose? Well, they have put together a tax bill for the simple purpose of defeating us to provide a political victory for themselves. And that's not good enough for the people.

Now, if there's any question about that, let me point something out. It was only a few months ago that they derided and denounced the very idea of a tax cut at all.

They said it would be wildly inflationary in these times. Then as we persisted, and as the voice of the people began to be heard, why, suddenly they also were for a tax cut. But they were just against ours. They wouldn't hear of a 3-year tax cut, no, sir. You couldn't do that. But one day we learned that they thought a 2-year cut might be practical. [*Laughter*] And now it's 2 years and maybe 3 if some economic standard is met 2 years from now.

Well, as I said the other day, I think the American people have enough cynicism that they don't think that trigger will ever work if you leave that much of an opening for 3 years from now. What we need is for people to look ahead 3 years and be able to plan on the knowledge of a sure thing.

My final word this morning is let us gently point out to the people that the alternative to what we propose was written by people who are better at increasing taxes than they are at reducing them. And no matter how much they call this one a tax cut, it's another increase.

Thank you very much.

Note: The President spoke at 9:47 a.m. in the Cannon Caucus Room, Room 345, Cannon House Office Building.

Remarks of the President and Prime Minister Robert D. Muldoon of New Zealand Following Their Meeting
July 24, 1981

The President. Ladies and gentlemen of the press, this has been a very great pleasure and honor for us to have Prime Minister Muldoon of New Zealand here with us today.

New Zealand is a longtime friend and ally in the closest relationship with the United States. They've been by our side in every war that has taken place that we've been involved in in this century. And we've had a very good meeting in getting acquainted, discussing the trade relations between us, and they're numerous and of mutual advantage to all of us.

We've discussed the world situation, our

own proposals for a project in the Caribbean and Central America, but they have had such a project for a number of years in the island nations of the South Pacific. So all in all, it has been a very, very warm and helpful experience. We're delighted, as I say, to have the Prime Minister here, and I hope that this is just the first of many meetings in the years to come.

Mr. Prime Minister, thank you for being here with us.

The Prime Minister. Thank you, Mr. President. I've been delighted to have this opportunity of making the acquaintance of

President Reagan and some of the members of his Cabinet who hold responsibilities that are particularly important to the bilateral relationship between New Zealand and the United States.

I don't think that there are closer friends than New Zealand and the United States. We see so many things alike, and we admire so much the way in which this country shoulders the burden of leadership of the free world. And today, in some of the early months of a new administration, I'm delighted to have had the opportunity of spending some time with the President and members of his Cabinet, making an acquaintance which I'm sure will be fruitful in the years to come in further cementing the great friendship between our two nations.

Note: The exchange began at 1:20 p.m. at the North Portico of the White House. Earlier, the President and the Prime Minister had a meeting in the Oval Office, followed by a luncheon in the Blue Room.

White House Statement and Telegram to Ambassador Philip C. Habib on the Cessation of Hostilities Between Lebanon and Israel
July 24, 1981

The President welcomes this as a hopeful and encouraging sign on the road to achieving a permanent peace in this critical region of the world.

We all applaud your consummate skill and tireless efforts on behalf of peace. You have my deep appreciation and admiration. Well done.

RONALD REAGAN

Note: Deputy Press Secretary Larry M.

Speakes read the statement to reporters (9:15 a.m. in his office at the White Hous(Assistant to the President for Communica tions David R. Gergen read the text of the President's telegram to Ambassador Habib at the daily news briefing, which began at 2:40 p.m. in the Briefing Room at the White House.

Earlier in the day, Ambassador Habib reported to the President from Israel on the cessation of hostilities between Lebanon and Israel.

Remarks About Federal Tax Reduction Legislation at a Meeting With Trade Association Representatives
July 27, 1981

Thank you, very much. And the gentleman accompanying me you will meet later, after my few minutes of remarks, our Secretary of the Treasury, Don Regan. I found out that if you go far enough back in Irish history, we're cousins. [*Laughter*] And I didn't know there was any nepotism involved, though, when I asked him to take this job. [*Laughter*]

Well, thank you for coming today. It gives us a chance to bring you up to date on the progress of our economic programs, and it also give us a chance to ask you for a little help. And it isn't the kind of help—don't reach for your checkbooks—this time we want blood. [*Laughter*] But we know that you're an interest group for free enterprise, and you know full well what is at stake as

Photographic
Portfolio

Overleaf: Horseback riding with Secretary of Commerce Baldrige at Quantico Marine Base, Va., June 17. *Left:* Congratulating Master Sergeant Roy P. Benavide on receiving the Congressional Medal of Honor, at the Pentagon February 24. *Below:* Greeting families of the freed American hostage in the State Dining Room, January 25. *Above right:* Addressing a joint session of the Canadian Parliament in Ottawa, March 11. *Below right* Leaving George Washington University Hospital following his recovery from the attempted assassination, April 11.

Left: With the Vice President during an awards ceremony in the Oval Office for *Columbia* astronauts John W. Young and Capt. Robert L. Crippen, May 19. *Below:* On board the U.S.S. *Constellation* off the coast of California, August 20. *Right:* Discussing the situation in Lebanon with reporters on the South Lawn, May 27.

Right: Participating in the bicentennial observance of the Battle of Yorktown with French President François Mitterrand, at Yorktown, Va., October 19. *Below:* With Secretary of State Haig at the International Meeting on Cooperation and Development in Cancún, Mexico, October 22.

we struggle to put in place our program for economic recovery.

We've accomplished a great deal. The Congress is completing work on the largest budget cuts that body has ever considered in the history of this country. We've done much to reduce the burden of overregulation, and we're going to continue along that line. And someday, maybe, the blizzard of paperwork will just be a light snowstorm each year on Washington.

We're working closely with the Federal Reserve Board to maintain a slow and steady monetary growth. But the last and the most crucial item on our agenda for prosperity still lies ahead. We must cut taxes.

The day after tomorrow, the Members of the Congress will choose between the bipartisan tax cut called for in our program for recovery, a bill coauthored by a Republican and a Democrat, and a tax increase proposed by the House leadership. They don't call it that, but it is. And the choice will determine the future of our economy, of your business or organization, and of your family.

Now, I'm afraid that as the tax debates come down to the wire, so much has been said that some very simple differences have gotten lost. For example, the Speaker of the House boasts that the leadership bill gives a higher cut to working Americans. And that's true, if you're only planning on living for 2 more years. [*Laughter*]

Tonight on television, I'll be on at 8 o'clock tonight on television, talking about this tax program, and I'm going to have some charts pointing out that, yes, with their 2-year cut and our 3-year cut, theirs seems to be a deeper cut as we go down. But their line then starts steeply upward at the end of those 2 years; ours keeps on going down for the third year, and then levels off, because we're indexing the tax brackets to stop government's illicit profiteering on the basis of inflation.

And you know, of course, what bracket creep is. That's when inflation causes your salary to go up, the taxes go up as well. It's been estimated that a worker who was earning $10,000 in 1972, to keep even today, has to earn nearly $20,000—$19,850. That's to keep even with inflation, but that's before taxes. After taxes, he hasn't kept even at all. His taxes have gone up 33 percent.

A sad trick has been played on the working people of this country, and our bill will make that right. By indexing taxes for inflation, we make a permanent commitment.

Now, we want to cut taxes for tomorrow as well as today. For the majority leadership to talk about a tax cut at all is puzzling, because the taxes will go up by nearly 22 percent over the next 3 years and continue going up beyond that period, due to that bracket creep that I mentioned, plus the tax increases already built into the system, four more tax increases to take place in social security payroll tax between now and 1990—and not only will there be increases in the rate, they will also increase the amount of earnings against which that rate will apply.

Now, their 15-percent cut will still leave a sizable tax increase. We counter that 22-percent climb with a 25-percent cut, and then we stop that increase that I mentioned that will be on that graph tonight by stopping bracket creep.

But when the details of the debate are cleared away, let everyone remember this: The concepts at the heart of our first tax proposal, the first thing that we came out with, remain intact today. There had been compromises and changes made, and the compromises weren't in principle at all. Actually, it proved that more cooks were better than just one, because we found legitimate proposals made that could benefit the package although we stayed within the same rough figure as to amount.

Our bill cuts taxes across the board, for 3 years, as I said, and cuts them by the same percentage for everyone who pays them and has a 3-year guarantee to let the people know where they stand. The independent businessman, the farmer, the shopkeeper— they will be able to look ahead for 3 years and see what their tax situation is going to be and thus be able to plan ahead.

Now, as you probably know, the bipartisan bill has business provisions such as the accelerated cost recovery system. And last week, we added incentives to further encourage investment in research and development. We've been lowest among all the industrial nations in that for a number of years. And our bill will almost eliminate estate taxes, ensuring that family farms and family-owned businesses will stay in the family and won't have to be sold to pay the tax.

The bipartisan proposal was designed to encourage small businesses that provide 80 percent of the new jobs that we must have. And, incidentally, in that estate tax, the thing that I'm happiest about of all is we do end that tax on a surviving spouse. There won't be any estate tax leveled when the inheritor is a husband or wife.

As you consider the two options, remember that the majority leadership in the House has given us five tax cuts in the last 10 years, and in these same 10 years, our taxes have gone up by more than $400 billion. Now, that's a kind of talent we don't possess. [*Laughter*] We do ask, "When is a tax cut not a tax cut?" And the answer is, "When they wind up as a tax increase." And if we don't act now, they'll do it again.

Only a few months ago, remember, the same people who are presenting that alternative tax bill, the so-called committee bill, made fun of the idea of trying to cut taxes at all. The voters didn't think it was so funny, so before the month of January was out, they suddenly discovered that they, too, were for a tax cut—just not for our tax cut. Of course, 3 years were out of the question, to see if you could plan for a tax cut 3 years ahead. But then in February, they discovered that, well, a 2-year tax cut might be practical. And now they say that's 2 years and maybe 3, if some economic standard is met 2 years from now, that if we've achieved that goal, then that would trigger the third year's tax cut.

Well, the bottom line is simply this: Ours is a permanent commitment, and theirs is not. And tonight I will be telling the people that their tax bill is so rigged, by the end of the second year, the deficit will be $7 billion or more bigger than it will be under our program, which will automatically ensure that they will never pull that trigger that would bring about the third year's tax cut.

We want to restore individual incentive; they do not. We offer a real tax cut, and they do not. And the choice is clear. For our country to have real chance at renewal, we must have economic recovery. And tonight, I'm going to appear, as I said, to discuss these taxes. But what I'm really going to be talking about is what I think is our plan to renew American prosperity. That was the mandate of the people last November, and I would like to have your help and be able to count on it to pass the kind of legislation needed to give that recovery a chance.

I think up on the Hill, there are a great many Representatives who want to know how you feel, who want to know how the folks back home feel in making their decision on behalf of the people.

And now, I'm going to turn this meeting over to Don Regan for further explanation in detail and for your questions that you might have on these tax programs, because I've got a meeting with a fellow that just came back from the Middle East, named Habib, and I think all of us are kind of interested in finding out a few things we need to know there, too.

So, if you will excuse me now, and may I present Don Regan, the Secretary of the Treasury.

Note: The President spoke at 11:43 a.m. in the East Room at the White House.

Statement by Ambassador Philip C. Habib Following His Report to the President on the Cessation of Hostilities Between Lebanon and Israel
July 27, 1981

I have just reported to the President on the mission which he directed me to undertake not long ago. This is a satisfying moment. An end to hostile military actions and the consequent bloodshed in the Israel-Lebanon area has now taken place. The situation, however, remains fragile and sensitive. That is normal and in the nature of such things. The progress achieved so far must not be lost. Everyone involved must exercise the greatest care and caution.

The end of armed attacks, which has been achieved, could be a first, important step on the road to greater calm and security in the area. This will be indispensable if future progress is to be made toward a broad and lasting peace in the Middle East. What has been accomplished could not have been done without the help and understanding of many people. The final result, I believe, is in the interest of all the parties involved.

Thank you.

Note: Ambassador Habib made the statement to reporters at 12:37 p.m. outside the Diplomatic Entrance on the South Lawn of the White House. Prior to his statement, Ambassador Habib met with the President in the Map Room and reported on the cessation of hostilities between Lebanon and Israel.

Message to the Senate Transmitting an Amendment to Annex II of the International Convention on Load Lines
July 27, 1981

To the Senate of the United States:

I transmit herewith, for the advice and consent of the Senate to acceptance, an amendment to regulation 49(4)(b) of Annex II of the International Convention on Load Lines, 1966. The report of the Department of State is also transmitted for the information of the Senate in connection with its consideration of this amendment.

The International Convention on Load Lines established uniform principles governing the safe loading of ships on international voyages. The annexes, which form an integral part of the Convention, embody the regulations for determining the location of ships' load lines and divide the world's oceans into regions in which particular load lines must be observed depending upon the season of the year in which they operate. The amendment to regulation 49(4)(b) of the Convention, which was proposed by the Government of Australia, would redefine the seasonal tropical area in the South Indian Ocean to include waters in the new offshore oil development area off the northwest coast of Australia.

I believe that the proposed amendment will not be detrimental to American shipping and should be accepted. I recommend that the Senate give early and favorable consideration to this amendment.

RONALD REAGAN

The White House,
July 27, 1981.

Address to the Nation on Federal Tax Reduction Legislation
July 27, 1981

Good evening.

I'd intended to make some remarks about the problem of social security tonight, but the immediacy of congressional action on the tax program, a key component of our economic package, has to take priority. Let me just say, however, I've been deeply disturbed by the way those of you who are dependent on social security have been needlessly frightened by some of the inaccuracies which have been given wide circulation. It's true that the social security system has financial problems. It's also true that these financial problems have been building for more than 20 years, and nothing has been done. I hope to address you on this entire subject in the near future.

In the meantime, let me just say this: I stated during the campaign and I repeat now, I will not stand by and see those of you who are dependent on social security deprived of the benefits you've worked so hard to earn. I make that pledge to you as your President. You have no reason to be frightened. You will continue to receive your checks in the full amount due you. In any plan to restore fiscal integrity of social security, I personally will see that the plan will not be at the expense of you who are now dependent on your monthly social security checks.

Now, let us turn to the business at hand. It's been nearly 6 months since I first reported to you on the state of the nation's economy. I'm afraid my message that night was grim and disturbing. I remember telling you we were in the worst economic mess since the Great Depression. Prices were continuing to spiral upward, unemployment was reaching intolerable levels, and all because government was too big and spent too much of our money.

We're still not out of the woods, but we've made a start. And we've certainly surprised those longtime and somewhat cynical observers of the Washington scene, who looked, listened, and said, "It can never be done; Washington will never change its spending habits." Well, some-

thing very exciting has been happening here in Washington, and you're responsible.

Your voices have been heard—millions of you, Democrats, Republicans, and Independents, from every profession, trade and line of work, and from every part of this land. You sent a message that you wanted a new beginning. You wanted to change one little, two little word—two letter word, I should say. It doesn't sound like much, but it sure can make a difference changing "by government," "control *by* government" to "control *of* government."

In that earlier broadcast, you'll recall I proposed a program to drastically cut back government spending in the 1982 budget, which begins October 1st, and to continue cutting in the '83 and '84 budgets. Along with this I suggested an across-the-board tax cut, spread over those same 3 years, and the elimination of unnecessary regulations which were adding billions to the cost of things we buy.

All the lobbying, the organized demonstrations, and the cries of protest by those whose way of life depends on maintaining government's wasteful ways were no match for your voices, which were heard loud and clear in these marble halls of government. And you made history with your telegrams, your letters, your phone calls and, yes, personal visits to talk to your elected representatives. You reaffirmed the mandate you delivered in the election last November—a mandate that called for an end to government policies that sent prices and mortgage rates skyrocketing while millions of Americans went jobless.

Because of what you did, Republicans and Democrats in the Congress came together and passed the most sweeping cutbacks in the history of the Federal budget. Right now, Members of the House and Senate are meeting in a conference committee to reconcile the differences between the two budget-cutting bills passed by the House and Senate. When they finish, all Americans will benefit from savings of approximately $140 billion in reduced government costs over just the next 3 years. And that doesn't include the additional savings from the hundreds of burdensome regulations already cancelled or facing cancellation.

For 19 out of the last 20 years, the Federal Government has spent more than it took in. There will be another large deficit in this present year which ends September 30th, but with our program in place, it won't be quite as big as it might have been. And starting next year, the deficits will get smaller until in just a few years the budget can be balanced. And we hope we can begin whittling at that almost $1 trillion debt that hangs over the future of our children.

Now, so far, I've been talking about only one part of our program for economic recovery—the budget-cutting part. I don't minimize its importance. Just the fact that Democrats and Republicans could work together as they have, proving the strength of our system, has created an optimism in our land. The rate of inflation is no longer in double-digit figures. The dollar has regained strength in the international money markets, and businessmen and investors are making decisions with regard to industrial development, modernization and expansion—all of this based on anticipation of our program being adopted and put into operation.

A recent poll shows that where a year and a half ago only 24 percent of our people believed things would get better, today 46 percent believe they will. To justify their faith, we must deliver the other part of our program. Our economic package is a closely knit, carefully constructed plan to restore America's economic strength and put our nation back on the road to prosperity.

Each part of this package is vital. It cannot be considered piecemeal. It was proposed as a package, and it has been supported as such by the American people. Only if the Congress passes all of its major components does it have any real chance of success. This is absolutely essential if we are to provide incentives and make capital available for the increased productivity required to provide real, permanent jobs for our people.

And let us not forget that the rest of the world is watching America carefully to see how we'll act at this critical moment.

I have recently returned from a summit meeting with world leaders in Ottawa, Canada, and the message I heard from them was quite clear. Our allies depend on a strong and economically sound America. And they're watching events in this country, particularly those surrounding our program for economic recovery, with close attention and great hopes. In short, the best way to have a strong foreign policy abroad is to have a strong economy at home.

The day after tomorrow, Wednesday, the House of Representatives will begin debate on two tax bills. And once again, they need to hear from you. I know that doesn't give you much time, but a great deal is at stake. A few days ago I was visited here in the office by a Democratic Congressman from one of our southern States. He'd been back in his district. And one day one of his constituents asked him where he stood on our economic recovery program—I outlined that program in an earlier broadcast—particularly the tax cut. Well, the Congressman, who happens to be a strong leader in support of our program, replied at some length with a discussion of the technical points involved, but he also mentioned a few reservations he had on certain points. The constituent, a farmer, listened politely until he'd finished, and then he said, "Don't give me an essay. What I want to know is are you for 'im or agin 'im?"

Well, I appreciate the gentleman's support and suggest his question is a message your own representatives should hear. Let me add, those representatives honestly and sincerely want to know your feelings. They get plenty of input from the special interest groups. They'd like to hear from their home folks.

Now, let me explain what the situation is and what's at issue. With our budget cuts, we've presented a complete program of reduction in tax rates. Again, our purpose was to provide incentive for the individual, incentives for business to encourage production and hiring of the unemployed, and to free up money for investment. Our bill calls for a 5-percent reduction in the income tax rates by October 1st, a 10-percent reduction beginning July 1st, 1982, and another 10-percent cut a year later, a 25-percent total reduction over 3 years.

But then to ensure the tax cut is permanent, we call for indexing the tax rates in 1985, which means adjusting them for inflation. As it is now, if you get a cost-of-living raise that's intended to keep you even with inflation, you find that the increase in the number of dollars you get may very likely move you into a higher tax bracket, and you wind up poorer than you would. This is called bracket creep.

Bracket creep is an insidious tax. Let me give an example. If you earned $10,000 a year in 1972, by 1980 you had to earn $19,700 just to stay even with inflation. But that's before taxes. Come April 15th, you'll find your tax rates have increased 30 percent. Now, if you've been wondering why you don't seem as well-off as you were a few years back, it's because government makes a profit on inflation. It gets an automatic tax increase without having to vote on it. We intend to stop that.

Time won't allow me to explain every detail. But our bill includes just about everything to help the economy. We reduce the marriage penalty, that unfair tax that has a working husband and wife pay more tax than if they were single. We increase the exemption on the inheritance or estate tax to $600,000, so that farmers and family-owned businesses don't have to sell the farm or store in the event of death just to pay the taxes. Most important, we wipe out the tax entirely for a surviving spouse. No longer, for example, will a widow have to sell the family source of income to pay a tax on her husband's death.

There are deductions to encourage investment and savings. Business gets realistic depreciation on equipment and machinery. And there are tax breaks for small and independent businesses which create 80 percent of all our new jobs.

This bill also provides major credits to the research and development industry. These credits will help spark the high technology breakthroughs that are so critical to America's economic leadership in the world. There are also added incentives for small businesses, including a provision that will lift much of the burden of costly paperwork that government has imposed on small business.

In addition, there's short-term but substantial assistance for the hard pressed thrift industry, as well as reductions in oil taxes that will benefit new or independent oil producers and move our nation a step closer to energy self-sufficiency. Our bill is, in short, the first real tax cut for everyone in almost 20 years.

Now, when I first proposed this—incidentally, it has now become a bipartisan measure coauthored by Republican Barber Conable and Democrat Kent Hance—the Democratic leadership said a tax cut was out of the question. It would be wildly inflationary. And that was before my inauguration. And then your voices began to he heard and suddenly, in February, the leadership discovered that, well, a 1-year tax cut was feasible. Well, we kept on pushing our 3-year tax cut and by June, the opposition found that a 2-year tax cut might work. Now it's July, and they find they could even go for a third year cut provided there was a trigger arrangement that would only allow it to go into effect if certain economic goals had been met by 1983.

But by holding the people's tax reduction hostage to future economic events, they will eliminate the people's ability to plan ahead. Shopkeepers, farmers, and individuals will be denied the certainty they must have to begin saving or investing more of their money. And encouraging more savings and investment is precisely what we need now to rebuild our economy.

There's also a little sleight of hand in that trigger mechanism. You see, their bill, the committee bill, ensures that the 1983 deficit will be $6½ billion greater than their own trigger requires. As it stands now, the design of their own bill will not meet the trigger they've put in; therefore, the third year tax cut will automatically never take place.

If I could paraphrase a well-known statement by Will Rogers that he had never met a man he didn't like, I'm afraid we have some people around here who never met a tax they didn't hike. Their tax proposal, similar in a number of ways to ours but differing in some very vital parts, was passed out of the House Ways and Means Committee, and from now on I'll refer to it as the committee bill and ours as the bipartisan bill. They'll be the bills taken up Wednesday.

The majority leadership claims theirs gives a greater break to the worker than ours, and it does—that is, if your're only planning to live 2 more years. The plain truth is, our choice is not between two plans to reduce taxes; it's between a tax cut or a tax increase. There is now built into our present system, including payroll social security taxes and the bracket creep I've mentioned, a 22-percent tax increase over the next 3 years. The committee bill offers a 15-percent cut over 2 years; our bipartisan bill gives a 25-percent reduction over 3 years.

Now, as you can see by this chart,[1] there is the 22-percent tax increase. Their cut is below that line. But ours wipes out that increase and with a little to spare. And there it is, as you can see. The red column—that is the 15-percent tax cut, and it still leaves you with an increase. The green column is our bipartisan bill which wipes out the tax increase and gives you an ongoing cut.

Incidentally, their claim that cutting taxes for individuals for as much as 3 years ahead is risky, rings a little hollow when you realize that their bill calls for business tax cuts each year for 7 years ahead. It rings even more hollow when you consider the fact the majority leadership routinely endorses Federal spending bills that project years into the future, but objects to a tax bill that will return your money over a 3-year period.

Now, here is another chart which illustrates what I said about their giving a better break if you only intend to live for 2 more years. Their tax cut, so called, is the dotted line. Ours is the solid line. As you can see, in an earning bracket of $20,000, their tax cut is slightly more generous than ours for the first 2 years. Then, as you can see, their tax bill, the dotted line, starts going up and up and up. On the other hand, in our bipartisan tax bill, the solid

---

[1] *At this point, the President referred to two charts which were shown on the televised broadcast of his address.*

line, our tax cut keeps on going down, and then stays down permanently. This is true of all earning brackets—not just the $20,000 level that I've used as an example—from the lowest to the highest. This red space between the two lines is the tax money that will remain in your pockets if our bill passes; and it's the amount that will leave your pockets if their tax bill is passed.

Now, I take no pleasure in saying this, but those who will seek to defeat our Conable-Hance bipartisan bill as debate begins Wednesday are the ones who have given us five "tax cuts" in the last 10 years. But, our taxes went up $400 billion in those same 10 years. The lines on these charts say a lot about who's really fighting for whom. On the one hand, you see a genuine and lasting commitment to the future of working Americans; on the other, just another empty promise.

Those of us in the bipartisan coalition want to give this economy and the future of this Nation back to the people, because putting people first has always been America's secret weapon. The House majority leadership seems less concerned about protecting your family budget than with spending more on the Federal budget.

Our bipartisan tax bill targets three-quarters of its tax relief to middle-income wage earners who presently pay almost three quarters of the total income tax. It also then indexes the tax brackets to ensure that you can keep that tax reduction in the years ahead. There also is, as I said, estate tax relief that will keep family farms and family-owned businesses in the family, and there are provisions for personal retirement plans and individual savings accounts.

Because our bipartisan bill is so clearly drawn and broadly based, it provides the kind of predictability and certainty that the financial segments of our society need to make investment decisions that stimulate productivity and make our economy grow. Even more important, if the tax cut goes to you, the American people, in the third year, that money returned to you won't be available to the Congress to spend, and that, in my view, is what this whole controversy comes down to. Are you entitled to the fruits of your own labor or does government have some presumptive right to spend and spend and spend?

I'm also convinced our business tax cut is superior to theirs because it's more equitable, and it will do a much better job promoting the surge in investment we so badly need to rebuild our industrial base.

There's something else I want to tell you. Our bipartisan coalition worked out a tax bill we felt would provide incentive and stimulate productivity, thus reducing inflation and providing jobs for the unemployed. That was our only goal. Our opponents in the beginning didn't want a tax bill at all. So what is the purpose behind their change of heart? They've put a tax program together for one reason only: to provide themselves with a political victory. Never mind that it won't solve the economic problems confronting our country. Never mind that it won't get the wheels of industry turning again or eliminate the inflation which is eating us alive.

This is not the time for political fun and games. This is the time for a new beginning. I ask you now to put aside any feelings of frustration or helplessness about our political institutions and join me in this dramatic but responsible plan to reduce the enormous burden of Federal taxation on you and your family.

During recent months many of you have asked what can you do to help make America strong again. I urge you again to contact your Senators and Congressmen. Tell them of your support for this bipartisan proposal. Tell them you believe this is an unequalled opportunity to help return America to prosperity and make government again the servant of the people.

In a few days the Congress will stand at the fork of two roads. One road is all too familiar to us. It leads ultimately to higher taxes. It merely brings us full circle back to the source of our economic problems, where the government decides that it knows better than you what should be done with your earnings and, in fact, how you should conduct your life. The other road promises to renew the American spirit. It's a road of hope and opportunity. It places the direction of your life back in your hands where it belongs.

I've not taken your time this evening merely to ask you to trust me. Instead, I ask you to trust yourselves. That's what America is all about. Our struggle for nationhood, our unrelenting fight for freedom, our very existence—these have all rested on the assurance that you must be free to shape your life as you are best able to, that no one can stop you from reaching higher or take from you the creativity that has made America the envy of mankind.

One road is timid and fearful; the other bold and hopeful.

In these 6 months, we've done so much and have come so far. It's been the power of millions of people like you who have determined that we will make America great again. You have made the difference up to now. You will make the difference again. Let us not stop now.

Thank you. God bless you, and good night.

Note: The President spoke at 8:01 p.m. from the Oval Office at the White House. His remarks were broadcast live on radio and television.

Message to the Senate Transmitting the United States-Sweden Supplementary Convention on Extradition
July 28, 1981

To the Senate of the United States:

With a view of receiving the advice and consent of the Senate to ratification, I transmit herewith the Supplementary Convention on Extradition between the United States of America and Sweden, signed at Washington on May 27, 1981.

I transmit also, for the information of the

Senate, the report of the Department of State with respect to the treaty.

The supplementary extradition treaty updates an existing extradition treaty with Sweden of October 24, 1961. It expands the list of extraditable offenses to include: tax evasion, obstruction of justice, offenses relating to the international transfer of funds, and conspiracy to commit extraditable offenses. Upon entry into force it will amend the extradition convention between the United States and Sweden.

This treaty will improve upon our current extradition treaty with Sweden and will thus contribute to international cooperation in law enforcement. I recommend that the Senate give early and favorable consideration to the treaty and give its advice and consent to ratification.

RONALD REAGAN

The White House,
July 28, 1981.

Nomination of Jack F. Matlock To Be United States Ambassador to Czechoslovakia
July 28, 1981

The President today announced his intention to nominate Jack F. Matlock, of Florida, to be Ambassador to the Czechoslovak Socialist Republic, vice Francis J. Meehan.

In 1953–56 Mr. Matlock was an instructor in Russian language and literature at Dartmouth College. He entered the Foreign Service in 1956 and was intelligence research analyst in the Department. He was consular officer in Vienna (1958–60), attended Russian language and area training in Oberammergau (1960–61), political officer in Moscow (1961–63), in Accra (1963–67), principal officer in Zanzibar (1967–69), and Deputy Chief of Mission in Dar es Salaam (1969–70). In 1970–71 he attended the Executive Seminar in National and International Affairs at the Foreign Service Insti-

tute. In the Department he was country director for Soviet affairs (1973–74). He was Deputy Chief of Mission, Minister-Counselor, in Moscow, in 1974–78. He was diplomat in residence at Vanderbilt University in 1978–79. In 1979–80 he was Deputy Director of the Foreign Service Institute, Department of State. Since 1980 he has been Deputy Chief of Mission and Chargé d'Affaires, Moscow.

He graduated from Duke University (A.B.) and Columbia University (M.A.). His languages are Czech, French, German, Russian, and Swahili. Mr. Matlock is married, has five children, and resides in Coconut Creek, Fla. He was born October 1, 1929, in Greensboro, N.C.

Nomination of Robert P. Paganelli To Be United States Ambassador to Syria
July 28, 1981

The President today announced his intention to nominate Robert P. Paganelli, of New York, to be Ambassador to the Syrian Arab Republic, vice Talcott W. Seelye.

Mr. Paganelli entered the Foreign Service in 1958 as intelligence research special-

ist in the Department. He attended Arabic language training in the Department and in Beirut in 1959–61. He was Foreign Service officer-general in Basra (1961–62) and in Baghdad (1962–63). He was economic officer in Beirut (1963–65), political officer in

669

Damascus (1965–67) and in Amman (1967–68). In 1968–71 he was in the Department as desk officer for Jordan, then personnel officer. He was political officer in Rome in 1971–74 and Ambassador to the State of Qatar in 1974–77. He attended the Executive Seminar in National and International Affairs at the Foreign Service Institute in 1977–78 and was Director of the Office of Western European Affairs in 1978–79. Since 1979 he has been Deputy Chief of Mission in Rome.

Mr. Paganelli graduated from Hamilton College (B.A.). He served in the United States Air Force in 1951–54. He is married, has two children, and resides in Albion, N.Y. He was born November 3, 1931, in New York, N.Y.

Nomination of Richard Murphy To Be United States Ambassador to Saudi Arabia
July 28, 1981

The President today announced his intention to nominate Richard Murphy to be Ambassador to the Kingdom of Saudi Arabia, vice Robert Neumann who has resigned.

Mr. Murphy, a career Foreign Service officer, is currently concluding his assignment as Ambassador to the Philippines. He has had extensive experience in the Middle East, previously serving as Ambassador to Syria. Mr. Murphy also served as Ambassador to Mauritania in 1971–73. His other assignments include Aleppo, Jidda (political officer), and Amman.

Mr. Murphy graduated from Harvard (1951) and Cambridge University (1953). He is married to the former Anne Cook.

Executive Order 12315—Amendments to the Manual for Courts-Martial, United States, 1969 (Revised Edition)
July 29, 1981

By the authority vested in me as President by the Constitution of the United States and by Chapter 47 of Title 10 of the United States Code (the Uniform Code of Military Justice), in order to prescribe amendments to the Manual for Courts-Martial, United States, 1969 (Revised edition), prescribed by Executive Order No. 11476, as amended by Executive Order No. 11835, Executive Order No. 12018, Executive Order No. 12198, Executive Order No. 12233, and Executive Order No. 12306, it is hereby ordered as follows:

Section 1. The fifth paragraph of paragraph 70*a* of the Manual for Courts-Martial, United States, 1969 (Revised edition), is amended by inserting the following after the first sentence: "If the plea is accepted, such evidence shall be introduced during the presentencing proceedings under paragraph 75, except when the evidence is otherwise admissible on the merits.".

Sec. 2. Paragraph 75 of the said Manual for Courts-Martial is amended to read as follows:

"*75. Presentencing Procedure. a. General.* (1) *Procedure.* After findings of guilty have been announced, the prosecution and defense may present appropriate matter to aid the court in determining an appropriate sentence. Such matter shall be presented pursuant to this paragraph and, when presented, shall ordinarily follow the following sequence:

"(a) Presentation by the trial counsel of service data relating to the accused taken from the charge sheet.

"(b) Presentation by the trial counsel of personal data relating to the accused and of the character of the accused's prior service as reflected in the personnel records of the accused.

"(c) Presentation by the trial counsel of evidence of prior convictions, military or civilian.

"(d) Presentation by the trial counsel of evidence of aggravation.

"(e) Presentation by the defense of evidence in extenuation or mitigation or both.

"(f) Rebuttal.

"(g) Argument by the trial counsel on sentence.

"(h) Argument by the defense counsel on sentence.

"(i) Rebuttal arguments in the discretion of the military judge or the president of a special court-martial without a military judge.

"(2) *Imposition of sentence.* Sentencing will be imposed in all cases without unreasonable delay.

"(3) *Sentencing matter and findings.* Evidence that is presented to the court after findings of guilty have been announced may not be considered as evidence against the accused in determining the legal sufficiency of the findings of guilty upon review. If any matter inconsistent with the plea of guilty is received or if it appears from any matter received that a plea of guilty was entered improvidently, action should be taken as outlined in paragraph 70.

"*b. Matter to be presented by the prosecution.*

"(1) *Service data from the charge sheet.* The trial counsel shall inform the court of the data on the charge sheet relating to the age, pay, and service of the accused and the duration and nature of any restraint imposed upon the accused before trial. Subject to the discretion of the military judge or president of a special court-martial without a military judge, this may be accomplished by reading the material from the charge sheet or by supplying the court with an appropriate statement of such matter. If the defense objects to the data as being materially inaccurate or incomplete or as containing specified objectional matter, the military judge or president of a special court-martial without a military judge shall determine the issue. Objections not asserted are waived.

"(2) *Personal data and character of prior service of the accused.* Under regulations of the Secretary concerned, the trial counsel may obtain and introduce from the personnel records of the accused evidence of the marital status of the accused and the number of dependents, if any, of the accused, and evidence of the character of prior service of the accused. Such evidence includes copies of reports reflecting the past military efficiency, conduct, performance, and history of the accused and evidence of any disciplinary actions to include punishments under Article 15. See paragraph 75*b* (3) for evidence of prior convictions of the accused. Personnel records of the accused include all those records made or maintained in accordance with departmental regulations that reflect the past military efficiency, conduct, performance, and history of the accused. If the accused objects to the information as being inaccurate or incomplete in a specific respect, or as containing matter that is not admissible under the Military Rules of Evidence as applied to the issue of sentencing, the matter shall be determined by the military judge or president of a special court-martial without a military judge. Objections not asserted are waived.

"(3) *Evidence of prior convictions of the accused.* (a) *Generally.* The trial counsel may introduce evidence of prior military or civilian convictions of the accused. Although such convictions need not be similar to the offense of which the accused has been found guilty, they must be for offenses committed during the six years next preceding the commission of any offense of which the accused has been found guilty. In computing the six-year period, periods of unauthorized absence demonstrated by the findings in the case or by evidence of previous convictions should be excluded. A vacation of a suspended sentence is not itself a conviction and is not admissible as such, but may be admissible under paragraph 75*b*(2) as reflected of the character of the prior service of the accused.

"(b) *Finality.* Before a conviction is admissible under this paragraph, all direct review and appeals must be completed.

(See Article 44(b) and paragraph 68*d*). The following do not constitute direct review or appeal under this paragraph and do not affect the admissibility of a court-martial conviction under this paragraph: a pending collateral attack on a conviction in a federal court; a pending extraordinary writ to a Court of Military Review or to the Court of Military Appeals; a request to the Judge Advocate General to vacate or modify the findings or sentence of a court-martial under Article 69 "on the ground of newly discovered evidence, fraud on the court, lack of jurisdiction over the accused or the offense, or error prejudicial to the substantial rights of the accused"; or a pending petition to the Judge Advocate General under Article 73. Before a civilian conviction is admissible under this paragraph, it must be considered a final conviction under the laws of the jurisdiction in which it occurred; unless specifically provided otherwise by such laws, the conviction will be considered final upon completion of all direct appeals. For example, pending collateral attack or an extraordinary writ does not affect the admissibility of a civilian conviction under this paragraph unless the laws of the jurisdiction in which the conviction occurred specifically provide that the conviction is not final under such circumstances.

"(c) *Method of proof.* Previous convictions may be proven by any evidence admissible under the Military Rules of Evidence. Normally, previous convictions may be proven by use of the personnel records of the accused, by the record of the conviction, or by the order promulgating the result of trial.

"(4) *Evidence in aggravation.* If a finding of guilty of an offense is based on a plea of guilty and available evidence as to any aggravating circumstances relating to the offenses of which the accused has been found guilty was not introduced before findings, the prosecution may introduce such evidence after the findings are announced. A written or oral deposition taken in accordance with paragraph 117 is admissible for purposes of evidence in aggravation, subject to Article 49.

"(5) *Access of the defense to information to be presented by the trial counsel.* The defense has the right upon request to receive prior to arraignment copies of such written material as will be presented by the prosecution on sentencing, along with a list of prosecution witnesses, if any. In the event that requested material is not provided, the defense shall have the right when such material is introduced on sentencing to obtain a recess or continuance to inspect and reply to the material.

"*c. Matter to be presented by the defense.* (1) *In general.* The defense may present matters in rebuttal of any material presented by the prosecution and may present matters in extenuation and mitigation regardless of whether the defense offered evidence before findings.

"(a) *Matter in extenuation.* Matter in extenuation of an offense serves to explain the circumstances surrounding the commission of an offense, including those reasons for committing the offense which do not constitute a legal justification or excuse.

"(b) *Matter in mitigation.* Matter in mitigation of an offense is introduced to lessen the punishment to be adjudged by the court, or to furnish grounds for a recommendation of clemency. It includes the fact that nonjudicial punishment under Article 15 has been imposed for an offense growing out of the same act or omission that constitutes the offense of which the accused has been found guilty (see paragraph 68*g*), particular acts of good conduct or bravery, and evidence of the reputation or record of the accused in the service for efficiency, fidelity, subordination, temperance, courage, or any other trait that is desirable in a good service-member. The accused may thus, for example, introduce evidence of the character of former military service in the form of former discharges from military service.

"(2) *Statement by the accused.* (a) *Generally.* The accused may testify, make an unsworn statement, or both in extenuation, in mitigation, or to rebut matters presented by the prosecution, or for all three purposes whether or not the accused testified prior to findings. Such statement may be limited to any one or more of the specifications of which the accused has been found guilty. This provision does not permit the filing of an affidavit of the accused.

"(b) *Testimony of the accused.* The accused may give sworn oral testimony under this paragraph and shall be subject to cross-examination concerning it by the trial counsel or examination on it by the court, or both.

"(c) *Unsworn statement.* The accused may make an unsworn statement under this paragraph and may not be cross-examined by the trial counsel upon it or examined upon it by the court. The prosecution may, however, rebut any statements of facts therein. The unsworn statement may be oral or written and may be made by the accused, by counsel, or both. An unsworn statement ordinarily should not include what is properly argument, but inclusion of such matter by the accused when personally making an oral statement normally should not be grounds for stopping the statement.

"(3) *Rules of evidence relaxed.* The military judge or president of a special court-martial without a military judge may, with respect to matters in extenuation or mitigation or both, relax the rules of evidence. This may include receiving letters, affidavits, certificates of military and civil officers, and other writings of similar authenticity and reliability.

"d. *Rebuttal and surrebuttal.* The prosecution may present evidence to rebut evidence presented by the defense. The defense in surrebuttal may then rebut any rebuttal evidence offered by the prosecution. Rebuttal and surrebuttal may continue, subject to the discretion of the military judge or president of a special court-martial without a military judge (see for example, Military Rule of Evidence 403), as appropriate. The Military Rules of Evidence may be relaxed during rebuttal and surrebuttal to the same degree as in paragraph 75c(3).

"e. *Production of witnesses.* (1) *In general.* The requirement for the personal appearance testimony in the presentencing proceeding differs substantially from that when the testimony of a witness is offered on the merits. During the presentence proceedings, there is much greater latitude to receive information by means other than testimony presented through the personal appearance of witnesses. See paragraph 115 for determination of availability of witnesses

prior to trial. The determination at trial as to whether a witness shall be produced to testify during presentence proceedings is a matter within the sound discretion of the military judge or the president of a special court-martial without a military judge, subject to the limitations in paragraph 75e(2).

"(2) *Limitations.* A witness may be produced to testify during presentence proceedings through a subpoena or travel orders at Government expense only if—

"(a) The testimony expected to be offered by the witness is necessary for consideration of a matter of substantial significance to a determination of an appropriate sentence, including evidence necessary to resolve an alleged inaccuracy or dispute as to a material fact;

"(b) The weight or credibility of the testimony is of substantial significance to the determination of an appropriate sentence;

"(c) The other party is unwilling to stipulate to the facts to which the witness is expected to testify, except in an extraordinary case when such a stipulation would be an insufficient substitute for the testimony;

"(d) Other forms of evidence, such as oral depositions, written interrogatories, or former testimony would not be sufficient to meet the needs of the court-martial in the determination of an appropriate sentence; and

"(e) The significance of the personal appearance of the witness to the determination of an appropriate sentence, when balanced against the practical difficulties of producing the witness, favors production of the witness. Factors to be considered in relation to the balancing test provided in paragraph 75e(2)(e) include, but are not limited to, the costs of producing the witness, the timing of the request for production of the witness, the potential delay in the presentencing proceeding that may be caused by the production of the witness, or the likelihood of significant interference with military operational deployment, mission accomplishment, or essential training.

"f. *Argument.* After introduction of matters relating to sentence under this paragraph, counsel for the prosecution and defense may make arguments for an appropriate sentence. Trial counsel may not in argument purport to speak for the convening authority or any higher authority, refer to the views of such authorities or any policy directive relative to punishment, or to any punishment or quantum of punishment in excess of that which can be lawfully imposed in the particular case by that particular court. Trial counsel may, however, recommend a specific lawful sentence and may also refer to any generally accepted sentencing philosophy, to include rehabilitation of the accused, general deterrence, specific deterrence of misconduct by the accused, and social retribution.".

Sec. 3. The fourth paragraph of paragraph 115 of the said Manual for Courts-Martial is amended as follows:

a. Insert the following after the second sentence: "With respect to a witness for the prosecution on the issue of sentencing, he will not take such action unless further satisfied that it will not cause a subpoena or travel orders at Government expense to be issued, except as authorized in paragraph 75*e*.".

b. Strike out the fourth sentence and insert the following in place thereof: "A request for the personal appearance of a witness will be submitted in writing, together with a statement signed by counsel requesting the witness. A request for a witness on the merits shall contain (1) a synopsis of the testimony that it is expected the witness will give, (2) full reasons that necessitate the personal appearance of the witness, and (3) any other matter showing that the expected testimony is necessary to the ends of justice. A request for a witness in a presentencing proceeding shall contain (1) a synopsis of the testimony that it is expected the witness will give and (2) the reasons why the personal appearance of the witness is necessary under the standards set forth in paragraph 75*e*.".

c. Strike out the words "the request" in the fifth sentence and insert the following in place thereof: "a request for a witness on the merits".

d. Insert the following after the fifth sentence: "The decision on a request for a witness in a presentencing proceeding shall be made under the standards set forth in paragraph 75*e*.".

Sec. 4. The second sentence of paragraph 117*b*(2) of the said Manual for Courts-Martial is amended as follows:

a. Insert "(a)" after "unless"; and

b. Strike out the period at the end of the sentence and insert the following: "; (b) the accused consents to appointment of assistant counsel at the site of the deposition; or (c) the deposition is ordered in lieu of production of a witness on the issue of sentencing under paragraph 75*e* and the authority ordering the deposition determines that the interests of the parties and the court-martial can be served adequately by (1) an oral deposition without the presence of the accused or (2) a written deposition without the presence of the accused or counsel at the site of the deposition.".

Sec. 5. Rule 1101(c) of Chapter 27 of the said Manual for Courts-Martial is amended by striking out "75*c*" and inserting "75*b*(4), 75*c*(3), 75*d*," in place thereof.

Sec. 6. These amendments shall take effect on August 1, 1981. These amendments apply to all court-martial processes taken on or after that date: Provided, that nothing contained in these amendments shall be construed to invalidate any investigation, trial in which arraignment has been completed, or other action begun prior to that date; and any such investigation, trial, or other action may be completed in accordance with applicable laws, Executive Orders, and regulations in the same manner and with the same effect as if these amendments had not been prescribed.

Sec. 7. The Secretary of Defense, on behalf of the President, shall transmit a copy of this Order to the Congress of the United States in accord with Section 836 of Title 10 of the United States Code.

Ronald Reagan

The White House,
July 29, 1981.

[Filed with the Office of the Federal Register, 4:13 p.m., July 29, 1981]

Remarks and a Question-and-Answer Session With Reporters Following Congressional Action on Federal Tax Reduction Legislation
July 29, 1981

The President. From the bottom of my heart, I want to express my thanks to the Congress for responding this afternoon to the pleas of millions of taxpayers. The victory we've just won doesn't belong to any one individual or one party or one administration. The victories—as a matter of fact, because there have been more than one today—are for all the people. A strong bipartisan coalition of Congress, Republicans and Democrats together, has virtually assured the first real tax cut that this country has had in nearly 20 years. And it has also removed one of the most important remaining challenges on our agenda for prosperity.

I believe this first 6 months of 1981 is going to mark the beginning of a new renaissance in America. Now we can face the future with confidence and courage, because we know we're united, and we know that we are a government of the people, by the people, and for the people.

No one should doubt the difficulties that we still face, but we have made a new beginning. We're back on the right road; we're making progress. And if we keep working together, we can reach that new era of prosperity that we all want. And as we do, we'll be showing the world that our democratic system of government works because you, the people, make it work.

Thank you very much.

Q. Sir, have you now got your program in place? Ought it now to work the way you envision it?

The President. Yes. Because of the bipartisan nature, there have been changes from the original program that we submitted, but the bulk of that program, the theme as we wanted it put together, is there. And as you know, the vote was completely bipartisan—238 to 195 in the House and in the Senate this afternoon, 89 to 11.

Q. When is all this prosperity going to come about, and did you make any promises today that will cost the American people a lot of money?

The President. No, not a bit. As a matter of fact, I had several of the—even those gentlemen that I called who didn't feel that they could go with our plan have remarked that they'll testify there's been no arm-twisting or anything of that kind.

Q. When will we see the prosperity, Mr. President?

The President. Well, I said that there were difficulties that we face. We've been a long time—we've been decades coming to the point where we are, and you're not going to cure this overnight. But I think this program—as a matter of fact, I think the very fact of its passage before the program begins to show the results is going to have a psychological effect that we will see in the expectation of the people here and in the business community. But it's going to take—that's why it's a 3-year program, it's going to take those 3 years.

Q. How about by the end of the year, Mr. President, will Americans start to feel relief by the end of the year?

The President. I think that we should be seeing some signs by then. But remember, it's a 3-year program because that was our target, that we wouldn't be reaching our goal for 3 years. The effect of the tax cuts in putting money back into the economy, well, those can't be seen until that money is invested in the economy. And of course, the budget cuts in government are going to be felt as they begin to take place in the 1982 budget year that begins October 1st.

Q. What are you going to focus on next?

The President. I think there are a lot of things that maybe are, you might say, in the beginnings, in the works now, but matters that have to be dealt with that we're talking about that have to do with our relations with other countries. There's the Middle East situation and this, too, is looking better. At least we've stopped the bulk of the violence there. But our building up of our defenses, our going forward with the plans for discussing reduction of armaments with the Soviet Union—there are many social issues to be settled, also. I don't think that we'll close up the desk and go fishing.

Q. The Senate Intelligence Committee seems to have cleared Mr. Casey. What's your reaction to that?

The President. They didn't seem to, they unanimously said they wanted him to remain as Director of the CIA. I'm not surprised, because we knew that those first wild charges and accusations had no substantiation behind them. And we're very pleased with that.

Q. Any personal message for Speaker O'Neill? Any last words? [*Laughter*]

The President. No, the Speaker and I have decided that after 6 o'clock, we're friends.

Q. Well, when you're the winner it's easy to be kind. [*Laughter*]

Q. If you didn't arm-twist, what brought them all along?

The President. Actually, Helen, [Helen Thomas, United Press International] what we did was when we talked to them, we said, "Remember, in 6 months we have come from tax cut versus no cut at all." That was the first position against us. And now it came to a choice of which tax cut. And what we discussed was, in every meeting and every phone call, I said that I hap-

pened to believe that our plan was better geared to getting the economy going again; did they have any questions, any particular concerns that I could speak to? And many of them did and would take a point or two, and I would give them what I thought was the proper answer to the questions they raised.

And I had some outstanding help from a number of people, but particularly from a very fine salesman named Secretary Don Regan. We were able to clarify points that, for many of them, that did put them on our side. In some instances, there were those who sincerely felt the other way, and there was never any animus or anything else. I understood their position, and that's what the game's all about.

Q. There were absolutely no secret promises at all?

The President. Nope. No.

Mr. Speakes. Okay, let's stop there. Thank you.

Q. Are you going to invite O'Neill over for a glass of champagne?

The President. He's sure welcome.

Q. Thank you, sir.

Note: The President spoke at 5:35 p.m. in the Oval Office at the White House.

Larry M. Speakes is Deputy Assistant to the President and Deputy Press Secretary.

Statement on United States Immigration and Refugee Policy
July 30, 1981

Our nation is a nation of immigrants. More than any other country, our strength comes from our own immigrant heritage and our capacity to welcome those from other lands. No free and prosperous nation can by itself accommodate all those who seek a better life or flee persecution. We must share this responsibility with other countries.

The bipartisan select commission which reported this spring concluded that the Cuban influx to Florida made the United States sharply aware of the need for more

effective immigration policies and the need for legislation to support those policies.

For these reasons, I asked the Attorney General last March to chair a Task Force on Immigration and Refugee Policy. We discussed the matter when President López Portillo visited me last month, and we have carefully considered the views of our Mexican friends. In addition, the Attorney General has consulted with those concerned in Congress and in affected States and localities and with interested members of the public.

The Attorney General is undertaking administrative actions and submitting to Congress, on behalf of the administration, a legislative package, based on eight principles. These principles are designed to preserve our tradition of accepting foreigners to our shores, but to accept them in a controlled and orderly fashion:

• We shall continue America's tradition as a land that welcomes peoples from other countries. We shall also, with other countries, continue to share in the responsibility of welcoming and resettling those who flee oppression.

• At the same time, we must ensure adequate legal authority to establish control over immigration: to enable us, when sudden influxes of foreigners occur, to decide to whom we grant the status of refugee or asylee; to improve our border control; to expedite (consistent with fair procedures and our Constitution) return of those coming here illegally; to strengthen enforcement of our fair labor standards and laws; and to penalize those who would knowingly encourage violation of our laws. The steps we take to further these objectives, however, must also be consistent with our values of individual privacy and freedom.

• We have a special relationship with our closest neighbors, Canada and Mexico. Our immigration policy should reflect this relationship.

• We must also recognize that both the United States and Mexico have historically benefited from Mexicans obtaining employment in the United States. A number of our States have special labor needs, and we should take these into account.

• Illegal immigrants in considerable numbers have become productive members of our society and are a basic part of our work force. Those who have established equities in the United States should be recognized and accorded legal status. At the same time, in so doing, we must not encourage illegal immigration.

• We shall strive to distribute fairly, among the various localities of this country, the impacts of our national immigration and refugee policy, and we shall improve the capability of those agencies of the Federal Government which deal with these matters.

• We shall seek new ways to integrate refugees into our society without nurturing their dependence on welfare.

• Finally, we recognize that immigration and refugee problems require international solutions. We will seek greater international cooperation in the resettlement of refugees and, in the Caribbean Basin, international cooperation to assist accelerated economic development to reduce motivations for illegal immigration.

Immigration and refugee policy is an important part of our past and fundamental to our national interest. With the help of the Congress and the American people, we will work towards a new and realistic immigration policy, a policy that will be fair to our own citizens while it opens the door of opportunity for those who seek a new life in America.

Memorandum Directing Improvements in Federal Travel Management
July 30, 1981

Memorandum for the Heads of Executive Departments and Agencies

Subject: Strengthening Federal Travel Management

The Federal Government will spend almost $4 billion in fiscal year 1981 on travel. Although most of this travel is required to carry out agency programs, instances of mismanagement and wasteful spending have continued to surface over the years. To improve the management of federal travel, I am directing that the following changes be made to travel policies and practices and would urge that the lead agencies work with the rest of the Executive Branch as they implement these recommendations:

—Separate travel regulations for civilian employees, foreign service, and uniformed services will be simplified, standardized, and updated to assure consistent treatment of all federal travelers.

—Travel authorization policies will be tightened, including a reduction in the use of general travel authorizations.

—Travel services for agency employees will be improved at headquarters and principal field locations, including greater use of commercial ticketing and travel services and available discounts.

—Greater efforts will be made in cooperation with the travel industry to expand the availability and use of transportation, lodging, and other travel-related discounts for federal travelers.

—Travel reimbursement policies will be streamlined to include adoption of locality-based flat per diem rates for subsistence costs, improved controls over travel advances, and simplified voucher processing.

Effective implementation of these improvements will require a coordinated effort by those agencies with travel policy and oversight responsibilities. Accordingly, I am directing the Secretary of State, the Secretary of Defense, the Director of the Office of Personnel Management, and the Administrator of General Services to implement the necessary changes to the regulations they promulgate. I have asked the Director of the Office of Management and Budget to coordinate the implementation activities.

These improvements are an important part of this Administration's economic reform program and its efforts to reduce wasteful federal spending. I expect the results of the improvement to include:

—annual cost savings of over $200 million, consisting of $116 million in direct travel expenditures and $85 million in travel-related administrative costs;

—improved control and management of agency travel expenditures; and

—accelerated reimbursements to travelers and payments to carriers.

RONALD REAGAN

Remarks to Members of the Future Farmers of America
July 30, 1981

The President. I know you've been well-treated here. I know that Elizabeth and Secretary Bell and all have taken good care of you—and I'm a ringer. [*Laughter*]

But some of you spotted me in there, and I wasn't loafing. [*Laughter*] I had one brief spot in there, and I was trying to get some mail answered. Yesterday was a busier day. You probably read about that.

When you spotted me, I couldn't resist coming out here and saying hello to all of you and welcoming you to the Capital. I think, though, that I should make it very short—not keep you standing any longer out in the sun. Some of you turned your backs momentarily and I saw "Iowa" on the backs of some of them. I imagine there are some from Illinois also—[*cheers*]—and California. [*Cheers*] I'm a three-State man—born and raised in Illinois, started my career in Iowa as a sports announcer, and wound up in California——

Future Farmer. Did you ever go through Nebraska? [*Laughter*]

The President. Oh, yes, many times. I think I've been in all the States and now—this isn't a State, so I guess this is the fourth locale for my life.

But it's good to see you all here, and God bless all of you. Just looking at you makes the job a little easier. There are some people—you know, here in Washington you're subjected to the doomcriers and the people that think that the world is all going downhill. Don't you believe it. You're going to have greater opportunities, you're going to see more, you're going to know more, you're going to be able to live longer and be healthier, and the only credit we can take is that maybe we had a little something to do with that in bringing you along to this point.

But there's a great big world out there, and this Nation is not going to go downhill or continue on the present path. There isn't anything that we cannot do if we set our minds to it, and we're going to set them to

it, and I take courage from you.

Note: The President spoke at 10:56 a.m. in the Rose Garden at the White House.

In his remarks, the President referred to Assistant to the President for Public Liaison Elizabeth H. Dole and Secretary of Education Terrel H. Bell.

Remarks in Atlanta, Georgia, at the Annual Convention of the National Conference of State Legislatures
July 30, 1981

Mr. President and President-elect, from a President that hopes he can stick around for a while, I want to thank you and thank all of you for a most warm welcome and for this opportunity.

You know, as a former Governor standing before so many State legislators, I feel as though I should either ask for an appropriation or veto something. [*Laughter*] Some of my fondest memories are of my years in Sacramento, so I'm very pleased to be surrounded once again by those who believe in State government as devoutly as I do.

I also want to thank you for your support of our administration's economic program. I don't know who's happier about yesterday's events, me or Prince Charles.[1] [*Laughter*]

All of you in State government know full well what is at stake as we struggle to put in place our program for economic recovery. That program has four pillars: budget cuts, deregulation, monetary control, and tax reduction.

On the spending reductions, the Congress is finishing up the largest budget cuts that body has ever considered in the history of this country. The conference committee has completed its work and now, as you know better than anyone else, their work will go

back to the House and the Senate for approval.

On regulatory relief, the entire Government is working to ease the burden. And someday, maybe the blizzard of paperwork will be just a light snowstorm for the private sector, for education, and for State and local governments.

We're working closely with the Federal Reserve Board to maintain slow and steady monetary growth. But let me hasten to point out: The Fed is completely autonomous, and the present interest rates are not part of our economic recovery program. [*Laughter*]

And last night, the most crucial and the most exciting item on our agenda for prosperity passed in the House and now will go with the Senate version to a conference committee. I've been thinking over and over what this tremendous vote on taxes will mean to our nation and to our future. America is better off today than she was yesterday. America is more confident today. And the economic possibilities for all Americans are greater than they were 24 hours ago.

America now has an economic plan for her future. We know where we're going. We're going forward; we're going onward, and we're going upward. And as I said before, we're leaving no one behind. The outpouring of support from the people has been one of the most inspiring events I can remember. Since Tuesday morning, Washington has been filled with the voices of the

---

[1] *Charles Philip Arthur George, Prince of Wales and heir apparent to the throne of the United Kingdom of Great Britain and Northern Ireland, married Lady Diana Frances Spencer on July 29.*

people, the voices of democracy. They've been ringing throughout the Capitol. The Congress and the White House have been flooded with calls and telegrams from thousands and thousands of Americans in support of our economic program that crossed party lines and is truly bipartisan.

I believe our campaign to give the government back to the people hit a nerve deeper and quicker than anyone first realized. The government in Washington has finally heard what the people have been saying for years: "We need relief from oppression of big government. We don't want to wait any longer. We want tax relief and we want it now."

The people of this country are saying that we've been on a road that they don't want to stay on. Now we're on a road that leads to growth and opportunity, to increasing productivity and an increasing standard of living for anyone. It was a road once that led to the driveway of a home that could be afforded by all kinds of Americans, not just the affluent.

The tax vote yesterday means that the independent businessman, the farmer, the shopkeeper will be able to look ahead for 3 years and see what the tax situation is going to be and thus be able to plan. The families who are struggling to keep up will not fall further and further behind while being pushed into higher and higher income tax brackets because of inflation. And as a result of this vote, the government will not be able to tax away more of the people's money without voting on the record to do so.

When the details have been cleared away, let everyone remember this: The concepts at the heart of our first tax proposal remain intact. Yes, there were changes made, but not changes in principle. Actually, as I said Monday night, it just proved that more cooks were better than one, because we found legitimate proposals that could benefit the package even though we stayed within the total amount that we had thought was necessary to be reduced.

[Our bill cuts] the rates across the board for 3 years, and we cut them by the same percentage for everyone who pays them. This bipartisan bill has business provisions such as the accelerated cost recovery

system, and last week we added incentives to further encourage investment in research and development. The bill will almost eliminate estate taxes, ensuring that family farms and family-owned businesses will stay in the family and won't have to be sold to pay the tax. And, incidentally, the thing that I'm happiest about of all is we end completely the estate or inheritance tax on a surviving spouse. There won't be any tax leveled when the inheritor is a husband or wife. And, of course, once those cuts are in effect, we've indexed them so that people won't be earning more and more but keeping less and less.

Yet, this isn't just an economic victory. It's a victory for our political system. It proves that our government and our institutions are capable of change when the people speak forcefully enough.

The American people have achieved a great victory for themselves with this vote. You know, there was much in the news about lobbying and arm-twisting and every kind of pressure, but what really sold this bill was the lobbying of the American people. They contacted their elected representatives in Washington, and it was plain they were ready to chart a new course to get this country moving again. My gratitude to the American people is as deep as my respect for what they can do when they put their minds to it.

With the help of these same Americans and with the help of the States, one of our next goals is to renew the concept of federalism. The changes here will be as exciting and even more profound in the long run than the changes produced in the economic package.

This Nation has never fully debated the fact that over the past 40 years, federalism—one of the underlying principles of our Constitution—has nearly disappeared as a guiding force in American politics and government. My administration intends to initiate such a debate, and no more appropriate forum can be found than before the National Conference of State Legislatures.

My administration is committed heart and soul to the broad principles of American federalism which are outlined in the Federalist Papers of Hamilton, Madison, and Jay and, as your President told you, they're in that tenth article of the Bill of Rights.

The designers of our Constitution realized that in federalism there's diversity. The Founding Fathers saw the federal system as constructed something like a masonry wall: The States are the bricks, the National Government is the mortar. For the structure to stand plumb with the Constitution, there must be a proper mix of that brick and mortar. Unfortunately, over the years, many people have come increasingly to believe that Washington is the whole wall—a wall that, incidentally, leans, sags, and bulges under its own weight.

The traumatic experience of the Great Depression provided the impetus and the rationale for a government that was more centralized than America had previously known. You had to have lived then, during those depression years, to understand the drabness of that period.

FDR brought the colors of hope and confidence to the era and I, like millions of others, became an enthusiastic New Dealer. We followed FDR because he offered a mix of ideas and movement. A former Governor himself, I believe that FDR would today be amazed and appalled at the growth of the Federal Government's power. Too many in government in recent years have invoked his name to justify what they were doing, forgetting that it was FDR who said, "In the conduct of public utilities, of banks, of insurance, of agriculture, of education, of social welfare—Washington must be discouraged from interfering."

Well, today the Federal Government takes too much taxes from the people, too much authority from the States, and too much liberty with the Constitution.

Americans have at last begun to realize that the steady flow of power and tax dollars to Washington has something to do with the fact that things don't seem to work anymore. The Federal Government is overloaded, musclebound, if you will, having assumed more responsibilities than it can properly manage. There's been a loss of accountability as the distinction between the duties of the Federal and State governments have blurred, and the Federal Government is so far removed from the people

that Members of Congress spend less time legislating than cutting through bureaucratic redtape for their constituents.

Our economic package, which consists of tax cuts, spending cuts, block grants, and regulatory relief, is a first phase in our effort to revitalize federalism. For too long, the Federal Government has preempted the States' tax base, regulatory authority, and spending flexibility. It has tried to reduce the States to mere administrative districts of a government centralized in Washington. And with our economic proposals, we're staging a quiet federalist revolution. It's a revolution that promises to be one of the most exciting and noteworthy in our generation.

The bipartisan tax plan which passed the House yesterday is not only a critical element of our economic recovery, it's an essential element of our federalist plan, because the rate of taxation is closely linked to the power of the Federal Government. We're strengthening federalism by cutting back on the activities of the Federal Government itself.

Our budget proposal is a dramatic shift in the growth of government. Without a structural shift of this kind, there's little hope for a long-term resistance to the burgeoning of Federal powers. Yet, our budget is more than a slowing of the growth rate of government; it reorders national priorities, seeking to return discretion, flexibility and decision-making to the State and local level.

As State legislators, I know that you're tired of the Federal Government telling you what to do, when to do and how to do it, and with no thought of the whys or wherefores of it at all.

Well, a major aspect of our federalism plan is the eventual consolidation of categorical grants into block grants. Today there are too many programs with too many strings offering too little a return. In 1960 there were approximately 132 intergovernmental grants. The programs were in existence, costing slightly more than $7 billion. By 1980, 20 years later, the number had grown to 500 programs costing $91.5 billion.

Take just one area. In 1978, there were 35 programs for pollution alone. Now, the real costs of all this are just beginning to sink in. The State of Wyoming turned down a juvenile justice grant because it would have cost the State $500,000 in compliance to get a $200,000 grant. You remember the old gag we used to pull, "Have you got two tens for a five?" [*Laughter*] The city of San Diego built a 16-mile trolley without Federal assistance, which is probably why it was accomplished within the budget and on time. [*Laughter*] I wish I could interest San Diego in taking over Amtrak. [*Laughter*]

You know, there's a joke that's almost too true to get a laugh, and that was the city that decided that it was going to elevate, raise its traffic signs. They were 5-feet high, and they were going to raise them to 7. And the Federal Government stepped in and volunteered with a program that they'd do it, and they did. They came in and lowered the streets 2 feet. [*Laughter*]

Block grants are designed to eliminate burdensome reporting requirements and regulations, unnecessary administrative costs, and program duplication. Block grants are not a mere strategy in our budget as some have suggested; they stand on their own as a federalist tool for transferring power back to the State and to the local level.

In normal times, what we've managed to get through the Congress concerning block grants would be a victory. Yet, we did not provide the States with the degree of freedom in dealing with the budget cuts that we had ardently hoped we could get. We got some categorical grants into block grants, but many of our block grant proposals are still up on the Hill, and that doesn't mean the end of the dream. Together, you and I will be going back and back and back until we obtain the flexibility that you need and deserve.

The ultimate objective, as I have told some of you in meetings in Washington, is to use block grants, however, as only a bridge, leading to the day when you'll have not only the responsibility for the programs that properly belong at the State level, but you will have the tax sources now usurped by Washington returned to you, ending that roundtrip of the peoples' money to Washington, where a carrying charge is deducted, and then back to you.

Now, we also are reviving the cause of federalism by cutting back on unnecessary regulations. The *Federal Register* is the road atlas of new Federal regulations, and for the past 10 years, all roads have led to Washington. As of December 1980 there were 1,259 Federal regulations imposed on State and local governments. Of these, 223 were direct orders and the remaining 1,036 were conditions of aid; 59 of the requirements were so-called crosscutting rules that applied to virtually all Federal grants. Accepting a government grant with its accompanying rules is like marrying a girl and finding out her entire family is moving in with you before the honeymoon. [*Laughter*]

Our regulatory task force, chaired by Vice President Bush, has already taken some 104 regulatory relief measures in the first 100 days of the administration. And of these measures, 34 provided significant relief to State and local governments on a range of regulations ranging from Medicaid to pesticides.

Secretary of Education Bell withdrew proposed rules that would have required a particular form of bilingual education—at a cost to school boards of over a billion dollars over the first 5 years. But while there's a need for bilingual education, it's absolutely wrong-headed to encourage and preserve native languages instead of teaching the language of our land to the non-English speaking, so they can have the keys to opportunity.

Just recently, on another front, Secretary of Transportation Drew Lewis modified transit accessibility rules that would have cost an estimated $7 billion. Rather than imposing specific, rigid regulations, Secretary Lewis has allowed local communities themselves to decide how best to meet the transportation needs of the handicapped people in their areas. And that, my fellow citizens, is how federalism should work.

The job of relieving the Federal Government of the powers that it has so jealously built up over the years is a difficult one. Consequently, I asked Senator Paul Laxalt, who's been a Governor, to chair both an administrative task force and a Presidential advisory committee on federalism. These groups have been asked to examine ways to reduce the Federal Government's overshadowing power in our society and to do so as soon as possible.

Now, one of their goals will be recommending allowing States to fulfill the creative role they once played as laboratories of economic and social development. North Dakota enacted one of the country's first child labor laws. Wyoming gave the vote to women decades before it was adopted nationally. And California, during the term of a Governor Reagan—I wonder whatever became of him—[*laughter*]—we enacted a clear air act that was tougher than the Federal measure that followed years later.

And, incidentally, while it's true that I do not believe in the equal rights amendment as the best way to end discrimination against women, I believe such discrimination must be eliminated. And in California, we found 14 State statutes that did so discriminate. We wiped those statutes off the books. Now, if you won't think me presumptuous, may I suggest that when you go back to your statehouses you might take a look at the statutes and regulations in your respective States.

The constitutional concept of federalism recognizes and protects diversity. Today, federalism is one check that is out of balance as the diversity of the States has given way to the uniformity of Washington. And our task is to restore the constitutional symmetry between the central Government and the States and to reestablish the freedom and variety of federalism. In the process, we'll return the citizen to his rightful place in the scheme of our democracy, and that place is close to his government. We must never forget it. It is not the Federal Government or the States who retain the power—the people retain the power. And I hope that you'll join me in strengthening the fabric of federalism. If the Federal Government is more responsive to the States, the States will be more responsive to the people, and that's the reason that you, as State legislators, and I, as President, are in office—not to retain power but to serve the people.

That great commentator on America that so many of us have quoted in speeches, de Tocqueville, once wrote: "There is an amazing strength in the expression of the will of the people, and when it declares itself, even the imagination of those who wish to contest it is overawed."

Well, de Tocqueville would still be awed by the will of the American people. As we've recently seen, even in our society of 225 million people scattered across an entire continent and complex in makeup, the people made their will known, and their elected representatives listened.

This final investment in the power of the people—this is the great drama, the great daring of the American experiment. It sparked our Revolution, it formed our Constitution.

Thomas Jefferson wrote, "I know of no safe depository of the ultimate powers of society but the people themselves." And it was Jefferson who reminded us that against the invasion of the people's liberty, the only "true barriers . . . are the state governments."

So today, fresh from our victories together, I ask you to join me in another great cause, another great revolution, and a great experiment.

Our intention, again, is to renew the meaning of the Constitution. Our aim is to rescue from arbitrary authority the rights of the people. Together then, let us restore constitutional government. Let us renew and enrich the power and purpose of States and local communities and let us return to the people those rights and duties that are justly theirs.

Now, after all this, let me say there are legitimate and very important functions of the Federal Government, of course—the maintaining of national security, for one; and for another, the protection of the constitutional rights of even the least individual among us, if that person's rights are being unjustly denied. In such a case, it is the responsibility of the Federal Government to restore those rights. And that is a responsibility that I will gladly accept, even as I do all I can to restore your autonomy under that same Constitution.

Thank you very much. God bless you.

Note: The President spoke at 2:04 p.m. in the Grand Ballroom at the Atlanta Hilton Hotel.

Remarks at a Republican Party Reception in Atlanta, Georgia
July 30, 1981

Thank you very much, and thank you all also for more than that and for all that I know you did to help. I have to tell you, it wasn't any one single victory. The victory goes to everyone, and I mean everyone in this country, as well as a great team there in Washington, and people on both sides of the aisle in Washington, who worked as hard as they could work. This truly was a bipartisan thing. Yesterday, they weren't Republicans or Democrats in the halls of Congress; they were Americans.

When I say you the people, just let me tell you a little bit of what it was like and what happened. Monday night in the Oval Office I went on with the television program. And an hour later, I got the first count on the calls that had come in just to the White House in that hour. By morning, we had received four times as many calls as we have received at any time in these 6 months on any of the other appearances that I've made or issues that we've discussed.

But up on the Hill, the Capitol switchboards were jammed. [*Laughter*] The calls were coming in. The wires were coming in from all over the country. And you'd be amazed how many, because I'm very proud of the fact that there wasn't any real arm-twisting. I can tell you that people that I called—Congressmen that I called and who had to tell me that, well, no, they thought they were going, leaning the other way. Many of them responded with the "but thanks"—because what can you do but say to them: "Well, I'm sorry. If there's anything I could tell you to change your mind, I would, but I understand." And they have commented and thanked for the fact that we didn't try to pressure them or threaten them or do anything else to get them.

This, I think, reflects that there is a change going on in this country. And the things that we used to say and wonder if we could ever get accomplished, now, we're on the side of the people. They feel that way, too.

So, now we go forward from here. I think this is the dramatic turn in the direction the government's taking, but it also means now the responsibility's on us. We've got to prove that what we said about it is true; it'll work. And I happen to believe that very definitely, that leaving more of the people's earnings in their hands and reducing government spending as we have, it will work.

But, all of us together are going to have to make sure that what we call "the safety net" remains, and that is no one must fall between the cracks. We have no intention of any of those cuts ever reflecting against or making it difficult for some person with real need, some person truly handicapped, some person who through no fault of his own must depend on his neighbors for help. And we all together, in our communities and every place else, have got to see that it works that way and that no one is cast aside.

Now, a few months ago—then I'm going to come down because I haven't got much time here—a few moments ago in there speaking to the legislators, I quoted a former Democratic President, and I think it's only fair that I quote a Republican President—[*laughter*]—something on the order of what this is all about and what I think we're trying to undo in Washington. This former President said, while he was a President, "No method or procedure has ever been devised by which liberty could be divorced from local self-government. No plan of centralization has ever been adopted which did not result in bureaucracy, tyranny, inflexibility, reaction, and decline. Of all forms of government, those administered by bureaus are about the least satisfactory to an enlightened and progressive people. Being irresponsible, they become autocratic, and being autocratic, they resist all development. Unless bureaucracy is constantly resisted, it breaks down representative government and overwhelms democracy. It is the one element of our institution—that our institutions set up—they set up the pretense of having autonomy over everybody and being responsible to nobody." And old, silent Cal Coolidge said that at William and Mary in 1926. [*Laughter*]

Well, I know that if I get down off here I have at least a few minutes to mingle. If I didn't have any other reason for getting home, Nancy has just arrived home from the wedding. And it's the longest separation since we've been married, and I want to make sure that she hasn't gone royal on me. [*Laughter*]

Okay. Thank you all very much.

Note: The President spoke at 2:43 p.m. to Georgia Republicans and Republican State legislators in the Galleria area of the Atlanta Hilton Hotel. Following the reception, the President returned to the White House.

Nomination of William Courtney Sherman To Be Deputy United States Representative in the Security Council of the United Nations
July 31, 1981

The President today announced his intention to nominate William Courtney Sherman to be Deputy Representative of the United States of America in the Security Council of the United Nations, with the rank of Ambassador. He would succeed Richard Wilson Petree.

Mr. Sherman served in Seoul as instruction administrator with the United States Army (1946–48) and as research assistant with the Economic Cooperation Administration (1948–50). He entered the Foreign Service in 1951 as research analyst with the Bureau of Intelligence and Research. In 1952–54 he was vice consul in Yokohama and political officer in Tokyo in 1954–56. In the Department he was intelligence research specialist (1956–58) and Belgian desk officer (1958–60). He was political officer in Rome in 1960–65. He was in the Depart-

ment as supervisory personnel officer (1965–66) and special assistant to the Deputy Under Secretary of State for Administration (1966–67). In 1967–68 he attended the National War College. He was principal officer in Kobe-Osaka in 1968–70 and counselor for political affairs in Tokyo in 1970–73. In the Department he was supervisory personnel officer (1973–74) and director of Japanese affairs (1974–77). In 1977–81 he was Deputy Chief of Mission in Tokyo.

Mr. Sherman graduated from the University of Louisville (B.A., 1946). He served in the United States Navy in 1943–46 and in 1950–51. He is a recipient of the Department of State's Superior Service Award (1980). He is married, has three children, and resides in Reston, Va. He was born September 27, 1923, in Edmonton, Ky.

Nomination of Ronald I. Spiers To Be United States Ambassador to Pakistan
July 31, 1981

The President today announced his intention to nominate Ronald I. Spiers, of Vermont, to be Ambassador to Pakistan. He would succeed Arthur W. Hummel, Jr., who has been named Ambassador to the People's Republic of China.

In 1950–55 Mr. Spiers was foreign affairs analyst with the United States Atomic Energy Commission. In 1955 he came to the Department of State as foreign affairs officer in the Bureau of International Organization Affairs. In 1957–61 he was officer in charge of disarmament affairs in the Office of the Special Assistant to the Secretary of State. He was Director of the Office of Political Affairs with the Arms Control and Disarmament Agency in 1961–62. In the Department, in 1962–66 he was Deputy Director, then Director, of NATO Affairs in the Bureau of European Affairs. He was counselor for political affairs in London in 1966–69 and Director of the Bureau of Politico-Military Affairs in the Department in 1969–73. In 1973–74 he was Ambassador to the Commonwealth of the Bahamas. He was Deputy Chief of Mission (Minister) in London in 1974–77 and in 1977–80, Ambassador to the Republic of Turkey. Since 1980 he has been Director of Intelligence and Research in the Department.

Mr. Spiers graduated from Dartmouth College (A.B., 1948) and Princeton University (M.P.A., 1950). He served in the United States Navy in 1943–46. He is married, has four children, and resides in South Londonderry, Vt. He was born July 9, 1925, in Orange, N.J.

Appointment of Stanton D. Anderson as a Member of the Advisory Committee for Trade Negotiations
July 31, 1981

The President today announced the appointment of Stanton D. Anderson as a member of the Advisory Committee for Trade Negotiations. He will succeed Myer Rashish.

Mr. Anderson is currently senior partner with the law firm of Anderson, Hibey, Nauheim and Blair of Washington, D.C. During the transition period, he served as director of the economic affairs group. During the Presidential campaign, he served as couselor to the Reagan-Bush Committee. He also served as general counsel to the 1980 Republican National Convention. In 1973–75 he was Deputy Assistant Secretary of State, and in 1971–73 he was Staff Assistant to the President. Mr. Anderson was with the law firm of Surrey and Morse, of Washington, D.C., in 1968–80, except for his time in government service. He has also served as assistant traffic manager of Pacific Northwest Bell, in Salem, Oreg., in 1965–66.

Mr. Anderson graduated from Westmore College, Santa Barbara, Calif. (1962) and Willamette University School of Law, Salem, Oreg. (1969). He has two children and resides in Washington, D.C. He was born October 18, 1940, in Portland, Oreg.

Appointment of Henry G. Cisneros as a Member of the Presidential Advisory Committee on Federalism
July 31, 1981

The President today announced the appointment of Henry G. Cisneros as a member of the Presidential Advisory Committee on Federalism.

Since May 1981 Mr. Cisneros has served as mayor of the city of San Antonio, Tex. In 1975–81 he was a member of the City Council of San Antonio. He has been a faculty member, Division of Environmental Studies, University of Texas at San Antonio, since 1974. In 1971 he was White House fellow and assistant to the Secretary of Health, Education, and Welfare. Mr. Cisneros was assistant to the executive vice president, National League of Cities, in 1970.

Mr. Cisneros is a member of the board of the National League of Cities and the Council on Urban Economic Development.

He graduated from Texas A & M University (B.A., 1968; M.A., 1970); John F. Kennedy School of Government, Harvard University (M.A., 1973); and George Washington University (Ph. D., 1975).

He is married, has two children, and resides in San Antonio, Tex. He was born June 11, 1947.

Statement and a Question-and-Answer Session With Reporters on the Air Traffic Controllers Strike
August 3, 1981

The President. This morning at 7 a.m. the union representing those who man America's air traffic control facilities called a strike. This was the culmination of 7 months of negotiations between the Federal Aviation Administration and the union. At one point in these negotiations agreement was reached and signed by both sides, granting a $40 million increase in salaries and benefits. This is twice what other government employees can expect. It was granted in recognition of the difficulties inherent in the work these people perform. Now, however, the union demands are 17 times what had been agreed to—$681 million. This would impose a tax burden on their fellow citizens which is unacceptable.

I would like to thank the supervisors and controllers who are on the job today, helping to get the nation's air system operating safely. In the New York area, for example, four supervisors were scheduled to report for work, and 17 additionally volunteered. At National Airport a traffic controller told a newsperson he had resigned from the union and reported to work because, "How can I ask my kids to obey the law if I don't?" This is a great tribute to America.

Let me make one thing plain. I respect the right of workers in the private sector to strike. Indeed, as president of my own union, I led the first strike ever called by that union. I guess I'm maybe the first one to ever hold this office who is a lifetime member of an AFL–CIO union. But we cannot compare labor-management relations in the private sector with government. Government cannot close down the assembly line. It has to provide without interruption the protective services which are government's reason for being.

It was in recognition of this that the Congress passed a law forbidding strikes by government employees against the public safety. Let me read the solemn oath taken by each of these employees, a sworn affidavit, when they accepted their jobs: "I am not participating in any strike against the Government of the United States or any agency thereof, and I will not so participate while an employee of the Government of the United States or any agency thereof."

It is for this reason that I must tell those who fail to report for duty this morning they are in violation of the law, and if they do not report for work within 48 hours, they have forfeited their jobs and will be terminated.

Q. Mr. President, are you going to order any union members who violate the law to go to jail?

The President. Well, I have some people around here, and maybe I should refer that question to the Attorney General.

Q. Do you think that they should go to jail, Mr. President, anybody who violates this law?

The President. I told you what I think should be done. They're terminated.

The Attorney General. Well, as the President has said, striking under these circumstances constitutes a violation of the law, and we intend to initiate in appropriate cases criminal proceedings against those who have violated the law.

Q. How quickly will you initiate criminal proceedings, Mr. Attorney General?

The Attorney General. We will initiate those proceedings as soon as we can.

Q. Today?

The Attorney General. The process will be underway probably by noon today.

Q. Are you going to try and fine the union $1 million per day?

The Attorney General. Well, that's the prerogative of the court. In the event that any individuals are found guilty of contempt of a court order, the penalty for that, of course, is imposed by the court.

Q. How much more is the government prepared to offer the union?

The Secretary of Transportation. We think we had a very satisfactory offer on the table. It's twice what other Government employees are going to get—11.4 percent. Their demands were so unreasonable there was no spot to negotiate, when you're talking to somebody 17 times away from where you presently are. We do not plan to increase our offer to the union.

Q. Under no circumstances?

The Secretary of Transportation. As far as I'm concerned, under no circumstance.

Q. Will you continue to meet with them?

The Secretary of Transportation. We will not meet with the union as long as they're on strike. When they're off of strike, and assuming that they are not decertified, we will meet with the union and try to negotiate a satisfactory contract.

Q. Do you have any idea how it's going at the airports around the country?

The Secretary of Transportation. Relatively, it's going quite well. We're operating somewhat in excess of 50 percent capacity. We could increase that. We have determined, until we feel we're in total control of the system, that we will not increase that. Also, as you probably know, we have some rather severe weather in the Midwest, and our first priority is safety.

Q. What can you tell us about possible decertification of the union and impoundment of its strike funds?

The Secretary of Transportation. There has been a court action to impound the strike fund of $3.5 million. We are going before the National Labor Relations Authority this morning and ask for decertification of the union.

Q. When you say that you're not going to increase your offer, are you referring to the original offer or the last offer which you've made? Is that still valid?

The Secretary of Transportation. The last offer we made in present value was exactly the same as the first offer. Mr. Poli[1] asked me about 11 o'clock last evening if he could phase the increase in over a period of time. For that reason, we phased it in over a longer period of time. It would have given him a larger increase in terms of where he would be when the next negotiations started, but in present value it was the $40 million originally on the table.

Q. Mr. Attorney General, in seeking criminal action against the union leaders, will you seek to put them in jail if they do not order these people back to work?

The Attorney General. Well, we will seek whatever penalty is appropriate under the circumstances in each individual case.

Q. Do you think that is an appropriate circumstance?

The Attorney General. It is certainly one of the penalties that is provided for in the law, and in appropriate cases, we could very well seek that penalty.

Q. What's appropriate?

The Attorney General. Well, that depends upon the fact of each case.

Q. What makes the difference?

Q. Can I go back to my "fine" question? How much would you like to see the union fined every day?

The Attorney General. Well, there's no way to answer that question. We would just have to wait until we get into court, see what the circumstances are, and determine what position we would take in the various cases under the facts as they develop.

Q. But you won't go to court and ask the court for a specific amount?

The Attorney General. Well, I'm sure we will when we reach that point, but there's no way to pick a figure now.

Q. Mr. President, will you delay your trip to California or cancel it if the strike is still on later this week?

The President. If any situation should arise that would require my presence here,

---

[1] *Robert Poli, president, Professional Air Traffic Controllers Organization.*

naturally I will do that. So, that will be a decision that awaits what's going to happen. May I just—because I have to be back in there for another appointment—may I just say one thing on top of this? With all this talk of penalties and everything else, I hope that you'll emphasize, again, the possibility of termination, because I believe that there are a great many of those people—and they're fine people—who have been swept up in this and probably have not really considered the result—the fact that they had taken an oath, the fact that this is now in violation of the law, as that one supervisor referred to with regard to his children. And I am hoping that they will in a sense remove themselves from the lawbreaker situation by returning to their posts.

I have no way to know whether this had been conveyed to them by their union leaders, who had been informed that this would be the result of a strike.

Q. Your deadline is 7 o'clock Wednesday morning for them to return to work?

The President. Forty-eight hours.

The Secretary of Transportation. It's 11 o'clock Wednesday morning.

Q. Mr. President, why have you taken such strong action as your first action? Why not some lesser action at this point?

The President. What lesser action can there be? The law is very explicit. They are violating the law. And as I say, we called this to the attention of their leadership. Whether this was conveyed to the membership before they voted to strike, I don't know. But this is one of the reasons why there can be no further negotiation while this situation continues. You can't sit and negotiate with a union that's in violation of the law.

The Secretary of Transportation. And their oath.

The President. And their oath.

Q. Are you more likely to proceed in the criminal direction toward the leadership than the rank and file, Mr. President?

The President. Well, that again is not for me to answer.

Q. Mr. Secretary, what can you tell us about the possible use of military air controllers—how many, how quickly can they get on the job?

The Secretary of Transportation. In answer to the previous question, we will move both civil and criminal, probably more civil than criminal, and we now have papers in the U.S. attorneys' offices, under the Attorney General, in about 20 locations around the country where would be involved two or three principal people.

As far as the military personnel are concerned, they are going to fundamentally be backup to the supervisory personnel. We had 150 on the job, supposedly, about a half-hour ago. We're going to increase that to somewhere between 700 and 850.

Q. Mr. Secretary, are you ready to hire other people should these other people not return?

The Secretary of Transportation. Yes, we will, and we hope we do not reach that point. Again as the President said, we're hoping these people come back to work. They do a fine job. If that does not take place, we have a training school, as you know. We will be advertising. We have a number of applicants right now. There's a waiting list in terms of people that want to be controllers, and we'll start retraining and reorganizing the entire FAA traffic controller group.

Q. Just to clarify, is your deadline 7 a.m. Wednesday or 11 o'clock?

The Secretary of Transportation. It's 11 a.m. Wednesday. The President said 48 hours, and that would be 48 hours.

Q. If you actually fire these people, won't it put your air traffic control system in a hole for years to come, since you can't just cook up a controller in—[*inaudible*]?

The Secretary of Transportation. That obviously depends on how many return to work. Right now we're able to operate the system. In some areas, we've been very gratified by the support we've received. In other areas, we've been disappointed. And until I see the numbers, there's no way I can answer that question.

Q. Mr. Lewis, did you tell the union leadership when you were talking to them that their members would be fired if they went out on strike?

The Secretary of Transportation. I told Mr. Poli yesterday that the President gave me three instructions in terms of the firmness of the negotiations: one is there would be no amnesty; the second there would be no negotiations during the strike; and third is that if they went on strike, these people would no longer be government employees.

Q. Mr. Secretary, you said no negotiations. What about informal meetings of any kind with Mr. Poli?

The Secretary of Transportation. We will have no meetings until the strike is terminated with the union.

Q. Have you served Poli at this point? Has he been served by the Attorney General?

The Attorney General. In the civil action that was filed this morning, the service was made on the attorney for the union, and the court has determined that that was appropriate service on all of the officers of the union.

Q. My previous question about whether you're going to take a harder line on the leadership than rank and file in terms of any criminal prosecution, can you give us an answer on that?

The Attorney General. No, I can't answer that except to say that each case will be investigated on its own merits, and action will be taken as appropriate in each of those cases.

Q. Mr. Lewis, do you know how many applications for controller jobs you have on file now?

The Secretary of Transportation. I do not know. I'm going to check when I get back. I am aware there's a waiting list, and I do not have the figure. If you care to have that, you can call our office, and we'll tell you. Also, we'll be advertising and recruiting people for this job if necessary.

Q. Mr. Secretary, how long are you prepared to hold out if there's a partial but not complete strike?

The Secretary of Transportation. I think the President made it very clear that as of 48 hours from now, if the people are not back on the job, they will not be government employees at any time in the future.

Q. How long are you prepared to run the air controller system—[*inaudible*]?

The Secretary of Transportation. For years, if we have to.

Q. How long does it take to train a new controller, from the waiting list?

The Secretary of Transportation. It varies; it depends on the type of center they're going to be in. For someone to start in the system and work through the more minor office types of control situations till they get to, let's say, a Chicago or a Washington National, it takes about 3 years. So in this case, what we'll have to do if some of the major metropolitan areas are shut down or a considerable portion is shut down, we'll be bringing people in from other areas that are qualified and then start bringing people through the training schools in the smaller cities and smaller airports.

Q. Mr. Secretary, have you definitely made your final offer to the union?

The Secretary of Transportation. Yes, we have.

Q. Thank you.

Note: The President read the statement to reporters at 10:55 a.m. in the Rose Garden at the White House.

Memorandum on Federal Budget Review Procedures
July 13, 1981

Memorandum for Heads of Executive Departments and Agencies

Subject: Budget Review Procedures

Historically the budget process has been an annual cycle with the Executive Branch proposing early in the year and the Congress disposing during the rest of the year. More recently the budget process has changed. It is now a complex year-round process which involves virtually continuous adjustment.

For example, right now we have pending a second round of rescissions and deferrals for FY 81 and a Reconciliation Bill for FY 82. We have simultaneously begun the Spring Review which leads to our budget marks for FY 83.

The Mid-session report on the budget just released shows that our overall position has not significantly changed. However, this small overall net change obscures the many program level budget threats which have developed and the increased strain they place on our abilities to make our overall budgetary objectives. We cannot make any decisions—foreign, domestic or defense—unless their budgetary impact is fully considered.

Because of the need to evaluate the budget continuously, I have established a Budget Review Board composed of Ed Meese, Jim Baker and Dave Stockman.

Any situation, decision or impending emergency, which you feel could lead to unbudgeted expenditures or to an increase in budgeted allocations must be reported promptly to the Budget Review Board. Authorization from the Budget Review Board must be obtained *prior* to incurring or obligating any such expenditure or increase.

Once I have set a budget projection, each of you must extend every effort to make sure we achieve that projection. It should be clear that achieving our budget objectives is something that must be a personal priority of each of us.

Bringing federal spending under control and keeping it there is our most urgent priority. This is the only way we will be able to achieve our objective of giving the American people the strong, healthy economy which they demanded in last fall's election, and it is the fundamental precondition for achieving many of the other important objectives that we have established to restore our Nation at home and abroad.

RONALD REAGAN

Note: The text of the memorandum was made available by the Office of the Press Secretary on August 4.

Remarks on Receiving Unspent Fiscal Year 1981 Funds From the Agency for International Development
August 4, 1981

The President. Ladies and gentlemen, back in the beginning of our administration, I talked a great deal about eliminating waste in government. And right now, I would like to introduce to you our Administrator for the Agency for International Development—AID—who has a statement to make and a presentation to make.

Peter McPherson. I said the title and not the name; I'm sorry.

Mr. McPherson. Thank you, Mr. President. It's certainly very nice to be here. In keeping with your commitment to the American people to reduce waste and inefficiency, I'm happy to announce today our initial results at the Agency for International Development. These results will save millions of dollars for the American taxpayer. We've identified $28 million that we do not need to spend. These cuts come from projects from around the world. Some are from money which is being returned because

local conditions have changed, some because of management problems, and some because of insufficient local government support.

Returning this money demonstrates that we will not hesitate to make changes in AID programs whenever they fall short of our expectations. Our reviews are not yet finished, but already we know there'll be millions of dollars additionally that we will return to the Treasury.

This effort is strongly supported by Secretary Haig, as evidenced by his presence here today. We hope to better serve you, Mr. President, and the American public by this effort.

Mr. President, I'd like to present to you our check for $28 million to be returned to the U.S. Treasury.

The President. Peter McPherson, I'm very proud to accept this. And I think that anyone who's familiar with the Washington

691

scene—as so may of you are—knows that it is far more normal at this stage of the fiscal year, only a couple months to go, that anyone that finds $28 million unspent in their department says to everyone, "Rush out and buy new furniture or do something. We must spend this money before the end of the fiscal year."

Twenty-eight million dollars—I can't wait to hand this to Don Regan, Secretary of the Treasury. Peter McPherson, thank you very much.

Note: The President spoke at 3:15 p.m. at the presentation ceremony in the Rose Garden at the White House.

The White House press release also contains Mr. McPherson's question-and-answer session with reporters which followed the presentation ceremony.

Remarks at the Welcoming Ceremony for President Anwar el-Sadat of Egypt
August 5, 1981

President Reagan. It's an honor and a very great pleasure to welcome President and Mrs. Sadat, those who've accompanied them here from their country, and for their family. Egypt and the United States enjoy a warm and a strong relationship, testimony to the honest good will of the people of both nations and recognition of President Sadat's foresight and leadership.

We are today friends and partners. We've come to trust each other so much that the bonds of unity grow stronger each day. We are a young country; Egypt a nation mature and rich with the blessings of time, a nation which cradled Western civilization in its arms. History will record that in the last half of the twentieth century, Egypt re-emerged as a significant force among the nations—not by conquest, but because one man with the courage that it took set out to lead mankind toward peace.

In 1799 the Rosetta Stone was discovered, a tablet that served as a key to the understanding of Egypt's history. Well, like that famous stone, President Sadat serves as a key to understanding the depth and character of the Egyptian people, opening the eyes of the world to new opportunities for peace.

Mr. President, earlier this year you said, "The answer to our present anxiety and fears in the world is not for us to cling to the past, with all its negative aspects, but to forge ahead toward a happier future."

Those words exemplify the values that speak well of your roots, roots planted deeply in the great and ancient culture of Egypt, roots planted deeply in the village culture of which you have spoken so often and so eloquently. We know, President Sadat, what you have done was not intended to bring the blessing of peace just to your own nation, itself a laudatory goal, but to all the people of the Middle East, something smaller minds had discarded as impossible.

There are those who claim the ingrained hatred can never be overcome. To them I assert, President Sadat has shown the way. There are those who think that distrust will always submerge and suffocate faith. To them I assert, President Sadat has shown the way. And there those who say that peace is impossible and are afraid to reach out. And again I assert, President Sadat has shown the way.

Mr. President, you were a soldier, but your greatest victory came in preventing bloodshed and thereby capturing the hearts of peace-loving people everywhere. Your courage in taking the first step, your good faith in pursuing a tangible agreement with a former enemy, your maturity and moderation in the face of frustration since Camp David—all of these are worthy of a man whom history will undoubtedly label one of the twentieth century's most courageous peacemakers.

I welcome this opportunity to get to know you personally and to discuss ways to strengthen our bilateral relations. We want you to know that although the Americans have changed Presidents, we have not altered our commitment to peace or our desire to continue building upon the achievements of Camp David.

Our mutual concern for the regional stability of the Middle East is a timely matter for discussion. External threats and foreign-inspired subversion menace independence. As we both know, the only beneficiary of violence, chaos, and blind hatred will be our adversaries.

But, good men, with the help of God, cooperating with one another, can and will prevail over evil. We're anxious to explore with you the road ahead and to see that the Egyptian people enjoy the fruits of peace and security from aggression. You have taken the first steps on a long, arduous journey with many obstacles to overcome. But today I assure you and the Egyptian people that we will walk that road together and that we will not be deterred from reaching our destination.

Welcome, President Sadat.

President Sadat. Mr. President, thank you for your very kind words. It is with pleasure and happiness that I met with you, and I'm going to hold a dialog which is certain to strengthen the structure of peace and enrich our perception of the world today. We look upon you with admiration and esteem. You are a man of faith and determination. Your leadership is inspiring, and your commitment is unwavering. Since you assumed your awesome responsibility as the leader of this great Nation, you set an admirable record of achievement and fulfillment.

You vowed to work for a stronger America, capable of confronting the challenges of our age. You pledged to exert tireless efforts in order to make the world more secure and just. You promised to introduce a better international equilibrium for the benefit of free nations. Within a few months, much has been achieved through your vigor and determination. We remain hopeful that much more will be attained in the months and years ahead.

Mr. President, we are holding our talks at a crucial moment. It is crucial for our region, for the Middle East, for the United States, and for the world at large. The rising tension and violence which we witnessed during the past few weeks in our area is a living evidence of the urgent need for a comprehensive peace in the Middle East.

No other goal is more pressing or crucial. At the same time, no other nation is more qualified to serve and safeguard the noble cause than your great nation. I'm confident that you will assume this responsibility with a sense of purpose and history, and I'm sure also that you will continue to play the role of the full partner willingly and vigorously.

Mr. President, we are equally committed to the cause of peace. No event or development can shake our belief that peace is the word of God and the only road to a happy future. It is a sacred mission that doesn't belong to a few persons or to one nation; rather, it belongs to mankind.

While I look forward to our talks today and in the days ahead with optimism and confidence, I'm sure much will depend on our common strategy for peace and stability. Much needs to be done to strengthen peace in the Arab world, in Africa, and in the Third World. New steps have to be taken to introduce a global balance that does not leave small nations under the mercy of those who possess the means of pressure and intervention.

Mr. President, I would like to address a word of appreciation and gratitude to the gallant American people. We are proud of our friendship and cooperation. You are a great companion and a most reliable friend and, like us in Egypt, you are a nation of believers. We shall do all that we can to bolster this friendship and intensify our cooperation in all fields. May God Almighty illuminate our way and guide our steps.

Together, Mr. President, we shall overcome.

Note: President Reagan spoke at 10:10 a.m. on the South Lawn of the White House, where President Sadat was given a formal welcome with full military honors.

Following the ceremony, the two Presidents met in the Oval Office. Also present at that meeting were the Vice President, Secretary of State Alexander M. Haig, Jr., and Assistant to the President for National Security Affairs Richard V. Allen, and, on the Egyptian side, Minister of Foreign Affairs Kamal Hasan 'Ali, Minister of State for Culture and Information Mansur Muhammad Mahmud Hasan, and Ambassador Osama al-Baz, First Under Secretary in the Foreign Ministry. President Reagan and President Sadat then met in the Cabinet Room with their delegations.

Letter to Congressional Leaders on the Sale of AWACS and Other Air Defense Equipment to Saudi Arabia
August 5, 1981

One of the essential elements of the Administration's Southwest Asia strategy will come before Congress for review in the near future. It is to provide Saudi Arabia with a package of equipment and training to improve its air defense capabilities. The package will include five E3A AWACS aircraft as well as enhancements for the F–15 aircraft which we have agreed to provide.

I am convinced that providing Saudi Arabia with this equipment will improve the security of our friends, strengthen our own posture in the region, and make it clear both to local governments and to the Soviet leadership that the United States is determined to assist in preserving security and stability in Southwest Asia.

We have not previously submitted this package to the Congress, although it was decided upon in principle some time ago, for two reasons: the priority we needed to place on securing passage of our economic program, and the necessity of working out a set of understandings with the Saudi leadership which will ensure that the equipment provided will be employed to our mutual benefit and that the U.S. technology and systems involved will be fully protected.

I am aware that information from a variety of sources has been circulating on Capitol Hill regarding this sale and that many Members have been under some pressure to take an early position against it. I hope that no one will prejudge our proposal before it is presented. We will make a strong case to the Congress that it is in the interest of our country, the Western Alliance and stability in the Middle East. Meanwhile, as the Congress prepares for its August recess, I would appreciate your support and assistance in urging that Members do not prejudge this important issue until they have had the opportunity to hear the Administration's views.

Sincerely,

RONALD REAGAN

Note: This is the text of identical letters addressed to Senate Majority Leader Howard H. Baker, Jr., Senate Minority Leader Robert C. Byrd, Speaker of the House of Representatives Thomas P. O'Neill, Jr., and House Minority Leader Robert H. Michel.

Nomination of George Southall Vest To Be United States Representative to the European Communities
August 5, 1981

The President today announced his intention to nominate George Southall Vest to be Representative of the United States of America to the European Communities, with the rank and status of Ambassador. He will succeed Thomas O. Enders, who has resigned.

Mr. Vest entered the Foreign Service in 1947 as consular officer in Hamilton. He served as consular officer in Quito (1949–51) and political officer in Ottawa (1951–53). In 1954–58 he was in the Department as Canadian desk officer, then special assistant to the Assistant Secretary for European Affairs. He was political officer in Paris (SHAPE, 1959–60), (USRO, 1960–61), and chief of private office for Secretary General in Paris (NATO, 1961–63). He attended the National War College in 1963–64. In 1965–67 he was Deputy Director of the Office of Atlantic Political-Military Affairs in the Department. He was Deputy Chief of Mission

in Brussels (USEC, 1967–69) and (NATO, 1969–71). In 1972–73 he was special assistant to the Secretary for negotiations on CSCE in Helsinki and Geneva. In the Department he was Deputy Assistant Secretary for Press Relations (1973–74), Director of the Bureau of Politico-Military Affairs (1973–76), and Assistant Secretary of State for European Affairs (1977–81).

Mr. Vest graduated from the University of Virginia (B.A., 1941; M.A., 1947). He served in the U.S. Army in 1941–46. He is married, has three children, and resides in Bethesda, Md. He was born December 25, 1918, in Columbus, Va.

Nomination of John Gunther Dean To Be United States Ambassador to Thailand
August 5, 1981

The President today announced his intention to nominate John Gunther Dean, of New York, to be Ambassador to Thailand. He will succeed Morton I. Abramowitz, who has resigned.

In 1950 Mr. Dean entered government service as economic analyst with the Economic Cooperation Administration in Paris. In 1951–53 he was industrial analyst in Belgium and assistant economic commissioner in Saigon, Phnom Penh, and Vientiane in 1953. He was with the Foreign Operations Administration in Saigon in 1953–54 and in 1955 with the International Cooperation Administration.

He was political officer in Vientiane (Department of State) in 1956–59, consular officer in Lomé (1959–60), and Chargé d'Affaires in Bamako (1960–61). In the De-

partment, he was officer in charge of Mali-Togo affairs (1961–64) and international relations officer (1964–65). In 1965–69 he was political officer in Paris. He attended the Harvard Center for International Affairs in 1969–70. He was on detail to the Agency for International Development as Deputy Regional Director in Saigon in 1970–72. In 1972–74 he was Deputy Chief of Mission in Vientiane. He was Ambassador to the Khmer Republic (1974–75), to Denmark (1975–78), and to Lebanon (1978–81).

Mr. Dean graduated from Harvard University (B.S., 1947; M.A., 1950) and the University of Paris (Ph. D., 1949). He served in the U.S. Army in 1944–46. Mr. Dean is married, has three children, and resides in New York, N.Y. He was born February 24, 1926, in Germany.

Nomination of Richard J. Bishirjian To Be an Associate Director of the International Communication Agency
August 5, 1981

The President today announced his intention to nominate Richard J. Bishirjian to be Associate Director of the International Communication Agency (Educational and Cultural Affairs). He will succeed Alice Stone Ilchman.

Dr. Bishirjian received his Ph. D. from the University of Notre Dame Department of Government and International Studies in 1972. He is the author of two books, "A Public Philosophy Reader" and "The Development of Political Theory," as well as 19 scholarly essays and reviews. He is former senior editor of Arlington House Publishers.

His academic career included chairmanship of the Department of Political Science at the College of New Rochelle, New York,

since 1972. In 1969–72 he was assistant professor of politics at the University of Dallas, Texas.

Dr. Bishirjian is a trustee of the Philadelphia Society and a member of the International Seminar for Philosophy and Political Science. Recently, he served as team leader of the National Endowment for the Humanities transition team.

Dr. Bishirjian is married, has two children, and resides in Tarrytown, N.Y. He was born June 5, 1942, in Pittsburgh, Pa.

Note: Mr. Bishirjian's nomination, which was submitted to the Senate on September 10, was withdrawn by the President on November 12.

Remarks at a Meeting With Congressional Leaders Following Passage of Federal Budget Reconciliation and Tax Reduction Legislation
August 5, 1981

The President. In the past several days, the Congress has acted with great wisdom and foresight in passing two bills that will help put us on the road to economic recovery. These bills—the reconciliation bill and the tax bill—are not yet here for signing, so we'll save that occasion for later. But before many of us leave Washington, I just wanted to ask all of these gentlemen down here for a few brief moments together.

In my view, the passage of this legislation marks the single most important achievement of the past 200 days. It represents the first serious step taken in decades to stop the growth of government, to end government's unwarranted intrusion into our lives, and to rebuild the foundations of our economy.

Now, those of you who are here now are among the chief architects and the builders of these bills. And your political skills, your

legislative talents, your insights, your hard work are responsible for their success. And I don't think I have to elaborate on the remarkable role that each one of you has played in this. This can be safely left to history. But I would be remiss if I didn't say a few simple or totally inadequate but heartfelt words to each of you, and the words are "thank you, thank you all." And they came not just from me but from the American people.

During the last 200 days, you've provided your countrymen with an example of representative democracy at its best. Those of you in the Republican leadership in the face of extraordinary pressures have forged a political unity that has rarely been equaled in Washington, and you did it first and foremost because you believed you were acting in the best interests of the country. And those of you here today who are members of the Democratic Party had the personal strength to put principle above partisan or special interests, and yours has been a special courage.

I think we can all agree that today our bipartisan coalition is becoming a strong and vibrant one. But I think we can also agree that we'll need this strength and vibrancy, because the challenges we must face together are by no means over. The struggle against government's irresistible urge to grow and grow is a continuing one. The fight to control the Federal budget is just beginning. But on this front, I think we can be very clear: There will be no falling back, no call for retreat.

We've stood together. We've fought together for what we believed was right. I know that we'll do so again. But today I wanted you to know how grateful I am to you and how grateful the American people are for your selflessness and your statesmanship.

Thank you.

Reporter. What's next, Mr. President?

The President. Oh, we've got a lot of goodies. [*Laughter*]

Q. Sir, the controllers are staying out and are being fired. What's next there?

The President. Well, we're up to about 75 percent of the normal air traffic. And there is still room for more to come back, because the 48 hours included until their shifts. So, there is an afternoon shift due in, there's a night shift and so forth, and we'll see what the total is in. As I understand, it's up to about 38 percent now are back in.

Q. Are you disappointed that after your speech—what was your reaction when only about 33 percent reported?

The President. Well, I was sorry, and I am sorry for them. I think that these are fine people out there who have been misled and who don't quite understand that our position has to be irreversible. There is a law and an oath that they signed, and I don't think any of them would hold still if any of us here took an oath, decided that we didn't mean to keep that oath.

Q. As a former union president, do you feel any pangs about firing people who strike for higher wages?

The President. Well, you bet. Anyone who went through the Great Depression thinks that's the worst thing in the world that can happen to anyone. And I do feel badly; I certainly take no joy out of this. And I was hoping that more of them would recognize the obligation they have. But there just is no other choice.

Q. Sir, when are we going to start feeling the effects of recovery?

The President. Well, you've got to wait till October 1st before the tax cut begins— [*laughter*]—and so we have to wait till that money begins showing up in the private sector and being returned to investment. And you have to wait until the end of the next fiscal year—or during the fiscal year for the effect of the lower government spending. But I think that those things together—no one promised this is instant. I think that we're going to have to wait till we actually feel the effect of those things that have been adopted, going into action.

On the other hand, I do think that there is an immediate kind of psychological thing that is happening among the people that will have some effect.

Q. Mr. President, do you think that the country will be seriously harmed by this walkout in terms of so few really experienced air controllers on the job now?

The President. Well, as I say, if we're up already to 75 percent of normal air traffic, under the present situation, I think this is an indication that we're not faced with disaster. But I still think that if those people would recognize that their responsibility, not only in their personal oath but in obeying the law, there's still some time today for more of them to come back to work.

Q. You're not worried about flying tomorrow?

The President. For an old ex-horse cavalryman, I'm always worried about flying. [*Laughter*]

Reporters. Thank you.

Note: The President spoke at 3:38 p.m. to reporters assembled in the Oval Office at the White House.

Toasts of President Reagan and President Anwar el-Sadat of Egypt at the State Dinner
August 5, 1981

President Reagan. Ladies and gentlemen, tonight we welcome a man who leads a nation recognized for its magnificent contributions to mankind. His depth of character and hard-won accomplishments suggest that Egypt's contributions will not be limited to those of antiquity. In the recent past, there have been few foreign leaders who have truly captured the hearts of the American people. And Anwar Sadat is one of those rare exceptions.

Historians often argue about whether events are shaped by people or people by events. There's little doubt that the man we honor this evening is an individual who shaped history. President Sadat, Mrs. Sadat, it's truly an honor to have you with us.

Now, Mr. President, I know that you struggled many years and played a prominent role in creating an organization which brought independence to your country. But then on the night of the revolution, when it actually began, you were in a movie theater watching a picture with your family. Now, you wouldn't by chance remember who happened to be in that movie, would you? [*Laughter*] I never won an Oscar, but a revolution would do. [*Laughter*]

But seriously, those charged with enormous responsibility are, after all, people and must have a very human quality of flowing with events. Nevertheless, some, like the man we honor tonight, do more than live through history; they make it. You, Mr. President, could have let the flow of events continue unchecked. Instead, with brilliant insight, you recognized an opportunity and seized the moment.

During your historic journey to Jerusalem you explained, "There come moments when it becomes imperative for those endowed with wisdom and lucidity of vision to penetrate beyond the past with all its complications and vestiges to usher in an undaunted move toward new horizons." Well, more than wisdom, it takes courage to make fundamental decisions—the kind that you, Mr. President, talked about.

Time and time again, he has demonstrated that vital courage as well as a majestic sense of decency and dedication to universal human principles. Instead of pounding on podiums and romanticizing the illusionary glory of conflict, President Sadat set goals for his people of peace, prosperity, and freedom. As your people have strived for these ends, Americans and Egyptians have unavoidably been drawn together—unavoidably, because we share the same goals. And as many who have visited both nations point out, we, the Egyptians and the Americans, are similar people. Certainly our love of freedom and independence unites us.

In a passage reminiscent of our own Thomas Jefferson, President Sadat penned his definition of freedom in his autobiography. "Freedom," he said, "is the most beautiful, holy, and precious fruit of our culture. An individual should never be made to feel that he's at the mercy of any force or coercion or that his will is subordinated to that of others."

Well, we're grateful to have in Egypt a full partner in achieving our mutual goals, which includes our common determination to making the blessings of peace available to all the people of the Middle East. We will sincerely endeavor to help where possible, and we want you to know that all of your efforts, your forbearance in times of frustration, and, most of all, your good will, is appreciated. You're following a path that is natural for us. You've said, "No man can be honest with others unless he is true to himself."

The ancient pharaohs built pyramids to their glory. Your monuments are strong and healthy young men, alive today because you pursued peace—symbols to all mankind that there is a better way.

So, I ask all of our friends who are with us here tonight to join me in a toast to the Egyptian people and to their gallant President and his lovely wife.

President Sadat. Mr. President, Mrs. Reagan, dear friends:

We are overwhelmed by your genuine hospitality and warmth.

The sentiments President Reagan expressed toward me and the Egyptian people clearly reflect the bonds of friendship and amity which exist today between our nations. For years we worked hand in hand to set our relations on the course which is compatible with the long history of mutual respect and admiration between our peoples. We are determined to cement this friendship even further.

Our meeting today was a historic one by any measure. Let me state first that I was delighted to meet you, Mr. President, and strike an everlasting friendship with you. You are a statesman of conviction and compassion. You have a clear vision of the world and our duty to make if safer and happier for the living generations and those to come. Your priorities are rightly set. I was pleased that we are in full agreement over the issues we discussed.

Your nation, Mr. President, has played a pivotal role to bring about peace in the Middle East. No progress, as I told you in the morning, Mr. President, would have been made without such an active and dynamic role; no result would have been achieved. But with your help we have taken gigantic steps on the road to peace.

When we launched our peace initiative, we had in mind the support of the American people. And as we prepare for the second stage, we count on your continued interest and backing. Together we shall continue to work vigorously until the sacred mission is fulfilled. What I heard from you today, Mr. President, was very encouraging indeed.

We believe that the time is right for the resumption of the peace process. Recent events in the area demonstrated beyond any doubt that we cannot wait long if we are to spare the region further destruction and devastation. We must take additional steps promptly and without delay in order to maintain the momentum for peace. We are determined to complete our mission. We will not be deterred or discouraged by any development.

A new initiative, Mr. President, a bright side of this event was the willingness of the Palestinians to accept a cease-fire in Lebanon and uphold it. This is a turning point that should not escape our notice. In effect, it means that for the first time the Palestinians have come close to endorsing the peaceful solution. Those who are genuinely interested in peace in the Middle East should recognize this positive development and build upon it for the good of all nations.

At the same time, this is an added ammunition for our goal for mutual and simultaneous recognition between the Israelis and the Palestinians. As I have repeatedly said, the answer to persisting fears and suspicions is a real willingness to coexist and live together as good neighbors. We have set a good example with the establishment of peace between Egypt and Israel within the context of a comprehensive settlement. That model applies to the relations between Israel and the other parties.

You can help this process of reconciliation, Mr. President, by holding a dialog with the Palestinians through their representatives. This is certain to strengthen the forces of moderation among them. It would also undermine the designs of those who exploit the present state of affairs for their own selfish ends. It would be an act of statesmanship and vision.

If we succeed to achieve tangible progress with respect to the Palestinian problem, a whole new situation will emerge. We will be able to confront the real challenges we face. They are challenges which involve the survival of many nations and the protection of the vital interests of the West. I am confident that we will meet these challenges decisively and without hesitation.

I came here hopeful and optimistic, Mr. President. After our first session, I have become most confident and certain, under your upright and under your inspiring leadership, this great country can realize its dreams and reach its goals.

On behalf of the Egyptian people, I invite you, Mr. President, and your family to visit Egypt. This will give our people an opportunity to express to you directly their feelings of gratitude and respect. Such a visit will also serve the cause of peace and stability in the Middle East. It will enable us to pursue this stimulating dialog and bolster the bonds of friendship and mutual understanding.

Dear friends, allow me to invite you to rise in a tribute to President Reagan, Mrs. Reagan, and the friendly people of the

United States.

Thank you very much.

Note: President Reagan spoke at 9:32 p.m. in the State Dining Room at the White House.

Remarks of President Reagan and President Anwar el-Sadat of Egypt Following Their Meetings
August 6, 1981

President Reagan. Ladies and gentlemen, sadly the time has come for a farewell. I hope it'll only be an *au revoir* and that we'll be meeting again soon.

My meetings with President Sadat have now ended, and I want to say how valuable our exchanges have been and how encouraged I am with the progress that has been made and how much I personally have learned from President Sadat about the complexities of the problems that we all face in seeking a just and lasting peace in the Middle East. I'm greatly impressed with his intimate knowledge and his passionate concern.

Our talks covered three general areas: first, the growing strategic threat to the region posed by the growth of Soviet military power and the activities of Soviet surrogates in the Near East, Southwest Asia, and Africa. The second issue, discussed in great detail, was the peace process—and here, to be completely candid, I was a willing listener. We're both anxious to ensure the the the negotiating process stemming from that Camp David agreements will resume and succeed.

President Sadat has urged that the United States continue to play an important role in this process, and this we will do. I'll be meeting with other Middle East leaders in the coming months to continue the process of sharing views with our friends about our common goals of peace, stability, and security in the area.

The third area we discussed—Congress isn't in session, is it? [1]

The third area we discussed had to do with the growing bilateral relations between the United States and Egypt. We covered issues of mutual security, military cooperation, and economic matters. President Sadat shares our belief that a strong defense and a strong economy go hand in hand. We will work closely with Egypt as full partners in our search for peace and stability in the Middle East.

And finally, let me add another personal note. I had, of course, heard a great deal about President Sadat and was optimistic that we would establish a close rapport. My optimism was justified. I respected him for all that he has done, and getting to know him has vastly increased that respect. I share his belief that with courage, determination, and foresight, and a bold vision of the future, we can succeed in our common endeavors.

We've been delighted to have President Sadat and his family here with us, and we look forward to meeting again.

President Sadat. Thank you. I have a few words after the President.

I quite agree—full agreement with what President Reagan said. If I am to add anything, it is expressing my deep gratitude to President Reagan for this kind invitation to meet with him and to survey all the prob-

---

[1] *The President was momentarily distracted by the sound of nearby fire engine sirens.*

lems that we are facing together and then to meet again with the American people with whom I cherish really the full pride to be friends, to be understanding. And I'm happy to tell the American people, as always as I told them, I'm very happy, because after this visit I can say that I enjoy the friendship of President Reagan as a great leader of a great nation.

Again, I shall end like I have always ended: I shall never let you down.

Thank you very much.

Note: President Reagan spoke at 10:08 a.m. to reporters assembled at the North Portico of the White House.

Earlier the two Presidents held a breakfast meeting in the Red Room.

Message to the Senate Transmitting the United States-Netherlands Treaty on Mutual Legal Assistance
August 6, 1981

To the Senate of the United States:

With a view to receiving the advice and consent of the Senate to ratification, I transmit herewith the Treaty on Mutual Legal Assistance between the United States of America and the Kingdom of the Netherlands, together with a related exchange of notes, signed at The Hague on June 12, 1981.

I transmit also, for the information of the Senate, the report of the Department of State with respect to the treaty.

The treaty is one of a series of modern mutual assistance treaties being negotiated by the United States. The treaty is self-executing and utilizes existing statutory authority.

The new treaty provides for a broad range of cooperation in criminal matters. Mutual assistance available under the treaty includes: (1) executing requests relating to criminal matters; (2) taking of testimony or statements of persons; (3) effecting the production, preservation, and authentication of documents, records, or articles of evidence; (4) returning to the requesting Party any objects, articles, or other property or assets belonging to it or obtained by an accused through offenses; (5) serving judicial documents, writs, summonses, records of judicial verdicts, and court judgments or decisions; (6) effecting the appearance of a witness or expert before a court of the requesting Party; (7) locating persons; and (8) providing judicial records, evidence, and information.

I recommend that the Senate give early and favorable consideration to the treaty and give its advice and consent to ratification.

RONALD REAGAN

The White House,
August 6, 1981.

Nomination of Edward A. Curran To Be Director of the National Institute of Education
August 6, 1981

The President today announced his intention to nominate Edward A. Curran to be Director of the National Institute of Education, Department of Education. He will succeed Michael Timpane.

Since February 1981 Mr. Curran has been an Associate Director in the Office of Presidential Personnel. He served on the Department of Education transition team. During the 1980 Presidential campaign, Mr. Curran was director of Professionals for

701

Reagan-Bush. He was headmaster, National Cathedral School, Washington, D.C., in 1968–80; teacher, assistant dean of middle school, dean of student affairs, college guidance officer, and assistant director of admissions, St. John's School, Houston, Tex., in 1957–68.

Mr. Curran graduated from Yale University (B.A., 1955) and Duke University (M.A.T., 1968). He is married, has two children, and resides in Rock Hall, Md. He was born August 22, 1933, in North Adams, Mass.

Appointment of 25 Members of the President's Export Council, and Designation of Chairman
August 6, 1981

The President today announced the selection of the following individuals to serve as members of the President's Export Council. In addition, the President announced the selection of J. Paul Lyet as Chairman.

J. Paul Lyet, chairman of the board and chief executive officer, Sperry Corp.

Donald R. Beall, president and chief operating officer, Rockwell International Corp.

Robert A. Beck, chairman of the board and chief executive officer, Prudential Insurance Co. of America

Richard M. Bressler, president and chief executive officer, Burlington Northern, Inc.

George D. Busbee, Governor, State of Georgia

Jesse M. Calhoon, president, National Marine Engineers Beneficial Association, AFL–CIO

Robert Dickey III, chairman of the board, president, and chief executive officer, Dravo Corp.

James A. D. Geier, chairman of the board, president, and chief executive officer, Cincinnati Milacron, Inc.

Douglas F. Glant, president and chief executive officer, Pacific Iron & Metal Co.

Allan Grant, immediate past president, American Farm Bureau Federation

James R. Greene, president, American Express International Banking Corp.

John V. James, chairman of the board and chief executive officer, Dresser Industries, Inc.

K. Gordon Lawless, senior vice president, Phifer International Sales, Inc.

Donald E. Lukens, State senator, State of Ohio

Wales H. Madden, Jr., attorney, Amarillo, Tex.

Dudly C. Mecum II, managing partner, Peat, Marwick, Mitchell of New York, N.Y.

Irene W. Meister, vice president, International American Paper Institute

Edmund T. Pratt, Jr., chairman of the board and chief executive officer, Pfizer, Inc.

Philip Saxon, attorney, Wilmington, Del.

Henry B. Schacht, chairman of the board and chief executive officer, Cummins Engine Co., Inc.

David C. Scott, chairman of the board and chief executive officer, Allis Chalmers Corp.

Howard G. Sloane, president, the New York Colosseum Exhibition Corp.

Charles Thone, Governor, State of Nebraska

Robert C. Warren, chairman of the board and chief exeuctive officer, Cascade Corp.

Henry Zenzie, senior vice president, Prescott, Ball & Turben of New York

Nomination of John E. Dolibois To Be United States Ambassador to Luxembourg
August 6, 1981

The President today announced his intention to nominate John E. Dolibois, of Ohio, to be Ambassador to Luxembourg. He will succeed James G. Lowenstein, who is resigning.

Mr. Dolibois served in the United States Army as captain from 1942 to 1946. He was with Procter and Gamble of Cincinnati, Ohio, as industrial engineer in 1942 and from 1946 to 1947. Since 1947 he has been vice president (development and alumni affairs) at Miami University, Oxford, Ohio. He served as a member of the Board of Foreign Scholarships in 1969–1977.

Mr. Dolibois graduated from Miami University (A.B., 1942). He is married, has three children, and resides in Oxford, Ohio. He was born December 4, 1918, in Luxembourg.

Proclamation 4851—National Blinded Veterans Recognition Day
August 6, 1981

By the President of the United States of America

A Proclamation

Among those Americans who have answered their country's call to service in defense of its freedoms, there are thousands who, as a result of service in our Nation's military forces, have suffered the catastrophic disability of blindness. Despite the extreme severity of this disability, these veterans have succeeded in leading useful and productive lives, in part through Federal programs for their readjustment but, more significantly, by drawing upon a special brand of heroism.

Our country now enjoys the blessing of peace, and it is appropriate that all Americans recognize the special debt owed to those who have been blinded in the defense of our freedoms during the wars of this century.

We must acknowledge also the example they have provided to those blinded veterans whose equally catastrophic disability occurred after their separations from military service, and to other blinded Americans. Few are more worthy of national recognition than the disabled American veterans who have honored their commitments to their country and serve as a source of pride for us all.

I would also like to single out for praise those employers who have provided blinded veterans with the opportunity to develop rewarding private-sector careers. This promise of a future with challenge and fulfillment is particularly meaningful.

It is fitting that the Congress has, by enactment of Senate Joint Resolution 64, designated August 13, 1981, as "National Blinded Veterans Recognition Day."

Now, Therefore, I, Ronald Reagan, President of the United States of America, call upon all Americans to observe Thursday, August 13, 1981, as National Blinded Veterans Recognition Day. I urge my fellow citizens and all interested groups and organizations to set aside this day to honor the sacrifices and service of our Nation's blinded veterans by means of appropriate programs, ceremonies, and activities.

In Witness Whereof, I have hereunto set my hand this sixth day of August, in the year of our Lord nineteen hundred and eighty-one, and of the Independence of the

United States of America the two hundred and sixth.

[*Filed with the Office of the Federal Register, 4:56 p.m., August 6, 1981*]

RONALD REAGAN

Statement on the Death of Ray Bliss
August 6, 1981

Ray Bliss, the son of German immigrants, was an American who believed in the political process on which this Nation's freedom rests. As chairman of the Republican National Committee from 1965 to 1969, he helped to rejuvenate and unify the party during a critical period of its development.

He understood that the strength of our democracy and the responsiveness of our government were dependent upon the vitality of the party system. He respected his party and those in his party respected him. Nancy and I convey our deepest sympathy to his family.

Statement on Signing the Maritime Act of 1981
August 6, 1981

On several occasions during my campaign for the Presidency, I expressed my support for a strong merchant marine and maritime industry. We must have a strong merchant marine capable of meeting both our peacetime need for transportation of resources and products and our need for logistical support in time of national emergency.

The merchant marine and the maritime industry of our country need effective leadership and direction. I have promised that my administration will provide the leadership and direction for a strong merchant marine. The process of correcting the problems of the maritime industry, however, will be difficult and will take time. There are no quick fixes. Vision and innovation accompanied by a spirit of cooperation, sacrifice, and compromise by all segments of the industry, labor, and government are essential if we are to succeed.

I am pleased to sign H.R. 4074, a bill which transfers the Maritime Administration to the Department of Transportation. This organizational change is a significant achievement and will be of assistance in considering the maritime industry as part of a comprehensive national transportation system. This is of particular importance in view of the recent innovations in marine transportation that have resulted in greater integration of land and water transportation modes.

Associated with this transfer of the Maritime Administration, I have designated the Secretary of Transportation, Drew Lewis, as my administration's spokesman on maritime matters. Not only do I consider this designation essential to addressing effectively the problems of the industry but also to resolving a frequently expressed desire of both the Congress and the industry for a single focal point for maritime matters within the executive branch.

I extend my thanks to all those who cooperated to develop and enact this legislation in less than two months. I would particularly like to recognize the efforts of Senator Packwood, chairman of the Senate Commerce Committee, and Congressman Jones, chairman of the Merchant Marine and Fisheries Committee, for their invaluable assistance and cooperation, and would like to acknowledge as well the significant contributions of Senator Slade Gorton, Senator Daniel Inouye, Congressman Gene Snyder, Congressman Mario Biaggi, and Congressman Paul McCloskey, whose work on this legislation was an outstanding example of bipartisan cooperation. I thank those members of the industry who expressed their strong support for this legislation and hope that we can continue to build on this cooperative spirit to resolve the pressing problems of the industry.

lems of the industry.

Note: As enacted, H.R. 4074 is Public Law 97–31, approved August 6.

Statement on Signing a Bill Amending the International Investment Survey Act of 1974
August 7, 1981

I have approved S. 1104, an act which amends the International Investment Survey Act of 1974.

One of my responsibilities under that act is to assure that the information needed is collected with a minimum of burden on business and other respondents. To fulfill this responsibility, I am asking the Congress to make a technical amendment to the act as amended by this bill. Specifically, I request the Congress to remove the reference to calendar year data, because many business firms would find it much less burdensome to report on the basis of their fiscal accounting year. I believe that a determination of the specific reporting period should be left to the technical experts who manage the program and have been charged with the responsibility for balancing the need for collecting accurate data with that of minimizing the burden on respondents.

Note: As enacted, S. 1104 is Public Law 97–33, approved August 7.

Nomination of Raymond C. Ewing To Be United States Ambassador to Cyprus
August 12, 1981

The President today announced his intention to nominate Raymond C. Ewing, of Virginia, to be Ambassador to the Republic of Cyprus. He would succeed Galen L. Stone.

In 1957 Mr. Ewing entered the Foreign Service as staff assistant to the Assistant Secretary of State for Economic Affairs. In 1959–62 he was staff aide in Tokyo and political officer in Vienna (International Atomic Energy Agency) in 1962–64. He was on detail to the International Communication Agency as executive assistant in Lahore in 1964–65. He was international economist of the Trade Division in the Department in 1966–69. In 1969–70 he attended advanced economic studies at Harvard University. He was financial economist in Rome (1970–73) and counselor for economic and commercial affairs in Bern (1973–75). In the Department he was special assistant to the Assistant Secretary of State for European Affairs (1975–76) and Deputy Director, then Director, of the Office of Southern European Affairs (1976–79). In 1979–80 he attended the Executive Seminar in National and International Affairs at the Foreign Service Institute. Since 1980 he has been Deputy Assistant Secretary of State for European Affairs.

Mr. Ewing graduated from Occidental College (B.A., 1957) and Harvard University (M.P.A., 1970). He is married, has three children, and resides in Annandale, Va. He was born September 7, 1936, in Cleveland, Ohio.

Remarks on Signing the Economic Recovery Tax Act of 1981 and the Omnibus Budget Reconciliation Act of 1981, and a Question-and-Answer Session With Reporters
August 13, 1981

The President. Good morning.

Q. Typical California weather.

The President. Yes, since this is the first day of this kind of weather, of fog, since we've been here, I shall refrain from saying that you're all responsible—[*laughter*]—for bringing it up with you. The Sun has been shining brightly here.

These bills that I'm about to sign—not every page—this is the budget bill, and this is the tax program—but I think they represent a turnaround of almost a half a century of a course this country's been on and mark an end to the excessive growth in government bureaucracy, government spending, government taxing.

And we're indebted for all of this—I can't speak too highly of the leadership, Republican leadership in the Congress and of those Democrats who so courageously joined in and made both of these truly bipartisan programs. But I think in reality, the real credit goes to the people of the United States who finally made it plain that they wanted a change and made it clear in Congress and spoke with a more authoritative voice than some of the special interest groups that they wanted these changes in government.

This represents $130 billion in savings over the next 3 years. This represents $750 billion in tax cuts over the next 5 years. And this is only the beginning, because from here on now we are going to have to implement all of these, and it's going to be a job to make this whole turnaround work. It's going to be the number one priority—or continue to be the number one priority of our administration.

And again, I express my gratitude to the Congress, the 97th Congress, and to the administration, the people who worked so hard to make these come about.

And, Joe,[1] I guess it is traditional that I have to use a lot of pens in these signatures.

---

[1] *Joseph W. Canzeri, Deputy Assistant to the President.*

[*At this point, the President began signing H.R. 4242.*]

Oops, one letter too many. I'll have to catch up here someplace.

Q. One letter a pen, Mr. President?

The President. That's the way it works out. There's a number that we have to have. Just think, if my name had had three more letters in it, we'd——

Q. Who gets the pens?

The President. Some of those people that helped.

There. That is the tax program.

[*The President began signing H.R. 3982.*]

I figured how to do it, Joe, on this one to come out even—on the "n"—I'll make one part of the "n," and then the other part.

They are signed, and now all we have to do is implement them.

If you have any questions, perhaps, on any of the features of this, fire away.

Q. How about another subject, Mr. President? [*Laughter*]

The President. You mean in the face of all of this, you want to change the subject? Does someone have a question on the subject, first?

The Nation's Economy

Q. Yeah, I do. Mr. President, the Wall Street Journal carried a story yesterday that the revenue projections which you will be getting are going to be lower than your administration previously thought, and that means we're headed for a more severe economic downturn with higher interest rates. Are you ready to revise your own projections about the economy downward? Are we headed for a recession?

The President. I don't know whether you'd call it a recession or not, but they're not saying anything that we haven't said over and over again. Our own projections have been that for the next several months this soft and soggy economy is going to continue and that we shouldn't be fooled by these last couple of months of seeming upturn, that this means a continued climb. We think that we are in a soggy economy and it's going to go on.

Remember that it won't be until October that any of this will begin to be implemented. This is the budget that begins for the year in October. The tax programs, of course, won't be into effect until then either. And what we're counting on is when these, and these begin to take effect, that we will see the results when people begin to have the more money in their pockets from their earnings and when the lowered expenditures of government begin taking effect.

But, no, we're not differing that. We've said, ourselves, to watch for a sagging economy for the next few months.

Air Traffic Controllers

Q. Mr. President, on the air controllers strike, the International Association of Air Controllers has called on you to negotiate with PATCO. Why do you continue to believe that you should not negotiate with them?

The President. Well, now, this has changed the subject already, but—Sam [Sam Donaldson, ABC News], you'll be next, since you wanted to change the subject.

On that, there is no strike. There is a law that Federal unions cannot strike against their employers, their employers being the people of the United States. There was in addition to that an oath that is taken by each employee that he or she will not strike, and we warned in advance in the negotiations—there were 7 months of negotiations. They resulted on June 22d in a settlement that was deemed satisfactory to the union negotiators. Then they came back several weeks later with demands that were—said that this was not suitable and with demands that increased by 17 times what had been agreed to in June. It would have amounted to a $40,000 increase per year per controller. But we warned, under the threat of a strike, that there could not be a strike against the law, that this would be breaking the law, and that there, therefore, could be no negotiations.

Now, in effect, what they did was terminate their own employment by quitting. And our obligation now—or to the several thousand who are keeping this system working and who did abide by their oath——

Q. Wouldn't it be worth it, Mr. President, to go ahead and rehire these 12,000 people rather than have the American people suffer the inconvenience and the damage to the economy this is going to cause?

The President. Well, how much inconvenience is there? Yesterday, flights were 80 percent of normal. And with regard to international flights, yesterday 117,000 people were carried on over-water flights, international flights.

So, we feel that we are rebuilding the system now in view of the action of those controllers who decided to violate their oath and to violate the law. And I just don't see any way that it could be expected that we could now just go back and pretend that they weren't breaking the law or breaking their oath.

Q. Are you absolutely ruling out use of Presidential pardon or amnesty?

The President. Our obligation is to those several thousand that are in there working. And I must say they have my utmost gratitude and admiration, and I think they should have of all the people for what they're doing.

Q. But you have the power of Presidential pardon and amnesty. Are you absolutely ruling that out with regard to the air traffic controllers?

The President. Yes, although we have said that those—and some have already—those who come back and can show that they were, you might say, coerced or harassed, pressured into doing what they did and it was not their will, we have taken some of those back.

U.S.-Soviet Relations

Q. Mr. President, let me ask you about the Soviet Union's commentary today that your policy is one of sheer insanity and that relations between Moscow and Washington are now at the lowest ebb that they've been in modern times, since the cold war ended. Are we now in a new cold war, and do you fear that it may lead to an actual shooting war?

The President. No, I don't fear the actual shooting war. And whatever they may want to term it, "cold war" or not, what we are in is a situation where we're being realistic about their military buildup, which has gone on unchecked in spite of all of the meetings having to do with arms control and so forth. And I can understand their anguish. They are squealing like they're sitting on a sharp nail simply because we now are showing the will that we're not going to let them get to the point of dominance, where they can someday issue to the free world an ultimatum of "surrender or die," and they don't like that.

But, no, I have made it plain—and it isn't just language—we are going to meet with them with regard to the theater nuclear weapons in Europe, but we are also going to meet, and I have asked that we meet to legitimately discuss the reduction of armaments on both sides, particularly in strategic weapons.

Neutron Warhead

Q. Mr. President, you made the decision to go ahead and manufacture the neutron weapon. Is this not an escalation on our part?

The President. No, not really. The neutron weapon—incidentally, we have information that the Soviet Union spent about a hundred million dollars in Western Europe alone a few years ago when the announcement was first made of the invention of the neutron warhead, and I don't know how much they're spending now, but they're starting the same kind of propaganda drive.

The neutron warhead is a defensive weapon. It is a deterrent to a conflict. But we didn't start manufacturing it. The previous administration had authorized its manufacture quite some time ago, and what we have been doing—they, however, did not put the actual neutron part of the warhead in the 8-inch shell of the Lance missile. And so you stored here, warehoused that and the casing that in time of need and necessity would be then put together. Well, this doesn't make very much sense.

All we've done is simply say that we're going to continue warehousing this, but we're going to put that in the casing and warehouse it as a unit instead of two separate parts.

Air Traffic Controllers

Q. Mr. President, can I go back to PATCO for one minute, please?

The President. Yes.

Q. There is a report that you are considering offering controllers a Presidential pardon or an amnesty, giving them back their jobs if they admit that they were wrong. Is there any such consideration, and would you consider amnesty if they did?

The President. No, and that goes with my answer again. No, there's never been—I don't know where that could have started, because there has been no change in our feelings about this at all.

Situation in Poland

Q. Mr. President, there's been a report today that the Soviet Union will begin wargames next month in the Baltic States and the Baltic Sea under the direct direction of the Soviet Defense Minister. Do you consider that a reaction to your neutron bomb announcement, and is that something that surprises the administration, that we didn't know about?

The President. No, because they—we're not surprised—they were preparing long before this news leaked out about the assembly of the neutron warhead. It leaked out that—or we had the information that they were preparing for these wargames, so they couldn't have been dependent on the neutron warhead at all.

Q. You don't consider those wargames any particular new threat to Poland, since they're in that area?

The President. They might be directed against that, but I would have no way of knowing what's in their mind. But apparently they're going to include amphibious landings, coastal landings, and so forth.

Neutron Warhead

Q. Mr. President, do you foresee the eventual deployment of the neutron warhead in Western Europe?

The President. No. Our intention is to simply stockpile it, warehouse it, you might say, as we do with other weapons, in the event that, heaven forbid, there ever is a necessity, a war that brings them about.

This weapon was particularly designed to offset the great superiority that the Soviet Union has on the western front against the NATO nations, a tank advantage of better than four to one, and it is purely, as I say, a defensive weapon. And maybe this is why it's so painful to the Soviet Union, to realize that this could offset their great advantage there.

But there is no question of deployment, and if ever there seemed to be a necessity for that, deployment would only follow full consultation with our NATO allies.

Weapons Sales to Israel

Q. Mr. President, what is the reason for continuing to withhold fighter planes from Israel that they have bought or are purchasing from us?

The President. Well, the decision is going to be made very soon, and it is just some last details in the review that has been going on that started with the incident in the Middle East. And then I will be announcing a decision, probably next week.

Q. It sounds as if you're moving toward a decision to go ahead and release them.

The President. Well, if I answered that then I might be announcing a decision. I'll tell you, I'll announce what the decision is next week.

Federal Spending

Q. Back on the budget, many Governors, particularly Democratic Governors, say it's a shell game, that you've got to help them on the so-called safety net more, or they're not going to be able to take up the slack.

The President. Well, some Governors did say that and yet I noticed that the whole Governors conference did support and vote for a resolution of continued cooperation with us in these packages.

Now, it is true, we were not able to get all that we wanted in the line of real block grants and autonomy for local and State government. You know, one level of government—they even have that conflict between local and State government, that each level is a little reluctant to give up autonomy and authority. We're going to continue to work with the Congress and

work with the States and local government representatives to give them the autonomy they can have to make these programs work.

It is true we did not get all that we had wanted in that regard.

Q. I gather, sir, it's not autonomy so much as money that they need.

The President. Well, the difference is— and what our reductions were based on is that the block grant, giving them the flexibility at that level to use this as they saw fit, setting the priorities, really would result in a savings, and our reductions were based on those estimated savings in unnecessary administrative overhead, direction, and restrictions that caused unnecessary spending at the local level. And as a Governor I can testify that that was true, that in many of the categorical grant programs we could see how much more efficiently they could have been run without the redtape imposed by the Federal Government.

Now, there was a hand over here, and then I'll go over there.

U.S.-Soviet Relations

Q. Secretary Haig recently called on the Russians to show restraint and reciprocity if they wanted better relations with the United States. In your communications with Brezhnev, what suggestions have you made to the Soviets of ways they can improve their behavior, or how would you suggest now the Soviets could improve so that you could get back to détente and reduce this war of words?

The President. Well, I made a suggestion at one time in correspondence with Mr. Brezhnev that sometimes it seems that the governments sometimes get in the way of the people and that I think that the people of all countries have a great many things in common—a desire to raise their families, a desire to choose the occupation or profession they want to work at, to have some control over their lives. And I suggested that maybe we might sit down sometime and see what it was the people really wanted.

I doubt that the people have ever started a war. So, I made that suggestion.

Q. Would you like to meet Brezhnev soon?

The President. Well, when we are ready to come forward with a program of proposals for the—and that will take some preliminary meetings at the ministerial level before we're ready to come in and actually negotiate, as I've said, legitimate arms reductions to remove this nightmare that hangs over the world today of the strategic weapons.

Neutron Warhead

Q. Mr. President, I wonder about the neutron bomb perhaps changing nuclear doctrine. If the Soviets attacked with tanks, might we become the first to use—would we engage in first strike with that weapon?

The President. Well, this is something that seems to be overlooked in all the propaganda that's now being uttered about this weapon, and that is that the present tactical battlefield weapons stationed in Europe are nuclear weapons, far more destructive, far longer in rendering areas uninhabitable because of radioactivity, than the neutron weapon. So, those tactical nuclear weapons are there on both sides already, and this, we think, is a more moderate but more effective version.

You also have to remember that those who are crying the loudest, the Soviet Union, and many of those who under the name of pacifism in Western Europe, who are opposing things like this and opposing the theater nuclear forces and so forth, maybe some are sincere—I'm sure they are—but I think others are really carrying the progaganda ball for the Soviet Union, because there's no mention made of 200 SS–20's, strategic nuclear weapons of medium range, that are aimed at the cities of all of Europe today, and that are not being considered in any of the talk of reduction of theater forces, East and West—just as in SALT II the Soviet Union called our aging B–52 a strategic weapon but did not call their Backfire, modern bomber, a strategic weapon.

So, let's remember the SS–20's before we start worrying too much about what we're thinking about. But remember also that our present 8-inch guns and our present Lance missiles over there are tactical nuclear weapons.

Federal Deficits

Q. Mr. President, back on the budget for a minute. Given the so-called soggy conditions, it seems that you're going to have greater deficits over the next few years, less revenues, more deficits. What are those deficits now? How much more in budget cuts are you going to have to make over the next couple of years, and will you still be able to balance the budget in '84?

The President. Well, this has always been our goal and will continue to be our goal. But remember that we always said that there were further budget cuts for the coming years, for '83 and '84. These are the ones that go into effect in '82.

Q. How much more, though?

The President. Well, we know, of course, that we will have a sizable deficit for '81. There was nothing we could do about that. And, as you know, the Government has been operating in '81 without a budget, just on appropriations, and we have tried to limit once we got into management what we could, but the die was already cast as to the amount of this deficit.

Now, the possibility of increased deficits in the coming years over our previous figures are due in part to not getting totally what we had asked for in the budget cuts, but also that the tax package finally came out with additional reductions. As I say, those have possibly called for some reductions simply to recognize the realities of these two packages now, but we are going to continue to work on this and work for more budget cuts. And it just means that we're going to have to try to get more additional cuts than we might have had to get before.

I'm not sure that we might not have been, however, too conservative in our estimates on the tax program, because, remember, our tax proposals were based on the belief that the cut in tax rates would not mean a comparable cut in tax revenues, that the stimulant to the economy would be such that the Government might find itself getting additional revenues, as it did last year in the cut of the capital gains tax.

Interest Rates

Q. Mr. President, are you still confident that high interest rates will come down toward the end of the year?

The President. Yes. I noticed this morning's report in the paper, about a headline that said, "Interest Rates Up." But then when you read the story, you found that that was simply in the bond market in New York and was reflecting bond buyers' competition for the limited amount of capital that was there for investment. That's part of what's in that tax program, is to make less limited that amount of money that's available for capital investment.

MX and B–1 Bomber Programs

Q. Mr. President, do you expect to make a decision on the MX and the B–1 before you return to Washington?

The President. No. As a matter of fact, not before I return to Washington, but the MX and the B–1 programs are—we've still been discussing these and the various options, and very possibly we may wait for the return of Congress.

Defense Spending

Q. Mr. President, in view of your hard line against the Soviets, are you going to be willing to make a substantial scale-down in your defense spending plans, if that's necessary?

The President. That would depend on the negotiating table and how willing they were to actually discuss arms reductions. You will recall that the previous President tried to introduce that once, and our Secretary of State was on his way home in 24 hours from Moscow, because they wouldn't even hear of a reduction. But they are the ones, with all of the talk that's going on, the Soviet Union has been engaged in the greatest military buildup in the history of man, and it cannot be described as necessary for their defense. It is plainly a buildup that is offensive in nature.

Q. Then it'll lead to war.

The President. What?

Q. You said earlier you didn't think it would lead to war, but you're describing something that inevitably has——

The President. Well, no, not if they could achieve such a superiority by conning everyone else into being quiescent, that they could then say, "Look at the difference in our relative strengths. Now, here's what we want." This is what I mean by an ultimatum, "Surrender or die." And I think maybe they see that plan losing some of its potency now with our own plans.

Secretary of the Interior

Q. Are you ever going to let Jim Watt up here? [*Laughter*]

The President. Yes. As a matter of fact, he would be very welcome here or anyplace else.

Jim Watt has been doing what I think is a common sense job in the face of some environmental extremism that we've suffered from. And I can assure you Jim Watt does not want to destroy the beauty of America. He just wants to recognize that people are ecology, too. We have some needs, and there has to be provision for us to live.

But if he does come up, I'd welcome his help, because we've got a woods back here that is full of downed limbs from trees, the result of a freak 8-inch snowstorm.

Q. What if he strikes oil in the corral? [*Laughter*]

The President. I'll cut him in. [*Laughter*]

Bubonic Plague

Q. Have you seen any evidence of the plague since you've been here other than the signs? [*Laughter*]

Q. Killer rats!

The President. No. No, I don't know where that was found—they say someplace a mile from the ranch here. But we all have to recognize that that is not something startlingly new in California, and maybe in other parts of the country, but it was only a few years ago that we had a State park just east of Los Angeles that had to be closed for a period because of bubonic plague threat, carried by ground squirrels that were littering the place with their dead. And it was only a few years ago that we had—I believe there was a petty officer in the Navy that was on a fishing trip down in the Ojai area and was brought in to the hospital desperately ill and was dead before they could diagnose that it was bubonic plague. And they went back into that area and found again the evidence that rodents had carried it, so it's——

Q. Do you really tuck your pants in your boots as a precaution?

The President. No.

Q. Let's see. [*Laughter*]

The President. No.

Q. That's what your Deputy Press Secretary has been telling us.

The President. No, we've been out there in the woods working very hard at cleaning up, as I say, some of that brush. I wish the fog would lift so you could see some of the brush piles around here. Lee Clearwater, who was here the night that the snowfall came, said it sounded like an artillery barrage, hearing the limbs snapping off all over in the woods. And we had it pretty park-like around here until then.

We'll be cutting for the next 10 years. If anyone wants some firewood—[*laughter*]—just bring a truck and a chainsaw, and we'll point you to all kinds of good oak firewood that you can have.

Q. Will Mrs. Reagan be coming out to say hello?

The President. I think she's back over there with——

Q. What are you going to do for the rest of your vacation?

The President. What's that?

Q. What are you going to do for the rest of the week while you're here?

The President. Oh, the same thing we've been doing. This is the first morning we haven't ridden—decided instead that we'd come out and *be* ridden. [*Laughter*]

Q. Is it foggy like this every day?

The President. No. This is the first day. As I say, I think you brought it with you.

Q. What's the truth of this story? Does Mrs. Reagan like it up here, or does she just come up here because you want to do it? [*Laughter*]

The President. I don't think after 29 years she could fool me that much. I think she likes it. We ride together every morning.

Q. Women have been fooling men since Adam and Eve. [*Laughter*]

Deputy Press Secretary Speakes. On that note, thank you.

The President. Wait a minute. Do you want to answer for yourself? [*Referring to Mrs. Reagan*]

Q. We have the best witness over there.

The President. Speak for yourself.

Q. Do you like it up here, Mrs. Reagan?

Mrs. Reagan. I love it.

The President. There.

Q. Does she have a card in her hand? [*Laughter*]

The President. Well, that does it there.

Q. Thank you, sir.

The President. Thank you all. I'm sorry that we couldn't have given you one of the mornings that we've had up here before. It's just been absolutely beautiful.

Q. What's the name of the dog, by the way?

The President. This was Lassie—oh, Lassie. Millie! [*Laughter*]

Q. No, that was an old movie.

The President. Millie. Millie's her name. And if the golden retriever comes around, his name is Victory. That's the one that was given to Nancy as a little pup when we were back on the campaign trail. And he's now a big dog.

Q. May we see your boots on this side?

The President. You didn't get—excuse me. This side was cheated. They want a shot of the boot up. [*Laughter*]

The Cabinet

Q. Can I ask you one more question? There have been specific reports that your Secretary of State and Secretary of Defense are not getting along and that they argue in front of you. Can you comment on those reports?

The President. The whole Cabinet argues in front of me. [*Laughter*] That was the system that I wanted installed. Instead of the traditional Cabinet meeting with each Cabinet member making a brief report on how things were going in his agency, I wanted this operation where I have the benefit of the thinking of all of them, because most problems do overlap. There's hardly a problem that doesn't touch other Cabinet agencies and other departments of government.

And so, what we do is we have an agenda, and it goes out on the table and there have been numerous differences. And the thing is, when there's been enough discussion and enough argument and I've joined in and I've heard enough, I make the decision.

But no ill will and no feuds or turf battles of any kind have been going on. I've made it plain that I want each department to explain from that department's standpoint, such as State and Defense, what is their thinking and their reasoning as to why they take a certain position. And then I have to decide and weigh which way to go and which way is best for the national interest.

Q. Is Maureen going to run for the Senate?

The President. I hope not. [*Laughter*] I don't know. I know she's talked of it. I don't know how serious she is about it.

Q. How much will you take for the place?

The President. Oh, you can't sell heaven. [*Laughter*]

Mrs. Reagan. Where did Sam go? What ever gave you the idea that I didn't like it?

Q. Well, these reporters have been writing these stories like that. You'd be surprised what they say.

Mrs. Reagan. Oh. Well, you can straighten them all out.

Q. Well, they say, for instance, that you come up here and stay on the phone talking to your friends in Los Angeles while the President's out chopping wood and clearing grass and all of that.

Mrs. Reagan. I don't chop wood. But I don't stay on the phone all the time either.

Q. Do you really like it up here?

Mrs. Reagan. I really like it up here.

The President. I've got to be honest and tell you some of those phone calls are to make it possible for me to go out and chop the brush.

Q. You only have one line, is that it? [*Laughter*] Well, don't cut your leg off. [*Laughter*]

Mrs. Reagan. "Where's the rest of me?" [*Laughter*]

The President. You shouldn't have mentioned it. [*Laughter*]

Q. Are you going to go in to Santa Barbara at all?

The President. Not on this trip, not on this particular stretch here. I think next week—I mean the week after next, I go down there.

Note: The President spoke at 10:32 a.m. outside his residence at Rancho del Cielo.

As enacted, H.R. 4242, the Economic Recovery Tax Act of 1981, is Public Law 97–34, and H.R. 3982, the Omnibus Budget Reconciliation Act of 1981, is Public Law 97–35, both approved August 13.

Statement on the Twentieth Anniversary of the Berlin Wall
August 13, 1981

Twenty years ago the city of Berlin was divided by barriers erected to seal off East Berlin from the rest of the city. Those barriers were soon replaced by a massive concrete wall—a wall that today symbolizes the imprisonment of millions of Germans under Communist rule.

Although this wall stopped the flow of more than 3,000 persons a day who were escaping just before it was built, it could not completely stifle the human longing for freedom—tragically, more than 70 people have lost their lives trying to climb across the Berlin Wall to safety and freedom.

The Berlin Wall is a dramatic example of the desperate and cruel extremes to which totalitarian regimes will go to deny their subjects contact with other Europeans. From the Baltic Sea to Southeastern Europe, a murderous barrier of minefields and barbed wire, manned by guards who shoot to kill, stands as a monument to the inhumanity of those who would make the individual the servant of the state.

All who treasure freedom and human dignity should never accept nor take for granted this lethal barrier to freedom that stands today in the heart of Europe.

The regimes responsible for the barrier must be constantly reminded that their elaborate efforts to stifle human freedom with walls, mines, gunfire, and barbed wire are a colossal admission of failure.

What can the world think of rulers who must build prison walls around their own nation? What can the world think of leaders who fear that their own people will flee their homeland at the first opportunity?

Today throughout the world men and women who cherish freedom pray for the day when the Berlin Wall and other such monuments to tyranny are only a bitter memory—a day when the people of East Europe can once again enjoy free contact with their neighbors in the West.

Nomination of Lenora Cole-Alexander To Be Director of the Women's Bureau of the Department of Labor
August 14, 1981

The President today announced his intention to nominate Lenora Cole-Alexander to be Director of the Women's Bureau, Department of Labor. She would succeed Alexis M. Herman.

Since 1978 Dr. Cole-Alexander has been vice president for student affairs, University of the District of Columbia. She was vice president for student life at the American University in 1973–77; assistant to the vice president for student affairs and interim director, Cooperative College Center, State University of New York (Buffalo) in 1969–73; research assistant, department of educational administration, State University of New York (Buffalo) in 1968–69; and teacher with the board of education, Chicago, Ill., in 1961–68.

Dr. Cole-Alexander has been involved in many community activities, including serving as a member of the steering committee of the National Council of Negro Women; member of the board of directors, Washington Opportunities for Women; and member, board of trustees, Legal Aid Society of Washington.

Dr. Cole-Alexander graduated from the State University College at Buffalo (B.S., 1957; M.Ed., 1969; Ph. D., 1974). She is married and resides in Washington, D.C. She was born March 9, 1935, in Buffalo, N.Y.

Proclamation 4852—National Schoolbus Safety Week
August 14, 1981

By the President of the United States of America

A Proclamation

Our country's greatest resource is its children; their education is our investment in the future.

Currently, more than 20 million students are transported by schoolbus to and from school each day. The safety of these students deserves the highest priority.

To remind all Americans of the importance of schoolbus safety, the Congress, by House Joint Resolution 141, has requested the President to proclaim the week beginning October 4, 1981, as "National Schoolbus Safety Week."

Now, Therefore, I, Ronald Reagan, President of the United States of America, do hereby designate the period from October 4, 1981 through October 10, 1981, as National Schoolbus Safety Week. I call upon all Americans to recognize and contribute to the imperative of providing safe transportation for our schoolchildren.

In Witness Whereof, I have hereunto set my hand this 14th day of August, in the year of our Lord nineteen hundred and eighty-one, and of the Independence of the

United States of America the two hundred and sixth.

RONALD REAGAN

[*Filed with the Office of the Federal Register, 1:22 p.m., August 18, 1981*]

Executive Order 12316—Responses to Environmental Damage
August 14, 1981

By the authority vested in me as President of the United States of America by Section 115 of the Comprehensive Environmental Response, Compensation, and Liability Act of 1980 (94 Stat. 2796; 42 U.S.C. 9615), it is hereby ordered as follows:

Section 1. National Contingency Plan. (a) The National Contingency Plan, hereinafter referred to as the NCP and which was originally published pursuant to Section 311 of the Federal Water Pollution Control Act, as amended (33 U.S.C. 1321), shall be amended to contain the implementing procedures for the coordination of response actions to releases of hazardous substances into the environment.

(b) The NCP shall contain a concept of a national response team composed of representatives of appropriate Executive agencies for the coordination of response actions. The national response team shall, in addition to representatives of other appropriate agencies, include representatives of the following: Department of State, Department of Defense, Department of Justice, Department of the Interior, Department of Agriculture, Department of Commerce, Department of Labor, Department of Health and Human Services, Department of Transportation, Department of Energy, Environmental Protection Agency, Federal Emergency Management Agency, and United States Coast Guard.

(c) The responsibility for the amendment of the NCP and all of the other functions vested in the President by Section 105 of the Comprehensive Environmental Response, Compensation, and Liability Act of 1980, hereinafter referred to as the Act (42 U.S.C. 9605), is delegated to the Administrator of the Environmental Protection Agency.

(d) In accord with Section 111(h)(1) of the Act and Section 311(f)(5) of the Federal Water Pollution Control Act, as amended (33 U.S.C. 1321(f)(5)), the following shall be among those designated in the NCP as Federal trustees for natural resources:

(1) Secretary of Defense.
(2) Secretary of the Interior.
(3) Secretary of Agriculture.
(4) Secretary of Commerce.

(e) Amendments to the NCP shall be coordinated with members of the national response team prior to publication for notice and comment. Amendments shall also be coordinated with the Federal Emergency Management Agency and the Nuclear Regulatory Commission in order to avoid inconsistent or duplicative requirements in the emergency planning responsibilities of those agencies.

(f) All amendments to the NCP, whether in proposed or final form, shall be subject to review and approval by the Director of the Office of Management and Budget.

Sec. 2. Response Authorities. (a) The functions vested in the President by the first sentence of Section 104(b) of the Act relating to "illness, disease, or complaints thereof" are delegated to the Secretary of Health and Human Services who shall, in accord with Section 104(i) of the Act, perform those functions through the Public Health Service.

(b)(1) The functions vested in the President by Section 101(24) of the Act, to the extent they require a determination by the President that "permanent relocation of residents and businesses and community facilities" is included within the terms "remedy" or "remedial action" as defined in Section 101(24) of the Act, are delegated to the Director of the Federal Emergency Management Agency.

715

(2) The functions vested in the President by Section 104(a) of the Act, to the extent they require permanent relocation of residents, businesses, and community facilities or temporary evacuation and housing of threatened individuals not otherwise provided for, are delegated to the Director of the Federal Emergency Management Agency.

(c) The functions vested in the President by Section 104 (a) and (b) of the Act are delegated to the Secretary of Defense with respect to releases from Department of Defense facilities or vessels, including vessels owned or bare-boat chartered and operated.

(d) Subject to subsections (a), (b), and (c) of this Section, the functions vested in the President by Sections 101(24) and 104 (a) and (b) of the Act are delegated to the Secretary of the Department in which the Coast Guard is operating, hereinafter referred to as the Coast Guard, with respect to any release or threatened release involving the coastal zone, Great Lakes waters, ports, and harbors.

(e) Subject to subsections (a), (b), (c), and (d) of this Section, the functions vested in the President by Sections 101(24) and 104 (a) and (b) of the Act are delegated to the Administrator of the Environmental Protection Agency, hereinafter referred to as the Administrator.

(f) The functions vested in the President by Section 104 (c), (d), (f), (g), and (h) of the Act are delegated to the Coast Guard, the Secretary of Health and Human Services, the Director of the Federal Emergency Management Agency, and the Administrator in order to carry out the functions delegated to them by subsections (a), (b), (d), and (e) of this Section. The exercise of authority under Section 104(h) of the Act shall be subject to the approval of the Administrator of the Office of Federal Procurement Policy.

(g) The functions vested in the President by Section 104(e)(2)(C) of the Act are delegated to the Administrator; all other functions vested in the President by Section 104(e) of the Act are delegated to the Secretary of Defense, the Secretary of Health and Human Services, the Coast Guard, the Director of the Federal Emergency Man-

agement Agency, and the Administrator of the Environmental Protection Agency, in order to carry out the functions delegated to them by this Section.

Sec. 3. Abatement Action. (a) The functions vested in the President by Section 106(a) of the Act are delegated to the Coast Guard with respect to any release or threatened release involving the coastal zone, Great Lakes waters, ports, and habors.

(b) Subject to subsection (a) of this Section, the functions vested in the President by Section 106(a) of the Act are delegated to the Administrator.

Sec. 4. Liability. (a) The function vested in the President by Section 107(c)(1)(C) of the Act is delegated to the Secretary of Transportation.

(b) The functions vested in the President by Section 107(c)(3) of the Act are delegated to the Coast Guard with respect to any release or threatened release involving the coastal zone, Great Lakes waters, ports, and harbors.

(c) Subject to subsection (b) of this Section, the functions vested in the President by Section 107(c)(3) of the Act are delegated to the Administrator.

(d) The functions vested in the President by Section 107(f) of the Act are delegated to each of the Federal trustees for natural resources set forth in Section 1(d) of this Order for resources under their trusteeship.

Sec. 5. Financial Responsibility. (a) The functions vested in the President by Section 107(k)(4)(B) of the Act are delegated to the Secretary of the Treasury. The Administrator will provide the Secretary with such technical information and assistance as the Administrator may have available.

(b) The functions vested in the President by Section 108(a) of the Act are delegated to the Federal Maritime Commission. Notwithstanding Section 1(d) of Executive Order No. 12291, the regulations issued pursuant to this authority shall be issued in accordance with that Order. The Commission shall be responsible, in accord with Section 109 of the Act, for the enforcement of civil penalties for violations of the regulations issued under Section 108(a) of the Act.

(c) The functions vested in the President by Section 108(b) of the Act are delegated to the Secretary of Transportation with respect to all transportation related facilities, including any pipeline, motor vehicle, rolling stock, or aircraft.

(d) Subject to subsection (c) of this Section, the functions vested in the President by Section 108(b) of the Act are delegated to the Administrator.

Sec. 6. Employee Protection and Notice to Injured. (a) The functions vested in the President by Section 110(e) of the Act are delegated to the Secretary of Labor.

(b) The functions vested in the President by Section 111(g) of the Act are delegated to the Secretary of Defense with respect to releases from Department of Defense facilities or vessels, including vessels owned or bare-boat chartered and operated.

(c) Subject to subsection (b) of this Section, the functions vested in the President by Section 111(g) of the Act are delegated to the Administrator.

Sec. 7. Management of the Hazardous Substance Response Trust Fund and Claims. (a) The functions vested in the President by Section 111(a) of the Act are delegated to the Administrator, subject to the provisions of this Section and applicable provisions of this Order.

(b) The Administrator shall transfer, to transfer appropriation accounts for other agencies, from the Hazardous Substance Response Trust Fund, out of sums appropriated, such amounts as the Administrator may determine necessary to carry out the purposes of the Act. These allocations shall be consistent with the President's Budget, within the amounts approved by the Congress, unless a revised allocation is approved by the Director of the Office of Management and Budget.

(c) The Administrator shall chair a budget task force composed of representatives of agencies having responsibilities under this Order or the Act. The Administrator shall also, as part of the budget request for the Environmental Protection Agency, submit a budget for the Hazardous Substance Response Trust Fund which is based on recommended allocations developed by the budget task force. The Administrator may prescribe reporting and other forms, procedures, and guidelines to be used by the agencies of the Task Force in preparing the budget request.

(d) The Administrator and each agency head to whom funds are allocated pursuant to this Section, with respect to funds allocated to them, are authorized in accordance with Section 111(f) of the Act to designate Federal officials who may obligate such funds.

(e) The functions vested in the President by Section 112 of the Act are delegated to the Administrator for all claims presented pursuant to Section 111.

Sec. 8. General Provisions. (a) Notwithstanding any other provision of this Order, any representation pursuant to or under this Order in any judicial or quasijudicial proceedings shall be by or through the Attorney General. The conduct and control of all litigation arising under the Act shall be the responsibility of the Attorney General.

(b) Notwithstanding any other provision of this Order, the President's authority under the Act to require the Attorney General to commence litigation is retained by the President.

(c) The functions vested in the President by Section 301 of the Act are delegated as follows:

(1) With respect to subsection (a), to the Administrator in consultation with the Secretary of the Treasury.

(2) With respect to subsection (b), to the Secretary of the Treasury.

(3) With respect to subsection (c), to the Secretary of the Interior.

(4) With respect to subsection (f), to the Administrator.

(d) The Attorney General shall manage and coordinate the study provided for in Section 301(e) of the Act.

(e) The performance of any function under this Order shall be done in consultation with interested agencies represented on the national response team, as well as with any other interested agency.

717

(f) Certain functions vested in the President by the Act which have been delegated or assigned by this Order may be redelegated to the head of any agency with his consent; those functions which may be redelegated are those set forth in Sections 2, 3, 4(b), 4(c), and 6(c) of this Order.

(g) Executive Order No. 12286 of January 19, 1981, is revoked.

RONALD REAGAN

The White House,
August 14, 1981.

[Filed with the Office of the Federal Register, 1:23 p.m., August 18, 1981]

Executive Order 12317—President's Commission on Hostage Compensation
August 14, 1981

By the authority vested in me as President by the Constitution and statutes of the United States of America, in accordance with the Federal Advisory Committee Act, as amended (5 U.S.C. App. I), and to give the President's Commission on Hostage Compensation additional time to prepare its report, it is hereby ordered that the first sentence of Section 1–202 of Executive Order No. 12285, as amended, is further amended to read: "The Commission shall submit a final report to the President no later than September 21, 1981.".

RONALD REAGAN

The White House,
August 14, 1981.

[Filed with the Office of the Federal Register, 1:24 p.m., August 18, 1981]

Nomination of Michael H. Newlin To Be United States Ambassador to Algeria
August 17, 1981

The President today announced his intention to nominate Michael H. Newlin, of Maryland, to be Ambassador to the Democratic Popular Republic of Algeria. He would succeed Ulric St. Clair Haynes, Jr.

Mr. Newlin served as a civilian expert with the Department of the Air Force in 1951–52. In 1952 he entered the Foreign Service as economic and consular officer in Frankfurt and was political officer in Oslo in 1954–58. In the Department he was foreign affairs officer in the Office of United Nations Political Affairs in 1958–63. He was deputy chief of the political section in Paris/USNATO (1963–67) and in Brussels/USNATO (1967–68). He was counselor for political affairs at the United States Mission to the United Nations in New York in 1968–72. In 1972–75 he was Deputy Chief of Mission in Kinshasa and principal officer in Jerusalem in 1975–80. In 1980–81 he was Deputy Assistant Secretary of State for International Organization Affairs in the Department.

Mr. Newlin graduated from Harvard College (B.A., 1949) and Harvard Business School (M.B.A., 1951). He is married, has one child, and resides in Bethesda, Md. He was born May 16, 1926, in Greensboro, N.C.

Remarks at a Target '82 Republican Fundraising Reception in Los Angeles, California
August 17, 1981

You know, being back here and seeing all of you, I just wish one thing about George Washington. [*Laughter*] He set so many precedents, why didn't he set one that the capital would henceforth be where the President lived? [*Cheers*]

Well, I thank all of you for being here. I know the cause that brings you together, and I think it is doubly important, more important than it has ever been. Next year, '82, that's an election year for all of our assemblymen, the administration, for the Senate. And if I have my figures correct, we would only have to hold our own in the assembly, where all are up for election, and win 10 of their seats, and we'd have a majority there. And in the Senate, there are 14 of them up for reelection, and only 6 Republicans—we'd only have to hold our own and win 4, and we would control that house.

Then, of course, we want the administration also. And the reason it's doubly important is because of some of the things that have been going on in Washington. I am determined that we're going to do everything we can to restore federalism to this land, to make this once again a federation of sovereign States, in which State governments, local governments would have more autonomy than they've had for 50 years. And while we didn't get all we wanted in the block grant process—to take off the backs of State and local government the redtape and the regulations, the strings that go with categorical grants—we'll keep on trying and fighting, because my dream is that the block grants are only a means to an end. And the end would be when the Federal Government turns back to the States and local governments sources, actual tax sources, of revenue, allowing the States and the local governments to perform those functions which are theirs by the Constitution and that they would have the tax resources with which to support those functions.

The other day up in the fog—[*laughter*]—on the hill,[1] we signed those two bills. And I got so mad, because I kept looking and looking—they wouldn't show enough of the size of them. The budget cuts alone were a stack of paper that high. I've read every page. [*Laughter*] And the tax cuts were only that high. [*Laughter*] But even so, in those tax cuts, it's going to amount to hundreds of billions of dollars over the next few years. It's going to reverse a tax increase built into the system that was going to take $92 billion more out of your pockets next year and $300-and-some billion out of your pockets over the next 3 years.

But the budget cuts, I think, have reversed a trend of the last half century—the idea that government can voluntarily reduce itself in size. And what we have actually done with those budget cuts is reduce the growth of government, reduce it by more than half, from more than 14 percent, almost 16 percent, some say, depending on who's doing the figuring, down to 6½-percent increase in the annual spending. And we still have a job to do. That's only the beginning.

This fall, when we start in on the 1983 budget, we have to find tens of billions of dollars of additional cuts. And in 1984 we're going to find more tens of billions of dollars of additional cuts. And then we're going to depend on those tax reductions that we've made to do what we've always said they would and that is to stimulate the economy, to create employment, and to make everyone, even including the government, more prosperous because of the increase—[*applause*].

Nancy is signaling me that I should get away from here—[*laughter*]—and we could get down there for the little bit of time that we have and say hello to you.

There are a couple of other things going on at the national level, also; one of course,

---

[1] *Rancho del Cielo.*

that's caused a lot of comment. Maybe I could seriously just say something. The air controllers strike in violation of the law and in violation of an oath taken individually by each member—and I've seen myself heralded as setting out to union bust. I'm the first union president that ever got elected President of the United States. [*Laughter*]

But you know, some years ago, when public employees first started to unionize, Phillip Murray—some of you here will remember that name. He was the head of the CIO. And John L. Lewis of the United Mine Workers, and Eleanor Roosevelt said that, "Yes, they could organize to bargain, but they could not strike against their fellow citizens." Franklin Delano Roosevelt said a strike by public employees would be insurrection against the people and the Government of the United States. And we know what Cal Coolidge said. He says, "If they go on strike, they're out of a job."

Seriously, I am sorry. I'm sorry those people were misled, and I'm sure they're nice people. But I don't think there was any choice but to do what we've done. Public employees cannot strike against the public. Well, I just knew you'd be wondering what we've been doing back there. [*Laughter*]

Well, God bless you all for being here and make sure that we have the kind of a government in California in 1982 that'll be ready and willing to accept the responsibilities that heretofore have been usurped by the Federal Government. And we'll try to see that they've got the resources to make them work without all that administrative overhead.

You know, the difference between local government and Washington is very simple. Recently, there was a little town. Their traffic signs were only 5 feet high, and they decided to raise them, for better visibility for the motorists, to raise them to 7 feet above the ground. And the Federal Government came in and said they had a program that would do that for them. They lowered the pavement 2 feet. [*Laughter*]

Thank you all very much.

Note: The President spoke at 7:08 p.m. in the Westside Room at the Century Plaza Hotel.

Nomination of Arthur Adair Hartman To Be United States Ambassador to the Union of Soviet Socialist Republics
August 18, 1981

The President today announced his intention to nominate Arthur Adair Hartman, of New Jersey, as Ambassador to the Union of Soviet Socialist Republics. He would succeed Thomas J. Watson, Jr., who has resigned.

Mr. Hartman served in the United States Army Air Force in 1944–46. He was in Paris as economic officer with the Economic Cooperation Administration (1948–52) and with the United States delegation to the European Army Conference (1952–54). He entered the Foreign Service in 1954 as politico-military officer in Paris/USRO. From 1956 to 1958, he was economic officer in Saigon. In the Department he was international relations officer in the Bureau of European Affairs (1958–61) and special assistant to the Under Secretary of State for Economic Affairs (1961–63). He was chief of the economic section in London in 1963–67. In the Department he was Director of the Inter-Departmental Group (1967–69) and Deputy Director for Coordination (1969–72). From 1972 to 1974, he was Deputy Chief of Mission and Minister Counselor in Brussels/USEC. He was Assistant Secretary of State for European Affairs in the Department in 1974–77, and since 1977 he has been Ambassador to France.

Mr. Hartman was born March 12, 1926, in New York, N.Y. He graduated (A.B.) in 1947 from Harvard University and attended Harvard Law School in 1947–48. He is married, has five children, and resides in Haddonfield, N.J.

Nomination of Harry G. Barnes, Jr., To Be United States Ambassador to India
August 18, 1981

The President today announced his intention to nominate Harry G. Barnes, Jr., of Maryland, to be Ambassador to India. He would succeed Robert F. Goheen.

In 1951 Mr. Barnes entered the Foreign Service as consular officer in Bombay and was head of the consular section in Prague in 1953–55. He attended Russian language training in Oberammergau, Germany, in 1955–56. He was publications procurement officer in Moscow in 1957–59. In 1959–62 he was political officer in the Office of Soviet Affairs in the Department of State. He attended the National War College in 1962–63. In 1963–67 he was Deputy Chief of Mission in Kathmandu. He attended Romanian language training at the Foreign

Service Institute in 1967–68 and was Deputy Chief of Mission in Bucharest in 1968–71. In the Department he was supervisory personnel officer (1971–72) and deputy executive secretary (1972–74). In 1974–77 he was Ambassador to Romania. In 1977–81 he was Director General of the Foreign Service and Director of Personnel in the Department.

Mr. Barnes was born June 5, 1926, in St. Paul, Minn. He graduated (B.A.) summa cum laude in 1949 from Amherst College and received his M.A. in 1968 from Columbia University. He served in the United States Army in 1944–46. Mr. Barnes is married, has four children, and resides in Bethesda, Md.

Remarks on Board the U.S.S. *Constellation* off the Coast of California
August 20, 1981

[*The President arrived at the U.S.S. Constellation via Marine One at approximately 10:50 a.m. He was met by Capt. Dennis M. Brooks, Commanding Officer, and Capt. William Carlson, Chief of Staff, Carrier Group Seven.*

The President, escorted by Captain Brooks, proceeded to the flag bridge where he was presented with a U.S.S. Constellation jacket and cap. He then entered the navigation bridge and spoke to the crew via the ship's public address system at approximately 11:02 a.m. His remarks follow.]

Remarks to the Crew of the U.S.S.
Constellation

Captain Brooks and crew of the *Constellation*, thank you for extending me this opportunity. This ship represents a powerful force in an uncertain world, and we all sleep a little better at night knowing that you're on duty. Everything we as Americans hold dear is safer because of what all

of you are doing. I'd like to especially greet those who will be in the air department, the combat direction center, in engineering and communication later on. Although you won't be with us later, you're certainly not forgotten.

The engineering unit, I understand, faces a major recertification examination tomorrow, and a September readiness evaluation is also rapidly approaching. These are two of the major challenges for which you've been preparing, so can I just express my confidence that you're going to come through with flying colors?

So, for those who will be standing watch, my very best wishes. For the rest of the officers and crew, I look forward to meeting you and getting to know more about the job that you're doing. After all, this is quite an experience for an ex-horse cavalryman. So, I wish all aboard "a good Connie day."

721

[*Following his remarks, the President proceeded to the auxiliary conning station to view a demonstration refueling operation. When the U.S.S.* Fletcher *came alongside the aircraft carrier, the President spoke to the crew of the destroyer at approximately 11:15 a.m., via the* Constellation's *public address system. His remarks follow.*]

Remarks to the Crew of the U.S.S. Fletcher

Officers and men of the *Fletcher*, it's my privilege and I'm greatly honored to have this opportunity to say hello to you but also to tell you how grateful all of us are for all that you're doing. We are truly grateful. I have just finished telling the crew here of the *Constellation* that this is really kind of an earth-shattering experience for me, since my military experience was as a horse cavalryman. This is somewhat different.

But, we are proud of all of you, and while there may be some people who think that the uniform is associated with violence, you are the peacemakers. It's because of what you're doing that we can be sure of peace.

So, again, thank you for giving me this opportunity to greet you and to tell you how proud we are.

[*At this point, the President toured the navigation bridge, stopping briefly to take the helm. He then held an informal question-and-answer session with reporters at approximately 11:30 a.m. The excerpts included in the White House press release follow.*]

Question-and-Answer Session on the Downing of Libyan Planes by U.S. Pilots

Q. Mr. President, why did we have to conduct training exercises so close to Libya?

The President. It is an area in which we have conducted training exercises rather regularly—not only us but others. And Libya has created an artificial line, claiming waters that are actually international waters. And we just felt that we gave the routine notice that is always given for such maneuvers, and we conducted those maneuvers on the basis of what are international waters and not that artificial line that had been created. This foray by the Libyans was nothing new. Over the last couple of years, they have frequently harassed our aircraft out beyond that line in the Mediterranean; French aircraft. There have even been incidents of threats of fire, and we decided it was time to recognize what are the international waters and behave accordingly.

Q. But why did we feel we had to challenge them at this particular time?

The President. We didn't challenge them. This was the scheduled time for the maneuvers. We've been holding them every year and in that area. And this time we didn't restrict ourselves on the basis of what, as I say, is an artificial line. We utilized the international waters there for the training exercise.

Q. Are you trying to destabilize Qadhafi's government, Mr. President?

The President. No. We responded as we will respond anywhere when any of our forces are attacked. They're going to defend themselves.

Q. Mr. President?

The President. Yes.

Q. There is some feeling that perhaps your aides should have awakened you earlier, because most of the country knew about the incident before you did.

The President. Well, no, there was no—everything was going forward and everything that had to be done—and there was no decision to be made or they would have. They would have awakened me if there had been a decision. But it was—the incident had taken place; there was no other reason, so they waited to call me when they had all the full information.

Q. Do you think that was right?

The President. What?

Q. Do you think that was proper?

The President. Yes. Yes.

Q. As you sit here in the bridge of this ship, what do you think the message should be from yesterday's event and your appearance here today?

The President. Well, that we're determined, that we are going to close that window of vulnerability that has existed for some time with regard to our defensive capability.

Q. Sir, your message wasn't just to the Libyans, but the Soviets as well?

The President. The message to the Libyans was brought on by the Libyans. We didn't go there to shoot down a couple of Libyan planes. They came out and fired on ours when we were holding maneuvers, and which everyone had been notified, all of our allies. All of the countries there in the area had been notified that we were going to hold those maneuvers, which we do every year in that same place.

Q. You wouldn't be sorry to see Qadhafi fall, would you?

The President. Well, I would think that diplomacy would have me not answer that question.

Q. We're a little confused as to whether you deliberately ordered a test of Qadhafi's challenge.

The President. No, the maneuvers have been planned for a long time.

Q. So, there was no deliberate——

The President. No. We were, as I say, faced with the knowledge that you could not go on recognizing this violation of international waters and that we were going to plan our maneuvers as we would have planned them without that rule, without his artificial line.

Now, if I could call to your attention that periodically we send some ships into the Black Sea just for the same reason, just as the Soviet Union sends ships into the Caribbean, to assure that everyone is observing international waters and the rules pertaining to them.

Q. But it sounds like you're saying, no, it wasn't a test, but you aren't sorry you've bloodied Qadhafi's nose.

The President. This is a rule that has to be followed. If our men are fired on, they're going to fire.

[*Following the question-and-answer session, the President viewed an aircraft launch and recovery exercise from the navigation bridge and then went to the flight deck to watch a weapons training exercise. He then had lunch with enlisted personnel in the mess.*

Following lunch, the President proceeded to the hangar deck for a reenlistment ceremony. Adm. James D. Watkins, Chief of Staff, Pacific Fleet, administered the oath, and the President congratulated the reen-

listed men individually as they crossed the dais.

Captain Brooks then presented the President with several mementos of his visit to the ship and introduced the President, who addressed the crew at approximately 1:25 p.m. as follows.]

Remarks to Crew and Signing of John Barry Day Resolution

Thank you all very much for this warm hospitality and this greeting. Admiral Watkins, Captain Brooks, the officers and men of the *Constellation:*

You know, Presidents are permitted to experience a great many things, but I can assure you, this day will be long remembered as a most special experience that I have had. It is my first time to ever be on a carrier. As I told many of you on the horn this morning when I arrived, I'm an old ex-horse cavalryman. But then I'll remind you that there was an admiral of the Navy that rode a horse into Tokyo at the end of World War II, so maybe we have something in common.

But this ship, what I've seen today and the officers and crew, you all make me very proud to be able to say I'm the Commander in Chief of all of you. The demonstration of firepower and efficiency by the air wing was impressive, but what's most important, it is also impressive to the enemies of freedom in the world. And we had an example of that just night before last on the carrier *Nimitz.*

But this carrier and its air wing represent the cutting edge of our naval power. It takes an extra bit of dedication to do this job. I know it's rough. It's rough on you, rough on your families, but it's never been more necessary at any time in our history than it is right now. Without someone willing to put in the long hours, willing to suffer the frustrations, willing to risk the dangers, our country wouldn't be sure of continued peace and freedom. There's no greater gift that you can give to your family, your community, or your country than the protection that you afford all of them by this job that you're doing.

I know there've been times when the military has been taken for granted. It won't happen under this administration. We're going to make sure to the best of our ability that your pay is fair and that you have the equipment that is needed to do the job right, from spare parts to new ships.

Today, military adventurism and subversion threaten in faraway areas of the world. Providing security for the United States is the greatest challenge and a greater challenge than ever, but we'll meet that challenge. We're committed to a 600-ship Navy, a Navy that is big enough to deter aggression wherever it might occur. Let friend and foe alike know that America has the muscle to back up its words, and ships like this and men like you are that muscle.

Of course, more than equipment is needed. You deserve compensation worthy of the sacrifices you're making, and you'll get it. We're taking the steps necessary to encourage you to stick with the service, because you're needed. And I am so proud and so thrilled by the evidence of that that we've seen here today.

But you know that it takes more than money to keep you out here. The word "patriotism" is defined as love for or devotion to one's country, and that can't be bought. But it's present on this great ship, on the destroyer *Fletcher* and the cruiser *Jouett*, the frigate *Wadsworth* as well.

There's a new spirit, I can tell you, sweeping America, and you're part of it. The Navy's pride and professionalism campaign is part of it. The push for quality by American workers is part of it. That young Marine sergeant, Jimmy Lopez, and the naval aviator, Commander Don Scherer, who wouldn't bend to their Iranian captors during the days of the hostages, were part of it. Maybe some of you don't know that Sergeant Jimmy Lopez, before he left his place of confinement in Iran, wrote on the wall in Spanish—which evidently they could not understand, "Long live the red, white, and blue."

Your country won't forget that while those people were held hostage, you were nearby, ready to help, setting a new record for the number of continuous days any conventional ship has been at sea. And your countrymen knew what that meant—long hours, strenuous effort, the pain of being away from loved ones. And yet, there were many out here that were a part of that long stretch who reenlisted and are still here with the *Constellation*.

I don't know whether you've read the book. There's a book by the novelist, James Michener, "The Bridges at Toko-Ri." He wrote very movingly of the men who had fought in that Korean conflict. But in the final scene of the book, Michener writes of the admiral, standing on the darkened bridge of his carrier, waiting for the pilots who had flown off the carrier's deck that day to bomb the Toko-Ri bridges and who now must try to find that deck, big as it is when you're on it, but a postage stamp when it's out there in an ocean in the dark for men trying to find it.

The admiral wondered at their selflessness, standing there alone in the darkness, and then in the book he asked aloud, "Where do we get such men?" Well, you're the answer to that question. Those men he was speaking of came from cities and towns, as you have come, from farms and villages, all a product of the freest and the greatest society that man has ever known. When you and I seek together peace, you're doing it with what you are doing here. And you are, as I said to the crew of the *Fletcher* when they went by this morning, you are ensuring peace just by doing what you're doing, because any potential enemy has to see that the price of aggression is just more than he might want to pay, and that's the greatest service that can be performed.

You know, today your ship's motto, "The Spirit is Old; The Pride is New," fits this Nation as well as the vessel. And I have a little chore that I'm going over here for just a second to do, and then I'll just finish with a few remarks.

There was a Commodore John Barry in the United States Navy back in the days of the Revolution, and he has been called by many the Father of the United States Navy. So, I'm going to go over here and tell you a little bit of what it is that I'm signing, and then I'll finish telling you something, a story that I think you might like to hear.

I'll just go to the table.

This is a proclamation [resolution]. It was passed by the 97th Congress of the United States authorizing and requesting me to designate September 13th, 1981, as Commodore John Barry Day. He was a hero of the American Revolution, holder of the first commission in the United States Navy. He was born in 1745 in County Wexford, Ireland. He was commissioned to command the brig *Lexington*, equipped for the Revolution, and became a national hero with the capture of a British man-of-war, the *Prince Edward*, April 1776.

Following the Revolution, when the sovereignty of this new nation was threatened by pirates, Commodore Barry was placed in command of the first ships authorized under the new Constitution and was named Senior Captain of the United States Navy in 1794. As I said, he's considered by many as the father of the United States Navy. He was honored in 1906 when the Congress had a statue of him erected in Lafayette Square in Washington, D.C., and since then a statue has also been erected by our Government in County Wexford, Ireland.

"So, now, therefore, be is resolved that the President is authorized and requested to designate September 13th as Commodore John Barry Day as a tribute to the Father of the United States Navy and to call upon Federal, State, and local government agencies and the people of the United States to observe such day with appropriate ceremonies and activities." It is signed by Congressman Thomas O'Neill, the Speaker of the House, and by George Bush, the Vice President of the United States and President of the Senate.

I'm going to use about four pens. I could have signed this at the hotel, but I just thought with this chance, I had to sign it right out here where the Navy is.

[*At this point, the President signed the bill. As enacted, S.J. Res. 87 is Public Law 97–43, approved August 20.*]

If I could take another moment of your time, there's a little story maybe known to some of you about the United States Navy. Back in about 1840, around there, when this Nation of ours was so little that the great powers of Europe still were planning to come—they didn't think the experiment would work and they would eventually take us over and colonize various parts of this country—there was a revolution in the

Austro-Hungarian Empire. And a Hungarian by the name of Kostia, one of the lieutenants of that revolution, fled to the United States, and he took out his first papers to become a citizen here.

Then he became an importer by trade, and he was in a port on the Mediterranean when someone tipped off the admiral in command of an Austrian warship in the harbor that he was there. And he was kidnaped in the night and taken aboard that ship to be returned to Austria—because the revolution had failed—where he would be hung.

The man who he had had working for him there—he had told him about his new country and about that flag, described the flag. And that man was down on the waterfront the next morning, knowing what had happened, and he saw an American flag. It was on a tiny warsloop, an American warsloop. And he went aboard and told Captain Ingraham of the United States Navy what had happened.

Ingraham went to the American Consul in that port. The Consul was reluctant to do anything when he learned that the man had only taken out his first papers, was not yet a citizen. But Captain Ingraham said, "I believe I am the senior officer in this port. I believe that my oath of office requires that I do something for this man who has announced his intention to be a citizen."

He had himself rowed out to the Austrian warship. He demanded to see our citizen. They were amused at the affrontery of this captain of the tiny warsloop, but they brought him on deck in chains. Captain Ingraham said, "I can understand him better without those chains." So they struck the chains, still amused. And then he said, "I'm going to ask you one question. Consider your answer carefully. Do you ask the protection of the American flag?" And Kostia, who had been badly beaten, nodded yes. And he said, "You'll have it."

He went back to his own ship, and in the meantime, three more Austrian warships sailed into the harbor. There were now four. He sent a message over to the admiral again that said, "Any attempt to leave this harbor with our citizen on board will be resisted with appropriate force. And I will expect an answer by 4 o'clock."

Well, at 4 o'clock that afternoon everyone was looking at everyone else through those long spyglasses. No evidence of motion, but it was evident that the four ships were getting ready to sail. He ordered that the guns be rolled into the sally ports. Now it was just seconds until 4 o'clock, and he ordered the men to light those tapers with which they touched off the cannons. They did. And then the lookout called down and said, "They're lowering a boat." And they rowed Kostia over and turned him over to Captain Ingraham. One sloop against four warships. He then went below and wrote his resignation to the United States Navy. He said, "I did what I thought my oath of office required, but if I have embarrassed my country, I tender my resignation."

The United States Senate turned down his resignation with these words: "This battle that was never fought may turn out to be the most important battle in our Nation's history."

For many, many years, indeed for more than a century, there has been a U.S.S. *Ingraham* in the United States Navy. I have just learned that with the reduction of forces that has taken place in recent years, there is not one now. I promise you there soon will be.

Now, speaking for all your fellow citizens, I want to say how proud you have made all of us. In the weeks ahead when the "Connie" sails into the Western Pacific, remember wherever you are, there also is America and there goes the pride and the good wishes of all your fellow citizens.

Well, men of the *Constellation*, it's been an honor for me to be here with you. Thank you very much, and God bless all of you.

Note: The President left the U.S.S. Constellation *on Marine One and traveled to the Santa Ana Marine Air Facility in Tustin, Calif., where he boarded the motorcade for the ride to Costa Mesa, Calif.*

Proclamation 4853—Commodore John Barry Day
August 20, 1981

By the President of the United States of America

A Proclamation

Commodore John Barry, hero of the American Revolution and holder of the first commission in the United States Navy under the Constitution, was born in 1745, in County Wexford, Ireland. Commodore Barry was commissioned to command the brig Lexington, one of the first ships bought and equipped for the Revolution, and became a national hero with the engagement and capture of the British warship Edward on April 7, 1776. He distinguished himself throughout the Revolution and again shortly thereafter in the Quasi-War with France as a fighter and seaman.

In 1797, with the advice and consent of the Senate, President Washington appointed Commodore Barry Captain in the Navy of the United States and Commander of the Frigate United States. In so doing, the

President said that he placed "special Trust and Confidence in (Commodore Barry's) Patriotism, Valour, Fidelity, and Abilities".

Commodore Barry was honored by the United States Congress in 1906, when a statue was commissioned and later placed in Lafayette Park, Washington, District of Columbia, and honored again some fifty years later when President Eisenhower caused a statue of Commodore Barry to be presented on behalf of the people of the United States to the people of Ireland, at County Wexford, Ireland.

Now, Therefore, I, Ronald Reagan, President of the United States of America, do hereby designate September 13, 1981, as "Commodore John Barry Day", as a tribute to one of the earliest and greatest American Patriots, a man of great insight who perceived very early the need for American power on the sea. I call upon Federal, state, and local government agencies and the people of the United States to observe such day with appropriate ceremonies and activities.

In Witness Whereof, I have hereunto set my hand this twentieth day of August, in the year of our Lord nineteen hundred and eighty-one, and of the Independence of the United States of America the two hundred and sixth.

RONALD REAGAN

[*Filed with the Office of the Federal Register, 3:06 p.m., August 21, 1981*]

Remarks and a Question-and-Answer Session With Orange County Republicans at a Target '82 Fundraising Reception in Costa Mesa, California
August 20, 1981

The President. Thank you very much. Stu [Spencer], that's going to be a hard act to follow. [*Laughter*]

Well, I am delighted to be back here, and I've had a day in which it's just fitting that I should be here in the place that I've often described as "where the Republicans go before they die." [*Laughter*] And the victory that Stu spoke of in those two pieces of legislation, the budget cuts and the tax program—I think I have to confess now, you all know that I once was a Democrat and that all these years, you see, I've been a subversive agent in the Republican Party—[*laughter*]—because I remember my first vote as a Democrat. And I voted for a Democratic platform that called for reducing the size and cost of the Federal Government, eliminating useless bureaus and agencies, turning authority and autonomy back to local and State government, and reducing the cost of government. And finally, after all these years since 1932, we're making good on that Democratic promise.

But, no, I'm delighted with the victory. But I have to be honest and say, you did that. You've no idea what it was like in Washington—not that I'm that familiar with the place, even after 8 months—but there was such a flood of phone calls, there was such a response from the people. That's what silenced the voices of the special interest groups and got the bipartisan victory that we had. And it was bipartisan, and it was a wonderful thing to see. And now, of course, that's only the beginning. Now we've got to make it work. And we still have more budget cuts to go in the off years, the years yet to come, to bring government down to the proper share of the gross national product that it should be. I think if we all stay together, we're going to do it.

And now, I'd like to talk a little bit about the purpose of this meeting and thank you all for being here. I've talked a lot about restoring federalism, putting us back to where we are a federation of sovereign States and not 50 administrative districts of the Federal Government. And to do that, you have to have governments at the State level that are willing to accept those responsibilities, as well as the sources of revenue to help pay for them. And this meeting is gathered to start raising what must be the campaign fund for the legislative and the administrative races, but this is particularly for the legislative races here in State government.

When you stop to count, 80 assemblymen, assembly persons, will be up for election, and we have 31. If we hold our own, we only need to get 10 of theirs to have a majority. And in the Senate, there will be, out of the 40 senators, there will be 20 up for reelection. Six will be Republican and 14 will be Democrat. We have 17 now. If we hold our own, all we have to do is get four and we will control the Senate.

Now, how important is that? Let me just tell you something. Only one year while I was Governor did we have a majority in both houses of the legislature, and it was barely a one-vote majority. But in that one year where we could create the majority in the committees by being the majority party, in the criminal justice committee of the Assembly, 41 crime-fighting bills came out of that committee to the floor where they were successfully voted into action in California.

Just recently you saw where that same criminal justice committee, now in the hands of the other party, killed in committee several crime-fighting bills. We found, if they ever get to the floor, then Democrat and Republican, out there in the open, they have to vote for them. But they can be killed in that committee, and they were.

Now, those same crime-fighting bills, just like the 41 in our time, those same crime-fighting bills can come back again if in '82 we get the majority. And then it'll be a Republican majority in the committee and those bills will reach the floor and they'll become tools that we need to restore law and order here in our neighborhoods and in our cities and our homes. So, I hope that you will all do everything you can to get that legislative majority and then, of course, to get the administration that goes with it.

Now, there is another little thing that I'd like to mention. You'd be interested to know that a former Supreme Court Justice of California, who's now Deputy Assistant Secretary of State, is the fellow that talked the Japanese into lifting their boycott on California fruits—Bill Clark. And he's doing a great job. But while that was going on, Carol Hallett and her colleagues there on the Republican side in the Assembly have been doing, I think, the greatest amount of work in getting some common sense into the program to aid the farmers who've been beset by this pest and who should not be in the position that they're in now. And they are the ones that are getting some practical work done, and I think that that's another reason why Carol and all those colleagues of hers deserve your support.

But I'm not going to go on talking more now about this, because this is the first time back here. This morning I started the day by helicoptering out to the *Constellation.* And there on that great carrier—and it is great, the crew of several thousand—I saw a display of planes being catapulted off into the air, and planes coming back and landing, and bombing and firing practice off the ship, and finally met with most of the ship's crew. And I have to tell you it was one of the most thrilling experiences. All of this talk that there isn't morale there—the sentiment among those young fellows out there on that is, "Okay, so we're not the biggest navy in the world anymore, but we're the best." And that's the way they feel.

Now, that was enough to start the day. I tell you, it was a really yankee-doodle day so far. But now to come to Orange County and here, and I want to do something we used to do when I was Governor now and then when we got together. I know I haven't got very much time because there's still another place to go yet, but rather than me going on with a monolog here, you must have wondered about a few things that happened in Washington, and now you've got a chance to hear it from the horse's mouth. [*Laughter*] Why don't we have a little dialog, and if you've got some questions, at least for a few minutes that remain, why don't you fire away?

Q. Have you been doing any horse riding?

The President. Am I doing any horseback riding? Yes. Yes, I am. At the ranch, of course. Every day. There in Washington, believe it or not, I have found out—I said that I was going to restore the cavalry. [*Laughter*] I didn't have to. At Quantico, just 20 minutes away from the White House, they've got a stable all filled with horses. And every once in a while, I slip away on one of these long summer afternoons, before the afternoon's quite over, and go down there for a horseback ride with the Marines. So I am. I'm doing some riding.

Q. Mr. President, will you return to California to participate personally in the gubernatorial and senatorial races?

The President. Well, I would like to help, but not in the primaries. [*Laughter*] I learned that as the Governor of California. Yes, I want to help, here and every place that I can.

Q. Mr. President, are you aware that if we use acupuncture for the senior citizens, we don't have to cut their benefits and we can still provide very good treatment for patients?

The President. Well, you're asking me now for a medical opinion, and I've learned better than to answer that. [*Laughter*]

Q. [*Inaudible*]

The President. Yes, we can run with the White House. Is there one that you'd want back? I mean is there one that you'd want me to send back to you when I'm finished? Will somebody get that? I'd be happy to run it.

Q. The Libyan situation is on everybody's mind.

The President. The Libyan situation is on everyone's mind. Well, it's very simple. We have annually held Sixth Fleet exercises in the Mediterranean. And you hold them—and other countries do, too—hold them in a certain portion of the Mediterranean. And that is opposite what is called the Gulf of Sidra. Now, the Gulf of Sidra is a great indentation in the coast of Africa. And we all know the laws about what are territorial waters and what are international waters open to all. But Qadhafi has drawn a line from the two points of land farthest out straight across that Gulf. It's as if we drew a line from the tip of Florida over to the Rio Grande River, the border of Texas, and then said, "That whole Gulf is our water. That's not international waters."

And so he has said that is the line. Now, in the last couple of years, for whatever reason, I don't know, our Navy has been ordered to hold its maneuvers, but to stay on the other side of that line and not challenge that. And I was given the briefing on the maneuvers before they were held, quite some time ago. And these are international waters. And I approved the idea that, while we don't want to be provocative or anything else, good Lord, we send our ships into the Black Sea, just as the Russians send theirs into the Caribbean to establish the fact that they are international waters. So, the exercises properly required crossing, to a certain extent, that line. And as I say, it's still international waters, and I approved that—that we would do that.

Now, we were aware that there might be some harassment, because for the last couple of years, Libyan planes have come out and harassed not only our planes out in

international waters but French planes, and in one instance or two have even fired. Whether they were firing directly at the plane or not, we don't know, but this was the kind of harassment tactics they were following. And in the briefing the question came up with regard to if they actually became hostile and fired on our forces' ships or planes, what would our response be in these maneuvers? We notified everyone in advance that we were going to hold the maneuvers, and there was only one answer to that question. If our men are fired on, our men are going to shoot back.

So, they shot back, as you know. [*Laughter*] And there's been a lot of talk, and the press has been very concerned, because 6 hours went by before they awoke me at 4:30 in the morning to tell me about it. And there's a very good answer to that. Why? If our planes were shot down, yes, they'd wake me up right away; if the other fellow's were shot down, why wake me up? [*Laughter*]

They tell me our dialog is over, but there is a lady, and no lady has asked a question yet.

Q. What would your answer be to [Governor of California] Jerry Brown, who is now writing his white paper and stating that the Federal Government—[*inaudible*].

The President. What was that? I didn't hear all of that.

Q. Jerry Brown is writing a white paper on Medflies [Mediterranean fruit flies] and blaming it on the Federal Government.

The President. He's blaming Medflies on the Federal Government? [*Laughter*] I'd be very interested in seeing that paper. I haven't read fiction for a long time. [*Laughter*]

This has to be the last one, I'm sorry, because I want to come down and say hello to some of you.

Q. Mr. President, what is your next most important program?

The President. Next most important program? Well, of course, we go back to the implementing of what has been passed, this economic recovery program. I would think, however, it has to be now, and this goes with another campaign promise, the restoring of the integrity of social security. And in contrast to what some people have tried to say, I promised, and this still holds, we have to restore that integrity. In 1977 they passed the biggest single tax increase in our nation's history in the payroll tax for social security. And the President told us then that that had made social security safe and sound financially until the year 2030. And as it now stands, the social security fund will be out of money before 1982 is over. So, something obviously has to be done.

But again, I will repeat the promise I made during the campaign that is in contrast to all the things that have been said about our proposals for social security. We will restore the integrity, but we are not going to endanger the checks that are going to those people dependent on social security. They're going to continue to get their checks, and there's no intention on our part to stop that.

This is awful hard to stop here. [*Laughter*]

Q. What can we do for you?

The President. Well, as I've said before, you've done it already with that program.

But just keep on supporting what I think is a 180-degree turnaround in government to bring it back to the proper size and to give back to the people a bigger share of their own earnings with the tax reductions. And we believe that this program will stimulate prosperity, create jobs. That's what it's designed to do. It isn't a step backward at all. It's a step forward toward ending this round that we've had of the excessive interest, of the excessive inflation.

And already there are evidences—I don't know whether you saw this, but the other day Bethlehem Steel took out a full-page ad, kind of addressed to us, that on the basis of this plan which is yet to be implemented—they're going forward with three-quarters of a billion dollars in modernization and expansion of plant to get back their place in the world steel market.

Thank you.

Note: The President spoke at 5:05 p.m. at the South Coast Plaza Hotel. Following the reception, he returned to the Century Plaza Hotel in Los Angeles.

Executive Order 12318—Statistical Policy Functions
August 21, 1981

By virtue of the authority vested in me as President by the Constitution and statutes of the United States, including Reorganization Plan No. 2 of 1970 (5 U.S.C. App. II), Section 202 of the Budget and Accounting Procedures Act of 1950 (31 U.S.C. 581c), Section 3(a) of the Paperwork Reduction Act of 1980 (Public Law 96–511, 94 Stat. 2825, 44 U.S.C. 3503 note), and Section 301 of Title 3 of the United States Code, and in order to transfer, redelegate, and reassign certain statistical policy functions from the Secretary of Commerce to the Director of the Office of Management and Budget, and to require redelegation of certain functions to the Administrator for the Office of Information and Regulatory Affairs, it is hereby ordered as follow:

Section 1. Sec. 1(c) of Executive Order No. 11541 of July 1, 1970, as amended, is amended by deleting the last phrase "is terminated on October 9, 1977" and substituting therefor "shall be implemented in accord with Section 3(a) of the Paperwork Reduction Act of 1980 (94 Stat. 2825; 44 U.S.C. 3503 note), to the extent that provision is applicable".

Sec. 2. Executive Order No. 10253 of July 11, 1951, as amended, is further amended as follows:

(a) "Secretary of Commerce" is deleted in Section 1 and "Director of the Office of Management and Budget" is substituted therefor.

(b) "Secretary" is deleted wherever it appears in Sections, 1, 2, 4, 5, and 6 and "Director" is substituted therefor.

(c) "Department of Commerce" is deleted in Section 6 and "Office of Management and Budget" is substituted therefor.

(d) Section 7 is deleted and a new Section 7 is substituted therefor as follows:

"Sec. 7. As required by Section 3(a) of the Paperwork Reduction Act of 1980 (94 Stat. 2825; 44 U.S.C. 3503 note), the Director shall redelegate to the Administrator for the Office of Information and Regulatory Affairs, Office of Management and Budget, all functions, authority, and responsibility under Section 103 of the Budget and Accounting Procedures Act of 1950 (31 U.S.C. 18b) which have been vested in the Director by this Order.".

(o) Section 8 is revoked.

Sec. 3. Executive Order No. 10033, as amended, is further amended as follows:

(a) "Secretary of Commerce, hereinafter referred to as the Secretary,", is deleted in Section 1 and "Director of the Office of Management and Budget, hereinafter referred to as the Director,", is substituted therefor.

(b) "Secretary" is deleted wherever it appears in Sections 2(a), 2(b), 2(c), 3, 4, and 5 and "Director" is substituted therefor.

(c) Section 7 is revoked.

Sec. 4. (a) Executive Order No. 12013 is revoked.

(b) Section 4 of Executive Order No. 11961, as amended, is further amended by deleting "the Secretary of Commerce shall perform the functions set forth in Sections 4(a)(3) and 5(c) of the Act", and substituting therefor "the Secretary of Commerce shall perform the function of making periodic reports to the Committees of the Congress as set forth in Section 4(a)(3) of the Act".

Sec. 5. The records, property, personnel, and unexpended balances of appropriations, available or to be made available, which relate to the functions transferred or reassigned from the Secretary of Commerce to the Director of the Office of Management and Budget by the delegations made in this Order, are hereby transferred to the Director of the Office of Management and Budget.

Sec. 6. The Director of the Office of Management and Budget shall make such determinations, issue such orders, and take all steps necessary or appropriate to ensure or effectuate the transfers or reassignments provided by this Order, including the transfer of funds, records, property, and personnel.

Sec. 7. Any rules, regulations, orders, directives, circulars, or other actions taken pursuant to the functions transferred or reassigned from the Secretary of Commerce to the Director of the Office of Management and Budget by the delegations made in this Order, shall remain in effect until amended, modified, or revoked pursuant to the delegations made in this Order.

Sec. 8. This Order shall be effective August 23, 1981.

RONALD REAGAN

The White House,
August 21, 1981.

[*Filed with the Office of the Federal Register, 3:44 p.m., August 21, 1981*]

Proclamation 4854—Women's Equality Day, 1981
August 24, 1981

By the President of the United States of America

A Proclamation

On August 26, 1920, the 19th Amendment to the Constitution became law, granting women the right to vote. On this, the 61st anniversary of that milestone, all Americans should reflect on the progress we have made toward the goal of equal opportunity.

Since ratification of the 19th Amendment, women have played increasingly important roles in guiding the Nation's basic institutions. While women continue to fulfill the irreplaceable and vitally important roles of wife and mother, increasing numbers of them have entered the professions and the work place as well, making steady, significant progress over the years.

Today, women faithfully shoulder responsibilities at all levels of government and in every area of employment and education and are opening up new opportunities every day. On this occasion, it is fitting that we honor the contributions women have made to every aspect of our development as a Nation and rededicate ourselves to maintaining a society in which the rights of all citizens are protected.

Now, Therefore, I, Ronald Reagan, President of the United States of America, do hereby proclaim August 26, 1981, as Women's Equality Day.

In Witness Whereof, I have hereunto set my hand this twenty-fourth day of August, in the year of our Lord nineteen hundred and eighty-one, and of the Independence of the United States of America the two hundred and sixth.

RONALD REAGAN

[Filed with the Office of the Federal Register, 2:11 p.m., August 27, 1981]

Letter to the Speaker of the House and the President of the Senate Transmitting the Annual Report on the Implementation of the Privacy Act of 1974
August 25, 1981

Dear Mr. Speaker: (Dear Mr. President:)

Forwarded herewith is the sixth annual report on the implementation of the Privacy Act of 1974.

This year's report focuses on the use of exemption provisions by Executive branch agencies and meets the reporting requirements specified in Section 3(p) of the Act.

We plan to continue our monitoring of agencies' use of these provisions during the coming year.

Sincerely,

RONALD REAGAN

Note: This is the text of identical letters addressed to Thomas P. O'Neill, Speaker of the House of Representatives, and George Bush, President of the Senate.

The report is entitled "Sixth Annual Report of the President on the Implementation of the Privacy Act of 1974—for Calendar Year 1980."

Message to the Congress Transmitting for Review a Department of Energy Loan Guarantee Commitment Agreement
August 25, 1981

To the Congress of the United States:

The Defense Production Act of 1950 (50 U.S.C. App. 2061 *et seq.*), as amended, provides that loan guarantees in excess of $38 million be transmitted to the Congress for its review.

The Department of Energy has negotiated a loan guarantee commitment agreement; identified as Synthetic Fuel Action 1981–1, with The Oil Shale Corporation in the amount of $1.112 billion for its participation in the Colony Project pursuant to the authority of Section 305 of the Defense Production Act. I am pleased to transmit for review:

1. an Executive Summary of the transaction;
2. a Major Terms and Condition sheet;

3. the loan guarantee transaction documents; and

4. the Operating Agreement between The Oil Shale Corporation and Exxon

Corporation for the Colony Project.

RONALD REAGAN

The White House,
August 25, 1981.

Nomination of John S. Herrington To Be an Assistant Secretary of the Navy
August 26, 1981

The President today announced his intention to nominate John S. Herrington to be an Assistant Secretary of the Navy (Manpower and Reserve Affairs). He would succeed Joseph A. Doyle.

In 1965–67 Mr. Herrington served as a deputy district attorney in the Ventura County District Attorney's Office, Ventura, Calif. In 1967 he opened his own law office in Walnut Creek, specializing in real estate, corporate law, taxation, and contracts. In 1967 he became partner and general manager of Herrington, Herrington and Herrington. The following year he founded the Quail Hill Ranch Co.

Mr. Herrington served as first lieutenant in the United States Marine Corps. He is presently attached to the Marine Corps Retired Reserves. He graduated from Stanford University (A.B., 1961) and the University of California, Hastings College of the Law (LL.B., J.D., 1964).

Mr. Herrington has recently served as Deputy Assistant to the President for Presidential Personnel. He is married, has two children, and resides in Walnut Creek, Calif. He was born May 31, 1939, in Los Angeles, Calif.

Nomination of Cameron M. Batjer To Be a Commissioner of the United States Parole Commission, and Designation as Chairman
August 26, 1981

The President today announced his intention to nominate Cameron M. Batjer to be a Commissioner on the United States Parole Commission, Department of Justice, for a term of 6 years. Upon confirmation, the President intends to designate Mr. Batjer Chairman.

Mr. Batjer is currently a justice on the Nevada Supreme Court, where he has been serving since 1967. He was chief justice on the Court in 1977–78. Previously he was in

the private practice of law in Carson City, Nev., in 1959–67 and served as district attorney and city attorney in Carson City in 1954–59. He was legal assistant to the late Senator George W. Malone in 1952–53.

Mr. Batjer graduated from the University of Nevada at Reno (B.A., 1941) and the University of Utah (J.D., 1950). He is married, has three children, and resides in Carson City, Nev. He was born August 24, 1919, in Smith, Nev.

Nomination of M. Virginia Schafer To Be United States Ambassador to Papua New Guinea and the Solomon Islands
August 26, 1981

The President today announced his intention to nominate M. Virginia Schafer, of Washington, as Ambassador to Papua New Guinea and to serve concurrently as Ambassador to the Solomon Islands. She would succeed Harvey J. Feldman.

Miss Schafer was with the General Electric Co. of Richland, Wash., in 1952–54. She entered the Foreign Service in 1954 as a clerk-typist in the Office of Security. She was clerk in Manila (1955–57), finance officer in Moscow (1957–60), in Vienna (1960–62), budget officer in Bucharest (1962–63), and finance officer in Conakry (1963–65). In 1966–67 she was budget officer in the Department and training officer at the Foreign Service Institute in 1967–69. She was administrative officer in Sydney in 1969–73 and budget officer in Beijing in 1973–74. In the Department she was program officer in the Bureau of Educational and Cultural Affairs (1974–75) and deputy executive officer in the Bureau of Near Eastern and South Asian Affairs (1975–77). She attended the Industrial College of the Armed Forces from 1977 to 1978. In 1978–79 she was special assistant to the Assistant Secretary of State for Administration and since 1979 has been Deputy Assistant Secretary of State for Operations.

Miss Schafer graduated from Washington State University (B.A., 1952) and also attended the University of Virginia, Iowa State University, and Georgetown University. She resides in Washington, D.C., and was born March 26, 1931, in Iowa City, Iowa.

Nomination of Clinton Dan McKinnon To Be a Member of the Civil Aeronautics Board, and Designation as Chairman
August 27, 1981

The President today announced his intention to nominate Clinton Dan McKinnon to be a member of the Civil Aeronautics Board for the term expiring December 31, 1985. Upon confirmation, the President intends to designate him Chairman.

Since 1962 Mr. McKinnon has owned radio station KSON in San Diego, Calif. In 1964 he acquired radio station KSON–FM (San Diego) and KIII–TV (Corpus Christi, Tex.). In 1976 he acquired KMBT–TV in Beaumont, Tex. He also owns House of Hits Music Publishing Firm and was publisher of the La Jolla Light Journal Newspaper in 1969–73.

Mr. McKinnon graduated from the University of Missouri (B.A., 1956) and attended Harvard Graduate School of Business (1968–69). He served in the U.S. Navy in 1956–60 as a naval aviator. He holds a Navy rescue record of 62 air/sea rescues in his career.

Mr. McKinnon has three children and resides in San Diego, Calif. He was born January 27, 1934, in San Bernardino, Calif.

Remarks and a Question-and-Answer Session at a Target '82 Fundraising Reception in Santa Barbara, California
August 27, 1981

The President. Thank you. Thank you for your, as always, generous words. I think that we're all very appreciative to our host and hostess for making this beautiful place available to us for this gathering. For those who are too far away to see, I want you to know that those spots on my tie are elephants. [*Laughter*] I think something in the oriental tradition—let this be the year of the elephant. [*Laughter*]

The year I'm thinking about is 1982, because of those fine members of the legislature who are here with us tonight. And the purpose of this—and it ties in so much with what we've been trying to do in Washington, because behind everything that Holmes was talking about, behind all the changes in the budget and the taxing, is the desire I've had for so long—to reverse course in this country and return us to a system that is so responsible for our freedom, and that is that we are a federation of sovereign States.

We want to return authority and autonomy that has been seized by the Federal Government to the levels of government closer to the people. And to do that, we're going to have to have people in charge in State and local government who believe in that, who will accept the responsibilities of those functions that have been taken over by the Federal Government that should be returned, can be better run at the State and local level. And it is my hope that through the system of block grants—we didn't get nearly all that we asked for in that. We're not going to stop trying, because I think of block grants as only a stepping stone to returning sources of taxation to the State and local governments that have been seized by the Federal Government.

Now, we didn't get all that we asked for in our budget cuts either, so in the appropriation process that will now go on we're going to keep trying for that also, because it is a world in which there are certain compromises. And so we didn't get all that we

wanted, but I think we sure got a big chunk.

Incidentally, I'm indebted to Bill Campbell and his fellows in the legislature for giving me some figures that I'm going to relay to you. They have already worked out that our tax cutting bill, or the reduction of Federal tax rates, will leave over the next 3 years more than $38½ billion in the hands of the people of California to spend as they would spend it rather than the way the Federal Government would spend it. And over 5 years, it will amount to more than $100 billion left in the hands of the people. So, now——

Participant. That will make Governor Brown happy. [*Laughter*]

Participant. Did you hear what he said?

The President. Yes, I did. I heard that.

Participant. Mr. President, we're going to get rid of Brown.

The President. Yes, I remember when I was running for Governor the first time and they were having trouble up in the orchards then. It was called "brown rot." [*Laughter*]

Well, listen, I'd like to do something, and I know that I can only take a few, because I know the time is very limited and very pressing here. But it's been—we have so little opportunity to visit or to have a dialog, and I just have been hungry to do this, and that is instead of me going on up here and talking about what we've done or tried to do in Washington, I would like that maybe a few of you and, as I say, it would have to be just a few, if you have some questions that I might not think of to touch on—there's a young lady already.

Q. [*Inaudible*]

Q. Interest rates. She sells real estate.

The President. Oh. A real estate salesman and interest rates. [*Laughter*] Well, yes.

Let me point out one thing. The Fed, Federal Reserve System, is independent, and they're hurting us in what we're trying to do as much as they're hurting everyone else. But, I have to point out also that this is something inherited by the situation we've had and is created somewhat by the market. Now, this year, 1981, when it ends in October, the fiscal year, we're going to have a tremendous deficit. That was built in. That was there before we arrived. And so when I say "the market," the market for capital, private capital out there is strained by the fact that the Federal Government is going into that market and competing for this investment capital. And when you have industry doing it, when you have people who want to have mortgages doing it, when you have the government going in there for a chunk that's going to be bigger than $60 billion for 1981, just the plain law of supply and demand pushes those interest rates up, because there isn't that much private capital.

This is one of the reasons why we wanted the tax cut and think it will be beneficial. We think that more people, with more of their own money in their own hands, will have it available to put in a bank or an insurance policy, to invest, to make more capital available for our needs. And then as we cut the government spending and reduce the need for government to go into that market, those interest rates, we think they will be coming down before the first of the year. But remember, nothing in our program starts until October 1st, and most of it doesn't start until January 1st.

Q. [*Inaudible*]

The President. The gentleman wants to know if we went on the gold standard, would interest rates be 3 percent?

Well, I'm old enough to remember when they were, and we were on a gold standard. But I don't think I have the answer to that, although we have a commission that is studying that very subject of gold and its place in our economy.

Q. Have you had any word from President Qadhafi?

The President. Have I had any word from President Qadhafi? No, but I notice he hasn't gone home yet. [*Laughter*] He's still traveling. Incidentally, lest someone think that I'm being macabre about any loss of life or anything, as far as we have been able to learn, both of their pilots were picked up from the sea and there was no loss of life in that incident. But it wasn't the first time

that they have done things of this kind. We just feel that a principle was involved.

Q. I'm an entomologist, and I'd like to know when we're going to start overhauling one of the biggest bureaucracies of all, the Environmental Protection Agency.

The President. We have a young lady that is director now of the Environmental Protection Agency, and she is introducing as fast as she can common sense in an area that I think has been yielding to environmental extremists. Of course, we've got a fellow named [Secretary of the Interior James G.] Watt, and he's got a few people excited. And I want to tell you, he——

Q. [*Inaudible*]

The President. Yes, yes we are.

Q. What about the MX missiles? I'm from Vandenberg.

The President. The gentleman from Vandenberg wants to know what about the MX missiles.

I have so much—I can't really call it fun—but interest every day in reading about what decisions I've made about the MX. [*Laughter*] The only answer I have for you is that I don't know where we're going to put it, but we're going to have it. Let me make [it] plain. Seriously, I have had presented to me a number of options with regard to our strategic policy, and those options—I have to choose between those options and make a decision, and that decision has not been made yet.

Q. What surprises you the most?

The President. What surprises me the most? I think the biggest surprise are the leaks. [*Laughter*] I tell you, I've gotten so that I address some things in the Cabinet meetings to the chandelier. I'm sure it must have a microphone in it. [*Laughter*] But there just isn't anything—it's not only the leaks of certain information but, then, suppositions are made or conclusions are drawn and printed as being what's going to be the result of this. And as I say, just like this last question about the MX, we haven't even made a decision, and we're reading in the paper what the decision is supposed to be.

But that's been a surprise. I guess maybe the other surprise has been that, to tell you the truth, after all the horror stories about the job. I'm kind of enjoying myself. [*Laughter*]

Participant. Don't you think we have a very beautiful, lovely lady serving in the White House? Wouldn't somebody like to ask our lovely lady a question?

The President. You pick the question, Holmes [Tuttle].

Participant. What would you like to ask our First Lady?

Q. [*Inaudible*] [*Laughter*].

The First Lady. I don't think he really meant that for me.

Q. Mr. President, do you remember when your nickname was "Dutch" and you knew the—[*inaudible*]—sisters?

The President. For heaven's sake, yes. [*Laughter*]

Q. Mary Ann Foster retired—[*inaudible*].

The President. Yes. Please give her my very best regards.

Mr. Tuttle. Mr. President and Nancy, I'd like for you to know that just a little over 3 weeks ago when your office called and said that you'd like to help here, that these great, wonderful workers that you have here went to work. And tonight, in the baseball jargon, we have over 1,200 but we have over 1,100 paid. [*Laughter*] So, they've come from all the counties, and here they are to say hello to you and thank you for the great job that you're doing for our great country.

The President. On behalf of Nancy and myself, Holmes, let me—they tell me that we've got to get down from here, and I wish we didn't have to. Well, we do. And I just want to, again, thank all of you. And again, if I can say, 1982, here in this State, we only have to get about four, I think it is, in the Senate. Isn't it? And that will give us a majority there. And 10 in the assembly will give us a majority in that house. Let me just give you a little comparison of what that difference can be.

The other day just coming out here, I picked up the paper and read where in the assembly criminal justice committee, five crime-fighting bills were buried and killed in committee, never got to the floor for a vote. Well, the party that is in the majority names the majority and the chairmen of the committees. And just 1 year, while I was Governor, we had a majority. It was a bare majority. In that 1 year, 41 anticrime bills came out of that committee to the floor, and even the opponents didn't dare vote against them once they were on the floor. That's what can happen.

There's a lady down here that——

Q. [*Inaudible*]

The President. Oh, thank you very much.

This young lady was just—I can't take any questions. This young lady was just speaking about the "up" feeling that has been prevalent in the land for the last few months. Let me tell you where I had the greatest thrill of that, and then we will leave.

Several days ago, before we came back up to the ranch, we were just out there on the other side of the big island, on the other side of Santa Cruz, on the *Constellation*—a crew of 5,000 on that aircraft carrier. We saw a demonstration of all that they can do. But something else, to those who have lost faith and don't believe that our volunteer military can do it. I want to tell you that was the biggest morale booster that I've ever had in my life, was to see those young men, probably average age of 19, and to hear a sailor say to me, "We may not be the biggest navy in the world; we're the best." That's the way they feel. It was great.

Well, thank you all.

Q. [*Inaudible*]

The President. The question was from the young man, "Are we going to spend government money on the Medfly? I think it is government that is funding the spraying, finally, of that. And it is a very real problem, and maybe the problem was we didn't start spending the money soon enough on the part of government.

I've got to tell you, you ought to see how wonderful that public housing we live in looks now, thanks to what she has done with the help of so many of you that helped and sent money in. You'd really be very proud.

Thank you.

Note: The President spoke at 6:45 p.m. at the Klinger residence, Hope Ranch.

As printed above, the transcript follows the text of the White House press release.

Message to the Congress Transmitting the Final Report on the Impact of New Military Facilities on Communities
August 28, 1981

To the Congress of the United States:

Section 803(b) of the Military Construction Authorization Act, 1981 (P.L. 96–418) called for "a thorough study of the adverse impact on communities in areas in which major, new military facilities are constructed with a view to determining the most effective and practicable means of promptly mitigating such impact." On March 23, 1981, I submitted a preliminary report on this study which has been conducted by an interagency task force of the Economic Adjustment Committee. At that time, I indicated that additional portions of the study were underway and would be reflected in a final report which would be forwarded to the Congress as early as practicable. I am herewith submitting the final report of this study.

The final report augments the preliminary report by including further analysis of the ability of communities to absorb growth; analyzing an additional budgeting and organizational alternative; and updating information on existing Federal assistance programs to reflect the Administration's budgetary revisions.

The report examines various organizational and budgeting mechanisms for providing assistance to communities impacted by the nearby construction of major, new military bases. The report concludes that, with rare exceptions, local and State resources and normal Federal domestic agency assistance should be used to provide public facilities and services supporting military bases. Special Federal assistance should only be warranted in highly unusual circumstances where a sudden population influx and the resulting demand for public services from a major, new military base could overwhelm State-local fiscal capacities

and impede achievement of critical national security objectives. As the reports states, the need for any special Federal assistance must be evaluated on a case-by-case basis.

In those rare circumstances where special Federal assistance would be warranted, we will want to attain a high degree of responsiveness to State and local concerns together with sufficient accountability and control of Federal funds associated with critical national security projects. In this regard, the Special Impact Assistance alternative appears to be a promising approach. However, the selection of the preferred organizational and budgetary mechanism will depend upon the particular circumstances in each case. I will look to the Secretary of Defense and the Director of the Office of Management and Budget, in consultation with affected States and communities, to advise me in this regard. I will request additional statutory authority when it is required.

I have been gratified by the excellent cooperation among all levels of Government in the preparation of this study. We intend to continue working closely with affected States and communities to reach satisfactory outcomes on national security projects which affect their interests.

RONALD REAGAN

The White House,
August 28, 1981.

Note: The report is entitled "Community Impact Assistance Study—Report Prepared By: Intergovernmental/Interagency Task Force on Community Impact Assistance, President's Economic Adjustment Committee—July 1981" (174 pages plus appendices).

Nomination of Malcolm R. Lovell, Jr., To Be Under Secretary of Labor
August 28, 1981

The President today announced his intention to nominate Malcolm R. Lovell, Jr., to be Under Secretary of Labor. He would succeed John N. Gentry.

Mr. Lovell has been president of the Rubber Shippers Association and chairman of the Tire Industry Safety Council. Before entering the rubber industry, he was Manpower Administrator and Assistant Secretary of Labor for Manpower in 1969–73. Prior to that he held a number of executive positions under Governor Romney, including director of the Michigan Employment Security Commission, director of the Michigan Economic Opportunity Office, and chairman of the Michigan State Labor Mediation Board. Earlier he served both the Ford Motor Co. and American Motors in a variety of executive capacities in industrial relations.

Mr. Lovell serves on the board of directors for the Highway Users Federation, the Equal Employment Advisory Council, and the Travelers Aid Association of America and is a member of the Mayor's Employment and Training Services Advisory Council in the District of Columbia. He was appointed by President Ford to the National Advisory Council on Vocational Education and served until 1979. He was a member of the National Commission for Manpower Policy in 1975–79.

Mr. Lovell graduated from the Harvard Business School with a masters degree in business administration in 1946. He is married, has four children, and resides in Washington, D.C. Mr. Lovell was born January 1, 1921, in Greenwich, Conn.

Nomination of Frank V. Ortiz, Jr., To Be United States Ambassador to Peru
August 28, 1981

The President today announced his intention to nominate Frank V. Ortiz, Jr., of New Mexico, as Ambassador to Peru. He would succeed Edwin G. Corr.

Mr. Ortiz was liaison officer at the United States Senate in 1943–44 and served in the United States Army Air Force in 1944–46. In 1951–53 he was assistant officer in charge of Egypt and Anglo-Egyptian Sudan in the Department of State. He was economic officer in Addis Ababa (1953–56) and political officer in Mexico City (1956–57). In the Department he was special assistant to the operations coordinator in the Office of Under Secretary (1957–60) and special assistant to the Assistant Secretary of State for Inter-American Affairs (1960–61). He was special assistant to the Ambassador in Mexico City in 1961–63. In 1963–66 he was country desk officer for Spain in the Department. He attended the National War College from 1966–67. He was counselor for political affairs in Lima (1967–70) and deputy chief of mission (chargé d'affaires for 1 year) in Montevideo (1970–73). In the Department he was country director for Argentina, Uruguay, and Paraguay (1973–75) and deputy executive secretary (1975–77). In 1977–79 he was Ambassador to Barbados and to Grenada and Special Representative to Dominica and St. Lucia and to the Associated States. In 1979–80 he was Ambassador to Guatemala, and since 1980 he has been political adviser to the Commander in Chief of the United States Southern Command in Panama.

He graduated (B.S.) in 1950 from Georgetown University and received his M.S. in 1967 from George Washington University.

He attended the University of Madrid (1950) and the University of Beirut (1952). Mr. Ortiz was born March 14, 1926, in Santa Fe, N. Mex. He is married, has four children, and resides in Santa Fe, N. Mex.

Nomination of David B. Funderburk To Be United States Ambassador to Romania
August 28, 1981

The President announced today his intention to nominate David B. Funderburk, of North Carolina, as Ambassador to the Socialist Republic of Romania. He would succeed O. Rudolph Aggrey.

Mr. Funderburk was instructor of history and government at Wingate College, Wingate, N.C., in 1967–69 and instructor of history (part-time) at the University of South Carolina, Columbia, S.C., in 1969–70. In 1972–78 he was assistant-associate professor of history at Hardin-Simmons University, Abilene, Tex., and since 1978 he has been associate professor of history at Campbell University, Buies Creek, N.C. In 1975 he was guide-interpreter at the United States Photography Exhibit in Sibiu, Romania, as Foreign Service staff officer with the International Communication Agency.

He received his B.A. (1966) and M.A. (1967) from Wake Forest University and his Ph. D. in 1974 from the University of South Carolina. He also attended the University of California at Los Angeles and the University of Washington.

Mr. Funderburk was born April 28, 1944, in Langley Field, Va. He is married, has two children, and resides in Buies Creek, N.C.

Statement on the 41st Birthday of Press Secretary James S. Brady
August 29, 1981

Nancy and I join Jim Brady's family and many friends in wishing him a happy 41st birthday. We continue to pray for his full and speedy recovery.

Jim Brady is a talented and dedicated public servant. He is my friend, and I am proud to have him as my Press Secretary. Nancy and I salute "The Bear" and Sarah today, and we look forward to celebrating his next birthday in his office at the White House.

Note: Deputy Press Secretary Larry M. Speakes read the statement to Mr. Brady during a birthday celebration in the Press Secretary's honor at the press center in Santa Barbara, Calif. Members of the White House press corps delivered birthday messages to Mr. Brady through a communications hook-up with the George Washington University Hospital. The White House also announced that the President telephoned Mr. Brady from Rancho del Cielo to wish him a happy birthday.

Message to the Congress Transmitting an Alternative Plan for Federal Civilian Pay Increases
August 31, 1981

To the Congress of the United States:

Under the Pay Comparability Act of 1970, an adjustment in Federal white collar pay will be required in October, 1981.

That Act requires that calculations be made annually of the adjustments that would be required in Federal statutory pay systems to achieve comparability with private sector pay for the same levels of work. My pay advisers have made those calculations and indicated that an average 15.1 percent increase would be required to achieve comparability as the concept and process were defined in the Pay Comparability Act of 1970.

While I fully support the comparability principle as the best basis for determining Federal pay, I believe that significant changes are required in the way that principle is currently defined and implemented. Therefore, last March we transmitted to the Congress proposed legislation to revise and strengthen the comparability process. At that time, we estimated that the revised process would result in an average increase in Federal pay of 4.8 percent in October, 1981.

The reform proposal has not yet been acted upon in Congress, but in accordance with our economic recovery program, the Congress included in the Omnibus Budget Reconciliation Act of 1981 (P.L. 97–35) a provision which limits this October's Federal white collar pay adjustment to the same 4.8 percent. Accordingly, I am submitting to the Congress an alternative plan which would implement that limitation on Federal white collar increases.

Current law provides that the annual increase for the military be the same as the average Federal white collar increase. This year, however, the Congress is expected to provide for a larger military pay increase as a part of the Defense Authorization Act for FY 82. The larger increases proposed under that legislation will supersede the increases that military personnel would otherwise receive under the alternative plan.

RONALD REAGAN

The White House,
August 31, 1981.

Report on Federal Pay Adjustments for October, 1981

Because of economic conditions affecting the general welfare, and in accordance with Sec. 1701(a) of Title XVII of the Omnibus Budget Reconciliation Act of 1981 (P.L. 97–35) and 5 U.S.C. 5305(c)(1), I hereby transmit to Congress the attached Alternative Plan. The overall percentage of the adjustment in the rates of pay under the General Schedule will be a 4.8 percent increase. The overall percentages of the adjustments in the rates of pay under the other statutory pay systems, the Foreign Service Schedule and the schedules for the Department of Medicine and Surgery of the Veterans' Administration, will also be 4.8 percent increases.

In accordance with 5 U.S.C. 5382(c) the following rates of basic pay for the Senior Executive Service shall become effective on the first day of the first applicable pay period that begins on or after October 1, 1981:

ES–1	$54,755
ES–2	56,936
ES–3	59,119
ES–4	61,300
ES–5	62,950
ES–6	64,600

ALTERNATIVE PLAN

Schedule 1—THE GENERAL SCHEDULE

	1	2	3	4	5
GS–1	$8,342	$8,620	$8,898	$9,175	$9,453
GS–2	9,381	9,603	9,913	10,178	10,292
GS–3	10,235	10,576	10,917	11,258	11,599
GS–4	11,490	11,873	12,256	12,639	13,022
GS–5	12,854	13,282	13,710	14,138	14,566
GS–6	14,328	14,806	15,284	15,762	16,240
GS–7	15,922	16,453	16,984	17,515	18,046
GS–8	17,634	18,222	18,810	19,398	19,986
GS–9	19,477	20,126	20,775	21,424	22,073
GS–10	21,449	22,164	22,879	23,594	24,309
GS–11	23,566	24,352	25,138	25,924	26,710
GS–12	28,245	29,187	30,129	31,071	32,013
GS–13	33,586	34,706	35,826	36,946	38,066
GS–14	39,689	41,012	42,335	43,658	44,981
GS–15	46,685	48,241	49,797	51,353	52,909
GS–16	54,755	56,580	58,405	60,230	62,055
GS–17	64,142	66,280	68,418	70,556	72,694
GS–18	75,177				

	6	7	8	9	10
GS–1	$9,615	$9,890	$10,165	$10,178	$10,439
GS–2	10,595	10,898	11,201	11,504	11,807
GS–3	11,940	12,281	12,622	12,963	13,304
GS–4	13,405	13,788	14,171	14,554	14,937
GS–5	14,994	15,422	15,850	16,278	16,706
GS–6	16,718	17,196	17,674	18,152	18,630
GS–7	18,577	19,108	19,639	20,170	20,701
GS–8	20,574	21,162	21,750	22,338	22,926
GS–9	22,722	23,371	24,020	24,669	25,318
GS–10	25,024	25,739	26,454	27,169	27,884
GS–11	27,496	28,282	29,068	29,854	30,640
GS–12	32,955	33,897	34,839	35,781	36,723
GS–13	39,186	40,306	41,426	42,546	43,666
GS–14	46,304	47,627	48,950	50,273	51,596
GS–15	54,465	56,021	57,577	59,133	60,689
GS–16	63,880	65,705	67,530	69,355	
GS–17					
GS–18					

NOTE.—Notwithstanding the salary rates shown, the maximum rate of basic pay legally payable to employees under this schedule may not exceed the rate payable for level V of the Executive Schedule, currently $50,112.50.

Schedule 2—THE FOREIGN SERVICE SCHEDULE

	1	2	3	4	5	6	7
Class 1	$46,685	$48,086	$49,528	$51,014	$52,544	$54,121	$55,744
Class 2	37,829	38,964	40,133	41,337	42,577	43,854	45,170
Class 3	30,653	31,573	32,520	33,495	34,500	35,535	36,601
Class 4	24,838	25,583	26,351	27,141	27,955	28,794	29,658
Class 5	20,126	20,730	21,352	21,992	22,652	23,332	24,031
Class 6	17,992	18,532	19,088	19,660	20,250	20,858	21,483
Class 7	16,084	16,567	17,064	17,575	18,103	18,646	19,205
Class 8	14,379	14,810	15,255	15,712	16,184	16,669	17,169
Class 9	12,854	13,240	13,637	14,046	14,467	14,901	15,348

	8	9	10	11	12	13	14
Class 1	$57,417	$59,139	$60,689	$60,689	$60,689	$60,689	$60,689
Class 2	46,525	47,921	49,358	50,839	52,364	53,935	55,553
Class 3	37,699	38,830	39,995	41,195	42,431	43,704	45,015
Class 4	30,548	31,464	32,408	33,380	34,382	35,413	36,475
Class 5	24,752	25,495	26,260	27,048	27,859	28,695	29,556
Class 6	22,128	22,792	23,475	24,180	24,905	25,652	26,422
Class 7	19,781	20,375	20,986	21,616	22,264	22,932	23,620
Class 8	17,684	18,215	18,761	19,324	19,904	20,501	21,116
Class 9	15,809	16,283	16,772	17,275	17,793	18,327	18,877

NOTE.—Notwithstanding the salary rates shown, the maximum rate of basic pay legally payable to employees under this schedule may not exceed the rate payable for level V of the Executive Schedule, currently $50,112.50.

Schedule 3—DEPARTMENT OF MEDICINE AND SURGERY SCHEDULES, VETERANS' ADMINISTRATION

	Minimum	Maximum
Scc. 4103 schedule:		
Chief Medical Director	([1])	[2] $84,304
Deputy Chief Medical Director	([1])	[3] 80,871
Associate Deputy Chief Medical Director	([1])	[4] 77,460
Assistant Chief Medical Director	([1])	[4] 75,177
Medical Director	[1] $64,142	[4] 72,694
Director of Nursing Service	[4] 64,142	[4] 72,694
Director of Podiatric Service	[4] 54,755	[4] 69,355
Director of Chaplain Service	[4] 54,755	[4] 69,355
Director of Pharmacy Service	[4] 54,755	[4] 69,355
Director of Dietetic Service	[4] 54,755	[4] 69,355
Director of Optometric Service	[4] 54,755	[4] 69,355
Physician and dentist schedule:		
Director grade	[4] 54,755	[4] 69,355
Executive grade	[4] 50,559	[4] 65,724
Chief grade	46,685	[4] 60,689
Senior grade	39,689	[4] 51,596
Intermediate grade	33,586	43,666
Full grade	28,245	36,723
Associate grade	23,566	30,640

Schedule 3—DEPARTMENT OF MEDICINE AND SURGERY SCHEDULES, VETERANS'
ADMINISTRATION—Continued

	Minimum	Maximum
Nurse schedule:		
Director grade	46,685	[4] 60,689
Assistant Director grade	39,689	[4] 51,596
Chief grade	33,586	43,666
Senior grade	28,245	36,723
Intermediate grade	23,566	30,640
Full grade	19,477	25,318
Associate grade	16,761	21,792
Junior grade	14,328	18,630
Clinical podiatrist and optometrist schedule:		
Chief grade	46,685	[4] 60,689
Senior grade	39,689	[4] 51,596
Intermediate grade	33,586	43,666
Full grade	28,245	36,723
Associate grade	23,566	30,640

[1] Single rate.
[2] Notwithstanding the rate shown, the maximum rate payable at this level may not exceed the rate payable for level III of the Executive Schedule, currently $55,387.50.
[3] Notwithstanding the rate shown, the maximum rate payable at this level may not exceed the rate payable for level IV of the Executive Schedule, currently $52,750.
[4] Notwithstanding the rates shown, the maximum rate payable at this level may not exceed the rate payable for level V of the Executive Schedule, currently $50,112.50.

Message to the Congress Transmitting a Report on the Federal Merit Pay System
September 1, 1981

To the Congress of the United States:

Supervisors and management officials in GS–13, 14, and 15 positions throughout the Federal Government will be converted to merit pay this October as required by Chapter 54, Title 5, U.S. Code, unless otherwise excluded by law.

Upon proper applications from the heads of affected agencies and upon the recommendation of the Director of the Office of Personnel Management, I have, pursuant to 5 U.S.C. § 5401(b)(2)(B), excluded 44 agencies and units of agencies from coverage under the Merit Pay System on account of size and efficiency, emergency conditions, and comity with the Legislative and Judicial branches.

Attached is my report describing the agency or unit to be excluded and the reasons therefor.

RONALD REAGAN

The White House,
September 1, 1981.

Note: The 6-page report, prepared by the Office of Personnel Management, is entitled "Report of the President to Congress on Agencies and Units of Agencies Excluded From the Federal Merit Pay System."

Remarks at the Illinois Forum Reception in Chicago
September 2, 1981

The President. Thank you very much, [Illinois State] Senator Don Totten, and thank you for going through a lot of wars together, as we have. Governor Jim Thompson, the Congressmen who have been up here—Bob Michel, John Porter, Bob McClory, Lynn Martin, Tom Railsback—but let me say one thing about—and I think the other Congressmen here will agree with me—if there's any justice in the world, when 1982 is over, Bob Michel, Minority Leader of the House, will be Bob Michel, Majority Leader of the House.

If ever there was a George Patton and Douglas MacArthur put together in our battles for the budget and the tax bills, it was Bob Michel.

I'm happy that our Secretary of Labor is here. He's going to break in the audience for me tomorrow morning. [*Laughter*] Depending on how he does is whether I'm going to run or stay. [*Laughter*]

Governor Thompson. I broke them in this morning, Mr. President. You're all right.

The President. Oh, okay. All right.

And our national committeeman, Harold Smith, and our State chairman, Don Adams, it's a great pleasure to be back here again. And I know that our time is limited, but I would like to just say a few things to you. I've told a few outside before we came in here that I'm surprised—I've been taking that vacation at the ranch, part vacation, you know, the job goes with you—but I've been surprised at all the things that I read that I've decided. [*Laughter*] I haven't decided any of them. [*Laughter*] That's what I'm going back to Washington for.

But, particularly right now, with all of the confusion and the trouble with the stock market and so forth, I was a little confused when I knew that a short time ago they said that the big surge in the stock market was due to their optimism about our economic package. That was before it was passed. And then it was passed after a lot of work. Now there's been a slump, and they say, "Well, the slump is because the program

isn't working." Well, it isn't. It doesn't start until October 1st. [*Laughter*]

Also, there is—and seriously—there is that question in people's minds, "Can you cut taxes and fight inflation by so doing?" Well, I believe very much that you can. Let me just read you something. "Our true choice is not between tax reduction on the one hand and avoidance of large Federal deficits on the other. An economy stifled by restrictive tax rates will never produce enough revenue to balance the budget, just as it will never produce enough jobs or enough profits." John F. Kennedy said that back in 1962, when he was asking for a tax decrease, a cut in tax rates across the board. And he was proven right, because that—the last tax cut, literally, that we've had—actually produced more revenue for government, because the economy was stimulated and more people were working and there was more industry and productivity in America. And this is why we didn't just stop at cutting the budget, and we're not through cutting it yet.

Lost in the conversation about the budget cuts we have secured for 1982 was our constant reminder that we had to go about $70 billion more in cuts in 1983 and 1884 [1984]. And I can tell you now, we're going to do it, because we have no choice. It has to be done.

But when John Kennedy said those words, he was echoing the words of Ibn Khaldun, a Moslem philosopher back in the 14th century, who said, "At the beginning of the dynasty taxation yields large revenues from small assessments. At the end of the dynasty taxation yields small revenue from large assessments." We're going to get back to the beginning of the dynasty. This was why we had to have the tax program as well as the budget cuts, because budget cuts, yes, would reduce government spending, but what was going to get American productivity and American industry rolling again and able to compete in the world market? It was to get government out of the people's pockets to the extent that it was in there, create private capital that could meet the needs for business investment. And to those in business here tonight, let me urge: Invest, expand.

I've just received something that gladdened my heart. I received a statement that is going out to all the members of the iron and steel industry. And based on their optimism about our economic program, the steel industry is embarking on $5 billion worth of expansion, modernization and building of new plant, rehabilitating of old. All the member companies—there has never been such an expansion in such a short period of time in the history of the steel industry. This, I believe, if it can be done simply on the promise of what the tax cuts will do and the budget cuts, ought to give us some indication of what's going to happen when they actually begin to be implemented.

But the fight isn't over, and that's why in 1982 coming up—seriously I mean it—we must send more people to Washington who believe, as we do, that there is a need for a turnaround in the country's policies. Send people there that will help and then be prepared for every kind of pressure from pressure-spending groups, from the bureaucracy that doesn't give up and has got a million tricks yet to be exposed as to how they're going to try to obstruct the progress and prove that this program won't work.

But we've had enough of roller coaster economics, and so we're going forward with this program. And we couldn't have gone forward with it without you. When the chips were down and the issue was in doubt, and believe me, it was—I woke up on that fatal morning for the last passage and had already been told how many votes there were against us. But in the meantime, all of you had been busy, and the phones were ringing, and the wires were coming in—not to us, but to the people who needed to get them, over there on the Hill. And when the vote was finally counted, as you know, we had won that battle.

There's one other thing I'd like to touch on because, as I say, I know the time is limited, and I do want to at least get down and be able to say hello to some of you here before we have to break up. But let me, if I could, tell you about the other thing. This morning, I understand that the Washington Post had a lead article to the effect that I was retreating with regard to national defense. Well, now let me state something here. When we say we have to make further cuts, this is across the board, and we realize there's no department of government that doesn't have waste in it that can be eliminated or reduced. And we're going to set out—and that includes the Department of Defense.

That does not mean that we are retreating from the program we adopted of an annual 7-percent increase in defensive spending to restore our defensive capability and close that window of vulnerability that has been opened in recent years with the superiority of the Soviet forces. We're going to continue, at the same time we are going to continue to urge them to sit down with us in a program of realistic strategic arms reduction. But it will be the first time that we have ever sat on our side of the table and let them know that there's a new chip on the table. And that chip is: There will be legitimate arms reduction, verifiable arms reduction, or they will be in an arms race which they can't win.

Now, one last thing. I know there's been a lot of concern about the volunteer military and would it work or were we going to have to resort to a draft. And as you all know, I've been campaigning up and down the country that I'm opposed to a peacetime draft. We never had had one until the years following World War II. And we've taken some steps. We've taken some steps for a realistic pay scale that we want for the men in the military. And I'm happy to tell you tonight that the enlistments are up, higher than they've ever been. The educational and quality level of the men enlisting is higher than it has ever been. The percentile of the lowest in education that we take in the military is the lowest that it has ever been.

And I've received a couple of letters, one on the domestic situation and one on the military, that made me very proud. One was from a lady here in Illinois. She was working in a Federal program on the Federal payroll. And she wrote to tell me frankly that she was one of four who were working in this particular task, and she said there isn't enough work for one. And she said, "When we came close to the end of the fiscal year, I was one who was told, 'Quick. Go out and spend the money that was left over.' " And so she said, "I sit at a magnificent new executive desk and a brand new typewriter. The only thing they could do to spend the money was to buy new furniture." Well, that's a bygone era. That isn't going to happen anymore in Washington, D.C. If there's money left over, it's going to be returned.

And we've already had one department head, international aid, AID, who presented me with a big facsimile of a check, about that high and that wide, which was for several hundred million dollars which was not going to be spent and which he was returning to the Secretary of the Treasury. Well, this letter from this lady in California [Illinois]—and incidentally, we're doing our best to try and find her some employment that will fully utilize her character and her abilities.

The second one came from a young man in the service—submarine duty, an enlisted man. He said he was really speaking on behalf of 180 shipmates, and he told me how good it was to be an American. And then he said, "We may not be the biggest navy in the world; we're the best."

I had the pleasure a few days ago of standing on the deck of the *Constellation,* our great carrier out there with a crew of nearly 5,000, and see all these young men and see their teamwork as they were getting planes off the deck, into the air, on the catapults, three at a time, then see the demonstration of the air power while it was in the air and then, finally, to speak to them, and then was privileged to stand there and watch 40 men step forward and sign up for re-enlistment. And incidentally, we have a new high also in the volunteer military of re-enlistments now.

So, I think things are going pretty well. And I have every confidence in the world, as I said all during the campaign, that all we had to do was get government out of the way and turn you, the people of this country, loose to do what you can do so well, and our problems would go away. And I'm positive that they are going to go away and that they've begun to go away already, even if our program doesn't start until October and some of it in January. [*Laughter*]

But God bless all of you. And now I'm going to get off of here. I've talked too long, but I've wanted the chance—oh, one point. I'll have a postscript. [*Laughter*] High interest rates. I heard Jim [Governor James R. Thompson of Illinois] talking about them, and he was absolutely right. High interest rates aren't something that someone deliberately imposes on the people or the economy. They are the result of inflation, not the cause. And that's why we're going forward with this battle against inflation to bring those interest rates down, because until we do, there are industries in this country that cannot exist or prosper. And they will come down. But as long as inflation is continuing and as long as there is a belief that there are going to be huge deficits, the interest rates are going to stay up, because there are too many people trying to borrow too little money—and the biggest borrower of all is the United States Government—to pay off those deficits.

So, we're going to whittle at those deficits, and when you hear the screams of anguish from some whose toes are being stepped on, just think that they can't be half as bad as the moans of the unemployed in this country today. And we're going to put them back to work.

God bless you, and thank you very much.

Note: The President spoke at 6:11 p.m. at the Republican fundraiser in the Empire Room at the Palmer House.

Remarks in Chicago, Illinois, at the Annual Convention and Centennial Observance of the United Brotherhood of Carpenters and Joiners
September 3, 1981

The President. Reverend clergy, distinguished gentlemen here on the dais with me, President Konyha and all of you:

It's an honor for me to be here with you today and even more of an honor to be asked to serve with your president, Bill Konyha, as the cochairman of your Centennial Observance Committee.

This union has a proud history. Just 100 years ago, having only a few thousand members, you opened your first convention in Chicago. Now, it's not true that I attended that convention, also. [*Laughter*] Since then, you've grown to more than 800,000 members. You've served as a bulwark in America's free union movement.

Over the years, this union was responsible for improving the well-being of its members as they labored building this Nation. And through the collective bargaining system, you improved images—or wages, I should say—benefits, and working conditions. More than that, the United Brotherhood of Carpenters and Joiners has shown time and time again that it supports our free market system and the fundamental tenets of American democracy. It was this belief in representative government and free enterprise that gave the working people of this country unequaled freedom and prosperity.

We forget this at our peril. In these recent years when advocates of collectivism and government intervention have held sway, we should recall the wisdom of that greatest of labor statesmen, the founder of the American labor movement, Samuel Gompers. He said, "Doing for people what they can and ought to do for themselves is a dangerous experiment. In the last analysis, the welfare of the workers depends on their own initiative. Whatever is done under the guise of philanthropy or social morality which in any way lessens initiative is the greatest crime that can be committed against the toilers. Let social busybodies and professional 'public morals experts' in their fads reflect upon the perils they rashly invite under this pretense of social welfare."

Samuel Gompers believed with all his heart that if a worker was properly and fairly paid for his work, he could provide for himself without having to hold out this hand to a caseworker for government-provided benefits. He was a champion of collective bargaining.

Collective bargaining in the years since has played a major role in America's economic miracle. Unions represent some of the freest institutions in this land. There are few finer examples of participatory democracy to be found anywhere. Too often, discussion about the labor movement concentrates on disputes, corruption, and strikes. But while these things are headlines, there are thousands of good agreements reached and put into practice every year without a hitch.

Part of successful collective bargaining is honest, straightforward exchanges. A number of Presidents have observed that of all the meetings in the Oval Office, the most direct, productive, and useful have been with the leaders of organized labor. Straight talk has always been a feature of these exchanges, and that's a tradition I want to continue here today. You and I may not always agree, as President Konyha said, on everything, but we should always remember how much we have in common.

I can guarantee you today that this administration will not fight inflation by attacking the sacred right of American workers to negotiate their wages. We propose to control government, not people. Now, today I want to express again my belief in our American system of collective bargaining and pledge that there will always be an open door to you in this administration.

During my 8 years as Governor of California, I was proud of my relationship with organized labor. Yes, we had disagreements over such things as welfare reform and budget allocation, but we followed the advice of a one-time mayor of Boston who said, "We can disagree without being disagreeable."

Some people would have forgotten— except your president very graciously reminded you—that I am the first man to attain this high office who was formerly president of an AF of L–CIO union.

Now, I know that there are some who read of the pay scale of top stars and wonder why a bunch of actors need a union. Well, it's true that a handful of superstars have an individual bargaining power based on their box office rating. But what's little known is the fact that taken as a whole, the membership of the Screen Actors Guild averages about the same annual income level as members of the craft unions. As for those in the high brackets, let it be understood that they have always used their star status and individual bargaining power to help their lower paid fellow actors in the Screen Actors Guild achieve gains at the collective bargaining table.

I participated as a negotiator at that table for some 20 years and as president led the Guild in its first major strike. We followed one rule in our demands. We asked ourselves a question about each thing that we demanded at the bargaining table: Is it fair to the other fellow, and is it fair to the customer, and is it good for our people? If we were satisfied on these three points, we fought our heads off, and we secured a fair pay scale, greatly improved working conditions and fringe benefits, including a pension and welfare plan for our members.

I remember one interunion squabble in which I faced your big Bill Hutcheson.[1] It's kind of ironic to look back on that because Bill was a Republican then. As a matter of fact, he served on the National Republican Committee, and at that time I was a Democrat. [*Laughter*] Now, if there's one challenge that I have for organized labor today, it is that they, in the footsteps of Bill Hutcheson, recognize that organized labor should

---

[1] *William L. Hutcheson, former general president of the United Brotherhood of Carpenters and Joiners.*

not become the handmaiden of any one political party.

Working people in America value family, work, and neighborhood. These are the things we have in common socially and politically. When it comes to the bottom line, all of us are striving for the same thing—a strong and healthy America and a fair shake for working people. But we weren't getting a fair shake, any of us in these recent years when it appeared that we were making more money—and we were with regard to the number of dollars—but the value of those dollars was shrinking by one-third just between 1975 and 1980.

The same forces that chipped away at your purchasing power ravaged the American economy with a severity unseen since the Great Depression, with the worst inflation in 60 years, almost 8 million unemployed, and skyrocketing interest rates.

I've taken the election of 1980 to be a demand by the working people of America for a change in the policies that caused their adversity. From Inauguration Day on, nothing has been more important to this administration than restoring the prosperity and freedom that is every American's birthright.

Today it's appropriate for me to thank you and working men and women throughout this land for the support that you gave to the recent economic reform struggles in the Congress. It was phone calls and letters that Americans like you made that made our economic plan a bipartisan measure. One Democratic Governor recently explained: "The old liberal approach that more money, a few Ph. D's, and a lot of new programs will cure what ails the nation is gone in our era." And he's right.

Now, one of my only regrets is that some in the labor movement oppose the recovery program because they may not fully understand what we are for, what we're trying to do, and that our program is designed to improve the well-being of all the people.

In his first inaugural address, Jefferson warned government not to "take from the mouth of labor the bread it has earned." But what we experienced in the last decade was bloated government feasting at the expense of the people, growing beyond all reason, and taxing away the American way of life.

Over the last 20 years, playing ward politics on a national scale, the Congress enacted for one group or another ever-increased spending plans and entitlement programs. "Entitlement programs" means the redistribution of your earnings. In 1967, my first year as Governor of California, these open-ended programs siphoned $57 billion from the pockets of the American taxpayer. By the end of my first year as President, that $57 billion would have been $428 billion had we not passed the economic recovery program. Is this uncontrolled spending really in the interests of the American workers?

The Federal budget has almost tripled in the last 10 years. To some of those who have opposed our proposed budget reductions, let me point out that we haven't cut spending back to less in 1982 than it was in the year of 1981. We have reduced the increase in spending from 14 percent each year to 6½ percent. Now, this is hardly cruel and inhuman deprivation. We are not, as some have said, trying to turn back the clock. We are just trying to make the rate of increase in spending about half of what it has been.

Similarly, our tax program is aimed at helping everyone. I've told you how inflation reduced the value of your dollar by one-third during the last 5 years. Well, in those same 5 years, your taxes went up by two-thirds—67 percent. Even those with cost-of-living clauses in the contracts found the taxes rising faster than their wages. This is why inflation is a tax. As you earned more to keep pace with the cost of living, you moved up to a higher tax bracket. You had a tax increase just as surely as if the Congress had voted to increase the tax rate. Now, that's something our tax bill, through indexing, is going to fix. After the three annual tax cuts, the income tax brackets each year will be adjusted to compensate for inflation. This is an historic reform. For the first time, it takes from government the hidden profit that government makes from inflation.

The central part of our tax program, however, is, as you know, an across-the-board, 25-percent rate reduction for every American taxpayer over a 3-year period. Without that tax rate reduction, taxes would have gone up $91½ billion in 1982 and $321 billion in the next 3 years. Now is this kind of confiscatory taxation really in the interest of the American workers?

Most of our critics didn't try to answer that question. Instead, appealing to greed and envy, they held that those paying more taxes would get a larger reduction. Well, you know, Teddy Roosevelt had something to say about a situation like this. "We must," he said, "decide that it is a great deal better that some people should prosper too much than no one should prosper enough." Now, of course, those having a larger tax will get a larger reduction in the number of dollars. The fellow paying a $10,000 tax will get a $1,000 reduction. The fellow paying a $1,000 tax will get $100 off. But the first one will still be paying 10 times as much as the other one.

The tax rate reduction is the same percentage across the board. What is most important, three-quarters of the tax reduction will go to middle-income wage earners who presently pay three-quarters of the total income tax.

Representative government is still alive and well in the United States. Even with powerful special interest groups fighting reform, the voice of the people was heard. The status quo—that's Latin for "the mess we're in"—was giving the American people a lower standard of living and ever higher taxes. Now the foundation has been laid for an American renaissance which will astound the world, a new era of good feeling in America; a time when jobs will be plentiful and the richness of the country can be shared by anyone who is willing to work.

Having gotten control of government spending and taxes, we will now concentrate on putting America back to work and making sure that there are jobs and opportunity available to all. The number of jobs will expand, and real take-home pay will increase. And while that battle in the Congress may have been won, the war for a healthier economy is not over. The struggle for more jobs and less inflation will continue to be the focus of this administration in the months ahead. There will be the need to further trim the budget, to monitor Capitol Hill closely to ensure that what has been accomplished is not eroded.

But restoring fiscal integrity to the Federal Government and health to our economy will require more than budget reductions. A number of important projects have been sitting on the back burner until the tax and spending cuts were in place.

An attack on waste and fraud will now be given the attention it deserves. In March we established a Council on Integrity and Efficiency to coordinate this effort. It can be expected to set in motion several new strike forces to make certain that we get solid results. This drive will include every part of the Federal Government, including the Department of Defense. The private sector will face scrutiny, too.

We will announce shortly the establishment of a National Productivity Advisory Committee. It will be composed of labor leaders, management, academia, and will make recommendations aimed at keeping American business and the American worker ahead of the competition, which is the real way to secure jobs for the future.

The aggressive deregulation drive Vice President Bush is leading will continue. We've made headway here and are beginning to feel the dividends. Within days of entering office, the price of oil was decontrolled. Critics howled that it contributed to inflation. Now that half a year has passed, the news media talks about how lucky we are to have an oil glut. Well, maybe chance had something to do with it, but the increase in domestic oil exploration unleashed by decontrol didn't hurt. In the first half of this year, more than 16,000 oil wells were successfully completed, almost double the 1979 figure.

In the area of industrial deregulation, we came forward with a plan to help the automobile industry, proposing changes or elimination of 34 specific regulations which, over a 5-year period, will save the American motorist $9.3 billion and release $1.4 billion in company funds which have been invested in federally mandated equipment and facilities. And we've just begun.

We've now talked about three of the pillars of our economic program—control of spending, reduced taxes, and regulatory relief. There is a fourth pillar—a stable monetary policy. Over the past decade, we've heard a great deal about fine-tuning the economy with the use of interest rates and money supply. We tried it and went on a financial roller coaster from which we still haven't recovered.

During the last 10 years, as a result of runaway inflation, savings plummeted to the lowest point in recent history. With savings down, the pool of money available for loans dried up. Simultaneously, the Federal Government ran large deficits. We haven't balanced the budget in the last 10 years. This reduced the resources available for building loans, because Uncle Sam was out competing in the money market, borrowing to fund those deficits. Is it any wonder the interest rates burst through the ceiling?

The administration is dedicated to licking inflation and bringing down interest rates permanently, and we've taken the first steps toward that goal. The dollar is strong, and our tax program gives tremendous new incentives to save. The Federal Reserve is following a conservative and careful approach to the money supply, which will ensure that once recovery begins it won't kick off another round of inflation.

Interest rates will come down. And when they do, they'll stay down because the underlying economic problems that caused them to skyrocket in the first place will be cured. And that's when genuine prosperity will begin.

Nowhere is there a greater need for a good dose of prosperity than in the construction industry. Unemployment in your industry is running roughly double that of other segments of the economy, with 768,000 out of work.

You know, a speaker always hopes that he can identify in some way with his audience. Well, my first summer job, when I was 14 years old, was with an outfit remodeling old homes for resale. And before the summer ended, I'd laid hardwood floors, shingled roof, painted ceilings, and dug foundations. There wasn't a very clear distinction in those days between craft lines in a small town. There also weren't any bulldozers or skip loaders in those days, so the grading was pretty much pick and shovel. I started with that and moved up to those other things I just mentioned. I remember one hot morning. I'd been swinging a pick for about 4 hours. I heard the noon whistle blow. I'd been waiting for that sound. I had the pick up over my shoulder ready for the next blow, and when I heard that whistle, I just let go and walked out from underneath it, let it fall behind me. And I heard a loud scream and then some very strong, profane language, and I turned around. And the boss was standing right behind me, and that pick was embedded in the ground right between his feet. Two inches either way and I'd have nailed him. [*Laughter*]

I remembered that incident when I heard some of the screams about our budget cuts. The screams sounded about the same.

But you know, I don't need to tell you the housing construction is in a pit. In 1972, a great year for the housing industry, there were 2.4 million housing starts. Eight years later, 1980, there were only 1.3 million. At the time of the passage of our tax and spending reforms this year, the housing industry was still sinking. This administration is committed to getting America building again, and that means more business and more jobs.

Second, we're moving forward with particular attention to your needs. In June I established a Presidential commission whose only job is solving the housing problem. Some of the best minds in the country are on that commission, and I can assure you that we'll take their recommendations as seriously as we did our effort to cut spending and taxes. They've found that up to 20 percent of the cost of a home is due to redtape, bureaucratic delays, and government regulation. We'll do everything we can to eliminate these impediments at the Federal level and plan to work with the State and local communities to see what can be done there to clear away some of the damaging web of controls, regulations, codes, and other restrictions.

I have told before of a neighbor of mine out in California who is building a home for himself. He got so frustrated with the paperwork that he glued all the pages together and he put up two poles in front of the house he was building and strung this ribbon of paper between the two poles. It was 250 feet long, just for permission to build his own home.

Last month Secretary of Housing and Urban Development Samuel Pierce announced that the redtape which clogged the pipeline preventing the construction of 50,000 low-income housing units had been cleared away. It took an agreement between HUD and the Office of Management and Budget on a financial adjustment factor. Now, this may not represent new allocation, but it certainly represents progress.

And finally, our tax program contains numerous provisions which will encourage building. The reduction in time needed for the depreciation of plant and equipment will quickly free cash for industrial construction, which will translate into more jobs in short order.

As for long-term needs, we're committed to providing the raw materials and energy sources you need to get the job done. To grow and prosper the country needs energy, especially those of you in the construction industry. The mismanagement of this vital component of American progress would be funny if it weren't so damaging. It's a monument to the inefficiency and confusion of the bureaucratic marketplace.

We're advancing on a broad front to ensure that our energy needs and those of the next generation of Americans are met. We started with oil control, but we're also taking the necessary steps to ensure a steady flow of energy from natural gas, nuclear power, coal, and other sources.

What is important for us now is not to be tempted again by those promising a quick fix or something for nothing. We'll come out of our current financial difficulties because, like every generation before us, we're going to knuckle down and work our way out. What our tax bill does is ensure it'll be profitable to do that work. Nevertheless, energy and dedication are still necessary to reach our goal.

Now, you know, it isn't true that I fought at Gettysburg; I didn't even go up San Juan Hill. But as a small boy, I saw Americans march off to war to save the world for democracy. I cast my first vote for Franklin

Roosevelt in the depths of the Great Depression. And when totalitarian forces threatened to send civilization into a new dark age, I saw this Nation put itself together and in 44 short months strike a mighty blow for freedom.

I mention these traumatic events only because they illustrate how time and again Americans have met the challenges. I don't believe Americans of today are any different from those doughboys of World War I or the GI's of World War II. And certainly our domestic problems are no greater today than those we overcame in the Great Depression we went through between those two wars.

I would like to speak of one more thing. Earlier in my remarks, I spoke of the history of organized labor in our country and quoted Samuel Gompers, the founder of the American Federation of Labor. The United Brotherhood of Carpenters was a mainstay of that early crusade and of the federation. The AF of L supported municipal, county, State, and Federal employees when they began to unionize. But from the very first, organized labor predicated its help and support on the condition that public employees could never be allowed to strike. Indeed, they insisted that unions of government employees would recognize this in their constitutions.

They were the first to point out the difference between public employment and private employment—that government could not close up shop, that government workers were employed by the people, and the people could not give any group the right to coerce the people's elected representatives. However, to protect the rights of government employees, labor offered to support legislation to ensure wages and working conditions comparable to those for similar work in the private sector.

When the National Labor Relations Act, known to most of us as the Wagner Act, was ratified in 1935, even liberal labor leaders such as Phillip Murray and John L. Lewis proclaimed they had no intention of allowing any segment of government to be organized with the right to strike.

President Franklin Delano Roosevelt declared: "Militant tactics have no place in the functions of any organization of government employees. A strike of public employees manifests nothing less than an intent on their part to prevent or obstruct the operations of government until their demands are satisfied. Such action, looking toward the paralysis of government by those who have sworn to support it, is unthinkable and intolerable." He likened public employee strikes to insurrection.

Reflecting these views, the Federal Government has a law prohibiting strikes by public employees. Some other levels of government have adopted similar statutes and ordinances. Yet in recent years some in labor have retreated from labor's earlier stand against public employee strikes. Strikes against the public safety by public employees have increased over the last many years, and many, like this last strike in PATCO, were in violation of the law and of oaths sworn to by individual union members.

Our very freedom is secure because we're a nation governed by laws, not by men. We have the means to change the laws if they become unjust or onerous. We cannot, as citizens, pick and choose the laws we will or will not obey. And I hope that organized labor today and its leadership will recognize that you, the rank and file they represent, are the supreme authority in our land, that you are the employers of all who serve in government, elected or appointed, and none of us in government can strike against you and the interests of you, the sovereign people.

I thank you once again for allowing me to be here.

Mr. Konyha. President Reagan, we're so thrilled that you took the time to come here to speak to this assembly. Now, I want to present you with a gift from the assemblage, and if nothing else, it will be a token of appreciation for attending our 100th anniversary. Thank you very kindly.

The President. Thank you.

Note: The President spoke at 10:27 a.m. at McCormick Place. Following the address, the President left Chicago and returned to the White House.

Exchange With a Reporter on Defense Spending
September 3, 1981

Reporter. Mr. President, Secretary Weinberger says that he does not expect there to be cuts of $30 billion in the defense budget. Do you expect them to be at that magnitude?

The President. All I know is that no department is going to be exempt, but we are not retreating from our program of building up our defenses.

Reporter. Thank you.

Note: The exchange took place on the South Lawn of the White House at 2:18 p.m. as the President returned from his stay in California.

Nomination of Thomas Aranda, Jr., To Be United States Ambassador to Uruguay
September 4, 1981

The President today announced his intention to nominate Thomas Aranda, Jr., of Arizona, to be Ambassador to Uruguay. He would succeed Lyle Franklin Lane.

Mr. Aranda served in the United States Air Force as lieutenant colonel in 1955–60. He was an attorney with law firms in Phoenix, Ariz.—Hiser and Aranda (1968–69), DePrima and Aranda (1969–70), DePrima, Aranda and DeLeon (1970–76), Thomas Aranda, Jr., private practice (1977–79), and Aranda and Fisher (1979 to present). In 1976–77 he was Special Assistant to President Ford. He also served as special adviser to the Chairman of the Inter-American Defense Board. He was appointed by President Ford as a member of the National Advisory Council on Extension and Continuing Education and the National Advisory Council on Equality of Educational Opportunity. He served as legal counsel for the Department of Foreign Relations of the Republic of Mexico and for the Arizona State Republican Party.

Mr. Aranda graduated from the University of Arizona (B.S., 1946; J.D., 1967). He is married, has two children, and resides in Phoenix, Ariz. He was born April 9, 1934, in Nogales, Ariz.

Nomination of Joseph Verner Reed, Jr., To Be United States Ambassador to Morocco
September 4, 1981

The President today announced his intention to nominate Joseph Verner Reed, Jr., of Connecticut, to be Ambassador to the Kingdom of Morocco. He would succeed Angier Biddle Duke.

Mr. Reed was an assistant to the President of the International Bank for Reconstruction and Development in 1961–63. Since 1963 he has been with the Chase Manhattan Bank of North America in New York, N.Y., serving successively as assistant to the director (1963–68), vice president and executive assistant to Chairman David Rockefeller in (1969–81), and vice president and adviser to the chairman (1981 to present). Since February 1981 he has also been senior adviser to the Chairman of the United States Business Committee for Jamaica. He is a member of the Council on Foreign Relations.

Mr. Reed graduated from Yale University (B.A., 1961). He is married, has two children, and resides in Greenwich, Conn. He was born December 17, 1937, in New York, N.Y.

Nomination of Faith Ryan Whittlesey To Be United States Ambassador to Switzerland
September 4, 1981

The President today announced his intention to nominate Faith Ryan Whittlesey, of Pennsylvania, to be Ambassador to Switzerland. She would succeed Richard David Vine.

Mrs. Whittlesey was a substitute teacher in the Philadelphia School District of Pennsylvania in 1962–64. She was with the Pennsylvania Department of Justice as special assistant attorney general (1964–65) and as special assistant attorney general in the Department of Public Welfare (1967–70). In 1965 she was law clerk to the Honorable Francis L. Van Dusen of the United States District Court (Eastern District of Pennsylvania). In 1972–76 she served in the Pennsylvania House of Representatives. Since 1976 she has been a member of the Delaware County Council in Media, Pa. Also, since 1980 she has been an attorney in the law firm of Wolf, Block, Schorr and Solis-Cohen of Philadelphia.

Mr. Whittlesey graduated from Wells College (B.A., 1960) and the University of Pennsylvania Law School (J.D., 1963). In 1962 she attended the Academy of International Law at The Hague, Netherlands. Mrs. Whittlesey is a widow and has three children. She resides in Haverford, Pa., and was born February 21, 1939, in Jersey City, N.J.

Appointment of Nancy Clark Reynolds as United States Representative on the Commission on the Status of Women of the Economic and Social Council of the United Nations
September 4, 1981

The President today announced his intention to appoint Nancy Clark Reynolds to be Representative of the United States of America on the Commission on the Status of Women of the Economic and Social Council of the United Nations. She would succeed Koryne Kaneski Horbal.

Following graduation from Goucher College (B.A., 1949), Ms. Reynolds became the assistant director of admissions in 1949–50. In 1954–58 she was a news reporter and panelist for WBAL–TV and radio in Baltimore, Md. In 1958 she moved to Boise, Idaho, and hosted and produced "Periscope" at KTVB. She became the first woman coanchor of KPIX–TV in San Francisco in 1962, and while there she was employed by the CBS television network as a floor correspondent for the Republican and Democrat conventions in 1964. In 1966–75 she was assistant press secretary to the Governor of California and served 4 years as a special assistant to the Governor, responsible for press conferences and special events. After leaving the Governor's office, she became an account executive with Deaver and Hannaford, a Los Angeles public relations firm. In 1966–67 she was the associate director of national affairs for the Boise Cascade Corp. She is currently serving as vice president of national affairs at the Bendix Corp. in Washington, D.C.

Ms. Reynolds is a recipient of America's Outstanding Women in Business and Labor Award from the Women's Equity Action League. She resides in Alexandria, Va., and was born June 26, 1927, in Pocatello, Idaho.

Announcement Concerning the U.S. Delegation to the United States-Nigeria Bilateral Talks
September 4, 1981

The President has asked Vice President George Bush to lead the U.S. delegation to the sixth round of U.S.-Nigeria bilateral economic talks, September 8 and 9, in Washington, D.C. Nigerian Vice President Alex Ekwueme will chair his country's delegation to the annual consultations. The talks will explore issues of mutual concern in the areas of agriculture, energy, trade and investment, health, education, and science and technology.

In addition to presiding over the talks, the two Vice Presidents will have a private meeting during Vice President Ekwueme's stay.

Announcement of the Vice President's Foreign Travel
September 4, 1981

The President has asked Vice President George Bush to represent the United States on an official visit to Brazil, Colombia, and the Dominican Republic. The Vice President has accepted the invitation of the Dominican Republic and will visit there on October 11 and 12 and has accepted the invitation of President Turbay to visit Colombia on October 13 and 14. The Vice President's trip will conclude with a visit to Brazil, at the invitation of the Brazilian Government, on October 14, 15, and 16.

[On the same day, Deputy Press Secretary Larry M. Speakes read the following information to reporters at his daily press briefing in Room 450 of the Old Executive Office Building.]

The purpose of the trip is to demonstrate the importance this administration places on our relationships with Latin America. In his visits to Brazil, Colombia, and the Dominican Republic, the Vice President will have an opportunity to exchange views with the heads of state and other high-level officials in these countries. The trip is being made at the invitation of the countries involved, and the times were worked out at a mutually convenient time to both countries.

Statement by Deputy Press Secretary Speakes on the Assassination of the French Ambassador to Lebanon
September 4, 1981

The President was shocked and saddened by the news this morning that the French Ambassador to Lebanon was killed as a result of an attack in Beirut. The President feels strongly that the violence and terror in many areas of the world constitutes a grave danger to the fabric of society. He would like to extend his deepest sympathies to the family, colleagues, and friends of Ambassador Delamar.

In addition, the President is sending a personal message to President Mitterrand [of France].

Note: Deputy Press Secretary Larry M. Speakes read the President's reaction to reporters during his daily press briefing, which began at 12:11 p.m., in Room 450 of the Old Executive Office Building.

Nomination of Donald James Quigg To Be Deputy Commissioner of Patents and Trademarks
September 4, 1981

The President today announced his intention to nominate Donald James Quigg to be Deputy Commissioner of Patents and Trademarks, Department of Commerce. He would succeed Lutrelle F. Parker.

Since 1945 Mr. Quigg has been employed in the patent division of the Phillips Petroleum Co. He was technical assistant specialist in 1945–46, staff patent attorney in 1946–50, senior patent attorney, section chief, in 1950–54, associate patent counsel

and chief, legal branch, in 1954–71, and patent counsel since 1971. Previous to 1945, he was in the private practice of law.

Mr. Quigg graduated from Oklahoma University (B.A., 1937) and Kansas City University (now University of Missouri at Kansas City) (J.D., 1940). He served in the U.S. Army in 1942–45. Mr. Quigg is married, has two children, and resides in Bartlesville, Okla. He was born April 28, 1916, in Kansas City, Mo.

Nomination of Charles Timothy Hagel To Be Deputy Administrator of Veterans Affairs
September 4, 1981

The President today announced his intention to nominate Charles Timothy Hagel to be Deputy Administrator of Veterans Affairs.

Mr. Hagel is presently serving as deputy commissioner general of the 1982 World's Fair (Energy Expo '82) to be held in Knoxville, Tenn. In 1977–81 he was manager, Government Affairs Office, Firestone Tire and Rubber Co., in Washington, D.C. In 1971–77 he was administrative assistant to U.S. Representative John Y. McCollister (R-Nebr.).

Mr. Hagel served in the U.S. Army for 2 years, when he won the American Spirit

Honor Medal. While with the Ninth Infantry Division in South Vietnam in 1968, he was awarded the Purple Heart with one Oak Leaf Cluster, Combat Infantry Badge, and Army Commendation Medal. He is a member of the American Legion and Veterans of Foreign Wars.

Mr. Hagel graduated from Brown Institute for Radio and Television in Minneapolis, Minn. He then graduated from the University of Nebraska at Omaha (B.S.). He was born October 4, 1946, in North Platte, Nebr. He currently resides in Washington, D.C.

Nomination of Susan Meredith Phillips To Be a Commissioner of the Commodity Futures Trading Commission
September 4, 1981

The President today announced his intention to nominate Susan Meredith Phillips to be a Commissioner of the Commodity Futures Trading Commission for the term expiring April 13, 1985. She would succeed Read P. Dunn, Jr.

Since 1978 Dr. Phillips has been an associate professor with the finance department of the University of Iowa. She served as interim assistant vice president of finance and university services in 1979–80. Since 1980 she has been associate vice president of finance and university services. Dr. Phillips was a Brookings economic policy fellow in 1976–77, an SEC economic fellow in 1977–78, and directorate of economic and policy research, Securities and Exchange Commission. She was an assistant professor at the University of Iowa in 1974–78 and at Louisiana State University in 1973–74.

Dr. Phillips graduated from Agnes Scott College (B.A., 1967) and Louisiana State University (M.S., 1971; Ph. D., 1973). She resides in Iowa City, Iowa. She was born December 23, 1944, in Richmond, Va.

Nomination of Jeffrey S. Bragg To Be Federal Insurance Administrator
September 4, 1981

The President today announced his intention to nominate Jeffrey S. Bragg to be Federal Insurance Administrator, Federal Emergency Management Agency. He would succeed Gloria Cusumano Jimenez.

Since 1976 Mr. Bragg has been director of public affairs, Ohio Medical Indemnity Mutual Corp., Blue Cross and Blue Shield of Central Ohio. In 1973–76 he was legislative representative with the Nationwide Insurance Companies and Affiliates. He was clerk, Ohio House of Representatives, in 1972–73.

Mr. Bragg graduated from Ohio State University (B.A., 1971). In 1981 he was elected to the executive board of the Industry Advisory Committee, Conference of Insurance Legislators. He is a member of the board of governors of the Ohio Medical Professional Liability Underwriting Association.

Mr. Bragg resides in Columbus, Ohio. He was born January 21, 1949, in Northampton, Mass.

Appointment of Rodney N. Searle as Chairman of the Upper Mississippi River Basin Commission
September 4, 1981

The President today announced his intention to appoint Rodney N. Searle to be Chairman of the Upper Mississippi River Basin Commission. He would succeed Neil S. Haugerud.

Mr. Searle has been a member of the Minnesota House of Representatives since 1956. He served on the House Appropriations Committee for 22 years and was chairman of the education division of the

House Appropriations Committee for 10 years. He was minority leader in 1975–78 and speaker of the House of Representatives in 1979.

Mr. Searle graduated from Mankato State College (B.A., 1960). He is married, has three children, and resides in Waseca, Minn. He was born July 17, 1920, in Camden, N.J.

Proclamation 4855—National Hispanic Heritage Week, 1981
September 4, 1981

By the President of the United States of America

A Proclamation

The Hispanic peoples, their traditions, language and culture are a vital part of the American heritage. Their influence on our nation began with the Spaniards long before our revolution brought independence from England. This heritage can today be found almost everywhere in our daily lives: the arts and music we enjoy, the architecture of the homes and buildings in which we live and work, the history we read, and the language we use.

The Hispanic peoples today add to our strength as a nation with their strong devotion to family, deep religious convictions, pride in their language and heritage and commitment to earning a livelihood by hard work. Outstanding Hispanic men and women have advanced our nation in science and technology, business and public service. From the Southwest to the Northeast of the United States, they carry on their tradition of service to the communities in which we all live. This year, San Antonio has joined Miami and other American cities in electing a prominent Hispanic citizen as its mayor. Hispanic Americans bring to us, as well, a tradition of respect for the role of women both at home and in the workplace. Hispanic Americans serve with distinction in our military services today as they have served with leadership and courage on the battlefield in defense of this nation in the past.

Their contributions all too often go unrecognized. It is, therefore, fitting that we set aside this week to honor the Hispanic peoples that are among us as a nation of Americans.

Now, Therefore, I, Ronald Reagan, President of the United States of America, do hereby proclaim the week beginning September 13, 1981, as National Hispanic Heritage Week in honor of the Hispanic peoples who have enriched our daily lives, our traditions and our national strength. In this spirit, I ask all of our citizens to reflect on the sense of brotherhood that binds us together as one people.

In Witness Whereof, I have hereunto set my hand this fourth day of September, in the year of our Lord nineteen hundred and eighty-one, and of the Independence of the United States of America the two hundred and sixth.

RONALD REAGAN

[*Filed with the Office of the Federal Register, 11:26 a.m., September 8, 1981*]

Message on the Observance of Labor Day
September 4, 1981

Samuel Gompers, one of the first labor leaders in this country, said that Labor Day was a time to pledge ourselves to an even greater effort in the coming year. Samuel

Gompers knew that the key to a prosperous future is to have faith in it, and that's why for him, Labor Day stood for a celebration of tomorrow's promise and possibilities.

Today, as we set our minds to a new season of work, we begin what I hope will be a new age of the American worker, an age in which all of us again are free to prosper.

Together, we've swept away many government-created obstacles to our prosperity. In our fight against inflation and high interest rates, we enacted the largest budget cuts ever considered by the Congress. We produced the first real tax cut for working men and women in nearly 20 years. We slowed the pace of Federal rulemaking. We saw to it our money supply followed a pattern of slow, stable growth.

These dramatic changes in economic policy—the tax and budget legislation I signed a few weeks ago—are the dynamic result of millions of individuals coming together, committed to preserving a society where we can each seek our own goals, assured of the freedom to climb as high as our own drive, ambition, and talent can take us.

Let me make our goal in this program very clear: jobs, jobs, jobs, and more jobs. I see the creation of 3 million more jobs by 1986, in addition to the 10 million already expected. I see an era in which wage earners will be taking home more money in real dollars and an era in which fewer of us will be looking for work. Our policy has been and will continue to be: What is good for the American worker is good for America.

We built this great Nation, built it to surpass the highest standards ever imagined, through the hard work of our people. I would match the American worker against any in the world. The people whose labor fuels our industry and economy are among the most productive anywhere.

But too many Americans don't have a job, and too many Americans who do, don't have the tools they need to compete. Past, stagnated policies have made it too difficult to modernize and too risky to expand. Our people, our workers, have cried out for change, and in the last 7 months have achieved an historic reversal of the failed policies of an era gone by. We returned to the principles that made us great.

Legislation now in effect has dawned a new age for American workers, an age in which once again we are free to achieve all that we can. To cite one example: This recent legislation passed by the Congress as part of our economic recovery plan makes it possible for American workers currently participating in company pension plans to expand this coverage with their own individual retirement plans. This is only one of many new exciting possibilities opened for American workers.

All of us must take advantage of the incentives for savings, investment, and hard work that have been restored. I urge American workers who traditionally saved to make their families secure to do so again. I urge American investors who traditionally took risks to make a profit to do so again. I urge American workers to save and invest, because I believe that when our economic program takes full effect, Americans again will be rewarded for working extra hours or assuming more responsibility.

In a few short months we've accomplished much. But merely signing legislation is not going to bring about an instant cure. We're only beginning a recovery that will take many long months. We're only beginning to emerge from an economic crisis still gripping the rest of the world.

In Poland, where the grocery shelves are bare, the state ideology dictates more rationing of scarcity while workers take to the streets in protest over these restrictions. It is a stifled economy. A government official there said the crisis of depression is deepening in Poland, and they still do not have a way out.

Well, as President Eisenhower told us once: A crisis can be deadly when inert men are smothered in despair. But a crisis also can be the sharpest goad to our creative energies, particularly when we recognize it as a challenge and move to meet it in faith, in thought, and in courage. We must act today in the name of generations still to come.

As we work to solve our economic problems, let us tap that well of human spirit. We'll find more than strength of numbers and strength of resources, we'll find strength of individual determination. We will find the strength of mutual trust. For too many years now, we've trusted numbers and computers. We've trusted balance sheets, organizational charts, policies and systems. We've placed trust in rules, regulations, and government dictates. Well, I think it's about time that we placed trust in ourselves and in each other.

I'm confident in our ability to work together, to meet and surmount our problems and accomplish the goals we all seek. Now, I know that we can't make things right overnight—but we will make them right. Our destiny is not our fate; it is our choice. I ask all Americans, in these first, crucial months of recovery, to join me with confidence as we strike out on this new path to prosperity.

Note: The message was taped on Friday, September 4, for use on radio on Sunday, September 6.

Remarks on Presenting a Check for the Westway Highway Project to Mayor Edward I. Koch in New York, New York
September 7, 1981

Mayor Koch, I want to thank you for a very warm and gracious introduction. I have known the hospitality of the mayor before, here at Gracie Mansion, and I'm highly honored to be here today.

Lieutenant Governor Cuomo, our two Senators from New York, Moynihan and D'Amato, the Members of the House of Representatives representing this great State, the State and city officials and representatives of organized labor who are here, and members of my Cabinet, Secretaries Donovan and Pierce and Lewis—Secretary of Interior Jim Watt would have been here, but he's working on a lease for strip mining of the Rose Garden—[*laughter*]—you, ladies and gentlemen:

You know, it's always a pleasure to be here in the company of another chief executive. I think the mayor and I have both learned there's a difficult thing about cutting expenses—the expenses can vote. [*Laughter*] But, we also have learned, I know, as I've watched him and the magnificent job he's done in restoring fiscal stability here to this city, that if you always do what you believe in your heart is right, you'll please some of the people and astound the rest.

There have been moments in the past months when I, looking at the mayor's battle, I thought that he was a little bit like the Quaker who was milking his cow, and the cow kept kicking the bucket over. And he finally stood up and faced the cow and he said, "Thou knowest I cannot beat thee. Thou knowest I cannot even curse thee. But dost thou know I can sell thee to someone who will?" [*Laughter*]

I used to find, when I was Governor myself, sometimes, that I'd go home and make very eloquent speeches in the shower. But then there were days like this Labor Day, here in New York City, when there's nothing like it in all the world. On a day like today, we prove that the American people control their government. We have silenced bureaucrats, cut through the red-tape, and kept our promises, as the mayor so graciously said.

The Westway project begins today. Now, people tell me that the name Westway has become a code word for a bureaucracy strangling in its own regulations. From this day forward, let Westway symbolize opportunity and enterprise, and let it remind each of us, as we watch Westway become a reality, that our government works for us, not the other way around.

Now, some of us here have come from another Labor Day celebration; some have not. But next year we should all come back and march together, knowing that because of what was done here today, tens of thousands of working people who are out of jobs will be working again.

Yes, it was 10 years ago that this project was first proposed, and for 10 years nothing happened while hundreds of thousands of New Yorkers needed work. This city's unemployment rate is more than 20 percent higher than the national average. Eleven months ago, as the mayor said, when I campaigned in New York City, I pledged my support. And today, because of the leadership of Mayor Koch and Members of the Congress, because of the close cooperation between New York City and New York State, and because of the persistent efforts of people like Frank Handley and Tom McGuire and Bill Finneran and so many of the rest of you who have worked so hard, Westway is going to be a reality. The project will, as the mayor said, create parkland and new areas for commerce and industry. It'll save millions by easing the flow of people and goods. But most important, it will create jobs.

And today, as we begin a new season of work, we begin what I hope will be a new age for the American workers. The key to everything we're trying to accomplish is jobs, and as I said yesterday: jobs, jobs, and more jobs. Promises and programs, subsidies and studies, welfare and make-work have all been tried by well-meaning individuals. But any worker knows a job is the best social program there is.

I see the creation of 3 million more jobs in this country by 1986, in addition to the 10 million that are already normally expected in our growth. I see an era in which wage earners will be taking home more money in real dollars, and an era in which fewer of us will be looking for work. Our policy has been and will continue to be: What is good for the American worker is good for America.

There's a new spirit sweeping this country, a spirit born from the values, energies, and dreams of our working people. It is the dynamic result of millions of individuals coming together, committed to preserving a society where we can each seek our own goals, assured of freedom to climb as high and as far as our own drive and ambition and talent can take us. For too many years now we've placed trust in regulations and government dictates. Well, I think it's about time we placed trust in ourselves and in each other.

But we have to give ourselves a chance. We have to have jobs. Franklin Delano Roosevelt said, when he spoke to a nation that was gripped by the economic woes of the Great Depression, "For more than three centuries we've been building on this continent a free society, a society in which promise of the human spirit may find fulfillment. Comingled here," he said, "are the blood and genius of all the people of the world who have sought this promise."

We have every right to be proud of what we've accomplished and to have confidence in what lies ahead. There's no crisis our people can't rise above, no problem we can't solve, and no challenge too great.

Mayor Koch and the people of New York have turned this city around, proving that she can live within her means. The Westway project is another step in the revitalization of this great American city.

So, as I present this check for $85 million for the purchase of the right-of-way, the first installment of a $1.3 billion Federal commitment, let us all take heart in this country from New York's example and from this victory over the inertia of bureaucracy. And on this Labor Day of 1981, let each of us commit ourselves again to the renewal of America.

Note: The President spoke at 2:12 p.m. on the East Lawn of Gracie Mansion in New York City.

In his remarks, the President referred to Frank Handley, executive vice president, International Union of Operating Engineers; Tom McGuire, business manager of the Operating Engineers of New York, N.Y.; and Bill Finneran, executive director, General Contractors Association of New York.

Exchange With Reporters on Defense Spending
September 7, 1981

Q. Have you made any decision yet on the defense budget? How much has [Secretary of Defense Casper W.] Weinberger said he will cut?

The President. That's going to be my evening reading.

Q. When are you going to make a decision?

The President. Well, I have to make one soon, but I'm going to get all the viewpoints.

Q. Do you think that there will have to be some cuts in defense?

The President. I think there can be some cuts every place, but it does not mean there's any retreat from our determination to rebuild the military.

Q. But he doesn't want to cut at all, does he?

The President. Well, I'll know that better when I read his report. [*Laughter*]

Q. Does the kind of bickering that has been going on upset you inside?

The President. No, there's not really any bickering. That loses something in translation. No, everybody's got their ideas and opinions, and we openly debate them. But I think you will find there's a great simpatico and a great accord among them.

Q. No problems between [Director of the Office of Management and Budget David A.] Stockman and Weinberger?

The President. No, no, they're defending their points, but they'll all go along with the decision.

Q. They'd better. [*Laughter*]

Q. Thank you.

Note: The exchange began at 4:10 p.m. on the South Lawn of the White House as the President returned from his trip to New York City.

Appointment of Six Members of the Advisory Commission on Intergovernmental Relations
September 8, 1981

The President today announced his intention to appoint the following named individuals to be members of the Advisory Commission on Intergovernmental Relations for terms of 2 years:

Ross O. Doyen, president of the Kansas State Senate. He was first elected to the Kansas House of Representatives in 1958, served five terms in the House, and has been in the Senate for 12 years. Mr. Doyen served as chairman of several committees, including the Senate Ways and Means Committee, before being elected to an unexpired term as president of the senate. Mr. Doyen is president of the National Conference of State Legislatures and has served in leadership roles on the executive committee and governing boards at the Council of State Governments. Mr. Doyen graduated from Kansas State University and served in the U.S. Navy during World War II. He is married, has two children, and was born in Cloud County, Kans., on October 1, 1926.

Margaret T. Hance, mayor of the city of Phoenix, Ariz. She was elected mayor in 1975, after serving two terms as as a city councilman, including one term as vice mayor. She is a member of the U.S. Conference of Mayors' board of trustees and chairman of the Air Quality Subcommittee. In addition, she has served on the U.S. Conference of Mayors' Task Force on Aging. Mayor Hance is a member of the board of directors of the National League of Cities and is a former chairman of the NLC Transportation Policy Committee. She is serving her second term as vice chairman of the Republican Mayors and Elected Officials Caucus. Mayor Hance graduated from Scripps College, Claremont, Calif., in 1945. She is widowed, has three children, and was born in Spirit Lake, Iowa, on July 2, 1923.

James Inhofe, mayor of the city of Tulsa, Okla. He was elected mayor in 1978 and is serving in his second term. He is also currently president of the Quaker Life Insurance Co. and president of Fly Riverside, Inc. Previously Mr. Inhofe was the Republican nominee for Governor of Oklahoma in 1974; chairman, First Congressional District campaign for Senator Dewey F. Bartlett in 1972; member of the Oklahoma State Senate in 1968–76; and member of the Oklahoma House of Representatives in 1966–68. He is a member of the executive committee of the U.S. Conference of Mayors. Mr. Inhofe graduated from the University of Tulsa. He is married, has four children, and was born in Des Moines, Iowa, on November 17, 1934.

Forrest Hood James, Jr., Governor of the State of Alabama. While at Auburn University, the Governor was an All-American halfback and was selected the most valuable player in the Southeastern Conference. After graduation in 1955, the Governor played professional football in Canada. In 1958 he returned to Alabama where he worked as a construction superintendent until 1962. In that year he founded his own company, Diversified Products Corp., a manufacturer of consumer and industrial products. He is married, has three children, and was born in Lanett, Ala., on September 15, 1934.

Joseph P. Riley, Jr., mayor of the city of Charleston, S.C. He was elected mayor in 1975 and is currently serving in his second term. He was elected to the South Carolina House of Representatives in 1968 and served for 6 years. He was a partner in the law firm of Riley and Barr before being elected mayor. Mr. Riley currently serves on the board of directors of the National League of Cities and the advisory board of the U.S. Conference of Mayors. He is chairman of the Governor's Committee on Criminal Justice, Crime and Delinquency, and president of the Municipal Association of South Carolina. Mr. Riley graduated from The Citadel and the University of South Carolina School of Law. He is married, has two children, and was born in Charleston, S.C., on January 19, 1943.

Peter F. Schabarum, a member of the Los Angeles County Board of Supervisors, Los Angeles, Calif. He has served in that position since 1972 when he was appointed, while a State assemblyman, by then Governor Ronald Reagan. He was returned to office by the voters in 1974 and 1978. He currently serves on the Air Quality Management District, the Los Angeles County Transportation Commission, and is a member of the executive committee of the California Supervisors' Association. In 1967–72 Mr. Schabarum served three terms in the California Assembly. He served on the Transportation, Ways and Means, and Revenue and Taxation Committees. He graduated from the University of California at Berkeley. He is married, has three children, and was born on January 9, 1929.

Message to the Senate Transmitting a Protocol to the United States-Jamaica Convention on Taxation and Fiscal Evasion
September 8, 1981

To the Senate of the United States:

I transmit herewith, for the advice and consent of the Senate to ratification, the Protocol amending the Convention between the Government of the United States of America and the Government of Jamaica for the Avoidance of Double Taxation and the Prevention of Fiscal Evasion with Respect to Taxes on Income, together with a related exchange of notes, signed at Kingston on July 17, 1981. I also transmit the report of the Department of State with respect to the Protocol.

The Protocol was negotiated subsequent to Prime Minister Seaga's visit to this country in January, 1981. It strengthens the provisions of the Convention in order to limit potential abuse of the treaty in certain situations and to make more effective the means of denying treaty benefits to residents of third countries who establish a corporation in one Contracting State in order to obtain treaty benefits from the other Contracting State. The Protocol also permits United States citizens to deduct expenses incurred while attending business conventions in Jamaica.

I recommend that the Senate give early and favorable consideration to the Protocol and Convention and give its advice and consent to ratification.

RONALD REAGAN

The White House,
September 8, 1981.

Recess Appointments of and Intention To Nominate United States Representatives and Alternate Representatives to the 36th Session of the General Assembly of the United Nations
September 8, 1981

The President today announced the recess appointments of, and his intention to nominate, the following individuals to serve as Representatives and Alternate Representatives of the United States of America to the Thirty-Sixth Session of the General Assembly of the United Nations:

Representatives:

Jeane J. Kirkpatrick, Representative of the United States to the United Nations;

Kenneth L. Adelman, Deputy Representative of the United States to the United Nations;

Andy Ireland, Representative from Florida;

Benjamin A. Gilman, Representative from New York;

John Sherman Cooper, attorney.

Alternate Representatives:

Charles M. Lichenstein, Alternate Representative of the United States for Special Political Affairs to the United Nations;

Jose S. Sorzano, Representative of the United States on the Economic and Social Council of the United Nations;

William Courtney Sherman, Deputy Representative of the United States in the Security Council of the United Nations;

Bruce Caputo, former Representative from New York;

George Christopher, former mayor of San Francisco, Calif.

Recess Appointments of Six Members of the Board of Directors of the National Railroad Passenger Corporation
September 8, 1981

The President today announced the recess appointments of the following individuals to be members of the Board of Directors of the National Railroad Passenger Corporation (AMTRAK):

Darrell Trent, Deputy Secretary of Transportation;

John M. Fowler, General Counsel, Department of Transportation;

Lee L. Verstandig, Assistant Secretary, Government Affairs, Department of Transportation;

Arthur E. Teele, Urban Mass Transportation Administrator;

Charles Swinburn, Deputy Assistant Secretary of Transportation (Policy and International Affairs);

Mark S. Knouse, Executive Assistant to the Secretary of Transportation.

Statement on the Death of Roy Wilkins
September 8, 1981

Roy Wilkins worked for equality, spoke for freedom, and marched for justice. His quiet and unassuming manner masked his tremendous passion for civil and human rights.

He once said, "The heritage of a man of peace will endure and shine into the darkness of this world." Although Roy's death darkens our day, the accomplishments of his life will continue to endure and shine forth.

I convey my deepest sympathy to his family, to the NAACP [National Association for the Advancement of Colored People] that he helped to build, and to all people who shared his devotion to the dignity of human life.

Proclamation 4856—Death of Roy Wilkins
September 8, 1981

By the President of the United States of America

A Proclamation

To the People of the United States:

With sadness, I announce the death of Roy Wilkins who died today in New York City.

Roy Wilkins worked for equality, spoke for freedom, and marched for justice. His quiet and unassuming manner masked his tremendous passion for civil and human rights.

He once said, "The heritage of a man of peace will endure and shine into the darkness of this world." Although Roy Wilkins' death darkens our day, the accomplishments of his life will continue to endure and shine forth.

As a mark of respect for the memory of Roy Wilkins, I hereby order that the flag of the United States shall be flown at half-staff upon all public buildings and grounds, at all military posts and naval stations, and on all naval vessels of the Federal Government in the District of Columbia and throughout the United States and its Territories and possessions until his interment. I also direct that the flag shall be flown at half-staff for the same length of time at all United States embassies, legations, consular offices, and other facilities abroad, including all military facilities and naval vessels and stations.

In Witness Whereof, I have hereunto set my hand this eighth day of September, in the year of our Lord nineteen hundred and eighty-one, and of the Independence of the United States of America the two hundred and sixth.

RONALD REAGAN

[*Filed with the Office of the Federal Register, 10:15 a.m., September 9, 1981*]

Note: The text of the proclamation was released by the Office of the Press Secretary on September 9.

Remarks at the Welcoming Ceremony for Prime Minister Menahem Begin of Israel
September 9, 1981

The President. Prime Minister Begin, on behalf of the American people, Nancy and I are honored and delighted to welcome you and all those accompanying you.

We're proud to stand beside you this morning, joining a tradition of hospitality for Israel observed by our Presidents for more than three decades. Your visit is testimony to the warm friendships, mutual respect, and shared values that bind our people. Today and tomorrow, we'll have an opportunity to meet, to come to know each other, and to discuss in detail the vital issues of peace and security that concern both our countries.

I welcome this chance to further strengthen the unbreakable ties between the United States and Israel and to assure you of our commitment to Israel's security and well-being.

Israel and America may be thousands of miles apart, but we are philosophical neighbors sharing a strong commitment to democracy and the rule of law. What we hold in common are the bonds of trust and friendship, qualities that in our eyes make Israel a great nation. No people have fought longer, struggled harder, or sacrificed more than yours in order to survive, to grow, and to live in freedom.

The United States and Israel share similar beginnings as nations of immigrants, yearning to live in freedom and to fulfill the dreams of our forefathers. We have both sought to establish societies of law, to live in peace, and to develop the full potential of our lands. We share a devotion to democratic institutions, responsible to the wills of our citizens. Our peoples embrace common ideals of self-improvement through hard work and individual initiative. Together, we seek peace for all people. In partnership, we're determined to defend liberty and safeguard the security of our citizens. We know Israelis live in constant peril. But Israel will have our help. She will remain strong and secure, and her special character of spirit, genius, and faith will prevail.

The prophet Ezekiel spoke of a new age—when land that was desolate has become like the Garden of Eden and waste and ruined cities are now inhabited. We saw how miraculously you transformed and made the desert bloom. We see how, despite dangers every day, your families continue working together to build a better place to live and to prosper in peace and freedom.

Our dream, our challenge, and, yes, our mission, is to make the golden age of peace, prosperity, and brotherhood a living reality in all countries of the Middle East. Let us remember that whether we be Christian or Jew or Moslem, we are all children of Abraham; we are all children of the same God.

Mr. Prime Minister, you come at a time of testing and of hope. The challenges we face are great with the forces of aggression, lawlessness, and tyranny intent on exploiting weakness. They seek to undo the work of generations of our people, to put out a light that we've been tending for these past 6,000 years. But we understand their designs, and we're determined to oppose them. Working with all our friends in the Middle East, we seek to reinforce the security of the entire region. As we consult about these problems, rest assured that the security of Israel is a principal objective of this administration and that we regard Israel as an ally in our search for regional stability.

Equally important in our discussions is the commitment of our two countries to advance the cause of peace. Mr. Prime Minister, your strong leadership, great imagination, and skilled statesmanship have been indispensable in reaching the milestones of the past few years on the road toward a just and durable peace in the Middle East.

You and the members of your coalition have earned our respect and admiration. Many cynics said Israel would never make peace with Egypt, but you did. Then they said you would not honor your commitment to return the Sinai to Egypt, but you have. Now they say you cannot go forward to work out a just and durable peace with all your neighbors; we know you will.

I look forward to receiving the benefit of your views and advice on the great tasks that remain before us. I'm confident that the United States and Israel will continue their close partnership as difficult negotiations toward peace are pursued. Let me also thank you, Mr. Prime Minister, for helping our special Ambassador, Philip Habib, to arrange a cessation of hostilities across your border with Lebanon—still another considered step for peace and one well taken.

Prime Minister Begin, I know your entire life has been dedicated to security and the well-being of your people. It wasn't always easy. From your earliest days you were acquainted with hunger and sorrow, but as you've written, you rarely wept. On one occasion, you did—the night when your beloved State of Israel was proclaimed. You cried that night, you said, because "truly there are tears of salvation as well as tears of grief."

Well, with the help of God, and us working together, perhaps one day for all the people in the Middle East, there will be no more tears of grief, only tears of salvation.

Shalom, shalom: to him that is far off and to him that is near. And again, Mr. Prime Minister, welcome to America.

The Prime Minister. Mr. President, my colleagues and I are grateful to you and to Mrs. Reagan for your kind invitation, for having given us the opportunity to discuss with you and your advisers international problems, bilateral issues, the danger to freedom resulting from Soviet expansionist policy in our region and its periphery and elsewhere, and the defense of human liberty, which is the essence of our lives, demotive of our efforts, the reason of our labors.

Our generation, Mr. President, lived through two World Wars, with all the sacrifices, the casualties, the misery involved. But the two wars also created and left after them, regrettably, two illusions. In the early twenties, the saying went around the world, "that was the war to end all the wars." It was not so to be. Only 25 years later another World War broke out, the most horrifying of all in the annals of mankind, not only with the sacrifices in tens of millions of human beings but also with atrocities unheard of in history. Ultimately, mankind crushed the darkest tyranny which ever arose to enslave the human soul, and then people believed that it is the end of tyranny of man over man. It was not to be.

After May 1945, there were 56 so-called local wars in a period of 36 years alone. In other words, blood-letting and enslavement are going on. Country after country is being taken over by totalitarianism. In nearly 8 years, eight countries were so taken over, either by proxy or directly. So, it is obvious that liberty is in danger, and all free women and men should stand together to defend it and to assure its future for all generations to come.

Mr. President, Israel is a small country, but a free one. Its democracy was proved time and again—true democracy. It is an integral part of the free world. It is a faithful and, through each democratic regime, a stable ally of the United States. We shall stand together, and Israel will give its share in defending human liberty.

Mr. President, out of those 56 local wars, five were thrust upon little Israel since its inception. We waged them out of necessity to defend our people and to save its existence and to sustain our independence. This is the simple reason why we not only want peace, but we yearn for peace. And therefore, as you rightly said, Mr. President, at a price of great sacrifices and admittedly undertaken—those are very serious risks—we made peace. We signed a peace treaty on this very lawn with our southern neighbor, but we strive to sign peace treaties and make peace forever on all our borders with all our neighbors. And with God's help, this noble aim will be achieved, too.

Mr. President, thank you for your heartwarming remarks about my people and my country and touching words about my life, which is only one of the uncountable thousands and millions who have suffered and fought and resisted and saw, after a long night, the rise of the Sun, the day. I am one of them because this is our generation. But your appreciation of our motives, our efforts, our sacrifices is very dear to all of us because, Mr. President, we see in you not only the President of the United States but also the defender of freedom throughout the world.

May I, Mr. President, extend to you on behalf of the people and Government of Israel, our invitation to come and visit our country and its capital, Jerusalem. Then we hope that we shall be able to reciprocate the wonderful hospitality, indeed, in the spirit of all Abraham, whom you mentioned, which was accorded to my colleagues and to myself. Be assured, Mr. President, the people of Israel will receive you not only with utmost respect but with deep cordiality.

Thank you.

Note: The President spoke at 10:09 a.m. on the South Lawn of the White House, where Prime Minister Begin was given a formal welcome with full military honors.

Following the ceremony, the President and the Prime Minister met in the Oval

Office. Also present at that meeting were the Vice President, Secretary of State Alexander M. Haig, Jr., Assistant to the President for National Security Affairs Richard V. Allen, Samuel Lewis, U.S. Ambassador to Israel and, on the Israeli side, Foreign Minister Yitzhak Shamir and Israeli Ambassador to the United States Ephraim Evron. President Reagan and Prime Minister Begin then held an expanded meeting with members of their delegations.

Nomination of James F. Goodrich To Be Under Secretary of the Navy
September 9, 1981

The President today announced his intention to nominate James F. Goodrich to be Under Secretary of the Navy. He would succeed Robert J. Murray.

In 1975–78 Mr. Goodrich was chairman of the board of directors of the Bath Iron Works Corp. He was president and chief executive officer, and previously vice president and director, of the Congoleum Corp. (formerly Bath Industries, Inc.) in 1965–75. In 1964–65 Mr. Goodrich was executive vice president of Bath Industries, Inc. Pre-

viously, in 1948–64, Mr. Goodrich held various positions with Todd Shipyards Corp. in Seattle, Wash., and Los Angeles, Calif.

Mr. Goodrich graduated from the University of Michigan (B.S., 1937). He attended the University of Washington (graduate courses in engineering and management) and received an honorary degree from Bowdoin College in 1973.

Mr. Goodrich resides in Cumberland Foreside, Maine. He was born January 24, 1913, in Fennville, Mich.

Toasts of the President and Prime Minister Menahem Begin of Israel at the State Dinner
September 9, 1981

The President. Ladies and gentlemen:

Prime Minister Begin, it's a genuine pleasure to welcome you to the White House this evening—I should say, welcome you back, because the Prime Minister is no stranger to this room. As a matter of fact, I have a funny feeling that he may have dined here more often than I have. [*Laughter*]

Be that as it may, once again, he's an honored guest. But this time Nancy and I have the privilege, and we're delighted. I'm not sure whether you saw it or not, Mr. Prime Minister, but in the play "Fiddler on the Roof," one of the townspeople asked

the rabbi if he had a proper blessing for the czar. The rabbi answered, "Why, of course. May God bless and keep the czar—far away from us." [*Laughter*]

Prime Minister Begin, as you know, the Jewish people have never been far away from sorrow and depression during their long and troubled history. And now—I don't believe your own influence on Jewish history goes as far back as the time of the czars. Now, you understand that there wouldn't be anything wrong with that; you will hear no criticism of age tolerated in this house. [*Laughter*] Lately, I've been heartened to remember that Moses was 80 when God commissioned him for public service, and he lived to be 120. [*Laughter*] And Abraham was 100 and his wife, Sarah, 90, when they did something truly amazing. [*Laughter*] He survived to be 175. So, Mr. Prime Minister, we haven't even hit our full stride yet. [*Laughter*]

But to be serious a moment: After our conversations today, very warm and productive, I'm convinced that we're on the way to the right road, that we really can draw closer to that golden age of peace, prosperity, and brotherhood and reason. And I think this is clear: Providence has blessed us at this critical time with two leaders—one in Israel and one in Egypt— uniquely capable of the great decisions that are required.

Prime Minister Begin, I remember reading in your book, "White Nights," how as a young man being held inside Soviet prisons, you longed to return with your people to the Middle East. And even then, you told your captors there would be plenty of room for the Arabs, for millions of Jews, and for peace. And you've been working ever since to make that dream come true. Though trained as a lawyer, you passed up the quiet life of a private attorney. From your earliest days, the spirit of freedom burned within you, leading you to make great personal sacrifices for the Jewish people.

As a political inmate in those Soviet dungeons, you learned the horrors of totalitarian abuse. You fought against Hitler, and you spent your early adult years helping create a haven for your people in a new Israel. Devoted to democratic traditions, you served as leader of your country's loyal opposition for nearly 30 years. Consistent in your views and skillful in presenting them, you were elected leader of a free people who recently reaffirmed their esteem for you. Called as a peacemaker, you boldly seized the opportunity for peace with Egypt and skillfully pursued it to a successful conclusion.

Mr. Prime Minister, the commitment you're making is a commitment to future generations. In the Talmud, there is a story about a man—and I should have asked you whether the pronunciation was "Ho-nee" or "Ho-ni," but one of the two—and one day

he was walking along and he saw an old man planting carob trees. It's said that the carob tree doesn't produce fruit for 70 years. And Honei commented to the old man, "Certainly, you don't expect to see the fruit from this tree." And the old man answered, "I came into this world and people had planted trees for me. I am planting for those who will come after me."

Well, thank you, Mr. Prime Minister, for planting these seeds of peace.

Ladies and gentlemen, I ask all of you to join me in a toast to Prime Minister Begin and his friends and the Israeli people. And, if I may refer to that rabbi from "Fiddler on the Roof" once again, "May the good Lord bless and keep you always close to us."

The Prime Minister. Mr. President, may I be allowed first of all to thank you for a good day. Our lives were harsh; the difficult days were many. The few ones, we remember them, we count them. You gave us today a good day, one of the few, through the warmth of your heart, your deep humanity, your friendship, understanding. And I believe all my friends and colleagues here assembled join me in the expression of that gratitude to you for a good day in our lives.

Both our nations, Mr. President, are built on vision. Vision is no utopia; it is the prerequisite for changing reality. Your Founding Fathers expressed their vision in the Declaration of Independence, mainly written by Jefferson, proclaiming self-evident truths. But if they are self-evident, why proclaim? But that proclamation called upon people to go into battle, poorly armed against professional soldiers, and after great suffering, win the day and create the greatest republic ever known in history.

Your Founding Fathers wrote a constitution—original, unknown in those days, and it works for more than 200 years. There are some crises from time to time, but out of every crisis democracy comes out stronger, deeper in the United States. And the Constitution works, with some amendments.

Then you had the vision of building real democracy. Perhaps this is the greatest achievement of the American people, proving in the 18th century, that it is not so that one man should inherit a throne and a crown and rule millions of people at his will. The people should decide who should form the government, and they should accept the government willingly. This, all nations learned from you. And perhaps the greatest vision of all was the acceptance of so many people of various origins from many countries. Here I would like to stress, because I believe in Divine Providence with all my heart, that as far as the Jewish people are concerned, a real miracle happened to them. In 25 years, at the turn of the two centuries, 2½ million Jews crossed the ocean and came to the hospitable shores of this country. If they hadn't done that, they would have been lost—their children and their grandchildren. Not a third of the Jewish people would have been wiped out, perhaps two-thirds of them would have been destroyed. Who knows whether we would have been able to recreate our statehood.

This is one of the great miracles in human history—those 25 years, 100,000 people every year coming to these shores. There is no wonder that Emma Lazarus wrote from her heart, "Give me your tired, your poor, your huddled masses yearning to breathe free." They came here without knowing one word of English. They worked i5sweatshops, and they wer peddlers. But the second generation learned perfect Eng lish. And the third, together with all the other natimnalities—or ethnic groups as you call them in America—built up this great country. A miracle, indeed. And I want now after so many years to express, may I say morally, historically, our deep gratitude that this great country made it possible for 2½ million of my brethren to come here and save their lives and the lives of three other generations.

We also build on vision, Mr. President— on a smaller scale, of course, because we are a New Hampshire more or less, no more, a small country. But when we won our freedom in the same way you did, fighting for it, not getting it as a gift, we were only 600,000. Now we are 3½ million. Relatively, proportionately perhaps, it is very close. And so that was the vision—to bring people from the four corners of the world as the prophet really foresaw in his vision in the ancient times, from the four corners of the world back to the land of the forefathers, back, return, old and young and limping and sick and everyone, so as the prophets wrote exactly. And of course we still keep the gates open for everyone who feels that he is persecuted, like in Russia, or humiliated, like in any other country which may happen, for everyone, as you did for so many years, actually for nearly two centuries.

We also had the vision of democracy. As we are a small country, ours is a parliamentary regime. I am not ashamed to say we copied it from the British. The British built up a beautiful home in their own country— real democracy. And we adopted this system, but it is also real democracy.

Mr. President, the election day in Israel— it was only 2 months ago—was one of the most beautiful days in our lives. Everybody a free citizen, went to the polls, put in the ballots. No pressure was asserted; it was impossible. The campaign was perhaps to some extent lively. [*Laughter*] But the day of the election, the quiet—it's the most beautiful day of the year. But of 4 years— real democracy.

And out of those ballots came a government. Not everybody is happy. Well, that is human nature. And therefore, believe it when we say we are your stable ally. We mean it completely, because only through the inherent stability of democracy you can keep that stability.

All the other regimes—something happens and there is upheaval. Not in a democracy. We still have division of peace, Mr. President. Yes, we made peace with Egypt, with our southern neighbor, the largest, the strongest Arab nation. But we want peace with all our neighbors.

Why isn't it so simple to achieve? Because for us, security is not a word, it's not even a concept. It is life itself. With our experience, surrounded on the northern, on the eastern front, still, after the peace, after the sacrifices we gave, we must be so careful. We bear so grave a responsibility, not only a great one in our generation in the wake of the Holocaust, to make sure that our children and our children's children will first of all live, and then live freely.

Security to us is so unique that we cannot only proclaim. Peace without security is hollow for us. Peace must be based on security. And we still bear in our hearts the prophets' vision of eternal peace, of complete disarmament, "neither will they learn or teach war."

It is difficult now to believe that it is realistic. All the world is arming to the teeth. Every disarmament conference brings more arms to the world. But our faith is unshakeable. This vision of the prophets will be realized, perhaps exactly as a result of that danger, which is looming over all mankind, of complete destruction. Out of that evil will come real peace and disarmament, and people will live together in good neighborhood—all of them.

We didn't have one day of peace. Nations fought. There was a war of 100 years between England and France. Ultimately, there was *entente cordiale*—a union or alliance—unwritten, that played so great a role in the years of 1914 and 1918. There was a 30-years war in Europe. In Europe, the saying went around about "eternal enemies," and the eternal enemies are now friends. War can be avoided. Peace is inevitable. But we didn't deviate even one day of peace. What my colleagues and I would like to do for our people is to give them an historic period of peace—two or three generations at least. Let them have peace and let there be no bereavements. That is our vision, and I believe it will bring us nearer a different reality.

Mr. President, today we achieved much in Washington, thanks to you. I shall leave town knowing that our cooperation in the field of security and strategy—in the face of a world danger to lose all the values we believe in, which make life worthwhile to live—will be concrete and close. This is a real achievement, again, thanks to you, Mr. President, to your wisdom and the warmth of your heart.

Now, before I raise my glass, I would like to tell a story. I cannot but tell at least one story after hearing your speech, Mr. President. At least one story. But I must caution my respected listeners that detect a chauvinistic Israeli undertone. [*Laughter*] I don't like it, and I don't mean it, and I apologize in advance; but the story is interesting, so I will tell it.

It goes like this: The President brought me into the Oval Office, and he showed me on the table three phones—one white and one blue. And he explained to me: "The white is the direct line to Mrs. Thatcher; the blue to President Mitterrand." And then I asked him, "What is the red phone?" "That is a direct line to God." So, I asked the President, "Mr. President, do you use it often?" And the President said, "Oh, no, very rarely. It's very expensive. Long distance—so long a distance. And I cannot afford it. I have to cut the budget and——" [*Laughter*]

So, then the President visited Jerusalem, and I showed him my office, and there are three phones. One was white, one was blue. And I said, "The white is a direct line to President Sadat." By the by, I have such a line, and he has such a line. "And the other, well, to Mrs. Thatcher." And there is a red phone. And the President asked, "What is the red phone for?" And I said, "This is a direct line to God." So, the President asked me, "Do you use it often?" I say, "Every day." "How can you afford it?" And I said, "Here, in Jerusalem, it is being considered a local call." [*Laughter*]

Now, Mr. President, neither of us has direct lines to God. I only believe that God listens to the prayer of a Jew and a Christian and of a Moslem—of every human being. But, if I have to continue with the story, then I will say that when you come, as I do believe, to Jerusalem, I will immediately put at your disposal the red phone. [*Laughter*] On the house. [*Laughter*] A local call.

I raise my glass to the President of the United States—a man of principle, a wonderful man whom we respect and love, the first day we met. [*Referring to Mrs. Reagan:*] Madam, the first sight. And to a great, devoted friend of the Jewish people and the State of Israel, and to the defender of freedom throughout the world.

To the President.

Note: The President spoke at 9:36 p.m. in the State Dinning Room at the White House.

Executive Order 12319—River Basin Commissions
September 9, 1981

By the authority vested in me as President by the Constitution and laws of the United States, in order to ensure the orderly termination of the six river basin commissions established pursuant to the Water Resources Planning Act (42 U.S.C. 1962 *et seq.*), it is hereby ordered as follows:

Section 1. In accord with the decision of the Water Resources Council pursuant to Section 203(a) of the Water Resources Planning Act (42 U.S.C. 1962b–2(a)), the following river basin commissions shall terminate on the date indicated:

(a) Pacific Northwest River Basins Commission, terminated on September 30, 1981.

(b) Great Lakes Basin Commission, terminated on September 30, 1981.

(c) Ohio River Basin Commission, terminated on September 30, 1981.

(d) New England River Basins Commission, terminated on September 30, 1981.

(e) Missouri River Basin Commission, terminated on September 30, 1981.

(f) Upper Mississippi River Basin Commission, terminated on December 31, 1981.

Sec. 2. All Federal agencies shall cooperate with the commissions and the member States to achieve an orderly close out of commission activities and, if the member States so elect, to carry out an orderly transition of appropriate commission activities to the member States.

Sec. 3. To the extent permitted by law, the assets of the commissions which the Federal Government might otherwise be entitled to claim are to be transferred to the member States of the commissions, or such entities as the States acting through their representatives on the commissions may designate, to be used for such water and related land resources planning purposes as the States may decide among themselves. The terms and conditions for transfer of assets under this Section shall be subject to the approval of the Director of the Office of Management and Budget, or such Federal agency as he designates, before the transfer is effective.

Sec. 4. Federal agency members of river basin commissions are directed to continue coordination and cooperation in future State and inter-State basin planning arrangements.

Sec. 5. (a) Effective October 1, 1981, the following Executive Orders are revoked:

(1) Executive Order No. 11331, as amended, which established the Pacific Northwest River Basins Commission.

(2) Executive Order No. 11345, as amended, which established the Great Lakes Basin Commission.

(3) Executive Order No. 11371, as amended, which established the New England River Basins Commission.

(4) Executive Order No. 11578, as amended, which established the Ohio River Basin Commission.

(5) Executive Order No. 11658, as amended, which established the Missouri River Basin Commission.

(b) Effective January 1, 1982, Executive Order No. 11659, as amended, which established the Upper Mississippi River Basin Commission, is revoked.

RONALD REAGAN

The White House,
September 9, 1981.

[*Filed with the Office of the Federal Register, 2:30 p.m., September 10, 1981*]

Note: The text of the Executive order was released by the Office of the Press Secretary on September 10.

Message to the Congress Reporting Budget Deferrals
September 10, 1981

To the Congress of the United States:

In accordance with the Impoundment Control Act of 1974, I herewith report two new deferrals totaling $6.7 million and revisions to three previously reported deferrals.

The deferrals affect programs in International Development Assistance, the Department of Health and Human Services, the Department of Transportation, the Pennsylvania Avenue Development Corporation, and the Motor Carrier Ratemaking Study Commission.

The details of each deferral are contained in the attached reports.

RONALD REAGAN

The White House,
September 10, 1981.

Note: The attachments detailing the deferrals are printed in the Federal Register *of September 16, 1981.*

Remarks of the President and Prime Minister Menahem Begin of Israel Following Their Meetings
September 10, 1981

The President. Well, ladies and gentlemen, the Prime Minister and I have had 2 days of friendly and useful and productive talks. I'm greatly encouraged by the common purpose that I have sensed throughout our discussions, and especially pleased by the friendship and complete candor that has developed between us from the very outset of our meetings.

Your views, Mr. Prime Minister, have been invaluable, and your grasp of issues that concern us is truly impressive. We've made progress in charting a course that we'll be following in the peace process in the months ahead. We'll work together to maintain the peace that was concluded between Israel and Egypt and to build on that peace and broaden it.

The United States stands ready to help advance the peace process in any way that is useful to the parties concerned. In our discussions about the strategic situation in the Middle East, it's only natural that we've found much common ground. As friends and as partners in peace, we share a determination to oppose all forces that threaten the freedom, integrity, and peace of our nations.

The United States will remain committed to Israel's security and well-being. We will work together with you and with our other friends in the region to counter Soviet aggression and to strengthen security of all the countries in the area.

Mr. Prime Minister, this is the first of what I know will be many warm and productive meetings between us. I'm delighted to have had this opportunity to come to know you and to discuss the partnership between our two countries. Through our conversations, I believe we've created new bonds of understanding between the United States and Israel, renewed and strengthened our very special friendship.

So, while I know that you are going to continue a few days longer, and while we part, but you will be here longer, I wish you a very pleasant, continued stay in the United States and, above all, a very safe return to Israel.

The Prime Minister. Mr. President, ladies and gentlemen of the press, I subscribe without any qualification to the appreciation of the talks we held in Washington with the President and his advisers. The

American delegation and the Israeli delegation spoke with candor, in detail.

All of us made our work well-prepared, and, therefore, the results can really be considered unanimously by both the President and his advisers and my colleagues and myself as very fruitful. We draw a distinction, a clear distinction, between problems of defending our country when it becomes necessary and the community of moral values and of direct interests between the United States and Israel, as far as the threat to freedom of many nations in the Middle East and elsewhere is concerned.

As far as defense of Israel is concerned, it is our problem. We will never ask any nation to send its soldiers to defend us. Our army will do its duty. We hate war. We hate bloodshed. We want peace. We gave great sacrifices for the sake of peace. We hope to achieve that peace with the other neighbors. But if it should come at any moment when we will have to defend our independence and our liberty and our land, then our young people will do so as they did in the past, in the spirit of self-sacrifice and, I don't hesitate to say, in heroism.

But, there is another problem in our time: a clear community of interests vis-a-vis a clear and present danger to every free nation by a totalitarian and an expansionist regime. On this issue, we work together, we will plan together, we will execute those plans together, in agreement, for the benefit both of the United States and Israel and the free world at large.

Mr. President, we are all grateful to you for the wonderful hospitality you accorded to us. To you and to your gracious lady, Mrs. Reagan, I can only repeat again, "We will be awaiting your visit to our country and to Jerusalem." With God's help you will come. And we shall give you the heartiest reception by a people who have got so great a respect for you as anybody who came to see you, to listen to you, to feel your warmth, your friendship, your readiness to give brotherhood to human beings, can feel.

So, I do not say goodby, Mr. President. I say next time, *au revoir*, in Jerusalem.

Note: The President spoke at 10:12 a.m. on the South Lawn of the White House. Earlier, the President and the Prime Minister held a breakfast meeting in the Oval Office.

Remarks at the Dedication of the General of the Army Douglas MacArthur Corridor at the Department of Defense
September 10, 1981

Mr. Secretary,[1] Mrs. MacArthur, the guests here on the platform, and you ladies and gentlemen, and you of the Armed Forces:

We honor today the memory of Douglas MacArthur and the legend that was his life. It was a legend that began on cavalry outposts in the Old West, where the son of a Civil War hero and Medal of Honor winner first heard the sound of drums and shout of cadence. He would hear those sounds again when he was graduated from West Point with one of the highest academic averages

---

[1] *Secretary of Defense Caspar W. Weinberger.*

in history and with the Academy's greatest honor, First Captain of the Corps, Douglas MacArthur.

As a young officer on a secret and highly dangerous intelligence mission in Mexico, he would win his first recommendation for a Congressional Medal of Honor. Wounded twice in France during World War I, he would be decorated repeatedly for his gallantry under fire and become one of the youngest and most popular generals in American history. As a superintendent of the Military Academy he would bring much needed reform to the West Point curriculum, upgrading scholastic standards while emphasizing the importance of sports.

Words he spoke then are even now inscribed at West Point in stone, "Upon the fields of friendly strife are the seeds that upon other fields, on other days, will bear the fruits of victory."

In the early thirties, as the youngest Army Chief of Staff in history, he warned the Congress of the need for military readiness and a modern army featuring strong armored and air forces. While bearing the brunt of the Japanese attack in 1942, he would win the Congressional Medal of Honor for his heroic defense of the Philippines. And when ordered by President Roosevelt to leave the Islands, he would thrill the Free World with his defiant pledge, "I shall return."

During his brilliant military campaigns in the South Pacific, his island-hopping, hit-'em-where-they-ain't strategy won quick victories with limited resources, victories that saved thousands of American lives, electrified his countrymen, and confounded the enemy. As a post-war ruler of Japan, he showed himself a wise and compassionate statesman who won forever the affection of the Japanese people, even as he brought about one of the most remarkable achievements in the history of self-government. Then in Korea, in the face of brutal aggression, he accomplished one of the most brilliant maneuvers in military history, the Inchon Landing. And in 1951, before a Joint Session of Congress, he would give one of the most memorable speeches in American history, a speech in which he warned, and we must always remember, "In war, indeed, there can be no substitute for victory."

It is true this brilliant career sometimes aroused envy in lesser men. But the General sought to leave intrigue to headquarters staff and politicians. He was always a frontline general, a leader of fighting men. Once at a remote airfield in New Guinea, an officer spotted him near the frontlines and rushed up to him. In a worried voice he pointed to a spot of jungle 50 yards away and said, "Excuse me, sir, but we killed a sniper in there only a few minutes ago." The General answered, "Fine, son, that's the best thing to do with them." [*Laughter*]

Even at the age of 82, he was giving the same inspiring example to young soldiers.

The class of 1962 at West Point will never forget the words they heard from him one May afternoon, words that he began with a bit of humor. He said, "As I was leaving the hotel this morning, a doorman asked me, 'Where you headed for, General?' And when I replied 'West Point,' he remarked 'Beautiful place. Have you ever been there before?' " [*Laughter*]

But then came that unforgettable speech, a speech in which he reminded those young soldiers that duty, honor, country were three hallowed words that reverently dictate what you ought to be, what you can be, and what you will be. "They are your rallying points," he said, "to build courage when courage seems to fail, to regain faith when there seems to be so little cause for faith, to create hope when hope becomes forlorn."

He spoke of his pride in the Long Gray Line that has never failed us. He told the cadets that his last waking thoughts would be of the corps and the corps and the corps. He was extraordinarily proud of his country's uniform. He said of it once, "I suppose in a way this has become a part of my soul. It is a symbol of my life. Whatever I've done that really matters, I've done wearing it. When the time comes, it will be in these that I journey forth. What greater honor could come to an American and a soldier?"

Well, today, a new generation of young officers are asked to defend our nation, just as a new generation of young Americans—to whom World War II, Korea, and even Vietnam are not even within memory—seek to define their own ideals and search for their own answers to ageless questions. Surely, as the tide of time recedes from his era, this new generation will see in Douglas MacArthur an unflinching idealist, an eloquent warrior, a visionary soldier, a gentle conqueror, an authentic American hero.

The General had some words for you young men. He said once that, "Being young meant a temperamental predominance of courage over timidity, and an appetite for adventure over love of ease." He added that, "Nobody grows old by merely living a number of years. People grow old by deserting their ideals."

As long as America affords her brave a place of honor, as long as we as a people seek to keep alive the ideals of selflessness and freedom, as long as we look to the wise and the just for inspiration, our thoughts will turn to the General and the General and the General.

Thank you.

Note: The President spoke at 2:23 p.m. at *the Pentagon.*

The new MacArthur Corridor contains an exhibit area which consists of 4 display cases and 10 story panels. The display cases are dedicated to the Civil War, Corregidor, the return to the Philippines, and West Point. The story panels generally correspond to the 10 parts of the General's book, "Reminiscences."

Nomination of Langhorne A. Motley To Be United States Ambassador to Brazil
September 10, 1981

The President today announced his intention to nominate Langhorne A. Motley, of Alaska, to be Ambassador to Brazil. He would succeed Robert Marion Sayre.

Mr. Motley served in the United States Air Force in 1960–70, successively as launch authentication officer (England), Deputy Combat Crew Commander, Aide to Commander of Air War College, and Aide and Executive Assistant to Commander in Chief (Alaska Command). In 1970–74 he was in real estate development in Anchorage, Alaska, as vice president of Area Realtors, Inc., president of Crescent Realty, Inc., and vice president of RODMAR, Inc. He was Commissioner of Commerce and Economic Development of the State of Alaska at Juneau, Alaska, in 1975–77. He was executive vice president of Citizens for the Management of Alaska Lands, Inc., in 1977–80. Since 1981 he has been president of Valeria, Inc., of Anchorage.

Mr. Motley graduated from The Citadel (B.A., 1960). He is married, has two children, and resides in Anchorage, Alaska. He was born June 5, 1938, in Rio de Janeiro, Brazil.

Nomination of Richard F. Staar To Be United States Representative for Mutual and Balanced Force Reductions Negotiations
September 10, 1981

The President today announced his intention to nominate Richard F. Staar to be Representative of the United States of America for Mutual and Balanced Force Reductions Negotiations, and his intention to nominate Mr. Staar for the rank of Ambassador. He would succeed Jonathan Dean.

In 1949–50 Dr. Staar was an intelligence officer with the Central Intelligence Agency and intelligence research specialist with the Department of State in 1951–54. He was library assistant at the University of Michigan in 1950–51. Dr. Staar was professor of political science at Harding College (1954–57), at Arkansas State College (1957–58), and Emory University (1959–69). In 1958–59 he was also chief of program analysis with Radio Free Europe in Munich, Germany. Since 1969 he has been principal associate director of the Hoover Institution at Stanford University.

He is the author of "Communist Regimes in Eastern Europe; Poland 1944–1962," and coauthor of "Long Range Environmental

Study of the Northern Tier of Eastern Europe in 1990–2000," and many articles and book reviews.

Dr. Staar graduated from Dickinson College (B.A., 1948), Yale University (M.A., 1949), and the University of Michigan (Ph. D., 1954). He is married, has two children, and resides in Stanford, Calif. He was born January 10, 1923, in Warsaw, Poland.

Nomination of Harold Edson Shear To Be Administrator of the Maritime Administration
September 10, 1981

The President today announced his intention to nominate Harold Edson Shear to be Administrator of the Maritime Administration, Department of Commerce.

Admiral Shear is vice president of the Norton Lilly Co., Inc., of New York, N.Y. He was Commander in Chief, Allied Forces, Southern Europe, with headquarters in Naples, Italy, in 1977–80. Previously he was Vice Chief of Naval Operations in 1975–77, Commander in Chief, U.S. Naval Forces, Europe, with headquarters in London, England, in 1974–75, Director of Anti-Submarine Warfare, Department of the Navy, in 1971–74, Director of Submarine Warfare in 1969–71, and Chief of the U.S. Naval Mission to Brazil in 1967–69. Admiral Shear specialized in submarines for 25 years. He commanded the U.S.S. *Becuna* in 1952–54, the U.S.S. *Patrick Henry* in 1959–62, and the Navy's fast combat support ship, U.S.S. *Sacramento*, in 1965–66.

Admiral Shear joined the Navy in 1941 and graduated from the U.S. Naval Academy in 1942. He retired as a four-star admiral in 1980. He is married, has two grown children, and resides in Cambridge, Md. He was born December 6, 1918, in New York, N.Y.

Remarks Following the "Salute to Lionel Hampton" Jazz Concert
September 10, 1981

Aren't we glad that we grew up in the era of the big bands? [*Applause*] Pearl, I don't know why, but as time has gone by I just appreciate old folks more than ever. [*Laughter*]

I'm going to remind her of a little something—I wasn't supposed to say this—that she might not remember. But some years ago, there was a young fellow that at age 21 had just a meteoric rise and skyrocketed in show business. The Friar's Club in Los Angeles was giving a testimonial dinner—a banquet, one of their famous roasts—to this young man. The biggest stars in the entertainment world were all there to entertain and to perform, and he was having a great time at the gathering before the dinner, mingling and so forth. Pearl was sitting over there, and I went over there and sat down beside her, and we watched this for a minute. And then the words of wisdom that have always characterized her came out. She turned to me and said—this was before we all had to go on in this big, star-studded evening—and she said, "I wish he were half as scared as I am." [*Laughter*]

Well, I think this has been a treat, Lionel, that Nancy and I will long remember, and I think we're speaking for everyone here when we say that.

What makes it really special is that it was all put together to honor a truly great American, Lionel Hampton. And the gathering here on the South Lawn of the White House is more than appropriate. This house, I've said before, belongs to the people of the United States. And it's fitting that a man who has contributed so much to the enjoyment and cultural betterment of his fellow citizens should be honored here.

Lionel stands for what's best about America. With raw talent and hard work he became one of the most respected men in American music. I understand when back in his younger days, before he went on to the vibraharp, the older musicians liked to play in groups with Lionel because he was a good-time drummer—he knew how to keep a beat. Well you know, Lionel, I don't think you've missed a beat in all these years. And this happens to be especially true when it comes to courage and decency. This man has always been an example for all of us. He's used his talent and his energy tirelessly, to advance the cause of brotherhood. And I think his strength of character and integrity come through in his music.

Of course, he's a real institution here in Washington. He played for the inaugural celebrations of six Presidents, and Nancy and I are happy that last January we happened to come in under the wire as number six. [*Laughter*]

When I was discussing this event with one of our fellows here on the team, he said, "Lionel Hampton—why he has played with all of the greats." And I said, "My friend, he *is* one of the greats." [*Laughter*]

There are many ways that people make contributions to their country. What you've given to America over these many years can never be taken away. What you've done is make this country a happier place and, I think, speaking for all of us, it's deeply appreciated.

Tonight, as you enjoy yourselves, all of you and those wonderful performers who have been up here with you and those that you introduced in the audience, at the Kennedy Center, the hearts of your fellow citizens are with you, hearts that are a little lighter because of the music you've provided.

Now, I'm going to stop making a speech because, unfortunately, the clean air board wouldn't give us permission to light the barbecue—[*laughter*]—so you're all invited inside for refreshments. Please join us in there.

Note: The President spoke at 6:30 p.m. on the South Lawn of the White House, where the Lionel Hampton Ensemble performed jazz variations of the past, present, and future. They were joined by other entertainers, including Pearl Bailey, Tony Bennett, Dave Brubeck, Woody Herman, Stephanie Mills, and Charlie Pride.

Remarks on Presenting the Young American Medals for Bravery and Service
September 11, 1981

The President. Attorney General Smith, Bill Webster of the FBI, families and friends who are here with these young people, and these young people who are going to be honored today—Senator, we're delighted to have you here:

They come to the White House as already citizen heroes to be honored by their government and their fellow citizens for their courage, their character, and their service.

The true test of civilization, it's been said, is not the census or the size of cities or the crops, but the kind of people the country turns out. And ours is a country that was born of heroes. And now in the first decade of our third century, tried by all the challenges those years could hold, our moral fiber is stronger still.

These nine young Americans are proof of that fiber and that strength. It's now my honor and my privilege to be able to present the Young American Medals for Bravery and Service to nine of our citizens who make all Americans very proud.

The Attorney General is going to present them to me.

The Attorney General. First, Mr. President, let me present Darryl Gregory and Wade Cornick of Virginia Beach, Virginia.

The President. You're Darryl? Wade? Turn around and let these people see you here. Let me tell you what's on the citation just briefly. These two young men here are awarded the Medal of Bravery for their exceptional courage, presence of mind, and swiftness of action. On the fourth day of March 1975, regardless of their personal safety, they rescued Mrs. Isaiah Carr in actual imminent danger of losing her life in a fire in Virginia Beach, Virginia.

Darryl, I'm very proud to present that to you, and congratulations—and to you. Congratulations to you both, and thank you.

The Attorney General. Next, may I present David and Robert Christie, brothers, from Eau Claire, Wisconsin.

The President. The citation there, in greater length than I'm reading here today, determines that these two young men were given the Medal of Bravery for having exhibited exceptional courage, presence of mind, and swiftness of action, and again, regardless of their own personal safety, on the fifth day of August 1975, they rescued nine injured occupants from a burning vehicle near Thorp, Wisconsin.

Is this the one that exploded just after you got them out?

Mr. Christie. Yes.

The President. There you are, and congratulations.

And I left one thing out I should have added. The measure of their heroism is that only a few seconds after they had completed the rescue, the vehicle exploded.

The Attorney General. Next, the winner of the 1976 Young American Medal for Bravery is Donna Lee Slack, of West Bloomfield, Michigan.

The President. Donna Lee Slack is awarded this medal for the same courage and the same swiftness of action and the same disregard for her own personal safety on the 20th day of March 1976, in rescuing three small children when a tornado demolished their home in Bloomfield, Michigan.

Here's your medal, and thank you, and congratulations.

The Attorney General. Next, I would like to present Tim Hoover of Hot Springs, Arkansas, winner of the 1978 Young American Medal for Service.

The President. Just a minute here. Somehow, I have lost a paper. But anyway, we know what it is for, and it is no less heroic: young people that are willing to give of their time and their effort in public service to their fellow man, the young people and those who need our help on a voluntary basis. This is one of the things that we hope we are going to see revived in America, more voluntarism, more effort expended by people in a neighbor-to-neighbor way and less of the officialdom of government intervening in that field.

The medal that he is given is, as I say, for that kind of service that he has rendered. He's from Hot Springs, Arkansas.

The Attorney General. Next, the 1978 Young American Medal for Bravery is to be conferred on Joel Peterson, of Eau Claire, Wisconsin.

The President. Joel, welcome up here. This was December 1978, 3 years ago. Joel, in great danger and risk to himself, laid down on the ice and pulled himself across the ice to rescue his friend who had fallen through the ice on the Eau Claire River and was in imminent danger of drowning, and certainly was disregarding his own personal safety in doing this.

Joel, congratulations. I'm very proud to give you that.

The Attorney General. Mr. President, the winner of the 1979 Young American Medal for Bravery is Jerome Dale of Baltimore, Maryland.

The President. Jerome, congratulations. And here again is a young man who demonstrated that bravery, that disregard for his own welfare, in rescuing two small children from a burning house in Baltimore, Maryland.

Congratulations.

The Attorney General. And finally, may I present the winner of the 1979 Young American Medal for Service, Carmen Maria Hernandez Rodriguez, of Caguas, Puerto Rico.

The President. And here again, Carmen Maria Hernandez Rodriguez is recognized again for that equally heroic task, the long hours in devoting her full time in service to her fellow man. We're deeply grateful to you.

Congratulations.

That concludes our ceremony today. I think all of us should go away a little more inspired. There's nothing wrong with our country when we've got young people doing things like that.

Thank you.

Note: The President spoke at 11:34 a.m. at the presentation ceremony in the Rose Garden at the White House. The ceremony was attended by friends and relatives of the award winners, Justice Department officials, and several Members of Congress.

The awards program, administered by the Department of Justice, was created by an act of Congress in 1950.

Statement on Food Aid for Poland
September 11, 1981

Today's shipment by Catholic Relief Services will provide food for thousands of children, the aged, and the infirm who have experienced severe shortages during the past months. Through the initiative of Catholic Relief Services, the spirited people of Poland will feel the compassion of the American people, who have frequently demonstrated their willingness to lend a hand to the needy around the world.

The milk shipped today was purchased by Catholic Relief Services from the U.S. Government at a favorable price using funds collected in Catholic churches throughout the United States. The distribution in Poland will be handled by the Catholic bishops there and will be based solely on need, rather than on religious or political considerations. I am happy that we are able to be a part of this important humanitarian effort. It is through voluntary agencies like Catholic Relief Services that the American people can express their concern for those who suffer the indignities of hunger and poverty.

Appointment of the Chairman, Vice Chairman, and Members of the Native Hawaiians Study Commission
September 11, 1981

The President today announced his intention to appoint the following individuals as members of the Native Hawaiians Study Commission. The President intends to designate Kina'u Boyd Kamali'i as Chairman and Stephen P. Shipley as Vice Chairman. In addition, he announced that he is calling for the first meeting to be held on September 23, 1981.

Kina'u Boyd Kamali'i is minority leader of the Hawaii House of Representatives. She was elected to the House of Representatives in 1974. She served as State chairman of the Reagan-Bush campaign in Hawaii in 1980. Mrs. Kamali'i was born October 24, 1930, in Honolulu, Hawaii.

Stephen P. Shipley is executive assistant to the Secretary of the Interior. Previously he was vice president of the Mountain States Legal Foundation in Denver, Colo., and assistant manager of the Bonneville Power Administration, Department of Energy. Mr. Shipley was born June 27, 1945, in Jackson, Wyo.

Winona K. D. Beamer is currently retired from Kamehameha Schools in Hawaii. She is a Hawaiian scholar of music and dance with an extensive background in the composition of Hawaiian music (contemporary and ancient). Mrs. Beamer was born August 15, 1923, in Honolulu, Hawaii.

H. Rodger Betts is corporation counsel for the County of Maui. Previously he was General Counsel of the Community Services Administration and an aide to Senator Hiram Fong (R-Hawaii). Mr. Betts was born July 18, 1924, in Waipahu, Oahu, Hawaii.

Carol E. Dinkins is currently Assistant Attorney General, Land and Natural Resources Division, Department of Justice. Prior to her present post, she was principal associate and adjunct assistant professor of law at the University of Houston. Mrs. Dinkins was born November 9, 1945, in Corpus Christi, Tex.

James C. Handley is special assistant to the Secretary of Agriculture. Previously he was assistant director of the Office of Personnel, Governor's Office, State of Illinois. Mr. Handley was born December 28, 1943, in Tuscola, Ill.

Diane K. Morales is Deputy Assistant Secretary for Policy, Territorial and International Affairs, Department of the Interior. Previously she worked with a marketing firm in Houston, Tex. Miss Morales was born July 11, 1946, in Houston, Tex.

Glenn R. Schleede is Executive Associate Director, Office of Management and Budget. Prior to this position, he was senior vice president of the National Coal Association. Mr. Schleede was born June 12, 1933, in Lyons, N.Y.

Memorandum on Defense Spending
September 12, 1981

Memorandum for the Secretary of Defense, the Director of the Office of Management and Budget

Subject: Defense Budget Outlay Ceilings

I am pleased that following our meetings on this subject, your further discussions have resulted in agreed defense budget outlay ceilings for fiscal years 1982–84. I hereby approve your agreement and direct that defense planning and programming be consistent with these outlay ceilings:

Revised defense outlay ceiling:
Fiscal year:

1982	181.8
1983	214.9
1984	242.6

I appreciate the spirit in which you have reached this agreement, and firmly believe that we have struck the balance necessary to assure both an increasingly strong defense and the economic health on which defense and wellbeing depend.

RONALD REAGAN

Statement on Defense Spending by Assistant to the President for Communications David R. Gergen
September 12, 1981

After extensive discussions, President Reagan this afternoon sent a directive to the Secretary of Defense and the Director of the Office of Management and Budget regarding future defense outlays. The President's decision calls for a reduction in defense outlays of $13 billion over fiscal years 1982 through 1984. Based upon initial analyses, Secretary of Defense Caspar Weinberger reported this afternoon that those outlay reductions are likely to result in reductions in total obligational authority of some $21 to $22 billion over the 3-year period.

The Secretary indicated that those figures are preliminary. The final reductions in obligational authority—and I would stress the difference between obligational authority and outlays; the outlay figure of $13 billion is firm—will depend upon the ultimate choice among specific, programmatic, and management alternatives for achieving the outlay reductions.

In the discussions that have occurred over the past several days, the President and his advisers have also considered the defense budgets for fiscal years 1985 and 1986, as previously submitted. The President decided that he would not seek any reductions in those budgets.

After signing this directive at Camp David this afternoon, the President reemphasized that his decision reflects his continuing commitment to two major goals or his administration—a strong economy and a strong national defense.

These changes in the defense budget are, of course, the first reductions on plans previously announced by the President to identify savings in the overall spending that will help to bring the Federal budget into balance by 1984 and, in the process, achieve economic recovery. I might note that this is the defense increment with regard to those reductions. The reductions with regard to other departments will be those that will be forthcoming in the near future. In other words, this is the defense portion of those additional savings that were to be identified.

At the same time, as he reemphasized at Camp David this afternoon, the President believes that it is essential to the security of the nation to embark upon a major, long-term buildup in American defense forces. The President's decision today is intended to ensure that as the nation moves toward a sounder economy, we also restore the margin of safety for the United States.

Note: Mr. Gergen read the statement to reporters at a briefing, which began at 5:55 p.m. in Room 450 of the Old Executive Office Building.

Mr. Gergen also announced that the President had met in the Oval Office on September 11 with Secretary of Defense Caspar W. Weinberger and David A. Stockman, Director of the Office of Management and Budget. A tentative decision as to the size of the defense budget outlays was reached at that meeting. The President telephoned Secretary Weinberger and Mr. Stockman after making his final decision on September 12.

Remarks on Signing a Proclamation Commemorating the 200th Anniversary of the British Surrender at Yorktown, Virginia
September 14, 1981

Good morning, and welcome to the White House. Nancy and I and Vice President Bush and Mrs. Bush are delighted that you could all join us here today for the signing of this proclamation and for the opening of the exhibit appropriately called "The Bicentennial Victory at Yorktown." Now, we don't plan to fire any cannons, although we did offer you fife and drum corps. But this little ceremony is our way of, if you will, of kicking off the big celebration that culminates in Yorktown October 19th—the 200th anniversary date of the American victory there.

Yorktown, of course, represents, as we know, much more than just a military victory. It meant the end of the revolutionary struggle, the beginning of independence, and the gateway to the Constitution. And this triumph pointed the way toward a bright and exciting new future for the rest of the world as well.

So, given the importance of Yorktown, we thought it fitting to invite some special people to be with us today, including the Governors of the Original Thirteen Colonies and the Ambassadors from Ireland, Great Britain, Spain, the Netherlands, Canada, Venezuela, Germany, and, of course, our old friend and valued ally, France. Now, I'm not sure that all of them made it, but I believe a good number are here.

Also, I want to be sure and thank all those in the Federal Government and in the many State and local groups and private organizations across the country who contributed so much to bring the Yorktown Bicentennial to fruition. It would be impossible to name you all, but let me at least single out a few. There's the Vice President, of course, Caspar Weinberger, the Secretary of Defense, and I have to look here because I thought somebody said Jim Watt was going to make it; but I know that he's out on a tour. But his Deputy, Don Hodel, is here, John Marsh, Secretary of the Army, John Lehman, Secretary of the Navy, Verne Orr, the Secretary of the Air Force, John Dalton, the Governor of Virginia, and the Virginia congressional delegation, Bill Fitzgerald, founder of Yorktown International Bicentennial Committee, Lewis McMurran, the chairman of the Virginia Independence Bicentennial Commission, and Richard Maeder, the president of the Yorktown Bicentennial Committee.

Now, I hope I haven't gotten confused or mixed up on any of those, but our thanks to all of them for what they've done.

You know, the historian Douglas Southall Freeman wrote something about this famous battle that we should always remember. He said, "Wheresoever men read history, Yorktown symbolized the inspiring truth that resolution works revolution."

The days ahead will be filled with colorful parades and music and fireworks and great fanfare. But amidst all this celebrating, let's not forget Freeman's message, and let's not forget that our Revolution lasted 8 long years and that it was an uphill battle all the way.

Our soldiers faced overwhelming odds. They endured disaster, and right up to the moment of Yorktown their cause seemed hopeless. But these men were no sunshine patriots. It was their bold vision of liberty and their resolve to win it that filled them with courage to endure, and ultimately to prevail.

History tells us that 56 men signed the original Declaration of Independence in '76, pledging their lives, their fortunes, and their sacred honor. By the Battle of Yorktown in 1781, some had given their lives, most had given their fortunes, but all had preserved their honor.

We Americans today are not often asked to make such sacrifices. Most never have known the kind of winter that our forefathers suffered through at Valley Forge. Nevertheless, it will take new determination, new resolve, to preserve the treasures of our Revolution.

We live in a precarious world threatened by totalitarian forces who seek to subvert and destroy freedom. The peace we enjoy is maintained only by our strength and resolve, and it's our duty to fortify both.

At home, our enemy is no longer Redcoats but red ink. You figured that I'd get to that, didn't you? [*Laughter*] You know, this is a little bit like the fellow at the wedding when the minister got to that portion of the ceremony where he said, "If any one can show just cause why these two should not be wed, let him speak now or forever hold his peace." And in the moment of silence that followed, a voice in the back says, "well, if no one wants to say nothing about the bride and groom, I'd like to say a few words about my home State of Texas." [*Laughter*] I'm going to say it: After 19 deficits in the last 20 years, with a national debt of nearly a trillion dollars, we face a choice of taking drastic action or inviting economic calamity.

Our administration, and I think the American people, have the resolve to do what we know is right and what we know must be done. And make no mistake—we will. But for those in and out of government so quick to carp and complain, so ready to retreat even before the program has begun, I have just two questions: If not us, then who? And if not now, when?

I believe the spirit of Yorktown, the spirit of our Revolution, is still alive and well in America. I'm confident that if we work together, reason together, and stick together, then just like our forefathers, we'll be all right.

That phrase, "reason together," was a favorite of President Lyndon Johnson. It's from a verse in the Bible that begins: Come, let us reason together. It's probably just as well that he left unspoken the rest of the verse. The next line is: If thou refuse, thou shalt be devoured by the sword. [*Laughter*]

Now, I'm going to stop talking long enough to sign this proclamation, if you'll just hold for a second.

[*At this point, the President signed the proclamation.*]

And now we invite you to get in out of the hot Sun and join us in the East Foyer for the official opening of the White House exhibit commemorating the Yorktown Bicentennial. We hope it will be an additional indication to citizens visiting the White House of the historical significance of this event in our nation's birth. So, we shall go and cut the ribbon and see the exhibit.

Thank you all again for being here.

Note: The President spoke at 11 a.m. at the signing ceremony in the First Lady's Garden at the White House.

Proclamation 4857—Yorktown Bicentennial
September 14, 1981

By the President of the United States of America

A Proclamation

On October 19, 1781, the British forces under Lord Cornwallis surrendered at Yorktown, Virginia, to General Washington and our French allies. That surrender signified the practical end of the struggle by our forefathers for liberty and independence. The impossible dream of those patriots was about to be transformed into the reality of a bright new Nation.

As the King's troops came slowly down the road to the surrender field, legend has it that they struck up the tune, "The World Turned Upside Down." And, indeed, the old order was to be turned upside down, for the creative powers of democracy were about to be released on an unsuspecting world.

This year marks the two hundredth anniversary of the surrender. October 19, 1781, was a major date in the development of America and her freedoms; and today, two centuries later, it remains an important reminder of our identity as a nation. The anniversary is also an appropriate time to recall the assistance France gave to America's revolutionary struggle. We, as Americans, are the product of many victories, many sacrifices, and many hopes. The campaign at Yorktown is a historic example.

The Congress has enacted a joint resolution (Public Law 96–414) designating October 19, 1981, as a "Day of National Observance of the Two Hundredth Anniversary of the Surrender of Lord Cornwallis to General George Washington at Yorktown, Virginia." It is fitting that we reflect upon our victory at Yorktown and commemorate it in such a manner as to inspire love of country and devotion to ideals by recalling to this generation the struggles of the past. We can do this at the same time as we give thanks for the great bond of friendship which exists between ourselves and Great Britain.

Now, Therefore, I, Ronald Reagan, President of the United States of America, do hereby proclaim Monday, October 19, 1981, as a day of national observance to remember and to honor the sacrifice of our ancestors in their quest for the political freedom that we enjoy today. I urge all Americans to celebrate again the joyous victory of our forefathers and I urge appropriate officials of the Federal, State, and local governments, as well as private organizations, to observe this day with appropriate ceremonies and activities.

In Witness Whereof, I have hereunto set my hand this 14th day of Sept, in the year of our Lord nineteen hundred and eighty-one, and of the Independence of the United States of America the two hundred and sixth.

RONALD REAGAN

[*Filed with the Office of the Federal Register, 3:45 p.m., September 14, 1981*]

Appointment of Joseph W. Canzeri as Assistant to the President and Assistant to the Deputy Chief of Staff
September 14, 1981

The President today announced the appointment of Joseph W. Canzeri to be Assistant to the President and Assistant to the Deputy Chief of Staff. Mr. Canzeri will serve as a general-purpose assistant to the Deputy Chief of Staff, while continuing to coordinate White House scheduling and advance operations and all Presidential travel. He will also serve as liaison with former Presidents.

Mr. Canzeri, 51, is presently a Deputy Assistant to the President, having joined the White House staff on January 20, 1981. He served as tour director of the 1980 Reagan Presidential campaign.

In 1966–72 Mr. Canzeri served as assistant to the Governor of New York, and in 1974–76 he served as Assistant to the Vice President for Special Events. In 1976–79 he served as personal assistant to Nelson A. Rockefeller. Mr. Canzeri has also served as president of the Greenrock Corp. He has held executive positions with hotels in Cooperstown and Lake Placid, N.Y., and in the Bahamas.

Mr. Canzeri received a degree in hotel administration from Paul Smith's College in 1953. He served in the United States Army in 1949–51. He has one son and resides in the District of Columbia.

Appointment of Richard G. Darman as Assistant to the President and Deputy to the Chief of Staff
September 14, 1981

The President today announced the appointment of Richard G. Darman to be Assistant to the President and Deputy to the Chief of Staff.

In his new position, Mr. Darman will have increased responsibility for the coordination and integration of White House staff activities. He will at the same time continue to serve as Deputy to the Chief of Staff, as White House Staff Secretary, and as coordinator of the Legislative Strategy Group. He will also retain overall management responsibility for the White House operating units.

Mr. Darman joined the White House staff on January 20, 1981, as a Deputy Assistant to the President and Deputy to the Chief of Staff. He served from November 1980 to January 1981 as executive director of the White House transition.

In 1977–80 Mr. Darman was a principal in ICF Inc., a Washington-based consulting firm. He served at the same time as a member of the faculty of Harvard University's Graduate School of Government, from which he is on leave of absence.

Mr. Darman served previously in the Federal Government in five Cabinet departments, including service as Assistant Secretary of Commerce (for Policy) in the Ford administration.

Mr. Darman, 38, was raised in Massachusetts and graduated with honors from Harvard College (B.A., 1964) and Harvard Business School (M.B.A., 1967). He is a former fellow of the Woodrow Wilson International Center for Scholars and the author of several publications in the field of public policy and management. Mr. Darman is married to the former Kathleen Emmet, Ph. D. They live with their sons William (age 5) and Jonathan (age 7 months) in McLean, Va.

Appointment of Craig L. Fuller as Assistant to the President for Cabinet Affairs
September 14, 1981

The President today announced the appointment of Craig L. Fuller to be Assistant to the President for Cabinet Affairs. Mr. Fuller will advance from his present position as Deputy Assistant to the President and Director of the Office of Cabinet Administration. He will continue to coordinate Cabinet activities and will report directly to Presidential Counsellor Edwin Meese.

Prior to joining the White House staff in January, Mr. Fuller served as a vice president and corporate secretary of Deaver & Hannaford, Inc., a Los Angeles-based public affairs consulting firm.

Mr. Fuller received his B.A. degree in political science from the University of California at Los Angeles in 1973 and his master's degree in urban studies from Occidental College in 1974. He was a Coro Foundation public affairs fellow in 1974.

In 1973 he served as a consultant to Governor Reagan's Local Government Reform Task Force. Also, in 1973 he served as a member of the California Housing and Community Development Commission. In 1974 he chaired the California Advisory Commission on Youth and became a public affairs officer for the Pacific Mutual Life Insurance Co. in Los Angeles. In 1977 he joined Deaver & Hannaford, Inc.

Mr. Fuller is married to the former Norine Leas of Los Angeles. They reside in Washington, D.C. Mr. Fuller is 30.

Appointment of Helene von Damm as Deputy Assistant to the President and Director of Presidential Personnel
September 14, 1981

The President today announced the appointment of Helene von Damm as Deputy Assistant to the President and Director of Presidential Personnel. Mrs. von Damm, currently Special Assistant to the President, will succeed John Herrington who is assuming the post of Assistant Secretary of the Navy.

As Director of Personnel, Mrs. von Damm will be responsible for the day-to-day internal management of the complex White House appointments process. In addition, the President intends to continue to rely on her personal assistance as may be required.

Mrs. von Damm has been associated with President Reagan since his first campaign for Governor in California in 1966. She has served him as personal secretary during his two terms as Governor, executive assistant during his business years, and as northeast regional finance director in the 1980 Presidential campaign. After the election, she worked with E. Pendleton James during the transition as associate director of personnel before assuming her present duties in the White House.

Helene von Damm was born and raised in Austria, where she received her formal education before immigrating to the United States in 1959. She recently married Byron Leeds, a New Jersey businessman.

Appointment of Karna Small as Director of White House Media Relations and Planning
September 14, 1981

The President today announced the appointment of Karna Small to be Director, Media Relations and Planning.

Ms. Small, Deputy Assistant to the President and currently serving as Deputy Press Secretary, will direct the Office of Media Relations and Planning, which will have responsibility for long-range planning in communicating the President's programs, media liaison with editors and broadcasters across the country, and the White House Speakers' Bureau.

In her new post, she will be reporting to the Assistant to the President for Communications, David Gergen.

Prior to joining the administration in January 1981, Ms. Small was the writer and moderator of a public affairs television program, produced by the U.S. Chamber of Commerce, which was syndicated in 135 television markets nationwide. She also hosted a 3-hour radio program on WRC Radio (NBC) in Washington on political and economic issues, with guests from the current administration, the House and Senate, business, labor, and academia.

Previously, from 1976 to 1978, she anchored the 10 p.m. news on WTTG–TV in Washington, D.C. From 1972 to 1976, Ms. Small anchored the early evening news on KGO–TV (ABC) in San Francisco, and from 1968 to 1972, she was featured on three newscasts per day on KRON–TV (NBC). During this time, she also commuted to Los Angeles to appear on the 6 p.m. news on KNBC–TV (NBC). Before this, she appeared in many freelance films in the San Francisco Bay area.

Ms. Small received her B.A. degree (with honors) from the University of Michigan and studied journalism and television news in the graduate schools at Stanford and San Francisco State Universities.

She is married to Dan Stringer, executive vice president of The Interface Group, and she has three sons. Ms. Small is a native of Wilmette, Ill.

Appointment of Peter Roussel as Deputy Press Secretary to the President
September 14, 1981

The President today announced the appointment of Peter Roussel to be Deputy Press Secretary to the President.

Mr. Roussel's primary duties will be in the domestic area, providing guidance on issues both to the Press Office and the press. He will also have other duties as assigned. Mr. Roussel will report directly to Larry Speakes, the Principal Deputy Press Secretary.

Mr. Roussel joins the White House from the Houston Chamber of Commerce, where he has served as director of governmental relations.

Mr. Roussel's career in Washington began in 1969, when he was named press secretary to U.S. Congressman George Bush. In 1970 he returned to Texas to serve as campaign press secretary to Mr. Bush in the U.S. Senate race of that year.

Following Mr. Bush's appointment as U.S. Ambassador to the United Nations in 1971, Mr. Roussel was named his personal press officer. When Mr. Bush was appointed Chairman of the Republican National Committee in 1973, Mr. Roussel returned to Washington as his personal press officer until 1974, when Bush reentered the diplomatic service. At that point, Mr. Roussel began a period of service at the White House as Staff Assistant to President Gerald

Ford. In 1975 he was appointed assistant to Chief of Staff Donald Rumsfeld, former U.S. Ambassador to NATO. Mr. Roussel served in a similar capacity to Richard Cheney, Mr. Rumsfeld's successor.

In 1976 Mr. Roussel served on the President Ford Campaign Committee as special assistant to James A. Baker III, national campaign director. In 1978 he was codirector of Mr. Baker's campaign for Attorney General.

Prior to his Washington service, Mr. Roussel was affiliated with the Houston advertising/public relations firm of Rives, Dyke and Co., and worked in numerous Texas political campaigns, including serving as media adviser in Senator John Tower's successful 1966 reelection effort. He has written and produced national award-winning documentary films and published articles.

Mr. Roussel graduated in 1965 from the University of Houston (B.S.). He was born October 23, 1941, in Houston, Tex., and resides in Houston

Appointment of Kathleen Osborne as Personal Secretary to the President
September 14, 1981

The President today announced the appointment of Kathleen Osborne to be Personal Secretary to the President.

Since 1975 Mrs. Osborne has been self-employed with Sacks Howe Avenue in Sacramento, Calif. She worked as a volunteer in the Reagan-Bush campaign headquarters in Sacramento during the 1980 Presidential campaign.

Mrs. Osborne was assistant to Helene von Damm in the Office of the Governor in 1969–72 and was secretary to Mrs. Reagan in 1972–73.

Mrs. Osborne has two children and was born December 4, 1943.

Appointment of Lyndon K. (Mort) Allin as Deputy Press Secretary to the President
September 14, 1981

The President today announced the appointment of Lyndon K. (Mort) Allin to be Deputy Press Secretary to the President.

Mr. Allin's responsibilities will be in the area of foreign affairs, providing guidance on issues and assisting in the coordination with the National Security Council, the State Department, and the Defense Department. He will also continue to serve as Press Office liaison with members of the foreign press corps. Mr. Allin will report to Larry Speakes, Principal Deputy Press Secretary.

A Foreign Service Reserve officer with the U.S. International Communications Agency, Mr. Allin has been Associate Press Secretary since January 20, 1981. In December 1980, he was transferred from the U.S. Embassy in Lagos, Nigeria, to assist the Office of the President-elect in working with foreign correspondents. He went to Lagos as assistant information officer in February 1979. He joined the United States Information Agency in 1975 and has earned Meritorious Service Awards both from USIA and its successor, USICA.

In 1975 Mr. Allin was deputy director of the American Council of Young Political Leaders. From 1968 to 1974, he was editor of the Daily News Summary for Presidents

Nixon and Ford, and Special Assistant to the President in 1973–74. In 1967–68 Mr. Allin was national director of Youth for Nixon. Previously he was a high school social studies instructor in Janesville, Wis.

Mr. Allin graduated from the University of Wisconsin (B.A., 1963). He is married, has two children, and resides in Washington, D.C. He was born February 7, 1941, in Detroit, Mich.

Appointment of Michael E. Baroody as Director of the White House Office of Public Affairs
September 14, 1981

The President today announced the appointment of Michael E. Baroody as Director of the Office of Public Affairs at the White House.

The Public Affairs Office will have the responsibility for the coordination of public affairs offices in the various departments and agencies of the administration, as well as the operation of a central research and information center to serve the White House staff.

The Public Affairs Office will be one of four reporting directly to the Assistant to the President for Communications, David Gergen.

Mr. Baroody, 35, joined the White House staff as Deputy Director of Communications in April 1981, leaving another position as Executive Assistant to the U.S. Trade Representative, Bill Brock.

Mr. Baroody has been public affairs director, and before that research director, at the Republican National Committee from 1977 to 1981. At the RNC, he founded and edited "Commonsense: A Republican Journal of Thought and Opinion," and directed the RNC's involvement in the Republican Party's unprecedented institutional advertising campaign, "Vote Republican. For a Change." He also served as editor-in-chief of the 1980 Republican platform.

Prior to 1977 Mr. Baroody had held various political and governmental positions, including service as executive assistant to Senator Bob Dole (R-Kans.) and legislative assistant to Senator Roman Hruska (R-Nebr.).

A native of the Washington, D.C., area, Mr. Baroody served in the U.S. Navy from 1968 to 1970 and is a graduate of the University of Notre Dame. He and his wife Muff and their six children reside in Alexandria, Va.

Appointment of James S. Rosebush as Special Assistant to the President in the Office of the Deputy Chief of Staff
September 14, 1981

The President today announced the appointment of James S. Rosebush as Special Assistant to the President in the Office of the Deputy Chief of Staff.

His responsibilities include the development of a private sector initiatives strategy for the President. Mr. Rosebush joined the administration on May 1, 1981, as Director of the Office of Business Liaison, U.S. Department of Commerce. To assume the role, Mr. Rosebush resigned his position with the Standard Oil Co. (SOHIO), where he had responsibility for a $10 million corporate contributions program.

Prior to this association with SOHIO, he was vice president for two affiliates of the Chamber of Commerce of the United States—the National Chamber Foundation, a public policy research group, and Citizens Choice, a national grassroots taxpayers lobby. Prior to his experience with the U.S. Chamber, he was a management consultant in Boston, specializing in corporate community affairs and organizational development. He also worked for two private foundations—the C. S. Mott Foundation in Flint, Mich., and the Associated Foundation of Greater Boston, in Boston, Mass.

Mr. Rosebush has a B.A. in business administration from the Principia College in Elsah, Ill., and an M.A. in public affairs from Boston University. He has taught at Georgetown University and George Washington University on the subject of corporate/public issues management and the history of philanthropy.

Originally from Flint, Mich., Mr. Rosebush now resides in Washington, D.C., with his wife, the former Nancy Paull, and his two daughters. He is 32 years old.

Appointment of the Chairman, Executive Director, and Membership of the President's Commission on Executive Exchange
September 14, 1981

The President today announced his intention to appoint the following individuals to be members of the President's Commission on Executive Exchange. Robert E. Kirby will also serve as Honorary Chairman and June Grace Walker will serve as Executive Director.

Samuel Armacost, president and chief executive officer, Bank of America

James A. Baker III, Assistant to the President and Chief of the White House staff

Malcolm Baldrige, Secretary of Commerce

William M. Batten, chairman, New York Stock Exchange

A. George Battle, partner, Arthur Andersen and Co.

Roger E. Birk, chairman, president, and chief executive officer, Merrill-Lynch and Co.

Thornton F. Bradshaw, chairman and chief executive officer, RCA Corp.

James E. Burke, chairman and chief executive officer, Johnson and Johnson

Willard C. Butcher, chairman and chief executive officer, Chase Manhattan Corp.

William P. Clark, Deputy Secretary of State

David W. Christopher, partner, Price Waterhouse and Co.

Donald J. Devine, Director, Office of Personnel Management

Coy G. Eklund, president and chief executive officer, Equitable Life Assurance Society

Max L. Friedersdorf, Assistant to the President for Legislative Affairs

Harry J. Gray, chairman and chief executive officer, United Technologies Corp.

Edwin L. Harper, Deputy Director, Office of Management and Budget

David T. Kearns, president and chief operating officer, Xerox Corp.

James L. Ketelsen, chairman and chief executive officer, Tenneco, Inc.

John F. McGillicuddy, chairman, president, and chief executive officer, Manufacturers Hanover Corp.

John K. McKinley, chairman and chief executive officer, Texaco, Inc.

Ruben F. Mettler, chairman and chief executive officer, TRW, Inc.

Betty Southard Murphy, partner, Baker and Hostetler

Frederick W. O'Green, president and chief operating officer, Litton Industries, Inc.

John R. Opel, president and chief executive officer, IBM Corp.

Donald T. Regan, Secretary of the Treasury

David Rockefeller, chairman, Chase International Advisory Committee, Chase Manhattan Bank

David M. Roderick, chairman and chief executive officer, United States Steel Corp.

James Roosevelt, president, James Roosevelt and Co.

Spyros S. Skouras, chairman, president, and chief executive officer, Prudential Lines, Inc.

Helene A. von Damm, Deputy Assistant to the President

William B. Walsh, chairman, Project HOPE

John C. Whitehead, senior partner, Goldman, Sachs and Co.

Marina v. N. Whitman, vice president, General Motors Corp.

Remarks at a White House Reception for Members of the Davis Cup and Wightman Cup Tennis Teams
September 14, 1981

The President. First of all, I think on behalf of all of us, I want to thank the two gentlemen who gave us this exhibition and then to welcome all of you here.

We're delighted to have you here, and we had originally planned, you know, to have some of our White House staff also do an exhibition, and I was preparing some remarks——

Mrs. Reagan. They chickened out.

The President. What?

Mrs. Reagan. They chickened out.

The President. Yes, they chickened out, Nancy said. [*Laughter*]

I was preparing some remarks, and I didn't know whether to have some facetious remarks in which I would say, "They were better at their jobs than they are on the court," or whether I was to be generous and say, "Well, they're just as good at their jobs as they are here,"—and that could be taken wrong. So, anyway they settled that for me.

We are pleased to have you here. Tennis, of course, in recent years, beginning about 1968, really, has stepped off and become one of the great national sports. There are now, as I believe, 92 tournaments. And we're very proud to have the Davis Cup team, the Wightman Cup players, team, here. We were very proud of what our ladies in the Wightman Cup did to the British, and we were proud of the Davis Cup team in defeating last year's champions, the good Czechoslovakian team, in New York. And we're all going to be watching them next month and rooting for them in that.

Tennis not only belongs to the expert players of the kind that are on those teams and that are in the tournaments and that we've been seeing the last couple of days on television. Tennis has become such a general sport. It is estimated that there are some 32 million people playing it, and it's become a family sport. We can now believe that a family that plays together stays together, and parents and children can be found playing. Sometimes the parents win. I was going to take up tennis again until I found out you couldn't get the horse on the court. [*Laughter*]

Now, I just want to say that with regard to your first suggestion about the net here, that "appropriation" was the wrong word. Dave Stockman, wherever he was, flinched. [*Laughter*] "Contribution," yes, that would be acceptable.

But again, we want to thank you all for being here. And now I'm going to quit talking, because I understand all of us are to go up there on the West Lawn.

Mrs. Reagan. Arthur wanted to introduce the players.

The President. Oh! Fine, you do that. And then I'll make the announcement I was going to make.

These Izod shirts say "White House Tennis Court" on them. And speaking of contributions, each member of the Wightman Cup and the Davis Cup are going to receive one of these shirts.

Mr. [Arthur] Ashe. Before we depart, Mr. President, I would like to introduce the members of the Davis Cup and the Wightman Cup teams who are here. Here she comes, one more. To Mrs. Reagan's immediate left, newly crowned 1981 U.S. Open Champion and a Davis Cup stalwart who has never failed us when we've asked, John McEnroe.

His partner in crime on the doubles court, Wimbledon and U.S. Open Doubles Champion, Peter Fleming.

Former Wightman Cup player, now Wightman Cup captain, Rosie Casals.

Fresh from her victory 2 days ago, the 1981 U.S. Open Champion for the second time now, Tracy Austin.

Next to her, 3 years ago I think it was, runner-up U.S. Open to Chris Evert Lloyd, Pam Shriver.

And she threw away her bubble gum today, Andrea Jaeger, 15 years old—sorry, 16.

Next to her, of course, our two players, Stan Smith and Marty Riessen.

And I'd also like to introduce—because it is appropriate and this is a national team, the two national teams that we are representing here today—president of the USTA, Marvin Richmond, and chairman of the USTA Davis Cup Committee, Gordon Jorgensen. Gordon, where are you? There he is. Thank you very much.

The President. All I have left to say is that there are going to be refreshments up there on the West Lawn, and we'll all just head that way right now. Thank you all again.

Ms. Shriver. Just one more moment, please. If Mr. President cannot bring a horse onto the tennis court, at least maybe he can bring a Prince, so I'd like to give him a Prince tennis racquet.

The President. Well, thank you very much.

Ms. Shriver. Thank you for having us.

Ms. Jaeger. And if he doesn't want to start tennis again, he can just stick with his jellybeans. [*Laughter*]

[*At this point, Ms. Jaeger presented the President with a gift of jellybeans.*]

The President. Well, that beats one of those boats in a bottle. [*Laughter*] Thank you very much, and you're almost forcing me into it now. I can see the Attorney General down there now. Mr. Smith is looking up. He is one of our tennis-playing set here in the Capital. You realize that I could win almost from the very first by Executive order. [*Laughter*]

Well, shall we go up for the refreshments?

Note: The President spoke at 5:36 p.m. at the White House tennis courts.

Executive Order 12321—Foreign Assistance and Arms Export Control
September 14, 1981

By the authority vested in me as President of the United States of America by Section 515(f) of the Foreign Assistance Act of 1961, as amended (22 U.S.C. 2321i(f)), Section 29 of the Arms Export Control Act, as amended (94 Stat. 3133; 22 U.S.C. 2769), and Section 301 of Title 3 of the United States Code, it is hereby ordered as follows:

Section 1. Section 1–701(d) of Executive Order No. 12163 of September 29, 1979, is amended by deleting "515(f),".

Sec. 2. Section 1(d) of Executive Order No. 11958 of January 18, 1977, is amended

to read as follows: "Those under Sections 22(a) and 29 of the Act to the Secretary of Defense.".

RONALD REAGAN

The White House,
September 14, 1981.

[*Filed with the Office of the Federal Register, 4:02 p.m., September 15, 1981*]

Note: The text of the Executive order was released by the Office of the Press Secretary on September 15.

Executive Order 12320—Historically Black Colleges and Universities
September 15, 1981

By the authority vested in me as President by the Constitution of the United States of America, in order to advance the development of human potential, to strengthen the capacity of historically Black

colleges and universities to provide quality education, and to overcome the effects of discriminatory treatment, it is hereby ordered as follows:

Section 1. The Secretary of Education shall supervise annually the development of a Federal program designed to achieve a significant increase in the participation by historically Black colleges and universities in Federally sponsored programs. This program shall seek to identify, reduce, and eliminate barriers which may have unfairly resulted in reduced participation in, and reduced benefits from, Federally sponsored programs. This program will also seek to involve private sector institutions in strengthening historically Black colleges.

Sec. 2. Annually, each Executive Department and those Executive agencies designated by the Secretary of Education shall establish annual plans to increase the ability of historically Black colleges and universities to participate in Federally sponsored programs. These plans shall consist of measurable objectives of proposed agency actions to fulfill this Order and shall be submitted at such time and in such form as the Secretary of Education shall designate. In consultation with participating Executive agencies, the Secretary of Education shall undertake a review of these plans and develop an integrated Annual Federal Plan for Assistance to Historically Black Colleges for consideration by the President and the Cabinet Council on Human Resources (composed of the Vice President, the Secretaries of Health and Human Services, Agriculture, Labor, Housing and Urban Development, and Education, the Attorney General, the Counsellor to the President, and the White House Chief of Staff).

Sec. 3. Each participating agency shall submit to the Secretary of Education a mid-year progress report of its achievement of its plan and at the end of the year an Annual Performance Report which shall specify agency performance of its measurable objectives.

Sec. 4. Prior to the development of the First Annual Federal Plan, the Secretary of Education shall supervise a special review by every Executive agency of its programs to determine the extent to which historically Black colleges and universities are given an equal opportunity to participate in Federally sponsored programs. This review will examine unintended regulatory barriers, determine the adequacy of the announcement of programmatic opportunities of interest to these colleges, and identify ways of eliminating inequities and disadvantages.

Sec. 5. The Secretary of Education shall ensure that each president of a historically Black college or university is given the opportunity to comment on the proposed Annual Federal Plan prior to its consideration by the President, the Vice President, and the Cabinet Council on Human Resources.

Sec. 6. The Secretary of Education, to the extent permitted by law, shall stimulate initiatives by private sector businesses and institutions to strengthen historically Black colleges and universities, including efforts to further improve their management, financial structure, and research.

Sec. 7. The Secretary of Education shall submit to the President, the Vice President, and the Cabinet Council on Human Resources an Annual Federal Performance Report on Executive Agency Actions to Assist Historically Black Colleges. The report shall include the performance appraisals of agency actions during the preceding year to assist historically Black colleges and universities. The report will also include any appropriate recommendations for improving the Federal response directed by this Order.

Sec. 8. The special review provided for in Section 4 shall take place not later than November 1, 1981. Participating Executive agencies shall submit their annual plans to the Secretary of Education not later than January 15, 1982. The first Annual Federal Plan for Assistance to Historically Black Colleges developed by the Secretary of Education shall be ready for consideration by the President, the Vice President, and the Cabinet Council on Human Resources not later than March 31, 1982.

Sec. 9. Executive Order No. 12232 of August 8, 1980, is revoked.

RONALD REAGAN

The White House,
September 15, 1981.

[Filed with the Office of the Federal Register, 1:25 p.m., September 15, 1981]

Remarks at a White House Luncheon for Officials of Black Colleges and Universities
September 15, 1981

Thank you all very much. And, Reverend, thank you very much for your suggestion earlier which we should have thought of. I don't know of a place where prayer is more appropriate than in Washington, D.C. [*Laughter*]

But we're gathered today because all of us want to nourish and protect an American institution that has served this Nation well. And I am, of course, referring to the traditional black colleges and universities. Hundreds of thousands of young Americans received training at these schools over the last 100 years, expanding their opportunities as individuals and laying the foundation for social progress.

It should never be forgotten that when educational opportunities were denied elsewhere, these institutions offered hope to black Americans—hope for a better life and hope that someday they would break the bonds of prejudice and discrimination.

These educational institutions did their job well. They have produced 50 percent of the black business executives, 75 percent of the black military officers, 80 percent of the black judges, and 85 percent of black physicians in this country.

The Black colleges and universities in America have offered black citizens a variety of opportunities to develop their skills and talents, and it's through such diversity that freedom flourishes. And it is through education, the education they offer, that individuals can make themselves into the type of people they choose to be and not what some central planner says they should be.

In pursuit of equal opportunity for black Americans, economics becomes as important as education. For a long period of our history, black people were prevented the chance of bettering themselves not only because they were denied the opportunity to learn, but because job opportunities were limited as well. It will do no good to educate young people if there are no jobs for them once they get out of school. And you,

more than any of our citizens, know how important a vibrant economy is to the progress of black Americans, particularly, and all Americans as well.

America's declining economy cut black family income. From 1959 to 1969, the median family income of blacks after adjusting for inflation rose at 5 percent per year. But from 1969 to 1979, it stopped going up, and that median income actually dropped.

Now I believe that our economic program will provide more opportunity for all Americans, including black college graduates. Most black progress has occurred during times of prosperity in America, and we're working to create a new era of prosperity for everyone.

Economic dislocation hurts institutions as well as individuals. America's colleges and universities have been hard-pressed to maintain standards in the face of inflation that increases the cost of everything from books to typewriters. It doesn't help very much when government regulations have multiplied to the point that a president of a modest-sized college or small university told me one day that just complying with government regulation paperwork had increased his administrative overhead in that department from $50,000 a year to $650,000 a year. That will buy a lot of courses and a lot of teaching and training—that kind of money.

With this in mind, with a serious commitment to protecting these unique educational institutions, we've made certain that in an era of budget cuts, black colleges and universities will actually receive a $9.6 million increase in Federal title III funds. Now, this is a jump of almost 8 percent. In our continuing review of Executive orders, we found a need to improve upon an existing order on historically black colleges, and that's why I was happy today to sign that new order that will strengthen the Federal commitment to the historic black colleges, while seeking new ways for the private sector to increase its support for these vital institutions.[1]

Our commitment takes several forms. First, the Executive order commits us to increase black college participation in federally sponsored programs. Secondly, this order mandates governmentwide coordination to ensure that these colleges and universities are given a full opportunity to participate in federally sponsored programs. Now, we all know that the Federal Government has a troublesome history of issuing reports with no teeth in them. Well, this administration believes in setting measurable objectives and then turning loose the creative resources to meet them. To ensure that the annual Federal plan called for in this order gets results, I am directing Secretary of Education Bell to submit an annual performance report on executive agency actions to carry out their plans. This is management by objectives in action. And the report card prepared by Secretary Bell will be reviewed by the Cabinet Council on Human Resources, the Vice President, and me.

You know, I've never forgotten the President who once stood in this room and said

---

[1] *Prior to the luncheon, the President signed Executive Order 12320 in a brief ceremony in the Blue Room at the White House. The President made the following remarks to the black college and university officials who viewed the signing:*

I'm very happy to sign this Executive order which commits the Federal Government to more support with regard to our historic black colleges, and also it commits us to a program of encouraging more private support with those same educational institutions. So, without further ado—because I'll be talking to you later—[laughter]—I'm going to put my name on the Executive order.

that sometimes he had wanted to find out when he issued an Executive order where out there in the bureaucracy did it just sink into the sand like water and disappear and never be heard from again. Well, this one is going to be heard from again with an annual report card, as I say—and they better pass.

Now, to reinforce this administration's commitment, I'm asking Vice President Bush to play a special role. He will work with the heads of Federal agencies to help ensure the fullest cooperation possible in conducting a special policy review to serve as a basis for all our future planning on black colleges and universities. He will then discuss the findings with the presidents of the historically black colleges.

And finally, this Executive order breaks new ground by calling on the Secretary of Education to encourage private sector initiatives in assisting these historic black institutions. The Federal Government's role can be to provide equal opportunity, but the private sector has an even greater potential and a challenging responsibility to provide direct assistance to these institutions.

We should remember that just as in the past, the future of these schools will depend more than anything else on the efforts of black Americans. What has been accomplished already is a tremendous source of pride, but now is not the time to rest on past accomplishments. The future depends on an even stronger commitment to excellence and diversity in education. And to paraphrase the motto of the United Negro College Fund: Let us recognize that America's historic black college is a "terrible thing to waste." And we're not going to allow it to be wasted.

Thank you very much.

Note: The President spoke at 1:10 p.m. in the State Dining Room at the White House.

Nomination of James J. Carey To Be a Commissioner of the Federal Maritime Commission
September 15, 1981

The President today announced his intention to nominate James J. Carey to be a Federal Maritime Commissioner for the remainder of the term expiring June 30, 1985.

He would succeed Peter N. Teige.

Since 1980 Mr. Carey has been business development manager with Telemedia, Inc. He was a management consultant to Telemedia in 1978–79. Mr. Carey is currently responsible for the development and implementation of major international training and technology transfer programs involving Navy/seagoing training projects. Previously Mr. Carey was president, Coordinated Graphics, in 1976–78; executive vice president, Total Graphic Communication, Inc., in 1974–76; and president of the Chicago Offset Corp. in 1972–74.

Mr. Carey served in the U.S. Navy in 1962–65 as an officer in the First and Seventh Fleets and held three commands. He graduated from Northwestern University. He has two children and resides in Lake Bluff, Ill. He was born April 9, 1939, in Berlin, Wis.

Nomination of Joseph Wentling Brown To Be a Member of the Foreign Claims Settlement Commission of the United States
September 15, 1981

The President today announced his intention to nominate Joseph Wentling Brown to be a member of the Foreign Claims Settlement Commission of the United States, Department of Justice, for the term expiring September 30, 1983. He would succeed Francis Leon Jung.

Mr. Brown was an associate attorney with Laxalt, Bell, Berry, Allison and LeBarron in Las Vegas from 1969 to 1971, when Bell and LeBarron formed their own firm which Mr. Brown joined. In 1973 the firm of Bell and LeBarron merged and became known as Jones, Jones, Bell, Close and Brown, Ltd. Since 1979 he has been commissioner of the Nevada Department of Wildlife. Mr. Brown is a member of the Nevada, District of Columbia, and American Bar Associations.

Mr. Brown graduated from the University of Virginia (B.A., 1965) and Washington and Lee University (LL.B., 1968). He served in the U.S. Marine Corps Reserve in 1963–69. Mr. Brown is married, has four children, and resides in Las Vegas, Nev. He was born July 31, 1941, in Norfolk, Va.

Nomination of the United States Representative and Alternate Representatives to the 25th Session of the General Conference of the International Atomic Energy Agency
September 15, 1981

The President today announced his intention to nominate the following individuals to be the Representative and Alternative Representatives of the United States of America to the Twenty-fifth Session of the General Conference of the International Atomic Energy Agency, which is scheduled to be held in Vienna, Austria, from September 21 through September 25, 1981:

Representative

W. *Kenneth Davis* is currently Deputy Secretary of Energy. Previously he was adjunct professor of engineering and applied science, University of California at Los Angeles, in 1980–81; vice president for development, Bechtel Group, Inc., in 1958–81; and chief development engineer, California Research and Development Co., in 1950–54. He was born July 26, 1918, in Seattle, Wash.

Alternate Representatives

Richard T. Kennedy is currently United States Representative to the International Atomic Energy Agency, with the rank of Ambassador. He is also Under Secretary of State for Manage-

ment. Previously he was Commissioner, United States Nuclear Regulatory Commission, in 1975–80 and Deputy Assistant to the President for National Security Council Planning in 1969–75. He was born December 24, 1919, in Rochester, N.Y.

Roger Kirk has been in the Foreign Service since 1949. He is currently Deputy Representative of the United States to the International Atomic Energy Agency, with the rank of Ambassador. He was born November 2, 1930, in Newport, R.I.

Thomas M. Roberts is currently a member of the Nuclear Regulatory Commission. Previously he was president and chief executive officer of Southern Boiler and Tank Works, Inc., in Memphis, Tenn. He was born April 14, 1937, in Memphis, Tenn.

Appointment of Three Members of the President's Commission on Housing
September 15, 1981

The President today announced his intention to appoint the following individuals to be members of the President's Commission on Housing:

Myra Goldwater is a realtor in Palm Springs, Calif. Mrs. Goldwater has served as director of the National Association of Realtors since 1978. She was president of the Palm Springs Board of Realtors in 1973–74, and was director of the California Association of Realtors in 1973–78. She has been a member of the Palm Springs Chamber of Commerce for 10 years and has served as a member of the Chamber's board of directors for 3 years. Mrs. Goldwater is married, has one daughter, and resides in Palm Springs. She was born in St. Louis, Mo.

Jasper Stillwell Hawkins is an architect and partner in the firm of Hawkins, Lindsey, Wilson Associates of Phoenix, Ariz. He founded the firm in 1978. He was appointed by President Ford to the Board of Directors of the National Institute of Building Sciences in 1976. He was a member of the U.S. Delegation to the U.N. Economic Commission for Europe's Working

Party on the Building Industry since 1978, and a member of the American Institute of Architects National Codes and Standards Committee since 1970. He is also a member of the California Council of the American Institute of Architects Task Force on Factory Built Housing. Mr. Hawkins graduated from the University of Southern California. He is married, has four children, and resides in Phoenix, Ariz. He was born November 10, 1932, in Orange, N.J.

George Peter Shafran is president and chief executive officer of the Realty Programming Corporation/Homes for Living Network. Mr. Shafran has been in the real estate profession since 1950. He founded Better Homes Realty, Inc., in 1951. The firm now has 23 offices in northern Virginia, Maryland, and the District of Columbia. He received the "Realtor of the Year" award in 1965 and is president of the Northern Virginia Board of Realtors. Mr. Shafran attended Bucknell University, Brown University, American University, and George Washington University. He is married, has four children, and resides in Arlington, Va. He was born May 4, 1926, in Atlas, Pa.

Nomination of Sonia Landau To Be a Member of the Corporation for Public Broadcasting
September 15, 1981

The President today announced his intention to nominate Sonia Landau to be a member of the Corporation for Public Broadcasting for the remainder of the term expiring March 26, 1986. She would succeed Melba Pattila Beals.

Ms. Landau served on the Presidential transition team on the National Endowment for the Arts in 1981. Previously she was executive director of the New York State Republican Finance Committee in 1980. In 1978-79 she was employed with J. Walter Thompson of London, England. Ms. Landau was director of corporate affairs, The Drey-

fus Corp., New York, N.Y., in 1977-78. She was the Republican nominee for the U.S. Congress for the 18th Congressional District in New York in 1976. In 1973-75 Ms. Landau was a media specialist with Roger Ailes and Associates, Inc., of New York. She was director of radio and television at the National Republican Congressional Campaign Committee in 1969-72.

Ms. Landau graduated from the University of Denver (B.A., 1958) and the University of California. She resides in New York, N.Y., and was born on July 14, 1937, in Wichita, Kans.

Nomination of R. Kenneth Towery To Be a Member of the Corporation for Public Broadcasting
September 15, 1981

The President today announced his intention to nominate R. Kenneth Towery to be a member of the Corporation for Public Broadcasting for the remainder of the term expiring March 26, 1986. He would succeed Reuben W. Askanase.

Mr. Towery is president and founder of the Sentinel Corp., a business and political consulting firm in Austin, Tex. He is also managing partner with the firm of Towery, Schulle and Associates. Previously Mr. Towery was assistant to the chancellor, the University of Texas System, in 1976-79; Assistant Director, and Deputy Director, of the United States Information Agency in 1969-76; press secretary, and then administrative assistant, to Senator John Tower in 1963-69; Capitol correspondent with Newspapers, Inc., in 1956-63; and reporter and

managing editor for Cuero Daily Record, a small daily newspaper in Cuero, Tex., in 1951-56. He was awarded the Pulitzer Prize in 1955 for a series of stories exposing fraud and corruption in the Texas Veterans Land Program.

Mr. Towery attended Southwest Texas Junior College and Texas A&M University. He entered the U.S. Army as a volunteer during World War II and served in the Philippines where he was captured and imprisoned for 3½ years. He was awarded the Purple Heart, the Presidential Unit Citation with two Oak Leaf Clusters, and other decorations.

Mr. Towery is married, has two children, and resides in Austin, Tex. He was born January 25, 1923, in Smithville, Miss.

Remarks at a White House Reception for Representatives of the Business Community
September 15, 1981

Thank you, thank you all very much. It's a privilege to welcome you here to the White House this evening. You and those you represent were not only the key to the successes of our bipartisan coalition, you're the key to economic recovery of this Nation.

I see many familiar faces—just as we hurried through the crowd here—and I met with many of you as we pushed for the largest tax and budget cuts in our history. But I know that all of you here worked very hard to make those goals a reality. You and your neighbors and coworkers wrote letters and made phone calls and visited your Congressmen to get them passed. And Members of Congress later spoke of being overwhelmed by the outpouring of support. They spoke of it; they screamed about it. [*Laughter*] They said no one could get through on their phone lines.

But we do owe you a great vote of thanks. But you didn't do all of that work for a thank you, as you better than most see the necessity of restoring free enterprise to American life. You understand the bottom line of profit and loss, and you know that people, businesses, and governments must live within their means. Representing all aspects of American life, you know the opportunity in store for all of us if we reawaken our entrepreneurial spirit.

For too long there's been an adversary relationship between government and its own business community. The freedom to take a risk, to reap its rewards, to work harder for a better wage, to climb as high as your own ambition and effort will take you—that kind of freedom is basic to the dream that is America and essential for the return of economic health in this country.

After decades of big government spending, there were some who didn't believe that the American people would take action to change that—but they did. And when I first came to office there were some who said the people didn't care enough to insist if Congress went along—but they did. And

now there are those who doubt the staying power of the American people, who don't understand our commitment. And for those doubting Thomases, I have a message—they're wrong again.

I think what must have been a thrill to you, and has been the biggest thrill to me in all these months, was to discover how the American people believe in America and in themselves. There's a great deal of confusion at the moment, I know. Yes, our economic recovery program has been passed by the Congress, signed into law, but it's not yet in effect.

The legislation that was passed this summer was historic, but that was only a beginning. We've only started on the long, hard road toward recovery, yet suddenly we hear some saying that our programs aren't working. Well, of course they're not; they don't start until October 1st. [*Laughter*] And when they do start, they're aimed at reversing three decades or more of mistaken economic policy, and they're not offered as a quick fix. It isn't going to happen overnight. But they will work.

I'm as committed today as on the first day I took office to balancing the budget, freeing the people from punitive taxation, and making America once again strong enough to safeguard our freedom. And I'm surer today than I ever was that we can achieve all three of those things. We'll continue to make budget adjustments as needed, and we'll hold the line. And I hope we have the same kind of bipartisan support that we had in passing the program, as we now have a need to resist the efforts to increase spending through appropriation bills. As for myself, with regard to that, I will not hesitate to use the veto to block any such efforts.

And let me silence those, those who would scare our older Americans. The budget will not be balanced at the expense of those dependent on social security. That system has serious problems; but we have sent our proposals to the Congress, and we have no plans to change them.

Now, I thank all of you for all that you've done to give our country a new beginning, but I remind you there are many trials yet ahead. I hope we can count on your help, the help that was so invaluable in the past. Together, I think that we're equal to our challenges, and together, we'll surmount them. So again, it's just a heartfelt thanks.

And now I have a couple of presentations to make. You know, there were a lot of people—you and all the help, as I've said, that you gave—but here in Washington, there were a few people that before the fight was over must have wondered why they made the decision to come here in the first place. And so I have a couple of presentations to make.

Two people that had to have worked as hard as anyone in the world were Dave Stockman, Office of Management and Budget—and he put in more hours than there really are—[*laughter*]. And this is just a little souvenir we thought that you might like. It contains the first page and the last page of that great reduction in government spending, the one where you put your name and make it legal, and one of the pens that was used to sign it. Dave? There you are.

And then someone else who must have wondered if he shouldn't have second thoughts, but he was one of the heroes of getting this done, equal in the number of hours, day after day, and doing a great job of selling all the time. This is the front page and this is that last one, the bottom line, where the signatures go. To Don Regan. And this is the tax program that reduced our taxes.

There's a double signature on there. I thought there ought to be a little personalized note on each one of them. [*Laughter*]

Well, there is no way to measure what they did and the work that they put in, and it's a shame to just have to say that that was only a battle—the war still goes on. [*Laughter*] So, they'll be still at it for months and months to come, not only in getting this '82 budget passed, but then, as we said before, we are working on the unspecified cuts that must be made in the budget for '83 and '84, and we're going to now make them specific.

But again, and I know they'll agree with me, there will be no retreat. So, I'll turn you over now to this memorable gathering.

Thank you very much.

Note: The President spoke at 5:33 p.m. on the South Lawn of the White House.

Nomination of C. Everett Koop To Be Surgeon General of the Public Health Service
September 16, 1981

The President today announced his intention to nominate C. Everett Koop to be Surgeon General of the Public Health Service for a term of 4 years. He would succeed Julius Benjamin Richmond.

Dr. Koop is currently serving as Deputy Assistant Secretary of Health, Department of Health and Human Services. He was surgeon-in-chief of Children's Hospital of Philadelphia, Pa., and professor of pediatric surgery at the University of Pennsylvania Medical School. He has been associated with the University of Pennsylvania since 1941.

He graduated from Dartmouth College (A.B., 1937), Cornell Medical School (M.D., 1941), Graduate School of Medicine of the University of Pennsylvania (Sc. D., 1947). He has received many honorary degrees and is the author of more than 170 articles and books on the practice of medicine.

Dr. Koop is a member of the Commission on Cancer, American College of Surgeons; the Surgical Steering Committee, Children's Cancer Study Group; Cancer Committee, American Pediatric Surgical Association; Arbitration Panel for Health Care, Commonwealth of Pennsylvania.

He is married, has four children, and re-

sides in Gladwyne, Pa. He was born on October 14, 1916, in New York City.

Nomination of Edgar F. Callahan To Be a Member of the National Credit Union Administration, and Designation as Chairman
September 16, 1981

The President today announced his intention to nominate Edgar F. Callahan to be a member of the National Credit Union Administration. Upon confirmation, the President intends to designate Mr. Callahan Chairman. He would succeed Harold A. Black.

Mr. Callahan is serving in his third term as director, Department of Financial Institutions, State of Illinois. Previously he was deputy secretary of state (Illinois), in 1975–

77; superintendent, Rockford Area Catholic Board of Education, in 1971–75; principal, vice principal, and instructor, Boyland Central Catholic High School, Rockford, Ill., in 1960–75.

He graduated from Marquette University (B.S., 1951; M.A., 1952). He is married, has eight children, and resides in Springfield, Ill. Mr. Callahan was born March 23, 1928, in Youngstown, Ohio.

Proclamation 4858—Citizenship Day and Constitution Week, 1981
September 16, 1981

By the President of the United States of America

A Proclamation

Daniel Webster once wrote, "We may be tossed upon an ocean where we can see no land—nor, perhaps, the sun or stars. But there is a chart and a compass for us to study, to consult, and to obey. The chart is the Constitution."

September 17, 1981, marks the 194th anniversary of our Constitution. Its Framers scarcely could have conceived of the timelessness of the document they so carefully drafted. They prepared a Constitution to meet the needs of a fledgling nation. Yet today, amid the complexities of the twentieth century, that same Constitution, with only several amendments, serves a nation whose territory spans a continent and whose population exceeds two hundred and twenty-five million. With the passing of each year, it becomes increasingly evident that, in the words of Chief Justice John Mar-

shall, our Constitution will "endure for ages to come."

The Constitution establishes the Congress, the Executive, and the Judiciary, and through a deliberate allocation of authority, it defines the limits of each upon the others. It particularizes the liberties which, as free men and women, we insist upon, and it constrains both Federal and State powers to ensure that those precious liberties are faithfully protected. It is our blueprint for freedom, our commitment to ourselves and to each other.

It is by choice, not by imposition, that the Constitution is the supreme law of our Land. As we approach the bicentennial of this charter, each of us has a personal obligation to acquaint ourselves with it and with its central role in guiding our Nation. While a constitution may set forth rights and liberties, only the citizens can maintain and guarantee those freedoms. Active and informed citizenship is not just a right; it is a duty.

In recognition of the paramount importance of the Constitution to our Nation, and in recognition of all who have attained the status of United States citizens, the Congress by joint resolution on February 29, 1952 (36 U.S.C. Section 153), designated September 17th as Citizenship Day, and by joint resolution of August 2, 1956 (36 U.S.C. Section 159), requested the President to proclaim the week beginning September 17th and ending September 23rd of each year as Constitution Week.

Now, Therefore, I, Ronald Reagan, President of the United States of America, call upon appropriate Government officials to display the flag of the United States on all Government buildings on Citizenship Day, September 17, 1981. I urge Federal, State and local officials, as well as leaders of civic,

educational and religious organizations to conduct ceremonies and programs that day to commemorate the occasion.

I also proclaim the week beginning September 17th and ending September 23rd, 1981 as Constitution Week, and I urge all Americans to observe that week with appropriate ceremonies and activities in their schools, churches and other suitable places.

In Witness Whereof, I have hereunto set my hand this 16th day of Sept. in the year of our Lord nineteen hundred and eighty-one, and of the Independence of the United States of America the two hundred and sixth.

RONALD REAGAN

[Filed with the Office of the Federal Register, 4:22 p.m., September 16, 1981]

Remarks at a White House Luncheon for Representatives of the Hispanic Community
September 16, 1981

Thank you very much, and *buenas tardes.* I had to say that because the reason I was late today—and I apologize to all of you—is because I had a very distinguished visitor in the office. And he had a presentation to make, and it did run over the time, but it was the Patriarch of Antioch—I'm trying to think again exactly what his title is—but of the Maronite Christian people in Lebanon. It was fascinating, the story that he was telling. But what fascinated me the most was that he conducted the almost 30 minutes of message to me in our language, in English, and he had simply just sat down and learned English in order to make this trip. And I had to confess that if I was going to Lebanon—*[laughter]*—I couldn't do what he did. But anyway, it couldn't be interrupted, so I was late.

But as a Californian, it's a special pleasure for me to welcome you here to the White House. And I know it probably wouldn't be technically proper for me to say *mi casa es su casa,* because this is already *su casa*— *[laughter]*—I just am a temporary tenant here. But all of us from the West have a

special place in our hearts for Hispanic culture. Incidentally, as long as I was talking about language, the day after tomorrow, I'm going to be speaking to an audience in Denver, Colorado, and I was going to tell them a little story that happened to deal with a visit that, when I was Governor of California, I made to Mexico on behalf of the then administration in Washington.

I made a speech, and I sat down to rather unenthusiastic and scattered applause, and I was a little embarrassed; I didn't know that I might have said that was wrong, and I was doubly embarrassed when the next man up, speaking in Spanish which I didn't understand, was getting enthusiastic applause every other sentence. So to hide my embarrassment I was clapping before anyone else and clapping after everyone else had finished, until our ambassador leaned over to me and said, "I wouldn't do that if I were you—he is interpreting your speech." *[Laughter]*

But coming from the West and having Hispanic culture in our hearts, it's so much a tradition in the Southwest that moving here to Washington was a bit of a culture shock. I understand that whenever there's Federal business to be done in any of the Southwestern States there is fierce competition among the Californians on my staff to get the assignment. It has something to do with enchiladas and refried beans and the fact that you don't just get those every day in Washington, D.C. In fact, I don't know where you can get them. Somebody, I'm sure, will tell me there is a place when I leave here.

But seriously, all of this has given me a deep appreciation for Hispanic culture, including its music, food, and qualities, but more than that, the qualities of character that it engenders, especially the sense of personal honor and integrity.

In the past election, I talked about five important values—family, neighborhood, work, peace, and freedom. Campaigning in Hispanic areas, I never felt more comfortable about those values. During the last two decades, when our traditions and values were under attack as never before, Hispanic Americans held firm to their beliefs like a solid rock amidst a stormy sea. They demonstrated a commitment to family, a reverence for God, as well as the pride and self-respect that comes from hard work.

Today, all of us are rediscovering those values, but the Hispanic community never lost them. And this dedication is beginning to bear fruit. Progress made by Hispanics can be described as nothing less than phenomenal. After years of adversity and, yes, discrimination, there is no doubt that Hispanics are taking their rightful place in American society. In my own administration, they're playing an invaluable role. Eighty Hispanics have already received appointments at all levels, and 18 of them in major positions. And I'm happy to say in looking back over the records to see how we're doing, that these first few months tops anything that has happened in the entire administrations that have preceded us. But across this land, in the private sector you're making your way into positions of influence and leadership. And all of this is a tremendous source of pride for a people that have worked so hard to overcome the obstacles before them.

A most admirable quality is the sense of honor and duty that is rooted so firmly in that culture. Few others can claim the patriotism demonstrated by our Hispanic citizens. Consistent with this, they've received awards for heroism and bravery far in excess to their proportion of the population. Two of my first ceremonial functions as President were, interestingly enough, directly related to heroism of Hispanic Americans.

First, I was honored to welcome back the hostages from Iran, and two of the Marines had been especially heroic. Both of them were Hispanic Americans. One of them, Jimmy López, is remembered not only for risking his life to help several Embassy employees escape but also for his spirit of defiance in captivity. Before they left to come home, he wrote on his cell wall, in Spanish, which the Iranians did not understand: *"Viva la roja, blanca, y azul."* [Long live the red, white, and blue.] His devotion will not be forgotten.

And then on February 24th, we discovered that there had been neglected for several years the presentation of a Congressional Medal of Honor, given only for service above and beyond the call of duty. And it was to go to a brave man, Master Sergeant Roy Benavidez, raised on a farm down near the border in Texas. His heroism in Vietnam earned him that highest award, the Congressional Medal of Honor, and I had the honor to present it to him. I had the honor to sit and visit with him for awhile about this, and let me just say a word or two about it. If you tried to put it in a television show, no one would believe it.

He was manning a desk when helicopters came in from an attempted rescue mission of a patrol surrounded by the enemy. The crews were shot up; the helicopters were shot up. They were readying others to go back in and try again. And he just walked away from his desk and climbed in the first helicopter, and he was the first man to— he's the only man to drop down from the only helicopter to get in. And he went 75 yards through heavy fire to get to this patrol of 12 men, 4 then dead and 8 wounded. And one by one, he carried the 8 out through that fire—wounded, shot four times. And after he'd been shot four times, he had to put down one of the men he was carrying and draw his bayonet and engage in hand-to-hand combat with a Vietnamese, who had clubbed him with a rifle and then was trying to stab him with a bayonet. And I think you would appreciate this when I tell you that he said, "I know we're taught to pary the bayonet by shoving it aside." "But," he said, "you don't always think of that." [*Laughter*] And he said, "So I grabbed it and held it against him." And in the sawing effort to get it loose, his left arm was totally disabled. But what I loved most of all was—he had been shot, remember, four times when this happened—he said to me, "That's when I got mad." [*Laughter*]

Well, the proclamation that we celebrate today about the strength that the Hispanic people have given to this country—all of this is based on the strength of character which I spoke of earlier. Recognizing this, I am proud to have proclaimed this "National Hispanic Heritage Week." In doing so, I hope that all Americans will reflect on how lucky we are to have such a wonderful people as a part of our country and a part of ourselves.

I could confess something, and my people of my own background wouldn't hold it against me: I think that if the country were just left to us Anglos, it would be kind of dull. [*Laughter*]

Thank you all very much, and God bless you.

Note: The President spoke at 1:05 p.m. in the State Dining Room at the White House.

Nomination of Thomas R. Pickering To Be United States Ambassador to Nigeria
September 17, 1981

The President today announced his intention to nominate Thomas R. Pickering, of New Jersey, to be Ambassador to the Federal Republic of Nigeria. He would succeed Stephen Low.

Mr. Pickering entered the Foreign Service in 1959 as intelligence research specialist in the Department of State, and was political officer (Test Ban Treaty) in Geneva on detail to the Arms Control and Disarmament Agency in 1961–64. He attended Swahili language training at the Foreign Service Institute in 1964–65. In 1965–67 he was principal officer in Zanzibar and Deputy Chief of Mission in Dar es Salaam in 1967–69. In the Department of State, he was Deputy Director of the Bureau of Po-litico-Military Affairs (1969–73), and Special Assistant to the Secretary of State and Executive Secretary of the Department (1973–74). In 1974–78 he was Ambassador to the Hashemite Kingdom of Jordan, and Assistant Secretary of State for Oceans and International Environmental and Scientific Affairs in the Department in 1978–81.

Mr. Pickering graduated from Bowdoin College (A.B., 1953); Fletcher School of Law (M.A., 1954); and the University of Melbourne (M.A., 1956). He served in the United States Navy in 1956–59. He is married, has two children, and resides in Rutherford, N.J. He was born November 5, 1931, in Orange, N.J.

Nomination of Rickey Dale James To Be a Member of the Mississippi River Commission
September 17, 1981

The President today announced his intention to nominate Rickey Dale James to be a member of the Mississippi River Commission for a term of 9 years. He would succeed Wilmer R. Hall.

Mr. James is a self-employed farmer and manager of cotton gins and grain elevators for the A.C. Riley Co. Since 1972 he has worked with various levee and drainage boards in Missouri and was employed with the Kentucky Department of Water Resources engineering office while attending the University of Kentucky in 1971.

He graduated from the University of Kentucky with a degree in civil engineering in 1971. Mr. James is married, has two children, and resides in New Madrid, Mo. He was born January 29, 1948, in Fulton County, Ky.

Proclamation 4859—National Cystic Fibrosis Week
September 17, 1981

By the President of the United States of America

A Proclamation

Cystic fibrosis is an hereditary, metabolic disease primarily affecting the respiratory and digestive systems. Tragically, the disease attacks the young. It imposes enormous economic, physical and emotional burdens on both victim and family. The disease is the leading genetic killer of young Americans; yet, its cause and cure are unknown. In addition, there is no test for determining who is a carrier—and there are up to 10 million sympton-free individuals who might pass cystic fibrosis on to their children.

Nevertheless, there is ample reason for hope. There have been important advances in the treatment of cystic fibrosis. Twenty-five years ago, children affected by the disease seldom reached school age. Today, half of those afflicted with the disease will live into their twenties, and the quality of life during these additional years has been significantly improved.

Supported by the National Institutes of Health and private voluntary agencies, researchers throughout the world are focusing their efforts on cystic fibrosis. Improved methods of diagnosis, detection, treatment and control are being examined and attention, as never before, is being paid to this cruel disease.

Since early diagnosis can prolong life, public awareness is critical. To increase this awareness and commemorate the progress being made in controlling cystic fibrosis, and to emphasize the need for a continued effort to defeat it, the Congress has, by Senate Joint Resolution 62, designated the week of September 20 through September 26, 1981, as National Cystic Fibrosis Week.

Now, Therefore, I, Ronald Reagan, President of the United States of America, do hereby proclaim the week of September 20 through September 26, 1981, as National Cystic Fibrosis Week. I call upon the people of the United States to observe that week with appropriate ceremonies and activities.

In Witness Whereof, I have hereunto set my hand this seventeenth day of September in the year of our Lord nineteen hundred and eighty-one, and of the Independence of the United States of America the two hundred and sixth.

RONALD REAGAN

[*Filed with the Office of the Federal Regis-*

ter, 10:35 a.m., September 18, 1981]
Note: The text of the proclamation was re-

leased by the Office of the Press Secretary
on September 18.

Executive Order 12322—Water Resources Projects
September 17, 1981

By the authority vested in me as President by the Constitution and laws of the United States of America, and in order to ensure efficient and coordinated planning and review of water resources programs and projects, it is hereby ordered as follows:

Section 1. Before any agency or officer thereof submits to the Congress, or to any committee or member thereof, for approval, appropriations, or legislative action any report, proposal, or plan relating to a Federal or Federally assisted water and related land resources project or program, such report, proposal, or plan shall be submitted to the Director of the Office of Management and Budget.

Sec. 2. The Director of the Office of Management and Budget shall examine each report, proposal, or plan for consistency with, and shall advise the agency of the relationship of the project to, the following:

(a) the policy and programs of the President;

(b) the Principles and Standards for Water and Related Land Resources Planning (Part

711 of Title 18 of the Code of Federal Regulations (45 FR 64366)), or other such planning guidelines for water and related land resources planning, as shall hereafter be issued; and

(c) other applicable laws, regulations, and requirements relevant to the planning process.

Sec. 3. When such report, proposal, or plan is thereafter submitted to the Congress, or to any committee or member thereof, it shall include a statement of the advice received from the Office of Management and Budget.

Sec. 4. Executive Order No. 12113, as amended, is revoked.

RONALD REAGAN

The White House,
September 17, 1981.

[*Filed with the Office of the Federal Register, 10:36 a.m., September 18, 1981*]

Note: The text of the Executive order was released by the Office of the Press Secretary on September 18.

Remarks at the Dedication of the Gerald R. Ford Presidential Museum in Grand Rapids, Michigan
September 18, 1981

Reverend clergy, President and Mrs. Ford, the distinguished people that you have met up here and those that are in the audience:

Millions of Americans will follow us to this place, and like us, they will find history here. They will relive in their own minds or through their children's eyes dramatic and

critically important moments in our nation's life. Here they will reflect on the achievements of the 38th President of the United States. They will dwell on what Gerald Ford brought to this Nation and what he gave to his country and his people. Some of those who come here will bring, just as many of us have today, personal memories. I have my own.

I couldn't help but recall, as we prepared for this trip, that the first time he and I encountered each other was in Michigan. Well, it wasn't exactly an encounter, and we certainly didn't have any awareness of each other. I was a young sports announcer for station WHO of Des Moines, Iowa. I was broadcasting an Iowa-Michigan football game. The center on that Michigan team was a fellow named Jerry Ford. Candor and a decent regard for history force me to admit that was about 47 years ago, and Michigan won.

I have some other unique memories; one in particular is more recent, but serves to highlight our mutual interest in sports and politics. In 1976 we were engaged in another kind of game. He won that one, too. But you observed one day that we had something in common. He said that we both played football, and he said that he had played for Michigan, and I played for Warner Brothers. [*Laughter*] Well, let me add that playing the Gipper did get more attention than my 3 years in the line for Eureka College, which maybe proved something us linemen have always felt, and that is that it's pretty easy for the backs to get the glory. I was a guard—right guard, that is. [*Laughter*]

Mr. President, other, less humorous similarities between us have occurred recently. This came home to me when I ran across this description of the American economy: "the worst inflation in the country's peacetime history, the highest interest rates in a century, the consequent severe slump in housing, sinking and utterly demoralized securities markets, a stagnant economy with large-scale unemployment in prospect, and a worsening international trade and payments position." That description comes from the New York Times, and I thought you would like to know the date was the summer of 1974. Gerald Ford had just become President of the United States.

During his first few months in office, he made the battle against inflation, growing unemployment, and a stagnant economy his first priority. He didn't hesitate to point to the causes of this economic crisis. He noted that in a 10-year period, Federal spending had increased from over 100 billion to over 300 billion dollars; in a 15-year period, direct and indirect Federal payments to individuals had gone from 24 percent of the Federal budget to 46 percent, while spending for defense fell from 49 percent of the budget to 26 percent.

President Ford asked his countrymen to choose: "To put it simply," he said, "we must decide whether we shall continue in the direction of recent years—the path toward bigger government, higher taxes, and higher inflation—or whether we shall now take a new direction, bringing to a halt the momentous growth of government, restoring our prosperity, and allowing each of you a greater voice in your own future."

Well, as President, Gerald Ford made his choice. And when he left office, the economy was again moving in the right direction with inflation shrunk to a yearly rate of 4.8 percent. And his decision to carefully rebuild America's defense and his willingness to protect American interest and lives abroad began to reestablish our international prestige. He showed it can be done.

Well, these are the facts, the objective criteria by which the success of the Ford Presidency can be judged. Yet the legacy left his countrymen by General [President] Gerald Ford is something deeper and something more profound.

In 1787, shortly after the Constitutional Convention concluded its work, Benjamin Franklin was asked what had been accomplished, and we all know he said: "We've given you a Republic, if you can keep it." For two centuries this has been the challenge before all Americans, a challenge that has always been met, but not without uncertainty, moments of doubt and danger.

During the first transition of Federal power from one party to the other in 1800, fierce acrimony, vows of retribution, and even talk of succession filled the Nation's Capital. And in 1861 another great internal crisis shook our nation. And this time the dissolution of the Union was not only threatened; it was, for a time, a reality. In both cases the steadiness, the fortitude, the personal ease, and quiet confidence of our Presidents saw us through.

On August 9th, 1974, when the nation was experiencing another traumatic test of its institutions, Gerald Ford, as it's been said several times here today, took the oath of office in the East Room of the White House and spoke of the "extraordinary circumstances never before experienced by Americans." He spoke of a time of "trouble" and "hurt," and he told us "our long national nightmare is over." He woke us from that nightmare. We've heard repeated here today dramatic statements that were made as evidence of that. He did heal America, because he so thoroughly understood America. His was and is an unquestioning belief in the soundness of our way of governing and in the resiliency of our people.

And when he was about to step down from the Presidency, he took note of our remarkable tradition of peaceful transitions of power. He said: "There are no soldiers marching in the streets except in the Inaugural Parade; no public demonstrations except for some of the dancers at the Inaugural Ball; the opposition party doesn't go underground, but goes on functioning; and a vigilant press goes right on probing and publishing our faults and our follies."

And during our Bicentennial, he reminded the American people of the collective wisdom of their ways and the remarkable achievements of their past and the fact that we can meet in solemn gatherings like this and go right on without being bothered a bit by a few raucous voices from beyond.

"In the space of two centuries," Gerald Ford said, "we have not been able to right every wrong, to correct every injustice, to reach every worthy goal. But for 200 years we have tried and we will continue to strive to make the lives of individual men and women in this country and on this Earth better lives—more hopeful and happy, more prosperous and peaceful, more fulfilling, and more free. This is our common dedication," he said, "and it will be our common glory as we enter the third century of the American adventure."

Gerald Ford healed America, because he understood the adventure of America—her way of governing, her people, and the source of her strength as a nation. And on the night he learned that he was likely to be the next President of the United States,

he and Betty recited a favorite prayer from the Book of Proverbs: "Trust in the Lord with all thine heart; and lean not unto thine own understanding. In all thy ways acknowledge him, and he shall direct thy paths."

Today many of us in public life, from this country and others, have come here to speak words of tribute to Gerald Ford. The millions of Americans who will soon hear or read these words will not long remember them, but can be sure that in their minds and hearts there will be a flash of recognition and a swell of gratitude, feelings that if put into words would result in a simple statement by his countrymen about Gerald Ford: He was a good President who led us well, a good man who sought to serve others.

Mr. President, I noted recently that your confidence in our nation's future is not at all diminished. You said that the nation again faces difficult moments, but that "there's a good feeling in the country despite the problems." You said our plans for economic recovery will work, because the American people will make them work. You noted that the will of the people "is more important than all the technical things, all the micro- and macro-economics. There is just no way to equate that," you said, "with the will of 229 million Americans."

I am, of course, grateful for your support and counsel on this matter, but I would remind you that if today 229 million Americans can look forward to that future you speak of, it is because you brought us through difficult and trying times and helped us to believe again in ourselves.

Not too long ago, on the 200th anniversary of Paul Revere's famous ride, you offered a prayer, Mr. President, in the Old North Church in Boston. You said you hoped that those who follow us might say of our generation, "We kept the faith, freedom flourished, liberty lived." That's a worthy prayer, Mr. President, and we offer it again today in a spirit of gratitude for your Presidency and affection for you.

Ladies and gentlemen, it is now my honor to introduce to you the 38th President of the United States, a man of decency, a man of honor, a man of healing, Gerald R. Ford.

Note: The President spoke at 12:15 p.m. outside the Gerald R. Ford Presidential Museum.

Prior to the dedication ceremony, the *President and Mrs. Reagan, Prime Minister Pierre Elliott Trudeau of Canada, President José López Portillo of Mexico, and former President Valéry Giscard d'Estaing of France accompanied former President and Mrs. Ford on a tour of the museum.*

Remarks in Denver, Colorado, at the Biennial Convention of the National Federation of Republican Women
September 18, 1981

Mrs. Reagan. I've been asked to introduce my husband. I don't think I've ever been asked to do that before. I was trying to remember on the plane coming out here. I think this is a first. He looks pretty confident that I'm going to give him a good introduction, doesn't he? [*Laughter*]

I'll tell you a little secret. He didn't look so confident when I was going to introduce him to my father. [*Laughter*]

But instead of introducing the dynamic leader that we all admire, I'd like to present a kind, loving husband, a pushover of a father, and the President of the United States.

The President. Ladies, thank you very much. I want to tell a little secret, too. Madam Chairman, Nancy, and I want you ladies to know that she isn't really that much taller than me; they've taken the box away that she was standing on. [*Laughter*]

And all of you here, Jim Watt from our Cabinet, the ladies here, and all of you, I just want to thank you for your most generous applause. Denver is known as the Mile-High City, and you certainly have made Nancy and me feel a mile high today with your greeting. Last month in California, when people applauded, I didn't know if they were clapping or swatting Medflies. [*Laughter*]

I think I may have told some of you this before, but I've just come from Michigan, where I met with our friend from below the border, President López Portillo, and it reminded me of this. I'm going to tell it again, just in case. And that was how I once addressed a very large audience, distinguished audience in Mexico City and then sat down to rather scattered and unenthusiastic applause. And I was somewhat embarrassed, even more so when the next man who spoke, a representative of the Mexican Government speaking in Spanish, which I don't understand, was being interrupted virtually every other line with the most enthusiastic kind of applause. To hide my embarrassment, I started clapping before anyone else and clapped longer than anyone else until our Ambassador leaned over and said to me, "I wouldn't do that if I were you; he's interpreting your speech." [*Laughter*]

But today you're the ones who deserve the applause for the support that you gave us in passing the recent budget and the tax bills. When I signed that legislation, I used 24 pens. And the reason it took 24 pens was not because they were government issued— [*laughter*]—they were for some of the people who had helped get the bills through the Congress. But, you know, if I had pens for everyone who assisted us, there would be thousands and thousands of Americans who would have received them—who phoned and contacted their Congressmen. They worked in our behalf, and ultimately they won a great victory for our country.

The National Federation of Republican Women was a vital part of that effort. I know of your two hotlines and what they accomplished. So, each of you here today deserves a pen, an engraved pen that reads:

"In deep appreciation for your generous service to your party and your Nation."

When you think about it, that should really be a surprise—or no surprise, I should say, because long ago the great philosopher and commentator, De Tocqueville, came here to America from France, and after a long look at our country he wrote: . . . if anyone asks me what I think the chief cause of the extraordinary prosperity and growing power of this Nation is due to, I should answer, it is due to the superiority of their women. I would add, especially our Republican women.

We've tapped many fine Republican women to serve in the administration. And in spite of the mistaken notions we are somehow lagging in women appointments, the truth is just the opposite. After 8 months in office, we have selected as many women to serve in top policymaking posts as the previous administration had at the end of the first entire year, and more appointments will follow. What this means is that for a comparable period of time, we've appointed more women to substantive jobs than any other administration in history. And let me assure you this is only the beginning.

Of course, one accomplishment that I'm especially proud of as President is the appointment to the Supreme Court of Sandra O'Connor. [*Applause*] Thank you. Thank you very much. She is an outstanding example of the qualified women living all across this country whose talents and energies are so helpful in Washington. And let me say that one of her good qualities is the fact that she was a member of this organization before she joined the bench.

I can tell you I firmly believe that she is imbued with the philosophy that we put into our platform at the convention in Detroit. And I'm convinced she'll make a fine Justice, not just because she's the first woman on the Court but she also brings, as I say, a philosophy with her that I believe is especially appropriate for the Court. As she said in her testimony before the Senate, ". . . the proper role of the judiciary is one of interpreting and applying the law, not making it." I believe that Mrs. O'Connor's commitment to judicial restraint will help to redefine the Court's role in our daily life.

Sandra O'Connor is a new Justice for a new American era.

Today I want to discuss an issue, though, that affects you as Republicans, as women, and as Americans. During last year's campaign, I made a pledge to the American people, a pledge to return this Nation to economic health and vitality. I have never taken a commitment more seriously, with the possible exception of the one I made nearly 30 years ago to you know who. [*Laughter*] This afternoon let me review the progress that we've made in meeting that economic commitment to the people and what we must still accomplish.

Eight months ago we were bogged down with Federal regulations, heavier and heavier taxation, and the lowest level of investment and savings in the industrialized world. Few of us could keep our heads above the rising inflation rate. Our economy was sinking and taking most Americans with it.

With bipartisan support, we passed the largest spending and tax reductions in the history of this Nation. We also launched one of the largest regulatory relief rescues ever attempted. The economic recovery package is a dramatic contrast to years of bland, halfhearted, and ineffective efforts.

This summer I received a letter from a young black man in Los Angeles who had just become the proud father of a little girl. I well know that feeling. And he said that even though he grew up in a Democratic family, he was now wholeheartedly supporting our recovery program for the sake of his daughter's future. And he said, "Our livelihoods depend on the total economic viability of America." Well, we're determined to make the economy viable for all Americans, and we're determined that his little girl's economic opportunities are going to be abundant.

As I've said before and I'll say again, America now has an economic plan for her future. We know where we're going: We're going onward, we're going upward, and we're not leaving anyone behind.

Our economic plan is to begin with the 1982 fiscal year on October 1st. I'm as convinced today as I was when we introduced the package that this economic plan is as good as money in the bank, and if I were a betting man, I would wager the rent money on it.

Now, I've listened to those Chicken Littles who proclaim the sky is falling and those others who recklessly play on high interest rates for their own narrow political purpose. But this concern about a plan not even in effect yet is nothing more than false labor. [*Laughter*]

Yes, the persistence with which high interest rates go on has made our task more difficult, and yes, additional budget cuts must be made in the years ahead, but we've known that and spoken of it for months, ever since we submitted the program. We referred to those unspecified cuts that we were later to specify, which we're going to do. Let me say that we did not sweat and bleed to get the economic package passed only to abandon it when the going gets a little tough.

We will not practice dilettante economics. We're committed to the economic plan, and we're committed to achieving it by holding to a firm, steady course for the long run. I told the American people we were going to turn this economy around, and we're going to do it.

Some of those Chicken Littles I mentioned got that way because over the past decades they've heard government talk of economy and saving, but at the end of each fiscal year, spending had exceeded revenues, and we went deeper and deeper into debt. Well, this is what we're going to change.

Let me give you some economic facts of life—what we intend to do about them and where they will lead us.

We're rapidly approaching a trillion dollar debt, a debt so large that it can only be compared to the universe because it, too, is incomprehensible in its dimensions. Think of it: The government owes a thousand billion dollars and must pay interest every day on that gargantuan amount. The interest on the debt was $74.8 billion last year alone. That's better than a billion dollars a week.

This enormous debt has been built up year by year by Congresses that consistently promised that they were—well, they promised more money than they had to give.

The Federal budget has been something like a runaway truck coming down a steep mountain road. Obviously, we can't stop it all at once without doing a great deal of damage, but what we have done is get ready to apply the brakes on October 1st, when the new fiscal year begins. There will be more pressure added on January 1st, and in fiscal 1983 we'll shift to a lower gear, and in the following years we intend to bring it completely under control.

Now, as some of you know, I've traveled the mashed potato circuit for years speaking of the need for fiscal responsibility and a balanced budget, and I'm not about to stop this long crusade after only 8 months in Washington. This administration is committed to a balanced budget, and we will fight to the last blow to achieve it by 1984.

Now, in attempting to slow the budget, we estimated that the 1982 deficit would be $42½ billion. But since that deficit, some things have changed. The interest rates have risen, increasing the cost of borrowing to fund the deficit and the debt that we've inherited. The Congress didn't give us quite all the deductions that we asked for, although we were very happy to get what they did pass after a long struggle. So, that leaves our $42½ figure bigger than that if nothing is done.

But something will be done. We will not sit on our hands and watch helplessly as the deficit swells and swells. We'll make further reductions in the 1982 budget and millions of dollars of additional spending cuts in the '83 and '84 budgets.

The cutbacks in spending will be shared by all departments of government, including the Department of Defense. But let me assure you, the defense budget will still increase significantly. There is no alternative to a stronger defense. Study after study and expert after expert have testified to our nation's need for a more muscular military.

The Soviet Union is the most massive and menacing—they had that buildup—in history. It is spilling over with military hardware. The Soviets have not built a society; they've built an arsenal. And we in the West can no longer turn our head or avert our eyes. For too many years the Pentagon was treated as the Federal Government's poor relation while domestic programs thrived and grew fat. We simply must rectify that imbalance. We will not cut defense spending to the point that it interferes or slows our plan for our national security.

All of us—the administration, the Congress, and the American people—are going to be bone-tired from the budget battles over the next few years. But these battles, no matter how exhausting, must be fought and must be won for the sake of our future. We cannot falter in our resolve and see the progress already made turn to dust. We must have the determination and patience.

And let me say to our friends in the financial markets, I hope the people on Wall Street will pay attention to the folks on Main Street. If they do, they'll see there's a rising tide of confidence in the future of America. It took us years of fiscal mismanagement to get where we are today, and our economic recovery program is not designed to provide instant gratification.

I've actually read statements that our plan isn't working. And yesterday on one of the morning television shows, former Vice President Mondale said, "Well, it was an interesting idea, but it just didn't work." Well, of course it didn't work. It doesn't go into effect until October 1st.

As I said before, I can understand the pessimism of those who remember past promises that were never kept. May I just interject here, the debt, the deficit that we will know of on the last day of this month when the fiscal year ends could, with the off-budget items, be as much as $80 billion—the '81 budget. That was the budget that the previous administration told us was going to be balanced. So, until people out there in the financial market know the annual debits are reduced and eventually eliminated, I guess the interest rates will remain high; so will inflation. And it isn't easy to reduce Federal spending, but we're going to do it. And when the financial markets see the evidence of this, their tune will change.

I remember the fears and the cries of disapproval by those who opposed our decision last January to decontrol oil prices, and they said that inflated energy prices would be the result. But what has been the result? Americans have curbed their driving, their

demand for oil. This in turn has helped the nation's balance of trade, which in turn has strengthened the value of the dollar overseas. And these benefits have occurred with very little effect on the consumer. The price of gas in July was the same as it was last February, and in some places it was even lower. And today's paper, the business section said, "We've reduced again our imports of oil." And we can do that because there has been a great increase in exploration and discovery of more oil here in our own land without going abroad.

The economic recovery program will prove as successful as the oil decontrol decision. I firmly believe that our tax incentives will act as a new battery for the American economy, recharging and energizing the nation with economic opportunity. The across-the-board tax cuts will result in across-the-board improvement in our economic health. Without that tax rate reduction, the taxes would have gone up $91½ billion in 1982 and nearly $300 billion over the next 3 years. The Federal Government was turning the taxpayer into an economic sharecropper, with the rewards earned by the sweat of the taxpayer's brow going to government. It simply had to stop.

We also passed various incentives for saving and investment, like reduced capital gains tax, the all-savers certificates, and various stimuli for business. These measures are going to spark jobs, an estimated 3 million more jobs by 1986, in addition to the 10 million that are already expected by way of natural growth. And productive jobs not only provide take-home pay; they provide self-respect.

I'm really optimistic about the individual retirement accounts. These are savings accounts that will be opened to those also covered by an employer pension plan, where the individual wants to contribute something above that pension plan to his own retirement nest egg. This will be deductible earnings that he can put aside. It will provide people with the feeling of security that, according to the polls, social security is not providing.

Now, I noticed that the theme for this convention is "We're changing—changing the future." Well, that's exactly what our economic program aims to do as well—change the future, change it so that our people and industry will have the incentive to be productive again.

Now, you've assisted us already with the initial spending and tax efforts, but I'm going to ask for your help again. I know what the members of this federation can do when you put your minds to it. The National Federation of Republican Women is known for raising the banner of the Republican Party, by raising campaign funds as well as candidates. You're also known for raising your voice to speak out on the issues vital to America.

In the weeks and months ahead, the Congress will need to hear your voice. There are great pressures building to stop our economic program while it's still taxing down the runway. Yet once we clear the fenceposts at the end of the field, this economy is going to soar. We'll have restored a healthy balance between government and free enterprise.

Now, I know I've talked a lot this afternoon about the dry, dusty figures of budgets and deficits, economic matters. It's essential to do so, of course. But I would like to take a moment and talk about somethng else. I'd like to speak of the heart of America.

I don't know whether I can explain or Nancy can explain what we feel living there in that great historic house. In Washington, surrounded and imbued with that history, there are moments when you feel that you're very close to the great heart of America. You can hear the sound of its beat. You're aware of its great depth and steady strength.

A young sailor on duty in a submarine writes to me, and he says that he's writing on behalf of his shipmates to express his pride in what he's doing. He said in his letter, "We're not the biggest navy, no; but we're the best."

A very elderly man writes very sincerely and volunteers to give up a portion of his limited pension if that would help the country.

And then there was another gentleman that wrote to me just the other day—I spoke of regulations. He attached a form to his regulation that he had received. He's one of those citizens that is picked for a four-times-a-year personal interview by the Census Bureau to get statistics on people and how things are going. And he says, "They've been to see me four times this last year." And he said, "Here's the form they sent me." Well, this form says they're going to come and see him again four times this year. The questions on that form that they're going to ask: Has he changed his mind about retirement? Is he thinking about maybe going back to work? And then he told me, he said, "I'm 84 years old. I've been living for years in a retirement home." [Laughter]

Well, there is another letter that just a few days ago reached my desk. It's from a small town in Iowa—speaking of that heart of America. I just thought I'd like to read it to you and share it with you.

"Dear Mr. President:

"Tonight I am alone in my son's bedroom. He no longer lives here. These are supposed to be the years to which I've been looking forward, but I don't seem to handle empty bedrooms very well. This is my third. A week ago, my son was still enrolled in the college of his choice. Tonight he's in a strange motel somewhere. Tomorrow he steps onto an airplane which will take him far away. He has selected and enlisted in a branch of the United States Armed Forces.

"During these past weeks, I've sensed and seen him about the process of pulling away, cutting the cord, getting ready to leave the nest. I saw him bequeath some valuable possessions like his penny collection and his baseball cards. They went to a couple of small boys in his Pied Piper following on the block. Lately I've noted that comments and remarks directed to family members have taken on a gentle tone of voice. I saw him wax his car again, and he told me I'm a great cook.

"And so, I now take my place among the thousands of other mothers who, through the years, have watched a son leave home to serve his country. Surely, their feelings were not so different from mine tonight.

"Actually, it's all quite appropriate. This is a guy who grew up in a room wallpapered with flags and muskets and drums. He regularly ran Old Glory up the flagpole in the backyard before breakfast in those days. He and his big brother had G.I. Joe uniforms, sizes four and six. And I remember seeing them sneaking up the little hill in the neighbor lady's backyard on their stomachs. I wonder how many times I've picked little plastic army men up from under the furniture. All those toys and memories have been packed away for years, but I feel like the need to bring them out and handle them tonight.

"He has examined the options, as I suggested, and the choices he's made are taking him far away from me. He believes there are opportunities for him in education, travel, and experience. No doubt there are. There's a stack of thirsty terry towels I bought for a college basketball player. He left them here. He left the shampoo and soap and cords and sweaters, too. He won't need those things. His country will now provide for all his needs. He thinks he's getting a good deal. No doubt he is. Personally, I'm inclined to believe the country is getting the good deal. In exchange for all their provisions, they are getting one tall, tanned fellow with summer bleached hair, a sharp young mind, more potential and possibility than I have the space here to describe.

"And so tonight, here in the shadows, here in the quiet, a dumb orange stuffed tiger and I sit together absorbing the intensity of this special day. I stepped over a tread-worn pair of size 13 Nikes, and there were trophies, photos of pretty girls, a dusty Bible, and a tape deck with the volume finally turned down.

"I've already marked the 9 weeks on the point on the calendar and have a picture in my mind of him coming home, with presents, in a uniform, at Christmas. I'm feeling especially thankful for the Hardy Boys mysteries I did get read, the chocolate marble cakes I did get baked, and the long quiet talks that did happen. There were other memories I'll try and forget.

"Thank you for taking the time while running a nation to listen to the passions of a mother's heart. I feel better now having shared my feelings tonight. And please, will you be especially careful with the country just now?"

I will be very careful with the country just now.

Thank you very much.

Note: The President spoke at 2:40 p.m. in Currigan Hall A at the Denver Convention Complex. Following his remarks, he went to Camp David, Md., for a weekend stay.

Remarks at a Breakfast Meeting With Representatives From the Private Sector Engaged in Volunteer Work
September 21, 1981

May I, ladies and gentlemen, first of all thank you very much for being here. You know, it's unusual for someone who grew up in politics—you're not supposed to reach for your checkbook; I want blood this time—[*laughter*]—new blood.

We need to pick your brains very much. All of you here are engaged, in addition to your own work, in volunteer work with organizations of various kinds that are serving the public. And I have a distinct feeling, and have for a long time, that we have drifted, as a people, too far away from the voluntarism that so characterized our country for so many years. And we have, in a sense, abdicated and turned over to government things that used to be functions of the community and the neighborhood. And now with what we're doing here in our economic plan, there is a great need to return to that.

That often-quoted-by-afterdinner speakers Frenchman, De Tocqueville, who came to this country so long ago to find out what was the secret of our greatness and all—there was one line in his book, when he went back and wrote a book for his fellow citizens, in which he said, "You know, there's something strange in the United States." He said, "Some individual sees a problem." And he said, "They walk across the street to a friend or a neighbor and they tell them of the problem, and they talk about it. And pretty soon, a committee is formed. And the next thing you know, they are solving the problem." And you won't believe this: He wrote, "But not a single bureaucrat was involved." [*Laughter*]

From the old raising-of-the-barn when someone's barn went up in flames, in the farm days, to every kind of activity in recent days, more modern times, I remember—now that government has gotten so greatly involved, and with the best of intentions—I don't fault their intentions—but we know, and you know better than anyone else with what you're doing, that if you take the various ways of helping people, the one with the least overhead is the private effort; next is the community or local effort if it is a public effort, but the highest of all is the Federal Government.

In addition to that, trying to form rules and regulations that will fit all of the various problems around the country ignores the diversity of this land of ours. I can tell you of an example when I was Governor. In our neighboring State of Oregon, up in Portland, Oregon, people like yourselves in the business community, dealing with the very real problem of high school dropouts, had formed an organization that was tremendously successful in preventing and reducing this rate of dropout. And then the Federal Government adopted a program, and one of the first places they dropped in on was Portland, Oregon. And the first task was to drive that private organization out of business and take over, and they weren't nearly as successful as the private group had been.

There's one of you here at this table, Mr. Monson[1]—I don't know how many of you are familiar with what, in his church, has occurred, with the literally providing of a welfare program that I believe is far superior to anything the government has been able to manage—taking care of their people, but based also on the work ethic.

---

[1] *Elder Thomas S. Monson, Church of Jesus Christ of Latter-Day Saints.*

Because one of the other things that government has done with its good intentions is violate that old rule that you can give a hungry man a fish and he'll be hungry tomorrow, or you can teach him to fish and he'll never be hungry again.

In California there is an aircraft plant that all on its own, in a nearby high school, heard about the dropout problem, instituted a program of its own, where young people who have to be imminent dropouts in their school are given afterschool work at this plant and training, on-the-job training, because they found that one of the great causes of dropouts is lack of money, need for money.

It's a two-way street for the company by this time, because not only do they prevent the dropouts—because the requirement is they can only have those jobs as long as they stay in high school; they can't drop out—then, diploma in hand, they have a pretty well-trained cadre of young people coming along who get permanent jobs after graduation in their company. I didn't mean to deal so much on dropouts. There are any other number of things.

I've talked to some clergymen who are beginning to recognize that the churches have stood back and let government do, in the realm of neighbor-helping-neighbor, what really should be the individual function of their members. Some are investigating the idea of child care centers. How easy it would be. Working mothers within a church and other mothers and women who would like to volunteer and do some good work, the church has the facilities to bring them together and say: Let's establish that with volunteer care here in our own church.

The possibilities are limitless for what we can take over that government has once been doing. Why you're here is, as I say, for us to find out from you who are already engaged in that, how we can work out a plan. We intend to go forward. Jim Rosebush is going to remain here with you after I have to leave. He's going to be the executive secretary of the commission that we will form, the committee, for the very purpose of finding out plans and ways that voluntarism in the community can take over and do many of the things that are not being very well done by the government today.

I have one last example of what can happen when it begins officially, other than doing it the community way—again, while I was Governor, and again, I'm sorry that the example has to do with dropouts. There was a Federal program where they paid students who would be given jobs in the school doing work that needed to be done, washing the blackboards and all that sort of thing, after school was over. And then they came in and found that some of the students weren't juvenile delinquents, and therefore they were fired. They couldn't have those jobs. Now, if anyone can think of a better temptation for a kid to go out and break a window simply to get back on the job and get paid, I don't know what it would be. No reward for those who were doing what they should do; plenty of reward for those who weren't.

Well, that's enough of that. Now I'm going to sit back for the time that's left, and I'd like to hear from you on the ideas and the thoughts that you might have. And when the schedule says that I have to go, Jim will remain here as long as you can give of your time to this. But we are going to make it a major project. I intend to be speaking, making a major address on this, very shortly, to the business community to find out how we can step in and resolve some of these problems.

So, thank you again very much for being here.

Note: The President spoke at 9 a.m. in the Family Dining Room at the White House, where he met with representatives from 17 private sector organizations.

James S. Rosebush is Special Assistant to the President, Office of the Deputy Chief of Staff.

Nomination of Beverly E. Ledbetter To Be an Assistant Attorney General
September 21, 1981

The President today announced his intention to nominate Beverly E. Ledbetter to be an Assistant Attorney General, Department of Justice.

Since 1978 Ms. Ledbetter has served as general counsel of Brown University. Previously she was legal counsel at the University of Oklahoma in 1973–78. She also served as adjunct professor, Center for Higher Education, College of Education, University of Oklahoma, in 1977–78; special lecturer, College of Nursing, University of Oklahoma, in

1976–78; adjunct professor, College of Law, University of Oklahoma, in 1977; and was a special instructor at the University of Colorado.

Ms. Ledbetter graduated from Howard University (B.S., 1964) and the University of Colorado (J.D., 1972). She is admitted to practice before the United States Supreme Court.

Ms. Ledbetter resides in Providence, R.I., and was born August 23, 1943, in Alto, Tex.

Nomination of John F. Cogan To Be an Assistant Secretary of Labor
September 21, 1981

The President today announced his intention to nominate John F. Cogan to be an Assistant Secretary of Labor (Policy, Evalua-

tion and Research). He would succeed Arnold H. Packer.

Since 1980 Dr. Cogan has been senior

research fellow and assistant professor of economics at the Hoover Institution, Stanford University. Previously he was associate economist, the Rand Corp., in 1975–80. He was visiting scholar, National Bureau of Economic Research, in 1978–79; consultant with Atwater and Associates in 1975–79; consultant, Foundation for Research in Eco-nomics and Education, in 1975; and resident consultant at the Rand Corp. in 1971–74.

Dr. Cogan graduated from the University of California at Los Angeles (A.B., 1969; Ph. D., 1976). He is the author of many publica-tons on labor and the economy.

He resides in Portola Valley, Calif., and was born April 6, 1947, in New York, N.Y.

Nomination of Carlos Salman To Be a Member of the Board of Directors of the Overseas Private Investment Corporation
September 21, 1981

The President today announced his inten-tion to nominate Carlos Salman to be a member of the Board of Directors of the Overseas Private Investment Corporation for a term expiring December 17, 1982. He would succeed James M. Friedman.

Since 1972 Mr. Salman has been a real estate broker and investor in Miami, Fla. Previously he was assistant comptroller, Wo-metco Enterprises, Inc., in Miami, in 1960–72; assistant treasurer, Iberia Machinery Co., Havana, Cuba, in 1957–60; and assist-ant to the vice president in charge of sugar exportation, Ward Garcia Line, Havana, in 1954–57.

Mr. Salman graduated from Villanova College (B.A., M.B.A.). He was cochairman of the Reagan-Bush committee for Dade County and Hispanic chairman of the Reagan-Bush committee of Florida.

Mr. Salman is married, has four children, and resides in Miami, Fla. He was born Oc-tober 3, 1932, in Havana, Cuba.

Letter to the Chairmen of the House and Senate Judiciary Committees Transmitting Documents Concerning Refugee Admissions Into the United States
September 21, 1981

Dear Mr. Chairman:

I am pleased to transmit the information required by the Refugee Act of 1980 in preparation for the consultations on refugee admissions for Fiscal Year 1982. As noted in my July 30 statement, immigration and ref-ugee policy is an important part of our past and fundamental to our national interest. With other countries, we will continue to share in the responsibility of welcoming and resettling those who flee oppression. At the same time, we will seek new ways to inte-grate refugees into our society without nur-turing their dependence on welfare.

The documents transmitted today include proposed admission levels and allocations among groups of special humanitarian con-cern to the United States or whose admis-sion is otherwise in the national interest. My final determination on admission levels and allocations will be made after taking Congressional and other views expressed at the consultations into consideration.

Sincerely,

RONALD REAGAN

Note: This is the text of identical letters

addressed to Strom Thurmond, chairman of the Senate Judiciary Committee, and Peter *W. Rodino, Jr., chairman of the House Judiciary Committee.*

Statement on Senate Confirmation of Sandra Day O'Connor as an Associate Justice of the Supreme Court of the United States
September 21, 1981

I want to express my gratitude to the Senate for unanimously approving today the nomination of Judge Sandra Day O'Connor as an Associate Justice of the United States Supreme Court.

Judge O'Connor is, as I have come to know personally, a very warm and brilliant woman who has had an outstanding career in Arizona. I know the Court and the nation will benefit both from her lifetime of work, service, and experience in the legal profession, and from her solid grasp of our Constitution, which she reveres. This truly is a happy and historic day for America.

Judge O'Connor's judicial philosophy is one of restraint. She believes, as she said in her Senate testimony, that a judge is on the bench to interpret the law, not to make it. This philosophy of judicial restraint needs representation in our courtrooms and especially on the highest court in our land.

Let me also say that Judge O'Connor's confirmation symbolizes the richness of opportunity that still abides in America—opportunity that permits persons of any sex, age, or race, from every section and every walk of life to aspire and achieve in a manner never before even dreamed about in human history.

Remarks on Signing a Petition for a California Referendum on Reapportionment
September 22, 1981

Today, I'm taking a break from my normal duties to do something that every private citizen I think should do, and that is to take an interest in his home State politics.

Protecting the integrity of our electoral system and the voting franchise, I think, is of concern to all Americans. What is happening in California, if not corrected, could damage fairness at the polls for a generation of Californians, attacking the heart of our system of representative government. While all States struggle with reapportionment, the situation in California seems to have gotten out of hand. For this reason, I'm signing petitions today that will place the issue of reapportionment before the voters of California. I do so sadly, because I feel that had members of the California Legislature met their responsibility, this petition drive would be unnecessary.

In June of 1980, the people passed Proposition 6, which became article 21 to the California constitution. This article requires to the extent possible that redistricting respect city and county integrity, as well as regional integrity. It also mandated a reasonable equality of population, sequential numbering, and the contiguity of districts. The plan that emerged from the Democratic-controlled legislature violates the spirit and the letter of this article of the California constitution. Under the current plan, there's even one congressional district up in the San Francisco area that travels across the bay twice—without a bridge—incorporating parts of three counties solely for political purposes. [*Laughter*]

The reapportionment plan as it now stands effectively disenfranchises large numbers of California voters. It is not just unfair to Republicans, it's unfair to the people. Given the opportunity, we're certain the voters will reject this power play and opt for fairness. And that's exactly what this drive is—an appeal for fairness. This signature drive wouldn't be necessary if the majority of the California Legislature had done their duty to enact a reasonable reapportionment plan.

I can't help but wonder if the time hasn't come to take reapportionment out of politics and have it done by a blue ribbon citizen committee on the basis of what is good for the people, not just the party that happens to be in power.

And with that said, I will sign these petitions and, in doing so, I ask all fair-minded citizens, Republicans, Democrats, and Independents in California, to join with me.

Note: The President spoke at 11:21 a.m. in the Rose Garden at the White House. The petition signing ceremony was attended by national and California State Republican leaders and members of the California congressional delegation.

Message to the Congress Reporting on Developments Concerning the Declaration of a National Emergency With Respect to Iran
September 22, 1981

To the Congress of the United States:

Pursuant to Section 204(c) of the International Emergency Economic Powers Act (IEEPA), 50 U.S.C. Section 1703(c), I hereby report to the Congress with respect to developments since my report of February 24, 1981, concerning the declaration of national emergency with respect to Iran in Executive Order No. 12170 of November 14, 1979. This declaration and previous actions under it were described in earlier reports submitted to the Congress.

1. Pursuant to my decision, reflected in Executive Order No. 12294 of February 24, 1981, that the January 19, 1981 agreements with Iran should be implemented, the Department of the Treasury, acting under my delegation of authority to the Secretary of Treasury, issued a series of regulations to implement Executive Orders Nos. 12276–12285, signed by President Carter on January 19, 1981, and my Order of February 24. Among other things, these regulations revoked certain trade and financial sanctions against Iran, provided for the transfer of blocked Iranian assets to Iran and to a security account for U.S. claimants against Iran, and suspended certain claims of U.S. nationals against Iran pending review by the Iran-U.S. Claims Tribunal. With the exception of regulations issued July 6 and August 17, which are attached herewith, regulations issued since February 24, 1981 have been provided to Congress in accordance with the National Emergencies Act, 50 U.S.C. Section 1641(b).

2. On July 2, 1981 the Supreme Court in the case of *Dames & Moore* v. *Regan*, 49 U.S.L.W. 4969 (U.S. July 2, 1981) (No. 80–2078), upheld the President's authority to nullify attachments and other judicial orders with respect to assets of Iran, to order the transfer of those assets pursuant to the agreements with Iran, and to suspend certain claims of U.S. nationals against Iran and Iranian entities.

3. Following the Supreme Court decision and pursuant to certain of the Executive Orders mentioned above, financial assets exceeding two billion dollars held by persons within the United States were transferred to the Federal Reserve Bank of New York in mid-July. The agreements provided that a total of one billion dollars of the assets formerly held by domestic banks was to be transferred to an interest-bearing security account in a foreign bank to be used for payment of Claims Tribunal awards to U.S. nationals against Iran. The remainder

of the assets was to be transferred through a foreign bank to Iran.

The technical arrangements for the establishment of the security account were concluded on August 17 by the Central Bank of Algeria, Bank Markazi Iran, the Federal Reserve Bank of New York, and the N.V. Settlement Bank of the Netherlands, a subsidiary of the Netherlands Central Bank. In connection with the arrangements, the U.S. agreed to provide special liquidity support of up to $500 million to the Netherlands Central Bank if lawsuits or other proceedings involving the security account impair the bank's ability to defend the guilder.

On August 18, the funds were transferred by the Federal Reserve Bank of New York to the Settlement Bank. Because of the delay in concluding arrangements for the security account, this transfer was delayed one month from the original transfer date of July 19 contemplated under the agreements.

4. Certain questions concerning the security account which were not resolved in our negotiations with Iran will be referred to the Claims Tribunal, which is expected to decide the issues shortly. These questions concern (1) the disposition of the interest accruing in the funds in the security account; (2) indemnification of the Settlement Bank of the Netherlands and the Netherlands Central Bank, as manager of the funds deposited with the Settlement Bank, against any claims relating to the security account; (3) payment of the administrative fees of the Settlement Bank; and (4) payment of settlements with U.S. claimants worked out directly between the U.S. claimants and Iran.

As now constituted, the Claims Tribunal consists of three Iranian, three U.S., and three neutral arbitrators (two from Sweden and one from France). The Tribunal has held preliminary organizational meetings and is expected to receive claims during the three-month period beginning October 20.

5. Other financial questions remain unresolved. U.S. banks and Bank Markazi Iran are continuing to negotiate concerning the repayment of non-syndicated loans and disputed interest from the $1.418 billion escrow account which is held by the Bank of England. To date, no payments have been made out of this account.

6. Pursuant to the January 19 agreements, the transfer of certain nonfinancial Iranian property, such as tangible merchandise, is to be made in accordance with directions from Iran. In many cases, there are questions concerning the exact nature of Iran's interest in these properties. Under my delegation of authority, the Treasury Department is reviewing those cases brought to its attention in which the entitlement of Iran is challenged or in which Iran has not paid claims or charges against the properties. In exercise of its discretion, Treasury has the power to license various transfers involving these properties.

7. Although the hostages have been released and certain assets returned to Iran, several financial and diplomatic aspects of the crisis with Iran have not yet been resolved and continue to present an unusual and extraordinary threat to the national security and foreign policy of the United States. I shall continue to exercise the powers at my disposal to deal appropriately with these problems and will continue to report periodically to Congress on significant developments.

RONALD REAGAN

The White House,
September 22, 1981.

Remarks at a Fundraising Event for the Phillips Art Gallery
September 22, 1981

Thank you very much. It's a pleasure for Nancy and myself to be here, to stop by and be able to see these beautiful paintings. This gallery is a tribute to something that I look forward to seeing improve in our country, and that is private initiative.

Duncan Phillips built this collection, and when he died, he left it for our enjoyment—over 2,500 paintings, 200 of which are on display here at any one time while the others are circulated to museums and galleries throughout the United States. And thanks to Mr. Phillips' kindness, people from all over the world, since the museum opened in 1921, have come here to see this collection of American moderns and French impressionists.

It's often overlooked that Americans like Duncan Phillips who made money in steel, in that industry, have a keen interest in the arts. This particular museum was left an endowment to take care of its needs. However, inflation and other economic problems have taken a toll, and that's why we're all here tonight.

You are individually doing your part, making your contribution to art, and that's the kind of effort that's in keeping with the spirit that we're trying to recapture in these days. I met with a group of our citizens the other day, one of whom is involved in addition to his own particular career, in heading up some very worthwhile, nonprofit endeavor in the country. And I hope that we can stimulate that and see a great increase in that sort of thing. Personal involvement—it makes this a better place to live.

I'm particularly proud of the role that Carolyn Deaver is playing to keep this gallery going. It's an admirable project, and I wish her and all of you the best, and just, I think on behalf of everyone in this country who wants to see things like this go on, to say a "thank you" to all of you.

And now I'll get off of here so the party can go on. [*Laughter*]

Note: The President spoke at 8:20 p.m. at the Gallery.

Remarks at the Annual Ambassadors Ball To Benefit the Multiple Sclerosis Society
September 22, 1981

Well, ladies and gentlemen here on the dais, and you ladies and gentlemen out there, first of all, let me apologize for not being properly dressed for the occasion. But the way this day has been going, I would have had to dress to fit the occasion this morning. [*Laughter*]

Anyway, it's a pleasure for Nancy and me to be with you here tonight and to honor and assist the Multiple Sclerosis Society. It's also a pleasure to welcome Washington's new Ambassadors.

Much attention has been focused on our budget proposals as of late. I don't know why; it's just something that happens every year. [*Laughter*] But this event and similar

efforts to directly involve the private sector in solving problems are the flip side of reducing the growth of government.

We advocate more than budget cuts. We advocate personal commitment and a tapping of a vast under-used resource—human compassion. For too long the American people have been told that they are relieved of responsibility for helping their fellow man because government's taken over the job. Now, we don't believe in totally eliminating government's role in humanitarian efforts, but we are trying to recapture that spirit of generosity that suffocates under heavy taxation and bureaucratic redtape.

Over our history, Americans have always been willing to lend a hand. In the aftermath of earthquakes, floods, plagues, typhoons and other natural disasters, Americans were there to help. Helping one another is a part of our heritage: The government was so far away, our earlier settlers depended on each other. And often people forget that the religious convictions of our forefathers went a little beyond puritanism. The Bible talks of faith, hope, and charity, and the greatest of these is charity.

Americans took this admonition seriously, just as they did the parable of the Good Samaritan. If you remember, the Samaritan walking along on the other side of the road from the beaten pilgrim didn't take a look and then hurry on to the nearest town where he could find a local official and tell him there was someone out there that needed help. He crossed the road and went to the aid of the fallen traveler. The real meaning of the parable has always been not so much the benefit that was done to the beaten man, but the good that accrued to the Samaritan.

Well, tonight we're gathered together to help those afflicted by multiple sclerosis—another of those brutal diseases that has yet to be conquered. Support by private companies and corporations for fighting this disease is in the finest tradition of which I just spoke. The Multiple Sclerosis Society has been collecting voluntary contributions to support research and patient services since 1945. Eighty clinics and 134 multiple sclerosis chapters throughout the United States are helping those who have contracted the disease as well as their families.

I'm especially proud of the involvement of Ursula Meese in this effort. She's a woman of tremendous energy and dedication. And far too often, people with such talent think the only way to better their country is to immerse themselves in politics. Some even delude themselves into thinking that political contributions are gifts of charity. [*Laughter*] In fact, some of the politicians think that. [*Laughter*]

But this degrades the meaning of charity and is counterproductive to efforts to help those in need. And today, as I've said, we seek to re-ignite that spirit of direct involvement, to recapture the energy that comes when people are helping because that's what they want to do, and to encourage people to care about each other.

This banquet is a fine example of what can be done. And although many people can't afford to give money, everyone has a role to play, even if it's a contribution of time instead of dollars.

Thanks to the diplomatic community for what you've done tonight to help fight this dreaded disease. And a very great "thank you" to those who organized this event for letting Nancy and me, at least for a few minutes, come here and play a part.

We've just been to one place where they hadn't had dinner yet; we've now interrupted you in the middle of dinner; and now we'll move on. [*Laughter*] It's quite a switch for a fellow that's been on the mashed-potato circuit as an afterdinner speaker for so many years.

But again, God bless you, and thank you all for what you're doing.

Note: The President spoke at approximately 9 p.m. in the International Ballroom at the Washington Hilton Hotel.

Executive Order 12323—Presidential Commission on Broadcasting to Cuba
September 22, 1981

By the authority vested in me as President by the Constitution of the United States of America, in accordance with the Federal Advisory Committee Act, as amended (5 U.S.C. App. I), and in order to create a commission to develop recommendations with respect to broadcasting of information and ideas to Cuba, it is hereby ordered as follows:

Section 1. Establishment. (a) There is established the Presidential Commission on Broadcasting to Cuba.

(b) The Commission shall be composed of 11 members appointed by the President from among citizens of the United States.

(c) The President shall designate one of the members to be the Chairman.

(d) There shall be a three member Executive Committee of the Commission which shall be composed of the Chairman and two other members elected by the Commission.

Sec. 2. Functions.

(a) The Commission shall develop a recommended plan for radio broadcasting intended for transmission to Cuba. The purpose of the plan shall be to promote open communication of information and ideas to Cuba and in particular broadcasting to the Cuban people of accurate information about Cuba.

(b) The Commission shall examine issues related to effectively carrying out such a plan for radio broadcasting to Cuba. These shall include, but not be limited to, possible program content, information gathering, writing and editing needs, staffing requirements, legal structure for a broadcasting organization, proposed legislation, sample budgets, and the location, structure and function of possible broadcasting stations.

(c) The Commission may conduct studies, inquiries, hearings, and meetings as it deems necessary. It may assemble and disseminate information, and issue reports and other publications. It may also coordinate, sponsor, or oversee projects, studies, events and other activities that it deems necessary or desirable for development of a recommended program of broadcasting to Cuba.

(d) The Executive Committee may coordinate the work of the Commission and may act on behalf of the whole Commission.

(e) The Commission shall submit its recommendations and final report to the President and the Secretary of State no later than October 1, 1982.

Sec. 3. Administration.

(a) Members of the Commission who are not otherwise Government employees shall serve without any compensation for their work on the Commission. However, all members shall be entitled to travel expenses, including per diem in lieu of subsistence, as authorized by law (5 U.S.C. 5701–5707).

(b) The heads of Executive agencies shall, to the extent permitted by law, provide the Commission such information and advice with respect to radio broadcasting to Cuba as the Commission may require for the purpose of carrying out its functions.

(c) Expenses of the Commission shall be paid from funds available to the Secretary of State.

Sec. 4. General.

(a) Notwithstanding any other Executive order, the functions of the President under the Federal Advisory Committee Act, as amended (5 U.S.C. App. I), which are applicable to the Commission, except that of reporting annually to the Congress, shall be performed by the Secretary of State in accordance with guidelines and procedures established by the Administrator of General Services.

(b) The Commission shall terminate on October 1, 1982, or 60 days after submitting its final report, whichever is earlier.

RONALD REAGAN

The White House,
September 22, 1981.

[Filed with the Office of the Federal Register, 10 a.m., September 24, 1981]

Note: The text of the Executive order was released by the Office of the Press Secretary on September 23.

Remarks at a Ceremony Commemorating the 10th Anniversary of the Retired Senior Volunteer Program
September 23, 1981

First of all, welcome to the White House. Nancy and I are most delighted that you're here, and we have a chance to say what a wonderful job that you and—I think it's wonderful the initials for your title, RSVP, what you are doing, Retired Senior Volunteer Program. But we also know that RSVP means, kind of, come again.

But even though the "R" stands for retired, that's not quite the way to describe you. Someone said that the only true retirement is of the heart, and you certainly haven't retired in that regard. You've given not only your heart to volunteer activities but your minds and hands as well.

Some here today have been doing volunteer work for RSVP since its inception 10 years ago. And I know this anniversary is especially meaningful for those of you who have been in since the beginning. But it's also meaningful to this administration because it shows that voluntarism can work. There are some 300,000 senior volunteers right now who are proving it in a number of ways—counseling runaway youth, juvenile offenders; giving disadvantaged children extra reading help; providing legal assistance in public defender offices. I'm told that you even have volunteers who counsel on how to fill out Medicare forms, which puts some of you in the genius category. [*Laughter*]

But wherever there's a need, you have the expertise to fill it. Now I, myself, have some volunteer work for you. When you return to your hometowns, would you tell your fellow volunteers that we intend to keep our promise to restore social security's fiscal integrity? In addition to that, the system can only be as strong as the economy, and we're attempting to make the economy strong so that social security will also be strong.

Thomas Carlisle said that the work of an unknown good man—or woman, I might add—is like a vein of water flowing hidden underground, secretly making the ground green. Well, you are making so many things green and growing with your volunteer work. And I imagine your work has probably made your lives a little greener, too.

Someone else once said that life begins when you begin to serve, and I've found there's some truth in that, also. [*Laughter*] But let me also just add this one thing: that with all the hard things that we have to do to restore this economy, the cuts of many things that we wish didn't have to be cut, we at the same time are just embarking on a program where, from the White House, we are going to take action and form a task force throughout the country to mobilize volunteers and the force of the public sector—or the private sector, I should say—to contribute, to take up the slack in many of the things that government perhaps shouldn't have been doing in the first place, that should have been left to that kind of work. And we're going to see if we can't mobilize that kind of a voluntarism back in our society again.

So, thank you for inviting Nancy and myself to share in the RSVP celebration.

Note: The President spoke at 10:16 a.m. in the Rose Garden at the White House. RSVP, the largest Federal volunteer program, is a part of ACTION.

Letter to the Speaker of the House and the Chairman of the Senate Foreign Relations Committee Reporting on the Cyprus Conflict
September 23, 1981

Dear Mr. Speaker: (Dear Mr. Chairman:)

In accordance with the provision of Public Law 95–384, I am submitting the following report on progress made during the past sixty days toward reaching a negotiated settlement of the Cyprus problem.

The intercommunal negotiations between Greek Cypriot and Turkish Cypriot representatives under the chairmanship of the United Nations Secretary General's Special Representative on Cyprus, Ambassador Hugo Gobbi, are continuing to explore issues of mutual concern. Following an interrupted schedule earlier this year when both Greek and Turkish Cypriots prepared for and held elections, intercommunal negotiations have resumed on a more frequent schedule with weekly sessions since July 29. The negotiating atmosphere has remained congenial and constructive.

This period has been marked by substantive presentations in the negotiations by both sides. The Turkish Cypriot negotiator submitted proposals on August 5 and the Greek Cypriot representative on September

9. These proposals are comprehensive in scope addressing the basic constitutional and territorial questions that lie at the core of the disagreements dividing Cyprus.

We have welcomed developments of this nature as indicative of a continuing commitment by both communities to resolve their differences by peaceful negotiation and a spirit of compromise. We hope that during the period ahead the discussion under the *aegis* of United Nations Secretary General Waldheim will lead to a just, fair and lasting resolution of the Cyprus problem. The intercommunal negotiations have now passed the one-year mark, and it is time for the parties to reinvigorate their efforts to bring the hopes stimulated by their inception to fruition.

Sincerely,

RONALD REAGAN

Note: This is the text of identical letters addressed to Thomas P. O'Neill, Jr., Speaker of the House of Representatives, and to Charles H. Percy, chairman of the Senate Foreign Relations Committee.

Statement by Assistant to the President for National Security Affairs Richard V. Allen Concerning Radio Broadcasting to Cuba
September 23, 1981

For more than 20 years, the Cuban people have been controlled and manipulated by a totalitarian Marxist-Leninist dictatorship dedicated to promoting armed violence and undermining the interests of the Free World. The standard of living of the Cuban people has deteriorated since 1975 as the Cuban leadership has broadened and intensified these efforts, sending tens of thousands of troops to Africa, bringing violent revolutionaries and terrorists from dozens of countries to Cuba for training,

and stepping up its subversion in Latin America.

Cuba's extensive international troublemaking is made possible by, and is all the more dangerous because of, its alliance with and dependence on the Soviet Union, which provides Cuba with massive economic and military support in exchange for Cuban promotion of Soviet interests. Cuba's Communist leaders have kept the Cuban people ignorant of this campaign of international violence by systematic manipulation of information. The regime in Cuba, like all totalitarian regimes, has in large measure governed the Cuban people through its control of the media. The Cuban revolution, in fact, has often been described as a revolution through the media.

One of the boasts of the Cuban Government is that the Cuban media never lie. The Cuban media, however, have lied throughout the two decades of the revolution, they lie today, and will continue to lie to the Cuban people. The truth about the costs borne by the Cuban people as a result of their government's grandiose international involvement and repression of basic human rights has been shrouded in lies and half-truths. The truth about underdevelopment and mismanagement despite massive Soviet subsidies and direction of the economy is not known in Cuba.

Cubans, like all peoples, yearn for the truth. Even Cuba's leaders rely on the Western press and wire services, the Voice of America, and BBC for factual, unbiased information about the world they live in.

But these sources, because they cover events around the world, cannot satisfy the Cuban people's thirst for reliable information about their own country.

This administration has decided to break the Cuban Government's control of information in Cuba. It will do this by supporting establishment of Radio Broadcasting to Cuba. In Spanish, it will be called *Radio Marti*, after José Marti, the father of Cuban independence. This radio service will tell the truth to the Cuban people about their government's domestic mismanagement and its promotion of subversion and international terrorism in this hemisphere and elsewhere. It will tell the Cuban people that these activities cost in terms of living standards for them and their children and will correct the false image they have been given of Cuba's international reputation.

Note: Mr. Allen read the statement on behalf of the President at approximately 4:40 p.m. during a briefing for the press in Room 450 of the Old Executive Office Building.

Remarks at a White House Reception and Barbecue for the California and Texas Congressional Delegations
September 23, 1981

They're darned good at that for Easterners. [*Laughter*] Well, I think everyone out here has told you how grateful we are. We have been superbly entertained. We've been superbly entertained, but I think everyone would agree, also, we've also tonight been inspired. Thank you.

I want you to know the truth: We're all guests. Not only the Statler Brothers but that wonderful dinner. Our friends, the Santa Ynez Barbecuers from Santa Ynez, California—[*applause*]—I don't know whether the custom exists anyplace else, but out in California in a number of communities, there are people like themselves for whom this is a hobby. But I don't think they've gone quite so far as this group has gone, because they came here as volunteers, and they brought the meat, and they

brought the stuff to burn to cook it, and everything else, and we're all—[*applause*].

Of course, I was a little surprised. I thought finally something had happened in Washington in which I could leave off a necktie, and I came here and everybody looks like lawyers from the East. [*Laughter*] Well, let's pretend they all just came here directly from the office. All right. And a lot of them are nodding, "Yes, we did." [*Laughter*]

Well, to all of you, Nancy and I are delighted that you have been here. We've enjoyed this, and I know from the way you've reacted that you have also. [*Applause*] And I think that for that lady they sang about, that if we just remember that every once in a while we cross a lot of State lines and we cross a lot of party lines, but if we just remember that if every once in a while we get together and break bread and realize how much we have in common, we'll discover that everything will be all right as long as we talk to each other instead of about each other.

So again, just a heartfelt thanks to all of you for the wonderful entertainment and a heartfelt thanks to all of you for coming and to those who fed us so well. And with that, I'll get off of here because I haven't got an encore. [*Laughter*] As a matter of fact, I haven't even got a get-off line except, "Good night."

Thank you all.

Note: The President spoke at 8:45 p.m. following a performance by the Statler Brothers on the South Lawn of the White House.

Remarks at a White House Reception for District and Appellate Court Judges and Supreme Court Justices
September 24, 1981

Well, Nancy and I are honored to welcome you all to the White House today—you who have met the exacting standards of integrity, fairness and intellect required for Federal judgeship. You provide reassurance for all of us that our ideals of liberty and justice are alive and well in the United States of America.

Wisdom is the quality we look for most in our judges. In an age of mounting judicial workloads and increasing technicality, we demand of our judges a wisdom that knows no time, has no prejudice, and wants no other reward. The challenge seems impossible, and yet you've dedicated your lives to it.

Every time I talk about wisdom, I think of the old legend of the three wise men on an island that was threatened with being flooded as the result of a hurricane. One of them decided that he would do all the things that he had never been able to do in his life in the limited time that was left. And the second one decided that he would just devote himself to further study. And I think the third one was a good pattern for everyone—he retreated with his closest advisers to the highest point on the island and set out to find out if they could live under water. [*Laughter*]

We've entrusted you with our ideals and our freedom, and our future depends on the way you define it today. It's a sacred trust whose burden can only be carried by the highest quality of men and women. Your determined commitment to the preservation of our rights is a commitment that often requires the lonely courage of a patriot. On behalf of all Americans, I want to express our often-neglected thanks. I assure you, your commitment is returned. I pledge to do everything in my power to enhance the prestige and quality of the Federal Bench.

In a society founded on law, we must take all reasonable steps to ensure that the best among us accept the call to serve and are able to serve for life. Our heritage of individual liberty is dependent on the rule of law. As the inscription over the door of the Department of Justice says, just a few blocks from here, it reminds us, "Law alone can give us freedom." You who interpret it, who administer it, are the guardians of freedom for generations yet unborn. It's a privilege to welcome you here today.

And that was the concluding line, except that now I ask again, "Why is it that they always fly out of National [Airport] just when we're doing something like this?" [*Laughter*] Well, thank you again for being here and I know we shall all see each other in a few moments. Thank you.

Note: The President spoke at 11:55 a.m. in the Rose Garden at the White House.

Nomination of David Charles Miller, Jr., To Be United States Ambassador to Tanzania
September 24, 1981

The President today announced his intention to nominate David Charles Miller, Jr., of Maryland, to be Ambassador to the United Republic of Tanzania. He would succeed Richard Noyes Viets.

In 1962 Mr. Miller was a summer intern with the Department of Commerce and with the Department of Justice in 1965. He was research associate with Simulmatics Corp. (for advanced research projects agency) in Vietnam in 1967–68. In 1968–69 he was a White House Fellow at the Department of Justice and was special assistant to the Attorney General in 1969–70. He was Director of the White House Fellowship Commission in 1970–71. In 1971–81 he was with Westinghouse Electric Corp., serving successively in Pittsburgh, Pa., as assistant to executive vice president for defense and public systems, director of planning of Westinghouse world regions, and director of corporate international relations. Following service in Lagos, Nigeria, as general manager of TCOM Corp. and Westinghouse country manager for Nigeria, he was deputy of international business operations of Westinghouse defense group in Baltimore, Md. He is currently special assistant to the Assistant Secretary of State for African Affairs in the Department of State.

Mr. Miller graduated from Harvard College (B.A., 1964) and the University of Michigan Law School (J.D., 1967). He is married, has three children, and resides in Baltimore, Md. He was born July 15, 1942, in Cleveland, Ohio.

Nomination of Ralph Ball To Be a Member of the Federal Farm Credit Board
September 24, 1981

The President today announced his intention to nominate Ralph Ball to be a member of the Federal Farm Credit Board, Farm Credit Administration, for a term expiring March 31, 1987. He would succeed Ralph N. Austin.

Mr. Ball is a farmer in Sterling, Kans., where he owns and operates a 2,100-acre corn, milo, wheat, and alfalfa farm. He is vice chairman of the board of Farmland Industries, Inc., and serves on the board of Far Mar Co., Inc., and Farmland Insurance. He is director of the Kansas Association of Wheat Growers and was a member of the White House Conference on Food, Health, and Nutrition.

Mr. Ball was born January 18, 1916, in Stafford, Kans.

Announcement of the Resumption of the Micronesian Status Negotiations
September 24, 1981

The President has authorized the resumption of negotiations with the Governments of Palau, the Marshall Islands, and the Federated States of Micronesia, which are intended to result in the termination of the last United Nations Trusteeship—one under which the United States has administered the Trust Territory of the Pacific Islands since 1947.

The President's decision marked the completion of a 6-month-long policy review conducted by an interdepartmental group under the chairmanship of James L. Buckley, Under Secretary of State for Security Assistance, Science and Technology. Mr. Buckley will head the United States delegation at a meeting in Hawaii proposed to begin October 3, which will mark the resumption of negotiations with the three Micronesian Governments.

The policy review concluded that the United States should move promptly to terminate the United Nations Trusteeship on terms satisfactory to itself and to the Government and peoples of Micronesia. It also endorsed a new political status in which the three Micronesian Governments would enter into relationships of free association with the United States. The three Micronesian Governments had earlier indicated their preference for that status by initialing with the United States, in late 1980, a Compact of Free Association. The political status of free association is distinguishable both from independence and from an extension of United States sovereignty; under it, plenary defense rights and responsibilities would remain vested in the United States, and the Micronesian Governments would enjoy full internal self-government and substantial authority in foreign affairs.

The Micronesian political status negotiations began under the Nixon administration and continued through each of the two subsequent administrations. They have been in a state of informal suspension, however, pending the completion of the Reagan administration's policy review.

In deciding to go forward on the basis of the Compact of Free Association and five agreements subsidiary to it which were also initialed late last year, the administration stipulated that 11 remaining subsidiary agreements would have to be completed to the mutual satisfaction of the negotiating parties before any of the documents could be considered complete.

Secretary Buckley's delegation to the proposed Hawaii meeting will present and explain these and other administration decisions to the chief executives and political status negotiators of the Micronesian Governments. Administration representatives will also seek to establish a schedule for completing work on the remaining subsidiary agreements, a process which is expected to require several months.

The delegation also plans to discuss with Micronesian officials the procedures by which the negotiated documents will ultimately be approved. The process envisions a plebiscite by the voters of Micronesia under U.N. observation, action by their governments in accordance with constitutional processes, and approval by both Houses of the United States Congress and enactment of the Compact into public law.

Palau and the Federated States of Micronesia together constitute the Caroline Islands. They and the Marshalls have a combined population of about 120,000. The Marshalls and the Carolines extend for almost 3,000 miles across the mid-Pacific between Hawaii and Guam and are located just north of the Equator. The Federated States of Micronesia and the Marshall Islands established elected constitutional governments in May 1979. Palau followed suit on January 1, 1981.

The Northern Mariana Islands, a fourth component of the Trust Territory, voted in 1975 after similar negotiations to become a commonwealth in political union with the United States. The Northern Marianas are now self-governing, but U.S. sovereignty will extend to those islands—and the island-ers will become U.S. citizens—only when the Trusteeship Agreement is terminated.

Address to the Nation on the Program for Economic Recovery
September 24, 1981

Good evening.

Shortly after taking office, I came before you to map out a four-part plan for national economic recovery: tax cuts to stimulate more growth and more jobs, spending cuts to put an end to continuing deficits and high inflation, regulatory relief to lift the heavy burden of government rules and paperwork, and, finally, a steady, consistent, monetary policy.

We've made strong, encouraging progress on all four fronts. The flood of new governmental regulations, for example, has been cut by more than a third. I was especially pleased when a bipartisan coalition of Republicans and Democrats enacted the biggest tax cuts and the greatest reduction in Federal spending in our nation's history. Both will begin to take effect a week from today.

These two bills would never have passed without your help. Your voices were heard in Washington and were heeded by those you've chosen to represent you in government. Yet, in recent weeks we've begun to hear a chorus of other voices protesting that we haven't had full economic recovery. These are the same voices that were raised against our program when it was first presented to Congress. Now that the first part of it has been passed, they declare it hasn't worked. Well, it hasn't; it doesn't start until a week from today.

There have been some bright spots in our economic performance these past few months. Inflation has fallen, and pressures are easing on both food and fuel prices. More than a million more Americans are now at work than a year ago, and recently there has even been a small crack in interest rates. But let me be the first to say that our problems won't suddenly disappear next week, next month, or next year. We're just starting down a road that I believe will lead us out of the economic swamp we've been in for so long. It'll take time for the effect of the tax rate reductions to be felt in increased savings, productivity, and new jobs. It will also take time for the budget cuts to reduce the deficits which have brought us near runaway inflation and ruinous interest rates.

The important thing now is to hold to a firm, steady course. Tonight I want to talk with you about the next steps that we must take on that course, additional reductions in Federal spending that will help lower our interest rates, our inflation, and bring us closer to full economic recovery.

I know that high interest rates are punishing many of you, from the young family that wants to buy its first home to the farmer who needs a new truck or tractor. But all of us know that interest rates will only come down and stay down when government is no longer borrowing huge amounts of money to cover its deficits.

These deficits have been piling up every year, and some people here in Washington just throw up their hands in despair. Maybe you'll remember that we were told in the spring of 1980 that the 1981 budget, the one we have now, would be balanced. Well, that budget, like so many in the past, hemorrhaged badly and wound up in a sea of red ink.

I have pledged that we shall not stand idly by and see that same thing happen again. When I presented our economic recovery program to Congress, I said we were aiming to cut the deficit steadily to reach a balance by 1984. The budget bill that I signed this summer cut $35 billion from the 1982 budget and slowed the growth of spending by $130 billion over the next 3 years. We cut the government's rate of growth nearly in half.

831

Now, we must move on to a second round of budget savings to keep us on the road to a balanced budget.

Our immediate challenge is to hold down the deficit in the fiscal year that begins next week. A number of threats are now appearing that will drive the deficit upward if we fail to act. For example, in the euphoria just after our budget bill was approved this summer, we didn't point out immediately, as we should, that while we did get most of what we'd asked for, most isn't all. Some of the savings in our proposal were not approved, and since then, the Congress has taken actions that could add even more to the cost of government.

The result is that without further reductions, our deficit for 1982 will be increased by some 18—or, pardon me—$16 billion. The estimated deficit for '83 will be increased proportionately. And without further cuts, we can't achieve our goal of a balanced budget by 1984.

Now, it would be easy to sit back and say, "Well, it'll take longer than we thought. We got most of what we proposed, so let's stop there." But that's not good enough.

In meeting to discuss this problem a few days ago, Senator Pete Domenici of New Mexico, chairman of the Senate Budget Committee, recalled the words of that great heavyweight champion and great American, Joe Louis, just before he stepped into the ring against Billy Conn. There had been some speculation that Billy might be able to avoid Joe's lethal right hand. Joe said, "Well, he can run but he can't hide." Senator Domenici said to me, "That's just what we're facing on runaway Federal spending. We can try to run from it, but we can't hide. We have to face up to it."

He's right, of course. In the last few decades we started down a road that led to a massive explosion in Federal spending. It took about 170 years for the Federal budget to reach $100 billion. That was in 1962. It only took 8 years to reach the $200 billion mark, and only 5 more to make it $300 billion. And in the next 5, we nearly doubled that. It would be one thing if we'd been able to pay for all the things government decided to do, but we've only balanced the budget once in the last 20 years.

In just the past decade, our national debt has more than doubled. And in the next few days, it'll pass the trillion dollar mark. One trillion dollars of debt—if we as a nation needed a warning, let that be it.

Our interest payments on the debt alone are now running more than $96 billion a year. That's more than the total combined profits last year of the 500 biggest companies in the country; or, to put it another way, Washington spends more on interest than on all of its education, nutrition, and medical programs combined.

In the past, there have been several methods used to fund some of our social experiments—one was to take it away from national defense. From being the strongest nation on Earth in the post World War II years, we steadily declined while the Soviet Union engaged in the most massive military buildup the world has ever seen.

Now, with all our economic problems, we're forced to try to catch up so that we can preserve the peace. Government's first responsibility is national security, and we're determined to meet that responsibility. Indeed, we have no choice.

Well, what all of this is leading up to is, "What do we plan to do?" Last week I met with the Cabinet to take up this matter. I'm proud to say there was no handwringing, no pleading to avoid further budget cuts. We all agreed that the "tax and tax, spend and spend" policies of the last few decades lead only to economic disaster. Our government must return to the tradition of living within our means and must do it now. We asked ourselves two questions—and answered them: "If not us, who? If not now, when?"

Let me talk with you now about the specific ways that I believe we ought to achieve additional savings, savings of some $6 billion in 1982 and a total of $80 billion when spread over the next 3 years. I recognize that many in Congress may have other alternatives, and I welcome a dialog with them. But let there be no mistake: We have no choice but to continue down the road toward a balanced budget, a budget that will keep us strong at home and secure overseas. And let me be clear that this cannot be the last round of cuts. Holding down spending must be a continuing battle for several years to come.

Now, here's what I propose. First, I'm asking Congress to reduce the 1982 appropriation for most government agencies and programs by 12 percent. This will save $17½ billion over the next several years. Absorbing these reductions will not be easy, but duplication, excess, waste, and overhead is still far too great and can be trimmed further.

No one in the meeting asked to be exempt from belt-tightening. Over the next 3 years, the increase we had originally planned in the defense budget will be cut by $13 billion. I'll confess, I was reluctant about this because of the long way we have to go before the dangerous window of vulnerability confronting us will be appreciably narrowed. But the Secretary of Defense assured me that he can meet our critical needs in spite of this cut.

Second, to achieve further economies, we'll shrink the size of the non-defense payroll over the next 3 years by some 6½ percent, some 75,000 employees. Much of this will be attained by not replacing those who retire or leave. There will, however, be some reductions in force simply because we're reducing our administrative overhead. I intend to set the example here by reducing the size of the White House staff and the staff of the Executive Office of the President.

As a third step, we propose to dismantle two Cabinet Departments, Energy and Education. Both Secretaries are wholly in accord with this. Some of the activities in both of these departments will, of course, be continued either independently or in other areas of government. There's only one way to shrink the size and cost of big government, and that is by eliminating agencies that are not needed and are getting in the way of a solution.

Now, we don't need an Energy Department to solve our basic energy problem. As long as we let the forces of the marketplace work without undue interference, the ingenuity of consumers, business, producers, and inventors will do that for us.

Similarly, education is the principal responsibility of local school systems, teachers, parents, citizen boards, and State governments. By eliminating the Department of Education less than 2 years after it was created, we cannot only reduce the budget but ensure that local needs and preferences, rather than the wishes of Washington, determine the education of our children.

We also plan the elimination of a few smaller agencies and a number of boards and commissions, some of which have fallen into disuse or which are now being duplicated.

Fourth, we intend to make reductions of some $20 billion in Federal loan guarantees. Now, these guarantees are not funds that the government spends directly. They're funds that are loaned in the private market and insured by government at subsidized rates. Federal loan guarantees have become a form of back door, uncontrolled borrowing that prevent many small businesses that aren't subsidized from obtaining financing of their own. They are also a major factor in driving up interest rates. It's time we brought this practice under control.

Fifth, I intend to forward to Congress this fall a new package of entitlement and welfare reform measures, outside social security, to save nearly $27 billion over the next 3 years. In the past two decades, we've created hundreds of new programs to provide personal assistance. Many of these programs may have come from a good heart, but not all have come from a clear head—and the costs have been staggering.

In 1955 these programs cost $8 billion. By 1965 the cost was $79 billion. Next year it will be $188 billion. Let there be no confusion on this score: Benefits for the needy will be protected, but the black market in food stamps must be stopped, the abuse and fraud in Medicaid by beneficiaries and providers alike cannot be tolerated, provision of school loans and meal subsidies to the affluent can no longer be afforded.

In California when I was Governor and embarked upon welfare reform, there were screams from those who claimed that we intended to victimize the needy. But in a little over 3 years, we saved the taxpayers some $2 billion at the same time we were able to increase the grants for the deserving and truly needy by an average of more than 40 percent. It was the first cost-of-living increase they'd received in 13 years. I believe progress can also be made at the national level. We can be compassionate about human needs without being complacent about budget extravagance.

Sixth, I will soon urge Congress to enact new proposals to eliminate abuses and obsolete incentives in the tax code. The Treasury Department believes that the deficit can be reduced by $3 billion next year and $22 billion over the next 3 years with prompt enactment of these measures. Now that we've provided the greatest incentives for saving, investment, work, and productivity ever proposed, we must also ensure that taxes due the government are collected and that a fair share of the burden is borne by all.

Finally, I'm renewing my plea to Congress to approve my proposals for user fees—proposals first suggested last spring but which have been neglected since.

When the Federal Government provides a service directly to a particular industry or to a group of citizens, I believe that those who receive benefits should bear the cost. For example, this next year the Federal Government will spend $525 million to maintain river harbors, channels, locks and dams for the barge and maritime industries. Yacht owners, commercial vessels, and the airlines will receive services worth $2.8 billion from Uncle Sam.

My spring budget proposals included legislation that would authorize the Federal Government to recover a total of $980 million from the users of these services through fees. Now, that's only a third of the $3.3 billion it'll cost the government to provide those same services.

None of these steps will be easy. We're going through a period of difficult and painful readjustment. I know that we're asking for sacrifices from virtually all of you, but there is no alternative. Some of those who oppose this plan have participated over the years in the extravagance that has brought us inflation, unemployment, high interest rates, and an intolerable debt. Now, I grant they were well-intentioned, but their costly reforms didn't eliminate poverty or raise welfare recipients from dependence to self-sufficiency, independence, and dignity. Yet, in their objections to what we've proposed, they offer only what we know has been tried before and failed.

I believe we've chosen a path that leads to an America at work, to fiscal sanity, to lower taxes, and less inflation. I believe our plan for recovery is sound, and it will work.

Tonight, I'm asking all of you who joined in this crusade to save our economy to help again, to let your representatives know that you will support them in making the hard decisions to further reduce the cost and size of government.

Now, if you'll permit me, I'd like to turn to another subject which I know has many of you very concerned and even frightened. This is an issue apart from the economic reform package that we've just been discussing, but I feel I must clear the air. There has been a great deal of misinformation and, for that matter, pure demagoguery on the subject of social security.

During the campaign, I called attention to the fact that social security had both a short- and a long-range fiscal problem. I pledged my best to restore it to fiscal responsibility without in any way reducing or eliminating existing benefits for those now dependent on it.

To all of you listening, and particularly those of you now receiving social security, I ask you to listen very carefully: first to what threatens the integrity of social security, and then to a possible solution.

Some 30 years ago, there were 16 people working and paying the social security payroll tax for every 1 retiree. Today that ratio has changed to only 3.2 workers paying in for each beneficiary. For many years, we've known that an actuarial imbalance existed and that the program faced an unfunded liability of several trillion dollars.

Now, the short-range problem is much closer than that. The social security retirement fund has been paying out billions of dollars more each year than it takes in, and it could run out of money before the end of 1982 unless something is done. Some of our critics claim new figures reveal a cushion of several billions of dollars which will carry the program beyond 1982. I'm sure it's only a coincidence that 1982 is an election year.

The cushion they speak of is borrowing from the Medicare fund and the disability fund. Of course, doing this would only postpone the day of reckoning. Alice Rivlin of the Congressional Budget Office told a congressional committee, day before yesterday, that such borrowing might carry us to 1990, but then we'd face the same problem. And as she put it, we'd have to cut benefits or raise the payroll tax. Well, we're not going to cut benefits, and the payroll tax is already being raised.

In 1977 Congress passed the largest tax increase in our history. It called for a payroll tax increase in January of 1982, another in 1985, and again in 1986 and in 1990. When that law was passed we were told it made social security safe until the year 2030. But we're running out of money 48 years short of 2030.

For the nation's work force, the social security tax is already the biggest tax they pay. In 1935 we were told the tax would never be greater than 2 percent of the first $3,000 of earnings. It is presently 13.3 percent of the first $29,700, and the scheduled increases will take it to 15.3 percent of the first $60,600. And that's when Mrs. Rivlin says we would need an additional increase.

Some have suggested reducing benefits. Others propose an income tax on benefits, or that the retirement age should be moved back to age 68. And there are some who would simply fund social security out of general tax funds, as welfare is funded. I believe there are better solutions.

I am asking the Congress to restore the minimum benefit for current beneficiaries with low incomes. It was never our intention to take this support away from those who truly need it. There is, however, a sizable percentage of recipients who are adequately provided for by pensions or other income and should not be added to the financial burden of social security.

The same situation prevails with regard to disability payments. No one will deny our obligation to those with legitimate claims, but there's widespread abuse of the system which should not be allowed to continue.

Since 1962 early retirement has been allowed at age 62 with 80 percent of full benefits. In our proposal we ask that early retirees in the future receive 55 percent of the total benefit, but—and this is most important—those early retirees would only

have to work an additional 20 months to be eligible for the 80-percent payment. I don't believe very many of you were aware of that part of our proposal.

The only change we proposed for those already receiving social security had to do with the annual cost-of-living adjustment. Now, those adjustments are made on July 1st each year, a hangover from the days when the fiscal year began in July. We proposed a one-time delay in making that adjustment, postponing it for 3 months until October 1st. From then on it would continue to be made every 12 months. That one-time delay would not lower your existing benefits but would, on the average, reduce your increase by about $86 one time next year.

By making these few changes, we would have solved the short- and long-range problems of social security funding once and for all. In addition, we could have canceled the increases in the payroll tax by 1985. To a young person just starting in the work force, the savings from canceling those increases would, on the average, amount to $33,000 by the time he or she reached retirement, and compound interest, add that, and it makes a tidy nest egg to add to the social security benefits.

However, let me point out, our feet were never imbedded in concrete on this proposal. We hoped it could be a starting point for a bipartisan solution to the problem. We were ready to listen to alternatives and other ideas which might improve on or replace our proposals. But, the majority leadership in the House of Representatives has refused to join in any such cooperative effort.

I therefore am asking, as I said, for restoration of the minimum benefit and for inter-fund borrowing as a temporary measure to give us time to seek a permanent solution. To remove social security once and for all from politics, I am also asking Speaker Tip O'Neill of the House of Representatives and Majority Leader in the Senate Howard Baker to each appoint five members, and I will appoint five, to a task force which will review all the options and come up with a plan that assures the fiscal integrity of social security and that social security recipients will continue to receive their full benefits.

I can not and will not stand by and see financial hardship imposed on the more than 36 million senior citizens who have worked and served this Nation throughout their lives. They deserve better from us.

Well now, in conclusion, let me return to the principal purpose of this message, the budget and the imperative need for all of us to ask less of government, to help to return to spending no more than we take in, to end the deficits, and bring down interest rates that otherwise can destroy what we've been building here for two centuries.

I know that we're asking for economies in many areas and programs that were started with the best of intentions and the dedication to a worthwhile cause or purpose, but I know also that some of those programs have not succeeded in their purpose. Others have proven too costly, benefiting those who administer them rather than those who were the intended beneficiaries. This doesn't mean we should discontinue trying to help where help is needed. Government must continue to do its share. But I ask all of you, as private citizens, to join this effort, too.

As a people we have a proud tradition of generosity. More than a century ago, a Frenchman came to America and later wrote a book for his countrymen, telling them what he had seen here. He told them that in America when a citizen saw a problem that needed solving, he would cross the street and talk to a neighbor about it, and the first thing you know a committee would be formed, and before long the problem would be solved. And then he added, "You may not believe this, but not a single bureaucrat would ever have been involved."

Some years ago, when we were a young nation and our people began visiting the lands of their forefathers, these American tourists then were rather brash, unsophisticated by European standards, but blessed with a spirit of independence and pride. One such tourist, an elderly, smalltown gentleman, and his wife were there in Europe listening to a tour guide go on about the wonders of the volcano, Mt. Aetna. He spoke of the great heat that it generated, the power, the boiling lava, et cetera.

Finally the old boy had had enough of it, turned to his wife, and he said, "We've got a volunteer fire department at home that'd put that thing out in 15 minutes." Well, he was typical of those Americans who helped build a neighbor's barn when it burned down. They built the West without an area redevelopment plan, and cities across the land without Federal planning.

I believe the spirit of voluntarism still lives in America. We see examples of it on every hand—the community charity drive, support of hospitals and all manner of nonprofit institutions, the rallying around whenever disaster or tragedy strikes. The truth is we've let government take away many things we once considered were really ours to do voluntarily, out of the goodness of our hearts and a sense of community pride and neighborliness. I believe many of you want to do those things again, want to be involved if only someone will ask you or offer the opportunity. Well, we intend to make that offer.

We're launching a nationwide effort to encourage our citizens to join with us in finding where need exists, and then to organize volunteer programs to meet that need. We've already set the wheels of such a volunteer effort in motion.

As Tom Paine said 200 years ago, "We have it within our power to begin the world over again." What are we waiting for?

God bless you, and good night.

Note: The President spoke at 9 p.m. from the Oval Office at the White House. His address was broadcast live on radio and television.

Remarks of the President and President Daniel T. arap Moi of Kenya Following Their Meeting
September 25, 1981

President Reagan. Ladies and gentlemen, we've been very pleased today to have with us a man who has two most important posts—President Moi, of Kenya, but also Chairman of the Organization of African Unity. The President has ably served in the demanding position as Chairman, and his work has helped bring about solutions to some grievous problems. Let me express my appreciation, Mr. President, for your wise thoughts and candid insights during our discussions, and let me assure you of this administration's interest in and the deep concern for Africa.

I hope our meeting today will be taken as a sign of that interest and concern. We seek the closest of ties with the nations of Africa, and with our allies, are determined to press on in our efforts to find an internationally accepted settlement for Namibia. We've contributed to the African Refugees Conference in Geneva, to the Zimbabwe Donor's Conference, and despite our own domestic belt-tightening, I've asked Congress for significant assistance levels for Africa. We look forward to cooperating with you on many additional initiatives.

And I also want to take this final opportunity to publicly thank your government and nation for its continuing cooperation with the United States. The United States and Kenya have an impressive list of cooperation—or history, I should say—of cooperation and good relations. Under President Moi's leadership this has continued and been strengthened. We share common interests and values, a belief in the democratic form of government, a belief in the free market processes. And Mr. President, your continuing commitment to these values merits emulation and holds the promise to the Kenyan people of continued freedom and increasing prosperity.

In our discussions today, we touched on several areas of common concern and interest. I believe these talks have laid a foundation for expanding cooperation in which the United States can continue its contribution to peace and economic well-being not only in Kenya but elsewhere in Africa. I understand that following talks with Vice President Bush, Secretary Haig, Secretary Weinberger, and others, that you will be quickly moving on to the Commonwealth Conference, so let me wish you, as you leave for Australia, Godspeed and our best wishes.

President Moi. Mr. President, ladies and gentlemen, we have had very useful discussions with the President of the United States, President Reagan, on a number of issues ranging from bilateral to the continent of Africa. We have discussed those matters which are of great concern not only for the two nations but also of international concern. We have discussed those matters that are of urgent concern, that is, the southern part of Africa and elsewhere, including economics and matters touching developing countries in Africa, the continent I represent as Chairman of the Organization of African Unity.

We have reached a greater understanding on these matters, and the United States of America being a great nation, cherishing those ideals of human dignity and human rights and other related matters, I feel that a solution now may be found in that part of Africa. I wish him and the other five nations a success in their discussions.

I thank him for receiving us in this great country, and I hope that the cooperation between not only us, Kenya and the United States, will prosper for the welfare and prosperity of the peoples of the two nations, and also that of Africa and the world at large.

Thank you, Mr. President.

Note: President Reagan spoke at 1 p.m. at the North Portico of the White House. Earlier in the day, the two Presidents held a meeting with their advisers in the Oval Office. The meeting was followed by a luncheon in the Family Dining Room.

Statement of Signing the Product Liability Risk Retention Act of 1981
September 25, 1981

I have today signed into law H.R. 2120, the Product Liability Risk Retention Act of 1981. I am pleased to have the opportunity to approve this much-needed legislation.

During the 1970's many businesses, especially smaller ones, experienced severe increases in their product liability insurance premiums. Others had difficulty obtaining needed coverage. The Interagency Task Force on Product Liability, chaired by the Department of Commerce, and its successor, the Task Force on Product Liability and Accident Compensation, thoroughly studied the problems. The Product Liability Risk Retention Act is an outgrowth of the Federal Government's efforts to address the concerns identified by the Federal task forces and numerous citizen groups.

This act is a marketplace solution designed to provide product manufacturers, distributors, and sellers with affordable product liability insurance. In keeping with this administration's policies, this goal is accomplished without imposing any new Federal regulations or expenditures. The act, respecting the rights of States to regulate the insurance industry within their borders, utilizes existing mechanisms of State insur-

ance departments, streamlined to address the specific needs for regulating this type of insurance. In particular, the act removes selected State regulatory barriers so that product sellers can form self-insurance cooperatives or purchase product liability insurance from commercial insurers on a group rate basis.

By making product liability insurance more easily available and affordable, the best interests of the consumer are also served. Not only will participating companies have lower insurance costs, and hence lower operating costs, but consumers will also benefit by the added protection provided to them through more widespread utilization of product liability insurance.

In short, the act is a good example of how the Federal Government can resolve a nationwide problem without creating additional programs or agencies.

This has been a bipartisan effort. Members of both the House and Senate deserve a great deal of credit for forging a solution which is so widely supported by the small business, insurance, and legal communities.

Note: As enacted, H.R. 2120 is Public Law 97–45, approved September 25.

Exchange With Reporters on Departure for Camp David, Maryland
September 25, 1981

Q. Why do you think the market is dropping?

The President. I don't know, but it started down yesterday. It rose six points yesterday morning, then before the end of the day, it started down, and I guess it is continuing on down. I don't know what the reason is, but I'm sure not going to take the blame.

Q. Why not?

The President. Because I'm going to go by the phone calls and the telegrams and so forth that have been coming in since last

night's speech, and they are running three and four to one and better in our favor on the speech, in support of what we advocated.

Q. What can you do to be sure that no one who is needy suffers if the cuts are made?

The President. We're going to do everything we can. And what we're aiming at mostly is what we have found by experience is true, and that is that there are programs that are being abused by people, who through technicalities and loopholes in the structure of the program are getting benefits they are not entitled to. In the school lunch program, we're simply trying to direct toward those who are in need, and not provide it to families with more affluence that don't really need it. And this is true of all of the other programs.

Q. Would you accept more defense cuts if Congress decides to change your program as long as they give you $13 billion in cuts?

The President. I am going to depend on Secretary Weinberger, because my own experience with him as my finance director in California—I know that if there is any place he can find, he would propose it, if it would be one that would not hurt the program of building that we are going forward with. And I want to point out to you that long before this, he found several billion dollars that reduced the amount of increase that we would have to have, that he translated from fat to muscle. So, he was busy at getting at that angle in the Defense Department long before we came to this point of additional cuts.

Q. Would you go along with it if Congress finds some space for more defense cuts?

The President. I would rather take my judgments from Secretary Weinberger because of the absolute necessity of redressing the imbalance in our defensive standpoint.

Q. Are you negotiating a compromise on the AWACS sale in order to get it through? And is it possible to get it through?

The President. I don't know whether it is possible. I don't really think that we have been to bat yet on this. I'm surprised at the attitude of a number of the Senators about this program, because I think if they reverse this decision to sell, they are literally doing away with our ability to continue to try to bring peace to the Middle East. This is what we're trying to do, and I believe that Saudi Arabia is essential to that process.

Q. Could we have an American in the airplane? Could Saudi Arabia agree to that, sir?

The President. We have Americans now that are maintaining it. We're talking about planes that won't be delivered for 4½ years. In that 4½ years, having kept faith with them, I believe that they can be persuaded as they were in the Lebanon crisis. There would have been no ceasefire had they not heeded our plea and injected themselves into a temporary cessation.

Q. Are you negotiating a compromise?

The President. We are going to find out if there is anything that can persuade these people up there without in any way presuming upon the good will of the Saudi Arabians, anything that can persuade some of these people to see common sense in this.

Q. Thank you.

Note: The exchange began at 3:30 p.m. on the South Lawn of the White House as the President was departing for Camp David.

As printed above, the transcript follows the text of the White House press release.

Remarks in New Orleans, Louisiana, at the Annual Meeting of the International Association of Chiefs of Police
September 28, 1981

Governor Treen, I appreciate those kind words. Mr. Chairman, and the other guests here on the dais, and you ladies and gentlemen:

It's a privilege to stand here today with those who command the front lines in America's battle for public order. You have a tough job and a dangerous one. Believe me, I know. I mean no irreverence when I mention that I once played a sheriff on TV who thought he could do the job without a gun. [*Laughter*] I was dead in the first 27 minutes of the show. [*Laughter*] And I should have included in my greeting here, and I know, the sheriffs, also, who are present.

You and I have a few things in common. Harry Truman once said about the job that

I have that being President is like riding a tiger: A man has to keep on riding or he'll be swallowed. [*Laughter*] Well, that's a pretty good description of what you do for a living. Society asks you simultaneously to protect the innocent, ensure the legitimate rights of property; that you must converse with the multitude, and oversee them, of social services that police captains provide and sheriffs provide for the public, and all the while balance the interests of your department with those of your community, the government, and its citizens. And none of this is easy. The pressures are enormous. You must be administrator, financier, social worker, public relations expert, even politician, and still, somehow, always be a cop.

Well, you do have one of the toughest jobs in America. And let me assure you today that I speak for millions of Americans who, if they could stand here now, would say simply and directly to you, "Thank you for all the always remembered things that you do each day. And remember you do have our support and our unfailing gratitude."

In preparing these remarks, I had an opportunity to go back and look over some of the comments I've made to law enforcement officials on other occasions. The topic of those discussions was a subject with which you have more than a passing familiarity—the steady, ominous growth of crime in our Nation.

In one speech some years ago in Las Vegas, I once wondered about what was happening to America, and I noted the fear and the anger of the citizenry as they locked themselves in their homes or refused to walk the streets at night. I spoke, too, about a phenomenon known as the "youthful offender," the astonishing percentage of crimes that they were estimated to be responsible for.

Then there was a speech in Dallas where I mentioned the effect of narcotics on the crime rate and the appalling estimates that drug addicts were responsible for the economic increase of certain crimes.

I don't mention these speeches now because they show any gift of insight on my part; the truth is, what I said then was well known at the time, certainly by you. The speech in Dallas was delivered in 1974; the speech in Las Vegas in 1967. The frightening reality—for all of the speeches by those of us in government, for all of the surveys, studies, and blue ribbon panels, for all of the 14-point programs and the declarations of war on crime, crime has advanced and advanced steadily in its upward climb, and our citizens have grown more and more frustrated, frightened, and angry.

You're familiar enough with the statistics. The cases that make them up cross your desk every day. In the past decade violent crime reported to police has increased by fifty-nine percent. Fifty-three percent of our citizens say they're afraid to walk the streets alone at night. Eighty-five percent say they're more concerned today than they were 5 years ago about crime.

Crime is an American epidemic. It takes the lives of 25,000 Americans, it touches nearly one-third of American households, and it results in at least some 6 billion—I think I said that figure wrong right there—it results in at least $8.8 billion per year in financial losses.

Just during the time that you and I are together today, at least 1 person will be murdered, 9 women will be raped, 67 other Americans will be robbed, 97 will be seriously assaulted, and 389 homes will be burglarized. This will all happen in the span of the next 30 minutes, or while I'm talking. Now, if by stopping talking I could change those figures, I'd stop. But you know that they will continue at the same rate throughout every 30 minutes of the 24 hours of the day. And I don't have to tell you, the men and women of your departments will be the first to cope with the mayhem, the wreckage, the suffering caused by those who consider themselves above the law with the right to prey on their fellow citizens.

Crime has continued on the upswing. It has gone on regardless of the efforts that we make. Crime has increased in that thing that I mentioned, of the youthful offender, between 18 and 21. And that other problem I mentioned years ago, the incredible impact of drug addiction on the crime rate, continues. Studies of prison inmates have found that at least half admitted to using drugs in the month prior to their arrest.

And it's still estimated that 50 to 60 percent of property crimes are drug-related.

From these statistics about youthful offenders and the impact of drug addiction on crime rates, a portrait emerges. The portrait is that of a stark, staring face, a face that belongs to a frightening reality of our time—the face of a human predator, the face of the habitual criminal. Nothing in nature is more cruel and more dangerous.

Study after study has shown that a small number of criminals are responsible for an enormous amount of the crime in American society. One study of 250 criminals indicated that over an 11-year period, they were responsible for nearly half a million crimes. Another study showed that 49 criminals claimed credit for a total of 10,500 crimes. Take one very limited part of the crime picture, subway crime in New York City: The transit police estimate that 500 habitual offenders are actually responsible for 40 percent of those offenses.

Now, I fully realize that the primary task for apprehending and prosecuting these career criminals, indeed, for dealing with the crime problem itself, belongs to those of you on the State and local level. But there are areas where the Federal Government can take strong and effective action, and today I want to outline for you some of the steps that we're going to take to assist you in the fight against crime.

First, this administration intends to speak out on the problem of crime. We will use this, what Teddy Roosevelt called a "bully pulpit" of the Presidency, to remind the public of the seriousness of this problem and the need to support your efforts to combat it. I believe that this focusing of public attention on crime, its causes, and those trying to fight it, is one of the most important things that we can do.

Second, in talking out about crime, we intend to speak for a group that has been frequently overlooked in the past—the innocent victims of crime. To this end I will soon be appointing a Task Force on the Victims of Crime to evaluate the numerous proposals now springing up regarding victims and witnesses. We will support legislation that will permit judges to order offenders to make restitution to their victims. The victims of crime have needed a voice for a

long, long time, and this administration means to provide it.

Third, law enforcement is already an important area in our effort to restore and renew federalism. We seek to end duplication and bring about greater cooperation between Federal, State, and local law enforcement agencies with the following steps:

—U.S. attorneys will seek to establish law enforcement coordinating committees, which will be composed of the district heads of Federal agencies as well as key State and local officials. These committees will stimulate an exchange of views and information that will lead to a more flexible, focused, and efficient attack against crime.

—We will seek to extend the cross-designation program now working with success in several localities. These programs permit Federal, State, and local prosecutors to enter each other's courts and grand jury rooms to pursue investigations and prosecutions of serious crimes when they cross jurisdictional lines.

—Closer cooperation with the States and localities on penal and correctional matters: We've recently established a Bureau of Prisons Clearinghouse, which will locate surplus Federal property that might be used as sites for State or local correctional facilities.

Fourth, this administration will support a number of statutory reforms that will redress the imbalance between rights of the accused and rights of the innocent.

—To this end we will be working with the Congress to achieve a sweeping revision of the Federal Criminal Code. This matter is now pending before both Houses. A revised Criminal Code will help in our fight against violent crime, organized crime, narcotics crime, and fraud and corruption. I cannot stress too strongly the need for prompt passage of legislation that revises the Federal Criminal Code, and this will be the foundation of an effective Federal effort against crime.

—We will push for bail reform that will permit judges, under carefully limited conditions, to keep some defendants from using bail to return to the streets, never to be seen in court again until they're arrested for another crime.

—We also support the reform of the exclusionary rule. I don't have to tell you, the people in this room, that this rule rests on the absurd proposition that a law enforcement error, no matter how technical, can be used to justify throwing an entire case out of court, no matter how guilty the defendant or how heinous the crime. The plain consequence of treating the wrongs equally is a grievous miscarriage of justice. The criminal goes free, the officer receives no effective reprimand, and the only ones who really suffer are the people of the community.

But I pause and interject here one incident, maybe known to a great many of you, because it is a famous case. But it occurred, back while I was Governor of California, in San Bernardino. Two narcotics officers, with enough evidence to warrant a search, get a search warrant, entered a home where they believed heroin was being peddled. A married couple lived there. They searched. They found no evidence. As they were leaving, one of them, on a hunch, went over to the crib where the baby lay sleeping and removed its diapers, and there was the heroin. The case was thrown out of the court because the baby hadn't given its permission to be searched. [*Laughter*] It became known as the diaper case. I told that story once, and one of the Secret Service agents assigned to the Presidential detail came up later and said, "I was one of those narcotics officers. That's why I quit." [*Laughter*]

—We also support an exception of the Posse Comitatus Act that will allow the military to assist in identifying and reporting the drug traffic.

—We will ask for revision of the Tax Reform Act that will make it easier for Federal departments to cooperate in making income tax cases against major organized crime figures and drug pushers.

—And we will support mandatory prison terms for those who carry a gun while committing a felony.

Fifth, one of the single most important steps that can lead to a significant reduction in crime is an effective attack on drug trafficking. Let me outline the major points in our narcotics enforcement strategy:

—A foreign policy that vigorously seeks to interdict and eradicate illicit drugs, wherever cultivated, processed, or transported. This includes the responsible use of herbicides. I will also be establishing a Special Council on Narcotics Control, consisting of the Attorney General and the Secretaries of State, Defense, Treasury, and others, to coordinate efforts to stop the drug flow into this country.

—A border policy that will improve detection and interception of illegal narcotics imports. This will include the use of available military resources for detection when necessary.

—A domestic policy that will more effectively coordinate efforts among Federal agencies as well as between these agencies and those at the State and local level. This will be a first priority of the Law Enforcement Coordinating Committee. We have already taken a step in this direction by significantly improving cooperation between the FBI and the Drug Enforcement Agency on drug investigations.

—A legislative program featuring the statutory reforms dealing with bails, sentencing, and admission of evidence that I have already mentioned.

Now, let me also emphasize that our efforts will not be confined to law enforcement. The problem of drug abuse is one that reaches deeply into American society. We need to mobilize our religious, educational, and fraternal groups in a national educational program against drug abuse.

One of the most effective groups in this effort has been more than 1,000 parent groups. And these groups have worked closely with the law and law enforcement agencies. They have recently formed a national federation to spread their work. This administration will do all in its power to encourage such efforts.

Let us recognize that important as intercepting the drug traffic might be, it cannot possibly equal the results in turning off the customers, the users, and making them take a different course in deciding to no longer be customers.

Sixth, violent crime is a major priority. But we fully understand that crime doesn't come in categories; all crime is related, and an effective battle against street crime can hardly be waged in a vacuum. The street criminal, the drug pusher, the mobster, the corrupt policeman or public official—they form their own criminal subculture; they share the climate of lawlessness. They need each other; they use each other; they protect each other.

We will continue to focus Federal efforts on sophisticated forms of crime, similar to those emphasized by the FBI under Judge Bill Webster. And that's why I want to say a word today to those Federal agents and prosecutors who have done so much in recent years to expose the problem of organized crime and public corruption. The existence of syndicates of highly organized criminals and public officials who peddle their sacred trust are blots on American history. I can assure you, no administration has ever been more anxious to work toward wiping away these blots. So, to those in the field who fight this frustrating, sometimes disheartening battle against highly sophisticated forms of crime: This administration stands behind you.

In discussing these forms of sophisticated crimes, we see again the emergence of the problem of career criminals—those who make a conscious decision to pursue illicit professions, a decision based on a belief that crime does pay. I believe the emergence of this problem of career criminals has seriously undermined the notion that criminals are simply products of poverty or underprivileged backgounds.

At the very same time that crime rates have steadily risen, our nation has made unparalleled progress in raising the standard of living and improving the quality of life. It's obvious that prosperity doesn't decrease crime, just as it's obvious that deprivation and want don't necessarily increase crime. The truth is that today's criminals for the most part are not desperate people seeking bread for their families; crime is the way they've chosen to live.

A few weeks ago, Esquire magazine published an article that gained widespread attention. Possibly some of you saw it. It was written by a young novelist who, with his psychiatrist wife, had moved into a section of Venice, California, that had become crime-ridden. In explaining why his wife

and he—two educated, urbane people—ultimately decided to arm themselves, he described in chilling terms the burglaries, rapes, holdups, gang fights, and murders that have become commonplace in their neighborhood.

"Let's face it," he said of the criminals, "some of these people are poor. Some of them are driven crazy with desire for stuff they'll never be able to afford. But not all of them are poor, not by a long shot. A lot of them are making as much money, or a great deal more, than you or I do. They do it because it's easy. They do it because they believe no one will stop them, and," he added, "they're right."

Well, let's face it: There is an arrogance to the criminal mind, a belief in its own superiority over the rest of humanity. The slang of organized crime is instructive here. It isn't surprising that some of these criminals habitually refer to themselves as "wise guys," and the honest people are "working stiffs." They do really believe that they're better than the rest of us, that the world owes them a living, and that those of us who lead normal lives and earn an honest living are a little slow on the uptake.

How accurate those words by that young novelist about career criminals: "They do it because they believe no one will stop them, and they're right." The truth is that criminals in America today get away with plenty, and sometimes, quite literally, they get away with murder. Only 40 percent of the murders ever end with a suspect being imprisoned. In New York City, less than 1 percent—no, I'm sorry, one-sixth—of reported felonies even end in arrests. And 1 percent of these felonies end in a prison term for an offender.

I would suggest the time has come to look reality in the face. American society is mired in excessive litigation. Our courts today are loaded with suits and motions of every conceivable type. Yet, as our system of justice has become weighed down with lawsuits of every nature and description, as the courts have become the arbiters of all kinds of disputes they were never intended to handle, our legal system has failed to carry out its most important function—the

843

protection of the innocent and the punishment of the guilty.

It's time for honest talk, for plain talk. There has been a breakdown in the criminal justice system in America. It just plain isn't working. All too often, repeat offenders, habitual law-breakers, career criminals, call them what you will, are robbing, raping, and beating with impunity and, as I said, quite literally getting away with murder. The people are sickened and outraged. They demand that we put a stop to it.

What is especially disturbing about our failure to deal with crime is the erosion it has caused in public confidence in our judicial system. In one recent poll, 70 percent of the people said they had little or no confidence in the ability of our courts to sentence and convict criminals.

The legal profession, one of the most highly regarded in this country, is now in deep trouble with the public. One ABC-Harris poll found that law firms finished last, after the Congress, the press, and the labor unions, in a list of 13 institutions which the public was asked to rate. Similarly, lawyers received favorable mentions from only 13 percent of those interviewed, half the percentage that did so in a 1973 survey.

This decline in public confidence in our courts and in the legal profession remains a threat to one of our most important traditions, traditions as Americans: the heritage of our independent judiciary, free from public or political influence, and a legal profession with a reputation for high, unassailable ethics.

Let me quote what one lawyer-policeman had to say recently about how criminal cases are handled today. He said, "In the criminal courts, cases are being trivialized in ways independent of the evidence." New York Police Commissioner Robert McGuire recently said, "Instead of the system being geared to treat each individual case as a manifestation of antisocial behavior, the main impetus is to dispose of it. No one is talking about the morality of crime."

Commissioner McGuire has put his finger on the problem. Controlling crime in American society is not simply a question of more money, more police, more courts, more prosecutors; it's ultimately a moral dilemma, one that calls for a moral or, if you will, a spiritual solution. In dealing with crime, new programs may help; more law-and-order rhetoric may be justified; the studies and surveys may still be needed; the blue ribbon panels may keep investigating. But in the end, the war on crime will only be won when an attitude of mind and a change of heart takes place in America, when certain truths take hold again and plant their roots deep in our national consciousness, truths like: Right and wrong matters; Individuals are responsible for their actions; Retribution should be swift and sure for those who prey on the innocent.

We must understand that basic moral principles lie at the heart of our criminal justice system, that our system of law acts as the collective moral voice of society. There's nothing wrong with these values, nor should we be hesitant or feel guilty about furnishing [punishing] those who violate the elementary rules of civilized existence. Theft is not a form of political or cultural expression; it is theft, and it is wrong. Murder is not forbidden as a matter of subjective opinion; it is objectively evil, and we must prohibit it. And no one but the thief and murderer benefits when we think and act otherwise.

Again, let me point to something that I hadn't included in my remarks but I am reminded of—the whole problem of capital punishment. Well, I had an answer to that on my desk for several years while I was Governor. It was a list of the names of 12 criminals, 12 murderers, who had all been sentenced to prison, who had all served their terms or been paroled, and released. And at the time the list was on my desk, their total number of victims then was 34, not 12. I think capital punishment in the beginning might have reduced that figure considerably.

A tendency to downplay the permanent moral values has helped make crime the enormous problem that it is today, one that this administration has, as I've told you, made one of its top domestic priorities. But it has occurred to me that the root causes of our other major domestic problem, the growth of government and the decay of the economy, can be traced to many of the same sources of the crime problem. This is because the same utopian presumptions about human nature that hinder the swift administration of justice have also helped fuel the expansion of government.

Many of the social thinkers of the 1950's and '60's who discussed crime only in the context of disadvantaged childhoods and poverty-stricken neighborhoods were the same people who thought that massive government spending could wipe away our social ills. The underlying premise in both cases was a belief that there was nothing permanent or absolute about any man's nature, that he was a product of his material environment, and that by changing that environment—with government as the chief vehicle of change through educational, health, housing, and other programs—we could permanently change man and usher in a great new era.

Well, we've learned the price of too much government: runaway inflation, soaring unemployment, impossible interest rates. We've learned that Federal subsidies and government bureaucrats not only fail to solve social problems but frequently make them worse.

It's time, too, that we acknowledge the solution to the crime problem will not be found in the social worker's files, the psychiatrist's notes, or the bureaucrat's budgets. It's a problem of the human heart, and it's there we must look for the answer. We can begin by acknowledging some of those permanent things, those absolute truths I mentioned before. Two of those truths are that men are basically good but prone to evil, and society has a right to be protected from them.

The massive expansion of government is related to the crime problem in another, less obvious way. Government interference in our lives tends to discourage creativity and enterprise, to weaken the private economic sector, and preempt those mitigating institutions like family, neighborhood, church, and school—organizations that act as both a buffer and a bridge between the individual and the naked power of the state.

A few years ago, Supreme Court Justice Lewis Powell noted that we had been cut adrift from the "humanizing authority" that had in the past "shaped the character of our people." He noted that governmental authority had grown large and regretted the weakening of the most "personal forms that we've known in the home, church, school, and community which once gave direction to our lives."

Charles Malik, a former President of the U.N. General Assembly, wondered about the weakening of moral authority in our places of learning. He said he had sought "in vain for any reference to the fact that character, personal integrity, spiritual depth, the highest moral standards, the wonderful living values of the great tradition, have anything to do with the business of the university or with the world of learning."

Well, as for the weakening of family values, Michael Novak, theologian and social critic, recently said that: "The family nourishes 'basic trust.' And from this springs creativity, psychic energy, social dynamism. Familial strength that took generations to acquire can be lost in a single generation, can disappear for centuries. If the quality of family life deteriorates," he said, "there is no 'quality of life.'"

What these commentators are saying is that for all our science and sophistication, for all of our justified pride in intellectual accomplishment, we must never forget the jungle is always there waiting to take us over. Only our deep moral values and our strong social institutions can hold back that jungle and restrain the darker impulses of human nature.

In order to return to this sense of self-imposed discipline, this concept of basic civility, we need to strengthen those private social institutions that nurture them. Our recent emphasis on voluntarism, the mobilization of private groups to deal with our social ills, is designed to foster this spirit of individual generosity and our sense of communal values. For this reason, we have moved to cut away many of the Federal intrusions of the private sector that were preempting the prerogatives of our private and independent institutions. That's why we've been willing to make some hard decisions in Washington about the growth of government. We've laid out a program for economic recovery. We'll stand by that program and see it through. We are determined to put an end to the fiscal joyride in Washington, determined to bring America back to prosperity and stability.

Assuring this kind of lawful society is an individual responsibility and one that must be accepted by all of us. This, too, is a matter of attitude—the way we live our lives, the example we set for youngsters, the leadership that we show in our profession.

I'd like to tell a little story here that I think illustrates this point. It was a few years back when Bud Wilkinson had those great national champion Oklahoma football teams. And one of those teams was playing against Texas Christian. Now, TCU was having some pretty mediocre seasons, but on this particular day, as sometimes any team will, they rose to the heights. And in a critical moment, a pass receiver for TCU made a diving catch in the end zone, what could have been the winning touchdown over the national champions. The people in the stadium were going wild, when the captain of TCU walked over to the referee and said, "No, sir. The ball touched the ground before he caught it."

Now, what was your first reaction? Did you just say to yourself, remembering your own times sitting in the grandstand, "Why didn't he keep his mouth shut? He could have gotten away with it." But should he have kept his mouth shut? Some day he may represent you in the Congress or in the White House or even the statehouse. He might even be on the Supreme Court. And what then? Do you want him to keep his mouth shut, to make a decision on the basis of political expediency, or do you want him to be guided by the same kind of inner moral conviction that made him tell the referee the truth? Where does it start?

I think every one of us would like to think that maybe his son has a chance to play football someday under that young man, who has now grown up and is a coach.

But where does it start? I think it starts inside each one of us. If each of us lives up to our responsibilities in our personal lives, professional capacity, we can foster a greater respect for the law, for the principle of truth and justice. You have to make decisions every day that require moral courage—the courage not to ignore that rumor of corruption about someone under your command, or to refuse a favor for a powerful politician or influential attorney, or just give in to weariness and not pursue a criminal case you know should be vigorously prosecuted.

When we took our oaths of office, you and I, we made certain promises. We said we would uphold the law, whether those who violate it are common criminals or misguided members of a public employees union. It may be old-fashioned, but nothing sums up this personal commitment more than the simple word, "honor."

When Thomas Jefferson was advising his nephew what path he should follow to achieve success, he told him that men must always pursue their own and their country's interests with the purest integrity, the most chaste honor. "Make these then your first object," Jefferson said. "Give up money, give up fame, give up science, give up the earth itself and all it contains rather than do an immoral act. And never suppose that in any possible situation or under any circumstances that it is best for you to do a dishonorable thing, however slightly so it may appear to be."

Again, I commend you for manning the thin blue line that holds back a jungle which threatens to reclaim this clearing we call civilization. No bands play when a cop is shooting it out in a dark alley.

God bless you, and thank you.

Note: The President spoke at 11:03 a.m. in Penn Hall at the Rivergate Convention Center. Following his remarks, the President was presented with a plaque by William F. Quinn, outgoing president of the association and chief of the Newton Police Department, West Newton, Maine.

Remarks at a Louisiana Republican Fundraising Reception in New Orleans
September 28, 1981

Well, Dave brought up—the Governor brought up a little nostalgia here. And I've been sitting here feeling a little nostalgia, also, to see here in this place a group like you, who, as he said, have paid the tab that you've paid for a Republican fundraiser. My nostalgia was going back to 1964, when there was no thought in my mind of ever being in public life or holding public office at all. But I came down here to help a man named Charleton Lyons, who said that his goal—he knew the election was impossible—but his goal was to see if we could not establish a two-party system here. And how happy he'd be to see how well it has been established here.

I've just spoken to a national meeting here in your city a few moments ago, the police chiefs of not only the Nation but internationally—sheriffs—tremendous crowd. I spoke to them about crime, and I'm happy to tell you that they're against it. [*Laughter*]

But you know, talking about some of the problems in Washington right now is a little like the Irish landlady who put up a lunch every day for one of her boarders that he took to work. And he was always unhappy about that lunch and let her know when he came home. So, she put two slices of bread in, and the next day she put in four, and he was still unhappy. And then she put in six, and he was unhappy. She got up to about 10, and he was still griping about the quality of the lunch, so she split a loaf of bread, put ham between the two halves, and put that in the lunch. He came home, and she was waiting for him and said, "How was the lunch?" He said, "Well, all right. But I see you're back to two slices again." [*Laughter*]

And you know, government's been doing that for a long time. They've been slicing away at our bread, more and more, and they've gotten all the way up to where they're just on the verge of grabbing the whole loaf. And I think that we have gone back to two slices, just recently, with the changes that have been made.

We had a great victory with the passage of that budget and that tax bill, and yet I think we should remember a Japanese proverb: "After a victory, tighten your helmet strap." Well, I started tightening ours Thursday night, because you've all got to be bone tired. We couldn't have had that victory without you. Believe me, it was for quite some time the talk of Washington of the extent to which the Capitol heard from the people of this country, and that's what made the victory possible.

And yet we're all going to be bone tired before we get through, because we have to continue, and we have to do more. And we made no secret of that fact. We said at the time it was passed that there had to be tens of billions of dollars more cut out in the next 2 years before we could get down to what should be the normal thing in our country, and that is a balanced budget. Our States have to do it; there's no reason why the Federal Government shouldn't have to do it. And we're going to keep going until we do.

And yet some of our opponents, those who dug in their heels and fought the hardest against what we were trying to do, are those who over the years have persisted in this system we've had of spending more than we take in. Before next week is out, our national debt will be over a trillion dollars. That's 16—not 16—but that's a thousand billion dollars. It's incomprehensible.

I told some of the crew the other night when we were doing that television speech, I said, "I was going to do an example here and hold, if I could get from the Treasury, a 4-inch stack of thousand dollar bills and tell the people, 'That's a million dollars.' And I was going to then show them what a trillion dollars was in a stack of bills, but I couldn't, because that would be about 63 miles high." I may be wrong with my arithmetic, but I did it very hastily in my head. [*Laughter*] But it would be up to about that size.

Anyway, those people who opposed that didn't offer any alternative, and now that it's passed, they're insistent on saying that it won't work. As a matter of fact, a couple of them have even said it hasn't worked. Well, it hasn't; it doesn't start until Thursday, and much of it doesn't start until January 1st, the beginning of the new year—many of the most important tax incentives that were built into the structure.

So, one thing that I think we have to remember is that the budget deficit at the end of 1982, whether we meet our target exactly or not—and we're determined to keep on trying that we will—would have been $35 billion bigger than it will be because that's how much we got in the package of cuts that have already been adopted. And the same thing is true of the years it would be $130 billion—those cuts spread over the next 3 years.

So, I think we have made a start, and yes, we are asking for more cuts, as I said. And I believe that our program will work. I believe it with all my heart. It's based on sound principles of a free marketplace, providing incentive for the entrepreneur, for the working person, for all the way up, yes, to the corporations, so that they can provide the jobs our people must have, and to remove the excessive interference by government in our personal and private lives.

And we've made a big start in that. George Bush is heading up a task force that has already cut the increase in government regulations in half. And we're not going to be satisfied until we have cut the existing regulations—I don't know whether in half or what it will be—but we're going to get rid of all the unnecessary, the complicated, the duplicative regulations.

Let me just tell you of a letter that I got. I'm going to quit talking in a minute, so that I can come down and say hello to some of you in the limited time we've got here. But I got a letter the other day from a gentleman, and he sent me a form that he'd received from the Census Bureau. And he said that he and the people living in the same place where he was had been under a program of the Census Bureau to have a continuing survey of the people—they had been chosen as some. And so he said, "We were interviewed four times this last year."

And he said, "This notice I've attached is the notice that they'll be coming back four more times this year. Now," he said, "I don't know how much this foolishness costs, but," he said, "among the questions—" and I looked at the form where four times they'll come back, on top of last year's four times, to ask them if they changed their minds about retiring, are they thinking about going back to work. And he said to me, "I'm 84 years old. I live in a retirement home. All of us here are retired, and they're going to come here and ask us four times in the coming year whether we're still retired or not." [*Laughter*]

Well, we're going to find out how much that costs, and we're going to do something about it.

But I'll say one last thing. As you know, we'd tried to do something that I had promised to do about the integrity of social security. We had hoped that our opponents would join us and make this a bipartisan effort because, as the program stands now, there is a long-term collapse of the program simply on the basis of the actuarial imbalance that exists within it. But there is an immediate problem in which the trust fund from which the benefits are paid will be out of money before the end of next year, if something isn't done.

Now, it is true that temporarily we can stave that off by borrowing from the other funds, as I said Thursday night in the broadcast. But I also said—and I don't think this was really a retreat—again, one last effort to get the kind of bipartisan cooperation we need, and that is if they will join us in establishing a task force to come up with a settlement that will do two things: that will restore the fiscal integrity of social security, but at the same time will guarantee that no one presently dependent on social security is going to suffer any loss or any harm or change in the benefits that they're presently receiving.

Now, the reason we have to hurry away— a couple of my neighbors up there and myself—is because there's a limit to how long we can leave those fellows alone. [*Laughter*]

But whatever speculation you've read or seen or heard or anything else, I was only built with one gear. We are not going to retreat from this program, because we know it is going to restore America to the economic stability that this nation——[*applause*].

Thank you all very much. And as Dave said, if you really want to do something for us in 1982, in addition to continuing to help as you have in the past, you send them some more teammates and give us the people that we need up there to continue with these programs. And we'll be forever grateful to you for that. They're very much needed, although I must say, we have had great cooperation from some people who are certainly spiritual brothers of ours, even if they do have a different party affiliation, and I think we can hold that group together to continue what we're doing.

God bless all of you, and thank you very much.

Note: The President spoke at 12:09 p.m. in the Galvez Room at the International Trade Center, following remarks and an introduction by Governor David C. Treen of Louisiana.

Nomination of Howard Kent Walker To Be United States Ambassador to Togo
September 28, 1981

The President today announced his intention to nominate Howard Kent Walker, of New Jersey, to be Ambassador to the Republic of Togo. He would succeed Marilyn Priscilla Johnson.

Mr. Walker was a teaching assistant at Boston University in 1960–62 and assistant professor at George Washington University in 1966–68. He served in the United States Air Force as first lieutenant in 1962–65. In the Department of State he was research analyst (1965–68) and international relations officer of the Office of Inter-African Affairs and principal officer in Kaduna in 1971–73.

In 1973–75 he was in the Department as international relations officer of the Office of West African Affairs. He was counselor for political affairs in Amman (1975–77), Deputy Chief of Mission in Dar es Salaam (1977–79), and since 1979, Deputy Chief of Mission in Pretoria.

Mr. Walker graduated from the University of Michigan (A.B., 1957; M.A., 1958) and Boston University (Ph. D., 1968). He is married, has two children, and resides in Atlantic City, N.J. He was born December 3, 1935, in Newport News, Va.

Nomination of Alan M. Hardy To Be United States Ambassador to Equatorial Guinea
September 28, 1981

The President today announced his intention to nominate Alan M. Hardy, of Virginia, to be Ambassador to the Republic of Equatorial Guinea. He would succeed Hume A. Horan.

Mr. Hardy entered the Foreign Service in 1956 as intelligence research specialist in the Department of State. He served in the United States Army in 1957–59. He was consular officer in Toronto (1959–61), administrative officer in Tananarive (1961–63), consular officer and economic officer in Milan (1963–65), and economic officer in Mogadishu (1965–67). In 1967–68 he was country officer for Nigeria in the Department. He attended African area studies at the University of California at Los Angeles in 1968–69. In the Department he was foreign affairs political analyst (1969–71) and country officer for Kenya and Tanzania (1971–73). From 1973 to 1975, he was political officer in Dakar. He attended Hungarian language training at the Foreign Service Institute in 1975–76. He was political officer in Budapest in 1976–78. In the Department he was personnel officer in 1978–79, and since 1979, he has been country officer for Mozambique and Namibia.

Mr. Hardy graduated from the University of Cincinnati (B.A., 1959) and the University of California at Los Angeles (M.A., 1969). He is married, has six children, and resides in Arlington, Va. He was born May 26, 1934, in Orange, N.J.

Nomination of Norman Braman To Be Commissioner of Immigration and Naturalization
September 28, 1981

The President today announced his intention to nominate Norman Braman to be Commissioner of Immigration and Naturalization, Department of Justice. He would succeed Leonel J. Castillo.

Since 1972 Mr. Braman has served as president of several automobile dealerships in Tampa and Miami, Fla. Previously, in 1964, Mr. Braman organized Philadelphia Pharmaceuticals and Cosmetics, a manufacturer of pharmaceuticals, and was president and chief executive officer. In 1959 he founded a chain of self-service department stores named Keystone Stores, Inc., in Philadelphia, Pa.

Mr. Braman has been very active in community affairs, including serving on the board of directors of the Greater Miami Chamber of Commerce, vice president of the Greater Miami Jewish Federation, and founder of the American-Israel Public Affairs Committee of the University of Miami. He graduated from Temple University (B.S., 1955).

Mr. Braman is married, has two children, and resides in Miami Beach, Fla. He was born August 23, 1932, in West Chester, Pa.

Note: Mr. Braman's nomination, which was sent to the Senate on September 29, was withdrawn by the President on November 18.

Proclamation 4860—Fire Prevention Week
September 28, 1981

By the President of the United States of America

A Proclamation

Every year this Nation experiences needless loss of life and property. America's fire losses are a great waste of our precious resources and must be minimized. Destruction of property and what we pay for fire protection totals over $21 billion each year. But even worse, 7,500 American deaths annually can be attributed to fire.

With a concerted effort by individual citizens, our Nation can curtail its needless fire losses.

Installing and properly maintaining smoke detectors and practicing fire escape plans can reduce loss of life and property. If each of us would take a few simple precautions, fewer Americans would suffer disfigurement, the agony of injury, or the mental anguish of the sudden loss of loved ones.

Now, Therefore, I, Ronald Reagan, President of the United States of America, do designate the week of October 4 through October 10, 1981, as Fire Prevention Week.

Furthermore, I congratulate the fire service for their fire prevention efforts and support their continued work. The National Fire Protection Association, the Fire Marshals Association of North America, fire chiefs, and fire fighters deserve our thanks for their sponsorship of this year's fire safety observance.

I direct the Federal Emergency Management Agency to work with all levels of government, industry, service organizations and volunteers to encourage the broadest possible use of smoke detectors across the Nation.

In Witness Whereof, I have hereunto set my hand this 28th day of Sept., in the year of our Lord nineteen hundred and eighty-one, and of the Independence of the United States of America the two hundred and sixth.

RONALD REAGAN

[Filed with the Office of the Federal Register, 4:02 p.m., September 29, 1981]

Note: *The text of the proclamation was released by the Office of the Press Secretary on September 29.*

Proclamation 4861—National Diabetes Week
September 28, 1981

By the President of the United States of America

A Proclamation

Diabetes is a serious and widespread public health problem, resulting from the inability of the body to convert nutrients into energy. This debilitating and often fatal disease affects about 10 million Americans and is occurring among all age and socio-economic groups at an increasing rate. More than 35,000 people die from diabetes every year, and the disease contributes to deaths from heart attack, stroke, kidney failure and blood vessel disorders. It is the leading cause of new blindness. The cost of diabetes is measured in the billions of dollars, but by far the highest price is paid in the suffering and shortened life span of its victims.

Fortunately, there is hope. Through advances in medical research, we are learning more about diabetes, its cause, and improved methods for its control and management. Prospects for better prevention and treatment appear brighter than at any time since the discovery of insulin more than 50 years ago.

I am pleased that in cooperation with private, voluntary organizations, the Federal Government plays a valuable role in support of this research. It is my fervent hope that continued efforts will improve the quality of life for all our Nation's diabetics and eventually lead to the prevention and cure of this difficult and cruel disease.

Now, Therefore, I, Ronald Reagan, President of the United States of America, do hereby proclaim the week beginning October 4 through October 10, 1981, as National Diabetes Week, and I call upon the people of the United States to observe that week with appropriate ceremonies and activities.

In Witness Whereof, I have hereunto set my hand this twenty-eighth day of September, in the year of our Lord nineteen hundred and eighty-one, and of the Independence of the United States of America the two hundred and sixth.

RONALD REAGAN

[Filed with the Office of the Federal Register, 4:03 p.m., September 29, 1981]

Note: *The text of the proclamation was released by the Office of the Press Secretary on September 29.*

Proclamation 4862—Child Health Day
September 28, 1981

By the President of the United States of America

A Proclamation

We have all heard the saying, "As the twig is bent the tree inclines." This maxim is especially true for the minds and bodies of our children. The physical and mental health of the child prepares the way for the physical and mental health of the adult.

Our future as a Nation lies in the healthy development of our children. That development must be fostered from the earliest stages so that our twigs and saplings will grow into straight and strong trees.

We must actively promote child health through the positive approach of preventive care, such as early prenatal care for mothers, assured immunization against dangerous childhood illnesses and early identification of handicapping conditions.

In this effort to improve the well-being and future of our children, I earnestly call for cooperative and voluntary action from all those who make maternal and child health their profession, from the States through their health care resources, from the organizations of private citizens who devote themselves to the health of mothers and children, and particularly from parents themselves, whose attention to their children's needs and personal examples of healthful behavior are vital factors in the protection of child health.

Now, Therefore, I, Ronald Reagan, President of the United States of America, pursuant to a joint resolution of May 18, 1928, as amended (36 U.S.C. 143), do hereby proclaim Monday, October 5, 1981, as Child Health Day.

In Witness Whereof, I have hereunto set my hand this 28th day of Sept., in the year of our Lord nineteen hundred and eighty-one, and of the Independence of the United States of America the two hundred and sixth.

RONALD REAGAN

[*Filed with the Office of the Federal Register, 4:04 p.m., September 29, 1981*]

Note: The text of the proclamation was released by the Office of the Press Secretary on September 29.

Proclamation 4863—White Cane Safety Day
September 28, 1981

By the President of the United States of America

A Proclamation

For blind Americans, the white cane is an important sign of independence, symbolizing their ability to travel in our Nation's cities and towns with great confidence and safety. For motorists, the white cane symbolizes caution, and reminds them that their courtesy and consideration insure the safety of the visually disabled.

We should always be aware of the significance of the white cane and extend every courtesy to those who carry it. By doing so, we will respect and ensure the right to independence of the visually disabled as they pursue a productive and fulfilling life.

In recognition of the significance of the white cane, the Congress, by a joint resolution of October 6, 1964 (78 Stat. 1003), authorized the President to proclaim October 15 of each year as White Cane Safety Day.

Now, Therefore, I, Ronald Reagan, President of the United States of America, do hereby proclaim October 15, 1981, as White Cane Safety Day.

I urge all Americans to mark this occasion by giving greater consideration to the special needs of the visually disabled, and, particularly, to observe White Cane Safety Day with activities that contribute to maximum independent use of our streets and public facilities by our visually handicapped population.

In Witness Whereof, I have hereunto set my hand this 28th day of Sept., in the year of our Lord nineteen hundred and eighty-one, and of the Independence of the United States of America the two hundred and sixth.

RONALD REAGAN

[*Filed with the Office of the Federal Register, 4:05 p.m., September 29, 1981*]

Note: The text of the proclamation was released by the Office of the Press Secretary on September 29.

Proclamation 4864—United Nations Day, 1981
September 28, 1981

By the President of the United States of America

A Proclamation

The United Nations rose from the ashes of the Second World War. As we observe another United Nations Day on October 24, 1981, we are thankful that the world has since been spared another major conflagration.

The United Nations has assisted in bringing stability to troubled areas and will surely do so again. United Nations peacekeeping forces are on duty in the volatile Middle East and have contributed to maintaining the peace in other places.

The problems addressed in this world forum are diverse, and the United Nations cannot resolve all matters it considers. But it has helped. This year it held a major conference for the purpose of pledging assistance to refugees in Africa. The United States made a substantial pledge, consistent with our historic support for United Nations refugee programs.

The United Nations is the world's meeting place. It brings together representatives of virtually all countries to discuss a multitude of subjects. These meetings afford opportunities for bilateral discussions, often at a high level, as an extra benefit. Today, much of the world's diplomacy takes place under the aegis of the United Nations.

The United States will continue to play a prominent role and champion the values and ideals that originally inspired the United Nations. We will further those activities that strengthen the capacity of the institution to serve the good of mankind.

Now, Therefore, I, Ronald Reagan, President of the United States of America, do hereby designate Saturday, October 24, 1981, as United Nations Day. I urge all Americans to use this day as an opportunity to better acquaint themselves with the activities and accomplishments of the United Nations.

I have appointed Mr. Robert Anderson to serve as 1981 United States National Chairman for United Nations Day, and welcome the role of the United Nations Association of the United States of America in working with him to celebrate this special day.

In Witness Whereof, I have hereunto set my hand this 28th day of Sept., in the year of our Lord nineteen hundred and eighty-one, and of the Independence of the United States of America the two hundred and sixth.

RONALD REAGAN

[*Filed with the Office of the Federal Register, 4:06 p.m., September 29, 1981*]

Note: The text of the proclamation was released by the Office of the Press Secretary on September 29.

Remarks at the Annual Meeting of the Boards of Governors of the World Bank Group and International Monetary Fund
September 29, 1981

Mr. Chairman, President Clausen, the Managing Director, Mr. de Larosière, Governors of the International Monetary and the World Bank group, and distinguished colleagues:

On behalf of the American people, I am delighted to welcome you to Washington for your 36th annual meeting. It seems that your deliberations take on added importance each year, and this year will be no exception.

I believe your meeting can strengthen the national resolve and international cooperation required for the global economic recovery and growth that we're all striving to achieve, and I'm very grateful for this opportunity to address your distinguished group.

It's customary to begin a speech before this annual meeting with a portrait of the serious problems and challenges we face in the world economy. Those problems and challenges are certainly there in force, and I will get back to them in a minute and review them. But first, let me just take a moment to salute the institutions that you represent. The IMF and the World Bank group have contributed enormously to the spread of hope of a better life throughout the world community. In the process, they have proved themselves capable of change, of adapting to new circumstances and the needs of new members.

Your institutions have worked tirelessly to preserve the framework for international economic cooperation and to generate confidence and competition in the world economy. They have been inspired by the ideal of a far better world in which economic growth and development would spread to all parts of the globe. For more than three decades, they have worked toward these goals and contributed to results that are now clearly visible to all.

This past decade in particular has tested the mettle and demonstrated the strength and merit of the World Bank and IMF. As the development report of the World Bank itself notes, "The 1970's witnessed international economic convulsions at least as serious as any that may be thought highly probable in the next 10 years. The world's economy, it's capacity to withstand shocks, has been severely tested, and the tests were not passed with entire success. But parts of the developing world have come through remarkably well."

We need to recognize our progress and talk about it more in our conversations with one another. This in no way denies the immense problems that we face. But without some sense of what we've achieved, without some encouragement to believe in our mission, we will succumb to defeatism or surrender to ill-advised solutions to problems that can never yield to grandiose schemes.

To look at the challenges before us, let us recall that vision we originally set out to reach through international cooperation. The Second World War had left us with the realization, born out of the suffering and the sacrifices of those years, that never again must human initiative and individual liberties be denied or suppressed.

The international political and economic institutions created after 1945 rested upon a belief that the key to national development and human progress is individual freedom—both political and economic. The Bretton Woods institutions and the GATT established generalized rules and procedures to facilitate individual enterprise and an open international trading and financial system. They recognized that economic incentives and increasing commercial opportunities would be essential to economic recovery and growth.

We who live in free market societies believe that growth, prosperity and, ultimately, human fulfillment are created from the bottom up, not the government down. Only when the human spirit is allowed to invent and create, only when individuals are given a personal stake in deciding economic policies and benefiting from their success—only then can societies remain economically alive, dynamic, prosperous, progressive, and free.

Trust the people. This is the one irrefutable lesson of the entire post-war period, contradicting the notion that rigid government controls are essential to economic development. The societies which have achieved the most spectacular broad-based economic progress in the shortest period of time are not the most tightly controlled, not necessarily the biggest in size, or the wealthiest in natural resources. No, what unites them all is their willingness to believe in the magic of the marketplace.

Everyday life confirms the fundamentally human and democratic ideal that individual effort deserves economic reward. Nothing is more crushing to the spirit of working people and to the vision of development itself than the absence of reward for honest toil and legitimate risk. So let me speak plainly: We cannot have prosperity and successful development without economic freedom; nor can we preserve our personal and political freedoms without economic freedom. Governments that set out to regiment their people with the stated objective of providing security and liberty have ended up losing both. Those which put freedom as the first priority find they have also provided security and economic progress.

The United States is proud of its contributions to the goals and institutions of post-war development. You can count on us to continue to shoulder our responsibilities in the challenges that we face today. We see two of overriding importance: restoring the growth and vitality of the world economy and assuring that all countries, especially the poorest ones, participate fully in the process of growth and development. But let us remember, the most important contribution any country can make to world development is to pursue sound economic policies at home.

Regrettably, many industrial countries, including my own, have not made this contribution in the recent past. We've overspent, overtaxed, and overregulated, with the result being slow growth and soaring inflation. This "stagflation," as the IMF annual report notes, is one of the two basic problems we must quickly overcome. The United States has set its course to economic recovery. Our program is comprehensive, and as I reminded the American people last Thursday evening, it will require effort and patience, but the reward is worth working for.

By reducing the rate of government spending, honoring our commitment to balance the budget, reducing tax rates to encourage productive investment and personal savings, eliminating excessive government regulation, and maintaining a stable monetary policy, we are convinced that we will enter a new era of sustained, noninflationary growth and prosperity, the likes of which we haven't seen for many years. And as the world's largest single market, a prosperous, growing U.S. economy will mean increased trading opportunities for other nations.

America now receives half of all non-OPEC, developing country exports of manufactured goods to all the industrialized countries, even though we account for only one-third of the total gross national product of those industrialized countries. Lower U.S. inflation and interest rates will translate into increased availability of financial resources at affordable rates. Already, capital markets in the United States are more accessible to the developing countries than capital markets anywhere else in the world. No American contribution can do more for development than a growing, prosperous United States economy.

The domestic policies of developing countries are likewise the most critical contribution they can make to development. Unless a nation puts its own financial and economic house in order, no amount of aid will produce progress. Many countries are recognizing this fact and taking dramatic steps to get their economies back on a sound footing. And I know it's not easy—I have a few scars to prove that fact—but it must be done.

Only with a foundation of sound domestic policies can the international economic system continue to expand and improve. My own government is committed to policies of free trade, unrestricted investment, and open capital markets. The financial flows generated by trade investment and growth capital flows far exceed official development assistance funds provided to developing countries. At the same time, we're sensitive to the needs of the low-income countries. They can benefit from international trade and growth in the industrial countries because they export many raw materials and primary products the industrial world needs. But they also depend upon our aid to strengthen their economies, diversify their exports, and work toward self-sufficiency.

The United States recognizes this. Over three decades, we've provided more than $130 billion in concessional assistance. The American people have proven themselves to be as compassionate and caring as any on Earth, and we will remain so.

We strongly support the World Bank. And because of our strong support, we feel a special responsibility to provide constructive suggestions to make it more effective. We believe these suggestions will permit it to generate increased funds for development and to support the efforts developing countries are making to strengthen their economies.

Taking into account our budgetary constraints, we are committed to providing the Bank and IDA resources for them to continue and improve their contributions to development. We know that stimulating private investment is also critically important. The International Finance Corporation plays the leading role in the Bank family in support of such investment. Given the importance of this role, we hope it can be enhanced. We believe all facets of the Bank can play a more active role in generating private resources and stimulating individual initiative in the development effort.

The IMF also plays a critical role in establishing conditions to encourage private capital flows to deficit countries. By reaching agreements with the IMF on a sound, comprehensive stabilization program and by demonstrating its determination to implement that program, a borrowing country signals private markets of its intent to solve its own economic problems.

We're committed to a pragmatic search for solutions to produce lasting results. Let us put an end to the divisive rhetoric of "us versus them," "North versus South." Instead, let us decide what all of us, both developed and developing countries, can accomplish together.

Our plans for the Caribbean Basin are one example of how we would like to harness economic energies within a region to promote stronger growth. The design and success of this undertaking depends upon the cooperation of many developed and developing countries. My colleagues and I also look forward to the upcoming summit meeting at Cancún, Mexico. That occasion will provide us with fresh opportunities to address the serious problems we face and encourage each other in our common mission.

In conclusion, each of our societies has a destiny to pursue. We've chosen ours in light of our experience, our strength, and our faith. We, each, are ultimately responsible for our actions and the successes and failures that they bring. But while individually responsible, we're also mutually interdependent. By working together through such institutions as the IMF and World Bank, we can all seek to collaborate on joint problems, share our insights, and encourage the common good.

These institutions have reflected a shared vision of growth and development through political freedom and economic opportunity. A liberal and open trade and payment system would reconstruct a shattered world and lay the basis for prosperity to help avoid future conflicts. This vision has become reality for many of us. Let us pledge to continue working together to ensure that it becomes reality for all.

Thank you very much.

Note: The President spoke at 10:03 a.m. at the Sheraton Washington Hotel at the opening session of the annual meeting of the International Monetary Fund, the International Bank for Reconstruction and Development (World Bank), the International Development Association, and the International Finance Corporation.

In his opening remarks, the President referred to Valentin Aris Mendi Elgue, Minister of Finance of Uruguay and Chairman of the annual meeting, A. W. Clausen, President of the International Bank for Recon-

struction and Development, and J. de Larosière, Managing Director and Chairman of

the Board of Executive Directors of the International Monetary Fund.

Statement on the Death of Former President Rómulo Betancourt of Venezuela
September 29, 1981

I speak for all Americans in expressing our heartfelt sadness at the death of Rómulo Betancourt. While he was first and foremost a Venezuelan patriot, Rómulo Betancourt was an especially close friend of the United States. During the 1950's he considered the United States a refuge while he was in exile, and we were proud to receive him. We are honored that this courageous man whose life was dedicated to the principles of liberty and justice—a man who fought dictatorships of the right and the left—spent his final days on our shores. We join the Venezuelan people and those who love freedom around the world in mourning his death.

Note: Rómulo Betancourt, 73, was President of Venezuela from 1945 to 1948 and from 1959 to 1964. He died on September 28 in Doctors Hospital in New York City.

On September 30, the White House announced the members of the U.S. Delegation to the funeral services for former President Betancourt in Venezuela on October 2. They are:

The Vice President, Head of Delegation

Mrs. Barbara Bush

Ambassador William H. Luers, U.S. Ambassador to Venezuela

Senator Jesse A. Helms (R-N.C.)

Senator Edward Zorinsky (D-Nebr.)

Representative Robert K. Dornan (R-Calif.)

Ambassador Thomas O. Enders, Assistant Secretary of State for Inter-American Affairs

Ambassador Teodoro Moscoso, former U.S. Ambassador to Venezuela (1961–62)

Ambassador Edwin M. Martin, former Assistant Secretary of State for Inter-American Affairs

Moises Garcia, U.S. International Communication Agency; former TIME correspondent

Robert J. Alexander, professor, Rutgers University

Nomination of John Dimitri Negroponte To Be United States Ambassador to Honduras
September 29, 1981

The President today announced his intention to nominate John Dimitri Negroponte, of New York, as Ambassador to Honduras. He would succeed Jack Robert Binns who is resigning.

Mr. Negroponte entered the Foreign Service in 1960 and served in Hong Kong as consular officer (1960–61) and commercial officer (1961–63). In the Department he was administrative assistant in the Bureau of African Affairs (1963) and studied the Vietnamese language at the Foreign Service Institute (1963–64). From 1964 to

1968, he was political officer in Saigon, and a member of the United States Delegation to the Paris Peace Talks on Vietnam from 1968 to 1969. He attended Stanford University from 1969 to 1970 and was a member of the staff at the National Security Council from 1970 to 1973. In 1973 he studied the Spanish language at the Foreign Service Institute. He was counselor for political affairs in Quito (1973–75) and consul general in Thessaloniki (1975–77). In the Department he was Deputy Assistant Secretary of State for Oceans and Fisheries Affairs, with rank of Ambassador from 1977 to 1979, and since 1980 he has been Deputy Assistant Secretary of State for East Asian and Pacific Affairs.

Mr. Negroponte was born July 21, 1939, in London, England. He graduated (B.A.) in 1960 from Yale University. His foreign languages are French, Spanish, and Vietnamese. He received the Department's Superior Honor Award in 1975.

Message to the Senate Transmitting the United States-Mexico Convention on Stolen or Embezzled Vehicles and Aircraft
September 29, 1981

To the Senate of the United States:

With a view to receiving the advice and consent of the Senate to ratification, I transmit herewith the Convention between the United States of America and the United Mexican States for the Recovery and Return of Stolen or Embezzled Vehicles and Aircraft, signed at Washington on January 15, 1981.

I transmit also, for the information of the Senate, the report of the Department of State with respect to the Convention.

The Convention represents an effort by the two Governments to confront the serious law enforcement problems posed by the theft of vehicles and aircraft, primarily along our shared border, and the subsequent use of some of them in the commission of felonies in the two countries. It would supersede the 1936 Convention for the Recovery and Return of Stolen or Embezzled Motor Vehicles, Trailers, Airplanes or Component Parts of Any of Them, which has been found inadequate to meet present law enforcement needs. I recommend that the Senate give favorable consideration to this treaty at an early date.

RONALD REAGAN

The White House,
September 29, 1981.

Proclamation 4865—High Seas Interdiction of Illegal Aliens
September 29, 1981

By the President of the United States of America

A Proclamation

The ongoing migration of persons to the United States in violation of our laws is a serious national problem detrimental to the interests of the United States. A particularly difficult aspect of the problem is the continuing illegal migration by sea of large numbers of undocumented aliens into the southeastern United States. These arrivals have severely strained the law enforcement resources of the Immigration and Naturalization Service and have threatened the welfare and safety of communities in that region.

As a result of our discussions with the Governments of affected foreign countries and with agencies of the Executive Branch of our Government, I have determined that new and effective measures to curtail these unlawful arrivals are necessary. In this regard, I have determined that international cooperation to intercept vessels trafficking in illegal migrants is a necessary and proper means of insuring the effective enforcement of our laws.

Now, Therefore, I, Ronald Reagan, President of the United States of America, by the authority vested in me by the Constitution and the statutes of the United States, including Sections 212(f) and 215(a)(1) of the Immigration and Nationality Act, as amended (8 U.S.C. 1182(f) and 1185(a)(1)), in order to protect the sovereignty of the United States, and in accordance with cooperative arrangements with certain foreign governments, and having found that the entry of undocumented aliens, arriving at the borders of the United States from the high seas, is detrimental to the interests of the United States, do proclaim that:

The entry of undocumented aliens from the high seas is hereby suspended and shall be prevented by the interdiction of certain vessels carrying such aliens.

In Witness Whereof, I have hereunto set my hand this twenty-ninth day of September, in the year of our Lord nineteen hundred and eighty-one, and of the Independence of the United States of America the two hundred and sixth.

RONALD REAGAN

[Filed with the Office of the Federal Register, 11:37 a.m., September 30, 1981]

Executive Order 12324—Interdiction of Illegal Aliens
September 29, 1981

By the authority vested in me as President by the Constitution and statutes of the United States of America, including Sections 212(f) and 215(a)(1) of the Immigration and Nationality Act, as amended (8 U.S.C. 1182(f) and 1185(a)(1)), in view of the continuing problem of migrants coming to the United States, by sea, without necessary entry documents, and in order to carry out the suspension and interdiction of such entry which have concurrently been proclaimed, it is hereby ordered as follows:

Section 1. The Secretary of State shall undertake to enter into, on behalf of the United States, cooperative arrangements with appropriate foreign governments for the purpose of preventing illegal migration to the United States by sea.

Sec. 2. (a) The Secretary of the Department in which the Coast Guard is operating shall issue appropriate instructions to the Coast Guard in order to enforce the suspension of the entry of undocumented aliens and the interdiction of any defined vessel carrying such aliens.

(b) Those instructions shall apply to any of the following defined vessels:

(1) Vessels of the United States, meaning any vessel documented under the laws of the United States, or numbered as provided by the Federal Boat Safety Act of 1971, as amended (46 U.S.C. 1451 *et seq.*), or owned in whole or in part by the United States, a citizen of the United States, or a corporation incorporated under the laws of the United States or any State, Territory, District, Commonwealth, or possession thereof, unless the vessel has been granted nationality by a foreign nation in accord with Article 5 of the Convention on the High Seas of 1958 (U.S. TIAS 5200; 13 UST 2312).

(2) Vessels without nationality or vessels assimilated to vessels without nationality in accordance with paragraph (2) of Article 6 of the Convention on the High Seas of 1958 (U.S. TIAS 5200; 13 UST 2312).

(3) Vessels of foreign nations with whom we have arrangements authorizing the United States to stop and board such vessels.

(c) Those instructions to the Coast Guard shall include appropriate directives providing for the Coast Guard:

(1) To stop and board defined vessels, when there is reason to believe that such vessels are engaged in the irregular transportation of persons or violations of United States law or the law of a country with which the United States has an arrangement authorizing such action.

(2) To make inquiries of those on board, examine documents and take such actions as are necessary to establish the registry, condition and destination of the vessel and the status of those on board the vessel.

(3) To return the vessel and its passengers to the country from which it came, when there is reason to believe that an offense is being committed against the United States immigration laws, or appropriate laws of a foreign country with which we have an arrangement to assist; provided, however, that no person who is a refugee will be returned without his consent.

(d) These actions, pursuant to this Section, are authorized to be undertaken only outside the territorial waters of the United States.

Sec. 3. The Attorney General shall, in consultation with the Secretary of State and the Secretary of the Department in which the Coast Guard is operating, take whatever steps are necessary to ensure the fair enforcement of our laws relating to immigration (including effective implementation of this Executive Order) and the strict observance of our international obligations concerning those who genuinely flee persecution in their homeland.

RONALD REAGAN

The White House,
September 29, 1981.

[*Filed with the Office of the Federal Register, 11:38 a.m., September 30, 1981*]

Message on the Observance of the Jewish High Holy Days
September 29, 1981

In Jewish places of worship the world over, the stirring call of the ram's horn, the shofar, will be heard symbolizing as it has for centuries the observance of Rosh Hashanah. On this most solemn occasion, Nancy and I express our warmest greetings to the Jewish people and join with you in your prayers for the New Year.

The High Holy Days are a time for introspection, atonement, and renewal—a time when those of the Jewish Faith pause to reflect upon the year which has passed and pray for the year which lies ahead. We join with you in the spirit of this holiday, for it is only by seeking the truth within our own hearts and acknowledging the sacred purpose of human life that we may, in the words of your tradition, "be inscribed and sealed in the book of life."

You have our every good wish that this new year, 5742, will advance your cherished hopes that human understanding and peace take the place of terrorism and violence, that the needs of the hungry and the poor be satisfied meaningfully throughout the world, and that there be progress toward the prophetic ideal that "nation shall not lift up sword against nation, neither shall they learn war anymore."

RONALD REAGAN

Note: The text of the message was made available by the Office of the Press Secretary. It was not issued as a White House press release.

Remarks on the Program for Economic Recovery at a White House Reception for Members of Congress
September 29, 1981

Well, Nancy and I are very pleased to have you here with us. During our time in Washington I've been to the Hill so frequently that I thought maybe it was fitting to have you as our guests over here for a change.

During the days immediately before the summer break there was such a flurry of legislative activity—you probably remember that—[*laughter*]—there was no time to thank you properly for supporting the economic recovery package. Just to make it official, the whole country is grateful to you for what you accomplished this summer, and that includes us.

For the last few years, we've all faced an ever more grave economic situation with dismay and frustration—sort of a truck on the way downhill, as I said the other night, without any brakes. Many of our citizens were resigning themselves to permanent economic hardship. But what you achieved this summer, I think, has put us in a position to get control of the situation. And for the first time in years, there are signs of hope and renewed confidence emerging among our people.

After you got back from your break and I got back from mine, some people developed a bad case of the jitters. Of all things, they were blaming the high interest rates and the other economic ills on the program that you'd just passed a few weeks before. Of course, they had a little help in arriving at that idea; most of those making the fuss never supported the program in the first place. [*Laughter*] And they also knew darn well that it doesn't even go into effect until the day after tomorrow. I suppose by sundown the day after tomorrow they'll be saying, "See, we told you so." [*Laughter*]

What we accomplished—the spending and the tax rate reduction—I think were proud and historic moments. In the last two decades the Federal Government has grown almost 500 percent, and that's several times as much as the country has grown.

And so did the income tax payments of individual Americans.

Every generation faces its responsibility and ours, I think, is bringing government growth and taxation under control before it destroys everything that we hold dear. Now, you knew something had to be done, so did the people.

There are those who underestimate the American people. I was in an industry that I thought did that for years. I used to think that most producers, the only time they ever saw America was from 30,000 feet on their way back and forth from New York to Hollywood. And I thought they underestimated a great deal. And that was a big mistake. But I think there have been accounts recently of citizens all over the country who are willing to sacrifice a bit now to get America back on the right track. Some of the press in reporting this seemed to be astounded by that fact. There shouldn't be any surprise on our part or theirs.

If there's one thing the American people aren't lacking, it is courage. At times they've been misled, but they can be counted on to do what has to be done. And right now from what I'm hearing, they're happy that you're making some tough decisions rather than taking the easy way out. The public knows that it took a number of years to get us into the economic mess, and it'll take time and hard work to set things right. So, when others start to panic, remember that the people are still on our side. And as long as we're sincerely trying to put America's house in order, they'll stay on our side.

Now, I expect some good economic signs within a few months of the start of our program. There's got to be a pony in here somewhere. [*Laughter*] I think with the tax incentives, there's going to be a dramatic jump in the money available to loan. And coupled with some of the new budget proposals—you didn't think I was going to let you out of here without mentioning them—

[*laughter*]—coupled with the budget proposals, the interest rates should come down. As a matter of fact, we've seen some nibbling on that already.

In this first 8 months, we moved forward with a multipronged approach, and I think it is beginning to show results. Now, the Vice President—he spearheaded the most vigorous attacks on redtape and overregulation that have ever been conducted. And by the end of our first year, the growth in the *Federal Register* will be 50 percent of what it was in 1980. And I know what he's aiming at: He wants to get it down to pamphlet size. [*Laughter*]

Furthermore, I think the oil situation looks good. Spurred on by decontrol—you remember, that was going to destroy everything—we've witnessed the biggest spurt in exploration in the nation's history. In an astonishing reversal, oil production in the lower 48 States has just increased for the third month in a row. And coupled with a more manageable inflation rate, the growth in total employment—you know that there are a million more Americans working now than there were just a year ago at this time—we're as confident today that the Nation's economic problems can and will be overcome as the day we proposed our program.

Now, I know it's not always going to be clear sailing, but we've come a long way and there's still much to do. So, let's never lose sight of the common goal—a healthy and a strong America. And I just want each of you to know what an honor it's been for me to work with all of you and a great pleasure.

And I'm happy to see that there's a young lady right here in front who's really, I think, a pretty good reason for everything that we're doing, to see if this country won't be as good to her and her friends her age as it's been to all of us.

Thank you all, and thanks for being there. And—[*turning to Mrs. Reagan*]—let's go down and say hello.

Note: The President spoke at 5:29 p.m. in the East Room at the White House at the reception for congressional supporters of the President's program for economic recovery.

Nomination of James R. Ambrose To Be Under Secretary of the Army
September 30, 1981

The President today announced his intention to nominate James R. Ambrose to be Under Secretary of the Army. He would succeed Harry Spiro, Jr.

Mr. Ambrose was employed during World War II and until 1955 at the Naval Research Laboratory (NRL), where he was involved in the early development of ship and airborne radar systems, semiconductors, nuclear weapons and reactors. In 1955 he joined the Lockheed Corp., missile systems division, where he studied and proposed efforts on satellites and ballistic missile projects. In late 1955 he became one of the principals in a new systems engineering firm, Systems Research Corp., which was subsequently acquired by Ford Motor Co. This acquisition was later merged with Philco Corp., and is currently operated as a wholly owned subsidiary of Ford, called Ford Aerospace and Communications Corp. Mr. Ambrose has spent over 36 years in these organizations in technical management assignments primarily related to defense equipment and systems, space programs, and major communications, command, and control systems. For the last 13 years of his career prior to retirement, he was vice president for technical affairs for Ford Aerospace and Communications Corp.

Mr. Ambrose graduated from the University of Maine (1943) and attended Georgetown, Catholic University, and the University of Maryland. He is a widower and has four married sons. Mr. Ambrose was born August 16, 1922, in Brewer, Maine.

Nomination of Jay Raymond Sculley To Be an Assistant Secretary of the Army
September 30, 1981

The President today announced his intention to nominate Jay Raymond Sculley to be an Assistant Secretary of the Army (Research, Development and Acquisition). He would succeed Percy Anthony Pierre.

Since 1978 Mr. Sculley has been head of the department of civil engineering at Virginia Military Institute (VMI). Previously he was associate professor of civil engineering at VMI in 1975–78 and assistant professor of civil engineering in 1970–73. In 1974–75 he was general manager, Corrugated Services, Inc., in Dallas, Tex. He was a design engineer and engineering consultant in 1965–69. Mr. Sculley was a civil engineer in the United States Air Force in 1962–65.

Mr. Sculley graduated from Virginia Military Institute (B.S., 1962) and Johns Hopkins University (M.S.E., 1970; Ph. D., 1974). He was born August 6, 1940, in Englewood, N.J., and resides in Lexington, Va.

Appointment of Christopher C. DeMuth as Administrator for Information and Regulatory Affairs and as Executive Director of the Presidential Task Force on Regulatory Relief
September 30, 1981

Christopher C. DeMuth was today appointed Administrator for Information and Regulatory Affairs at the Office of Management and Budget. The President also announced the appointment of Mr. DeMuth to be Executive Director of the Presidential Task Force on Regulatory Relief.

Since 1977 Mr. DeMuth has been lecturer in public policy at the Harvard School of Government and director of the Harvard Faculty Project on Regulation, which has conducted research on health, environmental, and economic regulation. He is the author of several articles on regulation and other aspects of government policy.

Following college, he served as staff assistant to the President in 1969–70, working first on urban policy matters and then as chairman of a White House task force on environmental policy. After leaving the White House in September 1971 to attend law school, he served as a member of the Legal Advisory Committee to the Council on Environmental Quality and of the Secretary of State's Advisory Committee for the United Nations Conference on the Human Environment.

He practiced regulatory, antitrust, and general corporate law with the firm of Sidley & Austin, in Chicago, in 1973–76. In 1976–77 he was Associate General Counsel of the Consolidated Rail Corp. (Conrail) in Philadelphia.

Mr. DeMuth graduated from Harvard College (A.B., 1968) and the University of Chicago Law School (J.D., 1973). He was admitted to the Illinois Bar in 1973. He is a member of the American Bar Association, the American Economic Association, and the Council on Foreign Relations, and is a contributing editor of the American Spectator. He is married to Susan Ann DeMuth, M.D. They have two children and reside in the District of Columbia. He was born August 5, 1946, in Kenilworth, Ill.

Executive Order 12325—Presidential Task Force on the Arts and Humanities
September 30, 1981

By the authority vested in me as President by the Constitution of the United States of America, and in order to extend the time for the Task Force to complete its work, Executive Order No. 12308 is hereby amended as follows:

Section 1. Section 1 is amended by deleting "No more than one member shall be a full-time Federal officer or employee. The remaining members shall not represent Executive agencies.".

Sec. 2. Section 4(b) is amended to read, "The Task Force shall terminate on October 31, 1981.".

RONALD REAGAN

The White House,
September 30, 1981.

[Filed with the Office of the Federal Register, 10:54 a.m., October 1, 1981]

Note: The signing of the Executive order was announced by the Office of the Press Secretary on October 1. It was not issued as a White House press release.

Executive Order 12326—Central Intelligence Agency Retirement and Disability System
September 30, 1981

By the authority vested in me as President of the United States of America by Section 292 of the Central Intelligence Agency Retirement Act of 1964 for Certain Employees, as amended (50 U.S.C. 403 note), and in order to conform further the Central Intelligence Agency Retirement and Disability System to certain amendments in the Civil Service Retirement and Disability System, it is hereby ordered as follows:

Section 1. Section 221(b)(1) of the Central Intelligence Agency Retirement Act of 1964 for Certain Employees, as amended, shall be deemed to be amended by inserting the following after the last sentence of that paragraph:

"Any written notification (or designation) by any participant under this section shall not be considered valid unless the participant establishes to the satisfaction of the Director (a) that the spouse has been notified of the loss of or reduction in survivor benefits or (b) that the participant has complied with such notification requirements as the Director shall, by regulation, prescribe.".

Sec. 2. Section 231(a) of the Central Intelligence Agency Retirement Act of 1964 for Certain Employees, as amended, shall be deemed to be amended by deleting the first sentence thereof, and inserting in lieu thereof the following:

"Any participant who has five years of service credit toward retirement under the system, excluding military or naval service that is credited in accordance with provisions of section 251 or 252(a)(2), and who has become disabled shall, upon his own application or upon order of the Director, be retired on an annuity computed as prescribed in section 221. A participant shall be considered to be disabled only if the participant is found by the Director to be unable, because of disease or injury, to render useful and efficient service in the participant's position and is not qualified for reassignment, under procedures prescribed by the Director, to a vacant position which is in the Agency at the same grade or level and in which the participant would be able to render useful and efficient service.".

Sec. 3. Section 221 of the Central Intelligence Agency Retirement Act of 1964 for Certain Employees, as amended, shall be deemed to be amended by inserting after subsection (l) thereof the following new subsection:

"(m) If a participant retiring under section 231 of this Act is receiving retired pay or retainer pay for military service (except that specified in section 252(e)) or Veterans Administration pension or compensation in lieu of such retired or retainer pay, the annuity of that participant shall be computed under subsection (a) of this section, excluding credit for such military service from that computation. If the amount of the annuity so computed, plus the retired or retainer pay which is received, or which would be received but for the application of the limitation in Section 5532 of Title 5 of the United States Code, or the Veterans Administration pension or compensation in lieu of such retired or retainer pay, is less than the annuity that would otherwise be payable under section 231, an amount equal to the difference shall be added to the annuity payable under subsection (a) of this Section.".

Sec. 4. Section 291 (a) and (b)(1) of the Central Intelligence Agency Retirement Act of 1964 for Certain Employees, as amended, shall be deemed to be amended to read as follows:

"(a) On the basis of determination made by the Director pertaining to per centum change in the Price Index, the following adjustments shall be made:

"(1) Except as provided in subsection (b) of this Section, effective March 1 of each year each annuity payable from the Fund having a commencing date not later than such March 1 shall be increased by the percent change in the Price Index published for December of the preceding year, adjusted to the nearest one-tenth of one percent.

"(b) Eligibility for an annuity increase under this Section shall be governed by the commencing date of each annuity payable from the Fund as of the effective date of an increase, except as follows:

"(1) The first cost-of-living increase (if any) made under subsection (a) of this Section to an annuity which is payable from the Fund to a participant who retires or to the widow or widower of a deceased participant whose annuity has not been increased under this subsection or subsection (a) of this Section, shall be equal to the product (adjusted to the nearest one-tenth of one percent) of—

(A) one-twelfth of the applicable percent change computed under subsection (a) of this Section, multiplied by

(B) the number of months (counting any portion of a month as a month)—

(i) for which the annuity was payable from the Fund before the effective date of the increase, or

(ii) in the case of a widow or widower of a deceased annuitant whose annuity was first payable to the deceased annuitant.".

Sec. 5. For the purpose of ensuring the accuracy of information used in the administration of the Central Intelligence Agency Retirement and Disability System, the Director of Central Intelligence may request, from the Secretary of State and the Administrator of Veterans Affairs such information as the Director deems necessary. To the extent permitted by law:

(a) The Secretary of Defense shall provide information on retired or retainer pay provided under Title 10 of the United States Code; and

(b) The Administrator of Veterans Affairs shall provide information on pensions or compensation provided under Title 38 of the United States Code.

The Director, in consultation with the officials from whom information is requested, shall ensure that information made available under this Section is used only for the purposes authorized.

Sec. 6. Section 221 of the Central Intelligence Agency Retirement Act of 1964 for Certain Employees, as amended, shall be deemed to be amended by adding thereto a new subsection (e) as follows:

"(e)(1) The Director shall, in accordance with this subsection, enter into an agreement with any State within 120 days of a request for agreement from the proper State official. The agreement shall provide that the Director shall withhold State income tax in the case of the monthly annuity of any annuitant who voluntarily requests, in writing, such withholding. The amounts withheld during any calendar quarter shall be held in the Fund and disbursed to the States during the month following that calendar quarter.

"(2) An annuitant may have in effect at any time only one request for withholding under this subsection, and an annuitant may not have more than two such requests in effect during any one calendar year.

"(3) Subject to paragraph (2) of this subsection, an annuitant may change the State designated by that annuitant for purposes of having withholdings made, and may request that the withholdings be remitted in accordance with such change. An annuitant also may revoke any request of that annuitant for withholding. Any change in the State designated or revocation is effective on the first day of the month after the month in which the request or the revocation is processed by the Director, but in no event later than on the first day of the second month beginning after the day on which such request or revocation is received by the Director.

"(4) This subsection does not give the consent of the United States to the application of a statute which imposes more burdensome requirements on the United States than on employers generally, or which subjects the United States or any annuitant to a penalty or liability because of this subsection. The Director may not accept pay from a State for services performed in withholding State income taxes from annuities. Any amount erroneously withheld from an annu-

ity and paid to a State by the Director shall be repaid by the State in accordance with regulations issued by the Director.

"(5) For the purpose of this subsection, 'State' means a State, the District of Columbia, or any territory or possession of the United States.".

Sec. 7. The amendments made by Sections 1, 2, 3, 4, 5, and 6 of this Order shall be effective as follows:

(a) Section 1 shall be effective as of January 5, 1981;

(b) Section 2 shall be effective as of March 5, 1981;

(c) Section 3 shall be effective as of this date for all participants who retire under Section 231 of the Central Intelligence Agency Retirement Act of 1964 for Certain Employees, as amended, on or after December 5, 1980.

(d) Section 4 shall be effective as of the date of this Order.

(e) Section 5 shall be effective as of August 13, 1981, and shall apply to annuities which commence before, on, or after such date.

(f) Section 6 shall be effective as of October 1, 1981.

RONALD REAGAN

The White House,
September 30, 1981.

[*Filed with the Office of the Federal Register, 8:45 a.m., October 2, 1981*]

Note: The text of the Executive order was released by the Office of the Press Secretary on October 1.

Message to the Congress Reporting Budget Deferrals
October 1, 1981

To the Congress of the United States:

In accordance with the Impoundment Control Act of 1974, I herewith report twenty-six deferrals of fiscal year 1982 funds totaling $737.2 million. The deferrals are primarily routine in nature and do not, in most cases, affect program levels.

The deferrals are for programs in the Departments of Agriculture, Commerce, Defense, Energy, Health and Human Services, Interior, Labor, State, Transportation, and Treasury, the Pennsylvania Avenue Development Corporation, and the Motor Carrier Ratemaking Study Commission, as well as

for Appalachian regional development programs.

The details of each deferral are contained
in the attached reports.

RONALD REAGAN

The White House,
October 1, 1981.

*Note: The attachments detailing the defer-
rals are printed in the* Federal Register *of
October 7, 1981.*

The President's News Conference
October 1, 1981

The President Well, welcome to my first
annual press conference. [*Laughter*]

Program for Economic Recovery

Last night I signed a bill that raised the
debt ceiling to more than $1 trillion. It was
necessary to do that to continue government operations. But it heightens the significance of this first day of the 1982 fiscal
year, because on this day our economic recovery program begins.

The $1 trillion debt figure can stand as a
monument to the policies of the past that
brought it about—policies which as of today
are reversed. Tax cuts and spending cuts
that take effect today will put America back
on the road to economic recovery. In the
next several years, we can create 13 million
jobs, reduce inflation, and reward the spirit
of liberty and enterprise that were responsible for our Nation's economic might. Our
programs won't be instantaneous. The mistakes of four decades can't be turned
around in 8 months.

There's recently been some improvement
in the area of short-term interest rates. The
prime rate has begun to turn down. Rates
on treasury bills that were almost 16 percent when I took office are down to 14½.
Fluctuations in the various economic indicators such as inflation and unemployment
rates will probably continue for several
months, but we will not be swayed from
our plan by every changing current, every
passing trend, or every short-term fluctu-
ation.

In times past, administrations have failed
to come even close to their spending targets, and the Congress has ignored its own
announced spending ceilings. Those times
are over. I will sign no legislation that

would "bust the budget" and violate our
commitment to hold down Federal spending.

New subject.

*Sale of AWACS Planes and F–15
Enhancement Items to Saudi Arabia*

This morning Congress was notified of
our intention to sell AWACS aircraft and F–
15 enhancement items to Saudi Arabia. I
have proposed this sale because it significantly enhances our own vital national security interests in the Middle East. By building confidence in the United States as a
reliable security partner, the sale will greatly improve the chances of our working constructively with Saudi Arabia and other
states of the Middle East toward our
common goal—a just and lasting peace. It
poses no threat to Israel, now or in the
future. Indeed, by contributing to the security and stability of the region, it serves
Israel's long-range interests.

Further, this sale will significantly improve the capability of Saudi Arabia and the
United States to defend the oil fields on
which the security of the free world depends.

As President, it's my duty to define and
defend our broad national security objectives. The Congress, of course, plays an important role in this process. And while we
must always take into account the vital interests of our allies, American security interests must remain our internal responsibility. It is not the business of other nations to
make American foreign policy. An objective
assessment of U.S. national interest must
favor the proposed sale. And I say this as
one who holds strongly the view that both a

secure state of Israel and a stable Mideast peace are essential to our national interests.

Jim [Jim Gerstenzang, Associated Press].

Economic Recovery Program: Support and Effects

Q. Mr. President, one of the original arguments for your budget and tax cuts was that they would have an immediate psychological impact, that the economy would get better once the people saw these cuts coming. That hasn't really happened yet, and the drop in interest rates, while it has happened as you pointed out, hasn't been major. With the program taking effect today, when will the actual dollar impact be felt and when will the social safety net catch the people who depend on it for health care and school lunches and so on? When will they start feeling the impact of this net under them?

The President. Well, I believe the answers to all those questions have to do with the fact that there has been some psychological improvement. It has been commented on in a number of places across the country, of a different feeling on the part of the people themselves. But also, there are material evidences of it: the announcement which I have referred to before by the Iron and Steel Institute, on behalf of that industry, that it is going to embark on the largest program of expansion and modernization in the briefest period of time in the history of that industry. And they have stated flatly that they are doing it on their optimism, based on their optimism with regard to our program. I have heard from other business sources—the National Chamber of Commerce and their wholehearted support of the program and what we're doing.

But you must remember that for the practical effect beyond that—today begins, for example, the tax cut for individuals, but since the first year's tax cut is only 5 percent, that's going to be reflected in a somewhat increased take-home pay for most people, but it is not going to be overwhelming to begin with. And it's going to take some time before that's reflected in increased savings and an increase in the capital pool and so forth. Now, some of our

business taxes are retroactive and go back to January 1st, but, of course, they won't be felt until tax-paying time.

But I am encouraged and do believe that there is a trust on the part of most of the people in this. As a matter of fact, the polls show, and the results of the response to my own address of last Thursday on TV has been running 3 to 1 in support of the program. But the other day in this room, Congressmen and Senators of both sides of the aisle told me that their own calls and wires were running 95 to 98 percent in support of our program.

Helen [Helen Thomas, United Press International].

U.S. Foreign Policy: AWACS and the Middle East

Q. Mr. President, since Saudi Arabia has agreed to an American presence on AWACS, what do you think is the possibility now of Senate acceptance of the sale? And you seem to have been telling us right now that Israel should keep her hands off what we consider American national security matters in the Middle East.

The President. Well, or anyone else. [*Laughter*] No, and let me hasten to add, I don't mean that in any deprecating way, because my meeting with Sadat and my meeting with Prime Minister Begin, President Sadat and the Prime Minister, both of them were fine meetings. I think we've arrived at a very great understanding, and we're going forward with strategic discussions of our relations with Israel. But I don't think that anyone—I suppose what really is the most serious thing is the perception, that other countries must not get a perception that we are being unduly influenced one way or the other with regard to foreign policy, and I——

Q. What about the chance of the sale going through in the Senate?

The President. I believe that the chance is good. I think that many of the things that we've had to report now, on the terms of that sale, meet most of the objections that some of those have had.

Economic Recovery Program: Block Grants and the Safety Net

Q. Mr. President, you made clear in your opening statement your intention of staying on course with a program that you articulated when you came into office. It assumes that if certain things happen that the States will be able to gear up and take over responsibilities which are being diminished in the Federal Government. It assumes that persons, people, will be able to fill in and do things on their own. Have you seen anything in the early signs on this fiscal new year that not everything is happening so smoothly, that there may be some temporary dislocations, some suffering and, if so, would that cause you to give any second thought to the short-range effects of your program?

The President. No, and I think that what you might be referring to is the somewhat obvious effort to portray these programs, already, as being harmful to people. And I have to think that we have to expect that there are certain areas in which those who administer the programs might—as I experienced in California—deliberately impose them in such a way that, justifying themselves as going by the book, they then pick out the cases that the programs were never intended to affect.

But let me just say that—for example, we asked for 88 categorical grant programs to be consolidated into block grants for State and local governments. We only succeeded in getting 57, but those 57 were integrated into six block grant programs. Now, the effect of that is going to be—well, I can show you. Knowing that I was going to be asked about some of this [*holding up the two stacks of regulations for the press and the cameras*], here are the regulations for those categorical grant programs—318 pages. And here are the six pages of regulations that will now apply to the nine block grants.

Granted that any program of any size, and certainly any government programs, are going to have some fallout and some errors and confusion. But what we've called the safety net is still in place, and the benefits are still maintained.

The programs are spending an average of over $15,000 per elderly couple. Over 102 million meals are going to be served and are being served every day under this program, and that's 15 percent of all the meals served in the country. Twenty-two million people were eligible for food stamps before the reform; some 21 million will still be eligible today. Now, some of those may have a reduction in the amount, the number of food stamps, but those will be based on their means and their outside income. And about 40 million individuals are still provided with over $50 billion in cash and in in-kind benefits in eight major public assistance programs other than social security.

So, whatever the fallout may be, I believe that—well, for example, in administering the block grants, I think it's something like 105 million man-hours of labor and paperwork by local government officials will be eliminated by making those block grants.

Black Concerns: Economic Policies and the Voting Rights Act

Q. Mr. President, as I think you're aware, a number of black leaders in this country have expressed some reservations about your policies, not only economic policies, but other policies. And I wonder if you might have something to say today to reassure the blacks in this country concerning your attitude and your policy? And specifically, sir, whether or not you're in favor of extending the Voting Rights Act as it is now constructed?

The President. Well, I have not had an opportunity—the report that I've been waiting for is on its way to my office and didn't get here before the press conference. But I am wholeheartedly in favor, let's say, in principle of the Voting Rights Act, because I believe very deeply that we've had experiences in this country—and not alone on a racial basis—of vote fraud and discrimination. And that's a sacred right that must be upheld, and I will uphold it.

I think that possibly there are some leaders of organizations in the black community who have followed the lead of others and have been attacking, from the very beginning, our programs. But I have been gratified by the support that is evidenced to me through mail, through calls, through personal meetings with members of the black community, that have told me they believe in the program.

I had one letter just a few days ago from a 16-year-old boy who identified himself as black. And he said, "I am wholeheartedly behind what you're trying to do, and I think it means much for my own future." I had another from a young black man who had just become the father of a baby girl. And he was telling that he—and he had come all the way over from being a diehard Democrat to support this program because, he said, "I think it means a better world for my daughter."

Lesley [Lesley Stahl, CBS News].

Economic Recovery Program: Effects on Individuals

Q. Mr. President, thank you. You've talked about the effect of your economic program being mainly something that will affect or be adverse to administrators, and I wonder if you could talk about some specific individuals in the country who may be getting some of their eligibility—or you have programs reducing the eligibility requirements in some programs. What do you say to the single working mother whose eligibility for Medicaid and for food stamps has been cut? What would you like to say to her today about how she cannot provide medical care for her children or feed them with food stamps?

The President. I don't believe that we're actually doing that. I don't say that there won't be some cutbacks and reductions. And I think to any of us, if there's any reduction in income, it forces us to change some of our plans and reorder our priorities.

Where the cuts have come is around the periphery—and some may be hurt more than others—but where we have tried to find those areas where people have other income, in addition to their public grants, and therefore we can reduce some of that public grant. But those people that are totally dependent on government, that is our obligation, and nothing is going to happen to them.

Economic Recovery Program: Defense Budget Cuts

Q. Mr. President, would you be willing to accept larger cuts in your '82 defense budget if the Congress prepares a proposal along those lines?

The President. I would hesitate to say that I would or that they should do this, because these cuts were not just made on a basis of saying, "Oh, let's take a percentage of their money away from them." We went into what—in the planned military buildup—that we believe is essential to our national security. What does each cut mean? What must we eliminate?

I would like to call to your attention that before the program even went into effect or before this $2 billion cut for 1982, Caspar Weinberger, the Secretary there, had already come up himself with $3½ billion in cuts in defense spending.

Q. Why didn't you go for that?

The President. What?

Q. Why didn't you go for $3½ billion?

The President. Well, we found—because he was able to find where he believed he could make the additional cuts, trying to be helpful, without any important setback to our military buildup.

AWACS Sale: Saudi Arabia and Iran

Q. Mr. President, are you aware that the same people at the Pentagon and the State Department who now want you to sell AWACS planes to Saudi Arabia, 4½ years ago wanted that very same weapons system sold to the Shah of Iran just before the Shah fell?

Given the fact that when the Shah fell, the United States lost much top secret military equipment in Iran—[*inaudible*]—missiles, F–15 fighters—can you now guarantee the Congress and the people of the United States that the AWACS system, if it's sold to the Saudis, will not compromise American security or would not fall into the wrong hands?

The President. I can make that guarantee that it will not compromise our security. I don't believe that it'll fall into enemy hands, but it would not compromise our security even if it had.

Now, with regard to 4½ years ago, I wasn't here then. And Iran—I have to say that Saudi Arabia, we will not permit to be an Iran.

Economic Recovery Program: Presidential Vetoes

Q. Mr. President, do you still have to honor the commitment to Congressman English that you will veto any windfall profits tax on natural gas?

The President. Well, I have always hesitated to say—I'll talk about vetoing in general principles, such as I will veto generally attempts to bust the budget. But I have always refrained from, and it's long before I came here, from talking of specifics. I would have to see a bill and what finally winds up on my desk before I would give an answer as to veto or not.

Nuclear War and Arms Reduction Talks

Q. Mr. President, there's been talk about limited nuclear war. Do you believe that either the Soviet Union or the United States could win a nuclear war? Is there a winnable nuclear war?

The President. It's very difficult for me to think that there's a winnable nuclear war, but where our great risk falls is that the Soviet Union has made it very plain that among themselves, they believe it is winnable. And believing that, that makes them constitute a threat, which is one of the reasons why I'm dedicated to getting them at a table not for arms limitation talks, but for arms reduction talks.

Yes, Sam [Sam Donaldson, ABC News].

Strategic Weapons: Window of Vulnerability

Q. Sir, on that same subject, that same general subject. Can you reassure our European allies and anyone else—*[inaudible]*—that you're not seeking military superiority over the Soviet Union or, in fact, is that the policy?

The President. We're seeking whatever is necessary to ensure that that "window of vulnerability" I've spoken of has been closed and that the risk has been reduced of there being a war at all. And I think our allies, largely in Europe, do know that. I also do think that there is—or there are

groups among our allies, as there is here in America, who are increasingly vocal in carrying their own message, and it is one there of pacifism and neutrality and so forth. I think they're very unrealistic, and if we listen to them, I think we'd all be in trouble.

Economic Recovery Program: Tax Reductions

Q. Mr. President, some of your critics are saying that by cutting taxes and at the same time spending more for the military you are, like Lyndon Johnson, saying it was possible to have guns and butter at the same time, and that it won't work for you any more than it did with Johnson and that it will, indeed, damage the economy. What do you say to that?

The President. Well, the great difference is the tax portion of our program, because when we say cutting taxes, we're really leaving a word off. There is a difference between reducing rates and reducing tax revenues. And we only have to look back just shortly before Lyndon Johnson's term to when John F. Kennedy was President and when he followed the policy across the board, against the same kind of economic advice that we've been getting, that he couldn't do that. But he cut those tax rates, and the government ended up getting more revenues, because of the almost instant stimulant to the economy. Now, that's what's being called today—they didn't use the term then—"supply-side economics."

And you don't even have to stop at that one. If you look at our reductions in capital gains tax, if you go back to the twenties when Mellon was the Secretary of the Treasury under Coolidge and was doing this, every time, that kind of a tax cut brings us back—I've told, I think, some of you before—to a principle that goes back at least, I know, as far as the fourteenth century, when a Moslem philosopher named Ibn Khaldun said, "In the beginning of the dynasty, great tax revenues were gained from small assessments. At the end of the dynasty, small tax revenues were gained from large assessments." And we're trying to get down to the small assessments and the great revenues.

Economic Recovery Program: Taxes and Revenues

Q. Mr. President, well you've just sounded a theme that you've sounded many times, that the tax cuts will, in effect, be self-replenishing and produce more revenues than they take away. If that's true, why do you have these huge spending cuts? Some of your colleagues, like Congressman Kemp, say they won't be necessary because revenues will grow. If you think revenues will grow, why are you cutting the budget?

The President. We're cutting the budget because the Federal Government is taking too high a percentage of the gross national product to allow for prosperity. And if the government is taking money out of the people's pockets which they could use as they saw fit, to continue to support things that are not properly government's business or that are not cost effective, then you have an obligation to do away with those things and let the people retain their own money.

Q. May I follow up?

The President. Yes.

Q. Your own projections show that revenue won't grow. Are they wrong?

The President. No, our projections don't show that. There are two things. I mentioned the gross national product. We are also taking in taxes a higher percentage of the gross national product than has been taken in, other than in war time, in our entire history. And if you go back to the beginning of this century and the classic economists, you'll find that they, themselves, tied business slumps to those moments when government went beyond a certain level in its taking money from people.

Administration's Image

Q. Mr. President, the style of your administration is being called "millionaires on parade." Do you feel that you are being sensitive enough to the symbolism of Republican mink coats, limousines, thousand-dollar-a-plate china at the White House, when ghetto kids are being told they can eat ketchup as a vegetable?

The President. Well, we changed that. Somebody got over ambitious in the bureaucracy with their ketchup for a vegetable, and we had to pull back on some regulations that were suggested.

On the other, I don't think it's a "millionaire's parade," and I haven't counted any of the mink coats that have been around.

But also, you mentioned the china. Let's set that straight once and for all, because Nancy's taken a bit of a bum rap on that. There has been no new china for the White House since the Truman administration—some partial augmentation under Lyndon Johnson, but not a full set of china. Now, breakage occurs even in the White House. I know that everyone's supposed to be walking around on feathers and that doesn't happen, but it does. And the truth of the matter is, at a state dinner, we can't set the tables with dishes that match. We have to have them mixed, so don't look too closely at other tables in there. And this was the result of an anonymous contribution, and the company making the china made it at cost. So there was nothing out of the taxpayers.

Federal Reserve Board: Interest Rates and Inflation

Q. Sir, you have been told by a number of Members of Congress, who say they have proof from intelligence they have, that the big central banks are totally responsible for influencing Paul Volcker of the Federal Reserve Board to keep the interest rates high. Now, they tell you that you can do something about this, despite the fact, we know, how separate the Federal Reserve is supposed to be from the executive and all that. Now, they say that the rates are now 10 percent above the inflation rate and that there's no ordinary reason for that. Now, will you do something about this?

The President. Well, those who say that, without trying to move in on the Federal Reserve, that we could do something are ignoring the simple truth of the marketplace. Those interest rates are based on the amount of money that is available for borrowing and the competition, the amount of people who want to borrow. And the truth

of the matter is we will bring down inflation—or bring down interest rates, when
we bring down inflation, and when we can
once and for all get the government out of
the financial market and end its excessive
borrowing, which is taking too great a percentage of the money that is available.

Q. But, sir, the inflation rate is lower than
the interest rates—10 percent, 10 points.

The President. Yes. But out in the open
market where you go into sell bonds and so
forth, and where corporations must go
when they want to expand and borrow
money, and individuals must go to borrow
for a mortgage on a house, it is supply and
demand and the competition that is generated by that. And we're hurt as much as
anyone else. What has thrown our budget
estimates off is the excessive interest we
have to pay to borrow the money to pay for
the deficit left us by other Congresses.

Saudi Arabia and Iran

Q. Mr. President, you said a few minutes
ago that you would not allow, you would
not permit what happened in Iran several
years ago to happen in Saudi Arabia. How
would you prevent that? Would you take
military intervention if that was necessary
to prevent it?

The President. I'm not going to talk about
the specifics of how we would do it, except
to say that in Iran, I think the United States
has to take some responsibility for what
happened there—with some very short-
sighted policies that let a situation come to
a boiling point, that there was no need to
do that.

But in Saudi Arabia, I just would call to
your attention that it's not only the United
States, it's the whole Western World. There
is no way, as long as Saudi Arabia and the
OPEC nations there in the East—and Saudi
Arabia's the most important—provide the
bulk of the energy that is needed to turn
the wheels of industry in the Western
World, there's no way that we could stand
by and see that taken over by anyone that
would shut off that oil.

Economic Recovery Program: Wall Street Reaction

Q. Mr. President, if you're so certain that
the American people are in back of your

economic program, why the over concern
on the part of the administration on how
Wall Street reacts to it—I mean, the constant banging away at Wall Street?

The President. Gary [Gary Schuster, Detroit (MI) News], we haven't been so constantly—I just thought that somebody would
ask a question about Wall Street. [*Laughter*]
And I have a letter here from the Securities
Industry Association, signed by the president, Edward O'Brien, and by the chairman
of the board, Ralph DeNunzio. And he said,

"Dear Mr. President,

"Widespread interpretation of recent weakness in securities prices as an indication of
significant disenchantment with the
Administration's economic program has
become a source of major concern within
the securities industry. Therefore, as
chairman and president of the Securities
Industry Association, which represents
more than 500 firms accounting for approximately 90% of the securities business done in this country, we want to
assure you that this interpretation is not
correct.

"The SIA Board, comprised of senior officers of brokerage and investment banking firms from all parts of the nation, has
just concluded a quarterly meeting in
Dallas, Texas." ". . . we can assure you
that the thrust of your economic program—reduced federal spending, major
tax reductions for business and individuals, business deregulation and slow but
steady growth in the money supply—
enjoys overwhelming support in the stock
brokerage and investment banking community.

"Just as it will take time for this program to
achieve its goals, it also will take time for
the millions of investors whose multiple
concerns and perceptions determine
stock and bond prices to recognize the
magnitude and the potential of the fundamental change in economic policy you
have set in motion.

"Concerns have, of course, been expressed
over the extent of future . . . deficits, as
well as the prolonged effects of present
high interest rates. We know that you

share these concerns and are addressing the problem[s]. . . . continued evidence of your determination to impose budgetary discipline will surely exert a positive influence on securities markets over a reasonable period."

Well, I'm very grateful for that. I left out a few lines—modesty caused me to do that. [*Laughter*]

Q. I'm sorry I asked, Mr. President. [*Laughter*]

The President. I'm not, because I've been carrying that letter all day. [*Laughter*] I was beginning to think none of you would get to it.

Social Issues Agenda

Q. Mr. President, the New York Times Sunday Magazine almost 3 weeks ago reported that unnamed Presidential strategists do not want you to give more than rhetorical support to the so-called social issues agenda; that is, such issues as abortion, busing, and voluntary school prayer. My question, sir, is do you plan to do more than give rhetorical support to the social issues agenda and, if so, what is it you plan to actually do?

Thank you.

The President. Well, I think I've made, over the months and even years, my position clear on most of those social issues. And I shall be happy to see them come to my desk for signature.

Economic Recovery Program: Wall Street Reaction

Q. Mr. President, there has been—despite your letter that you enjoyed there—a feeling in the administration that the financial markets have not shown the proper optimism, the kind of support that you would think they would have had for a man of your economic policies. Do you have no disappointment or no feeling of something of a letdown from the high interest rates——

The President. Well, if I had some I have less now that I've gotten that letter. But— and that's sort of what Gary's question was, also—it is true that we had had difficulty reconciling the stock market with the evidence that we were getting from business and industry, all the way from retail to manufacturing, about their optimism, their plans for expansion, and their outright support. Business organizations ranging from the National Chamber [of Commerce] on to various industry-type groups have been wholehearted in their support of us and what we were doing. So, it was hard to understand. But as they pointed out, if you really look at it, on Wall Street, these are people that are basing their own investment on what they see in the future.

Frankly, I think that it reflected less of a lack of confidence in us than it did in a pessimism that we wouldn't be able to get through the Congress the things we were trying to get. And that was based on long, sad experience. But now, I think that with a $35-billion cut in one package, asking for continued cuts, I think that they've got reason to be optimistic.

People's Republic of China: Possibility of Visit

Q. Mr. President, I'd like to take you pretty far from Wall Street to the People's Republic of China. There is a standing invitation here for you, as the American President, to go to China. In Peking they are talking about that possibility. In Cancún at that summit conference later this month, you will be there, and the head of government of the People's Republic of China will be there. What is your thinking now about traveling to Peking?

The President. Well, that's something that I look forward to with interest, but I don't think for a while yet.

Q. They think in the spring of next year. Is that possible?

The President. Well, that may be a little earlier than it should happen. And then I remember that all of you say that Presidents only travel when they're in trouble, and I don't want to be in trouble next spring. [*Laughter*]

Ms. Thomas. Thank you.

The President. Thank you, Helen.

Note: The President's fourth news conference began at 2 p.m. in the East Room at the White House. It was broadcast live on radio and television.

Executive Order 12327—Exemption for Fort Allen
October 1, 1981

By the authority vested in me as President by the Constitution and statutes of the United States of America, including Section 313 of the Federal Water Pollution Control Act, as amended (33 U.S.C. 1323), Section 118 of the Clean Air Act, as amended (42 U.S.C. 7418), Section 4 of the Noise Control Act of 1972 (42 U.S.C. 4903), and Section 6001 of the Solid Waste Disposal Act, as amended (42 U.S.C. 6961), and in order to provide for the immediate relocation and temporary housing of Haitian nationals, who are located in the State of Florida and presently in the custody of the United States, at a Federal facility known as Fort Allen, located in the Commonwealth of Puerto Rico, and having determined it to be in the paramount interest of the United States to exempt Fort Allen from all the requirements otherwise imposed on it by the said statutes, it is hereby ordered as follows:

1–101. Consistent with the provisions of subsection (a) of Section 313 of the Federal Water Pollution Control Act, as amended (33 U.S.C. 1323(a)), each and every effluent source located at Fort Allen is exempted from compliance with the provisions of that Act; except that no exemption is hereby granted from Sections 306 and 307 of that Act (33 U.S.C. 1316 and 1317).

1–102. Consistent with the provisions of subsection (b) of Section 118 of the Clean Air Act, as amended (42 U.S.C. 7418(b)), each and every particular emission source located at Fort Allen is exempted from compliance with the provisions of that Act; except that no exemption is hereby granted from Section 111 and 112 of that Act (42 U.S.C. 7411 and 7412).

1–103. Consistent with the provisions of subsection 4(b) of the Noise Control Act of 1972, as amended (42 U.S.C. 4903(b)), each and every single activity or facility, including noise emission sources or classes thereof, located at Fort Allen, are exempted from compliance with the provisions of that Act; except that no exemption is hereby granted from Sections 6, 17 and 18 of that Act (42 U.S.C. 4906, 4916 and 4917).

1–104. Consistent with the provisions of Section 6001 of the Solid Waste Disposal Act, as amended (42 U.S.C. 6961), each and every solid waste management facility located at Fort Allen is exempted from compliance with the provisions of that Act.

1–105. The exemptions granted by this Order shall be for the one-year period beginning October 2, 1981, and ending October 1, 1982.

RONALD REAGAN

The White House,
October 1, 1981.

[*Filed with the Office of the Federal Register, 8:46 a.m., October 2, 1981*]

Statement on Signing a Joint Resolution Providing Continuing Appropriations for Fiscal Year 1982
October 1, 1981

I have signed today the continuing resolution (House Joint Resolution 325) passed last night by the Congress to provide funds for the first 50 days of the new fiscal year starting today.

While I am signing this resolution, I want to make clear that it is only a stop-gap measure to keep the government running for the next few weeks, until the Congress acts upon regular 1982 appropriations bills.

The pattern of spending that is permitted by this resolution is far different from what the Congress or I would recommend. For example, defense spending will be held well below the levels I have requested. Spending for many other programs could, under this resolution, be far higher than I requested last March.

Furthermore, 1 week ago I outlined the steps needed to keep the Nation on the path to economic recovery. These steps include substantial reductions in 1982 budget requests so as to hold down spending and prevent a large increase in deficits. The new requests are below the levels I proposed last March and well below levels provided in the 1982 appropriations bills acted upon thus far by the House and Senate. My new proposals would reduce budget authority $26 billion below the levels proposed last March.

The Congress has made it clear during consideration of this resolution that the executive branch is expected to keep a tight rein on spending under the resolution so that we do not reduce the ability of Congress to consider fully the lower budgets I have proposed. The legislative history states that the amounts allowed to be obligated under the continuing resolution are to be considered as ceilings and not minimums. I expect all departments and agencies to follow this clear directive.

Note: As enacted, H.J. Res. 325 is Public Law 97–51, approved October 1.

Proclamation 4866—American Enterprise Day
October 2, 1981

By the President of the United States of America

A Proclamation

One of America's great strengths is its private enterprise system. The personal and economic freedom enjoyed by our people turned our fledgling nation, in a few short years, into an economic dynamo that astounded the world.

Today, the unique blend of individual opportunity, incentive and reward that is the free enterprise system provides Americans with an unparalleled standard of living.

As the foundation of our economic life, free enterprise depends on and serves every American. It is the enemy of poverty. It permits Americans to be the most compassionate of people, at home and to those in need abroad.

Through their insistence on the free enterprise system, our forefathers unleashed the creative energies of a people, built the foundation of our unparalleled political and economic freedom, and brought forth a vital force in the world.

In recognition of the importance of our free enterprise system, the Congress has, in Senate Joint Resolution 78, designated October 2, 1981, as American Enterprise Day.

Now, Therefore, I, Ronald Reagan, President of the United States of America, do hereby proclaim October 2, 1981, as American Enterprise Day. I urge all Americans to observe this occasion with appropriate activities, and in particular to encourage in our youth an appreciation and enthusiasm for the role of free enterprise in our nation's life.

In Witness Whereof, I have hereunto set my hand this second day of October, in the year of our Lord nineteen hundred and eighty-one, and of the Independence of the United States of America the two hundred and sixth.

RONALD REAGAN

[*Filed with the Office of the Federal Register, 12:05 p.m., October 2, 1981*]

Proclamation 4867—National Port Week
October 2, 1981

By the President of the United States of America

A Proclamation

Much of our history as a nation has been shaped by the ports of our sea coasts and inland waterways. Our early harbors fostered industry and trade and helped build many of America's great cities.

Today, our ports are an important resource in the Nation's economy. In 1980, the port industry handled almost two billion short tons of waterborne commerce in foreign and domestic trade. This commerce contributed over $35 billion to the gross national product and generated an additional $1.5 billion in services sold to users.

Recognizing their vital importance to America's economic health, State and local port authorities and private industry have continued to invest financial resources to improve port facilities to meet ever-increasing needs.

The growing demand for coal and other energy sources to fuel the economic growth of the United States and the rest of the industrialized world has presented the ports of this Nation with a unique challenge.

Many port authorities have begun and others have plans for the construction or expansion of harbor facilities. Some 70 million tons of annual capacity now under construction will result in a 50 percent increase over current capacity. By 1985 total investment in new or expanded facilities is expected to meet the projected demand of our industrial trading partners and to decrease our dependence on foreign oil.

In recognition of the importance of our ports to the Nation's economy, the Congress has, by Senate Joint Resolution 103, designated the week beginning October 4, 1981, as National Port Week.

Now, Therefore, I, Ronald Reagan, President of the United States of America, do hereby designate the seven calendar days beginning October 4, 1981, as National Port Week. I invite the Governors of the several States, the chief officials of local governments, and the people of the United States to observe this week with appropriate ceremonies and activities.

In Witness Whereof, I have hereunto set my hand this second day of October, in the year of our Lord nineteen hundred and eighty-one, and of the Independence of the United States of America the two hundred and sixth.

RONALD REAGAN

[*Filed with the Office of the Federal Register, 12:06 p.m., October 2, 1981*]

Appointment of Armand Hammer as a Member of the President's Cancer Panel, and Designation as Chairman
October 2, 1981

The President today announced his intention to appoint Armand Hammer to be a member of the President's Cancer Panel. The President also intends to designate Dr. Hammer Chairman.

Dr. Hammer acquired the Occidental Petroleum Corp. in 1957 and currently serves as chairman of the board and chief executive officer. Previously, Dr. Hammer was involved in the distilling and cattle businesses.

He is active in community and civic affairs and has been a strong supporter of cancer research. He serves on the board of directors of the Eleanor Roosevelt Cancer Foundation and is a trustee of the Eleanor Roosevelt Memorial Foundation. In 1969 he established the Armand Hammer Center for Cancer Biology at the Salk Institute in California. He is an art patron and founded the Hammer Galleries, Inc. (New York City), and continues to be a major supporter of the Los Angeles County Museum of Art.

Dr. Hammer graduated from Columbia University (B.S., 1919; M.D., 1921). He is married, has one son, and resides in Los Angeles, Calif. He was born May 21, 1898, in New York City.

Remarks and a Question-and-Answer Session With Reporters on the Announcement of the United States Strategic Weapons Program
October 2, 1981

The President. As President, it's my solemn duty to ensure America's national security while vigorously pursuing every path to peace. Toward this end, I have repeatedly pledged to halt the decline in America's military strength and restore that margin of safety needed for the protection of the American people and the maintenance of peace.

During the last several years, a weakening in our security posture has been particularly noticeable in our strategic nuclear forces—the very foundation of our strategy for deterring foreign attacks. A window of vulnerability is opening, one that would jeopardize not just our hopes for serious productive arms negotiations, but our hopes for peace and freedom.

Shortly after taking office, I directed the Secretary of Defense to review our strategy for deterrence and to evaluate the adequacy of the forces now available for carrying out that strategy. He and his colleagues, in consultation with many leaders outside the executive branch, have done that job well. And after one of the most complex, thorough, and carefully conducted processes in memory, I am announcing today a plan to revitalize our strategic forces and maintain America's ability to keep the peace well into the next century.

Our plan is a comprehensive one. It will strengthen and modernize the strategic triad of land-based missiles, sea-based missiles, and bombers. It will end longstanding delays in some of these programs and introduce new elements into others. And just as important, it will improve communications and control systems that are vital to these strategic forces.

This program will achieve three objectives:

—It will act as a deterrent against any Soviet actions directed against the American people or our allies;

—It will provide us with the capability to respond at reasonable cost and within adequate time to any further growth in Soviet forces;

—It will signal our resolve to maintain the strategic balance, and this is the keystone to any genuine arms reduction agreement with the Soviets.

Let me point out here that this is a strategic program that America can afford. It fits within the revised fiscal guidelines for the Department of Defense that I announced last week. And during the next 5 years, the entire cost of maintaining and rebuilding our strategic forces will take less than 15 percent of our defense expenditures. This is considerably below the 20 percent of our defense budget spent on strategic arms during the 1960's, when we constructed many of the forces that exist today. It is fair to say that this program will enable us to modernize our strategic forces and, at the same time, meet our many other commitments as a nation.

Now, let me outline the five main features of our program.

First, I have directed the Secretary of Defense to revitalize our bomber forces by constructing and deploying some 100 B–1 bombers as soon as possible, while continuing to deploy cruise missiles on existing bombers. We will also develop an advanced bomber with "stealth" characteristics for the 1990's.

Second, I have ordered the strengthening and expansion of our sea-based forces. We will continue the construction of Trident submarines at a steady rate. We will develop a larger and more accurate sea-based ballistic missile. We will also deploy nuclear cruise missiles in some existing submarines.

Third, I've ordered completion of the MX missiles. We have decided, however, not to deploy the MX in the racetrack shelters proposed by the previous administration or in any other scheme for multiple protective shelters. We will not deploy 200 missiles in 4,600 holes, nor will we deploy 100 missiles in 1,000 holes.

We have concluded that these basing schemes would be just as vulnerable as the existing Minuteman silos. The operative factor here is this: No matter how many shelters we might build, the Soviets can build more missiles, more quickly, and just as cheaply.

Instead, we will complete the MX missile which is much more powerful and accurate than our current Minuteman missiles, and we will deploy a limited number of the MX missiles in existing silos as soon as possible.

At the same time, we will pursue three promising long-term options for basing the MX missile and choose among them by 1984, so that we can proceed promptly with full deployment.

Fourth, I have directed the Secretary of Defense to strengthen and rebuild our communications and control system, a much neglected factor in our strategic deterrent. I consider this decision to improve our communications and control system as important as any of the other decisions announced today. This system must be foolproof in case of any foreign attack.

Finally, I have directed that we end our long neglect of strategic defenses. This will include cooperation with Canada on improving North American air surveillance and defense, and as part of this effort, I've also directed that we devote greater resources to improving our civil defenses.

This plan is balanced and carefully considered—a plan that will meet our vital security needs and strengthen our hopes for peace. It's my hope that this program will prevent our adversaries from making the mistake others have made and deeply regretted in the past—the mistake of underestimating the resolve and the will of the American people to keep their freedom and protect their homeland and their allies.

Now, I can only remain here for a few minutes. And I will do so for just a few questions that might deal with the statement or with policy. But for all the technical matters, I am going to turn you over to Secretary [of Defense] Cap Weinberger.

Yes, Helen [Helen Thomas, United Press International].

Q. On that, would we be ready to use these new systems as bargaining chips in arms talks with the Soviets?

The President. Oh, I think everything having to do with arms, Helen, would have to be on the table.

Q. Mr. President, when exactly is this "window of vulnerability?" We heard yesterday the suggestion that it exists now. Earlier this morning, a defense official indicated that it was not until '84 or '87. Are we facing it right now?

The President. Well, I think in some areas we are, yes. I think the imbalance of forces, for example, on the Western front, in the NATO line—we are vastly outdistanced there. I think the fact that right now, they have a superiority at sea.

Q. Mr. President, if there is or will be a "window of vulnerability," why is the MX any less vulnerable if it's in silos, the location of which the Soviets presumably already know, unless we were going to launch on their attack?

The President. I don't know but what maybe you haven't gotten into the area that I'm going to turn over to the Secretary of Defense.

I could say this: The plan also includes the hardening of silos so that they are protected against nuclear attack. Now, we know that is not permanent. We know that they can then improve their accuracy, their power, and their ability, but it will take them some time to do that, and they will have to devote a decided effort to doing that.

Q. So this is a way then of buying time, sir?

The President. In a way, of narrowing that "window of vulnerability."

Q. Mr. President, some people already are saying that your decisions are based to a large extent on politics, domestic politics, so let me ask you about two points: One, that you never considered the racetrack system because it was proposed by Jimmy Carter, and you didn't want to have anything to do with something that he had proposed; and, two, that you're not basing the MX in Utah and Nevada because of opposition from the Mormon Church and your good friend, Senator Paul Laxalt.

The President. Sam [Sam Donaldson, ABC News], I can tell you now, no, the entire study of the basis for basing—I got tangled up there with two words that sounded so much alike—the MX missile was a very thorough study of all those proposals that had been made. And actually, I could refer you to the Townes Commission [Panel], their study and their report that we would not have an invulnerable missile basing by doing that; that all they would have to do is increase the number of targeted warheads on that particular area and take out the whole area; and while it would force them to build additional missiles, we would be just as vulnerable as we are in the present Minutemen.

Q. Laxalt didn't persuade you, sir?
The President. No, no.

Q. Mr. President, your predecessor killed the B–1 manned bomber because he said it couldn't penetrate Soviet air defenses. The Soviets can make a lot of progress in radar between now and 1986. Can you guarantee that the B–1 could penetrate Soviet air defenses, and is it the best plane as a cruise missile launch platform?

The President. I think, again, you're getting in—I think that my few minutes are up—[*laughter*]—and I'm going to turn that question over to Cap. I think I know the answer to it, but I do believe that you are getting into the kind of questions that he is properly——

Q. Well, could you tell us why you decided to build the B–1 as opposed to your predecessor's decision not to build it? Do you think it can penetrate Soviet air space?

The President. We have to have it, because between the aging B–52 and the bomber we are developing, the newer bomber, there is too long a time gap in there and would leave us a very lengthy, vulnerable period. And the B–1 is designed not just to fill that gap, but it will then have a cruise missile carrying capacity later, in which it will still be worth the cost of building and worth having.

But now, I'm going to turn it over to Cap here for the rest of the questions.

Note: The President spoke at 2 p.m. in the East Room at the White House.

The Townes Panel was organized by the Department of Defense to study alternative basing modes for the MX missile system.

Nomination of Jean Broward Shevlin Gerard To Have the Rank of Ambassador While Serving as United States Permanent Representative to the United Nations Educational, Scientific and Cultural Organization
October 2, 1981

The President today announced his intention to nominate Jean Broward Shevlin Gerard to have the rank of Ambassador while serving as United States Permanent Representative to the United Nations Educational, Scientific and Cultural Organization.

In 1977–81 Mrs. Gerard was an attorney with the law firm of Cadwalader, Wickersham and Taft of New York, where she specialized in international law.

She graduated from Vassar College (A.B., 1959) and Fordham University School of Law (J.D., 1977). She is a member of the New York, District of Columbia, Florida, and American Bar Associations. Mrs. Gerard is married, has two children, and resides in New York City. She was born March 9, 1938, in Portland, Oreg.

Proclamation 4868—National Employ the Handicapped Week, 1981
October 2, 1981

By the President of the United States of America

A Proclamation

Communities across the land have formed partnerships—between disabled and non-disabled, labor and industry, employers and employees—to assure that disabled people might share fully in the American dream. There is a real need for such partnerships and for these ties to continue and expand.

Employers throughout the country are opening their doors to qualified disabled workers. This is happening not just because of existing laws, but because disabled men and women have been establishing such fine work records. Yet not all employers have opened their doors equally wide. We must therefore continue our efforts to find more and better jobs for people with disabilities.

Gains have also been made in education, training, housing, transportation and accessibility. We need to make the 1980s years in which disabled individuals achieve the greatest possible access to our society, maximum independence, and full opportunity to develop and use their capabilities.

The Congress, by joint resolution of August 11, 1945, as amended (36 U.S.C. 155), has called for the designation of the first full week in October each year as National Employ the Handicapped Week. Recognition of this special week presents the opportunity to dedicate ourselves to meeting the goal of expanded opportunity for disabled Americans.

Now, Therefore, I, Ronald Reagan, President of the United States of America, do hereby designate the week beginning October 4, 1981, as National Employ the Handicapped Week. I urge all Governors, Mayors, other public officials, leaders in business and labor, and private citizens to help meet the challenge of the future in which all disabled Americans will participate fully in our country's many opportunities.

In Witness Whereof, I have hereunto set my hand this second day of October, in the year of our Lord nineteen hundred and eighty-one, and of the Independence of the United States of America the two hundred and sixth.

RONALD REAGAN

[*Filed with the Office of the Federal Register, 4:38 p.m., October 2, 1981*]

Remarks at the Annual Meeting of the National Alliance of Business
October 5, 1981

Thank you very much for a very warm welcome.

Your organization is concerned with jobs. I heard of a fellow who had been unemployed for a long time, and a few days ago he found a job at a china warehouse. He'd only worked there a couple of days when he smashed a large oriental vase. The boss told him in no uncertain terms that the money would be deducted from his wages every week until the vase was paid for. And the fellow asked, "How much did it cost?"

He told him $300. And the fellow cheered and said, "At last, I've found steady work." [*Laughter*]

Seriously, I'm aware that the National Alliance of Business was formed to reduce the despair of unemployment, to provide opportunities where they would otherwise not exist. You've set for yourselves a noble and necessary goal. You know that a job at $4 an hour is priceless in terms of the self-respect it can buy. Many people today are economically trapped in welfare. They'd like nothing better than to be out in the work-a-day world with the rest of us. Independence and self-sufficiency is what they want. They aren't lazy or unwilling to work, they just don't know how to free themselves from that welfare security blanket.

After we undertook our welfare reforms in California, I received a letter from a woman with several children who had been on Aid to [Families With] Dependent Children. She wrote that she had become so dependent on the welfare check that she even turned down offers of marriage. She just could not give up that security blanket that it represented. But she said that she'd always known that it couldn't go on, couldn't last forever. So when our reforms began, she just assumed that the time had come and that somehow she would be off welfare. So she took her children and the $600 she had saved from her, as she put it, so-called "poverty," and went to Alaska, where she had relatives. And she was writing the letter now not to complain about our reforms, but to tell me that she had a good job and that working now had given her a great deal of self-respect, for which she thanked me, and then one line that I'll never forget. She said, "It sure beats daytime television." [*Laughter*]

Our economic program is designed for the very purpose of creating jobs. As I said on Labor Day, let us make our goal in this program very clear—jobs, jobs, jobs, and more jobs. And what is more, our program will reduce inflation so the wages from these jobs will not decrease in earning power.

Part of that economic package also includes budget cuts. Now, some of these cuts will pinch, which upsets those who believe the less fortunate deserve more than the basic subsistence which the governmental safety net programs provide. Well, the fact is, I agree. More can be done; more should be done. But doing more doesn't mean to simply spend more. The size of the Federal budget is not an appropriate barometer of social conscience or charitable concern.

Economic problems or not, isn't it time to take a fresh look at the way we provide social services? Not just because they cost so much and waste so much, but because too many of them just don't work? Even if the Federal Government had all the money it wished to spend on social programs, would we still want to spend it the way we have in the past?

In all my years as Governor, and now as President, I have never found an agency, a program, a piece of legislation, or a budget that was adequate to meet the total needs of human beings. Something is missing from such an equation. I believe that something is private initiative and community involvement—the kind the NAB exemplifies.

There is a legitimate role for government, but we musn't forget: Before the idea got around that government was the principal vehicle of social change, it was understood that the real source of our progress as a people was the private sector. The private sector still offers creative, less expensive, and more efficient alternatives to solving our social problems. Now, we're not advocating private initiatives and voluntary activities as a halfhearted replacement for budget cuts. We advocate them because they're right in their own regard. They're a part of what we can proudly call "the American personality."

The role of voluntarism and individual initiative has been misunderstood. Federal loan guarantees will not be restored by charity alone, nor will we replace the Department of Health and Human Services. Voluntarism is a means of delivering social services more effectively and of preserving our individual freedoms. John F. Kennedy knew this when he said, ". . . only by doing the work ourselves, by giving generously out of our own pockets, can we hope in the long run to maintain the authority of the people over the state, to insure that the people remain the master; the state, the servant. Every time that we try to lift a problem from our own shoulders, and shift that problem to the hands of the government, to the same extent we are sacrificing the liberties of our people."

There are hardheaded, no-nonsense measures by which the private sector can meet those needs of society that the government has not, can not, or will never be able to fill. Volunteer activities and philanthropy play a role, as well as economic incentives and investment opportunities. To be certain, we're talking about America's deep spirit of generosity. But we're also talking about a "buck for business" if it helps to solve our social ills.

With the same energy that Franklin Roosevelt sought government solutions to problems, we will seek private solutions. The challenge before us is to find ways once again to unleash the independent spirit of the people and their communities. That energy will accomplish far, far more than government programs ever could. What federalism is to the public sector, voluntarism and private initiative are to the private sector. This country is bursting with ideas and creativity, but a government run by central decree has no way to respond.

Having been a Governor, Franklin Roosevelt knew something of the dangers of overcentralization. In a message to the Congress, he wrote, "continued dependence upon relief"—it hadn't yet been given the name welfare—"induces a spiritual and moral disintegration fundamentally destructive to the national fibre. To dole out relief in this way is to administer a narcotic, a subtle destroyer of the human spirit. . . . The Federal Government must and shall quit this business of relief."

Well, what exactly is voluntarism? I guess Gary Cooper did about the best job describing it in the movie, "Mr. Deeds Goes to Town."

"From what I can see," he said, "no matter what system of government we have, there will always be leaders and always be followers. It's like the road out in front of my house. It's on a steep hill. And every day I watch the cars climbing up. Some go lickety-split up that hill on high;

some have to shift into second; and some sputter and shake and slip back to the bottom again. Same cars, same gasoline, yet some make it and some don't. And I say the fellas who can make the hill on high should stop once in a while and help those who can't."

Over our history, Americans have always extended their hands in gestures of assistance. They helped build a neighbor's barn when it burned down, and then formed a volunteer fire department so it wouldn't burn down again. They harvested the next fellow's crop when he was injured or ill, and they raised school funds at quilting bees and church socials. They took for granted that neighbor would care for neighbor.

When the city of Chicago was leveled by fire, urban renewal programs didn't exist; the people simply got together and rebuilt Chicago. The great French observer of America, de Tocqueville, wrote, "Whenever at the head of some new undertaking you see the government in France, or a man of rank in England, in the United States you will be sure to find an association of individuals."

The association of Americans has done so much and is so rich in variety. Churches once looked after their own members, and during the Depression, the Mormon Church undertook its own welfare plan based on the work ethic—a plan that is still successful today. With no disrespect intended, one can't help but wonder if government welfare would exist at all if our churches had at that same time, all of them, picked up that task.

Before World War I, the Rockefeller and Carnegie Foundations together spent twice as much as the government for education and social services—simply because there was a need. The National Foundation for Infantile Paralysis set out to conquer polio with dimes—and did it. And in a fitting symbol of America, our own Statue of Liberty was built with the nickels and dimes of French schoolchildren and the contributions of their parents.

We all know countless stories of individual and personal generosity. There was an incident in Los Angeles a couple of years ago involving a man named José Salcido, whose wife had died of cancer, leaving him both father and mother of 13 children. In an accident only the Lord can explain, one day the brakes on his truck didn't hold and he was crushed against a brick wall as he walked in front of the vehicle. The children who had lost their mother now had lost their father. But they were not orphaned by their neighbors or even complete strangers, who immediately began collecting contributions. The parish church started a drive. Finally, a fund was set up at the bank and a committee was formed of citizens to take care of it. They also discovered how kind the people of this land can be.

One letter accompanying a check said it all. "This is for the children of José Salcido. It is for them to know there are always others who care; that despite personal tragedy, the world is not always the dark place it seems to be; that their father would have wanted for them to go on with courage and strength and still open hearts."

Now, I know there are cynics who dismiss the notion of Americans helping other Americans. They say that I speak of an America that never was and never can be. They believe voluntarism is a mushy idea, the product of mushy thinking. They say that our society today is too complex or that we're trying to repeal the 20th century.

Well, the cynics who say these things have been so busy increasing Washington's power that they've lost sight of America. Have they forgotten the great national efforts before there ever was a thing called "foreign aid"? The American people organized to help Japan in the great earthquake, famine in India, "Bundles for Britain." The spirit is not dead.

I wish the cynics would visit David and Falaka Fattah in Philadelphia. I don't know whether I pronounced their name right, but the Fattahs decided to put their hearts and minds into reducing the gang violence in west Philadelphia, which killed up to 40 persons a year in the early 1970's. They were instrumental in negotiating a city-wide peace treaty among gangs, that reduced the number of deaths from 40 to about 1 a year. This one couple did something that all the social welfare and law enforcement agencies together had been unable to accomplish. They replaced the gang structure with a family structure. They actually took a gang of 16 into their home. Their House of Umoja has helped more than 500 boys now develop into self-sufficient and productive young men. And today, they're establishing what might be called an urban Boys Town.

I wish the doubters would visit Detroit, where a few years ago hundreds of children awaiting adoption were in the foster care system. Potential black parents were judged by arbitrary income standards and not whether they could offer a warm, loving, secure family to a homeless child. But a community group called Homes for Black Children challenged the adoption practices of the local agencies with astounding results. In its first year, Homes for Black Children placed more kids in permanent homes than all 13 of the traditional placement agencies combined.

There is the DeBolt family in California that began adopting only children who were grievously handicapped—at one time, 19 in their home.

I wish the cynics would call on New York City, the New York City Partnership, an association of 100 business and civic leaders, which this past summer found jobs for about 14,000 disadvantaged youths, the majority of whom would not have otherwise found jobs.

Talk to the Honeywell people who are training prison inmates in computer programing. Those inmates who reach an employable skill level before leaving prison have a recidivism rate of less than 3 percent, compared to a national rate estimated at 70 percent.

Or look at the marvelous work McDonald's is doing with it's Ronald McDonald Houses. These are places, homes, really, usually near children's hospitals, where families can stay while their children are treated for serious diseases. Currently, 28 homes are open and another 32 are in some stage of development. Since the homes are funded mainly by the local McDonald operators and the staff is all volunteer, no taxpayer money is spent.

The cynics should ask the Fattahs if the spirit is dead. They should ask the families who have been helped by the McDonald Houses and the Homes for Black Children if the spirit is dead. They should ask the disadvantaged New York youths who have summer jobs, or the prison inmates who are developing skills for the outside world. Why can't the skeptics see the spirit is there where it's always been—inside individual Americans?

Individual Americans like Father Bruce Ritter. Father Ritter's Covenant House in the heart of Times Square offers youths who are runaway or exploited a sanctuary from the pressures of modern life and an escape from those who would prey on them. With the help of 200 part-time and 65 full-time volunteers, Father Ritter last year aided nearly 12,000 youths.

Perhaps the doubters should consider how empty and gray our society would be right now if there were no such thing as volunteer activity. Erma Bombeck, that witty woman who appears in our newspapers, once wrote a more sober article on what it would be like if the volunteers all set sail for another country. And if you don't mind, let me read a part of what she said:

"The hospital was quiet as I passed it. Rooms were void of books, flowers, and voices. The children's wing held no clowns . . . no laughter. The reception desk was vacant.

"The Home for the Aged was like a tomb. The blind listened for a voice that never came. The infirm were imprisoned by wheels on a chair that never moved. Food grew cold on trays that would never reach the mouths of the hungry.

"All the social agencies had closed their doors, unable to implement their programs of scouting, recreation, drug control, Big Sisters, Big Brothers, YW, YM, the retarded, the crippled, the lonely, and the abandoned.

"The health agencies had a sign in the window, 'Cures for cancer, muscular dystrophy, birth defects, multiple sclerosis, emphysema, sickle cell anemia, kidney disorders, heart diseases, have been cancelled due to lack of interest.'

"The schools were strangely quiet with no field trips, no volunteer aides on the playground or in the classrooms . . . as were the colleges where scholarships and financial support were no more.

"The flowers on church altars withered and died. Children in day nurseries lifted their arms but there was no one to hold them in love."

Well, her article told a very much unrecognized truth: Volunteer cuts would be much more disruptive to the Nation than Federal budget cuts. Because they are so important, this administration seeks to elevate voluntary action and private initiative to the recognition they deserve. We seek to increase their influence on our daily lives and their roles in meeting our social needs. For too long, the American people have been told they are relieved of responsibility for helping their fellow man because government has taken over the job. Now we seek to provide as much support for voluntarism, without federalizing, as possible.

Today, I am announcing the creation of a Presidential Task Force on Private Sector Initiatives, comprised of 35 leaders from corporations, foundations, and voluntary and religious organizations. Its purpose will be to promote private sector leadership and responsibility for solving public needs, and to recommend ways of fostering greater public-private partnerships. I have asked Bill Verity, the chairman of Armco Steel, to chair the task force and act as my personal representative in expanding private sector initiatives and in recognizing outstanding examples of corporate and community efforts.

I'm instructing the Cabinet to review agency procedures and regulations and identify barriers to private sector involvement. We want to deregulate community service. For example, mothers and grandmothers have been taking care of children for thousands of years without special college training. Why is it that certain States prohibit anyone without a college degree in early childhood education from operating a day care facility?

I'm also asking the Cabinet to develop pump priming and seed money programs that offer incentives for private sector investment. In addition, the Cabinet will provide technical knowledge to develop private incentives. Furthermore, existing programs will be examined to determine those which could be more productively carried out in the private sector.

Voluntarism is an essential part of our plan to give the government back to the people. I believe the people are anxious for this responsibility. I believe they want to be enlisted in this cause. We have an unprecedented opportunity in America in the days ahead to build on our past traditions and the raw resources within our people. We can show the world how to construct a social system more humane, more compassionate, and more effective in meeting its members' needs than any ever known.

After I spoke of volunteerism several days ago, I received this mailgram: "At a breakfast this morning, 35 chief executive officers of the largest employers and financial institutions of San Antonio met and committed to: 1) support of you and your commitment of returning the responsibility of support of many worthy, previously federally funded programs to the local level; 2) committing themselves individually and corporately to do more in being a part of continuing or establishing that safety net of services each community needs; 3) as a first step, committing to achieving a minimum 20-percent increase in our local United Way campaign which represents 60 agencies included within that safety net; and finally, committing themselves that the programs supported are needed and efficiently and effectively administered. You have our support." And it was signed by Harold E. O'Kelley, chairman of the board and president of Datapoint Corporation, Tom Turner, Sr., chairman of the board and president of Sigmor Corporation, Dr. Robert V. West, Jr., chairman of the board of Tesoro Petroleum Corporation, and H. B. Zachry, Sr., chairman of the board of the H. B. Zachry Company.

And just this weekend, I received a letter from the insurance industry promising to undertake new budget initiatives to reduce unemployment, especially among minority youths. The insurance companies plan to direct their financial resources—which are in the hundreds of billions of dollars, as we know—to further this goal. They also plan to increase their dollar contributions to these programs affecting basic human needs.

The private sector can address the tough social problems of special concern to minority Americans, and I believe that we will soon see a torrent of private initiatives that will astound the advocates of big government.

The efforts of you at this conference also show what can be done when concerned people in businesses join in partnership with government. You are a model of future action, and I'm calling upon you today to help in the cause to enlarge the social responsibility of our citizens. The spirit that built this country still dwells in our people. They want to help. We only need to ask them.

All of us, and particularly we who are parents, have worried about whether the youth of today have absorbed some of the traditions with which we're so indoctrinated. Well, a few years ago, in Newport Beach, California, there were some lovely beachfront homes that were threatened by an abnormally high tide and storm-generated heavy surf—in danger of being totally undermined and destroyed. And all through the day and the cold winter night—and it does get cold in California at night; sometimes in the daytime—the volunteers worked filling and piling sandbags in an effort to save these homes. Local TV stations, aware of the drama of the situation, covered the struggle and went down there in the night to see what was happening, catch the damage being done and so forth.

And it was about 2 a.m. when one newscaster grabbed a young fellow in his teens, attired only in wet trunks, even at that hour. He'd been working all day and all that night—one of several hundred of his age group. And in answer to the questions—no, he didn't live in one of those homes they were trying to save; yes, he was cold and tired. And the newscaster finally wanted to know, well, why were he and his friends doing this? And he stopped for a minute and then he answered, and the answer was so poignant and tells us something so true about ourselves that it should be printed on a billboard. He said, "Well, I guess it's the first time we ever felt like we were needed."

Americans are needed. They're needed to keep this country true to the tradition of voluntarism that's served us so well. And they're needed to keep America true to her values. In the days following World War II when a war-ravaged world could have slipped back into the Dark Ages, Pope Pius XII said: The American people have a genius for great and unselfish deeds; into the hands of America, God has placed an afflicted mankind.

Let those words be true of us today. Let us go forth from this conference and say to the people: Join us in helping Americans help each other. And I assure you, I'm not standing here passing this off to you as solely your task, and the government will wash its hands of it. We intend a partnership in which we'll be working as hard as we can with you to bring this about.

Thank you, and God bless you.

Note: The President spoke at 10:35 a.m. at the Sheraton Washington Hotel.

Proclamation 4869—General Pulaski Memorial Day
October 5, 1981

By the President of the United States of America

A Proclamation

As we pay homage again to the memory of General Casimir Pulaski, we are reminded of his dedication to freedom, his selfless service to our Nation, and his contributions to the achievement of American independence. His tireless devotion to democratic ideals continues to inspire us, his adopted countrymen, today. His name and deeds remain similarly alive in the hearts of the people of his native Poland, and indeed of people the world over. His is a model we can all emulate.

Upon his arrival in America in 1777, General Pulaski was appointed by Congress as Commander of the Horse in the Continental Army. He fought at the battle of Germantown, conducted expeditions to obtain provisions for the Continental soldiers during their harsh winter at Valley Forge, Pennsylvania and, as the Revolutionary War continued, saw service in New Jersey and Delaware. Following a gallant attempt to wrest Savannah, Georgia from British con-

trol, this valiant patriot died on October 11, 1779.

Now, Therefore, I, Ronald Reagan, President of the United States of America, do hereby designate October 11, 1981 as General Pulaski Memorial Day.

Furthermore, in recognition of the supreme sacrifice General Pulaski made for his adopted country and for the cause of freedom, I do hereby designate October 11 of each succeeding year as General Pulaski Memorial Day.

I invite the people of the United States to honor the memory of General Pulaski by holding appropriate exercises and ceremonies on this date in suitable places throughout our land.

In Witness Whereof, I have hereunto set my hand this fifth day of October, in the year of our Lord nineteen hundred and eighty-one, and of the Independence of the United States of America the two hundred and sixth.

RONALD REAGAN

[*Filed with the Office of the Federal Register, 4:23 p.m., October 5, 1981*]

Message to the Senate Transmitting the Constitution of the United Nations Industrial Development Organization
October 5, 1981

To the Senate of the United States:

With a view to receiving the advice and consent of the Senate to ratification, I transmit herewith a copy of the Constitution of the United Nations Industrial Development Organization (UNIDO). This Constitution was adopted by the United Nations Conference on the Establishment of the United Nations Industrial Development Organization as a Specialized Agency on April 8, 1979, and signed on behalf of the United States of America on January 17, 1980. The report of the Department of State with respect to the Constitution is also transmitted for the information of the Senate.

The Constitution would establish UNIDO as an independent specialized agency of the United Nations system. It does not create a new entity, but rather revises UNIDO's existing legal framework in a way that significantly improves the position of the United States and other major donors in budget, program and assessment determinations.

UNIDO's principal purpose is to foster the industrialization of developing countries. It is currently the third largest executing agency for the United Nations Development Program. UNIDO's wide-ranging activities are geared to aid developing countries in establishing the technical and institutional skills necessary for industrialization. Many of these activities are consonant with United States development priorities, including development of indigenous entrepreneurial and productive capabilities in the private sector. United States commercial and academic interests also benefit from UNIDO activity.

In recent years, there has been growing recognition of the need to formulate more effective institutions within the United Nations system to deal with the problems of development in an increasingly interdependent world. Such institutions need to serve the interests of all member nations and to be governed in a manner that realistically reflects the political and economic situation in the world today.

The Constitution would give UNIDO a new governing machinery that will make it more responsive to its member governments and that will give greater recognition to the special role of major donors, including the United States, other industrial democracies, and the Soviet bloc. If they act together, the major donors will be able to block decisions on UNIDO's program and budgets. In this respect, the Constitution is a precedent-setting document.

The Constitution would also provide a specific right of withdrawal from UNIDO if the United States should ever determine that its interests are not served by continued membership. This could not be accomplished under UNIDO's current statute without withdrawal from the United Nations.

While the Constitution refers to the objective of helping establish a new international economic order, the United States has made clear its view that this does not refer to any preconceived notion of such an order as outlined in some UN resolutions to which the United States has taken exception.

The Constitution offers the United States important advantages over UNIDO's current status. It provides an opportunity to increase UNIDO's effectiveness in promoting economic development in the developing countries and, thus, its contribution to a more equitable and peaceful international environment. In addition to helping create a better institutional framework, ratification of the Constitution by the United States will be a strong reaffirmation of our commitment to the industrial development of the less developed countries and demonstrate our political will to pursue beneficial relations with these countries.

I recommend that the Senate give prompt consideration to the Constitution and advise and consent to its ratification.

RONALD REAGAN

The White House,
October 5, 1981.

Remarks Following a Meeting With Former National Security Officials on the Sale of AWACS Planes and Other Air Defense Equipment to Saudi Arabia
October 5, 1981

The President. This distinguished bipartisan group of former national security officials have agreed to the following statement of support for the sale of AWACS and other air defense equipment to Saudi Arabia. After reading this statement, both Harold Brown and Henry Kissinger would like to make a further statement of their own.

The statement is:

"The sale of AWACS and other air defense equipment to Saudi Arabia would make a substantial contribution to the national security interests of the United States in a vital part of the world. The rejection of this sale would damage the ability of the United States to conduct a credible and effective foreign policy, not only in the Gulf region, but across a broad range of issues."

I want to thank each one of these gentlemen who are here for their recognition that this sale is in the national security interests of the Nation. Their public appearance at this time is an indication of the broad bipartisan support this sale has among knowledgeable former national security officials from both Republican and Democratic administrations, going all the way back to the Eisenhower administration.

And we believe, as I've said before, that not only is what we're talking about in the interest of our national security, but it is in the best interests of the national security of our friend and ally, Israel.

Now, Henry. Dr. Kissinger.

Dr. Kissinger. Mr. President, I'm aware of the intense debate that is going on on this issue, and I can sympathize with many of the concerns that have been expressed. It is my strong conviction, however, that these concerns cannot be met by rejecting the sale of AWACS. I believe the sale is in the national interests of the United States; it is compatible with the security of Israel; it is essential for the peace process in the Middle East; and it is important for the President's ability to conduct an effective and credible foreign policy. And so, I would urge those who have legitimate concerns to meet them in conversation with the administration, and to vote for the AWACS package without attaching conditions that are incompatible with the dignity of Saudi Arabia and with the effective conduct of our foreign policy.

The President. Thank you very much. And now, former Secretary Brown.

Mr. Brown. Thank you, Mr. President. I believe that American national security depends very strongly on the preservation of peace and of a favorable situation in Southwest Asia. One can understand the arguments that well-meaning opponents of the AWACS transfer make. I believe that when these are weighed against the advantages that this sale brings to U.S. national security, that the conclusion is that it would not help U.S. security, it would not help Israeli security, to have this sale rejected.

I think that both from a military point of view and from a diplomatic point of view the transfer is advantageous to the United States—from a military point of view in terms of the ability it gives us to have information on air movements in the area, and from a diplomatic point of view because the United States needs, if it is to continue to contribute to the peace process, to have close relations with Israel, with Saudi Arabia, and with other countries in the region. I think that would be severely damaged if this sale were overturned.

I hope that the Members of Congress who are going to consider this matter take into full consideration these facets of the issue. And when they do, I believe that they should come out in favor.

Thank you.

The President. Well, this concludes, but I think you can all see that there's a who's who roster here of men who have served this country over a great many years and have proven today they continue to serve any time they're needed.

And on behalf of all the people of this country, I just want to express my heartfelt thanks to all of you for being here today and doing this. Thank you very much.

Note: The President spoke at 1:10 p.m. at the North Portico of the White House. Earlier, the President hosted a reception in the Rose Garden and a luncheon in the State Dining Room for the former government officials.

In addition to former National Security Adviser and Secretary of State Henry A. Kissinger and former Secretary of Defense Harold Brown, the statement on the sale of AWACS planes and other equipment to Saudi Arabia was issued by former Defense Secretaries Melvin R. Laird, Robert S. McNamara, Elliot L. Richardson, Donald Rumsfeld, and James R. Schlesinger; former National Security Advisers Zbigniew Brzezinski, McGeorge Bundy, Gordon Gray, Walt W. Rostow, and Brent Scowcroft; former Chairmen of the Joint Chiefs of Staff Gen. Lyman L. Lemnitzer, Adm. Thomas H. Moorer, and Gen. Maxwell D. Taylor; and former Secretary of State William P. Rogers.

Remarks on Signing a Bill Proclaiming Honorary United States Citizenship for Raoul Wallenberg of Sweden
October 5, 1981

Not only a distinguished gathering here on the platform but a distinguished audience out here. Today we're here for—I'm signing the bill to make Raoul Wallenberg an honorary citizen of the United States. But in making him a United States citizen, I think we're the ones that are being honored.

Raoul Wallenberg is the Swedish savior of almost 100,000 Jewish men, women, and children. What he did, what he accomplished was of biblical proportions. Sir Winston Churchill, another man of force and fortitude, is the only other person who has received honorary United States citizenship. And as John F. Kennedy said at that signing ceremony, "Indifferent himself to danger, he wept over the sorrows of others."

That compassion also exemplifies the man we are gathered here for today. In 1944 the United States requested Sweden's cooperation in protecting the lives of Hungarian Jews facing extermination at the hands of the Nazis. In the months that followed, the United States supplied the funds and the directives, and Raoul Wallenberg supplied the courage and the passion. How can we comprehend the moral worth of a man who saved tens and tens of thousands of lives, including those of Congressman and Mrs. Lantos?

In 1945, in violation of diplomatic immunity and international law, he was seized by the Soviet Union. The Nazis were gone, and the Soviets had come in as an ally. And yet today, there is evidence that he is still imprisoned by the Soviets. Wherever he is, his humanity burns like a torch.

I heard someone say that a man has made at least a start on understanding the meaning of human life when he plants shade trees under which he knows he will never sit. Raoul Wallenberg is just such a man. He nurtured the lives of those he never knew at the risk of his own. And then just recently, I was told that in a special area behind the Holocaust Memorial in Israel, Hungarian Jews, now living in Sweden, planted 10,000 trees in Raoul's honor.

Mrs. Lagergren, Mr. von Dardel, we're going to do everything in our power so that your brother can sit beneath the shade of

890

those trees and enjoy the respect and love that so many hold for him.

Note: The President spoke at 2:35 p.m. at the signing ceremony in the Rose Garden at the White House. Participants in the ceremony included the Swedish Ambassdor and Mrs. Wilhelm Wachtmeister, Members of the Senate and House of Representatives, representatives of the Jewish community, and Mr. Wallenberg's sister and brother,

Nina Lagergren and Guy von Dardel, who came from Sweden for the ceremony. Also in attendance were Representative Tom Lantos of California, the principal sponsor of the resolution in the House of Representatives, and his wife. While a 16-year-old youth working for the Hungarian Underground, Representative Lantos was saved in Budapest by Mr. Wallenberg.

As enacted, S.J. Res. 65 is Public Law 97–54, approved October 5.

Remarks and a Question-and-Answer Session With a Group of Out-of-Town Editors
October 5, 1981

The President. Well, thank you all very much, and welcome. And believe me, it is a pleasure to welcome you to the White House and the opportunity to meet—we call both these buildings the White House—and talk with you in these special briefings. This is something that all of us in the administration have looked forward to.

And you don't need me to tell you the tremendous influence that you of the press and the media have on public opinion. I think that you are the first to agree that diversity of interpretation and opinion is very important to your work and to our robust tradition of press freedom.

This diversity, as you know, has been threatened recently with the sad demise of several important institutions in the newspaper field. This came home to us here in Washington recently, when the Washington Star closed up shop after more than a century of publication.

So, we do look forward to this opportunity to talk with you. You all know the fresh perspective that a new reporter can bring to an old beat, and that's why we hope these briefings will lead to some new insights and perspectives for both of us, and that the ultimate beneficiaries will be the members—or the readers, the listeners, and the viewers in your hometowns.

Administration's Policies and Programs

This last month has been a rather busy one. It's also been a very satisfying one. We think we've brought about a sea-change in national policy. You may detect a feeling of zest and buoyancy around the Capitol, and certainly around this area on Pennsylvania Avenue where the White House is.

For all of us, this has been an exciting, invigorating and—I think that just about sums up these 9 months—satisfying could also go in there.

In the last month, there was a radio address to the Nation on Labor Day, a TV address on the economy, a news conference that covered the waterfront of issues. I've had an opportunity to do some traveling, to talk to union members in Chicago about the housing industry, to help get Westway started in New York City, assist at the dedication of President Ford's museum in Grand Rapids, Michigan, and to talk to the Republican women leaders in Denver about Wall Street and Main Street. Last week in New Orleans, I announced some major initiatives on crime and also spoke to the World Bank conference about our new development policy. And when I leave you—and I regret that I have to be here so briefly—I'm going to be speaking to the National Alliance of Business about mobilizing the private sector to assist the underprivileged.

Now, during all of this, we've had the usual round of White House activities, ranging from a luncheon for black college leaders to some very fruitful diplomatic discussions, including a visit from Prime Minister Begin of Israel. Now, I think that's pretty good for a fellow that only works 2 or 3 hours a day. [*Laughter*]

We've made economic recovery, as you know, a first priority, but the approach of this administration is hardly one-dimensional. We've been moving systematically to deal with that broad range of problems we promised to do something about in the campaign last year.

There's a good bit of discussion now about our plans to sell the AWACS system to Saudi Arabia. This issue is not simply a question of balancing the interests of two nations in the Middle East; it has to be seen in the larger context of the strategic importance of the Persian Gulf area. I think this message is beginning to get through to Members of the Congress. The truth is, we intend to stand by an old and trusted ally, and we mean that for all our allies. But we also intend to look for new and dramatic ways to protect and solidify the security and peace of the Middle East.

In our recent decision to rebuild our strategic force, we've also attempted to show some balance and flexibility. Our plans for the MX and the B–1 have these advantages: we can afford them; we keep our options open so that we can respond adequately and in time to any new Soviet buildup; and we send to the Soviets that signal that Winston Churchill once said was critical for any successful negotiations with the Soviet Union—strength of purpose and strength of resolve.

In the area of the economy, we're now pressing for the additional budget cuts needed to keep our promise of a balanced budget. I think we've managed to take the social security problem out of partisan politics with the appointment of a bipartisan commission that is charged with one task—finding a solution to social security's deep financial problems.

These two initiatives should be seen in the context of what else we've done in the last 9 months. When we entered office, the Federal budget was growing by some 14

percent a year. That growth has been cut in half. Federal tax revenues were scheduled to increase by more than $300 billion over the next 3 years. We've now passed the largest tax rate cut in history and almost entirely thwarted this increase. We've also indexed taxation to the rate of inflation, another historic reform.

On the regulatory front, more than 180 Federal regulations have been modified or canceled, with an estimated savings of more than $15 billion. The flow of new regulations has been cut in half. And we've also worked hard to assure a stable monetary policy.

It's been an exciting time, and I admit that sometimes a painful and a difficult one. This came home to me when I was discussing our belt-tightening measures with President Ford, while we were also talking about his new library and museum in Michigan. I found myself feeling very envious of him. So I came back, and with an eye on the future, I spoke to Dave Stockman about that subject. He tells me he's been pricing bookmobiles. [*Laughter*]

Well, I hope that you'll find your day here a useful and productive one, and I hope you will also relax and enjoy yourselves. Don't relax too much—as you know, my staff is rather reluctant about waking people up. [*Laughter*]

But now I have a little bit of time left here, and I'll take the easy questions first, and then I'm going to turn you over to Don Regan and Dave Stockman for the tough ones.

U.S. Immigration Policy

Q. Mr. President, we in Florida are having a tremendous problem with the influx of illegal immigrants. Do you see any way that the White House or the Congress, the administration, can spread the influx throughout the rest of the 50 States, rather than this—[*inaudible*]?

The President. So that we can spread the immigrants, do you mean, throughout the States?

Well, I think that our immigration policy is perhaps going to give us a better handle on that and put us back in a position of being able to control our own borders. You know that we've issued orders with regard to the interception of some who are not truly refugees, in the sense that we take those people who are fearing persecution and death in their own lands. We have been trying to diversify and spread the people that do come in, and that we take in to other areas of the country. But I believe that basically, the problem—that we'll get a handle on it with the new immigration program if the Congress will support us on that.

User Fees

Q. Mr. President, part of your economic recovery program calls for user fees, including user fees for dredging and—[*inaudible*]—rivers and canals. My town—and once your town—Sacramento, is among the hundred or so American port cities that would be seriously—[*inaudible*]—by the charge, by the canceling of this program.

My question, sir, is that since back about 1787, the Federal Government took from the States the privilege of collecting customs duties; and since the Federal Government now collects around $8 million a year in customs duties, in return for a variety of services, isn't it fair, sir, is it not a possibility that the Federal Government intended to provide those services to American ports?

The President. You slipped the question in that I wish you'd waited for Dave Stockman. [*Laughter*] No, I believe—and I don't believe that what we have in mind is going to be onerous or going to be destructive to anyone that's involved in that. But the basic principle of good tax policy, and one we've departed too far from in the past, is that wherever possible, assess a charge or assess a tax basically to those who are receiving the service or the benefit of the government service.

The gasoline tax, for example, at the State level—I know, in California—is a good example of this. The people who are out on the highways and driving on the streets and so forth are the ones who are paying for it. And they've got that ability to make a direct connection—are they getting their money's worth or not? Is the highway system up to par? Are the streets kept repaired, and so forth? And again, as I say, in a little while you can try again with this,

and I think get some more specific ideas to what we have in mind. But I think it is just one of, again, shifting a burden from the general public that may not be particularly benefiting from that, to those that are getting the benefit of the service.

Tax Reductions

Q. Mr. President, what percentage of the tax cut do you assume will go to savings and investment? And will not the—[*inaudible*]—if it doesn't go to savings and investment—be, in your clearly delightfully simple phrase, "more money chasing the same amount of goods" and, therefore inflationary, until the results of this investment allow business and industry to increase production?

The President. Well, I think there are two answers to that. First of all, the polls that we have seen indicate that below $15,000 of income, yes, most people, the majority of people answer that there are things they need that they would buy with the increased money, although there is a percentage, a pretty good percentage that says no, they would save. Above $15,000 it shifts dramatically—the majority of people saying they would use that money for savings and investment.

The other part of the answer to that is that at the same time in our tax policy, the business taxes and the changes there—we have indications already of corporate expansion and modernization and so forth. The Iron and Steel Institute is a classic example that is going to be spending—they have already announced—more than $5 billion. And they claim this is the largest modernization and expansion plan in the history of that industry in the limited period of time. They're going forward, and they've announced that it is basically on the basis of our plan.

So, maybe we're going to increase the goods that that money will be chasing.

Steel Industry Lay-Offs

Q. People in Pittsburgh are concerned about the increasing numbers of the lay-offs that are not only caused by the economy but by foreign imports. Is there anything you can do to help us?

The President. Well, we have the triggering device with regard to the dumping of
steel. We don't think that that has been
exercised in recent years the way it should.
And this is where someone comes in and
dumps on our market a steel at a less-than-
production cost, because their government
is subsidizing them in order to get that
market.

We intend to enforce that. But again, as I
say, it is the iron and steel industry—yes,
right now they're suffering and have been
suffering over the last year or more—
beyond that, to be honest. But again, they
are in the forefront of the ones that were
optimistic about what our policy is going to
do and are announcing this great expansion,
which after some temporary pain and suffering due to this, should result in an increase and in the return of those idle workers to their jobs.

Block Grants for the State of New Hampshire

Q. Mr. President, last week the New
Hampshire legislature met and acted on
only two of the seven block grants that will
be coming in under the new Federal program. And there was some concern that by
not acting on the five others, that the State
of New Hampshire would stand to lose
money from the Federal Government on
those other five programs. Is that so?

The President. Well now, I don't know. I
wasn't aware of what you were just saying,
what actions some of the States have taken
already on that. Are you aware of that,
Dave? He'll take care of that one when he
gets up.

The President's Programs and Voluntarism

Q. Mr. President, I hope I'm not breaking
the tradition by not asking a question. But
after confirming my visit here, last Thursday and Friday I went knocking on doors in
our circulation area to ask our readers what
they might say to you if they had the opportunity to talk with you face to face.
There were three things that came through,
and I thought I'd like to share them with
you, from our readers.

They're encouraged that there seem to
be signs in Washington that there is someone here who's finally doing something

about the economy. They're not sure yet
whether it's working or going to work, but
they're pleased that there is movement.

Number two, they feel comfortable with
your style, but there's still a healthy amount
of skepticism about where your administration is going and where it will wind up.

And number three, I thought was a poignant remark from a woman who said that
in deciding where to make budget cuts,
that you think of all of us as a family, and
make the decisions as a loving father. And
almost universally, they wish you the very
best in a very tough job.

The President. Well, thank you very
much. As to that lady, I'd like to fulfill her
request, and we are trying to do it in that
way.

There is something in the group that I
told you I was speaking to in a little while,
the national business association. We are
starting—in addition to our economic program and the cuts that we feel have to be
made, we believe that we have got to
reduce the percentage that government is
taking from the private sector, reduce the
share of cost. When you stop to think that
today, the biggest single cost item in the
average American family budget is government, that it amounts to more than food,
shelter, and clothing, all put together. Now
government, I don't think, was ever intended to have that—to be that proportionate.
There is the intervention by government
that has moved not only just from attempting to control business and industry but
right into the lives of every one of us by
way of regulations. We want to bring those
things back in hand.

But, to this group that I am going to be
speaking, the gist of my speech is—and they
have already taken up this matter, I might
add, in their meetings before I get there—
and that is to appeal to the business and
industrial community of America, and to
the private sector in general, to go back to
an America that we had where we didn't
automatically say, "Well, government
should do something about that," but where
we the people do something about that.
And I have to tell you that I'm going to tell
them that Bill Verity, chairman of Armco,
has accepted the chairmanship of what will

be a nationwide task force to go into communities, go into industrial and business groups, and find the areas where the private sector can pick up slack and do things that it once did.

How many of us have forgotten that when this country went in the all-out great rescue effort to Japan back in the early thirties [twenties] at the time of the great earthquake. That wasn't government; that wasn't a foreign aid program; the people did that. "Bundles for Britain," the famine in India—the people of this country used to come together. I remember when I was a sports announcer—the floods in Ohio—and we held an all-night radio program for people to volunteer help for the people in Ohio.

We think that that spirit of voluntarism is still out there among the American people. And we believe there's a place for government—to help coalesce this and to help point out where need is and those functions that could properly belong to the private sector. And maybe that's what a loving father would do, also.

Social Security

Q. Mr. President, it seems that some of the—[*inaudible*]—even within your own party, have convinced the administration to stray away from the unpopular cuts in social security at this time. With 60 percent of the Federal budget over the next couple of years tied up with the debt interest and defense and social security, is it just a matter of time before the administration has to make deep cuts in the elderly's benefits if you're going to satisfy your budget-balancing requirements by 1984? Are the elderly in real trouble when it comes to social security?

The President. Yes, social security has been in a state of actuarial imbalance for more—well, back more than a couple of decades, and we knew it then. I remember making a speech in 1964, in the Presidential campaign, pointing out that at that time, actuarially, the program was some $300 billion out of balance. In this last campaign, I pointed out that it was $4 trillion out of actuarial balance. Nothing has been done.

Over the years, Congresses have yielded to politics and increased benefits and spread them and so forth, and at the same time they have increased taxes. We now have and are under the ongoing biggest single tax increase ever passed in our Nation's history. It is scheduled for further tax increases, the payroll tax—one is in January, and then in '85 and '86—no, in '85, '87, I believe it is, and '90. And by this time, instead of that 2 percent of $3,000 of earnings, by the time these are all in place, it'll be over 15 percent of more than $60,000 in earnings. And it still—when this tax increase passed in '77, we were told that this squared social security until the year 2015. We will be out of money in 1982 if something isn't done.

Now, we introduced a plan that did not penalize in anything that was really measurable, anyone who's presently collecting the program. The only thing that changed for them was, once, making the cost of living adjustment go 15 months instead of 12. And yet, with what we had proposed—and really clearing up some things on the periphery, such as people getting disability in social security that weren't entitled—doesn't it sort of strike you strange that Son of Sam, serving that 75-year sentence up there for all his murders, is getting $350 a month from disability, social security, because they say he's incapable of holding a job? And this is going on all over the country. We have people in California that I know of, in mental institutions for the criminally insane, who are drawing regular payments because, due to their mental illness, they had been judged incapable of holding jobs. But now, we're paying their room, board, medical care, and laundry, housing, and yet they're getting that payment.

These are the things that need correcting. When we introduced our plan, we felt—because it was the majority party that had asked us to get our plan up there because they wanted to start working on this problem. We introduced the plan, and all we got was an attack and never one offer of cooperation. And we resubmitted now, after the recess, and again were informed that there was going to be no bipartisan approach to this problem.

And this is why the other night in my speech, I have withdrawn the plan and said—it doesn't mean that I don't believe in it, but all right, if this will bring a bipartisan approach, will they join us then in appointing a bipartisan task force? And we can get by 1982 if we borrow, inter-fund borrowing of the three basic funds of social security, because two of the funds, disability and the hospital benefits, Medicare, are not in the same trouble that the basic fund is, and to do that temporarily, simply while the task force comes back to us with something that we can, in a bipartisan way, get done, because there's no way we can do it without the bipartisan help.

The Prime Rate

[*Turning to Secretary Regan*] Do you want to give that line to me?

Secretary Regan [*laughing*]. Why not?

The President. Gee, Don, thank you. That's pretty generous.

[*Speaking to the editors*] Chase Manhattan has just cut its prime rate to 19 percent. And the Secretary of the Treasury says this is just a sign of what's coming.

MX Missile System

Q. Mr. President—[*inaudible*]—hearings, Defense Secretary Weinberger said the MX missile system clearly would not work unless it were in fact mobile. How do you square that position with your position, sir, that it can now be stationary?

The President. The first 36 that are produced are going to be put, as we've said, in the Minuteman and the Titan silos which are going to be hardened. Now, this does not render them invulnerable in perpetuity. But it does buy us some time in which the Soviet Union would have to increase its ability at targeting, and its power, in order to overcome this hardening. But by that time, we will have continued with our program. And during this time that we're installing the 36, we are studying the different modes, including airborne, seaborne.

There is one thing that we have to remember—unless technology improves, and possibly it will in these few years, the time that we're buying—and that is that you lose some accuracy when they are airborne or seaborne that you have when they're land-based.

Now, all right, except I've got to take one more, because a lady stood up, and there hadn't been one before.

Block Grants

Q. Mr. President, I've talked to several local and municipal officials before coming here, also, and I asked them what they would ask you. Most of them said that they would like to know how—[*inaudible*]—realistically meet their responsibilities with so little money coming from Washington?

The President. You mean local and State governments feel that way? Well, I don't think it's going to be easy. You could ask the same question about us, but I believe we can. And having been Governor of the largest State in the Union—or the most populous State in the Union, I've had some experience with Federal grant programs. And basically, what we're trying to do is eliminate the administrative overhead that was occasioned by unnecessary redtape and regulations. This is what's back of the block grant concept. And as I showed the other day in the press conference, when we could take that thick packet of paper that were the regulations that surrounded some 57 categorical grant programs, and by putting them into the nine block grant programs, reduce it to six pages of regulations, we think that they will find that they've got more flexibility with assessing priorities and with their method of delivering the aid, and that this—in other words, this will leave, we think, more of the money available for those that it is supposed to help.

The trouble with the Federal Government programs in recent years has been that, believe me, much more than half of this money, in many of the programs, goes simply to administer the program and not to the people it's intended to help.

Let me cite one job training program of a few years ago that graduated some 5,500 young people from the job training program at an average cost of $55,000 per graduate. I got a little trouble with the bureaucracy as Governor, when I vetoed a program that sounded on the face of it great. It was going to take some people from welfare, able-bodied people, and put them to work in the parks in this particular area of California. I vetoed it, which a Governor could do, and if his veto wasn't overridden in 60 days, it stuck. Mine wasn't overridden, because I was able to go before the people and tell the people the reason for the veto, and that is that it was going to put 11 people to work in the parks, with 17 people handling the administrative functions of this program to see that they all got to work on time.

I've just been told that my time's up. I've got to get to the national business alliance. I want to thank you very much. And I don't know which of you gentlemen here is scheduled first, but, Don Regan, Secretary of Treasury Don Regan, will take your questions and speak to you, and then Dave Stockman.

Thank you very much. Now you can ask the hard questions.

Note: The President spoke at approximately 9:30 a.m. in the Treaty Room at the Old Executive Office Building. The transcript of the interview was released by the Office of the Press Secretary on October 6.

Toast at a Luncheon Honoring Prime Minister Prem Tinsulanonda of Thailand
October 6, 1981

Prime Minister Prem, on behalf of the American people, it is a pleasure and an honor to welcome you and your colleagues to the White House today. I have enjoyed this opportunity to get to know you. Our conversations reinforced for me the importance of maintaining the security, stability, and national development of Thailand. Let me assure you that we value your counsel and views on trends and developments in your region.

Your country, Mr. Prime Minister, is truly named "Land of the Free." Blessed by nature, the Thai people are peaceful, hardworking, and have never menaced their neighbors. Blessed equally by brilliant and dynamic leaders, their nation has remained independent for more than seven centuries.

Thailand's relations with our own country date back more than 100 years and have been characterized by warm friendship and close cooperation. Our sons and daughters have studied side by side in each other's schools and universities; our soldiers have fought and died together in two wars. We share a relationship that's truly rare between two countries, especially since we're separated by 12,000 miles of ocean.

Your open society and free enterprise system are a shining example for the rest of Asia. The other day I had the great privilege of addressing the 36th annual meeting of the International Monetary Fund and the World Bank that was held here in Washington. And one of the points I made to that distinguished audience was: the societies which have achieved the most spectacular, and broad-based economic progress, in the shortest period of time, are not the most tightly controlled, not necessarily the biggest in size or the wealthiest in natural resources—what units them all is their willingness to believe in the magic of the marketplace.

I could have been speaking about your Thailand, Mr. Prime Minister. You can be very proud of what you and your government and your people have achieved. The American people are very proud to have contributed in a small way to your success. And let me just add that we intend, within our means, to maintain this contribution.

Now a menacing shadow threatens your country. We've talked about that this morning—threatens the world, for that matter—the aggressive actions of the Vietnamese Communists, backed by Soviet sponsors, and they pose a menace to your security, stability, and territorial integrity. Supported by your ASEAN [*Association for South East Asian Nations*] partners, you stand in the front lines of the great ideological struggle

897

of our century—one between free people who wish to live in peace in societies of law, and on the other side, the totalitarians who despise human freedom and seek to subvert or destroy it everywhere they can.

With Vietnamese occupation of Cambodia, you and your ASEAN partners buried your differences and joined together to face the common danger. The outcome of the International Conference on Cambodia, in the overwhelming vote to prevent the Vietnamese puppet regime in that country from gaining a U.N. seat, and the continuing efforts to rally the Khmer people against the illegal occupation of their country, all prove to be noble resources of the ASEAN endeavor.

The nations in your region are cooperating to defend their security, and the way is open for ultimate success. I can assure you that America is ready to help you and ASEAN to maintain your independence against Communist aggression. The Manila Pact in its clarification of our bilateral communique of 1962 is a living document. We will honor the obligations that it conveys.

Mr. Prime Minister, the American people join me, I'm sure, in conveying a warm greeting to the royal family and the people of Thailand. Nancy, my wife, would also like you to convey a message. She looks forward with great pleasure to the visit of Her Majesty, Queen Sirikit, to the White House on November 5th.

Now, I'm going to depart a little bit from normal custom here in proposing a toast. In view of the tragedy that has just happened, there is a—normally, you know, we rise for a toast. In one city in our land, Philadelphia, they have had a tradition for years that you only stand to toast the dead. So therefore, I'm going to propose a toast today with all of us still seated. And it is to you, Mr. Prime Minister, to Their Royal Highnesses, Their Majesties, the King and Queen, and to the people, and to the continuation of close relations between our two countries.

Note: The President spoke at approximately 12:48 p.m. in the State Dining Room at the White House. At the time of the luncheon, the Egyptian Government had not officially announced the death of President Sadat, so the President remained seated for his toast. Prime Minister Prem responded to the President's toast. His remarks were not included in the White House press release.

Remarks Announcing the Death of President Anwar el-Sadat of Egypt
October 6, 1981

Today the people of the United States join with the people of Egypt and all those who long for a better world in mourning the death of Anwar Sadat.

President Sadat was a courageous man whose vision and wisdom brought nations and people together. In a world filled with hatred, he was a man of hope. In a world trapped in the animosities of the past, he was a man of foresight, a man who sought to improve a world tormented by malice and pettiness.

As an Egyptian patriot, he helped create the revolutionary movement that freed his nation. As a political leader, he sought to free his people from hatred and war. And as a soldier, he was unafraid to fight. But most important, he was a humanitarian unafraid to make peace. His courage and skill reaped a harvest of life for his nation and for the world.

Anwar Sadat was admired and loved by the people of America. His death today—an act of infamy, cowardly infamy—fills us with horror.

America has lost a close friend; the world has lost a great statesman; and mankind has lost a champion of peace. Nancy and I feel that we have lost a close and dear friend; and we send our heartfelt sympathy to Mrs. Sadat, to his children, who were here such a short time ago.

Thank you very much.

Note: The President spoke at 2:28 p.m. at the North Portico of the White House. His remarks were broadcast live on radio and television.

Message to the Congress Transmitting a Report on the Naval Petroleum Reserves
October 6, 1981

To the Congress of the United States:

In accordance with section 7422(c) of the Naval Petroleum Reserves Production Act of 1976 (10 U.S.C. 7422(c)), I wish to inform you of my decision to extend the period of maximum efficient rate production of the naval petroleum reserves for a period of three years from April 4, 1982, the expiration of the current statutorily mandated period of production.

I am transmitting herewith a copy of the report investigating the necessity of continued production of the reserves as required by section 7422(c)(2)(B) of the Naval Petroleum Reserves Production Act of 1976. In light of the findings contained in that report, I hereby certify that continued production from the naval petroleum reserves is in the national interest.

RONALD REAGAN

The White House,
October 6, 1981.

Proclamation 4870—National Guard Day
October 6, 1981

By the President of the United States of America

A Proclamation

Three hundred and forty-five years ago, the first settlers organized militia units to defend their homes and lives in Massachusetts Bay Colony. With these first units the tradition of the citizen-soldier was born and took root in America, a tradition exemplified by the willingness of private citizens to leave their civilian occupations, don the uniform of their country, and serve their States and their Nation when the need arises.

These citizen-soldiers camped with Washington at Valley Forge and charged up San Juan Hill. They fought in the Meuse-Argonne and on Omaha Beach. Since World War II, the National Guard has played a role in every major American crisis or conflict including Korea, Berlin, and Vietnam. When called upon by their country, the men and women of the Guard have always responded.

When disaster has struck in times of peace, the Guard has been equally ready to serve, whether in the flood waters of Johnstown, or on the slopes of Mount St. Helens. The Guard has been responsible for saving countless lives and millions of dollars of property and equipment by its quick responses and efficiency.

Now, Therefore, I, Ronald Reagan, President of the United States of America, ask all Americans to celebrate Wednesday, October 7, 1981, as National Guard Day and to honor the Army and Air National Guard of the United States for service to their communities, to their States and to their Nation.

In Witness Whereof, I have hereunto set my hand this 6th day of October, in the year of our Lord nineteen hundred and eighty-one, and of the Independence of the United States of America the two hundred and sixth.

RONALD REAGAN

[*Filed with the Office of the Federal Register, 10:14 a.m., October 7, 1981*]

Note: The text of the proclamation was released by the Office of the Press Secretary on October 7.

Proclamation 4871—Leif Erikson Day, 1981
October 6, 1981

By the President of the United States of America

A Proclamation

Nordic stories passed through the ages tell us of the Viking Leif Erikson and his explorations across the North Atlantic. One of the most daring of the great Norse adventurers, he may have been the first European to discover our continent. Scandinavian tales tell us of a cargo of timber and wild grapes he brought from North America to his home in Greenland more than four centuries before Columbus.

Above all, Leif Erikson was an explorer, and he has come to symbolize mankind's efforts to push back his frontiers, master the elements, and conquer his fear of the unknown.

In honoring him, and in honoring the Nordic people whose achievements have continuously enriched the Western world, we also honor the act of discovery.

As a mark of respect to the courage of Leif Erikson and his Viking followers, the Congress of the United States, by joint resolution approved September 2, 1964 (78 Stat. 849, 36 U.S.C. 169c), authorized the President to proclaim October 9 in each year as Leif Erikson Day.

Now, Therefore, I, Ronald Reagan, President of the United States of America, do hereby designate Friday, October 9, 1981, as Leif Erikson Day, and I direct the appropriate Government officials to display the flag of the United States on all Government buildings that day.

I also invite the people of the United States to honor the memory of Leif Erikson on that day by holding appropriate exercises and ceremonies in suitable places throughout the land.

In Witness Whereof, I have hereunto set my hand this 6th day of October, in the year of our Lord nineteen hundred and eighty-one, and of the Independence of the United States of America the two hundred and sixth.

RONALD REAGAN

[*Filed with the Office of the Federal Register, 10:15 a.m., October 7, 1981*]

Note: The text of the proclamation was released by the Office of the Press Secretary on October 7.

Nomination of Geoffrey Swaebe To Be United States Representative to the European Office of the United Nations
October 7, 1981

The President today announced his intention to nominate Geoffrey Swaebe, of California, to be the Representative of the United States of America to the European Office of the United Nations, with the rank of Ambassador. He would succeed Gerald Bernard Helman.

Mr. Swaebe was executive officer with Florsheim Shoe Co., in Chicago, Ill., in 1936–38, and divisional merchandise manager with Thalhimers Department Store in

Richmond, Va., in 1938–48. He was general merchandise manager with Pizitz Department Store in Birmingham, Ala., in 1948–50; general manager, director, and vice president of the Hecht Co., in Baltimore, Md., in 1950–62; and chairman of the board and president of the May Department Stores of California in Los Angeles, Calif., in 1962–72. Since 1972 he has been self-employed as a business and management consultant in Los Angeles.

Mr. Swaebe served as commissioner of the Community Redevelopment Agency of the City of Los Angeles, and as a member of the Mayor's Advisory Committee. He served in the United States Army in 1942–46 and attended Boston University. Mr. Swaebe is married, has one son, and resides in Los Angeles, Calif. He was born March 23, 1911, in London, England.

Remarks at a White House Luncheon for the Governors' Representatives to the Fifty States Project for Women
October 7, 1981

Nancy and I are delighted to have this opportunity to meet with you today and to be able to tell you that the project that you're working on is of great importance to this administration.

You know, there's a great deal of misunderstanding, I think, that exists over some of the problems today, and it was ever thus, because back long before there was a question about discrimination, there should have been some forewarnings. And the late Will Rogers many years ago commented on this. I hope you wouldn't disapprove of what he said. He said that women were going to try and become more and more like men till pretty soon they wouldn't know any more than the men did. [*Laughter*]

But some critics have expressed concern that we're not addressing women's issues. So, let's set the record straight right now: That charge is a bum rap. With respect to our economic program, the well-being of women, like all Americans, depends on a healthy economy. And certainly, women won't benefit from continued inflation and unemployment.

As for appointments, as you've learned already in the meetings that you've been having so far, we've appointed women to high-level positions throughout the administration, and I've directed that we continue the effort to place qualified women in positions of responsibility. The quality of leadership and the contributions made by these women are an irreplaceable part of our effort to chart a new course for our Nation. Many of them are here today, as you well know by this time. And I'm particularly proud of one who is not—Sandra O'Connor, who now sits on the United States Supreme Court.

Then there's the question of the ERA and, while it's true that I do not believe that it is the best way to end discrimination against women, I do believe with all my heart that such discrimination must be eliminated.

There are numerous methods of rectifying the problem of sex discrimination. In California, we achieved a measure of success, perhaps more than some people give us credit for. As Governor of California, I signed 14 pieces of legislation eliminating regulations and statutes that discriminated against women. We passed legislation prohibiting sexual discrimination in employment and business matters, established the right of a married woman to obtain credit in her own name, and revised the property and probate laws to give the wife equal rights concerning community property.

And any number of these bread-and-butter issues, ones that were important to many individuals, and particularly women, when you read the list today—I won't read all of them, but if you did in 1981, it's hard to believe that those laws could have been on the books in the first place. And it's possible that similar discriminatory statutes and regulations may exist today in other States.

So, in my acceptance speech at the Republican National Convention in 1980 I pledged that, as President, I would establish a liaison with the 50 Governors to encourage them to eliminate discrimination against women wherever it exists. And that's why you are here today. You are the result of that. The Governors responded as I knew they would. And Judy Peachee, who serves as my Special Assistant for Intergovernmental Affairs, will be my personal liaison with you and your Governors on this important undertaking.

It's my hope that through the Fifty States Project we can alter or eliminate those State laws that continue to deny equality to women. And we will be working on the same thing here at the Federal level where that is needed, as we have done on our tax program, eliminating the marriage tax penalty. And we yet have to get at the discrimination against working wives in social security and some other things. We plan to help you focus public attention on the project and assist in developing support for the initiatives taken by your Governors and your legislatures.

At the National Conference of State Legislatures meeting in Atlanta on July 1st, I talked about this initiative and, I must say, got my biggest applause. I thought at the time I should have quit speaking right there—I couldn't top that. [*Laughter*] But we've received encouraging expressions of support since then, but the progress is going to depend on your efforts. When you go back to your States, I hope that you will think of yourselves not only as your Governor's representative, but also as representing the women in your States.

You'll be the key to making this project work. And the Fifty States Project is only a beginning. There's much to be done, but by inviting you here today, I want to reaffirm my commitment to the equality of all of our citizens and my commitment to this project. And I know it can be successful because it's already very apparent that the Governors made very good choices in their representatives.

Thank you all for being here again. I appreciate it.

Note: The President spoke at 1:10 p.m. in the State Dining Room at the White House.

Proclamation 4872—Death of Anwar el-Sadat
October 7, 1981

By the President of the United States of America

A Proclamation

America has lost a close friend; the world has lost a great statesman and mankind has lost a champion of peace.

President Sadat was a courageous man whose vision and wisdom brought nations and people together.

In a world filled with hatred, he was a man of hope. In a world trapped in the animosities of the past, he was a man of foresight, a man who sought to improve a world tormented by malice and pettiness.

He was admired and loved by the people of America. His death yesterday—an act of infamy, cowardly infamy—fills us with horror.

As a mark of respect for the memory of Anwar Sadat I hereby order that the flag of the United States shall be flown at half-staff upon all public buildings and grounds, at all military posts and naval stations, and on all naval vessels of the Federal Government in the District of Columbia and throughout the United States and its Territories and possessions until his interment. I also direct that the flag shall be flown at half-staff for the same length of time at all United States embassies, legations, consular offices, and other facilities abroad, including all military facilities and naval vessels and stations.

In Witness Whereof, I have hereunto set my hand this 7th day of October, in the year of our Lord nineteen hundred and eighty-one, and of the Independence of the United States of America the two hundred and sixth.

RONALD REAGAN

[Filed with the Office of the Federal Register, 4:50 p.m., October 7, 1981]

Nomination of Robert C. McEwen To Be a United States Commissioner on the International Joint Commission—United States and Canada, and Designation as Chairman
October 8, 1981

The President today announced his intention to nominate Robert C. McEwen to be a Commissioner on the part of the United States on the International Joint Commission—United States and Canada. Mr. McEwen will also serve as Chairman. He would succeed Robert J. Sugarman.

In 1964–80 Mr. McEwen served eight terms in the United States Congress, representing northern New York's 30th Congressional District. He was first elected to public office in 1954, when he began serving in the New York State Senate. He was a member of the American delegation to the Canada-United States Interparliamentary Group and was a member of the steering committee of the Northeast-Midwest Congressional Coalition and the Great Lakes Conference of Congressmen.

He graduated from the University of Vermont (B.S.), Albany Law School (LL.B.) and St. Lawrence University and Clarkson College of Technology (LL.D.). He is married, has two grown children, and resides in Ogdensburg, N.Y. He was born in Ogdensburg on January 5, 1920.

Statement Announcing a Series of Policy Initiatives on Nuclear Energy
October 8, 1981

A more abundant, affordable, and secure energy future for all Americans is a critical element of this administration's economic recovery program. While homeowners and business firms have shown remarkable ingenuity and resourcefulness in meeting their energy needs at lower cost through conservation, it is evident that sustained economic growth over the decades ahead will require additional energy supplies. This is particularly true of electricity, which will supply an increasing share of our energy.

If we are to meet this need for new energy supplies, we must move rapidly to eliminate unnecessary government barriers to efficient utilization of our abundant, economical resources of coal and uranium. It is equally vital that the utilities—investor-owned, public, and co-ops—be able to develop new generating capacity that will permit them to supply their customers at the lowest cost, be it coal, nuclear, hydro, or new technologies such as fuel cells.

One of the best potential sources of new electrical energy supplies in the coming decades is nuclear power. The United States has developed a strong technological base in the production of electricity from nuclear energy. Unfortunately, the Federal Government has created a regulatory environment that is forcing many utilities to rule out nuclear power as a source of new generating capacity, even when their consumers may face unnecessarily high electric rates as a result. Nuclear power has become entangled in a morass of regulations that do not enhance safety but that do cause extensive licensing delays and economic uncertainty. Government has also failed in meeting its responsibility to work with industry to develop an acceptable system for commercial waste disposal, which has further hampered nuclear power development.

To correct present government deficiencies and to enable nuclear power to make its essential contribution to our future energy needs, I am announcing today a series of policy initiatives:

(1) I am directing the Secretary of Energy to give immediate priority attention to recommending improvements in the nuclear regulatory and licensing process. I anticipate that the Chairman of the Nuclear Regulatory Commission will take steps to facilitate the licensing of plants under construction and those awaiting licenses. Consistent with public health and safety, we must remove unnecessary obstacles to deployment of the current generation of nuclear power reactors. The time involved to proceed from the planning stage to an operating license for new nuclear powerplants has more than doubled since the mid-1970's and is presently some 10–14 years. This process must be streamlined, with the objective of shortening the time involved to 6–8 years, as is typical in some other countries.

(2) I am directing that government agencies proceed with the demonstration of breeder reactor technology, including completion of the Clinch River Breeder Reactor. This is essential to ensure our preparedness for longer-term nuclear power needs.

(3) I am lifting the indefinite ban which previous administrations placed on commercial reprocessing activities in the United States. In addition, we will pursue consistent, long-term policies concerning reprocessing of spent fuel from nuclear power reactors and eliminate regulatory impediments to commerical interest in this technology, while ensuring adequate safeguards.

It is important that the private sector take the lead in developing commercial reprocessing services. Thus, I am also request-

ing the Director of the Office of Science and Technology Policy, working with the Secretary of Energy, to undertake a study of the feasibility of obtaining economical plutonium supplies for the Department of Energy by means of a competitive procurement. By encouraging private firms to supply fuel for the breeder program at a cost that does not exceed that of government-produced plutonium, we may be able to provide a stable market for private sector reprocessing and simultaneously reduce the funding needs of the U.S. breeder demonstration program.

(4) I am instructing the Secretary of Energy, working closely with industry and State governments, to proceed swiftly toward deployment of means of storing and disposing of commercial, high-level radioactive waste. We must take steps now to accomplish this objective and demonstrate to the public that problems associated with management of nuclear waste can be resolved.

(5) I recognize that some of the problems besetting the nuclear option are of a deep-seated nature and may not be quickly resolved. Therefore, I am directing the Secretary of Energy and the Director of the Office of Science and Technology Policy to meet with representatives from the universities, private industry, and the utilities, and requesting them to report to me on the obstacles which stand in the way of increased use of nuclear energy and the steps needed to overcome them in order to assure the continued availability of nuclear power to meet America's future energy needs, not later than September 30, 1982.

Eliminating the regulatory problems that have burdened nuclear power will be of little use if the utility sector cannot raise the capital necessary to fund construction of new generating facilities. We have already taken significant steps to improve the climate for capital formation with the passage of my program for economic recovery. The tax bill contains substantial incentives designed to attract new capital into industry.

Safe commercial nuclear power can help meet America's future energy needs. The policies and actions that I am announcing today will permit a revitalization of the U.S.

industry's efforts to develop nuclear power. In this way, native American genius, not arbitrary Federal policy, will be free to provide for our energy future.

Executive Order 12328—Federal Employees Contracting or Trading With Indians
October 8, 1981

By the authority vested in me as President of the United States of America by Section 437(b) of Title 18 of the United States Code (94 Stat. 544; Public Law 96–277), and Section 301 of Title 3 of the United States Code, it is hereby ordered as follows:

Section 1. The functions vested in the President by Section 437(b) of Title 18 of the United States Code (94 Stat. 544; Public Law 96–277) to prescribe rules and regulations under which any officer, employee, or agent of the Bureau of Indian Affairs may purchase from or sell to any Indian any service or any real or personal property or any interest therein, are delegated to the Secretary of the Interior.

Sec. 2. The functions vested in the President by Section 437(b) of Title 18 of the United States Code (94 Stat. 544; Public Law 96–277) to prescribe rules and regulations under which any officer, employee, or agent of the Indian Health Service may purchase from or sell to any Indian any service or any real or personal property or any interest therein, are delegated to the Secretary of Health and Human Services.

Sec. 3. Until rules and regulations are issued pursuant to Sections 1 and 2 of this Order, those rules and regulations previously applicable to Federal employees contracting or trading with Indians are hereby adopted as the rules and regulations of the President pursuant to, and to the extent not inconsistent with, Section 437(b) of Title 18 of the United States Code (25 CFR 251.5 and 252.31).

RONALD REAGAN

The White House,
October 8, 1981.

[*Filed with the Office of the Federal Register, 3:33 p.m., October 8, 1981*]

Remarks on the Departure of the United States Delegation to Funeral Services in Cairo for President Anwar el-Sadat of Egypt
October 8, 1981

On behalf of the country, I want to express a heartfelt thanks to Presidents Nixon, Ford, and Carter, and Mrs. Carter, for undertaking this sad mission. Their presence in Cairo will express to the Egyptian people the depth of America's grief and sorrow at the loss of a great leader and a beloved friend.

Today the American people stand beside the Egyptian people—the people of a new nation with the people of an ancient land; people of the West with the people of the East. We stand together in mourning the loss of Anwar Sadat and rededicating ourselves to the cause for which he so willingly gave his life.

There are times, there are moments in history, when the martyrdom of a single life can symbolize all that's wrong with an age and all that is right about humanity. The noble remnants of such lives—the spoken words of an Illinois lawyer who lived in this House, the dairy of a young Dutch schoolgirl, the final moments of a soldier-statesman from Mit Abu el-Qum—can gain the force and power that endures and inspires and wins the ultimate triumph over the forces of violence, madness, and hatred.

Anwar Sadat, a man of peace in a time of violence, understood his age. In his final moments, as he had during all his days, he stood in defiance of the enemies of peace, the enemies of humanity. Today, those of us who follow him can do no less. And so to those who rejoice in the death of Anwar Sadat, to those who seek to set class against class, nation against nation, people against people, those who would choose violence over brotherhood and who prefer war over peace, let us stand in defiance and let our words of warning to them be clear: In life you feared Anwar Sadat, but in death you must fear him more. For the memory of this good and brave man will vanquish you. The meaning of his life and the cause for which he stood will endure and triumph.

Not too long ago, he was asked in an interview if he didn't fear the possibility of the kind of violence that has now just taken his life. And he said, "I will not die 1 hour before God decides it is time for me to go."

Again, a heartfelt thank you to these men here, these three who are making this mission on behalf of our country. I thank you, and if I may, in the language of my own ancestry, say: Until we meet again, may God hold you in the hollow of His hand.

Note: The President spoke at 7:15 p.m. on the South Lawn at the White House. Prior to his remarks, the President and Mrs. Reagan met with former Presidents Richard M. Nixon, Gerald R. Ford, and Jimmy Carter and Mrs. Carter in the Blue Room.

On the same day, the White House announced the members of the official U.S. Delegation to the funeral services. In addition to the three former Presidents and Mrs. Carter, they are:

Alexander M. Haig, Jr., Secretary of State (Head of Delegation)

Mrs. Patricia Haig

Caspar W. Weinberger, Secretary of Defense

Jeane J. Kirkpatrick, U.S. Representative to the United Nations

Gen. Edward C. Meyer, Chief of Staff, U.S. Army

Joseph W. Canzeri, Assistant to the President

Strom Thurmond, United States Senator

Charles H. Percy, United States Senator

Claiborne Pell, United States Senator

Jim Wright, Member of Congress

Clement J. Zablocki, Member of Congress

William S. Broomfield, Member of Congress

Lenore Annenberg, Chief of Protocol

Dr. Henry A. Kissinger, former Secretary of State

Sol Linowitz, former Ambassador

Sam Brown, friend of President Sadat

Stevie Wonder, entertainer

Remarks at the Presentation Ceremony for the Presidential Medal of Freedom
October 9, 1981

The President. Ladies and gentlemen, I don't know why I should think of this at this lovely luncheon with all of you here today, but I did think of it. Many years ago in the days of austerity in England, after the Labor government had just gotten in, I'd arrived for the royal command performance at the Savoy Hotel. I went down to the dining room and knew that there was rationing and you couldn't get food such as we've had today, but then on the menu I saw pheasant. And I thought, well, you can't go wrong if you can get pheasant. So,

I ordered pheasant. I didn't know about their custom of serving game birds. And the waiter came in and with a flourish removed the silver lid, and I was looking at a bird that was looking back at me. [*Laughter*] The head and the ruff were on, the eyes were open, the big yellow legs were there attached to him. So, it did kind of curb my appetite a little. [*Laughter*]

But the very next day, Virginia Mayo and her husband, Michael O'Shea, arrived. And we went down to the dining room together. And I saw his eyes stop—I just knew, at the same place on the menu. I knew what was in his mind, and he ordered. Then I waited and didn't say a word. [*Laughter*] And the same flourish and the silver lid removed and there was that bird looking at him, but he topped me. As the waiter started away, he grabbed him by the coattail, and the waiter, surprised, stopped. And Mike said, "Bring me liniment and I'll have that bird flying again in 15 minutes." [*Laughter*]

Now, that story has absolutely nothing to do with today's luncheon. [*Laughter*] Well, maybe if I reach a little it does, because we have some high fliers here with us today who have flown, in the line of achievement in their own lives and in their service to humanity, very high.

The President's medal of freedom is the highest civilian honor that's given in the United States. What the Olympic Gold Medal is to athletes, what the Congressional Medal of Honor is to the military, the Presidential Medal of Freedom is to the private United States citizen. The names of those who have received this honor are stars in the American sky—Helen Keller, Aaron Copland, Walt Disney, Carl Sandburg, General Omar Bradley, Dr. Jonas Salk, Jessie Owens. The list goes on through the most illustrious and prominent of our citizens.

And today, we're adding the names of Charles (Tex) Thornton, a man whose energy and enterprise are symbolic of America herself; Morris Leibman, an honored American possessing a fine legal mind and a true humanitarian heart; Walter Judd, a doctor who ministered to the world's need for freedom and liberty; Bryce Harlow, an architect of public policy whose contributions have strengthened our democracy's political process; Ella Grasso, a genuine public servant who fought against death as she fought for political principle, with dignity; and Eubie Blake, an historical figure in American performing arts and one of the greatest ragtime composers and pianists.

Now, let me tell you how these six recipients have strengthened our freedom by reading to you something the historian Edward Gibbon wrote about ancient Athens, the first democracy and the fountainhead of Western culture. He wrote that when the Athenians finally wanted not to give to society but for society to give to them, when the freedom they wished for was freedom from responsibility, then Athens ceased to be free.

The recipients today have given greatly to our society in music, public service, and humanitarian activities. They've met their responsibilities to freedom. By giving of themselves and their energies, they've kept this society diverse, and in diversity there is liberty.

Perhaps this award is called the Medal of Freedom also because our Nation allowed these great Americans to pursue their interests unhindered. And when individuals are free to follow their hearts and talents, the common good benefits. America has given these honorees freedom, and they've discharged that responsibility with brilliant distinction.

Let me read the citation and present the medal to each recipient who will then, we hope, say a few words to us.

To Charles B. (Tex) Thornton:

[*At this point, the President read the citation, the text of which follows:*]

Industrialist, warrior and humanitarian, Tex Thornton's life has embodied all that is best in the worlds of commerce, military service and civic duty. In all three realms, Tex Thornton has never failed to give generously of his boundless energy, his unfailing courage, and his deep love of country. In war and peace, in public service and the private sector, Tex Thornton has earned the esteem of all Americans who value patriotism, enterprise and compassion as cornerstones of our nation's greatness.

And we regret in sorrow that because of his health, he cannot be here to accept this in person. But we're pleased that his son, Charles Bates Thornton, Jr. is here to accept for his father.

Mr. Thornton. Thank you, Mr. President. I'm privileged to accept this award on behalf of my father who, as you know, could not be here today. He wanted very much to come, however. He asked me to tell you though that he feels very fortunate to have had the opportunities afforded by this great country of ours and to have been able to serve it and to strive to contribute to its success.

Perhaps only those who matured in the last Depression, as he did, can best appreciate just how far we, as a Nation, have come in the last half century and the effort and the sacrifice it took to get here.

Even though his active role is drawing to a close, he is grateful to have played a part. He recognizes that the challenges before us remain enormous, yet is confident that this Nation's new leadership will guide us on the proper course—a course which does not reject the past in which he has played a part, but which lets us build on our accomplishments and learn from our mistakes.

I can think of no one more respected by him than you, Mr. President. It is therefore deeply touching that you have honored him in this way. And that makes this award all the more meaningful to him, to our mother, and to the two younger generations of our family here today.

Thank you.

The President. Morris I. Leibman:

[At this point, the President read the citation, the text of which follows:]

Attorney, teacher, scholar and philanthropist, Morris Leibman is living proof that a full career in the private sector can flourish hand in hand with civic and humanitarian duties. As a generous patron of the arts and charities, as a legal scholar as well as practitioner, as a founding member of the Georgetown University Center for Strategic and International Studies and as chairman of the American Bar Association's Standing Committee on Law and National Security, Morris Leibman has served selflessly to make America a just, healthy society within and a strong, secure nation without.

Mr. Leibman. Thank you, Mr. President. In the shadow of the assassination of recent hours, we thank the Lord that you, Mr. President, are here with us today. And we continue to be inspired by your courage and total commitment.

I and the other awardees, I feel certain, are humbled by the privilege of participating in this ceremony. We understand that on this occasion, we represent millions of citizens dedicated to our free society. This is an occasion of remembrance and rededication—remembrance of America's uniqueness, the noble experiment of government by melting pot of free people; rededication to your leadership and guidance to mean-

ingful patriotism, to national purpose, to national will and strength and credibility.

Our great American ideals and goals lose vitality without vibrant expression. You, Mr. President, have established yourself as the great communicator, a most important aspect of leadership in this world of competing and conflicting ideologies. A number of us present here today have struggled with the problem of improving the systems, forms, and structures for communicating American foreign policy, nationally and internationally. Under your leadership and under your Presidency, we eagerly renew our dedication to this effort and look forward to working with you in your great responsibility for continuing the dialog of Western civilization and the preservation of the free world.

Thank you, Mr. President.

The President. Walter H. Judd:

[At this point, the President read the citation, the text of which follows:]

Legislator, physician, missionary and orator, Walter Judd has served his nation and mankind with unfailing courage and distinction—as a youthful medical missionary in China, as a highly respected Member of Congress for two decades, and as a lifelong foe of tyranny and friend of freedom both at home and abroad. The skills of a healer, the eloquence of a great communicator, and his firm grasp of domestic and international affairs have made Walter Judd an articulate spokesman for all those who cherish liberty and a model for all Americans who aspire to serve mankind as physicians, spiritual leaders and statesmen.

Dr. Judd. To respond, of course, Mr. President, to your conferring on me so extraordinary an honor as this means that I must borrow Mr. Shakespeare's words: I can no other answer make save thanks and thanks and ever thanks.

I'm glad that this medal is called the Medal of Freedom. Concern for that greatest of all our blessings in this beautiful land has been, I think, a consistent and at least a major influence in my own life and motivation.

Freedom has been central to the efforts I made as a missionary in China, and as a political missionary in the House of Representatives and, in these last 19 years, as what might perhaps be called, "missionary-at-large," expecially to the colleges and high schools of our country, working with the youth to help develop a deeper understanding of what freedom makes possible—as has been demonstrated in these other awards—and what freedom requires.

Whenever I find my battery is running down, I like to go over to the monument, not so far from here, erected to the memory of that great American patriot who wrote down in immortal words the fundamental faith and philosophy which gave our Nation its birth and its greatness, Thomas Jefferson.

You've been there. And on the corona, in giant letters above his head, are these words of his personal declaration: "I have sworn upon the altar of God eternal hostility against every form of tyranny over the mind of man."

Now, that, to the best of my ability, has been the basic standard by which I tried to judge which of the various solutions being offered for this, that, or the other difficult problem for our country was right or nearest right. And that's what we're trying to do in retirement.

If followed, those principles and policies, would they strengthen the oppressor or would they strengthen the oppressed? Where does the United States stand—with wisdom and a recognition of timing and what's appropriate and what is possible at a given moment?

Now, I believe, Mr. President, that you and I and all of us in this blessed land were born to be free. And if we were born to be free, then so were the Czechs and the Poles and the Cubans and the Chinese and the Cambodians and the Afghans. And if they weren't born to be free, neither were we.

Now, this is not a note, I hope, a note of gloom or despair. On the contrary, it's the main basis for confidence and hope for our future. Surely the universe is on the side of human freedom, including the nature of the man and the nature of the woman. They can be arrested human beings. They can be in prison. They can be starved and brainwashed and beaten and sent to concentration camps and liquidated. But they cannot be separated in the end from that which is in them from their Creator—the urge to be free.

So, Mr. President, it's an honor not only for me, but for all of us in this land, to be joined with you in this noblest of crusades: Freedom.

The President. Thank you, Walter.

And now, ladies and gentlemen, Bryce N. Harlow:

[At this point, the President read the citation, the text of which follows:]

Counsellor to Presidents and sage observer of nearly half a century of Washington history, Bryce Harlow's vision, integrity, and persuasiveness have helped to shape his nation's destiny as leader of the Free World. Never a candidate for elected office himself, his experience and advice have helped bring out the best in countless public servants of both parties, in the White House, in the Congress and across the nation. Bryce Harlow is a sterling example of the positive side of politics—a life spent reconciling divergent interests, serving high moral principles, and channeling the forces of public policy toward the public good.

Mr. Harlow. Mrs. Reagan, please don't consider me discourteous, I'm standing up. *[Laughter]*

I thank you, Mr. President, very, very much. And that eloquent citation—I wish I had said it. I love every word in it. Thank you. *[Laughter]* The Harlow contingent here very deeply appreciates the great honor paid us, both by this very special award and by your personal participation. I mean that particularly, your *personal* participation in these proceedings, because we all know the vast energy and time drain on the President of the United States.

Now, this has come, of course, this award and all, the whole affair, as a tremendous surprise to me, as I guess it has perhaps to the others. When Mike Deaver called me about it last week, to alert me to it, I said, interrupted him, and I said, "Mr. Deaver, you've got a bad mistake on your hands. You have the wrong man and the wrong telephone number and you'd better hang up and start over." *[Laughter]* But then he said the nicest thing in my life, he said, "Oh, no. No," he said, "I've got the right man. It's you, Bryce Harlow." And I think that was music. I was afraid I was right and he was wrong. [*Laughter*]

The best I can figure it, Mr. President, the part of this award that is concerned with me, is my public service not my private service to the private sector. And that's the part that concerns me most—the public service started when you were 27 years old. This is when I came to Washington from Oklahoma City. I came here to spend 1 year and to complete my education and then go back to Oklahoma and teach school. Well, that never did happen. Things happened to me instead. The war came—that's for one. And then came Truman and Eisenhower and all the rest and a whole phantasmagoria of spectaculars. We all remember the gigantic events of our country and the world.

Somehow, and for reasons I don't to this day understand, I got entangled, embroiled, enmeshed in those activities, in those issues of those times. And in the course of that, I got involved and entangled with a great host of our national leaders, like the great Walter Judd and many others. And so, I spent nearly all of those years, Mr. President, working with the leaders of our country in the Congress and in the executive branch, including here at the White House, and the leadership of the Armed Forces during the war in the high command.

Now, the point that's relevant about that to this meeting is just simply this: It's not that I come—[*inaudible*]—but that I was never a leader in any of that. I was never the front man. I was never the boss or the chief. I was always the behind-the-scenes fellow. I was always the assistant, the counsellor, if you will.

Well now, if that's true, and it is, what am I doing here? I think that's a good question. Why would one with a career so unobtrusive, retiree, be here, receiving an award so utterly prestigious? That fascinated me greatly when I was called by Mike Deaver. And I came to this thought. Apparently here somewhere, and I hope it's you, Mr. President, came to the idea, "Well, this little "go-fer" for Uncle Sam—[*laughter*]— and all his wanderings for four decades, did, in his own right, perhaps working for and through and around the great people, help-

ing them, enough for our country to make him worthwhile."

Now, if that is true, if that's the reason that this comes to me, then I say it's absolutely marvelous—not because of me, Mr. President, but because I am projected across the country in millions of people who are working their tails off, getting little attention at all, who are working, who are loyal, who have the integrity, who are doing for their bosses, and doing for their bosses causes, expecting no recognition whatever.

And here's what I think may happen. Some of them will see about this award, maybe. Some of them may even see it some way or hear about it or read about it. And he'll say, "Hey, Joe, did you see where President Reagan gave a kind of a medal to this little fellow Harlow?" [*Laughter*] And he'll say, "No, what for?" He'll say, "For doing what we're doing." "Oh, we'd better work harder, hadn't we? We might get one." Mr. President, if it works like that, how beautiful it fits in with your program to constantly improve the quality, the standards, the productivity of American life.

Thank you, sir.

The President. Bryce, you know it's been common language that this particular job must be a very lonely place. It isn't really all that lonely, and now we all know why.

To Ella T. Grasso, to be accepted by her husband, Dr. Thomas A. Grasso.

[*At this point, the President read the citation, the text of which follows:*]

Long before the women's movement had gained prominence, Ella Grasso had already begun the long, hard ascent to distinction as an elected public servant. A fond wife and mother, she proved that it is possible to reconcile a full family life with a long and eventful political career. As a champion of moral as well as political principle, Mrs. Grasso won the respect of fellow citizens of both parties and served as the first woman governor to be elected to office in her own right. Tireless in the pursuit of duty and courageous in the face of illness, Ella Grasso has earned the admiration of all Americans as a legislator, a governor and a woman of outstanding character and achievement.

Dr. Grasso. Mr. President, I thank you very much for this signal honor. I haven't prepared anything officially; I'd like to speak to you from my heart.

Today is a bittersweet day in my life. We have been here under five Presidents, President Kennedy, President Johnson, President Nixon, President Ford, President Carter, and now you, Mr. President. I know this is the last time that I'll be here, because it was through the good fortune of Ella, my dear wife, that we were invited here. Ah, bittersweet, I say. It's bitter because of the loss of Ella. However, it's a happy occasion because she has been selected, or was selected as a recipient of this medal. It's unfortunate that the other brand has to present it to us. [*Laughter*] Let me go over that again. [*Laughter*] Very good.

Ella was an adviser to Presidents, U.S. Senators, Congressmen, and women and people interested in politics. She was a strange mixture of many, many things. She had integrity, sympathy, understanding. She was straight as an arrow. She was a good wife, an excellent mother and, above all, brought to politics a certain integrity that our good President is attempting to bring.

I think that this country lacks that type of person. And I, personally, and I know Ella, admired President Reagan very much. You know, in politics you have to do many things. The first thing you must do is get elected. And many times in getting elected, you know, you have to get elected.

And you fill in the valleys about what I am trying to say. Ella lived courageously. She died courageously. She died with a prayer on her lips.

And I am indeed honored to receive this medal, and I shall take it home and, of all the credits she has received, my son and daughter will not get this medal—I'm keeping it myself. [*Laughter*] Thank you.

The President. Now, I'm going to switch microphones, if you will bear with me for a moment.

This last one is to James H. (Eubie) Blake:

[*At this point, the President read the citation, the text of which follows:*]

Last of the great ragtime composers and pianists, the son of slaves, and a pioneer crusader for Black Americans in the world of arts and enter-tainment, Eubie Blake is a national treasure. As pianist, showman and, above all, as composer, he has added immeasurably to America's musical heritage and helped to clear the way for succeeding generations of talented artists who, but for his example, might have been denied access to the artistic mainstream.

And I understand that Eubie is going to respond in his own inimitable and unique way. He is 98 years old, he told me.

Mr. Blake. Ninety-eight and a half!

The President. Ninety-eight and a half! [*Laughter and applause*]

Mr. Blake. Mr. President, I thank you from the bottom of my heart.

The President. There just happens to be a piano here. [*Laughter*]

[*At this point, Mr. Blake played a ragtime version of "Memory of You" on the piano.*]

Mr. Blake. All I ever wanted to do was play the piano. You know, my mother used to say that, "You ain't ever going to be nothing but a piano plunker." And you know, that's what I am, a piano plunker. [*Applause*]

The President. Eubie, thank you very much.

Ladies and gentlemen, I think because of six Americans, some of whom couldn't be here, but were represented, all of us go away a little bit better, and better Americans because of them. And now my saddest words: I have to say I have to leave you because I am scheduled to sign a proclamation for the fellow that I guess made it all possible—the Columbus Day Proclamation. [*Laughter*] And the time has caught up with me, so I'm going to go and say a thank you to Christopher Columbus, with the Spanish Ambassador in attendance, too, because they did it together. [*Laughter*]

Thank you all very much for being here. God bless you all.

Note: The President spoke at 1:12 p.m. at a luncheon honoring the medal recipients in the East Room at the White House. Prior to the luncheon and presentation ceremony, the President hosted a reception for the award winners in the Blue Room.

Nomination of Robert A. Jantzen To Be Director of the United States Fish and Wildlife Service
October 9, 1981

The President today announced his intention to nominate Robert A. Jantzen to be Director of the United States Fish and Wildlife Service, Department of the Interior. He would succeed Lynn Adams Greenwalt.

Since 1968 Mr. Jantzen has been director of the Arizona Game and Fish Department. Previously he was chief of the Game Management Division in 1964–68; big game supervisor in 1959–63; and research biologist in 1957–58. He is a member of the International Association of Fish and Wildlife Agencies and served as president in 1980. He was chairman of the National Waterfowl Council in 1977–78 and served on the U.S. Forest Service Multiple Use Advisory Councils.

Mr. Jantzen graduated from the University of Arizona (B.S., 1953) and attended the University of Arizona Graduate College in 1957–58. He is married and resides in Scottsdale, Ariz. He was born October 15, 1928, in Phoenix, Ariz.

Remarks on Signing the Columbus Day Proclamation
October 9, 1981

Ladies and gentlemen, we are here for the signing of the proclamation with regard to Columbus Day. And I am delighted that here on the platform with us, we have the Italian Ambassador to the United States, Ambassador Rinaldo Petrignani; Ambassador José Lladó, the Spanish Ambassador to the United States—I think that we, all of us, understand the connection between Spain and Italy with regard to Columbus Day—[*laughter*]—Frank D. Stella, the president of the National Italian American Foundation; Donald J. Senese, president of Amerito, who is also our Assistant Secretary of Education; Anthony Giampapa, vice president of UNICO; and Mr. Aldo Caira, president of the Sons of Italy.

You know, just the other day, I learned that the Marine Band is known as the President's own, and it makes me very proud to be able to say that, because it is one of the great concert bands of the world. But it also has some Italian blood in its background. Apparently, Thomas Jefferson was not pleased with the Marine Band that he found at the White House when he arrived as President. Jefferson told the Marine Commandant that he should look for musicians in Italy, which was noted then, as now, for its musical talent. The Commandant, taking Mr. Jefferson's remarks as an order, sent a representative to Italy, where the fellow persuaded Italian musicians of all ages to join the Marines and return with him to America. [*Laughter*] And this Italian excellence has been the standard for the band ever since. And I can tell you that even after 183 years, the band hasn't lost its Italian love and heart for music.

Incidentally, that same search continues to later days. I knew a man in Hollywood, when I was there, who was an actor only long enough to save money so that he could study for his chosen career, which was opera. And having enough money, he left Hollywood and went to Milan, Italy. And there he studied for 2 years and finally received that great honor—was invited to sing at La Scala, the very spiritual fountainhead of opera. They were doing *Pagliacci*, and he sang the very beautiful aria, *Vesti la guibba*, and when he had finished singing the applause from the orchestra seats and the galleries and the balconies was so sustained and so thunderous, that they couldn't continue the opera until he stepped back and repeated the aria as an encore. And again, the same sustained and thunderous applause, and again, he sang *Vesti la guibba*. And finally, he motioned for quiet. And he said, "I have sung *Vesti la guibba* now nine times." He said, "My voice is gone. I cannot sing it again." And a voice from the balcony said, "You'll do it till you get it right." [*Laughter*]

But if I had thought of all of this sooner, I would have had that Marine Band come to play for us today, because we really should have music, because this is not just a solemn proclamation signing. It's a celebration of what the great mariner, Christopher Columbus, accomplished. And in recent years, Columbus Day has also become a day to celebrate what Italian Americans have accomplished.

Columbus is symbolic of the millions of Italians who have come to the New World since its discovery. They, too, possessed courage, and they, too, sought opportunity and endured hardship. For many, their journey was just as personally demanding as the one that Columbus undertook. I remember John Volpe telling me that it took his parents 6 weeks to cross the Atlantic in

steerage, and all they had was a battered suitcase when they arrived.

Our immigrant ancestors worked long and hard. They adhered to solid, decent values, and they consequently prospered. Today, if it were not for a rightful pride of heritage, there would be no reason to identify Italian Americans as any kind of separate ethnic group, for Italian Americans are integrated into every aspect of American life—business, labor, arts, the professions, as well as high posts in this administration. Indeed, time would not permit me to list those who are here as a part of this administration.

And I'm going to sign the proclamation now, but as I sign it, I am commemorating not only the great navigator and explorer, Christopher Columbus, but those who centuries later followed him to the New World and helped make this the great nation that it is today.

Note: The President spoke at 1:45 p.m. at the signing ceremony in the Rose Garden at the White House.

Proclamation 4873—Columbus Day
October 9, 1981

By the President of the United States of America

A Proclamation

Christopher Columbus, whose life and exploits we commemorate each October, is one of the true heroes of our Nation's history.

He is justly admired as a brilliant navigator, a fearless man of action, a visionary who opened the eyes of an older world to an entirely new one. Above all, he personifies a view of the world that many see as quintessentially American: not merely optimistic, but scornful of the very notion of despair.

Nearly five centuries have passed since the fateful day on which Columbus changed the course of history. But his adventurous spirit lives on among us, challenging us to

emulation and abiding with us as we too press forward on our voyage of discovery.

In tribute to the achievement of Columbus and to the many sons and daughters of Italy who have helped to shape our life and destiny as a people, the Congress of the United States of America has requested the President to proclaim the second Monday in October of each year as Columbus Day.

Now, Therefore, I, Ronald Reagan, President of the United States of America, do hereby designate Monday, October 12, 1981, as Columbus Day; and I invite the people of this Nation to observe that day in schools, churches, and other suitable places with appropriate ceremonies in his honor.

I also direct that the flag of the United States of America be displayed on all public buildings on the appointed day in memory of Christopher Columbus.

In Witness Whereof, I have hereunto set my hand this ninth day of October, in the year of our Lord nineteen hundred and eighty-one, and of the Independence of the United States of America the two hundred and sixth.

RONALD REAGAN

[*Filed with the Office of the Federal Register, 3:27 p.m., October 9, 1981*]

Statement on Signing a Bill Concerning the Protection of Marine Mammals
October 9, 1981

I have today approved H.R. 4084, a bill designed to improve the operation of the Marine Mammal Protection Act of 1972.

H.R. 4084 authorizes appropriations to carry out the act and amends it in several respects, principally by revising the procedures for returning to the States responsibility for management of marine mammals and by establishing a cooperative Federal-State procedure for managing marine mammals in ocean waters from 3 to 200 miles offshore. Specifically, H.R. 4084 provides for the Secretary of Commerce or the Secretary of the Interior to adopt State regulations applicable to the territorial waters and extend them by regulation to the federally controlled Fishery Conservation Zone. The bill, however, makes inapplicable to this process Executive Order 12291, the Regulatory Flexibility Act, the Paperwork Reduction Act, and the 30-day notice requirement under the Administrative Procedure Act, all of which are important to this administration's efforts to control the proliferation of Federal regulations.

I must express my concern over these exemptions. While I fully support the notion of encouraging and reinforcing State initiative in the management of marine mammals, I remain concerned that our important Federal regulatory review processes not be overlooked in.this instance. The exemption of these regulatory actions from the regulatory review processes circumvents our regulatory relief efforts. I oppose that exemption, no matter how well intended.

Moreover, the Department of Justice has advised me that the exemption of these regulatory actions from Executive Order 12291 should not be read to infringe in any way on the President's constitutional responsibility to supervise the Secretary of Commerce and the Secretary of the Interior in their execution of the law. I have requested the Attorney General to advise the Secretaries and the Director of the Office of Management and Budget on the actions they should take to carry out this provision of the bill consistent with the President's constitutional responsibilities.

Note: As enacted, H.R. 4084 is Public Law 97–58, approved October 9.

Message to the Senate Transmitting an Agreement on the Extension of the United States-Spain Treaty of Friendship and Cooperation
October 9, 1981

To the Senate of the United States:

With a view to receiving the advice and consent of the Senate to ratification, I herewith transmit an agreement, effected by an exchange of notes at Madrid on September 4, 1981, extending for a period of eight months commencing September 21, 1981, the rights, duties, and obligations of the Parties under the Treaty of Friendship and Cooperation of January 24, 1976 between the United States of America and Spain, 27 U.S.T. 3005, T.I.A.S. 8360 (the Treaty).

I transmit also, for the information of the Senate, the report of the Department of State with respect to the agreement.

The agreement would extend, until May 21, 1982, the rights, duties, and obligations of the Treaty, which by its terms expired on September 21, 1981. During that time, negotiations will continue on a successor agreement to the Treaty; it is expected that, by the time these negotiations are concluded, Spain will have completed the process of accession to the North Atlantic Treaty

of April 4, 1949 (63 Stat. 2241; T.I.A.S. 1964). The agreement would preserve in force on an interim basis United States rights regarding access to and use of important military facilities in Spain, and otherwise continue the significant cooperative relationship now existing between the two countries under the provisions of the Treaty. This action is necessary in order to regularize the legal relationship between the United States and Spain in the post-September 21 period, and thereby to facilitate the current negotiations. I recommend that the Senate give prompt and favorable consideration to this agreement.

RONALD REAGAN

The White House,
October 9, 1981.

Proclamation 4874—National Forest Products Week, 1981
October 9, 1981

*By the President of the United States
of America*

A Proclamation

The first settlers arriving in our land looked to the forests as their key to survival in an untamed and often forbidding land. The forests gave them wood for shelter, fuel for warmth, and meat for their table. Since those early times, our Nation's bountiful forests have provided for the welfare of generations of Americans. Yet, there are almost as many trees in our forests today as when the first tree was felled by our forefathers.

Although the daily lives of most Americans are now far removed from the forest environment, forests still supply lumber for homes, paper for disseminating information, fuel for stoves and fireplaces, and thousands of other uses that have become so commonplace they are often taken for granted.

Forests play a vital role in maintaining a healthy economy—more than 3 million Americans are employed in wood-dependent occupations, and their combined production is valued at about $100 billion each

year. Moreover, our forests provide us with a wealth of other treasures that can carry no price tags—water, wildlife, outdoor recreation, and wilderness.

The contribution forests must make to our Nation's welfare will remain just as great in the years ahead as in the past. To meet the needs of the future, our forests must benefit from effective timber management and from continuing research to find better ways to utilize forest products. Improved wood growth and usage will make more wood products available at affordable prices while helping to stimulate our entire economy.

America has been greatly blessed with the resources of our forests. To allow them to waste away, when they could benefit so many, would be to ignore our responsibilities of stewardship. Our forests must be managed in ways that are environmentally safe and that ensure they will be available for the enjoyment and use of future generations.

If we act intelligently, our forests will continue to benefit the economy, even as they nourish the human spirit. The need and opportunity to commune with nature, to seek solitude, and to appreciate the beauty and grandeur of America's forests must be respected and preserved. With wise forest management, the demands of aesthetics and economics will remain compatible.

To promote greater awareness and appreciation for our forest resources, the Congress has by Public Law 86–753, 36 U.S.C. 163, designated the week beginning on the third Sunday in October as National Forest Products Week.

Now, Therefore, I, Ronald Reagan, President of the United States of America, do hereby proclaim the week of October 18 through October 24, 1981, as National Forest Products Week and ask that all Americans express their appreciation for the Nation's forests through suitable activities.

In Witness Whereof, I have hereunto set my hand this 9th day of October, in the year of our Lord nineteen hundred and eighty-one, and of the Independence of the United States of America the two hundred and sixth.

RONALD REAGAN

[*Filed with the Office of the Federal Register, 3:38 p.m., October 9, 1981*]

Announcement of the Presentation of the National Medal of Science to Dr. Philip Handler
October 9, 1981

The President today awarded the National Medal of Science to Dr. Philip Handler, an outstanding American biochemist and former president of the National Academy of Sciences, the Nation's most prestigious scientific organization.

The National Medal of Science, created by an Act of Congress in 1959, is the Nation's highest scientific award. The award is made by the President "to individuals who, in his judgment, are deserving of special recognition by reason of their outstanding contributions to knowledge in the physical, biological, mathematical, or engineering science."

In awarding the National Medal of Science to Dr. Handler, the President has cited his "outstanding contribution to biochemical research, resulting in significant contributions to mankind, including research that led to a clearer understanding of pellagra." The award also cites Dr. Handler for his national leadership in furthering the state of American science.

Dr. Handler served as president of the National Academy of Sciences from 1969 to 1981, where he was a leading spokesman for excellence in American scientific endeavors. His strong and eloquent leadership of the Academy during turbulent times for science was praised widely by the scientific community on the occasion of his recent retirement.

In addition to his Academy presidency, Dr. Handler served as a member, and subsequently as Vice Chairman and Chairman of the National Science Board from 1962 to 1970, where he wisely upheld the cause of science and the development of the National Science Foundation.

In awarding this high honor to Dr. Handler, the President extended his best wishes to him as a scientist and individual who had devoted himself so completely to the advancement of American science, to intellectual freedom in international science, and to human progress and well-being everywhere.

Announcement Concerning the President's Review of the Civil Aeronautics Board's Decision on the Texas International Airlines-Continental Airlines Acquisition Case
October 12, 1981

The President today advised the Civil Aeronautics Board that he has determined not to disapprove the Board's decision in the Texas International Airlines-Continental Airlines acquisition case.

The Board's decision had been submitted to the President for review under section 801(a) of the Federal Aviation Act of 1958, as amended, under which the President has the authority to disapprove Board actions only upon the basis of foreign relations or national defense considerations. The President examined the Board's decision in light of these considerations, which are the only factors he is authorized by the statute to take into account, and determined not to disapprove the Board's decision within the 60 days the statute allows.

The President's letter notifying the Board of this decision also states that no foreign relations or national defense consideration underlies his determination not to disapprove the Board's decision.

The President is aware that the proposed acquisition of Continental Airlines by Texas International Airlines has led many to express concern about future levels of air service to Pacific islands, including those within the Trust Territory of the Pacific Islands. The President reaffirms the commitment of the United States to the economic development of the Trust Territory islands and recognizes the importance of commercial air service to that development.

In this regard, the Board's decision approving the acquisition includes safeguards designed to prevent unilateral reduction of air service to these islands. Consistent with the Board's action and sharing its concern, the President encourages efforts by the interested executive departments to develop, as appropriate, additional safeguards to assure that the islands of the Trust Territory will continue to receive adequate air service.

Question-and-Answer Session With Reporters on Middle East Issues
October 12, 1981

Q. Ford and Carter think that it's necessary for the U.S. to deal directly with the PLO [Palestine Liberation Organization].

The President. Well, there would be a condition—always has been. There's never been any refusal, only until they will recognize Israel's right to exist as a nation, which they still have never done.

Q. Mr. President, Mr. McFarlane [Robert C. McFarlane, Counselor of the Department of State] says we're going to be sending U.S. servicemen to the Sudan. Can you assure us that they're not there to take part in combat?

The President. I can assure you that we have no intention of any Americans engaging in combat.

Q. Sir, if Colonel Qadhafi [Mu'amaar al Qadhafi, Chief of State of Libya] is such a bad man, why don't we stop buying his oil and financing his activities?

The President. Well, someone else would buy the oil and finance his activities, and so we wouldn't be gaining anything there.

Q. Why not just cut him off?

The President. Well, as I say, I don't think that it would make any difference on that. We might be cutting off our own nose to spite our face.

Q. What do you think of the AWACS outlook right now?

The President. Well, I continue to be cautiously optimistic. I hope that some of the Senators who are opposed will recognize that even more than before it is essential that we show the Middle East that we are prepared to participate there in trying to bring peace and in aligning ourselves with the moderate Arab states, as well as we have with Israel.

Q. What about the speedup in arms delivery to Egypt and to the Sudan?

The President. I think that that's called for, yes.

Q. Are we going to make certain that Qadhafi does not invade the Sudan and take over the Sudan?

The President. Egypt and the Sudan have a treaty with regard to that. And Egypt has made it plain that they're going to stand by

that treaty. And I think if you compare Libya to Egypt, that should restrain—to beat Qadhafi.

Q. Are we drawing a line in the sand?

The President. Well, maybe along that border there of the Sudan. Maybe they have.

Q. Are *we* drawing it, sir?

The President. Well, as I've tried to point out, I don't think it's necessary for us to.

Q. Thank you very much, sir.

Note: The exchange began at 3:20 p.m. on the South Lawn of the White House as the President returned from a weekend stay at Camp David, Md.

Remarks at the Welcoming Ceremony for King Juan Carlos I of Spain
October 13, 1981

The President. Your Majesty, it gives me great pleasure to welcome you and Queen Sophia to the United States. We welcome you as monarch of Spain and as a champion of democracy.

Yesterday, we celebrated Columbus Day. Some 489 years ago, three ships sailing under the Spanish flag and commissioned by King Ferdinand and Queen Isabella made a discovery that irreversibly altered the course of history and marked the emergence of Spain as a world power. It's fitting that one who traces his lineage to Ferdinand and Isabella now leads Spain into a new era of democracy and freedom. We applaud the sensible path toward political liberty that you've chosen and the skill, and if I may add, personal courage, that you've demonstrated in reaching your goal.

On July 1st, I met with your Foreign Minister, José Pedro Pérez Llorca, and he emphasized that Spain is moving toward joining the major European institutions. This, too, we applaud. We look forward to Spain's complete integration into the Western community of nations. Already, the Spanish Government is playing a leading role in the struggle to combat terrorism on the Euro-

pean continent. Such initiative is well-appreciated here.

Spain's growing presence cannot help but strengthen the bond that exists between our two people. Americans will never forget the all important assistance Spain was during our struggle for independence and freedom.

So now, when we offer the Spanish people our hands and our hearts, we do so out of gratitude for all that Spain has done for us. Those of us from the western United States understand perhaps more than other Americans the magnitude of Spain's contribution. Spaniards explored the length and breadth of the southern and western United States, settling or passing through 16 of the present States of the Union. My own California is a wonderful example of Spain's lasting cultural gift. Catholic missions still stand in testimony to this magnificent cultural and spiritual contribution to the world. Spanish architecture is everywhere, and California's constitution was written in two languages—Spanish and English.

At my first inauguration as Governor of California, I took the oath of office with my hand on a Bible brought to California by Father Junipero Serra, a Spaniard whose unselfish devotion to God is an inspiration to all Americans. These things and our many citizens whose family trees are rooted in Spain have had a major impact on the American character.

In 1883, one of our great poets, Walt Whitman, commented on Hispanic traits and the American identity. He said, "No stock shows a grander historic retrospect— grander in religiousness and loyalty, or for patriotism, courage, decorum, gravity, and honor."

Well, today we know that the traits Walt Whitman described a century ago well characterize the leadership of King Juan Carlos. We welcome you, Your Majesties, and are grateful for your dedication to your country and to your ideals. You have the admiration and respect of the American people, and you honor us with your visit.

The King. Mr. President, the Queen and I offer our sincere thanks for your very warm greetings. It has given us great pleasure to be able to accept your most kind invitation and to be here today in your great country.

We officially begin our visit at this ceremony with our hearts and spirits working towards the pleasant task of bringing our peoples and our two countries together in a felicitous and productive cooperation based on our common interests and goals.

From the vantage points afforded us by our respective national characteristics and destinies, we are witnessing an increasingly closer weave in the fabric of our relationship—a relationship whose goal is the progress and well-being of our people within the global context of the noble principles of peace, understanding, freedom, and prosperity for all mankind.

We also wish at this time to express to the American people the Spanish people's message of sincere friendship. Mr. President, for the world and for my country, you embody the great American democracy which during its two centuries of existence, in times of peace as well as times of hardship, has succeeded in defending and upholding the timeless values of justice and the dignity of man.

In this task, you will always have the understanding and support of my country, which with its new democratic vitality, with faith and hope, has set out upon the path leading to full integration in the Western World to which it belongs.

Mr. President, here at the portico of the White House, whose architecture reflects the austere solemnity, the traditional virtue of the pioneers who founded the American nation, the Queen and I thank you and Mrs. Reagan for your cordial welcome.

Note: The President spoke at 10:12 a.m. on the South Lawn of the White House, where King Juan Carlos and Queen Sophia were given a formal welcome with full military honors.

Following the ceremony, the President and the King met in the Oval Office. Also present at that meeting were Secretary of State Alexander M. Haig, Jr., Assistant to the President for National Security Affairs Richard V. Allen, and Terence A. Todman, U.S. Ambassador to Spain, and, on the Spanish side, Foreign Minister José Pedro Pérez Llorca, General Sabino Fernandos Campo, Secretary General of the Palace, Jorge del Pino, Director General for U.S. and Pacific Affairs, and José Lladó, Spanish Ambassador to the United States. President Reagan and King Juan Carlos were then joined by an expanded group of their advisers for a second meeting in the Cabinet Room.

Remarks of the President and King Juan Carlos I of Spain Following Their Meetings
October 13, 1981

The President. His Majesty Juan Carlos and I have just completed a stimulating and instructive session of talks, during which we touched on some of the most critical international issues of the day.

We discussed the East-West situation, the importance of forging even closer Western unity and cohesion in the face of a determined Soviet challenge. We spent considerable time comparing notes on the Middle East and the interest which our two countries share in promoting peace and stability in that troubled region, so recently shaken by the tragic death of Egyptian President Sadat. We talked about Latin America and the Caribbean Basin, an area where, owing to the wealth of Hispanic culture and historical ties, Spanish insights are especially valuable.

Most important, my talks with His Majesty merely confirmed that—well, what I and millions of my fellow Americans already knew, that Spain has a wise and courageous chief of state, whose leadership in developing his country's democratic institutions has earned the world's profound respect.

Your Majesty, I take this opportunity to reiterate in public what I have expressed to you in private. The U.S. enormously admires the strides which you and your countrymen have taken toward creating a vital and vibrant democracy in so short a time. In fully supporting that democracy, we consider Spain not only a major strategic partner but a close friend, and we look forward even more closely to working with your government as Spain continues to pursue full integration with Europe and the West.

I speak for all Americans when I say that I hope you and your gracious Queen will soon return to our shores. You'll be particularly welcome not only here in Washington but in those many parts of our country where Spanish culture and language have contributed so enduringly to our own history and heritage.

Adios and *buen viaje.*

The King. First of all, Mr. President, I want to thank you for those kind words for which I am extremely grateful. But I want to tell you and publicly to tell you that without the help of the Spanish people, I would not have been able, in the beginning, to do what Spain achieved and what I achieved with them.

I want to express again to the President and Mrs. Reagan our gratitude for the invitation and for the hospitality we are receiving. Our visit to Washington couldn't have started better. I'm not referring to the weather, but to the most cordial and personal relationship that has developed in this, our first visit.

As the President told you, we discussed different matters around the world and, above all, the relationship between Spain and the United States, that can't be in a better way and in a better moment.

Thank you.

Note: The President spoke at 11:55 a.m. on the South Lawn of the White House.

Appointment of James H. Cavanaugh and Steve M. Jeong as Members of the President's Export Council
October 13, 1981

The President today announced his intention to appoint James H. Cavanaugh and Steve M. Jeong to be members of the President's Export Council. They will succeed Robert B. Washington, Jr., and Stephen P. Yokich.

Dr. Cavanaugh recently served as Special Consultant to the President in Presidential Personnel. Presently he is president of Allergan International, a unit of the Allergan Pharmaceutical Co. in Irvine, Calif. He was senior vice president for science and planning, having joined the company in 1977. In 1971 he joined the White House staff as Staff Assistant to the President for Health Affairs and was named Associate Director of the Domestic Council Staff in 1973. He later became Deputy Director of the Domestic Council Staff, and in 1976, was named Deputy Assistant to the President for Domestic Affairs and served as Deputy Chief of the White House staff. Prior to his White House service, Dr. Cavanaugh was Deputy Assistant Secretary of Health and Scientific Affairs, Department of Health, Education and Welfare. He was a member of the faculty of the Graduate College at the University of Iowa. He graduated from Fairleigh Dickinson University (B.S., 1959) and the University of Iowa (M.A., 1961; Ph. D., 1964). He is married, has two children, and resides in Newport Beach, Calif. He is 43 years old.

Mr. Jeong is a real estate broker and tax consultant and is owner of Steve M. Jeong Realty in San Francisco, Calif. He has been very active in civic and community affairs of the San Francisco Chinese community. He is the former president of the Chinese Consolidated Benevolent Association, the official representative organization of Chinese in the United States; former president of the Lung Kong Association; former president and member of the board of directors of the Sue Hing Benevolent Association; and serves on the boards of directors of the Chinese Hospital and the Chinese Chamber of Commerce. Mr. Jeong has served on the board of directors of the Chinatown-North Beach English Language Center (an agency of the Economic Opportunity Council of San Francisco). In 1971 he obtained a grant from the Department of Commerce to train non-English-speaking Chinese immigrants in a saleable skill, enabling them to be self-supporting. Mr. Jeong was born in Canton, China, on June 21, 1919. He has degrees in accounting from Kong Tai College in Hong Kong and Golden Gate University in San Francisco. He is married, has two grown children, and resides in San Francisco.

Nomination of Robert M. Garrick To Be a Member of the Board of Directors of the Communications Satellite Corporation
October 13, 1981

The President today announced his intention to nominate Robert M. Garrick to be a member of the Board of Directors of the Communications Satellite Corporation (COMSAT).

Mr. Garrick recently served as Deputy Counsellor to the President and resigned his full-time position to return to his public relations business in California.

Mr. Garrick, a retired rear admiral in the U.S. Navy Reserve, has been on leave from his position as senior vice president of Doremus & Co., an international public relations firm. He served on the transition organization as deputy director for public affairs and was director of research and policy development for the Reagan-Bush campaign committee.

Mr. Garrick attended Los Angeles City College, the University of Southern California, and the University of Hawaii, where he majored in journalism, radio and aeronautical engineering. During World War II, he served as an enlisted combat correspondent in the U.S. Navy on the staff of Fleet Admiral Chester W. Nimitz. During his 4 years in the Navy, he advanced from yeoman 3/C to chief yeoman. He was commissioned a lieutenant junior grade in the Naval Reserve in 1948, and in 1973 was promoted to the rank of rear admiral, as the Naval Reserve's first public affairs flag officer.

Following World War II, he returned to the Los Angeles Times-Mirror Corp. and served as assistant director of public relations. In 1947 he became director of public relations and advertising for the A. F. Gilmore Co. and the Hollywood Farmer's Market. He founded Robert M. Garrick Associates, a public relations consulting firm, in 1951, serving industrial and commercial firms and associations. In 1973 the firm was incorporated as Garrick Associates, Inc., and in 1975 the corporation merged with Doremus & Co.

Mr. Garrick retired from the Naval Reserve in March 1980 and was awarded the Legion of Merit. His other awards include two Navy Commendation Medals, the Asia-Pacific ribbon with 16 combat stars, and the World War II Victory, American Theatre, Naval Reserve Good Conduct, Philippines Liberation medals and other citations. He is a member of the Public Relations Society of America and has been awarded the Society's Silver Anvil, the highest recognized award in the public relations field.

Mr. Garrick is married to the former Billie Clair Welsh of Kansas City, Mo. They have two children, Martin Welsh Garrick and Patti Kathleen Garrick. The Garricks reside in Pasadena and Bonsall, Calif.

Toasts of the President and King Juan Carlos I of Spain at the State Dinner
October 13, 1981

The President. Your Majesties, welcome to the White House. In the epic poem, "El Canto de Mio Cid," it is pointed out that *el que en buena hora nacio,* el Cid was born in a favorable moment. Historically, he actually came into a world desperate for leadership. With courage that inspired a nation, el Cid, turning despair into hope and weakness into strength, won a series of battles against the foreign invaders who occupied much of Spain.

Tonight we honor a man who, like el Cid, was born in a favorable moment. Mankind is in desperate need of leaders with courage and wisdom. We watch the progress in Spain, the magnificent strides toward political freedom, with a sense of awe. In a world that seems to be drowning under a wave of authoritarianism, Spain shines as a beacon of hope.

This kind of progress requires of the people and of their leader a certain strength of character neither necessary nor natural in despotic regimes. Building a free society is every bit as perplexing and at times threatening as the struggle that faced el Cid. Such times as these and such challenges as those facing your country separate great leaders from lesser men, who by circumstances find themselves in positions of political power.

King Juan Carlos, Queen Sophia, and the Spanish people have risen to the task God has placed before them, and the world is being given a majestic gift—a truly free and prosperous Spain. Over the centuries, Spain has contributed so much. Whether one talks of the great Cervantes and the development of modern literature, or refers to the painting of Goya or El Greco, certainly Spain has provided Western civilization with a multitude of priceless gifts. And now, King Juan Carlos, with the courage of el Cid and the skill of the great Spanish masters, is creating a masterpiece of democracy.

In America we recognize that even with the proper leadership, a nation must have great people to maintain liberty. And in the case of Spain, we have total confidence.

So tonight, I ask you to join me in a toast to Their Majesties, to King Juan Carlos, Queen Sophia, and to the people of Spain. May they live in peace and freedom benefiting such a great people.

The King. Mr. President, Mrs. Reagan, I have followed the ideas expressed in your toast with keen interest and should like now, for my part, to tell you that it is a great pleasure for the Queen and for me to visit your great country once again and to listen to your warm and cordial words.

Five years ago, when I first visited your nation as King of Spain, it was my honor to tell your Congress that the restored Spanish monarchy had undertaken the commitment to be the institution under which all Spaniards would find ample scope for political participation, with no discrimination whatsoever. Today, 5 years later, I am proud to confirm that what was then a statement of intention is now a palpable and profound reality—a constitution approved by the people and by the freely elected parliament.

My country, Mr. President, a pioneer in the forging of the fundamental values of what we call the West, supported by its historic credentials and its Western and European vocation, which it will not renounce, wishes to occupy once again the place to which it is entitled in the international community. At the same time, it would like to offer as in years past its collaboration and its effort in the defense of the principles which are the very shared essence of our two nations.

On no scale of values can there be a more important goal for our two peoples than that of the defense of the principles in which the West finds its roots. Through this defense, consisting in the permanent safeguarding of the sovereignty and freedom of all the peoples of the Earth, Spain wishes to contribute to maintaining international peace and security.

We are fully aware that the peoples and nations which place moral and spiritual values above ambition for power and things material do freely express their will to live in peace with dignity. And we know that their freely elected governments heed these aspirations and join their efforts in order to attain the same goal.

Like your country, Spain defends peace and the rule of law, opposes threats and the use of force, and rejects all outside interference in its own affairs. It is in these terms that we conceive our international relations, which we wish to maintain peacefully with all peoples.

Our friendship with the American nation is as old as its origins. Yesterday, the day of our arrival in your country, was the 489th anniversary of the arrival of the Spaniards to this continent. With that magnificent event a new era began in world history, and through that heroic exploit, which was followed up by explorers and colonizers, the lands of America, from Alaska to Tierra del Fuego, came to form part—and still do

form a fundamental part of our Western World.

You also know, Mr. President, better than I, what the Spanish presence has meant in the American West—the tremendous work carried out by the Spanish explorers, missionaries, and colonizers in that region; the founding of dozens of towns and cities which even today form a rosary of names echoing with the sounds of Spain.

These are links, Mr. President, which nothing and nobody can break; very strong ties which transcend the vicissitudes of the moment and serve to reinforce the mutual understanding and friendship of our two peoples. This friendship now takes on a new dimension in view of our will to reinforce our progressive participation in the European and Western effort, aimed at achieving a world that is ever freer and more just and in which our sister nations may fully participate.

To the relations between Spain and the United States, that in the future they may produce abundant fruit and that the ties which unite our two countries may intensify and become ever closer, I raise my glass tonight. With my good wishes for the wellbeing of the great American people, and for your own personal happiness, Mr. President and Mrs. Reagan.

And I should like to express one other hope, that is that the invitation that the Queen and I have extended to you, on behalf of Spain and of the Spanish people, to visit us in Spain during your term of office at a mutually convenient time can be accepted by you. I think we can provide for you a welcome which you would like.

Note: The President spoke at 9:23 p.m. in the State Dining Room at the White House. King Juan Carlos spoke in Spanish, and his remarks were translated by an interpreter.

Nomination of Evan Griffith Galbraith To Be United States Ambassador to France
October 14, 1981

The President today announced his intention to nominate Evan Griffith Galbraith, of Connecticut, to be Ambassador to France. He would succeed Arthur A. Hartman.

Mr. Galbraith was a lawyer with the firm of Shearman and Sterling of New York in 1957–60. In 1960–61 he was Special Assistant to the Secretary of Commerce and was with the Morgan Guaranty Trust Co. (New York) in 1961–69, serving as assistant vice president (1961–63); administrator and director of Morgan and Cie, Paris, France (1963–68); and vice president of Morgan Guaranty Trust Co. in 1968–69. In 1969 Mr. Galbraith was an independent financial con-

sultant in New York, N.Y. In 1969–75 he was managing director and chairman of Bankers Trust International in London, England. He was chairman of Dillon Read Overseas Co. in London in 1975–80. Since 1980 he has been managing director of Dillon, Read and Co., Inc., New York.

Mr. Galbraith served in the United States Navy in 1953–57. He graduated from Yale University (B.A., 1950) and Harvard Law School (LL.B., 1953). He is married, has four children, and resides in Greenwich, Conn. He was born July 2, 1928, in Toledo, Ohio.

Remarks on Awarding the Rank of Distinguished Executive to Certain Members of the Senior Executive Service
October 14, 1981

The President. The ability of this or any administration to succeed depends in no small degree upon the energy, the dedication, and the spirit of our nation's civil servants. The granting of Presidential rank awards provides the opportunity to recognize a select group of these employees for extraordinary service.

America is passing into a new era, reversing a long trend of government expansion. Government must limit what it does, yet still perform its rightful task with utmost skill and professionalism. Meeting this difficult challenge will require the determination and imagination which this year's Rank Award recipients have amply demonstrated.

There are 6,500 Federal employees in the Senior Executive Service, and this year only 25 were selected to receive this distinguished executive award. These men are being honored for the contributions they've made during their careers as public servants. Over the years, they've maintained a level of accomplishment head and shoulders above many of their fellows. While their

talents have long been recognized by those with whom they work, this award gives us the opportunity to thank them in the name of the people of the United States who are the beneficiaries of their diligence.

There is a small stipend that accompanies this award. Yet, it in no way represents the enormous sums that they have saved the taxpayers. In looking over their backgrounds, I was impressed beyond words at the services they've performed. Some excelled in science or engineering projects, saving tax dollars by designing equipment that works well. In the case of Henry Harris, he developed a new weapons system of joint logistics that will be of considerable savings. This is an extraordinary list. Clyde Jeffcoat, for example, designed an accounting and billing system that eliminates the need for thousands of employees and saves millions of dollars. Better than focusing on new construction, Peter Kimm led an effort to upgrade current housing units and promote a self-help program for the units' underprivileged occupants. And David Menotti has a remarkable record—mediated difficult conflicts between the EPA, industry, and environmental groups.

Time won't permit me to detail all of their accomplishments, but let me just say that we're very proud to have all of you working with us. And for the people of this country, I offer you a hearty thank you and a well done. And now, I shall turn it over to you.

Mr. Devine. Thank you. Mr. President, I'm proud as your chief bureaucrat, the director of your civil service, to honor 25 outstanding government executives who express the true degree of patriotism by proving their commitment to the country every day as they've carried out their assignments for the public over their long periods of service.

As you mentioned, the decade of the eighties presents new challenges, and we very much need the support of all our civil servants. As you said in your acceptance speech—and probably the only time a politician has done this in an acceptance speech—you asked for the ideas and the efforts of Federal employees to help you make government work. Through the 98-year history of the civil service, you haven't been let down. And these 25 have responded in an extraordinary way to show that their support is with you and the country as we make these changes.

So, Mr. President, I'd like to present to you these 25 truly outstanding civil servants.

Note: The President spoke at 11:40 a.m. at the ceremony in the Rose Garden at the White House. Donald J. Devine, Director of the Office of Personnel Management, read the names of the recipients, who received a framed certificate signed by the President, a gold lapel pin, and a check for approximately $20,000.

The rank of Distinguished Executive is the most prestigious recognition that can be given to a member of the Senior Executive Service. The 1981 award recipients are: Alan G. Forssell, Henry H. Harris, Donald P. Hearth, Jimmie D. Hill, George O. Hipps, Jr., Clyde E. Jeffcoat, Peter M. Kimm, Lester P. Lamm, R. Kenneth Lobb, John W. Lyons, David G. Mathiasen, Harold A. McGuffin, David E. Menotti, Robert L. Morgan, Frederick T. Rall, Jr., Glenn Allan Rudd, Joseph H. Sherick, Richard G. Smith, William L. Smith, Earl R. Stadtman, Henning E. G. von Gierke, William C. Watson, Jr., Harvey J. Wilcox, Walter C. Williams, and A. Thomas Young.

Remarks at a White House Luncheon for Members of the Presidential Task Force on the Arts and Humanities
October 14, 1981

The President. Ladies and gentlemen, I've just received notification here—if suddenly in the midst of my remarks or anything else that's going on here, you see some individuals getting up and leaving, don't think that they're against the arts and humanities. [*Laughter*] They are Congressmen going to the House, because there is a vote up there coming shortly. All those who are against my side in the vote stay here. [*Laughter*]

Well, I want to welcome all of you here today to the White House on behalf of the American people, and I want to thank you for the important work that you've undertaken in these past few months. You're here because of your love for art, culture, and learning. You care deeply about things of the mind and spirit. Indeed, many of you are cultural leaders and you have proven what I have just said already, in the activities that you have undertaken on your own.

When Nancy inaugurated the Young Artists in Performance at the White House program here in this room, she quoted a line from Henry James: "It is art that *makes* life, makes interest, makes importance, . . . and I know of no substitute whatever for the force and beauty of its process." Well, those words can truly be applied to art, to the humanities, and their scholarly pursuit. As you know, our tradition of arts and scholarship in America is like most of our traditions—a pluralistic one. There are many wellsprings of support here for works of creativity and culture. I like to believe that's why artists and scholars continue to flock to our shores from other countries. Today we're seen as a great center of Western culture, a place where the artist and the scholar can find enrichment and excitement.

And I would like now to call on Dr. Hanna Gray, president of the University of Chicago, to present a report on your work.

Dr. Gray.

Dr. Gray. Thank you. Mr. President, Mrs. Reagan, members of the Task Force, distinguished guests:

It is with a very deep sense of appreciation that we are presenting to you, Mr. President, the report of your Task Force on the Arts and Humanities. We are, above all, grateful for the concern you have shown for the health and the vigor of our nation's cultural life.

You provided us with a stimulating occasion to consider the opportunities and the obligations which all of us share to sustain and to strengthen this country's commitment to the arts and to the humanities. The hallmark of that commitment lies in a devotion to the essential freedoms of thought and expression.

A society that recognizes the enduring significance of the arts and the humanities to the quality and to the future of our civilization will set high value also on diversity and on independence of initiative. This conviction asserts a confidence in the power and possibilities of scholarship and of education at their best, a dedication to the values and to the varieties of the creative and performing arts at their most vital. It rests on a regard for the cultivation of inherited tradition and also for encouraging the risk-taking that gives rise to new forms of learning and artistic accomplishment.

It is a difficult task, the task of leadership, to balance so many pressing needs and complex goals, to assess the claims of the future against those of the present, to stimulate the distinctive and cooperative roles of the public and the private sectors. In that context, we know that you will give consideration to those activities which over the generations will shape the capacities and the potential of an educated and creative people. We hope very much that the work of our task force will be of some use as you direct that process.

And in saying that, I know that I speak not only for the members of the Task Force, for the staff which has served the Task Force so ably, but also for the two Cochairmen who were not able to be present today—for Ambassador Terra who had to be absent today, and for Chuck Heston who has, however, written a statement.

And perhaps I could close with that. His statement says, "I regret that the film I'm shooting in British Columbia keeps me from joining you to second the convictions I know Hanna will express. I've been preaching the independence and perseverance of the artist all summer. Now I'm trying to practice it." [*Laughter*] "My thoughts are very much with you. I am grateful for your trust in us." Signed, Chuck Heston.

Mr. President, we thank you again. This is our report.

[At this point, Dr. Gray presented the President with the report of the Task Force.]

The President. Well thank you, Dr. Gray, very much. And now I think I'd like to conclude by pointing out that we hope your work will be very much a part of that era of national renewal I spoke of last January, an era we hope to make a reality in the next few years.

The challenge before us is to find ways once again to unleash the independent spirit of the people in their communities. And that energy will accomplish far, far more than just government programs alone ever could. It was in this context that I asked William (Bill) Verity, the chairman of Armco Steel, to chair a new Task Force on Private Sector Initiatives. Bill, since you so graciously accepted—I caught him in the middle of the Atlantic Ocean on a boat; I'd never done that before—won't you stand please and—[*applause*]. But then he told me he'd never been called on a boat before—[*laughter*]—so it was a first for both of us.

But the Task Force is going to be comprised of 35 leaders from corporations, foundations, and voluntary and religious organizations. And I'm delighted that he's here with us today, for the thrust of our new efforts in the arts and humanities is very much in the spirit of our overall private sector initiative. We hope in this area, as in others, to assure pump priming and seed money in partnership with private giving.

Now, we've done some talking recently about how our economic problems are the result of too much government intrusion into the economy. The danger of too much government was very much on the mind of the men who framed our Constitution, constructed our government, and built this public housing—[*laughter*]—and if you think about it, their fear of government has a special meaning for our century. It's important for us to continue to resist the intrusions of government. As John Updike has said so well, "I would rather chance my personal vision of truth striking home here and there in the chaos of publication, than attempt to filter it through a few sets of official, honorably public-spirited scruples." [*Laughter*]

Fostering arts and scholarship, not stifling it, not filtering it, has been the goal of the National Endowments for the Arts and Humanities. It has also been the goal of your work on the Task Force to act as a catalyst, to encourage the arts and humanities, to find for them new outlets and more generous sources of support. Unlike many other countries, American support for the arts and humanities comes primarily from the private sector—$3 billion in 1980. The Endowments, which began in 1965, account for only 10 percent of the donations to art and scholarship. Nonetheless, they have served an important role in catalyzing additional private support, assisting excellence in arts and letters, and helping to assure the availability of art and scholarship.

Our primary goal in the arts and humanities is to strengthen that public and private partnership. We hope to encourage a variety of private support and involvement and to ensure responsiveness of Federal programs to the real needs. To assure an effective dialog between government and the private sector, we will explore with the Congress the expansion of our Federal Council on the Arts and Humanities to include private membership.

I would like to announce now my nomination of Frank Hodsoll as our proposed Chairman of the National Endowment for the Arts. Frank, as many of you know, is now Deputy to Jim Baker on our White House staff. He's worked with you on the Task Force, and I've charged him to encourage additional private support for the arts in States and communities across the land, to assure that Federal programs are responsive to needs. Frank, why don't you stand up so they can see you?

He ran out a little while ago and I thought he was running out on the job, but it turns out he just had a telephone call and he's back. [*Laughter*] Telephone calls take on a new meaning since we've been in this job back here. [*Laughter*] I got one, as you all know—it was widely heralded in the press—at 4:30 in the morning. [*Laughter*] And everyone hailed it as that they were reluctant to wake me up. What did they think they were doing at 4:30 in the morning? [*Laughter*]

The arts and humanities have always been something of great personal importance to Nancy and to me. Nations are more often than not remembered for their art and thought. As I stated at the time of establishing the Task Force, our cultural institutions are an essential national resource. They must be kept strong.

So, I thank you all once again for being here, and I thank you all for this report. And I will read it. Thank you all.

Note: The President spoke at 1:10 p.m. in the East Room at the White House. The three Cochairmen of the Task Force are Dr. Hanna H. Gray (Chairman for the Humanities), Charlton Heston (Chairman for the Arts), and Ambassador at Large for Cultural Affairs Daniel J. Terra (Chairman for the Federal Government).

Nomination of Francis S. M. Hodsoll To Be Chairman of the National Endowment for the Arts
October 14, 1981

The President today announced his intention to nominate Francis S. M. Hodsoll to be Chairman of the National Endowment for the Arts for a term of 4 years. He would succeed Livingston L. Biddle, Jr.

Mr. Hodsoll is currently Deputy Assistant to the President and Deputy to Chief of Staff James A. Baker III. He has served in this capacity since January 20, 1981. His responsibilities have included a variety of White House policy assignments and serving as White House liaison for the Presidential Task Force on the Arts and Humanities.

Prior to joining the White House, Mr. Hodsoll served in the Reagan-Bush campaign as staff coordinator of preparation for the debates. He was previously a Foreign Service officer and Deputy U.S. Special Representative for Nonproliferation at the Department of State (1978–80). In the Ford administration, Mr. Hodsoll was Deputy Assistant Secretary of Commerce for Energy and Strategic Resource Policy and assistant to the Under Secretary of Commerce. He had previously been a special assistant to the Administrator of EPA.

Mr. Hodsoll is a member of the New York Bar and was formerly associated with Sullivan and Cromwell. He has managed a British trading company in the Philippines and has acted (with his wife) as general contractor of two houses in McLean. Originally from California, Mr. Hodsoll has degrees from Yale, Cambridge, and Stanford Law School. As an undergraduate, he was active in college theater and radio.

Mr. Hodsoll is married to the former Margaret McEwen of Winnetka, Ill. He has two children and resides in McLean, Va. He was born May 1, 1938.

Executive Order 12329—President's Task Force on Private Sector Initiatives
October 14, 1981

By the authority vested in me as President by the Constitution of the United States of America, and in order to establish, in accordance with the provisions of the Federal Advisory Committee Act, as amended (5 U.S.C. App. I), a task force on private sector initiatives policy of the United States, it is hereby ordered as follows:

Section 1. Establishment. (a) There is established the President's Task Force on Private Sector Initiatives. The Task Force shall be composed of members who shall be appointed by the President from among private citizens of the United States, public officials from State and local governments, and members of the Legislative and Executive Branches of the Federal government. No more than one member shall be a full time officer or employee of the Executive Branch. The members shall serve at the pleasure of the President.

(b) The President shall designate a Chairman from among the members of the Task Force.

Sec. 2. Functions. (a) The Task Force shall advise the President, the Secretary of Commerce, and other Executive agency heads with respect to:

(1) Methods of developing, supporting and promoting private sector leadership and responsibility for meeting public needs.

(2) Recommendations for appropriate action by the President to foster greater public-private partnerships and to decrease dependence on government.

(b) The Task Force shall serve as a focal point for private sector action addressing public problems.

Sec. 3. Administration. (a) The heads of Executive agencies shall, to the extent permitted by law, provide the Task Force with such information with respect to private sector initiatives issues as may be necessary for the effective performance of its functions.

(b) Members of the Task Force shall serve without any compensation for their work on the Task Force. However, they may be allowed travel expenses, as authorized by law for persons serving intermittently in the government service (5 U.S.C. 5701–5707), to the extent funds are available therefor.

(c) The Department of Commerce shall, to the extent permitted by law and subject to the availability of funds, provide the Task Force with such administrative services, funds, facilities, staff and other support services as may be necessary for the effective performance of its functions.

Sec. 4. General Provisions. (a) Notwithstanding the provisions of any other Executive order, the responsibilities of the President under the Federal Advisory Committee Act, as amended, except that of reporting annually to the Congress, which are applicable to the Task Force established by this Order, shall be performed by the Secretary of Commerce in accordance with the guidelines and procedures established by the Administrator of General Services.

(b) The Task Force shall terminate on December 31, 1982, unless sooner extended.

RONALD REAGAN

The White House,
October 14, 1981.

[*Filed with the Office of the Federal Register, 4:17 p.m., October 14, 1981*]

Remarks to Reporters Following a Meeting With Representative Eugene V. Atkinson of Pennsylvania
October 14, 1981

The President. Representative McDade, Secretary Drew Lewis, and the guest for the occasion, Eugene Atkinson:

I've invited you here today for what I think is an historic occasion, to welcome the 193d and newest Republican Member of the House of Representatives—the Honorable Eugene Atkinson of Pennsylvania.

Congressman Atkinson is changing his registration from Democrat to Republican. He's undertaken an act of outstanding political courage that symbolizes the beginning of a new coalition and a new era in American politics. As many of you know, Gene and I first became acquainted April 21st, when I telephoned him seeking support for the Gramm-Latta budget proposal. And I put on my best pitch on the telephone and then he said to me, "I am fully supportive of your programs." And it was then that I discovered that they had put the call through to him where he was the guest on a talk show, on radio, and he was doing this before a live radio audience, and my call had caught him there. Since then, we've gotten to know each other much better.

I've profited immeasurably from Gene's knowledge of the steel industry, which is so vitally important to the working men and women of his 25th district in Pennsylvania. In another sense, Gene and I actually go back well before last April, as his odyssey from Democrat to Republican is so strikingly parallel to my own.

Both Gene and I have long shared the same concerns for the plight of the working man in America. I was president of a labor union, while Gene lived and worked his entire life in an area that embodies the blue collar wage earner as much as anywhere in the United States. As Democrats, both Gene and I did the hard volunteer chores for the candidates of our choice. But as the time went on, we both came to the realization that our party, the party we belonged to, had drawn away from the concerns that we shared—the size of the Federal Government, the extent of its regulations, the nature of Federal income taxes and how they affect America's wage earners, and the decline of America's defenses. Those were the concerns uppermost in my mind in 1962, when I ended 30 years as a registered Democrat to join the Republican Party.

Those are the concerns that have led Gene Atkinson to do so today. In both cases, we followed the courage of action characterized so eloquently by Winston Churchill: "Some men change principle for party and some men change party for principle." More than any other recent development, I believe that Gene Atkinson's decision will send a loud and clear message to America that our party, the Republican Party, stands for the working men and women of this country. And that's why Gene is here today.

And now, Congressman Gene Atkinson, Republican of Pennsylvania.

Representative Atkinson. Thank you very much, Mr. President. I appreciate your kind words, and I also value the friendship that we've established and which you spoke of here today. I also appreciate the support of my good friends, Secretary Drew Lewis, and my colleague, the chairman of the Pennsylvania delegation, Joseph McDade.

You know, Mr. President, throughout my 20 years in public life, I've always been a Democrat. I have served as a Federal Government official, a county commissioner, and now as a United States Congressman from the 25th District of Pennsylvania. I've also served as Democratic county chairman and as a member of the Pennsylvania Democratic State Committee.

The modern Democratic Party bears no resemblance to the one I proudly joined many years ago, a party that stood for tax cuts and a national defense second to none. I'm not in tune with the modern Democratic Party which has, in my view, left behind the principles upon which it was founded—Jefferson's concept of less government and Jackson's idea of a party by and for the working men.

I do not put party labels on the President nor on programs. I think that's meaningless. What counts is purpose, and what counts is performance. It's encouraging to me, Mr.

President, that a true effort is being made to reduce Federal spending and curb runaway inflation.

Mr. President, Republicans and Democrats and Independents alike know of your commitment to the working men and women of America, who have been hit hardest by the tremendous impact of runaway spending and the high cost of living. That's why I voted down the line to support the budget programs and the tax cuts contained in your economic recovery program.

It's interesting to note that the House Democratic Caucus recently granted amnesty to those Congressmen who voted their convictions. It is painful that those of us who speak our minds and vote our conscience are now forgiven for these sins by the Democratic Caucus. I resent them granting me amnesty and the veiled threat that to continue to vote independently could cause a loss of seniority in committee assignments. How can Members of Congress across the Nation determine how I should vote?

Again, Mr. President, I am honored to join with you, for we share the same hopes and concerns for America. We have both lived the American dream and want a nation that is strong, that is prosperous, and that is free—for our children and for future generations. I will work with you to do for our Nation what President Kennedy, who first appointed me to public office, started to do, and that's to get America moving again.

It's a pleasure to be with you today, Mr. President. I respect you very much. I look forward to working with you as a Republican Member of the United States Congress.

The President. Gene, thank you very much. Thank you.

Secretary Lewis. I really have no comments. As a former politician from Pennsylvania, now public servant, I welcome, you, Gene, to the Republican Party.

Representative Atkinson. Thank you, Drew.

Representative McDade. Mr. President, and our newest Republican from Pennsylvania, I certainly want to express my thanks to Gene on behalf of the entire delegation and of the people of the United States.

I should say I have a personal reason for thanking him, because his switch of voting today makes me chairman of the Pennsylvania delegation rather than ranking member. [*Laughter*] So, we're especially delighted. I've known Gene. I'm delighted to see his act of courage toward making this Nation what we all want it to be—more prosperous, stronger, better for the men and women of America, who work everyday in the factories to make this a great nation.

We look forward to working together, and on behalf of the Pennsylvania delegation, we welcome our newest member, Gene Atkinson.

The President. I have to go back in and go to work, and this is my way of telling you that these gentlemen have graciously agreed to stay here for a few moments for any questions that you might have, and you can direct them to them.

Reporter. Do you think you'll win AWACS, Mr. President? [*Laughter*]

The President. I have to go back to work, and what I have to go back to work on is AWACS. [*Laughter*] I'm cautiously optimistic.

Q. Mr. President, the House is saying no on AWACS today.

The President. Well, that was expected. We knew that. But it takes both Houses to say no.

Q. Can you win in the Senate?

The President. Ask them.

Note: The President spoke at 1:45 p.m. in the Rose Garden at the White House. Following the President's return to the Oval Office, Representatives McDade and Atkinson answered reporters' questions. The transcript of the question-and-answer session is included in the White House press release.

Proclamation 4875—World Food Day, 1981
October 14, 1981

By the President of the United States of America

A Proclamation

The well-being of all people depends fundamentally upon an adequate and reliable supply of food.

The United States is blessed with abundant land, fertile soil, adequate water, and a favorable climate. Upon this natural base, Americans have erected a sound system of agriculture, founded on the right of private property ownership, the opportunity to earn rewards for honest toil and investment, the freedom to exchange in the marketplace, the availability of essential credit, the application of new scientific discoveries and technologies, and the primacy of the independent family farm. The result has been an unparalleled agricultural bounty, capable of feeding our own people and millions of people around the world.

Today, many nations lack either the natural endowments or the system of incentives to private enterprise that are critical to successful agriculture. Many millions of people, particularly in the Third World, and where government policies have denied land ownership and market incentives to their farmers, are suffering from hunger and malnutrition.

Americans have traditionally been generous in sharing our agricultural abundance and technology with those less fortunate than ourselves. Since the beginning of the Food for Peace program in 1954, more than 387 million tons of American food aid, valued at more than $30 billion, have been provided to the hungry peoples of the world. American agricultural development assistance programs have helped peoples all over the world to improve their food production.

Our efforts to alleviate hunger have complemented those of other members of the international community. We salute particularly the tireless efforts of the Food and

Agriculture Organization which, on World Food Day, celebrates thirty-six years of service in the effort to alleviate hunger and malnutrition.

To focus worldwide public attention on the world's food problem, 147 member nations of the Food and Agriculture Organization have unanimously urged individual nations to commemorate October 16 as World Food Day. The Congress of the United States has responded by adopting a Joint Resolution in support of this objective.

On this occasion, let us rededicate ourselves to continuing and strengthening our efforts to assist the people of other lands to work toward the elimination of hunger, to develop strong agricultural bases built upon sound principles, and to engage in mutually beneficial commercial trade between our countries.

Now, Therefore, I, Ronald Reagan, President of the United States of America, do hereby proclaim October 16, 1981, as "World Food Day", and do call upon the people of the United States to observe this day with appropriate ceremonies and activities.

In Witness Whereof, I have hereunto set my hand this fourteenth day of October, in the year of our Lord nineteen hundred and eighty-one, and of the Independence of the United States of America the two hundred and sixth.

RONALD REAGAN

[*Filed with the Office of the Federal Register, 10:05 a.m., October 15, 1981*]

Statement on Signing the Uniformed Services Pay Act of 1981
October 14, 1981

I am pleased to be signing into law today S. 1181, the Uniformed Services Pay Act of 1981. The legislation will provide to all of our men and women in uniform a richly deserved average increase of 14.3 percent in basic pay, basic allowance for quarters, and basic allowance for subsistence. The bill also contains increases in a number of special and incentive pays which are designed to attract and retain those highly skilled personnel who are so vital to the efficient operation of our Armed Forces.

Attracting and retaining well-motivated, high quality military personnel is a critical element of my commitment to strengthen America's defenses. This bill will enable us to do that. For too long our dedicated military personnel have been undercompensated for the sacrifices and family disruptions they have had to endure in protecting the freedom of all of us.

I am particularly pleased that this legislation received such strong bipartisan support in the Congress. In that regard, I want to personally thank Senators Roger Jepsen and James Exon and Congressmen Bill Nichols and Donald Mitchell for their hard work and skill in guiding this bill through the Congress.

Note: As enacted, S. 1181 is Public Law 97–60, approved October 14.

Remarks at the Swearing-In Ceremony for Members of the President's Export Council
October 15, 1981

Thank you all very much. I'm pleased to greet you this morning as members of the Export Council, Mr. Secretary and Mr. Chairman, Madam Chairman.

There is much to be done, and each of you has been selected because you have a contribution to make. In a message to Congress in 1957 President Eisenhower said, "International commerce is beneficial to the community of nations and conducive to the establishment of a just and lasting peace in the world."

Well, maybe that's even more true today. We see free and expanded trade between people and nations because this form of human activity is beneficial to everyone. It solidifies bonds of friendship and increases the standard of living of those on both sides of the transaction. The America of the 1980's is far more dependent on exports than during Eisenhower's time. Since 1960, our export business has grown from $19.6 billion per year to $220.6 billion in 1980. More than five million jobs in the United States are now directly tied to our thriving export industry. Our exports have played a key role in offsetting this Nation's increased import of foreign oil.

As a group, you possess a wealth of experience and knowledge. Under the leadership of Paul Lyet and Anna Chennault, we plan to tap this resource by asking you to help direct your country's policies in this vital area. We're relying on you to help improve America's competitive position in international trade.

The previous council did an excellent job in identifying regulations that impede the export industry. We are counting on you to expand upon this and further reduce such disincentives. Competition is good. You may have heard that somewhere before. [*Laughter*] Seriously, whether it's domestic or international, competition provides better quality and lower-priced products.

Nevertheless, we must ensure that our businessmen are not unintentionally hobbled by government. You will be of invaluable service if you will help us identify and correct government-related problems that hamper our exporters. This is a great example of how the private sector and government can work together. And when they do, everyone is a winner.

Now, thanks to all of you in advance for the time and the effort that you will put into this. It's well appreciated, I can assure you of that. And you will find that the administration, policywise, is in favor of the things that I have suggested that you give your attention to.

And now, you may not believe this—I'm only going to have a few minutes, because I want to say hello to all of you down there—but then, I'm finally going to get to Philadelphia.

Note: The President spoke at 10:17 a.m. at the ceremony in the Rose Garden, where the private sector members of the Council were sworn in by Secretary of Commerce Malcolm Baldrige.

J. Paul Lyet is Chairman and Anna C. Chennault is Vice Chairman of the Council.

Executive Order 12330—Adjustments of Certain Rates of Pay and Allowances
October 15, 1981

By the authority vested in me as President by the Constitution and the laws of the United States of America, it is hereby ordered as follows:

Section 1. Statutory Pay Systems. Pursuant to the provisions of subchapter I of Chapter 53 of Title 5 of the United States Code, the rates of basic pay and salaries are adjusted, as set forth at the schedules attached hereto and made a part hereof, for the following statutory pay systems:

(a) The General Schedule (5 U.S.C. 5332(a)) at Schedule 1;

(b) The Foreign Service Schedule (22 U.S.C. 3963) at Schedule 2;

(c) The Schedules for the Department of Medicine and Surgery, Veterans Administration (38 U.S.C. 4107) at Schedule 3; and

(d) The rates of basic pay for the Senior Executive Service (5 U.S.C. 5382) at Schedule 4.

Sec. 2. Pay and Allowances for Members of the Uniformed Services. Sections 101 and 102 of the Uniformed Services Pay Act of 1981 provides for adjustments in the rates of monthly basic pay (37 U.S.C. 203(a) and (c)), the rates of basic allowances for subsistence (37 U.S.C. 402), and the rates of basic allowances for quarters (37 U.S.C. 403(a)), as set forth at Schedule 5 attached hereto and made a part hereof, for members of the uniformed services.

Sec. 3. Executive Salaries. The Executive Salary Cost-of-Living Adjustment Act (Public Law 94–82, 89 Stat. 419) provides for adjustments in rates of pay and salaries, as set forth at the schedules attached hereto and made a part hereof, for the following:

(a) The Vice President (3 U.S.C. 104) and the Executive Schedule (5 U.S.C. 5312–5316) at Schedule 6;

(b) Congressional Salaries (2 U.S.C. 31) at Schedule 7; and

(c) Judicial Salaries (28 U.S.C. 5, 44(d), 135, 173, 213, 252, 792(b), and 11 U.S.C. 68(a), and Section 401(a), 404(a), 404(b), and 404(d) of Public Law 95–598) at Schedule 8.

Sec. 4. Effective Date. The adjustments in rates of monthly basic pay and allowances for subsistence and quarters for members of uniformed services shall be effective on October 1, 1981. All other adjustments of salary or pay shall be effective on the first day of the first applicable pay period beginning on or after October 1, 1981.

Sec. 5. Superseded Executive Orders. Executive Order No. 12248 of October 16, 1980 and Executive Order No. 12249 of October 25, 1980 are superseded.

RONALD REAGAN

The White House,
October 15, 1981.

[*Filed with the Office of the Federal Register, 10:52 a.m., October 15, 1981*]

Note: The schedules are printed in the Federal Register *of October 16, 1981.*

Message to the Congress Submitting a Proposed Waiver of Law Concerning the Alaska Natural Gas Transportation Act of 1976
October 15, 1981

To the Congress of the United States:

The Alaska Highway Pipeline route for the Alaska Natural Gas Transportation System was chosen by President Carter and approved by Congress in 1977. There was a strong Congressional endorsement that the pipeline should be built if it could be privately financed. That has been my consistent position since becoming President, as communicated on numerous occasions to our good neighbors in Canada and I am now submitting my formal findings and proposed waiver of law.

As I stated in my message to Prime Minister Trudeau informing him of my decision to submit this waiver:

My Administration supports the completion of this project through private financing, and it is our hope that this action will clear the way to moving ahead with it. I believe that this project is important not only in terms of its contribution to the energy security of North America. It is also a symbol of U.S.-Canadian ability to work together cooperatively in the energy area for the benefit of both countries and peoples. This same spirit can be very important in resolving the other problems we face in the energy area.

This waiver of law, submitted to the Congress under Section 8(g) of the Alaska Natural Gas Transportation Act, is designed to clear away governmental obstacles to proceeding with private financing of this important project. It is critical to the energy security of this country that the Federal Government not obstruct development of energy resources on the North Slope of Alaska. For this reason, it is important that the Congress begin expeditiously to consider and adopt a waiver of those laws that impede private financing of the project.

RONALD REAGAN

The White House,
October 15, 1981.

Findings and Proposed Waiver of Law

Pursuant to the provisions of the Alaska Natural Gas Transportation Act of 1976 (ANGTA) 15 U.S.C. § 719, *et seq.*, a transportation system to transport Alaska natural gas to consumers in the continental United States was selected and approved by Congress in 1977.

I find that certain provisions of law applicable to the Federal actions to be taken under Subsections (a) and (c) of Section 9 of ANGTA require waiver in order to permit expeditious construction and initial operation of the approved transportation

system. Accordingly, under the provisions of Section 8(g)(1) of ANGTA, I hereby propose to both Houses of Congress a waiver of the following provisions of law, such waiver to become effective upon approval of a joint resolution under the procedures set forth in Section 8(g)(2), 8(g)(3), and 8(g)(4) of ANGTA.

Waive P.L. 95–158 †[Joint Resolution of approval,* pursuant to Section 8(a) of ANGTA, incorporating the President's *Decision*] in the following particulars:

Section 1, Paragraph 3, and Section 5, Conditions IV–4 and V–1, of the President's *Decision*, in order to permit producers of Alaska natural gas to participate in the ownership of the Alaska pipeline segment and the gas conditioning plant segment of the approved transportation system; *Provided, however,* that any agreement on producer participation may be approved by the Federal Energy Regulatory Commission only after consideration of advice from the Attorney General and upon a finding by the Federal Energy Regulatory Commission that the agreement will not (a) create or maintain a situation inconsistent with the antitrust laws, or (b) in and of itself create restrictions on access to the Alaska segment of the approved transportation system for nonowner shippers or restrictions on capacity expansion; and

Section 2, Paragraph 3, First Sentence, of the President's *Decision*, to include the gas conditioning plant in the approved transportation system and in the final certificate to be issued for the system; and for application to be issued for the system; and the application of Section 5, Condition IV–2 of the President's *Decision* to the gas conditioning plant; and

---

†See: Executive Office of the President, Energy Policy and Planning, *Decision and Report to Congress on the Alaska Natural Gas Transportation System* (September 1977) (hereinafter referred to as President's *Decision*); and see H.J. Res. 621, Pub. L. No. 95–158 (1977), wherein the President's *Decision* was incorporated and ratified by Congress pursuant to Section 8(a) of ANGTA.
* 15 U.S.C. § 719f nt.

Section 5, Condition IV–3, of the President's *Decision; provided,* however, that such waiver shall not authorize the Federal Energy Regulatory Commission to approve tariffs except as provided herein. The Federal Energy Regulatory Commission may approve a tariff that will permit billing to commence and collection of rates and charges to begin and that will authorize recovery of all costs paid by purchasers of Alaska natural gas for transportation through the system pursuant to such tariffs prior to the flow of Alaska natural gas through the approved transportation system—

(a) to permit recovery of the full cost of service for the pipeline in Canada to commence—

(1) upon completion and testing, so that it is proved capable of operation; and

(2) not before a date certain, as determined (in consultation with the Federal Inspector) by the Federal Energy Regulatory Commission in issuing a final certificate for the approved transportation system, to be the most likely date for the approved transportation system to begin operation; and

(b) to permit recovery of the actual operation and maintenance expenses, actual current taxes and amounts necessary to service debt, including interest and scheduled retirement of debt, to commence—

(1) for the Alaska pipeline segment—

(A) upon completion and testing of the Alaska pipeline segment so that it is proved capable of operation; and

(B) not before a date certain, as determined (in consultation with the Federal Inspector) by the Federal Energy Regulatory Commission in issuing a final certificate for the approved transportation system, to be the most likely date for the approved transportation system to begin operation; and

(2) for the gas conditioning plant segment—

(A) upon completion and testing of the gas conditioning plant segment so that it is proved capable of operation; and

(B) not before a date certain, as determined (in consultation with the Federal Inspector) by the Federal Energy Regulatory Commission in issuing a final certificate for the approved transportation system, to be the most likely date for the approved transportation system to begin operation.

Waive Pub. L. No. 688,* 75th Cong., 2d Sess. [Natural Gas Act] in the following particulars:

Section 7(c)(1)(B) of the Natural Gas Act to the extent that section can be construed to require the use of formal evidentiary hearings in proceedings related to applications for certificates of public convenience and necessity authorizing the construction or operation of any segment of the approved transportation system; *provided,* however, that such waiver shall not preclude the use of formal evidentiary hearing(s) whenever the Federal Energy Regulatory Commission determines, in its discretion, that such a hearing is necessary; and

Sections 4, 5, 7, and 16 of the Natural Gas Act to the extent that such sections would allow the Federal Energy Regulatory Commission to change the provisions of any final rule or order approving (a) any tariff in any manner that would impair the recovery of the actual operation and maintenance expenses, actual current taxes, and amounts necessary to service debt, including interest and scheduled retirement of debt, for the approved transportation system; or (b) the recovery by purchasers of Alaska natural gas of all costs related to transportation of such gas pursuant to an approved tariff; and

Sections 1(b) and 2(6) of the Natural Gas Act to the extent necessary to permit the Alaskan Northwest Natural Gas Transportation Company or its successor and any shipper of Alaska natural gas through the Alaska pipeline segment of the approved transportation system to be deemed to be a "natural gas company" within the meaning of the Act at such time as it accepts a final certificate of public convenience and necessity authorizing it to construct or operate the Alaska pipeline segment and the gas conditioning plant segment of the approved

*15 U.S.C. § 717.

transportation system or to ship or sell gas that is to be transported through the approved transportation system; and

Section 3 of the Natural Gas Act as it would apply to Alaska natural gas transported through the Alaska pipeline segment of the approved transportation system to the extent that any authorization would otherwise be required for—

(1) the exportation of Alaska natural gas to Canada (to the extent that such natural gas is replaced by Canada downstream from the export); and

(2) the importation of natural gas from Canada (to the extent that such natural gas replaced Alaska natural gas exported to Canada); and

(3) the exportation from Alaska into Canada and the importation from Canada into the lower 48 states of the United States of Alaska natural gas.

Waive P.L. 94–163* [Energy Policy and

Conservation Act] in the following particulars:

Section 103 as it would apply to Alaska natural gas transported through the Alaska pipeline segment of the approved transportation system to the extent that any authorization would otherwise be required for—

(1) the exportation of Alaska natural gas to Canada (to the extent that such natural gas is replaced by Canada downstream from the export); and

(2) the importation of natural gas from Canada (to the extent that such natural gas replaced Alaska natural gas exported to Canada); and

(3) the exportation from Alaska into Canada and the importation from Canada into the lower 48 states of the United States of Alaska natural gas.

---

*42 U.S.C. § 6201, *et seq.*

Remarks at a Luncheon of the World Affairs Council of Philadelphia in Philadelphia, Pennsylvania
October 15, 1981

Drew Lewis, thank you very much for an introduction that—I couldn't have written it for myself, but—*[laughter]*—thank you. Governor Thornburgh, Mayor Green, Mr. Chairman, the distinguished guests here on the dais and you, ladies and gentlemen:

All in all, I really rather would be in Philadelphia.

I'm grateful for this opportunity to appear before your distinguished group and to share with you our administration's views on an important, upcoming event. I'll be traveling next week to Cancún, Mexico, to participate in a summit that will bring together leaders of two-thirds of the world's population. And the subject of our talks will be the relationships among the developed and the developing nations and, specifically, I hope we can work together to strengthen the world economy and to promote greater economic growth and prosperity for all our peoples.

U.S. foreign policy proceeds from two important premises: the need to revitalize the United States and world economy as a basis for the social and economic progress of our own and other nations, and the need to provide adequate defenses to remain strong, safe, in a precarious period of world history. In this context, U.S. relations with developing countries play a critical role. These countries are important partners in the world economy and in the quest for world peace.

We understand and are sensitive to the diversity of developing countries. Each is unique in its blend of cultural, historical, economic, and political characteristics, but all aspire to build a brighter future. And they can count on our strong support.

We will go to Cancún ready and willing to listen and to learn. We will also take with us sound and constructive ideas designed to help spark a cooperative strategy for global

937

growth to benefit both the developed and developing countries.

Such a strategy rests upon three solid pillars:

—First, an understanding of the real meaning of development, based on our own historical experience and that of other successful countries;

—Second, a demonstrated record of achievement in promoting growth and development throughout the world, both through our bilateral economic relations and through the concentration—or cooperation with our partners in the specialized international institutions, such as the World Bank, the International Monetary Fund;

—And third, practical proposals for cooperative actions in trade, investment, energy, agriculture, and foreign assistance, that can contribute to a new era of prosperity and abundance exceeding anything we may dream possible today.

We very much want a positive development dialog, but sometimes this dialog becomes oversimplified and unproductive. For example, some people equate development with commerce, which they unfairly characterize as simple lust for material wealth. Others mistake compassion for development and claim massive transfers of wealth somehow miraculously will produce new well-being. And still others confuse development with collectivism, seeing it as a plan to fulfill social, religious, or national goals, no matter what the cost to individuals or historical traditions.

All of these definitions miss the real essence of development. In its most fundamental sense, it has to do with the meaning, aspirations, and worth of every individual. In its ultimate form, development is human fulfillment, an ability by all men and women to realize freely their full potential to go as far as their God-given talents will take them.

We Americans can speak from experience on this subject. When the original settlers arrived here, they faced a wilderness where poverty was their daily lot, danger and starvation their close companions. But through all the dangers, disappointments, and setbacks, they kept their faith. They never stopped believing that with the freedom to try and try again, they could make tomorrow a better day.

[Referring to demonstrators shouting in the background] You know, I spoke here in 1975 and there wasn't an echo. [Laughter]

In 1630, John Winthrop predicted that we would be a city upon a hill with the eyes of all people upon us. By 1836, Alexis de Tocqueville was calling America "a land of wonders," where every change seems like an improvement, and what man has not yet done was simply what he hadn't yet attempted to do. And in 1937, Walter Lippmann could draw the lesson that America, for the first time in history, gave men "a way of producing wealth in which the good fortune of others multiplied their own."

Free people build free markets that ignite dynamic development for everyone. And that's the key, but that's not all. Something else helped us create these unparalleled opportunities for growth and personal fulfillment: a strong sense of cooperation, free association among individuals, rooted in institutions of family, church, school, press, and voluntary groups of every kind. Government, too, played an important role. It helped eradicate slavery and other forms of discrimination. It opened up the frontier through actions like the Homestead Act and rural electrification. And it helped provide a sense of security for those who, through no fault of their own, could not support themselves.

Government and private enterprise complement each other. They have, they can, and they must continue to coexist and cooperate. But we must always ask: Is government working to liberate and empower the individual? Is it creating incentives for people to produce, save, invest, and profit from legitimate risks and honest toil? Is it encouraging all of us to reach for the stars? Or does it seek to compel, command, and coerce people into submission and dependence?

Ask these questions, because no matter where you look today, you will see that development depends upon economic freedom. A mere handful of industrialized countries that have historically coupled personal initiative with economic reward now produce more than one-half the wealth of the world. The developing countries now growing the fastest in Asia, Africa, and Latin America are the very ones providing more economic freedom for their people—freedom to choose, to own property, to work at a job of their choice, and to invest in a dream for the future.

Perhaps the best proof that development and economic freedom go hand-in-hand can be found in a country which denies freedom to its people—the Soviet Union. For the record, the Soviets will not attend the conference at Cancún. They simply wash their hands of any responsibility, insisting all the economic problems of the world result from capitalism, and all the solutions lie with socialism.

Well, the real reason they're not coming is they have nothing to offer. In fact, we have just one question for them: Who's feeding whom? I can hardly remember a year when Soviet harvests have not been blamed on "bad weather," and I've seen a lot of harvest seasons, as the press keeps reminding me. [*Laughter*] They've had quite a long losing streak for a government which still insists the tides of history are running in its favor.

The Soviets, of course, can rely on farmers from America and other nations to keep their people fed. But ironically, they have a reliable source of nourishment right in their own country—the 3 percent of all cultivated land that farmers in the Soviet Union are allowed to farm on their own and market. Those who farm that 3 percent of land produce nearly 30 percent of the meat, milk, and vegetables in Russia, 33 percent of the eggs, and 61 percent of the potatoes.

Now, that's why this isn't a question of East versus West, of the U.S. versus the Soviet Union. It's a question of freedom versus compulsion, of what works versus what doesn't work, of sense versus nonsense. And that's why we say: Trust the people, trust their intelligence and trust their faith, because putting people first is the secret of economic success everywhere in the world.

Now I want to talk about the second part of our message at Cancún—our record and that of the international economic system itself in helping developing countries generate new growth and prosperity. Here again, it's time to speak out with candor. To listen to some shrill voices, you'd think our policies were as stingy as your Philadelphia Eagles' defense. [*Laughter*] There is a propaganda campaign in wide circulation that would have the world believe that capitalist United States is the cause of world hunger and poverty.

And yet each year, the United States provides more food assistance to developing nations than all the other nations combined. Last year, we extended almost twice as much official development assistance as any other nation.

The spirit of voluntary giving is a wonderful tradition that flows like a deep, mighty river through the history of our Nation. When Americans see people in other lands suffering in poverty and starvation, they don't wait for government to tell them what to do. They sit down and give and get involved; they save lives. And that's one reason we know America is such a special country.

All that is just one side of the coin. The other, only rarely acknowledged, is the enormous contribution we make through the open, growing markets of our own country. The United States buys approximately one-half of all the manufactured goods that non-OPEC developing countries export to the industrialized world, even though our market is only one-third of the size of the total industrialized world's. Last year, these same developing countries earned twice as much from exports to the United States than they received in aid from all other countries combined. And in the last 2 years alone, they earned more from exports to the United States than the entire developing world has received from the World Bank in the last 36 years.

Even as we work to strengthen the World Bank and other international institutions, let us recognize, then, the enormous contribution of American trade to development.

The barriers to trade in our markets are among the lowest in the world. The United States maintains few restrictions on our custom procedures, and they are very predictable. In 1980, 51 percent of our imports from developing countries entered this country duty free. American capital markets are also more accessible to the developing countries than capital markets anywhere else in the world.

From all this, two conclusions should be clear: Far from lagging behind and refusing to do our part, the United States is leading the way in helping to better the lives of citizens in developing countries. And a major way that we can do that job best, the way we can provide the most opportunity for even the poorest of nations, is to follow through with our own economic recovery program to ensure strong, sustained noninflationary growth. And that's just what we're determined to do.

Every 1 percent reduction in our interest rates, due to lower inflation, improves the balance of payments of developing countries by $1 billion. By getting our own economic house in order, we win, they win, we all win.

Now, just as there is need for a clearer focus on the real meaning of development and our own development record, there's a similar need to be clear about the international economic system. Some argue that the system has failed; others that it's unrepresentative and unfair. Still others say it is static and unchanging, and then a few insist that it's so sound it needs no improvement. Well, we need a better understanding than that.

As I recalled recently before the annual meeting of the World Bank and the IMF, the post-war international economic system was created on the belief that "the key to national development and human progress is individual freedom—both political and economic." This system provided only generalized rules in order to maintain maximum flexibility and opportunity for individual enterprise and an open international trading and financial system.

The GATT, the World Bank, the International Monetary Fund represent free associations of independent countries who accept both the freedom and discipline of a competitive economic system. Let's look at the record of international growth and development under their auspices.

From 1950 to 1980, gross national product, per capita, in 60 middle-income countries increased twice as fast as in the indus-

trial countries when real purchasing power is taken into account. In 1951 to 1979, industry and manufacturing in developing countries also expanded at a faster rate than their counterparts in the industrial countries. Since 1960, export volume for the developing countries, excluding OPEC, grew between 6 and 7 percent a year. Growth was particularly strong in manufactured exports, and even some low-income oil importers participated in this trend. And, concessional assistance grew by 50 percent in real items during the 1970's.

By any standard, this is a remarkable record. It's not a basis for complacency, however. We recognize that despite the progress, many developing nations continue to struggle with poverty, minorities, and the lack of infra-structure, and are seriously affected by disruption in the international economy.

But while much progress remains to be made, we can take pride in what has been accomplished—pride in the efforts of those countries that did most to utilize effectively the opportunities of the system and pride in the system itself for being sufficiently flexible to ensure that the benefits of international commerce flow increasingly to all countries.

Progress is also evident in the evolution of the international institutions themselves. Today approximately two-thirds of the members of GATT are developing countries, whereas only one-half were developing countries when it was created. Also, the resources of both the World Bank and the IMF have increased dramatically, as has the participation of developing country members.

Certainly, the record of the international system is not perfect, but people flirt with fantasy when they suggest that it's a failure and unfair. We know that much must still be done to help low-income countries develop domestic markets, strengthen their exports. But the way to do that is not to weaken the system that has served us so well, but to continue working together to make it better.

Now, this brings me to the third and final part of our message in Cancún—a program for action. This summit offers the leadership of the world an opportunity to chart a domestic course for—a strategic course, I should say, for a new era of international economic growth and development. And to do this, all countries, developed and developing alike, demonstrate the political will to address the real issues, confront the obstacles, and seize the opportunities for development wherever they exist.

To cite that old proverb: "Give a hungry man a fish and he'll be hungry tomorrow; teach him how to fish and he'll never be hungry again."

The principles that guide our international policies can lead to the cooperative strategy for global growth that we seek. The experience of our own country and others confirms the importance of strategic principles:

—first, stimulating international trade by opening up markets, both within individual countries and between countries;

—second, tailoring particular development strategies to the specific needs and potential of individual countries and regions;

—and third, guiding assistance toward the development of self-sustaining productive capacities, particularly in food and energy;

—fourth, improving in many of the countries the climate for private investment and the transfer of technology that comes with such investment;

—and fifth, creating a political atmosphere in which practical solutions can move forward, rather than founder on a reef of misguided policies that restrain and interfere with the international marketplace or foster inflation.

Developing countries cannot be lumped together under the title as if their problems were identical. They're diverse, with distinct resource endowments, cultures, languages, and national traditions. The international system is comprised of independent, sovereign nations, whose separate existence testifies to their unique qualities and aspirations.

What we will seek to do at Cancún and elsewhere in subsequent meetings is examine cooperatively the roadblocks which developing countries' policies pose to development and how they can best be removed. For example: Is there an imbalance between public and private sector activities? Are high tax rates smothering incentives and precluding growth in personal savings and investment capital? And then we must examine the obstacles which developed countries put in the way of development and how they, in turn, can best be removed. For example: Are industrial countries maintaining open markets for the products of developing countries? Do they permit unrestricted access by developing countries to their own capital markets? And finally, we must decide how developed and developing countries together can realize their potential and improve the world economy to promote a higher level of growth and development.

Our program of action includes specific, practical steps that implement the principles I've outlined.

First, stimulating international trade by opening up markets is absolutely essential. Last year, non-OPEC developing nations, by selling their products in American markets, earned $63 billion—just last year. This is more than twice the amount of total development assistance provided to all developing countries in that same year. It's time for all of us to live up to our principles by concrete actions and open markets and liberalized trade.

The most meaningful action that we could take to promote trade with developing nations in the early 1980's is to strengthen the GATT. It is through a shared, reciprocal effort within GATT that further liberalization of industrial nations' trade regimes is most likely to be achieved. This will benefit developing countries more than any other single step.

The United States will work for a successful GATT ministerial meeting in 1982. We'll launch an extensive round of consultations with all countries, including developing countries, to prepare for that GATT meeting. We will join with developing countries in working for an effective safeguards code that reflects our mutual concerns and interests. In addition, we'll continue to support the generalized system of preferences, and we'll take the lead in urging other developing countries to match us in expanding developing nations' access to markets.

Trade's contribution to development can be magnified by aligning trade opportunities more closely with private investment, development assistance, technology sharing. At Cancún, we will make it clear that we're ready to cooperate with other nations in putting in place this kind of integrated, complementary effort.

Actually, we're already doing so, which brings me to the second part of our program—tailoring particular development strategies to the specific needs and potential of individual countries and regions. In our own hemisphere, the United States has joined together with Mexico, Venezuela, and Canada to begin developing flexible, imaginative, and cooperative programs linking trade, investment, finance, foreign assistance, and private sector activities to help the nations in the Caribbean and to help them help themselves.

We met initially in Nassau in July. Consulting then took place with the Central American countries and Panama in Costa Rica, and with the Caribbean countries in Santo Domingo. By year end, we expect to complete consultation and move forward with efforts that are tailored to specific situations in individual countries.

Third, guiding our assistance toward the development of self-sustaining productive activities, particularly in food and energy.

Increasing food production in developing countries is critically important; for some, literally, it's a matter of life or death. It's also an indispensable basis for overall development. The U.S. has always made food and agriculture an important emphasis of its economic assistance programs. We have provided massive amounts of food to fight starvation, but we have also undertaken successful agricultural research, welcomed thousands of foreign students for instruction and training at our finest institutions, and helped make discoveries of the high-yielding varieties of the Green Revolution available throughout the world.

Looking to the future, our emphasis will be on the importance of market-oriented policies. We believe this approach will create rising agricultural productivity, self-sustaining capacity for research and innovation, and stimulation of job-creating entrepreneurship in rural areas.

Specifically, we've encouraged policies which reduce or eliminate subsidies to food consumers and provide adequate and stable price incentives to their agricultural sectors to increase production. We'll emphasize education and innovative joint research and development activities throughout the United States and developing countries' institutions. We will also encourage rural credit, improved storage and distribution facilities, and roads to facilitate marketing.

Now, that's a lot. But we need to do more. The focus will be on raising the productivity of the small farmer, building the capacity to pursue agricultural research, and stimulating productive enterprises that generate employment and purchasing power.

We will emphasize: new methods of plant improvement to develop crops that tolerate adverse soils and climatic conditions, insects, and diseases; research to increase the efficiency of using irrigation water; systems for the production of several crops per year in the humid tropics; and methods of human and animal disease control to remove such serious problems as the tsetse fly in Africa, which bars agricultural production on vast areas of potentially productive land.

Addressing the energy problems of developing countries is also vital to their sustained economic growth. Their net oil bill in 1980 was $46 billion, up from only $4 billion in 1973. This puts tremendous pressure on their balance of payments and threatens development.

The U.S. will emphasize funding for energy-related activities in the years ahead, especially for private efforts and the mobilization of developing countries' resources. Our energy bilateral aid program must stress technical assistance rather than resource transfers. We will support energy lending by multilateral institutions, provided the projects are economically viable and they expand developing country energy production through greater private investment.

We will also support selected elements of the programs of action of the U.N. conference on new and renewable resources of energy. They include intensified energy training programs for technicians from developing countries and efforts to help developing countries assess and more efficiently utilize their resources.

Fourth, improving the climate for private capital flows, particularly private investment. Investment is the lifeblood of development. Private capital flows—commercial lending and private investment—can account for almost 70 percent of total financial flows to developing countries. It's impractical, not to mention foolish, to attack these flows for ideological reasons.

We call upon all our partners in finance and development—business, banks, and developing countries—to accelerate their cooperative efforts. We seek to increase co financing and other private financing with the multilateral development banks. We want to enhance the international activities which foster private sector debt and equity financing of investments in the developing countries. Its program is increasing in both size and diversity and the bulk of IFC [International Finance Corporation] projects are privately financed in the developing countries from domestic and external sources.

We will explore the development of further safeguards for multilateral investment and ways to build upon successful bilateral experiences with these countries. We believe it is important to identify impediments to investment and trade such as conditions of political instability and the threat of expropriation. Working in concert with our trading partners, we'll seek to remove these impediments.

We will attempt to promote a general agreement of investment allowing countries to harmonize investment policies and to negotiate mutually beneficial improvements in the investment climate. Finally, we'll make an effort to identify developed and developing country tax measures which might increase market-oriented investment from both external domestic sources and in the developing countries.

Fifth, and finally, let me turn to the question of how we work together. To a remarkable degree, many nations in the world have now entered into an economic dialog. The choice before us is how to organize and conduct it. Do we persist in contentious

rhetoric, or do we undertake practical tasks in a spirit of cooperation and mutual political will? I think our country has signaled the answer to that question.

We go to Cancún with a record of success and contributions second to none—determined to build on our past, ready to offer our hand in friendship as a partner in prosperity. At Cancún we will promote a revolutionary idea born more than 200 years ago, carried to our shores in the hearts of millions of immigrants and refugees, and defended by all who risked their lives so that you and I and our children could still believe in a brighter tomorrow. It's called freedom, and it works. It's still the most exciting, progressive, and successful idea the world has ever known.

In closing, I want to tell you about something a friend of yours and mine said in a speech in Washington not too long ago. Being a man of vision, with a great admiration for America, he explained that he had come on a mission from his native land—a mission to secure economic progress for his people. And he told his audience:

I am dreaming. Really I am dreaming of a drive like the drive of your grandfathers, the drive to the West. Water we have, land we have, climate we have, farming we have. But we need technology, we need know-how, new ways of irrigation, new ways of agriculture. All this one can find here in America.

And then he pleaded:

Come and be my partners . . . be pioneers like your grandfathers who opened the West and built in 200 years the most powerful country, the richest country, the great United States of America.

Those words were spoken at the U.S. Chamber of Commerce in March 1979, by Anwar Sadat. This courageous man of peace and hope and love has now been taken from us. But his mission, his dream remain. As we proceed to Cancún, can we not join together so that the good he wanted for all people of the world would finally become theirs and his to share? Thank you very much.

Note: The President spoke at 1:50 p.m. in the Grand Ballroom of the Bellevue Stratford Hotel. In his opening remarks, he referred to Secretary of Transportation Drew L. Lewis, Pennsylvania Governor Richard L. Thornburgh, Philadelphia Mayor William J. Green, and Donald E. Meads, chairman of the Council.

Exchange With Reporters on the Sale of AWACS and Other Air Defense Equipment to Saudi Arabia
October 15, 1981

Q. Sir, it looks like you may have lost in the Committee, 9–8.

The President. Yes, that's what I was just going to speak to you about. Frankly, I'm gratified that it was that close. I, of course, would have wished that it would have been the other way. If one of them had a headache and had to go home early or something, it might have. But to be that close—and I still am going to continue believing that we can get it in the Senate vote on the floor.

And Lesley [Lesley Stahl, CBS News], in your earlier question here, I think I left the wrong impression. I was conscious that the press, the media had talked of the possibility of another way of doing this, and that's what I was really commenting on, that we hadn't had any meetings, conferences on it. And we haven't. So I don't know what any possibility there would be on anything of that kind or whether we would consider it or not.

We're going to continue believing that we can get the vote, that the Senate is going to see that this is not only essential—as three former Presidents have been saying for the last few days—to the United States, it's essential to the security of Israel.

We have totally protected the technology; there's no risk to that, and certainly no risk to Israel. And I just have to believe that there will be enough Senators that will recognize the importance to us of having the relationship that this can lead to, where we can continue the peace-making process.

Q. By not ruling out that waiver, sir, don't you leave the inference that if you win in the Senate, fine, but if you don't win, then you'll take it up?

The President. No, this is what I was trying to correct, because we hadn't even considered this. And it's a hypothetical question as it is. And I was commenting because when you asked, I thought, well, this was in connection with the stories that have appeared in the press.

Q. But you will not rule it out completely either, right?

The President. Well, it's a hypothetical question, and I'm not going to—I can't even answer that yet, because I don't know whether I would or not.

Q. Secretary Haig said once a few days ago that he thought you'd do what needed to be done under any circumstances, and it led everyone to believe that you'd use it if you had to.

The President. Well, it's something, as I say, it's hypothetical at the moment because I haven't even—there hasn't been any discussion with me on it.

Q. Did Senator Zorinsky ever call you back?

The President. No. Maybe they called the vote too soon.

Note: The exchange began at 4:25 p.m. at the Bellevue Stratford Hotel, as the President was preparing to depart Philadelphia for the trip to New Jersey.

The discussion concerned the vote of the Senate Foreign Relations Committee on the waiver provision of section 36(b) of the Arms Export Control Act and section 614 of the Foreign Assistance Act.

Remarks at a Republican Fundraising Reception in Whippany, New Jersey
October 15, 1981

Thank you very much. And thank all of you and Ray Donovan for all that you did to get rid of that word "next." [*Laughter*] And the gentleman who said, "Give them hell," that was—someone said that to Harry Truman. He said, "I'll just tell the truth and they'll think it's hell." [*Laughter*] And to Mrs. Kean and to—if the people of New Jersey do what they should—Governor Kean——[*applause*].

Let me clear the air on a misunderstanding that evidently exists with Tom Kean's opponent. It's not true that I'm running for Governor of New Jersey. [*Laughter*] He doesn't seem to know that. And it's not true that I was going to take the social security away from that little old lady on television. [*Laughter*] I'm just trying to keep the program from going bankrupt so she would get her check. But there's one thing about doing a political commercial, she won't get residuals. [*Laughter*]

New Jersey is known as the Garden State, and I'm happy to see the New Jersey Republican Party is about to blossom. Historians will note that in 1980, that was the year that America's working people finally realized that it is the Republican Party that advocates the things they believe in. Nowhere is this political realignment more apparent than right here in New Jersey. A man from New Jersey who was just up here is now my Secretary of Labor, and you can be proud of the job that he's doing. He's a major asset for our administration, and we're proud to have him with us.

During the campaign, you know, we were in here New Jersey, and Ray decided to offer me a chance to get direct feedback from some working people. So one night he took me over to Barrett's Tavern. And I'll have to admit it was one of the more memorable moments of the campaign. [*Laughter*] We not only couldn't get in on the floor of the barroom, they were standing on the bar. [*Laughter*] Finally, it was so jammed there that we had to go out on the

steps and speak to the people outside. But it was a wonderful evening.

Tonight we're here to help the Republican Party, but we're also here to get behind another citizen of New Jersey that you can be proud of, and you know that, too—Tom Kean. Tom exemplifies the common sense that's making the Republican Party the majority party.

One of Tom's heros happens to be Teddy Roosevelt. Well, Teddy is one of my favorites, too. And there's a room named after him in the White House. It's just across the hall from the Oval Office, and on the wall is a plaque with a quote from Teddy. It says, "Aggressive fighting for the right is the noblest sport the world affords."

Well, I think Tom Kean is a regular in that noble sport. Tom is aggressively campaigning on a concrete and specific program. We couldn't ask for a better spokesman for our cause.

I met Tom last year at the Ukranian Festival, during the campaign, and he proved he was resourceful. Because I was a candidate, and Nancy and I were there together, and naturally we couldn't be on the platform at a non-partisan function like that. But Tom just happened to recognize us out there in the audience and thought the people would be happy to see us if we'd stand and take a bow, which we did. [*Laughter*]

He's willing to tell you what he stands for. He wants to cut taxes. He wants to trim excessive spending, create real jobs, and encourage growth. Now, you may think that sounds a little familiar, that you've heard it before. Well, it is. And it's not some complicated formula; it's common sense.

This year, New Jersey is being offered a clear-cut choice between those who think government spending and taxes are the solution to our problems and those, like Tom, who understand that government spending and over taxation are the problems.

At the national level, we're trying to do our part. Tom's courageous support of our

945

economic recovery program is certainly appreciated.

Our tax cut will put $2 billion, or I should say leave $2 billion in the pockets of the people of New Jersey. But in the Congress, Tom's opponent voted no on the tax cut bill. And he voted no on the $35 billion of spending cuts, budget spending cuts. Voting for him would be voting for more of the same thing that got us in this mess that we've been in in the first place.

Now, no one knows better than those of us here in this Republican gathering that the people of New Jersey may be overwhelmingly registered in the other party. But I think they want to vote for candidates who offer positive programs and have faith that we can lick any problem.

The other party gave us inflation, unemployment, sky-high interest rates, and pessimism. We offer monetary and fiscal integrity, lower taxes, more jobs, and hope for a better future. The other party exploits the natural division between business and labor. Republicans are trying to bring all our citizens together in a campaign for economic progress.

We're working closely with a small group of courageous Democrats in the Congress who want to put America back on the right track. With their help, we've accomplished more than any of us thought possible only a year ago. But there's much more to do.

Our economic problems have been building for years, and it'll take time and hard work to set things straight. It'll also require us to enlist others to help us in the struggle at the national and the State levels. And that isn't impossible. Don't be afraid to reach out. You can't get elected in New Jersey without some Democrat help, and they're ready to help.

The day before—well, yesterday—I was going to say the day before yesterday, but yesterday, I had the supreme thrill and pleasure of escorting a gentleman out into the Rose Garden and there, with the press assembled, I presented the 193d Republican Congressman. He was the 193d without a single election. He was Democratic Congressman Atkinson from Pennsylvania, who came with me into the Rose Garden to announce publicly that he had just become a Republican.

And very frankly, I think we're going to see more of that in the days ahead. Having been a Democrat for most of my adult life, I can vouch for the pain that is involved in changing registrations. [*Laughter*] But they're going to do it. Some of them are very resentful for the fact that after they supported us for the budget cuts and the tax cuts, they were then taken into the leadership of their party and castigated and told, "Don't do it again. Maybe we'll forgive you this time, but we'll watch how you behave yourselves." That isn't the way we run things in the United States, and there are a number of them that are ready to say so, and that will soon happen.

I firmly believe there are a host of Democrats out there ready to jump on board if we stand firm in our principles and offer them a chance to join us in putting America's house back in order. You've got a tremendous potential here in New Jersey to build this new coalition, and the whole country is watching. You know, you're one of only three States that has a gubernatorial election this year. And I know, of course, you have other elections, too, and your candidates are here for the assembly, those other candidates, and if you're going to send Tom Kean up there, don't send him alone. Send him with that help that he's going to need.

And why is this so important? Well, part of one thing I haven't mentioned here, in connection with our program of economic recovery—I believe that part of our troubles are because back over the years, the leadership of the opposing party has step-by-step taken us away from the constitutional principle that we are a federation of sovereign States, and they have tried to reduce the States to administrative districts of an all-powerful Federal Government. And the Federal Government has tried to do things that the Federal Government is not able to do. We're going to give this country back the way the Constitution intended, that as many things as possible are going to be in the authority and the autonomy of the State and local governments, not in the power of the Federal Government.

And to do that, you're going to need a Governor that isn't a stooge for the Federal Government taking over more power. And he's going to need those other candidates to help him bring this about, and then to responsibly manage those programs that we're going to turn back—and to the greatest extent possible, along with the sources of revenue, as we progress, to help pay for those programs.

Now, I believe our program will work, but I also believe it will work better if Tom Kean is the Governor of New Jersey and these people are here to help him.

Thank you very much.

Note: The President spoke at 6:57 p.m. in the Grand Ballroom at Birchwood Manor. In his opening remarks, he referred to Secretary of Labor Raymond J. Donovan and Tom Kean, Republican candidate for Governor of New Jersey.

In introducing the President, Secretary Donovan referred to the many times in the past when he had introduced Mr. Reagan as the "next" President of the United States.

Statement on the Death of Moshe Dayan of Israel
October 16, 1981

We are deeply saddened to learn of the death of Moshe Dayan—a courageous soldier and a great Israeli statesman. Dayan provided his nation with military leadership that was the envy of the world. His bold strategies brought him victory on the battlefield and respect from friend and foe alike.

His service as a statesman was no less distinguished. He demonstrated those inner qualities of goodwill and integrity that are essential for peace and security.

Seldom does a foreign general and a statesman receive such admiration from Americans as did Moshe Dayan. His image became to many the symbol of Israeli resolve—the resolve of a great people to be free and independent, and a resolve shared by the people of the United States.

Reflecting on his passing and other recent tragic events, we must note that the Middle East may be entering a new era. Let us pray this will be an era of peace, when all nations and people in that region will live together in harmony. This, after all, was the cause of Moshe Dayan.

Remarks and a Question-and-Answer Session at a Working Luncheon With Out-of-Town Editors
October 16, 1981

The President. Well, I am grateful to Joe Sterne[1] for putting this group together, issuing the invitations and being so helpful to Karna[2] in arranging this briefing.

And now that I've gotten—[*inaudible*]— to recognize someone who's familiar with

---

[1] *Joe Sterne, Baltimore Sun.*
[2] *Karna Small, Director of Media Relations and Planning.*

the locale. They keep me busy reading a lot of other things, but I still manage to keep up with the papers. And the White House News Summary includes editorials from all of the papers that are represented here, as well as others.

And I know that on the editorial page, usually, the cartoons run. And there was one from a paper the other day that I was very happy to see, because it was for all those people that want instant results for changes in something that have taken several decades to be installed here in government. I don't know how many carried it. It's this cartoon of the group. I'll pass it around the table so you can see it. And the radio reporter, so you'll be happy to know, or TV reporter is saying, "And so it seems clear to this reporter that Reaganomics has failed, failed to thrive in a climate of optimism, failed to blossom into a viable economic alternative, failed to bear the fruit of prosperity—at least in these first five disappointing minutes." [*Laughter*]

Well, I think we should, because it is a working lunch, get to the questions. And as I said the other day when we had a briefing with some people from the Defense Department over here, I said that we will decide that etiquette does not prevail, and speaking with your mouth full will be considered a military necessity. [*Laughter*]

Ms. Small. Something else, Mr. President. This afternoon, as soon as they leave here, they will be meeting with David Stockman and with Secretary Drew Lewis on transportation issues, and they will also be hearing from Secretary Schweiker from HHS. So, you know, if they ask you something really technical and—you know, they will be hearing from those people on those issues later on this afternoon.

The President. All right.

Virginia Gubernatorial Campaign

Q. Mr. President, may I ask you a Virginia question? As you know, we have one of the two Governors' races, I think, in the country this year, between Chuck Robb, otherwise known as "LBJ's son-in-law," and Marshall Coleman. Have you made specific plans to come into Virginia to campaign for Marshall?

The President. I understand I am scheduled to. I was scheduled there for a reception, and it had to be canceled because of the live broadcast. Yes, I am scheduled now for an appearance in his behalf.

Mr. Meese.[3] I think it's week after next.

The President. Yes.

Q. Do you know when it is exactly?

_____

[3] *Counsellor to the President Edwin Meese III.*

Mr. Meese. I think it's the 27th of October. That's my belief. But, Karna, we could find out for sure. Is that right, Pete?[4]

Mr. Roussel. Yes.

Q. Is that in Tidewater—Norfolk, Virginia Beach area?

Mr. Roussel. I don't know about the locations they worked out——

President's Talks With Senators on AWACS

Q. Mr. President, did you make any converts this morning?

The President. Usually, I've found out they don't tell you whether you have or not when they go out. They wait, and you find out what they say to your people when they get outside whether they have or not. And some of them, very honestly, are really undecided and have heard this, and they want to take it back with everything else that they've heard on the other side and make their decision by themselves later.

So I don't press for that, and every one of them—there are no wrinkles in his sleeve when he goes out. [*Laughter*]

Q. You've got 51 names on that little list you have in your pocket. [*Laughter*]

The President. I wish I did. I wish I had a list in my pocket.

I don't know; I'm confident. And I think we're going to get it, because there are a number of them that have expressed themselves that regardless of their own personal feelings, they are concerned about interfering with the foreign policy effort that we're putting forth. Because we see this as very definitely a part of our ability to help in the peacemaking process over there in the Middle East; that the Saudi Arabians are very key to this. And we've had their help already, and so on, in things that lead us to believe that going forward at this and establishing this kind of a relationship with them will bear fruit.

The Palestinian Question

Q. Another Middle East question, sir. I see President Eisenhower's picture hanging in here. And I was in the Middle East last year for my newspaper and talked to a lot

_____

[4] *Deputy Press Secretary Peter Roussel.*

of people, including a lot of Palestinian Arabs, and they would often say that, "We remember Mr. Eisenhower with fondness. He seemed to understand the Arab cause."

We have the Palestinian problem in the news again with the comments by Presidents Carter and Ford. The autonomy talks are starting up again soon. Just interested in your general view of the Palestinian question. Do you think that these are people with a legitimate grievance? Is it something that goes back to the late forties and the founding of Israel? How do you see that problem?

The President. Well, I think wherever it may come from, you've got a million and a half people who are living there as homeless and refugees. I don't mean homeless in the sense of no shelter; that's being taken care of. But I think that problem—they have to be a part of the problem. And as those two gentlemen said, one of the keys is that you can't deal with someone or negotiate with someone as long as they maintain that position that they don't recognize Israel's right to exist as a nation.

Now, here again is one of the reasons we believe the Saudi Arabians can be a great help in changing that, changing that position, just as Egypt once changed their position. And, at the same time, I think that maybe they could be of help in broadening the representation of the Palestinians.

You know, the PLO is a self-announced voice for the Palestinians; no one elected them. And I think that it would be—that if this other takes place, if they acknowledge Israel's right to exist, that it ought to be broadened and there ought to be people—perhaps you could find leadership among some of the mayors of those communities on the West Bank and so forth. But that has to be a part of it.

Saudi Arabia's Role in the Middle East

Q. What kind of expectations do you have about what the Saudis might be willing to say about Israel's right to exist?

The President. Well, the best evidence that we have that—first of all, they're as concerned about the threat to the Middle East by the Soviet Union as, I think, we are.

They have seen those puppet governments installed around them with the proxy troops and so forth. They have seen the ability of—now, with Iran in chaos and the Soviets in Afghanistan, they've seen the ease with which the Kuwait oil installations were bombed. They know that they're vulnerable, their oil fields are vulnerable to such an attack.

But I think they want to be a part of the West. They associate more with our views and our philosophy.

In the Lebanon situation, when we'd sent Phil Habib over there, there came a point in which it was close to blowing up. The triggers were ready to be pulled. And he called us, and he told us of a gentleman from part of the establishment in Saudi Arabia who was here in the United States. He wasn't here on any official mission. He wasn't here in Washington. And we contacted him, that man, and on a Saturday afternoon, late afternoon, he was here in the White House, or in the Oval Office. We told him what it was we wanted and what we believed might forestall this blowup. And by evening, he was on a plane headed for Saudi Arabia, and he delivered our message to Prince Fahd. And within 12 hours, Prince Fahd was dealing with the Syrians and with the PLO. And Habib says there would have been no cease-fire without their intervention.

Now, this is what leads us to believe that with that kind of leadership and position in the Arab world, that if we go forward with this AWACS deal, that we will have further strengthened our credibility with them and our peacemaking ability in the Middle East. If we don't, I believe we could lose all credibility. And what could I say in trying to negotiate with them in the future? They could say, "Well, we don't know whether anything you tell us is right, because you may not be able to deliver."

And we think it's vital. This is why Sadat was so strong in support of this. And it's why the other day that group of 17 gentlemen that we had over in the White House for lunch, ranging from Henry Kissinger all the way back to people who'd been associated with administrations as far back as before Eisenhower, Democrat and Republican—all of them willing to go forward and stand out on the Portico with me and announce that they were in support of the AWACS sale on the belief that it was essential to Israel's security and essential to our security. And so this is why we're putting up the fight.

President's Talks With Senators on AWACS

Q. Mr. President, there have been some reports that you and/or Mr. Meese are giving away everything but Mrs. Reagan's new china to seal this bargain with the Senate. [*Laughter*] Would you comment on that generally and on, specifically, some charges that you either would run or would not run against Democrats who sided with you on this?

The President. I am delighted with that question and a chance to answer it. And incidentally, I'm going to preface it by taking Nancy off the spot. She didn't buy any china—[*laughter*]—and she didn't even get any contributions to buy china. The china itself was a gift from a foundation to the White House, as is most of the furniture in the White House—all the antiques and the paintings and so forth. And the company, a New Jersey company agreed to, because this foundation was buying it, to sell it at cost to them. So, the china is being a gift to the White House and, incidentally, the first new set of full china since Harry Truman's time.

But now, to get back to the other. No, we don't make deals. And I've said pretty much to everyone that we have over, and to the last four which made me late here, I said pretty much just what I've said to you about the necessity of this, plus the fact that I feel we can guarantee the security of the technology and the security of Israel in this. As a matter of fact, when Mr. Begin left here after his visit, and I told him what we were going to do, he told me he was going to maintain his position but he was not upset at all. And he left saying to others, not to us, but to others, that he believed he had the best understanding with us that he has had with any administration in Washington.

I don't know where these stories came from. Well, I know one that I will be honest about. This was back in the budget battle when the Boll Weevils were so stalwart in their support, it made it a bipartisan pack-

age. One day, one of them said, "You know, some of us, we wonder now after we've all been together on this," and this was before it had been passed even, he said, "We wonder if you're going to come down into our districts and campaign against us." And they didn't ask anything at all, but I volunteered how I actually feel. I said, "There's no way that I could go down and have any respect for myself and campaign against any of you individuals that have been doing what you've been doing."

Q. Would that presumably hold true for those who have sided with you on AWACS——

The President. I never said that about the AWACS deal.

Q. Would you care to say something now?

The President. No, it's never been asked and I'm quite sure that—there was a bond; those Boll Weevils kind of—there was almost a total agreement on ideology, on policy, and everything else with them. I think the AWACS deal can find people who could vote yes on that, then be against us on the budget and the tax program and everything else. We're still representing two differing policies.

MX Missile System

Q. Mr. President, let me bring up the MX issue if I might. Since your proposals were announced, General Jones and Senator Tower, among others, have questioned the survivability of missiles even in super-hardened sites. Since strategic weapons really get down to a question of perceptions in international affairs, is there a danger that this kind of reaction could undercut the credibility of your MX program with the rest of the world, particularly with Moscow?

The President. No, I don't believe so, because, first of all, the Air Force itself—there's been, I know, a lot of reporting of General Jones' opposition to this, his favoring the multiple shelters—but the Air Force is divided on that. Now, I agree that there is a vulnerability even in the hardened silos, but there is also the same vulnerability in the multiple shelters. It's as simple as this: What we're buying is some time while we try to narrow that window of vulnerability.

The Soviet Union—it will take them a few years to improve the accuracy and the power of their missiles, enough to make them vulnerable in those hardened silos. By the same token, if we put them in the multiple shelters, all they'd have to do there is build enough warheads to cover the whole area of shelters. They wouldn't try to pick out which one's got the missiles in it. They'd just destroy them all.

So, in either way, there is an ultimate vulnerability to either system. We feel that the other was so costly and so destructive, you might say, of the countryside and all, that as long as it was also going to be vulnerable, that we would proceed with this one which will buy us the time to, as I say, narrow the gap.

The only real defense so far that either side has with regard to intercontinental ballistic missiles is the threat that we both represent. In other words, if we balance them enough that they know that our retaliation could be more than they want to afford, then they'll restrain from a first strike. And I suppose the same thing holds with us, although we've never taken a position that we'd ever make a first strike.

In the meantime, we really mean that we're going to go forward with them and try to persuade them into a program of not limitation, but a program of actual reduction of these strategic weapons.

We will start in November the negotiation on theatre nuclear forces. Now, that doesn't mean the tactical weapons that will be used, soldiers against soldiers. Those are the theatre nuclear weapons like their SS–20's, that are targeted in on every city in Europe. And there's no defense and nothing comparable on the NATO side to that.

So, we're hopeful that maybe some of the systems, the very systems we're talking about, won't ever have to be completed. But right now, all we've committed to is 36—those missiles going into the old Titan silos and some of the Minuteman 3 silos. And we're still studying what might be the way to use the other 64 or the way to base them. And we haven't ruled anything out or anything in on that.

European Peace Movement

Q. One other thing. You mentioned the theatre nuclear weapon negotiations in Europe. How great a danger do you perceive of the European peace movement that's growing up and that had a quarter of a million people gathered in Bonn last weekend? How can the United States capture the peace issue instead of having it used against our country?

The President. Well, I think that we're up against the result of a long-time propaganda campaign. I think that some of those—while some are maybe very well meaning, I think a great many of those demonstrators represent the same kind of people we've seen in some demonstrations in our own country, whose philosophy is a little different than most of ours. And I think the propaganda that has led to this, the ability to turn it on, can be traced back to the Soviet Union. But still, we haven't had any result as far as the Europeans—our allies, their governments, falling back or falling away from the installation of these weapons.

Farm Price Supports

Q. Mr. President, the farmers back home are bringing in very big crops now, and they're facing also very low prices—prices that are lower than the cost of production. And your administration is fighting the higher farm price supports. What do you say to farmers who are confronting this problem?

The President. Well, I know this in a non sequitur, but I grew up in an era in which the only thing the farmer ever worried about was not getting a good crop. And it seemed kind of strange to me that today they can get a bumper crop, and it destroys them instead of help[s] them.

One thing, I think that—and I've said this before—I believe that we need to cooperate in the creation of more world markets, so that a farmer can look forward to a bumper crop and know that there's a market out there for it. I think that you can't pull the rug out from under them in a program that's been instituted for about four decades or more. But what I would like to see us work toward is a free marketplace and let them be governed by the marketplace.

If we go back to the days when this started—grew out of the Great Depression—you'll find that only about 20 to 25 percent of agriculture was ever in the system of supports and limitations. And the other 75 to 80 percent of farming was showing, year after year, a per capita increase in the consumption of what it produced. The government-subsidized part was showing a reduction in the per capita consumption. And I think it's significant that prior to the Carter administration, under Earl Butz, the support program got down from several billion dollars to only about $600 million, and net farm increase in the country increased by 16 percent. And under the Carter administration when we went back—and it went back up to about $6½ billion of price supports, net farm income decreased 14 percent.

So, I think the marketplace has proven itself if given a chance. But as I say, you can't just instantly say, "Well, you're out there on your own," not when they've based everything they do and all their planning on this other system. So, what we're trying to do is work with them toward a program that will, if we can, get back to the free marketplace. But at the same time, as I say, I believe the government has a function it can perform in helping to bring about an expansion of markets worldwide.

Saudi Arabia and Iran

Q. Mr. President, could you tell us in some more detail what you meant in your last press conference when you said that we would not permit Saudi Arabia to become another Iran?

The President. Yes, I said that because the question was asked in the sense of, "Well, what if Saudi Arabia went like Iran and they had our planes there and so forth?"

What I had in mind was that I don't believe that the Shah's government would have fallen if the United States had made it plain that we would stand by that government and support them in whatever had to be done to curb the revolution and let it be seen that we still felt that we were allied with them. But I think that the United States made it very evident that we weren't going to. As a matter of fact, we gave him very bad advice at the time and restrained him for some time.

I have been told by someone very knowledgeable and involved at that time, that there was a point at which the revolution, so-called, could have been headed off with the arrest of 500 individuals—just the arrest. They weren't executing people like they are now. And we advised against that.

And I suppose what I meant was that if we will make it plain that we recognize we have a stake in the Middle East and that we are going to stand by our friends and allies there, both Israel and those nations like Egypt and the Sudan and so forth, that I don't think that the same thing will happen, that kind of an overthrow would take place.

I think that if we, on the other hand, retreat and step back fearfully and say, "Well, we don't know what's going to happen in the Middle East, to Egypt or anyone else, and we better stay clear," then I think that we can bring about——

Saudi Arabia and AWACS

Q. Would you be prepared to side openly with the ruling Saudis in case of a revolution there and help suppress it?

The President. My belief is that it won't happen if we're evident there. But again, as I should have said earlier, the fear that prompted that question was a fear of our technology falling into strange hands. Well, that is a groundless fear also, because the technology that will be involved in this sale is not the ultimate technology that we ourselves possess; that is equipment that is not part of the sale. It is an effective, sophisticated radar system, but it is nothing that can't be found in the British Nimrod, in the planes that Israel itself has put into that service, their own surveillance planes. And I think the Warsaw Pact with the Soviets is making progress with the same type of thing.

The thing that makes our own AWACS plane, when we use it, exceptional, is an additional piece of equipment. So, I think there wasn't really any need for their worrying about that or that question.

The Budget's Impact on Older Industrial Cities

Q. Mr. President, there's some concern in older industrial cities like Chicago that they're really going to get hit with a double whammy by your budget. First, they're going to be losing a lot in some domestic programs and second, that the great bulk of defense spending will be going to the South and to the West. And all the tax advantages for businesses will apply equally to the South and the West, and also that the severance taxes that energy-rich States are charging are reaping so many billions that they'll be able to give incentives to industry that a city like Chicago just can't give. Do you have any program for counteracting—[*inaudible*]?

The President. Well, I think we're conscious of where we can—without increasing the cost or lowering the quality—where we can give contracts. The Northeast is going to get them up there—particularly by way of the Navy buildup—is going to get additional work out of the defense program. It is true that the missiles and the planes are basically built both in the South and the West. That's been true of the airplane industry for quite some time, and yet not exclusively—there are subcontracts in the building of all of those planes and things that are spread around the country somewhat.

Actually, we can't pretend that this whole program—that everyone isn't going to have to share a little bit in what happens. But at the same time, we think that continued inflation is a bigger threat than anything we're doing and could be the ultimate destruction for all of us.

And we believe that our program is going to be successful. It already is bringing inflation down. It's in single digits now, and I was interested to see that our Nobel economics prize winner, Milton Friedman, has just been quoted as saying that he believes it'll be down to 6 percent next year.

Federal Reserve Board

Q. Mr. President, are you satisfied with the performance or the policies of the Federal Reserve Board now, in managing the money supply and the interest rates?

The President. Well, we know that we have to have a consistent monetary policy that doesn't do what we've done over the last few decades, of the roller coaster effect—of when unemployment gets out of hand and it looks like hard times, they flood the market with paper money. And then when that brings on inflation, then all of a sudden you pull in and tighten it down and you go the other way. This is what's been happening.

I do have one little criticism, and yet I can see how it happened. You realize that we can visit with them, but we can't impose on them. They're totally autonomous. But it is true, recently, that they have two lines going up, a kind of a bracket, following productivity in the country, and they are trying to keep the money supply between those two lines. It may fluctuate a little bit, but staying between those two lines. And sometime back, they fell below their bottom line in this. And then they were faced with the prospect of trying to have a stable monetary policy to help in the fight against inflation. They didn't know how to just get back up where they should be without it looking like when on Wall Street they would look at the money supply and see this surge, they'd say, "Oh, oh, here we go again," and start acting as if, well, it was the same old game being played.

But I think that gradually they have moved back up into that, and that's why you've seen two and a half points drop in the prime rate just in recent weeks—the last one being just a few days ago. I think you're going to see some of that kind of nibbling away at the high rates for the next few months. But I believe as we go through next year, we are going to see a definite fall, because there will be that fall in inflation.

The other part, of course, I could say, also, that we're penalized a little bit, too, because those interest rates have thrown our figures off somewhat on what the budget cuts will do or what our deficits will be because of the price we have to pay to pay for the deficits that are already there.

And may I remind you that in 1981, the year we've just concluded, fiscal year, was the year that we were promised the budget was going to be balanced. And the deficit is somewhere in the neighborhood of 55 to 60 billion dollars. I don't know just what the figure is for the off-budget deficits. Now, that's money that you have to go into the capital market and borrow, and I don't claim any responsibility for it, because we weren't running the show.

You know, something that none of you have mentioned very much that I think you might be interested in is that not only did they say that it would be balanced, but we've operated—and I believe this is probably the first time, maybe I'm wrong— we've operated a whole fiscal year without a budget. And right now, the leadership in the House side is making it look as if they're going to start onto the second year. There has been no budget for 1981. They have simply passed continuing resolutions of spending, and in this way there was no way to get the handle on the spending in '81, and that's why we have that size deficit.

But right now, we're now into 1982, and we still don't have a budget. And the first continuing resolution that came down came down at a rate that was higher than the rate that they themselves passed when they passed the budget cuts, which means that they're ignoring their own action in passing those budget cuts. And—[inaudible]—now, that if we continue on with these spending resolutions. And at the same time, they've taken away from the President the right to impound or hold back any of that spending.

Now, you ladies and gentlemen wouldn't like to start an editorial campaign to give the President the right of line item veto, would you? [Laughter]

Your Governors all have it; I had it as a Governor. And the States, most of them, have a balanced budget clause in their constitution, and it works. Why should Uncle Sam think it's above all of that?

The Line Item Veto

Q. Do you think you inherently have that right, Mr. President, not to spend money, as President?

The President. I think that as long as—I think the whole budget policy, let me answer it this way: The whole budget policy of the Federal Government is a kind of a Rube Goldberg thing that doesn't make as much sense as it does in any State in the Union, and that is, it's called the President's budget. But about 80 percent of it is mandated on the President by actions of Congress. And then the President sends over a suggested budget, and the Congress, with no regard for what the estimated revenues are going to be in the coming year, does whatever they want to do to it. And again, the President doesn't have line item. He has to accept the whole budget or none at all.

And let me just cite what seems to me to make sense. As Governor of California, it was called the Governor's budget. Every year a group of experts from the private sector and government met and estimated the revenues. And over 25 years of this custom in California, that group never missed by more than 1 percent their estimate of what the revenues would be in the coming year, and then that 1 percent was on estimating them too low. Never did they go overboard and say, "Oh, we're going to have a lot more money" than we ended up having.

Then the Governor—with all the requests from the various departments coming in, programs from the Congress—the Governor worked out the budget with his people and submitted it to the legislature. The legislature could take out anything they wanted to take out, and the Governor could not put it back in. But by the same token, the legislature could put in things and the Governor could veto those things out, line item. Then it went back, and the Congress, if they could get a two-thirds vote to override the veto, could put them back in, so that you had a double control working back and forth between Congress, or the legislature, and the Governor.

And the system, why something of that kind couldn't work—I suggested it to Tip O'Neill when I first came here, and he acted as if I was threatening the very province of Congress and taking away all their rights. Well, all their rights have given us a $1 trillion deficit. Now, why couldn't such a system of that kind at the Federal level be just as effective as it is at the State level?

After all, the State of California is 10 percent of the population of the Nation.

But when you say that, yes, I think there should be some method of checking. There is no restraint on Congress passing any spending program they want. I could veto that program, but how many of the spending items are hung on as amendments to a bill that you can't veto? And some of the things that have been performed in the past, of hanging an amendment on, let's say, the social security payments—that's so farfetched an example, it didn't—but I mean like a welfare program that's very essential. And you can't veto the amendment, and you can't say no, and suddenly shut off the welfare checks.

Ms. Small. Mr. President, I just want to make one comment. The President hasn't had an opportunity to eat his lunch yet, and I thought if anybody had a question, maybe to direct to Mr. Meese just for a moment, to give the President an opportunity to eat.

The President. You ate your lunch. That's cheating. [*Laughter*]

Government Intrusion Into the People's Lives

Q. I can direct this question to Mr. Meese, as well, and perhaps if the President disagrees he can say so.

The President campaigned on a platform of getting the government off the backs of people, and yet we find the administration trying to make it more difficult to get information out of the government under the Freedom of Information Act. There are proposals advocated by the administration for preventive detention and for modifying the exclusionary rule to make it possible for government agents to break the law and to have their evidence admitted. There's talk about a change in the Executive order governing the CIA to enlarge the CIA's area of activity in domestic matters. Now, does this seem to you a contradiction to this pledge to get the government off the backs of people?

The President. I'm sorry; I'm eating. [*Laughter*] Go ahead.

Mr. Meese. I'm sure the President would answer it much better than I would.

The President. No.

Mr. Meese. Let me just say, first of all, a lot of the premises that you state are incorrect. We have actually gotten the government off of the backs of people amazingly well in just the first 10 months. For example, on regulations, the regulatory reform package I guess can best be summed up by looking at the *Federal Register,* which is about a third less the number of pages just because there are less than half as many proposed regulations this year than there were at this time a year ago. So that in terms of the kinds of regulations that impose upon individuals, labor and management, business and industry, we think we've made major strides in that regard.

Now, on the specifics you're talking about. The Freedom of Information Act, I think most people who have examined it would agree, can use some reform. We have—it has actually imposed a tax burden upon the public, and it's been misused by a lot of people. You take a person like Philip Agee, the renegade ex-CIA person. It's cost the government $500,000 to provide information to him under the Freedom of Information Act, which he then uses against our country. And I don't think this is what was intended by those of you—and I suspect most of you supported the Freedom of Information Act—and I don't think it's what was intended by Congress.

So, it's the reforms in this direction. As a matter of fact, some of the reforms are designed to make it easier for the news media to obtain information. And I think there's a great interest—I don't know whether Jon Rose[5] has talked with you yet?

Q. Yes, sir.

Mr. Meese. But I think there's a great interest in working out with responsible members of the news media any problems that you have with the proposed reforms. That's one item.

Let's talk about the CIA, because that's easy. There is absolutely nothing in the proposed intelligence order which will expand the ability of the CIA to engage in domestic spying. That is totally false, and it's propa-

---

[5] *Jonathan Rose, Assistant Attorney General, Office of Legal Policy, Department of Justice.*

ganda being put out by some staffers on the Hill who were part of Frank Church's infamous intelligence committee that was so destructive of our intelligence authorities some years ago.

Take the preventive detention, which is a name put upon a bail provision. The Constitution provides that bail shall be reasonable. What we're suggesting, what the Attorney General's task force has brought up, is that there would be a reasonable standard of bail. And we think that to take a person who has proved, by committing another crime while out on bail for a first crime, that they should be let out on bail again and again, we don't think that's reasonable. So, we're looking for some modifications of bail, to look at the protection of society, along with the ability of people to get out prior to their trial.

And finally, on the exclusionary rule, I don't think anybody who's studied the exclusionary rule would believe that that's been beneficial to society. It does not allow illegal acts by police. What it does is, it provides a good faith rule. Many times a police officer has to make a decision in 30 seconds, or at least in 5 minutes at the most, on whether he will make a search or a stop or something like that. And he does it under all the applicable law at that time. Two years later, by a 4–3 decision in a State court or a 5–4 decision of the United States Supreme Court, they decide that he was wrong, and they change the law. And it applies retroactively to what that officer did. So, what we're suggesting is that a rule of reason be established to say that if the officer was acting in good faith under the applicable laws of that time, then he should not be penalized and the evidence should not be excluded against an obviously guilty person.

So, in essence, I don't think any of these moves are inconsistent with our ideas of getting the government off the backs of the people.

The President. May I add—and incidentally, because I saw you noticing that was saccharin I put in there, and I have pledged I will not give any of it to Canadian rats. [*Laughter*]

Just one example, and I'm going to take this, on the exclusionary rule, because Cali-

fornia had a classic case of this a few years ago. Two narcotics agents in San Bernardino, California, had enough evidence to get a warrant to search a home, a couple living there that they believed was peddling heroin. And they searched the home and they didn't find the heroin. But as they were leaving, one of them, on a hunch, went back to the baby's crib. There was a baby. He took its diapers off and there was the heroin, stashed inside the diapers. And they went to court. And the judge threw the case out of court on the basis that the baby's constitutional rights had been violated by taking its diapers off without its permission. [*Laughter*]

And I told that story publicly once, and one of the Secret Service agents assigned to me came up afterward, and he said, "I thought you'd like to know, I was one of those narcotic agents, and that's when I quit, changed jobs, and became a Federal agent." [*Laughter*]

Strategic Nuclear Weapons

Q. Mr. President, I'd like to take you back to strategic weapons in Europe again, a couple of things you said. I guess I think that some of the people in Europe who are opposed to some of our policies are afraid that they may wind up as kind of proxy victims in a war between us and the Soviet Union, which—a fear that may be a little more, seem a little more plausible because of all the conversation about integrated battlefields and limited use of nuclear weapons. And I wonder—you must think about this—do you believe that there could be a limited exchange of nuclear weapons between us and the Soviet Union, or that it would simply escalate inevitably?

The President. I don't honestly know. I think, again, until someplace—and I know that all over the world there's research going on to try and find the defensive weapon against strategic nuclear weapons. There never has been a weapon that someone hasn't come up with a defense. But except in this one, the only defense is, "Well, if you shoot yours, we'll shoot ours." And if you still had that kind of a stalemate, I could see where you could have the exchange of tactical weapons against troops in the field without it bringing either one of the major powers to pushing the button.

The intermediate thing—and this is to call your attention to where SALT was so much at fault—is that we have our allies there who don't have an ocean between them, so it doesn't take intercontinental ballistic missiles, it just takes ballistic missiles of the SS–20 type. Well, the SS–20's will have, with what they're adding, 750 warheads—one of them capable of pretty much leveling a city. And they can sit right there and that's got all of Europe, including England and all, targeted. And the only comparable thing that has come along is now our proposal. And this is what's at argument there, is to provide and put on European soil the Pershings and the cruise missiles, so that, again, you've got this same kind of a stalemate, although, even so, ours do not have the range to really reach the depths of Russia. Russia's too far expanded, and the rest of Europe is too concentrated, so they can destroy where we can't.

And the SS–20's were not even considered a strategic weapon, because they didn't cross an ocean. In that SALT treaty there was no restriction on them, just as there was no restriction where they called our old B–52's strategic bombers, they didn't call their Backfire bombers, and we agreed to that in that treaty.

But these are the weapons, these—now what I call strategic, these theatre weapons, that are in the theatre of war, potential war, but would be used strategically, that we want to limit, and that's what we're going to start talking about on November 20th. This does not touch upon the actual tactical weapon, the thing that's fired out of one of our 8-inch guns, a shell that would be fired. And there we would kind of be on the other side of the fence, because the conventional supremacy of the Soviet Union is so great at this point that if—and I wouldn't be surprised if they would throw this at us in the negotiations—that if they should say, "Well, let's do away with the tactical weapons, too," then what's to stop them? You know they outnumber us in every conventional weapon, thousands of tanks, more than the NATO defense can have. At the moment, the only stalemate to them is the tactical nuclear weapon that

would be aimed at those tanks, if they ever started to roll forward.

Q. Do you think there could be a battlefield exchange without having buttons pressed all the way up the line?

The President. Well, I would—if they realized that we—if we went back to that stalemate, only because our retaliatory power, our seconds, or our strike at them after their first strike would be so destructive that they couldn't afford it, that would hold them off.

I do have to point out that everything that has been said and everything in their manuals indicates that, unlike us, the Soviet Union believes that a nuclear war is possible. And they believe it's winnable, which means that they believe that you could achieve enough superiority, then your opponent wouldn't have retaliatory strike capacity.

Now, there is a danger to all of us in the world as long as they think that. And this, again, is one of the things that we just want to disabuse them of. I feel very strongly about the negotiations for reduction. But I also feel that one of the things that's been lacking in the last several years in any negotiations was they sat on their side of the table and had nothing to lose. And we had nothing to threaten them with. Now, I think that we can sit down and maybe have some more realistic negotiations because of what we can threaten them with.

There's one thing sure. They cannot vastly increase their military productivity because they've already got their people on a starvation diet as far as consumer products are concerned. But they know our potential capacity industrially, and they can't match it. So, we've got the chip this time, that if we show them the will and determination to go forward with a military buildup in our own defense and the defense of our allies, they then have to weigh, do they want to meet us realistically on a program of disarmament or do they want to face a legitimate arms race in which we're racing.

But up until now, we've been making unilateral concessions on our side, allowing ours to deteriorate, and they've been building the greatest military machine the world has ever seen. But now they're going to be faced with that we could go forward with an arms race and they can't keep up.

Arms Sales to Foreign Countries

Q. Mr. President, if I could go back to the AWACS issue for a moment.

The President. All right.

Q. You were discussing earlier restrictions, legislative restrictions on the powers of the Presidency. Do you think it's a good idea that the present legislation gives Congress a veto power over major foreign arms sales by the President, or do you think this is an encroachment, intrusion on the President's flexibility to conduct these affairs?

The President. Well, I think out of what happened in the aftermath of Vietnam, I think the Congress has gone too far. It's always been recognized in this country that the executive branch is more or less entrusted with foreign policy, because you can't run foreign policy through legislation. And while there may be some safeguards that should remain—I wouldn't be averse to that; we do have a multiple kind of government—I do think that the President has got to have some leeway with regard to negotiating and some ability to say, across a table, this is what we will do or what we won't do. And those that he's dealing with know that he has the authority to say that.

What I meant would happen to us now, if they do this, is that how, how do I then go forward with this quiet diplomacy of trying to bring the Arab states into a peacekeeping process in which they can sit there and say, "Well, we don't know whether you can deliver on what you're talking about. You're not the fellow that's in charge; Congress is."

Supreme Court Jurisdiction

Q. Mr. President, speaking of separation of powers, a lot of lawyers and judges have worried about bills in Congress to limit the jurisdiction of the Federal courts in areas like busing and school prayer, affirmative action. How do you feel about that, because they might come to your desk? And what sort of advice will you seek from people in deciding whether to sign or veto that sort of legislation if it does pass?

The President. Well, I could quote Thomas Jefferson, who even back in his time warned that the courts were getting out of hand and that the courts, if they did take powers that properly belonged to the legislature, could upset the whole balance. And I think there's evidence that that's happened.

Let me give you an example and throw one at you right now, without getting into the specifics of those particular issues. We have an election—fair elections commission now, and we have rules and regulations with regard to contributions and the declaration of the same. And a Federal judge has just ruled that one political party in the United States does not have to obey those rules, the Communist Party.

The Communist Party does not have to reveal its list of contributors because those contributors might be politically harassed by our own government. This was his reasoning. And therefore, any Democrats and Republicans, they've got to sign up and their names go in to the [Federal] Election Commission, but the Communist Party can get its money any way it can get it, and no one knows where or how.

Well now, how can we recognize that? If their support is such that it would be so embarrassing, then maybe they shouldn't be a political party. And yet, we've never said that. We've always recognized the right of anyone to be [in] a political party. But then, if they're going to be, then don't they have to live by the same rules the other parties do?

And these are the type of things apropos of the things we were talking about in the exclusionary rule. How many people really stop to think that that's no law, that that is nothing but a case law? That was a decision handed down by a judge, and then other judges felt bound by precedent, and so it has become a matter of case law. But no legislature and no Congress ever passed that law. For example, I happen to believe that the court ruled wrongly with regard to prayer in schools, for example. The first amendment doesn't say anything about that. The first amendment says the Congress shall do nothing to abridge the practice of religion or to create a religion. And yet, we're still a country where it says "In God We Trust" on our coins and over the doors of the Supreme Court. Wasn't this a case, maybe, of the court going beyond what the Constitution actually says?

Busing. Again, I think this whole thing maybe has grown out of the extent to which the Federal Government has injected itself into something that traditionally was believed to belong at the lowest local level, the school district, that there, where the parents and those hired to teach their children could get together and work out how they wanted their children educated. To say nothing of the fact that I think busing has proven a failure. Now, I support fully the theory behind busing or what prompted it, the idea of equality of opportunity, no segregation. And yet, we've got a reverse segregation.

I think it's significant that Mrs. Brown, the woman who brought about the desegregation of schools with her decision, her personal story—maybe you're all aware of it. It's, I think, very interesting. When she was a little girl they lived next to a school. But then, in the racial prejudice of the times in areas in the United States, she had to walk about ½ mile beyond that school to go to the school that she was permitted to go to. And on cold and wet days and so forth, she told of crying in this long walk when the school was right next door. So, she—the Brown decision—she started this fight after she grew up so that her little girl wouldn't have to do this. And not too long ago, she said, "What I didn't have in mind is that my little girl now is picked up in a bus and taken past the school near our home and taken to a school several miles away." And she said, "I didn't have that in mind." [*Laughter*]

Ms. Small. Mr. President, I know that your schedule is very tight here. You have a meeting coming up in just a couple of minutes, and——

The President. Yes, but I want to finish my dessert. [*Laughter*]

Ms. Small. I know you do. I just thought by way of summary, it would be kind of nice to make this a two-way street. Maybe one of you could tell the President some of the concerns in your area. Jerry, we haven't heard from you. Could you just tell us— some of your readers down there in the San Diego area, what they're maybe saying

about some of the administration programs? We could hear from your side.

Q. I'd much rather ask the questions. [*Laughter*]

Ms. Small. Oh, I know. I just wanted him to have a chance to finish up here.

The President. I must say I enjoyed reading in the Cleveland Plain Dealer the other day the page of letters to the editor that was contained in our news summary.

Ms. Small. We are getting some feedback. I just thought someone might have some comments to feed back to us.

Voting Rights Act

Q. Well, I would say that in Virginia, Mr. President, we are very concerned about the Voting Rights Act which has deprived the citizens of the city of Richmond the right to run their own government for about 10 years now. And I think, generally speaking, the prevailing mood of the people in Virginia is to hope that you will continue to oppose extension of the Voting Rights Act in anything like its present form. That's my message for the day. [*Laughter*]

The President. Well, I had always believed and somehow I thought the Voting Rights Act should have been nationwide, rather than picking out certain areas and so forth. But then, I must say it was brought to my attention recently after I'd made a statement about this again, that some said that they were opposed to this because it would make it so cumbersome—and I hadn't thought about this—that it might be impossible to enforce. So, we dropped that position. But I know that the House is working on one and, I think, has maybe been pretty extreme in what it's done. I'm hopeful that the Senate is going to be more reasonable in what's done.

It has become a great symbol, I must say, to the minority communities, and I think this should be taken into consideration. But I agree with you that the perpetuating of punishment for sins that are no longer being committed is pretty extreme.

Ms. Small. Mr. President, I'm told that people are waiting for you for your next appointment——

The President. Yes.

Ms. Small. ——and I know things have been kind of delayed, but we certainly do appreciate your taking this much time to be with us today and answer all of our questions.

The President. Well, I am most grateful to all of you for the opportunity and sorry to rush away, but just between us, Mr. Kohl, the leader of the opposition party in Germany is waiting in the lobby out there.

Q. Thank you, Mr. President.

The President. Thank you all. We ought to schedule one of these for all afternoon sometime. [*Laughter*] Everybody else has the fun.

Note: The interview began at 12:15 p.m. in the Cabinet Room at the White House. The transcript of the interview was released by the Office of the Press Secretary on October 17.

Nomination of Ronald P. Wertheim To Be an Associate Judge of the Superior Court of the District of Columbia
October 17, 1981

The President today announced his intention to nominate Ronald P. Wertheim to be an Associate Judge of the Superior Court of the District of Columbia for a term of 15 years. Mr. Wertheim will fill the vacancy created by the elevation of James A. Belson to the D.C. Court of Appeals.

Mr. Wertheim is currently a member of the Merit Systems Protection Board. Previously, he was in the private practice of law with the firm of Ginsburg, Feldman and Bress in Washington, D.C.

Wertheim was Adviser to the Secretary of Defense for Law of the Sea Negotiations and Alternate U.S. Representative at the United Nations Conference on the Law of the Sea from May to October 1977.

He was Deputy General Counsel of the Peace Corps from 1964 to 1966 and Peace Corps Director in northeast Brazil from 1966 to 1968. Mr. Wertheim practiced trial law in Philadelphia from 1957 to 1959 and was assistant public defender in Philadelphia from 1959 to 1961. After that, and until he joined the Peace Corps, he was associate professor of law at the University of Virginia.

In 1962 Mr. Wertheim received a diploma from The Hague Academy of International Law. He was graduated from the University of Pennsylvania Law School in 1957, where he was editor in chief of its Law Review and received prizes for the highest grades in constitutional law and labor law. He also is a 1954 graduate of the Wharton School of Finance and Commerce at the University of Pennsylvania, where he was in the top 5 percent of his class.

Mr. Wertheim, 48, resides in Washington, D.C., with his wife and two children.

Statement on Signing the Veterans' Disability Compensation, Housing, and Memorial Benefits Amendments of 1981
October 17, 1981

Today, I am pleased to sign S. 917, the "Veterans' Disability Compensation, Housing, and Memorial Benefits Amendments of 1981." This bill will provide some 2.3 million service-disabled veterans and their survivors an 11.2 percent average cost-of-living increase in compensation benefits, retroactive to October 1 of this year.

At a time when we are striving to restore the economic stability that is essential to the overall strength of this Nation, we cannot lose sight of the nation's debt to those brave veterans who have sacrificed their life and limb for the defense of their country. In my budget last March, I proposed an 11.2 percent increase in compensation benefits. I am gratified that an increase now has become a reality.

S. 917 will benefit veterans in many other ways. For example, it contains increases in the amount of life insurance our service members can buy and strengthens the Veterans Administration's home loan and automobile assistance programs.

Although this bill is laudable in most respects, it contains two provisions that represent unwarranted intrusions on executive branch management. The first of these would require lengthy delays in reorganizations of VA activities designed to achieve more economical and effective operation. I am pleased that the final provision, unlike some earlier versions of it considered by the Congress, respects the constitutional princi-

ple of the separation of powers. It will, however, unwisely restrict executive flexibility in achieving managerial improvements.

The second provision that I find troublesome would effectively preclude the VA from conducting cost comparisons under OMB Circular A–76 to determine the most economical means of performing selected functions within its medical facilties—by contract or by the use of Federal employees in VA. Over the next few months, my administration will work with the Congress to allay its concerns and to find a mutually agreeable approach to the application of the Circular's provisions to the VA.

I want to commend both Chairman Alan Simpson and Chairman Sonny Montgomery of the Senate and House Veterans' Affairs Committees for their skillful and dedicated stewardship of this bill.

Note: As enacted, S. 917 is Public Law 97–66, approved October 17.

Exchange With Reporters on Economic and Foreign Policy Issues
October 18, 1981

Q. Mr. President, are you considering now a cutoff or a boycott, of oil from Libya?

The President. No, I heard a statement about—that would have to be a worldwide boycott, because there are plenty of customers for oil, and you've got to make sure that none of them would take the place.

Q. What do you hear about the Polish Government resigning?

The President. Well, all I've heard is that we are waiting for more details and that Kania is out. We have to find out what that means and we'll probably know more when we know who's going to replace him.

Q. Mr. President, if Congress is unwilling to give you your rescission and impoundment authority, what makes you think you can gain the support of Tip O'Neill and his cult of followers on your new line legislation, who at this moment are probably turning over in bed unable to wait to get to work on Monday morning to do everything

in the realm of their power to provide you with more?

The President. That's the result of the meeting with the editors from all over the country, and in answer to their question, I was telling them how most States ran and balanced their budgets on authority that was given to Governors of States, as was given to me when I was Governor of California. And I was pointing out the great weaknesses in the budgetary systems at the Federal level. And there are weaknesses, or we wouldn't have a trillion dollar deficit.

Q. Do you think you would be able to pass that legislation?

The President. No, I doubt if Congress would ever give up that power, and I think they're wrong.

Q. What do you think of Richard Nixon's proposal for an economic boycott of Libya——

Q. Do you think we are in a recession?

The President. I think there's a slight and, I hope, a short recession. Yes, I think everyone agrees on that.

Q. ——Richard Nixon's proposal for an economic boycott—[*inaudible*].

The President. I know, I just answered that a moment ago. I heard that. No, as I say, that would have to be worldwide. No one country could affect them by having a boycott.

Q. Did you talk to him about his plan?

The President. No, I haven't talked to anyone.

Q. Thank you, Mr. President.

Note: The exchange began at 11:51 a.m. on the South Lawn of the White House, as the President was departing for his visits to Yorktown and Williamsburg, Va.

Exchange of Remarks at a Luncheon Hosted by President François Mitterrand of France in Yorktown, Virginia
October 18, 1981

President Mitterrand. Mr. President, Madam, dear friends:

It is unusual to be able to live historical moments in a setting such as this one, and yet that is what has happened on this very fine and sunny day of Franco-American friendship.

The age-old traditions of the navy, when they receive illustrious guests, the vocal welcome and the bosun's whistle, which remind us of the glorious times of sail and all the soldiers of the sea that were lined in order to welcome you with the greatest possible dignity, Mr. President, on a few square meters of French territory—all this has brought us into this dining room of the commanding officer of the *De Grasse,* where we have just had our lunch with some of the best officers of the French Navy.

Now today, I would like, with your permission, to remain in the sort of intimate note that has already been struck in order to say that this has enabled me, Mr. President, to get to know you even better and to appreciate the humor of your conversation and the way you can tell a story, and also the very cheerful vigor with which you carry the burden, one of the heaviest burdens that exists on Earth, that is, being the leader of the great American people.

Now, I think our mutual knowledge of each other and a more profound knowledge will, I'm quite sure, help us and enable us to get over the inevitably difficult times that do sometimes inevitably exist in political discussions between two men who've come from different horizons and who've reached the same supreme responsibilities.

Now, we may not always be able to convince the other of what we're trying to do and achieve, but we're absolutely sure that in any case we will on all occasions enlighten our discussions in the, shall we say, the powerful sun of real frankness. And I'm quite sure, also, that we will also find that the areas of agreement would, in fact, always prove far broader, far wider than any possible differences.

And you can, at any rate, be assured, Mr. President, that we in France, we feel very close to the United States and the American people on the main issues that concern the world, and this we will always be able to talk about in a spirit of great friendship.

May I also, Mr. President, say on behalf of my wife and myself and all those who are present here today that we are very much struck to see the way you, in fact, demonstrated one of, perhaps the rarest virtues, and yet one of the most necessary for a statesman—the courage of someone who has just paid, paid dearly, paid with his own blood—his total commitment to the service of his country. And it is therefore, with deep emotion and very great joy, that we have seen you again here today, Mr. President, in, if I may say so, in such very good shape.

And I would like to raise my glass, Mr. President, to your health and to the generous smile of Mrs. Reagan and to the prosperity of the noble American people.

President Reagan. Well, Mr. President, Madam Mitterrand, thank you for your hospitality and again let me welcome you to the United States—but since we're currently on French territory, maybe I should welcome you to our waters. [*Laughter*] And I'm particularly pleased that I can introduce today our new Ambassador to France, Evan Galbraith, distinguished and learned businessman who has spent many years in your country developing a great appreciation and affection for it.

I think you would agree it's slightly unusual for France as the visiting nation to host the first meal between our two countries. Actually, this is symbolic and fitting. During our revolution, when we were destitute of resources, France gave us the monetary and military sustenance to continue and eventually win our struggle for independence. So, at this lunch we remember and thank the French people for the nourishment they gave to our cause 200 years ago as well as thanking you, Mr. President, for the sustenance that you have provided today.

It is also appropriate that we're on the French frigate, the *De Grasse,* as a reminder of the contribution of the great admiral, the same name, made to American free-

dom. The United States has honored the Count De Grasse for his essential service to our Republic. And our own *Count De Grasse* is anchored only a short distance away. These two ships lie anchored in peace and friendship, yet each is vigilant and ready to defend the other if threatened, for France and the United States are old, firm allies. You came to America when we needed you, and we went to France when you had need of us.

Tomorrow—well, the commitment still holds. This old alliance would prove just as young and strong and victorious as it did in 1781, 1918, and 1945. Tomorrow marks the anniversary of Cornwallis' surrender. I'm certain that 200 years ago, many an American was raising his glass to salute his French friends for their crucial aid in that victory.

Today, in the same spirit, Mr. President, Madam Mitterrand, I would like to toast our French friends a long alliance and our many victories together.

President Mitterrand. Thank you very much.

Note: President Mitterrand spoke at 2:52 p.m. on board the battleship De Grasse. *Earlier, President Reagan was accorded a welcoming ceremony with full military honors on arriving at the* De Grasse *from the U.S. Coast Guard Station in Yorktown.*

President Mitterrand spoke in French, and his remarks were translated by an interpreter.

Remarks at a Dinner Hosted by Governor John Dalton of Virginia in Williamsburg
October 18, 1981

President Mitterrand. Mr. Governor, dear friends, the warmth and the courtesy of your welcome here goes straight to my heart. And my wife and myself, we would like to thank you for the simplicity that one finds among old friends in exchanging sincere compliments at the end of the good and warm day.

Now, I know that you employ an expression which is a popular one in France and

that you would recognize. I would say that here we feel entirely at home, here in Virginia, where we find the best of America and we find everything that we dreamed about in our youth and which still fills our imagination with so many beautiful images.

Now, you have not had time to grow old. We were already an old nation in 1781 when Lafayette and Rochambeau came to help you in the first war of liberation of modern times. But in order to quote something that was said by one of my predecessors, General De Gaulle, about the French Revolution, the flame of which was going to be lit by the flame of yours. Those were times when France was still young although she had already lived a lot. So, let us recover today this mutual youth which led to victory here when arm in arm, as we say, we went together, the youngest republic and the oldest monarchy of the world.

There are so many suffering, there is so much distress and anguish and violence on this unfortunate planet that we must recover the spirit of youth—well, the spirit of our youth, I would say—the guilelessness, the courage, the generosity which inspired here and very near here, yes, some of the most noble accents of the minds and conscience of men.

I have come here to ask you to give me the secrets that lie in the heart of Patrick Henry and Jefferson. And you have never kept those secrets to yourselves, and I'm sure that they will help me to find the words and to take the action that is required in order to respond to the new will of a France which is moving.

Long live Franco-American alliance forever and long live Williamsburg and Virginia.

President Reagan. Thank you, Governor Dalton. And good evening to all of you.

President Mitterrand, Madam Mitterrand, I know that I speak for everyone here when I say how much we appreciate your remarks, not to mention your timely visit coinciding with this historic occasion. This day has already been wonderful, and there's still more to come tonight and tomorrow.

I couldn't leave here this evening without giving a special word of praise and thanks to Governor Dalton and Lewis McMurran, the chairman of the Virginia Independence Bicentennial Commission. The planning and the work that both of you and all of your associates put into these festivities is more than we'll ever know, but sometimes the spirit, the significance of an event is of such importance that it demands a celebration no one will ever forget, and that's what this bicentennial is all about. And believe me, you have acquitted yourselves with highest honors.

I wish I could take the time to salute all the rest of you individually, but where would I begin? If I may paraphrase a former President, this is the most extraordinary collection of human talent ever to gather in Williamsburg since Thomas Jefferson walked these streets alone.

Now, I know we're not supposed to take up too much of your time, so let us wish you an enjoyable evening and get on our way, and thank you again so much for your reception.

Thank you.

[*At this point, Governor Dalton presented President Reagan and President Mitterrand with gifts on behalf of the people of Virginia and the Nation's Governors. President Reagan resumed speaking as follows.*]

I shouldn't do this, but I just wanted to tell you that on the *De Grasse* today, having lunch with President and Mrs. Mitterrand, I learned a little bit of American history that maybe all of us or none of us know. I was told by the commander of the vessel there that when Washington went aboard that ship to speak to Rochambeau, who was a very tall man, and George Washington was tall, but not quite as tall—and as they met, in the amusement of everyone who then laughed at it, Admiral Rochambeau approached Washington, put his arms around him, embraced him and said, *"Mon petit General."* [*Laughter*]

Note: President Mitterrand spoke at 7:30 p.m. in the Virginia Room at the Williamsburg Lodge. He spoke in French, and his remarks were translated by an interpreter.

Earlier in the afternoon, President Reagan and President Mitterrand met at the Lightfoot House in Williamsburg, where President Reagan stayed during his visit to Virginia.

Toasts at a Dinner Honoring President François Mitterrand of France in Williamsburg, Virginia
October 18, 1981

President Reagan. President and Mrs. Mitterrand, Lord Hailsham, and distinguished guests:

Nancy and I are pleased and honored to welcome you into this historic residence this evening.

We want to thank you again, Mr. President, for that lovely luncheon on board the *De Grasse* this afternoon. We want to thank you again, as I say you learned more about the triumph of the American Revolution, and I learned more about the triumph of French cuisine. [*Laughter*] This evening, Nancy and I wanted to return the favor by preparing something truly special for you. *Formidable* is the word I believe you use in France—[*laughter*]—and I think our friends have done their job well.

Tomorrow morning, you and I have a rendezvous on the battlefield. Fortunately, we will not meet as enemies. [*Laughter*] France and America never have been and, I pray, never will. We're friends and allies and we must always remain that way, because just like 200 years ago, we need each other to protect something much bigger than ourselves: first the creation and now the preservation of those magnificent institutions of Western civilization, constitutional government, the rule of law, economic liberty, and the right to worship God. They are the foundation of human freedom and social progress, and they bind our countries in a common heritage.

Yorktown, too, represents something bigger than a Virginia town, delightful though it may be. It's a page turned in history like the Place de la Bastille and the landing beaches of Normandy. For here, France and America solidified their friendship with a military victory that would bring peace and independence to our tiny nation, an enduring vision of freedom and hope to the entire world.

And I'm now going to say something that isn't in the script that you have, but simply because I think in deference to some of our guests, I should point out that probably the most accurate description of the American Revolution was given to me by an Englishman who said that they understood it was just an argument between two groups of Englishmen. [*Laughter*]

Mr. President, I can think of no more appropriate occasion than here and now for your first visit to the United States as leader of the French Republic. Your nation faces many serious challenges and so does mine. But just as our ancestors did before and their descendents have done since, we can stand tall and stand firm by standing together. The durability of Franco-American friendship proves there is constancy in change. The world's oldest alliance has survived, and we can join together to strengthen the Atlantic Alliance for the future.

Actually, the alliance began in 1778 when France signed a treaty and became the first nation to recognize the United States of America as a nation. And the date was February 6th, which happens to be my birthday, but it's not true that I was there for the signing of the treaty. [*Laughter*]

France and America may not always see eye to eye on every issue, but we usually can, and like true friends, we know we can count on each other in times of peril.

Mr. President, we worked together in Ottawa, and in a few days we'll have another opportunity to do so in Cancún. I look forward to cooperating with you in a constructive spirit of friendship, trust, and good will.

And as for now here in Yorktown, I ask you all to join me in saluting François Mitterrand, a leader of vision and courage, and Mrs. Mitterrand.

Vive la France and *vive l'Amerique—amis ce soir, demain, et toujours.* Long live France and America—friends this evening, tomorrow, and always.

Lord Hailsham. Mr. President, Monsieur le President la République Française, Chief Justice, Excellencies, ladies and gentlemen:

I can see that as the representative of a former colonial power, I'm on the hiding to nothing. Now translate that into French, if you can. [*Laughter*] Oh, well. [*Laughter*]

I am very pleased and proud to be present here on this historic occasion. I am able, I think, to take a somewhat philosophical view of the matter. [*Laughter*] I had a direct ancestor who fought at this battle. He fought on the American side.

And you have laid upon me, Mr. President, the task in a flat three minutes of proposing any toast I like. And so I shall propose the toast. Of the heads of state here present or represented, and to the eternal friendship between their peoples, *je lève mon verre, Monsieur le President: Vive la France, notre amie et notre alliée* [I raise my glass, Mr. President: Long live France, our friend and our ally], and God bless America and God bless my own country, too. [*Laughter*]

President Mitterrand. Mr. President, Madam, dear Lord Hailsham, dear American and French friends:

Now, in the words that we've just been listening to, even beyond the point of humor, I have felt the powerful wind of America, the wind of the modern times that was 8 years after Yorktown, was going to in fact give rise to the wind of change and make France also a sort of new world.

We, the French—we, perhaps, were most attentive in listening to the bells of freedom that were ringing in response to Patrick Henry. First, we responded by coming to take our place by your sides in the first battlefields of freedom. And secondly, by putting almost immediately into effect in our own country and in our own way the great lesson that you had just given us.

Stirring news spread the world over as soon as Jefferson included the right to happiness as one of the main requirements of your Declaration of Independence. And at that time men of all continents and men of all countries gradually began to understand that this concerned them, each one of them, and all of them.

Now, a number of them, and indeed some of us, still have to appreciate that there can be no possible happiness where there is neither justice nor liberty. Like many others, I devoted part of my life, the best part of my life, to freedom, true freedom—the freedom for which Washington's

volunteers and also the French soldiers of year two of the French Revolution fought. And I felt in my own flesh and in my mind the inestimable price of such liberty for having lived in the French Resistance, those terrible years when our country was deprived of such freedom.

I learned in those dark days in France, a country that was hurt and humiliated and that owes you so much, that our main duty towards the others and towards ourselves is to struggle with all our might, always and ever, for freedom.

Now, how would I not feel, so to speak, in fact, as if I were one of your cousins in a way when I hear others, such as yourselves, use the plain and sound language of freedom? It is a language that we have in common. It is a code of expression for the mind and the heart, which allows a simple exchange to take place among us, even though some of them, and I'm afraid I am one of them, some of us, in fact, will speak the American language in such an imperfect fashion that it would not be safe to try to use it, and I wish to ask you to forgive me for this.

At least I did hear, and I have remembered, as many, many of my compatriots, the two words that the insurgents were shouting when they were rushing the trenches in Yorktown and which were the—for some of them—the last words of their life, "God and liberty."

May I say that I have this very much in mind when I'm raising my glass, Mr. President, to your excellent and powerful health, to Mrs. Reagan, and to the good health of Franco-American friendship, which I have certainly not found in any way endangered by our divergencies or differences of opinion during our talks, where the frankness among us was the kind of thing that old friends can demonstrate in order to be able to talk to each other without having to take too many precautions.

I would like to associate here in our gathering a thought for the millions of men and women who are in danger of famine and who are in fact listening, listening to what will come out of Cancún, where you and I, Mr. President, we will, with the other participants in the North-South conference, have an opportunity to pursue and to continue in greater depth our conversations of today.

We have other trenches, in fact, to overcome with the cry of "liberty." And the entrenchments of suffering and sorrow of man are more abrupt even than those of Yorktown or the walls of our Bastille. But the cry, our cry will be the same, "liberty."

I will raise my glass to your health, Mr. President, and to thank you for the very warm welcome that we have received in this city and in this country. And I know that all the French who have been guests of your country have always been received with the same warm welcome.

And to you, Madam, I would like to say how much I enjoyed our conversations in London and here in Williamsburg, and thanks to them I have learned to know more who you are. I have learned better to appreciate your charm and the presence of the First Lady of the United States.

I would also like to raise my glass to my good friend Lord Hailsham and through him to his country, because though between our two countries there have over the centuries been a lot of quarreling, since then another friendship and a very strong

friendship was born, has been born, and I will say more about this tomorrow.

And we do not forget that in 1940, the knight—the fighter for freedom was and was alone the United Kingdom.

I would like to raise my glass to all our American hosts. The French who are here know that we are in fact speaking with the same heart.

And I would like our American hosts to know that France is a country that wishes to achieve more justice and that will choose the parts in order to achieve that, according to its tastes. And France is a country who wishes by her experience to prolong the civilization, the civilization that was born two centuries ago, and that if it is to prolong itself and continue to act and act with power, it must learn to adapt and to change itself and to evolve while always remaining faithful to the original message.

Thank you.

Note: President Reagan spoke at 10 p.m. at the Royal Governor's Palace. President Mitterand spoke in French, and his remarks were translated by an interpreter.

The Rt. Honorable Lord Hailsham is the Lord Chancellor of the United Kingdom.

Remarks at the Bicentennial Observance of the Battle of Yorktown in Virginia
October 19, 1981

Mr. President, Mrs. Mitterand, Lord Chancellor,[1] Governor John Dalton—and I thank you very much for that most gracious introduction—Members of the Congress, members of the Cabinet, distinguished guests, and my fellow citizens:

I open with something of an announcement before my remarks. Since today is a day to celebrate freedom, I feel it only appropriate that I exercise one of the more pleasant powers of the Presidency. After consultation with Governor Dalton and with his approval, by the power vested in

me as President of the United States, I hereby grant amnesty to the corps of cadets of the Virginia Military Institute under the terms and conditions to be specified by the superintendent. [*Laughter*]

And now, this field, this ceremony, and this day hold a special meaning for people the world over, whether free in their lives or only in their dreams. Not long after the battle of Yorktown, Lafayette wrote home to France. "Here," he said, "humanity has won its battle, liberty now has a country."

It was an extraordinary moment in history. The Continental Army, as you've been told, had marched more than 400 miles from the Hudson River in New York to the

---

[1] *Rt. Honorable Lord Hailsham, Lord Chancellor of the United Kingdom.*

tidewaters of Virginia. They surprised and stranded Lord Cornwallis on the tip of this peninsula. When Admiral de Grasse and his French fleet blockaded the Chesapeake, the trap was sprung. There could be no rescue by land or by sea.

Nearly 8,000 British soldiers had swept from Charleston to Richmond to this spot between the York and the James Rivers, with far more victories than defeats. But as they were encircled and besieged by the Continentals, as they withstood day after day of grueling bombardment, they must have known in their hearts they were fighting for a cause they could not win.

Their enemies were a band of colonists with bandaged feet and muskets that couldn't be counted on to fire, but the British were thousands of miles from home and the Americans were fighting where they lived. Those rebels may not have had fancy uniforms or even adequate resources, but they had a passion for liberty burning in their hearts.

In a masterly execution of a textbook siege, General Washington and his grab-bag army defeated the finest troops King George could field.

The morning of the surrender must have been very much like this one today. The first real chill of autumn was in the air. The trees were turning brilliant with the hues of red and gold and brown. The sky was bright and clear. Quiet had finally returned to this lovely countryside. How strange the silence must have seemed after the thundering violence of war.

And then the silence was broken by a muffled beat of British drums, covered with black handkerchiefs, as the Redcoats marched to surrender. The pageantry was spectacular. The French in their spotless white uniforms lined one side of the road. The ragged Continentals were brown and dreary on the other side. But the journals of those who were present mention that the Americans stood every bit as straight and equally as proud as any army could. They had, on that day, a military bearing that was not to be outdone by their comrades in white and blue nor by King George's men in their brilliant red.

As the British marched between the allied armies to the field of surrender, tears streamed down many of their faces. Their musicians played a tune popular in England at the time, yes, "The World Turned Upside Down." And that's just what the colonists had done.

But those Americans were not professional soldiers at all. They had fought for freedom from Quebec to Saratoga, from Camden and Cowpens to Germantown, Valley Forge, and Monmouth—towns and countrysides once so anonymous that King George complained he could neither pronounce them nor find them on the map.

By Yorktown, they were veterans, but they were still not soldiers. They were farmers, backwoodsmen, tradesmen, clerks, and laborers—common men from all walks of life, anxious to return to their families and the building of a nation. On that day in 1781 a philosophy found a people, and the world would never be the same.

We who have traveled here today—and I'm told we number more than 60,000—did not come just to admire the strategies, battlements, and trenches of a siege. We did not come to idealize human suffering.

The wounds of this battle have long since healed. Our nations have matured, and bonds of friendship now exist between onetime enemies. The same has been true of other wars since, which makes you wonder if after all the hatred, all the pain, and all the sacrifice, we find ourselves able to be friends and allies, why couldn't we find ourselves able to be friends without first going to war?

We have come to this field to celebrate the triumph of an idea—that freedom will eventually triumph over tyranny. It is and always will be a warning to those who would usurp the rights of others: Time will find them beaten. The beacon of freedom shines here for all who will see, inspiring free men and captives alike, and no wall, no curtain, nor totalitarian state can shut it out.

The commemoration of this battle marks the end of the revolution and the beginning of a new world era. The promise made on July 4th was kept on October 19th. The dream described in that Pennsylvania hall was fulfilled on this Virginia field. Through courage, the support of our allies, and by the gracious hand of God, a revolution was won, a people were set free, and the world witnessed the most exciting adventure in the history of nations: the beginning of the United States of America.

But we didn't win this battle or this war by ourselves. From your country, Mr. President, came men and ships and goods. Generals Rochambeau and Lafayette and Admirals de Grasse and de Barras were among those without whose help this battle and this war could never have been won. France was first to our side, first to recognize our independence, and steadfast in friendship ever since. We are bonded in spirit and, in fact, by freedom. "Entre vous, entre nous, a la vie, a la mort," Rochambeau said—Between you, between us, through life, or death.

And others came to our aid—Poles, Spaniards, Scots, Canadians, Swedes, Germans, Dutch, Irish, and still more.

Our Revolution was won by and for all who cherish the timeless and universal rights of man. This battle was a vindication of ideas that had been forming for centuries in the Western mind.

From the Mediterranean had come the philosophies of Greece and the laws of Rome. England contributed representative government, and the French and the Poles shared their dreams of equality and liberty. On our own frontier, we learned dependence on family and neighbors, and in our Revolution free men were taught reliance on other free men.

We of the West have lived the central truths, the values around which we now must rally—human dignity, individual rights, and representative democracy. Our nations share the foundation of common law, separation of powers, and limited government. We must unite behind our own common cause of freedom.

There are those in the world today, as there always have been, who recognize human rights as only selective favors to be doled out by the state. They preach revolution against tyranny, but they intend to replace it with the tyranny of totalitarianism.

Once again, today, thousands of free men and women have gathered on this battlefield in testimony to their beliefs. Let the struggle that took place here remind us all: The freedom we enjoy today has not always

existed and carries no guarantees. In our search for an everlasting peace, let all of us resolve to remain so sure of our strength that the victory for mankind we won here is never threatened.

Will we meet the challenge, will we meet the challenge Joseph Warren put forth to Americans 200 years ago? Will we act worthy of ourselves?

Each generation before us has struggled and sacrificed for freedom. Can we do any less?

The men and boys who fought on this field somehow understood that government must be close to people and responsive to them; that if all men are free to prosper, all will benefit.

Today in our country those concepts are threatened by government's bloated size and the distortion of its true functions. Our people are struggling under a punishing tax burden many times heavier than that which ignited our first rebellion. Regulations that inhibit our growth and prosperity would be incomprehensible to the colonists who revolted because of the Stamp Act.

Our Founding Fathers devised a system of government unique in all the world—a federation of sovereign States, with as much law and decisionmaking authority as possible kept at the local level. This concept of federalism has been the secret of America's success and will be a priority again as we restore the balance between the Federal, State, and local levels that was intended in the Constitution.

But of equal concern to me is the uncertainty some seem to have about the need for a strong American defense. Now, that is a proper task for the National Government. Military inferiority does not avoid a conflict, it only invites one and then ensures defeat. We have been trusted with freedom. We have been trusted with freedom and must ensure it for our children and for their children. We're rebuilding our defenses so that our sons and daughters never need to be sent to war.

Where are the voices of courage and vision that inspired us in the past? Are we ever to hear those voices again? Yes. Thomas Paine, a voice of patriotism, said, "Those who expect to reap the blessings of freedom must, . . . , undergo the fatigue of supporting it." We always have, and we always will. That's just part of being an American.

Our Declaration of Independence has been copied by emerging nations around the globe, its themes adopted in places many of us have never heard of.

Here in this land, for the first time, it was decided that man is born with certain God-given rights. We the people declared that government is created by the people for their own convenience. Government has no power except those voluntarily granted to it by we the people.

There have been revolutions before and since ours, revolutions that simply exchanged one set of rulers for another. Ours was a philosophical revolution that changed the very concept of government.

John Adams wrote home from Philadelphia shortly before signing the Declaration of Independence, and he said, "I am well aware of the Toil and Blood and Treasure, that it will cost Us to maintain this Declaration, and support and defend these States. Yet through all the Gloom, I can see the Rays of ravishing Light and Glory. I can see that the End is more than worth all the Means—and that Posterity will triumph—".

It is that vision we recall today. We have economic problems at home, and we live in a troubled and violent world. But there is a moral fiber running through our people that makes us more than strong enough to face the tests ahead. We can look at our past with pride, and our future can be whatever we make it. We can remember that saying Thomas Paine said, "We have it within our power to begin the world over again." We only have to act worthy of ourselves.

And as has been said already today, God bless America.

Note: The President spoke at 12:23 p.m. from a reviewing stand overlooking the battlefield.

Following his remarks, the President returned to the White House.

Remarks at a Dinner Marking the 40th Anniversary of United Service Organizations, Inc.
October 17, 1981

Bob, that was a great one-liner. [*Laughter*]

President Ford, Madam Chairman, Mr. President, and all you distinguished ladies and gentlemen here tonight:

It is a great pleasure for Nancy and myself to be here to celebrate this 40th anniversary of USO and the 40 years of Bob Hope's association with USO.

I don't think any of us realize that there probably isn't anyone who loves his work as much as Bob Hope. I discovered that once when he was up at our ranch and I took him over to the paddock fence to show him our horses. And then I got a telephone call. When I came back, he was doing a monolog to the horses. And they were laughing. [*Laughter*]

And, of course, as has been made so very evident here tonight, his other love is golf. When we met tonight, I said, "Hello, how are you?" And he says, "Hello, what's your handicap?" I said, "The Congress." [*Laughter*]

But here with all the nice people like you I have to say I've discovered how nice people can be. I got a letter from an environmentalist the other day, and he was thanking me. He said it's the first time he's ever been able to make his children behave. He now scares them into being good by telling 'em James Watt will get 'em. [*Laughter*]

Of course, all your mail isn't that good. I've been getting some flak about ordering the production of the B-1. How did I know it was an airplane? I thought it was vitamins for the troops. [*Laughter*]

Now, tomorrow Nancy and I are going to Virginia to commemorate the Battle of

Yorktown. And let me lay to rest an ugly rumor. It isn't true that Bob entertained the troops there. [*Laughter*] He was still at Valley Forge. [*Laughter*]

But seriously, we are very proud to be here tonight, and I'm very proud to be the Honorary Chairman of the USO. The USO is the very epitome of the voluntary spirit, and it came into being 40 years ago, to meet a real need in the first few months of World War II. It continues because 40,000 volunteers give their time and effort to helping our men and women in uniform, and people like you give your help to them in what they're doing.

Now, this 40th anniversary is also the anniversary of Leslie Townes Hope with the USO. That's Bob. In fact, the USO had to catch up with him. Many of us have forgotten that he'd been entertaining the GI's for quite some time before there was a USO. And it was practically a solo act, wherever they were in the world. But now the USO goes on helping not only men and women in uniform but their families as well. And it does all this without government funding, depending on the great heart of a great people.

Let me tell you just one story—and this is not a joke. There were two sailors, undoubtedly with our fleet there in the Mediterranean, who had a leave, and they were going to try and see Italy. And they were hiking their way around, and they were camped one night sleeping in sleeping bags, south of Rome. And they were mugged, set upon and robbed of everthing including their identification papers and the clothing of one of them. And the next day, being resourceful Yankee sailors, they hitchhiked their way to Rome, one of them zipped up in his sleeping bag, as he was the one who'd lost his clothes. Now, you can imagine what it would have been like if they'd had to tell their story to a chief petty officer, but instead, they landed on the doorstep of the USO in Rome. And the USO got clothing for them, got identity papers for them, and then, because they were trying to see Italy, took them on a tour of Rome.

Just about anywhere in the world that the American military men and women find themselves, they also find the USO. Noah Webster said, "Wherever public spirit prevails, liberty is secure." Well, the public spirit of the USO and the public spirit of Bob Hope have been pretty evident for four decades now, and like everyone else up here, on behalf of all Americans, we thank the USO and Bob Hope for our liberty and for the men and women in the service.

And then, since I know that Bob hasn't got much to do these days, I have a job for him that he doesn't know about.

This is addressed to Bob Hope of California.

[*At this point, the President read a commission, the text of which follows.*]

Ronald Reagan
The President of the United States of America

To Bob Hope, of California, Greetings:

For more than half a century, under eleven Presidents, you have raised the spirits of the American people. Your unmatched patriotism, integrity, stamina, and sense of humor have contributed to the well-being of your country in countless ways. As an entertainer, you have brought new meaning to the art of comedy and laughter to our hearts. During hard times, your comedy has uplifted the spirits of millions at home and reassured those in our armed forces overseas. Your years of selfless service and dedication have made you an American legend. For all that you have done, I do hereby appoint you Ambassador of Good Will to the entire World, and authorize you to do and perform all such matters and things as to the said Office do appertain or as may be duly given you in charge hereafter.

Done at the City of Washington this seventeenth day of October in the year of our Lord one thousand nine hundred and eighty-one, and of the Independence of the United States of America the two hundred and sixth.

Note: The President spoke at approximately 10:15 p.m. in the International Ballroom at the Washington Hilton Hotel. In his opening remarks, he referred to former President Gerald R. Ford, Mrs. Charles H. Sethness, Jr., chairman of the dinner, and James E. Barrett, USO World President.

The transcript of the President's remarks was released by the Office of the Press Secretary on October 20.

Nomination of William Coskrey Plowden, Jr., To Be an Assistant Secretary of Labor
October 20, 1981

The President today announced his intention to nominate William Coskrey Plowden, Jr., to be Assistant Secretary of Labor for Veterans Employment.

Since 1976 Mr. Plowden has been State director, Veterans Employment and Services (South Carolina). He was appointed to the Americanism Commission of the American Legion National Organization in 1961 and served as Americanism chairman, State of South Carolina American Legion. He is a member of the Veterans of Foreign Wars (VFW) and the Disabled American Veterans (DAV).

Mr. Plowden served in World War II in the China-Burma Theatre, attaining the rank of lieutenant colonel, and retired from the reserve as a full colonel in 1965. He graduated from the Citadel Military College (B.A., 1939). He is married, has three children, and resides in New Zion, S.C. Mr. Plowden was born July 15, 1918, in New Zion.

Appointment of Charles S. Gubser as Chairman of the Permanent Joint Board on Defense—United States and Canada
October 20, 1981

The President today announced his intention to appoint Charles S. Gubser to be Chairman, Permanent Joint Board on Defense—United States and Canada.

Mr. Gubser was a Member of the United States House of Representatives for 22 years in 1953–74. He recently served as Chairman of the Permanent Joint Board on Defense, United States and Canada, in 1975–78.

He graduated from the University of California (B.A.). He is married and resides in Monument, Colo. He was born February 1, 1916, in Gilroy, Calif.

Message to the Congress Transmitting a Report of the United States Sinai Support Mission
October 20, 1981

I am pleased to transmit herewith the Twelfth Report of the United States Sinai Support Mission. It covers the Mission's activities during the six-month period ending October 1, 1981. This report is provided in accordance with Section 4 of Public Law 94–110 of October 13, 1975.

The Sinai Support Mission and its overseas arm, the Sinai Field Mission, have since 1976 made unique contributions to the peace process in that part of the Middle East, first by establishing and operating the tactical early warning system that made possible the second disengagement agreement between Egypt and Israel, and when that mission was successfully completed in January 1980, by undertaking during the interim withdrawal period the verification of Egyptian and Israeli adherence to the military limitations called for in their 1979 Peace Treaty.

This second peacekeeping role will end on April 25, 1982, the date established under the Treaty for the completion of Israeli withdrawal from the Sinai. At that time, the Sinai Field Mission will relinquish its verification responsibilities to the new Multinational Force and Observers being established to supervise implementation of the Treaty's security arrangements after Israel's withdrawal.

Funding for the Sinai Support Mission for Fiscal Year 1981 was authorized at $16 million. Only $10 million is being requested for Fiscal Year 1982, a level that will fund the Mission's operations during its final months and the projected costs of its phase out after April 25, 1982.

The role of the Sinai Support and Field Missions has been a concrete example of the United States' commitment to the achievement of a just and lasting peace in the Middle East. Our participation in the Multinational Force and Observers will be the next crucial step in the further promotion of that peace. I am counting on the continuing support of the Congress for our role in the peace process.

RONALD REAGAN

The White House,
October 20, 1981.

Executive Order 12331—President's Foreign Intelligence Advisory Board
October 20, 1981

By virtue of the authority vested in me as President by the Constitution and statutes of the United States of America, and in order to enhance the security of the United States by improving the quality and effectiveness of intelligence available to the United States, it is ordered as follows:

Section 1. There is hereby established within the White House Office, Executive Office of the President, the President's Foreign Intelligence Advisory Board (the "Board"). Members of the Board shall serve at the pleasure of the President and shall be appointed by the President from among trustworthy and distinguished citizens outside the Government who are qualified on the basis of achievement, experience, and independence. The President shall designate a Chairman and Vice Chairman from among the members. The Board shall utilize full-time staff and consultants as authorized by the President. Such staff shall be headed by an Executive Director, appointed by the President.

Sec. 2. The Board shall assess the quality, quantity, and adequacy of intelligence collection, of analysis and estimates, of counterintelligence, and other intelligence activities. The Board shall have the authority to continually review the performance of all agencies of the Government that are en-

gaged in the collection, evaluation, or production of intelligence or the execution of intelligence policy. The Board shall further be authorized to assess the adequacy of management, personnel, and organization in the intelligence agencies.

Sec. 3. The Board shall report directly to the President and advise him concerning the objectives, conduct, management, and coordination of the various activities of the agencies of the intelligence community. The Board shall report periodically, but at least semi-annually, concerning findings and appraisals and shall make appropriate recommendations for actions to improve and enhance the performance of the intelligence efforts of the United States.

Sec. 4. The Board shall receive, consider, and take appropriate action with respect to matters, identified to the Board by the Director of Central Intelligence, the Central Intelligence Agency, or other Government agencies engaged in intelligence or related activities, in which the support of the Board will further the effectiveness of the national intelligence effort. With respect to matters deemed appropriate by the President, the Board shall advise and make recommendations to the Director of Central Intelligence, the Central Intelligence Agency, and other Government agencies engaged in intelligence and related activities, concerning ways to achieve increased effectiveness in meeting national intelligence needs.

Sec. 5. The Board shall have access to the full extent permitted by applicable law to all information necessary to carry out its duties in the possession of any agency of the Government. Information made available to the Board shall be given all necessary security protection in accordance with applicable laws and regulations. Each member of the Board, each member of the Board's staff, and each of the Board's consultants shall execute an agreement never to reveal any classified information obtained by virtue of his or her service with the Board

except to the President or to such persons as the President may designate.

Sec. 6. Members of the Board shall serve without compensation, but may receive transportation, expense, and per diem allowances as authorized by law. Staff and consultants to the Board shall receive pay and allowances as authorized by the President.

RONALD REAGAN

The White House,
October 20, 1981.

[*Filed with the Office of the Federal Register, 3:31 p.m., October 20, 1981*]

Appointment of 19 Members of the President's Foreign Intelligence Advisory Board, and Designation of the Chairman and Vice Chairman
October 20, 1981

The President today announced his intention to appoint the following individuals to serve on the President's Foreign Intelligence Advisory Board. The President also announced his intention to designate Anne Armstrong as Chairman and Leo Cherne as Vice Chairman.

Anne Armstrong is currently chairman of the Advisory Board of the Georgetown University Center for Strategic and International Studies. She was United States Ambassador to Great Britain in 1976–77 and served as Counsellor to the President in 1973–74. She is married, has five children, and resides in Armstrong, Tex.

Leo Cherne is an economist and currently serves on the Advisory Board of the Georgetown University Center for Strategic and International Studies. He was a member of the President's Foreign Intelligence Advisory Board in 1973–76 and served as Chairman in 1976–77. He resides in New York City and was born September 8, 1912.

David Abshire was executive director of the Center for Strategic and International Studies, Georgetown University, in 1962–70 and has served as chairman since 1973. He was Chairman of the Board for International Broadcasting in 1974–77. He is married, has five chil-

dren, and resides in Washington, D.C. He was born April 11, 1926.

William O. Baker is a research chemist and was chairman of the board of Bell Telephone Laboratories. He was a member of the President's Foreign Intelligence Advisory Board in 1959–77. He is married, has one son, and resides in Morristown, N.J. He was born July 15, 1915.

Alfred S. Bloomingdale is a corporation executive in New York City. He was chairman of the board of directors of Diners' Club in 1964–70. He is married, has two children, and resides in New York. He was born April 15, 1916.

Frank Borman is chairman, president, and chief executive officer of Eastern Airlines. Colonel Borman was commander of the Apollo 8 space flight, the first lunar orbital mission, in December 1968. He is married, has two sons, and resides in Miami, Fla. He was born March 14, 1928.

W. Glenn Campbell has been director, Hoover Institution on War, Revolution and Peace, Stanford University, since 1960. He was a member of the National Science Board, National Science Foundation, in 1972–78. He is married, has three children, and resides in Stanford, Calif. He was born April 29, 1924.

John B. Connally is an attorney with the firm of Vinson & Elkins in Houston, Tex. He was Governor of Texas in 1963–69 and a candidate for President of the United States in 1980. He was Secretary of the Navy in 1961 and Secretary of the Treasury in 1971–72. He was a member of the President's Foreign Intelligence Advisory Board in 1971, 1972–74, and 1976–77. He is married, has three children, and resides in Houston, Tex. He was born February 27, 1917.

John S. Foster, Jr., is vice president, science and technology, TRW, Inc. He was Director of Defense Research and Engineering for the Department of Defense in 1965. Mr. Foster served as a member of the President's Foreign Intelligence Advisory Board in 1973–77. He is married, has five children, and resides in Cleveland, Ohio. He was born September 18, 1922.

Leon Jaworski is an attorney with the firm of Fulbright & Jaworski of Houston, Tex. He was Director of the Office of the Watergate Special Prosecution Force in 1973–74 and special counsel in President Kennedy's assassination investigation. He is married, has two children, and resides in Houston, Tex. He was born September 19, 1905.

Claire Boothe Luce was a member of the President's Foreign Intelligence Advisory Board in 1973–77. She is a playwright and journalist. She was also a Member of Congress in 1943–47 and Ambassador to Italy in 1953–57. She resides in Honolulu, Hawaii, and was born in New York City.

Thomas H. Moorer was Chief of Naval Operations in 1967 and Chairman of the Joint Chiefs of Staff in 1970–74. He recently retired from the Navy with the rank of admiral. He is a member of the board of advisers of the Georgetown University Center for Strategic and International Studies. He was born February 9, 1912.

Peter O'Donnell, Jr., is director of the First National Bank in Dallas, Tex., and was a member of the board of trustees and board of governors of Southern Methodist University in 1973–80. He was an adviser to the Deputy Secretary of Defense in 1973. He is married, has three chil-

dren, and resides in Dallas, Tex. He was born April 21, 1924.

H. Ross Perot is chairman of the board of Electronic Data Systems Corp. in Dallas, Tex. He was formerly with the IBM Corp. and is active in many community affairs including the Boy Scouts of America. He is a recipient of the highest civilian award by the Department of Defense, the Distinguished Civilian Service Award. He resides in Dallas, Tex., and was born in 1930.

Joe M. Rodgers is president of JMR Investments and American Constructors, Inc. He is past national president of the Associated Builders and Contractors, Inc. He was also finance chairman of the Republican National Committee in 1979–80. He is married, has two children, and resides in Nashville, Tenn. He was born November 12, 1933.

Paul Seabury is professor of political science at the University of California at Berkeley and specializes in international relations and U.S. foreign policy. He is married, has two children, and resides in Berkeley, Calif. He was born May 6, 1923.

Robert F. Six, an aviation pioneer and innovator, is founder and chairman of the board of Continental Airlines. He is married and resides in Los Angeles, Calif. He was born June 25, 1907.

Seymour Weiss was Ambassador to the Bahamas in 1974–76 and Director of the Office of Politico-Military Policy, Department of State, in 1973. He was also Director of the Office of Strategic Intelligence and Research, with the rank of Assistant Secretary of State. He is married, has three children, and resides in Bethesda, Md. He was born May 15, 1925.

Edward Bennett Williams is a partner with the firm of Williams & Connolly in Washington, D.C. He taught criminal law at Georgetown Law School in 1946–58 and was a lecturer at Yale Law School in 1971. He was a member of the President's Foreign Intelligence Advisory Board in 1976–77. He is married, has seven children, and resides in Potomac, Md. He was born May 31, 1920.

Appointment of Three Members of the Intelligence Oversight Board, and Designation of Chairman
October 20, 1981

The President today announced his intention to appoint the following individuals to be members of the Intelligence Oversight Board. The President also announced his intention to designate W. Glenn Campbell as Chairman.

W. Glenn Campbell has been director, Hoover Institution on War, Revolution and Peace, Stanford University, since 1960. He was a member of the National Science Board, National Science Foundation, in 1972–78. He is married, has three children, and resides in Stanford, Calif. He was born April 29, 1924.

Frank D. Stella is president and founder of the F. D. Stella Products Co. in Detroit, Mich. He also serves on the board of directors of Peoples Federal Savings & Loan Association of Detroit. He was appointed by President Nixon to serve on the Presidential Commission on Federal Statistics in 1970. He is married, has seven children, and resides in Detroit, Mich. He was born January 21, 1919.

Charles Tyroler II was president of Quadri-Science, Inc., in 1961–80. He is currently a business consultant on national problems. Since 1976 he has been director of the Committee on the Present Danger. In 1950–53 he was Assistant to the Secretary of Defense. He was born January 2, 1915.

Message to the Congress Reporting Budget Deferrals
October 20, 1981

To the Congress of the United States:

In accordance with the Impoundment Control Act of 1974, I herewith report 59 deferrals of fiscal year 1982 funds totaling $147.0 million.

Fifty-six of the deferrals, totaling $95.1 million, constitute the first group of deferrals of fiscal year 1982 funds made available for the period through November 20, 1981, by the Continuing Resolution, P.L. 97–51. These deferrals are intended to preserve Congressional options to act favorably on the proposals for reductions in FY 1982 budget authority that I announced on September 24, 1981, and subsequently transmitted to the Congress. These deferrals recognize the intent of Congress, reaffirmed during House and Senate action on the Continuing Resolution, that amounts provided in Continuing Resolutions are ceilings, not mandatory spending levels.

Accordingly, where the Continuing Resolution provides amounts in excess of my requests for the period of the resolution, deferrals are being proposed to restrain spending to levels in my requests until action on regular appropriations is complete. However, exceptions have been made in this general policy to avoid major administrative or personnel problems or to avoid serious disruption of an agency's missions.

Deferrals under the Continuing Resolution are included in this special message for the Executive Office of the President and twenty-two departments and agencies. Additional deferrals under the Continuing Resolution will be transmitted during the next week.

Three other deferrals, totaling $51.9 million, included in this special message report on amounts routinely carried forward from fiscal year 1981 in the Department of Health and Human Services that cannot be used immediately or are withheld pending completion of a review.

The details of each deferral are contained in the attached reports.

RONALD REAGAN

The White House,
October 20, 1981.

Note: The attachments detailing the deferrals are printed in the Federal Register *of October 26, 1981.*

Proclamation 4876—Suspension of the Application of Obligations Under an Agreement Between the Governments of the United States of America and Argentina Concerning Hide Exports and Other Trade Matters
October 20, 1981

By the President of the United States of America

A Proclamation

1. On August 10, 1979, the Governments of the United States of America and the Argentine Republic entered into an Agreement Concerning Hide Exports and Other Trade Matters (the Agreement). The Agreement was implemented by Proclamation 4694 of September 29, 1979, and became effective October 1, 1979.

2. The Agreement provides in pertinent part that Argentina adopts a 20% ad valorem tax on exports of cattle hides, effective October 1, 1979, to replace its existing embargo on exports of such products, and then to phase out the tax in accordance with the following schedule:

	Percent ad valorem
April 1, 1980	15
October 1, 1980	10
April 1, 1981	5
October 1, 1981	Free

The United States, inter alia, agreed to reduce its 5 percent ad valorem duty on bovine leather provided for in item 121.61 of the Tariff Schedules of the United States (TSUS) in accordance with the following schedule:

	Percent ad valorem
October 1, 1979	2
October 1, 1980	1
October 1, 1981	Free

3. The United States has complied with the terms of the Agreement. In October 1980, Argentina reduced its export tax to 10 percent, but has failed to reduce it further as required by the Agreement. The Government of Argentina has informed the United States that it does not intend to meet its obligations for further reductions in the export tax.

4. Argentina's breach of the Agreement constitutes a suspension of the application of trade agreement obligations of benefit to the United States. Adequate compensation has not been received therefor. The action taken by this proclamation is necessary to protect the economic interest of the United States.

5. Section 125(d)(1) of the Trade Act of 1974 (the Trade Act) (19 U.S.C. 2135(d)(1)) authorizes the President to withdraw, suspend, or modify the application of trade agreement obligations which are substantially equivalent to those which have been withdrawn, suspended, or modified by a foreign country, and to proclaim under section 125(c) of the Trade Act such import restrictions as are appropriate to effect adequate compensation from that foreign country or instrumentality.

6. Section 125(f) of the Trade Act requires the President to provide the opportunity for interested parties to present views at a public hearing prior to taking action pursuant to Section 125(d)(1). Such an opportunity was presented by scheduling such a hear-

ing for September 28, 1981, at the Office of the United States Trade Representative (USTR).

7. I have decided, pursuant to section 125(d)(1) of the Trade Act, to suspend the application of the Agreement insofar as it requires the United States to reduce its duty on bovine leather imports provided for in item 121.61 of the TSUS to free, and to modify the TSUS pursuant to Section 125(c) of the Trade Act to provide a one percent ad valorem column 1 rate of duty on such bovine leather imports.

Now, Therefore, I, Ronald Reagan, President of the United States of America, acting under the authority vested in me by the Constitution and the statutes of the United States, including Sections 125 and 604 of the Trade Act of 1974 (19 U.S.C. 2135 and 2483), do proclaim that:

(1) The application of the obligation of the United States pursuant to the Agreement to reduce its column 1 rate of duty on certain bovine leather imports to free as implemented by Proclamation 4694, is hereby suspended for and until such time as the USTR makes a determination (published in the *Federal Register*) that Argentina is in compliance with the Agreement or has otherwise granted adequate compensation for the breach thereof.

(2) The column 1 rate of duty applicable to item 121.61 of the TSUS is modified to read "1% ad val." effective as to articles entered, or withdrawn from warehouse for consumption, on or after the third day following the date of publication of this proclamation in the *Federal Register* and until such time as the USTR makes the determination referred to in paragraph (1) above, at which time the column 1 rate of duty would be free.

(3) The modification of the TSUS and the determination made by the USTR under the above paragraphs shall be published in the *Federal Register.*

In Witness Whereof, I have hereunto set my hand this twentieth day of October, in the year of our Lord nineteen hundred and eighty-one and of the Independence of the United States of America the two hundred and sixth.

RONALD REAGAN

[*Filed with the Office of the Federal Register, 10:41 a.m., October 21, 1981*]

Remarks to Reporters Upon Departure for the International Meeting on Cooperation and Development in Cancún, Mexico
October 21, 1981

The President. Good morning.

This summer, I had the privilege of representing the United States in Ottawa, at an economic summit attended by nations representing more than two-thirds of the world's wealth. Well, this morning I leave for Cancún, Mexico, to attend another economic summit, this one attended by 22 industrial and developing nations that comprise more than two-thirds of the world's population.

Together, these summits reflect a commitment by the peoples in nearly every part of the globe, and the United States is a part of this commitment. We believe a stronger domestic and world economy are vital to peace and stability. This objective is a top priority of American foreign policy, but we go to Cancún with no illusions. The problems of hunger and poverty are severe and deeply rooted. They cannot be solved overnight, nor can massive transfers of wealth somehow miraculously produce new well-being.

Our message at Cancún will be clear. The road to prosperity and human fulfillment is lighted by economic freedom and individual incentive. As always, the United States will be a friend and an active partner in the search for a better life.

We take with us a solid record of support for development and a positive program for the 1980's. Free people build free markets that ignite dynamic development for everyone. We will renew our commitment to strengthen and improve international trading, investment, and financial relations, and we will work for more effective cooperation to help developing countries achieve greater self-sustaining growth.

Cancún is a unique undertaking in world affairs. Never have so many nations gathered from so many parts of the globe for a summit conference on economic growth. With cooperation and good will, this summit can be more than just another shattered dream. It can be the beginning of new hope and a better life for all.

Q. Mr. Reagan, you said that you expected to find a hostile environment. Are you still expecting it, and why?

The President. No, not really, and maybe that was a harsh word for it. I think that there's been—there's kind of a wave of propaganda about the United States. But when you really analyze the facts, the United States has provided food for the developing world—more than all the rest of the world has provided put together.

We have more than half the trade. We import the products from the non-OPEC developing countries. More than half is imported by this country. And we have duty laws and so forth that encourage that trade. And I think that we have something to offer and have quite a record.

Q. How much of a partner will the United States be?

The President. Well, we're certainly not going to go backward. We hope that we will be able to suggest going forward with more of what we have done so well. What is needed is development of those countries to the point of being self-sustaining.

Q. Thank you, Mr. President.

Note: The President spoke at 8:31 a.m. to reporters assembled at the South Portico of the White House.

Statement on United States Strategic Policy
October 21, 1981

In the past few days, the Soviet Union has issued several propaganda statements that seek to drive a wedge between the United States and some of our closest friends in Europe. I do not intend to let these gross distortions of our policies go unchallenged.

American policy toward deterring conflict in Europe has not changed for over 20 years. Our strategy remains, as it has been, one of flexible response: maintaining an assured military capability to deter the use of force—conventional or nuclear—by the Warsaw pact at the lowest possible level.

As all Presidents have acknowledged, any use of nuclear weapons would have the most profound consequences. In a nuclear war, all mankind would lose. Indeed, the awful and incalculable risks associated with any use of nuclear weapons themselves serve to deter their use.

The suggestion that the United States could even consider fighting a nuclear war at Europe's expense is an outright deception. The essence of U.S. nuclear strategy is that no aggressor should believe that the use of nuclear weapons in Europe could reasonably be limited to Europe. Indeed it is the joint European-American commitment to share the burden of our common defense which assures the peace. Thus, we regard any military threat to Europe as a threat to the United States itself. Three hundred seventy-five thousand U.S. servicemen provide the living guarantees of this unshakable U.S. commitment to the peace and security of Europe.

Statement at the First Plenary Session of the International Meeting on Cooperation and Development in Cancún, Mexico
October 22, 1981

I am honored to be with all of you on this historic occasion.

In many ways, this summit is not ours alone. It belongs to the millions who look to us for help and for hope. If they could speak to us today, I believe they might tell us that words are cheap, that cooperative action is needed—and needed now. In their name, let us join together and move forward. Let us meet the challenge of charting a strategic course for global economic growth and development for all nations.

Each of us comes to Cancún from a different domestic setting, where our major responsibilities are found. My own government has devoted much of the past year to developing a plan of action to strengthen our economy. For years, our government has overspent, overtaxed, and overregulated, causing our growth rates to decline and our inflation and interest rates to rise. We have taken bold measures to correct these problems, and we are confident they will succeed—not tomorrow, nor next week, but over the months and years ahead.

We believe restoring sound economic policies at home represents one of the most important contributions the U.S. can make to greater growth and development abroad. The actions we are taking will renew confidence in the dollar, strengthen our demand for imports, hold down inflation, reduce interest rates and the cost of borrowing, and increase resources for foreign investment.

I have also had a chance to study and discuss with various leaders the domestic problems you face. I know how diverse and serious they are. For the poorest countries, more food and energy are urgently needed, while raising productivity through education, better health and nutrition, and the acquisition of basic facilities such as roads and ports represent longer-term goals.

Middle-income countries need foreign capital, technical assistance, and the development of basic skills to improve their economic climate and credit worthiness in international capital markets. The more advanced developing nations, which already benefit from the international economy, need increasing access to markets to sustain their development.

And across the income spectrum, many among you who are oil importers face acute financial difficulties from the large debt burdens resulting from the oil price shocks of the 1970's. High interest rates are exacerbating these problems, such that debt servicing and energy costs are making excessive claims on your foreign exchange earnings.

We recognize that each nation's approach to development should reflect its own cultural, political, and economic heritage. That is the way it should be. The great thing about our international system is that it respects diversity and promotes creativity. Certain economic factors, of course, apply across cultural and political lines. We are mutually interdependent, but, above all, we are individually responsible.

We must respect both diversity and economic realities when discussing grand ideas. As I said last week in Philadelphia, we do not seek an ideological debate; we seek to build upon what we already know will work.

History demonstrates that time and again, in place after place, economic growth and human progress make their greatest strides in countries that encourage economic freedom.

Government has an important role in helping to develop a country's economic foundation. But the critical test is whether government is genuinely working to liberate individuals by creating incentives to work, save, invest, and succeed.

Individual farmers, laborers, owners, traders, and managers—they are the heart and soul of development. Trust them. Because whenever they are allowed to create and build, wherever they are given a personal stake in deciding economic policies and benefiting from their success, then societies become more dynamic, prosperous, progressive, and free.

With sound understanding of our domestic freedom and responsibilities, we can construct effective international cooperation. Without it, no amount of international good will and action can produce prosperity.

In examining our collective experience with development, let us remember that international economic institutions have also done much to improve the world economy. Under their auspices, the benefits of international commerce have flowed increasingly to all countries. From 1950 to 1980, GNP per capita in 60 middle-income countries increased twice as fast as in the industrial countries when real purchasing power is taken into account.

Despite the mid-seventies recession, we were able to liberalize the international trading system under the leadership of the GATT. This created new trading opportunities for a number of developed and developing countries.

The IMF remains the centerpiece of the international financial system. It has adjusted its programs and increased its resources to deal with the major pressures and problems of our era. The World Bank and other multilateral development banks have dramatically increased their resources and their overall support for development.

Much remains to be done to help low-income countries develop domestic markets and strengthen their exports. We recognize that. But we are just as convinced that the way to do this is not to weaken the very system that has served us so well, but to continue working together to make it better.

I am puzzled by suspicions that the U.S. might ignore the developing world. The contribution America has made to development—and will continue to make—is enormous.

We have provided $57 billion to the developing countries in the last decade—$43 billion in development assistance and $14 billion in contributions to the multilateral development banks. Each year, the U.S. provides more food assistance to developing nations than all other nations combined. Last year, we extended almost twice as much official development assistance as any other nation.

Even more significant is the U.S. contribution in trade. Far too little world attention has been given to the importance of trade as a key to development.

The U.S. absorbs about one-half of all manufactured goods that non-OPEC developing countries export to the industrialized world, even though our market is only one-third the total industrialized world market. Last year alone, we imported $60 billion worth of goods from non-OPEC developing countries. That is more than twice the official development assistance from all OECD countries. Our trade and capital markets are among the most open in the world.

The range and breadth of America's commitment extend far beyond concessional assistance. We believe in promoting development by maximizing every asset we have.

As the world's largest single market, we can be a powerful conductor for economic progress and well-being. We come to Cancún offering our hand in friendship as your partner in prosperity. Together, we can identify the roadblocks to development and decide the best ways to stimulate greater growth everywhere we can. We have yet to unleash the full potential for growth in a world of open markets.

The U.S. is here to listen and learn. And when we leave Cancún, our search for progress will continue. The dialog will go on. The bonds of our common resolve will not disappear with our jet trails.

We are prepared to carry out the commitment in the Ottawa summit declaration to conduct a more formal dialog—bilaterally, with regional groups, in the United Nations, and in specialized international agencies. We take seriously the commitment at Ottawa "to participate in preparations for a mutually acceptable process of global negotiations in circumstances offering the prospects of meaningful progress."

It is our view that "circumstances offering the prospect of meaningful progress" are future talks based upon four essential understandings among the participants:

—The talks should have a practical orientation toward identifying, on a case-by-case basis, specific potential for or obstacles to development which cooperative efforts may enhance or remove. We will suggest an agenda composed of trade liberalization, energy and food resource development, and improvement in the investment climate.

—The talks should respect the competence, functions, and powers of the specialized international agencies upon which we all depend, with the understanding that the decisions reached by these agencies within respective areas of competence are final. We should not seek to create new institutions.

—The general orientation of the talks must be toward sustaining or achieving greater levels of mutually beneficial international growth and development, taking into account domestic economic policies.

—The talks should take place in an atmosphere of cooperative spirit, similar to that which has brought us together in Cancún, rather than one in which views become polarized and chances for agreement are needlessly sacrificed.

If these understandings are accepted, then the U.S. would be willing to to engage in a new preparatory process to see what may be achieved. I suggest that officials of our governments informally confer in the months ahead as to appropriate procedures.

But our main purpose in coming to Cancún is to focus on specific questions of substance, not procedural matters. In this spirit, we bring a positive program of action for development, concentrated around these principles:

—stimulating international trade by opening up markets, both within individual countries and among countries;

—tailoring particular development strategies to the specific needs and potential of individual countries and regions;

—guiding our assistance toward the development of self-sustaining productive activities, particularly in food and energy;

—improving the climate for private capital flows, particularly private investment; and

—creating a political atmosphere in which practical solutions can move foward, rather than founder on a reef of misguided policies that restrain and interfere with the international marketplace or foster inflation.

In our conversations, we will be elaborating on the specifics of this program. The program deals not in flashy new gimmicks, but in substantive fundamentals with a track record of success. It rests on a coherent view of what's essential to development—namely political freedom and economic opportunity.

Yes, we believe in freedom. We know it works. It's just as exciting, successful, and revolutionary today as it was 200 years ago.

I want to thank our hosts for arranging this historic opportunity. Let us join together and proceed together. Economic development is an exercise in mutual cooperation for the common good. We can and must grasp this opportunity for our people and together take a step for mankind.

Note: The President read the statement at the 2-day meeting which began at 10 a.m. at the Cancún Sheraton Hotel. In the inaugural session, President José López Portillo of Mexico, host and Cochairman of the meeting, made welcoming remarks. Prime Minister Pierre Elliott Trudeau of Canada, honorary Cochairman, also made introductory remarks.

The first plenary session began at 10:30 a.m. The leaders of the 22 participating nations and Secretary-General Kurt Waldheim of the United Nations made statements.

Proclamation 4877—Hungarian Freedom Fighters' Day
October 22, 1981

By the President of the United States of America

A Proclamation

Twenty-five years ago the Hungarian people rose to challenge foreign domination of their country and to assert their right to freedom and democratic self-determination.

Today, many of those same people are citizens of the United States. Their experiences, and their continuing devotion to the ideals for which they fought, have brought new strength and meaning to this Nation's commitment to freedom and justice for all people.

The Congress of the United States by joint resolution has authorized and requested the President to honor the memory of the brave Hungarian men and women who fought so courageously to achieve the realization of their aspirations in the face of overwhelming military force.

Now, Therefore, I, Ronald Reagan, President of the United States of America, do hereby designate October 23, 1981, as Hungarian Freedom Fighters' Day. I call upon the people of the United States to reaffirm our belief and hope that all nations will one day achieve through peaceful means the goals of democratic freedom and self-determination for which these gallant people sacrificed so much.

In Witness Whereof, I have hereunto set my hand this twenty-second day of October, in the year of our Lord nineteen hundred and eighty-one, and of the Independence of the United States of America the two hundred and sixth.

RONALD REAGAN

[*Filed with the Office of the Federal Register, 10:40 a.m., October 23, 1981*]

Note: *The text of the proclamation was released by the Office of the Press Secretary on October 23.*

Question-and-Answer Session With Reporters During the International Meeting on Cooperation and Development in Cancún, Mexico
October 23, 1981

The President. Good morning.

Q. You came here to listen and learn.

The President. Yes.

Q. What did you hear and what do you know now and what did you learn?

The President. Well, I think more about the specific problems of some of the nations that we're here to find a way to help—more specifics as to their particular problems. All in all, I think they've been fine meetings, and I think great progress has been made.

Q. Have any of the delegates, Mr. President, said anything to cause you to change your thinking about foreign aid or how you could help the poor people of the world?

The President. No, but you have to remember that there's no one at that table that has done more in the line of foreign aid than has the United States. And we're concerned, have been for some time, that our foreign aid would be as effective as it can be. And many times for a program that gigantic, and over the years, you know that it can fall into ruts. And the aid is being delivered, but you want to make sure that it's getting to the people that it's intended to help.

So, we had a very good discussion yesterday on food and agriculture for the countries that have that problem. And I think we've made a contribution to them, in proposals as to how we could go in—you might say that that's a task force route—and find out exactly how their own agricultural output could be improved.

Q. You said great progress was made. How do you interpret that, in what way?

The President. We had a very open discussion, identifying the point at which possibly aid isn't being as effective as it might be.

Q. There have been various interpretations as to whether you went for the global negotiations or you didn't—couldn't quite tell by the speech.

The President. Helen [Helen Thomas, United Press International], I think that it's a term and what the term means to various people. If there are those there, and possibly there are, who by global negotiations interpret that to mean some gigantic new international bureaucracy to be in charge, that we would be opposed to that.

If global negotiations means that we continue negotiations as to how all of us can help resolve these problems, we're perfectly willing to——

Q. How about the United Nations? Would that be a good place for global negotiations?

The President. Well, we think in some of the organizations that are already existing in the United Nations, that we direct our efforts and their efforts more specifically to doing things that need doing—for example, such things as the World Bank and the International Monetary Fund, other U.N. organizations that are being directed toward being helpful—and from out of this to learn the specifics, that we can go and work with them to make them more effective.

Q. [*Referring to the sale of AWACS and other air defense equipment to Saudi Arabia*] Are you going to give the bad news to [Prince] Fahd today?

The President. What bad news? [*Laughter*]

Q. Good news?

The President. No, we're going to keep on fighting. I look foward to getting back Monday morning and going to work some more.

Q. You're not discouraged then?

The President. I'm cautiously optimistic.

Q. We've heard that before.

The President. Well, the last time you heard it, it worked. [*Laughter*]

Q. Thank you.

Note: The session began at 8:22 a.m. in the President's suite at the Cancún Sheraton Hotel.

Nomination of Robert L. Barry To Be United States Ambassador to Bulgaria
October 23, 1981

The President today announced his intention to nominate Robert L. Barry, of New Hampshire, to be Ambassador to Bulgaria. He would succeed Jack Richard Perry.

Mr. Barry served in the United States Navy in 1957–60. He entered the Foreign Service in 1962 and was vice counsul in Zagreb in 1963–65. In 1965–67 he was in the Department of State as international relations officer in the Office of Soviet Union Affairs. He studied the Russian language at Munich (Garmisch) in 1967–68. He was consular officer, then political officer in Moscow (1968–70), political officer at the United States Mission to the United Nations in New York 1970–71, and deputy principal officer in Leningrad (1971–73). He was on detail to the International Communication Agency as Director of the U.S.S.R. Division of the Voice of America in 1973–75. In the Department of State he was Deputy Director of the Office of Soviet Union Affairs (1975–77), Director of the Office of United Nations Political Affairs (1977–78), Deputy Assistant Secretary of State for International Organization Affairs (1978–79), and since 1979 he has been Deputy Assistant Secretary of State for European Affairs.

Mr. Barry graduated from Dartmouth College (B.A., 1956) and Columbia University (M.A., 1962). He is married, has three children, and resides in Rindge, N.H. He was born August 28, 1934, in Pittsburgh, Pa.

Nomination of Melvyn R. Paisley To Be an Assistant Secretary of the Navy
October 23, 1981

The President today announced his intention to nominate Melvyn R. Paisley to be Assistant Secretary of the Navy for Research, Engineering and Systems. He would succeed David E. Mann.

Mr. Paisley is currently vice president of Boeing International and manager of international operations. During the past 27 years at Boeing, Mr. Paisley has filled numerous management and engineering positions. In 1954 he was responsible for the design and test on the BOMARC missle. In 1959 he became manager of the electronics staff for the Minuteman missile system where he directed early development of a radio launch control system.

In 1961 Mr. Paisley was appointed engineering manager of the Minuteman system at Wing I in Great Falls, Mont., where he was responsible for the engineering aspects of deploying the first Minuteman Wing.

Following that assignment, he was manager of the Safeguard anti-ballistic missle implementation project and was then assigned as the B-1 electronics proposal manager. In 1971 he became the 747 Tankers program manager. His last assignment before taking his present position was director of planning for Boeing Aerospace Co.

Mr. Paisley graduated from the American Institute of Technology (1953) and MIT (1954). He is married, has four children, and resides in Kent, Wash. He was born October 9, 1924, in Portland, Oreg.

Message to the Congress Reporting Budget Deferrals and Rescissions
October 23, 1981

To the Congress of the United States:

In accordance with the Impoundment Control Act of 1974, I herewith report 72 deferrals of fiscal year 1982 funds totaling $482.9 million. I am also reporting two new proposals to rescind $88.2 million in budget authority previously provided by the Congress.

Seventy-one of the deferrals totaling $391.6 million represent the second in a series of messages that I am transmitting deferring fiscal year 1982 funds made available by the Continuing Resolution, P.L. 97–51.

These actions are being taken in accord with the stated intent of the Congress to provide minimal and temporary funding for the duration of the Continuing Resolution which expires November 20, 1981. As indicated in my last special message of October 20, I plan to restrain spending to insure that the Congress has the opportunity to enact regular appropriations for the entire fiscal year at levels that are consistent with my revised budget request.

Deferrals under the Continuing Resolution are included in this special message for the Executive Office of the President and 20 departments and agencies.

I am also reporting in this message a deferral of $91.3 million for Veterans Administration construction pending completion of a project review and two rescission proposals for programs in the Department of Defense that are consistent with amendments to the Defense budget sent to the Congress on October 15.

The details of each rescission proposal and deferral are contained in the attached reports.

RONALD REAGAN

The White House,
October 23, 1981.

Note: The attachments detailing the deferrals and proposed rescissions are printed in the Federal Register *of October 30, 1981.*

Remarks and a Question-and-Answer Session With Reporters Upon Returning From the International Meeting on Cooperation and Development in Cancún, Mexico
October 24, 1981

The President. Throughout these 3 days in Cancún, I have participated in a unique and highly productive exchange of views with leaders of developed and developing nations. I hope that I speak for the many other world leaders there in saying that Cancún was a substantial success.

The spirit of this conference, as the Co-chairman described it, was extremely constructive and positive. The exchange was direct, frank, wide-ranging, and free of recrimination. We dealt with hard issues, and yet succeeded in finding many areas of shared priorities and of common ground.

The fact that we could suceed demonstrates the possibility for a more fruitful dialog conducted with candor and mutual respect. I believe that all those who attended found our expectations fulfilled and even exceeded. Together we succeeded in creating a spirit of new hope, which we want to translate into progress to revitalize the world economy and accelerate the growth of developing countries.

Last week in Philadelphia, I spoke of the goal that motivates our effort: the enhancement of human freedom and economic opportunity. We evaluated the record of what succeeds and proposed a program to address the fundamental problems facing the developing countries and the world economy.

At Cancún, we stressed many of those same important themes and the commitment of the United States to work with those countries in their development efforts. There was broad agreement on steps which had to be taken by the developing countries themselves, and by developed and developing countries together, to stimulate the process of growth. There was broad acceptance of many of the approaches proposed in Philadelphia and a strong desire to work with the United States in these areas.

All participants recognized the fact that economic prosperity in any country or group of countries depends both on individual countries own efforts and on close international economic cooperation. We didn't waste time on unrealistic rhetoric or unattainable objectives. We dealt with pragmatic solutions to the problems of growth—efforts to improve food security and agricultural development.

There was agreement with our proposal that task forces should be sent to developing countries to assist them in finding new agricultural techniques and transmitting to farmers techniques now in existence. I have directed the Agency for International Development to coordinate these U.S. efforts and to report to us on the progress made.

We also discussed ways to increase trade and industrialization, and there was strong support for working together at the GATT Ministerial. In addition, ways were discussed in which the developing nations can increase their energy production, and monetary and financial issues were reviewed.

I return home reminded again of the importance of American leadership in the world. At Cancún, we made a good beginning toward more constructive and mutually beneficial relations among developed and developing nations and toward a more prosperous world. We have an enormous opportunity now to advance mutually beneficial economic relations with our developing country partners.

I look foward to continuing our efforts in the constructive spirit that characterized the Cancún discussions. By sustaining that spirit, the American people, the people of the developing nations, and the entire world will be better.

End of statement.

Q. Mr. President, do you foresee any problems—when you were gone, a number of Senators have expressed the way they will vote on AWACS. And do you see any further problems for you in that area? Are you still expected to win?

The President. Well, I will repeat my cautious, but optimistic, statement, but say that's what I am back to get busy with again, and see if we can't continue to get some of those who are undecided to realize that the greatest security for the United States and the greatest security for Israel rests with the sale of the AWACS to Saudi Arabia. And those Senators who refuse to see this, I'm afraid, are not doing their country a service.

Q. Were there any futher discussions with Prince Fahd while you were there? Did you discuss AWACS at all?

The President. Never mentioned it.

Q. Is there any possibility that you will withdraw the sale from the Senate?

The President. No.

Q. In what ways are the Senators not doing the country a service?

The President. Because I don't think they're being realistic about the dangerous situation in the Middle East, the threat of the Soviet Union there, and the need for the United States and our allies to make their presence felt in that area.

Q. [*Inaudible*]

The President. We discussed that, discussed Egypt, and what we view as Egypt's progress now. And all in all, it was a very optimistic discussion.

Q. Do you think that Saudi Arabia has gone as far as it can go in terms of assurances and guarantees, and do you think they are sufficient enough to convince the 18 Senators you are going to meet next week?

The President. Helen [Helen Thomas, United Press International], they certainly should be, because I can say that with all my heart, we have guaranteed the security of the technology and the security of Israel.

Q. Mr. President, do you still leave open the option—or do you leave open the option of bypassing the Senate if they do not go along with the sale?

The President. Well, that's something that I refuse to even think about or discuss while we are still talking to Senators who are honestly uncommitted and undecided and waiting to make up their minds.

Q. Thank you very much.

The President. Thank you all.

Note: The President spoke at 4:22 p.m. at Andrews Air Force Base, Md. Following the question-and-answer session, the President returned to the White House on Marine One.

Nomination of Reynaldo Philip Maduro To Be an Assistant Director of ACTION
October 26, 1981

The President today announced his intention to nominate Reynaldo Philip Maduro to be Assistant Director for the Office of Compliance at ACTION. He would succeed Mary Frances Cahill Leyland.

Since 1977 Mr. Maduro has been president of RPM & Associates, a public relations and marketing service in Washington, D.C. He was vice president of B & C Associates, Inc., in 1977. Mr. Maduro was Deputy Spe-

cial Assistant to the President in the Office of Liaison at the White House in 1976–77. He served as Director, Executive Secretariat, Law Enforcement Assistance Administration, Department of Justice, in 1975–76. In 1975 he was staff assistant, Office of the Deputy Commissioner, Immigration and Naturalization Service; consultant to the President in 1974–75; principal adviser to the Chairman of the Cabinet Committee on

Opportunities for Spanish Speaking People in 1972–74; Deputy Manpower Administrator and Director, Equal Employment Opportunity Program in 1971–72.

He attended Modesto Junior College (Modesto, Calif.) in 1955–57; Drake University (Des Moines, Iowa) in 1957–58; and Los Angeles State University in 1958. He served in the United States Marine Corps in 1952–55. He has three children and resides in Bethesda, Md. He was born October 10, 1931, in New York, N.Y.

Nomination of Edward W. Ray To Be a Commissioner of the Copyright Royalty Tribunal
October 26, 1981

The President today announced his intention to nominate Edward W. Ray to be Commissioner of the Copyright Royalty Tribunal for the unexpired term of 5 years from September 27, 1977. He would succeed Clarence L. James, Jr.

Since 1979 he has been president of California Multiple Industries, a real estate investment-management firm in Los Angeles, Calif. He was vice president and general manager of Cream-Hi Records (Memphis Division) in 1976–79; president and owner of Eddie Ray Music Enterprises, Inc. (Memphis), in 1974–79; vice president of artist and repertoire, MGM Records (Los Angeles) in 1970–74; executive vice president and chief operating officer of the record/music division, Burt Sugarman/Pierre Cossette Television Production Co., in 1969–70; vice president for artist and repertoire, Capitol Records in 1964–69; and executive assistant to the president, Imperial Records (Los Angeles) in 1955–64.

He graduated from Los Angeles City College and Memphis State University. He has two children and resides in Los Angeles, Calif. He was born December 21, 1926, in Franklin, N.C.

Nomination of W. Proctor Scarboro To Be a Member of the Federal Farm Credit Board
October 26, 1981

The President today announced his intention to nominate W. Proctor Scarboro to be a member of the Federal Farm Credit Board, Farm Credit Administration, for a term expiring March 31, 1987. He would succeed David C. Waldrop.

Mr. Scarboro has managed and supervised farms during most of his lifetime. He has 30 years experience working on the Wilson, N.C., tobacco market and since 1972, has worked as sales manager of Smith Warehouse in Wilson.

He has been active in the Production Credit Association in North Carolina, including serving as a member, stockholder, and member of the nominating committee. He is also a charter member of the Farm Bureau of North Carolina. In 1973–77 Mr. Scarboro served on the State Highway Commission, State of North Carolina.

He is married and resides in Zebulon, N.C. He was born February 23, 1916, in Wake County, N.C.

Nomination of Bobby Jack Thompson To Be Administrator of the United States Fire Administration
October 26, 1981

The President today announced his intention to nominate Bobby Jack Thompson to be Administrator of the United States Fire Administration at the Federal Emergency Management Agency. He would succeed Gordon Vickery.

Since 1980 Mr. Thompson has been superintendent, National Fire Academy, at Emmitsburg, Md. He was city manager, city of Santa Ana, Calif., in 1976–80, fire chief in 1970–76, assistant fire chief in 1968–70, battalion chief in 1966–68, chief (fire prevention) in 1963–66, captain in 1961–63, engi-

neer in 1959–61, and fireman in 1958–59.

In 1955–58 he was a fireman and fire inspector in Redondo Beach, Calif. In 1965–79, he was also an instructor at California State University in Los Angeles, San Diego State University, Rio Hondo Community College (Whittier, Calif.), and California State University at Long Beach. He graduated from Rio Hondo Community College and California State University.

He is married, has five children, and resides in Cazenovia, N.Y. He was born March 26, 1930, in Perry, Okla.

Proclamation 4878—Veterans Day, 1981
October 26, 1981

By the President of the United States of America

A Proclamation

The willingness of our citizens to give freely and unselfishly of themselves, even their lives, in defense of our democratic principles, gives this great Nation continued strength and vitality. From Valley Forge to Vietnam, through war and peace, valiant Americans have answered the call to duty with honor and dignity.

Americans throughout this great land set aside Veterans Day for special remembrance of the men and women who have served to protect our freedom. The sound of bugles playing taps will pierce the air at countless ceremonies around the country and at our bases overseas in tribute to those who gave their lives in order to safeguard human liberty.

On this special day, our hearts and thoughts also turn to those who were disabled while serving their country. Their sacrifices and hardships endure, and daily earn anew the honor and compassion of a grateful nation.

With a spirit of pride and gratitude, we honor all our veterans, and especially those who have fought on the battlefields of Europe and the beaches of the Pacific, in the jungles and mountains of Asia, in hostile waters and skies around the globe.

Now, Therefore, I, Ronald Reagan, President of the United States of America, do hereby invite the American people to join with me in a fitting salute on Veterans Day, Wednesday, November 11, 1981. I urge all Americans to recognize the valor and sacrifice of our veterans through appropriate public ceremonies and private prayers.

I ask that we devote special attention to those veterans who are sick and disabled. Let us show them through our actions that we remember and honor them. There could be no better nor more tangible expression of our gratitude.

I also call upon Federal, state, and local government officials to display the flag of the United States and to encourage and participate in patriotic activities throughout the country. I invite the business community, churches, schools, unions, civic and fraternal organizations, and the media to support this national observance with suitable commemorative expressions and programs.

In Witness Whereof, I have hereunto set my hand this 26th day of Oct. in the year of our Lord nineteen hundred and eighty-one, and of the Independence of the United States of America the two hundred and sixth.

RONALD REAGAN

[*Filed with the Office of the Federal Register, 2:27 p.m., October 27, 1981*]

Note: The text of the proclamation was released by the Office of the Press Secretary on October 27.

Question-and-Answer Session With Reporters on the Sale of AWACS and Other Air Defense Equipment to Saudi Arabia
October 27, 1981

Q. How about telling us about the AWACS?

Q. Yes, Mr. President. I understand you've got it won. Is that right?

The President. I'm not going to say that. I'm cautiously optimistic, but I feel good.

Q. How about a count? If you won't say you'll win, why don't you give us your estimated count?

The President. Well, you know how it is. Those things can go one way or the other. But we've been busy, and I think it looks good.

Q. Do you feel that you've convinced some of the Senators that you've seen in the last couple of days to come to your side?

The President. Well, I think some have, yes.

Q. What's the argument that you've been using that's persuaded most?

The President. That it is good for the United States, good for peace in the Middle East, and good for the security of Israel.

Q. And good for President Reagan?

The President. No. I've never been in an AWACS myself. [*Laughter*]

Q. No, sir. I mean the argument is being made that if they don't support you, they weaken your hand in the conduct of foreign policy.

The President. I think that would be a natural assumption to make, yes. But that isn't the argument I have been using.

Q. What exactly has made you so optimistic tonight? I mean why do you feel good?

The President. Well, I just think that it's much closer than has been reported in the last few days.

Q. You need three votes?

The President. I don't know how many.

Q. Well now, when Ms. Thomas [Helen Thomas, United Press International] said in Cancún, "We have heard that before," you said, "Yes, before we have always won." Remember? You have won this one, haven't you?

The President. I don't know, really. No, you couldn't get me to say that if you threw a bomb at me—and don't. [*Laughter*]

Q. Would you consider an emergency arms—invoking the emergency powers?

The President. We haven't considered that. We haven't talked about that yet, and I seriously doubt it.

Q. You wouldn't rule it out though?

Q. You are expecting some more Senators to jump on the bandwagon now?

The President. Jump on or climb on or——

Q. Are you going to send the letter tomorrow to the Senate?

The President. I think that the letter has gone, hasn't it?

Deputy Press Secretary Speakes. It goes tomorrow.

The President. It is tomorrow? Yes, the letter is going up tomorrow.

Q. Have you made any deals? Have you been giving anything away?

The President. No, I don't make deals.

Q. What happens if you lose, Mr. President?

The President. I lie me down and bleed awhile and then get up and fight again. [*Laughter*]

Q. Which is closer, Marshall Coleman's victory or AWACS?

The President. On both, I am cautiously optimistic.

Q. Thank you.

Note: The session began at 5:17 p.m. on the South Lawn of the White House as the President was preparing to depart for Richmond, Va.

Remarks at a Rally in Richmond, Virginia, for Gubernatorial Candidate Marshall Coleman
October 27, 1981

The President. I have on other occasions spoken a line that I'm going to speak again, but I've never meant it more than I do now: "That is a hard act to follow." [*Laughter*]

Governor Dalton, Governor Godwin, Senator Warner, Congressman Bliley, Nathan Miller, Wyatt Durrette, the lovely wives of these gentlemen who are up here, Helen Obenshain, our good Virginia friends, the man who brought us here tonight, of course, and his wife, Marshall Coleman—Governor Coleman, if the people of Virginia do what I think they're going to do:

You know, I have a warm feeling about Virginia, and I feel like I'm among old friends tonight.

Audience. You are! [*Applause*]

The President. Thank you. I've discovered that somehow living in Washington leads to an emotional attachment to Virginia.

Audience. We love you.

The President. Thank you. I can run down to Quantico and ride horseback through your beautiful countryside. And why not? After all, according to what I read, I only work 2 or 3 hours a day. [*Laughter*]

Of course, I've had some experiences. Some years ago in World War II, I was a reserve officer in the Cavalry, and I was called to active duty. And I found myself assigned to Colonel Phillip Booker, 34 years Regular Army, Virginia Military Institute. A little later in the day, he passed by and says, "Reagan, Mrs. Booker and I'd be delighted to have you for dinner tonight." And I'll confess that I thought, "Oh, oh, this isn't bad." I was scared to death, a second "lieuie" first time out, and I thought, "but here maybe Hollywood has had some effect or something."

I didn't realize at the time that he'd had a bad experience when he first was assigned to active duty, and from that time on had always invited to dinner, on the first day, a new officer assigned to his command. But that night, in the company of a couple of admirals and a general or two, and their wives, and after a cocktail or two, there was a moment of silence. And I said, "Colonel Booker, I think you and I have something in common." And he says, "What's that, Reagan?" And I said, "Well, you're a graduate of Virginia Military Institute, and I was in a picture once called 'Brother Rat.'" [*Laughter*] And he said, "Yes, Reagan, I saw that picture. Nothing ever made me so mad in my life." [*Laughter*]

But seriously, there's much more about Virginia. It stands, as you have been told already tonight, as a hallmark of sound, responsible government. And this was demonstrated by your support during the recent budget and the tax battles. In keeping with Virginia's fine tradition of fiscal integrity, our program received the unanimous backing of your congressional delegation and of both of your fine Senators.

With the urging of Governor Dalton and Marshall Coleman, Virginia put itself on the line to get Federal spending and taxes under control, and your Commonwealth has been, as Governor Godwin told you, a shining example of the meaning of federalism— a testament to the principles of conservatism that provide opportunities, jobs, and hope for all citizens.

When I'm talking to Virginians, I say again, I know I'm talking to friends. We have much to be thankful for in America. The most precious gift we have is our political freedom—the legacy left us by Virginians like Jefferson, Madison, and Patrick Henry. But all of Virginia's great leaders are not found in past history. In the last two decades, you've been blessed with dynamic leadership that well represented the conservative convictions of the men and women of this Commonwealth.

Virginia's leaders, proud and independent, provided you with progress while maintaining your traditions and heritage. Seven days from now, you and your fellow Virginians will chart the future of this State. You will determine more than just who will be Virginia's next Governor, lieutenant governor, and attorney general, you'll reflect Virginia's commitment to preserving the tried and true concepts of shared power between the Federal and State governments.

Now, I believe that's one of the most important things that we're attempting in our economic program and all the other things in Washington. You will choose between time-honored beliefs, and an uncharted course of conduct which has led us far from the concept of sovereign states assembled together in a federation without losing their sovereignty.

Now, it would be inappropriate for me to tell the people of this State for whom they should vote, so I won't. [*Laughter*] However, since I just happen to be passing through town—[*laughter*]—I thought I might say a few words about a man who's been a strong supporter of our economic program, a man whom I tremendously respect—a fellow by the name of Marshall Coleman. He certainly is qualified to be the Governor of Virginia. His roots run deep. He has the depth and background necessary to do what needs to be done to keep this State on an even keel. And as the election draws near, people should carefully examine the records of the two candidates, examine them as they were pointed out to you just a few moments ago. And I hope they would do so free of the glare of advertising, in quiet reflection, ignoring the image-building that has characterized this campaign. And if they do, then Marshall Coleman will be the next Governor of the Commonwealth of Virginia.

You know, as an ex-Democrat myself, I never cease to be amazed at how conservative liberals can sound during election years. Well, Marshall Coleman not only sounds conservative, he is conservative in the finest meaning of that word. He understands how to deal with crime and how to keep budgets under control. He's got the experience and the qualifications to do the job. I'm looking forward to working closely with him once he's elected Governor of the State of Virginia, just as I have with Governor John Dalton.

It isn't going to do us any good to clean up the mess in Washington unless the right kind of public officials are elected at the State level, and not just our gubernatorial candidates. We need the right kind of people in the legislature. And don't send Marshall Coleman to the Capitol alone, he's going to need Nathan Miller and Wyatt Durette. He's going to need them to ensure that Virginia keeps moving in the right direction.

These men are committed to the principles in which we believe; they're conservative, independent, qualified for the jobs they seek, and willing to work hard once they're elected. They're the kind of public officials I'm counting on to make our economic program work. It'll only work if we have people in State government who believe in federalism, who believe as the Constitution says that certain powers are reserved to the States and the people, and not to an all-powerful central government.

I appreciate this chance to talk with you because nothing would make me happier than to know when I call the Governor of Virginia, I'm going to get someone on the line who believes that we should restore the tenth amendment of the Constitution.

Your election next week is important to Virginia's future and to the Nation. I'm going to talk a little of my own shop for a minute here.

I'm sure many of you are aware that there's a vote tomorrow in the United States Senate concerning the sale of radar planes to Saudi Arabia. I'm deeply concerned about this—not about whether or not the Saudis will actually get radar planes; they'll get such aircraft, whether we provide them or not—what concerns me is how a rejection by the Senate will affect peace in the Middle East and what it will do to our ability to provide the leadership so necessary for the security of our Nation and the free world.

We need the good will of the Saudis. They provide us with a significant amount of our oil, yes, but more than that they represent a moderate force in the Middle East. A rejection tomorrow, I'm afraid, will be a step toward closing them out of any peace initiative, and that's why I've suggested that tomorrow's vote is as important to the ultimate security of Israel as it is to our own interest.

I would never risk the security of Israel. And that security depends on a stable peace in that troubled part of the world. And peace can only come by drawing the moderate Arab nations into the peacemaking process, along with Egypt and Israel, who are already hard at work at that.

Your Senators know this. Bless them both. And they know what this vote will do to our ability to provide leadership not only in the Middle East but in the rest of the world.

Now, this is a vote that's vital—vital to the West, vital to America, vital to Israel and the cause of peace in the Middle East. But tonight—I just had to talk a little shop for a minute—tonight let's get concerned about the vote Virginians are going to cast on November 3d.

You have 7 more days. Don't let down. Buttonhole your friends and neighbors, yes, and a few strangers. I agree with everything that's been said here about postcard registration. That isn't our problem with people not turning out to vote. The reason that we've declined year after year in the number of people going to the polls is because the Federal Government year after year has usurped so much power and au-

thority that government seemed farther and farther away from the people.

When you buttonhole those people to make sure they get to the polls, remind them of the new course that's being charted for this Nation and how important it is to have Virginia involved in this crusade to restore fiscal responsibility to government, freedom to the individual, and autonomy to the Commonwealth of Virginia—the autonomy authorized by the Constitution, which for too many decades has been usurped by Washington.

Spend these 7 days making sure that Marshall Coleman will be the next Governor of Virginia and give him the team to do what has to be done.

You know, it's been a wonderful experience, this battle that's been going on in Washington the last few months. First of all, there was putting up with the shock of those who found out that you were going to try to do what you said you were going to try to do. [*Laughter*] Sometimes you felt like you had to wave your hand in front of their glazed eyes to get their attention. But the biggest miracle has been hearing from the people. Oh, yes, the people like yourselves—the floods of telephone calls when we mentioned it on television, the mail, the wires, the things that told our elected representatives what you, the people, wanted them to do.

But other calls that were so thrilling and so exciting:

—To get a call from a union worker before Solidarity Day in Washington, to tell me that he not only wasn't going to go but to show me or send to me a copy of the letter that he had sent to the head of his union explaining why the union shouldn't go and why they should be in support of what we were trying to do. The courage of a man to do that and stick his neck out that far.

—But then to get a letter from a 16-year-old boy who said, "From what's going on there, I'm sure that you're going to save the country for kids like me."

—To get a letter from an enlisted man on a submarine that says he knows he's speaking for his 180 shipmates, and he wound up saying, "We may not have the biggest navy in the world anymore; we've got the best."

—To get letters like the letter from a lady down in New Orleans who told me that she was black, told me her age—and I won't reveal it here, but she was very elderly—and then to tell me, "Thanks for destroying the war on poverty." She said, "Maybe now, we at last can get back to growing our own muscles and taking care of ourselves the way we should."

—To get a letter from a lady in Illinois who told me that she was one of three CETA employees at the time when we were changing that program. And she said, "I just want you to know I only have—really, there's only enough work for one of us. We don't need three." She said, "As we came to the end of last year, the last fiscal year, there was money left over." She said, "I was ordered to go out and buy new office furniture because we couldn't have any money left over or the grant might be reduced for the coming year." So, she said, "Here I sit at my great new executive desk with nothing to do." And I thought that was too much. I happened to have been born in Illinois myself. So, I called in some of our people, and I read them that letter. And I said, "I think she deserves better than what she's got." And you know something? She is now employed in a $25,000 a year job out in the private sector and happy with her work.

She says it beats daytime television—[*laughter*]—which gets me to the final thing that I just want to mention here that's part of all of this and part of why we need these gentlemen who are on the platform and need them in your State Capitol; and that is, I have believed for a long time that the history of America is based on voluntarism, that we have done good works.

I remember when I was a young man and the great earthquake virtually destroyed the cities of Japan—and America came to the rescue. It wasn't a government program or foreign aid. The people of America mobilized, and a national chairman was appointed by the President, and the people raised the money and went to the rescue. And it was true with the famines in India, it was true with the floods and the storms here in our own country. The first act wasn't to declare something a state of emergency. The first act was people in the rest of the area or around got together and created funds to send help to their neighbors, even though they didn't know those neighbors that lived in some other part of the country.

Well, the biggest thrill I'm getting today is, as we have set out and appointed a national committee to encourage voluntarism, the letters I am getting from communities, from organizations, from people all over this country that are already engaged in such programs. Do you know that in five States, there is a program where with private enterprise, they go in with volunteers to the high schools and they seek out the high school students who are about to graduate who are the least likely to succeed. They don't look for the prizes; they look for the ones who will have the least chance of getting a job. And in those five States they have had a tremendous success in putting those young people into jobs. The young people stay in the jobs and progress in the jobs, and before that, their high school graduates averaged 2 years out of high school before they went on welfare.

This, all being done by Americans like yourselves who still have faith in their neighbors and faith in this system and faith in freedom. And I am so excited and thrilled by what I'm seeing of America that says, "You bet. Just point to what you want solved, we'll do the rest."

So, we're going to get along just fine, and you're going to get along just fine, and I'm going to get along just fine with Governor Marshall Coleman. Thank you very much.

Note: The President spoke at 7:03 p.m. in the Virginia Room at the John Marshall Hotel, after being introduced by Senator John W. Warner.

Following the rally, the President returned to the White House.

Remarks and a Question-and-Answer Session With Reporters Following Senate Approval of the Sale of AWACS and Other Air Defense Equipment to Saudi Arabia
October 28, 1981

The President. I want to express my gratitude to the Members of the United States Senate for their approval of the sale of the AWACS defense system to Saudi Arabia. Today, I think, we've seen the upper Chamber at its best. The United States Senate has acted with statesmanship, with foresight, and with courage.

I can't fully express my gratitude to Senator Baker and the other Senate leaders, Democrats as well as Republicans, who played such a crucial role in this decision.

Today's action by the Senate will not only strengthen Saudi-American relations but will also protect our economic lifeline to the Middle East, win favor among moderate Arab nations, and most important, continue the difficult but steady progress toward peace and stability in the Middle East.

We've acted in concert to demonstrate that the United States is indeed a reliable security partner. Our friends should realize that steadfastness to purpose is a hallmark of American foreign policy, while those who would create instability in this region should note that the forces of moderation have our unequivocal support in deterring aggression.

This vote alone doesn't mean that our security problems in that part of the world have been completely solved. This package is but a part of our overall regional security strategy. Our strategy seeks to enhance the capacity of friendly states to defend themselves and to improve our own ability to project our own forces into the region should deterrence fail. We'll continue to pursue efforts in both areas.

Our support for the security of Israel is, of course, undiminished by today's vote. The United States will maintain its unshakeable commitment to the security and welfare of the State of Israel, recognizing that a strong Israel is essential to our basic goals in that area.

Much work still remains ahead. I trust that all of us who disagreed openly and vigorously in recent days can now put aside our honest differences and work together for common goals—friendship, security, and peace at last, in the cradle of our civilization. Because of actions like today's by the Senate, the cause of peace is again on the march in the Middle East. For this, all of us can be grateful.

Q. When did you know that you had won?

The President. When they came in and handed me the votes.

Q. Didn't you know earlier today that you could count it up?

The President. A little while ago, this afternoon, I felt that the count was—that at least we were going to be assured of a tie. And that would have been a victory, because it required a majority vote to stop this.

Q. Do you think this will be an inducement to get the Saudis into the Middle East peace process now?

The President. Yes, I do. I think that, as a matter of fact, the Saudis have shown by their own introduction of a peace proposal that they are willing to discuss peace in the Middle East.

Q. With Egypt and Israel?

The President. Yes, they submitted a plan. We couldn't agree with all the points, nor could the Israelis, but it was the first time that they had recognized Israel as a nation, and it's a beginning point for negotiations.

Q. What do you think this vote means for your ability to conduct the office of the Presidency?

The President. I think that it's going to have a very good effect. We had heard from many leaders who had expressed their concern about what this could mean in the whole world scene, if it had not turned out the way it did.

Q. Do you think it will help you put the budget fight ahead? The next budget round?

The President. I don't know. I don't know whether the two are connected at all.

Q. What aspect of what you told the Senators did you think was the convincing aspect, and what final thing do you think turned the tide in the last few days?

The President. Well, contrary to some of the things that have been said, there have been no deals made. None were offered. I talked strictly on the merits of the proposal. And basically I tried to point out, in every instance, the progress that has been made so far in the Middle East towards stability and peace and the part that was played in that by Saudi Arabia and Prince Fahd, beginning with the cease-fire that we were able to secure in Lebanon, in which they played a major role. And I simply played on that; that this, I felt, was essential for the security of Israel, for the entire Middle East, and for ourselves on the world scene.

Q. Do you foresee any circumstance under which, by 1985, this sale might be canceled if the Saudis aren't cooperating in the Middle East?

The President. Well, I would think that the only thing that could happen to make us not fulfill that would be if by some chance, the radical elements that we know are there and that have made themselves tragically evident in the last few weeks, that if they should gain control in the Middle East and gain control of all of those governments we're talking about, I think the very fact of what we've done and the knowledge now that the United States and our allies are not walking away from the Middle East is going to contribute to the stability and make it very unlikely that the other can happen.

Q. A big smile, Mr. President.

The President. I'm trying to smile with dignity. I don't want to look jubilant. [*Laughter*]

Note: The President spoke at 5:25 p.m. in the Oval Office at the White House.

Exchange With Reporters and Senate Majority Leader Baker Following Senate Approval of the Sale of AWACS and Other Air Defense Equipment to Saudi Arabia
October 28, 1981

Senator Baker. That's what campaigning in Virginia does for you, Mr. President. [*Laughter*] Mr. President, that was quite a vote.

Q. How do you think he did it, Senator?

Senator Baker. Well, I had one Senator today who told me he was going to vote for the proposal. He said, "You know, that man down at the White House could sell refrigerators to an Eskimo." I said, "Well, I'm glad he could sell AWACS to you."

The President did a tremendous job. He really did. We worked him very hard, I'm afraid, talking to Senator after Senator, but it paid off handsomely, and it was a good operation.

The President. Well, let me interject and say that there's a lineup of gentlemen here who worked very hard also, to whom I'm very indebted.

Senator Baker. We thank you. We appreciate it. And we're relieved. [*Laughter*]

Q. Any hidden tactics you want to reveal?

Senator Baker [*laughing*]. No hidden tactics. It was one vote at a time.

Q. What do you think did it? What pushed it over the top?

Senator Baker. I don't know if there was any one thing. I think that the weight of logic and time for people to think about it and to weigh the arguments pro and con—I think we had the better arguments, and I think in the final analysis, that's what one would make of it.

Q. You don't think it was the meeting with the President?

Senator Baker. Oh, yes, but you know, the President was our chief negotiator. And at one time or the other I expect the President saw, virtually, maybe every Member of the Senate or almost every Member of the Senate. And with some of them he met more than once. I sometimes got ashamed of myself for calling down here and asking him if he would meet with so-and-so. And sometimes Mr. President would say, "Well, I already did that." I'd say, "Well, I know, but you've got to do it again." [*Laughter*]

Q. Was it excruciating?

The President. No. And I must say it was very impressive, also, because many of the Senators that I talked to, in fact most of them, were honestly trying to find what they thought was the right answer for the country.

Reporters. Thank you.

Note: The session began at 6:10 p.m. in the Oval Office at the White House, where Senators Howard H. Baker, Jr., Paul Laxalt, Sam Nunn, John Tower, and John W. Warner met with the President after the Senate vote.

Nomination of H. Eugene Douglas To Be United States Coordinator for Refugee Affairs
October 28, 1981

The President today announced his intention to nominate H. Eugene Douglas to be United States Coordinator for Refugee Affairs, Department of State, and to be Ambassador at Large while so serving. He would succeed Victor H. Palmieri.

Since February, Mr. Douglas has been senior member of the Policy Planning Staff at the Department of State. Previously, he was corporate director, international trade and government affairs, Memorex Corp., in Santa Clara, Calif. In this position he was responsible for the conduct of the corporation's relations with the United States Government, State governments, and foreign governments, the corporation's international trade policy positions, overseas negotiations, and special projects.

Mr. Douglas served in the United States Navy in 1966–71. He graduated from the University of Texas (B.A., 1963) and Columbia University (M.A., 1966). He is married and resides in Vienna, Va. He was born October 5, 1940, in Wichita Falls, Tex.

Proclamation 4879—Silver Anniversary Year of the National System of Interstate and Defense Highways
October 29, 1981

By the President of the United States of America

A Proclamation

A quarter of a century ago, on June 29, 1956, President Dwight D. Eisenhower approved legislation which launched one of the most significant and far-reaching domestic programs in the history of the United States—the 42,500-mile National System of Interstate and Defense Highways.

Now more than 94 percent completed, with over 40,000 miles in use, the Interstate System has profoundly affected the life-styles of all Americans. Crisscrossing the Nation from ocean to ocean and from border to border, it links more than 90 percent of our cities that have populations of 50,000 or more, as well as many smaller cities and towns. The system comprises little more than one percent of the Nation's total road and street mileage, yet carries 20 percent of the traffic.

The Interstate System is modern America's paramount asset. By drastically cutting travel time it has drawn diverse sections of the country together. It expedites the movement of goods and produce, reducing costs and promoting competition. These and other economic benefits of the Interstate System have had a lasting impact on the standard of living of every American. At the same time, it provides us the means for the movement of military forces and supplies in the event of a national emergency.

The Interstate System is a magnificent undertaking in which all Americans can justifiably take great pride, and one which will return rich dividends to the American people for many decades to come.

Now, Therefore, I, Ronald Reagan, President of the United States of America, do hereby proclaim 1981 as The Silver Anniversary Year of the National System of In-

terstate and Defense Highways. I urge Federal, State and local government officials, as well as highway industry and other organizations, to hold appropriate observances during the remainder of this year, recognizing the benefits that the Interstate System has provided for our country during the past 25 years and reflecting upon how we can best continue to realize those benefits in the future.

In Witness Whereof, I have hereunto set my hand this 29th day of Oct. in the year of our Lord nineteen hundred and eighty-one, and of the Independence of the United States of America the two hundred and sixth.

RONALD REAGAN

[*Filed with the Office of the Federal Register, 3:48 p.m., October 29, 1981*]

Proclamation 4880—American Education Week, 1981
October 29, 1981

By the President of the United States of America

A Proclamation

Among the most precious gifts a child can receive is a good education. Historically, the primary responsibility for educating our youth has rested with parents. State and local educators stand to assist parents in achieving educational goals. The cooperative effort between parents and educators is the irreplaceable ingredient for American education.

In a free society, we are fortunate to have the right to oversee our children's education. The success of our educational system depends upon the exercise of this right by parents. It is thus fitting that mothers and fathers throughout the Nation should be encouraged to be involved with their local schools and to participate in supportive activities.

It is appropriate that the theme of this year's American Education Week is "American Education and You: Partners in Our Children's Future." Increased teamwork be-

tween school, home, church or synagogue, and the community cannot help but add to the quality of our children's education.

As a Nation, we are dedicated to excellence in education. It means a better life for our children as individuals, and it further secures the liberty which we cherish. As James Madison said, "Knowledge will forever govern ignorance: And a people who mean to be their own Governors, must arm themselves with the power which knowledge gives."

Now, Therefore, I, Ronald Reagan, President of the United States of America, do hereby designate the week beginning November 15, 1981, as American Education Week.

I invite all Americans to form education partnerships in shaping our children's future.

In Witness Whereof, I have hereunto set my hand this 29th day of Oct., in the year of our Lord nineteen hundred and eighty-one, and of the Independence of the United

States of America the two hundred and sixth.

RONALD REAGAN

[*Filed with the Office of the Federal Register, 3:49 p.m., October 29, 1981*]

Proclamation 4881—National Farm-City Week, 1981
October 29, 1981

By the President of the United States of America

A Proclamation

American agriculture is a modern-day miracle. In the last 30 years, United States farmers have increased productivity by 50 percent. Now, fewer than 4 percent of our population provides our Nation's agricultural products—and enough more to feed millions of people overseas.

The trust, reliance, and interdependence of farms and cities is a basic strength of this great Nation. Farm and city people have long been partners in economic and social progress. Without farms to provide food and fiber, cities would be barren; without the products and services of cities, farms would be primitive.

A close partnership between farm and city people in the productive use of land, labor, and capital is paramount if our Nation is to continue to have an abundance of safe, wholesome food as well as an abundance of goods and services at reasonable prices.

To achieve a deeper appreciation of the contributions and cooperation of farms and cities, the Nation has set aside a week in November as National Farm-City Week. The theme is: Partners in Progress—Key to the Future.

Now, Therefore, I, Ronald Reagan, President of the United States of America, do hereby designate the period November 20 through November 26, 1981, as National Farm-City Week.

In Witness Whereof, I have hereunto set my hand this 29th day of Oct. in the year of our Lord nineteen hundred and eighty-one, and of the Independence of the United States of America the two hundred and sixth.

RONALD REAGAN

[*Filed with the Office of the Federal Register, 3:50 p.m., October 29, 1981*]

Message to the Congress Reporting Budget Deferrals
October 29, 1981

To the Congress of the United States:

In accordance with the Impoundment Control Act of 1974, I herewith report 51 deferrals totaling $1,260.6 million.

Forty-nine of the deferrals totaling $763.7 million represent the third group in a series that I am transmitting deferring fiscal year 1982 funds made available by the Continuing Resolution, P.L. 97–51. The other two deferrals, totaling $496.9 million, represent withholdings of funds carried over from 1981 that will not be needed until later this fiscal year.

The 49 deferrals of funds made available by P.L. 97–51 are being taken in accord with the stated intent of the Congress to provide minimal and temporary funding for the duration of the Continuing Resolution which expires November 20, 1981. As indicated in my special message of October 20, I plan to restrain spending to insure that the Congress has the opportunity to enact regular appropriations for the entire fiscal year at levels that are consistent with my revised budget request.

Deferrals under the Continuing Resolution are included in this special message for Funds Appropriated to the President and ten departments and agencies. The deferrals of funds carried over from 1981 affect Funds Appropriated to the President and the Federal Emergency Management Agency.

The details of each deferral are contained in the attached reports.

RONALD REAGAN

The White House,
October 29, 1981.

Note: The attachments detailing the deferrals are printed in the Federal Register *of November 3, 1981.*

Exchange With Reporters on Domestic and Foreign Policy Issues
October 29, 1981

Q. Are you going to fire Allen [Richard V. Allen, Assistant to the President for National Security Affairs]?

The President. All I can tell you is whoever wrote that report not only was blowing smoke, they were also doing a disservice to this country. I am very happy with the team we have, and the country should be. And Al Haig is Secretary of State and, I think, one of the finest we've had in a very long time.

Q. How about Dick Allen?

The President. And Dick Allen is doing his job and we're all getting along fine and there's going to be no musical chairs being played.

Q. There's no conflict between the two of them?

The President. No.

Q. So the team stays in place?

The President. Yes, you bet.

Q. How are you feeling?

The President. Hungry. [*Laughter*]

Q. Any additional arms for Israel?

The President. Nothing except the agreements that we've always had with them. Our relationship has not changed at all, and they're still an ally.

Q. Saudi Arabia says it was a victory against Zionism, a defeat for Zionism.

The President. Well, it was a victory for peace in the Middle East.

Q. What about the Saudi peace plan? What are the best parts of that? You mentioned it last night.

The President, Well, I think the most significant part is the fact that they recognize Israel as a nation to be negotiated with.

Q. That recession is deepening, is it not? Those indicators today seemed to suggest it.

The President. I don't know. I'm on my way to a physical check-up, so I can answer his question of how I feel.

Q. Are we going to get an honest report afterwards? I mean, by that, they won't cover up anything, any problem that might develop?

The President. I haven't got any problems.

Q. We hope not. Thank you.

Note: The exchange began at 1:45 p.m. on the South Lawn of the White House as the President and Mrs. Reagan were departing for their annual physical examinations at the National Naval Medical Center in Bethesda, Md.

Nomination of Francis Terry McNamara To Be United States Ambassador to Gabon and Sao Tome and Principe
October 30, 1981

The President today announced his intention to nominate Francis Terry McNamara, of Vermont, to be Ambassador to the Gabonese Republic and to the Democratic Republic of Sao Tome and Principe. He would succeed Arthur T. Tienken.

Mr. McNamara served in the United States Navy in 1944–46 and 1950–51. In 1954–55 he was with the State Bank of Albany, Albany, N.Y., and served as a management intern with the United States Army at Watervliet, N.Y. in 1955–56. He entered the Foreign Service in 1956 and was an economic officer in Salisbury in 1957–59. In 1959–61 he served as a research analyst in the Department, departing in 1961 to become political officer in Lumbumbashi until 1964. From there he served as political officer in Dar es Salaam until 1967, when he was assigned to the Armed Forces Staff College. At the end of 1967 he became an economic officer in the Bureau of African Affairs in the Department, where he served until 1968 when he went on detail for the Agency for International Development to serve as Chief of Rural Development and Deputy Provincial Senior Adviser in Saigon. Thereafter he became principal officer in Da Nang until 1971, when he was assigned for a year to the Naval War College. In 1972–74 Mr. McNamara was Deputy Chief of Mission in Cotonou and in 1974–75 was consul general in Can Tho. For a time in 1975 Mr. McNamara was Associate Director of the Task Force for Resettlement of Indochinese Refugees in the Department before being assigned as consul general in Quebec until 1979. In early 1980 he became Deputy Assistant Secretary of State for Public Affairs where he has been serving until recently.

Mr. McNamara graduated from Russell Sage College (B.A., 1953) and George Washington University (M.S., 1972). He is married, has seven children, and resides in Manchester, Vt. He was born November 2, 1927, in Troy, N.Y.

Nomination of Benjamin F. Baer To Be Commissioner of the United States Parole Commission
October 30, 1981

The President today announced his intention to nominate Benjamin F. Baer to be Commissioner of the United States Parole Commission for a term of 6 years. He would succeed Joseph A. Nardoza.

Since 1972 Mr. Baer has been associated with the United States Parole Commission. He was hearing examiner in 1972–74 and later was appointed Administrative Hearing Examiner, Western Region, in 1974–79. Since 1979 he has been conducting parole hearings of Federal prisoners in the 14 Western institutions. Previously he was chairman, Youth Conservation Commission, Department of Corrections, St. Paul, Minn., and deputy commissioner, Minnesota Department of Corrections, in charge of the juvenile institutions of the State, in 1967–72. In 1965–67 he was codirector of the Correctional Decisions Information Project in Sacramento, Calif., and was director of corrections, State of Iowa, in 1960–64. Mr. Baer was associate warden of San Quentin Prison in 1954–60.

Mr. Baer graduated from San Diego State College (B.A., 1941) and the University of Southern California (M.A., 1947). He is married, has three children, and resides in San Mateo, Calif. He was born January 2, 1918, in Peoria, Ill.

Appointment of Warner M. Depuy as the Alternate Federal Member of the Susquehanna River Basin Commission
October 30, 1981

The President today announced his intention to appoint Warner M. Depuy to be the Alternate Federal member of the Susquehanna River Basin Commission. He would succeed Patrick Delaney.

Since 1968 Mr. Depuy has served as president and chief executive officer of the First National Bank of Pike County, Pa. Previously he was director of the bank since 1949. He was director, Intercounty Trust Co., Monticello, N.Y., in 1957–66; member of the board of directors, Bank of New York

(Port Jervis, N.Y.) in 1966–75; secretary of revenue, Commonwealth of Pennsylvania, in 1966–71; and served as a member of the General Assembly of Pennsylvania in 1942–50. He has served as a member of the Board of County Commissioners, Pike County, Pa., since 1956.

He graduated from Dartmouth College (A.B., 1939). He is married, has four children, and resides in Milford, Pa. He was born December 18, 1917.

Appointment of Charles L. Hardwick as a Member of the Presidential Advisory Committee on Federalism
October 30, 1981

The President today announced his intention to appoint Charles L. Hardwick to be a member of the Presidential Advisory Committee on Federalism. He would succeed Ross O. Doyen.

Since 1977 Mr. Hardwick has served in the New Jersey General Assembly. He is a member of the Joint Committee on Appropriations and a member of the Labor Committee. He has also served as director, civic information, Pfizer, Inc., of New York, since 1966.

Mr. Hardwick is president of the National Republican Legislators Association and vice chairman of the National Conference of State Legislatures Committee on Law and Justice.

He graduated from Florida State University at Tallahassee (B.S., M.B.A.). Mr. Hardwick is married, has two children, and resides in Westfield, N.J. He was born November 8, 1941, in Somerset, Ky.

Nomination of 10 Members of the Federal Council on the Aging, and Designation of Chairman
October 30, 1981

The President today announced his intention to nominate the following individuals to serve as members of the Federal Council on the Aging. The President also announced his intention to designate Adelaide Attard Chairman.

Margaret Long Arnold, of Washington, D.C., is

presently coordinator, women's activities, National Retired Teachers Association of the American Association of Retired Persons.

Adelaide Attard, of New York, is presently Nassau County Commissioner and member of the National Advisory Committee, 1981 White House Conference on Aging.

Nelda Ann Lambert Barton, of Kentucky, is presently president and chairman of the board of Health Systems, Inc., in Corbin, Ky.

Edna Bogosian, of Massachusetts, is presently principal insurance examiner, Department of Banking and Insurance of the Commonwealth of Massachusetts.

Syd Captain, of Florida, is presently involved with a local talk show on the aged and is a member of the Governor's Conference on Aging.

Charlotte W. Conable, of Washington, D.C., is presently Coordinator of Public Policy Projects, Women's Studies, George Washington University, and a member of the National Advisory Commmittee, 1981 White House Conference on Aging.

Katie G. Dusenberry, of Arizona, is presently a member, Board of Supervisors, Pima County, Ariz., and is president of the National Association of County Agency Programs. She is also president of the Affiliate on Aging Program, National Association of Counties.

Frances (Peg) Lamont, of South Dakota, is a Republican State senator who has authored and passed legislation dealing with the aging. She has twice served on the White House Conference on Aging.

Josephine K. Oblinger, of Illinois, is a State Representative who has drafted legislation regarding issues pertaining to the aging in the areas of care and insurance.

Edna Bonn (Bonny) Russell, of California, is presently director, education and training, at San Jose State University. She is a past member of the California Committee on Aging and was chairman during Governor Reagan's term.

Appointment of the Chairmen of the 10 Federal Regional Councils
October 30, 1981

The President today announced the appointments of the following individuals to be Chairmen of the 10 Federal Regional Councils:

Region I, Boston—Frederick L. Ahearn, Secretary's Representative, Department of Labor;

Region II, New York—Joseph D. Monticciolo, Regional Administrator, Department of Housing and Urban Development;

Region III, Philadelphia—Linda Z. Marston, Regional Director, Department of Health and Human Services;

Region IV, Atlanta—Clifton G. Brown, Regional Administrator, Department of Housing and Urban Development;

Region V, Chicago—Wayne A. Stanton, Regional Director, Department of Health and Human Services;

Region VI, Dallas—John A. Daeley, Regional Director, Department of Health and Human Services;

Region VII, Kansas City—Patricia S. Keyes, Regional Representative of the Secretary, Department of Transportation;

Region VIII, Denver—Derrell P. Thompson, Western Representative, Department of the Interior;

Region IX, San Francisco—George E. Miller, Regional Director, Department of Health and Human Services;

Region X, Seattle—John R. Spencer, Regional Administrator, Environmental Protection Agency.

Federal Regional Councils are comprised of nine Federal domestic agencies located in 10 standard Federal regions. Each Council is composed of the principal regional officials representing the following departments and agencies: Department of Agriculture, Department of the Interior, Department of Labor, Department of Health and Human Services, Department of Housing and Urban Development, Department of Transportation, Department of Energy, Department of Education, and the Environmental Protection Agency.

Nomination of Elliott Abrams To Be an Assistant Secretary of State
October 30, 1981

The President today announced his intention to nominate Elliott Abrams to be Assistant Secretary of State for Human Rights and Humanitarian Affairs. He would succeed Patricia M. Derian. Mr. Abrams will resign his current position as Assistant Secretary of State for International Organizations effective upon his assumption of this new position.

In making today's announcement, the President said "the promotion of liberty has always been a central element of our Nation's foreign policy. In my administration, human rights considerations are important in all aspects of our foreign policy. We will speak up against the enemies of freedom, and we will try to help its friends. We will encourage those who seek freedom, not least by telling the simple truth about their efforts and the efforts of those who seek to oppress them.

As Assistant Secretary for Human Rights and Humanitarian Affairs, Elliott Abrams will have a key role in this effort. He will give policy advice on human rights issues not only within the State Department but also to the U.S. International Communication Agency and other government agencies. In so doing, he will help this administration remind both Americans and our friends abroad that liberty is our Nation's greatest strength and our deepest wish for all mankind."

Before assuming his current post at the State Department, Mr. Abrams was an attorney with the law firm of Verner, Lipfert, Bernhard and McPherson of Washington, D.C. He was special counsel to Senator Daniel Moynihan (D-N.Y.) in 1977–79. In 1973–75 he was an attorney with the firm of Breed, Abbott and Morgan of Boston, Mass.

Mr. Abrams graduated from Harvard University (B.A., 1969); The London School of Economics (M.Sc., 1970); and Harvard Law School (J.D., 1973).

He was born January 24, 1948, in New York, N.Y. He currently resides in Washington, D.C.

Nomination of Milan D. Bish To Be United States Ambassador to Barbados, Dominica, St. Lucia, St. Vincent and the Grenadines, Antigua and Barbuda and Representative to St. Christopher-Nevis
October 31, 1981

The President today announced his intention to nominate Milan D. Bish, of Nebraska, to be Ambassador to Barbados, Commonwealth of Dominica, Saint Lucia, and Saint Vincent and the Grenadines, Antigua and Barbuda. The President also intends to designate Mr. Bish to be United States Representative to the State of St. Christopher-Nevis. He would succeed Sally Angela Shelton.

Mr. Bish is president of Mid-Continent Enterprises, a company engaged in land development, property management, and residential construction. Prior to founding this company, Mr. Bish was associated with and served as president of the Bish Machinery Co., a distributor of material-handling equipment and farm machinery. Since 1979 he has been a partner in the Bish and Son Cattle Co., and highway commissioner for the State of Nebraska. He was a member of the Presidential transition team at the Department of the Interior in November 1980 to January 1981.

He graduated from Hastings College (B.A., 1950). He is married, has three children, and resides in Grand Island, Nebr. He was born July 1, 1929, in Harvard, Nebr.

Nomination of Janet J. McCoy To Be High Commissioner of the Trust Territory of the Pacific Islands
October 31, 1981

The President today announced his intention to nominate Janet J. McCoy to be High Commissioner of the Trust Territory of the Pacific Islands. She would succeed Adrian P. Winkel.

Mrs. McCoy is currently retired and was director of the Reagan for President press office in Los Angeles, Calif., in 1976 and 1980. She has been extensively involved in California politics and has held press office positions in the Reagan for Governor campaign in 1966, Rockefeller for President in

1964, and Nixon for Governor in 1962.

In 1970–73 she was executive director of the Western American Convention & Travel Institute. Mrs. McCoy was director of the Office of Tourism and Visitor Services, State of California, in 1967–70.

Mrs. McCoy attended Wayne State University in Detroit, Mich. She is married, has two grown children, and resides in Scottsburg, Oreg. She was born July 13, 1916, in Saginaw, Mich.

Remarks at the Welcoming Ceremony for King Hussein I of Jordan
November 2, 1981

The President. It is a distinct pleasure and an honor to welcome Your Majesties to Washington. I've been looking forward to meeting King Hussein longer than I've been President. One of the advantages of age is the perspective it gives to looking back. I've watched King Hussein from a distance for many years, watched as he ascended the throne and accepted great responsibility while still in his teens. And in the years since, he's proved himself time and again a brave man and, I might add, a wise leader.

Our friendship with King Hussein has stood the test of time. It's based on shared interests, but also on common values and mutual respect. During the three decades that he has led Jordan, America has maintained an unwavering dedication to the search for Middle East peace. And over these many years, King Hussein has been our friend. Such loyalty is not lightly regarded by the people of the United States.

Let it be understood that America seeks peace with honor and security for all the states and people of the region, undoubtedly a similar goal to your own. Yet at this moment, Your Majesty, there's much to dis-

cuss about how to reach our mutual goal. Recent tragic events make it even more imperative that we work together if solutions are to be found.

Today, let us achieve an understanding about ourselves and then reaffirm to the world that there are no differences between us that we cannot overcome and none that will lessen the friendship between the United States and the Hashemite Kingdom of Jordan.

For our part, no one should doubt that the preservation of Jordan's security, integrity, and its unique and enduring character remains a matter of highest importance. Your Majesty, over the years your concern for the well-being of your people, your creative statesmanship, and your good sense have enriched Jordan. Under your leadership, King Hussein, the Jordanian economy has yielded fruit, literally and figuratively, to all the citizens of Jordan. And in Jordan today, the private sector is thriving and the standard of living is increasingly a model for developing nations.

In the last two decades, the literacy rate rose from 32 to 70 percent. Educated Jordanians now fill skilled jobs all over the

Middle East. Meanwhile, unemployment has almost disappeared, and Jordan boasts an average annual economic growth rate of 9 percent. Your success offers hope that people who've known grievous adversity can rise above their conflicts to build a new life. Similarly, there are tremendous opportunities for economic betterment in your region, while political problems work themselves out.

Given freedom to do so, people who live in such proximity will interact to better themselves, even though divided by politics. Such peaceful interactions should be applauded. Furthermore, the United States encourages any mutually beneficial economic cooperation between nations. The problems of water and transportation, for example, are areas of potential benefit to you and your neighbors if a farsighted approach is taken.

Your Majesty, there are, however, other forces which seek to widen and exploit the divisions among the peoples of the Middle East. Tension and conflict both reflect and increase the power and influence of such hateful forces. When focusing on the internal problems of the region, we must never lose sight of the role of external powers in aggravating those problems.

In your book, "Uneasy Lies the Head," you proclaimed, "I fear only God." Well, in your life you've demonstrated this courage in so many ways—as a pilot, as a soldier and, most important, as a statesman. But the point of that statement is not alone that you are brave, but that you are devout. It highlights your belief in and respect for the Supreme Being who's Father of us all. Americans admire such values.

Years ago, your grandfather, King Abdullah, a giant in the Arab world, in his memoirs wrote, "It is the duty of all Arabs to bear witness to the world that they possess a place and constitute an entity among the nations of the world and that they stand today at the side of the democracies in the contest between fear-inspiring communism and popular democracy."

Your Majesty, during your reign you have demonstrated the wisdom of your grandfather by maintaining a perspective on potential dangers while still providing leadership on the immediate issues confronting you and your neighbors.

The United States is concerned about outside threats to the Middle East, as well as those issues which most directly affect the people of the Middle East. We're sincerely attempting to do all that can be done to end the ongoing tragedy that has plagued that area of the world. A lasting peace is in our interest, just as it is in the interest of all people of good will. Respecting our differences and knowing you as we do, we're confident that you share our heartfelt desire for peace and stability. Your courage and integrity earned this trust and respect long ago.

The story is told that early in your reign, you decided to stay the night at a Bedouin encampment which was under threat of attack. And while walking in the darkness, you heard the voice of an elder tribesman proclaim from inside a tent, "Abdullah would be proud of his grandson." Well, we think that's even truer today, and we want you to know that we, too, are proud, proud to have you as a friend.

Welcome to our country.

The King. Mr. President, Mrs. Reagan, dear friends, it's indeed a moving moment for me as I express my sincere gratitude for the warm welcome to both Noor and myself and to our Jordanian colleagues who are with us today.

It is a great pleasure for us to be once again in the United States of America in response to your kind invitation, and to visit with you, the leader of this great nation. This year indeed marks the 25th anniversary of a unique relationship between the United States and Jordan, unique in its length and durability. It is a relationship seasoned by time and trouble. I recognized, as the leader of Jordan, 25 years ago, that the values and principles on which your nation's foundations were created were the same ones which are so dear to the Arabs and which were the foundations of the Arab awakening and resolve from the beginnings of this century.

It was my commitment to those ideals and principles that prompted me to proudly seek the establishment and consolidation of a friendship between our nations a quarter of a century ago. Meaningful and dynamic relations must always be based on mutual understanding. Throughout these eventful years, I've been totally committed to both the cause of the Arab people, which is my cause and motivation, and to a realization that it is an honorable and just cause. I deemed it my duty to present it and defend it and explain it to the best of my ability.

I'm a firm believer in the proverb that says you can hide the truth from all the people half the time, half the people all the time, but not all of the people all of the time, and that justice must inevitably, finally prevail. We must not permit the distortions of others to become a barrier to the understanding on which our relationship is based.

I know you, Mr. President, to be a man of honor, dedicated to the highest of ideals and principles. I know also that you have the courage of your convictions. You have displayed this throughout your public life and, because of it, have the respect of those who know you. I am confident that working together with all who truly seek peace and security for the people of the Middle East, that these qualities will provide the source of strength which that goal requires.

At this most turbulent and critical of times, I see in jeopardy not only Arab rights and legitimate interests but a threat to the very Arab identity and the rights of future Arab generations. I also see the larger threats to world peace, as well as to the vital interests of all those concerned with the security of our region, including the United States of America.

I hope that at this time I shall be able to present our case convincingly in the interest of us all, and thus achieve greater mutual understanding. In doing so, we can pave the way towards formulating proper policies and build once more lasting and strengthened relations between us, based on clear and solid foundations. It's a great task and a great challenge. It is, indeed, a duty. Despite the difficulties that surround us at this most critical juncture, I am optimistic, and I am determined. I am hopeful that upon my return home, I shall be able to carry to my people and to my colleagues at the next Arab summit, promising impressions and favorable news.

I can but do my best in these coming days. I hope it will be adequate, for what is at stake is both of our national interests and the future of so many. I am confident that on the basis of our long, close friendship and with courage, dedication, and God's blessing, we can—and indeed, must—successfully meet the challenge before us.

Mr. President, we are deeply in your debt for your friendship and the warmth of your welcome. May God bless you, protect you, guide your steps in leading the great American people towards a brighter future and in serving the cause of all mankind.

Thank you, sir.

Note: The President spoke at 10:13 a.m. on the South Lawn of the White House, where King Hussein was given a formal welcome with full military honors.

Following the ceremony, the President and the King met in the Oval Office. Also present at that meeting were the Vice President, Secretary of State Alexander M. Haig, Jr., Assistant to the President for National Security Affairs Richard V. Allen, and Richard N. Viets, U.S. Ambassador to Jordan. That meeting was followed by an expanded session which included, in addition to the above participants, Counsellor to the President Edwin Meese III, Assistants to the President James A. Baker III and Michael K. Deaver and, on the Jordanian side, Prime Minister Mudhir Badran, Foreign Minister Marwan al-Kasim, Chief of the Royal Court Ahmad Lawzi, 'Abd al-Hadi 'Atallah al-Majali, Jordanian Ambassador to the United States, and Lt. Gen. Sharif Zaid Bin Shaker, Commander in Chief of the Jordanian Armed Forces.

Nomination of John R. McKean To Be a Governor of the United States Postal Service
November 2, 1981

The President today announced his intention to nominate John R. McKean to be Governor of the United States Postal Service for the remainder of the term expiring December 8, 1986. He would succeed Richard R. Allen.

Mr. McKean is currently president of John R. McKean Accountants of San Fran-cisco, Calif. He founded this certified public accounting firm in 1958.

He attended the University of San Francisco (B.S., 1951) and Golden Gate University (M.B.A., 1977). Mr. McKean is married, has three children, and resides in San Leandro, Calif. He was born May 30, 1930, in Evanston, Ill.

Toasts of the President and King Hussein I of Jordan at the State Dinner
November 2, 1981

The President. Your Majesties and distinguished guests:

King Hussein once explained the three virtues upon which Bedouin life is based, saying, "We believe to be an honorable man, you must have the courage to defend your honor; we believe you must always show hospitality; and what is yours belongs to your guests." Tonight it gives me great pleasure to extend American hospitality to King Hussein and lovely Queen Noor. We cannot hope to match the graciousness of the Bedouins, but we do hope you'll consider what is ours is yours.

Having been a longtime friend of this country and the guest of many Presidents, His Majesty probably has been to dinner in this room more often than I have. [*Laughter*]

I've been told that early in his reign, King Hussein decided that he should know exactly what was on the minds of his people. So one night he commandeered a taxicab and then took over and posed as the cabdriver and ventured into Amman. It turned out to be a lively night. He picked up a fellow carrying a heavy bag of vegetables and then engaged him in conversation. And being modest and wanting to find out what they really thought, cabdriver Hussein was not exactly complimentary about King Hussein. [*Laughter*] And not knowing to whom he was talking, the faithful subject, the passenger in the cab, told the cabdriver that he'd beat him black and blue with a stick if he heard anything more said against the King. That fellow is probably still wondering why the cabdriver tipped him. [*Laughter*]

There can be little wonder, however, about why this citizen loved his monarch. King Hussein well represents the character of his people. His grandfather described this character. "The Arab," King Abdullah wrote, "has a penchant for unfettered liberty and cannot abide restriction or restraint. This is the reason why he has associated with the desert and the steppe and exhibits an incomparable bravery in defending his possessions. He is courageous and fond of oratory as well as poetry and love."

Tonight, we honor a man for whom liberty has personal as well as political meaning. Heads of state often find themselves restricted by their own staffs. King Hussein, for example, was once told that he could pilot airplanes as long as he didn't fly solo. His aides now know better. [*Laughter*] Today when many Americans think of King Hussein, an image of a swashbuckling pilot strapping himself into a jet comes to mind. And however attractive that image may be, it's Hussein's integrity that captures the hearts of Americans.

We are here to honor a head of state who's been a leader in the search for a just and lasting Middle East peace. Such a peace has been one of the most vexing international problems in the post-war world. Yet His Majesty has never abandoned the belief that people of good will, through dedication and vision, can find the means to bring peace with dignity, justice, and security to his region.

Our talks today ranged over numerous issues. The path ahead is fraught with both danger and opportunity. After our conversation, I remain certain we will walk this path as friends. Where we differed, we did so in that spirit and discussed how we can work together in complementary ways to achieve our shared goals.

Your Majesty, I learned much from our discussions. Furthermore, it's been a great delight getting to know you.

And now, I would ask all of you to join me in a toast to Their Majesties, King Hussein and Queen Noor, and to the long-abiding friendship between our two peoples.

The King. Mr. President, Mrs. Reagan, no words would adequately express the warmth of feelings that I have within me, the pride in a friendship that has meant so much, between our nations, and which has weathered storms and which has lasted for only a fraction of the time, I hope, it will last. For I am convinced, sir, that what is between us in terms of the ideals that are dear to us, the principles we uphold, the hopes and dreams, aspirations for a better tomorrow, the dedication to those ideals and principles, and the commitment to the cause of a better tomorrow with peace and dignity in our part of the world, or anywhere else, are elements that will always keep us together as brethren and as friends, proud of this friendship, ever determined to make our contribution to the fullest possible extent.

Sir, you have kindly spoken of some of the Bedouin traditions. I am proud to belong to the oldest tribe in Arabia, but I would like to say very frankly and sincerely that if we were to be outdone, you have succeeded in that respect in the warmth of your reception and the feelings that I have felt on this day that I shall always remember. Twenty-five years, sir, and then, many an occasion when I visited the United States and had the privilege of meeting with the

leaders of this great Nation, yet no visit has been more important than this one, at this time, at this point in history.

I am one of many in this world who have had a very deep admiration for you and respect for your courage, for the fact that you have always stood in defense of principles and ideals. And throughout these many years, we have been proud to belong to the family of free nations, and the cause of freedom and justice is very dear to us.

I must say, sir, I have been looking forward to this privilege and pleasure of meeting you. And before we met this morning, I was feeling the weight of the responsibility I bore, because there is so much at stake in terms which I can't even express, in terms of all that is important, for now and for tomorrow.

I can only say, sir, that having had this privilege, I feel more encouraged than I have felt for a long, long period of time; a greater faith that all will eventually be right; pride in knowing you, pride in our friendship. You, to us, are an example—all the human, wonderful qualities that are yours.

There are many areas where we have common treasured possessions as well, sir. I was reminded today of the fact, when we were having lunch, that we were talking and sitting "Philadelphia style," I believe was the expression used. I was reminded of the fact that we came from another Philadelphia. That is the name of the capital of Jordan, its ancient name. And Philadelphia here for you is the beacon for freedom and the beginnings of the creation of this, one of the greatest nations of all times, the City of Brotherly Love.

There is much that we share. There is faith in our hearts. There is a commitment to do our best and to work together to obtain our common goals and objectives. I pray to God to grant you always good health and every continued success, sir, in your great duties as the head of this great Nation and its leader and in fulfilling your tasks and facing up to the challenge for a better future for all mankind.

I'll carry back with me, as will Noor and all the Jordanian friends, colleagues who have come with us on this trip to the

United States, very treasured memories of this day.

Thank you both so much for your kindness, for this wonderful opportunity to be with friends, for the warmth of your welcome. God bless you, sir.

Ladies and gentlemen, I'd like you to join me in making a toast to President Reagan, President of the United States, to Mrs. Reagan, and to brotherly love, to friendship everlasting, and to a better tomorrow.

Note: The President spoke at 9:35 p.m. in the State Dining Room at the White House.

Remarks of the President and King Hussein I of Jordan Following Their Meetings
November 3, 1981

The President. Your Majesty and ladies and gentlemen, let me say a few words about the frank and very constructive meetings that I've just completed with His Majesty. We had wide-ranging discussions about the dangers and the opportunities we face in the Middle East.

His Majesty was generous to share a perspective that he alone can bring to bear on these matters. His long and unique experience now assumes all the greater importance in this troubled area.

We agree on much—on the necessity of making progress toward a just, lasting, and comprehensive Middle East peace, on the profound dangers which threaten the security of the region, and on the necessity to work in complementary ways to address these serious issues.

We also discussed bilateral matters. The security and well-being of the Hashemite Kingdom of Jordan is a matter of historic and enduring concern to the United States. We agreed that reinforcing this friendship is a primary goal and discussed how our relations can be strengthened.

We end this meeting on a note of optimism, realizing that today our friendship remains essential to the future of both our countries.

And, Your Majesty, we've been more than delighted with this visit and to have you here.

The King. Thank you, sir. Mr. President, ladies and gentlemen, I would like to reiterate my feelings of very deep gratitude to you, sir, for the unique opportunity through which you enabled me to have the privilege and pleasure of meeting with you and visiting with friends in the United States of America at this critical juncture, critical time, which has a bearing and an effect on the future of our part of the world and on many common goals and interests that we share with you.

I thank you, sir, for the opportunity to be with a friend whom I admire and respect. Now more than before, I value our friendship. And it has been a very moving experience for me to meet you, sir, and to have the chance to talk with you frankly, openly on all matters of mutual interest.

I'll go back with impressions I will convey to my people and colleagues in the area. I can assure you that we stand together in our hopes for a better future, for a just and comprehensive peace in the Middle East, and from our vantage point, for the freedom of the Arab people, the safeguarding of their identity, and for a better future for generations to come.

Ever proud of the relations that exist between us, a deep-rooted friendship, our commitment to the same ideals and principles, and having had the chance to meet you, sir, I am very, very proud to look into the future with hope and conviction that we will work together and make our contribution for a better future and a better tomorrow.

We wish you, sir, every continued success, good health. God bless you. We are proud to be your friends, sir. And rest assured that we will be on our way home shortly, realizing that this particular meeting at this particular time, in comparison with all my previous visits to Washington, has left me more reassured than any in the past and more confident of the future.

Thank you very, very much.

Note: The President spoke at 11:15 a.m. on the South Lawn of the White House, following a meeting with the King in the Oval Office.

Statement on Signing the Veterans' Health Care, Training, and Small Business Loan Act of 1981
November 3, 1981

I am today signing H.R. 3499, the "Veterans' Health Care, Training, and Small Business Loan Act of 1981."

This bill extends a number of programs for Vietnam-era veterans, including eligibility of educationally disadvantaged veterans for special noncompetitive appointments to the Federal civil service and for vocational training and secondary school education. It also extends the Vietnam-era veterans readjustment counseling program, with provision for shifting this program into regular Veterans Administration medical facilities at the end of fiscal year 1984.

In addition, H.R. 3499 extends certain health care activities in Puerto Rico, the Virgin Islands, other U.S. territories, and the Republic of the Philippines, and permits the Veterans Administration to recover costs of providing certain non-service-connected health care.

The bill contains other major provisions on which I wish to comment.

The bill would grant eligibility for Veterans Administration medical care to veterans who may have been exposed to Agent Orange and certain other toxic substances in Vietnam and also to veterans exposed to ionizing radiation from nuclear weapons testing or the U.S. occupation of Nagasaki and Hiroshima following World War II. Eligibility would be provided without regard to financial need and on a priority basis.

Extension of medical services for exposure to Agent Orange and other substances in Vietnam must not prejudice the results of Federal studies we now have under way on this question.

I note, however, that the Congress has put a time limit of approximately 3 years on the new medical care eligibility, so that it can be reexamined after the initial results of the Agent Orange study are available. Moreover, I expect this provision to be implemented in a manner that will not add to budgetary costs of Veterans Administration medical care and treatment.

Another section of H.R. 3499 would establish the number of hospital and nursing home beds in Veterans Administration medical facilities at not more than 125,000 and not less than 100,000, and require the Veterans Administration to operate and maintain not less than 90,000 such beds. Such a limitation must not restrict the ability of the Veterans Administration to use an appropriate mix of health care services, including ambulatory care, to treat the maximum number of veterans.

This provision would also require that the President include in the budget transmitted to Congress for each fiscal year amounts for medical care and construction to enable the Veterans Administration to operate and maintain the required minimum number of hospital and nursing home beds. I interpret this language to mean what it says. This language does not, and in my view could not, require the President to request of Congress any specific amounts, for it is the President's constitutional duty to make recommendations to Congress of such measures as he judges necessary and expedient.

Finally, H.R. 3499 authorizes a new small business loan program in the Veterans Administration for disabled and Vietnam-era veterans. Because this program might duplicate a similar program in the Small Business Administration and would involve the Veterans Administration in an area in which it has no expertise, I intend to weigh carefully any efforts to fund this program.

Many of the provisions of H.R. 3499 are desirable and have been supported by the administration. A number of them will be particularly helpful to Vietnam-era veterans. In view of my strong commitment to the welfare of America's veterans, particularly Vietnam-era veterans, I am approving this measure despite some of the concerns I have noted.

Note: As enacted, H.R. 3499 is Public Law 97–72, approved November 3.

Proclamation 4882—National Family Week
November 3, 1981

By the President of the United States of America

A Proclamation

The family is the basic unit of our society, the heart of our free democracy. It provides love, acceptance, guidance, support, and instruction to the individual. Community values and goals that give America strength also take root in the home. In times of change and challenge, families keep safe our cultural heritage and reinforce our spiritual foundation.

As the mainstay of our national life, family life must be preserved. When a family needs external assistance to help it to perform its unique role, this assistance should not interfere with the family's fundamental responsibilities and prerogatives. Rather, aid should be supportive and purposeful in strengthening the family's stability, self-sufficiency and permanence.

National Family Week is a time to be thankful for the family as a national heritage and resource. It is a time to recommit ourselves to the concept of the family—a concept that must withstand the trends of lifestyle and legislation. Let us pledge that our institutions and policies will be shaped to enhance an environment in which families can strengthen their ties and best exercise their beliefs, authority, and resourcefulness. And let us make our pledge mindful that we do so not only on behalf of individual family members, but for America.

Now, Therefore, I, Ronald Reagan, President of the United States of America, in accordance with Senate Joint Resolution 4, do hereby proclaim the week beginning November 22, 1981, as National Family Week. I call upon the people of the United States to observe this week with appropriate activities in their homes and communities.

In Witness Whereof, I have hereunto set my hand this 3rd day of November, in the year of our Lord nineteen hundred and eighty-one, and of the Independence of the United States of America the two hundred and sixth.

RONALD REAGAN

[*Filed with the Office of the Federal Register, 4:32 p.m., November 3, 1981*]

Appointment of James W. Cicconi as Special Assistant to the President
November 5, 1981

The President today announced the appointment of James W. Cicconi to be Special Assistant to the President. Mr. Cicconi will also serve as Special Assistant to the Chief of Staff, James A. Baker III, and will assist Mr. Baker generally in management and policy execution.

Since July 1980 Mr. Cicconi has served as

general counsel to the secretary of state of Texas. He had previously served on the staff of Governor William Clements of Texas as administrative assistant. Prior to joining the Governor's office, Mr. Cicconi served as issues coordinator for James A. Baker III in his 1978 campaign for attorney general of Texas.

Mr. Cicconi graduated from the University of Texas at Austin and holds a law degree from the University of Texas Law School.

He is married to the former Patricia Burgess, has one child, and resides in Austin, Tex. He was born in Elmira, N.Y., and is 29 years old.

Appointment of James E. Jenkins as Deputy Counsellor to the President
November 5, 1981

The President today announced the appointment of James E. Jenkins to be Deputy Counsellor to the President, serving under Counsellor to the President Edwin Meese III.

Since 1975 Mr. Jenkins has been executive vice president and cofounder of Mark Briggs and Associates, Inc., a local government and economic development consulting firm headquartered in Sacramento, Calif. He was secretary of health and welfare, State of California, in 1974–75. He served concurrently as a member of the Governor's cabinet and was responsible for supervisory authority over the Department of Health, Department of Benefit Payments (Welfare), Department of Corrections, Youth Authority, Rehabilitation, Employment Development, and Office of Aging. In

1971–74 he was assistant to the Governor and director of public affairs, State of California, with responsibility for all State-Federal relations. He was deputy director of finance, State of California, in 1969–71.

Previously, in 1966–69, Mr. Jenkins was Washington representative for the city of San Diego, Calif. He served in the United States Navy as Director of Public Affairs, 11th Naval District, in 1964–66. In 1959–64 he was Public Affairs Assistant to four Secretaries of the Navy.

Mr. Jenkins attended the United States Merchant Marine Academy (Class of 1944); Armed Forces Information School (1946–47); and Naval War College (1957–58). He is married, has three sons, and resides in Carmichael, Calif. He is 57.

Nomination of Glenn L. Archer, Jr., To Be an Assistant Attorney General
November 5, 1981

The President today announced his intention to nominate Glenn L. Archer, Jr., to be an Assistant Attorney General (Tax Division), Department of Justice. He would succeed M. Carr Ferguson.

Since 1956 Mr. Archer has been a member of the law firm of Hamel, Park, McCabe and Saunders of Washington, D.C. As senior tax partner in the firm, he has

participated in many contested and litigated tax cases at every level, as well as consultation, tax planning, and administrative and legislative matters for a variety of clients.

Mr. Archer graduated from Yale University (B.A., 1951) and George Washington University Law School (J.D., 1954). He is admitted to practice in the U.S. Supreme Court, Court of Appeals for the District of

Columbia, U.S. District Court for the District of Columbia, U.S. Tax Court, and U.S. Court of Claims.

He is married, has four children, and resides in Falls Church, Va. He was born March 21, 1929, in Densmore, Kans.

Nomination of Peter McCoy To Be an Under Secretary of Commerce
November 5, 1981

The President today announced his intention to nominate Peter McCoy to be Under Secretary of Commerce for Travel and Tourism (new position).

Since January 1981 Mr. McCoy has served as Deputy Assistant to the President and Staff Director for the First Lady. During the 1980 Presidential campaign, he served as Mrs. Reagan's staff director, accompanying her on all campaign trips and supervising the operation of her staff. Previously, since 1972, Mr. McCoy was president of

Sotheby Parke Bernet of Los Angeles, Calif. A former management consultant, he also spent 8 years with the William Morris Theatrical Agency.

Mr. McCoy served as president of the Southern California Auctioneers' Association and has lectured on art at auctions around the country, including participating as a faculty member in the Practicing Law Institute series "Workshops on the Arts."

He is married, has two children, and resides in Los Angeles. He is 39.

Letter to the Chairmen of the Senate Foreign Relations Committee and the House Foreign Affairs Committee on the Situation in Zimbabwe
November 5, 1981

Dear Mr. Chairman:

In accordance with the provisions of Section 720 of the International Security and Development Cooperation Act of 1980, I am submitting the following report on the internal situation in Zimbabwe.

Zimbabwe is well into its second year of independence, and in the period which has elapsed since the last report to the committees, the state of the nation can be described as basically stable politically. The disarmament and integration of the two former guerrilla groups continued on schedule and is expected to be completed in the very near future. This process represents one of this young nation's most significant achievements.

Prime Minister Mugabe's position within the government and within his party is still strong and his overall position in the coun-

try was enhanced by his skillful handling of the dismissal of former Minister of Manpower, Planning and Development, Edgar Tekere. While Mr. Mugabe is still lobbying for the creation of a one-party state, he has stated that he will not move in this direction without a popular mandate. The Prime Minister is also becoming a more prominent spokesman among Front Line leaders and within the OAU. Of obvious concern, however, is the increasing sensitivity Prime Minister Mugabe and other government officials are beginning to display over what they perceive as unfavorable press. The government recently fired the editor of the Umtali *Post* allegedly for questioning the military arrangement with the North Koreans.

In making public the government's decision to conclude a military agreement with

North Korea, the Prime Minister stated that the brigade to be trained and equipped by the North Koreans would be used for internal security only. He also said that the acceptance of military assistance has no political or ideological significance so far as Zimbabwe's non-alignment policy goes, but rather this action, balancing British military aid, is an affirmation of that non-alignment.

Economically, Zimbabwe appears to be going through a period of defining what government's policy and role in the economic sphere should be. This could be a lengthy process, and it is already generating considerable concern in the private sector about its own role in the country's plans for economic development. Zimbabwe's economic policymakers remain very realistic, however, and, for the most part, seem inclined to approach structural changes in the economy with caution and gradualism, recognizing the importance of relating ideology to attainable goals.

The government has attempted to maintain a favorable investment climate. However, in keeping with its commitment to the implementation of socialist goals, the government wants the private sector to become more responsive to its development concerns as well as to Zimbabwe's overall development goals. The recent decision to create a minerals marketing authority to control the production and marketing of the country's minerals and metals no doubt represents an attempt to manifest these concerns.

Although the new budget reflects a moderately socialist path, it contains no references to drastic income redistribution programs or plans for nationalization of the private sector. Tax hikes called for in the budget are high by Zimbabwean standards; they are designed to increase government revenue and will have the added effect of allowing the government to increase expenditures in the fields of health services, schooling and other social programs.

While there is no question that Zimbabwe is continuing to make economic progress and that the economy is growing, the rate of growth is slowing somewhat and inflation is up for both high and low-income families. Key factors contributing to the economic slow-down include constraints in foreign exchange and labor and transportation problems. The emigration of whites is continuing, but there has been no significant increase or decrease in the numbers leaving.

There are also indications that recent tensions between South Africa and Zimbabwe may be having a negative impact on the economy. Also, the Zimbabwe Government has acknowledged that the country cannot cut off commercial relations with its neighbor. South Africa's decision to cancel the preferential trade agreement and to phase out Zimbabwean contract workers presently in the Republic will certainly aggravate an already difficult foreign exchange situation. The reclaiming by South Africa of 25 of its railroad locomotives is also causing serious transport problems for Zimbabwe, particularly with respect to the transport of petroleum products and to the movement of surplus grain from Zimbabwe's record maize harvest.

Land distribution is being carried out very cautiously and carefully, to insure that the basic infrastructure is either in place or under construction before settlement takes place. Present plans call for the resettlement of 18,000 families by the end of this year on presently unused land.

Sincerely,

RONALD REAGAN

Note: This is the text of identical letters addressed to Charles H. Percy, chairman of the Senate Foreign Relations Committee, and Clement J. Zablocki, chairman of the House Foreign Affairs Committee.

Nomination of Five Members of the National Commission on Libraries and Information Science, and Designation of Chairman
November 5, 1981

The President today announced his intention to nominate the following individuals to be members of the National Commission on Libraries and Information Science. Upon confirmation, the President intends to designate Elinor M. Hashim Chairman.

Elinor M. Hashim is assistant manager, corporate library, Perkin-Elmer Corp., of Norwalk, Conn. Since 1976 she has served as chairman of the Connecticut State Library Board after being appointed in 1974. Miss Hashim has been a member of the American Library Association since 1975. She graduated from the University of Vermont (B.A., 1955) and Southern Connecticut State College (M.S., 1970). She resides in Bridgeport, Conn., and was born December 13, 1933, in Pittsfield, Mass.

John E. Juergensmeyer is a lawyer with the firm of Smith & Leahy of Elgin, Ill. He is currently serving as special assistant attorney general, State of Illinois, and was previously assistant State's attorney and public defender for Kane County. Dr. Juergensmeyer also is professor of constitutional law and political science at Judson College in Elgin, Ill. He is the author of many publications on law and government. He graduated from the University of Illinois (B.A., 1955; J.D., LL.B., 1963) and Princeton University (M.A., 1957; Ph. D., 1960). He is married, has two children, and resides in Elgin. He was born May 14, 1934, in Stewardson, Ill.

Byron Leeds is a member of the board of directors and executive officer of Publishers Prototype, a computer composition company he founded in 1963. Publishers Prototype has specialized in worldwide satellite communications for the publishing industry. He attended Tulane University (1950–52) and graduated from New York University (B.A., 1954) and New York University Graduate School (1955–56). He is married and resides in Secaucus, N.J. He was born September 6, 1932, in New Jersey.

Jerald Conway Newman is executive vice president of Bank Leumi Trust Co. of New York. He joined the bank in 1973. Previously he was vice president of National Bank of North America. In 1972 he was appointed as consultant to the Secretary of Health, Education, and Welfare on matters of higher education and civil rights. He is currently an adjunct professor of business administration at the Graduate School of Business, Long Island University. He graduated from New York University (B.S., 1953; M.B.A., 1954). Mr. Newman is married, has three children, and resides in North Woodmere, N.Y. He was born January 10, 1932, in New York, N.Y.

Julia Wu is head librarian at Virgil Junior High School in Los Angeles, Calif. She is also a member of the Task Force on Minority Library Needs, National Commission on Libraries and Information Science (NCLIS). She has served on the NCLIS in 1973–78. In 1980–81 Mrs. Wu was coordinator, Indochinese Refugee Children's Assistance Program, Los Angeles City School District. She graduated from Taiwan National Normal University (B.A., 1958); Immaculate Heart College (M.A., 1962); and California State University (M.A., 1976). She is married, has three children, and resides in Los Angeles. She was born July 2, 1936, in Nanking, China.

Nomination of James Daniel Theberge To Be United States Ambassador to Chile
November 6, 1981

The President today announced his intention to nominate James Daniel Theberge, of the District of Columbia, to be Ambassador to Chile. He would succeed George W. Landau.

Mr. Theberge served in the United States Marine Corps as first lieutenant in 1952–54. He was with the Department of State as economic adviser in Buenos Aires (1961–64), and head of the lending coordination staff (1965–66). In 1966–69 he was adviser and senior economist at the Inter-American Development Bank, Washington, D.C., and in 1970–75, was director of Latin American Studies, Center for Strategic and International Studies, at Georgetown University. He was Ambassador to Nicaragua in 1975–77. Mr. Theberge was president of the Institute for Conflict and Policy Studies, Washington, D.C., in 1977–79, and senior development adviser of the Planning Research

Corp., New York, N.Y., in 1979–81. Since 1981 he has been special adviser on inter-American affairs, Department of Defense.

Mr. Theberge graduated from Columbia University (B.A., 1952); Oxford University (M.A., 1960); and Harvard University (M.P.A., 1965). He is married, has three children, and resides in Washington, D.C. He was born December 28, 1930, in Oceanside, N.Y.

Nomination of Melvin Herbert Evans To Be United States Ambassador to Trinidad and Tobago
November 6, 1981

The President today announced his intention to nominate Melvin Herbert Evans, of the Virgin Islands, to be Ambassador to the Republic of Trinidad and Tobago. He would succeed Irving G. Cheslaw.

Dr. Evans was physician in charge of Frederiksted Municipal Hospital at St. Croix, V.I. in 1945–48 and in 1950–51. In 1948–50 he was senior assistant surgeon, teaching fellow in medicine, at Howard University, and in 1951–59 he was chief municipal physician at St. Croix. He was commissioner of health of the Virgin Islands in 1959–67. Dr. Evans was chairman of the Governor's Commission on Human Resources in 1962–

66, and member of the Selective Service Board of Appeals (Virgin Islands) in 1967–69. He was Governor of the Virgin Islands in 1969–75 (appointed 1969–71, elected 1971–75). In 1979–81 he was Delegate to Congress from the Virgin Islands. He has practiced medicine at St. Croix from 1967 to 1969, from 1976 to 1978, and since 1981.

Dr. Evans graduated from Howard University (S.B., 1940; M.D., 1944) and the University of California at Berkeley (M.P.H., 1967). He is married, has four children, and resides in St. Croix, V.I. He was born August 7, 1917, in the Virgin Islands.

Appointment of Four Members of the National Commission on Student Financial Assistance, and Designation of Chairman
November 6, 1981

The President today announced his intention to appoint the following individuals to be members of the National Commission on Student Financial Assistance. The President also intends to designate David R. Jones as Chairman.

David R. Jones is currently executive director of development, Vanderbilt University, a position he has held since 1976. He was executive director of the Tennessee Republican Party in 1975–76. He was administrative assistant to Senator James L. Buckley (R–N.Y.) in 1971–74.

Mr. Jones was executive director of the Charles Edison Memorial Youth Fund in 1968–70. Previously he was an instructor of history in St. Petersburg, Fla., in 1961–63, and Clearwater, Fla., in 1960–61. He attended West Liberty State College in West Virginia (A.B., 1960); L.M.U. (1956–57); and George Williams College in Chicago, Ill. (1955–56). He is married, has three children, and resides in Nashville, Tenn. He was born January 1, 1938, in Buffalo, N.Y.

Richard E. Kavanagh is senior vice president and manager of the Chicago Municipal Finance Group, A.G. Becker Inc., Chicago, Ill. Previously he was Chief of the Finance Branch, Chicago Region, Department of Housing and Urban Development. In 1977 he was appointed member, Governor's Ad Hoc Financial Advisory Committee for Bond Offerings, State of Illinois. He attended DePaul University (B.S.). He is married, has four children, and resides in Naperville, Ill. He was born November 14, 1931, in Chicago, Ill.

Marilyn D. Liddicoat is vice chairman of the Santa Cruz County Board of Supervisors, Santa Cruz, Calif. She was first elected to the Board in 1976. Previously she was president of the Santa Cruz County Board of Education and was judge pro tempore of the Santa Cruz Municipal Court. She maintained a private civil legal practice for many years. She graduated from the University of California (B.A.) and the University of Southern California (J.D.). She is married, has three children, and resides in Watsonville, Calif. She was born October 24, 1931, in Los Angeles, Calif.

Kenneth R. Reeher is executive director of the Pennsylvania Higher Education Assistance Agency, where he has served since 1964. He developed the first State scholarship and student loan program in the country to be completely automated. Previously he was coordinator, Division of Testing of the Pennsylvania Department of Public Instruction, 1961–64, and guidance specialist, Department of Public Instruction, in 1960–61. Mr. Reeher graduated from Villanova University (B.S., 1948); Westminster College (M.S., 1952); and Allegheny College (LL.B., 1975). He is married, has one child, and resides in Camp Hill, Pa. He was born August 7, 1922, in Sharon, Pa.

Statement About Extension of the Voting Rights Act
November 6, 1981

Several months ago in a speech, I said that voting was the most sacred right of free men and women. I pledged that as long as I am in a position to uphold the Constitution, no barrier would ever come between a secret ballot and the citizen's right to cast one. Today I am reaffirming that commitment.

For this Nation to remain true to its principles, we cannot allow any American's vote to be denied, diluted, or defiled. The right to vote is the crown jewel of American liberties, and we will not see its luster diminished.

To protect all our citizens, I believe the Voting Rights Act should and must be extended. It should be extended for 10 years—either through a direct extension of the act or through a modified version of the new bill recently passed by the House of Representatives. At the same time, the bilingual ballot provision currently in the law should be extended so that it is concurrent with the other special provisions of the act.

As a matter of fairness, I believe that States and localities which have respected the right to vote and have fully complied with the act should be afforded an opportunity to "bail-out" from the special provisions of the act. Toward that end, I will support amendments which incorporate reasonable "bail-out" provisions for States and other political subdivisions.

Further, I believe that the act should retain the "intent" test under existing law, rather than changing to a new and untested "effects" standard.

There are aspects of this law, then, over which reasonable men may wish to engage in further dialog in coming weeks. As this dialog goes forward, however, let us do so in a spirit of full and total commitment to the basic rights of every citizen.

The Voting Rights Act is important to the sense of trust many Americans place in their government's commitment to equal rights. Every American must know he or she can count on an equal chance and an equal vote. The decision we are announcing today benefits all of our citizens by making our democracy stronger and more available to everyone.

Nomination of Edwin Gharst Corr To Be United States Ambassador to Bolivia
November 6, 1981

The President today announced his intention to nominate Edwin Gharst Corr, of Oklahoma, to be Ambassador to Bolivia. He would succeed Marvin Weissman.

Mr. Corr served in the United States Marine Corps in 1957–60, and was a teaching assistant at the University of Oklahoma in 1960–61. He entered the Foreign Service in 1961 and was international affairs officer in the Office of Mexican and Caribbean Affairs in the Department. He was Foreign Service officer, then administrative assistant to the Ambassador in Mexico City (1962–66), and associate representative of the Peace Corps in Cali (1966–68). He attended Latin American Area Studies at the University of Texas in 1968–69. In 1969–71 he was desk officer in the Office of Panamanian Affairs in the Department, and program officer at the Inter-American Foundation in 1971–72. He was political officer in Bangkok (1972–75), counselor for political affairs in Quito (1975–76), and Deputy Chief of Mission in Quito (1976–78). In 1978–80 he was Deputy Assistant Secretary of State for International Narcotics Matters in the Department. He was Ambassador to Peru in 1980–81.

Mr. Corr graduated from the University of Oklahoma (B.S., 1957; M.A., 1961). He is married, has three children, and resides in Norman, Okla. He was born August 6, 1934, in Edmond, Okla.

Message to the Congress Reporting Budget Deferrals and A Rescission
November 6, 1981

To the Congress of the United States:

In accordance with the Impoundment Control Act of 1974, I herewith report nine deferrals totaling $132.0 million and one proposal to rescind $20.5 million in budget authority previously provided by the Congress.

This group of deferrals constitutes the final in a series of actions taken to restrain spending of funds made available by the Continuing Resolution, P.L. 97–51. As I stated in my special messages of October 20, 23, and 29, these actions are not only in accord with Congressional intent to view the amounts provided by the Resolution as a ceiling, but are also necessary to preserve the Congress' options to enact regular appropriations consistent with my revised budget request levels for fiscal 1982.

Deferrals under the Continuing Resolution are included in this special message for the Departments of Agriculture, Health and Human Services, and Transportation.

I am also proposing to rescind advance 1983 funds for the Corporation for Public Broadcasting.

The details of the rescission proposal and the deferrals are contained in the attached reports.

RONALD REAGAN

The White House,
November 6, 1981.

Note: The attachments detailing the rescission proposal and the deferrals are printed in the Federal Register *of November 12, 1981.*

Exchange With Reporters About Extension of the Voting Rights Act
November 6, 1981

Q. How did you make the voting rights decision?

The President. I made it.

Q. I said "how." What made you come down in favor of the "bail out"?

The President. I came down in favor of a present, proved piece of legislation that has been most successful over the years and do think, however, after all this time, there could be the possibility of a better bail out opportunity for those who have abided by the election laws.

Q. Won't the blacks be angry at you?

Q. What year will we balance the budget?

The President. What?

Q. What year will we balance the budget now?

The President. I'll answer that further down the road.

Q. Won't the blacks be angry at you, sir?

The President. Why?

Q. Because you're supporting provisions that they oppose. For example, the intent provision.

The President. Well, I just think that the one that we have is tried and proven——

Q. ——the aim of the Supreme Court. It isn't the tried and true. The tried and true is not the intent provision.

The President. ——the voting rights for quite some time, and I think that it has worked and that it has resolved many of the problems——

Q. Are you disappointed, sir, that the balanced budget seems out of reach?

The President. No, and if there may be some delay we'll know that later down the road. But that's still our goal, and we think this program will achieve it.

Q. Thank you.

Note: The exchange began at 4:20 p.m. on the South Lawn of the White House as the President was departing for New York.

Remarks at a Republican Fundraising Reception in New York, New York
November 6, 1981

Thank you very much, Chairman—George, I'm very delighted to be here. I'd be more delighted if Nancy were here with me, but she's temporarily grounded by the bug.

George Clark, let me just say I thank you and the Empire State. I think that you were made for each other, because George stands as tall as any man I know. George was a friend and a supporter from the very beginning. And then when others advised us to write off New York in 1980, George stood up and said, "No, we can win this State." And we listened to him, and you know the rest.

Now, right down here we have some other people that you can be very proud of

that have been giving us invaluable support in our economic recovery program. One of them, and a real leader in that support, was Jack Kemp, along with Barber Conable. Now, Barber Conable isn't here tonight, but your Senator D'Amato is and Representative Jerry Solomon and Norman Lent and other Congressmen are here. And they've been having more fun up on the Hill than they've had in years past, I think.

Our goal is to bring all the people together in a campaign for economic progress. I don't know if anyone has pointed out to you what the tax bill we passed will actually mean to the people of the Empire State. Forty-two billion dollars that otherwise would have gone to Washington will remain in the pockets of your taxpayers. Nearly $2,500 for every man, woman, and child in the State of New York.

Our party believes in growth, in spending restraints, a sound dollar, lower taxes, and getting rid of inflation. We want to create more permanent jobs and real hope for a better future.

Now, a neighbor of yours recently delivered this same message. He told his fellow citizens that he would work to put the future of their State back where it belongs, back in their hands. And while we may have to wait a few weeks, I guess, for a recount to take place, just a formality, we just may be able, in a few weeks, to salute Tom Kean, the second Republican in 28 years to be elected Governor of New Jersey.

And we don't have to stop there. George was absolutely right. If we keep working together, we can plan for a reunion one year from now, a reunion to celebrate economic recovery, new legislative victories, and the election of your new Governor, the new Republican Governor of New York.

Much is riding on our economic program, and we can succeed if we remember a few facts. First, we came to Washington with a plan to rebuild this economy. And that plan is on track, even though the train was a little late leaving the station, later than we had planned or wanted.

What we call supply side economics is just now being born. If you listen closely, you can hear the spank and then the cry. But only one-fifth of the personal income tax rate reductions are in place, and they will not be fully in place before 1983. The incentives to stimulate new savings, in IRA and Keogh retirement accounts, will not go into effect before January 1982, nor will the reduction of the maximum tax on income, intended to coax investors out of their tax shelters. Important incentives for business to stimulate new investment and production will also begin in the next few months of 1982, and then they'll be phased in over the next several years.

Those Monday morning quarterbacks who insist our program hasn't worked are a little too anxious. They're Monday morning quarterbacks, but they are doing the quarterbacking on Friday night; they're not

waiting. It makes you wonder if some people just don't really want our program to fail, if they're not really rooting for recession and misery on Main Street. They just can't face discovering that their tax and tax, spend and spend philosophy over all these years didn't work, doesn't work, and won't work.

Whenever I hear these rhetorical attacks made against our program, a question pops into my mind. Where on Earth have these people been? Who controlled the Congress for 26 straight years? Who passed every law, every tax, and piled up the major part of our trillion dollar national debt? It wasn't us.

Our economic problems didn't begin on January 20th, 1981, but we can start to solve them if we stick to our plan. Now, I've been disturbed lately by a lot of talk that our administration is thinking of changing that plan, that some of the new estimates, born of high interest rates and the fact that reducing inflation faster than we'd anticipated has actually reduced our revenue, has caused us to at least think of pushing the panic button. Well, don't you believe it. We're going to keep right on asking the Congress for more spending cuts until we get government costs down to within government's revenues.

A balanced budget has never been an end in itself, justifying any means. We never agreed to balance the budget on the backs of the taxpayers the way the last administration tried to do it. We have always believed that a balanced budget must result from our spending and tax reductions, which together will shrink the size of government and expand the private economy, generating new tax revenues. Maybe it'll take a little longer than we'd planned, but we're not retreating 1 inch.

Now some people, many of them well-intentioned, have proposed a different way to reduce the deficit—through tax increases. The Congress has already raised taxes to record levels during the last two decades. Yet, during this entire period, the government just managed to balance one budget. The tax reductions we just passed, the largest in history, will do little more than offset the built-in increases already scheduled between now and 1984 by our opponents when they were there.

Let's be honest. If the deficit continues to grow, it will not be because the Congress cut taxes too much, but because it refused to cut spending enough. And there is room for more cuts. Let's get something straight. With the massive $35 billion budget cut, Federal spending is not less in 1982 than it was in 1981. We didn't cut the spending back to less than has been going on. It's almost $100 billion more. Our cuts were greater than any that have ever been made in the history of this country, but that seems that they're hardly horrendous or austere.

The Congress, we're told, can't significantly cut spending further, so we must dismantle our own program of needed incentives to accommodate them. Well, we made a commitment to the American people, and we're going to honor that commitment. Your tax reduction will not be rescinded. It will not be delayed, and it will not be reduced. We didn't select our program because it would be easy or quick or politically expedient. We chose it because it's the right solution to cure the economic mess that we're in.

You know, if you ask people in sports what enables them to come back late in the game and win it all, invariably their answer is the same. Some may call it desire or mental toughness or second effort or unfailing determination. What they're all talking about really can be summed up in one word—character.

Well, for nations in history, just as for individuals in everyday life, character determines destiny. America faces a test of character that may well decide its destiny. As I say, we never said it would be easy and we never said it would be quick. But if we make up our minds to pull together the American economy and all that we hold dear, we'll prevail.

So, let me leave you with the words of Herb Brooks, who was coach of the gold medal Olympic hockey team—and I think all of us remember that thrilling win in Canada—and now your New York Rangers, the coach of them. He was in the locker room at Lake Placid. His team was about to take the ice against the Russians. And Brooks told them they were born to play that game. He said, "You were meant to be here at this time. This is your moment."

And my fellow Republicans, I believe that we are here to lead this struggle to save our economy, that this is our moment, yours and mine.

With hard work, faith in God and in each other, we can and will rebuild this wonderful land. I wish I could make public or show all of you or tell you of some of the letters that I've been receiving that make you realize how much we can trust each other. One of them, just a little, short letter that I got the other day, that I had to have translated because it was written in braille. This man, in World War II, lost his eyesight in Germany 37 years ago, but he was writing a short letter to tell me that if it required cutting the benefits to people like himself, he was in favor of it if it would help our country get back to fiscal responsibility.

I've had letters from people telling me about the volunteer efforts that are going forth in their community, where they're picking up the slack. They see the things that need to be done, and they're writing letters and thanking us for having reminded them that they have this capacity to do these things on their own.

Now, I've had faith in all of you for a long time. And I know that we're going to do what has to be done, and I know it's going to work. So, thank you all for being here tonight in the cause that brings you together, and God bless you because we're on our way.

Note: The President spoke at 6:15 p.m. in the Hilton Room at the Waldorf Astoria Hotel.

Remarks in New York, New York, at the 84th Annual Dinner of the Irish American Historical Society
November 6, 1981

Dr. Cahill, I thank you and all those who are responsible for this great honor. And I want to say that I happen to know that there is one among us here who has known, also, today, the same joy and even greater, if possible, than I could feel. And that is Dr. Cahill, himself, who this morning was presented by Cardinal Cooke, on behalf of the Pope, the Grand Cross Pro Merito Melitensi. He is the first American to ever receive this award.

Your Eminence, the other clergy here at the head table, the other distinguished guests, and one in particular that I might pick out and mention, Teddy Gleason of the International Longshoremen's Association. And I mention him because on Sunday he is going to celebrate the 42d anniversary of his 39th birthday. Teddy, I've found that for some time, that makes it much easier to greet each one of these annual occasions.

But I do thank you very much. You know, there is the legend in Ireland of the happy colleen of Ballisodare who lived gaily among the wee people, the tiny people, for 7 years, and then when she came home discovered that she had no toes. She had danced them off. I feel happy enough—when I get home tonight I'm going to count mine. [*Laughter*]

Nancy is sorry that she couldn't be here, and so am I. She sent her warm regards and her regrets. Unfortunately, on the last trip into town she picked up the bug.

Now, I'm happy to say that's not a situation for me, like the two sons of Ireland, who were in the pub one evening and one asked the other about his wife. And he said, "Oh, she's terribly sick." He said, "She's terribly ill." And the other one says, "Oh, I'm sorry to hear that." But he said, "Is there any danger?" "Oh," he said, "No. She's too weak to be dangerous anymore." [*Laughter*]

A writer for the Irish press who was based in Washington, a correspondent for the press there, stated to me the other day—or stated the other day about me—that I have only recently developed a pride

in my Irish heritage or background, and that up till now I have had an apathy about it. Well, let me correct the record. That is not so. I have been troubled until fairly recently about a lack of knowledge about my father's history.

My father was orphaned at age 6. He knew very little about his family history. And so I grew up knowing nothing more beyond him than an old photograph, a single photo that he had of his mother and father, and no knowledge of that family history. But somehow, a funny thing happened to me on the way to Washington. [*Laughter*] When I changed my line of work about a year ago, it seemed that I became of a certain interest to people in Ireland, who very kindly began to fill me in. And so I have learned that my great grandfather took off from the village of Ballyporeen in County Tipperary to come to America. And that isn't the limit to all that I have learned about that.

Some years ago, when I was just beginning in Hollywood in the motion picture business, I had been sentenced for the few years I'd been there to movies that the studio didn't want good, it wanted them Thursday. [*Laughter*]

And then came that opportunity that every actor asks for or hopes for, and that was a picture that was going to be made and the biography of the late Knute Rockne, the great immortal coach of Notre Dame. Pat O'Brien was to play Rockne. And there was a part in there that from my own experience as a sports announcer I had long dreamed of, the part of George Gip. And generously, Pat O'Brien, who was then a star at the studio, held out his hand to a young aspiring actor, and I played Gip. Pat playing Rockne, he himself will say, was the high point of his theatrical career. My playing "The Gip" opened the door to stardom and a better kind of picture.

I've been asked at times, "What's it like to see yourself in the old movies, the reruns on TV?" It's like looking at a son you never knew you had. [*Laughter*] But I found out—in learning about my own heritage, going back to Ballyporeen—that, believe it or not, what a small world it is, Pat O'Brien's family came from Ballyporeen.

But I've been filled-in much more since. An historian has informed me that our family was one of the four tribes of Tara, and that from the year 200 until about 900 A.D., they defended the only pass through the Slieve Bloom Mountains. They held it for all those centuries and adopted the motto, "The Hills Forever." And that, too, is strange, because for the better part of 9 months now, I've been saying much the same thing, only in the singular: "The Hill Forever." Capitol Hill, that is. [*Laughter*]

I do remember my father telling me once when I was a boy, and with great pride he said to me, "The Irish are the only people in the country, in America, that built the jails and then filled them." [*Laughter*] I was a little perturbed even then, at that tender age, because at the sound of pride in his voice and from the way I'd been raised, I couldn't quite understand why that was something to be proud of, until I then later learned, which he had never explained to me, that he was referring to the fact that the overwhelming majority of men wearing the blue of the police department in America were of Irish descent.

You know, those weren't the only jobs that were open to the Irish. Back in the high day of vaudeville, long before sound pictures drove it out, there were, very popular in this country, comedians who would reach great stardom in vaudeville with a broad German accent. German comedians coming on "*Ach und Himmel Sie der.*" What is little known in show business is that almost without exception, they were Irish. Their wit and humor that made them comedians, they came by naturally and honestly.

I was on a mission to England for our government some 10 years ago. I should say to Europe, to several countries, and finally wound up and the last country was Ireland.

On the last day in Ireland, I was taken to Cashel Rock. I didn't know at that time that it's only 25 miles from Ballyporeen. But I do know that the young Irish guide who was showing us around the ruins of the an-

cient cathedral, there on the rock, finally took us to the little cemetery. We walked with great interest and looked at those ancient tombstones and the inscriptions.

And then we came to one and the inscription said: "Remember me as you pass by, for as you are, so once was I. But as I am, you too will be, so be content to follow me." And that was too much for the Irish wit and humor of someone who came after, because underneath was scratched: "To follow you I am content, I wish I knew which way you went." [*Laughter*]

But the Irish, like many, a great many of the people and like my grandfather, great-grandfather, were driven to the New World by famine and by tragedies of other kinds. The Irish—they built the railroads, they opened the West wearing the blue and gold of the United States Cavalry. There was John L. Sullivan, the heavyweight champion of the world, writers like Eugene O'Neill, clergy like Cardinal Cooke, and even physicians to the Pope like Dr. Cahill.

And it goes all the way back in our history. George Washington said, "When our friendless standard was first unfurled, who were the strangers who first mustered around our staff? And when it reeled in the fight, who more brilliantly sustained it than Erin's generous sons?" And a century and a half later, who else than George M. Cohan would write of the Grand Old Flag, the Stars and Stripes, and Yankee Doodle Dandy with the line, "I'm a real live nephew of my Uncle Sam."

There must have been a Divine plan that brought to this blessed land people from every corner of the Earth. And here, those people kept their love for the land of their origin at the same time that they pledged their love and loyalty to this new land, this great melting pot. They worked for it, they fought for it and, yes, they died for it—and none more bravely than Erin's generous sons.

Tragedy, as I've said, very often was the impetus that sent many to America. Today, as has been said here already tonight, there is tragedy again in the Emerald Isle. The Cardinal prayed and His Holiness, the Pope, plead for peace when he visited Ireland. I think we all should pray that responsible leaders on both sides and the governments of the United Kingdom and the Republic of Ireland can bring peace to that beautiful Isle once again. And once again, we can join John Locke in saying, "O Ireland, isn't it grand you look—Like a bride in her rich adornment? And with all the pent-up love in [of] my heart, I bid you top o' the mornin'!"

No, I have no apathy, no feeling at all, I am just so grateful that among the other things that happened when I was allowed to move into public housing—[*laughter*]—I had a chance, finally, to learn of the very rich heritage that my father had left me.

And I can only say once again, with heartfelt thanks, I wear this and take it home with a feeling of great honor, and say

something that I know to all of you is as familiar as "top o' the mornin' " or anything else. That is: "May the road rise beneath your feet, the sun shine warm upon your face, and the wind be always at your back, and may God, until we meet again, hold you in the hollow of his hand."

Thank you.

Note: The President spoke at 9:36 p.m. at the Seventh Regiment Armory in New York City. He was introduced by Dr. Kevin Cahill, president of the Society, who presented the President with a medal representing the Society's highest award.

Following the dinner, the President returned to the White House.

Remarks at the Reopening of the Press Briefing Room at the White House
November 9, 1981

Mr. Brady. It's nice to be back. I was told I was going to say hello to you and that was it. Hello, good friends. [*Cheers*]

Reporters. Hi, Jim. Good to see you.

Mr. Brady. We tried to run over Sam [Sam Donaldson, ABC News] out in the street. [*Laughter*]

Mr. Donaldson. If you can't beat 'em, run 'em down. [*Laughter*]

Mr. Brady. That's right.

[*At this point, the President and Mrs. Reagan entered the Briefing Room.*]

The President. Well, aren't we overwhelmed by the grandeur of the place? First, let me welcome all you orphans home. You know, we sort of missed you. It's been quiet over here, kind of like when the kids go back to school. [*Laughter*] You know, of course, this press room is still built over a swimming pool. Now, it isn't true, however, that the floor has been hinged——

Mr. Brady. Yes, it is. [*Laughter*]

The President. ——and can be sprung like a trap. Not that you would ever ask the wrong questions. [*Laughter*] But if you

should, we have installed one new feature. The place is wired for sound. We can press a button here on the podium and get instant helicopter noise in here. [*Laughter*]

No, seriously, we have added one feature that will help Larry and David in answering your questions. This microphone now has a built-in scrambler, and before you say— don't say, "Are you using it now?" I'm not. But knowing your great interest in one subject, you'll have plenty to write about. We have new china at the snack bar. [*Laughter*]

Although this press room is often filled with lightheartedness, I don't need to stress the serious and essential role you play in our democracy. The public depends on you to keep them informed about what we're really doing here and expects you to keep an eye on the Presidency. And, Sam, that doesn't mean you can put a ladder up to the third floor windows. [*Laughter*]

As happy as we are about reopening today, we are even more elated by the presence of a man who truly belongs in this room, a man whose courage has been an inspiration to all of us. And I'm proud that Jim Brady is my Press Secretary. Jim, we're all waiting for the day that you're back for good. [*Cheers*]

Mr. Brady. I am, too, Mr. President.

The President. Jim says he is, too. So, in dedicating these new facilities, let me just say that I hope this room is always filled with as much integrity and good humor as Jim Brady has brought to it. And now, I've been looking forward to cutting this ribbon. I've been practicing all morning on Ed Meese's tie. [*Laughter*]

And, of course, you know that with us here is Jim's wife, Sarah, and his mother, Dorothy Brady, and Sarah's mother, Francie Kemp. And we're delighted that you could be here for this.

Now, are you ready, Jim?

Mr. Brady. I'm ready when you are, sir.

The President. Here we go.

[*At this point, the President and the Press Secretary cut the ribbon.*]

Mr. Brady. Nice job.

The President. Now, I was told that I had to get right out of here and go back to work. It seems that you and I are going to be meeting in the next 24 hours or so.

Reporter. When is that press conference, Mr. President?

The President. It's tomorrow, I think, isn't it? [*Laughter*] At 2 o'clock, tomorrow.

Reporter. You can't give us an advance word on your budget-cut package? A little something for the overnights? [*Laughter*]

The President. Why, you all know from the way you act about it, I can't say anything until they tell me what I'm supposed to say. [*Laughter*]

Reporter. We'll say it's an unnamed source. [*Laughter*]

The President. Jim, good, good to see you. And I'm going to have to run along here now.

Mr. Brady. All right. Take care, Mr. President. Thank you.

The President. Bless you.

Mr. Brady. [*Speaking to Mrs. Reagan*] Am I still your "Y and H"?

The President. The husband is always the last to know. [*Laughter*]

Mrs. Reagan. Do you know what the "Y and H" is? You know when there was that story going around that—well, I'm not even going to go into it. [*Laughter*]

Reporters. Oh, come on. [*Laughter*]

Mrs. Reagan. Well, anyway, I kept calling Jim my "Y and H"—my young and handsome. [*Laughter*] He's still my "Y and H."

Mr. Brady. Thank you.

Mrs. Reagan. See you later, "Y and H." [*Applause*]

Mr. Brady. All right.

Reporter. It is all under review. [*Laughter*]

Reporter. Jim, you come back and see us, okay?

Mr. Brady. I'll come back.

Reporter. Real soon.

Reporter. Good show, Bear.

Mr. Brady. Helen [Helen Thomas, United Press International] said all is forgiven. I can come back. [*Laughter*]

Ms. Thomas. Thank you, Mr. Press Secretary.

Mr. Brady. You're welcome.

Reporters. We miss you. We all miss you, Jim.

Mr. Brady. I miss you, too.

Reporter. Yeah, these other guys aren't as tough. [*Laughter*]

Mr. Brady. I miss *most* of you. [*Laughter*]

Note: The ribbon-cutting ceremony began at 12 noon in the Briefing Room at the White House, which had been closed for repair and renovation since August. During the 3-month period, reporters and several White House staff members were moved to the Old Executive Office Building, where the daily press briefings were held.

The dedication ceremony marked the first public visit to the White House Briefing Room by Press Secretary to the President James S. Brady since March 30, 1981, when he was wounded during the attempted assassination of the President outside the Washington Hilton Hotel.

Appointment of Robert W. Searby as United States Representative on the Governing Body of the International Labor Office
November 9, 1981

The President today announced his intention to appoint Robert W. Searby to be United States Representative on the Governing Body of the International Labor Office.

Mr. Searby was appointed Deputy Under Secretary of Labor for International Relations by Secretary of Labor Raymond J. Donovan on May 11, 1981.

Previously, he worked as a consultant to several corporations, including Westinghouse and the Edison Electric Institute. He specialized in developing cooperative union-business ventures in the private sector with primary focus on energy policies and projects.

Mr. Searby graduated from Iona College in New York (B.S., 1968) and St. John's University in New York (M.A., 1973). He is married, has five children, and resides in Vienna, Va. He was born November 2, 1946, in New York, N.Y.

Appointment of Three Members of the Marine Mammal Commission, and Designation of Chairman
November 9, 1981

The President today announced his intention to appoint the following individuals to be members of the Marine Mammal Commission. The President also announced he intends to designate James C. Nofziger as Chairman.

James C. Nofziger has a broad background and formal training in the zoological sciences as well as a longstanding interest in marine matters. Since 1961 Dr. Nofziger has been an agricultural consultant for commercial corporations relative to their animal interests. Among his present consulting interests is mariculture. Previously, he was an instructor and researcher at Washington State University in 1959–61; sales manager and manager of technical services, California Cattle Supply Co., in Bellflower, Calif., in 1955–58; and feed commodity salesman with N. V. Nootbaar & Co., Pasadena, Calif., in 1958–59. He graduated from the University of California at Los Angeles (B.A., 1948) and Washington State University (M.S., 1952; Ph. D., 1961). He is a member of the American Institute of Biological Sciences. He is married and resides in Canoga Park, Calif. He was born February 1, 1923, in Bakersfield, Calif.

Donald Kenneth MacCallum is an anatomist and cell biologist and has retained an active interest in the marine ecology of the southern and central California coastal regions, an area of study and research he began as an undergraduate zoologist at the Kerckhoff Marine Biology Laboratory, Newport Beach, Calif. Since 1975 Dr. MacCallum has been an associate professor of anatomy, University of Michigan Medical School and, since 1973, associate professor of dentistry (oral biology), University of Michigan. He was research scientist, Laboratory of Biochemistry, National Institute of Dental Research, N.I.H., Bethesda, Md., in 1977–78; assistant professor of anatomy, University of Michigan Medical School, in 1969–73; and assistant professorial lecturer in anatomy, George Washington University School of Medicine, in 1967–68. He is an instructor, researcher, and writer on anatomy. He graduated from Pomona College (B.A., 1961) and the University of Southern California (M.S., 1964; Ph. D., 1966). He is married, has two children, and resides in Ann Arbor, Mich. He was born April 13, 1939, in Los Angeles.

Robert B. Weeden has been professor of resource management, School of Agriculture and Land Resource Management, University of Alaska, since 1976. He was director of the Division of Policy Development and Planning, Office of the Governor, State of Alaska, in 1975–76; professor of wildlife management, University of Alaska, in 1970–75; associate in wildlife, University of Alaska, in 1967–70; and a game biologist, Alaska Department of Fish and Game, in

1959–69. He was an instructor of zoology at Washington State University. He was a member of the Alaska Environmental Advisory Board and the Marine Fisheries Advisory Committee. He graduated from the University of Massachusetts (B.Sc., 1953); the University of Maine (M.Sc., 1955); and the University of British Columbia (Ph. D., 1959). He is married, has three children, and resides in Fairbanks, Alaska. He was born January 8, 1933, in Fall River, Mass.

Remarks at a Ceremony Commemorating the Initiation of the Vietnam Veterans Leadership Program
November 10, 1981

On this eve of Veterans Day in 1981, we meet to inaugurate a program that's aimed at helping a group of veterans who have never received the thanks they deserved for their extraordinary courage and dedication. A long, dragged-out tragedy, Vietnam, divided our nation and damaged America's self-image. And part of that tragedy, a major part, was the sacrifice by men who fought as bravely as any American fighting men have ever fought. Millions of young Americans, when they were called upon, did their duty and demonstrated courage and dedication in the finest tradition of the American military in a war they were not allowed to win.

I want to express appreciation, on behalf of all Americans, to these veterans who are here today, not only for their service during the war but for their continued voluntary service to their comrades in arms and to the nation. Contrary to an unjust stereotype, the vast majority of Vietnam veterans readjusted quickly after returning from Southeast Asia. And many of these fine young people here have succeeded and excelled in their post-war endeavors. Those here with us today are outstanding examples of this fact.

At the same time, however, there are those who found it difficult to come to grips with problems that can be traced to their wartime experiences. The Vietnam Veterans Leadership Program is designed to draw volunteers from the pool of successful Vietnam veterans in order to provide guidance for those with lingering problems. This volunteer, self-help program is within the spirit of camaraderie that has characterized American veterans of every war, and it's even more important for those who've fought in Vietnam.

Those of you who will be doing your part to make this program a success deserve a special thanks. I hope that every American will follow your example and reach out individually to extend a helping hand, where needed, to all our fine Vietnam veterans. Recognition and appreciation for all they went through is long overdue.

We should always remember that in a hostile world, a nation's future is only as certain as the devotion of its defenders, and the nation must be as loyal to them as they are to the nation.

This program is one way of expressing our commitment not only to Vietnam veterans but to all those who now serve our country in the military. So, thanks to all of you for participating in this fine effort. I think you're going to find your fellow citizens will want to help.

Now, Tom Pauken.

Note: The President spoke at 11:48 a.m. at the ceremony in the Rose Garden at the White House.

The program is a new Federal initiative, begun at the beginning of this fiscal year and administered by ACTION. The remarks of Thomas W. Pauken, Director of ACTION, were not included in the White House press release.

Executive Order 12332—Establishment of the National Productivity Advisory Committee
November 10, 1981

By the authority vested in me as President by the Constitution of the United States of America, and in order to establish in accordance with the provisions of the Federal Advisory Committee Act, as amended (5 U.S.C. App. I), an advisory committee on strategies for increasing national productivity in the United States, it is hereby ordered as follows:

Section 1. Establishment. (a) There is established the National Productivity Advisory Committee. The Committee shall be composed of distinguished citizens appointed by the President, only one of whom may be a full-time officer or employee of the Federal Government.

(b) The President shall designate a Chairman from among the members of the Committee.

Sec. 2. Functions. (a) The Committee shall advise the President and the Secretary of the Treasury through the Cabinet Council on Economic Affairs on the Federal Government's role in achieving higher levels of national productivity and economic growth.

(b) The Committee shall advise the President, the Secretary of the Treasury and the President's Task Force on Regulatory Relief with respect to the potential impact on national productivity of Federal laws and regulations.

(c) The Committee shall advise and work closely with the Cabinet Council on Economic Affairs (composed of the Secretaries of the Treasury, State, Commerce, Labor, and Transportation, the United States Trade Representative, the Chairman of the Council of Economic Advisers, and the Director of the Office of Management and Budget), the Assistant to the President for Policy Development, and other governmental offices the President may deem appropriate.

(d) In the performance of its advisory duties, the Committee shall conduct a continuing review and assessment of national productivity and shall advise the Secretary of the Treasury and the Cabinet Council on Economic Affairs.

Sec. 3. Administration. (a) The heads of Executive agencies shall, to the extent permitted by law, provide the Committee such information with respect to productivity as it may require for the purpose of carrying out its functions.

(b) Members of the Committee shall serve without compensation for their work on the Committee. However, members of the Committee who are not full-time officers or employees of the Federal Government shall be entitled to travel expenses, including per diem in lieu of subsistence, as authorized by law for persons serving intermittently in government service (5 U.S.C. 5701–5707).

(c) Any administrative support or other expenses of the Committee shall be paid, to the extent permitted by law, from funds available for the expenses of the Department of the Treasury.

(d) The Executive Secretary of the Cabinet Council on Economic Affairs shall serve as the Executive Secretary to the National Productivity Advisory Committee.

Sec. 4. General. (a) Notwithstanding any other Executive Order, the responsibilities of the President under the Federal Advisory Committee Act, as amended, except that of reporting annually to the Congress, which are applicable to the advisory committee established by this Order, shall be performed by the Secretary of the Treasury in accordance with guidelines and procedures established by the Administrator of General Services.

(b) The Committee shall terminate on December 31, 1982, unless sooner extended.

RONALD REAGAN

The White House,
November 10, 1981.

[*Filed with the Office of the Federal Register, 3:28 p.m., November 10, 1981*]

Appointment of the Membership of the National Productivity Advisory Committee, and Designation of the Chairman and Executive Secretary
November 10, 1981

The President today announced the appointment of the following individuals to be members of the National Productivity Advisory Committee. The President also announced that William E. Simon will serve as Chairman. Roger B. Porter, Counselor to the Secretary of the Treasury, will serve as Executive Secretary.

Lamar Alexander, Governor, State of Tennessee.

Lewis M. Branscomb, vice president and chief scientist, IBM Corp., Armonk, N.Y.

Jesse M. Calhoon, president, National Marine Engineers Beneficial Association, AFL–CIO, Washington, D.C.

Nicholas T. Camicia, chairman, president, and chief executive officer, The Pittston Co., Greenwich, Conn.

Justin Dart, chairman and chief executive officer, Dart Industries, Inc., Los Angeles, Calif.

Michael K. Deaver, Assistant to the President and Deputy Chief of Staff, The White House, Washington, D.C.

John T. Dunlop, Lamont University professor, Harvard University, Boston, Mass.

Martin Feldstein, president, National Bureau of Economic Research, Belmont, Mass.

Clifton C. Garvin, Jr., chairman of the board and chief executive officer, Exxon Corp., New York, N.Y.

Harvey A. Goldstein, managing partner, Singer, Lewak, Greenbaum & Goldstein, Los Angeles, Calif.

J. Peter Grace, chairman of the board and chief executive officer, W. R. Grace & Co., New York, N.Y.

C. Jackson Grayson, chairman, American Productivity Center, Houston, Tex.

Robert E. Hall, professor of economics, Stanford University, Palo Alto, Calif.

David T. Kearns, president and chief executive officer, Xerox Corp., Stamford, Conn.

Alfred H. Kingon, editor in chief, Saturday Review Financial World View; vice chairman, Macro Communications, Inc., New York, N.Y.

Charles F. Knight, chairman and chief executive officer, Emerson Electric Co., St. Louis, Mo.

William Konyha, president, United Brotherhood of Carpenters and Joiners of America, Cleveland, Ohio.

Laurence William Lane, Jr., chairman of the board, Lane Publishing Co.; publisher, Sunset magazine, Menlo Park, Calif.

Paul MacAvoy, professor, Yale School of Organization and Management, New Haven, Conn.

Donald S. MacNaughton, chairman and chief executive officer, Hospital Corporation of America, Nashville, Tenn.

Ruben F. Mettler, chairman and chief executive officer, TRW, Inc., Redondo Beach, Calif., and Cleveland, Ohio.

John J. O'Donnell, president, Air Line Pilots Association, Washington, D.C.

Paul H. O'Neill, vice president, corporate planning, International Paper Co., New Canaan, Conn.

Gerald L. Parsky, partner, Gibson, Dunn & Crutcher, Washington, D.C.

John H. Perkins, president, Continental Illinois National Bank & Trust Co., Chicago, Ill.

Richard F. Schubert, vice chairman, Bethlehem Steel, Easton, Pa.

Maurice R. Schurr, international vice president, Local 929, International Brotherhood of Teamsters, Chauffeurs, Warehousemen and Helpers of America, Philadelphia, Pa.

Donald V. Seibert, chairman and chief executive officer, J. C. Penney Co., New York, N.Y.

L. William Seidman, vice chairman, Phelps-Dodge Corp., New York, N.Y.

William E. Simon, chairman, Crescent Diversified Ltd., New York, N.Y.

Roger B. Smith, chairman and chief executive officer, General Motors Corp., Detroit, Mich.

Jayne Baker Spain, executive in residence, George Washington University, Washington, D.C.

Arnold R. Weber, president, University of Colorado, Boulder, Colo.

The President's News Conference
November 10, 1981

The President. Ladies and gentlemen, I have an opening statement.

Program for Economic Recovery

From the day our administration took office, our top priority has been to rescue this economy from years of government mismanagement. We inherited the highest rates since the Civil War, the first back-to-back years of double-digit inflation since World War I, rising budget deficits, and a national debt ready to break through the trillion dollar barrier.

For years, government spending and taxation have grown faster than the underlying economy. The American people elected us to reverse that trend, and that's what we've begun to do. Our program has only been in effect for some 40 days, and you can't cure 40 years of problems in that short time. But we've laid a firm foundation for economic recovery in 1982.

We said we would cut taxes, and we've enacted the biggest tax reductions in history. And let's remember, those reductions will barely offset the built-in tax increases, already scheduled between now and 1984, that were adopted in 1977. We've slowed the growth of Federal spending. We've cut the growth of regulations by a third. Interest rates and inflation are both heading down.

Our reforms can stimulate new savings, new investments, new jobs, and a new America. But one condition must still be met. This government must stiffen its spine and not throw in the towel on our fight to get Federal spending under control.

The budget savings, despite all the talk of austerity, have been accomplished without sacrificing necessary government functions and services. Even with a $35 billion cut so far, Federal spending is still rising far too rapidly. The Federal budget has doubled since 1975, tripled since 1970. Who can honestly look Americans in the eye and tell them spending is under control?

Fiscal '82 is already 5 weeks old, but I have not received a single, regular appropriations bill. Most of the bills pending are over budget. It is imperative that the Congress meet its own spending target and move quickly to pass appropriation bills or a second continuing resolution that fits our September 24th request. I stand ready to veto any bill that abuses the limited resources of the taxpayers.

It's ironic that those who would have us assume blame for this economic mess are the ones who created it. They just can't accept that their discredited policies of tax and tax, spend and spend are at the root of our current problems.

We will not go back to business as usual. Our plan for economic recovery is sound. It was designed to correct the problems we face. I am determined to stick with it and stay on course, and I will not be deterred by temporary economic changes or short-term political expediency.

Now, for the first question. Helen [Helen Thomas, United Press International].

President's Foreign Policy

Q. Mr. President, your recent statements on limited nuclear war, State Department memos, interviews, have all hinted at possible intervention against Qadhafi, Castro. A high state of belligerency seems to personify your foreign policy, and people say it's in disarray.

My question is, were you misunderstood on the question of nuclear war? Are we going to intervene in the Caribbean or anywhere else? Are we going to provide a military shield for Egypt if it goes into Libya?

The President. I have been just as disturbed as you are and just as confused by some of the things that I've been reading about our supposed foreign policy. Let me say that that statement that started the whole thing with regard to the possibility of the spread of nuclear war, I can't say that it was misunderstood. I don't think it was misunderstood by the editors who were in the room. I was having lunch with a group of editors, and I made a statement that I've made a number of times. I won't repeat it here, but it was an explanation of the whole strategic concept. And then, evidently hearing it secondhand, because it wasn't written by anyone who was in that room, to my knowledge, it appeared in an entirely different context. And we could go back and get the transcript of what was actually said, and I would stand by that.

We have no plans for putting Americans in combat any place in the world. And our goal is peace; it has always been. And at the end of this month, we will go into negotiations with the Soviet Union on what I hope will be reduction of the theatre nuclear weapons in Europe to the lowest point possible.

The Caribbean

Q. Well, are you repudiating those memos that have been publicized in connection with Libya and the Caribbean?

The President. We are interested, of course, in the Caribbean. This is why we've been helping Salvador, because we believe that revolution has been exported to that area and with design. Again, as I say, our economic help to El Salvador is three times the military assistance we're giving. And that military assistance is not in the nature of combat forces of ours, nor do we have any plans to make it that way.

But, yes, we continue our interest in preserving the Americas from this kind of exported revolution, this expansionist policy that is coming by way of, I think, the Soviets and the Cubans.

Q. Mr. President.

The President. Yes, Jim [Jim Gerstenzang, Associated Press].

The Federal Budget

Q. With the budget deficit continuing to grow, have you decided—are you going to try to raise taxes in some way in '82, '83, or '84, or are you going to seek further budget cuts? And, also, now having said that your promise of a balanced budget by '84 can't be met, when do you expect to see a balanced budget, and what assurances do we have that this time it can be met?

The President. With the uncertainty, Jim, of when we can bring ourselves out of this recession which, I think, will take place in the first half of '82, I would hesitate to try and make a specific—set a date or an amount with regard to budget deficits or when a balanced budget would take place. That is still our goal. That has to be our goal. Government has to return to staying within its revenues. Our goal remains the same. We recognize now that the likelihood of meeting it on the 1984 date has become an unlikelihood, because of unforeseen changes. And again, as I say, we can't predict when that will be. But we stay on target, that is our eventual goal.

I don't think, however, that just the balancing of a budget could justify any means to attain it. You could always balance a budget if you put it on the backs of the people with tax increases. I don't favor that at all, because every time you do that you find that it's like getting addicted to a drug, because of the very fact that those tax increases then reduce the prosperity and the productivity of the Nation further, and you find that you need more of the same and more of the same. You'll reach a point of no return.

The reduction of government spending is the answer, and the thing that we are going to attempt. And we have before the Congress now, requests for further budget reductions. And in January when we present the figures for the '83 budget and the out year of '84, we will be asking for more of the same. Whether there will be any changes in revenue procedures or not, that is a decision to be made, and that, too, will be addressed in January when we present the other budget.

El Salvador

Q. Mr. President, I'd like to followup Helen's question. You mentioned El Salvador and the importance that El Salvador has to the United States and this region. Yet, the El Salvador Government is rapidly losing ground, and guerrillas already control almost one-fourth of the land there. How far will the United States go to keep the Duarte government in power?

The President. Well, first of all, let me say that there's some disagreement, a great deal of disagreement, about who is mostly in power or what the guerrillas might control. We have been urging, and hopefully cooperating with, a solution that would lead to an election and settle this dispute by peaceful means. It is true the guerrillas have switched their tactics now. Unable to win a military victory, they have switched them to hit-and-run tactics against the infrastructure of industry and the economy, trying to bring down the government by destroying the economy. But I don't believe that we could accept without question that there may be something of a stalemate in the inability to bring about a quick military solution to this, but we would prefer the other.

How far are we prepared to go? As I've said, we're giving economic aid. I think we should continue to do that. I don't believe this requires in any way, nor have we considered, aid of the kind of actual military intervention on our part. But we are hopeful, still, that with the help of some of the other neighbors in Central America who feel as we do, that we can bring about the idea of an election and a peaceful settlement.

It is true about one thing: It cannot be denied, the guerrillas, with their terrorist tactics in El Salvador, have failed miserably in an attempt to bring the population over on their side. The populace is still in support of the government.

NATO's Strategic Planning

Q. Mr. President, in your exchange with the editors—I happen to have the transcript—I'd like to read you what you said. You said, "I could see," you said, "where you could have the exchange of tactical weapons against troops in the field without it bringing either one of the major powers to pushing the button." Then, Secretary Haig last week talked of the possibility of a nuclear warning shot as part of NATO's contingency plans.

I would like to ask you, first, if you endorse still what you said to the editors and, second, if you believe that the nuclear warning shot should be a part of NATO's plans.

The President. Well, I have not been a party to the contingency planning of NATO that has gone on now for approximately 30 years and which, I think, has proven itself a deterrent to military action in Europe and for all this period of time.

What you've just quoted that I said there, the discussion was in the area of—and I suppose it's hypothetical—where you're talking about is it possible to ever use a nuclear weapon without this spreading automatically to the exchange of the strategic weapons from nation to nation. And I gave as what I thought was something that was possible, that the great difference between theatre nuclear weapons, the artillery shells and so forth that both sides have, that I could see where both sides could still be deterred from going into the exchange of strategic weapons if there had been battlefield weapons, troop-to-troop exchange there.

I think there's high risk, there's no question of that. I think the thing we have to recognize and why our goal must be able to seek peace is what someone said the other day: "If war comes, is any nation—would the opponents, faced with inevitable defeat, take that defeat without turning to the ultimate weapon?" And this is part of the danger and why we're going to pursue arms reductions as much as we can and do what we can to ensure peace. And I still believe that the only real insurance we have with that is deterrent power.

Possibility of a Nuclear Warning Shot

Q. Sir, if I may follow up. Could there be a nuclear warning shot? And I take it that you do endorse what you said in the context that you said it.

The President. Well, I endorse only that I said it was offered as a possibility, and I think you'd have to still say that that possibility could take place. You could have a pessimistic outlook on it or an optimistic, and I always tend to be optimistic. Your other question——

Q. Nuclear warning shot?

The President. Oh. Well, there seems to be some confusion as to whether that is still a part of NATO strategy or not, and so far I've had no answer to that.

Saudi Eight-Point Peace Plan

Q. Mr. President, I wonder if there's any portion of the Saudi eight-point peace plan that could be incorporated in the American peace initiative or that could be added on to the Camp David accords?

The President. Well, one in particular. I know that there's also some dispute about what I'm going to say between the parties concerned, but I believe—and I have stated previously that I believe—that it's implicit in the offering of that plan, recognition of Israel's right to exist as a nation. And this has been one of the sticking points so far, with the Arab world refusing to make that acknowledgement. This was why I have referred to it as a hopeful sign that here was an offer of a plan, whether you agreed with it or not, but indicated the willingness to negotiate, which does imply.

The other point in the plan is that one of the eight points calls for all of the states of the region living together in peace, and I think we all endorse that.

Q. Any other parts of it beside those two?

The President. Well, let me answer it this way. I think that the most realistic approach is the one that we are taking, which is, the attempt to bring peace in the Middle East must be based on the Camp David accords and 242 Resolution of the United Nations.

The Economic Outlook

Q. Mr. President, your Secretary of the Treasury, Donald Regan, yesterday gave a rather pessimistic view of the Nation's economy. I think he called it a "real downer" that we're facing. Do you share his pessimistic view of the economy? Are we in for a "real downer" in your opinion?

The President. Well, now, I don't know what his definition is of a "real downer." I think that we're going to have some hard times for the next few months. I think we're going to see a pickup in the economy—and I think that Don Regan believes this also—in spring or at the latest, early summer of 1982. The interest rates, as you know, have come down 3½ points since September, and this has been one of the major causes of our stepping into a recession; that while we had predicted, as you well know, a stagnant economy—and we refer to it as a "soggy economy"—and so forth throughout the year, none of us had predicted the stepping over into recession. And it has changed some of the estimates,

obviously, as witness our second question here about where we're going.

But I think all of us are agreed that we are going to come out of it in the next several months. And we believe as our economic program starts to work and has more than 40 days behind it, the oncoming tax cuts will take place that are scheduled for next July, and so forth, we think are going to bring about the reduction of unemployment and the stimulation of productivity. And we've had some pretty hopeful signs already with regard to the producer's cost index that has just recently come to us.

B–1 Bomber

Q. Sir, some Members of Congress say that this B–1 bomber you want to build is a "flying Edsel." The Congressional Budget Office says that it will cost twice as much as your people think it will cost. Your own Secretary of Defense calculates that its useful time—before the Soviets could keep it from penetrating Soviet airspace—would be about 4 years. Are you going to reconsider? Do we really need the B–1?

The President. Sam [Sam Donaldson, ABC News], yes, we do. I believe that this and the MX are both important parts of strengthening our weakened triad of strategic nuclear power.

The B–52, which has been hailed at the moment as the one that could be our craft for carrying missiles and penetrating, was never built for that. It would have to be rebuilt. So, you're not home free by using that older plane. There's a cost to that. The B–1 carries anywhere from one and a half to two times the payload that it carries. The B–1 has a target on radar that's only a fraction of that of the B–52. And it has greater speed.

But the problem that has necessitated that is a gap that remains between what has to be the ultimate use of the B–52, with their age, and the development of the new tactical bomber. That is only in a state of research and study right now. We cannot guarantee the date that it will be ready. It is that gap when we would have nothing that the B–1 would fill. But the very fact that its one mission of penetrating enemy airspace might be eliminated in a few years time, at the end of that gap as, hopefully, the other plane comes on line, does not mean that you scrap it. There will be other purposes and functions for which it can be used. So, it isn't a total loss.

As to the figure given by Congress, Cap Weinberger was my finance director for a while in California, and I trust his figures better than I trust theirs. And I think that we go ahead, and I think that's a worst-case situation that they're taking with regard to cost.

Minority Unemployment

Q. Mr. President, recently we've looked at unemployment that has nearly increased 20 percent and a minority portion of our economy that has experienced an unemployment problem of three times that. Is there any program, including your Urban Enterprise Zone Program, that you feel will add some measure of decreasing the unemployment and the depressive economic state for blacks and other minorities in this country?

The President. There is, and that problem is not new with this administration. As you know, the unemployment of minorities has been greater always than it is with the majority, the white community. And I don't think—we've lumped the figures together into one figure, say, for black unemployment, ignoring the fact that that figure has been heightened by the excessive amount of youthful or teenage unemployment. It is not totally reflective of the earner for the household.

But we think that our economic program is designed to rectify, over the long haul, this problem which has been with us for these 40 years that I've been talking about and needs correction. It didn't just come into being in these last few months.

But also, we are looking at, very seriously, the idea of urban renewal—well, that's the wrong name for it; I've criticized that too much to use it—the enterprise zone, the specialized zones to hit targets of very high unemployment in our cities. And we are going forward with that.

Entitlements Cuts and the Social Safety Net

Q. Mr. President, while you have made no decisions yet on your entitlements cuts

for 1983 and '84, what is your feeling in principle about the cuts that have been proposed to reduce Medicaid and Medicare benefits and to also force welfare mothers to go out and seek jobs. Does that mean that the social safety net is really in tatters?

The President. No, it isn't. And the main goal of any of these reductions is still aimed at correcting those abuses that come about through the interpretation of regulations, to allow people who do not have real need that justifies their imposing on their fellow citizens for sustenance, for them to still be able to take advantage of these programs. The person with real need, we still want to help.

At the same time, when you say to force someone to go out and seek work, I think that the whole target of some of our social reforms, like welfare, always should have been to find a way to salvage those people and make them self-sustaining, instead of perpetuating them unto the third and fourth generation as wards of the government. And let me just give an example here of the type of thing that goes on that has to be corrected.

We just recently received word of a little girl who has spent most of her life in a hospital. The doctors are of the opinion that if she could be sent home and receive her care at home, it would be better for her; this spending most of her life there and away from the home atmosphere is detrimental to her. Now, it would cost $1,000 a month for her particular ailment to send her home. Her parents have no way that they can afford that, and the regulations are such that Medicaid now cannot pay for that if she goes home. The alternative is Medicaid continues to pay $6,000 a month to keep her in a hospital, when the doctors say she would receive better treatment and be better off at home. But her parents can't afford to have her taken off Medicaid.

Now, by what sense do we have a regulation in government that says we'll pay $6,000 a month to keep someone in a hospital that we believe would be better off at home, but the family cannot afford one-sixth of that amount to keep them at home?

Q. To follow that, sir, do you endorse the Schweiker proposals?

The President. The what?

Q. Do you endorse the proposals made by your Health and Human Services Secretary?

The President. I have to tell you that those, again, are going to be presented as options which will be considered in an upcoming Cabinet meeting, so I can't give you an answer on that yet.

Q. Well, how do you feel about them?

The President. I feel that we have to look at these programs to see what we can do. But as I say, these will be presented as options that we have yet to go over and consider and see, make sure, that they're not going to unnecessarily hurt people that we don't intend to hurt.

Yes, George [George Skelton, Los Angeles Times].

Budget Issues and the Congress

Q. Mr. President, you say you want to stay on course with your September 24th program, but there's some confusion about what remains of that program which has never really been detailed to the public or to Congress.

Your entitlement program, for instance, you haven't—are you going to drop that, as reported, until January? The $3 billion in tax increases, is that going to be postponed?

The President. George, we'll be talking about whether there's going to be or should be any revenue changes in January, but also the entitlements. And it doesn't mean dropping them in any way. Those two will be presented in January with the budgeting process for '83, but those programs were never intended to go into effect until late in 1982 anyway. So even in January, we will be—if that is the route we take—they will be in time for when they were originally scheduled.

The problem has been, with the Christmas holidays coming, after all our discussions with our leaders in Congress, that we just can't produce or get anything done by Congress in this interim period. And so it's the best advice, that since they don't have to be set back by delaying their presentation until January, that's when we're going to do it.

Q. Can I follow up on that? Precisely what will you be asking Congress to do between now and January 1st?

The President. Well, we've got that 12-percent cut before them. They've got about 14 appropriation bills up there. Not one has come to my desk as yet. Now they're discussing a second continuing resolution of the kind that took us all the way through 1981, and here we go into 1982 and, as I say, we are waiting. Most of the appropriation bills that they're considering are above budget, the budget that we set. And as I've said, I will not stand still for budget-busting bills.

But whether they send those up or whether, in this interim period, they send up another continuing resolution, I don't know. But if they do, I hope that it is within our budgeted figures. The first one was not, which means that they enforced spending through a continuing resolution that was above our budget.

Foreign Policy Advisers and U.S. Foreign Relations

Q. Mr. President, what adjustments are you planning in your foreign policy structure or in your staff to avoid situations such as that last week, when your Secretaries of Defense and State were making conflicting statements on nuclear policy and which made it necessary for you to call your Secretary of State and your National Security Adviser into the Oval Office for a private meeting?

The President. Well, I called them in, actually, to find out and to urge that they, with their staffs, just as I have with my own, ensure that we're a little more careful. There seems to be too much just loose talk going around, but it has been exaggerated out of all reality. There's no animus, personal animus, and there is no bickering or back-stabbing going on. We're a very happy group. [*Laughter*]

The picture that has been given of chaos and disarray is a disservice to the country and to other countries and allies as well. We are not in disarray with regard to foreign policy. I think our accomplishments have been rather astounding.

I have had 70 meetings with—bilateral and multilateral—with heads of state, foreign secretaries, ranging from Southeast Asia, to Asia, to Europe, Africa, and certainly here within the Americas. We have a better rapport established now between the three North American countries than I believe we've ever had. We have—our allies—I don't think we've ever had a stronger relationship than we have with them in Europe.

We were supposed to be destroyed at the Ottawa summit, and suddenly you decided that by some fluke we weren't. And then came Cancún, and I was not burned at the stake. [*Laughter*] Everything turned out just fine, and I had bilateral meetings there with 17 individual heads of state that were there. They were very pleased with the presentation we made about how to meet some of their problems.

I think in the Middle East, we've progressed there. I think that we've made great progress and rectified some things that had been giving the country problems for a time. And tied with this, is our economic plan and our defense program to refurbish our defenses, so that I am greatly encouraged. Our meetings here with heads of state in every instance have—they have responded with statements to the effect that they have better relations than they've ever had before with our country, better understanding of where we stand with relation to each other.

And I think that Al Haig has done a remarkable job as Secretary of State. He is trusted and approved of in every country that we do business with. And the only thing that seems to be going wrong is, I think sometimes that the District of Columbia is one gigantic ear. [*Laughter*]

Q. One followup. You've criticized the press for circulating what you've called reports of disarray. I'm wondering if you think that Mr. Haig's behavior may have been at play in these reports also?

The President. All that I meant by that—I must say, there have been times when we've checked on "Is this story correct?" and we have been able to refute that the story is not correct, and then see it, still, appear and be made public. But all I would ask is—I know you've got a job to do and

you're trying to do a job—but all I'd ask is all of us, I think it behooves all of us to recognize that every word that is uttered here in Washington winds up, by way of Ambassadors and Embassies, in all the other countries of the world. And we should reflect on whether it's going to aid in what we're trying to do in bringing peace to troublespots like the Middle East, or whether it's going to set us back.

Federal Medical Programs

Q. Mr. President, you gave a rather dramatic example of a person who could be better treated for $1,000 at home or $6,000 of Medicaid funds in the hospital. Can that be taken to mean that you would approve the use of Medicaid funds for home treatment? And let me just add to that, when you talked about protecting the needy, are you aware that Secretary Schweiker's memorandum would permit for the first time since Medicaid started that the States levy charges on the poor for their Medicaid treatment?

The President. Well, the idea in government medical programs of putting some minimum charge in which the recipient, unless they're totally needy, pays some share has been found to be very successful in reducing overuse of some programs. Now, again, you're citing something that has not yet come to me, if it is going to come, as an option. So, we'll wait and see.

On the first part of your question, which I think is the main question, yes. Let me give an example. In California, we have some programs in which the choice could be between home care for the individual or institutionalizing them. I'm speaking of such things—mental retardation and so forth. And we have a program where a family that elects to go the one way—and there's certain means tests connected with this—gets a grant, which is far more economical, just as this hospital bill is, than in institutionalizing the person. And I think that when we see a case of this kind it reveals that hidebound regulations can be a tremendous expense to the taxpayers and doing no good to the patient.

Ms. Thomas. Thank you, Mr. President.

The President. Thank you, Helen.

Note: The President's fifth news conference began at 2 p.m. in the East Room at the White House. It was broadcast live on radio and television.

Announcement of the Decision To Use Federal Facilities at Fort Drum, New York, as a Temporary Holding Facility for Illegal Aliens
November 10, 1981

The Federal facilities at Fort Drum near Watertown, N.Y., will be utilized as a temporary holding facility for aliens arriving illegally in this country, pending construction of a permanent facility. A thorough search was conducted by the Departments of Justice, Health and Human Services, and Defense. All these Departments agreed Fort Drum was the one site that met the key criteria, including capacity, availability, and minimal impact on defense operations.

Use of this site will allow the Immigration and Naturalization Service to continue the administration's policy of detaining aliens arriving illegally in the United States, pending resolution of their status.

In connection with this decision, the President today met with Representative David Martin of New York who has been particularly concerned with the preservation of Fort Drum's role in national defense plans. The President reassured him of the administration's commitment to the long term development and use of the base as a key defense installation. The President also indicated that the temporary use of Fort Drum as a detention facility will in no way compromise current activities at the base. No decision has been made for the location of a permanent facility.

Remarks at the Dedication of the New ABC Washington Bureau Building
November 12, 1981

The President. Thank you all very much. It is a pleasure for me to be here, and am I impressed now when I stop to think that I used to go walking on the beach with Elton Rule in California. [*Laughter*]

I knew that I wanted to bring something to you today, so I have a news flash. Chase Manhattan has lowered the prime rate to 16½—[*laughter*]—the 3-month bill is down to 10–5–0, having opened at 11, and the long bond has improved two points on par in the first hour of the market. [*Laughter*] Oh, yes, and I think you should know that the space shuttle got off. [*Laughter*] That's the only thing my administration favors in going up. [*Laughter*]

Seriously, to see this, the largest building, as I understand, devoted totally to electronic news, is really something—and to know

that in the late fifties, your entire staff here in Washington consisted of four TV commentators and one for radio. But I'd just like to take you back a little further, being the only one here, I think, that's old enough to do it. But, yes, in those WHO days in Des Moines, Iowa, 50,000 watts, another network in the middle thirties, even the four and the one that were here in the fifties sounds pretty extravagant.

Now, I can't claim—maybe it isn't true if we look far enough—that we were the first to do radio news. But we had a kind of free soul that owned our company, B. J. Palmer. The Fair Trade Practices Act said that radio could not do news in those days because it was unfair to the printed media. And our boss came to a day in which he said we were going to do it. UPI was the only one that would sell us a news service. We hired a newspaper reporter who later became H. R. Gross, the conscience of the United States Congress in his many years as a Congressman here. But he did the news, and I did the sports, and the only other news source we had, legally—[*laughter*]—was a Western Union ticker that in the appropriate season would bring in whatever scores there were. And Charlie Gross and I—that was it.

There was an illegal source. I had a 10:30 at night sports summary, and I found that it went much easier if I ducked out of the studio a little before 10 and picked up the early morning edition of the Des Moines Register and Tribune—[*laughter*]—and from which I would ad lib a very entertaining sports summary.

But we've come a long way in all of this, and I am very proud and happy to be here. I understand there's going to be an unveiling of the plaque and all. And I'm not going to go into any great dissertation about freedom of the press, and you know how I feel about regulations. Let me just say that in our efforts to reduce them, cut them down and get rid of the unnecessary ones, your industry is included. We'd like to go to work on that, too, and free you up as citizens.

Mr. Donaldson. Mr. President, what would a newsroom be—[*laughter*]—try to make a little news from you. Let me ask you, sir, can David Stockman continue to be effective after saying such damaging things about your economic program?

The President. Sam [Sam Donaldson], when I leave here today I'm going back to have a meeting with Dave Stockman. That's all I can tell you.

Mr. Donaldson. Well, we were told by Republican Senators that he got a round of applause during a Cabinet Room meeting with you this morning.

The President. Well, he made a statement in there that did, yes. But I'm not going to say anything more until he and I meet this afternoon.

Mr. Donaldson. One final question as we say in—[*laughter*]—as H. R. Gross would have said, "One final question, please." You don't agree that your plan is a trickle-down, aid-the-rich program?

The President. No. As a matter of fact, if anyone wants to look closely, our original tax plan did not contain the reduction of the 70-percent bracket. That was suggested by the Democrats.

Thank you. [*Laughter*]

Mr. Arledge. I was only joking when I said the first question would be by Sam Donaldson. [*Laughter*]

Mr. Donaldson. So, fire me.

Mr. Arledge. You know, that's not a bad idea. [*Laughter*]

Note: The President spoke at 12:09 p.m. at the ABC News Washington Bureau. Elton Rule is president and chief operating officer of ABC, Inc., Roone Arledge is president of ABC News, and Sam Donaldson is a White House correspondent for ABC News.

Message to the Congress Concerning the Continuation of the Iran Emergency
November 12, 1981

To the Congress of the United States:

Section 202(d) of the National Emergencies Act (50 U.S.C. 1622(d)) provides for the automatic termination on the anniversary date of a declaration of emergency, unless prior to the anniversary date the President publishes in the *Federal Register* and transmits to Congress a notice that the emergency authority is to continue in effect beyond such anniversary date. On November 12, 1980 President Carter caused to be published in the *Federal Register* and transmitted to the Congress a notice that the emergency declared on November 14, 1979 with respect to Iran was to continue in effect beyond the November 14, 1980 anniversary date. I have sent to the *Federal Register* for publication the attached notice stating that the Iran emergency is to continue in effect beyond the November 14, 1981 anniversary date.

Although the crisis which existed in the fall of 1979 and throughout 1980 between the United States and Iran has substantially abated, the internal situation in Iran remains uncertain. The war between Iran and Iraq continues and the Soviet Union still occupies Afghanistan. In January 1981, Iran and the United States entered into agreements for release of the hostages and the settlement of opposing claims. An international arbitral tribunal has been established for the adjudication of claims of U.S. nationals against Iran and by Iranian nationals against the United States; but it must decide four disputes between the United States and Iran over the proper interpretation of the agreements before it can address private party claims. It appears that full normalization of commercial and diplomatic relations between the U.S. and Iran will require more time. In these circumstances, I have determined that it is necessary to maintain in force the broad authorities that may be needed to respond to the process of implementation of the January 1981 agreements with Iran and the eventual normalization of relations.

I will see that the Congress is kept informed of significant developments.

RONALD REAGAN

The White House,
November 12, 1981.

Notice of the Continuation of the Iran Emergency
November 12, 1981

On November 14, 1979, by Executive Order No. 12170, President Carter declared a national emergency to deal with the threat to the national security, foreign policy and economy of the United States constituted by the situation in Iran. Notice of the continuation of the national emergency beyond November 14, 1980 was transmitted by President Carter to the Congress and published in the *Federal Register* on November 12, 1980. Because our relations with Iran have not yet been normalized and the process of implementing the January 19, 1981 agreements with Iran is still under way, the national emergency declared November 14, 1979 must continue in effect beyond November 14, 1981. Therefore, pursuant to section 202(d) of the National Emergencies Act (50 U.S.C. 1622(d)), I am signing this notice of the continuation of the national emergency declared November 14, 1979, and causing such notice to be published in the *Federal Register* and transmitted to the Congress.

RONALD REAGAN

The White House,
November 12, 1981.

[*Filed with the Office of the Federal Register, 12:43 p.m., November 12, 1981*]

Appointment of Edward J. Rollins, Jr., as Assistant to the President for Political Affairs
November 12, 1981

The President today announced his intention to appoint Edward J. Rollins, Jr., to be Assistant to the President for Political Af- fairs. He would succeed Franklyn C. "Lyn" Nofziger, who is resigning.

Mr. Rollins was appointed Deputy Assistant to the President for Political Affairs on January 21, 1981. Previously he served as the Republican staff director for the California State Legislature. He also served as the principal staff assistant to the Speaker of the California Assembly, in addition to other legislative staff positions.

Mr. Rollins has been involved in managing many legislative and congressional races in California and other Western States. During the second Nixon and the Ford administrations, he served as Deputy Assistant Secretary for Congressional Affairs, and as a special assistant in the Office of the Secre-

tary at the Department of Transportation.

He has received undergraduate and graduate degrees from the California State University system in political science and public administration. He has also held teaching and administrative positions at California State University (Chico) and Washington University (St. Louis, Mo.). He also served as dean of the faculty and deputy superintendent at the National Fire Academy in Washington.

Mr. Rollins was born March 19, 1943, in Boston, Mass. He resides in Alexandria, Va.

Proclamation 4883—Thanksgiving Day, 1981
November 12, 1981

By the President of the United States of America

A Proclamation

America has much for which to be thankful. The unequaled freedom enjoyed by our citizens has provided a harvest of plenty to this Nation throughout its history. In keeping with America's heritage, one day each year is set aside for giving thanks to God for all of His blessings.

On this day of thanksgiving, it is appropriate that we recall the first Thanksgiving, celebrated in the autumn of 1621. After surviving a bitter winter, the Pilgrims planted and harvested a bountiful crop. After the harvest they gathered their families together and joined in celebration and prayer with the native Americans who had taught them so much. Clearly our forefathers were thankful not only for the material well-being of their harvest but for this abundance of goodwill as well.

In this spirit, Thanksgiving has become a day when Americans extend a helping hand to the less fortunate. Long before there was a government welfare program, this spirit of voluntary giving was ingrained in the American character. Americans have always understood that, truly, one must give in order to receive. This should be a day of giving as well as a day of thanks.

As we celebrate Thanksgiving in 1981, we should reflect on the full meaning of this day as we enjoy the fellowship that is so much a part of the holiday festivities. Searching our hearts, we should ask what we can do as individuals to demonstrate our gratitude to God for all He has done. Such reflection can only add to the significance of this precious day of remembrance.

Let us recommit ourselves to that devotion to God and family that has played such an important role in making this a great Nation, and which will be needed as a source of strength if we are to remain a great people.

Now, Therefore, I, Ronald Reagan, President of the United States of America, do hereby proclaim Thursday, November 26, 1981, as Thanksgiving Day.

In Witness Whereof, I have hereunto set my hand this twelfth day of November, in the year of our Lord nineteen hundred and eighty-one, and of the Independence of the United States of America the two hundred and sixth.

RONALD REAGAN

[*Filed with the Office of the Federal Register, 3:58 p.m., November 12, 1981*]

Appointment of Six Members of the Board of Directors of the Student Loan Marketing Association, and Designation of Chairman
November 12, 1981

The President today announced his intention to appoint the following individuals to serve as members of the Board of Directors, Student Loan Marketing Association. The President also intends to designate Edward A. McCabe as Chairman.

Judith M. Chambers has been vice president for student life, University of the Pacific, Stockton, Calif., since 1975. She also serves as affirmative action officer and was dean of students in 1973. She serves on the Northern California advisory committee of the National Association of Student Personnel Administrators. She was born April 14, 1945, in Philadelphia, Pa.

Edward A. McCabe has been a partner with the firm of Hamel, Park, McCabe & Saunders in Washington, D.C. since 1960. He was general counsel, Committee on Education and Labor, U.S. House of Representatives, in 1953–55. Mr. McCabe was Counsel and Administrative Assistant to the President in 1956–60. He is a trustee of Immaculata College (Washington) and Allentown College (Center Valley, Pa.). He was born March 4, 1917, in Ireland.

Donald E. Roch has been with the Metropolitan Insurance Co. in West Warwick, R.I., since 1958. From January 1979 until March 1981, he was Republican State chairman in Rhode Island. He served in the Rhode Island Senate in 1971–75 and 1977–81. He was named one of the Nation's 50 most outstanding legislators in 1973 by the Eagleton Institute of Politics at Rutgers University. He was born September 12, 1931, in West Warwick, R.I.

Richard D. Shelby is president of Thompson Well Servicing, Inc., Tulsa, Okla. Previously, he was Deputy Director, Office of Presidential Personnel, the White House. He served in the Presidential transition effort and was State chairman of the Oklahoma Republican State Committee. He was the recipient of the Distinguished Alumnus Award, Southwestern Oklahoma State University, and was president of the student body. He was born April 29, 1946, in Santa Marie, Calif.

Irby Clifford Simpkins, Jr., is president of the Nashville Banner, Nashville, Tenn., and is owner of Irby C. Simpkins Investments. He was a member of the Tennessee Higher Education Commission in 1979 and is a trustee of Meharry Medical College. He was born March 17, 1944, in Nashville, Tenn.

Earl S. Smittcamp has been chairman of the board of Wawona Frozen Foods since 1964 and Lyons-Magnus (food processing) since 1971. He is chairman, board of trustees, Dry Creek School District. He is an Outstanding Alumnus of Fresno State University. He was chairman of the Fresno State University President's Advisory Board. He was born May 15, 1918, in Fresno, Calif.

Memorandum Concerning the Fiscal Year 1983 Budget
November 12, 1981

Memorandum for Heads of Departments and Agencies

Subject: 1983 Budget

During the next six weeks, I expect to make final decisions on nearly all aspects of the 1983 budget that I must submit to the Congress in January. This budget will reflect my firm commitment to hold down government spending and reduce the serious adverse effect that government spending and government-stimulated borrowing is having on the national economy.

In September, you were advised of the outlay ceilings for 1983 and 1984 that I approved for your department or agency for the purpose of guiding the development of the request that you have submitted to the Office of Management and Budget. There will be very few, if any, cases where it will be possible for us to exceed those outlay ceilings. In some cases, it will be necessary to go even lower.

The Office of Management and Budget is reviewing your requests, and you will begin receiving the results of these reviews. I hope that there will be very few appeals but, if you find that an appeal is absolutely necessary, you should submit that appeal within 72 hours of the time you are notified of the initial decision. I have instructed Dave Stockman and his staff to work with you to resolve as many appeals as possible.

If some unresolved issues remain, I will look to the Budget Review Board that I established last July (consisting of Ed Meese, Jim Baker and Dave Stockman) to meet with you to consider any remaining appeal. You should be prepared to submit any matter unresolved at that level to me within 24 hours after you are advised of the Board's decision.

We have made good progress in bringing the size and cost of government under control, but we have a long way to go. Your continued cooperation in this effort is sincerely appreciated.

RONALD REAGAN

Note: The text of the memorandum was released by the Office of the Press Secretary on November 13.

Message to the Congress Reporting a Budget Deferral
November 13, 1981

To the Congress of the United States:

In accordance with the Impoundment Control Act of 1974, I herewith report one deferral of $108 thousand in fiscal year 1982 funds.

This action is taken to restrain spending of funds made available by the Continuing Resolution, P.L. 97–51.

The deferral contained in this message is for the Department of Interior's Historic Preservation Fund.

The details of the deferral are contained in the attached report.

RONALD REAGAN

The White House,
November 13, 1981.

Note: The attachment detailing the budget deferral is printed in the Federal Register of November 19, 1981.

Nomination of C. T. Conover To Be Comptroller of the Currency
November 13, 1981

The President today announced his intention to nominate C. T. Conover to be Comptroller of the Currency, Department of the Treasury, for a term of 5 years. He would succeed John Gaines Heimann.

Since 1978 Mr. Conover has been a partner with the firm of Edgar, Dunn & Conover, Inc., of San Francisco, Calif. During this time he designed an electronic funds transfer system for banking institutions and worked with California banks on projects involving operations improvement and float control. Previously he was a partner with Touche Ross & Co., management services and national services director for banks, in 1974–78. In 1972–74 he was vice president, corporate development, U.S. Bancorp, in Portland, Oreg. Mr. Conover was management consultant with McKinsey & Co., Inc., San Francisco, Calif., in 1965–72.

He graduated from Yale University (B.A. 1960) and the University of California Graduate School of Business Administration (M.B.A., 1965). He is married, has two children, and resides in Lafayette, Calif. He was born October 13, 1939, in Bronxville, N.Y.

Appointment of Lawrence F. "Pat" Kramer as a Member of the Advisory Council on Historic Preservation
November 13, 1981

The President today announced his intention to appoint Lawrence F. "Pat" Kramer to be a member of the Advisory Council on Historic Preservation for the remainder of the term expiring January 17, 1985. He would succeed Dianne Feinstein.

Mr. Kramer is serving in his fourth term as mayor of Paterson, N.J. (1966–71 and 1974 to present). He is on the executive board of the National Conference of Republican Mayors and is also a member of the National League of Cities and the U.S. Conference of Mayors.

He is married, has three children, and resides in Paterson, N.J. He was born February 24, 1933, in Paterson.

Appointment of Eight Members to the Council of the Administrative Conference of the United States, and Designation of Vice Chairman
November 13, 1981

The President today announced the appointment of the following individuals to be members of the Council of the Administrative Conference of the United States. The President also designated Richard S. Williamson as Vice Chairman.

Mark S. Fowler, Chairman, Federal Communications Commission

Michael R. Gardner, partner, Bracewell & Patterson of Washington, D.C.

Edith Dinneen Hakola, vice president, general counsel, and treasurer of the National Right to Work Legal Defense Foundation, Springfield, Va.

James C. Miller III, Chairman, Federal Trade Commission

T. Timothy Ryan, Jr., Solicitor, Department of Labor

Edward C. Schmults, Deputy Attorney General, Department of Justice

Edward L. Weidenfeld, partner, McKenna, Conner & Cuneo of Washington, D.C.

Richard S. Williamson, Assistant to the President for Intergovernmental Affairs, The White House

Exchange With Reporters Concerning Assistant to the President Richard V. Allen
November 13, 1981

Q. Mr. President, what about Allen taking all that money?

The President. One question, one answer.

Q. What about Allen?

The President. One answer.

Q. Okay.

The President. As far as I know, there is no evidence of any wrongdoing.

Q. You're satisfied completely? You're completely satisfied?

The President. I said, on the basis of all that I know.

Q. Does he stay at work, sir? He stays in the job?

The President. On the basis of what I know, yes.

Q. Thank you very much.

Q. What about Stockman?

The President. One question; three parts.

Q. What's wrong?

Note: The exchange began at 3:42 p.m. on the South Lawn of the White House as the President was departing for Texas.

Remarks to the Astronauts On Board the Space Shuttle *Columbia* During its Second Voyage
November 13, 1981

The President. Joe and Dick, this is Ronald Reagan.

Astronauts. Hello, Mr. President.

The President. Hello. I wanted to make a request. I just wondered if when you go over Washington before your landing at Edwards Air Force Base, could you pick me up and take me out? I haven't been to California since last August. [*Laughter*]

Astronauts. We'd be proud to, sir.

The President. Okay. Thank you. Thank you very much.

Let me just say, I'm sure you know how proud everyone down here is and how this whole nation—I'm sure the world—but certainly America, has got its eyes and its heart on you.

Astronauts. Thank you very much, Mr. President. We're awfully honored that we got the opportunity to take part in this, and I'm sure that we're very glad that you're getting a chance to meet all the people there in Houston that are making it happen.

The President. Well, I've enjoyed meeting them. I told them when I came in this was a rare experience for an old horse cavalry officer.

Astronauts. Mr. President, we certainly do appreciate your taking the trouble to show all the people working on the space shuttle how much you care, and it makes us mighty proud.

The President. I care. And, again, God bless you both. All of us here are watching with great pride.

Astronauts. Thank you very much, sir. Thank you, sir, very much.

The President. Thank you.

Note: The President spoke from the Mission Control area of the Lyndon B. Johnson Space Center in Houston, Tex., to astronauts Joe Henry Engle and Richard H. Truly, who were in their second day of the space voyage.

Remarks at a "Salute to a Stronger America" Republican Fundraising Dinner in Houston, Texas
November 13, 1981

Mr. Chairman, Governor Bill Clements, Rita, I can't thank you enough for that introduction and for what you said about this. I'm kind of sorry that we can't steal you for California—[*laughter*]—because I know how well you did in redistricting here. [*Laughter*] They redistricted California from the other side, and the only Republican district left is just south of Tijuana. [*Laughter*]

Governor John Connally, Nellie, Congressman Bill Archer and Jim Collins, Ron Paul, Jack Fields, Tom Leoffler, our State chairman, our national committeemen who are here, the guests here at the head table,

1045

and those that we honor tonight and who, I can assure you, are serving so well in your Nation's Capital. I, like Mike—yes, we both came from the office, so no black tie. But I would like to call to your attention that I am wearing a tie tack that is the seal of the State of Texas. And I think my cuff links make up for no black tie because they're a map of the State of Texas, and they were given to me by your Sam Hall. [*Laughter*]

Now, Mike Deaver and Jim Baker, it's true, told me that they're taking me on a turkey shoot tomorrow. And when they brought this up, I asked them, "Why are we going all the way to Texas to shoot turkeys?" [*Laughter*] And they said that, well, down here you had a different kind than the turkeys I'd been seeing. [*Laughter*]

And you know, Bill, when you said something about if I were a Texan or not—I don't know, I love Texas, too, and I love all the people of Texas who've been so wonderful to me every time I've ever been here. And I remember a story about Lyndon Johnson when he was President, and maybe it applies to States, too. But he was leaving the South Lawn of the White House, and the two helicopters were there, and he happened to be going toward the wrong one. And one of the security stepped up and didn't want to, with all the press covering this, make it obvious, said, "Mr. President, that's your helicopter over there." And Lyndon stopped and said, "Son, they're all mine." [*Laughter*]

I don't know whether that works with States or not, but anyway, I suppose you've been wondering what we've been doing up there these last 9 months or so. Well, this dinner, as you've been told, expresses what we've been trying to do, and that is to make America strong again—I'm so grateful for John's generous words about that—to make it strong economically, militarily, and spiritually. And I believe we're on the right track for all three.

Yes, the interest rates are high. We have a recession. But those interest rates have dropped 3½ percent since September. Inflation is just a little more than half what it was when we took office.

And to show you how it's going, this morning in one of the last meetings we had before we left to come here, the Secretary of Agriculture was waiting for me at a Cabinet Council meeting and presented me with a giant replica of a check. It was for $27 million that the Department of Agriculture has saved on personnel and travel costs—not a budget item, just saved by management.

Yes, I know that recently it's been announced that we have 500,000 more unemployed than we had a year ago. And I haven't been able to figure it out yet, because we have 260,000 more employed than we had when we took office.

Militarily—military enlistments are up, so are reenlistments. The educational level of those enlisting is higher than it has ever been, and the morale of our Armed Forces is something that makes you proud every time you see it.

I received a letter from a young lad who's a sailor on one of our submarines. He said he was writing, and he was writing on behalf of his 180 shipmates. And he said he just wanted us to know how good it felt to be an American. And he said, "We may not have the biggest Navy in the world, but we've got the best."

Spiritually—I have things happen almost every day that turn me inside out. And you'd be surprised how many of them have come from Texas: messages from associations, from individuals, groups, clubs, telling me that with regard to the call for voluntarism what they're doing to now step in and do the things that, as they say, "We always should have been doing except we got in the habit of thinking government should do them."

And one of your cities here—to tell me how the leading corporate heads and business heads in the city had met, the special projects they were engaged on, that they had decided to increase their United Way campaign target by 20 percent, just because there was more need now to do things voluntarily.

The letters from individuals—from an elderly lady in New Orleans who explained, told me her age and I won't repeat it, but it was considerable. She was black, but she said, "Thank you for doing away with the war on poverty." She said, "Thank you for letting us once again try our own muscle and not become helpless dependents."

Then I received a letter from a man who said he is on—he lives and is supported by the government. And he said, "If it means cutting what I receive in order to restore fiscal integrity to this land," he said, "you cut what I receive." His letter was written in braille. Thirty seven years ago as a GI in World War II, he lost his eyesight.

Somebody once told me before I became Governor—I think maybe I repeated it to Bill once when he was getting ready to take over as Governor here—that some days you'd go home feeling 10 feet tall. Well, I want to tell you, yesterday—you know, George Bush is heading up a task force to cut away and hack away at those regulations which have tied the hands of local government, which have tied the hands of business and industry in this country, and they're having great success.

But a couple of days ago, we ran into another regulation, and I told the press about it, because I learned about it in time for a press conference we were having— about a little girl in the Midwest, 3½ years old, who couldn't live at home. She has been ill virtually since birth. Maybe you saw it on television. We never intended that; I did not give her name or anything. But the enterprising press found out and on the news that night publicized it. She has spent her entire life in a hospital, requiring a care that costs about $12 thousand a month, and she could be cared for at home for $1 thousand per month. The doctors think she'd be better off at home. Her parents, a lovely couple, want her at home, but they can't afford that, and so the $10 thousand or $12 thousand a month is being paid by the government—but under a regulation that would cease if she went home.

Well, when they made it public and who it was, yesterday when I came to the office, Dick Schweiker over at HHS was happy to tell me that that regulation no longer applies to her and she's going home. Some days this job is more fun than other days.

Well, right now the economy—of course there's a lot of second-guessing about the economic plan that we adopted. We were determined to reduce government spending, to reduce the percentage of the gross national product that the government was taking in taxes, and some with the best intentions now would reject tax reduction as being financially unsound while there is a Federal budget deficit. But a deficit can result from waste and the weakness of the economy. And we can try to eliminate the deficit by raising taxes which further weakens the economy, or we can restore to full prosperity this nation and balance the budget with the revenues that such an economy would generate.

In the 14th century there was a Moslem philosopher—I've told about this a few times—who knew this about the economy. He said in the beginning of the dynasty, the dynasty reaps large tax yields from small assessments; at the end of the dynasty, it is reaping small tax yields from large assessments. Well, John F. Kennedy knew this in the 20th century. And he said our true choice is not between tax reduction on the one hand and avoidance of large Federal deficits on the other: An economy stifled by restrictive tax rates will never produce enough revenue to balance the budget, just as it will never produce enough jobs or enough profits.

Well, President Kennedy was selling a tax cut proposal against all the advice of the leadership of his own party and against that kind of economist that has got a Phi Beta Kappa key at one end of his watch chain and no watch on the other. [*Laughter*] Well, he had his way, and he got his tax cut. And he was asked by, again, those same people, "Well, what if it doesn't work?"

Well, I'm being asked now the same question by the Democratic leadership of Congress. And John Connally told you who has been responsible all these years for the problems that we're now in. Perhaps we should just refer them to the history of those years just prior to the Kennedy tax cut, when employment in America was increasing by 1.19 percent a year, and how in the years immediately following, the rate of increase in employment was almost doubled. The real gross national product, the rate of growth, went from a little over 3½ percent before the tax cut to over 5 percent after the tax cut. The savings, the growth rate of personal savings, jumped from 2⅓ percent to 8 percent of the American people's earnings.

Now, this is not only evidence of recent history of what can happen when more money rather than less is left in the hands of the people. There is more: 1969—there were 698 American business firms, each one with a net worth under $5 million, who were in the stock market, raising by way of that marketplace $1.4 billion to fund expansion and continued growth. And then in '69, the capital gains tax was doubled. And shortly thereafter, there were only four such firms in the stock market raising a mere $15 million.

With the help of your Congressmen and, yes, with the help of you, because, believe me, when the phone started ringing in Washington when we asked for it, and the telegrams and the letters—there were an awful lot of them that were coming from the State of Texas. With their help and your help, we have passed the greatest reduction in Federal spending in history. We didn't get all we asked for; we got about $35 billion worth.

And now the recession, brought on by high interest rates and the increased cost of government borrowing to pay for the built-in deficits that we inherited, has altered our estimates of revenues and deficits for the next few years ahead. And so immediately, someone pushed the panic button and says we should call off the tax cuts or we should pass new increases in taxes so that we could take back with one hand what we'd given with the other.

The Democratic leadership in September proclaimed that our plan doesn't work. Well, as John told you, it didn't start until October. [*Laughter*] But they were like Monday morning quarterbacks who were sounding off on Friday night. Our plan, as I say, didn't start till later, and we won't really feel the effects of it, as John indicated, for some time now, because additional tax cuts will go into effect in January, more in next July, and so forth.

Now, in the meantime, we are asking for additional cuts in spending, and that isn't new. When we got the first package, we told them that there were at least 70-odd billion dollars in unspecified cuts that we would require over the next 3 years to

make this plan work. But there's one thing I don't believe we need and one thing I'm against: We're not going to have a tax increase.

Our program was designed to stimulate the economy, increase productivity, and create jobs.

Now, let me give you a figure that doesn't appear, static numbers that are used in estimating the future deficits. They're all related to the budget. We must cut the budget *x* amount or we must get more tax revenue by a tax increase to meet this size budget.

Well, let me tell you some figures that aren't static. If our belief in improving the economy is correct, by just reducing unemployment by 1 percentage point, you will reduce the deficit by $25 billion. And you can take it from there as to having a goal. What should it be? To stifle the economy with increasing the taxes on the people's backs, or to improve the economy by placing not only 1 but 2 and 3 percentage points of those unemployed back to work in an industrial America that is once again leading the world? That's what our target is.

You know, Senator Kennedy at a dinner just recently, the 90th birthday party was being celebrated for former Governor and Ambassador Averell Harriman. Teddy Kennedy said that Averell's age was only half as old as Ronald Reagan's ideas. And you know, he's absolutely right. The Constitution is almost 200 years old, and that's where I get my ideas.

Marie Montessori, when she was asked why she didn't reply to her critics, replied if she were climbing a ladder and the dog came yapping at her heels, she would have two choices. She could either stop and kick the dog, or she could continue to climb the ladder. And she preferred to climb.

Well, I'll confess, I'm awfully tempted every once in a while to do some kicking. [*Laughter*] But I think that all of you sent us up there to climb. And with the help of these people that you've sent from your State, and those others from other States up there, I think we have a great team. And no matter how much they pick on us, we do enjoy each other. We're working together. And we're doing just exactly what you sent us up there to do: We're going to make a stronger America, with your help.

Thank you very much.

Note: The President spoke at approximately

9:45 p.m. in the Imperial Ballroom at the Hyatt Regency Hotel. The dinner was sponsored by the Texas Republican Congressional Committee and the Texas Republican Campaign Committee.

Proclamation 4884—Continuation of Temporary Duty Increase on the Importation Into the United States of Certain High-Carbon Ferrochromium
November 13, 1981

By the President of the United States of America

A Proclamation

1. Presidential Proclamation 4608 of November 15, 1978, issued pursuant to section 203(a)(1), of the Trade Act of 1974 (the Act) (19 U.S.C. 2253(a)(1)), provided for a temporary increase in the duty on imports of ferrochromium containing over 3 percent by weight of carbon provided for in item 607.31 of the Tariff Schedules of the United States (TSUS), when valued at less than 38 cents per pound of chromium content. This temporary increase was for the period from November 17, 1978, through November 16, 1981.

2. The United States International Trade Commission (the Commission), pursuant to sections 203(i)(2) and 203(i)(3) of the Act (19 U.S.C. 2253(i)(2) and 2253(i)(3)) and following an investigation, advised the President (United States International Trade Commission, Report TA–203–8) that termination of the temporary increase in the duty on certain high-carbon ferrochromium would have a significant adverse economic effect on the domestic high-carbon ferrochromium industry and recommended that the increased duty be extended.

3. Pursuant to section 203(h)(3) of the Act and (19 U.S.C. 2253(h)(3)), after taking into account the advice of the Commission and the considerations required by section 202(c) of the Act (19 U.S.C. 2252(c)), I have determined that extension for one year of the increased duty is in the national interest.

Now, Therefore, I, Ronald Reagan, President of the United States of America, acting under the authority vested in me by the Constitution and the statutes of the United States, including sections 203(h)(3) of the Act (19 U.S.C. 2253), do proclaim that—

(1) Part 1 of Schedule XX to the GATT shall remain modified to conform to the extension of the duty increase provided by the proclamation.

(2) Subpart A, part 2 of the Appendix to the TSUS shall remain modified as set forth in the Annex to this proclamation.

(3) This proclamation shall be effective as to those articles entered, or withdrawn from warehouse for consumption, on or after November 16, 1981, and before the close of November 15, 1982, unless the period of effectiveness is modified or terminated earlier.

In Witness Whereof, I have hereunto set my hand this thirteenth day of November, in the year of our Lord nineteen hundred and eighty-one, and of the Independence of the United States of America the two hundred and sixth.

RONALD REAGAN

[*Filed with the Office of the Federal Register, 8:59 a.m., November 16, 1981*]

Note: The text of the proclamation was released by the Office of the Press Secretary on November 14.

The annex to the proclamation is printed in the Federal Register *of November 17, 1981.*

Nomination of Three Judges of the United States Tax Court
November 14, 1981

The President today announced his intention to nominate the following individuals to be Judges of the United States Tax Court for terms expiring 15 years after they take office. These are new additional judgeships created by Public Law 96–439 of October 13, 1980, effective February 1, 1981.

Meade Whitaker is currently Federal tax director, office of general counsel, Ford Motor Co. Between September 1973 and January 1977, Mr. Whitaker was Chief Counsel of the Internal Revenue Service. Prior to that, between July 1969 and October 1970, Mr. Whitaker was Tax Legislative Counsel at the Treasury Department. He is 62.

Jules G. Korner III is a practicing lawyer in Washington, D.C., specializing in Federal and State taxation, since 1947. Mr. Korner was nominated by President Ford to be a Judge of the United States Tax Court in June of 1976, but his nomination expired on December 31, 1976, with no action having been taken by the United States Senate. Mr. Korner is 59.

Perry Shields is a practicing attorney, specializing in tax law, in Knoxville, Tenn., and served with the Internal Revenue Service as a Revenue Agent in 1950–56. Previously he was a claims attorney and a civil advisory and trial attorney in the office of the Regional Counsel in Atlanta, Ga., and Greensboro, N.C. He is 56.

Exchange With Reporters at the Winston Ranch in Sabinal, Texas
November 14, 1981

Q. I know who you are. [*Laughter*]

The President. You realize that after seeing this [*referring to his camouflage outfit*], we don't think that there may be very many turkeys left around. [*Laughter*]

Q. Mr. President, how does it feel to be out of Washington for a few days?

The President. Just fine. This is nice.

Q. Are you going to really shoot at a turkey?

The President. I hate to make that pledge. It's been a long time since I've—I've never gone turkey shooting. So, I'm looking forward to this.

Q. Have you got a license, Mr. President?

The President. You bet. Yes, I have.

Q. Is Mr. Allen going to stay on the job while he's under investigation?

The President. I can't comment on that while it's still under review.

Note: The exchange began at 12:20 p.m. outside the ranchhouse, where the President spent the weekend as a guest of the family of Assistant to the President and Mrs. James A. Baker III.

Message to the Congress Transmitting Reports Concerning Civilian and Military Pay Increases
November 16, 1981

To the Congress of the United States:

In accordance with the provisions of section 5305 of Title 5 of the United States Code, I hereby report on the pay adjustments I ordered for the Federal statutory

pay systems in October 1981.

The Secretary of Labor, the Director of the Office of Management and Budget, and the Director of the Office of Personnel Management, who serve jointly as my Pay

Agent, found that an overall increase of about 15.1 percent in General Schedule rates of pay would be required to achieve comparability with private sector pay as that concept and process are defined in the Pay Comparability Act of 1970. The Advisory Committee on Federal Pay agreed with that finding.

While I fully support the comparability principle as the best basis for determining Federal pay, I believe that significant changes are required in the way that principle is currently defined and implemented. Therefore, last March, the Administration transmitted to the Congress proposed legislation to revise and strengthen the comparability process. At that time, it was estimated that the revised process would result in an overall increase in Federal pay of about 4.8 percent in October 1981.

The reform proposal has not yet been acted upon in Congress, but in accordance with our economic recovery program, the Congress included in the Omnibus Budget Reconciliation Act of 1981 (Public Law 97–35) provisions that limited this October's Federal civilian pay adjustments to the same 4.8 percent. Accordingly, on August 31, 1981, I sent to the Congress an alternative plan which called for an increase of 4.8 percent at each grade. Neither House of Congress disapproved this alternative plan, so on October 15, 1981, I signed Executive Order No. 12330 implementing it.

Under that Executive Order:

—The scheduled rates of pay under the statutory pay systems (the General Schedule, the Foreign Service Schedule, and the schedules for the Department of Medicine and Surgery of the Veterans' Administration) were increased by 4.8 percent in accordance with the alternative plan.

—The scheduled rates of pay for the Vice President and the Executive Schedule and Congressional and Judicial salaries were increased, under the provisions of Public Law 94–82, by the overall 4.8 percent in rates of pay under the General Schedule.

—The scheduled rates of pay for the Senior Executive Service were increased under the provisions of section 5382 of Title 5 of the United States Code based on the new rate of pay for GS-16, step 1, of the General Schedule and the new rate of pay for level IV of the Executive Schedule.

—The scheduled rates of pay and allowances for members of the Uniformed Services were increased by amounts ranging from 10 percent to 17 percent depending on pay grade in accordance with the provisions of sections 101 and 102 of the Uniformed Services Pay Act of 1981 (Public Law 97–60) approved October 14, 1981.

The Order also reflects the effect of section 101(c) of Public Law 97–51 (the continuing resolution approved October 1, 1981), which contains limitations on payable salaries for certain top level Government positions.

I am transmitting herewith copies of the reports of my Pay Agent and the Advisory Committee on Federal Pay, the alternative plan, and the Executive Order I promulgated to put these pay adjustments into effect.

RONALD REAGAN

The White House,
November 16, 1981.

Nomination of Kenneth Lee Brown To Be United States Ambassador to the Congo
November 16, 1981

The President today announced his intention to nominate Kenneth Lee Brown, of California, to be Ambassador to the People's Republic of the Congo. He would succeed William Lacy Swing.

Mr. Brown served in the United States Army Reserve as second lieutenant in 1960–61. He entered the Foreign Service in 1961 as consular, economic, and political officer in Algiers. In 1963–65 he was research analyst in the Department and political officer in Kinshasa in 1965–67. He was a fellow at the Center for International Studies at New York University in 1967–69. Mr. Brown was program officer at the Department of State Reception Center in New York City in 1969–70, and desk officer for Zambia and Malawi in the Department in 1970–72. He was political officer (1972–75) and information officer (1975–77) in Brussels. In the Department of State he was Deputy Director of the Press Office and Associate Spokesman (1977–79), Deputy Director of United Nations Political Affairs (1979–80), and since 1980 he has been Director of the Office of Central African Affairs.

Mr. Brown graduated from Pomona College (B.A., 1959); Yale University (M.A., 1960); and New York University (M.A., 1975). He is married, has two sons, and resides in Van Nuys, Calif. He was born December 6, 1936, in Seminole, Okla.

Nomination of Two Members of the Commission on Civil Rights, and Designation of Chairman and Vice Chairman
November 16, 1981

The President today announced his intention to nominate Clarence M. Pendleton, Jr., and Mary Louise Smith to be members of the Commission on Civil Rights. The President also announced his intention to designate Mr. Pendleton as Chairman and Mrs. Smith as Vice Chairman.

Since 1975 Mr. Pendleton has been president of the Urban League of San Diego, Calif. He is also president of the San Diego County Local Development Corp., a nonprofit subsidiary of San Diego Urban League, Inc., and president of Building for Equal Opportunity (B.F.E.O.), a profit-making subsidiary of the San Diego Urban League. He was director of the Model Cities Department, city of San Diego, in 1972–75; director, urban affairs, National Recreation and Parks Association, in 1970–72; recreation coordinator, Model Cities Agency, city of Baltimore, Md., in 1968–70; and instructor in physical education and recreation, Howard University, Washington, D.C., in 1958–68. He has served on the Community Education Advisory Council, U.S. Office of Education, since 1979 and the Governor's Task Force on Affordable Housing, State of California, since 1978. Mr. Pendleton graduated from Howard University (B.S., 1954; M.A., 1962). He is married and resides in La Jolla, Calif. He was born November 10, 1930, in Louisville, Ky.

In 1961 Mrs. Smith became a member of the advisory board of the Iowa Federation of Women, a position she still holds. She served as vice chairman of the Wright County, Iowa, Republican Central Committee in 1962–63 and was an alternate delegate to the Republican National Convention in 1964 and a delegate and member of the platform committee at the Republican Convention in 1968. She served as chairman of the Republican National Committee in 1974–77, and was the first woman of either major political party to organize and call to order a national convention in August of 1976. She is presently a member of the executive committee of the Republican National Committee and served as chairperson for the women's policy advisory board for the Reagan-Bush campaign. She graduated from the University of Iowa (A.B., 1935). She is widowed, has three children, and resides in Des Moines, Iowa. She was born October 6, 1914, in Eddyville, Iowa.

Remarks at the Welcoming Ceremony for President Luis Herrera Campíns of Venezuela
November 17, 1981

President Reagan. Ladies and gentlemen, it's indeed an honor to welcome His Excellency, the President of Venezuela, and Mrs. Herrera Campíns to Washington.

President Herrera and I had the opportunity to get to know each other at last month's summit in Cancún. While we were there, we reaffirmed that our two nations share common goals and mutual concerns, especially about liberty and progress in the American family of nations. The challenges facing the people of the Americas are greater than ever before. Maintaining independence and freedom will require the same dedication demonstrated during the struggle for independence that is common to every American nation.

Venezuela played a unique role in America's struggle for independence. Its role in the future of the region is no less important. The great liberator Simón Bolívar once said, "It is harder to maintain the balance of liberty than to endure the weight of tyranny." He lamented that all too often mankind is willing to rest unconcerned and accept things as they are.

President Herrera, if Bolívar were alive today, he would be proud indeed of the current generation of Venezuelans and what it has accomplished. In two decades, you have built a free nation that is a beacon of hope for all those who suffer oppression. After courageously casting off the chains of dictatorship, Venezuelans rejected the tyranny of left and right and held firm in their commitment to dignity and freedom.

While still in its infancy, your young democracy withstood a serious challenge from an external force that still threatens other emerging nations, undermining legitimate attempts at social change in order to exploit chaos and promote tyranny. But, clearly, in a tribute to the decency and values of your people, the love of liberty has prevailed. It is to Venezuela's credit and in keeping with Bolívar's dream that you are now helping others overcome similar challenges to their freedom and prosperity.

I know that we will stand together, Mr. President, in our opposition to the spread to our shores of hostile totalitarian systems and in our dedication to true liberty and democracy.

Venezuela's development program, particularly in the Caribbean region, is an example of humanitarianism and farsightedness that has the highest respect and admiration of the people of the United States. Your recognition of the private sector's role in development is much appreciated here, but this, too, is in your tradition.

Over a century ago, Andres Bello, an intellectual giant and a Venezuelan, noted a relationship between liberty and enterprise. "Liberty," he suggested, "gives wings to the spirit of enterprise wherever it meets it. It breathes breath into where it does not exist."

We have much to learn from the people of Venezuela. Your knowledge of developing nations is invaluable and, President Herrera, I'm personally looking forward to your counsel on this vital subject.

Venezuela reaches out today, in the spirit of Bolivar and Bello, the liberator and the educator, to better mankind and to unite the freedom-loving peoples of this hemisphere.

Just a few months ago, President Herrera, you spoke to the United Nations and eloquently outlined your nation's commitment to principle. There you stated, "Venezuelans believe in and practice democracy. We do not attempt to impose our own values and concepts of society on anyone, but we know that freedom is the road of history." Let me say to you as clearly and directly as I can, in this expression of Venezuela's cherished goals, you have the firm and lasting support of the people of the United States of America.

Mr. President, our two peoples will walk that road together as equals, as friends who share common values. And so, as one American to another, we bid you a heartfelt welcome.

President Herrera. Your Excellency, Mr. Ronald Reagan, President of the United States, distinguished guests:

Mr. President, thank you on behalf of my wife, the people who accompany me, and in my own name, for your kind words of welcome. The United States and Venezuela have enjoyed throughout their history friendly and cordial relations with inevitable coincidence and divergences, but with the unalterable constant of friendship and understanding in a spirit of mutual and strict respect for the national dignity of our countries.

Venezuela has acquired a growing weight in international affairs. Today, we constitute an obligatory point of reference for all issues related to hemispheric dialog and relations between the industrialized and the developing worlds. We follow an honorable, independent, and serious international policy, attempting at all times to project the image of our democratic institutions, observant of the demands of freedom.

We have attained and consolidated since 1958 our democratic stability, following the effort made by our democratic organizations and the national armed forces to achieve mutual understanding and respect and after overcoming the threats of a Marxist-inspired subversion that meant to destabilize our process of democratization.

The presence of Venezuela in the hemisphere and in the world is enhanced by our position as a producer and exporter of strategically valuable energy resources, our status of promoter and founder of the Organization of Oil [Petroleum] Exporting Countries, and holder of a privileged geographical position in a region afflicted by international tensions. We labor indefatigably so that peace will not suffer impairment or wrong.

Mr. President, the foreign policy actions of my government are not characterized by any kind of notion against, anti, anything. They are governed by an unyielding purpose of acting in favor of, pro, in favor of the interests of Venezuela, of Latin America, of the developing world, and of all of mankind.

In our observance of this principle, when we coincide with other nations, we do not do so in submission. And when we disagree, it is not because of aversion. When we coincide, it is without complexes. When we differ, it is without fear. We are not, and shall not be, passive subjects or instruments in the struggle between the superpowers over the issue of world supremacy.

Our foreign policy is, as you well know, autonomous and sovereign, as is fit for a country that is the birthplace of Simón Bolívar, the liberator, father of our independence and fighter of Latin American integration. It is this intellectual and political legacy that inspires our domestic and foreign policies.

My visit to this great nation, Mr. President, comes at a precarious moment in world affairs. I hope that the talks we will hold will produce more points of coincidence than discrepancy both on the political and the social-economic issues.

We shall speak on the tense reality of the Central American and the Caribbean regions, all the complex factors that affect it and serve as breeding ground for convulsions resulting from social imbalances which are seized upon by political hegemonic aspirations and destabilizing ideological radicalisms. We want to preserve this region from the tensions of bloc politics.

We shall pursue, led by the same constructive spirit, the dialog begun in Cancún on the urgency of making substantial changes in the present international economic relations. The peoples of the world continue to hope to see global negotiations held within the framework of the United Nations. And even if they are to be initially frail, they will build up gradually as trade develops.

We shall discuss the improvement and expansion of bilateral relations between our two countries, both of which enjoy systems of freely elected democratic governments and a historical commitment to defend the freedom of mankind.

Our conversations will be clear in their wording, specific in their subject matter, and positive in their results. That is the deepest hope I harbor on the occasion of my visit here.

Mr. President, I thank you, your government, and your people, for this invitation you have extended to me to hold a dialog on the future of our countries, of our continent, and of peace. Thank you.

Note: President Reagan spoke at 10:18 a.m. in the East Room, where President Herrera was given a formal welcome. The ceremony was not held on the South Lawn, as is customary, due to inclement weather. President Herrera spoke in Spanish, and his remarks were translated by an interpreter.

Following the ceremony, the two Presidents met in the Oval Office. Also present at that meeting were, on the American side, *the Vice President, Secretary of State Alexander M. Haig, Jr., Assistant to the President for National Security Affairs Richard V. Allen, and U.S. Ambassador to Venezuela William H. Luers and, on the Venezuelan side, Foreign Minister José Alberto Zambraon Velasco, Minister, Secretariat of the Presidency, Gonzalo García Bustillos, and Venezuelan Ambassador to the United States Marcial Perez Chiriboga. President Reagan and President Herrera were then joined by an expanded group of their advisers for a second meeting in the Cabinet Room.*

Statement on America's All-Volunteer Armed Forces
November 17, 1981

Fiscal year 1981 was an important milestone in the history of America's all-volunteer armed forces. It demonstrated that, in a healthy, just society, men and women will serve their country freely, when given the proper encouragement, incentives, and respect.

All of the services met their recruiting goals in fiscal 1981; test scores improved dramatically; recruits included the highest proportion of high school graduates ever; and enlistment rates were up for all services.

Working with the Congress, we have begun to reverse the negative trends of the last few years in the standard of living of our military personnel. We have done this through more competitive pay, increased enlistment and reenlistment bonuses, and enhanced educational benefits. Just as important, we have fostered an attitude of increased appreciation and respect for the men and women who wear their country's uniform.

There is a new spirit of pride and patriotism alive in the land, and the impressive manpower record of the armed forces during fiscal year 1981 reflects this. Just as volunteer warriors won American independence more than two centuries ago, they stand as proud guardians of our freedom today. The success of this past year shows that the voluntary system can work and represents the best way to meet our manpower requirements in times of peace.

Nomination of Alan C. Nelson To Be Commissioner of the Immigration and Naturalization Service
November 17, 1981

The President today announced his intention to nominate Alan C. Nelson to be Commissioner of Immigration and Naturalization, Department of Justice. He would succeed Leonel J. Castillo. Norman Braman, who was announced on September 29, 1981, has asked that his name be withdrawn from consideration due to personal reasons.

Mr. Nelson is currently serving as Deputy Commissioner of the Immigration and Naturalization Service. Prior to his appointment as Deputy Commissioner, he was an attorney with Pacific Telephone and Telegraph Co. in San Francisco (1975–81); director, Department of Rehabilitation for the State of California (1972–75); assistant director, Department of Human Resources Development for the State of California (1969–72); deputy district attorney for Alameda County (1964–69); and an attorney with the firm of Rogers, Clark & Jordan (1958–64).

He graduated from the University of California (B.S., 1955) and the University of California School of Law (J.D., 1958). He is married, has three children, and resides in Lafayette, Calif. He was born October 18, 1933, in Oakland, Calif.

Appointment of Stephen E. Palmer, Jr., as State Department Member of the Commission on Security and Cooperation in Europe
November 17, 1981

The President today announced his intention to appoint Stephen E. Palmer, Jr., to be the Department of State member of the Commission on Security and Cooperation in Europe. He would succeed Patricia M. Derian.

Mr. Palmer is currently Senior Deputy Assistant Secretary for Human Rights. He entered the Foreign Service in 1951. Mr. Palmer served as vice consul in Nicosia, as political officer in Belgrade, consul in Sarajevo, chief of political section in Tel Aviv, political officer for Middle Eastern and North African Affairs in London, political counselor in Rawalpindi/Islamabad, and as consul general in South India, at Madras. In 1959–63 he was in the Department of State's Office of United Nations Political Affairs. He was a fellow of the Center for International Affairs at Harvard University during the 1973–74 academic year. In 1974–78 Mr. Palmer was the Director of Regional Affairs for the Near Eastern and South Asian Affairs Bureau. He served concurrently as Staff Director of the National Security Council's Interdepartmental Group for that area. In 1979 he was assigned to the U.S. Mission in Geneva as Minister-Counselor for Humanitarian Affairs.

He graduated from Princeton University (B.A.) and Columbia University (M.A.). He is married, has three children, and resides in Washington, D.C. He was born July 31, 1923, in Superior, Wis.

Appointment of Richard Norman Perle as Defense Department Member of the Commission on Security and Cooperation in Europe
November 17, 1981

The President today announced his intention to appoint Richard Norman Perle to be the Department of Defense member of the Commission on Security and Cooperation in Europe. He would succeed David E. McGiffert.

Mr. Perle is currently Assistant Secretary of Defense for International Planning. Previously, he was professional staff member, Senate Permanent Subcommittee on Investigations, and a staff member, Subcommittee on Arms Control, in 1972–80. He was with Senator Henry M. Jackson (D–Wash.) in 1972, and was a member, professional staff, Senate Subcommittee on National Security and International Operations, in 1969–72. He was a consultant to the Special Assistant to the Secretary of Defense in 1969 and was employed with the Westinghouse Electric Corp., 1967–69.

He graduated from the University of California (B.A., 1964) and Princeton University

(M.A., 1967). He is married, has one son, and resides in Chevy Chase, Md. He was born September 16, 1941, in New York, N.Y.

Appointment of William H. Morris, Jr., as Commerce Department Member of the Commission on Security and Cooperation in Europe
November 17, 1981

The President today announced his intention to appoint William H. Morris, Jr., to be the Department of Commerce member of the Commission on Security and Cooperation in Europe. He would succeed Herta L. Seidman.

Mr. Morris is currently Assistant Secretary of Commerce for Trade Development. Previously, he was president of William Morris and Associates, consultants in business management, government relations, and international marketing in 1980–81. In 1979–80

he was deputy commissioner of economic and community development for the State of Tennessee. Mr. Morris was executive vice president, Southern Supply Co., Jackson, Tenn., in 1977–79. He was with the Gooch-Edenton Wholesale Hardware Co., Jackson, Tenn., in 1950–76.

He attended the University of Tennessee. He is married, has two children, and resides in Nashville, Tenn. He was born January 5, 1929, in Memphis, Tenn.

Message to the Congress on a Proposed Amendment to the Internal Revenue Code Regarding a Canadian Tax Law Provision
November 17, 1981

To the Congress of the United States:

On September 9, 1980, President Carter sent a message to the Congress concerning the Canadian tax law which denies a deduction for Canadian income tax purposes for the cost of advertising placed with a foreign broadcast undertaking and directed primarily at the Canadian market. President Carter determined that this provision within Canadian law is an unreasonable practice which burdens U.S. commerce within the meaning of section 301(a)(2)(B) of the Trade Act of 1974, as amended (19 U.S.C. 2411(a)(2)(B)). President Carter further determined that the Canadian practice resulted in the loss of access by U.S. broadcasters to more than $20 million in advertising revenues annually.

President Carter, under provisions of the Trade Act of 1974, proposed legislation which would amend the Internal Revenue Code to deny a deduction, otherwise allow-

able under the Code, for expenses of an advertisement placed with a foreign broadcast undertaking and directed primarily to a market in the United States. This restriction would apply only if a similar deduction is denied to advertisers in the country in which such station is located for the cost of advertising directed primarily to a market in that country when placed with a U.S. broadcast undertaking. It would, therefore, be applicable to Canada.

Section 301 of the Trade Act of 1974 requires that if the President determines that action by the United States is appropriate to respond to any act, policy, or practice of a foreign country that is unjustifiable, unreasonable or discriminatory and burdens or restricts United States commerce, he shall take all appropriate and feasible action within his power to obtain the elimination of such act, policy or practice. The intent of section 301 is to resolve disputes and thereby eliminate the unjustifiable, unreasonable or discriminatory trade practices which burden or restrict United States commerce. The Canadian tax law is the subject of one such dispute. Notwithstanding a good faith effort on the part of the United States Trade Representative to resolve the dispute and have the offending practice eliminated, this dispute has not been resolved. Therefore, I am acting under the authority of section 301 to recommend legislation similar to the amendment proposed by President Carter. This amendment to the Internal Revenue Code would mirror the Canadian law as it applies to broadcast undertakings, i.e., it would deny a tax deduction for expenses of advertisements placed with a foreign broadcast undertaking and directed primarily to a market in the U.S. This restriction would apply only if the laws of the country in which such foreign broadcast undertaking is located deny a similar deduction to advertisers in that country. Thus, the legislation will establish a disincentive to the transfer of U.S. advertising revenues to foreign broadcast undertakings only if the laws of the country in which such broadcast undertakings are located create a similar disincentive vis-a-vis U.S. broadcast undertakings. Thus, if Canada

should repeal its law, the amendment will cease to apply to Canada. It would be effective with respect to deductions attributable to transactions entered into on or after the date of introduction of this bill.

At this time, the mirror image legislation is an appropriate response to the Canadian practice. The intent of such legislation is not to erect new barriers to trade, but rather to encourage the Canadians to eliminate their unreasonable and restrictive practice. I recognize, however, that this amendment by itself may not cause the Canadians to resolve this dispute. Therefore, I note that I retain the right to take further action, if appropriate, to obtain the elimination of the practice on my own motion under the authority of section 301(c)(1). Hopefully, this will not be necessary.

This legislative proposal is being submitted at this time because I feel it is imperative that the Government of Canada be made to realize the importance the U.S. Government attaches to the resolution of this issue. I urge its early passage.

Ronald Reagan

The White House,
November 17, 1981.

Appointment of Aram Bakshian, Jr., as Special Assistant to the President and Director of the Presidential Speechwriting Office
November 17, 1981

The President today announced the appointment of Aram Bakshian, Jr., to be Special Assistant to the President and Director of the Presidential Speechwriting Office.

Since February Mr. Bakshian has served as Special Assistant to the President in the Office of Public Liaison with responsibility for the arts, humanities, and academia.

A native of Washington, D.C., Mr. Bakshian, 37, is an author, critic, and essayist, whose writing has been published in over 10 languages on historical, political, humorous, and cultural subjects. He is the author or coauthor of several books, including "The War Game," "The Candidates 1980,"

"The Future Under President Reagan" and, in German, "Servus Du," the memoirs of Robert Stolz, Austria's last waltz and operetta master.

Besides his writing activities, Mr. Bakshian has served as a corporate consultant to leading American businesses and has occupied several political and governmental positions, serving as a consultant to Treasury Secretary William Simon in 1976–77, a speechwriter and aide to Presidents Nixon and Ford in 1972–75, a special assistant to the chairman of the Republican National Committee in 1971, and an aide to Representative (later Senator) Bill Brock (R–

Tenn.) in 1966–70.

Mr. Bakshian was educated in Washington public and private schools and in 1975 became a fellow of Harvard University's Institute of Politics. He is a member of the National Press Club in Washington and the Reform Club in London.

His writing has appeared in leading American and foreign newspapers and periodicals including Wall Street Journal, National Review, New York Times, Boston Globe, American Spectator, National Observer, the Washingtonian, Los Angeles Herald-Examiner, History Today (England), Spectator (England), and many international editions of Reader's Digest. He was assistant editor of the 1980 Republican platform.

Appointment of Anthony R. Dolan as Special Assistant to the President and Chief Speechwriter
November 17, 1981

The President today announced the appointment of Anthony R. Dolan to be Special Assistant to the President and Chief Speechwriter at the White House.

Mr. Dolan graduated from Yale University (1970) where he was an editorial board member and columnist for the Yale Daily News. He was a deputy press secretary for Buckley for Senate (1970) and then served as a consultant on several political campaigns for F. Clifton White Associates. He has also served in the Office of Economic Opportunity, Executive Office of the President.

He was a reporter for the Stamford (Conn.) Advocate (1974–80). He won five journalism awards, including the 1978 Pulitzer Prize for investigative reporting. His investigations into government corruption and organized crime led to the dismissal or resignation of more than 12 city and State officials and a number of indictments and convictions.

Mr. Dolan served as a speechwriter and a special research director for the Reagan-Bush Committee and the office of the President-elect.

He was born in Norwalk, Conn., on July 7, 1948. For the past 7 months, Mr. Dolan has served as Acting Director of Speechwriting.

Toasts of the President and President Luis Herrera Campíns of Venezuela at the State Dinner
November 17, 1981

President Reagan. President Herrera, Mrs. Herrera, distinguished guests, and friends:

President Herrera once said, "History shows that only those human actions which are based on ethical principles have a truly lasting significance." Tonight, we honor a man and a country that has chosen a path of principle, one that will have lasting significance.

Democracy and respect for human rights is not the easiest course, but it is the most moral. President Herrera, a man of deep religious and moral convictions, long ago decided to stand for what is right. As a boy, he witnessed a chain gang composed of political prisoners. This sight frightened lesser men; it instead strengthened Herrera Campíns' resolve to fight dictatorship. Later this love of freedom led to his own arrest and exile, yet he stood firm with the other brave individuals and, eventually, they and the principles of human freedom triumphed.

Such dedication is deeply admired here, but politics is not the only way to catch a glimpse of one's soul. Now, to many Americans, Venezuela has come to mean excellence in sports. David Concepcion and Tony Armas and many other fine baseball players have come to us from Venezuela. And interestingly, President Herrera and I both were sports journalists at one time.

In welcoming President Herrera to Washington, I recalled the portion of his magnificent statement to the United Nations. What I didn't mention was that after delivering it, he went to Yankee Stadium to see a ballgame. [*Laughter*]

Now, Mr. President, you probably don't know that your dinner partner tonight, my wife, Nancy—her birthday is July 6th, but her mother has told me it would have been July 4th, except she didn't want to miss the doubleheader at Yankee Stadium. [*Laughter*]

Mr. President, you're a man, and Venezuelans are a people, whose love of life and of freedom are something with which the people of the United States can identify. You and your country stand for those values and those principles that reflect the best of mankind. You honor us by this visit, and Venezuela honors us by its friendship.

Now, I ask all of you to join with me in a toast to President Herrera Campíns, his lovely wife, and to the people of Venezuela. May our bonds be always so strong.

President Herrera. Your Excellency, Mr. President of the United States, Mrs. Reagan, distinguished guests:

Mr. President, thank you for such a pleasant dinner, for your kind words, and the friendship and cordiality extended to us during this visit to the United States.

The ideals of liberty, human respect, and democratic government inspire our two countries. These principles are the fundamental basis of the good relations between Venezuela and the United States: mutual respect, the desire to understand each other's realities, and the conviction that dialog and negotiation enable us to overcome differences when inspired by a sincere willingness to achieve understanding.

We shall soon commemorate 250 years of George Washington's birth and, in 1983, the bicentennial of the birth of our liberator, Simón Bolívar. In the example of these two great men, we can and must seek and find the common source of our ideals of liberty and human dignity, those profound roots of friendship and cooperation between our two countries.

Allow me, Mr. President, to recall that in May of 1781, Francisco de Miranda, forerunner of Latin American independence, fought in Pensacola the battle that paved the way for Cornwallis' surrender in Yorktown. Between the 18th and the 19th centuries, the first Venezuelan cosmovisionary, Miranda, acted thus on all the great stages where freedom of man was at stake: the American Revolution, the French Revolution, and the Latin American Revolution— three related political processes of undeniable projection to the rest of the world.

It was thus on North American soil that Miranda began his journey to freedom. After Pensacola he would later say, "My first thought as a man was a feeling of national fervor. When participating in the emancipation of the United States, the first surge of my spirit was a yearning for the liberation of the places which saw me, coming to the world, for I did not dare to call America a homeland. This feeling of love for liberty acted so much upon me that ever since all my thoughts referred to it, and it became the motive for all my actions and the reason for all my journeys."

We are faithful to the Bolivarian teachings on the achievement of continental integration in a world of peace. Latin America is a region that feels a natural calling to multilateral relations. The Organization of American States, CARICOME, the subregional Andean Pact, the Amazonian Pact, the Latin American Organization for Energy, the Latin American Economic System, the Central American Common Market, the Latin American Integration Association are but part of those multilateral organizations where Latin American plurality is of the continental scope.

Multilaterality is both our inclination and our strength, notwithstanding the importance of bilateral ties which in no way deny and basically reinforce multilateral relations. More and more do we strive for oneness in a united comprehension of our diversities, so we will not go separate and divided, drifted by discord, disparity, and anarchy.

We wish to achieve a comprehensive, harmonious development. There are still many needs to be provided for, much want to be met, and social injustice to be redressed. The evils of underdevelopment resist all efforts to dislodge them and strike root by singular lack of understanding. The path that is to guide us at a lower social cost towards the future is that of cooperation based on solidarity.

Such a cooperation must range from the cultural to the economic. We aspire not only to a numerical increase of per capita income, but also to a fair distribution of wealth so that well-being and prosperity can be placed at everyone's reach and the population be guaranteed an access to the goods basic to human dignity. This must be the result of a joint effort, that of the government and that of the people. Education and work are the tools of progress and self-improvement. Personal, individual, and combined efforts must be encouraged. We believe in the promoting role of the state, a promoter state that fosters individual and social initiatives, yet does not waive its social function of intervention, regulation, and control.

We believe in foreign investments to be measured according to national convenience when they constitute financial injections and not simple patent permits that will absorb national savings and derive from them their profits without incurring the risk of investing their own capital. We act in this respect within the framework of Decision 24 of the Andean Pact because we wish to strengthen our own sources of financing.

We know that in many cases foreign capital, without losing sight of its profit-making goals, attempts to create wealth and employment in our countries. If it comes to us with that purpose, we welcome it. However, we have suffered exploitation and exaction from transnational companies whose doubtful procedures and excessive pursuit of profit forced the United States to legislate against monopolies.

We desire as much as you do a democratic Latin America—peace loving and respectful of human rights. Liberty must be supported on social justice if it wants to overcome critical poverty, disease, lack of culture, and backwardness. It is on the basis of nonintervention and respect for free self-determination of nations that we shall be able to achieve collective security and protect our region from the great world tensions where threatening language can trigger conflicts capable of destroying peace.

We are committed to democracy. Neither the traditional dictatorships nor the new leftist totalitarianisms represent valid solutions to nations whose vocation is liberty. In this line of conduct, we give active political and moral support to the government junta of El Salvador, presided by our distinguished friend José Napoleón Duarte, who is trying to offer a democratic and institutional way out of the situation of violence and terrorism existing in his country.

We have stretched out a hand to Nicaragua, as Latin America awaits its conversion to democracy after it supported its struggle against a dynastic dictatorship. As long as there remains any rational hope for a pluralistic society to be achieved there, we shall maintain our attitude of cooperation.

We are aware of the existence of destabilizing tensions and predications in the Caribbean, but we must weigh wisely our actions there so as to prevent conflicts from expanding and endangering world peace. We oppose any kind of foreign intervention and reject all provocative action taken by underpowers that act as mandataries in the Central American region and in the Caribbean.

The summit conference of Cancún took place a few weeks ago, and we had there the opportunity to exchange views on the international situation. You were witness to the seriousness, the dignity, and independence of Venezuela's position as stated in my speeches.

We did our best so that this unique, historical, momentous dialog between industrialized countries and developing nations would not end in failure. We all made a joint effort to avoid confrontation and seek foremost the positive coincidences that would lead to the necessary cooperation. The step taken was yet a modest one, but it brought out the political will of the 22 attending chiefs of state and government to pursue global negotiations within the framework of the United Nations.

Upon your return from Mexico you said that the efforts and constructive spirit which characterized the discussions at Cancún must continue. And the American Ambassador to the United Nations declared recently that every one of us bears the responsibility for transplanting the spirit of Cancún to all the forums of the United Nations system. This time we cannot fail. These words bring optimism to the developing world, which trusts the understanding and the good disposition of the United States.

Mr. President, Venezuela projects democracy and freedom in its foreign policy and has made its energetic wealth act as a concrete instrument of negotiation, cooperation, and international solidarity. A great many coincidences with the United States enable us to march side by side on the road of human freedom.

In your two speeches today, Mr. President, you referred first to Venezuelans such as Simón Bolívar, and in your speech tonight to young compatriots of mine who are in this world of sports, who, at a time not too far away nor too near this day, were people that were of interest to you and me when we were sports journalists.

You have called our compatriots, David Concepcion and Tony Armas, who today are excellent players in the big leagues. And if you allow me this association of ideas, perhaps you might have believed in

the talks I had today with you and with high representatives of your government that my position as was stated on Central America and the Caribbean is too optimistic. But I am an optimist, and I believe you are one, too.

When you were a candidate for the Presidency, on our television we saw many of the films in which you acted years ago, and I remember one very specially which is related to baseball.

You were playing the role of a pitcher, a great pitcher, who suddenly felt, let's say, a drop in his physical conditions, and it was the trust of his friends and his moral conviction that he had to play to have his team win that made the team win.

And I am sure that your quarry of optimism has not run dry. And although perhaps the situation might seem sometimes dramatic, we can be certain that it is people—men and people like those of the United States and Venezuela who love freedom—those are the ones that will win.

To reiterate, allow me to reiterate my gratitude and that of Betty and the persons who accompany me for all your kindness, and as I do so, I raise my glass in a toast to your personal happiness, that of your distinguished wife, to the democratic success of your government, and the prosperity and happiness of the people of the United States, a people forever committed to liberty.

Note: President Reagan spoke at 9:44 p.m. in the State Dining Room at the White House. President Herrera spoke in Spanish, and his remarks were translated by an interpreter.

Remarks to Members of the National Press Club on Arms Reduction and Nuclear Weapons
November 18, 1981

Officers, ladies and gentlemen of the National Press Club and, as of a very short time ago, fellow members:

Back in April while in the hospital I had, as you can readily understand, a lot of time

for reflection. And one day I decided to send a personal, handwritten letter to Soviet President Leonid Brezhnev reminding him that we had met about 10 years ago in San Clemente, California, as he and

President Nixon were concluding a series of meetings that had brought hope to all the world. Never had peace and good will seemed closer at hand.

I'd like to read you a few paragraphs from that letter. "Mr. President: When we met, I asked if you were aware that the hopes and aspirations of millions of people throughout the world were dependent on the decisions that would be reached in those meetings. You took my hand in both of yours and assured me that you were aware of that and that you were dedicated with all your heart and soul and mind to fulfilling those hopes and dreams."

I went on in my letter to say: "The people of the world still share that hope. Indeed, the peoples of the world, despite differences in racial and ethnic origin, have very much in common. They want the dignity of having some control over their individual lives, their destiny. They want to work at the craft or trade of their own choosing and to be fairly rewarded. They want to raise their families in peace without harming anyone or suffering harm themselves. Government exists for their convenience, not the other way around.

"If they are incapable, as some would have us believe, of self-government, then where among them do we find any who are capable of governing others?

"Is it possible that we have permitted ideology, political and economic philosophies, and governmental policies to keep us from considering the very real, everyday problems of our peoples? Will the average Soviet family be better off or even aware that the Soviet Union has imposed a government of its own choice on the people of Afghanistan? Is life better for the people of Cuba because the Cuban military dictate who shall govern the people of Angola?

"It is often implied that such things have been made necessary because of territorial ambitions of the United States; that we have imperialistic designs, and thus constitute a threat to your own security and that of the newly emerging nations. Not only is there no evidence to support such a charge, there is solid evidence that the United States, when it could have dominated the world with no risk to itself, made no effort whatsoever to do so.

"When World War II ended, the United States had the only undamaged industrial power in the world. Our military might was at its peak, and we alone had the ultimate weapon, the nuclear weapon, with the unquestioned ability to deliver it anywhere in the world. If we had sought world domination then, who could have opposed us?

"But the United States followed a different course, one unique in all the history of mankind. We used our power and wealth to rebuild the war-ravished economies of the world, including those of the nations who had been our enemies. May I say, there is absolutely no substance to charges that the United States is guilty of imperialism or attempts to impose its will on other countries, by use of force."

I continued my letter by saying—or concluded my letter, I should say—by saying, "Mr. President, should we not be concerned with eliminating the obstacles which prevent our people, those you and I represent, from achieving their most cherished goals?"

Well, it's in the same spirit that I want to speak today to this audience and the people of the world about America's program for peace and the coming negotiations which begin November 30th in Geneva, Switzerland. Specifically, I want to present our program for preserving peace in Europe and our wider program for arms control.

Twice in my lifetime, I have seen the peoples of Europe plunged into the tragedy of war. Twice in my lifetime, Europe has suffered destruction and military occupation in wars that statesmen proved powerless to prevent, soldiers unable to contain, and ordinary citizens unable to escape. And twice in my lifetime, young Americans have bled their lives into the soil of those battlefields not to enrich or enlarge our domain, but to restore the peace and independence of our friends and Allies.

All of us who lived through those troubled times share a common resolve that they must never come again. And most of us share a common appreciation of the Atlantic Alliance that has made a peaceful, free, and prosperous Western Europe in the post-war era possible.

But today, a new generation is emerging on both sides of the Atlantic. Its members were not present at the creation of the North Atlantic Alliance. Many of them don't fully understand its roots in defending freedom and rebuilding a war-torn continent. Some young people question why we need weapons, particularly nuclear weapons, to deter war and to assure peaceful development. They fear that the accumulation of weapons itself may lead to conflagration. Some even propose unilateral disarmament.

I understand their concerns. Their questions deserve to be answered. But we have an obligation to answer their questions on the basis of judgment and reason and experience. Our policies have resulted in the longest European peace in this century. Wouldn't a rash departure from these policies, as some now suggest, endanger that peace?

From its founding, the Atlantic Alliance has preserved the peace through unity, deterrence, and dialog. First, we and our Allies have stood united by the firm commitment that an attack upon any one of us would be considered an attack upon us all. Second, we and our Allies have deterred aggression by maintaining forces strong enough to ensure that any aggressor would lose more from an attack than he could possibly gain. And third, we and our Allies have engaged the Soviets in a dialog about mutual restraint and arms limitations, hoping to reduce the risk of war and the burden of armaments and to lower the barriers that divide East from West.

These three elements of our policy have preserved the peace in Europe for more than a third of a century. They can preserve it for generations to come, so long as we pursue them with sufficient will and vigor.

Today, I wish to reaffirm America's commitment to the Atlantic Alliance and our resolve to sustain the peace. And from my conversations with allied leaders, I know that they also remain true to this tried and proven course.

NATO's policy of peace is based on restraint and balance. No NATO weapons, conventional or nuclear, will ever be used in Europe except in response to attack. NATO's defense plans have been responsible and restrained. The Allies remain strong, united, and resolute. But the momentum of the continuing Soviet military buildup threatens both the conventional and the nuclear balance.

Consider the facts. Over the past decade, the United States reduced the size of its Armed Forces and decreased its military spending. The Soviets steadily increased the number of men under arms. They now number more than double those of the United States. Over the same period, the Soviets expanded their real military spending by about one-third. The Soviet Union increased its inventory of tanks to some 50,000, compared to our 11,000. Historically a land power, they transformed their navy from a coastal defense force to an open ocean fleet, while the United States, a sea power with transoceanic alliances, cut its fleet in half.

During a period when NATO deployed no new intermediate-range nuclear missiles and actually withdrew 1,000 nuclear warheads, the Soviet Union deployed more than 750 nuclear warheads on the new SS-20 missiles alone.

Our response to this relentless buildup of Soviet military power has been restrained but firm. We have made decisions to strengthen all three legs of the strategic triad: sea-, land-, and air-based. We have proposed a defense program in the United States for the next 5 years which will remedy the neglect of the past decade and restore the eroding balance on which our security depends.

I would like to discuss more specifically the growing threat to Western Europe which is posed by the continuing deployment of certain Soviet intermediate-range nuclear missiles. The Soviet Union has three different type such missile systems: the SS-20, the SS-4, and the SS-5, all with the range capable of reaching virtually all of Western Europe. There are other Soviet weapon systems which also represent a major threat.

Now, the only answer to these systems is a comparable threat to Soviet threats, to Soviet targets; in other words, a deterrent preventing the use of these Soviet weapons by the counterthreat of a like response against their own territory. At present, however, there is no equivalent deterrent to these Soviet intermediate missiles. And the Soviets continue to add one new SS–20 a week.

To counter this, the Allies agreed in 1979, as part of a two-track decision, to deploy as a deterrent land-based cruise missiles and Pershing II missiles capable of reaching targets in the Soviet Union. These missiles are to be deployed in several countries of Western Europe. This relatively limited force in no way serves as a substitute for the much larger strategic umbrella spread over our NATO Allies. Rather, it provides a vital link between conventional shorter-range nuclear forces in Europe and intercontinental forces in the United States.

Deployment of these systems will demonstrate to the Soviet Union that this link cannot be broken. Deterring war depends on the perceived ability of our forces to perform effectively. The more effective our forces are, the less likely it is that we'll have to use them. So, we and our allies are proceeding to modernize NATO's nuclear forces of intermediate range to meet increased Soviet deployments of nuclear systems threatening Western Europe.

Let me turn now to our hopes for arms control negotiations. There's a tendency to make this entire subject overly complex. I want to be clear and concise. I told you of the letter I wrote to President Brezhnev last April. Well, I've just sent another message to the Soviet leadership. It's a simple, straightforward, yet, historic message. The United States proposes the mutual reduction of conventional intermediate-range nuclear and strategic forces. Specifically, I have proposed a four-point agenda to achieve this objective in my letter to President Brezhnev.

The first and most important point concerns the Geneva negotiations. As part of the 1979 two-track decision, NATO made a commitment to seek arms control negotiations with the Soviet Union on intermediate range nuclear forces. The United States has been preparing for these negotiations through close consultation with our NATO partners.

We're now ready to set forth our proposal. I have informed President Brezhnev that

when our delegation travels to the negotiations on intermediate range, land-based nuclear missiles in Geneva on the 30th of this month, my representatives will present the following proposal: The United States is prepared to cancel its deployment of Pershing II and ground-launch cruise missiles if the Soviets will dismantle their SS–20, SS–4, and SS–5 missiles. This would be an historic step. With Soviet agreement, we could together substantially reduce the dread threat of nuclear war which hangs over the people of Europe. This, like the first footstep on the Moon, would be a giant step for mankind.

Now, we intend to negotiate in good faith and go to Geneva willing to listen to and consider the proposals of our Soviet counterparts, but let me call to your attention the background against which our proposal is made.

During the past 6 years while the United States deployed no new intermediate-range missiles and withdrew 1,000 nuclear warheads from Europe, the Soviet Union deployed 750 warheads on mobile, accurate ballistic missiles. They now have 1,100 warheads on the SS–20s, SS–4s and 5s. And the United States has no comparable missiles. Indeed, the United States dismantled the last such missile in Europe over 15 years ago.

As we look to the future of the negotiations, it's also important to address certain Soviet claims, which left unrefuted could become critical barriers to real progress in arms control.

The Soviets assert that a balance of intermediate range nuclear forces already exists. That assertion is wrong. By any objective measure, as this chart indicates, the Soviet Union has developed an increasingly overwhelming advantage. They now enjoy a superiority on the order of six to one. The red is the Soviet buildup; the blue is our own. That is 1975, and that is 1981.

Now, Soviet spokesmen have suggested that moving their SS–20s behind the Ural Mountains will remove the threat to Europe. Well, as this map demonstrates, the SS–20s, even if deployed behind the Urals, will have a range that puts almost all of Western Europe—the great cities—Rome,

Athens, Paris, London, Brussels, Amsterdam, Berlin, and so many more—all of Scandinavia, all of the Middle East, all of northern Africa, all within range of these missiles which, incidentally, are mobile and can be moved on shorter notice. These little images mark the present location which would give them a range clear out into the Atlantic.

The second proposal that I've made to President Brezhnev concerns strategic weapons. The United States proposes to open negotiations on strategic arms as soon as possible next year.

I have instructed Secretary Haig to discuss the timing of such meetings with Soviet representatives. Substance, however, is far more important than timing. As our proposal for the Geneva talks this month illustrates, we can make proposals for genuinely serious reductions, but only if we take the time to prepare carefully.

The United States has been preparing carefully for resumption of strategic arms negotiations because we don't want a repetition of past disappointments. We don't want an arms control process that sends hopes soaring only to end in dashed expectations.

Now, I have informed President Brezhnev that we will seek to negotiate substantial reductions in nuclear arms which would result in levels that are equal and verifiable. Our approach to verification will be to emphasize openness and creativity, rather than the secrecy and suspicion which have undermined confidence in arms control in the past.

While we can hope to benefit from work done over the past decade in strategic arms negotiations, let us agree to do more than simply begin where these previous efforts left off. We can and should attempt major qualitative and quantitative progress. Only such progress can fulfill the hopes of our own people and the rest of the world. And let us see how far we can go in achieving truly substantial reductions in our strategic arsenals.

To symbolize this fundamental change in direction, we will call these negotiations START—Strategic Arms Reduction Talks.

The third proposal I've made to the Soviet Union is that we act to achieve equality at lower levels of conventional forces in Europe. The defense needs of the Soviet Union hardly call for maintaining more combat divisions in East Germany today than were in the whole Allied invasion force that landed in Normandy on D-Day. The Soviet Union could make no more convincing contribution to peace in Europe, and in the world, than by agreeing to reduce its conventional forces significantly and constrain the potential for sudden aggression.

Finally, I have pointed out to President Brezhnev that to maintain peace we must reduce the risks of surprise attack and the chance of war arising out of uncertainty or miscalculation.

I am renewing our proposal for a conference to develop effective measures that would reduce these dangers. At the current Madrid meeting of the Conference on Security and Cooperation in Europe, we're laying the foundation for a Western-proposed conference on disarmament in Europe. This conference would discuss new measures to enhance stability and security in Europe. Agreement in this conference is within reach. I urge the Soviet Union to join us and many other nations who are ready to launch this important enterprise.

All of these proposals are based on the same fair-minded principles—substantial, militarily significant reduction in forces, equal ceilings for similar types of forces, and adequate provisions for verification.

My administration, our country, and I are committed to achieving arms reductions agreements based on these principles. Today I have outlined the kinds of bold, equitable proposals which the world expects of us. But we cannot reduce arms unilaterally. Success can only come if the Soviet Union will share our commitment, if it will demonstrate that its often-repeated professions of concern for peace will be matched by positive action.

Preservation of peace in Europe and the pursuit of arms reduction talks are of fundamental importance. But we must also help to bring peace and security to regions now torn by conflict, external intervention, and war.

The American concept of peace goes well beyond the absence of war. We foresee a flowering of economic growth and individual liberty in a world at peace.

At the economic summit conference in Cancún, I met with the leaders of 21 nations and sketched out our approach to global economic growth. We want to eliminate the barriers to trade and investment which hinder these critical incentives to growth, and we're working to develop new programs to help the poorest nations achieve self-sustaining growth.

And terms like "peace" and "security", we have to say, have little meaning for the oppressed and the destitute. They also mean little to the individual whose state has stripped him of human freedom and dignity. Wherever there is oppression, we must strive for the peace and security of individuals as well as states. We must recognize that progress and the pursuit of liberty is a necessary complement to military security. Nowhere has this fundamental truth been more boldly and clearly stated than in the Helsinki Accords of 1975. These accords have not yet been translated into living reality.

Today I've announced an agenda that can help to achieve peace, security, and freedom across the globe. In particular, I have made an important offer to forego entirely deployment of new American missiles in Europe if the Soviet Union is prepared to respond on an equal footing.

There is no reason why people in any part of the world should have to live in permanent fear of war or its spectre. I believe the time has come for all nations to act in a responsible spirit that doesn't threaten other states. I believe the time is right to move forward on arms control and the resolution of critical regional disputes at the conference table. Nothing will have a higher priority for me and for the American people over the coming months and years.

Addressing the United Nations 20 years ago, another American President described the goal that we still pursue today. He said, "If we all can persevere, if we can look beyond our shores and ambitions, then surely the age will dawn in which the strong are just and the weak secure and the peace preserved."

He didn't live to see that goal achieved. I invite all nations to join with America today in the quest for such a world.

Thank you.

Note: The President spoke at 10 a.m. at the National Press Club Building. His address was broadcast live on radio and television.

Remarks of President Reagan and President Luis Herrera Campíns of Venezuela Following Their Meetings
November 18, 1981

President Reagan. President Herrera and I have just concluded a series of productive meetings in which we reviewed the relations between our two countries and the international situation.

The overall relations between the United States and Venezuela are excellent, and we've discovered that both nations share similar concerns about the international situation. We took a close look at development in the Caribbean Basin Region and discussed what can be done to promote peace, freedom, and representative government in that part of the world.

We agreed to pursue the initiative begun by Venezuela, Mexico, Canada, and the United States for the Caribbean Basin Region. We will continue, and strengthen where possible, our individual assistance programs and encourage other states to do likewise. And furthermore, we agreed that we must promote the economic and social development of the hemisphere through international cooperation. We can be expected to continue our opposition to any interference in the internal affairs of Western Hemisphere countries.

We agreed that efforts must be made to strengthen democracy, liberty, and pluralism against extremism and totalitarianism. We continued discussions we started at Cancún about global economic relations and exchanged views on the alternative paths to Third World development.

Finally, we conducted a comprehensive and forthright review of the relations between Venezuela and the United States. We found that there is a high level of cooperation and respect between our nations and pledged to continue this friendly relationship.

In addition to the usefulness of reviewing these issues, I want to emphasize how much I enjoyed sharing the past 2 days with my friend President Herrera, with Mrs. Herrera, and the distinguished delegation that accompanied them. We expect to remain in close contact on matters of crucial importance to peace and to the well-being of the hemisphere.

President Herrera. Allow me first of all to thank very heartily the President of the United States, my friend Ronald Reagan, for the kind invitation he extended to me to visit this great democracy. Allow me to thank him for the excellent organization of this visit, for having made possible for us to have contacts not only at the highest level, that of the Presidency of the country, but also at the level of high officials and personalities coming from the executive and the legislative powers of the United States.

We shall return to Venezuela with our hearts filled with the attentions and the kindness shown to us by President Reagan, Mrs. Reagan, and all the Americans we saw and talked to.

I wish to say that I believe that this is a fortunate coincidence—the fact that I was here in Washington the morning of the extraordinary speech made by President Reagan. And I believe that this speech will have a great impact throughout the world, especially in regard to the need of limiting nuclear armament in Europe both by the United States and the Soviet Union. I believe that the four points you stated, Mr. President, in your speech to the National Press Club will be a great contribution to détente. And I must say I am very happy to have been here this morning.

We studied the bilateral relations between Venezuela and the United States, relations which, I must say, are presently at an optimal level. And we reviewed the need to continue implementing agreements, signed in the past between our two countries, most of them related to matters of technical exchange.

We also analyzed the difficult political situation existing in the Central American area and the Caribbean. And I must say that I expressed the independent, dignified, and serious position of our foreign policies with frankness, and I expressed in this way the views of my government. And allow me to say also, that I was listened to with respect and not only with respect but also with cordiality and understanding. And the concepts of peace, liberty, and democracy were ever present, were like a backdrop to our talks on the area.

As you know, the line of action of my government, the one we have always followed, is a line of non-intervention and respect for the self-determination of nations and the projection of the good of democracy and of freedom. And when we spoke about such a delicate situation as the one existing in Salvador, we coincided in the need to encourage the achievement of a democratic way out that will enable that country to overcome the subversion coming from Marxist radical movements.

We know of the great efforts made by the junta of the government, presided by José Napoleón Duarte in El Salvador, surrounded by so many difficulties in order to achieve an institutional way out to the situation there.

We have ratified the will of the Governments of the United States, Venezuela, Mexico, and Canada, to promote an ambitious program of cooperation in the area of the Caribbean and Central America and also a program where not only we would participate, but also we would encourage other governments to cooperate in the political, cultural, and economic, social development of this crucial area.

It has been of utmost importance for us and the developing nations of the world to have heard throughout my talks with President Reagan, and again in the speech he made this morning, a ratification of the political will expressed in Cancún, favoring global negotiations to be held soon, and thus bringing hope for peace through concrete and effective actions to all developing countries.

And finally, let me insist in extending my thanks again for all the kindness shown by President Reagan, Mrs. Reagan, and the team working with them, to me, my wife, the members of the Venezuelan party, and the special guests on this trip I made to Washington. And allow me to say that I appreciate greatly the generous concepts you have formulated time and again for my own person, for the government, democratic government I preside [over]—a government that tries to search for peace, development, participation, and respect of human rights everywhere.

Thank you.

Note: President Reagan spoke at 12:05 p.m. on the South Lawn of the White House.

Remarks to Reporters Upon Receiving a Thanksgiving Turkey from the National Turkey Federation
November 18, 1981

The President. This, of course, is a great tradition, of Thanskgiving in our country, and I'm very happy—we used to do this all the time in California, with the California association. And they came to the office, and I had a few adventures there, too. Finally one day they turned to the custom of actually bringing it in cooked, and we would have a lunch right there with the staff in the office. But I had to carve it for all those gentlemen and ladies of the press with their cameras on me. And I remember one day I was carving, and I thought they hadn't cooked it very well, because there was a lot of blood appearing, which didn't look very appetizing. I found out I'd cut my thumb. [*Laughter*] Sort of spoiled lunch.

Mr. Walts. Sort of spoiled lunch, yeah. Have you been in touch lately with Merv Amerine, who used to fly you around down——

The President. Oh, the turkey plane? I haven't seen Merv for a long time.

Mr. Walts. Haven't you?

Mr. McClain. I've seen Merv in April. I was out to the California board meeting.

The President. What we're talking about here is a sort of in-house—a gentleman named Merv Amerine in California in the '66 campaign when I was running for Governor. We chartered his plane, a DC–3, for part of the campaign, and found out that when he hasn't chartered it to us—he was a turkey grower and was using it to haul turkeys. And now I don't want anyone to say the obvious thing that comes to mind, that he hadn't really changed—[*laughter*]—in that new charter.

Well, thank you very much.

Mr. Walts. Oh yes, Mr. President. We're delighted to be here, and it's certainly a pleasure to see you again. And I think you know that the National Turkey Federation is very solidly behind your programs and you.

The President. Well, thank you very much.

I'm sorry to be so late for all of you in this, but on the other hand, I was just getting even, because down in Texas there, I sat for 3 hours before any of *them* showed up——

Mr. Walts. And still didn't get one. [*Laughter*]

The President. And still didn't get one.

Reporter. What are you going to do with him?

The President. Eat him.

Q. Why don't you pet him first?

The President. Well—[*laughter*]——

Mr. Walts. He's all right.

The President. I'll sneak up on him, kind of.

Mr. Walts. Sneak up on him.

The President. Hey, look over there.

Didn't think it would work, did you? [*Laughter*]

Mr. McClain. Yeah, I didn't think it would work.

The President. Well, over the years you get used to turkeys. [*Laughter*] [*To the turkey*] But you're the real thing.

Q. What are you going to do about your personnel problems, Mr. President?

The President. I don't have any personnel problems.

Q. What about Mr. Allen [*Richard V. Allen, Assistant to the President for National Security Affairs*]? Do you still have confidence in Mr. Allen?

The President. Answered all those questions and all that needs to be said.

Q. Sir, we're just not sure what you know.

You say on the basis of what you know you think he has done nothing wrong.

The President. But you know that it would be—there's no way that you can comment now while this is still evidently under review. So, I just feel that I'm not in a position to comment.

Q. But you first learned about it last September, we understand.

The President. Yes, and then it was investigated. And it was reported that everything was fine.

Note: The President spoke at 12:43 p.m. to reporters assembled in the Rose Garden at the White House. Lew Walts, executive vice president, and Hugh McClain, president, National Turkey Federation, also participated in the ceremony.

Nomination of William J. Bennett To Be Chairman of the National Endowment for the Humanities
November 18, 1981

The President today announced his intention to nominate William J. Bennett to be Chairman of the National Endowment for the Humanities, National Foundation on the Arts and the Humanities. He would succeed Joseph D. Duffey.

Since 1979 Dr. Bennett has been president and director of the National Humanities Center, Research Triangle Park, N.C. He is also an adjunct associate professor of philosophy at the University of North Carolina (Chapel Hill) and at North Carolina State University (Raleigh). He was executive director of the National Humanities Center in 1976–79. Previously he was assistant to the president and assistant professor of philosophy in the College of Liberal Arts, Boston University, in 1972–76. He has taught law and philosophy at the University of Southern Mississippi, the University of Texas, Harvard University, the University of Wisconsin, and Boston University.

Dr. Bennett has written a number of articles in professional journals such as the Harvard Civil Rights and Stanford Law Review, and for major news magazines on subjects pertaining to social issues. He is a trustee of the Institute for Educational Affairs and the Committee for a Free World, a member of the National Research Council of the National Science Foundation and a special panel of the National Academy of Education.

He graduated from Williams College, Williamstown, Mass. (B.A., 1965); the University of Texas, Austin, Tex. (Ph. D., 1967); and Harvard Law School (J.D., 1971). He resides in Chapel Hill, N.C., and was born July 31, 1943.

Nomination of Danny Lee McDonald To Be a Member of the Federal Election Commission
November 18, 1981

The President today announced his intention to nominate Danny Lee McDonald to be a member of the Federal Election Commission for a term expiring April 30, 1987. He would succeed Robert O. Tiernan.

Since 1979 Mr. McDonald has been general administrator, Oklahoma Corporation Commission, responsible for the management of 10 regulatory divisions. He was secretary of the Tulsa County Election Board in 1974–79 and a member of the Federal

Elections Commission Advisory Panel to the Federal Election Commission Clearinghouse. Mr. McDonald was clerk chief, Tulsa County Election Board, in 1979.

He graduated from Oklahoma State University (B.A., 1971) and attended the John F. Kennedy School of Government at Harvard University. He resides in Oklahoma City, Okla. He was born August 26, 1946, in Tulsa, Okla.

Remarks at a Dinner Honoring the Republican Majority in the Senate
November 18, 1981

Thank you very much. Look, if we're a family, I'm the father, sit down.

Howard, thank you very much. And incidentally, I think everyone here would agree with me, thank you also for being a magnificent leader of this majority in the Senate.

Now, last Sunday I called Howard out in Tennessee, because it was his birthday. And tonight I think, if we're a family we should recognize it's Ted Stevens' birthday today. Happy Birthday.

Now, I don't know whether you're to this age or not, but I gave Howard a suggestion that I've found very useful over the years, and that is if you are past 39, subtract 39 from you present age and refer to this as whatever that anniversary would be of your 39th birthday from here on. [*Laughter*] And that way we'll all stay in trim.

I hadn't realized, Howard, that it was exactly a year ago. I was about to stand up here tonight and say "about a year ago." I was here, we were all here under much the same circumstances—with a couple of important changes. I had not yet checked in at the timeclock, and your majority had not yet attained voting status in the Senate. But we were all both looking forward to those things taking place.

It isn't strange that I hadn't realized that it was 1 year ago exactly tonight. Nancy and I only found out the next morning about the parties that were held on the anniversary of the election. We went to bed early. [*Laughter*] No one could have convinced me anyway that it had been only a year. I thought it was a year 6 weeks after inauguration. [*Laughter*]

Let me just take a few minutes here to say what, in my mind, has happened in this year. "Family" is not a bad word to describe it. I served 8 years as a Governor. During only 1 of those 8 years did I have a bare majority. The rest of the time I was up against pretty much what we're up against with regard to the other House. And many times I've said I'll go to my grave wondering what it could have been like in that State if we had had our party in control of the legislature as well as the executive branch. And now I have a second chance. Many of you do, too.

I remember we discussed the last time a year ago when we were here, that there was only one among us who had ever served on a Republican majority before. He is still in the Senate. And I've already issued an Executive order that those fellows that are up for reelection are going to be re-elected—[*laughter*]—we'll accept no change in that.

As I look back over these months and what we've accomplished, it's been kept a secret by the Washington Post—[*laughter*]—the rest of the country knows what we've done. And I just have to say a thank you to all of you, because when the chips were down, always you were there. And I know it's going to continue that way.

When I say we've accomplished much, I'm not going to go into details of the things that you know better than anyone else. And probably each of you, from your mail count, could match the very things that I have received in the mail from those people we represent out there—letters that have made me so proud at times of what you've done and what we've accomplished together.

A young man in college who writes to tell me that he's been going to college on government loans, but he is going to drop out a year and work and save, because he doesn't think under the circumstances it would be right to impose another year on the government of his country by accepting another government loan. The man that wrote to me a letter that had to be translated for me because it was written in braille—he lost his eyesight 37 years ago in Germany in World War II—and he wrote to tell me that if cutting his benefit would help his country, then go ahead and cut that benefit.

The incident of just a few days ago that I know you're all aware of—that almost accidentally came to our attention—of the little 3½-year-old girl who had never lived at home with her parents and couldn't, actually, because of a regulation with regard to the government grant they had to have for medical expenses of 10 to 12 thousand dollars a month. And Dick Schweiker found out within 24 hours after we made it public that, by golly, he could change that regulation and got it changed. And I had the pleasure of calling those parents and speaking to them and their unspeakable happiness that the fact that their little girl was going to come home. The doctors had said she would be better off at home, and it

would only cost a thousand dollars a month at home.

I could go on picking out letters like this of people expressing their willingness—the young sailor that wrote to tell me that he was writing for 180 of his crewmates on a submarine, and he said, "We just want you to know how good it feels to once again be Americans." And he said, "We may not be the biggest navy, but we're the best." And I don't think we've been hearing things like that for quite some time around here. And I'll get maudlin if I keep on going, so I'd better not.

You each are sent here, and one of your principal responsibilities in addition to that of the country itself, is to your State. And then I've always thought that I'm the only one that's elected in which I'm the lobbyist for all 50 of the States. And therefore I promise you that anything that I in my heart believe is right for California, that's what I'll recommend to you. [*Laughter*]

I hope that we'll be here many more times for anniversaries of this and with a larger majority every time. And maybe after the next election we'll be able to invite a few representatives from the other House simply because they're a majority too, and when we have them both, then I think this country will go forward faster than it has. But I have to say, even with that handicap, thanks to all of you, we've made gains that I don't think any of us could ever have believed possible when we were here just a year ago today. With one House and the executive branch—somehow we've managed to make it work over on the other side. It's just that it'll be easier when they're a majority as you're a majority.

So, God bless you all. Thank you all for the relationship that we've had. If there's anything lacking in it and I don't know about it, well, please let me know about it, because, so far, I've felt nothing but warmth and a kindred spirit and feeling from all of you.

Thank you.

Note: The President spoke at approximately 10 p.m. in the Great Hall of the Library of Congress.

Nomination of John Hathaway Reed To Be United States Ambassador to Sri Lanka and the Maldives
November 19, 1981

The President today announced his intention to nominate John Hathaway Reed, of Maine, to be Ambassador to the Democratic Socialist Republic of Sri Lanka and to the Republic of Maldives. He would succeed Donald R. Toussaint.

Mr. Reed served in the United States Navy as lieutenant in 1942–46. In 1946–59 he was officer, director, and stockholder of Reed Farms, Inc., in Fort Fairfield, Maine. He served in the Maine State Legislature (1955–57), Maine State Senate (1957–59), and was Governor of Maine (1960–66). In 1967–75 he was a member of the Board, then Chairman, of the National Transportation Safety Board in Washington, D.C. He was Ambassador to Sri Lanka and to the Republic of Maldives in 1976–77. Since 1978 Mr. Reed has been director of government relations of the Associated Builders and Contractors, Inc., in Washington, D.C.

He graduated from the University of Maine (B.S., 1942) and has received two honorary LL.D. degrees from the University of Maine and Ricker College. He is married, has two children, and resides in Fort Fairfield, Maine. He was born January 5, 1921, in Fort Fairfield.

Appointment of Three Members of the National Air and Space Museum Advisory Board
November 19, 1981

The President today announced his intention to appoint the following individuals to be members of the National Air and Space Museum Advisory Board:

Donald M. Koll has been president of the Koll Co., a California general contractor, since 1962. He was vice president of K.W. Koll Construction Co. in 1958–62. He served in the United States Air Force as a pilot with the rank of captain in 1955–58. He graduated from Stanford University (B.A.). He is married, has six children, and resides in Newport Beach, Calif. He was born March 29, 1933, in Santa Monica, Calif. He will succeed Elwood R. Quesada.

James P. Moore, Jr., was legislative assistant and counsel to Representative Charles Pashayan, Jr. (R-Calif.) in 1979–81 and legislative assistant to Representative William M. Ketchum (R-Calif.) in 1977–81. He graduated from Rutgers College (B.A., 1975) and the University of Pittsburgh (M.A., 1976). He also attended Georgetown University. He resides in Ford City, Pa., and was born April 24, 1953, in Joliet, Ill. He will succeed William Hall.

Jacqueline A. Ponder is a homemaker in Colorado Springs, Colo. She has been involved in Republican Party activities, serving as chairman, Colorado Presidential Inaugural Committee in 1981, executive director, Colorado Reagan-Bush Committee in 1979–80, and has served as a precinct committeewoman since 1974. She was a delegate to the Republican National Convention in 1980. She graduated from Vanderbilt University (B.E., 1968). She is married, has two children, and resides in Colorado Springs, Colo. She was born November 29, 1946, in Tampa, Fla. She will succeed Olive Anne Beech.

Remarks at the Dedication of the James Madison Memorial Building of the Library of Congress
November 20, 1981

We live with history in this community, and Nancy and I never cease marvelling at actually living in the history of that home. Madison was the second to occupy it; the picture of Washington that Dolley saved hangs in the East Room. And there's a portion outside of the White House, not seen by too many people, where you can see the smudges of smoke on the stone from the fire when the Executive Mansion was burned.

I feel a great affinity with James Madison. I'm told that his worry over the size of the national debt drove him to distraction. [*Laughter*] I could sympathize; the debt was not of his making either. [*Laughter*] But I am proud to participate in this dedication of the first national memorial to James Madison.

The leadership of men like Madison gave shape to a nation that would become the greatest the world has ever seen. Our Founding Fathers began the most exciting adventure in the history of nations. In their debates with the principles of human dignity, individual rights, and representative democracy, their arguments were based on common law, separation of powers, and limited government. Their victory was to find a home for liberty.

Madison knew and we should always remember that no government is perfect, not even a democracy. Rights given to government were taken from the people, and so he believed that government's touch in our lives should be light, that powers entrusted to it be administered by temporary guardians. He wrote that "government was the greatest of all reflections on human nature." He wrote that "if men were angels, no government would be necessary. If angels were to govern men, neither external nor internal controls on government would be necessary. In framing a government," he said, "which is to be administered by men over men, the great difficulty lies in this: you must first enable the government to control

the governed, and next oblige it to control itself."

Led by Madison and Jefferson and others, the authors of the Constitution established a fragile balance between the branches and levels of government. That concept was their genius and the secret of our success— that idea of federalism. The balance of power intended in the Constitution is the guarantor of the greatest measure of individual freedom any people have ever known. Our task today, this year, this decade, must be to reaffirm those ideas. Our Founding Fathers designed a system of government that was unique in all the world—a federation of sovereign states with as much law and decisionmaking authority as possible kept at the local level. They knew that man's very need for government meant no government should function unchecked.

We the people—and that is still the most powerful phrase—created government for our own convenience. It can have no power except that voluntarily granted to it by the people. We founded our society on the belief that the rights of men were ours by grace of God. That vision of our Founding Fathers revolutionized the world. Those principles must be reaffirmed by every generation of Americans, for freedom is never more than one generation away from extinction. It can only be passed on to a new generation if it has been preserved by the old. And that's what I meant last January when I spoke of an American renewal—a rededication to those first principles.

Let it be said of this generation of Americans that when we pass the torch of freedom onto the new generation, it was burning as brightly as when it was handed to us. Then we will have kept faith with Madison and those other remarkable men we call the Founding Fathers. And we will have kept faith with God.

Thank you.

Note: The President spoke at 11:20 a.m. in the James Madison Memorial Hall.

Nomination of Franklin S. Forsberg To Be United States Ambassador to Sweden
November 20, 1981

The President today announced his intention to nominate Franklin S. Forsberg, of Connecticut, to be Ambassador to Sweden. He would succeed Rodney O'Gliasain Kennedy-Minott.

Mr. Forsberg was a teacher at Pace College and New York University in 1931–37, and publisher with Street and Smith Publications in New York City in 1937–42. He served in the United States Army in 1942–46 with the rank of colonel. In 1946–48 he was publisher and consultant with Forsberg and Church in New York City. He was publisher of Liberty Magazine in New York City (1948–50) and publisher and consultant with Forsberg, Merritt, Harrity and Church

in New York City (1950–55). Mr. Forsberg was publisher of Popular Mechanics Publishing Co., in Chicago, Ill., in 1955–59. In 1959–72 he was a publisher with Holt, Rinehart and Winston in New York City. Since 1972 he has been president of Forsberg Associates, Inc., of New York City. In 1973 he was appointed by the President as a member of the Air Quality Advisory Board.

Mr. Forsberg graduated from the University of Utah (B.A., 1930) and New York University (M.B.A., 1931). He is fluent in Swedish. He is married, has three children, and resides in Greenwich, Conn. He was born October 21, 1905, in Salt Lake City, Utah.

Nomination of Rear Adm. Herbert R. Lippold, Jr., To Be a Member of the Mississippi River Commission
November 20, 1981

The President today announced his intention to nominate Rear Adm. Herbert R. Lippold, Jr., National Oceanic and Atmospheric Administration, to be a member of the Mississippi River Commission. He would succeed Allen L. Powell.

Rear Adm. Herbert R. Lippold, Jr., is Director of the National Ocean Survey, National Oceanic and Atmospheric Administration. He joined the Coast and Geodetic Survey 30 years ago and has done research and surveying on land and sea in the Atlantic, Pacific, and Arctic Oceans, and in most of the conterminous United States, Alaska, and Hawaii. His service was highlighted by 9 years of sea duty on eight vessels, three of which he commanded. He surveyed the north Arctic coast by cat train, spent 8

years in geodesy, accomplishing basic surveys, established a satellite triangulation worldwide network, and served as liaison with the Air Force, bringing horizontal and vertical control to intercontinental ballistic missile sites in the United States. He conducted liaison with the Navy at Pearl Harbor on the Pacific tide and seismic sea wave warning system, supervised ship construction at Pt. Pleasant, W. Va., served as Director, Office of Fleet Operations in Rockville, Md., and directed the operations of NOAA's research and hydrographic survey fleet of 25 vessels. In 1965–66 he was a Department of Commerce Scientific and Technical Fellow, assigned to the National Bureau of Standards.

He graduated from New England College, Henniker, N.H. (B.S., 1949) and the University of New Hampshire (B.E., 1950). He was born April 9, 1926.

Interview With Reporters on Federalism
November 19, 1981

Q. Mr. President, a lot of the local government officials who have been listening to you talk about your dream of returning responsibilities and resources are saying that they've received the responsibilities, and now they are wondering when the next shoe is going to fall. Will your 1983 budget have a definite source of revenue for the local government?

The President. Well, we've been meeting with them, and they have been here in meetings with our people at OMB and with Don Regan of Treasury about these. And I can't say that any actual or final decisions have been made. I know that there has to be some pain for them also. But during these 10 months, I have met with over 1,200 State and local officials, going from Governors on down through counties and mayors and so forth, legislators, on all of these. And we have a commission, as you know, appointed to see how we can turn back tax sources to the local government.

This is what it comes down to. We wanted and asked the Congress for far more block grants than we got, a block grant where they can set the priorities within that and the method of using it. I'd learned as Governor that the categorical grants—where the government ties the red strings to it and tape to it and says this is exactly the way you have to spend it and so forth—results in a large administrative overhead cost. And we didn't get all that we wanted. We did get a certain number of categoricals into block grants, but there still remains too many categoricals.

And, then—maybe this is more than you bargained for in this answer, but let me get it all in—my dream is that the block grants are only a means to an end. And the end is that the government, which has preempted over the years so much of the tax revenue potential in this country, that we could turn back not only the responsibility to governments of tasks that I think they can perform better than the Federal Government can perform, but turn back tax sources so that the tax source itself goes to them. And they, therefore, then have the responsibility for collecting the money which they're going to spend for this by way of the tax.

And this isn't original with me. This was first suggested when the first proposal for Federal aid to education was made. Norris Cotton, then Senator from New Hampshire, looking at the amount of money that was suggested—and the Federal Government was protesting that it meant no interference; just wanted to help by giving money—and he said, "Well, if that's really true," he said, "why don't we turn the tobacco tax over to the States and the only restriction is that it be used for education?" And you know how they defeated him? They said, "Well, it wouldn't be right to educate our children with a sin tax." So the Federal Government got its foot in the door and went on from there. That's all we want to stop or change.

Q. Realistically, is it possible that there will be room in the fiscal 1983 budget for some turnback of a tax source to the States and local governments?

The President. I don't know yet. We have a task force, as I say, working on that under Ed Gray, that's to work and see how this could be done, what the mechanics of it would entail, and whether we could do this at the same time we give the responsibility that goes with it. But it just seems to me that there's an awful lot of money lost, simply in the process of bringing it to Washington and then sending it back out there minus a carrying charge that comes off the top here in Washington. It would make a lot more sense if it was there in the first place.

Q. Mr. President, the Governors have suggested a sorting-out process of what the Federal Government should have and what the States and locals should have. One of the things they suggested is, as you know, that the Federal Government pick up most of the welfare costs and that they would then pick up more schooling costs and more transportation costs. Would you go along with that? And if not, what sort of sorting out would you like to see? What functions do you think the Federal Government should have on the domestic side, and what would you pass on to them?

The President. Well, we have, again, a Presidential commission that is made up of representatives of State and local government, only their own people on this, to sort this out. But I would think that we might start with the tenth article of the Bill of Rights, the 10th amendment, which says that the Federal Government—those powers which are granted to the Federal Government are in the Constitution, and all others shall remain with the States or with the people.

I think that over the years, probably coming out of the Great Depression and the traumatic experience of that, the Federal Government has gradually involved itself in areas that were never before thought of as the Federal Government's province.

And so, yes, there has to be some sorting out. I'm not sure that I agree with some of the suggestions they've made because—let's take one, such as welfare, for example.

This is a very diverse country. The problems of a welfare client in New York City are far different than those from out in some small town in the rural areas in the Middle West, or something in more rural States. I believe that there's much more chance of waste and of fraud in trying to run it from the national level than there is in running it at the local level.

Now, when we reformed welfare in California—and it was the most successful reform that's ever been attempted while I was Governor there—we found that our biggest difficulty was getting waivers from the Federal Government in order to do some of the things that we felt had to be done.

And when we finished, we not only over a 3-year period had saved the taxpayers of California $2 billion, we were able to give the welfare recipients the first cost-of-living increase they'd had since 1958—and average increase of 43 percent in their grants. And it was simply just the application of common sense and the fact that these are your neighbors there that you're trying to help, and you're better able to know what to do for them than Washington is 3,000 miles away.

Q. Mr. President, in your dream of the future of American federalism, what domestic functions do you believe should be Federal, as opposed to State and local responsibilities?

The President. Well, the first one, of course, is national security. That is the prime responsibility of the National Government. You would have me doing the sorting out that we've got a commission trying to do.

But I would think that first of all, education—we built the greatest school system the world has ever seen and built it at the local level and the local school district level. And then the Federal Government got into the school business only by having preempted so much of the tax resources, and those tax resources that grew with the economy faster than something like the property tax, which is the principal basis for educational funding. Then they got into it through that money thing, having preempted the money, created the problem, and then they said, "Well, now we want to help you." But in return for the help, they wanted to also regulate, and have interfered to a large extent.

Welfare—welfare is presently administered at the local level. It is, in most States, done at the county level. They have a county welfare department, but they do it under regulations imposed from Washington. And I can tell you, those regulations would line the walls of this room, and they're constantly changing. They have got employees at the county level that do nothing but try to keep up and inform the workers of what the new regulations are.

Incidentally, we've already been pretty successful here with something of that kind.

The regulations that govern HHS grants out there used to fill 318 pages of the *Federal Register*; they now only fill 6.

Q. Do you continue to oppose such things as increasing the gasoline tax and perhaps then giving the States a part of that increase?

The President. Again, you're getting to the area that we haven't thought of—nothing should be ruled out until you see if it'll work. I have spoken of such things as, "What if the Federal income tax had a provision that *x* percent of that tax would not even come to Washington, would be retained in the States where it is collected for the States to use as they see fit?"

Excise taxes of the kind you've mentioned might be a way, as the example I gave of Norris Cotton when he suggested one. I think it would depend a lot on what is the revenue that's going to be gained, compared to the responsibility that you want it to cover. Is it one that is going to grow as the economy grows? Or is it going to be a static kind of tax that might meet the situation now, but won't meet it down the road a ways?

Q. So, as of now, you wouldn't rule out possibly increasing the Federal gas tax and giving some of that increase to the States?

The President. Oh, I won't rule anything out. Right now there is a sizable Federal gas tax, and most States—like our own has a gas tax also. The Federal gas tax came into being for the Federal interstate highway system—and I'm wondering if that's ever going to be completed—and it was supposed to be a temporary thing.

Q. Mr. President, towards the sorting out, there seems to be a new mood of great impatience among the Governors, combined with this year's budget situation, the growth of the entitlements, the defense budget, the tax cut, which the Governors perceive as being negative to the interest of the State and local government, which took a large portion of the cuts in the first round and then will be hit again by the 12 percent that you proposed in September. And as a matter of fact, they're so angry, the Western Governors' meeting in Scottsdale 12 days ago passed a resolution saying they would flatly oppose further cuts in the domestic discretionary budget proposed by your administration unless negotiation begins for a significant sorting out of functions between the Federal Government and the States.

Could you give us your reaction to their position?

The President. Yes. I think most of those Western Governors are Democrats now—[*laughter*]—it might have had something to do with it. No, we recognize that we have to straighten out this financial situation on the Federal level. They will benefit, also, to a great extent by the fact that inflation will come down. And indeed, it has come down faster than we had anticipated right now. Now that's got to be reflected somewhat in their costs. And as I say, we didn't get all that we wanted with regard to the switch to block grants, and I'm still going to continue striving for that because, again, the savings to them—we can reduce the amount of money in a block grant to less than a categorical grant because of the savings in administrative overhead.

Q. Along the same line of sorting out, would you like to see a continuing role or a continuing relationship between the cities and counties and the Federal Government?

The President. Oh, yes. I think it's vital. You know, if we remember back some years to—I think it was around 1914 or something, that was recognized in the fact that Senators were not popularly elected. They were chosen by State legislatures to represent the State. The House of Representatives represented the people. And then they made the change in the Constitution and changed it to make them all popularly elected. That was why in the whole bill of impeachment, the Senate had been picked to be the trial court and the judge, because they would not be bound by political considerations. Now that they're elected, they're just as bound as the other House would be.

But yes, that relationship has to exist. And I hope that not just on these things of budget and so forth, that bring in the people that we've met with—the 1,200 or so—that we would have ongoing meetings. And I should, while I'm here, have a department for that purpose.

Q. Do you think it's at all the responsibility of the National Government to redistribute resources between the States that are relatively well off and the States that are not?

The President. No, I think that is up to the States. My first reaction to that is that this is one of the—the built-in guarantee of freedom is our federalism that makes us so unique, and that is the right of the citizen to vote with his feet. If a State is badly managed, the people will either do one of two things: They will either use their power at the polls to redress that, or they'll go someplace else. And we've seen industries driven out of some States by adverse tax policies and so forth.

Q. But Mr. President, on that very point, Senator Durenberger has made quite an issue in the last few months that some States are energy rich and some energy poor; that there's a transfer of hundreds of billions of dollars within this decade going from the energy poor to the energy rich States. So he asks whether it's in any way fair to expect the States and localities that suffer from a declining economy to provide the same level of public services, including new services devolved from the Federal Government, as to expect from those States that are flush with energy generated revenues?

The President. Well now, if you take it that way, just in energy, then couldn't you make the same argument with regard to the great agricultural States that provide the food for the people of this country? California, for example—I hope it still prevails in spite of the fruit fly—but California, over the years, puts about 40 percent of all the fruits and nuts and vegetables that are on the tables of America, puts them on those tables. And the same thing might be said. There is a great natural and rich resource and a production. I just think the marketplace regulates that.

Q. How do you feel about States putting fairly steep taxes on the resources that they extract from the ground—whether it's food or minerals or oil—and ship to other States and thereby in effect pass on that additional tax burden to the consumers in those other States.

The President. Well, you're speaking of severance taxes that come on. Well again, doesn't that balance out with everything else? I once asked an automobile manufacturer several years ago that what if they put out a price tag that incorporated all the taxes that were paid in the manufacture of an automobile, and put the price tag out there like the gasoline pump does—*x* amount for tax, price of the automobile here—and I said, "Have you ever figured out what would it look like?" And he said, "Yes, we could tell you what it would look like." And he told me then of some model of car that they had that was about $3,800. And he said it would be $800 for the automobile and $3,000 tax. Because if you stop to think of the social security taxes and—all the way, the taxes that are in the steel that they buy by the time it gets there, and the glass and the rubber and all of this—well, as I've used the example many times in speeches and it's absolutely true: By the time you go to the market and buy an egg, there's 100 taxes in that egg; none of them put there by the chicken.

Q. In the Senate hearings that were held on the 5th of November, Governors Snelling and Busbee and Matheson made a point that the State budgets were in a condition of disarray and chaos because of the deep and the continuing Federal budget cuts. They pointed again to the inflation-driven entitlements, defense spending, the extent of the tax cut, feeling that more should be seen in that area in terms of the next economies. And Governor Snelling, for the Governors, proposed a 2-year moratorium on further cuts and discretionary grants to the States and localities so they would have a chance to catch their breath, institute some rational budgeting and planning, perhaps start some discussions with you about more block grants and a sorting out of responsibilities.

Could you give your reaction to the proposal of the moratorium for 2 years?

The President. I think it would be great if we could afford it. And I know that part of their problem—which you didn't mention there—it was not just the change, it's the fact that the States all have varying budget or fiscal years and in many States were caught with their budget already determined. And then we, by doing something at the Federal level, changed their—or ordered their estimates of revenues and so forth. And I just think our emergency is so great, I don't know how we could hold back and wait for all of this.

What we've tried to do and now with these meetings, and with Rich[1] in continued contact with them, is try to not throw any surprises at them, but to keep them informed so that, for example, in planning the next budget, they will know what we are considering and they can make allowance that in case we get what we ask for, why, they'll know what it's going to be like.

Q. Mr. President, the idea that Americans can, as you say, vote with their feet, if necessary, we've heard this from some of your other spokesmen in the government. If someone, say, in New York City were caught—I'm talking about in a pocket of poverty—*[inaudible]*. I mean, what can you say to them? They have no money to move, really. They are now trapped. I mean, in the best of all possible worlds, perhaps they could move—*[inaudible]*. But now they're trapped. What do you say to them? How do they get out of this—*[inaudible]*?

The President. Well, I never said that anyone tells them to move out.

Q. No, I know that.

The President. I think that as the people—we've been and still are a very migrant people. I think Americans move more than anyone else. And in many instances, it's the job holder; something happens and he starts exploring for work some place else and maybe goes and then sends for the family. But whatever means they have to use they do it. I can't see any way that the Federal Government could set up a program for moving people, because then you get into the element of would there be something compulsory about it, would the government decide that somebody had to move. And many people—during the campaign I talked to people out in Ohio and Michigan there, and the great unemployment in the automobile industry, and you talk to someone who'd say, "I'm third gen-

---

[1] *Richard S. Williamson, Assistant to the President for Intergovernmental Affairs.*

eration in my family living here. I don't want to live anywhere else." So he's going to sweat it out until jobs open up and he can get a job there.

And then on the other hand, you find particularly younger people here that—in the Sunbelt right now, for example, they're not having some of the same problems, and how Houston is a kind of a boom city because of the people that have gone there because it didn't have unemployment——

Q. Mr. President, I know that there are not many final decisions on the budget, but I assume that you're probably far enough into that process that you have some general idea where you stand.

Is it going to be possible, for example, to hold general revenue sharing at its present level? Is it going to be possible to hold the new block grants at their present funding level, or are all of those programs at this point still subject to further reductions in fiscal 1983?

The President. The suggested 12-percent cut—we didn't see how—and I think all of us recognize that this was going to be a blow to many communities, particularly the local level, not the State level, and again I'd seen it in our own State work. But we felt we had to go across the board, and we were asking other equally important programs to take that cut. There were only a few exceptions, such as hospital medical care for veterans. You couldn't cut that. But it extended to every place, including the White House, and so we felt that we had to do it.

Now realistically, the question is are you doing to get 12 percent—and I doubt it— from the Congress? But again, as I say, we had to hope that if we get control of this economy at this end, that this might be a temporary setback to some communities—a painful one, but the off-setting thing of reducing inflation and interest rates and, hopefully, having a surge in the economy would also begin to offset that.

I think one of their concerns when they came here—I've just met with a large group of both city and county and State officials, Governors, on this. And a lot of them, it was a fear—they'd been led to believe that maybe we were phasing it out entirely. And I could assure them that there was no such thing in our minds, that the only way it would ever be phased out is if we had an alternate source, a tax that we were going to give to them for their own use.

Q. Referring specifically to general revenue sharing.

The President. Yes.

Q. Mr. President, could the economic recession delay your plans for implementing some of the—[*inaudible*].

The President. I'm not sure that it could, because I believe that in the federalism thing that we're approaching or approving, I believe that there is, in the long run, the reduction of government cost, as I say, the administrative overhead that is involved in the Federal Government doing so many of these things.

This little case—you know an example of what we're trying to cure is this one that, God bless him, Dick Schweiker grabbed a hold of after I made it public the other day of the little girl out in Iowa, and how quickly we made this change. To think that our government—and I was wrong; I had old-fashioned figures when I said $6,000. It was costing between $10,000 and $12,000 a month for Medicaid, and even the doctors said she should be home, that she'd be better off at home, and it would only cost $1,000 a month at home. But that was more than her family could afford, so they couldn't take her home because they couldn't take over the cost. But here was the government shelling out $10,000 or $12,000 every month, when a silly regulation stood in the way of them getting it for $1,000 a month. Dick found a way to ignore that, make an exception to that regulation, but you wonder how many more cases are out there in the country like that. It's another example.

If the people in that community had been in charge of that program, you know darn well they wouldn't have stood still for a moment for that cost differential.

Q. The opinion of the Governors and the local officials seems to be that deregulation isn't going to get them where they need to be quickly enough to run their own operations properly. In the same Senate hearings I was referring to on November 5th, Governor Busbee, for example, expressed

such distress about the current national and State and local fiscal dilemma and the lack of legitimate Federal reform, as the Governors see it, that he said it is time that we had a domestic economic summit involving the President, the bipartisan leadership of the Congress, and our, that is the Governor's leadership, so that we might gain general agreement on ultimate prime responsibilities for government programs, the budget targets we should all plan for, and the timeframe in which we are going to reach these goals.

It seems to be the Governors would like a much larger role—not to be informed, but to be in at an early point of taking part in the decisions.

The President. Listen, I will buy that, because those Governors, and led by Busbee, were the greatest help in the world in our getting the economic package that was passed. But where we all were helpless was, we could not convince the majority leadership in the House, particularly, to give up Federal strings on so many—particularly the block grants.

So here was Busbee and the Governors who had helped us get this, and they were helping because they want the block grants. They know how it would benefit them. And we just had to stand here, and we were helpless to get them. Washington doesn't give up authority very easily. All I could say to them is, "Look, I'm going to continue to fight for them and please help."

In a thing of this kind, maybe they could, because there is a feeling among a great many people in the Congress—well, let's say less a feeling than a lack of understanding—of the State problem. In fact, some of the Governors told me that at the Inaugural, when I made a statement to this effect, and they were—the Governors were seated right behind many of the House of Representatives—they said that many of them, when I made that statement about the States' powers and so forth, turned around to them and mouthed, "Over our dead bodies." [*Laughter*]

Q. Mr. President, without being too general, I wonder if you could sum up for us some sort of philosophical thing, just what you see as the new federalism? Just a brief—[*inaudible*].

The President. Again, as I say, start with the Constitution and eliminate first of all those functions that properly belong at the Federal Government—interstate commerce and the national defense and things of this kind. Then find those functions—maybe we'd do well if we looked at the past. I know that everyone used to say I'm trying to take the country back—no, only as far as the Constitution. Find out those things that are, today, more or less administered in partnership at the local level and yet under Federal control, and see if you need that extra layer of bureaucracy on top.

I would think that this would include such things as welfare; certainly, it would include education. And then with this, under this federalism, review again what legitimately and honestly belongs at the Federal level and at the local level in the system of taxes.

Back when I was growing up, the governments of the United States, between them, only took a dime out of every dollar earned. Only a third of that or less went to the Federal Government; two-thirds to local and State government. Today, they are taking more than 40 cents out of every dollar, and two-thirds of that goes to the Federal Government. It's just reversed; the other way around.

And have this fairness in revenues so that wherever possible, you can have the responsibility for raising the money and the responsibility for performing the function in the hands of the same government.

Q. Thank you, Mr. President.

Note: The interview began at 5 p.m. in the Oval Office at the White House. The transcript of the interview was released by the Office of the Press Secretary on November 22.

The President was interviewed by five reporters from the Gannett News Service, the National Journal, the New York Times, the Wall Street Journal, and the Washington Post.

Remarks Following a "Young Artists in Performance at the White House" Concert
November 22, 1981

I hope you've enjoyed the program as much as we have here.

This concert and those that will follow bring the accomplished talents of master performers together with artists of the new generation waiting to be recognized. Together, they represent the best of mind and spirit that America has to offer. They add to our tradition of creativity and freedom.

The grand designs of soldiers and statesmen are often forgotten by history. More often than not, people are remembered for the quality of their ideas and the beauty of their art. We in this country have a cultural record to be proud of. Through private and voluntary contributions, the American people maintain more orchestras, more opera, more ballet, more nonprofit theater, more libraries and other cultural activities than all the rest of the world put together.

And, as Nancy said earlier, art is no stranger to our national house. Many who lived here have filled it with civilizing beauty. John Fitzgerald Kennedy, who died on this day 18 years ago, certainly did so. A month before his death, President Kennedy spoke of his vision for American culture. He said, "I look forward to an America which will not be afraid of grace and beauty . . . which commands respect not only for its strength but for its civilization as well."

As the White House Young Artist series demonstrates, the arts in America are rich, diverse, and growing—a vital creative expression of our free society. American artists, like the ones we have seen tonight, guarantee that we will indeed be remembered for our civilization as well as for our strength.

Note: The President spoke at 5:59 p.m. in the East Room at the White House. The concert, featuring pianist Rudolph Serkin and *violinist Ida Levin, and the President's remarks were filmed for later broadcast on the Public Broadcasting Service.*

Exchange With Reporters on the Continuing Resolution for Fiscal Year 1982 Appropriations
November 22, 1981

Q. Mr. President, are you going to come and talk to us?

Q. Are you going to tell us about the veto?

Q. Can you come just a little closer?

Q. Are you going to veto?

The President. Well, I'm hoping that I won't have to. I have suggested that perhaps we have an extension of the present continuing resolution, so that they can all go home for their planned holidays and we'll take this up when they come back. But I just did not feel that I could pass what has finally been decided, which was several billion dollars more than we had suggested for the budget.

Q. What do you particularly—what has made you particularly unhappy? Is there any area where you think they should have kept the cuts?

The President. Well, it's just that it is several billion dollars. I haven't had too much of an opportunity in the late-night rush there to know what has been done within the overall framework of moving funds here and there, which I would also be bound by in this continuing resolution.

Q. Aren't you concerned about the country running out of money? Congress has sent you the bill that they think they compromised on, and you indicated they won't sign it. Won't that have a very harmful effect?

The President. I think it'd have a more harmful effect on the country if the country got the idea that we're going to continue going down the road of lavish deficit spending. Now, I know we can't solve that all in one year; that's been made very plain. But I think the people have made it very clear that they want control of the budget; they want us to get back on to the road of fiscal

sanity. And I think that's far more important than——

Q. Mr. President?

The President. May I just say that there are many necessary services which are not bound by that. Social security checks go out; health, national security—those things go on.

Q. Did they indicate that they would extend the present budget during the holidays?

The President. Well, that's what's now under consideration up there.

Q. How long have you asked in terms of the extension, sir?

The President. Oh, I would think just until we get past the holidays.

Q. Are you going to be on the phone this afternoon now working the Hill, trying to get that through?

The President. What's that?

Q. What are you going to do this afternoon to try and urge them to pass it? Are you going to be making phone calls to Congressmen about this?

The President. No, I don't believe there'd be any purpose in that. I've spoken to the leadership on both sides, and I think——

Q. Mr. President, may I ask a question on the visit of the King of Sweden? How do you think we Swedes treated the submarine case?

The President. Well, obviously, with your King I did not discuss that.

Q. No, but in general, what do you think of us?

The President. I thought you did very well.

Q. Mr. President, will you be going to California this evening?

The President. That depends. Obviously, if there is no choice but to veto and then the country is left in the situation of coming to a halt at the end of this, no, I would not go. And they wouldn't go home, either.

Deputy Press Secretary Speakes. Thank you very much.

Q. What do you think of this whole budget process? Does it frustrate you the way this government runs?

The President. Yes. The fact that this country has gone on now for a year without a budget and is 2 months into the second year without a budget—that is no way to run a railroad. And it's even less of a way to run a country.

The beginning of the fiscal year you should have a budget in place in which you know what the cost for each department is going to be. This continuing resolution is a process whereby the Congress can add to the spending, and the only choice left to a President is to literally close down the government by veto, unlike vetoing a budget figure. And it's time for us to get legitimate appropriations bills passed and to have a budget. We haven't had one. There wasn't one when I came here, and they're continuing down the same path.

Q. How long did you say you asked for an extension? Would it be till January sometime?

The President. Well, I left it a little bit—no, I—some outside have suggested going beyond January, but I suggested 15 to 20 days.

Q. Speaker of the House John McCormack will have passed away a year today, and today is the day that Jack Kennedy was assassinated. Do you have any comment at all about these great people—just like they are great, they were great?

The President. Yes, I think that this country will be marked for a long time by the tragedy of John F. Kennedy's assassination.

Q. Mr. President.

The President. Oh, I've got to go now.

Q. Thank you, Mr. President.

Note: The exchange began at 2:20 p.m. at the South Portico of the White House following the departure of King Carl Gustaf XVI and Queen Silvia of Sweden, who had earlier visited the President and Mrs. Reagan in the Residence.

Remarks to Reporters Announcing the Veto of the Continuing Resolution for Fiscal Year 1982 Appropriations
November 23, 1981

The President. Good morning, and I do mean morning. [*Laughter*] It's funny how much scanter the audience is this early in the morning.

Well, I just wanted to tell you I am returning to the Congress without my signature House Joint Resolution 357, the continuing resolution providing appropriations for fiscal year 1982.

This resolution presented me with a difficult choice: either to sign a budget-busting appropriations bill that would finance the entire government at levels well above my recommendations—and thus set back our efforts to halt the excessive Government spending that has fueled inflation and high interest rates, and destroyed investments for new jobs—or to hold the line on spend-

ing with a veto but risk interruption of government activities and services.

I have chosen the latter. The failure to provide a reasonable resolution means that some citizens may be inconvenienced and that there is a possibility of some temporary hardship. Nevertheless a far greater threat to all Americans is the sustained hardship they will suffer by continuing the past budget-busting policies of big spending and big deficits.

When reports came to us in September that spending and the deficit for fiscal year 1982 were rising, we took action to stem the tide.

On September 24th I asked for a reduction of 12 percent in the appropriations for nearly all nondefense discretionary programs and a modest reduction in our planned program to strengthen the national defense. The 12-percent cut would have saved $8½ billion—a significant contribution to reducing the deficit, but a modest sum in a budget which will total more than $700 billion.

By refusing to make even this small saving to protect the American people against overspending, the Congress has paved the way for higher interest rates and inflation, and a continued loss of investment, jobs, and economic growth. At the same time, the continuing resolution fails to provide sufficient security assistance to allow America to meet its obligations.

The practice of loading the budget with unnecessary spending and then waiting until after the eleventh hour to pass a continuing resolution, on the assumption that it was safe from a Presidential veto, has gone on much too long. It's one of the principal reasons why the growth of government spending is still not under control.

For much of the past fiscal year, most of the domestic budget was funded in this manner—through a continuing resolution, without regular appropriations bills subject to Presidential approval or disapproval. These so-called stopgap resolutions are actually budgetbusters that can last for an entire year and create the kind of economic mess we inherited last year.

A few days ago I offered to meet the Congress halfway. But the continuing resolution the Congress has now passed provides less than one-quarter of the savings that I requested. This represents neither fair compromise nor responsible budget policy.

In the hours ahead the Congress has the opportunity to reconsider, and I urgently request that it do so. In the meantime we are making every effort to avoid unnecessary dislocations and personal hardship.

I can give assurance that social security and most other benefit checks will be paid on schedule. The national security will be protected. Government activities essential to the protection of life and property, such as the treatment of patients in veterans hospitals, air traffic control, and the function of the Nation's banks, will also continue. But in order to prevent unnecessary inconve-

nience and hardship as Thanksgiving approaches, I must urge the Congress to act promptly and responsibly.

Now, that's the end of the veto message. But I can't take any of your questions, because I have the Cabinet waiting for me over there so that we can begin discussions.

Q. What do you want Congress to do now, Mr. President? What do you think the best thing to do in the next few days?

The President. They can do one of two things: They could continue—and then this is all I can take—they could continue a brief continuing resolution until after the holidays—continuing the present continuing resolution—extension is what I should say—of that and then come back and take this up and arrive at a settlement. Or they could come in and pass what I said in the first place, that I would split the difference with them between our request for help and their budget figure, instead of doing what they did.

Q. You won't take less than that, is that true? You won't take less than that? You won't reconsider?

The President. I don't think the people should take less than that.

Q. You don't think this is theatrics?

The President. What?

Q. You've been accused of putting on a stage show here by Wright,[1] that it's theatrics.

The President. No, I just think that it is time that we recognize we have been—we're into the second year without a budget with the government running on continuing resolutions, which heretofore a President has felt—and it's very difficult for me to see how you could veto that with all the ramifications. And now here we go again. And I think it's time someplace along the line that we've got to say let's quit this and do what 50 States manage to do on time every year, and that is have a budget.

Q. So, it's Congress fault, sir?

The President. I'm not going to get challenged by a statement like that. That would be writing a lead for you, Sam [Sam Don-

---

[1] *House of Representatives Majority Leader Jim Wright.*

aldson, ABC News], and I'm not going to do that.

Note: The President spoke at 8:03 a.m. in

the Briefing Room at the White House. His remarks were broadcast live on radio and television.

Message to the House of Representatives Returning Without Approval the Continuing Resolution for Fiscal Year 1982 Appropriations
November 23, 1981

To the House of Representatives:

I am returning to the Congress without my signature H.J. Res. 357, the Continuing Resolution providing appropriations for Fiscal Year 1982.

This Resolution presented me with a difficult choice:

—Either to sign a budget-busting appropriations bill that would finance the entire Government at levels well above my recommendations, and thus set back our efforts to halt the excessive Government spending that has fueled inflation and high interest rates, and destroyed investments for new jobs;

—Or, to hold the line on spending with a veto, but risk interruption of Government activities and services.

I have chosen the latter. The failure to provide a reasonable Resolution means that some citizens may be inconvenienced and that there is a possibility of some temporary hardship. Nevertheless, a far greater threat to all Americans is the sustained hardship they will suffer by continuing the past budget-busting policies of big spending and big deficits.

When reports came to us in September that spending and the deficit for Fiscal Year 1982 were rising, we took action to stem the tide.

On September 24, I asked for a reduction of 12 percent in the appropriations for nearly all non-defense descretionary programs and a modest reduction in our planned program to strengthen the national defense. The 12 percent cut would have saved $8.5 billion—a significant contribution to reducing the deficit, but a modest

sum in a budget which will total more than $700 billion.

By refusing to make even this small saving to protect the American people against over-spending, the Congress has paved the way for higher interest rates and inflation, and a continued loss of investment, jobs and economic growth. At the same time, the Continuing Resolution fails to provide sufficient security assistance to allow America to meet its obligations.

The practice of loading the budget with unnecessary spending—and then waiting until after the eleventh hour to pass a Continuing Resolution on the assumption that it was safe from a Presidential veto—has gone on much too long. It is one of the principal reasons why the growth of Government spending is still not under control.

For much of the past fiscal year, most of the domestic budget was funded in this manner—through a Continuing Resolution, without regular appropriations bills subject to Presidential approval or disapproval. These so-called stop-gap resolutions are actually budget-busters that can last for an entire year and create the kind of economic mess we inherited last year.

A few days ago I offered to meet the Congress half-way. But the Continuing Resolution the Congress has now passed provides less than one quarter of the savings I requested. This represents neither fair compromise nor responsible budget policy.

In the hours ahead the Congress has the opportunity to reconsider, and I urgently request that it do so. In the meantime, we are making every effort to avoid unnecessary dislocations and personal hardship. I can give asssurance that:

—Social Security and most other benefit checks will be paid on schedule.

—The national security will be protected.

—Government activities essential to the protection of life and property, such as the treatment of patients in veterans hospitals, air traffic control and the functioning of the Nation's banks, will also continue.

But in order to prevent unnecessary inconvenience and hardship as Thanksgiving approaches, I must urge the Congress to act promptly and responsibly.

RONALD REAGAN

The White House,
November 23, 1981.

Note: The House of Representatives reconsidered H.J. Res. 357 on November 23, and the legislation was referred to the House Committee on Appropriations.

Exchange With Reporters on the Extension of the Continuing Resolution for Fiscal Year 1982 Appropriations
November 23, 1981

Q. Mr. President, was this a manufactured crisis to make the point you wanted to make?

The President. Not at all. I could not sign the bill as it came down last night, yesterday, and I so informed them that there would be a veto message.

Q. And yet you signed the continuing legislation now?

The President. And I asked for an extension, and of course, we now must come back and do the work all over again in the Congress on a bill that can be signed. But I'm glad for this extension so that no one's holidays were disrupted.

Q. What's going to happen after Thanksgiving?

The President. Well, we will come back and start to negotiate a bill that I can sign.

Q. Did you just sign it right now?

Q. Do you still have confidence in Richard Allen [*Assistant to the President for National Security Affairs*]?

The President. I have just signed this extension just now, yes.

Q. Have you seen the Brezhnev proposals on pulling out missiles out of Europe?

The President. What?

Q. The Brezhnev proposal to pull out hundreds of missiles.

The President. I haven't heard any word of that.

Q. Did you have fears that you might have to carry out the trash yourself?

The President. Carry out what?

Q. Did you have any fears that you might have had to carry out the garbage yourself? [*Laughter*]

The President. No, no. Happy Thanksgiving.

Mrs. Reagan. Happy Thanksgiving.

Note: The exchange began at 6:43 p.m. at the South Portico of the White House as the President and Mrs. Reagan were leaving for a visit to their ranch near Santa Barbara, Calif., for the Thanksgiving holiday.

Remarks by Telephone to the Republican Governors Conference in New Orleans, Louisiana
November 23, 1981

The President. Hello.

Governor Dalton. Mr. President, this is John Dalton. How are you tonight?

The President. John, I'm just fine, and sorry we're late. We're up here in Air Force One, and we've been having a time getting through to you. And, Dave Treen, our host there, and all of you, I've been looking forward to saying hello to all of you at the Republican Governors Conference, friends and former colleagues.

I would have called, not only just being late now, but, earlier, but I had a little problem there. I'm probably the first President to reach a Governors conference by direct long-distance dialing. All the White House telephone operators were furloughed today because of the veto.

You know, I thought I was going to turn out earlier today to be the first President to have to carry out the trash himself and mow the South Lawn. At noon, Washington was quite a ghost town. The last time I remember that much peace and quiet was when I was doing a "Death Valley Days" segment in Death Valley.

But, listen, I want to thank all of you for the resolution you adopted today in support of my veto and the support that you've given me all this time on the economic program. It was very heartwarming for me to find this out.

Last night, when I informed them that I would veto what they had passed, I suggested that after the veto an extension of the present continuing resolution, just for 20 days until December 15th, when we could come back from the Thanksgiving holidays and really settle this issue.

I don't know whether you're aware of this or not, or have heard the news, but this morning the House met, and then at noon the Senate convened, and before we left, the House had a solid victory for this 20-day extension. The House leadership had tried to get an extension all the way into the middle of February, which would have come after we'd even tried to get a 1983 budget, let alone find a solution to the 1982 budget.

And then, well, all the Republicans in the House stuck together and were aided by 43 Democrats, and they passed it. It went over to the Senate, where it passed 88 to 1. I signed it and, 10 minutes later, was on the plane heading for my own Thanksgiving.

This was my first veto, and as I mentioned in my statement this morning, the failure of the Congress to agree to a reasonable compromise, I felt, had left me no choice. The only alternative would have been to cave in to the big spenders.

I think that Congress has fallen into a bad habit when, if you stop to think that we didn't have a budget all the way through 1981 and now we're 2 months into 1982 and we still don't have a budget—they just wait until the 11th hour to force through unnecessary spending. It's a kind of legislative game of chicken because for a Governor to veto—a President to veto—see, I'm getting right back in the swing of things, I still think I'm a Governor—but it is a game of chicken, and someone just had to bring it to a halt.

There's no reason on Earth why the National Legislature can't act with the same responsibility as its counterparts at the State level. You've all had to make hard calls. It's a part of the job. And as Republicans, I know you share my commitment to making government at all levels less wasteful and more responsive to the American people.

Your meeting there in New Orleans couldn't have come at a more important time. In the year ahead, 36 States will hold gubernatorial elections, including 16 States with Republican incumbents up for reelection. A lot is at stake. And I hope that I can be of help to you and will be in every way I can.

Right now, of course, I think that means standing firm against those people, the sharpest critics, the ones who tried to pass this lengthy resolution today who really are the ones who took us down the path that has led to the trillion-dollar deficit over these last few decades. And they've offered nothing except a repeat of going down that same road. Well, I think it's time to choose a different road and to bring spending relief and tax relief for our overburdened citizens.

I know that I've talked to so many of you about federalism and my belief that we've drifted away from that concept. My dream is that we can return more authority, more autonomy and responsibility to you at the State level and, at the same time, turn back to you tax sources that have been preempted by the Federal Government and which they should no more have than the responsibilities that they have also preempted.

I think the people voted for a change in 1980. I think they'll be voting for much the same thing if we stay with this plan, and that's just what we're going to do in the congressional and State elections across the country in November of '82.

So, please believe that I'm not going to give up the fight for the block grants, for getting to you more flexibility in spending the money that comes from the national level. And we'll do this while we work and continue to work to get to that point that we can turn actual tax sources over to you.

Governor Dalton. Mr. President, we appreciate your calling. We've got 21 Republican Governors here, and we read a unanimous resolution there this morning. And Governor Dave Treen of Louisiana is here to speak to you also.

The President. Well, all right. And I appreciate that resolution also.

Governor Treen. Mr. President, there are several hundred people here, members of the Republican Governors Association Club, hosts, supporters of you, and supporters of the Republican Governors that I think at this point would like to stand up and give you a standing ovation for standing tough on an issue of vital importance to our country. [*Applause*]

Mr. President, I hope that you can hear that.

The President. I heard that——

Governor Treen. It is from the heart of these people.

The President. ——and, believe me, I think, from the way it sounded, if I'd have put down the phone, I could have heard it up here in the plane without the phone. Thank you all very much.

Governor Treen. Thank you, Mr. President, and Godspeed and have a good rest in California.

The President. Okay, David. I hope to see you all soon.

Governor Treen. We look forward to having you here, sir. Thank you. Good night.

The President. Okay. Good night, and——

Governor Treen. And good night to Mrs. Reagan.

The President. ——God bless all of you.

Governor Treen. Thank you, sir.

Governor Dalton. Good night. Mr. President.

Note: The President spoke at approximately 8:30 p.m. on board Air Force One, while en route to Santa Barbara, Calif.

Governor John Dalton of Virginia is chairman of the conference.

Statement on the Procurement of Additional Stocks of Bauxite for the National Defense Stockpile
November 24, 1981

I am today directing the Federal Emergency Management Agency (FEMA) to procure approximately 1.6 million tons of Jamaican-type, metal grade bauxite for the National Defense Stockpile during the current fiscal year.

Our nation's potential vulnerability to raw material supply disruptions during a period of emergency mobilization is well known. In answer to this, last March we began the first major purchase program for the Defense Stockpile in over 20 years with the expectation of implementing a long-term, fiscally responsible program to redress stockpile deficiencies.

This bauxite acquisition program represents another necessary step. Bauxite is a raw material used to produce aluminum, a major element in almost all modern military weapons systems such as the B–1 bomber and F–18 aircraft. It is a critical input to industries that are essential to support a mobilization effort. During World War II a substantial portion of our bauxite ore-carrying ships was sunk in the South Atlantic by enemy submarines, thus pointing up the need for wartime resources of bauxite within our nation's boundaries. Currently the stockpile is critically deficient in Jamaican-type bauxite, with an inventory 12 million tons below requirements.

This large and cost-effective acquisition program will be accomplished through a combination of direct cash purchase and exchange with excess materials from our stockpile by General Services Administration, and barter, using agricultural commodities with the Department of Agriculture. Agricultural barter to require needed raw materials will thus be used for the first time in almost 15 years. This barter arrangement follows from the congressional mandate contained in section 6 of the Stockpiling Act of 1979.

While improving our own defense posture, this program will contribute to Prime Minister Seaga's strategy for Jamaica to rely to the maximum extent possible on production and exports to fuel its economic recovery. The stability and economic strength of Jamaica are important to our national security interests in the Caribbean.

Message to the Senate Transmitting the Radio Regulations (Geneva, 1979)
November 24, 1981

To the Senate of the United States:

With a view to receiving the advice and consent of the Senate to ratification, I transmit herewith the Radio Regulations (Geneva, 1979) and a final Protocol signed on behalf of the United States at Geneva on December 6, 1979, with several reservations.

I transmit also, for the information of the Senate, the report of the Department of State with respect to the 1979 Radio Regulations.

The 1979 Regulations constitute a revision of, and a complete replacement for, the Radio Regulations (Geneva, 1959), as amended by six Partial Revisions, to which the United States is a party. The primary purpose of the present revisions is to update the existing Regulations to take into account technical advances and the rapid development of certain services and to harmonize the decisions taken at specialized radio conferences since 1959. The new Reg-

ulations, with the few exceptions noted below, are consistent with the proposals of and positions taken by the United States at the 1979 World Administrative Radio Conference.

At the time of signature, the United States Delegation submitted reservations to several of the decisions included in the Regulations. It was felt in these few cases, that the decisions could adversely affect an important national interest. In addition, the Administration considers it necessary to maintain in force the reservation of the United States associated with a frequency allotment plan included in the Partial Revision adopted by the 1974 World Maritime Administrative Radio Conference. The specific reservations, with reasons, are given in the report of the Department of State.

The 1979 Radio Regulations will enter into force on January 1, 1982 for Governments which, by that date, have notified the Secretary General of the International

Telecommunication Union of their approval thereof. Subject to the reservations mentioned above, I believe the United States should be a party to the Regulations from the outset, and it is my hope that the Senate will take early action on this matter

and give its advice and consent to ratification.

RONALD REAGAN

The White House,
November 24, 1981.

Nomination of William Robert Casey, Jr., To Be United States Ambassador to Niger
November 24, 1981

The President today announced his intention to nominate William Robert Casey, Jr., of Colorado, to be Ambassador to the Republic of Niger. He would succeed James Keough Bishop.

Mr. Casey was a systems analyst with the Kennecott Cooper Corp. in Salt Lake City, Utah, in 1969–71. He was a mining engineer with the Hudson Bay Mining and Smelting Co. in Flin Flon, Manitoba, Canada, in 1971–72 and a project engineer with Fluor Utah, Inc., in San Mateo, Calif., in 1973–74. He was chief field engineer with Arthur G. McKee in Salt Lake City, Utah, in 1973–74, and was senior mining

engineer with Morrison-Knudson Co. in Boise, Idaho, in 1974–75 and with Dravo in Denver, Colo., in 1975–77. In 1977–79 he was project manager with CONOCO in Denver, Colo., and Paris, France. Since 1979 he has been manager of Rocky Mountain Energy Co. in Broomfield, Colo.

Mr. Casey graduated from Colorado School of Mines (B.E., 1969) and is a member of the American Institute of Mining Engineers and the Colorado Mining Association. He is married, has four children, and resides in Longmont, Colo. He was born December 15, 1944, in Denver, Colo.

Announcement of the United States Trade and Investment Mission to Africa
November 25, 1981

The President today announced that Secretary of Commerce Malcolm Baldrige and Secretary of Agriculture John R. Block will lead a U.S. trade and investment mission to Africa January 8–22, 1982, in support of the administration's commitment to advance U.S. economic relations with developing countries.

The mission will include the chief executive officers of 30 U.S. firms interested in doing business in Africa. Other government members of the mission will be Lionel H. Olmer, Under Secretary of Commerce for International Trade; Robert Hormats, Assistant Secretary of State; William H. Draper

III, President and Chairman of the U.S. Export-Import Bank; Craig A. Nalen, President and Chief Executive Officer of the Overseas Private Investment Corporation; and Elise duPont, Assistant Administrator, Bureau of Private Enterprise, Agency for International Development.

The mission will visit Cameroon, Ivory Coast, Nigeria, and Morocco. Participants will meet with government officials and business executives in the four countries.

United States exports to Africa now account for 4 percent of total U.S. exports, and U.S. investment in Africa is 3.2 percent of total U.S. foreign investment.

Appointment of Five Members of the National Advisory Committee on Oceans and Atmosphere, and Designation of Chairman and Vice Chairman
November 25, 1981

The President today announced his intention to appoint the following individuals to be members of the National Advisory Committee on Oceans and Atmosphere. The President also announced that he intends to designate Mr. Knauss as Chairman and Mr. Singer as Vice Chairman.

Fitzgerald Bemiss is president of Fitzgerald & Co. and vice president of Golden Crescent Petroleum, Inc., in Richmond, Va. He has served as a consultant to the Department of Commerce (extended fisheries jurisdiction) in 1976–77 and to the Department of Defense (international security affairs) in 1973. He was on the board of directors of the James River Corp. of Virginia. He served in the Virginia House of Delegates in 1955–59 and the Virginia Senate in 1960–67. He attended the University of Virginia. Mr. Bemiss is married, has two children, and resides in Richmond, Va. He was born October 2, 1922, in Richmond. He would succeed Evelyn F. Murphy.

Carl Franklin Brady, Sr., is president, ERA Helicopters, Inc., in Anchorage, Alaska. He operated the first commercial helicopter in Alaska in 1948. He has served as president of the Helicopter Association of America and is past president of the Greater Anchorage Chamber of Commerce. He served in the Army Air Corps during World War II and the Alaska House of Representatives and State Senate. Mr. Brady is married, has three children, and resides in Anchorage, Alaska. He was born October 29, 1919, in Chelsea, Okla. He would succeed Charles H. Warren.

John A. Knauss is provost for marine affairs at the University of Rhode Island, Kingston, R.I. He was appointed a member of the National Advisory Committee on Oceans and Atmosphere in 1977, was appointed Vice President in 1979, and is currently serving as Acting Chairman. He was a member of the Presidential Commission on Marine Sciences Engineering and Resources in 1967–68. Dr. Knauss organized the first National Sea Grant Conference in 1965 and worked on passage of the sea grant legislation in 1966. Since 1962 he has been dean of Graduate School of Oceanography, University of Rhode Island. He graduated from MIT (B.S.); University of Michigan (M.S.) and University of California (Ph. D.). He is married, has two children, and resides in Saunderstown, R.I. He was born September 1, 1925, in Detroit, Mich.

Vernon E. Scheid has been professor of mineral economics in the department of mining engineering at the Mackay School of Mines, University of Nevada, since 1972. For more than 20 years (1951–72), Dr. Scheid was dean of the Mackay School of Mines. He was chairman and director of the Nevada Oil and Gas Conservation Commission, director of the Nevada Mining Analytical Laboratory, and director of the Nevada Bureau of Mines and Geology. He graduated from the Johns Hopkins University and the University of Idaho. He is married, has two children, and resides in Reno, Nev. He was born September 5, 1906, in Baltimore, Md. He would succeed John Arthur Biggs.

S. Fred Singer is professor, department of environmental sciences, University of Virginia, a position he has held since 1971. He was Deputy Assistant Administrator, Environmental Protection Agency, in 1970–71; Deputy Assistant Secretary for Scientific Programs, Department of the Interior, in 1967–70; professor of atmospheric science and dean, School of Environmental and Planetary Sciences, University of Miami, in 1964–67; Director, National Weather Satellite Center, U.S. Weather Bureau, in 1962–64; and associate professor and professor, physics department, University of Maryland, in 1963–64. He graduated from Ohio State University and Princeton University. Dr. Singer is married, has three children, and resides in Alexandria, Va. He was born September 27, 1924, in Vienna, Austria. He would succeed Louis J. Battan.

Appointment of Two Members of the Board for International Food and Agricultural Development
November 25, 1981

The President today announced his intention to appoint the following individuals to be members of the Board for International Food and Agricultural Development, for a term of 3 years.

Daryl Arnold is president of the Western Growers Association, which represents nearly 60 percent of the fresh vegetable, melon, and potato shipments in the United States. He farmed in west Los Angeles, Calif., in 1946–51. He later moved his farming operation to Ventura County and formed Cee Dee Ranch Co. In 1960 he incorporated Ocean View Farms, a packing and shipping company. He merged Ocean View Farms with Freshpict Foods, Inc., a wholly owned subsidiary of the Purex Corp., in 1969. He attended the University of Southern California and served in the United States Navy. He is married, has three children, and resides in Corona del Mar, Calif. He was born November 12, 1924, in Los Angeles. Mr. Arnold would succeed Johnnie W. Prothro.

Ernest T. Marshall is an independent businessman and vice president of Montgomery Associates, merger and executive search consultants. He established the first full-time national office of the National Agri-Marketing Association in 1974 and has served as executive director. Mr. Marshall was with the Biddle Co. (1967–74); Potts Woodbury Advertising, Inc. (1957–67); and Continental Oil Co. (1950–57). He graduated from Iowa State University (B.S.) and Boston University (M.S.). He is married, has six children, and resides in Mission Hills, Kans. He was born August 5, 1925, in Des Moines, Iowa. Mr. Marshall would succeed David Garst.

Statement on Food Assistance for Poland
November 25, 1981

I have authorized a $30 million food grant to the people of Poland. The food, consisting of flour, grain products, milk, and oil, will be donated by the United States through Public Law 480 (Title II), the "Food for Peace Program," to food programs managed by CARE and the Catholic Relief Services over the next 6 months. The groups within Poland to be primarily assisted by this food aid are those that have been affected by the severe shortage of staple goods. These groups include preschool children, pregnant women, the elderly, the hospitalized, and orphans.

This food grant reflects the humanitarian concern of this Nation for the well-being of the people of Poland. It demonstrates U.S. recognition of longstanding ties and friendship between the American and Polish people and the administration's commitment to the peaceful resolution of the current Polish situation.

Nomination of Clarence E. Hodges To Be Chief of the Children's Bureau
November 27, 1981

The President today announced his intention to nominate Clarence E. Hodges to be Chief of the Children's Bureau, Department of Health and Human Services. He would succeed John A. Calhoun III.

Mr. Hodges is Assistant Director, Community Services Administration, and Director of Community Action. He was staff assistant to Senator Richard G. Lugar (R-Ind.) in 1977–81; employed with the Indianapolis Housing Authority in 1976–77; director, Department of Human Resources, and assistant to the mayor in 1973–76; Executive Director, Concentrated Employment Program, U.S. Department of Labor, St. Louis, Mo., in 1967–73; director of social services, Kinloch School District, St. Louis County, Mo., in 1966–67; and casework supervisor, Division of Welfare, State of Missouri, in 1962–66.

Mr. Hodges was a candidate for the United States House of Representatives from the 11th District of Indiana in 1980. He graduated from Upper Iowa University (B.A.) and Occidental College (M.A.). He is married, has four children, and resides in Silver Spring, Md. He was born October 1, 1939, in Princeton, N.C.

Nomination of James N. Broder To Be a Member of the Federal Council on the Aging
November 27, 1981

The President today announced his intention to nominate James N. Broder to be a member of the Federal Council on the Aging for a term expiring June 5, 1983. He would succeed Fernando M. Torres-Gil.

Since 1979 Mr. Broder has been senior resident partner with the law firm Thaxter, Lipez, Stevens, Broder & Micoleau in Washington, D.C. Previously he was partner in the law firm of Millman, Broder & Curtis in 1975–79; field director, Steele for Governor committee, Berlin, Conn., in 1974–75; staff director, Republican Task Force on Aging, U.S. House of Representatives, in

1973–74; and served on the legislative staff of Representative Robert H. Steele (R-Conn.) in 1973.

He graduated from the University of Virginia (B.A., 1968) and the Georgetown University Law Center (J.D., 1975). He also attended the Graduate School of Arts and Sciences at the University of Maryland. He is a member of the District of Columbia and Maryland Bar Associations.

Mr. Broder is married, has two children, and resides in Rockville, Md. He was born October 2, 1946.

Appointment of Seven Members of the National Commission for Employment Policy, and Designation of Chairman
November 27, 1981

The President today announced his intention to appoint the following individuals to be members of the National Commission for Employment Policy. The President also announced his intention to designate Kenneth M. Smith as Chairman.

Kenneth M. Smith is president and chief executive officer, International Management and Development Group Ltd., a management consulting firm in Washington, D.C. He is also president and chief executive officer, Jobs for America's Graduates, Inc., a national public service corporation designed to replicate the Delaware comprehensive youth employment program in five other States. Previously he was president and chief executive officer, Jobs for Delaware Graduates, Inc., in 1978–80. Mr.

Smith was special assistant for education to Gov. Pierre S. du Pont IV (R-Del.) in 1977–78; founder, president, and chief executive officer, 70001, Ltd., a national job training program for high school dropouts, in 1976–77; and director of 70001 and director of special projects for Distributive Education Clubs of America in 1973–76. He was staff assistant to Patrick J. Buchanan, Special Assistant to the President, in 1969–71. He graduated from American University (B.S., 1970). He is married, has one child, and resides in Queenstown, Md. He was born April 5, 1949, in Auburn, N.Y. He would succeed George L. Jenkins.

Roberto Cambo is sole owner and president of Rocam Produce Co., Inc., in Miami, Fla. He began the business in 1960 selling fruits and vegetables, effecting deliveries in his own car.

With increased sales he acquired delivery trucks and purchased his first warehouse in 1964. In 1973 he acquired a second warehouse and currently employs 14 people. He is also former president of Loveland Estates, Inc. Mr. Cambo was educated in Cuba and came to the United States in 1960. He is married, has three children, and resides in Key Biscayne, Fla. He was born April 15, 1937, in Cuba. He would succeed Sam Lena.

Michael D. Caver is an associate with the firm Heidrick and Struggles, Inc., an international consulting firm in executive search, located in Chicago, Ill. Previously he was director of personnel and manager of employee relations, Travelnol International, Inc., in Deerfield, Ill. (1977–79), and held various positions with the Procter & Gamble Co. (1965–77). He was manager of personnel administration for Procter & Gamble in Canada in 1973–76 and personnel services manager (international division) in 1976–77. He graduated from Hampden-Sydney College, Virginia (1964) and attended Yale University (1964–65). He is married, has three children, and resides in Deerfield, Ill. He was born April 7, 1942, in Washington, D.C. He would succeed Austin P. Sullivan, Jr.

Jack A. Gertz is public affairs and media relations manager with AT&T (Bell System) in Washington, D.C. He has served with AT&T since 1961. Previously he was National Director of Public Affairs and Press Relations, Federal Aviation Agency, in 1959–61; Washington news bureau chief and national director of public affairs, Mutual Broadcasting System, in 1954–59; and Director of Public Affairs at the State Department in 1951–53. He is a graduate of the United States Naval War College. He is married, has one child, and resides in Potomac, Md. He was born April 10, 1916, in Chugwater, Wyo. He would succeed Pedro R. Garza.

Paul R. Locigno is research director, Ohio Conference of Teamsters. He is also serving as legislative agent of Ohio D.R.I.V.E., the political voice of the Ohio Conference of Teamsters. He

is a member of the Ohio Commission on Aging; Economic Development Group, Ohio House of Representatives, Committee on Business and Economic Development; and chairman, Private Industry Council, Employment and Training Consortium of Cuyahoga and Geauga County. He graduated from Case Western Reserve University, Cleveland, Ohio (B.A., 1976). He is married, has one child, and resides in Windham, Ohio. He was born September 17, 1948, in Cleveland. He would succeed Eli Ginzberg.

Roderick R. Paige is professor of health and physical education, Texas Southern University. Previously he was athletic director, professor of health and physical education, in 1975–80, and head football coach in 1971–75. He served at the University of Cincinnati as assistant football coach and assistant professor of health and physical education in 1969–71. He was head football coach at Jackson State University in 1962–69. He graduated from Jackson State University (B.S., 1955) and Indiana University (M.S., 1964; Ph. D., 1969). He is married, resides in Houston, Tex., and was born June 17, 1933, in Monticello, Miss. He would succeed Leon H. Sullivan.

Kenneth O. Stout is self-employed and involved with real estate investment programs. He was business manager, Alaska Methodist University, in 1975–76; professor of business administration in 1974–75; Chief, J-6 Military Secretariat Organization of the Joint Chiefs of Staff, in 1973–74; Commander, U.S. Army Security Detachment Headquarters, U.S. Army, Alaska, in 1971–73; Commander, Intelligence Detachment, Office of the Chief of Staff for Intelligence, in 1969–70; and Operations Officer, Communications Intelligence, U.S. Army Security Agency, in 1965–67. He graduated from the University of Nebraska (1964) and the University of Alaska (1973). He is married, has two children, and resides in Anchorage, Alaska. He was born October 5, 1929, in Wheatland, Mo. He would succeed Ruth Love.

Remarks by Telephone to the Plenary Session of the Caribbean and Central America Action Conference in Miami, Florida
November 29, 1981

Doctor West, Governor Graham, it's a pleasure to be able to talk to all of you there tonight. It would be a greater pleasure if I could be there with you. I'm most

grateful to Prime Minister Seaga for his invitation, which I couldn't accept. I'd like to express greetings to all of you and to my friend, President Duarte, who is present, and I wish you success in this work that you're doing. With such a group of distinguished and talented business and government officials, I expect the conference could be a turning point in the economic development of a large region.

I share the spirit and the dream and the task that we've all set before us. The enormous importance of the program that we're jointly developing—strengthening cooperation with our neighbors in the Caribbean Basin—this is one of my highest priorities.

We're neighbors. We share not only opportunities for mutual benefits but also each others' troubles. I know that economic success is crucial to resolving problems of political instability, and I know that economic and social progress occur most often and most vigorously in societies that protect individual freedoms and democratic processes.

Each nation's approach to development should reflect its own cultural, political, and economic heritage. But there are common problems; therefore, an opportunity as well as the need for a regional approach.

We seek to formulate a regional approach which is genuinely cooperative. We have consulted closely with both government and private leaders in the region. This has included discussions with Puerto Rico and the Virgin Islands, whose development needs must be taken into account in any comprehensive set of measures. And it's on this basis that we're developing a program. Because we seek an innovative program, we've already begun discussions with our Congress, where approval for some of the contemplated actions will rest.

Let me just touch, if I can for a moment, on the principles underlying the program. Action must be cooperative. External sup-port will be very important, but internal efforts are indispensable. The people of the Caribbean Basin themselves must decide what needs to be done and how to do it.

Second, governments and the private sector complement each other. Governments set the framework within which economic activities can flourish, but governments can't do it alone. The private sector has formidable powers of creativity and risk-taking, and it requires and deserves more support than we've given it over the past several years.

Third, our program will integrate trade, investment, and financial assistance to spur self-sustaining growth. In this sense, the program is tailored to the modern period and shouldn't be confused with more simplistic approaches that were pursued in earlier periods.

Alone, each of these tools makes an important contribution, and when each supports the others in a well-focused program, the effects are going to be multiplied. From such a program, the region will be able to secure relief for its most pressing problems, but will enjoy larger benefits from the cumulative impact of the measures.

I'm delighted that former Senator Bill Brock, and now our United States Trade Representative, is there with you and, I know, will give a more detailed outline of what it is we're talking about in this plan for the Caribbean and for Central America.

Again, I appreciate more than I can say, this opportunity to speak to you, and regret, equally, that I couldn't be there in person with you.

God bless you all.

Note: The President spoke to the Conference participants from his ranch near Santa Barbara, Calif., at approximately 6:05 p.m.

Remarks at an Ohio State Republican Fundraising Reception in Cincinnati
November 30, 1981

Thank you all very much. It's always a pleasure to be here in Ohio and have a chance to acknowledge the great help that your Governor has been to me over the years. It seems now a long time back, but I turned to him for counsel and advice when I was a brand new Governor. We didn't know each other. We met, and I had his unstinting and very effective support then, and counsel and advice, and I had it last year in the election, and I'm having that same kind of support now for our economic program.

I'm also delighted as I see—and I know that some of your Congressmen are here: Del Latta, Bob McEwen, Clarence "Bud" Brown, Ed Weber, Clarence Miller, Ralph Regula, John Ashbrook, and Willis Gradison. And the only thing I want to ask of them is: Are you sure the other fellows went home? [*Laughter*] I'd hate to leave them back there without us.

These are exciting times. The *Columbia* has been orbiting the Earth, Senator Glenn is in orbit around New Hampshire—[*laughter*]—and the Federal budget is off somewhere in the wild blue yonder. You know, we're completing 14 months without a budget. Your State isn't run that way, and we didn't run California that way. In fact, I don't believe I can remember any State ever practicing the fiscal irresponsibility that has characterized the majority party leadership in Washington over these past three or four decades.

In the debate over the continuing resolution the weekend before Thanksgiving, some of those who must share responsibility for our economic situation protested that I was making a theatric gesture over a mere $1 or $2 billion. Well, in the first place, they must be practitioners of the new math. The figure in dispute was nearer $10 billion over and above the budget that I'd asked for in September.

But aside from that, how does one use the word "mere" in talking about a billion or $2 billion? A few years ago, one of that same spendthrift fraternity, trying to explain the increase in government spending, said in all seriousness, "Well, you know, a billion here and a billion there; it adds up." [*Laughter*] Well, he was right. Their billion here and a billion there have added up to a national debt of more than $1 trillion. Now, that's an unimaginable figure. Just think, if we started paying off that debt at $1 billion a year, it would take us a thousand years to lift the mortgage.

Speaker O'Neill says that I know less about the budget than any President he's ever known. Well, maybe we're not talking about the same kind of budgets. [*Laughter*] I presided over eight balanced budgets as Governor of California, and he's only seen a balanced budget once in his 27 years in Congress. And I could point out that since I became President, there hasn't been a Federal budget for me to look at. [*Laughter*]

But let me state something that I know about the Federal budgets of the past few decades. Thanks to the tax-and-tax and spend-and-spend policy of our opponents, those budgets are always much bigger at the end of the fiscal year than they were at the beginning, and they were too big at the beginning.

Now they've found an easier way to spend. It's called the continuing resolution. Now, let me explain what such a resolution really is. It's a means whereby spending can go on out of control. The resolution simply says that government can continue at a prescribed spending level while it goes on talking about a budget for 14 months.

Well, in the fiscal year that ended October 1st, the continuing resolutions came in way over the budget figure announced by the previous administration in 1980. And now the same process appears to be starting and is going on for 1982.

Let me give an example of how the spenders can assure themselves of a free hand. Within the total amount passed in the resolution, they can short change, shift funds around, and apply them—well, deny them to necessary things like health care, for example. Then they add that money that should have gone for that purpose to some pet program of their own. They do this knowing that health care will run out of funds before the year end, making a supplemental appropriation necessary, because no one can stand by and allow people who are ill to not have medical treatment. Now, I wonder sometimes if the Speaker thinks I don't know that. [*Laughter*]

The other thing they like about continuing resolutions is that if they're vetoed, all but a few government functions grind to a halt. It is against the law for government to go on without funding. Checks can't be issued, and government employees can't even volunteer to work a day without pay. Now, there, the Speaker was right about the things I don't know. I didn't know that it was considered impossible to veto a continuing resolution, so I vetoed one. [*Laughter*]

Now Nancy and I have flown to California for the holidays, and now we've flown back here, and I'm still waiting for the sky to fall, and it hasn't. You know, if it goes on like this, a fellow might be tempted to try doing some of those other things they say are impossible, like reducing the size of government, eliminating inflation, reducing tax rates, and even maybe having a budget, before we're finished.

Yes, we're in a recession, and its causes go way back beyond January 20th, 1981. Tax policies and inflation reduce the ability of the people to save. This reduced the pool of capital needed by industry to modernize and keep abreast of new production methods. One hundred dollars in a savings account from 1960 to 1980, 20 years, plus compound interest, has after those 20 years a purchasing power of only $83—$100 plus interest combined.

In 1960 the average weekly earnings for a worker with three dependents was $73, after deducting income and social security taxes. By 1970 it had increased to $80. By 1980 it had fallen back to only $74.

When this administration began, interest rates were the highest they'd been since the Civil War—21½ percent. Taxes were taking a higher percent of the workers wage than food, shelter, and clothing all put together. Yes, we've had an increase in the number of unemployed, but there already was great unemployment in the auto industry, in steel, and in construction. While there are more unemployed today, there are also more working. There are 266,000 more people working today in the work force than there were when we took office.

There have been other changes. Inflation is a little more than half of what it was, and interest rates have fallen by more than 4 percent in the last few months. Some banks now are at 15¾ percent, and on the way in here—I didn't have time to write it down—someone just told me outside that the prime rate of the Fed has dropped today and gone down again.

We've already cut the rate of increase in government spending to less than half of what it had been. We said unnecessary regulations must be eliminated. Well, last year the Health and Human Services Department, the old HEW, the regulations filled 316 pages of the *Federal Register*. Now they fill six.

And we've just begun to phase in the biggest single tax cut in history. In 1977, you will remember we were handed the biggest single tax *increase* in history. It hasn't all gone into effect. That legislation passed increases in the social security payroll tax that will go on from now till 1987, the next increase will be in January coming up.

Now many of those responsible for that increase are now the most vocal opponents of our economic program, both the cuts in spending and the reduction in tax rates. With all their opposition to what we proposed doing, they have yet to suggest anything other than a return to their bankrupt policies of higher spending and higher taxes. All they can say is they're against what we're trying to do, but they haven't anything new to offer against those things that have gotten us into the mess we're in.

What we don't need is more spending, and what we don't need are taxes, and what we do need is a lot less of both. Our programs are designed to encourage savings, investment, and productivity. They'll get this economy moving again, growing again, and lift the standard of living for all Americans.

John Kennedy knew this 20 years ago when he proposed a tax cut based on the same principle. He knew an economy stifled by restrictive tax rates can never produce enough revenue to balance the budget, just as it can never produce enough jobs or enough profits. History proved him right. After enactment of the Kennedy tax cut, the rate of increase in employment almost doubled. The rate of growth in gross national product went from a little over 3 percent before the tax cut to 5 percent after the tax cut, and personal savings jumped from 2.3 percent to 8 percent of the American people's earnings. If our tax policies result in an increase of only 2 percentage points in the level of savings, that will mean $40 billion more in the money available for investment and mortgages.

In November of 1980, the American people voted overwhelmingly for change, for a new beginning. Together we've set a new course for freedom and prosperity. I believe that America can and will heal itself as it has so often in our past history.

Ours is a special destiny, both as Republicans and as Americans. Abraham Lincoln once said, "We Americans, the freest people in the world, will determine our own fate. If it is to be greatness, we will have built it," he said. "If it is destruction, then we will have wrought it. As a nation of free men," he said, "we must live through all time or die by suicide." That responsibility is now ours. Let it never be said that ours was the first generation of Americans to falter.

You're gathered here as a kind of headstart on preparing for the 1982 campaign. Well, let me tell you, we need more Republican Governors if we're to realize the great strength built into our Federal system of 50 sovereign States. We need our Republican Congressmen returned to Washington. In the recent battle, they stood together 100 percent in the final vote that brought us more time to work out the budget. We need more like them. We need a majority in the House to match our majority in the Senate. And I could point out, you'll have an opportunity to send a new Senator to increase our narrow majority there.

And if you need encouragement, let me tell you just one thing. There's one Democrat Congressman already that has announced that he will seek reelection as a Republican. And in announcing that, he said he believes in our Republican principles and he believes in our economic program. And he has supported it all the way. Well, I promised him for what he's doing, and I will promise you for what you're doing—just because of what you are—we will not retreat 1 inch in our determination to proceed with our program and to restore fiscal integrity, productivity in the industry of America. We're going to stick with it.

Thank you all very much. And let me just close with one thing. A lot of wonderful things happen, and there are some days when you go home feeling 10 feet tall. And part of it is what I'm hearing from all of you, the people of this country, wonderful letters that are just unbelievable, ranging from a sailor in a submarine that goes to the trouble to write and tell me—he says, "Okay. So we're not the biggest navy in the world, but we're the best." And then the other day I received a letter that I thought was one for all time. It had to be translated from the braille. A GI that had lost his sight in World War II in Germany wrote, in braille, to tell me that if cutting his pension would help get this country back on its feet, he'd like to have me cut his pension. But we're not going to cut his pension. But we're sure going to get this country back on its feet.

Thank you.

Note: The President spoke at 6:25 p.m. in the Presidential Ballroom at the Westin Hotel. He was introduced by Governor James A. Rhodes of Ohio.

Following the reception, the President attended a meeting at the hotel with major Ohio Republican contributors and then returned to the White House.

Remarks at the 1981 White House Conference on Aging
December 1, 1981

Mr. Secretary, distinguished guests here at the head table, you, ladies and gentlemen—and I understand there is another room where others of you are seeing this on closed circuit television. And that's kind of a kick for me, because I've been on the late, late show so long it's good to be on daytime TV. [*Laughter*]

I've been looking forward to this meeting with you for a number of reasons, but probably the best one is my belief that most problems can be solved when people are talking to each other instead of about each other.

Now, you know a speaker usually tries to establish in his own mind some relationship between himself and his audience or, put another way, why he or she is addressing a particular group. Well, I could say it is traditional for the President to address the White House Conference on Aging, but there's in my case a better answer. We're of the same generation. And we have met to counsel together on matters of mutual interest.

You know, when we were much younger, we defined a generation in a rather narrow sense. We perceived it as almost limited to our classmates. And then, as the number of candles on the birthday cakes increased, so did the breadth of our generation. As longtime adults, we now perceive our generation, as we call it, as including all those within several years on either side of our own age. And that is as it should be, for as adults, we've worked together to achieve common goals in our work, in our communities, and in our nation.

Just a few weeks ago at a White House luncheon for the Medal of Freedom recipients, one of those recipients was Eubie Blake. Eubie's one of the last of the great ragtime composers and pianists. We sat there at the luncheon table as contemporaries, because as I looked at him, his songs, his music were very much a part of my life. And yet, in my remarks about him and his accomplishments I mentioned that he was

98 years old, and he interrupted me and said "Ninety-eight and a half." [*Laughter*]

Well now, having established the parameters of our generation, let me say a few words about us. It's right that each generation looks at the preceding one and is critical of its shortcomings. We were when it was our turn, and as a young generation will challenge our mores and customs, will question our values, as we did before them when we were young. But as the years pass, we learn not to cast aside proven values simply because they're old. At least we should learn that if civilization is to continue.

A few years ago, in the rebellious sixties and early seventies, we did see such a discarding of basic truths. It was a time when at least a part of the generation of our sons and daughters declared that no one over 30 could be trusted. One wonders what they think now that they themselves have passed that 30-year mark. [*Laughter*]

In those troubled times when no one was boasting about only living a stone's throw from the campus, I, as Governor, couldn't go on our campuses in California without causing a demonstration. And then one day the student body presidents of our nine university campuses and some of their other student officers asked to have a meeting with me. Well, I was delighted. I said yes, because I was anxious to establish some kind of communication. They arrived, some of them were barefoot, all of them were in T-shirts and jeans. And when we were all seated—maybe I should say slouched—[*laughter*]—their spokesman opened the meeting.

"Governor," he said, "it's impossible for you to understand us, to understand our generation." Well, I tried to establish some base for conversation, and I said, "Well, we know more about being young than we do about being old." And he said, "No, I'm serious. You can't understand your own sons and daughters. You didn't grow up in a world of instant electronic communications, of cybernetics, of men computing in seconds what it once took months and even years, of jet travel, nuclear power, and journeys into space to the Moon."

Well, you know, usually in a situation of that kind you don't think of the right answer until the meeting's over and you're at home, and then it's too late. But he went on in that vein just long enough for the Lord to provide the right words. And when he finished I said, "You're absolutely right. We didn't have those things when we were· growing up. We invented them." And I was right, because almost everything he was talking about had come into being in our adult lifetime.

Yes, our generation has made mistakes and possibly fallen short at times. But we need apologize to no one. Only a few times in history is a single generation called upon to preside over a great period of transition, and our generation, yours and mine, has been one of those rare generations. We have gone literally, in our lifetime, from the horse and buggy to journeys to the Moon. We've known four wars and a great worldwide depression in our lifetime. We have fought harder and paid a higher price for freedom and done more to advance the dignity of man than any people who ever lived.

Having said what I have, maybe you can understand my frustration over the last couple of years—during the campaign and now in this office I hold—to be portrayed as somehow an enemy of my own generation. Most of the attack has been centered around one issue, social security. There's been political demagoguery and outright falsehood, and as a result, many who rely on social security for their livelihood have been needlessly and cruelly frightened. And those who did that frightening either didn't know what they were talking about or they were deliberately lying.

In October of 1980, as a candidate, I pledged that I would try to restore the integrity of social security and to do so without penalty to those dependent on that program. I have kept that pledge and intend to keep it—both parts of it. We will not betray those entitled to social security benefits, and we will—indeed, we must—put social security on a sound financial base.

A recent poll showed that 59 percent of the people were willing to pay a higher tax in order to be sure of social security's continuation. Almost as many, 54 percent, have expressed mistrust and a lack of confidence that the program will be there when their time comes.

Well, let me take up that matter of increased tax. The answer to the problem isn't that simple. We already have an increase. It was passed in 1977, and I don't think very many people are aware that it calls for a series of increases—one in this coming January and several more, automatically, over the next 5 years.

The payroll tax has increased 2,000 percent since 1950, and even with the increases yet to come, the accumulated deficit could still be $111 billion in the next 5 years.

In 1982 the maximum tax will be $2,170.80, matched of course by an equal amount by the employer. For the self-employed, that payment will be $3,029.40. The 1980 top rates are 6.7 percent and 9.35 percent for the self-employed on the first $32,400 of earnings. Now both the rates and the amount of earnings taxed will go up in the several increases that are already scheduled and that I have mentioned.

When the program started in 1936 it was $20 a year—1 percent of $2,000. Thirty years ago there were about 16 workers for each recipient. Now there are only 3.2, and in the next 40 years that's projected to fall to only 2.1.

Now, I'm not pointing out these facts because I want to scare anyone. I agree with what Congressman Claude Pepper has said, that this country is big enough and able enough to provide for those who have served it and who now have come to their time of retirement. But we can't afford— and what we were trying to correct in our original proposal—we can't afford to support, as disabled, people who are not disabled or educate from social security funds young people who come from families of great affluence and wealth. And this we've been doing. I had hoped that our proposal would have been taken as a beginning point for bipartisan solution of the problem. I was led to believe by others that it would. Well, that didn't happen.

Social security can and will be saved. It will require the best efforts of both parties and of both the executive and legislative branches of government. The future is too important—the future of social security for it to be used as a political football.

It's for this reason that I have withdrawn our proposal and have established a bipartisan Task Force on Social Security Reform. The Task Force will consist of 15 members—5 appointed by the President, 5 by the Senate Majority Leader Baker, and 5 by Speaker of the House Tip O'Neill. The mandate of the Task Force is an important one. Time and again in the past, studies of the social security system have been made that pointed out the problems—but nothing further was done. This must not happen again.

The charge of the Task Force will be to work with the Congress and the President, not only to propose realistic, long-term reforms to put social security back on a sound financial footing but also to forge a working, bipartisan consensus so that the necessary reforms will be passed into law.

The business of the Task Force on Social Security Reform is urgent. I will shortly be announcing appointments to it, and I hope that Majority Leader Baker and Speaker O'Neill will act promptly to select the remaining members. And I pledge my fullest cooperation to make the Task Force's mission a success.

We want the elderly needy, like all needy Americans, to know that they have a government and a citizenry that cares about them and will protect them. Their basic human needs must be met with compassion as well as efficiency. This, too, is a goal that I have set for our administration.

It's fashionable just now to talk about the graying of America. And if you go by the numbers, we are indeed a people growing older in years. Today, one American in five, more than 45 million in all, is over 55. By the year 2000, there will be another 10 million of us. But the American people are not just growing older; we're also growing healthier. Our years of full, active life are increasing—thanks to the countless historic breakthroughs our nation has made in science, medicine, technology, economic op-

portunity, and education in this century. And here again our generation can take pride in the contributions we made to bring that about.

Today's young people, many instances, don't even know the names of diseases that plagued mankind when we were young and that have been eliminated by discoveries made again in our adult lifetime. Many of these breakthroughs were made by senior citizens who are still with us and will be for many years to come, enjoying the well-earned fruits of their own labor as researchers, educators, inventors, businessmen, or average men and women whose work in shops, factories, and farms helped make America possible.

Since 1979 [1970][1] the national mortality rate has dropped 2 percent each year. There are already more Americans over 65 than the entire population of Canada. Today's typical 65-year-old will live another 16 years, and our median national age will go up another 3 years in the next decade. I'm already ahead of that, and—[*laughter*]—that's a cause of great distress to a number of people. [*Laughter*]

But make no mistake, this growing older of Americans is an asset. The so-called senior market plays a key role in consumer spending and saving. One-fifth of the population, the over 55's, account for 27 percent of all consumer spending. Internal Revenue Service figures show that almost half, 46 percent of all the reported saving account interest is earned by people over 65 although they are only 11 percent of the population. Senior savers and senior spenders are a vital and positive part of the economy and are playing a positive role in our program for economic recovery. It couldn't succeed without us.

This administration is dedicated to the kinds of programs and policies that will allow the vast majority of older Americans to continue to live independent lives. This is not just a matter of economic common sense; it's a matter of basic human dignity.

Here, as elsewhere, the state of the aging is bound together with the state of the nation. We cannot have a healthy society

---

[1] *White House correction.*

without a healthy economy. Young and old alike, Americans have suffered too long from the combined burden of runaway inflation and an ever heavier tax burden. This destructive cycle has fed on itself. The same taxes and inflation that directly undermine the earning power of individual Americans also drive down productivity and economic growth nationwide.

Because of the graduated tax rate, each 10-percent increase in inflation pushes tax receipts up 17 percent. The taxpayers have that much less money to spend; Washington has that much more to squander; and the economy suffers another blow from the twin evils of inflation and stagnation. The only way to put an end to this disastrous cycle, a cycle that hits Americans on fixed incomes the hardest, is to make real cuts in spending and taxes.

And this administration has made a beginning. It's only a beginning, but the initial signals are encouraging. The inflation rate, as measured by the Consumer Price Index, has fallen from 12.4 percent in 1980 to 9.6 percent in the first 10 months of this year. And last month's figures marked the lowest rate of increase in 15 months. If we could hold to last month's increase cost, we would be down to a 4.4 percent inflation rate.

There was also improvement at the wholesale level, with prices rising at a 7½-percent annual rate, down from 11.8 in 1980. Now, this is especially important, because a decline in wholesale prices now usually means further relief for the consumer as wholesale goods reach the retail market down the line a ways.

Interest rates have also begun to drop. The prime lending rate of 16 percent has reached a 12-month low. Some banks have already dropped to below 16. A year ago, they were at 21½.

Now, these are only early signs. But they are all positive indicators that our economic policy is beginning to work.

Older Americans have also begun to benefit from our tax relief measures. The Economic Recovery Tax Act of 1981 will mean further relief from inflation and taxation, amounting to a 25-percent cut in personal income taxes over 3 years. And starting in 1985, personal tax rates and exemptions will be indexed to keep up with the cost of living so that just a cost-of-living increase won't move you into a higher tax bracket. Inflation will no longer push old and young Americans into ever-higher tax rates through bracket creep.

Other tax reforms of special benefit to older Americans include liberalizations in the capital gains tax, tax exclusions for older Americans selling their homes, and estate tax provisions.

None of this relief from taxation and inflation would be possible if we ignored the problem of runaway government spending. This administration is serious. We have cut back the increased rate of government spending. We're convinced that the Nation's economy cannot heal itself unless the Federal Government begins to put its own house back in order.

But while cutting spending, we have safeguarded services to those poor and elderly who depend on the Government. In the field of health care and human services, Federal spending is actually up by over 15 percent in 1981 and about another 10 percent in 1982. Elderly Americans making up 11 percent of our population will receive 28 percent of the Federal budget in this present fiscal year.

Our administration has also supported reauthorization of the Older Americans Act. The act helps older Americans keep up their independence through a wide variety of home- and community-based services, such as home health care, transportation, meals, and counseling. We're also working on improvements to the program that'll make it an even more effective means of strengthening the dignity and independence of the elderly.

Ours is a generation rich in experience as well as in years. We've been tried and tested. And we've also benefited from a surge of human progress that our parents and our grandparents could never even have imagined.

Now, I happen to be an optimist. I believe attitudes toward the elderly are getting better, not worse. And the polls seem to bear this out. One recent survey revealed that 65 percent of the younger work force now rejects the notion of requiring older workers to retire. Well, this is a dramatic turnaround from just 7 years ago. Then a plurality of younger workers took the opposite view. So, as some Americans grow older, America itself seems to be growing a little bit wiser and a little more tolerant.

You know, Cicero said, "If it weren't for elderly citizens correcting the errors of the young, the state would perish." In those days of the generation gap that I mentioned earlier, it was almost as if our young rebels saw the generations as horizontal, each generation separated from the other like slices from a sausage. Well, humankind is vertical. Each generation sees farther than the one before, because it's standing on the shoulders of those who have gone before.

I look forward to receiving the results of your work here in this Conference. Now, I've been dwelling on the problems of con-

cern for the members of our generation, problems I know that you will be considering. But may I ask also—and maybe it isn't necessary to ask—that you give your counsel with regard also to how we of our generation, in this time of danger to our nation and to the world, can be of help to this blessed land that we've already served so faithfully and so well.

We have much to offer, a great deal to offer. Let our children and our children's children one day say of us, the world that they live in is better because we were here before them.

Thank you very much.

Note: The President spoke at 12:30 p.m. in the Grand Ballroom at the Sheraton Washington Hotel. In his opening remarks, he referred to Secretary of Health and Human Services Richard S. Schweiker.

Nomination of Gerald E. Thomas To Be United States Ambassador to Guyana
December 1, 1981

The President announced today his intention to nominate Gerald E. Thomas, of California, to be Ambassador to the Cooperative Republic of Guyana. He would succeed George B. Roberts, Jr.

In 1951 Mr. Thomas began his career with the United States Navy, serving on the U.S.S. *Newman K. Perry* (1951–54) and U.S.S. *Worcester* (1954–56). He attended naval school in 1956–57 and was assigned to the National Security Agency in 1957–60. He was executive officer on the U.S.S. *Lowe* (1960–62) and assistant head of the college training programs section in the Bureau of Naval Personnel in 1963–65 and attended the Naval War College in 1965–66. In 1966–67 he was commanding officer on the U.S.S. *Bausell*. He was executive officer of the NROTC Unit of Prairie View A & M

College at Prairie View, Tex., in 1967–69 and professor of naval science in 1969–70. He attended the NROTC Unit at Yale University in 1970–73. He was Commander of Destroyer Squadron NINE (1973–74) and of Cruiser Destroyer Group FIVE (1974–76). In 1976–78 he was Director of the Near East and South Asia Region of the Office of the Assistant Secretary of Defense and was Commander of Training Command of the Pacific Fleet in 1978–81. He retired as rear admiral in 1981.

Mr. Thomas is married, has three children, and resides in San Diego, Calif. He graduated from Harvard University (B.S. 1951), George Washington University (M.S., 1966), and Yale University (Ph. D., 1973). He was born June 23, 1929, in Natick, Mass.

Nomination of Mark Evans Austad To Be United States Ambassador to Norway
December 1, 1981

The President today announced his intention to nominate Mark Evans Austad, of Arizona, to be Ambassador to Norway. He would succeed Sidney Anders Rand.

Mr. Austad was a missionary of the Church of Latter-Day Saints in Norway in 1936–39 and served in the United States Army in 1941–45. He was an announcer with KSL Radio in Salt Lake City, Utah (1941–43); commentator, newsman, and broadcaster with WWDC in Washington, D.C. (1945–50); and commentator–morning man with WTOP–CBS in Washington, D.C. (1950–60). In 1960–75 and since 1977, he has been vice president for public affairs with Metromedia, Inc. He hosted his own television program "The Mark Evans Show," and was anchorman of an award-winning documentary on pollution called "1985."

In 1973 Mr. Austad was United States Alternate Representative to the 28th Session of the General Assembly of the United Nations. In 1975–77 he was Ambassador to Finland.

He graduated from Weber State College. Mr. Austad is married, has three children, and resides in Scottsdale, Ariz. He was born April 1, 1917, in Ogden, Utah.

Designation of Fred M. Zeder II To Serve as Personal Representative of the President During Negotiations on the Status of the Trust Territory of the Pacific Islands
December 1, 1981

The President today designated Fred M. Zeder II to serve as Personal Representative of the President to conduct negotiations on the future political status of the Trust Territory of the Pacific Islands. In addition, the President also announced his intention to nominate Mr. Zeder for the rank of Ambassador while serving in that capacity. He would succeed Peter R. Rosenblatt.

Since 1978 Mr. Zeder has been president, Paradise Cruise, Ltd., and Paradise Holdings Corp. in Honolulu, Hawaii. He was president and chairman, Hydrometals, Inc., in New York, N.Y., and Dallas, Tex., in 1959–75. In 1975–77 Mr. Zeder was Director, Office of Territorial Affairs, Department of the Interior.

Mr. Zeder attended Detroit University, the University of Michigan, the University of California at Los Angeles, and Northwood Institute. He is married, has five children, and resides in Honolulu, Hawaii. He was born March 14, 1921.

Nomination of Eugene V. Lipp To Be a Member of the National Transportation Safety Board
December 1, 1981

The President today announced his intention to nominate Eugene V. Lipp to be a member of the National Transportation Safety Board, for a term expiring December 31, 1986. He would succeed James B. King.

Mr. Lipp is a self-employed contractor

and political consultant in Pasadena, Calif. He served as a member of the Alcoholic Beverage Control Appeals Board, State of California, in 1971–78 and was assistant state finance director, Committee to Re-elect Governor Reagan, in 1970. Previously he was an independent contractor in 1968–69; coordinator/administrative assistant, Department of Housing & Community Development, State of California, in 1967–68; public relations and business development

officer, Community Bank, Los Angeles, Calif., in 1955–67. He was in advance sales and marketing, Rheingold Brewing Co., Los Angeles, in 1953–55, and a research assistant, Secret Weapons Development, Cal Ord Research Corp., Pasadena, in 1952–53.

Mr. Lipp is married and resides in Pasadena, Calif. He was born July 19, 1919, in Avon, Pa.

White House Statement on a Meeting Between President Reagan and President Mobutu Sese Seko of Zaire
December 1, 1981

President Reagan met for 45 minutes this afternoon with President Sese Seko Mobutu of Zaire in the Oval Office. He welcomed the opportunity to learn more about the interests and concerns of this important African country and friend of the United States. The meeting was friendly and open. Among the issues discussed were Namibia and Chad, where the President praised Zaire's contribution to a peaceful solution. They also discussed Zaire's need for the cooperation of friendly states, including the United States and our European allies, as well as international organizations in working to develop its economy and reinforce its national security.

There was a mutual understanding of the need for strengthening Zaire's economic institutions and the armed forces. The President told President Mobutu that the United States is prepared to help Zaire achieve its development and security goals while recognizing that those goals require some diffi-

cult decisions, such as those now being taken and planned by the Zairian Government, particularly in improved administration. There was agreement on the importance of the private sector as a force for economic development.

The President wished President Mobutu well during his meetings with Members of Congress and the business community and visits to other parts of the United States.

Present at the meeting in addition to the two Presidents were: Zaire's Foreign Minister Yoka, Zaire's Ambassador to the United States Kasongo, Vice President Bush, Secretaries Haig and Weinberger, Counsellor to the President Meese, Deputy Assistant to the President for National Security Affairs Nance, U.S. Ambassador to Zaire Oakley, Assistant Secretary of State for African Affairs Crocker, Assistant to the Vice President for National Security Affairs Dyke, and Fred Wettering, senior NSC staff member on Africa.

White House Statement on Discharged Air Traffic Controllers
December 1, 1981

There has been no change in the President's fundamental position regarding air traffic controllers.

The President suggested to the Teamsters

leaders today that he was considering the question of whether or not the controllers who have been fired should continue to be barred from any Federal employment for a

3-year period, as is currently the case. Before making any decision, the President wishes to confer with the Secretary of Transportation.

The President emphasized in the meeting this morning: "Our first responsibility is to the controllers who stayed on the job, work-ing long hours to keep the planes flying safely."

Note: The President met with members of the general board of the International Brotherhood of Teamsters at 10:45 a.m. in the Cabinet Room at the White House.

Appointment of 44 Members of the President's Task Force on Private Sector Initiatives, and Designation of Chairman
December 2, 1981

The President today announced the appointment of the following individuals to be members of the President's Task Force on Private Sector Initiatives. The President has announced that C. William Verity, Jr., will serve as Chairman.

William Aramony, president, United Way of America, Alexandria, Va.

William J. Baroody, Jr., president, American Enterprise Institute, Washington, D.C.

Helen G. Boosalis, mayor, city of Lincoln, Nebr.

William R. Bricker, national director, Boys Clubs of America, New York, N.Y.

Barber B. Conable, Jr., Member, U.S. House of Representatives, Washington, D.C.

J. Richard Conder, president, National Association of Counties, Rockingham, N.C.

Terence Cardinal Cooke, archbishop of New York.

Walter G. Davis, director, Department of Community Services, AFL–CIO, Washington, D.C.

Kenneth N. Dayton, chairman of the executive committee, Dayton-Hudson Corp., Minneapolis, Minn.

Pierre S. du Pont IV, Governor, State of Delaware.

David Durenberger, Member, U.S. Senate, Washington, D.C.

Luis A. Ferre, former Governor of Puerto Rico.

John H. Filer, chairman, Aetna Casualty & Life Co., Hartford, Conn.

Max M. Fisher, Detroit, Mich.

John Gardner, chairman, Independent Sector, Washington, D.C.

Daniel Gilbert, president, Eureka College, Eureka, Ill.

Jean L. Harris, secretary of human resources, Commonwealth of Virginia, Richmond, Va.

James S. Henry, president, Center for Public Resources, New York, N.Y.

E. V. Hill, pastor, Mt. Zion Baptist Church, Los Angeles, Calif.

Dee Jepsen, advisory board member, STEP Foundation (Strategies to Eliminate Poverty), Washington, D.C.

Michael S. Joyce, executive director, John M. Olin Foundation, New York, N.Y.

Edward J. Kiernan, president, International Union of Police, Washington, D.C.

Arthur Levitt, Jr., chairman, American Stock Exchange, New York, N.Y.

Robert D. Lilley, chairman, Local Initiatives Support Corp., New York, N.Y.

Henry Lucas, Jr., chairman, New Coalition for Economic and Social Change, San Francisco, Calif.

Leslie L. Luttgens, chairman, Council on Foundations, the Rosenberg Foundation, San Francisco, Calif.

Richard W. Lyman, president, Rockefeller Foundation, New York, N.Y.

Cornell C. Maier, chairman, Kaiser Aluminum & Chemical Corp., Oakland, Calif.

Thomas S. Monson, elder, Church of Jesus Christ of Latter-Day Saints, Salt Lake City, Utah.

Robert Mosbacher, Jr., vice president, Mosbacher Production Co., Houston, Tex.

Franklin D. Murphy, chairman of the executive committee, Times Mirror Co., Los Angeles, Calif.

William C. Norris, chairman and chief executive officer, Control Data Corp.

Frank Pace, Jr., chairman and chief executive officer, National Executive Service Corp., New York, N.Y.

Thomas Pauken, Director, ACTION, Washington, D.C.

George Romney, chairman, National Center for Citizen Involvement, Arlington, Va.

James W. Rouse, chairman, the Rouse Co., Columbia, Md.

Andrew C. Sigler, chairman and chief executive officer, Champion International, Stamford, Conn.

Ellen Sulzberger Straus, president, WMCA Radio, New York, N.Y.

Leon Sullivan, founder, Opportunities Industrialization Center, Zion Baptist Church, Philadel-phia, Pa.

Alexander Trowbridge, president, National Association of Manufacturers, Washington, D.C.

C. William Verity, Jr., chairman, Armco Steel, Inc., Middletown, Ohio.

William S. White, president, C. S. Mott Foundation, Flint, Mich.

Jeri J. Winger, first vice president, General Federation of Womens Clubs, Washington, D.C.

Thomas H. Wyman, president, CBS, Inc., New York, N.Y.

Appointment of 13 Members of the President's Council on Physical Fitness and Sports
December 2, 1981

The President today appointed the following individuals to be members of the President's Council on Physical Fitness and Sports. The President has previously announced the appointment of George Allen as Chairman.

Bernard R. Cahill, M.D., medical director, Great Plains Sports Medicine Foundation, Peoria, Ill. Dr. Cahill is an orthopedic surgeon and an authority on athletic injuries.

Donald L. Cooper, M.D., director, Oklahoma State University Hospital and Clinic, Stillwater, Okla. A general practitioner, Dr. Cooper is team physician for the Oklahoma State University Cowpokes.

Tom J. Fatjo, Jr., president, the Houstonian Foundation, Houston, Tex. He is founder of Criterion Capital Corp., Browning-Ferris Industries, Inc., and the MortageBanque, Inc.

Warren K. Giese, Ph. D., professor, University of South Carolina, Columbia, S.C. He is currently president of the United States Collegiate Sports Council. Dr. Giese was formerly athletic director, head football coach, and dean of the school of health and physical education at South Carolina.

Dorothy Hamill, special guest star of the Ice Capades, from Riverside, Conn. She was the Olympic world and national figure skating champion in 1976 and is a frequent television performer.

William E. LaMothe, chairman of the board and chief executive officer, the Kellogg Co., Battle Creek, Mich. He joined Kellogg in 1950 and is a member of the boards of directors of several colleges, foundations, and corporations.

Donn D. Moomaw, D.D., senior pastor, Bel Air Presbyterian Church, Los Angeles, Calif. An All-American lineman at UCLA, Dr. Moomaw is a member of the Collegiate Football Hall of Fame and was one of the organizers of the Fellowship of Christian Athletes.

Wayne Newton, singer-entertainer, Flying Eagle, Inc., Las Vegas, Nev. He is a recording star, an actor, owner of the Aladdin Hotel in Las Vegas, and proprietor of one of the world's largest Arabian horse breeding farms.

Mark Lee Saginor, M.D., director, Internal Medicine and Endocrinology, Metabolic Research Medical Group, Inc., Los Angeles, Calif. Dr. Saginor is an authority on eating disorders.

Roger Staubach, president, Holloway-Staubach Realtors, Dallas, Tex. He won the Heisman Trophy during his junior year at the United States Naval Academy, served 4 years in the Navy, and quarterbacked the Dallas Cowboys from 1969 to 1979, leading them to the Super Bowl championships in 1971 and 1977.

Ronald H. Walker, managing vice president and senior partner, Korn/Ferry International, Washington, D.C. He is a former Director of the National Park Service and former associate director of World Championship Tennis.

Leon J. Weil, general partner, Herzfeld and Stern, New York, N.Y. He is a member of the New York Stock Exchange and is an accomplished marathon runner, skier, cyclist, and squash player.

David A. (Sonny) Werblin, president and chief executive officer, Madison Square Garden Corp., New York, N.Y. He is a former president

of both the Music Corp. of America and the New York Jets football team and a former chairman of the New Jersey Sports and Exposition Authority.

Remarks at a Luncheon Meeting With Members of the President's Task Force on Private Sector Initiatives
December 2, 1981

I think I got up here too soon. I think I'm supposed to wait until they're all ready. You said 2 minutes? I don't know whether I've got enough ad lib material to go for 2 minutes—*[laughter]*—until we get down to the important message.

Well, I can say that I can spend some time thanking all of you for being here and for doing what you're doing. I think it's of great importance, and I have been telling some audiences here and there around the country of the response that we're getting and the mail that we're getting and the spirit of the people out there and their desire to participate in something of the kind that you are bringing together here. And I see that one camera's on. *[Laughter]* We shall proceed.

So, again, good afternoon to all of you and welcome to the White House. I think most of you know the story about President Kennedy, who was welcoming a delegation of Nobel Prize winners to the White House in this very room. And he called it the most impressive collection of talents assembled here since Thomas Jefferson dined alone. *[Laughter]*

Looking over this distinguished group today, I'm not sure Thomas Jefferson could match this team. I know I can't. We're glad that you're here and thankful that leaders of your caliber strongly support our administration's commitment to strengthen private sector initiatives.

What we're asking you to do is to help rediscover America—not the America bound by the Potomac River, but the America beyond the Potomac River, the America whose initiative, ingenuity, and industry made our country the envy of the world, the America whose rich tradition of

generosity began with simple acts of neighbor caring for neighbor.

We're asking you to build on this heritage to encourage greater contributions of voluntary effort and personal involvement, to form a partnership between the private and public sector for the good of America. We want you to seek out models for private sector initiatives—schools, churches, civic groups, businesses, unions, the foundations—and give them the recognition that they deserve. Help us identify the obstacles government has placed in the way of private initiative and make recommendations to me for the removal of those obstacles and the introduction of needed incentives.

Finally, we think a wonderful legacy of this task force could be the creation of thousands of local task forces just like yours, one for every town in America, to carry on the work that you will begin today. And I've learned enough just sitting here at lunch to know that some of you on your own have already been doing just exactly that same thing, even—with regard to the Federated Women—internationally.

You can help revive the sense of community which has been the hallmark of America but which recently has been weakened by the growth of big government. Americans should never have to consider themselves wards of the state. They're members of their communities, and the answers to their problems can be found on the streets where they live.

Your job, as I see it, is not to try to solve these problems or to spend a lot of time writing one of those thick reports, although I know that there is going to be a report, so I won't say that I don't want any report at all. No, I'm very curious; I'd like to know. But also, I'm going to be settling for results. And that's why each one of you was enlisted—leaders from every walk of life who have to solve these problems every day.

Government can provide opportunity. It can pave the way. But ultimately, it is individuals like yourselves who brave new horizons, expand freedom, and create better lives for us all.

Your success will be measured by how much and how well you marshall the private resources of America in the service of community development. I'm told that Americans perform some $100 billion worth of labor every year for volunteer organizations across the country, and that's in addition to the $47 billion they contribute in cash to charitable and religious organizations.

The country is bursting with ideas and creativity, but a government run by central decree has no way to respond. People want to play a part in building a better America, and you can show the way. You are their colleagues, their friends, and you can talk with them and work with them just as I want to talk and work with you.

I will also be speaking out on this subject, working with the Cabinet to refocus the resources of government so they encourage private initiatives instead of discouraging them.

When I spoke to the National Alliance of Businessmen [Business], I mentioned several outstanding models of corporate responsi-bility and community spirit. But for every one I mentioned, I know there are a hundred more, just as good. Find them. Spread the word. Help 230 million Americans get organized. Help us create new leadership at the State and local level, a new Alliance for Progress here at home. Help us put America's future back in the people's hands.

I know your Chairman, Bill Verity, has excellent ideas on how these things can be done. And each of you brings expertise and experience to our enterprise as well. We look to you, we appreciate you and, most of all, we're counting on you. We're confident that this task can be done and that your task force is the group to do it.

So, again, a heartfelt thanks. And maybe you can cure the misconception that has existed since a few years ago, when an immigrant to this country who had become a very successful farmer, died and left his estate—it was not in seven figures at all—but left his estate to the government, the United States Government, for what this country had done for him.

And when the State took its share of the estate in estate taxes, the Federal Government sued that it was tax-free and that this shouldn't be allowed. And what you can cure is the fact that the Federal Government won that case on the basis that it was a charitable organization. [*Laughter*]

Thank you.

Note: The President spoke at 1:02 p.m. in the State Dining Room at the White House.

Interview With Joseph Rice of the Cleveland Plain Dealer
November 30, 1981

Libya

Mr. Rice. Mr. President, there were reports recently that Libya had sent people to the United States to assassinate both yourself and other top government officials. Do you give any credence to these reports? And exactly how far will your administration go in dealing with people, such as Qadhafi, who obviously hate the United States?

The President. Well, we're studying right now our economic relations with them. I think he has made it obvious that he is against most of the things that we're trying to achieve, such as peace in the Middle East, appealing to the moderate Arab nations, and so forth.

As to his threats personally against me, I think in view of the record, you can't dismiss them out of hand. On the other hand, they're not going to change my life much.

Beyond that, I never comment on security matters.

Mr. Rice. There has not been any hard evidence, though, to substantiate the rumors, has there?

The President. Well, I can't go beyond what I've said.

Richard Allen

Mr. Rice. Ed Meese said today that there was no guarantee that Richard Allen would return to the White House if, in fact, the investigation cleared him. I wonder how you personally feel about the entire Allen affair, and would you like to see him back there if he is given a clean bill of health?

The President. I think that we have to wait and see. And, again, as long as this is under review, or it is, again, it's one of those things I don't think I can or should comment.

So far, most of it has just simply been innuendo and accusation. And what I'm hoping a review will do will be what we've always held as a fair thing in our system, and that is wait until the facts are in and then make a judgment and a decision.

Mr. Rice. But could he still function effectively in your administration after this cloud, even if, in fact, the investigation had him cleared?

The President. That certainly would reveal that there was no wrongdoing.

Mr. Rice. That's not to say he would necessarily keep the position, though?

The President. What?

Mr. Rice. That's not to say that he would necessarily keep his job, though, the fact he's cleared?

The President. Again, as I say, I can't comment beyond the fact that, obviously, they all hope that the review will be favorable.

Economic Recovery Program

Mr. Rice. You said at your October news conference that it was unrealistic to expect to cure in 40 days problems that developed over 40 years. Now, at what time do you think it will be fair for the American people to make a judgment on whether or not your economic program has been a success, and

what goals would you set in your own mind in terms of inflation, unemployment, home interest rates?

The President. Well, we ourselves had evolved a plan that was to go into effect over a period of 3 years to try and bring spending down within reason. Our tax program is implemented over a 3-year span. I think at least we should wait until that program is actually functioning and that there has been time to see some indication of whether the tax program, for example, has contributed to an increase in productivity, a broadening of the economy. I couldn't pin a particular time on it. I think that we have to go by trends.

Now, there are so many imponderables. We made, in good faith, some projections based at 1984 on the basis of things as they were. Well, the interest rates stayed up longer than had been anticipated. And I'm sure they had something to do with the recession, which, while no one ruled it out as a possibility, everyone was hopeful that while the economy was—well, the economy we inherited was down, with great unemployment, steel and the automobile industries and construction hurting. We still had thought that we knew the economy would be soft. But the recession came, and this has obviously changed our own estimates.

Mr. Rice. You think it might not be possible to see this recovery by the congressional elections next year?

The President. Well, it's what you call economic recovery.

No, I would think that we're going to begin to see a turn in the economy before then. But that's it. It's got to be a progressive thing. But the direction is set, and you see the direction that we're going, that it is up and not down. And right now, we see the interest rates are going down. We certainly have had an impact on inflation.

And, as I said in my remarks tonight, even though recently the figures in what I think is a rather haphazard way of determining unemployment in this country, you know, there's no real hard and fast count. It's taken by a telephone poll of some thousands of households. But, even so, when they came up with the word that there were 500,000 more unemployed than there had been, you can count the figures of the employed much more accurately. And there are 266,000 more people working, in the work force, than there were when I took office.

Mr. Rice. But in your own mind you had some goal as to what the inflation rate, the unemployment rate should be by next year, you'd call successes?

The President. Well, I'll say single digit.

Mr. Rice. On the annual rate of inflation.

The President. But let me—Don Regan pointed something out one day, when someone was challenging, "Well, you made estimates and then you had to change the estimates."

When you're talking about, over the next few years, getting to a $4 trillion gross national product, if you make a 1-percent error, if you're 99 percent right, that 1 percent can throw you off by $40 billion.

Now, the error can go either way. If you were ultraconservative, were off 1 percent, you'd be $40 billion better off. If you go the opposite way, such as this recession could have done to us, you could be $40 billion off in your estimates and under what your projections had been.

Mr. Rice. What about home interest rates? Do you have any guess as to what you'd like to see them down to?

The President. Oh, sure. I want to see them down. I think that if we can get down to around 10 percent it would be a great boon to the construction industry particularly and to the automobile industry.

Mr. Rice. Is that a realistic expectation, though, for next year? Or do you have a goal——

The President. No, I can't really tell you on this. I do know this: People have to be aware that with the interest rates starting to come down, a lull in these industries that are affected can continue. Because once they start down, history shows us people then tend to wait, thinking, well, they're going down; I'll wait till they get lower.

Federal Revenue Sharing

Mr. Rice. You said in 1975 that the Federal Government should shift some of the Federal programs back to the States and at the same time give them the tax resources to finance these programs. Now, we're faced with the budget deficit now, and given the current Federal financial situation, how far in the future do you think it might be before we might see some of these tax sources transferred back to the States? And do you envision the government being able to do anything in the next year or two to cushion the impact that the budget cuts have had on the cities and the States?

The President. We have a task force working right now on this whole front, men working with local and State governments. You see, it isn't—when I say a total loss to the Federal Government, if the Federal Government could find a tax, let's say a tax of an excise nature, and turn it over to local government along with a function that it's to perform, it simply replaces grants, where the Federal Government is taking the money in taxation from the people, taking it to Washington, then going through the administrative process of doling it out again. Well, if you turn the tax source over to that other level of government, then you would cancel the grant that it is replacing. And the idea is that there would be a lot less administrative overhead.

We have been working—and not as successfully as I wish we could have been with the Congress—to transfer what are called categorial grants to block grants. Now, having been a Governor, I can tell you what the categorical grants do. They come to you with Federal money, but with enormous amounts of redtape and regulation prescribing exactly what the priorities are and how this money must be spent. Well, no one in Washington can set rules of that kind that will fit New York City and some small town in the urban area or a city in the South that doesn't have the same problems or the West. So, it makes those programs needlessly extravagant.

As I say, we haven't been able to persuade Congress to change as many as we'd like, but we have—as one thing, this answers the part of your question about helping local and State government—we have been able to get some of those changed into block grants. And in so doing, they will have the flexibility to make better use of the money.

Mr. Rice. Is there any promise of immediate relief, though, for the States and the local governments who are now faced in situations such as Ohio where they had to raise taxes to offset a budget deficit?

The President. Well, you've got several States like Ohio that have abnormal unemployment rates because of the industries that were predominant here and in Michigan, other States like that. And so, they have the abnormal unemployment rate, their revenues are down because of that, and costs are greater.

One of the things that we're talking about is the program we're trying to get underway of the free enterprise zones in cities, that we should, if we get those operating—I hope we can soon—that we should put those into States that have these problems that we're talking about, and on a kind of an experimental basis before you're actually going nationwide with a program.

Mr. Rice. But there's no immediate relief, though, in sight, though?

The President. No. You know, as bad off as many of the States are, who's worse off than the Federal Government? We've got a trillion dollar debt. Any program of help to these States would be coming out of the pockets of the same people that they must tap for taxes.

Corporate Mergers

Mr. Rice. Mobil Oil Company is now trying to take over Marathon Oil Company, which is an Ohio-based company, against the wishes of the officers of Marathon. My question is, do you feel that it's in the best interests of the public to have a large conglomerate such as Mobil take over a smaller, locally based company, and what position might your Justice Department take in terms of any antitrust action?

The President. Well, let me say on this one that I understand there are several companies now that are in the bidding for this takeover, and we try to leave that to the private marketplace unless there is violation of the antitrust laws and unless it is felt that under the fair trade practices and the Justice Department that there is some violation of those. Then the Federal Government has to intervene. But other than that, I don't think it's the place of the Federal Government to intervene in the marketplace.

Mr. Rice. So, you wouldn't make a judgment whether or not it's a good thing?

The President. No.

El Salvador

Mr. Rice. Mr. President, approximately a year ago four American churchwomen, two of them from Cleveland, were killed in El Salvador. Since then the Salvadoran Government has been holding some soldiers for questioning. Now, they recently released a report that contained little new and did not contain anything on the events after February 17th, which was before the soldiers were arrested. Are you satisfied with the way the Salvadoran Government has handled this situation?

The President. I have to tell you that I don't have an answer to that. This doesn't mean I haven't been interested and we haven't been trying to keep track. I haven't had the latest report back on this situation. I do know that earlier we were informed that there was no real hard evidence with regard to the people who had been arrested. Now, I would have to—and will, of course—attempt to find out what we know about this, and we have been keeping close track of it.

I think that the Duarte government is trying very hard to have a democratic regime and to bring about a political settlement of this war that's going on down there, not a military settlement. And I think that they are doing what we ourselves have advocated, which is, they are in the middle and they are opposed to both extremists of the right and left.

Air Traffic Controllers

Mr. Rice. Mr. President, you're meeting at the White House, Wednesday, with Lane Kirkland and some other labor leaders who have been somewhat critical of you in the past. There is some speculation among labor leaders that you might offer some kind of an olive branch, possibly on the PATCO situation, to organized labor. Is there anything in the works on PATCO, or what do you expect to come out of this meeting?

The President. No, I can't say that there is. I intend to, before this meeting, talk to the Department of Transportation, Secretary of Transportation, about PATCO. I have to call your attention again that they had plenty of warning. They were informed in the negotiations that the strike, if they took one after they'd threatened, it was illegal, that they themselves had taken personal oaths, and that there was no way that we could stand by and not recognize that the law had been broken. So, what we informed them was that they might call it a strike, but in reality they were quitting their jobs.

Now, I think a great consideration we must have—we're not trying for vengeance or anything else of that kind, but I do think that there must be great consideration given to those who did continue to work.

Mr. Rice. You cannot see then offering any PATCO striker his job back then?

The President. I'd be very happy to hear any suggestions that they may have, but I also feel that they ought to recognize that the people they represent, the members of their unions, are the employers of public servants. And when there's a strike, it's a strike against them, the people.

And labor once recognized that. I've a little background in labor myself, but when public employees first began to organize, unionize, organized labor said they would help them only if public employee unions put in their constitutions that they would not strike.

Mr. Rice. Mr. President, are you ruling out then any chance that they might get a job back, if that's brought up by labor?

The President. No.

1984 Candidacy

Mr. Rice. You made a reference tonight to the senior Senator from Ohio, John Glenn, who has been in New Hampshire and other States testing the waters. I wonder in your own mind, sir, what your current thinking is about whether you'll run for reelection and exactly how formidable an opponent you view Senator Glenn as.

The President. Oh, I don't know. He's very popular in his own State. I meant my line humorously.

As for myself in 1984, I don't think about it, because I set a policy for myself when I was Governor for 8 years—well, the second 4 years didn't matter. But I said that there would be no consideration of political matters in any decision that our administration had to make, because the minute you do that then you begin compromising in your own mind. And I said we would meet every issue simply on the basis of was it right or wrong for the people.

So, as far as 1984 is concerned, the only time I consider it is when I'm worrying about what the deficit will be by 1984.

Nuclear Force Negotiations

Mr. Rice. The arms control talks, sir, began today in Geneva. Do you expect the current round of negotiations to produce anything substantive, or is it more likely to lead to a summit meeting with yourself and President Brezhnev?

The President. Well, I don't think the two are related in that way. I've not ruled out a summit meeting. As a matter of fact, I think that's something that has to be thoroughly prepared for. But I am very hopeful about these negotiations.

It is the first time in a great many years that we will have met with them on supposed arms limitation—I prefer to call it arms reduction—when we ourselves were not unilaterally disarming. The Russians could sit at the negotiating table, and they didn't have to give up anything. We were doing it to ourselves. And this time, with our determination to rebuild our military, I think they may find they have a reason to want to meet us halfway on disarmament.

And so, as I say, I'm hopeful that—I think it would be wonderful for the world and for Europe if those missiles planted there near the NATO border, in that vicinity—able to hit every population center in Europe—if those were taken out and we did not have to counter them by poising the same kind of missiles aimed at their country.

Mr. Rice. Mr. President, thank you very much.

Deputy Press Secretary Speakes. You know, one thing we ought to point out on this State—money for the State governments, that the first relief that they will begin to feel is when the economic program starts to work. And that'll benefit State governments as well as their own citizens.

The President. Yeah, it sure will. I just talked to a man tonight that's starting a new plant in Ohio. But the other thing also I should have mentioned—one thing for the States. You've got to remember that they also benefit a little in the reduction of their costs as inflation comes down. Governments spend money, too, and then feel inflation.

Mr. Rice. Mr. President, thank you so much.

The President. You bet.

Note: The interview was conducted on board Air Force One as the President was returning to Washington, D.C., from Cincinnati, Ohio.

The transcript of the interview was released by the Office of the Press Secretary on December 2.

Letter Accepting the Resignation of Max L. Friedersdorf as Assistant to the President for Legislative Affairs
December 3, 1981

Dear Max:

December 3, 1981

It is with deep regret that I accept your resignation as Assistant to the President for Legislative Affairs. Your energy, ability, and dedication have played a key role in translating our economic recovery program into legislative reality. We could not have done it without you, and I am sure that the members and leaders of the Congress share my admiration for the excellent job you have performed over the past ten months.

Of course, I do plan to keep your phone number in Bermuda close by, and I hope you will not mind an occasional call for consultation about matters on the Hill.

We have been through some historic times together; your contribution will long be remembered. I know that you will bring the same outstanding qualities to bear on your new duties as Consul General to Bermuda. Nancy and I wish you and Priscilla all the best in this new phase of a distinguished public service career.

Sincerely,

RONALD REAGAN

[The Honorable Max L. Friedersdorf, Assistant to the President for Legislative Affairs, The White House, Washington, D.C. 20500]

Dear Mr. President:

I wish to advise you that I am herewith submitting my resignation as Assistant to the President for Legislative Affairs effective January 2, 1982.

It has been one of the most significant and pleasurable years of my life to have served you in this capacity during a session of Congress which I believe will rank historically as one of major and longlasting significance for our country.

Under your leadership, the nation has embarked on a course leading again to full economic health, and I consider the passage of your Economic Recovery Program to be a milestone in the course you have charted for the United States.

I believe that we have one of the finest White House congressional relations staffs in the history of this office and one that will continue to produce satisfactory results during the remainder of your term of office.

You have my heartfelt thanks for the opportunity to serve you in this capacity, and I look forward to continuing my contribution to this Administration in my new assignment.

With warmest thanks and cordial regard,

I am

Sincerely,

MAX L. FRIEDERSDORF
Assistant to the President

[The President, The White House, Washington, D.C. 20500]

Nomination of Gilbert G. Pompa To Be Director of the Community Relations Service
December 3, 1981

The President today announced his intention to nominate Gilbert G. Pompa for reappointment as Director, Community Relations Service, Department of Justice, for a term of 4 years.

Mr. Pompa has served as Director, Community Relations Service, since 1978. Prior to his appointment he had served in various levels within the Community Relations Service since 1967. He was assistant district attorney, Bexar County, Tex., in 1963–67; assistant city attorney, San Antonio, Tex., in 1960–63; and in the private practice of law in 1958–60.

He is cofounder and member, National Conference of Hispanic Law Enforcement Officers Association, and a member of the National Hispanic Corrections Association. He is also cofounder and member, Involvement of Mexican Americans in Gainful Endeavors.

Mr. Pompa graduated from St. Mary's University School of Law (J.D., 1958). He is married, has three children, and resides in Fairfax, Va. He was born October 1, 1931, in Devine, Tex.

Appointment of Brigadier General Calvin G. Franklin as Commanding General of the Militia of the District of Columbia
December 3, 1981

The President today announced his intention to appoint Brig. Gen. Calvin G. Franklin to be Commanding General of the Militia of the District of Columbia. He would succeed Maj. Gen. Cunningham C. Bryant.

Brigadier General Franklin began his military career by enlisting in the California Army National Guard in November 1948. He entered on active duty in 1950 with the 1402d Combat Engineers when the California National Guard was mobilized. He served with the 1402d at Fort Lewis and in Germany. Receiving his release in 1952, he rejoined the California National Guard, 765th Transportation Company, in San Diego, Calif., in 1953. In late 1953 he entered the State OCS program, and upon graduation in 1954, he was commissioned as a second lieutenant and served as Platoon Leader, 765th Transportation Company.

In 1961 he was promoted to captain, serving as Commanding Officer of the 118th Signal Company and later Commander of Company B, 240th Signal Battalion, 40th Armor Division. He served as the Division Radio Officer in 1965–66. Promoted to major in 1968, he served as Communications Officer, 111th Army Group, and was Commander, 3d Battalion, 185th Armor, 40th Division, after being promoted to lieutenant colonel in 1972. He was subsequently assigned as Assistant Chief of Staff, G5, 40th Division, in 1974–75, and in 1975 he assumed command of the 240th Signal Battalion (40th Division). He was promoted to colonel in 1976.

After completing training at the United States Army War College in 1977, Brigadier General Franklin remained on active duty and was assigned to Headquarters Forces

Command, DCSOPS, as Chief, Mobilization Improvement, and Director of NIFTY NUGGET/MOBEX 78. Upon completion of that assignment, he served as Assistant Chief of Staff, G3, for the D.C. National Guard in 1979. He is currently assigned as the Assistant Adjutant General, State of California National Guard.

He graduated from San Diego City College (A.A., 1955), National University of San Diego (B.A., 1972), and United States International University (M.A., 1974). He resides in San Diego, Calif., and was born March 31, 1929, in DeQueen, Ark.

Appointment of Colonel Ernest Roland Morgan as Adjutant General of the Militia of the District of Columbia
December 3, 1981

The President today announced his intention to appoint Col. Ernest Roland Morgan to be Adjutant General of the Militia of the District of Columbia. He would succeed Brig. Gen. Wayne W. Bridges.

Colonel Morgan was Chief of Operations and Training, Artillery Brigade, Europe, in 1965–66; Executive Officer, 94th Artillery Group, Europe, in 1966–67; School Secretary, Division Chief, United States Army Intelligence School, Fort Holabird, Md., in 1967–69; Assistant Inspector General, United States Army, Vietnam, in 1969–70; Commander, 4th Nike Hercules Battalion, Fort Bliss, Tex., in 1971–72; Chief, Tactical ADP Branch/Staff Officer, Office of the Assistant Chief of Staff, Force Development, Army Staff, Washington, D.C., in 1972–73.

In 1973–74 he attended the Army War College. He was Chief, Plans & Programs Branch, U.S. Army Element JUSMMAT, Ankara, Turkey, in 1974–75; Director, National Security Seminar, U.S. Army War College, in 1975–77; professor of military science, Prairie View A&M University (Texas) in 1977–79; and Deputy Assistant Chief of Staff, J–5 Plans, Headquarters, U.S. Forces in Korea/Eighth Army, in 1979–81. He is currently Deputy Assistant Commander, J–5, Headquarters, U.S. Forces Korea/Eighth Army.

He graduated from the University of Maryland (B.A.) and Shippensburg State College (M.S.). He resides in Houston, Tex., and was born March 29, 1932, in Petersburg, Va.

Statement About the 1981 White House Conference on Aging
December 3, 1981

I would like to extend my heartfelt thanks to the more than 4,000 delegates and observers who traveled from across the country and around the world to participate in the 1981 White House Conference on Aging.

Above all, this Conference has been a forum for the open exchange of ideas. For the past 3 days, an impressive cross section of older Americans has grappled with the many critical problems which affect the aging. Their goal has not necessarily been to reach unanimous agreement on every issue, but rather to share diverse views and arrive at recommendations for the common good.

The challenge before us is to develop policies for older Americans which are constructive, comprehensive, and compassionate. I know that all White House Conference delegates have taken this responsibility seriously. However, their work does not stop with the adjournment of the final plenary session of the 1981 Conference. They will continue their constructive analysis upon return to their communities by completing a unique system of post-Conference reports to be submitted to Secretary Schweiker within 30 days of adjournment. This period of analysis will provide delegates an opportunity for an in-depth, detailed study of the individual Conference reports prior to the submission of thoughtful commentary and specific views.

I salute all the Conference delegates and observers for their unselfish contributions and for making the 1981 Conference a productive, memorable event. I look forward to receiving the final Conference report.

Letter to the Speaker of the House of Representatives and the Chairman of the Senate Foreign Relations Committee Reporting on the Cyprus Conflict
December 3, 1981

Dear Mr. Speaker: (Dear Mr. Chairman:)

In accordance with the provision of Public Law 95–384, I am submitting the following report on progress made during the past 60 days toward reaching a negotiated settlement of the Cyprus problem.

The intercommunal negotiations between Greek Cypriots and Turkish Cypriots have taken a significant step. Both sides accepted presentation of a United Nations "evaluation" of the status of the intercommunal talks on November 18. The "evaluation," although not a formal proposal, embodies ideas and concepts which may prove useful for the parties in their discussion of outstanding issues.

Following the presentation of proposals earlier this summer by the Turkish Cypriots (August 5) and the Greek Cypriots (September 9), the development of the United Nations "evaluation" signals continuing progress towards a negotiated settlement of the Cyprus problem. The United Nations, the Special Representative of the Secretary General, Ambassador Hugo Gobbi, and the participating parties are to be commended for their efforts. We hope that both parties will seize the opportunity offered by the United Nations "evaluation" to devote renewed energy to resolving their differences by peaceful negotiation in a spirit of compromise.

Sincerely,

RONALD REAGAN

Note: This is the text of identical letters addressed to Thomas P. O'Neill, Jr., Speaker of the House of Representatives, and Charles H. Percy, chairman of the Senate Foreign Relations Committee.

Interview With Managing Editors on Domestic Issues
December 3, 1981

The President. Well, I'm happy to have a chance to say welcome, and particularly when there are at least six here from California. But all of you are just as welcome. I know you've been briefed on a number of subjects, and so almost anything that I might say would be plowing ground that's already been plowed. And yet I will do that, just to put emphasis on one, and that is what I think is the overall problem here of trying to get control of Federal spending and a realistic approach to the budget.

We're now into the 14th month that we've been without a budget. Our entire year of '81 went through with nothing but continuing resolutions and no budget. And we're now 2 months into this fiscal year, and still no budget. And I frankly don't know of a State that has ever run itself that way. Part of it is evident reluctance of some to see any curb put on Federal spending. So, we're still working on that.

And now I'm going to save all of the rest of the time here for whatever questions you may have.

Let me just say that with regard to our program, which has only just now begun to be put into effect, contrary to the impression that a lot of people seem to have had that it's been tried and found wanting and is a failure, and that was decided before it started—we don't believe it is, and we think that some of the signs are very encouraging already.

And that is that a year ago, or when we took office, inflation was above 12 percent, around 12½ percent. For the first 10 months of this year, it's down to 9.6 and last month came in at 4.4. Interest rates, which were 21½ [percent], have of late begun to drop and are down to 15¾, and we think are going to continue coming down. The wholesale inflation rate has been running 7½ [percent], which means that I think we can look forward to further drops in the days ahead, because the wholesale inflation rate determines, in advance, what the regular cost-of-living index is going to be just a ways down the road.

But I know that you must have some questions, and I'd rather try that than continuing, as I say, plowing this already plowed ground.

Q. Mr. President, you talked about the great need to cut spending, yet on this emphasis of the need to get a budget, you've appeared before a veterans' group and you've said that you're not going to make them make any sacrifices. You appeared before a council on aging and you told them you're not going to make them make any sacrifices. What groups are you prepared to appear before and say, "You have to make the sacrifices?"

The President. No, I think with regard to the veterans, we were talking about medical benefits for the veterans and so forth. And I do believe that this is a contract that you have to take care of those who have served their country. Social security—what I said to them was—and this was the basis of the plan that we submitted, but which

was widely distorted in the debate that followed and I think for pure political demagoguery—that all the way through the campaign I cited the immediate problem of social security, of its running out of funds, and the long-range actuarial imbalance which is in the trillions of dollars, if you look on down the road, for those people who are just beginning their working years.

What I pledged to do was to have a social security—to put it on a sound fiscal basis, and yet not at the expense of those people who are presently retired; that you pull the rug out from under them and reduce their benefits. The only thing that could be called a reduction in any way in the proposal we made, of those existing benefits, was we were going to try and get social security onto the fiscal year basis with regard to the cost-of-living adjustment. That would mean that for 1 year alone, they would go 15 months instead of 12 before their cost-of-living adjustment was computed. And that would, as we figured it out, average probably a $90 reduction of increase, not a reduction of existing benefits, reduction of their increase over their lifetime. That would be the only single thing.

The other things that we had suggested in that program were not aimed at deserving and eligible recipients. They were aimed at the abuses in the program, people that are collecting disability benefits and are not disabled. A recent story of a family, a heartbreaking story, that made it look as if we had suddenly taken this family off disability benefits—and we looked into it to find out if this was true. We found out they were taken off of their disability benefits under the previous administration, and they were taken off because for 3 years, the disabled household head had been working. And now the question is, working, moonlighting on the side—a check is being made to see whether he was paying income tax all that time.

This is the type of thing that we think there's much more of it than anyone realizes, as was evidenced in Chicago a couple of years ago with the—or a few years ago— with the welfare queen who went on trial. And it was found that in addition to collecting welfare under 123 different names, she also had 55 social security cards. So, this is where we were going to try and make some of the changes.

Q. Mr. President, a regional question. What do you see as the Federal role with regard to California in terms of the Medfly, which is a terribly expensive battle, and also the vast number of refugees from Asia that have moved into, particularly, Los Angeles? What do you see as the role there to perform?

The President. Well, we've been dealing with a reform of the immigration laws on all of this, except that with regard to the refugees—people who are fleeing persecution and who, if they were made to return to their own country, would probably face death or imprisonment—I think that our traditions—there's no way that we can abandon those traditions or the words that are on the base of the Statue of Liberty. And we have a particular problem, I know, with our neighbor to the South. But we think that this program is going to meet our needs and the needs of the refugees coming in, so that we won't be abandoning that. We are also looking at how we can handle these and probably a fairer distribution in our country.

I know, in 1980—the administration then was caught by the great exodus from Cuba in addition to the Haitian overflow and so forth. No planning had been made for that. We're also looking at available sites and facilities for a detention center for those who are apprehended and are illegal aliens, who will probably be returned.

Q. Mr. President, one of the potential detention centers that you're considering is in northern New York, where I'm from, where the climate is about as different as you can get from the Haitian climate and still be in the country. How humane is it to consider that, a site like that?

The President. Well, I know the climate problem, and we've thought about that and talked about it. One of our problems is finding a facility that would have all the factors and the capacity that we need for estimated larger numbers, and also finding one that the inhabitants of the State would be willing—you'd be surprised how difficult it is to find some State that wants it.

We think that the one that we have settled on not only meets the needs but also happens to be in an area that would benefit economically from having an installation of that kind there because of the abnormally high unemployment rate, economic problems.

Q. Mr. President, the State of Florida claims the Federal Government owes a lot of money to the State because of the refugee problem. Although you didn't inherit it, are you considering additional funds, or——

The President. To tell you the truth, I can't answer that right now. We have not come in with the—we have not had our meeting yet with the new presentation from OMB of suggested budget cuts for '83, so until we do, I don't know just how some of these problems have been treated.

Q. Mr. President, is there any thought being given to changing the make-up or the limits of your safety net in light of the recession? Any thought being given to changing any of the benefits that have been cut or restoring any?

The President. Well, again, this would be something that we'll face when we see the '83 budget, although I don't believe that the so-called safety net has been much changed.

This recession—remember that when we came here, January 20th, we had a great unemployment problem, severe in several areas far more than in others. It's easy to look at, say, an 8 percent inflation rate and think of that as the nation as a whole. That isn't true. We have States, and some of you are probably from those States, where inflation is approaching the 20 percent mark. That's like the Great Depression of the thirties, due to the particular industries that have been affected—in addition to construction, the steel industry, automobiles, and so forth.

We think that the best thing that we can do is to go forward with this plan, which we think is going to stimulate the economy. I think we're due, for several months yet, of hard times, but I think that in '82 we're going to see—later in the year—a change in the situation. The falling interest rates indicate that—the inflation rates that I mentioned—so that I think the safety net is still there for those people of real need.

Q. Is there an unemployment level at which you rethink that?

The President. Well, I think it would be based on if there's actual distress. I don't think anyone is going to stand by and see people in actual distress.

Let me just say one thing about that particular problem. I was as surprised as anyone when suddenly the announcement was made that in a month we've increased the unemployed by 500,000. Now, as you know, there's no accurate way of counting the unemployed. There is an accurate way of counting the people who are in the work force. And it's difficult for me to understand this sudden surge of unemployment when, at the same time, there are 266,000 more people employed in the work force than there were on January 20th, when this administration started. I can't believe that we've suddenly added three-quarters of a million people to our population.

But let me point out one reason why there could be some fluctuations. First of all, any unemployed, other than those who are voluntarily between jobs, is too much. So, I don't want to sound callous about that. As a matter of fact, there's nothing that is harder for me to do than to think of putting somebody out of a job. I came into the work force myself in the depths of the Great Depression. I saw what took place there.

But unemployment is determined by some 60-odd thousand telephone calls, like a Nielsen rating on a TV show, throughout the country—random. And the question is, "Is anyone in the household looking for work?" If the answer is "yes," that's a statistic—unemployed. If the answer is "no," they pass on. And on the basis of these calls and the percentage, the percentage of unemployed is determined. But there's room for discretion there and shading, depending on the callers.

Suppose it's a housewife who says to you on the phone, "Well, you know, the children are getting along now and if I could find something that didn't interfere with family and was right, yes." Well, the person can put that down as she's looking for work, or the person from this end of the phone can put that down as "no." Nor are we dividing between all those teenagers, that

on the other end of the phone someone might answer and say, "Well, my son would love to have an after-school job if he could find one, and so you can put him down unemployed."

The millions of unemployed are not, all of them, heads of household, leading a family without earnings. Maybe I'm overly suspicious, but I keep remembering that when I was Governor of California, they decided to do some changing in counting the unemployed, here in Washington. I protested as loud as I could, but didn't get anyplace with it. Our unemployment rate in California at the time was 5.2 [percent], and in 24 hours, our unemployment rate went to 7.2, just based on a little change in the procedures here in Washington.

So, I've been a little worried here that sometimes we—and I don't mean to do any less about trying to get them the work, we're going to—but I think that our program is aimed at that. I'm aware that—I know somebody is waiting to tell me I have to leave—*[laughter]*—but I'm also aware that when Kennedy had his across-the-board tax cuts, aimed at the same thing, to stimulate the economy, and the same economists and many of the same voices were raised, advising against it and saying that was absolutely the wrong thing to do, he persisted. And immediately thereafter the rate of savings, personal savings in the country—the percentage went up from 2.9 percent of the earnings in the country to 8 percent. The rate of increase in employment—not unemployment, in employment—doubled. The percentage of the gross national product or, I mean, the gross national product increased sizeably, and the government's revenues increased at the lower rate of taxation.

Now, one of the economists who has previously, and all these past months, been opposed to our proposal, Walter Heller, a very distinguished economist, when the recession was announced a short time ago, Walter Heller said how lucky we were that our tax reduction was just going into effect and that that just turned out to be exactly the right medicine for a recession. Well, if it's the right medicine to maybe help cure the recession, why wouldn't it have been good medicine to have prevented the recession?

If we, taking those personal savings—if we could increase by 2 percentage points the rate of savings in this country, through these tax cuts, that adds $40 billion to the capital pool that is available for investment and for people for mortgages and so forth. And incidentally, since the construction industry is one of the hard hit things right now in this recession, we have taken action—and I maybe sticking——

Mr. Gergen. It's out.

The President. It's out. All right, it's been announced. I don't want to be one of the White House leaks. [*Laughter*]

This morning we had a group from the construction industry in, and we have—over in the Labor Department—made some definite changes in regulations. Those changes are going to free up the billions and billions of dollars in pension funds for—that they can now be invested in home mortgages. Previous to this, they have not been able to. The total pension money available for investment in this country is over a trillion dollars—will be 3 trillion by 1984—and for the first time, this money will be made available for that kind of investment, which we think should go a long way toward beginning the revival of the housing industry.

You know, part of the lull in housing construction right now is the lowering of interest rates. The slump was caused by the high interest rates, but when the high interest rates start down, there's a lull while everybody says, "Well, let's wait till they get lower." That's going on right now, too. Maybe we can, with this new decision, maybe we can increase the speed with which those rates come down.

Q. What would be your advice, Mr. President, to Americans who want to know how to volunteer their time and their effort in a program that you have talked about—voluntarism?

The President. Oh! Listen—[*laughter*]—we just had a meeting yesterday of our national task force. That's exactly what they are set up to do—is to not only spread the word of where volunteer efforts have been tried someplace and are working successfully, and then spread that so that other people can do it, but also to answer that question of the many people who are trying to volunteer.

There is an estimated $100 billion worth of time and effort right now being contributed in this country in work in voluntary causes, in addition to $47 billion in actual cash contributed in volunteer efforts. And some of the things we're finding—and the mail that I'm getting is the most inspiring thing in the world—of communities that have just moved and said, "Why have we been sitting here, letting government do this? We should have been doing it long ago."

I believe this is beginning to sweep the country. So, people like that, I think will find that they're being sought out by the task force. If they don't get their volunteering in beforehand, somebody will be around to see if they want to volunteer.

Ms. Small. Thank you, Mr. President.

The President. Thank you all very much for being here.

Note: The President spoke at 3:55 p.m. in the Roosevelt Room at the White House. David R. Gergen is Assistant to the President for Communications, and Karna S. Small is Director, Media Relations and Planning.

Appointment of Kenneth M. Duberstein as Assistant to the President for Legislative Affairs
December 4, 1981

The President today announced his intention to appoint Kenneth M. Duberstein to be Assistant to the President for Legislative Affairs. He would succeed Max L. Friedersdorf.

Mr. Duberstein is currently serving as Deputy Assistant to the President for Legislative Affairs. In this position, he has served as the President's chief deputy liaison with the United States House of Representatives.

Prior to his appointment, Mr. Duberstein had served for 4 years as vice president of the Committee for Economic Development and director of business-government relations. He was responsible for directing CED's contacts with government and administering its research program. CED is a nonprofit, public policy organization comprised of 200 prominent business leaders and university presidents.

He was Deputy Under Secretary of Labor during the Ford administration and was responsible for all legislative and intergovernmental activities of the Department. He was Director of Congressional and Intergov-

ernmental Affairs for the U.S. General Services Administration in 1972–76. Prior to entering government, he was administrative assistant to the president of Franklin and Marshall College, Lancaster, Pa. In 1965–67 Mr. Duberstein was an intern and then a research assistant to Senator Jacob Javits (R-N.Y.).

Mr. Duberstein graduated from Franklin and Marshall College (A.B., 1965) and American University (M.A., 1966). He studied for 1 year at the New York Law School. He resides in Alexandria, Va., and has one daughter. He was born April 21, 1944, in Brooklyn, N.Y.

Remarks on Signing the Energy and Water Development Appropriation Act, 1982
December 4, 1981

The President. Good morning.

I'm signing the first regular appropriations bill for 1982, the energy and water development appropriations act. This bill should be a model for a responsible approach to reducing budget deficits. It provides nearly three-fourths of the additional savings for 1982 that I requested. So, on behalf of the taxpayers, please accept my gratitude.

There are good reasons for these savings, why they were achieved, and those reasons are standing right here around me. The two Appropriations Committee chairmen, Mark Hatfield and Tom Bevill, and one of the ranking minority members, John Myers, all worked hard, well, and together. Under their leadership, along with the other ranking minority member, Senator Johnston, the Conference Committee agreed to a bill that actually provided less spending than either the House or the Senate version.

I think it's particularly important that spending for the nondefense programs in this bill is lower than in 1981. For example, water resources construction and maintenance is 5 percent below 1981, but funding for all essential needs has been maintained. The bill provides funds for a number of initiatives of the administration, and it will strengthen the atomic energy defense programs of the Department of Energy.

The American people understand that every dollar we save of unnecessary spending means not only a lower deficit but also a chance to expand the pool of capital needed by industry to modernize and keep abreast of new production methods, so we can create more jobs and more economic opportunity for the people we serve. That's our goal, and thanks to the skill and dedication of these gentlemen, this bill is a significant step in the right direction. If we keep working together, I know we can make bigger and better progress in the days ahead.

And I shall now——

[*At this point, the President signed the bill into law, handing the pens to the three Members of Congress.*]

Representative Bevill. I have that luck when I write, too. [*Laughter*]

Senator Hatfield. Thank you.

Representative Myers. Thank you.

Reporter. Mr. President, how about the '82 spending bill? Have you made a decision on this compromise of 4 billion?

The President. Right now we're working up on the Hill with that. And we'll have a statement later on it, but we're working on it, and——

Q. Is it acceptable?

The President. Well, I'm very pleased with the progress that's been made, and we'll let you know.

Q. Mr. President, with Christmas coming, we now have 9 million Americans out of work. Are you alarmed at this sudden jump in the unemployment rate?

The President. I'd be alarmed if there were only half that many. And it's not a—well, maybe "alarm" isn't the proper word to be used here. We've known that the economy was going to be in the doldrums for the latter part of this year; we talked about it a great deal. And while none of us had used the word "recession" or projected that, it is now technically a recession.

But I'd like to point out that this has been a long-time unemployment that I was talking about clear back in the campaign, and this is one of the reasons for the economic program, is to restore our productivity and our ability to compete in the world market so that these people can be put back to work. But having grown up and entered the work force in the depths of the Great Depression, I can assure you I do not take unemployment lightly. I think it's a very great tragedy for our country and for the people involved.

Q. Mr. President, why have you assigned extra security protection for some of your top aides?

The President. Well, I think that the press had carried the story pretty well, that there is a threat to them that has been made rather obvious.

Q. Are you concerned about the terrorist squad?

The President. Well, obviously you have to be concerned about everyone and all the people that have been named in this.

Q. Have you tried to contact Libyan leader Qadhafi to tell him of your concern, or what are we saying to Libya?

The President. Oh, I think he figures that I'm concerned. But no—as you know, I hope you'll understand, we don't talk about security measures and situations of this kind.

Q. But you are taking them seriously?

The President. I think you have to. I think it safe to say that in any security case, even sometimes when security gets what they think is a crank call, why, they can't take that for granted.

Q. Thank you very much, Mr. President.

Q. But Speakes hasn't had any security. [*Laughter*]

The President. What?

Q. Speakes doesn't have any security.

The President. Who?

Q. Larry Speakes. [*Laughter*]

Deputy Press Secretary Speakes. I'll need that with regard to you. [*Laughter*]

The President. He's told me that he's assured of protection because of the warmth and the relationship with all of you. [*Laughter*]

Q. He's in a lot of trouble then, Mr. President. [*Laughter*]

Q. Thank you.

Note: The President spoke at 10:06 a.m. to reporters assembled in the Oval Office at the White House.

As enacted, H.R. 4144 is Public Law 97–88, approved December 4.

Nomination of Richard W. Heldridge To Be a Member of the Board of Directors of the Export-Import Bank of the United States
December 4, 1981

The President today announced his intention to nominate Richard W. Heldridge to be a member of the Board of Directors of the Export-Import Bank of the United States. He would succeed Margaret W. Kahliff.

Mr. Heldridge was president and chief executive officer, California Commerce Bank of San Jose, from 1975 until his retirement in 1980. Previously he was president and chief executive officer, Ammex Bank Holding Co., a subsidiary of Banco Nacional de Mexico, in 1977–80. Mr. Heldridge was executive vice president, Crocker National Bank, San Francisco, and directed and managed the assimilation of headquarters and 63 branches of U.S. National Bank, San Diego, into Crocker National Bank. He worked for Northwest Bancorporation, Minneapolis, Minn., in various capacities, in 1946–61.

He graduated from the University of Iowa (1940) and attended the Command and General Staff College (1948–49) and Columbia University. He is married, has four children, and resides in Los Gatos, Calif. He was born September 18, 1918, in Wessington Springs, S. Dak.

Appointment of Two Members of the Board of Visitors of the United States Military Academy
December 4, 1981

The President today announced his intention to appoint the following individuals to be members of the Board of Visitors, United States Military Academy:

Bernard J. Lasker has been a senior partner with the firm Lasker, Stone & Stern of New York, N.Y., since 1968. He joined his present firm's predecessor, E. H. Stern & Co., as a partner in 1947. He became a partner in the firm of Kaufmann, Alsberg & Co. and a member of the New York Stock Exchange in 1939. Mr. Lasker was elected chairman of the board of governors of the New York Stock Exchange in 1969 and 1970, after having served 2 years as vice chairman and 2 years as Governor. He was elected a director of the Stock Exchange in 1972. In 1969 Mr. Lasker was appointed by Governor

Nelson Rockefeller to serve as a commissioner of the Port Authority of New York and New Jersey. He is married, has two children, and resides in New York City. He was born August 10, 1910, in New York.

Clyde H. Slease is an attorney with the firm of Watt, Tieder, Killian, Toole & Hoffar of Washington, D.C. He was labor counsel, assistant to the president, and vice president and general counsel of the Dravo Corp., Pittsburgh, Pa., in 1948–78. He was an attorney with Paul, Lawrence & Wills, in 1946–48. He graduated from Haverford College (B.S., 1938) and the University of Pennsylvania (LL.B., J.D., 1941). He is married, has two children, and resides in Edgewater, Md. He was born July 25, 1916, in Hackensack, N.J.

Appointment of Two Members of the Board of Visitors of the United States Naval Academy
December 4, 1981

The President today announced his intention to appoint the following individuals to be members of the Board of Visitors, United States Naval Academy:

Edward R. Borcherdt, Jr., has been president, Borcherdt & Co. (financial consultants), in Los Angeles, Calif., since 1966. In addition, he was president, Darnell Corp., Ltd. in 1980–81; chairman, the Monterey Vineyard, Inc., in 1976–77; chairman, West Bay Financial Corp., in 1972–74; vice president, the Wolper Organization, Inc., in 1971–72; president, Western

Video Industries, Inc., 1968–71; and director, General Services, Western Division, Fry Consultants, Inc., in 1960–66. He is founder and chairman of the California Small Business Development Co. He served in the United States Marine Corps in 1953–57 and attained the rank of captain. Mr. Borcherdt graduated from Stanford University (A.B., 1953; M.B.A., 1957). He is married, has two children, and resides in Los Angeles, Calif. He was born July 12, 1930, in Butte, Mont.

Bernard E. Smith, Jr., is a partner with the firm of Lawrence O'Donnell & Co. of New York,

N.Y. Previously he was a partner with the firm Lasker, Stone and Stern in 1967–78 and a partner with LaMorte Maloney & Co. in 1950–67. He served in the United States Navy and Naval Reserve as assistant navigator and aide to executive officer, U.S.S. *Midway.* He graduated from the United States Naval Academy (B.S., E.E., 1946). He is married, has 11 children, and resides in New York, N.Y. He was born December 20, 1924, in New York City.

Appointment of Two Members of the Board of Visitors of the United States Air Force Academy
December 4, 1981

The President today announced his intention to appoint the following individuals to be members of the Board of Visitors, United States Air Force Academy:

Terrence O'Donnell is an attorney with the firm of Williams & Connolly, Washington, D.C. He was staff assistant and later Special Assistant to the President in 1972–77 and was a commissioned officer in the United States Air Force in 1966–72. He was a legal officer, Office of the Judge Advocate General, in 1971–72. He was a counterintelligence officer in South Vietnam in 1969–70 and assigned to Headquarters, USAF, Washington, D.C., in 1966–69. He attained the rank of captain. Mr. O'Donnell graduated from the United States Air Force Acade-my (B.S., 1966) and Georgetown University Law Center (J.D., 1971). He is married, has three children, and resides in Bethesda, Md. He was born March 3, 1944, in New York, N.Y.

Henry B. Sayler is chairman of the Republican Party of Florida. He was a member of the Florida State Senate in 1966–78 and is director of the Community Bank of Pinellas. He served in the United States Air Force in 1943–55 as a fighter pilot in the 8th Air Force. He was awarded the Distinguished Flying Cross and the Air Medal with 7 Clusters. He graduated from the United States Military Academy (B.S., 1943). He is married, has four children, and resides in St. Petersburg, Fla. He was born January 16, 1921, in Savannah, Ga.

Statement on United States Intelligence Activities
December 4, 1981

Today I am issuing two Executive orders, one to govern the activities of our intelligence agencies and one to reestablish the Intelligence Oversight Board, which works to ensure that our intelligence activities are lawful. These orders are designed to provide America's intelligence community with clearer, more positive guidance and to remove the aura of suspicion and mistrust that can hobble our nation's intelligence efforts.

This action is consistent with my promise in the campaign to revitalize America's intelligence system. The American people are well aware that the security of their country—and in an age of terrorism, their personal safety as well—is tied to the strength and efficiency of our intelligence-gathering organizations.

These orders have been carefully drafted—in consultation with the intelligence committees of both Houses of the Congress—to maintain the legal protection of all American citizens. They also give our intelligence professionals clear guidelines within which to do their difficult and essential job. Contrary to a distorted image that emerged during the last decade, there is no inherent conflict between the intelligence community and the rights of our citizens. Indeed, the purpose of the intelligence community is the protection of our people.

This is not to say mistakes were never made and that vigilance against abuse is unnecessary. But an approach that emphasizes suspicion and mistrust of our own intelligence efforts can undermine this Nation's ability to confront the increasing challenge of espionage and terrorism. This is particularly true in a world in which our adversaries pay no heed to the concerns for individual rights and freedoms that are so important to Americans and their government. As we move into the 1980's, we need to free ourselves from the negative attitudes of the past and look to meeting the needs of the country.

To those who view this change of direction with suspicion, let me assure you that while I occupy this office, no intelligence agency of the United States, or any other agency for that matter, will be given the authority to violate the rights and liberties guaranteed to all Americans by our Constitution and laws. The provisions of these Executive orders make this abundantly clear.

Most Americans realize that intelligence is a good and necessary profession to which high caliber men and women dedicate their lives. We respect them for their honorable and often perilous service to our nation and the cause of freedom. For all our technological advances, the gathering of information and its analysis depend finally on human judgment; and good judgment depends on the experience, integrity, and professionalism of those who serve us in the intelligence community.

Let us never forget that good intelligence saves American lives and protects our freedom. The loyalty and selflessness of our intelligence community during hard times are testimony to its commitment to the principles on which our country is based. I have faith in our intelligence professionals and expect each and every one of them to live up to the ideals and standards set by these Executive orders.

These orders charge our intelligence agencies to be vigorous, innovative, and responsible in the collection of accurate and timely information—information essential for the conduct of our foreign policy and crucial to our national safety. The country needs this service and is willing to allocate the resources necessary to do the job right.

It is not enough, of course, simply to collect information. Thoughtful analysis is vital to sound decisionmaking. The goal of our intelligence analysts can be nothing short of the truth, even when that truth is unpleasant or unpopular. I have asked for honest, objective analysis, and I shall expect nothing less. When there is disagreement, as there often is, on the difficult questions of our time, I expect those honest differences of view to be fully expressed.

These orders stipulate that special attention be given to detecting and countering the espionage and other threats that are directed by hostile intelligence services against us at home and abroad. These hostile services respect none of the liberties and rights of privacy that these orders protect. Certainly the same can be said of international terrorists, who present another important area of concern and responsibility for our intelligence professionals.

I want to stress that the primary job of the CIA is to conduct intelligence activities overseas and to deal with certain foreign persons who come into this country. The FBI takes primary responsibility for security activities within the United States, directed against hostile foreigners and those Americans who seek to do damage to our national security.

These orders do not alter this basic division of labor; they reaffirm it. They also encourage the fullest possible cooperation among the CIA, the FBI, and other agencies of the intelligence community as they seek to deal with fundamental challenges to our national security—challenges that respect neither national boundaries nor citizenship.

As these Executive orders are issued, I again want to express my respect and admiration for the men and women of our intelligence community: They run the risks; they bear the tensions; they serve in silence. They cannot fully be thanked in public, but I want them to know that their job is vital and that the American people, and their President, are profoundly grateful for what they do.

Executive Order 12333—United States Intelligence Activities
December 4, 1981

Table of Contents

		Page
	Preamble..	[1]*1128*
Part 1.	Goals, Direction, Duties and Responsibilities With Respect to the National Intelligence Effort.	*1128*
1.1	Goals..	*1128*
1.2	The National Security Council ...	*1129*
1.3	National Foreign Intelligence Advisory Groups.	*1129*
1.4	The Intelligence Community	*1129*
1.5	Director of Central Intelligence.	*1130*
1.6	Duties and Responsibilities of the Heads of Executive Branch Departments and Agencies..	*1131*
1.7	Senior Officials of the Intelligence Community.	*1131*
1.8	The Central Intelligence Agency.	*1132*
1.9	The Department of State	*1132*
1.10	The Department of the Treasury.	*1132*
1.11	The Department of Defense.......	*1133*
1.12	Intelligence Components Utilized by the Secretary of Defense.	*1133*
1.13	The Department of Energy	*1135*
1.14	The Federal Bureau of Investigation.	*1135*
Part 2.	Conduct of Intelligence Activities.	*1135*
2.1	Need..	*1135*
2.2	Purpose	*1135*
2.3	Collection of Information	*1135*
2.4	Collection Techniques..................	*1136*
2.5	Attorney General Approval	*1137*
2.6	Assistance to Law Enforcement Authorities.	*1137*
2.7	Contracting	*1137*
2.8	Consistency With Other Laws....	*1137*
2.9	Undisclosed Participation in Organizations Within the United States.	*1137*
2.10	Human Experimentation.............	*1137*
2.11	Prohibition on Assassination........	*1137*
2.12	Indirect Participation..................	*1137*
Part 3.	General Provisions........................	*1138*
3.1	Congressional Oversight.............	*1138*
3.2	Implementation............................	*1138*
3.3	Procedures	*1138*

Table of Contents—Continued

		Page
3.4	Definitions......................................	*1138*
3.5	Purpose and Effect	*1139*
3.6	Revocation......................................	*1139*

Timely and accurate information about the activities, capabilities, plans, and intentions of foreign powers, organizations, and persons, and their agents, is essential to the national security of the United States. All reasonable and lawful means must be used to ensure that the United States will receive the best intelligence available. For that purpose, by virtue of the authority vested in me by the Constitution and statutes of the United States of America, including the National Security Act of 1947, as amended, and as President of the United States of America, in order to provide for the effective conduct of United States intelligence activities and the protection of constitutional rights, it is hereby ordered as follows:

Part 1 *Goals, Direction, Duties and Responsibilities With Respect to the National Intelligence Effort*

1.1 *Goals.* The United States intelligence effort shall provide the President and the National Security Council with the necessary information on which to base decisions concerning the conduct and development of foreign, defense and economic policy, and the protection of United States national interests from foreign security threats. All departments and agencies shall cooperate fully to fulfill this goal.

(a) Maximum emphasis should be given to fostering analytical competition among appropriate elements of the Intelligence Community.

(b) All means, consistent with applicable United States law and this Order, and with full consideration of the rights of United

---

[1] *Editorial note: The page numbers in the original text have been changed to those of this book.*

States persons, shall be used to develop intelligence information for the President and the National Security Council. A balanced approach between technical collection efforts and other means should be maintained and encouraged.

(c) Special emphasis should be given to detecting and countering espionage and other threats and activities directed by foreign intelligence services against the United States Government, or United States corporations, establishments, or persons.

(d) To the greatest extent possible consistent with applicable United States law and this Order, and with full consideration of the rights of United States persons, all agencies and departments should seek to ensure full and free exchange of information in order to derive maximum benefit from the United States intelligence effort.

1.2 *The National Security Council.*

(a) *Purpose.* The National Security Council (NSC) was established by the National Security Act of 1947 to advise the President with respect to the integration of domestic, foreign and military policies relating to the national security. The NSC shall act as the highest Executive Branch entity that provides review of, guidance for and direction to the conduct of all national foreign intelligence, counterintelligence, and special activities, and attendant policies and programs.

(b) *Committees.* The NSC shall establish such committees as may be necessary to carry out its functions and responsibilities under this Order. The NSC, or a committee established by it, shall consider and submit to the President a policy recommendation, including all dissents, on each special activity and shall review proposals for other sensitive intelligence operations.

1.3 *National Foreign Intelligence Advisory Groups.*

(a) *Establishment and Duties.* The Director of Central Intelligence shall establish such boards, councils, or groups as required for the purpose of obtaining advice from within the Intelligence Community concerning:

(1) Production, review and coordination of national foreign intelligence;

(2) Priorities for the National Foreign Intelligence Program budget;

(3) Interagency exchanges of foreign intelligence information;

(4) Arrangements with foreign governments on intelligence matters;

(5) Protection of intelligence sources and methods;

(6) Activities of common concern; and

(7) Such other matters as may be referred by the Director of Central Intelligence.

(b) *Membership.* Advisory groups established pursuant to this section shall be chaired by the Director of Central Intelligence or his designated representative and shall consist of senior representatives from organizations within the Intelligence Community and from departments or agencies containing such organizations, as designated by the Director of Central Intelligence. Groups for consideration of substantive intelligence matters will include representatives of organizations involved in the collection, processing and analysis of intelligence. A senior representative of the Secretary of Commerce, the Attorney General, the Assistant to the President for National Security Affairs, and the Office of the Secretary of Defense shall be invited to participate in any group which deals with other than substantive intelligence matters.

1.4 *The Intelligence Community.* The agencies within the Intelligence Community shall, in accordance with applicable United States law and with the other provisions of this Order, conduct intelligence activities necessary for the conduct of foreign relations and the protection of the national security of the United States, including:

(a) Collection of information needed by the President, the National Security Council, the Secretaries of State and Defense, and other Executive Branch officials for the performance of their duties and responsibilities;

(b) Production and dissemination of intelligence;

(c) Collection of information concerning, and the conduct of activities to protect against, intelligence activities directed against the United States, international terrorist and international narcotics activities, and other hostile activities directed against the United States by foreign powers, organizations, persons, and their agents;

(d) Special activities;

(e) Administrative and support activities within the United States and abroad necessary for the performance of authorized activities; and

(f) Such other intelligence activities as the President may direct from time to time.

1.5 *Director of Central Intelligence.* In order to discharge the duties and responsibilities prescribed by law, the Director of Central Intelligence shall be responsible directly to the President and the NSC and shall:

(a) Act as the primary adviser to the President and the NSC on national foreign intelligence and provide the President and other officials in the Executive Branch with national foreign intelligence;

(b) Develop such objectives and guidance for the Intelligence Community as will enhance capabilities for responding to expected future needs for national foreign intelligence;

(c) Promote the development and maintenance of services of common concern by designated intelligence organizations on behalf of the Intelligence Community;

(d) Ensure implementation of special activities;

(e) Formulate policies concerning foreign intelligence and counterintelligence arrangements with foreign governments, coordinate foreign intelligence and counterintelligence relationships between agencies of the Intelligence Community and the intelligence or internal security services of foreign governments, and establish procedures governing the conduct of liaison by any department or agency with such services on narcotics activities;

(f) Participate in the development of procedures approved by the Attorney General governing criminal narcotics intelligence activities abroad to ensure that these activities are consistent with foreign intelligence programs;

(g) Ensure the establishment by the Intelligence Community of common security and access standards for managing and handling foreign intelligence systems, information, and products;

(h) Ensure that programs are developed which protect intelligence sources, methods, and analytical procedures;

(i) Establish uniform criteria for the determination of relative priorities for the transmission of critical national foreign intelligence, and advise the Secretary of Defense concerning the communications requirements of the Intelligence Community for the transmission of such intelligence;

(j) Establish appropriate staffs, committees, or other advisory groups to assist in the execution of the Director's responsibilities;

(k) Have full responsibility for production and dissemination of national foreign intelligence, and authority to levy analytic tasks on departmental intelligence production organizations, in consultation with those organizations, ensuring that appropriate mechanisms for competitive analysis are developed so that diverse points of view are considered fully and differences of judgment within the Intelligence Community are brought to the attention of national policymakers;

(l) Ensure the timely exploitation and dissemination of data gathered by national foreign intelligence collection means, and ensure that the resulting intelligence is disseminated immediately to appropriate government entities and military commands;

(m) Establish mechanisms which translate national foreign intelligence objectives and priorities approved by the NSC into specific guidance for the Intelligence Community, resolve conflicts in tasking priority, provide to departments and agencies having information collection capabilities that are not part of the National Foreign Intelligence Program advisory tasking concerning collection of national foreign intelligence, and provide for the development of plans and arrangements for transfer of required collection tasking authority to the Secretary of Defense when directed by the President;

(n) Develop, with the advice of the program managers and departments and agencies concerned, the consolidated National Foreign Intelligence Program budget, and present it to the President and the Congress;

(o) Review and approve all requests for reprogramming National Foreign Intelligence Program funds, in accordance with guidelines established by the Office of Management and Budget;

(p) Monitor National Foreign Intelligence Program implementation, and, as necessary, conduct program and performance audits and evaluations;

(q) Together with the Secretary of Defense, ensure that there is no unnecessary overlap between national foreign intelligence programs and Department of Defense intelligence programs consistent with the requirement to develop competitive analysis, and provide to and obtain from the Secretary of Defense all information necessary for this purpose;

(r) In accordance with law and relevant procedures approved by the Attorney General under this Order, give the heads of the departments and agencies access to all intelligence, developed by the CIA or the staff elements of the Director of Central Intelligence, relevant to the national intelligence needs of the departments and agencies; and

(s) Facilitate the use of national foreign intelligence products by Congress in a secure manner.

1.6 *Duties and Responsibilities of the Heads of Executive Branch Departments and Agencies.*

(a) The heads of all Executive Branch departments and agencies shall, in accordance with law and relevant procedures approved by the Attorney General under this Order, give the Director of Central Intelligence access to all information relevant to the national intelligence needs of the United States, and shall give due consideration to requests from the Director of Central Intelligence for appropriate support for Intelligence Community activities.

(b) The heads of departments and agencies involved in the National Foreign Intelligence Program shall ensure timely development and submission to the Director of Central Intelligence by the program managers and heads of component activities of proposed national programs and budgets in the format designated by the Director of Central Intelligence, and shall also ensure that the Director of Central Intelligence is provided, in a timely and responsive manner, all information necessary to perform the Director's program and budget responsibilities.

(c) The heads of departments and agencies involved in the National Foreign Intelligence Program may appeal to the President decisions by the Director of Central Intelligence on budget or reprogramming matters of the National Foreign Intelligence Program.

1.7 *Senior Officials of the Intelligence Community.* The heads of departments and agencies with organizations in the Intelligence Community or the heads of such organizations, as appropriate, shall:

(a) Report to the Attorney General possible violations of federal criminal laws by employees and of specified federal criminal laws by any other person as provided in procedures agreed upon by the Attorney General and the head of the department or agency concerned, in a manner consistent with the protection of intelligence sources and methods, as specified in those procedures;

(b) In any case involving serious or continuing breaches of security, recommend to the Attorney General that the case be referred to the FBI for further investigation;

(c) Furnish the Director of Central Intelligence and the NSC, in accordance with applicable law and procedures approved by the Attorney General under this Order, the information required for the performance of their respective duties;

(d) Report to the Intelligence Oversight Board, and keep the Director of Central Intelligence appropriately informed, concerning any intelligence activities of their organizations that they have reason to believe may be unlawful or contrary to Executive order or Presidential directive;

(e) Protect intelligence and intelligence sources and methods from unauthorized disclosure consistent with guidance from the Director of Central Intelligence;

(f) Disseminate intelligence to cooperating foreign governments under arrangements established or agreed to by the Director of Central Intelligence;

(g) Participate in the development of procedures approved by the Attorney General governing production and dissemination of intelligence resulting from criminal narcotics intelligence activities abroad if their departments, agencies, or organizations have intelligence responsibilities for foreign or domestic narcotics production and trafficking;

(h) Instruct their employees to cooperate fully with the Intelligence Oversight Board; and

(i) Ensure that the Inspectors General and General Counsels for their organizations have access to any information necessary to perform their duties assigned by this Order.

1.8 *The Central Intelligence Agency.* All duties and responsibilities of the CIA shall be related to the intelligence functions set out below. As authorized by this Order; the National Security Act of 1947, as amended; the CIA Act of 1949, as amended; appropriate directives or other applicable law, the CIA shall:

(a) Collect, produce and disseminate foreign intelligence and counterintelligence, including information not otherwise obtainable. The collection of foreign intelligence or counterintelligence within the United States shall be coordinated with the FBI as required by procedures agreed upon by the Director of Central Intelligence and the Attorney General;

(b) Collect, produce and disseminate intelligence on foreign aspects of narcotics production and trafficking;

(c) Conduct counterintelligence activities outside the United States and, without assuming or performing any internal security functions, conduct counterintelligence activities within the United States in coordination with the FBI as required by procedures agreed upon by the Director of Central Intelligence and the Attorney General;

(d) Coordinate counterintelligence activities and the collection of information not otherwise obtainable when conducted outside the United States by other departments and agencies;

(e) Conduct special activities approved by the President. No agency except the CIA (or the Armed Forces of the United States in time of war declared by Congress or during any period covered by a report from the President to the Congress under the War Powers Resolution (87 Stat. 855)) may conduct any special activity unless the President determines that another agency is more likely to achieve a particular objective;

(f) Conduct services of common concern for the Intelligence Community as directed by the NSC;

(g) Carry out or contract for research, development and procurement of technical systems and devices relating to authorized functions;

(h) Protect the security of its installations, activities, information, property, and employees by appropriate means, including such investigations of applicants, employees, contractors, and other persons with similar associations with the CIA as are necessary; and

(i) Conduct such administrative and technical support activities within and outside the United States as are necessary to perform the functions described in sections (a) through (h) above, including procurement and essential cover and proprietary arrangements.

1.9 *The Department of State.* The Secretary of State shall:

(a) Overtly collect information relevant to United States foreign policy concerns;

(b) Produce and disseminate foreign intelligence relating to United States foreign policy as required for the execution of the Secretary's responsibilities;

(c) Disseminate, as appropriate, reports received from United States diplomatic and consular posts;

(d) Transmit reporting requirements of the Intelligence Community to the Chiefs of United States Missions abroad; and

(e) Support Chiefs of Missions in discharging their statutory responsibilities for direction and coordination of mission activities.

1.10 *The Department of the Treasury.* The Secretary of the Treasury shall:

(a) Overtly collect foreign financial and monetary information;

(b) Participate with the Department of State in the overt collection of general foreign economic information;

(c) Produce and disseminate foreign intelligence relating to United States economic policy as required for the execution of the Secretary's responsibilities; and

(d) Conduct, through the United States Secret Service, activities to determine the existence and capability of surveillance equipment being used against the President of the United States, the Executive Office of the President, and, as authorized by the Secretary of the Treasury or the President, other Secret Service protectees and United States officials. No information shall be acquired intentionally through such activities except to protect against such surveillance, and those activities shall be conducted pursuant to procedures agreed upon by the Secretary of the Treasury and the Attorney General.

1.11 *The Department of Defense.* The Secretary of Defense shall:

(a) Collect national foreign intelligence and be responsive to collection tasking by the Director of Central Intelligence;

(b) Collect, produce and disseminate military and military-related foreign intelligence and counterintelligence as required for execution of the Secretary's responsibilities;

(c) Conduct programs and missions necessary to fulfill national, departmental and tactical foreign intelligence requirements;

(d) Conduct counterintelligence activities in support of Department of Defense components outside the United States in coordination with the CIA, and within the United States in coordination with the FBI pursuant to procedures agreed upon by the Secretary of Defense and the Attorney General;

(e) Conduct, as the executive agent of the United States Government, signals intelligence and communications security activities, except as otherwise directed by the NSC;

(f) Provide for the timely transmission of critical intelligence, as defined by the Director of Central Intelligence, within the United States Government;

(g) Carry out or contract for research, development and procurement of technical systems and devices relating to authorized intelligence functions;

(h) Protect the security of Department of Defense installations, activities, property, information, and employees by appropriate means including such investigations of applicants, employees, contractors, and other persons with similar associations with the Department of Defense as are necessary;

(i) Establish and maintain military intelligence relationships and military intelligence exchange programs with selected cooperative foreign defense establishments and international organizations, and ensure that such relationships and programs are in accordance with policies formulated by the Director of Central Intelligence;

(j) Direct, operate, control and provide fiscal management for the National Security Agency and for defense and military intelligence and national reconnaissance entities; and

(k) Conduct such administrative and technical support activities within and outside the United States as are necessary to perform the functions described in sections (a) through (j) above.

1.12 *Intelligence Components Utilized by the Secretary of Defense.* In carrying out the responsibilities assigned in section 1.11, the Secretary of Defense is authorized to utilize the following:

(a) *Defense Intelligence Agency,* whose responsibilities shall include:

(1) Collection, production, or, through tasking and coordination, provision of military and military-related intelligence for the Secretary of Defense, the Joint Chiefs of Staff, other Defense components, and, as appropriate, non-Defense agencies;

(2) Collection and provision of military intelligence for national foreign intelligence and counterintelligence products;

(3) Coordination of all Department of Defense intelligence collection requirements;

(4) Management of the Defense Attaché system; and

(5) Provision of foreign intelligence and counterintelligence staff support as directed by the Joint Chiefs of Staff.

(b) *National Security Agency,* whose responsibilities shall include:

(1) Establishment and operation of an effective unified organization for signals intelligence activities, except for the delegation of operational control over certain operations that are conducted through other elements of the Intelligence Community. No other department or agency may engage in signals intelligence activities except pursuant to a delegation by the Secretary of Defense;

(2) Control of signals intelligence collection and processing activities, including assignment of resources to an appropriate agent for such periods and tasks as required for the direct support of military commanders;

(3) Collection of signals intelligence information for national foreign intelligence purposes in accordance with guidance from the Director of Central Intelligence;

(4) Processing of signals intelligence data for national foreign intelligence purposes in accordance with guidance from the Director of Central Intelligence;

(5) Dissemination of signals intelligence information for national foreign intelligence purposes to authorized elements of the Government, including the military services, in accordance with guidance from the Director of Central Intelligence;

(6) Collection, processing and dissemination of signals intelligence information for counterintelligence purposes;

(7) Provision of signals intelligence support for the conduct of military operations in accordance with tasking, priorities, and standards of timeliness assigned by the Secretary of Defense. If provision of such support requires use of national collection systems, these systems will be tasked within existing guidance from the Director of Central Intelligence;

(8) Executing the responsibilities of the Secretary of Defense as executive agent for the communications security of the United States Government;

(9) Conduct of research and development to meet needs of the United States for signals intelligence and communications security;

(10) Protection of the security of its installations, activities, property, information, and employees by appropriate means, including such investigations of applicants, employees, contractors, and other persons with similar associations with the NSA as are necessary;

(11) Prescribing, within its field of authorized operations, security regulations covering operating practices, including the transmission, handling and distribution of signals intelligence and communications security material within and among the elements under control of the Director of the NSA, and exercising the necessary supervisory control to ensure compliance with the regulations;

(12) Conduct of foreign cryptologic liaison relationships, with liaison for intelligence purposes conducted in accordance with policies formulated by the Director of Central Intelligence; and

(13) Conduct of such administrative and technical support activities within and outside the United States as are necessary to perform the functions described in sections (1) through (12) above, including procurement.

(c) *Offices for the collection of specialized intelligence through reconnaissance programs,* whose responsibilities shall include:

(1) Carrying out consolidated reconnaissance programs for specialized intelligence;

(2) Responding to tasking in accordance with procedures established by the Director of Central Intelligence; and

(3) Delegating authority to the various departments and agencies for research, development, procurement, and operation of designated means of collection.

(d) *The foreign intelligence and counterintelligence elements of the Army, Navy, Air Force, and Marine Corps,* whose responsibilities shall include:

(1) Collection, production and dissemination of military and military-related foreign intelligence and counterintelligence, and information on the foreign aspects of narcotics production and trafficking. When collection is conducted in response to national foreign intelligence requirements, it will be conducted in accordance with guidance from the Director of Central Intelligence. Collection of national foreign intelligence, not otherwise obtainable, outside the United States shall be coordinated with the CIA, and such collection within the United States shall be coordinated with the FBI;

(2) Conduct of counterintelligence activities outside the United States in coordination with the CIA, and within the United States in coordination with the FBI; and

(3) Monitoring of the development, procurement and management of tactical intelligence systems and equipment and conducting related research, development, and test and evaluation activities.

(e) *Other offices within the Department of Defense appropriate for conduct of the intelligence missions and responsibilities assigned to the Secretary of Defense.* If such other offices are used for intelligence purposes, the provisions of Part 2 of this Order shall apply to those offices when used for those purposes.

1.13 *The Department of Energy.* The Secretary of Energy shall:

(a) Participate with the Department of State in overtly collecting information with respect to foreign energy matters;

(b) Produce and disseminate foreign intelligence necessary for the Secretary's responsibilities;

(c) Participate in formulating intelligence collection and analysis requirements where the special expert capability of the Department can contribute; and

(d) Provide expert technical, analytical and research capability to other agencies within the Intelligence Community.

1.14 *The Federal Bureau of Investigation.* Under the supervision of the Attorney General and pursuant to such regulations as the Attorney General may establish, the Director of the FBI shall:

(a) Within the United States conduct counterintelligence and coordinate counterintelligence activities of other agencies within the Intelligence Community. When a counterintelligence activity of the FBI involves military or civilian personnel of the Department of Defense, the FBI shall coordinate with the Department of Defense;

(b) Conduct counterintelligence activities outside the United States in coordination with the CIA as required by procedures agreed upon by the Director of Central Intelligence and the Attorney General;

(c) Conduct within the United States, when requested by officials of the Intelligence Community designated by the President, activities undertaken to collect foreign intelligence or support foreign intelligence collection requirements of other agencies within the Intelligence Community, or, when requested by the Director of the National Security Agency, to support the communications security activities of the United States Government;

(d) Produce and disseminate foreign intelligence and counterintelligence; and

(e) Carry out or contract for research, development and procurement of technical systems and devices relating to the functions authorized above.

Part 2 *Conduct of Intelligence Activities*

2.1 *Need.* Accurate and timely information about the capabilities, intentions and activities of foreign powers, organizations, or persons and their agents is essential to informed decison-making in the areas of national defense and foreign relations. Collection of such information is a priority objective and will be pursued in a vigorous, innovative and responsible manner that is consistent with the Constitution and applicable law and respectful of the principles upon which the United States was founded.

2.2 *Purpose.* This Order is intended to enhance human and technical collection techniques, especially those undertaken abroad, and the acquisition of significant foreign intelligence, as well as the detection and countering of international terrorist activities and espionage conducted by foreign powers. Set forth below are certain general principles that, in addition to and consistent with applicable laws, are intended to achieve the proper balance between the acquisition of essential information and protection of individual interests. Nothing in this Order shall be construed to apply to or interfere with any authorized civil or criminal law enforcement responsibility of any department or agency.

2.3 *Collection of Information.* Agencies within the Intelligence Community are authorized to collect, retain or disseminate information concerning United States persons only in accordance with procedures established by the head of the agency concerned and approved by the Attorney General, consistent with the authorities provided by Part 1 of this Order. Those procedures shall permit collection, retention and dissemination of the following types of information.

(a) Information that is publicly available or collected with the consent of the person concerned;

(b) Information constituting foreign intelligence or counterintelligence, including such information concerning corporations or other commercial organizations. Collection within the United States of foreign intelligence not otherwise obtainable shall be undertaken by the FBI or, when significant foreign intelligence is sought, by other authorized agencies of the Intelligence Community, provided that no foreign intelligence collection by such agencies may be undertaken for the purpose of acquiring information concerning the domestic activities of United States persons;

(c) Information obtained in the course of a lawful foreign intelligence, counterintelligence, international narcotics or international terrorism investigation;

(d) Information needed to protect the safety of any persons or organizations, including those who are targets, victims or hostages of international terrorists organizations;

(e) Information needed to protect foreign intelligence or counterintelligence sources or methods from unauthorized disclosure. Collection within the United States shall be undertaken by the FBI except that other agencies of the Intelligence Community may also collect such information concerning present or former employees, present or former intelligence agency contractors or their present or former employees, or applicants for any such employment or contracting;

(f) Information concerning persons who are reasonably believed to be potential sources or contacts for the purpose of determining their suitability or credibility;

(g) Information arising out of a lawful personnel, physical or communications security investigation;

(h) Information acquired by overhead reconnaissance not directed at specific United States persons;

(i) Incidentally obtained information that may indicate involvement in activities that may violate federal, state, local or foreign laws; and

(j) Information necessary for administrative purposes.

In addition, agencies within the Intelligence Community may disseminate information, other than information derived from signals intelligence, to each appropriate agency within the Intelligence Community for purposes of allowing the recipient agency to determine whether the information is relevant to its responsibilities and can be retained by it.

2.4 *Collection Techniques.* Agencies within the Intelligence Community shall use the least intrusive collection techniques feasible within the United States or directed against United States persons abroad. Agencies are not authorized to use such techniques as electronic surveillance, unconsented physical search, mail surveillance, physical surveillance, or monitoring devices unless they are in accordance with procedures established by the head of the agency concerned and approved by the Attorney General. Such procedures shall protect constitutional and other legal rights and limit use of such information to lawful governmental purposes. These procedures shall not authorize:

(a) The CIA to engage in electronic surveillance within the United States except for the purpose of training, testing, or conducting countermeasures to hostile electronic surveillance;

(b) Unconsented physical searches in the United States by agencies other than the FBI, except for:

(1) Searches by counterintelligence elements of the military services directed against military personnel within the United States or abroad for intelligence purposes, when authorized by a military commander empowered to approve physical searches for law enforcement purposes, based upon a finding of probable cause to believe that such persons are acting as agents of foreign powers; and

(2) Searches by CIA of personal property of non-United States persons lawfully in its possession.

(c) Physical surveillance of a United States person in the United States by agencies other than the FBI, except for:

(1) Physical surveillance of present or former employees, present or former intelligence agency contractors or their present or former employees, or applicants for any such employment or contracting; and

(2) Physical surveillance of a military person employed by a nonintelligence element of a military service.

(d) Physical surveillance of a United States person abroad to collect foreign intelligence, except to obtain significant information that cannot reasonably be acquired by other means.

2.5 *Attorney General Approval.* The Attorney General hereby is delegated the power to approve the use for intelligence purposes, within the United States or against a United States person abroad, of any technique for which a warrant would be required if undertaken for law enforcement purposes, provided that such techniques shall not be undertaken unless the Attorney General has determined in each case that there is probable cause to believe that the technique is directed against a foreign power or an agent of a foreign power. Electronic surveillance, as defined in the Foreign Intelligence Surveillance Act of 1978, shall be conducted in accordance with that Act, as well as this Order.

2.6 *Assistance to Law Enforcement Authorities.* Agencies within the Intelligence Community are authorized to:

(a) Cooperate with appropriate law enforcement agencies for the purpose of protecting the employees, information, property and facilities of any agency within the Intelligence Community;

(b) Unless otherwise precluded by law or this Order, participate in law enforcement activities to investigate or prevent clandestine intelligence activities by foreign powers, or international terrorist or narcotics activities;

(c) Provide specialized equipment, technical knowlege, or assistance of expert personnel for use by any department or agency, or, when lives are endangered, to support local law enforcement agencies. Provision of assistance by expert personnel shall be approved in each case by the General Counsel of the providing agency; and

(d) Render any other assistance and cooperation to law enforcement authorities not precluded by applicable law.

2.7 *Contracting.* Agencies within the Intelligence Community are authorized to enter into contracts or arrangements for the provision of goods or services with private companies or institutions in the United States and need not reveal the sponsorship of such contracts or arrangements for au-

thorized intelligence purposes. Contracts or arrangements with academic institutions may be undertaken only with the consent of appropriate officials of the institution.

2.8 *Consistency With Other Laws.* Nothing in this Order shall be construed to authorize any activity in violation of the Constitution or statutes of the United States.

2.9 *Undisclosed Participation in Organizations Within the United States.* No one acting on behalf of agencies within the Intelligence Community may join or otherwise participate in any organization in the United States on behalf of any agency within the Intelligence Community without disclosing his intelligence affiliation to appropriate officials of the organization, except in accordance with procedures established by the head of the agency concerned and approved by the Attorney General. Such participation shall be authorized only if it is essential to achieving lawful purposes as determined by the agency head or designee. No such participation may be undertaken for the purpose of influencing the activity of the organization or its members except in cases where:

(a) The participation is undertaken on behalf of the FBI in the course of a lawful investigation; or

(b) The organization concerned is composed primarily of individuals who are not United States persons and is reasonably believed to be acting on behalf of a foreign power.

2.10 *Human Experimentation.* No agency within the Intelligence Community shall sponsor, contract for or conduct research on human subjects except in accordance with guidelines issued by the Department of Health and Human Services. The subject's informed consent shall be documented as required by those guidelines.

2.11 *Prohibition on Assassination.* No person employed by or acting on behalf of the United States Government shall engage in, or conspire to engage in, assassination.

2.12 *Indirect Participation.* No agency of the Intelligence Community shall participate in or request any person to undertake activities forbidden by this Order.

Part 3 *General Provisions*

3.1 *Congressional Oversight.* The duties and responsibilities of the Director of Central Intelligence and the heads of other departments, agencies, and entities engaged in intelligence activities to cooperate with the Congress in the conduct of its responsibilities for oversight of intelligence activities shall be as provided in title 50, United States Code, section 413. The requirements of section 662 of the Foreign Assistance Act of 1961, as amended (22 U.S.C. 2422), and section 501 of the National Security Act of 1947, as amended (50 U.S.C. 413), shall apply to all special activities as defined in this Order.

3.2 *Implementation.* The NSC, the Secretary of Defense, the Attorney General, and the Director of Central Intelligence shall issue such appropriate directives and procedures as are necessary to implement this Order. Heads of agencies within the Intelligence Community shall issue appropriate supplementary directives and procedures consistent with this Order. The Attorney General shall provide a statement of reasons for not approving any procedures established by the head of an agency in the Intelligence Community other than the FBI. The National Security Council may establish procedures in instances where the agency head and the Attorney General are unable to reach agreement on other than constitutional or other legal grounds.

3.3 *Procedures.* Until the procedures required by this Order have been established, the activities herein authorized which require procedures shall be conducted in accordance with existing procedures or requirements established under Executive Order No. 12036. Procedures required by this Order shall be established as expeditiously as possible. All procedures promulgated pursuant to this Order shall be made available to the congressional intelligence committees.

3.4 *Definitions.* For the purposes of this Order, the following terms shall have these meanings:

(a) *Counterintelligence* means information gathered and activities conducted to protect against espionage, other intelligence activities, sabotage, or assassinations conducted for or on behalf of foreign powers, organizations or persons, or international terrorist activities, but not including personnel, physical, document or communications security programs.

(b) *Electronic surveillance* means acquisition of a nonpublic communication by electronic means without the consent of a person who is a party to an electronic communication or, in the case of a nonelectronic communication, without the consent of a person who is visably present at the place of communication, but not including the use of radio direction-finding equipment solely to determine the location of a transmitter.

(c) *Employee* means a person employed by, assigned to or acting for an agency within the Intelligence Community.

(d) *Foreign intelligence* means information relating to the capabilities, intentions and activities of foreign powers, organizations or persons, but not including counterintelligence except for information on international terrorist activities.

(e) *Intelligence activities* means all activities that agencies within the Intelligence Community are authorized to conduct pursuant to this Order.

(f) *Intelligence Community* and *agencies within the Intelligence Community* refer to the following agencies or organizations:

(1) The Central Intelligence Agency (CIA);

(2) The National Security Agency (NSA);

(3) The Defense Intelligence Agency (DIA);

(4) The offices within the Department of Defense for the collection of specialized national foreign intelligence through reconnaissance programs;

(5) The Bureau of Intelligence and Research of the Department of State;

(6) The intelligence elements of the Army, Navy, Air Force, and Marine Corps, the Federal Bureau of Investigation (FBI), the Department of the Treasury, and the Department of Energy; and

(7) The staff elements of the Director of Central Intelligence.

(g) *The National Foreign Intelligence Program* includes the programs listed below, but its composition shall be subject to review by the National Security Council and modification by the President:

(1) The programs of the CIA;

(2) The Consolidated Cryptologic Program, the General Defense Intelligence Program, and the programs of the offices within the Department of Defense for the collection of specialized national foreign intelligence through reconnaissance, except such elements as the Director of Central Intelligence and the Secretary of Defense agree should be excluded;

(3) Other programs of agencies within the Intelligence Community designated jointly by the Director of Central Intelligence and the head of the department or by the President as national foreign intelligence or counterintelligence activities;

(4) Activities of the staff elements of the Director of Central Intelligence;

(5) Activities to acquire the intelligence required for the planning and conduct of tactical operations by the United States military forces are not included in the National Foreign Intelligence Program.

(h) *Special activities* means activities conducted in support of national foreign policy objectives abroad which are planned and executed so that the role of the United States Government is not apparent or acknowledged publicly, and functions in support of such activities, but which are not intended to influence United States political processes, public opinion, policies, or media and do not include diplomatic activities or the collection and production of intelligence or related support functions.

(i) *United States person* means a United States citizen, an alien known by the intelligence agency concerned to be a permanent resident alien, an unincorporated association substantially composed of United States citizens or permanent resident aliens, or a corporation incorporated in the United States, except for a corporation directed and controlled by a foreign government or governments.

3.5 *Purpose and Effect.* This Order is intended to control and provide direction and guidance to the Intelligence Community. Nothing contained herein or in any procedures promulgated hereunder is intended to confer any substantive or procedural right or privilege on any person or organization.

3.6 *Revocation.* Executive Order No. 12036 of January 24, 1978, as amended, entitled "United States Intelligence Activities," is revoked.

RONALD REAGAN

The White House,
December 4, 1981.

[*Filed with the Office of the Federal Register, 4:09 p.m., December 4, 1981*]

Executive Order 12334—President's Intelligence Oversight Board
December 4, 1981

By the authority vested in me as President by the Constitution and statutes of the United States of America, and in order to enhance the security of the United States by assuring the legality of activities of the Intelligence Community, it is hereby ordered as follows:

Section 1. There is hereby established within the White House Office, Executive Office of the President, the President's Intelligence Oversight Board, which shall be composed of three members. One member, appointed from among the membership of the President's Foreign Intelligence Advisory Board, shall be designated by the President as Chairman. Members of the Board shall serve at the pleasure of the President and shall be appointed by the President from among trustworthy and distinguished citizens outside the Government who are qualified on the basis of achievement, experience and independence. The Board shall utilize such full-time staff and consultants as authorized by the President.

Sec. 2. The Board shall:

(a) Inform the President of intelligence

activities that any member of the Board believes are in violation of the Constitution or laws of the United States, Executive orders, or Presidential directives;

(b) Forward to the Attorney General reports received concerning intelligence activities that the Board believes may be unlawful;

(c) Review the internal guidelines of each agency within the Intelligence Community concerning the lawfulness of intelligence activities;

(d) Review the practices and procedures of the Inspectors General and General Counsel of the Intelligence Community for discovering and reporting intelligence activities that may be unlawful or contrary to Executive order or Presidential directive; and

(e) Conduct such investigations as the Board deems necessary to carry out its functions under this Order.

Sec. 3. The Board shall, when required by this Order, report directly to the President. The Board shall consider and take appropriate action with respect to matters identified by the Director of Central Intelligence, the Central Intelligence Agency or other agencies of the Intelligence Community. With respect to matters deemed appropriate by the President, the Board shall advise and make appropriate recommendations to the Director of Central Intelligence, the Central Intelligence Agency, and other agencies of the Intelligence Community.

Sec. 4. The heads of departments and agencies of the Intelligence Community shall, to the extent permitted by law, provide the Board with all information necessary to carry out its responsibilities. Inspectors General and General Counsel of the Intelligence Community shall, to the extent permitted by law, report to the Board concerning intelligence activities that they have reason to believe may be unlawful or contrary to Executive order or Presidential directive.

Sec. 5. Information made available to the Board shall be given all necessary security protection in accordance with applicable laws and regulations. Each member of the Board, each member of the Board's staff, and each of the Board's consultants shall execute an agreement never to reveal any classified information obtained by virtue of his or her service with the Board except to the President or to such persons as the President may designate.

Sec. 6. Members of the Board shall serve without compensation, but may receive transportation, expense, and per diem allowances as authorized by law. Staff and consultants to the Board shall receive pay and allowances as authorized by the President.

RONALD REAGAN

The White House,
December 4, 1981.

[Filed with the Office of the Federal Register, 4:10 p.m., December 4, 1981]

Statement on Signing the Intelligence Authorization Act for Fiscal Year 1982
December 4, 1981

I am pleased today to sign into Law H.R. 3454, the Intelligence Authorization Act for Fiscal Year 1982. This act represents a significant first step toward achieving revitalization of our nation's intelligence community. The President of the United States must have timely, accurate, and insightful foreign intelligence in order to make sound national defense and foreign policy decisions. This act helps to assure that we will have the necessary intelligence information to make these difficult decisions.

The Congress has with this act authorized appropriations sufficient to assure that we continue to have the world's best and most professional intelligence service. The Congress has also provided new administrative authorities to the heads of the nation's three major intelligence agencies to assure that they can perform their missions more effectively. I hope that the spirit of cooperation between the legislative and executive branches which resulted in this act will continue as we move to rebuild our nation's intelligence capabilities.

I would also note my hope that I will soon be able to sign the Intelligence Identities Protection Act, which has passed the House and is awaiting floor action in the Senate. I strongly support enactment of this measure, preferably in the form in which it was passed by the House of Representatives; we must act now to protect our intelligence personnel, who serve our nation under what are often difficult and dangerous circumstances.

Note: As enacted, H.R. 3454 is Public Law 97–89, approved December 4.

Nomination of Walter Leon Cutler To Be United States Ambassador to Tunisia
December 4, 1981

The President today announced his intention to nominate Walter Leon Cutler, of Maryland, to be Ambassador to the Republic of Tunisia. He would succeed Stephen Warren Bosworth.

Mr. Cutler served in the United States Army in 1954–56, prior to entering the Foreign Service. He was consular officer in Yaounde in 1957–59. In the Department, he was foreign affairs officer in the Executive Secretariat (1959–61) and Staff Assistant to the Secretary of State (1961–62). He was political officer in Algiers (1962–65), principal officer in Tabriz (1965–67), political officer in Seoul (1967–69), and in Saigon (1969–71). In 1971–73 he was international rela-

tions officer in the Department. He attended the Senior Seminar at the Foreign Service Institute in 1973–74. He was country director of Central African Affairs in the Department in 1974–75 and served as Ambassador to the Republic of Zaire in 1975–79. He was Deputy Assistant Secretary of State for Congressional Relations in 1979–81.

Mr. Cutler graduated from Wesleyan University (B.A., 1953) and Fletcher School of Law and Diplomacy (M.A., 1954). He is married, has three children, and resides in Chevy Chase, Md. He was born November 25, 1931, in Boston, Mass.

Nomination of Maurice H. Stans To Be a Member of the Board of Directors of the Overseas Private Investment Corporation
December 4, 1981

The President today announced his intention to nominate Maurice H. Stans to be a member of the Board of Directors of the Overseas Private Investment Corporation. He would succeed William M. Landau.

Mr. Stans served for 10 years under two Presidents, 6 of those years in Cabinet-level positions. He became Secretary of Commerce on January 22, 1969, and held that post until February 1972. Mr. Stans is cur-

rently a business consultant in Los Angeles, Calif.

Previously he was president of Gore Forgan Staats, Inc., investment bankers, New York, in 1961 and 1962. He served as Vice Chairman and a Director of the Bureau of the Budget under President Eisenhower in 1958–61 and had been Deputy Director for 6 months.

For 2 years before the budget bureau post, Mr. Stans had been Deputy Postmaster General. In 1953 he served on a task force which assisted the House Appropriations Committee in reviewing the Federal budget for fiscal year 1954. Prior to 1955 he was executive partner in the national accounting firm of Alexander Grant & Co.

He attended Northwestern University and Columbia University. Mr. Stans is married, has four adopted children, and resides in Los Angeles, Calif. He was born March 22, 1908, in Shakopee, Minn.

Appointment of Two Members of the Council of the Administrative Conference of the United States
December 4, 1981

The President today announced his intention to appoint the following individuals to be members of the Council of the Administrative Conference of the United States:

Walter Gellhorn is professor emeritus, Columbia School of Law, New York, N.Y. He has been on the staff of the Columbia University since 1933. He graduated from Amherst College (A.B., 1927), Columbia University (L.H.D., 1952; LL.B., 1931), and the University of Pennsylvania (LL.D., 1953). He is married, has two children, and resides in New York, N.Y. He was born September 18, 1906, in St. Louis, Mo.

Otis M. Smith has been associated with the General Motors Corp. since 1967. He is currently vice president and general counsel. Previously he was Justice, Supreme Court, State of Michigan, in 1961–66. He graduated from Catholic University (J.D., 1950). He is married, has four children, and resides in Detroit, Mich. He was born February 20, 1922, in Memphis, Tenn.

Statement on Mr. and Mrs. Andrei Sakharov's Hunger Strike
December 4, 1981

Academician Andrei Sakharov, a leading Soviet scientist and Nobel Peace Prize Laureate, and his wife have been for over a week on a hunger strike. They are protesting the repeated refusal of the Soviet authorities to grant an exit visa to Mr. Sakharov's daughter-in-law, Elizaveta Alekseyeva, to join her husband, Mr. Aleksei Semionov, a student at an American university. The young couple has been separated for a long time. I am concerned for the health of Mr. and Mrs. Sakharov and strongly urge the Soviet Government to allow Mrs. Alekseyeva to join her husband.

Proclamation 4885—Bill of Rights Day, Human Rights Day and Week, 1981
December 4, 1981

By the President of the United States of America

A Proclamation

On December 15, 1791, our Founding Fathers rejoiced in the ratification of the first ten amendments to the Constitution of the United States—a Bill of Rights which has helped guarantee all Americans the liberty which we so cherish.

One hundred and fifty-seven years later, on December 10, 1948, the United Nations adopted the Universal Declaration of Human Rights, an effort aimed at securing basic human rights for the people of all nations.

Each of these great documents was born after the bloodshed of a bitter war. We remember the great sacrifices Americans have made for 200 years, from the Revolutionary War, in which our ancestors pledged "their lives, their fortunes, and their sacred honor," to the wars of this century, in which hundreds of thousands of young Americans and millions of others gave their lives on the battlefields of Europe, Asia, and Africa in the struggle for freedom. And, yet, even today, as we celebrate Bill of Rights Day and Human Rights Day, we all are only too well aware that the individual rights declared in these documents are not yet respected in many nations.

We have learned that the lesson our Founding Fathers taught is as true today as it was two centuries ago—liberty depends not upon the state but upon the people. Liberty thrives in the free association of citizens in free institutions: families, churches, universities, trade unions, and a free press.

Mankind's best defense against tyranny and want is limited government—a government which empowers its people, not itself, and which respects the wit and bravery, the initiative, and the generosity of the people. For, above all, human rights are rights of individuals: rights of conscience, rights of choice, rights of association, rights of emigration, rights of self-directed action, and the right to own property. The concept of a nation of free men and women linked together voluntarily is the genius of the system our Founding Fathers established.

We will continue to strive to respect these rights fully in our own country and to promote their observance abroad. We could have no greater wish for mankind than that all people come to enjoy these rights.

This year, after nearly 20 years of effort, the United Nations Human Rights Commission and the UN General Assembly have approved a declaration on the elimination of all forms of discrimination based on religion. It begins with words Americans will find familiar, "Everyone will have the right to freedom of thought, conscience and religion." It declares that parents must have the right to teach their children to worship God and that all religions must have the right to teach their faith, to train their clergy, and to observe their customs and holidays.

We in America are blessed with rights secured for us by the sacrifices of our forefathers, but we yearn for the day when all mankind can share in these blessings. Never is there any excuse for the violation of the fundamental rights of man not at any time or in any place, not in rich countries or poor, not under any social, economic or political system.

Now, Therefore, I, Ronald Reagan, President of the United States of America, do hereby proclaim December 10, 1981 as Human Rights Day and December 15, 1981 as Bill of Rights Day, and call on all Americans to observe the week beginning December 10, 1981 as Human Rights Week. During this week, let each of us give special thought to the blessings we enjoy as a free people and let us dedicate our efforts to making the promise of our Bill of Rights a living reality for all Americans and, whenever possible, for all mankind.

In Witness Whereof, I have hereunto set my hand this 4th day of December, in the year of our Lord nineteen hundred and eighty-one, and of the Independence of the United States of America the two hundred and sixth.

RONALD REAGAN

[Filed with the Office of the Federal Register, 3:35 p.m., December 7, 1981]

Note: The text of the proclamation was released by the Office of the Press Secretary on December 5.

Exchange With Reporters on Reports on Libyan Assassination Squads
December 7, 1981

The President. Now, let me state in advance that I'm going to make a statement, and it's going to be hit and run because——

Q. Oh, no.

The President. Yes. [*Laughter*] I have to. No, this was not on the schedule, and I've got the astronauts who took the *Columbia* around the globe several times waiting for me. And I've already delayed them, so——

Q. Don't you want to answer Qadhafi before you start? [*Laughter*]

Q. Mr. President, he says you're a liar and silly and a child for believing that he's trying to assassinate you.

The President. I wouldn't believe a word he says if I were you.

Q. He says he wants the evidence; that if you don't have any evidence then you must be a liar.

The President. We have the evidence, and he knows it.

Q. Mr. President, are the reports of the assassination squads exaggerated? Are they exaggerated? The reports of the assassination squads, are they accurate—the things that have been in the press?

The President. I just—I won't comment on security matters. I really won't.

Q. Do you feel you're adequately protected?

The President. Yes. If I didn't think I was adequately protected, I wouldn't come in this room. [*Laughter*]

Note: The exchange began at 10:45 a.m. in the Briefing Room at the White House, where the President had gone to make a statement to reporters on his meeting with the Inspectors General and members of the President's Council on Integrity and Efficiency. The exchange preceded his statement.

Remarks to Reporters on Integrity and Efficiency in Federal Programs
December 7, 1981

I've just met with the Inspectors General to receive their 6-month consolidated report on this administration's drive against fraud, waste, and mismanagement in the Federal Government. And I am happy—and I really mean happy—to announce that their report contains some very good news for the American taxpayer.

Last March, I signed an Executive order establishing the Council on Integrity and Efficiency. Its purpose was to form a new and more effective strike force against corruption and inefficiency in government by pooling the resources of the Inspector General, the FBI, the Department of Justice, the Office of Management and Budget, and the Office of Personnel Management. And in just 6 months, these gentlemen here and the others, their colleagues, in joint efforts authorized by our Executive order, have saved the taxpayers over $2 billion.

Now, you've heard me talk about the billions of dollars in delinquent debt that have been costing the honest taxpayers of this country $14 million a day. We're making progress now in collecting that debt, thanks to these gentlemen. Just this year in one department, we have collected $1 billion in delinquent debt. Now, I hope the Congress will act on the legislation that I have proposed that will enable us to collect $½ billion a year, which is presently beyond our reach.

The great majority of Federal employees are honest, hardworking, and dedicated to public service. But over the last 6 months, 145 Federal employees have been discharged as a result of the 16 investigations. Others may have voluntarily resigned to avoid the embarrassment of being fired.

In establishing the Council, I assured the American people that this was no cosmetic gesture but a serious, substantial step toward restoring government efficiency and thereby rebuilding public confidence in our political institutions. I promised that we'd follow every lead, root out every incompetent, and prosecute every crook that we found cheating the people of this Nation.

Well thanks to the dedication of these Inspectors General, this pledge has been and will continue to be kept. We're reduc-

ing fraud, improving management controls, eliminating errors in government programs and, by doing so, also providing a growing deterrent against future abuses.

I have just come from a meeting with this entire group and discovered that the few facts that I have in here only scratch the surface of what has actually been accomplished. Integrity and efficiency in managing government programs not only save the government money, they mean better service for those the programs are designed to serve the American people.

It's on behalf of the people that I extend my thanks to the Inspectors General for their valuable work and urge them to keep on being as mean as junkyard dogs when it comes to protecting the taxpayers. I again repeat my thanks and my congratulations to these men and women who have been doing this job. And as I say, I've only scratched the surface.

And now I've got to go meet the astronauts and ask why they didn't pick me up on their way around and take me to California. [*Laughter*]

Note: The President spoke at 10:49 a.m. in the Briefing Room at the White House following a meeting with the Inspectors General and members of the President's Council on Integrity and Efficiency. The 92-page report is entitled, "Addressing Fraud, Waste and Abuse, A Summary Report of Inspectors General Activities—President's Council on Integrity and Efficiency, FY 1981 II."

Remarks at a Ceremony Honoring the Pilots of the Second Flight of the Space Shuttle *Columbia*
December 7, 1981

The President. We're here, ladies and gentlemen, with these two gentlemen and their wives, who, I think, thrilled all of us in flying the *Columbia* and for a ceremony. And I now turn it over to the Colonel.

Lieutenant Colonel Muratti. Attention to orders.

"The National Aeronautics and Space Administration awards Joe H. Engle the NASA

Distinguished Service Medal, for distinguished service as Commander of the Second Orbital Flight Test of the Space Shuttle *Columbia*, the first demonstration of shuttle reusability. His exceptional skills facilitated the accomplishment of major mission objectives despite an abbreviated mission.

"Signed and sealed at Washington, D.C.,

this 7th day of December, 1981."

Signed, James M. Beggs, Administrator, NASA.

The President. Sir, we are glad to do this, and congratulations.

Colonel Engle. Thank you, Mr. President. Thank you, it's a tremendous honor. Thank you, sir.

The President. You thrilled all of us.

Lieutenant Colonel Muratti. "The National Aeronautics and Space Administration awards Richard H. Truly the NASA Distinguished Service Medal, for distinguished service as pilot of the Second Orbital Flight Test of the Space Shuttle *Columbia*, the first demonstration of shuttle reusability. His exceptional skills facilitated the accomplishment of major mission objectives despite an abbreviated mission.

"Signed and sealed at Washington, D.C., this 7th day of December, 1981."

Signed, James M. Beggs, Administrator, NASA.

The President. And thank you on behalf of the people, and congratulations.

Captain Truly. Thank you, Mr. President.

The President. I was just sharing with— oh, we're not through yet.

Colonel Engle. Well, Mr. President, it's our honor on behalf of all the people at NASA to present you with this American flag and crew emblem that was flown aboard the space shuttle *Columbia*. We want to thank you again for your support of the program and for taking the time to come down and talk with us during the flight. It was an honor and a thrill to us.

The President. Well, it was a thrill to me. I'd never made a long distance call like that. [*Laughter*] Well, thank you very much. I'm very proud to have this, and I accept it on behalf of the people. Thanks very much.

I was just telling them that—and if it's of interest to any of you—that I learned while I was there, something that I can't quit talking about, and that is the miracle that takes place. Their approach to Edwards Air Force Base in California begins out over the Hawaiian Islands, and when the plane levels off and starts into the runway, just envision that kind of an approach. It only takes 20 minutes.

Note: The President spoke at 11 a.m. to reporters assembled in the Oval Office at the White House. Lt. Col. Jose A. Muratti is the Army Aide to the President.

On November 13, the President spoke to astronauts from the Mission Control area at the space center in Houston, Tex., see page 1045 for his remarks.

Nomination of Cathie A. Shattuck To Be a Member of the Equal Employment Opportunity Commission
December 7, 1981

The President today announced his intention to nominate Cathie A. Shattuck to be a member of the Equal Employment Opportunity Commission for the term expiring July 1, 1985. She would succeed Ethel Bent Walsh.

Miss Shattuck is self-employed in the private practice of law, representing both plaintiffs and defendants in labor-employment related matters and business. She is also special hearing officer, State Personnel Board, State of Colorado. She is a lecturer and trainer in the field of employment and employee relations, including teaching courses for continuing legal education in Colorado, Inc. She has been a trial attorney for the U.S. Equal Employment Opportunity Commission in Denver.

Previously Miss Shattuck was a law clerk, Office of the Attorney General, State of Nebraska, in 1969–70; assistant law librarian, Nebraska University College of Law, in 1967–70; and legislative aide to the speaker of the Nebraska Unicameral (Legislature).

She graduated from the University of Nebraska at Lincoln (B.A., 1967; J.D., 1970). She resides in Boulder, Colo., and was born July 18, 1945, in Salt Lake City, Utah.

Statement on the Death of Thomas Corcoran
December 7, 1981

Thomas Corcoran, known as Tommy to his legion of friends, was one of those bright young men of the 1930's who helped to light America's way through the dark years of the Great Depression. He generated ideas, enthusiasm, and the confidence that something could be done about the problems that beset this country. "Tommy the Cork" was one of those individuals America cannot do without—he was an indomitable doer and an irrepressible advocate.

Throughout his years, he remained a valued counselor to Presidents and statesmen. I convey my deepest sympathy to his family and to all Americans who, indeed, have lost a source of vitality and a voice of experience.

Message to the Congress Transmitting a Report on United States Participation in the United Nations
December 7, 1981

To the Congress of the United States:

I am pleased to transmit herewith a report of the activities of the United States Government in the United Nations and its affiliated agencies, as required by the United Nations Participation Act (Public Law 264, 79th Congress). The report covers calendar year 1980, the last year of the previous Administration.

The United Nations remains an important institution for the foreign policy of the United States, and the United States will uphold the ideals upon which the United Nations was founded.

RONALD REAGAN

The White House,
December 7, 1981.

Note: The report is entitled "United States Participation in the UN—Report by the President to the Congress for the Year 1980" (Government Printing Office, 407 pages).

Message to the Congress Transmitting the Chugach Region Study Report
December 8, 1981

To the Congress of the United States:

Pursuant to the provisions of Section 1430 of the Alaska National Interest Lands Conservation Act (ANILCA), I hereby transmit the Chugach Region Study. The participants to the study failed to agree upon a settlement of the land claims of Chugach Natives, Incorporated. However, the Chugach Natives, Incorporated, may elect to satisfy their land entitlements pursuant to existing law under Section 1429 of ANILCA, or pursuant to land exchanges in accordance with a federal proposal dated November 13, 1981.

RONALD REAGAN

The White House,
December 8, 1981.

Note: The 3-volume study is entitled "Chugach Region Study Report—November 1981."

White House Statement on a Meeting Between President Reagan and President Spyros Kyprianou of Cyprus
December 8, 1981

President Reagan and Cypriot President Spyros Kyprianou met in a working visit today and held discussions on recent developments on Cyprus and the intercommunal talks. Vice President Bush and Secretary Haig also attended the meeting along with Cypriot Foreign Minister Rolandis and Ambassador Jacovides. President Reagan stressed U.S. hopes for a just and lasting settlement of the Cyprus problem and emphasized his support for the United Nations-supervised intercommunal talks. The United States believes that recent developments in the negotiations, including presentation of a U.N. "evaluation" of the talks, suggest the potential for progress toward a mutually beneficial agreement.

Satement on Federal Employment of Discharged Air Traffic Controllers
December 9, 1981

For the past 4½ months we have kept the airways safe and the Nation's air traffic moving despite a strike by members of the Professional Air Traffic Controllers Organization.

We faced a choice last August: concede to the demands of a union engaged in an illegal strike—or dismiss the controllers who violated their oath and walked off their jobs, and keep the airways operating with the resources available to us.

We made the only choice we could. While we regret the loss of an experienced work force, we have an even greater commitment to the people of America to uphold the principles on which this country is built—principles of law, due process, and respect for the public trust.

Those principles have been honored, and our commitment to them remains firm. But at the same time there is another principle we honor in America—the tradition that individuals deserve to be treated with compassion. In that spirit, I am today extending to the air traffic controllers discharged because of their actions in striking against the Federal Government, an opportunity to reapply for Federal employment, in departments and agencies other than the Federal Aviation Administration. I do not believe that those who forfeited their jobs as controllers should be foreclosed from other Federal employment. I am sure that many of those who were misled or badly advised regret their action and would welcome an opportunity to return to Federal service.

So, today I am issuing this directive to the Office of Personnel Management.

First, when the Office of Personnel Management receives applications for Federal employment from former FAA controllers terminated by their strike action, it will apply the same suitability standards as it applies to all other candidates for jobs with the Federal Government. This means that each application will be considered fairly and on a case-by-case basis.

Second, because returning the striking controllers to their former positions would adversely affect operational efficiency, damage morale, and perhaps impair safety, the former controllers will be eligible for employment consideration in any Federal agency except the Federal Aviation Administration.

I realize that these conditions prevent the ex-controllers from returning to their former jobs. But in considering an applicant for a position of public responsibility, we must take into account not only the ability to perform that job but the effect that his or her employment may have on others within the agency. This is particularly true where the effectiveness of the nation's air traffic control system and the safety of the airways are at stake.

Memorandum on Federal Employment of Discharged Air Traffic Controllers
December 9, 1981

Memorandum for the Director of the Office of Personnel Management
Subject: Federal Employment of Discharged Air Traffic Controllers

The Office of Personnel Management has established the position that the former air traffic controllers who were discharged for participating in a strike against the Government initiated on August 3, 1981 shall be debarred from federal employment for a period of three years. Upon deliberation I have concluded that such individuals, despite their strike participation, should be permitted to apply for federal employment outside the scope of their former employing agency.

Therefore, pursuant to my authority to regulate federal employment, I have determined that the Office of Personnel Management should permit federal agencies to receive applications for employment from these individuals and process them according to established civil service procedures.

Your office should perform suitability determinations with respect to all such applicants according to established standards and procedures under 5 CFR, Part 731.

After reviewing reports from the Secretary of Transportation and the Administrator of the Federal Aviation Administration, I have further determined that it would be detrimental to the efficiency of operations at the Federal Aviation Administration and to the safe and effective performance of our national air traffic control system to permit the discharged air traffic controllers to return to employment with that agency. Therefore, these former federal employees should not be deemed suitable for employment with the Federal Aviation Administration.

I direct you to process their applications for reemployment with the federal government accordingly.

RONALD REAGAN

Message About March of Dimes Birth Defects Prevention Month, January 1982
December 9, 1981

Birth defects represent the nation's number one child health problem and in 1982 will strike one out of every twelve newborn infants with some form of mental or bodily damage.

Through the March of Dimes Birth Defects Foundation, remarkable progress is being made in discovering the causes and preventing and treating birth defects in the newborn and the unborn.

During 1981, laboratory research and medical science produced new ways to treat birth defects in the mother's womb. Actual cases made medical history, and because of its funding and support, the March of Dimes shares in these accomplishments.

The work of the March of Dimes is made possible through the generosity of millions of our citizens and the dedicated efforts of tens of thousands of volunteers. This uniquely American volunteer spirit is a hall-mark of the March of Dimes, for the people of our great nation accept personal responsibility for the health of children today and in the future.

I urge all Americans to observe January as March of Dimes Birth Defects Prevention Month.

RONALD REAGAN

Note: The President signed the message during an Oval Office ceremony where he greeted 1982 March of Dimes National Poster Child Richard T. Wagner and his family. Also attending the ceremony were James Roosevelt, trustee, and Charles L. Massey, president, March of Dimes Birth Defects Foundation.

Nomination of Kalo A. Hineman To Be a Commissioner of the Commodity Futures Trading Commission
December 10, 1981

The President today announced his intention to nominate Kalo A. Hineman to be a Commissioner of the Commodity Futures Trading Commission for a term expiring June 19, 1986. He would succeed Robert L. Martin.

Since 1947 Mr. Hineman has been a cattleman, rancher, and wheat and milo farmer in Dighton, Kans. He is president and owner of Kalo Hineman Cattle Co. and Kalo Hineman Farm Co. He has also been director, First National Bank of Dighton, since 1955 and a member of the Kansas House of Representatives since 1974.

Mr. Hineman is a member of the Kansas Livestock Association (president, 1972), the National Cattlemen's Association (member, board of directors, 1971–72), American Farm Bureau Federation, and the National Association of Wheat Growers.

He graduated from Kansas State University (D.V.M., 1943). He served in the United States Army, Veterinarian Corps, as a captain in 1943–46. He is married, has four children, and resides in Dighton, Kans. He was born March 4, 1922, in Dighton.

Nomination of Anthony J. Calio To Be Deputy Administrator of the National Oceanic and Atmospheric Administration
December 11, 1981

The President today announced his intention to nominate Anthony J. Calio to be Deputy Administrator of the National Oceanic and Atmospheric Administration. He would succeed James Patrick Walsh.

Since 1977 Dr. Calio has served as Associate Administrator for Space and Terrestrial Applications at the National Aeronautics and Space Administration (NASA). He was the Deputy Associate Administrator for

Space Science in 1975–77 and began his NASA career in 1963, when he joined the Electronics Research Task Group in the NASA Headquarters Office of Advanced Research and Technology.

In 1964 he was appointed Chief of Research and Engineering at the newly established Electronics Research Center in Boston. He returned to NASA Headquarters, Manned Space Science Program Office, in 1965. Dr. Calio transferred to the Johnson Space Center in 1968 and was named Director of Science and Applications in 1969. During this period, he was a member of NASA's Apollo management team specifically responsible for implementing and directing all aspects of the

program's science activities for all missions from Apollo 7 through Apollo 17.

Prior to joining NASA, he was employed as a nuclear physicist with the Westinghouse Atomic Power Division in Pittsburgh, Pa. He served in the United States Army Chemical Corps in 1954–56.

Dr. Calio graduated from the University of Pennsylvania (B.S., 1953), did graduate work in physics at the University of Pennsylvania and the Carnegie Institute of Technology, and in 1974, received an honorary D. Sc. from the Washington University of St. Louis. He is married, has four children, and resides in Bethesda, Md. He was born October 27, 1929, in Philadelphia, Pa.

Statement on Congressional Action Concerning Fiscal Year 1982 Appropriations
December 11, 1981

The continuing resolution just passed by the Congress represents another difficult step forward in this Nation's struggle to restore responsible economic and fiscal policy. It is a step away from the big spending that wreaked havoc in the past and toward our goal of once again living within our means.

This vote represents, however, only another installment in a long and hard program to get the Federal budget under control. We must not rest. The nation expects continued followthrough.

Together with excessive taxation, overspending in Washington has led to the re-

duced saving and investment, high inflation, and crippling interest rates that created today's recession. Only continued commitment to the joint goals of lower taxes, reduced spending and borrowing, fewer regulations, and a stable monetary policy will pave the way for recovery in 1982 and a return to economic prosperity in the 1980's.

I thank the Members of the House and Senate for a responsible vote. I look forward to future victories of economic sanity we can win together for the American people.

Announcement of the Creation of the President's Volunteer Action Awards Program
December 12, 1981

The President today announced the creation of the President's Volunteer Action Awards to honor outstanding volunteer achievement by individual citizens and their organizations.

The awards program is cosponsored by VOLUNTEER, the National Center for Citizen Involvement, and ACTION in a unique cooperative effort between the private sector and government.

1151

The President will present the awards at a White House ceremony in April. Awards will be made in seven categories: jobs, health, material resources, education, recreation and the environment, public safety, the arts and humanities.

In announcing the program, the President said, "Throughout our history, Americans have always extended their hands to neighbors in assistance. The energy expended by our citizens in problemsolving is absolutely imperative to maintain and improve the quality of life for all Americans. I believe this program of recognition is vital to call attention both to what is being done by American volunteers and to what can be done through voluntary action."

VOLUNTEER is the primary national organization supporting greater citizen involvement in problemsolving. It provides a broad range of technical assistance services to volunteer-involving organizations, public agencies, unions, and corporations. It works closely with a network of approximately 200 associated Voluntary Action Centers and over 1,000 other local, State, and national organizations.

ACTION, the national volunteer agency, serves to stimulate voluntarism and to demonstrate the effectiveness of volunteers in addressing social problems. Its major programs include the Foster Grandparent, Retired Senior Volunteer, and Senior Companion programs for the elderly and a variety of programs for youth.

The announcement of the program followed the first meeting of the President's Task Force on Private Sector Initiatives, chaired by William Verity, chairman of Armco Steel. Two of VOLUNTEER's board members, George Romney and Senator David Durenberger (R-Minn.), sit on that task force, as does Tom Pauken, Director of ACTION.

Official nomination forms are available by writing to the President's Volunteer Action Awards, P.O. Box 37488, Washington, D.C., 20013. The deadline for receipt of nominations is February 7.

Nomination of Kenneth E. Moffett To Be Director of the Federal Mediation and Conciliation Service
December 14, 1981

The President today announced his intention to nominate Kenneth E. Moffett to be Federal Mediation and Conciliation Director. He would succeed Wayne Horvitz.

Mr. Moffett has been Acting Director since January 1, 1981. He was appointed Deputy Director of the Federal Mediation and Conciliation Service in 1977. Previously he served as the Director of Mediation Services for 5 years. In 1969 Mr. Moffett was special assistant to former Director J. Curtis Counts. During this time, he was also named Executive Secretary of the Atomic Energy Labor-Management Relations Panel. Commissioned a mediator with FMCS in 1961, Mr. Moffett served in Washington, D.C., and in Cleveland, Ohio, for 5 years. In 1957–61 he was an international representative for District 50, United Mine Workers of America.

He graduated from the University of Maryland (1958). He resides in Adelphi, Md., with his three children. He was born September 11, 1931, in Lykens, Pa.

Nomination of Herbert E. Ellingwood To Be Chairman of the Merit Systems Protection Board
December 14, 1981

The President today announced his intention to nominate Herbert E. Ellingwood to be a member of the Merit Systems Protection Board for the remainder of the term expiring March 1, 1986. The President also intends to nominate Mr. Ellingwood to serve as Chairman.

Mr. Ellingwood is currently Deputy Counsel to the President. He was a partner with the firm of Caldwell and Toms of Sacramento, Calif. He was deputy assistant attorney for Alameda County, Calif., in 1960–66 and legislative advocate for law and legislative committees, District Attorneys' and Peace Officers' Associations, in 1966–69. Mr. Ellingwood was the legal affairs secretary to then Gov. Ronald Reagan in 1969–74 and served as special assistant to the attorney general, State of California, in 1975–79. He served in the United States Army in 1953–56.

He graduated from Yale University (B.A., 1953) and Stanford University Law School (LL.B., 1960). Mr. Ellingwood is married, has two children, and resides in Sacramento, Calif. He was born on March 5, 1931, in Ordway, Colo.

Appointment of M. B. Oglesby, Jr., To Be Deputy Assistant to the President for Legislative Affairs
December 14, 1981

The President today announced his intention to appoint M. B. Oglesby, Jr., to be Deputy Assistant to the President for Legislative Affairs. He would succeed Kenneth M. Duberstein.

Mr. Oglesby is currently serving as Special Assistant for Legislative Affairs. In his new position, he will serve as the President's chief deputy liaison with the United States House of Representatives.

Previously he had served as minority staff associate for the House Energy and Commerce Committee, dealing principally with railroad, environmental, and commerce-related legislation. Mr. Oglesby also served as deputy and acting director of the State of Illinois Washington office and as executive assistant to Congressman Edward Madigan (R-Ill.). Prior to coming to Washington, he served in Illinois State government as an assistant to Gov. Richard B. Oglivie and as executive assistant to the speaker of the house. Mr. Oglesby also spent 3½ years in management positions with Illinois Bell Telephone Co.

He attended the University of Illinois at Champaign. He is married, resides in Bethesda, Md., and was born October 1, 1942, in Flora, Ill.

Excerpts From a Telephone Conversation With Pope John Paul II About the Situation in Poland
December 14, 1981

The President. "Your Holiness, I want you to know how deeply we feel about the situation in your homeland."

"I look forward to the time when we can meet in person."

"Our sympathies are with the people, not the government."

"Our country was inspired when you visited Poland, and to see their commitment to religion and belief in God. It was an inspiration to the whole world to watch on television. All of us were very thrilled."

Note: The telephone conversation began at approximately 12:15 p.m.

As printed above, the transcript of the remarks follows the press release and a portion of the daily press briefing.

Proclamation 4886—Wright Brothers Day, 1981
December 14, 1981

By the President of the United States of America

A Proclamation

Since the dawn of civilization, men have dreamed of conquering the air. History is filled with tales of those who tried to emulate the flight of birds, but not until the early days of this century did that dream become a reality.

On December 17, 1903, near Kitty Hawk, North Carolina, the age of aviation began when Orville and Wilbur Wright launched man's first successful flight in a mechanically propelled aircraft. Orville Wright remained aloft in a flying machine for just 12 seconds, covering a distance of only 120 feet, but the inventiveness and daring of these two brothers changed our lives for all time.

Today, aviation is vital to the American way of life and to our economy and national defense. The air transportation network enables us to travel for business or pleasure with unequalled speed and convenience while providing for the rapid and efficient transfer of our nation's commercial goods.

The pioneering spirit exhibited by the Wright brothers and fostered by our system of free enterprise has kept America in the forefront of innovative aeronautics—a spirit dramatically demonstrated again this year with the two successful missions of the United States Space Shuttle COLUMBIA. As it glided to perfect landings in the California desert, COLUMBIA gave us pause to reflect on another triumph in American aviation and on the creative genius of the American people.

To commemorate the historic achievements of the Wright brothers, the Congress, by a joint resolution of December 17, 1963 (77 Stat. 402, 36 U.S.C. 169), designated the seventeenth day of December of each year as Wright Brothers Day and requested the President to issue a proclamation annually inviting Americans to observe that day with appropriate ceremonies and activities.

Now, Therefore, I, Ronald Reagan, President of the United States of America, do hereby call upon the people of this nation and their local and national governmental officials to observe Wright Brothers Day, December 17, 1981, with appropriate ceremonies and activities, both to recall the accomplishments of the Wright brothers and to provide stimulus to aviation in this country and throughout the world.

In Witness Whereof, I have hereunto set my hand this 14th day of Dec., in the year of our Lord nineteen hundred and eighty-one, and of the Independence of the United

States of America the two hundred and sixth.

RONALD REAGAN

[*Filed with the Office of the Federal Register, 5:04 p.m., December 14, 1981*]

Nomination of John R. Bolton To Be an Assistant Administrator of the Agency for International Development
December 15, 1981

The President today announced his intention to nominate John R. Bolton to be an Assistant Administrator of the Agency for International Development (Program and Policy Coordination). He would succeed Alexander Shakow.

Mr. Bolton has been General Counsel, Agency for International Development, since February 1981. Previously he was an attorney with the firm of Covington and Burling in Washington, D.C., in 1974–81. He served on the personnel management transition team during the Presidential transition effort in 1980–81.

Mr. Bolton graduated from Yale College (B.A., 1970) and Yale Law School (J.D., 1974). He is married and resides in Vienna, Va. He was born October 20, 1948, in Baltimore, Md.

Nomination of Otto J. Reich To Be an Assistant Administrator of the Agency for International Development
December 15, 1981

The President today announced his intention to nominate Otto J. Reich to be an Assistant Administrator of the Agency for International Development (Latin America and the Caribbean), United States International Development Cooperation Agency. He would succeed Abelardo Lopez Valdez.

Mr. Reich has been special assistant to the Administrator, Agency for International Development, since September 1981. He was director of Washington operations, Council of the Americas, in 1976–81; community development coordinator, city of Miami, Fla., in 1975–76; international representative, Florida Department of Commerce, in 1973–75; vice president for international development, Cormorant Enterprises, Miami, in 1972–73; research fellow, Center for Strategic and International Studies, in 1971–72; and staff assistant to Representative W. R. Hull, Jr., of Missouri, in 1970–71.

He graduated from the University of North Carolina (B.A., 1966) and Georgetown University (M.A., 1973). He is married, has one child, and resides in McLean, Va. He was born October 16, 1945, in Havana, Cuba.

Nomination of James Jay Jackson To Be a Member of the Federal Home Loan Bank Board
December 15, 1981

The President today announced his intention to nominate James Jay Jackson to be a member of the Federal Home Loan Bank Board for the remainder of the term expiring June 30, 1982. He would succeed John N. Dalton.

Since 1974 Mr. Jackson has been executive vice president, Fidelity Savings & Loan Association, Port Arthur, Tex. Previously he was loan officer, Beaumont Savings & Loan Association, Beaumont, Tex., in 1973 and branch manager, Republic of Texas Savings Association, Port Arthur, Tex., in 1972.

Mr. Jackson is president of the Greater Port Arthur Chamber of Commerce and is a member of the National Energy Conference of the U.S. League of Savings Associations.

He graduated from Louisiana College (B.A., 1970). He is married, has two children, and resides in Port Neches, Tex. He was born on July 31, 1948, in Jennings, La.

Remarks on Signing the Continuing Resolution for Fiscal Year 1982 Appropriations
December 15, 1981

The President. Well, we have a signing of a bill here. I'm signing House Joint Resolution 370, the continuing resolution providing appropriations for most of the government until March 31st.

The Congress, with strong leadership from these gentlemen here—Senators Baker and Hatfield and Congressman Conte and Michel—is now addressing the problem of excessive spending generated through the appropriations process.

I would prefer—I know they would—that the gbe financed by separate appropriation bills subject to Presidential approval or disapproval, as has been the case for most of our history. But the continuing resolution I'm signing today is far better than those of recent years and better than the one I vetoed 3 weeks ago.

This resolution represents a genuine effort at spending restraint and embodies substantial savings for taxpayers. It is $49 billion in appropriations below the original request of the previous administration last January and $8½ billion below my own much reduced request of last March.

This lower level of appropriations will cut spending both in the immediate fiscal year 1982 and in later years. The bill is somewhat above my September request, but it's a big change from the business-as-usual appropriations of the past.

I hope shortly to receive and be able to sign the individual appropriations bills. These appropriations measures would then supersede the provisions of this continuing

resolution. I've already signed one such appropriations bill, the energy and water development bill.

Getting control of government spending, reducing inflationary expectations, and restoring jobs, growth, and prosperity for our people is a slow and difficult process. We don't want and the economy can't stand another rollercoaster recovery. We need a lasting recovery, and that will require a wealth of cooperation, courage, and determination. We took our first big step forward last summer when I signed the Omnibus Reconciliation Act.

This resolution marks another significant step. But let's not stop here. If we continue working together, we can bring the rate of inflation down further, and we can keep it down as the recovery begins.

And now, I do this with——

[At this point, the President signed the bill, handing the pens to the three Members of Congress.]

Senator Hatfield. Thank you very much.

The President. I ought to have a middle name or put a middle name in here so I can make it go to the end of the pens.

Senator Baker. Thank you.

Representative Conte. Thank you, Mr. President.

The President. You're more than welcome. And thank all of you for what you've done to bring this about.

Note: The President spoke at 3:37 p.m. to reporters assembled in the Oval Office at the White House.

As enacted, H.J. Res. 370 is Public Law 97–92, approved December 15.

Statement Announcing the Establishment of the National Commission on Social Security Reform
December 16, 1981

In recent years inflation has created great uncertainty about our social security system. Time and again we've been reassured the system would be financially sound for decades to come, only to find that recalculations of receipts and benefits forecast a new crisis. Current and future retirees now question the system's ability to provide them the benefits they've been led to expect. Americans look to us for leadership and for answers.

As a candidate in 1980 I pledged that I would do my utmost to restore the integrity of social security and do so without penalty to those dependent on that program. I have honored that pledge and will continue to do so. We cannot and we will not betray people entitled to social security benefits.

In September I announced that I would appoint a bipartisan task force to work with the President and the Congress to reach two specific goals: propose realistic, long-term reforms to put social security back on a sound financial footing and forge a working bipartisan consensus so that the necessary reforms will be passed into law.

Senate Majority Leader Baker, Speaker O'Neill, and I agreed we would each select five members for a new national commission on social security. Today I am pleased and honored to announce the formation of the commission and that Alan Greenspan has agreed at my request to serve as Chairman of that commission.

I'm asking the commission to present its report to the American people at the end of next year. I can think of no more important domestic problem requiring resolution than the future of our social security system.

Let me make one thing plain: With bipartisan cooperation and political courage, social security can and will be saved. For too long, too many people dependent on social security have been cruelly frightened by individuals seeking political gain through demagoguery and outright falsehood, and this must stop. The future of social security is much too important to be used as a political football.

Saving social security will require the best efforts of both parties and of both the executive and legislative branches of government. I'm confident this can be done and that in its deliberations this commission will put aside partisan considerations and seek a solution the American people will find fiscally sound and fully equitable.

That's the end of the statement.

Note: The President spoke at 12:03 p.m. to reporters assembled in the Briefing Room at the White House.

Executive Order 12335—National Commission on Social Security Reform
December 16, 1981

By the authority vested in me as President by the Constitution of the United States of America, and to establish, in accordance with the provisions of the Federal

Advisory Committee Act, as amended (5 U.S.C. App. I), the National Commission on Social Security Reform, it is hereby ordered as follows:

Section 1. Establishment. (a) There is established the National Commission on Social Security Reform. The Commission shall be composed of fifteen members appointed or designated by the President and selected as follows:

(1) Five members selected by the President from among officers or employees of the Executive Branch, private citizens of the United States, or both. Not more than three of the members selected by the President shall be members of the same political party;

(2) Five members selected by the Majority Leader of the Senate from among members of the Senate, private citizens of the United States, or both. Not more than three of the members selected by the Majority Leader shall be members of the same political party;

(3) Five members selected by the Speaker of the House of Representatives from among members of the House, private citizens of the United States, or both. Not more than three of the members selected by the Speaker shall be members of the same political party.

(b) The President shall designate a Chairman from among the members of the Commission.

Sec. 2. Functions. (a) The Commission shall review relevant analyses of the current and long-term financial condition of the Social Security trust funds; indentify problems that may threaten the long-term solvency of such funds; analyze potential solutions to such problems that will both assure the financial integrity of the Social Security System and the provision of appropriate benefits; and provide appropriate recommendations to the Secretary of Health and Human Services, the President, and the Congress.

(b) The Commission shall make its report to the President by December 31, 1982.

Sec. 3. Administration. (a) The heads of Executive agencies shall, to the extent permitted by law, provide the Commission such information as it may require for the purpose of carrying out its functions.

(b) Members of the Commission shall serve without any additional compensation for their work on the Commission. However, members appointed from among private citizens of the United States may be allowed travel expenses, including per diem in lieu of subsistence, as authorized by law for persons serving intermittently in the government service (5 U.S.C. 5701–5707), to the extent funds are available therefor.

(c) The Commission shall have a staff headed by an Executive Director. Any expenses of the Commission shall be paid from such funds as may be available to the Secretary of Health and Human Services.

Sec. 4. General. (a) Notwithstanding any other Executive Order, the responsibilities of the President under the Federal Advisory Committee Act, as amended, except that of reporting annually to the Congress, which are applicable to the Commission, shall be performed by the Secretary of Health and Human Services in accordance with the guidelines and procedures established by the Administrator of General Services.

(b) The Commission shall terminate thirty days after submitting its report.

RONALD REAGAN

The White House,
December 16, 1981.

[*Filed with the Office of the Federal Register, 2:22 p.m., December 16, 1981*]

Appointment of the Membership of the National Commission on Social Security Reform
December 16, 1981

The President today announced his intention to appoint/designate the following individuals to serve on a 15-member bipartisan National Commission on Social Security Reform. Alan Greenspan will serve as Chairman.

Establishment of the Commission fulfills a pledge made by the President in September to create a bipartisan task force to work with the President and Congress to reach two specific goals:

—To propose realistic, long-term reforms to put social security back on a sound financial footing, and

—To forge a working, bipartisan consensus so that the necessary reforms can be passed into law.

Robert A. Beck, chairman of the board and chief executive officer, Prudential Insurance Co. of America, Newark, N.J. He is a member of the President's Export Council.

Mary Falvey Fuller, vice president, finance, Shaklee Corp., San Francisco, Calif. Previously she was senior vice president and director, Blyth Eastman Dillon & Co., Inc., New York, N.Y.

Alan Greenspan, chairman and president, Townsend-Greenspan and Co., Inc., New York, N.Y. He is a member of the President's Economic Policy Advisory Board.

Alexander B. Trowbridge, president, National Association of Manufacturers, Washington, D.C. He is a member of the President's Task Force on Private Sector Initiatives.

Joe D. Waggonner, Jr., consultant, Bossier Bank & Trust Co., Plain Dealing, La. He represented the Fourth Congressional District of Louisiana during the 87th to 95th Congresses.

Senate Majority Leader Howard Baker, in consultation with Senate Minority Leader Robert Byrd, selected the following individuals to serve on the Commission:

William Armstrong, United States Senate (R-Colo.), chairman of the Subcommittee on Social Security of the Senate Finance Committee.

Robert Dole, United States Senate (R-Kans.), chairman of the Senate Finance Committee.

John Heinz, United States Senate (R-Pa.), chairman of the Senate Special Committee on Aging.

Lane Kirkland, president of the American Federation of Labor-Congress of Industrial Organizations.

Daniel Patrick Moynihan, United States Senate (D-N.Y.), ranking minority member of the Subcommittee on Social Security of the Senate Finance Committee.

House Speaker Thomas P. O'Neill, in consultation with House Minority Leader Robert Michel, selected the following individuals to serve on the Commission:

William Archer, United States House of Representatives (R-Tex.), ranking minority member of the Subcommittee on Social Security, House Ways and Means Committee.

Robert M. Ball, was Commissioner of Social Security in 1962–73. He is senior scholar, Institute of Medicine, National Academy of Sciences.

Barber Conable, United States House of Representatives (R-N.Y.), ranking minority member, House Ways and Means Committee.

Martha E. Keys, former Assistant Secretary of Health and Human Services. She served in the 94th and 95th Congresses.

Claude D. Pepper, United States House of Representatives (D-Fla.), chairman, House Select Committee on Aging.

Appointment of Three Members of the Board of Foreign Scholarships
December 16, 1981

The President today announced his intention to appoint the following individuals to be members of the Board of Foreign Scholarships:

Jeffrey B. Gayner has served as director of foreign policy studies, the Heritage Foundation, since 1974. In this position, he has taken research trips to Chile, Vietnam, Thailand, Malaysia, Korea, Taiwan, Laos, Nicaragua, Panama, East Asia, Iran, Europe, U.S.S.R., South Africa, and other countries. He was a member of the International Development Cooperation Agency transition team during the Presidential transition effort in 1980–81. Mr. Gayner graduated from Washington & Lee University (B.A., 1967) and attended the University of North Carolina at Chapel Hill. He served in the United States Army in Vietnam (1969–71). He resides in Washington, D.C., and was born February 27, 1945, in Cleveland, Ohio.

E. Victor Milione has been president of the Intercollegiate Studies Institute, Inc., since 1962. ISI was founded in 1953 and assists students, through publications, seminars, and lectures, in apprehending the values and knowledge necessary to the preservation of the free society. He is publisher of the Intercollegiate Review and a member of the board of visitors of Thomas Aquinas College. Mr. Milione was a senior adviser to the National Endowment for the Humanities transition team, and he has served as a trustee of the Philadelphia Society. He graduated from St. Joseph's University in Philadelphia. He is married, has one child, and resides in Ardmore, Pa. He was born May 12, 1924, in Havertown, Pa.

Gerhart Niemeyer is professor emeritus of government, University of Notre Dame. He has held many academic positions, including serving as visiting professor at Yale University (1942, 1946, 1954–55), Columbia University (1952), Vanderbilt University (1962–66), Japan National Defense Academy (1980); and distinguished visiting professor, Hillsdale College (1976 to present). He was foreign affairs officer, Department of State, (1950–53). Dr. Niemeyer emigrated from Germany in 1933 and became a U.S. citizen in 1943. He attended Cambridge University (1925–26), Munich University (1926–27), and Kiel University (1927–30). He is married, has five children, and resides in South Bend, Ind. He was born in Germany in 1907.

Statement About the Plan Selected To Dismantle the Department of Energy
December 17, 1981

Last September in my economic message I announced that we would develop a plan for dismantling the Department of Energy. In the intervening months, a group led by the Secretary of Energy developed a number of proposals to carry out that commitment.

I have selected a plan that will divide the current responsibilities of the Department of Energy between the Department of the Interior and the Department of Commerce. This would fulfill my campaign promise to make government more efficient and reduce the cost of government to the taxpayers.

Under the plan I have approved, the Interior Department will take on those functions of DOE that bear on the management of natural resources, such as supervision of the national petroleum reserves and the hydroelectric dams operated by the power marketing administrations.

The Commerce Department will be responsible for ensuring that energy is given full consideration in national economic policy; for developing plans for responding to energy supply emergencies, including our relations with international energy organizations; and for the collection of statistical data on energy.

In addition, we will establish an agency to carry out the important research programs now operated by DOE. This agency will report to me through the Secretary of Commerce and will also have responsibility for operating the atomic energy defense program that develops and produces nuclear weapons for our strategic forces.

I believe that this plan will result in a strong Federal effort in basic research in energy that avoids the excessive regulation that led me to call for dismantling DOE. Under this plan, we will limit the role of the Federal Government in energy. The government will no longer try to manage every aspect of energy supply and consumption.

I have directed that a task force composed of representatives from the White House Office of Policy Development, the Office of Management and Budget, and the Departments of Energy, Commerce, and Interior get to work immediately on the detailed legislation and plans needed to carry out the decision I made yesterday.

We will of course be consulting with the Congress on the detailed plan, which I anticipate submitting to the Congress with the fiscal year 1983 budget.

By dismantling a bureaucracy while keeping intact its essential functions, we are moving ahead with our promise to make government serve the people—and do it more efficiently. This is a big step, but there is more to be done, and we are pledged to do it.

Statement Concerning Parking Fees for Federal Employees
December 17, 1981

Recently the U.S. Court of Appeals ruled that the government had acted lawfully in imposing market-oriented rates for parking facilities used by Federal employees. The regulation, which took effect on November 1, 1979, directed agencies to develop procedures to charge fees based on the ongoing commercial rate of the area. A legal challenge resulted in a March 1981 decision by the U.S. District Court blocking further implementation of the fee schedule and ordering the refunding of fees already collected.

The government can now resume collection of parking fees. After consulting a delegation of Members of Congress, including Marjorie Holt, Stan Parris, and Frank Wolf, I have decided, however, not to do so. To resume those fees would impose yet another financial burden upon thousands of hard-pressed Federal employees who have had only 4.8 percent increases in their pay.

Many employees have limited access to public transportation and appreciate the flexibility and security of automobiles. I feel that energy conservation goals will not be affected by this decision, since existing car pool and van pool priorities at parking facilities will remain in effect.

The President's New Conference
December 17, 1981

The President. Good afternoon. I have a statement which is being handed out, but I will read it for the sound media.

The Situation in Poland

All the information that we have confirms that the imposition of martial law in Poland has led to the arrest and confinement, in prisons and detention camps, of thousands of Polish trade union leaders and intellectuals. Factories are being seized by security forces and workers beaten.

These acts make plain there's been a sharp reversal of the movement toward a freer society that has been underway in Poland for the past year and a half. Coercion and violation of human rights on a massive scale have taken the place of negotiation and compromise. All of this is in gross violation of the Helsinki Pact, to which Poland is a signatory.

It would be naive to think this could happen without the full knowledge and the support of the Soviet Union. We're not naive. We view the current situation in Poland in the gravest of terms, particularly the increasing use of force against an unarmed population and violations of the basic civil rights of the Polish people.

Violence invites violence and threatens to plunge Poland into chaos. We call upon all free people to join in urging the Government of Poland to reestablish conditions that will make constructive negotiations and compromise possible.

Certainly, it will be impossible for us to continue trying to help Poland solve its economic problems while martial law is imposed on the people of Poland, thousands are imprisoned, and the legal rights of free trade unions—previously granted by the government—are now denied. We've always been ready to do our share to assist Poland in overcoming its economic difficulties, but only if the Polish people are permitted to resolve their own problems free of internal coercion and outside intervention.

Our nation was born in resistance to arbitrary power and has been repeatedly enriched by immigrants from Poland and other great nations of Europe. So we feel a special kinship with the Polish people in their struggle against Soviet opposition to their reforms.

The Polish nation, speaking through Solidarity, has provided one of the brightest, bravest moments of modern history. The people of Poland are giving us an imperishable example of courage and devotion to the values of freedom in the face of relentless opposition. Left to themselves, the Polish people would enjoy a new birth of freedom. But there are those who oppose the idea of freedom, who are intolerant of national independence, and hostile to the European values of democracy and the rule of law.

Two Decembers ago, freedom was lost in Afghanistan; this Christmas, it's at stake in Poland. But the torch of liberty is hot. It warms those who hold it high. It burns those who try to extinguish it.

And now, the first question will come from Jim Gerstenzang of the Associated Press.

Q. Mr. President, with the apparent, in your words, "Soviet involvement," how will this affect our relations both with Poland in the future as a consequence and with the Soviet Union, including trade and arms talks?

The President. Well, Jim, you're getting into the area there that I just don't feel that I can discuss—the area of initiatives and options that might be available as conditions develop that we may not be able to foresee. So, I just am not going to answer questions or discuss what those initiatives might be or what our reaction might be.

Q. If I could follow up, have you made it clear to the Soviet Union how there might be some impact?

The President. Well, I think not only we but our allies in Western Europe have made it very plain how seriously we will consider Russian intervention there.

Israeli Annexation of the Golan Heights

Q. Mr. President, there are repressions in other areas in the world. In recent days the newspapers have been filled with reports of oppressions by the Israelis in the occupied zones against the people there, even killing children, shooting and killing children, and annexing the Golan Heights.

My question is, very simply, how can the American taxpayer in good conscience continue to support aid to Israel with arms and money under those circumstances?

The President. Well, Helen [Helen Thomas, United Press International], we have no observation—or information, I should say, on any violence or anything that's been happening there.

Q. It's been in the newspapers.

The President. We have registered our disagreement and the fact that we do deplore this unilateral action by Israel, which has increased the difficulty of seeking peace in the Middle East under the terms of the U.N. Resolutions 242 and 338. And we continue to address them with the idea, hopefully, that this action can be ameliorated.

Q. Mr. President, following up Helen Thomas' question concerning the Israeli action on the Golan Heights. Mr. President, did you get any indications whatsoever from the Israelis that they were about to annex the Golan Heights before, indeed, they very quickly took that action and, secondly, Mr. President, I was wondering what effect you felt this unilateral annexation will have on the Camp David peace process and your hopes for peace in that part of the world?

The President. Well, I partially answered that with regard to the difficulties now with 242 and 338. We were caught by surprise. This was done without any notification to us. But apparently, other than a few hours interruption, the peace process is going forward. Egypt and Israel are continuing to work on the subject of autonomy. And we still continue to be optimistic about the Middle East, although we recognize that difficulties can arise.

Q. But, sir, doesn't it make your job a little more difficult in trying to bring the parties there together?

The President. Yes—[*laughing*]—but then I've come to the conclusion that there is a worldwide plot to make my job more difficult in almost any day that I go to the office.

Yes, it is. It introduces a factor that has complicated things.

States' Rights and the Voting Rights Act

Q. Mr. President, blacks perceive you as resurrecting States' rights through your block grant programs without any guidelines, and as being against affirmative action, and your wanting to prove intent in the Voting Rights Act. They see all of this as a setback to civil rights. Now, doesn't this hurt the Republican Party as well as hurt-

ing blacks? There was evidence in the Virginia election.

The President. Well, thank you very much. I have to say that I think this may be an impression that some are trying to give because they're in disagreement with many of our policies, but I can assure you that this administration is dedicated and devoted to the principle of civil rights. And in spite of the fact that I do believe in returning more to our system of federalism, recognizing that there are functions that can be better performed at the State and local level, I recognize also that one of the prime responsibilities of the Federal Government is to assure that not one single citizen in this country can be denied his or her constitutional rights without the Federal Government coming in and guaranteeing those rights.

Q. I have a followup on that. You know blacks fought very hard and long to overthrow States' rights. I'm from Virginia; we had a pretty tough time. And now, in your Voting Rights Act, you're asking to prove intent. And when the government testified before the African Affairs [Sub]committee on the investment proposal, it said that while the intent of this bill may be good, we cannot accept the effect. So, why, then? In some instances, you're accepting the effect and disregarding the intent, and then vice versa.

The President. No, we believe that the intent was a useful thing in that bill because there have been communities and areas of the country who have proven, without question, their total adherence to voting rights for all their people, and yet the difficulty of them then escaping the provisions of the law which impose a burden on them are still denied.

Effect—to use that instead of intent—the effect rule could lead to the type of thing in which effect could be judged if there was some disproportion in the number of public officials who were elected at any governmental level, and so forth. And we don't think that that was what the bill intended or that that would be a fair test. You could come down to where all of society had to have an actual quota system.

Sam [Sam Donaldson, ABC News].

The Situation in Poland

Q. Mr. President, there are reports today of killings in Poland and more violence. What do you think the people of Poland should do? Should they acquiesce quietly to this martial law? Should they resist it? And if they resist it, what help will the United States give them?

The President. Well again, Sam, you're getting into the area that I've said I cannot discuss, of what our initiatives might be, what our options might be. I don't think those should be discussed in advance of any need for action. We have the report, also, but we have no confirmation as yet with regard to today's violence, and we're waiting to get that confirmation.

Q. Well, sir, aren't we letting the Russians get away with it? With each passing day, aren't they solidifying their position, and, in fact, there's nothing we can do about it?

The President. No, we're not letting them get away with it, and I thought that I indicated that in my remarks. But again, you are leading in another way into the area that I just don't feel would be proper for me to discuss.

Libyan Assassination Squad

Q. Mr. President, Jimmy Carter said that when he was in office he also was the subject of perceived death threats from Libya, but he thought it was unwise to discuss it publicly. Can you tell us your reasoning behind making the charge public? And secondly, sir, can you comment on the concern of some people that your dialog with Colonel Qadhafi has resulted largely in enhancing his stature in the world?

The President. Well, I haven't had any dialog with Mr. Qadhafi, and we did not make it public. The news, claiming leaks from unidentified sources, made it public at a time when we had held this entire matter confidential and secret for a long time, because we believed that we had a better opportunity of apprehending any terrorists or terrorist squads if it were not made public. And so we're sorry that it was. And for anyone to suggest, as has been suggested lately, that we had some reason for making this public, we don't put that shoe on. And, as a matter of fact, we made an effort at

one point to call in some leaders in the media and ask for their cooperation in restraint in talk on this, and that then became the story on the news for that evening.

Secretary of Labor Donovan

Q. Mr. President, can you say at this point, despite the fact that you can't comment about the investigation, whether you think it would be proper as a matter of principle for your Labor Secretary to take an administrative leave if a special prosecutor is appointed and, secondly, whether you have sought some assurances from him that these allegations are not true?

The President. The matter of appointing a special prosecutor under the present act is one that does not connote guilt or any evidence of wrongdoing. And therefore only under such circumstances as that maybe an individual would find they would not have time to perform their duties—and that is not true in the case of Secretary Donovan— I see no reason why they should step down while such a review is going forward. And, yes, I have had assurances that there is no ground to these charges.

Q. Have you had assurances from the Secretary, sir?

The President. What?

Q. Have you had assurances from the Secretary that there are no grounds to these charges?

The President. Yes.

Syria and the Golan Heights

Q. Mr. President, on the Golan Heights, do you believe that the Golan Heights should be returned to Syria, given Syria's record of bombarding the Israeli farms for so many years?

The President. Well, now you are getting into the area of what is trying to be settled in the talks under 242 and 338 and the peacemaking talks regarding all of the territory that might be held. And therefore, it's not proper for me to comment on this. This is the very matter that's being negotiated.

Q. To follow that up, sir, your own opinion—did you ever object to the Arab legion's occupation of the West Bank or the shelling of the Israeli farms?

The President. Well, you're going back a long way, and it's hard for me to remember what my position was. I know where I was during the Six Days War; I was in the Hollywood Bowl at a mass meeting in support of Israel. And at that time, there were only two political figures or officeholders there that I recall—former Senator George Murphy, then a Senator, and myself as Governor of California.

Balanced Budget and the Economy

Q. Mr. President, during your campaign you didn't use many "ifs" or "maybes" when you said that you would balance the budget by 1983, possibly by 1982. Now with deficits of $100 billion possibly in store for the coming years, why shouldn't the American people judge your campaign promises as harshly as they did that of your predecessor?

The President. Well, because in the first place, I said what was our goal, not a promise. But when I first announced our economic plan—and this is when those dates were used—was in September of 1980 during the campaign. The deterioriation in the economy was so great between September and January that, taking office, we had to revise our own estimates and our own figures and plan. And I have confidence in our plan, that it is the right solution to the present problem.

But again, like so many, we were caught. While we always said that the economy would be sluggish and soft for the balance of the year and into 1982, we did not foresee a recession, and I don't think anyone else did. But we also did not foresee the interest rates remaining at the extremely high level for as long as they did. And may I point out, those interest rates did not just get high under our administration. They were up at that pitch before we got here, higher than they've ever been since the War Between the States. And in the brief time that our program has been in effect, I have to point out that there's every evidence that we are on the right track.

Now, I will be the first to tell you that I think it's highly unlikely that the budget could be now, in these new circumstances, could be balanced by 1984, which was our goal, the target that we were aiming at—

difficult, because when you start predicting figures, a change of 1 percentage point in the unemployment rate can result in $25 billion either way, depending whether it's up or down in your estimated figures for a deficit.

But the evidence that our program is succeeding is the fact that since September, the interest rates have come down some 6 or 6½ points. Inflation has come down to single digit, when it had averaged 14 or it had averaged around 14 or better at the time that we took office. And we have cut the rate of increase in the cost of government just about in half.

Now, we believe that these are signs—the control of interest rates or bringing them down, the reducing of the percentage of gross national product that the government is taking out of the private sector—all of these things, we think, are on the path of what will cure this recession. We can't do it instantly. You can't undo in 11 weeks what it took several decades to create.

But this is not a case of a broken promise. This is a case of circumstances beyond our control, whose foundation has been laid over the last several decades.

Libyan Assassination Squad

Q. Mr. President, I wonder if I could get back to a question on the Libyan hit squad. Yesterday, Senator Baker said that the chances of an assassination attempt on you by this hit squad have been diminished. I wonder, sir, is that true and, secondly, is this hit squad still on the loose?

The President. Well, I understand that words come out from the Senator's office— that he did not have any intelligence information that would give rise to such a statement or such an assumption. Now, maybe he was giving an opinion and believed that things are cooling down a little bit.

I think it would be very foolish of us to relax any of the security measures. And I can only tell all of you that our information on this entire matter has come from not one but several widespread sources, and we have complete confidence in it, and that the threat was real.

The Situation in Poland

Q. Mr. President, I don't want to really just re-ask the same question, but I think it's something that is on the public's mind. What prospect do you see that the Soviet Union could become involved militarily in Poland, and that consequently the United States could have to have some kind of military involvement, too? Should we be relaxed about it or concerned about it?

The President. We are concerned about it, and beyond that, again, I can't say as to initiatives. And we have in no unmistakable terms, with our allies, let the Soviet Union know how the free world would view and how seriously we would take any overt interference or military interference in Poland.

Justice Department Investigations of Administration Officials

Q. Mr. President, you said that you didn't see any reason for Secretary Donovan to step down if a special prosecutor is named, because the appointment of a special prosecutor doesn't necessarily mean that he's guilty.

But I'm wondering, sir, that—it's not only Secretary Donovan who's under investigation by the Justice Department but also the CIA Director, Mr. Casey, and your national security adviser, Mr. Allen. And I'm wondering that—regardless of whether, eventually, we find out these men engaged in any wrongdoing or not—if you think that the fact that you're not taking action to disassociate them from your administration is going to hurt your administration or hurt your ability to lead?

The President. I believe in the fairness of the American people. And I believe that in recent years, there's been a very dangerous tendency in this country for some to jump to the conclusion that accusation meant guilt and conviction. And I think it is high time we recognized that any individual is innocent until proven guilty of any wrongdoing, and that's what we're going to do.

I think that I cheated over here. [*Referring to Bill Groody, Mutual Broadcasting System*] I had recognized you and someone else took the place, and I kind of nodded that you'd be next, and I forgot about that.

The Situation in Poland

Q. In your statement on Poland, I was wondering, you seemed to imply that there will be no more food shipments or other aids to Poland until martial law ends. Is that the intent?

The President. I can only say with regard to that—and again, we're getting dangerously close to initiatives—we have suspended the shipments that we were going to make, because those were intended [as], and we've had quite a record of, humanitarian aid to the people of Poland. We'd like to continue that. But under the present circumstances, we cannot go forward with that if it can be used by the government as a measure to further oppress and control the people of Poland. So, we've suspended such shipments.

Libyan Assassination Squad

Q. Mr. President, there's been a report recently that that so-called Libyan assassination squad was not really under the sponsorship of Mr. Qadhafi but that they were Shiite Moslems who themselves were opposed to Mr. Qadhafi and, secondly, that the U.S. Government paid the informers or at least one of them, a quarter of a million dollars for his information. Can you confirm those reports? And are you still determined to go ahead with the evacuation of American citizens from Libya?

The President. I cannot confirm—I know nothing of anything of the kind that you said or that they are not the terrorist groups that we were led to believe they were. As I said, I'm confident of our information. I don't know anything about anyone being paid or not.

And the last part of your question was?—oh, the American people. Here again, I regret very much the disrupting of their lives, and I know that they probably had the greatest relationship with the people of Libya, their own friends and neighbors that surrounded them, and their fellow workers. But also, our information was such that it would have been irresponsible for us to not think forward to a possible hazard for them as this situation developed, and we didn't have any choice. The only choice we had was that if we didn't do what we have done, there could have come a moment in which you all would have been asking me, "Why were we so irresponsible?"

U.S.–Soviet Relations

Q. Mr. President, during the campaign and in the early months in office, you used harsh, even strident terms to criticize the Soviet Union's policies and positions on any number of issues. But last month you turned statesman in your message to the Russians about negotiating deployment of missiles. And last week you intentionally used words about the situation in Poland that wouldn't rouse the Russian Bear, so to speak. Should these alterations be interpreted as a change in tactics, or should they be interpreted as a softening in your policy towards Moscow?

The President. No. If I may remind you, in the first press conference that I held, over across the street in the Executive Office Building, I did not volunteer any information about the Soviet Union; I was asked a question. And I answered the question to the best of my ability. And I think you will find that the teachings of Marxist-Leninism confirm what I said. And at that time, what I spelled out was that they recognize as immoral only those things which would delay or interfere with the spread of socialism and that otherwise, anything that furthers socialism is moral.

Now, I didn't set out to talk harshly about them. I just told the truth, and it's what Harry Truman said it was once for some people when they hear the truth.

Budget Deficits and Tax Cuts

Q. Mr. President, some of the supply-side economists have been saying lately that budget deficits don't matter, at least the size of the budget deficit doesn't matter. Some of your aides refer to you as the supply-side mole in the White House. I'm wondering if you agree that the size of the Federal deficit doesn't really matter to an economic recovery, and how large a deficit are you willing to swallow in the fiscal '83 budget?

The President. Again—and I think that those economists who were quoted as saying that, what they were trying to explain was not that a deficit is all right, and

not that we shouldn't continue a program to eventually to get us back, as I've said, within our means, but the important thing is whether you are following a program, consistent program, that will get us there; not whether changing conditions, such as we've had now with this recession, have delayed the day by which you can do this.

You have two lines that must converge. And they are the line of increase of government spending, the line of normal increase in government revenues; an increase that is regulated by the growth of the economy, increase in prosperity, not by increasing the rates.

And we are embarked, and the figures indicate that we are achieving this, even though we've had a cut in the tax rates. It is that cut which is going to stimulate the productivity. And I think what they're pointing out is, you can balance the budget by robbing the people, by imposing a punitive tax system on the people which maybe once will give you the benefits you want, but then you will also find you've torpedoed your economy, and you go right back into recession and lack of productivity and so forth, because of what you're doing.

The only proper way to balance the budget is through control of government spending, which we haven't had for some 30-odd years or more, and increasing prosperity and productivity for all. And that's what our program has aimed to do, and I have every confidence it is going to do it.

Decontrol of Natural Gas

Q. Mr. President, back to your statement about the recession and circumstances beyond your control. I'm from Buffalo, where the unemployment rate is even higher than the national average because of steel and autos. I'd like to ask you about something under your control. The people there are most concerned now, in the cold months, about the prospect of decontrol of natural gas and estimates that it could double, triple, or even quadruple their fuel bills in the winter. I'm wondering if, in light of the recession that you might reconsider the idea of decontrolling natural gas?

The President. Well, we haven't made a decision on that as yet. But let me also point out that everybody seemed to think the same thing would happen to the price of gasoline if we decontrolled oil. We decontrolled oil and the only increase that took place, and that was temporary, was one because of a, at the same time, a current increase in OPEC oil prices, and it only amounted to a few cents.

Now, I happen to believe in accelerating the decontrol of natural gas. It is scheduled to be decontrolled a few years down the road. I think that there might be advantages in accelerating that. I also find it difficult to believe that the price would double or triple or quadruple, because the price that the retail buyer of natural gas pays, only 15 percent of that has to do with the gas itself. The rest of that bill—I think you'll find these figures are correct—is made up of the processing, the transportation, the delivery of the gas to the house, and that would not be affected by a change in the wellhead price of the gas.

Q. Well, just to follow up, you say there are some advantages in accelerating. What are they to the consumers?

The President. In the longrun, to the consumer, they're the same thing they were with regard to oil, that you stimulate the production of natural gas to the point that competition then—which has always been the thing that brings prices down—that competition enters the arena. And with a greater supply competing for customers, the price comes down.

Now, the gentleman right there and then the young lady behind him.

Q. Thank you, Mr. President. Staying with natural gas, if you do accelerate the decontrol, do you plan to go with options your advisers are now discussing to tax it and possibly raise any other taxes to help balance the budget or at least to hold down spending? And there's a second part to that. Can you now promise the American people and the American businesses that they, the tax cuts they just got, will not be pulled back or somehow delayed?

The President. I sure can promise the American people that. And I think you all should know that I have met with some of the leading managers of investment firms in the United States. I have met with our Council of Economic Advisers that crosses

the spectrum; Milton Friedman, George Schultz, Arthur Burns returned from Germany briefly for this, Alan Greenspan, Arthur Laffer, Paul McCracken, any number. I should stop because I know I won't name them all, and I apologize to them for that. All of them are of a single mind with me: We stick with our tax program; we go forward with the reduction in tax rates. And I have no plans for increasing taxes in any way.

Q. Can I follow up——

The President. Everybody has a follow up. [*Laughter*]

Q. ——on the oil decontrol tax? Do you now state that you will not increase or impose a tax on decontrolled natural gas?

The President. I'm saying that my consideration of the decontrol of natural gas is on decontrol only.

Air Traffic Controllers

Q. Mr. President, it's the season to be jolly, and I wonder if you might reconsider hiring the air controllers to get travel in this country back on line? You did let them go back to work for the Federal Government, and it seems a bit ludicrous that they can't go into their own trained field. Would you reconsider?

The President. I think that the conduct or the plan that we've had and what we have done is correct. There is a law that those who were fired under some kind of a cloud cannot seek Federal employment for 3 years. We did ask for the waiver on that. We thought that was unnecessary—the pressure that they should not have. And that was waived.

With regard to any of them coming back, I think our first obligation is to those who stayed in the towers and who have kept the planes flying. But a number of the controllers have, under the civil service regulations, appealed their firing. And I suppose it is possible that some may win their appeals and thus would go back. So, that is the procedure and other than that, why, I can't comment.

Q. Mr. President——

The President. What?

Q. Which one of us?

The President. Him, and then I'll take you. [*Referring to Bill Plante, CBS News*] I was pointing to you.

I must have the worst-aimed finger in the world. [*Laughter*] That's because Mama taught me not to point. [*Laughter*]

National Security Adviser to the President

Q. Mr. President, can you say unequivocally that if Richard Allen is cleared in the investigation by the Justice Department that he will be rehired or reappointed to his position? And are you considering changing the role of your national security adviser so that the reports he gives you on foreign policy, as well as those from the State Department, come directly to you instead of being filtered through your Big Three?

The President. Well, the answer to the first question is that I can't and won't answer while an investigation is in process. I'm not going to comment in any way on that.

On the second, it's not just a particular department. At about this stage, when you're new here and have put together an administration and it's been a very busy one—and I must say a most successful one with regard to what we have obtained. Virtually all of our campaign promises have been kept with regard to cutting spending, lowering tax rates, eliminating useless regulations, for the first time in a few decades putting into operation a strategic defense program that I think is adequate to our needs—all of these things, including last night's farm bill, we have manged to do. And at the same time, I think you've come to a pause like this where you review your processes and see where—not only just one agency or department but all of them— where you can facilitate things, where you can perhaps loosen something that might have been a bottleneck. I still haven't found an answer to leaks. But this kind of a review is going on, yes, but not only of one agency but several.

Affirmative Action Programs

Q. Mr. President, do you agree with William Bradford Reynolds in the Civil Rights Division of the Justice Department that the Weber decision, which allowed firms to conduct voluntary affirmative action, that

that decision should be overturned? And if you do agree with him, why do you agree with him?

The President. I have to confess to you, just to throw the thing at me—the Weber decision: I can't bring that to mind as to what it pertains to and what it calls for.

Q. It's a decision ruled on by the Supreme Court, which allows specifically—in that particular case, it was a labor union and a firm which entered into a voluntary agreement to conduct affirmative action programs for training minorities and moving them up in the work force. William Bradford Reynolds, the Assistant Attorney General for Civil Rights, said that that decision should be overturned and that he was looking for future Supreme Court cases in which that decision could be overturned. Apparently that was——

The President. Well, if this is something that simply allows the training and the bringing up so there are more opportunities for them, in voluntary agreement between the union and management, I can't see any fault with that. I'm for that.

Q. Mr. President, I want to get back to——

[*At this point, Ms. Thomas signaled the end of the news conference.*]

Q. ——if I may, Helen?

The President. Are you letting him? [*Laughter*]

Ms. Thomas. Yes.

The President. All right. Helen says she'll let you. [*Laughter*]

Budget Deficits and Inefficient Government Programs

Q. I'm sorry. The second part of Tom DeFrank's [Newsweek magazine] question, I don't believe you answered, which had to do with how much of a budget deficit you are willing to swallow. Specifically, are you willing to accept a 1982 deficit of about $100 billion and perhaps that high in 1983 rather than ask for higher taxes?

The President. I thought I had answered it by saying that I don't believe that in all the figures that are being kicked around, number one, I don't believe that anyone could make a proper estimate of that, but I also don't believe that that is the goal, to simply set a figure and say you try to reach it.

The goal is the one that I outlined in my answer about making progress in the reduction of the rate of increase in government spending and so forth. And we're dedicated to that.

I don't think that there's any way that you could say what you would be satisfied with. The goal has to be this: That you eliminate every bit of unnecessary spending that you can, with an—*unnecessary*—that you do not, in pursuit, just single-minded pursuit of reducing the deficit, eliminate functions which would find the government being irresponsible and not performing the services that it is supposed to perform for the people. And so this has to be your watchword and, in maintaining those essential services at the same time, that you seek to control the other kind of spending.

And may I point out that with no regard to the budget or budget figures, we have had a commission for 6 months tied in with the Inspectors General, and I believe it was yesterday that I tried to—no, yesterday was social security, and I didn't see much of that, either. You had other things in your mind.

But a few days ago, I announced that these Inspectors General, in these first 6 months, have saved $2 billion. They have found 8,500 social security recipients who are still receiving grants and have been dead for an average of almost 7 years. And that has been eliminated. And we're going nationwide in the pursuit of this kind of investigation.

Now, those are the type of things that you can't, in advance, put in the budget and say, "We'll meet this figure in the budget because we're going to do this." No, these are the things that you, at the end of the year, or 6 months, as they came in with their 6-month report. They also found quite a number, several hundred black lung recipients who have also been dead for several years but are continuing to receive their payments.

And I think that there is a wealth of savings out there that are to be made in this particular area. But, again, this is the danger of saying, "Well, I'll settle for this or settle for that." I just don't think anyone knows.

And I'm very heartened by the fact that Alice Rivlin, the economist with the Congressional Budget Office, has said that our program is going to show results and a growth in the economy and recovery next year.

Helen has told me I've got to get out.

Ms. Thomas. Thank you.

Note: The President's sixth news conference began at 2 p.m. in the East Room at the White House. It was broadcast live on radio and television.

Letter to the Chairmen of the Senate Foreign Relations Committee and the House Foreign Affairs Committee Reporting on the Situation in Zimbabwe
December 17, 1981

Dear Mr. Chairman:

In accordance with the provisions of Section 720 of the International Security and Development Cooperation Act of 1980, I am submitting the following report on the internal situation in Zimbabwe.

One of the more significant events to take place since the submission of the last Report to the Congress was the unanimous decision handed down by the Zimbabwe Supreme Court which held that the War Victims Act, introduced shortly after independence to replace the Victims of Terrorism Act, was constitutional. The latter Act had been introduced by the former government to encourage commercial farmers to stay in the country by providing compensation in the event they suffered property damage as a result of military action. The new law which provides for relief only in case of death or injury, but not property loss, was enacted because of government's fear of being financially overwhelmed by new claims for compensation—loss of cattle by peasant farmers for example—which would have had to be honored under the old Act. This landmark decision was precipitated by a suit in which the plaintiff argued that application of the War Victims Act constituted an unconstitutional acquisition by the government of property (a claim for compensation that had occurred under the old Act) without adequate compensation.

This court case, like the one in which former Cabinet Minister Edgar Tekere was acquitted, again demonstrated the government's resolve to adhere to the Lancaster House Constitution and to the due process of law. Owing to the importance of this case the government selected a renowned South African attorney to represent it in the proceedings.

Some whites will no doubt see the Court's decision as eroding the protection of their property rights. This in turn, will lead to increased speculation on the part of many that the stage has now been set for the government to deprive large land owners of their property and give it to squatters. Any such government action, however, would clearly constitute an unjustifiable extension of the precedent in this case and would directly conflict with explicit constitutional prohibitions against the acquisition and redistribution of land without adequate compensation.

On the economic side the agricultural sector continues to lead the field in terms of output and is followed by construction and retail sales. The government, however, is still faced with a difficult balance of payment situation and foreign exchange deficiencies, and there are still serious shortages of skilled and experienced manpower.

Zimbabwe's banking and financial institutions have repeatedly demonstrated the ability to adapt to changed circumstances. They have continued to do so since independence and the phenomenon is evidenced by the speed with which these institutions have taken advantage of recent opportunities to participate in international arrangements with foreign banks. Mainly because of government's strict management of its external debt and its tight-fisted spending policies, Western banking institutions have come to regard Zimbabwe as one of the more creditworthy countries in Africa. Citibank recently became the second U.S. bank to open an office in Salisbury.

After hitting record lows the Zimbabwe stock market, long considered one of the key indexes of business confidence in the country, is presently enjoying a modest recovery. This development was probably triggered by increases in fuel supplies and the prospects for considerable improvements in economic and commercial relations with South Africa, which continues to be Zimbabwe's main trading partner. The realization by the government that the country has attracted very little foreign investment since independence and the resulting efforts to create a more favorable investment climate could be strong catalysts for restoring investor confidence in the future of private enterprise in Zimbabwe. This in turn, could lead to the long-term recovery of the stock market.

Politically, it appears that post-election euphoria is beginning to wane, and with it, some of ZANU's early popularity. The government's very deliberate and pragmatic approach to land resettlement and the rising cost of living are primarily responsible for much of the criticism being directed at it. The government, believing that it is being judged too harshly, is sensitive to criticism and has shown little tolerance for its critics, Ian Smith and Bishop Abel Muzorewa in particular.

A recently introduced order requiring prior notification to the Minister of Home Affairs of the intent to hold public political gatherings has the potential for seriously restricting the opposition's ability to present dissenting views. The Minister of Home Affairs, acting on the strength of this new measure, recently refused permission for a Muzorewa-sponsored rally to be held in Bulawayo, but granted permission to ZANU–PF and ZAPU, partners in the government coalition, to hold political meetings in Bulawayo on the same day. This order was also recently cited as justification for preventing ZAPU-oriented youth from carrying out a demonstration in support of the anniversary of the Soviet revolution.

These new restrictive measures appear unwarranted unless there is evidence not yet made public that Prime Minister Mugabe's government is being more threatened than it appears to be by opposition politicians. From all outward appearances, the Prime Minister is still firmly in control and the threat of political instability continues to diminish.

Prime Minister Mugabe has continued to take steps to reassure the whites by reaffirming his commitment to reconciliation and by stressing the point that Zimbabwe's brand of socialism would not be built on the basis of destroying the present economic infrastructure, but by preserving that structure. At the same time, however, he does not hesitate to castigate those whites who, according to him, have not changed their negative racial attitudes. His decision to fire Health Minister Herbert Ushewokunze, considered one of the more provocatively radical Cabinet members, has been a significant boost to white morale.

The exercise designed to integrate the two former guerrilla armies and the former Rhodesian forces into a single army, which was organized and directed by the British, has been successfully completed. The entire operation took 18 months and involved approximately 58,000 troops. The success of this operation reflects credit on the British, Prime Minister Mugabe, Joshua Nkomo and the white leadership of the former Rhodesian forces. It has also laid to rest the problem of force amalgamation which was one of the most intractable issues in the Anglo-American and Lancaster House settlement efforts.

Prime Minister Mugabe continues to view a Namibian settlement as an urgent issue, and he has stated publicly that Zimbabwe supports recent Contact Group efforts to bring about independence. Zimbabwe's balanced position on key regional issues is important to us in seeking a Namibian settlement and pursuing other U.S. objectives in Africa.

Sincerely,

RONALD REAGAN

Note: This is the text of identical letters addressed to Senator Charles H. Percy, chairman of the Senate Foreign Relations Committee, and Representative Clement J. Zablocki, chairman of the House Foreign Affairs Committee.

Remarks on Lighting the National Community Christmas Tree
December 17, 1981

Ladies and gentlemen and fellow Americans:

This is a wonderful occasion, an annual occasion here in Washington, when we turn on the nation's Christmas tree.

Christmas, of course, is, I think for all of us, is a time of memories of our own childhood, of our children, grandchildren—but anyway, it is a time of children. And so, here tonight we're surrounded by children, I'm happy to say, here in the East Room of the White House.

Maybe it's fitting that children should be here and that Christmas is a time for children, because the man whose birthday we celebrate in this season came to us the Prince of Peace, not in a chariot, but as a babe in a manger. I know there are some who celebrate this day, the Christmas Day, as the birthday of a great teacher and philosopher. To others of us, he is more than that; he is also divine. But to all of us, he taught us the way that we could have peace on Earth and good will to men, and that is if we would do unto others as we would have others do unto us.

Now, this button here and this box has been used for turning on the national

Christmas tree since 1923, I believe it was, when President Coolidge first did it. It didn't always get turned on here in the White House. Sometimes it was outdoors and down where the tree is and sometimes it wasn't even in Washington. Harry Truman turned the tree on once with this same switch from Independence, Missouri. Franklin Delano Roosevelt turned it on at times from Hyde Park. But it's going to be turned on here from Washington.

I had hoped that—in fact, I one day said that our grandchild, Cameron Michael, might be able to push the button, but he's 3,000 miles away. All these children are here, and I couldn't pick one of them out of all of this number to push the button, so I'm going to have to do it myself.

And in doing it, we all know that this Christmas is not as happy for some Americans as it could be, not as happy for some people out in other parts of the world. We've had other Christmases in our land—the first one when we were a nation in 1976 [1776], and Washington led his men across the Delaware River in a battle that set the stage for our independence. And legend has it that the path of their march through the snow was one of blood-stained footprints. But we shall live with the hope and the promise of the man of Galilee that Christmases will be better and that we will have peace and good will among men.

And now—[*pressing the button*]—the tree is lighted.

Do you want to look around and you can see the tree over there on the monitor? There it is. All lighted up.

Note: The President spoke at 5:40 p.m. in the East Room at the White House where he pressed the button which lighted the National Christmas tree at the annual Christmas Pageant of Peace ceremonies on the Ellipse.

Excerpt From an Exchange With a Reporter Concerning the Kidnaping of Brigadier General James Dozier
December 18, 1981

Q. Mr. President, can we do anything to try to find General Dozier and free him from the Red Brigades?

The President. Well, I think that everything is being done that can be done. This is, I think, a terrible situation. And it's a most frustrating situation, because I would like to be able to stand sometime—I'm sure that we all would—and say to the people that do these things, they are cowardly bums. They aren't heroes, they don't have a cause that justifies what they're doing.

They're cowards. They wouldn't have the guts to stand up to anyone individually in any kind of a fair contest. And I think it is—well, I can't say any more than that.

Yes, we're doing everything we can.

Note: The exchange began at approximately 12:30 p.m. as the President was beginning a luncheon meeting with American automobile industry representatives in the Cabinet Room at the White House.

Nomination of J. J. Simmons III To Be a Member of the Interstate Commerce Commission
December 18, 1981

The President today announced his intention to nominate J. J. Simmons III to be a member of the Interstate Commerce Commission for the remainder of the term expiring December 31, 1985. He would succeed Thomas A. Trantum.

Since 1970 Mr. Simmons has been vice president, government relations, Amerada Hess Corp., New York, N.Y. He was Administrator, Oil Import Administration, Department of the Interior, in 1969–70; Deputy Administrator, Oil Import Administrator, in 1968–69; Assistant Director, Office of Oil and Gas, Department of the Interior, in 1961–68; and vice president, secretary-treasurer, Geologist Simmons Royalty Co., Muskogee, Okla., in 1949–61.

He graduated from St. Louis University (B.S., 1949) and attended the University of Detroit. He is married, has five children, and resides in Scotch Plains, N.J. He was born March 26, 1925, in Muskogee, Okla.

Remarks on Signing Executive Order 12336, Establishing the Task Force on Legal Equity for Women
December 21, 1981

The President. Welcome to the White House.

The decisions that are made in this room mold and shape the Federal policy, and today we are here to reaffirm, or affirm again, that discrimination of any kind will not be tolerated in the Federal Government.

During the campaign I stated that while I was opposed to the ERA, I was dedicated to eliminating discrimination against women. We've made progress in fulfilling this commitment. Judy Peachee has been appointed as my special assistant to vigorously pursue this objective. With her help, in October we launched the Fifty States Project to ferret out any remaining discriminatory laws at the State level. Judy is keeping me advised on the progress that's being made there.

Admittedly, most of our attention in these first months has been focused on putting America's economic house in order, and I don't think anything could be more helpful to American women than reducing inflation and laying the foundation for solid economic progress. We've accomplished more in this area than anyone, I'm sure, would have predicted. At the same time, however, specific steps other than the Fifty States Project have been taken.

To assist the task force we're establishing today, the Attorney General is systematically reviewing laws and regulations with an eye to identifying gender-based discrimination. Also, I think, we can take a little credit for making Sandra O'Connor the first female Supreme Court Justice.

Today we meet to move forward one more step. The Task Force on Legal Equity for Women will work to ensure that current and future Federal regulations do not discriminate because of sex. For the first time, there will be a working Task Force, with a clear Presidential mandate, for this express purpose. The people who will carry out this mandate were selected because of their ranking positions in the departments and agencies. Demonstrating the seriousness of our effort, members of the Task Force hold the rank of Assistant Secretary or the equivalent, in the Cabinet departments, and the rank of Deputy Administrator in the independent agencies. Fourteen of the 21 members are women. All are in positions to effect change.

I've asked Carol Dinkins of the Justice Department to chair the Task Force. She has impressive legal experience in dealing with regulations and has chaired two regulatory review task forces in Texas. Furthermore, in her current position as an Assistant Attorney General, she has the responsibility for examining and analyzing laws and regulations. I believe she's ideally suited to manage the functions of the Task Force and will take this responsibility with the seriousness it deserves.

So now, in pursuing our goal of equal opportunity for all Americans, it gives me sincere pleasure to sign this Executive order establishing the Task Force on Legal Equity for Women.

It is signed, the Task Force is in existence, and, Carol, you can have the pen. [*Laughter*]

Ms. Dinkins. Thank you.

Reporter. Mr. President, when you talk about eliminating discrimination, might it not be easier to just, with one point, have the ERA and take care of it at one level federally?

The President. Well, I know that that is the way many think. My objections have been not because of opposition to what it was supposed to accomplish, but to the fact that it would take out of the legislature and put in the hands of the courts this matter. And it wouldn't be just simple; it would mean people believing that the constitutional right had been violated, taking their case to court, and long litigation on many points. And it offers an opportunity for mischiefmaking, not on the part of women, but on the part of men who would seek to take advantage of it for their own benefit. And with our own experience in California, where we eliminated by statute 14 outright discriminations against women, this was where, I believe, that there was a better way.

The truth of the matter is—I'm not a lawyer, and as the poet says, "I'm not so smart as these lawyer guys"—strictly between us two—I believe that, actually, we have a constitutional provision now. The 14th amendment specifically uses the word "persons"—that all persons are equal in this country. And, indeed, some cases have been brought in the context of the 14th amendment.

Again, as I say, it leaves it up to lengthy litigation, and it seems to me that it's just far simpler to change the regulations and to change the existing statutes, and that does it.

Note: The President spoke at 11:55 a.m. at the Cabinet Room ceremony attended by the members of the Task Force and reporters.

On the same day, the Office of the Press Secretary announced the 21 members of the Task Force. They are:

Carol E. Dinkins, Assistant Attorney General, Land and Natural Resources Division, Department of Justice (Chairman of the Task Force);

Arlene Triplett, Assistant Secretary for Administration, Department of Commerce;

Lawrence J. Korb, Assistant Secretary of Defense (Manpower, Reserve Affairs and Logistics);

Jean Tufts, Assistant Secretary for Special Education and Rehabilitative Services, Department of Education;

Robert C. Odle, Jr., Assistant Secretary, Congressional, Intergovernmental, and Public Affairs, Department of Energy;

Dorcas Hardy, Assistant Secretary of Health and Human Services;

Judith Tardy, Assistant Secretary for Administration, Department of Housing and Urban Development;

J. Robinson West, Assistant Secretary—Policy, Budget and Administration, Department of the Interior;

Mary C. Jarratt, Assistant Secretary, Food and Consumer Services, Department of Agriculture;

Lenora Cole-Alexander, Director, Women's Bureau, Department of Labor;

Joan M. Clark, Director General of the Foreign Service and Director of Personnel, Department of State;

Katherine M. Anderson, Director, Executive Secretariat, Department of Transportation;

Angela Buchanan, Treasurer of the United States, Department of the Treasury;

Winifred Pizzano, Deputy Director, ACTION;

W. Antoinette Ford, Assistant Administrator for Near East, Agency for International Development;

Joseph A. Cannon, Acting Associate Administrator for Policy and Resource Management, Environmental Protection Agency;

James T. Hackett, Associate Director for Management, International Communication Agency;

Linda L. Smith, Assistant to the Director for Administration, Office of Management and Budget;

Loretta Cornelius, Deputy Director, Office of Personnel Management;

Carolyn D. Schoenberg, Director, Women's Business Enterprise, Small Business Administration;

Elizabeth Flores Burkhart, Associate Deputy Administrator for Information Resources Management, Veterans Administration.

Executive Order 12336—Task Force on Legal Equity for Women
December 21, 1981

By the authority vested in me as President by the Constitution of the United States of America, and in order to provide for the systematic elimination of regulatory and procedural barriers which have unfairly precluded women from receiving equal treatment from Federal activities, it is hereby ordered as follows:

Section 1. Establishment. (a) There is established the Task Force on Legal Equity for Women.

(b) The Task Force members shall be appointed by the President from among nominees by the heads of the following Executive agencies, each of which shall have one representative on the Task Force.

(1) Department of State.
(2) Department of the Treasury.
(3) Department of Defense.
(4) Department of Justice.
(5) Department of the Interior.
(6) Department of Agriculture.
(7) Department of Commerce.
(8) Department of Labor.
(9) Department of Health and Human Services.
(10) Department of Housing and Urban Development.
(11) Department of Transportation.
(12) Department of Energy.
(13) Department of Education.
(14) Agency for International Development.
(15) Veterans Administration.
(16) Office of Management and Budget.
(17) International Communication Agency.
(18) Office of Personnel Management.
(19) Environmental Protection Agency.
(20) ACTION.
(21) Small Business Administration.

(c) The President shall designate one of the members to chair the Task Force. Other agencies may be invited to participate in the functions of the Task Force.

Sec. 2. Functions. (a) The members of the Task Force shall be responsible for coordinating and facilitating in their respective agencies, under the direction of the head of their agency, the implementation of changes ordered by the President in sex-discriminatory Federal regulations, policies, and practices.

(b) The Task Force shall periodically report to the President on the progress made throughout the Government in implementing the President's directives.

(c) The Attorney General shall complete the review of Federal laws, regulations, policies, and practices which contain language that unjustifiably differentiates, or which effectively discriminates, on the basis of sex. The Attorney General or his designee shall, on a quarterly basis, report his findings to the President through the Cabinet Council on Human Resources.

Sec. 3. Administration. (a) The head of each Executive agency shall, to the extent permitted by law, provide the Task Force with such information and advice as the Task Force may identify as being useful to fulfill its functions.

(b) The agency with its representative chairing the Task Force shall, to the extent permitted by law, provide the Task Force with such administrative support as may be necessary for the effective performance of its functions.

(c) The head of each agency represented on the Task Force shall, to the extent permitted by law, furnish its representative such administrative support as is necessary and appropriate.

Sec. 4. General Provisions. (a) Section 1–101(h) of Executive Order No. 12258, as amended, is revoked.

(b) Executive Order No. 12135 is revoked.

(c) Section 6 of Executive Order No. 12050, as amended, is revoked.

RONALD REAGAN

The White House,
December 21, 1981.

[*Filed with the Office of the Federal Register, 2:43 p.m., December 21, 1981*]

Exchange With Reporters About Former Polish Ambassador Romuald Spasowski
December 22, 1981

Q. Mr. President, can you make any comment on the Polish situation today, any reports, any word of options on our part?

The President. No. It's too early in the day. We haven't had any meeting yet on it for any update on the progress that we might be making.

Q. What is your feeling about the Ambassador and what he represents to us as Americans and to the Polish people?

The President. I'm very proud that he's here in this office. I think we're in the presence of a very courageous man and woman who have acted on the highest of principle. And I think the people of Poland are probably very proud of them also.

Q. Can you give him any encouragement about options that this country might take?

The President. Well, the Ambassador is aware of the things that we've been talking about and what we're trying to do.

Q. Are you at all concerned that your remarks may incite the Poles to take to the streets and then they, in fact, be crushed by it?

The President. No, no one is suggesting that.

Q. Thank you.

Note: The exchange began at 9:45 a.m. as the President was meeting with the former Ambassador and his wife, who were seeking political asylum in the United States, in the Oval Office at the White House.

Statement on Signing the Agriculture and Food Act of 1981
December 22, 1981

I am pleased to sign today a bipartisan farm bill that recognizes both our reliance on the American farmer and the limits of government.

This legislation is the result of many months of hard work, both in the Congress and in the administration. There are many in the House and Senate who deserve credit for their efforts, but in particular I would like to thank Senators Jesse Helms,

Bob Dole, and Dee Huddleston, and Representatives Kika de la Garza, Bill Wampler, and Tom Foley for their leadership. This bill provides needed assistance to our farmers and ranchers, benefits consumers, and is responsible from a budget perspective.

The strength of our economy is our reliance on the marketplace. All Americans are gripped today by a painful recession. Our agricultural producers—the farmers and ranchers who are our mainstay—feel the sting of high interest rates and inflation the same as any other business man or woman. Returning to the principles of free enterprise will return us all to prosperity.

The Agriculture and Food Act of 1981 recognizes the importance of the marketplace and emphasizes the great export potential of American agriculture. This bill will help farmers expand foreign markets and enhance our already positive agricultural balance of trade. I would like to challenge America's agricultural community to take full advantage of these export incentive provisions. I believe we can increase our agricultural exports 42 percent by 1984. That would mean $64 billion in agricultural trade—an increase of $19 billion pouring directly into our agricultural economy.

Funding for significant programs such as food stamps, agricultural research and extension services, and Food for Peace are also authorized in this bill.

We should never forget that American farmers and ranchers are the most productive in the world. On behalf of all Americans, I thank them for the abundance we enjoy even in these difficult days. I sign this bill in the belief that it will yield benefits to both producers and consumers. Working together, sensitive to the needs of each in the marketplace, we can restore prosperity to all our people.

Note: The President signed the bill at a ceremony in the Cabinet Room at the White House.

As enacted, S. 884 is Public Law 97–98, approved December 22.

Statement About Distribution of the Cheese Inventory of the Commodity Credit Corporation
December 22, 1981

The Dairy Price Support program in this country has resulted in the stockpiling of millions upon millions of pounds of cheese by the Commodity Credit Corporation. At a time when American families are under increasing financial pressure, their government cannot sit by and watch millions of pounds of food turn to waste.

I am authorizing today the immediate release of 30 million pounds from the CCC inventory. The cheese will be delivered to the States that request it and will be distributed free to the needy by nonprofit organizations.

The 1981 farm bill I signed today will slow the rise in price support levels, but even under this bill, surpluses will continue to pile up. A total of more than 560 million pounds of cheese has already been consigned to warehouses, so more distributions may be necessary as we continue our drive to root out waste in government and make the best possible use of our nation's resources.

Nomination of Michael Hayden Armacost To Be United States Ambassador to the Philippines
December 22, 1981

The President today announced his intention to nominate Michael Hayden Armacost, of Maryland, to be Ambassador to the Philippines. He would succeed Richard W. Murphy.

Mr. Armacost was instructor in government (1962–65) and assistant professor of government (1965–68) at Pomona College in Claremont, Calif. In 1968–69 he was visiting professor of international relations at the International Christian University in Tokyo, Japan. He was lecturer in international relations at Johns Hopkins University in Baltimore, Md. (1970–71) and at Georgetown University in Washington, D.C. (1971–72).

He was a member of the Policy Planning Staff at the Department of State in 1969–72 and in 1974–77. In 1972–74 he was special assistant to the Ambassador to Japan in Tokyo. In 1977–78 he was senior staff member for East Asia at the National Security Council. He was Deputy Assistant Secretary of Defense in 1978–80, and since 1980 he has been Deputy Assistant Secretary of State for East Asian and Pacific Affairs at the Department of State.

Mr. Armacost graduated from Carleton College (B.A., 1958) and Columbia University (M.A., 1961; Ph. D., 1965). He is married, has three children, and resides in Bethesda, Md. He was born April 15, 1937, in Cleveland, Ohio.

Appointment of Carl A. Anderson as a Member of the Native Hawaiians Study Commission
December 23, 1981

The President today announced his intention to appoint Carl A. Anderson to be a member of the Native Hawaiians Study Commission. He would succeed Charles D. Ferris.

Mr. Anderson is Counselor to the Under Secretary of Health and Human Services. He was legislative assistant to Senator Jesse Helms in 1976–81. He is president of the American Family Institute, a nonpartisan, tax-exempt, independent research and educational organization supporting studies and publications concerning the impact of public policy upon the family and its role in a free society. Mr. Anderson is also a practicing attorney in the State of Washington and the District of Columbia.

He graduated from Seattle University (B.A., 1972) and the University of Denver, College of Law (J.D., 1975). He is married, has three children, and resides in Arlington, Va. He was born February 27, 1951, in Torrington, Conn.

Designation of Five Members of the Board of Directors of the Rural Telephone Bank
December 23, 1981

The President today announced his intention to designate the following individuals to be members of the Board of Directors of the Rural Telephone Bank:

Seeley G. Lodwick is Under Secretary of Agriculture for International and Commodity Programs. Previously Mr. Lodwick served as Iowa administrator for Senator Roger W. Jepsen (R-Iowa), while managing a family-owned corn and soybean farm in southeast Iowa. He was born October 19, 1920.

Frank W. Naylor, Jr., is Under Secretary of Agriculture for Small Community and Rural Development. Previously Mr. Naylor was senior vice president of the 11th Farm Credit District, Sacramento, Calif. He was born February 7, 1939.

Ruth A. Reister is Deputy Under Secretary of Agriculture for Small Community and Rural Development. Previously Mrs. Reister was assistant vice president of the Federal Reserve Bank of Minneapolis, Minn. She was born May 3, 1936.

William F. Stake is president, Stake Construction Co., Lennox, S.D. He founded the company in 1948. Mr. Stake was a member of the Minnesota Telephone Association in 1973–77. He was born August 28, 1920.

Don C. Stansberry, Jr., is senior partner, Baker, Worthington, Crossley, Stansberry and Wolf of Huntsville, Tenn. Previously Mr. Stansberry was general counsel for the Highland Telephone Cooperative, Inc., with headquarters in Sunbright, Tenn. He was born February 7, 1939.

Proclamation 4887—Import Fees on Certain Sugars, Sirups and Molasses
December 23, 1981

By the President of the United States of America

A Proclamation

1. The Secretary of Agriculture has advised me that he has reason to believe that certain sugars, sirups and molasses derived from sugarcane or sugar beets, classified under items 155.20 and 155.30, of the Tariff Schedules of the United States (TSUS) (19 U.S.C. 1202), are being, or are practically certain to be, imported into the United States under such conditions and in such quantities as to render or tend to render ineffective, or to materially interfere with the price support operations being conducted by the Department of Agriculture for sugarcane and sugar beets.

2. I agree that there is reason for such belief by the Secretary of Agriculture, and, therefore, I am requesting the United States International Trade Commission to make an immediate investigation with respect to this matter pursuant to section 22 of the Agricultural Adjustment Act, as amended (7 U.S.C. 624), and to report its findings and recommendations to me as soon as possible.

3. The Secretary of Agriculture has also determined and reported to me with regard to such sugars, sirups and molasses that a condition exists which requires emergency treatment and that the import fees hereinafter proclaimed should be imposed without awaiting the report and recommendations of the United States International Trade Commission.

4. I find and declare that the imposition of import fees hereinafter proclaimed, without awaiting the recommendations of the United States International Trade Commission with respect to such action, is necessary in order that the entry, or withdrawal from warehouse, for consumption of certain sugars, sirups and molasses described below by value, use and physical description and classified under TSUS items 155.20 and

155.30 will not render or tend to render ineffective, or materially interfere with, the price support operations being conducted by the Department of Agriculture for sugarcane or sugar beets.

Now, Therefore, I, Ronald Reagan, President of the United States of America, by the authority vested in me by section 22 of the Agricultural Adjustment Act, as amended, and the Statutes of the United States including Section 301 of Title 3 of the United States Code, do hereby proclaim that Part 3 of the Appendix to the Tariff Schedules of the United States is amended as follows:

1. Headnote 4 is continued in effect and amended, effective 12:01 a.m. (Eastern Standard Time) December 24, 1981, by changing paragraph (c) to read as follows:

(c)(i) The quarterly adjusted fee provided for in items 956.05 and 957.15 shall be the amount of the fee for item 956.15 plus .15 times the amount by which the applicable market stabilization price exceeds the 20 day average of the daily spot (world) price quotations for raw sugar as calculated in paragraph (ii) hereof.

(ii) The quarterly adjusted fee provided for in item 956.15 shall be the amount by which the average of the daily spot (world) price quotations for raw sugar for the 20 consecutive market days immediately preceding the 20th day of the month preceding the calendar quarter during which the fee shall be applicable (as reported by the New York Coffee, Sugar and Cocoa Exchange or, if such quotations are not being reported, by the International Sugar Organization), expressed in United States cents per pound, Caribbean ports, in bulk, adjusted to a United States delivered basis by adding applicable duty and attributed costs, is less than the applicable market stabilization price: *Provided,* That whenever the average of such daily spot price quotations for 10 consecutive market days within any calendar quarter, adjusted to a United States delivered basis as provided herein, plus the fee then in effect (1) exceeds the market stabilization price by more than one cent, the fee then in effect shall be decreased by one cent, or (2) is less than the market stabilization price by more than one cent, the fee then in effect shall be increased by one cent: *Provided further,* That the fee may not be greater than 50 per centum of the average of such daily spot price quotations for raw sugar.

(iii) The market stabilization price for the first, second, and third calendar quarters of 1982 shall be 19.0800 cents per pound. The market stabilization price that shall be applicable to each subsequent fiscal year shall be determined and announced by the Secretary of Agriculture (hereafter the "Secretary") in accordance with this headnote no later than 30 days prior to the beginning of the fiscal year for which such market stabilization price shall be applicable. The market stabilization price shall be equal to the sum of: (1) the price support level for the applicable fiscal year, expressed in cents per pound of raw cane sugar; (2) adjusted average transportation costs; (3) interest costs, if applicable; (4) an amount adequate to compensate for the estimated value of duty reductions to be granted under the Generalized System of Preferences on imported raw cane sugar, as determined by the Secretary and (5) 0.2 cents. The adjusted average transportation costs shall be the weighted average cost of handling and transporting domestically produced raw cane sugar from Florida to Atlantic Coast ports north of Cape Hatteras, as determined by the Secretary. Interest costs shall be the amount of interest that would be required to be paid by a recipient of a price support loan for raw cane sugar upon repayment of the loan at full maturity. Interest costs shall only be applicable if a price support loan recipient is not required to pay interest upon forfeiture of the loan collateral.

(iv) Attributed costs for the first, second, and third calendar quarters of 1982 shall be 1.5032 cents per pound of imported raw cane sugar. The attributed costs that shall be applicable to each subsequent fiscal year shall be determined and announced by the Secretary in accordance with this headnote no later than 30 days prior to the beginning of the fiscal year for which such attributed costs shall be applicable. Attributed costs shall be equal to the sum of the costs, as estimated by the Secretary, of freight, insurance, stevedoring, financing, weighing, sampling, and International Sugar Agreement fees which are attributable to the importation of raw cane sugar from Caribbean ports.

(v) The Secretary shall determine the amount of the quarterly fees in accordance with this headnote and shall announce such fees not later than the 25th day of the month preceding the calendar quarter during which the fees shall be applicable. The Secretary shall certify the amount of such fees to the Secretary of the Treasury and file notice thereof with the *Federal Register* prior to the beginning of the calendar quarter during which the fees shall be applicable. The Secretary shall determine and announce any adjustment in the fees made within a calendar quarter in accordance with the first proviso of paragraph (ii) hereof, shall certify such adjusted fees to the Secretary of the Treasury, and shall file notice thereof with the *Federal Register* within 3 market days of the fulfillment of that proviso.

(vi) If an adjustment is made in the fee in accordance with the first proviso of paragraph (ii) hereof, any subsequent adjustment made within that quarter shall only be made on the basis of the average adjusted spot price for any 10 consecutive market day period following the effective date of the immediately preceding fee adjustment. No adjustment shall be made in any fee in accordance with the first proviso of paragraph (ii) hereof during the last fifteen market days of a calendar quarter.

(vii) Any adjustment made in a fee during a quarter in accordance with the first proviso of paragraph (ii) hereof shall be effective only with respect to sugar entered or withdrawn from warehouse for consumption after 12:01 a.m. (local time at point of entry) on the day following the filing of notice thereof with the *Federal Register:* Provided, That such adjusted fee shall not apply to sugar exported (as defined in section 152.1 of the Customs Regulations) on a through bill of lading to the United States from the country of origin before such time.

2. Items 956.05, 956.15 and 957.15 are continued in effect and amended to read as follows:

Item	Articles	Rates of duty (Section 22 Fees)
	Sugars, sirups and molasses derived from sugarcane or sugar beets, except those entered pursuant to a license issued by the Secretary of Agriculture in accordance with headnote 4(a): .	
	Principally of crystalline structure or in dry amorphous form, provided for in item 155.20 part 10A, schedule 1: .	
956.05	Not to be further refined or improved in quality.	3.1104 per lb. adjusted quarterly beginning January 1, 1982, in accordance with headnote 4(c), but not in excess of 50% ad val.

Item	Articles	Rates of duty (Section 22 Fees)
956.15	To be further refined or improved in quality.	2.1418 per lb., adjusted quarterly beginning January 1, 1982 in accordance with headnote 4(c), but not in excess of 50% ad val.
957.15	Not principally of crystalline structure and not in dry amorphous form, containing soluble nonsugar solids (excluding any foreign substance that may have been added or developed in the product) equal to 6% or less by weight of the total soluble solids, provided for in item 155.30, part 10A, schedule 1.	3.1104 per lb. of total sugars, adjusted quarterly beginning January 1, 1982, in accordance with headnote 4(c), but not in excess of 50% ad val.

3. The provisions of this proclamation shall terminate upon the filing of a notice in the *Federal Register* by the Secretary of Agriculture that the Department of Agriculture is no longer conducting a price support program for sugar beets and sugarcane.

4. The provisions of paragraph (c)(v) of Headnote 4 of Part 3 of the Appendix to the TSUS, as added herein, requiring the determination and announcement by the Secretary of Agriculture not later than the 25th day of the month preceding the calendar quarter during which the fees shall be applicable, shall not apply to the fees to become effective January 1, 1982.

5. The provisions of Proclamation 4631 of December 28, 1978 are hereby terminated, except with respect to those articles which are exempted from the provisions of this proclamation under paragraph 6 below.

6. This proclamation shall be effective as of 12:01 a.m. (Eastern Standard Time) on the day following its signing. However, the provisions of this proclamation shall not apply to articles entered, or withdrawn from warehouse, for consumption prior to January 1, 1982, which are imported to fulfill forward contracts that were entered into

prior to June 1, 1981 between (a) an exporter and an end user of such articles; or (b) an importer, broker, or operator and an end user of such articles.

In Witness Whereof, I have hereunto set my hand this twenty-third day of December, in the year of our Lord nineteen hundred and eighty-one, and of the Independence of the United States of America the two hundred and sixth.

RONALD REAGAN

[*Filed with the Office of the Federal Register, 5:01 p.m., December 23, 1981*]

Proclamation 4888—Modification of Tariffs on Certain Sugars, Sirups and Molasses
December 23, 1981

By the President of the United States of America

A Proclamation

1. Headnote 2 of Subpart A of Part 10 of Schedule 1 of the Tariff Schedules of the United States, hereinafter referred to as the "TSUS", provides, in relevant part, as follows:

"(i) . . . if the President finds that a particular rate not lower than such January 1, 1968, rate, limited by a particular quota, may be established for any articles provided for in item 155.20 or 155.30, which will give due consideration to the interests in the United States sugar market of domestic producers and materially affected contracting parties to the General Agreement on Tariffs and Trade, he shall proclaim such particular rate and such quota limitation, . . ."

"(ii) . . . any rate and quota limitation so established shall be modified if the President finds and proclaims that such modification is required or appropriate to give effect to the above considerations; . . ."

2. Headnote 2 was added to the TSUS by Proclamation No. 3822 of December 16, 1967 (82 Stat. 1455) to carry out a provision in the Geneva (1967) Protocol of the General Agreement on Tariffs and Trade (Note 1 of Unit A, Chapter 10, Part I of Schedule XX; 19 U.S.T., Part II, 1282). The Geneva Protocol is a trade agreement that was entered into and proclaimed pursuant to section 201(a) of the Trade Expansion Act of 1962 (19 U.S.C. 1821(a)). Section 201(a) of the Trade Expansion Act authorizes the President to proclaim the modification or continuance of any existing duty or other import restriction or such additional import restrictions as he determines to be required or appropriate to carry out any trade agreement entered into under the authority of that Act.

3. I find that the modifications hereinafter proclaimed of the rates of duty applicable to items 155.20 and 155.30 of the TSUS are appropriate to carry out a trade agreement and give due consideration to the interests in the United States sugar market of domestic producers and materially affected contracting parties to the General Agreement on Tariffs and Trade.

Now, Therefore, I, Ronald Reagan, President of the United States of America, by the authority vested in me by the Constitution and statutes, including section 201 of the Trade Expansion Act of 1962, and pursuant to General Headnote 4 and Headnote 2 of Subpart A of Part 10 of Schedule 1 of the TSUS, do hereby proclaim until otherwise superseded by law:

A. The rates of duty in rate columns 1 and 2 for items 155.20 and 155.30 of Subpart A of Part 10 of Schedule 1 of the TSUS are modified and the following rates are established:

155.20.............. 2.98125¢ per lb. less 0.0421875¢ per lb. for each degree under 100 degrees (and fractions of a degree in proportion) but not less than 1.9265625¢ per lb.

155.30.............. Dutiable on total sugars at the rate per lb. applicable under Item 155.20 to sugar testing 100 degrees.

B. Those parts of Proclamation 4334 of November 16, 1974, Proclamation 4463 of September 21, 1976, Proclamation 4466 of October 4, 1976, Proclamation 4539 of November 11, 1977, and Proclamation 4720 of February 1, 1980, which are inconsistent with the provisions of paragraph (A) above are hereby terminated.

C. The provisions of this Proclamation shall apply to articles entered, or withdrawn from warehouse, for consumption after 12:01 a.m. (Eastern Standard Time) on the day following the date of this Proclamation. However, the provisions of this proclamation shall not apply to articles entered, or withdrawn from warehouse, for consumption prior to January 1, 1982 which are imported to fulfill forward contracts that were entered into prior to June 1, 1981 between: (a) an exporter and an end user of such articles; or (b) an importer, broker, or operator and an end user of such articles.

In Witness Whereof, I have hereunto set my hand this twenty-third day of December, in the year of our Lord nineteen hundred and eighty-one and of the Independence of the United States of America the two hundred and sixth.

RONALD REAGAN

[*Filed with the Office of the Federal Register, 5:02 p.m., December 23, 1981*]

Statement on Signing Proclamations Concerning Imports of Sugar and Sugar Products
December 23, 1981

I have today signed two proclamations imposing import fees and increasing duties on sugar. The proclamations were made necessary by enactment of the 1981 Agriculture and Food Act's price support program for domestic sugar.

The high price support level for domestic sugar (16.75¢ in FY 82) creates an opportunity for foreign producers to export sugar to this country. Under present world market conditions, foreign sugar can be delivered in the United States at a price less than the domestic support price. Unless duties are increased and import fees imposed, the Federal Government would have to take ownership of large quantities of sugar at a tremendous cost to the taxpayers of this country.

The import fee imposed by one of these proclamations results in a market stabilization price for sugar of 19.08¢ per pound. This price consists of the 16.75¢ purchase price plus 2.33¢ to cover adjusted average freight and related marketing costs of raw sugar.

The other proclamation raises the basic duty for raw sugar from the current level of 0.625¢ per pound to 2.8125¢, the maximum permitted by law.

The proclamations allow a limited exemption for sugar imports which were contracted for prior to June 1, 1981, and which will be brought into this country before January 1, 1982. This exemption was made as a matter of equity for foreign traders who had made contracts to sell us sugar well before congressional acceptance of the sugar provisions of the farm bill.

I personally regret the necessity for signing these proclamations. The sugar program enacted by Congress to protect higher cost domestic producers will result in higher costs for all American sugar consumers. I have directed that the import fees imposed by these proclamations be adjusted at least quarterly, so that they can be revised downward whenever possible, without incurring significant government purchases of sugar or encouraging forfeiture of sugar loans beginning in FY 83.

In addition, I realize that the sugar duties and fees may have adverse effects on our major foreign sugar suppliers, particularly those in the Caribbean Basin. I have thus asked appropriate agencies to review this question on a priority basis to see what we can do to mitigate the effects.

Address to the Nation About Christmas and the Situation in Poland
December 23, 1981

Good evening.

At Christmas time, every home takes on a special beauty, a special warmth, and that's certainly true of the White House, where so many famous Americans have spent their Christmases over the years. This fine old home, the people's house, has seen so much, been so much a part of all our lives and history. It's been humbling and inspiring for Nancy and me to be spending our first Christmas in this place.

We've lived here as your tenants for almost a year now, and what a year it's been. As a people we've been through quite a lot—moments of joy, of tragedy, and of real achievement—moments that I believe have brought us all closer together. G. K. Chesterton once said that the world would never starve for wonders, but only for the want of wonder.

At this special time of year, we all renew our sense of wonder in recalling the story of the first Christmas in Bethlehem, nearly 2,000 year ago.

Some celebrate Christmas as the birthday of a great and good philosopher and teacher. Others of us believe in the divinity of the child born in Bethlehem, that he was and is the promised Prince of Peace. Yes, we've questioned why he who could perform miracles chose to come among us as a helpless babe, but maybe that was his first miracle, his first great lesson that we should learn to care for one another.

Tonight, in millions of American homes, the glow of the Christmas tree is a reflection of the love Jesus taught us. Like the shepherds and wise men of that first Christmas, we Americans have always tried to follow a higher light, a star, if you will. At lonely campfire vigils along the frontier, in the darkest days of the Great Depression, through war and peace, the twin beacons of faith and freedom have brightened the American sky. At times our footsteps may have faltered, but trusting in God's help, we've never lost our way.

Just across the way from the White House stand the two great emblems of the holiday season: a Menorah, symbolizing the Jewish festival of Hanukkah, and the National Christmas Tree, a beautiful towering blue spruce from Pennsylvania. Like the National Christmas Tree, our country is a living, growing thing planted in rich American soil. Only our devoted care can bring it to full flower. So, let this holiday season be for us a time of rededication.

Even as we rejoice, however, let us remember that for some Americans, this will not be as happy a Christmas as it should be. I know a little of what they feel. I remember one Christmas Eve during the Great Depression, my father opening what he thought was a Christmas greeting. It was a notice that he no longer had a job.

Over the past year, we've begun the long, hard work of economic recovery. Our goal is an America in which every citizen who needs and wants a job can get a job. Our program for recovery has only been in place for 12 weeks now, but it is beginning to work. With your help and prayers, it will succeed. We're winning the battle against inflation, runaway government spending and taxation, and that victory will mean more economic growth, more jobs, and more opportunity for all Americans.

A few months before he took up residence in this house, one of my predecessors, John Kennedy, tried to sum up the temper of the times with a quote from an author closely tied to Christmas, Charles Dickens. We were living, he said, in the best of times and the worst of times. Well, in some ways that's even more true today. The world is full of peril, as well as promise. Too many of its people, even now, live in the shadow of want and tyranny.

As I speak to you tonight, the fate of a proud and ancient nation hangs in the balance. For a thousand years, Christmas has been celebrated in Poland, a land of deep religious faith, but this Christmas brings little joy to the courageous Polish people. They have been betrayed by their own government.

The men who rule them and their totalitarian allies fear the very freedom that the Polish people cherish. They have answered the stirrings of liberty with brute force, killings, mass arrests, and the setting up of concentration camps. Lech Walesa and other Solidarity leaders are imprisoned, their fate unknown. Factories, mines, universities, and homes have been assaulted.

The Polish Government has trampled underfoot solemn commitments to the UN Charter and the Helsinki accords. It has even broken the Gdansk agreement of August 1980, by which the Polish Government recognized the basic right of its people to form free trade unions and to strike.

The tragic events now occurring in Poland, almost 2 years to the day after the Soviet invasion of Afghanistan, have been precipitated by public and secret pressure from the Soviet Union. It is no coincidence that Soviet Marshal Kulikov, chief of the Warsaw Pact forces, and other senior Red Army officers were in Poland while these outrages were being initiated. And it is no coincidence that the martial law proclamations imposed in December by the Polish Government were being printed in the Soviet Union in September.

The target of this depression [repression] is the Solidarity Movement, but in attacking Solidarity its enemies attack an entire people. Ten million of Poland's 36 million citizens are members of Solidarity. Taken together with their families, they account for the overwhelming majority of the Polish nation. By persecuting Solidarity the Polish Government wages war against its own people.

I urge the Polish Government and its allies to consider the consequences of their actions. How can they possibly justify using naked force to crush a people who ask for nothing more than the right to lead their own lives in freedom and dignity? Brute force may intimidate, but it cannot form the basis of an enduring society, and the ailing Polish economy cannot be rebuilt with terror tactics.

Poland needs cooperation between its government and its people, not military oppression. If the Polish Government will honor the commitments it has made to human rights in documents like the Gdansk agreement, we in America will gladly do our share to help the shattered Polish economy, just as we helped the countries of Europe after both World Wars.

It's ironic that we offered, and Poland expressed interest in accepting, our help after World War II. The Soviet Union intervened then and refused to allow such help to Poland. But if the forces of tyranny in Poland, and those who incite them from without, do not relent, they should prepare themselves for serious consequences. Already, throughout the Free World, citizens have publicly demonstrated their support for the Polish people. Our government, and those of our allies, have expressed moral revulsion at the police state tactics of Poland's oppressors. The Church has also spoken out, in spite of threats and intimidation. But our reaction cannot stop there.

I want emphatically to state tonight that if the outrages in Poland do not cease, we cannot and will not conduct "business as usual" with the perpetrators and those who aid and abet them. Make no mistake, their crime will cost them dearly in their future dealings with America and free peoples everywhere. I do not make this statement lightly or without serious reflection.

We have been measured and deliberate in our reaction to the tragic events in Poland. We have not acted in haste, and the steps I will outline tonight and others we may take in the days ahead are firm, just, and reasonable.

In order to aid the suffering Polish people during this critical period, we will continue the shipment of food through private humanitarian channels, but only so long as we know that the Polish people themselves receive the food. The neighboring country of Austria has opened her doors to refugees from Poland. I have therefore directed that American assistance, including supplies of basic foodstuffs, be offered to aid the Austrians in providing for these refugees.

But to underscore our fundamental opposition to the repressive actions taken by the Polish Government against its own people, the administration has suspended all government-sponsored shipments of agricultural and dairy products to the Polish Government. This suspension will remain in force until absolute assurances are received that distribution of these products is monitored and guaranteed by independent agencies. We must be sure that every bit of food provided by America goes to the Polish people, not to their oppressors.

The United States is taking immediate action to suspend major elements of our economic relationships with the Polish Government. We have halted the renewal of the Export-Import Bank's line of export credit insurance to the Polish Government. We will suspend Polish civil aviation privileges in the United States. We are suspending the right of Poland's fishing fleet to operate in American waters. And we're proposing to our allies the further restriction of high technology exports to Poland.

These actions are not directed against the Polish people. They are a warning to the Government of Poland that free men cannot and will not stand idly by in the face of brutal repression. To underscore this point, I've written a letter to General Jaruzelski, head of the Polish Government. In it, I outlined the steps we're taking and warned of the serious consequences if the Polish Government continues to use violence against its populace. I've urged him to free those in arbitrary detention, to lift martial law, and to restore the internationally recognized rights of the Polish people to free speech and association.

The Soviet Union, through its threats and pressures, deserves a major share of blame for the developments in Poland. So, I have also sent a letter to President Brezhnev urging him to permit the restoration of basic human rights in Poland provided for in the Helsinki Final Act. In it, I informed him that if this repression continues, the United States will have no choice but to take further concrete political and economic measures affecting our relationship.

When 19th century Polish patriots rose against foreign oppressors, their rallying cry was, "For our freedom and yours." Well, that motto still rings true in our time. There is a spirit of solidarity abroad in the world tonight that no physical force can crush. It crosses national boundaries and enters into the hearts of men and women everywhere. In factories, farms, and schools, in cities and towns around the globe, we the people of the Free World stand as one with our Polish brothers and sisters. Their cause is ours, and our prayers and hopes go out to them this Christmas.

Yesterday, I met in this very room with Romuald Spasowski, the distinguished former Polish Ambassador who has sought asylum in our country in protest of the suppression of his native land. He told me that one of the ways the Polish people have demonstrated their solidarity in the face of martial law is by placing lighted candles in their windows to show that the light of liberty still glows in their hearts.

Ambassador Spasowski requested that on Christmas Eve a lighted candle will burn in the White House window as a small but certain beacon of our solidarity with the Polish people. I urge all of you to do the same tomorrow night, on Christmas Eve, as a personal statement of your commitment to the steps we're taking to support the brave people of Poland in their time of troubles.

Once, earlier in this century, an evil influence threatened that the lights were going out all over the world. Let the light of millions of candles in American homes give notice that the light of freedom is not going to be extinguished. We are blessed with a freedom and abundance denied to so many. Let those candles remind us that

1187

these blessings bring with them a solid obligation, an obligation to the God who guides us, an obligation to the heritage of liberty and dignity handed down to us by our forefathers and an obligation to the children of the world, whose future will be shaped by the way we live our lives today.

Christmas means so much because of one special child. But Christmas also reminds us that all children are special, that they are gifts from God, gifts beyond price that mean more than any presents money can buy. In their love and laughter, in our hopes for their future lies the true meaning of Christmas.

So, in a spirit of gratitude for what we've been able to achieve together over the past year and looking forward to all that we hope to achieve together in the years ahead, Nancy and I want to wish you all the best of holiday seasons. As Charles Dickens, whom I quoted a few moments ago, said so well in "A Christmas Carol," "God bless us, every one."

Good night.

Note: The President spoke at 9 p.m. from the Oval Office at the White House. The address was broadcast live on nationwide radio and television.

Christmas Message
December 24, 1981

Nancy and I are very happy to send our warmest greetings and best wishes to all those who are celebrating Christmas. We join with Americans everywhere in recognizing the sense of renewed hope and comfort this joyous season brings to our nation and the world.

The Nativity story of nearly twenty centuries ago is known by all faiths as a hymn to the brotherhood of man. For Christians, it is the fulfillment of age-old prophecies and the reaffirmation of God's great love for all of us. Through a generous Heavenly Father's gift of His Son, hope and compassion entered a world weary with fear and despair and changed it for all time.

On Christmas, we celebrate the birth of Christ with prayer, feasting, and great merriment. But, most of all, we experience it in our hearts. For, more than just a day, Christmas is a state of mind. It is found throughout the year whenever faith overcomes doubt, hope conquers despair, and love triumphs over hate. It is present when men of any creed bring love and understanding to the hearts of their fellow man.

The feeling is seen in the wondrous faces of children and in the hopeful eyes of the aged. It overflows the hearts of cheerful givers and the souls of the caring. And it is reflected in the brilliant colors, joyful sounds, and beauty of the winter season.

Let us resolve to honor this spirit of Christmas and strive to keep it throughout the year.

Nancy and I ask you to join us in a prayer that prudence, widsom, and understanding might descend on the people of all nations so that during the year ahead we may realize an ancient and wondrous dream: "peace on earth, goodwill toward men."

RONALD REAGAN

Interview With the President
December 23, 1981

The President. Knowing that after you get asking your questions I might not feel as good as I feel now, let me, while I feel good, say that this being a kind of a year-end roundup, I have a very good feeling about the year past and, thus, a hope for the year to come.

I think we have had a most successful year and a lot of it due to the fact that we did put together a working, bipartisan coalition to cope with the problems of spending and taxes and so forth. And I think the accomplishments that have us with, domestically, an economic program now in place to deal with the crisis, makes me feel good, and I'm optimistic about that.

Also, on the world scene, I think that with all the troubles that we have, we have a relationship with our neighbors here in the Western Hemisphere and with our allies abroad that—we've made progress toward easing the strain in some of the trouble spots of the world. Poland, of course, was an emergency situation that we couldn't have planned for very far in advance, but I mean such things as Middle East peace, the Caribbean and Central America, and so forth. And all in all, I think we have made some good progress.

So, now, go ahead and make me feel bad. [*Laughter*]

Tax Program

Q. Mr. President, the question of taxes. So many of your advisers now are suggesting that you have to go through some sort of a tax increase. Where do you stand at this point?

The President. Well, there certainly will be no change in taxes in 1982, I guarantee you. We have put a program in place that I believe will increase government's revenues simply by broadening the base of the economy, stimulating increase in productivity, offering incentives that the program does offer.

I learned a long time ago that putting your feet in concrete was dangerous, because I have among my mementos a round cement block with a pair of shoes imbedded in it that was given me by the Capitol Press Corps in Sacramento after I had put my feet in concrete and then, one day, had to stand before them and say the sound you hear is the sound of concrete breaking around my feet. So, they gave me that, but I would like to see what happens with this program.

Of course, there is the one thing with regard to taxes, that from the very first I did always speak of, and that was we continue the review of where there are places where people are getting undeserved tax breaks, the so-called closing of loopholes. Now, in that I do not include as loopholes the legitimate deductions that—without which the whole program would have failed a long time ago—but actual loopholes where, as I say, there is an unjust break. This we continue to review, and I am not opposed to that. But I think that until we see this program in operation—and then, what other circumstances can arise.

For example, we, as everyone else—we were all caught by surprise with the recession. We knew the economy was not going to be healthy for a while, but a recession, which I think was precipitated by the overlong continuation of high interest rates, brought that on. And when you just add one percentage point to the unemployment, you add $25 billion to the deficit. And until we see what begins to happen with this program, because, by the same token, you can reduce a projected deficit by $25 billion if you lower the unemployment rate.

Q. At what point will you expect to make a decision?

The President. With—

Q. On taxes—what point do you expect to make a decision?

The President. After I see what happens. You can't—the tax reform or reduction has only been in existence now for about 12 weeks, since October 1st, and that's only the smallest part. Next July we're slated for another 10-percent reduction, and I think you have to wait until you see the—what this program is going to bring about—what changes. And I am optimistic about it, myself.

Q. Mr. President——

Q. Can I follow that, on taxes? You flatly ruled out, you said, absolutely no tax increase in 1982, except for loophole closing, which leaves open the possibility that you might accept tax increases in 1983. And the second part of that—or do you want to address that first? What about '83?

The President. Well, let me say here that in no way will I—do I look kindly upon anything that is contrary to the stimulative part of our tax program, that was designed to improve productivity. No, what I was trying to say with my story about the cement block was that with the unexpected things that can happen, I just feel that I'm in no position to comment on those ideas. My leaning would be against a tax increase, but again, I don't want another block of concrete.

Q. Even in '82 you don't want another block of concrete as far as taxes are concerned?

The President. No, I believe in '82, I think that we can see far enough ahead to know, and I want to see this program and what its results will be.

Q. Mr. President, you said that you—and Dave Gergen[1] told us much the same thing—that you don't want anything that would be contrary to the stimulative part of that program?

The President. That's right, yes.

Q. Would an increase in excise taxes on tobacco, alcohol, or gasoline be in such conflict? Or might they be acceptable, if you find it necessary to increase revenue in 1983?

The President. Well, let me just say that things of that kind, and excise taxes, are not as contrary, granted that all taxes are paid by the people. But I don't think that consumption taxes are in direct opposition to the tax program that we've instituted.

Q. So that you would look a little bit more kindly on consumption taxes rather than a windfall profits tax?

The President. Let me just say, if necessity could convince me that they had to be put into effect, I'd be more tolerant of those. I would not look kindly on any tax increase.

Economic Recovery Program

Q. Let me ask another part of that. You said your feet are not in concrete, and you've also said that the problem with tax increases at this time is that it would aggravate a recession. With the skepticism that

---

[1] *Assistant to the President for Communications.*

you're well aware of about supply-side economics and the economic program, at what point, Mr. President, if the unemployment rate continues to go up, do you begin to rethink this, the supply-side economics, which seems to get such skepticism on the outside?

The President. Well, but you see, I never had heard the term before, you know, "supply-side," but I had long been a believer in this idea of reducing the share, the percentage that government takes from the private sector. My own degree was in economics, and I remember back in those days, on those dark Depression days, that one of the things that you learned was that around the turn of the century the classical economists theorized that business ups and downs, the recurrent business cycles and so forth, that invariably the business or the economic slowdown was accompanied by government going beyond a certain point with regard to the money that it took out of the private sector—in other words, that government can be a drag on the economy.

And if you look at what has happened in this century, the last being the Kennedy tax cuts, economists by and large opposed him on that and said, oh, this was a terrible thing. I think their figure averaged out that he would lose $83 billion in tax revenue. Well, he went ahead with that tax cut, and the government didn't lose 83, it got 54 billion extra.

Now, we look at every time that there has been a reduction or an increase in the capital gains tax, an increase in that tax, the government winds up getting less money at the higher rate. And by the reverse thing, every time that they have reduced that tax, in the very first year the government gets additional revenue at the lower rate. So, I happen to believe this.

In California, when we began giving back the surpluses to the people in the form of a one-time tax rebate, like a bonus to employees or something, gave it back, California's economy showed a reaction to that. We were—normally we had a higher unemployment rate than the national average and a higher inflation rate. In both instances that changed, and we had lower rates.

Q. But, Mr. President, those were soaring times in the sixties, and with California. The economy was in great shape for reasons other than the government action. For the first time, this recession, you're cutting back on budget, which also has in some degree a recessionary effect. And what I'm trying to find out is, if unemployment goes to 10 percent and seems to not be abating, would you then consider the possibility of some change in direction of the economic program?

The President. I see our economic program as the best hope we've got for solving the unemployment problem. Nothing that's been done in the past has any long-range effect. If you will look at government spending its way out of, say, a recessionary cycle, the artificial stimulation of the money supplies, government spending. This was done, oh, along about, before the '68 campaign—sometimes that stimulated spending is timed to meet an election year—and in '70 we had a recession, and we elected a Republican administration in '68. But in '70 the repercussion was so bad, because up went inflation and up went unemployment at the same time. Then, for the '72 election, the same thing had happened, the stimulating of the economy artificially instead of working our way out. Then in '74 we had a deeper recession, where unemployment was greater, inflation was greater.

Now, the same thing has gone on. We now have, with one difference—and I think due to the policies, even though the program is actually not gone into effect until now—but even with the reductions, the several billions of dollars that we've managed to cut out of the budget that was already—well, I almost said, in existence, but it wasn't, because we haven't had a budget since quite some time ago—but we cut several billion dollars out of the '81 spending. But today—and this, now, is one of our factors—inflation has not accompanied the increase in unemployment. Inflation is going down.

And, incidentally, that has caused another reduction in tax revenues that we hadn't counted on. We didn't think we were going to be as successful so quickly in lowering inflation. But inflation is a tax, and when it

went down faster than we'd planned, our estimates of revenues were thrown off.

But I believe that what we're aimed at is the answer to unemployment, is not a quick fix with some gerry-built programs that government programs and government spending that increases the size and the power of government. What is needed is a stimulant to the private sector, which provides the bulk of the jobs, the employment.

Q. And if private sector doesn't provide, by some chance?

The President. What?

Q. And if the private sector doesn't provide, by some chance?

The President. Well, then you find out what more you can do that will stimulate that private sector.

Views on the Presidency

Q. Considering some of the problems with the economy as well as the problems in Poland, has this year taught you anything about the limits of what a President can do?

The President. About the——

Q. Limits of what a President can do?

The President. The limits, yes. Well, I must say, it was not too much of a surprise after 8 years, Governor of California. I was aware that things don't instantly change and that the wheels of government grind slowly—and perhaps by good intent, that government is prevented from doing things too hastily.

But, yes, there are limitations. There are probably more because of the events of the last few years.

Q. Particularly in Poland.

The President. Well, no, there are actions, and there are actions that I will be talking about tonight on television that we can take, are taking, and additional things that will be taken.

Now, I won't go into specific detail, let me warn you, on those, because I've never believed that you can do that without tipping your hand and showing the other fellow your cards.

Q. If I could follow up on that question. You came to office with a more well-formed viewpoint of the Presidency and what you wanted to do in the Presidency than many of your predecessors. And yet, as you pointed out, with Poland, with the high interest rates, with the unanticipated recession, much of your time is really spent in what might be called "crisis management."

The President. Yes.

Q. Do you have any ideas for next year on how you can reimpose, if you will, the Reagan agenda on top of all of the intrusions from outside so that your Presidency has some stamp of your own ideas, rather than reacting to what the world is doing?

The President. It looks to me as if we will be building on what we have already done. We have a 1983 budget that must be presented in January, even before a 1982 budget is approved. And so, we've been working on that, because at the same time that we got our billions of dollars of reductions—the biggest single reduction in the increase in government—we've cut the rate of increase in government spending in half. It had averaged 14 percent or better the preceding 3 years. It's down to about 7½ percent now. But at the same time, we said there will be additional savings that must be made in '83, '84. So, now we'll be coming in, they won't be as easy to get, because we made a pretty good slice there the first time around. But we're going to be asking for additional cuts. We're going to go forward faster with what I talked about for so long as federalism. We're working on the program of how to transfer back to other levels of government programs and revenue sources to pay for them. We'll be going forward with that.

We have the commission finally appointed which will be——

Q. The '83 budget? Excuse me. You'll do that in the '83 budget?

The President. Well, not entirely. This is going to take some phase-in to transfer——

Q. Right, I'm sorry. Excuse me for interrupting.

The President. ——on that. Then we've got the commission to come in with a plan to restore social security in spite of the efforts that made that a political football—and disgracefully so—this past year.

We still, all of us in government, have to meet the problem that is imposed by social security's fiscal situation. It is actuarily out of balance and must be corrected. And, at the same time, that does not mean, as they've charged, nor have we ever suggested taking benefits away from those people now dependent on them. We're not going to do that.

On the world scene, we'll be going forward with our Caribbean plan, which includes, of course, Central America, also. We'll be continuing in the process that started at Cancún on how to help the lesser developing nations, pursuing the peace process in the Middle East, and, of course, working to do what we can with this present unanticipated situation in Poland. And yet, that in a way is a part of the whole East-West problem, because Poland didn't bring this on itself. The Soviet Union had a very large hand in there.

But in connection with that, we'll also be pursuing the thing I talked about earlier, arms reductions with the Soviet Union—not arms limitations that allow both sides to go on adding to their arsenals, but to see if we cannot get an actual cutback, particularly in the strategic nuclear weapons.

The Middle East

Q. Back to the world scene. One of the earlier things you mentioned here, pursuing a peace process in the Middle East, is the latest incident with Israel over the Golan Heights and our reaction to that part of an overall reassessment of our Middle East policy in which we intend to take a stronger line with Israel?

The President. No, it's just friends sometimes have some arguments, and I guess this is one of them. We had no——

Q. Do you object to the language of those arguments of the past few days?

The President. Well, I think maybe more of that will be temperate now. There was a little harsh tone to that. But, no, we're still committed as we've always been to our relationship with Israel, to the assurance, the obligation that I think this country feels that Israel shall exist as a nation and, we hope, in peace with its neighbors.

And maybe part of the, oh, the momentary distractions that have occurred are because we believe that in striving for peace we have to make the Arab states there understand and realize that we want a just and a fair peace, and we're not just intervening as the ally of one country, even though we are allied and have been in this moral obligation to Israel which we'll continue to be. But we want them to know that we want fairness for them, also, and here's where I think we've made great progress.

Q. Do you think we'll see the reinstitution of the strategic agreement or do you consider it canceled? Do you think it will be——

The President. No, it isn't canceled. We just held it up here until—no, I don't believe it's canceled. We don't consider it so.

Q. Do you believe that it will be reinstituted?

The President. Yes.

Q. At what point? Do you have any idea?

The President. Well, let me say I hope sooner rather than later.

Formulation of U.S. Policy and Programs

Q. One of the problems, I suppose, that I gather from Prime Minister Begin, is—and several of us have come across this on other occasions—and that is there seems to be differences of opinion between you and your staff on some basic issues—and I'll use Israel as an example. I think that in Prime Minister Begin there's a suspicion that there may be a difference of opinion as to the commitment to Israel between, say, you and your feelings and those of, say, your, many have used the expression, "more pragmatic," let us say, advisers.

The President. No. Let me say I can assure you that is not so, and I can address myself to that appearance in just a second. But remember that some of the things—for example, the Iraqi incident: We were bound by law. The law in delivering American weapons says for defensive purposes only, and they cannot be used in any other way. And without warning here was, apparently, an attack on a neighboring country using the weapons that we had provided. And the law was very specific. There had to be an investigation of this.

Now, Israel's defense was that it had information that led it to believe that this was a defensive move, a preemptive strike in their own defense.

Q. Suggested it came from you, too.

The President. What?

Q. Begin suggested it came from you, the information.

The President. Well, it didn't. [*Laughter*] As a matter of fact, I understand why now, too. We had never known that there was any talk with regard to the supplying of material to that nuclear reactor in the files or that any had ever taken place involving the previous administration. Now, I'm quite sure that he probably felt that once we were in we must have had access to that information. We didn't. No one had ever mentioned it. So, we were surprised to learn that.

But the thing about differences appearing, I think, is perhaps because it's the first time that there has really been in operation what I call Cabinet government. I did this in California and was so satisfied with the result that we instituted it here.

Now, what do we mean by that? There's always been a Cabinet, but usually the Cabinet heads or Secretaries in the perfunctory Cabinet meetings which would be held, it was a case of each one kind of reporting a little bit on his own situation. My idea of Cabinet government was that you recognize that there are very few problems that don't really overlap in a lot of areas, and I'm the fellow who has to make the decision. So, we meet.

We've met 29 times so far as a full Cabinet, and the issues that come up and are put out on the table—there is debate entered into by everyone present, like a board of directors would debate something. The only difference between that and a board of directors meeting is, we don't take a vote. When I've heard enough to make a decision, I know that I have to make the decision.

But the result is, when you have that kind of meeting—yes, you're going to have different views presented, and it finally has to come down to options that, well, this way, that way—then I make the decision, and there's been no animus in any of this. There's been total acceptance of the final decisions. But I think that this is so unusual in Washington, this method of doing this, that this has led to the assumption on the part of some that there's somehow some disarray or friction going on. The very contrary is true.

I am more than pleased with the team that we've brought here and the way they have functioned. And we're going to continue that system of government.

Richard V. Allen

Q. Speaking of that team, now that the Justice Department has cleared Richard Allen, will you accept him back as the national security adviser?

The President. Well, I can't comment yet on that. I'm delighted that they found there was no need for a special prosecutor—delighted, not surprised—but at the same time, there is a review procedure, internal in the White House, with regard to ethical standards and so forth. And that review is in process, so——

Q. How long is that going to last?

The President. I don't think that'll take long, so——

Q. Have you asked for a quick decision?

The President. Everybody understands that, yes, but——

Q. A couple of days? A week? The first of the year?

The President. Well, never having done it before, I can't tell you, but Dick Hauser, the deputy in Fielding's [2] office, is going to be in charge of that.

Mrs. Reagan

Q. Mr. President, your own popularity has held up quite well during this first year, but polls indicate that Mrs. Reagan has aroused a higher rate of disapproval than other Presidents' wives, mainly because of a perception that she likes expensive things—clothes and mink coats and jewelry and costly china. Does she, in fact, have expensive taste? Is that bad? What are your thoughts on this?

The President. No, and let me tell you that in regard to that, I think she's taken a lot of abuse that she did not in any way and in the slightest deserve. First of all, she is a very conservative and saving soul, and I kid her that she's even still got the middy blouses she had in gym class at school.

---

[2] *Fred F. Fielding, Counsel to the President.*

Sometimes some of these attacks are leveled, and she's wearing a dress that's 10 or 12 years old—and I don't know how many ladies do that. But she likes quality and good things, as I think we all do.

But she's not extravagant. She's not dedicated to that. She is very dedicated to the causes that interest her—the Foster Grandparents program, the drug programs. Some people have even indicated that somehow there isn't a sincerity in that. Well, there is. And it was her interest in that program, which really got started in California, that spread—it not only spread it nationally but when we were sent on a mission to Australia once for a preceding President—not the preceding President, but another President, while I was Governor—before we left Australia, the Foster Grandparents program was given birth there, thanks to her.

But all of this talk, all of these things that she has done—we found—and it probably could have been true if anyone else was here—that there was a lot of long-delayed maintenance due in the house. Coupled with that was something that was best expressed, I think, by Jackie Kennedy when she was President—Mrs. Onassis. She said at the time that this is the house that belongs to all of America. Therefore, it should be the prettiest house. And she, as you know, set out herself—and people through the years have contributed wonderful pieces and furniture and antiques and so forth to the White House.

We found many of those were moldering away in a warehouse—Nancy found. And learning from the staff and the people who were there the things that the White House actually possessed and weren't there, she went, and many of them had deteriorated badly. The warehouse people were delighted that she—they said, "We can't take care of them. They don't belong here." But there were people then who volunteered and helped refinish them, refurbish them.

The dishes? She didn't buy any dishes. An entire set of dishes was contributed to the White House. Now, I think Margaret Truman has expressed herself on that and said that even that far back, you couldn't set a dinner in the State Dining Room without a mixture of dishes, because there's a certain thing called breakage that takes place over the years.

Q. You seem to be warming to the subject, Mr. President. [*Laughter*]

The President. I am. I think the people that have been doing this really have been aiming at me, and maybe found it easier to do it by getting——

Q. Has anything made you more angry——

The President. What?

Q. Has anything made you more angry in this past year than——

The President. Not very much.

Q. Could you regard her as an adviser, as a, perhaps, a silent member, silent partner of that Cabinet government?

The President. No, she does not attend Cabinet meetings, and she does not project herself that way. But for all of you who might be married—we've been married almost 30 years now, and certainly we talk about things, and she has a viewpoint. But never has she tried to play a role in government. And many times I respect her woman's intuition.

But in regard to unpopularity, I just heard earlier today—and maybe Larry can tell me if this is true—I just heard that some poll or something has revealed that she's the most popular woman in the world.

Deputy Press Secretary Speakes. I haven't seen that, Mr. President. I'll have to get it. [*Laughter*]

The President. I tell you, if it isn't true, it should be. I'm on her side.

Employment Programs

Q. I hate to leave the subject, because it's a good one, but let me ask on behalf of some papers I have in the Midwest and Detroit, where things are really tough economically, and it looks like they're going to get tougher. This is going to be a very tough winter for a lot of people in the part of the country that you came from, and it's going to be a while, as you say, before the economic program takes hold. Are there any plans at all to help, aid some of these people in some of these areas in this coming winter, in this next, very tough 6 months or so?

The President. Well, this is a subject of much of our discussion because we get—

you know, people look at the national figures, unemployment rate such and such and so forth. We forget that unemployment is not spread evenly across the country, that what we call a recession in some areas is actually what I said it was in the campaign, a depression. You can have some areas with an 18- , 15-percent unemployment rate, and this is true. It is that spotted. We also have some other parts of the country where there isn't even a recession at the moment.

And yes, we think—for example, we're discussing this whole program of enterprise zones, and we're looking at this from the standpoint of, could those be—it's an experimental program—could those be launched more in the heart of those areas where they're having problems, in those cities such as you've named, where the steel industry and the automobile industry is so much a part of their economy, and it is down so low.

Q. But you expect a recovery in the economy by next spring. Won't it take a long time to launch something like an enterprise zone?

The President. That's again one of those frustrations you asked about, that you can think of something good that doesn't happen all at once. But we've—that, and I know that now and then, with regard to the defense program, where defense has got to be the first priority—what is the best way to arm the country—at the same time, now and then there is a situation where a decision can be made with regard to that defense program that will not reduce the quality in any way, but can be directed toward some place in the country where the economic situation could be benefited by it.

Anything, everything that we can do, we want to do in helping that. The programs in the past that have been—well, like job training programs and so forth—not that we're doing away with those. There's certainly a need for them. But to use those as a substitute for legitimate employment when the very fact of those programs and their cost was slowing down the reinvigoration of the economy, we're not going to do it.

Q. Then you would see some special programs or adjustments or other methods used in this kind of winter——

The President. Whatever we can legitimately do to help in that regard. There's nothing that's going to benefit us more, and benefit them, than getting those industries back on their feet, the steel industry—and there we've met with them. And I just met with the heads of the automobile companies on what can government do for those industries. And there have been a number of suggestions and things that we're looking at that can help them with their problems.

The steel industry, as you know, has now a program for modernization of plant equipment. This has been one of the big factors that has made us become noncompetitive with other countries that we helped rebuild in the Marshall plan and who now have more modern facilities than we do. I think our workers are the best in the world, but we've got to give them the tools to match those other workers.

And so, we are seeking every way that we can to get those industries rolling again.

Q. Mr. President? Oh, I'm sorry, go ahead.

Mr. Speakes. We ought to let Ben and Loye get one in here since our time is running out.

U.S.–Soviet Relations

Q. I want to take you back to foreign affairs. When the Soviet Union rolled into Afghanistan, President Carter said he was shocked that the Soviets would behave as they did. Prior to the crackdown in Poland, you made it quite clear to Moscow how you viewed the situation and what your wishes were for their behavior. And yet, as you stated last week at the press conference, Moscow is clearly behind what has happened in Poland. Does this demonstrate to you, to use Ann's phrase, "the limits" of the American Presidency to shape events in certain parts of the world?

The President. Well, let me answer that, as best I can, is that at 9 o'clock tonight I will be talking on that particular subject and about some of the actions that we have already taken and that there are other actions that we can take. This is both with regard to Poland and the Soviet Union.

Q. Were you surprised that despite communication with the Soviet Union, both public and private, prior to December 12, that this has occurred in Poland?

The President. Well, surprised to the extent that we knew that there were plans laid for this. We knew that it was a very risky situation with the Polish Government wanting to be able to handle the situation themselves with the knowledge that if they didn't, the Soviet Union could very conceivably come in, as it's done before in Hungary and in Czechoslovakia. That we wanted least of all.

I suppose the actual timing of this, yes, we had no warning of the actual timing, and I think that probably it was precipitated by the proposal of Solidarity to let the Polish people vote on whether they wanted the kind of government they have. And if ever—and I appeal to the media on this—if ever there was an example of the moral bankruptcy of communism, it was that this could happen, people could be imprisoned, people could be killed, violence could take place as has, martial law declared, simply over whether the people have a right to vote on the kind of government they want. And apparently, as I'm sure we all knew down inside but we just don't give it much thought in our day-to-day lives, communism doesn't dare let the people vote, because they know——

Q. Are you suggesting that Solidarity went too far in asking for such a vote?

The President. Well, I'm not going to say that. I'd defend the right of the people to vote. I am going to say that maybe they should have realized that they were asking the one thing that a Communist government cannot allow.

Q. On that score, you've talked in more conciliatory terms about the possibility of a summit with the Russian leader, Premier Brezhnev—President Brezhnev. Has this changed thinking about the possibility that——

The President. No, no. I still feel that sometime in the coming year, properly prepared for—and I noticed that Mr. Brezhnev the other day, in answer to a question, said that there would have to be careful planning for such a meeting—but yes, and I think a meeting is likely.

Q. Have you changed your opinion, then, of what you said in your first press conference, that the Russians, that, really, their article of faith is the reserving unto themselves the right to commit any crime, to lie, to cheat in order to obtain that and that is moral and not immoral. That was pretty strong talk from you at the beginning of——

The President. Well, it was an answer to a question. Someone asked me something about whether or not I thought they were lying or telling the truth on some—I can't remember what incident it was—and I just pointed out what is a part of Communist dogma going all the way back to Marx, and that is that if you look at their dogma, they say that the only moral—that morality is anything that furthers the spread of socialism and the cause of socialism and that the only immorality is anything that counters that or works against that.

Well, we should always remember from the very beginning that that is their philosophy, it's their religion. And as long as they adhere to that, we're fools if we do not negotiate, recognizing that they claim that right for themselves.

Q. Well, that and some other statements and, specifically, on the subject of the summit, if not from you, from some of your top advisers, were—until very recently the summit seemed to be ruled out or put far, far away. And yet, in the present situation when, in your own words, the Soviets have committed more offenses in relation to the Polish thing than at any time in your administration, you're talking more reasonably about a summit within the foreseeable future, within possibly the next year or so, which is——

The President. Yes, I think we're in the world together, and this doesn't mean that you can't talk and try to resolve your differences. But I think you go at it with some realism. So, I have no objection to talking.

Q. I take it, though, Mr. President, that if you were a candidate right about now or a private citizen right about now, I think you probably would take a different view. Your stand against communism—and it's well known—is tough and has always been

tough. But I gather that since you've become President, you've sort of run into the new realism of, "We're in this world together."

The President. No, not at all. I had my earliest experience with communism, and it is pretty much the same.

I know that it sounds kind of foolish maybe to link Hollywood, an experience there, to the world situation, and yet, the tactics seemed to be pretty much the same. But that much rewritten history of Hollywood and distorted history has hidden from many people what actually took place back there in the late forties after World War II. It was a Communist attempt to gain control of the motion picture industry, because at that time the Hollywood motion picture industry provided the film for 75 percent of the playing time in all the theaters of the world. It was the greatest propaganda device, if someone wanted to use it for that, that's ever been known.

And they used the device of the jurisdictional strike. And I found myself not a bystander; I was right in the middle of it as president of the Screen Actors Guild. We were the one union that, if they could persuade us to participate in that strike—and you know, there's no way in a jurisdictional strike—it isn't like someone striking for better conditions or wages. This is an argument between two, in this instance, it was two groups of unions—all of them, by the way, aligned in the AFL–CIO at the time, some 43 unions and guilds in the picture business all told. But this was the device that was being used.

Where we were, the key is that as long as one side could keep enough people in to keep the cameras turning, they'd turn as long as there were actors in front of the cameras. So, the whole key was to try and prevent the actors from going in because then the business would be closed. And we met for 7 months, virtually daily and many times twice daily, with both factions, because being in the spot we were in, it was decided that we would invite both factions and management to sit at a table with us, and we, as the noninvolved, would ensure fairness in the discussion, but to try and find a method that would keep the business open and not throw 30,000 people out of jobs. And this was how we got into it.

This is how I know it from the inside, and I think I learned a lot there. And the funny thing is, I didn't start with a bias. As a matter of fact, I started the other way, because I'd also been in Hollywood at the time that Browne and Bioff were turned up in the opposite side as being extortionists and so forth, in labor. But I learned the hard way, at that table, in all those months, who was really to blame and what the purpose of the strike was.

No, I don't think that I talked more harshly than I do now. And at the same time, I've always recognized that ultimately there's got to be a settlement, a solution. The other way, if you don't believe that, then you're going to find yourself trapped in the back of your mind, the inevitability of a conflict some day. So, that kind of conflict is going to end the world.

So, I believe, yes, in talking, but talk with some knowledge of what the other fellow's aims are and what his tactics are and what you're going to do. As a matter of fact, I have met Brezhnev. I met him 10 years ago. And lying in the hospital last April, after March 30, I wrote a handwritten letter recalling that meeting to Mr. Brezhnev, and sent it to him, because, as I say, no, we must find a solution.

Assessment of Administration

Q. Mr. President, if we could very quickly transport you back to January 20th, what would you do that you haven't done? What mistakes had you made in the last 10 or 12 months?

The President. I suppose maybe there were some mistakes someplace along the line. On the other hand, as I said in my opening remarks, I feel very good about the seven great victories that we had. The defense program has been put in place, interest rates coming down—the things that we've accomplished.

But I would have to say, probably the one thing that we were induced to do was present our program for straightening out the fiscal situation with social security. And it was a leader in the majority party in the House who just told us that if we did not submit our proposal, they were going to go

ahead with hearings and have a proposal of their own. Well, we had not wanted to submit it at the time, because we were working hard for those budget cuts. We didn't want any confusion that somehow social security's financial problem was a part of the budget-balancing process, because it isn't. And yet that's what was done.

With their challenge we had reason to believe then that there would be a bipartisan getting-together on this problem, with whoever submitted a proposal. And instead, it was used as a demagogic attack with distortions and outright falsehood as to what was in our program and what we were trying to do—and not one single move made toward trying to come to a meeting of the minds on how we solve the problem. And I regret now that we didn't just brazen it out and tell them, "Well, okay, if you want to go ahead, you go ahead, but we're not going to tie social security into this other situation." And now we have a commission formed, with a year to try and work it out.

Mr. Speakes. We're going to have to quit, because we've got to go over and——

Reporters. Thank you very much.

The President. I wanted to say one last thing on that question that, when I was talking earlier about Nancy and I said it was maintenance, you'd be surprised how much of what went on up there was restoring of the floors, the beautiful mahogany doors which looked just like a flat, solid, dirty black instead of a beauty of the wood—all of those things refurbished. Drapes that were tattered, with holes in them, probably from the sunlight coming in. And painting—there had been no painting, internal painting, for 20 years or more.

Q. So, that money that was donated, you're saying was used primarily for that rather than for things like china and the——

The President. Oh, the china itself was donated, not the money for it.

Q. No, I understand that.

The President. They donated a set of china and——

Q. Have you eaten off of it, Mr. President?

The President. No, it hasn't come yet. [*Laughter*] We're still using the mixed dishes.

Q. The other thing you said you wouldn't have done last year was go to the Washington Hilton. [*Laughter*]

The President. Yeah, if a fellow could know what he knows now. But anyway—oh, I should also tell you, the plumbing. [*Laughter*]

The plumbing was actually so old that if something went wrong, you could no longer get parts. And there was a fellow in town who would hand-forge, at quite some expense, the parts that you needed. Also, there was a danger that one day we might find ourselves wading. [*Laughter*] So, a part of all of that was the plumbing.

Q. It's not as good as the Pacific, I'll bet.

The President. What?

Q. The surf here would not be as good as the Pacific.

The President. No, I'm quite sure of that.

Reporters. Thank you very much. Thank you and a Merry Christmas.

The President. Thank you. The same to all of you. Merry Christmas.

Note: The President spoke at 2 p.m. in the Oval Office at the White House. Participating in the interview were Andrew J. Glass of Cox Newspapers, Benjamin Shore of Copley News Service, Ann Devroy of Gannett News Service, Robert E. Thompson of Hearst Newspapers, Saul Friedman of Knight-Ridder Newspapers, Loye W. Miller, Jr., of Newhouse News Service, and Ted Knap of Scripps-Howard News Service.

The transcript of the interview was released by the Office of the Press Secretary on December 27.

Statement on the Situation in Afghanistan
December 27, 1981

Our current concern regarding Poland should not cause us to forget that 2 years ago today, massive Soviet military forces invaded the sovereign country of Afghanistan and began an attempt to subjugate one of the most fiercely independent peoples of the world. Despite the presence of 90,000 Soviet combat troops, a recent increase of some 5,000, the courageous people of Afghanistan have fought back. Today they effectively deny Soviet forces control of most of Afghanistan. Efforts by the Soviets to establish a puppet government in the Soviet image, which could govern a conquered land, have failed. Soviet control extends little beyond the major cities, and even there the Afghan freedom fighters often hold sway by night and sometimes even by day. The battle for Afghan independence continues.

But the gallant efforts of the people of Afghanistan to regain their independence have come at great cost. Almost 3 million Afghan refugees, a fifth of the pre-invasion population of Afghanistan, have fled their homes and have taken refuge across the border, largely in Pakistan. Those who have remained at home have become the unfortunate victims not only of the dislocations of war but also of indiscriminate Soviet attacks on civilians. So, while we express our admiration for those who fight for the freedom we all cherish, we must also express our deep sympathy for those innocent victims of Soviet imperialism who, because of the love of freedom of their countrymen, have been forced to flee for their lives.

On three separate occasions, most recently on November 18, 1981, the United Nations General Assembly passed by overwhelming margins resolutions aimed at Soviet aggression in Afghanistan. The U.S. Government and the American people join in the broad international condemnation of the Soviet invasion and occupation of Afghanistan. Just as in Poland we see the use of intimidation and indirect use of power to subjugate a neighboring people, in Afghanistan we see direct aggression in violation of the United Nations Charter and other principles governing the conduct among nations.

While extending our admiration and sympathy to the people of Afghanistan, we also call upon the Soviet Union to avail itself of proposals set forth by the community of nations for the withdrawal of Soviet forces from Afghanistan so that an independent and nonaligned nation can be reestablished with a government responsive to the desires of the people, so that the millions of Afghans who have sought refuge in other countries can return with honor to their homes. As long as the Soviet Union occupies Afghanistan in defiance of the international community, the heroic Afghan resistance will continue, and the United States will support the cause of a free Afghanistan.

Announcement of the Establishment of the Emergency Mobilization Preparedness Board
December 29, 1981

The President today announced the formation of an Emergency Mobilization Preparedness Board to improve mobilization capabilities and interagency cooperation within the Federal Government to respond to major peacetime or war-related emergencies. The Board will develop and recommend national preparedness policies.

The Board consists of the representatives of 22 key Federal agencies at the Deputy Secretary or Under Secretary level and is chaired by the Assistant to the President for National Security Affairs. A full-time Secretariat has been established to support the Board and monitor the implementation of the Board's recommendations by Federal agencies. The Secretariat is chaired by a senior official of the Federal Emergency Management Agency.

Eleven working groups, each organized to address a functional area of mobilization planning, are included in the Board structure. Each working group, with the chairing agency shown in parenthesis, is as follows:

—Industrial Mobilization (Department of Commerce)
—Military Mobilization (Department of Defense)
—Food and Agriculture (Department of Agriculture)
—Government Operations (Federal Emergency Management Agency)
—Emergency Communications (Departments of Defense and Commerce)
—Economic Stabilization and Public Finance (Department of the Treasury)
—Law Enforcement and Public Safety (Department of Justice)
—Civil Defense (Federal Emergency Management Agency)
—Social Services (Department of Health and Human Services)
—Human Resources (Department of Labor)
—Health (Department of Health and Human Services)

With the establishment of the Emergency Mobilization Preparedness Board, the President formalized his commitment to achieve a credible and effective capability to harness the mobilization potential of America. This potential will support the Armed Forces, while meeting the needs of the national economy and the preparedness requirements for domestic emergencies.

Nomination of James W. Sanderson To Be an Assistant Administrator of the Environmental Protection Agency
December 29, 1981

The President today announced his intention to nominate James W. Sanderson to be an Assistant Administrator of the Environmental Protection Agency (Policy and Resource Management).

Since 1977 Mr. Sanderson has been an attorney with the firm Saunders, Snyder, Ross & Dickson in Denver, Colo. He was Regional Counsel, Environmental Protection Agency, Region VII, in 1973–77; legislative assistant to Senator Gordon Allott (R-Colo.) in 1970–73; and was employed by the Office of Chief Counsel, Interpretative Division, Internal Revenue Service, in 1969–70.

Mr. Sanderson has specialized in environmental law, with an emphasis on water and air quality, solid and hazardous waste management, and natural resource project development. He has written several publications on environmental law and water pollution.

He graduated from the University of Nebraska (B.A., 1966); the University of Denver, College of Law, (J.D., 1969); and attended Georgetown University School of Law in 1970–72. Mr. Sanderson is married, has one child, and resides in Englewood, Colo. He was born in Scotts Bluff, Nebr. He is 37 years old.

Appointment of 11 Members of the American Battle Monuments Commission
December 29, 1981

The President today announced his intention to appoint the following individuals to be members of the American Battle Monuments Commission:

Francis J. Bagnell is resident manager of Fahnestock & Co. (investment bankers) in Bala Cynwyd, Pa. He was senior vice president, New York Stock Exchange, in 1967–70.

Esther "Kitty" Bradley is an author and television writer. She is the widow of former General of the Army Omar N. Bradley. She resides in Los Angeles, Calif.

Gen. Mark Wayne Clark, U.S. Army (Retired). He is president emeritus of The Citadel Military College and was Commanding General of U.S. Armed Forces in the Far East in 1949–52. He resides in Charleston, S.C.

Aubrey O. Cookman was formerly director of public affairs, Universal Oil Products Co., Des Plaines, Ill. He is currently retired and resides in Albuquerque, N. Mex.

Rexford C. Early is secretary-treasurer, Mid-States Engineering Co., Indianapolis, Ind. He resides in Indianapolis, Ind.

William E. Hickey is an attorney in Quincy, Mass., specializing in real estate law and estate planning and probate law. He resides in Quincy, Mass.

Armistead Jones Maupin is senior partner, Maupin, Taylor & Ellis (attorneys) in Raleigh, N.C. He resides in Raleigh, N.C.

John C. McDonald is senior partner, McDonald, Keller & Brown (attorneys) in Dallas Center, Iowa. He resides in Dallas Center, Iowa.

Freda J. Poundstone is a homemaker in Englewood, Colo. She is an active Republican and was involved in the Reagan for President campaign in 1980.

Maj. Gen. Edwin Bliss Wheeler, U.S. Marine Corps (Retired). He was deputy secretary of health and welfare, State of California, in 1972–74. He resides in Hot Springs, Ark.

Lawrence A. Wright is senior partner, Gravel, Shea & Wright, Ltd., in Burlington, Vt. He resides in South Burlington, Vt.

Excerpt From an Exchange With Reporters on the Situation in Poland
December 29, 1981

Q. What effect do you anticipate that the sanctions that will be announced today against the Soviet Union are going to have on the situation in Poland?

The President. Well, the measures are directed at the Governments of Poland and of the Soviet Union, and the purpose is to convey to those regimes how strongly we feel about their joint efforts to extinguish liberty in Poland. And they're not meant to increase the hardship on the victims of repression, the Polish people—quite the contrary. By our actions, we expect to put powerful doubts in the minds of the Soviet and Polish leaders about this continued repression. And in addition, we are going to continue assisting the flow of food, medicines, and other necessities to the Polish people, not to the governments.

And the whole purpose of our actions is to speak for those who have been silenced and to help those who've been rendered helpless.

Q. Sir, let's say they don't respond in the way that you hope they will. What next?

The President. Well, there are further actions that could be taken that we have withheld.

Note: The exchange began at approximately 11:15 a.m. as the reporters were assembled in the Executive Suite at the Century Plaza Hotel to observe the President signing bills into law.

Statement on Signing International Security and Foreign Assistance Legislation
December 29, 1981

Today I am signing into law S. 1196, the International Security and Development Cooperation Act of 1981, and H.R. 4559, the Foreign Assistance and Related Programs Appropriations Act, 1982. S. 1196 authorizes appropriations for fiscal year 1982 and 1983 for security and development assistance programs and related activities and makes certain substantive changes in the statutory standards, procedures, and requirements governing such programs. H.R. 4559 makes appropriations for fiscal year 1982 for foreign assistance and related programs.

The programs and activities for which funds are authorized and appropriated by this legislation are vital to important United States foreign policy and national security interests. They are the principal means by which the United States contributes to the security and economic development needs

of a wide range of countries less favored than our own.

Foreign aid suffers from a lack of domestic constituency, in large part because the results of the programs are often not immediately visible and self-evident. Properly conceived and efficiently administered, however, security assistance programs, an essential complement to our defense effort, directly enhance the security of the United States. Development assistance also contributes to this effort by supplementing the indigenous efforts of recipients to achieve economic growth and meet the basic needs of their peoples. Progress in both of these areas will contribute to regional stability and to a more peaceful world, both of which are central U.S. policy objectives.

It has been a major objective of this administration to subject all Federal programs to continuous and rigorous scrutiny to ensure that they directly serve United

States interests and that each dollar is effectively used. My administration undertook a thorough and careful review of foreign assistance when we assumed office. We have worked closely with the Congress on this legislation. It reflects the considered judgment of both branches that our national interests are inextricably tied to the security and development of our friends and allies.

Last spring I proposed several major initiatives and substantive changes to the laws governing foreign assistance programs. My proposals were intended to restore needed flexibility to enable the United States to utilize foreign assistance in a timely and effective manner and to be able to respond to changes in the international environment. I am grateful that the bills I am approving today contain many of those proposals and that Congress generally shares my view that excessive rigidities in the law hamper the effectiveness of these programs. The authorization of a Special Defense Acquisition Fund to permit advance procurement in anticipation of foreign sales, the authority to begin a security assistance program for Pakistan, and the repeal of the absolute prohibitions on security assistance to Argentina and Chile are major steps forward in this regard. I regret, however, that H.R. 4559 does not contain language necessary to permit the Special Defense Acquisition Fund to begin operations. This will severely hamper our ability to meet the military needs of allies and friends on a timely basis, degrading U.S. force capabilities.

I welcome the authorization of appropriations for two fiscal years, 1982 and 1983. I shall, of course, transmit to the Congress in the near future any additional substantive or budgetary recommendations for fiscal year 1983 that I believe are necessary to promote or sustain our foreign policy interests. I must note, however, my deep concern about the 52-percent reduction from my request in the appropriated level for grant financing of foreign military sales to 14 countries. This level is inadequate to meet minimum requirements and will have a severe impact on those countries that have legitimate defense needs, but whose economies cannot sustain financing at or near commercial rates.

Finally, I have serious reservations about sections 109 and 737 of S. 1196, and the section of H.R. 4559 limiting use of Economic Support Funds for Special Requirements and section 514 of that bill.

Section 109 of S. 1196 permits the Congress to disapprove, by adoption of a concurrent resolution certain proposed leases of defense articles. Section 737 would permit the Congress, also by concurrent resolution, to disapprove a Presidential waiver necessary to continue certain foreign military and economic assistance following transfers of certain nuclear technology covered by sections 669 and 670 of the Foreign Assistance Act.

H.R. 4559 requires the prior written approval of the appropriations committees of both Houses before funds may be obligated or expended for the Special Requirements Fund. In addition, section 514 requires similar committee approval before funds may be transferred, pursuant to statutory authority, between appropriations accounts.

The Attorney General has advised me that these four provisions are unconstitutional in light of the express requirements of Article I, section 7 of the Constitution that legislative measures having the force and effect of law must be presented to the President for approval, and because of the potential for involving the Congress in the day-to-day implementation of the law, a responsibility allocated solely to the President under the Constitution. These provisions can be expected to inject an unnecessarily disruptive element by subjecting proposed programs to disapproval, congressional or even committee, even after they have been examined by the executive branch and found to be compatible with congressionally adopted standards and supportive of the national interests of the United States.

While I am signing S. 1196 and H.R. 4559 into law because of the overall importance to the foreign policy and national security of the United States of the programs for which funds are authorized and appropriated, I must express my deep concern about these provisions, and my action today does not imply my acceptance of their constitutional validity.

The ultimate importance to the United States of our security and development assistance programs cannot be exaggerated. The programs and activities provided for in these bills will enable the United States to continue its contribution to the achieve-

ment of a secure and stable international environment.

Note: As enacted, S. 1196 is Public Law 97–113, and H.R. 4559 is Public Law 97–121, both approved December 29.

Statement on Signing the Department of Defense Appropriation Act, 1982
December 29, 1981

I am pleased to sign into law H.R. 4995, the Department of Defense Appropriation Act, 1982. This legislation is a significant step in this administration's commitment to enhancing the defense posture of the United States and of maintaining our responsibilities to the nations of the free world. This is just a beginning, and in the years ahead we will need to sustain the effort mandated by the American people and supported by the Congress so that we will succeed in strengthening the nation's defense.

In addition to containing funds for essential strategic programs of the Department of Defense, the legislation provides funds to support the military and civilian personnel of the Department of Defense. I would like

to express my appreciation for the strong bipartisan support that this legislation received and wish to personally thank the dedicated members of the Committees on Appropriations of the Senate and the House who supported my budget requests and did so much to see that this legislation was enacted.

Finally, I would like to take the opportunity to commend the dedicated men and women of the Armed Forces and to express, on behalf of the American people, the gratitude of us all for the dedication and sacrifice they exhibit in the defense of our Nation.

Note: As enacted, H.R. 4995 is Public Law 97–114, approved December 29.

Statement on Signing Social Security Legislation
December 29, 1981

I have signed into law H.R. 4331, a bill that substantially incorporates the social security changes which I urged in my address of September 24 to the nation—restoration of the minimum benefit for people receiving that benefit, and interfund borrowing to tide the system over while the new National Commission on Social Security Reform develops a bipartisan plan to achieve long-lasting solutions to social security's financing problems.

I commend the Congress for its action on this bill, especially the chairmen and mem-

bers of the House Committee on Ways and Means and Senate Committee on Finance.

There is no more important domestic issue on which we have to have a national consensus than social security, because it affects just about all of us either as current beneficiaries or current taxpayers. Continuing the minimum benefit for present beneficiaries reflects a bipartisan consensus, which I strongly support.

We all know that interfund borrowing is just a temporary solution to the financing difficulties ahead for social security, which are real and serious. The bill authorizes interfund borrowing until the end of 1982, the same time the new National Commission on Social Security Reform is scheduled to report its recommendations.

I am determined that we put social security back on a sound financial footing and restore the confidence and peace of mind of the American public in its social security system. That is the reason for the National Commission which I proposed in September and the members of which Majority Leader Baker, Speaker O'Neill, and I have just selected. I am confident that after they have reviewed all the options and agreed on a plan to assure the fiscal integrity of social security, the administration and the Congress will work together swiftly to enact legislation to restore the financial soundness of the social security system.

I believe that we should build any social security rescue plan around three very basic principles:

First, we must preserve the integrity of the trust funds and the basic social security benefit structure.

Second, we must eliminate abuses within the system and elements of the system which duplicate other programs, both of which could rob beneficiaries of their hard-earned benefits.

Third, we must hold down the tax burden on current and future workers.

I believe in those principles, and I think that a great majority of the American people believe in them, too.

I believe in the social security system. I believe that it will survive and keep its promise to this generation of beneficiaries and those to come.

Note: As enacted, H.R. 4331 is Public Law 97–123, approved December 29.

Statement on Signing Black Lung Program Reform Legislation
December 29, 1981

I am pleased to sign into law H.R. 5159, which contains the "Black Lung Benefits Revenue Act of 1981" and the "Black Lung Benefits Amendments of 1981". This bill embodies this administration's comprehensive black lung reform proposals.

I commend the Members of the Congress on both sides of the aisle who steered this bill to passage. I am gratified that the bill represents the combined efforts of the coal industry, the insurance industry, and organized labor, especially the United Mine Workers, in working with the administration to achieve needed improvements in the black lung program.

A major purpose of this legislation is to restore solvency to the Black Lung Disability Trust Fund. At present, the Fund has a deficit of approximately $1.5 billion. With no change in the law, the deficit would climb to $7 billion over the next 10 years.

The bill addresses the revenue side of this problem by temporarily doubling the excise taxes on coal producers, but requiring that those rates revert to their present levels when the Fund becomes fully solvent, and in no case later than the end of 1995.

The bill also addresses eligibility criteria and benefit payments for the black lung program. These changes are needed to assure that the black lung program will provide adequate workers compensation benefits to coal miners suffering from black lung disease, while reducing the potential for substantial abuses.

I hope and expect that the spirit of cooperation between labor, industry, and the administration in enacting this important bill will continue in the coming months.

Note: As enacted, H.R. 5159 is Public Law 97–119, approved December 29.

Statement on Signing Legislation Concerning Water Resources Development Projects
December 29, 1981

I have before me today two enrolled enactments: H.R. 779, an Act "To authorize the Secretary of the Army to contract with the Tarrant County Water Control and Improvement District Numbered 1 and the City of Weatherford, Texas, for the use of water supply storage in Renbrook Lake, and for other purposes," and S. 1493, an Act "To deauthorize several projects within the jurisdiction of the U.S. Army Corps of Engineers."

These two bills are linked together by the fact that they both contain similar, though not identical, provisions dealing with removal of certain structures at water resources development projects administered by the U.S. Army Corps of Engineers. Inadvertently, one of the provisions, section 8 of

S. 1493, as enrolled, is broader than its sponsors intended. Because of this, the Congress passed another, somewhat narrower provision in the form of section 6 of H.R. 779. It is clear from statements on the floor of both the House and Senate that the narrower provision, section 6 of H.R. 779, was intended to govern the Corps management practices. Therefore, in order to accomplish that intent, I will sign enrolled enactment S. 1493 before I sign H.R. 779, thereby making section 6 of H.R. 779 the provision to govern Corps management practices.

Note: As enacted, H.R. 779 is Public Law 97–140, and S. 1493 is Public Law 97–128, both approved December 29.

Statement on Signing the Municipal Wastewater Treatment Construction Grant Amendments of 1981
December 29, 1981

I am pleased to sign into law H.R. 4503, the Municipal Wastewater Treatment Construction Grant Amendments of 1981. To date, this is the most significant piece of environmental protection legislation enacted by this Congress and represents the combined efforts of both the Congress and this administration to ensure that the goals of our construction grants program will be the improvement of water quality, the enhancement of our environment, and an emphasis on effectiveness in federally funded treatment works. This legislation represents a rededication to environmental goals and a turn away from public works for the sake of public works.

Although it is impossible to single out all the people responsible for H.R. 4503, I want to take this opportunity to congratulate some of those individuals whose guidance on this bill was indispensable. Senator

John H. Chafee, with support from Senator Robert T. Stafford, provided strong leadership in this environmental legislation. Also vital to this success in the House were the concerted efforts of Full Committee Chairman James J. Howard, Ranking Minority Member Don H. Clausen, Subcommittee Chairman Robert A. Roe, and Ranking Minority Member John Paul Hammerschmidt.

With the critical support of these key legislators and the unselfish efforts for reform from those involved from the private sector, we have, together, achieved a significant redirection of the construction grants program in a record period of time. The consultation and cooperation from State and local officials was especially helpful in focusing attention on key areas of concern. The efforts of Governor Scott Matheson, on behalf of the National Governors' Association, were particularly worthy of note.

In April of this year, we proposed reforms to the construction grants program. Our proposal refocused the program on those projects necessary to meet existing high priority water quality improvement needs. H.R. 4503 substantially incorporates our recommendations.

H.R. 4503 focuses Federal funds on treatment-related needs, giving the States a high degree of flexibility to address local needs. In addition, it allows for a 3-year phase-in of these major reforms. In this way there should be very little disruption in ongoing construction. States and localities will have ample time to plan rationally for their en-

larged role in planning for improved water quality.

The primary objectives of this administration's construction grants reform proposal were to emphasize the need for water quality improvement, to incorporate greater cost-effectiveness, and to provide more flexibility to the States and localities. The agreement reached by the Congress achieves the administration's fundamental objectives while ensuring minimum dislocation to the program.

For all these reasons, I am pleased to sign H.R. 4503.

Note: As enacted, H.R. 4503 is Public Law 97–117, approved December 29.

Statement on Signing the Union Station Redevelopment Act of 1981
December 29, 1981

I am pleased to sign into law today S. 1192, the Union Station Redevelopment Act of 1981. I know that the leadership in the House and Senate and Secretary Lewis at the Department of Transportation have worked hard to develop this legislation. This legislation will help to turn the Union Station complex into a successful commercial center with access to several modes of transportation. It is especially noteworthy that the Senate and House committees were able to develop compromises so that the House could pass the Senate bill without further amendment. I am aware that previous attempts in recent years to enact such legislation were not successful.

The legislation provides that the Department of Transportation will be responsible to rehabilitate and develop the Union Station complex as a commercial center and multi-use transportation terminal. Secretary Lewis has expressed his enthusiasm for the challenge this bill presents to the Department to encourage private commercial de-

velopment of the complex and make it a successful venture.

While I am signing S. 1192, it contains a legislative veto provision which the Attorney General advises is unconstitutional. Section 114(e) of the bill would purport to authorize either of two committees of Congress to pass a resolution disapproving the expenditure of any sums in excess of $29 million from certain rail programs for the rehabilitation of Union Station. However, committees of Congress cannot bind the executive branch in the execution of the law by passing a resolution that is not adopted by both Houses of Congress and presented to the President for approval or veto. Accordingly, this language of section 114(e) must be objected to on constitutional grounds. The Secretary of Transportation will not, consistent with this objection, regard himself as legally bound by any such resolution.

Note: As enacted, S. 1192 is Public Law 97–125, approved December 29.

Statement on Signing the Multinational Force and Observers Participation Resolution
December 29, 1981

It gives me great pleasure to sign into law the Multinational Force and Observers Participation Resolution. The Multinational Force and Observers is an international organization established by the protocol signed by Egypt and Israel on August 3, 1981. This organization will have the important function of supervising the implementation of key security aspects of the treaty of peace between Egypt and Israel. It will thus help ensure that the timetables established in the peace treaty are met. The legislation I have signed today ensures that the United States will be in a position to participate in this organization along with other nations that are interested in contributing to the peace process in the Middle East.

The peace treaty between Egypt and Israel is an extraordinary achievement, and its continuing implementation will constitute a further major advance in the peace process. I am confident that U.S. participation in this critical step will contribute to our broader efforts to bring about a just and lasting peace in the region.

I am signing this joint resolution with the understanding that when U.S. agencies provide property, support, or services to the MFO on a reimbursable basis, they shall not seek to recover from the MFO amounts in excess of the cost to the U.S. Government of acquisition of the property, support, or services so provided, and, in accordance with section 4(c) of the joint resolution, such costs of acquisition shall not be considered to include administrative or similar surcharges.

Finally, I wish to commend the Congress for its responsible approach to this critical legislation. I am gratified that both the executive and legislative branches addressed this matter which is so vital to our nation's foreign policy in a spirit of close consultation and cooperation. This legislation demonstrates the results that can be achieved through working together in that spirit.

Note: As enacted, S.J. Res. 100 is Public Law 97–132, approved December 29.

Memorandum of Disapproval of Legislation Concerning a Uniform Law on Bankruptcies
December 29, 1981

I am withholding my approval of H.R. 4353, to amend the Act entitled "An Act to Establish a Uniform Law on the Subject of Bankruptcies."

This bill would benefit the creditors of a single large asset bankruptcy. The debtor's estate has disputed the amount which it must pay to the Referees' Salary and Expense Fund. While I am aware that the Fund has been abolished with respect to recent cases, nothing except this debtor's dispute of the assessment distinguishes this one case from all others where the plan of arrangement was confirmed prior to September 30, 1978. I cannot support this effort to confer special relief in the guise of general legislation at a possible loss to the Treasury of $1.6 million. I believe the judicial process should be allowed to run its course.

RONALD REAGAN

The White House,
December 29, 1981.

Statement on U.S. Measures Taken Against the Soviet Union Concerning its Involvement in Poland
December 29, 1981

The Soviet Union bears a heavy and direct responsibility for the repression in Poland. For many months the Soviets publicly and privately demanded such a crackdown. They brought major pressures to bear through now public letters to the Polish leadership, military maneuvers, and other forms of intimidation. They now openly endorse the suppression which has ensued.

Last week I announced that I had sent a letter to President Brezhnev urging him to permit the restoration of basic human rights in Poland as provided for in the Helsinki Final Act. I also informed him that, if the repression continued, the United States would have no choice but to take further concrete political and economic measures affecting our relationship.

The repression in Poland continues, and President Brezhnev has responded in a manner which makes it clear the Soviet Union does not understand the seriousness of our concern, and its obligations under both the Helsinki Final Act and the U.N. Charter. I have, therefore, decided to take the following immediate measures with regard to the Soviet Union:

—All Aeroflot service to the United States will be suspended.
—The Soviet Purchasing Commission is being closed.
—The issuance or renewal of licenses for the export to the U.S.S.R. of electronic equipment, computers and other high-technology materials is being suspended.
—Negotiations on a new long-term grains agreement are being postponed.

—Negotiations on a new U.S.-Soviet Maritime Agreement are being suspended, and a new regime of port-access controls will be put into effect for all Soviet ships when the current agreement expires on December 31.
—Licenses will be required for export to the Soviet Union for an expanded list of oil and gas equipment. Issuance of such licenses will be suspended. This includes pipelayers.
—U.S.-Soviet exchange agreements coming up for renewal in the near future, including the agreements on energy and science and technology, will not be renewed. There will be a complete review of all other U.S.-Soviet exchange agreements.

The United States wants a constructive and mutually beneficial relationship with the Soviet Union. We intend to maintain a high-level dialog. But we are prepared to proceed in whatever direction the Soviet Union decides upon—towards greater mutual restraint and cooperation, or further down a harsh and less rewarding path. We will watch events in Poland closely in coming days and weeks. Further steps may be necessary, and I will be prepared to take them. American decisions will be determined by Soviet actions.

Secretary Haig has been in communication with our friends and allies about the measures we are taking and explained why we believe such steps are essential at this time.

Once again I call upon the Soviet Union to recognize the clear desire of the overwhelming majority of the Polish people for a process of national reconciliation, renewal, and reform.

Proclamation 4889—Staged Reduction of Rates of Duty on Certain Products To Carry Out a Trade Agreement With Japan, and Technical Corrections in the Tariff Schedules of the United States
December 29, 1981

By the President of the United States of America

A Proclamation

1. I have determined, pursuant to section 124(a) of the Trade Act of 1974 (the Trade Act) (19 U.S.C. 2134(a)) that certain existing duties of the United States are unduly burdening and restricting the foreign trade of the United States and that one or more of the purposes of the Trade Act would be promoted by entering into the trade agreement with Japan identified in the third recital of this proclamation.

2. Sections 131(a), 132, 133, 134, 135, and 161(b) of the Trade Act (19 U.S.C. 2151(a), 2152, 2153, 2154, 2155, and 2211(b)) and section 4(c) of Executive Order No. 11846 of March 27, 1975 (3 CFR 1971–1975 Comp. 974) have been complied with.

3. Pursuant to Title I of the Trade Act (19 U.S.C. 2111 *et seq.*), I have, through my duly empowered representative, on September 30, 1981, entered into a trade agreement with Japan pursuant to which United States rates of duty on certain products would be modified as hereinafter proclaimed and as provided for in Annexes I and II to this proclamation, in exchange for certain measures which will benefit United States interests.

4. Pursuant to the Trade Act, I determine that the modifications or continuance of existing duties hereinafter proclaimed are required or appropriate to carry out the trade agreement identified in the third recital of this proclamation.

Now, Therefore, I, Ronald Reagan, President of the United States of America, acting under the authority vested in me by the Constitution and the statutes, including but not limited to sections 124 and 604 of the Trade Act (19 U.S.C. 2134 and 2483), do proclaim that:

(1) The TSUS is hereby modified as provided in Annex I to this proclamation;

(2) Annexes II and III to Presidential Proclamation 4707 of December 11, 1979, are amended as provided in Annex II to this proclamation;

(3) Annex IV of Proclamation 4707 of December 11, 1979, is superseded to the extent inconsistent with this proclamation.

(4) Whenever the column 1 rate of duty in the TSUS for any item specified in Annex I to this proclamation is reduced to the same level as, or to a lower level than, the corresponding rate of duty inserted in the column entitled "LDDC" by Annex I of this proclamation, the rate of duty in the column entitled "LDDC" for such item shall be deleted from the TSUS.

(5) Each of the modifications made by this proclamation shall be effective as to articles entered, or withdrawn from warehouse for consumption, on and after January 1, 1982.

In Witness Whereof, I have hereunto set my hand this twenty-ninth day of December, in the year of our Lord nineteen hundred and eighty-one, and of the Independence of the United States of America the two hundred and sixth.

RONALD REAGAN

[*Filed with the Office of the Federal Register, 4:20 p.m., December 30, 1981*]

Note: The text of the proclamation was released by the Office of the Press Secretary on December 30.

Annexes I and II to the proclamation are printed in the Federal Register *of January 4, 1982.*

Nomination of Four Members of the Board of Directors of the National Railroad Passenger Corporation
December 30, 1981

The President today announced his intention to select the following individuals to be members of the Board of Directors of the National Railroad Passenger Corporation:

Crete B. Harvey is owner and operator of Harvey Arabian Farms in Sterling, Ill. Her farming interest began in 1961 with the purchase of a horse farm, then expanded to include grain and livestock production. She was born July 10, 1929, in Butte, Mont.

Samuel H. Hellenbrand is vice president of real estate operations of International Telephone and Telegraph Corp. and has held that position since 1971. He was vice president for real estate and industrial development for the Penn Central Corp. in 1968–71. He was born November 11, 1916, in New York.

Frank W. Jenkins is an attorney in Ambler, Pa. He was a member of the Pennsylvania House of Representatives and serves on the board of the Southeastern Pennsylvania Transportation Authority. He was born May 8, 1926, in Philadelphia, Pa.

Ralph Thomas Kerchum is a transportation consultant in Oakland, Calif. He has also served with the National Park Service since 1955. He was born November 12, 1911, in Oakland.

Appointment of Seven Members of the Legal Services Corporation, and Designation of Acting Chairman
December 31, 1981

The President has granted recess appointments to the following individuals as members of the Board of Directors of the Legal Services Corporation. The President has also designated William J. Olson as Acting Chairman.

Howard H. Dana, Jr., of Cape Elizabeth, Maine, is a partner in the Portland, Maine, law firm of Verrill & Dana. Mr. Dana is 41 years old and is married, with three children. He succeeds Robert J. Kutak.

Marc Sandstrom, of La Jolla, Calif., is the executive vice president of the San Diego Federal Savings and Loan. He is 46 years old and is married, with four children. Mr. Sandstrom succeeds Richard Allan Trudell.

William F. Harvey, of Indianapolis, Ind., is Carl M. Gray Professor of Law with the Indianapolis University. He is also on the board of advisors of the Pacific Legal Foundation's College of Public Interest Law. He is 49 years old. He succeeds Howard R. Sacks.

William J. Olson, of Falls Church, Va., is currently a partner with the law firm of Smiley, Murphy, Olson & Gilman located in Washington, D.C. Mr. Olson is 32 years old and is married. He succeeds F. William McCalpin.

George E. Paras, of Sacramento, Calif., is currently in the private practice of law with the firm of Johnson, Greve, Clifford, and Diepenbrock in Sacramento. Prior to that, Justice Paras was appointed to the Superior Court of Sacramento County and later elevated to the California District Court of Appeal for the Third Appellate District. He is 47 years old and is married, with two children. He succeeds Michael Kantor.

Robert Sherwood Stubbs II, of Waleska, Ga., is executive assistant attorney general for the State of Georgia. Mr. Stubbs is 59 years old and is married, with two children. He succeeds Ramona Toledo Shump.

David E. Satterfield III, of Richmond, Va., is a lawyer with the firm of Cook, Purcell, Hansen and Henderson in Washington, D.C. Mr. Satterfield is 61 years old and is married. He succeeds Revius O. Ortique, Jr.

Appendix A—Digest of Other White House Announcements

The following list includes the President's public schedule and other items of general interest announced by the Office of the Press Secretary and not included elsewhere in this book.

January 20

Following the Inaugural luncheon at the Capitol, the President and Mrs. Reagan went by motorcade along the parade route to the White House, where they viewed the Inaugural parade from the reviewing stand.

January 21

In the morning, the President received his national security briefing in the Oval Office.

The White House announced the following members of the White House staff:

Edwin Meese III, Counsellor to the President

James A. Baker III, Chief of Staff and Assistant to the President

Michael K. Deaver, Deputy Chief of Staff and Assistant to the President

Richard V. Allen, Assistant to the President for National Security Affairs

Martin Anderson, Assistant to the President for Policy Development

James Scott Brady, Assistant to the President and Press Secretary

Elizabeth Hanford Dole, Assistant to the President for Public Liaison

Max L. Friedersdorf, Assistant to the President for Legislative Affairs

David R. Gergen, Assistant to the President and Staff Director

Edward L. Harper, Assistant to the President

E. Pendleton James, Assistant to the President for Presidential Personnel

Franklyn C. Nofziger, Assistant to the President for Political Affairs

Robert M. Garrick, Deputy Counsellor to the President

Joseph W. Canzeri, Deputy Assistant to the President and Assistant to the Deputy Chief of Staff

Red Cavaney, Deputy Assistant to the President for Public Liaison

Richard G. Darman, Deputy Assistant to the President and Deputy to the Chief of Staff

Kenneth M. Duberstein, Deputy Assistant to the President for Legislative Affairs

Craig L. Fuller, Deputy Assistant to the President and Director of the Office of Cabinet Administration

Edwin J. Gray, Deputy Assistant to the President and Director of the Office of Policy Development

Edward V. Hickey, Jr., Deputy Assistant to the President and Director of Special Support Services

Francis S. M. Hodsoll, Deputy Assistant to the President and Deputy to the Chief of Staff

Peter McCoy, Deputy Assistant to the President and Director of Staff for the First Lady

Powell Allen Moore, Deputy Assistant to the President for Legislative Affairs

James W. Nance, Deputy Assistant to the President for National Security Affairs

Edward Rollins, Deputy Assistant to the President for Political Affairs

Karna Small Stringer, Deputy Assistant to the President and Deputy Press Secretary

Edwin W. Thomas, Jr., Assistant Counsellor to the President

Richard Salisbury Williamson, Assistant to the President for Intergovernmental Affairs

Douglas Leighton Bandow, Special Assistant to the President for Policy Development

Richard Smith Beal, Special Assistant to the President

David C. Fischer, Special Assistant to the President

Kevin Randall Hopkins, Special Assistant to the President for Policy Development

Dennis E. Le Blanc, Special Assistant to the President and Deputy Director of Special Support Services

Helene A. von Damm, Special Assistant to the President

Melvin Bradley, Senior Advisor, Office of Policy Development

Paul Russo, Deputy Assistant for Legislative Affairs

Larry M. Speakes, Deputy Press Secretary

Dr. Daniel Ruge, Personal Physician to the President

M. Peter McPherson, Acting Counsel to the President

The President held a luncheon meeting in the Oval Office with Counsellor to the President Edwin Meese III and Assistants to the President James A. Baker III and Michael K. Deaver.

The White House announced that former President Jimmy Carter telephoned the President from Air Force One prior to landing in Wiesbaden, Germany, to visit the freed American hostages. The President asked President Carter to express his joy and pleasure at their release.

The White House announced that at the invitation of the President, Prime Minister Edward Philip George Seaga of Jamaica will visit Washington on January 28. The official visit will provide the two leaders with an opportunity to discuss bilateral relations and regional issues affecting the Caribbean.

The White House announced that at the invitation of the President, President Chun Doo Hwan of the Republic of Korea will visit Washington on February 2. The official visit will afford the two Presidents an opportunity to discuss bilateral political, economic, and security aspects of relations between the United States and the Republic of Korea, as well as regional issues affecting Northeast Asia.

The White House announced several previously scheduled meetings of the President with foreign leaders. On February 17 and 18 King Juan Carlos I of Spain will visit the United States, and on February 25 and 28 Prime Minister Margaret Thatcher of the United Kingdom will visit. In addition, the White House expects to schedule a visit between the President and Prime Minister Pierre Elliott Trudeau of Canada, possibly in Canada. It also is anticipated that the President will meet with Foreign Minister Jean François-Poncet of France, who will visit the United States February 23–25 for meetings with Secretary of State Alexander M. Haig, Jr.

January 22

The President met at the White House with:
—Counsellor to the President Edwin Meese III and Assistants to the President James A. Baker III and Michael K. Deaver;
—members of the Cabinet and their families;
—the economic policy group, to discuss energy issues;
—the Vice President;
—Representative Dan Rostenkowski of Illinois, chairman of the House Ways and Means Committee;
—Representative James R. Jones of Oklahoma, chairman of the House Budget Committee;
—Representatives Jack Brooks of Texas, chairman, and Frank Horton of New York, ranking minority member, House Government Operations Committee;
—Representative John D. Dingell of Michigan, chairman of the House Energy and Commerce Committee;
—representatives of "The March for Life."

The White House announced that the President met at the White House with former Vice President Walter F. Mondale, who delivered President Carter's letter to the President reporting on his visit with the freed American hostages in Wiesbaden, Germany.

In reference to the United States–Iran agreement on release of the American hostages, the White House announced that the agreements negotiated by the Carter administration and the related Executive orders issued by it are very detailed and complicated. An in-depth review of what they entail and require on the part of all involved has begun and will be conducted as expeditiously as possible. The administration fully intends to carry out the objectives of these agreements consistent with international and domestic law. It must be recognized, however, that the implementation of these agreements will be complex and time consuming and that good-faith actions will be required on the part of the parties concerned as well as a cooperative spirit on the part of all.

The White House announced that January 21 the President telephoned Prime Minister Pierre Elliott Trudeau of Canada, Prime Minister Arnoldo Forlani of Italy, Prime Minister Margaret Thatcher of the United Kingdom, President Valéry Giscard d'Estaing of France, Chancellor Helmut Schmidt of the Federal Republic of Germany, and Prime Minister Zenko Suzuki of Japan, to say that he looked forward to working with them on problems of mutual concern to the United States and their countries.

January 23

The President met at the White House with:
—the Republican congressional leadership;
—members of the Cabinet.

In the morning, the President received his daily national security briefing in the Oval Office.

The President attended a luncheon with Secretary of the Treasury Donald T. Regan, Paul A. Volcker, Chairman of the Board of Governors of the Federal Reserve System, Murray L. Weidenbaum, Chairman-designate of the Council of Economic Advisers, and Assistant to the President for Policy Development Martin Anderson in the Secretary's office at the Department of the Treasury.

January 24

The President received his national security briefing in the Oval Office.

The President met with the Cabinet in the Cabinet Room. The meeting focused on economic issues. Secretary of State Alexander M. Haig, Jr., briefed the Cabinet members on the condition of the freed American hostages.

The President met in the Oval Office with Gen. Bernard W. Rogers, U.S. Army, Supreme Allied Commander, Europe, and Secretary of Defense Caspar W. Weinberger.

The President had lunch at the Alibi Club and dinner at the Alfalfa Club.

January 26

In the morning, the President met with members of the White House staff and then received his national security briefing from Assistant to the President for National Security Affairs Richard V. Allen in the Oval Office.

The President met in the Oval Office with Secretary of State Alexander M. Haig, Jr., who reviewed the condition of the freed American hostages. Participants in the meeting included the Vice President, Secretary of Defense Caspar W. Weinberger, and other administration officials.

The President met with his national security advisers in the Oval Office. Participants included the Vice President, Secretary of State Alexander M. Haig, Jr., Secretary of Defense Caspar W. Weinberger, Attorney General William French Smith, William J. Casey, Director of Central Intelligence, William H. Webster, Director of the Federal Bureau of Investigation, and other administration officials.

The President held a series of meetings in the Oval Office with Members of Congress. The President discussed national defense and security issues in meetings with Representatives Clement J. Zablocki, William B. Broomfield, Melvin C. Price, and William L. Dickinson, and Senator Barry Goldwater. The President discussed the economy with Senators Jesse Helms, James McClure, and William Armstrong.

Late in the afternoon, the President met with members of the White House staff in the Oval Office.

January 27
The President met with members of the White House staff in the Oval Office.

The President met in the Oval Office with Senator Howard H. Baker, Jr., Representative Robert H. Michel, Secretary of the Treasury Donald T. Regan, David A. Stockman, Director of the Office of Management and Budget, and Assistant to the President for Legislative Affairs Max L. Friedersdorf.

The President met with the Cabinet in the Cabinet Room.

Late in the afternoon, the President met with members of the White House staff in the Oval Office.

In the evening, the President and Mrs. Reagan hosted a reception at the White House for the diplomatic corps. Guests included Ambassadors to the Organization of American States, the Vice President and Mrs. Bush, and Secretary of State Alexander M. Haig, Jr., and Mrs. Haig.

January 28
In the morning, the President met with members of the White House staff and then received his national security briefing in the Oval Office.

The President met in the Oval Office with John B. Connally, former Governor of Texas.

The President discussed economic issues in an Oval Office meeting with Secretary of the Treasury Donald T. Regan, David A. Stockman, Director of the Office of Management and Budget, and Murray L. Weidenbaum, Chairman-designate of the Council of Economic Advisers.

January 29
The President received his national security briefing and then met with members of the White House staff in the Oval Office.

The President held meetings in the Oval Office with:
—Senators Robert Dole, Russell B. Long, Bob Packwood, and Harry F. Byrd, Jr.;
—Representative Barber B. Conable, Jr.

January 30
The President received his national security briefing and then met with members of the White House staff in the Oval Office

The President held a series of meetings in the Oval Office with:
—Representative Jamie L. Whitten;
—Representative Richard Bolling;
—Representative Charles W. Stenholm;
—Representative Robert H. Michel, Trent Lott, Hank Brown, and James A. Courter;
—Senator Mark O. Hatfield.

The White House announced that the President has accepted the resignations of the Chairman and members of the Board of Directors of the United States Synthetic Fuels Corporation.

The President had lunch in the Oval Office with the Vice President.

The President met in the Oval Office with Secretary of Health and Human Services Richard S. Schweiker

The President discussed his economic program with representatives of the National Federation of Independent Business, the National Association of Manufacturers, the Chamber of Commerce, the Business Roundtable, and the Business Council. Participants in the Cabinet Room meeting included Secretary of the Treasury Donald T. Regan, Secretary of Commerce Malcolm Baldrige, Assistant to the President for Public Liaison Elizabeth H. Dole, and Murray Weidenbaum, Chairman-designate of the Council of Economic Advisers.

In the afternoon, the President left the White House for a weekend stay at Camp David, Md.

February 1
The President returned to the White House from Camp David, Md.

February 2
The President met with members of the White House staff and then received his national security briefing in the Oval Office.

The President met with former Secretary of State Henry A. Kissinger in the Oval Office.

The White House announced that the visit to the United States of King Juan Carlos I of Spain, scheduled for February 17 and 18 has been postponed to a date to be determined.

February 3

The President met with members of the White House staff and then received his national security briefing in the Oval Office.

The President met at the White House with:
—Representative Thomas B. Evans, Jr., of Delaware;
—Attorney General William French Smith.

The President met with Mayors Marion Barry, Jr., of Washington, D.C., Tom Bradley of Los Angeles, Calif., Richard E. Carver of Peoria, Ill., Wyeth Chandler of Memphis, Tenn., Margaret Hance of Phoenix, Ariz., Richard G. Hatcher of Gary, Ind., William H. Hudnut III of Indianapolis, Ind., Edward I. Koch of New York, N.Y., Jim McConn of Houston, Tex., William H. McNichols of Denver, Colo., Tom Moody of Columbus, Ohio, Pete Wilson of San Diego, Calif., and administration officials in the Cabinet Room. Following the meeting, he lunched with the mayors in the Family Dining Room.

The President met with members of the Congressional Black Caucus in the Cabinet Room.

February 4

The President met with members of the White House staff and then received his national security briefing in the Oval Office.

The President met at the White House with:
—civil rights leaders Reverend Ralph Abernathy, Mayor Charles Evers of Fayette, Miss., and Hosea L. Williams;
—the Cabinet, to discuss the Soviet grain embargo and other subjects;
—Senator Paul Laxalt of Nevada.

The President met with the bipartisan congressional leadership in the President's Room at the Capitol.

The President announced his intention to nominate Secretary of the Treasury Donald T. Regan to be U.S. Governor of the International Monetary Fund for a term of 5 years, U.S. Governor of the International Bank for Reconstruction and Development for a term of 5 years, Governor of the Inter-American Development Bank for a term of 5 years, and U.S. Governor of the Asian Development Bank and U.S. Governor of the African Development Fund.

February 5

The President met with members of the White House staff and then received his national security briefing in the Oval Office.

The President received the annual report to the Nation of the Boy Scouts of America in a ceremony in the Oval Office.

February 6

The President met with members of the White House staff and then received his national security briefing in the Oval Office.

The President met at the White House with:
—the Vice President, Secretary of Agriculture John R. Block, chief officers of the American Farm Bureau Federation, National Farmers Organization, National Grange, National Cattlemen's Association, National Pork Producers Council, National Association of Wheat Growers, National Corn Growers Association, American Soybean Association, National Milk Producers Federation, National Cotton Council, American Agricultural Movement, National Council of Farmers Cooperatives, National Broiler Council, Cooperative League of the USA, and Women Involved in Farm Economics, and other administration officials;
—the Vice President, for lunch;
—the National Security Council.

In the morning, Mrs. Reagan hosted a gathering to celebrate the President's birthday in the Oval Office. Attending the event were Members of Congress and members of the White House staff.

February 7

The President announced the designation of former Governor and Mrs. John Davis Lodge as his personal representatives to the funeral services for former Connecticut Governor Ella T. Grasso to be held on Monday, February 9.

February 9

The President met with members of the White House staff and then received his national security briefing in the Oval Office.

The President met at the White House with:
—Secretary of the Treasury Donald T. Regan and David A. Stockman, Director of the Office of Management and Budget;
—Representative Robert McClory of Illinois.

February 10

The President had breakfast with Frank Fitzsimmons, president of the International Brotherhood of Teamsters, Shannon Wall, president of the National Maritime Union, Jesse Calhoon, president of the Marine Engineers Beneficial Association, and Robert Poli, president of the Professional Air Traffic Controllers, in the Family Dining Room. Also attending the breakfast were the Vice President, Secretary of Labor Raymond J. Donovan, and Counsellor to the President Edwin Meese III.

The President received his national security briefing in the Oval Office. The President met with the Cabinet to discuss the progress of Presidential appointments, the Inspectors General program, the economic program, and other subjects.

The President met in the Roosevelt Room with Governors George Busbee of Georgia, John V. Evans of Idaho, James R. Thompson, Jr., of Illinois, William G. Milliken of Michigan, George Nigh of Oklahoma, John Dalton of Virginia, Lee Sherman Dreyfus of Wisconsin, Pierre S. Du Pont IV of Delaware, John Carlin of Kansas, Richard Thornburgh of Pennsylvania, Robert List of Nevada, Richard Snelling of Vermont, James B. Hunt, Jr., of North Carolina, Brendan T. Byrne of New Jersey, John D. Rockefeller IV of West Virginia, Harry Hughes of Maryland, Lamar Alexander of Tennessee, and Robert D. Ray of Iowa, executive and standing committee chairmen of the National Governors' Association. Following the meeting, he lunched with the Governors in the Family Dining Room.

The President met with his economic advisers in the Cabinet Room.

The President met with Lane Kirkland, president of the AFL-CIO, Douglas Fraser, president of the United Auto Workers, Sam Church, Jr., president of the United Mine Workers, and Frank Fitzsimmons, president of the International Brotherhood of Teamsters, in the Oval Office. Also attending the meeting were the Vice President, Secretary of the Treasury Donald T. Regan, Secretary of Labor Raymond J. Donovan, Counsellor to the President Edwin Meese III, and Murray L. Weidenbaum, Chairman-designate of the Council of Economic Advisers.

The President and Mrs. Reagan attended a performance by the Dance Theatre of Harlem at the John F. Kennedy Center for the Performing Arts.

February 11

The President met with members of the White House staff and then received his national security briefing in the Oval Office.

The President met in the Cabinet Room with a budget working group composed of Secretary of the Interior James G. Watt, Secretary of Health and Human Services Richard S. Schweiker, Secretary of Agriculture John R. Block, Secretary of Energy James B. Edwards, and David A. Stockman, Director of the Office of Management and Budget. Also participating in the meeting were the Vice President, Secretary of the Treasury Donald T. Regan, Assistant to the President James A. Baker III, Counsellor to the President Edwin Meese III, and other administration officials.

The President had lunch with the National Security Council.

February 12

The President met with members of the White House staff and then received his national security briefing in the Oval Office.

The President met in the Cabinet Room with a budget working group composed of Secretary of Commerce Malcolm Baldrige, Secretay of Labor Raymond J. Donovan, and the heads of several independent agencies. Also participating in the meeting were David A. Stockman, Director of the Office of Management and Budget, and other administration officials.

The President had lunch in the Family Dining Room with the chief officers of the following Hispanic organizations: American Association of Spanish Speaking Certified Public Accountants, American G. I. Forum of the United States, ASPIRA of America, Cuban National Planning Council, IMAGE, League of United Latin American Citizens, Mexican American Women's National Association, National Coalition of Hispanic Mental Health and Human Services Organizations, National Conference for Puerto Rican Women, National Puerto Rican Forum, Operation SER/Jobs for Progress, Secretariat for Hispanic Affairs of the U.S. Catholic Conference, National Association of Latinos Elected Officials, National Council of Law Raza, U.S. Hispanic Chamber of Commerce, Puerto Rican Legal Defense and Educational Fund, National Association of Spanish Broadcasters, National Association of Farmworkers Organization, TELACU, and Mexican American Legal Defense and Educational Fund. The Vice President, Counsellor to the President Edwin Meese III, and Assistant to the President James A. Baker III also attended the luncheon.

The President met in the Oval Office with:
—Italian Foreign Minister Emilio Colombo, Vice President Bush, Secretary of State Alexander M. Haig, Jr., and Assistant to the President for National Security Affairs Richard V. Allen;
—Omani Foreign Minister Qais Abdul Munim Al-Zawawi, Vice President Bush, Secretary of State Alexander M. Haig, Jr., and Assistant to the President for National Security Affairs Richard V. Allen.

The White House announced that the President and President José López Portillo of Mexico have decided to meet in Tijuana and in San Diego on April 27 and 28 for an exchange of views on bilateral and regional issues. Their decision was in accordance with the understanding reached in Ciudad Juarez on January 5 that the two leaders meet again soon, at the border, to review in depth issues of interest to the United States and to Mexico, and to strengthen the personal friendship they have established.

The President and Mrs. Reagan dined with the Vice President and Mrs. Bush at the Vice President's residence.

February 13

The President met with members of the White House staff and then received his national security briefing in the Oval Office.

The President met in the Cabinet Room with a budget working group composed of Secretary of Defense Caspar W. Weinberger, Secretary of Housing and Urban Development Samuel R. Pierce, Secretary of Education Terrel H. Bell, Secretary of Transportation Drew L. Lewis, Jr., Secretary of Commerce Malcolm Baldrige, Secretary of State Alexander M. Haig, Jr., and the heads of several independent agencies. Also participating in the meeting were David A. Stockman, Director of the Office of Management and Budget, and other administration officials.

The President had lunch with the economic working group in the Roosevelt Room to discuss revenue and tax issues. Included in the group were Secretary of the Treasury Donald T. Regan and David A. Stockman, Director of the Office of Management and Budget.

The President met with the Cabinet in the Cabinet Room.

The President spoke by telephone in the afternoon with President Valéry Giscard d'Estaing of France. President Reagan initiated the call, and the 5-minute conversation enabled the two Presidents to discuss bilateral and European regional policy matters.

The President left the White House for a weekend stay at Camp David, Md.

February 16

The President returned to the White House from Camp David, Md.

The President met with members of the White House staff in the Oval Office.

The President and Mrs. Reagan dined with the Speaker of the House and Mrs. Thomas P. O'Neill, Jr., in the Family Dining Room at the White House.

February 17

The President met with members of the White House staff and then received his national security briefing in the Oval Office.

The President met at the White House with:
—Richard A. Viguerie and representatives of the following conservative coalition groups: Citizens for the Republic; National Right to Work Committee; National Conservative Political Action Committee; Eagle Forum; the Conservative Caucus; National Rifle Association; Committee for the Survival of a Free Congress; Coalition for Peace Through Strength; National Pro-Life Political Action Committee; National Tax Limitation Committee; American Legislative Exchange Council; Free Congress Foundation; Young Americans for Freedom; Human Events; Gun Owners of America; A.C.U. Educational and Research Institute; Citizens Committee for the Right to Keep and Bear Arms; Maupin, Taylor & Ellis; Life Amendment Political Action Committee; Lincoln Institute; and the Conservative Majority Committee; and members of the White House staff;
—Senator Bob Packwood of Oregon and Representative Guy Vander Jagt of Michigan, for lunch;
—participants in National Patriotism Week;
—Secretary of State Alexander M. Haig, Jr., Secretary of Agriculture John R. Block, and a group of Congressmen, to discuss the Soviet grain embargo;
—former State chairmen of the Reagan-Bush campaign.

The White House announced that the President has decided, in light of the economic conditions, not to seek increases in Federal executive salaries. He directed David A. Stockman, Director of the Office of Management and Budget, to inform the Congress that the status of the economy requires that efforts be concentrated on achieving substantial budget reductions and that Federal executives, the Congress, and the judiciary should forgo salary increases at this time.

February 18

The President met with members of the White House staff and then received his national security briefing in the Oval Office.

The President met at the White House with:
—the bipartisan congressional leadership;
—a bipartisan group of congressional leaders to discuss the program for economic recovery;
—the National Security Council.

In a joint announcement, Prime Minister Pierre Elliott Trudeau of Canada announced that the President of the United States and Mrs. Reagan have accepted the invitation of the Governor General of Canada and Mrs. Schreyer to pay a state visit to Canada on March 10 and 11.

February 19

The President had breakfast with a group of newspaper and television news editors in the East Room at the White House. Also attending the breakfast were Secretary of the Treasury Donald T. Regan, Murray L. Weidenbaum, Chairman-designate of the Council of Economic Advisers, and David A. Stockman, Director of the Office of Management and Budget.

The President left the White House for a visit to his ranch, Rancho del Cielo, near Santa Barbara, Calif.

February 20

In the morning, the President received his national security briefing at his ranch, Rancho del Cielo, near Santa Barbara, Calif.

The President spoke by telephone with the Vice President. They discussed the situation in Atlanta and the establishment of a Federal on-site task force which the Vice President announced in Washington at the President's request. The task force will be headed by Charles Rinkevich of the Law Enforcement Assistance Administration and will coordinate Federal efforts with Mayor Maynard Jackson and local officials in the investigation of the disappearance and deaths of youth in Atlanta. Attorney General William French Smith, Secretary of Health and Human Services Richard S. Schweiker, and Secretary of Education Terrel H. Bell will combine services from their departments for the task force.

The White House announced that the President also telephoned Representative James R. Jones, chairman of the House Budget Committee, to discuss the prospects for the economic recovery program in the Congress.

The White House announced that the President has invited Prime Minister Zenko Suzuki of Japan to visit Washington on May 7 and 8. The Prime Minister has accepted the invitation. Prime Minister Suzuki will travel to other cities in the United States in conjunction with this visit.

February 21

In the morning, the President received his national security briefing at his ranch, Rancho del Cielo, near Santa Barbara, Calif.

The White House announced that the President has designated Mike Mansfield, U.S. Ambassador to Japan, as his personal representative to welcome Pope John Paul II on his arrival in Guam on February 22. The President has also designated Secretary of Labor Raymond J. Donovan as his personal representative to meet with the Pope in Anchorage, Alaska, on February 26. The following people will accompany Secretary Donovan when he meets with the Pope: Senators Ted Stevens, Frank H. Murkowski, Jeremiah Denton, Mack Mattingly, and their wives, Representatives William Carney, Vin Weber, Don Young, Henry J. Hyde, and their wives, Representatives John Hiler, Toby Roth, and Lindy (Mrs. Hale) Boggs, and Governor Jay S. Hammond of Alaska.

February 22

The President returned to the White House from a visit to his ranch, Rancho del Cielo, near Santa Barbara, Calif.

February 23

The President met with members of the White House staff and then received his national security briefing in the Oval Office.

The President met at the White House with:
—Counsellor to the President Edwin Meese III and Assistants to the President James A. Baker III and Michael K. Deaver, for lunch;
—Senator Robert T. Stafford of Vermont;
—Representative Clint Roberts of South Dakota;
—Senator Jake Garn of Utah;
—Representative James H. Quillen of Tennessee.

Senator Barry Goldwater met with the President in the Oval Office and presented him with two statues sculpted by Raymond Renfroe, an Arizona artist. Mr. Renfroe and his wife attended the meeting.

February 24

The President met in the Cabinet Room with the Republican congressional leadership.

The President met with members of the White House staff and then received his national security briefing in the Oval Office.

The President met in the Oval Office with Foreign Minister Yitzhak Shamir of Israel. Secretary of State Alexander M. Haig, Jr., and Israeli Ambassador Ephraim Evron also attended the meeting.

The White House announced that the President telephoned King Juan Carlos I of Spain.

In a ceremony in the Oval Office, the President received diplomatic credentials from Ambassadors Charles A. T. Skeete of Barbados, Keith Johnson of Jamaica, and Saud Nasir Al-Sabah of Kuwait.

February 25

The President met with members of the White House staff and then received his national security briefing in the Oval Office.

The President met at the White House with:
—Foreign Minister Jean François-Poncet of France;
—Senators Howard H. Baker, Jr., of Tennessee and James A. McClure of Idaho;
—Bowie Kuhn, commissioner of the American Baseball Association.

The President attended a special meeting of his economic advisers to discuss the Office of Management and Budget's finding that budget outlay figures used by OMB to date had been underestimated by several billion dollars. Participants in the meeting included the Vice President, Secretary of the Treasury Donald T. Regan, David A. Stockman, Director of the Office of Management and Budget, Murray L. Weidenbaum, Chairman of the Council of Economic Advisers, Assistant to the President for Policy Development Martin Anderson, Counsellor to the President Edwin Meese III, and Assistant to the President James A. Baker III. Later, the President had a luncheon meeting in the Cabinet Room with Secretary Regan, Mr. Weidenbaum, and Mr. Stockman.

The President attended a reception in the Blue Room for members of the Congressional Core Group.

February 26

The President met with members of the White House staff and then received his national security briefing in the Oval Office.

The President met at the White House with:
—the Vice President, for lunch;
—Representative Trent Lott and his Republican whip staff;
—the Cabinet.

February 27

The President met with members of the White House staff and then received his national security briefing in the Oval Office.

The President met at the White House with:
—Senator John Tower of Texas;
—Representative Bill Frenzel of Minnesota;
—Representative W. Henson Moore of Louisiana;
—the National Security Council.

The President met with members of the Cabinet Council on Economic Affairs to discuss the situation resulting from the finding by the Office of Management and Budget that budget outlay figures had been underestimated by several billion dollars.

The White House announced that the President has directed that a Cabinet task force on immigration and refugee policy be established to review the report of the Select Commission on Immigration and Refugee Policy, which was presented to the Vice President today. The members of the task force will be Attorney General William French Smith (Chair), Secretary of State Alexander M. Haig, Jr., Secretary of Health and Human Services Richard S. Schweiker, and Secretary of Labor Raymond J. Donovan.

February 28

The President met with Prime Minister Margaret Thatcher of the United Kingdom in the Residence.

The President announced the members of a delegation from the United States who will

attend the inauguration of Chun Doo Hwan as President of the Republic of Korea on March 3. The delegation will include Senator Charles H. Percy of Illinois; William Gleysteen, Jr., U.S. Ambassador to the Republic of Korea; Senator S. I. Hayakawa of California; Representative Clement Zablocki of Wisconsin; Representative Edward J. Derwinski of Illinois; Gen. John W. Vessey, Jr., Vice Chief of Staff, U.S. Army; Michael H. Armacost, Acting Assistant Secretary of State for East Asian and Pacific Affairs; Robert G. Rich, Director of the Office of Korean Affairs; Mrs. Anna Chennault, president, TAC International, chairman, National Republican Heritage Groups Council, and cochairman, Republican National Finance Committee; and Haydon Williams, president of the Asia Foundation. The delegation will depart Washington February 28 and return March 4.

March 2

The President met with members of the White House staff and then received his national security briefing in the Oval Office.

The President met separately in the Oval Office with:
—Senator Henry M. Jackson of Washington;
—Senator Bob Packwood of Oregon;
—Representative Silvio O. Conte of Massachusetts;
—Representative James T. Broyhill of North Carolina.

March 3

The President met with members of the White House staff and then received his national security briefing in the Oval Office.

The President met at the White House with:
—members of the Automotive Task Force, including Secretary of Transportation Drew L. Lewis, Jr., Secretary of State Alexander M. Haig, Jr., Secretary of the Treasury Donald T. Regan, Secretary of Commerce Malcolm Baldrige, Secretary of Labor Raymond J. Donovan, Ambassador William E. Brock, U.S. Trade Representative, David A. Stockman, Director of the Office of Management and Budget, Murray L. Weidenbaum, Chairman of the Council of Economic Advisers, Counsellor to the President Edwin Meese III, and Assistant to the President James A. Baker III;
—former President Gerald R. Ford.

The President attended a Veterans of Foreign Wars reception at the Sheraton Washington Hotel.

The President and Mrs. Reagan dined with Senate Majority Leader and Mrs. Howard H. Baker, Jr., in the Family Dining Room at the White House.

March 4

The President attended a breakfast meeting with freshmen Republican Members of the House of Representatives and members of the White House staff.

The President met in the Oval Office with members of the 1981 Inaugural Committee to receive his copy of the Inaugural Book.

The President received his national security briefing in the Oval Office and then met with the National Security Council in the Cabinet Room.

The President greeted Colleen Finn, the 1981 Easter Seal Poster Child, her parents, and officials of the National Easter Seal Society in the Oval Office.

The President and Mrs. Reagan attended a private dinner at the Jockey Club to celebrate their 29th wedding anniversary.

The President has designated the following individuals as Acting Chairmen of their agencies: J. Clay Smith, Jr., Equal Employment Opportunity Commission; Leslie L. Kanuk, Federal Maritime Commission; David A. Clanton, Federal Trade Commission; Joseph M. Hendrie, Nuclear Regulatory Commission; Frank R. Barnako, Occupational Safety and Health Review Commission; and Philip A. Loomis, Jr., Securities and Exchange Commission.

March 5

The President attended a breakfast meeting with members of the Congressional Conservative Democratic Forum and members of the White House staff.

The President met with members of the White House staff and then received his national security briefing in the Oval Office.

The President met at the White House with:
—Ann McGill Gorsuch, Administrator-designate of the Environmental Protection Agency;
—Cystic Fibrosis Poster Children Jennifer Lynn Haninger, Attilio "Otto" D'Agostino, and Douglas Leon Mohler, their parents, and officials of the Cystic Fibrosis Foundation;
—the Vice President, for lunch;
—Senators Russell B. Long and J. Bennett Johnston and Representatives Jerry Huckaby and Buddy Roemer, all of Louisiana.

The President met briefly with reporters in the Roosevelt Room to select by way of a lottery the questioners for his second news conference, to be held on March 6.

The President met with the Cabinet in the Cabinet Room.

March 6

The President met with members of the White House staff and then received his national security briefing in the Oval Office.

The President met with Governors Christopher Bond of Missouri, Lee Sherman Dreyfus of Wisconsin, Pierre S. Du Pont IV of Delaware, William G. Milliken of Michigan, Robert Orr of Indiana, James Rhodes of Ohio, James R. Thompson, Jr., of Illinois, and Richard L. Thornburgh of Pennsylvania, and the Vice President, Secretary of the Treasury Donald T. Regan, Secretary of Commerce Malcolm Baldrige, Ambassador William E. Brock, United States Trade Representative, David A. Stockman, Director of the Office of Management and Budget, and Murray L. Weidenbaum, Chairman of the Council of Economic Advisers, to discuss the automobile industry.

The White House announced that the President has designated Benjamin Huberman as Acting Director of the Office of Science and Technology Policy within the Executive Office of the President.

The President left the White House for a weekend stay at Camp David, Md.

March 8

The President returned to the White House following a weekend stay at Camp David, Md.

March 9

The President met at the White House with:
—members of the White House staff;
—Max Fisher, Gordon Zacks, Ted Cummings, George Klein, and Jacob Stein, who are current and former leaders of Jewish organizations;
—Foreign Minister Hans-Dietrich Genscher of the Federal Republic of Germany, Vice President George Bush, and Secretary of State Alexander M. Haig, Jr.;
—award winners of the 1981 White House News Photographers Association's photography contest.

The White House announced that the President has designated Janet Dempsey Steiger as Acting Chairman of the Postal Rate Commission.

March 11

The White House announced that at the invitation of the President and Mrs. Reagan, the Chancellor of the Federal Republic of Germany and Mrs. Schmidt will pay an official visit to Washington on May 20–23. The meetings which the Chancellor will have with President Reagan and other senior administration officials are part of the continuing process of consultations between the Federal Republic of Germany and the United States of America aimed at coordinating their policies in response to problems of mutual interest throughout the world. The consultations which the Chancellor will have with President Reagan and other senior administration officials will provide an opportunity for an exchange of views on a broad variety of issues of mutual interest to both countries. The President and the Chancellor last met in Washington on November 20, 1980.

March 12

The President held a breakfast meeting with sophomore Republican Members of the House of Representatives in the State Dining Room at the White House. The Vice President and members of the White House staff attended the meeting.

The President met with members of the White House staff and then received his national security briefing in the Oval Office.

The President had lunch with the Vice President in the Vice President's office in the Old Executive Office Building.

The President went by helicopter to Walter Reed Army Medical Center to visit Senator Robert Dole of Kansas, who was recuperating from surgery.

The President attended a reception for members of the National Newspaper Association in the East Room.

March 13

The President met with members of the White House staff and then received his national security briefing in the Oval Office.

The President met at the White House with:
—Spencer W. Kimball, president of the Church of Jesus Christ of Latter-Day Saints;
—the Cabinet.

The President left the White House for a weekend stay in New York City.

March 14

The President left the Waldorf Astoria and went to the offices of the New York Daily News for an interview.

Following the interview, the President went to Angelo's Restaurant for a luncheon meeting with local community leaders. Guests at the luncheon included Senator and Mrs. Alfonse M. D'Amato and Representative and Mrs. Guy V. Molinari.

Following the luncheon, the President returned to the Waldorf Astoria, where he met in his suite with Mayor Edward I. Koch, Commissioner Charles J. Hynes of the New York City Fire Department, and James Bingham, New York City Budget Director.

Later in the afternoon, the President attended a reception in the Vanderbilt Suite at the Waldorf Astoria for New York State Republican leaders.

In the evening, he President and Mrs. Reagan went to the Mark Hellinger Theatre for a performance of "Sugar Babies." Following the performance, they dined at Le Cirque restaurant and then returned to the Waldorf Astoria.

March 15

In the evening, the President and Mrs. Reagan went to the Metropolitan Opera House, Lincoln Center for the Performing Arts, for a performance by the Joffrey Ballet. During intermission they met with members of the cast, including their son, Ron.

Following the conclusion of the performance, the President and Mrs. Reagan returned to the White House.

March 16

The President received his national security briefing and then met with members of the White House staff in the Oval Office.

In the afternoon, the President met in the Oval Office with Jerry Lewis, national chairman, and Christi Bartlett, National Poster Child, of the Muscular Dystrophy Association.

March 17

Following the meeting with the Republican congressional leadership on Capitol Hill, the President received his national security briefing and then met with members of the White House staff in the Oval Office.

March 18

The President met in the Map Room with Ms. Janet Collins and students from the Chadwick School in California. The President congratulated Ms. Collins, a former teacher of Maureen and Mike Reagan, on her upcoming retirement.

The President held a breakfast meeting in the Family Dining Room with freshmen Republican Members of the Senate. The Vice President and other administration officials also attended the meeting.

The President met with members of the White House staff and then received his national security briefing in the Oval Office.

The President met in the Oval Office with Representative Guy Vander Jagt of Michigan, Mrs. Lieske Van Kessel of the Netherlands, Mandy Evans of Michigan, and Wally Phillips of "The Wally Phillips Show" in Chicago. Ms. Evans recently won a "Fantasy Wish" contest sponsored by Mr. Phillips' show, and as a result, she has been reunited with Mrs. Van Kessel, who was a member of the Dutch Underground during World War II and hid downed fliers and refugees on her houseboat.

The President met in the Oval Office with Representative Jim Wright of Texas, who presented the President with jalapeño jellybeans from Texas. Representative Wright was given the candies for presentation to the President by the cast of the Grandbury Opera in Texas.

The President met in the Oval Office with Senators David L. Boren and Don Nickles and Representative Glenn English, of Oklahoma, and Karie Kaye Ross, the 1981 Maid of Cotton.

The White House announced that the President yesterday declared a major disaster for the Commonwealth of Kentucky as a result of sewer explosions in Loiusville, on February 13, 1981, which caused extensive property damage.

March 19

The President met with members of the White House staff and then received his national security briefing in the Oval Office.

The President met at the White House with:
—the Vice President, for lunch;
—the Cabinet;
—the National Security Council;
—Ambassador Chai Zemin and Deputy Director Ji Chao Zhu of the American and Oceanic Department of the Ministry of Foreign Affairs of the People's Republic of China.

In a ceremony in the Oval Office, the President presented the Merchant Marine Trophy to Walter James Amoss, president of the Lykes Brothers Steamship Co. The trophy is awarded annually by the Robert L. Hague American Legion Post No. 1242.

In the evening, the President and Mrs. Reagan attended a performance of "The Little Foxes" at the John F. Kennedy Center for the Performing Arts.

March 20

The President met with members of the White House staff and then received his national security briefing in the Oval Office.

The President met at the White House with:
—Jacob K. Javits, former Senator from New York;
—Takeo Fukuda, former Prime Minister of Japan;
—Jack Brickhouse, announcer for the Chicago Cubs baseball team, who interviewed the President;
—representatives of the National Conference of State Legislatures, the Vice President, and other administration officials.

The White House announced that at the invitation of the President, Prime Minister Andreas A. M. van Agt of the Netherlands will make a working visit to Washington to meet with the President on April 1. Foreign Minister Christoph Van Der Klaauw will accompany Prime Minister van Agt, who is the current chairman of the European Council.

March 23

The President met with members of the White House staff and then received his national security briefing in the Residence Library.

The President greeted 1981 March of Dimes Poster Child Mary Melissa Jablonski, former Poster Children, and officials of the March of Dimes Birth Defects Foundation in the East Room.

The President met with the executive board of the National Association of Realtors in the Cabinet Room.

The President received the Inaugural flags and medals from Senator Mark O. Hatfield of Oregon and other members of the 1981 Presidential Inaugural Committee in the Oval Office.

The President met in the Oval Office with Comptroller General of the United States and Mrs. Elmer B. Staats on the occasion of Mr. Staats' retirement. During the meeting the President presented Mr. Staats with the Presidential Citizens Medal in honor of his career as a civil servant and his "honesty, industry, initiative and commitment to make government the efficient servant, not the overbearing master."

The President met with the Cabinet Council on Economics Affairs in the Cabinet Room.

March 24

The President met at the White House with:
—the bipartisan congressional leadership;
—members of the White House staff;
—Senators Howard H. Baker, Jr., of Tennessee and John C. Danforth of Missouri;
—Foreign Minister Masayoshi Ito of Japan and Secretary of State Alexander M. Haig, Jr.;
—Governor Forrest James, Jr., of Alabama;
—the California State Legislature leadership group, including State Treasurer Jesse Unruh, Senators David A. Roberti and William Campbell, and Assemblymen Willie L. Brown, Jr., Carol Hallett, and Mike Roos.

The President attended a reception in the Blue Room for Senators David L. Boren of Oklahoma, Dale Bumpers of Arkansas, John H. Chafee of Rhode Island, J. James Exon of Nebraska, Wendell H. Ford of Kentucky, Mark O. Hatfield of Oregon, Ernest F. Hollings of South Carolina, Paul Laxalt of Nevada, David Pryor of Arkansas, Robert Stafford of Vermont, and Strom Thurmond of South Carolina, all former State Governors. Also attending the reception were the Vice President and Secretary of Energy James B. Edwards.

The White House announced that the working visit to Washington of Prime Minister Andreas A. M. van Agt of the Netherlands, originally scheduled for April 1, will take place on March 31.

March 25

The President met with members of the White House staff and then received his national security briefing in the Oval Office.

The President met with the President's Economic Policy Advisory Board in the Cabinet Room.

The President has declared a major disaster for the Teritory of American Samoa as a result of Typhoon Esau on March 2, which caused extensive property damage.

March 26

The President met with members of the White House staff and then received his national security briefing in the Oval Office.

The President met at the White House with:
—Representative Barber B. Conable, Jr., of New York;
—the Vice President, for lunch;
—the National Security Council.

The President attended the Radio and Television Correspondents Association dinner at the Washington Hilton Hotel.

March 27

The President met with members of the White House staff and then received his national security briefing in the Oval Office.

The President met at the White House with:
—the Vice President, Secretary of the Treasury Donald T. Regan, David A. Stockman, Director of the Office of Management and Budget, and Republican members of the House Ways and Means Committee;
—representatives of ethnic groups who had supported the President's 1980 campaign.

The White House announced that the President has asked the Vice President to head the United States delegation to the International Conference on Assistance to Refugees in Africa to be held in Geneva, April 9 and 10. This Conference is sponsored by the Organization of African Unity, the United Nations High Commissioner for Refugees, and the Secretary General of the United Nations. Its purpose is to mobilize international action to meet the urgent and growing problem of refugees in Africa.

The President and Mrs. Reagan dined with Senator and Mrs. Paul Laxalt of Nevada in the Residence.

March 28

In the evening, the President attended the Gridiron Dinner at the Capital Hilton Hotel.

March 30

The President attended an administration leadership breakfast in the East Room at the White House.

The President received his national security briefing in the Oval Office.

The President met with a group of Hispanic leaders and several administration officials in the Cabinet Room.

The White House announced that Chancellor Helmut Schmidt of the Federal Republic of Germany telephoned the President at 9:15 a.m. They discussed the situation in Poland, and both the President and the Chancellor, on behalf of their own countries, felt that in the event suppression be applied either externally or internally in Poland, it would be impossible to render further economic assistance to Poland.

At approximately 2:25 p.m. outside the Washington Hilton Hotel, after addressing the national conference of the Building and Construction Trades Department, AFL-CIO, an assassination attempt was made on the President. The President was taken immediately to George Washington University Hospital. Press Secretary James S. Brady, Secret Service Agent Timothy J. McCarthy, and District of Columbia policeman Thomas K. Delahanty also were wounded in the incident. The Office of the Press Secretary issued daily medical reports and press briefings by Dr. Dennis O'Leary, dean for clinical affairs, George Washington University Hospital, on the condition of those hospitalized. Excerpts from these reports follow each day's activities.

Later in the evening at a press briefing, Dr. Dennis O'Leary, dean for clinical affairs, George Washington University Hospital, gave the following medical report:

The President is in the recovery room. He is in stable condition, and he is awake. He was at no time in any serious danger. He was alert and awake with stable vital signs up until the time he underwent anesthesia. He was in the operating room for approximately 2 hours. Part of that time was spent ascertaining that he did not have any blood in his abdominal cavity. Indeed, he did not. It was a single bullet wound that entered slightly underneath the left armpit. It traversed about 3 inches of the chest wall and then ricocheted off the seventh rib into the left lower lobe of the lung and moved about 3 inches into the lung substance itself. The operative incision was about 6 inches in width, a relatively simple procedure. The bullet was removed, and then the incision was closed. He is stable and in good condition. The prognosis is excellent.

Secret Service Agent Timothy J. McCarthy had a single bullet wound also. It entered the posterior right chest and passed through the lung tissue, causing virtually no damage at all except for the passage tract. It passed through the diaphragm into the dome of the liver and passed through the liver into the lateral side of the chest where it lodged against the end of the eleventh rib. Mr. McCarthy did have blood in his abdominal cavity. The same test that was performed on the President was also performed on him, and it was positive. The abdominal cavity was carefully explored, and the only damage was the bullet through the liver itself. A drain was placed in this area, and he is doing extremely well; has been in the intensive care unit now for about 45 minutes.

Press Secretary James S. Brady is still in surgery. His condition is critical. We don't have any further information at this time.

March 31

The President met at George Washington University Hospital with the Vice President and members of the White House staff. He was also visited by Mrs. Reagan and members of his family.

During a morning press briefing, Dr. Dennis O'Leary, dean for clinical affairs, George Washington University Hospital, gave the following medical report:

The President had an excellent night. The endotrachial tube which was placed in his surgery was removed at 3:00 this morning. He was moved from the recovery room to a private area at about 5:00 this morning. He did not get a lot of sleep last night; busy night. He maintained a constant dialog with the nurses and doctors who were in constant attendance with him, maintaining an excellent sense of humor. I'm sure you'll hear many of his remarks. My favorite one is, he said, "If I got this much attention in Hollywood, I'd never have left." This went on all night. I had an opportunity to see him this morning. He is in excellent spirits. All of his vital signs are entirely normal. He's on almost no medication, and at this point in time, he really probably does not require an intensive level of medical care. He's doing extremely well.

Secret Service Agent Timothy J. McCarthy is also doing extremely well. He is complaining a little bit of soreness in the liver area, which is a little bit understandable. He has a mild elevation of his temperature and of his white blood count, which would be expected after a liver injury. But he otherwise is doing extremely well.

Press Secretary James S. Brady is much improved over his initial prognosis. He still has his endotrachial tube in. However, he is responsive and is moving the right side of his body in response to command. It is anticipated his tube will be removed later today. We are guarded as to his prognosis, but his progress thus far has really been extraordinary.

The White House issued the following medical report:

Morning

At 6:15 this morning, the President left the recovery room for the intensive care ward. Dr. Daniel Ruge, the President's personal physician, said, "The President's vital signs are all in the normal range. He's in exceptionally good condition." Dr. Ruge indicated that the President was talking and writing notes.

On James Brady's condition, Dr. Ruge said, "It is serious, but improving. It's too early to make a prognosis. He is somewhat responsive."

Dr. Ruge also said that Secret Service Agent Timothy McCarthy's condition is "very fine."

Doctors at the Washington Hospital Center said the condition of D.C. policeman Thomas Delahanty is serious, but the prognosis is good.

Afternoon

Physicians at George Washington University Hospital report that Press Secretary James S. Brady remains in critical but stable condition. He is being observed closely for possible complications for which he is at significant risk. Mr. Brady is responsive and continues to move the right side of his body in response to voice command. It is clear that Mr. Brady understands voice command, implying retention of significant brain function. Physicians are encouraged by Mr. Brady's progress thus far, but he remains in guarded condition.

Physicians at George Washington University Hospital report that Secret Service Agent Timothy J. McCarthy continues in good condition as his vital signs remain stable. He is awake and alert and is receiving routine care. His prognosis is excellent, and he will most likely be moved to a surgical ward within the George Washington University Hospital sometime tomorrow.

Evening

Dr. Daniel Ruge, Physician to the President, made the following statement at 5 p.m.:

The President continues on the road to recovery. He is doing extremely well. After sleeping this morning, he has spent the day reading newspapers. From time to time he is sitting up in bed. He is converting from non-oral to oral feeding and tolerating it very well. He has had clear liquids such as soup and gelatin. He continues on intravenous fluids and antibiotics. His vital signs are in the normal range.

The President was informed about Jim Brady, Agent Tim McCarthy, and Officer Thomas Delahanty shortly after noon. He was very saddened and expressed sorrow.

The physicians attending Jim Brady are pleased he has continued to be more responsive. Although he is seriously ill, they are optimistic.

Secret Service Agent Tim McCarthy continues to improve.

Officer Thomas Delahanty is improving at the Washington Hospital Center. He is listed in fair condition and will be moved from intensive care today. There are no plans as of today to remove the bullet from his neck.

April 1

The President met with members of the Whte House staff and received his national security briefing in his room at George Washington University Hospital.

Mrs. Reagan visited the President at the hospital.

On behalf of the President, the Vice President presided over a meeting of the National Security Council at the White House.

The White House announced that in view of the need for the Vice President to remain in Washington to assist the President during his period of recovery, the Vice President will be unable to lead the U.S. delegation to the International Conference on Assistance to Refugees in Africa to be held in Geneva on April 9 and 10. The President has, therefore, asked Ambassador Jeane J. Kirkpatrick, U.S. Permanent Representative to the United Nations, to replace the Vice President as head of the U.S. delegation.

The White House issued the following medical report:

Morning

Following surgical rounds at the George Washington University Hospital, physicians report the President's condition continues to improve as well as can be expected. The President was moved from the intensive care unit to a surgical ward last evening. The President will increase his food intake beginning today, as his diet is changed from liquid to solid food. The President is in good condition but is experiencing some pain and fatigue in response to his injury. The President slept well during the night and is up and walking this morning.

Following surgical rounds at the George Washington University Hospital, physician's report Press Secretary James S. Brady's condition continues to improve as he remains in critical condition. Mr. Brady is able to speak, can move his left arm and leg, and it is anticipated that he may be able to sit up in his hospital bed in a few days. During Mrs. Brady's visit last night, she and Mr. Brady played catch, demonstrating his ability to move in spite of his weakened condition. Physicians continue to be cautiously optimistic as Mr. Brady's neurological condition continues to im-

prove. Mr. Brady is breathing well without the assistance of a respirator.

Secret Service Agent Timothy J. McCarthy's condition continues to improve. He will undergo some diagnostic liver scanning tests this morning, and it is anticipated that he will be relocated within the hospital to a surgical ward later today.

Afternoon

Dr. Daniel Ruge, Physician to the President, said at 3:30 p.m. the President continues to make excellent progress toward full recovery. His condition remains the same as it was this morning. He has experienced some pain during the day, which is normal for one experiencing an injury and surgery of this type. He is now resting comfortably.

Evening

Dr. Dennis O'Leary, dean for clinical affairs, George Washington University Hospital, reported at 5 p.m. that Press Secretary James S. Brady continues to make very satisfactory progress. Mr. Brady continues to play catch and is responsive to command. There was no evidence of complications at this time.

Dr. O'Leary also reports that Special Agent McCarthy is in good condition. Agent McCarthy was transferred out of intensive care this morning and is in a private room. Agent McCarthy underwent a scan of his liver to exclude the possibility of blood collection there, and Dr. O'Leary reports that everything looks very good. Agent McCarthy is doing extremely well and is stable.

April 2

The President met in his room at George Washington University Hospital with:
— Senators Howard H. Baker, Jr., and Paul Laxalt;
— the Vice President and members of the White House staff;
— Senator Strom Thurmond.

The President received his national security briefing at the hospital.

Mrs. Reagan visited with the President at the hospital. In the evening, she brought Deputy Assistant to the President and Director of Special Support Services Edward V. Hickey, Jr., and John Simpson, Assistant Director of Protective Operations, and Jerry S. Parr, Special Agent in Charge of the Presidential Protection Division, U.S. Secret Service, to the President's room for a brief visit.

On behalf of the President, the Vice President met at the White House with:
— Dr. Leon Sullivan, chairman, and members of the executive board of the Opportunities Industrialization Centers of America, Inc.;
— the Cabinet;

—Republican members of the House Ways and Means Committee;

—Republican members of the House Budget Committee.

The White House issued the following medical report:

Morning

Following morning surgical rounds at George Washington University Hospital, physicians report the President's progress to be satisfactory. He remains in good condition with vital signs and temperature well within normal limits. The President is experiencing some pain as anticipated in response to his injury and surgical care, but he is able to walk around the Presidential surgical suite. His appearance reflects the effect of a peaceful night's sleep. Chest X-rays show that the President's injured lung is expanded, and he is coughing well, a favorable indication of his continued progress and recuperation.

Following morning surgical rounds at George Washington University Hospital, physicians report that Press Secretary James S. Brady's post-operative progress continues to improve, and his vital signs are stable. He remains in critical condition in the intensive care unit. A routine post-operative CT scan confirms Mr. Brady's steady progress, physicians report, and rudimentary vision and cognitive test results are satisfactory. The post-operative drainage tubes placed at the sight of the injury at surgery have been removed. Mr. Brady is able to cooperate in his nursing care through working with the nurses to position himself for standard treatment.

Following morning surgical rounds at George Washington University Hospital, physicians report Secret Service Agent Timothy J. McCarthy's condition as good, as he experiences some anticipated "third day" soreness. X-rays show Mr. McCarthy's chest to be clear, and his vital signs are stable.

Evening

Following afternoon surgical rounds at the George Washington University Hospital, physicians report the President continues to make excellent progress. His condition is good, with respiration, heart rate, and other vital signs well within normal limits. The President is now exercising regularly by walking in the Presidential surgical suite four times each day. He continues to receive briefings in person and in writing.

Following afternoon surgical rounds, physicians report that Press Secretary James S. Brady's post-operative status continues to improve and that he appears clearer mentally. He held a restricted conversation with his physician this afternoon. When asked how he was feeling, Mr. Brady replied with a thumbs-up sign and said, "Fine,

fine." Mr. Brady is also now performing breathing exercises on instructions and has gained some minimal voluntary movement of the proximal muscles of his left arm and leg.

Following afternoon surgical rounds, physicians report that Secret Service Agent Timothy J. McCarthy's condition is good and that his vital signs remain stable. Mr. McCarthy's chest tube has been removed, and his injured lung remains fully expanded. He is now obtaining some mild exercise by walking around his hospital room.

April 3

The President met with members of the White House staff and received his national security briefing in his room at George Washington University Hospital.

Mrs. Reagan visited the President at the hospital.

The President met at the hospital with the Vice President and Secretary of State Alexander M. Haig, Jr., who left today for a trip to the Middle East. They discussed the Secretary's visits to Egypt, Israel, Saudi Arabia, and Jordan.

The President met at the hospital with the Vice President and Secretary of Defense Caspar W. Weinberger. They discussed the Secretary's trip to London to meet with the NATO Nuclear Planning Group.

The President transmitted to the Congress the sixth annual report of the Nuclear Regulatory Commission.

On behalf of the President, the Vice President presided over a meeting of the Cabinet Council on Natural Resources and the Environment at the White House.

The White House issued the following medical report:

Morning

Following morning surgical rounds at George Washington University Hospital, physicians report the President continues to recover from his injury in a satisfactory manner. Over the past several hours, the President has developed a moderate temperature elevation, an occurrence which is considered commonplace at this stage for patients recovering from injuries and surgery of this nature. The President's chest X-ray continues to show the left lung to be fully expanded with no evidence of new changes. Mr. Reagan's surgical incisions are clean, and he feels refreshed and appears well rested after a good night's sleep. The temperature elevation is being appropriately evaluated, and the frequency of chest therapy has been increased.

Following morning surgical rounds at the George Washington University Hospital, physicians report that Press Secretary James S. Brady's level of consciousness continues to improve as he remains in the intensive care unit in critical condition. There is no apparent change since yesterday in Mr. Brady's overall motor function. When asked by his physician how he was feeling this morning, Mr. Brady replied, "I'm feeling fine." During the night Mr. Brady experienced a transient temperature elevation which readily resolved.

Following morning surgical rounds at George Washington University Hospital, physicians report that Secret Service Agent Timothy J. McCarthy's condition is good; his vital signs remain stable. His general recovery from surgery has been progressive and without complication.

According to Washington Hospital Center's director of public affairs, last night's operation on Officer Thomas Delahanty went very well. His vital signs are stable, and he is in good condition. Officer Delahanty spent the night in intensive care, resting well. The microsurgery procedure took 3 hours.

Evening

Following afternoon surgical rounds, physicians at George Washington University Hospital report that President Reagan's condition is satisfactory. The previously reported temperature elevation again became moderately elevated. A fiberoptic bronchoscopy was then performed, and several small bronchial plugs as well as some dormant blood were successfully removed. The President has been restarted on the broad spectrum antibiotic which he had received following surgery, pending the results of specific cultures. All blood and urine studies performed thus far are normal. The President has received several visitors through the day and remains alert and generally comfortable.

Following afternoon surgical rounds, physicians at George Washington University Hospital report that Press Secretary James S. Brady's condition continues to improve. He has now been removed from the critical list but remains in the intensive care unit. His vital signs are stable, and there have been no further temperature elevations. This afternoon when Mr. Brady's physician asked him what his job was, he replied, "Press Secretary at the White House."

Following afternoon surgical rounds, physicians at George Washington University Hospital report that Secret Service Agent Timothy J. McCarthy continues to do well. His digestive system appears to be functionally normal, and his chest X-ray is clear.

April 4

Mrs. Reagan and members of the White House staff visited with the President in his room at George Washington University Hospital.

The President announced his intention to appoint the following individuals to the Advisory Commission on Intergovernmental Relations: Secretary of the Interior James G. Watt, Secretary of Housing and Urban Development Samuel R. Pierce, Jr., and Assistant to the President for Intergovernmental Affairs Richard S. Williamson. Secretary Watt will be designated as Chairman.

The White House issued the following medical report:

Morning

Following morning surgical rounds, physicians at George Washington University Hospital report that the President's condition is good. He is responding very well to routine chest physical therapy, and his temperature is only mildly elevated. The last chest tube was removed this morning, and his chest X-ray has improved. The President is very alert, telling stories and laughing. The President met with Physician to the President Dr. Daniel Ruge, Assistant to the President Dave Fischer, and Secret Service Agent Jerry Parr at 9:25. He was given an update on the condition of the others. He said, "That's great news, just great, especially about Jim." He also said, "We'll have to get four bedpans and have a reunion."

Following morning surgical rounds, physicians at George Washington University Hospital report that Press Secretary James S. Brady continues to make excellent progress. He is now trying to open his eyes, and mild intermittent temperature elevations have been easily controlled. When asked this morning by his physicians what his job involved, he replied, "I answer questions." His physician said, "Who for?" Brady responded, "Anyone who asks for them." In followup to earlier FBI reports that the bullet which struck Mr. Brady may have exploded on impact, physicians agree that the entry wound is compatible with such a thesis but doubt that much if any of the lead azide explosive actually penetrated the skull. Physicians also comment that surgical debridement of the missile track was sufficiently thorough to assure that any remaining chemical would have been removed at surgery.

Following morning surgical rounds, physicians at George Washington University Hospital report that Secret Service Agent Timothy J. McCarthy's condition remains good. He has been started on a liquid diet. Mr. McCarthy is scheduled for further routine post-operative tests early next week.

Evening

Following afternoon surgical rounds, physicians at the George Washington University Hospital report that the President continues to progress satisfactorily. His temperature has slowly ebbed through the day and is normal at this time. Although all culture results are still negative, the President continues on antibiotic coverage as a precautionary measure. At 12:12 p.m., the President was visited by Secret Service Agent Timothy J. McCarthy and his wife, Carolyn. Mrs. Reagan visited with the President at that time. When Special Agent McCarthy arrived, the President was seated in a chair having lunch and rose to shake hands with Mr. McCarthy. They discussed their treatment in the hospital for about 10 minutes. As the McCarthys were preparing to leave, Mrs. McCarthy mentioned their children would be visiting their father on Sunday. The President said: "You tell them their father put himself between me and that guy. I'm glad there are guys around to do those kind of jobs." The President has otherwise spent the day napping occasionally and visiting with Mrs. Reagan and her brother, Dr. Richard Davis. He has also taken several walks during the day.

Following afternoon surgical rounds, physicians at the George Washington University Hospital report that Press Secretary James S. Brady's general level of alertness has improved further and that he has been transferred from the intensive care unit to a private room on the neurosurgery service. With effort, he can now partially open his right eye. He has also begun to speak spontaneously.

Following afternoon surgical rounds, physicians at the George Washington University Hospital report that Secret Service Agent Timothy J. McCarthy continues to recuperate uneventfully. His condition remains good.

Officer Thomas Delahanty's condition is good, and he is making satisfactory progress. He was moved from the intensive care unit last night. He has some pain, which is to be expected, but the prognosis is good. He has been walking around. His vital signs are stable.

April 5

Mrs. Reagan visited the President at George Washington University Hospital.

The President met in his room at the hospital with:

—the Vice President;
—Vernon E. Jordan, Jr., president of the National Urban League.

The White House issued the following medical report:

After morning surgical rounds at the George Washington University Hospital, physicians report that the President continues his convalescence after sleeping most of the night. His temperature was intermittently elevated to moderate levels through the evening but is again normal this morning. Earlier this morning, the President was transported to the radiology department for

standard posterior-anterior and lateral chest X-rays. These films show persistent lung infiltrates along the bullet track, findings which would be expected to resolve quite slowly. Physicians continue to monitor the President's clinical course carefully. The President remains alert and in good spirits. It is anticipated that no further reports concerning the President's condition will be issued today.

After morning surgical rounds at the George Washington University Hospital, physicians report that Press Secretary James S. Brady spent a good night and continues to make satisfactory progress. He is now eating solid foods and sipping water. Although intermittent temperature elevations continue, all cultures performed thus far are negative. Mr. Brady has been informed by his wife as to the President's injury and is aware that the President is also hospitalized at George Washington. Mr. Brady's speech is becoming more sophisticated, and he clearly recognizes his wife both by sound and vision. Last night Mr. Brady commented on his injury by remarking, "The 'Bear' was certainly in the wrong place that time."

Secret Service Agent McCarthy continues to make excellent progress.

Officer Thomas Delahanty is in good condition at George Washington Hospital Center. He was walking around today and took a shower. The hospital spokesman said that Officer Delahanty had a moderate elevation in temperature and is receiving antibiotics although there is no evidence of infection.

April 6

The President met with members of the White House staff and received his national security briefing in his room at George Washington University Hospital.

Mrs. Reagan and the President's daughter Maureen visited him at the hospital.

The President met with Speaker of the House of Representatives Thomas P. O'Neill, Jr., in his room at the hospital.

The White House announced that the President has invited Prime Minister Malcolm Fraser of Australia to make an official visit to Washington June 29 to July 1 and that the Prime Minister has accepted the President's invitation.

The White House issued the following medical report:

Following morning surgical rounds, physicians at George Washington University Hospital report that the President spent a restful night as he continues to recuperate. Intermittent moderate temperature elevations have persisted through the past 24 hours. A portable chest X-ray this morning shows modest clearing of the previously described lung infiltrates when compared to earlier portable chest film. Existing cultures and review of specimen smears show no evidence of bacterial infection. However, as a precautionary measure, antibiotic coverage was broadened further yesterday. The President continues to be alert and in good spirits.

Following morning surgical rounds, physicians at George Washington University Hospital report that Press Secretary James S. Brady continues his thus far uncomplicated recovery. Vital signs, including temperature, are normal. Motor function is essentially unchanged, but Mr. Brady is able to open both eyes, the left still with some difficulty. The facial swelling is gradually receding. Mr. Brady's thinking processes and speech continue to improve. He now makes quips and jokes spontaneously. After his first look at his neurosurgeon, Dr. Arthur Kobrine, Mr. Brady remarked, "Not a bad job, Doc."

Secret Service Agent Timothy J. McCarthy continues to make excellent progress.

Physicians at the Washington Hospital Center report that Officer Thomas Delahanty's condition continues good. He is up and around and eating well. His temperature is normal.

April 7

The President met with members of the White House staff and received his national security briefing in his room at George Washington University Hospital.

Mrs. Reagan visited the President in his room at the hospital.

The President met in his room at the hospital with:

—H. Stuart Knight, Director, John R. Simpson, Assistant Director (Protective Operations), and Jerry S. Parr, Special Agent in Charge of the Presidential Protective Division, U.S. Secret Service;

—the Vice President.

The President met with Counsellor to the President Edwin Meese III, William H. Webster, Director of the Federal Bureau of Investigation, and two FBI agents. The agents then conducted a private interview with the President as part of the investigation of the assassination attempt.

On behalf of the President, the Vice President met with Republican members of the House Appropriations Committee.

The White House issued the following medical report:

Following morning surgical rounds, physicians at George Washington University Hospital report that the President's condition has improved further. His temperature returned to near normal last night and has remained at this level. Stand-

ard X-ray facilities were temporarily established in the Presidential suite yesterday. Posterior-anterior and lateral chest X-rays since that time show some apparent clearing of the lung infiltrates, although radiographic abnormalities related to the injury and surgery persist, as expected. All cultures remain negative, and the President continues to receive broad spectrum antibiotic coverage. The President is in excellent spirits. His color is good, and he is eating well.

Following morning surgical rounds, physicians at the George Washington University Hospital report that Press Secretary James S. Brady had a restful night and continues to recuperate uneventfully. Mr. Brady sat up in a chair twice yesterday. He can now drink by himself and is eating solid foods on a regular basis. Yesterday Mr. Brady was evaluated by the physical therapy and occupational therapy staffs, who have initiated appropriate treatment programs.

Secret Service Agent Timothy J. McCarthy was discharged from the hospital this morning in good condition and is scheduled for a routine followup visit with his surgeon next week. The President visited with Agent McCarthy, his wife Carolyn, Jerry Parr, and Dave Fischer at 10:04 a.m. They shook hands, exchanged pleasantries and chatted briefly about the incident. Mr. McCarthy told the President about an offer by W. Clement Stone for the use of his condominium in Acapulco. The President urged Mr. McCarthy to go and have fun. As Mr. McCarthy was leaving, the President said to him, "I wish you well on your vacation and trip to Mexico, and I thank you from the bottom of my heart."

Physicians at Washington Hospital Center report that Officer Thomas Delahanty's condition continues good. His temperature is normal. He is expected to remain on antibiotics for another 24 hours as a precautionary measure.

April 8

The President met with members of the White House staff and received his national security briefing in his room at George Washington University Hospital.

Mrs. Reagan visited the President at the hospital.

The President met in his room at the hospital with:

—Senator Paul Laxalt of Nevada;

—the Vice President and Senate Majority Leader Howard H. Baker, Jr.;

—John B. Connally, former Governor of Texas;

—Mike Reagan, his son.

The White House issued the following medical report:

Following morning surgical rounds, physicians at George Washington University Hospital report that the President continues his progressive improvement. His temperature, which was mildly elevated last evening, is essentially normal this morning. Chest X-rays today show significant clearing of the previously described lung infiltrates, which are now barely perceptible. Although antibiotic coverage is being continued, the President is no longer receiving any oxygen therapy. The President has been ambulating with increasing vigor and is described as animated in his conversations with physicians and visitors.

Following morning surgical rounds, physicians at George Washington University Hospital report that Press Secretary James S. Brady continues to make satisfactory progress. Mr. Brady spent much of yesterday napping but sat up in his chair for dinner. A further routine CT scan was performed last evening. It shows continued resolution of the injury site with no evidence of complications.

Physicians at Washington Hospital Center report that Officer Thomas Delahanty is progressing nicely. Antibiotics have been discontinued, and he has no fever. He is up and around. No discharge date has been determined.

April 9

The President met with members of the White House staff and received his national security briefing in his room at George Washington University Hospital.

Mrs. Reagan visited the President at the hospital.

The President met in his room at the hospital with:

—Senate Minority Leader Robert C. Byrd and House Minority Leader Robert H. Michel;

—Secretary of the Treasury Donald T. Regan;

—Attorney General William French Smith.

On behalf of the President, the Vice President chaired a meeting of the Cabinet Council on Economic Affairs.

The White House issued the following medical report:

Following morning surgical rounds, physicians at George Washington University Hospital report that the President continues to make highly satisfactory progress. His temperature has stayed down for the past 24 hours and remains normal this morning. Chest X-rays show steady post-operative resolution. One antibiotic, Topramycin, has been discontinued. Chest physical therapy has also been terminated. The President continues to be active and in good spirits.

Press Secretary James S. Brady continues his uneventful recuperation. His temperature has been normal, and antibiotic therapy was stopped this morning. Mr. Brady naps occasionally through the day, but has been receiving a limited number of visitors, including the Vice President, who met with Mr. Brady yesterday afternoon.

April 10

The President met with members of the White House staff and received his national security briefing in his room at George Washington University Hospital.

Mrs. Reagan visited the President at the hospital.

The President met with the Vice President in his room at the hospital.

The White House announced that the bilateral border summit meeting between Presidents Reagan and José López Portillo, originally scheduled for April 27–28, has had to be postponed and that the Governments of the United States and Mexico will seek to reschedule the meeting at the earliest, mutually convenient time.

Counsellor to the President Edwin Meese III announced that the administration is forming an interdepartmental task force on Puerto Rico. The Task Force will be composed of Assistant Secretaries from Treasury, Defense, State, Justice, Commerce, Agriculture, and Health and Human Services, and representatives of the Office of the Vice President, Office of Management and Budget, and the White House policy development staff. The task force will be chaired by Assistant to the President for Intergovernmental Affairs Richard S. Williamson, and overall coordination of task force activities will be the responsibility of the White House Intergovernmental Affairs Office. The task force will consider the development of policy options on economic, social, and geopolitical issues.

The President today declared a major disaster for the State of Alabama as a result of tornadoes, severe storms, and flooding in Russell County, beginning on March 31, which caused extensive property damage.

During a morning press briefing, Dr. Dennis O'Leary, dean for clinical affairs, George Washington University Hospital, gave the following medical report:

[The President is] doing extremely well. He had another excellent day. Yesterday was still yet his best day. He has no temperature elevation, I think, by any criterion. His white blood cell count is now within the normal range, and he looks excellent. I had a chance to chat with him a couple of minutes this morning. I see a lot of patients in hospitals, and on a relative basis, I think he looks really outstanding. On the chest X-ray this morning, in the area of the bullet track—which is an area that will eventually scar down—there's a little lucent or transparent area that's a little bit less than a half inch in diameter, and it's an area that we would like to watch for another 24 hours or so before we definitively commit ourselves to a discharge time. The greatest likelihood is that that's an area that had a little bit of blood in it, that that blood became liquified and that he coughed it up. And now we're seeing just a little tiny pocket there. Our overall plan is to take another chest X-ray in the morning. If that looks stable, he will probably be discharged tomorrow. If there's any reason to be concerned about that at all, we'll probably take a few more sophisticated X-rays in the afternoon and evaluate those. If those are all right, he'll probably still leave the hospital tomorrow. If there's, again, any significant concern at all, we'll probably keep him until Sunday and get one more chest X-ray to evaluate it. The chances of his hospital stay extending beyond Sunday are really quite remote, because by all measures he's doing extremely well.

[Press Secretary James S.] Brady's doing fine again this morning. I think at this juncture, we all ought to keep our expectations at a reasonable level. His progress from here on out is going to be slower, and we're talking now weeks, months of recuperation and a lot of hard work for Jim Brady to regain as much function as possible. We feel very optimistic about his mental state, about the return of his personality. He may not be precisely the way he was before, and undoubtedly there will be some subtle changes. But they may be so subtle that even the people who are very close to him are going to have trouble identifying those.

April 11

The President met with members of the White House staff in his room at George Washington University Hospital. Mrs. Reagan and his daughter Patti accompanied him on his return to the White House.

April 12

On behalf of the President, the Vice President spoke at the Founder's Day and Centennial Celebration ceremonies at Tuskegee Institute in Tuskegee, Ala.

April 13

The President met with members of the White House staff and received his national security briefing in the Residence.

The President met in the Residence with:
—the Vice President and Secretary of State Alexander M. Haig, Jr.;

—the Vice President and Secretary of Defense Caspar W. Weinberger.

The White House announced that physicians at George Washington University Hospital said that Press Secretary James S. Brady, who was wounded during the attempted assassination of the President on March 30, continues to make satisfactory progress. He is more talkative and in good spirits.

April 14

The President met with members of the White House staff and received his national security briefing in the Residence.

The President met with the Vice President, David A. Stockman, Director of the Office of Management and Budget, and members of the White House staff to discuss legislative strategy.

The President spoke by telephone with Press Secretary James S. Brady.

The Vice President represented the President at funeral services for Gen. Omar N. Bradley held at the National Cathedral. Mrs. Reagan and Mrs. Bush accompanied the Vice President.

April 15

The President met with the Vice President and members of the White House staff and received his national security briefing in the Residence.

On behalf of the President, the Vice President chaired a meeting of the Cabinet Council on Commerce and Trade.

April 16

The President met with members of the White House staff and received his national security briefing in the Residence.

The President met with Joseph M.A.H. Luns, Secretary General of the North Atlantic Treaty Organization, the Vice President, and Secretary of State Alexander M. Haig, Jr., in the Residence.

On behalf of the President, the Vice President chaired meetings of:
—the Cabinet Council on Economic Affairs;
—the Cabinet.

The White House announced that physicians at George Washington University Hospital reported that Press Secretary James S. Brady is continuing his steady recuperation. There is slow but significant recovery of the hip and thigh muscles of his left leg. All medications have now been discontinued.

April 17

The President met with members of the White House staff and received his national security briefing in the Residence.

The President met in the Residence with:
—speechwriter Kenneth Khachigian;

—Terence Cardinal Cooke, Archbishop of New York.

April 20

The President met with members of the White House staff and received his national security briefing in the Residence.

The President spoke by telephone with Members of Congress to discuss the program for economic recovery.

The President spoke by telephone with former President Gerald R. Ford to discuss the former President's participation in speeches he will deliver during the congressional recess.

The White House announced that physicians at George Washington University Hospital reported that Press Secretary James S. Brady, who was wounded during the attempted assassination of the President on March 30, remains in satisfactory condition. It was noted that the announcement of April 16 overlooked the fact that Mr. Brady was continuing to receive standard antiseizure and antihypertensive medication. This information is germane to the management of his care over the past weekend. Early in the weekend, Mr. Brady developed a generalized rash and temperature elevation, which eventually reached high levels. Appropriate culture and specimen smears, including spinal fluid, were obtained, and following infectious diseases consultation, broad spectrum antibiotic coverage was initiated. Because no evidence of infection has been identified and Mr. Brady's white blood cell count is normal, it is believed that his rash and temperature elevations were due to a drug reaction. Therefore, the previous antiseizure and antihypertensive medications were discontinued, and acceptable alternative medications have been started. This morning Mr. Brady's rash has faded, and his temperature is only slightly elevated. He remains alert and in good spirits.

April 21

The President met with members of the White House staff and received his national security briefing in the Residence.

The President spoke by telephone with Members of Congress to discuss the program for economic recovery. One call announced by the White House was to Representative Eugene V. Atkinson of Pennsylvania, who was appearing on the radio broadcast "A.M. Connection" in Beaver Falls, Pa.

The President met with Governors James A. Rhodes of Ohio, Richard L. Thornburgh of Pennsylvania, Pierre S. du Pont IV of Delaware, Bill Clements of Texas, David Treen of Louisiana, Robert Orr of Indiana, Frank White of Arkansas, and Forrest D. James, Jr., of Alabama, to discuss the program for economic recovery.

The White House announced that the President has made a decision on the sale of military equipment to Saudi Arabia. The United States has made a commitment to Saudi Arabia to move forward with the enhancement of the F-15 aircraft, which include conformal fuel tanks, AIM-9L air-to-air missiles, which will augment the defense role of the F-15's, and to respond to the Saudis' request for air refueling capability. In addition the United States has approved the sale of five airborne warning and control system (AWACS) aircraft, subject to congressional approval. The administration has been and will continue to consult with the congressional leadership. A decision has not been made as to when and how the package will be submitted to Congress.

Secretary of Defense Caspar W. Weinberger represented the President at funeral services for former heavyweight boxing champion Joe Louis, held in the Memorial Chapel at Fort Myer, Va.

The White House announced that physicians at George Washington University Hospital reported that Press Secretary James S. Brady continues his slow but steady neurologic improvement. The drug reaction which developed over the past weekend is resolving satisfactorily as Mr. Brady's rash and temperature elevation continue to diminish.

April 22

The President met with members of the White House staff and received his national security briefing in the Residence.

The President spoke by telephone with Members of Congress to discuss the program for economic recovery.

The President met with Assistant to the President for Presidential Personnel E. Pendleton James, and members of his staff to discuss pending personnel announcements.

April 23

The President met with members of the White House staff and received his national security briefing in the Residence.

The President spoke by telephone with Members of Congress to discuss the program for economic recovery.

The President met with Senate Majority Leader Howard H. Baker, Jr., and members of the White House staff to discuss the sale of the AWACS aircraft to Saudi Arabia and the F-15 enhancement package. They also discussed the President's plans to address a joint session of the Congress on April 28. The White House later announced that the President had spoken by telephone with Speaker of the House Thomas P.

O'Neill, Jr., on April 22 to discuss the planned address on the program for economic recovery.

The President met with Assistant to the President for Presidential Personnel E. Pendleton James and members of his staff to discuss pending personnel announcements.

The White House announced that physicians at George Washington University Hospital reported that Press Secretary James S. Brady was transferred back to his hospital room from the recovery room earlier in the morning. His vital signs, including temperature, are normal, and he remains in satisfactory condition following additional surgery. He has slept intermittently through the night as the usual effects of anesthesia wear off, but he is readily awakened and responds normally to questions. Comprehensive cultures were obtained during the course of last night's 5-hour surgical procedure. Physicians caution that several days of careful monitoring will be required before the effectiveness of the surgery can be adequately assessed. Mr. Brady continues to receive broad spectrum antibiotic coverage.

The President announced the designation of Joseph Coors of Golden, Colo., to represent the United States at the annual Australia-America Friendship Week celebrations in Australia April 30-May 8. Mr. Coors will be accompanied on his trip by his wife, Holly Coors, and the Department of State's Director of Australian and New Zealand Affairs, Frank Bennett, Jr.

April 24
The President met with members of the White House staff and received his national security briefing in the Residence.

The President met at the White House with:
—the Cabinet;
—Senator Paul Laxalt of Nevada.

The White House announced that physicians at George Washington University Hospital reported that Press Secretary James S. Brady continues to progress satisfactorily in his recovery from surgery Wednesday evening. His vital signs remain stable, and his temperature, which was slightly elevated last evening, is normal this morning. He is eating well, is alert, and is talking. A postoperative CT scan performed yesterday afternoon shows good resolution of the intracranial air and is otherwise satisfactory. While there remains no evidence of infection, Mr. Brady continues to be carefully monitored by the neurosurgical and infectious diseases staffs.

April 25
The President left the White House for a weekend stay at Camp David, Md.

The White House issued a medical report on Press Secretary James S. Brady, who was wounded during the attempted assassination of the President on March 30. Mr. Brady continues his satisfactory recovery from surgery earlier in the week.

April 27
The President returned to the White House from Camp David and met with speechwriter Kenneth Khachigian.

The White House issued a medical report on Press Secretary James S. Brady, who continues an uneventful recovery from last week's surgery.

April 28
The President met in the Roosevelt Room with the Vice President, Secretary of the Treasury Donald T. Regan, David A. Stockman, Director of the Office of Management and Budget, Murray L. Weidenbaum, Chairman of the Council of Economic Advisers, Richard Richards, chairman of the Republican National Committee, and Republican congressional leaders, to discuss the program for economic recovery.

The President met with members of the White House staff, received his national security briefing, and discussed his address before the Congress with speechwriter Kenneth Khachigian in the Oval Office.

The President has transmitted to the Congress the 15th annual report of the National Endowment for the Humanities for fiscal year 1980 and the annual report for fiscal year 1980 of the National Endowment for the Arts and the National Council on the Arts.

April 29
The President met with members of the White House staff and then received his national security briefing in the Oval Office.

The White House announced that President Reagan and President José López Portillo will meet in Washington, D.C., on June 8 and 9, to continue their close consultations on matters of interest to both countries. President Reagan has accepted the gracious offer of President López Portillo to come to Washington, D.C., for the working visit originally scheduled to be held this month in Tijuana and San Diego. During the visit, the two Presidents will confer privately at Camp David.

The White House issued a medical report on Press Secretary James S. Brady, who remains in satisfactory condition.

April 30
The President met with members of the White House staff and then received his national security briefing in the Oval Office.

The President met at the White House with:
—Kurt Waldheim, Secretary General of the United Nations, and the Vice President;

—the National Security Council;
—Members of the House of Representatives to discuss the program for economic recovery.

The President transmitted the following reports to the Congress:

—the annual report of the Corporation for Public Broadcasting for fiscal year 1980;
—the 13th annual report of the U.S.-Japan Cooperative Medical Science Program, covering calendar year 1980;
—the 14th annual report on the Operation of the Automotive Products Trade Act of 1965;
—the 1980 annual report of the Federal Council on the Aging;
—the annual report for fiscal year 1980 of the Administration on Aging.

May 1

The President met with members of the White House staff and then received his national security briefing in the Oval Office.

The President met at the White House with:
—speechwriter Kenneth Khachigian;
—Members of the House of Representatives to discuss the program for economic recovery;
—Prince Charles of the United Kingdom.

The White House issued a medical report on Press Secretary James S. Brady, who remains in satisfactory condition.

May 2

The President announced the appointment of George H. Aldrich to serve on the Iran-U.S. Claims Tribunal, pursuant to the Claims Settlement Agreement of January 19, 1981. Ambassador Aldrich will replace Judge Malcolm R. Wilkey, who was appointed on April 17 but who, on May 2, requested that the President replace him on the Tribunal because of the heavy caseload of his own court, the U.S. Court of Appeals for the District of Columbia Circuit. Ambassador Aldrich is the former Deputy Special Representative of the President for the Law of the Sea Conference, 1977–81. In April 1981 he was nominated by the Secretary of State to be the new U.S. member of the United Nations International Law Commission.

May 4

The President met with members of the White House staff and received his national security briefing in the Oval Office.

Throughout the morning, the President met with the Vice President and Members of the House of Representatives in the Oval Office to discuss the program for economic recovery.

The White House issued a medical report on Press Secretary James S. Brady, who was wounded during the attempted assassination of the President on March 30. Mr. Brady remains in satisfactory condition.

May 5

The President met with members of the White House staff and received his national security briefing in the Oval Office.

The President met with Ambassador Philip C. Habib in the Oval Office. The President has asked Ambassador Habib to travel to the Middle East as his emissary to consult with and seek the views of the leaders of Lebanon, Syria, and Israel in exploring ways to reduce tensions produced by recent developments surrounding the situation in Lebanon.

The President and Mrs. Reagan had lunch with Senator and Mrs. Robert Dole, Assistants to the President James A. Baker III and Michael K. Deaver.

In the afternoon, the President met with the Vice President and Members of the House of Representatives in the Oval Office to discuss the program for economic recovery.

The President met with Ambassador Ephraim Evron of Israel in the Oval Office.

The White House issued a medical report on Press Secretary James S. Brady, who remains in satisfactory condition following a third surgical procedure on Monday night to prevent the passage of large blood clots into his lungs from his legs or pelvis.

May 6

The President met with members of the White House staff and received his national security briefing in the Oval Office. The Vice President was present for the briefing.

The President met with the Vice President and Members of the House of Representatives in the Oval Office to discuss the program for economic recovery.

The President, the Vice President, and other administration officials met in the Cabinet Room for a working luncheon to prepare for the visit of Prime Minister Zenko Suzuki of Japan.

In a ceremony in the Rose Garden, the Vice President accepted on behalf of the President the honorary chairmanship of the Freedoms Foundation at Valley Forge.

The President announced the appointment of seven government officials as members of the Board of Directors of the National Consumer Cooperative Bank. They are:

Deputy Secretary of Commerce Joseph R. Wright, Jr.
Assistant Secretary of Housing and Urban Development Philip D. Winn
Assistant Attorney General Carol E. Dinkins
Assistant Secretary of Labor Albert Angrisani
Assistant Secretary of the Treasury Roger W. Mehle, Jr.

Assistant Secretary of Agriculture William G. Lesher
Deputy Secretary of Transportation Darrell M. Trent

The White House issued a medical report on Press Secretary James S. Brady, who remains in satisfactory condition.

May 7

The President met with members of the White House staff and received his national security briefing in the Oval Office. The Vice President was present for the briefing.

The President met in the Oval Office with Representatives Phil Gramm of Texas and Delbert L. Latta of Ohio to discuss the upcoming House vote on the fiscal year 1982 budget resolution.

May 8

The President met with members of the White House staff and received his national security briefing in the Oval Office.

The President met with House Minority Leader Robert H. Michel in the Oval Office to discuss the House of Representatives approval of the fiscal year 1982 budget resolution.

The President met in the Oval Office with U.S. Ambassador-designate to the United Kingdom John J. Louis, Jr., and Senator S. I. Hayakawa of California.

The President left the White House for a weekend stay at Camp David, Md.

The White House issued a medical report on Press Secretary James S. Brady, who remains in satisfactory condition.

May 10

The President returned to the White House from Camp David, Md., and then observed Mother's Day with members of his family.

May 11

The President met with members of the White House staff and then received his national security briefing in the Oval Office.

The President met at the White House with:
—the Cabinet Council on Human Resources;
—House Minority Leader Robert H. Michel and ranking Republican members of the standing committees of the House.

The White House issued a medical report on Press Secretary James S. Brady, who was wounded during the attempted assassination of the President on March 30. Mr. Brady is in good condition after another uneventful weekend.

May 12

The President met in the Cabinet Room with the Vice President, Secretary of the Treasury Donald T. Regan, David A. Stockman, Director of the Office of Management and Budget, Deputy Secretary of Defense Frank C. Carlucci,

Murray L. Weidenbaum, Chairman of the Council of Economic Advisers, and Republican congressional leaders.

The President met with members of the White House staff and received his national security briefing in the Oval Office.

The President met at the White House with:
—Secretary of the Treasury Donald T. Regan and David A. Stockman, Director of the Office of Management and Budget;
—members of the executive committee and standing committee chairmen of the National Governors' Association.

May 13

The President met with members of the White House staff and then received his national security briefing in the Oval Office.

The President met in the Cabinet Room with the Vice President, a group of Democratic Senators, and members of the White House staff.

The President announced his intention to nominate Frank Sato to be Inspector General of the Veterans Administration. Mr. Sato was originally announced to be Inspector General of the Environmental Protection Agency on March 26.

The White House issued a medical report on Press Secretary James S. Brady, who remains in good condition as his activities continue to be gradually increased.

May 14

The President met with members of the White House staff and then received his national security briefing in the Oval Office.

The President met at the White House with:
—Senator Larry Pressler of South Dakota and Representatives Thomas B. Evans, Jr., of Delaware and John LeBoutillier of New York;
—Deputy Secretary of State William P. Clark, John A. Gavin, U.S. Ambassador to Mexico, and Assistant to the President for National Security Affairs Richard V. Allen;
—the Cabinet for a working lunch to discuss economic conditions and the legislative situation.

The President announced that he is according Herbert B. Thompson the personal rank of Ambassador while serving as head of the U.S. delegation to the meeting of the Inter-American Council for Education, Science and Culture to be held at Buenos Aires, Argentina, June 8–15, and the meeting of the Inter-American Economic and Social Council scheduled for Caracas, Venezuela, in September 1981. Mr. Thompson is Deputy U.S. Permanent Representative to the Organization of American States.

The President declared a major disaster for the State of Alabama as a result of severe storms and flooding in Mobile County during May 5–6, which caused extensive property damage.

May 15

The President met at the White House with:
—members of the White House staff;
—Minister of Foreign Affairs and Information F. Roelof Botha of South Africa, Secretary of State Alexander M. Haig, Jr., and Assistant to the President for National Security Affairs Richard V. Allen;
—the National Security Council;
—Minister of Foreign Affairs Stefan Andrei of Romania, Secretary of State Alexander M. Haig, Jr., and Assistant to the President for National Security Affairs Richard V. Allen.

The President transmitted to the Congress the second annual report of the Powerplant and Industrial Fuel Use Act of 1978.

The White House issued a report on Press Secretary James S. Brady, who continues to make satisfactory progress and remains in good condition.

May 16

The President met in the Oval Office with Prince Turki al-Faisal, adviser to King Khalid bin Abd al-Aziz Al-Sa'ud of Saudi Arabia, to discuss the situation in the Middle East.

May 17

On his return flight to Andrews Air Force Base, Md., after addressing graduates at commencement ceremonies at the University of Notre Dame in South Bend, Ind., the President telephoned Senator Robert Dole, chairman of the Senate Finance Committee, from Air Force One, to discuss the President's tax cut proposals.

May 18

The President met with members of the White House staff and then received his national security briefing in the Oval Office.

The President met in the Oval Office with Paul A. Volcker, Chairman of the Board of Governors of the Federal Reserve System. Also attending the meeting were Counsellor to the President Edwin Meese III, Assistant to the President James A. Baker III, David A. Stockman, Director of the Office of Management and Budget, and Assistant to the President for Policy Development Martin Anderson.

The President has transmitted the 1981 budget supplemental of the District of Columbia to the Congress and has asked the Congress to consider the proposed supplemental for fiscal year 1981 in the amount of $17 million from the District of Columbia's own revenues.

The White House issued a medical report on Press Secretary James S. Brady, who was wounded during the attempted assassination of the President on March 30. Mr. Brady remains in good condition after a quiet weekend.

May 19

The President met with members of the White House staff and then received his national security briefing in the Oval Office.

May 20

The President met with members of the White House staff and then received his national security briefing in the Oval Office.

The President met at the White House with:
—Secretary of the Treasury Donald T. Regan;
—the Cabinet Council on Commerce and Trade;
—members of the White House staff, for a working lunch.

May 21

The President met with members of the White House staff and then received his national security briefing in the Oval Office.

The White House issued a medical report on Press Secretary James S. Brady, who remains in good condition as he progresses into a more active physical therapy program.

May 22

The President met in the Cabinet Room with the National Security Council and then met with members of the White House staff in the Oval Office.

The President left the White House for a visit to his ranch, Rancho del Cielo, near Santa Barbara, Calif.

May 23

In the morning, the President received his national security briefing at his ranch, Rancho del Cielo, near Santa Barbara, Calif.

The President announced the appointments of the following Department of Defense personnel:

Gen. Richard L. Lawson, USAF, for reassignment to the position of Chief of Staff, Supreme Headquarters Allied Powers Europe. General Lawson is presently serving as U.S. Representative to the NATO Military Committee.

Lt. Gen. Paul X. Kelley, USMC, nominated for promotion to the grade of general and assignment as Assistant Commandant of the Marine Corps and Chief of Staff, Headquarters, U.S. Marine Corps. General Kelley is currently serving as Commander, Rapid Deployment Joint Task Force, MacDill A.F.B., Fla.

Gen. William Y. Smith, USAF, for reassignment to the position of Deputy Commander-in-Chief, United States European Command. General Smith is currently serving as Chief of Staff, Supreme Headquarters, Allied Powers, Europe.

Gen. James R. Allen, USAF, for reassignment to the positon of Commander-in-Chief, Military Airlift Command. General Allen is currently assigned as Deputy Commander-in-Chief, United States European Command.

Rear Adm. James A. Lyons, Jr., USN, nominated for promotion to the grade of vice admiral and assignment as Commander, Second Fleet. Admiral Lyons is currently serving as Commander, Naval Surface Group, Western Pacific.

Maj. Gen. John W. McEnery, USA, nominated for promotion to the grade of lieutenant general and assignment as Chairman, Inter-American Defense Board. General McEnery is currently serving as Chief of Staff, United States Army Forces Command, Fort McPherson, Ga.

May 25

In the morning, the President received his national security briefing at his ranch, Rancho del Cielo, near Santa Barbara, Calif.

May 26

The President returned to the White House from his visit to California.

The White House issued a medical report on Press Secretary James S. Brady, who was wounded during the attempted assassination of the President on March 30. Mr. Brady remains in good condition as he continues to show steady neurological improvement.

May 28

The President met with members of the White House staff and then received his national security briefing in the Oval Office.

The President met at the White House with:
—members of the White House staff;
—Avital Shcharanskiy, wife of Soviet dissident Anatoly Shcharanskiy, Soviet Jewish dissident Iosif Mendelevich, and the Vice President;
—the Vice President, for lunch;
—the National Security Council;
—the Cabinet.

The President transmitted to the Congress the 1980 annual report on the Administration of the Radiation Control for Health and Safety Act.

The President has declared a major disaster for the State of Montana as a result of severe storms and flooding, beginning on or about May 19, which caused extensive property damage.

The White House issued a medical report on Press Secretary James S. Brady, who has developed moderate to high temperature elevations over the past 48 hours, but remains in good condition.

May 29

The President met with members of the White House staff and received his national security briefing in the Oval Office.

The President met at the White House with:
—Ambassador Philip C. Habib, the President's emissary in consultations in the Middle East;
—the Cabinet Council on Commerce and Trade;
—U.S. Ambassadors Robert D. Nesen (Australia), John A. Burroughs (Malawi), and Arthur H. Woodruff (Central African Republic).

The White House issued a medical report on Press Secretary James S. Brady, who, having now been diagnosed as having lower left lobe pneumonia, is responding satisfactorily to antibiotic therapy and remains in good condition.

The White House announced that the President has appointed Representative Clement J. Zablocki, chairman of the House Foreign Affairs Committee, and Representative William S. Broomfield, ranking minority member of the House Foreign Affairs Committee, to serve as Special Representatives of the President and Cochairmen of the Presidential delegation to the funeral of Stefan Cardinal Wyszynski. Other members of the delegation are: John Cardinal Krol, Archbishop of Philadelphia; Aloysius Mazewski, president of the Polish American Congress; the Honorable Francis J. Meehan, Ambassador to Poland; and the Honorable William Wilson, Personal Envoy of the President to the Holy See. They will arrive in Warsaw May 30 and will participate in the funeral services for Cardinal Wyszynski in Warsaw's Victory Square on May 31.

May 30

The White House issued a medical report on Press Secretary James S. Brady, who was wounded during the attempted assassination of the President on March 30. Mr. Brady, who has now been diagnosed as having left lower lobe pneumonia, has responded well to antibiotic therapy.

June 1

The President met with members of the White House staff and then received his national security briefing in the Oval Office.

The President met at the White House with:
—Senator Alan K. Simpson of Wyoming;
—Senator Edward M. Kennedy of Massachusetts;
—Democratic congressional leaders, the Vice President, Secretary of the Treasury Donald T. Regan, and members of the White House staff;

—the Vice President and a group of Governors and mayors, to discuss the program for economic recovery;

—the National Security Council.

The White House issued a medical report on Press Secretary James S. Brady, who spent a quiet weekend and remains in good condition.

June 2

The President met in the Cabinet Room with Republican congressional leaders, the Vice President, Secretary of the Treasury Donald T. Regan, David A. Stockman, Director of the Office of Management and Budget, Under Secretary of Health and Human Services David B. Swoap, and Richard Richards, chairman of the Republican National Committee.

The President met with members of the White House staff and then received his national security briefing in the Oval Office.

The President met with the Cabinet in the Cabinet Room.

The President visited Press Secretary James S. Brady in his room at George Washington University Hospital.

The President announced that he has instructed the Administrator of the Small Business Administration to provide assistance under programs administered by that agency in the flood-stricken area of Austin, Tex. That action will make available long-term, low-interest rate loans to aid homeowners and businesses in repairing flood damage. In addition, insurance claims are already being processed under a federally subsidized program administered by the Federal Insurance Administration. The President expressed appreciation for the timely and humane assistance being rendered by the Red Cross and other voluntary organizations, as well as the excellent cooperation on the part of State and local officials. While recognizing the fine work by such groups, the President also praised the efforts of the citizens and local businesses. The President realizes the suffering and hardship occasioned by this serious event and has instructed the designated Federal agencies to provide help in a timely manner.

June 3

The President met with members of the White House staff and then received his national security briefing in the Oval Office.

The President met at the White House with:

—orchestral conductor Dimri Shostakovich;

—a group of mayors to discuss the program for economic recovery;

—the graduating class of the Congressional Page School;

—Representative Tom Loeffler of Texas;

—Representative Sam B. Hall, Jr., of Texas;

—Senate Minority Leader Robert C. Byrd;

—Anita Wagner and Jan Smith, the Multiple Sclerosis Mother and Father of the Year, and Frank Sinatra, national campaign chairman of the National Multiple Sclerosis Society;

—Senate Majority Leader Howard H. Baker, Jr., Senators Jesse Helms of North Carolina, and Strom Thurmond of South Carolina, and the Vice President.

The President attended a White House reception for representatives of TIME, Inc., and European businessmen.

The President has announced that he has accorded the personal rank of Ambassador to James Stromayer during the period of June 1 through August 31, while he serves as the United States Coordinator for the United Nations Conference on New and Renewable Sources of Energy. The conference will be held in Nairobi, Kenya, August 10–12.

The President announced his intention to nominate the following to be members of the Board of Directors of the Commodity Credit Corporation:

Richard E. Lyng, Deputy Secretary of Agriculture;

Frank W. Naylor, Jr., Under Secretary of Agriculture for Small Community and Rural Development;

Mary Caliborne Jarratt, Assistant Secretary of Agriculture for Food and Consumer Services.

The President transmitted to the Congress the 1980 annual report of the Federal Prevailing Rate Advisory Committee.

The White House announced that Secretary of the Navy John F. Lehman, Jr., represented the President at the funeral of former Representative Carl Vinson in Milledgeville, Ga., on June 3.

June 4

The President met with members of the White House staff and then received his national security briefing in the Oval Office.

The President met at the White House with:

—Representative Jack F. Kemp of New York;

—a group of mayors and city officials to discuss the program for economic recovery;

—Republican members of the House Ways and Means Committee;

—Republican members of the Senate Finance Committee;

—members of the House Conservative Democratic Forum;

—the National Security Council;

—Secretary of Agriculture John R. Block.

In a ceremony in the Oval Office, the President received diplomatic credentials from Ambassadors Mohamoud Haji Nur of the Somali Democratic Republic, Salah Hadji Farah Dirir of the Republic of Djibouti, Henricus A. F. Heidweiller of the Republic of Suriname, Dr. José

Rafael Molina Morillo of the Dominican Republic, and Dr. Joseph Saye Guannu of the Republic of Liberia.

The President met with members of the President's Commission on White House Fellowships in the Rose Garden at the White House.

At the invitation of the President, the following foreign leaders will visit Washington, D.C., at the times indicated:

Prime Minister Malcolm Fraser of Australia, June 30, for an official visit;

President Anwar el-Sadat of Egypt, August 5–6, for a state visit;

Prime Minister Menachem Begin of Israel, September 9–10, for an official visit;

King Hussein of Jordan, November 2–3, for a state visit;

Queen Beatrix and Prince Claus of the Netherlands, April 19–22, 1982, for a state visit.

The President has asked Senators Barry Goldwater of Arizona and Paul Laxalt of Nevada and Representative Barry M. Goldwater, Jr., of California to represent him at the Paris Air Show, June 4–10.

The White House issued a medical report on Press Secretary James S. Brady, who remains in good condition as he continues to make satisfactory progress in his recovery.

June 5

The President met with members of the White House staff and received his national security briefing in the Oval Office.

The President met at the White House with:
— members of the White House staff for a working luncheon to discuss the upcoming visit of President José López Portillo of Mexico;
— Ambassador William E. Brock, United States Trade Representative;
— a group of mayors and city officials to discuss the program for economic recovery;
— Minister of External Relations Claude Cheysson of France and the Vice President.

The President transmitted to the Congress the 1976 annual report on Occupational Safety and Health as prepared by the Department of Labor.

The President left the White House for a weekend stay at Camp David, Md.

June 7

The President returned to the White House from Camp David, Md.

June 8

The President met with members of the White House staff and then received his national security briefing in the Oval Office.

June 9

The President met with members of the White House staff in the Oval Office.

The President announced his intention to nominate William R. Gianelli, Assistant Secretary of the Army (Civil Works), to be a member of the Board of the Panama Canal Commission.

The White House issued a medical report on Press Secretary James S. Brady, who was wounded during the attempted assassination of the President on March 30. Mr. Brady remains in good condition and continues his satisfactory progress.

June 10

The President met with members of the White House staff and then received his national security briefing in the Oval Office.

The President met at the White House with:
— the Vice President and Senator William V. Roth, Jr., of Delaware;
— the National Security Council;
— George Shultz, Chairman of the President's Economic Policy Advisory Board;
— Senate Majority Leader Howard H. Baker, Jr., and Senator Pete V. Domenici of New Mexico;
— former Secretary of State Henry A. Kissinger.

The President announced his intention to nominate Under Secretary of State for Management Richard T. Kennedy to be Representative of the United States of America to the International Atomic Energy Agency, with the rank of Ambassador.

The White House announced that the President and Mrs. Reagan will serve as honorary chairmen of the Save the Children's 50th Anniversary Committee.

June 11

The President met with members of the White House staff and received his national security briefing in the Oval Office.

The President met at the White House with:
— a group of labor union presidents;
— the President's Economic Policy Advisory Board;
— Secretary of Agriculture John R. Block.

The President attended the Evening Parade at the Marine Barracks in Washington, D.C.

The White House announced that King Juan Carlos I and Queen Sofia of Spain have accepted an invitation from the President and Mrs. Reagan to pay a state visit to Washington. The visit will take place in September at a date to be announced.

June 12

The President met with members of the White House staff and received his national security briefing in the Oval Office.

The President met at the White House with:

—the Cabinet Council on Commerce and Trade;
—a group of mayors;
—the National Security Council;
—the Vice President, for lunch.

In a ceremony in the Oval Office, the President received diplomatic credentials from Ambassadors Arturo J. Cruz of Nicaragua, Nelson Thompson Mizere of Malawi, Ernesto Rivas Gallont of El Salvador, Georges N. Leger, Jr., of Haiti, and Vasco Luis Caldeira Coelho Futscher Pereira of Portugal.

June 15

The President met with members of the White House staff and then received his national security briefing in the Oval Office.

The President met at the White House with:
—the Presidential Task Force on the Arts and Humanities;
—Republican members of the House Ways and Means Committee to discuss tax legislation;
—Members of the Senate to discuss footwear imports;
—Democratic Members of the Senate to discuss tax legislation;
—President El Hadj Omar Bongo of the Gabonese Republic.

The President has asked the Congress to consider proposed amendments to the requests for appropriations for fiscal year 1982 for the Department of Defense (Military) and for the Department of State.

The President has declared a major disaster for the Commonwealth of Pennsylvania as a result of severe storms and flooding, beginning on June 8, which caused extensive property damage.

June 16

The President met with Republican congressional leaders in the Cabinet Room at the White House.

The President met with members of the White House staff and then received his national security briefing in the Oval Office.

The President attended a reception given for former State Governors who are now U.S. Senators in the Blue Room at the White House.

The White House issued a medical report on Press Secretary James S. Brady, who was wounded during the attempted assassination of the President on March 30. Mr. Brady is making steady progress in recovering from his injury. He continues in an active physical therapy program in his hospital room. His vital signs remain normal, and he is in excellent spirits.

The President declared a major disaster for the State of Ohio as a result of severe storms, tornadoes, and flooding, beginning on June 13, which caused extensive property damage.

June 17

The President met with members of the White House staff and then received his national security briefing in the Oval Office.

The President spoke by telephone with Speaker of the House of Representatives Thomas P. O'Neill, Jr.

The President met at the White House with:
—members of Broadcast Pioneers, an organization of persons who developed and worked in the early broadcasting industry;
—U.S. Ambassador-designate to Lebanon Robert Sherwood Dillon, U.S. Ambassador to Egypt Alfred L. Atherton, and U.S. Ambassador-designate to Canada Paul Heron Robinson, Jr., for a courtesy visit prior to leaving for their posts.

The President and Secretary of Commerce Malcolm Baldrige went to Quantico Marine Base, Va., for several hours of horseback riding.

The President named the Vice President to head the U.S. delegation to the June 30 inauguration of President Ferdinand E. Marcos of the Philippines.

June 18

The President met with members of the White House staff and received his national security briefing in the Oval Office.

The President met in the Oval Office with Kansas State Senator Ross Doyen, president-elect of the National Conference of State Legislatures. He then met with Senator Doyen and other members of the executive board of the organization in the Cabinet Room.

The President met at the White House with:
—Loret M. Ruppe, Director of the Peace Corps;
—Members of Congress at a luncheon to discuss Federal budget and tax reduction legislation;
—the Cabinet.

The President nominated the following persons to be members of the Board of Directors of the National Consumer Cooperative Bank for the terms indicated:

For the remainder of the term expiring September 23, 1982

Assistant Attorney General Carol E. Dinkins
Assistant Secretary of Agriculture William Gene Lesher
Assistant Secretary of the Treasury Roger William Mehle, Jr.
Deputy Secretary of Transportation Darrell M. Trent
Assistant Secretary of Housing and Urban Development Philip D. Winn
Deputy Secretary of Commerce Joseph Robert Wright, Jr.

For the remainder of the term expiring June 10, 1983

Assistant Secretary of Labor Albert Angrisani

The President has asked the Congress to consider proposed supplemental appropriations for the fiscal year 1981 in the amount of $646,075,000 for the Department of Agriculture and a reduction in the request for appropriations for the fiscal year 1982 in the amount of $249,911,000 for the Postal Service.

June 19

The President met with members of the White House staff and then received his national security briefing in the Oval Office.

The President met at the White House with:

—Virginia State Republican candidates J. Marshall Coleman (Governor), Nathan H. Miller (Lieutenant Governor), and Wyatt B. Durrette (Attorney General);

—Secretary of Transportation Drew L. Lewis.

The President left the White House for a weekend stay at Camp David, Md.

June 21

The President returned to the White House from Camp David, Md.

June 22

The President met with members of the White House staff and then received his national security briefing in the Oval Office.

The President spoke by telephone with Secretary of Transportation Drew L. Lewis, who reported on the government's tentative contract agreement with the Professional Air Traffic Controllers Organization.

The President met with Governors George Busbee of Georgia, Richard A. Snelling of Vermont, Lamar Alexander of Tennessee, James R. Thompson, Jr., of Illinois, Pierre S. du Pont IV of Delaware, and Scott M. Matheson of Utah, to discuss the block grant proposals of the program for economic recovery.

The President met in the Oval Office with Senate Majority Leader Howard H. Baker, Jr., and House Minority Leader Robert H. Michel.

June 23

The President met with members of the White House staff and received his national security briefing in the Oval Office.

The President met at the White House with:

—Benjamin Hooks, executive director, and Margaret Bush Wilson, chairperson, National Association for the Advancement of Colored People;

—U.S. Ambassador to Italy Maxwell M. Rabb and U.S. Ambassador to Haiti Ernest Henry

Preeg, for a courtesy visit prior to leaving for their posts;

—oceanographer Jacques Cousteau;

—Republican members of the Senate Finance Committee to discuss Federal tax reduction legislation;

—the Cabinet Council on Commerce and Trade to discuss footwear imports;

—the Cabinet to discuss Federal budget and tax reduction legislation, the agreement with the air controllers, the President's Commission on Housing, and the Davis-Bacon Act;

—the Presidential Advisory Committee on Federalism.

The President announced the designation of three government officials to be members of the Board of Directors of the Overseas Private Investment Corporation. They are:

Assistant Secretary of State for Economic and Business Affairs Robert D. Hormats;

Assistant Secretary of Commerce for International Economic Policy Raymond J. Waldman;

Assistant Secretary of the Treasury (International Affairs) Marc E. Leland.

June 24

The President met with members of the White House staff and received his national security briefing in the Oval Office.

The President met in the Oval Office with Mayor Maynard Jackson of Atlanta, Ga.

The President left the White House for visits to San Antonio, Tex., Los Angeles and Santa Barbara, Calif., and Denver, Colo. Following his remarks to the United States Jaycees in San Antonio, Tex., the President went to Los Angeles, Calif., where he remained overnight at the Century Plaza Hotel.

June 25

In the morning, the President received his national security briefing in his suite at the Century Plaza Hotel. Later in the day, the President met at the hotel with Secretary of State Alexander M. Haig, Jr., who reported to the President on his trip to Asia, including meetings in Beijing with leaders of the People's Republic of China, the meeting of ASEAN in Manila, and the ANZUS meeting in New Zealand.

The White House announced that Prime Minister Pierre Elliott Trudeau of Canada will visit Washington on July 10. He will meet with the President to discuss issues related to the Ottawa summit which will be held July 20–21.

The White House announced that the President has invited Prime Minister Robert D. Muldoon of New Zealand to meet with him in Washington on July 24, and that the Prime Minister has accepted the President's invitation.

June 26

In the morning, the President received his national security briefing in his suite at the Century Plaza Hotel. The President and Mrs. Reagan then left Los Angeles for a visit to their ranch, Rancho del Cielo, near Santa Barbara, Calif.

The President announced the United States delegation which will accompany the Vice President to the inaugural ceremonies of President Ferdinand Marcos of the Philippines on June 30. Members of the delegation are:

Ambassador Richard Murphy, U.S. Ambassador to the Philippines

Gov. Robert Ray, of Iowa

Adm. Robert Long, Commander in Chief, Pacific

Adm. Daniel J. Murphy, USN (Ret.), Chief of Staff to the Vice President

Ambassador Clare Booth Luce

Van Cliburn

Efrem Zimbalist, Jr.

June 27

The Vice President visited the President at his ranch, Rancho del Cielo, near Santa Barbara, Calif., to report on his trip to France and the United Kingdom and his upcoming trip to the Philippines and Southeast and East Asia.

June 28

The President left his ranch, Rancho del Cielo, near Santa Barbara, Calif., for an overnight stay in Los Angeles, Calif.

June 29

The President left Los Angeles for Denver, Colo., where he addressed the annual convention of the National Association for the Advancement of Colored People. Following his remarks, the President returned to Washington, D.C.

June 30

The President met with members of the White House staff and then received his national security briefing in the Oval Office.

The President met at the White House with:
—Representative Jack H. Kemp of New York;
—Representative James T. Broyhill of North Carolina;
—Representative Joel H. Deckard of Indiana;
—Representative Christopher H. Smith of New Jersey;
—Representative David Michael Staton of West Virginia;
—Senator Strom Thurmond of South Carolina.

The White House announced that, acting upon recommendations of his Cabinet-level Trade Policy Committee, the President decided he would not seek an extension of the current restrictions on imports of nonrubber footwear from Taiwan and the Republic of Korea. The Orderly Marketing Agreements which limited the imports expired at midnight on June 30.

The President declared a major disaster for the State of Illinois as a result of severe storms, tornadoes, and flooding, beginning on June 13, which caused extensive property damage.

July 1

The President received his national security briefing and then met with members of the White House staff in the Oval Office.

The President met at the White House with:
—members of the board of directors of the National Association of Counties;
—the Cabinet to discuss a report of the Cabinet Task Force on Immigration and Refugee Policy.

July 2

The President met with members of the White House staff and then received his national security briefing in the Oval Office.

The President met at the White House with:
—George A. Keyworth, Director-designate of the Office of Science and Technology Policy;
—the National Security Council;
—members of the U.S. Business Committee on Jamaica and chairmen of the counterpart committees in Canada, Venezuela, and Jamaica;
—former regional Reagan State campaign chairmen.

In response to questions about the administration's policy of U.S. arms shipments to Israel following that country's attack on the Osirak nuclear facility near Baghdad, Iraq, on June 7, Deputy Press Secretary Larry M. Speakes made the following points to reporters:
—The suspension of arms sales to Israel announced on June 10 applies to the four F-16's which were scheduled to be shipped June 12.
—The review on whether there was a violation of the arms sale agreement continues, and no decisions have been made.
—The review is expected to be completed prior to any decision which is necessary on the future arms shipments of F-16's.

July 4

The President and Mrs. Reagan attended a birthday party for Mrs. Reagan at Woodlawn Plantation in Virginia. Following their return to the White House, they viewed the holiday fireworks display from the Residence.

July 6

The President met with members of the White House staff and received his national security briefing in the Oval Office.

The President met at the White House with:

—the Vice President;

—the National Security Council;

—Ambassador Philip C. Habib, the President's emissary in consultations in the Middle East, the Vice President, Secretary of State Alexander M. Haig, Jr., and members of the White House staff, for lunch;

—Secretary of Labor Raymond J. Donovan, who reported on his recent trip abroad;

—members of the executive committee of the Council of State Governments, to discuss block grant proposals and transportation matters.

The President has appointed M. Peter McPherson, Administrator of the Agency for International Development, as Special Coordinator for International Disaster Assistance.

The President transmitted to the Congress the annual report of the Commodity Credit Corporation for fiscal year 1980 and the annual report on the operation and activities of the Alaska Railroad for fiscal year 1980.

July 7

The President met with members of the White House staff and received his national security briefing in the Oval Office.

The President met at the White House with:

—members of the President's Commission on Housing;

—the Cabinet, to discuss the illegal aliens at Fort Chaffee, Ark.;

—Senator Jesse Helms of North Carolina.

During the day the President spoke by telephone with Chief Justice of the United States Warren E. Burger, Reese Smith, Jr., president of the American Bar Association, Senator Strom Thurmond, chairman of the Senate Judiciary Committee, former Associate Justice Potter Stewart, and Senate Majority Leader Howard H. Baker, Jr., to inform them of his intention to nominate Judge Sandra Day O'Connor to be an Associate Justice of the Supreme Court.

The President announced the appointments of the following officials to serve on the board of governors of the American National Red Cross Corporation for a term of 3 years:

Secretary of State Alexander M. Haig, Jr.

Secretary of Defense Caspar W. Weinberger

Secretary of Health and Human Services Richard S. Schweiker

Secretary of Education Terrel H. Bell

Assistant Secretary of Health and Human Services Edward N. Brandt, Jr.

Louis O. Giuffrida, Director, Federal Emergency Management Agency

Gen. David C. Jones, USAF, Chairman of the Joint Chiefs of Staff

July 8

The President met with members of the White House staff and received his national security briefing in the Oval Office.

The President attended the swearing-in ceremony in the Oval Office for Charles H. Dean, Jr., Chairman of the Board of Directors of the Tennessee Valley Authority.

The President and Deputy Secretary of State William P. Clark went to Quantico Marine Base, Va., for several hours of horseback riding.

July 9

The President met with members of the White House staff and received his national security briefing in the Oval Office.

The President met at the White House with:

—Senator Robert Dole of Kansas and a group of independent oil producers;

—Senator Jesse Helms of North Carolina and Duke University football coach Wallace Wade;

—Representative Paul S. Trible, Jr., of Virginia, and Rev. Michael David Anglin, former senior minister of 26 Washington-area Churches of Christ, who presented the President with a Bible;

—Representative Don Young of Alaska;

—Representative G. William Whitehurst of Virginia and Skip Wilkins, a community leader of Virginia Beach, Va., who presented the President with a copy of his book, "The Real Race," an inspirational account of his life following his paralysis caused by an accident;

—Spanish Minister of Foreign Affairs José Pedro Pérez Llorca;

—James E. Cheek, president of Howard University;

—the Vice President, for lunch;

—black supporters of the 1980 Reagan-Bush campaign;

—the National Security Council.

The President attended two receptions in the East Room at the White House for the Eagles, financial contributors to the Republican National Committee.

July 10

The President met with members of the White House staff and received his national security briefing in the Oval Office.

The President met at the White House with:

—members of the executive committee of the National Black Caucus of State Legislators;

—Republican Members of the Senate and House of Representatives.

In a ceremony in the Oval Office, the President received diplomatic credentials from Ambassadors Lawrence Mfama Mncina of Swaziland,

Rinaldo Petrignani of Italy, Chief Abudu Yesufu Eke of Nigeria, Atanraoi Baiteke of Kiribati, and Rafik Jweijeti of Syria.

The President left the White House for a weekend stay at Camp David, Md.

July 12

The President returned to the White House following a weekend stay at Camp David, Md.

July 13

The President met with members of the White House staff in the Oval Office.

The President met at the White House with:
Assistant to the President Michael K. Deaver, designated as Presidential Liaison to the 1984 Olympic Games, the U.S. Olympic Committee, and the International Olympic Committee;
—a group of Polish-American leaders to discuss the tax reduction legislation and other issues concerning Polish Americans;
—a group of Italian-American leaders to discuss the tax reduction legislation and other issues concerning Italian Americans.

The President held a working luncheon with the Cabinet. The topics discussed included the overall U.S. immigration policy and the economic mid-session review, which was reported on by David A. Stockman, Director of the Office of Management and Budget.

The White House announced that the President will receive his daily national security briefing in written format and continue to meet with his national security advisers several times a week.

July 14

The President met at the White House with:
—members of the White House staff;
—Senator Thad Cochran of Mississippi;
—Willie Stargell, of the Pittsburgh Pirates baseball team;
—Dr. Daniel D. Gilbert, president of Eureka College, Eureka, Ill.;
—his national security advisers.

The White House announced that the President has invited Indonesian President Suharto to make a state visit to the United States. President Suharto has accepted the invitation, and the visit will take place at a time to be determined later by the two Governments.

In the afternoon, the President and Mrs. Reagan attended a ceremony at the Irish Embassy where Dr. Loyal Davis, Mrs. Reagan's stepfather, was made an honorary fellow of the Royal College of Surgeons in Ireland. Following a White House reception in the Blue Room, the President went to Decatur House for a dinner honoring Dr. Davis.

July 15

The President met at the White House with:
—members of the White House staff;
—Judge Sandra Day O'Connor;
—Senator Paul Laxalt of Nevada;
—leaders of the small business community;
—James Roosevelt, to discuss observances in connection with the 100th anniversary of the birth of President Franklin D. Roosevelt;
—David Anderson, U.S. Ambassador to Yugoslavia, Monteagle Stearns, U.S. Ambassador to Greece, and Richard L. Walker, U.S. Ambassador to the Republic of Korea, prior to their departure for their overseas posts.

The President telephoned Thomas P. O'Neill, Jr., Speaker of the House of Representatives, to discuss the timetable for congressional action on the budget and tax reduction legislation.

In the evening, the President attended a reception for labor union leaders at Tayloe House.

July 16

The President met at the White House with:
—members of the White House staff;
—Secretary of State Alexander M. Haig, Jr., and Secretary of the Treasury Donald T. Regan;
—the Cabinet, to discuss U.S. immigration policy;
—Governors William G. Milliken of Michigan, Al Quie of Minnesota, and Robert D. Ray of Iowa;
—Paul A. Volcker, Chairman of the Board of Governors of the Federal Reserve System, the Vice President, Secretary of the Treasury Donald T. Regan, Murray L. Weidenbaum, Chairman of the Council of Economic Advisers, David A. Stockman, Director of the Office of Management and Budget, and Assistant to the President for Policy Development Martin Anderson.

The President attended a working luncheon on the Ottawa summit meeting with the Vice President, Secretary of State Alexander M. Haig, Jr., Secretary of the Treasury Donald T. Regan, Murray Weidenbaum, Chairman of the Council of Economic Advisers, Assistant to the President for Policy Development Martin Anderson, Counsellor to the President Edwin Meese III, Assistants to the President James A. Baker III and Michael K. Deaver, Assistant to the President for National Security Affairs Richard V. Allen, and Deputy Assistant to the President Richard G. Darman.

The President today asked the Congress to consider requests for supplemental appropriations for the fiscal year 1981 in the amount of $600,000 in transfer authority and $16,800,000 in budget authority and an amendment to the request for appropriations for fiscal year 1982 in the amount of $201,000.

July 17

The President met at the White House with:
—members of the White House staff;
—his national security advisers, including the Vice President, Secretary of State Alexander M. Haig, Jr., Secretary of Defense Caspar W. Weinberger, Counsellor to the President Edwin Meese III, Assistant to the President Michael K. Deaver, Assistant to the President for National Security Affairs Richard V. Allen, and Adm. Daniel J. Murphy, Chief of Staff for the Vice President;
—leaders of veterans groups and military organizations;
—participants in yesterday's working luncheon on the Ottawa summit meeting for a second working luncheon;
—Secretary of State Alexander M. Haig, Jr., and Secretary of the Treasury Donald T. Regan;
—Representatives Dan Glickman of Kansas, Ralph M. Hall of Texas, Sam Hall of Texas, Buddy Roemer of Louisiana, Billy Lee Evans of Georgia, Richard C. Shelby of Alabama, and Richard C. White of Texas, to discuss tax reduction legislation.

In response to the Israeli raid into Lebanon, the White House made available a statement made by Dean E. Fischer, Assistant Secretary of State (Public Affairs) at the State Department. The statement reads as follows:

For the past weeks, there has been progressive escalation of violence across the Lebanon-Israel border. The toll of innocent civilians killed and wounded in Lebanon and Israel has mounted steadily as the extent of the violence has spread to wider areas on both sides of the border. The United States deplores this intensified violence and deeply regrets the civilian casualties and the loss of innocent lives.

The United States believes these recent tragic events underscore the essential fact that only peace can provide for the long-term security and well-being of all in the area. At the present time, it is imperative that a ceasefire be established in this volatile area. President Reagan has requested Ambassador Habib to work quickly to help achieve this objective and has directed that he go to Israel as the first step in this effort.

July 18

In the morning, the Reverend Billy Graham left the White House after having dinner with the President the previous evening and remaining overnight at the Residence.

The President declared a major disaster for the State of Kansas as a result of severe storms, tornadoes, and flooding beginning on June 14, 1981, which caused extensive property damage.

July 19

In the afternoon, the President left the White House and traveled to Canada to attend the Ottawa Economic Summit Conference, which was held at the Chateau Montebello, 62 miles east of Ottawa. The President was greeted on arrival by Prime Minister Pierre Elliott Trudeau, Chairman of the summit conference.

Later in the day, the President had separate meetings with Chancellor Helmut Schmidt of the Federal Republic of Germany and President François Mitterrand of France. He attended a dinner for the Heads of State and Government in the Ontario Room at the Chateau.

July 20

In the morning, the President had a breakfast meeting with Prime Minister Margaret Thatcher of the United Kingdom. He then attended the first plenary session of the summit, where the participants discussed macroeconomics, including monetary, financial, and trade issues.

At the luncheon meeting, the Heads of State and Government were joined by their Foreign Ministers for a discussion of political issues. The afternoon session of the summit conference focused on North-South relations and energy.

In the evening, the President met with Prime Minister Giovanni Spadolini of Italy and attended a barbeque dinner with the summit participants.

The President met with his national security advisers to discuss the situation in the Middle East. On behalf of the President, Secretary of State Alexander M. Haig, Jr., announced that the President decided to defer the shipment of F-16's to Israel and that the matter remains under review.

July 21

In the morning, the President had a breakfast meeting with Prime Minister Zenko Suzuki of Japan. He then attended the morning session of the summit conference, where the participants discussed East-West economic relations and the final declaration of the summit.

Following the morning session, the President and other summit participants left the Chateau Montebello and went to Ottawa. There they attended a luncheon hosted by Edward R. Schreyer, Governor General of Canada, at Government House, also known as Rideau Hall, the residence and office of the Governor General.

The final session of the summit conference was held in the Committee Conference Room of the East Block, on Parliament Hill. Following the session, the summit participants went to the National Arts Center for their concluding statements.

Following a reception hosted by Prime Minister Trudeau at the National Arts Center, the

President left Canada and returned to the White House in the evening.

July 22

The President met at the White House with:
—members of the White House staff;
—a group of his national security advisers;
—Secretary of Defense Caspar W. Weinberger, to discuss national defense matters;
—the Cabinet Council on Natural Resources and the Environment, to discuss synthetic fuels.

In the evening, the President attended the annual House Gymnasium Association Supper in tho Longworth House Office Building.

July 23

The President met at the White House with:
—members of the White House staff;
—Mr. and Mrs. Jim McKinzie and football coach Ralph McKinzie of Eureka College, Eureka, Ill.;
—House Minority Leader Robert H. Michel, Republican Whip Trent Lott, and Republican members of the House Ways and Means Committee;
—Representatives Charles W. Stenholm, Phil Gramm, Kent R. Hance, and G. V. (Sonny) Montgomery.

July 24

In the morning, the President met with members of the White House staff in the Oval Office.

In the afternoon, the President toured the George Catlin exhibit at the National Museum of American Art.

July 25

The President left the White House in the morning for a weekend stay at Camp David, Md.

July 26

The President invited a group of Congressmen to Camp David for a discussion of Federal tax reduction legislation. The President returned to the White House in the evening.

July 27

The President met at the White House with:
—members of the White House staff;
—Governor Forrest James of Alabama, to discuss the trip the Governor is taking to several States on behalf of the President's tax bill;
—a group of corporate representatives, to discuss the tax legislation.

Throughout the day, the President met at the White House with Members of Congress to discuss the tax legislation.

Pursuant to the requirements of section 10 of the Saint Lawrence Seaway Act of May 13, 1954, the President transmitted the Saint Lawrence Seaway Development Corporation's annual report of 1980.

In accordance with section 411(c) of the Trade Act of 1974, as amended (19 U.S.C. 2441), the President transmitted the report on East-West trade. The report discusses United States trade relations with the Soviet Union, the People's Republic of China, and the Eastern European countries.

July 28

The President met at the White House with:
—members of the White House staff;
—Representative Eugene Johnston of North Carolina;
—Representative Michael Oxley of Ohio;
—Representative Robert E. Badham of California;
—Jeane J. Kirkpatrick, U.S. Representative to the United Nations.

The President met in the Oval Office with John Cardinal Krol, Archbishop of Philadelphia, to discuss the Cardinal's trip to Poland. The President indicated strong interest in the Cardinal's request to buy surplus food, held by the U.S. Government, at concessionary prices for distribution in Poland. This food would be paid for by the Catholic Relief Service. The President instructed Assistant to the President for National Security Affairs Richard V. Allen to look into the feasibility of such a plan. Mr. Allen and other members of the NSC staff are coordinating with the Department of Agriculture and the State Department on this matter, and Mr. Allen will report his findings to the President and to Cardinal Krol.

During the afternoon, the President held a series of meetings with Members of Congress to discuss the tax legislation.

July 29

The President met at the White House with Representative Norman D. Dicks of Washington. Throughout the day, the President spoke by telephone with Members of Congress to discuss the tax legislation.

July 30

The President met at the White House with members of the White House staff before departing for Atlanta, Ga.

July 31

The President met at the White House with:
—members of the White House staff;
—the Cabinet Council on Economic Affairs;
—the National Security Council.

In the afternoon, the President left the White House for a weekend stay at Camp David, Md.

August 2

The President returned to the White House following a weekend stay at Camp David, Md.

August 3

The President met at the White House with:
—members of the White House staff;
—Senator Malcolm Wallop of Wyoming;
—a group of State legislators and elected local officials from 13 Western States;
—the National Security Council.

The President announced the members of the official delegation to the funeral of Gen. Omar Torrijos Herrera of Panama. They are:

Gen. David C. Jones (Head of Delegation), Chairman, Joint Chiefs of Staff

Mrs. George Bush

Ambassador Ambler Moss, U.S. Ambassador to Panama

Ambassador Thomas O. Enders, Assistant Secretary of State for Inter-American Affairs

William R. Gianelli, Assistant Secretary of the Army (Civil Works) and Chairman of the Board of Directors of the Panama Canal Commission

Ambassador Ellsworth Bunker

Ambassador Sol Linowitz

Lt. Gen. Wallace Nutting, USA, Commander in Chief of Southern Command

Dennis P. McAuliffe, Administrator of the Panama Canal Commission

The President transmitted the 1982 budget amendments of the District of Columbia and asked the Congress to consider the proposed amendments for fiscal year 1982 in the amount of $73,041,900 from the District of Columbia funds.

The President asked the Congress to consider a request for additional appropriation language for fiscal year 1982 for the Department of Health and Human Services.

The White House announced that physicians at George Washington University Hospital reported that Press Secretary James S. Brady, who was wounded during the attempted assassination of the President on March 30, had a grand mal seizure in his room immediately after breakfast this morning. The seizure was promptly treated with intravenous medication and anesthesia, and he remained under observation throughout the day. His vital signs were reported as normal.

August 4

The President met at the White House with:
—members of the White House staff;
—Secretary of Transportation Drew L. Lewis, who reported on the air traffic controllers strike;
—the Cabinet, to discuss debt collection by the government, waste and fraud in government, and amendments to the Clean Air Act.

The President went to the Washington Star Building for a luncheon and discussion with members of the editorial board and reporters for the newspaper, which is ceasing publication on August 7.

The President appointed Assistant Secretary of State for Oceans and International Environmental and Scientific Affairs James L. Malone as Special Representative of the President and Chief of Delegation to the Law of the Sea Conference. The President also accorded Mr. Malone the personal rank of Ambassador.

The White House announced that physicians at George Washington University Hospital reported that Press Secretary James S. Brady is in good condition this morning after an uneventful evening. The seizure problem has responded satisfactorily to barbiturate anesthesia, and he is now responsive.

August 5

The President met at the White House with;
—members of the White House staff;
—the Cabinet Council on Natural Resources, to discuss synthetic fuel production and natural gas deregulation;
—Secretary of Transportation Drew L. Lewis, who reported on the air traffic controllers strike;
—former President Gerald R. Ford.

The White House announced that physicians at George Washington University Hospital reported that Press Secretary James S. Brady remains in good condition, having experienced no further seizure activity since the evening of August 3.

August 6

The President met at the White House with:
—members of the White House staff;
—the Vice President, for lunch.

The President left the White House for a month-long stay in southern California. He arrived at his ranch, Rancho del Cielo, near Santa Barbara in the evening.

The White House announced that physicians at George Washington University Hospital reported that Press Secretary James S. Brady remains in good condition following transfer to his hospital room yesterday afternoon. There has been no further seizure activity.

August 7

The President received his national security briefing, which was written and sent electronically from Washington, D.C.

The White House announced that Prime Minister Prem Tinsulanonda of Thailand will visit the United States and meet with the President on October 6 to exchange views on the U.S.-Thai relations and other issues of mutual interest.

The President signed the recess appointment of Terry Chambers, of California, to be Alternate Federal Cochairman of the following:

Coastal Plains Regional Commission
Four Corners Regional Commission
New England Regional Commission
Old West Regional Commission
Ozarks Regional Commission
Pacific Northwest Regional Commission
Southwest Border Regional Commission
Upper Great Lakes Regional Commission

August 10

The President spoke by telephone with Philadelphia Phillies baseball player Pete Rose, who earlier in the evening had broken the National League's all-time record for hits set by Stan Musial.

August 11

The President spoke by telephone with Secretary of Transportation Drew L. Lewis, who reported on the air traffic controller situation.

The White House announced that physicians at George Washington University Hospital reported that Press Secretary James S. Brady, who was wounded during the attempted assassination of the President on March 30, remains in good condition and is alert and in good spirits. Physicians continue to make minor dosage adjustments in his antiseizure medications in order to achieve optimum blood concentrations of these drugs.

August 12

The President spoke by telephone with Secretary of State Alexander M. Haig, Jr.

In the evening, the President and Mrs. Reagan hosted a reception for military personnel who assisted with construction of the temporary structures at their ranch, Rancho del Cielo, near Santa Barbara, Calif.

August 13

The President granted recess appointments to John R. Van de Water and Robert P. Hunter to be members of the National Labor Relations Board. The President also designated Mr. Van de Water as Chairman. Both individuals have been nominated to the Senate. The President announced his intention to nominate them on June 18.

August 14

The White House announced that President José López Portillo of Mexico has invited the Vice President to attend Mexico's Independence Day celebrations on September 16 in Mexico City. At the request of President Reagan, the Vice President will attend the celebrations.

August 16

The President met at his ranch, Rancho del Cielo, near Santa Barbara, Calif., with Secretary of State Alexander M. Haig, Jr.

August 17

In the morning, the President left his ranch, Rancho del Cielo, near Santa Barbara, Calif., and went to Los Angeles for the remainder of the week.

At the Century Plaza Hotel in Los Angeles the President met with:

—Secretary of State Alexander M. Haig, Jr., and Secretary of Defense Caspar W. Weinberger;
—the National Security Council to discuss defense and strategic weapons;
—Charles Z. Wick, Director of the International Communication Agency.

The President announced the appointment of Michael Novak, of the District of Columbia, as the Representative of the United States on the Human Rights Commission of the Economic and Social Council of the United Nations.

In the evening, the President attended a Republican Party fundraiser at the Century Plaza Hotel in Los Angeles.

August 18

The President met at the Century Plaza Hotel in Los Angeles with:

—Assistant to the President for Presidential Personnel E. Pendleton James;
—a group of his advisers for a meeting on defense budget matters;
—a group of his advisers for a working luncheon to review the 1982 fiscal year budget and begin preparations for the 1983 and 1984 budgets;
—representatives of the California Waterfowl Association, who presented him with an oil painting by Harry Adamson which will be on loan to the White House;
—Representatives of the Southern California Chinese Businessmen's Association, who presented him with an inscribed plaque;
—members of the family of the late actor John Wayne and representatives of the U.S. Repeating Arms Company, who presented him with Serial Number 1 of the deluxe version of the John Wayne Winchester Commemorative Rifle.

The White House announced that physicians at George Washington University Hospital reported that Press Secretary James S. Brady, who was wounded during the attempted assassination of the President on March 30, is scheduled for elective surgery on August 20 to resolve the problem of leakage of small amounts of spinal fluid. Mr. Brady remains in good spirits and has been receiving a limited number of visitors on a regular basis.

The White House announced that the President has designated Leonard Silverstein as Chairman of the United States Advisory Commission on Public Diplomacy.

The White House announced that the Department of Agriculture has agreed to sell 9,000 metric tons of dairy products from the inventories of the Commodity Credit Corporation to the Catholic Relief Service at the best price obtainable. They will be for noncommercial use in Poland. The President telephoned John Cardinal Krol, Archbishop of Philadelphia, on Saturday, August 15, to advise him of the decision.

August 19
The President met at the hotel with Counsellor to the President Edwin Meese III and Assistant to the President for National Security Affairs Richard V. Allen to discuss the incident involving two Libyan fighter planes which were shot down by U.S. Navy jets after one of them fired on the Navy F-14's which were conducting exercises in the Gulf of Sidra.

The White House announced that the President granted a recess appointment to Richard M. Murphy as U.S. Ambassador to the Kingdom of Saudi Arabia. The President announced his intention to nominate Mr. Murphy for that position on July 20.

The White House announced that the President has appointed Warren Clark, Jr., as the Deputy Representative of the United States on the Economic and Social Council of the United Nations. He will succeed Robert Kaufman. Mr. Clark is currently financial attaché and Treasury Department representative at the American Embassy in Ottawa. He was born November 7, 1936, in Bronxville, N.Y.

August 20
The White House announced that physicians at George Washington University Hospital reported that Press Secretary James S. Brady underwent surgery to seal off a persistent spinal fluid leak, and that they are cautiously optimistic that the surgical procedure has achieved its intended purpose.

August 21
The President met at the Century Plaza Hotel in Los Angeles with:
—Senator John Tower, chairman of the Senate Armed Services Committee, and Representative William L. Dickinson, ranking Republican member of the House Armed Services Committee;
—members of the American Medical Association to discuss health issues.

The White House announced that physicians at George Washington University Hospital reported that Press Secretary James S. Brady is stable and in good condition following Thursday's surgery. He returned to his hospital room late Thursday afternoon, and is fully alert and in excellent spirits.

August 22
The President left Los Angeles and returned to his ranch, Rancho del Cielo, near Santa Barbara, Calif., for the remainder of the week.

August 26
The President met at the ranch with Secretary of Defense Caspar W. Weinberger and Counsellor to the President Edwin Meese III to discuss the Secretary's recent trip to London and a wide range of defense matters.

August 27
The President announced the following individuals to represent the United States at the celebrations to be held in Swaziland on September 2–6, to mark the Diamond Jubilee of King Sobhuza II:

George Verne Orr, Secretary of the Air Force, and Mrs. Orr (Secretary Orr will head the delegation);

Representative Arlen Erdahl and Mrs. Erdahl;

Loret Miller Ruppe, Director, Peace Corps;

Ambassador Earl Smith, former Ambassador to Cuba, and Mrs. Smith;

Lannon Walker, Deputy Assistant Secretary for African Affairs, Department of State, and Mrs. Walker;

Max Binswanger, businessman, and Mrs. Binswanger;

Don Defore, actor, and Mrs. Defore;

Jewell LaFontant, former Deputy Solicitor General;

Ambassador Richard C. Matheron, Ambassador to Swaziland, and Mrs. Matheron.

The President and Mrs. Reagan hosted a reception for members of the White House press corps on the lawn of the Santa Barbara Biltmore Hotel.

August 28
The White House announced that the President intends to nominate the following: Malcolm R. Lovell, Jr., to be Under Secretary of Labor; David B. Funderburk to be United States Ambassador to Romania; and Frank V. Ortiz, Jr., to be United States Ambassador to Peru.

The President declared a major disaster for the State of Nevada as result of severe storms and flooding beginning on or about August 10, 1981, which caused extensive property damage.

August 29
The President met at his ranch, Rancho del Cielo, near Santa Barbara, Calif., with Assistant to the President James A. Baker III.

August 30

The President left his ranch , Rancho del Cielo, near Santa Barbara, Calif., and went to Los Angeles, where he stayed at the Century Plaza Hotel.

August 31

At the Century Plaza Hotel in Los Angeles, the President received his national security briefing and met with Assistant to the President James A. Baker III to discuss the bombings in the vicinity of the American Embassy in Lima, Peru.

The President met at the the the Century Plaza Hotel in Los Angeles with:
—Wilson Riles, California State Superintendent of Education, to discuss education and youth unemployment matters;
—Rex Allen, a country and western singer, and Tony Lama, Jr., who presented the President with a pair of boots manufactured by Mr. Lama's company in El Paso, Tex.

September 1

The President met at the Century Plaza Hotel with Assistant to the President James A. Baker III.

September 2

The President left Los Angeles, Calif., and went to Chicago, Ill. Following his remarks to the Illinois Forum, the President met with Mayor Jane Byrne at the Palmer House, where the President remained overnight.

September 3

Following his address to the United Brotherhood of Carpenters and Joiners, the President left Chicago and returned to the White House.

September 4

The President met at the White House with:
—members of the White House staff;
—Secretary of State Alexander M. Haig, Jr.;
—Secretary of the Interior James G. Watt
The President transmitted the following reports to the Congress:
—the 17th annual report on the status of the National Wilderness Preservation System, for the calendar year 1980;
—the fiscal year 1980 annual report of the Rehabilitation Services Administration;
—the fiscal year 1979 annual report on mine safety and health activities.

September 8

The President met at the White House with:
—members of the White House staff;
—his economic advisers, including Secretary of the Treasury Donald T. Regan, Secretary of Commerce Malcolm Baldrige, David A. Stockman, Director of the Office of Management and Budget, Murray L. Weidenbaum,

Chairman of the Council of Economic Advisers, Assistant to the President for Policy Development Martin Anderson, the Vice President, and other administration officials to discuss the Federal budget and the economy;
—Secretary of State Alexander M. Haig, Jr., and Secretary of Defense Caspar W. Weinberger, for a luncheon meeting to discuss tomorrow's visit by Prime Minister Menahem Begin of Israel;
—Senators Paul Laxalt and Howard H. Baker, Jr., and Representative Robert H. Michel, to discuss the congressional agenda for the next several months;
—Attorney General William French Smith, to discuss possible initiatives in the area of law enforcement and crime.

September 9

The President met at the White House with:
—members of the White House staff;
—David A. Stockman, Director of the Office of Management and Budget, Counsellor to the President Edwin Meese III, Assistants to the President James A. Baker III and Michael K. Deaver, and other administration officials for a luncheon meeting on budget issues;
—Secretary of Defense Caspar W. Weinberger, David A. Stockman, Director of the Office of Management and Budget, and members of the defense budget planning group, including the Vice President, Secretary of the Treasury Donald T. Regan, Secretary of State Alexander M. Haig, Jr., William J. Casey, Director of the Central Intelligence Agency, Chairman of the Joint Chiefs of Staff Gen. David C. Jones, Assistant to the President for National Security Affairs Richard V. Allen, Counsellor to the President Edwin Meese III, and Assistants to the President James A. Baker III, Michael K. Deaver, and Martin V. Anderson, to discuss issues concerning defense spending for fiscal years 1983 and 1984.

September 10

The President met at the White House with:
—members of the President's Economic Policy Advisory Board;
—the Cabinet at a working luncheon on the economy and the budget;
—George Allen, Chairman of the President's Council on Physical Fitness and Sports.

September 11

In the morning, the President met with members of the White House staff.

In a ceremony in the Oval Office, the President met with officials of Sertoma, a service organization with headquarters in Kansas City, Mo., and Mr. and Mrs. Nick Haywood of Kansas City. Mr. Haywood is the recipient of the Sertoma Humanitarian Award presented in recognition of his help to underprivileged children in that city.

In the afternoon, the President left the White House for a weekend stay at Camp David, Md.

September 13
The President returned to the White House following a weekend stay at Camp David, Md.

September 14
The President met at the White House with:
—members of the White House staff;
—members of the House Conservative Democratic Forum for a general discussion on the need for further budget cuts;
—members of the new class of White House fellows to present them with certificates;
—Speaker of the House Thomas P. O'Neill, Jr., and House Minority Leader Robert H. Michel at a luncheon meeting to discuss the upcoming congressional agenda;
—Senators Paul Laxalt of Nevada and Jake Garn of Utah to discuss the MX missile system;
—Members of the Senate to discuss the sale of AWACS planes to Saudi Arabia.

September 15
The President met at the White House with:
—members of the White House staff;
—the Republican congressional leaders to discuss budget matters;
—participants in the President's Executive Exchange Program;
—the National Security Council;
—the Governing Mayor of West Berlin, Richard von Weizacker.

The White House announced that at the invitation of the President and Mrs. Reagan, Their Majesties King Juan Carlos and Queen Sophia of Spain will pay a state visit to Washington on October 13. Following their stay in the Capital, the King and Queen will visit various cities with Spanish traditions in the western part of the United States.

In accordance with Section 411(c) of the Trade Act of 1974, as amended (19 U.S.C. 2441), the President transmitted to the Congress the quarterly report on East-West trade covering the first quarter of 1981. The report discusses U.S. trade relations with the Soviet Union, the People's Republic of China, and the Eastern European countries.

September 16
The President met at the White House with:
—members of the White House staff;
—His Beatitude Anthony Peter Khoraiche, Maronite Catholic Patriarch of Antioch and All The East, who was accompanied by Terence Cardinal Cooke, Archbishop of New York.

In a ceremony in the Roosevelt Room, the President met with the Boys Clubs of America's "National Boy of the Year" regional finalists and the executive directors of the Boys Clubs. The President made the official presentation of the award to John Harrison Magee II, of North Little Rock, Ark.

The President participated in the Cabinet Room swearing-in ceremony for members of the President's Commission on Executive Exchange.

In the evening, the President hosed a reception for contributors to the Republican Senatorial Trust.

September 17
The President met at the White House with:
—members of the White House staff;
—a group of bipartisan congressional leaders, including Speaker of the House Thomas P. O'Neill, Jr., House Majority Leader Jim Wright, House Minority Leader Robert H. Michel, Senate Majority Leader Howard H. Baker, Jr., Senate Minority Leader Robert C. Byrd, and Senate president pro tem Strom Thurmond, to discuss the sale of AWACS planes to Saudi Arabia and the budget;
—the Cabinet, to review several of the options for further budget cuts.

In the afternoon, the President left the White House to attend ceremonies in Grand Rapids, Mich., related to the dedication of the Gerald R. Ford Presidential Museum. Upon arrival in Grand Rapids, the President was greeted by the former President.

Prior to the dinner honoring President Ford, the President held separate meetings at the Amway Grand Plaza Hotel with Valéry Giscard d'Estaing, former President of France, Prime Minister Pierre Elliott Trudeau of Canada, and President José López Portillo of Mexico, who were in Grand Rapids to attend the dedication ceremonies.

The White House announced that President José Napoleón Duarte Fuentes of El Salvador will pay a 10-day visit to the Unitd States beginning September 19. President Duarte will call on President Reagan on Monday, September 21, and will meet with high-level administration officials and congressional leaders to discuss issues of mutual interest.

The White House announced that the President will meet with Daniel T. Arap Moi of Kenya on Friday, September 25. President Moi will be in the United States in connection with his speech before the United Nations General Assembly.

September 18

In the morning, the President hosted a breakfast meeting for Prime Minister Pierre Elliott Trudeau of Canada and President José López Portillo of Mexico at the Amway Grand Plaza Hotel. Following the dedication of the Ford Museum, the President went to Denver, Colo., to address the National Federation of Republican Women. Following his address in Denver, the President went to Camp David, Md., for the weekend.

In accordance with the Civil Service Reform Act of 1978 (Public Law 95-454, Sec. 701) (5 U.S.C. 7104(e)), the President transmitted to the Congress the Second Annual Report of the Federal Labor Relations Authority for the fiscal year ended September 30, 1980.

September 20

The President returned to the White House following a weekend stay at Camp David, Md.

September 21

The President met at the White House with:
—members of the White House staff;
—President José Napoleón Duarte Fuentes of El Salvador;
—Governor William Clements of Texas;
—Senator Jesse Helms of North Carolina, to receive a replica of the Cape Hatteras Lighthouse;
—Representatives Sid Morrison of Washington, Denny Smith of Oregon, Gene Chappie of California, Larry E. Craig of Idaho, George Hansen of Idaho, Joel Pritchard of Washington, and Norman D. Shumway of California, to discuss the impact of the current economy on the timber industry as a result of slow housing starts;
—Clement J. Zablocki, chairman, and William S. Broomfield, ranking minority member, of the House Foreign Affairs Committee, to discuss the legislative timetable for the consideration of the sale of AWACS planes to Saudi Arabia.

In a ceremony in the Oval Office, the President received diplomatic credentials from Ambassadors Ejaz Azim of Pakistan, Lew Byong Hion of the Republic of Korea, Enrique Valenzuela of Chile, Faernando Gaviria of Colombia, John Wycliffe Lwamafa of Uganda, and Leslie N. Agius of Malta.

The President met with Representatives Albert Lee Smith, Jr., of Alabama, and Richard T. Schulze of Pennsylvania, who presented him with a petition signed by 155 Members of Congress pledging support for Presidential vetoes of bills in order to achieve the President's budgetary aggregate.

September 22

The President met at the White House with:
—members of the White House staff;
—Secretary of the Treasury Donald T. Regan, David A. Stockman, Director of the Office of Management and Budget, Counsellor to the President Edwin Meese III, and Assistants to the President James A. Baker III and Michael K. Deaver, to discuss details for the President's address to the nation on the economic recovery program;
—Dr. Ralph Abernathy, civil rights leader.

The President announced the appointment of James F. Burke as Chairman of the President's Commission on Executive Exchange. Mr. Burke is currently chairman and chief executive officer of Johnson & Johnson.

The President declared a major disaster for the State of Texas as a result of severe storms and flooding beginning on or about August 30, 1981, which caused extensive property damage.

Late in the afternoon, the President hosted a reception for the Eagles, $10,000 contributors to the Republican National Committee.

September 23

The President met at the White House with:
—members of the White House staff;
—David A. Stockman, Director of the Office of Management and Budget to discuss budget matters;
—Sugar Ray Leonard, welterweight boxing champion.

September 24

The President met at the White House with:
—members of the White House staff;
—Senate Majority Leader Howard H. Baker, Jr., to discuss the sale of AWACS planes to Saudi Arabia;
—Langhorne A. Motley, U.S. Ambassador to Brazil, Richard Murphy, U.S. Ambassador to Saudi Arabia, and Michael H. Newlin, U.S. Ambassador to Algeria, prior to their departure for their overseas posts;
—members of the executive committee of the National Governors Association, including Governors Richard A. Snelling of Vermont, George Busbee of Georgia, John V. Evans of Idaho, Robert D. Ray of Iowa, James R. Thompson, Jr., of Illinois, Joseph E. Brennan of Maine, and William G. Milliken of Michigan;
—the Cabinet, to discuss details of the address to the nation on the economic recovery program;
—Republican congressional leaders to discuss details of the address to the nation.

The President hosted a luncheon in the Family Dining Room for Justices of the United States Supreme Court and their spouses.

September 25

In the morning, the Pesident met in the Oval Office with members of the White House staff.

The President and Mrs. Reagan went to the Supreme Court to attend the swearing-in ceremony for Sandra Day O'Connor as an Associate Justice.

In the afternoon, the President left the White House for a weekend stay at Camp David, Md.

The White House announced that on the occasion of the Yorktown Bicentennial Celebration, the President has invited President François Mitterrand of France to meet with him at Williamsburg, Va., on Sunday, October 18. Following the meeting, the President and Mrs. Reagan will host a dinner at the historic Governor's Palace in commemoration of the Bicentennial. President and Mrs. Mitterrand will be guests of honor. The President has also accepted an invitation from President Mitterrand to have lunch that same day on board the French warship *de Grasse*, anchored in the York River. They will be accompanied by their wives. On Monday, October 19, the two Presidents will attend the military review at the Yorktown Battlefield, and will speak at the ceremony.

September 26

The White House announced that the President has accorded the personal rank of Ambassador to William E. Schuyler, Jr., in his capacity as Head of the U.S. Delegation to the Diplomatic Conference on the Revision of the Paris Industrial Property Convention in Nairobi, September 24 through October 24, 1981.

The White House announced that the President has asked the Congress to consider amendments reducing requests for appropriations for fiscal year 1982 by a total of $365,900,000 for foreign assistance.

September 27

The President returned to the White House following a weekend stay at Camp David, Md.

September 29

The President met at the White House with:
—members of the White House staff;
—Ambassador Jeane J. Kirkpatrick, U.S. Representative to the United Nations, who reported on her trips to Latin America and Asia;
—J. Richard Conder, president of the National Association of Counties.

The White House announced that the President has designated Elizabeth E. Bailey as Vice Chairman of the Civil Aeronautics Board for the period ending December 31, 1981.

September 30

The President met at the White House with:
—members of the White House staff;
—Republican congressional leaders to receive a report on pending legislation.

The President declared a major disaster for the Marshall Islands of the Trust Territory as a result of a major fire on August 24, 1981, which caused extensive property damage.

The President asked the Congress to consider amendments reducing requests for appropriations for fiscal year 1982 by $18,070,934,000 and an off-budget request in the amount of $3,217,991,000 for the Strategic Petroleum Reserve.

October 1

The President met at the White House with:
—members of the White House staff;
—the Cabinet Council on Economic Affairs;
—a group of Members of Congress.

October 2

The President met at the White House with:
—members of the White House staff;
—Vice President Mohamed Hosni Mubarak of Egypt.

In the afternoon, the President left the White House for a weekend stay at Camp David, Md.

October 4

The President returned to the White House following a weekend stay at Camp David, Md.

October 5

The President met at the White House with:
—members of the White House staff;
—Senators Robert C. Byrd and Jennings Randolph and Representative Cleve Benedict of West Virginia, who accompanied the West Virginia Strawberry Queens for 1980 and 1981;
—Senator Harrison Schmitt of New Mexico;
—Representative Ronald M. Mottl of Ohio;
—Senator Ted Stevens of Alaska;
—Representatives Daniel Coats of Indiana, Larry J. Hopkins of Kentucky, Bob McEwen of Ohio, Ron Marlenee of Montana, and Dan Marriott of Utah.

October 6

The President met at the White House with:
—members of the White House staff;
—Senator Charles McC. Mathias, Jr., of Maryland to discuss the sale of AWACS and other air defense equipment to Saudi Arabia;
—Senator Alan K. Simpson of Wyoming to discuss the AWACS sale;
—Senator Orrin G. Hatch of Utah to discuss the AWACS sale;

—Republican members of the Senate Foreign Relations Committee to discuss the AWACS sale;

—members of the National Security Planning Group, including the Vice President, Secretary of State Alexander M. Haig, Jr., Secretary of Defense Caspar W. Weinberger, William J. Casey, Director of Central Intelligence, Gen. David C. Jones, Chairman of the Joint Chiefs of Staff, Assistant to the President for National Security Affairs Richard V. Allen, Counsellor to the President Edwin Meese III, and Assistants to the President James A. Baker III and Michael K. Deaver, to review the events of the day concerning the assassination of President Sadat of Egypt and discuss their meaning for the future.

October 7

The President met at the White House with:

—members of the White House staff;

—43 Republican Members of the Senate to discuss the AWACS sale;

—Senator Dale Bumpers of Arkansas;

—Governors Pierre (Pete) S. Du Pont IV of Delaware and Lamar Alexander of Tennessee.

The President accorded the personal rank of Ambassador to Robert J. Ryan, Jr., in his capacity as Coordinator for the Caribbean Basin Initiative.

The President announced his intention to appoint William J. Baroody, Jr., as Chairman of the Board of Trustees of the Woodrow Wilson International Center for Scholars. Mr. Baroody's appointment as a member of the Board was announced on March 2, 1981.

The President and Mrs. Reagan went to the National Cathedral for a memorial service for President Anwar el-Sadat of Egypt.

The White House announced that the President has decided to send to the Congress waivers to the Alaska Natural Gas Transportation Act, passed by the Congress in 1976. The waiver package is being assembled and will be transmitted to the Congress later this week. If approved by the Congress, it would facilitate private financing of the Alaska Natural Gas Transportation System.

October 8

The President met at the White House with:

—Senator Nancy Landon Kassebaum of Kansas, who announced her support of the AWACS sale to reporters following the meeting;

—the Vice President, for a luncheon meeting;

—the Cabinet Council on Natural Resources and the Environment;

—Egyptian Ambassador to the United States Ashraf A. Ghorbal, to express to the Ambassador, and through the Ambassador to the Egyptian people, the deep sense of grief he and Mrs. Reagan and the people of the United States feel concerning the death of President Sadat;

—Harry G. Barnes, Jr., U.S. Ambassador to India, John Gunther Dean, U.S. Ambassador to Thailand, John E. Dolibois, U.S. Ambassador to Luxembourg, David B. Funderburk, U.S. Ambassador to Romania, Jack F. Matlock, Jr., U.S. Ambassador to Czechoslovakia, Frank V. Ortiz, Jr., U.S. Ambassador to Peru, Robert P. Paganelli, U.S. Ambassador to Syria, M. Virginia Schafer, U.S. Ambassador to Papua New Guinea and the Solomon Islands, Ronald I. Spiers, U.S. Ambassador to Pakistan, Faith Ryan Whittlesey, U.S. Ambassador to Switzerland, and David E. Zweifel, U.S. Ambassador to the Yemen Arab Republic, prior to their departure for their overseas posts.

In a ceremony in the Oval Office, the President began this year's Combined Federal Campaign, the annual fundraising drive, by signing a pledge card. Participants in the ceremony included Secretary of Commerce Malcolm Baldrige, chairman of the drive, William Schaeffler, director of the Combined Federal Campaign of the National Capital Area, Barbara Lett Simmons, representative of the National Service Agencies, Dr. William B. Walsh, representative of the International Service Agencies, Robert L. Montague III, chairman of the Council of National Health Agencies, Edwin W. Pfeiffer, president, and Kent T. Cushenberry, chairman, 1981 United Way Campaign of the National Capital Area.

October 9

The President met at the White House with:

—members of the White House staff;

—Senator Thad Cochran of Mississippi;

—members of the National Commission on Excellence in Education

In a ceremony in the Oval Office, the President met with Dr. Eli Goldensohn, president, and William M. McLin, executive director, of the Epilepsy Foundation of America, and Brenda Jo Buckley, age 6, the 1982 Poster Child. Also present were Brenda's parents, Mr. and Mrs. Lonn L. Buckley, and her brother, Lonn. The Buckleys are from Bountiful, Utah.

In the afternoon, the President left the White House for a weekend stay at Camp David, Md.

October 12

The President returned to the White House following a weekend stay at Camp David, Md.

October 13

The President met at the White House with:

—members of the White House staff;

—the National Security Council, where Secretary of State Alexander M. Haig, Jr., and Secretary of Defense Caspar W. Weinberger reported on their trip to the funeral services for President Anwar el-Sadat of Egypt in Cairo;

—Senator Larry Pressler of South Dakota to discuss the sale of AWACS and other air defense equipment to Saudi Arabia;

—former President Jimmy Carter to discuss world affairs and particularly the situation in the Middle East.

October 14

The President met at the White House with:

—members of the White House staff;

—William (Bill) Verity, Chairman of the President's Task Force on Private Sector Initiatives;

—William F. Bolger, Postmaster General.

The President held a series of meetings at the White House to discuss the sale of AWACS and other air defense equipment to Saudi Arabia with the following Senators:

—James S. Abdnor of South Dakota;

—John P. East of North Carolina;

—David Pryor of Arkansas;

—Mack Mattingly of Georgia and Dan Quayle of Indiana;

—Walter D. Huddleston of Kentucky;

—William S. Cohen of Maine;

—Charles E. Grassley of Iowa;

—Ernest F. Hollings of South Carolina.

October 15

In the morning, the President met with members of the White House staff in the Oval Office.

The President asked the Congress to consider amendments reducing requests for appropriations for fiscal year 1982 by $7,607,332,000. These requests would implement the fall budget program proposals that the President announced to the nation on September 24, 1981.

Before leaving the White House for a trip to Philadelphia, the President telephoned the new Prime Minister of Norway, Kaare Willoch.

While in Philadelphia, the President met at the Bellevue Stratford Hotel with Governor Richard L. Thornburgh of Pennsylvania to discuss a Federal partnership with the State in funding projects concerning the Three Mile Island nuclear facility.

The President then met at the Bellevue Stratford Hotel with John Terry, a 16-year-old who, for the past 6 years, has been cleaning up his neighborhood twice a week at his own expense. He was accompanied by his sister, Lucille Blake. The President brought Mr. Terry into another meeting at the hotel, where the President discussed private sector initiatives with a group of corporate and civic leaders from the Philadelphia area. Participants in that meeting included Robert Dee, chairman, Smith Kline Corp.; William Eagleson, chairman, Girard Bank; Robert I. Smith, president, Pew Memorial Trust; Sister Falaka Fattah, founder, House of Umoja; James Bodine, director, Greater Philadelphia Partnership; Lee Driscoll, president, ARA Food Service and president, United Way; and the Rt. Rev. Lyman C. Ogilby, Episcopal Bishop of the Diocese of Pennsylvania.

October 16

The President met at the White House with:

—members of the White House staff;

—Sir Seewosagur Ramgoolam, Prime Minister of Mauritius;

—Helmut Kohl, leader of the Christian Democratic Party in the Federal Republic of Germany;

—the National Security Council.

The President met at the White House with the following independent agency officials to discuss the budgets for their agencies:

—M. Peter McPherson, Administrator, Agency for International Development;

—James M. Beggs, Administrator, National Aeronautics and Space Administration;

—John B. Slaughter, Director, National Science Foundation;

—Robert P. Nimmo, Administrator, Veterans Administration;

—Gerald P. Carmen, Administrator, General Services Administration;

—Donald J. Devine, Director, Office of Personnel Management;

—Michael Cardenas, Administrator, Small Business Administration;

—Charles Z. Wick, Director, International Communication Agency;

—William H. Draper III, Chairman, Export-Import Bank of the United States;

—Nancy Harvey Steorts, Chairman, Consumer Product Safety Commission;

—Thomas A. Pauken, Director, ACTION;

—Eugene Victor Rostow, Director, U.S. Arms Control and Disarmament Agency;

—Louis O. Giuffrida, Director, Federal Emergency Management Agency;

—William Giannelli, Chief of Engineers, Department of Defense;

—Richard T. Pratt, Chairman, Federal Home Loan Bank Board;

—Loret Ruppe, Director, the Peace Corps.

The President held a series of meetings at the White House to discuss the sale of AWACS and other air defense equipment to Saudi Arabia with the following Senators:

—J. Bennett Johnston of Louisiana;
—Patrick J. Leahy of Vermont;
—Dennis DeConcini of Arizona;
—Quentin N. Burdick of North Dakota;
—David L. Boren of Oklahoma;
—John Heinz of Pennsylvania;
—Howell Heflin of Alabama;
—Russell B. Long of Louisiana.

The President transmitted to the Congress the annual report of the Railroad Retirement Board for fiscal year 1980.

October 17

The White House announced that the President has designated the following to be members of the U.S. delegation attending the funeral services for former Israeli Foreign Minister Moshe Dayan:

Attorney General and Mrs. William French Smith
Senator and Mrs. Roger W. Jepsen of Iowa
Representative and Mrs. Richard Cheney of Wyoming
Representative Mickey Edwards of Oklahoma
Senator Edward Zorinsky of Nebraska
Mr. and Mrs. Jack Stein

October 20

The President met at the White House with:
—members of the White House staff;
—Secretary of State Alexander M. Haig, Jr., and Secretary of the Treasury Donald T. Regan;
—representatives of the American Business Conference;
—Senator Spark Matsunaga of Hawaii;
—Senator Malcolm Wallop of Wyoming;
—Senator Alan Dixon of Illinois;
—Senator Roger W. Jepsen of Iowa;
—Senator Jennings Randolph of West Virginia;
—Senator John Melcher of Montana;
—Senator Daniel Inouye of Hawaii.

October 21

The President arrived at Cancún International Airport, Mexico, for the 2-day International Meeting on Cooperation and Development, which was attended by heads of state and government and foreign ministers of 22 nations and the Secretary General of the United Nations. The President was greeted at the airport by President José López Portillo of Mexico, Cochairman of the Meeting. Following the arrival ceremony, the two Presidents held a bilateral meeting with their advisers at the airport and then went to the Cancún Sheraton Hotel, where the President and other foreign leaders stayed during the sessions.

At the Cancún Sheraton Hotel, the President and his advisers held a luncheon meeting with Premier Zhao Ziyang and Vice Premier and For-

eign Minister Huang Hua of the People's Republic of China, and other members of the Chinese delegation.

In the afternoon, the President and his advisers held separate bilateral meetings at the Cancún Sheraton Hotel with Prime Minister Indira Gandhi of India and members of the Indian delegation; President Alhaji Shehu Shagari of Nigeria and members of the Nigerian delegation; and President Luis Herrera Campíns of Venezuela and members of the Venezuelan delegation.

October 22

Prior to the inaugural session of the International Meeting on Cooperation and Development, the President and his advisers held separate meetings at the Cancún Sheraton Hotel with President Sergej Kraigher of Yugoslavia and members of the Yugoslavian delegation and Foreign Minister Willibald Pahr of Austria and members of the Austrian delegation.

Following the first plenary session of the International Meeting on Cooperation and Development, the President and his advisers held separate meetings at the Cancún Sheraton Hotel with President Ferdinand E. Marcos of the Philippines and members of the Philippine delegation and Foreign Minister Hans-Dietrich Genscher of the Federal Republic of Germany and members of the German delegation.

In the afternoon, the President attended the second plenary session of the International Meeting on Cooperation and Development at the Cancún Sheraton Hotel, at which the participants discussed food and agricultural issues.

In the evening, the President met at the Cancún Sheraton Hotel with Secretary of State Alexander M. Haig, Jr., and then attended a dinner at the hotel hosted by President José López Portillo for the heads of state and government and foreign ministers.

October 23

In the morning, the President met at the Cancún Sheraton Hotel with Secretary of State Alexander M. Haig, Jr., Secretary of the Treasury Donald T. Regan, and Assistants to the President James A. Baker III and Michael K. Deaver.

Prior to the morning session of the International Meeting on Cooperation and Development, the President and his advisers held separate meetings at the Cancún Sheraton Hotel with President Chadli Bendjedid of Algeria and members of the Algerian delegation and President Julius K. Nyerere of Tanzania and members of the Tanzanian delegation.

The President attended the third plenary session of the International Meeting on Cooperation and Development, at which the participants discussed trade, energy, and investment and financial matters.

Following the third plenary session, the President and his advisers held a meeting and luncheon at the Cancún Sheraton Hotel with Prince Fahd of Saudi Arabia and members of the Saudi Arabian delegation.

The President attended the fourth and final session of the International Meeting on Cooperation and Development.

In the evening, the President attended a dinner at the Cancún Sheraton Hotel in honor of President José López Portillo.

October 24

In the morning, the President and his advisers held separate meetings at the Cancún Sheraton Hotel with Prime Minister Azizur Rahman of Bangladesh and members of the Bangladeshi delegation; Executive President Forbes Burnham of Guyana and members of the Guyanan delegation; and Secretary General Kurt Waldheim of the United Nations.

The President left the Cancún Sheraton Hotel and, following a departure ceremony at the Cancún International Airport, returned to the United States.

The President declared a major disaster for the State of Texas as a result of severe storms and flooding beginning on or about October 12, 1981, which caused extensive property damage.

October 26

The President met at the White House with:
—members of the White House staff;
—the Cabinet, for a working luncheon.

The President held a series of meetings at the White House to discuss the sale of AWACS and other air defense equipment to Saudi Arabia with the following Senators:

—Frank H. Murkowski of Alaska;
—William L. Armstrong of Colorado;
—Mark N. Andrews of North Dakota;
—Roger W. Jepsen of Iowa;
—Robert W. Kasten of Wisconsin;
—John C. Danforth of Missouri;
—Howard W. Cannon of Nevada.

In a ceremony in the Oval Office, the President received diplomatic credentials from Ambassadors Ernest Corea of Sri Lanka, Inacio Semedo, Jr., of Guinea-Bissau, Ahmad Salim Al-Mokarrab of the United Arab Emirates, Esteban Arpad Takacs of Argentina, Mohammad Abdallah al-Iryani of the Yemen Arab Republic, Janos Petran of Hungary, and Abdul Hadi Majali of Jordan.

October 27

The President met at the White House with:
—members of the White House staff;

—several Senators to discuss the sale of AWACS and other air defense equipment to Saudi Arabia.

The President attended the Outdoor Life Magazine Conservation Award presentation ceremony in the Map Room at the White House.

October 28

The President met at the White House with:
—members of the White House staff;
—several Senators to discuss the sale of AWACS and other air defense equipment to Saudi Arabia.

The White House announced that the President has transmitted to the Congress the 1980 annual report as submitted by the Secretary of Health and Human Services and the 1977 through 1980 annual reports as submitted by the Secretary of Labor on occupational safety and health.

October 29

The President met at the White House with:
—members of the White House staff;
—Huang Hua, Vice Premier and Foreign Minister of the People's Republic of China.

The President went to the National Naval Medical Center in Bethesda, Md., for his annual physical examination.

October 30

The President left the National Naval Medical Center and went to Camp David, Md., for the weekend.

The White House released the following statement by Dr. Daniel Ruge, Physician to the President:

"The President was thoroughly examined at Bethesda Naval Hospital on October 29–30, 1981, by a team of 14 specialists in five medical fields. Preliminary oral reports have been provided, pending complete written reports which will be submitted within the next few days. There are a number of routine laboratory tests which will be analyzed over the weekend.

The President is in excellent health. His blood pressure, pulse, and respiratory functions are normal. He is fully recovered from gunshot wounds suffered on March 30.

The President was accompanied by Mrs. Reagan for their annual physicals. Mrs. Reagan is also in excellent health."

November 1

The President returned to the White House following a weekend stay at Camp David, Md.

November 2

The President met during the day at the White House with members of the White House staff. In an afternoon session, they discussed matters relating to the budget and the economy.

November 3

The President met at the White House with:
—members of the White House staff;
—members of the White House staff for a luncheon meeting to discuss matters relating to the budget and the economy;
—Archbishop Iakovos, Primate of the Greek Orthodox Church in North and South America;
—the Cabinet Council on Commerce and Trade;
—Senators Howard H. Baker, Jr., Pete V. Domenici, and James A. McClure, and Representatives James T. Broyhill, Robert H. Michel, and Clarence J. Brown, to discuss natural gas deregulation.

November 4

The President met at the White House with:
—members of the White House staff;
—members of the House and Senate Agriculture Committees to discuss farm legislation;
—the Cabinet to discuss the Voting Rights Act;
—George Shultz, Alan Greenspan, Paul McCracken, and Walter Wriston, to discuss the economy;
—the Vice President.

The President announced his intention to nominate Under Secretary of State for Economic Affairs Myer Rashish to be U.S. Alternate Governor to the International Bank for Reconstruction and Development, the Inter-American Development Bank, the Asian Development Bank, and the African Development Bank. He would succeed Richard N. Cooper.

The White House announced that at the invitation of the President, President Luis Herrera Campíns of Venezuela will make a state visit to the United States November 16–19. He will meet with the President at the White House on November 17.

November 5

The President met at the White House with:
—members of the White House staff;
—Secretary of State Alexander M. Haig, Jr., and Assistant to the President for National Security Affairs Richard V. Allen to discuss foreign policy operations;
—a group of leaders from the financial community;
—members of the White House staff to discuss matters relating to the budget and the economy.

The White House announced that the President has declared a major disaster for the State of Oklahoma as a result of severe storms and flooding beginning on October 10, 1981, which caused extensive property damage.

The President accorded the personal rank of Ambassador to John Warlick McDonald, Jr., during his tenure of service as U.S. Coordinator for the United Nations World Assembly on Aging during the period from November 1981 to April 1982.

November 6

The President met at the White House with:
—members of the White House staff;
—Senate Republican leaders, including Howard H. Baker, Jr., Ted Stevens, Robert Dole, Pete V. Domenici, Mark O. Hatfield, James A. McClure, John G. Tower, Jake Garn, Paul Laxalt, and Strom Thurmond, to discuss matters relating to the budget and the economy;
—House Republican leaders, including Robert H. Michel, Trent Lott, Barber B. Conable, Jr., Delbert L. Latta, Jack Kemp, Dick Cheney, and Silvio O. Conte, to discuss matters relating to the budget and the economy.

The President asked the Congress to consider amendments to the requests for appropriations for fiscal year 1982 by $72,700,000 and a reduction of $16,500,000 in a request for advance fiscal year 1984 appropriations.

The President went to New York City to attend a State Republican fundraising reception and the 84th annual dinner of the American Irish Historical Society. Following the dinner, he returned to the White House.

November 9

The President met at the White House with:
—members of the White House staff;
—a group of Presidential appointees for a breakfast meeting;
—a group of local elected officials, including Mayors Robert Isaac of Colorado Springs, Colo., William H. Hudnut III of Indianapolis, Ind., Helen Boosalis of Lincoln, Nebr., George Latimer of St. Paul, Minn., Jane Byrne of Chicago, Ill., George Voinovich of Cleveland, Ohio, George Israel of Macon, Ga., William Donald Schaefer of Baltimore, Md., Henry Cisneros of San Antonio, Tex., Patience Latting of Oklahoma City, Okla., Lewis Murphy of Tucson, Ariz., and Richard Carver of Peoria, Ill., and County Commissioners Richard Conder of Richmond County, N.C., and Virgil Brown of Cuyahoga County, Ohio, to discuss revenue sharing.

The President met in the Oval Office with 11-year-old Ricky Schroeder, star of "The Champ," and members of his family, in a ceremony marking the opening of this year's Christmas Seal campaign, an annual event sponsored by the

American Lung Association. The ceremony was also attended by officials of the association and Dr. Samuel Spagnolo, a pulmonary medicine specialist.

November 10

The President met at the White House with:
—members of the White House staff;
—the Cabinet Council on Human Resources.

The President hosted a reception in the Residence for members of the Presidential transition group.

November 12

The President met at the White House with:
—members of the White House staff;
—a group of Republican Senators and Congressmen to discuss the second continuing resolution and funding for the B–1 bomber and the MX missile;
—David A. Stockman, Director of the Office of Management and Budget, for a luncheon meeting;
—the Cabinet Council on Natural Resources and the Environment to discuss coal slurry;
—Mrs. Rose Kennedy.

In a ceremony in the Oval Office, representatives of the European Rodeo Association presented the President with a silver belt buckle.

The President accorded the personal rank of Ambassador to Louis G. Fields, Jr., in his capacity as the Department of State's representative to the first committee meetings on disarmament during the 36th Session of the United Nations General Assembly now in progress, and for the spring session of the Committee on Disarmament which will open in Geneva, Switzerland, on February 2, 1982.

The President announced his intention to nominate the following individuals to be members of the Board of Directors of the Inter-American Foundation:

Thomas O. Enders, Assistant Secretary of State for Inter-American Affairs;

Marc E. Leland, Deputy Under Secretary of the Treasury (International Affairs);

M. Peter McPherson, Administrator, Agency for International Development.

November 13

The President met at the White House with:
—members of the White House staff;
—Senator John C. Stennis of Mississippi;
—Paul Hartling, United Nations High Commissioner for Refugees;
—Representative James V. Hansen of Utah;
—Representative Arlen Specter of Pennsylvania;
—the Cabinet Council on Human Resources to discuss the future of the Department of Education.

The President left the White House in the afternoon for a weekend stay in Texas.

November 15

The President returned to the White House following his weekend stay at the Winston Ranch in Sabinal, Tex. He flew from Kelly Air Force Base, Tex., to Andrews Air Force Base, Md., aboard the E–4A, a modified Boeing 747B jet transport, which is currently utilized by the Joint Chiefs of Staff as the National Emergency Airborne Command Post.

November 16

The President met at the White House with:
—members of the White House staff;
—members of the executive board of the American Association of Minority Enterprise Business Investment Companies;
—the National Security Council.

November 17

The President met at the White House with:
—members of the White House staff;
—a group of local elected officials, including Mayors Ferd Harrison of Scotland Neck, N.C. (first vice president, National League of Cities), Tom Moody of Columbus, Ohio, James Ryan of Arlington Heights, Ill., Jayne Plank of Kensington, Md., Arthur Trujillo of Santa Fe, N. Mex., Fred Turnage of Rocky Mount, N.C., Corinne Freeman of St. Petersburg, Fla., and Richard Berkley of Kansas City, Mo., City Council members Thomas Clark of Long Beach, Calif., and Anne Gresham of Grand Prairie, Tex., County Executive Lawrence Hogan of Prince Georges County, Md., County Commissioners Fred McIlhattan of Clarion County, Pa., Bob Eckels of Harris County, Tex., and Earl Baker of Chester County, Pa., and Councilman George Akahane of Honolulu County, Hawaii, to discuss revenue sharing;
—Senators Warren Rudman of New Hampshire and J. Bennett Johnston of Louisiana, and Representatives Robert L. Livingston of Louisiana, Don Ritter of Pennsylvania, Floyd Spence of South Carolina, Jim Jeffries of Kansas, and James H. Quillen of Tennessee.

The President went to the Department of Defense for a tour of the Pentagon and luncheon with officials.

The White House announced that the President has asked Congress to consider an amendment to the request for appropriations for fiscal year 1982 in the amount of $50,000,000 for foreign assistance.

The White House announced that at the invitation of the President, President Spyros Kyprianou of Cyprus will meet with the President on December, 8, for a working visit.

November 18

The President met at the White House with:
—members of the White House staff;
—Milan D. Bish, U.S. Ambassador to Barbados, Dominica, St. Lucia, St. Vincent and the Grenadines, Antigua and Barbuda, Edwin C. Corr, U.S. Ambassador to Bolivia, Robert L. Barry, U.S. Ambassador to Bulgaria, and Evan G. Galbraith, U.S. Ambassador to France, prior to their departure for their overseas posts.

Early in the evening, the President and Mrs. Reagan attended a reception hosted by the White House Historical Association for contributors to the White House restoration project. The reception was held in the East Room, following a tour of the restored White House rooms by the contributors.

November 19

The President met at the White House with:
—members of the White House staff;
—a group of representatives of the Jewish community;
—the Vice President, for a luncheon meeting;
—the Cabinet;
—a group of leaders of Jewish organizations.

The White House announced that the President and Mrs. Reagan have invited Their Majesties, the King and Queen of Sweden, to visit with them on Sunday, November 22. King Carl XVI Gustaf and Queen Silvia are in the United States on a private visit.

The White House announced that the President has invited Chancellor Helmut Schmidt of the Federal Republic of Germany to meet with him at the White House on January 5, 1982. The Chancellor plans to be in the United States on a vacation at that time and the President is taking advantage of this opportunity for them to have wide-ranging discussions on issues of mutual interest.

The President announced his intention to appoint Counsel to the President Fred F. Fielding to be a member of the President's Commission on White House Fellowships. He will succeed Francis S. M. Hodsoll, who was recently appointed Chairman of the National Endowment for the Arts.

November 20

The President met at the White House with:
—members of the White House staff;
—President Gaafar Mohamed Nimeiri of the Sudan;
—Governors William G. Milliken of Michigan, James R. Thompson, Jr., of Illinois, Albert

Quie of Minnesota, and Lee S. Dreyfus of Wisconsin, to discuss how budget cuts will affect those four Midwestern States;
—Governor Paul Calvo of Guam;
—Members of the Idaho congressional delegation.

The White House announced that the President has asked the Congress to consider offsetting amendments to requests for appropriations for the Federal Emergency Management Agency.

The President accorded the personal rank of Ambassador to Paul H. Nitze while serving as Head of the U.S. Delegation to the Intermediate Range Nuclear Force Negotiations and also announced his intention to nominate Mr. Nitze for the rank of Ambassador while serving as Head of the Delegation.

November 23

The President met with the Cabinet at the White House.

November 25

The White House announced that the President telephoned Ambassador Philip C. Habib, the President's emissary to consultations in the Middle East, to discuss the Ambassador's forthcoming return to the region. The United States is pleased that the Lebanon-Israel area has remained relatively quiet and stable since the July cessation of hostilities. The United States remains committed to reenforcing that situation. For that reason, the President has asked Ambassador Habib to return to the region to determine how the United States could be helpful in reducing tensions further and in improving basic conditions in Lebanon. The Ambassador left after Thanksgiving.

The White House announced that the President called Ambassador Paul H. Nitze, head of the U.S. delegation to the Intermediate Range Nuclear Force Negotiations. He emphasized that Ambassador Nitze has the United States highest confidence as he leaves for Geneva, Switzerland, to present the constructive U.S. proposal on Theater Nuclear Forces. They discussed the seriousness of the U.S. proposal, the U.S. commitment to negotiate in good faith, and the firm support which we have from our allies. In view of the Thanksgiving Day departure, the President expressed the Nation's thanks, hopes, and good wishes to Ambassador Nitze.

The White House announced that the President received a telephone call from Chancellor Helmut Schmidt of the Federal Republic of Germany. Chancellor Schmidt gave the President his assessment of his recent meeting with President

L. I. Brezhnev of the Soviet Union and other matters of mutual interest.

November 26

The White House announced that, upon learning of the injury to Israeli Prime Minister Menahem Begin sustained during a fall, the President sent a message expressing his hopes for a quick and full recovery.

November 28

The White House announced that the President received a telephone call from Assistant to the President for National Security Affairs Richard V. Allen who requested administrative leave until such time as the Department of Justice has completed its investigation. The President granted his request. Deputy Assistant to the President for National Security Affairs James W. Nance will assume Mr. Allen's duties during his absence.

November 30

The President left his ranch, Rancho del Cielo, near Santa Barbara, Calif., where he had spent the Thanksgiving holiday, and following a stop in Cincinnati, Ohio, he returned to the White House.

December 1

The President met at the White House with:
—members of the White House staff;
—members of the general board of the International Brotherhood of Teamsters.

December 2

The President met at the White House with:
—members of the White House staff;
—a group of leaders of agricultural organizations;
—members of the executive council of the AFL–CIO.

December 3

The President met at the White House with:
—members of the White House staff;
—members of the President's Commission on Housing; and a group of housing industry leaders;
—a group of presidents and executive directors of State municipal leagues and county associations;
—the Vice President, for lunch;
—a group of managing editors.

The President declared a major disaster for the Commonwealth of Massachusetts as a result of a fire which began on November 28, 1981, causing extensive property damage.

December 4

The President met at the White House with:

—members of the White House staff;
—Secretary of the Treasury Donald T. Regan, David A. Stockman, Director of the Office of Management and Budget, Murray L. Weidenbaum, Chairman of the Council of Economic Advisers, and members of the White House staff to discuss the 1983 budget;
—representatives of the steel industry, including William DeLancey, chairman, Republic Steel Corp., David Roderick, chairman, United States Steel, Donald Trautlein, chairman, Bethlehem Steel Corp., and Robert Peabody, president, American Iron and Steel Institute.

The President transmitted to the Congress the Sixteenth Annual Report of the Department of Housing and Urban Development covering the calendar year 1980.

December 7

The President met at the White House with:
—members of the White House staff;
—local Republican officials;
—the National Security Council;
—representatives of the National Rifle Association, who presented the President with a replica of a Kentucky rifle;
—Members of Congress who were early supporters of the President.

December 8

The President met at the White House with:
—members of the White House staff;
—the National Security Council;
—the Vice President, Secretary of the Treasury Donald T. Regan, David A. Stockman, Director of the Office of Management and Budget, Murray L. Weidenbaum, Chairman of the Council of Economic Advisers, and members of the White House staff, to discuss the fiscal year 1983 budget;
—members of the White House staff to discuss foreign assistance for fiscal years 1983 and 1984;
—Anne Armstrong, Chairman of the President's Foreign Intelligence Advisory Board.

In an Oval Office ceremony, the President was presented with diplomatic credentials from Ambassadors Hubert Ondias-Souna of Gabon, Tiemoko Marc Garango of Upper Volta, Habib Ben Yahia of Tunisia, Tadhg F. O'Sullivan of Ireland, Allan Ezra Gotlieb of Canada, and Hudson Kemul Tannis of St. Vincent and the Grenadines.

The President transmitted to the Congress the 19th annual report of activities under the Comprehensive Employment and Training Act.

December 9

The President met at the White House with:
—members of the White House staff;
—Secretary of Transportation Drew L. Lewis to discuss the air traffic controllers;
—Republican congressional leaders;
—Melvin H. Evans, U.S. Ambassador to Trinidad and Tobago, Francis T. McNamara, U.S. Ambassador to Gabon, Jean Gerard, U.S. Permanent Representative to UNESCO, and James Lilley, Director of the American Institute in Taiwan, prior to departing for their posts;
—Speaker of the House of Representatives Thomas P. O'Neill, Jr., and Mr. and Mrs. Tom Geoghegan, who presented the President and Speaker O'Neill with Blackthorn walking-sticks;
— Speaker of the House of Representatives Thomas P. O'Neill, for lunch.

The President greeted a group of senior citizens who were touring the White House.

The White House announced that the President is gratified by the decision to grant an exit visa to Elizaveta Alekseyeva, Andrei Sakharov's daughter-in-law. He is pleased to hear reports that the Sakharovs' hunger strike is ended, and it is the administration's hope that they will be allowed to lead a normal life.

December 10

The President met at the White House with:
—members of the White House staff;
—R. William Taylor, president, and James P. Low, immediate past president, American Society of Association Executives;
—the U.S. Business Committee on Jamaica;
—the President's Economic Policy Advisory Board;
—the Vice President, for lunch;
—members of the White House staff and officials from the Departments of Labor and Energy to discuss the fiscal year 1983 budget;
—the National Security Council.

The President attended a reception for Republican legislators attending the State-Federal assembly of the National Conference of State Legislatures.

The White House announced that at the invitation of the President, the Crown Prince and First Deputy Prime Minister of Saudi Arabia will make an official visit to Washington on January 19, 1982.

December 11

The President met at the White House with:
—members of the White House staff;

—Republican Members of the House of Representatives;
—George M. White, Architect of the Capitol;
—former President Gerald R. Ford;
—Col. Frank Kurtz, president of the U.S. Olympians, who presented the President with a medal making him an honorary Olympian;
—Ambassador Philip C. Habib, the President's emissary in consultations in the Middle East, to discuss his mission to the region.

The White House announced that the President has invited President Alessandro Pertini of Italy to pay a state visit to Washington in March 1982. President Pertini has accepted the President's invitation and will meet with the President in March 1982.

The President left the White House for a weekend stay at Camp David, Md.

December 13

The President returned to the White House from Camp David, Md.

The President met at the White House with the Vice President and members of the White House staff to discuss the situation in Poland.

December 14

The President met at the White House with:
—members of the White House staff;
—Paul A. Volcker, Chairman of the Board of Directors, Federal Reserve System, Secretary of the Treasury Donald T. Regan, and members of the White House staff;
—members of the American Legislative Exchange Council;
—Archbishop Pio Laghi, Apostolic Delegate to the United States, William A. Wilson, Personal Representative of the President to the Holy See, and representatives of the academic community, who presented the President with a study on nuclear arms;
—the Vice President, Secretary of State Alexander M. Haig, Jr., and members of the White House staff, to discuss the situation in Poland.

The White House announced that the President designated T. Timothy Ryan, Jr., Solicitor for the Department of Labor, to serve as a member of the Board of Directors of the Overseas Private Investment Corporation.

The President and Mrs. Reagan hosted a Christmas party for members of the White House press corps on the State Floor of the White House.

December 15

The President met at the White House with:
—members of the White House staff;

—a group of Republican Members of the House of Representatives;

—members of the White House staff and officials from the National Aeronautics and Space Administration and the Environmental Protection Agency to discuss the fiscal year 1983 budget;

—Agostino Cardinal Casaroli, Secretary of State of the Vatican City State, the Vice President, Secretary of Alexander M. Haig, Jr., Archbishop Pio Laghi, Apostolic Delegate to the United States, and William A. Wilson, Personal Representative of the President to the Holy See;

—the Presidential Advisory Committee on Federalism;

—the Cabinet Council on Natural Resources and the Environment to discuss the Department of Energy;

—Governor Richard A. Snelling of Vermont.

The President and Mrs. Reagan hosted a Christmas party for members of the White House press corps on the State Floor of the White House.

The President transmitted to the Congress the following reports:

—the 15th annual report on the Automotive Products Trade Act for calendar year 1980;

—the 1980 Aeronautics and Space Report;

—the annual report on Pipeline Safety for calendar year 1980;

—the 11th annual report on Hazardous Materials Transportation for calendar year 1980.

December 16

The President met at the White House with:

—members of the White House staff;

—Governor-elect Thomas H. Kean of New Jersey;

—leaders of the Associated General Contractors of America;

—Charles H. Price II, U.S. Ambassador to Belgium.

The President and Mrs. Reagan hosted a Christmas party for Members of Congress on the State Floor of the White House.

The President transmitted to the Congress the 12th annual report of the National Science Board for calendar year 1979 and the 13th annual report of the National Science Board for 1980.

December 17

The President met at the White House with:

—members of the White House staff;

—members of the White House staff and officials from the Department of Energy to discuss the fiscal year 1983 budget;

—Representatives Marjorie S. Holt of Maryland and Stan Parris and Frank R. Wolf of Virgin-

ia, to discuss parking fees for Federal employees.

The President announced the recess appointments of the following three persons as members of the Federal Election Commission:

Joan D. Aikens, nominated on November 24. She would succeed Vernon W. Thomson.

Lee Ann Elliott, nominated on November 24. She would succeed Joan D. Aikens.

Danny Lee McDonald, nominated on December 14. He would succeed Robert O. Tiernan.

The President announced the recess appointment of Herbert E. Ellingwood as a member and Chairman of the Merit Systems Protection Board.

December 18

The President met at the White House with:

—members of the White House staff;

—Lane Kirkland, president of the AFL–CIO, and Secretary of State Alexander M. Haig, Jr.;

—members of the White House staff and officials from the Department of Defense to discuss the fiscal year 1983 budget;

—House Minority Leader Robert H. Michel and Representatives Barber B. Conable, Jr., of New York, Delbert L. Latta of Ohio, Jack F. Kemp of New York, Richard Cheney of Wyoming, and Jack Edwards of Alabama, to discuss the fiscal year 1983 budget and 1982 legislative initiatives;

—the National Security Council;

—Senate Majority Leader Howard H. Baker, Jr., and Senator Paul Laxalt of Nevada, to discuss the fiscal year 1983 budget and 1982 legislative initiatives;

—Senators Howard H. Baker, Jr., Paul Laxalt, Pete V. Domenici of New Mexico, Robert Dole of Kansas, and Mark O. Hatfield of Oregon, to discuss the fiscal year 1983 budget and 1982 legislative initiatives.

The President announced the recess appointment of Cathie A. Shattuck as a member of the Equal Employment Opportunity Commission. She would succeed Ethel Bent Walsh.

The White House announced that President Mohamed Hosni Mubarak of Egypt has accepted the invitation of President Reagan to make a state visit to Washington beginning on February 3. The President and Mrs. Reagan look forward to welcoming President and Mrs. Mubarak on behalf of all Americans on that occasion. The visit will underscore the continuity of the broad and profound relations between the two countries and the friendship of our two peoples.

December 21

The President met at the White House with:

—members of the White House staff;

—members of the White House staff to discuss the foreign assistance appropriations portion of the fiscal year 1983 budget;

—the National Security Council;

—the Vice President, John Cardinal Krol, Archbishop of Philadelphia, Aloysius Mazewski, president of the Polish-American Congress, Joseph Drobot, president of the Roman Catholic Union, and Helen Zielinski, president of the Polish Women's Alliance, to discuss the situation in Poland;

—members of the White House staff to discuss the entitlements portion of the fiscal year 1983 budget and the economic forecast in connection with the budget;

—Mark Evans Austad, U.S. Ambassador to Norway, Franklin S. Forsberg, U.S. Ambassador to Sweden, Ronald D. Palmer, U.S. Ambassador to Malaysia, and Harry Thayer, U.S. Ambassador to Singapore, prior to their departure for their overseas posts.

Deputy Press Secretary Larry M. Speakes announced that during a meeting between the President and Egyptian Ambassador to the United States Ashraf A. Ghorbal, the President stressed the U.S. commitment to the peace process and emphasized that all relevant and outstanding issues should be resolved by neogtiations between the parties.

The President announced the recess appointment of William J. Bennett as Chairman of the National Endowment for the Humanities. He would succeed Joseph D. Duffey.

December 22

The President met at the White House with:

—members of the White House staff;

—members of the White House staff to discuss the fiscal year 1983 budget;

—the National Security Council;

—the Cabinet Council on Commerce and Trade.

The White House announced that the President signed a memorandum to heads of departments and agencies encouraging them to excuse from duty any employee whose services could be spared for the last half of the scheduled workday on December 24.

The White House made available copies of "The Reagan Presidency—A New Beginning: A Review of the First Year, 1981," a report compiled and edited by the White House Office of Public Affairs.

December 23

The President met at the White House with:

—members of the White House staff;

—members of the White House staff to discuss the fiscal year 1983 budget;

—the National Security Council.

The White House announced that the President and Crown Prince Fahd of Saudi Arabia have agreed to the postponement of the visit of the Crown Prince to Washington scheduled for January 19. This decision was reached in the light of current developments in the Middle East in particular and in the world in general and the Crown Prince's determination that these developments require his presence in Saudi Arabia. The President and the Crown Prince look forward to the rescheduling of the visit at an early, mutually agreed upon time.

The President has transmitted to the Congress the Aggregate Report on Personnel pursuant to title 3, United States Code, section 113, for fiscal year 1981.

December 25

The President and Mrs. Reagan celebrated Christmas in the Residence with members of their family and friends.

December 27

The President left the White House for a weeklong visit to California. Upon arrival in Los Angeles, the President went to the Century Plaza Hotel where he stayed overnight.

December 28

In the morning, the President went to his ranch, Rancho del Cielo, near Santa Barbara, Calif. While at the ranch, he spoke by telephone with the Vice President, Counsellor to the President Edwin Meese III, and Deputy Assistant to the President for National Security Affairs James W. Nance. Following the meeting of the Special Situation Group in Washington, D.C., to review the current situation in Poland, they presented the President with recommendations on options discussed with the President before he left for California.

Early in the evening, the President left his ranch and returned to the Century Plaza Hotel in Los Angeles.

December 29

The President met at the Century Plaza Hotel in Los Angeles with Governor Robert D. Ray of Iowa and D. C. Spriestersbach, acting president, and James Freedman, president-elect, of the University of Iowa.

December 30

In the morning, the President left Los Angeles and went to Palm Springs. He spent the remainder of his visit to California at the residence of Walter and Lenore Annenberg.

Appendix B—Nominations Submitted to the Senate

The following list does not include promotions of members of the Uniformed Services, nominations to the Service Academies, or nominations of Foreign Service officers.

Submitted January 20

Alexander Meigs Haig, Jr.,
of Connecticut, to be Secretary of State.

Donald T. Regan,
of New Jersey, to be Secretary of the Treasury.

Caspar Willard Weinberger,
of California, to be Secretary of Defense.

William French Smith,
of California, to be Attorney General.

James Gaius Watt,
of Colorado, to be Secretary of the Interior.

John R. Block,
of Illinois, to be Secretary of Agriculture.

Malcolm Baldrige,
of Connecticut, to be Secretary of Commerce.

Raymond J. Donovan,
of New Jersey, to be Secretary of Labor.

Richard S. Schweiker,
of Pennsylvania, to be Secretary of Health and Human Services.

Samuel R. Pierce, Jr.,
of New York, to be Secretary of Housing and Urban Development.

Andrew L. Lewis, Jr.,
of Pennsylvania, to be Secretary of Transportation.

James B. Edwards,
of South Carolina, to be Secretary of Energy.

T. H. Bell,
of Utah, to be Secretary of Education.

Jeane J. Kirkpatrick,
of Maryland, to be the Representative of the United States of America to the United Nations with the rank and status of Ambassador Extraordinary and Plenipotentiary, and the Representative of the United States of America in the Security Council of the United Nations.

Submitted January 20—Continued

David A. Stockman,
of Michigan, to be Director of the Office of Management and Budget.

William J. Casey,
of New York, to be Director of Central Intelligence, vice Stansfield Turner.

Darrell M. Trent,
of California, to be Deputy Secretary of Transportation, vice William J. Beckham, Jr.

William Emerson Brock III,
of Tennessee, to be United States Trade Representative, with the rank of Ambassador Extraordinary and Plenipotentiary, vice Reubin O'D. Askew.

Withdrawn January 21

Dorothy Sellers,
of the District of Columbia, to be an associate judge of the Superior Court of the District of Columbia for a term of 15 years, vice Edmond T. Daly, deceased.

Ricardo M. Urbina,
of the District of Columbia, to be an associate judge of the Superior Court of the District of Columbia for a term of 15 years, vice Normalie Holloway Johnson, elevated.

John A. Gronouski,
of Texas, to be a member of the Board for International Broadcasting for a term expiring April 28, 1983 (reappointment).

Thomas R. Donahue,
of the District of Columbia, to be a member of the Board of Directors of the Communications Satellite Corporation until the date of the annual meeting of the Corporation in 1981, vice George Meany.

Lynn R. Coleman,
of the District of Columbia, to be Deputy Secretary of Energy, vice John C. Sawhill, resigned, to which office he was appointed during the last recess of the Senate.

Walter Meheula Heen,
of Hawaii, to be United States District Judge for the District of Hawaii, vice Dick Yin Wong, de-

ceased, to which office he was appointed during the last recess of the Senate.

Ralph W. Emerson,
of the District of Columbia, to be a member of the Foreign Claims Settlement Commission of the United States for the term expiring September 30, 1981 (new position—P.L. 96–209), to which office he was appointed during the last recess of the Senate.

Thomas W. Fredericks,
of Colorado, to be an Assistant Secretary of the Interior, vice Forrest J. Gerard, resigned, to which office he was appointed during the last recess of the Senate.

Alex P. Mercure,
of New Mexico, to be Under Secretary of Agriculture for Small Community and Rural Development (new position), to which office he was appointed during the last recess of the Senate.

Joseph S. Bracewell,
of Texas, to be President of the Solar Energy and Energy Conservation Bank (new position), to which office he was appointed during the last recess of the Senate.

The following-named persons to be Assistant Directors of the Community Services Administration, to which offices they were appointed during the last recess of the Senate:

Laird F. Harris, of Michigan, vice Frank Jones, resigned.

Harold Lafayette Thomas, of the District of Columbia, vice John B. Gabusi, resigned.

The following-named persons to be members of the Board of Directors of the Corporation for Public Broadcasting for terms expiring March 26, 1986, to which offices they were appointed during the last recess of the Senate:

Reuben W. Askanase, of Texas, vice Donald E. Santarelli, term expired.

Melba Pattillo Beals, of California, vice Lucius Perry Gregg, Jr., term expired.

Vernon W. Thompson,
of Virginia, to be a member of the Federal Election Commission for the remainder of the term expiring April 30, 1983, vice Max L. Friedersdorf, resigned, to which office he was appointed during the last recess of the Senate.

Alice Coig McDonald,
of Kentucky, to be a member of the National Council on Educational Research for a term expiring September 30, 1982, vice John Corbally,

term expired, to which office she was appointed during the last recess of the Senate.

John C. Truesdale,
of Maryland, to be a member of the National Labor Relations Board for the term of 5 years expiring August 27, 1985 (reappointment), to which office he was appointed during the last recess of the Senate.

The following-named persons to be members of the National Museum Services Board for terms expiring December 6, 1985, to which offices they were appointed during the last recess of the Senate:

John Connell, of California, vice Gary K. Clarke, term expired.

Dorothy Graham-Wheeler, of North Carolina, vice George Horse Capture, term expired.

Albert T. Klyberg, of Rhode Island, vice Charlotte Ferst, term expired.

Wallace Nathaniel Hyde,
of North Carolina, to be a Governor of the United States Postal Service for the term expiring December 8, 1989, vice M. A. Wright, term expired, to which office he was appointed during the last recess of the Senate.

John C. Sawhill,
of the District of Columbia, to be Chairman of the Board of Directors of the United States Synthetic Fuels Corporation for a term of 7 years (new position), to which office he was appointed during the last recess of the Senate.

The following-named persons to be members of the Board of Directors of the United States Synthetic Fuels Corporation for the terms indicated, to which offices they were appointed during the last recess of the Senate:

John D. DeButts, of Virginia, for a term of 1 year (new position).

Catherine Blanchard Cleary, of Wisconsin, for a term of 2 years (new position).

Frank Savage, of New York, for a term of 3 years (new position).

Joseph Lane Kirkland, of the District of Columbia, for a term of 5 years (new position).

Maj. Gen. William Edgar Read,
240–28–5638, United States Army, to be a member and President of the Mississippi River Commission, under the provisions of Section 2 of an Act of Congress, approved 28 June 1879 (21 Stat. 37) (33 U.S.C. 642).

Submitted January 22

Frank C. Carlucci,
of Virginia, to be Deputy Secretary of Defense.

Submitted January 23

John O. Marsh, Jr.,
of Virginia, to be Secretary of the Army, vice
Clifford L. Alexander, Jr., resigned.

John F. Lehman, Jr.,
of Virginia, to be Secretary of the Navy, vice
Edward Hidalgo.

Verne Orr,
of California, to be Secretary of the Air Force,
vice Hans Michael Mark.

Submitted January 26

William P. Clark,
of California, to be Deputy Secretary of State,
vice Warren M. Christopher, resigned.

Submitted January 30

Edward C. Schmults,
of Connecticut, to be Deputy Attorney General,
vice Charles B. Renfrew.

Donald I. Hovde,
of Wisconsin, to be Under Secretary of Housing
and Urban Development, vice Victor Marrero.

Murray L. Weidenbaum,
of Missouri, to be a member of the Council of
Economic Advisers, vice Charles L. Schultze.

Edwin L. Harper,
of Missouri, to be Deputy Director of the Office
of Management and Budget, vice John Patrick
White.

Submitted February 2

R. T. McNamar,
of California, to be Deputy Secretary of the
Treasury, vice Robert Carswell.

W. Dennis Thomas,
of Maryland, to be a Deputy Under Secretary of
the Treasury, vice Gene E. Godley, resigned.

Donald P. Hodel,
of Oregon, to be Under Secretary of the Interior,
vice James Alfred Joseph, resigned.

Submitted February 3

James L. Buckley,
of Connecticut, to be Under Secretary of State
for Coordinating Security Assistance Programs,
vice Matthew Nimetz, resigned.

Submitted February 3—Continued
Richard T. Kennedy,
of the District of Columbia, to be Under Secretary of State for Management, vice Benjamin H.
Read, resigned.

Walter J. Stoessel, Jr.,
of California, to be Under Secretary of State for
Political Affairs, vice David D. Newsom.

Richard Fairbanks,
of the District of Columbia, to be an Assistant
Secretary of State, vice J. Brian Atwood, resigned.

Robert Carl McFarlane,
of Maryland, to be Counselor of the Department
of State, vice Rozanne L. Ridgway.

M. Peter McPherson,
of Maryland, to be Administrator of the Agency
for International Development, vice Douglas J.
Bennet, Jr., resigned.

Richard E. Lyng,
of Virginia, to be Deputy Secretary of Agriculture, vice James H. Williams.

Vice Admiral B. R. Inman,
U.S. Navy, to be Deputy Director of Central Intelligence, and to have the rank of Admiral while
so serving.

Submitted February 5

Donald T. Regan,
of New Jersey, to be United States Governor of
the International Monetary Fund for a term of 5
years and United States Governor of the International Bank for Reconstruction and Development
for a term of 5 years; a Governor of the Inter-American Development Bank for a term of 5
years; and United States Governor of the Asian
Development Bank and United States Governor
of the African Development Fund.

Ray A. Barnhart,
of Texas, to be Administrator of the Federal
Highway Administration, vice John S. Hassell, Jr.

Submitted February 19

Charles M. Lichenstein,
of the District of Columbia, to be the Alternate
Representative of the United States of America
for Special Political Affairs in the United Nations,
with the rank of Ambassador.

Submitted February 23

Roscoe L. Egger, Jr.,
of the District of Columbia, to be Commissioner of Internal Revenue, vice Jerome Kurtz, resigned.

Robert W. Blanchette,
of Maryland, to be Administrator of the Federal Railroad Administration, vice John McGrath Sullivan, resigned.

Submitted February 24

John M. Fowler,
of Pennsylvania, to be General Counsel of the Department of Transportation, vice Thomas George Allison, resigned.

Thomas W. Pauken,
of Texas, to be Director of the ACTION Agency, vice Samuel Winfred Brown, Jr., resigned.

Submitted February 26

John E. Chapoton,
of Texas, to be an Assistant Secretary of the Treasury, vice Donald Cyril Lubick, resigned.

Paul Craig Roberts,
of Virginia, to be an Assistant Secretary of the Treasury, vice Curtis Alan Hessler, resigned.

Albert Angrisani,
of New Jersey, to be an Assistant Secretary of Labor, vice Ernest Gideon Green, resigned.

Submitted February 27

William Francis Baxter,
of California, to be an Assistant Attorney General, vice Sanford M. Litvack, resigned.

Submitted March 2

James L. Malone,
of Virginia, to be Assistant Secretary of State for Oceans and International Environmental and Scientific Affairs, vice Thomas R. Pickering, resigned.

T. Timothy Ryan, Jr.,
of Virginia, to be Solicitor for the Department of Labor, vice Carin Ann Clauss.

Judith T. Connor,
of New York, to be an Assistant Secretary of Transportation, vice William B. Johnston, resigned.

Submitted March 2—Continued
Lee L. Verstandig,
of the District of Columbia, to be an Assistant Secretary of Transportation, vice Susan J. Williams, resigned.

Submitted March 5

The following-named persons to be Associate Judges of the Superior Court of the District of Columbia for terms of 15 years as follows:
Henry F. Greene, of the District of Columbia, vice Edmond T. Daly, deceased.
Ricardo M. Urbina, of the District of Columbia, vice Norma Holloway Johnson, elevated.

Angela M. Buchanan,
of the District of Columbia, to be Treasurer of the United States, vice Azie Taylor Morton, resigned.

Thorne G. Auchter,
of Florida, to be an Assistant Secretary of Labor, vice Eula Bingham.

Donald J. Devine,
of Maryland, to be Director of the Office of Personnel Management for a term of 4 years, vice Alan Keith Campbell, resigned.

Submitted March 6

David B. Swoap,
of Virginia, to be Under Secretary of Health and Human Services, vice Nathan J. Stark, resigned.

The following-named person to the positions indicated:
C. W. McMillan, of Virginia, to be an Assistant Secretary of Agriculture, vice P. R. Smith.
C. W. McMillan, of Virginia, to be a member of the Board of Directors of the Commodity Credit Corporation, vice P. R. Smith.

Submitted March 17

Myer Rashish,
of the District of Columbia, to be Under Secretary of State for Economic Affairs, vice Richard N. Cooper, resigned.

Elliott Abrams,
of the District of Columbia, to be an Assistant Secretary of State, vice Richard Lee McCall, Jr., resigned.

Chester A. Crocker,
of the District of Columbia, to be an Assistant Secretary of State, vice Richard M. Moose, resigned.

Submitted March 17—Continued
John H. Holdridge,
of Maryland, to be an Assistant Secretary of State,
vice Richard Holbrooke, resigned.

Norman B. Ture,
of Virginia, to be Under Secretary of the Treasury, vice Bette Beasley Anderson, resigned.

Beryl Wayne Sprinkel,
of Illinois, to be Under Secretary of the Treasury for Monetary Affairs, vice Anthony Morton Solomon, resigned.

Philip D. Winn,
of Colorado, to be an Assistant Secretary of Housing and Urban Development, vice Lawrence B. Simons, resigned.

Raymond A. Peck, Jr.,
of the District of Columbia, to be Administrator of the National Highway Traffic Safety Administration, vice Joan Buckler Claybrook, resigned.

Arthur E. Teele, Jr.,
of Florida, to be Urban Mass Transportation Administrator, vice Theodore Compton Lutz, resigned.

Loret M. Ruppe,
of Michigan, to be Director of the Peace Corps, vice Richard Frank Celeste, resigned.

Rudolph W. Guiliani,
of New York, to be Associate Attorney General, vice John H. Shenfield, resigned.

Carol E. Dinkins,
of Texas, to be an Assistant Attorney General, vice James W. Moorman, resigned.

D. Lowell Jensen,
of California, to be an Assistant Attorney General, vice Philip B. Heymann, resigned.

Theodore B. Olson,
of California, to be an Assistant Attorney General, vice John M. Harmon, resigned.

Fred Charles Ikle,
of Maryland, to be Under Secretary of Defense for Policy, vice Robert W. Komer, resigned.

Willian H. Taft IV,
of Virginia, to be General Counsel of the Department of Defense, vice Togo D. West, Jr., resigned.

William H. Coldiron,
of Montana, to be Solicitor of the Department of the Interior, vice Clyde O. Martz, resigned.

Submitted March 17—Continued
Seeley Lodwick,
of Iowa, to be Under Secretary of Agriculture for International Affairs and Commodity Programs, vice Dale Ernest Hathaway, resigned.

John B. Crowell, Jr.,
of Oregon, to be an Assistant Secretary of Agriculture, vice Malcolm Rupert Cutler, resigned.

Willian Gene Lesher,
of Virginia, to be an Assistant Secretary of Agriculture, vice Alex P. Mercure.

To be members of the Board of Directors of the Commodity Credit Corporation:
    Seeley Lodwick, of Iowa, vice Dale Ernest Hathaway, resigned.
    William Gene Lesher, of Virginia, vice Ray V. Fitzgerald, resigned.

Emanuel S. Savas,
of New Jersey, to be an Assistant Secretary of Housing and Urban Development, vice Donna Edna Shalala, resigned.

Submitted March 19

John J. Knapp,
of New York, to be General Counsel of the Department of Housing and Urban Development, vice Jane McGrew.

R. Tenney Johnson,
of Maryland, to be General Counsel of the Department of Energy, vice Lynn R. Coleman.

Michael Cardenas,
of California, to be Administrator of the Small Business Administration, vice Arthur Vernon Weaver, Jr., resigned.

Submitted March 23

Robert D. Hormats,
of Maryland, to be an Assistant Secretary of State, vice Deane R. Hinton.

Joseph Robert Wright, Jr.,
of New York, to be Deputy Secretary of Commerce, vice Luther H. Hodges, Jr., resigned.

Lionel H. Olmer,
of Maryland, to be Under Secretary of Commerce for International Trade, vice Robert E. Herzstein, resigned.

G. Ray Arnett,
of California, to be Assistant Secretary for Fish and Wildlife, Department of the Interior, vice Robert L. Herbst, resigned.

Submitted March 23—Continued
J. Lynn Helms,
of Connecticut, to be Administrator of the Federal Aviation Administration, vice Langhorne McCook Bond.

Submitted March 25

Nicholas A. Veliotes,
of California, a Foreign Service officer of the Class of Career Minister, to be an Assistant Secretary of State, vice Harold H. Saunders, resigned.

Submitted March 26

Robert L. Brown,
of Virginia, to be Inspector General of the Department of State and the Foreign Service (new position).

Submitted March 27

Gerald P. Carmen,
of New Hampshire, to be Administrator of General Services, vice Rowland G. Freeman III, resigned.

Submitted April 1

Lawrence S. Eagleburger,
of Florida, a Foreign Service officer of the Class of Career Minister, to be an Assistant Secretary of State, vice George S. Vest, resigned.

Lawrence J. Korb,
of Virginia to be an Assistant Secretary of Defense, vice Robert Burns Pirie, Jr., resigned.

Garrey Edward Carruthers,
of New Mexico, to be an Assistant Secretary of the Interior, vice Guy Richard Martin, resigned.

William H. Morris, Jr.,
of Tennessee, to be an Assistant Secretary of Commerce, vice Herta Lande Seidman, resigned.

Dorcas R. Hardy,
of California, to be an Assistant Secretary of Health and Human Services, vice Cesar A. Perales, resigned.

Richard T. Pratt,
of Utah, to be a member of the Federal Home Loan Bank Board for the remainder of the term expiring June 30, 1981, vice Jay Janis, resigned.

Richard T. Pratt,
of Utah, to be a member of the Federal Home Loan Bank Board for the term of 4 years expiring June 30, 1985 (reappointment).

Submitted April 1—Continued
John S. R. Shad,
of New York, to be a member of the Securities and Exchange Commission for the remainder of the term expiring June 5, 1982, vice Harold Marvin Williams, resigned.

John S. R. Shad,
of New York, to be a member of the Securities and Exchange Commission for the term of 5 years expiring June 5, 1986, vice Stephen J. Friedman, term expiring.

Submitted April 3

John J. Louis, Jr.,
of Illinois, to be Ambassador Extraordinary and Plenipotentiary of the United States of America to the United Kingdom of Great Britain and Northern Ireland.

Robert F. Burford,
of Colorado, to be Director of the Bureau of Land Management, vice Frank Gregg, resigned.

Edward N. Brandt, Jr.,
of Texas, to be an Assistant Secretary of Health and Human Services, vice Julius Benjamin Richmond, resigned.

John A. Svahn,
of Maryland, to be Commissioner of Social Security, vice William J. Driver, resigned.

William Stewart Heffelfinger,
of Virginia, to be an Assistant Secretary of Energy (Management and Administration), vice William Walker Lewis, resigned.

Ann McGill Gorsuch,
of Colorado, to be Administrator of the Environmental Protection Agency, vice Douglas M. Costle, resigned.

Raymond J. Waldmann,
of Maryland, to be Assistant Secretary of Commerce, vice Abraham Katz, resigned.

Louis O. Giuffrida,
of California, to be Director of the Federal Emergency Management Agency, vice John W. Macy, Jr., resigned.

Submitted April 6

Arthur H. Woodruff,
of Florida, a Foreign Service officer of Class two, to be Ambassador Extraordinary and Plenipotentiary of the United States of America to the Central African Republic.

Submitted April 6—Continued

Deane R. Hinton,
of Illinois, a Foreign Service officer of the Class of Career Minister, to be Ambassador Extraordinary and Plenipotentiary of the United States of America to El Salvador.

John A. Burroughs, Jr.,
of Maryland, to be Ambassador Extraordinary and Plenipotentiary of the United States of America to the Republic of Malawi.

John A. Gavin,
of California, to be Ambassador Extraordinary and Plenipotentiary of the United States of America to Mexico.

Roger William Mehle, Jr.,
of New York, to be an Assistant Secretary of the Treasury, vice Roger C. Altman, resigned.

Frederick Morris Bush,
of Texas, to be Assistant Secretary of Commerce for Tourism, vice Fabian Chavez, Jr., resigned.

Donald Allan Derman,
of the District of Columbia, to be an Assistant Secretary of Transportation, vice Mortimer L. Downey III, resigned.

Robert C. Odle, Jr.,
of Virginia, to be an Assistant Secretary of Energy (Congressional, Intergovernmental and Public Affairs), vice Ruth M. Davis, resigned.

Submitted April 13

Marc E. Leland,
of California, to be a Deputy Under Secretary of the Treasury, vice C. Fred Bergsten, resigned.

Kenneth L. Smith,
of Oregon, to be an Assistant Secretary of the Interior, vice Thomas W. Fredericks, resigned.

A. James Barnes,
of the District of Columbia, to be General Counsel of the Department of Agriculture, vice Daniel Marcus, resigned.

Charles Z. Wick,
of California, to be Director of the International Communication Agency, vice John E. Reinhardt, resigned.

Submitted April 22

Ernest W. Lefever,
of Maryland, to be Assistant Secretary of State for Human Rights and Humanitarian Affairs, vice Patricia M. Derian, resigned.

Submitted April 22—Continued

Robert Dean Nesen,
of California, to be Ambassador Extraordinary and Plenipotentiary of the United States of America to Australia and to serve concurrently and without additional compensation as Ambassador Extraordinary and Plenipotentiary of the United States of America to the Republic of Nauru.

Henry E. Catto, Jr.,
of Virginia, to be an Assistant Secretary of Defense, vice Thomas B. Ross, resigned.

Russell A. Rourke,
of Maryland, to be an Assistant Secretary of Defense, vice Russell Murray II, resigned.

Kenneth A. Gilles,
of North Dakota, to be Administrator of the Federal Grain Inspection Service, vice Earl Leland Bartelt, resigned.

Sherman E. Unger,
of Ohio, to be General Counsel of the Department of Commerce, vice Homer E. Moyer, Jr., resigned.

Gerald J. Mossinghoff,
of Virginia, to be Commissioner of Patents and Trademarks, vice Sidney A. Diamond, resigned.

Antonio Monroig,
of Puerto Rico, to be an Assistant Secretary of Housing and Urban Development, vice Sterling Tucker, resigned.

Joseph J. Tribble,
of Georgia, to be an Assistant Secretary of Energy (Conservation and Renewable Energy), vice Thomas Eugene Stelson, resigned.

Rosslee Green Douglas,
of South Carolina, to be Director of the Office of Minority Economic Impact, vice Louis F. Moret, resigned.

Vincent E. Reed,
of the District of Columbia, to be Assistant Secretary for Elementary and Secondary Education, Department of Education, vice Thomas Kendall Minter, resigned.

Loren A. Smith,
of Delaware, to be Chairman of the Administrative Conference of the United States for the term of 5 years, vice Reuben B. Robertson, resigned.

Edward E. Noble,
of Oklahoma, to be Chairman of the Board of
Directors of the United States Synthetic Fuels
Corporation for a term of 7 years, vice John C.
Sawhill.

Lawrence J. Brady,
of New Hampshire, to be an Assistant Secretary
of Commerce, vice Frank Alan Weil, resigned.

Arlene Triplett,
of Virginia, to be an Assistant Secretary of Commerce, vice Elsa Allgood Porter, resigned.

Paul A. Vander Myde,
of Virginia, to be an Assistant Secretary of Commerce, vice Andrew E. Manatos, resigned.

Richard D. DeLauer,
of California, to be Under Secretary of Defense
for Research and Engineering, vice William J.
Perry, resigned.

Submitted April 27

Robert Gerhard Neumann,
of California, to be Ambassador Extraordinary
and Plenipotentiary of the United States of
America to the Kingdom of Saudi Arabia.

Frank W. Naylor, Jr.,
of California, to be Under Secretary of Agriculture for Small Community and Rural Development, vice Alex P. Mercure, resigned.

W. Kenneth Davis,
of California, to be Deputy Secretary of Energy,
vice Lynn R. Coleman, resigned.

William C. Clohan, Jr.,
of West Virginia, to be Under Secretary of Education, vice Steven A. Minter, resigned.

Daniel Oliver,
of Connecticut, to be General Counsel, Department of Education, vice Betsy Levin, resigned.

Mark S. Fowler,
of Virginia, to be a member of the Federal Communications Commission for the unexpired term
of 7 years from July 1, 1979, vice Tyrone Brown,
resigned.

Alex Kozinski,
of California, to be Special Counsel of the Merit
Systems Protection Board for a term of 5 years,
vice Haywood Patrick Swygert, resigned.

Submitted April 29

Jonathan C. Rose,
of Virginia, to be an Assistant Attorney General,
vice Maurice Rosenberg, resigned.

Robert J. Rubin,
of Massachusetts, to be an Assistant Secretary of
Health and Human Services, vice John L. Palmer,
resigned.

Stephen J. Bollinger,
of Ohio, to be an Assistant Secretary of Housing
and Urban Development, vice Robert Campbell
Embry, Jr.

James R. Harris,
of Indiana, to be Director of the Office of Surface
Mining Reclamation and Enforcement, vice
Walter N. Heine, resigned.

Winifred Ann Pizzano,
of Virginia, to be Deputy Director of the
ACTION Agency, vice Mary Elizabeth King, resigned.

Submitted May 1

Mary Claiborne Jarratt,
of Virginia, to be an Assistant Secretary of Agriculture, vice Carol Tucker Foreman, resigned.

John V. Byrne,
of Oregon, to be Administrator of the National
Oceanic and Atmospheric Administration, vice
Richard Asher Frank, resigned.

Pamela Needham Bailey,
of Virginia, to be an Assistant Secretary of Health
and Human Services, vice Billy M. Wise, resigned.

Stephen May,
of New York, to be an Assistant Secretary of
Housing and Urban Development, vice Horace
Dicken Cherry, resigned.

David R. MacDonald,
of Illinois, to be a Deputy United States Trade
Representative, with the rank of Ambassador,
vice Robert D. Hormats.

Fred Joseph Villella,
of California, to be Deputy Director of the Federal Emergency Management Agency (new position).

Submitted May 4

John Whitlock Hernandez, Jr.,
of New Mexico, to be Deputy Administrator of the Environmental Protection Agency, vice Barbara Blum, resigned.

Submitted May 5

Carleton S. Coon, Jr.,
of New Hampshire, a Foreign Service officer of Class one, to be Ambassador Extraordinary and Plenipotentiary of the United States of America to the Kingdom of Nepal.

Robert A. McConnell,
of Arizona, to be an Assistant Attorney General, vice Alan A. Parker, resigned.

Richard P. Kusserow,
of Illinois, to be Inspector General, Department of Health and Human Services, vice Thomas D. Morris, resigned.

Reese H. Taylor, Jr.,
of Nevada, to be a member of the Interstate Commerce Commission for the term of 7 years from January 1, 1977, vice Robert J. Corber.

Submitted May 11

Henry Dargan McMaster,
of South Carolina, to be United States Attorney for the District of South Carolina for the term of 4 years, vice Thomas E. Lydon, Jr., deceased.

Submitted May 12

Tidal W. McCoy,
of Virginia, to be an Assistant Secretary of the Air Force, vice Joseph Charles Zengerle III, resigned.

Shelby Templeton Brewer,
of Maryland, to be an Assistant Secretary of Energy (Nuclear Energy), vice George W. Cunningham, resigned.

Charles M. Butler III,
of Maryland, to be a member of the Federal Energy Regulatory Commission for the remainder of the term expiring October 20, 1983, vice Charles B. Curtis, resigned.

Philip F. Johnson,
of Illinois, to be a Commissioner of the Commodity Futures Trading Commission for the term expiring April 13, 1984, vice Gary Leonard Seevers, resigned.

Philip F. Johnson,
of Illinois, to be Chairman of the Commodity Futures Trading Commission, vice James M. Stone.

Submitted May 12—Continued
Mary Ann Weyforth Dawson,
of the District of Columbia, to be a member of the Federal Communications Commission for a term of 7 years from July 1, 1981, vice Robert E. Lee, term expiring.

Thomas O. Enders,
of Connecticut, a Foreign Service officer of the Class of Career Minister, to be an Assistant Secretary of State, vice William Garton Bowdler, resigned.

Daniel J. Terra,
of Illinois, to be Ambassador at Large for Cultural Affairs.

Lawrence F. Davenport,
of California, to be an Associate Director of the ACTION agency, vice John Robert Lewis, resigned.

Fred Joseph Villella,
of California, to be an Associate Director of the Federal Emergency Management Agency, vice Frank A. Camm, resigned.

Paul Robert Boucher,
of Virginia, to be Inspector General, Small Business Administration (reappointment).

Donald E. Sowle,
of Virginia, to be Administrator for Federal Procurement Policy, vice Karen Hastie Williams, resigned.

Withdrawn May 12

Fred Joseph Villella,
of California, to be Deputy Director of the Federal Emergency Management Agency (new position), which was sent to the Senate on May 1, 1981.

Submitted May 14

Craig A. Nalen,
of Florida, to be President of the Overseas Private Investment Corporation, vice J. Bruce Llewellyn, resigned.

Georgiana H. Sheldon,
of Virginia, to be a member of the Federal Energy Regulatory Commission for a term expiring October 20, 1984 (reappointment).

Francis Anthony Keating II,
of Oklahoma, to be United States Attorney for the Northern District of Oklahoma for the term of 4 years, vice Hubert H. Bryant, resigning.

David L. Russell,
of Oklahoma, to be United States Attorney for
the Western District of Oklahoma for the term of
4 years, vice Larry D. Patton, resigning.

Submitted May 19

Ronald DeWayne Palmer,
of Maryland, a Foreign Service officer of Class
one, to be Ambassador Extraordinary and Plenipotentiary of the United States of America to
Malaysia.

James A. Belson,
of the District of Columbia, to be an Associate
Judge of the District of Columbia Court of Appeals for the term of 15 years, vice George R.
Gallagher, retired.

Submitted May 20

James B. Conkling,
of California, to be an Associate Director of the
International Communication Agency, vice Mary
C. F. Bitterman, resigned.

William A. Niskanen, Jr.,
of California, to be a member of the Council of
Economic Advisers, vice George C. Eads, resigned.

Submitted May 22

Eugene Victor Rostow,
of Connecticut, to be Director of the United
States Arms Control and Disarmament Agency,
vice Ralph Earle II, resigned.

Joel E. Bonner, Jr.,
of Virginia, to be an Assistant Secretary of the
Army, vice Alan J. Gibbs.

William R. Gianelli,
of California, to be an Assistant Secretary of the
Army, vice Michael Blumenfeld, resigned.

Warren Roger King,
of the District of Columbia, to be an Associate
Judge of the Superior Court of the District of
Columbia for a term of 15 years, vice Fred L.
McIntyre, retired.

Richard Stephen Salzman,
of the District of Columbia, to be an Associate
Judge of the Superior Court of the District of
Columbia for a term of 15 years, vice William S.
Thompson.

Reggie Barnett Walton,
of the District of Columbia, to be an Associate
Judge of the Superior Court of the District of

Submitted May 22—Continued
Columbia for a term of 15 years, vice Leonard
Braman.

Daniel N. Miller, Jr.,
of Wyoming, to be an Assistant Secretary of the
Interior, vice Joan Mariarenee Davenport.

Judith L. Tardy,
of Virginia, to be an Assistant Secretary of Housing and Urban Development, vice William Antonio Medina, resigned.

Alan Green, Jr.,
of Oregon, to be a Federal Maritime Commissioner for the term of 5 years expiring June 30,
1986, vice Leslie Lazar Kanuk, term expiring.

James Montgomery Beggs,
of Missouri, to be Administrator of the National
Aeronautics and Space Administration, vice
Robert Alan Frosch, resigned.

A. Alan Hill,
of California, to be a member of the Council on
Environmental Quality, vice James Gustave
Speth, resigned.

Submitted May 27

J. William Middendorf II,
of Virginia, to be the Permanent Representative
of the United States of America to the Organization of American States, with the rank of Ambassador.

Jose S. Sorzano,
of Virginia, to be the Representative of the
United States of America on the Economic and
Social Council of the United Nations, with the
rank of Ambassador.

Ernest Henry Preeg,
of Virginia, a Foreign Service officer of Class one,
to be Ambassador Extraordinary and Plenipotentiary of the United States of America to Haiti.

Charles L. Dempsey,
of Virginia, to be Inspector General, Department
of Housing and Urban Development (reappointment).

Kent Lloyd,
of California, to be Deputy Under Secretary for
Management, Department of Education, vice
John B. Gabusi.

James Bert Thomas, Jr.,
of Virginia, to be Inspector General, Department
of Education (reappointment).

James T. Hackett,
of Virginia, to be an Associate Director of the
International Communication Agency, vice James
David Isbister, resigned.

Submitted May 28

Theodore E. Cummings,
of California, to be Ambassador Extraordinary
and Plenipotentiary of the United States of
America to Austria.

Clarence Thomas,
of Maryland, to be Assistant Secretary for Civil
Rights, Department of Education, vice Cynthia
G. Brown, resigned.

O. Evans Denney,
of Delaware, to be United States Marshal for the
District of Delaware for the term of 4 years, vice
Irvin B. Smith, Jr., resigning.

Submitted May 29

Edward L. Rowny,
of Virginia, to be Special Representative for Arms
Control and Disarmament Negotiations, and to
have the rank of Ambassador while so serving,
vice Ralph Earle II, resigned.

Richard D. Erb,
of Virginia, to be United States Executive Director of the International Monetary Fund for a
term of 2 years, vice Sam Young Cross, Jr., resigned.

Harry N. Walters,
of New York, to be an Assistant Secretary of the
Army, vice William Eldred Peacock, resigned.

Robert G. Dederick,
of Illinois, to be an Assistant Secretary of Commerce, vice Robert Thallon Hall, resigned.

Bernard J. Wunder, Jr.,
of Virginia, to be Assistant Secretary of Commerce for Communications and Information, vice
Henry Geller, resigned.

Joseph P. Welsch,
of Virginia, to be Inspector General, Department
of Transportation, vice Frank Saburo Sato.

Robert Melvin Worthington,
of Utah, to be Assistant Secretary for Vocational
and Adult Education, Department of Education,
vice Daniel B. Taylor, resigned.

Dwight A. Ink,
of Maryland, to be Director of the Community
Services Administration, vice Richard John Rios.

Submitted May 29—Continued

Frank Saburo Sato,
of Virginia, to be Inspector General, Veterans
Administration, vice Allan L. Reynolds.

Submitted June 1

Charles W. Bray III,
of Maryland, a Foreign Service officer of Class
one, to be Ambassador Extraordinary and Plenipotentiary of the United States of America to the
Republic of Senegal.

Jane Abell Coon,
of New Hampshire, a Foreign Service officer of
Class two, to be Ambassador Extraordinary and
Plenipotentiary of the United States of America
to the People's Republic of Bangladesh.

Robert Sherwood Dillon,
of Virginia, a Foreign Service officer of Class one,
to be Ambassador Extraordinary and Plenipotentiary of the United States of America to the Republic of Lebanon.

Charles H. Price II,
of Missouri, to be Ambassador Extraordinary and
Plenipotentiary of the United States of America
to Belgium.

Maxwell M. Rabb,
of New York, to be Ambassador Extraordinary
and Plenipotentiary of the United States of
America to Italy.

Richard Mulberry,
of Texas, to be Inspector General, Department of
the Interior, vice June Gibbs Brown.

Sherman Maxwell Funk,
of Maryland, to be Inspector General, Department of Commerce, vice Mary P. Bass.

Thomas F. McBride,
of the District of Columbia, to be Inspector General, Department of Labor, vice Marjorie Fine
Knowles, resigned.

Joseph A. Sickon,
of Virginia, to be Inspector General, General
Services Administration, vice Kurt W. Muellen-
berg.

Submitted June 2

Ann Dore McLaughlin,
of the District of Columbia, to be an Assistant
Secretary of the Treasury, vice Joseph Laitin, resigned.

Submitted June 2—Continued
John M. Walker, Jr.,
of New York, to be an Assistant Secretary of the Treasury, vice Walter J. McDonald, resigned.

Peter J. Wallison,
of New York, to be General Counsel for the Department of the Treasury, vice Robert H. Mundheim, resigned.

Donald L. Dotson,
of Pennsylvania, to be an Assistant Secretary of Labor, vice William P. Hobgood.

Herman E. Roser,
of New Mexico, to be an Assistant Secretary of Energy (Defense Programs), vice Duane C. Sewell, resigned.

Jay F. Morris,
of Maryland, to be an Assistant Administrator of the Agency for International Development, vice Donald Gordon MacDonald, resigned.

Submitted June 3

Russell D. Hale,
of Virginia, to be an Assistant Secretary of the Air Force, vice Charles Willian Snodgrass, resigned.

The following-named persons to be members of the Board of Directors of the Commodity Credit Corporation:
　Richard E. Lyng, of Virginia, vice James H. Williams, resigned.
　Frank W. Naylor, Jr., of California, vice Malcolm Rupert Cutler.
　Mary Claiborne Jarratt, of Virginia, vice Carol Tucker Foreman.

J. Erich Evered,
of Nevada, to be Administrator of the Energy Information Administration, vice Lincoln E. Moses, resigned.

Submitted June 5

Donna Pope,
of Ohio, to be Director of the Mint for a term of 5 years, vice Stella B. Hackel.

Thomas Patrick Melady,
of Connecticut, to be Assistant Secretary for Postsecondary Education, Department of Education, vice Albert H. Bowker.

John H. Rodriguez,
of Virginia, to be Deputy Under Secretary for Intergovernmental and Interagency Affairs, Department of Education, vice Elizabeth S. Carpenter, resigned.

Submitted June 9

Dean E. Fischer,
of Virginia, to be an Assistant Secretary of State.

Vernon A. Walters,
of Florida, to be Ambassador at Large.

H. Monroe Browne,
of California, to be Ambassador Extraordinary and Plenipotentiary of the United States of America to New Zealand, and to serve concurrently and without additional compensation as Ambassador Extraordinary and Plenipotentiary of the United States of America to Western Samoa.

Edward J. Philbin,
of California, to be Deputy Assistant Secretary of Defense for Reserve Affairs, vice Harold W. Chase, resigned.

George A. Sawyer,
of New Jersey, to be an Assistant Secretary of the Navy, vice George A. Peapples, resigned.

John V. Graziano,
of Virginia, to be Inspector General, Department of Agriculture, vice Thomas F. McBride.

Warren T. Lindquist,
of New York, to be a member of the Board of Directors of the New Community Development Corporation, vice A. Russell Marane.

James R. Richards,
of Virginia, to be Inspector General of the Department of Energy, vice John Kenneth Mansfield.

K. William O'Connor,
of Virginia, to be Inspector General, Community Services Administration, vice Frankie Muse Freeman.

William H. Draper III,
of California, to be President of the Export-Import Bank of the United States, vice John Lovell Moore, Jr.

William R. Gianelli,
an Assistant Secretary of the Army, to be a member of the Board of the Panama Canal Commission, vice Michael Blumenfeld.

Submitted June 10

Richard T. Kennedy,
of the District of Columbia, to be the Representative of the United States of America to the International Atomic Energy Agency, with the rank of Ambassador.

Submitted June 10—Continued

W. Ernst Minor,
of Ohio, to be a member of the Council on Environmental Quality, vice Robert H. Harris.

June Gibbs Brown,
of Virginia, to be Inspector General, National Aeronautics and Space Administration, vice Eldon D. Taylor, resigned.

Submited June 11

Rex E. Lee,
of Utah, to be Solicitor General of the United States, vice Wade Hampton McCree, Jr., resigning.

William Bradford Reynolds,
of Maryland, to be an Assistant Attorney General, vice Drew S. Days III, resigned.

Michael J. Fenello,
of Florida, to be Deputy Administrator of the Federal Aviation Administration, vice Quentin Saint Clair Taylor.

Hans Michael Mark,
of Virginia, to be Deputy Administrator of the National Aeronautics and Space Administration, vice Alan M. Lovelace, resigned.

Nunzio J. Palladino,
of Pennsylvania, to be a member of the Nuclear Regulatory Commission for the term of 5 years expiring June 30, 1986, vice Joseph Mallam Hendrie, term expiring.

Submitted June 15

Jose Manuel Casanova,
of Florida, to be Executive Director of the Inter-American Development Bank for a term of 3 years, vice Ralph Anthony Dungan, resigned.

Francis J. West,
of Rhode Island, to be an Assistant Secretary of Defense, vice David E. McGiffert, resigned.

Harold V. Hunter,
of Oklahoma, to be Administrator of the Rural Electrification Administration for a term of 10 years, vice Robert W. Feragen, resigned.

Donald J. Senese,
of Virginia, to be Assistant Secretary for Educational Research and Improvement, Department of Education, vice F. James Rutherford, resigned.

Thomas L. Lias,
of Iowa, to be an Assistant Director of the ACTION Agency, vice Irene Tinker, resigned.

Submitted June 15—Continued

Gilbert A. Robinson,
of New York, to be Deputy Director of the International Communication Agency, vice Charles W. Bray III, resigned.

Danford L. Sawyer,
of Florida, to be Public Printer, vice John J. Boyle, resigned.

Charles H. Dean, Jr.,
of Tennessee, to be a member of the Board of Directors of the Tennessee Valley Authority for the term expiring May 18, 1990, vice Robert N. Clement, term expired.

Submitted June 16

Paul Heron Robinson, Jr.,
of Illinois, to be Ambassador Extraordinary and Plenipotentiary of the United States of America to Canada.

Arthur F. Burns,
of the District of Columbia, to be Ambassador Extraordinary and Plenipotentiary of the United States of America to the Federal Republic of Germany.

Joan M. Clark,
of New York, a career member of the Senior Foreign Service, to be Director General of the Foreign Service (new position).

Edward C. Prado,
of Texas, to be United States Attorney for the Western District of Texas for the term of 4 years, vice Jamie C. Boyd, resigned.

James G. Stearns,
of Nevada, to be Director of the Office of Alcohol Fuels (new position).

Withdrawn June 16

Ernest W. Lefever,
of Maryland, to be Assistant Secretary of State for Human Rights and Humanitarian Affairs, vice Patricia M. Derian, resigned, which was sent to the Senate on April 22, 1981.

Submitted June 18

The following-named persons to be members of the Board of Directors of the National Consumer Cooperative Bank for the terms indicated:
> *For the remainder of the term expiring September 23, 1982*
>> Carol E. Dinkins, an Assistant Attorney General, vice William A. Clement, Jr.

Submitted June 18—Continued

William Gene Lesher, an Assistant Secretary of Agriculture, vice Carol Tucker Foreman.

Roger William Mehle, Jr., an Assistant Secretary of the Treasury, vice Roger C. Altman.

Darrell M. Trent, Deputy Secretary of Transportation, vice Graciela (Grace) Olivarez.

Philip D. Winn, an Assistant Secretary of Housing and Urban Development, vice Geno Charles Baroni.

Joseph Robert Wright, Jr., Deputy Secretary of Commerce, vice Sam W. Brown, Jr.

For the remainder of the term expiring June 10, 1983

Albert Angrisani, an Assistant Secretary of Labor, vice Alexis Herman.

Submitted June 19

Jerry L. Jordan,
of New Mexico, to be a member of the Council of Economic Advisers, vice Stephen M. Goldfeld, resigned.

Submitted June 22

W. Antoinette Ford,
of Michigan, to be an Assistant Administrator of the Agency for International Development, vice Joseph Coolidge Wheeler.

Francis Stephen Ruddy,
of Texas, to be an Assistant Administrator of the Agency for International Development, vice Goler Teal Butcher, resigned.

William E. Mayer,
of California, to be Administrator of the Alcohol, Drug Abuse, and Mental Health Administration, vice Gerald L. Klerman, resigned.

Robert P. Nimmo,
of California, to be Administrator of Veterans' Affairs, vice Joseph Maxwell Cleland, resigned.

The following-named persons to be members of the Board of Directors of the United States Synthetic Fuels Corporation for the terms indicated:

Robert A. G. Monks,
of Maine, for a term of 3 years, vice Frank Savage, resigned.

Victor M. Thompson, Jr.,
of Oklahoma, for a term of 4 years (new position).

C. Howard Wilkins,
of Kansas, for a term of 5 years, vice Joseph Lane Kirkland, resigned.

Submitted June 22—Continued

Victor A. Schroeder,
of Georgia, for a term of six years (new position).

Submitted June 25

Parker W. Borg,
of the District of Columbia, a Foreign Service officer of Class two, to be Ambassador Extraordinary and Plenipotentiary of the United States of America to the Republic of Mali.

Robert Strausz-Hupé,
of Pennsylvania, to be Ambassador Extaordinary and Plenipotentiary of the United States of America to the Republic of Turkey.

Kenneth W. Gideon,
of Texas, to be an Assistant General Counsel in the Department of the Treasury (Chief Counsel for the Internal Revenue Service), vice N. Jerold Cohen, resigned.

Bevis Longstreth,
of New York, to be a member of the Securities and Exchange Commission for the remainder of the term expiring June 5, 1982, vice John S. R. Shad, resigned.

Robert A. Rowland,
of Texas, to be a member of the Occupational Safety and Health Review Commission for a term expiring April 27, 1987, vice Frank R. Barnako, term expired.

Sarah Evans Barker,
of Indiana, to be United States Attorney for the Southern District of Indiana for the term of 4 years, vice Virginia Dill McCarty, resigning.

Submitted June 30

Julius Waring Walker, Jr.,
of Texas, a Foreign Service officer of Class one, to be Ambassador Extraordinary and Plenipotentiary of the United States of America to the Republic of Upper Volta.

Richard L. Walker,
of South Carolina, to be Ambassador Extraordinary and Plenipotentiary of the United States of America to the Republic of Korea.

Davis Rowland Robinson,
of the District of Columbia, to be Legal Adviser of the Department of State, vice Roberts Bishop Owen, resigned.

Richard N. Perle,
of Maryland, to be an Assistant Secretary of Defense, vice Gerald Paul Dinneen, resigned.

Submitted June 30—Continued

Nora Walsh Hussey,
of South Dakota, to be Superintendent of the Mint of the United States at Denver, vice Evelyn T. Davidson, resigned.

Robert W. Karpe,
of California, to be President, Government National Mortgage Association, vice Ronald P. Laurent.

Anthony G. Sousa,
of Hawaii, to be a member of the Federal Energy Regulatory Commission for a term expiring October 20, 1984, vice George R. Hall, term expired.

J. Robinson West,
of Pennsylvania, to be an Assistant Secretary of the Interior, vice Larry E. Meierotto.

Submitted July 1

William C. Lee,
of Indiana, to be United States District Judge for the Northern District of Indiana, vice a new position created by P.L. 95–486, approved October 20, 1978.

Daniel K. Hedges,
of Texas, to be United States Attorney for the Southern District of Texas for the term of 4 years, vice Jose Antonio Canales, resigned.

Frank H. Conway,
of Massachusetts, to be a member of the Foreign Claims Settlement Commission for the remainder of the term expiring September 30, 1981, vice Ralph W. Emerson.

Frank H. Conway,
of Massachusetts, to be a member of the Foreign Claims Settlement Commission for the term expiring September 30, 1984 (reappointment).

George A. Conn,
of Maryland, to be Commissioner of the Rehabilitation Services Administration, vice Robert R. Humphreys, resigned.

Anne Graham,
of Virginia, to be Assistant Secretary for Legislation and Public Affairs, Department of Education, vice Martha Keys.

Jon D. Holstine,
of Virginia, to be an Assistant Administrator of the Agency for International Development, vice John H. Sullivan, resigned.

Submitted July 1—Continued

George A. Keyworth II,
of New Mexico, to be Director of the Office of Science and Technology Policy, vice Frank Press, resigned.

Submitted July 6

Kathleen M. Bennett,
of Virginia, to be an Assistant Administrator of the Environmental Protection Agency, vice David G. Hawkins, resigned.

Everett Alvarez, Jr.,
of Maryland, to be Deputy Director of the Peace Corps, vice William G. Sykes.

Submitted July 7

Robert John Hughes,
of Massachusetts, to be an Associate Director of the International Communication Agency, vice John William Shirley.

Submitted July 8

Arthur W. Hummel, Jr.,
of Maryland, a Foreign Service officer of the Class of Career Minister, to be Ambassador Extraordinary and Plenipotentiary of the United States of America to the People's Republic of China.

Monteagle Stearns,
of California, a Foreign Service officer of Class one, to be Ambassador Extraordinary and Plenipotentiary of the United States of America to Greece.

John R. Countryman,
of the District of Columbia, a Foreign Service officer of Class two, to be Ambassador Exraordinary and Plenipotentiary of the United States of America to the Sultanate of Oman.

William Lacy Swing,
of North Carolina, a Foreign Service officer of Class two, to be Ambassador Extraordinary and Plenipotentiary of the United States of America to the Republic of Liberia.

J. Raymond Bell,
of the District of Columbia, to be Chairman of the Foreign Claims Settlement Commission of the United States for the term expiring September 30, 1982 (new position—P.L. 96–209).

Rear Adm. Herbert R. Lippold, Jr.,
NOAA, to be Director of the National Ocean Survey, National Oceanic and Atmospheric Administration, vice Rear Adm. Allen L. Powell, retired.

Jan W. Mares,
of Connecticut, to be an Assistant Secretary of
Energy (Fossil Energy), vice George Fumich, Jr.,
resigned.

Alvin W. Trivelpiece,
of California, to be Director of the Office of
Energy Research, vice Edward Allan Frieman,
resigned.

John P. Horton,
of New Jersey, to be an Assistant Administrator of
the Environmental Protection Agency, vice William Drayton, Jr.

James H. Quello,
of Virginia, to be a member of the Federal Communications Commission for the unexpired term
of 7 years from July 1, 1977, vice Charles D.
Ferris, resigned.

Henry M. Rivera,
of New Mexico, to be a member of the Federal
Communications Commission for a term of 7
years from July 1, 1980, vice James H. Quello,
term expired.

Submitted July 9

David Anderson,
of New York, a Foreign Service officer of Class
one, to be Ambassador Extraordinary and Plenipotentiary of the United States of America to the
Socialist Federal Republic of Yugoslavia.

Marshall Brement,
of Arizona, a Foreign Service officer of Class one,
to be Ambassador Extraordinary and Plenipotentiary of the United States of America to Iceland.

Richard Noyes Viets,
of Vermont, a Foreign Service officer of Class
one, to be Ambassador Extraordinary and Plenipotentiary of the United States of America to the
Hashemite Kingdom of Jordan.

David Eugene Zweifel,
of Maryland, a Foreign Service officer of Class
two, to be Ambassador Extraordinary and Plenipotentiary of the United States of America to the
Yemen Arab Republic.

D. Brook Bartlett,
of Missouri, to be United States District Judge for
the Western District of Missouri, vice John W.
Oliver, retired.

John R. Gibson,
of Missouri, to be United States District Judge for
the Western District of Missouri, vice Elmo B.
Hunter, retired.

Joseph E. Stevens, Jr.,
of Missouri, to be United States District Judge for
the Eastern and Western Districts of Missouri,
vice William R. Collinson, retired.

William W. Wilkins, Jr.,
of South Carolina, to be United States District
Judge for the District of South Carolina, vice
Robert W. Hemphill, retired.

Richard S. Cohen,
of Maine, to be United States Attorney for the
District of Maine for the term of 4 years, vice
Thomas E. Delahanty II, resigning.

Thomas Morgan Roberts,
of the District of Columbia, to be a member of
the Nuclear Regulatory Commission for the term
expiring June 30, 1985, vice Richard T. Kennedy,
term expired.

Submitted July 10

John Langeloth Loeb, Jr.,
of New York, to be Ambassador Extraordinary
and Plenipotentiary of the United States of
America to Denmark.

Keith Foote Nyborg,
of Idaho, to be Ambassador Extraordinary and
Plenipotentiary of the United States of America
to Finland.

Julia Chang Bloch,
of the District of Columbia, to be an Assistant
Administrator of the Agency for International
Development, vice Calvin H. Raullerson, resigned.

Submitted July 13

Abraham Katz,
of Florida, a Foreign Service officer of Class one,
to be the Representative of the United States of
America to the Organization for Economic Cooperation and Development, with the rank of Ambassador.

A. Melvin McDonald,
of Arizona, to be United States Attorney for the
District of Arizona for the term of 4 years, vice
Michael D. Hawkins, resigned.

R. Lawrence Steele, Jr.,
of Indiana, to be United States Attorney for the
Northern District of Indiana for the term of 4
years, vice David T. Ready, resigning.

Submitted July 13—Continued
Thomas E. Dittmeier,
of Missouri, to be United States Attorney for the Eastern District of Missouri for the term of 4 years, vice Robert D. Kingsland.

Richard A. Stacy,
of Wyoming, to be United States Attorney for the District of Wyoming for the term of 4 years, vice Charles E. Graves, resigned.

Nancy Harvey Steorts,
of Maryland, to be a member of the Consumer Product Safety Commission for the remainder of the term expiring October 26, 1984, vice Susan B. King.

Nancy Harvey Steorts,
of Maryland, to be Chairman of the Consumer Product Safety Commission (new position).

Alfred F. Eckes, Jr.,
of Virginia, to be a member of the United States International Trade Commission for the remainder of the term expiring June 16, 1990, vice Italo H. Ablondi.

Eugene J. Frank,
of Pennsylvania, to be a member of the United States International Trade Commission for the remainder of the term expiring December 16, 1982, vice George M. Moore, resigned.

Submitted July 15

Kenneth L. Adelman,
of Virginia, to be the Deputy Representative of the United States of America to the United Nations, with the rank and status of Ambassador Extraordinary and Plenipotentiary.

William Jennings Dyess,
of Alabama, a Foreign Service officer of Class one, to be Ambassador Extraordinary and Plenipotentiary of the United States of America to the Kingdom of the Netherlands.

Frederic L. Chapin,
of New Jersey, a Foreign Service officer of Class one, to be Ambassador Extraordinary and Plenipotentiary of the United States of America to Guatemala.

Bruce Chapman,
of Washington, to be Director of the Census, vice Vincent P. Barabba, resigned.

William M. Otter,
of Kentucky, to be Administrator of the Wage and Hour Division, Department of Labor, vice Xavier M. Vela, resigned.

Submitted July 15—Continued
Marie P. Tolliver,
of Oklahoma, to be Commissioner on Aging, vice Robert Clyde Benedict.

William Addison Vaughan,
of Michigan, to be an Assistant Secretary of Energy (Environmental Protection, Safety and Emergency Preparedness), vice Ruth C. Clusen, resigned.

Elise R. W. du Pont,
of Delaware, to be an Assistant Administrator of the Agency for International Development, vice Genta A. Hawkins, resigning.

Submitted July 16

Clifford M. Barber,
of New York, to be Superintendent of the United States Assay Office at New York, New York, vice Manuel A. Sanchez, Jr.

Henry E. Thomas IV,
of Virginia, to be an Assistant Secretary of Energy (International Affairs), vice Leslie J. Goldman.

Robert F. Chapman,
of South Carolina, to be a United States Circuit Judge for the Fourth Circuit, vice Clement F. Haynsworth, Jr., retired.

John C. Bell,
of Alabama, to be United States Attorney for the Middle District of Alabama for the term of 4 years, vice Barry E. Teague.

J. B. Sessions III,
of Alabama, to be United States Attorney for the Southern District of Alabama for the term of 4 years, vice William A. Kimbrough, Jr., resigned.

Joseph J. Farnan, Jr.,
of Delaware, to be United States Attorney for the District of Delaware for the term of 4 years, vice James W. Garvin, Jr.

James A. Rolfe,
of Texas, to be United States Attorney for the Northern District of Texas for the term of 4 years, vice Kenneth J. Mighell.

James C. Miller III,
of the District of Columbia, to be a Federal Trade Commissioner for the term of 7 years from September 26, 1981, vice Paul Rand Dixon, term expiring.

Submitted July 23

Anthony H. Murray, Jr.,
of Pennsylvania, to be Superintendent of the Mint of the United States at Philadelphia, vice Shallie M. Bey, Jr.

Edward C. Aldridge, Jr.,
of Virginia, to be Under Secretary of the Air Force, vice Antonia Handler Chayes, resigned.

J. Paul McGrath,
of New Jersey, to be an Assistant Attorney General, vice Alice Daniel, resigned.

Dallas Lynn Peck,
of Virginia, to be Director of the Geological Survey, vice H. William Menard.

Charles Wilson Shuman,
of Illinois, to be Administrator of the Farmers Home Administration, vice Gordon Cavanaugh, resigned.

Thomas R. Donnelly, Jr.,
of Virginia, to be an Assistant Secretary of Health and Human Services, vice William Brownlee Welsh, resigned.

Juan A. del Real,
of Maryland, to be General Counsel of the Department of Health and Human Services, vice Joan Zeldes Bernstein, resigned.

James Eugene Burnett, Jr.,
of Arkansas, to be a member of the National Transportation Safety Board for the term expiring December 31, 1985, vice Elwood Thomas Driver, term expired.

James Eugene Burnett, Jr.,
of Arkansas, to be Chairman of the National Transportation Safety Board for a term of 2 years, vice James B. King, term expiring.

Rayburn D. Hanzlik,
of California, to be Administrator of the Economic Regulatory Administration, vice Hazel Reid Rollins.

Matthew Norman Novick,
of the District of Columbia, to be Inspector General, Environmental Protection Agency, vice Inez Smith Reid.

William M. Bell,
of Michigan, to be a member of the Equal Employment Opportunity Commission for the term expiring July 1, 1986, vice Eleanor Holmes Norton.

Submitted July 23—Continued
L. Keith Bulen,
of Indiana, to be a Commissioner on the part of the United States on the International Joint Commission, United States and Canada, vice Jean Lande Hennessey, resigned.

Robert P. Hunter,
of Virginia, to be a member of the National Labor Relations Board for the term of 5 years expiring August 27, 1985, vice John C. Truesdale.

Paul J. Manafort, Jr.,
of Virginia, to be a member of the Board of Directors of the Overseas Private Investment Corporation for a term expiring December 17, 1983, vice Wallace F. Bennett, term expired.

Frank S. Swain,
of the District of Columbia, to be Chief Counsel for Advocacy, Small Business Administration, vice Milton David Stewart, resigned.

Submitted July 24

Elizabeth Jones,
of New Jersey, to be Engraver in the Mint of the United States at Philadelphia, Pennsylvania, vice Frank Gasparro, resigned.

Alton Gold Keel, Jr.,
of the District of Columbia, to be an Assistant Secretary of the Air Force, vice Robert Jay Hermann.

Michael R. Spaan,
of Alaska, to be United States Attorney for the District of Alaska for the term of 4 years, vice Alexander O. Bryner, resigned.

Jean Tufts,
of New Hampshire, to be Assistant Secretary for Special Education and Rehabilitative Services, Department of Education, vice Edwin W. Martin, Jr.

The following-named persons to be members of the California Debris Commission:
Brig. Gen. Homer Johnstone, Jr., Corps of Engineers
Col. Paul Bazilwich, Jr., Corps of Engineers
Col. Paul Frederick Kavanaugh, Corps of Engineers

Clarence Eugene Hodges,
of Indiana, to be an Assistant Director of the Community Services Administration, vice Michael T. Blouin, resigned.

Maj. Gen. William Edgar Reed,
United States Army, to be a member and president of the Mississippi River Commission.

The following-named persons to be members of the Mississippi River Commission:
  Maj. Gen. Hugh Granville Robinson, United States Army
  Brig. Gen. Richard Samuel Kem, United States Army

John R. Van de Water,
of California, to be a member of the National Labor Relations Board for the remainder of the term expiring August 27, 1981, vice John A. Penello, resigned.

John R. Van de Water,
of California, to be a member of the National Labor Relations Board for the term of 5 years expiring August 27, 1986 (reappointment).

Submitted July 28

Jack F. Matlock, Jr.,
of Florida, a Foreign Service officer of Class one, to be Ambassador Extraordinary and Plenipotentiary of the United States of America to the Czechoslovak Socialist Republic.

Roger J. Miner,
of New York, to be United States District Judge for the Northern District of New York, vice James T. Foley, retired.

Submitted July 29

Robert P. Paganelli,
of New York, a Foreign Service officer of Class one, to be Ambassador Extraordinary and Plenipotentiary of the United States of America to the Syrian Arab Republic.

Donald L. Totten,
of Illinois, to be a Commissioner on the part of the United States on the International Joint Commission, United States and Canada, vice Charles R. Ross, resigned.

Joseph M. McLaughlin,
of New York, to be United States District Judge for the Eastern District of New York, vice a new position created by P.L. 95–486, approved October 20, 1978.

John E. Sprizzo,
of New York, to be United States District Judge for the Southern District of New York, vice Charles H. Tenney, retired.

Frank W. Donaldson,
of Alabama, to be United States Attorney for the Northern District of Alabama for the term of 4 years, vice Jesse Roscoe Brooks, resigned.

J. Frederick Motz,
of Maryland, to be United States Attorney for the District of Maryland for the term of 4 years, vice Russell T. Baker Jr., resigned.

W. Stephen Thayer III,
of New Hampshire, to be United States Attorney for the District of New Hampshire for the term of 4 years, vice William H. Shaheen, resigned.

Charles M. Girard,
of Virginia, to be an Associate Director of the Federal Emergency Management Agency, vice Richard J. Green.

Submitted July 31

William Courtney Sherman,
of Virginia, a Foreign Service officer of Class one, to be the Deputy Representative of the United States of America in the Security Council of the United Nations, with the rank of Ambassador.

Ronald I. Spiers,
of Vermont, a Foreign Service officer of the Class of Career Minister, to be Ambassador Extraordinary and Plenipotentiary of the United States of America to the Islamic Republic of Pakistan

Ben J. Wattenberg,
of the District of Columbia, to be a member of the Board for International Broadcasting for a term expiring April 28, 1983, vice John A. Gronouski, term expired.

Joseph Robert Wright, Jr.,
of New York, to be Federal Cochairman of the following:
  1. Coastal Plains Regional Commission
  2. Four Corners Regional Commission
  3. New England Regional Commission
  4. Old West Regional Commission
  5. Ozarks Regional Commission
  6. Pacific Northwest Regional Commission
  7. Southwest Border Regional Commission
  8. Upper Great Lakes Regional Commission

Thomas K. Turnage,
of California, to be Director of Selective Service, vice Bernard Daniel Rostker, resigned.

Submitted August 11

Henry R. Wilhoit, Jr.,
of Kentucky, to be United States District Judge for the Eastern District of Kentucky, vice Howard David Hermansdorfer, resigned.

Conrad K. Cyr,
of Maine, to be United States District Judge for the District of Maine, vice George J. Mitchell, resigned.

John C. Coughenour,
of Washington, to be United States District Judge for the Western District of Washington, vice Morell E. Sharp, deceased.

Glen H. Davidson,
of Mississippi, to be United States Attorney for the Northern District of Mississippi for the term of 4 years, vice Hosea M. Ray, resigned.

George Landon Phillips,
of Mississippi, to be United States Attorney for the Southern District of Mississippi for the term of 4 years, vice Robert E. Hauberg, retired.

Gary L. Jones,
of Virginia, to be Deputy Under Secretary for Planning and Budget, Department of Education, vice Carl William Fischer, resigned.

Edward A. Curran,
of Maryland, to be Director of the National Institute of Education, vice P. Michael Timpane.

Submitted August 18

Dominick L. DiCarlo,
of New York, to be Assistant Secretary of State for International Narcotics Matters.

George Southall Vest,
of Maryland, a Foreign Service officer of the Class of Career Minister, to be the Representative of the United States of America to the European Communities, with the rank and status of Ambassador Extraordinary and Plenipotentiary.

Robert Carlton Horton,
of Colorado, to be Director of the Bureau of Mines, vice Lindsey D. Norman, Jr.

Charles A. Bowsher,
of Maryland, to be Comptroller General of the United Sates for a term of 15 years, vice Elmer Boyd Staats, term expired.

John Gunther Dean,
of New York, a Foreign Service officer of the Class of Career Minister, to be Ambassador Extraordinary and Plenipotentiary of the United States of America to Thailand.

Submitted August 18—Continued
John E. Dolibois,
of Ohio, to be Ambassador Extraordinary and Plenipotentiary of the United States of America to Luxembourg.

Raymond C. Ewing,
of Virginia, a Foreign Service officer of Class one, to be Ambassador Extraordinary and Plenipotentiary of the United States of America to the Republic of Cyprus.

Submitted August 19

Sandra Day O'Connor,
of Arizona, to be an Associate Justice of the Supreme Court of the United States, vice Potter Stewart, retired.

Michael H. Newlin,
of Maryland, a Foreign Service officer of Class one, to be Ambassador Extraordinary and Plenipotentiary of the United States of America to the Democratic and Popular Republic of Algeria.

Submitted August 28

Harry G. Barnes, Jr.,
of Maryland, a Foreign Service officer of the Class of Career Minister, to be Ambassador Extraordinary and Plenipotentiary of the United States of America to India.

Arthur Adair Hartman,
of New Jersey, a Foreign Service officer of the Class of Career Minister, to be Ambassador Extraordinary and Plenipotentiary of the United States of America to the Union of Soviet Socialist Republics.

Guy W. Fiske,
of Missouri, to be Under Secretary of Energy, vice John Mark Deutch, resigned.

John Augustus Bohn, Jr.,
of California, to be United States Director of the Asian Development Bank, vice Lester E. Edmond, resigned.

Charles Edwin Lord,
of the District of Columbia, to be First Vice President of the Export-Import Bank of the United States, vice H. K. Allen, resigned.

Lee M. Thomas,
of South Carolina, to be an Associate Director of the Federal Emergency Management Agency, vice William H. Wilcox, resigned.

Submitted August 28—Continued

Nyle C. Brady,
of New York, to be an Assistant Administrator of the Agency for International Development, vice Sander Martin Levin, resigned.

H. Franklin Water,
of Arkansas, to be United States District Judge for the Western District of Arkansas, vice Paul X. Williams, retiring.

John Ernest Lamp,
of Washington, to be United States Attorney for the Eastern District of Washington for the term of 4 years, vice James J. Gillespie, resigning.

Emery R. Jordan,
of Maine, to be United States Marshal for the District of Maine for the term of 4 years, vice Richard D. Dutremble.

Submitted September 4

M. Virginia Schafer,
of Washington, a Foreign Service officer of Class two, to be Ambassador Extraordinary and Plenipotentiary of the United States of America to Papua New Guinea, and to serve concurrently and without additional compensation as Ambassador Extraordinary and Plenipotentiary of the United States of America to the Solomon Islands.

Frank V. Ortiz, Jr.,
of New Mexico, a Foreign Service officer of Class one, to be Ambassador Extraordinary and Plenipotentiary of the United Sates of America to Peru.

David B. Funderburk,
of North Carolina, to be Ambassador Extraordinary and Plenipotentiary of the United States of America to the Socialist Republic of Romania.

Faith Ryan Whittlesey,
of Pennsylvania, to be Ambassador Extraordinary and Plenipotentiary of the United States of America to Switzerland.

Luis Victor Hurtado,
of California, to be Assayer of the Mint of the United States at Denver, vice Michael E. Witt.

Robert N. Smith,
of Ohio, to be an Assistant Secretary of Defense, vice John Howard Moxley III, resigned.

Cameron M. Batjer,
of Nevada, to be a Commissioner of the United States Parole Commission for a term of 6 years, vice William E. Amos, term expired.

Submitted September 4—Continued

Everett George Rank, Jr.,
of California to be a member of the Board of Directors of the Commodity Credit Corporation, vice Howard W. Hjort.

Lawrence Y. Goldberg,
of Rhode Island, to be an Assistant Director of the Community Services Administration, vice Robert Stern Landmann, resigned.

John A. Todhunter,
of Maryland, to be Assistant Administrator for Toxic Substances of the Environmental Protection Agency, vice Steven D. Jellinek.

Donald Eugene Santarelli,
of Virginia, to be a member of the Board of Directors of the Overseas Private Investment Corporation for a term expiring December 17, 1983, vice Edward L. Marcus, term expired.

Submitted September 8

Lawrence W. Pierce,
of New York, to be United States Circuit Judge for the Second Circuit, vice Murray I. Gurfein, deceased.

Submitted September 10

Richard W. Murphy,
of Maryland, a Foreign Service officer of the Class of Career Minister, to be Ambassador Extraordinary and Plenipotentiary of the United States of America to the Kingdom of Saudi Arabia, to which office he was appointed during the last recess of the Senate.

Thomas Aranda, Jr.,
of Arizona, to be Ambassador Extraordinary and Plenipotentiary of the United States of America to Uruguay.

Joseph Verner Reed, Jr.,
of Connecticut, to be Ambassador Extraordinary and Plenipotentiary of the United States of America to the Kingdom of Morocco.

Donald James Quigg,
of Oklahoma, to be Deputy Commissioner of Patents and Trademarks, vice Lutrelle F. Parker.

Susan Meredith Phillips,
of Iowa, to be a Commissioner of the Commodity Futures Trading Commission for the term expiring April 13, 1985, vice Read P. Dunn, Jr., term expired.

Jeffrey S. Bragg,
of Ohio, to be Federal Insurance Administrator,
Federal Emergency Management Agency, vice
Gloria Cusumano Jimenez.

Richard J. Bishirjian,
of New York, to be an Associate Director of the
International Communication Agency, vice Alice
Stone Ilchman.

Submitted September 11

Langhorne A. Motley,
of Alaska, to be Ambassador Extraordinary and
Plenipotentiary of the United States of America
to Brazil.

Richard F. Staar,
of California, for the rank of Ambassador during
his tenure of service as Representative of the
United States of America for Mutual and Balanced
Force Reductions Negotiations.

James F. Goodrich,
of Maine, to be Under Secretary of the Navy,
vice Robert J. Murray, resigned.

Loretta Cornelius,
of Virginia, to be Deputy Director of the Office
of Personnel Management, vice Jule M. Sugarman,
resigned.

Submitted September 14

John S. Herrington,
of California, to be an Assistant Secretary of the
Navy, vice Joseph A. Doyle.

Harold E. Shear,
of Connecticut, to be Administrator of the Maritime
Administration (new position).

Tom C. Korologos,
of Virginia, to be a member of the United States
Advisory Commission on Public Diplomacy for a
term expiring July 1, 1984, vice John Hope
Franklin, term expired.

Frederic V. Malek,
of Virginia, to be a Governor of the United States
Postal Service for a term expiring December 8,
1989, vice Wallace Nathaniel Hyde.

Submitted September 15

The following-named persons to be the
Representative and Alternate Representatives of
the United States of America to the Twenty-fifth
Session of the General Conference of the
International Atomic Energy Agency:

Submitted September 15—Continued
  Representative:
    W. Kenneth Davis, of California

  Alternate Representatives:

    Richard T. Kennedy, of the District of Columbia
    Roger Kirk, of the District of Columbia
    Thomas M. Roberts, of Tennessee

John Augustus Bohn, Jr.,
of California, for the rank of Ambassador, while
serving as United States Director of the Asian
Development Bank.

Sonia Landau,
of New York, to be a member of the Corporation
for Public Broadcasting for the remainder of the
term expiring March 26, 1986, vice Melba Patillo
Beals.

R. Kenneth Towery,
of Texas, to be a member of the Corporation for
Public Broadcasting for the remainder of the
term expiring March 26, 1986, vice Reuben W.
Askanase.

Submitted September 16

Vernon R. Wiggins,
of Alaska, to be Federal Cochairman of the
Alaska Land Use Council (new position).

James J. Carey,
of Illinois, to be a Federal Maritime Commissioner
for the remainder of the term expiring June
30, 1985, vice Peter N. Teige, resigned.

Submitted September 17

William L. Garwood,
of Texas, to be United States Circuit Judge for
the Fifth Circuit, vice a new position created by
P.L. 95–486, approved October 20, 1978.

Hayden Wilson Head, Jr.,
of Texas, to be United States District Judge for
the Southern District of Texas, vice Owen D.
Cox, retired.

James R. Nowlin,
of Texas, to be United States District Judge for
the Western District of Texas, vice Jack Roberts,
retired.

William H. Kennedy,
of California, to be United States Attorney for the
Southern District of California for the term of 4
years, vice Michael H. Walsh, resigned.

Submitted September 17—Continued
Guy Gordon Hurlbutt,
of Idaho, to be United States Attorney for the District of Idaho for the term of 4 years, vice M. Karl Shurtliff, resigning.

Jim J. Marquez,
of Kansas, to be United States Attorney for the District of Kansas for the term of 4 years, vice James P. Buchele, resigned.

John A. Smietanka,
of Michigan, to be United States Attorney for the Western District of Michigan for the term of 4 years, vice James S. Brady, resigned.

Kenneth W. McAllister,
of North Carolina, to be United States Attorney for the Middle District of North Carolina for the term of 4 years, vice Henry M. Michaux, Jr., resigned.

Samuel T. Currin,
of North Carolina, to be United States Attorney for the Eastern District of North Carolina for the term of 4 years, vice George M. Anderson, resigned.

Rodney Scott Webb,
of North Dakota, to be United States Attorney for the District of North Dakota for the term of 4 years, vice James R. Britton, resigned.

Brent D. Ward,
of Utah, to be United States Attorney for the District of Utah for the term of 4 years, vice Ronald L. Rencher, resigned.

George W. F. Cook,
of Vermont, to be United States Attorney for the District of Vermont for the term of 4 years, vice William B. Gray, resigned.

Thomas C. Greene,
of Alabama, to be United States Marshal for the Northern District of Alabama for the term of 4 years, vice Ralph C. Bishop.

Melvin E. Jones,
of Alabama, to be United States Marshal for the Middle District of Alabama for the term of 4 years, vice Rufus A. Lewis, resigning.

P. A. Mangini,
of Connecticut, to be United States Marshal for the District of Connecticut for the term of 4 years, vice Anthony G. Dirienzo, resigned.

Lynn H. Duncan,
of Georgia, to be United States Marshal for the Northern District of Georgia for the term of 4 years, vice Ronald E. Angel, resigned.

Submitted September 17—Continued
Ralph D. Morgan,
of Indiana, to be United States Marshal for the Southern District of Indiana for the term of 4 years, vice Frank J. Anderson, resigning.

Submitted September 18

Rickey Dale James,
of Missouri, to be a member of the Mississippi River Commission for a term of 9 years, vice Wilmer Richard Hall, resigned.

Submitted September 21

Thomas R. Pickering,
of New Jersey, a Foreign Service officer of the Class of Career Minister, to be Ambassador Extraordinary and Plenipotentiary of the United States of America to the Federal Republic of Nigeria.

Beverly E. Ledbetter,
of Rhode Island, to be an Assistant Attorney General, vice a new position created by P.L. 95–598, approved November 6, 1978.

Malcolm R. Lovell, Jr.,
of the District of Columbia, to be Under Secretary of Labor, vice John N. Gentry.

John F. Cogan,
of California, to be an Assistant Secretary of Labor, vice Arnold H. Packer.

Lenora Cole-Alexander,
of the District of Columbia, to be Director of the Women's Bureau, Department of Labor, vice Alexis M. Herman.

C. Everett Koop,
of Pennsylvania, to be Medical Director in the Regular Corps of the Public Health Service, subject to qualifications therefor as provided by law and regulations, and to be Surgeon General of the Public Health Service, for a term of 4 years, vice Julius Benjamin Richmond, term expired.

Mark Goode,
of California, to be a member of the Board for International Broadcasting for a term expiring April 28, 1983, vice Rita E. Hauser, resigned.

James Ernest Yonge,
of Florida, to be a member of the Board of Directors of the Export-Import Bank of the United States, vice Thibaut de Saint Phalle, resigned.

Rosemary M. Collyer,
of Colorado, to be a member of the Federal Mine Safety and Health Review Commission for the

Submitted September 21—Continued
term of 6 years expiring August 30, 1986, vice
Jerome R. Waldie.

Joseph Wentling Brown,
of Nevada, to be a member of the Foreign
Claims Settlement Commission of the United
States for the term expiring September 30, 1983,
vice Francis Leon Jung, term expired.

Edgar F. Callahan,
of Illinois, to be a member of the National Credit
Union Administration Board for the term expiring August 2, 1987, vice Harold Alonza Black,
term expired.

Carlos Salman,
of Florida, to be a member of the Board of Directors of the Overseas Private Investment Corporation for a term expiring December 17, 1982, vice
James M. Friedman, term expired.

Submitted September 23

Joe E. Whitley,
of Georgia, to be United States Attorney for the
Middle District of Georgia for the term of 4
years, vice D. Lee Rampey, Jr., resigned.

Dan K. Webb,
of Illinois, to be United States Attorney for the
Northern District of Illinois for the term of 4
years, vice Thomas P. Sullivan, resigned.

Ronald E. Meredith,
of Kentucky, to be United States Attorney for the
Western District of Kentucky for the term of 4
years, vice J. Albert Jones, resigned.

Stanford O. Bardwell, Jr.,
of Louisiana, to be United States Attorney for the
Middle District of Louisiana for the term of 4
years, vice Donald L. Beckner, term expired.

Leonard R. Gilman,
of Michigan, to be United States Attorney for the
Eastern District of Texas for the term of 4 years,
vice James K. Robinson, resigned.

Robert J. Wortham,
of Texas, to be United States Attorney for the
Eastern District of Texas for the term of 4 years,
vice John H. Hannah, Jr., resigned.

Submitted Sepember 24

Michael Joseph Connally,
of Michigan, to be General Counsel of the Equal
Employment Opportunity Commission for a term
of 4 years, vice Leroy D. Clark, resigned.

Submitted Sepember 24—Continued
Frederic N. Andre,
of Indiana, to be a member of the Interstate
Commerce Commission for the term of 7 years
from January 1, 1981, vice Charles L. Clapp,
term expired.

Malcolm M. B. Sterrett,
of Maryland, to be a member of the Interstate
Commerce Commission for the term of 7 years
from January 1, 1981, vice George M. Stafford,
resigned.

Submitted September 28

Paul A. Magnuson,
of Minnesota, to be United States District Judge
for the District of Minnesota, vice Edward J.
Devitt, retired.

Samuel J. Cornelius,
of the District of Columbia, to be Deputy Director of the Community Services Administration,
vice William Whitaker Allison.

Submitted September 29

John Dimitri Negroponte,
of New York, a Foreign Service officer of Class
one, to be Ambassador Extraordinary and Plenipotentiary of the United States of America to
Honduras.

Alan M. Hardy,
of Virginia, a Foreign Service officer of Class one,
to be Ambassador Extraordinary and Plenipotentiary of the United States of America to the Republic of Equatorial Guinea.

David Charles Miller, Jr.,
of Maryland, to be Ambassador Extraordinary
and Plenipotentiary of the United States of
America to the United Republic of Tanzania.

Howard Kent Walker,
of New Jersey, a Foreign Service officer of Class
two, to be Ambassador Extraordinary and Plenipotentiary of the United States of America to the
Republic of Togo.

Pedro A. Sanjuan,
of the District of Columbia, to be an Assistant
Secretary of the Interior, vice John Henry Kyl,
resigned.

Ford Barney Ford,
of California, to be Assistant Secretary of Labor
for Mine Safety and Health, vice Robert B. Lagather.

Submitted September 29—Continued

Norman Braman,
of Florida, to be Commissioner of Immigration
and Naturalization, vice Leonel J. Castillo, resigned.

Ralph Ball,
of Kansas, to be a member of the Federal Farm
Credit Board, Farm Credit Administration, for a
term expiring March 31, 1987, vice Ralph N.
Austin, term expired.

L. Ebersole Gaines,
of Idaho, to be Executive Vice President of the
Overseas Private Investment Corporation, vice
Dean R. Axtell, resigned.

Submitted October 1

Richard J. Cardamone,
of New York, to be United States Circuit Judge
for the Second Circuit, vice William H. Mulligan,
resigned.

Robert D. Potter,
of North Carolina, to be United States District
Judge for the Western District of North Carolina,
vice a new position created by P.L. 95–486, approved October 20, 1978.

James R. Ambrose,
of North Carolina, to be Under Secretary of the
Army, vice Robert Harry Spiro, Jr., resigned.

Jay Raymond Sculley,
of Virginia, to be an Assistant Secretary of the
Army, vice Percy Anthony Pierre, resigned.

Submitted October 5

William H. Ewing, Jr.,
of Tennessee, to be United States Attorney for
the Western District of Tennessee for the term of
4 years, vice W. J. Michael Cody, resigned.

Robert W. Foster,
of Ohio, to be United States Marshal for the
Southern District of Ohio for the term of 4 years,
vice Roy A. Smith, resigned.

Submitted October 6

Geoffrey Swaebe,
of California, to be the Representative of the
United States of America to the European Office
of the United Nations, with the rank of Ambassador.

Clinton Dan McKinnon,
of California, to be a member of the Civil Aeronautics Board for the remainder of the term expiring December 31, 1985, vice Marvin S. Cohen,
resigned.

Submitted October 7

Robert N. Miller,
of Colorado, to be United States Attorney for the
District of Colorado for the term of 4 years, vice
Joseph F. Dolan, term expired.

Alan H. Nevas,
of Connecticut, to be United States Attorney for
the District of Connecticut for the term of 4
years, vice Richard Blumenthal, term expired.

Ronald D. Lahners,
of Nebraska, to be United States Attorney for the
District of Nebraska for the term of 4 years, vice
Edward G. Warin, resigned.

Robert D. Olson, Sr.,
of Alaska, to be United States Marshal for the
District of Alaska for the term of 4 years (reappointment).

Ralph L. Boling,
of Kentucky, to be United States Marshal for the
Western District of Kentucky for the term of 4
years, vice Robert L. Wright, resigned.

Charles Pennington, Jr.,
of Kentucky, to be United States Marshal for the
Eastern District of Kentucky for the term of 4
years, vice Billie Lykins, resigning.

Laurence C. Beard,
of Oklahoma, to be United States Marshal for the
Eastern District of Oklahoma for the term of 4
years, vice Rex O. Presley, resigning.

Kernan H. Bagley,
of Oregon, to be United States Marshal for the
District of Oregon for the term of 4 years, vice
Wallace P. Bowen, resigned.

Jean Broward Shevlin Gerard,
of New York, for the rank of Ambassador during
the tenure of her service as the United States
Permanent Representative to the United Nations
Educational, Scientific, and Cultural Organization.

Submitted October 9

Robert A. Jantzen,
of Arizona, to be Director of the United States
Fish and Wildlife Service, vice Lynn Adams
Greenwalt, resigned.

Carlos C. Campbell,
of Virginia, to be an Assistant Secretary of Commerce, vice Jerry Joseph Jasinowski, resigned.

Submitted October 9—Continued
Lilla Burt Cummings Tower,
of Texas, to be Director of the Institute for Museum Services, vice Leila I. Kimche, resigned.

Robert C. McEwen,
of New York, to be a Commissioner on the part of the United States on the International Joint Commission, United States and Canada, vice Robert J. Sugarman, resigned.

Gerald D. Fines,
of Illinois, to be United States Attorney for the Central District of Illinois for the term of 4 years (reappointment).

W. Hunt Dumont,
of New Jersey, to be United States Attorney for the District of New Jersey for the term of 4 years, vice Robert J. Del Tufo, resigned.

Charles R. Brewer,
of North Carolina, to be United States Attorney for the Western District of North Carolina for the term of 4 years, vice Harold M. Edwards, re-signed.

Lincoln C. Almond,
of Rhode Island, to be United States Attorney for the District of Rhode Island for the term of 4 years, vice Paul F. Murray.

John Perry Alderman,
of Virginia, to be United States Attorney for the Western District of Virginia for the term of 4 years, vice John S. Edwards, resigning.

Blaine Skinner,
of Idaho, to be United States Marshal for the District of Idaho for the term of 4 years, vice Anthony Skoro, resigning.

J. Jerome Perkins,
of Indiana, to be United States Marshal for the Northern District of Indiana for the term of 4 years, vice Joseph N. Novotny.

Donald W. Wyatt,
of Rhode Island, to be United States Marshal for the District of Rhode Island for the term of 4 years, vice John J. Partington, resigning.

Delaine Roberts,
of Wyoming, to be United States Marshal for the District of Wyoming for the term of 4 years, vice James W. Byrd, term expired.

Submitted October 14

Emmett Ripley Cox,
of Alabama, to be United States District Judge for the Southern District of Alabama, vice Virgil Pittman, retired.

Cynthia Holcomb Hall,
of California, to be United States District Judge for the Central District of California, vice Harry Pregerson, elevated.

Clarence A. Beam,
of Nebraska, to be United States District Judge for the District of Nebraska, vice Robert V. Denney, deceased.

Elsie L. Munsell,
of Virginia, to be United States Attorney for the Eastern District of Virginia for the term of 4 years, vice William B. Cummings, resigned.

Frank Shakespeare,
of Connecticut, to be a member of the Board for International Broadcasting for a term expiring May 20, 1983, vice Frank Markoe, Jr., term expired.

Submitted October 15

John W. Gill, Jr.,
of Tennessee, to be United States Attorney for the Eastern District of Tennessee for the term of 4 years, vice John H. Cary, resigned.

Submitted October 16

The following-named persons to be Representatives and Alternate Representatives of the United States of America to the Thirty-sixth Session of the General Assembly of the United Nations, to which offices they were appointed during the last recess of the Senate:

Representatives:
Kenneth L. Adelman, of Virginia
John Sherman Cooper, of Kentucky
Benjamin A. Gilman, United States Representative from the State of New York
Andy Ireland, United States Representative from the State of Florida
Jeane J. Kirkpatrick, of Maryland

Alternate Representatives:
Bruce F. Caputo, of New York
George Christopher, of California
Charles M. Lichenstein, of the District of Columbia
William Courtney Sherman, of Virginia
Jose S. Sorzano, of Virginia

Submitted October 16—Continued

Robert M. Garrick,
of California, to be a member of the Board of Directors of the Communications Satellite Corporation until the date of the annual meeting of the Corporation in 1984, vice George Meany.

Evan Griffith Galbraith,
of Connecticut, to be Ambassador Extraordinary and Plenipotentiary of the United States of America to France.

John R. Van de Water,
of California, to be a member of the National Labor Relations Board for the term of 5 years expiring August 27, 1986 (reappointment), to which position he was appointed during the last recess of the Senate.

Submitted October 19

Ronald P. Wertheim,
of the District of Columbia, to be an Associate Judge of the Superior Court of the District of Columbia for a term of 15 years, vice James B. Belson, elevated.

F. Keith Adkinson,
of West Virginia, to be a Federal Trade Commissioner for the unexpired term of 7 years from September 26, 1975, vice Robert Pitofsky, resigned.

Francis S. M. Hodsoll,
of Virginia, to be Chairman of the National Endowment for the Arts for a term of 4 years, vice Livingston L. Biddle, Jr., term expiring.

Submitted October 20

Jesse E. Eschbach,
of Indiana, to be United States Circuit Judge for the Seventh Circuit, vice Luther M. Swygert, retired.

John Bailey Jones,
of South Dakota, to be United States District Judge for the District of South Dakota, vice Fred J. Nichol, retired.

James C. Cacheris,
of Virginia, to be United States District Judge for the Eastern District of Virginia, vice a new position created by P.L. 95–486, approved October 20, 1978.

Denny L. Sampson,
of Nevada, to be United States Marshal for the District of Nevada for the term of 4 years, vice Richard J. Dunn, term expired.

Submitted October 21

Joseph P. Russoniello,
of California, to be United States Attorney for the Northern District of California for the term of 4 years, vice G. William Hunter, resigning.

James M. Rosenbaum,
of Minnesota, to be United States Attorney for the District of Minnesota for the term of 4 years, vice Thomas K. Berg, resigned.

Philip N. Hogen,
of South Dakota, to be United States Attorney for the District of South Dakota for the term of 4 years, vice Terry L. Pechota, resigned.

Submitted October 27

Robert L. Barry,
of New Hampshire, a career member of the Senior Foreign Service, Class of Minister-Counselor, to be Ambassador Extraordinary and Plenipotentiary of the United States of America to Bulgaria.

Melvyn R. Paisley,
of Washington, to be an Assistant Secretary of the Navy, vice David Emerson Mann, resigned.

Richard A. Posner,
of Illinois, to be United States Circuit Judge for the Seventh Circuit, vice Philip W. Tone, resigned.

William Coskrey Plowden, Jr.,
of South Carolina, to be Assistant Secretary of Labor for Veterans' Employment (new position).

Submitted October 30

William F. Weld,
of Massachusetts, to be United States Attorney for the District of Massachusetts for the term of 4 years, vice Edward F. Harrington, resigning.

Submitted November 2

Joseph P. Stadtmueller,
of Wisconsin, to be United States Attorney for the Eastern District of Wisconsin for the term of 4 years, vice Joan F. Kessler, resigned.

John Robert Byrnes,
of Wisconsin, to be United States Attorney for the Western District of Wisconsin for the term of 4 years, vice Frank M. Tuerkheimer, resigned.

Reynaldo Philip Maduro,
of Maryland, to be an Assistant Director of the ACTION agency, vice Mary Frances Cahill Leyland, resigned.

Submitted November 2—Continued

Edward W. Ray,
of California, to be a Commissioner of the Copyright Royalty Tribunal for the unexpired term of 5 years from September 27, 1977, vice Clarence L. James, Jr., resigned.

W. Proctor Scarboro,
of North Carolina, to be a member of the Federal Farm Credit Board, Farm Credit Administration, for a term expiring March 31, 1987, vice David C. Waldrop, term expired.

Bobby Jack Thompson,
of New York, to be Administrator of the United States Fire Administration, vice Gordon Vickery, resigned.

Submitted November 3

Frederick N. Falk,
of Wisconsin, to be United States Marshal for the Western District of Wisconsin for the term of 4 years, vice Robert M. Thompson.

William S. Vaughn,
of Missouri, to be United States Marshal for the Eastern District of Missouri for the term of 4 years, vice Franklin Payne, resigning.

Submitted November 4

Francis Terry McNamara,
of Vermont, a career member of the Senior Foreign Service, Class of Counselor, to be Ambassador Extraordinary and Plenipotentiary of the United States of America to the Gabonese Republic, and to serve concurrently and without additional compensation as Ambassador Extraordinary and Plenipotentiary of the United States of America to the Democratic Republic of Sao Tome and Principe.

Myer Rashish,
of the District of Columbia, to be United States Alternate Governor of the International Bank for Reconstruction and Development for a term of 5 years; United States Alternate Governor of the Inter-American Development Bank for a term of 5 years; United States Alternate Governor of the Asian Development Bank; and United States Alternate Governor of the African Development Fund, vice Richard N. Cooper, resigned.

John H. Moore II,
of Florida, to be United States District Judge for the Middle District of Florida, vice a new position created by P.L. 95–486, approved October 20, 1978.

Submitted November 4—Continued

Jackson L. Kiser,
of Virginia, to be United States District Judge for the Western District of Virginia, vice a new position created by P.L. 95–486, approved October 20, 1978.

John C. Shabaz,
of Wisconsin, to be United States District Judge for the Western District of Wisconsin, vice James E. Doyle, retired.

Donald B. Ayer,
of California, to be United States Attorney for the Eastern District of California for the term of 4 years, vice Herman Sillas, Jr., resigned.

Hinton R. Pierce,
of Georgia, to be United States Attorney for the Southern District of Georgia for the term of 4 years, vice William T. Moore, Jr., resigned.

Louis G. DeFalaise,
of Kentucky, to be United States Attorney for the Eastern District of Kentucky for the term of 4 years, vice Patrick H. Molloy, resigned.

Robert G. Ulrich,
of Missouri, to be United States Attorney for the Western District of Missouri for the term of 4 years, vice Ronald S. Reed, Jr., resigned.

Byron H. Dunbar,
of Montana, to be United States Attorney for the District of Montana for the term of 4 years, vice Robert T. O'Leary, resigned.

Joe B. Brown,
of Tennessee, to be United States Attorney for the Middle District of Tennessee for the term of 4 years, vice Harold D. Hardin, resigned.

Benjamin F. Baer,
of California, to be a Commissioner of the United States Parole Commission for the term of 6 years, vice Joseph A. Nardoza, term expired.

Janet J. McCoy,
of Oregon, to be High Commissioner of the Trust Territory of the Pacific Islands, vice Adrian Paul Winkel, resigned.

The following-named persons to be members of the Federal Council on the Aging for the terms indicated:

For a term expiring June 5, 1982:
Adelaide Attard, of New York, vice Walter L. Moffett, term expired.
Charlotte W. Conable, of New York, vice James T. Sykes, term expired.

Submitted November 4—Continued

For a term expiring June 5, 1983:

Nelda Ann Lambert Barton, of Kentucky, vice Fannie B. Dorsey, term expired.

Edna Bogosian, of Massachusetts, vice Mary A. Marshall, term expired.

Frances Lamont, of South Dakota, vice Bernice L. Neugarten, term expired.

For a term expiring June 5, 1984:

Margaret Long Arnold, of the District of Columbia, vice John B. Martin, term expired.

Syd Captain, of Florida, vice Cyril Hilary Carpenter, term expired.

Katie Dusenberry, of Arizona, vice Mary Crowley Mulvey, term expired.

Josephine K. Oblinger, of Illinois, vice Jean Jones Perdue, term expired.

Edna Bonn Russell, of California, vice Shimeji Kanazawa, term expired.

John R. McKean,
of California, to be a Governor of the United States Postal Service for the remainder of the term expiring December 8, 1986, vice Richard R. Allen, resigned.

Stanley S. Harris,
of the District of Columbia, to be United States Attorney for the District of Columbia for the term of 4 years, vice Charles F. C. Ruff, resigning.

Howard V. Adair,
of Alabama, to be United States Marshal for the Southern District of Alabama for the term of 4 years, vice Tyree A. Richburg.

John W. Roberts,
of Arizona, to be United States Marshal for the District of Arizona for the term of 4 years, vice Lee A. Limbs, Jr., term expired.

Warren D. Stump,
of Iowa, to be United States Marshal for the Southern District of Iowa for the term of 4 years, vice Richard W. Nehring, resigning.

Kenneth L. Pekarek,
of Kansas, to be United States Marshal for the District of Kansas for the term of 4 years, vice Bert D. Cantwell, term expired.

John L. Meyers,
of Louisiana, to be United States Marshal for the Middle District of Louisiana for the term of 4 years, vice Thomas A. Grace, Jr., retired.

Robert L. Pavlak, Sr.,
of Minnesota, to be United States Marshal for the District of Minnesota for the term of 4 years, vice Wesley D. Lane, resigning.

Submitted November 4—Continued

Lee Koury,
of Missouri, to be United States Marshal for the Western District of Missouri for the term of 4 years, vice Emmett W. Fairfax, term expired.

Ronald D. Daniels, Jr.,
of New Hampshire, to be United States Marshal for the District of New Hampshire for the term of 4 years, vice Robert E. Raiche, resigned.

Kenneth B. Muir,
of North Dakota, to be United States Marshal for the District of North Dakota for the term of 4 years, vice Harold C. Warren, resigned.

Paul R. Nolan,
of Washington, to be United States Marshal for the Eastern District of Washington for the term of 4 years, vice Archie P. Sherar.

Submitted November 5

Milan D. Bish,
of Nebraska, to be Ambassador Extraordinary and Plenipotentiary of the United States of America to Barbados, and to serve concurrently and without additional compensation as Ambassador Extraordinary and Plenipotentiary of the United States of America to the Commonwealth of Dominica, Ambassador Extraordinary and Plenipotentiary of the United States of America to Saint Lucia, Ambassador Extraordinary and Plenipotentiary of the United States of America to Saint Vincent and the Grenadines, and Ambassador Extraordinary and Plenipotentiary of the United States of America to Antigua and Barbuda.

Robert G. Doumar,
of Virginia, to be United States District Judge for the Eastern District of Virginia, vice Richard B. Kellam, retired.

David V. O'Brien,
of the Virgin Islands, to be United States District Judge for the District of the Virgin Islands for the term of 8 years, vice Warren H. Young, deceased.

Submitted November 9

Elliott Abrams,
of the District of Columbia, to be Assistant Secretary of State for Human Rights and Humanitarian Affairs, vice Patricia M. Derian, resigned.

Glenn L. Archer, Jr.,
of Virginia, to be an Assistant Attorney General, vice M. Carr Ferguson, resigned.

John R. Kendall,
of Michigan, to be United States Marshal for the Western District of Michigan for the term of 4 years, vice Andrew L. Metcalf, resigning.

Harry Connolly,
of Oklahoma, to be United States Marshal for the Northern District of Oklahoma for the term of 4 years, vice Carl W. Gardner, term expired.

The following-named persons to be members of the National Commission on Libraries and Information Science for the terms indicated:
For the remainder of the term expiring July 19, 1982;
John E. Juergensmeyer, of Illinois, vice Frances Healy Naftalin.
Jerald Conway Newman, of New York, vice Joan Helene Gross.
Julia Li Wu, of California, vice Clara Stanton Jones.
For a term expiring July 19, 1986:
Elinor M. Hashim, of Connecticut, vice Robert W. Burns, Jr., term expired.
Byron Leeds, of New Jersey, vice Horace E. Tate, term expired.

Submitted November 10

Edwin Gharst Corr,
of Oklahoma, a career member of the Senior Foreign Service, Class of Counselor, to be Ambassador Extraordinary and Plenipotentiary of the United States of America to Bolivia.

Melvin Herbert Evans,
of the Virgin Islands, to be Ambassador Extraordinary and Plenipotentiary of the United States of America to the Republic of Trinidad and Tobago.

James Daniel Theberge,
of the District of Columbia, to be Ambassador Extraordinary and Plenipotentiary of the United States of America to Chile.

Withdrawn November 12

Richard J. Bishirjian,
of New York, to be an Associate Director of the International Communication Agency, vice Alice Stone Ilchman, which was sent to the Senate on September 10, 1981.

Submitted November 13

Clyde H. Hamilton,
of South Carolina, to be United States District Judge for the District of South Carolina, vice Robert F. Chapman, elevated.

Submitted November 16

C. T. Conover,
of California, to be Comptroller of the Currency for a term of 5 years, vice John Gaines Heimann, resigned.

Charles Timothy Hagel,
of the District of Columbia, to be Deputy Administrator of Veterans' Affairs (new position).

Edward R. Becker,
of Pennsylvania, to be United States Circuit Judge for the Third Circuit, vice Max Rosenn, retired.

Jules G. Korner III,
of Maryland, to be a Judge of the United States Tax Court for a term expiring 15 years after he takes office (new position—P.L. 96–439 of October 13, 1980).

Perry Shields,
of Tennessee, to be a Judge of the United States Tax Court for a term expiring 15 years after he takes office (new position—P.L. 96–439 of October 13, 1980).

Meade Whitaker,
of Michigan, to be a Judge of the United States Tax Court for a term expiring 15 years after he takes office (new position—P.L. 96–439 of October 13, 1980).

Christopher K. Barnes,
of Ohio, to be United States Attorney for the Southern District of Ohio for the term of 4 years, vice James C. Cissell.

Richard C. Turner,
of Iowa, to be United States Attorney for the Southern District of Iowa for the term of 4 years, vice Roxanne Barton Conlin, resigned.

James P. Jonker,
of Iowa, to be United States Marshal for the Northern District of Iowa for the term of 4 years, vice John A. Roe, resigned.

Wallace L. McLendon,
of Florida, to be United States Marshal for the Northern District of Florida for the term of 4 years, vice Emmett E. Shelby, term expired.

Submitted November 17

Alvin I. Krenzler,
of Ohio, to be United States District Judge for the Northern District of Ohio, vice Don J. Young, retired.

Submitted November 18

Ralph K. Winter, Jr.,
of Connecticut, to be United States Circuit Judge
for the Second Circuit, vice Walter R. Mansfield,
retired.

Withdrawn November 18

Norman Braman,
of Florida, to be Commissioner of Immigration
and Naturalization, vice Leonel J. Castillo, resigned, which was sent to the Senate on September 29, 1981.

Submitted November 19

Kenneth Lee Brown,
of California, a career member of the Senior Foreign Service, Class of Counselor, to be Ambassador Extraordinary and Plenipotentiary of the
United States of America to the People's Republic of the Congo.

Marc E. Leland,
of California, to be a member of the Board of
Directors of the Inter-American Foundation for
the remainder of the term expiring September
20, 1982, vice Guy Feliz Erb, resigned.

Thomas O. Enders,
of Connecticut, to be a member of the Board of
Directors of the Inter-American Foundation for a
term expiring September 20, 1984, vice Viron P.
Vaky, resigned.

M. Peter McPherson,
of Maryland, to be a member of the Board of
Directors of the Inter-American Foundation for
the remainder of the term expiring September
20, 1986, vice Paula Stern, resigned.

Submitted November 23

Franklin S. Forsberg,
of Connecticut, to be Ambassador Extraordinary
and Plenipotentiary of the United States of
America to Sweden.

Israel Leo Glasser,
of New York, to be United States District Judge
for the Eastern District of New York, vice Jacob
Mishler, retired.

James L. Meyers,
of Louisiana, to be United States Marshal for the
Middle District of Louisiana for the term of 4
years, vice Thomas A. Grace, Jr., retired.

Joseph S. Cage, Jr.,
of Louisiana, to be United States Attorney for the
Western District of Louisiana for the term of 4
years, vice Joseph Ransdell Keene.

Submitted November 23—Continued
Gene S. Anderson,
of Washington, to be United States Attorney for
the Western District of Washington for the term
of 4 years, vice John C. Merkel, Jr., term expired.

David A. Faber,
of West Virginia, to be United States Attorney for
the Southern District of West Virginia for the
term of 4 years, vice Robert B. King, resigned.

William I. Berryhill, Jr.,
of North Carolina, to be United States Marshal
for the Eastern District of North Carolina for the
term of 4 years, vice Hugh Salter, term expired.

Wayne D. Beaman,
of Virginia, to be United States Marshal for the
Western District of Virginia for the term of 4
years, vice Paul J. Puckett, term expired.

Rear Adm. Herbert R. Lippold, Jr.,
National Oceanic and Atmospheric Administration, to be a member of the Mississippi River
Commission, vice Rear Adm. Allen L. Powell, retired.

Withdrawn November 23

John L. Meyers,
of Louisiana, to be United States Marshal for the
Middle District of Louisiana for the term of 4
years, vice Thomas A. Grace, Jr., retired, which
was sent to the Senate on November 4, 1981.

Submitted November 24

John Hathaway Reed,
of Maine, to be Ambassador Extraordinary and
Plenipotentiary of the United States of America
to the Democratic Socialist Republic of Sri
Lanka, and to serve concurrently and without
additional compensation as Ambassador Extraordinary and Plenipotentiary of the United States
of America to the Republic of Maldives.

J. Owen Forrester,
of Georgia, to be United States District Judge for
the Northern District of Georgia, vice Newell
Edenfield, retired.

Sam A. Crow,
of Kansas, to be United States District Judge for
the District of Kansas, vice Frank G. Theis, retired.

Peter McCoy,
of California, to be Under Secretary of Commerce for Travel and Tourism (new position).

Submitted November 24—Continued

Joan D. Aikens,
of Pennsylvania, to be a member of the Federal Election Commission for the remainder of the term expiring April 30, 1983, vice Max L. Friedersdorf, resigned.

Lee Ann Elliott,
of Illinois, to be a member of the Federal Election Commission for a term expiring April 30, 1987, vice Joan D. Aikens, term expired.

Gerald E. Thomas,
of California, to be Ambassador Extraordinary and Plenipotentiary of the United States of America to the Cooperative Republic of Guyana.

William Robert Casey, Jr.,
of Colorado, to be Ambassador Extraordinary and Plenipotentiary of the United States of America to the Republic of Niger.

Mark Evans Austad,
of Arizona, to be Ambassador Extraordinary and Plenipotentiary of the United States of America to Norway.

Clarence Eugene Hodges,
of Maryland, to be Chief of the Children's Bureau, Department of Health and Human Services, vice John A. Calhoun III.

Eugene V. Lipp,
of California, to be a member of the National Transportation Safety Board for a term expiring December 31, 1986, vice James B. King, term expiring.

Submitted December 2

Paul H. Nitze,
of Maryland, for the rank of Ambassador while serving as Head of the United States Delegation to the Intermediate Range Nuclear Force Negotiations.

Fred M. Zeder II,
of Hawaii, for the rank of Ambassador during the tenure of his service as Personal Representative of the President to conduct negotiations on the future political status of the Trust Territory of the Pacific Islands.

Submitted December 4

Walter Leon Cutler,
of Maryland, a career member of the Senior Foreign Service, Class of Career Minister, to be Ambassador Extraordinary and Plenipotentiary of the United States of America to the Republic of Tunisia.

Submitted December 4—Continued

Maurice H. Stans,
of California, to be a member of the Board of Directors of the Overseas Private Investment Corporation for a term of 3 years expiring December 17, 1984, vice William M. Landau, term expiring.

Michael S. Kanne,
of Indiana, to be United States District Judge for the Northern District of Indiana, vice Phil M. McNagny, Jr., deceased.

James T. Moody,
of Indiana, to be United States District Judge for the Northern District of Indiana, vice Jesse E. Eschbach, elevated.

David L. Russell,
of Oklahoma, to be United States District Judge for the Northern, Eastern and Western Districts of Oklahoma, vice Frederick A. Daugherty, retired.

Lamond Robert Mills,
of Nevada, to be United States Attorney for the District of Nevada for the term of 4 years, vice B. Mahlon Brown III, resigned.

Thomas A. O'Hara, Jr.,
of Nebraska, to be United States Marshal for the District of Nebraska for the term of 4 years, vice Mack A. Backhaus.

Bruce R. Montgomery,
of Tennessee, to be United States Marshal for the Eastern District of Tennessee for the term of 4 years, vice Harry D. Mansfield.

Robert T. Keating,
of Wisconsin, to be United States Marshal for the Eastern District of Wisconsin for the term of 4 years, vice William L. Brown, term expired.

Submitted December 7

Robert H. Bork,
of the District of Columbia, to be United States Circuit Judge for the District of Columbia Circuit, vice Carl E. McGowan, retired.

Harold L. Ryan,
of Idaho, to be United States District Judge for the District of Idaho, vice Ray McNichols, retired.

Submitted December 8

Evan L. Hultman,
of Iowa, to be United States Attorney for the Northern District of Iowa for the term of 4 years, vice James H. Reynolds, term expired.

Submitted December 16—Continued

Cathie A. Shattuck,
of Colorado, to be a member of the Equal Employment Opportunity Commission for the term expiring July 1, 1985, vice Ethel Bent Walsh, term expired.

Richard W. Heldridge,
of California, to be a member of the Board of Directors of the Export-Import Bank of the United States, vice Margaret W. Kahliff, resigning.

Submitted December 9

Stephen S. Trott,
of California, to be United States Attorney for the Central District of California for the term of 4 years, vice Andrea M. Sheridan Ordin, term expired.

Submitted December 11

J. William Petro,
of Ohio, to be United States Attorney for the Northern District of Ohio for the term of 4 years, vice James R. Williams.

Kalo A. Hineman,
of Kansas, to be a Commissioner of the Commodity Futures Trading Commission for the term expiring June 19, 1986, vice Robert L. Martin, resigned.

William J. Bennett,
of North Carolina, to be Chairman of the National Endowment for the Humanities for a term of 4 years, vice Joseph D. Duffey, term expired.

Anthony J. Calio,
of Maryland, to be Deputy Administrator of the National Oceanic and Atmospheric Administration, vice James Patrick Walsh, resigned.

Submitted December 14

Danny Lee McDonald,
of Oklahoma, to be a member of the Federal Election Commission for a term expiring April 30, 1987, vice Robert O. Tiernan, term expired.

Kenneth E. Moffett,
of Maryland, to be Federal Mediation and Conciliation Director, vice Wayne L. Horvitz, resigned.

Herbert E. Ellingwood,
of California, to be a member of the Merit Systems Protection Board for the remainder of the

Submitted December 14—Continued

term expiring March 1, 1986, vice Ruth T. Prokop, resigned.

Herbert E. Ellingwood,
of California, to be Chairman of the Merit Systems Protection Board, vice Ruth T. Prokop, resigned.

Submitted December 15

John R. Bolton,
of Virginia, to be an Assistant Administrator of the Agency for International Development, vice Alexander Shakow, resigned.

Otto J. Reich,
of Virginia, to be an Assistant Administrator of the Agency for International Development, vice Abelardo Lopez Valdez.

James Jay Jackson,
of Texas, to be a member of the Federal Home Loan Bank Board for the remainder of the term expiring June 30, 1982, vice John H. Dalton, resigned.

Submitted December 16

Alan C. Nelson,
of California, to be Commissioner of Immigration and Naturalization, vice Leonel J. Castillo, resigned.

George L. McBane,
of North Carolina, to be United States Marshal for the Middle District of North Carolina for the term of 4 years, vice George L. Miller, term expired.

Stuart E. Earnest,
of Oklahoma, to be United States Marshal for the Western District of Oklahoma for the term of 4 years, vice Coy W. Rogers, resigning.

William J. Jonas, Jr.,
of Texas, to be United States Marshal for the Western District of Texas for the term of 4 years, vice Rodolfo A. Garza, term expired.

Eugene H. Davis,
of Utah, to be United States Marshal for the District of Utah for the term of 4 years, vice William E. Pitt, resigned.

Christian Hansen, Jr.,
of Vermont, to be United States Marshal for the District of Vermont for the term of 4 years, vice Earle B. McLaughlin, term expired.

Appendix C—Checklist of White House Press Releases

The following list contains releases of the Office of the Press Secretary that are not included in this book.

Released January 20

Advance text:
Inaugural address of President Ronald Reagan

Fact sheet:
Federal employee hiring freeze

Transcript:
Exchange with reporters during a photo session in the Oval Office

Released January 21

Announcement:
Appointment of David R. Gergen as an Assistant to the President and Staff Director of the White House

Released January 22

Transcript:
Remarks to members of the Cabinet and their families during a photo session

Fact sheet:
The President's memorandum on actions to reduce Federal spending

News conference:
On the Presidential Task Force on Regulatory Relief—by the Vice President

Released January 23

News conference:
On the President's meeting with the Republican congressional leadership—by Senate Majority Leader Howard H. Baker, Jr., and House Minority Leader Robert H. Michel

News conference:
Announcing Presidential nominees—by Deputy Press Secretary Karna Small

Announcement:
Appointment of Linda Faulkner as Assistant Social Secretary—by Press Secretary to the First Lady Sheila Patton

Released January 23—Continued
News conference:
On economic issues—by Murray L. Weidenbaum, Chairman-designate of the Council of Economic Advisers

Announcement:
Appointment of Glenn R. Schleede as Executive Associate Director of the Office of Management and Budget

Announcement:
Appointment of Helene von Damm as Special Assistant to the President

Announcement:
Appointment of M. Peter McPherson as Acting Counsel to the President

Released January 24

Announcement:
Appointment of John F. W. Rogers as Special Assistant for Management and Acting Director of the Office of Administration

Released January 26

Biographical data:
Richard Smith Beal, appointed as Special Assistant to the President and Director of the Office of Planning and Evaluation

Announcement:
Appointment of Margaret D. Tutwiler as Special Assistant to the Chief of Staff

Announcement:
Appointment of Mitchell F. Stanley as Special Assistant to the Counsellor to the President

Released January 27

Announcement:
Appointment of Donald W. Moran as Associate Director of Health and Human Services in the Office of Management and Budget

Announcement:
Appointment of William Gene Lesher as Director of Economics, Policy Analysis and Budget, Department of Agriculture

Released January 28

Fact sheet:
Executive Order 12287, decontrol of oil

News conference:
On Executive Order 12287, decontrol of oil—by Secretary of Energy James B. Edwards

Biographical data:
Melvin L. Bradley, appointed as Senior Policy Adviser to the President

Announcement:
Appointment of Gregory J. Newell as Special Assistant for Scheduling

Announcement:
Appointment of Anne Higgins as Director of Presidential Correspondence

Released January 29

Announcement:
Appointment of James C. Miller as Associate Director, Office of Management and Budget

Fact sheet:
Executive Order 12288, Council on Wage and Price Stability

Fact sheet:
Memorandum on postponement of pending Federal regulations

Released January 30

Announcement:
Appointment of Richard D. Shelby and A. Wayne Roberts as Deputy Directors for Presidential Personnel

Transcript:
Exchange with reporters on departure for Camp David, Md.

News conference:
On the President's meeting with business leaders—by Wilson S. Johnson, president, National Federation of Independent Business, James S. Binns, chairman, National Association of Manufacturers, and C. William Verity, Jr., chairman, U.S. Chamber of Commerce

Released February 3

Announcement:
Appointment of Annelise G. Anderson as Associate Director for Economics and Government in the Office of Management and Budget

Released February 3—Continued

News conference:
On their meeting with the President—by Mayors Pete Wilson of San Diego, Calif., Edward I. Koch of New York, N.Y., Jim McConn of Houston, Tex., and William H. Hudnut III of Indianapolis, Ind.

News conference:
On their meeting with the President—by Representatives Shirley Chisholm of New York and William H. Gray III of Pennsylvania and Delegate Walter E. Fauntroy of Washington, D.C., members of the Congressional Black Caucus

Released February 5

Advance text:
Address to the nation on the economy

Released February 6

News conference:
On their meeting with the President—by Secretary of Agriculture John R. Block, Robert Delano, president, American Farm Bureau Federation, Merlyn Carlson, president, National Cattlemen's Association, Jim Billington, president, National Association of Wheat Growers, William Mullins, president, National Corn Growers Association, and Morgan Williams, president, Cooperative League of the USA

Released February 9

Announcement:
Appointment of Dodie T. Livingston as Director of the Office of Special Presidential Messages and Carol S. McCain as Director of the White House Visitors Office

News conference:
On their meeting with the President—by State Senator Don Totten of Illinois, State Representatives Richard Hodes of Florida and Marilyn Lewis of Pennsylvania, and County Executive Robert Eckels of Harris County, Tex.

Released February 10

News conference:
On their meeting with the President—by Governors George Busbee of Georgia, John Dalton of Virginia, and Lamar Alexander of Tennessee

Released February 12

Text:
Audit of the U.S. economy

Released February 12—Continued
News conference:
On the audit of the U.S. economy—by Murray L. Weidenbaum, Chairman-designate of the Council of Economic Advisers

Transcript:
Exchange with reporters on balancing the fiscal year 1983 budget

News conference:
On the White House Office for Legislative Affairs and the nation's economic situation—by Assistant to the President for Legislative Affairs Max L. Friedersdorf

Released February 17

Transcript.
Exchange at a meeting with conservative coalition group representatives

News conference:
On the Presidential Task Force on Regulatory Relief and Executive Order 12291, Federal regulation—by the Vice President

Released February 18

Advance text:
Address before a joint session of the Congress on the program for economic recovery

Summary fact sheet:
Program for economic recovery

Fact sheet:
The President's initiatives to reduce regulatory burdens

Released February 23

News conference:
On the program for economic recovery—by David A. Stockman, Director of the Office of Management and Budget, Secretary of Agriculture John R. Block, Secretary of Transportation Drew L. Lewis, and Ambassador William E. Brock, U.S. Trade Representative

News Conference:
On their meeting with the President and White House staff members—by Governors George Busbee of Georgia, Lamar Alexander of Tennessee, and John Dalton of Virginia

Released February 24

News conference:
On the program for economic recovery—by Edwin L. Harper, Deputy Director-designate of the Office of Management and Budget, Secretary

Released February 24—Continued
of Health and Human Services Richard S. Schweiker, and Secretary of Education T. H. Bell

News conference:
On their meeting with the President—by Secretary of State Alexander M. Haig, Jr., and Foreign Minister Yitzhak Shamir of Israel

Released February 25

News conference:
On the program for economic recovery—by Secretary of Housing and Urban Development Samuel R. Pierce, Jr., Secretary of Labor Raymond J. Donovan, and David A. Stockman, Director of the Office of Management and Budget

News conference:
On their meeting with the President—by Secretary of State Alexander M. Haig, Jr., and Foreign Minister Jean François-Poncet of France

Statement:
On the January Consumer Price Index figures— by Murray L. Weidenbaum, Chairman of the Council of Economic Advisers

Released February 26

News conference:
On the program for economic recovery—by Secretary of Energy James B. Edwards, Secretary of the Treasury Donald T. Regan, and Murray L. Weidenbaum, Chairman of the Council of Economic Advisers

Released February 27

News conference.
On the program for economic recovery—by Secretary of Commerce Malcolm Baldrige, Secretary of the Interior James G. Watt, Secretary of State Alexander M. Haig, Jr., and David A. Stockman, Director of the Office of Management and Budget

Released March 2

Advance text:
Remarks at the Mid-Winter Congressional City Conference of the National League of Cities

Released March 3

News conference:
On his meeting with the President—by former President Gerald R. Ford

Released March 4

Transcript:
Opening remarks at a meeting with freshmen Republican Members of the House of Representatives

News conference:
On their meeting with the President—by Representatives Hank Brown, president, Bill McCollum, vice president, Bob McEwen, secretary-treasurer, Sid Morrison, whip, and John P. Hiler, all of the Republican freshman class

Released March 5

News conference:
On their meeting with the President—by Representatives Charles W. Stenholm of Texas, Phil Gramm of Texas, G. V. Montgomery of Mississippi, Carroll Hubbard, Jr., of Kentucky, Kent Hance of Texas, and Tom Bevill of Alabama

Transcript:
Remarks on drawing the names of the questioners for the March 6 news conference

Released March 6

News conference:
On the President's meeting with Governors to discuss the automobile industry—by Governor William G. Milliken of Michigan and Secretary of Transportation Drew L. Lewis

Announcement:
Appointment of Anthony R. Dolan, Dana Rohrabacher, and Mari Maseng as Presidential speechwriters

Released March 9

News conference:
On their meeting with the President—by Roy Orr, president, and Bob Eckels, chairman of the Republican Caucus, National Association of County Officials

News conference:
On their meeting with the President—by Foreign Minister Hans-Dietrich Genscher of the Federal Republic of Germany and Secretary of State Alexander M. Haig, Jr.

News conference:
On their meeting with the President—by Max Fisher, chairman of the Jewish Agencies, and Gordon Zacks, of the American-Israeli public affairs committee of the board of National United Jewish Appeal

Released March 10

Fact sheet:
The fiscal year 1982 budget

Released March 11

Advance text:
Address before a joint session of the Canadian Parliament in Ottawa

News conference:
On the U.S.-Canadian discussions—by Secretary of State Alexander M. Haig, Jr., and Secretary of State for External Affairs Mark MacGuigan of Canada

Released March 13

Advance text:
Remarks on the additional Federal aid for the investigation of murdered and missing youth in Atlanta, Ga.

Released March 17

Transcript:
Exchange with reporters following the meeting with Republican congressional leaders on Capitol Hill

Released March 20

News conference:
On his meeting with David A. Stockman, Director of the Office of Management and Budget—by Mayor Edward I. Koch of New York, N.Y.

News conference:
Following the President's meeting with members of the National Conference of State Legislatures—by Richard Hodes, president, and Ross Doyen, president-elect, National Conference of State Legislatures

Advance text:
Remarks at the Conservative Political Action Conference dinner

Released March 23

News conference:
On his meeting with the President—by Elmer B. Staats, retiring Comptroller General of the United States

Released March 24

News conference:
On their meeting with the President—by Secretary of State Alexander M. Haig, Jr., and Foreign Minister Masayoshi Ito of Japan

Released March 26

News conference:
On governmentwide anti-fraud and waste efforts—by Edwin L. Harper, Deputy Director of the Office of Management and Budget, and William H. Webster, Director of the Federal Bureau of Investigation

Fact sheet:
President's Council on Integrity and Efficiency

Released March 30

Advance text:
Remarks to the national conference of the Building and Construction Trades Department, AFL-CIO

Transcripts:
Press briefings following the attempted assassination of the President
  —by Assistant to the President David R. Gergen;
  —by Deputy Press Secretary Larry M. Speakes (2 releases);
  —by Secretary of State Alexander M. Haig, Jr.;
  —by Assistant to the President for Political Affairs Franklyn C. (Lyn) Nofziger (2 releases);
  —by Assistant to the President for Political Affairs Franklyn C. (Lyn) Nofziger, Dr. Dennis O'Leary, dean for clinical affairs, George Washington University Hospital, and Press Secretary to the First Lady Sheila Patton;
  —by the Vice President, Deputy Press Secretary Larry M. Speakes, and Assistant to the President David R. Gergen

Released March 31

Transcript:
Press briefing on the President's surgery and his post-operative condition—by Dr. Dennis O'Leary, dean for clinical affairs, George Washington University Hospital, and Deputy Press Secretary Larry M. Speakes

Transcript:
Question-and-answer session with reporters following the Vice President's meeting with the bipartisan congressional leadership—by Senators Paul Laxalt, Howard H. Baker, Jr., Robert C. Byrd, and Alan Cranston

Transcript:
Press briefing on the coordination by government officials following the attempted assassination of the President—by Assistants to the President James A. Baker III and David R. Gergen

Released April 2

Transcript:
Press briefing on the President's recovery—by Dr. Dennis O'Leary, dean for clinical affairs, George Washington University Hospital

Released April 3

Statement:
On Senate passage of the Federal budget legislation—by the Vice President

Released April 6

News conference:
On actions to help the U.S. auto industry—by the Vice President

Fact sheet:
Actions to help the U.S. auto industry

Announcement:
Membership of the U.S. team sent to Japan to brief Japanese Government leaders on domestic actions to help the U.S. auto industry

Released April 7

News conference:
On a comparison of the President's program for economic recovery with a plan proposed by Representative Jim Jones, chairman of the House Budget Committee—by Secretary of the Treasury Donald T. Regan and David A. Stockman, Director of the Office of Management and Budget

Fact sheet:
Comparison of the President's program for economic recovery with a plan proposed by Representative Jim Jones, chairman of the House Budget Committee

Released April 8

News conference:
On the Presidential Advisory Committee on Federalism—by Senator Paul Laxalt, Chairman of the Committee

Released April 9

Statement:
On tax reduction proposals of Representative Dan Rostenkowski, chairman of the House Ways and Means Committee—by Secretary of the Treasury Donald T. Regan

News conference:
On tax reduction proposals of Representative Dan Rostenkowski, chairman of the House Ways

Released April 9—Continued
and Means Committee—by Secretary of the
Treasury Donald T. Regan

Released April 10

News conference:
On the recovery of the President and Press Secretary James S. Brady—by Dr. Dennis O'Leary,
dean for clinical affairs, George Washington University Hospital

Released April 11

Transcript:
The President's exchange with reporters on his
departure from George Washington University
Hospital

Released April 13

Transcript:
Telephone conversation between the Vice Presi-
dent from his office in the Old Executive Office
Building and astronauts John W. Young and Capt.
Robert L. Crippen aboard the space shuttle *Co-
lumbia*

Transcript:
The Vice President's exchange with reporters following his telephone conversation with the astronauts

Photocopy:
The President and Mrs. Reagan's U.S. Individual
Tax Return for 1980

Released April 15

Text:
Letter to the President from Marine Cpl. Ishmael
Franco of California, who sent the President a
Purple Heart the corporal had been awarded for
service in Vietnam

Transcript:
Remarks and a briefing for regional reporters,
editors, and news directors on the program for
economic recovery—by the Vice President

Transcript:
Briefing for regional reporters, editors, and news
directors on the program for economic recovery—by Secretary of the Treasury Donald T.
Regan

Released April 16

Transcript:
Remarks and a question-and-answer session with
reporters on NATO Secretary General Joseph
M.A.H. Luns' meetings with the President and

Released April 16—Continued
other U.S. officials—by Secretary of State Alexander M. Haig, Jr., and Secretary General Luns

Transcript:
Press briefing on actions to eliminate waste,
fraud, and abuse in the Federal Government—by
Edwin L. Harper, Deputy Director of the Office
of Management and Budget

Fact sheet:
On actions to eliminate waste, fraud, and abuse
in the Federal Government

Transcript:
Press briefing on a Congressional Budget Office
study of the program for economic recovery—by
David A. Stockman, Director of the Office of
Management and Budget

Released April 17

Transcript:
Remarks to reporters following his meeting with
the President—by Terence Cardinal Cooke,
Archbishop of New York

Released April 20

Statement:
On the gross national product figures for the first
quarter of 1981—by Murray L. Weidenbaum,
Chairman of the Council of Economic Advisers

Fact sheet:
Federal audiovisual aids and publications

Transcript:
Press briefing on Federal audiovisual aids and
publications—by Edwin L. Harper, Deputy Director of the Office of Management and Budget

Released April 21

Transcript:
Exchange between the President and Representative Eugene V. Atkinson on the radio broadcast "A.M. Connection" in Beaver Falls, Pa.

Transcript:
The Vice President's remarks at a briefing on the
program for economic recovery given for regional reporters, editors, and news directors

Transcript:
Press briefing on their meeting with the Presi-
dent—by Governors James A. Rhodes of Ohio,
Richard L. Thornburgh of Pennsylvania, Pierre S.
du Pont IV of Delaware, Bill Clements of Texas,
David Treen of Louisiana, Robert Orr of Indiana,
Frank White of Arkansas, and Forrest D. James,
Jr., of Alabama

Released April 22

Transcript:
The Vice President's remarks at a briefing on the program for economic recovery given for State and local officials

Released April 23

Fact sheet:
Federal credit management

Statement:
On the Consumer Price Index figures for March—by Murray L. Weidenbaum, Chairman of the Council of Economic Advisers

Transcript:
Press briefing on the Consumer Price Index figures for March and the program for economic recovery—by Murray L. Weidenbaum, Chairman of the Council of Economic Advisers

Announcement:
Designation of Joseph Coors to represent the United States at the annual Australia-America Friendship Week celebrations

Transcript:
Remarks of Counsellor to the President Edwin Meese III and Assistant to the President James A. Baker III at the American Society of Newspaper Editors luncheon

Released April 28

Transcript:
Remarks of the Vice President at a breakfast meeting at the Associated Builders and Contractors Annual Legislative Conference

Transcript:
Press briefing on their meeting with the President—by Senate Majority Leader Howard H. Baker, Jr., and House Minority Leader Robert H. Michel

Advance text:
The President's address before a joint session of the Congress

Released April 30

Transcript:
Remarks of Elie Wiesel, Chairman of the United States Holocaust Memorial Council, at the White House commemoration ceremony

Transcript:
Remarks of the Vice President to members of the American Legislative Exchange

Released May 10

Transcript:
Question-and-answer session with reporters on the program for economic recovery (conducted on May 8)—by Assistant to the President James A. Baker III and Assistant to the President for Legislative Affairs Max L. Friedersdorf

Released May 11

Announcement:
Appointment of Bently T. Elliott and Landon Parvin as Presidential speechwriters

Announcement:
Nomination of Henry Dargan McMaster to be United States Attorney for the District of South Carolina

Released May 13

Announcement:
Nomination of Francis Anthony Keating II to be United States Attorney for the Northern District of Oklahoma

Announcement:
Nomination of David L. Russell to be United States Attorney for the Western District of Oklahoma

Released May 15

Fact sheet:
The President's trip to the University of Notre Dame on May 17

Released May 17

Advance text:
Address at commencement exercises at the University of Notre Dame

Released May 27

Advance text:
Address at commencement exercises at the United States Military Academy, West Point, N.Y.

Released May 28

Announcement:
Nomination of O. Evans Denney to be United States Marshal for the District of Delaware

Released May 29

Transcript:
Exchange with reporters following his meeting with the President to discuss the situation in Lebanon—by Ambassador Philip C. Habib, the

Released May 29—Continued
President's emissary in consultations in the Middle East

Transcript:
Question-and-answer session with reporters on the President's June 1 meeting with the Democratic congressional leadership to discuss Federal tax reductions—by Assistant to the President James A. Baker III

Released June 1

Transcript:
Press briefing following the President's meeting with Democratic congressional leaders on tax reductions—by Secretary of the Treasury Donald T. Regan

Transcript:
Press briefing following the President's meeting with a group of Governors and mayors—by Governors Robert D. Orr of Indiana and Edward J. King of Massachusetts, and Mayors William H. Hudnut III of Indianapolis, Ind., and Jayne Plank of Kensington, Md.

Released June 2

Transcript:
Press briefing following the President's meeting with Republican congressional leaders on tax reductions—by Senator Robert Dole, chairman of the Senate Finance Committee, and Representative Barber B. Conable, Jr., chairman of the House Ways and Means Committee

Released June 4

Statement by the President:
On Federal tax reductions (as read to reporters following meetings with congressional leaders)

Released June 5

Transcript:
Excerpt from a press briefing on the nomination of Ernest W. Lefever to be Assistant Secretary of State for Human Rights and Humanitarian Affairs—by Counsellor to the President Edwin Meese III and Assistant to the President James A. Baker III

Released June 8

Statement:
Press advisory on information concerning the Israeli bombing of the nuclear facility in Iraq—by Deputy Press Secretary Larry M. Speakes

Statement:
Activities of President Reagan and President José López Portillo of Mexico during their stay at

Released June 8—Continued
Camp David, Md.—by Deputy Press Secretary Larry M. Speakes (two releases)

Released June 10

Biographical data:
Under Secretary of State for Management Richard T. Kennedy, nominated to be U.S. Representative to the International Atomic Energy Agency

Text:
Letter to the chairman of the Senate Foreign Relations Committee on the Israeli bombing of the nuclear facility in Iraq—by Secretary of State Alexander M. Haig, Jr.

Released June 16

Announcement:
Nomination of Edward C. Prado to be United States Attorney for the Western District of Texas

Statement by the President:
On the program for economic recovery (as read at his news conference in Room 450 of the Old Executive Office Building)

Released June 24

Advance text:
Remarks at the annual convention of the United States Jaycees in San Antonio, Tex.

Released June 25

Announcement:
Nomination of Sarah Evans Barker to be United States Attorney for the Southern District of Indiana

Transcript:
Question-and-answer session with members of the press following his meeting with the President to report on his trip to Asia—by Secretary of State Alexander M. Haig, Jr.

Released June 27

Transcript:
Press briefing on the program for economic recovery—by Counsellor to the President Edwin Meese III, David A. Stockman, Director of the Office of Management and Budget, and Assistant to the President for Legislative Affairs Max L. Friedersdorf

Transcript:
Press briefing on his visit with the President—by the Vice President

Released June 29

Advance text:
Remarks at the annual convention of the National Association for the Advancement of Colored People in Denver, Colo.

Released July 1

Announcement:
Nomination of William C. Lee to be United States District Judge for the Northern District of Indiana

Announcement:
Nomination of Daniel K. Hedges to be United States Attorney for the Southern District of Texas

Released July 7

Statement by the President:
Intention to nominate Judge Sandra Day O'Connor to be an Associate Justice of the Supreme Court (as read to reporters in the Briefing Room)

Transcript:
Question-and-answer session with reporters on the President's nomination of Judge O'Connor—by Attorney General William French Smith

Advance text:
Remarks at the Citizens for Thompson Dinner in Chicago, Ill.

Released July 9

Announcement:
Nomination of D. Brook Bartlett to be United States District Judge for the Western District of Missouri

Announcement:
Nomination of John R. Gibson to be United States District Judge for the Western District of Missouri

Announcement:
Nomination of Joseph E. Stevens, Jr., to be United States District Judge for the Eastern and Western Districts of Missouri

Announcement:
Nomination of William W. Wilkins, Jr., to be United States District Judge for the District of South Carolina

Announcement:
Nomination of Richard S. Cohen to be United States Attorney for the District of Maine

Released July 10

Transcript:
Press briefing on the President's meeting with members of the executive committee of the National Black Caucus of State Legislators—by Clarence Mitchell, president of the National Black Caucus of State Legislators

Released July 13

Announcement:
Nomination of A. Melvin McDonald to be United States Attorney for the District of Arizona

Announcement:
Nomination of Raymond Lawrence Steele, Jr., to be United States Attorney for the Northern District of Indiana

Announcement:
Nomination of Thomas E. Dittmeier to be United States Attorney for the Eastern District of Missouri

Announcement:
Nomination of Richard A. Stacy to be United States Attorney for the District of Wyoming

Released July 15

Announcement:
Nomination of Robert F. Chapman to be a United States Circuit Judge for the Fourth Circuit

Announcement:
Nomination of John C. Bell to be United States Attorney for the Middle District of Alabama

Announcement:
Nomination of J. B. Sessions III to be United States Attorney for the Southern District of Alabama

Announcement:
Nomination of Joseph J. Farnan, Jr., to be United States Attorney for the District of Delaware

Announcement:
Nomination of James A. Rolfe to be United States Attorney for the Northern District of Texas

Transcript:
Press briefing following the President's meeting with representatives of the small business community—by John Sloan of Nashville, Tenn., Carolyn Gaudry of Portland, Oreg., and William M. Burckhart of Williamsville, N.Y.

Released July 16

Fact sheet:
United States nonproliferation and peaceful nuclear cooperation policy

Released July 20

Transcript:
Press briefing on the President's decision to defer the shipment of F–16's to Israel—by Secretary of State Alexander M. Haig, Jr.

Released July 21

Transcript:
Press briefing on the Ottawa Economic Summit Conference—by Assistant to the President for National Security Affairs Richard V. Allen

Statement by the President:
On the Ottawa Economic Summit Conference (concluding statement made at the National Arts Center in Ottawa)

Released July 24

Announcement:
Nomination of Michael R. Spaan to be United States Attorney for the District of Alaska

Released July 27

Excerpts:
President's address to the nation on Federal tax reduction legislation

Advance text:
President's address to the nation on Federal tax reduction legislation

Released July 28

Announcement:
Nomination of Roger J. Miner to be United States District Judge for the Northern District of New York

Transcript:
Press briefing following his meeting with the President to discuss food for Poland—by John Cardinal Krol, Archbishop of Philadelphia

Released July 29

Announcement:
Nomination of Joseph M. McLaughlin to be United States District Judge for the Eastern District of New York

Announcement:
Nomination of John E. Sprizzo to be United States District Judge for the Southern District of New York

Released July 29—Continued

Announcement:
Nomination of Frank W. Donaldson to be United States Attorney for the Northern District of Alabama

Announcement:
Nomination of J. Frederick Motz to be United States Attorney for the District of Maryland

Announcement:
Nomination of W. Stephen Thayer III to be United States Attorney for the District of New Hampshire

Statement by the President:
On congressional action on the Federal tax reduction legislation (as read to reporters in the Oval Office)

Released July 30

Advance text:
Address to the annual convention of the National Conference of State Legislatures in Atlanta, Ga.

Released August 1

Transcript:
Press briefing on Federal tax reduction legislation—by Secretary of the Treasury Donald T. Regan, Counsellor to the President Edwin Meese III, and Assistant to the President James A. Baker III

Released August 3

Statement by the President:
Air traffic controllers strike (as read to reporters in the Rose Garden)

Released August 5

Statement by the President:
Federal budget reconciliation and tax reduction legislation (as read to reporters in the Oval Office)

Released August 6

Announcement:
Nomination of John C. Coughenour to be United States District Judge for the Western District of Washington

Announcement:
Nomination of Conrad K. Cyr to be United States District Judge for the District of Maine

Announcement:
Nomination of Henry R. Wilhoit, Jr., to be United States District Judge for the Eastern District of Kentucky

Released August 6—Continued

Announcement:
Nomination of Glen H. Davidson to be United States Attorney for the Northern District of Mississippi

Announcement:
Nomination of George Landon Phillips to be United States Attorney for the Southern District of Mississippi

Released August 12

Fact sheet:
Economic Recovery Tax Act of 1981

Fact sheet:
Omnibus Budget Reconciliation Act of 1981

Released August 19

Fact sheet:
U.S.S. *Constellation*

Released August 20

Announcement:
Nomination of H. Franklin Waters to be United States District Judge for the Western District of Arkansas

Announcement:
Nomination of Emery R. Jordan to be United States Marshal for the District of Maine

Announcement:
Nomination of John Ernest Lamp to be United States Attorney for the Eastern District of Washington

Released August 29

Transcript:
Birthday messages delivered to Press Secretary James S. Brady through a communication hookup with George Washington University Hospital—by members of the White House press corps during a celebration in the Press Secretary's honor at the press center in Santa Barbara, Calif.

Released September 3

Advance text:
Remarks to the annual convention of the United Brotherhood of Carpenters and Joiners in Chicago, Ill.

Released September 8

Announcement:
Nomination of Lawrence W. Pierce to be United States Circuit Judge for the Second Circuit

Released September 16

Announcement:
Nomination of William L. Garwood to be United States Circuit Judge for the Fifth Circuit

Announcement:
Nomination of Hayden Wilson Head, Jr., to be United States District Judge for the Southern District of Texas and nomination of James R. Nowlin to be United States District Judge for the Western District of Texas

Announcement:
Nomination of George W. F. Cook to be United States Attorney for the District of Vermont; Samuel T. Currin to be United States Attorney for the Eastern District of North Carolina; Guy Gordon Hurlbutt to be United States Attorney for the District of Idaho; William H. Kennedy to be United States Attorney for the Southern District of California; Jum J. Marquez to be United States Attorney for the District of Kansas; Kenneth W. McAllister to be United States Attorney for the Middle District of North Carolina; John A. Smietanka to be United States Attorney for the Western District of Michigan; Brent D. Ward to be United States Attorney for the District of Utah; and Rodney Scott Webb to be United States Attorney for the District of North Dakota

Announcement:
Nomination of Lynn H. Duncan to be United States Marshal for the Northern District of Georgia; Thomas C. Greene to be United States Marshal for the Northern District of Alabama; Melvin E. Jones to be United States Marshal for the Middle District of Alabama; Pasquale Arnold Mangini to be United States Marshal for the District of Connecticut; and Ralph D. Morgan to be United States Marshal for the Southern District of Indiana

Released September 18

Advance text:
Remarks at the dedication of the Gerald R. Ford Presidential Museum in Grand Rapids, Mich.

Advance text:
Remarks to the 21st biennial convention of the National Federation of Republican Women in Denver, Colo.

Released September 22

Announcement:
Nomination of Stanford O. Bardwell, Jr., to be United States Attorney for the Middle District of Louisiana; Leonard R. Gilman to be United States Attorney for the Eastern District of Michigan;

Released September 22—Continued

Ronald E. Meredith to be United States Attorney for the Western District of Kentucky; Dan K. Webb to be United States Attorney for the Northern District of Illinois; Joe D. Whitley to be United States Attorney for the Middle District of Georgia; and Robert J. Wortham to be United States Attorney for the Eastern District of Texas

Released September 24

Advance text:
Address to the nation on the program for economic recovery

Fact sheet:
Fall budget program, program for economic recovery

Released September 25

Transcript:
Press briefing on details of the President's address to the nation on the program for economic recovery

Released September 28

Advance text:
Remarks to the International Association of Chiefs of Police in New Orleans, La.

Announcement:
Nomination of Paul A. Magnuson to be United States District Judge for the District of Minnesota

Released September 29

Advance text:
Remarks to the annual meeting of the Boards of Governors of the International Monetary Fund and the World Bank Group

Released September 30

Announcement:
Nomination of Richard J. Cardamone to be United States Circuit Judge for the Second Circuit

Announcement:
Nomination of Robert D. Potter to be United States District Judge for the Western District of North Carolina

Released October 1

Announcement:
Nomination of Robert W. Foster to be United States Marshal for the Southern District of Ohio

Released October 2

Announcement:
Nomination of William H. Ewing, Jr., to be United States Attorney for the Western District of Tennessee

Statement by the President:
U.S. strategic weapons policy (as read to reporters in the East Room)

Transcript:
Press briefing on the U.S. strategic weapons policy—by Secretary of Defense Caspar W. Weinberger

Released October 5

Advance text:
Remarks at the annual meeting of the National Alliance of Business

Statement:
Sale of AWACS planes and other air defense equipment to Saudi Arabia—issued by former national security officials (as read by the President following his meeting with the officials)

Announcement:
Details of the Presidential Medal of Freedom ceremony to be held at the White House on Friday, October 9

Released October 6

Statement by the President:
Death of President Anwar el-Sadat of Egypt (as read to reporters at the North Portico of the White House)

Released October 7

Announcement:
Nomination of Ronald D. Lahners to be United States Attorney for the District of Nebraska; Robert N. Miller to be United States Attorney for the District of Colorado; and Alan H. Nevas to be United States Attorney for the District of Connecticut

Announcement:
Nomination of Kernan H. Bagley to be United States Marshal for the District of Oregon; Laurence C. Beard to be United States Marshal for the Eastern District of Oklahoma; Ralph L. Boling to be United States Marshal for the Western District of Kentucky; Robert D. Olson, Sr., to be United States Marshal for the District of Alaska; and Charles Pennington to be United States Marshal for the Eastern District of Kentucky

Released October 8

Transcript:
Press briefing on nuclear energy policy initiatives, following the President's meeting with the Cabinet Council on Natural Resources and the Environment—by Secretary of Energy James B. Edwards

Released October 9

Announcement:
Nomination of John Perry Alderman to be United States Attorney for the Western District of Virginia; Lincoln C. Almond to be United States Attorney for the District of Rhode Island; Charles R. Brewer to be United States Attorney for the Western District of North Carolina; W. Hunt Dumont to be United States Attorney for the District of New Jersey; and Gerald D. Fines to be United States Attorney for the Central District of Illinois

Announcement:
Nomination of J. Jerome Perkins to be United States Marshal for the Northern District of Indiana; Delaine Roberts to be United States Marshal for the District of Wyoming; Blaine Skinner to be United States Marshal for the District of Idaho; and Donald W. Wyatt to be United States Marshal for the District of Rhode Island

Released October 11

Transcript:
Interview with former Presidents Jimmy Carter and Gerald R. Ford aboard the aircraft 26000, during the return trip after attending funeral services for President Anwar el-Sadat of Egypt in Cairo—by Steve Bell, ABC News, Jim Anderson, United Press International, and Haynes Johnson, the Washington Post (interview dated October 10)

Released October 13

Announcement:
Nomination of Clarence A. Beam to be United States District Judge for the District of Nebraska; Emmett Ripley Cox to be United States District Judge for the Southern District of Alabama; and Cynthia Holcomb Hall to be United States District Judge for the Central District of California

Announcement:
Nomination of Elsie L. Munsell to be United States Attorney for the Eastern District of Virginia

Released October 14

Announcement:
Nomination of John W. Gill, Jr., to be United States Attorney for the Eastern District of Tennessee

Transcript:
Press briefing on the report of the Presidential Task Force on the Arts and Humanities—by Dr. Hanna H. Gray, Cochairman, and W. Barnabas McHenry, Vice Chairman, of the Task Force

Released October 15

Fact sheet:
Federal employee pay increase

Advance text:
Remarks to the World Affairs Council of Philadelphia

Released October 16

Transcript:
Press briefing on the history of the Yorktown, Va., celebration—by Special Assistant to the President for Intergovernmental Affairs Judy F. Peachee

Released October 19

Transcript:
Interview with David A. Stockman, Director of the Office of Management and Budget, on NBC's "Today"

Advance text:
Remarks at the bicentennial observance of the Battle of Yorktown at Yorktown, Va.

Released October 20

Transcript:
Press briefing on the International Meeting on Cooperation and Development in Cancún, Mexico—by Secretary of State Alexander M. Haig, Jr., and Secretary of the Treasury Donald T. Regan

Announcement:
Nomination of Jesse E. Eschbach to be United States Circuit Judge for the Seventh Circuit

Announcement:
Nomination of James C. Cacheris to be United States District Judge for the Eastern District of Virginia and John Bailey Jones to be United States District Judge for the District of South Dakota

Released October 20—Continued

Announcement:

Nomination of Denny L. Sampson to be United States Marshal for the District of Nevada

Released October 21

Announcement:

Nomination of Philip N. Hogen to be United States Attorney for the District of South Dakota, James M. Rosenbaum to be United States Attorney for the District of Minnesota, and Joseph P. Russoniello to be United States Attorney for the Northern District of California

Transcript:

Remarks with reporters on the President's statement concerning Europe and the U.S. strategic policy—by Secretary of State Alexander M. Haig, Jr.

Transcript:

Press briefing on the President's bilateral meetings with foreign leaders at the International Meeting on Cooperation and Development in Cancún, Mexico—by Secretary of State Alexander M. Haig, Jr.

Released October 22

Transcript:

Interview with Secretary of the Treasury Donald T. Regan on the International Meeting on Cooperation and Development in Cancún, Mexico—by Steve Bell, ABC News, on "Good Morning America"

Transcript:

Interview with Assistant to the President for National Security Affairs Richard V. Allen on the Cancún meetings—by Marvin Kalb, NBC News, on "Today"

Transcript:

Interview with Secretary of the Treasury Donald T. Regan on the Cancún meetings—by Diane Sawyer, CBS News, on the "CBS Morning News"

Transcript:

Press briefing on the first session of the Cancún meetings—by Secretary of State Alexander M. Haig, Jr., and Secretary of the Treasury Donald T. Regan

Transcript:

Press briefing on the day's Cancún meetings—by Secretary of the Treasury Donald T. Regan and Assistant to the President James A. Baker III

Released October 22—Continued

Transcript:

Interview with Secretary of the Treasury Donald T. Regan on the Cancún meetings—by Ted Koppel, ABC News, on ABC's "Nightline"

Released October 23

Transcript:

Interview with Assistant to the President James A. Baker III on the International Meeting on Cooperation and Development in Cancún, Mexico—by John Palmer, NBC News, on "Today"

Transcript:

Interview with Secretary of State Alexander M. Haig, Jr., on the Cancún meetings—by Diane Sawyer, CBS News, on the "CBS Morning News"

Statement:

September's consumer price index—by Murray L. Weidenbaum, Chairman of the Council of Economic Advisers

Released October 24

Transcript:

Press briefing on the International Meeting on Cooperation and Development in Cancún, Mexico—by Secretary of State Alexander M. Haig, Jr., and Secretary of the Treasury Donald T. Regan

Advance text:

Remarks of the President upon arrival at Andrews Air Force Base, Md., following his return from the Cancún meetings

Released October 27

Announcement:

Nomination of Richard A. Posner to be United States Circuit Judge for the Seventh Circuit

Released October 28

Transcript:

Question-and-answer session with reporters following the Senate vote on the sale of AWACS and other air defense equipment to Saudi Arabia—by Assistant to the President James A. Baker III

Released October 29

Announcement:

Nomination of William F. Weld to be United States Attorney for the District of Massachusetts

Released October 29—Continued

Statement:
Response to press inquiries concerning the OPEC price decision, the Saudi role in the decision, and U.S. arms transfers to Saudi Arabia

Transcript:
Press briefing on the sale of AWACS and other air defense equipment to Saudi Arabia—by Assistants to the President Richard V. Allen and James A. Baker

Released October 30

Announcement:
Nomination of John Robert Byrnes to be United States Attorney for the Western District of Wisconsin and nomination of Joseph P. Stadtmueller to be United States Attorney for the Eastern District of Wisconsin

Released November 2

Announcement:
Nomination of Frederick N. Falk to be United States Marshal for the Western District of Wisconsin and nomination of William S. Vaughn to be United States Marshal for the Eastern District of Missouri

Released November 4

Announcement:
Nomination of Jackson L. Kiser to be United States District Judge for the Western District of Virginia; John H. Moore II to be United States District Judge for the Middle District of Florida; and John C. Shabaz to be United States District Judge for the Western District of Wisconsin

Announcement:
Nomination of Donald B. Ayer to be United States Attorney for the Eastern District of California; Joe B. Brown to be United States Attorney for the Middle District of Tennessee; Louis G. DeFalaise to be United States Attorney for the Eastern District of Kentucky; Byron H. Dunbar to be United States Attorney for the District of Montana; Hinton R. Pierce to be United States Attorney for the Southern District of Georgia; and Robert G. Ulrich to be United States Attorney for the Western District of Missouri

Announcement:
New appointments for five members of the staff of the White House Office of Policy Development

Statement:
Details of the results of the President's annual physical examination—by Dr. Daniel Ruge, Physician to the President

Released November 4—Continued

Announcement:
Nomination of Howard V. Adair to be United States Marshal for the Southern District of Alabama; John W. Roberts to be United States Marshal for the District of Arizona; Warren D. Stump to be United States Marshal for the Southern District of Iowa; Kenneth L. Pekarek to be United States Marshal for the District of Kansas; John L. Meyers to be United States Marshal for the Middle District of Louisiana; Robert L. Pavlak, Sr., to be United States Marshal for the District of Minnesota; Lee Koury to be United States Marshal for the Western District of Missouri; Ronald D. Daniels, Jr., to be United States Marshal for the District of New Hampshire; Kenneth B. Muir to be United States Marshal for the District of North Dakota; and Paul R. Nolan to be United States Marshal for the Eastern District of Washington

Announcement:
Nomination of Stanley S. Harris to be United States Attorney for the District of Columbia

Released November 5

Transcript:
Press briefing on the President's proposals for Federal credit/loan guarantee reductions—by Lawrence Kudlow, Assistant Director for Economic Policy, Office of Management and Budget

Fact sheet:
President's proposals for Federal credit/loan guarantee reductions

Announcement:
Nomination of Harry Connolly to be United States Marshal for the Northern District of Oklahoma and nomination of John R. Kendall to be United States Marshal for the Western District of Michigan

Announcement:
Nomination of Robert G. Doumar to be United States District Judge for the Eastern District of Virginia and nomination of David V. O'Brien to be United States District Judge for the District of the Virgin Islands

Statement:
NATO strategy and considerations of nuclear employment—issued by the Department of Defense

Released November 10

Transcript:
Press briefing on the Vietnam Veterans Leadership Program—by Thomas W. Pauken, Director

Released November 10—Continued
of ACTION, and other representatives involved in the program

Announcement:
Establishment of the National Productivity Advisory Committee

Statement by the President:
Economic recovery program (as read at the beginning of his news conference in the East Room)

Released November 12

Transcript:
Press briefing on his meeting with the President to discuss the issues raised by an article in The Atlantic magazine concerning the President's economic recovery program—by David A. Stockman, Director of the Office of Management and Budget

Statement:
The President's meeting with David A. Stockman, Director of the Office of Management and Budget, to discuss The Atlantic magazine article—by Deputy Press Secretary Larry M. Speakes

Released November 13

Announcement:
Nomination of Clyde H. Hamilton to be United States District Judge for the District of South Carolina

Released November 14

Announcement:
Restriction of White House comments relating to Assistant to the President for National Security Affairs Richard V. Allen and the handling of funds from the Japanese magazine *Shufu no Tomo* while the matter is under review by the Department of Justice, together with a statement by Mr. Allen

Announcement:
Nomination of Edward R. Becker to be United States Circuit Judge for the Third Circuit

Announcement:
Nomination of Christopher K. Barnes to be United States Attorney for the Southern District of Ohio, and nomination of Richard C. Turner to be United States Attorney for the Southern District of Iowa

Announcement:
Nomination of James P. Jonker to be United States Marshal for the Northern District of Iowa,

Released November 14—Continued
and nomination of Wallace L. McLendon to be United States Marshal for the Northern District of Florida

Released November 16

Announcement:
Nomination of Alvin I. Krenzler to be United States District Judge for the Northern District of Ohio

Released November 18

Advance text:
Address to the National Press Club on arms reduction and nuclear weapons

Announcement:
Nomination of Ralph K. Winter, Jr., to be United States Circuit Judge for the Second Circuit

Released November 19

Announcement:
Nomination of Israel Leo Glasser to be United States District Judge for the Eastern District of New York

Announcement:
Nomination of Gene S. Anderson to be United States Attorney for the Western District of Washington, Joseph S. Cage, Jr., to be United States Attorney for the Western District of Louisiana, and David A. Faber to be United States Attorney for the Southern District of West Virginia

Announcement:
Nomination of Wayne D. Beaman to be United States Marshal for the Western District of Virginia, and William I. Berryhill, Jr., to be United States Marshal for the Eastern District of North Carolina

Released November 23

Statement:
On his departure from George Washington University Hospital—by Press Secretary James S. Brady

Released November 24

Transcript:
Interview with Counsellor to the President Edwin Meese III on the President's veto of the continuing resolution for fiscal year 1982 appropriations—by Leslie Stahl, CBS News, on "Morning"

Released November 24—Continued
Transcript:
Interview with Assistant to the President James A. Baker III on the President's veto of the continuing resolution for fiscal year 1982 appropriations—by Richard Valeriani and Tom Brokaw, NBC News, on "Today"

Statement by Deputy Press Secretary Larry M. Speakes:
Establishment of a Republican task force representative of the Senate, the House of Representatives, and the White House to develop a package that can be supported by the leadership of the Senate, the Republican leadership of the House, and the White House with regard to the next continuing resolution

Released November 25

Announcement:
Nominations of Sam A. Crow to be United States District Judge for the District of Kansas and J. Owen Forrester to be United States District Judge for the Northern District of Georgia

Announcement:
Invitation by the President to President Mobutu Sese Seko of the Republic of Zaire to meet with him at the White House on December 1

Released November 29

Transcript:
Interview with Assistant to the President for National Security Affairs Richard V. Allen on NBC's "Meet the Press"

Announcement:
Meeting of the President and Mrs. Reagan, upon their arrival on November 30 at Pt. Mugu Naval Air Station, Calif., with Capt. and Mrs. James Hickerson and their son, Todd. As Governor of California, the President wore a bracelet which bore the name of Todd's father, Capt. Stephen Hanson, USMC, who served as a helicopter pilot during the Vietnam conflict and was shot down over Laos on June 3, 1967. When the American prisoners of war were granted freedom in 1973, Captain Hanson's status was changed from missing in action to killed in action.

Released December 1

Advance text:
Address to the 1981 White House Conference on Aging

Fact sheet:
The Reagan administration and the elderly—10-month update

Released December 1—Continued
Announcement:
Completion of Justice Department investigation concerning the discovery of an envelope containing 10 $100 bills in a safe in an office occupied at one time by Assistant to the President for National Security Affairs Richard V. Allen, and restriction of White House comments on other matters concerning Mr. Allen pending completion of other Justice Department inquiries

Released December 3

Biography:
Max L. Friedersdorf, who is resigning as Assistant to the President for Legislative Affairs

Released December 4

Fact sheet:
H.R. 4144—Energy and Water Development Appropriation Act, 1982

Announcement:
Meeting of members of the White House staff with representatives of major news organizations to request restraint by the news organizations in reporting and televising specific security measures utilized in the protection of the President and others

Statement:
Executive orders on United States intelligence activities—by Counsellor to the President Edwin Meese III

Statement:
Executive orders on United States intelligence activities—by Adm. B.R. Inman, Deputy Director of the Central Intelligence Agency

Statement:
Executive orders on United States intelligence activities—by Richard K. Willard, Counsel Office of Intelligence Policy and Review, Department of Justice

Announcement:
Nomination of Michael S. Kanne to be United States District Judge for the Northern District of Indiana; James T. Moody to be United States District Judge for the Northern District of Indiana; and David L. Russell to be United States District Judge for the Northern, Eastern, and Western Districts of Oklahoma

Announcement:
Nomination of Lamond Robert Mills to be United States Attorney for the District of Nevada

Released December 4—Continued

Announcement:
Nomination of Thomas A. O'Hara, Jr., to be United States Marshal for the District of Nebraska; Bruce R. Montgomery to be United States Marshal for the Eastern District of Tennessee; and Robert T. Keating to be United States Marshal for the Eastern District of Wisconsin

Released December 7

Announcement:
Nomination of Robert H. Bork to be United States Circuit Judge for the District of Columbia

Announcement:
Nomination of Harold L. Ryan to be United States District Judge for the District of Idaho

Transcript:
Press briefing on the second summary report of the Inspectors General activities—by Edwin L. Harper, Deputy Director of the Office of Management and Budget

Released December 8

Announcement:
Nomination of Evan L. Hultman to be United States Attorney for the Northern District of Iowa

Released December 9

Announcement:
Nomination of Stephen S. Trott to be United States Attorney for the Central District of California

Transcript:
Press briefing on the President's decision regarding the discharged air traffic controllers—by Secretary of Transportation Drew L. Lewis and Donald J. Devine, Director of the Office of Personnel Management

Statement:
The President's decision regarding the discharged air traffic controllers—by Secretary of Transportation Drew L. Lewis (as read at his press briefing)

Released December 10

Statement:
Department of State actions concerning Americans in Libya—by Deputy Secretary of State William P. Clark (as read at a press briefing at the Department of State)

Text:
Cable to chief executive officers of U.S. companies employing Americans in Libya from Deputy Secretary of State William P. Clark

Released December 11

Announcement:
Nomination of J. William Petro to be United States Attorney for the Northern District of Ohio

Transcript:
Remarks to reporters on his meeting with the President—by Ambassador Philip C. Habib, the President's emissary in consultations in the Middle East

Released December 15

Statement by the President:
Approval of H.J. Res. 370, continuing resolution for fiscal year 1982 appropriations (as read at the bill signing ceremony in the Oval Office)

Released December 16

Statement:
Establishment of the National Commission on Social Security Reform (as read to reporters by the President)

Transcript:
Press briefing on the National Commission on Social Security Reform—by Alan Greenspan, Chairman of the Commission

Announcement:
Nominations of Eugene H. Davis to be United States Marshal for the District of Utah, Stuart E. Earnest to be United States Marshal for the Western District of Oklahoma, Christian Hansen, Jr., to be United States Marshal for the District of Vermont, William J. Jonas, Jr., to be United States Marshal for the Western District of Texas, and George L. McBane to be United States Marshal for the Middle District of North Carolina

Released December 17

Transcript:
Press briefing on the planned dismantling of the Department of Energy—by Secretary of Energy James B. Edwards and Edwin L. Harper, Deputy Director of the Office of Management and Budget

Transcript:
Press briefing on the President's decision not to reimpose parking fees for Federal employees—by Representatives Marjorie S. Holt of Maryland and Stan Parris and Frank R. Wolf of Virginia

Released December 21

Announcement:
Nomination of Julio Gonzales to be United States Marshal for the Central District of California

Released December 22

Press briefing on the administration's end-of-the-year report—by Counsellor to the President Edwin Meese III and Chief of Staff James A. Baker III

Released December 23

Advance text:
Address to the nation about Christmas and the situation in Poland

Released December 29

Remarks before the World Affairs Council in San Francisco, Calif.—by Secretary of State Alexander M. Haig, Jr.

Appendix D—Acts Approved by the President

Approved January 26

S.J. Res. 16 / Public Law 97–1
A joint resolution designating January 29, 1981, as "A Day of Thanksgiving To Honor Our Safely Returned Hostages".

Approved February 7

H.R. 1553 / Public Law 97–2
An act to provide for a temporary increase in the public debt limit.

Approved February 10

S. 253 / Public Law 97–3
An act to increase the number of members of the Commission on Wartime Relocation and Internment of Civilians.

Approved February 17

S. 272 / Public Law 97–4
An act to increase the membership of the Joint Committee on Printing.

Approved March 13

H.R. 2166 / Public Law 97–5
An act to amend the Energy Policy and Conservation Act to extend certain authorities relating to the international energy program.

Approved March 31

S. 509 / Public Law 97–6
An act to amend section 201 of the Agricultural Act of 1949, as amemded, to delete the requirement that the support price of milk be adjusted semiannually.

Approved April 9

S. 840 / Public Law 97–7
An act to continue in effect any authority provided under the Department of Justice Appropriation Authorization Act, Fiscal Year 1980, for a certain period.

S.J. Res. 61 / Public Law 97–8
A joint resolution to authorize and request the President to issue a proclamation designating April 9, 1981, as "African Refugee Relief Day".

Approved April 14

H.J. Res. 182 / Public Law 97–9
A joint resolution to designate April 26, 1981, as "National Recognition Day for Veterans of the Vietman Era".

Approved May 1

H.J. Res. 155 / Public Law 97–10
A joint resolution to authorize and request the President to issue a proclamation designating May 3 through May 10, 1981, as "Jewish Heritage Week".

Approved May 22

S 730 / Public Law 97–11
An act to ensure necessary funds for the implementation of the Federal Crop Insurance Act of 1980.

Approved June 5

H.R. 3512 / Public Law 97–12
Supplemental Appropriations and Rescission Act, 1981.

Approved June 12

S.J. Res. 50 / Public Law 97–13
A joint resolution designating July 17, 1981, as "National P.O.W.-M.I.A. Recognition Day".

Approved June 16

S. 1070 / Public Law 97–14
Youth Employment Demonstration Amendments of 1981.

Approved June 17

H.R. 2156 / Public Law 97–15
An act to amend title 38, United States Code, to extend by twelve months the period during which funds appropriated for grants by the Veterans Administration for the establishment and support of new State medical schools may be expended.

Approved June 23

S. 1213 / Public Law 97–16
An act to amend title I of the Marine Protection, Research, and Sanctuaries Act, as amended.

Approved June 29

H.J. Res. 288 / Public Law 97–17
A joint resolution to correct Public Law 97–12 due to an error in the enrollment of H.R. 3512.

Approved June 30

H.R. 3991 / Public Law 97–18
An act to amend the Food Stamp Act of 1977 to increase the authorization for appropriations for fiscal year 1981, and to amend Public Law 93–233 to continue, through August 1, 1981, the cash-out of food stamp program benefits of certain recipients of Supplemental Security Income.

Approved July 6

S. 1123 / Public Law 97–19
An act to permit certain funds allocated for official expenses of Senators to be utilized to procure additional office equipment.

S. 1124 / Public Law 97–20
An act to authorize the Sergeant at Arms and Doorkeeper of the Senate, subject to the approval of the Committee on Rules and Administration, to enter into contracts which provide for the making of advance payments for computer programing services.

Approved July 9

H.J. Res. 238 / Public Law 97–21
A joint resolution to approve a Constitution for the United States Virgin Islands.

Approved July 10

H.R. 3807 / Public Law 97–22
Defense Officer Personnel Management Act Technical Corrections Act.

Approved July 17

H.R. 3520 / Public Law 97–23
Steel Industry Compliance Extension Act of 1981.

Approved July 23

S. 1395 / Public Law 97–24
An act to extend the time for conducting the referendum with respect to the national marketing quota for wheat for the marketing year beginning June 1, 1982, and to eliminate the requirement that the Secretary of Agriculture waive interest on loans made on 1980 and 1981 crops of wheat and feed grains placed in the farmer-held grain reserve.

Approved July 27

H.R. 31 / Public Law 97–25
Cash Discount Act.

Approved July 29

H.J. Res. 308 / Public Law 97–26
A joint resolution making an urgent supplemental appropriation for the Department of Health and Human Services for the fiscal year ending September 30, 1981.

Approved August 4

H.J. Res. 84 / Public Law 97–27
A joint resolution designating the week of October 4 through October 10, 1981, as "National Diabetes Week".

S.J. Res. 28 / Public Law 97–28
A joint resolution designating the week beginning March 7, 1982, as "Women's History Week".

Approved August 6

H.J. Res. 191 / Public Law 97–29
A joint resolution designating August 8, 1982, as "National Children's Day".

S. 1040 / Public Law 97–30
An act to amend the District of Columbia Self-Government and Governmental Reorganization Act to increase the amount authorized to be appropriated as the annual Federal payment to the District of Columbia.

H.R. 4074 / Public Law 97–31
Maritime Act of 1981.

S.J. Res. 64 / Public Law 97–32
A joint resolution designating August 13, 1981, as "National Blinded Veterans Recognition Day".

Approved August 7

S. 1104 / Public Law 97–33
An act to amend the International Investment Survey Act of 1976 to provide an authorization for futher appropriations, to avoid unnecessary duplication of certain surveys, and for other purposes.

Approved August 13

H.R. 4242 / Public Law 97–34
Economic Recovery Tax Act of 1981.

H.R. 3982 / Public Law 97–35
Omnibus Budget Reconciliation Act of 1981.

Approved August 14

H.J. Res. 141 / Public Law 97–36
A joint resolution authorizing and requesting the President to issue a proclamation designating the period from October 4, 1981, through October 10, 1981, as "National Schoolbus Safety Week".

H.R. 1100 / Public Law 97–37
Former Prisioner of War Benefits Act of 1981.

S. 547 / Public Law 97–38
An act to enable the Secretary of the Interior to erect permanent improvements on land acquired for the Confederated Tribes of Siletz Indians of Oregon.

S. 694 / Public Law 97–39
Department of Defense Supplemental Authorization Act, 1981.

S. 640 / Public Law 97–40
An act to amend the District of Columbia Self-Government and Governmental Reorganization Act to extend the authority of the Mayor to accept certain interim loans from the United States and to extend the authority of the Secretary of the Treasury to make such loans.

S. 875 / Public Law 97–41
An act to authorize the generation of electrical power at Palo Verde Irrigation District Diversion Dam, California.

S. 1278 / Public Law 97–42
Saccharin Study and Labeling Act Amendment of 1981.

Approved August 20

S.J. Res. 87 / Public Law 97–43
A joint resolution to authorize and request the President to designate September 13, 1981, as "Commodore John Barry Day".

Approved September 17

S.J. Res. 62 / Public Law 97–44
A joint resolution to authorize and request the President to designate the week of September 20 through 26, 1981, as "National Cystic Fibrosis Week".

Approved September 25

H.R. 2120 / Public Law 97–45
Product Liability Risk Retention Act of 1981.

H.R. 4416 / Public Law 97–46
An act to enable the Secretary of Agriculture to assist, on an emergency basis, in the eradication of plant pests and contagious or infectious animal and poultry diseases.

Approved September 30

H.R. 2903 / Public Law 97–47
An act to extend by one year the expiration date of the Defense Production Act of 1950.

H.J. Res. 266 / Public Law 97–48
A joint resolution to provide for a temporary increase in the public debt limit.

H.J. Res 265 / Public Law 97–49
A joint resolution to provide for a temporary increase in the public debt limit.

S. 1475 / Public Law 97–50
An act to extend the expiration date of section 252 of the Energy Policy and Conservation Act.

Approved October 1

H.J. Res. 325 / Public Law 97–51
A joint resolution making continuing appropriations for the fiscal year 1982, and for other purposes.

Approved October 2

S.J. Res. 78 / Public Law 97–52
A joint resolution to provide for the designation of October 2, 1981, as "American Enterprise Day".

S.J. Res. 103 / Public Law 97–53
A joint resolution to authorize and request the President of the United States to issue a proclamation designating the seven calendar days beginning October 4, 1981, as "National Port Week".

Approved October 5

S.J. Res. 65 / Public Law 97–54
A joint resolution proclaiming Raoul Wallenberg to be an honorary citizen of the United States, and requesting the President to ascertain from the Soviet Union the whereabouts of Raoul Wallenberg and to secure his return to freedom.

Approved October 6

H.R. 618 / Public Law 97–55
An act to convey certain interests in public lands to the city of Angels, California.

H.R. 2218 / Public Law 97–56
An act to direct the Secretary of Agriculture to convey certain National Forest System lands in the State of Nevada, and for other purposes.

Approved October 9

H.J. Res. 263 / Public Law 97–57
A joint resolution to designate May 6, 1982, as "National Recognition Day for Nurses".

H.R. 4084 / Public Law 97–58
An act to improve the operation of the Marine Mammal Protection Act of 1972, and for other purposes.

S. 1033 / Public Law 97–59
An act granting the consent of Congress to the agreement between the States of North Carolina and South Carolina establishing their lateral seaward boundary.

Approved October 14

S. 1181 / Public Law 97–60
Uniformed Services Pay Act of 1981.

S.J. Res. 98 / Public Law 97–61
A joint resolution to authorize and request the President to issue a proclamation designating October 16, 1981, as "World Food Day".

S. 1712 / Public Law 97–62
An act to extend the time for conducting the referendum with respect to the national marketing quota for wheat for the marketing year beginning June 1, 1982.

Approved October 16

S. 304 / Public Law 97–63
National Tourism Policy Act.

H.R. 4048 / Public Law 97–64
An act granting the consent of Congress to the agreement between the States of Kansas and Missouri establishing their mutual boundary in the vicinity of the French Bottoms near Saint Joseph, Missouri, and Elwood, Kansas.

H.R. 3136 / Public Law 97–65
Overseas Private Investment Corporation Amendments Act of 1981.

Approved October 17

S. 917 / Public Law 97–66
Veterans' Disability Compensation, Housing, and Memorial Benefits Amendments of 1981.

Approved October 20

H.R. 4612 / Public Law 97–67
An act to temporarily delay the October 1, 1981, increase in the price support level for milk and to extend the time for conducting the referendum with respect to the national marketing

Approved October 20—Continued
quota for wheat for the marketing year beginning June 1, 1982.

Approved October 26

S. 1191 / Public Law 97–68
An act to extend for three additional years the provisions of the Fishermen's Protective Act of 1967 relating to the reimbursement of United States commercial fishermen for certain losses incurred incident to the seizure of their vessels by foreign nations; and for other purposes.

S. 1224 / Public Law 97–69
An act to amend the provisions of title 39, United States Code, relating to the use of the frank, and for other purposes.

S. 1687 / Public Law 97–70
An act to make a technical amendment to the International Investment Survey Act of 1976.

H.J. Res. 268 / Public Law 97–71
A joint resolution to designate October 23, 1981, as "Hungarian Freedom Fighters Day".

Approved November 3

H.R. 3499 / Public Law 97–72
Veterans' Health Care, Training, and Small Business Loan Act of 1981.

S. 1209 / Public Law 97–73
An act authorizing appropriations to the Secretary of the Interior for services necessary to the nonperforming arts functions of the John F. Kennedy Center for the Performing Arts, and for other purposes.

S. 1000 / Public Law 97–74
Independent Safety Board Act Amendments of 1981.

S.J. Res. 4 / Public Law 97–75
A joint resolution to authorize the President to issue a proclamation designating the week beginning November 22, 1981, as "National Family Week".

Approved November 5

H.R. 4608 / Public Law 97–76
An act to continue in effect any authority provided under the Department of Justice Appropriation Authorization Act, Fiscal Year 1980, for a certain period, and for other purposes.

Approved November 13

S. 1322 / Public Law 97–77
An act to designate the United States Department of Agriculture Boll Weevil Research Laboratory building, located adjacent to the campus of Mississippi State University, Starkville, Mississippi, as the "Robey Wentworth Harned Laboratory"; to extend the delay in making any adjustment in the price support level for milk; and to extend the time for conducting the referenda with respect to the national marketing quotas for wheat and upland cotton.

H.R. 661 / Private Law 97–1
An act for the relief of Blanca Rosa Luna de Frei.

H.R. 688 / Private Law 97–2
An act for the relief of Junior Edmund Moncrieffe.

H.R. 783 / Private Law 97–3
An act for the relief of Roland Karl Heinz Vogel.

H.R. 1469 / Private Law 97–4
An act for the relief of Madeleine Mesnager.

H.R. 1480 / Private Law 97–5
An act for the relief of Omar Marachi.

H.R. 1550 / Private Law 97–6
An act for the relief of Aurora Isidra Rullan Diaz.

H.R. 1785 / Private Law 97–7
An act for the relief of Gladys Belleville Schultz.

H.R. 2010 / Private Law 97–8
An act for the relief of Kai-Mee Chen.

H.R. 2185 / Private Law 97–9
An act for the relief of Hanife Frantz.

H.R. 2573 / Private Law 97–10
An act for the relief of Moses Bank.

H.R. 2975 / Private Law 97–11
An act for the relief of Yuk Yee Li.

Approved November 16

H.R. 3975 / Public Law 97–78
An act to facilitate and encourage the production of oil from tar sand and other hydrocarbon deposits.

S. 736 / Public Law 97–79
Lacey Act Amendments of 1981.

Approved November 20

S. 999 / Public Law 97–80
An act to amend the Earthquake Hazards Reduction Act of 1977 and the Federal Fire Prevention and Control Act of 1974 to authorize the appro-

Approved November 20—Continued
priation of funds to the Director of the Federal Emergency Management Agency to carry out the earthquake hazards reduction programs and the fire prevention and control program, and for other purposes.

H.R. 4792 / Public Law 97–81
Military Justice Amendments of 1981.

H.R. 4734 / Public Law 97–82
An act to recognize the organization known as the Italian American War Veterans of the United States.

S. 195 / Public Law 97–83
An act to recognize the organization known as the United States Submarine Veterans of World War II.

S. 1672 / Public Law 97–84
An act to expand the membership of the United States Holocaust Memorial Council from sixty to sixty-five and for other purposes.

Approved November 23

H.J. Res. 368 / Public Law 97–85
A joint resolution making further continuing appropriations for the fiscal year 1982.

Approved December 1

S. 815 / Public Law 97–86
Department of Defense Authorization Act, 1982.

S. 1133 / Public Law 97–87
An act to amend the National Advisory Committee on Oceans and Atmosphere Act of 1977 to authorize appropriations to carry out the provisions of such Act for fiscal year 1982, and for other purposes.

Approved December 4

H.R. 4144 / Public Law 97–88
Energy and Water Development Appropriation Act, 1982.

H.R. 3454 / Public Law 97–89
Intelligence Authorization Act for Fiscal Year 1982.

H.R. 3413 / Public Law 97–90
Department of Energy National Security and Military Applications of Nuclear Energy Authorization Act of 1982.

H.R. 4522 / Public Law 97–91
District of Columbia Appropriation Act, 1982.

Approved December 15

H.J. Res. 370 / Public Law 97–92
A joint resolution making further continuing appropriations for the fiscal year 1982, and for other purposes.

S.J. Res. 115 / Public Law 97–93
A joint resolution to approve the President's recommendation for a waiver of law pursuant to the Alaska Natural Gas Transportation Act of 1976.

Approved December 17

H.R. 4591 / Public Law 97–94
An act to amend the mineral leasing laws of the United States to provide for uniform treatment of certain receipts under such laws, and for other purposes.

S.J. Res. 136 / Public Law 97–95
A joint resolution to validate the effectiveness of a plan for the use or distribution of funds appropriated to pay a judgment awarded to the San Carlos Tribe of Arizona.

Approved December 21

S. 1098 / Public Law 97–96
National Aeronautics and Space Administration Authorization Act, 1982.

H.R. 4845 / Public Law 97–97
An act to designate the building known as the Lincoln Federal Building and Courthouse in Lincoln, Nebraska, as the "Robert V. Denney Federal Building and Courthouse".

Approved December 22

S. 884 / Public Law 97–98
Agriculture and Food Act of 1981.

Approved December 23

H.R. 3455 / Public Law 97–99
Military Construction Authorization Act, 1982.

H.R. 4035 / Public Law 97–100
An act making appropriations for the Department of the Interior and related agencies for the fiscal year ending September 30, 1982, and for other purposes.

H.R. 4034 / Public Law 97–101
Department of Housing and Urban Development—Independent Agencies Appropriation Act, 1982.

H.R. 4209 / Public Law 97–102
Department of Transportation and Related Agencies Appropriation Act, 1982.

Approved December 23—Continued
H.R. 4119 / Public Law 97–103
An act making appropriations for Agriculture, Rural Development, and Related Agencies programs for the fiscal year ending September 30, 1982, and for other purposes.

H.R. 3484 / Public Law 97–104
George Washington Commemorative Coin Act.

H.R. 4910 / Public Law 97–105
An act to amend the District of Columbia Self-Government and Governmental Reorganization Act and the charter of the District of Columbia with respect to the provisions allowing the District of Columbia to issue general obligation bonds and notes and revenue bonds, notes, and other obligations.

H.R. 4241 / Public Law 97–106
Military Construction Appropriation Act, 1982.

H.R. 5273 / Public Law 97–107
An act to allow the George Washington University Higher Education Facilities Revenue Bond Act of 1981 of the District of Columbia to take effect immediately.

H.R. 1465 / Public Law 97–108
State and Local Government Cost Estimate Act of 1981.

Approved December 26

S. 1003 / Public Law 97–109
An act to amend title III of the Marine Protection, Research, and Sanctuaries Act of 1972, as amended, to authorize appropriations for such title for fiscal years 1982 and 1983, and for other purposes.

H.R. 4879 / Public Law 97–110
International Banking Facility Deposit Insurance Act.

S. 1948 / Public Law 97–111
An act to permit to become effective certain Farm Credit Administration regulations which expand the authority of financing institutions, other than farm credit system institutions, to borrow from and discount with Federal intermediate credit banks.

Approved December 29

H.R. 4894 / Public Law 97–112
An act to authorize the Secretary of the Interior to disburse certain trust funds of the Lac Courte Oreilles Band of Lake Superior Chippewa Indians of Wisconsin, and for other purposes.

S. 1196 / Public Law 97–113
International Security and Development Cooperation Act of 1981.

H.R. 4995 / Public Law 97–114
Department of Defense Appropriation Act, 1982.

S. 1086 / Public Law 97–115
Older Americans Act Amendments of 1981.

H.R. 4327 / Public Law 97–116
Immigration and Nationality Act Amendments of 1981.

H.R. 4503 / Public Law 97–117
Municipal Wastewater Treatment Construction Grant Amendments of 1981.

H.R. 4506 / Public Law 97–118
An act to name the lock and dam authorized to replace locks and dam 26, Mississippi River, Alton, Illinois, as "Melvin Price Lock and Dam".

H.R. 5159 / Public Law 97–119
An act to amend the Internal Revenue Code of 1954 to provide a temporary increase in the tax imposed on producers of coal, and for other purposes.

S. 657 / Public Law 97–120
An act to designate the Department of Commerce Building in Washington, the District of Columbia, as the "Herbert Clark Hoover Department of Commerce Building".

H.R. 4559 / Public Law 97–121
Foreign Assistance and Related Programs Appropriations Act, 1982.

H.R. 4431 / Public Law 97–122
An act to provide for the designation of the E. Michael Roll Post Office.

H.R. 4331 / Public Law 97–123
An act to amend the Omnibus Reconciliation Act of 1981 to restore minimum benefits under the Social Security Act.

H.R. 3799 / Public Law 97–124
An act to extend the Federal tort claims provisions of title 28, United States Code, to acts or omissions of members of the National Guard, and to provide that the remedy under those provisions shall be exclusive in medical malpractice actions involving members of the National Guard.

S. 1192 / Public Law 97–125
Union Station Redevelopment Act of 1981.

H.R. 2494 / Public Law 97–126
An act to designate the John Archibald Campbell United States Courthouse.

S. 1946 / Public Law 97–127
Czechoslovakian Claims Settlement Act of 1981.

S. 1493 / Public Law 97–128
An act to deauthorize several projects within the jurisdiction of the Army Corps of Engineers.

S. 1211 / Public Law 97–129
An act to amend the Toxic Substances Control Act to authorize appropriations for fiscal years 1982 and 1983.

S. 271 / Public Law 97–130
Record Carrier Competition Act of 1981.

S.J. Res. 34 / Public Law 97–131
A joint resolution to provide for the designation of the week commencing with the third Monday in February 1982 as "National Patriotism Week".

S.J. Res. 100 / Public Law 97–132
Multinational Force and Observers Participation Resolution.

H.J. Res. 377 / Public Law 97–133
A joint resolution providing for the convening of the second session of the Ninety-seventh Congress.

H.R. 3210 / Public Law 97–134
Federal-Aid Highway Act of 1981.

S.J. Res. 57 / Public Law 97–135
A joint resolution to provide for the designation of February 7 through 13, 1982, as "National Scleroderma Week".

S. 831 / Public Law 97–136
An act to authorize appropriations for the Coast Guard for fiscal year 1982, and for other purposes.

H.R. 2241 / Public Law 97–137
An act to provide for the establishment of the Bandon Marsh National Wildlife Refuge, Coos County, State of Oregon, and for other purposes.

S.J. Res. 84 / Public Law 97–138
A joint resolution to proclaim March 19, 1982, "National Energy Education Day".

S.J. Res. 121 / Public Law 97–139
A joint resolution to provide for the designation of the year 1982 as the "Bicentennial Year of the American Bald Eagle" and the designation of June 20, 1982, as "National Bald Eagle Day".

Approved December 29—Continued
H.R. 779 / Public Law 97–140
An act to authorize the Secretary of the Army to contract with the Tarrant County Water Control and Improvement District Numbered 1 and the city of Weatherford, Texas, for the use of water supply storage in Benbrook Lake, and for other purposes.

S. 1551 / Public Law 97–141
Federal Physicians Comparability Allowance Amendments of 1981.

H.R. 4926 / Public Law 97–142
An act to authorize the Secretary of the Army to acquire, by purchase or condemnation, such interests in oil, gas, coal, and other minerals owned or controlled by the Osage Tribe of Indians as are needed for Skiatook Lake, Oklahoma, and for other purposes.

Approved December 29—Continued
S. 1976 / Public Law 97–143
An act to amend the Act of July 31, 1946, as amended (40 U.S.C. 193a).

S.J. Res. 117 / Public Law 97–144
A joint resolution to authorize and request the President to designate the week of January 17, 1982, through January 23, 1982, as "National Jaycee Week".

H.R. 3567 / Public Law 97–145
Export Administration Amendments Act of 1981.

H.R. 1797 / Private Law 97–12
An act to direct the Secretary of the department in which the United States Coast Guard is operating to cause the vessel Capt Tom to be documented as a vessel of the United States so as to be entitled to engage in the coastwise trade.

Subject Index

ABC Washington Bureau building dedication—1038

AFL–CIO—137, 306

ASEAN. *See specific member countries*

AWACS sale to Saudi Arabia. *See* Arms and munitions

Abortion—212, 597

Academy Awards presentation ceremonies—315

Accident Compensation, Task Force on Product Liability and. *See* Product Liability and Accident Compensation, Task Force on

ACTION
  Assistant Directors—334, 987
  Associate Director—374
  Budget—388
  Deputy Director—327, 1175
  Director—73, 1028, 1108
  Peace Corps—99, 420
  President's Volunteer Action Awards program—1151
  Retired Senior Volunteer Program—825
  Vietnam Veterans Leadership Program—1028

Administration. *See other part of title*

Administrative Conference of the U.S.—267, 1044, 1142

Advertising Council—446

Advisory commissions, committees, councils, etc. *See other part of title*

Aeronautics Board, Civil. *See* Civil Aeronautics Board

Aeronautics and Space Administration, National. *See* National Aeronautics and Space Administration

Affirmative action programs. *See* Civil rights

Afghanistan, Soviet occupation—192, 194–196, 313, 382, 455, 1186, 1199

Africa
  Administration policies—837
  U.S. trade and investment mission—1091

Africa, southern, U.S. consultations—314

African Refugee Relief Day—347

African Refugees Conference—837

African Unity, Organization of—837

Afro-American (Black) History Month, National. *See* National Afro–American (Black) History Month

Aged persons
  See also Social security system
  Administration policies—110

Agency. *See other part of title*

Agent Orange—530, 1011

Aging, Administration on. *See* Health and Human Services, Department of

Aging, Federal Council on the. *See* Federal Council on the Aging

Aging, White House Conference on. *See* White House Conference on Aging

Agricultural Development, Board for International Food and. *See* International Food and Agricultural Development, Board for

Agricultural Stabilization and Conservation Service. *See* Agriculture, Department of

Agriculture, Department of
  Agricultural Stabilization and Conservation Service—284
  Assistant Secretaries—52, 89, 91, 245, 303, 1175
  Budget—388, 547, 631, 866, 1019
  Commodity Credit Corporation—623, 1178
  Cost savings—1046
  Deputy Secretary—34
  Emergency mobilization planning—1200
  Environmental damage, release of hazardous substances—715
  Farmers Home Administration—215, 284, 378, 485
  Federal Grain Inspection Service—345
  Federal Regional Councils—654
  General Counsel—266
  Inspector General—24, 289, 405
  National Defense Stockpile, role—1090
  Price support operations—1180, 1182
  Rural Electrification Administration—345
  Rural Telephone Bank—1180
  Secretary—5, 9, 63, 151, 167, 216, 265, 290, 382, 383, 715, 1046, 1091, 1180
  Under Secretary—74

Agriculture and agricultural sector
  Cancún summit. *See* International Meeting on Cooperation and Development
  Dairy price support program (cheese)—1178
  Farm price supports—951
  Food aid and sales to Poland—320, 781, 1093, 1187
  Fruit, exports to Japan—728
  Grain embargo against Soviet Union—58, 195–196, 212, 382, 383
  Loans—215, 378
  Pricing—216
  Soviet farming—196, 939
  Sugars, price support operations—1180–1185

Agriculture Day, National. *See* National Agriculture Day

Agriculture and Food Act of 1981—1177

Air Force, Department of the
Assistant Secretaries—356, 361, 480
Intelligence activities—1134
Secretary—32, 610, 784
Under Secretary—486
Air Force Academy, U.S. *See* U.S. Air Force
Academy
Air and Space Museum Advisory Board, National. *See* National Air and Space Museum
Advisory Board
Air traffic controllers. *See* International Association of Air Controllers; Professionsal Air
Traffic Controllers Organization
Airline industry—917
Alaska, Chugach Region Study—1147
Alaska Land Use Council—589
Alaska Pipeline—232, 237, 934
Alcohol, Drug Abuse, and Mental Health Administration. *See* Health and Human Services, Department of
Alcohol, excise tax. *See* Taxation
Alcohol Fuels Office. *See* Energy, Department of
Algeria, U.S. Ambassador—718
Aliens. *See* Immigration and naturalization
Ambassadors. *See specific country*
Ambassadors Ball—822
American Bar Association—329
American Battle Monuments Commission—1201
American Cancer Society—323
American Conservative Union—275
American Education Week—998
American Enterprise Day—876
American Samoa, U.S.-New Zealand maritime
boundary treaty—287
American States, Organization of—247, 517
Amerito—912
Amtrak. *See* National Railroad Passenger Corporation
Andean Group. *See specific member countries*
Antigua and Barbuda, U.S. Ambassador—1004
Appalachian regional development programs,
budget—223, 867
Appellate and district court judges, White
House reception—828
Argentina
Human rights—197
President—264
Security assistance, U.S.—1203
Taxation and fiscal evasion, convention
with U.S. *See* Taxation
Trade with U.S.—977
Arizona, Phoenix, mayor—342
Armed Forces, U.S.
See also Defense and national security
Administration policies—724
Courts-Martial Manual. *See* Manual for
Courts-Martial
Dependents' education—525
European peace protection—979
Intelligence activities—136

Armed Forces, U.S.—Continued
Law enforcement efforts—842
Manpower review—610
Medals. *See specific medals*
National Guard—463
North American Aerospace Defense Command Agreement, renewal—232
Pay—741, 746, 932, 934, 1050
Travel—678
USO. *See* United Service Organizations,
Inc.
Veterans. *See* Veterans
Vietnam war, role. *See* Vietnam
Volunteer military—463, 464, 746, 747,
1055
Armed Forces Day—429
Arms Control and Disarmament Agency, U.S.
See U.S. Arms Control and Disarmament
Agency
Arms Control Negotiations, U.S. Delegation—398
Arms and munitions
AWACS sale to Saudi Arabia—694, 839,
867, 868, 870, 889, 892, 917, 931, 944,
948–950, 952, 984, 987, 990, 993, 995,
996, 1000
B-1 bomber—880, 1034
MX missiles—736, 880, 896, 950
Conventional arms transfers—615
Export controls—793
Foreign countries, sales policy—958
Israel, weapons sales—709, 1000, 1193
Modernization efforts, U.S.—313, 711, 1114
Neutron weapons—708, 710
Nuclear nonproliferation—160, 521, 630,
956, 979, 1031, 1034
Nuclear weapons, reduction and limitation—112, 152, 153, 194, 195, 313, 448,
454, 708, 710, 711, 746, 871, 878, 951,
957, 1032, 1062, 1114, 1192
Nuclear weapons testing, radiation exposure—1011
Soviet buildup—57, 112, 309, 448, 708, 711,
746, 812, 832, 871, 878, 879, 892, 896,
957
Strategic arms limitation talks (SALT)—57,
454, 957
Strategic arms reduction talks (START)—1066
Strategic weapons program—878
Theater nuclear forces—454, 708, 951, 957,
1031
Turkey, U.S. assistance—211
Army, Department of the
Assistant Secretaries—317, 367, 435, 863
Chief of Staff—460, 464n., 906n.
Corps of Engineers—1206
Intelligence activities—1134
Secretary—31, 461, 610, 784, 1206
Under Secretary—862

Arts and humanities
Administration policies—110
National Portrait Gallery—547ftn.
Phillips Art Gallery—822
President's Volunteer Action Awards program—1152
Young Artists in Performance at the White House—1082
Arts and the Humanities, Federal Council on the. *See* National Foundation on the Arts and the Humanities
Arts and the Humanities, National Endowments for the. *See* National Foundation for the Arts and the Humanities
Arts and the Humanities, National Foundation on the. *See* National Foundation on the Arts and the Humanities
Arts and Humanities, Presidential Task Force on the. *See* Presidential Task Force on the Arts and Humanities
Asian Development Bank—517
Asian/Pacific American Heritage Week—365
Assassination attempt on President—310, 311, 312, 350, 370–373, 524
Assets, President's personal, blind management trust—65
Associated General Contractors—255
Association. *See other part of title*
Astronauts. *See* Space shuttle
Ataturk Centennial Year. *See* Turkey
Atlanta, Ga., murdered and missing young people. *See* Georgia
Atlantic Alliance. *See* North Atlantic Treaty Organization
Atmosphere, National Advisory Committee on Oceans and. *See* National Advisory Committee on Oceans and Atmosphere
Atomic energy. *See* Energy, nuclear
Atomic Energy Agency, International. *See* International Atomic Energy Agency
Atomic Energy Community, European. *See* European Atomic Energy Community
Atomic energy defense program. *See* Energy, Department of
Attorney General. *See* Justice, Department of
Australia
Minister for Foreign Affairs—582n.
Prime Minister—580, 583, 584
Relations with U.S.—580
Secretary, Department of Prime Minister and Cabinet—582n.
U.S. Ambassador—363
Austria
Polish refugees, assistance—1187
U.S. Ambassador—465
Auto Task Force—269, 333n.
Automobiles and automobile industry
Domestic industry, assistance—332, 1112
Industry representatives, meeting with President—1173n.
Japanese imports—208, 269
Regulatory reform. *See* Regulatory reform

Automobiles and automobile industry—Continued
Unemployment—333, 1195, 1196
Aviation Administration, Federal. *See* Transportation, Department of
Aviation Organization, Council of the International Civil. *See* International Civil Aviation Organization, Council of the

B-1 bomber. *See* Arms and munitions
Bahrain, Ambassador to U.S.—505n.
Bangladesh
President—473
U.S. Ambassador—472
Banks and banking
See also specific banks
Bankruptcies, uniform law, veto—1208
Federal loan guarantees—833
Savings and loans, relationship to economic recovery program. *See* Economic recovery program
Barbados, U.S. Ambassador—1004
Barbuda. *See* Antigua and Barbuda
Baseball Hall of Fame—297
Battle Monuments Commission, American. *See* American Battle Monuments Commission
Bauxite stockpiles—1089
Belgium, U.S. Ambassador—470
Berlin Wall. *See* Germany, Federal Republic of
Bilingual education. *See* Education
Bill of Rights Day—1143
Black history month. *See* National Afro-American (Black) History Month
Black lung program reform legislation. *See* Health and medical care
Blacks
See also specific organizations
Administration policies—513, 523, 574, 869
Businesses, black-owned—578
Colleges, aid. *See* Colleges and universities
Murdered and missing young people in Atlanta. *See* Georgia
Unemployment. *See* Employment and unemployment
Blinded Veterans Recognition Day, National. *See* National Blinded Veterans Recognition Day
Block grants, Federal. *See* State and local governments
Board. *See other part of title*
Boating Week, National Safe. *See* National Safe Boating Week
Bolivia
Generalized System of Preferences—264
U.S. Ambassador—1019
Brazil
U.S. Ambassador—777
Vice President's visit—756
British Virgin Islands, taxation and fiscal evasion convention with U.S. *See* Taxation

Broadcasters, National Association of. *See* National Association of Broadcasters

Broadcasting, Board for International. *See* International Broadcasting, Board for

Broadcasting, Corporation for Public. *See* Public Broadcasting, Corporation for

Broadcasting to Cuba, Presidential Commission on. *See* Presidential Commission on Broadcasting to Cuba

Brotherhood Week, National. *See* National Brotherhood Week

Bubonic plague—711

Budget, Federal
  Balanced budget targets—1032
  Fiscal year 1981—5, 216, 223
  Fiscal year 1982—5, 85, 207, 216, 220–223, 233, 324, 335, 390, 410, 421, 745, 875, 1080, 1083–1089, 1097, 1098, 1123, 1151, 1156, 1169, 1192
  Fiscal year 1983—745, 1042, 1076, 1192
  Fiscal year 1984—223, 745
  Line item veto—954, 961
  Recovery program, relationship. *See* Economic recovery program
  Rescissions and deferrals—62, 100, 223, 263, 269, 388, 496, 547, 631, 774, 866, 976, 985, 999, 1019, 1043
  Review procedures—690
  Statistics—1103

Budget Reconciliation Act of 1981, Omnibus. *See* Omnibus Budget Reconciliation Act of 1981

Budget Review Board—691, 1043

Building and Construction Trades Department, AFL–CIO—306

Building temperature restrictions, emergency—103

Bulgaria, U.S. Ambassador—984

Bureau. *See other part of title*

Business, National Alliance of. *See* National Alliance of Business

Business Committee on Jamaica, U.S. *See* U.S. Business Committee on Jamaica

Business and industry
  See also specific businesses and industries; Small businesses
  Black-owned firms—578
  Corporation mergers—1113
  Federal Government relationship—800
  Intelligence activities, U.S.—1129
  International investment survey, reporting requirements—705
  Loans, Government—378
  Minority-owned firms—523
  Recovery program, relationship. *See* Economic recovery program
  Subsidies, Federal—110

Busing. *See* Education

CIA. *See* Central Intelligence Agency

Cabinet
  Functions—712, 1193
  Meeting with President—27

Cabinet—Continued
  Voluntarism, role—885

Cabinet Administration Office. *See* White House staff

Cabinet Councils
  Commerce and Trade—167
  Economic Affairs—167, 183, 1029
  Food and Agriculture—167
  Formation—166
  Human Resources—167, 794, 796, 1176
  Natural Resources and Environment—167

Cabinet Task Force on Immigration and Refugee Policy—676

California
  Congressional delegation, White House reception and barbecue—827
  Elections—719, 727, 728, 737
  Lake Tahoe—238
  Mayor, Santa Fe Springs—300
  President's visits—140, 563, 706, 719, 727, 735
  Reapportionment referendum—819

California Debris Commission—653

Canada
  Air defense cooperation with U.S.—879
  Ambassador to Iran, former—527
  Ambassador to U.S.—527, 622n., 783
  Caribbean Basin Initiative—942
  Fishing and maritime treaties. *See* Maritime industry
  Governor General—224, 226, 237
  Immigration to U.S. *See* Immigration and naturalization
  Joint session of Parliament—229
  Natural gas pipeline—232, 237, 934
  Oil production—210
  Ottawa Summit. *See* Ottawa Summit
  President's visit—224–226, 231, 235
  Prime Minister—225, 228, 231, 235, 237, 620, 637, 639–646, 810n., 935, 982n.
  Relations with U.S.—209, 210, 224, 226, 231, 237, 1057
  Speaker of the House of Commons—225, 231
  Speaker of the Senate—225, 231
  Under Secretary—622n.
  U.S. Ambassador—487

Canada, International Boundary Commission, U.S. and. *See* International Boundary Commission, U.S. and Canada

Canada, International Joint Commission—U.S. and. *See* International Joint Commission—U.S. and Canada

Canada, Permanent Joint Board on Defense—U.S. and. *See* Permanent Joint Board on Defense—U.S. and Canada

Cancer Control Month—282

Cancer Courage Award—323

Cancer Panel, President's. *See* President's Cancer Panel

Cancún summit. *See* International Meeting on Cooperation and Development

Candidacy for second term, President's—522, 523, 1114

Capital punishment. *See* Law enforcement and crime

Captive Nations Week—586

Caribbean Basin—856, 942, 1189, 1192

Caribbean and Central America Action Conference—1095

Caroline Islands. *See* Micronesia

Carpenters and Joiners, United Brotherhood of. *See* United Brotherhood of Carpenters and Joiners

Categorical grants, Federal. *See* State and local governments

Catholic Relief Services—781

Census Bureau. *See* Commerce, Department of

Center for Citizen Involvement, National. *See* National Center for Citizen Involvement

Central African Republic, U.S. Ambassador— 329

Central America. *See* Latin America

Central America Action Conference. *See* Caribbean and Central America Action Conference

Central City and California Taxpayers' Associations—563

Central Intelligence Agency—5, 15, 36, 676, 864, 955, 973, 1127, 1129–1132, 1136, 1138, 1166

Chamber of Commerce, U.S.—868, 874

Champions of American Sport—547

Cheese, distribution to disadvantaged persons—1178

Chief Justice of U.S. *See* Supreme Court of the U.S.

Chief of Protocol for White House. *See* State, Department of

Chiefs of Police, International Association of. *See* International Association of Chiefs of Police

Child Health Day—852

Children and youth
  Atlanta murders. *See* Georgia
  Employment—110
  Senate youth program—78
  Young American Medals for Bravery and Service—779
  Young Artists in Performance at the White House—1082

Children's Bureau. *See* Health and Human Services, Department of

Children's Diabetes Foundation—578n.

Chile
  Security assistance, U.S.—1203
  Trade with U.S.—580
  U.S. Ambassador—1016

China, People's Republic of
  Arms sales, U.S.—526
  President's visit—874

China, People's Republic of—Continued
  Relations with U.S.—524
  Trade with U.S.—478, 479
  U.S. Ambassador—512

Chinese New Year—71

Christmas message—1185, 1188

Christmas Tree, National Community. *See* National Community Christmas Tree

Chugach Natives, Inc.—1147

Chugach Region Study—1147

Church of Jesus Christ of Latter-Day Saints— 816ftn.

Citibank—1171

Cities, National League of. *See* National League of Cities

Citizen Involvement, National Center for. *See* National Center for Citizen Involvement

Citizenship Day and Constitution Week—802

Civil Aeronautics Board—734, 917

Civil Aviation Organization, Council of the International. *See* International Civil Aviation Organization, Council of the

Civil rights
  See also Blacks; Equal rights amendment; Human rights
  Administration policies—2, 58, 217, 242, 573, 1163
  Affirmative action programs—1169
  Intelligence activities, U.S.—1126, 1128, 1135
  Voting Rights Act—513, 869, 959, 1018, 1020

Civil Rights, Commission on—1052

Classified information. *See* Defense and national security

Clean-Up and Flag-Up America's Highways Week, National. *See* National Clean-Up and Flag-Up America's Highways Week

Cleveland Plain Dealer—1110

Coast Guard, U.S. *See* Transportation, Department of

Code of Federal Regulations—113, 178

Coffee. *See* International Coffee Agreement, 1976

Colleges and universities
  See also Education
  Black colleges, aid—578, 793, 795, 796n.
  Student loans—378, 833

Colombia
  Extradition treaty with U.S.—469
  Generalized System of Preferences—264
  Legal assistance treaty with U.S.—504
  Vice President's visit—756

Colorado
  Denver Mint—436, 623
  President's visits—573, 810

Colored People, National Association for the Advancement of. *See* National Association for the Advancement of Colored People

Columbia. *See* Space shuttle

Columbus Day—912, 913

Combined Federal Campaign—593

Commerce, Department of
Assistant Secretaries—141, 142, 184, 245, 368, 386, 629, 1057, 1175
Budget—223, 388, 631, 866
Census Bureau—622
Deputy Secretary—52
Economic Development Administration—110, 111
Emergency mobilization planning—1200
Energy Department functions—1160, 1161
Environmental damage, release of hazardous substances—715
General Counsel—270
Inspector General—24, 289, 373
Maritime Administration—704, 778
National Ocean Survey, NOAA—514
National Oceanic and Atmospheric Administration—362, 514, 1150
Patent and Trademark Office—273, 757
Product liability insurance study—838
Secretary—5, 10, 63, 127, 151, 167, 290, 319, 333n., 382, 383, 593, 715, 730, 791, 914, 928, 929, 933, 1091
Statistical policy functions, redelegation—730
Under Secretary—95, 1014, 1091
Commerce, international
Administration policies—855
Africa, trade and investment mission—1091
Agricultural commodities, foreign markets—216
Automobile industry—269
Canadian government, discussions—237
Cancún summit. *See* International Meeting on Cooperation and Development
Disputes settlement agreement—517
Exports, U.S.—103, 382, 383, 728, 793, 1178
General Agreement on Tariffs and Trade (GATT)—940, 941, 981, 1049
Generalized System of Preferences for developing countries—263, 315, 579, 941
Imports, U.S.—208, 316, 353, 415, 977, 1049, 1180–1185
International investment survey, reporting requirements—705
Ottawa Summit. *See* Ottawa Summit
Poland, sale of U.S. dairy products—320
Socialist nations, bilateral trade agreements—478–480
Tariff Schedules of the U.S.—316, 353, 579, 977, 978, 1049, 1180–1185, 1210
Commercial Arbitration, Inter-American Convention on. *See* Inter-American Convention on Commerical Arbitration
Commission. *See other part of title*
Committee. *See other part of title*
Commodity Credit Corporation. *See* Agriculture, Department of
Commodity Futures Trading Commission—190, 758, 1150
Commodore John Barry Day—724–726

Communication Agency, International. *See* International Communication Agency
Communications, radio broadcasting to Cuba—823, 826
Communications Commission, Federal. *See* Federal Communications Commission
Communications Satellite Corporation—921
Communism—434, 519, 958, 1167, 1197
Community development—180
Community Relations Service. *See* Justice, Department of
Community Services Administration
Assistant Director—495, 515
Deputy Director—495
Director—290, 400
Inspector General—24, 289, 404
Comptroller of the Currency. *See* Treasury, Department of the
Comptroller General of the U.S. *See* General Accounting Office
Conference. *See other part of title*
Congo, U.S. Ambassador—1051
Congress
See also Republican Party
Annual salute dinner—76
House Speaker. *See* Speaker of the House of Representatives
Intelligence activities, oversight responsibilities—1138
Leaders, meeting with President—696
Salaries—934, 1051
Congressional Budget Office—1170
Congressional Gold Medal—527
Congressional Medal of Honor—155
Congressional Space Medal of Honor—441
Conservative Political Action Conference—275
Constellation, U.S.S. *See* U.S.S *Constellation*
Constitution Week. *See* Citizenship Day and Constitution Week
Construction industry—1112, 1122
Construction Trades Department, Building and, AFL–CIO. *See* Building and Construction Trades Department, AFL–CIO
Consumer Cooperative Bank, National. *See* National Consumer Cooperative Bank
Consumer Product Safety Commission—614
Continental Airlines acquisition case. *See* Texas International Airlines-Continental Airlines acquisition case
Coordinating Task Force on Federalism—147, 342, 682
Copyright Royalty Tribunal—988
Corporation. *See other part of title*
Council. *See other part of title*
Counties, National Association of. *See* National Association of Counties
Courts, U.S.
See also specific U.S. Courts
Judicial salaries—934, 1051
Jurisdictional powers—958, 959

Courts-Martial Manual. *See* Manual for Courts-Martial

Credit management. *See* Federal departments and agencies

Credit Union Administration, National. *See* National Credit Union Administration

Crime. *See* Law enforcement and crime

Crime, Task Force on the Victims of. *See* Victims of Crime, Task Force on the

Criminal Code, Federal. *See* Federal Criminal Code

Cuba
  El Salvador, role. *See* El Salvador
  Human rights—196
  Immigration to U.S. *See* Immigration and naturalization
  Latin America, role. *See* Latin America
  Radio broadcasting, U.S.—826
  Soviet role—826

Cuba, Presidential Commission on Broadcasting to. *See* Presidential Commission on Broadcasting to Cuba

Cyprus
  Ambassador to U.S.—1148
  Conflict resolution—322, 438, 655, 826, 1118, 1148
  Foreign Minister—1148
  Missing persons—439
  President—1148
  U.S. Ambassador—705

Cystic Fibrosis Week, National. *See* National Cystic Fibrosis Week

Czechoslovakia, U.S. Ambassador—660

Dairy products and subsidies. *See* Agriculture and agricultural sector

Davis Cup Tennis Team—792

Days of Remembrance of Victims of the Holocaust—375, 396

Defense, Department of
  See also specific military departments
  Assistant Secretaries—246, 271, 316, 537, 562, 610, 1056, 1175
  Budget—112, 180, 223, 547, 631, 812, 839, 866, 985, 1204
  Defense Intelligence Agency—1133
  Deputy Assistant Secretary—485
  Emergency mobilization planning—1200
  Environmental damage, release of hazardous substances—715
  General of the Army Douglas MacArthur Corridor—775
  General Counsel—101
  Intelligence activities—1133
  Joint Chiefs of Staff—610, 950
  National Security Agency—1133
  Secretary—4, 7, 68, 152, 156, 158n., 180, 213, 289, 290, 344, 464, 476, 610, 678, 712, 715–717, 738, 763, 775, 782, 783n., 784, 833, 837, 839, 842, 865, 870, 878–880, 906n., 1036, 1106, 1129, 1131, 1133, 1138
  Under Secretary—86, 185

Defense highways, silver anniversary. *See* Silver Anniversary Year of the National System of Interstate and Defense Highways

Defense Intelligence Agency. *See* Defense, Department of

Defense Manpower Task Force—464

Defense and national security
  See also Armed Forces, U.S.; Arms and munitions
  Administration policies—461, 711, 746, 783, 812, 832, 839, 867, 870, 871, 878, 892, 896, 1195, 1198
  Canadian-American defense production sharing agreements—237
  Expenditures—112, 250, 253, 307, 309, 392, 754, 763, 782
  Information classification and protection—736, 955, 956
  Intelligence activities, U.S.—1126, 1128
  National Defense Stockpile—242, 1089
  New military facilities, impact on local communities—283, 738
  Nuclear defense activities—708, 710, 979

Defense Transportation Day, National. *See* National Defense Transportation Day and National Transportation Week

Delaware, Governor—342, 1107

Denmark, U.S. Ambassador—618

Department. *See other part of title*

Department of Defense Appropriation Act—1204

Developing countries
  Administration policies—855
  Cancún summit. *See* International Meeting on Cooperation and Development
  Generalized System of Preferences. *See* Commerce, international
  Industrialization—888
  Ottawa Summit. *See* Ottawa Summit

Development Association, International. *See* International Development Association

Diabetes Foundation, Children's. *See* Children's Diabetes Foundation

Diabetes Week, National. *See* National Diabetes Week

Disabled persons. *See* Handicapped persons

Disadvantaged persons
  Administration policies—110, 207, 250, 251, 870
  Cheese distribution—1178

District and appellate court judges, White House reception—828

District of Columbia budget, fiscal year 1982—65

District of Columbia Court of Appeals—443

District of Columbia Judicial Nomination Commission—430

District of Columbia Militia—1116, 1117

District of Columbia Superior Court—205, 456, 960

Domestic Policy Staff. *See* Policy Development, Office of
Dominica, U.S. Ambassador—1004
Dominican Republic, Vice President's visit—756
Draft registration. *See* Selective Service System
Drug Enforcement Administration. *See* Justice, Department of
Drugs and narcotics. *See* Law enforcement and crime

ERA. *See* Equal rights amendment
EURATOM. *See* European Atomic Energy Community
Easter—361
Economic Adjustment Committee, President's. *See* President's Economic Adjustment Committee
Economic Advisers, Council of—35, 94, 127, 133, 167, 302, 458, 610
Economic Cooperation and Development, Organization for—620
Economic Development Administration. *See* Commerce, Department of
Economic Policy Advisory Board, President's. *See* President's Economic Policy Advisory Board
Economic recovery program—2–5, 56, 59, 61, 64, 79–83, 87, 94, 108–140, 152, 153, 177–182, 197–201, 206–208, 211, 214, 216, 220–223, 232, 233, 244, 250, 251, 253–255, 257, 294, 308, 324, 333, 336–339, 343, 390–393, 419, 423, 447, 462, 465, 472, 482, 501, 505, 510, 519, 523, 525, 526, 529, 530, 540, 544, 546, 549, 553, 556, 560, 561, 563, 571, 574, 602, 604–606, 626, 627, 649–651, 656–662, 664–668, 675, 676, 679–685, 696, 697, 706, 710, 711, 719, 729, 730, 736, 741, 745, 747, 749–752, 760, 783, 784, 795, 800, 810, 811, 831, 838, 846, 847, 855, 861, 867, 868, 871, 873, 874, 876, 882, 892–894, 1020–1022, 1031, 1036, 1039, 1047, 1048, 1098, 1099, 1102, 1103, 1111, 1119, 1120, 1123, 1124, 1151, 1156, 1165, 1167, 1170, 1174, 1185, 1189, 1190, 1191, 1198
Economic Recovery Tax Act of 1981—706
Economic Regulatory Administration. *See* Energy, Department of
Economy, international
    Cancún summit. *See* International Meeting on Cooperation and Development
    Ottawa Summit. *See* Ottawa Summit
Economy, national
    Audit—79, 94
    Economic report—115, 116
    Gross national product—121, 137, 872, 940
    Public debt ceiling—55
    Recession—962, 1000, 1034
    Recovery program, relationship. *See* Economic recovery program
    World War I era, comparison—61

Ecuador
    Generalized System of Preferences—264
    Minister of Defense—458
    President—458
Education
    See also Colleges and universities
    Bilingual programs—181, 682
    Blacks—578
    Busing—959
    Federal assistance—110, 218
    Federalism, relationship. *See* State and local governments
    Military dependents. *See* Armed Forces, U.S.
    Prayer in schools—958
    President's Volunteer Action Awards program—1152
    School meals—110
    Veterans education assistance program. *See* Veterans
Education, Department of
    Abolition—60, 833
    Assistant Secretaries—240, 326, 346, 348, 355, 400, 417, 912, 1175
    Atlanta, murdered and missing young people, Federal assistance—204, 241
    Black colleges, funding—578
    Budget—223, 547
    Deputy Under Secretaries—327, 331, 351
    Federal Regional Councils—654
    General Counsel—239
    Inspector General—24, 289, 293
    Institute of Museum Services—514
    National Institute of Education—701
    National Institute of Handicapped Research—440
    Rehabilitation Services Administration—347
    Secretary—5, 13, 60, 63, 167, 218, 290, 343, 678, 679n., 682, 794, 796
    Under Secretary—185
Education Week, American. *See* American Education Week
Egypt
    First Under Secretary—694n.
    Foreign Affairs Minister—694n.
    Middle East peace efforts. *See* Middle East
    Minister of State—694n.
    Nuclear energy agreement with U.S.—594
    President—692, 698, 700, 868, 898, 902, 905, 943, 949
    Sinai Support Mission. *See* U.S. Sinai Support Mission
    Sudan, role. *See* Sudan
El Salvador
    Cuban role—192, 193
    Human rights—209, 1113
    Nicaraguan role—193
    President—192, 1095
    Right-wing takeover—206
    Soviet role—153, 192

El Salvador—Continued
U.S. Ambassador—329
U.S. role—153, 191–193, 206, 207, 209, 313, 1032
Elderly persons. *See* Aged persons
Election Commission, Federal. *See* Federal Election Commission
Emergency Management Agency, Federal. *See* Federal Emergency Management Agency
Emergency Mobilization Preparedness Board—1200
Employment and unemployment
Autoworkers—333
Blacks—576, 1035
Federal employees, reduction. *See* Federal employees
National Alliance of Business goals—882
President's Volunteer Action Awards program—1152
Recovery program, relationship. *See* Economic recovery program
Statistics—307, 749, 1121
Trade adjustment assistance. *See* Labor
Urban enterprise zones—1035, 1113, 1195
Youth. *See* Children and youth
Energy
Canadian energy program—210, 237
Cancún summit—942
Conservation—103, 135, 455
Gasoline excise tax. *See* Taxation
Iran, American business relationship—57
National policy plan—633
Natural gas—58, 232, 237, 934, 1167, 1168
Nuclear energy—160, 416, 521, 594, 903
Oil—44, 45, 127, 128, 134, 210, 211, 455, 751, 752, 813, 862, 867, 873, 961, 962, 1168
Ottawa Summit. *See* Ottawa Summit
Regulatory reform. *See* Regulatory reform
Synthetic fuels—110, 138
Energy, Department of
Abolition—60, 833, 1160
Alcohol Fuels Office—397
Assistant Secretaries—220, 247, 272, 317, 386, 437, 515, 562, 1175
Atomic energy defense programs—1123
Budget—223, 388, 631, 866
Deputy Secretary—263, 798
Economic Regulatory Administration—111, 551
Energy Information Administration—387
Energy Research Office—496
Environmental damage, release of hazardous substances—715
Federal Energy Regulatory Commission—335, 359, 418, 935, 936
Federal Regional Councils—654
General Counsel—97
Inspector General and Deputy—25, 288, 424
Military Liaison Committee—589

Energy, Department of—Continued
Minority Economic Impact Office, Director—271
Nuclear energy, role. *See* Energy
Oil Shale Corporation, loan guarantee agreement—732
Secretary—5, 13, 44, 60, 63, 167, 290, 595, 633, 904, 1135
Synthetic fuels program—110
Under Secretary—608
Energy Information Administration. *See* Energy, Department of
Energy Regulatory Commission, Federal. *See* Energy, Department of
Energy and Water Development Appropriation Act, 1982—1123
England. *See* United Kingdom
Enterprise zones, urban. *See* Employment and unemployment
Entitlement programs
See also specific programs
Administration policies—109, 110, 179, 180, 199, 200, 556, 565, 1035
Environment
Administration policies—711
Hazardous substance releases—715
President's Volunteer Action Awards program—1152
Environmental Protection Agency
Acting Associate Administrator—1176
Administrator—63, 146, 290, 715–717, 736
Assistant Administrators—507, 588, 591, 1201
Budget—496, 547
Deputy Administrator—146
Environmental damage, release of hazardous substances—715
Federal Regional Councils—654, 1003
Hazardous Substance Response Trust Fund—717
Inspector General—24, 289, 293, 425, 654
Regulatory reform—333
Environmental Quality, Council on—335, 426, 427
Equal Employment Opportunity Commission—507, 599, 1146
Equal rights amendment—214, 683, 901, 1174
Equatorial Guinea, U.S. Ambassador—849
Europe, Commission on Security and Cooperation in—1056, 1057
Europe, Madrid Conference on Security and Cooperation in—1066
Europe, nuclear weapons. *See* Arms and munitions
European Atomic Energy Community—160
European Communities, Commission of—625, 645, 646n., 694
European Council, Chairman—313
Excise taxes. *See* Taxation

Executive Exchange, President's Commission on. *See* President's Commission on Executive Exchange
Executive Office of the President
See also specific units
Budget deferrals—976, 985
Export Council, President's. *See* President's Export Council
Export-Import Bank of the U.S.—110, 267, 444, 600, 1091, 1124, 1187
Exports, U.S. *See* Commerce, international

FBI. *See* Justice, Department of
Family Week, National. *See* National Family Week
Farm-City Week, National. *See* National Farm-City Week
Farm Credit Administration, Federal Farm Credit Board—829, 988
Farm Safety Week, National. *See* National Farm Safety Week
Farmers of America, Future. *See* Future Farmers of America
Farmers Home Administration. *See* Agriculture, Department of
Father's Day—445
Federal advisory committees, annual report to Congress—305
Federal Aviation Administration. *See* Transportation, Department of
Federal Bureau of Investigation. *See* Justice, Department of
Federal Communications Commission—240, 334, 492
Federal Council on the Aging—1002, 1094
Federal Council on the Arts and the Humanities. *See* National Foundation on the Arts and the Humanities
Federal Criminal Code—841
Federal departments and agencies
See also specific departments and agencies
Audiovisual aids and publications—364
Consultants and contract studies, reduction—29, 30
Credit management and debt collection—378, 379
Inspectors General—359, 612
Law enforcement efforts—842
Procurement—29, 30
Recovery program, relationship. *See* Economic recovery program
Regional Councils—654
Regulatory reform efforts. *See* Regulatory reform
Travel reduction—29, 30
Federal Election Commission—537, 538, 1071
Federal Emergency Management Agency
Associate Directors—562, 588
Budget—1000
Deputy Director—318
Director—154, 715, 716
Emergency mobilization planning—1200

Federal Emergency Management Agency—Continued
Environmental damage, release of hazardous substances—715
Federal Insurance Administration—445, 758
National Defense Stockpile, role—242, 1089
U.S. Fire Administration—989
Federal employees
Distinguished Executive rank awards—924
Fraud, waste, and mismanagement—25, 26, 112, 179, 287, 288, 290, 291, 307, 359, 612, 613, 751, 1144
Hiring freeze—4, 5, 27, 199, 200
Indians, contracting or trading—905
Merit Pay System—744
Noncareer, resignation request—28
Parking fees—1161
Pay increases—223, 741, 742, 744, 934, 1050
Reduction in force—205, 833
Security breaches—1131
Travel—677
Unionization and right to strike—753
Federal Energy Regulatory Commission. *See* Energy, Department of
Federal Farm Credit Board. *See* Farm Credit Administration
Federal Grain Inspection Service. *See* Agriculture, Department of
Federal grants. *See* State and local governments
Federal Highway Administration. *See* Transportation, Department of
Federal Home Loan Bank Board—260, 1155
Federal Housing Administration. *See* Housing and Urban Development, Department of
Federal Insurance Administration. *See* Federal Emergency Management Agency
Federal Judicial Officers, Committee on Selection of—404
Federal Maritime Commission—383, 716, 797
Federal Mediation and Conciliation Service—1152
Federal Mine Safety and Health Review Commission—551
Federal National Mortgage Association—624
Federal Pay, Advisory Committee on—1051
Federal procurement. *See* Federal departments and agencies
Federal Procurement Policy Office. *See* Management and Budget, Office of
Federal Railroad Administration. *See* Transportation, Department of
Federal Regional Councils—654, 1003
Federal Register—31, 63, 106, 108, 113, 178, 682, 955
Federal Republic of Germany. *See* Germany, Federal Republic of
Federal Reserve System—61, 114, 233, 735, 751, 872, 953

Federal spending. *See* Budget, Federal
Federal Trade Commission—209, 570
Federalism. *See* State and local governments
Federalism, Coordinating Task Force on. *See* Coordinating Task Force on Federalism
Federalism, Presidential Advisory Committee on. *See* Presidential Advisory Committee on Federalism
Federated Women—1109
Federation of Republican Women, National. *See* National Federation of Republican Women
Fellows, White House. *See* White House Fellows
Fellowships, President's Commission on White House. *See* President's Commission on White House Fellowships
Ferrochromium, U.S. imports—1049
Fifty States Project for Women—901
Finance Corporation, International. *See* International Finance Corporation
Finland, U.S. Ambassador—619
Fire Administration, U.S. *See* Federal Emergency Management Agency
Fire Prevention Week—850
Fish and fishing. *See* Maritime industry
Fish and Wildlife Service, U.S. *See* Interior, Department of the
Flag Day and National Flag Week—476
Flag-Up America's Highways Week, National Clean-Up and. *See* National Clean-Up and Flag-Up America's Highways Week
Fletcher, U.S.S. *See* U.S.S. *Fletcher*
Florida
    Haitian refugees—875
    Miami, Central American conference. *See* Caribbean and Central America Action Conference
    Refugee care, Federal compensation—1120
Food. *See* Agriculture and agricultural sector
Food Act of 1981, Agriculture and. *See* Agriculture and Food Act of 1981
Food and Agricultural Development, Board for International. *See* International Food and Agricultural Development, Board for
Food Day, World. *See* World Food Day
Food for Peace—1178
Food stamps—111, 556, 565, 833, 869, 1178
Ford Presidential museum. *See* Gerald R. Ford Presidential Museum
Ford's Theatre benefit gala—279, 280
Foreign Assistance and Related Programs Appropriations Act—1202
Foreign Claims Settlement Commission of the U.S. *See* Justice, Department of
Foreign Intelligence Advisory Board, President's. *See* President's Foreign Intelligence Advisory Board
Foreign Scholarships, Board of. *See* Scholarships, Board of Foreign
Foreign Service
    Director General—518, 1175

Foreign Service—Continued
    Pay—741, 743, 934, 1051
    Personnel system—151
    Travel—678
Foreign Service Act of 1980—149
Foreign Service Board of Examiners. *See* State, Department of
Foreign Service Retirement and Disability System—101, 151
Forest Products Week, National. *See* National Forest Products Week
Fort Allen, P.R. *See* Puerto Rico
Foster Grandparents Program—446, 1194
Foundation *See other part of title*
Fourth of July. *See* Independence Day
France
    Ambassador to Lebanon, assassination. *See* Lebanon
    Ambassador to U.S.—783
    President—418, 640, 646n., 962–969
    U.S. Ambassador—924, 963
Fraud, waste, and mismanagement in Federal government. *See* Federal employees
Freedom medal. *See* Presidential Medal of Freedom
Future Farmers of America—678

GATT. *See* Commerce, international
GNP. *See* Economy, national
Gabon, U.S. Ambassador—1001
Garrison project—237
Gas, natural. *See* Energy
Gasoline excise tax. *See* Taxation
General Accounting Office
    Comptroller General of the U.S.—289, 612, 614
    Fraud, waste, and mismanagement in Federal programs—291
General Agreement on Tariffs and Trade (GATT). *See* Commerce, international
General of the Army Douglas MacArthur Corridor. *See* Defense, Department of
General Contractors Association of New York—762n.
General Pulaski Memorial Day—887
General Services Administration
    Administrator—176, 183, 290, 678, 929, 1029
    Budget—223
    Inspector General—24, 289, 405
    National Defense Stockpile, role—1090
Generalized System of Preferences for developing countries. *See* Commerce, international
Geological Survey. *See* Interior, Department of the
Georgia
    Atlanta, murdered and missing young people—58, 204, 241, 248, 513, 573
    Governor—148, 162, 342, 1081
    President's visit—679, 684
Gerald R. Ford Presidential Museum—807

Germany, Federal Republic of
Ambassador to U.S.—783
Berlin Wall—713
Chancellor—448, 451–453, 639, 641, 646n.
U.S. Ambassador—442
Golan Heights—1162, 1163, 1164, 1192
Gold standard—736
Government National Mortgage Association.
See Housing and Urban Development, Department of
Government Printing Office—389
Government procurement. *See* Federal departments and agencies
Governors
See also specific States
Dinner honoring—162
Governors' Association, National. *See* National Governors' Association
Grain. *See* Agriculture and agricultural sector
Grain Inspection Service, Federal. *See* Agriculture, Department of
Grants, Federal. *See* State and local governments
Great Britain. *See* United Kingdom
Great Lakes—232, 237, 716
Great Lakes Basin Commission—773
Greece
Cyprus conflict. *See* Cyprus
President—285
Relations with U.S.—211
Turkish relations—322
U.S. Ambassador—592
Grenadines. *See* St. Vincent and the Grenadines
Gross national product. *See* Economy, national
Guatemala, U.S. Ambassador—619
Guinea, Equatorial. *See* Equatorial Guinea
Gun control. *See* Law enforcement and crime
Guyana, U.S. Ambassador—1104

Haiti
Immigration to U.S. *See* Immigration and naturalization
U.S. Ambassador—455
Handgun control. *See* Law enforcement and crime
Handicapped persons
Administration policies—110, 682
Central Intelligence Agency benefits—864
Disabled mountain climbers—607
Foreign Service benefits—101
Handicapped Research, National Institute of.
See Education, Department of
Handicapped Week, National Employ the.
See National Employ the Handicapped Week
Hawaiians Study Commission, Native. *See* Native Hawaiians Study Commission
Hazardous Substance Response Trust Fund.
See Environmental Protection Administration
Hazardous substances. *See* Pollution

Head Start—110
Health Day, Child. *See* Child Health Day
Health and Human Services, Department of
Aging, Administration on—457
Alcohol, Drug Abuse, and Mental Health Administration—420
Assistant Secretaries—98, 185, 304, 387, 627, 1175
Atlanta, murdered and missing young people, Federal assistance—204, 241
Budget—388, 547, 631, 774, 866, 976, 1019
Children's Bureau—1093
Emergency mobilization planning—1200
Environmental damage, release of hazardous substances—715
Federal Regional Councils—654, 1003
General Counsel—362
Indian Health Service—905
Inspector General—26, 289, 390
Public Health Service—715, 801
Secretary—5, 11, 63, 167, 290, 343, 450, 466, 715, 716, 905, 1036, 1047, 1072, 1081, 1100, 1104n., 1118, 1158
Social Security Administration—190
Under Secretary—73
Health and medical care
Administration policies—1103, 1170
Atlanta, Federal assistance—241
Black lung program reform, legislation—1205
Medicaid—111, 833, 1037
Medicare—110, 834, 896
President's Volunteer Action Awards program—1152
Veterans. *See* Veterans
Health Review Commission, Federal Mine Safety and. *See* Federal Mine Safety and Health Review Commission
Health Review Commission, Occupational Safety and. *See* Occupational Safety and Health Review Commission
Hearst Foundation. *See* William Randolph Hearst Foundation
Hide exports from Argentina—977
Highway Administration, Federal. *See* Transportation, Department of
Highways and highway systems
Interstate and defense highways, silver anniversary. *See* Silver Anniversary Year of the National System of Interstate and Defense Highways
Westway Highway. *See* New York
Highways Week, National Clean-Up and Flag-Up America's. *See* National Clean-Up and Flag-Up America's Highways Week
Hispanic Americans
Administration policies—61, 804
Representatives, White House luncheon—803
Hispanic Heritage Week, National. *See* National Hispanic Heritage Week

Historic Preservation, Advisory Council on— 550, 1044

Holocaust, Days of Remembrance of Victims of the. *See* Days of Remembrance of Victims of the Holocaust

Honduras, U.S. Ambassador—857

Hostage Compensation, President's Commission on. *See* President's Commission on Hostage Compensation

Hostages, Americans in Iran—16–23, 27, 31, 38, 39, 41, 43, 48, 58, 352, 527, 625, 804

Housing
Administration policies—529–531, 752, 1122
Government loans—378, 565
Regulatory reform. *See* Regulatory reform

Housing, President's Commission on. *See* President's Commission on Housing

Housing Administration, Federal. *See* Housing and Urban Development, Department of

Housing and Urban Development, Department of
Assistant Secretaries—90, 147, 203, 272, 301, 332, 1175
Budget—223, 547
Federal Housing Administration—378
Federal Regional Councils—654, 1003
General Counsel—186
Government National Mortgage Association—389
Inspector General—24, 289, 292
New Community Development Corporation—318
Secretary—5, 11, 63, 167, 290, 343, 529, 530, 531, 752, 761
Under Secretary—41

Human Events—275, 276

Human rights
See also specific countries; Civil rights
Administration policies—196

Human Rights Day and Week—1143

Humanities. *See* Arts and humanities

Humanities, Federal Council on the Arts and the. *See* National Foundation on the Arts and the Humanities

Humanities, National Endowments for the Arts and the. *See* National Foundation on the Arts and the Humanities

Humanities, National Foundation on the Arts and the. *See* National Foundation on the Arts and the Humanities

Humanities, Presidential Task Force on the Arts and. *See* Presidential Task Force on the Arts and Humanities

Hungarian Freedom Fighters' Day—982

Hungary, trade with U.S.—478–480

Iceland, U.S. Ambassador—609

Illegal aliens. *See* Immigration and naturalization

Illinois
Governor—342, 600, 601, 603, 745
President's visit—600, 745, 748

Immigration and naturalization
Aliens, illegal—201, 858, 859, 892, 1038, 1120
Canadians—677
Cubans—676, 1120
Haitians—875, 1120
Mexicans—201, 676, 677
Refugee admissions policy—818, 1120

Immigration and Naturalization Service. *See* Justice, Department of

Immigration task force. *See* Cabinet Task Force on Immigration and Refugee Policy

Imports, U.S. *See* Commerce, international

Inauguration
Address to Nation—1
Balls—17
Committee, reception—28
Luncheon—16

Independence Day—593

India, U.S. Ambassador—721

Indian Affairs Bureau. *See* Interior, Department of the

Indian Health Service. *See* Health and Human Services, Department of

Indiana
Governor—431
Mayor, Indianapolis—176, 179, 342
President's visit—431

Indians, contracting or trading with Federal employees. *See* Federal employees

Indonesia, Generalized System of Preferences—264

Industry. *See* Business and industry

Inflation, recovery program, relationship. *See* Economic recovery program

Information, classified. *See* Defense and national security

Information Science, National Commission on Libraries and. *See* National Commission on Libraries and Information Science

Inspectors General. *See* Federal departments and agencies

Institute. *See other part of title*

Insurance Administration, Federal. *See* Federal Emergency Management Agency

Insurance industry—838, 886

Integrity and Efficiency, President's Council on. *See* President's Council on Integrity and Efficiency

Intelligence activities, U.S.—1126, 1128, 1139, 1140

Intelligence Advisory Board, President's Foreign. *See* President's Foreign Intelligence Advisory Board

Intelligence Authorization Act for Fiscal Year 1982—1140

Intelligence Oversight Board, President's. *See* President's Intelligence Oversight Board

Interagency Task Force on Product Liability—838

Inter-American Convention on Commercial Arbitration—517
Inter-American Development Bank—459
Interest rates, recovery program, relationship. *See* Economic recovery program
Intergovernmental Relations, Advisory Commission on—477, 763
Interior, Department of the
  Assistant Secretaries—102, 304, 332, 511, 590, 1175
  Budget—223, 547, 866, 1043
  Energy Department functions—1160, 1161
  Environmental damage, release of hazardous substances—715
  Federal Regional Councils—654, 1003
  Geological Survey—497
  Indian Affairs Bureau—905
  Inspector General—24, 289, 474
  Land Management Bureau—187
  Mines Bureau—590
  Reclamation Bureau—438
  Secretary—5, 9, 63, 167, 217, 290, 343, 711, 715, 717, 736, 810, 905, 914
  Solicitor—239
  Surface Mining Reclamation and Enforcement Office—186
  Taxes, payments in lieu of—213
  Under Secretary—40
  U.S. Fish and Wildlife Service—912
Internal Revenue Service. *See* Treasury, Department of the
International Association of Air Controllers—707
International Association of Chiefs of Police—839
International Atomic Energy Agency—630, 797
International Bank for Reconstruction and Development—516, 856, 939, 940, 981
International Boundary Commission, U.S. and Canada—260
International Broadcasting, Board for—388, 569
International Brotherhood of Teamsters—408, 1106, 1107n.
International Civil Aviation Organization, Council of the—595
International Coffee Agreement, 1976—238
International Communication Agency—151, 213, 388, 407, 437, 459, 507, 696, 1176
International Development, Agency for. *See* U.S. International Development Cooperation Agency
International Development Association—856
International Development Cooperation Agency, U.S. *See* U.S. International Development Cooperation Agency
International Finance Corporation—856, 943
International Food and Agricultural Development, Board for—1093
International Joint Commission—U.S. and Canada—380, 635, 903

International Labor Office—1027
International Longshoremen's Association—1023
International Meeting on Cooperation and Development (Cancún, Mexico)—856, 937–943, 978, 980, 983, 986, 1192
International Monetary Fund—388, 854, 940, 981
International Security and Development Cooperation Act—1202
International Telecommunication Union—1090
International Trade Commission, U.S. *See* U.S. International Trade Commission
International Union of Operating Engineers—762n.
International Whaling Commission—634
International Wheat Agreement Conventions, 1971—502
International Year of Disabled Persons—83, 84
Interstate Commerce Commission—403, 516, 1174
Interstate highways, silver anniversary. *See* Silver Anniversary Year of the National System of Interstate and Defense Highways
Investigation, Federal Bureau of. *See* Justice, Department of
Iowa, Governor—162
Iran
  American hostages. *See* Hostages
  Litigation, suspension—158, 159
  President's views—56, 57, 59, 60, 873, 952
  U.S. national emergency declaration—820, 1039, 1040
Iran-U.S. Claims Tribunal—158, 159, 364, 820, 821
Iraq, Israeli bombing of nuclear facility—505, 520, 1193
Ireland
  Ambassador to U.S.—258, 783
  Minister of Finance—258
  U.S. Ambassador—258, 259
Ireland, Northern. *See* Northern Ireland
Irish American Historical Society—1023
Israel
  Ambassador to U.S.—505, 769
  AWACS sale to Saudi Arabia. *See* Arms and munitions
  Foreign Minister—769
  Former Defense Minister—947
  Golan Heights annexation—1162, 1192
  Iraqi nuclear facility bombing. *See* Iraq
  Middle East peace efforts. *See* Middle East
  Nuclear nonproliferation stance—521
  PLO, role. *See* Palestine Liberation Organization
  Prime Minister—766, 769, 774, 868, 892, 1193
  Sinai Support Mission. *See* U.S. Sinai Support Mission

Israel—Continued
 U.S. Ambassador—769
 Weapons sales, U.S. *See* Arms and muni-
  tions
Italian-Americans—912, 913
Italy
 Ambassador to U.S.—912
 Prime Minister—644, 646n.
 U.S. Ambassador—471

Jamaica
 Bauxite, U.S. stockpiles—1089, 1090
 Deputy Prime Minister—45
 Internal situation—59
 Minister of Foreign Affairs and Foreign
  Trade—45
 Prime Minister—45, 47, 59, 161, 1090, 1095
 Taxation and fiscal evasion, convention
  with U.S. *See* Taxation
 U.S. investment—161
Jamaica, U.S. Business Committee on. *See* U.S.
 Business Committee on Jamaica
Japan
 Prime Minister—409, 411, 413, 414, 643,
  646n.
 Trade with U.S.—208, 269, 333, 415, 1210
Jaycees, U.S. *See* U.S. Jaycees
Jaycees International—560n.
Jaycettes, U.S. *See* U.S. Jaycettes
Jesus Christ of Latter-Day Saints, Church of.
 See Church of Jesus Christ of Latter-Day
 Saints
Jewish Heritage Week—401
Jewish High Holy Days—860
Joint Chiefs of Staff. *See* Defense, Depart-
 ment of
Jordan
 Ambassador to U.S.—505n., 1007n.
 Chief of Royal Court—1007n.
 Commander in Chief of Armed Forces—
  1007n.
 Foreign Minister—1007n.
 King—1005, 1008, 1010
 Prime Minister—1007n.
 Queen—1008, 1009
 Relations with U.S.—1005
 U.S. Ambassador—487, 1007
Judges, district and appellate court. *See* Dis-
 trict and appellate court judges
Judicial Nominating Commission for the Dis-
 trict of Puerto Rico—404
Judiciary, Federal. *See* Courts, U.S.
Justice, Department of
 Assistant Attorneys General—89, 144, 145,
  395, 402, 470, 653, 817, 1013, 1169, 1175
 Associate Attorney General—144
 Atlanta, murdered and missing young
  people, Federal assistance—204, 241
 Attorney General—4, 8, 63, 127, 140, 167,
  290, 328, 329n., 333, 513, 574, 596, 597,
  676, 677, 687, 717, 779, 780, 842, 860,
  914, 935, 1129, 1137, 1138, 1174, 1176,
  1203, 1207

Justice, Department of—Continued
 Budget—223, 631
 Community Relations Service—204, 1116
 Counselor to Attorney General—58n.
 Deputy Attorney General—34, 58n., 288
 Drug Enforcement Administration—842
 Emergency mobilization planning—1200
 Environmental damage, release of hazard-
  ous substances—715
 Federal Bureau of Investigation—58, 204,
  241, 288, 358, 574, 596, 779, 842, 843,
  1127, 1135–1137
 Foreign Claims Settlement Commission of
  the U.S.—541, 797
 Immigration and Naturalization Service—
  850, 858, 1038, 1055
 Juvenile Justice and Delinquency Preven-
  tion Office—205
 Law Enforcement Assistance Administra-
  tion—204
 Solicitor General—457
 U.S. Parole Commission—733, 1001
 Voting Rights Act, assessment—513
Juvenile Justice and Delinquency Prevention
 Office. *See* Justice, Department of

Kenya
 President—837
 Relations with U.S.—837
Korea, Democratic People's Republic of, in-
 volvement in Zimbabwe—1014, 1015
Korea, Republic of
 Ambassador to U.S.—68
 Deputy Prime Minister—69
 Foreign Minister—69
 Minister of National Defense—68
 President—66–70
 Secretary General to President—69
 U.S. Ambassador—69, 571

Labor, trade adjustment assistance—111
Labor, Department of
 Assistant Secretaries—90, 91, 363, 444, 599,
  817, 972
 Autoworkers, assistance for unemployed—
  333
 Budget—223, 631, 866
 Emergency mobilization planning—1200
 Environmental damage, release of hazard-
  ous substances—715
 Federal Regional Councils—654, 1003
 Inspector General—289, 292, 612
 Secretary—5, 10, 63, 127, 151, 167, 290,
  717, 745, 761, 945, 947n., 1050, 1164,
  1166
 Solicitor—90
 Under Secretary—739
 Wage and Hour Division—497
 Women's Bureau—714, 1175
Labor Day—759
Labor Office, International. *See* International
 Labor Office

Labor Relations Board, National. *See* National
Labor Relations Board
Land Management Bureau. *See* Interior, Department of the
Lands, Federal, taxes. *See* Interior, Department of the
Latin America
See also specific countries; Caribbean Basin
Administration policies—191–193
Cuban role—207
Soviet role—207
Latter-Day Saints, Church of Jesus Christ of.
See Church of Jesus Christ of Latter-Day
Saints
Law Day, U.S.A.—321, 328
Law Enforcement Assistance Administration.
See Justice, Department of
Law enforcement and crime
Administration's policies—841, 956
Atlanta, murdered and missing young
people—204, 241, 248
Capital punishment—844
Crime prevention task force—328, 956
Drug abuse—210, 840, 842
Fraud, waste, and mismanagement in Federal programs. *See* Federal employees
Gun control—373, 521
Intelligence activities, U.S.—1129–1131,
1136, 1137
Mutual legal assistance treaty with U.S. *See*
Netherlands
Security breaches. *See* Federal employees
Statistics—307, 840
Treaties. *See specific countries*
Leather exports from Argentina—977
Lebanon
French Ambassador, assassination—756
Internal situation—504
Peace mission. *See* Middle East
Syrian missiles in—524
U.S. Ambassador—475
Legal profession—844
Legal Services Corporation—1211
Leif Erikson Day—900
Liberia, U.S. Ambassador—587
Libraries and Information Science, National
Commission on. *See* National Commission
on Libraries and Information Science
Library of Congress, James Madison Memorial
Building—1074
Libya
American citizens, evacuation—1166
Assassination squad in U.S. *See* Terrorism
Chief of State—723, 917, 918, 1110, 1124,
1144, 1164
Oil, U.S. boycott—961, 962
Relations with U.S.—722, 729, 736, 917,
918
Sudan, involvement. *See* Sudan
Load lines. *See* Maritime industry
Loan guarantees, Federal. *See* Banks and
banking

Longshoremen's Association, International.
See International Longshoremen's Association
Louisiana
Governor—847, 1088, 1089
New Orleans, Republican Governors Conference—1088
President's visit—839, 847
Loyalty Day—354
Luxembourg, U.S. Ambassador—703

M.I.A. Recognition Day. *See* National P.O.W.-
M.I.A. Recognition Day
MX missiles. *See* Arms and munitions
MacArthur Corridor. *See* Defense, Department of
Madrid conference. *See* Europe, Madrid Conference on Security and Cooperation in
Malawi, U.S. Ambassador—330
Malaysia
Generalized System of Preferences—264
U.S. Ambassador—438
Maldives, U.S. Ambassador—1073
Mali, U.S. Ambassador—542
Management and Budget, Office of
Assistant to Director—1176
Associate Director for Management—290
Audiovisual aids and publications, production and procurement—365
Budget studies, etc.—85, 86, 115, 120, 336,
1042
Credit management and debt collection—
379
Deputy Director—288, 290, 291, 612, 791
Director—5, 15, 30, 60, 63, 86, 104–108,
127, 133, 151, 167, 223, 290, 343, 510,
545, 610, 678, 691, 715, 730, 731, 738,
744, 763, 773, 782, 783n., 801, 807, 892–
894, 897, 914, 1039, 1043, 1050
Energy Department, task force for dismantlement—1161
Federal Procurement Policy Office—62,
268
Federal Regional Councils, role—654, 655
Federalism, role—1076
Fraud investigations. *See* Federal employees
Information and Regulatory Affairs Office—
128, 730, 731, 863
Regulatory reform role—128
Statistical policy functions—730
Manual for Courts-Martial—475, 670
Marathon Oil Company—1113
March of Dimes Birth Defects Foundation—
1150n.
March of Dimes Birth Defects Prevention
Month—1149
Marine Band—912, 913
Marine Corps, U.S., intelligence activities—
1134
Marine Mammal Commission—1027
Marine mammals. *See* Maritime industry

Maritime Act of 1981—704

Maritime Administration. *See* Commerce, Department of; Transportation, Department of

Maritime Commission, Federal. *See* Federal Maritime Commission

Maritime Day, National. *See* National Maritime Day

Maritime industry
Canadian-U.S. agreements—209, 235–237, 366, 587
Load lines, international convention—663
Marine mammals—914
New Zealand-U.S. agreement—287
Norwegian-U.S. agreement—154
Polish fishing fleet, operation in American waters—1187
Transportation system, integration into—704
Whaling industry—634

Marshall Islands. *See* Micronesia

Mass transportation, administration policy—215

Meal subsidies, Federal—833

Medals. *See other part of title*

Medfly—737

Mediation and Conciliation Service, Federal. *See* Federal Mediation and Conciliation Service

Medicaid. *See* Health and medical care

Medical care. *See* Health and medical care

Medicare. *See* Health and medical care

Memorial Day—383

Merit Systems Protection Board—303, 359, 1153

Meritorious Service Medal—592

Mexico
Cancún summit. *See* International Meeting on Cooperation and Development
Caribbean Basin Initiative—942
Convention with U.S. on stolen or embezzled vehicles and aircraft—858
Immigration to U.S. *See* Immigration and naturalization
President—202, 493, 497, 500, 511, 676, 810, 982n.
Relations with U.S.—201, 210
Secretary of Foreign Relations—500n.
U.S. Ambassador—328

Michigan, President's visit—807

Micronesia, status negotiations—830

Middle East
See also specific countries
Egyptian-Israeli peace treaty—767, 993, 1163, 1208
German-U.S. position—455
Palestinian autonomy issue—949
President's emissary in consultations—460, 504, 521, 660, 663, 949
Saudi Arabian peace plan—949, 995, 1000, 1034
Sinai Support Mission. *See* U.S. Sinai Support Mission

Middle East—Continued
U.S. peace efforts—460, 504, 520, 660, 663, 675, 949, 1110, 1189, 1192

Military Academy, U.S. *See* U.S. Military Academy

Military Liaison Committee to Energy Department. *See* Energy, Department of

Military Manpower Task Force—610

Militia of the District of Columbia. *See* District of Columbia Militia

Mine Safety and Health Review Commission, Federal. *See* Federal Mine Safety and Health Review Commission

Mines Bureau. *See* Interior, Department of the

Mining Reclamation and Enforcement Office, Surface. *See* Interior, Department of the

Minorities
See also specific minority groups
Administration policies—513, 523
Affirmative action programs—1169

Mint Bureau. *See* Treasury, Department of the

Missing Persons (Cyprus), Committee on—439

Mississippi River Basin Commission, Upper. *See* Upper Mississippi River Basin Commission

Mississippi River Commission—652, 806, 1075

Missouri River Basin Commission—773

Mobil Oil Company—1113

Molasses. *See* Sugars

Monetary Fund, International. *See* International Monetary Fund

Monetary policy, recovery program, relationship. *See* Economic recovery program

Mormons. *See* Church of Jesus Christ of Latter-Day Saints

Morocco, Ambassador to U.S.—505n., 754

Mortgage Association, Federal National. *See* Federal National Mortgage Association

Mortgage Association, Government National. *See* Housing and Urban Development, Department of

Mostly Mozart Festival Orchestra—611

Mother's Day—352

Motor Carrier Ratemaking Study Commission—774, 866

Mozambique, trade with U.S.—580

Multinational Force and Observers. *See* United Nations

Multiple Sclerosis Society—822

Municipal Wastewater Treatment Construction Grant Amendments—1206

Muscular Dystrophy Poster Child, National. *See* National Muscular Dystrophy Poster Child

Museum Services, Institute of. *See* Education, Department of

Mutual and Balanced Force Reductions Negotiations, U.S. Representative for—777

NAACP. *See* National Association for the Advancement of Colored People

NASA. *See* National Aeronautics and Space Administration

NATO. *See* North Atlantic Treaty Organization

Namibia—315, 837, 1172

Narcotics and drugs. *See* Law enforcement and crime

Narcotics Control, Special Council on. *See* Special Council on Narcotics Control

National Advisory Committee on Oceans and Atmosphere—1092

National Aeronautics and Space Administration
  Administrator—290, 379, 442n.
  Deputy Administrator—380
  Inspector General—24, 289, 477
  Space program. *See* Space program

National Aeronautics and Space Administration Distinguished Service Medal—442n., 1145, 1146

National Afro-American (Black) History Month—66

National Agriculture Day—99

National Air and Space Museum Advisory Board—1073

National Alliance of Business—881

National Association for the Advancement of Colored People—573

National Association of Broadcasters—447

National Association of Counties—213

National Association of State Departments of Agriculture—265

National Blinded Veterans Recognition Day—703

National Brotherhood Week—100

National Center for Citizen Involvement—1151

National Clean-Up and Flag-Up America's Highways Week—579

National Commission on Libraries and Information Science—1016

National Commission on Social Security Reform—1157, 1159

National Commission on Student Financial Assistance—1017

National Community Christmas Tree—1172

National Conference of State Legislatures—679

National Consumer Cooperative Bank, budget—223

National Credit Union Administration—802

National Cystic Fibrosis Week—806

National Day of Prayer—268

National Day of Recognition for Veterans of the Vietnam Era—381

National Defense Stockpile. *See* Defense and national security

National Defense Transportation Day and National Transportation Week—376

National Diabetes Week—851

National Employ the Handicapped Week—881

National Endowments for the Arts and Humanities. *See* National Foundation on the Arts and the Humanities

National Family Week—1012

National Farm-City Week—999

National Farm Safety Week—256

National Federation of Republican Women—810

National Flag Week. *See* Flag Day and National Flag Week

National Forest Products Week—915

National Foundation on the Arts and the Humanities
  Federal Council on the Arts and the Humanities—490, 547, 927
  National Endowment for the Arts—407, 490, 496, 927, 928
  National Endowment for the Humanities—407, 490, 496, 1070

National Governors' Association—147, 162, 1206

National Guard. *See* Armed Forces, U.S.

National Guard Day—899

National Highway Traffic Safety Administration. *See* Transportation, Department of

National Hispanic Heritage Week—759

National Institute of Education. *See* Education, Department of

National Institute of Handicapped Research. *See* Education, Department of

National Italian American Foundation—912

National Labor Relations Board—539

National Leadership Conference of Teen-Age Republicans—552

National League of Cities—176

National Maritime Day—377

National Medal of Science—916

National Mortgage Association, Federal. *See* Federal National Mortgage Association

National Mortgage Association, Government. *See* Housing and Urban Development, Department of

National Muscular Dystrophy Poster Child—560n.

National Nursing Home Week—420

National Ocean Survey. *See* Commerce, Department of, National Oceanic and Atmospheric Administration

National Oceanic and Atmospheric Administration. *See* Commerce, Department of

National Poison Prevention Week—243

National Port Week—877

National Portrait Gallery. *See* Smithsonian Institution

National P.O.W.-M.I.A. Recognition Day—508, 509

National Prayer Breakfast—77

National Press Club—76, 1062

National Productivity Advisory Committee—751, 1029, 1030

National Railroad Passenger Corporation—765, 1211

National Review—275

National Safe Boating Week—483

National Schoolbus Safety Week—714

National Science Foundation—388, 615

National Security Agency. *See* Defense, Department of

National Security Council—285, 286, 1128, 1129, 1131, 1138, 1139

National Transportation Safety Board—561, 1105

National Turkey Federation—1069

Native Hawaiians Study Commission—781, 1179

Natural gas. *See* Energy

Nauru, U.S. Ambassador—363

Naval Academy, U.S. *See* U.S. Naval Academy

Naval Petroleum Reserve—899

Navy, Department of the
Assistant Secretaries—436, 733, 985
Intelligence activities—1134
Secretary—32, 610, 784
Under Secretary—769
Vessels. *See specific vessels*

Nebraska, Lincoln, mayor—1107

Nepal, U.S. Ambassador—403

Netherlands
Ambassador to U.S.—783
Extradition treaty with U.S.—469
Mutual legal assistance treaty with U.S.—701
Prime Minister—313
Queen—313
U.S. Ambassador—628

Neutron weapons. *See* Arms and munitions

Nevada, Lake Tahoe—238

Nevis. *See* St. Christopher-Nevis

New Community Development Corporation. *See* Housing and Urban Development, Department of

New England River Basins Commission—773

New Guinea. *See* Papua

New Jersey
Election—945–947, 1021
President's visit—945

New York
Hostages from Iran—38n.
Illegal aliens, detention centers—1038, 1120
Lieutenant Governor—761
Mass transit—243
Mayor, New York City—181, 342, 761, 762
President's visit—243, 244, 460, 1020, 1023
Westway Highway—243, 244, 761

New Zealand
Maritime boundary treaty with U.S.—287
Prime Minister—659
U.S. Ambassador—480

Nicaragua, role in El Salvador. *See* El Salvador

Niger, U.S. Ambassador—1091

Nigeria
Economic talks with U.S.—756
U.S. Ambassador—805

Nimitz, U.S.S. *See* U.S.S. *Nimitz*

North American Aerospace Defense Command Agreement. *See* Armed Forces, U.S.

North Atlantic Treaty Organization
Foreign Ministers—408
Nuclear weapons—313, 709, 1033, 1063–1065
Poland—344
Theater nuclear forces. *See* Arms and munitions

North Carolina, Scotland Neck, mayor—342

North Korea, involvement in Zimbabwe—1014, 1015

Northern Ireland, condemnation of terrorist acts—258

Norway
Fishery agreement. *See* Maritime industry
U.S. Ambassador—1105

Notre Dame, University of. *See* University of Notre Dame

Nuclear energy. *See* Energy

Nuclear nonproliferation. *See* Arms and munitions

Nuclear Regulatory Commission—428, 495, 595, 631, 715, 904

Nuclear war—522, 1031–1033

Nuclear weapons. *See* Arms and munitions

Nursing Home Week, National. *See* National Nursing Home Week

OPEC. *See* Petroleum Exporting Countries, Organization of

Occupational Safety and Health Review Commission—445

Ocean Survey, National. *See* Commerce, Department of

Oceanic and Atmospheric Administration, National. *See* Commerce, Department of

Oceans and Atmosphere, National Advisory Committee on. *See* National Advisory Committee on Oceans and Atmosphere

Office. *See other part of title*

Ohio
Governor—1097, 1099n.
Mayor, Columbus—342
President's visit—1097

Ohio River Basin Commission—773

Oil. *See* Energy

Older Americans Month—394

Older persons. *See* Aged persons

Olympic Games, 1984—622

Oman, U.S. Ambassador—588

Omnibus Budget Reconciliation Act of 1981—706

Operating Engineers of New York—762n.

Organization. *See other part of title*

Ottawa Summit—237, 620, 621, 635, 637, 646, 981

Overseas Private Investment Corporation. *See* U.S. International Development Cooperation Agency

PATCO. *See* Professional Air Traffic Controllers Organization

PLO. *See* Palestine Liberation Organization

P.O.W.-M.I.A. Recognition Day, National. *See* National P.O.W.-M.I.A. Recognition Day

Pacific albacore tuna vessels—587

Pacific American Heritage Week. *See* Asian/Pacific American Heritage Week

Pacific Islands territory. *See* Trust Territory of the Pacific Islands

Pacific Northwest River Basins Commission—773

Pakistan
  U.S. aid—525, 1203
  U.S. Ambassador—685

Palau. *See* Micronesia

Palestine Liberation Organization—917, 949

Palestinian autonomy issue. *See* Middle East

Pan American Day and Pan American Week—281

Panama Canal Commission—395

Paperwork reduction. *See* Regulatory reform

Papua New Guinea, U.S. Ambassador—734

Parole Commission, U.S. *See* Justice, Department of

Passover—361

Patent and Trademark Office. *See* Commerce, Department of

Pay, Advisory Committee on Federal. *See* Federal Pay, Advisory Committee on

Peace Corps. *See* ACTION

Peanuts, import quota—353

Pennsylvania
  Governor—937, 944n.
  Mayor, Philadelphia—937, 944n.
  Philadelphia, World Affairs Council of—937
  Philadelphia Mint—458, 623
  President's visit—937

Pennsylvania Avenue Development Corporation—774, 866

People's Republic of China. *See* China, People's Republic of

Permanent Joint Board on Defense—U.S. and Canada—972

Personnel Management, Office of
  Air traffic controllers terminated by strike action, Federal employment—1148
  Deputy Director—540, 1176
  Director—98, 151, 288, 290, 678, 791, 925, 1050

Peru
  Generalized System of Preferences—264
  U.S. Ambassador—739

Petroleum (oil). *See* Energy

Petroleum Exporting Countries, Organization of—134

Petroleum Reserve, Naval. *See* Naval Petroleum Reserve

Philippines
  Generalized System of Preferences—264

Philippines—Continued
  U.S. Ambassador—1179

Phillips Art Gallery—822

Phosphate rock, exports to Soviet Union—382, 383

Physical Fitness and Sports, President's Council on. *See* President's Council on Physical Fitness and Sports

Poison Prevention Week, National. *See* National Poison Prevention Week

Poland
  Deputy Prime Minister—294, 319
  Food aid and sale—320, 781, 1093, 1187
  Former Ambassador—1177, 1187
  German-U.S. position—454
  Human rights—1162, 1186, 1187
  Internal situation—293, 309, 313, 520, 525, 760, 961, 1154, 1161, 1164, 1186, 1202, 1209
  NATO position—344
  Primate's death—469
  Relations with U.S.—319, 1162, 1164, 1166, 1187, 1189
  Solidarity movement—1186, 1196
  Soviet role—195, 244, 294, 525, 1162, 1164, 1166, 1186, 1187, 1192, 1196, 1202, 1209

Police, International Association of Chiefs of. *See* International Association of Chiefs of Police

Policy Development, Office of—167, 183, 655

Political action committees—524, 525

Pollution
  Canadian-U.S. discussions—237
  Hazardous substances—715

Poor. *See* Disadvantaged persons

Port Week, National. *See* National Port Week

Portrait Gallery, National. *See* Smithsonian Institution

Postal Rate Commission—319

Postal Service, U.S. *See* U.S. Postal Service

Postmaster General, U.S. *See* U.S. Postal Service

Prayer, National Day of. *See* National Day of Prayer

Prayer Breakfast, National. *See* National Prayer Breakfast

Prayer in schools. *See* Education

Presidency, President's views—202

President, Executive Office of the. *See specific units*

Presidential Advisory Board on Ambassadorial Appointments—266

Presidential Advisory Committee on Federalism—340–342, 682, 686, 1002

Presidential Citizens Medal—442n.

Presidential Commission on Broadcasting to Cuba—823

Presidential Medal of Freedom—906

Presidential museum. *See* Gerald R. Ford Presidential Museum

Presidential Task Force on the Arts and Humanities—407, 490, 491, 864, 925
Presidential Task Force on Regulatory Relief—30, 104–108, 113, 127–129, 179, 338, 434, 512, 682, 848, 862, 863, 1029, 1047
President's Advisory Committee for Women—214
President's Cancer Panel—877
President's Commission on Executive Exchange—791
President's Commission on Hostage Compensation—484, 718
President's Commission on Housing—528, 530, 531, 798
President's Commission on White House Fellowships—427
President's Council on Integrity and Efficiency—287, 288, 290, 291, 360, 613, 751, 1144, 1145n., 1170
President's Council on Physical Fitness and Sports—628, 1108
President's Economic Adjustment Committee—738
President's Economic Policy Advisory Board—88, 183, 241, 501, 631
President's Export Council—349, 702, 920, 933
President's Foreign Intelligence Advisory Board—973, 974
President's Intelligence Oversight Board—976, 1126, 1131, 1139
President's Task Force on Private Sector Initiatives—885, 894, 926, 928, 1107, 1109
President's Volunteer Action Awards—1151
Press Club, National. *See* National Press Club
Principe. *See* Sao Tome and Principe
Prisoners of war. *See* Hostages
Privacy Act implementation, annual report—732
Private Sector Initiatives, President's Task Force on. *See* President's Task Force on Private Sector Initiatives
Private sector voluntarism. *See* Voluntarism
Procurement, Federal. *See* Federal departments and agencies
Procurement Policy Office, Federal. *See* Management and Budget, Office of
Product Liability, Interagency Task Force on. *See* Interagency Task Force on Product Liability
Product Liability and Accident Compensation, Task Force on—838
Product Liability Risk Retention Act—838
Productivity, recovery program, relationship. *See* Economic recovery program
Productivity Advisory Committee, National. *See* National Productivity Advisory Committee
Professional Air Traffic Controllers Organization—687, 697, 707, 708, 720, 753, 1106, 1114, 1148, 1149, 1168

Project Head Start. *See* Head Start
Public Broadcasting, Corporation for—799, 1019
Public Diplomacy, U.S. Advisory Commission on. *See* U.S. Advisory Commission on Public Diplomacy
Public Health Service. *See* Health and Human Services, Department of
Puerto Rico
Development program—1096
Fort Allen—875
Puerto Rico, Judicial Nominating Commission for District of. *See* Judicial Nominating Commission for District of Puerto Rico
Pulaski Memorial Day. *See* General Pulaski Memorial Day

Radiation exposure from nuclear weapons. *See* Arms and munitions
Radio broadcasting to Cuba. *See* Cuba; President's Commission on Broadcasting to Cuba
Radio Regulations (Geneva, 1979)—1090
Railroad Administration, Federal. *See* Transportation, Department of
Railroad Passenger Corporation, National. *See* National Railroad Passenger Corporation
Railroad Retirement Board—631
Railway Association, U.S. *See* U.S. Railway Association
Recession. *See* Economy, national
Reclamation Bureau. *See* Interior, Department of the
Reconstruction and Development, International Bank for. *See* International Bank for Reconstruction and Development
Recovery program, economic. *See* Economic recovery program
Red Cross, International Committee of the—439
Red Cross Month—171
Refugee Affairs, U.S. Coordinator for. *See* State, Department of
Refugee Relief Day, African. *See* African Refugee Relief Day
Refugees. *See* Immigration and naturalization
Refugees Conference, African. *See* African Refugees Conference
Regional Councils, Federal. *See* Federal Regional Councils
Regulatory Impact Analysis—104–108, 128
Regulatory reform
Administration policies—63, 104, 114, 221, 233, 466, 512, 848, 862, 892, 955
Auto industry—208, 333, 751
Energy—111, 903
Freeze on pending regulations—56
Housing—752
Marine mammals—914
Recovery program, relationship. *See* Economic recovery program

Regulatory reform—Continued
  Vice President, role. *See* Vice President
Regulatory Relief, Presidential Task Force on.
  See Presidential Task Force on Regulatory
  Relief
Rehabilitation Services Administration. *See*
  Education, Department of
Republic. *See other part of title*
Republican National Committee—510
Republican Party
  Congressional leadership, meetings with
    President—257, 625, 1071
  Fundraisers—600, 719, 727, 735, 745, 847,
    945, 1020, 1045, 1097
  Governors conference—1088
  Reception—684
  Senate-House dinner—336
Republican Women, National Federation of.
  See National Federation of Republican
  Women
Republicans, National Leadership Conference
  of Teen Age. *See* National Leadership Con-
  ference of Teen Age Republicans
Research and development
  Atomic energy defense program—1161
  Energy Department programs—1161
  Intelligence systems and devices—1132–
    1135, 1137
Reserve System, Federal. *See* Federal Reserve
  System
Retired Senior Volunteer Program. *See*
  ACTION
Retirement
  Central Intelligence Agency benefits. *See*
    Central Intelligence Agency
  Foreign Service. *See* Foreign Service Re-
    tirement and Disability System
Revenue sharing. *See* State and local govern-
  ments
Rivers and harbors
  Hazardous substances, release—716
  River basin commissions
    See also specific commissions
    Termination and transfer of assets—773
Robert F. Kennedy Medal—488
Romania
  Trade with U.S.—478–480
  U.S. Ambassador—740
Rosh Hashanah. *See* Jewish High Holy Days
Rural Telephone Bank. *See* Agriculture, De-
  partment of

SALT. *See* Arms and munitions
START. *See* Arms and munitions
Safe Boating Week, National. *See* National
  Safe Boating Week
Safe Summer Parks and Recreation Pro-
  gram—513
Safety Board, National Transportation. *See*
  National Transportation Safety Board
Safety and Health Review Commission, Fed-
  eral Mine. *See* Federal Mine Safety and
  Health Review Commission

Safety and Health Review Commission, Occu-
  pational. *See* Occupational Safety and
  Health Review Commission
St. Christopher-Nevis, U.S. Representative—
  1004
St. Lucia, U.S. Ambassador—1004
St. Vincent and the Grenadines, U.S. Ambas-
  sador—1004
"Salute to Lionel Hampton" Jazz Concert—
  778
Samoa. *See* Western Samoa
Sao Tome and Principe, U.S. Ambassador—
  1001
Satellite Corporation, Communications. *See*
  Communications Satellite Corporation
Saudi Arabia
  Administration policy—873
  Ambassador to U.S.—505n.
  AWACS sale. *See* Arms and munitions
  Crown Prince and Deputy Prime Minis-
    ter—949, 996
  Middle East peace plan. *See* Middle East
  Palestinian autonomy issue, role. *See*
    Middle East
  Relations with U.S.—952
  U.S. Ambassador—366, 670
Save Your Vision Week—148
Savings and loans. *See* Economic recovery
  program
Scholarships, Board of Foreign—1160
Schoolbus Safety Week, National. *See* National
  Schoolbus Safety Week
Schools. *See* Education
Science, National Medal of. *See* National
  Medal of Science
Science Foundation, National. *See* National
  Science Foundation
Science and Technology Policy, Office of—
  443, 904
Secret Service, U.S. *See* Treasury, Depart-
  ment of the
Securities and Exchange Commission—154,
  542
Securities Industry Association—873
Security, national. *See* Defense and nationl
  security
Security Council, National. *See* National Secu-
  rity Council
Selective Service System—59, 591, 610
Senegal, U.S. Ambassador—471
Senior Volunteer Program, Retired. *See*
  ACTION
Service. *See other part of title*
Ships and shipping. *See* Maritime industry
Silver Anniversary Year of the National
  System of Interstate and Defense High-
  ways—997
Sinai Support Mission, U.S. *See* U.S. Sinai Sup-
  port Mission
Singapore
  Generalized System of Preferences—264

Singapore—Continued
  Prime Minister—543
Sirups. *See* Sugars
Sister Cities International—300
Small Business Administration
  Administrator—145, 290
  Budget—223
  Chief Counsel for Advocacy—486
  Director—1176
  Inspector General—24, 289, 292, 612
Small Business Week—283
Small businesses, administration policies—566
Smithsonian Institution
  National Portrait Gallery—547ftn.
  Woodrow Wilson International Center for Scholars—182
Social programs. *See* Entitlement programs
Social Security Administration. *See* Health and Human Services, Department of
Social Security Reform, National Commission on. *See* National Commission on Social Security Reform
Social Security Reform, Task Force on—1102
Social security system
  Administration policies—110, 450, 566, 634, 729, 800, 825, 834, 848, 892, 895, 1101, 1119, 1170, 1192, 1198, 1205
  Canadian-American benefits—232
  Legislation—1204
Solidarity movement. *See* Poland
Solomon Islands, U.S. Ambassador—734
Sons of Italy—912
South Africa
  Human rights—196
  Relations with Zimbabwe—598, 1015
South East Asian Nations, Association for (ASEAN). *See specific member countries*
South Korea. *See* Korea, Republic of
Soviet Union. *See* Union of Soviet Socialist Republics
Space Medal of Honor, Congressional. *See* Congressional Space Medal of Honor
Space program—111
Space shuttle—348, 353, 393, 441, 1045, 1145
Spain
  Ambassador to U.S.—783, 912, 919n.
  Director General for U.S. and Pacific Affairs—919n.
  Foreign Minister—918, 919n.
  King—918, 919, 922
  Queen—918, 919n., 922
  Secretary General of Palace—919n.
  Treaty with U.S.—914
  U.S. Ambassador—919n.
Spanish-speaking Americans. *See* Hispanic Americans
Speaker of the House of Representatives—1, 16, 24–26, 160, 223, 263, 394, 439, 450, 549, 635n., 656n., 658, 661, 676, 694n., 732, 835, 1097, 1102, 1118, 1157, 1159, 1205
Special Council on Narcotics Control—842
Spending, Federal. *See* Budget, Federal

Sports, President's Council on Physical Fitness and. *See* President's Council on Physical Fitness and Sports
Sri Lanka, U.S. Ambassador—1073
State, Department of
  See also Foreign Service
  Ambassadors at Large—92, 482, 927
  Ambassadors. *See specific country*
  Assistant Secretaries—50, 72, 92, 143, 188, 189, 204, 374, 481, 493, 627, 1004, 1091, 1106
  Budget—547, 866
  Chief of Protocol—93, 906
  Counselor—51
  Deputy Assistant Secretaries—728, 1056
  Deputy Secretary—33, 520, 625
  Director of Personnel—1175
  Environmental damage, release of hazardous substances—715
  Foreign Service Board of Examiners—151
  Holy See, President's Personal Representative—93
  Inspector General—289, 292
  Intelligence and Research Bureau—1138
  Legal Adviser—491
  Refugee Affairs, U.S. Coordinator—997
  Secretary—4, 6, 68, 151, 167, 192, 194, 197, 286, 290, 311, 313, 319, 344, 352n., 385, 408, 442n., 454, 479, 500, 503, 510, 517, 520, 582n., 595, 622n., 625, 631, 678, 694n., 769, 824, 837, 842, 859, 865, 906, 919n., 944, 1000, 1007n., 1036, 1037, 1055, 1066, 1106, 1132, 1135, 1148, 1209
  Treaty reports—503, 504, 587, 888
  Under Secretaries—49, 50, 69, 187, 527, 830
State Legislatures, National Conference of. *See* National Conference of State Legislatures
State and local governments
  Administration policies—2, 180–182, 1115, 1174
  Arts and humanities programs—407
  California elections—719, 727, 728, 737
  Cheese, distribution to disadvantaged persons—1178
  Crime prevention—328
  Defense contracts—953
  Education—833
  Employee unionization and right to strike—753
  Federal grants—110, 180, 207, 215, 216, 249, 339, 465, 467, 545, 546, 554, 557, 565, 681, 682, 709, 719, 735, 869, 894, 896, 1076, 1112, 1163
  Federalism—87, 111, 147, 182, 213, 215, 217, 249, 339–343, 433, 466, 655, 681–683, 709, 719, 727, 735, 841, 1076, 1163, 1192
  Military facilities, impact on local communities—283, 738

State and local governments—Continued
National Guard. *See* Armed Forces, U.S.
Private sector initiatives—1110
Regional economic disparities—1080
Revenue sharing—148, 467, 1112
River basin commissions, transfer of Federal assets—773
State attorneys general—329n.
Steel industry—549, 554, 565, 632, 746, 868, 894, 1195, 1196
Strategic arms limitation talks (SALT). *See* Arms and munitions
Strategic arms reduction talks (START). *See* Arms and munitions
Strategic weapons program, U.S. *See* Arms and munitions
Student Financial Assistance, National Commission on. *See* National Commission on Student Financial Assistance
Student Loan Marketing Association—1042
Sudan
Ambassador to U.S.—505n.
Libyan involvement—917, 918
Sugars, import fees—1180
Supreme Court of the U.S.
Associate Justices—538, 596, 597, 601, 811, 819, 901, 1174
Chief Justice—1, 4n., 27
White House reception—828
Surface Mining Reclamation and Enforcement Office. *See* Interior, Department of the
Susquehanna River Basin Commission—1002
Sweden
Ambassador to U.S.—891
Extradition treaty with U.S.—668
King—1083, 1084n.
Queen—1084n.
U.S. Ambassador—1075
Switzerland, U.S. Ambassador—755
Synthetic fuels. *See* Energy
Synthetic Fuels Corporation, U.S. *See* U.S. Synthetic Fuels Corporation
Syria
Golan Heights—1164
Missiles in Lebanon. *See* Lebanon
U.S. Ambassador—669

Tahoe Federal Coordinating Council—238
Tahoe Regional Planning Agency—238
Taiwan
Relations with U.S.—526
Trade with U.S.—580
Tanzania, U.S. Ambassador—829
Tariff Schedules of the U.S. *See* Commerce, international
Tariffs and Trade, General Agreement on. *See* Commerce, international
Task force. *See other part of title*
Tax Act of 1981, Economic Recovery. *See* Economic Recovery Tax Act of 1981
Tax Court, U.S. *See* U.S. Tax Court
Tax Court Nominating Commission, U.S. *See* U.S. Tax Court Nominating Commission

Taxation
Administration policies—357, 1168, 1189
Alcohol excise tax—1190
Argentina-U.S. taxation and fiscal evasion convention—503
British Virgin Islands-U.S. taxation and fiscal evasion convention—367
Canadian broadcast provision—1057
Federal payments to counties. *See* Interior, Department of the
Gasoline excise tax—1078, 1190
Jamaica-U.S. taxation and fiscal evasion convention—764
Oil decontrol tax—1168
Recovery program, relationship. *See* Economic recovery program
Social Security System—450
State and local government revenues—216
Statistics—308, 358
Tax code reform—834
Tobacco excise tax—1190
User fees—109, 222, 893
Teamsters, International Brotherhood of. *See* International Brotherhood of Teamsters
Teen Age Republicans, National Leadership Conference of. *See* National Leadership Conference of Teen Age Republicans
Telecommunication Union, International. *See* International Telecommunication Union
Telephone Bank, Rural. *See* Agriculture, Department of
Tennessee, Governor—342
Tennessee Valley Authority—397
Terrorism
Egypt, assassination of President—898, 902, 906
Intelligence activities, U.S.—1127, 1129, 1135–1137
Lebanon, assassination of French Ambassador—756
Libyan assassination squad in U.S.—1124, 1144, 1164–1166
Northern Ireland, violence—258
Ottawa Summit statement—637
Pope, assassination attempt—423
President's views—56, 396, 397
Turkish anti-terrorist activities, U.S. support—323
Texas
Congressional delegation, White House reception and barbecue—827
Governor—1045, 1047
President's visit—555, 1045, 1050, 1146n.
Texas International Airlines-Continental Airlines acquisition case—917
Thailand
Generalized System of Preferences—264
Prime Minister—897
Queen—898
Relations with U.S.—897
U.S. Ambassador—695

Thanksgiving Day—1041
Thanksgiving turkey—1069
Tobacco, excise tax. *See* Taxation
Tobago. *See* Trinidad and Tobago
Togo, U.S. Ambassador—849
Tokelau, U.S.-New Zealand maritime boundary treaty—287
Trade. *See* Commerce, international
Trade adjustment assistance. *See* Labor
Trade association representatives—660
Trade Commission, Federal. *See* Federal Trade Commission
Trade Commission, U.S. International. *See* U.S. International Trade Commission
Trade Negotiations, Advisory Committee for—686
Trade Representative, Office of the U.S. *See* U.S. Trade Representative, Office of the
Trade Week, World. *See* World Trade Week
Transportation. *See* Mass transportation
Transportation, Department of
    Assistant Secretaries—53, 141, 273
    Budget—223, 388, 774, 866, 1019
    Coast Guard, U.S.—715, 716
    Deputy Secretary—5
    Director, Executive Secretariat—1175
    Environmental damage, release of hazardous substances—715
    Federal Aviation Administration—191, 346, 687
    Federal Highway Administration—54
    Federal Railroad Administration—37
    Federal Regional Councils—654, 1003
    General Counsel—38
    Inspector General—24, 289, 368, 612
    Maritime Administration—704
    National Highway Traffic Safety Administration—53, 333
    Secretary—5, 12, 63, 167, 208, 290, 682, 688, 704, 716, 717, 929, 930, 937, 944n., 1207
    Union Station redevelopment—1207
    Urban Mass Transportation Administration—203
Transportation Day, National Defense, and National Transportation Week. *See* National Defense Transportation Day and National Transportation Week
Transportation Safety Board, National. *See* National Transportation Safety Board
Treasury, Department of the
    Assistant General Counsel—429
    Assistant Secretaries—40, 64, 96, 189, 219, 369, 422
    Budget—866
    Comptroller of the Currency—1043
    Deputy Secretary—33
    Deputy Under Secretary—219
    Emergency mobilization planning—1200
    General Counsel—424
    Internal Revenue Service—37

Treasury, Department of the—Continued
    Iran, U.S. national emergency declaration, regulations—820
    Mint Bureau—369, 436, 458, 623
    Secretary—4, 6, 55, 63, 88, 127, 132, 159, 167, 289, 290, 319, 343, 358, 472, 482, 625, 651, 660, 662, 676, 692, 716, 717, 791, 801, 820, 842, 896, 897, 1029, 1034, 1076, 1132
    Tax code reform—834
    Tax reduction report—115
    Treasurer of U.S.—96, 1175
    Under Secretary—36, 52
    U.S. Assay Office—440
    U.S. Secret Service—1132
Trinidad and Tobago, U.S. Ambassador—1017
Trust Territory of the Pacific Islands—830, 917, 1005, 1105
Tuna vessels, Pacific albacore. *See* Pacific albacore tuna vessels
Tunisia, U.S. Ambassador—1141
Turkey
    Ataturk Centennial Year—323
    Cyprus conflict. *See* Cyprus
    Foreign Minister—322, 323
    Relations with U.S.—323
    U.S. Ambassador—543
    U.S. assistance—211
Turkey Federation, National. *See* National Turkey Federation

UNICO—912
USO. *See* United Service Organizations, Inc.
Unemployment. *See* Employment and unemployment
Uniformed Services Pay Act—932
Union of Soviet Socialist Republics
    Afghanistan occupation. *See* Afghanistan
    Ambassador to U.S.—194
    Communist goals—57
    Cuba, relations. *See* Cuba
    Economic sanctions—212, 382, 383
    El Salvador, role. *See* El Salvador
    Farming. *See* Agriculture and agricultural sector
    Grain embargo. *See* Agriculture and agicultural sector
    Human rights—196
    Hunger strikers—1142
    Internal situation—520
    Latin America, role. *See* Latin America
    Military buildup. *See* Arms and munitions
    Nuclear weapons negotiations. *See* Arms and munitions
    Poland, role. *See* Poland
    President—152, 153, 194, 195, 510, 520, 1062, 1063, 1065, 1066, 1087, 1196, 1198, 1209
    Relations with U.S.—193–196, 1167, 1197
    U.S. Ambassador—720
Union Station Redevelopment Act—1207

United Brotherhood of Carpenters and Joiners—748
United Kingdom
  Ambassador to U.S.—783
  Economic situation—198
  Lord Chancellor—965, 967
  Prime Minister—153, 164, 165, 168, 172, 194, 197, 198, 642, 646
  Relations with U.S.—164, 165
  U.S. Ambassador—296
  Zimbabwe military force—1172
United Nations
  See also specific specialized organizations
  Afghanistan—1199
  Alternate Representative for Special Political Affairs—71
  Cyprus conflict resolution—438, 1148
  Economic and Social Council—406, 755
  European Office—900
  Multinational Force and Observers—1208
  Secretary-General—656, 826, 982n.
  Secretary-General's Special Representative on Cyprus—438, 655, 826, 1118
  Security Council, U.S. Deputy Representative—685
  U.S. Alternate Representative—765
  U.S. Deputy Representative—72, 608
  U.S. participation—1147
  U.S. Representative—5, 14, 765, 906
United Nations Conference on the Law of the Sea—455
United Nations Day—853
United Nations Educational, Scientific and Cultural Organization—880
United Nations Industrial Development Organization—888
United Service Organizations, Inc.—970
U.S. Advisory Commission on Public Diplomacy—599
U.S. Air Force Academy—1126
U.S. Arms Control and Disarmament Agency—377, 595
U.S. Assay Office. *See* Treasury, Department of the
U.S. Business Committee on Jamaica—161
U.S. Chamber of Commerce. *See* Chamber of Commerce, U.S.
U.S. Circuit Judge Nominating Commission—404
U.S. Council for International Year of Disabled Persons—83
U.S. Fire Administration. *See* Federal Emergency Management Agency
U.S. Fish and Wildlife Service. *See* Interior, Department of the
U.S. Foreign Claims Settlement Commission. *See* Justice, Department of
U.S. International Development Cooperation Agency
  Agency for International Development—51, 331, 356, 357, 375, 389, 398, 421, 618, 691, 986, 1091, 1155, 1175

U.S. International Development Cooperation Agency—Continued
  Director—151, 289, 290
  Overseas Private Investment Corporation—321, 422, 542, 629, 818, 1091, 1141
U.S. International Trade Commission—425, 426, 1049, 1180
U.S. Jaycees—555
U.S. Jaycettes—560n.
U.S. Military Academy
  Board of Visitors—1125
  Commencement exercises—460
  Hostages from Iran—38n.
  Superintendent—460, 462, 464n.
U.S. Naval Academy—1125
U.S. Parole Commission. *See* Justice, Department of
U.S. Postal Service
  Federal subsidies—111
  Governors—572, 1008
  Postmaster General—289
U.S. Railway Association—631
U.S. Secret Service. *See* Treasury, Department of the
U.S. Sinai Support Mission—355, 972
U.S. Supreme Court. *See* Supreme Court of the U.S.
U.S. Synthetic Fuels Corporation—322, 416, 487
U.S. Tax Court—1050
U.S. Tax Court Nominating Commission—404
U.S. Trade Representative, Office of the
  Argentinian leather exports—978
  Deputy—274, 275
  International Coffee Agreement of 1976, implementation—238
  Representative—16, 68, 167, 625, 1096
  Trade agreements with Hungary and Romania—480
U.S. Virgin Islands—617, 1096
U.S.S. *Constellation*—721, 723, 747
U.S.S. *Fletcher*—722
U.S.S. *Nimitz*—723
University of Notre Dame—431
Upper Mississippi River Basin Commission—758, 773
Upper Volta, U.S. Ambassador—572
Urban development—180
Urban enterprise zones. *See* Employment and unemployment
Urban Mass Transportation Administration. *See* Transportation, Department of
Uruguay
  Minister of Finance—856
  U.S. Ambassador—754
User fees. *See* Taxation
Utah, Governor—342

Venezuela
  Ambassador to U.S.—783, 1055
  Caribbean Basin Initiative—942
  Foreign Minister—1055

Venezuela—Continued
  Former President, death—857
  Generalized System of Preferences—264
  Minister, Secretariat of Presidency—1055
  President—1053, 1059, 1067
  U.S. Ambassador—857, 1055
Vermont, Governor—342
Vessels. *See specific vessels; Maritime industry*
Veterans
  Disability compensation, housing, and memorial benefits—960
  Education assistance program—473
  Medical care—530, 1119
  Pensions—110
  Vietnam-era—530, 1011, 1012
Veterans Administration
  Acting Administrator—163n.
  Administrator—152, 163, 290, 399, 472, 865
  Associate Deputy Administrator—1176
  Budget—223, 985
  Credit management and debt collection—378
  Deputy Administrator—163n., 757
  Inspector General—24, 289
  Medicine and Surgery Department, pay—741, 743, 934, 1051
Veterans Day—989
Veterans' Health Care, Training, and Small Business Loan Act of 1981—1011
Veterans Leadership Program, Vietnam. *See* Vietnam Veterans Leadership Program
Veterans Recognition Day, National Blinded. *See* National Blinded Veterans Recognition Day
Veterans of the Vietnam Era, National Day of Recognition for. *See* National Day of Recognition for Veterans of the Vietnam Era
Vice President
  Assassination attempt on President, statements concerning—311, 312
  Atlanta, murdered and missing young people, Federal assistance—204, 241, 248, 574
  Birthday—510
  Black colleges, Federal assistance plan consideration—794, 796
  Brazil, official visit—756
  Cabinet Councils, appointments—167
  Cancer Courage Award—323
  Colombia, official visit—756
  Cypriot President, meeting—1148
  Dominican Republic, official visit—756
  Dutch Prime Minister, meeting—313
  Egyptian officials, meeting—694n.
  European Communities President, meeting—625
  Federal budget—324, 482
  Israeli Prime Minister, meeting—769
  Jordanian officials, meeting—1007n.
  Kenyan President, meeting—837
  Korean President, meeting—68

Vice President—Continued
  Law Day, U.S.A.—328
  Local government regulatory relief task force—214
  National Security Council, crisis management team chairman—285, 286
  Nigeria, bilateral economic talks—756
  Polish Deputy Prime Minister, meeting—319
  President Reagan, meeting—627
  Regulatory reform, role—31, 127, 179, 338, 434, 512, 682, 751, 848, 862, 1047
  Republican Senate-House Dinner—336
  Salary—934, 1051
  Senate President, role—1, 24–27, 160, 263, 732
  Space shuttle astronauts—441, 442n.
  Turkish Minister of Foreign Affairs, meeting—322
  Venezuelan officials, meeting—1055
  Venezuelan President, former, funeral—857
  White House Correspondents Association, annual dinner—385
  Yorktown bicentennial—783, 784
  Zairian officials, meeting—1106
Victims of Crime, Task Force on the—841
Victims Rights Week—340
Vietnam
  Veterans. *See* Veterans
  U.S. Armed Forces, role—155–158
Vietnam Era, National Day of Recognition for Veterans of the. *See* National Day of Recognition for Veterans of the Vietnam Era
Vietnam Veterans Leadership Program—1028
Virgin Islands, British. *See* Taxation
Virgin Islands, U.S. *See* U.S. Virgin Islands
Virginia
  Election—948, 991
  Governor—784, 963, 967, 991, 992, 1088, 1089
  President's visit—783, 962–970, 991
  Yorktown bicentennial—783, 785, 962–970
Virginia Independence Bicentennial Commission—964
Virginia Military Institute—967
Vision Week, Save Your. *See* Save Your Vision Week
Voluntarism—110, 208, 241, 252, 447, 815, 825, 836, 845, 882, 894, 994, 1109, 1122
VOLUNTEER—1151, 1152
Volunteer Action Awards, President's. *See* President's Volunteer Action Awards
Volunteer military. *See* Armed Forces, U.S.
Voting Rights Act. *See* Civil rights

Wage and Hour Division. *See* Labor, Department of
Wage and price regulatory program, termination—62

Wage and Price Stability, Council on—56, 62, 127
Wall Street—873
Waste, fraud, and mismanagement in Federal Government. *See* Federal employees
Wastewater Treatment Construction Grant Amendments, Municipal. *See* Municipal Wastewater Treatment Construction Grant Amendments
Water Development Appropriation Act, 1982, Energy and. *See* Energy and Water Development Appropriation Act, 1982
Water Resources Council, Chairman—302
Water resources projects—807, 1206
Welfare—111, 136, 208, 466, 833, 882, 1077
Western Samoa, U.S. Ambassador—480
Westway Highway. *See* New York
Whaling. *See* Maritime industry
Whaling Commission, International. *See* International Whaling Commission
Wheat Agreement Conventions, 1971, International. *See* International Wheat Agreement Conventions, 1971
White Cane Safety Day—852
White House, Young Artists in Performance at the. *See* Young Artists in Performance at the White House
White House china—950, 1194, 1198
White House Conference on Aging—1100, 1117
White House Correspondents Association—384
White House Fellows—502
White House Fellowships, President's Commission on. *See* President's Commission on White House Fellowships
White House Intergovernmental Affairs Office—213
White House Press Briefing Room—1025
White House staff
 Army Aide to President—1145, 1146n.
 Assistant Counsellor—55
 Assistant to President and Assistant to Deputy Chief of Staff—786
 Assistant to President for Cabinet Affairs—787
 Assistant to President and Chief of Staff—68, 167, 182, 343, 353, 691, 791, 1007n., 1050
 Assistant to President for Communications—535, 660, 1122, 1190
 Assistant to President and Deputy Chief of Staff—68, 622, 786, 1007n.
 Assistant to President for Intergovernmental Affairs—88, 147, 343, 1174
 Assistant to President for Legislative Affairs—419, 791, 1115, 1122
 Assistant to President for National Security Affairs—68, 500, 582n., 610, 622n., 694n., 769, 826, 919n., 1000, 1007n., 1044, 1055, 1111, 1129, 1166, 1169, 1194, 1200

White House staff—Continued
 Assistant to President for Policy Development—88, 127, 183, 610, 1029
 Assistant to President for Political Affairs—1040
 Assistant to President for Presidential Personnel—172
 Assistant to President and Press Secretary—35, 76, 166, 280, 310, 311, 373, 385, 391, 601, 740, 1025, 1026
 Assistant to President for Public Liaison—678, 679n.
 Assistant to President and Staff Director—310, 782, 783n.
 Assistants to President—288, 906
 Associate Director of Presidential Personnel—172
 Cabinet Administration Office—167
 Chief of Staff. *See* Assistant to President and Chief of Staff
 Counsel to President—54
 Counsellor to President—68, 167, 343, 384, 610, 691, 948, 955, 1007n., 1106, 1111
 Deputies to Special Assistant to President for Intergovernmental Affairs—350
 Deputy Assistant to President and Deputy to Assistant to President for Intergovernmental Affairs—349
 Deputy Assistant to President and Deputy to Assistant to President for Public Liaison—261
 Deputy Assistant to President and Deputy to Chief of Staff—927
 Deputy Assistant to President and Director of Presidential Personnel—787
 Deputy Assistant to President for Legislative Affairs—1153
 Deputy Assistant to President for National Security Affairs—1106
 Deputy Assistant to President for Presidential Personnel—406
 Deputy Assistant to President and Principal Deputy Press Secretary—344, 460, 493n., 504, 513n., 536, 597n., 660, 756, 789, 990, 1114, 1124
 Deputy Assistants to President—706, 791
 Deputy Chief of Staff. *See* Assistant to President and Deputy Chief of Staff
 Deputy Counsellors to President—70, 1013
 Deputy Counsels to President—273, 274, 1194
 Deputy Press Secretaries—537, 788, 948ftn.
 Deputy Special Assistant to President for Public Liaison—261
 Deputy Staff Secretary—39
 Director of Communications Office—296
 Director of Media Relations and Planning—788, 947
 Director of Public Affairs Office—790

White House staff—Continued
  Director of Resources, Office of Public Liaison, and Deputy Director, Office of Consumer Affairs—262
  Intergovernmental Affairs Office—655
  Marine Corps Aide to President—528
  Personal Secretary to President—789
  Press Secretary. *See* Assistant to President and Press Secretary
  Reduction in force—833
  Special Assistant to President—86
  Special Assistant to Assistant to President for Intergovernmental Affairs—350
  Special Assistant to President for Administration and Director of Office of Administration—270
  Special Assistant to President and Chief Speechwriter—1059
  Special Assistant to President and Director of Advance Office—74
  Special Assistant to President and Director of Presidential Speechwriting Office—1058
  Special Assistant to President for National Security Affairs—401
  Special Assistant to President for Policy Development—75
  Special Assistant to President in Deputy Chief of Staff Office—790, 817n.
  Special Assistant to President and Special Assistant to Chief of Staff—1012
  Special Assistants to President and Deputy Directors for Public Liaison—261
  Special Assistants to President for Intergovernmental Affairs—349, 350
  Special Assistants to President for Public Liaison—261, 262
  Special Consultant to President—85
  Staff Assistant to President and Assistant Director of Office of Cabinet Administration—97
  Swearing-in ceremony—26
Wightman Cup Tennis Team—792
William Randolph Hearst Foundation—78
Wilson Center. *See* Smithsonian Institution
Women—214, 248, 462, 683, 811, 901, 1174
Women, Commission on the Status of, U.S. Representative on U.N. Economic and Social Council—755

Women, Federated. *See* Federated Women
Women, Fifty States Project for. *See* Fifty States Project for Women
Women, National Federation of Republican. *See* National Federation of Republican Women
Women, President's Advisory Committee for. *See* President's Advisory Committee for Women
Women, Task Force on Legal Equity for—1174–1177
Women's Bureau. *See* Labor, Department of
Women's Equality Day—731
Woodrow Wilson Center. *See* Smithsonian Institution
World Affairs Council of Philadelphia—937
World Bank. *See* International Bank for Reconstruction and Development
World Bank Group—854
World Food Day—931
World Trade Week—202
Wright Brothers Day—1154

Yemen Arab Republic, U.S. Ambassador—609
Yorktown Bicentennial. *See* Virginia
Young American Medals for Bravery and Service—779
Young Americans for Freedom—275
Young Artists in Performance at the White House—1082
Young Republican Leadership Conference—294
Youth. *See* Children and youth
Yugoslavia
  Trade with U.S.—580
  U.S. Ambassador—610

Zaire
  Ambassador to U.S.—1106
  Foreign Minister—1106
  President—1106
  U.S. Ambassador—1106
Zimbabwe
  Independence—581
  Internal situation—325, 598, 1014, 1170
  North Korea, involvement—1014, 1015
  Prime Minister—598, 1014, 1015, 1172
  South Africa, relations—598, 1015
Zimbabwe Donor's Conference—837

Name Index

Abdullah, King—1006, 1008
Abell, Richard—295
Abraham—767, 770
Abrams, Elliott—72, 1004
Abshire, David—974
Adams, Abigail—593
Adams, Don—745
Adams, John—593, 970
Adelman, Kenneth L.—608, 765
Adkinson, F. Keith—570
Ahearn, Frederick L.—1003
Aikens, Joan D.—537
Akaka, Repr. Daniel K.—527
Albert, Margo—491
Aldrich, Alexander—550
Aldridge, Edward C., Jr.—486
Alekseeva, Elizaveta—1142
Alexander, Grover Cleveland—297
Alexander, Kelly—573
Alexander, Gov. Lamar—342, 478, 1030
Alexander, Robert J.—857
Alhegelan, Sheikh Faisal—505
'Ali, Kamal Hasan—694n.
Allen, George—628
Allen, Richard V.—68, 500n., 582n., 610, 622n., 694n., 769n., 826, 827n., 919n., 1000, 1007n., 1036, 1044, 1055n., 1070, 1111, 1194
Allin, Lyndon K. (Mort)—789
Alvarez, Everett, Jr.—420
Ambrose, James R.—862
Amerine, Merv—1069
Anderson, Carl A.—1179
Anderson, David—610
Anderson, Karen Eakens—323
Anderson, Katherine M.—1175
Anderson, Martin—88, 343, 610
Anderson, Robert—853
Anderson, Stanton D.—686
Andre, Frederic—516
Angrisani, Albert—90
Annenberg, Leonore—93, 906
Applegarth, Paul V.—502
Aramony, William—1107
Aranda, Thomas Jr.—754
Archer, Repr. Bill—1045
Archer, Glenn L., Jr.—1013
Archer, William—1159
Arismendi, Valentín—854, 856n.
Arledge, Roone—1039
Armacost, Michael Hayden—1179
Armacost, Samuel—791
Armas, Tony—1060
Armitage, Constance D.—485

Armstrong, Anne—974
Armstrong, Raymond J.—65
Armstrong, William—1159
Arnett, G. Ray—102
Arnold, Daryl—1093
Arnold, Margaret Long—1002
Ashbrook, Repr. John M.—1007
Ashe, Arthur—792
Ataturk, Mustafa Kemal—323
Atkinson, Repr. Eugene V.—929, 930, 946
Attard, Adelaide—1002
Attlee, Clement R. P.—168
Auchter, Thorne G.—91
Austad, Mark Evans—1105
Austin, Tracy—792

Bach, Johann Sebastian—611
Badham, Repr. Robert E.—140
Badran, Mudhir—1007n.
Baer, Benjamin F.—1001
Bagnell, Francis J.—1201
Bailey, Pamela Needham—304
Bailey, Patricia—209
Bailey, Pearl—778, 779n.
Baker, Sen. Howard H., Jr.—1, 209, 257n., 324, 336, 338, 391, 421, 450n., 482, 625–627n., 635n., 694n., 835, 995, 996, 1071, 1102, 1156, 1157, 1159, 1165, 1205
Baker, Mrs. Howard H., Jr.—281
Baker, James A., III—68, 182, 343, 353n., 691, 791, 927, 1007n., 1043, 1046, 1050n.
Baker, Mrs. James A., III—1050n.
Baker, William O.—974
Bakshian, Aram, Jr.—261, 1058
Baldrige, Malcolm—5, 10, 319, 333n., 593, 791, 1091
Ball, Ralph—829
Ball, Robert M.—1159
Banfield, Edward C.—491
Barber, Clifford M.—440
Bark, Dennis L.—427
Barnes, A. James—266
Barnes, Harry G., Jr.—721
Barnhart, Ray A.—54
Baroody, Michael E.—790
Baroody, William J., Jr.—182, 1107
Barrett, James E.—970, 971n.
Barry, Commodore John—723–726
Barry, Robert L.—984
Bartlett, Christi—555, 560n.
Barton, Joe Linus—502
Barton, Nelda Ann Lambert—1003
Baskowitz, Eve—350
Bass, Anne—491

Batjer, Cameron M.—733
Batten, William M.—791
Battle, A. George—791
Baxter, William Francis—145
Baz, Osama al—694n.
Bazilwich, Col. Paul, Jr.—653
Beall, Donald R.—702
Beamer, Winona K. D.—781
Beatrix, Queen—313
Beck, Robert A.—702, 1159
Beecher, Henry Ward—476
Beggs, James Montgomery—379
Begin, Menahem—766, 769, 774, 868, 892, 950, 1193
Beilenson, Laurence—462
Bell, J. Raymond—541
Bell, Terrel H.—5, 13, 343, 678, 679n., 682, 796, 833
Bell, William M.—507
Bella, James Warner—17, 462
Bello, Andres—1053
Belson, James A.—443
Bemiss, Fitzgerald—1092
Benavidez, M. Sgt. Roy P.—155, 804
Bengelloun, Ali—505
Bennett, Kathleen M.—591
Bennett, Tony—779n.
Bennett, William J.—1070
Benson, Ezra Taft—265
Bentsen, Sen. Lloyd—482
Berkowitz, David—895
Berlin, Irving—505
Betancourt, Rómulo—857
Betts, H. Rodger—781
Bevill, Repr. Tom—1123
Bhumibol Adulyadej, King—898
Biaggi, Repr. Mario—704
Biley, Repr. Thomas J., Jr.—991
Binyon, Laurence—155
Birk, Roger E.—791
Birney, Richard Eugene—502
Bish, Milan D.—1004
Bishirjian, Richard J.—696
Blackwell, Morton C.—261
Blake, Eubie—907, 911, 1100
Blake, William—607
Blanchette, Robert W.—37
Bliss, Ray—704
Bloch, Julia Chang—618
Block, John R.—4, 9, 58, 216, 265, 500, 1046, 1091
Bloomingdale, Alfred S.—974
Bludhorn, Charles—161
Boggs, Repr. Lindy (Mrs. Hale)—251ftn.
Bogosian, Edna—1003
Bohn, John A., Jr.—517
Bolívar, Simón—1053
Bolling, Repr. Richard—342
Bollinger, Stephen J.—272
Bolton, John R.—1155
Bombeck, Erma—885

Bonitati, Robert F.—262
Bonner, Joel E.—367
Booker, Col. Phillip—991
Boone, Pat—23
Boorstin, Daniel J.—491
Boosalis, Helen G.—1107
Borcherdt, Edward R., Jr.—1125
Borcherdt, Wendy H.—172, 248
Boren, Sen. David L.—342, 482
Borg, Parker W.—542
Borman, Frank—161, 974
Bostic, James E., Jr.—427
Boucher, Paul R.—292, 612n.
Boucicault, Dion—259
Bowen, Otis R.—342, 431, 435n.
Bowen, William G.—491
Bower, Bruce L.—427
Bowsher, Charles A.—612, 614
Bradley, Esther (Kitty)—1201
Bradley, Gen. Omar N.—29, 343, 344, 907
Bradshaw, Thornton F.—791
Brady, Carl Franklin, Sr.—1092
Brady, Dorothy—1026
Brady, James S.—35, 76, 152, 161, 166, 280, 286, 310n., 312n., 337, 350, 373, 385, 391, 601, 740, 1025, 1026
Brady, Lawrence J.—184
Brady, Nyle C.—421
Brady, Sarah—385, 740, 1026
Bragg, Jeffrey S.—758
Braman, Norman—850
Brandt, Edward N., Jr.—98
Branscomb, Lewis M.—1030
Bray, Charles W., III—471
Brement, Marshall—72, 609
Bressler, Richard M.—702
Brett, George—336
Brewer, Shelby Templeton—317
Brezhnev, Leonid I.—152, 153, 194, 195, 510, 709, 1062, 1065, 1066, 1187, 1196, 1198, 1209
Bricker, William R.—1107
Broadbent, Robert N.—438
Brock, William E.—16, 68, 336, 625, 1096
Broder, James N.—1094
Brooke, Edward W.—532
Brooks, Capt. Dennis M.—721, 723
Brooks, Herb—1022
Brooks, Repr. Jack—342, 613
Broomfield, William S.—906
Brown, Repr. Clarence J. (Bud)—342, 1097
Brown, Clifton G.—1003
Brown, Gov. Edmund G., Jr. (Jerry)—76, 729
Brown, Garry E.—532
Brown, Harold—889, 890n.
Brown, Joseph Wentling—797
Brown, June Gibbs—477
Brown, Kenneth Lee—1051
Brown, Robert L.—292
Brown, Sam—906

Browne, H. Monroe—480
Brubeck, Dave—779n.
Bryant, William Cullen—348
Brzezinski, Zbigniew—890n.
Buali, Abdulaziz Abdulrahman—505
Buchanan, Angela M.—96, 1175
Buckley, James L.—50, 830
Bulen, L. Keith—380
Bundy, McGeorge—890n.
Bunyan, John—580
Burford, Robert F.—187
Burger, Warren E.—1, 4n., 27n.
Burgess, Jack—261
Burke, James E.—791
Burkhart, Elizabeth Flores—1176
Burnett, James E., Jr. 561
Burnham, James—276
Burns, Arthur F.—88, 241, 442, 1168
Burr, Raymond—231
Burroughs, John A., Jr.—330
Busbee, Gov. George—148, 162, 342, 702, 1081
Busch, Adolphus—451
Bush, Barbara—16, 41, 170, 248, 783, 857
Bush, Frederick Morris—245
Bush, George—1, 16, 27, 31, 41, 68, 81, 113, 127, 161n., 170, 174, 179, 204, 213, 214, 241, 242, 248, 264n., 297, 311–313, 319, 322–324, 328, 333, 336, 371, 391, 434, 441, 442n., 482, 498, 510, 512, 574, 625–627n., 657, 682, 725, 732n., 751, 756, 783, 784, 796, 837, 848, 862, 1007n., 1047, 1055n., 1106, 1148
Butcher, Willard C.—791
Butler, Charles M., III—335
Butler, Merrill—624
Butler, Samuel—505
Butz, Earl L.—952
Byrd, Sen. Harry F., Jr.—244, 482
Byrd, Sen. Robert C.—244, 450n., 627n., 635n., 694n., 1159
Byrne, John V.—362

Cahill, Dr. Bernard R.—1108
Cahill, Kevin—1023–1025n.
Caira, Aldo—912
Calhoon, Jesse M.—702, 1030
Calio, Anthony J.—1150
Callahan, Edgar F.—802
Cambo, Roberto—1094
Camicia, Nicholas T.—1030
Campbell, Carlos C.—629
Campbell, W. Glenn—974, 976
Campbell, William—735
Cannon, Joseph A.—1176
Canzeri, Joseph W.—706ftn., 786, 906
Captain, Syd—1003
Caputo, Bruce—765
Cardenas, Michael—145
Cardin, Benjamin L.—342
Carey, James J.—796
Carl, Bernard J.—532

Carl XVI, King Gustaf—1083, 1084n.
Carleson, Robert B.—75, 343
Carlisle, Thomas—825
Carlson, Capt. William—721
Carmen, Gerald P.—176, 551
Carnegie, Andrew—883
Carr, Mrs. Isaiah—780
Carrington, Lord—636
Carruthers, Garrey Edward—305
Carter, Anderson—485
Carter, Jimmy—1, 17, 27, 85, 160, 209, 435n., 820, 880, 905, 906n., 934, 952, 1057
Carter, Rosalynn—905, 906n.
Cartier, Jacques—228
Carver, Richard E.—532
Casals, Rosie—792
Casanova, Jose Manuel—459
Casey, William J.—5, 15, 676
Casey, William Robert, Jr.—1091
Castañeda de la Rosa, Jorge—500n.
Castro, Fidel—59
Catto, Henry E., Jr.—246
Cavanaugh, James H.—85, 920
Cavaney, Red—261
Caver, Michael D.—1095
Cervantes Saavedra, Miguel de—922
Chaffee, Sen. John H.—1206
Chambers, Judith M.—1042
Chambers, Whittaker—278
Chapin, Frederic L.—619
Chapman, Bruce—622
Chapoton, John E.—96
Charles, Prince—679ftn.
Charles, Ray—19
Cheney, Repr. Richard Bruce—658
Chennault, Anna C.—349, 933
Cherne, Leo—974
Chesterton, G. K.—1185
Choo Yong Bock—69
Christian X, King—617
Christie, David—780
Christie, Robert—780
Christopher, David W.—791
Christopher, George—765
Chun Doo Hwan—66, 68
Chun Doo Hwan, Madame—66, 68
Churchill, Sir Winston—3, 168, 175, 228, 259, 432, 890, 892, 930
Cianchette, Ival—255, 256n.
Cicconi, James W.—1012
Cicero—1104
Cisneros, Henry G.—686
Clark, Allen B., Jr.—472
Clark, George—1020
Clark, Joan M.—518, 1175
Clark, Joe—235n.
Clark, Gen. Mark Wayne—1201
Clark, William—228
Clark, William P.—33, 520, 625, 728, 791
Clausen, A. W.—854, 856n.

Clausen, Repr. Don H.—1206
Clearwater, Lee—712
Cleland, Max—163
Clements, Gov. Bill—1045–1047
Clements, Rita—1045
Clohan, William C., Jr.—185
Cobb, W. Montague—573
Cogan, John F.—817
Cohan, George M.—1024
Coldiron, William H.—239
Cole-Alexander, Lenora—714, 1175
Coleman, Marshall—948, 991
Coles, James B.—624
Collins, Repr. Cardiss—250ftn.
Collins, Repr. James M.—1045
Collins, Marva Nettles—427, 577
Collins, Wayne Dale—502
Collyer, Rosemary M.—551
Colson, Janet—401
Columbus, Christopher—911–913
Conable, Repr. Barber B., Jr.—482, 483, 501, 519, 558, 566, 658, 666, 1020, 1107, 1159
Conable, Charlotte W.—1003
Concepcion, David—1060
Conder, J. Richard—342, 1107
Conkling, James B.—437
Conn, Billy—832
Conn, George A.—347
Connally, John B.—974, 1045–1048
Connally, Michael J.—599
Connally, Nellie—1045
Connor, Judith T.—141
Conover, C. T.—1043
Conte, Repr. Silvio O.—1156
Conway, Frank H.—541
Cooke, Terence Cardinal—41, 423n., 1023, 1024, 1107
Cookman, Aubrey O.—1201
Coolidge, Calvin—137, 466, 468, 685, 720, 871, 1173
Coon, Carleton S., Jr.—403
Coon, Jane Abell—472
Cooper, Dr. Donald L.—1108
Cooper, Gary—883
Cooper, John Sherman—765
Coors, Holly—21
Coors, Joseph—21, 491
Copland, Aaron—907
Corbett, Jim—548
Corcoran, Thomas—1147
Cornelius, Loretta—540, 1176
Cornelius, Samuel J.—495
Cornick, Wade—780
Cornwallis, Lord Charles—785, 963, 968
Corr, Edwin Gharst—1019
Cotton, Norris—1076, 1078
Countryman, John R.—588
Cox, Beverly—547
Cribb, T. Kenneth, Jr.—97
Crippen, Capt. Robert L.—348, 353, 393, 441, 442n.

Crippen, Mrs. Robert L.—442
Crocker, Chester A.—188, 314, 1106
Cronkite, Walter—191
Crowell, John B., Jr.—91
Cummings, Lilla Burt—514
Cummings, Theodore E.—465
Cuomo, Lt. Gov. Mario M.—761
Curran, Edward A.—701
Cutler, Walter Leon—1141

Daeley, John A.—1003
Dale, Jerome—780
Dalton, Gov. John N.—784, 963, 967, 991, 992, 1088, 1089
D'Amato, Sen. Alfonse M.—76, 244, 761, 1020
Dames & Moore—820
Damocles—450
Dana, Howard H., Jr.—1211
Darman, Richard G.—786
Dart, Justin—1030
Davenport, Lawrence F.—374
Davies, Rev. A. Powell—100
Davis, Johnny (Scat)—23
Davis, Stuart A.—533
Davis, Walter G.—1107
Davis, Willard Kenneth—263, 798
Dawson, Mary Ann Weyforth—334
Dayan, Moshe—947
Dayton, Kenneth N.—1107
de Barras, Adm.—969
de Grasse, Comte François—968, 969
de la Garza, E. (Kika)—1177
de Larosière, J.—854, 856n.
de la Vega Domínguez, Jorge—500
de Tocqueville, Alexis—161, 683, 811, 815, 883, 938
de Valera, Eamon—259
Dean, Charles H., Jr.—397
Dean, Dizzy—298
Dean, John Gunther—695
Deaver, Carolyn—822
Deaver, Michael K.—69, 371ftn., 622n., 1007n., 1030, 1046
DeBolt family—884
DeConcini, Sen. Dennis—509
Decter, Midge—427
Dederick, Robert G.—368
Deer, Ada E.—427
Delahanty, Thomas K.—310n., 337, 350, 391
Delamar, Louis—756, 757
DeLauer, Richard D.—185
del Pino, Jorge—919n.
del Real, Juan A.—362
Dempsey, Charles L.—292
DeMuth, Christopher C.—863
Denton, Sen. Jeremiah—508, 509
DeNunzio, Ralph—873
Depuy, Warner M.—1002
Derman, Donald Allan—273
Deutsch, Armand S.—491, 550
Devine, Donald J.—98, 427, 791, 925n., 1149

DeVos, Richard—511
Devroy, Ann—1199
Diana, Princess—679ftn.
DiCarlo, Dominick L.—627
Dickens, Charles—1186, 1188
Dickey, Robert, III—702
Dillon, Robert Sherwood—475
Dinkins, Carol E.—89, 782, 1175
Disney, Walt—907
Dobrynin, A. F.—194
Dodd, Sen. Christopher J.—76
Dolan, Anthony R.—1059
Dole, Elizabeth H.—678, 679n.
Dole, Sen. Robert—265, 266n., 482, 509, 540, 563, 564, 604, 626, 1159, 1177
Dole, Mrs. Robert—265
Dolibois, John E.—703
Domenici, Sen. Pete V.—152, 324, 338, 342, 390, 392, 421, 626, 832
Donaldson, Sam—526
Donlon, Sean—258, 259n.
Donlon, Mrs. Sean—258
Donnelly, Thomas R., Jr.—627
Donovan, Raymond J.—5, 10, 745, 761, 945, 947n., 1164
Dornan, Repr. Robert K.—509, 857
Dotson, Donald L.—363
Douglas, H. Eugene—997
Douglas, Priscilla Harriet—502
Douglas, Rosslee Green—271
Doyen, Ross O.—342, 763
Dozier, Brig. Gen. James—1173
Draper, William H., III—267, 1091
Duarte Fuentes, José Napoleon—192, 209, 1095, 1113
Duberstein, Kenneth M.—1122
DuBois, F. E., III—444
Duggin, Thelma—261
Duncan, John C.—161
Duncan, Virginia B.—491
Dunlop, John T.—1030
Dunnels, G. Richard—533
du Pont, Elise R. W.—375, 1091
du Pont, Henry—463
DuPont, Gov. Pierre S., IV—342, 1107
Durenberger, Sen. David—342, 1107, 1152
Durette, Wyatt—991, 992
Dusenberry, Katie G.—1003
Dwight, James S., Jr.—484
Dyess, William J.—628
Dyke, Nancy Bearg—1106
Dymally, Repr. Mervyn M.—76

Eagleburger, Lawrence S.—204
Early, Rexford C.—1201
Eastman, Penny L.—350
Eckes, Alfred E., Jr.—425
Eddy, Nelson—279
Edison, Thomas—506, 556, 564
Edwards, James B.—5, 13, 60, 833, 904, 1160
Edwards, Repr. Mickey—275
Egger, Roscoe L., Jr.—37

Einstein, Albert—447, 506
Eisenhower, Dwight D.—168, 234, 301, 435n., 463, 594, 726, 760, 889, 933, 949
Eissa, Omer Salih—505
Eklund, Coy G.—791
Ekwueme, Alex—756
el Cid—922
El Greco—922
Eliot, T. S.—277
Elizabeth II, Queen—169, 584
Ellingwood, Herbert E.—273, 1153
Elliott, Lee Ann—538
Enders, Thomas O.—374, 857
Engle, Joe Henry—1045n., 1145, 1146
Erb, Richard D.—388
Erikson, Leif—900
Evans, Clifford—384, 385, 386n.
Evans, Melvin Herbert—1017
Evered, J. Erich—387
Evron, Ephraim—505, 769n.
Ewing, Raymond C.—705
Exon, Sen. J. James—932
Ezekiel—767

Fahd, Prince. *See* Sa'ud, Fahd ibn 'Abd al-'Aziz Al
Fairbanks, Richard—50
Falwell, Jerry—76
Fatjo, Tom J., Jr.—1108
Fattah, David—884
Fattah, Falaka—884
Faulknor, William—234, 434
Feldstein, Martin—1030
Felt, W. Mark—358
Fenello, Michael J.—346
Fenwick, Millicent—248ftn.
Ferdinand V, King—918
Fernandos Campo, Gen. Sabino—919n.
Ferre, Luis A.—1107
Ferst, Jeanne H.—485
Fiedler, Repr. Bobbi—252ftn.
Fielding, Fred F.—54, 1194ftn.
Fields, Repr. Jack—1045
Filer, John H.—1107
Findley, Repr. Paul—553
Finneran, Bill—762
Fischer, Dean E.—481
Fisher, Max M.—1107
Fiske, Guy W.—608
Fitzgerald, Bill—784
Fitzgerald, Eugene—258, 259n.
Fitzsimmons, Frank—408
Flanigan, Peter M.—241
Fleming, Peter—792
Foley, Repr. Thomas S.—1177
Ford, Betty—807, 809, 810n.
Ford, Ford Barney—599
Ford, Gerald R.—435n., 578n., 807–810, 891, 892, 905, 906n., 970, 971n.
Ford, Glenn—231
Ford, Henry—506, 568, 594

Ford, Toni—389
Ford, W. Antoinette—1175
Fore, Richard L.—533
Forsberg, Franklin S.—1075
Forssell, Alan G.—925n.
Foster, John S., Jr.—975
Foster, Mary Ann—737
Fountain, Repr. L. H.—342
Fowler, John M.—38, 765
Fowler, Mark S.—240, 1044
Frank, Eugene J.—426
Franklin, Benjamin—808
Franklin, Brig. Gen. Calvin G.—1116
Frantz, Cecilia Aranda—440
Fraser, J. Malcolm—580, 583, 584
Fraser, Mrs. J. Malcolm—580, 584
Freeman, Douglas Southall—784
Friedersdorf, Max L.—419, 791, 1115
Friedersdorf, Priscilla—1115
Friedman, Milton—88, 138, 241, 276, 953, 1168
Friedman, Saul—1199n.
Frisch, Frankie—277
Fryer, Robert—491
Fuelner, Edwin J.—427
Fuller, Craig L.—787
Fuller, Mary Falvey—1159
Fulton, Robert—506, 568, 594
Funderburk, David B.—740
Funk, Sherman Maxwell—373

Gaines, L. Ebersole—542
Galbraith, Evan Griffith—924, 963
Garcia, Ernest Eugene—262
Garcia, Moises—857
Garcîa Bustillos, Gonzalo—1055n.
Gardner, John—1107
Gardner, Michael R.—1044
Garrick, Rear Adm. Robert M.—70, 921
Garrow, Gilbert—555, 560n.
Garvin, Clifton C., Jr.—1030
Gavin, John A.—328
Gayner, Jeffrey B.—1160
Geier, James A. D.—702
Geldzahler, Henry—491
Gellhorn, Walter—1142
George, W. H. Krome—161
George III, King—968
Georgine, Robert A.—306, 310n.
Gerard, Jean Broward Shevlin—880
Gergen, David R.—310, 535, 660n., 782, 1025, 1122
Gerstenzang, Jim—370
Gertz, Jack A.—1095
Getz, Bert A.—624
Giampapa, Anthony—912
Gianelli, William R.—317
Gibbon, Edward—907
Gideon, Kenneth W.—429
Giese, Warren K.—1108
Gilbert, Daniel—1107
Gilles, Kenneth Albert—345

Gilman, Benjamin A.—765
Gingrich, Repr. Newt—658
Gipp, George—431, 432, 435n., 808, 1023
Girard, Charles M.—588
Giscard d'Estaing, Valéry—810n.
Giuffrida, Louis O.—154
Giuliana, Rudolph W.—144
Glant, Douglas F.—702
Glass, Andrew J.—1199n.
Gleason, Robert R., Jr.—350
Gleason, Teddy—1023
Glenn, Sen. John—1097, 1114
Gleysteen, William, Jr.—69
Gobbi, Hugo—438, 655, 826, 1118
Godwin, Mills E., Jr.—991, 992
Goldberg, Lawrence Y.—495
Goldberg, Rube—954
Goldstein, Harvey A.—1030
Goldwater, Sen. Barry—276
Goldwater, Myra—798
Gompers, Samuel—306, 307, 748, 753, 759
Goode, Mark—569
Goodpaster, Lt. Gen. Andrew Jackson—427, 460, 462, 464n.
Goodrich, James F.—769
Goodwin, Lee—533
Gorsuch, Ann McGill—146
Gorton, John—435
Gorton, Sen. Slade—704
Gottlieb, Allan—622
Gould, Charles—78, 79n.
Goya, Francisco de—922
Grace, Peter—1030
Gradison, Repr. Willis D.—1097
Graham, Anne—417
Graham, David—584
Graham, Gov. Robert—1095
Gramm, Repr. Phil—392, 557, 563, 565
Grant, Allan—702
Grasso, Ella T.—84, 907, 910
Grasso, Dr. Thomas A.—910
Gray, Bob—18-23, 28
Gray, Edwin J.—1076
Gray, Gordon—890n.
Gray, Hanna H.—407, 491, 926, 927n.
Gray, Harry J.—791
Grayson, C. Jackson—1030
Graziano, John V.—405
Green, Alan, Jr.—383
Green, Edith—428
Green, William J.—937, 944n.
Greene, Henry F.—205
Greene, James R.—702
Greenspan, Alan—88, 241, 1157, 1159, 1168
Gregory, Darryl—780
Gross, H. R.—1039
Gubser, Charles S.—972

Habib, Philip C.—460, 504, 602, 660, 663, 767, 949
Hackett, James T.—459, 1176

Hagel, Charles Timothy—757
Haig, Alexander M., Jr.—4, 6, 18, 68, 192, 286, 311, 314, 319, 320, 352, 385, 408, 442n., 500n., 510, 520, 582n., 622n., 694n., 769n., 837, 906, 919n., 1000, 1007n., 1036, 1037, 1055n., 1066, 1106, 1148, 1209
Haig, Mrs. Patricia—906
Hailsham, Rt. Hon. Lord—965, 967
Hainkel, John J., Jr.—342
Hakola, Edith Dinneen—1044
Halbouty, Michel T.—428
Hale, Russell D.—361
Hall, Robert E.—1030
Hall, Repr. Sam B., Jr.—1046
Hallett, Carol—728
Hamill, Dorothy—1108
Hamilton, Alexander—168, 680
Hammer, Dr. Armand—877
Hammerschmidt, Repr. John Paul—509, 1206
Hampton, Lionel—778, 779
Hance, Repr. Kent—482, 483, 501, 519, 558, 566, 666
Hance, Margaret T.—342, 763
Handler, Philip—916
Handley, Frank—762
Handley, James C.—782
Hanes, Gordon—491
Hanks, Nancy—491
Hanna, Paul R.—491
Hansen, Clifford—342
Hansen, George—200
Hanzlik, Rayburn D.—551
Hardwick, Charles L.—1002
Hardy, Alan M.—849
Hardy, Dorcas R.—185, 1175
Harlow, Bryce N.—907, 909, 910
Harper, Edwin L.—288, 612, 791
Harriman, Averell—1048
Harris, Henry H.—924, 925n.
Harris, James R.—186
Harris, Jean L.—1107
Harrison, Ferd—342
Hartman, Arthur Adair—720
Harvey, Crete B.—1211
Harvey, William F.—1211
Hasan, Mansur Muhammad Mahmud—694n.
Hasenkamp, Bruce H.—428
Hashim, Elinor M.—1016
Hatfield, Sen. Mark O.—1, 16, 1123, 1156
Hauser, Richard A.—274, 1194
Hawkes, Susan—350
Hawkins, Jasper Stillwell—798
Hawkins, Sen. Paula—248ftn.
Hawkins, Robert Boone, Jr.—342, 477
Haydn, Franz Joseph—611
Hayek, Friedrich—276
Hazlitt, Henry—276
Hearth, Donald P.—925n.
Heffelfinger, William S.—247
Hefner, Repr. W. G. (Bill)—77
Heine, Heinrich—451

Heineman, Lt. Comdr. Ellen Elizabeth—502
Heinz, Sen. John—336, 1159
Heldridge, Richard W.—1124
Hellenbrand, Samuel H.—1211
Heller, Walter—1121
Helmbrecht, Richard K.—533
Helms, J. Lynn—191
Helms, Sen. Jesse A.—76, 857, 1177
Hemingway, Ernest—234
Henderson, Mary—175
Henderson, Sir Nicholas—175
Hendon, Repr. Bill—509
Henry, James S.—1107
Honry, Patrick—002
Herder, Peter D.—533
Herman, Billy—298
Herman, Woody—779n.
Hernandez, John Whitlock—146
Herrera Campíns, Luis—1053, 1059, 1067
Herrera Campíns, Mrs. Luis—1053, 1059, 1068
Herrington, John S.—406, 733
Herter, Susan C.—428
Hesburgh, Rev. Theodore M.—431, 435n.
Heston, Charlton—407, 491, 927n.
Hewitt, Frankie—281
Hickey, William E.—1201
Hiler, Repr. John P.—431, 435n.
Hill, A. Alan—335
Hill, E. V.—1107
Hill, Jimmy D.—925n.
Hillis, Repr. Elwood H.—77, 78n.
Hills, Carla Anderson—530-532
Hinckley, John W., Jr.—311n., 372, 373
Hinckley, Mr. and Mrs. John W., Sr.—373
Hineman, Kalo A.—1150
Hinojosa, Richard—428
Hinton, Deane R.—329
Hipps, George O., Jr.—925n.
Hitler, Adolf—194, 770
Hodel, Donald P.—40, 784
Hodges, Clarence Eugene—515, 1093
Hodsoll, Francis S. M.—428, 927, 928
Holdridge, John H.—188
Hollenbeck, Repr. Harold C.—509
Hollings, Sen. Ernest F. (Fritz)—152, 324, 342
Holmer, Alan F.—349
Holstine, Jon D.—356
Holt, Repr. Marjorie S.—1161
Holtzmann, Howard M.—364
Honei—770
Hooks, Benjamin—573, 576
Hoover, Tim—780
Hope, Bob—156, 174, 970, 971
Hormats, Robert D.—188, 1091
Horton, Repr. Frank—342
Horton, John P.—507
Horton, Robert Carlton—590
Hovde, Donald I.—41
Howard, Repr. James J.—1206

Hoyt, Waite—298
Huddleston, Sen. Walter D.—1177
Hudnut, William H., III—176, 179, 342
Hughes, Author E.—428
Hughes, Langston—575
Hughes, Robert John—507
Hummel, Arthur W., Jr.—512
Hunter, Harold V.—345
Hunter, Robert P.—539
Hurtado Larrea, Oswaldo—458
Hurtado, Luis Victor—623
Hussein I, King—1005, 1008, 1010
Hussey, Nora Walsh—436
Hutcheson, William L.—749ftn.

ibn Khaldun—745, 871
Ikle, Fred C.—86
Ingels, Dianne E.—624
Ingraham, Capt. Duncan Nathaniel—725
Inhofe, James—764
Ink, Dwight A.—400
Inman, Vice Adm. B.R.—36
Inouye, Sen. Daniel K.—704
Ireland, Andy—765
Isabella I, Queen—918
Isaiah—397

Jackson, James Jay—1155
Jackson, Maynard—58ftn., 204, 241, 242, 574
Jackson, Samuel C.—533
Jacovides, Andrew J.—1148
Jaeger, Andrea—792, 793
Jagielski, Mieczyslaw—294, 319
James, Forrest Hood, Jr.—764
James, Henry—925
James, John V.—702
James, Rickey Dale—806
Jantzen, Robert A.—912
Jarratt, Mary Claiborne—245, 1175
Jaruzelski, Wojciech—1187
Jaworski, Leon—975
Jay, John—681
Jeffcoat, Clyde E.—924, 925n.
Jefferson, Thomas—3, 77, 168, 594, 657, 683, 698, 749, 846, 912, 958, 964, 992, 1074, 1109
Jenkins, Frank W.—1211
Jenkins, James E.—1013
Jensen, D. Lowell—145
Jeong, Steve M.—920
Jepsen, Dee—1107
Jepsen, Sen. Roger W.—22, 932
Jepsen, Mrs. Roger W.—22
Jeremiah—396
John Paul II, Pope—423, 434, 1023, 1024, 1154
Johnson, Lyndon—784, 871, 872, 1046
Johnson, Philip F.—190
Johnson, R. Tenney—97
Johnson, Samuel—463, 650
Johnson-Evans, Lt. Comdr. Marsha A.—428
Johnston, Sen. J. Bennett—1123

Johnstone, Brig. Gen. Homer, Jr.—653
Jonas, Allan K.—323
Jones, Gen. David C.—610, 950
Jones, David R.—1017
Jones, Elizabeth—623
Jones, Gary L.—327
Jones, Repr. Walter B.—704
Jordan, Jerry L.—458
Jorgensen, Gordon—793
Joyce, Michael S.—1107
Juan Carlos I, King—918, 919
Judd, Dr. Walter H.—907–909
Juergensmeyer, John E.—1016
Jurges, Billy—298

Kamali'i, Kina'u Boyd—781
Karamanlis, Constantine—285
Karmal, Babrak—637
Karnes, David Kemp—502
Karpe, Robert W.—389
Kasim, Marwan al—1007n.
Kasongo Mutuale—1106
Kassebaum, Nancy Landon—428
Katz, Abraham—620
Kauffmann, Howard C.—161
Kavanagh, Richard E.—1017
Kavanaugh, Col. Paul F.—653
Kean, Gov. Tom—945–947n., 1021
Kean, Mrs. Tom—945
Kearns, David T.—83, 791, 1030
Keel, Alton Gold, Jr.—480
Keller, Helen—907
Kem, Brig. Gen. Richard S.—652
Kemp, Francie—1026
Kemp, Repr. Jack F.—658, 1020
Kennedy, Sen. Edward M.—76, 489, 521, 1048
Kennedy, John F.—137, 200, 211, 468, 488, 510, 559, 567, 576, 605, 627, 745, 871, 882, 890, 1047, 1082, 1084, 1099, 1109, 1121, 1186, 1190
Kennedy, Jacqueline—1194
Kennedy, Joseph—488
Kennedy, Richard T.—49, 798
Kennedy, Robert F.—488
Kennedy, Mrs. Robert F. (Ethel)—488
Kerchum, Ralph Thomas—1211
Ketelson, James L.—791
Keyes, Patricia S.—1003
Keys, Martha E.—1159
Keyworth, George A.—443
Kiernan, Edward J.—1107
Kim Kyong Won—69
Kim Yong Shik—69
Kimm, Peter M.—924, 925n.
King. *See specific name*
King, Warren Roger (Willie)—456
Kingon, Alfred H.—1030
Kipling, Rudyard—462
Kirby, Robert E.—791
Kirk, Roger—798

Kirk, Russell—276
Kirkland, Lane—1159
Kirkpatrick, Jeane J.—5, 14, 765, 906n.
Kissinger, Henry A.—889, 890n., 906n., 949
Kline, Maj. John P., Jr.—528
Knap, Ted—1199n.
Knapp, John J.—186
Knauer, Virginia H.—262
Knauss, John A.—1092
Knight, Charles F.—1030
Knouse, Mark S.—765
Koch, Edward I.—181, 342, 761
Koehler, Heidi—578n.
Kohl, Helmut—960
Koll, Donald M.—1073
Konyha, William—748, 753, 1030
Koop, C. Everett—801
Korb, Lawrence J.—316, 610, 1175
Korner, Jules G., III—1050
Korologos, Tom C.—599
Kozinski, Alex—303
Kramer, Lawrence F. (Pat)—1044
Krents, Hal—607
Kristol, Irving—428
Kuhn, Bowie—299
Kulikov, Marshal—1186
Kump, Ernest J.—491
Kusserow, Richard P.—390
Kyprianou, Spyros—1148

Lacey, James—279n.
Lacovara, Philip A.—430
Lafayette, Marquis de—967, 969
Laffer, Arthur—88, 241, 1168
Lagergren, Nina—890, 891n.
Lagomarsino, Repr. Robert J.—140
Laingen, Bruce—42, 527
Laird, Melvin R.—890n.
Lamm, Lester P.—925n.
Lamont, Frances (Peg)—1003
LaMothe, William E.—1108
Landau, Sonia—799
Lane, Laurence William, Jr.—1030
Langhorn, Garfield—578
Lantos, Repr. Tom—509, 890, 891n.
Lantos, Mrs. Tom—890, 891n.
Larkin, June Noble—491
LaSalle, Robert Cavelier Sieur de—228
Lasker, Bernard J.—1125
Latta, Repr. Delbert L. (Del)—392, 1097
Lawless, K. Gordon—702
Lawrence, Carol—23
Lawzi, Ahmad—1007n.
Laxalt, Sen. Paul—258, 341, 343, 466, 657, 682, 997n.
LeBoutillier, Repr. John—509
Ledbetter, Beverly E.—817
Lee, Rex E.—457
Lee, Dr. Sammy—428
Lee Kuan Yew—543
Leeds, Byron—1016
Lefever, Ernest W.—143, 196, 493

Lehman, John F., Jr.—32, 610, 784
Leibman, Morris I.—907, 908
Leland, Marc E.—219
Lemnitzer, Gen. Lyman L.—890n.
Lemon, Bob—297
Lent, Repr. Norman F.—1020
Leoffler, Repr. Tom—1045
Lesher, William Gene—89
Levin, Ida—1083
Levitt, Arthur, Jr.—1107
Lewis, Drew L., Jr.—5, 12, 208, 551, 682, 688–690, 704, 761, 929, 930, 937, 944n., 1107, 1114, 1207
Lewis, John L.—720, 753
Lewis, Meriweather—228
Lewis, Samuel—769n.
Lho Shin Yong—69
Lias, Thomas L.—334
Lichenstein, Charles M.—71, 765
Liddicott, Marilyn D.—1018
Lide, Vinton DeVane—425
Lilley, Robert D.—1107
Lincoln, Abraham—3, 77, 78, 95, 162, 606, 1099
Lindbergh, Charles A.—568, 594
Lindeman, Sen. Ann—342
Lindquist, Warren T.—318
Linkletter, Art—231
Linowitz, Sol—906n.
Lipp, Eugene V.—1105
Lippmann, Walter—938
Lippold, Rear Adm. Herbert Rudolph, Jr.—514, 1075
Little, Rich—18, 38
Lladó, José—912, 919n.
Lloyd, Chris Evert—792
Lloyd, Kent—351
Lobb, R. Kenneth—925n.
Locigno, Paul R.—1095
Locke, Allen W.—39
Locke, John—168, 1025
Lodwick, Seeley G.—74, 1180
Loeb, John Langeloth, Jr.—618
Long, Sen. Russell B.—197
Longstreth, Bevis—542
Lopez, Sgt. James M.—41, 42, 724, 804
López Portillo, José—202, 493, 497, 511, 676, 810, 982n.
Lord, Charles E.—444
Lott, Repr. Trent—482, 658
Louis, Joe—351, 510, 548, 594, 832
Louis, Mrs. Joe—351n.
Louis, John J., Jr.—296
Lovelace, Alan M.—441, 442
Lovell, Malcolm R., Jr.—739
Lozano, Diana—261
Lucas, Henry, Jr.—485, 1107
Luce, Claire Boothe—975
Luce, Gordon C.—534
Luers, William H.—857, 1055n.

Lugar, Sen. Richard G.—431, 435n.
Lukens, Donald E.—702
Lumiansky, Robert M.—491
Luttgens, Leslie L.—1107
Lyet, J. Paul—702, 933
Lyman, Richard W.—1107
Lyng, Richard E.—34
Lynn, James T.—88, 241, 428
Lyon, James E.—624
Lyons, Charleton—847
Lyons, John W.—925n.

MacArthur, Gen. Douglas—66, 68, 464, 745, 775
MacArthur, Mrs. Douglas—775
MacAvoy, Paul—1030
MacCallum, Donald Kenneth—1027
MacDonald, Angus—491
MacDonald, David R.—274
Mackenzie, Sir Alexander—228
Macmillan, Harold—168
MacNaughton, Donald S.—1030
Madden, Wales H., Jr.—702
Madison, Dolley—1074
Madison, James—680, 992, 998, 1074
Maduro, Reynaldo Philip—987
Maeder, Richard—784
Maier, Cornell C.—161, 1107
Majali, 'Abd al-Hadi 'Atallah al—1007n.
Malek, Frederic V.—572
Malik, Charles—845
Malone, James L.—92
Manafort, Paul J., Jr.—422
Mann, Maurice—534
Mares, Jan W.—437
Mark, Hans M.—380
Marsh, John O., Jr.—31, 461, 610, 784
Marshall, Ernest T.—1093
Marshall, John—802
Marston, Linda Z.—1003
Marti, José—827
Martin, Repr. David O'B.—1038
Martin, Edwin M.—857
Martin, Lynn—745
Martin, Preston—534
Martinez, Samuel R.—357
Marx, Karl—1197
Massey, Charles L.—1150n.
Massey, Raymond—231
Matheson, Gov. Scott M.—342, 1206
Mathiasen, David G.—925n.
Mathison, Robert V.—534
Matlock, Jack F.—669
Maupin, Armistead Jones—1201
May, Stephen—203
Mayer, Martin P.—534
Mayer, William E.—420
Mayo, Virginia—906
McAvoy, James F.—426
McBride, Thomas F.—292, 612n.
McCabe, Edward A.—1042
McCann, William Edward—258, 259

McCarthy, Timothy J.—310n., 312n., 337, 350, 391
McClain, Hugh—1069, 1070
McClory, Repr. Robert—745
McCloskey, Repr. Paul N., Jr.—704
McConnell, Robert A.—402
McCoy, Janet J.—1005
McCoy, Peter—1014
McCoy, Tidal W.—356
McCracken, Paul W.—88, 241, 1168
McDade, Repr. Joseph M.—929–931n.
McDonald, Danny Lee—1071
McDonald, John C.—1201
McEnroe, John—792
McEwen, Repr. Bob—1097
McEwen, Robert C.—903
McFarlane, Robert C.—51
McFeatters, Ann—76, 77
McGillicuddy, John F.—791
McGrath, J. Paul—653
McGuffin, Harold A.—925n.
McGuire, Robert—844
McGuire, Tom—762
McHenry, W. Barnabas—407, 491
McKean, John R.—1008
McKenna, William F.—530, 531
McKerrow, Mr. and Mrs. Alan—611
McKerrow, Amanda—611
McKinley, John K.—791
McKinnon, Clinton Dan—734
McLaughlin, Ann Dore—369
McMahon, Ed—20
McMillan, C. W.—52
McMurran, Lewis—784, 964
McNamar, R. T.—33
McNamara, Francis Terry—1001
McNamara, Robert S.—890n.
McPherson, M. Peter—51, 691, 692n.
Mead, Dana G.—428
Meads, Donald E.—937, 944n.
Mecum, Dudly C., II—702
Medas, James M.—349
Meese, Edwin, III—68, 342, 384, 610, 691, 948, 1007n., 1026, 1043, 1106
Meese, Ursula—823
Mehle, Roger W., Jr.—189
Mehta, Nancy—491
Meister, Irene W.—702
Melady, Thomas Patrick—348
Mellon, Andrew William—871
Mennotti, David E.—925
Menzies, Sir Robert—581
Metkovitch, George—297
Mettler, Ruben F.—791, 1030
Meyer, Gen. Edward C.—460, 464n., 906n.
Meyer, Frank—276
Michel, Repr. Robert H.—253, 257, 337, 343, 450n., 482, 601, 603, 635n., 658, 694n., 745, 1156, 1159
Michener, James—156, 430, 724

Middendorf, J. William, II—247
Milione, E. Victor—1160
Mill, John Stuart—155, 168
Miller, Repr. Clarence—1097
Miller, Daniel N.—332
Miller, David Charles, Jr.—829
Miller, Edward S.—358
Miller, George E.—1003
Miller, James C., III—570, 1044
Miller, Loye W.—1199
Miller, Nathan—991, 992
Mills, Stephanie—779n.
Milstein, Seymour—161
Milton, John—445
Minor, W. Ernst—427
Mitchell, Arthur—170, 491
Mitchell, Repr. Donald J.—932
Mitterrand, François—418, 640, 757, 962–967
Mitterrand, Mrs. François—963–965, 967
Mobutu Sese Seko, Lt. Gen.—1106
Moffett, Kenneth E.—1152
Moi, Daniel T. arap—837
Molinari, Repr. Guy A.—244
Mondale, Walter F.—1, 27, 813
Monks, Robert A. G.—416
Monroig, Antonio—301
Monson, Thomas S.—816ftn., 1107
Montessori, Marie—1048
Montgomery, Repr. G. V. (Sonny)—961
Monticciolo, Joseph D.—1003
Moody, Tom—342
Moomaw, Rev. Donn D.—1, 4n., 1108
Moore, James P., Jr.—1073
Moorer, Adm. Thomas H.—890n., 975
Morales, Diane K.—782
Moreno, Rita—428
Morgan, Col. Ernest Roland—1117
Morgan, Robert L.—925n.
Morris, Jay Fleron—331
Morris, William H., Jr.—142, 1057
Mosbacher, Robert A., Jr.—182, 1107
Moscoso, Teodoro—857
Moses—770
Mosk, Richard M.—364
Mossinghoff, Gerald J.—273
Mother Teresa—481
Motley, Langhorne A.—777
Moynihan, Sen. Daniel P.—761, 1159
Mozart, Wolfgang Amadeus—611
Mugabe, Robert—325, 326, 598, 1014, 1015, 1172
Mulberry, Richard—474
Muldoon, Robert D.—659
Muratti, Lt. Col. Jose A.—1145, 1146
Murphy, Betty Southard—791
Murphy, Franklin D.—491, 1107
Murphy, George—1165
Murphy, Richard—670
Murphy, William—342
Murray, Anthony H., Jr.—458
Murray, Phillip—720, 753

Muskie, Edmund S.—27
Musso, George—548
Muth, Richard F.—535
Muths, Thomas B.—550
Muzorewa, Bishop Abel—1171
Myers, Repr. John T.—1123

Nagao, Genichi (Gary)—555, 560n.
Nalen, Craig A.—321, 1091
Nance, James W.—1106
Nast, Thomas—451
Naylor, Frank Wesley, Jr.—303, 1180
Negroponte, John Dimitri—857
Nelson, Alan C.—1055
Nelson, James R.—595
Nesen, Robert Dean—363
Nestande, Bruce—342
Neumann, Robert Gerhard—366
Nowlin, Michael H.—718
Newman, Jerald Conway—1016
Newton, Wayne—19, 1108
Nichols, Repr. Bill—932
Niemeyer, Gerhart—1160
Nimmo, Robert P.—399
Niskanen, William A., Jr.—302
Nixon, Richard M.—905, 906n., 1063
Nkomo, Joshua—1172
Noble, Edward E.—322
Nofziger, James C.—1027
Noor, Queen—1008, 1009
Norris, William C.—1107
Novak, Michael—845
Novick, Matthew N.—654
Nunn, Sen. Sam—997n.
Nyborg, Keith Foote—619

Oakley, Robert B.—1106
Obenshain, Helen—991
Oblinger, Josephine K.—1003
O'Brien, Chuck—607
O'Brien, Edward—873
O'Brien, Hugh—23
O'Brien, Pat—431, 432, 1023, 1024
O'Connor, K. William—404
O'Connor, Sandra Day—596, 597, 601, 811, 819, 901, 1174
Odle, Robert C., Jr.—220, 1175
O'Doherty, Kieran —319
O'Donnell, John J.—1030
O'Donnell, Peter, Jr.—975
O'Donnell, Terrence—1126
Oglesby, M. B., Jr.—1153
O'Green, Frederick W.—791
O'Kelley, Harold E.—886
O'Leary, Dr. Dennis—311
O'Leary, Gratin—228
Oliver, Daniel—239
Olmer, Lionel H.—95, 1091
Olmstead, Gen. George—294
Olson, Theodore Bevry—144
Olson, William J.—1211

O'Neill, Eugene—1024
O'Neill, Paul H.—1030
O'Neill, Repr. Thomas P., Jr.—1, 5, 16, 25n., 26n., 76, 115n., 161n., 223n., 258, 264n., 391, 394, 439n., 450n., 526, 545, 549, 635n., 650, 656n., 661, 676, 694n., 725, 732n., 826n., 835, 954, 1097, 1098, 1102, 1118n., 1157, 1159, 1205
O'Neill, Mrs. Thomas P., Jr.—281
Opel, John R.—791
Orr, Gov. Robert D.—431, 435n.
Orr, Roy—342
Orr, Verne—32, 610, 784
Ortiz, Frank V., Jr.—739
Osborne, Kathleen—789
O'Shea, Michael—906, 907
O'Toole, Dennis—547
Otter, William M.—497
Owens, Jessie—907

Pace, Frank, Jr.—1107
Pachter, Marc—547
Packard, David—491
Packwood, Sen. Bob—336, 704
Paganelli, Robert P.—669
Pahlavi, Mohammad Reza—952
Paige, Roderick R.—1095
Paine, Thomas—836, 969, 970
Paisley, Melvyn R.—985
Palladino, Nunzio J.—428
Palmer, B. J.—1038
Palmer, Ronald DeWayne—438
Palmer, Stephen E., Jr.—1056
Paras, George E.—1211
Parris, Repr. Stan—658, 1161
Parsky, Gerald L.—1030
Patton, Gen. George S., Jr.—462, 745
Pauken, Thomas Weir—73, 1028, 1108, 1152
Paul, Repr. Ron—1045
Peachee, Judy F.—86, 349, 902, 1174
Peary, Rear Adm. Robert Edwin—476
Peck, Dallas Lynn—497
Peck, Raymond A., Jr.—53
Pell, Sen. Claiborne—906n.
Pendleton, Clarence M., Jr.—1052
Pepper, Repr. Claude D.—1101, 1159
Percy, Sen. Charles H.—326, 439n., 598n., 600, 656n., 826n., 906n., 1015n., 1118n., 1172n.
Perez-Chiriboga, Marcial—1055n.
Pérez Llorca, José Pedro—918, 919n.
Perkins, John H.—1030
Perle, Richard N.—537, 1056
Perot, H. Ross—975
Perrault, Raymond J.—225, 231
Peterson, Joel—780
Peterson, Martha—428
Petrignani, Renaldo—912
Philbin, Edward J.—485
Phillips, Duncan—822
Phillips, Susan Meredith—758
Pickering, Thomas R.—805

Pickford, Mary—231
Pidgeon, Walter—231
Pierce, Samuel R., Jr.—5, 11, 343, 530, 551, 752, 761
Pierpoint, Robert C.—384–386n.
Pillsbury, Edmund—491
Pinard, Yvon—225, 231
Pius XII, Pope—396, 461, 887
Pizzano, Winifred Ann—327, 1175
Plowden, William Coskrey, Jr.—972
Poli, Robert—688
Pompa, Gilbert G.—1116
Ponder, Jacqueline A.—1073
Pontius Pilate—423
Pope. *See specific name*
Pope, Donna—369
Porter, Repr. John E.—745
Porter, Roger B.—1030
Poundstone, Freda J.—1201
Powell, Lewis—845
Pratt, Edmund T., Jr.—702
Pratt, Richard T.—260
Preeg, Ernest Henry—455
Prem Tinsulanonda, Gen.—897
Price, Charles H., II—470
Pride, Charlie—779n.
Prince. *See specific name*
Princess. *See specific name*
Pulaski, Gen. Casimir—887

Qadhafi, Col. Mu'ammar—191, 195, 722, 723, 729, 736, 917, 1124, 1144, 1164
Quayle, Sen. Dan—431, 435n.
Queen. *See specific name*
Quello, James Henry—492
Quetzalcoatl—498
Quigg, Donald James—757
Quinn, William F.—846n.

Rabb, Maxwell M.—471
Rahman, Ziaur—473
Railsback, Repr. Tom—745
Rall, Frederick T., Jr.—925n.
Rank, Everett George, Jr.—623
Rashish, Myer—69, 187
Ray, Edward W.—988
Ray, Gov. Robert D.—162
Read, Maj. Gen. William E.—652
Reagan, Cameron Michael—1173
Reagan, Maureen—713
Reagan, Nancy—16, 19, 20, 41, 43, 66, 68, 71, 76, 140, 168, 174, 224, 229n., 243, 254, 280, 294, 295, 385, 423, 431, 446, 448, 460, 580, 601, 685, 712, 713, 737, 778, 783, 792, 810, 822, 823, 825, 827, 828, 861, 872, 898, 901, 906n., 925, 927, 950, 965, 970, 1000n., 1025, 1026, 1060, 1074, 1082, 1087, 1098, 1194
Reagan, Neil—219
Reed, John Hathaway—1073
Reed, Joseph Verner, Jr.—754

Reed, Vincent E.—240
Reeher, Kenneth R.—1018
Regan, Donald T.—4, 6, 27, 55, 88, 132, 138,
    258ftn., 319, 343, 358n., 466, 472, 482, 483,
    551, 625, 651, 660, 662, 676, 692, 791, 801,
    820, 892, 896, 897, 1034, 1076, 1112
Regula, Repr. Ralph—1097
Reich, Alan—83
Reich, Otto J.—1155
Reister, Ruth A.—1180
Renfrew, Charles B.—58ftn.
Revere, Paul—809
Reynolds, David P.—161
Reynolds, Dean—526
Reynolds, Nancy Clark—428, 755
Reynolds, William Bradford—470
Rhee, Syngman—66
Rhoads, Dean—342
Rhodes, J. Steven—350
Rhodes, Gov. James A.—1099n.
Ricardo-Campbell, Rita—631
Ricci, Mary Elisabeth Lupo—502
Rice, Joseph—1110
Richards, Carol—76
Richards, James R.—424
Richards, Richard—336, 510
Richardson, Elliot L.—890n.
Richardson, Warren S.—304
Richmond, Marvin—793
Rickey, Branch—548
Riessen, Marty—792
Riles, Wilson—577
Riley, Joseph P., Jr.—764
Ritter, Father Bruce—885
Rivera, Henry M.—492
Rivlin, Alice—835, 1170
Roberts, James C.—428
Roberts, Paul Craig—64
Roberts, Thomas Morgan—495, 798
Robinson, Davis R.—491
Robinson, Gilbert A.—407
Robinson, Maj. Gen. Hugh G.—652
Robinson, Jackie—548
Robinson, Paul Heron, Jr.—487
Roch, Donald E.—1042
Rochambeau, Comte de Jean Baptiste—964,
    969
Roche, George C.—491
Rockefeller, David—161, 791
Rockefeller, John Davison—883
Rockne, Knute—431, 432, 435n., 1023
Roderick, David M.—791
Rodgers, Joe M.—336, 337, 975
Rodino, Repr. Peter W., Jr.—819n.
Rodriguez, Carmen Maria Hernandez—780
Rodriguez, John H.—331
Roe, Repr. Robert A.—1206
Roebling, Johann Augustus—449
Rogers, John F. W.—270
Rogers, Will—510, 557, 566
Rogers, William P.—890n.

Rolandis, Nikos A.—1148
Roldós Aguilera, Jaime—458
Roldós Aguilera, Mrs. Jaime—458
Rollins, Edward J., Jr.—1040
Romney, George—1108, 1152
Roosevelt, Eleanor—720
Roosevelt, Franklin D.—168, 194, 307, 435n.,
    446, 640, 681, 720, 753, 762, 776, 883, 1173
Roosevelt, James—791, 1150n.
Roosevelt, Theodore—393, 397, 750, 841, 945
Rose, Jonathan C.—395
Rosebush, James S.—790, 816, 817n.
Roser, Herman E.—386
Rostenkowski, Repr. Dan—472, 604
Rostow, Eugene V.—377
Rostow, Walt W.—890n.
Roth, Sen. William V., Jr.—342, 482, 613
Rourke, Russell A.—246
Rouse, James W.—1108
Roussel, Peter—537, 788, 948
Rowland, Robert A.—445
Rowny, Edward L.—398
Rubin, Robert J.—387
Rudd, Glenn Allan—925n.
Ruddy, Francis Stephen—398
Ruge, Dr. Daniel—312
Rule, Elton—1038, 1039n.
Rumsfeld, Donald—890n.
Ruppe, Loret M.—99
Russell, Edna Bonn (Bonny)—1003
Ruth, Babe—594
Ryan, Brock Vincent—578
Ryan, T. Timothy, Jr.—90, 1044

Sadat, Anwar el-—692, 698, 700, 868, 898,
    902, 905, 943, 949
Sadat, Mrs. Anwar el- (Jihan)—254, 692, 698,
    898
Saginor, Dr. Mark Lee—1108
Sakharov, Andrei—402, 1142
Sakharov, Mrs. Andrei—1142
Salcido, José—884
Salk, Dr. Jonas E.—907
Salman, Carlos—818
Salzman, Richard Stephen—456
Sandburg, Carl—394, 606, 907
Sanderson, James W.—1201
Sandstrom, Marc—1211
Sanjuan, Pedro A.—590
Santa Claus—451
Santarelli, Donald Eugene—487, 629
Sarah—770
Sato, Frank S.—293
Sattar, Abdus—473
Satterfield, David E., III—1211
Sa'ud, Fahd ibn 'Abd al-'Aziz Al—949, 987,
    996
Savage, Repr. Gus—76
Savas, Emanuel S.—147
Sawyer, Danford L.—389
Sawyer, George A.—436

Saxon, Philip—702
Sayler, Henry B.—1126
Scaife, Richard Mellon—491
Scanlon, Dr. Edward F.—323
Scarboro, W. Proctor—988
Schabarum, Peter F.—764
Schacht, Henry B.—702
Schafer, M. Virginia—734
Schaffner, Franklin—491
Schafran, George Peter—798
Schatz, Lee—527
Scheid, Vernon E.—1092
Scherer, Comdr. Don—724
Schleede, Glenn R.—782
Schlesinger, James R.—890n.
Schlichter, Sumner—419
Schmidt, Helmut—448, 451-453, 639, 641
Schmidt, Mrs. Helmut—448, 451, 453
Schmidt, Wilson E.—516
Schmults, Edward C.—34, 1044
Schoenberg, Carolyn D.—1176
Schreyer, Edward R.—224, 226, 237
Schroeder, Victor—416
Schubert, Richard F.—1030
Schultz, George—1168
Schulze, Repr. Richard T.—342
Schurr, Maurice R.—1030
Schweiker, Richard S.—5, 11, 343, 450, 466,
   1047, 1072, 1081, 1100, 1104n., 1118
Scott, David C.—702
Scowcroft, Brent—890n.
Sculley, Jay Raymond—863
Seabury, Paul—975
Seaga, Edward Philip George—45-47, 59,
   161, 764, 1090, 1095
Seaga, Mrs. Edward Philip George—45, 46
Searby, Robert W.—1027
Searle, Rodney N.—758
Seibert, Donald V.—1030
Seidman, L. William—1030
Seko, Toshihiko—409
Semionov, Aleksei—1142
Senese, Donald J.—326, 912
Serkin, Rudolph—1083
Serra, Father Junipero—918
Sethness, Mrs. Charles H., Jr.—970, 971n.
Shad, John S. R.—154
Shah of Iran. *See* Pahlavi, Mohammad Reza
Shaker, Lt. Gen. Sharif Zaid Bin—1007n.
Shakespeare, Frank—569
Shamir, Yitzhak—769n.
Sharaf, Al-Sharif Fawaz—505
Shattuck, Cathie A.—1146
Shear, Harold Edson—778
Sheardown, Mr. and Mrs. John—527
Shearer, Hugh Lawson—45ftn.
Shelby, Richard D.—1042
Sheldon, Georgiana—359
Shelley, Percy Bysshe—409
Sherick, Joseph H.—925n.
Sherman, William Courtney—685, 765

Shields, Perry—1050
Shin Byong Hyun—69
Shipley, Stephen P.—781
Shore, Benjamin—1199n.
Shriver, Pam—792, 793
Shull, Capt. Thomas Counter—502
Shultz, George P.—88, 241
Shuman, Charles Wilson—485
Sickon, Joseph A.—405
Siegan, Bernard H.—535
Sigler, Andrew C.—1108
Sills, Beverly—491
Silverstein, Leonard—491
Silvia, Queen—1084n.
Simmons, J. J., III—1174
Simon, William E.—88, 241, 1030
Simpkins, Irby Clifford, Jr.—1042
Simpson, Sen. Alan K.—961
Singer, S. Fred—1092
Sirikit, Queen—898
Six, Robert F.—975
Skouras, Spyros S.—791
Slack, Donna Lee—780
Slatkin, Leonard—611
Slaughter, John—615
Slease, Clyde H.—1125
Sloane, Howard G.—702
Small, Karna—788, 947ftn., 1122n.
Smith, Adam—168
Smith, Bernard E., Jr.—1125
Smith, Donald L.—342
Smith, Gladys—231
Smith, Harold—745
Smith, Ian—1171
Smith, Jean—428
Smith, Kenneth L.—304
Smith, Kenneth M.—1094
Smith, Linda L.—1176
Smith, Loren A.—267
Smith, Mary Louise—1052
Smith, Michael B.—275
Smith, Otis M.—1142
Smith, Richard G.—925n.
Smith, Robert I.—491
Smith, Dr. Robert N.—562
Smith, Roger B.—1030
Smith, Stan—792
Smith, William French—4, 8, 140, 328, 329n.,
   333, 500, 513, 520, 574, 596, 597, 625, 676,
   677, 687, 688, 690, 779, 780, 793, 914, 1203
Smith, William L.—925n.
Smith, William R.—329n.
Smith, Zane G., Jr.—239
Smittcamp, Earl S.—1042
Smoley, Sandra—218, 342
Snelling, Gov. Richard A.—342
Snyder, Repr. Gene—704
Solomon—446
Solomon, Repr. Gerald B. H.—1020
Son of Sam. *See* Berkowitz, David

Sophia, Queen—918–920, 922
Sorzano, Jose S.—406, 765
Sousa, Anthony G.—418
Sowell, Thomas—88, 241
Sowle, Donald E.—268
Spadolini, Giovanni—644
Spain, Jayne Baker—1030
Spasowski, Romuald—1177, 1187
Speakes, Larry M.—314, 344, 382, 460, 472,
    493, 504, 513n., 536, 660n., 712, 740n.,
    756n., 757n., 990, 1025, 1114, 1124, 1195,
    1196
Spencer, Lady Diana Frances. *See* Diana,
    Princess
Spencer, John R.—1003
Spencer, Stu—727
Spiers, Ronald I.—685
Spinkel, Beryl W.—52
Staar, Richard F.—777
Staats, Elmer B.—612
Stack, Edward W.—299
Stack, Robert—20
Stadtman, Earl R.—925n.
Stafford, Sen. Robert T.—1206
Stake, William F.—1180
Stans, Maurice H.—1141
Stansberry, Don C., Jr.—1180
Stanton, Wayne A.—1003
Starr, Kenneth—58ftn.
Statler Brothers—827
Staubach, Roger—1108
Stearns, James G.—397
Stearns, Monteagle—592
Steffens, Lincoln—613
Steiger, William A.—200
Stein, Herbert—88, 241
Steinway, Heinrich—451
Stella, Frank D.—912, 976
Steorts, Nancy H.—614
Sterne, Joe—947ftn.
Sterrett, Malcolm M. B.—516
Stevens, Roger—491
Stevens, Sen. Ted—626, 1071
Stevenson, Robert Louis—580
Stewart, James K.—502
Stewart, Potter—538, 539n., 596, 601
Stewart, Mrs. Potter—538
Stivers, Repr. T. W. (Tom)—342
Stockdale, Vice Adm. James B.—427, 502
Stockman, David A.—5, 15, 30, 60, 133, 138,
    221, 343, 384, 510, 545, 610, 691, 738, 763,
    783n., 792, 801, 892–894, 897, 914, 1039,
    1043
Stoessel, Walter J., Jr.—49, 527, 528n.
Stout, Kenneth O.—1095
Strand, Curt R.—161
Straus, Ellen Sulzberger—1108
Strauss, Levi—451
Strauss, Robert S.—428
Strausz-Hupé, Robert—543
Street, Anthony A.—582n.

Stuart, John—488
Stubbs, Robert Sherwood, II—1211
Studdert, Stephen M.—74
Subía Martínez, Maj. Gen. Marco—458
Subía Martínez, Mrs. Marco—458
Sullivan, John L.—548, 1024
Sullivan, Leon—1108
Sun Tzu—461
Suzuki, Zenko—409, 411, 413, 414, 643
Suzuki, Mrs. Zenko—409, 411, 414
Svahn, John A.—190
Swaebe, Geoffrey—900
Swain, Frank S.—486
Swearingen, John—491
Sweeney, Maj. Howard Patrick—502
Sweeney, Peter—391, 574
Swinburn, Charles—765
Swing, William Lacy—587
Swoap, David S.—73

Tacha, Deanell Reece—428
Taft, William Howard, IV—101
Tardy, Judith L.—332, 1175
Taylor, Elizabeth—22
Taylor, Kenneth—234, 527
Taylor, Gen. Maxwell D.—890n.
Taylor, Reese H., Jr.—403
Teele, Arthur E., Jr.—203, 765
Tekere, Sec. Gen. Edgar—326, 1014, 1171
Tennyson, Alfred Lord—488
Teresa, Mother—481
Terra, Daniel J.—92, 407, 491, 927n.
Thatcher, Carol—168, 170, 175
Thatcher, Dennis—168, 170, 175
Thatcher, Margaret—153, 164, 165, 168, 170,
    172, 174, 197, 198, 277, 642
Theberge, James Daniel—1016
Thomas, Clarence—400
Thomas, Edwin W., Jr.—55
Thomas, George Lee—502
Thomas, Gerald E.—1104
Thomas, Helen—76, 370
Thomas, Henry E., IV—562
Thomas, James B., Jr.—293
Thomas, Lee M.—562
Thomas, Tommy—511
Thomas, W. Dennis—40
Thompson, Bobby Jack—989
Thompson, Derrell P.—1003
Thompson, Gov. James R., Jr.—342, 600, 603,
    745, 747
Thompson, Robert E.—1199n.
Thompson, V. M., Jr.—417
Thone, Charles—702
Thorn, Gaston—625, 645
Thornburgh, Gov. Richard L.—937, 944n.
Thornton, Charles B. (Tex), Jr.—907
Thurmond, Sen. Strom—25n., 26n., 450n.,
    626, 627n., 818n., 906n.
Thygerson, Kenneth J.—535
Todhunter, John A.—588

Todman, Terence A.—919n.
Tolliver, Lennie-Marie P.—457
Tomlinson, Kenneth Y.—155
Tomseth, Victor—527
Totten, Donald L.—635, 745
Towe, Peter M.—527, 528n., 622n.
Tower, Sen. John—625, 627n., 997n.
Towery, R. Kenneth—799
Treen, Gov. David C.—839, 847, 849, 1088, 1089
Trent, Darrell M.—5, 765
Treptow, Martin—4
Tribble, Joseph J.—272
Triplett, Arlene—141, 1175
Trivelpiece, Alvin W.—496
Trowbridge, Alexander B.—1108, 1159
Trudeau, Pierre Elliott—210, 225, 228, 229, 235, 620, 637–646, 810n., 935, 982n.
Truly, Capt. Richard H.—1045n., 1146
Truman, Harry S—168, 839, 872, 945, 950, 1167, 1173
Truman, Margaret—1194
Tubman, Harriet—575
Tufts, Jean—346, 1175
Ture, Norman B.—36
Turkmen, Ilter—322
Turnage, Maj. Gen. Thomas K.—591, 610
Turner, Tom, Sr.—886
Tuttle, Holmes—737
Twain, Mark—384, 510, 584
Tyroler, Charles, II—976

Ullman, Myron Edward, III—502
Unger, Sherman E.—270
Updike, John—927
Urbina, Ricardo M.—205
Ursomarso, Frank A.—296
Urstadt, Charles J.—535
Ushewokunze, Herbert—1172

Valis, Wayne H.—262
van Agt, Andreas A. M.—313
Van de Water, John R.—539
Vander Jagt, Repr. Guy—336, 337
Vander Myde, Paul A.—184
Vaughan, William Addison—515
Veliotes, Nicholas A.—189
Verity, C. William, Jr. (Bill)—885, 894, 926, 1107, 1108, 1110, 1152
Verstandig, Lee L.—53, 765
Vest, George Southall—694
Viets, Richard Noyes—487, 1007
Villanueva, Danny—306
Villella, Fred Joseph—318
Viola, Roberto—264
Volcker, Paul—61
Volpe, John—913
von Braun, Werner—451
von Damm, Helene A.—787, 791
von Dardel, Guy—890, 891n.
von Gierke, Henning E. G.—925n.
von Mises, Ludwig—276

von Steuben, Baron Friedrich—448
Wachtmeister, Wilhelm—891n.
Wachtmeister, Mrs. Wilhelm—891n.
Waggonner, Joe D., Jr.—1159
Wagner, Richard L., Jr.—589
Wagner, Richard T.—1150
Waldheim, Kurt—656, 826
Waldmann, Raymond J.—142
Walesa, Lech—1186
Walker, Charls E.—88, 241
Walker, Howard Kent—849
Walker, John M., Jr.—422
Walker, Julius Waring, Jr.—572
Walker, June Grace—791
Walker, Richard L.—571
Walker, Ronald H.—1108
Wall, Shannon J.—428
Wallenberg, Raoul—890
Wallison, Peter J.—424
Walsh, William B.—791
Walters, Harry N.—435
Walters, Vernon A.—482
Walton, Reggie Barnett—456
Walts, Lew—1069, 1070n.
Wampler, William C.—1177
Ward, C. D.—342
Warner, Sen. John W.—22, 991, 994, 997n.
Warner, Rawleigh, Jr.—491
Warren, Joseph—3
Warren, Robert C.—702
Washington, George—3, 259, 461, 463, 476, 719, 785, 968, 1024
Watkins, Adm. James D.—723
Watson, William C., Jr.—925n.
Watt, James G.—4, 9, 217, 302, 343, 711, 736, 761, 784, 810, 970
Wattenberg, Ben J.—569
Weaver, Walter D.—445
Weber, Arnold R.—1030
Weber, Repr. Ed—1097
Webster, Daniel—802
Webster, Noah—971
Webster, William H.—288, 779, 843
Weeden, Robert B.—1027
Weicker, Lowell—76
Weidenbaum, Murray L.—35, 94, 133, 137, 138, 610
Weidenfeld, Edward L.—1044
Weil, Leon J.—1108
Weinberger, Caspar W.—4, 7, 68, 156, 158n., 180, 213, 309, 464, 610, 738, 763, 775ftn., 783n., 784, 833, 837, 839, 870, 878–880, 906n., 1035, 1106
Weiss, Seymour—975
Wells, Barbie—552ftn.
Welsch, Joseph P.—368, 612n.
Werblin, David A. (Sonny)—1109
Wertheim, Ronald P.—960
West, Francis J.—271
West, J. Robinson—511, 1175

West, Robert V., Jr.—886
Wettering, Fred—1106
Wheeler, Maj. Gen. Edwin Bliss—1201
Whetstone, Frank A.—260
Whitaker, Meade—1050
White, Col. Edward—463
White, F. Clifton—342
White, William S.—1108
Whitehead, John C.—791
Whitman, Marina v. N.—791
Whitman, Walt—919
Whitney, Eli—506
Whittier, John Greenleaf—441
Whittlesey, Faith Ryan—755
Wick, Charles Z.—18-23, 28, 213
Wick, Mary Jane—21, 22, 23, 29
Wiggins, Vernon R.—589
Wilcox, Harvey J.—925n.
Wilkey, Malcolm R.—364
Wilkins, C. Howard—417
Wilkins, Roy—766
Wilkinson, Bud—846
Williams, Edward Bennett—975
Williams, Walter C.—925n.
Williamson, Richard S.—88, 147, 213, 216, 343, 1044, 1080ftn.
Wilson, Betty—300, 301
Wilson, Margaret Bush—428, 573, 577
Wilson, Rufus H.—163n.
Wilson, William A.—93
Wilson, Woodrow—182, 552
Winger, Jeri J.—1108
Winn, Philip D.—90
Winthrop, John—938
Wolf, Repr. Frank R.—1161
Wonder, Stevie—906n.

Wood, Mary Anne O.—502
Wood, Robert E.—463
Woodruff, Arthur H.—329
Worthington, Robert Melvin—355
Wright, Repr. Jim—450n., 906n., 1085ftn.
Wright, Joseph F., Jr.—52
Wright, Lawrence A.—1201
Wright, Orville—568, 594, 1154
Wright, Wilbur—568, 594, 1154
Wriston, Walter B.—88, 241
Wu, Julia—1016
Wulsin, Lucien—491
Wunder, Bernard J., Jr.—386
Wyman, Thomas H.—1108
Wyszynski, Stefan Cardinal—469

Yeend, Sir Geoffrey—582n.
Yellis, Ken—547
Yoka Mangono—1106
Yonge, James E.—600
Young, A. Thomas—925n.
Young, Comdr. John W.—348, 353n., 393, 441, 442n.
Young, Mrs. John W.—442

Zablocki, Repr. Clement J.—326, 598n., 906n., 1015n., 1172n.
Zacharia, Michael Esa—502
Zachry, H. B., Jr.—886
Zambrano Velasco, José Alberto—1055n.
Zeder, Fred M., II—1105
Zenzie, Henry—702
Zia, Begum—473
Zook, Jan—555, 560n.
Zorinski, Sen. Edward—857, 944
Zweifel, David Eugene—609

U.S. GOVERNMENT PRINTING OFFICE : 1982 O – 87-400